Jane's Military Vehicles and Logistics 2011-2012

Shaun C Connors
and Christopher F Foss

Thirty-second Edition

Bookmark jmvl.janes.com today!

The title is also available on online, JDS (Jane's Data Services), Intra/Spex (offline), and Intel centres. Online gives the capability of real-time editing, permitting frequent updating. We trust our readers will use these facilities to keep abreast of the latest changes as and when they occur.

Updates online: Any update to the content of this product will appear online as it occurs.

Jane's Military Vehicles and Logistics online site gives you details of the additional information that is unique to online subscribers and the many benefits of upgrading to an online subscription. Don't delay, visit jmvl.janes.com today and view the list of the latest updates to this online service.

ISBN 978 0 7106 2952 4
"Jane's" is a registered trademark

Copyright © IHS Global Limited 2011
IHS Jane's, IHS Global Limited, Sentinel House, 163 Brighton Road, Coulsdon, Surrey, CR5 2YH, UK

In the US and its dependencies
Jane's Information Group Inc., 110 N. Royal Street, Suite 200, Alexandria, Virginia 22314, US

Copyright enquiries
e-mail: copyright@ihsjanes.com

MIX
Paper from
responsible sources
FSC® C018575
www.fsc.org

This book was produced using FSC® certified paper

Printed and bound in the UK by the MPG Books Group

Rheinmetall MAN Military Vehicles –
A new dimension in protected mobility

Jointly owned by the Rheinmetall Group and MAN Nutzfahrzeuge AG, the company is an important single-source maker of military wheeled vehicles, supplying the world's armed forces with a complete range of armoured and non-armoured transport, command, and mission-specific systems. The creation of Rheinmetall MAN Military Vehicles GmbH is an important step in the consolidation of Europe's tactical vehicle industry.

Rheinmetall MAN Military Vehicles GmbH · Dachauer Straße 655 · 80995 Munich · Germany

RHEINMETALL MAN

MILITARY VEHICLES

Contents

Jane's Military Vehicles and Logistics website: jmvl.janes.com

Alphabetical list of advertisers

EDITORIAL AND ADMINISTRATION

Managing Director: Michael Dell, e-mail: michael.dell@ihsjanes.com

Group Publishing Director: Sean Howe, e-mail: sean.howe@ihsjanes.com

Director EMEA Editing and Design: Sara Morgan,
e-mail: sara.morgan@ihsjanes.com

Director IHS Jane's Reference and Data Transformation: Chris Bridge,
e-mail: chris.bridge@ihsjanes.com

Compiler/Editor: Welcomes information and comments from users who
should send material to:
Research and Information Services
IHS Jane's, IHS Global Limited, Sentinel House, 163 Brighton Road,
Coulsdon, Surrey CR5 2YH, UK
Tel: (+44 20) 87 00 38 11 Fax: (+44 20) 87 00 39 59
e-mail: yearbook@ihsjanes.com

SALES OFFICES

Europe and Africa
IHS Jane's, IHS Global Limited, Lombard House, 3 Princess Way, Redhill,
Surrey RH1 1UP, UK
Tel: (+44 0) 17 37 37 97 40 Fax: (+44 0) 17 37 37 90 01
e-mail: customer.support@ihs.com

North/Central/South America
Jane's Information Group Inc., 110 N Royal Street, Suite 200, Alexandria,
Virginia 22314, US
Tel: (+1 703) 683 21 34 Fax: (+1 703) 836 02 97
Tel: (+1 800) 824 07 68 Fax: (+1 800) 836 02 97
e-mail: customerservices.us@ihsjanes.com

Asia
IHS Jane's, IHS Global Limited, 78 Shenton Way, #12–01, Singapore
079120, Singapore
Tel: (+65) 65 76 53 00 Fax: (+65) 62 26 11 85
e-mail: asiapacific@ihsjanes.com

Oceania
IHS Jane's, IHS Global Limited, Norwest Business Park, Suite 405, 14
Lexington Drive, Bella Vista, NSW 2153, Australia
Tel: (+61 0) 288 84 00 00 Fax: (+61 0) 288 84 00 11
e-mail: oceania@ihsjanes.com

Middle East
IHS Jane's, IHS Global Limited, PO Box 502138, Dubai, United Arab
Emirates
Tel: (+971 4) 390 23 36 Fax: (+971 4) 390 88 48
e-mail: mideast@ihsjanes.com

Japan
IHS Jane's, IHS Global Limited, CERA51 Bldg, 1-21-8 Ebisu, Shibuya-ku,
Tokyo 150-0013, Japan
Tel: (+81 3) 57 91 96 63 Fax: (+81 3) 54 20 64 02
e-mail: japan@ihsjanes.com

ADVERTISEMENT SALES OFFICES

UNITED KINGDOM
IHS Jane's, IHS Global Limited
Sentinel House, 163 Brighton Road,
Coulsdon, Surrey CR5 2YH, UK
Tel: (+44 20) 87 00 37 00 Fax: (+44 20) 87 00 38 59/37 44
e-mail: defadsales@ihsjanes.com

Janine Boxall, Global Advertising Sales Director,
Tel: (+44 20) 87 00 38 52 Fax: (+44 20) 87 00 38 59/37 44
e-mail: janine.boxall@ihsjanes.com

Richard West, Senior Key Accounts Manager
Tel: (+44 1892) 72 55 80 Fax: (+44 1892) 72 55 81
e-mail: richard.west@ihsjanes.com

Carly Litchfield, Advertising Sales Manager
Tel: (+44 20) 87 00 39 63 Fax: (+44 20) 87 00 37 44
e-mail: carly.litchfield@ihsjanes.com

Miles Torrent, Advertising Sales Executive
Tel: (+44 20) 87 00 37 27 Fax: (+44 20) 87 00 37 44
e-mail: miles.torrent@ihsjanes.com

UNITED STATES
Jane's Information Group Inc.
110 N Royal Street, Suite 200,
Alexandria, Virginia 22314, US
Tel: (+1 703) 683 37 00 Fax: (+1 703) 836 55 37
e-mail: defadsales@ihsjanes.com

Janet Berta, US Advertising Sales Director,
Tel: (+1 703) 236 24 10 Fax: (+1 703) 836 55 37
e-mail: janet.berta@ihsjanes.com

Sean Fitzgerald, South and Southeast USA
Tel: (+1 703) 836 24 46 Fax: (+1 703) 836 55 37
e-mail: sean.fitzgerald@ihsjanes.com

Dave Dreyer, Northeastern USA
Tel: (+1 703) 438 78 38 Fax: (+1 703) 836 55 27
e-mail: dave.dreyer@ihsjanes.com

Janet Murphy, Central USA
Tel: (+1 703) 836 31 39 Fax: (+1 703) 836 55 37
e-mail: janet.murphy@ihsjanes.com

Richard L Ayer, Western USA and National Accounts
127 Avenida del Mar, Suite 2A, San Clemente, California 92672, US
Tel: (+1 949) 366 84 55 Fax: (+1 949) 366 92 89
e-mail: ayercomm@earthlink.net

REST OF THE WORLD
Australia: *Richard West* (UK Office)

Benelux: *Miles Torrent* (UK Office)

Brazil: *Sean Fitzgerald* (USA office)

Canada: *Janet Murphy* (USA office)

Eastern Europe (excl. Poland): MCW Media & Consulting Wehrstedt
Dr Uwe H Wehrstedt
Hagenbreite 9, D-06463 Ermsleben, Germany
Tel: (+49 03) 47 43/620 90 Fax: (+49 03) 47 43/620 91
e-mail: info@Wehrstedt.org

Germany and Austria: *MCW Media & Consulting Wehrstedt* (see Eastern
Europe)

Greece: *Carly Litchfield* (UK Office)

Hong Kong: *Carly Litchfield* (UK Office)

India: *Carly Litchfield* (UK Office)

Israel: *Oreet International Media*
15 Kinneret Street, IL-51201 Bene Berak, Israel
Tel: (+972 3) 570 65 27 Fax: (+972 3) 570 65 27
e-mail: admin@oreet-marcom.com
Defence: Liat Heiblum
e-mail: liat_h@oreet-marcom.com

Italy and Switzerland: *Ediconsult Internazionale Srl*
Piazza Fontane Marose 3, I-16123 Genoa, Italy
Tel: (+39 010) 58 36 84 Fax: (+39 010) 56 65 78
e-mail: genova@ediconsult.com

Japan: *Carly Litchfield* (UK Office)

Middle East: *Miles Torrent* (UK Office)

Pakistan: *Miles Torrent* (UK Office)

Poland: *Miles Torrent* (UK Office)

Russia: *Anatoly Tomashevich*
1/3, appt 108, Zhivopisnaya Str, Moscow, 123103, Russia
Tel/Fax: (+7 495) 942 04 65
e-mail: to-anatoly@tochka.ru

Scandinavia: *Falsten Partnership*
23, Walsingham Road, Hove, East Sussex BN41 2XA, UK
Tel: (+44 1273) 77 10 20 Fax: (+ 44 1273) 77 00 70
e-mail: sales@falsten.com

Singapore: *Richard West* (UK Office)

South Africa: *Richard West* (UK Office)

Spain: *Carly Litchfield* (UK Office)

ADVERTISING COPY
Kate Gibbs (UK Office)
Tel: (+44 20) 87 00 37 42 Fax: (+44 20) 87 00 38 59/37 44
e-mail: kate.gibbs@ihsjanes.com

For North America, South America and Caribbean only:
Tel: (+1 703) 683 37 00 Fax: (+1 703) 836 55 37
e-mail: us.ads@ihsjanes.com

Executive Overview

The logical starting point for the Executive Overview of the 2011-2012 (32nd) edition of what is now titled *Jane's Military Vehicles and Logistics* (JMVL) is coverage of content changes that continue to evolve and take place within the title. Readers that follow the pattern of the world's biggest and most prestigious land-focusing defence exhibitions and exhibit a penchant for biannualism by opting to replace their JMVL hard copy in sync with the IDEX/DSEi exhibitions, will in this 2011-2012 edition notice that the Mine Warfare Equipment section is conspicuous by its absence. This of course will not be news to those that opt to replace their hard copy in sync with the Eurosatory exhibition, or to those that subscribe to the continuously updated electronic version of the title...

The removal of the Mine Warfare Equipment section from the 2010-2011 (31st) edition of JMVL concluded a process that began in the 2005-2006 edition of the title. The then Mine Laying, Mine Detection, Mine Clearing and Minefield Marking sections were culled, with the removal of anything not vehicle towed or mounted, and combined to form a new smaller and more vehicular focused Mine Warfare Equipment section. As projected at the time, the core content of JMVL has continued to grow and evolve; this primarily due to ongoing deployed operations and the doctrinal and equipment changes these have resulted in. The overall result of this process was to implement the planned decision to remove the no-longer core content Mine Warfare Equipment section from the 31st edition onwards.

Readers should note that the vast majority of JMVL's legacy mine-related sections have, since the creation of *Jane's Mines and Mine Clearance* (JMMC), always been near-duplicated in that title. Further, for JMVL's electronic subscribers, archive access to all former mine-related sections and any other recently removed sections, is still available.

The other area of significant change within JMVL is the inclusion and coverage of protected vehicles and vehicle protection solutions. As regular readers of title-related subject matter will know only too well, over recent years the continuing conflicts in Afghanistan and Iraq have caused a considerable greying of the area between what was once a softskin 'B' (or even 'C') vehicle and an armoured 'A' vehicle. Virtually all light utility vehicle and truck procurements ('B' vehicles) by armed forces that participate in deployed operations now include some form of protection requirement, as do an increasing number of plant/material handling equipment procurements ('C' vehicles). To reflect this almost step-change in policy, the content of both the current and more recent editions of JMVL has evolved to provide relevant coverage of this topic, with details of individual manufacturers armouring/protection solutions included in individual entries on a 'where relevant' basis. The subject of what may, or may not, fit the 'where relevant' caveat (and why) is addressed in detail throughout this Executive Overview.

The vehicles shown in this image, BAE's Caiman and Navistar's MaxxPro Plus, are both considered relevant as both are based on a military/militarised truck chassis (US DoD)   1391477

Bank Breaker

Before taking a selective look at some of the more significant vehicle and equipment developments of 2010, those anticipated for 2011 (and beyond in some cases), and providing an overview of the two main conflicts that have driven many of these developments, an acknowledgement of the global economic downturn/recession and the impact this is having on the defence sector is perhaps in order.

Up until early/mid-2010, the more optimistic of commentators would, if pressed on the subject, probably have concluded that in relation to the global economic downturn/recession, that global defence budgets and expenditure, while not proof to those events, were certainly demonstrating resistance to them. More recently, that view may have shifted slightly to the belief that for the majority of the world's armed forces (and the defence industries that support them) 2010 was in fact the year in which the effects of the global economic downturn/recession finally became a reality.

Headlines of most industry specific journals are currently rife with details of high-minded procurement projects that have been, or will be, cancelled or delayed, or of plans for modernisation that have or may be put on hold or even scrapped. For many armed forces the implications are this means soldiering on with ageing platforms and/or having to accept defence budgets that may not be able to maintain current inventories and/or levels of ambition.

However, when talking defence expenditure it quickly becomes apparent, that be it spender or recipient, the overall values involved bring into play considerable vested interest in both the political and industrial spheres. The smoke screen generated by such vested interest does nothing but impede anybody tasked with assessing what may be spent, has been spent, or by whom. Even after sifting through the maze of massaged statistics that purport to give an indication of defence spend, Global Domestic Product (GDP) and all manner of other related figures, what real chance is there of making sense of it all if some of our bigger-spending political leaders themselves appear incapable of keeping an accurate track of defence spend?

Ultimately though, no matter how optimistic your view may be, it must remain clear the world is in the midst of an economic crisis, the overall effects of which will be felt for years to come. That said, and even from highly variable figures, it is as clear that while it may be suffering the overall global defence spend has not been affected to the level of some other sectors by this economic crisis. Accepting that as with all things statistics-related the waters here can easily be muddied, if we take as an example of the global top 15 defence spenders, Italy, Japan and Spain, the defence budgets of these three countries have dropped in monetary/percentage GDP terms, but as armed force manpower levels have dropped also, the amount of spend per man has actually increased.

And it may also be the case that as one door appears to close partially, another may open slightly to compensate. It is true that post Cold War, defence spending in the bulk of European/NATO countries began an ongoing trend of stagnation, even decline, but to compensate this and perhaps the added effects of the current crisis, there is now a projected sizeable spending boom in Asia and the Middle East. Middle Eastern expenditure will always remain heavily influenced by oil and oil prices, but with regard to Asia, recent reports have suggested that irrespective of economic downturn, by 2016 Asia will account for 32 per cent of global military spending. Over the same timeline North America's share (currently approaching 50 per cent) will drop to around 30 per cent. Perhaps not a global reduction in spend, but more a global reallocation.

A US Army soldier surveys the terrain around the Kunar river in Afghanistan's Noorgal district. While in the broader sense the security situation in Iraq did steadily improve, throughout 2010 the security situation in Afghanistan continued to deteriorate at an alarming rate. However, the US currently plans to start reducing the 90,000 troops it presently has in Afghanistan from July 2011 (US Army)   1391478

Never Ending Story

In terms of mainstream media coverage the average man in the street could probably be forgiven for thinking the tempo of operations in Afghanistan and Iraq had dropped off quite considerably in recent months, perhaps even assuming these deployments could be nearing a satisfactory conclusion. Of course, those with any real knowledge of what the United States (US) refers to as Operation Enduring Freedom (OEF) and Operation New Dawn (previously Operation Iraqi Freedom (OIF)), will know 'satisfactory conclusion' is most certainly not the case.

In the broader sense, and despite some significant incidents during the writing of this Executive Overview, the security situation in Iraq does steadily improve, with total coalition fatalities down from a peak of 961 (904 US) in 2007 to 60 in 2010. Following the withdrawal of Australian troops from Iraq in July 2009, the only foreign combat troops in the country were from the US. The last of the UK's combat troops were withdrawn from Iraq in May 2009.

Operation Iraqi Freedom (OIF) in Iraq has been declared complete after seven years, the combat mission ostensibly ended. Under what since 1 September 2010 has been called Operation New Dawn (OND), about 50,000 US troops (down from around 112,000 early 2010) remain in Iraq, these with an advise-and-assist mission. They are structured into Advise-and-Assist Brigades (AABs) as opposed to Brigade Combat Teams (BCTs). These AABs retain the same combat capability as they did prior to being re-missioned and do still engage in combat. However, Iraqi forces now lead the operations and mainly partner with US personnel for logistic and Intelligence, Surveillance and Reconnaissance (ISR) support.

And while the security situation in Iraq may be showing signs of improvement, the security situation in Afghanistan continues to deteriorate

US Marines evacuate casualties onto a British CH-47 Chinook after an IED strike in the Sangin District, Afghanistan
(Lance Cpl Jorge A Ortiz (US DoD))   1391479

at an alarming rate. By mid-January 2011, a total of 2,301 OEF coalition troop fatalities had been recorded (1,461 US, 349 UK, 154 Canada, 53 France, 46 Germany, 40 Denmark and 198 others). Troop fatalities continue to increase annually, with a significant increase from 295 in 2008 to 521 in 2009 (317 US, 108 UK and 95 others). This figure again increased during 2010 to a record 711 (499 US, 103 UK and 109 others).

Completely over-matched in any conventional combat sense, the insurgents weapon of choice in Afghanistan continues to be the Improvised Explosive Device (IED). Throughout 2010, insurgent IED attacks wounded 3,366 US troops, this approaching 60 per cent of the total IED-wounded since the start of OEF. Equally as disturbing, of 711 non-US coalition troops killed in 2010, 368 of the 630 that were killed in action were by IEDs, this around 36 per cent of the total IED-killed since the start of OEF.

To help address the deteriorating security situation in Afghanistan, the US announced in December 2009 it would deploy an additional 30,000 troops to the country by mid-2010. At the time the US government announced the 30,000 surge in OEF troop numbers, it also stated that the draw-down of US troops in Afghanistan would begin in July 2011. This date was reaffirmed late 2010 by Chairman of the Joint Chiefs of Staff, Admiral Mike Mullen, who said during a 28 November interview on CNN: "We will start drawing down troops next July; there's no question about that." And while than may indeed happen, few analysts can actually agree on timelines, and most agree that multinational forces will be present in Afghanistan for a number of years yet, and certainly well beyond 2011.

The sun sets over Combat Outpost Ziohaq, Afghanistan in April 2010
(D Myles Cullen (US DoD))   1391480

Official International Security Assistance Force (ISAF) figures for January 2011 quote a total of 131,730 coalition troops in Afghanistan, 90,000 of those US, 9,500 British, with the remaining 32,230 contributed by some 44 other nations, with individual quantities ranging from three (Austria) to 4,877 (Germany).

Canada currently has 2,913 troops deployed to Afghanistan, having had a presence in the country continuously since 2002. In 2008 Canadian parliament announced the planned withdrawal of Canadian troops from Afghanistan in 2011. The forces were in the process of planning the withdrawal when in October the United Arab Emirates (UAE) complicated matters by advising Canada it would have to leave Camp Mirage: the staging base that the Canadian Forces (CF) have maintained in Dubai for the past nine years. The UAE took the decision, demanding Canada vacate within 30 days, after negotiations between the two countries failed to result in more landing rights in Canada for two UAE-based airlines.

At a reported cost of CAD300, Canada closed down the base on 4 November and moved its air cargo operations to Spangdahlem in Germany and its personnel staging area to Paphos, Cyprus.

In mid-November the Canadian government announced that it intends to keep up to 950 soldiers in Afghanistan until March 2014 as part of the NATO Training Mission, the estimated cost of this commitment being CAD700 million per year.

Changing Lanes

The way in which operations in Afghanistan and Iraq have necessitated an evolution away from a conventional armoured battle force with a softskin logistic support fleet for participating nations has, of course, been well documented. In what is now an urban/semi-urban, almost guerrilla war with no front line and essentially no rear echelon, every person and every vehicle is now a viable target in the eyes of insurgent forces. Not only are new and better-suited vehicles types required, but everything from ambulance to ammunition hauler must now be protected from small arms fire, mine blast and the insurgents' continuing weapon of choice, the IED.

This need for protection on what were traditionally softskin vehicles and the subsequent replacement in many roles (certainly on deployed operations) of softskin vehicles by protected ones and the impact this had on procurement strategy, have combined to create a grey area and some ongoing content conundra for the editors. It is hoped the following brief explanation will assist readers in determining what protected/armoured vehicles they may find included in JMVL, in what level of detail these may be covered, plus the rationale behind respective inclusion or exclusion decisions.

All HMMWVs (model shown is M1151) currently produced for US Armed Forces are manufactured to comply with the US Army's Long Term Armor Strategy (LTAS), and as such are armoured using an A-kit/B-kit principle; designed 'fitted for, but not with', protection
(Senior Airman Nathanael Callon (US DoD))   1391481

Taking the ubiquitous AM General High Mobility Multipurpose Wheeled Vehicle (HMMWV) as an example, excluding the armament carrier variants which, from the very first contract award have always been fitted with a very limited level of fragmentation protection, a fully protected variant has been available since the mid-1990s. This variant which is factory-delivered fully armoured (that is does not have a removable appliqué-type kit fitted) has always been covered in the JMVL HMMWV entry. From around 2003, and as the significance of this variant increased, so did the degree of coverage it received in JMVL's HMMWV entry. Such coverage, while increasing in word count and detail, has not increased (and will not) to include full technical specifications, but has increased to include an identifying image. There has always been a dedicated specific entry for fully protected HMMWV variants in *Jane's Armour and Artillery* (JAA).

Vehicles such as the Otokar Cobra, which utilise HMMWV automotives, but feature a purpose-designed monocoque (chassis-less) armoured hull, receive no more than an acknowledgement in the primary JMVL HMMWV entry, with readers referred to JAA for full details.

To confuse issues somewhat, virtually all current HMMWV production models enter service armoured. However, they are manufactured to comply with the US Army's Long Term Armor Strategy (LTAS) and as such are armoured using an A-kit/B-kit principle; they are designed 'fitted for, but not with', protection. Protection kits can be installed and uninstalled from vehicles in the field using only basic tools. The A-kit is fitted on the production line and is the combination of a limited amount of armouring (in difficult-to-access areas of the vehicle), together with a significant amount of armour installation attachments and required support structures. The bulk of the armour, the B-kit, is installed in the field on an 'as required' basis.

The LTAS principle is applied to all current production US tactical 'softskin' vehicles (HMMWV, Family of Medium Tactical Vehicles (FMTV), Medium Tactical Vehicle Replacement (MTVR) and Family of Heavy Tactical Vehicles (FHTV)) and is covered in detail in these vehicles' respective JMVL entries.

Other manufacturers offer similar armouring solutions, some adopting a benign in appearance approach. For load carrying trucks these solutions can also include fixed or interchangeable armoured cabs.

One armouring area that may cause more confusion than most is with heavier so-called Mine Resistant Ambush Protected (MRAP) class/type designs. MRAP is in fact a United States Marine Corps (USMC) programme, it is not a vehicle, nor is it a class of vehicle. However, given the prominence of the MRAP programme it is now a common occurrence for a mine and/or blast protected vehicle to be referred to as an MRAP (albeit sometimes spuriously), much the same as a backhoe loader produced by Case, Caterpillar (or others) can be referred to as a JCB, or a four-wheel drive vehicle produced by Mitsubishi, Nissan, Toyota (or others) can be

This Oshkosh M977A4 Heavy Expanded Mobility Tactical Truck (HEMTT), like all current US heavy tactical truck deliveries, is fitted with a Long Term Armor Strategy (LTAS) compliant armoured cab (Carl Schulze)   1391482

referred to as a Land Rover or Jeep. Throughout JMVL the descriptive terms MRAP-type or MRAP-class will be used to define vehicles that fall outside of the USMC MRAP procurement and that the editors believe qualify as significantly mine and/or blast protected designs.

Focusing on the USMC MRAP programme as an example, and specifically two of the vehicles selected for it, the include or not problems for the editors become clear. Navistar Defense's MaxxPro is covered in reasonable detail (in the Navistar Defense (International) range of military vehicles entry) as the type is based on the chassis and running gear of a militarised International truck chassis. The BAE Systems RG33, beyond references that may put MRAP awards or details into context, is not covered as the design uses a monocoque armoured hull and a 'parts box' selection of driveline components. Both vehicles are covered in *Jane's Armour and Artillery* (JAA).

Navistar's MaxxPro Mine Resistant Ambush Protected (MRAP) (this is the Dash variant) is covered in reasonable detail in the Navistar Defense (International) range of military vehicles entry as the type is based on the chassis and running gear of a militarised International truck chassis (Carl Schulze)   1391483

JMVL also covers load-carrying (logistic) variants of armoured vehicles, a long-standing example here being a South African family of vehicles based on the Casspir MPV that included cargo, tanker and recovery variants. More recently MRAP-class/type vehicles, which have primarily been procured for the transport of troops in high-threat areas, have evolved and increasing numbers of cargo and other specialist variants of this type of vehicle are now offered.

Recent examples here would include the Thales Copperhead (a flatbed variant of the monocoque-hulled Bushmaster Protected Mobility Vehicle (PMV)), a cargo/flatbed variant of the Krauss-Maffei Wegmann (KMW) Dingo 2, and recovery and tractor truck variants of the Navistar MaxxPro MRAP. Copperhead is currently competing for a segment of Australia's Land 121, while the cargo variant of the Krauss-Maffei Wegmann (KMW) Dingo All Protected Vehicle (APV) is competing for a segment of Germany's Gepanzertes TransportFahrzeug (GTF) requirement. Both of these requirements began as straight logistic vehicle programmes, but both have evolved to include significant protection requirements. Initial orders have been placed for the Navistar MaxxPro recovery and tractor truck variants.

Money Movers
In terms of global defence spending, perhaps unsurprisingly the US continues to lead the world, the projected spend for 2012 is USD544 billion, a figure that excludes the cost of ongoing Overseas Contingency Operations (OCO) in Afghanistan and Iraq. Putting US defence spending into some sort

of context, the 2009 spend (total USD663.26 billion) was over nine times that of China's estimated spend and was almost equal to that of the rest of the world's spend combined. However, in further context, in terms of military expenditure as a percentage of GDP (using the most recently available and accepted to be 'variable' in accuracy figures) the US falls just outside the top 20, a top 20 that includes only one NATO nation, Turkey. The world's biggest spender on defence (in terms of percentage of GDP) is Oman; estimated at 11.4 per cent.

However, and reflecting back to earlier comments on the global economic downturn/recession, US Defense Secretary Robert Gates announced plans early-2011 to reduce the Pentagon's budget by USD78 billion over the next five years, this including steep cuts in troop levels and the scrapping of several expensive weapons programmes.

The proposed defence budget for 2012 (at USD544 billion excluding OCO) would be a modest three per cent increase, but it is proposed that budgets will gradually reduce to reach zero percentage growth in 2015 and 2016. The proposed cuts include reducing the size of the Army and Marine Corps by 27,000 and 15,000-20,000, respectively. However, these changes will not be implemented until 2015 and are based on an assumption that America's ground combat commitment in Afghanistan will be significantly reduced by the end of 2014 in accordance with current plans.

A further USD100 billion is also targeted to be saved from non-war defence spending over the next five years.

Proposed budget cuts notwithstanding, the US currently has a number of big budget JMVL-related programmes running, including ongoing buys of High Mobility Multipurpose Wheeled Vehicles (HMMWVs), Family of Medium Tactical Vehicles (FMTVs) and the third iteration of the Family of Heavy Tactical Vehicles (FHTV) contract award. Also running is the ongoing MRAP-All-Terrain Vehicle (MRAP/M-ATV) procurement, and still in the system is the potential USD10 billion Joint Light Tactical Vehicle (JLTV) programme.

From the above-mentioned programmes, the one to have recently occupied the most column inches in periodicals will undoubtedly have been the FMTV. Oshkosh Defense announced in August 2009 that it had been awarded the FMTV A1P2 rebuy production contract. Following protests filed by the losing bidders (BAE Systems and Navistar), some elements of which were upheld by the US Government Accountability Office (GAO), the US Army confirmed in February 2010 that following a re-evaluation of the FMTV award in line with GAO recommendations, that the award remained with Oshkosh Defense.

Shown here is a BAE Systems-produced FMTV fitted with a Low Signature Armored Cab (LSAC)
(Mass Communication Specialist 2nd Class Walter M Wayman (US DoD))   1391484

The FMTV A1P2 rebuy is a five-year 'build-to-print' requirements-type award that has been quoted as allowing the US government to order from zero up to an estimated 12,400 trucks and 10,900 trailers. The award, which includes support services and engineering, could be worth approximately USD3 billion if all options are exercised.

The latest FMTV awards were announced in December 2010, these valued at USD513.3 million and calling for more than 2,050 FMTV trucks and more than 1,650 FMTV trailers. All deliveries under this award are destined for US Army National Guard units and will run from November 2011 until May 2013. These latest awards bring FMTV delivery order totals to at least 13,210 trucks and 4,800 trailers, with award totals currently in excess of USD2.6 billion.

Some FMTV variants were excluded from the rebuy competition, those excluded include specialist FMTV variants such as HIMARS, Patriot, MEADS and LVAD, plus all the armoured cabs developed by BAE Systems including the Low Signature Armored Cab (LSAC), over 4,000 of which are in-service, the Individual Crew Protection (ICP) cab fitted to current HIMARS, and the base LTAS cab, over 16,000 of which have been produced to date for the A1P2 variant. All Oshkosh FMTV vehicles will include the company's own Long-Term Armor Strategy (LTAS)-compliant armour solution.

BAE Systems continues deliveries of the specialist variants not covered by the rebuy award, the most recent specialist variant award announced in

November 2010. Under a contract valued at USD16.3 million an additional 44 HIMARS vehicles have been ordered, these to be equipped with BAE Systems' Increased Crew Protection (ICP) cab. Deliveries will be completed by December 2011.

BAE Systems will continue development and marketing of the FMTV for export, and at DSEi 2009 unveiled the FMTV General Tactical Vehicle (GTV), a EURO 5 emissions-compliant European-optimised FMTV that is currently being touted for at least one European country's requirement.

With the FMTV rebuy award remaining with Oshkosh, the US Army effectively now has a single supplier for its entire tactical truck fleet. Currently this appears to be working extremely well, however, should issues develop then these could have quite serious consequences for US heavy truck procurement.

US Army Oshkosh M1070 Heavy Equipment Transporters (HETs) at work in Iraq. The M1070 HET forms part of the Family of Heavy Tactical Vehicles (FHTV) awards to Oshkosh, this also including Heavy Expanded Mobility Tactical Truck (HEMTT) and Palletized Load System (PLS/PLST) trucks and trailers (US DoD)   1391485

Prior to the medium FMTV segment award, Oshkosh was already under contract to deliver approaching 13,000 new and recapitalised (Recap) Heavy Expanded Mobility Tactical Truck (HEMTT), Palletized Load System trucks and trailers (PLS/PLST) and Heavy Equipment Transporters (HET) to the US Army under the three-year FHTV-3 contract awarded in October 2008. The US government did request interest from competitors in this heavy (FHTV) area through a Market Survey in 2007, but opted to continue placing single source-contracts with Oshkosh. By early 2011 Oshkosh had delivered somewhere in the region of 60,000 trucks and trailers of types covered by the FHTV awards.

Additionally, Oshkosh is the sole supplier of tactical trucks to the US Marines, having delivered approaching 11,000 Medium Tactical Vehicle Replacement (MTVR) trucks since 1999, while most recently is under contract to deliver approaching 1,400 Logistic Vehicle System Replacement (LVSR).

Oshkosh has delivered approaching 11,000 of these Medium Tactical Vehicle Replacement (MTVR) trucks (in various configurations) to the US Marines since 1999. The company is the sole supplier of medium and heavy tactical trucks to the US Marines, and the sole supplier of heavy tactical trucks to the US Army (Spc Ian Schell (US DoD))   1391486

Oshkosh may have missed out on the lucrative circa 17,500-vehicle four-manufacturer split MRAP buy of recent years, but with its MRAP – All-Terrain Vehicle (M-ATV), it has secured the lucrative award to provide US forces with a vehicle that has protection equal to that of an MRAP, while being considerably more mobile. Since the initial delivery order placed in June 2009, Oshkosh has received orders for 8,329 M-ATVs, this figure

including the most recent (December 2010) order for 250 ambulance variants - 246 production; four test - and bringing contract value to date to around USD5.4 billion.

The Oshkosh M-ATV is not a vehicle covered in detail by JMVL, as while being chassis-based like some MRAPs that are covered, the Oshkosh M-ATV is based on an a designed-for-application chassis and not an in-production truck chassis. The M-ATV chassis does share some components with that of the Oshkosh MTVR and is fitted with a lighter version of the Oshkosh TAK-4 independent suspension as fitted to the Oshkosh MTVR and LVSR. The MTVR, and later LVSR, remain the only two tactical trucks in volume production that are equipped with fully independent suspension for all wheels.

In an attempt to enhance their mobility in the difficult terrain of Afghanistan, TAK-4 independent suspension is being retrofitted to around 2,900 Force Protection Cougar ((4 × 4) and (6 × 6)), around 350 BAE Systems RG33 (4 × 4) and around 130 General Dynamics Land Systems (GDLS) RG31 (4 × 4) MRAPs.

Additionally, the lighter Dash variant of Navistar's MaxxPro truck-based MRAP is also being upgraded to an independent suspension configuration. Orders placed in February 2010 (1,050) and December 2010 (175) received Navistar's DXM independent suspension at production stage, while the previously ordered 1,222 examples were retro-fitted in theatre. Eighty MaxxPro Dash for export customers (including Poland (20), Romania (20), and Singapore (15)) are also fitted with DXM independent suspension, bringing overall totals to 2,527.

Oshkosh may be the sole provider of medium and heavy tactical trucks to the US military, but for the equally important line haul role the entrenched sole provider is Daimler-owned Freightliner.

Since winning its first M915 series of line haul tractor contract in 1988, the now Daimler Trucks North America has been the incumbent supplier of M915 series trucks, having delivered at least 10,000 vehicles under the most recent contract, this awarded in 2000 and (with three one-year extensions) having recently concluded. It is understood that at the time of writing the award of a single-source two-year follow-on contract was pending.

Since winning its first M915 series of line haul tractor contract in 1988, the now Daimler Trucks North America has been the incumbent supplier of M915 series trucks. Current production standard is M915A5 (shown is an M915A2), and it is understood that at the time of writing the award of a single-source two-year follow-on M915 series contract was pending (US DoD)   1391487

Current M915 series deliveries are for the much-revised M915A5 series, this entering production in January 2010. In keeping with all US military trucks, the latest M915A5 is considerably uprated over earlier models and features an A-kit/B-kit Long Term Armor Strategy (LTAS) compliant cab; by early 2011, 2,166 vehicles (including options) were on contract.

The Lighthorsemen
At the lighter end of the vehicle scale, the ubiquitous and much-maligned by some HMMWV continues to soldier on. Written off by many as ever-bigger IEDs began taking their toll on early lightly armoured variants in Afghanistan and Iraq, it would appear that AM General has successfully beefed up and re-invented the vehicle.

With most lighter-weight vehicle detractors finally recognising that a trade off between size/weight, tactical/strategic mobility and ultimately protection has to made on occasion, the latest improved HMMWV variants appear to have given the type a new lease of life. However, in a surprise move and following continued extensions of AM General's 2000-awarded HMMWV production contract, in February 2010 the US Army stated that it had no plans to purchase new HMMWVs beyond FY10.

The USMC and other braches of US armed forces could continue to purchase new vehicles (as could export customers), but the US Army had rather abruptly concluded that it had reached its procurement target for HMMWVs. The intent appeared to be that future funds would be allocated to the recapitalisation (Recap) of the current fleet, however, this proved an unacceptable option (at the time) and in July 2010 AM General was awarded a new HMMWV production contract (W56HZV-10-C-0405).

This latest contract allows for the production of up to 8,995 HMMWVs and has a base year with two option years. The contract also provides for continuing HMMWV support such as service parts, supply chain management, training and field service. The first award under contract

W56HZV-10-C-0405 was announced on 30 July, it is valued at USD619 million and is a Foreign Military Sale (FMS) award covering vehicles for the Afghan police force and Afghan National Guard. The second award under contract W56HZV-10-C-0405 was announced on 15 December and is valued at USD211 million. This award covers 1,263 HMMWVs of various models for the US Army, with work scheduled for completion in June 2011.

Afghan border patrol force M1151 (Sgt Jeffrey Alexander (US DoD))

1391488

Current primary HMMWV production variants are the M1151, M1152, M1165 and M1167, the first of these to enter production being the M1152 in 2005. These models all follow the previously covered LTAS A-kit/B-kit philosophy. Standard A2-series HMMWV variants remain in production, but primarily for export. Recent HMMWV export customers (some of which have received M1151 series models including loaned vehicles and donations) have included Afghanistan, Bulgaria, Chile, Croatia, Egypt, Georgia, Hungary, Iraq, Kuwait, Latvia, Lithuania, Nepal, Peru, Poland, Portugal, Romania and Saudi Arabia.

As of early 2011 over 270,000 HMMWVs had been produced, that figure including over 230,000 for the US government, the remainder supplied to over 50 foreign governments.

Ultimately the HMMWV will have to be replaced in the US military's inventory, but with the Army having an estimated holding of 154,000 (around 40 per cent of these armoured) and the Marines around 20,000, the HMMWV is destined to be around for a number of years yet. The current vehicle touted for the task of replacing (or part-replacing) the HMMWV is the Joint Light Tactical Vehicle (JLTV).

The JLTV programme is an ambitious joint US Army/USMC effort to design a family of vehicles that will incorporate the latest advances in armour protection, fuel efficiency and crew survivability. Following false starts, stalls and the almost inevitable protests by disgruntled unsuccessful bidders, by February 2009 the three 27-month JLTV Technology Development (TD) contracts, originally awarded to teams led by Lockheed Martin, General Dynamics and BAE Systems in October 2008, were in place. Upon completion of the TD phase, it is currently anticipated that another full and open competition will be conducted, this resulting in the award of two contracts for further development and demonstration, with a Milestone C decision in FY13 and full production and fielding anticipated in 2015. At the time of writing (January 2011) there had been no further official JLTV timeline or Milestone-related announcements.

However, to cast doubts over JLTV achieving its original desired aim as a full and complete replacement for the HMMWV, it was reported in *Jane's*

The vehicle shown is one of the Lockheed Martin team led JLTV prototypes (Lockeed Martin)

1391489

Defence Weekly (JDW) that US government auditors have recommended that the Department of Defense (DoD) take steps to ensure its Tactical Wheeled Vehicle (TWV) programmes balance requirements with available resources and consider the future of legacy platforms, those steps including looking at the scaling back of the JLTV programme.

Currently US Army procurement officials plan to procure a portfolio of TWVs in the coming years that could cost up to USD3.7 billion a year, although the current estimates are that it can only afford to spend around USD2.5 billion annually on these accounts.

In a 5 November report the Government Accountability Office (GAO) suggested the Pentagon should, in formulating a TWV strategy, first resolve decisions on budgeting for long-term sustainment of MRAPs, producing new HMMWVs, recapitalising existing HMMWVs (the army has asked for funding in FY2011 to recapitalise some of its HMMWV fleet at Army depots and is also considering a possible competition for a HMMWV recapitalisation programme) and finalising the specific cost and capabilities for the JLTV programme.

The Army has estimated the cost per stock JLTV at about USD300,000, while the GAO estimates that unit costs could be over USD800,000 when mission equipment packages are added. Aside from costs, the GAO expressed concern that the JLTV: "has demanding projected requirements that necessitate technological and engineering advances." The Pentagon concurred with the GAO recommendations and noted that the JLTV programme is conducting an analysis of alternatives to: "explore potential offsets to JLTV quantities."

As previously mentioned, the Army is considering scaling back the JLTV programme and could do this by either reducing the procurement rate or the total buy. One possible option here might then be a HMMWV upgrade programme which could deliver more capable, mobile and survivable vehicles. However, according to Lieutenant General Robert Lennox, the Army's deputy chief of staff for programmes, the upgrade programme idea does not yet appear to be materialising despite the recent emergence of several industry developed upgrade packages.

Some Marine Corps officials have previously expressed trepidation regarding the overall size/weight of projected JLTV variants, and there remains the danger the Corps may ultimately opt out of the programme. However, the current view of Lieutenant General George Flynn, head of the USMC's Combat Development Command, is that his preferred strategy would be a combination of recapitalisation (there are more than 20,000 HMMWVs in the Marine Corps inventory of various types) and new buys like the JLTV.

On a broader note, the USMC's tactical wheeled vehicle strategy is still being formulated, but the Corps has already decided to reduce its overall inventory, including new buys, by 10,000 vehicles.

A further option for all arms might be the adoption of a two-tier replacement approach for the HMMWV, with a smaller/lighter, cheaper and possibly unprotected vehicle procured for selected roles. However, should this approach be adopted it must be hoped that it would be more successful than the previous attempt at such a strategy, the joint tactical HMMWV/ non-tactical Commercial Utility Cargo Vehicle (CUCV) procurement of the early/mid 1980s, the result of which was additional HMMWVs then procured to replace the wholly inadequate CUCV fleet.

Above and beyond any concerns regarding what JLTV may or may not replace and when, the major issue regarding JLTV for the editors of JMVL is ultimately one of inclusion or not. Clearly a HMMWV replacement or part-replacement would be a multipurpose, multirole 'light' utility vehicle. However, JLTV is from the ground up a purpose-designed armoured vehicle, and as such is not the remit of JMVL. Fortunately, with current full production not scheduled until 2015 (and there will inevitably be more slippage), the editors have a few years yet to ponder this particular subject, and in the belief that the content of JMVL will continue to evolve to include JLTV in some form when it (or what it may evolve into) finally becomes a reality.

The Europeans

Moving away from the US and the approaching 50 per cent of the world's defence expenditure it accounts for, we should take a look at some recent and pending developments in Europe and elsewhere. If we use the league table of big defence spenders as a starting point, we should begin with either France or the UK (depending on interpretation of figures). In contradiction of *Jane's Sentinel Security Assessments*, which ranks the UK above France in terms of defence spending, we will start a selective European overview with France, if only because as this Executive Overview was being written there was a development with France's long running major truck replacement program, *Porteur Polyvalente Terrestre* (PPT).

Since the issue of the initial Request For Quotation (RFQ) in 2004, PPT has been well documented in JMVL, but in brief this is a project to replace the French Army's *Vehicule de Transport Logistique* (VTL), the initial order for which was placed in 1988. PPT, which throughout its evolution has added a dump truck and recovery element, began as a requirement for around 2,500 load-carrying trucks, most equipped with a Demountable Rack Off-loading and Pick-up System (DROPS)/Palletized Load System (PLS)-type Load Handling System (LHS). Following stalls and false starts, PPT finally re-emerged in January 2010 with an initial requirement that was understood to be for 150 trucks with armoured cabs and more than 40 trailers. Additional batches and options totalling 2,350 trucks and 550 trailers could then follow between 2012-2017. Responses were due by March 2010, with respondents thought likely to be established PPT

Porteur Polyvalente Terrestre (PPT) is a project to replace the French Army's Véhicule de Transport Logistique (VTL) (shown), the initial order for which was placed in 1988. An initial order for 150 trucks fitted with a Load Handling System (LHS), 40 companion trailers, and 50 recovery trucks and valued at around EUR160 million was placed late 2010
(Shaun C Connors)   1391490

contenders Renault, Scania and SOFRAME, the latter offering an IVECO truck.

Ultimately only Renault and SOFRAME would respond, and while not officially reported initially, it became known in January 2011 that late November 2010 the French Direction Générale de l'Armement (DGA) had awarded the PPT contract to SOFRAME, a division of the Lohr Group. The losing bidder, Renault Trucks Defense had promptly filed a protest, the reasons cited being the length and clarity of the procurement process. This protest was not upheld and in January 2011 it was disclosed the contract had been ratified by French Defense Minister Alain Juppé in mid-December 2010.

The initial order placed under PPT is reportedly valued at EUR160 million and calls for 150 trucks fitted with a Load Handling System (LHS), 40 companion trailers, and 50 recovery trucks. The trucks, supplied by IVECO, will be delivered during 2013-2014 and be based on a purpose-designed (8 × 8) tactical chassis manufactured at IVECO's ASTRA plant, this fitted with a militarised driveline from the IVECO Trakker commercial range. The military pattern flat-panelled cab will be fitted with an IBD-developed appliqué armour kit.

Further orders for an additional 2,100 logistic trucks (variants including LHS, cargo with crane and dump), 550 companion trailers (est.) and 100 recovery vehicles can be placed with delivery running until 2021. The overall contract value is estimated to be just under EUR1 billion.

IVECO has also recently been awarded a Swiss army contract. This, the fourth award since 2000, is valued at EUR125 million and calls for up to 925 militarised Trakker range trucks. When deliveries under this latest award are complete, since 2000 IVECO will have delivered up to 1,700 militarised Cargo/Trakker range trucks to Switzerland's Armed Forces.

IVECO is also involved in a sizeable UK truck delivery, albeit a relatively low-profile Private Finance Initiative (PFI) award. As part of its 16-year PFI undertaking for the MoD's C-vehicle fleet, ALC is currently delivering 182 (6 × 6) Trakker range trucks. The bulk of the fleet will be tippers (MDT/SLDT) with the remainder split between Truck-Mounted Loader (TML) and small quantities of drilling rigs and flush capping system platforms. The 63 Medium Dump Trucks (MDTs) will replace the current Foden MDT, while the 71 Self-Loading Dump Trucks (SLDTs) will replace the Volvo SLDT. The TML, a flatbed with a rear-mounted materials handling crane, is a new capability. The to-be-replaced drilling rigs are currently mounted on IVECO Trakker and ASTRA chassis, while the to-be-replaced flush capping systems are currently mounted on Bedford TM (6 × 6) trucks.

Outside of this PFI procurement, IVECO will also supply the MoD direct with 15 (including a trials vehicle) (8 × 8) Trakker SLDTs fitted with a KMW-developed ballistic and blast protected cab.

Another UK PFI that is currently out to tender is that of the non-combat white fleet transport provision for UK Armed Forces in the UK at all but a small number of specified sites. Around 15,000 vehicles are involved in a contract that is currently understood to be worth in excess of GBP100 million per year to incumbent supplier ALC, and which expires in August 2011.

The UK's current major 'green fleet' truck procurement program, Support Vehicle, continues to run to schedule, with in excess of 5,000 of the 7,479 Support Vehicles and derivatives contracted to the MoD to date delivered by January 2011. The most recent Support Vehicle development was the announcement at Defence Vehicles Dynamics (DVD) 2010 that under a Urgent Operational Requirement (UOR) in excess of 300 examples were being upgraded to the latest Theatre Entry Standard (TES).

Further UK UORs are the ongoing/recently completed delivery of protected vehicles that occupy that ever-expanding grey area between JMVL and JAA content. These deliveries include 140 Jackal 2a long range patrol-type vehicles (complete), 89 additional Husky utility variants, 97 Wolfhound Tactical Support Vehicles (TSVs), plus over 100 Warthog tracked all-terrain vehicles.

Shown here Supacat's Coyote, support vehicle for the company's Jackal
(UK MoD)   1391492

Jackal (and its supporting Coyote) are essentially open vehicles, although underbody blast and some limited crew protection is provided. Husky is based on the much-modified chassis and driveline of an International light truck, while Wolfhound (and the Mastiff and Ridgback it supports) has a monocoque armoured hull. Warthog is a UK variant of the Singapore Technologies Kinetics (STK) Bronco.

The next 'big budget' non-UOR UK vehicle procurement was expected to be Operational Utility Vehicle System (OUVS) a programme that originally set out to replace the entire UK MoD fleet of around 16,000 light utility vehicles. OUVS has previously been covered in detail, the most recent official development being the December 2009 confirmation by Quentin Davies, then Minister for Defence Equipment and Support (DE&S), that the programme had been deferred for two years. Many analysts believed that OUVS would suffer further slippage, possibly re-invention and even cancellation, and that was before the 2010 Strategic Defence and Security Review (SDSR).

Post SDSR there has yet to be any announcement related specifically to OUVS, however, there is little if any chance that it will proceed in anything like its originally intended format. A formal announcement regarding the future structure of the UK MoD's light utility vehicle fleet (and other areas) is anticipated mid-2011, this likely to take into account (among other things) recent and ongoing fleet-wide refurbishment activities.

IVECO is supplying the UK MoD with 15 (including a trials vehicle) (8 × 8) Trakker SLDTs fitted with a KMW-developed ballistic and blast protected cab. As part of its 16-year PFI undertaking for the MoD's C-vehicle fleet, ALC is currently delivering 182 (6 × 6) Trakker range trucks to the MoD
(IVECO)   1391491

Under Project Remus 1 around 6,250 Defender XD (Wolf) Truck Utility Medium (TUM) could be refurbished, extending viable fleet life to around 2030 (Siete Meeter)   1391493

To remain a viable asset during the delay in OUVS some of the oldest Land Rover light vehicles in British Army service, the more than 20 year old pre-Defender XD fleet of Ninety, One-Ten and Defender models required some attention. To address this issue, it was disclosed in mid-2007 that under Project Tithonus, a GBP10 million, three-year programme, that around 3,500 of the 3,950 vehicles that remained in service would be refurbished by ABRO (now Defence Support Group (DSG)). At the conclusion of the project in March 2010 around 1,230 vehicles had been completed.

More recently, under Project Remus 1, plans to refurbish roughly 6,250 of approximately 7,500 Defender XD (Wolf) Truck Utility Light (TUL) and Medium (TUM) vehicles in service have been disclosed, these extending viable fleet service life from 2017 to 2030. At present only the longer (110 inch) wheelbase TUM variant will be refurbished, there being no current plans to refurbish the shorter (90 inch) wheelbase TUL variant. Under Project Shoehorn, around 3,300 TUM variants have earlier received a GVW upgrade from 3,350 to 3,500 kg.

Previously, under Project Epione, a Land Rover Defender XD (Pulse) ambulance fleet (quantity of less than 800) were converted from a four-stretcher to a two-stretcher configuration, while most recently it has been proposed that around 200 surplus XD ambulances could be converted under Project Hebe into a crew-cab utility configuration. Among other roles, these converted vehicles could replace the now-retired Reynolds Boughton RB-44 in the Mortar Section role. Under existing plans, from around 2015 up to a total of 300 XD ambulances may become available for conversion.

The pending replacement of the UK MoD's 2,000-vehicle Demountable Rack Off-loading and Pick-up System (DROPS) is one of a number of programmes that will be affected by the recent Strategic Defence and Security Review (SDSR) (Siete Meeter)   1391494

In addition to the previously covered OUVS, the SDSR will also likely impact on another sizeable UK MoD program that has suffered continued slippage as ongoing operations in Afghanistan place the defence budget under even greater strain. The former Heavy Load Distribution Capability (HLDC), now the 'Non-Articulated Vehicle' Programme (NAVP), is the project to replace the UK MoD's fleet of around 2,000 15,000 kg payload DROPS vehicles. The most recent pre-SDSR update for this programme suggested the service life of the current fleet might be extended a further four years, with the projected new capability due for delivery from 2022, by which time the bulk of the current fleet will be between 28 and 32 years old.

Ultimately though, those previous delays, while unfortunate at the time, will now likely contribute to delivering a NAVP capability better suited to a post-SDSR Army, as similar occurrences will with OUVS.

Running on Empty

Delays in procurement appear to now be almost a given, and with numbers ultimately ordered only ever a fraction of the originally stated requirement. Manufacturers are, of course, wise to this and plan for it when responding to tenders. However, the current economic crisis can only compound matters, further delaying, certainly reducing numbers even further, and doubtless causing the cancellation of some procurements.

The military market may be shrinking, but with the commercial truck sector affected to an even greater extent that the military one, most commercial truck manufacturers with military operations have recently shifted their military enthusiasm up at least one level. Further, some with very little or no military presence pre-downturn, are now actively involved in the sector.

The reasons for these sometimes step-changes in policy become clear when examining commercial truck markets. Despite showing signs of recovery in 2010, European Union (EU) commercial truck sales when compared to pre-crisis levels of 2008 sales were still down 35 per cent year-on-year, while US sales are still recovering from a 47-year low and 50 per cent sales drop between 2006 and 2008.

A good example of what can be achieved by a commercial manufacturer with the right approach to military business, which is generally perceived to be high risk but high return and something you have to be in for the long haul, can be seen in Navistar Defense's recent performance. Since a return to the defence sector in 2003 and receiving its first sizeable contract awards

An Afghan border police supply truck is cross-loaded from a USMC Oshkosh MTVR (Spc Ian Schell (US DoD))   1391495

in 2005, Navistar has accumulated USD7.8 billion worth of defence contracts, these covering an estimated total of 29,000 vehicles.

Another manufacturer that may be poised to make a return to the defence sector is Holland's DAF. DAF was acquired by defence market-shy Paccar of the US in 1996, and since that acquisition the defence market has been a virtual no-go area for DAF, the legacy supplier of trucks to Holland's Armed Forces. However, it should be noted that while defence market-shy, and despite current trading conditions, Paccar recently returned a net profit for the 71st successive year. However, with the delayed Dutch Defence Wide Replacement Operational Wheeled Vehicles programme possible seeing some movement this year, and with production capacity currently to spare, it has been suggested that DAF has again been talking military, if only in a partnering or assembly role.

The original Request For Information (RFI) for the Dutch Defence Wide Replacement Operational Wheeled Vehicles programme, which aims to replace around 8,000 vehicles ranging in size from Airmobile Brigade Light Strike Vehicles to tractor trucks and 10,000 kg-payload heavy trucks, was announced mid-2008, this being followed by a revised RFI in December 2008.

DAF supplied the Dutch military with around 13,000 medium and heavyweight trucks in the 1970s and 80s, these including the DAF YA4442 (4 × 4) 4,000 kg truck (shown) (Shaun C Connors)   1391496

Another European project behind schedule but one that saw movement the day after this Executive Overview was completed is the proposed joint Norwegian/Swedish heavy truck procurement. The initial step was taken in April 2008, when Norway released an RFI that was essentially an information-gathering exercise to determine the projects' feasibility as well as to define its technical and functional requirements, budget and time frame. A procurement RFQ from Norway/Sweden was then expected during 2009, this then deferred to late-2010/2011. The latest developments were the release of a Pre-Qualification Questionnaire (PQQ) to industry in January, with responses due by 8 March 2011. The programme will also be open to the armed forces of Denmark and Finland.

In Germany, GTF, the project to replace the German Army's fleet of MAN Kat 1 high-mobility tactical/combat trucks, originally began in the late 1980s, at which time it is understood to have called for 33,000 new vehicles. Since then the GTF programme has been re-evaluated at least three times and as part of ongoing Bundeswehr reforms which will help meet a required EUR8.3 billion reduction in the defence budget by 2014 and an overall decrease in personnel from 235,000 to 180,000, is likely to be re-evaluated again. This re-evaluation will almost certainly result in a further reduction to the currently required 2,500 new vehicles in four payload classes, and some progress may be made this year.

A large proportion of the German military's non-combat 'green fleet' vehicles are currently supplied PFI-style by BwFuhrparkservice. Deliveries under this arrangement have thus far been distributed with a degree of fairness between key German military suppliers IVECO, MAN and

Norwegian Army vehicles to be replaced under a currently evolving programme include around 1,700 Scania 3-Series delivered between 1986-1995 (Shaun C Connors)   1391497

Mercedes-Benz. The most recent deliveries have included initial batches (150 in 2009, 500 in 2010) of the Mercedes-Benz Unimog, however, few additional deliveries of any vehicle type are expected in the foreseeable future as BwFuhrparkservice is currently working on better utilisation of the current fleet.

Another programme likely to be influenced by recently announced budgetary constraints is Canada's CAD1.22 billion Medium Support Vehicle System (MSVS). MSVS has been covered in JMVL in recent years, and following the award to Navistar during 2008 of the CAD274 million MilCOTS segment, over 1,000 of the 1,300 MilCOTS trucks on order had been delivered by late 2010.

Navistar's MSVS partner, DEW Engineering, was awarded a contract for 895 MSVS Special Equipment Vehicle (SEV) Baseline Shelters (with an option for 110) in late-2009.

The Request For Proposal (RFP) for the MSVS Standard Military Pattern (SMP) fleet has yet to be released, this phase of the programme now running more than two years behind schedule. In a recent *Jane's Defence Weekly* (JDW) story, Colonel Mike Dixon, director of land requirements said the project "is in definition" and that the delay had been caused by "several factors...the main one being getting it right".

MSVS SMP is stated to call for 1,500 SMP trucks, up to 150 armour systems and up to 300 Load Handling System (LHS) equipped trailers. Bidders for MSVS SMP are likely to include BAE Systems, Mercedes-Benz (Daimler), Navistar, Oshkosh and Rheinmetall MAN Military Vehicles GmbH (RMMV), the latter being the 2010 formation by Rheinmetall AG and MAN Nutzfahrzeuge AG of a joint wheeled military vehicles company, a development that may have been financially driven, but one that in other ways certainly highlights the previously covered greying of the centreline between softskin and armoured vehicles.

The strong bias towards local content/participation, and so on, promoted by Canada's Canada First Defence Strategy appears to have backfired somewhat with MSVS. Navistar (which has teamed with TATRA for MSVS SMP) was the sole bidder for the MilCOTS segment and, despite IVECO, Renault and Sisu having proven and suitable vehicles, it appears they will not compete for the SMP requirement.

Down Under
Australia's Land 121 now appears to be back on track following a February 2010 announcement that a down-select to Mercedes-Benz, MAN and Thales had been made. An Offer Definition and Refinement Process (ODRP) then commenced and from that a final preferred bidder is now expected to be announced late 2011.

A total of 925 Mack Model RM6866RS (6 × 6) trucks were delivered to the Australian Army from 1986, these and a fleet of Mercedes-Benz Unimogs are scheduled to be replaced under the medium/heavy segments of Australia's Land 121 requirement (Carl Shulze)   1391498

Following its not insignificant issues, South Africa's Project Vistula also appears to now be back on track and is understood to be due for further movement in the near future. Previously covered in detail throughout JMVL, Vistula is set to relaunch mid-2011 following some five years of delays brought about by allegations of impropriety. Vistula has been revised and it is understood could now call for around 5,000 trucks, with a follow-in interlinked buy of specialist-role trucks, plus a requirement for the Vistula truck driveline to be installed in the approximately 4,000-strong new mine-protected Armoured Personnel Carrier (APC) fleet that could be procured under Project Sapula.

The bidders for the re-run of Vistula, and to a certain extent the product they offer, will most certainly be determined by the detailed wording of the Request For Offer (RFO) which may, or may not, favour those manufacturers and/or the products that were down-selected during the previous round of the competition. In a draft version of this Executive Overview the editors had exceeded 1,000 words simply speculating on the teaming options for Vistula. They therefore elected to act on the reasonably well-known Elizabeth Gaskell utterance of "speculation is the enemy of calm" by waiting until for the release of the previously mentioned RFO before making any further comment.

Specialised vehicles provide key support role
While the bulk of JMVL comprises trucks and other tactical support vehicles, details are also provided of the key Armoured Engineer Vehicles (AEV), Armoured Recovery Vehicles (ARV), unarmoured recovery vehicles and bridging systems without which no army today can operate.

The British Army has successfully deployed its BAE Systems Trojan Engineer Tank System (ETS) to Afghanistan where it has supported British and more recently Afghan and US forces in clearing mines.

Trojan is a multirole ETS that can not only clear minefields with its Python rocket propelled mineclearing system and front mounted plough type mine clearing system but also carry fascines to drop into ditches.

Its hydraulic arm can be fitted with various attachments such as a bucket to clear battlefield obstacles or prepare firing positions.

Prior to deployment to Afghanistan these Trojan ETS were upgraded in a number of key areas to enhance their survivability.

The British Army has also deployed a number of its truck mounted BR90 bridging systems based on a Unipower 8 × 8 truck chassis to Afghanistan and these were also upgraded prior to deployment. This included enhanced crew protection.

British Army BR90 Bridging Vehicle (8 × 8) upgraded for Afghanistan by BAE Global Combat Systems with enhanced crew protected cab (BAE Systems)   1364008

The US Army phased out its M728 Combat Engineer Vehicle (CEV) many years ago. This should have been replaced by the Grizzly vehicle but this was subsequently cancelled.

The US Marine Corps has now fielded its Assault Breacher Vehicle (ABV) based on a surplus General Dynamics Land Systems Abrams Main Battle Tank (MBT) chassis.

This can be rapidly fitted with various types of front mounted mine clearing devices or a combat dozer blade and is also fitted with a rocket propelled mine clearing system.

The ABV has been deployed to Afghanistan by the US Marine Corps and has also been adopted by the US Army providing a much needed boost to its combat engineer capability.

Another role for surplus M1 Abrams MBT chassis is the Joint Assault Bridge (JAB) that is also now a joint US Army/Marine Corps programme having originally been started by the latter.

The German Leopard 2 MBT has now been exported to 16 countries but of these only six countries have purchased new build Rheinmetall Büffel ARV to support these vehicles.

In addition to these six countries two Büffel have been loaned by the German Army to the Canadian Army for deployment to Afghanistan and prior to deployment these were upgraded by Rheinmetall in a number of areas including enhanced survivability.

In mid-2010 the German company of FFG unveiled their Wisent 2 Leopard 2 Support Vehicle as a more cost effective alternative to the procurement of brand new Büffel ARV.

Wisent 2 has been developed as a private venture by FFG who have considerable experience in the overhaul and upgrades of armoured fighting vehicles, including the Leopard 1 ARV.

Wisent 2 is based on a surplus Leopard 2 MBT chassis and has been converted into the specialised Support Vehicle role as an Armoured Recovery Vehicle (ARV).

This is fitted with a new well protected armoured crew compartment at the front left which has been provided with appliqué armour, hydraulic crane, winches and front mounted dozer/stabiliser blade.

Its design is such that it can be converted into the armoured engineer vehicle role in less than 24 hours.

Wisent 2 Leopard 2 Support Vehicle in baseline armoured recovery vehicle configuration and with dozer/stabiliser in travelling position (FFG) 1401380

China North Industries Corporation (NORINCO) continues to develop more specialised versions of their tracked and wheeled armoured vehicles.

To support export sales of their VN1 (8 × 8) amphibious Armoured Personnel Carrier (APC) NORINCO has developed an ARV to recover this and other vehicles.

This is provided with a range of recovery equipment including a roof mounted hydraulic crane for changing engines and powerpacks.

A version of the VN1 is in service with the Peoples Liberation Army as the ZBD-09 Infantry Fighting Vehicle (IFV) which made its first public appearance in Beijing in late 2009.

By late 2010 the German company of Kraus-Maffei Wegmann had built over 700 Dingo 2 (4 × 4) All Protected Vehicle (APV) for the home and export markets with production still underway at its Munich facility.

This is based on the Mercedes-Benz U-5000 (4 × 4) cross country chassis with a well protected central crew compartment that provides the occupants with a high level of protection against a wide range of battlefield threats especially mines and IED.

To recover this and similar vehicles Krauss-Maffei Wegmann has developed, as a private venture the Dingo 2 (6 × 6) recovery vehicle which was shown for the first time in mid-2010.

This is fitted with a full range of recovery equipment and is fitted with the two door protected cab which is also used for the 44 Dingo 2 (4 × 4) battle damage repair vehicles which have recently been delivered to the German Army.

Latest Dingo 2 (6 × 6) recovery vehicle towing a Dingo APV on a suspended tow (Kraus-Maffei Wegmann) 1364322

The Russian T-90 Main Battle Tank (MBT) is currently in service with Algeria, India, Libya, Russia and Turkmenistan and to support this vehicle

the BREM-1M Armoured Repair and Recovery Vehicle (ARRV) has been developed based on the same chassis.

For its specialised mission the BREM-1M ARRV is fitted with a front mounted dozer/stabiliser blade, winches and a hydraulic crane for changing complete vehicle power packs.

By late 2010, General Dynamics Land Systems facilities in Canada and the United States had delivered over 3,550 Stryker (8 × 8) Infantry Carrier Vehicles (ICV) and variants to the US Army with production expected to continue for some years to come.

In addition to the M1126 ICV there are nine specialised versions of the Stryker but no dedicated maintenance recovery vehicle. This means that the Stryker has to be recovered by other vehicles that may not have the same level of protection and mobility.

To meet the potential requirements of the US Army, General Dynamics Land Systems has designed and built the Stryker Maintenance and Recovery Vehicle which has the same level of protection and mobility as the Stryker ICV.

The People's Liberation Army (PLA) has been introducing much heavier tracked and wheeled armoured vehicles into service, hence the development and fielding of enhanced bridging systems.

NORINCO is now marketing this 60T Modified Heavy Mechanised Bridge which is transported and launched from a locally produced Mercedes-Benz (8 × 8) cross-country truck chassis.

When in position each bridge element has an overall length of 15 m and can take tracked vehicles weighing up to 60 tonnes. Five systems can be used to bridge a wet or dry gap up of up 75 m.

60T Modified Heavy Mechanised Bridge being positioned over an already deployed bridge starting (NORINCO) 1421662

NORINCO is also marketing the Light Companying Bridge (LCB) which is very similar in concept to the German Rapidly Emplaced Bridge System (REBS).

The latter is now in service with the US Army to support its Stryker Brigade Combat Teams which is based on a member of the Oshkosh Heavy Expanded Mobility Tactical Truck (HEMTT).

The three part bridge of the NORINCO LCB is transported and launched over the rear of a locally manufactured Mercedes-Benz cross-country truck chassis.

When fully extended the three part bridge can span a gap of up to 20.5 m and take tracked vehicles weighing up to 22 tonnes. The German REBS has a higher load capacity for tracked and wheeled vehicles than its German counterpart.

The Polish OBRUM MS-20 Daglezja Towed Support Bridge has been developed to meet the requirements of the Polish Army and is towed and launched over the rear of a 6 × 6 tractor truck.

The scissors type bridge has an overall length of 23 m when opened out and cap span wet or dry gaps of up to 21 m and take tracked vehicles weighing up to 63.5 tonnes.

Force Protection has built large quantities of Cougar (4 × 4) mine protected vehicles for the home and export markets and these provide their occupants with a high level of protection against a variety of battlefield threats, especially mines and IED.

The Cougar Tactical Support Vehicle has been developed as a private venture and is fitted with two door well protected crew compartment and to the rear of this is a flatbed on which cargo can be carried up to a maximum stated load of nine tonnes.

Shaun C Connors
Christopher F Foss

Acknowledgements

Acknowledgements

One of the last and most important parts of any Executive Overview preparation is remembering to extend thanks to the many individuals and corporate entities without whose invaluable help and assistance there would be no content and by default no requirement for any Executive Overview. Any attempt to name all those whose contributions have helped in the compilation of this edition of *Jane's Military Vehicles and Logistics* would certainly fail: people would inevitably be forgotten or overlooked, even assuming that page space could be found to list each and every individual, no matter the size of their contribution. Thus, to those not mentioned in the following shortlist of people whose continuing advice and assistance has proved invaluable to the editors, we offer our apologies together with our sincere thanks. There would be no *Jane's Military Vehicles and Logistics* without your continued support.

Our special thanks go to Gordon Arthur, Victor Manuel Saraiva Barreira, Scott R. Gourley, Inigo Guevara, José Higuera, Grzegorz Holdanowicz, Mitsuhiro Kadota, James Kinnear, Dzirhan Mahadzir, Stefan Marx, Martin Pagh, Pedro Paulo Rezende, Carl Schulze, Cesar Cruz Tantalean, Pierre Touzin, Dawei Xia, Ian C Young and Periklis Zorzovilis.

Additionally, we thank all those involved in the production and printing processes, especially Mel Rovery, Neil Gibson and the Content Editing team; Colin Maslin whose IT skills I only wish were mine; Patrick Allen for his superb images; and Sara Morgan, Director, EMEA Editing and Design, who is the first person to be yelled at when things go wrong. We must also thank the many *Jane's* reference and magazine editors and staff who readily made their individual research and material available for use in *Jane's Military Vehicles and Logistics*.

User comments

It is often written at the end of a Executive Overview in a factual title such as this, that the Editors would welcome any additional information, corrections, updates or comments regarding content. That is very much the case regarding all entries in this Yearbook and please direct any correspondence regarding content you may have to the Editors at *Jane's Military Vehicles and Logistics*, IHS Jane's, Sentinel House, 163 Brighton Road, Coulsdon, Surrey CR5 2YH, UK. Tel: (+44) 208 700 3700; Fax: (+44) 208 700 3900; e-mail: yearbook@janes.com

Shaun C Connors

Shaun Connors is one of the lucky few who have had the opportunity to turn a life-long interest and hobby into a career. From childhood through his early working years in a non defence-related section of industry his interest in military vehicles and logistics developed, and it was the by-chance commissioning of his first defence-related magazine article in 1991 that effectively began his transition from hobby to profession. There followed numerous further articles on military logistic vehicle-based subjects for a wide variety of international magazines (including a variety of *IHS Jane's* titles), national newspapers and contributions to books before Shaun took up the post of co-editor of *Jane's Military Vehicles and Logistics* from Terry Gander, in April 2001.

As Editor of *Jane's Armour and Artillery,* Christopher Foss will continue to be responsible for armoured repair vehicles, armoured recovery vehicles, mechanised bridges and all-terrain carriers and prime movers, leaving Shaun to concentrate on his core interests of transport and logistical support equipment.

In 20 years of industry involvement, and in addition to writing and professional photography, Shaun has also undertaken a number of industry and governmental consultations and gained 'hands-on' experience of a wide variety of in-service and developmental military vehicles and equipment, manufactured and in-service worldwide.

Christopher F Foss

Christopher F Foss is the Editor of *Jane's Armour and Artillery* and Co-Editor of *Jane's Armour and Artillery Upgrades, Jane's Land-Based Air Defence* and *Jane's Military Vehicles and Logistics*; he is also the Land Consultant for *Jane's Defence Weekly* and *Jane's International Defence Review.*

Christopher F Foss began his association with *Jane's* as early as 1970, when he began writing for *Jane's Weapon Systems.* Since 1979 he has acted as a self-employed contractor with the company and with a number of other organisations and companies throughout the world. His achievements have included conceiving and editing *Jane's Defence Review,* the first magazine ever produced by Jane's Information Group, and proposing and launching *Jane's Missiles and Rockets.*

He has written numerous books relating to armoured vehicles and weapons systems both for *IHS Jane's* and for other publishers. He has also lectured in a number of countries and has chaired many conferences.

IHS Jane's Users' Charter

This publication is brought to you by IHS Jane's, a global company drawing on more than 100 years of history and an unrivalled reputation for impartiality, accuracy and authority.

Our collection and output of information and images is not dictated by any political or commercial affiliation. Our reportage is undertaken without fear of, or favour from, any government, alliance, state or corporation.

We publish information that is collected overtly from unclassified sources, although much could be regarded as extremely sensitive or not publicly accessible.

Our validation and analysis aims to eradicate misinformation or disinformation as well as factual errors; our objective is always to produce the most accurate and authoritative data.

In the event of any significant inaccuracies, we undertake to draw these to the readers' attention to preserve the highly valued relationship of trust and credibility with our customers worldwide.

If you believe that these policies have been breached by this title, you are invited to contact the editor.

A copy of IHS Jane's Code of Conduct for its editorial teams is available from the publisher.

Glossary

AARADCOM	Army Armament Research and Development Command
AAT	All Arms Trencher
AAV	Assault Amphibian Vehicle
AAVP	Assault Amphibian Vehicle Personnel
AAVR	Assault Amphibian Vehicle Recovery
ABLE	Automotive Bridge Launching Equipment
ABS	Anti-lock Brake System
ABS(T)	Amphibious Bridging System (Tracked)
ACE	Armored Combat Earthmover
ACEATM	Aimed Controlled Effect Anti-tank Mine
ACP	Airfield Clearance Plough
ACPM	*Anti-Char à Pose Mecanique*
ACRV	Armoured Command and Reconnaissance Vehicle
ACT	Air-portable Cargo Trailer
ADAM	Area Denial Artillery Munition
ADS	Ammunition Delivery System
AEC	Associated Equipment Company
AEV	Armoured Engineer Vehicle
AFARV	Armored Forward Area Rearm Vehicle
AFB	Axial Folding Bridge
AFDE	Arctic Fuels Dispensing Equipment
AFV	Armoured Fighting Vehicle
Ah	Ampère hour
AHE	Ammunition Handling Equipment
AHM	Anti-Helicopter Mine
ALB	Automatic Load-dependent Brake
ALSV	Advanced Light Strike Vehicle
AMIDS	Airborne Minefield Detection System
AMMAD	Anti-Magnetic Mine Actuation Device
AMMAS	Advanced Minefield Marking System
AMS	Air Management System
AMTV	Armoured Medical Treatment Vehicle
AMV	Armored Maintenance Vehicle
AMX	*Atelier de Construction d'Issy-les-Moulineaux*
APC	Armoured Personnel Carrier
APFC	Air-Portable Fuel Container
APU	Auxiliary Power Unit
ARCE	Amphibious River Crossing Equipment
ARGES	Automatic Rocket Guardian with Electronic Sensor
ARM	Artillery Rearm Module
ARMS	Armoured Resupply Maintenance System
ARRV	Armoured Recovery and Repair Vehicle
ARV	Armoured Recovery Vehicle
ASF	Army Standard Family (shelters)
ASM	Armored Systems Modernization
ASTAMIDS	Airborne Standoff Minefield Detection System
AT	Anti-Tank
ATAC	All-Terrain All Climate
ATAC	All-Terrain Amphibious Carrier
ATGW	Anti-Tank Guided Weapon
ATIS	Anti-Tank Influence Sensor
ATLAS	All-Terrain Lifter Army System
ATMDS	Anti-Tank Mine-Dispensing System
ATMID	All-Terrain Mine Detector
ATMP	All-Terrain Mobile Platform
ATS	*Atelier de Construction de Tarbes*
ATTD	Advanced Technology Test Demonstrator
ATV	All-Terrain Vehicle
AV	American Version
AVE	Armoured Vehicle for Engineers
AVLB	Armoured Vehicle-Launched Bridge
AVRE	Assault Vehicle Royal Engineers
BAP	Bridge Adaptor Pallet
BARC	Beach Amphibious Resupply Cargo
BARV	Beach Armoured Recovery Vehicle
BBE	Bridge Boat Erection
BEML	Bharat Earth Movers Limited
BFTA	Bulk Fuel Tank Assembly
bhp	brake horse power
BLT	Bridge Laying Tank
BLU	Bomb Live Unit
BRE	Battlefield Recovery and Evacuation
BS	British Standard(s)
CALM	Crane Attachment Lorry Mounted
CAMIS	Computer Aided Munition Identification System
CBT	Common Bridge Transporter
CBU	Cluster Bomb Unit
CCFP	Competitive Concept Formulation Phase
CCE	Commercial Construction Equipment
CCSLEP	Chaparral Chassis Service Life Extension Program
cd	candela
CEC	*Couverture d'Emplacement de Combat*

CEE	Combat Emplacement Excavator
CEP	Concept Evaluation Program
CET	Combat Engineer Tractor
CFM	Crane, Field, Medium
CFRP	Carbon Fibre Reinforced Plastic
CFV	Cavalry Fighting Vehicle
CHU	Container Handling Unit
CIS	Commonwealth of Independent States
CKD	Component Knock-Down
CLAMS	Clear Lane Marking System
CLD	*Camion Lourd de Depannage*
CLEWP	Cleared Lane Explosive Widening Path charge
CLK	Container Lift Kit
CMV	Counter Mobility Vehicle
COCT	Cab-Over Cargo Truck
COE	Cab-Over Engine
COV	Counter Obstacle Vehicle
CP	Command Post
CPP	Cambridge Parallel Processing
CRB	Capsill Roller Beam
CRDA	Co-operative Research and Development Agreement
CRRC	Combat Rubber Raiding Craft
CSB	Combat Support Boat
CSF	Combined Service Forces
CST	Combat Support Trailer
CTIS	Central Tyre Inflation System
CUCV	Commercial Utility Cargo Vehicle
CVR(T)	Combat Vehicle Reconnaissance (Tracked)
DAP	Distributed Array Processor
DARPA	Defense Advanced Research Projects Agency
DAT	*Direction des Armements Terrestres*
dB	decibel
DBP	Draw Bar Pull
DCU	Dispenser Control Unit
DEF.STAN	Defence Standard
DERA	Defence Evaluation and Research Agency
DEU	Deployment and Emplacement Unit
DEUCE	Deployable Universal Combat Earthmover
DIN	*Deutsche Industrie Normen*
DMPI	Digital Magnetic Pulse Induction
DRES	Defence Research Establishment Suffield
DROPS	Demountable Rack Off-loading and Pick-up System
EBG	*Engin Blindé de Génie* (combat engineer tractor)
ECV	Expanded Capacity Vehicle
EFP	Explosively Formed Projectile
ELCAS	Elevated Causeway
EMD	Engineering and Manufacturing Development
EMI	ElectroMagnetic Interference
EMP	ElectroMagnetic Pulse
EMP	Engineering Mine Plough
EMS	Enhanced Mobility System
ENS	Explosive Neutralization System
EOD	Explosive Ordnance Disposal
EPP	Electric Power Plant
EPU	Electrical Power Unit
ERAM	Extended Range Anti-armor Munition
ERV	Electronic Repair Vehicle
ESAB	Extended Span Assault Bridge
ESBL	Extended Span BridgeLayer
ESMB	Explosive Standoff Minefield Breacher
ESP	Extended Service Program(me)
EWK	EisenWerke Kaiserslautern
EWT	Engineer Wheeled Tractor
FAALS	Forward Area Armored Logistic System
FAASV	Field Artillery Ammunition Support Vehicle
FAC	Fast Attack Craft
FAC	Forward Air Controller
FAE	Fuel-Air Explosive
FAMV	Forward Area Multipurpose Vehicle
FARE	Forward Area Refuelling Equipment
FARV-A	Fully integrated armored rearm
FASCAM	Family of Scatterable Mines
FAST	Forward Area Support Team
FAV	Fast Attack Vehicle
FAWPSS	Forward Area Water Point Supply System
FCS	Field-expedient mineclearing system
FCS	Fire-Control System
FCVP	Future Cargo Vehicle Project
FDC	Fire Direction Centre
FEBA	Forward Edge of the Battle Area
FFLAV	Future Family Light Armoured Vehicles
FFR	Fitted For Radio

FLIR	Forward Looking Infra-Red		**JSOR**	Joint Service Operation Requirement
FLPT	Fork Lift Pallet Trailer		**KERR**	Kinetic Energy Recovery Rope
FMS	Foreign Military Sales		**KHD**	Klockner-Humboldt-Deutz
FMTV	Family of Medium Tactical Vehicles		**KIFV**	Korean Infantry Fighting Vehicle
FMU	Folding Medical Unit		**kN**	kilonewton
FN	Fabrique Nationale		**kT**	kiloton
FNNH	Fabrique Nationale Nouvelle Herstal		**kW**	kilowatt
FOCOS	Foam Overhead Cover Support system		**LAA**	Light Anti-Aircraft
FOM	*Forces d'Outre Mer*		**LAAG**	Light Anti-Aircraft Gun
FOPS	Falling Object Protective Structure		**LAB**	Light Assault Bridge
FRG	Federal Republic of Germany		**LACH**	Lightweight Amphibious Container Handler
FRS-H	Forward Repair System Heavy		**LAD**	Light Aid Detachment
FSB	*Faltschwimmbrucke*		**LAF**	Light Assault Ferry
FUE	First Unit Equipped		**LAPES**	Low Altitude Parachute Extraction System
FV	Fighting Vehicle		**LAR**	Light Artillery Rocket
FVS	Fighting Vehicle System		**LARC**	Lighter Amphibious Resupply Cargo
FWAM	Full Width Attack Mine		**LAV**	Light Armoured Vehicle
FWD	Four-Wheel Drive		**LAW**	Light Anti-armour Weapon
FWMP	Full Width Mine Plough		**LCCV**	Light Cross-Country Vehicle
FY	Fiscal Year		**LCD**	Liquid Crystal Display
GCS	Ground Control Station		**LCP**	Line-Carrying Projectile
GCW	Gross Combination Weight		**LED**	Light-Emitting Diode
GDLS	General Dynamics Land Systems		**LFV**	Light Forces Vehicle
GEMSS	Ground-Emplaced Mine-Scattering System		**LHD**	Left-Hand Drive
GLCM	Ground-Launched Cruise Missile		**LIMAS**	Lightweight Marking System
GMC	General Motors Corporation		**LIME**	Light In-stride Mine Extractor
GPM	Gallons Per Minute		**LMD**	Light Mobile Digger
GPM	*Gepanzerte Pioniermaschine*		**LMG**	Light Machine Gun
GPMG	General Purpose Machine Gun		**LMMSA**	Lightweight Modular Multipurpose Spanning Assembly
GPR	Ground Penetrating Radar		**LMS**	Lightweight Multipurpose Shelter
GPS	Global Positioning System		**LMTV**	Light Medium Tactical Vehicle
GRP	Glass-Reinforced Plastic		**LMTVT**	Light Medium Tactical Vehicle Trailer
GV	Giant Viper		**LOTS**	Logistics Over The Shore
GVW	Gross Vehicle Weight		**LPC**	Launch Pod Container
GW	Guided Weapon		**LPDK**	Lightweight, Portable Demolition Kit
HAB	Heavy Assault Bridge		**LSA**	Logistic Support Analysis
HB	Heavy Barrel		**LSV**	Light Strike Vehicle
HDRV	Heavy-Duty Recovery Vehicle		**LSV**	Logistic Supply Vehicle
HDSB	Heavy Dry Support Bridge		**LSV**	Logistic Support Vehicle
HE	High Explosive		**LSVW**	Light Support Vehicle Wheeled
HEAT	High Explosive Anti-Tank		**LTRS**	Light Tactical Recovery System
HELBAT	Human Engineering Laboratory, Battalion Artillery Test		**LVS**	Logistic Vehicle System
HEMAT	Heavy Expanded Mobility Ammunition Trailer		**LVT**	Landing Vehicle Tracked
HEMTT	Heavy Expanded Mobility Tactical Truck		**LWB**	Long WheelBase
HESH	High Explosive Squash Head		**LWCSS**	LightWeight Camouflage Screen System
HESV	Heavy Engineer Support Vehicle		**MAB**	Medium Assault Bridge
HET	Heavy Equipment Transporter		**MAB**	Mobile Assault Bridge
HGMS	Heavy Ground Mobility System		**MACH**	Mechanically Assisted Construction by Hand
HGV	Heavy Goods Vehicle		**MACI**	Military Adaption of Commercial Items
HLVW	Heavy Logistic Vehicle - Wheeled		**MACI**	*Mine Anti-Char Indetectable*
HMBS	High-Mobility on Board System		**MACPED**	*Mine Anti-Char Pointable à Effet Dirigé*
HMD	Helicopter Mine Dispenser		**MACS**	Magnetic Countermine System
HMMHE	High-Mobility Material Handling Equipment		**MARRS**	Modular Armoured Repair and Recovery System
HMMWV	High-Mobility Multipurpose Wheeled Vehicle		**MARS**	Military Amphibious Reconnaissance System
HMRT	Heavy Material Recovery Team		**MAV**	Maintenance Assist Vehicle
HMT	High Mobility Trailer		**MBB**	Messerschmitt-Bölkow-Blohm (now part of DaimlerChrysler Aerospace)
HMTT	High Mobility Tactical Truck		**MBT**	Main Battle Tank
Hp	Horse power		**MCAP**	MineClearing/Armor Protection
HPD	*Haut Pouvoir de Destruction*		**MCBS**	MineClearing Blade System
HRV	Heavy Repair Vehicle		**MCESS**	Marine Corps Expeditionary Shelter System
HSEV	High-Speed Engineering Vehicle		**MCS**	Mobile Camouflage System
HTR	Heat Transfer Reduction		**MDK**	*Mashina dorozhnoy kopatelnoy*
HTT	Heavy Tracked Tractor		**MDR**	*Moyen de Deminage Rapide*
HUMS	Health Usage Monitoring System		**MDV**	Mine Detection Vehicle
HVSS	Horizontal Volute Spring Suspension		**MEDDS**	Mechem Explosive and Drug Detection System
Hz	Hertz		**MERADCOM**	Mobility Equipment Research and Development Command
IDA	Improved Dogbone Assembly		**MET**	Medium Equipment Transporter
IFAV	Interim Fast Attack Vehicle		**MEV**	Medical Evacuation Vehicle
IFP	ISO Compatible Palletised Flatrack		**MEXE**	Military Engineering Experimental Establishment
IFV	Infantry Fighting Vehicle		**MG**	Machine Gun
ILDP	Improved Landmine Detection Project		**MGB**	Medium Girder Bridge
ILS	Integrated Logistic Support		**MHAB**	MultiHop Assault Bridge
IMF	Improved Mine Fuze		**MHC**	Materials Handling Crane
IMMLC	Improved Medium Mobility Load Class		**MIACAH**	*Mine Anti-Char d'Action Horizontale*
IMR	*Inzhenernaia Maschina Razgrazhdeniia*		**MICLIC**	Mineclearing Line Charge
IOC	Initial Operational Capability		**MICV**	Mechanised Infantry Combat Vehicle
IOD	Improvised Ordnance Disposal		**MIDAP**	Minefield Detection Algorithm and Processor
IOTE	Initial Operational Test and Evaluation		**MIL**	Military
IPDS	Inland Petroleum Distribution System		**MIMID**	Miniature Mine Detector
IR	InfraRed		**MINDER**	Mine Detection, Neutralisation and Route Proving System
IRR	InfraRed Radiation		**MIRADOR**	Minefield Reconnaissance and Detector System
IRV	Improved Recovery Vehicle		**MiWS**	*Minenwerfersystem*
ISC	Infantry Section Carrier		**MLAB**	Manually Launched Assault Bridge
ISO	International Standards Organisation		**MLC**	Military Load Class
ITT	Invitation To Tender		**MLI**	Mid-Life Improvement
IVECO	Industrial Vehicle Corporation			
JGSDF	Japanese Ground Self-Defence Force			
JSFU	Joint Services Flail Unit			

MLRS	Multiple Launch Rocket System	RF	Radio Frequency
MLSV	Military Logistic Support Vehicle	RFI	Radio Frequency Interference
MLVW	Medium Logistic Vehicle Wheeled	RFI	Request For Information
MMD	Minimum Metal Detector	RFO	Request For Offer
MMLC	Medium Mobility Load Carrier	RFP	Request For Proposals
MMST	Multifunction Medium-Sized Tent	RFQ	Request For Quotation
MMSV	Multipurpose Maintenance and Shop Van	RHD	Right-Hand Drive
MMW	Medium Multipurpose Wheeled	RLC	Royal Logistical Corps
MoD	Ministry of Defence	RLT	Rolling Liquid Transporter
MOPMS	Modular Pack Mine System	RMDS	Robotic Mine Detection System
MoT	Ministry of Transport	RMID	Road Mine Detector
MR	Mine Roller	ROMANS	Rapid Operational Minefield Attack and Neutralisation System
MRAV	MultiRole Armoured Vehicle		
MRCV	MultiRole Combat Vehicle	ROPS	RollOver Protective Structure
MRT	Mobile Repair Team	RORS	Rapid Ordnance Removal System
MRTFL	Medium Rough Terrain ForkLift	ROWPU	Reverse Osmosis Water Purification Unit
MRV	Maintenance-Recovery Vehicle	RP	Route Proving
MSCD	MultiSpectral Camouflage Dress	rpm	revolutions per minute
MSG	*Minensuchgerat*	RPV	Remotely Piloted Vehicle
MSMW	*Minenstreumittel-Werfer*	RRR	Rapid Runway Repair
MT	MegaTon	RSH	*Reservoirs Souples Heliportable*
MTS	MultiTrack System	RSME	Royal School of Military Engineering
MTT	Medium Tactical Truck	RTE	Rail Transfer Equipment
MTU	*Motoren-und Turbinen-Union*	RTFL	Rough Terrain ForkLift
MTV	Medium Tactical Vehicle	SACC	Small Area Camouflage Cover
MTVT	Medium Tactical Vehicle Trailer	SAD	Safety and Arming Device
MVEE	Military Vehicles and Engineering Establishment	SAE	Society of Automotive Engineers
MVP	Motor Vehicle Plant	SAM	Surface-to-Air Missile
MWT	Medium Wheeled Tractor	SAPIR	Sensor Active Passive Infra-Red
NATO	North Atlantic Treaty Organisation	SAPLIC	Small Arms Projected Line Charge
NBC	Nuclear, Biological, Chemical	SAS	*Schnellbrucke Auf Stutzen*
NDI	Non-Developmental Item	SAVA	Standard Army Vectronics Architecture
OEF	Operation Enduring Freedom	SEE	Small Emplacement Excavator
OEM	Original Equipment Manufacturer	SEP	System Enhancement Package
OEW	Ordnance and Explosive Waste	SEV	Specially Equipped Vehicle
OFC	Overhead Foxhole Cover	SFC	Soldier Fighting Cover
OHC	OverHead Cam shaft	shp	shaft horse power
OHV	OverHead Valve	SICPS	Standardised Integrated Command Post Shelter
OIF	Operation Iraqi Freedom	SLEP	Service Life Extension Program(me)
OP	Observation Post	SLUFAE	Surface-Launched Unit, Fuel-Air Explosive
ORATMS	Off-Route Anti-Tank Mine System	SMP	Surface Mine Plough
OSV	Over-snow Strike/Support Vehicle	SMS	Scatterable Mine System
OVE	Onboard Vehicle Equipment	SOS	Switch On and Search
Pa	Pascal	SOV	Special Operations Vehicle
PAA	*Pont Automoteur d'Accompagnement*	SPB	Section Personnel Bridge
PADS	Position Attack Defence System	SPG	Self-Propelled Gun
PARM	*Panzerabwehr-Richtmine*	SRDE	Signals Research and Development Establishment
PBX	Plastic Bonded eXplosive		
PDM	Pursuit Deterrent Mine	SS	Surface-to-Surface
PE	Plastic Explosive	SSD	Sensor Safety Device
PETN	Pentaerythritetranitrate	SSM	Surface-to-Surface Missile
pF	picofarad	STB	Short Trackway Bridge
PF	Pocket Filter	STEFVS	Simplified Test Equipment Fighting Vehicle System
PFC	Parapet Foxhole Cover		
PFM	*Pont Flottant Motorisé*	STORM	Sensored Tactical Off-Road Mine
PFT	Prefabricated Foxhole - Twin	SUMMADE	System Universal Modular Mine And Demolition Explosives
PI	Product Improvement		
PIMD	Pulse Induction Mine Detector	SUSV	Small Unit Support Vehicle
PIP	Product Improvement Programme	SUU	Suspended Underwing Unit
PLS	Palletised Load System	SWB	Short WheelBase
POL	Petrol, Oil and Lubricants	SWG	Standard Wire Gauge
POMINS	Portable Mine Neutralisation System	SWL	Safe Working Load
POP	Pipeline Outfit, Petroleum	TAB	Towed Assault Bridge
PSA	Prefabricated Surface, Aluminium	TACOM	Tank Automotive and Armaments Command
psi	pounds per square inch	TAD	Trailing Arm Drive
PTO	Power Take-Off	TAR	Tactical Aircraft Refueller
pvc	polyvinyl chloride	TARADCOM	Tank Automotive Research and Development Command
RAAC	Royal Australian Armoured Corps		
RAAMS	Remote Anti-Armor Mine System	TBT	Tank Bridge Transporter
RAC	Royal Armoured Corps	TCC	Temporary Camouflage Coating
RACE	Rapid Area Clearance Equipment	TD	Tank Destroyer
RAE	Royal Aircraft Establishment	TDP	Technology Demonstration Programme
RAE	Royal Australian Engineers	TECOM	Test and Evaluation Command
RAMBS	Rapid Anti-personnel Minefield Breaching System	TEG	Thermo-Electric Generator
RAP	Regimental Aid Post	TEXS	Tactical Explosive System
RARDE	Royal Armament Research and Development Establishment	TFR	Tank Ferry Raft
		THAAD	Theatre High-Altitude Air Defense Missile
RARDE(C)	Royal Armament Research and Development Establishment (Christchurch)	TILOS	Tangram Integrated Logistic System
		TLB	Trailer-Launched Bridge
RATT	Rescue All-Terrain Transport	T/MDV	Towing/Mine Detection Vehicle
RBEB	Ribbon Bridge Erection Boat	TNA	Thermal Neutron Activation
RCATV	Remote Control, All-Terrain Vehicle	TNT	Trinitrotoluene
RCT	Royal Corps of Transport	TOC	Tactical Operations Centre
R&D	Research and Development	TPT	Tactical Petroleum Terminal
RDB	Rapid Deployment Bridge	TQG	Tactical Quiet Generator
RDV	Remote Detection Vehicle	TRACER	Tactical Reconnaissance Armoured Combat Equipment Requirement
RE	Royal Engineers		
REME	Royal Electrical and Mechanical Engineers	TRM	*Toutes Roues Motrices*
REMIDS	Remote Minefield Detection System	TROSS	Technical and Rear Operations Support System

TRTG	Tactical Radar Threat Generator	**VAMIDS**	Vehicular Array Mine Detection System
TU	Towed Unit	**VCG**	*Véhicule de Combat du Génie*
TUH	Truck, Utility, Heavy	**VCI**	*Véhicule de Combat d'Infanterie*
TUL	Truck, Utility, Light	**VCR-AT**	*Véhicule de Combat à Roues - Atelier Technique*
TUM	Truck, Utility, Medium	**VEMASID**	Vehicle Magnetic Signature Duplicator
TWDS	Tactical Water Distribution System	**VLRA**	*Véhicule Léger de Reconnaissance et d'Appui*
TWMP	Track Width Mine Plough	**VLSMS**	Vehicle-Launched Scatterable Mine System
TWVMP	Tactical Wheeled Vehicle Modernization Plan	**VLTT**	*Véhicule de Liaison Tout Terrain*
UAV	Unmanned Aerial (air) Vehicle	**VMB**	Vickers Modular Bridge
UBLE	Universal Bridge Launching Equipment	**VMMD**	Vehicle Mounted Mine Detector
UET	Universal Engineer Tractor	**VMRMDS**	Vehicle-Mounted Road Mine Detector System
UK	United Kingdom	**vpm**	vibrations per minute
ULC	Unit Load Container	**VRRTFL**	Variable Reach Rough Terrain ForkLift
ULCANS	Ultra Lightweight Camouflage Net System	**VRRTFLT**	Variable Reach Rough Terrain ForkLift Truck
ULCAS	Ultra Lightweight Camouflage Screen	**VSD**	Vehicle Signature Duplicator
UMIDS	Universal Mine-Dispensing System	**VSTOL**	Vertical Short Take-Off and Landing
UNPROFOR	United Nations Protection Force	**VTL**	Vehicle Tactical Logistic
UOR	Urgent Operational Requirement	**VVSS**	Vertical Volute Spring Suspension
USA	United States of America	**WAM**	Wide Area Mine
UV	Ultra-Violet	**WASPM**	Wide Area Side-Penetrating Mine
UWBSAR	Ultra Wide Band Synthetic Aperture Radar	**WCP**	Water Carriage Pack
UXO	Unexploded Ordnance/Object	**WHO**	World Health Organisation
VAB	*Véhicule de l'Avant Blindé*	**WMIK**	Weapons Mount Installation Kit
VAB	Vickers Armoured Bridgelayer	**ZF**	*Zahnradfabrik Friedrichshafen*

Other products available from IHS Jane's

defence

Aero-Engines
Aircraft Component Manufacturers
Aircraft Upgrades
Air-Launched Weapons
All the World's Aircraft
Ammunition Handbook
Amphibious and Special Forces
Armour and Artillery
Armour and Artillery Upgrades
Avionics
C4I Systems
Defence Equipment and Technology Intelligence Centre
Defence Forecasts – Combat Vehicle Programmes
Defence Forecasts – Military Aircraft Programmes
Defence Forecasts – Military Vessel Programmes
Defence Industry
Defence Industry and Markets Intelligence Centre
Defence Weekly
DS Forecast
Electronic Mission Aircraft
Electro-Optic Systems
Explosive Ordnance Disposal
Fighting Ships
Helicopter Markets and Systems
High-Speed Marine Transportation
Infantry Weapons
International ABC Aerospace Directory
International Defence Directory
International Defence Review
Industry Quarterly
Land-Based Air Defence
Marine Propulsion
Military Communications
Military Vehicles and Logistics
Mines and Mine Clearance
Missiles and Rockets
Naval Construction and Retrofit Markets
Naval Weapon Systems
Navy International
Nuclear, Biological and Chemical Defence
Radar and Electronic Warfare Systems
Simulation and Training Systems
Space Systems and Industry
Strategic Weapon Systems

defence, cont.

Underwater Warfare Systems
Unmanned Aerial Vehicles and Targets
Unmanned Ground Vehicles and Systems
Unmanned Maritime Vehicles and Systems
World Air Forces
World Armies
World Defence Industry
World Navies

law enforcement

The Beat Officer's Companion
Part 1 Promotion Crammer for Sergeants and Inspectors
Part 2 Pass for Promotion for Sergeants and Inspectors
Police and Homeland Security Equipment
Police Review
The Scottish Beat Officer's Companion
The Traffic Officer's Companion

security

Chemical, Biological, Radiological and Nuclear Assessments
Country Risk Daily Report
Homeland Security Review
Intelligence Review
Intelligence Weekly
Islamic Affairs Analyst
Military and Security Assessments Intelligence Centre
Sentinel Country Risk Assessments
Terrorism and Events Spatial Layer
Terrorism and Insurgency Centre
Terrorism and Security Monitor
Terrorism Watch Report
World Insurgency and Terrorism

transport

Air Traffic Control
Airport Review
Airports and Handling Agents
Airports, Equipment and Services
Merchant Ships
Transport Finance
Transport Library
Urban Transport Systems
World Railways

discover more

IHS Jane's

Asia	Europe and Africa	North/Central/South America
Tel: (+65) 65 76 53 00	Tel: (+44 20) 87 00 37 00	Tel: (+1 800) 824 07 68

How to use

Content
This product covers the full range of military vehicles in any way connected with the logistical effort of armed forces around the world, ranging from armoured engineer vehicles to mine warfare equipment, and from trucks to bridging systems.

Structure
This publication has been laid out in a series of principal sections grouped under main functional headings, each of which relates to a particular item of equipment or vehicle. The exact headings and groupings can be seen on the Contents page.

Record structure
The following main headings are used within each record:

Development
Where applicable this heading covers the history of the development of a specified item of equipment up to the point where it entered service and, in some instances, details of any major development after entry into service.

Description
Under this heading a detailed technical description is given of each system, in so far as military and commercial confidentiality allows. Where equipments integrate with other equipment or systems, this is noted.

Specifications
Under this heading the main technical parameters of systems are listed, including length and weight, operating parameters (where available) and, in the case of weapons, destructive charge and so on.

Status
This lists the current status of the system - that is, under development, on order, undergoing trials and so on and where known, a note of the users of the equipment.

Contractor
Brief details of main contractor(s).

Images
Photographs are provided for each equipment wherever possible. Line drawings and graphics are also provided in some cases. Images are annotated with a seven digit number which uniquely identifies them in IHS Jane's image database.

Other information
If any particular item of equipment or vehicle is needed, each heading is laid out in country order. In most cases the latest items are mentioned first, but when relating to vehicles, usually the payload weight order is followed, from the lightest up to the heaviest. If only a designation is available, the index should be consulted.

ARMOURED ENGINEER VEHICLES

ARMOURED ENGINEER VEHICLES

Austria

General Dynamics European Land Systems - Steyr Engineer Tank 4KH7FA-AVE Greif

Development

The Steyr-Daimler-Puch Engineer Tank 4KH7FA-AVE Greif, also known as the Steyr Armoured Vehicle for Engineers (AVE) is a further development of the Steyr 4KH7FA-B Greif ARV. Production of the Greif has been completed and it is no longer marketed.

The AVE entered Austrian Army service in 1988 where it is known as the Pionierpanzer 4KH7FA-Pi.

The Austrian Army took delivery of 19 vehicles with the only export customer being Tunisia who took delivery of two AVE. This vehicle is a member of the Steyr-Daimler-Puch 4KH7FA series of light tracked vehicles.

The Austrian Army still operates a number of the older generation 4K 4FA series of armoured personnel carriers, which were developed to meet their operational requirements.

It should be noted that production of this family of tracked armoured vehicles has been completed by Steyr-Daimler-Puch.

Marketing is now concentrating on the ASCOD infantry fighting vehicle which is in service with Austria (as the Ulan) and Spain (as the Pizarro).

The Spanish Army has ordered 47 engineer vehicles based on the Pizarro chassis. This is part of the second order for a total of 190 vehicles, with final deliveries due in 2013.

While the original prime contractor for the Greif was Steyr-Daimler-Puch Spezialfahrzeug, as a result of restructuring, the company is now called General Dynamics European Land Systems - Steyr.

Description

The hull of the Engineer Tank 4KH7FA-AVE is made of all-welded steel armour, which provides the occupants with protection from small arms fire and shell splinters with the fully enclosed crew compartment at the front.

Normal means of entry to the crew compartment is by two doors on the left side of the hull but there are additional hatches in the roof. The engine and transmission are at the rear of the hull.

The engine compartment is fitted with a fire detection and extinguishing system that can be operated manually or automatically. Over the engine decking is a stowage platform for engineer equipment.

The torsion bar suspension either side consists of five dual rubber-tyred roadwheels with the drive sprocket at the rear and the idler at the front. There are three track-return rollers and hydraulic shock-absorbers which are fitted at the first and fifth roadwheel stations.

Mounted on the right side of the superstructure at the front is a hydraulically operated excavation device (ditcher), the boom of which can be traversed through 234°. Earth-drilling equipment with a 350 mm diameter auger can be mounted in place of the bucket, as can a crane hook.

A hydraulically operated winch is situated in the lower part of the hull and leads out through the front part of the hull. It is provided with 60 m of 16 mm diameter cable and has a maximum pulling capacity of 8,000 kg.

A hydraulically operated dozer blade is mounted on the front of the hull. This has a straight motion mechanism and no earth-transporting capability. It is 2.5 m wide when travelling (3 m when working) and 0.9 m high.

A full range of engineer equipment is carried, including cutting and welding equipment. The Engineer Tank does not have an NBC system, although the crew compartment is provided with a ventilation and heating unit.

Austrian Army Engineer Tank 4KH7FA-AVE, with dozer blade raised and hydraulic boom extended (Michael Jerchel)　　0589686

Specifications

Engineer Tank 4KH7FA-AVE Greif
Crew: 4
Combat weight: 21,000 kg
Power-to-weight ratio: 15.23 hp/t (11.36 kW/t)
Length: 7.49 m
Width:
  (chassis) 2.5 m
  (dozer blade in transport position) 2.5 m
  (dozer blade in working position) 3 m
Height:
  (overall) 3.15 m
  (top of hull) 2.3 m
  (transported) 2.8 m
Ground clearance: (loaded) 0.4 m
Track: 2.12 m
Track width: 380 mm
Length of track on ground: 3.037 m
Ground pressure: 0.82 kg/cm²
Max speed: (road) 65.3 km/h
Range: (road) 600 km
Fuel capacity: 500 litres
Fording: 1 m
Gradient: 70%
Side slope: 40%
Trench: 2.1 m
Turning circle: 8 m
Engine: Steyr 7FA 6-cylinder water-cooled 4-stroke turbocharged diesel developing 320 hp (239 kW) at 2,300 rpm
Transmission: ZF type 6HP500 automatic with 6 forward and 1 reverse gears
Electrical system: 24 V
Batteries: 2 × 12 V, 180 Ah
Armament:
  1 × .50" (12.7 mm) M2 HB MG
  4 smoke grenade dischargers

Engineer equipment
Dozer blade
Width, operating: 3 m
Width, travelling: 2.3 m
Max operating depth: 300 mm

Crane winch
Winch pull: (1st gear/2nd gear) 80 kN/6.5 kN
Effective cable length: 57 m
Cable diameter: 16 mm

Ditcher
Digging depth: 2.2 m
Dumping height: 4.5 m
Radius of operation: 6.3 m
Area of swivel: 234°

Ground auger
Max torque: 2.17 kN.m
Max speed: 125 rpm
Boring diameter: 350 mm

Status

Production complete. In service with Austria (19) and Tunisia (two). No longer marketed. Marketing is now concentrating on the ASCOD infantry fighting vehicle which is in service with Austria (as the Ulan) and Spain (as the Pizarro).

A further development of ASCOD is the basis for the General Dynamics UK Specialist Vehicle for which the company was awarded a development contract in mid-2010.

Contractor

General Dynamics European Land Systems - Steyr

China

Type WZ763 mine clearing system

Development

The China Xinshidai Company is now marketing a number of Armoured Fighting Vehicles (AFV) for export including the Type WZ763 mine clearing system. It is understood that the system has already been deployed within the Peoples Liberation Army (PLA).

According to Chinese sources the Type WZ763 is based on the Type 79 (or Type 69) Main Battle Tank (MBT) chassis. At this stage it is not certain as to whether the Type WZ763 is a brand new build, or a conversion of surplus MBT chassis.

Chinese Type WZ763 mine clearing vehicle with full-width mine plough in the raised position and showing the magnetic signature duplicating devices extending over the front of the vehicle
(China Xinshidai Company)   1333777

While the Type WZ763 is being marketed as a dedicated mineclearing system, it could be possible to remove the front-mounted plough type mineclearing equipment and replace this with a dozer blade to carry out battlefield clearance operations.

As of October 2010 there are no known export sales of the WZ763 mine clearing system which as far as it is known has only been offered on the export market by the China Xinshidai Company.

Description

For the mineclearing application the existing three-person, 100 mm or 105 mm tank-gun armed turret has been removed. This has been replaced by a new raised, welded, armoured-steel superstructure, with the forward part being the crew compartment. This provides the crew with protection from small arms fire and shell splinters.

On the standard Type79/69 MBT the driver is seated at the front left side of the chassis. In the Type WZ763 it is possible that the driver's position has been moved upwards and to the rear for higher survivability.

To the immediate rear of the new crew compartment is the launcher for the rocket-propelled mineclearing system. This fires a rocket-propelled high explosive line-charge. The launcher is raised at an angle of 45° prior to rocket launch. When not required, this retracts into an armour protected box installed towards the rear of the chassis.

Mounted on the front of the chassis is an arrowhead shaped full-width mine plough, fitted with a depth-sensing device. The plough is claimed to be able to clear a path through a mine field up to a width of 4 m, this whilst the vehicle is travelling at a speed of between 4 and 7 km/h.

The vehicle is fitted with a two pole-like devices that extend over the front of the vehicle. These are understood to be magnetic signature duplicating devices able to neutralise (prematurely detonate) anti-tank mines fitted with magnetic-influence fuzes. The devices can neutralise anti-tank mines at a range of 5 m, again whilst the vehicle is travelling at speeds between 4 and 7 km/h.

When travelling between missions, the devices are lowered and stowed along either side of the chassis just above the level of the vehicle's suspension.

In a typical mine breaching mission, the vehicle would stop short of the minefield and fire a rocket-propelled mineclearing line-charge across the minefield. The charge falls to the ground and is then detonated. The charge is claimed to be able clear a path through the minefield 100 m long by 4 m wide. The vehicle then enters the minefield, with the mine plough lowered and magnetic signature duplicator enabled, clearing any remaining anti-tank mines.

The effectiveness of the rocket-propelled mineclearing system does depend on a number of factors, which includes the ambient weather conditions and so is not always effective in high wind-speed conditions.

As far as it is known the WZ763 system does not have any remote control capacity, nor is it fitted with a lane marking system to allow follow up vehicles to rapidly move forward through the cleared minefield.

Standard equipment fitted to the WZ763 includes an NBC system and a smoke screen generator. The smoke screen is generated by injecting diesel fuel into the exhaust outlet, which is situated on the left side of the hull towards the rear.

Variants

China North Industries Corporation (NORINCO) has developed and placed in production at least two other support vehicles based on the Type 59 MBT Chassis. These are the Type 84 Armoured Vehicle Launched Bridge (AVLB) and the Type 653 Armoured Recovery Vehicle (ARV). Details are provided on both of these vehicles in separate entries within *Jane's Military Vehicles and Logistics*. Production of both of these vehicles is undertaken on an as required basis.

Specifications

WZ763 mine clearing system
Crew: 3
Weight: (combat) 38,000 kg
Length: 7.49 m
Width: 4.07 m
Height: 4.13 m
Max speed: (road) 45 km/h
Range: (road) 400 km
Max gradient: 40%
Fording: 1.4 m
Trench: 2.0 m

Status

Production as required. In service with the PLA.

Contractor

Chinese state factories

Finland

Patria Land & Armament Heavy Mine Breaching Vehicle

Development

To operate with its fleet of 124 ex-German Army Leopard 2A4 MBTs, the Finnish Defence Force (FDF) has now fielded an Armoured Vehicle Launched Bridge (AVLB) and a Heavy Mine Breaching Vehicle (HMBV) based on the same chassis.

In 2006 the Finnish Defence Force carried out user trials of the first of six HMBV developed by Patria Land & Armament. These trials have now been completed and all six vehicles have now been delivered.

In mid-2010 Patria Land & Armament announced that they had teamed with the Spanish company of EXPAL to offer a mine clearing vehicle based on the chassis of the German Krauss-Maffei Wegmann Leopard 2A4 MBT to meet the potential requirements of the Spanish Army.

Under the terms of this agreement, EXPAL would be prime contractor with Patria Land & Armament being main subcontractor. This would be based on the Heavy Mine Breaching Vehicle already supplied to the Finnish Army.

Description

HMBV is based on a surplus German Krauss-Maffei Wegmann Leopard 2A4 MBT chassis. For its new role the turret has been removed and replaced by a new superstructure of welded armoured steel.

Vehicle commander and engineer are seated in this well-protected superstructure with each provided with day periscopes for all round observation and a single-piece hatch cover.

To carry out its mine breaching role the HMBV is fitted with a complete suite of mine clearing equipment supplied by Pearson Engineering of the UK.

Patria Land & Armament Heavy Mine Breaching Vehicle fitted with front-mounted Pearson Engineering Combat Dozer Blade
(Patria Land & Armament Oy)   1296005

Patria Land & Armament Heavy Mine Breaching Vehicle fitted with Pearson Engineering Full Width Mine Plough at the front and Cleared Lane Marking System either side at the rear (Patria Land & Armament Oy)
1296006

This consists of a Full Width Mine Plough or a Surface Mine Plough that is installed at the front of the vehicle and operated by the driver.

To enable it to carry out some combat engineer roles, a Pearson Engineering Combat Dozer Blade can also be installed at the front of the chassis. This can be used to clear battlefield obstacles, prepare firing positions or prepare sites for bridging operations.

The mine breaching and dozer blade can be rapidly installed on the front of the chassis using an interface system developed by Patria Land & Armament and Pearson Engineering.

This interface system includes an electro-hydraulic power pack installed inside of the crew compartment, external high lift adapter and a hydraulic emergency jettison system.

Mounted either side of the hull rear is a Pearson Engineering Clear Lane Marking System which vertically deploys pennants into the ground as the HMBV moves forwards.

HMBV is operated by a crew of three consisting of the commander, engineer and driver with space being provided for an additional crew member.

Internally an additional floor has been added to enhance crew survivability against anti-tank mines and all of the crew seats are attached to the roof rather than the floor for additional crew survivability.

Armament consists of a Russian 12.7 mm heavy Machine Gun (MG) mounted on the right side of the superstructure and a total of 16 × 76 mm electrically operated smoke grenade launchers that cover the frontal arc.

Standard equipment includes vehicle heater, NBC system, complete suite of forward facing cameras and passive night vision equipment.

Large equipment containers are provided over the rear engine decks to allow for additional specialised engineer equipment to be carried.

Specifications

Heavy Mine Breaching Vehicle
Crew: 3
Weight: depends on equipment fitted
Length: 7.92 m
Width: 3.75 m
Height: 2.88 m
Note: Automotive characteristics are similar to the German Rheinmetall Landsysteme Büffel ARV covered in a separate entry in *Jane's Military Vehicles and Logistics*.

Status

Production complete. Total of six systems supplied to Finnish Defence Force.

Contractor

Patria Land & Armament Oy

France

Nexter Systems AMX-30 combat engineer tractor (EBG)

Development

The AMX-30 *Engin Blindé du Génie* (EBG) was developed by Giat Industries (now Nexter Systems) to meet the requirements of the French Engineers and the prototype was shown for the first time in 1981.

The EBG entered production during 1987 with the first of a batch of 20 units being completed by the end of that year. A further 16 vehicles were funded in 1989. The French Army had a total requirement for 126 EBGs but production ceased after 71 had been produced. The last EBG was handed over to the French Army in early 1994.

Upgraded EBG combat engineer tractor of the French Army from the rear and fitted with RAFAEL Advanced Defense Systems Carpet rocket propelled mine clearing equipment (Pierre Touzin) 1333648

Development and production of the AMX-30 EBG was undertaken at the Nexter Systems facilities at Roanne. As the AMX-30 production line is closed it is not anticipated that there will be any further production of the EBG.

It should be noted that there are no AMX-30 MBTs left in front line service with the French Army although specialised versions such as ARV and EBG remain in service. For example, although the French Army has taken delivery of a total of 406 Leclerc MBTs and 20 Leclerc based ARV, many other support vehicles still remaining in service are based on the older AMX-30 chassis.

The French Army also has a potential requirement for a new armoured engineer vehicle with similar capabilities to that of the BAE Systems Global Combat Systems Terrier Combat Engineer Vehicle.

This has recently entered production for the British Army and is covered in detail in a separate entry in *Jane's Armour and Artillery*.

Description

The chassis of the EBG is almost identical to that of the AMX-30D ARV, but uses automotive components of the later AMX-30 B2 MBT including the engine, transmission, torque converter and suspension. The three-man crew consists of the vehicle commander, sapper and driver.

Mounted at the front of the hull is a hydraulically operated dozer blade with a capacity of 250 m³/h for transport and filling, or 120 m³/h for excavating. Mounted at the back of the lower part of the dozer blade are six scarifying teeth, these being used for ripping up the surface of roads to a depth of 200 mm when the vehicle is being driven in reverse. The dozer blade is 3.55 m wide when fully extended and 1.1 m high.

The hydraulic winch has a capacity of 20,000 kg, is provided with 80 m of cable and has a winching speed of 0.2 to 0.35 m/s irrespective of traction force. Automatic winding speed is from 0.2 to 1.4 m/s with traction capability interlocked with the speed of the vehicle. The winch, which leads out through the front of the vehicle, can be used during fording operations.

Pivoted at the front of the hull on the right side is a hydraulic arm with a maximum lifting torque of 15,000 kg/m; the double-jointed arm can be extended to 7.5 m and traversed through a full 360°. The arm is provided with a lifting hook and pincer-type grab. The arm can also be fitted with an auger which can drill 220 mm diameter holes in the ground to a depth of 3 m. A 220 mm cutting saw is carried and a 12.5 kW hydraulic Power Take-Off (PTO) is provided as standard.

Mounted in the centre of the hull, slightly offset to the right, is a two-tier turret. The upper part has a single-piece hatch cover that opens to the rear and is fitted with a 7.62 mm machine gun. To the rear of the turret, on either side, are two electrically operated smoke grenade dischargers.

Mounted on the forward part of the lower tier is a launching tube for 142 mm demolition charges and either side of this are two mine-launching tubes, each having a launching container of five anti-tank mines.

The 142 mm calibre demolition charge is 800 mm long, weighs 17 kg and contains 10 kg of explosive. The charge is fin-stabilised and fitted with a nose-mounted point-detonating fuze; range is between 30 and 300 m.

The anti-tank mines are 139 mm in diameter, weigh 2.34 kg and contain 700 g of explosive. The launcher discharges the mines to a distance of between 60 and 250 m and the mines are then triggered by any vehicle weighing over 1,500 kg. According to Nexter Systems, anti-tank mines will penetrate a tank floor equivalent to 50 mm of conventional steel armour plate at 500 mm stand-off distance and 60° incidence, or break up a tank's track if the mine is run over. The mines self-destruct after a preset time.

Standard equipment on the EBG includes provision for deep fording with the aid of a snorkel, passive night periscope for the driver, NBC system and a range-finder telescope for the sapper.

EBG upgrade

The French Army took delivery of a total of 71 AMX-30 *Engin Blindé de Genie* (EBG) combat engineer tractors with final deliveries taking place from Roanne in late 1993.

Upgraded EBG combat engineer tractor of the French Army fitted with the RAFAEL Advanced Defence Systems Carpet rocket propelled mineclearing equipment at the rear and dozer blade (lowered) at the front (RAFAEL)
1334217

Nexter Systems was awarded a contract to upgrade a total of 54 of these vehicles to an enhanced configuration. Of these, 12 were modified for the mineclearing role.

The upgrade was extensive and cover three key areas: protection, engineering functions and ergonomics. The gunner's station was removed and additional armour is fitted to provide a higher level of protection. Parts of the vehicle are fitted with Explosive Reactive Armour (ERA).

Vision devices are provided with laser protection while a Galix vehicle protection system is fitted which can launch a variety of grenades.

The excavator arm was improved and a 10-tonne winch and fuel air-explosive rocket-propelled mineclearing system installed. A new-generation magnetic mine-neutralisation system was fitted. The current engine has been replaced by the more modern Mack E9 diesel from Renault Trucks Defense.

For improved ergonomics the EBG is fitted with an air conditioning system, new driver's night vision system and the commander will be provided with new night vision and range-finding equipment.

Finally, the latest Thales PR4G series radio will be fitted, plus a battle management system and a global positioning system.

EBG with Carpet mine clearing system
It has been disclosed that a batch of French Army EBG combat engineer vehicles have been fitted with the RAFAEL Advanced Defense Systems Carpet fuel air explosive minefield breaching system.

This is mounted at the rear of the chassis and when travelling is in the horizontal position and traversed into the vehicle position prior to launch.

This launches unguided fuel air explosive type rockets over the mine field which are then detonated to create an overpressure to explode anti-tank mines.

Specifications
EBG combat engineer tractor
Crew: 3
Weight combat: 41,500 kg
Power-to-weight ratio: 13.48 kW/t (18.07 hp/t)
Ground pressure: 0.9 kg/cm²
Length: (overall) 8.29 m
Width:
   (overall) 3.55 m
   (without dozer blade extensions) 3.12 m
Height: (overall) 3.02 m
Ground clearance: 0.45 m
Track: 2.52 m
Track width: 570 mm
Length of track on ground: 4.12 m
Max speed: (road) 65 km/h
Fording:
   (without preparation) 2.5 m
   (with preparation) 4 m
Gradient: 60%
Side slope: 30%
Vertical obstacle: 0.9 m
Trench: 2.9 m
Engine: Mack E9 diesel developing 559 kW (750 hp)
Transmission: 5 SD with 5 gears in both directions, or ENC 200 gearbox with lock-up torque converter with 5 forward and 1 reverse gears
Electrical system: 24 V
Armament:
   1 × 7.62 mm MG
   2 × 2 smoke grenade dischargers
   1 × 142 mm demolition charge projector
   4 anti-tank mine projectors
Ammunition:
   (MG) 4,000 rounds
   (demolition charges) 5
   (mines) 40 (8 containers each holding 5)

Status
Production complete. In service with the French Army (71). The AMX-30 EBG is no longer marketed. A total of 54 of these vehicles have now been upgraded by Nexter Systems.

Enquiries to
Nexter Systems

Germany

FFG Wisent 2 Leopard 2 Support Vehicle

Development
The German company of Flensburger Fahrzeugbau Gesellschaft (FFG) has many years of experience in the overhaul and upgrade of tracked Armoured Fighting Vehicles (AFV), including Main Battle tanks (MBT).

In the second half of 2008 FFG started development, using company funding, of the Wisent 2 Leopard 2 Support Vehicle with the first prototype being completed in time for display at Eurosatory in June 2010.

Wisent 2 Leopard 2 Support Vehicle is already being offered on the world market as a cost effective alternative to a new build Leopard 2 Armoured Recovery Vehicle (ARV) or Armoured Engineer Vehicle (AEV).

As of November 2010, company trials of the Wisent 2 Leopard 2 Support Vehicle were underway and it was being marketed to a number of existing Leopard 2 MBT customers.

Description
For its new role the complete turret of the Leopard 2 MBT has been removed and a new all welded steel armour superstructure added at the front of the vehicle.

The fully enclosed crew compartment is at the front left side with the driver at the very front and commander to the immediate rear.

The driver is provided with a large one piece hatch cover that opens to the left with three integral periscopes providing observation over the frontal arc. The middle periscope can be replaced by an image intensification or thermal device for night driving.

In addition there is one access door in the left side of the hull for the crew and an additional access door for the toolbox.

As well as the commander/gunner and driver, space is provided for an additional crew member.

Commander/gunner is seated to the rear and provided with a cupola with ballistic windows that provide all round observation and a single piece hatch cover that lifts and swings to one side.

The vehicle has a new hydraulic and electronics system designed by FFG that allows for the rapid role switching.

The main hydraulic winch is located at the front of the vehicle and has a capacity of 40 tonnes and provided with 170 m of 33 mm diameter cable of which 160 m is usable with maximum winding speed being up to 90 m/min.

There is also an auxiliary winch with a maximum capacity of 3.5 tonnes and this is provided with 300 m of 9 mm diameter cable with maximum winch speed being up to 90 m/min.

Mounted at the front of the chassis is the hydraulically operated dozer blade that is also used to stabilise the vehicle when the winches are being used. This has a normal width of 3.54 m but with extensions this can be increased to 4.04 m.

Pivoted at the right side of the hull is the hydraulically operated crane which is traversed to the rear for travelling and this has a maximum lifting capacity of up to 32 tonnes.

Power pack consists of a MTU MB 873 Ka 501 diesel developing 1,500 hp coupled to a modified Renk HSWL 354 automatic transmission with four forward and two reverse gears.

A 17 Kw Auxiliary Power Unit (APU) has been installed in the right side of the hull at the rear. Series production Wisent 2 Leopard 2 Support Vehicles may have a different APU according to specific user requirements.

Wisent 2 Leopard 2 Support Vehicle can recover damaged and tow disabled vehicles such as the Leopard 2 MBT and in addition to carrying tools and other specialised equipment can also carry a replacement Leopard 2 power pack on the rear decking.

As the Wisent 2 Leopard 2 Support Vehicle will often operate in the forward battle area it is provided with a high level of ballistic protection.

Over the frontal arc is STANAG 4569 Level 5 with a spall liner being standard for the crew compartment.

Mine protection is currently being quoted as STANAG 4569 Level 4a and 4b which is claimed to provided protection against the TMRP-6 anti-tank mine.

Using standardised attachment points the base armour system can be quickly upgraded with bar armour to provide a higher level of protection against rocket propelled grenades such as the widely deployed Russian RPG-7.

Other armour alternatives include RUAG Land Systems SidePRO-LASSO or explosive reactive armour.

If required the vehicle can be fitted with a roof mounted remote weapon station armed with a 7.62 mm or .50 M2 HB machine gun or a 40 mm automatic grenade launcher.

Wisent 2 Leopard 2 Support Vehicle in travelling configuration with crane traversed to rear and dozer/stabiliser blade raised (FFG)   1401380

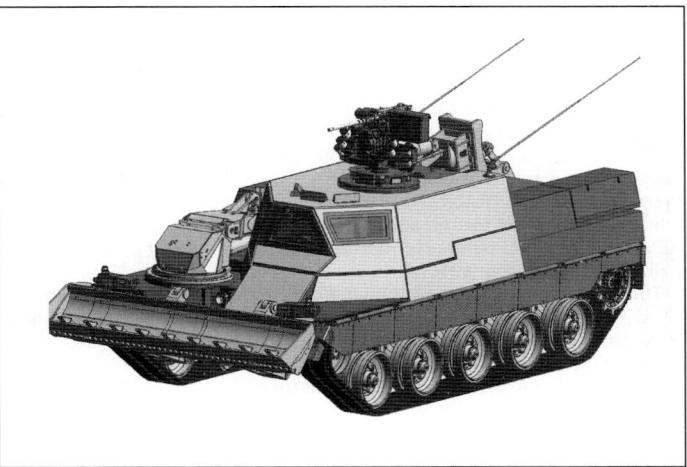

Artist's impression of RUFUS medium support vehicle with dozer blade raised (Rheinmetall)   1296007

On the prototype, eight 76 mm grenade launchers are mounted on the left side of the superstructure firing forwards but other alternatives are possible according to customer requirements.

A key feature of the Wisent 2 Leopard 2 Support Vehicle is that it can be re-rolled from the ARV to the AEV role in less than 24 hours.

The crane can be replaced by a scissors type hydraulic arm fitted with a bucket with a digging depth down to 5.3 m and a reach of 10.2 m.

This can excavate up to 200 m³ of soil in one hour, but this does depend on the type of terrain.

The hydraulic arm can also be fitted with an earth auger to or concrete cutting equipment.

The standard dozer blade can be replaced by a new one optimised for engineer role such as removing battlefield obstacles or preparing firing positions and weapon pits. This dozer blade is laser/global positioning system guided.

If required, the dozer blade can be rapidly removed and replaced by a Pearson Engineering mine plough system and lane marking equipped fitted either side of the hull towards the rear. Another alternative would be the installation of mine clearing rollers.

Specifications
Crew: 2-3
Weight:
  (unloaded) 55,000 kg
  (combat) 60,000 kg
Power-to-weight ratio: 27.27 hp/tonne
Length: 9.24 m
Width: 3.6 m
Height: 2.65 m
Ground clearance: 0.51 m
Track width: 635 mm
Max speed:
  (forwards) 70 km/h
  (reverse) 31 km/h
Fuel capacity: 1,620 litres
Fording: 1.2 m
Gradient: 60%
Side slope: 30%
Vertical obstacle: 0.92 m
Trench: 3 m
Engine: MTU MB 873 Ka-501 4-stroke exhaust-gas turbocharged diesel developing 1,500 hp (1,119 kW) at 2,600 rpm
Transmission: Renk HSWL 364, hydromechanical with 4 forward and 2 reverse gears
Suspension: Torsion bar
Electrical system: 24 V
Batteries: 8 × 12 V, 100 Ah, total capacity 400 Ah

Status
Prototype undergoing trials.

Contractor
FFG Flensburger Fahrzeugbau Gesellschaft GmbH

Rheinmetall Landsysteme RUFUS medium support vehicle

Development
In mid-2007 it was revealed that Rheinmetall Landsysteme was developing a new medium support vehicle called RUFUS (which is an abbreviation for Rheinmetall Universal Fahrzeug Fuer Unterstuetzings-Systeme).

RUFUS is being developed by the company as a private venture to meet emerging user requirements for an Armoured Engineer Vehicle (AEV) to support medium forces.

The company believe that there is a potential market for different armoured support vehicle types for the home and export markets. In the case of Germany, this would be used to support the new German Army Puma Armoured Infantry Fighting Vehicle.

To reduce development time and overall life cycle costs, the new RUFUS AEV will use proven Military-Off-The-Shelf (MOTS) and Commercial-Off-The-Shelf (COTS) wherever possible.

It is envisioned that RUFUS will have a crew of two or three people and have a combat weight of 30 to 31 tonnes with the maximum protection being provided for the crew compartment rather than other systems.

This weight would allow it to be transported in the A400M military transport aircraft similar to the new German Army Puma AIFV.

It is possible that a modular appliqué armour package could be developed along similar lines to that of the Puma AIFV that could be fitted after the vehicle has been delivered by the A400M.

It is understood that as of late 2010, design and development work was still underway and that no firm decision had been taken as to whether to build a prototype of the RUFAS medium support vehicle.

Description
The overall layout of the RUFUS AEV is similar to the Leopard 1 AEV with the fully enclosed crew compartment front left, hydraulic arm pivoted at the front right and the diesel powerpack at the rear.

The driver is provided with windows to the front and sides plus roof-mounted periscopes for observation over the frontal arc. Commander's cupola is to the immediate rear of the driver's position and has periscopes for all round observation and a remote-controlled weapon station armed with a machine gun. There is an emergency escape hatch to the rear of this position.

To carry out its mission, RUFUS would be fitted with a hydraulic arm which can be fitted with various attachments including bucket or auger. When travelling, this hydraulic arm is traversed to the rear.

Mounted at the front would be a hydraulically operated tiltable dozer blade that could be replaced by various types of mine clearing device. A nine-tonne hydraulically operated winch would be fitted as standard. RUFUS would be fitted with an NBC system and air conditioning system as standard.

RUFUS would be powered by a MTU 8V199 TE20 diesel developing 530 kW (711 hp), this coupled to an HSWL 106 automatic transmission.

Suspension would be hydropneumatic for improved cross-country mobility. This suspension either side has a total of five dual rubber tyred road wheels with the drive sprocket at the rear, idler at the front and track return rollers. The upper part of the suspension is covered by a skirt.

Space would be provided on the rear decking to transport specialised engineer equipment.

Variants
It is envisaged that the RUFUS chassis could also be used for other combat support roles such as Armoured Recovery Vehicle (ARV) or an Armoured Vehicle Launched Bridge (AVLB).

The latter would typically carry two Military Load Class (MLC) 45 bridges each 22 m long which would be launched over the front of the vehicle.

Specifications
Not released.

Status
Under development as a private venture.

Contractor
Rheinmetall Landsysteme GmbH

Rheinmetall Landsysteme Pionierpanzer 2 Dachs armoured engineer vehicle

Development
The now Rheinmetall Landsysteme (previously Mak), developed and produced three prototypes of the Pionierpanzer 2 Dachs (Badger) Armoured Engineer Vehicle (AEV) to meet the operational requirements of the German Army. The German Army designation for the vehicle is the Pionierpanzer 2 A1 Dachs.

A contract award for the conversion of a mix of Leopard 1 ARVs and AEVs was awarded by the German MoD during the early part of 1987 for delivery by December 1990.

The conversion price was DM1.3 million per unit. A further nine vehicles, known as the Badger, were produced for the Canadian Armed Forces using new armoured chassis and hulls. The Canadian contract was worth DM49 million and was completed in 1990.

The Canadian Army has a requirement for up to 18 new AEV based on a Leopard 2 chassis which will eventually replace the currently fielded Badger AEV, some of which have been deployed in Afghanistan.

Description
For the German conversion programme, Rheinmetall Landsysteme stripped down the original chassis, repaired them where necessary, fitted the dozer blade assembly and hydraulic system and completed the final assembly. Jung Jungenthal GmbH was responsible for hull modifications, Eisenwerke Kaiserslautern (today General Dynamics European Land Systems - Germany) for the excavator and traversing turntable and Wieger Maschinenbau for the telescopic arm assemblies.

The Pionierpanzer 2 is based on the hull, running gear and suspension of the Leopard 1 AEV and the Leopard 1 ARV.

According to Rheinmetall Landsysteme, typical roles of the Pionierpanzer 2 Dachs armoured engineer vehicle include dozing, scarifying, excavating, underwater dozing, load lifting, cutting and welding, excavating a slope, towing and recovery with the main winch.

The vehicles have an armoured steel superstructure situated towards the left-hand side of the vehicle, with a telescopic excavator arm located on the right and the traversing turntable situated forward. An extended dozer blade is mounted on the front of the vehicle. This is also used as a stabiliser when the hydraulic winch is being used.

The driver, seated at the front of the superstructure under a hatch cover, is provided with a number of periscopes and night driving aids and operates the dozer blade. Behind the driver is seated the commander with his own cupola and all-round day vision periscopes. Periscopes provided for the commander and driver can be tilted. The cupola has provision for mounting a 7.62 mm MG3 machine gun. The commander operates the telescopic excavator arm. There is a third crew member seated within the superstructure.

A bank of six electrically operated 76 mm smoke grenade launchers is mounted on the left side of the superstructure, firing forwards.

The telescopic excavator arm is hydraulically operated by a 300 bar system and is electrically controlled. It can be used in a variety of ways and can be elevated or depressed to an angle of ±60°. Its horizontal arc of operation is 196.5°. The bucket on the end of the arm has a capacity of 1.1 m³ and the arm can be extended to a maximum length of 8.3 m. It has an earth working capacity of 140 m³/h. The arm can also be used as a crane jib. If required, the excavator arm can be controlled from a remote dismounted position.

The dozer blade has a maximum width of 3.75 m with side extensions fitted and has scarifiers to rip up road surfaces to a maximum depth of 0.45 m. Maximum operating speed with the dozer blade in use is 8 km/h and the blade can shift up to 270 m³/h of spoil.

The Pionierpanzer 2 is equipped with a front-mounted hydraulic winch that can be used for self-recovery or the recovery of other vehicles, in which case the dozer blade can be lowered to improve operating stability. The hydraulic winch, which is sealed, has a cable tensioning system, is supplied with 90 m of 33 mm cable and has a straight pull capacity of 20,000 kg. This can be increased to 35,000 kg by multi-reeving the cable. The vehicle can be used to tow disabled vehicles. Canadian Badger vehicles are fitted with a 35,000 kg hydraulically operated capstan winch.

Pionierpanzer 2 of the German Army in travelling configuration deployed in Somalia (Andreas Warneke)   0105874

Badger AEV of the Canadian Army from the rear, showing appliqué armour on forward part of hull (Michael Jerchel)   0589688

By using a deep wading kit which includes a snorkel tower, the vehicle can be used to prepare underwater approach routes or clear obstacles at depths up to 4 m. Additional bilge pumps are provided for underwater operations.

Specialist equipment carried on the vehicle includes cutting and welding equipment with an operating voltage of 54 V. For operations in the Balkans some of the Canadian Badger AEV were fitted with an additional passive armour package. This was installed on the front and sides of the crew compartment. This was developed by the German Company, IBD.

Specifications
Dachs armoured engineer vehicle
Crew: 3
Weight:
    (empty) 42,500 kg
    (loaded) 43,000 kg
Power-to-weight ratio: 14.40 kW/t (19.3 hp/t)
Ground pressure:
    (combat weight) 0.92 kg/cm²
Length:
    (travelling, roads) 8.375 m
    (travelling, cross-country) 8.925 m
Width: 3.25 m
Width, dozer blade extended: 3.75 m
Height: (to top of MG mount) 2.57 m
Ground clearance: 0.44 m
Track: 2.7 m
Track width: 550 mm
Length of track on ground: 4.236 m
Max speed: (road) 62 km/h
Range: approx 650 km
Fuel capacity: 1,410 litres
Fording:
    (normal) 1.2 m
    (with preparation) 4 m
Gradient: 50%
Side slope: 30%
Vertical obstacle: 0.9 m
Trench: 2.5 m
Engine: MTU MB 838 Ca M-500 37.4 litres V-10 multifuel developing 619 kW (830 hp) at 2,200 rpm
Transmission: ZF 4 HP 250 planetary-gear shift with hydraulic torque converter, 4 forward and 2 reverse gears
Steering: regenerative double differential
Electrical system: 24 V
Batteries: 6 × 12 V, 300 Ah
Armament:
    1 × 7.62 mm MG3 MG (Canadian vehicles have different MG)
    6 × 76 mm smoke grenade dischargers
Dozing capacity: 270 m³/h
Excavating capacity: 140 m³/h
Excavator pull force: 125 kN
Excavator push force: 85 kN
Towing force main winch: 350 kN
Scarifying depth: 0.45 m
Dozing and scarifying speed: 8 km/h (max)
Traverse, excavator arm: 195°
Tilt angle, telescopic arm: ±60°

Status
Production complete. In service with Canada (nine) and Germany (140). As of late 2010 there were no known plans for Germany to replace their Pionieer Dachs 2 armoured engineer vehicles.

Contractor
Rheinmetall Landsysteme GmbH

Rheinmetall Landsysteme Leopard 1 armoured engineer vehicle

Development

The Leopard 1 Armoured Engineer Vehicle (AEV) is a direct development of the Krauss-Maffei Wegmann Leopard 1 ARV and differs from it only in minor details.

The first prototype, based on a design by Dr Ing P Porsche KG, was completed by the now Rheinmetall Landsysteme of Kiel in 1967, with the first production vehicles completed in 1968.

Wherever possible, standard Leopard 1 MBT components were used, for example the MTU engine, ZF transmission and torsion bar suspension.

Thirty-six Leopard 1 AEV were converted by the now Rheinmetall Landsysteme to Pionierpanzer 2 Dachs armoured engineer vehicles for the German Army while the Canadian Army took delivery of nine new vehicles which they call the Badger. For operations in the Balkans some of these have been fitted with additional passive armour for a higher level of battlefield survivability.

This passive armour package was provided by the German company of IBD.

Description

The hull of the Leopard 1 AEV is of all-welded steel armour construction with the crew compartment at the front and the engine and transmission at the rear.

The driver is seated at the front of the vehicle to the left of the crane and is provided with a single-piece hatch cover and three day periscopes for observation, one of which can be replaced by a passive night vision periscope.

The commander is seated to the rear of the driver and has a single-piece hatch cover and eight day periscopes, one of which can be replaced by a passive night vision periscope.

There is another hatch to the rear of the commander's position, and three day periscopes provide vision to the rear of the vehicle. There is a swivelling day periscope in the roof of the superstructure.

The crew of four (commander, driver and two mechanics) can enter the vehicle either through the roof hatches or through two doors in the left side of the hull.

The suspension is of the torsion bar type and consists of seven dual rubber-tyred road wheels either side with the drive sprocket at the rear and the idler at the front.

There are four track-return rollers. The first, second, third, sixth and seventh road wheel stations are fitted with hydraulic shock-absorbers. The Diehl tracks are of the double-pin type and have rubber pads.

The Leopard 1 AEV can carry out similar roles to the ARV including recovering disabled vehicles and changing vehicle components (although an auger is carried in place of the replacement power pack (comprising engine, transmission and cooling system) carried on the ARV).

The dozer blade is mounted at the front of the hull and operated by two hydraulic cylinders through two lever arms and is mechanically locked when not in use. The dozer blade has a maximum capacity of 200 m³/h and the width of the blade can be extended to 3.75 m by additional side attachments. It can be fitted with four scarifiers to rip up the surface of roads.

The installation of a heat exchanger enables the vehicle to perform unlimited bulldozing activities even at high ambient temperatures. In addition to being used for dozing operations, the dozer blade is also used to stabilise the AEV when the crane is in use or when vehicles are being recovered.

The hydraulic main winch, with its horizontal cable drum, is in the centre of the crew compartment under the floor. This winch is provided with a total of 90 m of 33 mm cable. The maximum tractive effort of the hydraulic main winch in the lowest cable position is 35,000 kg, which can be increased to 70,000 kg when using an appropriately located guide pulley.

Leopard 1 armoured engineer vehicle with earth auger in action   0554961

The exit opening for the main winch is located at the nose of the vehicle. A hydraulically driven cable-tensioning device is located immediately behind the opening and automatically extends or rewinds the cable.

The crane jib is mounted on a turntable on the front right side and when in the travelling position, lies horizontally along the right side of the hull. It has a maximum lifting capacity of 20,000 kg when used with the dozer blade as a stabiliser.

A scale on the side plate of the jib shows the allowed load: if it is exceeded the jib is stopped automatically. The two hydraulic cylinders for lifting the jib are arranged so that they are fully splinter-proof in the travelling position and extensively splinter-proof in the operating position. The jib is turned by the traversing gearbox directly underneath the console of the crane. If the hydraulics fail, the traversing gear can be operated by hand. The ladder mounted on the jib assists in the assembly of the earth-drilling equipment and can also be used for other work such as overhead lines.

The auger is mounted, when required, at the end of the jib crane and can drill holes 700 mm in diameter to a maximum depth of 2 m. The hydraulic oil is supplied to the radial piston motor of the earth drill through hoses which can be connected to the jib boom by means of quick-disconnect couplings.

The hydraulic hoisting winch with a vertical cable drum is mounted on the right side of the crew compartment. It is provided with 100 m of 13 mm diameter cable.

Equipment carried on the AEV includes a set of shackles, towbar, electric impact wrench, guide pull and electric welding and cutting equipment. For demolition work a total of 117 kg of explosives is carried.

Armament consists of a 7.62 mm MG3 machine gun mounted in the bow of the tank on the left side; this has an elevation of +15°, a depression of –15° and a traverse of 15° left and right. A similar 7.62 mm MG3 machine gun is mounted on the commander's hatch for anti-aircraft defence. Six 76 mm electrically operated smoke grenade dischargers are mounted on the left side of the hull.

The Leopard 1 AEV is also provided with an NBC system, crew compartment heater, fire warning and extinguishing system and a hull escape hatch. The basic model can ford to a depth of 2.1 m, but for deep fording operations, a snorkel can be quickly installed.

Variants

Wisent 2 Leopard 2 Support Vehicle

This has been developed as a private venture by the German Company of FFG and can be used as an ARV or rapidly reconfigured as an AEV.

Development of the Wisent 2 Leopard 2 Support Vehicle has been completed but as of November 2010 no contracts had been placed.

Specifications

Leopard 1 armoured engineer vehicle
Crew: 4
Weight:
  (empty) 40,200 kg
  (loaded) 40,800 kg
Power-to-weight ratio: 15.17 kW/t (20.34 hp/t)
Ground pressure: 0.86 kg/cm²
Length: (with dozer blade raised) 7.98 m
Width:
  (with side elements of blade fitted) 3.75 m
  (hull) 3.25 m
Height: (with AA MG) 2.69 m
Ground clearance: 0.44 m
Track: 2.7 m
Track width: 550 mm
Length of track on ground: 4.236 m
Max speed: (road) 62 km/h
Range:
  (road) 800 km
  (cross-country) 500 km
Fuel capacity: 1,410 litres

Leopard 1 armoured engineer vehicle using its front-mounted dozer blade
0554960

Fording: 2.1 m
  (with snorkel) 3 m
Gradient: 60%
Side slope: 30%
Vertical obstacle: 1 m
Trench: 3 m
Engine: MTU MB 838 Ca M-500 10-cylinder multifuel developing 619 kW (830 hp) at 2,200 rpm
Transmission: ZF 4 HP 250 with 4 forward and 2 reverse gears
Electrical system: 24 V
Batteries: 6 with total capacity of 300 Ah, charged by 3-phase generator driven from main engine
Armament:
  1 × 7.62 mm MG3 MG in bow
  1 × 7.62 mm MG3 MG on commander's hatch
  4,250 rounds of 7.62 mm ammunition
  6 × 76 mm smoke grenade dischargers

Status
Production complete. In service with Belgium (six), Germany (36), Italy (40) and Netherlands (25). Oto Melara built 28 Leopard 1 AEVs for the Italian Army. The Pionierpanzer 2 Dachs is in service with Canada (nine) and Germany (149); these are designated the Pionierpanzer 2 A1 in Germany.

It should be noted that the above figures are the quantities of vehicles delivered and in some cases, the numbers of vehicles in service is now smaller due to force structure reductions.

Contractor
Rheinmetall Landsysteme GmbH

Leopard 1 dozer blade unit

Description
The Leopard 1 dozer blade unit can be fitted as an optional extra to the Krauss-Maffei Wegmann designed and built Leopard 1 and 2 MBTs. The complete dozer blade unit consists of the dozer blade, two pivot-mounted push arms and a hydraulic unit for raising and lowering the blade. A floating capability is available to enable the dozer blade to follow ground contours. Add-on extension elements allow for the dozing of lanes wider than the width of the tank's running gear.

The complete dozer blade can be attached or removed from the front of the vehicle in approximately 10 minutes without recourse to cranes or other equipment and it can be mechanically locked in the raised position for travelling. All control elements are packaged into a watertight unit so that the dozer blade can be used during fording operations. A control panel is located in the driver's position and the power supply and control cable passes through one of the slots normally occupied by the vision blocks via a cable adaptor.

This Leopard 1 dozer blade system was used by Australia and Canada for their Leopard 1 MBTs. Australia has replaced their Leopard 1 with M1A1 Abrams.

The Canadian Army has deployed some of its Leopard C2 (Leopard 1 MBTs) to Afghanistan and these have been used with dozer blades and mine clearing attachments.

Status
Production as required. In service with several nations using Leopard 1 MBTs.

Contractor
Krauss-Maffei-Wegmann GmbH & Co KG

Danish Leopard 1A5 MBT fitted with Krauss-Maffei Wegmann dozer blade shown in lowered position (Richard Stickland)   1333650

India

Armoured Amphibious Dozer

Development
The Armoured Amphibious Dozer was designed by Indian government facilities for earthmoving operations in a battlefield environment coupled with good cross-country mobility.

The vehicle was jointly developed by the Research and Development Establishment (Engineers) at Pune and the Vehicle Research and Development Establishment at Ahmednagar.

The vehicle is based on the Russian Kurgan Machine Construction Plant BMP-2 IFV, licence-produced in India as the Sarath. Licence production of the BMP-2 is undertaken in India at the Ordnance Factory Medak. India has not exported any BMP-2 series IFV or variants.

Some of the features of this vehicle are very similar to the British BAE Systems Global Combat Systems (originally Royal Ordnance Factories) Combat Engineer Tractor (CET) of which 15 were delivered to the Indian Army.

Description
The Armoured Amphibious Dozer utilises a modified BMP-2 (Sarath) hull and chassis allied to various items of combat engineer equipment. The vehicle has a crew of two, with dual control for the driver and dozer bucket operator located back-to-back.

The dozer bucket is operated to the rear of the vehicle, having a capacity of 1.5 m³. An 8,000 kg capacity winch can be combined with a self-recovery rocket-propelled anchor, launched from a position over the front hull roof; cable lengths may be 50 or 100 m. Also provided is a 3 t/m jib crane. Hydraulic power for the dozer bucket, winch and suspension locks is provided by a 200 bar pressure self-contained hydraulic system.

The armoured and NBC protection, smoke generator and amphibious capabilities of the BMP-2 (Sarath) are retained. Bridge classification is MLC 16.

Specifications
Armoured Amphibious Dozer
Crew: 1 or 2
Bridge classification: MLC 16
Max speed:
  (road) 60 km/h
  (water) 7 km/h
Fording: amphibious
Gradient: 30°
Vertical obstacle: 0.7 m
Trench: 2 m
Bucket capacity: 1.5 m³
Winch capacity: 8,000 kg
Jib capacity: 3 t/m

Status
It is understood that a small production batch of these Armoured Amphibious Dozer have been delivered to the Indian Army.

Rear view of Armoured Amphibious Dozer in transport configuration
0512298

Armoured Amphibious Dozer showing rocket propelled anchor on the forward part of the hull   0554957

Contractor
Production of the basic BMP-2 IFV is undertaken in India at the Ordnance Factory Medak.

Development Establishment
Research and Development Establishment (Engineers), Defence Research and Development Organisation

---

Armoured Engineer Reconnaissance Vehicle (AERV)

Development
The Armoured Engineer Reconnaissance Vehicle (AERV) was developed jointly by the Research and Development Establishment (Engineers) at Pune and the Vehicle Research and Development Establishment at Ahmednagar.

The Armoured Engineer Reconnaissance Vehicle is based on a much-modified Russian-designed BMP-2 Infantry Fighting Vehicle (IFV) chassis. The BMP-2 IFV has been manufactured under licence in India at the Ordnance Factory Medak. India has not exported any BMP-2 IFV or variants.

The vehicle is capable of acquiring and recording engineer reconnaissance data such as river width, riverbank height, gradient, soil bearing capacity, underwater bed profiles and water current.

Description
The AERV, which is fully amphibious, utilises a modified BMP-2 (Sarath) armoured steel hull and chassis allied to various items of combat engineer reconnaissance equipment and land navigation instruments.

The vehicle has a small turret capable of mounting a machine gun and smoke generators are provided.

The Armoured Engineer Reconnaissance Vehicle is equipped with various reconnaissance and navigation instruments for carrying out engineer reconnaissance operations. These instruments operate on the internal power supply of the vehicle. All of the instruments are microprocessor based.

AERV has been equipped with a ring gyro-based advanced land navigation system with a built-in Global Positioning System (GPS) for navigation purposes.

Armoured Engineer Reconnaissance Vehicle from the rear with doors open   0069292

Indian design Armoured Engineer Reconnaissance vehicle showing its amphibious capabilities   0005008

Instruments such as a digital cone penetrometer and a inclinometer are used for surveying the terrain. Dry and wet gap slope measurement is done by electronic theodolite and other equipment includes a laser range-finder and a night ranging capability.

The underwater bed profile and water current are measured automatically when the vehicle is negotiating water obstacles. The operator seated under full armour protection can acquire all of the required reconnaissance data.

The data from all of the instruments are integrated and logged onto a ruggedised computer.

Trail-blazing equipment is provided in the vehicle. Explosive-based marker rods are driven into the ground at predetermined distances. The equipment contains two magazines, each containing 80 flagged marker rods.

The Armoured Engineer Reconnaissance is fully amphibious, being propelled in the water by its tracks. Before entering the water, the bilge pumps are activated and the trim vane erected at the front of the vehicle by remote control.

Status
In production for the Indian Army. As of late 2010 there are no known exports of the Indian AERV.

Contractor
Production of the basic BMP-2 is undertaken in India at the Ordnance Factory Nmedak. M/s Bharat Electronics, Pune, manufactures instruments for the AERV.

Development Establishment
Research and Development Establishment (Engineers), Defence Research and Development Organisation

---

International

Rheinmetall Landsysteme/RUAG Defence Kodiak armoured engineer vehicle

Development
The Kodiak Armoured Engineer Vehicle (AEV) was developed from 2002 by Rheinmetall Landsysteme of Germany and RUAG Land Systems (which from January 2011 will become RUAG Defence) of Switzerland using company funding to meet the operational requirements of the Swiss Army, which supplied the Leopard 2 chassis.

The first prototype was built in Germany in 2003 and has also been referred to as the Armoured Engineer Vehicle 3 (AEV 3).

The first prototype was put through a series of trials in Germany and then went to Switzerland for extensive user trials.

The Kodiak is based on a surplus Leopard 2 MBT chassis, which has been rebuilt for its specialised role.

It should be noted that all development costs of the Kodiak AEV were funded by Rheinmetall Landsysteme and the now RUAG Defence.

Main roles of the Kodiak AEV can be summarised as building and breaching any kind of obstacles on the battlefield, including minefields and the support of subsidiary tasks after natural disasters.

Early in 2007 the now RUAG Defence was awarded a contract covering the supply of 12 Kodiak AEV for the Swiss Army.

Rheinmetall Landsysteme of Germany is the main sub-contractor and has complete systems responsibility for the Kodiak AEV and will also take the lead in the international market place.

Production of the Kodiak is being undertaken at the now RUAG Defence facility in Thun, Switzerland with the Leopard 2 chassis coming from surplus Swiss Army stocks.

Under the terms of the contract, first production vehicles are being delivered to the Swiss Army in 2009 with final deliveries due in 2011.

Early in 2008 Rheinmetall was awarded a contract worth about EUR100 million to supply 10 of its Kodiak AEV to the Royal Netherlands Army and six to the Swedish Army.

Kodiak Armoured Engineer Vehicle with dozer blade lowered and excavator arm deployed to the front of the vehicle (Rheinmetall)   0530491

Kodiak Armoured Engineer Vehicle fitted with a plough type mineclearing system and clear lane marking system towards the rear (Rheinmetall)

1334218

Deliveries to the Netherlands and Sweden will run from 2011 through to 2012.

The Netherlands and Swedish vehicles will have about 95 per cent commonality and the vehicles will be fitted with the Norwegian Kongsberg Protector Remote Controlled Weapon Station (RCWS) armed with a .50 (12.7 mm) M2 HB machine gun.

The Netherlands, Sweden and Switzerland already operate the Leopard 2 MBT and the Büffel armoured recovery vehicle which share a similar chassis.

Description
Kodiak AEV is provided with a new, fully enclosed armour-protected crew compartment at the front with the driver and one other crew member in the left one and the vehicle commander, who also operates the remote-controlled .50 (12.7 mm) M2 HB machine gun, in the right one.

The driver has a single-piece hatch cover that opens to the rear and this has three integral day periscopes in its forward part. The middle periscope can be replaced by a passive periscope for driving at night.

The vehicle commander is seated on the right and has a cupola with a single-piece hatch cover that opens to the rear, which has a Krauss-Maffei Wegmann Gun Mount Model 2048 armed with a .50 (12.7 mm) M2 HB machine gun. There are two banks of eight electrically operated 76 mm smoke grenade launchers. The prototype is fitted with a simple cupola with a hatch cover that opens to the rear. This is also provided with periscopes for observation purposes.

Production vehicles are fitted with weapons specified by the customer. The Netherlands and Swedish vehicles will be fitted with a Kongsberg RCWS armed with a .50 M2 HB MG.

The 1,500 hp MTU power pack is mounted in the rear of the chassis and is identical to that used in the Leopard 2 MBT and the Rheinmetall Landsysteme Büffel armoured recovery vehicle.

Suspension is of the torsion bar type and either side consists of seven dual rubber-tyred road wheels with the drive sprocket at the rear, idler at the front and track-return rollers. The upper part of the suspension is covered by a skirt.

Mounted at the front of the hull in the middle is the turntable mounted hydraulic crane with an articulating jib, which is normally fitted with a bucket that can be replaced by a tree gripper or hydraulic hammer. When not required this is traversed to the rear and lays between the two parts of the crew compartment. The hydraulically operated excavator has a bucket volume of 1m³, maximum operating range of 9 m, maximum operating height of 8.2 m and a maximum operating depth of 3.9 m. Lifting capacity is about 3.5 tonnes.

Mounted at the front of the hull is a hydraulically operated tiltable blade, which can be used as a dozer blade or to stabilise the vehicle when the hydraulic crane and/or winch is being used.

The dozer blade can also be rapidly fitted with scarifiers to rip up the surfaces of roads. The dozer blade can also be removed and replaced with plough-type mineclearing equipment.

The dozer blade can be rapidly replaced by a Pearson Engineering full width mine plough with a cleared lane marking system being mounted either side at the rear.

It can also be fitted with a signature duplicator system to neutralise anti-tank mines fitted with advanced fuzes. Stowage is also provided for engineer stores and tools.

Two Rotzler hydraulic nine-tonne winches are also fitted and can be used to pull obstacles such as trees out of the way. The vehicle is fitted with a hydraulic interface for hand tools, which provides hydraulic pressure up to 700 bar. Different hydraulic Commercial-Off-The-Shelf (COTS) tools could be used such as a cutter.

For increased survivability, the chassis has been fitted with an anti-spall liner and the recently developed Leopard 2 MBT mine protection kit which has already been fitted to a small number of Leopard 2 MBTs of the German and Swedish armies, with first deliveries made in mid-2004. New mine-protected seats have also been provided for the crew of the Kodiak AEV.

The NBC system from the Leopard 2 ARV has been retained but the Kodiak AEV also has an air conditioning system, modified fire suppression system for the crew compartment and a camera for reverse driving.

Although developed to meet the requirements of the Swiss Army, which did not operate an AEV, Rheinmetall Landsysteme and RUAG Defence have a joint marketing agreement. The standard AEV of the German Army today is the Leopard 1 AEV.

Specifications
Kodiak armoured engineer vehicle
Crew: 3
Weight: (combat) 59,000 kg
Power-to-weight ratio: 19.00 kW/t (25.42 hp/t)
Power pack: MTU MB 873 Ka-501 diesel developing 1,119 kW (1,500 hp) coupled to Renk HSWL 354 automatic transmission
Length: 10.2 m
Width: 3.54 m
Height: 2.6 m
Max speed: 68 km/h
Range: 650 km
Armament 1 × .50 (12.7 mm) M2 HB MG
Smoke grenades 2 × 8 × 76 mm

Status
Production for Netherlands (10), Sweden (six) and Switzerland (12) with production running from 2009 through to 2012.

Contractor
Rheinmetall Landsysteme
RUAG Defence AG

Israel

Israel Military Industries bulldozer protection kit

Development
Operational experience gained by the Israeli Defense Forces demonstrated that there is a requirement for some form of protection for combat engineer bulldozers working in combat areas. Protection is required from small arms and artillery fire and also for vehicles operating in areas where chemical attack is possible.

Israel Military Industries Ltd designed an add-on kit for such situations, which has been fitted to the United States-designed and -built Caterpillar D9 bulldozers, but it can be adapted to suit other commercial engineer equipment.

According to Israel Military Industries, this system can be used for a wide range of full scale combat and low intensity conflicts.

These roles include battlefield demolition and construction, urban warfare support, engineering battalion support, explosive ordnance disposal and demolition support, creating access and egress routes for combat support and clearing lines of fire.

It can also be used in operations other than war including humanitarian demining, peacekeeping support, engineering tasks and disaster area support.

Description
The add-on passive armour kit requires no modifications to the basic vehicle structure. The armoured cab is mounted on the vehicle's standard safety frame mounts and provides the occupants with protection from small arms fire and shell splinters. The added weight is claimed to have no effect on overall performance characteristics.

The armoured cab has space for an operator/driver and a commander/assistant. Reinforced glass block windows for vision forward, to the sides and to the rear, may be removed, leaving an external hardened glass pane to maintain cab isolation and conditioning.

Two doors are provided at the front of the cab for entry and exit and an additional door at the rear doubles as a refuelling access point and an emergency exit. The commander has a roof cupola with a full 360° traverse and provision for mounting a 7.62 mm or similar machine gun and/or a grenade projector.

The cab armour is of a special layered type and armour plating is provided for the engine compartment on three sides complete with integral air vanes for engine compartment ventilation; servicing access is still possible. Protection is also provided for the hydraulic pistons and tubing and for the fuel and hydraulic fluid tanks.

The cab is equipped with an air conditioning unit driven by the vehicle diesel engine and with an internal and external communications system. Internal lighting is provided and an external light projector may also be fitted. Full convoy and blackout lights are provided and other external additions contained in the kit include weapon mountings, brackets for four fuel containers, a camouflage net and three window wipers.

Internal stowage includes water tanks, brackets for personal weapons and equipment, stowage for machine gun ammunition and four replacement reinforced glass window blocks. The cab is sealed for operations under NBC conditions.

In mid-2004, the Israel Defense Force stated that it was to increase its D9R armoured bulldozer fleet in the Gaza Strip in an effort to deal with Palestinian mines and roadside bombs.

Caterpillar D9T fitted with Israel Military Industries bulldozer protection kit and the Israel Aircraft Industries remote controlled kit
(Israel Aircraft Industries)
1405655

At that time it was stated that an additional 25 units had been ordered, which would bring the total Israel Defense Force D9R fleet up to about 100 units.

Since it was first introduced into service the DR9 has been upgraded. It has now been fitted with front and rear charge coupled cameras to give the operator a wider field of view.

During Operation Iraqi Freedom, the US Army acquired 14 DR9s from Israel Defense Force stocks. These were deployed to Iraq during the initial invasion.

Variants

Israel Aircraft Industries, Ramta Division, has developed a remote controlled kit for the D9 tractor which is already deployed with the Israel Defense Force.

When fitted with this kit, all functions of the D9 dozer can be carried out by remote control including full operation of the dozer blade and ripper.

This is controlled using the portable control panel from a line-of-sight/close support location or from any remote location using multiple integrated cameras.

The proprietary robotics suite also allows for rapidly switching between manned and unmanned operation of the dozer with only a few minutes preparation.

According to Israel Aircraft Industries, the remote controlled D9 series dozer can be operated up to 3 km (line of sight) or 500 to 700 m (non line of sight) when operating in a built up area.

It is fitted with six standard cameras for driving, operating and observation including day and night capability. It is also fitted with an additional look out camera. Up to four camera views can be displayed at the same time on the combat operators display.

An on board navigation system is provided which can integrate existing maps and diagrams. There is also the capability to have multiple control units combined in order to separate camera and operational functionality.

Total weight of the D9 series with protection kit and remote control capability is currently being quoted as 60 tonnes and is capable of up to four hours of continuous operations.

Specifications

Weight of attachment: (approx) 6,000 kg
Cab dimensions (internal):
  (length) 2 m
  (width) 2.6 m
  (height) 1.7 m
Air conditioner capacity: 7.03 kW (24,000 BTU/h)

Status

Production as required. In service with Israel and the US.

Contractor

Israel Military Industries Limited (IMI)

Israel Military Industries ABK-3 add-on bulldozer kit

Description

Israel Military Industries Ltd produces a hydraulically operated add-on bulldozer kit known as the ABK-3. This is suitable for use on a range of MBTs including the Centurion, M48, M60 and several other designs. The attachment is mounted on the front of the MBT using existing towing and other lugs. Installation takes about 20 minutes without requiring any special tools.

When fitted, the dozer blade can dig to a level 0.25 m below the track level. The blade is 0.99 m high and 3.96 m wide. Weight of the complete kit is approximately 3,400 kg and a 24 V DC power supply is required from the carrier vehicle to drive a 10 hp electric motor. The control box is located in the driver's compartment.

Israel Military Industries ABK-3 add-on bulldozer kit mounted on Centurion MBT with dozer blade in deployed position
0511460

The dozer blade operates in four modes: travelling; 'floating', with the blade resting on the soil surface; blade down for digging; and with blade routers lowered for surface ripping. Blade capacity is 3.1 m^3. The dozer blade can also be used for clearing scatterable mines from flat surfaces. Tank speed when digging is approximately 5 km/h.

Status

Production as required. In service with the Israeli Army. Although the photograph shows the ABK-3 add on bulldozer kit fitted to the Centurion MBT, it should be noted that none of these gun tanks remain in service with the Israel Defense Force as they have all been converted to specialist roles such as engineer vehicles or heavily armoured troop carriers. The M48 tank has also been phased out of service with the IDF, and the M60 tank fleet is to be reduced. In Israel Defense Force service the ABK-3 would be fitted to the Merkava MBT. The Israel Defense Force uses the Merkava Mk 1, 2, 3 and 4.

Contractor

Israel Military Industries Limited (IMI)

Urdan RKM bulldozer attachment

Development

The Urdan RKM bulldozer attachment was developed jointly by Urdan RKM Limited and the Israeli Army to provide every MBT with the ability to act as an earth-moving vehicle.

In Israeli Army service the RKM bulldozer attachment is fitted to specialist heavy engineer vehicles based on modified Centurion tank chassis as well as the locally built Merkava Mk 1, 2, 3 and 4. It should be noted that the current production model is the Merkava Mk 4.

It can be fitted to other MBTs and, according to the manufacturer, no modifications are required to the actual vehicle in order to carry the RKM bulldozer attachment. There are, however, no known exports of the Urdan RKM bulldozer attachment.

The Israel Defense Force currently deploys the Puma armoured engineer vehicle which is based on a much modified Centurion tank chassis.

This can be fitted with a front mounted dozer blade as well as various types of mine clearing system of the roller or plough type.

It can also deploy a rocket propelled mine clearing system which is fired over the minefield and then exploded to create a blast overpressure to hopefully neutralise anti-tank mines.

Description

The Urdan RKM bulldozer attachment has three main assemblies. The first is a standard bulldozer blade modified slightly to improve its performance when working in rocky terrain and sandy soils. The second part is the electrohydraulic unit, which is completely sealed to enable operation underwater. It is connected to the vehicle's electrical system to supply hydraulic power to the main cylinder; the unit can be easily and rapidly replaced for maintenance. The electrohydraulic system and the movements of the blade are controlled from a control box inside the driver's compartment. The third part of the RKM bulldozer attachment is the main structure, which includes the adaptor and the arms; it carries the bulldozer blade and the power unit.

The structure was designed to withstand vibrations caused by the higher MBT driving speeds when crossing difficult terrain. The attachment can be installed and removed from the MBT by the tank crew in about 15 minutes. If required, the blade can be locked in its upper (travel) position manually if the hydraulic system is damaged. The high folding geometry of the attachment enables the carrier tank to negotiate steep banks, terraces and vertical obstacles.

The RKM bulldozer attachment has several operating modes. One is the travel position with the blade in the maximum up position. The bulldozer blade can also be made to 'float' so that the blade rests on the soil, but in

Urdan RKM bulldozer attachment fitted to Merkava Mk 1 MBT showing angle of blade when fully lifted   0511459

the 'blade down' mode the hydraulic cylinder pushes the blade down into the soil for heavy earth-moving. The attachment has automatic hydrostatic locking at any given position and a mechanical safety lock (using the travel lock) at the highest position.

Typical roles of the Urdan RKM bulldozer attachment include clearing battlefield obstacles and preparing fire positions.

Status
Production as required. In service with the Israeli Army. As far as it is known, there have been no exports of the Urdan RKM bulldozer attachment in recent years.

Contractor
Urdan Industries Limited

Japan

Mitsubishi Type 75 armoured dozer

Development
Development of an armoured dozer, to meet the operational requirements of the Japanese Ground Self-Defence Force, commenced in 1964 and two prototypes were built during Fiscal Year 1972 by Komatsu, one with a straight dozer blade and another with an angled blade.

After extensive trials, the latter was standardised in 1975 and the dozer is in service with the Japanese Ground Self-Defence Force.

The Type 75 armoured dozer can carry out over 90 per cent of the tasks of the US Caterpillar D6 medium dozer but is armoured and has a much higher road speed, enabling it to keep up with the leading elements of a convoy.

Like all Japanese armoured vehicles, the Type 75 armoured dozer was never offered on the export market. Production of the Type 75 armoured dozer was completed some time ago, but no replacement for the vehicle has been announced.

Description
The crew compartment of the Type 75 armoured dozer is of all-welded steel armour that provides the occupants with protection from small arms fire and shell splinters.

Type 75 armoured dozers (Kensuke Ebata)   0512299

Type 75 armoured dozer with dozer blade raised (Kensuke Ebata) 0088563

When the Type 75 armoured dozer is travelling, the dozer blade is to the rear and the fully armoured crew compartment at the front. The two-man crew can enter either by a door on the right side of the hull or through two circular rear-opening roof hatches. The driver is seated on the left with a rectangular shutter hinged at the top immediately in front of him. This has an integral vision block and can be locked open.

The commander is seated to the right of the driver and has a small square shutter hinged at the top, which also has a vision block and can be locked open. Vision blocks are provided in each side of this compartment and there is a shutter with an integral vision block in the rear of the crew compartment for forward vision during dozing operations. There is also a single vision block to the left of the shutter.

The water-cooled diesel engine and radiator are at the rear of the vehicle. In a combat area they are protected by armoured plates, which are removed when the Type 75 is operating in a non-combat area.

The torsion bar suspension either side consists of five dual rubber-tyred road wheels with the drive sprocket at the front and the idler at the rear. There are also three track-return rollers. Hydraulic shock-absorbers are fitted at the first, second and fifth road wheel stations.

The hydraulically operated dozer blade is controlled by the driver from inside the armoured cab. The dozer blade is hinged in the middle and a hydraulic winch can be fitted in front of the cab if required.

The Type 75 armoured dozer in unarmed.

Specifications
Type 75 armoured dozer
Crew: 2
Weight: 19,200 kg
Power-to-weight ratio: 13.39 kW/t (17.97 hp/t)
Length:
(travelling) 6.84 m
(working) 6.3 m
Width:
(travelling) 2.7 m
(working) 3.45 m
Height: 2.79 m
Max speed: 45 km/h
Fording: 1 m
Gradient: 60%
Engine: water-cooled diesel developing 257 kW (345 hp) at 2,100 rpm on road, 119 kW (160 hp) at 1,850 rpm when carrying out dozing activities
Armament: none

Status
Production complete. No longer marketed. In service with the Japanese Ground Self-Defence Force.

It is considered that a new vehicle will be developed to eventually replace the Type 75 armoured dozer.

Contractor
Komatsu Ltd

Norway

Alvis Moelv Armoured Engineer Vehicle

Development
In 1995, Alvis Moelv was awarded a contract by the Norwegian Army for the conversion of 22 Leopard 1 MBT chassis into Armoured Engineer Vehicles (AEV).

Late in 1999, the first prototype was deployed to Kosovo by the Norwegian Army, with the first two production vehicles being handed over in mid-October 1999.

The main roles of this AEV can be summarised as: the repair and re-establishment of the axis of advance; the rapid construction of slit trenches for armoured vehicles and assault personnel; the construction of field locations and fire emplacements for MBTs and AIFVs; preparing

Alvis Moelv Armoured Engineer Vehicle in travelling configuration crossing a bridge (Alvis Moelv)   1405657

Alvis Moelv Armoured Engineer Vehicle with dozer blade partly raised and arm fitted with bucket traversed to the front of the vehicle (Richard Stickland)   0130965

access and egress sites or entry and exit ramps for water crossings and to make riverbeds traversable; recovery of MBTs and other vehicles; constructing and removing battlefield obstacles and barriers; and the destruction of roads.

Within the Royal Norwegian Army, the Alvis Moelv Armoured Engineer Vehicle is known as Project 5025 and all 22 vehicles were delivered to the Norwegian Army by 2001.

Alvis Moelv closed down late in 2004 but the Leopard 1-based AEV remain in service with the Norwegian Army.

Description

The conversion from the original Leopard 1 MBT included removing the complete three-person turret, installing a new all-welded steel superstructure for the crew of two and new engineer systems. The Leopard 1 MBT chassis has been modified by the addition of an anti-spall liner and mine protection.

Mounted at the front of the vehicle is a hydraulically operated dozer blade. This has three hydraulic cylinders; one pitch and two elevation. The primary mission of this is to clear and destroy roads, with the secondary mission being to use the dozer blade as a soil anchor when operating the winch or excavator boom.

The dozer blade is 3.6 m wide and 1.1 m high and can also be fitted with two scarifiers to dig up surfaces of roads to a maximum depth of 0.50 m. It has a maximum earth moving capacity of 270 m³/h. The unique hydraulic design allows the dozer blade to be tilted, elevated and skewed.

Pivoted at the front of the hull is a hydraulically operated arm, traversed to the rear when not required. This arm can be traversed through 175° and is fitted with a bucket with a capacity of 1 m³ for digging purposes. The arm is able to reach to a maximum of 8 m and has a maximum digging depth of 4 m. If required, it is possible to mount a soil drill in place of the bucket.

Two hydraulic capstan winches are provided for recovery purposes; they would normally be used in conjunction with the dozer blade. One winch has a towing force of 90 kN with a total theoretical force of 720 kN. Each winch is provided with a storage drum that has 200 m of cable with a diameter of 16 mm.

The configuration includes a Krauss-Maffei Wegmann Type 2038 overhead weapon station armed with a 1 × .50 (12.7 mm) M2 HB machine gun.

If required, the US-developed Mineclearing Line Charge (MICLIC) can be carried and launched from the roof of the AEV.

Variants

Armoured mineclearing vehicle
Under contract to the Norwegian Army, Alvis Moelv built a flail-type mineclearing system. This programme was cancelled.

Beach Recovery Vehicle (Hippo)
Alvis Moelv supplied four of these to the UK for use by the Royal Marines during amphibious operations. Details are provided in a separate entry in *Jane's Military Vehicles and Logistics*.

Specifications

Armoured Engineer Vehicle
Crew: 2
Weight: 46,000 kg (armour dependant)
Power-to-weight ratio: 13.46 kW/t (18.04 hp/t)
Length: 10 m
Width:
   (overall) 3.6 m
   (rail transport) 3.37 m
Height: 3 m
Max road speed: (approx) 60 km/h
Max road range: (approx) 450 km
Fuel capacity: 985 litres
Fording:
   (with preparation) 2.2 m
   (with snorkel) 4 m
Vertical obstacle: 1.3 m
Trench: 2.5 m
Gradient: 60%
Side slope: 30%
Engine: MTU MB 838 Ca M-500, 10-cylinder diesel developing 619 kW (830 hp) at 2,200 rpm
Transmission: ZF 4 HP 250 planetary-gear shift with hydraulic torque converter, 4 forward gears and 1 reverse
Steering: double differential
Clutch: torque converter with mechanical interlock
Suspension: torsion bar
Electrical system: 24 V
Batteries: 6 × 12 V, 100 Ah (each)
Armament: 1 × .50 (12.7 mm) M2 HB machine gun

Status

Production complete. In service with Norwegian Army (22 units). No longer marketed.

Contractor

Alvis Moelv AS (This company closed in 2004).

Poland

MID armoured engineering vehicle

Development

During 1992, the Research and Development Centre of Mechanical Appliances (OBRUM) at Gliwice developed and produced the prototype of an armoured engineering vehicle, based on the chassis of the Russian-designed T-72 MBT and incorporating many features of the Polish-designed WZT-3 armoured recovery vehicle.

In April 2003 Malaysia placed a USD375 million contract with Poland that included the supply of three enhanced models called the MID-M breacher.

The MID vehicles delivered to Malaysia have a different specification to the standard production MID including locally produced 1,000 hp diesel coupled to a Renk fully automatic transmission and upgraded suspension system. The Malaysian vehicles are designated the MID-M.

Description

The vehicle, known as the MID Road Engineering Machine (MID - *Maszyna Inzynieryjno-Drogowa)*, uses many engineering features and components from the T-72/WZT-3 chassis and automotive components.

The main difference from the WZT-3 Armoured Recovery Vehicle (covered in detail in a separate entry in *Jane's Military Vehicles and Logistics*) is the provision of a hydraulically powered heavy jib crane arm located on the right-hand side of the armoured superstructure. The crane arm is provided either with gripper claws intended for the grasping and removal of battlefield obstacles, or a digger bucket.

The jib crane arm has a lift capacity of 7,000 kg and can extend from 5.94 to 7.56 m over a horizontal working angle of 230°; the maximum vertical working angle is +60° and minimum −55°.

MID armoured engineering vehicle based on chassis of T-72 MBT/WZT 3 ARV with dozer blade lowered and arm with bucket extended   0554969

MID armoured engineering vehicle in travelling configuration (OBRUM)

0589696

The gripper claws fitted to the end of the jib arm can open to a maximum width of 1 m, lift 3,000 kg and turn through an angle of 180°. Maximum operating height is 7.5 m and depth 5.5 m. If required, the gripper claws can be replaced by a 0.96 m³ scoop bucket with a cutting width of 0.92 m and a maximum cutting depth of 5 m. When not in use the scoop bucket and other equipment can be carried on the hull rear.

Located on the front of the vehicle is a V-shaped dozer blade with removable side extensions; the maximum width is 4.2 m. Maximum dozing depth is 0.25 m.

The vehicle is provided with two hydraulically operated winches for recovery and other purposes. The main winch has a maximum capacity of 840 kN (with a cable pulley) and is provided with 200 m of rope. An auxiliary winch has a capacity of 20 kN and 400 m of cable.

Other special equipment carried includes a 60 to 250 A arc welding system. There are stowage bins on the rear upper decking.

The basic crew is the commander and driver, although there is internal provision for a combat engineer team of three men. They are provided with an NBC air filtration system and detection equipment.

Armament is one 12.7 mm NSW (NSV) air defence machine gun, a 7.62 mm RPK light machine gun for local defence and a shoulder-fired RPG-7 unguided rocket-propelled grenade launcher and a thermal smoke generator are provided. The latter injects diesel fuel into the exhaust outlet on the left side of the hull towards the rear.

If required, the vehicle can be provided with deep wading equipment enabling the vehicle to wade through water obstacles up to 5 m for distances up to 1,000 m. The normal wading depth without preparation is 1.2 m.

Specifications

MID armoured engineering vehicle
Crew: 2 + 3
Weight: 46,500 kg
Power-to-weight ratio: 12.51 kW/t (16.77 hp/t)
Ground pressure: 90 kPa
Length: 8.73 m
Width:
  (over mudguards) 3.6 m
  (dozer blade) 4.2 m
Height: 2.79 m
Ground clearance: 0.43 m
Max speed: (roads) 60 km/h
Range: 650 km
Fording:
  (normal) 1.2 m
  (with preparation) 5 m
Gradient: 60%
Side slope: 30%
Vertical obstacle: 0.7 m
Trench: 1.2 m
Engine: V-12 W46-6 diesel developing 582 kW (780 hp) at 2,000 rpm
Armament:
  1 × 12.7 mm NSW MG
  1 × 7.62 mm RPK MG
  1 × RPG-7 rocket launcher
  8 × electrically operated 81 mm smoke grenade launchers

Jib crane
Max lift capacity: 7,000 kg
Jib length:
  (max) 7.56 m
  (min) 5.94 m
Working slope angle: −55° to +60°
Working traverse: 230°

Jib scoop
Capacity: 0.96 m³
Cutting width: 0.92 m
Cutting depth: 5.5 m

Gripper jaws
Max opening: 1 m
Nominal turn angle: 180°
Lift capacity: 3,000 kg
Max operational height: 7.5 m
Max operational depth: 5.5 m

Dozer blade
Width: (with extensions) 4.2 m
Cutting depth: 0.25 m

Main winch
Max towing capacity: (with pulley) 840 kN
Pay-out speed: 0.3 to 0.7 m/s
Winding speed: 0.31 to 0.74 m/s
Rope length: 200 m

Auxiliary winch
Max towing capacity: 20 kN
Max winding and pay-out speed: 1.3 m/s
Rope length: 400 m

Status
Small batch supplied to Poland. A total of three MID-M have now been supplied to Malaysia together with PT-91M MBT, WZT-4 armoured recovery vehicles and armoured PMC vehicle launched bridges.

Contractor
Osrodek Badawczo-Rozwojowy Urzadzen Mechaniczynch (OBRUM)

_____

MT-LB armoured engineer reconnaissance vehicle

Development
The Polish Army utilises a version of the Russian-designed MT-LB multipurpose tracked vehicle developed specifically for the engineer reconnaissance role.

The vehicle is intended for the reconnaissance of roads, bridges and their approaches, structures and potential demolition sites, minefields, battlefield obstacles, structures, water resources and other locations likely to be of interest to combat engineers. The vehicle is also equipped with sensors to detect and plot chemical and nuclear radiation contamination.

Production of the MT-LB is undertaken in Poland on an as required basis.

Description
The vehicle uses the same general outlines as the conventional MT-LB; full details of which can be found in *Jane's Armour and Artillery*. As far as it is known only Bulgaria and Poland are still marketing the MT-LB family of vehicles. Russia and Ukraine also offer a number of upgrades for the MT-LB family of tracked armoured vehicles. As far as it is known, Russia has not exported any of these MT-LB upgraded vehicles.

The crew of the MT-LB reconnaissance vehicle comprises the commander and driver, with provision internally for a further six men. The additional crew members either operate the various items of reconnaissance or radio equipment, or dismount for the close inspection of specific objectives.

Polish armoured engineer reconnaissance vehicle based on Polish-produced MT-LB multipurpose tracked vehicle chassis

0511462

Polish built Kroton mine laying vehicle which is armed with a 12.7 mm machine gun and showing launchers either side of the rear chassis for anti-tank mines (HSW)
1365161

Most of the additional crew members are seated towards the rear of the vehicle where the specialised role equipment is either located or stowed.

The reconnaissance equipment includes photographic and other optical instruments, plus specialised instruments for determining the state or characteristics of roads, ground surfaces and levels, river banks and water obstacles. Reconnaissance data is relayed to higher formations via an R-173 radio system which utilises a rail-type antenna mounted over the right-hand side of the hull; the antenna can be dismounted when not required. This information can be analysed on board and can be passed to the next level in the chain of command.

The vehicle is amphibious, propelled in the water by its tracks at a maximum speed of 8 km/h, and is provided with NBC air filtration equipment. Under normal operations the vehicle's various NBC sensors are maintained in a permanently on condition. Automatic and hand-operated fire extinguishers are provided.

Mounted at the front right is the commander's one-person manually operated turret provided with vision devices. Mounted over the turret is a 12.7 mm NSW (NSV) machine gun for local and air defence; stowage is provided for 240 rounds. Other armament carried includes six RPG-7 unguided Rocket-Propelled Grenade (RPG) launchers and 20 F-1 hand grenades. Eight 81 mm NDG-2 smoke grenade launchers are mounted on the hull sides towards the rear, four each side.

Variants

Baseline MT-LB
This is currently being marketed by HSW with standard equipment including a turret mounted 7.62 mm MG, self-entrenching equipment mounted on the hull at the top rear, NBC system, intercom, heater, engine pre-heater and towing hook.

Optional equipment for the Polish MT-LB includes various communications equipment, drivers night vision device, dosimeter, NBC decontamination set and a 12.7 mm machine gun mounted externally on a turret as fitted to the Kroton mine laying vehicle and Hors engineering reconnaissance vehicle.

Kroton anti-tank mine laying vehicle
The anti-tank mine laying version has four square launchers each with 20 tubes with the system capable of rapidly laying 400 anti-mines each of which is fitted with a self-destruct mechanism.

Gross combat weight is being quoted as 15.87 tonnes and speed when laying the anti-tank mines is between 7.5 and 22 km/h. The anti-tank mines can be launched from the sides or rear of the vehicle.

This is based on the stretched chassis which has a total of seven road wheel stations either side which provide the vehicle with more internal volume and payload.

Specifications

MT-LB armoured engineer reconnaissance vehicle
Crew: 2 + 6
Weight: 12,900 kg ±250 kg
Power-to-weight ratio: 9.52 kW/t (13.0 hp/t)
Ground pressure: 0.46 kg/cm^2
Length: 6.625 m
Width: (transport condition) 3 m
Height:
(to antenna) 2.7 m
(antenna lowered) 2.35 m
Ground clearance: 0.43 m (max)
Max speed:
(road) 60 km/h
(dirt road) 26-32 km/h
(water) 8 km/h
Range: 500 km
Fording: amphibious
Engine: SW680/167/1 6-cylinder turbocharged diesel developing 183 kW (245 hp)

Armament:
1 × 12.7 mm NSW MG
6 × RPG-7 rocket launchers
8 × 81 mm smoke grenade launchers

Status
Production as required. In service with the Polish Army.

Contractor
Huta Stalowa Wola SA

Marketed by
CENZIN Co. Ltd

Russian Federation

IMR-2 combat engineer vehicle

Development
The IMR-2 series of combat engineer vehicles is based on the chassis of the T-72 MBT and is the replacement for the first-generation IMR based on the T-54/T-55 MBT chassis.

The original IMR-2 underwent several production changes, the final model carrying extended mineclearing charges in addition to mineclearing ploughs and combat engineer equipment.

This was replaced in 1982 by the IMR-2M1 on which the extended mineclearing charges were removed and extra protection for the hydraulic system was introduced.

This model remained in production from March 1987 until July 1990 when a slightly revised model, the IMR-2M2, was introduced.

The latest version of the IMR-2 is designated the IMR-2MA and is similar to the IMR-2M, but has a combat weight of 49.5 tonnes, has a travelling length of 9.32 m and a travelling height of 3.43 m.

It is possible that a number of IMR-2 vehicles are now surplus to requirements and are available for sale.

Production of the IMR-2 is now complete and marketing is now being concentrated on the latest IMR-3M that has similar capabilities but is based on a more recent chassis.

Description
The layout of the IMR-2 series of combat engineer vehicles is the same as the T-72 MBT with driver's compartment at the front, crew compartment in the centre and power pack (engine, transmission and cooling system) compartment at the rear. The chassis of the IMR-2M is known as the Objekt 637.

To carry out its combat engineer role, the turret of the T-72 MBT has been removed and a new all-welded steel armoured superstructure has been fitted with bulletproof windows for the commander/operator. Mounted on this is the telescopic arm, which can be fitted with various attachments.

To enable it to carry out its combat engineer role on the battlefield, the IMR-2M has the following equipment:

- Front-mounted, hydraulically operated dozer blade which is 1 m high and 3.38 m wide when being used in the V-blade configuration, 3.925 m wide when being used in the straight dozing position and 3.212 m wide when being used in the grading position;
- Maximum digging depth of dozer blade is 450 mm. When not required, the blade is folded upwards. The clearing rate of the dozer blade depends on the type of terrain, for example stone barriers can be cleared at the rate of 280 to 350 m^3/h while trenches and ditches can be filled in at the rate of 350 to 360 m^3/h. Digging gun pits and fire positions are accomplished at the rate of 200 to 250 m^3/h;
- Multipurpose operating element which can have a bucket with a maximum capacity of 0.35 m^3 and a pull-and-push shovel capacity of 0.17 m^3. The bucket has an operating width of 1.33 m and a penetration depth of 450 mm;
- The above uses a telescopic arm which can also be fitted with a manipulator and can be traversed through a full 360°. With a reach of 8.15 m it can lift 2,000 kg. When travelling this is normally traversed to the rear. On the IMR-2M2 the gripper-type manipulator tool normally used with this arm is replaced by a more versatile attachment. The telescopic arm can be operated by remote control as well as from within the vehicle;
- A KMT-R plough type mine clearing system complete with an electromagnetic device to activate anti-tank mines before they come into contact with the vehicle.

Standard equipment includes night vision equipment for the commander and driver, NBC system of the overpressure type, fire detection and suppression system and an engine starting pre-heater. The vehicle can lay its own smoke screen by injecting diesel fuel into the exhaust outlet on the left side of the hull.

Variants

IMR-3 series
Whereas the earlier IMR-2 series of combat engineer vehicles is based on the chassis of the T-72 series MBT, the latest IMR-3 series, which includes the IMR-3M, is based on the more recent T-90 series MBT. The equipment fitted to the IMR-3 is the same as that used on the older IMR-2.

IMR-2M combat engineer vehicle with dozer blade raised and KMT-8 plough type mineclearing equipment lowered   0512435

IMR combat engineer vehicle with dozer blade being used in 'V' configuration (Shaun C Connors)   0525506

The latest IMR-3M has a combat weight of 49.5 tonnes including the front mounted mine clearance attachment and is powered by a BM-84MC diesel developing 840 hp which gives a maximum quoted road speed of 50 km/h with a road range of up to 500 km.

As of late 2010 the T-90 was the only MBT in production in Russia and was in service with Algeria, India (local production), Libya, Russia and Turkmenistan.

Specifications

IMR-2M2 combat engineer vehicle
Crew: 2
Weight: 44,300 kg
Power-to-weight ratio: 14.14 kW/t (18.96) hp/t
Ground pressure: 0.98 kg/cm²
Length: 9.55 m
Width:
   (hull) 3.735 m
   (overall) 4.35 m
Height: 3.68 m
Ground clearance: 0.426 m
Max road speed: 50 km/h
Road range: 500 km
Max gradient: 25°
Fording: 1.2 m
Engine: V-84-1 V-12 multifuel liquid-cooled diesel developing 626 kW (840 hp) (IMR-2A is powered by a V-84MS engine)
Armament: 1 × 12.7 mm NSVT MG

Status

Production of the IMR-2 is complete. All future production would be to the IMR-3 configuration which is based on the latest T-90 MBT rather than the older T-72 MBT which is no longer in production in Russian. The IMR-2 is in service with the Russian Army and other undisclosed countries.

Contractor

Ural Transport Engineering Design Bureau (Uralvagonzavod)

IMR combat engineer vehicle

Development

The combat engineer vehicle IMR (*Inzhenernaya Maschina Razgrazhdeniia* - engineer vehicle for the removal of obstacles) was first seen in 1973 and is based on the Russian T-55 MBT chassis. It evolved from the Objekt 616A prototype first produced in 1969. In most front line Russian units the IMR has been replaced by the IMR-2, which is based on the more recent and more well protected and mobile T-72 MBT chassis.

Production of the IMR-2 combat engineer vehicle is complete and details of this are provided in a separate entry in *Jane's Military Vehicles and Logistics*. Marketing is now being concentrated on the latest IMR-3M combat engineer vehicle.

Description

For the manufacturing conversion from the original T-55 MBT, the turret was removed and replaced by a hydraulically operated crane which can be traversed through 360°. The jib of this crane is telescopic and when in the travelling position rests on a cradle at the rear of the hull. The cradle folds down against the engine deck when the crane is being used.

The crane is provided with a pair of pincer-type grabs, which are used to remove trees and other battlefield obstacles. The grab can be replaced by a small bucket which is normally carried above the left-rear track when not required.

The crane operator is provided with an armoured cupola, which has observation windows. A searchlight is mounted on the crane for night operations. At the front of the hull is a hydraulically operated dozer blade, which can be used in the straight or V-configuration, but cannot angle doze.

Standard equipment for the IMR includes night vision devices, NBC system and the ability to lay a smoke screen by injecting diesel fuel into the exhaust on the left side of the hull. Some vehicles carry an un-ditching beam, which is mounted at the rear of the hull when not required.

Variants

IWT
The IWT (*Inzynieryjny Woz Torujacy*) is the Polish equivalent of the IMR and shares many of the same features. However, the IWT can carry a PW-LWD rocket-launched mineclearing system identical to that carried by Polish Army T-72 MBTs.

Specifications

IMR combat engineer vehicle
Crew: 2
Weight: (combat) 37,500 kg
Power-to-weight ratio: 11.53 kW/t (15.47 hp/t)
Ground pressure: 0.76 kg/cm²
Length:
   (dozer blade in operating position and crane stowed) 10.6 m
   (hull) 6.45 m
Width:
   (hull) 3.27 m
   (over dozer blade) 3.48 m
Height:
   (crane operator's cupola) 2.48 m
   (crane in travelling position) 3.37 m
Ground clearance: 0.425 m
Track: 2.64 m
Track width: 580 mm
Length of track on ground: 3.84 m
Max speed: (road) 48 km/h
Range: 400 km
Fuel capacity: 812 litres
Fording: 1.4 m
Gradient: 60%
Vertical obstacle: 0.8 m
Trench: 2.7 m
Engine: Model V-55 V-12 water-cooled diesel developing 433 kW (580 hp) at 2,000 rpm
Transmission: manual with 5 forward and 1 reverse gears
Electrical system: 24 V
Batteries: 4 × 12 V, 280 Ah
Armament: nil

Armour
Hull front: 100 mm at 60°
Hull sides: 70 mm
Hull rear: 60 mm
Hull floor: 20 mm
Hull roof: 30 mm

Status

Production complete. No longer marketed. In service with Russia and many other countries. In the Russian Army it has been supplemented by the T-72 MBT based IMR-2 series combat engineer vehicle. Export marketing is now concentrated on the latest IMR-3 based on the latest T-90 MBT chassis. It is possible that the Russian Army has some IMR and IMR-2 surplus to requirements and these could be refurbished prior to export.

Contractor

Ural Transport Engineering Design Bureau (Uralvagonzavod)

IRM engineer reconnaissance vehicle

Development

The IRM engineer reconnaissance vehicle (IRM - *Inzhenernaya Rezvedivatel 'naya Maschina*) was originally known in the West as the IPR amphibious engineer vehicle. It is based on components from the Kurgan Machine Construction Plant BMP-1 Infantry Fighting Vehicle (IFV) tracked chassis.

Production of the BMP-1 was completed some time ago and it was replaced in production by the improved BMP-2 IFV. This in turn was replaced in production by the BMP-3 IFV which is a brand new design.

The IRM is intended for engineer and other reconnaissance over a wide variety of terrain and climatic conditions. It can be carried to its zone of operations by cargo aircraft, assault ships or hovercraft.

The IRM engineer reconnaissance vehicle is in service with the Russian Army and production is undertaken on an as required basis. Marketed by Rosoboronexport.

This IRM engineer reconnaissance vehicle is still be offered on the export by Rosoboronexport but as far as it is known there have been no export sales as of late 2010.

Description

The IRM is based on automotive components of the BMP-1 IFV but uses a longer all-welded steel armour hull with an extra road wheel, making seven road wheels each side; the diesel power pack is located at the rear. There are also five track-return rollers.

The all-welded steel-armoured hull of the IRM provides the occupants with protection from small-arms fire. The vehicle is fully amphibious and, when travelling, the hull superstructure may carry a folded-down snorkel mast approximately 10 m long which is erected when the vehicle operates fully submerged; this mast is not always carried.

When floating, the vehicle is driven and steered by two three-bladed, cowled propellers mounted one either side at the rear. A trim vane is fitted at the front of the vehicle and this is extended prior to amphibious operations.

Internally the IRM engineer reconnaissance vehicle is divided into three main compartments; driver's, fighting and power pack.

Four further sections include the bow, right- and left-hand sections for the diesel fuel tanks and the stern.

The driver's and fighting compartments are protected against nuclear warfare effects with a total radiation penetration reduction ratio of 2.78.

Vehicle services include: a sealed NBC system; an internal air regeneration system, which can switch on automatically, allowing the vehicle to remain airtight in contaminated areas for up to four hours; a fire extinguishing system; a bilge pump device; and a reusable smoke-generation system which injects diesel fuel into the engine exhausts.

The crew consists of up to six personnel, the basic crew being the commander, driver and one or two 'reconnaissance engineers'; extra personnel may be carried for dismounted reconnaissance operations.

The driver and commander are seated towards the front of the hull and are provided with circular hatches; more hatches are provided for the engineers. There is an emergency escape hatch under the hull. The commander is also provided with a small turret at the front of the hull, which mounts day and night vision devices and a 7.62 mm PKT machine gun; an infra-red searchlight is mounted next to the machine gun. The only other armament consists of the crew's personal weapons, although a smoke-generating apparatus is provided.

For closed-down observation the driver is provided with a TNPO-160 observation device for land use; this is changed to a TNP-370 for use when in water. Also provided is a TVN-2BM surveillance device.

For the reconnaissance role the IRM is provided with a variety of specialised equipment, such as:

- TNA-3 inertial land navigation system
- RShM-2 mine detection system
- auger-type sensor for determining the load-bearing capacities of various types of terrain (described as a PR-1 'penetrometer' and probably coupled to an onboard computer)

IRM engineer reconnaissance vehicle showing its amphibious characteristics with shrouded propellers at rear (Rosoboronexport) 1334220

- an EIR echo-sounder providing an accurate determination of water depth from 0.5 to 20 m (this system has an automatic recorder, three hydro-acoustic transducers and can be used to determine the firmness of river bottoms)
- an AGI-1s artificial horizon mounted on the driver's control panel
- clinometer to measure beach and other terrain angles for the driver
- PAB-2M aiming circle
- seven day plus two night vision devices.

Also carried are a PIR-451 retractable engineer reconnaissance periscope 1.5 m long (of which 0.75 m can be raised) and a DSP-30 range-finder to carry out basic survey operations from within the vehicle. Portable equipment carried for use outside the vehicle includes RVM-2M, IMP-2 and RVM-2 hand-held mine detectors, a device for measuring the thickness of ice and a portable terrain load-bearing measuring instrument. Also carried are two R-147 radio sets with a range of 20 km.

Mounted at the front of the vehicle, in line with the tracks, are two hydraulically operated arms, carrying spade-like units, which are mine detectors using the induction principle.

The detector units are held parallel to the ground surface by a hydraulic terrain-following mechanism mounted on the arms. If the detector senses a mine, the vehicle will stop automatically for the mine to be cleared manually. This can clear a path up to a depth of 3.6 m wide and to a depth of 0.30 m. The vehicle will also stop automatically if the detector strikes an obstacle such as an immovable tree or rock.

When not in use, the detector arms are folded back on to the roof and sides of the vehicle. The RShM-2 river-type wide-span mine detector can detect ferromagnetic materials at a depth of up to 300 mm with the vehicle moving at speeds of 3 to 5 km/h.

According to Russian sources, the IRM can carry out route reconnaissance at a typical speed of 8 to 10 km/h and mine fields at the rate of 5 km/h. A water barrier 100 m wide can be covered in five minutes.

Should an IRM engineer reconnaissance vehicle become stranded in soft or difficult terrain under hazardous circumstances, such as under enemy fire, the IRM can make use of a rocket-powered self-recovery system, which can be utilised with all crew members remaining under cover.

At the top of the hull rear are two banks of up to twelve 9M39 solid-propellant rockets which can be ignited to provide thrust to assist the vehicle from difficulties.

Each mass-produced 9M39 rocket engine weighs 6.3 kg, is 70 mm in diameter and 800 mm long. Each rocket motor can deliver a tractive force of 312 kg.

IRM engineer reconnaissance vehicle from the rear showing large ducted propellers for amphibious operations (Christopher F Foss)   1296013

IRM engineer reconnaissance vehicle with mine detection devices extended to the front of vehicle, periscope in raised position and crew hatches locked in the vertical position (Rosoboronexport)   1334219

Specifications

IRM engineer reconnaissance vehicle
Crew: up to 6
Weight: 18,000 kg
Power-to-weight ratio: 14.23 kW/t (16.67 hp/t)
Ground pressure: 0.69 kg/cm^2
Length: 8.30 m
Width: 3.15 m
Height: 2.42 m
Ground clearance: 0.40 m
Max speed:
(land) 52 km/h
(water) 10 km/h
Range: 500 km
Fuel capacity: 600 litres
Endurance afloat: 12 h
Max gradient: 36°
Vertical obstacle: 0.65 m
Fording: amphibious
Trench: 2.3 m
Engine: Type UTD-20 6-cylinder in-line water-cooled diesel developing 224 kW (300 hp) at 2,000 rpm
Transmission: manual, 5 forward gears and 1 reverse
Steering: clutch and brake
Suspension: torsion bar
Electrical system: 24 V
Armament: 1 × 7.62 mm PKT MG
smoke generator
Armour: (hull) steel

Status
Production as required. In service with the Russian Army and probably some other countries.

Contractor
Muromteplovoz JSC

MT-LB engineer vehicle

Development
The MT-LB engineer vehicle is a variant of the MT-LB multipurpose tracked vehicle. As far as it is known only Bulgaria and Poland are still marketing the MT-LB family of vehicles. The vehicle was originally designed and built in Ukraine.

As far as it is known there has been no recent production of brand new MT-LB vehicles by any of these countries. A number of countries have a number of ML-LB variants, including engineer vehicles, that are now surplus to requirements.

A number of contractors in Russia and the Ukraine are now offering automotive upgrades for the MT-LB multipurpose tracked vehicle and these are also applicable to the MT-LB engineer vehicle. These normally relate to the installation of a new engine and in some cases a new transmission.

Description
The MT-LB engineer vehicle is similar in appearance to the basic MT-LB but modified to carry a plough blade on the hull roof or side. This blade is manually fitted to two hydraulic arm assemblies on the hull rear to allow plough blade operations to the rear only. Other combat engineer equipment is carried internally.

MT-LB engineer vehicle with plough blade in travelling position alongside of hull 0511457

The MT-LB is fully amphibious, being propelled in the water by its tracks at a maximum speed of 8 km/h. Mounted at front-right side of the hull is a one-person manually operated turret that is armed with a 7.62 mm PKT machine gun.

The former East German Army used the MT-LB for combat engineer purposes but their version lacked the plough blade. A rectangular box on the rear upper hull carried engineer equipment.

Variants
Zabot
A prototype of an MT-LB based Czech Army engineer vehicle with a large dozer blade at the rear is known as Zabot. As far as is known this remained at the prototype stage and was not developed further.

Status
Production complete. The standard MT-LB is in service with the following countries, some of whom also operate the engineer variant: Armenia, Azerbaijan, Bangladesh, Belarus, Bulgaria, Finland, Hungary, Kazakhstan, Lithuania, Montenegro, Moldova, Russia, Serbia, Sweden and Ukraine.

Contractor
Bulgarian, Polish and Russian state factories. As far as it is known, there has been no recent production of the MT-LB vehicle in any of these three countries.

Muromteplovoz MT-LB Versatile Road Earth Moving Machine

Development
Based on its extensive experience in the design, development and production of a wide range of upgrade packages for the tracked and wheeled armoured fighting vehicles, Muromteplovoz has developed the Versatile Road Earth Moving Machine.

This is based on a modified and upgraded MT-LB multipurpose tracked armoured vehicle chassis which was built in large numbers in Ukraine.

Production of the MT-LB has been completed but large quantities remain in service in many parts of the world.

According to the manufacturer, typical missions of the MT-LB Versatile Road Earth Moving Machine includes preparing fire positions and clearing away battlefield obstacles.

It is understood that the Versatile Road Earth Moving Machine has been developed as a private venture but as of late 2010 it remained at the prototype stage.

Description
The overall layout of the vehicle is almost identical to the standard MT-LB with the driver front left and vehicle commander to the right. The power pack is to the rear of the driver's position which leaves the remainder of the vehicle clear to carry troops or cargo.

Above the commander's position is a manually operated one-person turret armed with one 7.62 mm PKT machine gun.

In this upgrade, mounted at the front of the chassis is a hydraulically operated dozer blade which is 3.09 m wide and 750 mm high. This blade has a maximum cutting depth of 390 mm and can be used as a conventional straight dozer blade or traversed 18° left and right.

Mounted on the roof at the rear is a hydraulic arm complete with a bucket that is normally used over the rear arc. For travelling however, this is normally traversed so that it lays over the top of the hull.

This excavator is operated by a person situated in a protected position at the right rear of the chassis with this position being provided with vision blocks.

The standard excavator bucket has a maximum capacity of 0.25 cubic meters, and with boom extended to 1 m, has a maximum load carrying capacity of one tonne.

MT-LB-based Versatile Road Earth Moving Machine from the rear with dozer blade raised and excavator arm stowed for travelling (Muromteplovoz) 1296010

Maximum excavating depth is 2 m with a maximum height discharge of 2.6 m and a total traverse of 270°.

The chassis has been upgraded in a number of areas including the installation of a YaMZ-238VM four-stroke diesel developing 240 hp.

It is claimed that the Versatile Road Earth Moving Machine can be transported by the Il-76 and An-22 transport aircraft as well as by heavy lift helicopters as an under slung load.

Specifications

MT-LB Versatile Road Earth Moving Machine
Crew: 2
Weight: (combat) 13,500 kg
Length: 7.44 m
Width: 3.09 m
Height:
  (with excavating equipment) 2.75 m
Max road speed: 60 km/h
Armament: 1 × 7.62 mm PKT MG
Armour:
  (hull) steel
  (turret) steel

Status

Development complete. Production as required.

Contractor

Muromteplovoz

TBS-86 tank-mounted dozer blade

Development

The TBS-86 hydraulically operated tank-mounted dozer blade is categorised by its manufacturers as a snow dozer but its applications extend to clearing debris from roads, surface scraping and preparing fire positions.

It can be attached to the front of Russian-designed and built T-54/55, T-62 and T-72 MBTs. It is understood that this TBS-86 tank mounted dozer blade can also be fitted to the more recent T-90 series of MBT.

As of late 2010 the T-90 was the only MBT in production in Russia and was in service with Algeria, India (local production), Libya, Russia and Turkmenistan.

Description

The complete TSB-86 tank-mounted dozer blade equipment consists of the dozer blade, pushing frame, hydraulic pump drive, electrical systems and two control panels in the driver's position. The time taken to attach the equipment to the front of the hull is from 1.5 to two hours.

The dozer blade is attached to the pusher frame in such a way that it can be configured to the optimum position for grading or dozing by altering the blade angle.

The optimum position is set automatically by a limit switch as the equipment is changed from the travelling to the working position. Blade angles are altered by two hydraulic cylinders protected inside telescopic armoured steel shrouds.

Electrical power for the hydraulics is taken from the host vehicle's electrical system and supplied to equipment inside the pusher frame via an armoured cable.

Specifications

TBS-86 tank-mounted dozer blade
Weight: (attached) 2,000 kg
Width: 3.38 m
Height: 0.9 m
Blade turning angle: 15°

TBS-86 tank-mounted dozer blade on T-72 MBT with system lowered into operating position, with dozer blade at an angle 0007333

Path clearing capacity:
  (anti-tank ditches) 170-200 m³/h
  (water crossing approaches) 350-400 m³/h
  (stone obstacles) 70-80 m³/h
  (trails through deep snow) 10-12 m³/h
Time required to prepare fire position: 0.5-0.7 h

Status

Production of the TBS-86 tank-mounted dozer blade is undertaken on an as-required basis. In service with the Russian Army and probably other countries.

Contractor

Russian State factories

Tank-mounted bulldozers BTU and BTU-55

Description

The BTU and BTU-55 hydraulically operated tank-mounted bulldozers can both be fitted to either the T-54 or T-55 series of MBTs. The BTU-55 is the more recent version and is an improvement in all aspects.

The original BTU took between 90 and 120 minutes to be installed on a tank and between 30 and 40 minutes to be removed.

The main drawback of the original BTU dozer blade was its weight so in 1955 the BTU-55 was developed which could be used on the T-54 and T-55 tanks. This weighed only 1,400 kg and had no effect on the performance of the tank.

A BTU-55M bulldozer unit for attachment to T-55 series tanks is also marketed by Bulgaria.

Typical uses of these tank-mounted dozers include clearing battlefield obstacles and preparing fire positions for tanks and artillery systems. The dozer blade has also been observed fitted to up-armoured T-55 series MBTs.

The T-54/T-55 has now been phased out of front-line Russian Army service but is still in widespread service with many other countries.

A number of countries have exported surplus T-54/T-55 MBTs in recent years and some of these may have been fitted with the BTU series of dozer blades.

Bulgarian BTU-55M bulldozer unit fitted to T-55AM tank which is also fitted with additional passive armour 0512295

Romanian tank fitted with dozer blade shown here raised into the travelling position 1162410

Variants

STU and STU-38 (STU-2) snow ploughs

These were developed in the early 1950s for clearing snow from roads with the equipment fitted to T-34/85 and T-54B tanks.

The STU snowplough was designed to clear convoy routes with a snow depth of up to 1.2 m at a speed of 5 to 8 km/h.

The STU-38 was designed to clear snow and the upper layer from slightly irregular terrain (terrain snow profiling). It could clear 800 mm to 1,000 mm of snow with a width of 3 to 3.2 m in one pass.

This was followed by the improved STU-2M in 1961 which was fitted with an electro-hydraulic control system which was standardised for use with the BTU dozer blade.

TBS-86 tank mounted dozer blade

This is covered in a separate entry in *Jane's Military Vehicles and Logistics* and can be installed on the more recent T-72 and T-90 MBTs.

As of late 2010 the T-90 was the only MBT in production in Russia and was in service with Algeria, India (local production), Libya, Russia and Turkmenistan.

Specifications

Model	BTU	BTU-55
Weight:	2,300 kg	1,400 kg
Width:	3.4 m	3.8 m
Clearing speed:	1.5-5 km/h	5-7 km/h
(in snow)	4-6 km/h	4-6 km/h
Digging performance:	100-200 m³/h	130-150 m³/h
Pushing performance:	350 m³/h	
Mounting time:	80-90 min	60 min
Dismounting time:	30-60 min	45 min

Status

Production complete in Russia but still marketed by Bulgaria. In widespread service. As far as it is known there has been no recent production of these tank-mounted bulldozers.

Contractor

Bulgarian state factories
Russian state factories

Spain

Peugeot Talbot CZ-10/25E Alacran armoured engineer vehicle

Development

During 1995, the Spanish Army requested Peugeot Talbot SA to manufacture for evaluation, a prototype of the CZ-10/25E Alacran armoured engineer vehicle based on the chassis of a modified ex-Spanish Army General Dynamics Land Systems M60 series MBT.

In 1997, Peugeot Talbot was awarded a (at the time of writing) Pta3,441 million (USD23.7 million) contract to convert 38 M60 MBTs into CZ-10/25E Alacran armoured engineer vehicles for the Spanish Army.

The first three conversions were delivered during 1997 with 15 following in 1998 and the remaining 20 during 1999.

Also competing for this contract was the GAMESA M60 VZ engineer tank also based on a modified M60 MBT chassis. This never passed the prototype stage.

Spain also uses an M60 series tank chassis fitted with a Krauss-Maffei Wegmann (previously Military Mobile Bridges) LEGUAN bridge, which is launched over the front of the vehicle.

Description

The conversion of the original M60 MBT to the CZ-10/25E Alacran involved the removal of the 105 mm M68 main gun from the turret and the replacement of elements of the power pack (engine, transmission and steering system) bearings, brakes and electrical system.

The M60 cast amour turret is retained, mounting a Case Poclain mechanical digger to be used over a full 360° traverse without having to move the vehicle. The hydraulic digger has an articulated arm with a reach of 7.21 m and a maximum depth of 2.65 m using a 430-litre capacity rear-excavating shovel, which can lift a maximum load of 7,000 kg. The shovel can be replaced by an NPK hammer or a Verachert VTC-30 cutting tool.

The conversion involved a new central hydraulic power take-off from the main L3 Combat Propulsion Systems AVDS-1790-2 series diesel engine to drive a front-mounted dozer blade 4 m wide and 0.8 m deep; excavation depth is up to 0.3 m. The blade, controlled from the driver's position, can also act as a stabilising anchor.

The dozer blade can be replaced by mineclearing ploughs or rollers. When mineclearing, a marking pole emplacement set can be added to the centre of the hull rear. A Global Positioning System (GPS) can be fitted for accurate minefield recording purposes.

Peugeot Talbot CZ-10/25E Alacran armoured engineer vehicle in action with dozer blade raised and arm with bucket attached traversed to the front
0007399

The CZ-10/25E Alacran armoured engineer vehicle also has a rear-mounted hydraulic winch with a continuous Citröen spool having a direct traction force of 25,000 kg; this can be increased to 50,000 kg by inserting a return block. The winch is provided with 80 m of 26 mm diameter cable having a maximum pulling speed of 5 m/min.

Armament involves a .50 (12.7 mm) M2 MB machine gun next to the commander's turret hatch. Eight 76 mm electrically operated smoke grenade dischargers are provided which are mounted four either side of the turret firing forwards.

The CZ-10/25E Alacran has a crew of three.

CZ-10/25E Alacran replacement

In the longer term, Spain will replace this vehicle with a new armoured engineer vehicle based on a Leopard 2A4 MBT chassis.

In mid-2010 Patria Land & Armament announced that they had teamed with the Spanish company of EXPAL to offer a mine clearing vehicle based on the chassis of the German Krauss-Maffei Wegmann Leopard 2A4 MBT to meet the potential requirements of the Spanish Army.

Under the terms of this agreement, EXPAL would be prime contractor with Patria Land & Armament being main subcontractor.

This would be based on the Heavy Mine Breaching Vehicle (HMBV) based on a much modified Leopard 2A4 chassis that has already been supplied to the Finnish Army by Patria Land & Armament.

The HMBV can also be used for limited engineer roles such as preparing fire positions. Details of the Patria Land & Armament HMBV are provided in a separate entry in *Jane's Military Vehicles and Logistics* and this is already in service with the Finnish Defence Force.

Other potential Leopard 2 based AEV solutions are the German FFG Wisent 2 Leopard 2 Support Vehicle and the German/Swiss Kodiak armoured engineer vehicle.

The former was shown for the first time in mid-2010 and as of late 2010 was still at the prototype stage. The Kodiak is now in production in Switzerland to meet the requirements of Netherlands, Sweden and Switzerland.

Details of both of these vehicles are provided in separate entries in *Jane's Military Vehicles and Logistics*.

Status

The conversion of 38 vehicles was undertaken between 1997 and 1999 for the Spanish Army. Production can be resumed if additional significant orders are placed. The Spanish Army received 50 M60A1 MBTs from the US of which 38 were converted to the CZ-10/25E Alacran standard and 12 to VLPD 26/70E AVLBs.

The bridge and launching system for Spain was provided by the then MAN Mobile Bridges which has now been taken over by Krauss-Maffei Wegmann.

Contractor

Peugeot Talbot SA, Spain

Turkey

Turkish M48 based armoured engineer vehicle

Development

The Turkish Land Forces Command (TLFC) has always relied on upgraded Armoured Fighting Vehicles (AFV) to meet its operational requirements including large quantities of US-manufactured M48 tanks.

The TLFC facility at Kayseri started upgrading M48 tanks with the assistance of the US as far back as 1983 with the Arifiye coming on stream the following year.

M48 armoured engineer vehicle based on a surplus M48T5 tank chassis
(Christopher F Foss)
1133924

In all over 2,000 M48 tanks were upgraded to the M48A5T1/M48A5T2 standard with all of these being armed with a 105 mm gun. The German company of Krauss-Maffei Wegmann also developed an upgrade package for the M48 tank which was almost identical to that supplied to the German Army under the designation of the M48A2GA2.

This had many improvements and is armed with a 105 mm gun and powered by an MTU MB 837 Ea-500 diesel. While the two prototypes were supplied by Germany, a total of 165 conversions were carried out in Turkey under the designation of the M48T5.

Recently two new vehicles, based on surplus M48T5 chassis, have been developed and placed in production at the Kayseri facilities of the TLFC, the Armoured Recovery vehicle (ARV) and the Armoured Engineer Vehicle (AEV).

It is understood that production has now been completed but it could be resumed if additional orders are placed by the Turkish Land Forces Command.

Description
Although these vehicles have a different battlefield role they both feature a lower hull of a M48T5 tank fitted with a brand new all-welded armoured superstructure. This provides protection from small arms fire and shell splinters.

Crew compartment is on the front left side, turntable mounted boom at front right and the power pack at the rear.

The M48-based AEV has a combat weight of 51 tonnes and is fitted with a hydraulically operated winch with a maximum rated capacity of 70 tonnes and an auxiliary winch with a capacity of two tonnes with both of these being deployed to the front of the vehicle.

The turntable mounted boom with a telescopic jib can be traversed through 195° and has a maximum lifting capacity of seven tonnes. The boom can be rapidly fitted with various attachments to meet specific battlefield engineer roles including a bucket which can excavate up to 140 m³ of soil an hour.

This can be rapidly replaced by auger for boring holes in the ground. This is about 25 cm diameter and 200 cm in length. When not required this is stowed on the rear decking. When travelling, the boom is traversed to the rear and lays along the right side of the hull.

Mounted under the front of the hull is a hydraulically operated dozer blade which can shift up to 270 m³ of soil an hour. In addition this is used when the vehicle is recovering heavier vehicles and as a stabiliser blade when the boom is being used.

A variety of other specialised equipment is carried including a 350 A electric welding system. Armament includes a roof-mounted 7.62 mm or .50 (12.7 mm) HB machine gun.

Specifications
M48 based AEV
Weight: (combat) 51,000 kg
Length: 8.375 m
Width: 3.666 m
Height: 3.195 m
Range: 280 km
Fuel capacity: 890 litres
Fording:
 (standard) 1.2 m
 (snorkel) 4 m
Max gradient: 60%
Max side slope: 30%
Vertical obstacle: 0.9 m
Trench: 2.50 m
Engine: MTU MB837 Ea 500 diesel
Armament: 1 × 7.62 mm or .50 (12.7 mm) M2 HB machine gun

Status
Production complete. In service with the Turkish Land Forces Command.

Contractor
See Development.

FNSS Savunma Sistemleri Armoured Combat Vehicle - Armoured Engineering Squad Vehicle (AESV)

Development
Following a competition, FNSS Savunma Sistemleri (previously FNSS Defense Systems) was awarded a contract to build 1,698 Armoured Combat Vehicles (ACVs) to meet the operational requirements of the Turkish Land Forces Command.

First production vehicles were delivered in 1991 and final vehicles were delivered under the original contract early in 2000.

Export marketing started at an early stage and in 1997 the United Arab Emirates placed a contract with FNSS Savunma Sistemleri for the supply of 136 specialised vehicles with the first of these being delivered early in 1999.

Included in this contract was a quantity of Armoured Combat Vehicle - Armoured Engineering Squad Vehicle (AESV), or AESV 350 as it is also referred to by the manufacturer, with the 350 indicating the output of the Detroit Diesel engine in horse power.

This has been designed by FNSS Savunma Sistemleri to move a team of combat engineers in and out of the combat zone while providing ballistic protection to the team and their equipment from enemy direct and indirect fire weapons.

By late 2010, sales of the ACV had been made to Malaysia (211 delivered with another 48 ordered early in 2008), Turkey (1,698 + 551 with all delivered) and UAE (136 delivered).

In April 2008, Malaysia placed an order through DRB-HICOM Defence Technologies, and its subsidiary, Defence Services to supply additional FNSS vehicles to the Malaysian Army.

This order covered the supply of 48 Adnan standard ACV and eight ACS-S armed with the French TDA 120 mm 120R 2M recoiling mortar, which have now been delivered.

The ACV-S is the latest version of the ACV to enter production and was developed by the company as a private venture to meet customer requirements for a vehicle with increased volume and payload.

It is in service with Malaysia and Saudi Arabia with the latter country using the vehicle in the command post configuration.

Description
The hull of the ACV-AESV is of all-welded aluminium construction with an additional layer of steel armour to provide a higher level of battlefield survivability.

The driver is seated at the front of the vehicle on the left side with the fully enclosed diesel power pack to the right. The driver has a single piece hatch cover and four-day periscopes that give observation over the front and sides. The central one of these can be replaced by an image intensification or thermal device for driving at night.

There is an additional raised cupola to the rear of the driver's position. It has a single roof hatch and day periscopes with the .50 (12.7 mm) M2 HB machine gun cupola being mounted on the right side of the roof.

The .50 (12.7 mm) M2 HB machine gun is mounted externally with the gunner aiming the weapon from within the cupola via periscope with a magnification of ×5. The cupola also has a single piece hatch cover that opens to the rear and three day periscopes that give observation to the front and sides.

The troop compartment is at the rear and is provided with a single piece hatch that opens to the rear with normal means of entry and exit being via the large power operated ramp at the rear that is also provided with an emergency access door.

The troops are seated either side on bench seats with two firing ports and associated vision devices being provided either side of the troop compartment.

Suspension is of the torsion bar type with either side consisting of five single rubber-tyred road wheels with the drive sprocket at the front and idler at the rear; there are no track return rollers.

The vehicle is fully amphibious, being propelled in the water by its tracks. Before entering the water the trim vane is erected at the front of the vehicle and the bilge pumps are switched on.

FNSS Armoured Engineering Squad Vehicle as supplied to the UAE
(FNSS)
0589692

FNSS Armoured Engineering Squad Vehicle from the rear as supplied to UAE showing external stowage (FNSS)
1039180

In addition to the .50 (12.7 mm) M2 HB machine gun, a bank of six 76 mm electrically operated smoke grenade launchers is mounted on the glacis plate firing forwards.

For its specialised AESV role, additional stowage is provided on the outside of the hull for demolition explosives and other combat engineer equipment.

The vehicle is air portable in a Lockheed Martin C-130 Hercules transport aircraft. Standard equipment on UAE vehicles includes an NBC overpressure and air-conditioning system and passive night vision devices.

Variants
These include an engineering command post vehicle and an engineering reconnaissance vehicle.

ACV-S
As previously stated, the ACV-S has a longer chassis with an additional road wheel station either side which provides for increased internal volume and more payload. This allows the vehicle to undertake a wider range of battlefield roles and missions.

Specifications
AESV
Crew: 3 + 8
Weight: (combat) 13,100 kg
Power-to-weight ratio: 19.92 kW/t (26.71 hp/t)
Ground pressure: 0.64 kg/cm²
Length: 5.26 m
Width:
  (overall) 3.32 m
  (tracks) 2.54 m
Height: (hull roof) 2.01 m
Ground clearance: 0.43 m
Track width: 381 mm
Length of track on ground: 2.68 m
Fuel capacity: 416 litres
Max road speed:
  (forwards) 65 km/h
  (reverse) 11 km/h
Max water speed: 6.3 km/h
Max road range: 490 km
Fording: amphibious
Gradient: 60%
Side slope: 30%
Vertical obstacle: 0.74 m
Trench: 1.83 m
Engine: Detroit Diesel Model 6V-53TA developing 261 kW (350 hp) (it is also offered with a 224 kW (300 hp) engine)
Transmission: Allison X-200-4B automatic crossdrive with 4 forward gears and 1 reverse
Steering: hydrostatic
Suspension: torsion bar
Electrical system: 24 V
Armament: (main) 1 × .50 (12.7 mm) M2 HB MG
Smoke laying equipment: 6 × 76 mm smoke grenade launchers
Armour:
  (hull) aluminium, 12-44 mm
  (cupola) steel

Gun control equipment
Turret power control: manual
Gun elevation/depression: +50°/–10°
Turret traverse: 360°
Gun stabiliser:
  (vertical) no
  (horizontal) no
NBC system: optional (standard on UAE vehicles)
Night vision equipment: optional (standard on UAE vehicles)

Status
Production as required. This variant is known to be in service with the United Arab Emirates. The Armoured Combat Vehicle is also in service in various configurations with Malaysia, Saudi Arabia (ACV-S) and the United Arab Emirates.

Contractor
FNSS Savunma Sistemleri AS

Turkish M113A2T2 Engineering Squad Armoured Vehicle (ESV)

Development
The Turkish Land Forces Command operates a fleet of over 3,000 now BAE Systems, US Combat Systems (previously United Defense) M113 series full tracked Armoured Personnel Carriers (APC).

The Turkish Land Forces Command's 109th Ordnance Factory at Kayserie developed an upgrade package for the M113 under the local designation of the M113A2T2.

This includes a new diesel powerpack and new fuel tanks positioned one either side at the rear of the chassis.

By late 2010 it is estimated that over 2,000 petrol powered M113 had been upgraded to the M113A2T2 standard. In addition to the basline APC, a number of specialised versions of the M113A2T2 have been developed and placed in production.

These include the M113A2T2 Engineering Squad Armoured Vehicle (ESAV) which is now in service with the Turkish Land Forces Command.

Description
The overall layout of the M113A2T2 ESAV is identical to the standard M113 with the driver front left and powerpack to the right with the troop compartment extending to the rear.

Suspension either side consists of five dual rubber tyred road wheels with the drive sprocket at the front and idler at the rear. There are no track return rollers and the upper part of the track is covered by a rubber skirt.

ESAV is fitted with the standard cupola armed with a .50 (12.7 mm) M2 HB MG and a bank of electrically operated 76 mm smoke grenade launchers on the front of the vehicle. It retains the full amphibious characteristics of the baseline vehicle.

Although there is a hatch over the rear crew compartment, the crew normally enter and leave via the large power-operated ramp in the hull rear which is fitted with an emergency door.

On the standard M113, the troops are seated on benches down either side facing inwards, but on the ESAV, they now sit in the middle of the troop compartment facing outwards and with stowage space under their seats.

This arrangement has left the sponsons clear for the stowage of specialist engineer equipment. In addition, special racks have been provided internally on either side of the hull to provide additional stowage space.

Specifications
Engineering Squad Armoured Vehicle
Crew: 2 + 8
Weight:
  (combat) 11,450 kg
  (unloaded) 9,900 kg
Power-to-weight ratio: 13.81 kW/t (18.52 hp/t)
Length: 5.30 m
Width: 3.416 m
Height: 2.54 m
Ground clearance: 406 mm
Max speed:
  (road) 65 km/h
  (water) 4.8 km/h
Fuel capacity: 360 litres
Range: 483 km
Fording: amphibious
Vertical obstacle: 0.61 m
Gradient: 60%
Side slope: 30%
Trench: 1.68 m
Engine: Detroit Diesel 6V-53 water-cooled diesel developing 158 kW (212 hp)
Transmission: Allison TX-100-1 automatic
Armament: (main) 1 × .50 (12.7 mm) M2 HB machine gun
Smoke grenade launchers: 8 × 76 mm
NBC system: yes
Night vision equipment: yes
Armour:
  (hull) aluminium, 12-44 mm
  (cupola) steel

Status
Production as required. In service with Turkish Land Forces Command.

Contractor
See Development.

Ukraine

BAT-2 combat engineer vehicle

Development
The BAT-2 (*Bul'dozer na Artilleriyskom Tygache 2*) combat engineer vehicle is intended to supplement the unarmoured BAT-M high-speed tractor-mounted bulldozers and similar vehicles, but is more readily described as a combat engineer vehicle.

The reason for this is that the BAT-2 is armoured and can undertake a wider range of roles and missions than the BAT-M type vehicle.

The BAT-2 development designation was Article 454, while that of the MDK high-speed excavating machine was the Article 453. The baseline MT-T tractor was Article 429AM. The BAT-2 was designed by the Kharkov Morozov Machine-building Design Bureau (KhMDB). Available details of the MT-T heavy tracked transporter are provided in a separate entry in *Jane's Military Vehicles and Logistics*.

Production of the MT-T heavy tracked transporter is now complete in the Ukraine.

Description
In addition to the large front dozer blade normally fitted, the BAT-2 has carrying capacity for combat engineer stores behind the fully enclosed forward control cab and also has a turntable-mounted hydraulic crane mounted at the rear of the cab to handle them.

The crane can be fitted with pincer-type grabs for clearing obstacles, has a maximum boom outreach of 7.3 m and a load-lifting capacity of 2,000 kg.

Mounted on the same platform as the crane is a 25-tonne capacity hydraulic winch provided with 100 m of cable.

The armoured cab has seating for a crew of two and a compartment for a combat engineer squad of eight. An NBC system is provided for the cab. The operating temperature range may be from −45 to +45°C.

The BAT-2 is based on the chassis of the MT-T tracked carrier, which uses suspension and running gear components from the T-64 tank, which was also designed and built in Ukraine, and is powered by a V-64-4 V-12 multifuel diesel engine developing 700 hp.

The BAT-2 has the large dozer blade of the earlier BAT-M vehicles mounted at the front but the hydraulic cylinder actuation system is more powerful and uses a different operating layout. There is also a different system to raise the blade vertically when not in use. The blade widths can be varied to suit the task. As a bulldozer the blade is 4.5 m wide, for road or track clearing it is 4.2 m wide, when grading it may have a width variable between 4.1 and 4.35 m. The blade may also be tilted through 10° for some operations, while a blade-mounted skid allows the blade to follow terrain contours.

The BAT-2 can be employed to drive graded tracks across 'ordinary' terrain at a speed up to 6.8 km/h; across snow the speed is 8.15 km/h. Scrubby terrain with trees up to 300 mm in diameter can be cleared at a rate of 2.3 km/h. When route-clearing or creating earth barriers the dozer blade has a clearing capacity from 350 to 450 m³/h. When digging ditches it is 200 to 250 m³/h. Solid or frozen ground can be loosened down to a depth of 500 mm.

Specifications
BAT-2 combat engineer vehicle
Crew: 2 + 8
Weight: (combat) 39,700 kg
Power-to-weight ratio: 13.15 kW (17.63 hp/t)
Ground pressure: 0.81 kg/cm²
Length: 9.64 m
Width: 4.2 m
Height: 3.69 m
Ground clearance: 0.425 m
Max speed: (roads) 60 km/h
Range: 500 km
Fording: 1.3 m
Engine: V-64-4 V-12 multifuel diesel developing 522 kW (700 hp)

Status
Production complete. Known to be in service with Hungary, Russia and Ukraine.

Contractor
Joint Stock Company Budshliakhmash

United Kingdom

BAE Systems Global Combat Systems TROJAN Engineer Tank System (ETS)

Development
Following a competition, early in 2001, the then UK Defence Procurement Agency (DPA) awarded Vickers Defence Systems (today known as BAE Systems Global Combat Systems) a GBP250 million plus contract to supply the British Army with a new Engineer Tank System (ETS), which was previously called the Future Engineer Tank (FET).

The contract covered the supply of 66 ETSs against the original requirement for 102 vehicles to replace the then current in-service Armoured Vehicle Royal Engineer (AVRE) and Armoured Vehicle Launched Bridge (AVLB) systems, based on the now obsolete Chieftain MBT chassis.

These are the first armoured engineer vehicles specifically designed for their role rather than adapted from battle tank chassis. They also incorporate the latest survivability features.

Major subcontractors include:
- AdVal - computer-based training applications
- Caterpillar (CAT) - use of Commercial-Off-The-Shelf (COTS) military equipment
- domnick hunter - vehicle regenerative NBC system, development and background technology
- Pearson Engineering - breaching and dozing capability developments, capability improvement, obstacle marking systems
- Parker - hydraulic system supplier, integrated solution
- Perkins - power pack design authority and power pack development
- Tyco - harness system suppliers
- Ultra Electronics - vetronics and indirect vision system design, development and integrated system approach
- ASTRUM - track development, safety, reduced maintenance times and increased durability.

Late in 2006, following extensive trials with prototype vehicles, the Engineer Tank System met its In Service Date (ISD) with a Full Operational Capability (FOC) in 2008.

In addition to the four prototype vehicles (two TITAN and two TROJAN), a total of 66 production vehicles have now been built for the Royal Engineers at Newcastle-upon-Tyne, 33 TITAN and 33 TROJAN.

At one time it was expected that the four prototype vehicles would be upgraded to a full production standard. A decision has been taken that this would no longer be a cost effective solution.

Since the contract was originally awarded, there have been a number of changes with the most significant being the installation of the General Dynamics UK Bowman digital communications system and second the integration of an enhanced armour package as a result of operational experience in the Middle East.

Prime contractor for the TROJAN Front End Equipment (FEE) is Pearson Engineering and this includes their Full Width Mine Plough (FWMP), Track Width Mine Plough (TWMP), dozer blade and a new 100-rod Obstacle Marking System (OMS) mounted one either side towards the rear.

The introduction of TITAN and TROJAN mark a number of firsts for the British Army including the first vehicles to be developed for world wide deployment as they are fitted with a complete environmental control system, first production vehicles to be fitted with Bowman, first vehicles (TROJAN) with a remote-controlled overhead weapon station, first purpose-built AVLB/breacher and can be fitted for but not with a remote-control capability for use in hazardous operations.

BAT-2 combat engineer vehicle in travelling configuration
(Shaun C Connors)   0525488

BAE Systems Land Systems TROJAN breacher (Patrick Allen/IHS Jane's)
                                                                    1198398

Royal Engineers TROJAN breacher deployed to Afghanistan and showing mine ploughs in raised position and hydraulic arm holding a roll of fascines (UK MoD) 1363924

Production the TROJAN and TITAN members of the Engineer Tank System has been completed and in June 2009 the Final Acceptance Build Standard (FABS) commenced at Newcastle-upon-Type.

The final FABS phase involves the return of all 66 production TITAN and TROJAN from the British Army for a series of upgrades to bring the fleet up to a common build standard.

Following work at Newcastle-upon-Tyne the FABS vehicles are sent to the Defence Support Group (DSG) at Bovington for final refurbishment and then sign-off back to the customer. The complete FABS programme is scheduled to be completed by December 2011.

Late in 2009 three TROJAN breacher vehicles were upgraded by BAE Systems, Global Combat Systems to meet an Urgent Operational Requirement (UOR) at their Newcastle-upon-Tyne facility.

These were deployed to Afghanistan early in 2010 and deployed by 28 Engineer Regiment. The upgrade included additional armour in the form of bar armour around the rear arc and upper part of the chassis for enhanced protection against rocket propelled grenades.

These TROJAN breacher vehicles were used to clear paths through mine fields using the trailer mounted Python rocket propelled mine clearing system and the Pearson Engineering full width mine clearing system mounted on the front of the chassis.

These were supported by two upgraded Challenger Armoured Repair and Recovery Vehicles which had previously been upgraded for deployed in Iraq.

Description

The TROJAN ETS, or obstacle/mine clearance vehicle, as it is also referred to, is based on a much-modified Challenger 2 MBT chassis, with the crew compartment at the front and the power pack at the rear.

It has the same level of armour protection as the Challenger 2 MBT that provides a very high level of protection against direct-fire weapons and it has enhanced protection against mines. The add-on armour is of a modular design so new packs can be fitted if the threat changes.

The driver and operator are seated at the front of the vehicle. Each is provided with a hatch cover above their position that opens to the rear and periscopes for observation to the front and sides.

The commander is seated in a raised position, to the rear of the driver and operator and is also provided with a single piece hatch cover that opens to the rear and periscopes for all round observation. There is also an emergency escape hatch in the rear of the superstructure.

The TROJAN is able to clear battlefield obstacles and clear a path through minefields. On the right side is a Caterpillar excavator arm with thumb that can take a number of attachments.

The bucket attachment has a capacity of 1 m³ and the arm has a lift capacity of 6.5 tonnes. Other attachments include an impact hammer/earth auger. These are run from a hydraulic power take-off that operates at 140 bar.

The excavator arm can be used for a number of roles, including unloading and placing fascines, grabbing and removal of obstacles as well as its main role of digging.

Electronic sensors monitor slew, boom and stick position to prevent contact with the hull and mine plough. The hoses are routed for maximum protection from sagging during cross-country operations.

TROJAN can be rapidly fitted with a Pearson Engineering front-mounted dozer blade or a full-width mine-plough system and can also clear mines using a trailer-mounted BAE Systems Python rocket-propelled mine clearance system.

The cleared mine breach can then be automatically marked using the on board Obstacle Marking System. It can also be fitted with a vehicle signature duplicator to neutralise anti-tank mines fitted with magnetic or other advanced fuzes.

TROJAN can also carry fascines to drop into ditches up to 8 m wide and tow various types of engineer trailer, including one with the Python rocket propelled mineclearing equipment.

Standard equipment on both vehicles includes an auxiliary power unit, climate-control system and an advanced NBC regenerative filtration system, developed by domnick hunter. The latter continually purifies air as it enters the vehicle.

It is also provided with direct and indirect vision devices with low light, image intensification and thermal imaging capabilities, which will allow operation in most conditions.

Armament comprises a Thales 7.62 mm SWARM Lite weapons station, electrically operated 66 mm smoke grenade launchers and hand-held, light anti-tank weapons. SWARM Lite is mounted to the left of the commander's position and can be aimed and fired with the commander under complete armour protection.

With the introduction of the TITAN and TROJAN ETSs, the British Army now has a common, heavy-platform family, with the other members being the Challenger 2 MBT, Challenger Driver Training Tank and the Challenger Armoured Repair and Recovery Vehicle.

Specifications

TROJAN Breacher
Crew: 3
Training weight: 57,300 kg
Power-to-weight ratio: 15.62 kW (20.94 hp/t)
Length: 8.949 m
Width: 3.506 m
Height: 3.035 m
Max speed: (road) 56 km/h
Range: 500 km
Power pack: Perkins Engines Company CV-12 8a developing 895 kW (1,200 hp) coupled to a modified David Brown Gear Systems TN54 transmission with 6 forward and 2 reverse gears
Armament: 1 × 7.62 mm machine gun
Electrical system: three sources (engine, APU and six batteries which provide 360 Ah capacity)
Nominal voltage: 24 V dc

Status

Two prototype TROJAN vehicles were completed in early 2003 and a total of 33 production vehicles delivered from late 2005 through to 2009.

Contractor

BAE Systems Land Systems

BAE Systems, Global Combat Systems Terrier Combat Engineer Vehicle

Development

The now BAE Systems, Global Combat Systems (at that time RO Defence) was awarded the original GBP290 million contract for design, development and production of the Terrier Combat Engineer Vehicle (CEV) in July 2002.

This contract covered one prototype CEV, four Demonstrator Vehicles (DV) and 65 production vehicles.

First prototype of the Terrier CEV was unveiled in May 2005 and this was followed by the four Demonstrator Vehicles (DV1, DV2, DV3 and DV4).

Delays incurred through Bowman integration and reliability of the single prototype vehicle used during the demonstration trials had a significant knock-on effect to the overall Terrier CEV programme.

Coupled with contractual changes to meet evolving theatre entry criteria, meant that the original requirement for the first 20 production Terrier CEV to be in service with the British Army by late 2008 could not be met.

Terrier CEV carrying gap-crossing fascines into position with an additional fascine being carried on the rear of the vehicle (BAE Systems) 1332890

Terrier CEV in travelling configuration with bucket and arm in stowed position (BAE Systems)   1332891

One of the Terrier CEV demonstrator vehicles being put through its paces during trials and showing front mounted bucket (Christopher F Foss)
1405658

Eventually Milestone 12, the entry criteria for production release and the start point for Reliability Growth Trials was declared in September 2008. This led to a formal MoD announcement for Terrier CEV production go-ahead in late March 2009.

As of 2010 the Terrier CEV was into Reliability And Maintainability (RAM) testing. The four DV have been engaged in an extensive series of trials manned by a mixture of BAE Systems and British Army crews from the Royal Engineers Trials and Development Unit (RETDU).

Production Terrier CEV will be to Theatre Entry Standard (TES), which is understood to include enhanced mine-blast protection, the latest General Dynamics Bowman digital communications system and electronic devices to counter Improvised Explosive Devices (IED).

The latest contract amendment to incorporate TES has added a further 16 months to the programme. This long delay period is due to these features having to be designed into the vehicles now, rather, as has occurred with a number of recently deployed UK armoured vehicles, being added at a later date.

One of the key requirements for Terrier is an air-transport weight of no more than 31.5 tonnes, enabling it to be transported in the future A400M transport aircraft. For several years that has pushed the boundaries of design.

A condition of the recent contractual change has been a reduction of weight to allow for more robust and reliable sub-components to be fitted in risk areas. Weight trades mean that Terrier CEV will not now be fitted with a winch or tow bar.

When fielded, the Terrier CEV will fill a major capability gap in the Royal Engineer's portfolio following the withdrawal of the Combat Engineer Tractor (CET) at the end of its service life late in 2008.

Main roles of the Terrier MSV CEV are as follows:
- Dig vehicle slots
- Dig, carry and load spoil and rubble
- Dig trenches
- Grab, grapple and carry two-tonne items over short distances
- Self recover and demolish structures using its integral 20-tonne winch.

The first Terrier CEV hull was completed late in 2010 and has been used for mine blast trials to demonstrate the improved protection levels being incorporated into the vehicle following operational experience in Iraq and Afghanistan, especially in the area of mine protection.

This hull will be followed by production standard Terrier CEV hulls which will allow for assembly, integration and test of the first production Terrier vehicles in the first half of 2011.

BAE Systems have invested GBP2 million in process and machinery equipment at Newcastle-upon-Type for the Terrier CEV and under current plans this will be the last tracked armoured vehicle to be built in the UK by BAE Systems, Global Combat Systems.

Original projected In Service Date (ISD) for the first batch of 20 Terrier was late 2008 and this has now slipped to 2013. Some of the delay has been due to the introduction of additional requirements.

The CET has already been withdrawn from service with the Royal Engineers and to provide a partial interim capability a number of JCB High Mobility Engineer Excavators have now been deployed.

Description

The hull of Terrier is of all-welded steel construction, which provides the crew of two with protection from small arms fire and shell splinters as well as mine blast.

The driver is seated front left with the vehicle commander to the right. Both have observation periscopes and a single piece hatch cover.

Standard equipment includes a full suite of day/thermal vision equipment to provide vision through a full 360°, General Dynamics Bowman digital communications system, AMETEK Aircontrol Technologies Environmental Control System/Nuclear Biological Chemical (ECS/NBC) protection system.

Terrier will have the ability to be operated by remote control in high risk areas up to a maximum range of 1,000 m and have route marking capabilities.

A high level of protection will be provided against small arms fire, splinters and mines. The armour package will be a modular design, so allowing for improved armour packages to be fitted as the threat evolves or as new armour technology becomes available.

One of the Terrier CEV demonstrator vehicles from the rear with hydraulic arm complete with bucket deployed to front of the vehicle (Christopher F Foss)   1405659

The power pack is at the rear of the vehicle and consists of a Caterpillar C18 diesel engine developing 700 hp coupled to an Allison X300 series fully automatic transmission with four forward and two reverse gears.

To meet the requirement for both high road speed and high tractive effort for digging, a new Caterpillar two-speed final drive was developed.

The suspension is of the Horstman hydrogas type with either side having five dual rubber-tyred road wheels with the drive sprocket at the rear and the idler at the front plus track return rollers. The upper part of the suspension is covered by a skirt. The suspension is based on that of the proven AS90 and also features a lock-out facility for use when digging.

To undertake its wide variety of battlefield missions, Terrier is fitted with a variety of specialised equipment including winch, extendable arm that can be fitted with a variety of attachments and a front mounted bucket/dozer blade.

To carry out its mission the CEV is fitted with a front mounted multirole hydraulically-operated bucket that can be used to doze, dig, load and grip large items. This bucket has a capacity of 2.8 m³ and a lifting capability of five tonnes.

The bucket can be rapidly replaced by forks, a ripper attachment, or the Pearson Engineering surface mine-clearance device.

Mounted on the right side is a hydraulic arm fitted with a bucket that has a lifting capability of 2.5 tonnes at maximum reach. Capable of mounting a variety of COTS equipment, Terrier CEV will be delivered with a bucket, earth auger and lifting hook.

Terrier CEV can tow an 18-tonne Armoured Vehicle Royal Engineer (AVRE) trailer, carrying either fascines or a rolled up trackway, either of which can be deployed direct from the vehicle under armour. Load rails are also fitted to the rear decks which allows up to five tonnes of engineer stores to be carried.

In addition to the AVRE trailer, the Python line-charge mineclearing device can also be towed, this giving the Terrier the capability to breach a 400 m minefield. This and all other trailers have a rapid jettison capability, which, if required can be while under armour.

The Terrier is fitted with a full range of day/thermal cameras enabling it to carry out it its missions under day and night conditions. It also has a regenerative Environmental Control System and NBC system which can be run individually or together.

Fitted with a Health and Usage Monitoring System (HUMS), a key part of the CANbus vetronics architecture, the vehicle has an integrated self diagnostic capability and on board electronic documentation. This electronic architecture will make it easier to 'plus and play' upgrades in the future.

All production vehicles will be fitted for, but not with, a remote control system that would allow an operator to drive and operate bucket and hydraulic arm from a safe distance of up to 1 km.

A 7.62 mm General Purpose Machine Gun (GPMG) is fitted on the roof for self defence and this can be operated by the commander or driver in the head out position.

Provision has been made for a remote controlled weapon station that would replace current 360° periscopic sight. Situational awareness is aided by five on board cameras. Two banks of four electrically operated smoke grenade launchers aid self defence.

Specifications

Terrier Combat Engineer Vehicle
Crew: 2
Armament: 1 × 7.62 mm machine gun
Combat weight: 31,500 kg
Power-to-weight ratio: 16.57 kW/t (22.22 hp/t)
Length: 9.3 m
Width: (incl armour) 2.96 m
Height: (incl cupola) 2.9 m
Track Width: 550 mm
Length of track on ground: 3.39 m
Max speed:
  (road) 70 km/h
  (cross-country) 40 km/h
Range: 600 km
Fuel capacity: 680 litres
Fording: 1.4 m
Gradient: 60%
Vertical obstacle: 0.75 m
Trench: 2.5 m
Suspension: hydropneumatic
Power pack: Caterpillar C18 diesel developing 522 kW (700 hp) coupled to an Allison X300-10 series fully automatic transmission
Electrical System: two sources (engine and six batteries) provide a 330 Ah capacity

Status

Final Development. A total of 65 production vehicles are due to be built with the first of these being completed in 2011, with an in service date of 2013.

Contractor

BAE Systems, Global Combat Systems

BAE Systems, Global Combat Systems Combat Engineer Tractor (FV180)

Development

In 1962, a General Staff Target (GST 26) was issued for an engineer equipment which would combine the characteristics of an armoured vehicle and an earthmover.

The following year, three companies, Caterpillar UK, GKN and Vickers, were invited to put forward their proposals for a vehicle to meet GST 26. GKN and Vickers responded but their proposals were not taken up. In 1965, the Military Engineering Experimental Establishment at Christchurch prepared a design to meet GST 26. At the same time discussions took place between the UK, France and Germany for the joint development of a Combat Engineer Tractor.

Subsequently, two prototypes were built by the then Royal Ordnance Factory at Leeds, based on a design prepared by the Military Engineering Experimental Establishment.

They were powered by a Cummins V-8 diesel, which developed 350 hp, were fully amphibious and incorporated some features of the US Universal Engineer Tractor.

FV180 Combat Engineer Tractor with bucket carrying roll of trackway
(BAE Systems)   1333653

They were delivered in 1968, but France had meanwhile dropped out of the project as it required a vehicle with a higher water speed and only limited earthmoving capabilities.

In 1970, after trials with the two test rigs in both Germany and the UK, the Germans withdrew from the programme as they required a heavier vehicle, without an amphibious capability, mainly for clearing river crossing points.

Meanwhile a major redesign of the vehicle had been carried out with two major objectives: to use standard commercial components wherever possible, (engine, transmission, steer unit and winch) and to make the vehicle amphibious with the minimum preparation. In 1969, a GST was issued and the following year Royal Ordnance Factory Leeds (which was subsequently taken over by Vickers Defence Systems) was nominated as the prime manufacturer with the then Military Vehicles and Engineering Establishment responsible for design work. A contract was awarded for seven prototypes, all delivered between February 1973 and January 1974.

Extensive trials were carried out in both the UK and Germany and in July 1975 the Combat Engineer Tractor (CET) was accepted for service with the British Army.

Production of the CET began at Nottingham in 1977 and the first production vehicle was accepted in May 1978. Production was completed in March 1981 after 143 had been built for the British Army, but in mid-1984 it was announced that India had ordered the CET. The initial order was for nine vehicles with options (since taken) on a further six. The first vehicle was delivered at the end of 1988 and was first shown publicly in January 1989.

In April 1993, the Singapore Armed Forces ordered 18 CETs with an option on a further 18, which was subsequently exercised. Late in 1995 an additional 18 vehicles were ordered bringing the total to 54. In service they are used for combat engineering duties plus logistics over-the-shore duties during joint operations with the Singapore Navy. Production of the CET was completed in December 1998.

Late production CETs incorporate some automotive assemblies, aluminium welded fabrications and machined components provided by the then Alvis Vehicles Limited.

All production of the CET was undertaken at the former Royal Ordnance Factory at Leeds, which has subsequently closed. The CET was phased out of service with the British Army in 2008.

In British Army service the replacement for the CET is the BAE Systems, Global Combat Systems Terrier Combat Engineer Vehicle (CEV) which is covered in a separate entry in *Jane's Military Vehicles and Logistics*.

Original projected In Service Date (ISD) for the first batch of 20 Terrier CEV was late 2008 and this has now slipped to 2013. Some of the delay has been due to the introduction of additional requirements.

Following the early withdrawal of the CET a partial interim capability has been achieved by the deployment of a number of JCB High Mobility Engineer Excavators.

Description

The CET was designed to provide integral engineer support for the battle group and typical roles include excavating vehicle and gun pits for defensive purposes, repairing and maintaining roads, preparation of river banks, recovering disabled vehicles and preparing or clearing obstacles.

The hull of the CET is made of all-welded aluminium armour, supplied by Alcan. The vehicle is normally driven with its bucket to the rear and in this position the crew is seated on the left side. The following description is for the vehicle in this condition.

The driver is seated at the front and also operates the winch, with the bucket operator to the rear. Both crew members can reverse their seats and essential controls are duplicated so that either crew member can operate the vehicle.

The crew compartment is provided with two hatch covers, which open to the right and a total of 10 vision blocks. The crew compartment is supplied with cooled air via the NBC system from an air conditioning unit, produced by Gallay Limited. The unit contains a refrigeration package with a compressor, driven from the main gearbox.

The engine and transmission are mounted at the right side of the hull with the final drives being mounted at the front of the hull. From the engine, power is passed through two gearboxes to a steering unit and final drives.

The first of these gearboxes, the transfer box, provides PTOs for the water propulsion units and hydraulic pumps. Controlled differential steering is used for road and cross-country drive and skid steering is used for bulldozing operations, with an independent clutch/brake system provided for this purpose.

The suspension is of the torsion bar type and consists of five road wheels either side, with the fifth road wheel acting as the idler. The drive sprocket is at the front. The tracks are of cast steel with rubber bushes and rubber pads are provided, reducing damage when operating on roads. Hydraulic double-acting ram-type dampers are mounted on the front and rear wheel stations and can be locked from the crew compartment if required.

The CET can ford to a depth of 1.83 m without preparation, but with preparation the vehicle is fully amphibious. It is propelled in the water by two 330 mm Dowty 40/40B water-jets which are mounted one either side of the hull.

When in the water, steering is accomplished by deflecting the thrust from the unit on the inside of the turn and deflecting both units gives reverse. The preparation required before entering the water is to unfold

FV180 Combat Engineer Tractor with bucket lowered and using winch for recovery operations (Ian V Hogg) 1365737

the trim board at the front of the hull and inflate two Hycafloat units to the rear of the trim board. The units were developed by FPT Industries of Portsmouth and replaced the original bellows-type units installed on the prototypes. Two plastic-cased polyurethane foam blocks are fitted into the bucket and held in place by retaining straps.

The bucket is of light alloy construction with steel cutting edges and tines and has a maximum capacity of 1.72 m³. Its maximum lift height is 1.829 m and its minimum lift height is 102 mm below the track line. This can be used for either digging or bulldozing and can also be used as an earth anchor. Its maximum capacity is 200 m³/h over a 50 m hauling distance.

The two-speed winch has a maximum pull of 8,000 kg and is provided with 113 m of 16 mm diameter rope; maximum winching speed is 1.9 m/s. For self-assistance, the winching speed is matched to the speed of the tractor. A high-speed winching facility is available for ferrying work. The rope can be led to the front or rear of the vehicle by direction-changing blocks.

A self-emplacing earth anchor is mounted on the top of the hull and this can be rocket-propelled over the front of the vehicle to a maximum distance of 91.4 m. The anchor is attached to the vehicle's winch rope and is used to assist the vehicle when leaving a river with a steep bank.

CETs could be provided with an NBC filtration pack installed at the front of the vehicle, providing clean air to the crew compartment. The filters are changed through an external hatch. If required, a passive night vision device can be installed at either crew position. Vehicles produced for India have air conditioning.

The CET can also be used to tow the trailer-mounted now BAE Systems (originally Royal Ordnance) Giant Viper or Python mine clearance systems. The CET vehicle is air-portable in Lockheed Martin C-130 Hercules aircraft.

The following ancillary equipment can be installed on the CET if required:
• Pusher bar for launching bridging
• Class 30 and Class 60 trackway laying equipment
• A jib crane attachment for handling palletised stores up to a maximum weight of 4,000 kg can be installed in the bucket.

Specifications

Combat Engineer Tractor
Crew: 2
Weight combat: 18,350 kg
Power-to-weight ratio: 13.00 kW/t (17.43 hp/t)
Length:
(overall) 7.3 m
(hull) 5.334 m
Width:
(bucket) 2.921 m
(hull) 2.87 m
(tracks) 2.769 m
Height:
(without RP anchor) 2.83 m
(with RP anchor) 3.41 m
Ground clearance: 0.425 m
Track width: 508 mm
Length of track on ground: 3.76 m
Ground pressure: 0.435 kg/cm²
Max speed:
(road) 52 km/h
(water) 9 km/h
Range: 320 km
Fuel capacity: 418 litres
Fording: 1.83 m (amphibious with preparation)
Gradient: 60%
Vertical obstacle: 0.61 m

Trench: 2.06 m
Engine: Perkins Engines Company E320TX 12.17 litre 6-cylinder in-line diesel developing 239 kW (320 bhp) at 2,100 rpm
Transmission: David Brown Gear Systems TN26 manually controlled power shift with 4 gears in each direction coupled to a Rolls-Royce CGS 312 steering system
Electrical system: 24 V
Batteries: 4 × 6TN rated at 100 Ah connected in series/parallel giving total capacity of 200 Ah
Armament:
1 × 7.62 mm MG (optional)
6 × 66 mm smoke grenade dischargers
Armour: aluminium

Status
Production complete. In service with India (15) and Singapore (54). No longer marketed.

A number of British Army CET are now surplus to requirements and available for sale.

Contractor
Production of the CET was undertaken at the RO Defence facility at Nottingham, which has now closed.

Pearson Engineering Combat Dozer UDK1

Development
The Pearson Combat Dozer UDK1 was developed by Pearson Engineering as an add-on attachment for MBTs or armoured engineer vehicles. It can carry out bulldozing tasks such as ground levelling, digging defensive 'tank scrapes', preparing ground for launching bridges, urban obstacle clearance, filling anti-tank ditches and so on.

All Challenger 1 MBTs (420 were built, of which 402 were transferred to Jordan where they are known as the Al Hussein) and Challenger 2 (Oman and UK) MBTs are fitted to receive the Pearson Engineering Combat Dozer UDK1. The first customer for this system was Jordan, who ordered 60 units and these were delivered ahead of the British Army systems.

Recent information has indicated that orders were subsequently placed for additional UDK1 dozers for Jordan.

Scale of issue of the UDK1 depends on mission but could be one per troop of Challenger 2 MBTs.

Description
The UDK1 incorporates its hydraulic power pack into the boom arm and is thus a totally self-contained unit. A wedge-block mounting system enables the bulldozer to be removed from one vehicle and fitted to another in under 15 minutes.

The bulldozer fits directly to the glacis plate by means of attaching two anchor blocks and lashing eyes pre-welded to the glacis plate. Electrical connection is made between a harness fitted permanently to the bulldozer and a glacis plate harness. The harness passes through armoured ducting to a control box in the driver's compartment. This control box can also be used to control the Pearson Mine Plough.

The UDK1 unit comprises a blade and boom fitted to a mounting plate, with the blade position controlled by a hydraulic cylinder and top link. The blade is a fabricated steel unit fitted with replaceable hardened steel cutting edges and corner tips. The blade has an extension in the centre that increases dozing capacity and reduces spillage. An electrohydraulic power pack is fitted within the boom, along with the drive motor and hydraulic oil reservoir.

The control box in the driver's compartment controls blade lift and lowering functions electrically, using a joystick lever. Cutout switches in the power pack provide protection against motor and oil overheating, oil filter blockage and low oil level.

Challenger 2 MBT fitted with Pearson Engineering Combat Dozer UDK1 (Richard Stickland) 1334222

These protective switches can be overridden under combat conditions by a 'Battle' switch. The full range of operations are: blade up, blade down, float on, float off, the 'Battle' override and a warning light test.

The Pearson Jacklift Pallet can be used with the UDK1 as well as other Pearson Engineering combat engineer equipment.

Specifications

Combat Dozer UDK1
Weight: 2,200 kg
Width: 3.69 m
Height: 1.225 m
Cutting depth: 175 mm
Fitting and removal time: 10 min
Power supply: 24-28 V, 250 A max
Operating pressure: 1,250 bar
Power requirements: 250 A at 24-28 V DC

Status

Production as required. In service with the British Army for Challenger 2 MBT. In service with a number of other countries including France and Jordan. All of Jordan's MBTs (Khalid, M60A1 and Tariq) are fitted to receive the UDK1 combat dozer. Jordan has now taken delivery of 402 of the British Army fleet of Challenger 1 MBTs.

It should be noted that the Tariq MBTs have now been phased out of service.

Contractor

Pearson Engineering Ltd

Pearson Engineering Combat Dozer UDK2

Development

The Pearson Engineering Combat Dozer UDK2 is a smaller and lighter version of the UDK1 (which is covered in a separate entry in *Jane's Military Vehicles and Logistics*) and normally installed on heavy vehicles such as tanks) and can be fitted to light tanks, self-propelled guns and infantry fighting vehicles. It was originally developed to meet the requirements of the British Army with the first application being for use with the BAE Systems, Golobal Combat Systems Warrior mechanised combat vehicle.

As far as it is known, there have been no exports of the UDK2 combat dozer.

Description

The UDK2 weighs 1,100 kg and has virtually no effect on vehicle mobility and does not interfere with any main armament. All working parts are identical to those of the UDK1. The main difference is that the actual blade is narrower and therefore lighter so enabling it to be fitted to smaller vehicles.

Specifications

Combat Dozer UKD2
Weight: 1,100 kg
Width: 3.27 m
Height: 1.1 m
Cutting depth: 160 mm
Fitting and removal time: 10 min
Power supply: 24-28 V, 250 A max
Operating pressure: 1,250 bar
Power requirements: 250 A at 24-28 V DC

Status

Production as required. In service with undisclosed countries. It is understood that a quantity of these were supplied to the British Army in 2004 for use on Warrior vehicles.

Contractor

Pearson Engineering Ltd

Pearson Combat Dozer UDK2 fitted to Warrior mechanised combat vehicle
0511463

United States

Assault Breacher Vehicle

Development

The Assault Breacher Vehicle (ABV) was originally developed to meet the operational requirements of the US Marine Corps for a vehicle capable of supporting its current fleet of armoured vehicles, including the General Dynamics Land Systems M1A1 Main Battle Tank.

To support development, trials and testing, a total of six Prototype and Pre-Production ABV were built between 2002 and 2006.

To support these vehicles Pearson Engineering Limited of the UK supplied a number of High Life Adaptors (HLA), Full Width Mine Ploughs (FWMP), Combat Dozer Blades (CDB), Surface Mine Ploughs (SMP), Rapid Ordnance Removal Systems (RORS), Lane Marking Systems (LMS) and remote-control systems.

To reduce time and cost, wherever possible proven sub-systems have been used in the ABV programme including Non Development Items (NDI) and Military-Off-The-Shelf (MOTS) equipment.

Following a four week Independent Operational test and Evaluation conducted at 29 Palms, California, a Full Rate Production decision was awarded for the ABV programme.

The chassis used for these ABV were supplied from surplus Army stocks and were refurbished to a common standard with the current M1A1 Abrams MBT used by the US Marine Corps. This included the same communications system and a deep fording capability.

The work is carried out at the US Army Anniston Depot in Alabama who has extensive experience in the overhaul and modernisation of armoured fighting vehicles and other equipment.

The US Marine Corps has ordered a total of 45 systems and by and all of these have now been delivered. It has already been deployed by the US Marine Corps in Afghanistan and saw action for the first time in December 2010.

Following the cancellation of the Grizzly Combat Mobility Vehicle and the phasing out of service of the M728 Combat Engineer Vehicle, the US Army had no specialised engineer vehicles to support its Heavy Brigade Combat Teams (HBCT).

The US Army has now joined the US Marine Corps Assault Breacher Vehicle Programme and is currently testing two vehicles. It has a requirement for a total of 183 platforms, funding permitting.

Recent information has indicated that Army requirement has increased to 280 units with a potential for an additional 180 units. In FY10 the US Army requested USD63.25 million for an initial 13 production ABV.

Description

For the ABV role, the turret of the M1A1 Abrams MBT has been removed and replaced by a new all-welded aluminium structure to which has been added the latest Explosive Reactive Armour (ERA) package.

This provides a higher level of protection against anti-tank weapons fitted with a High Explosive Anti-Tank (HEAT) warhead fitted to weapons such as the RPG-7 (Rocket Propelled Grenade).

The commander is seated in the new superstructure and provided with a cupola armed with a .50 (12.7 mm) M2 HB machine gun. A bank of standard electrically operated grenade launchers are fitted one either side of the superstructure to cover the frontal arc.

To enable it to carry out its counter mobility role, a variety of specialised equipment supplied by Pearson Engineering of the UK can be fitted.

The HLA, whilst providing an increased approach angle to the ABV, allows the rapid fitting and removal of the full suite of ABV front end equipment and sub-systems.

For clearing minefields, the FWMP can be swiftly installed at the front of the vehicle which can be rapidly replaced by the CDB that, in addition to clearing battlefield obstacles, can also be used to prepare firing positions.

US Marine Corps Assault Breacher Vehicle fitted with Pearson Engineering Full Width Mine Plough (US Marine Corps)
1296003

US Marine Corps Assault Breacher Vehicle fitted with Pearson Engineering Combat Dozer Blade (US Marine Corps)   1296004

Another alternative installation at the front of the vehicle is the Pearson Engineering ROBS or an SMP.

Mounted on the rear of the ABV turret structure is the Linear Demolition Charge System containing two launchers with an updated firing system. Each of these launchers is fitted with a MK 2 solid propellant rocket attached to a M58 linear charge that contains C-4 high explosive.

In a typical mine clearing operation, the ABV would come to a halt outside of the minefield and one of the line charges would be fired.

The explosive charge is then propelled across the minefield and falls to the ground. It is then detonated from the ABV electrically and the resultant explosion clears a path through the mines by sympathetic detonation (direct contact) and by the blast overpressure produced acting on the fuzes.

The ABV would then enter the minefield and the FWMP would clear any remaining mines. Mounted one either side of the rear is the Pearson Engineering Lane Marking System that dispenses pennants into the ground to show follow up vehicles the cleared path through the minefield.

A suite of day/thermal cameras for the driver and vehicle commander of the ABV allows for day and night mine-clearing operations.

The ABV can be put ashore by US Navy Landing Craft Air Cushion which has already been successfully demonstrated during extensive user trials.

The introduction of the ABV provided a significant increase in the US Marine Corps counter mobility capability. With the cancellation of the very expensive Grizzly breacher vehicle several years ago, the US Army has no dedicated breacher vehicle.

Specifications
Not available.

Status
In production. In service with US Marine Corps who have ordered a total of 45 vehicles, Undergoing trials with the US Army who has a total requirement for 183 units. All Assault Breacher Vehicles are conversions of surplus M1 MBT chassis, with conversion work being carried out at the Anniston Army Depot.

Contractor
See text.

General Dynamics Land Systems M728 Combat Engineer Vehicle (CEV)

Development
In 1959, the M60 was selected to become the standard MBT of the US Army. Design work on a new Combat Engineer Vehicle (CEV) based on the M60/M60A1 MBT was soon started and the first prototype was known as the T118E1.

After trials this was type classified as the M728 in 1963 and entered production in 1965, entering the US Army inventory in 1968. The M728 Combat Engineer Vehicle has now been phased out of service by the US Army without direct replacement. It was to have been replaced by the new Grizzly Combat Mobility Vehicle but this was cancelled early in 2000.

In mid-2009 the US Army was testing two Assault Breacher Vehicles that were originally developed to meet the requirements of the US Marine Corps who have ordered a total of 45 production vehicles. The US Army requirement is for 183 Assault Breacher Vehicles that will fill part of the gap left by the withdrawal of the M728 CEV.

Description
The M728 is based on the General Dynamics Land Systems M60A1 MBT. The hull is of cast sections welded together, while the turret is cast in one piece. The driver is seated at the front of the hull in the centre and is provided with a single-piece hatch cover. He has three M27 day periscopes for observation purposes, of which the centre one can be replaced by an image intensification periscope on a separate mount for night operations.

M728 in service with Singapore and fitted with Pearson Engineering Track Width Mine Plough (David Boey)   0038790

The other three crew members are in the turret, with the commander and gunner on the right and the loader on the left. The commander's cupola can be traversed through a full 360° and he is provided with a total of eight vision blocks and an M34 day periscope, which can be replaced by an image intensification periscope for night observation. The gunner has an M105 telescope and an M32C periscope. The loader is seated on the left side of the turret and is provided with a single-piece hatch cover that opens towards the rear and an M37 day periscope for observation purposes. The engine, transmission and diesel fuel tanks are at the rear of the hull.

The suspension of the M728 is of the torsion bar type consisting of six road wheels either side with the drive sprocket at the rear and the idler at the front; there are three track-support rollers. Hydraulic shock-absorbers are provided at the first, second and sixth road wheel stations.

The M728 is designed to carry out numerous roles on the battlefield, including the destruction of field fortifications and roadblocks, filling in gaps, craters and ditches, preparing fire positions and roadblocks.

Main armament of the M728 consists of an M135 165 mm demolition gun which has an elevation of +20° and a depression of –10°. Turret traverse is a full 360° at 1.6°/s; traverse and elevation are either powered or manual. A 7.62 mm M219 machine gun is mounted coaxially with the main armament (late production vehicles are equipped with an M240 coaxial machine gun). A .50 (12.7 mm) M85 machine gun is mounted in the commander's cupola; this has an elevation of +60° and a depression of –15°. In total 30 rounds of 165 mm, 3,600 rounds of 7.62 mm and 600 rounds of .50 (12.7 mm) ammunition are carried.

The 165 mm demolition gun fired only one type of war shot - the 165 mm High Explosive Plastic (HEP) M123/M123A1 - which has a muzzle velocity of 259 m/s (850 ft/s) and a maximum effective range of 914 m (1,000 yd). The associated training projectile was the M623 TP (Target Practice).

An A-frame is pivoted on the front of the turret and when not required lies back over the rear of the hull. This has a maximum lifting capacity of 15,876 kg; the two-speed winch, which is mounted at the rear of the turret, is provided with 61 m of 19 mm rope and is controlled by the vehicle commander.

The dozer blade is hydraulically operated and is mounted at the front of the hull. (Trials were carried out using a two-part mine plough in place of the dozer blade.) The M728 CEV used by Singapore can also be fitted with the Pearson Engineering (UK) Track Width Mine Plough system.

The M728 is provided with night driving equipment and most vehicles in service with the US Army were originally fitted with a Xenon infra-red searchlight mounted over the top of the main armament. A central air filtration system pipes fresh air to each crew member.

Side view of M728 combat engineer vehicle with A-frame stowed (Michael Jerchel)   0512152

Specifications

M728 Combat Engineer Vehicle
Crew: 4
Weight:
(empty) 50,439 kg
(loaded) 53,200 kg
Power-to-weight ratio: (empty) 11.09 kW/t (14.87 hp/t)
Length:
(with boom erected) 9.3 m
(with blade and boom in travelling position) 8.91 m
Width:
(including blade) 3.7 m
(hull) 3.631 m
Height:
(travelling) 3.2 m
(lowest operable) 3.257 m
Ground clearance: 0.381 m
Track: 2.921 m
Track width: 711 mm
Length of track on ground: 4.235 m
Ground pressure: 0.89 kg/cm²
Max speed: (road) 48.28 km/h
Range: 450 km
Fuel capacity: 1,420 litres
Fording: 1.219 m
(with kit) 2.438 m
Gradient: 60%
Vertical obstacle: 0.76 m
Trench: 2.51 m
Engine: L3 Combat Propulsion Systems AVDS-1790-2A or -2D, 12-cylinder diesel developing 559 kW (750 bhp) at 2,400 rpm
Transmission: General Motors Corporation (Allison Division) CD-850-6A with 3 ranges (low, high and reverse)
Suspension: torsion bar
Electrical system: 24 V
Batteries: 6 × 6TN
Armament:
1 × 165 mm M135 demolition gun
1 × 7.62 mm M240 MG coaxial with main armament
1 × .50 (12.7 mm) M85 AA MG
2 banks of smoke grenade dischargers, 6 in each

Armour

Turret: (steel)
(front) 120 mm
(sides) 76 mm
(rear) 50 mm
(top) 25 mm
Hull: (steel)
(front) 120 mm
(sides, front) 76 mm
(sides, rear) 51 mm
(top) 57 mm
(rear) 44 mm
(floor) 13.63 mm

Status

Production complete. In service with Portugal, Saudi Arabia (15) and Singapore (eight). The M728 CEV was withdrawn from US Army service without replacement.

Contractor

General Dynamics Land Systems

General Dynamics Land Systems - Canada, M1132 Engineer Squad Vehicle (ESV)

Development

In November 2000, following an international competition, the US Army Tank automotive and Armament Command selected the now General Dynamics Land Systems - Canada Light Armoured Vehicle III (LAV-III) (8 × 8) vehicle to meet its requirement for a Medium Interim Armored Vehicle (MIAV).

The initial contract was worth USD61.7 million in research, development, test and evaluation with a second contract worth USD578 million for an initial batch of 366 LAV-III production vehicles.

Production is undertaken by General Dynamics Land Systems - Canada as well as General Dynamics Land Systems facilities in Lima, Ohio (US) and Anniston, Alabama (US).

The first LAV-III (8 × 8) vehicles delivered were in the Infantry Carrier Vehicle (ICV) configuration and were handed over to the US Army in March 2002.

Deliveries of the M1132 Engineer Squad Vehicle commenced in late 2002. The first batch of M1132 ESV comprised 22 units. Each BGT is issued with nine M1132 ESV in the engineer company. This includes three combat mobility platoons each of which comprises two HMMWV (4 × 4) and three M1132 ESV.

General Dynamics Land Systems - Canada M1132 Engineer Squad Vehicle fitted with Rapid Ordnance Removal System (Pearson Engineering)
1127280

The latter can be fitted with front mounted Pearson Engineering roller type mine clearing systems or surface mine clearing ploughs. The M1132 ESV can also tow a trailer mounted Mineclearing Line Charge (MICLIC) system. It is also fitted with lane marking systems and mine detection systems.

The first Interim Brigade Combat Team (IBCT) is the 3rd Brigade, 2nd Infantry Division, which was ready for operations in May 2003.

By late 2010 the US Army had placed orders for 4,000 Stryker of which over 3,200 had been delivered.

Baseline M1126 Stryker ICV is fitted with a Norwegian Protector RCWS which is normally armed with a .50 M2 HB MG and banks of electrically operated smoke grenade launchers.

In addition to the baseline M1126 Stryker ICV and the M1132 ESV other versions of the Stryker are the M1127 reconnaissance, M1128 Mobile Gun System (MGS), M1129 120 mm mortar carrier, M1130 command vehicle, M1131 fire support, M1133 medical evacuation vehicle, M1134 anti-tank (armed with Raytheon TOW anti-tank guided missiles) and M1135 NBC (Nuclear, Biological and Chemical) reconnaissance.

Description

The overall layout of the Stryker is similar to the LAV-III. The hull is of all-welded steel armour to which an additional layer of appliqué passive armour is fitted to provide a higher level of protection.

According to General Dynamics Land Systems - Canada, the armour package provides protection against 14.5 mm armour piercing attack and shell splinters.

Since it was introduced into service with the US Army in 2003 the Stryker has been upgraded in a number of areas, especially survivability.

Vehicles deployed to Iraq have been fitted with an air conditioning system and slat armour to provide a higher level of protection against Rocket Propelled Grenades (RPG) fitted with a High Explosive Anti-Tank (HEAT) warhead.

Under contract to GDLS-C, General Dynamics Armaments and Technical Products have developed and type classified an Explosive Reactive Armour (ERA) package for the Stryker.

In May 2009 GDLS-C awarded the company a USD150 million contract for an undisclosed number of systems with first deliveries made in 2010.

The driver is seated at the front left and provided with a single piece hatch cover and three M17 day periscopes for forward observation and the centre one can be replaced by a passive periscope for driving at night.

The power pack is to the right of the driver and the remainder of the vehicle is taken up by the crew compartment. The roof to the immediate rear of the drivers position is raised for greater internal volume.

The crew enter and leave the vehicle via a power operated ramp in the hull rear which is also provided with an emergency door. Over the rear part of the troop compartment are two roof hatches that open left and right. There is no provision for the crew to use their weapons from within the vehicle.

Following a competition, the Remote Weapon Station developed by the Norwegian company of Kongsberg Protech AS was selected with first production batch being delivered from Norway to the US early in 2002.

The RWS consists of an externally mounted weapon (normally a .50 (12.7 mm) M2 HB machine gun) and a fire-control system and in its standard configuration the fire-control system includes a Charge Coupled Device fitted with a 2° to 45° zoom lens, an uncooled thermal camera from Thales and a flat panel display.

Traverse is a full 360° with weapon elevation from –20° to +60°. The RWS in not stabilised and not fitted with a laser range-finder. These could be added if required by the user. The commander is also provided with a single piece hatch cover and seven M45 day periscopes.

A team comprising BAE Systems and Northrop Grumman was selected by the US Army Communications & Electronics Command to provide the digital vehicle intercom system for the Stryker with first contract valued at USD4.5 million for 350 systems.

Standard equipment includes hydropneumatic suspension system with height management system, central tyre inflation system with runflats, power brakes with ABS on rear three axles and fire detection and suppression system for engine and crew compartments.

General Dynamics Land Systems - Canada M1132 Engineer Squad Vehicle fitted with front-mounted mineclearing rollers shown in lowered position (Pearson Engineering) 1127279

A hydraulic self-recovery winch is provided at the front of the vehicle and NBC detectors and ventilated face mask system is standard. Land navigation includes a global position system and a complete communications system and a squad leaders video display panel.

The climate control system includes two roof vent fans and a crew/engine heater. An air conditioning system can be fitted if required.

Specifications

M1132 Engineer Squad Vehicle
Crew: 2 + 7
Configuration: 8 × 8
Combat weight: 17,236 kg
Power-to-weight ratio: 15.14 kW/t (20.31 hp/tonne)
Length: 6.985 m
Width: 2.717 m
Height: 2.641 m
Ground clearance: n/avail
Track: n/avail
Wheelbase: n/avail
Angle of approach/departure: n/avail
Max speed: 96.56 km/h
Acceleration: 9 seconds to reach 50 m
Fuel capacity: 200 litres
Range: 531 km at 64.37 km/h
Fording: n/avail
Gradient: 60%
Side slope: 30%
Vertical obstacle: 0.584 m
Trench: 1.981 m
Turning radius: n/avail
Engine: Caterpillar 3126 diesel developing 261 kW (350 hp)
Transmission: Allison MD 3066 automatic with 6 forward and 1 reverse gears
Transfer case: 2 speed
Steering: power assisted, front two wheels either side
Suspension: hydropneumatic with height adjustment
Tyres: Michelin 1200R20 XML
Brakes:
  (main) power
  (parking) hydraulic
Electrical system: 24 V
Batteries: 4
Armament:
  1 × 40 mm MK 19 grenade launcher or
  1 × .50 (12.7 mm) M2 HB machine gun or
  1 × 7.62 mm M240 machine gun (with adapter)
Ammunition:
  (40 mm) 430 or
  (.50 (12.7 mm)) 2,000 or
  (7.62 mm) 3,200
Smoke grenade launchers: 4 × M6 each with four tubes
Gun control equipment
Weapon power control: powered/manual
Gun elevation/depression: –20° /+60°
Weapon traverse: 360°
Gun stabiliser:
  (vertical) no
  (horizontal) no
NBC system: yes
Night vision equipment: yes (passive)
Armour: (hull) steel plus appliqué

Status
Production. In service with US Army.

Contractor
General Dynamics Land Systems - Canada (but see Development)

BAE Systems, US Combat Systems M9 Armored Combat Earthmover (ACE)

Development
In 1958, the US Army Mobility Equipment Research and Development Center at Fort Belvoir began work on a vehicle called the All-purpose Ballastable Crawler (ABC). This eventually became known as the Universal Engineer Tractor (UET).

The first prototypes of the Universal Engineer Tractor were built by the Caterpillar Tractor Company and the International Harvester Company. In January 1975, the Pacific Car and Foundry Company completed a further four vehicles, two of which underwent field evaluation at Fort Hood.

The result of these trials was considered satisfactory and indicated the vehicle's superiority over available equipment. TECOM testing was completed in August 1976 and type classification (Standard A) was approved in February 1977.

Trials of the M9 were subsequently carried out in both Yuma and Alaska to test modifications made as a result of previous trials and new equipment, such as a winterisation kit.

In November 1982, a revised contract worth USD29 million was awarded for the purchase of 15 equipments, of which USD19.3 million was for the vehicle and the remainder for product improvements (the original contract was to have been USD40.4 million for 36 vehicles).

All 15 vehicles were delivered by the end of 1984. Trials with this first batch of vehicles demonstrated that further improvements were required in some areas. Seven of this first batch were modified by PCF Defense Industries and were delivered to the US Army during January 1985. Tests with this batch of vehicles were carried out at Fort Hood.

During April 1986, Request For Proposals (RFP) were issued to industry and resulted in offers from ADCOR, BMY, FMC, General Motors of Canada, Ingersoll-Rand and PCF Defense Industries.

BMY was ultimately awarded a production contract on 25 July 1986. By the end of 1992 434 M9s had been built. The first production examples were delivered to the training base at Fort Leonard Wood during the fourth quarter of FY89. US Army units in Europe started to receive their vehicles during the last quarter of 1990.

During 1991, two overseas orders were placed for M9s. The first, for 18 units, was from a customer in Asia. The second order was worth USD8 million, with deliveries starting in late 1992.

In September 1993, the then United Defense (which is today BAE Systems, US Combat Systems) was awarded a USD78 million, 114 vehicle contract, consisting of 80 vehicles for the US Marine Corps and 34 vehicles for the National Guard. US Marine Corps deliveries commenced during 1995 with National Guard deliveries starting in 1996.

Production for the US Armed Forces ended in 1996, but in November 1997, a further 51 ACE vehicles were ordered for the US Army. The contract contained an option for a further 51 vehicles and was worth USD40.4 million.

The US Army placed an order for an additional 51 M9 ACE vehicles with the first of these delivered in early 1999. Production continued until late 1999. There was also an option on an additional 51 vehicles but this was not exercised. Production can start again if required. The M9 ACE has seen service with the US Armed Forces in the Gulf in 1991 and 2003.

The latest M9 ACE vehicles incorporate six new system improvements including an all-steel dozer blade furnished by the US Government, new belly plate and an improved hydraulic system.

Previous production M9 ACE vehicles were overhauled and upgraded to the latest production standard, or Product Improvement Programme (PIP), at Anniston Army Depot.

The M9 ACE has been ordered by the South Korean Armed Forces. Licence production (the final in-service total is 207) was carried out in South Korea by the now Samsung Techwin, Defense Program Division.

As of November 2010 the US Army had not announced any plans for the replacement of the M9 ACE.

Description
The M9 Armored Combat Earthmover (ACE) is intended to operate in forward areas and, due to its high road speed, can be located with the lead tanks in a convoy, closer to where it is needed, rather than at the back, as is the case with vehicles (such as the Caterpillar D7 medium crawler) which the M9 was intended to replace.

The M9 ACE is a general purpose engineer vehicle and can carry out tasks in three critical areas: mobility, counter-mobility and survivability. Mobility tasks include: filling craters and ditches; assisting fighting

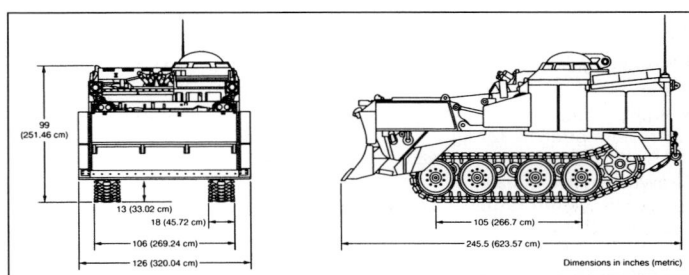

General arrangement drawing of M9 Armored Combat Earthmover which can be used for a variety of battlefield missions 0069297

M9 Armored Earthmover (Michael Jerchel)   0589690

vehicles (winching or towing); removing roadblocks, trees, rubble and other battlefield obstacles; preparing access/egress for fording sites and river crossings; preparing and maintaining combat routes; and preparing and maintaining assault airfields.

Counter-mobility tasks include: the construction of anti-armour obstacles; demolishing fords and bridge bypasses; participating in the digging of tank ditches; destroying landing fields and airfields; participating in the preparation of strong points and hauling obstacle materials.

Survivability tasks include: the digging of hull defilade positions for armour; construction of defensive positions for command-and-control operations; construction of earth berms for protection; hauling material for protective shelters; clearing fields of fire; and digging slots for vehicle-mounted TOWs and other battlefield weapons.

The M9 is air-portable in C-130, C-141B and C-5A transport aircraft. It is unarmed but has a smoke grenade launcher. Other equipment includes a standard NBC system (ventilated facepiece), a radio and the operator can utilise standard night vision goggles.

It has an amphibious capability after minimal preparation and armour protection is provided for the engine, power train and the operator.

The hull of the M9 is made of welded aluminium armour. At the front of the vehicle is the 6.7 m³ capacity scraper bowl (ballast compartment), hydraulically operated apron and positive load ejector.

The driver is seated towards the middle of the vehicle on the left side and is provided with a cupola providing 360° vision. A lighter hatch cover (weight 81.65 kg) than those fitted to early vehicles has been introduced; the hatch incorporates vision blocks in place of the earlier periscopic vision devices.

The Cummins V903C diesel engine is positioned to the right of the driver's compartment. The Clark Model 13.5 HR 3610-2 transmission is below the engine and the steer unit is to the rear, coupled to the final drives. On-vehicle equipment includes a 15.2 litre/s bilge pump and a Carco P30 planetary-winch with a line pull of 15,900 kg, using a 19 mm diameter wire rope 60 m long.

The M9 ACE can also be used to tow trailers and other equipment as it has a maximum drawbar pull of 14,059 kg. It is fully amphibious with preparation, being propelled in water by its tracks. The M9 is not suitable for operating in fast-flowing rivers.

The dozer blade is mounted on the apron and dozing and scraping are accomplished by raising and lowering the entire front of the vehicle by means of the hydropneumatic suspension.

This consists of eight sets of 711 mm diameter steel road wheels with the drive sprocket at the rear. The hydropneumatic suspension allows the M9 to be tilted to apply the dozing effort to one corner of the blade. The capability of the vehicle for operations such as dozing can be nearly doubled by self-loading the bowl with approximately 8,000 kg of earth, which is used as ballast.

Late production vehicles incorporate six new system improvements, including an all-steel dozer blade furnished by the US Government.

The US Army Anniston Army Depot has overhauled M9 ACE vehicles as well as incorporating a number of improvements as part of a Product Improvement Package (PIP).

Specifications

M9 Armored Combat Earthmover
Crew: 1
Weight:
(travel mode) 16,327 kg
(gross, ballasted) 24,490 kg
Drawbar pull: 14,059 kg
Power-to-weight ratio: 13.47 kW/t (18.06 hp/t)
Length: 6.248 m
Width:
(with dozer wings) 3.2 m
(without dozer wings) 2.79 m
(over tracks) 2.692 m

Height:
(windshield raised) 3 m
(windshield stowed) 2.7 m
Ground clearance:
(sprung, engine running) 0.343 m
(unsprung) variable
Track width: 457 mm
Length of track on ground: 2.67 m
Ground pressure: (empty) 0.68 kg/cm²
Max speed:
(road) 48.3 km/h
(water) 4.8 km/h
Range: (secondary roads) 322 km
Fuel capacity: 507 litres
Fording: 1.83 m (amphibious with minimal preparation)
Freeboard with load of 1,814 kg: 0.28 m
Gradient:
(kerb) 20%
(ballasted) 60%
Side slope: 20%
Vertical obstacle: 0.457 m
Trench: 1.575 m
Engine: Cummins V903C 14.8 litres 8-cylinder diesel developing 220 kW (295 hp) at 2,600 rpm
Transmission: Clark Model 13.5 HR 3610-2 with 6 forward and 2 reverse gears. Geared system for high-speed road and cross-country travel and, clutch and brake system for bulldozing operations
Suspension: hydropneumatic
Steering: hydraulic with gears and clutches
Turning radius:
(geared steer mode) 13.7 m
(clutch brake mode) pivots
Armament: none apart from smoke grenade launcher
Armour: aluminium, Kevlar and steel

Status
Production complete. Production can be resumed if significant export orders are placed. In service with the US Army, Marine Corps and National Guard. South Korea (207) where it was licence-produced by the now Samsung Techwin, Defense Program Division. The M9 ACE is also in service with Taiwan. At least part of the US Army fleet of M9 ACE have been upgraded in a number of key areas.

Contractor
BAE Systems, US Combat Systems

BAE Systems, US Combat Systems Mobile Tactical Vehicle Engineering (MTVE)

Development
To meet the operational requirements of the Canadian Army, the now BAE Systems, US Combat Systems (previously United Defense LP) developed a number of specific variants of the Mobile Tactical Vehicle Light (MTVL).

The Canadian MTVL and variants Mobile Tactical Vehicle Recovery (MTVR), Mobile Tactical Vehicle Engineer (MTVE), Mobile Tactical Vehicle Cargo (MTVC) and Mobile Tactical Vehicle Fitter (MTVF) are all rebuilds of existing vehicles with the work carried out in Canada.

Description
The Mobile Tactical Vehicle Engineer (MTVE) incorporates the Canadian Specially Equipped Vehicle (SEV) kit into the MTVL chassis and entered production in Canada in 2002.

All of the Canadian vehicles have been converted from existing M113 SEV vehicles.

A total of 28 production vehicles have now been delivered to Canada.

The MTVE provides integral light bulldozer, hydraulic auger and power tool capability to combat engineer sections in support of mechanised combat arms operations.

Equipped with a Cadillac Gage/Textron Marine & Land Systems power assisted .50 (12.7 mm) M2 HB turret, the MTVE provides under armour firing capability for the vehicle commander for both the .50 (12.7 mm) M2 HB heavy machine gun and the C6 7.62 mm light machine gun.

Two banks of four electrically-fired 76 mm multipurpose grenade launchers can fire a variety of munitions including smoke, white phosphorus and fragmentation.

The MTVE carries a crew of two, driver and vehicle commander and can accommodate an engineer section of eight soldiers with winter gear and rucksack.

Status
A total of 28 units delivered to Canada. Production has been completed for Canada but it could be placed back in production for the export market if additional orders were placed.

Contractor
BAE Systems, US Combat Systems

BAE Systems, US Combat Systems M113 with dozer blade kit

Description

The BAE Systems, US Combat Systems (previously United Defense Ground Systems) M113/M113A1/M113A2/M113A3/Mobile Tactical Vehicle Light armoured personnel carrier can be adapted for general bulldozing work by the addition of a dozer blade kit.

Once fitted, the kit does not impair the normal capabilities of the vehicle or its load-carrying ability. The vehicle can remain amphibious and the dozer blade acts as a trim vane in the water once the standard trim vane has been removed.

This dozer blade system is fitted to the Canadian upgraded M113 Specially Equipped Vehicle (SEV).

Status

Production as required. In service with the US Army and other countries, including Canada. This dozer blade kit is also applicable for other members of the M113 series family including the M113A1/M113A2/M113A3 Mobile Tactical Vehicle Light and the design can be applied to later models of the M113 series of vehicle. It is understood that there has been no recent production of this dozer blade for the home or export market.

Contractor

BAE Systems, US Combat Systems

US Army M113 APC fitted with hydraulically-operated dozer blade kit, with dozer blade being used
0512438

BAE Systems, US Combat Systems M113 with dozer blade kit

Description

Status

Contractor

BAE Systems, US Combat Systems

RECOVERY VEHICLES AND EQUIPMENT

ARMOURED RECOVERY VEHICLES

Austria

General Dynamics European Land Systems - Steyr Bergepanzer 4KH7FA-SB 20 Greif armoured recovery vehicle

Development

The Steyr-Daimler-Puch Bergepanzer 4KH7FA-SB 20 Greif armoured recovery vehicle is based on the chassis of the Jagdpanzer SK 105 light tank.

The first prototype of the Bergepanzer 4KH7FA-SB 20 was completed in 1974 with the first production vehicles following in 1976 to 1977.

Production of the Greif ARV was completed some time ago but started again in 1999/2000 with new vehicles being supplied to Botswana and Brazil.

Production of this family of vehicles has now been completed, and it is no longer marketed. It is possible that the Austrian Army may have some Greif ARV that are surplus to requirements.

In 2010 Steyr-Daimler-Puch became General Dynamics European Land Systems - Steyr GmbH.

Description

The hull of the Greif ARV is of all-welded steel armour construction, which provides the occupants with protection from small arms fire and shell splinters.

The hydraulic winch and crew compartment is at the front. Normal means of entry to the crew compartment is via two doors in the left side of the hull. In addition there are hatches in the roof.

The diesel engine and transmission are at the rear of the hull and there is a stowage platform over the engine decking which is used to carry replacement components.

The torsion bar suspension consists of five roadwheels either side, with the drive sprocket at the rear and the idler at the front. There are three track-return rollers. Hydraulic shock-absorbers are provided at the first and fifth roadwheel stations.

Mounted on the right side of the superstructure, at the front, is a hydraulic crane, which is traversed to the rear for travelling. This crane can be traversed through 234° and its boom elevated from 0° to +60°. The boom can be extended from its normal length of 3 to 3.9 m and has a maximum lifting capacity of 6,000 kg.

The crane is provided with 42 m of cable and is capable of lifting the complete two-person FL-12 series oscillating turret, armed with a 105 mm gun of the Jagdpanzer SK 105 light tank.

The hydraulic main winch is in the lower part of the hull and leads out through the front of the hull. This opening can be sealed for fording operations. The winch is provided with 95 m of 24 mm diameter cable and has a maximum pull of 20,000 kg. This enables the Greif ARV to recover both the Jagdpanzer SK 105 light tank and the 4K series of full tracked APC.

A rake blade is mounted at the front of the hull and is used in conjunction with the main winch. A full range of tools is carried, as is cutting and welding equipment. The Greif ARV does not have an NBC system, but the crew compartment is provided with a ventilation and heating unit.

Armament comprises a roof-mounted unprotected .50 (12.7 mm) M2 HB machine gun and four 80 mm electrically operated smoke grenade launchers.

Steyr-Daimler-Puch developed a pioneer vehicle based on the chassis of the Greif ARV. This vehicle is used by Austria (19) and Tunisia (two). Details of this vehicle are given in a separate entry in *Jane's Military Vehicles and Logistics*. Production of this vehicle is complete and it is no longer being marketed.

An upgrading programme involving the installation of a ZF 6HP 500 automatic transmission, hydraulically operated boom telescope arm and capstan-type recovery winch, has been completed for the Austrian Army Greif ARVs.

Bergepanzer 4KH7FA-SB 20 Greif armoured recovery vehicle
(Michael Jerchel)   1162440

Specifications

Greif ARV
Crew: 4
Weight: 19,800 kg
Power-to-weight ratio: 16.16 hp/t (12.05 kW/t)
Length: 6.705 m
Width: 2.5 m
Height:
  (max) 3.02 m
  (top of hull) 2.3 m
Ground clearance: 0.4 m
Track: 2.12 m
Track width: 380 mm
Length of track on ground: 3.037 m
Ground pressure: 0.75 kg/cm^2
Max speed: (road) 67.5 km/h
Range: (road) 625 km
Fuel capacity: 500 litres
Fording: 1 m
Gradient: 70%
Side slope: 40%
Vertical obstacle: 0.8 m
Trench: 2.1 m
Engine: Steyr Type 7FA 6-cylinder turbocharged diesel developing 320 hp (237 kW) at 2,300 rpm
Transmission: ZF manual with 6 forward and 1 reverse gears; upgraded to ZF 6HP 500 automatic (Austrian vehicles only)
Turning circle: 7.25 m
Electrical system: 24 V
Batteries: 2 × 12 V, 180 Ah
Armament:
  1 × .50 (12.7 mm) M2 HB MG
  4 × 80 mm smoke grenade dischargers
Ammunition: .50 (12.7 mm) - 1,500 rounds

Status

Production complete. In service with the following countries: Argentina (six), Austria (39), Bolivia (two), Botswana (two), Brazil (one), Morocco (10) and Tunisia (three). No longer being marketed.

Contractor

General Dynamics European Land Systems - Steyr GmbH (previously Steyr-Daimler-Puch Spezialfahrzeug AG & Co KG)

General Dynamics European Land Systems - Steyr Pandur I (6 × 6) Armoured Recovery and Repair Vehicle

Development

To support its growing family of Pandur (6 × 6) armoured personnel carriers and variants, the Austrian Company of Steyr-Daimler-Puch Spezialfahrzeug AG & Co KG (SFF) developed the Pandur Armoured Recovery and Repair Vehicle (ARRV).

By late 2010, six countries had adopted the Pandur I (6 × 6): Austria, Belgium, Gabon, Kuwait, Slovenia and the US. Of these, Belgium and Kuwait are known to use the armoured repair and recovery version of the Pandur. The vehicles for Kuwait were manufactured in the United States by AV Technology LLC.

Production of the Pandur has been completed in the US after a total of 70 vehicles had been built for the Kuwait National Guard and 12 for the US Army to meet its Armoured Ground Mobility System (AGMS) requirement. More recently additional vehicles have come from the Austrian production line for the US Army.

In 2010 Steyr-Daimler-Puch became General Dynamics European Land Systems - Steyr GmbH.

Description

The hull of the Pandur is of welded steel armour construction. It provides all-round protection against penetration from 7.62 × 51 mm Armour Piercing (AP) projectiles fired from a distance of 30 m and frontal arc penetration from 12.7 × 99 mm AP projectiles fired from a distance of 100 m (± 30°).

The driver is seated front left-side with the power pack to his right. The driver is provided with a left opening, single-piece hatch cover, in front of which are three day periscopes, of which the centre one can be replaced by a passive night vision device.

The Steyr WD 612 diesel engine is coupled to a fully automatic Allison MT 653DR transmission with torque converter and lock-up clutch. The air intake/outlets are in the roof of the vehicle with the exhaust outlet being on the right side.

There is a single-piece hatch cover to the rear of the drivers compartment, with the commander/machine gunner being seated on the right. This person is provided with a single-piece hatch cover that opens to the rear, day periscopes and an externally mounted 7.62 mm or .50 (12.7 mm) M2 HB machine gun.

Pandur I Armoured Recovery and Repair Vehicle as delivered to Kuwait in the travelling configuration   0121246

Unlike the standard Pandur APC, the Armoured Recovery and Repair Vehicle does not have any hatches over the rear part of the hull, although the two doors in the hull rear are retained.

To carry out its specialised ARRV role, the vehicle is fitted with a recovery winch and crane. The hydraulic recovery winch is a Rotzler TR-80 capstan type that is normally used to the front of the vehicle with a front-mounted spade lowered to the ground to provide vehicle stability during winching operations.

The crane is mounted on the left side of the hull over the last road wheel station and can be traversed through 250°. It can lift a maximum load of 3,000 kg between +20° and +47°. It can be operated by remote control up to a distance of 9 m using an umbilical cable.

When the crane is being used, four stabilisers are lowered to the ground, two either side of the hull to provide a more stable platform.

The vehicle is normally armed with a .50 (12.7 mm) M2 HB or 7.62 mm machine gun and banks of electrically operated smoke grenade launchers.

Optional equipment for the Pandur ARRV includes NBC protection, air conditioning, engine pre-heating, passive night vision equipment, fire detection and suppression system, arc welder and spare wheel. A more powerful diesel engine can be fitted as can a higher level of ballistic protection.

Pandur II family

Marketing is now being concentrated on the Pandur II family, which is available in 6 × 6 and 8 × 8 models.

The first customer is Portugal, which placed a contract for a total of 260 Pandur II (8 × 8) vehicles in early 2005, with deliveries to run from 2006 through to 2010. Included in this order are seven Repair and Recovery Vehicles (RRVs).

In mid-2006, the Czech Republic selected the Pandur II 8 × 8 and ordered 199 units with an additional 35 units making a total of 234. Of these 199 Pandur II vehicles, the first 21 were to come from the Austrian production line with the remainder being manufactured in the Czech Republic.

Early in 2008 the Czech Ministry of Defence cancelled the contract but in April 2008 an agreement had been reached that, subject to tests with two Pandur II vehicles, the Czech Army would take delivery of just 107 Pandur vehicles in six variants to be delivered by 2011.

Specifications

Pandur I Armoured Recovery and Repair Vehicle
Crew: 2 + 2
Configuration: 6 × 6
Max combat weight: 13,500 kg
Power-to-weight ratio: 19.3 hp/t (14.4 kW/t)
Length: 6.20 m
Width: 2.82 m
Height: (over crane) 2.794 m
Ground clearance: 0.43 m
Track:
  (first axle) 2.148 m
  (second axle) 2.148 m
  (third axle) 2.155 m
Wheelbase: 1.53 + 1.53 m
Angle of approach/departure: 45°/38°
Max road speed: 100 km/h
Fuel capacity: 275 litres
Range: >700 km
Fording: 1.5 m
Gradient: 70%
Side slope: 40%
Trench: 1.1 m
Vertical obstacle: 0.5 m
Turning radius: 8.5 m
Engine: Steyr WD 612 6-cylinder in-line diesel with direct injection, turbocharger and boost intercooler developing 260 hp (194 kW) at 2,400 rpm

Transmission: Allison MT 653DR automatic with torque converter and lock-up clutch with five forward and one reverse gears
Steering: ZF power assisted on first and second axles
Tyres: 12.5 R 20 on rims 11-20. Emergency run flat elements and central tyre pressure regulation system
Brakes:
  (main) pneumatically controlled ventilated disc, dual circuit, all wheels
  (parking) drum brake acting on transmission output shaft
Suspension: independent
Electrical system: 24 V
Batteries: 24 V, 100 Ah
Armament: 1 × .50 (12.7 mm) M2 HB or 7.62 mm machine gun
NBC system: optional
Night vision equipment: optional

Status

Production as required. In service with Belgium (these are actually repair vehicles as they do not have a winch) and Kuwait.

Contractor

General Dynamics European Land Systems - Steyr GmbH (previously Steyr-Daimler-Puch Spezialfahrzeug AG & Co KG)

Belgium

SABIEX Heavy Armoured Recovery Tank (HART)

Development

The Heavy Armoured Recovery Tank (HART) was developed by SABIEX in the late 1990s, based on its considerable experience in the overhauling and upgrading of a wide range of tracked and wheeled armoured fighting vehicles for the export market.

The first customer is Brazil, who took delivery of the small batch of HART vehicles to support its fleet of Leopard 1 series Main Battle Tanks (MBT). As of late 2010 Brazil was the only known customer for the HART.

Typical roles of the HART include the recovery and repair of damaged or disabled vehicles. The dozer blade can also be used to clear obstacles or prepare fire positions.

Description

HART is essentially a German-built Krauss-Maffei Wegmann Leopard 1 MBT chassis with its turret removed and a new all-welded armoured steel superstructure installed at the front of the vehicle. This provides protection from small arms fire and shell splinters.

The driver is seated at the front right and has a single-piece hatch cover and three day periscopes that give observation over the frontal arc. The middle periscope can be replaced by a passive periscope for driving at night.

The vehicle commander is seated to the left rear of the driver and has a large, single-piece hatch that opens to the rear. Additional seats are also provided for additional personnel.

To carry out its specialised role, a complete set of recovery equipment has been installed. Mounted at the front of the hull is a full width dozer blade that is also used to stabilise the vehicle when the winch or crane is being used. In addition to being operated from within the vehicle, the crane and winches installed in the HART can also be operated by remote control.

Mounted at the front left side of the hull is the crane with a telescopic jib which is traversed to the rear when not required. This has a capacity of 56 tonnes at 1 m and the telescopic jib can be extended from 6.1 to 8.6 m.

The vehicle is fitted with two winches, main and secondary and both of these lead out through the front of the vehicle. The main winch has a capacity of 45 tonnes while the auxiliary winch has a maximum capacity of 5.5 tonnes.

Mounted at the rear of the hull, on the left side, is the stabiliser leg which is lowered to the ground when required and has a maximum capacity of 40 tonnes.

SABIEX Heavy Armoured Recovery Tank (HART) in travelling configuration   0589493

An auxiliary power unit is fitted as standard, as is a variety of hydraulic and pneumatic equipment, tow bars and a tool box. A replacement power pack can be carried on top of the hull at the rear. The maximum power pack weight that can be carried by the HART is stated to be 4.54 tonnes.

The standard Leopard 1 power pack is at the rear. The suspension is of the torsion bar type with either side having seven dual rubber-tyred road wheels, idler at the front, drive sprocket at the rear and track return rollers. The upper part of the suspension is covered by a rubber skirt.

Specifications
SABIEX Heavy Armoured Recovery Tank
Crew: 2
Weight:
(combat) 42,000 kg
(unloaded) 41,000 kg
Ground pressure: 0.90 kg/cm²
Power-to-weight ratio: 19.8 hp/t (14.7 kW/t)
Length: 8.75 m
Width: 3.65 m
Height: 3.30 m
Ground clearance: 440 mm
Track: 2.57 m
Track width: 550 mm
Length of track on ground: 4.236 m
Max speed: 62 km/h
Range: 450 km
Gradient: 60%
Side slope: 30%
Vertical obstacle: 1.15 m
Trench: 3 m
Fording:
(without preparation) 1.2 m
(with preparation) 2.10 m
Turning radius: 4.96 m
Fuel capacity: 950 litres
Engine: MTU MB 838 Cam-500 diesel developing 830 hp (619 kW) at 2,200 rpm
Transmission: ZF 4 HP 250 automatic
Electrical system: 24 V
Batteries: 8

Status
Production as required. In service with Brazil.

Contractor
SABIEX International SA

SIBMAS (6 × 6) armoured recovery vehicle

Development
The SIBMAS (6 × 6) armoured recovery vehicle is a conversion of the basic SIBMAS (6 × 6) vehicle range and uses the same basic hull and drive train. The prototype armoured recovery vehicle was produced as the first production example in mid-1983, retaining much of its commonality with the rest of the SIBMAS (6 × 6) range.

Production of the SIBMAS range of vehicles was completed many years ago and it is no longer being marketed.

The Malaysian Army was the only customer for the SIBMAS range of 6 × 6 vehicles. Recently, three Malaysian companies have overhauled a single example of the SIBMAS vehicle.

In March 2008 it was stated that only about half of the 186 SIBMAS vehicles (including the 22 ARV models) delivered remained in service and that the other part of the fleet had been used for spares from 2006.

Under current plans it is expected that SIBMAS replacement vehicles will be procured under the 10th Malaysian Plan which covers the years 2011 through to 2015.

In April 2010 Malaysia announced that it was to order a total of 257 AV8 (8 × 8) armoured personnel carriers and variants under the 10th Malaysian Plan of 2011 through to 2015.

This will be based on the Turkish FNSS Pars family of wheeled combat vehicles with the prime contractor being the Malaysian company of Deftech.

Under current plans, the first prototype is required to be completed and ready for trials by January 2012 followed by first production vehicles is 2013 and all production vehicles delivered by 2016.

The AV8 will replace the currently deployed SIBMAS (6 × 6) vehicle as well as the now Rheinmetall MAN Military Vehicles Condor (4 × 4) vehicles currently deployed.

It is expected that the SIBMAS (6 × 6) ARV will be replaced by a variant of the AV8 (8 × 8) vehicle, probably towards the end of the production run.

Description
The hull of the SIBMAS ARV is all-welded steel armour and fully watertight. It provides the crew with full protection against 7.62 mm armour-piercing rounds. The driver is seated in the centre of the hull front behind three bulletproof windscreens.

SIBMAS (6 × 6) armoured recovery vehicle in travelling configuration
0589494

Behind the driver there is a circular hatch for the commander. Mounted on the hatch rail is a 7.62 mm machine gun which can be elevated 65° and depressed 10°.

Between the commander's hatch and crane support there is one large roof hatch and another entry hatch on the right of the hull rear. Internally there is rear-facing seating for three fitters, each side of the commander's position and next to the side doors.

The power pack, suspension and drive train are all identical to the rest of the SIBMAS (6 × 6) range.

Specialist recovery equipment is mounted externally and consists of two hydraulically operated spades, a hydraulic crane and two winches. The spades are mounted one at the front and the other at the rear and both can be fully folded, when required.

The hydraulic crane is mounted centrally on the hull roof and can be telescopically extended. It has a capacity of 10.5 tonnes at one metre and can lift loads of up to 3,000 kg at a radius of 3.5 m and 8,000 kg when used with the crane boom support for suspended towing operations. When extended, a crane jib support is used to secure heavy loads for towing.

Of the two winches one is used as the main multipurpose winch and is centrally mounted to enable the cable's guide pulleys to be extended front or rear. The hydraulically operated main winch has a direct pull of 20,000 kg. The other winch is used as an auxiliary and is mounted behind the main winch. It has a 1,500 kg capacity and is used to unwind the main winch cable.

Other external equipment includes:
- towing eyes front and rear
- 360° rotating searchlight on the hull roof
- emergency rotating warning light
- tow rope
- lifting bar
- vehicle tool kit and an axe
- shovel and pickaxe
- sand channels
- stowage box
- hydraulic lifting jack with an 8,000 kg capacity
- fuel and water jerrycans
- first aid kit
- compressor air outlet for tyre inflation
- two six-barrel 76 mm smoke launchers.

Internally, there is stowage capacity for a wide range of specialist equipment, including a portable gas welding kit and a hydraulic lifting jack with a 10,000 kg capacity. There is also a VHF communications radio set and full internal communications loudspeakers, only the driver and commander have headsets. The driver has a passive periscope for night driving and air conditioning is provided for the crew.

Specifications
SIBMAS Armoured Recovery Vehicle
Crew: 2 + 3
Configuration: 6 × 6
Length overall: (travelling) 7.63 m
Width: 2.54 m
Height: (top of crane) 3.2 m
Ground clearance: 0.4 m
Track: 2.066 m
Wheelbase: 2.8 m + 1.4 m
Angle of approach/departure: 35°/35°
Max road speed: 80 km/h
Fuel capacity: 410 litres
Max range: (road) 800 km
Fording: 1.07 m
Max gradient: 50%
Side slope: 30%
Vertical obstacle: 0.6 m

Trench: 1.8 m
Engine: MAN D 2566 MK 6-cylinder, in-line, water-cooled turbocharged diesel developing 320 hp (239 kW) at 1,900 rpm
Transmission: ZF fully automatic power-shift gearbox with hydrodynamic torque converter Type ZF 6 HP-500
Steering: power-assisted
Turning circle: 18 m
Tyres: 14.00 × 20
Electrical system: 24 V

Status
Production complete and no longer being marketed. In service with Malaysia (22).

Contractor
Belgian Mechanical Fabrication (BMF) SA

Bulgaria

MTP-1 armoured recovery vehicle

Development
The MTP-1 armoured recovery vehicle is a variant of the Russian vehicle known in the West as the Armoured Command and Reconnaissance Vehicle (ACRV - actual designation MT-LBus) as produced in Bulgaria for the home and export markets.

The MTP-1 is used for the recovery of damaged or disabled vehicles, changing vehicle components, preparing fire positions and vehicle hides and for general crane lift purposes.

It is understood that there has been no recent production of the MTP-1 armoured recovery vehicle in Bulgaria.

Description
The MTP-1 is virtually identical to the Russian designed ACRV but mounted on the front right-hand side is a turret identical to that fitted to the MT-LB multipurpose armoured vehicle. This manually operated turret is armed with a 7.62 mm PKT machine gun, although some turrets have been up-gunned to 12.7 mm.

The hull of the MTP-1 is of all-welded steel armour, which provides the occupants with protection from small arms fire and shell splinters.

Mounted on the roof is a crane with a telescopic jib. When travelling, the crane is traversed to the front and the hook is restrained by an eye on the front of the hull. The crane is mounted in a small, turret-like cupola, with the crane operator being provided with full armour protection. The crane has a lift capacity of 3,000 kg with the jib extended to 3.4 m, or 2,000 kg extended to the full 5 m.

Mounted at the rear of the vehicle is an entrenching blade similar to that fitted to the engineering variant of the MT-LB. This full-width blade is mounted on hydraulic arms and can prepare a vehicle scrape in about 110 minutes.

The blade can also act as an anchor and support when the vehicle's onboard winch is in operation. With the blade lowered the winch has a maximum capacity of 30 tonnes. With the blade raised, the winch capacity is lowered to 10 tonnes.

The MTP-1 is fully amphibious, being propelled in the water by its tracks. An NBC system is fitted. Combat weight is 14,000 kg.

Production of this vehicle and variants was undertaken in Bulgaria by BETA PLC. According to the United Nations arms transfer lists, there were no exports of this vehicle between 1993 and 2008.

Rear view of MTP-1 armoured recovery vehicle with entrenching blade lowered
0511464

Status
Production as required. In service with Bulgarian and other undisclosed countries.

Contractor
BETA PLC

China

NORINCO Type 654 Armoured Recovery and Repair Vehicle

Development
In 2008 it was revealed that China North Industries Corporation (NORINCO) had completed development of a new Armoured Recovery and Repair Vehicle (ARRV) called the Type 654.

This is based on the chassis of the MBT 2000 that has been developed by NORINCO specifically for the export market and shares many common components with this vehicle.

MBT 2000 is the latest MBT to be offered on the export market by NORINCO with the Type 98/Type 99 being reserved for the People's Liberation Army (PLA).

It is possible that the PLA has already fielded a new ARRV to support its more recently fielded heavier MBTs with similar capabilities to the ARRV Type 654.

It is also possible that the ARRV Type 654 was developed to meet the requirements of Pakistan as it has the same compact 6TD-2 diesel engine as installed in the T-80UD/T-84 MBTs.

According to NORINCO, main roles of the latest Type 654 ARRV can be summarised as follows:
- Recovery of tracked vehicles up to Military Load Class 50 (MLC 50) with main winch out
- Securing tracked vehicles during river crossing operations
- Towing of tracked vehicles up to MLC 50 on and off road
- Removal of complete power packs
- Removal of turrets.

Secondary applications of the Type 654 include:
- Recovery of tanks under combat conditions
- Carrying a replacement power pack for rapid installation into a disabled vehicle
- Carrying out dozing operations and preparing field works
- Battery charging
- Electric welding and cutting tasks
- Machining and repair using on board equipment.

NORINCO is still marketing the older Type 653 series ARV which are covered in detail in a separate entry in *Jane's Military Vehicles and Logistics*. The latest version is the NORINCO Type 653B.

Type 653 ARV series has been exported to a number of countries and has also been manufactured under licence by Heavy Industries Taxila (HIT).

Description
The Type 654 ARRV has a hull of all-welded steel armour that provides the occupants with protection from small arms fire and shell splinters. The crew and specialised recovery equipment is at the front of the vehicle with the power pack at the rear.

The vehicle is normally operated by a five-person crew which consists of commander, driver and three mechanics.

Mounted at the front of the vehicle is a hydraulically operated stabiliser blade that is operated by the driver from under complete armour protection.

This dozer blade is normally used when the winch or crane is being used but can also be used as a dozer blade to clear battlefield obstacles as well as preparing firing positions. It has a maximum capacity of 120 m³ of soil an hour.

Mounted on the right side of the chassis is a hydraulically operated crane that has a maximum lifting capacity of 25 tonnes. This is pivoted at the front of the chassis and is traversed to the rear when not required.

Type 654 ARRV in travelling configuration (NORINCO)
1334235

*Armoured Recovery and Repair Vehicle Type 654 towing a disabled MBT
(NORINCO)*   1303237

This crane can lift complete vehicles as well as being used to change
major vehicle components such as turrets and power packs.

The main hydraulic winch leads out through the front of the vehicle and
has a maximum pulling force of 82 tonnes which enables it to recover all of
the current armoured fighting vehicles deployed by China.

In addition to the bank of eight electrically operated smoke grenade
launchers located above the driver's position at the front left side of the
vehicle, the ARRV Type 654 is armed with a roof-mounted 12.7 mm
machine gun for self-defence purposes.

Variants

There are no known variants of the ARRV Type 654 but the vehicle could
also be used for a number of engineer support roles.

Specifications

Type 654 ARRV
Crew: 5
Weight: (combat) 47,500 kg
Power-to-weight ratio: 25.3 hp/t (18.8 kW/t)
Length: 8.830 m
Width: (with skirts) 3.52 m
Height: (crane in travelling configuration) 2.4 m
Ground clearance: n/avail
Track: n/avail
Length of track on ground: n/avail
Max speed:
  (road) 60 km/h
  (cross-country) 35-45 km/h
Range: 500 km
Fording: 1.8 m
Gradient: 60%
Side slope: 40%
Vertical obstacle: 0.85 m
Trench: 2.7 m
Engine: 6TD-2 6-cylinder opposed two-stroke super-charged multi-fuel
developing 1,200 hp (895 kW)
Transmission: planetary type mechanically and hydraulically operated
with 7 forward and 4 reverse gears
Suspension: torsion bar
Night vision equipment: yes
Armament: 1 × 12.7 mm machine gun
Smoke grenade launchers: 1 × eight-barrelled 76 mm

Status

Development complete. Ready for production.

Contractor

China North Industries Corporation (NORINCO)

NORINCO Type 653 and 653A armoured recovery vehicles

Development

The China North Industries Corporation (NORINCO) Type 653 Armoured
Recovery Vehicle (ARV) is based on the chassis and hull of the Type 69
MBT. The Type 653 bears no relationship to a recovery version of the Type
59 MBT which has a tractor-towing role only.

The Type 653A is basically a Type 653 with a more powerful crane. A
small batch of Type 653A ARVs has been supplied to Kuwait as part of a
complete NORINCO PLZ-45 155 mm/45-calibre self-propelled artillery
package.

Saudi Arabia has purchased a fleet of NORINCO PLZ-45 155 mm/45-
calibre self-propelled artillery systems and it is considered possible that
this deal could also have included a quantity of ARVs.

Although normally referred to as the NORINCO Type 653A/Type 653B
ARV, more recently NORINCO has also referred to the Type 653A simply as
the W653A recovery vehicle.

*NORINCO Type 653B armoured recovery vehicle with dozer/stabiliser
blade almost lowered to ground and crane elevated (NORINCO)*   1162436

Description

The Types 653 and 653A are intended for the field recovery and repair of
medium battle tanks and also have a limited combat engineering
capability. The basic hull and suspension of the Type 69 MBT are retained,
but in place of the turret, a fixed superstructure is fitted offset to the left and
the vehicle also carries a hydraulic crane and an earthmoving dozer blade
at the front. The main and auxiliary winches are located within the
superstructure.

The vehicle has a crew of five with the driver located forward on the
left-hand side in an armoured position, raised above the normal height of
the Type 69 MBT driver's position. The driver has a single forward-vision
aperture and a circular overhead access hatch. Infra-red lighting and vision
devices are provided for night driving.

Mounted on the front of the hull and operated by two hydraulic
cylinders, is the earthmoving dozer blade that can also act as an anchor for
heavy winching operations.

The full width dozer blade has an earthmoving capacity of 100 m³/h on
dry soil. The main winch access rollers are located between the twin
hydraulic cylinders for the dozer blade and the blade has to be in the lower
position for recovery. The main winch is hydraulic, with a maximum
pulling performance of up to 70,000 kg and the effective length of the cable
is 130 m (160 m on Type 653A).

To the right of the driver's position is the hydraulic crane jib with its full
360° turntable in line with the driver's position. The crane jib is telescopic
and is normally stowed to the rear for travelling. It can be extended to a
maximum lifting height of 6 m and has a rated lifting torque (static) of 392
to 686 kN.m (40 to 70 tonnes force metres) on Type 653A. The rated lifting
capacity is 10 tonnes on the Type 653 and 20 tonnes on the Type 653A.

Recovered vehicles can be towed behind the vehicles using a rigid
towing trail which is normally carried on the main hull superstructure side.
This superstructure has two circular roof hatches and there is provision for
a 12.7 mm Type 54 machine gun mounting on the roof.

The Type 653 can also lay its own smoke screen by injecting diesel fuel
into the exhaust outlet on the left side of the hull towards the rear.

The auxiliary winch is located to the left of the driver on the track fenders,
which also support a number of tool and other stowage boxes.

The Type 653 is stated to have a capability of carrying out field repairs
and the hydraulic crane can lift an entire tank turret complete main
armament. The main communications equipment is the Type 889 radio set
and the Type 803 is used as the intercom system.

Variants

Type 84 Medium Tank Recovery Vehicle

This is currently being offered on the export market by Poly Technologies
and appears to have similar capabilities to the earlier Type 653 series ARV
being marketed by NORINCO.

It is understood that the Type 84 designation is that used by the Peoples
Liberation Army (PLA) with the Type 653 designation being for the export
version.

According to Poly Technologies, the Type 84 has a crew of five and a
combat weight of 38.5 tonnes. The winch has a minimum capacity of 32 to
35 tonnes and is provided with 130 m of cable that has a diameter of
28.5 mm.

The hydraulic crane can be traversed through 360°, has a maximum
lifting height of 7.15 m and a rated capacity of 10 tonnes.

Upgraded Type 653A ARV

The Type 653A ARV is being marketed as part of the NORINCO PLZ-45 155
mm/45-calibre self-propelled howitzer system. This model has the winch
with a maximum capacity of 70 tonnes, crane with a lifting capacity of 20
tonnes, rigid towing equipment for a vehicle weighing 40 tonnes and a
dual purpose blade for dozing and anchoring.

NORINCO Type 653B ARV

This is the latest model of the Type 653 ARV to be marketed. The main
difference is the replacement of the original 580 hp diesel with a 730 hp
engine, which gives a higher speed of 55 km/h and greater mobility.

NORINCO Type 653A armoured recovery vehicle with jib stowed in the travelling position and stabiliser/dozer lowered at the front of the chassis (NORINCO)
1405666

NORINCO Type 654 ARRV

China North Industries Corporation (NORINCO) has completed development of a new Armoured Recovery and Repair Vehicle (ARRV) called the Type 654 and this is now being offered on the export market.

This is based on the chassis of the MBT 2000 that has been developed by NORINCO specifically for the export market and shares many common components with this vehicle. Full details of this ARRV are provided in a separate entry in *Jane's Military Vehicles and Logistics*.

The more capable Type 654 ARRV is being marketed alongside the older and less capable NORINCO Type 653.

Specifications

Type 653 armoured recovery vehicle
Crew: 5
Weight:
 (Type 653) 38,000 kg
 (Type 653A) 41,000 kg
Power-to-weight ratio:
 (Type 653) 15.26 hp/t (11.38 kW/t)
 (Type 653A) 14.15 hp/t (10.55 kW/t)
Length:
 (Type 653) 7.18 m
 (Type 653A) 7.87 m
Width: (over side skirts) 3.304 m
Height:
 (highest point) 3 m
 (top of superstructure) 2.34 m
Ground clearance: 0.425 m
Track: 2.64 m
Length of track on ground: 3.845 m
Max speed: 50 km/h
 (towing) 18 km/h
Range:
 (road, normal fuel tanks) 370 km
Fording: 1.4 m
Gradient: 58%
 (towing) 40%
Side slope: 40%
Vertical obstacle: 0.7 m
Trench: 2.6 m
Engine: Type 12150L-7BW V12 diesel developing 580 hp (433 kW) at 2,000 rpm
Suspension: torsion bar
NBC system: yes
Night vision equipment: yes
Armament: 1 × 12.7 mm Type 54 MG

Main winch
Max towing force: 628-686 kN (64,000-70,000 kgf)
Cable delivery and retract speed:
 (without load) 28-30 m/min
 (with load) 7 m/min

Crane - Type 653
Rated lifting capacity: 10,000 kg
Rated lifting torque: (static) 392 kN.m (40,000 kgf.m)
Max lifting height: 6 m

Dozer blade
Max digging depth: 200 mm
Digging capacity: (dry earth) 100 m³/h
Max supporting force: 686 kN (70,000 kgf)

Status

Production as required. In service with Bangladesh, China, Kuwait (used to support 155 mm PLZ-45 155 mm/45-calibre self-propelled artillery systems), Pakistan, Sri Lanka and Thailand. According to United Nations sources, between 1992 and 2008 China exported ARVs to just two countries. Pakistan took delivery of 20 units in 1995 with Sri Lanka taking delivery of two units in 1992. It is considered that these were Type 653

series vehicles. Chinese sources have also referred to this as the W 653A-1 ARV. China has exported quantities of other undisclosed types of armoured fighting vehicles, both tracked and wheeled, which could also have included ARVs.

Contractor
China North Industries Corporation (NORINCO)

NORINCO Type 85 armoured recovery and repair vehicle

Development
The China North Industries Corporation (NORINCO) Type 85 armoured recovery and repair vehicle is based on the chassis and hull of the NORINCO Type 85 APC (originally known as the YW 531 H). This vehicle is apparently intended only for light recovery and repair tasks on other vehicles in the Type 85 APC family. As it is not fitted with a winch, its recovery capabilities are very limited.

Description
The basic all-welded steel armour hull and chassis of the Type 85 APC are retained, along with the 12.7 mm machine gun turret, but a hydraulic jib crane has been installed on the left- hand side of the upper hull rear. Internal capacity for the commander and a crew of five is provided. The crane has a lift capacity of 1,000 kg. Among other equipment carried is a 5 kW generator, a welding kit and special recovery and repair tools. If required, all equipment can be powered by an external AC power source.

The vehicle is very similar to the NORINCO Type 85 armoured repair vehicle covered in a separate entry in *Jane's Military Vehicles and Logistics*. The roof mounted 12.7 mm Type 54 machine gun is provided with armour protection through about 330°. This machine gun installation is similar to that fitted onto other Chinese light armoured vehicles, tracked and wheeled.

Variants
NORINCO VP1 APC
In late-2010 NORINCO was only offering one tracked light Armoured Fighting Vehicle (AFV), on the export market, the VP1 full tracked Armoured Personnel Carrier (APC).

This is similar in appearance and capabilities to the NORINCO Type 90 APC which has a distinct chamfer to the upper part of the troop compartment and slightly different hull front.

The Type 90 APC is no longer being offered on the export market by NORINCO.

More specialised versions of the VP1 APC include ambulance, command post vehicle and self-propelled mortar.

As far as it is known there is not a dedicated ARV version of the NORINCO VP1 ARV. It is considered that this could be developed for the export market if there was a firm requirement.

NORINCO Type WZ551 (6 × 6) ARV
There is a repair and recovery version of the WZ551 (6 × 6) which features a power operated winch and a hydraulically operated crane at the rear of the roof which is fitted with a telescopic jib for changing armoured vehicle subsystems in the field.

NORINCO VN1 (8 × 8) Armoured Personnel Carrier (APC)
In 2008, NORINCO had started to market a new 8 × 8 wheeled Armoured Personnel Carrier (APC) called the VN1.

NORINCO Type 85 recovery vehicle showing roof-mounted crane elevated from the stowed position
0004987

This is now in service with the Peoples Liberation Army under the designation of the ZBD-09 (8 × 8) Wheeled Infantry Combat Vehicle.

There is also a recovery version of the VN1 (8 × 8) APC that has already been offered on the export market by NORINCO although there are no known sales as of late 2010.

Specifications

Type 85 armoured recovery and repair vehicle
Crew: 6
Weight: (combat) 15,000 kg
Power-to-weight ratio: 21.3 hp/t (15.9 kW/t)
Length: 6.125 m
Width: (overall) 3.06 m
Height: (overall) 2.949 m
Ground clearance: 0.46 m
Max speed:
    (roads) 65 km/h
    (water) 6 km/h
Fuel capacity: 450 litres
Range: (road) 500 km
Fording: amphibious
Gradient: 62.5%
Vertical obstacle: 0.6 m
Trench: 2.2 m
Engine: Deutz air-cooled diesel developing 320 hp (239 kW)
Transmission: manual, 4 forward and 1 reverse gears
Suspension: torsion bar
Electrical system: 24 V
Armament: 1 × 12.7 mm Type 54 MG

Status

Production as required. Small quantities of this vehicle may have been built for the home and export markets.

The United Nations arms transfer list for the period 1992 through to 2008 shows no exports of this vehicle.

Contractor

China North Industries Corporation (NORINCO)

NORINCO VN1 Armoured Recovery Vehicle

Development

China North Industries Corporation (NORINCO) is currently marketing the VN1 (8 × 8) Armoured Personnel Carrier (APC) on the export market.

This is the export version of the ZBD-09 (8 × 8) Infantry Fighting Vehicle (IFV) which is now in service with the Peoples Liberation Army and made its first public appearance in October 2009.

ZBD-09 is fitted with a two-person turret armed with a 30 mm cannon and a 7.62 mm co-axial Machine Gun (MG) with a Red Arrow 73 (HJ-73D) Anti-Tank Guided Weapon (ATGW) either side of the turret.

A number of export versions of the VN1 are being marketed including a Command Post Vehicle (CPV) with a higher roof line to the rear of the turret and an Armoured Recovery Vehicle (ARV).

As far as it is known, as of November 2010, no export sales of the VN1/ZBD-09 had been made and it is not known as to whether the ARV model had entered quantity production.

Description

The hull of the VN1 (8 × 8) ARV is of all-welded steel armour construction with appliqué armour that provides the occupants with protection from small arms fire and splinters.

The drivers compartment is at the front left with the power pack to the right which leaves the remainder of the vehicle free for the crew compartment.

Steering is power-assisted on the front four wheels and it is fully amphibious at a speed of up to 8 km/h being propelled in the water by two propellers mounted one either side of the lower part of the chassis towards the rear. Before entering the water a trim vane is erected at the front of the chassis and the bilge pumps are activated.

Standard equipment includes a central tyre pressure regulation system, run flat tyres, air conditioning system, NBC system and an automatic fire detection and suppression system.

No details of the specific recovery equipment fitted to the ARV have been released although pivoted at the rear of the chassis roof is a hydraulic crane with a telescopic jib. When travelling this is traversed towards the front of the chassis and held in a travel lock.

It is considered probable that a full range of tools and other specialised equipment is carried and a winch is probably mounted in the rear of the chassis to recover vehicles.

Specifications

Not available.

Status

Prototype. Not yet in production or service.

Contractor

China North Industries Corporation (NORINCO)

Croatia

M-84A1 Armoured Recovery Vehicle

Development

To support the M-84A1 Main Battle Tank (MBT), Croatia is now marketing the M-84A1 Armoured Recovery Vehicle (ARV).

Although the primary role of this vehicle is to recover damaged and disabled vehicles and change major subsystems such as power packs, it can also be used as a combat engineer vehicle.

This is essentially a local version of the Polish WZT-3 Armoured Recovery Vehicle (ARV), modified for use in high ambient temperatures.

In 1998, Kuwait ordered from the former Yugoslavia 200 M-84 series MBTs plus 15 command vehicles and 15 ARV. At that time Yugoslavia did not have an ARV version of the M-84 so plans were obtained of the Polish WZT-3 which became the M-84A1 ARV.

In the end only a small batch of M-84A1 ARV were built and these were subsequently taken into service by Croatia and Serbia and Montenegro. As far as it is known, there has been no recent production of the M-84A1 ARV for the home or export markets. The M-84A1 ARV is still being offered on the export market, together with locally built MBTs.

Description

The M-84A1 ARV is almost identical to the Polish WZT-3 ARV, which is covered in detail in a separate entry in *Jane's Military Vehicles and Logistics*.

To carry out its specialised role the M-84A1 ARV is fitted with a complete range of specialised equipment.

Mounted on the left side of the hull towards the front is a hydraulic crane with a telescopic jib which can be traversed through a full 360° and has a maximum capacity of 25 tonnes. The jib can be extended to a maximum reach of 8 m and when not required is traversed to the rear.

Mounted at the front of the hull is the hydraulically operated dozer blade, which is also used to stabilised the vehicle when the crane or winches are being used. The dozer blade is 3.605 m wide and has an average cutting angle of 30° and a cutting depth of 250 mm.

The main hydraulic winch is provided with 200 m of cable and has a maximum capacity of 300 kN which can be increased to 900 kN with a three part pully block.

The drum type hydraulically operated auxiliary winch has a maximum capacity of 20 kN and is provided with 400 m of cable.

Chinese VN1 (8 × 8) in armoured recovery vehicle configuration and showing roof mounted hydraulic crane in travelling configuration (NORINCO) 1353434

M-84A1 ARV using its dozer blade and with crane traversed to the rear (Duro Dakovic Specijalna Vozila) 0589495

A 12.7 mm machine gun is fitted for self-defence purposes and mounted either side at the front of the chassis is a bank of six electrically operated 81 mm grenade launchers.

Other more specialised equipment includes gas welding and cutting equipment, 220 V AC power supplier, full servicing and repair kit for the M-84AB tank, medical kit, tools, NBC system and provision to be fitted with a snorkel for deep fording operations.

Specifications
M-84A1 Armoured Recovery Vehicle
Crew: 4
Combat weight: 42,000 kg
Power-to-weight ratio: 23.81 hp/t (17.75 kW/t)
Length: 8.30 m
Width: 3.605 m
Height: 2.15 m
Ground clearance: 470 mm
Ground pressure: 0.813 kg/cm²
Max speed: 65 km/h
Range: (roads) 700 km
Fuel capacity: 1,450 litres
Fording:
(without preparation) 1.2 to 1.8 m
(with preparation) 5 m
Gradient: 58%
Side slope: 47%
Vertical obstacle: 0.85 m
Trench: 2.6 to 2.80 m
Engine: V-46TK 4 stroke, 12-cylinder multi fuel liquid-cooled diesel developing 1,000 hp (746 kW) at 2,000 rpm
Transmission: two-side epicyclic gearbox with 7 forward and 1 reverse gears, hydro-mechanical control
Suspension: torsion bar
Electrical system: 28.5 V
Main armament: 1 × 12.7 mm machine gun
Ammunition: 300 × 12.7 mm
Smoke grenade launchers: 12 × 81 mm

Status
Production as required. In service with Croatia, Montenegro and Serbia. As far as it is known there has been no recent production of the M-84A1 ARV in Croatia.

Contractor
Duro Dakovic Specijalna Vozila dd

Czech Republic

VT-55A armoured recovery vehicle

Development
Between 1967 and 1983, the former Czechoslovakia produced 2,321 Armoured Recovery Vehicles (ARVs). Of these, 1,820 were VT-55As for the Warsaw Pact (including Russia) and 501 were VT-55Ks for the export market.

The East German Army (NVA) took delivery of 250 VT-55As and these were designated the Panzerzugmaschine T-55T. These were fitted with a towing device in front (as per T-55T/TB), and from 1978, the lifting capacity of the crane was raised to two tonnes.

According to the United Nations, the following quantities of VT-55A series ARV were exported between 1992 and 2008 but there could be other undisclosed exports as well.

From	To	Quantity	Date	Comment
Czech Republic	Germany	1	2005	
Czech Republic	Hungary	1	2003	
Czech Republic	Slovakia	2	2002	
Hungary	Iraq	4	2005	2 × VT-55A, 2 × BT-55A
Slovakia	Sri Lanka	2	2002	
Ukraine	Iraq	3	2006	BTS-5B
Ukraine	Azerbaijan	4	2007	BTS-5M
Ukraine	Georgia	6	2007	BTS-5

Description
The VT-55A ARV is based on the hull and running gear of the Russian designed T-55A MBT. The hull of the VT-55A ARV is almost identical to that of the T-55A MBT and provides the same level of ballistic protection.

Mounted on the right of the hull is a hydraulic crane with a maximum lifting capacity of 1,500 kg and a maximum radius of 4 m. On the roof of the ARV towards the rear, is a 1.6 × 1.6 m platform that can carry a maximum load, such as a power pack of up to 3,000 kg.

VT-55A armoured recovery vehicle with dozer blade raised and crane on left side of the hull in the travelling position   0511466

The VT-55A has two winches. The main winch is mechanically driven by the main engine. It has a maximum capacity of 25,000 kg and is provided with 200 m of 28 mm diameter cable. The hydraulically operated auxiliary winch has a capacity of 800 kg and is provided with 400 m of 6.3 mm diameter cable. The seat of the winch operator rotates within a small turret.

At the front of the vehicle is a hydraulically operated, full-width dozer blade with a soil-shifting capacity of 150 m³/h. This is also used to stabilise the vehicle when the crane or winches are being used.

The vehicle can be fitted with a snorkel tube on top of the hull to allow operations in water obstacles up to 1,000 m wide and 5 m deep and with a stream velocity of 1.5 m/s. Under normal conditions, the vehicle can ford water obstacles up to 1.4 m deep.

All vehicles have several towbars and a tow cable 4.2 m long. Electric welding equipment, a workbench and a vice are mounted above one of the tracks and are pulled out when required. At the rear of the vehicle is a winch anchor spade which can also be used as a dozer blade.

The one-person machine gun turret can be traversed through 360° and the 7.62 mm machine gun can be used against ground and air targets. The vehicle has a three-man crew and standard equipment includes a crew compartment heater, NBC system and infra-red night vision equipment.

The VT-55A ARV can also lay its own smoke screen by injecting diesel fuel into the exhaust outlet on the left hand side of the hull towards the rear.

Variants
When fitted with a dozer blade BTU-55 or BTZ-55, the vehicle becomes the ZS-55A.

Specifications
VT-55A Armoured Recovery Vehicle
Crew: 3
Weight: 36,450 kg
Power-to-weight ratio: 15.91 hp/t (11.87 kW/t)
Length overall: 7.12 m
Width:
(overall) 3.275 m
(inside track) 2.04 m
Height: (top of stowed crane) 2.64 m
Ground clearance: 0.425 m
Max speed: 50 km/h
Average speed:
(road) 32-35 km/h
(towing) up to 18 km/h
Range:
(road) 270 km
(cross-country) 100 km
Gradient: 32°
Side slope: 30°
Fording:
(normal) 1.4 m
(with preparation) 5 m
Engine: V-55 water-cooled diesel developing 580 hp (433 kW) at 2,000 rpm
Transmission: manual with 5 forward and 1 reverse gears
Armament: 1 × 7.62 mm MG

Status
Production complete. Quantities of vehicles are available for export. The earlier MT-55 is in service with the armed forces of Czech Republic and Slovakia.

It is understood that Finland and Sweden have taken delivery of a quantity of T-55T series ARVs. A number of VT-55A ARV are now surplus to requirements and as stated in Development, small quantities of these have been exported.

Contractor
VOP 025 Novy Jicin sp

Egypt

Kader Fahd 240 Recovery and Repair Vehicle

Development
The Kader Factory for Developed Industries developed the Recovery and Repair Vehicle Fahd 240 which is based on the latest production Fahd 240 (4 × 4) Armoured Personnel Carrier (APC).

It is estimated that about 1,200 Fahd (4 × 4) series APCs and variants have now been built for the home and export markets.

It is not known as to whether any sales of the Fahd 240 Recovery and Repair Vehicle had been made but at least one example of the vehicle has been built and successfully tested.

According to the United Nations arms transfer lists covering 1999 through 2008, there was only one declared export of Fahd vehicles, and that was 53 to Algeria in 1992.

It is understood that there has been no recent production of any Fahd (4 × 4) APC or variants such as the repair and recovery vehicle.

Description
The overall layout of the Fahd 240 Recovery and Repair Vehicle is identical to that of the APC, with the driver and commander seated at the front of the vehicle with forward observation via large bulletproof windows. These can be rapidly covered by an armoured shutter hinged at the top.

The commander and driver enter the vehicle via a door in the forward part of the hull which opens forwards and is provided with a bulletproof window in the upper part.

There is also a door in the hull rear with the lower part folding down to form a step and with the upper part opening upwards, hatches in the roof and vision blocks in the sides and rear of the vehicle.

Mounted on the roof at the rear is a turntable-mounted hydraulic crane with a telescopic jib which can be traversed through 315° with the boom being elevated to +70°.

When the crane is being used, two hydraulic stabilisers are lowered to the ground to provide a more stable platform. The crane has the following capabilities:

Raised Mass	Boom Length	Torque
2,000 kg	2 m	39.2 kN.m
1,500 kg	2.7 m	39.7 kN.m
1,000 kg	4 m	39.2 kN.m

Specialised equipment carried includes an air compressor, electric power unit, battery charger, testing unit, portable drill and grinder, tyre repair set, radiator set, tool set, greasing equipment, hydraulic jack, oxy acetylene set, recovery equipment and a tent.

Specifications

Fahd 240 Recovery and Repair Vehicle
Configuration: 4 × 4
Weight: 12,500 kg
Power-to-weight ratio: 19.2 hp/t (14.32 kW/t)
Length: 6 m
Width: 2.45 m
Height: 2.8 m
Track: 2.126 m
Angle of approach/departure: 35/35°
Wheelbase: 3.2 m
Maximum road speed: 81 km/h
Road range: 700 km

Fording: 0.7 m
Gradient: 70%
Side slope: 30%
Trench: 0.8 m
Vertical obstacle: 0.5 m
Engine: Mercedes-Benz OM 366 LA 4 6-cylinder direct injection, turbocharged, water-cooled diesel developing 240 hp (179 kW) at 2,600 rpm
Transmission: manual with 5 forward and 1 reverse gears
Transfer case: 2 speed
Steering: power assisted
Turning radius: 7 m
Brakes: hydropneumatic
Suspension: leaf springs and shock-absorbers
Electrical system: 24 V
Armament: optional
NBC system: optional
Night vision equipment: optional

Status
Production as required. Sales of the Fahd APC have been made to the following countries but it is not known as to whether any of these have the recovery and repair vehicle in service. Algeria, Egypt, Kuwait, Oman and Sudan.

Contractor
Kader Factory for Developed Industries

France

Nexter Systems DNG armoured recovery vehicle

Development
The Depannage Nouvelle Generation (DNG) Armoured Recovery Vehicle (ARV) was developed by Nexter Systems (previously Giat Industries) to support the Leclerc MBT which cannot be recovered by the older Nexter Systems AMX-30D ARV.

The Roanne facility of the company built two prototypes of the Leclerc ARV and the UAE ordered 46 production vehicles.

The French Army selected the DNG to meet its future requirements in 1997 and placed a production order for a total of 20 units. First production Leclerc DNG were delivered to the French Army in 1999.

The French Army version of the DNG is called the Depanneur Chars Leclerc (DCL) and has the same MTU power pack as the UAE vehicles.

This is called the EuroPowerPack and consists of the MTU 883 V-12 diesel developing 1,500 hp coupled to a Renk HSWI 295 TM automatic transmission.

Most of the specialised recovery equipment for the DNG/DCL is supplied by Rheinmetall Landsysteme (previously MaK) of Germany and is the same as that used in the Büffel ARV, based on automotive components of the Leopard 2 MBT.

Due to its overall modular design, the DNG can also be produced configured as the EPG armoured engineer vehicle and can readily accept the K2D mineclearing kit.

The first prototype of the EBG armoured engineer vehicle was completed late in 2001, but as of late 2010 this remained at the prototype stage.

Production of the Leclerc MBT and the Leclerc ARV has been completed at the Nexter Systems Roanne facility but production could commence again if sufficient additional orders are placed.

Fahd (4 × 4) Recovery and Repair Vehicle from the rear with stabilisers lowered to the ground and crane traversed to the rear
(Kader Factory for Developed Industries)   0589496

Nexter Systems Leclerc DNG (ARV) modified for the breacher role and fitted with the K2D mine-clearing kit that includes a front mounted Pearson Engineering full width mine plough and two pods of rocket propelled mine clearing systems one either side at the rear (Nexter Systems)   1405667

Nexter Systems DNG undergoing automotive trials (Nexter Systems)
0011639

The United Arab Emirates have taken delivery of a total of 46 Leclerc ARV and a number of these are expected to be converted in the assault breacher role in the future.

Description
The DNG ARV is based on the armoured hull and running gear of the Leclerc MBT, although the chassis is longer, to accommodate seven road wheels and seven independent suspension units each side, instead of six.

The TRW Systems Aeronautiques hydropneumatic suspension system is retained, as is the track tensioning system, allowing the driver to adjust the track tension without leaving his protected position. The rear suspension units can be locked by actuators when the crane is in operation.

The vehicle is manned by a crew of three: commander, driver and operator/mechanic, with one extra foldable seat for a passenger. An air conditioning system is provided for the crew compartment together with an NBC protection system.

The Galix close defence system is provided and the commander has a .50 (12.7 mm) M2 HB machine gun mounted over his cupola.

Additional armour can be fitted if required. This can be of the Explosive Reactive Armour (ERA) type to provide a higher level of protection against anti-tank weapons fitted with a tandem High Explosive Anti-Tank (HEAT) warhead.

The vehicle has a fully armoured superstructure at the front of the hull, with a crane jib with a maximum capacity of 30 tonnes, on a turntable on the right of the vehicle. Crane jib traverse is 260° and maximum height below the hook is 7.9 m. A dozer blade with a width of 3.42 m is located at the front, to act as an anchor during recovery operations or to clear battlefield obstacles and debris.

The main capstan winch has a 34-tonne capacity and is provided with 160 m of cable; an auxiliary winch has a 15-tonne capacity and has 230 m of cable.

Also carried is a demountable diesel-electric power generator. The actual level of equipment involved, plus items such as tool kits and stowage bins, can vary according to end user requirements. A complete Leclerc power pack can be carried on the hull rear.

Crew and vehicle features include: an NBC system; an automatic fire detection and suppression system in the crew, power pack and hydraulic compartments; and the hydraulic compartment is isolated from the crew. Crew comforts include air conditioning and a chemical toilet.

One optional item of equipment is an auxiliary power unit and the Nexter Fast Information Navigation DEcision and Reporting System (FINDERS). This is standard on the Leclerc DNG supplied to the United Arab Emirates.

Specifications
DNG armoured recovery vehicle
Crew: 3 + 1
Weight: 59,000 kg
Bridge classification: MLC 65 to 70 according to equipment
Power-to-weight ratio: 25.42 hp/t (18.96 kW/t)
Length: (overall) 9.15 m
Width:
    (over tracks) 3.38 m
    (over dozer blade) 3.42 m
Height: (roof) 2.6 m
Ground clearance: (nominal) 0.485 m
Track width: 635 mm
Ground pressure: 0.82 kg/cm²
Max speed: 72 km/h
Fuel capacity: 1,500 litres under armour
Range: (road) 500 km
Fording: (without preparation) 1 m
Gradient: 60%
Side slope: 30%
Vertical obstacle: 0.8 m
Trench: 3 m
Engine: MTU EuroPowerPack with MTU 883 turbocharged V-12 diesel developing 1,500 hp (1,119 kW)

Transmission: Renk HLSW 295 TM automatic gearbox with integrated torque converter and hydrokinetic retarder; 5 forward and 3 reverse gears
Suspension: hydropneumatic, 2-cylinder
Electrical system: 24 V
Batteries: 8 × 12 V, 125 Ah
Armament:
    1 × .50 (12.7 mm) M2 HB MG
    Galix close defence system
Ammunition: .50 (12.7 mm) - 100 rounds of ready-use, 600 in reserve

Status
Production complete but can be resumed. In service with France (20) and the United Arab Emirates (46 delivered). Normally issued on the scale of one per squadron (French Army).

Contractor
Nexter Systems

Nexter Systems AMX-30D Armoured Recovery Vehicle

Development
The AMX-30D Armoured Recovery Vehicle (ARV) was designed by Nexter Systems (previously Giat Industries) to carry out three basic tasks: the recovery of disabled and damaged AFVs; major field repairs such as changing a complete power pack and engineer work.

Description
The full-tracked chassis of the AMX-30D ARV (or *Char AMX-30 Depanneur-Niveleur*) is identical to that of the basic AMX-30 MBT, but the all-welded steel armour superstructure is new. Its crew of four consists of commander, driver and two mechanics.

The driver is seated at the front of the hull, slightly to the left and is provided with three day periscopes for observation. One of these can be replaced by a passive night vision device. His single-piece hatch cover swings to the left.

The commander is seated to his rear and is provided with a TOP 7 cupola. This is similar to that installed on the AMX-30 MBT but does not have the infra-red searchlight or the contrarotating equipment. The cupola has 10 day periscopes for observation and a ×10 sight for aiming the 7.62 mm machine gun, which is externally mounted on the commander's cupola but aimed and fired from within the turret.

To the rear of the commander's cupola is the entrance hatch for the engineers which opens to the right. There is a single M336 day periscope fore and aft of this hatch cover.

The engine and transmission at the rear of the hull are separated from the crew compartment by a fireproof bulkhead. The suspension is of the torsion bar type and either side consists of five roadwheels with the drive sprocket at the rear and the idler at the front. The first, second, fourth and fifth roadwheels are mounted on bogies, which are provided with hydraulic shock-absorbers. Five rollers support the inside of the track.

At the front of the hull is a dozer blade, which is hydraulically operated by two cylinders. It is controlled by the driver and is used both for dozing operations and to stabilise the vehicle when the winch crane is being used.

The hydraulically operated Griffet crane is mounted at the front right side of the ARV and can lift a load of 12,000 kg through 240°, or 15,000 kg when the crane is towards the front and the dozer blade is in the support position. This crane is normally used for changing major AFV components such as power packs and turrets. A power pack can be carried on the rear of the hull for the rapid replacement of a AMX-30 power pack in the field.

The main hydraulic winch is mounted in the centre of the hull and consists of three sub-assemblies, frame, transfer gearbox and winch drum with integral reduction gear. The winch cable is led out through the front of the hull. The winch is provided with 100 m of 34 mm diameter cable and is also provided with a safety device which consists of two overload sensing

AMX-30D armoured recovery vehicle of the French Army in travelling configuration (Pierre Touzin)
0589498

French Army AMX-30D armoured recovery vehicle in travelling configuration with front mounted dozer blade in raised position
(Pierre Touzin)   1405668

cylinders operated by a pressure switch, which stops the winch automatically when the maximum load of 35,000 kg is reached. The winch has a maximum speed on external layer of 23 m/min and on internal layer of 18.8 m/min.

The auxiliary hydraulic winch is a Retel TRA 251 mounted at the front of the hull. It is provided with 120 m of 11.2 mm diameter cable and has a maximum capacity of 3,500 kg.

The AMX-30D is provided with an NBC system and a crew heater. A snorkel can be installed over the mechanic's hatch enabling the tank to ford to a depth of 4 m.

The AMX-30D is still used by the French Army as only 20 Leclerc ARV have so far been ordered and delivered. Due to being unable to recover the heavier Nexter Systems Leclerc MBT, it is supplemented by the new Nexter Systems DCL.

Variants

The AMX-30D(S) was a special export model for operations in the Middle East with sand shields over the top half of the tracks and a modified gearbox. The Hispano-Suiza HS-110 diesel engine develops 620 hp at 2,400 rpm.

The AMX-30DI was developed by the Pinguely Division of Creusot-Loire. The first prototype was completed in July 1974. This model has a boom, which can lift a maximum load of 15,000 kg and slew it through 240°.

Specifications

AMX-30D armoured recovery vehicle
Crew: 4
Weight: (loaded with diesel power pack) 40,000 kg
Power-to-weight ratio: 17.50 hp/t (13.05 kW/t)
Length: (dozer blade up, jib in travelling position) 7.53 m
Width: 3.15 m
Height: 2.65 m
   (with jib at max extension) 6.15 m
   (roof) 2.05 m
Ground clearance: 0.45 m
Track: 2.53 m
Track width: 570 mm
Length of track on ground: 4.12 m
Ground pressure: 0.8 kg/cm²
Max speed: (road) 60 km/h
Range: 650 km
Fuel capacity: 1,100 litres
Fording: 2 m
   (with preparation which takes 5 min) 4 m
Gradient: 60%
Vertical obstacle: 0.93 m
Trench: 2.9 m
Engine: Hispano-Suiza HS-110, 12-cylinder, water-cooled, multifuel developing 700 hp (522 kW) at 2,400 rpm
Transmission: automatic with 5 forward gears; reverse gear gives same speeds in reverse
Electrical system: 28 V
Batteries: 8 × 12 V, 100 Ah in 2 groups of 4
Armament:
   1 × 7.62 mm MG
   3 × 80 mm smoke grenade dischargers

Status

Production complete. Known users include Cyprus (two), France (134), Greece (14), Qatar (one), Saudi Arabia (57), Spain (10), UAE (four) and Venezuela (four). It should be noted that these figures relate to vehicles delivered and in some cases (e.g. Greece and Spain), they are no longer in front line service.

Contractor

Nexter Systems (Roanne)

Germany

Rheinmetall Landsysteme Büffel armoured recovery vehicle (Bergepanzer 3)

Development

Concept studies for a new armoured recovery vehicle, based on the Leopard 2 Main Battle Tank (MBT) chassis and capable of recovering up to MLC 60 loads, began in 1982, following a series of component studies that commenced in 1977.

In 1984, a finalised definition phase contract was placed. This phase was completed in 1986 with the completion of an experimental prototype. A further contract signed in 1987 called for a further two prototypes and the conversion of the experimental prototype.

By 1988, the three prototypes were undergoing technical, tactical and logistic testing. In mid-1990, after an invitation to tender by the Bundesamt für Wehrtechnik und Beschaffung, MaK System Gesellschaft mbH (today Rheinmetall Landsysteme) was selected as the main contractor for series production of the new Armoured Recovery Vehicle (ARV), named Büffel, for the German Bundeswehr and the Dutch Armed Forces. The Dutch Army contributed to the development costs.

The order was for 100 vehicles. The final allocation was 75 for the Bundeswehr and 25 for the Dutch Armed Forces. Manufacture was shared by Rheinmetall Landsysteme at Kiel (55) and the now Krauss-Maffei Wegmann at Munich.

All future production of the Büffel was subsequently undertaken by Rheinmetall Landsysteme. Current and future production of the Büffel ARV is undertaken at the Unterluss which is the main production unit for tracked vehicles.

In mid-1999, the Swedish Defence Material Administration (FMV) awarded Rheinmetall Landsysteme a contract worth SEK520 million for the supply of 14 Büffel (Buffalo) ARVs for the Swedish Army.

The contract included the maintenance system, training, technical documentation and project administration.

In June 2002 Rheinmetall Landsysteme handed over the first of 14 (10 + 4) Büffel ARV to the Swedish Army who has designated the vehicle the Bgbv 120. The first two vehicles were built in Kiel with the remaining 12 being built at Unterluss.

The Büffel ARV has been designed to recover the Leopard 2 which is used by the Swedish Army in two versions, Strv 121 and Strv 122. In addition, the Büffel ARV can carry out major repairs on this vehicle and other heavy armoured vehicles such as the rapid replacement of the complete powerpack under field conditions.

The Swedish version is an upgraded model of the Büffel that was originally designed by Rheinmetall Landsysteme. The company call this vehicle the Büffel 3.

Main improvements for the Swedish Bgbv 120 include improved ballistic protection which includes an integrated interior spall liner, reduced infra-red signature, command-and-control system incorporating a navigation system, a new weapon station (designated the 2048 HYM) and a Nexter Systems (previously Giat Industries) Galix self-protection launcher system which is already fitted to many other Swedish armoured vehicles.

In addition, the vehicle has a rear-view camera for recovery operations under-armour protection. The crane has an increased working range, an 1.5-tonne auxiliary winch and an increased triple-pull performance of the main winch (35-tonne single-pull).

Spain ordered 16 Büffel ARVs of which four came from the German production line and 12 were manufactured under licence in Spain by General Dynamics Santa Bárbara Sistemas.

The Spanish version features the following modifications, installation of the Lince integrated command-and-control system, spall liner for the crew compartment, stronger auxiliary winch, rear-mounted camera for the driver, nitrogen fire extinguisher installed in the power pack.

Büffel armoured recovery vehicle of the German Army in travelling configuration with dozer/stabiliser blade in raised position
(Christopher F Foss)   1405669

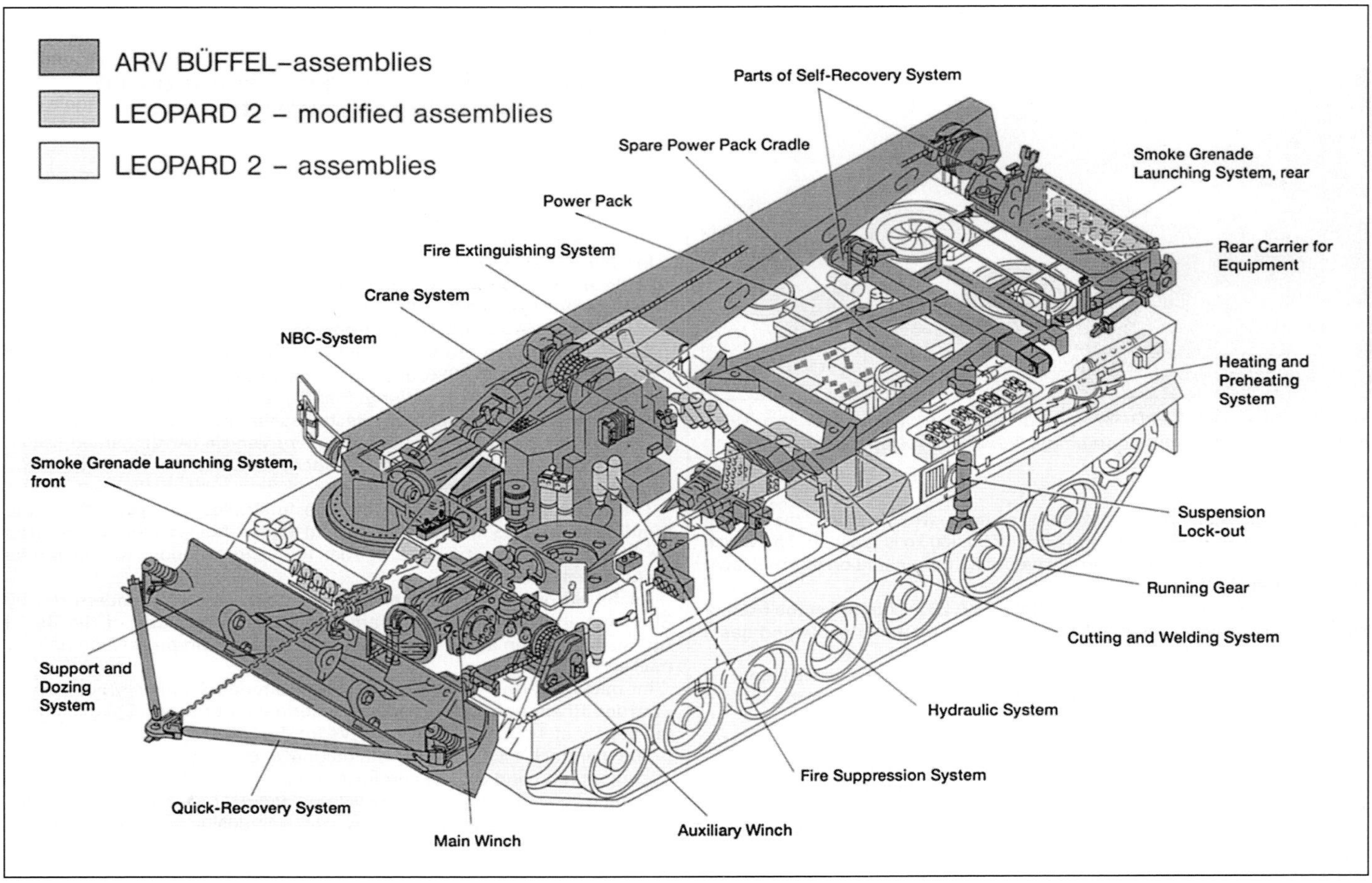

ARV BÜFFEL–assemblies

LEOPARD 2 – modified assemblies

LEOPARD 2 – assemblies

Parts of Self-Recovery System

Spare Power Pack Cradle

Smoke Grenade
Launching System, rear

Power Pack

Fire Extinguishing System

Rear Carrier for
Equipment

Crane System

NBC-System

Heating and
Preheating
System

Smoke Grenade Launching System,
front

Suspension
Lock-out

Running Gear

Cutting and Welding System

Support and
Dozing
System

Hydraulic System

Quick-Recovery System

Fire Suppression System

Main Winch

Auxiliary Winch

Cutaway drawing of Büffel armoured recovery vehicle showing position of main components   0536235

Late in 2001, Switzerland awarded Rheinmetall Landsysteme a EUR71 million contract for the supply of 25 Büffel vehicles, all of which were built in Germany although Swiss Industry did provide some subsystems.

These were delivered from 2004 through to 2005. Under the terms of the direct co-production agreement, the Swiss defence industry were responsible for a 10.5 per cent share of the manufacturing process.

The Swiss vehicle is the BPz Büffel CH and has the following additional features, spall liner for the crew compartment, a dual-circuit electrical system, rear-mounted camera to aid the driver, internally operated MG mount, dozer blade with lateral extension parts and scarifiers and a tactical recovery system mounted on the rear of the vehicle for recovery operations to be carried out under full armour protection.

To support its fleet of new Leopard 2 series MBTs, the Hellenic Army also placed an order for 12 Büffel ARVs and 12 AVLBs based on a Leopard 1 MBT chassis.

The Rheinmetall Landsysteme co-production for Greece included the assembly of the Büffel ARV in Greece by a local company, with the vehicle being designated the ARV Leopard 2 GR, as well as the production and delivery of major components and systems in Greece. These are fitted with the Rheinmetall Defence Electronics Iniochos command-and-control system that is fitted into the Greek Leopard 2 MBTs.

Upgraded Büffel ARV as supplied to Canada for deployment with its Leopard 2A6M CAN MBTs and clearly showing bar armour installation on front and sides of vehicle (Rheinmetall Defence)   1333595

The Rheinmetall Landsysteme offset programme to Greece included production know-how transfer to the Hellenic industry, modernisation of surplus ARV Leopard 1 to the more recent Bergepanzer 2 standard and grant of a number of modernised ARV Leopard 1 to the Hellenic Army.

As of late 2010 the following countries had taken delivery of the Büffel ARV: Canada (from German Army stocks for deployment to Afghanistan), Germany, Greece, Netherlands, Spain, Sweden and Switzerland.

Production has been completed and can be started again when additional orders are placed.

The actual recovery equipment installed in the Büffel ARV is also supplied to two export customers, France and the Republic of Korea, who integrate these into their own specialised ARVs.

France integrated this into the Leclerc ARV, of which 20 have been supplied to France and 46 to the UAE. In the case of South Korea, a total of 200 K1 ARVs have now been ordered.

Description

The Büffel ARV is based on the chassis of the Leopard 2 MBT. Its main purpose is the support of the Leopard 2 MBT family of vehicles and it can be used for recovery, towing, obstacle removal and crane operations of other vehicles in the same load class.

The general layout of the Büffel ARV follows that of the earlier Leopard 1 ARV.

The Büffel ARV features a traversing crane unit with a maximum capacity of 30 tonnes. Jib traverse is 270°. The crane has an electronic load momentum limiter which computes vehicle tilt, crane jib elevation, load mass and so on and prevents the crane from being overloaded. The crane has a maximum tilt angle of 70°.

The main winch is a Rotzler GmbH, Treibmatic TR650/3 dual capstan unit with an effective cable length of 180 m and a tractive capacity at a single pull of 35 tonnes. The winch is installed in the hull front plate with direct connection to the cable roller guide so that there is improved distribution of forces directly into the hull structure. The winch has several advanced features such as a constant maximum pulling force and cable speed over the entire cable length and an absence of cable friction, as the cable runs in grooves on the capstans, so that the windings do not touch each other.

Other features include reduced cable wear, increased cable life and safe pay-out and pull-in of the cable under all load conditions and varying loads. No cable tensioner is required. This winch is stated to cover 90 to 95 per cent of all military recovery operations as defined by the German Army.

The vehicle is provided with an enlarged (3.42 m wide and 880 mm high) dozer/support blade at the front to support and assist during recovery and for obstacle-clearing and dozing operations. Other recovery equipment includes: a Rotzler HZ 010/1-8 auxiliary winch with a capacity of 650 kg and 280 m of 7 mm diameter cable; a running gear blocking system; a self-recovery system; various couplings and towbars (including a rapid-recovery bar to be attached to the dozer/support blade); and rapid connect

Büffel armoured recovery vehicle of the German Army in travelling configuration with dozer/stabiliser blade in raised position
(Christopher F Foss)   1405670

and disconnect couplings for towing. Electrical cutting and welding equipment is carried. A complete Leopard 2 MBT power pack may be carried on a cradle over the engine compartment decking.

Support systems provided include fire extinguishing and suppression systems, a preheating and heating system, an NBC ventilation system and deep fording equipment with bilge pumps.

Armament carried includes a 7.62 mm MG3 machine gun mounted over the commander's cupola and 16 × 76 mm smoke grenade dischargers mounted on the front hull (eight) and rear (eight). The all-welded steel armour is capable of providing protection against 20 mm projectiles.

Variants

Canadian upgraded Büffel ARV
Canada has leased two Büffel ARV from the German Army for deployment to Afghanistan with its recently acquired Leopard 2A6M CAN MBTs.

Prior to deployment these were rapidly upgraded by Rheinmetall at their Kassel facility and fitted with Canadian communications equipment, cooling system for the crew, modified dozer blade and an increased drinking water capacity.

The most significant design change to the Büffel has been an armoured recovery vehicle, specific add-on armour and mine protection package.

This included an underbelly mine protection plate similar to the Leopard 2A6M MBT, additional side armour and bar armour fitted around the vehicle to neutralise weapons fitted with a High Explosive Anti-Tank (HEAT) type warhead.

FFG Wisent 2 Leopard 2 Support Vehicle
As a private venture the German company of FFG have developed to the prototype stage the Wisent 2 Leopard 2 Support Vehicle. This is based on a rebuilt Leopard 2 MBT chassis.

This vehicle is designed as an ARV but can be re-rolled in 24 hours to carry out the role of an armoured engineer vehicle.

Details of the Wisent 2 Leopard 1 Support Vehicle are provided in a separate entry in *Jane's Military Vehicles and Logistics*. As of November 2010 this vehicle was undergoing company trials.

Kodiak Armoured Engineer Vehicle
This has been developed as a private venture by Rheinmetall Defence of Germany and RUAG Land Systems of Switzerland and is covered in a separate entry in *Jane's Military Vehicles and Logistics*.

Specifications

Büffel Armoured Recovery Vehicle
Crew: 3
Combat weight: 54,300 kg
Bridge classification: MLC 60
Power-to-weight ratio: 27.62 hp/t (20.60 kW/t)
Length: 9.07 m
Width overall: 3.54 m
Height:
  (top of MG mount) 2.99 m
  (less MG) 2.735 m
Ground clearance: 0.51 m
Track width: 635 mm
Max speed: (road) 68 km/h
Range:
  (road) 650 km
  (off road) 325 km
Fuel capacity: 1,620 litres
Fording:
  (without preparation) 1.2 m
  (with preparation) 4 m
Gradient: 60%
Side slope: 30%
Vertical obstacle: 0.92 m

Trench: 3 m
Engine: MTU MB 873 Ka-501 4-stroke exhaust-gas turbocharged diesel developing 1,500 hp (1,119 kW) at 2,600 rpm
Transmission: Renk HSWL H354, hydromechanical
Suspension: torsion bar
Electrical system: 24 V
Batteries: 8 × 12 V/100 Ah, total capacity 400 Ah
Generator: 20 kW
Armament:
  1 × 7.62 mm MG3 MG
  16 × 76 mm smoke grenade dischargers
Main winch capacity: 35,000 kg
Cable length: 180 m
Cable diameter: 33 mm
Cable speed: (max) 16 m/min
Crane load:
  (lifting) 30,000 kg
  (pulling) 70,000 kg
Max hook height: 7.9 m
Max reach:
  (front) 4.7 m
  (right) 5.9 m
Crane traverse: 0-270°
Boom control range: 0-70°
Towing capacity: 62,000 kg (MLC 60)
Dozer blade width: 3.42 m
Dozer blade height: 880 mm

Status
Production as required. In service with the following countries:

Country	Quantity	Comment
Canada	2	leased from German Army
Germany	75	delivered
Greece	12	delivered
Netherlands	25	delivered
Spain	16	delivered
Sweden	14	delivered
Switzerland	25	delivered

Contractor
Rheinmetall Landsysteme GmbH

Rheinmetall Landsysteme Leopard 1 armoured recovery vehicle

Development
At an early stage in the development of the Leopard 1 MBT, Germany decided to develop an ARV based on its chassis and automotive components.

Design work was carried out by Porsche with the first prototype completed by a working group, consisting of Luther and Jordan, Jung Jungenthal and MaK of Kiel, in 1964.

The first production ARV (in Germany the Bergepanzer, or BPZ) was completed in September 1966. Production of the ARV and other specialised members of the Leopard 1 family was undertaken by Rheinmetall Landsysteme (at that time MaK) while most production of the Leopard 1 MBT was undertaken by the now Krauss-Maffei Wegmann of Munich.

Taurus ARV of the Canadian Army fitted with appliqué armour, in use in the Balkans (Michael Jerchel)   0589501

Upgraded Leopard ARV of the German Army with dozer blade in raised position (Stefan Marx)   1333597

Upgraded Leopard 1 ARV of the German Army, which is called the Dachs, with stabiliser lowered at the rear (Stefan Marx)   1127954

The Leopard 1 ARV was designed to undertake the following roles:
- recovering vehicles disabled through enemy action or mechanical failure, or that have become bogged down
- towing disabled vehicles
- changing components such as power packs and turrets. (A replacement Leopard 1 power pack is carried on the rear decking and a complete power pack change can be carried out in less than 30 minutes)
- carrying out dozing operations
- refuelling and defuelling other vehicles.

Up to 104 Leopard 1 armoured recovery vehicles were converted to Pionierpanzer 2 Dachs armoured engineer vehicles. Details of this vehicle are provided in a separate entry in *Jane's Military Vehicles and Logistics*.

In the German Army, the Leopard 1 ARV has been supplemented by the Büffel ARV based on the chassis of the Leopard 2 MBT with Rheinmetall Landsysteme being the prime contractor.

According to the United Nations Arms transfer lists for the period 1992 through to 2008 there were only the following identified transfers of Leopard ARV in this period.

In some cases however, it is possible that the ARV quantities were also included in the transfer figures for the Leopard 1 MBT.

From	To	Quantity	Date
Belgium	Brazil	2	2001 (HART)
Germany	Chile	7	2002
Germany	Romania	3	2008

Description

The Leopard 1 ARV is almost identical to the Leopard 1 AEV and the reader is referred to this entry for a detailed description of the vehicle. The main differences between the ARV and the AEV are: the ARV can carry a replacement power pack and no auger; the ARV carries no explosives for demolition work; no heat exchanger is installed; the support/dozer blade is not provided with scarifiers to rip up the surface of roads.

In 1978 the German Army took delivery of 100 product-improved Leopard 1 ARVs from Rheinmetall Landsysteme. The main improvement was the installation of a hydraulically operated rear support on the right side of the hull at the rear. This relieves the suspension on the crane side and enables the crane to lift a maximum load of 16,000 kg and traverse it through 270°.

In addition, the main winch has a higher cable pay-out speed (74 m/min) than the original vehicle's (22 m/min), which corresponds to that of the creeping speed of a Leopard 1 MBT.

The lifting capability of the product-improved Leopard 1 ARV compared with the original ARV is shown in the Specifications.

Variants

HART ARV

The Heavy Armoured Recovery Tank (HART) was developed as a private venture for the export market by the Belgian company of SABIEX. As of late 2010 the only export customer was Brazil, which took delivery of two vehicles based on surplus Leopard 1 MBT chassis. Full details of HART are given in a separate entry under Belgium.

ARV 2000

This is a private venture development by FFG for export and details are given in the 'FFG Armoured Recovery Vehicle 2000' in a separate entry in *Jane's Military Vehicles and Logistics*. A total of 20 of these vehicles have already been supplied to the Belgian Army.

Leopard 1 ARV with extra armour

IBD of Germany has developed an appliqué armour package for the Leopard 1 ARV. This has been sold to Canada and Norway with each country taking one upgrade package.

Specifications

Leopard 1 ARV
(Data in square brackets relates to product-improved version where different from basic vehicle)
Crew: 4
Weight:
   (with replacement power pack)
   (empty) 39,200 [39,980] kg
   (loaded) 39,800 [40,580] kg
Power-to-weight ratio: 20.85 [20.45] hp/t (15.55 [15.25] kW/t)
Length: (support/dozer blade raised) 7.57 [7.68] m
Width: 3.25 m
Height: (incl MG) 2.7 m
Ground clearance: 0.44 m
Track: 2.7 m
Track width: 550 mm
Length of track on ground: 4.236 m
Ground pressure: 0.83 [0.85] kg/cm²
Max speed: (road) 62 km/h
Range:
   (road) 850 km
   (cross-country) 500 km
Fuel capacity: 1,410 litres
Fording: 2.5 m
   (with snorkel) 4 m
Gradient: 60%
Side slope: 30%
Vertical obstacle: 1.15 [0.88] m
Trench: 2.5 m
Engine: MTU MB 838 Ca M-500 10-cylinder multifuel developing 830 hp (619 kW) at 2,200 rpm
Transmission: ZF 4 HP 250 with 4 forward and 2 reverse speeds
Electrical system: 24 V
Batteries: 6 with total capacity of 300 Ah, charged by 3-phase generator driven from main engine
Armament:
   1 × 7.62 mm MG3 MG in bow
   1 × 7.62 mm MG3 MG on commander's hatch
   6 × 76 mm smoke grenade dischargers
Ammunition: 7.62 mm - 4,250 rounds

Status

Production complete, although conversions from Leopard 1 MBTs are available - see separate entry. In service with Belgium (36), Brazil (two × HART), Canada (eight - called Taurus), Chile (seven), Germany (444 plus 100 product-improved versions; 104 converted to Pionierpanzer 2), Greece (four brand new, plus fouradditional vehicles from German Army stocks), Italy (137), Netherlands (52), Norway (six), Poland (10 from German Army stocks), Romania (three in 2008) and Turkey (12). Note that in some cases these figures have been reduced as surplus vehicles have been exported.

As part of the contract covering the supply of Leopard 2 series MBTs to the Hellenic Army, Rheinmetall Landsysteme has now supplied 12 Büffel ARV as well as a batch of surplus Leopard 1 ARV upgraded to the enhanced standard.

Contractor

Rheinmetall Landsysteme GmbH

FFG Armoured Recovery Vehicle 2000

Development

The Flensburger Fahrzeugbau Gesellschaft mbH (FFG) company have considerable experience in the upgrade and overhaul of armoured fighting vehicles of all types.

The company has also developed and placed in production an upgrade package for the now BAE Systems, US Combat Systems (previously United Defense) M113 series of armoured personnel carriers and this is now in service with Denmark and Germany with production being

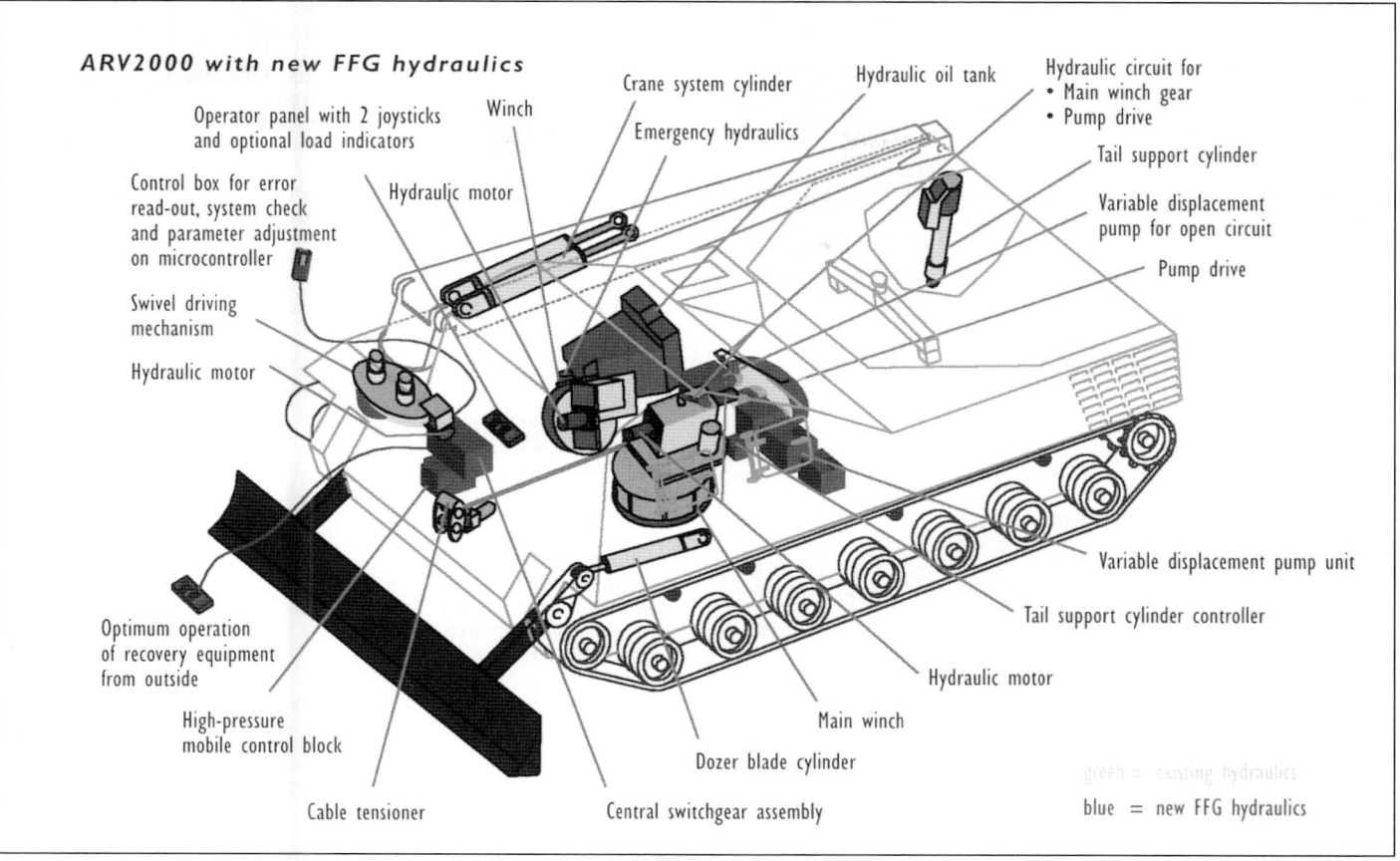

Key elements of the new hydraulic concept installed in the FFG ARV2000 and AEV2000 upgrades based on the Leopard 1 Armoured Recovery Vehicle (FFG)
1405671

undertaken on an as required basis. Elements of this upgrade are also used in the Australian Army M113 series upgrade for which the prime contractor is the now BAE Systems Australia. This is now in service with the Australian Army.

As a private venture, FFG has developed and placed in production an upgraded version of the Rheinmetall Landsysteme Leopard 1 ARV, called Armoured Recovery Vehicle 2000 (ARV 2000).

Following a competition in 2002, the Belgian Ministry of Defence awarded FFG a contract to upgrade 20 of its existing Leopard 1 ARV to the enhanced ARV2000 standard.

The second customer was Chile, which took delivery of seven Leopard 1 ARVs from German Army stocks. These were upgraded by FFG before delivery.

In addition, the Belgian Army has upgraded six Leopard 1 AEV to the ARV2000 standard and these are called the Leopard AEV2000 by FFG.

Description
The overall layout of the ARV 2000 is identical to the original Rheinmetall Landsysteme Leopard 1 ARV, which was originally developed in the 1960s, with first production vehicles being completed in 1966.

In the upgraded ARV 2000, older subsystems have been removed and replaced wherever possible by commercial off-the-shelf systems with the end result being a more reliable and capable vehicle.

These include micro controller control, new hydraulic components, a new high grade steel hydraulic oil tank, three dimension control by a joystick, the auxiliary hydraulics can now be operated without the main MTU engine running, key elements can now be run from outside of the vehicle, and emergency hydraulics have been fitted.

The new, high grade steel hydraulics oil tank features an integrated oil filter, installed auxiliary hydraulic pump and oil level and atmosphere monitoring.

The new hydraulic components include variable displacement pumps, A11VLO fitted with charge pump, pressure cut-off, load-sensing control valve, A4VG variable displacement pump, over centre, with all components needed for closed circuit operation, integrated auxiliary pump for boost and pilot oil supply, fixed displacement motors and axial tapered piston bent axis design.

In addition, an auxiliary 1.5-tonne hoist has been installed and a self-diagnostic and system check fitted.

The auxiliary hydraulics operate the front mounted dozer/stabiliser blade, rear support cylinder on the right side, crane arm, auxiliary hoist and main winch.

Security aspects have also been improved with emergency stop actuated separately from the engine and pumps, logical protective functions by intelligent software and start up of the hydraulics only at a number of revolutions lower than 1,000 rpm.

Variants

FFG Wisent 2 Leopard 2 Support Vehicle
As a private venture the German company of FFG have developed to the prototype stage the Wisent 2 Leopard 2 Support Vehicle. This is based on a rebuilt Leopard 2 MBT chassis optimised for its new role.

This vehicle is designed as an ARV but can be re-rolled in 24 hours to carry out the role of an armoured engineer vehicle.

Details of the Wisent 2 Leopard 2 Support Vehicle are provided in a separate entry in Jane's Military Vehicles and Logistics. As of November 2010 this vehicle was undergoing company trials.

Status
Production as required. In service with a number of countries including Belgium (20) and Chile (seven). The Belgian Army has taken delivery of six AEV2000 vehicles upgraded by FFG.

Contractor
FFG Flensburger Fahrzeugbau Gesellschaft GmbH

FFG Armoured Vehicle 2000 based on Leopard I chassis showing storage box on rear of chassis (FFG)
1333598

Krauss-Maffei Wegmann Dingo 2 Recovery Vehicle

Development
To meet the future potential requirements of the Germany Army and export customers, in mid-2010 Krauss-Maffei Wegmann completed company trials of the Dingo 2 (6 × 6) Armoured Recovery Vehicle (ARV) and this was shown for the first time in mid-June 2010.

The Dingo 2 (4 × 4) All Protected Vehicle (APV) is currently in full scale production at the Krauss-Maffei Wegmann facility in Munich, Germany and by late 2010 over 800 had been ordered.

Dingo 2 (6 × 6) recovery vehicle in the travelling configuration and showing the fully enclosed and fully protected two door cab (KMW)   1364323

Dingo 2 APV (4 × 4) in mobile workshop configuration for the German Army fitted with the FLW 100 RCWS (Krauss-Maffei Wegmann)   1401009

In addition to being deployed by the German Army, export sales of the Dingo 2 (4 × 4) APV vehicle have also been made to Austria, Belgium, Czech Republic, Germany, Luxembourg and Norway for a wide range of missions.

According to Krauss-Maffei Wegmann, the German Army has a potential requirement for between 10 and 20 Dingo ARV to support currently deployed vehicles in Afghanistan.

As of November 2010 no production contracts had been announced for the Dingo 2 (6 × 6) ARV.

Description
The Dingo 2 (6 × 6) ARV is based on an extended UNIMOG U-5000 (4 × 4) chassis and has the same three door fully enclosed cab as the Dingo 2 battle damage repair vehicle which provides a high level of protection against small arms fire, shell splinters and Improvised Explosive Devices (IED).

If required, on the cab roof can be mounted a FLW 100 Remote Controlled Weapon Station which is already in service with the German Army.

The crew can rapidly enter and leave the Dingo 2 ARV via a door in either side of the hull which has a bullet proof window in the upper part.

There is a large bullet proof window to the front and in the cab rear is a bullet/splinter proof window to give the crew observation through the rear arc.

An NBC system, air conditioning system, independent vehicle heating system, anti-skid braking system and central tyre inflation system are fitted as standard and gross vehicle weight is currently being quoted as 17.5 tonnes.

To carry out its specialised role the Dingo ARV is fitted with a 10-tonne hydraulic winch and a crane with a maximum lifting capacity of five tonnes.

This enables it to recover a damaged or disabled Dingo 2 APV as a suspended load as well as other wheeled vehicles with a combat weight of up to 14 tonnes.

Three cameras are provided, one on the crane, one on the back of the vehicle and one on the cab rear with images being displayed in the cab.

Stowage space is also provided for specialised tools and equipment and this includes a covered load area to the rear of the cab.

Variants
Dingo 2 Battle Damage Repair Vehicle
In March 2010 Germany awarded Krauss-Maffei Wegmann a contract for a batch of 44 Dingo APV optimised for the battle damage repair role and all of these were delivered by the end of 2010.

The Dingo 2 optimised for the battle damage repair role is the first production Dingo 2 to be fitted with the three person fully enclosed and protected cab.

This provides the same level of ballistic protection as the current four door eight person cab of the standard production Dingo 2 APV.

For self-defence purposes on the roof of the cab is fitted the Krauss-Maffei Wegmann FL 100 RCWS which can be armed with a 7.62 mm or .50 machine gun.

To the rear of the cab is fitted a flat bed on which is mounted the pod which has been fitted out as a mobile workshop complete with integrated storage system for tools and spare parts.

This version is supplied with its own generator to provide power for the on board equipment. When travelling the upper part of the pod is retracted to reduce the overall height of the vehicle.

Specifications
Crew: 3
Weight:
(combat) 17,500 kg
(towing) 18,000 kg
Length: 7.52 m
Width: 2.39 m
Height:
(cab roof) 2.87 m
(with RCWS FL 100) 3.56 m
Ground clearance: 0.48 m
Wheelbase: 3.85 + 1.40 m
Max road speed: 80 km/h
Range: 1,000 km
Fording: 1.2 m
Engine: Mercedes-Benz diesel developing 219 hp
Transmission: automatic

Status
Development complete. Ready for production.

Contractor
Krauss-Maffei Wegmann GmbH & Co KG

India

Vijayanta armoured recovery vehicle

Development
Little information is available regarding the Vijayanta armoured recovery vehicle other than it is based on the hull, power pack and running gear of the Vijayanta MBT which is based on the Vickers Mk 1 MBT chassis (Vickers is today part of BAE Systems Global Combat Systems).

Description
An armoured superstructure replaces the usual armoured gun turret of the Vijayanta and an A-frame lifting jib is located over the front hull. It is assumed that a recovery winch is located inside the hull. Spades are provided at the rear of the chassis and these are lowered to the ground prior to the start of recovery operations.

India has acquired significant quantities of ZTS VT-72B armoured recovery vehicles from Slovakia as the Vijayanta armoured recovery vehicle is unable to recover the latest Indian Arjun MBT. Some of these are being assembled locally in India. These are being used to support the locally produced T-72M1 and T-90 MBTs.

While India has purchased MBTs from Russia it has yet to purchase any of the more specialised vehicles and these have been produced from other sources.

Vijayanta armoured recovery vehicle   0511467

Status
Production complete. In service with the Indian Army. The Vijayanta MBT is now rapidly being phased out of service with the Indian Army. The Indian Army also has large quantities of the Polish WZT-3 and Slovakian VT-72B ARV which are based on T-72 MBT automotive components.

Contractor
Government of India

Israel

Merkava Armoured Recovery Vehicle

Development
To support its fleet of locally developed Merkava series of Main Battle Tank (MBT), an Armoured Recovery Vehicle (ARV) has been developed to the prototype stage.

Description
This essentially consists of a Merkava MBT chassis with the three-person turret removed and replaced by a turntable mounted crane fitted with a telescopic jib. When travelling this crane is traversed slightly to the right and locked in position.

The crane is believed to have a lifting arm with a capacity of 490 kN.m (50 tonnes force metres) and a pulling capacity of 343 kN (35 tonnes force). As far as it is known, the Merkava ARV is not provided with a winch, so cannot recover heavy armoured fighting vehicles.

In addition to hatches in the roof of the Merkava ARV, the crew can also enter the vehicle through a large door in the hull rear. A typical crew consists of commander, driver and up to eight mechanics.

The Merkava ARV can also carry a complete Merkava MBT replacement power pack (engine, transmission and cooling system) using a special cradle that is fitted on the roof of the vehicle.

In addition to an NBC system, the Merkava ARV is also provided with an Auxiliary Power Unit (APU) to provide power to various items of onboard equipment with the main diesel engine shut down.

Dedicated equipment carried on board includes an air pressure system to supply power to specialised tools and equipment.

It is understood that this Merkava ARV is based on the chassis of the Merkava Mk 3 MBT and is being used to support the latest production Merkava Mk 4 MBT that is now in service with the Israel Defence Force.

Components of the Merkava Mk 4 MBT are also used in the more recent Namer heavy infantry fighting vehicle which is now in low-rate production for the Israel Defense Force. The main production run will be undertaken in the US by General Dynamics Land Systems.

Status
Prototype vehicle undergoing trials. Not yet in production or service. The Merkava MBT has not been exported by Israel. Current production model is the Merkava Mk 4 MBT.

Contractor
Israel Ordnance Corps, facility at Tel a Shomer, near Tel Aviv, Israel
Enquiries to SIBAT - Foreign Defence Assistance and Defence Export

Japan

Mitsubishi Type 90 armoured recovery vehicle

Development
To support the Type 90 Main Battle Tank (MBT), Mitsubishi Heavy Industries developed and subsequently placed in production the Type 90 Armoured Recovery Vehicle (ARV).

As with all Japanese armoured fighting vehicles, production of the Type 90 ARV has been undertaken at a very low rate and it has never been offered on the export market.

The Type 90 ARV can also recover the latest Japanese Mitsubishi Type TK-X (or Type 10) MBT, which was shown for the first time in 2009.

Description
In overall layout the Japanese Type 90 ARV is very similar to the German Rheinmetall Landsysteme Büffel ARV with the crew compartment front left.

This is of all welded steel armour construction that provides the occupants with protection from small arms fire and shell splinters.

On the right side of the front of the upper hull is the pivot for a hydraulically operated crane, with a maximum capacity of 25 tonnes and a remote control facility.

For travelling, the crane is stowed facing the rear along the right-hand side of the hull top. Located beside the crane pivot is the superstructure with accommodation for the driver, commander and two other crew members. The crew commander's cupola is provided with a mounting for

Prototype of Type 90 armoured recovery vehicle　　0511469

a .50 (12.7 mm) M2 HB machine gun; the superstructure also carries electrically operated smoke grenade dischargers. These provide coverage over the frontal arc of the Type 90 ARV.

Mounted on the front of the vehicle is a hydraulically operated dozer blade that can also be used as a stabiliser during recovery operations. As far as it is known this dozer blade is of the straight type and cannot be used as an angle blade.

The vehicle is provided with a recovery winch capable of recovering the Mitsubishi Type 90 MBT which has a combat weight of 50 tonnes. After recovery, the Type 90 armoured recovery vehicle can tow a Type 90 MBT.

The Type 90 armoured recovery vehicle weighs 50 tonnes and has a maximum road speed of 70 km/h. It can pivot turn.

Variants
Armoured Engineer Vehicle
The Japanese Ground Self Defence Force has fielded a new Armoured Engineer Vehicle (AEV) which is believed to be based on a Type 90 chassis.

Status
Low-rate production for the Japanese Ground Self Defence Force. This vehicle has not been offered on the export market. Production is very low with normal procurement being one unit per year. In FY2003 and FY2004, the procurement rate remained the same at one Type 90 ARV per year.

Contractor
Mitsubishi Heavy Industries

Mitsubishi Type 78 armoured recovery vehicle

Development
The prototype of an Armoured Recovery Vehicle (ARV) based on the chassis of the Mitsubishi Type 74 Main Battle Tank (MBT) was completed in 1974 and subsequently standardised as the Type 78 ARV in 1978. The layout of the Type 78 ARV is very similar to that of the German Leopard 1 and French AMX-30D ARVs.

Production of the Type 78 ARV has been completed and it was replaced in production by the more capable Type 90 ARV.

Like all Japanese armoured fighting vehicles, the Mitsubishi Type 78 ARV was never exported or offered on the export market.

The Type 90 and Type 78 ARV can also recover the recently developed Mitsubishi Type TK-X (or Type 10) MBT.

Description
In overall layout the Japanese Type 78 ARV is very similar to the German Rheinmetall Landsysteme Büffel ARV with the crew compartment front left which extends about half way down the chassis to the engine compartment at the rear.

This is of all welded steel armour construction that provides the occupants with protection from small arms fire and shell splinters.

To carry out its battlefield mission, mounted on the right side of the hull at the front, is a hydraulically operated crane which is 3.5 m long and has a telescopic jib that can be extended a further 1.5 m. The jib can be traversed through 270° and lift a maximum load of 20,000 kg.

Mounted at the front of the hull is a hydraulically operated dozer blade which can be used both for dozing operations and as a stabiliser when the winch is being used. The Type 78 retains the hydropneumatic suspension of the Type 74 MBT.

The hydraulic winch has a maximum capacity of 38,000 kg, is provided with 60 m of 32 mm diameter cable and has two speeds: 6 and 15 m/min. A hydraulic motor is used to extract the cable from the winch at a maximum speed of 30 m/min and there is also a system to apply tension to the cable for rewinding smoothly into the winch when there is no load.

Armament of the Type 78 ARV consists of a pintle-mounted .50 (12.7 mm) M2 HB Browning machine gun and a bank of six electrically operated smoke grenade dischargers.

Type 78 ARV in travelling configuration (Kensuke Ebata)   0512302

Specifications

Type 78 Armoured Recovery Vehicle
Crew: 4
Weight: 38,900 kg
Power-to-weight ratio: 18.51 hp/t (13.80 kW/t)
Length: 7.95 m
Width: (overall) 3.38 m
Height: (to top of hull) 2.4 m
Ground clearance: 0.4 m
Max speed: 53 km/h
Gradient: 60%
Engine: Mitsubishi 10 ZF 2-cycle 10-cylinder air-cooled diesel, developing 720 hp (537 kW) at 2,200 rpm
Transmission: Mitsubishi power-shift with 6 forward and 1 reverse gears
Suspension: hydropneumatic with suspension lock at kneeled position
Crane capacity: 20,000 kg
Main winch capacity: 38,000 kg
Armament:
  1 × .50 (12.7 mm) M2 HB MG
  6 × smoke grenade dischargers

Status

Production complete. In service with the Japanese Ground Self Defence Force. The Type 78 ARV is now being supplemented by the more recent Type 90 ARV based on the Type 90 MBT chassis.

Contractor

Mitsubishi Heavy Industries

Jordan

King Abdullah II Design and Development Bureau Al Monjed Armoured Recovery Vehicle

Development

Based on its experience in the design, development and production of the M47 Armoured Recovery and Repair Vehicle for the Jordanian Armed Forces, the King Abdullah II Design and Development Bureau (KADDB) has developed the Al Monjed Armoured Recovery Vehicle (ARV).

This is based on the more recent US-supplied General Dynamics Land Systems M60A1 Main Battle Tank (MBT) which is currently in service with the Jordanian Armed Forces (JAF). As of late 2010 it is understood that production of the Al Monjed ARV had yet to commence.

Description

The Al Monjed ARV uses the complete lower hull, suspension and power pack of the General Dynamics Land Systems M60A1 MBT but has a brand new all-welded armoured superstructure that provides the occupants with protection from small arms fire and shell splinters.

Mounted at the front of the chassis is a hydraulically operated blade that can be used to stabilise the Al Monjed ARV when the crane or winch is being used.

This blade has been designed to withstand a main winch pull of the casualty of up to 80 tonnes and can also be used as a dozer blade.

Pivoted at the front right side of the chassis is the turntable mounted hydraulically operated crane that is fitted with a telescopic jib. When not required this is traversed to the rear and lays alongside of the chassis.

This crane can lift a maximum load of 6.5 tonnes at a reach of 4.9 m and can be traversed through 360°.

Al Monjed ARV carrying an MBT replacement power pack shown lifting the front end of an M113 series APC
(King Abdullah II Design and Development Bureau)   1333601

The hydraulically operated winch is located in the lower forward part of the chassis and leads out through the front of the vehicle. This has a maximum single line pull of 41 tonnes at a speed of 13 m/minute.

Maximum pay in and pay out speed is 40 m/minute and it is provided with 70 m of usable cable. Rope exit angles at maximum load are minus 35 to plus 10° vertically and 80° left and right.

The crew compartment is at the front of the vehicle on the left side with the driver at the front and commander and other crew members to the rear. As well as the crew of three, space is provided for an additional passenger.

The driver is provided with a single-piece hatch cover and periscopes for observation to the front and sides of the vehicle. The commander is seated to the rear of the driver and is provided with a single-piece hatch cover that opens to the left side and a pintle-mounted .50 (12.7 mm) M2 HB machine gun.

Hydraulics used in the crane, dozer blade and winch are powered by the power take-off from the main L3 Combat Propulsion Systems AVDS-1790-2DR series diesel engine or by the Auxiliary Power Unit (APU) as an auxiliary system.

This means that the vehicle can run its key subsystems with the main engine switched off.

In addition to the hydraulically operated crane, winch and dozer blade, it is also provided with cutting equipment and tools. A complete MBT power pack consisting of engine, transmission and cooling system can be carried over the rear engine deck of the Al Monjed.

According to KADDB, the Al Monjed ARV will tow vehicles up to 60 tonnes at speeds of up to 30 km/h.

Variants

There are no known variants of the Al Monjed ARV.

Specifications

Al Monjed ARV
Crew: 3 + 1
Weight:
  (combat) 49,000 kg
  (combat) 55,000 kg (with replacement powerpack)
Power-to-weight ratio: 15.3 hp/t (11.4 kW/t)
Ground pressure: 0.9 kg/cm^2
Length: 7.46 m
Width: 3.7 m
Height: 3.42 m
Max speed: 45 km/h
Fording: 1.25 m
Gradient: 60%
Side slope: 40%
Vertical obstacle: 0.914 m
Trench: 2.6 m
Engine: L3 Combat Propulsion Systems AVDS-1790-2DR 12-cylinder diesel developing 750 hp (599 kW) with growth potential to 900 hp (671 kW)
Transmission: General Motors Corporation, cross-drive, single stage with 2 forward and 1 reverse ranges
Suspension: hydropneumatic suspension on rear units with locking actuators during crane operation. Torsion bars on remaining units
Electrical system: 24 V
Armament: 1 × .50 (12.7 mm) M2 HB machine gun

Status

Development complete. Ready for production.

Contractor

King Abdullah II Design and Development Bureau

King Abdullah II Design and Development Bureau M47 Armoured Recovery and Repair Vehicle (ARRV)

Development

The King Hussein Military Workshop at Zarqa, near Amman, has developed an Armoured Recovery and Repair Vehicle (ARRV) based on the chassis of a former Iranian M47 Main Battle Tank (MBT) supplied via Iraq.

The vehicle was developed as a technical exercise to determine if a vehicle could be produced. It combined the attributes of the M88, Chieftain and Centurion Armoured Recovery Vehicles (ARVs), none of which has an inherent full repair and all-round recovery capability, capable of coping with the Jordanian Army's Khalid MBTs (an upgraded Chieftain MBT) under all conditions.

It will also recover the Al Hussein MBT, which is the local name for the ex-British Army, Challenger 1 series MBT. A total of 402 of these have now been delivered to Jordan, including non-runners. It is understood that only part of this quantity has been returned to service.

The M47 ARRV can remove a complete MBT power pack, carry a complete power pack above the rear engine deck in a universal cradle, recover disabled or damaged vehicles plus self-recovery and is capable of dozing and earth moving.

This is also referred to as the AB1 Armoured Recovery And Repair Vehicle (ARRV). In April 2001 the General Headquarters of the Jordanian Armed forces placed a contract with the King Abdullah Design and Development Bureau for the supply of 20 AB1 systems with first deliveries being made in 2002. Deliveries have now been completed.

More recently the Al Monjed ARRV has been designed and built based on the more recent M60 MBT chassis and details of this are given in a separate entry. As of late 2010 this is understood to remain at the prototype stage.

Description

Conversion of the M47 MBT to the ARRV involves removing the turret and plating over the turret well. A hydraulically-operated dozer blade is attached to the front of the vehicle to act as an earth dozer or as a stabiliser/anchor blade during recovery operations. The blade is 3.4 m wide and 0.75 m high.

An ATLAS crane taken from a BAE Systems Global Combat Systems Chieftain ARV is mounted on the front right side of the hull. The crane has a telescopic boom jib and can lift a maximum load of 6.5 tonnes at 3.2 m reach; maximum lift height is 4.4 m and full traverse 280°. When travelling, the crane is traversed to the rear and located along the right side of the hull. The crane is provided with a safety seat for the operator.

Mounted in the forward part of the hull is a hydraulically-operated winch provided with 157 m of usable cable. This winch was taken from a US BAE Systems, US Combat Systems (previously United Defense) M88A1 ARV and can be operated by the commander or the driver, having a single line pull up to 28 tonnes, increasing to 56 tonnes when a pulley block is introduced. Once recovered, tracked loads up to 60 tonnes can be towed.

The basic crew is two, although an extra member can be carried to assist in tasks such as paying out the recovery cable. The driver is seated at the left front of the vehicle with the commander behind and provided with a cupola assembly taken from a BAE Systems, US Combat Systems M113 APC, complete with the capacity to mount a .50 (12.7 mm) M2 HB machine gun.

The original power pack has been replaced by an L3 Combat Propulsion Systems AVDS-1790-2DR diesel taken from a M88A1 ARV. This is coupled to an Allison CD-850-6A fully automatic transmission. The existing suspension and tracks have been retained while the side skirts from a Centurion-series MBT (which is locally called the Tariq) have been added. With the introduction of the ex-British Army Challenger 1 MBTs into the Jordanian Army under the local name of Al Hussein, the older Tariq tanks are now being phased out of service. Some of these may be converted to other roles. These include the AB14 Temsah heavy infantry fighting vehicle and the Multipurpose Armoured Platform. As of late 2010 neither of these had entered quantity production.

Specifications

M47 Armoured Recovery and Repair Vehicle
Crew: 2 + 1
Weight:
  (combat) 42,000 kg
  (combat, with replacement power pack) 48,000 kg
Power-to-weight ratio: 18.7 hp/t (13.32 kW/t)
Ground pressure: 0.75 kg/cm²
Length: 7.1 m
Width: 3.5 m
Height: (overall) 2.8 m
Max speed: (roads) 56 km/h
Range: (roads) 590 km
Fuel capacity: 1,460 litres
Gradient: 40%
Trench: 2.4 m
Engine: L3 Combat Propulsion Systems AVDS-1790-2DR diesel developing 750 hp (599 kW) at 2,400 rpm
Transmission: Allison CD-850-6A fully automatic with 2 forward and 1 reverse gears
Suspension: torsion bar

M47 armoured recovery and repair vehicle (or AB1) in travelling configuration   0121243

Electrical system: 24 V
Batteries: 6 × 12 V, 100 Ah
Generator: 8.5 kW
Armament: 1 × .50 (12.7 mm) M2 HB MG

Main winch
Rated line pull: 275 kN (28 tonnes force)
Usable rope length: 157 m

Jib crane
Lift capacity: 204 kN.m (6,500 kg at 3.2 m)
Traverse: 280°

Dozer blade
Width: 3.4 m
Depth: 0.75 m

Status

Production as required. A total of 20 vehicles delivered to Jordanian Army.

Contractor

King Abdullah II Design and Development Bureau (KADDB)

Korea, South

ROTEM K-1 armoured recovery vehicle

Development

The ROTEM K-1 Armoured Recovery Vehicle (ARV) is based on the chassis of the K-1 MBT and was developed in co-operation with the now Rheinmetall Landsysteme of Germany. It uses an armoured superstructure and recovery system similar to the German Büffel armoured recovery vehicle.

These recovery subsystems include the crane, winch system, dozer system, hydraulics and electrics. These are also used in the Nexter

K1 armoured recovery vehicle (left) with dozer blade lowered lifting complete turret of K1 MBT (ROTEM)   1333599

Systems Leclerc ARV currently in service with France and the United Arab Emirates. The ROK has been manufacturing an increasing number of these subsystems.

The first two prototypes of the K1 ARV were completed in the late 1980s and by early 2004 a total of three batches of vehicles had been delivered to the ROK Army.

The first batch consisted of 96 vehicles and were delivered from 1993 with the second batch consisting of 59 vehicles which were delivered from 1997. Third batch consisted of 18 vehicles which were delivered in 2004.

The fourth order has now been placed for a total of 20 vehicles and these are being delivered from 2005 onwards and will bring the K1 ARV fleet up to a total of 200 units.

The K-1/M-1A1 MBT and its two specialised variants, the ARV and the AVLB, have been offered on the export market but as of late 2010 no sales have been made.

Production of the K1 and K1A1 MBTs is now understood to have been completed.

Production is now underway of the new generation K2 MBT which features a crew of three, a 120 mm L/55 smoothbore gun fed by a bustle mounted automatic loader and has a combat weight of 55 tonnes. This can be recovered by the current in service K1 ARV.

Description

The K-1 ARV is based on the chassis and running gear of the K-1 MBT.

There is a crew of four consisting of a commander, driver, operator and a mechanic. An integral crew heating system is provided but NBC protection is restricted to individual systems.

The main winch is of the capstan type and is provided with 150 m of usable cable. The winch capacity is 35 tonnes, or 70 tonnes with a guide pulley. There is also an auxiliary winch with 260 m of usable cable.

The hydraulic lifting crane mounted on a turntable to the right of the main superstructure has a maximum lifting capacity of 25 tonnes and can be elevated to an angle of 70°; the crane traverse is 270°.

If the permitted load is exceeded, an automatic cut-out system is activated. The crane can be operated by a remote-control joystick. A straight dozer blade is mounted at the front and can be used for obstacle clearing or for support when operating the main winch. The blade's soil moving capacity is 170 m³/h.

Standard equipment includes fire detection and suppression system, welding and cutting equipment, gas-turbine auxiliary power unit and an integrated test system. Other equipment includes refuel/defuel systems and an automatic chainsaw.

A pintle for a .50 (12.7 mm) M2 HB Browning machine gun is mounted over the commander's cupola on the superstructure roof and smoke grenade dischargers are mounted on the hull front.

The .50 (12.7 mm) M2 HB MG is called the K6 in the Republic of Korea Army.

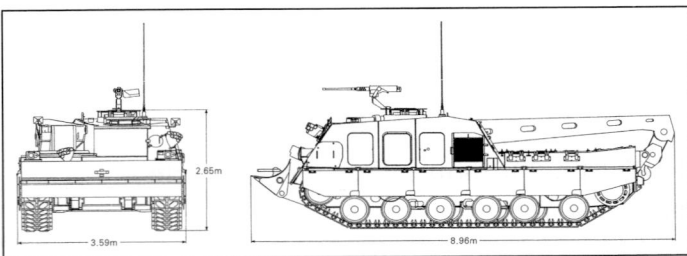

Front and side drawings of K1 armoured recovery vehicle (ROTEM) 1333600

K-1 armoured recovery vehicle with blade lowered and crane traversed to the front   0512441

Variants

Armoured engineer vehicle

Under development is a new combat mobility vehicle which has a hull similar to that used for the K1 ARV. Mounted at the front right side will be a hydraulic arm of which can be fitted a variety of attachments including a bucket.

The front of the vehicle can be fitted with dozer- or roller-type mine clearing equipment as well as a magnetic signature duplicator. Towards the rear of the hull, on either side, would be pennants that would be fired into the ground to show the clear path through the minefield to following units.

Specifications

K-1 Armoured Recovery Vehicle
Crew: 4
Weight:
  (combat) 51,100 kg
  (with replacement power pack) 56,000 kg
Power-to-weight ratio: 23.48 hp/t (17.55 kW/t)
Ground pressure: 0.87 kg/cm²
Length: 8.96 m
Width: 3.59 m
Height: 2.65 m
Ground clearance: 0.46 m
Max speed:
  (road) 65 km/h
  (cross-country) 40 km/h
Range: 600 km
Fording:
  (normal) 1.2 m
  (with kit) 2.2 m
Gradient: 60%
Side slope: 30%
Vertical obstacle: 1.0 m
Trench: 2.74 m
Engine: MTU MB 871 Ka-501 8 cylinder diesel developing 1,200 hp (895 kW) at 2,600 rpm
Transmission: ZF LSG 3000 automatic with 4 forward and 2 reverse gears
Suspension: hydropneumatic and torsion bar
Electrical system: 24 V
Batteries: 6 × 12 V, 100 Ah
Armament:
  1 × .50 (12.7 mm) M2 HB MG
  2 × 6 smoke grenade launchers

Status

Production. A total of 200 are being provided to the ROK Army. There have been no exports as of late 2010.

Contractor

ROTEM Ltd

Doosan K288A1 armoured recovery vehicle

Development

The Doosan Infracore Defense Products BG (previously Daewoo Heavy Industries) K288A1 Armoured Recovery Vehicle (ARV) is based on the chassis of the K200A1 APC and forms part of what has been known as the Korean Infantry Fighting Vehicle (KIFV) family of armoured vehicles. This family of vehicles was developed to meet the operational requirements of the Republic of Korea Army.

As of late 2010, the only export customer for the KIFV was Malaysia, which took delivery of over 100 units between 1993 and 1995. This included a small quantity of K288 series ARV.

The KIFV has been replaced in production by the Doosan K-21 NIFV, though no specialised ARV version has yet been announced.

Description

The hull of the Doosan K288A1 ARV is of all-welded aluminium armour with an additional layer of passive armour for a higher level of protection.

The K288A1 ARV is equipped with a hydraulically driven winch for the recovery of damaged and disabled vehicles. Mounted either side of the hull are spades which are lowered to the ground manually during recovery operations. An auxiliary spade unit, carried on the roof when not required, can be used between the two spades when operating in soft soil.

The hydraulic winch is located in the rear crew compartment and has a direct maximum capacity of 10,000 kg, although this can be increased to 20,000 kg by introducing a snatch block. Mounted on the left side of the hull roof is a 6,000 kg capacity crane with a full 360° traverse.

The crew of four consists of the commander, driver, operator and mechanic. There is provision for mounting a .50 (12.7 mm) M2 HB Browning machine gun by the commander's cupola on top of the superstructure. Six electrically operated smoke grenade launchers are mounted on the front of the hull.

The K288A1 ARV is fully amphibious, being propelled in the water by its tracks. Before entering the water, the trim vane is erected at the front of the hull and the bilge pumps switched on.

K288A1 armoured recovery vehicle in travelling configuration and armed with roof-mounted .50 (12.7 mm) M2 HB machine gun 0536238

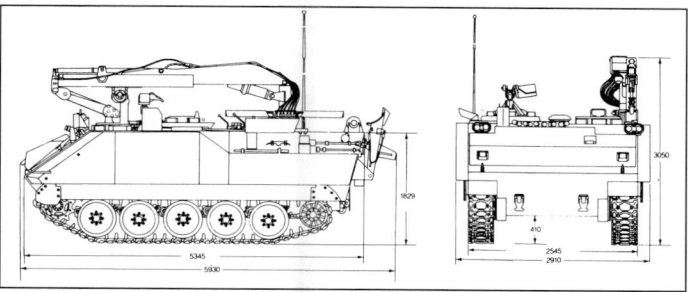

General arrangement drawing of the K288A1 armoured recovery vehicle in travelling configuration 0069306

Standard equipment includes an AN/VRC 946KE communications system, fixed fire extinguisher in the engine compartment and a portable fire extinguisher in the crew compartment.

The hull of the K288A1 armoured recovery vehicle is of all-welded aluminium armour construction with an additional layer of laminate armour for a higher level of protection. This provides protection from small arms fire and shell splinters.

Variants

The specifications in the table below relate to upgraded versions of the K288A1. The earlier version was powered by a Doosan Model D2848M 8V 4-cycle diesel developing 280 hp coupled to a Daewoo-produced, UK-developed, David Brown Gear Systems T-300 transmission.

Potential new ARV

Now in production for the Republic of Korea Army is the Doosan Next Infantry Fighting Vehicle (NIFV) which is a brand new design with a combat weight of about 26 tonnes and is also known as the K-21.

At the present time, no variants of this have been announced, but it is possible that in the future an ARV version of this could be developed together with other specialised versions to undertake some of the roles currently undertaken by the KIFV.

Specifications

K288A1 Armoured Recovery Vehicle
Crew: 4
Weight:
(combat) 14,500 kg
(empty) 12,800 kg
Power-to-weight ratio: 24.1 hp/t (18.00 kW/t)
Ground pressure: (combat) 0.75 kg/cm^2
Length:
(overall) 5.93 m
(hull) 5.345 m
Width:
(overall) 2.91 m
(over tracks) 2.545 m
Height:
(top of crane, stowed) 3.05 m
(hull roof) 1.829 m
Ground clearance: 0.41 m
Track width: 381 mm
Max speed:
(road) 70 km/h
(water) 6 km/h
Range: (cruising) 480 km
Fuel capacity: 400 litres
Fording: amphibious
Gradient: 60%
Side slope: 30%

Vertical obstacle: 0.63 m
Trench: 1.68 m
Engine: MAN (Daewoo) D2848T 14.62 litre V-8 4-cycle turbocharged diesel developing 350 hp (261 kW)
Transmission: Allison Transmission 200-5K automatic with 4 forward and 1 reverse gears
Suspension: torsion bar
Electrical system: 28 V
Batteries: 6TN, 2 of 100 Ah each
Armament: 1 × .50 (12.7 mm) M2 HB MG

Status

Production complete. In service with the ROK army and Malaysia (4+). Production can be resumed if additional orders are placed.

Contractor

Doosan Infracore Defense Products BG

Netherlands

RDM Technology Bulldog Beach Recovery Vehicle

Development

To meet the operational requirements of the Royal Netherlands Marine Corps, the Netherlands Army depot at Leusden designed and built a Beach Armoured Recovery Vehicle (BARV) based on a surplus Krauss-Maffei Wegmann Leopard 1 series Main Battle Tank (MBT) chassis. A small quantity of these were subsequently built and are now in service.

Further development of this vehicle by RDM Technology, which had considerable experience in the overhaul and upgrade of tracked armoured fighting vehicles and artillery systems for the export market, resulted in the RDM-T Bulldog Beach Recovery Vehicle.

This was offered to the UK to meet its requirement for a Future Beach Recovery Vehicle. This competition was won by the then Alvis Moelv company in Norway, which closed down in 2004.

The Bulldog Beach Recovery Vehicle remains in service, but is no longer marketed.

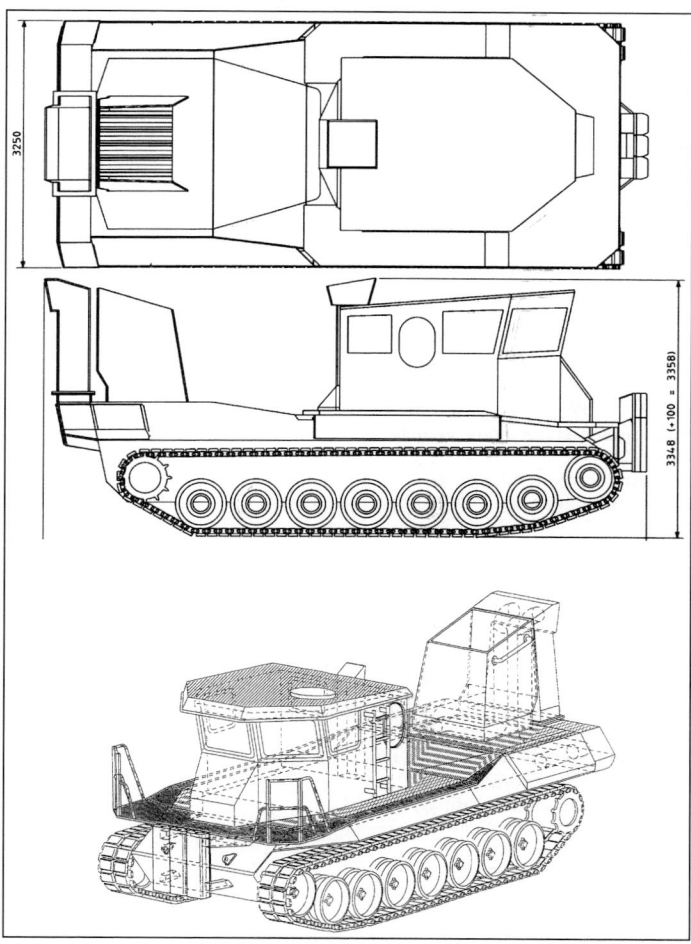

General arrangement drawings of Bulldog Beach Recovery Vehicle 0536237

Royal Netherlands Marines Beach Recovery Vehicle in Egypt
(Paul Beaver)   0568216

Description

The Bulldog Beach Recovery Vehicle is based on a much modified Krauss-Maffei Wegmann Leopard 1 MBT chassis which has had its turret removed. Mounted at the front of the hull is a push block, and towing fixtures are also provided.

Wherever possible the standard and well proven Leopard 1 MBT components are used, including the power pack and transmission, braking system, suspension, track, electric system and steering.

The raised crew compartment is at the front with a raised air inlet/exhaust outlet at the rear. The welded steel armour hull has been modified to allow for partly submerged operations.

The crew compartment is of welded steel with armoured glass windows with the crew working deck being provided with railings. The crew cabin is provided with an air conditioning system with a separate compressor.

To enable operations to be carried out in darkness, external flood lights are mounted on top of the cabin. There is also a stowage crate on the aft deck.

To improve tractive effort, some three tonnes of ballast have been added to the hull and steel fuel tanks have been fitted in place of the original fuel tanks. A heater system has been fitted to pre-heat the engine and heat the crew cabin.

The original road wheels have been replaced by corrosion resistant steel road wheels and the standard lubricating oils have been replaced by seawater resistant grease. A sludge-tank with pump has been fitted to preclude engine fluid spills.

The rear-mounted engine inlet and exhaust stacks allow for operation up to Sea State six. A new electrical system has been installed. A fog horn is also fitted as is corrosion-resistant protective coating system. Asbestos free liners are also installed for safety reasons.

Other RDM Leopard 1 conversions

In mid-2001, RDM Technology was awarded a contract by Chile for the supply of 11 specialised variants of the Leopard 1 MBT from surplus Royal Netherlands Army stocks. These included three bridgelayers, three armoured engineer vehicles and two mine clearing vehicles. The remaining three versions carry replacement bridges. These have now been delivered to Chile.

Chile has also taken delivery of 136 Leopard 2 MBTs but no specialised vehicles have yet been ordered. These were supplied from German Army stocks.

Specifications

Bulldog Beach Recovery Vehicle
Crew: 3
Weight: (combat) 42,500 kg
Power-to-weight ratio: 19.53 hp/t (14.56 kW/t)
Length: 7.09 m
Width: (without skirts) 3.25 m
Height: 1.50 m
Ground clearance: 0.44 m
Track: 2.7 m
Track width: 550 mm
Length of track on ground: 4.236 m
Fuel capacity: 985 litres
Engine: MTU MB 838 Ca M-500 10-cylinder diesel developing 830 hp (619 kW) at 2,200 rpm
Transmission: ZF 4 HP 250 with 4 forward and 2 reverse gears with hydraulic torque converter
Steering: double differential
Suspension: torsion bar
Electrical system: 24 V
Batteries: 8 × 12 V 100 Ah

Status

Production complete. No longer marketed. In service with Royal Netherlands Marines.

Contractor
RDM Technology BV (Closed down in 2004.)

Norway

Alvis Moelv Beach Recovery Vehicle (BRV)

Development

In January 2000, following an international competition, the Norwegian company of Hägglunds Moelv AS was awarded an initial GBP7.5 million contract from the then UK's Defence Procurement Agency (DPA) for the supply of four Future Beach Recovery Vehicle (FBRV) to replace the Centurion Beach Armoured Recovery Vehicle (CeBARV) then used by the Royal Marines.

The first BRV was delivered to the UK for an extensive series of trials by the Amphibious Trials and Training Unit Royal Marines in mid-2001. The remaining three production vehicles have now been delivered.

The BRV forms part of the Amphibious Beach Unit, Royal Marines, and typical missions include pushing landing craft off the beach by using its traction. In addition it will remove damaged and disabled tracked and wheeled vehicles from the beach.

In late 2002, Hägglunds Moelv was renamed Alvis Moelv as part of a corporate restructuring. This company was closed in 2004. On entering service, the word Future was dropped and it is now referred to as the Beach Recovery Vehicle (BRV).

This vehicle is no longer marketed.

Description

The BRV is based on a German Krauss-Maffei Wegmann Leopard 1 Main Battle Tank (MBT) chassis specially modified for new missions. The turret has been removed and replaced by a new all-welded steel armour superstructure which provides the occupants with protection from small arms fire and shell splinters. The BRV will be able to operate in water up to 2.95 m in depth.

In the standard Leopard 1 MBT the driver is seated at the front of the hull but in the BRV the drivers position is now in the raised superstructure to provide improved forward observation when operating in deep water. Bullet and splinter proof windows provide observation for the crew of four through the frontal arc.

Mounted at the front of the BRV is a protected push bar to push landing craft off the beach.

Working platforms have been located around the top of the crew compartment and an auxiliary power unit has been fitted to provide power for the subsystems when the vehicle is in a standby mode.

Some of the Leopard 1 series MBT subsystems have been modified to enable the BRV to operate in salt water up to a depth of 2.95 m.

The new vehicle is heavier than the standard Leopard 1 MBT with improved suspension and brakes and a gear reduction in order to provide the necessary traction. The roadwheels are made of coated steel instead of aluminium for improved corrosion resistance.

The air intakes for the main engine and crew compartment are located in the top rear end of the crew compartment with the exhaust outlets being positioned one either side at the rear

Specifications

Beach Recovery Vehicle
Crew: 3-4
Weight: 50,000 kg
Power-to-weight ratio: 16.6 hp/t (12.4 kW/t)
Length: 7.5 m
Width: 3.4 m
Height: 4.1 m
Max speed:
  (road, forwards) 32 km/h
  (road, reverse) 12 km/h
Fording depth: 2.9 m
Vertical obstacle: 0.75 m
Gradient: 60%
Turning circle: 9.6 m
Engine: MTU MB 838 Ca M-500 10-cylinder diesel developing 830 hp (619 kW) at 2,200 rpm
Transmission: ZF 4 HP 250 with 4 forward and 2 reverse gears
Electrical system: 24 V

Status

First of four BRV commenced trials with the Royal Marines in mid-2001. Main production run of three vehicles has now been completed. There was also the option of an additional vehicle, which was not exercised by the UK.

There will be no further production or marketing of this vehicle.

Contractor
Alvis Moelv AS (This company closed down late in 2004.)

Pakistan

HIT Al Hadeed Armoured Repair and Recovery Vehicle

Development
Based on its extensive experience in the local production and assembly of the now BAE Systems US Combat Systems M113 series of full-tracked Armoured Personnel Carrier (APC) and variants, Heavy Industries Taxila (HIT) developed and placed in production a new APC called the Tahla.

This is very similar in appearance to the US M113 APC but has a different shaped hull front with the upper part of the hull sides at the rear sloping inwards and provided with firing ports.

The first version of the Tahla APC had five road wheel stations but a version has also been developed with six road wheel stations which has greater internal volume and therefore greater payload.

This version forms the basis of the Al Hadeed Armoured Repair and Recovery Vehicle (ARRV). As of late 2010, it is understood that development of the ARRV was complete and production was expected to start soon.

Description
The hull of the Al Hadeed ARRV is of all-welded aluminium armour that provides protection from small arms fire and shell splinters. Unlike the Tahla APC the upper part of the hull sides of the Al Hadeed ARRV do not slope inwards but are vertical.

The layout of the Al Hadeed is similar to the M113 with the driver front left, diesel power pack to the right, which leaves the remainder of the vehicle free for the crew compartment. The diesel fuel tanks are mounted externally, one either side of the power operated ramp at the rear.

The driver is provided with a single-piece hatch cover and day periscopes for observation to the front and sides. One of the day periscopes can be replaced for driving at night.

The vehicle commander is also provided with a single-piece hatch cover and periscopes for all-round observation and a 12.7 mm machine gun is normally provided at the commander's station. There is also a hatch in the roof of the vehicle towards the rear.

Suspension either side consists of six dual rubber-tyred road wheels with the drive sprocket to the front, idler at the rear and no track return rollers.

To carry out its specialised mission, the Al Hadeed ARRV is fitted with a roof-mounted hydraulically-operated crane with a lifting capacity of three tonnes at a reach of 2.2 m. This has a telescopic jib that can be traversed through 360°.

Mounted in the rear of the vehicle is a hydraulic winch which leads out though the lowered rear ramp and can be used to recover vehicles weighing up to 20 tonnes when the two hydraulic stabilisers are lowered at the rear, one either side of the ramp. The winch is provided with 130 m of 16 to 20 mm diameter cable.

Internally, the Al Hadeed carries a number of specialised tools and equipment including a battery charger, compressor, drill, generator, grinder, hydraulic press, lathe, welding equipment and tools.

Optional equipment includes an NBC system, night vision equipment and smoke grenade launchers.

Specifications
Al Hadeed ARRV
Crew: 5
Combat wieght: 15,000 kg
Unloaded weight: 13,000 kg
Power-to-wieght ratio: 17.7 hp/t (13.2 kW/t)
Length: 6.048 m
Width: 2.54 m
Height:
 (with crane) 3.022 m
 (without crane) 1.854 m
Ground clearance: 0.431
Track width: 381 mm
Length of track on ground: n/avail
Maximum speed:
 (road) 75 km/h
 (water) 6 km/h (estimate)
Fuel capacity: 380 litres
Range: 300 km
Fording: amphibious
Gradient: 60%
Side slope: 40%
Vertical obstacle: 0.609 m
Trench: 1.676 m
Engine: Detroit diesel 6V-53T developing 265 hp (198 kW) at 2,800 rpm
Transmission: Allison TX-100-A automatic
Steering: differential or pivot brake
Suspension: torsion bar
Electrical system: 28 V
Batteries: 2 × 12 V, 100 Ah (each)
Armament: 1 × 12.7 mm MG
Ammunition: 2,000 × 12.7 mm
NBC system: optional
Night vision equipment: optional

Status
Development complete. Ready for production.

Contractor
Heavy Industries Taxila (HIT)

Poland

WZT-3 armoured recovery vehicle

Development
The WZT-3 Armoured Recovery Vehicle (ARV) is based on the chassis of the Russian- designed T-72 MBT as produced in Poland at the Zaklady Mechaniczne 'Bumar-Labedy' SA. The actual vehicle was developed by The Research and Development Centre of Mechanical Appliances (OBRUM). This has also been referred to as the PMC-90 ARV when being marketed as a complete package with MBTs and AVLBs.

In general layout and appearance it resembles the Russian BREM-1, which is described and illustrated in a separate entry within *Jane's Military Vehicles and Logistics*, but there are numerous differences to suit the requirements of the Polish Armed Forces.

In 2002, the Polish company of PHZ Bumar, acting on behalf of ZM Bumar Labedy the prime contractor, was awarded a contract by the Indian company of Bharat Earth Movers (BEM) for the supply of an additional 80 WZT-3 Armoured Recovery Vehicles (ARV) for the Indian Army.

Financial details of the contracts have not been revealed although sources in Warsaw estimate that it is worth between USD60 and 70 million. Bids for this Indian requirement were submitted late in February 2002 by two companies with the other contender being the Slovakian VT-72 ARV which is also based on a T-72 series MBT chassis.

The new batch of 80 WZT-3 ARV supplement the 44 vehicles delivered by Poland in 2001 which have the Indian Army designation of the ARV-3.

The first batch of 14 WZT-3 ARVs were delivered to the Bharat Earth Movers (BEM) Kolar Gold Field facility before the end of 2002 with the remainder being delivered from 2004.

The final batch of 40 WZT-3 ARVs has been assembled in India from kits supplied by ZM Bumar Labedy.

The new batch of 80 WZT-3 ARVs are powered by Indian-built V46.6 diesel engines developing 780 hp manufactured in India at the Avadi Engine Facility.

Al Hadeed armoured repair and recovery vehicle showing roof mounted hydraulic crane and longer chassis with six road wheels (HIT) 1333502

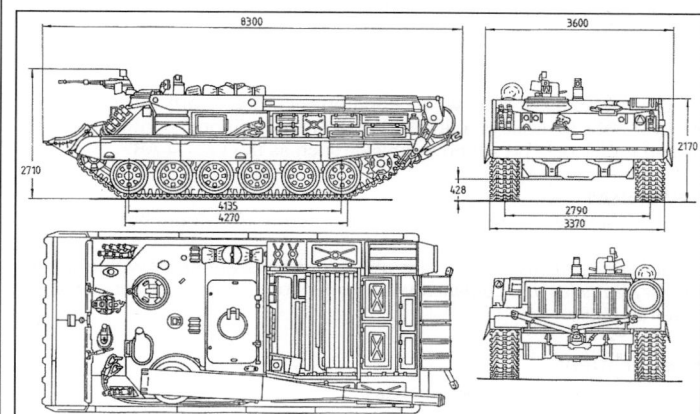
Detailed four-view drawing of Polish WZT-3 armoured recovery vehicle in travelling configuration 0512442

WZT-3 armoured recovery vehicle in travelling configuration
(Michael Jerchel)   0088548

These engines, originally manufactured for the locally-produced Russian T-72M1 series MBT, also power the first batch of 44 WZT-3 vehicles. In 2004, another 228 WZT-3s were ordered by India and up to 40 per cent of this work will be carried out in India.

The Polish Army has taken delivery of an additional batch of WZT-3M, all upgraded after the overhaul of the existing platforms. The first of these vehicles were delivered to the 10th Armoured Brigade in Swietoszow in December 2001.

The WZT-3 ARV is currently in production for the export market. The older WZT-2 ARV is similar to the VT-55A based on a modified chassis.

Production of the Polish WZT-3 and WZT-4 ARV is undertaken for the home and export markets on an as required basis.

Description

The WZT-3 ARV has a crew of up to four, although only two (the driver and commander) are required during operations. The driver is seated under a hatch cover to the left front of an armoured superstructure. The commander is seated on the right under a cupola provided with day vision periscopes and a 12.7 mm NSW (NSV) Heavy machine Gun (HMG) pintle. Both the commander and driver are provided with night vision devices. A further crew hatch is provided in the centre of the superstructure roof towards the rear of the superstructure.

Behind the superstructure is a load-carrying platform for replacement power packs or other components. The platform measures 1.91 m long by 2.16 m wide and has sidewalls 0.62 m high; the load capacity is 3,500 kg.

Mounted on a small turntable to the left front of the superstructure is a TD-50 extending jib crane with a lifting capacity of 15 tonnes, a maximum hook height of 8.6 m and a maximum reach of 5.8 m. This crane can be traversed through a full 360° and be elevated from 42.5 to +72.5 and has a maximum lifting speed of 2.7 m/min.

At the front of the vehicle is a 3.605 m wide dozer blade which can be used for earth-excavating or anchoring and support during recovery operations. It has a maximum cutting depth of 0.25 m.

The main recovery winch is mechanically driven and has a maximum pulling capacity, with tackle, of 840 kN; the winch has a usable 200 m of 28.5 mm diameter rope cable. Winch speed is 18.6 m/min at full load. There is also an auxiliary hydraulic winch with a pulling capacity of 20 kN and 400 m of 9 mm cable.

Other recovery equipment carried includes rigid towbars and towcables. Specialised repair equipment includes electrical and gas welding gear, impact wrenches, chain saws, a tool kit and various special tools, spares and mobile work benches.

Standard equipment includes a fire detection and suppression system in the engine and crew compartments, refuel/defuel pump and an auxiliary power unit.

The WZT-3 can be fitted with a deep wading kit for water obstacles up to 1,000 m wide. Extra diesel fuel can be carried in drums on the hull rear.

Variants

WZT-4 ARV

This is an enhanced version of the early WZT-3 and features a more powerful crane and an improved winch. Malaysia placed a contract for six WZT-4 ARVs to support its new PT-91M MBTs in 2003. These WZT-4 ARV were delivered to Malaysia in 2007 together with the other associated support vehicles. If and when additional contracts are placed for the PT-91M MBT by Malaysia, it is expected that additional contracts will be placed for associated support vehicles such as the WZT-4 ARV.

ARV M-84A1

This is produced in Croatia and is similar to the WZT-3 but based on T-84 MBT components.

Full details of this vehicle are given in a separate entry within *Jane's Military Vehicles and Logistics*, with production being undertaken on an as required basis.

Specifications

WZT-3 Armoured Recovery Vehicle
Crew: up to 4
Weight: (approx) 42,000 kg
Ground pressure: 0.85 kg/cm²

Power to weight ratio: 20.0 hp/t (14.9 kW/t)
Length: (overall) 8.5 m
Width:
  (overall) 3.6 m
  (over tracks) 3.37 m
Height:
  (overall) 2.71 m
  (hull roof) 2.17 m
Ground clearance: 0.395 m
Track: 2.79 m
Length of track on ground: 4.27 m
Max speed:
  (roads) 60 km/h
  (towing 42 t load, road or cross-country) 12 km/h
Range:
  (road) 650 km
  (dirt road) 420-600 km
Fuel capacity:
  (basic) 1,126 litres
  (with extra tanks) 1,526 litres
Fording:
  (normal) 1.2 m
  (with preparation) 5 m
Gradient: 60%
Side slope: 46%
Vertical obstacle: 0.7 m
Trench: 2.6-2.8 m
Engine: liquid-cooled multifuel supercharged diesel S12-U developing 840 hp (626 kW) at 2,000 rpm
Transmission: planetary gear, hydraulically assisted with 7 forward and 1 reverse gears
Steering: clutch and brake
Suspension: torsion bar
Electrical system: 27 V
Batteries: 4 × 12 V, 280 Ah
Armament: 1 × 12.7 mm NSW (NSV) HMG
Ammunition: 720 × 12.7 mm
Smoke grenade launchers:
  1 × 8-barrelled 81 mm
  1 × 4-barrelled 81 mm

Status

Production as required. In service with Croatia, India, Poland and other undisclosed countries. In 2003 Malaysia placed a contract with Poland for a complete PT-91M battalion that included six of the latest WZT-4 series of ARVs. First deliveries of the WZT-4 were made to Malaysia in 2007 to support the PT-91M MBT and variants.

Contractor

Zaklady Mechaniczne 'Bumar-Labedy' SA

Russian Federation

BREM-1M Armoured Repair and Recovery Vehicle

Development

To support its export sales of the T-90S series Main Battle Tanks (MBT), the Uralvagonzavod Joint Stock Company, located in Nizhny Tagil, has completed development of the BREM-1M Armoured Repair Recovery Vehicle (ARRV).

This is being marketed to customers who have purchased the T-90S MBT (including Algeria, India, Libya and Turkmenistan) as well as existing T-72 MBTs users.

The original BREM-1 ARRV was based on the older chassis of the T-72 MBT which is no longer manufactured by Uralvagonzavod, although quantities of these are available for sale.

The T-90 was followed in production by the T-90 with the export version being the T-90S which is currently being manufactured under licence in India for the Indian Army.

Typical roles of the BREM-1M ARRV include the recovery of damaged and disabled vehicles as well as carrying out minor repairs and replacement of key sub-systems such as a complete vehicle powerpack.

As of November 2010, development of the BREM-1M was completed but as far as it is known the vehicle had yet to enter production or service.

Description

BREM-1M ARRV is based on the lower chassis of a T-90S MBT and according to Uralvagonzavod has the same high level of protection over the frontal arc.

The chassis is of all welded steel armour with the driver in the middle for enhanced survivability if the vehicle goes over a anti-tank mine, crew compartment in the middle and powerpack at the rear.

The carry out its mission, mounted at the front of the BREM-1M chassis is a hydraulically operated dozer blade which is use to stabilise the vehicle when the winch or crane is being used as well as preparing firing positions and clearing battlefield obstacles.

Pivoted at the front left side of the hull is a hydraulically operated crane with a telescopic winch which when not required is traversed to the rear.

The BREM-1M has three hydraulic winches, main, secondary and towing. Some tools and other specialised equipment are carried including an electric welding system and a hydraulic jack.

On the roof of the vehicle to the rear of the commanders and gunners hatches is a load area that can carry a maximum load of 1.5 tonnes.

A 12.7 mm machine gun is fitted for air defence and local defence purposes and like the T-72 and T-90 MBTs the BREM-1M can lay its own smoke screen by injecting diesel fuel into to exhaust outlet on the left side of the hull.

As with the T-90S MBT, the BREM-1M ARRV is provided with an NBC system and night driving aids.

BREM-1M can ford to a depth of 1.2 m without preparation but with the aid of a snorkel which is carried on the right side of the chassis it can deep ford to a maximum depth of 5 m.

Like the T-90S, the BREM-1M ARRV is powered by a V-92S2 diesel engine which develops 1,000 hp and this gives a maximum road speed of 60 km/h.

Variants
None known.

Specifications
Not available.

Status
Development complete. Ready for production on receipt of orders.

Contractor
Ural Transport Engineering Design Bureau (Uralvagonzavod)

BREM-80U armoured recovery vehicle

Development
To support the T-80U Main Battle Tank (MBT), Russia developed to the prototype stage, a new Armoured Recovery Vehicle (ARV) called the BREM-80U. This was first seen in public late in 1998.

The BREM-80U ARV was developed by the Transport Machine Building Design Bureau, with the prototype being built by the Plant of Transport Machine Building. As far as it is known, as of late 2010, the BREM-80U remained at the prototype stage.

The BREM-80U ARV is a considerable advance over earlier vehicles of this type such as the BREM-1, which is based on the older T-72 MBT chassis.

Production of the T-80 MBT was undertaken in Russia and the Ukraine but has now been completed.

Further development of the T-80D (diesel version) by the Ukraine resulted in the T-84 MBT of which 320 have been sold to Pakistan.

The Ukraine has developed a new ARV based on T-84 MBT components called the BREM-84 and details of this are provided in a separate entry in *Jane's Military Vehicles and Logistics*. As of late 2010 the BREM-84 remained at the prototype stage.

As of late 2010, the only MBT in production in Russian was the T-90, which is itself a further development of the T-72.

Description
The baseline T-80U turbine powered chassis is retained in the BREM-80U ARV but a new all-welded steel-armoured superstructure has been added at the front for the crew and the winch equipment.

BREM-80U armoured recovery vehicle in travelling configuration (Steve Zaloga)   0069308

This provides protection from small arms fire and shell splinters. The tools and smaller spare parts are carried in fully enclosed stowage boxes located alongside the hull and extended to the rear.

The main hydraulic winch has a capacity of 35 tonnes but, using snatch blocks, this can be increased to 140 tonnes. The main winch can unwind at the rate of 50 m/min with two winding speeds being available, 17 and 50 m/min. A more powerful auxiliary winch is also provided. The main winch is provided with 120 m of wire rope while the auxiliary winch is provided with 320 m of wire rope.

The crew of four consists of the commander, mechanic/driver, fitter and welder/rigger, a fifth seat is provided for an additional crew member.

Mounted at the front of the hull is a hydraulically operated blade which can be used as a dozer blade or an anchor blade when the winch or crane is being used.

The hydraulically operated crane is pivoted at the left side of the hull and folds back along the right side of the hull when not required. The jib crane is of the telescopic type and has a maximum lifting capacity of 18 tonnes.

This enables it not only to lift complete MBT powerpacks and turrets as well as lifting many lighter armoured vehicles such as the Russian Kurganmashzavod Joint Stock Company BMP-2 infantry combat vehicle.

Armament consists of a 12.7 mm Heavy machine Gun (HMG), with a bank of eight electrically operated 81 mm smoke grenade launchers being mounted at the front of the vehicle on the left side. Personnel weapons carried include four AKS-47 assault rifles, an RPG-7 unguided rocket-propelled grenade launcher and a signal pistol.

Standard equipment includes an NBC system and night vision equipment for the commander and driver, plus an air conditioning system.

A complete range of tools is provided as well as an electric welding system. As the vehicle is fitted with an auxiliary power unit, the various items of equipment can be run while the main turbine engine is switched off to save fuel. A snorkel is carried on the right side at the rear and, when fitted, the BREM-80U can deep ford. The standard BREM-80U is fitted with steel tracks but as an option rubber pad type tracks can be fitted.

Variants
Projected variants based on the BREM-80U chassis include a command and staff vehicle and an ammunition resupply vehicle.

Specifications
Full details of the BREM-80U ARV have not yet been released although some data has been quoted by Russian sources collated in the following table.

BREM-80U
Weight: 46 tonnes
Max speed: (road) 70 km/h
Operational range: 500 km
NBC system: yes
Night vision equipment: yes
Armament:
   1 × 12.7 mm HMG
   8 × 81 mm smoke grenade launchers

Main hydraulic winch
Rated line pull:
   (single cable) 343 kN (35 tonnes)
   (with snatch blocks) 1.37 MN (140 tonnes)
Usable rope length: 120 m
Winding rate: 17-50 m/min

Status
Prototype. Not yet in production or service.

Contractor
Developed by the Transport Machine Building Design Bureau
Prototype produced by the Plant of Transport Machine Building

BREM-80U armoured recovery vehicle with stabiliser blade lowered and crane in use (Steve Zaloga)   0069309

BREM-1 armoured recovery and repair vehicle

Development
The BREM-1 (*Bronirovannaya Remontno-evakuatsionnaya-1*) Armoured Recovery Vehicle (ARV) was developed by the Ural Transport Engineering Design Bureau to support the widely deployed Russian-designed T-72 series MBT.

Following extensive trials with prototype vehicles, production commenced in 1983 with first production vehicles being completed in 1984. Production of the BREM-1 ARV is undertaken on an as required basis.

Description
The BREM-1 ARV is based on the chassis of the T-72 series MBT with the driver's compartment at the front, crew compartment in the centre and diesel powerpack at the rear.

It is understood that the hull has the same level of armour protection as the T-72 MBT with the highest level of protection being over the frontal arc. The glacis plate of the BREM-1 includes welded steel with additional layers of composites and other materials inside.

Suspension is of the torsion bar type with either side having six dual rubber-tyred roadwheels with the drive sprocket at the rear and idler at the front. The upper part of the suspension is supported by track-return rollers.

The BREM-1 has a crew of three: commander, driver and a vehicle mechanic. Each of the crew is provided with day and night observation equipment.

When towing another tank, the road range is reduced to 220 km without refuelling. Long-range diesel fuel tanks are mounted on the rear and can be jettisoned if required. An unditching beam is carried under the rear fuel drums.

For fording, an OPVT snorkel can be fitted over the crew compartment to enable fording of water obstacles up to 5 m deep and 1,000 m wide. When not in use, the OPVT snorkel tube is carried horizontally at the rear of the vehicle on the right.

On the left side of the vehicle is pivoted a 4.4 m hydromechanical crane, used for lifting damaged or ditched vehicles for access or repair. The crane has a lifting capacity of 3,000 kg at the full 4.4 m extension or 19,000 kg at 2 m extension. Hydraulic power for the crane is supplied by a pump driven from the vehicle's main engine via an auxiliary gearbox.

If the main V-84 MS V-12 engine is not running, an electrical pump driven from the vehicle's batteries may be used. The crane is controlled from an elevated position that is equipped with all the necessary controls for the operation. With the maximum load suspended from the crane hook the vehicle may be driven over level ground. If the load exceeds 3,000 kg the vehicle suspension is locked automatically. The crane turntable is also lockable. With the crane outrigger extended to 3 m the crane may be used through a full 360°. When extended 3 to 4 m the crane may only operate between +60° and −10° towards the rear and between +90° and −10° to the front, measured from a line fore and aft. For travelling, the outrigger is stowed along the side of the vehicle and held in a special clamp by a screw fitting.

The BREM-1 ARV is equipped with an electric welding system that comprises an SG-10-1S starter/generator, switch unit, working position, welding socket and a set of welding leads. The maximum welding current is 360 A. Controls for the welding equipment are located on a panel in a hermetically sealed container mounted on a shelf over the left-hand track. Other special tools carried include a universal fitter's tool, spanners and adaptors, all carried in two portable containers on a load platform. In the centre of the roof is a platform 1.706 m long and 1.4 m wide. It is provided with removable side flaps; and can accommodate a maximum load of 1,500 kg.

For recovery operations the BREM-1 ARV is equipped with hoisting and auxiliary winches, add-on plough and bulldozer blades, towing equipment and a full set of accessories. The mechanical main winch has a capacity of 25,000 kg but this may be increased by using snatch blocks to 100,000 kg. Normally this winch is used forward, in conjunction with the lowered dozer blade, but for self-recovery it may be used to the rear. The length of cable used is 220 m.

Russian BREM-1 ARV in travelling configuration from the rear. Note that the long range fuel tanks are not fitted and under the racks for these is the unditching beam (Steven Zaloga) 0569719

Russian BREM-1 ARV in travelling configuration with crane stowed and dozer/stabiliser blade raised at front of vehicle (Steven Zaloga) 0069545

The winch is power-driven from a 'swing frame' gear via a reduction gearbox. The winch is controlled from the elevated operator's position. A 530 kg auxiliary winch and 425 m of cable are used to pull the cable towards the winch hoist and the speed of winding and unwinding is controlled hydraulically. The winch controls are to the right of the operator's position.

A detachable device may be used to clean dirt from the cable. In use, this is placed on the fixed element of the cable feeder and comprises two round revolving brushes, a hydraulic motor, the cable guides and a reduction gear to transmit drive to the brushes. The device is switched on once the cable has been extended.

The bulldozer equipment is mounted on the front of the hull and is hydraulically driven, with control via two push-buttons on the driver's main control handles. The blade is 3.1 m wide and can be used to create an MBT firing position in 20 minutes in heavy soil or 12 minutes in light sandy soil. The dozer blade has a maximum digging depth of 450 mm.

The towing equipment consists of two towing rods, each 1.68 m long and with internal shock-absorbers, and two 5.5 m long tow lines. The vehicle can tow loads up to 50,000 kg for prolonged periods. Other special equipment carried includes a 30-tonne capacity hydraulic jack and ESA-1 welding equipment.

The BREM-1 ARV has an R-123U radio installation, a TPU tank telephone system and an overpressure NBC system.

The only armament carried by the BREM-1 ARV is a single 12.7 mm NSVT machine gun and 840 rounds of ammunition. Four forward-firing 81 mm smoke dischargers may be fitted but smoke screens can be produced by injecting diesel fuel into the exhaust outlet which is situated on left side of the hull towards the rear. An NBC protection system is provided for the crew. Night vision devices and a navigation system are also provided.

Variants
VT-72B
This ARV based on a T-72 chassis was developed in Slovakia. Details of this are given in a separate entry within *Jane's Military Vehicles and Logistics*. Production of this is undertaken on an as required basis.

WZT-3
This is a Polish armoured recovery vehicle based on the T-72 MBT chassis.

Further development of this has resulted in the improved WZT-4 for which the first export customer is Malaysia. Details of the WZT-3 and WZT-4 ARV are provided in a separate entry in *Jane's Military Vehicles and Logistics* with production of these being undertaken on an as required basis.

BREM-1M armoured repair and recovery vehicles
The BREM-1M Armoured Repair And Recovery Vehicle (ARRV) has been developed to support the T-90S export MBT which is already in service with Algeria, India, Libya, Russia and Turkmenistan.

As of November 2010, development of the BREM-1M ARRV was complete but as far as it is known the vehicle had yet to enter production or service.

Available details of the latest BREM-1M ARRV are provided in a separate entry in *Jane's Military Vehicles and Logistics*.

Specifications
BREM-1 armoured repair and recovery vehicle
Crew: 3
Weight: 41,000 kg
Power-to-weight ratio: 20.5-20.9 hp/t (15.28-15.59 kW/t)
Ground pressure: 0.826-0.808 kg/cm^2
Length: 7.98 m
Width:
 (over side skirts) 3.46 m
 (over tracks) 3.37 m
Height: (loaded) 2.425 m
Ground clearance: 0.457 m
Track: 2.79 m
Length of track on ground: 4.278 m

Average speed:
  (road) ≤50 km/h
  (earth road) 35-45 km/h
  (earth road towing tank) ≤12 km/h
Max speed: (road) 60 km/h
Range:
  (roads) 700 km
  (earth roads) 450-650 km
  (towing) 220 km
Fording:
  (normal) 1.2 m
  (with preparation) 5 m
Gradient: 60%
Side slope: 40%
Vertical obstacle: 0.85 m
Trench: 2.6-2.8 m
Engine: V-84 MS V-12 multifuel diesel developing 840 hp (626 kW) at 2,000 rpm
Armament: 1 × 12.7 mm NSVT MG
Ammunition: 12.7 mm - 840 rounds

Main winch
Rated line pull: 25,000 kg
With snatch blocks: 100,000 kg
Usable rope length: 200 m
Winding rate: 13 m/min

Auxiliary winch
Max line pull: 530 kg
Usable rope length: 425 m

Jib crane
Lift capacity:
  (at max 4.4 m extension) 3,000 kg
  (2-3 m extension) 12,000 kg
  (2 m extension) 19,000 kg
Max hook height: 4.36 m
Traverse: 360°

Status

Production complete but could be resumed for the export market. The T-72 is used by the following countries many of which use a T-72 based recovery vehicle: Algeria, Angola, Armenia, Azerbaijan, Belarus, Bulgaria, Croatia, Finland (reserve), Georgia, Hungary, India, Iran, Iraq, Kazakhstan, Kyrgyzstan, Libya, Macedonia, Montenegro, Morocco, Myanmar, Poland, Romania, Russian Federation, Serbia, Slovakia, Sudan, Syria, Tajikistan, Turkmenistan, Ukraine, Uzbekistan, Vietnam and Yemen. In some cases, such as Slovakia and Poland, they use locally developed ARVs based on a similar chassis.

Contractor

Ural Transport Engineering Design Bureau (Uralvagonzavod)

T-54/T-55 Armoured Recovery Vehicles (ARV)

Development

The first ARV, based on the chassis of the standard Russian T-54 Main Battle Tank (MBT), appeared in the 1950s and was designated the T-54-T. Since then at least seven other T-54/T-55 ARVs have been developed. Most of them have very limited capabilities compared with ARVs developed in the West and few are equipped with a winch, limiting their capabilities to towing damaged vehicles off the battlefield. These vehicles are known as BTS (medium armoured towers) in Russia. The T-55-TK is an improvement over the earlier models as it can lift tracked and wheeled vehicles weighing up to 20,000 kg.

Description

All these ARVs use a T-54 or T-55 MBT chassis with the turret removed. The driver is seated at the front of the hull on the left side and is provided with two day periscopes for observation and a single-piece hatch cover that lifts and swings to one side to open.

T-55-T armoured recovery vehicle (Michael Jerchel)   0512440

T-55-TK armoured recovery vehicle   0038811

The vehicle commander is normally seated to his right and is provided with a single-piece hatch cover which opens to the right. The other crew members normally sit in the cargo area, which is often cramped as the large snorkel and additional fuel drums are usually carried there. An unditching beam is carried on the right side of the hull and towbars of varying lengths are also carried.

The engine and transmission are at the rear of the hull, but unlike the T-54/T-55 MBT, there does not appear to be any provision for carrying additional diesel fuel tanks on the rear of the hull. It is assumed that most of these ARVs are provided with an NBC system.

The suspension is of the torsion bar type and either side consists of five dual rubber-tyred roadwheels with the idler at the front and the drive sprocket at the rear. There are no track-return rollers.

Like the T-54/T-55 tank chassis on which it is based, all of these vehicles can lay a smoke screen by injecting diesel fuel into the exhaust outlet on the left side of the hull.

Variants

T-54-T/T-55-T

This was the first model to enter service and performs a similar role to the older T-34-T (B) ARV but is based on a more powerful chassis. A loading platform is mounted in the centre of the vehicle, with sides that can be folded down to facilitate the loading or unloading of replacement components such as an engine or a transmission. A large spade is mounted at the rear of the hull and a large-diameter snorkel can be installed to the rear of the driver's position for deep fording operations. A jib crane which can lift a maximum weight of 1,000 kg is provided. There is no winch, so the vehicle is limited to towing operations.

It has been confirmed that development of this ARV commenced in 1947 under the designation of the Article 9 with the first prototype being completed in 1950.

This was followed by a further three vehicles that were built and tested between 1951 and late 1952.

It was recommended for acceptance into service in 1954 and was officially accepted for service as the BTS-2 in February 1955.

The first production batch of 10 vehicles was completed in 1956 and a total of 250 production vehicles were built with late production vehicles having a number of improvements.

BTS-4A armoured recovery vehicle

This was developed from 1965 and based on the T-54 Model 1949 chassis. It was accepted for service in November 1967 and all of these were built on surplus T-54 series tank chassis.

It is almost identical to the original BTS-2 but has a smaller crew, and different roof hatches as well as different access hatches for winch and fording equipment.

BREhM-3 armoured repair and recovery vehicle

This was developed based on the T-54 Model 1949 chassis and the first prototype was completed in Kiev (now in the Ukraine) in 1979 but it never entered service.

T-54 (A)

This was a former East German development and can be fitted with a snorkel for deep fording operations. Standard equipment includes a push/pull bar, full range of tools including both welding and cutting equipment, dismountable crane with a lifting capacity of 1,000 kg, radiation warning equipment and a chemical warfare agent detector. This model does not have a winch, nor a spade at the rear. If required, PT-54 or PT-55 roller type mineclearing equipment can be installed at the front.

T-54 (B)

This was also a former East German development. It is similar to the T-54 (A) but at the rear of the hull are brackets for securing tow ropes and on the glacis plate at the front of the hull is a protective plate. This model is not provided with a winch or a spade.

T-55-TK (previously known as T-54 (C))

This was another former East German development. It is provided with a stowage platform, snorkel, spade at the rear, dozer blade at the front and a heavy-duty crane which is mounted on the right side of the hull. This has a telescopic jib and can lift a maximum weight of 20,000 kg. When not required, the crane is traversed to the rear so that its jib rests along the left side of the hull.

BTS-2 armoured recovery vehicle clearly showing snorkel mounted on roof of the vehicle (Dirk Caemerlynck)   0536239

Czechoslovak VT-55A ARV

This was developed to meet the requirements of the then Czechoslovakia Army. Full details of this are given in a separate entry in *Jane's Military Vehicles and Logistics*.

Polish T-54/T-55 ARVs

Poland has developed at least two ARVs based on T-54 or T-55 MBT chassis, designated the WZT-1 and WZT-2. The later WZT-3 ARV is based on the more recent T-72 series MBT. Details of this are provided in a separate entry in *Jane's Military Vehicles and Logistics* with the latest version being the WZT-4. This has been sold to Malaysia to support the sale of Polish PT-91M series MBTs.

Exports of surplus ARV

According to the United Nations, the following quantities of Czechoslovakian-designed VT-55A series ARV were exported between 1992 and 2008, but there could be other undisclosed exports as well.

From	To	Quantity	Date	Comment
Czech Republic	Germany	1	2005	
Czech Republic	Hungary	1	2003	
Czech Republic	Slovakia	2	2002	
Hungary	Iraq	4	2005	2 × VT-55A, 2 × BT-55A
Slovakia	Sri Lanka	2	2002	
Ukraine	Iraq	3	2006	BTS-5B model
Ukraine	Azerbaijan	4	2007	BTS-5M model
Ukraine	Georgia	6	2007	BTS-5 model
Ukraine	Iraq	4	2008	BREM-4

Specifications

T-54-T
(Data in square brackets refers to T-54 (B) and T-55-TK where different)
Crew: 3-5
Weight: (empty) 36,000 [32,000], [34,000] kg
Power-to-weight ratio: 14.44 [16.25], [17.06] hp/t (10.77 [12.12], [12.72] kW/t)
Length: 7.12 [7.05], [9.74] m
Width: 3.23 m
Height: 1.89 [2.2], [2.65] m
Ground clearance: 0.425 m
Track: 2.64 m
Track width: 580 mm
Length of track on ground: 3.84 m
Ground pressure: 0.72 [0.72], [0.77] kg/cm^2
Max speed: (road) 48 km/h
Range: 400 km
Fuel capacity: 812 litres
Fording: 1.4 m
Gradient: 60%
Vertical obstacle: 0.8 m
Trench: 2.7 m
Engine:
   (T-54 chassis) Model V-54, V-12, water-cooled diesel developing 520 hp (388 kW) at 2,000 rpm
   (T-55 chassis) Model V-55, V-12, water-cooled diesel developing 580 hp (433 kW) at 2,000 rpm
Transmission: manual with 5 forward and 1 reverse gears
Electrical system: 24 V
Batteries: 4 with total capacity of 280 Ah
Armament: nil

Armour
Glacis plate: 100 mm at 60°
Upper hull sides: 70 mm at 0°
Hull rear: 60 mm
Hull floor: 20 mm
Hull roof: 30 mm

Status

Production complete. The T-54 and T-55 are in service with the following countries so it can be assumed that most of these use the T-54/T-55 ARV: Afghanistan (status uncertain), Albania, Algeria, Angola, Armenia, Azerbaijan, Bangladesh, Belarus, Bosnia-Herzegovina, Bulgaria, Cambodia, Central African Republic, Chad, China, Congo-Brazzaville, Congo (Democratic Republic) Croatia, Cuba, Ecuador, Egypt, Eritrea, Ethiopia, Georgia, Guinea, India, Iran, Iraq, Korea (North), Laos, Latvia, Lebanon, Libya, Macedonia, Malawi, Mali, Mauritania, Mongolia, Montenegro, Mozambique, Namibia, Nicaragua, Nigeria, Pakistan, Peru, Romania, Russia, Rwanda, Serbia, Slovenia, Somalia, Sri Lanka, Sudan, Syria, Tanzania, Togo, Uganda, Ukraine, Uruguay, Uzbekistan, Vietnam, Yemen and Zambia.

Contractor

Czech/Slovak Polish and Russian state factories.

BREhM-D repair and recovery vehicle

Development

The BREhM-D repair and recovery vehicle is based on the chassis of the BTR-D airborne Armoured Personnel Carrier (APC) designed and built at the Volgograd Tractor Plant and is equipped for the specific purpose of repairing and recovering BMD-1 Airborne Combat Vehicle (ACV) and similar vehicles. The BMD-1 ACV was followed in production by the BMD-2, BMD-3 and more recently the BMD-4. As far as it is known there are not any specialised repair and recovery vehicles based on these chassis.

Of these, the only one that is currently in production is the BMD-4 which has not been exported. Although designed at the Volgograd Tractor Plant, production of the latest BMD-4 is being undertaken at the Kurgan Machine Construction Plant. This is due to a commonality of components used in the BMD-4 and the latest BMP-3, both of which is also constructed at the Kurgan Machine Construction Plant.

Description

In order to carry out its specialised repair and recovery role, new line equipment carried on the BREhM-D includes a hydraulic crane, recovery winch, combination spade/dozer blade, towing equipment, welding kit, plus other tools and stowage points.

When not in use, the hydraulic crane boom is carried stowed in a retaining frame on the upper hull of the vehicle. The crane, which has a traverse of 150° and a reach of 2 m, has a capacity of 1,500 kg or more, depending on the number of cable runs, with the runs rigged to the top of the vehicle. The crane is operated from the commander's position using power from the vehicle hydraulic system, although a hand pump is provided for when the engine is not running.

For recovery tasks the vehicle uses the hydraulic recovery winch and the spade/dozer blade. Using the main cable, the winch has a capacity of 3,500 kg but this can be increased to 10,500 kg using extra cable runs. The winch is controlled from the commander's position. The winch cable is 100 m long and plays out forwards through a framework holding heavy rubber rollers to keep the cable free from mud or snow. When carrying out heavy recovery tasks the spade/dozer blade is lowered manually by two personnel to provide an anchor.

For towing there are two telescopic towbars with internal hydraulic shock-absorbers. When not in use, these are carried on the rear of the hull.

The electrical welding set is powered by a VG-7500 generator driven by the vehicle's main diesel engine. The vehicle also carries special repair and recovery tools, including tow rods, some of which are stowed in special compartments inside the hull. Folding seats for four passengers are provided inside the hull.

Armament consists of a roof mounted 7.62 mm PKT bow machine gun. Also carried are a radio, an intercom and a FTP-100M NBC and ventilation system.

The BREhM-D is fully amphibious with preparation, being propelled in the water by two water jets mounted at the rear of the hull.

Preparation includes activating the bilge pumps and erecting the trim vane at the front of the hull.

Specifications

BREhM-D Repair and Recovery Vehicle
Crew: 3 + 4
Weight: 8,000 kg
Power-to-weight ratio: 30.0 hp/t (22.4 kW/t)
Length: 5.885 m
Width: 2.63 m
Height: (max) 1.82 m
Ground clearance: 0.1-0.45 m
Max speed:
   (roads) 61 km/h
   (water) 9 km/h
Range:
   (roads) 450-500 km
   (water) 75-90 km
Fording: amphibious
Gradient: 60%
Side slope: 40%

Engine: Type 5D20-240 V-6 liquid-cooled diesel developing 240 hp (179 kW)
Armament: 1 × 7.62 mm PKT MG
Ammunition: 7.62 mm, 1,000 rounds

Status
Production complete. In service with Russian Army. The BMD-1 is also used by Angola, Armenia, Azerbaijan, Belarus, India, Moldova, Russia, Ukraine and Uzbekistan. Some of these countries may also use the BREhM-D repair and recovery vehicle.

Contractor
Volgograd Tractor Plant

Arzamas BREM-K armoured repair and recovery vehicle

Development
The BREM-K (*Bronirovannaya Remontno-evakuatsionnaya-K*) armoured repair and recovery vehicle is based on the hull and chassis of the Arzamas Machinery Plant BTR-80 (8 × 8) Amphibious Personnel Carrier (APC). The BREM-1K is also referred to by the company designation of the GAZ-59033.

More recently the Arzamas Machinery Plant has constructed the much larger BTR-90 (8 × 8) APC which has been produced in small quantities. As of late 2010 there is not a specialised repair and recovery model derived from the BTR-90 APC.

In the Russian Army service the BTR-80 APC will be supplemented by the latest BTR-82/BTR-82A (8 × 8) APC which is now undergoing trails and is expected to soon enter quantity production.

The BTR-82/BTR-82A features a new unified armament module with electric actuators and a digital two-plane stabilisation system coupled to a new day/night sighting system (TKN-4GA/TKN-4GA-02) for 24 hour operations.

Main armament consists of a 30 mm 2A72 cannon (BTR-82) or a 14.5 mm KPVT MG (BTR-82A) and a 7.62 mm PKTM co-axial MG.

Protection has been enhanced due to the installation of spall liners, new energy absorbing floor and suspended crew seats. It is understood that appliqué armour has also been installed.

Finally a more powerful 300 hp diesel engine, new transmission elements and new suspension have been fitted for enhanced mobility. It retains the full amphibious capability of the BTR-80 and BTR-80A series vehicles.

It is expected that eventually an armoured repair and recovery vehicle based on the BTR-82 chassis will be developed.

Description
The main change from the BTR-80 APC is that the one-person, manually operated turret is modified to mount a 7.62 mm PKT machine gun and act as the carrier for two cable drums, one each side. The standard BTR-80 APC is fitted with a one-person manually operated turret armed with one 14.5 mm and one 7.62 mm MG. The cable drums are used together with a collapsible jib crane which is erected on the front hull. When not in use the jib components are stowed along the sides of the hull; the jib takes about 20 minutes to install. The crane, which cannot be traversed, has a lifting capacity of 1.5 tonnes and is supplied by two 75 m lengths of cable from the drums behind the turret.

There is also an alternative, collapsible, manually operated jib crane which can be traversed; this has a lift capacity of 800 kg and is provided with two 5 m lengths of cable. The crane takes 20 minutes to be set up and 23 minutes to be taken down. A hinged table for vices and other tools is located on the left side of the hull.

Located inside the hull is the main recovery winch. This has a pull capacity from 4,400 to 6,000 kg, although this may be increased to 15,000 kg by the introduction of pulley blocks.

The winch is provided with 50 m of cable. When the winch and the crane are in operation, vehicle stability is improved by lowering two hydraulically operated, front-mounted earth spades located under the front of the hull. The hull interior contains folding seats for up to eight passengers.

The turret is armed with a 7.62 mm PKT machine gun, turret traverses is 360° with manual elevation from −4° to +60°.

Other special-to-role equipment carried by the BREM-K includes a 500 kg load capacity platform behind the turret, a GD-304UZ welding set, towing ropes and rods and special tools.

Standard equipment on the BREM-K includes a R-173 radio, R-173P radio receiver, two R-162-01 portable radio sets. Like other members of the BTR-80 (8 × 8) family of APC the BREM-K is fully amphibious being propelled in the water by a water jet mounted at the rear of the hull.

Before entering the water, the trim vane is erected at the front of the vehicle and the electrically operated bilge pumps are activated. An NBC system is also fitted as standard in the BREM-K ARV.

Specifications
BREM-K Armoured Repair and Recovery Vehicle
Crew: 4 + 8
Weight: 14,500 kg
Power-to-weight ratio: 17.9 hp/t (13.4 kW/t)
Length: 7.70 m
Width: 2.95 m
Height: 3 m
Ground clearance: 0.475 m
Track: 2.41 m
Wheelbase: 4.40 m
Max speed:
  (roads) 80 km/h
  (water) 9 km/h
  (water, towing) 5.2 km/h
Range: (roads) 600-800 km
Fording: amphibious
Gradient: 60%
Side slope: 40%
Vertical obstacle: 0.5 m
Trench: 2 m
Engine: KamAZ-7403 V-8 turbocharged diesel developing 260 hp (194 kW)
Transmission: manual 5 forward and 1 reverse gears
Transfer case: 2-speed
Steering: power assisted
Turning radius: 13.2 m
Tyres: 13.00 × 18 (tubeless)
Suspension: torsion bar with hydraulic shock absorbers
Brakes:
  (main) hydraulic on all wheels
  (parking) mechanical
Electrical system: 24 V
Armament: 1 × 7.62 mm PKT MG
Ammunition: 7.62 mm, 1,500 rounds

Status
Production as required. In service with Russian Army. Other users of the BTR-80 series of 8 × 8 APC include Afghanistan, Algeria, Angola, Armenia, Azerbaijan, Bangladesh, Belarus, Burundi, Chad, Colombia, Côte d'Ivoire, Djibouti, Estonia, Finland, Georgia, Hungary, Indonesia, Iraq, Kazakhstan, Korea (North), Korea (South), Kyrgyzstan, Macedonia, Moldova, Pakistan, Russian Federation, Sudan, Sri Lanka, Tajikistan, Turkey, Turkmenistan, Uganda, Ukraine and Uzbekistan. Some of these countries may well operate the BREM-K ARV.

Contractor
Arzamas Machinery Plant

Kurgan BREM-L armoured repair and recovery vehicle

Development
According to the Kurgan Machine Construction Plant, the BREM-L armoured repair and recovery vehicle has been designed to undertake the following missions on the battlefield:

- Recovering disabled vehicles
- Towing controlled and uncontrolled vehicles in various types of terrain on both land and water
- Carrying out repair work in the field such as electric welding, cutting and lifting operations
- Changing vehicle subsystems including the powerpack of the BREM-L armoured repair and recovery vehicle
- Transporting cargo on the jib crane within the repair depot
- Carrying out earth-moving operations when constructing repair bases and fortifications, as well as preparing vehicles for recovery
- Transporting infantry fighting vehicle (for example, BMP-1/BMP-2/BMP-3) spare parts and power packs.

Production of the BREM-L armoured repair and recovery vehicle is undertaken on an as required basis for the home and export markets.

BREM-K armoured repair and recovery vehicle with A-frame erected (T J Gander)
0007347

BREM-L armoured repair and recovery vehicle in travelling configuration and showing front mounted dozer blade in raised position
(Kurgan Machine Construction Plant)   1334237

Description

The BREM-L (*Bronirovannaya Remontno-evakuatsionnaya-L*) armoured repair and recovery vehicle is based on the hull and chassis of the amphibious Kurgan BMP-3 Infantry Fighting Vehicle (IFV).

It is manufactured from new and is intended to be a component in a proposed family of vehicles based on the hull and chassis of the BMP-3. Overall prime contractor for the complete family of BMP-3 vehicles is the Kurgan Machine Construction Plant.

The BREM-L does not have the main turret of the BMP-3 IFV but instead has a small one-man manually-operated turret offset to the right-hand side of the hull roof. This turret is occupied by the commander who has access to a 7.62 mm PKTM Machine Gun (MG) mounted over the turret hatch. A normal crew for the BREM-L is three personnel although there is seating for a further two.

The left-hand side of the hull roof is occupied by a five tonne capacity jib crane; the crane capacity can be doubled to 11 tonnes by introducing a pulley block.

A 15-tonne capacity winch is located inside the hull; the winch capacity can be doubled to 45 tonnes with a pulley block. The winch is provided with 150 m of useable cable. When the winch is in operation, a hydraulically operated dozer blade can be lowered at the front of the hull and this also acts as a stabiliser when the crane is in use.

This hydraulically operated dozer blade can be used when the BREM-L is ashore or afloat and is 3.150 m wide and has a maximum ground penetration depth of 340 mm.

A load area capable of carrying replacement power packs is located over the rear of the vehicle. On land, this load carrying area has a maximum capacity of 300 kg while when afloat it has a maximum capacity of 1,700 kg. Welding equipment is carried. Towbars and other recovery equipment and tools are stowed around the hull roof and sides.

An unditching beam is carried on top of the rear of the BREM-L hull.

Specifications

BREM-L armoured repair and recovery vehicle
Crew: 3 + 2
Weight: 18,700 kg
Power-to-weight ratio: 24.06 hp/t (17.94 kW/t)
Length: 7.64 m
Width: 3.15 m
Height:
(overall) 2.71 m
(turret roof) 2.35 m
Ground clearance: 0.45 m
Track: 2.76 m
Track width: 380 mm
Length of track on ground: 4.06 m
Ground pressure: 0.59 kg/cm²
Max speed:
(roads) 71.5 km/h
(dirt roads) 52 km/h
(water) 9 km/h
Range: (roads) 600 km
Fording: amphibious
Gradient: 60%
Side slope: 30%
Vertical obstacle: 0.8 m
Trench: 2.50 m
Engine: UTD-29T 4-stroke diesel developing 450 hp (336 kW)
Transmission: hydromechanical, 4 forward and 2 reverse gears
Steering: differential with hydrostatic drive
Suspension: hydropneumatic shock absorbers
Armament: 1 × 7.62 mm PKTM MG
Ammunition: 1,000 × 7.62 mm

Status

Production as required. There are seven known users of the BMP-3, Azerbaijan, Cyprus (two), Korea (South), Kuwait, Russia, Ukraine and the United Arab Emirates. Of these, Cyprus and the United Arab Emirates

(total of 65 units) are known to use the BMP-3 based BREM-L armoured repair and recovery vehicle. It is considered probable that some of these other countries, including Russia, also operate the BREM-L armoured repair and recovery vehicle.

Contractor

Kurgan Machine Construction Plant

Singapore

Singapore Technologies Kinetics Bionix Recovery Vehicle

Development

To support the Bionix Infantry Fighting Vehicle (IFV), the first battalion of which became operational with the Singapore Armed Forces early in 1999, the now Singapore Technologies Kinetics (previously known as Singapore Technologies Automotive) developed the Bionix Recovery Vehicle (RCV). This was revealed for the first time early in 2000.

Following extensive trials by the Singapore Armed Forces, the Bionix Recovery Vehicle was accepted for service and a production order placed with Singapore Technologies Kinetics. The vehicle is now in service with the Singapore Armed Forces who is the only user of the Bionix IFV.

The first version of the Bionix IFV is fitted with a two person turret armed with an ATK 25 mm M242 cannon and 7.62 mm Machine Gun (MG). More recent versions are fitted with a two person turret armed with an ATK 30 mm MK44 cannon and 7.62 mm MG.

There is also the 40/50 version which is fitted with a STK developed cupola armed with a STK developed .50 MG and 40 mm Automatic Grenade Launcher (AGL). This cupola is also fitted to some upgraded M113 series vehicles in service with the SAF.

In addition, there is a Bionix Armoured Vehicle Launched Bridge (AVLB) which is covered in a separate entry in *Jane's Military Vehicles and Logistics*. The latest variant of the Bionix to enter service is the Trailblazer flail type mine clearance system.

Description

To reduce procurement and operating costs, the Bionix RCV uses the same diesel powerpack, hydropneumatic suspension system and other automotive components as the standard Bionix IFV but has a new all-welded steel hull with an additional layer of passive armour for increased battlefield survivability.

No details of the protection levels of the Bionix recovery have been released but the highest level of protection is over the frontal arc.

The driver is seated at the front of the vehicle on the left with the powerpack to his right, other two crew members are in the middle of the vehicle with the rear of the vehicle being taken up with specialised recovery equipment.

The driver has a single-piece hatch that opens left rear and three day periscopes for forward observation, the centre one of these can be replaced by a night vision periscope for night driving. The vehicle commander, seated on the left has a rear opening hatch and three day periscopes for forward observation while the winch and crane operator, seated on the right, has a forward opening roof hatch.

Bionix RCV has been designed to carry out two main functions. First the recovery of tracked and wheeled vehicles bogged down in soft ground or trapped in ditches.

Second is the removal and replacement of Line Replaceable Units (LRU) of damaged and disabled vehicles by means of the 30 metric tonne crane so that they can return to duty as soon as possible. It can recover tracked and wheeled vehicles up to Military Load Class 30 (MLC 30).

In order to carry out its mission, the Bionix RCV is fitted with a crane and a recovery winch, both of which are hydraulically operated and run from a power take-off from the Detroit Diesel 6V-92TA engine. The crane is mounted on the hull roof towards the rear and when travelling is traversed to the front. The crane has a telescopic boom and a maximum lifting capacity of 30 metric tonnes and a maximum horizontal reach of 6.5 m.

Bionix recovery vehicle with telescopic jib of crane extended over front of vehicle   0073072

The crane can be traversed through a full 360°. It can be operated either directly from the operator's station or by remote control. This crane is not only capable of lifting complete power packs and the complete turret for replacement, it can also assist in the recovery of bogged down vehicles. When being used to lift heavy loads stabilisers are lowered manually at the front and rear of the Bionix RCV.

The Treibmatic recovery winch is provided with 90 m of cable and has a maximum pull on a single line of 25 tonnes which can be increased to 50 tonnes on a double line pull. The winch is used to the rear and a stabiliser is lowered to the ground when the winch is being used to recover bogged down vehicles.

The winch and crane can be used at the same time, which is of particular use when recovering vehicles from ditches. Other specialised equipment carried includes tools and tow bars.

The RCV is equipped with two pintle-mounted 7.62 mm MGs, mounted one each at the commander's and winch operator's station with a bank of three electrically operated 76 mm smoke grenade launchers being mounted on either side of the hull, firing forwards.

Specifications

Bionix Recovery Vehicle
Crew: 3
Combat weight: 24,000 kg
Power-to-weight ratio: 19.79 hp/t (14.76 kW/t)
Length: 6.10 m
Width: 2.78 m
Height: 2.82 m
Track width: 430 mm
Max road speed: 70 km/h
Cross-country: 25 km/h
Acceleration: 0 to 32 km/h in 9 s
Range: 415 km at 45 km/h
Gradient: 60%
Side slope: 30%
Vertical obstacle: 0.60 m
Trench: 2 m
Pivot turn: 3.1 m
Powerpack: Detroit Diesel 6V-92TA 2-cycle diesel developing 475 hp (354 kW) at 2,400 rpm
Transmission: L3 Combat Propulsion Systems HMPT 500-3EC fully automatic transmission
Steering: hydrostatic
Brakes: multidisc oil-cooled
Suspension: hydropneumatic
Electrical system: 28 V
Batteries: 4 × 12 V, 200 Ah
Alternator: 300 A
Armament: 2 × 7.62 mm MGs
Smoke grenade launchers: 2 × 3-barrelled 76 mm
NBC system: no
Night vision equipment: yes
Recovery system:
    (crane) 30 metric tonne with 12 tonnes lift
    (winch) constant torque with up to 25 tonnes single pull or 50 tonnes double pull

Status
Production as required. In service with Singapore Armed Forces.

Contractor
Singapore Technologies Kinetics

Slovakia

ZTS VT-72B armoured recovery vehicle

Development
The VT-72B Armoured Recovery Vehicle (ARV) was developed in the former Czechoslovakia and is based on the chassis of the Russian-designed T-72M1 MBT, which has been produced in Slovakia by the now ZTS Tees Defence (previously ZTS Tees Martin) with some input from concerns in the Czech Republic.

The VT-72B differs from the Russian BREM-1 (based on the Russian T-72 MBT chassis) armoured recovery and repair vehicle in many respects, not the least of which in having the swivelling hydraulic crane on the right-hand side of the superstructure at the front rather than the left.

Of the total of the vehicle's main assemblies, 13 are the same as the T-72M1 MBT, 23 assemblies have been adapted and 12 are of a new design.

In late 1993, India purchased 35 VT-72B at a unit cost of INR28.9 million each. The total order was valued at USD31.5 million, including spares and the free transfer of technology. There were 10 vehicles provided complete,

VT-72B armoured recovery vehicle (T J Gander)   0511465

the first being delivered in May 1994, with the remaining 25 vehicles delivered in semi-knocked-down kit form for assembly at the Bharat Heavy Electricals Limited (BHEL) plant in Trichy, southern India.

BHEL signed a contract to supply around 210 ARVs to the Indian Army, with an option to eventually double that number; at that stage it was anticipated that the total Indian requirement was some 400 vehicles. However, due to local production difficulties, a second order for 78 further complete VT-72Bs was placed with the Slovakian concern.

A variant known as the VT-72A has been reported with a lighter crane capable of lifting only 7,000 kg and some other changes. As far as can be determined this variant was not developed past the prototype stage.

As well as marketing the VT-72B ARV and updated versions of the Russian T-72M1 MBT, ZTS have also developed the MT-72 scissors type Armoured Vehicle Launch Bridge (AVLB). Details of the AVLB are provided in a separate entry in *Jane's Military Vehicles and Logistics*.

Production of all these vehicles is currently undertaken on an 'as required' basis by ZTS.

Description
The VT-72B ARV has a crew of two, commander and driver, although there is provision to carry a further three personnel, all housed in an armoured superstructure built on to the chassis based on the T-72M1 MBT.

The VT-72B can be used to recover stranded vehicles and tow them to a place of safety where the 19-tonne crane jib can be used to remove major components such as tank turrets and powerpacks. Further repair work can be accomplished using the tools and electric welding kit carried on the vehicle, while further spares and equipment can be carried on a load platform capable of bearing up to 4,000 kg and measuring 1.4 × 2 m.

The hydrostatic main recovery winch is located centrally with a usable 200 m of rope cable on a drum located over the forward part of the engine compartment. The winch has a main traction force of 300 kN with the cable led to the front through a pulley arrangement on the front hull. An auxiliary winch has a 10 kN capability and is provided with 400 m of rope cable.

The main winch is used in conjunction with a front-mounted straight dozer blade that can be used as an earth anchor for heavy recovery tasks. The blade is 3.36 m wide and can be lowered into the ground to a depth of 300 mm. As a secondary function, the blade may also be used to clear battlefield obstacles and debris or create scrapes to assist in the concealment of other vehicles.

The swivelling hydraulic crane is mounted on a small turntable on the right front of the hull next to the superstructure. The crane has a maximum lifting capacity of 19 tonnes and an arm radius of 7.6 m. Arm traverse is 360°; maximum lift angle is 72°. The operator can control the main and auxiliary winch and crane from within the vehicle or up to 7 m away from the vehicle with the aid of a remote-control device.

Racks located over the rear of the vehicle carry extra fuel in both drums and jerrycans.

The main armament for air defence is a 12.7 mm NSV Heavy machine Gun (HMG) provided with a K 10-T collimator sight.

The VT-72B can lay its own smoke screen by injecting diesel fuel into the exhaust outlet on the left side of the hull. An NBC system is fitted as standard.

Variants

VT-72M4 CZ armoured recovery vehicle
To support the upgraded T-72M4 CZ MBTs, three VT-72B Armoured Recovery Vehicles (ARV) have been upgraded to the enhanced VT-72M4 CZ ARV standard by VOP-25 with deliveries now complete.

In addition to the installation of the new NIMDA powerpack, other enhancements include fitting the BVIS vehicle information system, diagnostic and navigation system, DICOMs RF-1350 tactical and PR20 personal radios, new driver's instrument and controls, higher level of protection, installation of camouflage netting, infra-red masking matting, new vehicle intercom, NV-3P driver's night vision camera, protective paint, new tracks, three TV cameras for improved situational awareness and a TV camera for deep fording.

Upgraded VT-72M4 CZ armoured recovery vehicle in travelling configuration (Michal Zdobinsky)   1299253

Specifications
VT-72B Armoured Recovery Vehicle
Crew: 2 + 3
Combat weight: 46,500 kg
Ground pressure: 0.90 kg/cm^2
Power-to-weight ratio: 13.47 kW/t (18.06 hp/t)
Length: (with extra fuel tanks) 8.15 m
Width overall: 3.37 m
Height: (incl MG) 2.64 m
Ground clearance: 0.435 m
Max speed: (roads) 60 km/h
Range:
   (roads, basic fuel) 485 km
   (roads, with extra tanks) 620 km
   (dirt roads, basic fuel) 235-470 km
   (dirt roads, with extra tanks) 300-600 km
Fording:
   (normal) 1.2 m
   (with preparation) 1.8 m
   (with kit) 5 m
Engine: V-46-6 V-12 diesel developing 626 kW (840 hp)
Transmission: synchromesh, hydraulically assisted with 7 forward and 1 reverse gears
Steering: clutch and brake
Suspension: torsion bar
Armament: 1 × 12.7 mm NSV HMG

Main winch
Rated line pull: 300 kN
Usable rope length: 200 m

Auxiliary winch
Rated line pull: 10 kN
Usable rope length: 400 m

Jib crane
Lift capacity: 19,000 kg
Max crane arm radius: 7.59 m
Traverse: 360°

Dozer blade
Width: 3.36 m
Digging depth: 300 mm
Max load capacity: 900 kN

Status
Production as required. In service with Czech Republic, India (local assembly), Russia and Slovakia.

Contractor
ZTS Tees Defence as

Marketed by:
Kerametal

VPV armoured recovery vehicle

Development
The VPV *(Vyprost'ovaci Pásové Vozidlo)* tracked armoured recovery vehicle is a Czech modification of the Russian Kurgan Machine Construction Plant BMP-2 Infantry Fighting Vehicle (IFV). It has been licence-produced in the Czech Republic and Slovakia as the BVP-2.

The VPV is used to support Czech and Slovak armies' motorised infantry units and can recover, tow or push BMP-1, BRDM-2 (4 × 4), BTR-60 (8 × 8) and other tracked and wheeled vehicles with weights up to 15 tonnes. The VPV is very similar in layout and type of equipment to the Russian-equivalent BREM-2.

VPV armoured recovery vehicle from the front   0038809

Production of the VPV armoured recovery vehicle had been completed. It is probable that there are a number of surplus vehicles for export.

Description
The VPV has a crew of two or three: the commander, who also operates the vehicle's crane and winch; the driver; and an optional recovery fitter. Although the BMP-2 IFV chassis, running gear and engine have been retained, the turret is replaced by a cable drum with a hatch at its centre. An extendable traversing crane is installed on top of the hull rear.

It has a maximum lifting capability of 5,200 kg with the boom extended 1.35 m; maximum boom extension is 4.5 m. The crane can be operated by remote control. The vehicle's diesel fuel capacity has been increased to 480 litres.

The VPV has a recovery winch with a tractive force of a basic 125 kN although this can be increased to up to 345 kN by the use of return pulleys. The winch has 120 m of 19 mm diameter cable. There is also a spade which is hydraulically lowered when the winch is in use. Also carried are tool kits, a 300 A welding set and cutting devices; the commander and driver are both trained welders.

Other equipment carried on the VPV include a R-123M radio set, a R-124 intercom, fire extinguishers and smoke generating equipment. There are two PR-22 pocket type radio sets provided for dismounted use together with an associated battery charger.

The VPV retains the amphibious characteristics of the BMP-2 IFV but with some restrictions. It can ford water obstacles if the waves are not higher than 100 mm and in current velocities not more than 1.2 m/s.

When afloat the VPV is propelled in the water by its tracks. Before entering the water the trim vane is erected at the front of the hull and the electrically operated bilge pumps are switched on.

A version of this vehicle used by Hungary is known as the BMP- 1 VPV.

Specifications
VPV Armoured Recovery Vehicle
Crew: 2 or 3
Combat weight: 14,000 kg
Power-to-weight ratio: 20.36 hp/t (15.18 kW/t)
Length: 6.47 m
Width overall: 2.94 m
Height: (crane lowered) 2.5 m
Max speed:
   (road) 70 km/h
   (water) 7 km/h
Range: 500 km
Fuel capacity: 480 litres
Engine: UTD-20 water-cooled diesel developing 285 hp (213 kW)
Armament: 1 × 7.62 mm PKT MG
Ammunition: 7.62 mm - 2,000 rounds

Status
Production complete. In service with the Czech and Slovak armies, Hungary and Russia. A number of VPV ARVs care now surplus to requirements and could be available for export.

Contractor
Podpolianske Strojarne Detva

Marketed by:
Kerametal

South Africa

BAE Systems Land Systems South Africa Gemsbok (4 × 4) armoured recovery vehicle

Development
The Gemsbok (4 × 4) armoured recovery vehicle is a member of the Casspir family of vehicles based on a wheeled armoured personnel carrier, the Casspir Mark 2.

Gemsbok (4 × 4) armoured recovery vehicle in travelling configuration

0511471

These vehicles were originally designed to operate as internal security and riot control vehicles but can also operate over long periods in the bush and desert terrain conditions prevailing in southern Africa.

The Gemsbok and Casspir were originally developed and produced by TFM (Pty) Limited, who was subsequently taken over by Reumech OMC. Late in 1999 the latter company was taken over by Vickers Defence Systems of the UK and renamed Vickers OMC. Late in 2002, Alvis purchased Vickers Defence Systems and Vickers OMC was renamed Alvis OMC. In late 2004, BAE Systems took over Alvis PLC and Alvis OMC became BAE Systems Land Systems OMC. Today the company is officially know as BAE Systems Land Systems South Africa.

An increasing number of countries are now using surplus ex-South African Casspir vehicles but, as far as it is known, only South Africa has the Gemsbok in service.

Description
The Gemsbok uses the standard Casspir Mark 2 chassis, which in its turn is based on automotive components of a 15-tonne (4 × 4) commercial truck chassis. The armoured front cab uses a combination of armour plated and high-alloy steels and has a V-shaped monocoque hull to withstand land mine explosions.

The hull can withstand three simultaneous TM-57-type anti-tank mine explosions (or an equivalent of between 18 and 20 kg of TNT) without penetration, although mechanical component damage may occur. The armour is protection against NATO 7.62 and 5.56 mm ball ammunition and all windows use bullet-resistant glass. Mounted on the roof next to the driver's position is a one-man steel turret which can mount one 7.62 mm MG4 machine gun. A further 7.62 mm MG4 machine gun can be mounted in the front left windscreen.

The armoured cab has seating for three of the crew of a recovered vehicle as well as the recovery vehicle crew of driver and commander. The armoured cab also contains the 185-litre diesel fuel tank. Cab ventilation is provided by two impeller fans.

The Gemsbok recovery unit is mounted on the open chassis behind the fully enclosed armoured cab and consists of a twin boom, two service drum recovery hoist with a maximum capacity of 5,000 kg. Rectangular section-stabilising legs are provided on each side of the chassis when the hoist is in use. Tool box and other stowage is provided on the rear area for extra recovery equipment and special tools. A standard vehicle tool kit is carried inside the main cab.

Specifications
Gemsbok armoured recovery vehicle
Cab seating: 2 + 3
Configuration: 4 × 4
Weight:
　(empty) 9,600 kg
　(loaded) 14,800 kg
Max load: 5,000 kg
Towed load: 15,000 kg
Length: 6.74 m
Width: 2.5 m
Height: 3.12 m
Ground clearance: 0.355 m
Wheelbase: 4.3 m
Angle of approach: 46°
Max speed: 87 km/h
Range:
　(road) 850 km
　(cross-country) 560 km
Fuel capacity: 185 litres
Max gradient: 60%
Side slope: 30%
Vertical obstacle: 0.5 m
Trench: 0.95 m

Fording: 1 m
Engine: ADE 352 T 5.675 litre 6-cylinder vertical in-line turbocharged diesel developing 121 kW (162.5 hp) at 2,800 rpm
Gearbox: Mercedes-Benz DB G 3/60 - 5/7, 5 synchromesh with 5 forward and 1 reverse gears
Clutch: single dry plate
Transfer box: Mercedes-Benz 2 speed
Steering: ball and nut, power-assisted
Turning circle: 18.3 m
Suspension: semi-elliptic leaf springs on needle roller bearings with telescopic shock-absorbers front and rear (double spring pack at rear)
Tyres: 14.00 × 20
Number of tyres: 4 + 1 spare
Brakes:
　(main) dual-circuit air-assisted hydraulic with engine-mounted exhaust brake
　(parking) mechanical
Electrical system: 12 V
Battery: 1 × 12 V
Alternator: 55 A
Armament: 1 or 2 × 7.62 mm MG4 MG

Status
Production complete. In service with South African Police. No longer marketed.

In recent years export sales of surplus Casspir vehicles have been made to many countries including Angola, Djibouti, India, Indonesia, Mozambique, Nepal, Nigeria, Norway, Senegal, Sweden, United Nations and the US. It should be noted that in some cases these are used by private countries rather that government armed forces. As far as it is known there have been no sales of the Gemsbok.

Contractor
BAE Systems Land Systems South Africa (previously known as BAE Systems Land Systems OMC)

Spain

GAMESA M-47 VR armoured recovery vehicle

Development
Following a competition, in 1994 the Spanish Army selected GAMESA to convert 22 old M-47E1 (a modified version of the old US-supplied M47 tank originally armed with a 90 mm gun and upgraded in Spain with a new diesel engine and 105 mm gun) tanks into armoured recovery vehicles. Final deliveries to the Spanish Army were made late in 1996 under the designation M-47 VR.

Although the original intention was to use these vehicles to support US-supplied Spanish Army M48 and M60 tanks, experience has shown that they were capable of providing support for the German Krauss-Maffei Wegmann Leopard 2 series MBT which is now in service with the Spanish Army.

Between 1995 and 1996 the Spanish Army took delivery of a total of 108 ex-Germany Army Leopard 2A4 MBTs.

In addition, General Dynamics Santa Bárbara Sistemas built 219 Leopard 2A6 MBT opimised to meet the requirements of the Spanish Army.

These are designated the Leopard 2E by the Spanish Army and all vehicles have now been delivered.

It is expected that some of the Leopard 2A4 may now be converted into more specialised roles and replace existing vehicles based on obsolete tank chassis.

These will include armoured recovery vehicles, armoured engineer vehicles and armoured vehicle launched bridges currently deployed by the Spanish Army.

The Spanish Army has now taken delivery of a total of 16 German Rheinmetall Landsysteme Büffel ARV. Of these, four came from the German production line and the remaining 12 were manufactured under licence in Spain by General Dynamics Santa Bárbara Sistemas. These were manufactured at the Sevilla facilities of the company.

Description
The M-47 VR ARV conversion involved replacing the complete turret and part of the hull of the M-47. A new, welded, armoured superstructure houses the crew of four consisting of commander, driver, radio operator and the recovery equipment operator.

The driver's station has been moved with regard to the original vehicle to allow adequate visibility in the converted vehicle. The brakes, steering systems and power pack of the more recent M48 tank, have been incorporated in the M-47 VR.

The superstructure is of all-welded steel armour construction and provides protection from small arms fire up 12.7 mm in calibre as well as shell splinters.

The M-47 VR has been fitted with a front-mounted bulldozer-type blade driven by two hydraulic cylinders with two roles. The first is to stabilise the tank when the crane or winch are being used and second is to carry out dozing operations.

GAMESA M-47 VR recovery vehicle, with dozer blade lowered and telescopic jib of crane extended (GAMESA)   1127958

The blade is 3.7 m wide and 900 mm high which allows the front of the tank to be raised 300 mm. It is also equipped with three ripper-scarifiers located on the rear of the blade.

The hydraulic unit is housed inside the hull, the variable flow piston pump with load sensing is driven through an electromagnetic clutch and cardan joint, by an additional power-take-off built onto the L3 Combat Propulsion Systems AVDS-1790-2D diesel engine. It is also provided with a constant speed regulator which works when the hydraulic system is operative.

The main 35,000 kg constant pull winch is housed inside the hull and is provided with a cable 120 m long and 33 mm in diameter, this leaves the vehicle guided by means of an airtight roller box placed on the front of the tank. With the return pulley, which is included in the accessories of the tank, pulling can be doubled to 70,000 kg.

The release speed and rapid collection of the cable is adjustable from 0 to 40 m/min and working speed under load is adjustable from 0 to 8 m/min.

The auxiliary winch is located on the front of the vehicle and can be used to handle 33 mm diameter cable in lengths of 100 m.

Mounted on the front right side of the vehicle is a telescopic crane which can be traversed through a full 360° and has a torque capacity of 60 tons at one metre (598 kN.m). The crane is provided with 100 m of 16 mm diameter cable which allows it to raise 22,000 kg. An overload prevention system is fitted as standard.

The length of the jib is 6.1 m and the telescopic boom adds 2.5 m to its reach. Total length of the extended jib is 8.6 m and maximum height to hook is 9.75 m.

Armament comprises a .50 (12.7 mm) M2 HB Machine Gun (MG) on the tank commander's cupola and a 7.62 mm MG on the front of the vehicle. Two banks of four electrically operated 76 mm smoke dischargers cover an arc of 40° to the left and right of the vehicle.

Electrical and hydraulic intakes for the use of tools equipped with snap on connectors are located on the right side of the tank.

In case of an emergency, such as the breakdown of the main diesel engine or lack of main hydraulic power, the vehicle is fitted with an auxiliary electric pump which allows the crane, bulldozer blade and winch to be returned to the travelling position.

Standard equipment includes: engine smoke generator; NBC ventilation system; fire detection and suppression system for the engine compartment; fire and explosion suppression system for the crew compartment; and lifting points to enable it to be loaded on board ships.

If required, provision is made for the transport of a complete power pack (engine, transmission and cooling system) for a M48, M60 or Leopard 2 MBT.

Specifications

M-47 VR Armoured Recovery Vehicle
Crew: 4
Weight:
   (combat) 48,500 kg
   (empty) 46,450 kg
Power-to-weight ratio: 15.67 hp/t (11.69 kW/t)
Length: 8.4 m
Width: 3.7 m
Height: (without armament) 3.07 m
Ground clearance: 0.469 m
Max speed: 48 km/h
Max road range: 500 km
Fuel capacity: 1,420 litres
Fording: 1.2 m
Vertical obstacle: 0.9 m
Trench: 2.6 m
Gradient: 60%
Side slope: 30%
Engine: L3 Combat Propulsion Systems AVDS-1790-2D diesel developing.760 hp (567 kW) at 2,400 rpm
Electrical system: 24 V
Batteries: 6 × 12 V, 300 Ah

Armament:
   (main) 1 × .50 (12.7 mm) M2 HB MG
   (secondary) 1 × 7.62 mm MG
Smoke grenade launchers: 2 × 4-barrelled 76 mm
Ammunition:
   (main) 600 × 12.7 mm
   (secondary) 2,000 × 7.62 mm

Status
Production complete, no longer marketed. In service with the Spanish Army (22 units).

Contractor
GAMESA International

General Dynamics European Land Systems Santa Bárbara Sistemas Pizarro recovery combat vehicle

Development
To develop an Infantry Fighting Vehicle (IFV) to meet the requirements of the Austria and Spanish armed forces, a joint venture company called ASCOD (which stands for Austria Spanish Co-Operative Development) was formed by the now General Dynamics European Land Systems Santa Bárbara Sistemas and the new General Dynamics European Land Systems Steyr.

The Austrian Army call the vehicle the Ulan while the Spanish Army call this vehicle the Pizarro.

The now General Dynamics European Land Systems Steyr (at that time Steyr-Daimler-Puch) built a total of 112 Ulan for the Austrian Army at their Vienna, Austria, facility, but it is not expected that any additional vehicles will be ordered. There were no special versions of the Ulan supplied to the Austrian Army.

The now General Dynamics European Land Systems Santa Bárbara Sistemas was awarded the first Pizarro contract that covered the supply of 144 vehicles of which 122 were in the IFV configuration and the remaining 22 in the command post configuration. Production of this batch has been completed.

The company is now building a second batch of 190 Pizarro to a higher standard with production now underway at their Seville facility. This covers the supply of 106 Infantry Fighting Vehicle (IFV), 27 observer vehicles, 10 recovery vehicles and 47 armoured engineer vehicles.

Description
The Pizarro recovery combat vehicle's hull is of the all-welded steel armour construction that provides the occupants with protection from small arms fire and shell-splinters, with the highest level of protection over the frontal arc.

The driver is seated at the front on the left side and is provided with three forward-facing day-light periscopes. The middle periscope can, if required, be replaced by a night vision device. Ingress and egress for the driver is via a single-piece armoured hatch, which opens to the rear and left.

The powerpack is to the right of the driver, with the raised area to the rear being for the specialised recovery equipment and the remainder of the crew.

The commander is seated to the rear of the driver and is provided with a cupola fitted with periscopes to give full 360° vision and a 7.62 mm MG3 machine gun for self-defence purposes. Addition self-defence is provided by the 12 × 76 mm electrically operated smoke grenade launchers.

Computer generated drawing of the Pizarro recovery combat vehicle in travelling configuration with dozer/stabiliser blade raised and crane stowed
(General Dynamics European Land Systems Santa Bárbara Sistemas)   1296620

Suspension is of the torsion bar type with either side having seven dual rubber-rimmed road wheels, a drive sprocket at the front and idler at the rear. There are also four return rollers that support the inner portion of the track only.

Mounted at the front of the chassis is a hydraulically operated blade that can be used as dozer blade or a stabiliser when the crane or winch is being used. This blade is 3 m wide, 800 mm in height and has a maximum cutting depth of 400 mm.

The hydraulically operated crane is pivoted at the left rear of the chassis and is fitted with a telescopic jib which is retracted to the rear when travelling.

When heavy items of equipment are being lifted a single stabiliser-leg can be deployed at the left rear of the chassis.

The main hydraulic winch has a maximum direct pull of 25.5 tonnes and capable of two-speed operation; slow at 10 m/min and fast at 38 m/min. The winch is supplied with a total cable length of 100 m and is a nominal 26 mm in diameter.

Also fitted is a secondary hydraulic winch which is provided with 100 m of 5 mm diameter cable.

Other equipment installed includes an NBC system of the over pressure type, automatic fire detection and suppression system in the engine compartment, explosion detection and suppression system in the crew compartment, air conditioning and heating system, oxy-acetylene-based welding and cutting equipment, tools and an electrical power generator.

Variants

Common Base Platform
A further development of this chassis, called the ASCOD 2, is the Common Base Platform (CBP) for the General Dynamics UK Specialist Vehicle for the UK MoD.

The company was awarded a GBP500 million development contract in mid-2010 covering the design and construction of seven prototype vehicles for trials.

This is understood to include three scout vehicles, two protected mobility vehicles (armoured personnel carriers) and two repair and recovery vehicles.

Specifications

Pizarro Recovery Combat Vehicle
Crew: 4
Weight: 33,000 kg
Power-to-weight ratio: 21.85 hp/t (16.29 kW/t)
Length: 7 m
Width: 3.13 m
Height: 2.6 m
Ground clearance: 0.45 m
Track width: 500 mm
Max speed: 65 km/h
Range: 500 km
Fuel capacity: 860 litres
Fording: 1.2 m
Gradient: 75%
Side slope: 40%
Vertical obstacle: 0.95 m
Trench: 2.5 m
Engine: MTU 8V-199-TE-20 V-8 diesel developing 721 hp (538 kW)
Transmission: Renk HSWL 106C3 automatic hydro mechanical with 6 forward and 3 reverse gears
Suspension: torsion bar with hydraulic shock absorbers at 1st, 2nd and 6th road wheel stations
Electrical system: 24 V
Batteries: 6 × 24 V, 300 Ah
Armament: 1 × 7.62 mm MG3 MG
Smoke grenade launchers: 12 × 76 mm
NBC system: yes
Night vision equipment: yes

Status
In production for Spanish Army (10 units).

Contractor
General Dynamics European Land Systems Santa Bárbara Sistemas

---

General Dynamics European Land Systems Santa Bárbara Sistemas SA BMR 3560.55 armoured recovery and repair vehicle

Development
The General Dynamics Santa Bárbara Sistemas BMR 3560.55 armoured recovery and repair vehicle, is based on the hull and suspension of the BMR 3560.50 (6 × 6) armoured personnel carrier and has many components in common with the basic vehicle. It is intended for the recovery of other vehicles in the BMR 600 range (and similar vehicles) and also has some repair capabilities for immobilised vehicles in the field.

BMR 3560.55 armoured repair and recovery vehicle in travelling configuration (Pierre Touzin) 1127959

Late in 2007, it was stated that at least part of the Spanish Army's fleet of BMR-600 (6 × 6) IFV and variants would be replaced by a number of new vehicles including Mine Resistant Ambush Protected Vehicle (MRAP) models.

Late in 2007, Spain placed an order with IVECO Defence vehicles covering the supply of an initial batch of 40 Light Multipurpose Vehicles (LMV) (4 × 4) and these were all delivered by March 2008.

In September 2008, General Dynamics Santa Bárbara Sistemas of Spain was awarded a EUR64.6 million contract by the Spanish MoD to supply 100 RG32 Mk 5E mine protected vehicles to the Spanish Army.

This order comprised 85 APC, 10 ambulance vehicles and five command post vehicles and all vehicles have now been delivered, with first vehicles deployed to Afghanistan in October 2009.

General Dynamics Santa Bárbara Sistemas is the prime contractor and provides programme management, engineering and logistic support with BAE Systems Land Systems South Africa (previously BAE Systems Land Systems OMC) supplying vehicles as a sub-contractor.

In the longer term, the Spanish Army will field a replacement for the remaining BMR-600 vehicles and this is expected to be an 8 × 8 vehicle.

Description
The BMR 3560.55 armoured repair and recovery vehicle retains the basic 6 × 6 configuration and hull of the armoured personnel carrier virtually unchanged, the main alteration being the installation of a hydraulic crane on a roof-mounted turntable.

This hydraulically operated crane has a full 360° traverse and a lifting capacity of 12,000 kg at one metre (118 kN.m). The horizontal reach is 6 m and the maximum hook elevation is 8 m.

To stabilise the crane when deployed, the BMR 3560.55 has four hydraulically operated stabiliser jacks, one on each side between the first and second set of roadwheels and the other two at the rear behind the rear set of wheels.

Access to the interior of the vehicle is gained via a large single-piece rear ramp that opens downwards. The driver's position may be reached from inside the main cabin or through a roof hatch. There is another roof hatch for the commander and another for the crane operator towards the rear. The commander's position has a cupola with a machine gun mounting (.50 (12.7 mm) M2 HB or 7.62 mm MG1A1) that can be operated from within the vehicle.

The weapon ports of the basic BMR-600 are retained, allowing the crew to use their personal weapons from within the vehicle and a rack of six forward facing German designed Krauss-Maffei Wegmann 76 mm smoke dischargers is situated on the left-hand side of the hull.

Inside the main vehicle cabin there is provision for various tool cabinets and other special racks but the main space is occupied by a winch with a pulling capacity of 7,000 kg; by using double pulleys this can be increased to 14,000 kg. The cable length is 100 m. The normal front-mounted winch of the BMR-600 is retained. This has a pulling capacity of 4,500 kg. The controls for the main winch are located close to those of the crane, that is, inside the crane operator's turret hatch.

The crane and main winch can both be operated from within the main cabin with the rear door closed. When the rear ramp is closed, the main winch cable is passed through the rear door emergency hatch.

To enable the vehicle to be used in the repair role the BMR 3560.55 carries a canvas penthouse and supports on the roof and sides. For this purpose, lighting is supplied by a 50 m long string of lamps with power from a 1.5 kW generator.

A workshop tool kit, welding kit, slings, chains and other recovery and repair equipment are also carried. A lockable tool chest is located just inside the left of the rear door. Radio equipment is located against the engine bulkhead.

The original Pegaso diesel engine installed in the BMR (6 × 6) series of vehicles has been replaced by the more fuel efficient Scania D9 engine developing 310 hp at 2,200 rpm. A total of 700 engines were ordered in 1996 with first deliveries taking place late in the same year. This upgrade programme is now complete. This upgrade package has been offered on the export market but as of late 2010 there are no known sales.

Specifications

BMR 3560.55 Armoured Recovery and Repair Vehicle
Crew: 5
Configuration: 6 × 6
Weight: (combat - APC) 13,750 kg
Power-to-weight ratio: 22.54 hp/t (16.81 kW/t)
Length: 6.15 m
Width: 2.5 m
Height: (hull top) 2 m
Ground clearance: (adjustable) 0.45 m
Track: 2.08 m
Wheelbase: 1.65 m + 1.65 m
Angle of approach/departure: 50°/45°
Max speed: 100 km/h
Fuel capacity: 400 litres
Max range: 1,000 km
Gradient: 60%
Side slope: 30%
Vertical obstacle: 0.6 m
Trench: 1.2 m
Engine: Pegaso model 9157/8 6-cylinder in-line diesel developing 310 hp (231 kW) at 2,200 rpm (replaced in Spanish Army vehicles by a Scania D9 diesel developing 310 hp (231 kW) at 2,200 rpm)
Transmission: ZF 6 HP 500 automatic with 6 forward and 1 reverse gears
Steering: hydraulic
Turning radius: 7.5 m
Suspension: ZF hydropneumatic, independent each wheel
Tyres: 13.00 × 20
Electrical system: 24 V
Batteries: 1 × 12 V, 150 Ah
Armament:
    1 × .50 (12.7 mm) M2 HB or 7.62 mm MG1A3 MG
    6 × 76 mm smoke grenade dischargers

Status

Production complete. In service with the Spanish Armed Forces and the Saudi Arabian and Egyptian armies.

Contractor

General Dynamics Santa Bárbara Sistemas European Land Systems

Sweden

BAE Systems Global Combat Systems CV90 armoured recovery vehicle

Development

The Combat Vehicle 90 (CV90) infantry combat vehicle was developed to meet the operational requirements of the Swedish Army with BAE Systems Bofors being responsible for the turret armed with a 40 mm L/70 cannon and BAE Systems Hägglunds for the full-tracked chassis.

In addition, BAE Systems Hägglunds was also responsible for the design, development and production of the CV90 Armoured Recovery Vehicle (ARV).

First prototype of the CV90 armoured recovery vehicle was completed in 1991 with the Swedish Defence Material Administration placing the first production contract in 1993. First production vehicles were delivered to the Swedish Army in 1995 and it is understood that a total of 26 CV90 ARV vehicles were supplied.

As of late 2010 the only customer for the CV90 ARV was Sweden. Export customers for the CV90 include Denmark (45 delivered), Finland (57 + 45 delivered), Norway (104 delivered), Netherlands (184 being delivered) and Switzerland (186 delivered).

BAE Systems Hägglunds is today part of BAE Systems Global Combat Systems and the CV90 ARV continues to be marketed to current and future family customers.

The Swedish Army did take delivery of a total of 24 now BAE Systems Global Combat Systems Bargningsbandvagn Armoured Recovery Vehicles (ARV) which were delivered in 1973. These have now been phased out of service and scrapped.

Description

The CV90 ARV is based on the chassis, running gear, power pack and armoured steel hull of the CV90, but in place of the usual turret, there is a raised cupola for the commander. The crew of five consists of commander, gunner, driver, winch operator and one additional member. There is also provision for one passenger.

Standard equipment includes a front-mounted stabiliser blade, which can also be used for dozing operations. The hull contains two hydraulic capstan winches. Each winch has a constant pulling force and cable speed over the entire cable length. Using a four part pull on each winch, the CV90 ARV has a maximum recovery capability of 61 tonnes to the front. The pulling capacity to the rear is 33 tonnes and 8.4 tonnes to the side. A light crane with a telescopic jib is fitted on the left side of the hull roof towards the rear. As an option, this crane can be replaced by one able to lift a power pack.

BAE Systems Global Combat Systems CV90 armoured recovery vehicle in travelling configuration   0069311

The vehicle has an overpressure NBC system and an automatic Halon fire detection and suppression system.

A 7.62 mm machine gun with 4,000 rounds of ammunition is carried for local defence. A total of six smoke dischargers in two groups of three is provided.

Optional equipment is available for the CV90 ARV including enhanced armour protection and a defensive aids suite.

Specifications

CV90 armoured recovery vehicle
Crew: 4 + 1
Weight combat: 35,000 kg
Power-to-weight ratio: 15.71 hp/t (11.71 kW/t)
Ground pressure: 0.56 kg/cm²
Length: 7.9 m
Width: 3.2 m
Height:
    (over cupola) 2.7 m
    (roof) 1.73 m
Ground clearance: 0.4 m
Track: 2.47 m
Track width: 533 mm
Length of track on ground: 4.1 m
Max speed: (road) 70 km/h
Range: 600 km
Fuel capacity: 610 litres
Fording: 1.5 m
Gradient: 60%
Side slope: 40%
Vertical obstacle: 1.0 m
Trench: 2.6 m
Engine: Scania DS-14 diesel developing 550 hp (410 kW) at 2,200 rpm
Transmission: Perkins Engines Company X-300-5N fully automatic with torque converter and lock-up clutch; 4 forward and 2 reverse gears
Electrical system: 24 V
Batteries: 500 Ah
Armament:
    1 × 7.62 mm MG
    6 × smoke grenade dischargers
Ammunition: 7.62 mm - 4,000 rounds

Status

Production as required. A total of 26 have been delivered to the Swedish Army.

Contractor

BAE Systems, Global Combat Systems

Turkey

Turkish M48 based armoured recovery vehicle

Development

The Turkish Land Forces Command (TLFC) has always relied on upgraded Armoured Fighting Vehicles (AFV) to meet its operational requirements, including large quantities of M48 tanks.

The TLFC facility at Kayseri started upgrading M48 tanks with the assistance of the United States as far back as 1983 with the Arifiye facility coming on stream the following year.

M48 Armoured Recovery Vehicle based on a surplus M48T5 tank chassis (Christopher F Foss) 1123959

In all over 2,000 M48 tanks were upgraded to the M48A5T1/M48A5T2 standard with all of these being armed with a 105 mm gun.

The German company of Krauss-Maffei Wegmann also developed an upgrade package for the M48 tank which was almost identical to that supplied to the German Army under the designation of the M48A2GA2. This had many improvements and is armed with a 105 mm gun and powered by a MTU MB 837 Ea-500 diesel. While the two prototypes were supplied by Germany a total of 165 conversions were carried out in Turkey under the designation of the M48T5.

Two new vehicles based on surplus M48T5 chassis have been developed and placed in production at the Kayseri facilities of the TLFC, the Armoured Recovery vehicle (ARV) and the Armoured Engineer Vehicle (AEV).

The Turkish Land Forces Command has taken delivery of 298 ex-German Army Leopard 2A4 MBTs. As of late 2010, no Büffel ARV have been ordered to support these Leopard 2A4 MBTs.

Description

Although these vehicles have a different battlefield role they both feature a lower hull of a M48T5 tank fitted with a brand new all-welded armoured superstructure.

The crew compartment is on the front left side, turntable-mounted boom at front right and the engine powerpack at the rear.

The M48 based ARV has a combat weight of 52 tonnes and is fitted with a hydraulically operated winch with a maximum rated capacity of 70 tonnes and an auxiliary winch with a capacity of two tonnes with both of these being deployed to the front of the vehicle.

The turntable-mounted boom crane can be traversed through a full 270° and has a maximum lifting capacity of 20 tonnes. When travelling the boom is traversed to the rear and lays along the right side of the hull. Mounted under the front of the hull is a hydraulically operated dozer blade which can shift up to 270 m³ of soil per hour. In addition this is used when the vehicle is recovering heavier vehicles and as a stabiliser blade when the crane is being used.

A variety of other specialised equipment is carried including a 350 A electric welding system. Armament includes a roof-mounted 7.62 mm MG3 or .50 (12.7 mm) M2 HB Machine Gun (MG) and a complete replacement powerpack can be carried on the rear engine decks.

Specifications

M48 based armoured recovery vehicle
Weight: (combat) 52,000 kg
Length: 7.88 m
Width: 3.66 m
Height: 3.07 m
Track: 2.921 m
Track width: 711 mm
Length of track on ground: 4 m
Range: 280 km
Fuel capacity: 890 litres
Fording: 1.2 m
Gradient: 60%
Side slope: 30%
Vertical obstacle: 0.9 m
Trench: 2.50 m
Engine: MTU MB837 Ea 500 diesel
Armament: 1 × 7.62 mm MG3 or 50 (12.7 mm) M2 HB MG

Status

Production as required. In service with the Turkish Land Forces Command.

Contractor

See development.

FNSS Savunma Sistemleri Armoured Recovery Vehicle

Development

Following a competition, the now FNSS Savunma Sistemleri was awarded a contract to build 1,698 Armoured Combat Vehicles (ACVs) to meet the operational requirements of the Turkish Land Forces Command.

First production vehicles were delivered in 1991 and final vehicles were delivered under the original contract in 2000. Since then the Turkish Land Forces Command has placed an additional order for a further batch of 551, which have now been delivered.

Export marketing of the ACV started at an early stage and in 1997 the United Arab Emirates placed a contract for the supply of 136 specialised variants of the ACV with the first of these being delivered in 1999 with deliveries now complete. This order included eight of the ACV Armoured Recovery Vehicle model.

Late in 2000 Malaysia placed a contract for a total of 211 ACV in 11 variants including an unspecified quantity in the ARV configuration. First production vehicles were delivered to Malaysia in 2002.

Sometimes these ACV are referred to as the ACV 350, with the latter number relating to the output of the Detroit 350 hp engine.

In April 2008, Malaysia placed another order with the company covering the supply of another batch of 48 vehicles (Armoured Combat Vehicle 300) as well as eight 120 mm self-propelled mortar systems (Armoured Combat Vehicle - Stretched). The latter are armed with the French TDA 120 mm 120R 2M recoiling mortar.

This latest batch of 48 ACV-300 vehicles were delivered from 2009 through to 2010 and comprised the following versions:

- 12 × Infantry Fighting Vehicle I
- 8 × Infantry Fighting Vehicle II
- 8 × Infantry Fighting Vehicle III
- 4 × anti-armour vehicles
- 2 × armoured vehicle signals
- 4 × armoured recovery vehicle
- 10 × armoured vehicle fitter.

Description

The hull of the Armoured Combat Vehicle Armoured Recovery Vehicle (ACV ARV) is of all-welded aluminium construction with an additional layer of steel armour to provide a higher level of battlefield survivability. This provides the crew with protection from small arms fire and shell splinters.

This version of the ACV has a crew of three that consists of driver, machine gunner and equipment operator.

The driver is seated at the front of the vehicle on the left side, with the fully enclosed powerpack to the right. The driver has a single-piece hatch cover and day periscopes that give observation over the front and sides. The centre one of these periscopes can be replaced by an image intensification or thermal device for driving at night.

To the rear and right of the driver is a cupola armed with an externally mounted .50 (12.7 mm) M2 HB Machine Gun (MG) with the gunner aiming the weapon from within the cupola via a periscope with a magnification of ×5. The cupola also has a single-piece hatch cover that opens to the rear and three day periscopes that give observation to the front and sides.

The crew and winch compartment is at the rear and is provided with a single-piece hatch cover that opens to the rear with normal means of entry and exit being via the large power-operated ramp at the rear that is also provided with an emergency access door.

Suspension is of the torsion bar type with either side consisting of five single rubber-tyred road wheels with the drive sprocket at the front and idler at the rear, there are no track return rollers.

The vehicle is fully amphibious, being propelled in the water by its tracks. Before entering the water, a trim vane is erected at the front of the vehicle and the electrically operated bilge pumps are switched on.

In addition to the cupola-mounted .50 (12.7 mm) M2 HB MG, a bank of six 76 mm electrically operated smoke grenade launchers is normally mounted on the glacis plate firing forwards.

FNSS Armoured Recovery Vehicle in travelling configuration (FNSS) 1127960

Mounted on the left side of the hull roof, to the rear of the drivers position, is the HIAB Model 172R hydraulically operated crane which can be operated up to 10 m away using a remote control device.

The crane is used to lift powerpacks and other components and has the following capabilities:

- Tip hook, 1.68 m reach, 3,085 kg
- Semi-extended, 2.28 m reach, 2,270 kg
- Fully extended, 3.19 m reach, 1,360 kg.

Mounted in the rear of the hull is the Braden Model 03419 hydraulic winch with 90 m of cable and a total capacity of 9,070 kg. This is used through the rear of the hull with the ramp door lowered just below the horizontal position. Mounted either side of the rear door are two stabilisers/anchors that are lowered to the ground when the winch is being used.

The vehicle is air-portable in a Lockheed Martin C-130 Hercules transport aircraft and standard equipment includes an NBC overpressure and air conditioning system and passive night vision devices.

Specifications

Armoured Recovery Vehicle
Crew: 3
Combat weight: 13,900 kg
Power-to-weight ratio: 25.17 hp/t (18.78 kW/t)
Ground pressure: 0.68 kg/cm²
Length: 5.26 m
Width: 2.82 m
Height:
  (hull roof) 2.01 m
  (overall) 3.12 m
Ground clearance: 0.40 m
Track width: 318 mm (track is T-130 forged)
Length of track on ground: 2.68 m
Fuel capacity: 416 litres
Max road speed:
  (forwards) 65 km/h
  (reverse) 11 km/h
Max water speed: 6.3 km/h
Max road range: 490 km
Acceleration: 21 seconds (0 to 48 km/h)
Fording: amphibious
Gradient: 60%
Side slope: 30%
Vertical obstacle: 0.74 m
Trench: 1.83 m
Engine: Detroit Diesel 6V-53TA diesel developing 350 hp (261 kW)
Transmission: Allison X200-4B automatic cross drive with 4 forward and 1 reverse gears
Steering: hydrostatic
Suspension: torsion bar
Electrical equipment: 24 V
Armament: (main) 1 × .50 (12.7 mm) M2 HB MG
Smoke laying equipment: 6 × 76 mm smoke grenade launchers
NBC system: standard
Night vision equipment: standard

Gun control equipment
Turret power control: manual
Gun elevation/depression: +50°/–10°
Turret traverse: 360°
Gun stabiliser:
  (vertical) no
  (horizontal) no

Status

Production as required. In service with Malaysia and the United Arab Emirates. Malaysia has taken delivery of another batch of 48 ACV-300 between 2009 and 2010 which includes four ARV and 10 armoured fitter vehicles.

Contractor

FNSS Savunma Sistemleri AS

Ukraine

BREM-84 armoured recovery vehicle

Development

The Kharkov Morozov Design Bureau has developed an Armoured Recovery Vehicle (ARV) called the BREM-84 that can be based on the chassis of the diesel powered T-80UD or more recent locally developed T-84 Main Battle Tank (MBT).

The prototype of the BREM-84 ARV was built by the Malyshev Plant who will also undertake production of the vehicle.

Late in 1999, the Ukraine delivered the last of 320 T-80UD MBTs to Pakistan and the new BREM-84 ARV has been developed to support this and similar MBTs on the battlefield.

BREM-84 armoured recovery vehicle in travelling configuration on a low loader   1133926

The T-84 MBT is a further development of the T-80UD MBT by the Kharkov Morozov Design Bureau and has a number of improvements including an all welded steel turret with additional special armour.

Typical tasks of the BREM-84 ARV include the recovery of damaged and disabled heavy armoured vehicles and the repair of armoured vehicles as far forward on the battlefield as possible. It can also use its front dozer blade to clear obstacles or prepare fire positions.

The BREM-84 ARV has been demonstrated overseas but as of late 2010, there are no known export sales.

Description

The overall layout of the BREM-84 ARV is similar to modern western ARVs such as the German Büffel based on the Leopard 2 chassis. The fully enclosed crew and winch compartment is at the front with the powerpack at the rear.

The latter consists of a locally manufactured compact 6TF series diesel engine developing 1,000 hp coupled to a manual transmission.

The main mechanical winch leads out through the front of the vehicle and is provided with 130 m of cable and has a maximum traction force of 250 kN.

Cable winding and unwinding speed is 10 m/minute. The hydrostatic auxiliary winch has a maximum traction force of 9 kN and is provided with 260 m of cable.

Mounted at the front of the hull is the hydraulically operated dozer blade that is 3.40 m wide. This can be used as a stabiliser while the crane or winch is being used or can be used in the traditional earth moving role. It can dig to a maximum depth of 300 mm and in clay terrain can move 120 m³ of soil an hour.

Mounted on the right side of the hull is the hydraulically operated crane which can be traversed through 360° and lift a maximum weight of 25 tonnes.

The jib has a maximum radius of 6.8 m and can be used from 0° to 75° in elevation with hook lowering and hoisting speed being from 0.2 to 6 m/min. When not required the crane lays along the right side of the hull.

A loading platform is also provided which is 1.2 × 1.90 m and can carry a maximum load of 1,500 kg. A welding set is also installed as standard equipment and this operates on a current of 300 A with the electrode having a maximum diameter of 5 mm.

It can ford to a depth of 1.8 m but with preparation, including the fitting of a snorkel, it can cross rivers up to 1,000 m wide with a maximum depth of 5 m. Standard equipment includes an NBC system and night vision equipment.

Mounted on the roof is a 12.7 mm NSVT machine gun which can be aimed and fired with the gunner under complete armour protection and mounted on the front right side of the hull is a bank of eight 81 mm electrically operated smoke grenade launchers.

Standard equipment includes an NBC system and night vision equipment and the vehicle can also lay its own smoke screen by injecting diesel fuel into the exhaust outlet.

Specifications

BREM-84 armoured recovery vehicle
(T-84 chassis)
Crew: 3
Combat weight: 46,000 kg
Ground pressure: 0.93 kg/cm²
Power-to-weight ratio: 21.74 hp/t (16.21 kW/t)
Length: 8.89 m
Width: 3.56 m
Height: 2.74 m (including 12.7 mm machine gun)
Ground clearance: 0.515 m
Track: 2.80 m
Track width: 580 mm
Length of track on ground: 4.29 m
Max road speed: 60 km/h

Max range:
  (road) 450 km
  (cross-country) 360 km
Fuel capacity: 1,300 litres
Fording:
  (without preparation) 1.8 m
  (with preparation) 5 m
Gradient: 63%
Side slope: 36%
Trench: 2.85 m
Vertical obstacle: 1 m
Engine: 6TF series twin-stroke, multifuel, liquid-cooled 6-cylinder diesel, fuel-injected, developing 1,000 hp (746 kW)
Transmission: mechanical epicycle with 7 forward and 1 reverse gears
Steering: clutch and brake
Electrical system: 27 V
Armament:
  1 × 12.7 mm NSVT machine gun
  8 × 81 mm smoke grenade launchers

Status

Development complete. Ready for production on receipt of orders. As of late 2010 there were no known customers for the BREM-84 ARV.

Contractor

Malyshev Plant

BREM-64 armoured recovery vehicle

Development

The BREM-64 (*Bronirovannaya Remontno-evakuatsionnaya-64*) armoured recovery vehicle is a conversion based on the hull and chassis of the T-64 MBT. The latter was built at the Malyshev Plant in Ukraine and was only used originally by the Russian Army. While the T-64 is understood to have been phased out of service with the Russian Army, it remains in service with Ukraine which is upgrading part of its T-64 series MBTs to extend their operational lives.

Description

For the ARV application, the T-64 turret is removed from the T-64 and replaced by a new, all-welded, armoured steel superstructure that provides the crew with protection from small arms fire and shell splinters. There is also a raised cupola for the vehicle commander. A swivelling crane with a folding jib is located on the left-hand side of the superstructure; the crane has a lifting capacity of 2,500 kg. Two winches are provided, the main winch has a basic pulling capacity of 25 tonnes while the secondary winch has a capacity of 2.5 tonnes. When the main winch is in operation, vehicle stability is provided by a front-mounted hydraulically operated dozer blade which may also be utilised to clear battlefield obstacles and prepare sites.

The main power unit remains the Type 5DTF 700 hp diesel, as used on the T-64 MBT, but there is also a SMD 21 auxiliary power unit developing 145 hp which may be used to power dismounted welding equipment and other power tools.

The BREM-64 weighs approximately 40,500 kg and has a maximum road speed of 45 km/h. Armament is a 12.7 mm NSVT air defence machine gun. The crew comprises a commander, driver and a fitter.

Status

Production complete. In service with Russia and Ukraine. It is probable that quantities of these vehicles are held by Ukraine for export. At of late 2010, there were no known exports of the BREM-84 armoured recovery vehicle.

Contractor

Kharkov Armoured Repair Factory
Zhytomir Armoured Repair Factory

BREM-2 armoured repair and recovery vehicle

Development

The BREM-2 (*Bronirovannaya Remontno-evakuatsionnaya-2*) armoured repair and recovery vehicle is a conversion based on the hull and chassis of the Russian designed BMP-1 Infantry Fighting Vehicle (IFV).

Production of the original BMP-1 chassis was undertaken at the Kurgan Machine Construction Plant, in Russia. This was followed in production by the BMP-2 and, more recently, the BMP-3, which is a new design.

Production of the BREM-2 armoured repair and recovery vehicle is complete but quantities of surplus vehicles are probably available for export.

Description

The turret is removed from the BMP-1 and replaced by an armoured plate, while the upper hull is modified to accommodate a swivelling jib crane with a 1,500 kg lift capacity. It is capable of lifting a BMP-1/BMP-2 series power pack, various items of recovery equipment and a stowage area with a load capacity of 1,500 kg over the left rear roof area.

Other recovery equipment, including a VG-7500 welding kit and two tow rods, is stowed around the hull roof and sides. The resultant overall layout is very similar to that of the Czech/Slovak VPV armoured recovery vehicle.

The hull interior is rearranged to house a 6,500 kg capacity winch and the four-man crew; there are folding seats for up to five passengers. NBC protection for the crew is provided by a FTP-200M collective system.

With the aid of a pulley block the rated line pull is increased to 19.5 tonnes. The usable cable length is 150 m.

The engine remains the usual BMP-1 Type UTD-20 diesel developing 300 hp at 2,000 rpm. Armament is limited to a single 7.62 mm PKMB machine gun and six 81 mm smoke grenade launchers on the hull roof.

The vehicle can also lay its own smoke screen by injecting diesel fuel into the exhaust outlet on the right side of the hull. Some vehicles were also provided with an unditching beam.

Other ARV exports by Ukraine

Ukraine has considerable numbers of other surplus ARV for sale on the export market.

Known exports of ARV from the Ukraine include the following, but there may well be more:

From	To	Date	Type
Ukraine	Uganda	1995	2 × BTS-4
Ukraine	Iraq	2006	2 × BTR-5B
Ukraine	Azerbaijan	2007	4 × BTS-5M
Ukraine	Georgia	2007	6 × BTS-5

Specifications

BREM-2 Armoured Repair Vehicle
Crew: 4 + 5
Weight: 14,000 kg
Power-to-weight ratio: 21.4 hp/t (16.0 kW/t)
Length: 7.68 m
Width: 3.16 m
Height: (with cargo platform) 2.27 m
Track 2.75 m
Track width 300 mm
Length of track on ground 3.53 m
Max speed:
  (road) 65 km/h
  (water) 7 km/h
Range:
  (roads) 550-560 km
  (earth roads) 400-570 km
Fording: amphibious
Engine: Type UTD-20 diesel developing 300 hp (224 kW) at 2,000 rpm
Transmission: manual, 5 forward and 1 reverse gears
Steering: clutch and brake

Model of BREM-64 armoured recovery vehicle (T J Gander)   0007345

BREM-2 armoured repair and recovery vehicle in travelling configuration (SSFTIF)   1334241

Suspension: torsion bar
Electrical system: 24 V
Armament: 1 × 7.62 mm PKMB MG
Ammunition: 7.62 mm - 1,000 rounds

Main winch
Rated line pull: 6,500 kg
With snatch blocks: 19,500 kg
Usable rope length: 150 m

Jib crane
Lift capacity: 1,500 kg
Traverse: 270°

Status
Conversions of existing BMP-1 IFV available. The BMP-1 IFV is used by the following countries, some of which also use the BREM-2 armoured recovery vehicle: Algeria, Angola, Armenia, Azerbaijan, Belarus, Bulgaria, Cambodia, Congo (Democratic Republic), Côte d'Ivoire, Cuba, Czech Republic, Egypt, Eritrea, Ethiopia, Finland, Georgia, Greece, Hungary, India, Iran, Iraq, Kazakhstan, Korea (North), Kyrgyzstan, Libya, Mongolia, Mozambique, Poland, Romania, Russia, Slovakia, Sri Lanka, Sudan, Syria, Tajikistan, Turkmenistan, Ukraine, Uruguay, Vietnam and Yemen. As far as it is known there has been no recent production of this vehicle in Ukraine. Ukraine has quantities of refurbished BREM-2 armoured repair vehicles for sale.

Contractor
Kharkov Armoured Repair Factory
Zhytomir Armoured Repair Factory

BTR-3BR Armoured Repair and Recovery Vehicle (ARRV)

Development
This Armoured Repair and Recovery Vehicle (ARRV) has been developed based on the chassis of the locally developed BTR-3E (8 × 8) Armoured Personnel Carrier (APC).

The BTR-3E is very similar in appearance to the Russian-developed BTR-80 series of 8 × 8 APCs but has many improvements including greater internal volume owing to a higher roof line and more powerful and fuel efficient diesel engine.

To date, all production of the BTR-3 series of 8 × 8 amphibious APC has been for the export market with known sales of the APC to Azerbaijan (three delivered 2006), Kazakhstan (two delivered 2005), Myanmar (10 delivered 2003), Nigeria (10 delivered 2006) and the United Arab Emirates (24 for Marines). In mid-2007 it was reported that the Royal Thai Army would take delivery of 96 BTR-3 (8 × 8) series vehicles at a cost of USD120 million.

According to the United Nations Arms Transfer Lists, a total of eight BTR-3E series APCs were delivered to Chad in 2008.

The official designation for this vehicle is the BTR-3BR Armoured Repair and Recovery Vehicle but as of late 2010 there are no known export sales.

Description
The hull of the BTR-3BR ARRV is of all-welded steel armour construction that provides the occupants with protection from small arms fire and shell splinters.

According to the manufacturer, typical roles of the BTR-3BR ARRV include the recovery and towing of damaged and disabled armoured fighting vehicles, carrying out welding and excavation work and the transport of spare parts and other equipment up to a maximum weight of two tonnes.

The commander and driver are seated at the front of the vehicle and provided with a single-piece hatch cover above their position and vision blocks. To their front is a window that can be rapidly covered by an armoured shutter when the vehicle is in a combat area.

Mounted on the roof, to the rear of the drivers and commanders position, is a turntable mounted crane with a telescopic jib. This is traversed to the rear when not required. The crane has a maximum load of at least two tonnes when the jib is extended to 3.5 m. Maximum hook height is 4.5 m.

When the crane is being used, a hydraulically operated stabiliser blade is lowered to the ground on either side of the vehicle between the first and second road wheel stations.

The main winch has a maximum pulling force of six that can be increased to 15 tonnes with a triple pulley system. The cable has a maximum usable length of 50 m.

Mounted under the front of the hull is a dozer blade that can also be used as a stabiliser blade when the crane is being used. A loading platform is provided which can carry a maximum load of up to one tonne.

Other specialised equipment carried includes cutting and welding equipment which can be operated up to 50 m away from the vehicle and be used to cut steel up to 10 mm thick. An auxiliary power unit is fitted as standard with a capacity of at least 8 kW.

BTR-3BR (8 × 8) armoured repair and recovery vehicle in travelling configuration with two part side door open and 12.7 mm machine gun mounted above front crew compartment (Ukrspecexport)   1405673

The powerpack is located at the rear of the BTR-3BR ARRV and separated from the crew compartment by a bulkhead. Hatches are provided in the roof and there is also an entry door in each side of the vehicle between the second and third road wheels. This is similar to that on the BTR-80, with the lower part folding downwards to form a step and the upper part being a door that opens to the right.

Steering is power assisted on the front four wheels and standard equipment includes a central tyre pressure regulation system, NBC system, air conditioning system and smoke laying equipment.

Armament typically consists of one PKT 7.62 mm Machine Gun (MG) for which a total of 1,500 rounds (6 × 250) of ammunition are carried. The vehicle is normally operated by a crew of five.

New 8 × 8 APC from Ukraine
Ukraine has developed a new and larger 8 × 8 APC which will form the basis for a complete family of vehicles including an ARRV. This is called the BTR-4 with the first model being in the APC configuration which can be fitted with a wide range of turrets and weapons stations. A number of variants have been proposed including an armoured recovery and repair vehicle.

Specifications
BTR-3BR Armoured Repair and Recovery Vehicle
Crew: 3 + 2
Configuration: 8 × 8
Weight: 15,000 kg
Power-to-weight ratio: 21.73 hp/t (16.21 kW/t)
Length: 7.65 m
Width: 2.9 m
Height: 2.86 m
Max speed:
  (road) 85 km/h
  (water) 8 km/h
Cruising range: 600 km
Fording: amphibious
Gradient: 60%
Side slope: 40%
Vertical obstacle: 0.5 m
Trench: 2 m
Engine: diesel developing 326 hp (243 kW)
Transmission: automatic
Armament: 1 × 7.62 mm MG
NBC system: yes
Night vision equipment: yes

Status
Development complete. Ready for production on receipt of orders.

Contractor
Kharkov Morozov Machine Building Design Bureau

United Kingdom

BAE Systems Global Combat Systems Challenger Armoured Repair and Recovery Vehicle

Development
The Challenger Armoured Repair and Recovery Vehicle (CrARRV - named Rhino by the British Army) was designed and developed by Vickers Defence Systems to support the UK Ministry of Defence's Challenger MBT regiments.

Each Challenger 2 armoured regiment has five CrARRVs, one with the Royal Electrical and Mechanical Engineers (REME) Light Aid Detachment and one with each armoured squadron.

British Army Challenger ARRV from the rear (Christopher F Foss) 1133742

Production of the CrARRV was undertaken at Leeds and Newcastle-upon-Tyne with 81 being built for the British Army and four for Oman.

Vickers Defence Systems was taken over by Alvis PLC and renamed Alvis Vickers. Late in 2004, Alvis PLC was taken over by BAE Systems and Alvis Vickers then became BAE Systems Land Systems.

Today the company is known as BAE Systems Global Combat Systems, with the only remaining UK production facility for armoured fighting vehicles currently being at Newcastle-Upon-Tyne.

Production of the Challenger 2 MBT and Challenger ARRV had been completed and neither of these are now marketed by BAE Systems Global Combat Systems.

Late in 2009 three TROJAN breacher vehicles were upgraded by BAE Systems, Global Combat Systems to meet an Urgent Operational Requirement (UOR) at their Newcastle-Upon-Tyne facility.

These were deployed to Afghanistan early in 2010 by 28 Engineer Regiment. The upgrade included additional armour in the form of bar armour around the rear arc and upper part of the chassis for enhanced protection against rocket propelled grenades.

These TROJAN breacher vehicles were used to clear paths through mine fields using the trailer mounted Python rocket propelled mine clearing system and the Pearson Engineering full width mine clearing system mounted on the front of the chassis.

These were supported by two upgraded Challenger ARRV which had previously been upgraded for deployment in Iraq but were subsequently withdrawn in 2009.

Description

The Challenger ARRV uses the same hydrogas suspension and automotive components as the Challenger 2 MBT. With the David Brown Gear Systems TN54 automatic transmission and incorporating the Dowty Digital Automotive System Control Unit (DASCU), it carries out the functions of both the previous Main Engine Control Unit and the Gearbox Controller Automatic.

The Challenger ARRV has a basic crew of three (commander, driver and radio operator) but usually carries an additional two fitters. There is seating for a further two passengers in the L-shaped crew compartment. Integral crew heating and cooling facilities are provided, along with full NBC protection, automatic fire detection and suppression and a chemical toilet. The Challenger ARRV is equipped with welding and air-powered tools, plus onboard spares holding, allowing the vehicle to be used as a field repair vehicle as well as a recovery vehicle.

The Challenger ARRV can tow vehicles up to 68,000 kg weight on free tracks at speeds up to 30 km/h. Stability is maintained when retarding the load and when towing at low speeds.

According to the manufacturer, the hydraulic main winch of the Challenger ARRV enables it to undertake 80 per cent of recovery tasks on a 65-tonne MBT with a single line pull.

The commander's cupola is a modified (no contra-rotation) AV No 32 Mark 1 (known as the No 36 Mark 1) with a demountable quartz spotlight. For day vision there is a main ×1 wide-angle day periscope and a ring of six ×1 day periscopes. For night vision a single ×1 image intensifier periscope

British Army Challenger ARRV have been upgraded with additional armour (Christopher F Foss) 1308380

British Army Challenger ARRV (Richard Stickland) 1334238

is fitted in a rotatable mounting. The driver has a main ×1 day periscope and a ×1 auxiliary day periscope; for night vision a ×1 image intensifier periscope is fitted. The commander is also provided with a single 7.62 mm L37A2 machine gun on a sliding cradle mounted on a fixed rail around his hatch.

The main winch is a Rotzler Treibmatic hydraulically driven double capstan type with a single line pull of 510 kN. It is controlled from the driver's station and is operable in the closed-down position. The auxiliary winch, a Plumett TL 15, has a maximum line pull of 15 kN and it is also operated from the driver's position. It is independent of the main winch.

The front-mounted blade is a multipurpose item that can act as an earth anchor, dozer blade or stabiliser blade for the crane. It is controlled from the driver's compartment and, in its role as earth anchor, is capable of withstanding a double reeved main winch pull of 1,020 kN.

The hydraulically operated repair crane is an ATLAS AK6000M8. Hydraulically operated, it has a lift capacity of 6,500 kg and is capable of lifting a complete Challenger 2 MBT powerpack. It is driven by an electric motor in turn powering a self-contained hydraulic power system.

CrARRV trailer

In mid-2000 the Royal Electrical and Mechanical Engineers took delivery of the last of 24 trailers for use with the CrARRV and the Warrior repair and recovery vehicle.

Although the CrARRV was originally designed to carry a complete Challenger 2 MBT powerpack this was found to be impractical so the four-wheeled trailer was developed and built by Reynolds Boughton Ltd of the UK under a GBP2.5 million contract.

The trailer is an enhanced and more capable variant of the Armoured Vehicle Royal Vehicles trailer but fulfils a different role.

Up-armoured CrARRV

To support the squadron of British Army Challenger 2 MBTs deployed to Iraq, a small batch of Challenger Armoured Repair and Recovery Vehicles (CrARRV) have been upgraded under the leadership of BAE Systems Global Combat Systems.

This includes installation of Explosive Reactive Armour (ERA) on the hull sides, bar armour around the rear arc, wire cutters, modified air conditioner and driver's night vision devices.

They have also been fitted with a number of electronic devices to neutralise Improvised Explosive Devices (IEDs).

Omani CrARRV

This version of the CrARRV has been modified in such a way as to meet the customer's specific operational requirements. The vehicle's specification has been developed for operation in the climatic conditions of the Middle East. The powerpack cooling group was modified to allow operation without power cutback in ambient temperatures above +50°C. An air conditioning system is installed as standard equipment.

Remanufacture of CrARRV winch

Following a competition, late in 2005 Smith & Jewell Ltd were awarded a five year contract by Light Armoured Systems Support IPT of the Defence Logistics Organisation (DLO) which covered the remanufacture of the main hydraulic winch of the Warrior recovery vehicle and the auxiliary winch of the CrARRV.

Specifications

Challenger Armoured Repair and Recovery Vehicle (CrAAV)
Crew: 3 + 2 (plus 2 passengers)
Weight: (combat) 62,000 kg
Ground pressure: 0.99 kg/cm²
Power-to-weight ratio: 19.35 hp/t (14.43 kW/t)
Length: 9.59 m
Width:
(operating) 3.62 m
(transport, without blade) 3.51 m
Height: (overall) 3.005 m

Ground clearance: 0.5 m
Max speed:
  (road) 56 km/h
  (cross-country) 40 km/h
Towing speed: (towing 60 t casualty)
  (road) 30 km/h
  (cross-country, typical) 18 km/h
Range:
  (road) 450 km/h
  (cross-country) 250 km/h
Fording: 1.07 m
Gradient:
  (normal) 58%
  (towing 65 t) 25%
Vertical obstacle: 0.85 m
Trench: 2.3 m
Engine: Perkins Engines Company (today Caterpillar Defence Products) CV12 TCA 1200 26.1 litre V-12 direct injection 4- stroke diesel developing 1,200 bhp (895 kW) at 2,300 rpm
Transmission: David Brown Gear Systems TN54 automatic with 6 forward and 2 reverse gears
Suspension: hydrogas variable spring rate
Electrical system: 24 V
Main engine generator: 350 A continuous
Auxiliary power unit generator: 500 A continuous
Armament:
  1 × 7.62 mm L37A2 MG
  20 × 66 mm smoke grenade dischargers (10 front, 10 rear)

Main winch
Speed: ≤60 m/min
Max line pull:
  (9 m/min) 510 kN
  (60 m/min) 76 kN
Max pay-out rate: 60 m/min
Rope diameter: 35 mm
Rope min breaking load: 1,000 kN
Rope usable length: (when new) 150 m
Winch life: a minimum of 720 full load, full length pulls

Auxiliary winch
Max line pull: (60 m/min) 15 kN
Rope diameter: 7 mm
Rope min breaking load: 31.4 kN
Rope usable length: 300 m

Crane
Max lift capacity: 6,500 kg at 4.9 m reach
Max reach: 5.15 m with 5,000 kg
Max hook height of lift: 6.82 m above ground level
Max time to elevate boom without max load: 36 s
Max time to elevate boom with max load: 72 s
Lifting speed of hook, max load: 0-4 m/min
Lifting speed of hook without load: 0-8 m/min
Slewing range: (boom up) 360° continuous
Slew speed: (horizontal, no load) 0 to 6°/s
Max working slope: 6°, vehicle at any orientation to slope
Hook travel: 5 m
Rope diameter: 20 mm
Rope breaking load: 357 kN

Status
Production completed. In service with Oman (four) and UK (81). No longer marketed.

Contractor
BAE Systems Global Combat Systems

Chieftain armoured recovery vehicle

Development
The Chieftain armoured recovery vehicle (FV4204) was developed by the Military Vehicles and Engineering Establishment (which no longer exists) and the Royal Ordnance Factory at Leeds (which has since closed down as a tank production facility), as the replacement for the Centurion armoured recovery vehicle (FV4006).

The final requirement, issued late in 1964, called for a vehicle that could clear obstacles on the battlefield, tow an immobilised Chieftain Main Battle Tank (MBT) both on roads and cross-country and be fitted with a winch with a maximum capacity of 90,000 kg.

The first of two prototypes (designated R1 and R2) was built and delivered to the School of Electrical and Mechanical Engineering at Bordon late in 1971. Trials with the first prototype resulted in a complete redesign of the hydraulic system of the vehicle, undertaken by Lockheed Precision Products (now AP Precision Hydraulics).

Chieftain armoured repair and recovery vehicle in travelling configuration (T J Gander)   1158886

This redesign, with a few more modifications, was considered satisfactory and production was authorised. Production of the Chieftain armoured recovery vehicle was undertaken by Vickers Defence Systems at its Elswick facility and the vehicle entered service with the British Army in 1976.

Iran ordered 71 Chieftain ARVs, the last of which was completed early in 1980. About 21 vehicles had been delivered to Iran by the time of the revolution. The remaining 50 vehicles were purchased by Jordan.

Production total for the Chieftain ARV was 257. The Chieftain ARV is no longer used with British MBT regiments as they use the Challenger ARRV.

In October 2002, Alvis took over Vickers Defence Systems. The new company was named Alvis Vickers Limited.

Late in 2004, Alvis PLC was taken over by BAE Systems and Vickers Defence Systems became BAE Systems Land Systems. Today the company is known as BAE Systems, Global Combat Systems, with the only remaining UK production facility for armoured fighting vehicles currently being at Newcastle-Upon-Tyne.

Description
The Chieftain ARV is based on the chassis of the Chieftain Mk 5 MBT and has three main compartments. The hydraulic winch compartment is at the front of the vehicle on the right side, with the driver seated on the left.

To the rear of the driver is a single-piece hatch cover, with a single day periscope. The other three crew members are seated in the centre of the vehicle. Provision is made for carrying a fifth passenger.

The commander has a No 17 cupola that can be manually traversed through a full 360°. In the forward part of the cupola is a No 62 sight periscope with magnifications of ×1 and ×10 and seven No 40 day periscopes give the commander vision to the sides and rear. An image intensification sight can be fitted if required and a white/infra-red spotlight is mounted externally. The 7.62 mm L37A1 machine gun can be aimed and fired from inside the cupola. There is a second hatch in the roof of the vehicle, to the right of the commander's cupola.

The crew compartment has an NBC system and a heater. The engine and transmission at the rear of the hull are separated from the crew compartment by a fireproof bulkhead. The crew consists of commander, driver/winch operator, radio operator and a recovery mechanic.

The suspension is of the Horstmann type and consists of three bogies per side, each with two sets of roadwheels and a set of three horizontal springs. The first roadwheel station has a hydraulic shock-absorber. The drive sprocket is at the rear and the idler at the front, with three track-return rollers. The top half of the track is covered by armoured skirts, which can be removed for maintenance.

Standard equipment includes a Kidde Graviner fire warning, detection and extinguishing system, NBC system, heater and infra-red detection equipment.

The main winch is of the double capstan type with electrohydraulic controls. It is provided with 122 m of 28 mm diameter cable and has a maximum speed of 13.73 m/min. The auxiliary winch is also of the double capstan type and is hydraulically operated with 259 m of 11 mm diameter cable and a maximum speed of 61 m/min. Power for both winches is taken from a Power Take-Off (PTO) on the main engine.

The front-mounted dozer blade, which weighs 833 kg, is operated by two hydraulic arms. When lowered it allows the vehicle to exert a pull of up to 90,000 kg.

The vehicle is provided with a full range of recovery equipment including pulleys, cables and towbars. Some of the Chieftain ARVs for Iran were fitted with an ATLAS AK6000M hydraulic crane which, in this application, can lift a maximum load of 5,803 kg at a reach of 3.62 m. Distance from the hook to the ground at a radius of 3.62 m is 4.67 m and minimum radius with boom extended is 1.445 m. Maximum lifting speed is 3.4 m/min and maximum slewing speed is 9°/s.

Variants
Armoured Repair and Recovery Vehicle
With the introduction of the Challenger 1 MBT into service with the British Army, the FV434 was unable to service the new vehicle as it could not lift the power pack. This led to the introduction into service of the Chieftain

Armoured Repair and Recovery Vehicle (ARRV), which has a hydraulic crane boom mounted on the left side of the superstructure with the pivot mounted just behind the commander's hatch. A stand for a power pack is located on the rear deal over the vehicle's engine compartment. An additional six vehicles were delivered to Jordan in 2004 from British Army stocks.

Specifications

Chieftan armoured recovery vehicle
(Vehicle with crane)
Crew: 4 + 1
Weight: 55,640 kg
Power-to-weight ratio: 13.48 hp/t (10.05 kW/t)
Length: 8.57 m
Width:
   (incl blade) 3.53 m
   (tracks) 3.33 m
Height: 3.43 m
Ground clearance:
   (front) 0.5 m
   (rear) 0.58 m
Track: 2.72 m
Track width: 610 mm
Length of track on ground: 4.775 m
Ground pressure: 0.9 kg/cm²
Max speed: (road) 42.2 km/h
Range:
   (road) 400-500 km
   (cross-country) 200-300 km
Fuel capacity: 955 litres
Fording: 1.007 m
Gradient: 70%
Vertical obstacle: 0.90 m
Trench: 3.15 m
Engine: Leyland L60 No 4 Mark 8A, 2-stroke, compression ignition, 6-cylinder (12 opposed pistons) vertically opposed multifuel developing 750 hp (559 kW) at 2,250 rpm
Transmission: David Brown Gear Systems TN12 with 6 forward and 2 reverse gears plus emergency mechanical selector for second gear forward and low reverse
Electrical system: 28.5 V (24 V nominal) DC
Batteries: 4 × 12 V, 200 Ah
Armament:
   1 × 7.62 mm L37A1 MG
   2 × 6-barrelled 66 mm smoke grenade dischargers (front)
   2 × 4-barrelled 66 mm smoke grenade dischargers (rear)
Ammunition: 7.62 mm - 1,600 rounds

Status

Production complete. No longer marketed. In service with Iran, Jordan (another six Chieftain ARRV delivered in 2004) and the UK.

Contractor

BAE Systems Global Combat Systems

Vickers armoured repair and recovery vehicle

Development

Early in 1977, Kenya placed an order with Vickers Defence Systems for 38 Mk 3 Main Battle Tanks (MBTs) and three Armoured Recovery Vehicles (ARVs) based on the same chassis. The Vickers Mk 3 MBT is a further development of the Vickers Mk 1 MBT which was built for India and Kuwait. First production MBTs were delivered in 1979 and first production ARVs were delivered in 1981. Two of the ARVs have a hydraulically operated crane. In 1978, Kenya placed an additional order for 42 MBTs plus four ARVs, two with a crane and two without. In late 1981 Nigeria placed an order for 36 MBTs, five ARVs and six bridgelayers; since then two repeat orders have been placed. Tanzania has also taken delivery of four vehicles to support Chinese supplied armoured vehicles.

Late in 2002, Vickers Defence Systems was purchased by Alvis PLC who also owned Alvis Vehicles with the new and larger company known as Alvis Vickers Limited.

Late in 2004, Alvis PLC was taken over by BAE Systems and Vickers Defence Systems became BAE Systems Land Systems. Production of the Vickers Mk 3 MBT was completed some time ago and it and its specialised variants are no longer marketed.

Today the company is known as BAE Systems Global Combat Systems with the only remaining UK production facility for armoured fighting vehicles currently being at Newcastle-Upon-Tyne.

This facility is now manufacturing the Terrier combat engineer vehicle which is the replacement for the FV180 Combat Engineer Vehicle (CET) that has already been phased out of service with the British Army.

Description

The all-welded steel armour of the Vickers armoured repair and recovery vehicle provides the occupants with protection from small arms fire and shell splinters and is divided into three main compartments: front, centre

Vickers armoured repair and recovery vehicle   0512444

and rear. The front compartment is divided into two, with the driver's compartment on the right and the winch compartment on the left. The driver has a single-piece hatch cover which can be locked open. Mounted in the hatch is a single wide-angle day periscope. This can be replaced by a passive periscope for night driving.

The centre compartment accommodates the radio operator, commander and mechanic and also contains the radio sets, batteries, 7.62 mm machine gun ammunition stowage and recovery kit. The commander's cupola can be traversed manually through 360° and is provided with a single-piece hatch cover that opens to the rear, periscopes for all-round day observation and an externally mounted 7.62 mm L37A1 MG, which can be aimed and fired from inside the cupola and has an elevation of +90° and a depression of −10°.

The rear compartment houses the power and transmission units. Panniers above each track contain two bag-type fuel tanks. All production Vickers armoured repair and recovery vehicles built to date were fitted with the Detroit Diesel 12V-71T V-12 diesel coupled to the David Brown Gear Systems (previously Self Changing Gears) TN12 Mark V5 transmission, which combines the Wilson Epicyclic gear change principle with the Merritt steering system.

Suspension is the torsion bar type with each side consisting of six dual rubber-tyred roadwheels with the drive sprocket at the rear, idler at the front and three track-return rollers. All suspension stations mount a secondary torsion bar within the body of the axle and the first, second and sixth roadwheel stations have a hydraulic shock-absorber. The tracks are of manganese steel and, when new, each track comprises 96 links.

The main winch is operated by the driver and is mechanically driven through an input gearbox with hydraulically operated selector box. The engine Power Take-Off (PTO), mounted on the rear bulkhead of the winch/crew compartment, is engaged by the driver to provide a drive to the input gearbox and raise hydraulic pressure before the winch can be operated.

The twin capstan winch is equipped with 122 m of 28 mm diameter cable and has a nominal capacity of 25,000 kg when being used in conjunction with an earth anchor spade fitted to the front of the vehicle. The winch, when achieving 25,000 kg direct line pull, is capable of dealing with all normal recovery operations.

Where necessary, the line pull can be increased to a nominal figure of 75,000 kg by multireeving the cable using recovery equipment provided with the vehicle. The hydraulically operated earth anchor enables the maximum pull to be achieved without moving the vehicle.

The Vickers ARV hull is manufactured to accept a hydraulic crane with a lifting capacity of 4,000 kg. All vehicles produced to date, other than part of the batch delivered to Kenya, have been fitted with this crane.

Optional equipment for the Vickers ARV included: passive night vision equipment for both the commander and driver; cradle for transporting a complete power pack with TN12 transmission; auxiliary winch with a capacity of 4,060 kg and 250 m of 11 mm diameter cable; smoke grenade launchers; NBC system and a heater.

Specifications

Vickers armoured repair and recovery vehicle
Crew: 4
Weight: 38,000 kg
Power-to-weight ratio: 18.95 hp/t (14.13 kW/t)
Length:
   (vehicle) 7.56 m
   (vehicle with spade) 8.38 m
Width: 3.16 m
Height: (top of commander's sight) 2.89 m
Ground clearance: 0.432 m
Track: 2.52 m
Track width: 521 mm
Length of track on ground: 4.28 m
Ground pressure: 0.79 kg/cm²
Max speed: (road) 50 km/h

Range: (road, at 32.2 km/h) 600 km
Fuel capacity: 1,000 litres
Fording: 1.1 m
Gradient: 60%
Side slope: 30%
Vertical obstacle: 0.914 m
Trench: 3 m
Engine: Detroit Diesel 12V-71T V-12 diesel developing 720 bhp (537 kW) at 2,500 rpm
Transmission: David Brown Gear Systems TN12 Mark V5 automatic
Electrical system: 24 V
Batteries: 4 × 12 V 6TN
Armament: 1 × 7.62 mm L37A1 MG

Status
Production complete. In service with Kenya (seven), Nigeria (15) and Tanzania (four). No longer marketed.

Contractor
BAE Systems Global Combat Systems

BAE Systems Global Combat Systems Warrior repair and recovery vehicle

Development
The Warrior repair and recovery vehicle is a member of the Warrior mechanised combat vehicle family and uses a basically similar hull and superstructure and a common power train and running gear.

Two variants were ordered by the British Army, including 110 FV512 Mechanised Combat Repair Vehicles (MCRVs) with a crane but no winch and 67 FV513 Mechanised Recovery Vehicles (Repair) (MRV(R)s), with both a winch and crane.

The British Army took delivery of 789 Warrior vehicles while Kuwait has taken delivery of 254, including variants.

Production of the Warrior was undertaken by GKN Defence, which then became Alvis. This company took over Vickers Defence Systems and Alvis Vickers was formed. Late in 2004, BAE Systems took over Alvis PLC and Vickers Defence Systems became BAE Systems Land Systems.

Today the company is known as BAE Systems Global Combat Systems, with the only remaining UK production facility for armoured fighting vehicles currently being at Newcastle-upon-Tyne.

Production of the Warrior for the British Army and Desert Warrior for Kuwait was undertaken at Telford, which has now closed down as a production facility.

Production of the Warrior and its variants has now been completed and it is now longer being marketed by BAE Systems Global Combat Systems.

Current projected out of service date for British Army Warrior IFVis 2035.

Part of the British Army fleet of Warrior mechanised combat vehicles will be upgraded under the Warrior Capability Sustainment Programme (WCSP) for which there are two bidders, BAE Systems Global Combat Systems and Lockheed Martin UK.

The WCSP includes the Warrior Fightability & Lethality Improvement Programme (WFLIP), Warrior Enhanced Electronic Architecture (WEEA) and Warrior Modular Protection System (WMPS).

The latter is a mounting system for the armour package installed on the vehicle which is Government Furnished Equipment (GFE).

The British Army took delivery of 789 Warrior IFV and specialised variants and it was expected that up to 449 would be upgraded with the WFLIP and all vehicles with the WEEA and WMPS.

Due to British Army restructuring the figure of 449 is expected to be reduced, perhaps to between 300 and 350 vehicles.

Both contractors have partnered with the Defence Support Group (DSG) at Donnington who have already overhauled over 1,000 Warrior vehicles.

Description
The MCRV has a crew of five comprising commander, driver, gunner and two fitters. The main change to the superstructure is the addition of a hydraulically operated crane on the left of the superstructure and with the pivot to the rear. This has a capacity of 6,500 kg and a maximum reach of 4.52 m. The crane has a full 360° traverse and can lift and replace Challenger 2 or Warrior power packs or similar assemblies from other MBTs, AIFVs or self-propelled artillery. A hydraulically-actuated stabiliser leg at the left rear of the vehicle is lowered when the crane is in use.

On the MRV(R) a twin capstan winch is carried internally at the rear and has a 20,000 kg capacity, 38,000 kg when double-reeved. There is sufficient cable to enable a single line pull of 100 m. The winch can tow a Warrior Section Vehicle over rough terrain up a gradient of 40 per cent. For the recovery role an earth anchor is hydraulically lowered from the hull rear. A pilot winch is used to raise and lower the earth anchor and is provided with 200 m of cable to provide a capacity of 1,250 kg maximum pull.

Internally the vehicle is provided with a fully equipped workshop. The vehicle is fitted with a one-man turret armed with a single 7.62 mm L94A1 Chain Gun. There is also a collective NBC unit, along with an air conditioning system.

The Warrior MCRV can tow the High-Mobility Trailer. This trailer was specially designed to operate with the Warrior Mechanised Combat Repair Vehicle and has a gross weight of 10,500 kg. It can carry a Challenger 2 MBT power pack and employs a four-damper jacking system to maintain a safe level platform when not connected for towing.

The Warrior repair and recovery vehicle has now been fitted with the General Dynamics UK Bowman digital communications system.

Specifications
Warrior repair and recovery vehicle
Crew: 5
Weight: (combat, MRV(R)) 30,000 kg
Power-to-weight ratio: 18.33 hp/t (13.67 kW/t)
Length:
(overall) 6.675 m
(over tracks) 5.39 m
Width: 3.13 m
Height:
(over cupola) 2.302 m
(roof) 1.935 m
Ground clearance: 0.49 m
Track: 2.54 m
Track width: 460 mm
Length of track on ground: 3.817 m
Max speed: (road) 71 km/h
Range: (road) 500 km
Fuel capacity: 770 litres
Fording: 1.3 m
Gradient: 60%
Side slope: 40%
Vertical obstacle: 0.75 m
Trench: 2.5 m
Angle of approach/departure: 29°/34.5°
Engine: Perkins Engines Company (now Caterpillar Defence Products) CV8 TCA V-8 diesel developing 550 hp (410 kW) at 2,300 rpm
Transmission: Perkins Engines Company X-300-4B fully automatic with torque converter and lock-up clutch, 4 forward and 2 reverse gears
Turning radius: 6 m
Electrical system: 24 V
Armament:
1 × 7.62 mm L94A1 Chain Gun
up to 8 banks of 66 mm smoke grenade dischargers

British Army Warrior Mechanised Combat Repair Vehicle in travelling configuration from the rear (Richard Stickland)   1158884

British Army Warrior Mechanised Combat Repair Vehicle (MCRV) towing a High-Mobility Trailer (Michael Jerchel)   1296027

Ammunition: 7.62 mm - 4,000 rounds
Armour:
   (hull) aluminium alloy
   (turret) steel

Status
Production complete. In service with the British Army and Kuwait. No longer marketed.

Contractor
BAE Systems Global Combat Systems

Lockheed Martin UK MLRS Repair and Recovery Vehicle

Development
Following a competition, in 2004 the now Lockheed Martin UK was awarded a GBP2.4 million contract from the then UK's Defence Logistics Organisation (DLO) for the design, development and manufacture of a Repair and Recovery Vehicle (RRV) to support the tracked Multiple Launch Rocket System (MLRS) in service with the Royal Artillery.

Following trials with a prototype vehicle, a total of four MLRS RRV were supplied with final deliveries taking place in 2006. These are manned by the Royal Electrical and Mechanical Engineers.

While Lockheed Martin UK was the overall design authority, the actual vehicle integration work was carried out by sub-contractor JS Chin of Hinckley. The crane and recovery winch used in the MLRS RRV are Commercial-Off-The-Shelf (COTS) assemblies.

Scale of issue is typically one MLRS RRV per MLRS battery which normally consists of a total of nine launchers.

The UK took delivery of 63 M270 MLRS systems of which four came from the US production line with the remainder being manufactured under licence in Europe.

A total of 36 of these M270 are being upgraded to the M270B1 standard that includes the Improved Fire-Control System (IFCS) but not the Improved Launcher Mechanical System which is standard on the US Army M270A1 launchers.

The UK Royal Artillery have deployed five of the upgraded M270B1 MLRS to Afghanistan where they have seen extensive use firing Guided MLRS (GMLRS) which provide a precision strike capability out to over 60 km.

Description
The standard MLRS has the fully enclosed armour protected cab at the front and this can be tilted forwards to allow access to the diesel powerpack for maintenance role.

Cab is provided with an NBC system, a forward opening door in each side and a single roof hatch located in the right side of the roof and opening to the rear.

Bulletproof windows are provided in the front and sides that have the same level of ballistic protection as the welded aluminium armour.

The cab can be tilted forward to allow access to the diesel powerpack for maintenance purposes.

To the rear of the cab is the flatbed on which the complete 227 mm (12-round) rocket launcher is normally mounted. For the RRV the launcher has been removed and replaced by a repair and recovery modification kit developed by the company.

The kit includes a hydraulic crane and a hydraulic winch. The HIAB crane with deployable outriggers can lift 2.5 tonnes at a reach of 5.2 m, be traversed through a full 360° and used to lift sub-systems such as a complete MLRS diesel powerpack.

A complete MLRS replacement power pack can be carried between the cab and recovery equipments.

Front view of a British Army Multiple Launch Rocket System (MRLS) converted into Repair and Recovery Vehicle configuration (Lockheed Martin UK) 1333671

British Army MLRS Repair and Recovery Vehicle with stabilisers deployed and crane lifting a powerpack (Lockheed Martin UK) 1405672

The winch, which is provided with 100 m of wire cable, enables MLRS RRV to rapidly recover damaged and disabled MLRS vehicles under almost all situations and has a maximum double pull capacity of 40 tonnes.

When the winch is being used, two earth anchors are lowered at the rear of the vehicle to provide a more stable platform for recovery operations. An auxiliary winch with 200 m of wire cable and a 900 kg capacity is also fitted to the MLRS RRV to aid deployment of recovery equipment.

The MLRS RRV can recover and tow casualty vehicles weighing up to 26 tonnes over all terrain.

The MLRS RRV is equipped with other repair equipment including an air compressor, battery charger and stowage boxes for tools and other specialised recovery equipment.

An onboard integrated diesel driven auxiliary hydraulic back up pump is fitted as standard and this allows the MLRS RRV to replace its own powerpack in the field.

A stowage cage is provided at the front of the cab as are two banks of four electrically operated 66 mm smoke grenade launchers.

In addition to being used to recover MLRS and other armoured and wheeled vehicles, the MLRS RRV also has a self-recovery capability. All subsystems such as winch, crane and earth anchors can be operated by remote control or manual override.

Specifications
MLRS Repair and Recovery Vehicle (RRV)
Cab seating: 1 + 2
Weight: (loaded) 29,340 kg
Power-to-weight ratio: 20.45 hp/t (15.25 kW/t)
Length:
   (chassis) 6.97 m
   (overall) 7.57 m
Width: 2.97 m
Height:
   (overall) 2.87 m
   (cab) 2.59 m
   (chassis) 1.206 m
Ground clearance: 430 mm
Track width: 533 mm
Length of track on ground: 4.33 m
Max speed:
   (road) 65 km/h
   (10% gradient) 26 km/h
Range: (at 40 km/h) 473 km
Fuel capacity: 726 litres
Max gradient: 60%
Max side slope: 40%
Fording: 1.2 m
Vertical obstacle: 0.91 m
Trench: 2.36 m
Engine: Cummins VTA-903T 14.8 litre turbocharged 8-cylinder diesel developing 600 hp (447 kW) at 2,400 rpm
Transmission: L3 Combat Propulsion Systems HMPT 500-3EC hydropneumatic with electronic controller
Steering: hydrostatic
Suspension: steel torsion bar
Brakes: multidisc, oil-cooled
Electrical system: 28 V
Batteries: 4 × 12 V 6TN, 100 Ah
Alternator: 2 × 300A
Smoke grenade launchers: 2 × 4-barrelled 66 mm

Status
Production complete but can be restarted again. In service with the British Army (four units). These are operated by the Royal Electrical and Mechanical Engineers (REME).

Contractor
Lockheed Martin UK

BAE Systems Global Combat Systems Samson armoured recovery vehicle

Development

The Samson (FV106) is a member of the Scorpion range of light tracked vehicles developed by the then Alvis Vickers and the then Military Vehicles and Engineering Establishment. The first prototype was completed in the early 1970s but, as a result of trials, some redesign work had to be carried out and the final design entered production in 1977 to 1978.

Alvis PLC took over Vickers and a new company called Alvis Vickers was formed. In late 2004, BAE Systems took over Alvis Vickers and BAE Systems Land Systems was formed.

Today the company is known as BAE Systems Global Combat Systems with the only remaining UK production facility for armoured fighting vehicles currently being at Newcastle-upon-Tyne.

Production of the Scorpion range of light tracked armoured vehicles was undertaken at Coventry that has now closed.

Production of the Scorpion and its variants, including the Samson ARV has now been completed and it is now longer being marketed by BAE Systems Global Combat Systems.

Following a competition between General Dynamics United Kingdom (GD UK) and BAE Systems Global Combat Systems, the former announced on 1 July 2010 that it had been awarded a contract by the UK MoD worth GBP500 million for the demonstration phase of the British Army's Specialist Vehicle (SV) programme.

When fielded the SV Scout will replace the British Army's fleet of aging Combat Vehicle Reconnaissance (Tracked) which were first introduced as far back as 1972. In the past this programme has been called the Future Rapid Effect System (FRES) but this name was dropped in 2010.

The first vehicle to be replaced will be the Alvis Scimitar reconnaissance vehicle armed with an unstabilised 30 mm RARDEN cannon and 7.62 mm co-axial Machine Gun (MG).

Under the terms of this demonstration contract, GD UK will build a total of seven prototype SV Scout with the first of these due to be completed in 2013 to be followed by the production phase.

Under the demonstration phase, in addition to the SV Scout, a number of support vehicles will be built on the ASCOD (which is an abbreviation for the Austrian Spanish Co-Operative Development) Common Base Platform (CBP) which weighs about 23 tonnes.

For the first phase, seven vehicles will be integrated in Spain at the facilities of General Dynamics European Land Systems, Santa Bárbara Sistemas followed by progressive production transfer to the UK.

Eventual production and integration of the SV Scout will be undertaken at the Defence Support Group (DSG) facility at Donnington under an agreement already signed.

It is expected that the Samson ARV will be replaced a version of the CBP optimised for the ARV mission.

Samson armoured recovery vehicle (Michael Jerchel)   0038803

Description

The hull of the Samson is similar to that of the Spartan APC and is of all-welded aluminium armour construction. This provides the crew with protection from small arms fire and shell splinters. The driver is seated at the front of the hull on the left side and is provided with a single-piece hatch cover which opens to the front and a wide-angle periscope for driving in the closed-down position. This can be replaced by a passive night periscope. The powerpack, mounted to the right of the driver, is common to the Scorpion CVR(T) range.

To the rear of the driver, in the centre of the roof, is a one-person No 27 cupola. This has a single-piece hatch cover that opens to the left and can be traversed manually through 360°. Mounted in the forward part of the cupola is a day periscope with a magnification of ×1, which can be replaced by a passive night periscope. There are another five day periscopes for all-round vision. Mounted externally on the right side of the cupola is a 7.62 mm L7A2 GPMG.

The NBC unit, if carried, is on the right-hand sponson plate, with the radio in a corresponding position on the left side. Alternatively, an air cooling or through-flow air circulation system can be installed.

At the rear of the hull are the winch compartment and a small door with a built-in vision block. Over the winch compartment is a roof hatch.

The suspension is of the torsion bar type and either side consists of five roadwheels, with the drive sprocket at the front and the idler at the rear. The first and fifth roadwheel stations are provided with a hydraulic shock-absorber. The British Army fleet has been fitted with new dampers.

The Samson can ford to a depth of 1.067 m without preparation, but with the flotation screen erected it is fully amphibious, being propelled in the water by its tracks at a speed of 6.44 km/h. A propeller kit increases its water speed to 9.6 km/h. In British Army service the flotation screen has been removed and the vehicle no longer has an amphibious capability.

The hydraulic recovery winch is mounted in the rear of the hull and is driven from a Power Take-off (PTO) on the main engine. This winch is provided with 229 m of rope and has a variable speed up to 122 m/min. Maximum pull, with a 4:1 snatch block, is 12,000 kg. This enables the Samson to recover vehicles such as the British Army FV432 APC. The cable leads out over the top of the hull at the rear. Two spades at the rear of the hull are released manually. An additional strengthening piece is then added and the Samson is reversed on to the spades. An A-frame can be mounted at the rear of the vehicle enabling the Samson to change light components in the field. A full range of tools, towbars and blocks is carried.

British Army Samson ARV have now had their existing Jaguar petrol engines replaced by a more fuel efficient Cummins 6BT 5.9-litre diesel developing 235 hp. First vehicles with the new Cummins diesel engine were handed over in April 1999. Brunei, Oman and Jordan have also taken delivery of these repower packages from the original manufacturer.

Alvis Vickers, the then design authority for the CVR(T) converted the first batch of 200 vehicles with the Cummins diesel engine. Following a competition, the now Defence Support Group (at that time the Army Base Repair Organisation - ABRO) were awarded a contract to convert a further batch of at least 870 vehicles with the kits being provided by Alvis Vickers at Telford. Export contracts have been placed by Brunei, Jordan and Oman for CVR(T) upgrades.

Stormer ARV

For the export market, the company has developed an ARV version of the Stormer APC. The first customer for this vehicle is Indonesia who took delivery of a small quantity of vehicles in 1996. Production of the Stormer series of vehicles is complete and they are no longer marketed.

Specifications

Samson ARV
Crew: 3
Weight: (loaded) 8,738 kg
Power-to-weight ratio: 21.74 hp/t (16.21 kW/t)
Length: 4.788 m
 (incl vice and bench) 5.004 m
Width: 2.43 m

Stormer armoured recovery vehicle as supplied to Indonesia   0121236

Height:
 (top of hull) 1.718 m
 (incl MG) 2.254 m
 (incl A-frame) 2.83 m
Ground clearance: 0.356 m
Track: 1.7 m
Track width: 432 mm
Length of track on ground: 2.74 m
Ground pressure: 0.358 kg/cm²
Max speed:
 (road) 72.5 km/h
 (water) 6.44 km/h
Range: 483 km
Fuel capacity: 404.51 litres
Fording: 1.067 m
Freeboard with screen raised:
 (front) 0.965 m
 (rear) 0.815 m
Gradient: 60%
Vertical obstacle: 0.5 m
Trench: 2.057 m
Engine:
 (original) Jaguar J60 No 1 Mark 100B 4.2-litre 6-cylinder in-line petrol developing 190 hp (142 kW) at 4,750 rpm
 (upgrade) Cummins 6BT 5.9-litre 6-cylinder in-line diesel developing 235 hp (175 kW)
Transmission: David Brown Gear Systems TN15 cross-drive, 7 speeds in each direction
Electrical system: 28 V
Batteries: 4 × 6TN, 100 Ah; generator output is 140 A at 28 V
Armament:
 1 × 7.62 mm L7A2 GPMG
 4 × 66 mm smoke grenade dischargers on each side of hull front
Ammunition: 7.62 mm - 2,000 rounds

Status
Production complete. In service with Brunei (two), Oman, UK and Venezuela. No longer marketed.

Contractor
BAE Systems Global Combat Systems
Production of the Samson ARV was undertaken at the former Alvis facility at Coventry, which has now closed.

United States

BAE Systems US Combat Systems M88, M88A1, and M88A2 armoured recovery vehicles

Development
BMY was awarded a contract to build three prototype armoured recovery vehicles under the designation of T88, using as many components as possible of the M60 MBT.

These prototypes were followed by 10 pre-production vehicles for troop trials. The production contract was awarded to BMY in 1960 with the first production M88s completed in February 1961. Final vehicles were completed in 1964, by which time 1,075 had been built.

The M88 was powered by a Continental (now L3 Propulsion Systems) AVSI-1790-6A, 12-cylinder, air-cooled, supercharged, fuel injection petrol engine.

In April 1972, BMY received a contract from the US Army to design significant improvements for the M88. The basis for these improvements was to change the engine from petrol to diesel fuel, corresponding with the US Army's move towards converting all its armoured vehicles to diesel engines.

M88A1 ARV of the Austrian Army from the rear showing A-frame lowered (Michael Jerchel) 　　0589507

US Army M88A2 ARV with A-frame deployed at front of vehicle for lifting operations (BAE Systems, Global Combat Systems) 　　0098885

In 1973 an M88 was fitted with a variant of the engine fitted to the M60 MBT. The Teledyne Continental Motors (now L3 Propulsion Systems) AVDS-1790-2DR 12-cylinder diesel engine produced 750 bhp at 2,400 rpm and had a Power Take-Off (PTO) to facilitate operation of the hydraulic system.

Trials demonstrated an increase in operating range from 360 to 450 km. This vehicle also had a modified transmission, a diesel-fired personnel heater and auxiliary power unit and stowage space for a small quantity of LAW anti-tank weapons.

The hydraulic system was redesigned allowing the auxiliary power unit to operate the main winch cable as well as stow the boom and spade to prepare the vehicle for recovery, should the hydraulic system fail.

The converted vehicle was designated the M88E1 and BMY built five prototypes for accelerated evaluation. The M88A1 was type classified in March 1975. Due to an increased need for medium recovery vehicles and a desire to improve those already in the field, the US Army contracted in 1975 to reopen the M88 production line at the BMY plant in York, Pennsylvania.

Most of the original M88s (878 of the 1,075 produced) were returned to BMY's production facility for overhaul and conversion. Beginning in 1977, this overhaul/conversion process ran in parallel with new production until early 1982. Production of new M88A1s continued, with a total of 2,167 completed when production ended in early 1989.

When production ended at that stage and, taking into account the overhaul/conversions, the total of M88s was 3,244. Of these, 199 were basic M88s, most in service with overseas armies. Although most of the M88A1s are in service with the US Armed Forces, some 496 were then in service with NATO and allied countries.

In November 1990, it was announced that orders placed by a country in Asia for the M88A1 would involve the reopening of the production line.

During 1981 an Independent Research and Development (IR&D) programme was initiated to investigate improvements necessary for the recovery support of the heavier General Dynamics Land Systems M1-series Abrams MBT.

An initial result was the development of the M88AX automotive demonstrator (see under Variants in this entry), which led to the acceptance by the US Army of a revised version of the M88A1 known as the M88A1E1 (see also under Variants) following testing completed during 1988. The M88A1E1 was expected to be type classified as the M88A2.

The first production funding of USD79 million was scheduled for FY89, when 80 vehicles were projected. There was no FY90 funding, leading to further work on the M88A1E1 being terminated from April 1989 until early 1991.

It was expected that between 500 and 1,300 new M88A2s would be produced by BMY with no conversions from existing vehicles being involved. The M88A2 was to have been used to support US Army M60A3, M1 and M1A1 units. Existing US Army M88A1 assets were to have been transferred to supporting the Bradley Fighting System and M109 series self-propelled 155 mm howitzers.

In October 1991, it was announced that the US Army Tank Automotive Command (TACOM) had awarded BMY Combat Systems Division a contract worth USD12.8 million to complete the development and testing of the M88A1E1 Improved Recovery Vehicle (IRV). The five existing M88A1E1 prototypes were reconditioned and improved in a number of key areas.

Testing restarted during 1992 and continued into 1993. A contract, eventually worth USD30.6 million, was placed in October 1994 and involved 13 vehicles. The award was for Low Rate Initial Production (LRIP) and was completed by January 1996.

In August 1997, the M88A2 Hercules was type classified as Standard and the programme was raised from LRIP to Full Scale Production (FSP). By November 1998 the US Army had placed orders for 49 M88A2s.

Thailand had also placed an order for six brand new M88A2s with first deliveries taking place in the last half of 1999. The order, for the Royal Thai Army, was worth USD20.9 million with training and spares. Kuwait has taken delivery of 14 M88A2 vehicles.

The first US Army units were issued with the M88A2 in 1997 and fielding was scheduled to continue to the year 2013.

The name Hercules also stands for Heavy Equipment Recovery Combat Utility Lift and Evacuation System.

In March 1999, the company was awarded a contract for another 15 M88A2 vehicles for the US Army and at this time 80 vehicles had already been built. The 15 new vehicles were delivered between February and December 2000.

Late in 2000, the company was awarded a USD22 million long lead parts contract for the production of M88A2 vehicles for FY2001. This covered 27 M88A2 for the US Army and 17 M88A2 vehicles for the US Marine Corps.

This contract followed a USD54.4 million contract for 27 vehicles for the US Marine Corps which was placed in April 2000 with deliveries taking place between March 2001 and February 2002.

In April 2002 the company was awarded a contract worth USD58.4 million to cover the supply of 21 M88A2 for the US Army and six M88A2 for the US Marine Corps. These remanufactured vehicles were delivered from April 2003 through to May 2004.

By August 2004, the US Army had taken delivery of a total of 152 M88A2 ARV against a procurement objective of 607 vehicles.

The US Army funded a total of 152 M88A2 between FY94 and FY02, while the US Marine Corps funded a total of 55 vehicles between FY00 and FY02.

All US Army M88A2s are rebuilds of the older M88A1 under a joint programme between the then United Defense LP York facility and the US army's Anniston Army Depot. The latter facility strips down the older M88A1 and sends this to York, where the vehicle is fitted out, tested and then shipped to the customer.

Export sales of the M88A2 have been as follows:

Country	Quantity	Comment
Australia	7	Delivered 2006/2007
Egypt	66	Delivered, another 21 to be supplied
Kuwait	14	Delivered
Thailand	6	Delivered

Since then additional orders have been placed and in mid-2010 the US Army awarded the company a contract to convert another batch of 30 M88A1 to the enhanced M88A2 standard and these will be delivered from November 2012 through to March 2013.

As of July 2010 a total of 329 M88A2 had been fielded by the US Army and 57 by the US Marine Corps.

M88A2 enhancements

Block II Modifications

These are currently being incorporated into US Army and Marine Corps M88A2 in the future and include:
- Enhanced diagnostics
- Laser safe vision blocks
- Main winch power reduction and visibility improvements
- Brake modulation.

In mid-2005, United Defense was taken over by BAE Systems and the company became known as BAE Systems, Ground Systems. More recently the company has been renamed as BAE Systems, US Combat Systems.

Block III Modifications

These are planned for installation on US Army and Marine Corps M88A2s in the future:
- Increased stowage (incorporating the US Army's new machine gun mounts)
- Quick release for ballistic skirts
- Driver's viewer enhanced (night vision)
- Exothermic cutter.

Description

The hull of the M88 and M88A1 ARV is of cast armour and rolled armour welded together, with the crew compartment at the front and the engine and transmission at the rear.

The driver and mechanic are seated at the front of the hull, each with a single-piece hatch cover and periscopes. The commander was originally provided with a cupola with an internally mounted .50 (12.7 mm) M2 HB machine gun but this was subsequently replaced by a simple cupola with a pintle-mounted .50 (12.7 mm) M2 HB machine gun. There is an entry door in each side of the hull.

The suspension is similar to that used on the M60 MBT consisting of six roadwheels, with the drive sprocket at the rear and the idler at the front. There are three track-return rollers. Hydraulic shock-absorbers are provided for the first, second and sixth road wheel stations.

At the front of the vehicle is a hydraulically operated blade, which stabilises the vehicle when the winch is being used and assists in bulldozing operations.

An A-type boom pivoted at the front of the hull can lift a vehicle weighing up to 5,443 kg without using the blade or suspension lockout at the front, or 18,160 kg using lockout without using the blade. The vehicle can lift 22,700 kg when using the blade. The two winches are in the lower part of the hull.

M88A1 of the Austrian Army, with stabiliser blade lowered and A-frame in position (Stefan Marx)   1127951

The M88 is not provided with an NBC system (a kit exists for an M88A1 system incorporating a ventilated facepiece) and has no amphibious capability. A fording kit is available for use in water up to 2.6 m deep. Standard equipment includes tools, towbars and an auxiliary fuel pump, allowing the vehicle to transfer fuel to other AFVs at 95 litres/min.

The M88A1 is fitted with an Auxiliary Power Unit (APU) powered by an Onan 10.8 hp (8.1 kW) diesel, two-cylinder, four-cycle engine. The APU powers an auxiliary hydraulic system which can be used to power the boom, spade and main winch and hoist cables if the main hydraulic system is inoperative. It also provides power for the refuelling and fuel transfer pump, which allows the M88A1 to act as a mobile filling station. The hydraulic system also provides power to operate a 19 mm drive hydraulic impact wrench, used for track maintenance and other maintenance and recovery tasks.

Variants

M88AX/M88A1E1/M88 IRV/M88A2

In order to determine the growth potential of the basic M88A1 components, the company developed an M88AX automotive demonstrator in 1984-85. The demonstrator vehicle was increased in power and weight, powered by a 960 bhp Teledyne Continental Motors (now L3 Propulsion Systems) AVDS-1790-8DR diesel engine mated to a slightly modified transmission, the XT-1410- 5X. The final drive ratio was changed from 4.63:1 to 4.00:1. The primary purpose of the M88AX was to validate engineering predictions in connection with the US Army search for an armoured vehicle to recover the M1A1/M1A2 Abrams MBT.

In late 1985, the US Army decided to establish a Product Improvement Programme (PIP) that capitalised on the company's initial efforts. This programme was overtaken by the introduction of the M88A1E1.

The US Army awarded the company a research and development contract in January 1987. The fixed-price contract covered the design, construction and testing of five prototype vehicles plus a separate hull for ballistic testing. The prototype vehicles were designated the M88A1E1.

The M88A1E1 was the follow-on from the M88AX programme and featured a 1,050 hp AVDS-1790-8CR diesel engine coupled to an Allison XT-1410-5A transmission. Improved brakes were fitted along with a brake booster and the sprocket mounting was improved.

One of the main changes introduced was a new hydraulic main winch with a continuous line pull of 63,504 kg, provided with a nominal 100 m of cable. A 2,722 kg lead winch was incorporated to allow a single crew member to deploy the main winch cable. The hoist had a capacity (spade down and with a four-part line) of 31,752 kg and was used in conjunction with an A-frame, lengthened by 0.84 m to increase the lift height. The lengthened A-frame involved the introduction of increased diameter staylines and an increase in length to 8.65 m with the boom stowed.

Combat loaded weight was 63,050 kg, with most of the weight increase introduced by the addition of overlay passive spaced armour to the existing M88A1 hull armour, providing ballistic protection against up to 30 mm calibre direct fire and 152 mm indirect fire fragmentation. Ballistic skirts were also provided. The suspension torsion bars, shock-absorbers and snubbers were upgraded to cater for the weight increase.

Five of the six prototypes produced were used to support activities at Aberdeen Proving Ground.

In January 1991, at the request of the US Army Tank Automotive Command (TACOM), the company submitted a Phase I M88 Improved Recovery Vehicle (IRV) proposal. This would involve the tear-down and inspection of the five M88A1E1 prototypes and some limited engineering to further improve selected areas of the design. Phase II would complete the overhaul and upgrade of the prototypes, conduct the required testing and complete a Technical Data Package.

In October 1991, it was announced that the US Army Tank Automotive Command (TACOM) had awarded the company a contract worth USD12.8 million to complete the development and testing of the M88A1E1 IRV. The five existing M88A1E1 prototypes were reconditioned and improved in a number of key areas. Approximately 18,000 km of government testing was successfully completed by September 1993, demonstrating that the M88 IRV fully met all M1A2 Abrams MBT support requirements.

Subsequent contract modifications totalling USD6.3 million were awarded to the company to define interface drawings with Anniston Army Depot and complete Integrated Logistics Support activities (provisioning, training and technical manuals) that had been deferred due to lack of funding.

At a Special In-process Review conducted in January 1994 the US Army decided to move the programme into limited production. A contract award was made in September 1994 with first vehicle deliveries in early 1996. Type classification of the M88A1E1 to the M88A2 took place in August 1997.

Subsequent modifications to this contract were made in 1995 and 1996 which brought the total production quantity of M88 IRVs up from 13 to 63 vehicles of which 14 of these are for the Kuwait land forces.

Since then, additional orders have been placed for the US Army and Marine Corps.

The latest production figures for the M88A2 are provided earlier in this entry under development.

M88 with MTU diesel engine

This programme has now been cancelled and the M88A2 will retain its existing powerpack.

Egyptian M88A2 ARV co-production

In September 1998, the company was awarded a USD12.9 million Foreign Military Sales (FMS) contract by the US Army Tank-automotive and Armaments Command (TACOM) to provide Manufacturing Technical Assistance (MTA) to Egypt.

This contract was the first of two contracts which lead to the co-production of 50 M88A2 Hercules heavy Armoured Recovery Vehicles (ARV) at the Egyptian Tank Plant (ETP) near Cairo, Egypt.

In March 1999, the company was awarded the main USD102.3 million contract, which provided the necessary parts and kits for co-production as well as the manufacturing and support required to carry out hull machining and weld work at the main facility in York.

This facility, which is currently building M88A2s for US Army, sent hulls to the ETP who undertook final assembly and delivery to the Egyptian Land Forces with final deliveries taking place in 2003. Total value of the Egyptian contract, including spares, is around USD200 million.

The ETP is also known as Factory 200 and as well as assembling the M1A1 Abrams MBT, also carried out overhaul work on M88A1 ARVs and M60A1/M60A3 MBTs for the Egyptian Land Forces.

In the end, a total of 66 M8A2 were assembled in Egypt, and more recently, it has been announced that another 21 units will be produced in Egypt.

Israeli M88

Israeli M88 ARVs are fitted with a Blazer reactive armour package and additional anti-personnel weapons for self and local defence.

More recently some Israel Defense Force M88 series ARV have been provided with bar armour and a new commanders cupola for improved all round observation.

Specifications

M88A2 Hercules armoured recovery vehicle
Crew: 3 + 4
Weight: (combat) 63,050 kg
Power-to-weight ratio: 16.65 hp/t (12.42 kW/t)
Length: (dozer blade raised) 8.58 m
Width: 3.67 m
Height:
  (with MG) 3.22 m
  (top of commander's hatch) 2.97 m
Ground clearance: 0.406 m

Track: 2.717 m
Track width: 711 mm
Length of track on ground: 4.61 m
Ground pressure: 0.963 kg/cm²
Max speed: (road) 48.3 km/h
Range: 483 km
Fuel capacity: 1,628 litres
Fording: 1.42 m
Gradient: 60%
Vertical obstacle: 1.07 m
Trench: 2.62 m
Engine: L3 Propulsion Systems AVDS-1790-8CR, 29.3 litre, 12-cylinder, air-cooled, supercharged fuel injection diesel developing 1,050 bhp (783 kW) at 2,400 rpm
Transmission: Twin Disc XT-1410-5A cross-drive
Suspension: torsion bar
Electrical system: 24 V
Batteries: 6 × 12 V 6TN, 100 Ah
Armament:
  1 × .50 (12.7 mm) M2 HB MG
  2 × 6 smoke grenade dischargers
Ammunition: .50 (12.7 mm) - 1,500 rounds
Armour protection level: 30 mm direct fire AP
Boom capacity:
  (spade down, 4-part line) 31,752 kg
  (spade up, 4-part line, with lockout) 22,680 kg
Boom lift height:
  (at 2.4 m reach) 6.9 m
  (at 1.2 m reach) 7.6 m
Main winch capacity: 63,504 kg
Useable cable: 85.3 m
Auxiliary winch capacity: 2,722 kg
Useable cable: 201.2 m

Status

In production. Current production model is the M88A2. Anniston Army Depot provides the baseline chassis used for this conversion. The M88A1 is in service with Australia (seven), Bahrain (four), Egypt (221 M88A1 + 66 M88A2), Greece (66), Israel (25), Jordan (32), Korea (South) (38), Kuwait (10 + 14 M88A2), Morocco (18), Norway (three), Oman (two), Pakistan (52), Portugal (six), Saudi Arabia (139), Spain (one), Sudan (two), Taiwan (33), Thailand (21 + 6 M88A2), Tunisia (six) and the US (US Army 2,470, Marine Corps 81).

Contractor

BAE Systems US Combat Systems

BAE Systems US Combat Systems M578 light armoured recovery vehicle

Development

In 1956, the Pacific Car and Foundry Company of Renton, Washington, was awarded a US Army contract to design a new range of self-propelled artillery systems which would all use the same basic chassis.

One of the main requirements was to reduce the overall weight of the chassis so that it could be carried by transport aircraft then in service.

The following year the programme was expanded to include three Armoured Recovery Vehicles (ARV), designated the T119, T120 and T121. The T119 and T121 both had their cranes in an unarmoured mounting, but were not developed beyond the prototype stage.

Further development of the T120 (which had a petrol engine) resulted in the T120E1 ARV with a Detroit Diesel engine, which was accepted for service as the M578. The contract was awarded to the then FMC Corporation (today BAE Systems US Combat Systems), which produced the first production vehicle late in 1962. Production was originally completed in the late 1960s.

In 1971, Bowen-McLaughlin-York (which became United Defense and then in mid-2005 BAE Systems, Ground Systems) won a competitive contract to resume production of the M578 and began production the same year. BMY produced a total of 1,018 M578s by the end of 1983 and a total of 1,844 on completion.

Following a Special Mission Adaptation (SMA) a selected number of M578s were used with Combat Electronic Warfare Intelligence (CEWI) battalions.

There has been no production of the M578 for some years and it is no longer being marketed. In most countries the M578 has been supplemented by more capable vehicles.

Description

The hull of the M578 is similar to that of the 175 mm M107 and 203 mm/8 in M110 self-propelled guns, all of which are now phased out of United States Army service. The M107 and M110 are still used by some countries but in declining numbers.

The hull and crane turret of the M578 light armoured recovery vehicle is of all-welded cast armour and high tensile alloy steel which provides some protection against small arms fire and shell splinters.

The driver is seated at the front of the hull on the left side and is provided with a single-piece hatch cover and three M17 day periscopes for driving when closed down. The centre periscope can be replaced by a passive night vision periscope. The diesel engine is to his right and the transmission is at the front of the hull.

At the rear of the hull is mounted the turret and crane which can be traversed through 360°. The turret has a door in each side and double doors in the rear. Both the commander and operator are provided with a single-piece hatch cover that opens to the rear and six M17 day periscopes for observation.

The torsion bar suspension either side consists of five roadwheels with the drive sprocket at the front, the fifth roadwheel acting as the idler. Four of the roadwheels have a hydraulic bump-stop and during recovery operations the suspension can be locked providing a more stable platform.

Armament consists of an unprotected single .50 (12.7 mm) M2 HB Browning machine gun mounted at the commander's position.

The M578 is provided with night driving lights and has an NBC filter kit option for the driver and cab crew. The vehicle does not have an amphibious capability.

Equipment carried includes tools, towbars, hydraulic impact wrench, acetylene welding and cutting equipment. A spade is mounted at the rear of the hull. This is lowered to the ground for recovery and lifting operations. The vehicle has two winches: a tow winch with a maximum capacity of 27,000 kg on a bare drum and a hoisting winch with a maximum capacity of 6,750 kg.

Specifications

M578 light armoured recovery vehicle
Crew: 3
Weight:
(combat) 24,300 kg
(air transport) 20,443 kg
Power-to-weight ratio: 17.5 hp/t (13.5 kW/t)
Length:
(overall) 6.426 m
(hull) 5.588 m
Width: 3.149 m
Height:
(top of cupola) 2.921 m
(incl MG) 3.416 m
Ground clearance: 0.44 m
Track: 2.692 m
Track width: 457 mm
Length of track on ground: 3.758 m
Ground pressure: 0.7 kg/cm²
Max speed: (road) 55 km/h
Range: 725 km
Fuel capacity: 1,136 litres
Fording: 1.066 m
Gradient: 60%
Vertical obstacle: 1.016 m
Trench: 2.362 m
Engine: Detroit Diesel 8V-71T turbocharged V-8 liquid-cooled diesel developing 425 bhp (317 kW) at 2,300 rpm
Transmission: Allison XTG-411-2A cross-drive with 4 forward and 2 reverse gears (automatic)
Electrical system: 24 V with 300 A generator
Batteries: 4 × 6 TN
Armament: 1 × .50 (12.7 mm) M2 HB MG
Ammunition: .50 (12.7 mm) - 500 rounds
Armour: steel

Status

Production complete. In service with Bolivia, Brazil, Canada, Denmark, Egypt, Iran, Jordan, Morocco, Netherlands, Norway, Philippines, Saudi Arabia (88), Spain and US. Only a few M578 ARVs now remain in US Army service. The M578 ARV is no longer marketed.

Contractor

BAE Systems US Combat Systems

BAE Systems US Combat Systems ARVs and repair vehicles based on the M113 APC chassis

Development

The M113 is the most widely used full-tracked armoured personnel carrier in the world and, in addition to being produced in the US, was also built under licence in Italy by Oto Melara.

The first M113s were completed in 1960, followed by the M113A1 which has a diesel engine. In the late 1960s, a Fitter's Vehicle was developed, fitted with a hydraulic crane and the ability to change Armoured Fighting Vehicles (AFV) components.

The then FMC (which subsequently became United Defense and then in mid-2005 BAE Systems, Ground Systems) developed a recovery vehicle which became known as the XM806 (gasoline), followed by the XM806E1 (diesel), 24 of which were produced for export.

Upgraded Australian Army M806AS4 Armoured Recovery Vehicle in travelling configuration. This has an extended chassis with six road wheels either side and appliqué armour (BAE Systems Australia)   1333604

As the US Army did not purchase the XM806 type recovery vehicle, the company called a later version the M113A2 Recovery Vehicle.

It has an improved suspension and cooling system with a new dual-air personnel heater compatible with NBC protective systems. It is in service with several countries.

The company developed a further vehicle combining the features of the Recovery Vehicle with the Fitter's Vehicle. It is called the M113A2 Maintenance Recovery Vehicle (MRV) and uses the same crane and winch as the Fitter's Vehicle. The first prototype was ready early in 1982; since then it has been produced in Belgium and the US.

The MRV can swim without the need for a water barrier and it has a buoyant trim vane. The crane is hydraulically operated and has its own winch. The Royal Netherlands Army uses the AIFV recovery vehicle which is similar to the M113A2 Maintenance Recovery Vehicle but with torsion bar and tube suspension and a 265 hp turbocharged engine. The AIFV weighs approximately 113 kg more than the M113A2 Recovery Vehicle.

The Turkish company, FNSS Savunma Sistemleri is currently marketing two similar versions of its Armoured Combat Vehicle 300 (ACV 300), one armoured recovery vehicle and one fitters vehicle.

Details of the former are provided in a separate entry in *Jane's Military Vehicles and Logistics*. Both of these vehicles are still being marketed.

This latest batch of 48 ACV-300 vehicles for Malaysia were delivered from 2009 through to 2010 and comprises the following versions:
- 12 × Infantry Fighting Vehicle I
- 8 × Infantry Fighting Vehicle II
- 8 × Infantry Fighting Vehicle III
- 4 × anti-armour vehicles
- 2 × armoured vehicle signals
- 4 × armoured recovery vehicle
- 10 × armoured vehicle fitter.

Description

M113A2 recovery vehicle

The hull of the M113A1/A2 is made of all-welded aluminium armour construction which provides the occupants with protection from small arms fire and shell splinters.

The driver is seated at the front of the hull on the left side and is provided with a single-piece hatch cover that opens to the rear. For observation purposes the driver has four M17 day periscopes and an M19 infra-red

M113 series maintenance recovery vehicle with crane stowed and showing manually operated spades at the hull rear in the retracted position (BAE Systems US Combat Systems)   0568220

Fitters/armoured recovery vehicle on AIFV chassis showing additional buoyancy aids on hull front and sides
(BAE Systems US Combat Systems)
0589509

Upgraded M113AS4 Armoured Fitters Vehicle with extended chassis with six road wheels either side and appliqué armour
(BAE Systems Australia)
1333605

periscope in the roof hatch for night driving. Most countries have now replaced the infra-red based optical device with one using image intensification as its basis of operation.

The Detroit Diesel 6V-53 engine is mounted to the right of the driver. The commander's cupola has five day periscopes and a single-piece hatch cover that opens to the rear. A .50 (12.7 mm) Browning M2 HB machine gun is mounted on the commander's cupola with an elevation of +53° and a depression of −21°.

To the immediate rear of the commander is a rectangular hatch which opens to the rear. Normal means of entry and exit are by a power-operated ramp in the rear of the hull.

The torsion bar suspension either side consists of five roadwheels with the drive sprocket at the front and the idler at the rear. There are no track-return rollers.

The vehicle is fully amphibious, being propelled in the water by its tracks. Before entering the water, the trim vane is extended at the front of the hull and the bilge pumps are switched on. The basic vehicle does not have an NBC system, but this and a variety of other kits are available as optional extras.

The M113A2 recovery vehicle has a P30 (modified) hydraulic winch which is provided with 91.4 m of 16 mm diameter cable, with a capacity on a full drum of 5,103 kg and on a bare drum of 9,070 kg. A rotating fairlead that guides the cable is at the rear of the vehicle. A cable tensioner, built into the fairlead, allows free cable to be wound tightly. A level winder keeps the cable properly coiled on the winch drum and heavy shrouds over the winch assembly and a swing-up guard set into the ramp opening protect the operator during winching operations.

A single spade is mounted on each side of the hull at the rear and an additional spade unit can be mounted between the two outer ones for recovery in soft soil. The two spades are lowered to the ground manually.

A manually operated hydraulic crane is mounted on the left side of the vehicle with an extensible arm with two positions for flexibility of use. This crane has a maximum lifting capacity of 1,361 kg at a reach of 2.99 m.

Recovery vehicles produced in Belgium incorporated the M113A1 power train and modified (heavy-duty) torsion bars. These vehicles are unique to the Belgian Army. These are now being replaced by the MOWAG Piranha (8 × 8) vehicles.

M113A3 MRV

The most recent production version is designated the M113A3 and is powered by the Detroit Diesel 6V-53T turbocharged Reliability Improved Selected Equipment (RISE) unit developing 275 hp.

Fitter's vehicle

This vehicle has an almost identical hull to the M113A2 but does not have the small crane or heavy winch. Mounted on the left side of the roof is an Hiab hydraulic crane which can lift a maximum of 1,360 kg at a reach of 3.29 m. The commander's cupola and the hatch to the rear are mounted on a large top hatch that opens to the right. This is 2.39 × 1.37 m and enables a replacement M113 Detroit Diesel engine to be carried inside the vehicle and to be lifted out with the aid of the crane. The crane is provided with a hydraulic winch which has a maximum capacity on a full drum of 1,360 kg, or 1,770 kg on a bare drum. For this winch, 15.2 m of 11.1 mm cable is provided.

MTVR ARV

For the Canadian M113LE (Life Extension) programme, the company has developed a recovery vehicle based on the Mobile Tactical Vehicle Light (MTVL) chassis powered by the Detroit Diesel 6V-35TIA engine. Production of this vehicle commenced in 2002.

MTVF Fitter's Vehicle

The company has developed a Mobile Tactical Vehicle Light (MTVL) version of the Fitter's Vehicle. This version is powered by the Detroit Diesel 6V-53TIA and has a crane capacity of 1,590 kg at a reach of 6.3 m. The MTVF were co-produced in Canada starting in 2002.

Australian Army upgrades

The Australian Army deploys a fleet of M113 series vehicles including the M113 Armoured Fitters Vehicle (AFV) and the M806 Armoured Recovery Vehicle Light (ARVL).

These are being upgraded to the enhanced M113AS4 and M806AS4 standard under the leadership the now BAE Systems Australia.

Both of these are being upgraded in a number of key areas including the installation of a new diesel powerpack, driveline and protection which is common to all seven versions of the M113 used by Australia.

The AFV also features a new Hiab hydraulic crane with an enhanced 2.4-tonne lift at 4 m, while the ARVL has a Sepson winch with a capacity of 13 tonnes on a single line pull.

It was originally expected that Australia would have a mix of standard (five road wheel stations either side) and stretched (six road wheel stations either side), but a decision was taken that all variants would be in the stretched configuration as this offers more volume and payload.

A total of 431 vehicles of all types are being upgraded under the leadership of BAE Systems Australia, with final deliveries now due in 2012.

Specifications

M113A2 ARV

Crew: 3
Weight:
  (air transport) 11,991 kg
  (combat loaded) 12,896 kg
Power-to-weight ratio: 21.3 hp/t (15.9 kW/t)
Length: 5.34 m
Width: 2.69 m
Height: 3.15 m
Track: 2.159 m
Track width: 381 mm
Length of track on ground: 2.67 m
Ground pressure: 0.634 kg/cm^2
Max road speed: 66 km/h
Range: 483 km
Fuel capacity: 363 litres
Fording: amphibious
Gradient: 60%
Side slope: 40%
Vertical obstacle: 0.609 m
Trench: 1.68 m
Engine: Detroit Diesel 6V-53T developing 275 hp (205 kW)
Transmission: Allison X-200-4A hydrokinetic
Electrical system: 24 V
Batteries: 4 × 12 V
Armament: 1 × .50 (12.7 mm) M2 HB machine gun
Ammunition: 2,000 × .50 (12.7 mm)
Armour:
  (type) aluminium alloy
  (thickness) 12-38 mm

M113A2 recovery vehicle
(Data in square brackets relate to Fitter's Vehicle where different)
Crew: 3 [2 + 1 seating]
Weight:
  (air transport) 10,834 [10,275] kg
  (combat loaded) 11,637 [11,700] kg
Power-to-weight ratio: 18.5 [18.4] hp/t (13.8 [13.7] kW/t)
Length: 5.34 [4.87] m
Width: 2.69 m

Height: 2.46 [3.15] m
Ground clearance: 0.43 m
Track: 2.159 m
Track width: 381 mm
Length of track on ground: 2.67 m
Ground pressure: 0.57 [0.576] kg/cm²
Max speed:
  (road) 67.6 [67.5] km/h
  (water) 5.8 km/h
Range: 483 km
Fuel capacity: 363 [360] litres
Fording: amphibious
Gradient: 70%
Side slope: 30%
Vertical obstacle: 0.61 m
Trench: 1.68 m
Engine: Detroit Diesel Model 6V-53, 6-cylinder, water-cooled developing 215 bhp (160 kW) at 2,800 rpm
Transmission: Allison TX-100-1 with 3 forward and 1 reverse gears
Differential: DS200
Electrical system: 24 V
Batteries: 2 × 12 V
Armament: 1 × .50 (12.7 mm) Browning M2 HB MG
Ammunition: 2,000 rounds
Armour:
  (type) aluminium alloy
  (thickness) 12-38 mm

Status

Production as required. Both the M113A1/A2 armoured recovery vehicle and the Fitter's Vehicle are known to be in service with the Australian Army. In service with Bahrain (four M113A2 MRV delivered 1991), Belgium, Brazil, Egypt, Israel, Lebanon, Netherlands (based on AIFV), Sudan and Thailand (10 MRV), Jordan (18 ARV transferred from Belgium in 2008).

Contractor

BAE Systems US Combat Systems

BAE Systems US Combat Systems Assault Amphibian Vehicle, Recovery, Model 7A1

Development

The Assault Amphibian Vehicle, Recovery, Model 7A1 (AAVR7A1) was developed from the Landing Vehicle, Tracked, Recovery, Model 7 (LVTR7) and was renamed during 1985.

The original LVTR7 was developed by the FMC Corporation under contract to the US Naval Sea Systems Command to recover other members of the LVT7 family (the LVT7 is now known as the Assault Amphibian Vehicle or AAV). The FMC Corporation first became what was known as United Defense, in mid-2005 this became BAE Systems Ground Systems and in 2009 is presently known as BAE Systems US Combat Systems.

The first prototype, designated the LVTRX2, was completed in 1968 and after trials was standardised as the LVTR7.

Further development by the company resulted in the LVTR7A1, later known as the AAVR7A1. The AAVR7A1 has improvements to the hull, suspension and power train and changes to the fuel, hydraulic and electrical systems.

The recovery equipment also underwent major modification. Following the completion of US Marine Corps testing in 1981, a contract was awarded to the company to convert the AAVR7 vehicles to the AAVR7A1 configuration.

Since then additional vehicles have been built for the export market and the US Marine Corps has now upgraded a total of 680 vehicles over a four-year period under the Reliability, Availability and Maintainability/Rebuild to Standard (RAM/RS) programme. This will extend their operational life pending the introduction of the new General Dynamics Expeditionary Fighting Vehicle (EFV) (this was previously called the Advanced Amphibious Assault Vehicle) that is currently under development.

The introduction into service of the EFV has been delayed several times and for this reason the AAV7A1 and its many variants will stay in service for some years to come.

This upgrade applies to all US Marine Corps members of the AAV7A1 series of vehicles and was carried out jointly by the company and the US Marine Corps facilities at Albany and Barstow who carried out test and final assembly of the vehicles.

Spain has also recently upgraded its complete fleet of vehicles to the AAV7A1 standard and late in 1999 Italy decided to upgrade its complete fleet of vehicles to the latest RAM/RS configuration with the work being carried out in Italy.

For a higher level of protection most US Marine Corps and some foreign customers, for example South Korea, have fitted their vehicles with additional passive armour protection.

This passive armour system was originally developed by the now RAFAEL Advanced Defense Systems.

AAVR7A1 in travelling configuration   0511473

While the AAV7A1 is expected to be eventually replaced by the much delayed General Dynamics EFV, at present there is no dedicated recovery model of the vehicle.

Description

The hull, which is almost identical to that of the AAV, is made of all-welded aluminium alloy armour. The engine and transmission are at the front of the vehicle and can be removed as a complete unit. The crew compartment and repair area are at the rear of the vehicle.

The driver is seated at the front of the hull on the left side and is provided with a single-piece hatch cover that opens to the rear.

Seven vision blocks are provided for observation and for night driving an AN/VVS-2(V)1A periscope can be mounted in the hatch cover.

The commander is seated to the rear of the driver and also has a single-piece hatch cover that opens to the rear and seven direct vision blocks. The commander has an M27 day periscope that extends vertically, providing a view over the driver's position.

The winch/crane operator is seated on the right side and has nine direct vision blocks, with the hatch cover opening to the rear; when operating the crane the operator uses a seat mounted on the crane structure.

Over the top of the repair area is a large cargo hatch. Normal means of entry and exit are via the large power-operated ramp in the rear of the hull, which is provided with an integral door.

The torsion bar/tube suspension consists of six dual-rubber-tyred roadwheels, with the idler at the rear and the drive sprocket at the front. The first, second and sixth roadwheel stations are provided with a hydraulic shock-absorber. The AAVR7A1 is fully amphibious, being propelled in the water by two water-jets, one in each side of the hull at the rear. These water-jets are driven through right-angled gearboxes. Deflectors are used for steering and reverse. If these fail, the vehicle can be propelled in the water by its tracks at a slower speed.

Armament consists of a pintle-mounted 7.62 mm M240G machine gun. The AAVR7A1 is not provided with an NBC system but does have passive night vision equipment. Kits for the vehicle include a winterisation kit, visor kit for the driver and a navigation light kit for use when the vehicle is afloat at night.

On the right side of the hull is a hydraulic crane which can be elevated from 0° to +65°. Its boom is telescopic and can lift 2,722 kg at 6.553 m reach. A two-speed winch, with a maximum capacity of 13,608 kg on a bare drum at low speed and 1,878 kg on a full drum at high speed, is also installed. Equipment carried includes an air compressor, AC generator, workbenches, welding kit and a complete range of tools. If required, a tent can be erected at the rear of the vehicle to enable repairs to be carried out in bad weather or under blackout.

Specifications

AAVR7A1 recovery vehicle
Crew: 5
Weight:
  (empty) 22,731 kg
  (loaded) 23,643 kg
Power-to-weight ratio: 16.9 hp/t (12.6 kW/t)
Length: 8.14 m
Width: 3.27 m
Height: 3.28 m
Ground clearance: 0.406 m
Track: 2.609 m
Track width: 533 mm
Length of track on ground: 3.94 m
Ground pressure: 0.55 kg/cm²
Max speed:
  (road) 72.4 km/h
  (water) 12.9 km/h
Range: (land) 482 km at 40 km/h
Endurance: (water) 7 h at 2,600 rpm
Fuel capacity: 647 litres

Fording: amphibious
Gradient: 60%
Side slope: 40%
Vertical obstacle: 0.914 m
Trench: 2.44 m
Engine:
(LVTR7) Detroit Diesel Model, 8V-53T 8-cylinder, water-cooled, turbocharged diesel developing 400 hp (298 kW) at 2,800 rpm
(AAVR7A1) Cummins VT400, 8-cylinder, water-cooled, turbocharged diesel developing 400 hp (298 kW) at 2,800 rpm
Transmission: HS400-3A1 giving 4 forward and 2 reverse gears, manually operated but with power assistance
Electrical system: 24 V
Batteries: 4 × 12 V 6 TN
Armament: 1 × 7.62 mm M240G MG
Ammunition: 7.62 mm - 880 rounds
All US Marine Corps vehicles have the Cummins Diesel engine.

Armour
Material: aluminium alloy
Ramp outer: 25.4 mm
Ramp inner: 12.7 mm
Hull sides: 31-44.5 mm
Hull floor and roof: 30.1 mm
Hull rear: 35.4 mm

Status
The AAV7RA1 entered production again in 1996 for Brazil, which ordered 14 new vehicles including one AAV7A1, all of which were delivered early in 1997. The basic AAV is in service with Argentina, Brazil, Italy, South Korea, Spain, Thailand, US and Venezuela.

The AAVR7 and AAVR7A1 are in service with Argentina (one), Brazil (one), South Korea (three), Spain (one), Thailand (one), US (64) and Venezuela (one).

Late in 1995 South Korea signed a co-production programme for a total of 57 new AAV7A1 vehicles, including five AAVR7A1 vehicles, with deliveries taking place from 1997 through to 2000. As of late 2010 there was not a date as to when this vehicle would be phased out of service with the US Marine Corps.

Contractor
BAE Systems US Combat Systems

Cadillac Gage LAV-150S and LAV-300 Commando armoured recovery vehicles

Development
This range of 4 × 4 light armoured vehicles was developed as a private venture by Cadillac Gage (now Textron Marine & Land Systems) with the first production models being completed in 1964. These were designated the V-100 and were followed a few years later by the larger V-200. The V-200 was developed to meet the operational requirements of the Singapore Armed Forces, who are the only customer for the vehicle.

Late production was based on the V-150S, which has many improvements over the earlier V-100 and the similar V-150. More recently the V-150S and V-300 been renamed the LAV-150S and LAV-300. The latest model of the former is the LAV-150ST which is stretched and turbocharged.

These vehicles are also referred to by the manufacturer as the Commando family.

Production and marketing of the LAV-150S (4 × 4) and LAV-300 (6 × 6) Commando vehicles has now ceased and marketing is now being concentrated on the new Armored Security Vehicle (4 × 4), which has been developed for the US Army.

LAV-150S (4 × 4) recovery vehicle in travelling order 0512304

In 1999 the US Army Tank-automotive & Armaments Command placed a contract with Textron Marine & Land Systems worth USD50 million covering the supply of 94 production M1117 ASV for the US Army Military Police for delivery over a five-year period.

First production M1117 Guardian ASVs were completed at the Textron Marine & Land Systems facility in New Orleans in the second quarter of 2000.

In mid-2004, the US Army directed Textron to accelerate/ramp up production to monthly delivery objectives of 12,24,36 and ultimately 48 vehicles per month the latter figure has been maintained since 2006.

As a result of operational experience in Iraq, the US Army placed additional orders for the ASV and in mid-2009 the 2000th vehicle rolled off the production line.

By mid-November 2010 the US Army had ordered 3,030 M1117s and 414 M1200 Armored Knights, an ASV variant used by the US Army Field Artillery Combat Observation Lasing Teams (COLT) in both Heavy and Infantry Brigade Combat Teams (IBCT).

Under the current contract, production is expected to continue into at least 2012 and Textron Marine & Land Systems is currently building 48 vehicles a month with a built in surge capacity for additional home and export contracts.

In mid-2004 the US Project and Contracting Organization (PCO) acting on behalf of the Iraqi Ministry of the Interior, placed an order worth USD50 million covering the supply of 62 vehicles for the Iraqi Civil Intervention Force and all of these were delivered between late 2004 and mid-2005.

The order for 62 included 56 in the stretched Armoured Personnel Carrier (APC) configuration and armed with a roof mounted protected MG installation which can carry 10 people including commander, driver and gunner.

The remaining vehicles in the order included four in the command-and-control configuration with extensive communications equipment and two recovery vehicle configurations.

Since then the US Army has provided an additional 182 M1117 vehicles to Iraq and by late 2010 a Foreign Military Sales (FMS) case was established for a further 72 APCs and eight command-and-control variants.

Other export contracts have also been placed by Bulgaria (seven through a direct commercial sales) and Colombia (39 for USD45.6 million though FMS).

Description
The hull of the LAV-150S is of all-welded steel armour construction which provides the crew with protection from small arms fire. The driver is seated at the front of the hull on the left side with the co-driver to his right. Both are provided with vision blocks and a single-piece hatch cover that opens to the left or right. There is a further vision block on either side of their positions.

The remainder of the crew is seated to the rear of the driver's position. The gunner's hatch is in the centre of the roof and a 7.62 mm machine gun is mounted at this position.

There is a door in each side of the hull and a third door in the rear on the right side, both with a vision block and a firing port. These doors are in two parts, top and bottom; the bottom part opening downwards to form a step and the top half opening left or right. There is a further firing port and vision block in each side of the hull forward of the side doors. There is also a two-part roof hatch to the right of the engine compartment.

The engine and transmission are mounted at the rear of the hull on the left side with access hatches in the roof and side of the hull. The Cummins engine compartment is provided with a fire suppression system which is operated by the driver.

The suspension is of the solid axle type with semi-elliptical springs and heavy-duty shock-absorbers at each wheel station. The axles have automatic silent positive locking differentials. The steering is power assisted and the tyres are of the run-flat type and have a self-cleaning tread. Central tyre inflation is optional. If fitted, this allows the driver to adjust the tyre pressure to suit the terrain being crossed, to provide maximum traction. The LAV-150S is fully amphibious, propelled in the water by its wheels; two electric bilge pumps are provided.

The A-frame is supported when in operation by two cables attached to the rear of the vehicle. A hydraulically actuated spade is provided at the front of the hull and is operated through the same controls used for the winch and boom. The winch is mounted in the centre of the hull and leads out through an opening in the forward part of the commander's roof pod. The winch has a maximum capacity of 11,348 kg and has 61 m of 19 mm diameter cable. The boom has a maximum lifting capacity of 4,536 kg with the two jack stands in position. When not in use this rests on the rear of the hull.

Equipment carried on board includes 15.24 m of hose for the compressor, fuel transfer pump, jacks, gunner's platform/workbench, portable spotlight, slave cables, tools and towbars.

Variants

LAV-300 armoured recovery vehicle
A 6 × 6 armoured recovery vehicle, based on the LAV-300 armoured vehicle, was produced. This variant has no turret and has a raised and fixed superstructure at the rear. An A-frame jib is mounted on the hull roof front and a folding spade anchor is located under the vehicle front. An 11,348 kg capacity winch is fitted and provided with 61 m of cable. Gross weight of

the LAV-300 is 14,969 kg, length is 6.4 m, hull width is 2.54 m and hull height is 1.98 m. Power is provided by a Cummins 6 CTA.8.3 turbocharged, after-cooled in-line 6-cylinder diesel developing 206 kW (276 hp) at 1,900 rpm.

Textron Martin & Land Systems have ceased all marketing of the LAV-300 series of 6 × 6 light armoured vehicles.

Specifications

LAV-150S Commando Armoured Recovery Vehicle
Crew: 4
Configuration: 4 × 4
Combat weight: 10,886 kg
Power-to-weight ratio: 25.35 hp/t (18.91 kW/t)
Length: 6.14 m
Width: 2.26 m
Height: (hull) 1.98 m
Ground clearance: (under hull) 0.647 m
Track:
(front) 1.91 m
(rear) 1.94 m
Wheelbase: 3.12 m
Ground pressure: 1.5 kg/cm²
Max speed:
(road) 100 km/h
(water) 5 km/h
Range: 644 km
Fuel capacity: 302 litres
Fording: amphibious
Gradient: 60%
Side slope: 30%
Vertical obstacle: 0.91 m
Engine: Cummins 6 CTA 8.3 (turbocharged, after-cooled, in-line 6-cylinder diesel), 276 hp (206 kW) at 1,099 rpm (governed), torque 828 ft.lbf (1,122 N.m) at 1,300 rpm
Transmission: Allison automatic 6-speed
Transfer box: single speed with spline engagement clutch for front axle drive
Steering: variable ratio power
Turning radius: 8.5 m
Suspension: solid axles with semi-elliptic multileaf springs with telescopic direct- acting shock-absorbers at each wheel station
Tyres: 14.00 R 20
Electrical system: 24 V
Batteries: 2 × 12 V, 100 Ah
Alternator: 60 A
Armament: 1 × 7.62 mm MG
Ammunition: 7.62 mm - 2,200 rounds

Status

Production complete. No longer marketed. Users of the LAV-150 include Bolivia, Botswana, Cameroon, Chad, Dominican Republic, Gabon, Guatemala, Indonesia, Jamaica, Malaysia, Mexico (ARV confirmed), Philippines, Saudi Arabia (ARV confirmed), Singapore V-200 (ARV confirmed), Sudan, Taiwan, Thailand, Turkey, US and Venezuela. Marketing is now being concentrated on the Armored Security Vehicle (ASV) which is now in service with the US Army and Bulgaria (seven), Colombia (39) and Iraq (244).

Contractor

Textron Marine & Land Systems

General Dynamics Land Systems Stryker Maintenance Recovery Vehicle

Development

General Dynamics Land Systems (GDLS), prime contractor for the US Army's Stryker Family Of Vehicles (FOV) have developed as a private venture the Stryker Maintenance Recovery Vehicle (MRV).

The US Army currently deploys a complete family of Stryker Infantry Carrier Vehicles (ICV) and variants and by late 2010 General Dynamics Land Systems facilities in Canada and the United States had delivered 3,535 to the US Army with the total US Army order book being 4,074.

At the present time there is not a dedicated MRV version of the Stryker and this is currently supported and recovered by other vehicles.

Development of the Stryker MRV has been completed and it has been evaluated by the US Army but as of early 2011 no production orders had been placed for the vehicle.

The Stryker MRV has been designed to carry out a number of battlefield missions including the recovery of other members of the Stryker ICV FOV as well as other vehicles, tracked and wheeled.

It can also carry out battlefield repairs to members of the Stryker ICV FOV, for example changing a complete Stryker powerpack.

It has the same mobility characteristics as the Stryker and same level of protection.

Description

The hull of the Stryker MRV is all welded high hardness steel armour construction that provides the occupants with protection from small arms fire and shell splinters.

General Dynamics Land Systems Stryker Maintenance Recovery Vehicle with earth anchor deployed at front of vehicle, crane deployed to the rear and stabilisers extended to side of vehicle
(General Dynamics Land Systems)   1403725

The description below relates to the first prototype of the Stryker MRV but there is considerable flexibility in the design of the vehicle to meet users specific operational requirements.

Spall liners are fitted internally and appliqué armour can be fitted to the front and side of the chassis for a higher level of ballistic protection.

The driver is seated at the front left with the diesel power pack to the right.

Driver is provided with a single piece hatch cover above his position that opens to the rear with three standard M17 day periscopes providing situational awareness through the frontal arc. The middle periscope can be replaced by a passive device for night driving.

The vehicle commander is normally seated to the rear of the driver and has a single piece hatch cover that opens to the rear and five M17 day periscopes and the centre periscope can be replaced by a periscope for night driving.

There is an additional crew station to the rear of the commanders position on the right side of the hull and this also provided with a single piece hatch cover that opens to the rear and five standard M17 day periscopes.

Armament depends on users specific requirements but can include a standard Kongsberg Protector Remote Controlled Weapon Station (RCWS) that is mounted to the right of the commanders position.

This can be armed with a stabilised 7.62 mm or .50 (12.7 mm) Machine Gun (MG) or a 40 mm automatic grenade launcher which is laid onto the day using a flat panel display located in the hull.

In order to carry out its specialised role, the Stryker MRV is fitted with a range of specialist equipment.

Mounted at the front of the chassis is the earth anchor that is 2.585 m wide and is constructed of ballistic steel.

It is hydraulically operated and has up/down/float modes of operation. It also has an integral pintle mount, work surface and flood light mount.

The recovery winch is a Rotzler TR 200 that has a maximum line pull of 200 kN and a nominal line pull of 180 kN which is used to the front of the vehicle.

This winch is provided with 200 m of cable with a useable length of 190 m and a stated maximum breaking strength of 45,360 kg.

The winch has a maximum speed of 38 m/min and a nominal speed of 9 m/min and can be operated from within the vehicle or via remote control up to 400 m away from the vehicle.

General Dynamics Land Systems Stryker Maintenance Recovery Vehicle with earth anchor deployed at front of vehicle
(General Dynamics Land Systems)   1403726

Pivoted at the rear of the hull on the left side is a Magnum 210M hydraulically operated crane with a nominal rating of 21.3 meter/ton. When not required this is traversed to the front of the vehicle.

This hydraulic crane has the following reach and lift capacity:
4,460 kg at 4.71 m
6,075 kg at 3.5 m
7,000 kg at 3 m
7,480 kg at 2.5 m

The hydraulic crane has a maximum horizontal reach of 5.04 m and a vertical reach of 6.75 m and can be traversed through 365°.

To provide a more stable platform when the hydraulic crane is in use two hydraulically operated stabilisers legs are provided one either side at the rear of the chassis. These have a maximum extension of 0.8 m and a maximum spread of 3.21 m.

Standard equipment for the Stryker MRV includes powered steering, automatic fire detection and suppression system for the crew compartment, NBC system, air conditioning system with communications equipment and navigation system depending on users specific requirements. Stowage boxes are provided for tools and other equipment.

Optional equipment includes a central tyre pressure regulation system that allows the driver to adjust the tyre pressure to suit the terrain being crossed.

In addition to the winch, crane and earth anchor, a number of additional features can be provided according to customers requirements.

These include welding equipment, pioneer rack, tow bars, shackles, snatch blocks, specialised tools and a 45,360 kg towing pintle at the rear. A rear self-recovery winch can also be fitted.

Specifications

Stryker Maintenance Recovery Vehicle
Crew: 3
Configuration: 8 × 8
Combat weight: 24,948 kg
Power-to-weight ratio: 14.02 hp/tonne
Length: 8.224 m
Width: 2.715 m
Height: 2.759 m
Ground clearance: 0.47 m
Track: 2.27 m
Wheelbase: 3.86 m
Angle of approach/departure: 35°/35°
Max speed: 100 km/h
Fuel capacity: 200 litres
Range: 530 km
Fording: 1.7 m
Gradient: 60%
Side slope: 30%
Vertical obstacle: 0.58 m
Trench: 1.981 m
Turning radius: 17 m
Engine: Caterpillar 3126 diesel developing 350 hp
Transmission: Allison MD 3066 automatic with 6 forward and one reverse gears
Transfer case: two speed
Steering: power-asisted, front two wheels either side
Suspension: independant with optional height adjustment
Tyres: Michelin 1200R20 XML run flat
Brakes:
(main) power with ABS
    (parking) hydraulic
Electrical system: 24 V
Batteries: 4 × 12 V
Armament: 1 × .50 (12.7 mm MG) M2 MG (depends on customer requirement)
NBC system: yes
Night vision equipment: yes

Status

Prototype completed.

Contractor

General Dynamics Land Systems

ARMOURED REPAIR VEHICLES

Canada

General Dynamics Land Systems - Canada LAV (8 × 8) armoured repair and recovery vehicle

Development
With the award of a production contract to Diesel Division, General Motors of Canada, which subsequently became General Motors Defense, (today General Dynamics Land Systems - Canada) to produce the Light Armoured Vehicle (LAV) series of vehicles based on the MOWAG (8 × 8) Piranha, the company developed a repair and recovery version of the basic vehicle.

The LAV recovery was issued to the US Marine Corps, which had an initial requirement for 46 of these vehicles. They were delivered during 1986.

In July 1989, the Australian government purchased an LAV repair and recovery vehicle from the US Marine Corps as part of an initial purchase of 15 vehicles. The vehicles entered service with the Australian Army's 2nd Cavalry during 1990.

There is a separate entry in *Jane's Military Vehicles and Logistics* on the MOWAG Piranha (8 × 8) armoured repair vehicle, which is used by a number of countries.

The General Dynamics Land Systems - Canada LAV III (8 × 8) vehicle forms the basis of the US Army's Stryker Infantry Carrier Vehicle.

Description
The LAV (8 × 8) repair and recovery vehicle uses the basic hull configuration of the original Swiss developed MOWAG Piranha, but it is equipped with American-manufactured cranes and winches.

The vehicle has a crew of four: driver, commander, rigger and one additional crew member, with the driver seated forward on the left side and the commander behind him, seated under a cupola.

The roof level of the rear hull is raised and there is a hatch for the rigger, who controls the hydraulic crane by remote control. The HIAB crane has a 4,125 kg lift capacity (1,040 kg at maximum extension) and has a full 360° traverse with the pivoting point just forward and to the left of the rigger's cupola. The crane jib reach radius is from 1.37 to 4.7 m. Normally the crane rests on a support at the rear of the hull.

The additional crew member is seated in the rear compartment which also contains extra tools, floodlights and cutting equipment. The vehicle also carries a rear-mounted hydraulic winch with a 13,608 kg capacity. The vehicle is amphibious within about five minutes of preparation and in the water is driven by two propeller units at the rear.

All 8 × 8 versions of the LAV used by Canada have had their propellers and amphibious capability removed.

The LAV (8 × 8) repair and recovery vehicle has a fuel transfer subsystem and carries an auxiliary power unit. If required, the crane can be operated using a remote control box from outside the vehicle. The commander's cupola has a pintle for a 7.62 mm M60 machine gun; 1,000 rounds of 7.62 mm ammunition can be carried.

Two banks of M257 smoke grenade dischargers are carried, one on each side and are controlled from the commander's position. A towing hook is fitted at the rear. Outrigger legs are fitted for use when the crane jib is extended.

Variants
As a private venture General Dynamics Land Systems – Canada have built the prototype of a Stryker maintenance and recovery vehicle which has been developed to support the Stryker ICV and variants deployed by the US Army.

As of November 2010 the US Army had not placed any contracts for the Stryker ARV.

General Dynamics Land Systems - Canada LAV (8 × 8) armoured repair and recovery vehicle　　　　0511476

Specifications

LAV armoured repair and recovery vehicle
Crew: 4
Configuration: 8 × 8
Weight: (combat) 12,860 kg
Power-to-weight ratio: 21.38 hp/t
Length:
(normal) 7.376 m
(reduced) 6.39 m
Width: 2.5 m
Height:
(normal) 2.845 m
(reduced) 2.692 m
Max speed: (road) 100 km/h
Range: 660 km
Engine: Detroit Diesel 6V-53T, 6-cylinder diesel developing 275 hp at 2,800 rpm
Transmission: Allison MT-653 DR automatic, 5 forward and 1 reverse gears
Turning diameter: 15.5 m
Wheel travel: 0.33 m
Armament:
1 × 7.62 mm M60 MG
2 × M257 smoke grenade launchers
Ammunition: 7.62 mm - 1,000 rounds

Status
Production as required. In service with Australia (one), Saudi Arabia (67) and US Marine Corps (46). These are from the Canadian production line, other users have received these vehicles from Switzerland (MOWAG) or the now BAE Systems Global Combat Systems. The latter has built significant quantities of Piranha vehicles for the export market including Oman, Qatar and Saudi Arabia.

Contractor
General Dynamics Land Systems - Canada

General Dynamics Land Systems - Canada Bison (8 × 8) Mobile Repair Team vehicle

Development
In July 1989, the now General Dynamics Land Systems - Canada received an order from the Canadian government for 199 8 × 8 vehicles based on the US Marine Corps LAV, originally known as the Infantry Section Carrier (ISC) and named Bison. The Bison was designed by the now General Dynamics Land Systems - Canada during 1988.

Four versions of the vehicle were developed, including 16 maintenance vehicles for use by Mobile Repair Teams (MRT). The other Bison vehicles are the ISC, a command post and an 81 mm mortar fire support vehicle.

The Bison was developed from the LAV-L armoured logistics carrier by increasing the width of the vehicle at the roof line to create additional internal volume and by adding a hydraulically actuated ramp door at the rear. Other minor changes were made to meet unique Canadian requirements.

The Bison was designed as a common baseline vehicle. By the use of various kits, the ISC can be modified for other roles. Each kit is installed in the chassis with a minimum of changes to the hull through the use of a system of integral standard rails, to which various components and stowage items can be attached. The vehicle has a flat floor with integral tiedowns and can be used as a cargo carrier.

For operations in Bosnia, some of the Canadian Bison vehicles were fitted with appliqué passive armour.

With the introduction of the more recent General Dynamics Land Systems - Canada LAV - III, the Canadian Forces are now re-rolling their existing fleet of 199 Bison (8 × 8) vehicles and additional details are given under variants. During this re-role the amphibious capability of all Bison vehicles was removed.

Description
The Bison Mobile Repair Team vehicle follows the same general lines as the LAV armoured repair and recovery vehicle, but differs in many details to meet Canadian Forces requirements.

The Bison Mobile Repair Team vehicle is a basic Bison ISC chassis with the cargo hatch relocated to the rear and with the two troop hatches removed along with two of the four seats. Other additional items include a 265° traverse HIAB hydraulically operated crane and stabilisers (the crane is the same as that used on the LAV (8 × 8) US Marine Corps' repair and recovery vehicle, as are the stabilisers), two detachable floodlights, a utility air line, a machinist's vice and a quick-release hose for power tools. Provision is made for tool, camouflage net and other equipment stowage.

The vehicle is capable of self-loading and unloading spare wheel assemblies and can carry a complete diesel Bison powerpack internally.

Bison (8 × 8) Mobile Repair Team vehicle (Richard Stickland)   0007355

It is also capable of towing a similar vehicle and is equipped with a standard towbar. Although no heavy recovery winch is installed, all Bison vehicles are equipped with a front-mounted 6,800 kg dynamic pull hydraulic winch.

The vehicle has a crew of two, a driver and a commander, who also acts as a rigger. The driver is seated on the left of the vehicle and, when it is fully closed down, he is provided with three M17 day periscopes; the commander has five day periscopes for his position behind the driver. Night vision devices are optional. The vehicle is provided with an M8A1 ventilated face mask NBC system and a VHF radio. A Halon 1301 manual fire suppression system is provided for the crew and engine compartments.

There is provision for a 7.62 mm M60 machine gun mounting over the commander's hatch and two 76 mm Krauss-Maffei Wegmann smoke grenade launchers with eight grenades. An ATGW wire cutter is positioned in front of the driver's position.

Bison Re-role

This re-role will be completed by 2011 with the work being carried out by General Dynamics Land Systems - Canada and Ottawa based Dew Engineering and Development Limited.

When completed, the Bison will be re-rolled into the following specialised versions:
Ambulance (32)
Command, Control, Communications and Intelligence (C31) (83)
Electronic warfare (16)
Mobile Repair Team (32)
Maintenance and Recovery Vehicle (32)

Husky armoured repair vehicle

This is a member of the Armoured Vehicle General Purpose (AVGP) family of 6 × 6 LAV of which a total of 491 were delivered to the Canadian Army by 1982.

Within this total were 19 Husky armoured repair vehicles. These have all been withdrawn from service together with the Grizzly armoured personnel carrier and Cougar fire support vehicles.

Canada has loaned 105 AVGP (100 Grizzly APC and five Husky armoured repair vehicles) to three African Union countries for use in Sudan. The AVGP (6 × 6) is based on the Swiss MOWAG Piranha I (6 × 6) design.

In 2007, Uruguay took delivery of 40 surplus Cougar vehicles from Canada. It is not known as to whether any Husky armour repair vehicles were also included.

Specifications

Bison mobile repair team vehicle
Crew: 2
Configuration: 8 × 8
Weight:
 (kerb) 12,055 kg
 (max) 13,027 kg
Power-to-weight ratio: 21.11 hp/t
Max load: 973 kg
Length: 7.366 m
Width: 2.5 m
Height: 2.692 m
Max speed: (road) 100 km/h
Range: 665 km
Gradient: 60%
Side slope: 30%
Fording: 1.5 m
Trench: 2.06 m
Engine: Detroit Diesel 6V-53T 6-cylinder diesel developing 275 hp at 2,800 rpm
Gearbox: Allison MT-653 DR automatic, 5 forward and 1 reverse gears
Steering: power assisted
Turning radius: 15.5 m
Suspension: independent on all 8 wheels
Electrical system: 24 V
Batteries: 4
Armament: 1 × 7.62 mm M60 MG

Status

Production complete but can be resumed if further orders are placed. In service with the Canadian Forces.

Contractor

General Dynamics Land Systems - Canada

China

NORINCO Type 85 armoured repair vehicle

Development

The China North Industries Corporation (NORINCO) Type 85 armoured repair vehicle is based on the chassis and hull of the Type 85 APC (originally known as the YW531H series APC).

NORINCO is no longer marketing the Type 85 APC and its variants, including the Type 85 armoured repair vehicle.

In late-2010 NORINCO was only offering one tracked light Armoured Fighting Vehicle (AFV), on the export market, the VP1 full tracked Armoured Personnel Carrier (APC).

This is similar in appearance and capabilities to the NORINCO Type 90 APC which has a distinct chamfer to the upper part of the troop compartment and slightly different hull front.

The Type 90 APC is no longer being offered on the export market by NORINCO.

More specialised versions of the VP1 APC include ambulance, command post vehicle and self-propelled mortar.

As far as it is known there is not a dedicated ARV version of the NORINCO VP1 ARV. It is considered that this could be developed for the export market if there was a firm requirement.

Description

The basic hull and chassis of the Type 85 APC are retained, which along with the one-person 12.7 mm machine gun cupola providing lateral protection through about 340° but does not have any overhead protection for the gunner.

The main structural change is to the rear crew compartment where the roof is raised to form a box superstructure, providing more internal space for the crew of six (commander, driver and four fitters) and their repair tools and other equipment.

A hand-operated boom crane capable of lifting loads weighing up to 1,000 kg can be erected at the rear of the vehicle. Other specialised equipment carried includes a 36 kW electrical generator, air and oil filter cleaners, grease filters, an M30 impact wrench, recoil brake checking tools and a 200 bar air cylinder.

The vehicle can recharge armoured vehicle batteries and perform engine power measurements using its onboard equipment and a Type 883 or VRC-83 radio set is carried.

Specifications

Type 85 armoured repair vehicle
Crew: 6
Weight: (combat) approx 15,000 kg
Power-to-weight ratio: approx 21.3 hp/t
Length: 6.125 m
Width: (overall) 3.06 m
Height: (overall) 2.949 m
Ground clearance: 0.46 m
Track: 2.526 m
Track width: 360 mm
Length of track on ground: 3.275 m

NORINCO Type 85 armoured repair vehicle clearly showing raised roof line to rear of driver's compartment   0007356

Max speed:
 (roads) 60 km/h
 (water) 6 km/h
Fuel capacity: 450 litres
Range: (road) 500 km
Fording: amphibious
Gradient: 60%
Vertical obstacle: 0.6 m
Engine: KHD air-cooled diesel developing 320 hp
Transmission: manual, 4 forward and 1 reverse gears
Steering: clutch and brake
Suspension: torsion bar
Electrical system: 24 V
Armament: 1 × 12.7 mm Type 54 MG
NBC system: yes
Night vision equipment: yes

Status

Production complete. There are no known exports of the NORINCO Type 85 ARV. Some sources have indicated that this vehicle was developed for the export market and was not used by the People's Liberation Army.

Contractor

China North Industries Corporation (NORINCO)

France

Nexter Systems AMX-10 ECH repair vehicle

Development

The Nexter Systems (previously Giat Industries) AMX-10 ECH is the repair vehicle member of the AMX-10P Infantry Combat Vehicle (ICV) family. It entered service with the French Army in 1973. The vehicle was shown for the first time in 1977. It has no recovery capability and is limited to changing components of other AFVs, for example, the complete powerpack of the AMX-10P.

Production of the vehicle was undertaken at Roanne. The company is no longer marketing the AMX-10P family of armoured vehicles.

In French Army service the AMX-10P is to be replaced by the Nexter Systems VBCI (8 × 8) infantry fighting vehicle with first deliveries made to the French Army in 2008.

Under current plans, the French Army is to take delivery of a total of 630 VBCI (8 × 8) vehicles in two versions, 520 infantry fighting vehicle and 110 command post.

At the present time there are no plans to field a specialised armoured recovery vehicle or armoured repair vehicle model of the VBCI by the French Army.

In French Army service, the AMX-10P ICV has started to be replaced by the VBCI with a total of 630 ordered of which over 200 had been delivered by late 2010.

Of the 630 VBCI, 520 are in the VCI (*Vehicule de Combat d'Infanterie*) and remaining 110 in the VPC (*Vehicule Poste de Commandement*) command post configuration. some of the VCI carry MBDA Eryx Anti-Tank Guided Weapons (ATGW) or an 81 mm mortar carrier for dismounted use.

As of late 2010 no recovery version of the VBCI family of 8 × 8 vehicles had been ordered although Nexter Systems had studied this version.

Description

The hull of the AMX-10 ECH is almost identical to that of the AMX-10P and is of all-welded aluminium construction. This provides protection from small arms fire and shell splinters.

The driver is seated at the front of the hull on the left side and is provided with a single-piece hatch cover and three day periscopes for observation. The centre periscope can be replaced by a passive periscope for driving at night. The powerpack, consisting of a Renault HS 115-2 V-8 diesel engine, coupled to a pre-selective transmission, is mounted to the right of the driver.

The crew compartment is at the rear of the hull and entrance to it is by the large power-operated ramp at the rear, which is provided with a door in case the ramp fails to open.

The suspension is the torsion bar type and either side consists of five roadwheels with the drive sprocket at the front and the idler at the rear. There are three track-return rollers. Double-acting lever-type hydraulic shock-absorbers are provided for the first and fifth roadwheel stations.

The crew of five consists of the driver, the commander in the turret and three mechanics. The AMX-10 ECH is fully amphibious, propelled in water by either its tracks at a speed of 6 km/h, or by two water-jets, one in each side of the hull, giving a maximum water speed of 7.92 km/h. Before entering the water, a trim board is erected at the front of the hull.

The vehicle has a Nexter Systems Toucan I one-person turret, slightly offset to the left side of the hull, fitted with a 20 mm cannon and a coaxial 7.62 mm machine gun. The turret can be traversed through 360° and the armament elevated from −13° to +50°.

Nexter Systems AMX-10 ECH, a member of the AMX-10P family of tracked combat vehicles   0512447

Elevation and traverse are manual, maximum elevation speed is 16°/s and maximum traverse speed is 12°/s. Optical equipment for the turret includes six day periscopes, a day sight with a magnification of ×6 for engaging ground targets and a separate day sight for anti-aircraft fire. A total of 576 rounds of 20 mm and 2,000 rounds of 7.62 mm ammunition is carried.

On the right side of the roof, at the rear, is the hydraulically operated crane, with an extensible jib which can lift a maximum of 6,000 kg. The operator is provided with a small roof-hatch. When using this crane, jacks are placed under the rear of the hull to support the vehicle.

Other equipment carried include tools, two sheer legs and two jacks, which are used to replace suspension components (for example torsion bars) on other AFVs including the AMX-30 MBT.

Saudi Arabia has taken delivery of a total of 230 AMX-30S MBTs plus many specialised versions. It is understood that the former are now in reserve but many of the specialised versions remain in service.

Optional kits for the AMX-10 ECH included an NBC system and passive night vision equipment. The company have proposed a number of automotive upgrades for the AMX-10 ECH series of ICV.

Late in 2005, the company was awarded a contract to upgrade 108 AMX-10P ICVs of the French Army, with deliveries running from 2006 through to 2008. This did not include an upgrade to the specialised versions of the vehicle, such as the AMX-10 ECH.

Specifications

AMX - 10 ECH repair vehicle
Crew: 5
Weight:
 (empty) 11,300 kg
 (loaded) 13,800 kg
Power-to-weight ratio: 20.28 hp/t
Length: 5.76 m
Width: 2.78 m
Height:
 (top of hull) 1.92 m
 (overall) 2.62 m
Ground clearance: 0.45 m
Ground pressure: 0.53 kg/cm²
Max speed: (road) 65 km/h
Range: (road) 600 km
Fording: amphibious
Gradient: 60%
Vertical obstacle: 0.7 m
Trench: 1.6 m
Engine: Renault HS 115-2 V-8 water-cooled supercharged diesel developing 280 hp at 3,000 rpm
Transmission: pre-selective with 4 forward and 1 reverse gears
Electrical system: 24 V
Armament:
 1 × 20 mm cannon
 1 × 7.62 mm MG coaxial with main armament
 2 × smoke grenade dischargers either side of turret
NBC system: yes
Night vision equipment: yes

Status

Production complete. In service with Saudi Arabia. The AMX-10P or its variants is also in service with Bosnia, France, Qatar, Saudi Arabia and the UAE. This vehicle is no longer marketed.

Contractor

Nexter Systems

Renault Trucks Defense VAB ECH repair vehicle

Development
In 1969, the French Army issued a requirement for a new wheeled vehicle called the VAB (*Véhicule de l'Avant Blindé*).

The VAB was designed to undertake a wide range of roles including use as an APC, load carrier, ambulance and anti-tank vehicle. Prototypes were built by Panhard and Saviem and, after comparative trials, the Saviem model was adopted by the French Army in 1974.

The first production orders were placed the following year and first deliveries of the 4 × 4 version were made to the French Army late in 1976.

Production of the VAB was completed in 1993 after just over 5,000 had been built for the home and export markets. Product support and upgrade packages for the VAB series of 6 × 6 and 4 × 4 vehicles is now carried out by Renault Trucks Defense.

Production of the standard VAB has been completed but production could commence again if additional export orders are placed.

In mid-2010 Nexter Systems unveiled pre-production examples of the latest generation VAB Mk II in 6 × 6 and 4 × 4 versions and it is expected that any new build vehicles will be to this standard.

Qualification of the VAB Mk II is expected to be completed by Renault Trucks Defense in 2011 and the vehicle is already being offered on the export market by the company to both new and existing customers.

Description
The hull of the VAB ECH is of all-welded steel armour, with the driver seated at the front of the vehicle on the left and the commander, who also operates the externally mounted machine gun, to the right.

Both the driver and commander have a bulletproof windscreen to their front, which can be covered by an armoured plate if required, and a side door with a bulletproof window. The driver has a single-piece hatch cover in the roof, which opens to the rear. The armament installation is over the commander/gunner's position.

The engine and transmission are mounted to the rear of the driver's position and are removed as a complete unit through the roof. The engine compartment is provided with a fire extinguishing system.

The crew compartment is at the rear of the vehicle and there is a very small connecting corridor between the driver and commander's compartment at the front and the rear compartment on the vehicle's right-hand side. At the rear of the vehicle are two doors, which open outwards, each with a window which has armoured cover. There is no centre post, therefore bulky equipment can be easily loaded. There are two large roof hatches over the rear compartment which can be locked in the vertical position and on each side there are three bulletproof windows covered by an armoured shutter.

The steering is power-assisted on the front four wheels (in the case of the 6 × 6 model) and the suspension is of the torsion bar type with telescopic shock-absorbers. The tyres are of the run-flat type.

Power is transmitted from the engine to the wheels through a hydraulic torque converter and the gearbox. Gears are selected by means of a short pneumatically assisted lever which also operates the clutch.

The basic vehicle is fully amphibious, propelled in the water by its wheels but, if required, the VAB can be delivered with two water-jets mounted one in each side of the hull at the rear.

Other optional equipment includes: passive night vision equipment, NBC system, heater and a front-mounted winch with 60 m of cable and a maximum capacity of 7,000 kg.

The VAB ECH is provided with the following equipment: a welding station with cylinders of oxygen and acetylene; generator; grinding machine; hand drill; hoist; searchlight; storage cabinets and drawers; water tank; workbench; vice; and tool kit. To give the repair crew increased headroom a PVC roof extension can be quickly raised over the rear compartment.

Specifications
VAB ECH repair vehicle
Crew: 4
Configuration: 6 × 6
Weight:
  (empty) 12,000 kg
  (loaded) 14,000 kg
Power-to-weight ratio: 15.71 hp/t
Length: 5.98 m
Width: 2.49 m
Height: (top of hull) 2.06 m
Ground clearance: (axles) 0.4 m
Track: 2.035 m
Angle of approach/departure: 45/45°
Wheelbase: 1.5 + 1.5 m
Tyres: 14.00 × 20
Max speed:
  (road) 92 km/h
  (water) 7.2 km/h (with wheels)
Range: (road) 1,000 km
Fuel capacity: 300 litres
Fording: amphibious
Gradient: 60%
Side slope: 30%
Vertical obstacle: 0.5 m
Trench: 1 m (6 × 6 version only)
Engine: Renault MIDS 06.20.45 6-cylinder diesel developing 220 hp at 2,200 rpm
Transmission: semi-automatic with 5 forward and 1 reverse gears
Electrical system: 24 V
Armament: 1 × 7.62 mm MG (see text)

Status
Production complete, but can be resumed if further orders are placed. The baseline VAB is in service with the French Army and other countries including Brunei, Central African Republic, Chad, Cyprus, Indonesia, Italy (NBC model only), Ivory Coast, Lebanon, Mauritius, Morocco, Oman, Qatar, UAE and other undisclosed countries.

Contractor
Renault Trucks Defense

Poland

MT-LB technical support vehicle

Development
The Polish Army utilises a locally developed version of the Russian designed MT-LB multipurpose tracked armoured vehicle for the front-line technical support of armoured units. The vehicle is similar to the basic MT-LB, but is provided with various items of special equipment for its role.

In addition to its technical support role, the vehicle can also be used as a general or NBC reconnaissance vehicle.

Prime contractor for Polish production of the MT-LB and its many variants is Huta Stalowa Wola SA who are also involved in many other Polish vehicle and artillery programmes.

The baseline MT-LB is currently being marketed by HSW with standard equipment including a turret mounted 7.62 mm MG, self-entrenching equipment mounted on the hull at the top rear, NBC system, intercom, heater, engine pre-heater and towing hook.

Optional equipment for the Polish MT-LB includes various communications equipment, drivers night vision device, dosimeter, NBC decontamination set and a 12.7 mm machine gun mounted externally on a turret as fitted to the Kroton mine laying vehicle and Hors engineering reconnaissance vehicle.

Description
The MT-LB technical support vehicle has a basic crew of three but further seating is provided internally for up to four passengers. Its main role is the front-line repair and general support of other armoured vehicles, which includes the towing of disabled light vehicles, the evacuation of personnel (including the provision of medical first aid assistance), and the provision of earth hides or scrapes.

Renault Trucks Defense VAB ECH repair vehicle with hatches and rear doors open
0511477

Polish MT-LB technical support vehicle showing entrenching blade and A-frame crane stowed on hull roof
0511478

Polish PZP-WLWD which is used to tow trailer with rocket-propelled minecleaning equipment (Stefan Marx)   0536876

For the latter role the vehicle is provided with two hydraulic arms at the rear of the vehicle onto which a self-entrenching blade can be secured; when not in use, the blade is carried on the hull roof on the right-hand side.

Also provided for the support role is a light A-frame crane which can be erected over the rear of the hull to assist when handling vehicle components.

For transport the crane is stowed folded flat on the hull roof. A comprehensive suite of repair and other tools is carried. The vehicle can be used to tow a trailer carrying spare components or supplies.

Under normal operations the vehicle's various NBC sensors are maintained in a permanently on condition.

All standard production MT-LB vehicles are fully amphibious and are propelled in the water by their tracks only. When compared to the original MT-LB, this version has improved amphibious characteristics.

The commander's position is covered by a small, one-person manually operated turret provided with vision devices. Mounted over the turret is a 12.7 mm NSW (NSV) machine gun for local and air defence.

Variants
The Polish manufacturer of the MT-LB has proposed that this stretched version could be used for a number of other battlefield roles. Examples include a command post for air defence units (this is designated the LA-3 Command Automation Vehicle) and a flat bed for specialised roles such as mine layer. Poland also uses the stretched MTLB chassis to tow a trailer carrier rocket-propelled minecleaning equipment. This is called PZP-WLWD. A different version of this rocket-propelled minecleaning system is installed on tanks. For this application the pods of mine clearing rockets are normally carried one either side of the rear.

Kroton anti-tank mine laying vehicle
The anti-tank mine laying version has four square launchers each with 20 tubes with the system capable of rapidly laying 400 anti-mines each of which is fitted with a self-destruct mechanism.

Gross combat weight is being quoted as 15.87 tonnes and speed when laying the anti-tank mines is between 7.5 and 22 km/h. The anti-tank mines can be launched from the sides or rear of the vehicle.

This is based on the stretched chassis which has a total of seven road wheel stations either side which provide the vehicle with more internal volume and payload. This enables the vehicle to carry out a wider range of battlefield roles and missions.

Specifications

MT-LB technical support vehicle
Crew: 3 + 4
Weight: 12,900 kg (±200 kg)
Power-to-weight ratio: 18.99 hp/t
Ground pressure: 0.46 kg/cm²
Towed load:
  (trailer) 6,500 kg
  (vehicle) 14,000 kg
Length:
  (with blade) 7.378 m
  (without blade) 7.14 m
  (crane extended) 8.72 m
Width: 3.03 m
Height:
  (crane stowed) 2.305 m
  (crane extended) 4.14 m
Ground clearance: (max) 0.415 m
Max speed:
  (road, without trailer) 60 km/h
  (road, with trailer) 45 km/h
  (when towing vehicle) 6 km/h
  (water) 8 km/h
Range: 500 km
Fording: amphibious
Engine: SW680/167/1 6-cylinder turbocharged diesel developing 245 hp
Armament:
  1 × 12.7 mm NSW (NSV) MG
  smoke grenade launchers

Status
Production as required. In service with the Polish Army.

Contractor
Huta Stalowa Wola SA

Russian Federation

MTP-LB technical support vehicle

Development
Several variations of the MT-LB multipurpose tracked vehicle existed before the MTP-LB technical support vehicle was issued to the Russian Technical Emergency Service.

It had the responsibility of vehicle recovery and repair in the front line. The baseline MT-LB was actually designed and built in what is today the Ukraine.

The MT-LB series has also been manufactured under licence for the home and export markets in Bulgaria and Poland. Both of these countries have developed their own specialised versions of the MT-LB vehicle. As far as it is known, there has been no recent production of the baseline MT-LB vehicle in Bulgaria, Poland or Ukraine.

Description
The basic form of the MT-LB vehicle remains unchanged, but several alterations were made to adapt it for recovering armoured fighting vehicles by direct tow or winch and the recovery of amphibious vehicles from water obstacles.

One of the main fitments is an A-frame crane mounted on the front of the vehicle and powered by the winch to provide a 1,500 kg lift capacity. This has two working positions.

One is with the crane jib length at 2.15 m, giving a lift height of 3.6 m.

The other, with the jib length at 1.35 m, gives a lift height of 4.2 m. With the crane under load the vehicle can be driven at speeds up to 5 km/h and with a list of 5°.

The vehicle is also provided with a cable winch, a jacking device, a towing attachment, chocks and other arresting devices, waterborne salvage equipment and gas welding and oxy-acetylene cutting equipment for both steel and aluminium.

The hydraulic cable winch is driven by the auxiliary gearbox and drives a cable 80 m long; winching capacity is 60 kN. The winch may be operated manually but the maximum pull is then limited to 150 kg.

The jacking device on the front of the vehicle acts not only as an anchor when the cable winch is in use, but also as a metalwork workbench. A hand winch is provided for moving the jacking device from its normal transport position on the vehicle front to the cargo platform when the MTP-LB is afloat.

The towing attachment is used for towing armoured fighting vehicles with steering that is out of action. An electric welding kit is carried.

Other specialised changes to the MTP-LB are the removal of the one-person, manually operated, MT-LB machine gun turret and its replacement by an extra hatch and periscope over the commander's position for use when afloat.

Extra frames and containers have been fitted to carry the additional equipment and, apart from the recovery role, the MTP-LB carries the equipment required for observation, command, warning, reconnaissance, decontamination and camouflage. Interior lighting is also fitted.

Polish MT-LB technical support vehicle
Details of this vehicle, which has a longer chassis with six roadwheels either side, are given in a separate entry in *Jane's Military Vehicles and Logistics*. Prime contractor in Poland is Huta Stalowa Wola.

Details of this are provided in a separate entry in *Jane's Military Vehicles and Logistics*.

MTP-LB technical support vehicle (Michael Jerchel)   0512307

MT-LB upgrade

Russia and Ukraine are now offering automotive upgrades for the MT-LB range of vehicles. This upgrade includes the replacement of the existing diesel engine. As far as it is known none of these have entered quantity production or service.

Specifications

MTP-LB technical support vehicle
Crew: 2
Combat weight: 12,300 kg
Power to weight ratio: 19.5 hp/t
Ground pressure: 0.46 kg/cm²
Length: 6.8 m
Width: 2.85 m
Height:
　(hull roof) 1.865 m
　(recovery array) 2.3 m
Ground clearance: 0.395-0.415 m
Track: 2.3 m
Track width: 350 mm
Max speed:
　(land) 55 km/h
　(water) 6.5 km/h
Range: (roads) 500 km
Fording: amphibious
Engine: YaMZ 238 V V-8 cylinder diesel developing 240 hp at 2,100 rpm

Status

Production complete. The MT-LB is used by the following countries, some of whom also use the MTP-LB version: Armenia, Azerbaijan, Bangladesh, Belarus, Bulgaria, Eritrea, Finland, Georgia, Kazakhstan, Lithuania, Macedonia, Moldova, Nigeria (United Nations deployment), Russia, Serbia, Sweden, Ukraine and Uruguay.

Contractor

State factories.

RM-G tracked repair vehicle

Development

The RM-G tracked repair vehicle was developed by the Joint Stock Company (JSC) Rubtsovsk Machine Building Plant to undertake repairs to tanks and BMP-type Infantry Fighting Vehicle (IFV) in the forward combat area. The RM-G is also referred to as the Repair Tracked Vehicle (RTV).
　Typical roles of the RTV include:
- Towing BMP-1/2/3 IFVs
- Carrying out repairs and maintenance to MBTs and BMP-1/2/3 IFV
- Carrying out welding repairs
- Carrying out technical maintenance
- Carrying equipment and replacement subsystems up to a maximum weight of 1,000 kg
- Charging accumulator batteries
- Electric starting of MBT and BMP-1/BMP-2/BMP-3 diesel engines using onboard equipment.

Description

The Repair Tracked Vehicle is based on the chassis of the Kurgan Machine Construction Plant BMP-1 full tracked IFV and has a similar layout.
　The driver is seated front left with the vehicle commander to his rear and both are provided with a single-piece hatch cover and day periscopes.
　The engine compartment is to the right and the crew compartment at the rear. Mounted above the latter is an all-welded steel turret with an electrically operated crane, which can lift a maximum load of 3,000 kg. The crane turret can be traversed through 228° and has a maximum lifting height of 4.01 m.
　Mounted externally on top of the turret is a 7.62 mm PKT machine gun and standard equipment includes a VG-7500N welding system, repair set, tools, FVU-100N NBC system, night vision equipment, 81 mm electrically operated smoke grenade launchers and a diesel-engine driven smoke generating system. This creates a smoke screen via the exhaust outlet on the right side of the hull.
　The torsion bar suspension either side is the same as that of the BMP-1 IFV with six single rubber-tyred roadwheels, drive sprocket at the front, idler at the rear and track-return rollers. The upper part of the track is covered by a steel shroud and an unditching beam can be carried on the left side of the hull.
　Standard equipment includes an NBC system and night vision equipment. It is fully amphibious, being propelled in the water by its tracks. Before entering the water a trim vane is erected at the front of the vehicle and the bilge pumps are switched on.
　The first examples of the RM-G tracked repair vehicle were based on the chassis of the BMP-1 IFV manufactured at the Kurgan Machine Construction Plant. The BMP-1 IFV was subsequently replaced in production by the similar BMP-2 IFV with a 30 mm 2A42 cannon.
　This in turn was followed by the BMP-3, which is a brand new design. This has been built in limited numbers for the Russian Army and has also been exported to a number of other countries, including Cyprus, South Korea, Kuwait and the UAE. Production of the BMP-3 is still underway for the home and export markets.

RM-G tracked repair vehicle with crane traversed to left. This vehicle also carries an unditching beam on the left side of the hull　0038802

Specifications

RM-G tracked repair vehicle
Crew: 4
Combat weight: 13,800 kg
Power-to-weight ratio: 21.73 hp/t
Ground pressure: 0.65 kg/cm²
Length: 6.736 m
Width: 2.94 m
Height: (with 7.62 mm PKT machine gun) 2.4 m
Ground clearance: 0.37 m
Track: 2.55 m
Track width: 300 mm
Length of track on ground: 3.8 m
Max road speed: 65 km/h
Max water speed:
　(forward gear) 6 km/h
　(reverse gear) 2 km/h
Fuel capacity: 462 litres
Road range: 660 km
Gradient: 60%
Side slope: 30%
Vertical obstacle: 0.7 m
Trench: 2.5 m
Engine: Model UTD-20 6-cylinder, 4-stroke direct injection diesel developing 300 hp at 2,600 rpm
Transmission: manual, 5 forward and 1 reverse gears
Clutch: multiplate, dry, constant engagement
Suspension: torsion bar, hydraulic shock-absorbers on 1st, 2nd and 6th roadwheels
Electrical system: 22-29 V
Armament: 1 × 7.62 mm PKT machine gun
Smoke laying equipment: diesel fuel injected into exhaust; 2 × 2 81 mm smoke grenade launchers

Status

Production as required. In service with Russian Army. As far as it is known there has been no recent production of this vehicle. Future RM-G repair vehicles could be based on surplus BMP-1 or BMP-2 IFV chassis rather than new build vehicles.

Contractor

Joint Stock Company (JSC)

Switzerland

General Dynamics European Land Systems - MOWAG Piranha (8 × 8) armoured repair vehicle

Development

One of the Piranha series of vehicles developed by the Swiss MOWAG concern during the early 1970s was the 8 × 8 armoured repair vehicle, which may also be used if required as an armoured recovery vehicle.
　It follows the same general lines as the Husky (6 × 6) and Bison (8 × 8) armoured repair vehicles built in Canada by the now General Dynamics Land Systems - Canada.

UK built Piranha II (8 × 8) for Oman in armoured recovery vehicle
(BAE Systems Global Combat Systems)　　　　　0576084

Licensed production of the MOWAG Piranha has also been undertaken in Chile by the now FAMAE and the United Kingdom by the now BAE Systems Systems, Global Combat Systems (at that time GKN Defence).

The UK-built Piranha 8 × 8 variants for Kuwait, Qatar and Saudi Arabia at their Telford facility which has now closed down as a production site.

BAE Systems Global Combat Systems is no longer marketing the Piranha family of 8 × 8 vehicles on the export market.

Known users of the Piranha (8 × 8) armoured repair vehicle/recovery vehicle include:

Country	Quantity	Comment
Australia	11	called ASLAV – Recovery
Belgium	17	in three batches, 9, 5 and 3
Botswana	n/k	includes recovery version
Brazil	1	ordered 2006, delivered 2007
Ireland	1	
New Zealand	3	called maintenance recovery vehicle
Qatar	2	supplied by UK
Spain	n/k	for marines, amphibious version
Saudi Arabia	n/k	supplied by UK
Saudi Arabia	44	ordered 2009, delivery from 2011
US	46	US Marine Corps

In January 2006 the Belgian government selected the MOWAG Piranha IIIC (8 × 8) light armoured vehicle to meet the requirements of its Armoured Infantry Vehicle (AIV) programme.

A total of 242 Piranha IIIC units in three batches are were delivered from 2007 with the first batch to consist of 138 units. The order includes a total of 17 recovery vehicles in three batches each consisting of nine, five and three units. The C in the designation means that the vehicle has a conventional suspension system.

Late in December 2009 it was stated that the capability of the Saudi Arabian National Guard (SANG) is to be further enhanced by the acquisition of another 724 Light Armoured Vehicles (LAV) that are to be manufactured by General Dynamics Land Systems – Canada.

This contract, worth USD2.2 billion, was signed through the Canadian Commercial Corporation, a Crown Agency of the Canadian Government and placed with the US Army TACOM Life Cycle Management Command.

Under the terms of this contract, SANG will receive 10 different variants of the LAV II with first deliveries due in April 2011.

The 10 variants include 264 LAV-25 (armed with an ATK 25 mm M242 cannon), 48 ambulance, 72 anti-tank, 26 armoured personnel carrier, 114 command-and-control vehicles, 24 engineer, 44 recovery, 84 90 mm assault gun, 36 120 mm mortar systems and 12 ammunition carriers.

Description

The hull of the Piranha vehicle is of all-welded steel armour with the front, sides and rear proof against NATO 7.62 mm ball ammunition.

The driver is seated at the front of the hull on the left side and is provided with a single-piece hatch cover and three day periscopes. The centre one can be replaced by a passive periscope for driving at night. The Detroit Diesel 6V-53T diesel engine is mounted to the right of the driver and the personnel compartment is at the rear. Entry to this compartment is via two doors at the rear of the hull, each with a firing port. Roof hatches are provided.

The rear suspension is of the torsion bar type, and the front suspension has coil springs and wishbone. All wheels are fitted with hydraulic shock-absorbers.

When the crane is in use, the vehicle is stabilised by hydraulic and mechanical ground supports. All tyres have run-flat cores and the dual-circuit brakes are hydraulic, assisted by compressed air.

The vehicle is also available in a fully amphibious form, driven in the water by two propellers at the rear. Before entering the water, a trim vane is erected at the front of the vehicle.

Not all customers have 8 × 8 vehicles with the amphibious capability and Canada, for example, has removed this capability from its vehicles.

The usual crane fitted to the Piranha (8 × 8) is a HIAB hydraulic unit with a maximum capacity of 3,000 kg, although other cranes may be fitted.

The latest version of the MOWAG Piranha is an 8 × 8 vehicle with a revised superstructure to mount a 7,000 kg hydraulic crane centrally. This version has several layout changes from the original, one of which is the provision of stabiliser legs inset in the sides in a central position.

The centrally mounted crane position allows more internal storage space so that more tools and repair equipment can be carried.

Specifications

Piranha armoured repair vehicle
Crew: 4 +
Configuration: 8 × 8
Weight:
　(loaded) 12,300-13,000 kg
　(empty) 8,800 kg
Power-to-weight ratio: 23 hp/t
Length: 6.6 m
Width: 2.5 m
Height:
　(hull top, front) 1.85 m
　(hull top, rear) 2.7 m
Ground clearance: (under hull) 0.5 m
Track:
　(front) 2.18 m
　(rear) 2.205 m
Tyres: 11.00 × 16
Wheelbase: 1.1 + 1.335 + 1.04 m
Angle of approach/departure: 40/45°
Max speed:
　(road) 100 km/h
　(water) 10.5 km/h
Range: (road) 780-1,000 km
Fuel: 300 or 500 litres
Gradient: 60%
Side slope: 35%
Vertical obstacle: 0.5 m
Engine: Detroit Diesel 6V-53T developing 300 hp at 2,800 rpm (latest vehicles for US Army are powered by a Caterpillar 3126 diesel developing 350 hp)
Transmission: Allison MT-653 automatic, 5 forward and 1 reverse gears
Electrical system: 24 V
Armament: 1 × 7.62 mm MG

Status

Production as required. Known users of the Piranha, some of whom might use the Piranha repair vehicle, include: Australia, Belgium, Botswana, Brazil, Canada, Chile, Denmark, Ghana, Ireland, Liberia, New Zealand, Nigeria, Oman, Qatar, Romania, Saudi Arabia, Spain, Sweden, Switzerland and United States (Army called Stryker and Marine Corps).

Contractor

General Dynamics European Land Systems - MOWAG GmbH

RECOVERY VEHICLES

Austria

Steyr Type 14 M 22 K36 (4 × 4) recovery vehicle

Development
The Steyr Type 14 M 22 K36 12 (4 × 4) recovery vehicle is a development of the Steyr M2000 series of 4 × 4 trucks which are covered in detail in a separate entry in *Jane's Military Vehicles and Logistics*. It is essentially an M2000 series (4 × 4) truck modified for the recovery role.

Description
The Steyr Type 14 M 22 K36 (4 × 4) recovery vehicle uses a forward control cab-over-engine design and features a hydraulic tilting cab mechanism that provides maintenance access to the main MAN D0826LFL diesel engine coupled to an Eaton manual transmission.

The cab is provided with seats for the driver and two passengers. The chassis is constructed of low torsion U-section main members with riveted and bolted in tubular cross members.

A towing device in provided in the steel bumper. The front and rear suspension consists of trapezoidal springs with telescopic shock absorbers and stabiliser.

Mounted to the cab rear is the Type EH/TC 12000 hydraulic telescopic crane which is mounted on a turntable. According to Steyr, this crane has been especially designed for towing, salvage work, load lifting and all types of crane work.

The unit consists of a fully hydraulic telescopic crane, crane winch, hydraulic operated support legs in front and rear and different working accessories.

The boom has a maximum extension of 5.50 m with maximum hook height also being 5.50 m. The crane can be traversed through a rear arc of 270° with maximum lifting angle being 55° and minimum lowering angle being 9°.

With a double wire rope, the crane winch has a maximum lifting capacity of 6,000 kg and is provided with 50 m of wire rope. When the crane is being used, four outriggers are normally extended, two either side of the chassis to provide a more stable platform.

Standard equipment includes one triangular type towbar with towing ring, one floodlight mounted on the crane boom (or as an alternative at the operators position), one crow bar, one sledge hammer, one pick axe, two support planks, two wedges for the wheels, one set of special spanners, two lifting belts, one twin strand rope with two shackles, one polyester round sling, one rope set with ring and safety hook, one rope with two slings, two shackles rated at four tonnes and one tow bar.

A wide range of optional equipment is also available for this vehicle, including:
- an air compressor (special version for use in the tropics)
- reinforced engine brake
- various power take-offs
- front axle different lock
- permanent front wheel drive
- different gearboxes (including automatic)
- transfer case with automatic drive train management
- different axle ratios and tyres
- right hand drive
- rear of cab fitted with windows
- foldable roof-hatch (which could be fitted with a weapon station)
- different mirrors
- locking air suspended seats
- co-drivers bench (fitted for radio)

- auxiliary heater for cab and engine
- air conditioning
- additional 200 litre diesel fuel tank (which increases the range of the vehicle)
- trailer and towing couplings
- air and electric connections for trailer
- front protection
- speed limited
- different electrical installations
- self-recovery hydraulically operated winch
- five-tonne hydraulically-operated winch.

Specifications
Type 14 M 22 K36 recovery vehicle
Cab seating: 1 + 2
Configuration: 4 × 4
Weight: (gross vehicle weight) 13,500 kg
Length: 6.5 m
Width: 2.49 m
Height: (top of cab) 2.833 m
Ground clearance: 0.255 m
Wheelbase: 3.5 m
Max speed: 101 km/h
Fuel capacity: 150 litres
Gradient: 30%
Fording: 0.75 m
Engine: MAN D0826LFL 6.871 litre 6-cylinder in-line-water cooled direct injection diesel developing 220 hp at 2,400 rpm
Gearbox: Eaton manual model 5206 with 6 forward and 1 reverse gears
Clutch: single disc dry, hydraulic actuation
Transfer box: G1000/2
Steering: ZF 8095 power assisted
Suspension: trapezoidal springs with telescopic shock absorbers front and rear
Tyres: 10 R 22.5
Axle loadings:
  (front) 5,000 kg
  (rear) 9,000 kg
Brakes: dual circuit air
Electrical system: 24 V
Batteries: 2 × 12 V,88 Ah

Status
Development complete. Ready for production.

Contractor
Steyr Nutzfahrzeuge AG

Steyr Type 14 M 22 (4 × 4) recovery vehicle

Development
The Steyr Type 14 M 22 (4 × 4) recovery vehicle is a development of the Steyr M2000 series of 4 × 4 trucks which are covered in a separate entry in *Jane's Military Vehicles and Logistics*.

The first of these vehicles, fitted with recovery equipment, was produced in 1988 for the Nigerian Defence Forces and since then it is understood that sales have been made to a number of other countries.

Production of this specialised vehicle is undertaken on an as required basis.

Description
The vehicle uses a forward control cab over engine design and features a hydraulic tilting cab mechanism that provides maintenance access to the main MAN diesel engine coupled to a manual transmission.

The cab is provided with seats for the driver and two passengers. The chassis is constructed using open channel steel section having a parallel frame design for mounting the recovery equipment.

There is a heavy duty suspension to cater for a 9,000 kg rear-axle load and a 5,000 kg lifted towing.

The main recovery equipment is a 12 t/m crane manufactured by the Austrian company of Penz. Also installed, for recovery purposes, are two hydraulically operated Rotzler winches, one with a capacity of five tonnes and the other with a capacity of 3.5 tonnes. These are mounted to the rear of the forward control cab.

In addition there are four square outriggers that provide stability during crane operations and two support props for towing loads from the rear.

Tools and recovery equipment are carried in a large compartment under the crane boom.

A replacement wheel and tyre is also carried on the crane boom. A triangular towbar and lifting tackle are provided for lifted towing.

Steyr Type 14 M 22 K36 (4 × 4) recovery vehicle in travelling configuration (Steyr)
0567065

Steyr Type 14 M 22 (4 × 4) recovery vehicle in travelling configuration

0122601

Specifications

Type 14 M 22 recovery vehicle
Cab seating: 1 + 2
Configuration: 4 × 4
Weight:
(kerb) 10,000 kg
(gross vehicle weight) 14,000 kg
Length: 6.5 m
Width: 2.5 m
Height:
(top of crane) 3.5 m
(top of cab) 3.0 m
Ground clearance: 0.27 m
Track:
(front) 1.892 m
(rear) 1.792 m
Wheelbase: 3.6 m
Angle of approach/departure: 39/45°
Max speed: 90 km/h
Fuel capacity: 150 litres
Gradient: 30%
Fording: 0.8 m
Engine: MAN D0829LFL 6.871 litre 6-cylinder in-line water-cooled direct-injection diesel developing 220 hp at 2,400 rpm
Gearbox: Eaton model 5206 with 6 forward and 1 reverse gears
Clutch: single disc dry, hydraulic actuation
Transfer box: MAN G 1000/2, 2-speed
Steering: ZF 8095 power assisted
Suspension: semi-elliptic springs with double-acting hydraulic shock-absorbers front and rear, stabiliser bar rear
Tyres: 9.00 R 20
Axle loadings:
(front) 5,000 kg
(rear) 9,000 kg
Brakes: dual circuit air
Electrical system: 24 V
Batteries: 2 × 12 V,120 Ah
Alternator: 28 V, 35 A (55 or 80 A optional)

Status
Production as required. In service with Cyprus, Ghana, Greece and Nigeria.

Contractor
MAN Steyr AG

Steyr Type 33 M 37 (6 × 6) recovery vehicle

Development
The Steyr Type 33 M 37 (6 × 6) (33.373 DFAK) recovery vehicle is a Steyr-built version of the German F2000 truck, covered in detail in a separate entry in *Jane's Military Vehicles and Logistics*. The first of these vehicles fitted with recovery equipment was produced for the Hellenic Armed Forces.

For the latter customer, Hellenic Vehicle Industry SA (ELVO) was the local contractor.

Description
The vehicle uses a standard forward control cab-over-engine design and features a hydraulic tilting cab mechanism that provides maintenance access to the main MAN D2866 diesel engine coupled to a ZF transmission.

The cab is provided with seats for the driver and two passengers. The chassis is constructed using open channel steel section for mounting the recovery equipment. There is bogie suspension to cater for 2 × 13,000 kg rear-axle load and 7,500 kg lifted towing.

The main recovery equipment is a 30 t/m crane manufactured by Palfinger or Penz of Austria.

Also installed on the vehicle are two hydraulically operated Rotzler winches, one with a capacity of 10 tonnes and the other with a capacity of 6.5 tonnes.

In addition, there are four square outriggers that provide stability during crane operations and two support props for towing loads from the rear.

Tools and recovery equipment are located in a large compartment under the crane boom.

A replacement wheel and tyre is also carried on the crane boom. A triangular towbar and lifting tackle are provided for lifted towing.

Steyr 33 M 41 K35 (6 × 6) recovery vehicle
This is the more recent 6 × 6 recovery vehicle to be marketed by Steyr Nutzfahrzeuge AG, which is also known as Steyr Trucks.

It is very similar in appearance to the Steyr Type 33 M 37 (6 × 6) recovery vehicle and has a fully enclosed forward control cab with seats for two people.

It is powered by a MAN D2866LF31 6-cylinder diesel developing 410 hp at 1,700 rpm, coupled to a ZF 16 S 151 manual gearbox with 16 forward and 2 reverse gears.

To carry out its specialised role it is fitted with a turntable-mounted telescopic crane Model EH/TC 3000, which, with boom extended to a full 7.50 m, can lift a maximum load of 3.7 tonnes. With a boom extension of 4.35 m it can lift a maximum load of 6.70 tonnes.

When the crane is being used, four hydraulic stabilisers are lowered to the ground, two either side of the vehicle to provide a more stable platform.

In addition, the crane winch has a maximum capacity of 13 tonnes while the rear frame winch has a maximum pulling capacity of 10 tonnes.

Specifications

Type 33 M 37 recovery vehicle
Cab seating: 1 + 2
Configuration: 6 × 6
Weight:
(kerb) 20,000 kg
(gross vehicle weight) 32,000 kg
Length: 9.00 m
Width: 2.5 m
Height:
(top of crane) 3.7 m
(top of cab) 3.2 m
Ground clearance: 0.35 m
Track:
(front) 2.067 m
(rear) 1.8 m
Wheelbase: 3.5 m + 1.40 m
Angle of approach/departure: 23/25°
Max speed: 90 km/h
Fuel capacity: 400 litres
Gradient: 60%
Side slope: 30%
Fording: 0.8 m
Engine: MAN D2866, 11.967 litre 6-cylinder in-line water-cooled direct-injection diesel developing 370 hp at 1,800 - 2,000 rpm
Gearbox: ZF 16 S 151 synchromesh
Clutch: single disc, dry, hydraulic actuation
Transfer box: MAN VG 1700 single speed, 2 speed optional
Steering: ZF 8098 power assisted
Suspension: semi-elliptic springs with double-acting hydraulic shock-absorbers front and rear, stabilser bar rear
Tyres: 12.00 R 20
Axle loadings:
(front) 7,500 kg
(rear) 2 × 13,000 kg

Steyr Type 33 M 37 (6 × 6) recovery vehicle in travelling configuration with crane stowed and out riggers in raised position

0122602

Brakes: dual circuit air
Electrical system: 24 V
Batteries: 2 × 12 V,140 Ah
Alternator: 28 V, 35A (55 or 80 A optional)

Status
Production as required. In service with Greece and Zimbabwe.

Contractor
Steyr Nutzfahrzeuge AG

Steyr Type 19S25 (4 × 4) recovery vehicle

Development
The Steyr Type 19S25 (4 × 4) recovery vehicle is a development of the Steyr 1291 series of 4 × 4 trucks, developed some years ago. The first of these vehicles fitted with recovery equipment was produced in 1984 for the Saudi Arabian National Guard.

Production was completed some time ago and they are no longer being marketed. This was replaced in production by the Steyr 14 M 22 (4 × 4) recovery vehicle. Details of this are provided in a separate entry in *Jane's Military Vehicles and Logistics*. with production being undertaken on an as required basis.

Description
The Steyr Type 19S25 (4 × 4) recovery vehicle uses a forward control cab-over-engine design and features a hydraulic tilting cab mechanism providing maintenance access to the main Steyr diesel engine coupled to a ZF transmission.

The fully enclosed cab has seating for the driver and two passengers. The chassis is constructed using open channel steel sections, having a parallel frame design for mounting the recovery equipment. There is a heavy-duty suspension to cater for a 13,000 kg rear axle load and 6,500 kg lifted towing.

The main hydraulically operated recovery component is a 16 t/m crane manufactured by Penz (Austria). Also provided are two Rotzler hydraulically operated winches, one five-tonne, the other 3.5-tonne. There are four square-section outriggers providing stability during recovery operations and two crane jib support props for towing loads to the rear, each with a 10-tonne pulling capacity. When the crane is being used, the outriggers are deployed two either side of the vehicle.

Tools and recovery equipment are located in a large compartment under the crane boom. A spare wheel is carried on the left side (when the crane is traversed to the rear) of the crane boom. A triangular towbar and lifting tackle are provided for lifted towing.

Specifications
Type 19S25 recovery vehicle
Cab seating: 1 + 2
Configuration: 4 × 4
Weight:
(kerb) 13,000 kg
(GVW) 19,000 kg
Length: 7 m
Width: 2.5 m
Height:
(top of crane) 3.6 m
(top of cab) 3 m
Ground clearance: 0.35 m
Track:
(front) 1.958 m
(rear) 1.8 m
Wheelbase: 3.8 m
Angle of approach/departure: 23/25°
Max speed: 90 km/h
Fuel capacity: 380 litres
Gradient: 60%

Steyr Type 19S25 (4 × 4) recovery vehicle in travelling configuration 0511480

Side slope: 30%
Fording: 0.8 m
Engine: Steyr WD 615.74 10 litre 6-cylinder in-line water-cooled direct injection diesel developing 250 hp at 2,200 rpm or Steyr WD 615.73 diesel developing 290 hp at 2,200 rpm or Steyr WD 615.78 diesel developing 320 hp at 2,200 rpm
Gearbox: ZF 9 S 109 synchromesh or 16 S 130 (for 320 hp engine)
Clutch: single disc dry, hydraulic actuation
Transfer box: Steyr VG 1200 2 speed
Steering: ZF 8046 hydraulic
Suspension: semi-elliptic springs with double-acting hydraulic shock-absorbers front and rear
Tyres: 12.00 R 20
Axle loadings:
(front) 7,500 kg
(rear) 13,000 kg
Brakes: dual circuit air
Electrical system: 24 V
Batteries: 2 × 12 V, 120 Ah
Alternator: 28 V, 30 or 55 A

Status
Production complete. No longer marketed. In service with Cyprus, Ghana, Nigeria and the Saudi Arabian National Guard. This was followed in production by a new generation Steyr Nutzfahrzeuge recovery vehicle.

Contractor
Steyr Nutzfahrzeuge AG

Steyr Type 32S29 (6 × 6) recovery vehicle

Development
The Steyr Type 32S29 (6 × 6) recovery vehicle is a development of the Steyr 1491 series of 6 × 6 trucks.

The first of these vehicles fitted with recovery equipment was produced for the Saudi Arabian National Guard. Production was completed some time ago and they are no longer marketed. This has now been replaced in production by the Steyr 33 M 37 (6 × 6) recovery vehicle for which there is a separate entry in *Jane's Military Vehicles and Logistics*.

Production of the vehicle is undertaken on an as required basis.

Description
The vehicle uses a forward control cab-over-engine design and features a hydraulic tilting cab mechanism to provide maintenance access to the main Steyr diesel engine coupled to manual ZF transmission. The fully enclosed cab has seating for the driver and two passengers.

The chassis is constructed using open channel sections and a parallel frame design for mounting the recovery equipment. There is a bogie suspension to cater for a 2 × 13,000 kg rear load and 7,500 kg lifted towing.

The main recovery component is a hydraulically operated 30 t/m crane manufactured by ATLAS or Penz (Austria). Also provided, to the cab rear, are two hydraulically operated Rotzler winches, one winch has a capacity of 10-tonne, the other 6.5-tonne.

There are four outriggers providing stability during recovery operations and two crane jib support props for towing loads to the rear, each with a 20-tonne pulling capacity.

When the crane is being used, the two outriggers are lowered to the ground, either side of the vehicle, to provide a more stable lifting platform. Tools and recovery equipment are located in a large compartment under the crane boom. A replacement wheel and tyre are carried on or behind the crane boom. A triangular towbar and lifting tackle are provided for lifted towing.

Specifications
Type 32S29 recovery vehicle
Cab seating: 1 + 2
Configuration: 6 × 6
Weight:
(kerb) 18,000 kg
(GVW) 32,000 kg
Length: 9 m
Width: 2.5 m
Height:
(top of crane) 3.6 m
(top of cab) 3 m
Ground clearance: 0.35 m
Track:
(front) 1.958 m
(rear) 1.8 m
Wheelbase: 3.5 + 1.35 m
Angle of approach/departure: 23/25°
Max speed: 90 km/h
Fuel capacity: 380 litres
Gradient: 60%
Side slope: 30%
Fording: 0.8 m

Steyr Type 32S29 (6 × 6) recovery vehicle in travelling configuration with boom stowed and stabilisers in raised position   0511482

Engine: Steyr WD 615.73 10 litre 6-cylinder in-line water-cooled direct injection diesel developing 290 hp at 2,200 rpm or Steyr WD 615.78 diesel developing 320 hp at 2,200 rpm
Gearbox: ZF 9 S 109 synchromesh or 16 S 130 (for 320 hp engine)
Clutch: single disc dry, hydraulic actuation
Transfer box: Steyr VG 1200 2 speed
Steering: ZF 8046 hydraulic
Suspension: semi-elliptic springs with double-acting hydraulic shock-absorbers front and rear
Tyres: 12.00 R 20
Axle loadings:
  (front) 7,500 kg
  (rear) 2 × 13,000 kg
Brakes: dual circuit air
Electrical system: 24 V
Batteries: 2 × 12 V, 120 Ah
Alternator: 28 V, 30 or 55 A

Status
Production complete. No longer being marketed. In service with Cyprus, Ghana, Lebanon and the Saudi Arabian National Guard. Canada has a 6 × 6 recovery version of a Steyr 1491.6 × 6 M truck but production of this was completed some time ago after 124 recovery units had been delivered.

Contractor
Steyr Nutzfahrzeuge AG

Australia

Mack RM6866RS (6 × 6) heavy recovery vehicle

Development
The Mack Model RM6866RS (6 × 6) truck, covered in detail in a separate entry in *Jane's Military Vehicles and Logistics*, was produced in Australia by Mack Trucks Australia Pty Limited as the Truck, Cargo, Heavy, MC3.

It is a version of the basic US Mack R-series. Three prototypes were produced in Australia in 1978 and after extensive trials an order was placed in 1981 for 906 units. These were all delivered by the end of 1985 and in 1988 a further 19 units were built which brought the grand total to 925 units in all configurations.

During 1993 a contract to upgrade 542 of these trucks was awarded to Mack Trucks Australia Pty Limited. This AUD8.77 million contract included the replacement of mechanical suspension units with an SA441W air suspension system and was scheduled to take two years.

In 1994 there was an extension to the contract to cover the remainder of the Australian Army's Mack fleet together with modifications on cargo/cargo with winch variants to fit container twistlocks.

The RM6866RS heavy recovery vehicle was developed by the company to meet the requirements of the Australian Army which ordered a total of 64 units.

Off-road heavy recovery vehicle had previously been provided to deployed forces through the Truck Wrecker, Heavy, MC3 eight-tonne, Mack6866RS, (TWH) fitted with the Homes 750 twin boom recovery system.

Due to mechanical failure of the recovery module, associated operational restrictions, occupational health and safety limitations that have been in place since 1995, this recovery system was not providing the intended service required for the conduct of recovery tasks, route and battlefield clearance and rescue of deployed forces.

The HRV entered operational service with the Australian Army in April 2005 but will be replaced by a new vehicle as part of Project 121 Overlander for which BAE Systems, Protection & Mobility Systems, was selected late in 2007 as the preferred bidder for the heavier class of tactical wheeled vehicle.

BAE Systems, Protection & Mobility Systems preferred bidder status was subsequently withdrawn and the competition started again.

In the end three contractors were shortlisted for the Land 121 Phase 3 requirement for medium weight/heavy weight capability and these were the now Rheinmetall MAN Military Vehicles, Mercedes-Benz Australia Pacific and Thales a contract expected to be signed late in 2011.

Description
The Heavy Recovery Vehicle (HRV) is a Mack Model RM6866RS (6 × 6) forward control truck chassis modified for use in the specialised role.

Primary role of the HRV is to recover the heavy truck and medium truck variants, ASLAV (8 × 8), Bushmaster (4 × 4), M113 armoured personnel carrier and variants and the range of heavy commercial vehicles within the designed parameters of those vehicles' variants.

The HRV has undergone major modifications from the standard Mack RM6866RS chassis to increase its capability in the field.

This includes increasing the output of the engine from 285 hp up to 320 hp with torque range now at 1,600 rpm. The transmission has been upgraded to an Eaton RTXF-14710B which gives a wider operating range for the loads required to be towed. Major difference is the range change within the transmission to give five speeds in low range and five more speeds in high range.

The 'R' model cab has been substantially modified and the rear cab wall has been removed and a crew cab has been bolted to the rear allowing the carriage of the recovery crew (two people) along with their webbing. The complete cab set up has been placed on an air suspended sub-frame.

A new integrated recovery unit has been mounted to the rear of the vehicle. This is a modern recovery unit consisting of Material Handling Equipment (MHE), two retrieval winches with fairlead systems, a lift towing system, and stowage facilities for recovery stores and equipment as well as for crew personal weapons and kit.

There are two aluminium locker assemblies, one of either side of the vehicle and each of these comprises four key lockable lockers and one key lockable locker that contains the winch and lift tow control panels.

The lift tow system consists of three hydraulic rams, one for lifting and two for the alignment of the crossbar and assistance with the lifting. The MHE is a Palfinger model PK9501 crane which can be operated by both manual and remote controls.

The crane has maximum lifting capacity of 5,600 kg, an outreach of 5.7 m and a slewing angle of 210°. The crane is fitted with the Paltronic 50 overload protection device.

To provide a more stable platform when operating the crane, two hydraulically operated controlled stabiliser legs are lowered to the ground, one on either side of the cab rear.

The unit is fitted with two Sepson 63.02-009 winches which are hydraulically driven and are of the drum type, two-speed constant force winches.

Capacity in automatic mode is 13-tonne constant force on all layers and in manual mode 13 tonnes on the bottom layer which reduces to 9 tonnes on the top layer. There are a total of four rope layers with the rope used being Casar 17 mm IWRC, Grade G1960 and 98 m in length.

The walkways on top of the recovery body have a reduced slip coating on the lockers and a non-slip fold up and removable walkway between the lockers. A reduced slip coating has also been applied to the bonnet area.

A replacement tyre is located on top of the rear section of the recovery body and is removed by using the Palfinger crane.

A closed circuit TV monitor is fitted to the dash and two cameras are remote-fitted at the rear of the body to enable the driver to see the casualty vehicle when reversing for hook up and whilst travelling.

A tamper proof speed limiter is fitted to the vehicle to set the speed to 100 km/h. The two diesel fuel tanks have been replaced by one larger diesel fuel tank that is located in between the chassis rails, under the walkway.

Specifications
RM6866RS heavy recovery vehicle
Cab seating: 2 + 2
Configuration: 6 × 6
Weight: 18,990 kg
Length: 9.50 m (with lift tow rams raised)
Width: 2.5 m
Height:
  (overall unladen) 3.265 m
  (overall reducable) 3.075 m

Mack RM6866RS (6 × 6) heavy recovery vehicle of the Australian Army (Mack Trucks Australia)   1156190

Ground clearance: 200 mm (limiting feature air suspension equaliser beams)
Track: 1.911 m
Wheelbase: 5.465 m
Angle of approach/departure: 32.5/57°
Max speed: 100 km/h
Range:
    (first class road) 1,144 km
    (second class road with recovery trailer) 572 km
Fuel capacity: 498 litres
Gradient: 50%
Fording: 0.8 m
Engine: Mack EM6 diesel developing 320 hp
Gearbox: Eaton RTXF-14710B, 10 speed
Transfer box: Mack TC150
Steering: Sheppard model 92
Turning radius: 24.1 m between kerbs
Suspension: Neway ARDST 2446 air
Tyres: Goodyear Omnitrac 1200 × 20
Brakes: wedge type

Status
Production complete. No longer marketed. In service with the Australian Army.

Contractor
Mack Trucks Australia Pty Ltd

Belarus

Minsk Wheel Tractor Plant Volat MZKT-790986 (8 × 8) heavy duty recovery vehicle

Development
The Minsk Wheel Tractor Plant has designed and built a wide range of 8 × 8 heavy duty cross-country truck chassis for a variety of roles. These include the Volat 74135 (8 × 8) tractor truck, which is designed to tow a semi-trailer carrying an MBT, as well as towing a trailer carrying another MBT.

Details of this are given in a separate entry in *Jane's Military Vehicles and Logistics*. Development of these vehicles is complete and production can commence when orders are placed.

The company is also marketing the Volat MZKT-790986 (8 × 8) heavy duty recovery vehicle that shares a number of subsystems with the previously mentioned heavy duty tractor truck.

This has been demonstrated in a number of countries, including the United Arab Emirates where it successfully recovered and towed a Denel Land Systems 155 mm/45-calibre G6 (6 × 6) self-propelled artillery system, which weighs 47 tonnes.

Description
The fully enclosed four-door cab is at the front of the vehicle and is of the fibreglass suspended type. It is normally provided with a total of seven seats but as an option this can be changed to three seats, plus two sleeping births.

The turntable-mounted EMPL hydraulic telescopic crane Model EH/TC 53.000 is mounted in the middle of the hull between the second and third axles. When travelling, the crane is traversed to the rear and the telescopic jib held in a travel lock.

The crane has a maximum lifting capacity of nine to 10 tonnes, with a reach of 4 m. The crane winch is provided with 58 m of wire rope that is 14 mm in diameter.

The rear frame heavy duty recovery hydraulic winch has a maximum pulling capacity with a single wire rope of 20 tonnes, which can be increased to 40 tonnes on a double wire. This is provided with 60 m of cable and is hydraulically controlled from the driver's seat.

Minsk Wheel Tractor Plant Volat MZKT-790986 (8 × 8) heavy duty recovery vehicle (Christopher F Foss)   1334243

There is also an auxiliary winch with 100 m of cable for pulling out the wire rope of the heavy duty recovery winch.

To provide a more stable lifting platform a hydraulic telescopic stabiliser can be lowered to the ground either side of the second road wheel station. In addition, hydraulic spades can be lowered at the rear of the chassis.

It is also provided with a propeller pulley at the rear of the body with a rope brake for the rear frame winch and a triangular-type tow bar.

Standard equipment includes a central tyre-pressure regulation system that allows the driver to adjust the tyre pressure from the cab to suit terrain being crossed.

A tropical air conditioning system with automatic climate control is mounted in the roof of the cabin to allow the vehicle to operate in high ambient temperatures.

Specifications
Volat MZKT-790986 heavy duty recovery vehicle
Cab seating: 1 + 6 (see text)
Configuration: 8 × 8
Weight:
    (chassis) 23,700 kg
    (with recovery equipment) 39,700 kg
Length: 10.86 m
Width:
    (max) 3.65 m
    (chassis) 3.07 m
Height:
    (overall) 4 m
    (cab roof) 3.84 m
Ground clearance: 480 mm
Track: 2.415 m
Wheelbase: 2.20 + 3.40 + 1.70 m
Angle of approach/departure: 30/30°
Max speed: 85 km/h
Range: n/avail
Fuel capacity 2 × 385 litres
Gradient: 30°
Side slope: n/avail
Fording: 1.4 m
Engine: Deutz BF8M1015C 4-stroke V-8 turbocharged inter-cooled diesel developing 400 kW (544 hp) at 2,100 rpm
Transmission: Allison HD 4560P automatic with 6 forward and 1 reverse gears
Transfer box: Minsk Wheel Tractor Plant two speed with locking inter-bogie differential
Steering: hydraulic
Turning radius: 16 m
Suspension: independent
Tyres: Michelin 23.5R25 XLB TL 188E wide profile tubeless with Hutchinson beadlock
Brakes:
    (main) drum shoe type with pneumatic drive, two circuit
    (parking) spring type energy accumulator, actuating transfer case output shaft brake mechanism, pneumatically driven
    (additional) engine brake
Electrical system: 24 V
Batteries: n/avail
Alternator: n/avail

Status
Development complete. Ready for production.

Contractor
Minsk Wheel Tractor Plant

France

Renault Trucks Defense Kerax 385.40 (8 × 4) heavy recovery vehicle

Development
Early in 1998, following an international competition, the Belgian Armed Forces placed a contract with the now Renault Trucks Defense for the supply of 27 heavy recovery vehicles, based on the civilian Kerax 385.40 8 × 4 quarry vehicle.

These four-axle trucks are designed to be operated as road and all-terrain breakdown and service trucks and have been assembled at the Renault facility at Villaverde, Spain. The first unit was delivered in October 1998 and three units were then delivered each month.

The equipment package for the Kerax 385.40 was developed by JIGE International of France and was fitted onto the chassis in Belgium by Espace Mobile International (EMI) SA.

The second customer for the Renault Trucks Defense Kerax 385.40 (8 × 4) heavy recovery vehicle was the French Army, which has taken delivery of 17 units.

The Renault Trucks Defense Kerax 385.40 (8 × 4) chassis is being marketed for a wide range of applications and with various body, cab and engine options.

Renault Trucks Defense Kerax 385.40 (8 × 4) heavy recovery vehicle of Belgian Army with hydraulic crane to cab rear (M Pagh)   1296035

Renault Trucks Defense Kerax 385.40 (8 × 4) heavy recovery vehicle of the Belgian Army from the rear, with stabilisers lowered to the ground (M Pagh)   1129830

For the military market, production of the vehicle is undertaken on an as required basis.

Description
The Kerax 385.40 (8 × 4) heavy recovery vehicle has a fully enclosed two-door forward control cab, which has seats for the driver and four mechanics.

The vehicle is powered by a Renault 06.23.56 11-litre diesel engine developing 385 hp at 2,000 rpm. It is coupled to a ZF 16 S 221 mechanical gearbox with WSK torque converter and integrated hydraulic retarder.

The unit has a gross vehicle weight of 32 tonnes and a gross combination weight of 65 tonnes.

According to Renault Trucks Defense, the vehicle is equipped to handle every type of breakdown situation and carries a complete range of highly efficient service and repair equipment.

This includes a hydraulically powered crane with a telescopic jib, a central hydraulic winch with a traction capacity of 17 tonnes, a hydraulic arm for lifting or towing vehicles and an automatic hauling winch.

The payload of the hydraulic crane depends on the extension. At maximum extension of 10.72 m, it can lift 7.9 tonnes while at an extension of 2.89 m, it can lift 30 tonnes.

To provide a more stable platform during lifting and recovery operations, a hydraulic stabiliser can be lowered either side of the vehicle.

In addition to being used as a recovery vehicle it has also been designed to handle and carry standard 20 ft ISO containers.

Storage areas have been provided on both sides of the chassis for the tools and accessories required for recovery operations.

French Army version
Renault Trucks Defense was awarded a contract for the supply of 17 similar vehicles for delivery to the French Army from the year 2000.

These are similar to those used by the Belgian Army but are fitted with a ZF 6 HP 90 automatic transmission and have no crane mounted to the rear of the cab.

Status
Production as required. In service with Belgian Army (27 units) and France (17).

Contractor
Renault Trucks Defense

Renault Trucks Defense TRM 10 000 CLD (6 × 6) heavy wrecker

Development
The French Army had a requirement for a heavy wrecker truck capable of supporting the Nexter Systems (previously Giat Industries) Leclerc MBT operations as well as performing the usual range of heavy-duty recovery operations.

Using the Renault Trucks Defense TRM 10 000 6 × 6 truck as the basic chassis, trials were carried out with two types of hydraulic crane, both with a 15,000 kg lifting capacity and almost identical in appearance. One crane was a PPM product, the other, the GIC 156, a Pinguely product.

The Pinguely GIC 156 was selected by the French Army. In total, 300 CLD *(Camion Lourd de Dépannage)* crane and truck combinations were delivered to the French Army between 1992 and 1999.

Production of the TRM 10 000 family of 6 × 6 trucks, including the heavy wrecker, was completed early in 1999.

This family of specialised military 6 × 6 cross-country trucks is no longer manufactured by Renault Trucks Defense but the company continue to support these vehicles.

Description
The TRM 10 000 CLD (6 × 6) heavy wrecker has a five-seat tilting-forward control cab which can be fitted with a tarpaulin or removable hardtop.

It is understood all French Army TRM 10 000 CLD (6 × 6) heavy wrecker vehicles have tarpaulin-type cab covers.

Designed to take up all the forces supported by the CLD in all its operational configurations, the subframe is fixed on to the side members of the carrier and made up of high-yield strength steel-plate boxes, plus cross members connected to stabilisation beams.

The CLD is equipped with four separately controlled outriggers with sloped telescopic beams. They are actuated by four internal cylinders and are fully protected and equipped with aluminium removable support shoes that can be replaced by anchoring pads for hauling.

When the crane is being used to lift heavy loads (for example the complete power pack of the now Nexter Leclerc MBT), the wheels of the vehicle are clear of the ground with the complete weight of the system absorbed by the four outriggers.

When the CLD is moved whilst carrying a load, four hydraulic cylinders equipped with resilient limit switch dampers lock the suspension for the rear tandem of the carrier.

The hauling winch is actuated by a hydraulic motor driven from a power take-off on the vehicle's gearbox and is equipped with a rope tensioner with a wheel-type fray-proof device, a clutching out handle, an anti-drift brake and an unwinding safety device.

The winch has a maximum direct pull of 18 tonnes (this can be increased to 36 tonnes with a sheave), a maximum pulling speed of 14.5 m/min and is provided with 100 m of 20 mm diameter cable. The cable is carried in a special trough inside the subframe for unloading/loading using an auxiliary winch with a maximum pulling speed of 40 m/min and 200 m of 5 mm diameter cable.

The CLD is mounted on a constant-traverse turntable with a cab for the operator; maximum traversing speed is 2 rpm. When traversed to the front, the operator's cab is on the right side of the crane turntable. The telescopic box-section jib is raised by a double-acting cylinder equipped with a balancing valve and check valve.

The crane can lift 15 tonnes at 2.5 m, although it is possible to lift loads such as tank turrets weighing 20 tonnes at 4.2 m. Minimum jib length is 4.4 m and maximum 7 m. The crane can be traversed through 360° and elevated from –1° to +55°.

For towing, the CLD can pull a weight of up to 40 tonnes at 25 km/h. It is also possible to lift and tow a weight of 7.5 tonnes by the axle.

The CLD is provided with six toolboxes, a fixed vice and spirit level and working lights. Other equipment provided with the CLD includes four anchoring shoes, an opening sheave, two 36-tonne sheaves for hauling, a

Renault Trucks Defense TRM 9000 CLD (6 × 6) heavy recovery vehicles deployed by Morocco (Shaun C Connors)   1405678

Renault Trucks Defense TRM 10 000 CLD heavy wrecker of the French Army
1296036

safety sleeve used when removing tank turrets, ropes, chains, towing straps, towing triangle, adjustable connecting rods, hinged bar, welding and cutting equipment and various other tools.

Optional equipment included a hydraulically operated rear spade-type anchor. A replacement wheel and tyre are located to the rear of the cab.

Variants

TRM 9000 CLD wrecker
This is similar to the TRM 10 000 but has a shorter wheel base. It is in service with Morocco and UAE but is no longer marketed.

Specifications

TRM 10 000 CLD recovery vehicle
Cab seating: 1 + 3
Configuration: 6 × 6
Weight:
  (complete) 23,000 kg
  (crane equipment) 11,500 kg
Towed load: up to 40,000 kg
Length: (jib forward) 8.686 m
Width:
  (travelling) 2.48 m
  (stabilisers extended) 2.903 m
Height: (overall) 3.436 m
Track: 2.053 m
Wheelbase: 4.3 + 1.4 m
Max speed: 90 km/h
Range: 1,000 km
Fuel capacity: 500 litres
Angle of approach/departure: 45/33°
Engine: Renault MIDS 06.20-45 6-cylinder diesel developing 275 hp at 2,200 rpm
Transmission: ZF 6 HP 500 automatic with torque converter
Transfer box: 2 speed
Steering: hydraulic power-assisted
Tyres: 14.00 × 20
Electrical system: 24 V

Status
Production complete. In service with French Army (300 units). No longer marketed.

Contractor
Vehicle: Renault Trucks Defense
Crane: Pinguely Industries

Berliet TBC 8 KT (6 × 6) wrecker

Development
The Berliet TBC 8 KT (6 × 6) CLD (*Camion Lourd de Dépannage*) is a member of the Berliet GBC 8 KT (6 × 6) four-tonne truck family. For many years, this was the standard vehicle in its class of the French Army. Most of the fleet has now been upgraded to the Renault Trucks Defence GBC 180 (6 × 6) 5,000 kg truck standard. The reader is referred to the entry on the latter vehicle in the Trucks section for a detailed history of its development and a description of its technical characteristics.

Production of this vehicle was completed many years ago and Berliet was subsequently absorbed by Saviem, which in turn was taken over by Renault, with the military part of the business now being known as Renault Trucks Defense.

While no longer manufactured or marketed, Renault Trucks Defense continue to support this range of military vehicles.

Description
The rear hydraulically operated winch is provided with 60 m of cable and has a maximum capacity of 5,000 kg which can be increased to 7,000 kg with the aid of earth anchors.

Berliet GBC 8 KT (6 × 6) wrecker in travelling configuration
0511484

The crane mounted in the rear is hydraulically operated and slews through 270°; two stabilisers on each side are lowered to the ground manually. Equipment carried includes: two telescopic arm brackets to support the jib; two rear radius rods to support the jib on the ground; towbars; two earth anchor spades; tackles; one acetylene bottle and hose; one oxygen bottle and hose; and tools.

Part of the French Army fleet of Berliet TBC 8 KT (6 × 6) trucks has been upgraded in a number of key areas. This upgrade may include the wrecker. The upgraded cargo truck model is called the Renault Trucks Defence GBC 180 (6 × 6) 5,000 kg truck.

Variants
A light recovery version of the GBC 8 KT (6 × 6) truck is also in service. This has drop sides and an overhead rail and is provided with a 2,000 kg hoist which can be used to lift light vehicles and change components. A winch with a capacity of 5,000 kg (or 7,000 kg with earth anchors in use) is fitted and can be led out through the front or rear. Loaded weight is 12,600 kg and empty weight is 9,600 kg (for example 4,400 kg on the front axles and 2,600 kg on each of the rear axles).

Specifications
TBC 8 KT wrecker
Cab seating: 1 + 2
Configuration: 6 × 6
Weight: (empty) 13,650 kg
Length: 7.693 m
Width: 2.4 m
Height: 2.97 m
Ground clearance:
  (max) 0.515 m
  (axles) 0.28 m
Track: 1.86 m
Wheelbase: 3.31 + 1.28 m
Angle of approach/departure: 45/45°
Max speed: (road) 80 km/h
Range: 800 km
Fuel capacity: 200 litres
Max gradient: 50%
Side slope: 22%
Fording: 1.2 m
Engine: Berliet MK 520 5-cylinder multifuel developing 125 hp at 2,100 rpm
Transmission: Berliet BDSL with 6 forward and 1 reverse gears, 2-speed transfer case
Turning radius: 10.5 m
Steering: worm gear and nut with servo-assistance, turning circle indicator provided
Suspension:
  (front) longitudinal leaf springs with hydraulic shock-absorbers
  (rear) leaf springs

Light recovery version of Berliet GBC 8KT (6 × 6) in travelling configuration (Pierre Touzin)
0587620

Tyres: 12.00 × 20
Brakes: air with 3 circuits (1 for front, 1 for rear and 1 for trailer) with exhaust retarder
Electrical system: 24 V
Batteries: 4 × 12 V

Status
Production complete. No longer marketed. In service with the French Army. The cargo truck version was built and sold to Algeria, Austria, China, Morocco and Portugal, some of which may possibly use the recovery version. Renault Trucks Defense is now marketing an upgrade package for this chassis. As far as it is known, this upgrade package has only been adopted by the French Army.

Contractor
Automobiles M Berliet, Bourg (Berliet is now part of the Renault Group.)

ACMAT Type TPK 6.40 WRT recovery vehicle

Development
The Type TPK 6.40 WRT is the recovery member of the ACMAT series of VLRA (6 × 6) vehicles that are covered in detail in a separate entry. By late 2010 about 12,000 vehicles had been built with sales made to more than 40 countries. These were originally developed for use in the harsh conditions of North Africa.

This 6 × 6 ACMAT is, in turn, a development of the more widely deployed ACMAT VLRA series of 4 × 4 vehicles. These ACMAT 6 × 6 and 4 × 4 vehicles share many common components such as suspension, axles, drive line, engine and transmission which reduces operating and procurement costs.

In 2006, ACMAT was taken over by Renault Trucks Defense but still trades under the ACMAT brand name with the production facility still being in Saint-Nazaire.

Description
The layout of the ACMAT Type TPK 6.40 WRT recovery vehicle is similar to the standard VLRA (6 × 6) vehicle with the engine at the front, driver and two passengers to the rear and with the recovery equipment mounted to the rear of the cab.

The cab is of the military open type with the roof reinforced for the installation of a circular ring mount on which a variety of weapons can be mounted, including 7.62 and .50 (12.7 mm) M2 HB machine guns. The windscreen can be folded down or dismounted if required.

ACMAT Type TPK 6.40 WRT (6 × 6) recovery vehicle of the French Army (Pierre Touzin)   1333667

ACMAT Type TPK 6.40 WRT (6 × 6) recovery vehicle in travelling configuration   0536879

The rear platform is on scored plate 4 mm thick, which is reinforced by tubular cross pieces and a spacer, 8 mm thick and designed for the mounting of the hydraulic crane. A large storage compartment, with two doors, is fitted on the left side for tools and other equipment.

The vehicle is fitted with a Type HP 2860 T7 hydraulic crane with a lifting torque of 20,000 kg for all positions of the arm having a maximum elevation of +75° and a depression of −15°. The winch is provided with 74 m of 12 mm diameter cable.

Mounted either side of the rear are two telescopic arms on the ends of which are mounted stabilisers that are lowered to the ground by remote control when the crane is being used. These provide a more stable platform. A tow hook with a capacity of 10 tonnes is mounted at the rear.

Specifications
Type TPK 6.40 WRT recovery vehicle
Cab seating: 1 + 2
Configuration: 6 × 6
Weight:
  (empty) 10,500 kg
  (loaded) 22,000 kg
Length: 7.01 m
Width: 2.46 m
Height: 2.65 m (crane jib)
Ground clearance: 300 mm
Track:
  (front) 1.76 m
  (rear) 1.80 m
Wheelbase:
  4.10 m (front axle to middle of rear unit)
  1.20 m (middle of rear unit)
Angle of approach/departure: 45/41°
Max road speed: 85 km/h
Range: 800 km
Fuel capacity: 210 litres
Max gradient: 55%
Max side slope: 30%
Fording: 0.9 m
Engine: Perkins Phaser 6.354 6-cylinder diesel developing 160 hp at 2,800 rpm (latest production ACMAT vehicles have Cummins diesel engine)
Gearbox: Type TR 540 manual with 5 forward and 1 reverse gears
Clutch: single dry plate (356 mm)
Transfer box: ACMAT Type AL 660 2-speed
Steering: ACMAT Burman hydraulic power-assisted
Turning radius: 10.35 m
Suspension:
  (front) special Sahara type, heavy-duty shock-absorbers
  (rear) reversed springs mounted on flexible rotating bearing, with reaction rods
Tyres: 335/80 R 20
Brakes:
  (main) air/hydraulic
  (parking) mechanical
Electrical system: 24 V
Batteries: 2 × 12 V, 100 Ah

Status
Production as required. In service with many countries, including Botswana, France, Ireland and Zimbabwe.

Contractor
Ateliers de Construction Mécanique de l'Atlantique (ACMAT) (now part of Renault Trucks Defense)

Germany

FAUN BKF 35-4 recovery vehicle

Development
The BKF 35-4 is the latest in a long line of recovery vehicles developed by FAUN for the civil and military markets and a quantity of these have been supplied to the German Army. The vehicle is capable of being used as a crane or as a recovery vehicle. As of late 2010, there were no known exports of the FAUN BKF 35-4 recovery vehicle but it has been offered on the export market.

Description
The FAUN BKF 35-4 recovery vehicle has a similar layout to the other recently developed FAUN vehicles of this type with the fully enclosed cab at the front protruding well forwards of the first axle. The diesel powerpack is to the cab rear.

The cab is of composite construction (steel sheet metal and fibre glass) with safety glass, air cushioned adjustable seats and engine dependent hot water heater.

Steering is powered on the first, second and fourth axles and if required power to the third axle can be disengaged. Suspension is hydropneumatic with levelling and road wheel adjustment.

FAUN BKF 35-4 recovery vehicle of the German Army from the rear, in the travelling configuration 1159835

The turntable-mounted crane is in the middle of the chassis between the second and third sets of road wheels and for travelling can be traversed to the front or rear. When traversed to the front the fully enclosed cab is on the left side.

The recovery equipment is at the rear and when the crane is being used a total of four hydraulically operated stabilisers are lowered to the ground. Two of these are positioned at the front of the vehicle and two between the third and four sets of road wheels. All of these are on outriggers.

The crane is fitted with a telescopic boom, which can be extended from 6.9 m out to 22.50 m with a lifting capacity from 35 tonnes to 2.6 tonnes, this depends on the height and extension of the boom. The boom has an elevation from −1° to +80°.

According to the manufacturer, the BKF 35-4 recovery vehicle can tow vehicles up to a maximum weight of 40,000 kg. Mounted at the rear is the towing device, which consists of a cradle with a tilt cylinder, vertical telescope and two-stage extendable jib for pick up of the load. This has a vertical adjustment of 400 mm and the boom can be extended from 1.83 to 3.76 m.

It is fitted with a hydraulic rope winch with 75 m of 22 mm diameter cable with a rated load of up to 200 kN. This is used to the rear of the vehicle.

It is also capable of recovery operations using the crane boom and the hoist winch and this gives a maximum diagonal pull of 7.5 tonnes.

Optional equipment for the chassis includes a 12 V plug box at the rear, engine independent hot air diesel heating, air conditioning, remote control for towing cradle with 5 m cable, two portable searchlights and lifting cradle adjustable in width.

Optional equipment for the superstructure includes emergency crane controls, working light on boom, floodlight suspended from boom point and a central lubrication system.

Specifications

BKF 35-4 recovery vehicle
Cab seating: 2
Configuration: 8 × 8 (but third axle can be disengaged)
Weight:
    (unloaded) 31,960 kg
    (first axle) 9,100 kg
    (second axle) 9,100 kg
    (third axle) 6,930 kg
    (fourth axle) 6,930 kg
Length: 11.846 m (crane to rear)
Width: 2.75 m (travelling)
Height: 3.785 m
Wheelbase: 1.70 m + 3.14 m + 2.20 m
Angle of approach/departure: 23.5/23°
Max speed: 82.5 km/h
Engine: Mercedes-Benz 6-cylinder water-cooled diesel model OM 501 developing 394 hp at 1,800 rpm
Gearbox: automatic with 12 forward and 2 reverse gears
Steering: ZF powered on 1, 2 and 4 axles
Turning radius: n/avail
Suspension: hydropneumatic
Tyres: 16.00 R 25 with on/off road profile
Brakes:
    (main) dual circuit compressed air
    (parking) spring on 2, 3 and 4 axles
Electrical system: 24 V
Batteries: 2
Generator: 80 A

Status

Production as required. In service with German Army.

Contractor

FAUN GmbH

MAN Type 27.365 VFAE (8 × 8) recovery vehicle

Development

The MAN Type 27.365 VFAE (8 × 8) recovery vehicle is a development from the main line of MAN (8 × 8) 15-tonne high mobility, cross-country truck chassis and was first produced for use by the US Army in Europe and the Canadian Armed Forces Europe.

The first two examples of this recovery vehicle for the US Army were delivered between July and September 1981 under the designation XM1002. They were later approved for service as the M1002. Production ceased in 1987. The US Army vehicles, which were used to support Ground Launched Cruise Missiles, have been disposed of, while the Canadian vehicles are no longer based in Europe.

Description

The main D 2840 MFG V-10 water-cooled engine is situated just behind the fully enclosed tilt-forward cab, which has air-assisted suspension seating for the driver and two passengers. The entire chassis frame is constructed from all-welded steel and is a low torsion box structure. A replacement wheel and tyre are located to the right of the engine. Behind the MAN Diesel engine is an open equipment-carrying box with drop sides 2.3 m long. Behind the box is an ATLAS hydraulic crane with a capacity of 20,000 kg which is provided with a remote-control unit; outriggers can be mounted for stability. Directly over the third and fourth axles is a substructure which can either be used as a 'fifth wheel' load-carrying surface or as the position for a recovery assembly capable of lifting up to 11,340 kg and towing 38,556 kg. The recovery assembly may be fitted with a towing bar or other recovery equipment.

Other special equipment includes a heavy-duty recovery winch with a 20,412 kg capacity and a self-recovery winch with a 9,072 kg capacity. Power take-offs for all this equipment can be selected from the main power train. Additional replacement wheels and tyres can be carried over the main recovery assembly. When originally being marketed, a range of optional equipment was available including paint that was NBC decontaminant resistant and an arctic kit.

Variants

Following an international competition, MAN Truck and Bus of the UK were awarded a contract by the UK MoD for a complete fleet of 4 × 4, 6 × 6 and 8 × 8 tactical wheeled vehicles. Included in the latter are a total of 288 recovery vehicles and 69 recovery trailers. Some of these have been upgraded under Urgent Operational Requirement (UOR) funding for deployment to Afghanistan.

Specifications

Type 27.365 VFAE recovery vehicle
Cab seating: 1 + 2
Configuration: 8 × 8
Weight:
    (kerb) 20,180 kg
    (GCW) 45,300 kg
Axle loadings:
    (front) 2 × 7,500 kg
    (rear) 2 × 10,500 kg
Length: 8.996 m
Width: 2.5 m
Height:
    (top of crane) 3 m approx
    (top of cab) 2.921 m
Ground clearance: 0.457 m
Track:
    (front) 2.066 m
    (rear) 2.072 m
Wheelbase: 1.93 + 3.2 + 1.5 m or 1.93 + 2.77 + 1.5 m
Angle of approach/departure: 42.5/45°
Max speed: (approx) 90 km/h
Fuel capacity: 600 litres
Max gradient: (without towed load) 60%
Side slope: 40%
Fording: 1.22 m

MAN recovery vehicle on (8 × 8) Kat 1A1 chassis in travelling configuration 0511485

Engine: MAN D 2840 MFG V-10 water-cooled diesel developing 365 hp at 2,300 rpm
Gearbox: ZF synchromesh 4S-150 8 speed
Clutch: ZF torque converter clutch 400
Transfer box: ZF-GPA
Steering: recirculatory ball hydro-steering
Suspension: coil springs and telescopic shock- absorbers
Tyres: 16.00 × 20
Brakes: dual-circuit air and air over hydraulic
Electrical system: 24 V
Batteries: 4 × 12 V, 125 Ah
Alternator: 28 V, 95 A

Status
Production complete. In service with the Canadian Forces and other armies.

Contractor
MAN Nutzfahrzeuge AG

FAUN recovery crane Type RTF 25

Development
The FAUN recovery crane Type RTF 25 was developed for the recovery and repair of wheeled and tracked vehicles as well as for general crane lifting purposes. Production of the FAUN recovery crane Type RTF 25 is undertaken on an as required basis by the company. As far as it is known, as of late 2010 there have been no export sales of the Type RTF 25.

Description
The vehicle has a high degree of cross-country mobility using a 4 × 4 drive configuration and with steering on both power axles. Steering is power-assisted to reduce driver fatigue.

The FAUN recovery crane Type RTF 25 uses a forward control cab constructed from steel and glass fibre and with the crane turntable immediately behind the cab. The crane has a telescopic jib with a maximum extension of 22.34 m. Telescopic stabilisers are provided for use when the crane is operating. The crane is stated to have a lifting capacity of 25,000 kg at a reach of 7.54 m.

ATF 120-5 Crane
FAUN have supplied two of their ATF 120-5 all terrain cranes to the German Army. These have the military designation of the FKS 120 t gl FAUN.

They were integrated into the German Army's Field Camp Concept in order to facilitate transport and displacement of containers and other types of heavy loads in unprepared terrain conditions.

This vehicle features a five-axle chassis powered by a Mercedes-Benz Euro I 8-cylinder water-cooled diesel developing 503 hp at 2,100 rpm coupled to a ZF transmission with 16 forward and 2 reverse gears.

Suspension is of the hydropneumatic type with levelling adjustment. The turntable-mounted crane is operated by its own Euro I 6-cylinder diesel engine that develops 153 hp at 2,000 rpm. The crane is mounted in the centre of the chassis and when being used, hydraulic stabilisers are normally extended either side.

The main boom consists of five telescopic sections that are hydraulically extended under load from 12.5 to 40 m. The maximum lifting capacity is 130 tonnes with 3 m of boom and a counterweight of 29.4 tonnes.

Specifications
Type RTF 25 recovery crane
Cab seating: 1 + 1
Configuration: 4 × 4 (with steering on all wheels)
Weight: 21,600 kg

FAUN recovery crane Type RTF 25 showing steering on all four wheels
0511486

Length: approx 10.45 m
Width: 2.5 m
Height: 3.35 m
Wheelbase: 3.8 m
Max speed: 80 km/h
Fuel capacity: 300 litres
Engine: Mercedes-Benz OM 366 LA water-cooled diesel developing 240 hp at 2,600 rpm
Gearbox: ZF 6 WG 180 power shift with HN 500 converter providing 6 forward and 2 reverse gears
Steering: ZF semi-integral power, dual circuit
Tyres: 14.00 R 25
Brakes: compressed air, dual circuit

Status
Production as required. In service with a number of undisclosed countries.

Contractor
FAUN GmbH

FAUN BKF 30.40 recovery vehicle for Patriot/Roland SAMs

Development
The FAUN BKF 30.40 8 × 8 recovery vehicle for Raytheon Systems Company Patriot and the now MBDA (previously Euromissile) Roland Surface-to-Air Missile (SAM) system was developed in response to a requirement stated in 1985 by the German MoD.

A production contract was placed in 1990 and by 1995 two vehicles were undergoing troop trials. The only known user is the German Air Force, which has taken delivery of 10 vehicles for use with its Raytheon Patriot SAM as the shorter range MBDA Roland SAM have now been phased out of service.

Description
The FAUN BKF 30.40 recovery vehicle is based on the MAN 32.422 VFAEG chassis and is modified by fitting hydropneumatic suspension and larger tyres. These provide increased traction and a lower ground pressure. The main equipment fitted is a FAUN recovery crane with a capacity of 15.3 tonnes at a boom length of 4.8 m.

Also supplied is: a hydraulic jackplate; hydraulic four-point support plates; a Rotzler Treibmatic winch with a towing capacity of 20 tonnes over the entire cable length of 100 m; auxiliary cable with spooler for a 240 m long; 7 mm cable to tow the main cable; various other items of Rotzler towing and recovery equipment; and a Treibmatic-driven towing attachment with a 13-tonne lifting capacity for towed vehicles. Remote control is standard.

Standard equipment includes a rear-mounted stabiliser blade and four outriggers, two either side, which are normally deployed when the crane is in use. Steering is power-assisted on the front two axles.

FAUN BKF 30.40 recovery vehicle for Patriot/Roland SAMs   0512310

FAUN BKF 30.40 recovery vehicle for Patriot/Roland SAMs towing a MAN (8 × 8) truck   0512311

Specifications

BKF 30.40 recovery vehicle
Cab seating: 1 + 1
Configuration: 8 × 8
Weight: 29,500 kg
Max axle load, front/rear: 15,000/26,000 kg
Max tow weight: 30,000 kg
Length: approx 10.15 m
Width: 2.75 m
Height: 3.15 m
Wheelbase: 1.93 + 3.57 + 1.5 m
Engine: MAN Model D2866 LFG 6-cylinder water-cooled diesel developing 400 hp at 2,000 rpm
Transmission: ZF semi-automatic type 16 S 160 A
Suspension: hydropneumatic
Tyres:
    (front) 16.00 R 20 XZL
    (rear) 24 R 21 XZL
Max speed: (limited) 88 km/h
Fording: 1.2 m
Gradient: 60% (without towed load)
Side slope: 40%
Ditch crossing: 1.9 m
Fuel: 400 litres
Range: 800 km
Electrical system: 24 V
Batteries: 4×12 V 100 Ah

Status

Production as required. In service with German Air Force (10 units).

Contractor

FAUN GmbH

India

Ashok Leyland Light Recovery Vehicle (4 × 4)

Development

The Light Recovery Vehicle (LRV) (4 × 4) was originally developed by Ashok Leyland to meet the operational requirements of the Indian Army.

It is based on the Stallion (4 × 4) series of cross-country cargo truck but has a number of modifications for the recovery role, including a shorter wheelbase.

It is understood that total production of the Stallion (4 × 4) series of cargo truck has passed 22,500 units. At least 950 LRVs have been built for the Indian Army.

The LRV has been designed for the recovery and towing of wheeled vehicles with a payload of up to 7,500 kg. Vehicles can be towed by using tow bars or suspended towing. It can also be used as a mobile crane.

This vehicle has been offered on the export market but as of late 2010 there are no known sales.

Description

The forward control cab has seats for the driver and two passengers. To allow access to the power pack, the cab can be tilted forwards. To the immediate rear of the cab is a crew cabin, which is provided with side and roof protection but is open to the rear.

The chassis of the vehicle is of the all-steel ladder bolted type with a total of seven cross section members with each of these being 229 × 76 × 6 mm thick.

The propeller shaft is a 1600 series (three-part). The rear axle is a fully floating single-speed hypoid drive type, with cross-axle lock with a capacity of 10,000 kg and a ratio of 5.833:1.

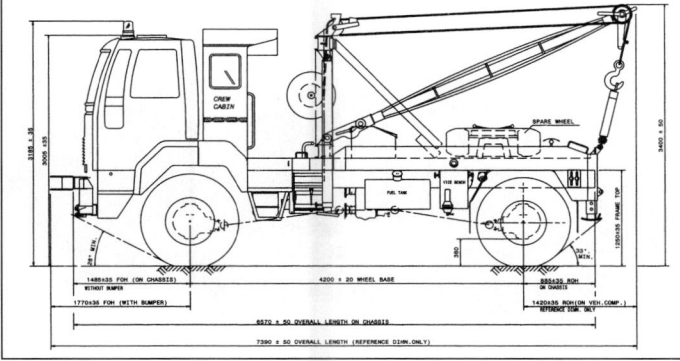

Detailed side drawing of the Ashok Leyland Light Recovery Vehicle (4 × 4)
(Ashok Leyland)   1129832

Ashok Leyland Light Recovery Vehicle (4 × 4) with stabilisers deployed
(Shaun C Connors)   1296038

The front axle is a fully floating single-speed hypoid drive type with a capacity of 7,500 kg and a ratio of 5.833:1. Tyres are 14.00 R20 XZL all round with single tyres on the rear wheels. A replacement wheel and tyre is carried in the horizontal position at the rear below the twin booms.

Mounted on the middle of the rear chassis is the twin boom recovery equipment, which has a reach of 3.5 m to the side and 450 mm to the rear. It is also fitted with two winches each with a capacity of 7.5 tonnes, which gives a combined winching capacity of 15 tonnes.

To provide a more stable platform during recovery operations, a stabiliser is lowered to the ground either side to the immediate rear of the rear crew cab.

Variants

There are no known variants of the Ashok Leyland LRV, although the chassis can be adopted for a wide range of roles and missions.

Specifications

Ashok Leyland Light Recovery Vehicle (LRV)
Cab seating: 1 + 2
Configuration: 4 × 4
Weight: 17,725 kg (7,000 kg payload)
    (kerb) 10,725 kg
    (GVW) 15,225 kg (4,500 kg payload)
Length: 7.39 m
Width: 2.50 m
Height:
    (cab roof) 3.005 m
    (cab warning lights) 3.185 m
    (top of jib travelling) 3.40 m
Ground clearance: 360 mm
Track:
    (front) 2.03 m
    (rear) 2.06 m
Wheelbase: 4.2 m
Angle of approach/departure: 28/33°
Max speed: 91 km/h
Range: n/avail
Fuel capacity: 320 litres
Max gradient: 60%
Side slope: 40%
Fording: 0.76 m
Engine: WO6DTI water-cooled turbocharged and inter-cooled diesel engine developing 117 kW (160 hp) at 2,400 rpm
Clutch: single dry plate, hydraulically operated, with a diameter of 353 mm
Transmission: ZF manual with 6 forward and 1 reverse gears
Transfer case: 2-speed with disengagable front drive
Steering: integral powered
Turning radius: n/avail
Suspension: semi-elliptical laminated multileaf and hydraulic telescopic shock absorbers
Tyres: 14.00 × 20
Brakes:
    (main) air, dual line
    (parking) n/avail
Electrical system: 24 V
Batteries: 110 Ah
Generator: n/avail

Status

Production as required. In service with India (950 units).

Contractor

Ashok Leyland

Israel

EYAL heavy recovery vehicles

Development
The EYAL Engineering and Industrial Company Limited developed five models of heavy-wheeled recovery vehicle. They are: the HRV 720 with a lifting ability of 20 t/m; the HRV 930 with a lifting ability of 30 t/m; the HRV 1236 with a lifting ability of 36 t/m; the HRV 1545 with a lifting ability of 45 t/m; and the heaviest model, the HRV 1760 with a lifting ability of 60 t/m.

Description
All these models are produced using a 6 × 6 chassis with the model and make of chassis according to customer choice; most examples used by the Israeli Armed Forces use locally modified US supplied M809 (6 × 6) series chassis. It should be noted that production of the US M809 (6 × 6) truck was completed many years ago.

The recovery hamper is produced as a bolt-on unit and consists of a hydraulic crane, four hydraulically operated outriggers, a main recovery hydraulic winch, towing hitch, operating cab and the hydraulic system.

The hydraulic crane has a full 360° traverse and is equipped with a planetary hydraulic hoisting winch mounted on the main boom. The winch has a built-in automatic brake. Boom operations are carried out by a hydraulic double-acting cylinder with built-in safety devices. The crane block may be assembled with one or two sheaves on a roller bearing and with a swivel hook.

The four outriggers are located with one pair at the front of the upper structure and the other pair at the rear. Each pair is operated separately under hydraulic control and with automatic built-in safety locking valves. When deployed, the stabilisers take the full weight of the vehicle with all of the wheels being raised clear of the ground.

The main recovery winch is mounted on the front of the upper structure and is equipped with 70 m of cable. The winch may have a line pull of 15, 20 or 25 tonnes depending on the model. The cable is drawn under the floor of the recovery unit.

The towing hitch is mounted at the rear and can tow suspended loads of six, seven, eight or 10 tonnes, depending on the EYAL model involved.

The operating cab is mounted on the right-hand side of the crane boom and levers are used to control the hydraulic system. A rainproof canvas cover is supplied for the operator who is seated on the right side of the crane turntable.

The hydraulic system is driven from the vehicle power take-off.

EYAL heavy recovery vehicle on US supplied 6 × 6 chassis lifting recovery frame complete with crane   0511487

Hellenic Army Oshkosh Defense MTVR (6 × 6) with recovery hamper provided by EYAL and with stabiliser outriggers in the raised position (Shaun C Connors)   1405679

EYAL also produces a range of hydraulic cranes with varying lift capacities. One of them, the Model 3501, was mounted on Israeli Army M3 half-tracks. Recent information has indicated that the IDF has phased out of front line service its half-track vehicles.

The company has also developed recovery packages for installation on full-tracked armoured vehicles such as the US M47 tank. These were for the export market as the Israel Defense Force has never used the M47 tank but it has used the later M48 and M60 in large numbers. It is understood that in the case of the M47/M48 tank based ARV conversions that these were based on foreign design.

It should be noted that while the upgraded M60 tank is still used in declining numbers by the Israeli Army there are no M48 tanks in front line service.

Variants
EYAL also provide their hampers to other contractors for installation on local chassis.

The Hellenic Army, for example has Oshkosh Defense MTVR (6 × 6) vehicles fitted with a EYAL rear hamper for use in the specialised recovery role.

The prime contractor for this is the local company of Hellenic Vehicle Industries (ELBO) who have extensive experience in tracked and wheeled vehicle integration.

Status
Production as required. In service with the Israeli Armed Forces.

Contractor
EYAL Engineering and Industrial Company Limited

Italy

IVECO M320.42 WM (8 × 8) mobile crane

Development
The IVECO M320.42 WM (8 × 8) mobile crane is a member of the IVECO M320.42 WM (8 × 8) family of tactical vehicles. Details of the baseline 15, 000 kg cargo truck, which has a nominal payload of 15,000 kg, are given in a separate entry in *Jane's Military Vehicles and Logistics*. It is included here because its crane can be used to lift and recover tracked and wheeled vehicles weighing up to 30 tonnes. As of late 2010, there were no known sales of the IVECO M320.42 WM (8 × 8) mobile crane.

Description
The IVECO M320.42 WM (8 × 8) mobile crane truck has a fully enclosed two-door forward control cab with the hydraulically operated crane positioned on the rear above the third axle.

When lifting heavier loads, four outriggers are lowered to the ground either side and, with these in position, the crane can lift 30 tonnes at 3.8 m to 10.5 tonnes at 11.6 m. Without outriggers deployed, the crane can lift from 8.5 tonnes at 3.8 m to 2.4 tonnes at 11.6 m.

Standard equipment includes powered steering on the front two axles; a wide range of optional equipment includes an anti-skid braking system, central tyre-pressure inflation system, run-flat tyres and a winch.

Specifications
M320.42 WM mobile crane
Crew: 1 + 2
Configuration: 8 × 8
Weight: 32,000 kg
Towing capability: 20,000 kg
Length: 10.03 m
Width: 2.50 m
Height:
(cab roof) 3.035 m
(with crane) 3.950 m
Wheelbase: 1.955 + 3.595 + 1.45 m
Angle of approach/departure: 45/35°

IVECO M320.42 WM (8 × 8) mobile crane in travelling configuration with crane traversed to the front and lowered into position   0092483

Max speed: 90 km/h
Gradient: 60%
Engine: diesel developing 420 hp
Transmission:
ZF 6 HP 900 automatic with 6 + 6 speed or
ZF WSK 400 torque converter, ZF 16S 221 synchromesh 16 + 16 speeds
Tyres: 14.00 R 20
Brakes: disc (front and rear)
Electrical system: 24 V
Batteries: 2

Status
Development complete. Ready for production.

Contractor
IVECO SpA, Defence Vehicles Division

IVECO 6605 AG (6 × 6) recovery vehicle

Development
The IVECO 6605 AG (6 × 6) is the recovery member of the 6605 range of 6 × 6 vehicles for which there is a separate entry. The first prototype of the vehicle was completed in 1972, with first production models following in 1974.

The Italian Army designation for the vehicle is the Autogru AG 70-5 t (6 × 6). Production of the IVECO 6605 series was completed many years ago and it is no longer being marketed.

The prime contractor for this family of vehicles is now IVECO SpA, Defence Vehicles Division. This vehicle is still deployed by the Italian Army.

Description
The chassis of the IVECO 6605 AG (6 × 6) recovery vehicle is the ladder type with two longitudinal pressed steel channels, to which are riveted the cross members, brackets and spring supports.

The four-door forward control cab is all-steel and has a removable canvas top and side screens and a windscreen which can be folded flat against the bonnet. Standard equipment includes a cab heater and ventilator.

Mounted at the rear of the vehicle is a hydraulically operated crane with an extendable jib, which can lift a maximum load of 5,000 kg. Before the crane is used, two stabilisers are extended either side and lowered to the ground to provide a more stable lifting platform.

The IVECO 6605 AG has two hydraulic winches, one front-mounted with a capacity of 9,200 kg and one rear-mounted with a capacity of 20,000 kg.

The transmission consists of a set of gears mounted on four shafts (input, primary, layshaft and reverse). Shifting from each gear is controlled by a lever through a pneumatic servo. Shifting from the high to the low range, or vice versa, is by electropneumatic control with a preselector switch, interlocked with the clutch pedal.

The transfer box is mechanical and consists of helical constant mesh gears mounted on three shafts (input, intermediate and output) of which the input one carries the dog clutch with a lockable divider differential distributing power to the front and rear axles.

Specifications

6605 AG recovery vehicle
Cab seating: 1 + 1
Configuration: 6 × 6
Weight:
(empty) 19,000 kg
(loaded) 25,000 kg
Max load: 5,000 kg
Towed load: 15,000 kg
Length: 8.32 m
Width: 2.5 m
Height:
(cab) 2.74 m
(top of crane in travelling position) 3.01 m
Ground clearance: 0.363 m
Track: 2.072 m
Wheelbase: 3.217 + 1.365 m
Angle of approach/departure: 45/40°
Max speed: (road) 80 km/h
Range: 700 km
Fuel capacity: 360 litres
Max gradient: 60%
Max side slope: 20%
Fording: 1.5 m
Engine: IVECO Model 8212.02 6-cylinder in-line water-cooled diesel developing 260 hp at 2,200 rpm
Gearbox: manual with 8 forward and 2 reverse gears
Clutch: dual dry plate
Transfer box: 2 speed
Steering: ZF hydraulic assisted
Turning radius: 8 m

IVECO 6605 AG (6 × 6) recovery vehicle showing front-mounted winch. The system is shown in the travelling configuration   0512448

Suspension:
(front) 2 semi-elliptic constant rate leaf springs with double-acting hydraulic shock-absorbers
(rear) rocker and torque arms with 2 constant rate leaf springs
Tyres: 14.00 × 20
Brakes:
(main) drum air-operated on all wheels, dual circuit with connections for trailer braking
(parking) drum, hand-operated, mounted on transfer rear output shaft
Electrical system: 24 V
Batteries: 4 × 12 V, 90 Ah

Status
Production complete. In service with the Italian Army. This vehicle is no longer being marketed.

Contractor
IVECO SpA, Defence Vehicles Division

IVECO 90 PM 16 (4 × 4) wrecker with 5-tonne crane

Development
The IVECO 90 PM 16 (4 × 4) was developed as a private venture and is essentially the standard vehicle modified to carry out the recovery role. Production is now completed an it is no longer marketed by IVECO. As far as it is known, the IVECO 90 PM (4 × 4) wrecker is not used by the Italian Army.

Description
The fully enclosed two door forward control cab is at the front with the FARID hydraulically operated boom crane mounted towards the rear of the chassis.

The IVECO 90 PM 16 (4 × 4) truck chassis was developed to mount a 5,000 kg capacity hydraulically operated FARID crane boom. The crane is mounted behind the vehicle cab on a sheet-steel subframe connected to the chassis by brackets.

On this subframe are mounted the superstructure, crane and outriggers; when the crane is in use, the entire vehicle is raised on to the outriggers for overall stabilisation.

The crane is a FARID model F 5 which is hydraulically operated. The maximum boom length is 5.7 m, the maximum boom elevation 75° and the traverse is a full 360°. The crane has a maximum pull to the rear of 5,000 kg but extra pull capability is provided by a rear-mounted auxiliary winch with a 4,000 kg capability.

A self-recovery winch is mounted at the front and this has a capacity of 3,000 kg. The four outriggers, one at each corner of the subframe, are hydraulically operated from a panel at the side of the vehicle; the crane controls are on a panel by the operator's seat.

Accessories include a drawbar, collapsible snatch blocks, a set of chains with hooks, spare wheel holder and tool boxes. The deck of the subframe, which is covered with a non-slip steel plate, measures 3.4 m long and 2.3 m wide and may be used for carrying extra equipment or cargo.

The fully enclosed forward control cab can be tilted forwards to allow access to the power pack for maintenance. A replacement wheel and tyre is carried to the rear of the cab.

Variant
IVECO 90.17 WM (4 × 4) wrecker
This uses a similar chassis to the IVECO 90 PM 16. It has a 6,000 kg capacity crane. Production of the 90.17 WM four-tonne (4 × 4) truck was complete some time ago and it is no longer being marketed.

IVECO 90 PM 16 (4 × 4) wrecker with five-tonne crane deployed in operating position with stabilisers lowered to the ground   0511488

Specifications

IVECO 90 PM 16 wrecker
Cab seating: 1 + 1
Configuration: 4 × 4
Weight:
   (gross) 9,700 kg
   (kerb) 8,200 kg
Payload: (load hang to hook) 1,500 kg
Towing capacity: 4,000 kg
Length: (incl crane overhang) 7.042 m
Width: 2.476 m
Height: (cab) 2.627 m
Ground clearance: 0.47 m
Track: 1.851 m
Wheelbase: 3.7 m
Angle of approach/departure: 42/42°
Max speed: 80 km/h
Range: 700 km
Power-to-weight ratio: 16.5 hp/t
Max gradient: 60%
Side slope: 30%
Fording: 0.7 m
Engine: IVECO Model 8062.24 6-cylinder supercharged direct injection water-cooled diesel developing 160 hp at 3,200 rpm
Gearbox: manual with 5 forward and 1 reverse gears
Clutch: single dry plate
Transfer box: 2 speed
Steering: recirculating ball with hydraulic servo
Turning radius: 7.5 m
Suspension: leaf springs (dual at rear) with hydraulic shock-absorbers (telescopic)
Tyres: 12.5 R20 PR22

Status
Production complete. No longer being marketed. In service with Venezuela (60).

Contractor
Chassis: IVECO SpA, Defence Vehicles Division

IVECO 230.35 WM (6 × 6) recovery vehicle

Development
The IVECO 230.35 WM (6 × 6) recovery vehicle is a variant of the IVECO 230.35 WM (6 × 6) 10,000 kg truck, which is covered in a separate entry in *Jane's Military Vehicles and Logistics* modified for the specialised recovery role. Production of this family of 10,000 kg series of trucks, including the recovery vehicle, is now completed and it is no longer marketed. As far as it is known the IVECO 230.35 WM (6 × 6) recovery vehicle was not deployed by the Italian Army.

Description
The recovery equipment is mounted on a welded steel subframe that is linked by brackets to the vehicle chassis, crane, winch outriggers and related control units. The upper part of the subframe carries the 360° rotating platform for the crane, which is an Isoli Model M 140 - 49.8 t/m with a maximum lifting capacity of 14,000 kg.

The crane hydraulics are powered from the main IVECO Model 8280.02 V-8 water-cooled diesel engine with the crane using a telescopic boom. The crane has a hook-lifting speed of 8 m/min and maximum elevation is 55°. The maximum boom length is 6.35 m and the minimum 3.55 m.

IVECO 230.35 WM (6 × 6) recovery vehicle in travelling configuration
0511489

The four outriggers are operated independently of each other and have independent controls for all movements. A hydraulic recovery winch is fitted to the side of the vehicle for front and rear operations. It has a maximum pulling capacity (on the first layer) of 15,000 kg.

The IVECO 230.35 WM (6 × 6) recovery vehicle is fitted with a torque converter to obtain the maximum tractive effort in any gear.

The vehicle has a two-door forward control cab with removable top and sides. The engine and transmission is the same as that installed in the IVECO 260.35 WM (6 × 6) recovery vehicle covered in detail in a separate entry in *Jane's Military Vehicles and Logistics*. Like the IVECO 230.35 WM (6 × 6) recovery vehicle, this is no longer marketed by IVECO.

Specifications

230.35 WM recovery vehicle
Cab seating: 1 + 2
Configuration: 6 × 6
Weight:
   (kerb) 19,000 kg
   (GVW) 25,000 kg
Load: (load hang to hook) 5,000 kg
Towed load: (off-road) 15,000 kg
Length: (overall) 8.48 m
Width:
   (overall) 2.5 m
   (cab) 2.494 m
Height:
   (overall) 3.06 m
   (cab) 3 m
Ground clearance: 0.35 m
Track:
   (front) 2.027 m
   (rear) 2.032 m
Wheelbase: 3.3 + 1.38 m
Angle of approach/departure: 45/30°
Max speed: 83 km/h
Range: 600 km
Fuel capacity: 300 litres
Max gradient: 60%
Side slope: 30%
Fording: 0.85 m
Engine: IVECO Model 8280.02 V-8 17.2 litre water-cooled diesel developing 352 hp at 2,400 rpm
Transmission: Type ZF 4 S 150 GPA with 8 forward and 1 reverse gears, with torque converter
Transfer box: electropneumatically lockable
Steering: power assisted, recirculatory ball
Turning radius: 9.5 m
Suspension:
   (front) single flexibility leaf springs with hydraulic telescopic shock-absorbers
   (rear) single flexibility leaf springs, reversed, fully articulated
Tyres: 14.00 × 20
Brakes:
   (main) drum, air on all wheels
   (parking) mechanical on rear wheels
   (exhaust) pneumatic, pedal control
Electrical system: 24 V
Batteries: 4 × 12 V, 143 Ah
Generator: 650 W

Status
Production complete. No longer marketed. In service with undisclosed countries.

Contractor
IVECO SpA, Defence Vehicles Division

IVECO 260.35 WM (6 × 6) recovery vehicle

Development
The IVECO 260.35 WM (6 × 6) recovery vehicle is a variant of the IVECO 260.35 WM (6 × 6) 10,000 kg truck, fitted with a 12,000 kg hydraulic crane. Production of this family of vehicles is now complete and is no longer marketed. As far as it is known, the IVECO 260.35 (6 × 6) recovery vehicle was not deployed by the Italian Army.

IVECO 260.35 (6 × 6) recovery vehicle with 12-tonne crane in travelling configuration 0511490

Description

The recovery equipment is mounted on a welded steel subframe, linked by brackets to the vehicle chassis, crane, winch, outriggers and related control units. The upper part of the subframe carries the 360° rotating platform for the crane, an Isoli Model M 120 - 42.8 t/m with a maximum lifting capacity of 12,000 kg.

The hydraulic system uses three pumps driven from the vehicle main IVECO Model 8280.02 V-8 diesel engine with the crane having a telescopic extendable boom. The crane has a hook lifting speed of 10 m/min with the maximum elevation angle of 50°. The maximum telescopic boom length is approximately 6.4 m and the minimum about 3.6 m.

The four hydraulic outriggers are operated independently of one other and have independent controls for all movements. Two of the hydraulic jacks are located to the rear of the front axles and the other two are at the very rear of the chassis.

An axle lock can lock the rear bogie, raising it off the ground for increased stability during crane operations. A hydraulic recovery winch is fitted to the side of the vehicle cab for front and rear operations. It has a maximum pulling capacity (on the first layer) of 15,000 kg.

The IVECO 260.35 WM (6 × 6) recovery vehicle is fitted with a torque converter to obtain the maximum tractive effort in any gear.

The IVECO 260.35 WM (6 × 6) recovery vehicle has a two-door fully enclosed forward control cab. Its IVECO engine and ZF transmission are the same as that installed in the IVECO 230.35 WM (6 × 6) recovery vehicle covered in a separate entry in *Jane's Military Vehicles and Logistics*.

Specifications

260.35 WM recovery vehicle
Cab seating: 1 + 1
Configuration: 6 × 6
Weight:
  (kerb) 20,600 kg
  (GVW) 25,600 kg
Load: (load hang to hook) 5,000 kg
Towed load: (off-road) 15,000 kg
Length: (overall) 8.86 m
Width: (overall) 2.5 m
Height:
  (overall) 3.03 m
  (exhaust over cab) 3.123 m
Ground clearance: 0.312 m
Track:
  (front) 1.927 m
  (rear) 1.809 m
Wheelbase: 3.85 + 1.38 m
Angle of approach/departure: 33/27°
Max speed: 94 km/h
Range: 600 km
Fuel capacity: 300 litres
Max gradient: 60%
Side slope: 30%
Fording: 0.65 m
Engine: IVECO Model 8280.02 V-8 17.2 litre water-cooled diesel developing 352 hp at 2,400 rpm
Transmission: ZF 4 S 150 GPA with 8 forward and 1 reverse gears, with torque converter
Transfer box: electropneumatically operated
Steering: power assisted, recirculatory ball
Turning radius: 9.5 m
Suspension:
  (front) single flexibility leaf springs with hydraulic telescopic shock-absorbers
  (rear) single flexibility leaf springs, reversed, fully articulated
Tyres: 12.00 × 20
Brakes:
  (main) drum, air on all wheels
  (parking) mechanical on rear wheels
  (exhaust) pneumatic, pedal control
Electrical system: 24 V
Batteries: 2 × 12 V, 143 Ah
Generator: 650 W

Status

Production complete. No longer marketed. In service with undisclosed countries.

Contractor

IVECO SpA, Defence Vehicles Division

Japan

Mitsubishi Model FX50MMY190 (6 × 6) recovery vehicle

Development

This Mitsubishi Model FX50MMY190 (6 × 6) recovery vehicle uses the same chassis as the Mitsubishi Type 74 (6 × 6) 10,000 kg cargo truck used by the Japanese Self-Defence Force. The baseline chassis is a commercial design that has been modified to meet military requirements. Production is complete and it is no longer marketed.

There are no known exports of this vehicle.

Description

The two-door all-steel fully enclosed control cab can be tilted forward to allow access to the powerpack for maintenance.

Mounted to the rear of the cab is a hydraulically-operated crane with a telescopic jib. When the recovery equipment is being used, two stabilisers are lowered each side of the recovery equipment. Winches are provided front and rear and earth anchors can be fitted to the rear of the vehicle if required.

This vehicle was previously referred to as the Mitsubishi Model FW419M1 (6 × 6) recovery vehicle.

Specifications

Model FX50MMY190 recovery vehicle
Cab seating: 1 + 2
Configuration: 6 × 6
Weight:
  (unladen) 19,290 kg
  (laden) 19,530 kg
Length: 9.515 m
Width: 2.49 m
Height: 3.230 m
Wheelbase: 4.17 + 1.350 m
Track:
  (front) 1.940 m
  (rear) 1.845 m
Max speed: (road) 95 km/h
Engine: Mitsubishi 8-cylinder diesel developing 355 hp at 2,200 rpm
Turning radius: 10.5 m
Tyres: 12R 22.5-16PR

Status

Production complete. In service with the Japanese Ground Self-Defence Force. As far as is known, there have been no exports of this vehicle.

Contractor

Mitsubishi Motors Corporation

Mitsubishi Model FX50MMY190 (6 × 6) recovery vehicle 0092481

Isuzu SKW (6 × 6) light wrecker

Development

The Isuzu SKW (6 × 6) light wrecker is based on the chassis of the Isuzu SKW (6 × 6) 3,500 kg truck used for a wide range of missions by the Japanese Ground Self-Defence Force. It was introduced into Japanese Self-Defence Force service in 1973.

Isuzu Type SKW (6 × 6) light wrecker in the travelling configuration 0512154

Production of this family of 6 × 6 tactical vehicles, including the Type SKW (6 × 6) light wrecker is now complete.

As far as it is known, this Isuzu SKW (6 × 6) light wrecker was never offered on the export market.

Description
The latest version of the SKW light wrecker (manufacturer's designation was SKW440MR but is now SKW464MR) has improvements to the Isuzu 8PE1 V-8 liquid-cooled diesel engine, axles, cab and so on. It has a two-man forward control cab with a canvas roof and a windscreen that can be folded forward on to the bonnet.

The load-carrying area behind the cab carries a hydraulic crane with a maximum lifting capacity of 4,800 kg. Stabilising jacks are lowered when the crane, which has a full 360° traverse, is in use. There is also a hydraulically operated recovery winch with a capacity of 4,500 kg.

Specifications
SKW light wrecker
Cab seating: 1 + 1
Configuration: 6 × 6
Weight:
  (unladen) 14,220 kg
  (laden) 14,380 kg
Towed load:
  (road) 6,000 kg
  (cross-country) 4,000 kg
Length: 7.81 m
Width: 2.49 m
Height: 3.06 m
Ground clearance: 0.33 m
Wheelbase: 3.395 + 1.31 m
Track:
  (front) 1.97 m
  (rear) 1.84 m
Angle of approach/departure: 44/46°
Max road speed: 95 km/h
Range: 500 km
Fuel capacity: 170 litres
Fording: 0.8 m
Engine: Isuzu 8PE1 V-8 liquid-cooled diesel developing 250 hp at 2,200 rpm
Transmission: Allison MD automatic. The earlier Isuzu SKW464 model had a manual gearbox with 5 forward and 1 reverse gears
Clutch: single dry plate
Transfer box: 2 speed
Steering: power assisted
Turning radius: 9.4 m
Suspension:
  (front) elliptic springs and hydraulic shock-absorbers
  (rear) semi-elliptic springs
Brakes:
  (main) air/hydraulic
  (parking) mechanical
Tyres: 11.00 × 20
Electrical system: 24 V
Winch capacity: 4,500 kg

Status
Production complete. In service with the Japanese Ground Self-Defence Force. As far as is known there have been no exports of any of the Isuzu SKW (6 × 6) series of vehicles.

Contractor
Isuzu Motors Limited

Korea, South

Kia Motors KM 1001 10 ton (8 × 8) wrecker

Development
The KM 1001 10 ton (8 × 8) wrecker was developed by Kia Motors to meet the operational requirements of the Republic of Korea (RoK) Army. Wherever possible, standard commercial parts have been used in the construction Kia Motors KM 1001 10 ton (8 × 8) wrecker. This is basically a civilian vehicle chassis which has been modified for its specialised military recovery/wrecker role.

There are no known exports of this KM 0001 (8 × 8) wrecker.

Description
The KM 1001 10 ton (8 × 8) wrecker has a fully enclosed forward control cab to the immediate rear of which is installed the hydraulically operated crane, which is mounted on a turntable.

The telescopic jib of the crane can be elevated to +70° and rotated through a full 360° and can lift 6.5 tonnes at a reach of 8 m, seven tonnes at a reach of 2.5 m, and 15 tonnes at a reach of 3 m.

Mounted one either side to the rear of the cab is a hydraulically operated stabiliser that is lowered to the ground when the crane is being used.

A hydraulically operated winch has a capacity of 10.34 tonnes when used to the front of the vehicle and 21.86 tonnes when used to the rear of the vehicle. The KM 1001 wrecker can tow a trailer or damaged vehicle weighing up to six tonnes.

Variants
The KM 1001 10 ton (8 × 8) wrecker is related to the KM 1002 (8 × 8) tractor truck, which is also used by the RoK Army and covered in detail in a separate entry in *Jane's Military Vehicles and Logistics*. This tows a locally developed semi-trailer carrying heavy armoured vehicles such as the Rotem K1/K1A1 MBT.

It could also be used to transport the latest K2 MBT now in production for the Republic of Korea Army.

Specifications
KM 1001 wrecker
Cab seating: 1 + 1
Configuration: 8 × 8
Weight:
  (unloaded) 27,500 kg
  (maximum) 35,500 kg
Payload: 8,000 kg
Length: 9.712 m
Width: 2.574 m
Height:
  (cab flashing lights) 3.46 m
  (top of crane) 3.441 m
Ground clearance: 349 mm
Track:
  (1st axle) 2.01 m
  (2nd axle) 2.10 m
  (3rd axle) 1.89 m
  (4th axle) 1.89 m
Wheelbase: 1.696 m + 3.201 m + 1.354 m
Angle of approach/departure: 33/34°
Max road speed: 103 km/h
Range: 819 km
Max gradient: 60%
Max side slope: 20%
Fording: 0.76 m
Engine: diesel developing 450 hp
Steering: power assisted on front two axles
Turning radius: 11.8 m
Electrical system: 24 V

Kia Motors KM 1001 10 ton (8 × 8) wrecker in travelling configuration
0536877

Status
Production as required. In service with Republic of Korea Army. There are no known exports of this vehicle.

Contractor
Kia Motors Corporation

KM502 5 ton (6 × 6) wrecker in travelling configuration   0511491

Kia Motors KM502 5 ton (6 × 6) wrecker

Development
The KM502 5 ton (6 × 6) wrecker is part of the KIA Motors KM50 series of 5 ton vehicles. The KM50 series of 5 ton (6 × 6) trucks are almost identical to the US M809 5 ton (6 × 6) trucks but are powered by a locally built MAN engine.

Production of this family of 6 × 6 vehicles is now complete and they are no longer being marketed by the Kia Motors Corporation.

Description
Mounted on the rear of the chassis is the hydraulically operated crane that can be traversed through a full 360° without stops and through 270° with stops. The telescopic boom of the crane can be extended from 305 to 549 cm and can be raised to an angle of 45°.

The power-operated winch is mounted at the front of the vehicle and has a maximum capacity of 9,070 kg. The rear power-operated winch has a maximum capacity of 20,400 kg. Cable roller guides allow winch operation at angles of up to 90° off-centre and 60° above or below the horizontal plane.

When the crane is being used, two stabilisers are lowered either side of the vehicle to provide a more stable platform. Late production models of the baseline KM500 (6 × 6) cargo truck are powered by a D6AZ six-cylinder in-line diesel developing 270 hp, which gives a maximum road speed of 88 km/h and a cruising range of 855 km.

Specifications
KM502 5 ton wrecker
Cab seating: 1 + 2
Configuration: 6 × 6
Weight:
  (kerb, front axle) 4,728 kg
  (kerb, rear axle) 11,404 kg
  (kerb, total) 16,132 kg
  (gross, front axle) 11,329 kg
  (gross, rear axle) 20,244 kg
  (gross, total) 21,537 kg
Payload:
  (road) 5,442 kg
  (off-road) 3,715 kg
Length: (overall) 9.048 m
Width: 2.477 m
Height:
  (top of cab) 2.689 m
  (top of crane) 2.692 m
Ground clearance: 0.27 m
Track:
  (front) 1.88 m
  (rear) 1.829 m
Wheelbase: 4.547 m
Angle of approach/departure: 34/43°
Max speed: 85 km/h
Range: (cruising) 805 km
Fuel capacity: 500 litres
Gradient: 45%
Fording: (without kit) 0.762 m
Engine: MAN D2156HM 10.35 litre 6-cylinder water-cooled diesel developing 236 hp at 2,200 rpm
Gearbox: manual with 5 forward and 1 reverse gears
Clutch: single dry disc
Transfer box: 2 speed
Steering: power assisted
Turning radius: 14.58 m
Suspension:
  (front) semi-elliptic leaf springs with shock absorbers
  (rear) semi-elliptic inverted leaf springs
Tyres: 11.00 × 20
Brakes: air over hydraulic
Electrical system: 24 V
Batteries: 4 × 12 V, 100 Ah
Alternator: 60 A

Status
Production complete. With the South Korean Armed Forces. As far as is known there have been no exports of this vehicle.

Contractor
Kia Motors Corporation

Malaysia

DRB-HICOM FTS 33H 6-tonne light recovery vehicle

Development
The FTS 33H 6-tonne light recovery vehicle (4 × 4) was developed by DRB-HICOM Defence Technologies (DEFTECH) to meet the operational requirements of the Royal Malaysian Army who have taken delivery of a total of 19 units.

It entered operational service with the Royal Malaysian Army in November 1999 but as far as it is known, as of late 2010, the Royal Malaysian Army remained the only user of this recovery vehicle.

Description
The FTS 33H 6-tonne light recovery vehicle is essentially a commercial Japanese Isuzu FTS 33H (4 × 4) forward control truck chassis modified for use in the specialised military recovery role.

The original commercial vehicle has twin rear wheels while this specialised recovery version has stronger RABA heavy duty double reduction axles with differential lock and is fitted with Michelin 365/80 R20 XZL tyres.

The drive train has been upgraded with the installation of an Allison 2500 SP fully automatic transmission with the braking system having been changed from air over hydraulic to a full air braking system with ABS.

The two-door fully enclosed forward control all steel cab can be tilted forwards to allow access to the power pack and the windscreen and forward opening side doors are fitted with wire mesh protection.

The recovery equipment is mounted at the rear and has been designed to recover vehicles with a gross weight of up to 7seven tonnes. In addition the vehicle is fitted with a hydraulically operated crane mounted to the cab rear which can lift a maximum load of 3.5 tonnes. This can be traversed through a full 360° and is fitted with an overload safety device.

To provide a more stable platform when the crane is being used two hydraulically operated stabilisers are lowered to the ground one either side of the cab rear.

Hydraulically operated winches are installed at the front and rear and have a maximum capacity of seven tonnes and are provided with 60 m of cable. There is also a safety cutout device and a rope tensioner. The recovery equipment can be operated by remote control.

Type FTS 33H six-tonne light recovery vehicle in travelling configuration (DEFTECH)   0587623

Finally there is a hydraulically operated wrecker bar capable of being extended up to 1.5 m from the rear of the vehicle. This has a lifting capacity of three tonnes with an extension of 1.5 m. Suspended tow capacity is seven tonnes.

It is also provided with a complete set of tools and other specialised equipment. A replacement 30 m cable is coiled in a storage drum.

Specifications
FTS 33H light recovery vehicle
Cab seating: 1 + 2
Configuration: 4 × 4
Weight:
  (unloaded) 10,000 kg
  (maximum) 16,500 kg
Payload: 7,000 kg
Length: 7.5 m
Width: 2.56 m
Height: 3.30 m
Ground clearance: 320 mm
Track:
  (front) 2.024 m
  (rear) 2.024 m
Wheelbase: 4.25 m
Angle of approach/departure: 26/24°
Max speed: 85 km/h
Range: n/avail
Fuel capacity: 200 litres
Gradient: 60%
Fording: 0.8 m
Engine: Isuzu type 6HH1S 4-cycle OHC, direct injection, water-cooled diesel developing 175 hp
Gearbox: Allison 2500 SP fully automatic with 4 forwards, 1 reverse gear and power take off
Transfer box: 2-speed, helical gear, high and low
Steering: re-circulating ball nut with integral power assisted
Turning radius: 9 m
Suspension:
  (front) semi-elliptical leaf springs of the shackle type with hydraulic double acting telescopic shock absorbers
  (rear) semi-elliptic alloy steel leaf springs of the shackle type
Tyres: Michelin 13.00 R 20-365/80 R20 (tubeless)
Brakes:
  (main) full air, dual circuit with ABS
  (parking) full air type, at end of transfer
  (auxiliary) engine exhaust brake with optional retarder
Electrical system: 24 V
Batteries: 2 × 12 V

Status
Production as required. In service with Malaysian Army (19 units). Has been offered on the export market but there are no known sales.

Contractor
DRB-HICOM Defence Technologies SDN BHD

Netherlands

DAF YBZ 3300 DKX 500 (6 × 6) heavy recovery vehicle

Development
During early 1990, the DAF YBZ 3300 DKX 500 (6 × 6) heavy recovery vehicle was chosen by the Dutch Ministry of Defence as the replacement for the older 6 × 6 DAF YB 616/626 recovery vehicles. Production was started in 1991, with deliveries made during 1992 and 1993. In total, 255 units were ordered.

The DAF YBZ 3300 DKX 500 (6 × 6) heavy duty recovery vehicle is still in service with the Royal Netherlands Army but its being replaced by new Scania trucks.

DAF trucks are no longer engaged in the design, development or production of military trucks.

Description
The DAF YBZ 3300 DKX 500 (6 × 6) recovery vehicle chassis is very similar to the DAF YAZ 2500 (6 × 6) family of trucks of which 1,500 were delivered to the Netherlands Armed Forces.

This family of 6 × 6 vehicles is covered in detail in a separate entry in *Jane's Military Vehicles and Logistics* and remains in service with the Netherlands forces in declining numbers.

The layout is conventional with the fully enclosed two door forward contract cab at the front and the recovery equipment installed at the rear.

The latter consists of a Norwegian-designed Alvis Moelv (previously known as Hägglunds Moelv) recovery crane which uses hydraulically operated outrigger arms and a large hoist arm at the rear. Three Rotzler hydraulic winches are provided.

DAF YBZ 3300 DKX (6 × 6) heavy recovery vehicle in travelling configuration (Shaun C Connors)   1405680

It should be noted that the Norwegian company of Alvis Moelv closed down in 2004.

The DAF YBZ 3300 DKX 500 (6 × 6) heavy recovery vehicle has a fully enclosed forward control cab that can be tilted forward to allow access to the diesel powerpack for maintenance purposes.

Stabilisers are lowered to the ground when the crane is being used.

Specifications
YBZ 3300 DKX 500 heavy recovery vehicle
Cab seating: 1 + 1 or 2
Configuration: 6 × 6
Weight:
  (empty) approx 11,000 kg
  (GVW) 27,500 kg
Towed load: (suspended) 6,000 kg
Length: 9.05 m
Width: 2.5 m
Height: (overall) 3.55 m
Ground clearance:
  (front) 0.36 m
  (rear) 0.9 m
Track:
  (front) 1.97 m
  (rear) 1.82 m
Wheelbase: 5 m
Angle of approach/departure: 30/37°
Max speed: 88 km/h
Range: 500 km
Max gradient: 50%
Side slope: 30%
Fording: 0.9 m
Engine: DAF DKX 1160 ATi 11.6 litre 6-cylinder turbocharged diesel developing 325 hp at 2,200 rpm
Gearbox: ZF 16 S-160 A with 8 forward and 1 reverse gears, with splitter on each gear
Dropbox: ZF A 800
Steering: ZF 8098 hydraulic, power assisted
Turning radius: 12 m
Suspension: DAF semi-elliptic with Koni hydraulic shock-absorbers on front
Tyres: 12.00 R 24 XL
Brakes:
  (main) air mechanical, dual line
  (parking) spring cylinders on front and 2nd axle
Electrical system: 24 V
Batteries: 2 × 12 V, 125 Ah
Alternator: 55 A

Status
Production complete. No longer being marketed. In service with Netherlands (a total of 255 units were delivered but less than this now remain in service).

Contractor
Military Sales Department DAF Trucks NV
It should be noted that this company is no longer involved in the design, development and production of military trucks.

Pakistan

Light Recovery Vehicle

Development
The Light Recovery Vehicle (LRV) has been developed to meet the requirements of the Pakistan Army by the Military Vehicles Research and Development Establishment (MVRDE) in Rawalpindi.

It is understood to be in service with the Pakistan Army and it is expected that a new and improved version will be introduced in the near future, which will be based on a new five-tonne cross-country chassis.

This is expected to be based on a 4 × 4 cross-country chassis modified for its new role.

As of late 2010 no details of this follow on vehicle were available.

Description
It is understood that the LRV is based on a modified commercial (4 × 4) chassis of foreign origin, perhaps from the Japanese company Isuzu.

The vehicle has a fully enclosed forward enclosed cab that can be tilted forwards to allow access to the power pack for maintenance purposes.

The recovery equipment is mounted in the centre of the rear chassis. This consists of two booms, which are capable of casualty handling, on site repairs and suspended tow operations.

Each of these booms has a rated capacity of four tonnes and can be used individually or in conjunction with each other.

According to MVRDE, the LRV has a towing capacity of up to 9,979 kg and the boom has a length of 2.489 m and a total of 60.7 m of 12.7 mm diameter cable is provided.

To provide a more stable platform when the recovery equipment is being used, a total of four stabilisers can be lowered to the ground. These are positioned one either side to the rear of the first road wheel and one either side to the rear of the last road wheel.

Specifications
Not available.

Status
Production as required. In service with Pakistan. There have been no known exports of this vehicle.

Contractor
Various but developed under the direction of Military Vehicles Research and Development Establishment (MVRDE)

Russian Federation

Ural-375D/Ural-4320 (6 × 6) recovery vehicle

Development
A recovery vehicle based on the Ural-375D/Ural-4320 (6 × 6) 4,000 kg truck was designed to recover vehicles weighing up to 8,500 kg in the half-loaded position. The vehicle can tow disabled vehicles weighing up to 5,000 kg on dirt roads and up to 10,000 kg on hard-surfaced roads.

Russia has developed a cab armour protection kit for their 6 × 6 cross-country trucks for use in high threat areas. This provides the occupants with protection from small arms fire and shell splinters.

Description
The vehicle is fitted with a winch, half-loaded towing gear, universal rigid towing blade and a trail spade at the rear. Standard equipment includes a repair kit, entrenching tools, fire extinguishers, searchlight and pivoting signal lamps. The repair kit is carried to enable a recovered vehicle to be made ready for towing or to make a vehicle ready for transporting.

The power-operated winch is mounted at the chassis rear and has a maximum capacity of 7,000 kg. In addition to recovering vehicles it can also load the recovered vehicle on to a transport unit.

The transport unit consists of a boom with cross-beam, linking chains and a longer on-frame extension with struts and upper frame members. To couple the recovered vehicle to the transport unit, the boom is lowered to the level of the front bumper and locked in place by a special mechanism. The vehicle is chained to the cross-beam and then raised half off the ground by the winch cable.

With the trail spade lowered and in position, the hydraulic winch capacity is increased from 7,000 to 14,000 kg. The boom is also intended to hold the recovery vehicle down while a vehicle is being recovered. The boom is lowered to the ground and attached to the trail spade which, in turn, is secured to the upper frame members by two cable braces.

The Ural-375D/Ural-4320 recovery vehicle retains the cab heater, engine heater and central tyre pressure regulation system of the standard 6 × 6 cargo truck. The latter allows the driver of the truck to adjust the tyre pressure to suit the type of terrain being crossed.

A closely allied variant using the Ural-4320 chassis is known as the MTP-A1.1 Technical Assistance Vehicle. This vehicle is used to carry out first- and second-line repairs and carries specialised repair equipment, tools, spare parts and materials for body repairs. Also carried are lubricants, electrical equipment and hydraulic jacks.

A cargo-lifting gantry protrudes over the cab and bonnet and can be used for lifting components. Towing bars and rigs can be used to tow disabled vehicles and a winch is provided.

Status
Production of the Ural-375D was completed in 1977 but production of the latest Ural-4320 (6 × 6) is undertaken as and when required. In service with the Russian Army and many countries which have received Russian military equipment.

Details of the current production Ural MTP-A2.1 recovery truck, based on the Ural 4320-31 (6 × 6) cross-truck are provided in a separate entry in *Jane's Military Vehicles and Logistics*.

Contractor
Chassis: Ural Motor Vehicle Plant Joint Stock Company

Ural MTP-A2.1 recovery truck

Development
The Ural MTP-A2.1 recovery truck is based on the latest Ural-4320-31 (6 × 6) truck chassis modified to undertake its specialised battlefield mission. The baseline cargo truck has been built in significant numbers for the Russian Army.

Main roles of the MTP-A2.1 have been summarised by the manufacturer as: the evacuation of damaged trucks; recovery of damaged vehicles; and refuelling vehicles with fuel, lubricants and special fuels.

Russia has developed a cab armour protection kit for their 6 × 6 cross-country trucks for use in high threat areas. This provides the occupants with protection from small arms fire and shell splinters.

Description
The layout of the MTP-A2.1 recovery truck is conventional with the YAMZ-238M2 diesel engine and transmission at the front, two-door fully enclosed cab in the centre and the recovery equipment at the rear.

Standard equipment includes an engine pre-heater, cab heater, powered steering to reduce driver fatigue and a central tyre-pressure regulation system that allows the driver to adjust the tyre pressure to suit the terrain being crossed.

Damaged or disabled vehicles can be transported in a half-loaded position at the rear using the rigid double tow hook.

Mounted to the rear of the cab is a hydraulically-operated crane, normally traversed to the front when not required. This crane has a maximum outreach of 8.2 m and the following lifting capacity:
5.4 m outreach 1,650 kg
3.8 m outreach 2,300 kg
2.1 m outreach 4,000 kg.

When this crane is being used, two hydraulically-operated stabilisers are normally lowered to the ground and these are positioned one either side of the vehicle between the first and second axles.

The winch has a maximum tracking effort of 10 to 11 tonnes without tackle block or 20 tonnes with tackle block.

Specifications
MTP-A2.1 recovery truck
Crew: 2 or 3
Configuration: 6 × 6
Combat weight: 17,600 kg
Maximum payload: 4,500 kg
Maximum load on transport device: 3,500 kg
Maximum weight of towed truck:
(half loaded position) 12,000 kg
(being towed) 15,500 kg
Fording: 1.2 m
Engine: YAMZ-238M2 V-8 liquid-cooled diesel developing 240 hp
Transmission: manual, five speed, two speed transfer box with inter-axle locked differential
Tyres: 14.00 - 20 series (fitted with central tyre pressure regulation system)
Note: Can also be supplied fitted with YAMZ-236BE2 diesel developing 250 hp or YAMZ-236NE2 engine developing 230 hp.

Status
Production as required. In service with Russian Federation and possibly other countries.

Contractor
Ural Motor Vehicle Plant Joint Stock Company

MTP-A2.1 recovery truck based on Ural-4320-31 (6 × 6) truck chassis in travelling configuration
0092482

KET-L (6 × 6) recovery truck

Development
The KET-L (6 × 6) recovery truck is based on the chassis of the Ural-375E (6 × 6) 4,000 kg truck. The original Ural-375 series trucks entered production in 1971 and were built in large numbers for the home and export markets.

Production of the Ural-375 (6 × 6) series of vehicles has now been completed and production is now concentrated on the latest Ural-4320-31 (6 × 6) cross-country truck.

Details of this are provided in a separate entry in *Jane's Military Vehicles and Logistics*. This provides the occupants with protection from small arms fire and shell splinters.

Description
For recovery operations, the KET-L is fitted with two hydraulic winches, which can be used to either the front or rear; it is recommended that vehicles are recovered when in line with the KET-L recovery truck.

The rear-mounted winch has a maximum capacity of 15,000 kg while the front winch has a capacity of 5,000 kg. Vehicles up to 1.5 times the weight of the KET-L can be recovered without using supports but for heavier vehicles, an anchor plate must be lowered from the rear of the vehicle.

Vehicles weighing up to 5,000 kg can be towed on dirt roads using the Type 3108 rigid towbar carried on the left rear top of the recovery hamper. Vehicles weighing up to 10,000 kg can be towed on paved roads. Mounted on the rear of the chassis is a jib crane with hydraulic power supplied from the main winch via a power take-off. The crane has a boom 2.4 m long and a hook lift height of 3.5 m. Maximum capacity is 1,500 kg.

Standard equipment carried by the KET-L recovery truck includes a floodlight at the rear for night recovery operations, timber baulks, a pulley block, two Type OU-2 manually operated fire extinguishers (one stowed each side of the cab rear), provision for radio communication systems and metal-cutting equipment.

An essentially similar but later vehicle based on the chassis of the Ural-4320 (6 × 6) truck is known as the KT-LM light recovery vehicle. The KT-LM lacks the crane jib of the KET-L and relies on a 7,000 kg capacity winch with 65 m of cable for recovery tasks. It can tow disabled vehicles by using rigid tow bars and is provided with an anchor spade for use during winching operations.

Standard equipment on the KET-L recovery truck includes a cab heater, engine heater and a central tyre pressure regulation system. The latter allows the driver to adjust the tyre pressure to suit the terrain being crossed.

Status
Production complete. In service with Russian Federation and many other countries. Marketing is currently being concentrated on the latest MTP-A2.1 recovery vehicle that is based on the more recent Ural-4320-31 (6 × 6) truck chassis.

Details of this are given in a separate entry with production being undertaken by the Ural Motor Vehicle Plant on an as required basis.

Contractor
Chassis: Ural Motor Vehicle Plant Joint Stock Company

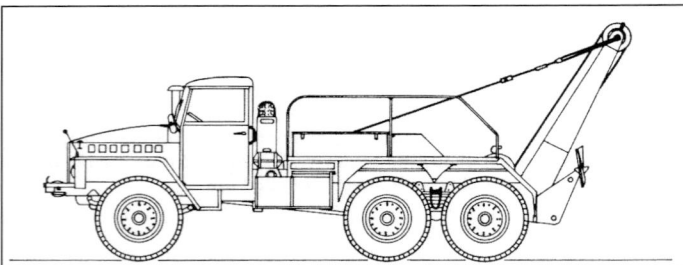

KET-L (6 × 6) recovery truck shown here in the travelling configuration

0511483

Slovakia

TATRA AV-15 (8 × 8) heavy recovery truck

Development
The TATRA AV-15 (8 × 8) heavy recovery truck is a variant of the TATRA T 815 8 × 8.1 R truck series which first entered production in 1982. For its specialised mission, it carries a telescopic boom jib and other equipment for heavy vehicle recovery. The vehicle is also intended to have a secondary role supporting construction and loading operations. Production of this is undertaken on an as required basis.

Description
The crane is mounted over the rear axles and has a traversing jib with one folding adapter for extended work. It has a maximum lift capacity of 12,000 kg, although with the adapter extended this is reduced to 4,000 kg.

TATRA (6 × 6) recovery vehicle built under licence in India by Bharat Earth Movers Limited

0038824

The main hydraulic recovery system is a winch supplied with a usable 150 m of cable. Maximum pulling capacity to the front of the vehicle is 270 kN, while to the rear it is 290 kN.

Stability during these operations is provided by a front-mounted dozer blade, which can be lowered 250 mm into the ground surface.

The dozer blade can also be used for clearing obstacles and preparing sites. Also provided is an auxiliary hydraulic winch with a capacity of 6.85 kN and 320 m of cable.

Once recovered, vehicles can be towed by the AV-15 using towbars, towing triangles or other devices. Loads weighing up to 65 tonnes can be pulled.

Other equipment carried includes a 230 A welding and cutting set and various special recovery tools.

Other TATRA trucks equipped with recovery or multipurpose cranes include: the 6 × 6 AD-20T, a multipurpose crane vehicle with a low-slung forward control cab; the 6 × 6 AD-28 crane truck; and the AVS 6 × 6 medium recovery vehicle.

Indian Tatra trucks
The Indian company of Bharat Earth Movers Limited manufactures TATRA 8 × 8 and 6 × 6 trucks for the Indian Armed Forces. They produce many specialised variants including a 6 × 6 recovery vehicle, a complete range of 8 × 8 used for bridging operations as well as missile resupply and transport/launch vehicles.

As far as it is known, India has not exported any Tatra trucks with all production being for the home market.

Specifications
AV-15 heavy recovery vehicle
Crew: 3
Configuration: 8 × 8
Weight: 30,000 kg
Max towed load:
  (road) 65,000 kg
  (cross-country) 15,000 kg
  (cross-country, short distance) 30,000 kg
Length: 12.3 m
Width with dozer blade: 2.57 m
Height overall: 3.36 m
Ground clearance: 0.32 m
Angle of approach: 18°
Angle of departure: 29°

TATRA AV-15 (8 × 8) heavy recovery truck (T J Gander)

0512153

Wheelbase: 1.65 + 2.87 + 1.45 m
Max road speed: 70 km/h
Min road speed: 1.7 km/h
Fuel capacity: 480 litres
Vertical obstacle: 0.6 m
Trench: 1.6 m
Fording: 1.3 m
Engine: TATRA 3-930-40 supercharged multifuel, 4-stroke, OHV, air-cooled with direct injection developing 360 hp at 2,200 rpm
Gearbox: manual, 20 forward, 4 reverse gears
Clutch: single plate
Steering: worm and roller, power assisted on front four wheels
Turning radius: 12.5 m
Suspension:
   (front) torsion bars, shock absorbers
   (rear) leaf springs

Status
Production as required. In service with the Czech and Slovak armed forces. The 6 × 6 model is believed to be in service with India.

Contractor
Chassis: TATRA a.s
Recovery hamper: Vychodoslovenske Strojarne as Kosice

Marketed by
Kerametal JSC

TATRA RV-20 SAS (8 × 8) heavy recovery truck

Development
The RV-20 SAS (8 × 8) heavy recovery vehicle is the most recent vehicle of its type to be developed by TATRA and is based on the latest production TATRA T816 (8 × 8) chassis. It is understood that the total UAE order was for some 1,100 trucks, including numerous configurations with deliveries now complete. It is understood that this contract did not include RV-20 SAS.

As of late 2010 it is understood that there had been no quantity production of this recovery vehicle.

Description
The RV-20 SAS heavy recovery vehicle is based on the TATRA T816 - 6ZVP8T (8 × 8) cross-country truck chassis that features all-wheel drive, independent swing semi-axle wheel suspension with leaf springs on the front wheels and leaf springs combined with air springs on the rear wheels.

The fully enclosed two-door cab is at the front and has four seats with the water-cooled, turbocharged, direct injection charged cooled diesel engine developing 400 kW coupled to a six-speed automatic transmission integrated into the chassis backbone tube.

The chassis also features a torque divider, two inter-axle and four inter-axle lockable differentials, hub reductions, tubeless tyres with beadlocks and a central tyre pressure regulation system that allows the driver to adjust the tyre pressure to suit the terrain being crossed.

Two circuit pneumatic brakes are provided with a two-line coupling for the trailer. Power steering is standard for the front two axles and a cooling system is located to the cab rear with a hydraulically driven fan.

The hydraulically-operated crane is mounted at the rear and has been specially designed for military purposes with steel coverings of all vital parts. It has a telescopic boom jib with one folding adapter for extended work. The crane can be used to lift armoured vehicle engines, complete power packs and containers up to a maximum weight of 15,000 kg.

When being used, two hydraulically-operated stabilisers are lowered to the ground either side. It can operate on slopes of up to 5° without any limitations by using an automatic self-levelling system.

The main hydraulic recovery equipment is a winch supplied with a usable 100 m of cable. Maximum pulling capacity to the rear of the vehicle is 24,500 kg.

The main hydraulic winch is also used for self-recovery from the front of the vehicle, with maximum pulling force restricted to 13,250 kg.

Stability when carrying out recovery operations is provided by a front-mounted dozer/stabiliser blade and a rear anchor plate. The dozer blade can also be used to clear obstacles and preparing sites.

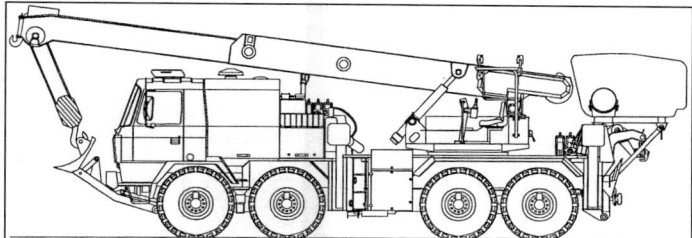

Detailed side drawing of TATRA RV-20 (8 × 8) heavy recovery truck with crane traversed to the front 0536880

TATRA RV-20 (8 × 8) heavy recovery truck in travelling configuration (T J Gander) 0079513

The vehicle is also provided with an auxiliary hydraulic winch with a capacity of 835 kg and 300 m of cable to tow the main cable. Various other items and recovery equipment are available including a towing attachment with 13,250 kg lifting capacity for towed vehicles. Winching can be carried out by remote control.

Designed space in the superstructure enables the vehicle to carry special recovery tools. The vehicle is equipped with a large variety of repair equipment including a welding and cutting set for field emergency repairs.

In addition, lubricants, electrical equipment and hydraulic jacks are carried. A platform to the rear of the vehicle has been designated to carry a power pack or other equipment up to a maximum weight of 7,000 kg.

Once recovered, vehicles can be towed by the RV-20 SAS using tow bars, towing angles or other devices, up to a maximum weight of 65,000 kg.

Specifications
RV-20 SAS heavy recovery truck
Crew: 1 + 3
Configuration: 8 × 8
Weight: 32,315 kg
Max towed load: 65,000 kg
Length:
   (chassis) 9.215 m
   (overall) 12.588 m
Width: 2.768 m
Height: 3.243 m
Ground clearance: 0.380 m
Wheelbase: 1.65 + 3.10 + 1.45 m
Max road speed: 100 km/h
Fuel capacity: 490 litres
Fording: 1.25 m
Vertical obstacle: 600 mm
Trench: 2 m
Gradient: 60%
Side slope: 30%
Engine: water-cooled turbocharged diesel developing 400 kW
Transmission: 6-speed automatic
Steering: power-assisted
Turning radius: 14 m

Status
Development complete. Ready for production.

Contractor
Chassis: TATRA a.s
Recovery hamper: Vychodoslovenske Strojarne as Kosice

Marketed by:
Kerametal

VSS Kosice Light Recovery Vehicle 7

Development
The Light Recovery Vehicle 7 (LRV 7) (4 × 4) has been developed for civil and military applications by VSS as Kosice of the Slovak Republic.

The system has been designed to recover and tow vehicles under a wide range of operational conditions within the temperature range of –50 to +40° C.

Specifically, roles of the LRV 7 include the following:
- Recovery of sunk, buried, overturned or crashed automotive or pioneer equipment and possibly light armoured vehicles with a tractive effort of up to 73.5 kN
- Towing of damaged vehicles and of pioneer equipment as well as wheeled armoured personnel carriers, by means of suspending their front or rear part on the lifting equipment in a semi-suspended state
- Towing of damaged vehicles and pioneer equipment as well as wheeled armoured personnel carriers by means of suspending their front or rear part on the towing triangle in a semi-suspended state.

Light Recovery Vehicle 7 (4 × 4) based on TATRA 815 chassis in travelling configuration 0536881

The vehicle can also be used for the permanent towing of recovered or damaged equipment up to the maximum weight of 15,000 kg, with the proportion of weight falling on the lifting equipment up to a maximum of 3,600 kg.

Description
The system is based on a TATRA T 815 (4 × 4) truck chassis, for which full details are given in a separate entry in *Jane's Military Vehicles and Logistics*. The TATRA T 815 entered production in 1982, alongside the TATRA T 815 series of 8 × 8 trucks. The recovery vehicle has a fully enclosed two-door cab. A replacement wheel and tyre is also carried to the immediate rear of the cab in the vertical position. The recovery equipment is mounted to the cab rear.

The latter includes the basic frame, the auxiliary frame with a platform, rear lifting equipment, landing gear, boom with extension arm, recovery equipment, hydraulic driving system, electrical installation, pneumatic system and the vehicle accessories. Stowage boxes are provided either side between the front and rear axles.

According to the manufacturer, the maximum carrying capacity of the fully retracted boom is 7,500 kg and fully extended is 4,500 kg. The maximum carrying capacity of the extended boom, without using the landing gear, is 3,000 kg while the maximum height of the boom end is 5.22 m.

The recovery winches have a maximum tractive effort using the stabilisers to the rear of 73.5 kN (2 × 36.75), while the maximum tractive effort without using stabilisers sideways is 19.13 kN.

The maximum average speed of rope winding is 4 m per minute, while the length of the hydraulic winch cables is 47.5 m.

Specifications
Light Recovery Vehicle 7 (LRV 7)
Configuration: 4 × 4
Gross vehicle weight: 11,500 kg
Length: 7.33 m
Width: 2.525 m
Height: 3.20 m
Ground clearance: 380 mm (unloaded)
Track:
(front) 2.034 m
(rear) 2.050 m
Wheelbase: 4.09 m
Angle of departure:
(front) 35°
(rear) 26°
Maximum road speed:
(without towed equipment) 90 km/h
(with towed equipment) 60 km/h
(when pulling the winch rope) 5 km/h

Status
Development complete. Production as required. As of late 2010, there were no known exports of the LRV 7 for military applications.

Contractor
VSS as Kosice

South Africa

SAMIL recovery vehicles

Development
SAMIL produced two types of recovery vehicle, one based on the chassis of the SAMIL 50 4 × 4 and the other based on the chassis of the 6 × 6 SAMIL 100.

SAMIL 100 (6 × 6) recovery vehicle with mineproof cab (T J Gander) 0007359

SAMIL 50 (4 × 4) recovery vehicle fitted with mineproof cab in travelling configuration (T J Gander) 0038820

The SAMIL range of 4 × 4 and 6 × 6 trucks are the standard cross-country trucks of the South African Army and were designed and built by Truckmakers, which no longer exists.

The SAMIL range of vehicles are based on a much modified Magirus Deutz design from Germany.

The now BAE Systems, Land Systems South Africa (previously BAE Systems Land Systems OMC and before that OMC) are the current design authority for the SAMIL range of 4 × 4 and 6 × 6 tactical vehicles, including those fitted with a Mine Protected Cab.

The South African National Defence Force (SANDF) has a requirement for a new family of cross-country trucks to replace the currently deployed SAMIL vehicles but as of late 2010 no contracts had been awarded.

Description
SAMIL 50 recovery vehicle
The SAMIL 50 (4 × 4) recovery vehicle could be provided fitted with a standard unarmoured cab or a fully protected cab for use against land mine fragments or small arms fire. Bulletproof vision blocks are provided in the front and sides of the protected crew compartment.

It has two hydraulic winches driven by a power take-off from the main gearbox with a combined pull of 20,000 kg and two booms, which extend to the rear for a suspended tow. The combined lifting capacity of the booms is 7,250 kg when retracted and 2,500 kg when fully extended. The rear platform is used for recovery equipment stowage and self-recovery rollers are fitted to each corner of the superstructure.

The fully enclosed steel armour protected cab, when fitted, has seating for four people and has doors, a roof hatch and bulletproof windows.

SAMIL 100 recovery vehicle
The SAMIL 100 (6 × 6) recovery vehicle may be fitted with the standard cab of the SAMIL 100 truck or with a mineproof cab; the standard cab can be enlarged to carry a crew of five. The recovery hamper is carried to the rear of the vehicle and consists of a twin jib structure on a flatbed heavy-duty body. The main winch is mounted centrally and much of the space at the rear is taken up with recovery equipment stowage.

Withings MK 1A (6 × 6) recovery truck
Details of this are provided in a separate entry in *Jane's Military Vehicles and Logistics*. Production is complete and it is no longer marketed.

Status
Production complete. In service with the South African National Defence Force. No longer marketed. A number of companies in South Africa are now offering surplus South African military vehicles for sale, including quantities of SAMIL (4 × 4) and (6 × 6) trucks in various models.

Enquiries to
BAE Systems, Land Systems South Africa (previously BAE Systems Land Systems OMC)

BAE Systems Land Systems South Africa
Withings MK 1A (6 × 6) recovery vehicle

Development

The Withings MK 1A (6 × 6) recovery vehicle is a member of the SAMIL family of military trucks originally developed by Truckmakers and based on a German design.

Truckmakers is no longer trading and, as of late 2010, BAE Systems Land Systems South Africa (previously BAE Systems Land Systems OMC) are the current design authority for the SAMIL range of 4 × 4 and 6 × 6 tactical vehicles, including those fitted with a Mine Protected Cab.

The South African National Defence Force (SANDF) has a requirement for a new family of cross-country trucks to replace the currently deployed SAMIL vehicles but as of late 2010 no contracts had been awarded.

Description

The Withings MK 1A (6 × 6) recovery vehicle is based on the chassis of the SAMIL 100 (6 × 6) 10,000 kg truck, suitably modified for the recovery role.

The vehicle is normally fitted with a fully enclosed mineproof cab which also protects the occupants from small arms fire and shell splinters. The cab is provided with bullet-proof windows in the front and sides.

The main recovery equipment is a centrally located heavy-duty winch, which is used to pull disabled vehicles and power a towing arm system. It can lift a mass of 8,000 kg from 0.75 to 1.6 m above ground level and lock it there for towing.

The main winch can also be utilised for forward self-recovery and may be used to provide lifting power for two demountable crane arms. These are normally stowed on top of the operating deck area and, in use, extend to a maximum of 4.5 m behind the vehicle; maximum lift height is 4 m.

Other recovery equipment carried includes four skid pans with chains, tools, sheaves, a cable guard and two adjustable spotlights.

The SAMIL 100 (6 × 6) truck on which this system is based was built by Truckmakers who ceased trading some time ago. The SAMIL 100 (6 × 6) truck is used for a wide range of roles in the South African National Defence Force. Typical roles include towing the now Denel Land Systems 155 mm/45-calibre G5 artillery system and being fitted with surface-to-surface unguided rockets.

Specifications

Withings Mk 1A recovery vehicle
Crew: up to 4
Configuration: 6 × 6
Axle rating:
 (front) 7,500 kg
 (rear) 10,000 kg/13,000 kg
Length: 9.77 m
Width: 2.495 m
Height: 3.35 m
Ground clearance: 0.355 m
Track:
 (front) 2.002 m
 (rear) 2.048 m
Wheelbase: 5.94 m
Angle of approach/departure: 30/35°
Engine: Deutz diesel Type F 10 L 413F air-cooled diesel
Gearbox: Fuller RT 14609
Clutch: Fichtel & Sachs 42 mm
Transfer box: Getrag Z90
Steering: ZF 8043 ball and nut
Suspension: semi-elliptic leaf springs
Brakes: drum front and rear
Tyres: 16.00 R 20
Electrical system: 24 V
Batteries: 2 × 12 V, 118 Ah
Alternator: 28 V, 55 A

Status

Production complete. No longer marketed. In service with the South African National Defence Force.

Contractor

BAE Systems, Land Systems South Africa (previously BAE Systems Land Systems OMC)

Withings MK 1A (6 × 6) recovery vehicle (T J Gander)   0512450

Sweden

Scania P113 HK (6 × 6) recovery vehicle

Development

The Scania P113 HK (6 × 6) recovery vehicle is based on the Scania P113 series of cross-country vehicles which were based on a modified commercial design and manufactured in 4 × 4, 6 × 4 and 6 × 6 configurations with different bodies.

Production of this series of vehicles was completed in 1995 when it was replaced by a new generation of vehicles.

Alvis Moelv of Norway was the main sub-contractor and provided the complete recovery equipment. This company is no longer trading.

Description

The Scania P113 HK recovery vehicle is based on the Scania 113 HK 6 × 6 Z truck chassis. The vehicle is equipped with a fully enclosed forward control CP19 cab with seating for the driver, a tilting passenger seat and a bench seat for three further passengers at the rear. The cab may be tilted forward hydraulically 60° for maintenance.

The recovery rig is a Norwegian designed Alvis Moelv (previously Hägglunds Moelv) BV 730 which consists of a hydraulic crane with a maximum lifting moment of 28 t/m. The maximum lifting capacity is 8,400 kg.

The vehicle is also provided with a towing lift boom with a maximum lift capacity of 7,000 kg and a hydraulic recovery winch with a maximum single cable pulling force of 20,000 kg.

The winch is provided with 85 m of cable and can be slewed through 300°. When the recovery rig is in use, four hydraulic outriggers are deployed for stability, two either side. The vehicle also has a self-recovery winch with a maximum pulling force of 10,000 kg equipped with 50 m of cable.

Ancillary equipment includes a rotating beacon, two working lights, an auxiliary heater for the cab and engine, an electrical engine heater, a 24 V emergency outlet and a spare wheel carrier.

Scania P113 HK (6 × 6) recovery vehicle deployed in the field, changing a Leopard 1 MBT powerpack   0092480

Scania P113 HK (6 × 6) recovery vehicle of the Finnish Defence Force in travelling configuration (Richard Stickland)   0536873

Specifications

P113 HK recovery vehicle
Cab seating: 1 + 4
Configuration: 6 × 6
Weight:
  (kerb) 21,000 kg
  (GVW) 28,000 kg
Length: 8.65 m
Height: (overall) 3.2 m
Wheelbase: 4.25 + 1.45 m
Max speed: 100 km/h
Fuel capacity: 300 litres
Engine: Scania DS11 75 11 litre 6-cylinder liquid-cooled turbocharged direct injection diesel developing 310 hp at 2,000 rpm
Gearbox: GRH871 10-speed full synchromesh with hydraulic torque converter acting in low range
Clutch: K432 single dry plate
Transfer box: GT811 2 speed
Steering: hydraulic power assisted
Suspension: semi-elliptic steel leaf springs
Tyres: 14.00 × R20
Brakes:
  (main) dual circuit air
  (parking) spring
Electrical system: 24 V

Status

Production completed during 1995. In service with Finland and Norwegian armies. Alvis Moelv has now closed down, so there can be no further production of this equipment.

Contractor

Scania Trucks and Buses

United Kingdom

Future Recovery Vehicle

Development

Until recently, the British Army did deploy three wheeled recovery vehicles:

- Reynolds Boughton (4 × 4) 6,000 kg based on a Bedford (4 × 4) chassis (small number);
- Scammell Crusader (6 × 4) recovery vehicle (130 delivered of which a few remain in service);
- Foden (6 × 6) recovery vehicle (333 delivered of which 322 remain in service).

In early 2001, the UK Defence Procurement Agency (DPA) issued Invitations To Tender (ITT) to five contractors for the acquisition of about 8,500 combat support vehicles for the UK armed forces. Most of these will be used by the British Army and replace vehicles which are now 20 years old or more.

The five contractors that were issued with an ITT were Leyland Trucks (UK), MAN Truck and Bus (UK), Mercedes-Benz (UK), Oshkosh Truck Corporation (US) and Stewart & Stevenson (US).

The ITTs were returned by four of the contractors in mid-2002 and in the end Leyland Trucks decided not to bid.

Of the 8,500 combat support vehicle requirement, it was originally expected that 8,000 would be cargo vehicles including:

- six-tonne medium mobility (off road) Light Cargo Vehicle (LCV)
- nine-tonne medium mobility and improved medium mobility (off road) Medium Cargo Vehicle (MCV)
- 15-tonne medium mobility (off road) Heavy Cargo Vehicle (HCV).

The nine-tonne vehicle also includes a 7,000 litre fuel tanker variant and the remainder of the buy will include recovery vehicles.

In October 2004, the UK Defence Procurement Agency (DPA) selected the MAN proposal for its Support Vehicle requirement with contract awarded in April 2005.

The contract is worth GBP1 billion for the supply of trucks to replace the current in tri-service fleet of four, eight and 14-tonne cargo vehicles and recovery trucks.

In April 2007 MAN ERF started delivering the first of 7,285 generation cross-country trucks and trailers to the British Army.

Chassis and forward control cab are supplied from the MAN production line in Vienna, Austria, and sent to the UK where the chassis is integrated with the specific to role body. All of the cargo bodies are manufactured and integrated by Marshall Specialist Vehicles at the dedicated facility at Mildenhall.

Complete vehicle is then sent to a MAN ERF facility at Ashchurch for its Pre-Delivery Inspection (PDI) prior to being supplied to the UK MoD.

The vast majority of the new fleet of vehicles are going to the British Army but some will also go to the Royal Marines and Royal Air Force. In Service Date (ISD) for the cargo version was June 2007 with ISD of the recovery version being February 2008.

Ashchurch supply between six and eight vehicles a day with deliveries expected to run through to 2013. Projected out of service date is currently 2034.

MAN (8 × 8) recovery vehicle of the British Army fitted with enhanced protection under a Urgent Operational Requirement (UOR) (Christopher F Foss)   1333669

All of the vehicles have a fully enclosed forward control cab which can be tilted forward to give access to the power pack, powered steering and automatic transmission (two versions, one fully automatic and one automated clutch operated transmission).

All of the vehicles are in right hand drive configuration and standard equipment includes air conditioning system.

Under the terms of the contract, MAN ERF have guaranteed a five years parts and labour agreement for each vehicle as well as a number of reliability assurances and key performance indicators.

The new fleet basically consists of two ranges, the HX Medium Mobility (MM) and the SX Improved Medium Mobility (IMM). The MM consists of 4 × 4, 6 × 6, and 8 × 8 vehicles while the IMMC consists of 6 × 6 and 8 × 8 vehicles only.

Within the IMV are 288 recovery vehicle (8 × 8) which are used with 69 recovery trailers. These have a full range of recovery equipment which includes a hydraulic crane and winches.

The recovery equipment being supplied by EKA includes three Rotzler hydraulic winches (main, auxiliary and self-recovery) and a crane supplied by Terex Atlas which is operated by remote control.

The main TR200 two speed winch has a capacity of 25 tonnes which can be increased to 50 tonnes at 50 m stand off with a snatch block.

A total of 120 m of cable is provided and an automatic cable system is fitted as standard.

The TR80 self-recovery winch has a minimum capacity of eight tonnes and is provided with 90 m of cable and is fitted with an automatic cable cleaning system.

The HZ010 auxiliary winch is provided with 250 m of 6 mm diameter cable with an automatic cable clearing system fitted as standard.

The crane is fitted with a telescopic jib with a maximum reach of 9.7 m with lift capability depending on reach. For example, maximum lift at 8.05 m radius is seven tonnes. To provide a more stable platform, stabiliser legs can be lowered to the ground before the crane is used.

Other equipment fitted includes compressed air supply, towing pintles, rear stiff legs, locker system, fuel transfer system and operator controls.

This equipment is supplied and fitted by EKA who have considerable experience in this area. The three axle turntable drawbar recovery trailers are supplied by Andover Trailers and have a gross vehicle weight of 30 tonnes which enables a payload in excess of 20 tonnes to be carried.

The first 161 production vehicles are used for training but from vehicle 162 all vehicles have the ability to be fitted with a recently developed Adaptive Protection Kit (APK).

MAN (8 × 8) recovery vehicle of the British Army fitted with enhanced protection under a Urgent Operational Requirement (UOR) (Christopher F Foss)   1405681

MAN (8 × 8) recovery vehicle of the British Army recovering a damaged truck (Christopher F Foss)

1333668

The UK MoD has ordered a total of 1,098 of these APK kits that can be rapidly installed on the cab to provide enhanced protection against small arms fire and some other battlefield threats. These kits and the run flat tyres will be held in depots and issued to vehicles when they are deployed on operations.

MAN ERF has a number of UK sub-contractors for the programme including Marshall SV (cargo bodies), HIAB (hydraulic cranes and subcontractor to Marshall SV), Fluid Transfer (fuel delivery systems), EKA (recovery systems), Andover Trailers (recovery trailer) and Quorum Logistics Services and VT (training and subcontractor to Quorum).

Description
Details of the German MAN HX range of 4 × 4, 6 × 6 and 8 × 8 tactical trucks, on which the UK MAN Support Vehicle range is based, are provided in a separate entry in *Jane's Military Vehicles and Logistics*.

Variants

Urgent Operational Requirement upgrades for MAN Support Vehicles
In mid-2008 the British Army started to deploy its latest generation MAN Support Vehicles (SV) to Iraq with a significant number of enhancements funded under an Urgent Operation Requirement (UOR) programme called project Fortress that started in January 2008.

This programme was run by the General Support Vehicle (GSV) Integrated Project Team (IPT) which is part of the recently formed Deference Equipment and Support (DE&S) organisation.

Under this UOR a total of 280 units of the MAN SV have been upgraded in a number of key areas with the main emphasis on crew survivability.

All of the 280 vehicles are fitted with enhanced electronic counter measures equipment in an effort to neutralise Improvised Explosive Devices (IED) which are now the main threat.

The forward control cab is fitted with applique passive armour that meets STANAG 4569 Level 2 ballistic protection and greater than Level 1 blast protection.

Front and sides of the cab have been fitted with bar armour to help neutralise Rocket Propelled Grenades (RPG) fitted with a single High Explosive Anti-Tank (HEAT) warhead before they impact the main armour.

Mounted on the roof of the cab is a Protected Weapon Station (PWS), which is protected to STANAG 4569 Level 2. This is fitted with a 7.62 mm General Purpose Machine Gun (GPMG) for self-defence purposes.

All UOR SV are fitted with infra-red headlights, rear position lights and night vision devices. Run flat tyres are standard on UOR vehicles and all are finished in desert camouflage paint.

In addition all vehicles are fitted with the General Dynamics UK Bowman VHF and HF clip-in digital communications equipment and vehicle intercom. All production MAN SV are fitted with a roof mounted air conditioning system as standard.

Vehicle types being upgraded under the UOR are the six-tonne (4 × 4) cargo light, nine-tonne (6 × 6) cargo medium, 15-tonne (8 × 8) cargo heavy, 7,000-litre Unit Support Tanker (UST) (6 × 6), Enhanced Palletised Load System (EPLS) 15-tonne (8 × 8), nine-tonne cargo medium (6 × 6) and recovery vehicle (8 × 8).

The last member of the SV family to enter service was the 8 × 8 recovery version fitted with an EKA recovery hamper which is the replacement for the older Foden (6 × 6) recovery vehicle.

There are two versions of RV, narrow and wide with the latter having 24 inch wheels on the rear bogie all allow recovery of the heaviest vehicles while maintaining vehicle stability and mobility.

Specifications
Not available at present.

Status
Production. In service in British Army.

Contractor
MAN Truck and Bus UK

Foden (6 × 6) recovery vehicle

Development
The British Army took delivery of a total of 333 Foden (6 × 6) recovery vehicles which share many components with the Foden 155 mm FH-70 gun tractor (6 × 6) and limber vehicles (6 × 6) that have now been phased out of service with the British Army.

Of the 333 vehicles supplied, a total of 332 remained in service late in 2007, of which about 250 vehicles and trailers were put through an In Depth Repair (IDR) programme at the now Defence Support Group (at that time the Army Base Repair Organisation) facility at Bovington, Dorset.

The original contract was for 132 vehicles, plus an initial eight which were used in the development of a strategy to develop workshop planning instructions, spares procurement and the manufacture of tooling.

Two of the initial eight vehicles required winterisation. This involved supplying a number of additional extras such as crew and battery heaters, as the vehicles were deployed to an environment of sub-zero temperatures.

During the first year 51 vehicles were completed, 40 in the second and 41 in the final year including the two armoured variants used in Northern Ireland. Final deliveries were made in 2002.

In 2008 the British Army started to deploy the first of the 288 MAN (8 × 8) recovery vehicles and 69 recovery trailers. These have started to replace the Foden (6 × 6) recovery vehicles.

Description
The Foden non-corrosive, fire-retardant glass-reinforced plastic tilting cab has seating for four men, bunk or stretcher facilities and is fully fitted for radio.

A strengthened roof incorporates both observation hatches and machine gun mountings. For service in Iraq, some Foden (6 × 6) recovery vehicles were fitted with a passive armour kit for the cab.

The vehicle has a maximum road speed of 97 km/h and is powered by a Perkins Engines Company Eagle 290 6-cylinder diesel engine, a Fuller main gearbox and GKN hub reduction axles and transfer gearbox. When equipped with its full complement of recovery equipment, it can climb, hold and restart on 33 per cent gradients.

A front-mounted 10-tonne winch provides a self-recovery capability. Recovery eyes and detachable NATO-pattern towing hooks are provided at both front and rear.

The vehicle is fitted with the EKA Limited hydraulically operated Compact recovery unit Model AK 6500 EA12/1. With its drawbar, support/suspend towing and winching facilities, this unit can recover all of the British Army's in-service logistic support and armoured wheeled vehicles up to a gross vehicle weight of 30,000 kg.

Foden (6 × 6) recovery vehicle in travelling configuration (Shaun C Connors)

1296040

Foden (6 × 6) recovery vehicle from the rear in travelling configuration (Shaun C Connors)

1334242

A Rotzler type 25000 HS/390 25,000 kg single line pull hydraulic main winch is fitted and two rear anchor spades provide anchorage for the vehicle.

A slewing crane with 220° of slewing angle and a maximum lift capacity of 12,500 kg provides optimum lifting facilities. For vehicle stability, two extensible hydraulically operated outriggers are fitted, one to each side of the vehicle. The boom has a straight lift capacity of 12,500 kg at 2.5 m extension and 5,800 kg at 7.7 m.

Detachable load-bearing feet are also provided for the rear ground anchors when these are used as stabilisers.

All recovery and lifting functions are controlled from a locker-mounted console or from a remote-control unit with 30 m of wander lead.

Scammell crusader (6 × 4) recovery vehicle

In the late 1970s, the former Scammell company supplied the British Army with 130 Crusader 6 × 4 recovery vehicles with a further two vehicles being supplied to the Royal Air Force. Some of these remain in service.

Specifications

Foden recovery vehicle
Cab seating: 1 + 3
Configuration: 6 × 6
Weight: (loaded) 25,338 kg
Length: 9.055 m
Width: 2.482 m
Height: (cab) 3.35 m
Ground clearance: 0.42 m
Track:
(front) 2.029 m
(rear) 2.06 m
Wheelbase: 3.97 + 1.516 m
Angle of approach/departure: 28/29°
Max road speed: 97 km/h
Fuel capacity: 360 litres
Max gradient: 33%
Engine: Perkins Engines Company Eagle 290 6-cylinder in-line turbocharged 4-stroke diesel developing 290 bhp at 1,950 rpm
Gearbox: Fuller RTX 11609B 9-speed constant mesh
Clutch: Spicer twin plate hydraulically operated
Transfer box: GKN/Kirkstall AGB 7000 Mark 11 2 speed with optional integral power take- off
Axles:
(front) Kirkstall SD66-11-1S 10 t with differential lock
(rear) Kirkstall D66-11-1SHF and D66-11-1S with differential locks on both axles, 6.64:1 overall axle ratio. Third differential on foremost axle
Steering: recirculatory ball with integral power assistance
Turning circle: (kerb to kerb) 25 m
Suspension: semi-elliptic laminated springs front, two-spring fully articulating rear spring
Brakes: air, split-circuit, trailer brake connection to front and rear of chassis
Wheels and tyres: 16.00 × 20 - 28 ply tyres, 11.25 rims
Electrical system: 24 V
Batteries: 2 × 12 V

Status

Production complete. In service with the British Army. No longer being marketed. Now being replaced by a new MAN (8 × 8) recovery vehicle.

Contractor

Foden Trucks a division of Paccar UK Limited (this company is no longer involved in the military vehicle business)

Reynolds Boughton (4 × 4) 6,000 kg recovery vehicle

Development

The Reynolds Boughton (4 × 4) 6,000 kg recovery vehicle was developed as a follow on to the much older Recovery Vehicle, Wheeled, Light, Bedford RL (4 × 4) which was developed in the 1950's and no longer in front line service.

The Reynolds Boughton (4 × 4) 6,000 kg recovery vehicle uses the later Bedford Trucks MJP chassis fitted with a recovery system developed by Reynolds Boughton.

Bedford Trucks as such no longer exist although small quantities of these remain in service with the UK and a number of overseas countries.

This vehicle is now being phased out of UK service.

Description

It uses a Bedford MJP2BMO chassis with a 3.962 m wheelbase and a Bedford TK style all-steel two-door fully enclosed steel cab. The hydraulically operated recovery unit is mounted on the rear and is constructed on load-carrying longitudinal main channels with cross-channel bearers gusseted at all intersections. Six stowage lockers are fitted, three to each side. The floor has a non-slip metal covering. Access steps are provided at the front and rear.

Reynolds Boughton (4 × 4) 6,000 kg recovery vehicle on Bedford chassis and with crane in stowed position   0007361

The recovery jib is mounted on a main turret tower. The jib has inner and outer rectangular box sections and a position stay is provided for use when carrying suspended loads. The winch is mounted on the hydraulically operated jib. The cable diameter is 14 mm and the lifting capacity 6,000 kg.

Four hydraulically powered stabiliser legs are provided, one at each corner of the recovery unit and each leg is independently operated for levelling. The hydraulic pump is driven from a power take-off on the vehicle gearbox.

All crane operations are carried out from the crane turret platform while stabiliser levelling is from the side of the vehicle. Most of the hydraulic piping is carried in flexible two-wire hose.

A recovery winch is mounted in the centre of the vehicle, having a capacity of 6,096 kg. The 14 mm winch cable is 65 m long and there is also a heavy-duty ground anchor centrally mounted between the axles.

An overload safety device is linked to the crane hydraulics to operate when the hook load exceeds 105 per cent of the safe working load. The crane functions can then only be moved into a safe condition.

In British Army service, these Bedford 4 × 4 trucks have been supplemented by the Leyland Trucks (4 × 4) 5,000 kg truck. To date, a recovery version of this truck has not been deployed by the British Army.

The UK is taking delivery of a total of 288 MAN (8 × 8) recovery vehicles and these will replace all currently deployed wheeled recovery vehicles used by the British Army.

Specifications

6,000 kg recovery vehicle
Cab seating: 1 + 2
Configuration: 4 × 4
Length: 6.579 m
Width: 2.438 m
Height: 2.667 m
Wheelbase: 3.962 m
Jib radius retracted: 3.327 m
Jib extension: 1.727 m
Max rear lift: (0.482 m jib overhang from body rear) 6,000 kg
Crane slewing speed: 270° in 40 s
Jib extension from retract to extension: 16 s

Status

Production complete. No longer marketed, as Bedford chassis on which it is based is no longer built. In service with the British Army (deliveries complete), Brunei and Oman.

Contractor

Reynolds Boughton Limited

United States

BAE Systems, Global Tactical Systems M1089 (6 × 6) recovery vehicle

Development

The M1089 (6 × 6) series is the recovery/wrecker member of the US Army's Family of Medium Tactical Vehicles (FMTV) which is produced in 4 × 4 and 6 × 6 configuration for the home and export markets.

The original prime contractor was Stewart & Stevenson which was subsequently taken over in 2006 by Armor Holdings, Tactical Vehicle Systems. This was subsequently taken over by BAE Systems and today the company is known as BAE Systems Global Tactical Systems which also includes BAE Systems, Land Systems South Africa (originally BAE Systems Land Systems OMC South Africa).

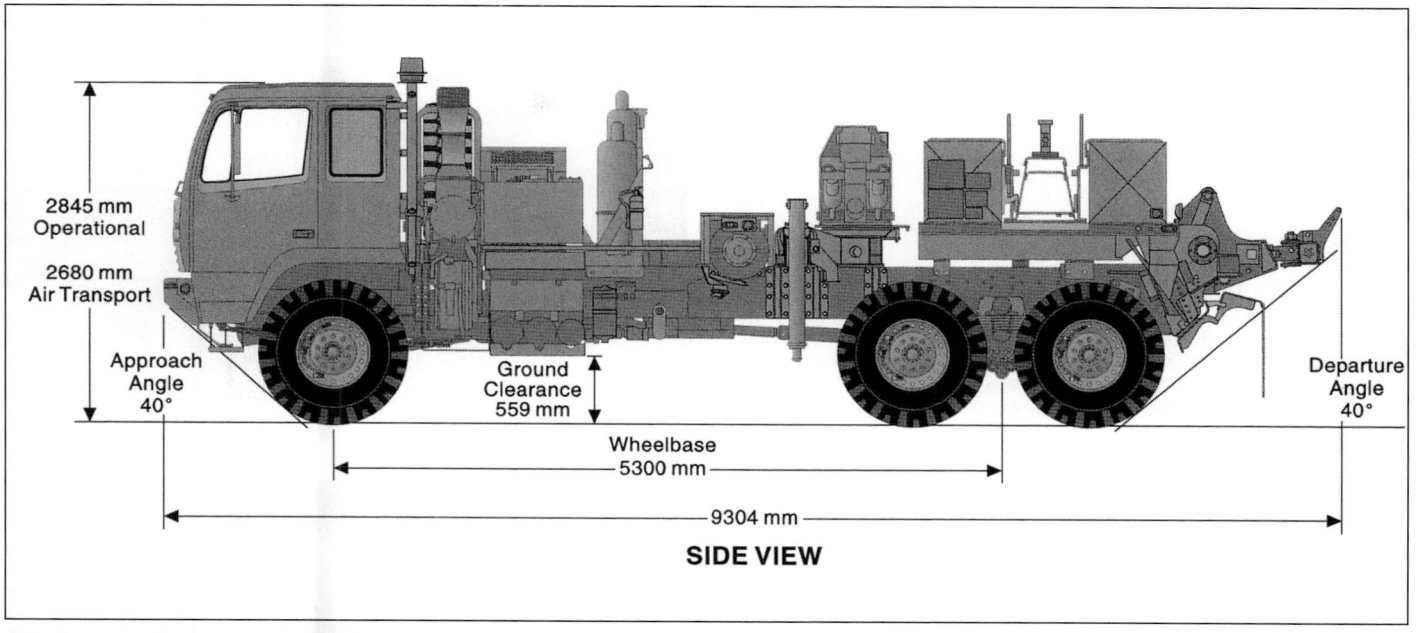

2845 mm Operational

2680 mm Air Transport

Approach Angle 40°

Ground Clearance 559 mm

Departure Angle 40°

Wheelbase 5300 mm

9304 mm

SIDE VIEW

Side drawing of latest M1089A1 5 ton wrecker in travelling configuration (BAE Systems, Global Tactical Systems)

1159837

In late 1999 the A1 version of the FMTV replaced the original model of the FMTV series of vehicle.

This has a number of new features including the installation of a new Caterpillar 3126B 7.2 litre diesel engine coupled to an improved Allison MD D7 automatic transmission, anti-lock brake system, databus for digital communications and enhanced diagnostic capabilities.

It is also fitted with the enhanced drive line already being fitted to the currently fielded FMTV fleet of vehicles in service with the US Army.

Under the original multiyear production contract the company built about 14,000 FMTVs in all versions (AO), with the first unit being equipped in 1996.

In 1998 the US Army signed a second multiyear contract with the company for a further 7,800 A1 series vehicles (6 × 6 and 4 × 4), plus 1,600 trailers. Since then additional orders have been placed.

The A1 vehicles incorporate a number of improvements including a more powerful electronically controlled diesel engine, exhaust brake and cold weather start-up.

In mid-2008 the US Department of Defense awarded the company a contract for the supply of up to 10,000 members of the FMTV worth up to USD2.2 billion of which USD1.645 billion already agreed.

This contracts also included a one year option for the procurement of an additional 10,000 FMTV.

This contract is for the Long Term Armor Strategy (LTAS) and vehicles supplied will be configured for cargo, wrecker, expansible vans, shop vans, load handing systems, High Mobility Artillery Rocket system support vehicles and Low Velocity Air Drop configured trucks.

LTAS is the newest version of the FMTV and is designed to accept an adaptable armour system offering high levels of protection when required.

By September 2009 BAE Systems Global Tactical Systems had built over 56,000 FMTV trucks and trailers and operational readiness rate of vehicles deployed to Afghanistan and Iraq is 94 per cent.

There was a competition for the next follow on FMTV contract for which BAE Systems Global Tactical Systems, Navistar Defense and Oshkosh Defense bid. The US DoD selected Oshkosh Defense for future FMTV contracts.

Under current contracts, BAE Systems, Global Tactical Systems, will continue FMTV production in the short term.

Following a competition, Oshkosh Defense was awarded the FMTV next five year rebid. BAE Systems, Global Combat Systems protested this rebid but in early 2010 Oshkosh Defense were awarded a contract by the US Army for the next five year procurement of the latest FMTV.

Over this period it is expected that Oshkosh Defense will deliver about 23,000 trucks and trailers in 17 models and 23 variants with payloads of 2.5- to 10-tonne.

Initial FMTV units were delivered for US Army trials in May 2010 with the first production vehicles being completed late in 2010.

In May 2010 the company was awarded a USD410 million contract that covered the supply of 2,634 FMTV and trailers for delivery from March through to December 2011.

In September 2010 the company was awarded a contract worth more than USD259 million for more than 1,300 trucks and 700 trailers for delivery through to June 2012.

In November 2010 another contract was awarded to Oshkosh Defense worth USD797 million to deliver more than 4,150 FMTV trucks and 590 trailers from September 2011 through to August 2012.

This brought the total Oshkosh Defense FMTV order book to more than 14,000 trucks and trailers, with additional contracts to be awarded in the future to complete the five year rebuy.

Description

Most of the chassis, forward-control cab, automotive components, drive train, central tyre-inflation system and other systems used on the M1089 MTV (6 × 6) 5 ton wrecker are identical to their equivalents on other FMTV variants.

The chassis has been provided with some extra stiffening panels but other modifications are few and minor. The main change from the other variants is the provision of a recovery hamper over the rear chassis and axles.

The main recovery component is a hydraulically operated recovery winch with a twin 13,608 kg line pull capacity. A lift and tow assembly provides front or rear recovery from the vehicle operator station or remote control. It can handle loads of 4,990 kg, including almost all wheeled military vehicles. Stabiliser jacks are provided each side for deployment during recovery operations.

Variants

M1089A1 (6 × 6) wrecker

This is the latest production model and according to the manufacturer has the following features:

- Fully automatic transmission
- Electronic Central Tyre Inflation System
- Anti-lock braking system
- Fully MANPRINT complaint
- C-130 transportable at gross-vehicle weight
- US Army certified 22-year corrosion protection.

Earlier vehicles were powered by a Caterpillar 3126B engine but the A1 model is powered by a Caterpillar C7 developing 330 hp coupled to an Allison MD 3700 SP fully automatic transmission.

Specifications

M1089A1 recovery vehicle
Cab seating: 1 + 2
Configuration: 6 × 6
Weight: (kerb) 15,954 kg
Length: 9.305 m

US Army M1089 MTVR (6 × 6) 5 ton wrecker from the rear in travelling configuration (Shaun C Connors)

1405682

Width: 2.438 m
Height:
  (operational) 2.845 m
  (for air transport) 2.68 m
Ground clearance: 0.559 m
Wheelbase: 5.3 m
Angle of approach/departure: 40/40°
Max speed: 94 km/h
Range: 483 km plus
Gradient: 60%
Side slope: 30%
Fording:
  (without kit) 0.914 m
  (with kit) 1.524 m
Engine: Caterpillar 3126B ATAAC 7.2 litre 6-cylinder turbocharged and after-cooled diesel developing 330 hp at 2,400 rpm
Gearbox: Allison MD-D7 automatic, 7 speed
Transfer box: Allison single speed integral to transmission with planetary inter-axle differential (lockable)
Steering: power assisted
Suspension: parabolic tapered leaf springs
Tyres: 395 R 20 XML
Electrical system: 12/24 V
Alternator: 100 or 200 A

Status

In production. In service with US Army. Known export sales of the M1089A1 (6 × 6) wrecker include Bangladesh (17 units) and Jordan (10 units).

Contractor

BAE Systems, Global Tactical Systems
Oshkosh Defense (five year re-bid confirmed in early 2010)

M62, truck, wrecker: Medium, 5 ton, (6 × 6)
M246, truck, tractor, wrecker: 5 ton, (6 × 6) M543, truck, wrecker: Medium, 5 ton, (6 × 6)

Description

These vehicles are all members of the M54 series of 5 ton (6 × 6) trucks which were developed after the Second World War. This series of vehicle is no longer used by the US Army. The last contractor AM General who are no longer involved in the production of 6 × 6 tactical vehicles and are currently in production of the HMMWV (4 × 4).

Variants

M62 wrecker
This has a hydraulically-operated crane, mounted at the rear with a maximum lifting capacity of 9,072 kg when used with the two stabilisers either side of the vehicle.

Truck, wrecker: Medium, 5 ton (6 × 6) M62 upgraded with a new diesel engine in Brazil (Christopher F Foss)   0079515

Truck, tractor, wrecker: 5 ton (6 × 6) M246 with front-mounted winch (US Army)   0511494

A winch is mounted at the front, with a maximum capacity of 9,072 kg when being used to the front and 18,144 kg when being used to the rear. Later models of the M62 are the M62A1 and M62A2.

A number of countries have modernised these vehicles with the original petrol engine being replaced by a more fuel-efficient diesel engine. A typical country is Brazil.

M246 wrecker
This was designed for use as both a recovery vehicle and for towing semi-trailers. The Austin-Western hydraulic crane at the rear has a jib which can be extended from 3.504 to 7.924 m. This crane can be slewed through 360° and its jib elevated to a maximum of 45°. Later models of the M246 are the M246A1 and the M246A2, which has a Continental LDS 465-1 or LDS 465-2 multifuel engine. The M246 was replaced in production by the similar M819, for which there is a separate entry in *Jane's Military Vehicles and Logistics*. Production of this vehicle is complete and it is no longer marketed.

Designation	M62	M246	M543
Chassis designation:	M40C	M63C	M40C
Configuration:	6 × 6	6 × 6	6 × 6
Towed load:			
(road)	13,608 kg	20,865 kg	13,608 kg
(cross-country)	9,072 kg	17,010 kg	9,072 kg
Weight: (empty)	15,275 kg	14,829 kg	15,603 kg
Length:	7.848 m	8.953 m	10.007 m
Width:	2.463 m	2.489 m	2.444 m
Height:	2.59 m	3.352 m	2.743 m
Ground clearance:	0.279 m	0.279 m	0.279 m
Wheelbase:	3.86 + 1.371 m	4.775 + 1.371 m	3.86 + 1.371 m
Angle of approach/departure:	37/38°	35/55°	37/38°
Max speed: (road)	84 km/h	84 km/h	84 km/h
Range:	344 km	369 km	360 km
Fuel capacity:	295 litres	295 litres	295 litres (some have 504 litres)
Max gradient:	36%	47%	61.4%
Fording:			
(without preparation)	0.762 m	0.762 m	0.762 m
(with preparation)	1.981 m	-	1.981 m
Engine:	Continental 6-cylinder petrol developing 196 hp at 2,800 rpm [1]		
Transmission:	5 forward and 1 reverse gears and 2-speed transfer case		
Turning radius:	12.648 m	14.325 m	14.5 m
Tyres:	11.00 × 20	11.00 × 20	11.00 × 20
Brakes:	all have hydraulic brakes, air-actuated		
Electrical system:	24 V	24 V	24 V
Batteries:	2 × 12 V	2 × 12 V	2 × 12 V

[1] In some cases, late production models are powered by a multifuel rather than a petrol engine.

M543 wrecker

This has a Gar Wood hydraulically operated crane at the rear, which can lift a maximum of 4,536 kg. Two stabilisers are provided each side and a winch is mounted at the front and rear.

The second production model M543A1 has a diesel engine. In 1963 the M543A2 was introduced. It has an LDS-465 multifuel engine, which develops 180 hp at 2,600 rpm and gives the vehicle a maximum road speed of 84 km/h and a range of 938 km. The M543A2 was replaced in production by the similar M816 for which there is a separate entry in *Jane's Military Vehicles and Logistics*. Production of this vehicle is complete and it is no longer marketed.

Specifications

See table at foot of facing page

Status

Production complete. No longer marketed. In service with a number of countries. In US Army service these have been replaced by the now BAE Systems, Global Tactical Systems M1089 series of 6 × 6 recovery vehicles.

The basic chassis has been manufactured by various companies since the early 1950s, including International Harvester, Kaiser Jeep (now AM General Corporation) and Mack Trucks. Last manufacturer was AM General Corporation.

Contractor

AM General Division

This company is no longer involved in the production of 5 ton (6 × 6) trucks and their specialised variants.

AM General M816, truck, wrecker, 5 ton, (6 × 6) M819, tractor, wrecker, 5 ton, (6 × 6)

Development

These vehicles are members of the AM General M809 series of 5 ton (6 × 6) trucks which were manufactured in large numbers for the home and export markets.

The M809 series of 5 ton 6 × 6 (US) trucks was followed in production by the much improved M939 series which were built by AM General and BMY - Wheeled Vehicles Division of HARSCO. The latter company is no longer involved in military vehicle production.

The recovery member of the M939 series was called the M936 with the winch-equipped model being the M936A2.

Production of the M939 series of 6 × 6 vehicles is now complete and they are no longer being marketed. In US Army service they are being replaced by the FMTV.

Description

The M816 wrecker is provided with a turntable-mounted hydraulic crane at the rear which has a self-supported extensible boom and boom to ground supports. Outriggers are provided to stabilise the vehicle when the crane is

AM General M816 5 ton (6 × 6) wrecker in travelling configuration 0512449

being used. Hydraulically operated winches are fitted. The M819 also has a hydraulic crane mounted on the rear but has a longer wheelbase. It can tow a trailer or vehicle weighing up to 13,608 kg on roads or 9,076 kg across country.

Optional kits for these vehicles when originally manufactured included an air brake kit, closure hardtop, deep water fording kit, slave receptacle, thermal barrier kit, winterisation personnel heater kit and a power plant kit.

Specifications

See table below

Status

M816 in service with the US Forces, Australia, South Korea, Philippines (36), Zaïre and many other forces. M819 production complete. In US Army service these are now being rapidly replaced by the now BAE Systems, Global Tactical Systems M1089 series of 6 × 6 recovery vehicles.

Following a competitive five-year re-bid, in 2010 Oshkosh Defense was awarded the contract for the FMTV but BAE Systems, Global Tactical Vehicles will continue production in the short term.

Contractor

AM General Division

This company is no longer involved in the production of 5 ton (6 × 6) trucks and their specialised variants.

Oshkosh Defense M984A1/M984A1 recovery vehicle 10 ton (8 × 8)

Development

The Oshkosh M984A1 recovery vehicle 10 ton (8 × 8) is the recovery component of the Oshkosh Heavy Expanded Mobility Tactical Truck (HEMTT) family of vehicles. The US Army fleet of HEMTT vehicles are now being upgraded by Oshkosh to extend their lives well into the 21st Century.

Designation	M816	M819
Chassis type:	M809A1	M811A1
Cab seating:	1 + 2	1 + 2
Configuration:	6 × 6	6 × 6
Weight:		
(unloaded)	16,385 kg	15,392 kg
(on front axle empty)	4,966 kg	6,304 kg
(on rear bogie empty)	11,418 kg	9,251 kg
Length:	9.042 m	9.124 m
Width:	2.484 m	2.489 m
Height:	2.69 m	3.352 m
Ground clearance:	0.295 m	0.295 m
Track:	1.88 m (front) and 1.829 m (rear)	1.88 m (front) and 1.829 m (rear)
Wheelbase:	4.547 + 1.371 m	4.125 + 1.371 m
Angle of approach/departure:	35/34°	36/55°
Max speed: (road)	84 km/h	83.6 km/h
Range:	805 km	563 km
Fuel capacity:	295 litres	295 litres
Max gradient:	31%	31%
Fording:		
(without preparation)	0.762 m	0.762 m
(with preparation)	1.879 m	1.879 m
Engine:	Model NHC-250 6-cylinder in-line diesel developing 240 hp (gross) at 2,100 rpm	
Transmission:	5 forward and 1 reverse gears, 2-speed transfer box	
Tyres:	11.00 × 20	12.00 × 20
Electrical system:	24 V	24 V

Oshkosh Defense M984A1 (8 × 8) recovery vehicle in travelling configuration 0511495

The US Department of Defense has awarded the Oshkosh Defense regular contracts for the HEMTT series of 8 × 8 trucks.

In June 2008 the company was awarded additional US Army contracts for the latest A4 HEMTT series which will bring total production of this variant up to 1,978 units worth USD658 million.

This contract covered the supply of 233 HEMTT A4 series vehicles, including fuel service vehicles, load handing system vehicles and wreckers.

In September 2008 Oshkosh delivered 20,000 HEMTT with production still underway in late 2010.

Description

The M984A1 recovery vehicle follows the same general construction lines as the rest of the HEMTT family. The M984A1 recovery system consists of a main recovery winch, a self-recovery winch and ground spades.

The main recovery winch has a capacity of 27,216 kg and is an automatic, two-speed, hydraulically operated winch drum with fully proportional controls. It has 56.4 m of usable wire rope. The winch automatically shifts to low speed when recovering heavy loads.

The main recovery winch system, which includes a fairlead/tensioner device, provides the capability of recovering stranded vehicles at up to 32° to the left or right, or 23° below the vehicle. The fairlead/tensioner also provides proper winding of the wire rope on the drum winch by maintaining an even rope tension between the rear of the vehicle and the drum.

The self-recovery winch is a standard HEMTT winch with forward deployment and a bare drum capacity of 9,072 kg. The ground spades are emplaced manually. The main hydraulic winch can be operated using a remote-control unit.

The M984A1 uses a lift and tow system that can be deployed and attached to a disabled vehicle in two to three minutes. The system consists of a crossbar that 'floats' on a 102 mm ball. The ball is supported by three hydraulic cylinders, which provide precise positioning of the crossbar during connection to the disabled vehicle. The ball system provides articulation and stability when travelling over uneven terrain and when cornering.

Based on testing by the US Army Combat Systems Test Activity (CSTA), the M984A1 recovery vehicle is approved for towing with towbar tracked vehicles up to 30 tons, which includes the BAE Systems US Combat Systems (previously United Defense) M2 Bradley infantry fighting vehicle and M3 cavalry fighting vehicle and their variants. The Bradley is only used by Saudi Arabia and the United States.

The M984A1 is equipped with a hydraulically operated material-handling crane with a lift capacity of 6,350 kg. The crane has the lift and reach capability to support the removal and replacement of power packs from a wide range of wheeled and tracked vehicles including the M1A1/M1A2, M2, M3, M109A2, M109A5, M109A6 and M88A1/M88A2 series tracked armoured vehicles. The hydraulic crane can be operated using a remote-control unit.

The M984A1 has an equipment body with stowage provisions for support equipment including oxygen/acetylene welding equipment, tow adapters, chain slings and snatch blocks.

The stowage provisions include 10 lockable and watertight individual compartments. The entire body can be removed for air transport weight reduction in less than 10 minutes.

M984A4 recovery truck (wrecker)

This is the latest version to be marketed by Oshkosh Defense and has a new powerpack consisting of a Caterpillar C-15 diesel developing 500 hp coupled to an Allison 4500 series five speed automatic transmission.

The A4 version also features a fully air conditioned and armour ready cab, improved suspension, safety improvements and structural changes to make the installation of add on armour in the field quicker and easier.

Curb weight is being quoted as 24,539 kg with a maximum road speed of 100 km/h. Front axles are Oshkosh 46K and rear axles are Dana DS650. Suspension is air ride with four height control valves.

Oshkosh MK48/15 recovery vehicle

To meet the requirements of the US Marine Corps, Oshkosh Defense developed the MK48 series logistic vehicle. The recovery version of this is the MK48/15. This is only used by the US Marine Corps.

Specifications

M984A1 recovery vehicle
Cab seating: 1 + 1
Configuration: 8 × 8
Weight:
  (chassis) 14,968 kg
  (kerb) 22,226 kg
  (GCW) 45,360 kg
Length: 9.957 m
Width: 2.438 m
Height:
  (travelling) 2.845 m
  (top of cab) 2.565 m
  (crane extended) 3.759 m
  (loading, flatbed) 1.6 m
Ground clearance: 0.33 m
Wheelbase: 4.85 m
Angle of approach/departure: 43/45°
Max speed: 88 km/h
Range: 483 km
Fuel capacity: 589 litres
Fording: 1.219 m
Engine: Detroit Diesel 8V-92TA V-8 developing 445 hp at 2,100 rpm
Gearbox: Allison HT740D with torque converter, 4 forward, 1 reverse speeds
Transfer box: Oshkosh 55000 2 speed
Steering: integral hydraulic main and booster gears
Suspension:
  (front) Hendrikson RT340
  (rear) Hendrikson RT500
Tyres: 16.00R × 20
Electrical system: 24 V
Batteries: 4 × 12 V

Status

Production as required. In service with the US Army and Saudi Arabia. US Army vehicles are going through a phased upgrade programme by Oshkosh to extend their operational life.

Contractor

Oshkosh Defense

Oshkosh Defense Forward Repair System - Heavy (FRS-H)

Development

The Forward Repair System - Heavy (FRS-H), originally known as the Heavy Repair Vehicle (HRV), was developed by the US Army Ordnance Center and School at Aberdeen Proving Ground, Maryland, to meet a need for a forward area maintenance vehicle.

The FRS-H is capable of supporting armoured, mechanised infantry, combat engineer, field artillery, armoured cavalry and forward support maintenance battalions.

It is intended for the repair of battle-damaged vehicles in the forward area and to operate forward of the brigade support areas at equipment breakdown sites and unit maintenance collection points.

The FRS-H carries tools, selected repair parts, cutting and welding equipment and small quantities of fuel and lubricants, along with the crew of four, their personal equipment and weapons.

Description

This has now been type classified by the US Army as the Forward Repair System - Heavy, M7.

Forward Repair System - Heavy (FRS-H) being used to remove a complete power pack of the General Dynamics Land Systems M1 series MBT 0121593

The FRS-H is based on the chassis of the Oshkosh Defense (10 × 10) M1074 series Palletized Load System (PLS) vehicle, which is used in large numbers by the US Army.

The standard (10 × 10) chassis has been modified to accept a repair module containing a work and storage area for a tool set suitable for the type of unit involved.

The chassis is further modified to accept a 7.5-tonne hydraulically operated lifting crane at the rear of the chassis; the hydraulic crane is the same as that used on the Oshkosh Defense M984A1 (8 × 8) recovery vehicle (see separate entry covered in *Jane's Military Vehicles and Logistics*) and can be used to lift and handle vehicle major components. The main repair/stowage module has a roof hatch to accept components for repair.

Stowage points around the vehicle are used to carry further tools and equipment and provision is made for a minimum of two NATO slave receptacles and a standard diagnostic connector assembly. Other external connectors provide 110 or 220 V power supplies produced by a 10 kW Tactical Quiet Generator (TQG). A spotlight is mounted on the top rear of the repair/stowage module.

The FRS-H is capable of towing other vehicles. To provide a more stable platform when the crane is being used two stabilisers are lowered to the ground at the rear.

The cab and repair/stowage modules are armoured against 7.62 mm small arms fire and 152 mm artillery fragments. Both areas also have a collective NBC protection system.

Weapons carried include one .50 (12.7 mm) M2 HB Browning machine gun mounted over a hatch in the cab roof, four 5.56 mm M16 rifles, a smoke grenade launcher and light anti-tank weapons.

At the end of 1993 one prototype, based at Fort Hood, had been produced for concept evaluation purposes. At that time it was intended that the FRS-H would be distributed at the rate of five per armoured battalion and armoured cavalry squadron, six to a mechanised infantry battalion, four to a field artillery or combat engineer battalion and three to a division cavalry squadron. In addition, one HRV would be distributed to each special howitzer, engineer and system support company.

The baseline chassis is supplied by Oshkosh Defense. These are supplied to Rock Island Arsenal to produce the actual module, install it on the PLS Truck and deliver the complete system back to the US Army.

Other equipment carried on the FRS-H includes air compressor, three hose reels, welder and compressed gases.

Two SINCGARS radios are provided for communication between repair crews with walkie talkies being provided to speed up repair tasks.

Specifications

FRS-H M7
Crew: 4
Configuration: 10 × 10
Weight: (kerb, with crane and module) 26,082 kg
Length: 10.973 m
Width: 2.44 m
Height:
(overall) 3.886 m
(top of load handing equipment) 3.251 m
Ground clearance: 0.39 m
Wheelbase: 5.71 m
Angle of approach/departure: 42/62°
Max speed: (laden) 90.1 km/h
Fuel capacity: 378.6 litres
Range: 540 km (road)
Fording: 1.22 m
Engine: Detroit Diesel Model 8V-92TA V-8 diesel developing 500 hp at 2,100 rpm
Transmission: Allison CLT-755 5-speed automatic with torque converter and equipped with Allison Transmission Electronic Controls (ATEC)
Transfer box: Oshkosh 55000 series 2-speed with 30:70 differential with lock
Steering: power assisted on 1st, 2nd and 5th axle
Suspension: Hendrikson walking beam front and rear
Electrical system: 12/24 V
Armament:
1 × .50 (12.7 mm) M2 HB MG
4 × 5.56 mm M16A1 rifles

Status

Production as required. In service with the US Army and fielded with 4th Infantry Division and III Corps. According to the US Army this is the replacement for the M113A2/M113A3 armoured personnel carrier 'maintenance track' currently used for the maintenance role in Force XXI Divisions and the Stryker Brigade Combat Teams of which seven have been formed.

Contractor

Oshkosh Defense

Development agency

US Army Ordnance Center and School
Directorate of Combat Development (Proponent Systems)

Oshkosh Defense (6 × 6) MK36 wrecker recovery vehicle

Development

The Oshkosh Defense MK36 wrecker recovery vehicle is a member of the Medium Tactical Vehicle Replacement (MTVR) programme for the US Marine Corps.

Following trials with preproduction vehicles, production of the MK36 wrecker was authorised. The first order was for a total of 308 units, with first production vehicles completed in 2004.

Today there are a total of seven base line chassis versions of the Medium Tactical Vehicle Replacement (MTVR) series of vehicles in service and these are listed below:-
- MK23 - standard cargo truck with a wheel base of 4.674 m
- MK25 - standard cargo truck with a wheel base of 4.674 m and fitted with a winch
- MK27 - long wheel base cargo truck with a wheel base of 5.486 m
- MK28 - long wheel base cargo truck with a wheel base of 5.486 m and fitted with a winch
- MK29 - dump truck with a wheel base of 4.674 m
- MK30 - dump truck with a wheel base of 4.674 m and fitted with a winch
- MK36 - wrecker with a wheel base of 5.486 m.

Under the original contract a total of 5,666 MTVR were to be delivered by late 1999 but in the end a total of 5,931 vehicles were delivered of which 5,393 were for the US Marine Corps and 538 to the US Navy.

In July 2004 a follow on contract was awarded to Oshkosh who is expected to cover an additional 2,000 vehicles including MK25,MK28, M28C, MK30, MK31 and MK36.

The latest version is the MK31 Medium Equipment Transporter (MET) tractor truck for towing semi-trailers. The MK37 is a MK27 with a Hiab crane for handle pods of MLRS rockets for the US Marine Corps High Mobility Artillery Rocket System (HIMARS) (6 × 6) surface-to-surface rocket system.

For operations in Iraq, many US Marine Corps series (6 × 6) MTVR trucks have been fitted with additional passive armour protection to provide the crew with a higher level of survivability.

In September 2008, a USD28 million contract was awarded for support work for the MTVR. Under the terms of this contract the company delivered nearly 200 reducible height Armour Protection Kits (APK), 200 fuel fire protection kits and 160 engines to support in theatre maintenance and repair of the MTVR.

The reducible height version of the armour kit allows the US Marine Corps to transport MTVR aboard ships by lowering the overall height of the vehicle. All of this work was completed by September 2009.

This followed a contract placed in mid-2008 for 480 APK which was fitted by June 2009 with the work being carried out in the US.

Production of the MTVR is undertaken by Oshkosh Defense on an as required basis and by late 2010 over 10,000 vehicles had been produced.

The Oshkosh Defense TAK-4 independent suspension on the MTVR family of vehicles is also used on the Oshkosh Defense (MRAP) All-Terrain Vehicle (M-ATV) which entered production and service with the US Army in mid-2009 and has already been deployed to Afghanistan.

The US Marine Corps Approved Acquisition Objective (AAO) is for a total of 9,924 MTVR that will be increased in FY 2012 to 10,139 units.

In addition the US Navy Sea Bees Construction Battalions deploy about 1,800 MTVR vehicles in various configurations.

Description

All versions of the Oshkosh Defense MTVR are based on the same 6 × 6 drive configuration with the engine under a forward bonnet. The chassis frame is constructed using bolted/huck bolted formed channel made of carbon manganese steel, while the three-seat cab is of welded aluminium extension construction with adhesive bonded aluminium skins.

The aluminium hinged windscreen, roof, side walls, door frames and rear wall can be quickly folded down to reduce the overall height of the vehicle to 2.489 m.

Oshkosh Defense MK36 wrecker recovery vehicle (6 × 6) with stabilisers lowered and crane extended to the rear 0536882

The power pack of the MK36 wrecker recovery vehicle consists of a Caterpillar C-12 electronic controlled ADEM III six-cylinder diesel developing 425 hp, coupled to an Allison 4070P electronically controlled seven speed transmission with a TC-541 torque converter.

Suspension uses a system known as the Oshkosh TAK-4 independent suspension, which utilises a coil spring and upper lower control arms at wheel position. This system provides each front wheel with a total vertical travel of 406 mm and a travel of 325 mm on the rear axles.

Mounted to the rear of the cab is a Manitowoc Boom Truck Model 1731 crane with a capacity of 9,979 kg at 2.75 m radius from the crane centre. This has a lift capacity of 1,796 kg at a maximum reach of 9.5 m.

Mounted at the rear of the chassis is a hydraulically operated spade with a capacity of 31,752 kg and mounted either side, between the first and second axle, is a hydraulically operated stabiliser which is lowered to the ground by remote control when the crane is being used.

The two main winches have a total capacity of 15,877 kg and are provided with 91.4 m of 19 mm diameter cable. In addition there is a self-recovery winch with a capacity of 11,340 kg.

The MK36 has a lift capacity of 6,350 kg and a flat tow capacity of 21,773 kg cross-country and 27,715 kg on roads. The MK36 can also tow a trailer up to a maximum capacity of 9,979 kg.

Provided as standard equipment on the MK36 vehicle is a Central Tyre-Inflation System (CTIS), anti-lock brakes and an On Board Diagnostics System (OBDS) for maintenance and repair purposes.

Optional equipment includes an arctic kit for the engine, roof-mounted machine gun mounting kit, NBC alarm and decontamination apparatus mounting kits.

The MK36 wrecker recovery vehicle is fitted with Command Zone electronics, which have been integrated with the existing electronics to provide a functional and intelligent auxiliary control system.

The Command Zone system uses PC-based diagnostic software to provide the operator with real-time diagnostics and prognostics of vehicle operations. According to Oshkosh, Command Zone electronics significantly reduces troubleshooting time and provides the user with a higher level of system availability.

Specifications

MK36 wrecker recovery vehicle
Cab seating: 1 + 2
Configuration: 6 × 6
Weight: (curb) 22,271 kg
Gross vehicle weight: 22,498 kg
Length: 9.835 m
Width: 2.489 m
Height: 3.556 m
Track: 2.052 m
Wheelbase: 5.486 m
Angle of approach/departure: 30/41°
Max speed, road: 105 km/h
Range, road: 458 km
Fuel capacity: 295 litres
Gradient: 60%
Side slope: 30%
Fording: 1.524 m (without kit)
Engine: Caterpillar C-12 11.9 litre electronically controlled diesel developing 425 hp at 1,800 rpm
Transmission: Allison HD 4070P automatic with 7 forward and 1 reverse gears
Transfer box: Oshkosh 30000 series, 3 shaft, single speed
Steering: power air-assisted
Turning radius: 13 m
Suspension: Oshkosh TAK-4 independent suspension, coil spring upper/lower control arms
Tyres: 16.00 R 20 Michelin XZL (with central tyre inflation system)
Brakes: spring brakes on axles 2 and 3
Electrical system: 24 V
Batteries: 2 × 12 V
Alternator: 150 A

Status
Production as required. In service with US Marine Corps.

Contractor
Oshkosh Defense

Freightliner (6 × 6) wrecker

Development
The Freightliner (6 × 6) wrecker is a member of the Freightliner military truck family. The M915A3 series has been produced for the US Army in the tractor truck configuration but not the wrecker.

This is essentially a commercial vehicle with the minimum of modifications for military use. Details of the M915/M916 series of vehicles

Freightliner (6 × 6) wrecker in travelling configuration   0511496

are provided in a separate entry in *Jane's Military Vehicles and Logistics*. Production of these vehicles is undertaken on an as required basis.

Description
The Freightliner military truck family is based on the M915A2 (6 × 4) and M916A1 (6 × 6) series of long-haul trucks which are used in significant numbers by the US Army and utilises many components and other items carried over from commercial models.

By using commercial components overall total life cycle costs are reduced. Many well-proven features of the family are used with the Freightliner (6 × 6) wrecker, including an aluminium cab and a Detroit Diesel DDE 6-cylinder engine of advanced fuel efficiency design, which is used for commercial applications.

The main recovery feature is a rotating hydraulic boom crane mounted on a turntable over the rear axle bogies. The boom has a capacity of 18,144 kg and can lift and tow loads up to 7,031 kg. When travelling, the boom is normally traversed to the front. A replacement wheel and tyre is carried on the left side of the crane at the rear.

Specifications
Freightliner wrecker
Cab seating: 1 + 1
Configuration: 6 × 6
Weight:
  (kerb) 18,080 kg
  (front axle, loaded) 7,258 kg
  (rear axles, loaded) 23,587 kg
Length: 9.32 m
Width: 2.49 m
Height:
  (overall) 3.24 m
  (cab) 2.97 m
Ground clearance: 0.23 m
Wheelbase: 5.79 m
Angle of approach: 26°
Max speed:
  (road) 85.3 km/h
  (3% gradient) 40.22 km/h
Fuel capacity: 379 litres
Fording: 0.51 m
Engine: Detroit Diesel DDE 12.7 litre 6-cylinder high torque rise diesel developing 400 hp at 2,100 rpm
Transmission: Allison HT-740 AT with torque converter, 4 forward, 1 reverse speeds
Transfer box: Oshkosh Series 55,000, 2 speed
Steering: Ross integral power
Turning radius: 26.33 m
Brakes: air/mechanical; Eaton front, Rockwell rear
Tyres: 315/80 R 22.5
Electrical system: dual 12/24 V
Batteries: 4 × 12 V

Status
Production as required. As far as is known this vehicle is not in service with the US Army but is in service with the Philippines which took delivery of 10 units.

Contractor
Freightliner LLC

BRIDGING SYSTEMS

MECHANISED BRIDGES

China

China Shipbuilding Trading Company heavy mechanised bridge Type 84A

Development
The heavy mechanised bridge Type 84A was designed and built by the China Shipbuilding and Trading Company to meet the operational requirements of the People's Liberation Army. This is also referred to as the Type 84A Heavy Duty Mechanised Bridge.

The company has also developed and markets the type 79A Ribbon Bridge which is also transported and launched from a Mercedes-Benz (6 × 6) chassis.

It should be noted that China North Industries Corporation (NORINCO) market a similar systems called the 60T Heavy Modified Mechanised Bridge and details of this are provided in a separate entry in *Jane's Military Vehicles and Logistics.*

Description
In concept the heavy mechanised bridge Type 84A is very similar to the Russian TMM truck mounted treadway bridge, which is based on a 6 × 6 chassis and covered in detail in a separate entry in *Jane's Military Vehicles and Logistics.*

The Type 84A system has been designed for use by tracked vehicles up to a maximum weight of 50 tonnes and by wheeled vehicles with a maximum axle load of 13 tonnes.

The bridge sections are carried and placed into position by an 8 × 8 (as shown in the photograph) or a 6 × 6 forward control type vehicle and the general laying sequence and operation are much the same as those for the Russian TMM truck-mounted treadway bridge system.

Each span is 10.5 m long and up to five of these can be coupled together to span a maximum gap of up to 50 m.

The Type 84A can be used in water up to a depth of 3.5 m and Type 84A bridges can also be connected with various types of pontoon bridges.

Specifications
Heavy mechanised bridge Type 84A
Weight of bridgelayer: (total) 20,000 kg
Configuration: 8 × 8
Length of single span: 10.5 m
Roadway width: 3.8 m
Total length of bridge: 50 m
Bridge height:
  (max) 3.8 m
  (min) 2.2 m

Heavy mechanised bridge Type 84A under construction with another section being laid over previously positioned bridges   0512316

Heavy mechanised bridge Type 84A on Mercedes-Benz (6 × 6) chassis in travelling configuration   1129585

Capacity:
  (tracked vehicles) 50,000 kg
  (three-axle truck) 39,000 kg
  (max single axle load) 13,000 kg

Status
The system is in service with the People's Liberation Army. Production as required. There are no known exports of this system.

Contractor
China Shipbuilding Trading Company Limited

NORINCO 60T Modified Heavy Mechanised Bridge

Development
China North Industries Corporation (NORINCO) is now marketing the 60T Modified Heavy Mechanised Bridge on the international market.

This appears to be a further development of the China Shipbuilding Trading Company Type 84A Heavy Mechanised Bridge which is covered in detail in a separate entry in *Jane's Military Vehicles and Logistics.*

The main difference is that the bridge not only has a greater tracked load capacity of 60 tonnes but when fully extended each span has an overall length of 15 m, this compares to 10.5 m of the older Type 84A.

In concept, both of these Chinese systems are very similar in concept and operation to the older Russian TMM truck mounted treadway bridge that is launched over the rear of a 6 × 6 cross-country truck chassis.

Description
The NORINCO 60T Modified Heavy Mechanised Bridge is transported and launched from a locally manufactured Mercedes-Benz (8 × 8) forward control cross-country truck chassis.

The features powered steering on the front four wheels and is probably fitted with a central tyre inflation system that allows the driver to adjust the tyre pressure from his cab to suit the terrain being crossed.

In a typical laying operation the truck backs up to the wet or dry gap to be crossed and the bridge is opened out.

When the bridge fully open the hydraulically operated outriggers are opened out and extend until they are in contact with the ground.

The outriggers are hydraulically operated and are claimed to be fully automatic with double acting cylinders and are fitted with a large shoe which contacts the river bed.

When opened out each bridge is 15 m long and five systems can be used to span a wet or dry gap up to 75 m wide.

A single span takes about 12 minutes to be positioned while a complete set of five spans takes up to 60 minutes to be positioned. This does however depend on a number of factors.

According to NORINCO, their 60T Modified Heavy Mechanised Bridge can be used in rivers with a maximum flow of up to 2 m/s up to a maximum depth of 5.5 m.

One set consists of a total of five vehicles each of which can transport and launch one bridge. This set has a total crew of 12 of which seven are required to position each span.

Specifications
Weight of bridgelayer: (total) 30,600 kg
Length: 10.89 m
Width: 3.15 m
Height: 3.66 m
Configuration: 8 × 8
Length of single span: 15 m
Roadway width: 3.8 m
Total length of bridge: 75 m (five transporters)
Max height: 5.5 m (from shoes to deck)
Capacity:
  (tracked vehicles) 60,000 kg
  (axle load) 13,000 kg

Status
Development complete. Understood to be in service with the People's Liberation Army.

Contractor
China North Industries Corporation (NORINCO)

NORINCO Type 84 armoured bridgelayer

Development
To provide a gap crossing capability for its Type 59 and Type 69 Main Battle Tanks (MBTs), the Type 84 Armoured Vehicle Launched Bridge (AVLB) was developed.

Type 84 AVLB in travelling configuration with bridge stowed and front mounted dozer/stabiliser blade in raised position (Poly Technologies)

1334248

The vehicle was originally marketed by China North Industries Corporation (NORINCO), but more recently it has also been marketed by Poly Technologies. The Poly Technologies version is based on the chassis of the Type 79 MBT.

The Type 84 AVLB launches a bridge with a weight capacity of 40,000 kg, but more recent Chinese MBTs, for example the Type 98 and Type 99, weigh far more than the bridge's current weight capacity.

It is therefore considered likely that China has developed an additional AVLB with increased capabilities to cope with these higher-weight MBTs.

Description

The China North Industries Corporation (NORINCO) Type 84 armoured bridgelayer uses the hull and suspension of the Type 69-II MBT. The vehicle has a crew of three with the driver in the normal position seated in the middle of the hull on the left side with a rear opening roof hatch above his position.

The other two are seated inside the hull with a small observation hatch provided for the commander. This is fitted with a periscope and an infra-red night vision device.

The hull of the Type 84 armoured bridgelayer is of all-welded steel armour construction with a high level of protection provided over the frontal arc. As far as it is known, the actual protection level and automotive aspects of the NORINCO type 84 AVLB are identical to those of the Type 69 series MBT.

A hydraulically operated stabiliser blade, used during the final stages of bridgelaying, is mounted under the front of the hull and can also be used for obstacle clearing and dozing operations.

The bridge is of the German Biber pattern with some alterations to the laying system. It is constructed of light steel and is in two halves, one half carried on top of the other. Total length, when deployed, is 18 m, of which 16 m can normally be used and the maximum weight carried on the main trackways is 40,000 kg.

A narrower internal auxiliary trackway is limited to 8,000 kg. The bridgelaying mechanism is driven using hydraulic actuators and rams carried on forward and rear operating assemblies and a rail framework is used to carry and move the bridge into position.

The laying sequence commences with the positioning of the carrier vehicle close to the obstacle to be bridged.

Operations commence with both halves of the bridge being moved backwards along the carrier frame. As this is carried out, the rear of the upper bridge half is raised slightly, followed by the front. This upper bridge half lifts clear of the lower part, allowing the hydraulic system to move the latter forward along the carrier frame as far as it will go on the forward positioning assembly. At this point the hydraulic ram system at the rear of the vehicle is swung downwards to the rear, after which the lower half is moved forward yet again by a ram on the forward assembly. This allows both halves of the welded steel bridge to be lowered to the same level and they can then be joined. The ram system at the rear is then disconnected allowing the forward assembly to push the entire bridge forward to its maximum extent. Before this operation is completed, the stabiliser blade at the front is lowered to the ground to provide support for the vehicle as the bridge is extended.

At the full extension point, the carrier frame is tilted forward by the forward hydraulic assembly until the far end of the bridge touches the ground. The carrier vehicle is then reversed slowly as the near end of the bridge is lowered, after which the carrier frame is disconnected to complete the operation. Recovery is carried out in the opposite sequence.

The bridge can be assembled and carried to the laying point positioned centrally on the carrier frame in order to save time at the actual bridging position.

The time required for a complete bridge launch operation is between four and five minutes and between four and six minutes for recovery. A height difference of 4 m between banks is possible, with the slope limit for the carrier vehicle being 10° under such conditions. The bridge can be launched with the carrier vehicle positioned on a side slope of between 8° and 10°.

The Type 84 armoured bridgelayer can lay its own smoke screen by injecting diesel fuel into the exhaust outlet on the left side of the hull. A 7.62 mm machine gun is provided for local defence.

Standard communications equipment on Chinese Type 84 AVLBs includes a Type 889 radio with a range of 20 to 25 km and a Type 803 intercom set.

Specifications

Type 84 AVLB
Crew: 3
Weight:
  (combat) 38,500 kg
  (without bridge) 30,000 kg
Power-to-weight ratio: 15.06 hp/t (11.23 kW/t)
Length: (with bridge) 9.879 m
Width: (overall) 3.27 m
Height: (with bridge) 2.978 m
Ground clearance: 0.35 m
Track: 2.64 m
Length of track on ground: 3.845 m
Ground pressure: 0.852 kg/cm²
Max speed: (road) 50 km/h
Range: 365 km
Fuel capacity: 930 litres
Fording: 1.1 m
Gradient: 25°
Side slope:
  (travelling) 15°
  (launching bridge) 8-10°
Engine: Model 12150 L-7BW V-12 water-cooled diesel developing 580 hp (433 kW) at 2,000 rpm
Transmission: manual, 5 forward and 1 reverse gears
Electrical system: 24 V
Batteries: 4 × Type 65
Armament: 1 × 7.62 mm MG
Ammunition carried: 1,500 rds

Bridge
Weight: 8,000 kg
Load capacity:
  (main bridge) 40,000 kg
  (auxiliary bridge) 8,000 kg
Length:
  (complete) 18 m
  (usable) 16 m
Width: 3.2 m
Height: 0.78 m
Track width:
  (main bridge) 0.6 m
  (auxiliary bridge) 0.55 m

Status

Production complete. In service with the People's Liberation Army (PLA) and Thailand. More recently Poly Technologies has been marketing the Type 84 AVLB based on a Type 79 MBT chassis, but at this stage it is not known as to whether these would be new build vehicles or surplus Peoples Liberation Army systems.

Contractor

China North Industries Corporation (NORINCO)

NORINCO Light Companying Bridge

Development

China North Industries Corporation (NORINCO) is now marketing the Light Companying Bridge (LCB) which may already be in service with the Peoples Liberation Army (PLA).

In concept, this Chinese bridge system is very similar to the General Dynamics European Land Systems - Germany Rapidly Emplaced Bridge System (REBS) which is currently in service with the US Army.

REBS is integrated on to Oshkosh Defense M1977 (8 × 8) truck chassis and launches a two part bridge over the rear.

When opened out this is 13.8 m long and can be used to span a wet or dry gap of up to 13 m and can take loads of up to Military Load Class 40 (MLC 40).

The NORINCO LCB is a three-part bridge and when opened out is 22.5 m long and can be used to span a wet or dry gap of up to 20.5 m and take tracked vehicles weighing up to 22 tonnes. Each element of the bridge is 7.5 m long.

Description

The NORINCO LCB is transported and launched from a locally manufactured NORINCO (6 × 6) Mercedes-Benz forward control cross-country truck chassis.

This is already used by the PLA for a wide range of roles and missions including towing 155 mm and other field artillery systems and the Type 90 series of NORINCO 122 mm (40-round) artillery rocket systems.

This chassis features powered steering on the front two wheels and is probably fitted with a central tyre inflation system that allows the driver to adjust the tyre pressure from his cab to suit the terrain being crossed.

Mounted to the rear of the chassis is the three part bridge system. On arriving at the gap to be crossed the lower and far bank element is extended over the rear with legs being unfolded.

The second central section is then lowered and mated with the far end bank element of the bridge and this is then moved to the rear.

Finally the near bank element is lowered in line with the first two elements and locked in position. The complete three-part bridge is then positioned over the gap, the launching system disconnected and the laying vehicle removed.

Maximum twist in erection is ±5° with the maximum allowed bank difference being 2 m.

The bridge takes about 10 minutes to position and a similar time to be withdrawn back into the travelling position. It is operated by a crew of three people.

Specifications

NORINCO Light Companying Bridge
Weight of bridgelayer: (total) 21,800 kg
Length: 10.96 m
Width: 3.2 m
Height: 3.64 m
Configuration: 6 × 6
Length of bridge: (overall) 22.5 m
Length of one bridge span: 7.5 m
Gap span of bridge: 20.5 m
Weight of bridge: 6,500 kg
Roadway width: 3.2 m
Track girder width: 1.16 m
Capacity:
   (tracked vehicles) 22,000 kg
   (axle load) 10,000 kg

Status

Development complete. Understood to be in service with the Peoples Liberation Army.

Contractor

China North Industries Corporation (NORINCO)

Czech Republic

MT-55A armoured bridgelayer

Development

The MT-55A armoured bridgelayer was originally a joint Czech/Soviet project designed to replace the earlier MT-34. The MT-34 was based on the World War Two era Russian-designed T-34 tank chassis, which was phased out of service many years ago.

The MT-55A armoured bridgelayer was subsequently adopted by Czechoslovakia, the Soviet Union and other countries. First produced in 1962, it is based on a T-55A tank chassis with the turret removed. The basic chassis is similar to that used for the T-54/T-55 ARVs and, as many vehicles are converted MBTs rather than 'new' vehicles.

Production of the MT-55A armoured bridgelayer was completed many years ago but some countries may have quantities of vehicles surplus to requirements.

Description

There are two types of scissors bridge. The first model has circular holes in the sides of the bridge, similar to those on the bridge carried by the earlier Russian designed MT-34 bridgelayer, while the most common model has solid panels.

MT-55A armoured bridgelayer of the Slovakian Engineer Battalion without bridge and showing laying mechanism (D Caemerlynck)   0092488

MT-55A armoured bridgelayer in travelling configuration (Stefan Marx)
1133701

It is possible to mistake the latter for the former East German BLG-60 armoured bridgelayer. The main feature distinguishing between the two is the bridge surface of the MT-55A, which has a pattern, whereas the BLG-60's is smooth with a plastic covering.

The steel bridge is launched over the front of the vehicle hydraulically by an automatically controlled electrohydraulic system. In an emergency, the hydraulic system can be operated with the aid of three mechanical levers and, if the main diesel engine fails, the tank's batteries can provide sufficient power to launch the bridge.

The launching procedure is as follows: the MT-55A stops short of the gap and raises the bridge slightly from its horizontal travelling position, the launching girder foot is lowered to the ground and the span is raised to the vertical. The bridge is then unfolded and lowered across the gap. The bridge takes three minutes to lay in position and from three to eight minutes to retrieve.

The MT-55A armoured bridgelayer can also be used to carry and launch the 20 m bridge normally used with the MT-72 (based on the more recent T-72 chassis) armoured vehicle launched bridge produced in the Slovak Republic and covered in a separate entry in *Jane's Military Vehicles and Logistics*.

Standard equipment on the MT-55A includes an NBC system, snorkel, inclinometer and other equipment for determining the width of the gap before the bridge is laid in position.

Additional diesel fuel drums can be carried on the rear of the hull and diesel fuel can be injected into the exhaust outlet on the left side of the hull to lay a smoke screen.

Specifications

MT-55 armoured bridgelayer
Crew: 2
Weight:
   (with bridge) 36,000 kg
Power-to-weight ratio: 16.11 hp/t (12.01 kW/t)
Length: (with bridge) 9.88 m
Width: (with bridge) 3.3 m
Height: (with bridge) 3.35 m
Ground clearance: 0.425 m
Track: 2.64 m
Track width: 580 mm
Length of track on ground: 3.84 m
Ground pressure: 0.82 kg/cm²
Max speed:
   (road) 32-35 km/h
   (cross-country) 16-20 km/h
Range: 485-500 km
Fuel capacity: 900 litres
Fording:
   (normal) 1.4 m
   (with preparation) 4 m
Gradient: 30°
Vertical obstacle: 0.7 m
Trench: 2.7 m
Engine: V-55, V-12, water-cooled diesel developing 580 hp (433 kW) at 2,000 rpm
Transmission: manual with 5 forward and 1 reverse gears
Electrical system: 24 V
Batteries: 4, 280 Ah

Bridge
Weight: 6,500 kg
Length:
   (extended) 18 m
   (folded) 9.6 m
Width: 3.34 m
Height: 0.9 m
Track width: (each) 1.15 m
Carrying capacity: 50,000 kg

Status
Production complete. In service with Croatia, Czech Republic, India, Montenegro, Russian Federation (CIS) (568 declared), Serbia and Slovakia. Production was completed some time ago but quantities of MT-55A vehicles are available for sale (from reserve stocks) as and when required.

Contractor
VOP 025 Novy Jicin sp

Finland

New Finnish Leopard 2 Bridging System

Development
Late in 2003 Patria Land & Armament was awarded a study contract by the Finnish Defence Forces (FDF) for a new bridging system for crossing wet and dry obstacles.

Following a competition, RUAG Land Systems of Switzerland, part of the RUAG technology group, was awarded a CHF10 million contract to supply one prototype Armoured Vehicle Launched Bridge (AVLB) based on a modified Krauss-Maffei Wegmann Leopard 2 MBT chassis for trials.

The contract to RUAG Land Systems was awarded by Patria Land & Armament who is the overall prime contractor for the system and acts on behalf of the FDF.

RUAG Land Systems of Switzerland is prime contractor for the sub-systems and the German company Krauss-Maffei Wegmann (previously Military Mobile Bridges) supplies the Leguan bridge and some elements of the launching system.

Under the terms of this contract, the first prototype of the Leopard 2 tank-based AVLB was delivered for extensive user trials in December 2006.

If these are successful then it is expected that a contract for production systems will be awarded. It is understood that the FDF has a requirement for at least six systems based on a Leopard 2 tank chassis.

It is expected that the Finnish defence industry will be involved in the production phase of the Leopard 2 based AVLB programme.

Today the only AVLB used by the FDF is based on the Russian T-54/T-55 tank chassis which has limited gap spanning capability and cannot carry the Leopard 2A4 MBTs used by the FDF which weigh over 55 tonnes.

Effective 1 January 2011, RUAG Land Systems and RUAG Electronics were merged to form a new company called RUAG Defence.

Description
For this armoured vehicle launched bridge application, the complete turret of the Leopard 2A4 MBT has been removed and the hull roof modified to accept the launching system for the LEGUAN bridge. Full details of the LEGUAN are provided in a separate entry in *Jane's Military Vehicles and Logistics*.

This two part Military Load Class 70 (MLC 70) bridge is launched over the front of the vehicle and when opened out is 26 m long and can span a gap of 24 m. Maximum downhill pitch bridge laying is 10 per cent and maximum transversal pitch bridge laying is five per cent.

Bridge laying time is being quoted as five minutes. Mounted at the front of the chassis is a hydraulically operated blade that can be used to clear a path for bridge laying operations and then acts as a stabiliser while the bridge is being launched in position. The vehicle has a crew of two people but space is provided in the armour-protected chassis for an additional crew member.

Specifications
Finnish Leopard 2 armoured bridgelayer

Crew:	2
Length:	13.37 m
Width:	4.01 m
Height:	4 m

Detailed drawing of Leopard 2 MBT chassis modified to accept a two-part bridge that is launched over the front of the vehicle (RUAG Defence)
1296074

Status
Prototype under going trials with Finnish Defence Forces.

Contractor
Patria Land & Armament

France

Nexter Systems AMX-30 armoured bridgelayer

Development
The prototype of the AMX-30 bridgelayer was built by the now Nexter Systems (previously Giat Industries) in 1966 to 1967, but there were initial technical problems and CODER-Industries was formed to take over the manufacturing activities for the bridge.

This bridgelayer was produced only for Saudi Arabia. Production of the base line AMX-30 MBT was completed many years ago and it is no longer marketed.

It should be noted that the AMX-30 MBT has been phased out of service with the French Army, but specialised versions remain in service.

Description
The Class 50 bridge is composed of two hinged elements with removable widening panels and wheel guides. When opened out, it is 22 m long and will span a gap up to 20 m.

The bridge is 3.1 m wide without the widening panels and 3.92 m with them. The bridge is launched hydraulically over the rear of the vehicle and takes about five minutes to lay into position. It can be recovered from either end. The bridge can be launched on relative slopes of 30 per cent with a relative slant reaching 15 per cent.

The basic chassis is almost identical to that of the standard AMX-30 MBT. The hull provides the crew with protection against small arms fire and artillery splinters and is fitted with the same NBC system as the AMX-30 series MBT.

The driver is seated at the front of the vehicle on the left side and is provided with a single-piece hatch cover and three-day periscopes for observation. The centre of these three periscopes can be replaced by a night periscope of the image intensification type.

The commander and bridge operator are seated to the rear of the driver. The diesel powerpack is at the rear of the tank and is separated from the crew compartment by a fireproof bulkhead.

AMX-30 bridgelayer laying its scissors bridge in position in a non-tactical situation
0092489

AMX-30 bridgelayer with scissors bridge starting to unfold over the rear of the vehicle
0064641

The suspension is of the torsion bar type and either side consists of five dual rubber-tyred roadwheels with the drive sprocket at the rear and the idler at the front.

There are five track support rollers which support the inside of the track only. The first two and last two roadwheels are mounted on bogies and are provided with hydraulic shock-absorbers. The upper part of the suspension either side is covered by a skirt that helps to reduce dust.

Nexter Systems Leclerc AVLB

Unlike most armies, the French Army does not deploy a full tracked AVLB to support its fleet of Nexter Systems Leclerc MBTs.

For the export market, Nexter Systems has proposed a Leclerc AVLB that would carry and launch the German Krauss-Maffei Wegmann (previously Military Mobile Bridges) 26 m long LEGUAN bridge which is covered in detail in a separate entry in *Jane's Military Vehicles and Logistics*.

The Nexter Systems Leclerc MBT production line is closed and as of late 2010 the Leclerc AVLB remains a concept.

Specifications

AMX-30 armoured bridgelayer
Crew: 3
Weight:
   (with bridge) 42,500 kg
   (without bridge) 34,000 kg
Power-to-weight ratio:
   (with bridge) 16.47 hp/t (12.28 kW/t)
   (without bridge) 20.59 hp/t (15.35 kW/t)
Length:
   (with bridge) 11.4 m
   (hull only) 6.7 m
Width:
   (with bridge) 3.95 m
   (without bridge) 3.15 m
Height: (with bridge) 4.29 m
Ground clearance: 0.4 m
Track: 2.53 m
Track width: 570 mm
Length of track on ground: 4.12 m
Ground pressure: (with bridge) 0.93 kg/cm^2
Max road speed:
   (with bridge) 50 km/h
   (without bridge) 60 km/h
Range: 600 km
Fuel capacity: 1,100 litres
Fording: 1 m
Gradient: 50%
Side slope: 25%
Vertical obstacle: 0.93 m
Trench: 2.9 m
Engine: Hispano-Suiza HS-110, 12-cylinder, water-cooled, multifuel diesel developing 700 hp (522 kW) at 2,400 rpm
Transmission: automatic with 5 forward gears; a reverse gear gives the same speeds in reverse
Electrical system: 28 V
Batteries: 8 × 12 V, 100 Ah in 2 groups of 4
Armament: nil

Status

Production complete. In service with Saudi Arabia. This system is no longer being marketed.

Contractor

Nexter Systems

CNIM PTA modular assault bridge

Development

To meet French Army requirements *Constructions Industrielles de la Mediterrannee* (CNIM) was awarded a EUR138 million contract in 2003 to develop the *Pont d'Assault Modulaire* (PTA) Modular Assault Bridge.

This is based on a new 10 x 10 cross-country truck chassis that will enable it to operate with the Leclerc MBT already in service with the French Army.

Baseline PTA 2 carries two 14.3 m long bridges one on top of the other that are launched over the front of the vehicle and can take vehicles up to Military Load Class 70 (MLC). As an alternative one 26 m bridge can be carried.

The French Army ordered a total of 18 PTA 2 systems but this has been cut back to 10 systems with first now due to de delivered in 2009 and all should be delivered by 2014.

Each PTA 2 system will consist of one 10 x 10 armoured launcher with two bridges and a semi-trailer truck carrying additional bridges.

Unlike many other countries, the French Army does not operate any tracked AVLB based on an MBT chassis.

CNIM PTA 2 and PTA 3 Modular Assault Bridges in Travelling configuration on their 10 × 10 wheeled chassis (CNIM)   1333643

Description

The PTA modular assault bridge is based on the 10 × 10 cross-country chassis, which is fitted with power steering, independent suspension and a central tyre pressure regulation system that provides a high level of mobility. This allows the driver to adjust the tyre pressure to suit the terrain being crossed.

The standard PTA 2 modular assault bridge carries two bridge sections, one above the other, that are launched over the front of the vehicle. The length of the bridge is decided upon launching. One PTA 2 can launch either two 14.3 m bridges or one 26 m bridge over wet and dry gaps.

All bridges used with the PTA are to Military Load Class 70 (MLC 70) and can be laid and recovered with the crew under complete NBC and armour protection within the launch vehicle.

The PTA 2 can launch one section in three minutes and two sections in five minutes, while the PTA 3 can launch one section in four minutes, two sections in six minutes and three sections in seven minutes.

Variants

PTA 3

Another proposed version is the PTA 3 that could carry three 10.5 m bridges or 1 × 10.5 m and 1 × 18,7 m or one 27 m bridge. In each case the bridge is launched with the crew under complete armour and NBC protection.

AMAB airportable modular assault bridge

CNIM has also studied a more compact version called Pont d'Assault Modulaire Aerotransportable (AMAB) which would be air transportable in an A400M aircraft.

This consists of an 8 × 8 chassis with two 10.5 m long bridges one above the other each of which can be laid in five minutes. The launching system and bridge are derived from the PTA 2.

Specifications

PTA modular assault bridge

Model	PTA 2	PTA 3
Crew:	2	2
Configuration:	10 × 10	10 × 10
Weight: (combat)	51,000 kg	53,000 kg
Power-to-weight ratio:	15.68 hp/t (11.70 kW/t)	15.09 hp/t (11.26 kW/t)
Length: (chassis)	15.09 m	15 m
Width:	4 m	4 m
Height:	4 m	4 m
Max speed:	70 km/h	70 km/h
Range: (approx)	900 km	900 km
Powerpack:	V-8 diesel developing 800 hp (597 kW)	V-8 diesel developing 800 hp (597 kW)
Number of sections:	2	3
Length of each section:	14.3 m	10.5 m
Bridging capacity:	2 × 14.3 m or 1 × 26 m	3 × 10.5 m or 1 × 18.7 m and 1 × 10.5 m or 1 × 27 m

Model	PTA 2	PTA 3
Launching time:		
(1 section bridge)	3 min	4 min
(2 section bridge)	5 min	6 min
(3 section bridge)	not applicable	7 min

Status

Development almost complete with deliveries running from 2009 through to 2014.

Contractor

Constructions Industrielles de la Méditerranée (CNIM)

Enquiries to

CNIM Head Office

CNIM PAR 70 towed support bridge MLC 70

Development

The CNIM PAR 70 towed support bridge MLC 70 is a recent development which involves many existing in-service and fully developed components. The intention is to produce a fast deployment close support bridge, 19.5 m long, with a bridging classification of MLC 70.

The launch/retrieve system involved is similar to the one on the *Pont Automoteur d'Accompagnement* (PAA) self-propelled bridge system.

The scissor bridge is the PAA bridge upgraded to MLC 70 and developed by CNIM under contract to the Delegation Generale pour l'Armement. The semi-trailer axle assembly is taken from the PFM floating bridge system which has been in French Army service since 1985.

The non-specific truck tractor involved may be a 6 × 6 or 6 × 4 unit. The Renault Trucks Defense TRM 10 000 (6 × 6), Astra BM 309, (6 × 6), Steyr 24M (6 × 6) and TATRA 815 (8 × 8) are typical examples. The only completely new elements in the system are a hydraulic power-generating set and the semi-trailer frame.

The Renault Trucks Defense TRM 10 000 (6 × 6) truck is used for a wide range of roles by the French Army including cargo carrier, towing 155 mm artillery, recovery and as a tractor truck towing elements of the PFM bridge system, covered in detail in a separate entry in *Jane's Military Vehicles and Logistics*. This has been in service with the French Army for some years. It should be noted that production of the TRM 10 000 (6 × 6) military truck is now complete.

Description

The CNIM PAR 70 towed support bridge MLC 70 has a twin trackway bridge formed from two folding symmetrical sections. When fully opened, the bridge is 19.5 m long and 3.6 m wide, enabling gaps up to 18 m wide to be bridged. Construction involves light alloys and the load classification of the PAA upgraded scissors bridge is MLC 70.

As the non-specific truck tractor prime mover involved provides a measure of stability during bridge-laying and recovery operations, it has to weigh a minimum of 12 tonnes; for towing 330 hp is required.

For laying, the semi-trailer carrying the system is reversed to the launch point. A hydraulic power-generating set located over the semi-trailer gooseneck provides the power to the launch/retrieve system.

This involves a stabiliser leg under the point of launch, a bridge-raising prism, a winch and two deployment jacks within the bridge to provide the power to open it once raised past the vertical. While the bridge unfolds, the prism continues its rotation until the bridge is fully unfolded in the horizontal position. In this condition, stabilisation is provided by the weight of the semi-trailer and the prime mover. The bridge is laid on the bank by a further rotation of the prism. The stabiliser leg is then retrieved and the bridge is positioned on the home bank by using the winch.

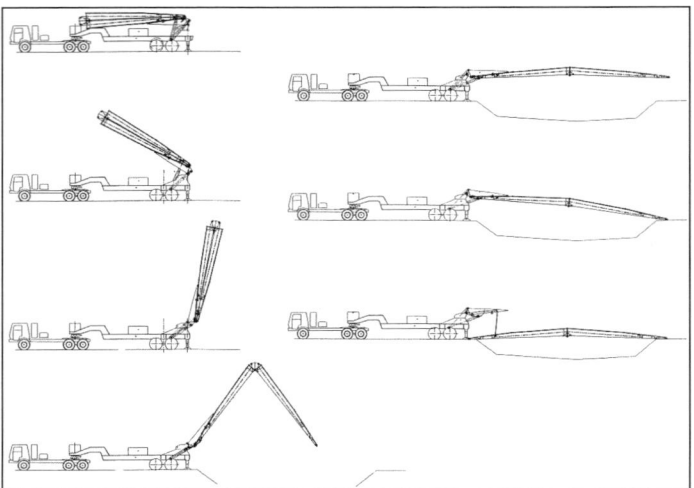

Laying sequence for the CNIM PAR 70 Towed Support Bridge MLC 70, from top left downwards and then from top right   0512322

Once the bridge is emplaced, two members of the three-person crew (the third member is the driver) can add extra side plates and guidance lamps on posts; these increase the overall emplaced bridge width to 4 m. The side plates and posts are carried on the semi-trailer. Each trackway is 1.523 m wide. Maximum difference in the level between banks is ±3 m.

The time required to deploy the bridge is six minutes. Recovery can be from either side of the gap involved.

Optional equipment for the semi-trailer can include an all-wheel drive (10 × 10) system (including trailer wheel motorisation) and a central tyre inflation system, where applicable. Another option is a pipeline crossing bridge version, which includes four raising supports that allow the bridge and access ramps to be raised manually.

CNIM Assault Treadway Bridge MLC 65

This was developed as a private venture by CNIM and was first shown in 1990 but never entered production or service. Marketing of this system by CNIM has now ceased.

Specifications

PAR 70 towed support bridge MLC 70
(Provisional)
Weight: 9,000 kg
Length: (unfolded) 19.5 m
Span: <19 m
Width:
  (overall, emplaced) 4 m
  (roadway) 4 m
  (trackways, each) 1.523 m
Height: (emplaced) 1.15 m
Max difference in bank levels: ±3 m
Load classification: MLC 70
Deployment time: 6 min

Bridge and vehicle, loaded
Crew: 3
Weight:
  (complete) approx 35,000 kg
  (semi-trailer) approx 23,000 kg
Length: <18 m
Width: 4 m

CNIM PAR 70 Towed Support Bridge MLC 70 deployed (two units) with AMX-30 MBT crossing   0092490

CNIM PAR 70 towed support bridge being launched from its semi-trailer towed by a Renault Trucks Defense TRM 10 000 (6 × 6) tractor trailer (CNIM)   1333644

Height: approx 3.9 m
Max speed:
  (road) 80 km/h
  (cross-country) 25 km/h

Status
Prototype. As of late 2010, production of this system had yet to commence.

Contractor
Constructions Industrielles de la Méditerranée (CNIM)

Enquiries to
CNIM Head Office

CEFA Engin de Franchissement de l'Avant (EFA)

Development
The *Engin de Franchissement de l'Avant* (EFA) was originally known as the *Matériel Amphibie de Franchissement* (MAF). It was under competitive development as the replacement for the Gillois system then used by the French Army (now withdrawn from service).

The Etablissement Technique d'Angers was in charge of the evaluation of two prototypes and overall project management was under the Direction Technique des Armements Terrestres.

CEFA and DCAN of Lorient each developed and built a prototype of the EFA and following extensive trials the EFA from CEFA was selected by the French Army. Final trials were completed in 1987 and the French Army ordered 80 units (later reduced to 39) to replace the Gillois bridge and ferry system.

The EFA is also referred to as the Forward Crossing Vehicle with first production units being delivered to the French Army in 1992.

In 2006 production of an enhanced version of the EFA commenced for a undisclosed country in the Middle East who placed an order for 10 units with all of these completed by 2009.

Description
The light alloy hull of the EFA contains the power pack, hydraulic generator, axles, propeller and the fully enclosed drivers cabin. When afloat, the four large rubber-tyred road wheels are retracted into the hull of the vehicle. This helps reduce drag and therefore improves the speed of the vehicle whilst afloat.

Compartmentalised floats, which are inflated by compressors, are fixed on lateral flats, which are hydraulically deployed.

At each end of the vehicle is a scissors type ramp, which allows for forward embarkation and disembarkation of vehicles.

The hull and ramps of the EFA are made of welded aluminium alloy. In the road configuration, a 12 m folded ramp is jointed on the top of the vehicle at each end.

Before entering the water, the unit deploys hinged flaps on each side and the floats are inflated. The vehicle has four driving and steering wheels. The tyre pressure can be adjusted by the driver while the vehicle is moving as a central tyre pressure system is fitted as standard.

When afloat the unit is propelled in the water by two Schottel swivelling propellers (pump jets) which are situated one at each end of the hull and rotatable through 360° to allow navigation lengthwise or crosswise.

The EFA can be used as a bridge, a ferry or as a raft. When being used as a bridge one unit has a span of 23.6 m. It can be used in rivers flowing at speeds of up to 2.5 m/s. A ferry (one unit) can carry an MLC 70 MBT.

A raft made up of two units can be loaded up to 150 tons provided that the load is distributed over the loading surface. The total area of each EFA is 96 m².

The required number of EFA can be connected together to provide an MLC 70 bridge as long as required. For example, a 100 m bridge requires four units and is built in under 10 minutes.

Engin de Franchissement de l'Avant EFA in road-travelling configuration
0121588

Engin de Franchissement de l'Avant (EFA) ferry carrying a Nexter Systems Leclerc MBT
0044086

A floating bridge formed by four Engin de Franchissement de l'Avant (EFA) units, with the lead vehicle being a EBG combat engineer tractor 0044089

The diesel power pack compartment of the EFA is provided with an automatic fire detection and suppression system while the fully enclosed cab has an NBC system.

Variants
The 10 EFA units recently built for the export market have a number of modifications to meet the specific operational requirements of the customer.

These include the installation of an MTU 8V 199 TE diesel developing 760 hp at 2,300 rpm, STANAG 4569 Level 2 armour protection for the cabin and the installation of an air conditioning system for the cab to allow the system to be operated in higher ambient temperatures.

The new export version has a combat weight of between 45 and 46 tonnes.

Specifications
Amphibious bridging system
Crew: 4
Weight: (total) 44,000 kg
Power-to-weight ratio: 16.59 hp/t (12.37 kW/t)
Length:
  (travelling) 12.60 m
  (as bridge) 23.68 m
  (as ferry) 34.55 m
Width:
  (travelling) 3.6 m
  (airbags in position) 6.8 m
Height: (travelling) 4.095 m
Track: 2.17 m
Wheelbase: 6.6 m
Max speed:
  (road) 85 km/h
  (water, with MLC 70 load) 3.1 m/s
  (water, empty) 3.8 m/s
Range:
  (road) approx 700 km
  (in water) approx 12 h
Fording: (without preparation) 1.2 m
Gradient: 50%
Side slope: 30%
Engine: Baudoin 12 F 120 SR water-cooled diesel developing 730 hp (544 kW) at 2,700 rpm
Suspension: hydropneumatic with level correction
Tyres: 26.5 × 25 XL
Electrical system: 24 V

Status
The French Army has taken delivery of 39 units and an undisclosed export customer in the Middle East is taking delivery of 10 units which have now been delivered.

Contractor
Chaudronnerie Et Forges d'Alsace (CEFA)

Germany

Krauss-Maffei Wegmann Panzerschnellbrücke 2/Bruglegger MLC 70 (PSB 2)

Development

To meet the operational requirements of the German and Royal Netherlands armies, Krauss-Maffei Wegmann (with the bridging element previously known as Military Mobile Bridges) has developed the Panzerschnellbrucke 2 (German Army designation)/Bruglegger (Royal Netherlands Army designation) Military Load Class 70 (MILC 70) Armoured Vehicle Launched Bridge (AVLB).

The first of two pre-production AVLB systems were completed late in 2002 and then delivered to the German Army for extensive trials.

The total German Army requirement is for 35 units plus 66 bridge sets while the Royal Netherlands Army requirement is for 14 units plus 28 bridge sets.

As of late 2010, no production orders had been placed for PSB 2 Leopard 2 based bridgelayer. It is understood that a more cost effective system, perhaps using the latest LEGUAN bridge system on a Leopard 2 chassis, may be under consideration.

This has already been developed and tested by Krauss-Maffei Wegmann. Details are provided in a separate entry in *Jane's Military Vehicles and Logistics.*

Description

The PSB 2/BRL MLC 70 system features three bridge modules carried on a redesigned Leopard 2 MBT chassis; each bridge module is 9.7 m long. The bridgelayer can lay the bridge modules either individually or coupled together with a normal load carrying capacity of MLC 70 (MLC 100 with caution).

The bridge modules are 4 m wide and form bridge lengths of 9.7 m (one module), 18.7 m (two modules) or 27.8 m (three modules). All three modules can be laid in about eight minutes.

The bridge modules are manufactured using a weldable aluminium alloy. Each module weighs approximately 4.8 tonnes.

Specifications

Bruglegger MLC 70 (PSB 2)
Weight:
    (bridgelayer) approx 61,800 kg
    (bridge modules) approx 4,800 kg
Length:
    (bridge modules) 9.7, 18.7 and 27.8 m
Width:
    (bridge) 4 m
Height:
    (bridge) 0.65 m
Classification: MLC 70/100

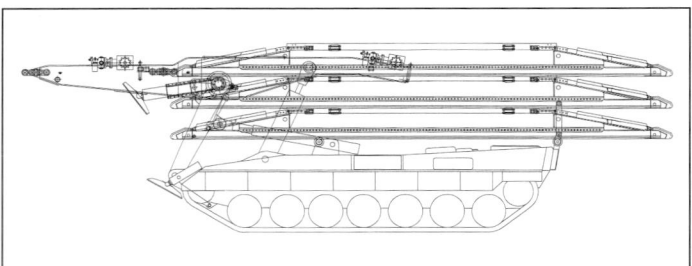

Outline drawing of Panzerschnellbrücke 2/Bruglegger MLC 70 in travelling configuration   0044088

PSB2 modular bridge system integrated onto a Leopard 2 MBT chassis in travelling configuration and showing three bridges stacked on top of each other (Christopher F Foss)   1330577

Status

Prototypes being tested. Total expected procurement was to be the order of 35 for Germany 35 and 14 for the Netherlands. As of late 2010 no production orders had been placed for the PSB 2, system. For more information please refer to the development section.

Contractor

Krauss-Maffei Wegmann GmbH & Co KG (previously known as Military Mobile Bridges (MMB) GmbH).

Krauss-Maffei Wegmann LEGUAN bridgelayer

Description

The LEGUAN mobile bridgelayer with its 26 m Military Load Class 70 (MLC 70) bridge can be transported and launched from a variety of chassis, tracked and wheeled.

The LEGUAN technical concept aims at higher efficiency, reliability and compatibility with different chassis types.

The standard chassis is a modified MAN ÖAF 36.422 VFAE 8 × 8 all-terrain truck chassis, with a low-set driver's cab. Other wheeled and tracked chassis can be used as carrier vehicles.

The LEGUAN bridge and bridgelayer are attached to the vehicle via an auxiliary frame on which the bridge can be pushed out over the rear of the vehicle.

The LEGUAN bridge consists of four interchangeable wheel tread girders with a flat ramp design, each 13 m long, 2 m wide and weighing 2,500 kg.

Bolt connections join the bridge girders and, when travelling, the bridge halves lie one on top of the other. The laying equipment consists of the laying arm at the rear of the shifting frame which moves the bridge longitudinally by means of a roller guide and a geared drive.

The top bridge half is taken up by an arm at the front end and is supported by an auxiliary arm at the rear. The bridge can be laid with a traverse and longitudinal inclination of up to 10 per cent.

Laying is carried out automatically with the two-person crew monitoring the sequence. No preparation of the crossing site is normally required.

The laying sequence commences with the vehicle reversing to the bank until the end of the shifting frame is approximately 7.5 m from the edge. After raising the top bridge half, which is suspended at the front in the slewing support arm and, with the roller at its rear resting on the top chord of the lower wheel girder, the lower bridge half is advanced and then lowered by 10 per cent.

It is held at the front by the slewing support arm and at the rear by the coupling support arm. The bridge halves are then coupled automatically by lowering the coupling supporting arm.

The bridge is then pushed back until its centre of gravity is over the two rear axles of the carrying vehicle, where it is held until the shifting frame has been moved under the bridge and the hydraulic supports have been lowered.

The next step is for the bridge to be fully advanced, at which point it is clamped in the laying arm by the roller carriage. At this stage the ramp tip is placed on the far bank. This removes the load from the rollers and the laying arm can then be removed to lower the bridge.

For the final stage, the supports are retracted and the shifting frame is moved back. The bridge is then ready for use. The entire laying process takes approximately eight minutes. Reloading the bridge is carried out in the reverse order and can be carried out from either bank.

The bridge is constructed from standard commercial aluminium alloy, grade Al/Zn/Mg (94.5/4.5/1 per cent) and is designed to meet US Standards for the bridge life.

Variants

Leopard 1 chassis with LEGUAN
Details are given in a separate entry in *Jane's Military Vehicles and Logistics.* This is tracked version currently being marketed by Krauss-

Sisu (10 × 10) cross-country truck chassis fitted with a Krauss-Maffei Wegmann LEGUAN bridge and associated launching system (Christopher F Foss)   1296064

Norwegian Army LEGUAN (8 × 8) bridgelayer in travelling configuration
(Krauss-Maffei Wegmann)   1296073

Maffei Wegmann. The most recent customer being the Turkish Land
Forces Command (TLFC) who have taken delivery of 36 systems.

M48/M60 with LEGUAN
Details of this are given in a separate entry in *Jane's Military Vehicles and
Logistics*. This version is in service with Spain under the name of Lanzador.

M1 with LEGUAN
Details of this model, which is only in service with the US Army, is
provided in a separate entry in *Jane's Military Vehicles and Logistics*.
Prime contractor for this programme, which is now complete, was General
Dynamics Land Systems. In US Army service, this is called the Wolverine
Heavy Assault Bridge.

Leopard 2 with LEGUAN
This has been developed under the leadership of Patria Land &
Armaments to meet the requirements of the Finnish Defence Force. Details
are provided in a separate entry in *Jane's Military Vehicles and Logistics*.

Finnish 10 × 10 truck launched LEGUAN
The Finish Defence Force deploys the LEGUAN bridge integrated onto a
locally developed SISU (10 × 10) cross-country truck chassis. This is fitted
with a mine and armour protected cab.

A total of nine chassis have been built with deliveries completed in 2008.
The complete system (chassis, launching system and bridge) has a gross
vehicle weight of 43 tonnes.

Norwegian LEGUAN upgrade
In July 2007 a EUR9 million contract was awarded to Krauss-Maffei
Wegmann by the Norwegian Defence Procurement Agency to upgrade the
LEGUAN bridgelaying systems currently deployed by the Norwegian
Army.

Under the terms of this contract, these LEGUAN systems have now
undergone a comprehensive modernisation programme that focused on
the installation of a new electronic control system for the launching
system.

Specifications
LEGUAN bridgelayer
Crew: 2
Configuration: 8 × 8
Weight:
   (vehicle) 25,200 kg
   (bridge - approx) 10,000 kg
   (total - approx) 35,600 kg
Power-to-weight ratio:
   (total - approx) 11.57 hp/t (8.42 kW/t)
Length:
   (overall, travelling with bridge) 15.3 m
   (overall, without bridge) 13.4 m
Width:
   (overall, with bridge) 4.01 m
   (without bridge) 3.15 m
Height:
   (overall with bridge) 4 m
   (overall without bridge) 2.73 m
   (top of cab) 2.285 m
Ground clearance: 0.45 m
Wheelbase: 1.6 + 3.25 + 1.55 m
Angle of approach/departure: 20/25°
Max road speed: 71.5 km/h
Range: 600 km
Fuel capacity: 400 litres
Max gradient: 60%

Engine: D 2866LD/422 water-cooled diesel developing 412 hp (307 kW) at
2,000 rpm
Transmission: WSK 400 + 16 S 151
Transfer box: 2-speed 1700-1
Steering: ball and nut, ZF Model 8046
Turning circle: 29 m
Suspension: Koni adjustable shock-absorbers with stabilisers on front
and rear axles
Brakes:
   (main) dual circuit air
   (parking) mechanical on rear wheels
   (engine) pneumatically actuated on exhaust
Tyres: Michelin 16.00 R 20
Electrical system: 24 V
Batteries: 2 × 12 V, 173 Ah each

Bridge
Classification: Class 70
Weight: (approx) 10,000 kg
Length:
   (bridge) 26 m
   (effective span) 25 m
Width:
   (bridge) 4.01 m
   (wheel tread girder) 1.555 m
Height:
   (bridge centre) 1.1 m
   (ramp tip) 0.075 m

Status
In production. In service with Belgium, Finland, Greece, Indonesia,
Norway, Singapore, South Africa, Spain, Turkey, United States (based on
M1 Abrams MBT chassis and called Wolverine), Venezuela and other
countries.

Contractor
Krauss-Maffei Wegmann GmbH & Co KG (previously known as Military
Mobile Bridges (MMB) GmbH).

Krauss-Maffei Wegmann Leopard 1 LEGUAN AVLB

Development
In December 1995, the Norwegian Army Matériel Command awarded the
then Military Mobile Bridges (now part of Krauss-Maffei Wegmann) a
contract to convert nine surplus Leopard 1 MBT chassis into the Armoured
Vehicle Launched Bridge configuration (AVLB). A total of 13 LEGUAN
bridges were also ordered, each bridge 26 m long, rated to the Military
Load Class 70 (MLC 70) load classification.

The bridges are fitted with special adapters allowing them to be
incorporated in ferries. Krauss-Maffei Wegmann undertook the Leopard 1
MBT conversions and the integration of the bridgelaying equipment.

The first example was handed over to the Norwegian Army in December
1997. Deliveries are now complete.

Under a contract placed in 1999, the Belgian Army has taken delivery of
nine surplus Leopard 1 MBT chassis converted into AVLBs. Also supplied
were a total of 16 LEGUAN bridges, each bridge 26 m long, rated to the
MLC 70 load classification.

*Norwegian Army Leopard 1 LEGUAN AVLB without bridge and showing
front-mounted dozer/stabiliser blade* (Richard Stickland)   1044341

Laying Phases

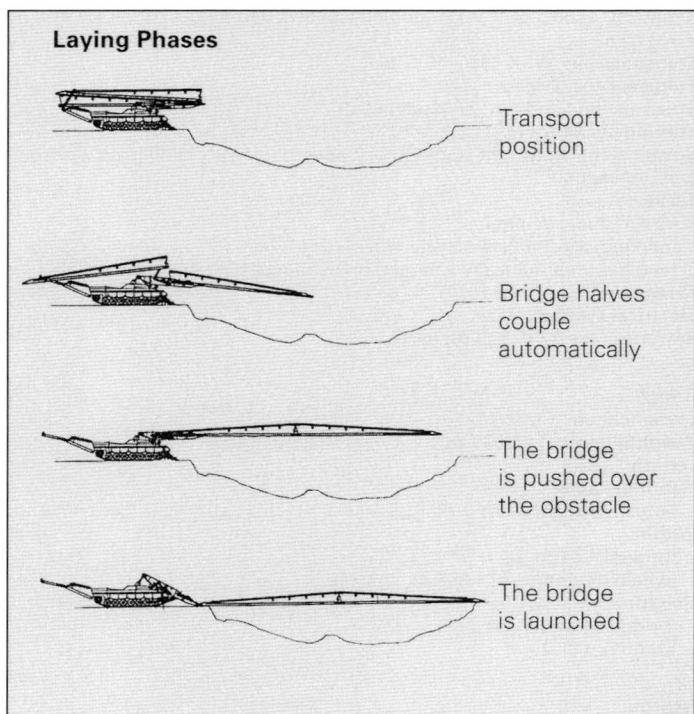

Transport position

Bridge halves couple automatically

The bridge is pushed over the obstacle

The bridge is launched

Leopard 1 MBT chassis fitted with LEGUAN 26 m bridge, showing method of launching 0569678

Leopard 1 LEGUAN AVLB in travelling configuration (Krauss-Maffei Wegmann) 1334254

The Hellenic Army has now placed a contract with Krauss-Maffei Wegmann of Germany for the supply of 170 Leopard 2A6 series Main Battle Tanks (MBTs) as well as 24 Büffel Armoured Recovery Vehicles (ARVs) and 12 Armoured Vehicle Launched Bridges (AVLBs).

The AVLB is based on surplus Leopard 1 series MBT chassis and fitted with a new LEGUAN bridge system that is already in service with a number of countries.

The Finnish Defence Force is currently testing a prototype of the Leopard 2A4 MBT chassis fitted with a LEGUAN system.

The Finnish Defence Force also has the LEGUAN bridge system integrated onto a locally designed and built SISU (10 × 10) cross-country truck chassis. This is also fitted with a mine and armour-protected cab.

A total of nine 10 × 10 chassis were built with deliveries completed in 2008. The complete system (chassis, launching system and bridge) has a gross vehicle weight of 43 tonnes.

The latest customer for the Leopard 1 based LEGUAN AVLB is the Turkish Land Forces Command (TLFC). The agreement signed in November 2008 was for a total of 36 Leopard 1 AVLB fitted with the LEGUAN bridge (26 m long, MLC 70).

Description

The Leopard 1 LEGUAN AVLB is based on the hull and chassis of the Krauss-Maffei Wegmann Leopard 1 MBT with all main and subcomponents unchanged. Various items from the removed turret and other components are modernised and integrated into the AVLB.

For the conversion, the driver's hatch remains unchanged while the commander's hatch is adopted from the MBT turret.

The driver's seat also remains unchanged, while the commander's seat is adopted from the Leopard 1 MBT turret. A hatch providing access to the hydraulic and stowage compartment is of a new form.

Leopard 1 LEGUAN AVLB of the Hellenic Army in travelling configuration and showing dozer/stabiliser blade raised at front of chassis (Krauss-Maffei Wegmann) 1405691

Leopard 1 LEGUAN AVLB laying its two part bridge over the front of the chassis and showing dozer/stabiliser blade lowered to the ground (Krauss-Maffei Wegmann) 1405690

The fording depth is 1.8 m while sealing, NBC protection, bilge pumps and heating remain the same as the Leopard 1 series MBT, as does most of the electrical system apart from extra lighting.

Other unchanged systems carried over include the power pack, although the dual-circuit braking system is reinforced to accommodate the increased overall weight of approximately 50 tonnes.

Some adjustments are necessary to the torsion bar suspension while the tracks are to Diehl 640 A standard.

Some extra passive ballistic protection is added externally and an anti-spall liner is provided for the crew compartment.

The 26 m LEGUAN aluminium alloy bridge follows standard LEGUAN construction and laying procedures. The main change from the standard procedures is that, before laying, a hydraulically-operated tiltable support blade is lowered under driver control from the front of the hull. The support blade can be deployed as a light dozer blade for light obstacle clearing.

For laying, a laying arm supports and guides the LEGUAN bridge during transport and launching. The arm is hinged to the hull and positioned by a hydraulic cylinder. The arm is a welded box-type structure carrying the roller carriages for guiding the bridge, the bridge advance unit and the mechanism for bridge unlocking.

A rear arm holds the bridge at the rear end during transport and guides it for coupling and uncoupling. This arm is connected to the hull by four bolts and is actuated by a hydraulic cylinder.

An electronic control system monitors the position of all drive units, operates the programmed laying/retrieval sequences and indicates any faults.

For laying, once the AVLB is in position with the support blade lowered, the rear arm swings into the vertical position. It raises the rear of the upper bridge half allowing the lower half to move forward until it reaches the coupling position. An auxiliary arm then rises to support the forward part of the upper bridge, as the laying arm moves down to move the lower half to the coupling position. The rear arm then swings down for the upper half to assume the coupling position, so that, when the auxiliary arm is lowered, the two bridge halves can be automatically coupled.

At this point the rear arm is unlatched allowing the entire bridge to be moved forward. Once fully extended, the far end is lowered on to the opposite bank. Tilting the laying arm lowers the nearest end of the bridge on to the near bank. Once the support blade is raised, the bridge is ready for use. Launching and retrieval times can be less than five minutes.

Variants

M48/M60 MBT chassis with LEGUAN
Details of this are given in a separate entry in *Jane's Military Vehicles and Logistics* and this version is in service with Spain under the name of Lanzador.

M1 MBT chassis with LEGUAN
Details of this model, which is only in service with the US Army are provided in a separate entry in *Jane's Military Vehicles and Logistics*.

Prime contractor for this programme, which is now complete, is General Dynamics Land Systems. In US Army service this is called the Wolverine Heavy Assault Bridge.

Leopard 2 MBT chassis with LEGUAN
This has been developed under the leadership of Patria Land & Armaments to meet the requirements of the Finnish Defence Force. Details are provided in a separate entry in *Jane's Military Vehicles and Logistics*.

Finnish 10 × 10 truck launched LEGUAN
The Finish Defence Force deploys the LEGUAN bridge integrated onto a locally developed SISU (10 × 10) cross-country truck. Details of this are provided in a separate entry in *Jane's Military Vehicles and Logistics*.

Specifications

Leopard 1 LEGUAN AVLB
Crew: 2
Weight:
   (with bridge - approx) 50,000 kg
Power-to-weight ratio: 16.60 hp/t (12.38 kW/t)
Length:
   (with bridge) 13.37 m
   (without bridge, rear arm in transport position) 12.705 m
Width:
   (with bridge) 4.01 m
   (without bridge) 3.37 m
   (dozer blade) 3.25 m
Height:
   (with bridge) 3.94 m
Fording: (approx) 1.8 m
Engine: MTU MB 838 CaM multifuel developing 830 hp (619 kW) at 2,200 rpm
Transmission: ZF 4 HP 250 with hydraulic torque converter
Suspension: torsion bar
Electrical system: 24 V
Bridge weight: 10,800 kg
Load classification: MLC 70
Bridge length: (extended) 26 m
Gap spanned: 24 m
Bridge width: 4.01 m
Roadway width: (each) 1.55 m

Status

Production as required. In service with Belgium (nine chassis plus 16 bridges), Finland (prototype on Leopard 2 chassis), Greece (12 on Leopard 1 MBT chassis), Malaysia (PT-91 chassis), Norway (nine chassis plus 13 bridges) and Turkey (36 on Leopard 1 MBT chassis).

Contractor

Krauss-Maffei Wegmann GmbH & Co KG (previously known as Military Mobile Bridges (MMB) GmbH).

Leopard 2 LEGUAN Armoured Vehicle Launched Bridge

Development

The Krauss-Maffei Wegmann (previously Military Mobile Bridges) LEGUAN bridge system has already been integrated onto a wide range of tracked and wheeled chassis.

Based on this prior extensive experience in the design, development, integration and production of the LEGUAN bridge system, Krauss-Maffei Wegmann have completed development of the Leopard 2 LEGUAN Armoured Vehicle Launched Bridge (AVLB).

Development of the Leopard 2 LEGUAN AVLB is now complete but as of late 2010 no production orders had been placed.

This is a potential replacement for the PSB2 AVLB also based on the Leopard 2 MBT chassis which is covered in detail in a separate entry in *Jane's Military Vehicles and Logistics*.

Description

The Leopard 2 LEGUAN AVLB is based on a Krauss-Maffei Wegmann Leopard 2 chassis with its turret removed and replaced by a bridge launching system. Launched over the front of the chassis, the bridges can be either of the standard LEGUAN bridge types; a single 26 m, or two 14 m bridges.

Leopard 2 MBT chassis modified to transport and launch two LEGUAN 14 m bridges. In this photograph one bridge has been laid over the front of the chassis with a second bridge being carried ready for launch (Krauss-Maffei Wegmann)   1334258

Leopard 2 MBT chassis modified to transport and launch one LEGUAN 26 m bridge shown in travelling configuration. Note front mounted dozer/stabiliser blade (Krauss-Maffei Wegmann)   1405689

Details of the launching method, which is identical to that of the Krauss-Maffei Wegmann Leopard 1 LEGUAN AVLB, is covered in a separate entry in *Jane's Military Vehicles and Logistics*.

Specifications

No specifications are at present available.

Status

Development complete. Ready for production on receipt of orders.

Contractor

Krauss-Maffei Wegmann GmbH & Co KG

Krauss-Maffei Wegmann M47/M60 LEGUAN armoured bridgelayer

Development

The Krauss-Maffei Wegmann (previously Military Mobile Bridges) M47/M60 LEGUAN armoured bridgelayer is an adaptation of a surplus M47 or M60 MBT chassis, designed to carry and launch the standard MLC 70 26 m LEGUAN bridge, which is covered in detail in a separate entry in *Jane's Military Vehicles and Logistics*.

One trial M47 was successfully tested in Spain in co-operation with Peugeot Talbot España SA. It is based on an M47 MBT chassis and known as the VLPD-26/70 E 'Lanzador'. Series production carried out together with Peugeot España started during 1997.

A total of 12 General Dynamics Land Systems-built units were built for the Spanish Army all based on a M60 series MBT chassis with final deliveries taking place in 1999. The conversion can also be carried out on MBTs such as the Centurion, Leopard 1/2, M1 Abrams and other MBTs.

In the longer term it is expected that Spain will replace this vehicle with a new AVLB based on a Leopard 2A4 MBT chassis.

The Spanish Army has now taken delivery of 219 locally built Leopard 2A6 MBTs which are called the Leopardo 2E by the Spanish Army. In addition it has taken delivery of a total of 16 Büffel Armoured Recovery Vehicles (ARV).

M47 LEGUAN armoured bridgelayer in its Spanish VLPD-26/70 E 'Lanzador' form in travelling configuration　　1133704

Prior to this Spain purchased 108 Leopard 2A4 from the German Army and it is expected that eventually some of these will be converted into specialised AVLB (to replace the Lanzador).

Some may also be used for a new armoured engineer vehicle (to replace the currently deployed CZ-10/25E Alacran based on a surplus M60 chassis).

Description

The M47/M60 LEGUAN conversion utilises as many standard LEGUAN components as possible. However, the overall bridge launch position is forward instead of to the rear as on the 8 × 8 wheeled LEGUAN.

This entails displacing the normal launch components through 180°, but the basic LEGUAN launch procedures are maintained.

The bridgelaying US designed and built surplus M47 or M60 tank chassis has to undergo some modifications in addition to the removal of the turret. The laying components include a traversing laying arm on the hull roof, roller carriages, bridge advance unit, auxiliary arms and a hydraulic cylinder supported by the hull.

A rear arm is used for coupling the bridge halves and there are hydraulic and electrical switching and control components inside the hull.

Modification to the tank hull includes removing the top frontal armour plate and front roofplate together with the turret ring. New armour and roofplates with hatches are welded into place and extra plates are added along the sidewalls and engine cover.

A new forward support blade, described as an outrigger system, is added to the front hull. Once lowered by two hydraulic cylinders, the support blade levels the laying vehicle on adverse slopes and provides support during bridgelaying operations.

The LEGUAN laying arm rests in a bearing welded to the hull roof, with its traversing cylinder pivoting on girders welded inside the hull. A line and cable bushing close to the bearing provides protection for electrical cables and hydraulic lines connecting the control unit inside the hull and the switches and actuators in the laying arm. Extra welded stiffening webs transmit loads from the bearing to the rear roofplate and the area around the traversing cylinder is kept watertight by a plastic cover.

A rear arm assembly is secured to baseplates welded to the top rear corners of the sidewalls. The laying arm is supported by the hull roof and controlled by a hydraulic cylinder inside the hull.

The laying arm accommodates the roller carriages for the bridge as well as the bridge advance unit and auxiliary arms, for use during the coupling of the bridge halves.

A two-element outrigger arm is provided at the hull rear to assist the coupling of the bridge sections; this arm can be lowered to a travelling position when a bridge is not being carried. The rear arm base also supports the bridge.

On arrival at a bridge launch site, the bridgelayer is driven to the point to be bridged and the support blade is lowered and extended to ensure the bridge is in a horizontal position. Forward slopes up to 20 per cent up and down can be accommodated, as can transverse slopes up to 10 per cent. The maximum downwards laying step is 0.8 m.

To commence the laying operation, the rear end outrigger arm is swung vertically to lift the bridge upper section. The bridge advance unit moves the lower bridge section forward towards the coupling position as the auxiliary arms move upwards to lift the upper section.

At that point the rear end outrigger arm is lowered and the laying arm swings the front section ready for coupling. Claw couplings then slide into each other and the rear end outrigger is disengaged. The laying arm swings upwards and coupling is complete.

The bridge advance unit can then move the complete bridge forward into position. Once fully extended, the laying arm lowers first the far end and then the near end, ready for the support blade to be raised and the laying arm disengaged from the bridge. The bridgelayer can then withdraw. Only two crew, the driver and commander, are involved in the laying operation, which takes between 3.5 and four minutes.

Specifications

VLPD-26/70 E 'Lanzador'
(M60 MBT chassis)
Crew: 2
Weight:
  (with bridge) 50,370 kg
  (without bridge) 43,000 kg
Power-to-weight ratio:
  (with bridge) 15.09 hp/t (11.25 kW/t)
  (without bridge) 17.67 hp/t (13.18 kW/t)
Ground pressure:
  (with bridge) 1.15 kg/cm²
  (without bridge) 0.93 kg/cm²
Length:
  (with bridge) 13.5 m
  (without bridge) 11.73 m
Width:
  (with bridge) 4.1 m
  (without bridge) 3.56 m
Height:
  (with bridge) 3.9 m
  (without bridge) 2.81 m
Ground clearance: 0.47 m
Angle of approach/departure:
  (with bridge) 24/30°
  (without bridge) 26/30°
Max speed: (with bridge) 50 km/h
Range: 600 km
Gradient: (with bridge) 45%
Side slope: 30%
Vertical obstacle: 0.48 m
Trench: 2.45 m
Engine: L3 Propulsion Systems AVDS-1790-2D turbo-charged diesel developing 760 hp (567 kW) at 2,400 rpm
Transmission: Allison CD-850-6A automatic
Bridge weight: 10,000 kg
Load classification: MLC 70
Bridge length:
  (extended) 26 m
  (folded) 13.5 m
Gap spanned: 24 m
Bridge width: 4.01 m
Roadway width: (each) 1.555 m
Bridge height: (max) 0.9 m

Status

Production complete . In service with Spanish Army (12 units on M60 MBT chassis). In the future these systems may be mounted on a Spanish Army Leopard 2 chassis.

Contractor

Krauss-Maffei Wegmann GmbH & Co KG (previously known as Military Mobile Bridges (MMB) GmbH).
Peugeot Talbot SA

Rheinmetall Landsysteme Brückenlegepanzer Biber armoured bridgelayer

Development

Development of an armoured bridgelayer based on the Leopard 1 MBT chassis (production of which was completed some time ago) commenced during 1965. In 1969, prototypes of two different types of armoured bridgelayer based on the chassis of the Leopard 1 MBT were built, known as Type A and Type B.

The Type A had a telescopic boom which was extended to the far bank; the bridge was then slid across and the telescopic boom removed. The Type B was of the cantilever type. The bridge was designed by Klöckner-Humboldt-Deutz, with Porsche in charge of overall development.

Biber AVLB of the Royal Netherlands Army with dozer/stabiliser blade lowered at front of vehicle (D Caemerlynck)　　0092493

Biber AVLB of the German Army laying its 22 m length two-part bridge across a wet obstacle (RLS)   0569069

German Army Biber armoured bridgelayer on Leopard 1 chassis crossing a bridge (General Dynamics Santa Bàrbara Sistemas - Germany)   1334252

After comparative trials, the Type B was selected for production by the now Rheinmetall Landsysteme (at that time MaK) of Kiel and the first production bridgelayers, known as the *Biber*, were completed in 1975. The official German Army designation is *Brückenlegepanzer Biber* or BRP-1.

In the longer term the *Biber* may be supplemented in Dutch and German Army service by the new Military Mobile Bridges Panzerschnellbrücke 2/Bruglegger MLC 70 system based on a new-build Leopard 2 chassis provided by Krauss-Maffei Wegmann in Munich. The first of two pre-production systems based on the Leopard 2 chassis were completed late in 2002 for German Army trials.

As of late 2010, Germany and the Netherlands had not placed any firm orders for the PSB 2 which is covered in detail in a separate entry in *Jane's Military Vehicles and Logistics*.

A more cost effective alternative to the PSB system could be the Krauss-Maffei Leopard 2 LEGUAN armoured vehicle launched bridge which is covered in detail in a separate entry in *Jane's Military Vehicles and Logistics*.

This has been developed as a private venture by Krauss-Maffei Wegmann and is considered to be a most cost effective solution.

Description

The hull of the *Biber* (Beaver) is almost identical to that of the Leopard 1 MBT. The driver is seated at the front of the hull on the right side, the commander in the centre and the power pack is at the rear. The torsion bar suspension either side consists of seven dual rubber tyred roadwheels, with the drive sprocket at the rear and the idler at the front. There are four track-return rollers.

The first, second, third, sixth and seventh roadwheel stations either side are provided with a hydraulic shock-absorber. The tracks are of the double-pin type and have rubber pads. Standard equipment includes an NBC system.

The bridge is of aluminium construction having a total span of 22 m, allowing a gap of up to 20 m to be spanned. The main advantage of the *Biber* is that its bridge is extended horizontally rather than vertically as with the majority of bridgelayers.

When travelling, the bridge is carried in two symmetrical 11 m halves, one above the other. It may be taken up from either end.

The bridge was designed to take tracked and wheeled vehicles up to MLC 50, or MLC 60 with care. The bridge can be laid on longitudinal and lateral slopes of 10 per cent; the opposite bank can be 2 m higher or lower, or have a difference in inclination of 10 per cent towards the bank on the laying vehicle's side.

Biber AVLB of the German Army laying its two part bridge over the front of the vehicle (Michael Jerchel)   1405685

When the *Biber* arrives at a gap or river, the vehicle first lowers the support blade (which can also be used for dozing operations such as preparing a river bank) at the front of the hull. The lower half of the bridge slides forward until its end is lined up with the end of the upper half and the two sections are then locked together and extended over the gap.

The bridge is lowered into position and the cantilever arm withdrawn. The *Biber* then raises the support blade and pulls away. The bridge can be retrieved from either end by performing the laying operations in reverse order.

Power for the bridgelaying operation comes from a central hydraulic system consisting of hydraulic pumps, an oil tank, valve blocks, control valves and hydraulic cylinders. All operations are controlled by electrical non-contact limit switches, using a sequence control system.

Elements of the *Biber* system are used in the General Dynamics Santa Bàrbara Sistemas - Germany, Rapidly Emplaced Bridge System (REBS) that is now in service with the US Army.

Details of the REMBS are provided in a separate entry in *Jane's Military Vehicles and Logistics*.

Specifications

Biber armoured bridgelayer
Crew: 2
Weight:
  (with bridge) 45,300 kg
  (without bridge) 35,100 kg
Power-to-weight ratio:
  (with bridge) 18.32 hp/t (13.66 kW/t)
  (without bridge) 23.65 hp/t (17.63 kW/t)
Length:
  (with bridge) 11.79 m
  (without bridge) 10.56 m
Width:
  (with bridge) 4 m
  (without bridge) 3.25 m
Height:
  (with bridge) 3.55 m
  (without bridge) 2.56 m
Ground clearance: 0.42 m
Track: 2.7 m
Track width: 550 mm
Length of track on ground: 4.236 m
Ground pressure: 0.97 kg/cm^2
Max speed: (road) 62 km/h
Range:
  (road - approx) 450 km
  (cross-country) 300 km
Fuel capacity: 995 litres
Fording:
  (without preparation) 1.2 m
  (with preparation) 1.65 m
Gradient: 60%
Side slope: 30%
Vertical obstacle: 0.7 m
Trench: 2.5 m
Engine: MTU MB 838 Ca M-500 10-cylinder multifuel turbocharged diesel developing 830 hp (619 kW) at 2,300 rpm
Transmission: ZF HP 250 planetary shift with 4 forward and 2 reverse gears
Electrical system: 24 V
Batteries: 6 × 300 Ah, charged by 3-phase 9 kW generator driven from main engine chassis
Armament: 8 × 76 mm smoke grenade dischargers

Armour
Nose: 70 mm at 55°
Glacis: 70 mm at 60°

Glacis top: 25 mm at 83°
Sides upper: 35 mm at 50°
Sides lower: 25 mm at 90°
Hull rear: 25 mm at 88°
Hull roof: 10 mm
Hull floor: 15 mm

Bridge
Weight: 9,940 kg
Length:
(total) 22 m
(effective) 20 m
Width: 4 m
Height: 0.96 m
Width of one track: 1.55 m
Classification: MLC 60

Status
Production complete. In service with Canada (nine), Denmark (10), Germany (104) and Netherlands (17). Production in Italy was undertaken by Oto Melara for the Italian Army (64) and is complete. These figures relate to total numbers of vehicles delivered, not actually in service.

Contractor
Rheinmetall Landsysteme GmbH

BLG-60, BLG-67 and BLG-67 M2 armoured bridgelayers

Development
The BLG-60 armoured bridgelayer was a joint development between the former East Germany and Poland. The bridge is launched in a similar fashion to the Czech/Slovak MT-55A and the reader is referred to the separate entry in *Jane's Military Vehicles and Logistics* for details of the bridge launching method.

It should be noted that the BLG-60 and BLG-67 armoured bridgelayers were used by the East German Army and not the West German Army who uses the Leopard 1 based Biber armoured bridgelayer.

A number of countries have purchased surplus BLG-60 series AVLBs. The Swedish Army, for example, purchased a total of 32 BLG-60 AVLB and as of 2010 a total of 12 remained in service under the local designation of the Brobv 971.

Following the withdraw from service of the older Hagglünds Brobv 941, these BLG-60 are the only AVLB currently deployed by the Swedish Army.

Description
In position, the bridge has a total length of 21.6 m, a width of 3.2 m and a height of 0.8 m. It can span a maximum gap of 20 m compared with the maximum span of 16 m of the MT-55A and has a maximum capacity of 50,000 kg.

The main external differences between the MT-55A and the BLG-60 are that the surface of the BLG-60's bridge is smooth and covered in plastic (the MT-55A has a patterned surface), the bridge girder ends are closed (on the MT-55A they are open) and the pulley wheels for the scissors-action operating gears are solid. The BLG-60 is provided with an NBC system and a snorkel.

There is also a BLG-67 bridgelayer, an updated version of the basic BLG-60, the main users being Bulgaria and Poland. The BLG-67 M2 is a special variant designed to lay two-span and three-span bridges.

All its main assemblies (chassis, track bridge, span-laying gear, span-fastening system, hydraulics, electrical control system and so on) have been modified, as have the bridges.

The base of the extendible arm of the span-laying gear has been lengthened and the surface on which this arm rests is lined with rubber. The edges of the roadway have been widened to provide a width of 3.47 m.

BLG-60 armoured bridgelayer (Michael Jerchel) 0511508

BLG-60 armoured bridgelayer (C R Zwart) 0512165

Anchorages are provided on the left- and right-hand side of the base span while the bridge is being laid. The BLG-67 M2 system was carried over to the Polish PMCz-90 armoured bridgelayer based on the Russian-designed T-72M1 MBT.

When two-span or three-span bridges are laid in water with a current speed above 0.2 m/s, a bridge anchorage system is employed. This uses a tie, reel and hoist with the reel holding 40 m of steel cable.

One end of the cable is attached to the front of a bridge while the other is passed through the hoist affixed to a tie driven into the ground. The hoist draws and grips the cable with two pairs of jaws operated by a hand lever. Each BLG-67 M2 carries two anti-current anchors.

Multispan bridges are formed by laying the first span with one end on a bank and the other at the bottom of the gap to be bridged. A second span is then laid from the first and, if necessary, a third span is then emplaced either to extend the span or to accommodate a difference in height on the far bank.

The span support points should be situated not more than 2.5 m from the span ends on which the next span rests. Once emplaced, the spans are connected and anchored by three grab links, two further links, a block and the hoist and line from the anti-current anchor system. A suitable track bridge or pontoons can be used as intermediate supports.

Multispan bridges have to be monitored for alignment after 10 vehicles have crossed (two spans) or, in the case of three spans, every three vehicles. Vehicles have to cross the multispan bridges in low gear at a constant speed.

A special training version of the BLG-67 M2 was introduced for trainee drivers. The vehicle is used for training in laying bridges, vehicle maintenance and repair.

Wojskowe Zaklady Inzynieryjne (Army Engineer Workshops) of Deblin offer a service to bring earlier BLG-60 and BLG-67 models up to full BLG-67 M2 standards.

These vehicles are fitted with an NBC system and can lay a smoke screen by injecting diesel fuel into the exhaust outlet on the left side of the hull.

Leopard 1 AVLB
For trials purposes the German company of NFW integrated a Krauss-Maffei Wegmann Leopard 1 chassis with a BLG scissors type bridge. This was first shown in 2000 but never entered production or service.

Specifications

BLG-60 armoured bridgelayer
Crew: 2 or 3
Weight:
(with bridge) 37,000 kg
(without bridge) 31,000 kg
Power-to-weight ratio:
(with bridge) 15.68 hp/t (11.69 kW/t)
(without bridge) 18.71 hp/t (13.95 kW/t)
Length: (with bridge) 10.57 m
Width: (with bridge) 3.48 m
Height: (with bridge) 3.4 m
Ground clearance: 0.425 m
Track: 2.64 m
Track width: 580 mm
Length of track on ground: 3.84 m
Ground pressure: 0.83 kg/cm^2
Max speed: (road) 50 km/h
Range: 500 km
Fuel capacity: 960 litres
Fording: 1.4 m
Gradient: 58%
Vertical obstacle: 0.8 m
Trench: 2.7 m
Engine: V-55 V-12 water-cooled diesel developing 580 hp (433 kW) at 2,000 rpm
Transmission: manual with 5 forward and 1 reverse gears

Electrical system: 24 V
Batteries: ×4, 280 Ah
Armament: nil

Armour
Glacis plate: 100 mm at 60°
Upper hull side: 70 mm at 0°
Hull rear: 60 mm
Hull floor: 20 mm
Hull roof: 30 mm

Status
Production complete. In service with the Indian and Polish armies (including BLG-67 M2). Bulgaria uses the BLG-67. The Swedish Army took delivery of 32 BLG-60 AVLB of which 12 remain in service under the local designation of the Brobv 071. It is possible that quantities of these AVLB are available for sale.

Contractor
Polish state factories (chassis).
Former East German State factories (bridge and conversion work).

General Dynamics European Land Systems - Germany M3 amphibious bridging and ferrying system

Development
The M3 amphibious bridging and ferrying system was developed by the now General Dynamics European Land Systems - Germany (originally EWK) as the replacement for the earlier M2 system. Four German Army M3 prototypes were produced, plus three for the British Army.

These prototypes, plus four pre-series vehicles, underwent trials with the German and British armies, completing reliability and other trials successfully prior to the production contract that was placed with the now General Dynamics European Land Systems - Germany, in August 1994. The first seven production examples were delivered by the end of 1996, with further deliveries being made until the end of 1999.

Initial total requirements were 64 units to be jointly procured for the German and British armies, with the British Army taking 38 (including four of the seven pre-production vehicles) and the German Army 30 vehicles. M3 vehicles, known as rigs, are a development based on experience gained from the existing M2. It should be noted that the M2 is no longer marketed.

In 1997 Taiwan placed an order for 22 M3 units. All 22 units are now in service.

The M3 units built for Taiwan are provided with an armoured cabin, an NBC protection and air conditioning system and some other special systems to suit the local climate.

The M3 has been action with the British Army in Iraq in 2003 when its performance was stated to be outstanding.

Singapore has ordered the latest M3 and first deliveries were made by the company in 2006.

Poland cancelled its order for 13 M3 units for budgetary reasons and the vehicles originally ordered by Poland have now been delivered to other undisclosed customers.

Production of the M3 amphibious bridging and ferrying system is undertaken by General Dynamics European Land Systems - Germany on an as required basis for the export market.

M3 amphibious bridging and ferry system in travelling configuration (General Dynamics European Land Systems - Germany) 1333636

M3 amphibious bridging and ferry system entering water with side floats unfolded (General Dynamics European Land Systems - Germany) 1333637

Four M3 amphibious bridging and ferry systems coupled together to form a ferry (General Dynamics European Land Systems - Germany) 1333638

Description
The M3 design is based on thirty years of experience by the now General Dynamics European Land Systems - Germany, with several major amphibious and floating bridge systems, such as the GILLOIS, the M2 and the FSB Folding Float Bridge.

The M3 incorporates advanced technology and has undergone many improvements to meet the users latest operational requirements. These include the ability to be driven on land and water from the same end (when the older M2 is in the water, the cab is at the rear) and improved cross-country and water manoeuvrability.

Three 8.35 m long bridging ramps are carried on each M3 (the M2 had four 5.88 m ramps). Additional buoyancy to carry MLC 85 standard loads is provided by the larger main hull and side pontoons and the inflatable wheel arches.

The M3 offers adjustable four wheel steering and a central tyre pressure adjusting system. Both axles can be lowered and lifted to provide a ground clearance of up to 0.70 m.

In addition to having an increased load carrying the M3 has a number of other enhancements including improved land and water performance and quicker construction times.

As an indication of the potential of the M3's bridging and ferrying performance, the following examples are provided: a 100 m bridge able to carry MLC 85 tracked or MLC 132 wheeled, constructed in less than 20 minutes; a two-bay ferry able to carry MLC 70 tracked (constructed in about 10 minutes); a three-bay ferry able to carry MLC 100 wheeled or two MLC 70 tracked (constructed in about 13 minutes); and the ability to operate in current velocities up to 3.5 m/s.

For standard configurations with an M3 bridge, the bridge length (L) is calculated based on the number (N) of units by using the formula: $L = (N \times 11.5) + 8.35 - (E \times 5.04)$ metres.

Each M3 rig carries three ramps in its standard configuration. Based on special requirements, General Dynamics European Land Systems - Germany also now offers a version with four ramps per rig and additional lightweight plates to allow bridging and rafting operations without carrying the additional required ramps on transport trucks.

Optional equipment
Late in 2003, the now General Dynamics European Land Systems - Germany stated that the following optional equipment was then (and still is) available for the M3 amphibious bridging and ferrying system: NBC

protected driver's cabin; air-conditioned driver's cabin; armoured driver's cabin; tropical climate kit; automatic fire detection and suppression system; anchoring system; and 4th ramp and additional ramp plates. Some of these options were included in the M3 systems already delivered to Taiwan.

Specifications

M3 amphibious bridging and ferry system
Crew: 3
Configuration: 4 × 4
Weight: (total - approx) 25,300 kg
Power-to-weight ratio: 13.36 hp/t (9.96 kW/t)
Front axle load: 12,300 kg
Rear axle load: 13,000 kg
Length: 13.03 m
Width:
   (side floats folded) 3.35 m
   (side floats unfolded) 6.57 m
Height: (wheels in normal position) 3.97 m
Ground clearance: (wheels in normal position) 0.7 m
Track: (front and rear) 2.4 m
Wheelbase: 6.5 m
Max speed:
   (road - approx) 80 km/h
   (cross-country - approx) 35 km/h
Range:
   (land) 725 km
   (as ferry) 6.25 h
Max gradient: 60%
Fording: amphibious
Engine:
   (current) Caterpillar C9, 9.3-litre diesel, in-line, six-cylinder
   (original) Deutz (KHD) BF 8 L 513 LC diesel, developing 338 hp (252 kW) at 2,100 rpm
Transmission: automatic, 6 speed
Turning circle diameter: (all-wheel steering) 24 m
Tyres: 605/30 R25

Performance

Immersion with wheel arch inflation:
   (one-bay ferry, without load) 0.54 m
   (two-bay ferry, with MLC 70 load) 1.02 m
Freeboard with wheel arch inflation:
   (one-bay ferry, without load) 0.81 m
   (two-bay ferry, with MLC 70 load) 0.33 m
Bridge, immersion average with MLC 70 load: 0.84 m
Useful bridge roadway width: 4.76 m (5.6 m with extension plates)
Water travelling speed:
   (one-bay ferry, without payload, approx.) 14 km/h
   (one-bay ferry with 12 t payload, approx.) 13 km/h
   (two-bay ferry with MLC 70 payload, approx.) 10 km/h
Average fuel consumption:
   (land) 55 litres/100 km
   (water) 64 litres/h

Status

Production as required. In service with:

Country	Quantity	Comment
Germany	30	M2 series re-built
Taiwan	22	Built as M3 standard
Singapore	number unknown	first deliveries made 2006
UK	38	M2 series re-built

Contractor

General Dynamics European Land Systems - Germany GmbH

General Dynamics European Land Systems - Germany M2 amphibious bridging and ferrying system

Development

The M2 amphibious bridging and ferrying system was developed by EisenWerke Kaiserslautern (EWK) (which is today called General Dynamics European Land Systems - Germany) and Klöckner-Humboldt-Deutz (KHD). First production units were delivered to German Army Pioneer battalions early in 1968.

There have been five versions of the M2, as follows:
- M2A - used for trials only
- M2B - production version for British and German armies, subsequently modified to M2D
- M2C - version for Singapore with Deutz Model F 8 L 413 F diesel engines. These systems were overhauled by the now Singapore Technologies Kinetics

British Army M2D in travelling configuration (Michael Jerchel)   0512454

Three units of the M2 amphibious bridging and ferrying system coupled together (General Dynamics European Land Systems - Germany)   1405686

- M2D - conversion of M2B to accommodate Class 70 (tracked) and Class 92 (wheeled) vehicles following the introduction of the Challenger 1 MBT (which has now been replaced by the latest Challenger 2 MBT) into British Army service. The extra load is accommodated by the use of engine-inflatable bags at the centre, front and rear along with some other modifications
- M2E - proposed interim updated version with a hydraulic crane and a more powerful diesel engine. Although one vehicle was fitted with a new engine, this version was not proceeded with.

Production of the M2 is complete; 385 units were produced.

Production of the latest generation M3 amphibious bridging and ferry system is undertaken on an as required basis. When compared to the M2, the latest generation M3 is a more capable system and can carry vehicles with an increased gross vehicle weight.

This is already in service with Germany, Singapore, Taiwan and the United Kingdom. Details of this system are provided in a separate entry in *Jane's Military Vehicles and Logistics*.

Description

The M2 has a chassis of welded high-alloy construction, with a crew of four seated in the cab at the front of the vehicle. All four wheels can be steered and the suspension is adjustable.

Before entering the water, the hydraulically operated hinged buoyancy tanks, which when travelling are on the top of the vehicle reducing the overall width, are swung through 180° into position. The decking is positioned in a few minutes by a light-alloy crane which, when travelling, is on the centreline of the vehicle.

When assembled, the roadway is 8.7 m long and 5.6 m wide. When the roadway has been positioned, the crane is traversed 90° to the centre of the unit. Once in the water, the units are coupled together to form a Class 50 bridge or ferry. For the latter, three M2s are required.

The M2 is fully amphibious: one of the main Deutz diesel engines drives two 600 mm propellers for sideways propulsion while the second Deutz engine powers the 650 mm diameter steering propeller. One of the two side propellers can also be used for steering. When swimming, the cab of the M2 is to the rear and the wheels are retracted into the hull to reduce drag.

Specifications

M2 amphibious bridging and ferrying system
Crew: 4
Configuration: 4 × 4
Weight: 22,000 kg
Power-to-weight ratio: 8.09 hp/t (6.03 kW/t)
Length: (travelling) 11.315 m
Width: (travelling) 3.579 m
Overall width: (with ramps and buoyancy tanks in position) 14.68 m
Height: (travelling) 3.579 m
Ground clearance: 0.6-0.84 m
Track:
   (front) 2.13 m

(rear) 2.161 m
Wheelbase: 5.35 m
Max speed:
  (road) 60 km/h
  (water, single unit) 14 km/h
Range:
  (road) 1,000 km
  (water) 6 h
Max gradient: 60%
Engines: Deutz Model F 8 L 714a V-8 diesels developing 178 hp (133 kW) at 2,300 rpm each (Singaporean vehicles have Deutz model F 8 L 413 F diesels developing 180 hp (134 kW) at 2,300 rpm)
Turning circle: 25.4 m
Tyres: 16.00 × 20

Status

Production complete. In service with Singapore where an upgrade and overhaul has now taken place. Marketing is now concentrating on the much-improved M3 system. The M3 is in service with Germany, Taiwan and the UK.

Contractor

General Dynamics European Land Systems - Germany GmbH

General Dynamics European Land Systems - Germany Rapidly Emplaced Bridge System (REBS)

Development

To move towards having more light, airmobile and fast-to-deploy forces, the US Army also brought up the requirement for a new light bridge system to equip the Brigade Combat Teams formed around the General Dynamics Land Systems - Canada Stryker Light Armoured Vehicle (LAV III) series of 8 × 8 vehicles.

The key US Army technical requirement was that of a bridge system than can be mounted on, transported by and launched from an in service truck or trailer.

The now General Dynamics European Land Systems - Germany proposed a new system based on the proven design of the *Biber* (Beaver) Armoured Vehicle Launched Bridge (AVLB) system and finally in 2002 the US Army Tank Automotive and Armaments Command (TACOM) awarded the company a contract for a total of 20 REBS.

For the US Army REBS programme, the company was teamed with AM General who integrated logistics support for the complete system.

Description

The REBS design is based on proven components and proven designs that have already been used on other bridge systems.

For example the REBS uses the same launching mechanism and launching procedure that the company designed and built for the *Biber* ALVB that has been in use with eight countries.

REBS consists of a US Government furnished Oshkosh Defense M1977 (8 × 8) cross-country Palletised Load System (PLS) truck chassis fitted with a so-called Bridge Adapter Pallet (BAP).

The M1977 is a member of the Heavy Expanded Mobility Tactical Truck (HEMTT) family which is used in large numbers by the US Army for a wide range of missions.

The BAP contains a two-part modular bridge that is launched horizontally over the rear of the vehicle, in process that takes approximately 10 minutes.

The system has a crew of two, of whom one is the operator who carries out the complete launching sequence using a remote control unit.

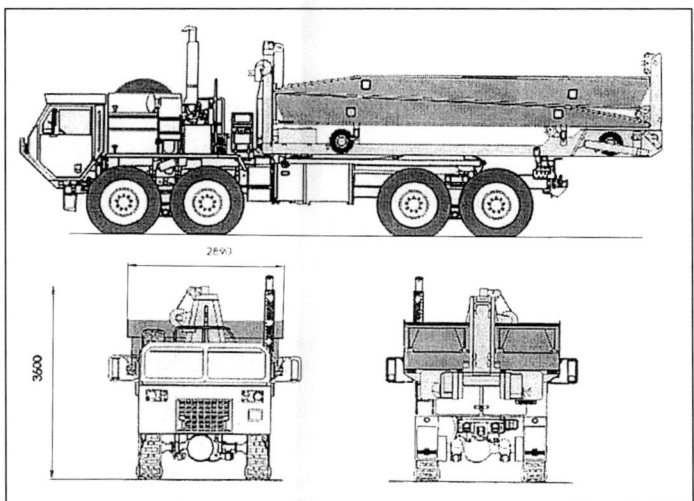

General arrangement drawing of Rapidly Emplaced Bridge System (REBS) on Common Bridge Transporter (CBT) M1977 (8 × 8) chassis   0533524

The aluminium bridge launched is 13.8 m long, 3.35 m wide and can be used to span gaps of up to 13 m. Each individual track is 1.2 m wide allowing it to be crossed by infantry.

The bridge can accommodate tracked and wheeled vehicles weighing up to Military Load Class 50 (MLC 50).

Main components of the REBS are the transport and launcher pallet, the latter having an integrated launcher and associated launch beam. When travelling the two bridge halves are carried one on top of the other.

The launcher pallet also has an electrical control system and independent diesel driven engine to supply the hydraulic system with power during launching operations.

On arrival at the wet or dry gap to be crossed, the REBS reverses into position and two hydraulic stabilisers are lowered to the ground at the rear. The launch rail is extended and the lower bridge is extended until it lines up with the other half of the bridge.

The two elements are then locked and the complete bridge is extended across the wet or dry gap and lowered into position. The launching arm is then withdrawn and traffic can start to cross. It can be retrieved from either end in about ten minutes.

While a number of countries use scissors type bridges, REBS is launched over the gap horizontally so has a much lower silhouette and is therefore more difficult to detect.

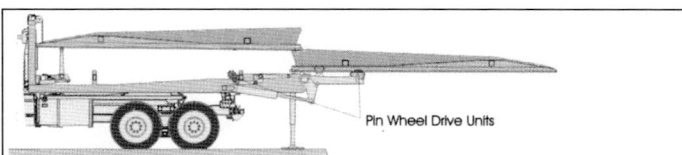

Pin Wheel Drive Unit moves the lower bridge half into coupling position.

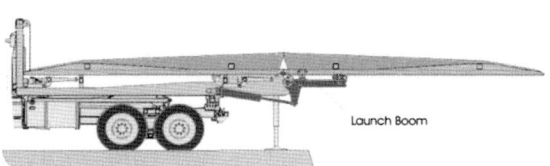

Bridge halves are coupled together.

Pin Wheel Drive Unit transports the bridge into launching position.

Launch Boom lowers the bridge to the far bank.

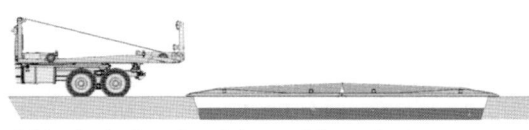

Bridge is deployed and the truck is ready to move.

Sequence of events showing the REBS being extended and positioned over the rear of the Common Bridge Transporter M1977   0569578

US Army REBS in travelling configuration complete with bridge (General Dynamics European Land Systems - Germany)   1334253

US Army REBS with assembled bridge being extended over gap
(Stefan Marx)   1334255

REBS bridge fully assembled being positioned over a wet gap by its Oshkosh Defense M1977 (8 × 8) chassis
(General Dynamics European Land Systems - Germany)   1405687

If required, once the PLS has completed its bridging mission, the pallet can be removed and the vehicle used for normal transport operations.

The inherent advantage in this design is the fact the enemy observation is impeded considerably due to the low profile signature.

The REBS is designed to be uploaded, deployed and transported using the Load Handling System (LHS) of the standard M1977 Common Bridge Transporter (CBT). The CBT is the same as that used to support of the Improved Ribbon Bridge (IRB).

Transport on other types of trucks is also possible if the latter are equipped with an adequate pallet-loading system and offer sufficient load carrying capacity.

The REBS design also provides for air transportability by a Lockheed Martin C-130 fixed wing aircraft. Similar to the road transport configuration, the bridge quarters will be hydraulically retracted to 2.87 metres for C-130 loading.

Transport of the deployed bridge by a Boeing CH-47 helicopter is accomplished by attaching the sling to the REBS tie down lugs.

Both REBS and the REBS vehicle combination (CBT + REBS) are also qualified, without any restrictions, for rail transport within Europe, Korea and the United States. In addition, both the REBS and REBS vehicle combination are marine transportable.

MOWAG Piranha with REBS
This was first shown in mid-2008 and is covered in detail in a separate entry in *Jane's Military Vehicles and Logistics*. As of late 2010 this remained at the prototype stage.

Specifications
Rapidly Emplaced Bridge System (REBS)
(Bridge system including pallet)
Weight: 9,450 kg
Length: 7.63 m
Width: 2.79 m
Height: 2.4 m

Bridge
Weight: 4,800 kg
Height: (deployed) 0.65 m
Length:
    (deployed) 13.80 m
    (effective) 13.00 m
Width: 3.35 m
Width of track: 1.20 m
Transport width: 2.79 m
Payload:

(standard) MLC 30
(caution) MLC 50

Status
Production as required. A total of 20 systems have been delivered to the US Army for use by its Brigade Combat Teams that use General Dynamics Land Systems - Canada (8 × 8) Stryker vehicles.

Contractor
General Dynamics European Land Systems - Germany GmbH

India

Kartik armoured bridgelayer

Development
During the 1989 Republic Day parade held in New Delhi, the Indian Army displayed the prototype of an armoured bridgelayer known as the Kartik.

Description
The Kartik is based on the chassis of the Catapult self-propelled 130 mm gun (SP-130), an Indian-produced version of the Vijayanta (or Vickers MBT) lengthened by the addition of an extra roadwheel each side. The vehicle has a crew of three, all of whom are seated in the chassis under full armour protection.

The Kartik uses a hydraulically operated scissors-type bridge apparently similar to that used on the German BLG-60 AVLB, also in service with India. The steel bridge has a total length of 20 m and a maximum load capacity of MLC 60; bridge weight is 8,500 kg.

Details of the BLG-60 AVLB are provided in a separate entry in *Jane's Military Vehicles and Logistics*.

Status
In service with the Indian Army. Production complete. Not offered on the export market. Production of this chassis was completed some time ago and no further production is expected. India is now building the Russian T-90S MBT under licence but as of late 2010 none of the specialised versions of this are being made in India.

Contractor
Government of India

Kartik armoured bridgelayer in travelling configuration   0511511

Bridge Layer Tank T-72 (BLT T-72)

Development
The Bridge Layer Tank T-72 (BLT T-72) is based on the turretless chassis of the T-72M1 MBT, which was licence-produced in India at the Heavy Vehicle Factory Avadi as the Ajeya.

In August 1998, a contract was awarded to LTM Limited and Chennai and Binny Engineering Limited, both of Chennai (Madras), for the limited series production of 12 BLT T-72s.

These are now understood to be in service with the Indian Army. India is now undertaking licensed production of the more recent T-90S MBT. It is considered possible that future production of the BLT T-72 AVLB could be based on the more recent T-90 series MBT chassis.

Bridge Layer Tank T-72 (BLT T-72) laying its scissors bridge over front of vehicle
0533529

Bridge Layer Tank T-72 (BLT T-72) in travelling configuration and with KMT-6 mine ploughs raised in the travelling configuration
0079521

The final phase of the launch of a Multi-Hop Assault Bridge (MHAB) with the trestle about to be lowered from its nesting position
0512328

A Centurion MBT chassis carrying a Multi-Hop Assault Bridge (MHAB) in its travelling configuration
0512329

A TATRA 815 (8 × 8) mat-laying vehicle crossing an emplaced Multi-Hop Assault Bridge (MHAB)
0512330

Description

The BLT T-72 can lay two types of bridge. One is the same steel 20 m MLC 60 scissors bridge as that already in service with the Kartik armoured bridgelayer which was only built in small numbers and is covered in a separate entry in *Jane's Military Vehicles and Logistics*.

The second bridge is aluminium, 22 m long and is also a scissors bridge, with an MLC 70 load classification. The gap between the trackways is capable of being filled with decking and end panels, once the bridge is emplaced. Both types of bridge are laid using a modular high-pressure hydraulic system and cylinders.

The 22 m bridge is constructed using a high-strength, weldable, self-ageing, aluminium zinc-magnesium alloy (RDE-40); weight of the bridge alone is 8,800 kg. Once emplaced the full roadway is 4 m wide, with each trackway 1.625 m wide.

A bridge takes between three and five minutes to launch using either manual or electronic control. The vehicle has a crew of three, including the driver, all provided with full NBC protection.

Armament is limited to the crew's personal weapons and a 7.62 mm or 12.7 mm machine gun for air defence, although a multibarrel smoke discharger is provided. Russian developed and built KMT-6 plough mine ploughs may be added at the front of the vehicle.

The vehicle can lay its own smoke screen by injecting diesel fuel into the exhaust outlet on the left side of the hull. It is possible that an unditching beam is also carried at the rear as on the original Russian T-72 MBT.

Status

Production as required. A total of 12 units are understood to be in service with Indian Army. It should be noted that the T-72M1 has now been completed in India. It was replaced by licensed production of the T-90S MBT.

Development agency

Research and Development Establishment (Engineers), Pune and the Combat Vehicles Research & Development Establishment - Chennai.

Tank-mounted Multi-Hop Assault Bridge (MHAB)

Development

For development and initial production purposes, the Multi-Hop Assault Bridge (MHAB) is based on the chassis of the Kartik armoured bridgelayer (see separate entry). It may eventually be carried on the turretless chassis of the Russian-designed T-72M1 series MBT which has been licence-produced in India by Heavy Vehicle Factory Avadi under the local name of the Ajeya (some test systems employed Centurion MBT chassis).

It is one component in an indigenous military bridging system encompassing all aspects of military bridging from bridge site reconnaissance to site preparation, various designs of assault bridging and line of communication bridges.

The Indian reconnaissance vehicle is based on a modified locally manufactured Russian BMP-2 Infantry Fighting Vehicle (IFV). This is called the Armoured Engineer Reconnaissance Vehicle (AERV) and is covered in a separate entry in *Jane's Military Vehicles and Logistics*.

Indian-built vehicles are known as the Sarath and many specialised versions have been developed to meet different operational requirements of the Indian Army. As far as it is know India has not exported any of these Sarath IFV or variants.

Description

The bridge used with the MHAB is constructed using a high-strength weldable self-ageing aluminium zinc-magnesium alloy (RDE-40). The bridge, which is flat-topped when emplaced, is 20 m long and 4 m wide with side kerbs and capable of carrying MLC 60 loads; with caution the bridge may carry MLC 70 loads.

A four-legged trestle is provided at the far end to support the bridge when it is employed as part of a multispan bridge. As the bridge is launched, it is lowered through a cradle and boom and scissored open using a 22 tonne winch and spreading cylinders.

In the final phases of the launch the trestle is released from its nesting position and telescoped to the required height using hydraulic motors.

Power for the modular high-pressure hydraulic controls and circuits is provided by the main carrier vehicle engine via a PTO. The trestle height can be varied from 1.7 to 2.7 m. This allows the bridge to be used over canals and river beds having channels up to 2.5 m deep.

A complete MHAB launch sequence can be completed in 7 to 8 minutes. Side folding decks on both sides of the bridge can be laid manually after launch in 10 to 15 minutes. The launch of each additional span, with docking, takes about 20 minutes by day or 30 minutes by night.

The MHAB can be employed as a ramp to negotiate bank heights up to 2.5 m.

Status
Development. Limited series production contract may be awarded in the near future.

Development agency
Research and Development Establishment (Engineers) and the Vehicle Research & Development Establishment - Ahmednagar.

Extended Span Assault Bridge (ESAB)

Development
The Extended Span Assault Bridge (ESAB) is carried on and launched from the chassis of the Kartik armoured bridgelayer (which is covered in a separate entry), which is then known as the Extended Span BridgeLayer (ESBL). Some early test systems employed Centurion MBT chassis.

It is one component in an indigenous military bridging system encompassing all aspects of military bridging from bridge site reconnaissance to site preparation, various designs of assault bridging and line of communication bridges.

Details of the specialised reconnaissance vehicles, based on the BMP-2 infantry fighting vehicle chassis manufactured in India, are given in a separate entry in *Jane's Military Vehicles and Logistics*. This is called the Armoured Engineer Reconnaissance Vehicle (AERV) and is in service with the Indian Army.

Description
The ESAB is constructed using a high-strength weldable self-ageing aluminium zinc-magnesium alloy (RDE-40). The bridge, which is flat-topped when emplaced, has three segments, two with lengths of 10 and one 8 m; when extended, it is 28 m long and 4 m wide with side kerbs and is capable of carrying MLC 24 loads.

When fully folded the bridge is 10.5 m long and 3.5 m wide; height when travelling is 3.96 m. The bridge could be redesigned for higher load classifications if a heavier carrier vehicle is available.

The launch of the ESAB follows the same lines as those of the MBT chassis-based Multi-Hop Assault Bridge (MHAB) More details of the MHAB can be found in a separate entry in *Jane's Military Vehicles and Logistics*.

As the bridge is launched, it is lowered through a cradle and boom and scissored open using a 22-tonne winch and spreading cylinders.

Scissoring of the third segment is carried out with the assistance of the winch and a hydraulic cylinder mounted on the second bridge segment, after which the entire bridge is lowered. Power for the modular high-pressure hydraulic controls and circuits is provided by the main carrier vehicle engine via a PTO. The entire launch sequence can be carried out under manual or electronic control.

A complete ESAB launch sequence can be completed in 7 to 8 minutes. Side folding decks on both sides of the bridge can be laid manually in 10 to 15 minutes after launch.

The initial phase of the launch of an Extended Span Assault Bridge (ESAB). The laying vehicle is a modified Centurion tank chassis for trials purposes
0512331

Extending the third segment of an Extended Span Assault Bridge (ESAB). The laying vehicle is a modified Centurion tank chassis for trials purposes
0512332

If required, the ESAB could be launched from a MHAB and docked with the MHAB. The ESAB can be employed as a ramp to negotiate bank heights up to 3 m.

Status
Development. Limited series production contract expected to be awarded in the near future.

Development agency
Research and Development Establishment (Engineers) and Vehicle Research & Development Establishment - Ahmednagar.

Sarvatra truck-mounted bridging system

Development
The Sarvatra Tatra (8 × 8) truck-mounted bridge is one component in an indigenous military bridging system. It encompasses all aspects of military bridging from bridge site reconnaissance to site preparation, various designs of assault bridging and line of communication bridges.

The Sarvatra was developed under the auspices of the Defence Research and Development Establishment (Engineers), Dighi, Pune, using what is described as a concurrent engineering approach.

This entails numerous advanced design and evaluation techniques involving several teams, including the co-operation of several commercial concerns involved in all design and development stages and that will eventually manufacture the fully developed system. Commercial concerns involved to date have been:

- Bharat Earth Movers Limited (responsible for the 8 × 8 locally produced Tatra cross-country truck chassis)
- Binny Limited
- L & T McNeil
- Oscar Equipments
- Badawe Engineers
- Tata Electric Companies
- Oilgear Towler Polyhydron Limited.

'Sarvatra' is the motto of the Indian Corps of Engineers. Translated it means the same as the motto of the British Royal Engineers, namely Ubique, or Everywhere. It may be termed a universal bridging system capable of overcoming gaps up to 100 m (following further development).

A Sarvatra truck-mounted bridging system with bridge partly extended over rear
0079522

The TATRA T 815 VNN (8 × 8) carrier vehicle has excellent cross-country mobility.

Description

Sarvatra has many concept features in common with the RFAS TMM series of truck-mounted (on a conventional 6 × 6 bonneted try chassis) treadway bridges (covered in detail in a separate entry) in that folded bridge sections are launched from the back of a carrier truck.

However, the two differ in design detail, the Sarvatra having, to name but one difference, five sections as opposed to the four of the TMM.

Each Sarvatra bridge section is 15 m long, 4 m wide and fully decked. A trestle is located at the far end of each section so that, as each bridge section is hydraulically launched from a re-engineered TATRA T 815 VVN 8 × 8 carrier vehicle (which is manufactured under licence in India by Bharat Earth Movers Limited and used for a wide range of roles by the Indian Army), the telescopic trestle can be adjusted in height before the next section is added (the fifthsection rests on the far bank).

To assist the laying operation, a fully enclosed auxiliary cab is added at the rear of the TATRA chassis, not only to control the laying process but to allow the vehicle to be driven safely in reverse along newly laid bridge sections.

Up to five 15 m sections may be laid at present, making an overall Sarvatra bridge length of 75 m. Following further development, each bridge section will eventually be extended to 20 m with only a marginal bridge weight increase overall, so 100 m Sarvatra bridges will be possible.

The bridge is fabricated out of aluminium alloy RDE-40 and is to MLC 70. The bridge can be deployed across wet gaps with a soil bearing capacity as low as 1 kg/cm², depth 2.5 to 6 m and a water current of up to five knots.

Status

Development complete. Limited series production contract expected to be awarded in the near future. This is already being offered on the export market.

Development agency

Research and Development Establishment (Engineers), Pune and Combat Vehicles Research & Development Establishment - Chennai.

International

BAE Systems Global Combat Systems/SEI bridgelayer system

Development

Some years ago, the now BAE Systems Global Combat Systems (at that time Alvis and subsequently Alvis Vickers) entered into an agreement with the US company of Systems & Electronics Incorporated (SEI), under which BAE Systems Global Combat Systems would offer the SEI Light Assault Bridge (LAB) for some export markets.

Types of chassis would include an 8 × 8 truck, the now BAE Systems Global Combat Systems Stormer flatbed chassis and a trailer based system that could be towed by a variety of tracked and wheeled chassis.

A part of a major export sale of BAE Systems Global Combat Systems Scorpion and Stormer light armoured vehicles to Indonesia in the late 1990s included a small batch, understood to be two, of these systems based on an BAE Systems Global Combat Systems Stormer flatbed vehicle.

Production of the Stormer is now complete and is no longer being marketed.

Description

BAE Systems Global Combat Systems/SEI bridgelayer system is based on a flatbed version of the Stormer APC with the crew of three (commander,

BAE Systems Global Combat Systems/SEI bridgelayer system on a Stormer chassis and laying bridge over rear of vehicle   0569068

driver and operator) under armour in the forward part of the welded aluminium hull. This provides the occupants with protection from small arms fire and shell splinters.

The bridge is launched over the rear of the hull, with stability during launching operations provided by two rear-mounted stabiliser jacks with circular pads.

Power for the launch sequence is provided by a 220 bar hydraulic system with a permanently engaged, engine-driven, variable displacement pump.

The LAB two-part scissors bridge is 15.24 m long overall, being formed from box structure 7.62 m long ramps. Once emplaced, the bridge can span gaps up to 14 m (subject to terrain) and has a load capacity of MLC 30; it is planned to increase this to MLC 35.

The bridge can be launched in one of three ways. The under-armour option is fully automatic taking approximately five minutes to launch. If required, the same sequence can be accomplished from outside the vehicle using remote control. The third option is a manual mode with direct control of the hydraulics. Recovery can be from either end of the bridge.

BAE Systems Global Combat Systems/SEI bridge layer system could be air transported in a Lockheed Martin C-130 Hercules aircraft but the bridge and carrier have to be separated.

Production of the Stormer was originally undertaken in Coventry, but this facility closed and production was transferred to Telford. Production of armoured fighting vehicles has now ceased at Telford and the only remaining facility is at Newcastle-upon-Tyne in the UK.

Specifications

Carrier vehicle
Crew: 3
Weight:
  (vehicle and launcher) 11,600 kg
  (loaded with bridge) 14,770 kg
Power-to-weight ratio: 16.93 hp/t (12.62 kW/t)
Length:
  (hull) 6.165 m
  (overall, bridge loaded) 8.13 m
Width: 2.8 m
Height: (loaded) 3.866 m
Max speed: 75 km/h
Engine: Perkins Engines Company T6.3544 water-cooled 6-cylinder turbocharged diesel developing 250 bhp (186 kW) at 2,600 rpm.
Transmission: David Brown Gear Systems T300 crossdrive, semi-automatic, hot-shift type, providing 7 speeds in each direction
Suspension: torsion bar
Electrical system: 28 V

Bridge
Load capacity: MLC 30
Weight: 3,170 kg
Bridge length: 15.24 m
Max gap width: 14 m
Load class: MLC 70/100
Laying time: (automatic) 5 mins

Status

Production complete. No longer marketed. In service with Indonesia (two).

Contractor

BAE Systems Global Combat Systems
Systems & Electronics Inc (SEI) (bridge)

BAE Systems Global Combat Systems/SEI bridgelayer system on Stormer chassis in travelling configuration (TJ Gander)   0554761

General Dynamics European Land Systems/Germany/General Dynamics European Land Systems - MOWAG Piranha III Armoured Vehicle Launched Bridge

Development
In 2008 the Swiss MOWAG Piranha III (8 × 8) Armoured Personnel Carrier (APC) was shown in an Armoured Vehicle Launched Bridge (AVLB) version.

This is a standard production Piranha III (8 × 8) APC fitted with the General Dynamics European Land Systems - Germany Rapidly Emplaced Bridge - Adaptable Bridge Launching Kit (REB - ABLK).

This is a further development of the Rapidly Emplaced Bridge System (REBS) originally developed by the company for the US Army's Stryker Brigade Combat Teams (BCT) and integrated onto a Oshkosh Defense M1977 Common Bridge Transporter (CBT). Full details of the REBS, currently in service with the US Army, are provided in a separate entry in *Jane's Military Vehicles and Logistics*.

Although the first example is based on the Swiss MOWAG Piranha III (8 × 8) chassis, its design is such that it can be fitted onto an wide range of other chassis, tracked and wheeled.

Development of this AVLB system is complete but as of late 2010 no production orders had been placed.

Description
The hull of the MOWAG Piranha III (8 × 8) APC is of all welded steel armour which provides the occupants with protection from small arms fire and shell splinters.

Driver is front left with the powerpack to the right which leaves the remainder clear for the troop compartment.

Mounted on the roof is the launching system and bridge. The system can rapidly launch a two part Military Load Class 50 (MLC 50) bridge over the front of the chassis which, when extended is 13.8 m long and can typically be used to span a gap up to 13 m.

The bridge takes two minutes to lay or recover with the REB weighing 4.8 tonnes while the ABLK weighs only 1.8 tonnes.

The bridge would normally be transported by a PLS truck and then lifted onto the Piranha III (8 × 8) which is rapidly fitted with a launching system which includes stabilisers at the front of the chassis. REB - ABLK is fitted with a laser rangefinder and camera to facilitate accurate placing of the bridge over the obstacle.

MOWAG Piranha III (8 × 8) fitted with REB - ABLK with bridge being launched over front of vehicle
(General Dynamics European Land Systems - Germany)   1330926

MOWAG Piranha III (8 × 8) fitted with REB - ABLK with bridge in travelling position (General Dynamics European Land Systems - Germany) 1330925

Once the bridge has been laid in position, Piranha III can be fitted with another bridge to carry out another mission or the ABLK can be removed from the Piranha III that can be used for its normal mission.

Specifications
Piranha III Armoured Vehicle Launched Bridge
Max payload: MLC 50
Length: 13.8 m
Gap span: 13.0 m
Weight:
  (REB) 4,800 kg
  (ABLK) 1,800 kg
  (total) 6,600 kg

Status
Development complete. Ready for production on receipt of orders.

Contractors
Bridge
General Dynamics European Land Systems - Germany GmbH

Piranha III
General Dynamics Santa Bárbara Sistemas - MOWAG GmbH

Israel

Israel Military Industries AVLB Upgrades

Development
Based on its wide experience in the design, development and production of assault bridging, Israel Military Industries is now offering modernisation programmes for the widely deployed US designed and built M48/M60 Armoured Vehicle Launched Bridge (AVLB).

According to Israel Military Industries, the original AVLB Military Load Class 60 (MLC 60) scissors type bridge, of all aluminium construction, requires a considerable amount of maintenance owing to its age and its mechanical structure.

Description
Israel Military Industries is now offering two unique and modern solutions for the existing US M48/M60 AVLB launcher without any change or modification to the launcher or its associated hydraulic launching system.

First is a new 20 m steel bridge of MLC 70 which is a direct replacement for the original scissor-type bridge with the launching mechanism and drills remaining the same.

Second is the new Tandem bridge which is covered in a separate entry in *Jane's Military Vehicles and Logistics*. This is already in service with the Israel Defense Force. This comprises two identical 11.7 m bridges carried by the original, US-developed M48/M60 AVLB launcher without any change.

These two steel bridges can multiply the bridging capability of a single bridgelayer whenever the anti-tank obstacles do not exceed a span of between 10 and 11 m.

In both of these Israel Military Industries proposals, the overall dimensions and weight of the tank launcher, with the 20 m/Tandem bridges, remains the same. Each of these bridges can be launched and recovered from either end.

All operations are carried out with the crew under complete protection.

Status
Development complete. Ready for production. The Tandem bridge system is known to be in service with the Israel Defense Force based modified M48/M60 tank chassis but as far as it is known there has been no production of this system for the export market.

Contractor
Israel Military Industries Limited (IMI), Slavin Facility.

Israel Military Industries Tandem M48/M60 Armoured Vehicle-Launched Bridge (AVLB)

Development
The Israel Military Industries Tandem Armoured Vehicle-Launched Bridge (AVLB) is based on the US-designed and built General Dynamics Land Systems M48/M60 AVLB.

It is adapted to carry two 11.7 m Military Load Class 70 (MLC 70) assault bridges transported and launched with the first bridge stacked over the second. No changes are required for an M48/M60 AVLB to accommodate the Tandem concept.

All production applications for the Tandem AVLB have been for the M48/M60 tank chassis, but its modular design is such that it can be integrated onto other tank chassis.

Israel Military Industries Tandem M48/M60 Armoured Vehicle Launched Bridge (AVLB) in transport configuration in the travelling configuration (Peter Felstead)   1334257

Description

Only the bottom (second) bridge remains mated to the launch vehicle, the second bridge being in effect the launcher for the first.

Tandem bridges can be launched and retrieved from either end. To launch the first bridge, both bridges are lifted from the transport position and lowered in an up-and-over motion allowing the first bridge to be placed in position to span gaps up to 11 m wide.

The first bridge is then mechanically disconnected from the second, which can then be returned to the transport position ready to be launched and emplaced in exactly the same manner as any other M48/M60 AVLB bridge.

Each Tandem MLC 70 bridge is constructed using high-strength steel so that it can, when necessary, be repaired in the field using standard equipment and tools. Each bridge has a roadway width of 4.26 m and weighs 6.75 tonnes.

When the Tandem AVLB vehicle is not being used for bridgelaying it can carry mine rollers or a front-mounted D9L-P dozer blade.

Specifications

Tandem M48/M60 AVLB
Weight: 6,750 kg
Length: 11.7 m
Span: 11 m
Roadway width: 4.26 m
Load classification: MLC 70

Status

Production as required. In service with Israel Defence Force. The IDF uses these bridges integrated onto a M48/M60 chassis but they can be integrated onto other tank chassis if required by the customer.

Contractor

Israel Military Industries Limited (IMI), Slavin Facility

Israel Military Industries Alligator Medium Assault Bridge (MAB)

Development

The Israel Military Industries Alligator Medium Assault Bridge (MAB) consists of three main components. One is the bridge set of two bridges, one 22 m long and the other 15 m long.

The second component is the launching mechanism, mounted on a French Nexter Systems (previously Giat Industries and before that Creusot-Loire) AMX-13 light tank chassis. The system is completed by the control system.

Deploying an Alligator Medium Assault Bridge (MAB) with the launching system based on an AMX-13 type chassis   0511512

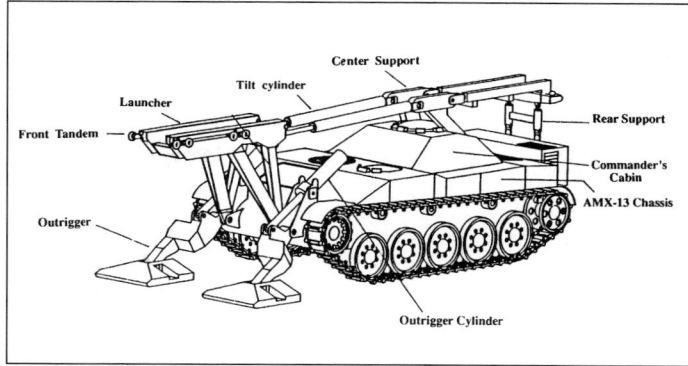

General arrangement drawing of the Alligator Medium Assault Bridge (MAB) based on a modified AMX-13 light tank chassis without the bridge fitted   0533528

As far as it is known the only production application has been for the older AMX-13 light tank chassis. It should be noted that the Israel did use the AMX-13 light tank, but these were phased out of service many years ago.

As of late 2010 the only remaining users of the AMX-13 light tank were Argentina, Cote d'Ivoire, Ecuador, Indonesia, Morocco, Peru, Singapore and Venezuela.

Description

The lightweight bridges are made of high-strength aluminium alloy with a load capacity of MLC 30. The bridges are constructed with two symmetric treadways transversely connected by beams. There is also a folding and locking mechanism. Each trackway has a centre-section and two ramps. There is no hydraulic system in the bridge.

The launch mechanism is carried on a modified AMX-13 light tank chassis with complete 75 mm/90 mm two-person turret removed and plated over.

An armoured superstructure protects the launch mechanism and has a position for the commander. Launching is carried out using a launcher and outriggers hydraulically operated to move and position the bridge using a flip cantilever mode.

Launch and retrieval can be carried out from either end. Launching takes three to four minutes and retrieval takes 4.5 to 5.5 minutes.

The control system controls the hydraulics in either an automatic or manual mode. The system can be operated by either member of the crew of two (driver and commander) or from outside the system vehicle.

If required, two identical bridges can be used in a tandem combination to increase the gap crossing capability. Two 15 m bridges can then be used to cross a 21 m gap while two 22 m bridges can cross a 32 m gap.

A bridge can be crossed even when one main structural chord is damaged. Vehicles crossing a bridge can do so at speeds up to 25 km/h in crosswinds of less than 20 km/h.

Specifications

Alligator Medium Assault Bridge - System

Bridge length	22 m	15 m
Weight:		
(complete system)	20,300 kg	18,500 kg
(vehicle with system)	16,000 kg	15,000 kg
(bridge)	4,300 kg	3,500 kg
Length:		
(overall)	9 m	9 m
(vehicle with system)	7.6 m	7.6 m
Width:		
(complete system)	3.2 m	3.2 m
(vehicle with system)	2.6 m	2.6 m
(bridge)	3.2 m	3.2 m
Height:		
(overall)	3.6 m	3.4 m
(vehicle with system)	3 m	3 m
Ground clearance:	0.4 m	0.4 m
Max speed:		
(road)	51 km/h	51 km/h
(cross-country)	30 km/h	30 km/h
Range: (road)	350 km	350 km
Fording:	0.8 m	0.8 m
Gradient:	50%	50%
Side slope:	30%	30%

Bridge length	22 m	15 m
Vertical obstacle:		
(forward)	0.65 m	0.65 m
(to rear)	0.45 m	0.45 m
Trench:	1.6 m	1.6 m

Alligator Medium Assault Bridge - Bridge

Bridge length	22 m	15 m
Load capacity:	MLC 30	MLC 30
Max gap capability:	20 m	14 m
Folded length:	9 m	9 m
Width:		
(overall)	3.2 m	3.2 m
(roadway)	3 m	3 m
(trackway)	1.2 m	1.2 m
Height:		
(folded)	1.47 m	1.24 m
(deployed)	0.735 m	0.735 m
Centre gap:	0.6 m	0.6 m
Ramp slope:	8%	12%
Max twist angle:	10%	10%
Transverse slope:	15%	15%
Uphill slope:	25%	25%
Downhill slope:	15%	15%

Status
Production as required. In service with unspecified export customers.

Contractor
Israel Military Industries Limited (IMI), Slavin Facility

Japan

Mitsubishi Type 91 Armoured Vehicle-Launched Bridge (AVLB)

Development
The Japanese Type 91 Armoured Vehicle Launched Bridge (AVLB) is based on the chassis of the Type 90 MBT.

Until the introduction of the Type TK-X (or Type T-10 MBT), the Type 90 was the most modern MBT in service with Japan.

Following trials with prototype vehicles it was type classified as the Type 91 AVLB but production has been undertaken at a very low rate. In FY1999 one vehicle was procured with another vehicle being procured in FY2000. One each Type 91 AVLB were procured in FY2003 and FY2004. Like other Japanese armoured fighting vehicles, the Type 91 AVLB has never been offered on the export market.

Description
The Type 91 AVLB is based on a modified Type 90 MBT with its turret removed and replaced by a launching mechanism for a two part bridge which, when in the travelling position are stowed one on top of the other.

Mounted at the front of the chassis is a dozer blade that can be used to stabilise the platform when the bridge is being launched or to clear a launching platform for the bridge.

On arrival at the crossing point the lower part of the bridge is extended over the gap followed by the upper part. The complete bridge is then extended across the wet or dry gap and lowered into position.

When extended the bridge is 20 m long and can be used to span a gap of up to 18 m and take tracked and wheeled vehicles weighing up to 50 tonnes.

Specifications
Type 91 AVLB
Crew: 2
Weight: 41,800 kg
Power-to-weight ratio: 16.99 hp/t (12.67 kW/t)
Length: 10.9 m
Width: 4 m
Height: 3.8 m
Ground clearance: (variable) 0.4 m
Max speed: (road) 50 km/h
Engine: Model 10ZF 10-cylinder air cooled diesel developing 710 hp (529 kW) at 2,200 rpm
Transmission: automatic
Suspension: torsion bar/hydropneumatic

Status
Production complete. In service with Japanese Ground Self-Defence Force. This has not been offered on the export market.

Contractor
Mitsubishi Heavy Industries

Mitsubishi Type 67 Armoured Vehicle-Launched Bridge (AVLB)

Development
To support its fleet of Type 67 MBTs the Japanese Ground Self-Defence Force deployed a number of support vehicles based on a similar chassis.

These included the Type 67 Armoured Vehicle Launch Bridge (AVLB) which was only built in small numbers. All of the Type 67 MBTs have now been replaced out of service with the introduction of the more recent Type 74 and Type 90 MBTs.

Description
The Mitsubishi Type 67 AVLB is basically a turretless Type 61 MBT carrying a scissors bridge and launching mechanism. The bridge is similar in design and construction to the US M48 AVLB bridge but is much shorter.

When opened out, it is 12 m long, compared with the M48's bridge which is 19.202 m long; it will span a wet or dry gap of up to 10 m. The bridge is opened out over the front of the Type 67 and can be retrieved from either end. Launching time is three to five minutes. The bridge has a maximum loading capacity of 40,000 kg.

The chassis is almost identical to that of the Type 61 MBT, with the driver seated at the front of the hull on the right side, having three day periscopes for observation and a single-piece hatch cover.

The middle day periscope can be replaced by a passive night vision device. The other two crew members are positioned in the centre of the hull, with the diesel power pack at the rear.

The suspension is of the torsion bar type and either side consists of six dual rubber tyred roadwheels, with the drive sprocket at the front and the idler at the rear, having three track-return rollers per side.

Hydraulic shock-absorbers are provided for the first, second, fifth and sixth roadwheel stations.

Specifications
Type 67 AVLB
Crew: 3
Weight: 35,000 kg
Power-to-weight ratio: 18.57 hp/t (13.85 kW/t)
Length:
(with bridge) 7.27 m
(hull) 6.32 m
Width:
(with bridge) 3.5 m
(without bridge) 2.95 m
Height: (with bridge) 3.5 m
Ground clearance: 0.4 m
Track: 2.45 m
Track width: 500 mm
Length of track on ground: 3.7 m
Ground pressure: 0.95 kg/cm²
Max speed: (road) 45 km/h
Range: 200 km
Fording: 1 m
Gradient: 60%
Vertical obstacle: 0.8 m
Trench: 2.7 m
Engine: Mitsubishi Type 12 HM 21 WT V-12 turbocharged air-cooled diesel developing 650 hp (485 kW) at 2,100 rpm
Transmission: mechanical with 5 forward and 1 reverse gears, with 2-speed auxiliary reduction unit
Electrical system: 24 V
Batteries: 4 × 12 V, 200 Ah
Armament: 1 × 7.62 mm MG

Armour
Hull front: 46 mm
Hull sides: 25 mm
Hull rear: 15 mm

Type 67 armoured vehicle-launched bridge in travelling configuration (Kensuke Ebata)
0512333

Status
Production complete. In service only with the Japanese Ground Self-Defence Force. Being supplemented by the Type 91 AVLB based on the more recent Type 90 MBT. Production of the Type 90 MBT is complete with the latest Japanese MBT being the Type TK-X (or Type T-10).

Contractor
Production was undertaken at the Maruko, Tokyo, plant of Mitsubishi Heavy Industries, but AFV production is undertaken at the Sagamihara Plant, near Tokyo.
Mitsubishi Heavy Industries

Type 70 self-propelled pontoon bridge

Development
During the early 1960s, the Japanese Ground Self-Defence Force issued a requirement for a self-propelled pontoon bridge system, which could also be used as a ferry.

Development of the Type 70 self-propelled pontoon bridge was under the leadership of the Hitachi Manufacturing Company and commenced in 1965 with the first prototype bridge was completed the following year. After further trials it was standardised as the Type 70 self-propelled pontoon bridge. Production of the Type 70 self-propelled pontoon bridge is now complete.

It is considered that some of these may have been upgraded to take into account the heavier armoured vehicles introduced into Japanese service since the Type 70 self-propelled pontoon bridge unit was first introduced into service.

Description
In concept, the Type 70 is very similar to the German General Dynamics Land Systems - Germany GmbH (previously known as EWK) M2. Before entering the water, a hydraulic mechanism rotates the floats from the deck through 180° so that they lie along the sides of the vehicle and provide extra flotation.

When afloat, the wheels, which have large low-pressure tyres, are retracted into the hull to reduce water resistance. To provide additional buoyancy the wheel wells are pressurised.

The vehicle is fitted with a central tyre pressure regulation system, allowing the tyre pressure to be adjusted to suit the type of ground being crossed. Typically the tyres would be inflated for road use and then deflated when travelling across rough terrain.

Once afloat, a built-in crane emplaces the three treadways and the units are joined to form a ferry bridge.

The crane is also used to emplace drive-on ramps. Three Type 70 units coupled together have a capacity of 40,000 kg and a roadway width of 3.9 m. It is possible that this system has been upgraded with an enhanced load capacity. This takes into account the heavier vehicles introduced into service.

Specifications
Type 70 self-propelled pontoon bridge
Configuration: 4 × 4
Weight: 26,000 kg
Power-to-weight ratio: 12.69 hp/t (9.46 kW/t)
Length: 11.4 m
Width:
   (without floats) 2.8 m
   (floats extended) 5.4 m
Height: 3.4 m
Superstructure length: 8.5 m
Superstructure width: 3.8 m
Engine: Nissan V-8 diesel developing 330 hp (246 kW) at 2,200 rpm
Max speed:
   (road) 56 km/h
   (water) 12 km/h
Gradient: 47%

Status
In service with Japanese Ground Self-Defence Force. Production complete. This system was not exported. Improvements to this system may be carried out.

Type 81 truck mounted bridgelayer

Development
The Type 81 bridgelayer is a Mitsubishi Type 74 (6 × 6) 10,000 kg cross-country truck chassis with a hydraulically launched bridge, mounted to the rear and laid from the rear of the cab.

Like all Japanese military equipment, the Type 81 truck mounted bridgelayer was never offered on the export market.

In concept, the Type 81 truck mounted bridgelayer is very similar to the Chinese Type 84A and Slovakian AM-50 systems, which are also truck mounted. These are covered in separate entries in *Jane's Military Vehicles and Logistics*.

Description
To lay a bridge, which can take tracked and wheeled armoured vehicles weighing up to 42,000 kg, two vehicles are required. Each vehicle carries a bridge span in two halves with one also carrying two telescopic pier legs.

The latter vehicle approaches the gap to be bridged tail first and the telescopic pier legs are attached to the end of the bottom pier half.

The bottom pier half is then hydraulically driven by rams out across the gap. As the bridge half is driven across the gap the two pier legs fall downwards and, when the full length of the first bridge half is reached, the top half is attached and the hydraulic rams then push the second half out to the full extent.

When the full extent of the bridge half is reached, the two are lowered with the telescopic pier legs resting on the ground. The legs can accommodate slight variations in level and the full weight of the two connected bridge halves is taken up by lowering the bridge to the ground at the truck end.

The weight of the span in the centre is then taken on to foot pads, each about 1 m². A ramp is then fitted to the truck end, ready for the second truck to approach backwards on to the bridge lowering the second half of the bridge span.

This is carried out in exactly the same way as the first, except that there are no pier legs. Once the second bridge section has been laid, a further drive-on ramp can be fitted to the far end and the bridge is ready for use. Some additional levelling may be required before heavy vehicles use the bridge.

The foregoing relates to a two-section bridge but extra sections, along with extra pier legs, may be employed to build longer bridges when necessary. The maximum bridging length is 60 m which requires ten bridging sets.

Specifications
Type 81 truck mounted bridgelayer
Crew: 2
Configuration: 6 × 6
Weight: 21,800 kg
Length: 9.6 m
Width: 2.85 m
Height: 3.4 m
Max road speed: 85 km/h
Vertical obstacle: 0.8 m

Bridge
Capacity: MLC 42
Length: 10 m
Width: 3.75 m
Max bridging height: 4 m
Bridging height variation: 2 m
Max bridging length: 60 m (10 sets)

Status
Production complete. In service with Japanese Ground Self-Defence Force. Production complete. This system was never offered on the export market.

Type 70 self-propelled pontoon bridge unit in travelling configuration
0512167

Type 81 truck mounted mechanised bridge in travelling configuration and showing stabiliser legs in horizontal position below the two elements of the bridge (K Nogi)
0511513

Korea, South

Rotem K1 Armoured Vehicle-Launched Bridge (AVLB)

Development

The K1 series of MBT was developed to meet the operational requirements of the Republic of Korea (ROK) Army in the early 1980s with much of the original development work being carried out by the now General Dynamics Land Systems in the United States.

Production of the 105 mm K1 MBT was undertaken in the ROK by the Hyundai Precision & Ind Co Ltd which is now known as Rotem.

To support the K1 series MBT a number of specialised support vehicles were developed including an Armoured Recovery Vehicle (ARV) and an Armoured Vehicle Launched Bridge (AVLB).

The latter was developed by Rotem in association with the then Vickers Defence Systems of the United Kingdom, which is, today, known as BAE Systems Global Combat Systems.

In 1989, the latter company was awarded a contract to develop a launching system and bridge for the K1 AVLB while the now Rotem developed the chassis based on the K1 MBT.

The first scissors bridge and associated launch system was built in the UK and in 1990 sent to Rotem who integrated this with the launch platform.

Late in 1993, a contract was placed with the now as BAE Systems Global Combat Systems, worth USD34.47 million for the supply of eight bridges and 41 launching systems which were integrated in the ROK on new build K1 chassis.

It is understood that the ROK Army has now taken delivery of a total of 56 K1 AVLB and associated bridges with production subsequently being undertaken in the ROK under a technology transfer deal.

The K1 series of MBTs and variants has been offered on the export market. Under development is the K2 MBT with first test beds undergoing trials. At this stage it is not expected that there will be any specialised variants based on the K2 chassis.

Description

The K1 AVLB is based on a modified chassis of the K1 MBT which is the standard MBT of the Republic of Korea Army. The chassis of the K1 AVLB has the same level of armour protection as the K1 MBT and has the same level of cross-country mobility.

The layout of the K1 AVLB has the driver compartment at the front of the chassis, commander's position in the centre and the diesel power pack at the rear.

The K1 AVLB has a crew of two, commander and driver. The commander is located under a cupola in the hull roof. An integral crew heating system is provided but NBC protection is restricted to individual systems. Automatic fire detection and suppression systems are provided in the power pack and crew compartments.

The bridge is of the scissors type and can bridge a gap with a clear span of 20.5 m; the load classification is Military Load Class 60 (MLC 60) and the bridge alone weighs 12,700 kg.

The anticipated service life is over 8,000 crossings. Launch time is three to five minutes and retrieval time 10 minutes. The bridge can be launched with a side slope of 3° and a longitudinal slope of ±10°; bank height difference is 2.4 m. The total length of the bridge when open is 22 m.

A pintle for a 7.62 mm M60 Machine Gun (MG) is mounted over the commander's cupola on the hull roof and two six-barrel smoke grenade dischargers are mounted on the hull front. Communications equipment includes a VRC-947K FM type, which has a range of 30 km.

Specifications

K1 AVLB
Crew: 2
Weight:
  (vehicle and bridge) 53,700 kg
  (bridge) 12,700 kg
Power-to-weight ratio: 22.35 hp/t (16.66 kW/t)
Ground pressure: 0.9 kg/cm²
Length overall: 12.56 m
Width overall: 4 m
Height overall: 4 m
Ground clearance: 0.46 m

K1 armoured vehicle-launched bridge laying the scissors bridge over front of the vehicle (Rotem)   1405688

Max speed:
  (road) 65 km/h
  (cross-country) 40 km/h
Range: 500 km
Gradient: 60%
Side slope: 30%
Vertical obstacle: 0.8 m
Trench: 2.66 m
Fording: 1.2 m
Engine: MTU MB 871 Ka-501 8-cylinder diesel developing 1,200 hp (895 kW) at 2,600 rpm
Transmission: Renk LSG 3000 automatic with 4 forward and 2 reverse gears
Suspension: hydropneumatic and torsion bar
Electrical system: 24 V
Batteries: 6 × 12 V, 100 Ah
Armament: 1 × 7.62 mm M60 MG

Status

Production complete. In service with the South Korean Army. There have been no exports of this system.

Contractor

Rotem Precision & Ind Co Ltd

Pakistan

M47M Armoured Vehicle-Launched Bridge (AVLB)

Development

The Pakistan Military Vehicle Research and Development Establishment at Rawalpindi developed an Armoured Vehicle-Launched Bridge (AVLB) based on the turretless chassis of a surplus US supplied M47M tank for the Pakistan Ministry of Defence.

The M47M tank is an upgraded version of the 90 mm armed M47 tank which was developed in the United States shortly after the end of the Second World War.

This was phased out of service with the US Army in the 1950s and large quantities were supplied to countries such as Pakistan.

So far the only production application is for a system based on the obsolete US M47 tank chassis, but the bridge and its laucher could be integrated onto other tank chassis.

It is known that China has supplied Pakistan with some Type 653 Armoured Recovery Vehicles (ARV) and it is possible that China could also have supplied Pakistan with some Type 84 AVLB.

Description

The bridge-launching mechanism is installed on the hull of the turretless M47M and is used to launch an aluminium alloy folding scissors bridge with a maximum span of 21.4 m.

The bridge has a maximum clear span of 20.3 m. The vehicle has a crew of two, a driver and a commander/operator who uses 13 hydraulic cylinders to launch the bridge in about three minutes. Power for the hydraulic system is provided by the M47M launch vehicle's main engine.

M47M Armoured Vehicle-Launched Bridge (AVLB) with 21.4 m bridge in transport position (Christopher F Foss)   0533520

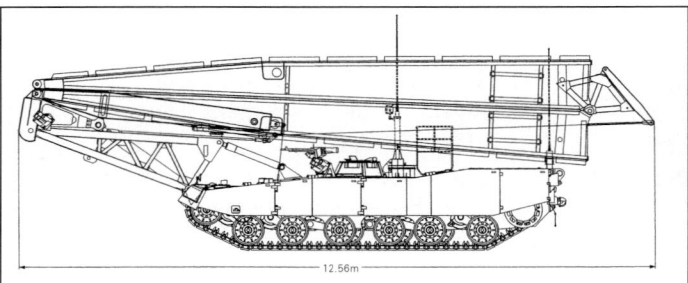

Side drawing of K1 AVLB in travelling configuration (Rotem)   1164669

M47 Armoured Vehicle-Launched Bridge laying its scissors bridge over a previously laid bridge (Military Vehicles Research and Development Establishment) 1044343

Polish PMCz-90 armoured bridgelayer in travelling configuration 0007678

Polish PMCz-90 armoured bridgelayer in action launching scissors bridge over front of vehicle 0007679

The bridge-launching sequence commences with the main launching cylinder lifting the main launching beam from its transport position.

When the bridge reaches an angle of 45°, the bridge unloading cylinder is operated and starts to retract. As it retracts it pulls a set of two steel ropes, passing over a system of pulleys and joined to the further part of the bridge. This initiates the bridge unfolding sequence. The travel of the main launching cylinder and the bridge-operating cylinder continues until the nearest part of the bridge rests on the ground in front of the launcher. In this position the launching cylinders block the movement of the launching frame and the bridge is pushed further by auxiliary cylinders.

The fulcrum of operation shifts and the operation of the bridge-opening cylinders continues until the bridge is fully open. The bridge is then lowered into position by the main operating cylinder. At this point the operator actuates three unlocking cylinders disengaging the launching beam from the bridge.

A mechanical lock is opened at the same time, allowing the launching vehicle to move away from the bridge. The bridge is recovered in the reverse sequence. If the launch vehicle engine or the hydraulic pumps fail, there is provision for the bridge to be launched manually.

The M47M launcher can also be used to lay a short single-span bridge. This bridge is one half of the folding 21.4 m bridge fitted with an extra set of folding ramps. No details are available regarding this variant, but it is assumed that it is launched in the same manner and sequence as the full-size folding bridge.

According to the Military Vehicle Research and Development Establishment, a major advantage of this system is that the laid bridge can be retrieved from either side. This permits the carrier vehicle to lay the bridge and recover the bridge from either end.

Specifications

M47M AVLB
Crew: 2
Weight: 54,000 kg
Width: 4 m
Height: 3.83 m

Bridge
Weight: 9,800 kg
Max span of bridge: 21.4 m
Max clear span: 20.3 m
Bridge width: 4 m
Distance between treadways: 0.96 m

Status

It is understood that a small production batch of M47M AVLB have been built. In service with Pakistan. As far as it is known, there are no exports of the M47M AVLB system.

Contractor

Military Vehicles Research and Development Establishment (MVRDE)

Poland

PMCz-90 armoured bridgelayer

Development

The PMCz-90 armoured bridgelayer, also known as the PMCz-94, is based on the turretless hull of a modernised T-72M1, or more recent Polish designed and built PT-91 MBT.

It closely follows the same lines as other similar T-72 based bridgelayers such as the Slovak ZTS MT-72. The German BLG-67 M2 series of Military Load Class 50 (MLC 50) load capacity steel-constructed scissors bridge and bridgelayer system are carried over to the PMCz-90.

It is, therefore, possible for up to three bridges to be placed one on the other to span extended gaps, although the load capacity is then reduced to MLC 40.

While the first examples of the PMCz-90 armoured bridgelayer were fitted with a scissors-type bridge, the first export customer, Malaysia, had their models fitted with the German Krauss-Maffei Wegmann 26 m LEGUAN bridge system.

Details of the LEGUAN bridge system, which is in service with a number of customers launched from a number of different tracked and wheeled chassis, are provided in a separate entry in *Jane's Military Vehicles and Logistics*.

Description

The scissors bridge takes three minutes to launch and four minutes to recover and can be laid with a maximum bank difference of 4.3 m. Maximum side slope for launching is 6° and maximum longitudinal bank difference is 15°.

It is fitted with a fire detection and suppression system as standard and can be fitted with various types of communications equipment according to customer requirements.

Armament of the PMCz-90 AVLB consists of a 12.7 mm machine gun and 76 mm (Western) or 81 mm (Eastern) electrically operated smoke grenades.

The vehicle can also lay its own smoke screen by injecting diesel fuel into the exhaust outlet on the left side of the hull at the rear.

The commander is provided with Type TNPO-160 and TNPA-65 day observation periscopes while the driver is provided with TNPO-168 and TNPA-65 day observation periscopes.

For night observation the driver is provided with a POD-72 passive device with a quoted range of up to 2,000 m while the driver is provided with a PNK-72 passive periscope with a range of up to 1,200 m.

Standard communications equipment is a RRC-9500 radio, although other types can be fitted.

Variants

Malaysian AVLB
In 2003, Malaysia placed a contract with Poland for the supply of 48 PT-91M MBTs, six of the latest WZT-4 Armoured Recovery Vehicles (ARV), five PMC Armoured Vehicle Launched Bridges (AVLB) and three MID-M obstacle breaching vehicles plus ammunition and training.

The Malaysian vehicles are fitted with a new power pack consisting of the Polish Wola S-1000R diesel engine developing 1,000 hp coupled to a German Renk 350 series automatic transmission with German Diehl tracks being installed.

While prototypes of the PMC-90 AVLB used a locally developed scissors bridge that is laid over the front of the vehicle, the Malaysian vehicles are fitted with the proven Krauss-Maffei Wegmann (previously Military Mobile Bridges) 26 m Leguan bridge system.

This is laid horizontally over the front of the vehicle and can span a gap of up to 24 m. It has already been built in large numbers for the export market.

The WZT-4 ARV is an enhanced version of the current WZT-3 but has a more powerful crane and improved winch. Brief details of the latest WZT-4 ARV are provided in the entry for the older WZT-3 ARV.

The first order placed by Malaysia will be sufficient to form one armoured regiment but funding permitting it is expected that additional orders will be placed for another two regiments to enable an armoured brigade to be formed.

As of late 2010 no additional contracts had been placed by Malaysia for additional quantities of PT-91M MBTs or variants.

Specifications
PMCz-90 AVLB
Crew: 2
Weight:
  (combat ready - approx) 37,000 kg
  (chassis) 30,000 kg
Power to weight ratio: 21.25 hp/t (17.13 kW/t)
Ground pressure: 0.75 kg/cm^2
Length:
  (overall) 10.84 m
  (chassis) 6.86 m
Width: 3.59 m
Height: (overall) 3.43 m
Ground clearance: 0.44 m
Max speed:
  (road) 60 km/h
  (cross-country) 40 km/h
Range: (cruising, road) 550 km
Gradient: 60%
Side slope: 30%
Vertical obstacle: 0.85 m
Trench: 2.6-2.8 m
Fording:
  (without preparation) 1.2 m
  (with 5 min preparation) 1.8 m
  (deep fording) 5 m
Engine: S12-U V-12 diesel developing 850 hp (634 kW) at 2,300 rpm
Transmission: planetary gear, hydraulically assisted with 7 forward and 1 reverse gears
Suspension: torsion bar
Electrical system: 24 V
Batteries: 4 × 12 V, 180 Ah

Bridge
Load capacity: 50,000 kg
Length: 20 m
Width: 3.47 m
Weight of bridge: 7,000 kg
Max bank difference: 4.3 m
Launching time: 3 mins
Retrieving time: 12 mins

Status
Production as required. First export customer is Malaysia who has taken delivery of five versions fitted with a German Krauss-Maffei Wegmann 26 m LEGUAN bridge. All of these were delivered in 2007 according to the United Nations Arms Transfer lists.

Contractor
Zaklady Mechaniczne 'Bumar-Labedy' SA

OBRUM MS-20 Daglezja Towed Support Bridge

Development
The Polish company of *Osrodek Badawczo-Rozojowy Urzaden Mechanicznych* (OBRUM) have developed the MS-20 Daglezja Towed Support Bridge.

This has been developed by OBRUM to meet the operational requirements of the Polish Army who funded development of the MS-20 Daglezja Towed Support Bridge.

The total Polish Army requirement is for up to 100 to 120 systems but it is expected that initial contracts will be for between 30 and 40 systems.

In concept, the OBRUM MS-20 Towed Support Bridge is very similar to the French CNIM PAR 70 towed Support bridge which is covered in detail in a separate entry in *Jane's Military Vehicles and Logistics.*

Description
The MS-20 Towed Support Bridge consists of the prime mover tractor (6 × 6) and a semi-trailer that carries the scissors type bridge and its associated launching system.

The current prime mover is the Polish Jelcz C662.D43-M Daglezja (6 × 6) tractor truck which is fitted with a forward control two door cab and is powered by an IVECO 430 kW diesel engine. Other cross-country chassis could also be used.

MS-20 Deglezja Towed Support bridge in travelling configuration (OBRUM)   1332001

MS-20 Deglezja Towed Support Bridge with scissors bridge being unfolded in position over rear of trailer launcher (OBRUM)   1332002

The scissors type bridge is transported and launched over the rear of the three axle trailer by remote control with the trailer being provided with an Auxiliary Power Unit (APU) to power the launching system.

Before laying the bridge hydraulically operated stabilisers are lowered to the ground to provide a more stable launch platform.

When opened out the scissors type bridge is 23 m long which allows it to span gaps of up to 21 m which depends on the conditions of the bank.

The bridge takes about 10 minutes to lay in position and can take tracked vehicles weighing up to 63.5 tonnes or wheeled vehicles up to 99.7 tonnes.

The use of intersections fills the space between the two elements to allow troops and small vehicles to rapidly cross the bridge.

It can also be laid across the Polish PP-64 heavy folding pontoon bridge which is covered in a separate entry in *Jane's Military Vehicles and Logistics.*

Variants
MG-20 Daglezja-G
This would be the baseline scissors bridge integrated onto the latest version of the locally developed PT-91 tank chassis.

M-20 Daglezja-S
This would be a similar concept but mounted on a wheeled chassis and capable of launching a MLC 70/MLC 100 bridge that could be used to span a gap of up to 40 m.

Specifications
OBRUM MS-20 Daglezja Towed Support Bridge
Weight of bridgelayer: (total) 48,000 kg
Length: 16.5 m
Width: 2.55 m
Height: 4 m
Configuration: 6 × 6
Max road speed: 80 km/h

Range: 650 km
Length of bridge: 23 m
Weight of bridge: 15,000 kg
Roadway width: 4 m
Capacity:
  (tracked vehicles) MLC 70
  (wheeled vehicles) MLC 110

Status
Development complete.

Contractor
OBRUM

SMT-1 truck-mounted treadway bridge

Development
The SMT-1 truck-mounted treadway bridge was developed in Poland to meet the specific requirements of the Polish Army and performs a similar function to the Russian-designed TMM and KMM treadway bridges which are covered in detail in a separate entries in *Jane's Military Vehicles and Logistics*. Production of both of the Russian systems is now complete.

Production of the SMT-1 truck mounted treadway bridge was completed many years ago and it is no longer manufactured or marketed. Production of the Star 660 series of 6 × 6 cross-country chassis, on which the SMT-1 treadway bridge is based, has also been completed.

Description
The SMT-1 truck-mounted treadway bridge consists of four 11 m spans, each of these spans is carried in the horizontal position on the rear of a Star 660 M1 or Star 660 M2 2,500 kg (6 × 6) cross-country truck chassis.

They are launched over the front of the vehicle, unlike the Russian TMM and KMM treadway bridges (which are also transported and launched from a 6 × 6 cross-country truck chassis), which are launched over the rear.

Unlike the TMM and KMM treadways, the SMT-1 treadways do not have to be spread before launching as they are fixed. Each treadway consists of tubular steel trusses welded together by struts, crosspieces and diagonal stiffeners, with steel mesh panels mounted on the top of the trusses to form the treadway.

The SMT-1 is much lighter than the TMM treadway: the TMM weighs 666 kg/m and the SMT-1, 210 kg/m.

Each span is launched in three to five minutes with the launching controlled from the forward control cab. Individual spans of the SMT are used for other purposes, for example as ramps on pontoon bridges. The SMT-1 is often used as a single-span bridge without the trestle legs. Additional spans are carried on a single-axle trailer, which has dual tyres.

The SMT-1 truck-mounted treadway bridge is used in conjunction with the PSMT-1 intermediate support, which is also used with other bridges such as the former East German BLG-60 AVLB. The PSMT-1 is positioned by crane or floated into position. It consists of a platform and four trestles adjustable in height.

SMT-1 bridges being operated during a training exercise   0512168

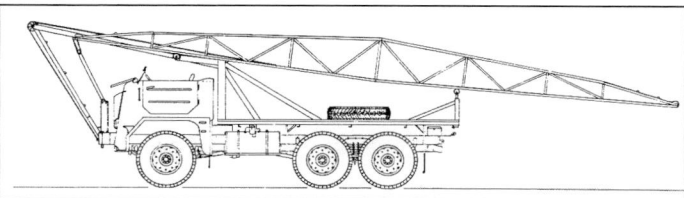

SMT-1 bridgelayer carried on Star 66 (6 × 6) truck chassis   0511515

The trestles are 5 m long and can be folded for travel. The PSMT-1 is capable of floating, primarily because of the plastic foam material used in its construction. It is transported on a single-axle trailer and can be floated directly by reversing the prime mover into the water.

Specifications
SMT-1 truck-mounted treadway bridge
(Bridge only)
Weight: 2,300 kg
Length: 11 m
Width: 3 m
Trestle leg height: adjustable to 3.5 m
Capacity: 40,000 kg

Status
Production complete. In service with the Polish Army. As far as is known, this system was not exported. Poland has offered surplus SMT-1 systems on the export market.

Contractor
Polish state factories.

Russian Federation

TMM (6 × 6) truck-mounted treadway bridge

Development
The Russian TMM (6 × 6) truck-mounted treadway bridge was developed as a follow on to the older Russian designed KMM truck mounted bridge which was carried and launched from a ZIL-157 (6 × 6) truck mounted chassis.

The KMM truck mounted bridge system has now been phased out of service with the Russian Army. More details on the system can be found in a separate entry in *Jane's Military Vehicles and Logistics*. Its replacement, the more recent TMM, is a much more capable system, primarily as it can be used to cross far wider gaps.

Details of this are provided in a separate entry in *Jane's Military Vehicles and Logistics*.

Description
The TMM (*Tyazhelo Mekhniznrovanny Most* - heavy mechanised bridge) consists of four 10.5 m spans, each of which is carried and launched from the rear of a modified KrAZ-214 (6 × 6) 7,000 kg cross-country truck or the more recent KrAZ-255B (6 × 6) 7,500 kg truck.

The latter model has improvements in the bridgelaying mechanism and is recognisable by the replacement wheel and tyre, carried on the roof of the cab rather than at the cab rear as on the KrAZ-214.

The model carried on the KrAZ-255B (6 × 6) truck is designated the TMM-3. Three of the spans have integrally mounted adjustable trestle legs; the fourth (or far-shore) span does not, as it is the link between the third span and the far bank.

The system operates as follows: before launching the treadway, the trestle legs must be adjusted to the correct height so the roadway is level when the bridge has been positioned. During transit, the legs are folded and stored beneath the folded scissors span. The treadways are then spread to the full roadway width of 3.8 m.

TMM-3 bridge carried on KrAZ-255B 7,500 kg truck (Michael Jerchel)   0512159

TMM-3 bridge carried on KrAZ-255B 7,500 kg truck (Michael Jerchel)

0512160

TMM-3 truck-mounted scissors bridge being lowered into position over a previously laid TMM-3 bridge which has its legs lowered in position (Shaun C Connors)

0533521

The truck backs up to the river and the hydraulic launching girder raises the folded span to the vertical position, the span is straightened by a cable and winch system and then lowered.

As it is lowered into position, the integral trestle legs swing into place. Once it is in position the cables are disconnected, the launching girder is brought back into the travelling position and the truck moves off. This procedure is repeated until the bridge is complete.

If required, the bridge can be extended past the basic four spans by further additions. The launched spans can be recovered from either end and recovery takes about the same time as launching.

A complete TMM truck-mounted treadway bridge system complete with four spans can cross a gap up to 40 m in 45 to 60 minutes in daylight, or 60 to 80 minutes at night.

These times are for an average crew and can be halved by a well-trained crew. To reduce the possibility of detection, the TMM can also be laid under the surface of the water, which takes 50 per cent longer than the normal method. Log and metal plate supports can be used to support the trestle legs when obstacles up to 5 m deep are encountered or when the slope is too great.

A Chinese-produced version of the TMM is known as the Heavy Mechanised Bridge Type 84A. Details of this system, which is currently being offered on the export market, are provided in a separate entry in *Jane's Military Vehicles and Logistics*.

The Chinese bridge has capabilities similar to the older Russian TMM bridge, but is transported and launched from a 8 × 8 (or a 6 × 6 chassis) forward control truck. This fully enclosed cab can be tilted forwards to allow access to the power pack.

The Indian Sarvatra bridging system employs many principles similar to those used on the TMM series. Details of this are given in a separate entry in *Jane's Military Vehicles and Logistics*. This is already being offered on the export market.

Funding permitting, the TMM truck-mounted treadway bridge will be supplemented by the new wheeled (8 × 8) Gusenitsa-2 heavy bridge building system. Details of this more capable system are given in a separate entry in *Jane's Military Vehicles and Logistics*.

Specifications

TMM truck-mounted treadway bridge
Cab seating: 1 + 2
Configuration: 6 × 6
Weight: 19,500 kg
Power-to-weight ratio: 10.51 hp/t (7.84 kW/t)
Length: 9.3 m

Width: 3.2 m
Height: 3.15 m
Ground clearance: 0.36 m
Track: 2.03 m
Wheelbase: 4.6 m + 1.4 m
Max speed: (road) 55 km/h
Range: 530 km
Fuel capacity: 450 litres
Fording: 1 m
Engine: YaMZ M206B 6-cylinder water-cooled diesel developing 205 bhp (153 kW) at 2,000 rpm
Transmission: manual with 5 forward and 1 reverse gears and 2-speed transfer box
Tyres: 15.00 × 20

Bridge
Weight: 7,000 kg
Length: 10.5 m
Width: 3.8 m
Trestle leg length: adjustable between 1.7-3.2 m
Capacity: 60,000 kg

Status

Production complete. In service with Bulgaria, Hungary and other armed forces including those of China, Montenegro, Nicaragua (20), Serbia. The Bulgarian Army developed a modified bridge using tubular section metal parts. It is not known if it was adopted or produced in quantity.

Contractor

Russian State factories.

KMM truck-mounted treadway bridge

Development

The KMM truck-mounted treadway bridge system entered service with the Russian Army in the 1950s and was also exported to a number of countries.

The KMM truck mounted bridge system has now been phased out of service with the Russian Army.

It has been replaced by the more recent and more capable TMM truck mounted treadway bridge, which can be used to cross much wider gaps. This is covered in a separate entry in *Jane's Military Vehicles and Logistics*. Production of this has been completed but surplus vehicles may be available from some countries such as the Ukraine.

Description

The KMM (mechanised treadway bridge) consists of five 7 m spans, each of which is carried and launched from the rear of a modified ZIL-157 (6 × 6) 2,500 kg truck or a similar vehicle.

Four of these spans have integral-mounted adjustable trestles while the fifth (or far-shore) span does not, as it is the link between the fourth span and the far bank.

Each trestle has a pair of octagonal shoes with a tip protruding about 0.6 m below the shoe. When buried in the soil, the tip provides additional stabilising strength to the bridge support. When travelling, the trestle shoes are detached from the trestle columns.

The system works as follows: before launching the treadway, the trestle legs must be adjusted to the correct height so the treadway is level when the bridge has been positioned; the treadway is spread to the full roadway width of 2.95 m.

Each clear span can bridge a gap of 6 m and a set of five spans can bridge 34 m. Bridge capacity is reported to be 15,000 kg. The truck then backs up to the river and the span is raised hydraulically to the vertical using the launching girder.

Once in this position, the launching girder serves as a brace for the cables, which support the downward movement of the span. Once the launch has been completed, the launching girder is lowered back to the

KMM truck-mounted treadway bridge on ZIL-157 (6 × 6) 2,500 kg truck with TMM truck-mounted treadway bridge on KrAZ-255B (6 × 6) 7,500 kg truck behind (Egyptian Ministry of Defence)

0511507

travel position. The procedure is repeated with more spans until the far bank has been reached. The launched spans can be recovered from either end, with recovery taking about the same time as launching.

A single KMM can span a gap up to 9.5 m and can be launched in about 15 minutes. A complete five-span KMM bridge can span a gap up to 34 m in 45 to 60 minutes in daylight, or 60 to 80 minutes at night. These times are for an average crew and can be halved by a well-trained crew.

If required, the KMM can also be laid under water reducing the possibility of detection, although this takes approximately 50 per cent longer than the normal method.

The main drawback of the KMM truck-mounted treadway bridge is its limited load bearing capability.

Specifications

KMM truck-mounted treadway bridge
(Vehicle with bridge)
Cab seating: 1 + 2
Configuration: 6 × 6
Weight: 8,800 kg
Power-to-weight ratio: 12.39 hp/t (9.24 kW/t)
Length: 8.3 m
Width: 3.15 m
Height: 3.36 m
Ground clearance: 0.31 m
Track:
   (front) 1.755 m
   (rear) 1.75 m
Wheelbase: 3.665 + 1.12 m
Max speed: (road) 40 km/h
Range: 430 km
Fuel capacity: 215 litres
Max gradient: 28%
Fording: 0.8 m
Engine: ZIL-157K 6-cylinder water-cooled petrol developing 109 hp (81 kW) at 2,800 rpm
Transmission: manual with 5 forward and 1 reverse gears and 2-speed transfer box
Tyres: 12.00 × 18

Bridge
Weight: 1,420 kg
Length: 7 m
Width:
   (without trestle leg) 2.95 m
   (with trestle leg) 3.95 m
Trestle leg height: (adjustable) 1-3 m
Capacity: 15,000 kg
Crossing speed:
   (tracked vehicles) 1 km/h
   (wheeled vehicles) 15-20 km/h
Min distance between crossing vehicles: 15 m

Status

Production complete; replaced in front-line Russian Army units by the TMM truck-mounted treadway bridge. May still be in service in limited numbers with other armed forces including those of China and Egypt. Quantities of surplus KMM truck mounted bridges may be available for sale by some countries.

Contractor

Russian State factories.

PMM-2 amphibious bridging and ferry system

Development

The Russian PMM-2, or *Paromno-Mostovaya Maschina-2*, floating bridging and ferry system was originally known in the West as the Amphibious Bridging System (Tracked), or ABS(T).

The vehicle has a tracked suspension based on the use of T-64 MBT suspension and roadwheel components. It uses a chassis similar to that employed with the PTS-2 amphibious carrier, the MDK-3 trench-digging machine and, what is probably the base vehicle for the series, the MT-T heavy tracked transporter.

It is most likely that the engine used to power the PMM-2 is the V-64-4 diesel. The T-64 MBT and the MT-T heavy tracked transporter were both designed and built in Ukraine.

An updated PMM-2M is known to exist; the available data provided in the Specifications table refers to this version. While this was developed to meet the requirement of the Russian Army, it was actually designed and built in Ukraine. There has been no recent marketing of this PMM-2 amphibious bridging and ferry system.

As far as it is known, production of the PMM-2 and PMM-2M is complete although it has been offered on the export market.

Its replacement could be a new tracked ferry system which has the industrial designation of the Izdeliye 561P, with the latter meaning amphibious. This may have the Western designation of the M-2007 Ferry.

PMM-2 amphibious bridging and ferry unit in travelling configuration

0079524

PMM-2 amphibious bridging and ferry unit with front units being employed prior to entering the water (INA)   1333642

Description

The PMM-2 amphibious bridging and ferry system is the replacement for the older Russian GSP heavy amphibious ferry system, this covered in a separate entry in *Jane's Military Vehicles and Logistics*. It uses a similar chassis and float layout, but the PMM-2 float units unfold for use and can be folded back for road transport. The PMM-2 is able to ferry loads up to around 42.5 tonnes.

In use the PMM-2 follows the same general lines as the earlier GSP but the float units are mechanically unfolded using hydraulic mechanisms just before or as the vehicle enters the water.

The top float unfolds to the right and the second section, which is slightly shorter than the top section as it is located behind the cab, to the left. Also unfolded mechanically are two two-section loading ramps each side. Once in the water, propulsion is provided by two propeller units at the rear.

These are lowered once the vehicle is in the water and the drive is taken from the main 710 hp diesel engine. The propellers are concealed within prominent cowls preventing damage; the cowls also support small steering rudders.

PMM-2 units can be connected together to form floating bridges by using latching mechanisms on the outer edges of the float units. Bridges up to 10 units wide have been reported and no bridging boats are apparently involved in the formation of such bridges. The PMM-2 system can operate in rivers with a flow rate of up to 2 m/s.

Individual PMM-2 units can also be used to bridge small water gaps. The overall width of the PMM-2 on the road is 3.36 m; once the side floats are lowered, the overall width is 10 m.

The loading ramps each have a usable length of at least 5 m so a single PMM-2 can probably be used to bridge water gaps almost 20 m wide. In practice this width is probably reduced to around 17 m.

It has been reported that the PMM-2 has a crew of five, but the cab appears to be too small to accommodate this number and the number of personnel required to operate the vehicle as a ferry would probably be limited to two or three. The PMM-2 probably has a collective NBC protection system for the cab, in common with other vehicles using the same or similar chassis.

Specifications

PMM-2 amphibious bridging and ferry system
Length: (overall) 13.35 m
Width: (overall) 3.36 m
Height: (overall) 3.65 m
Max speed:
   (road) 55 km/h
   (water) 10 km/h
Engine: diesel, 710 hp (529 kW)
Max load: 42,500 kg

Status
Production complete. In service with the Russian Army and probably some other members of the now disbanded Warsaw Pact.

Contractor
Kryukovskiy Vegonostroitel'nny Zavod

Gusenitsa-1 (MTU-90) armoured bridgelayer

Development
The MTU-72 armoured bridgelayer, covered in detail in a separate entry in *Jane's Military Vehicles and Logistics*, is based on the chassis of the widely deployed T-72 series Main Battle Tank (MBT).

Further development of the T-72 MBT resulted in the T-90 MBT which, in addition to being in service with the Russian Army, has also been exported to a number of other countries including Algeria, India, Libya and Turkmenistan.

To support the T-90 MBT, Russia has developed the Gusenitsa-1 (MTU-90) armoured bridgelayer which is based on a modified T-90 series MBT chassis which has been fitted with a three- part bridge that is launched over the front of the chassis.

Development of the MTU-90 armoured bridgelayer, which is also referred to as the Gusenitsa-1 (Caterpillar), is complete but as of late 2010 it is understood that production has yet to start.

The MTU-90 AVLB has been developed by the Uralvagonzavod Production Association located in Nizhny Tagil who is also prime contractor for the T-90 MBT as well as other armoured support vehicles such as the BREM-1M armoured recovery vehicle, IMR-2 and IMR-3 armoured engineer vehicles.

In addition to the MTU-90, Russia has developed a number of other specialised vehicles based on the chassis of the T-90 MBT.

This includes the BREM-1M Armoured Repair and Recovery Vehicle (ARRV) and the IMR-3 combat engineer vehicle.

Available details of the latest BREM-1M ARRV are provided in a separate entry in *Jane's Military Vehicles and Logistics*. As of late 2010 it is understood that production of the BREM-1M ARRV had yet to commence.

Description
The chassis of the MTU-90 armoured bridgelayer is the same as that of the T-90 MBT with a high level of protection for the crew, especially over the frontal arc. The driver is seated at the front, fighting compartment in the middle and the V-12 diesel power pack at the rear.

The bridge has a total gap crossing length of 24 m and can carry loads up to 50 tonnes. There are three bridge sections involved, two identical ramps and a centre section, to scissor open in an up-and-over sequence.

During this, a forward support frame is lowered to the ground to assume most of the bridge weight as it unfolds. Total laying time is 2.5 to three minutes.

An NBC protection system is provided for the crew of two. Other equipment includes a fire detection and extinguishing system, night driving equipment, unditching beam at the rear and the ability to lay its own smoke screen by injecting diesel fuel into the exhaust outlet, on the left side of the hull, towards the rear.

It is stated that 'special provisions are made to provide protection against armour-piercing, incendiary and hollow charge projectiles'.

The MTU-90 bridge is operationally compatible with the Gusenitsa-2 (TMM-6) system, which is based on a BAZ-7930 (8 × 8) cross-country truck chassis.

Specifications
(Provisional)
Crew: 2
Weight: 45,700 kg
Power-to-weight ratio: 18.38 hp/t (13.71 kW/t)
Ground pressure: 0.91 kg/cm²
Length: (with bridge) 9.6 m

Width: (with bridge) 3.52 m
Height: (with bridge) 3.92 m
Speed: (road, max) 60 km/h
Range:
 (road) 750 km
 (unpaved road) 350-515 km
Engine: V-84 V-12 multifuel developing 840 hp (626 kW) at 2,000 rpm
Transmission: synchromesh, hydraulically assisted with 7 forward and 1 reverse gears
Steering: clutch and brake
Suspension: torsion bar
Electrical system: 24 V

Bridge
Bridge capacity: 50,000 kg
Weight: 8,600 kg
Length: 25.01 m
Gap spanned: 24 m
Roadway width: 3.55 m
Track width: 1.25 m
Throughout per hour: 150 vehicles
Laying time: 2-2.5 min

Status
Development complete. Ready for production.

Contractor
Ural Transport Engineering Design Bureau (Uralvagonzavod)

MTU-72 armoured bridgelayer

Development
Commencing in 1974, a number of Russian T-72B MBTs were converted to the MTU-72 armoured bridgelayer configuration by removing the two-person turret and replacing it with a hydro-mechanical bridge-launching system and bridge.

The design bureau designation was Objekt 632. One reference mentions that a small number (nine) of these bridgelayers were manufactured from new, utilising the T-72S export chassis.

Production of the MTU-72 is now complete, with only the more recent MTU-90 armoured bridgelayer presently being marketed by Russia.

Development of the MTU-90 armoured Bridgelayer is now complete but it is understood that as of late 2010 it is understood production is yet to commence.

Details of the MTU-90 armoured bridgelayer, which shares a number of components with the TMM-6 heavy bridge building system are provided in a separate entry in *Jane's Military Vehicles and Logisitcs.*

Description
The single-span bridge involved has an overall length, when laid, of 20 m. The bridge, which is constructed of aluminium alloys, has a maximum capacity of 50,000 kg, is 3.3 m wide and can span a gap of 18 m. By itself the bridge weighs 6,400 kg. For transport, the overall length of the bridge can be reduced by folding both ends through 180°.

The overall layout and the operating method of the resultant MTU-72 are similar to those of the older Russian MTU-20 and MTU bridgelayers. These are covered in separate entries in *Jane's Military Vehicles and Logistics.*

The time required to lay a bridge is three minutes, and eight minutes for retrieval. It is possible to lay a second bridge over an emplaced bridge to span gaps up to 30 m wide.

The vehicle is fitted with a hydraulically operated front-mounted stabiliser blade. This can also double as a dozer blade to clear obstacles or prepare bridging sites.

The vehicle is provided with a NBC protection system, a fire suppression system and a thermal smoke generation unit for screening. This is achieved by the injection of diesel fuel into the exhaust outlet on the left side of the hull, towards the rear.

MTU-90 AVLB in travelling configuration and clearly showing three part folded bridge   1164668

Russian MTU-72 armoured bridgelayer with ends of bridge starting to unfold (Uralvagonzavod)   1296067

Armament is limited to a 7.62 mm PKMS light machine gun and crew weapons.

A bridging vehicle based on the chassis of the T-72 MBT, but using a scissors bridge and known as the BLP-72, was developed to the prototype stage by the former East German Army. Few details are available but it is believed to have been generally similar to the MTU-72.

Variants

In addition to the Russian MTU-72, a number of other countries have also developed and placed T-72 based Armoured Vehicle Launched Bridges (AVLBs) into production.

Some examples of which are listed below:
- Indian - Bridge Layer Tank T-72 (BLT T-72)
- Poland - PMCz-90 armoured bridgelayer
- Slovakia - ZTS MT-72 armoured bridgelayer.

Each of the examples mentioned previously are covered in greater detail in separate entries within *Jane's Military Vehicles and Logistics*.

Specifications

MTU-72 armoured bridgelayer
Crew: 2
Weight: (approx) 40,000 kg
Power-to-weight ratio: 21 hp/t (15.66 kW/t)
Ground pressure: 0.808 kg/cm²
Length with bridge: 11.64 m
Width: 3.46 m
Height: (with bridge) 3.38 m
Ground clearance: 0.492 m
Track width: 580 mm
Length of track on ground: 4.278 m
Ground pressure: 0.808 kg/cm²
Max speed: (road) 60 km/h
Range: (road) 500 km
Fuel capacity: 1,000 litres
Fording:
  (normal) 1.2 m
  (with preparation) 4.5 m
Gradient: 60%
Side slope: 40%
Vertical obstacle: 0.85 m
Trench: 2.8 m
Engine: V-84-1 multifuel diesel developing 840 hp (626 kW) at 2,000 rpm
Transmission: synchromesh, hydraulically assisted with 7 forward and 1 reverse gears
Suspension: torsion bar
Electrical system: 24 V
Armament: 1 × 7.62 mm PKMS MG

Bridge
Bridge capacity: 50,000 kg
Bridge weight: 6,400 kg
Bridge length:
  (extended) 20 m
  (folded) 9.42 m
Bridge width: 3.3 m
Bridge track: 1 m × 2
Gap spanned: 18 m

Status

Production complete. In service with the Russian Army and probably some other countries.

Contractor

Ural Transport Engineering Design Bureau (Uralvagonzavod)

MTU-20 armoured bridgelayer

Development

The MTU-20 armoured bridgelayer was introduced into the Soviet Army in 1967 as the replacement for the older MTU bridgelayer. It was based on the T-55 tank chassis rather than the T-54 tank chassis used for the MTU.

The original design bureau designation was Objekt 602. The MTU-20 armoured bridgelayer was replaced in production by the MTU-72 bridgelayer based on the later T-72 MBT chassis modified for its new role.

Russia has now ceased production and marketing of the MTU-72 and is now concentrating on marketing of the MTU-90 AVLB based on the current production T-90 MBT chassis.

Description

The MTU-20 was developed as the replacement for the older MTU-54. This was based on a modified T-54 chassis and is covered in a separate entry in *Jane's Military Vehicles and Logistics*.

The MTU-20 has a much longer bridge than the older MT-54 and can therefore be used to cross far wider gaps. The method of launching is the same as the MT-54, although stabilisers are fitted at the front of the chassis to provide a more stable platform when the bridge is being manoeuvred into position.

MTU-20 armoured bridgelayer in travelling configuration   0512158

The welded steel bridge weighs 7,000 kg and is of the box construction type. It has a maximum length of 20 m and can span a gap up to 18 m. It is 3.3 m wide, 1 m high and has a maximum capacity of 60,000 kg. When travelling, the ends of the bridge are folded back through 180° so that they lie on top of the bridge. They are lowered and locked in position before the bridge is launched. The bridge takes five minutes to lay in position and between five and seven minutes to recover.

As the MTU-20 is based on a T-55 chassis it is thought likely that an NBC system is installed.

The MTU-20 can also lay a smoke screen by injecting diesel fuel into the exhaust outlet on the left side of the hull towards the rear. The driver is provided with night vision equipment. An unditching beam is carried at the rear of the hull.

Specifications

MTU-20 armoured bridgelayer
Crew: 2
Weight: (with bridge) 37,000 kg
Power-to-weight ratio: 15.68 hp/t (11.69 kW/t)
Length: (with bridge) 11.64 m
Width: (with bridge) 3.306 m
Height: (with bridge) 3.4 m
Ground clearance: 0.425 m
Track: 2.64 m
Track width: 580 mm
Length of track on ground: 3.84 m
Ground pressure: 0.84 kg/cm²
Max speed: (road) 54 km/h
Range: 485-500 km
Fuel capacity: 960 litres
Fording: 1.4 m
Gradient: 40%
Vertical obstacle: 0.8 m
Trench: 2.7 m
Engine: V-55 V-12 water-cooled diesel developing 580 hp (433 kW) at 2,000 rpm
Transmission: manual with 5 forward and 1 reverse gears
Electrical system: 24 V
Batteries: 4 × 12 V, 280 Ah
Armament: nil

Armour
Glacis plate: 100 mm at 60°
Upper hull sides: 70 mm at 0°
Hull rear: 60 mm
Hull floor: 20 mm
Hull roof: 30 mm

Status

Production complete. The MTU-20 is known to be in service with Egypt, Finland, India, Israel, Nigeria, Russia (563 originally declared) and Syria. Russia may have quantities of the MTU-20 AVLB that are surplus to requirements.

Contractor

Russian State factories.

MTU-54 armoured bridgelayer

Development

The MTU-54 bridgelayer (*Mostoykladchik tankoviy ustroystvo* - MTU), entered service with the Russian Army in 1958 as the replacement for an older bridgelayer based on a T-34 MBT chassis.

The technical characteristics of the MTU were approved in October 1946, with original development being carried out by Factory Number 75. Following delays, some of the work was subsequently carried out by Factory Number 264.

MTU-54 armoured bridgelayer in travelling configuration   0511505

The first two prototypes of the vehicle, which had the development designation of the Article 421, were completed at Factory 75 in 1952 and sent for user trials, with a third vehicle being completed in 1954.

Following extensive trials, Article 421 was accepted for service with the Russian Army under the official designation of the MTU-54. Full-rate production was established at Factory Number 75 and 183 in 1956/1957.

All vehicles were built on new chassis and were not conversions of older vehicles.

The MTU-54 was supplemented in Russian Army service by the MTU-20. This vehicle was fitted with a new bridge able to span gaps of up to 20 m. Details of the MTU-20 are provided in a separate entry in *Jane's Military Vehicles and Logistics*.

When compared with more recent MTU-20 and MTU-90, the MTU-54 has limited capabilities. When compared to the latest MTU-90 (T-90 MBT chassis) and MTU-72 (T-72 MBT chassis), the MTU-54 based on the T-54/T-55 chassis has a lower level of protection and cross-country mobility.

Production of the MTU-72 armoured bridgelayer based on the T-72 MBT chassis is complete and details of this are provided in a separate entry in *Jane's Military Vehicles and Logistics*.

The latest Russian armoured bridgelayer is the MTU-90 which is based on the current production Russian T-90 MBT. Details of this are provided in a separate entry in *Jane's Military Vehicles and Logistics*.

Development of the MTU-90 armoured bridgelayer is now complete but it is understood that as of late 2010 production had yet to commence.

The MTU-90 armoured bridgelayer shares a number of components with the TMM-6 heavy bridge building system based on an 8 × 8 cross-country truck chassis.

Description

The MTU-54 was based on the chassis of the T-54 MBT with its turret removed. Later production models were based on the T-55 chassis, rather than the T-54 chassis used on earlier models.

The chassis of the T-54 was modified for the MTU-54 role, other changes include modifications to the cooling system and engine heater, fuel system and transmission.

The suspension is of the torsion bar type with either side of the vehicle having five roadwheels, an idler is fitted at the front and the drive sprocket at the rear. There are no track-return rollers.

The MTU-54 was crewed by three personnel, consisting of the driver, commander and gunner.

The driver was seated at the front of the hull on the left side and was provided with two day periscopes for observation and a single-piece hatch cover.

The commander was seated in the crew compartment to the rear of the driver with the V-54 V-12 engine and transmission at the rear of the hull.

A 12.7 mm DShKM machine gun, mounted in the centre of the hull between the two treadways, has to be removed before the bridge can be laid in position.

The MTU-54 was not fitted with an NBC system and had no deep fording capability. Auxiliary fuel drums were often carried at the rear of the hull.

The MTU-54 armoured bridgelayer was also lay its own smoke screen by injecting diesel fuel into the exhaust outlet on the left side of the hull towards the rear. Some vehicles had been observed with an unditching beam carried at the rear of the hull.

The bridge carried by the MTU-54 was 12.3 m long, 3.27 m wide and 1 m high and was able to span a gap of 11 m. The bridge's maximum loading capacity was 50,000 kg.

The bridge consisted of four box-truss panels. The outer treadways were used by tracked vehicles and the inner treadways by smaller vehicles. When travelling, the ramp sections of the inner treadways were folded on top of the main treadways.

The bridge was positioned as follows: a chain drive mechanism moves the bridge over the cantilever launching girder until the far bank was reached, the cantilever launching girder was depressed, lowering the span on to the near bank. Launching the bridge took between three and five minutes, retrieval could be from either side.

The chassis provided the same level of protection as the T-54 series MBT.

Specifications

MTU-54 armoured bridgelayer
Crew: 3
Weight: (with bridge) 34,000 kg
Power-to-weight ratio: 15.29 hp/t (11.40 kW/t)

Length: (with bridge) 12.3 m
Width: (with bridge) 3.27 m
Height: (with bridge) 2.87 m
Ground clearance: 0.425 m
Track: 2.64 m
Track width: 580 mm
Length of track on ground: 3.84 m
Ground pressure: 0.76 kg/cm²
Max speed: (road) 48 km/h
Range: 400 km
Fuel capacity: 812 litres
Fording: 1.4 m
Gradient: 60%
Vertical obstacle: 0.8 m
Trench: 2.7 m
Engine: V-54 V-12 water-cooled diesel developing 520 hp (388 kW) at 2,000 rpm
Transmission: manual with 5 forward and 1 reverse gears
Electrical system: 24 V
Batteries: ×4, 280 Ah each
Armament: 1 × 12.7 mm DShKM MG

Armour
Glacis plate: 100 mm at 60°
Upper hull sides: 70 mm at 0°
Hull rear: 60 mm
Hull floor: 20 mm
Hull roof: 30 mm

Status

Production complete. The T-54 is used by the following countries, some of which also use the MTU-54 bridgelayer: Afghanistan, Albania, Algeria, Angola, Armenia, Azerbaijan, Bangladesh, Belarus, Bosnia-Herzegovina, Bulgaria, Cambodia, Central African Republic, Chad, Congo (Democratic Republic), Côte d'Ivoire, Croatia, Cuba, Egypt (confirmed), Ethiopia, Finland (confirmed), Georgia, Guinea, India, Iran, Iraq, Israel (confirmed), Korea (North), Laos, Lebanon, Libya, Macedonia, Mali, Mauritania, Mongolia, Montenegro, Mozambique, Myanmar, Nicaragua, Nigeria, Pakistan, Peru, Romania, Russian Federation (confirmed), Rwanda, Serbia, Slovenia, Somalia, Sri Lanka, Sudan, Syria (confirmed), Tanzania, Togo, Uganda, Ukraine, Uruguay, Uzbekistan, Vietnam, Yemen, and Zambia.

Contractor

Russian state factories.

Gusenitsa-2 heavy bridge building system (TMM-6)

Development

The Russian Gusenitsa-2 (TMM-6) heavy bridge system was developed as a follow on to the older TMM truck-mounted treadway bridge which is still used by the Russian Army and covered in detail in a separate entry in *Jane's Military Vehicles and Logistics*.

When compared to the older TMM truck-mounted heavy bridge the latest TMM-6 is based on an 8 × 8 chassis with greater cross-country mobility.

It is understood that development of this system is complete but as of late 2010 quantity production had yet to commence.

Description

The Gusenitsa-2 (Caterpillar-2) heavy bridge building system, also known as the TMM-6, is based on a BAZ-7930 (8 × 8) truck chassis with a lengthened wheelbase and can be used to lay up to six bridge sections to form bridges with spans of from 17 to 102 m.

The Gusenitsa-2 system is compatible with the tracked Gusenitsa-1, and operates along the same general lines as the earlier TMM system (see separate entry in *Jane's Military Vehicles and Logistics*).

Each Gusenitsa-2 folded bridge section forms a 17 m bridge section when unfolded. The bridge load capacity is 60 tonnes. Each bridge section has a trestle support assembly that can unfold as each section is opened or can be kept folded if the far bank is reached; the depth the bridge trestle legs can negotiate is 5 m.

Gusenitsa-2 heavy bridge building system in travelling configuration
0079527

Gusenitsa-2 heavy bridge building system with another bridge being launched to the rear of a previously laid bridge   0092496

Gusenitsa-2 heavy bridge building system laying bridge over rear of three bridge units already in position (Steven Zaloga)   0079529

Six TMM-6 sections can form a bridge 102 m long within 55 minutes. Once emplaced, traffic can cross the finished bridge at speeds of 25 to 30 km/h.

A 102 m Gusenitsa-2 bridge may be further extended to 125 m by the use of a Gusenitsa-1 (MTU-90) armoured bridgelayer system. Full details of the T-90 based MTU-90 are provided in a separate entry in *Jane's Military Vehicles and Logistics*.

The TMM-6 system was designed by the Omsk Machine-Building Design Bureau with manufacture undertaken by the Omsk Transport Machine-Building Plant.

This facility was also involved in production of the T-64 and T-80 MBTs. No MBTs are currently in production in Omsk.

The bridge can be laid from within the cab or from outside using a remote control device. The bridge launching system is hydraulic with a power take off from the main diesel engine.

The BAZ-7930 (8 × 8) chassis on which the system is based is provided with powered steering and a central tyre pressure regulation system that allows the crew to adjust the tyre pressure from within the cab. The forward control, fully enclosed two-door cab is provided with an NBC system.

Specifications

TMM-6 heavy bridge building system
Crew: 2
Configuration: 8 × 8
Bridge length: 17 to 102 m (later figure is with six bridge units)
Bridge capacity: 60,000 kg
Depth of obstacle: 5 m
Launch time of six span bridge: 50 mins
Vehicle crossing speed: 20 to 30 km/h
Speed of 8 × 8 launcher: 35 to 40 km/h (average)
Max speed of launcher: 70 km/h
Max range of launcher: 1,100 km

Status
Prototypes. Troop tested by the Russian Army. There are no known exports of this system.

Contractor
Omsk Transport Machine Building Plant

Serbia and Montenegro

Truck-mounted scissors treadway bridge

Development
This truck-mounted scissors bridge consists of three 13 m spans carried and launched from the rear of a modified FAP 2220BDS (6 × 4) truck. Full details of the FAP 2220BDS can be found in a separate entry in *Jane's Military Vehicles and Logistics*.

As far as is it known, there has been no recent production of this system. This system was originally designed and manufactured in the former Yugoslavia.

Yugoimport market a wide range of defence products but as far as is known this truck mounted scissors bridge is no longer marketed.

It is not expected that there will be any future production of this truck-mounted scissors treadway bridge system.

Description
The system is laid in a similar manner to the older Russian TMM KrAZ-255 series (6 × 6) truck-mounted scissors treadway bridge and has similar capabilities.

The trestle legs on the Serbian truck-mounted scissors treadway bridge can be extended to a maximum length of 4 m, whereas the TMM's trestle legs can be extended to only 3 m, enabling the bridge to be used for deeper crossings.

The treadway bridge is laid as follows: before launching the treadway, the trestle legs are adjusted to the correct height so that the roadway is level when the bridge is in position; the truck then backs up to the gap; and the treadway is raised to the vertical position.

The span is then straightened and lowered into position while the trestle legs are simultaneously swung into place. Once this is complete, the truck drives off and the procedure is repeated until the bridge is complete. Each individual span takes five to six minutes to lay in position and can be recovered from either end. Recovery takes about the same time as launching. A complete three-span bridge will span a gap up to 36 m wide.

Specifications
Truck mounted scissors treadway bridge
Cab seating: 1 + 1
Configuration: 6 × 4
Weight: 20,000 kg
Power-to-weight ratio: 10.00 hp/t (7.46 kW/t)
Length: 8.2 m
Width: 2.5 m
Height: 2.56 m
Track:
  (front) 1.97 m
  (rear) 1.745 m
Wheelbase: 3.12 m + 1.2 m
Max road speed: 60 km/h
Range: (estimated) 300 km
Fuel capacity: 200 litres
Engine: Famos 2F/002A 6-cylinder water-cooled diesel developing 200 hp (149 kW)
Tyres: 11.00 × 20

Bridge
Length: 13 m
Width: 2.5 m
Trestle leg length: 4 m

Status
In service with Montenegro and Serbia and possibly in other parts of the former Yugoslavia. Production complete. No longer marketed.

Contractor
Yugoimport SDPR

Truck-mounted scissors treadway bridge in travelling position on FAP 2220BDS (6 × 4) truck   0511518

Singapore

Light Assault Bridge LAB 30

Development
The Light Assault Bridge (LAB 30) is essentially a French AMX-13 light tank chassis, originally developed in France in the late 1940's, modified for its new role. A few of these were issued to the French Army but these have now been withdrawn from service.

Description
The Light Assault Bridge LAB 30 is very similar to the French AMX-13 armoured bridgelayer (now withdrawn from service) and is based on a now Nexter Systems AMX-13 light tank chassis.

The bridgelayer is produced by removing the AMX-13 tank turret and replacing it with the mechanism to lay a folding or sliding assault bridge. The hydraulically-operated mechanism is incorporated on the front and rear of the tank chassis and operates in a manner very similar to that of the French AMX-13 system.

The folding bridge employed is manufactured entirely from aluminium alloy and weighs 3,200 kg; length is 14 m and width 2.9 m. The bridge can be launched within three to four minutes and will take loads up to Military Load Class 30 (MLC 30). The bridge can cross a gap of 12 m (on soft ground) or 13 m (on hard ground). With two bridges placed side by side, the load class can be increased to Military Load class 60 (MLC 60).

When travelling complete with its bridge the LAB 30 is 7.38 m long and 3.2 m high.

Singapore operates a fleet of over 350 AMX-13 SM1 light tanks and an undisclosed quantity of LAB 30 are understood to be in service.

As far as it is known, no other country operates the AMX-13 AVLB.

The original AMX-13 light tank was developed and produced in the late 1940s and this, and its many variants, were built in large numbers for the home and export markets.

Status
Production complete. In service with Singapore. No longer marketed.

Contractor
Singapore Technologies Kinetics

Singapore Technologies Kinetics Bionix AVLB

Development
In mid-2000 Singapore Technologies Kinetics revealed that for three years they had been developing an Armoured Vehicle-Launched Bridge (AVLB) version of their Bionix Infantry Fighting Vehicle (IFV) to meet the operational requirements of the Singapore Armed Forces (SAF).

This was the fourth version of the Bionix to be developed for the SAF; the first two versions, the Bionix 25 and 40/50 IFVs, became operational in 1999 with the third version, the Bionix recovery vehicle starting its trials in 1999.

Following extensive trials with prototype vehicles, the Bionix AVLB was type classified for service by the Singapore Armed Forces and a production contract placed with Singapore Technologies Kinetics. This is now in service with the Singapore Armed Forces.

According to Krauss-Maffei Wegmann (previously Military Mobile Bridges), key sub-contractor to Singapore Technologies Kinetics for the bridge and its associated launching system, the latter are also applicable to other types of tracked and wheeled chassis, armoured and unarmoured.

The Bionix family of tracked vehicles has been marketed overseas but as of late 2010 no sales had been made.

The Bionix chassis is also used for an ARV and the Trailblazer flail type mine clearing system which are also in service with the Singapore Armed Services.

Description
The hull of the Bionix AVLB is of all-welded steel to which an additional layer of passive armour is added to provide a higher level of battlefield survivability.

The driver is seated at the front left with the commander on the right and they enter the vehicle via two hatches above their position. The driver is provided with day periscopes, the centre one of which can be replaced by a passive periscope for driving at night.

Mounted on top of the Bionix hull is the Military Load Class 30 (MLC 30) two part bridge which, when open, is 22 metres long and can be used to span wet and dry gaps of up to 20 m. Two MLC 30 bridges can be used side by side to form a MLC 60 bridge to take heavier tracked vehicles.

The push-pull bridge is constructed of aluminium alloy and takes less than six minutes to launch with the crew of two being under complete armour protection. It can also be launched via remote control using a remote-operating panel and there are no hydraulic parts in the bridge.

Bridgelaying is carried out automatically, the laying sequence starting with the vehicle travelling forward to the near bank.

After raising the top bridge half, the lower bridge half is advanced. The top bridge half is held at the front by the slewing support arm and at the rear by the coupling support arm. The bridge halves are then coupled automatically by lowering the coupling support arm.

Bionix AVLB in the travelling configuration   0073178

Bionix AVLB with two part bridge being laid over the front of the vehicle   0129731

The bridge can then be advanced fully, at which point it is guided along the girder by the roller carriage. For the final stage, the girder is moved back. The bridge is then ready for use.

Krauss-Maffei Wegmann is known mainly for its heavy assault bridges carried on Leopard 1, Leopard 2 and M1 Main Battle Tank (MBT) chassis but the new 22 m medium assault bridge is adaptable to a wider range of other light tank and full-tracked chassis.

Variants

Bionix Recovery Vehicle
The Bionix Recovery Vehicle (RV) was developed by Singapore Technologies Kinetics to meet the requirements of the Singapore Armed Forces. It is covered in detail in a separate entry in *Jane's Military Vehicles and Logistics*.

Trailblazer mine clearing vehicle
The Trailblazer mine clearing vehicle is the latest member of the Bionix family to enter service with the Singapore Armed Forces. The Trailblazer has a flail-type mine clearing system fitted on the rear of its chassis.

Specifications
Bionix AVLB
Crew: 2
Weight: 28,000 kg
Power-to-weight ratio: 16.96 hp/t (12.65 kW/t)
Length: 11.2 m
Width: 3.2 m
Height: 3.77 m
Track width: 430 mm
Max speed:
(road) 65 km/h
(cross-country) 25-40 km/h
Acceleration: 0 to 32 km/h in 9 s
Fuel capacity:
(total) 562 litres
(usable) 527 litres
Range: 400 km
Gradient: 45%
Side slope: 30%
Vertical obstacle: 0.6 m

Trench: 1.6 m
Fording: 1 m
Engine: Detroit Diesel 6V-92TA 2-cycle diesel developing 475 hp (354 kW)
Transmission: L3 Combat Propulsion Systems HMPT-500-3RC fully automatic
Steering: hydrostatic
Brakes: multidisc oil cooled
Suspension: hydropneumatic
Electrical system: 28 V
Batteries: 4 × 12 V, 200 Ah
Alternator: 300 A

Bridge System
Capacity: MLC 30
Length: 22 m
Width: 3.2 m

Status
Production as required. In service with the Singapore Armed Forces. The Bionix family of tracked armoured vehicles have been offered on the export market but there are no known sales.

Contractor
Singapore Technologies Kinetics

Slovakia

ZTS MT-72 armoured bridgelayer

Development
The MT-72 armoured bridgelayer was developed using the chassis of the Russian-designed, Slovakian built T-72M1 MBT as a basis but otherwise follows the same general lines as the MT-55A armoured bridgelayer, covered in detail in a separate entry in *Jane's Military Vehicles and Logistics.*

The MT-55A deploys a scissors-type bridge that is 18 metres long when extended, while that of the more recent MT-72 has a total length of 22 metres.

The MT-55A can carry and launch the MT-72 bridge if required. As far as it is known there has been no recent production of the T-72M1 MBT or its variants in Slovakia.

Description
The MT-72 bridge is of the scissors type and is constructed using high-strength steel. The bridge has a carrying capacity of 50,000 kg and has a total length of 20 m, allowing gaps up to 18 m to be bridged.

When gaps longer than 20 m have to be bridged it is possible to lay a second bridge on the first. According to ZTS, the scissor type bridge can be laid on gradients of ±50° and side slopes ±6°.

The width of the bridge is 3.3 m while each bridge track is 1.15 m wide. Weight of the complete bridge is 6,000 kg. When folded the bridge is 10.6 m long.

The hydraulic bridgelaying mechanism used on the MT-72 is the same as that used on the older T-55 chassis based MT-55A; working pressure is 22 MPa (220 bar) and maximum pressure 28 MPa (280 bar). An automatic laying sequence lasts three minutes, with bridge retrieval from three to eight minutes.

The MT-72 is provided with a fording device, which allows water obstacles up to 4.2 m deep to be negotiated.

It can also lay its own smoke screen by injecting diesel fuel into the exhaust outlet at the left side of the hull rear. An unditching beam can also be carried on the hull rear. Standard equipment includes an NBC system and passive night driving aids.

The ZTS MT-72 AVLB can be provided by Slovakia as part of a complete package that also includes the ZTS VT-72B ARV and various models of the T-72 series MBT. There has been no recent marketing of these vehicles by ZTS Tees Martin.

Specifications
MT-72 armoured bridgelayer
Crew: 2
Weight: (approx, with bridge) 41,500 kg
Power-to-weight ratio: (approx, with bridge) 20.24 hp/t (15.09 kW/t)
Length: (with bridge) 10.6 m
Width: (with bridge) 3.59 m
Height: (max, with bridge) 3.8 m
Fording:
    (wading) 1.5 m
    (with preparation) 4.2 m
Vertical obstacle: 0.85 m
Trench: 2.6-2.8 m
Engine: V-64-4 V-12 diesel developing 840 hp (626 kW)

Bridge
Weight: 6,000 kg
Length:
    (extended) 20 m
    (folded) 10.6 m
Width: 3.30 m
Track width: (each) 1.15 m
Carrying capacity: 50,000 kg

Status
Development complete. Ready for production. A small production batch of MT-72 armoured bridgelayers may have been built.

Contractor
ZTS Tees Martin

AM-50 and AM-50B truck-mounted scissors bridges

Development
In 1972, Czechoslovakia introduced a scissors bridge launched over the rear of a Czech Republic-built TATRA 813 (8 × 8) cross-country truck chassis and known as the AM-50 *(Automobilni Most 50)* or AM-50A.

It is launched in a similar fashion to the Russian-designed and-built TMM treadway bridge, but the AM-50 system has the added advantage that the trestle columns have hydraulic rather than manual adjustment. This feature enables the system to be deployed more rapidly as well as providing a more stable platform.

Another feature is that the bridge has a full-width roadway rather than the two single tracks of the Russian TMM system.

Production of the AM-50/AM-50B is now undertaken on an as required basis. It may be possible to integrate this truck mounted scissors bridge system on other chassis.

Description
The AM-50B is an essentially similar bridge carried on the TATRA T 815 VP 19.28 265 8 × 8.1 R truck with a central tyre pressure control system; this was introduced in 1989. A complete AM-50 bridge system on the move weighs 25,900 kg when a dozer blade is included. Late production AM-50 and all AM-50B bridges are interchangeable.

A single AM-50B bridge weighs 5,700 kg and has a load capacity of 50 tonnes for tracked vehicles or 70 tonnes for multi-axle wheeled vehicles. Using a crew of three, each bridge can span a 12.5 m gap (the actual bridge length when opened is 13.5 m), the width with the bridge rims unfolded being 4 m.

As the bridge can be laid on to hydraulic trestle columns, extra bridges can be added to span large gaps. For instance, up to eight AM-50B bridges can be used to cross a water obstacle 106 m wide and up to 6 m deep.

The time it takes to lay a single AM-50B bridge is up to seven minutes and up to four can be laid in line in about 30 minutes. At night or in unfavourable conditions, the erection time is multiplied by a factor of 1.5. Each telescopic trestle leg can be varied in height from 1.988 to 6.052 m; each leg weighs 1,760 kg.

ZTS MT-72 armoured bridgelayer in travelling configuration from the front (Stefan Marx) 1133711

AM-50B truck-mounted scissors bridge in travelling configuration 0512319

AM-50B scissors bridges in position with unloaded TATRA T815 (8 × 8) laying vehicles crossing   0512320

BrüPz 68/88 armoured bridgelayer crossing a laid bridge   0044096

To prevent the front axles of the AM-50B carrier vehicle rising during the final stages of the laying operation, the front of the vehicle is anchored to the ground or to an existing bridge section by a rope or cable.

Once the bridge is in position, wheeled vehicles can cross at a maximum speed of 30 to 40 km/h; the maximum speed for tracked vehicles is from 15 to 20 km/h.

The fully enclosed two-door cab can be tilted forwards for maintenance purposes using a hydraulic system. As an option the cab can be fitted with an air conditioning system and/or an NBC system.

If required, a BZT T 815 dozer blade can be mounted at the front of the chassis. This is typically used to prepare bridging enter and exit points. A hydraulically operated winch with 15.94 m of 25 mm diameter cable is provided.

Specifications

AM-50B truck-mounted scissors bridge
Crew: 2 or 3
Weight:
  (AM-50B, vehicle and bridge, with dozer) 25,900 kg
  (AM-50, vehicle and bridge) 24,450 kg
  (bridge) 5,700 kg
  (trestle leg) 1,760 kg
  (ramp section) 70 kg
  (vehicle only) 17,400 kg
Bridge capacity:
  (tracked vehicles) 50,000 kg
  (multi-axle wheeled vehicles) 70,000 kg
Bridge span: 13.5 m
Bridge width:
  (rims unfolded) 4 m
Length of bridge travelling: (folded) 8.05 m
Width of bridge travelling: 3.15 m
Height of bridge travelling: 3.8 m
Angle of approach/departure:
  (with dozer blade) 18°/28°
  (without dozer blade) 32°/28°
Fording: 1.4 m
Length of trestle legs: 1.988-6.052 m
Time to lay one bridge: up to 7 min
Vehicle crossing speeds:
  (wheeled vehicles) 30-40 km/h
  (tracked vehicles) 15-20 km/h
Vehicle length with dozer: 12 m
Vehicle width with dozer: 3.15 m
Vehicle height: (loaded) 3.8 m
Max vehicle speed:
  (road, loaded) 80 km/h
  (cross-country, loaded) 30 km/h
Range: (road) 900 km

Status
Production as required. In service with the armies of the Czech Republic, India and Slovak Republic.

As far as it is known there has been no recent production of this system for the home or export markets.

Contractor
Vychodoslovenske Strojarne as Kosice

Switzerland

RUAG Defence Brückenlegepanzer 68/88 armoured bridgelayer

Development
The first prototype of the *Brückenlegepanzer* 68 (BrüPz 68) was based on the chassis of the Pz 61 MBT, but production vehicles were based on the chassis of the later Pz 68 MBT.

Prototype vehicles carried a steel bridge, which was replaced on production vehicles by an aluminium bridge. Production was completed in June 1977. Since then, several modifications have been introduced, including a fully automatic hydraulic bridgelaying system, resulting in a change of designation to BrüPz 68/88.

The bridgelaying system was developed by the Eidgenössische Konstruktionswerkstätte facility at Thun which subsequently became RUAG Land Systems and is the only tracked armoured fighting vehicle facility in Switzerland. The Pz 68 MBT chassis on which this vehicle is based was designed and built at Thun.

It should be noted that all of the Pz 61 and Pz 68 MBTs have now been phased out of service with the Swiss Army.

In January 2011, RUAG Land Systems and RUAG Electronics merged to form a new company called RUAG Defence.

In January 2005, following a competition, the now RUAG Defence was awarded a CHF10 million contract to supply the Finnish Defence Forces with one Leopard 2 armoured vehicle launched bridge system.

The bridge and some elements of the launching system have been provided by the German company Krauss-Maffei Wegmann (previously known as Military Mobile Bridges). Details of this system are provided in a separate entry in *Jane's Military Vehicles and Logistics*.

Description
The hull of the *Brückenlegepanzer* 68/88 (BrüPz 68/88) is almost identical to that of the Pz 68 MBT. The driver is seated at the front of the hull, in the centre, and is provided with three day periscopes for observation (the centre one of which can be replaced by a passive periscope) and a single-piece hatch cover. The commander and the bridge operator are seated in the centre of the vehicle with the power pack at the rear.

The suspension of the BrüPz 68 is the Belleville type and either side consists of six roadwheels with the drive sprocket at the rear and the idler at the front. There are three track-return rollers. Each roadwheel is independently sprung by layers of Belleville washers.

The bridge itself has an overall length of 18.23 m and a width of 3.79 m with maximum trackway width being 3.55 m. Its maximum capacity is 60,000 kg but it is normally limited to a maximum load of 50,000 kg.

The bridge is launched as follows: the bridgelayer approaches the obstacle and halts; the bridge is tilted forward and a beam slid across to the far bank; the bridge is slid across the beam until it reaches the far bank; and the beam is then withdrawn back into the horizontal position. The laying sequence is fully automatic, once initiated. A bridge takes about two minutes to lay and under five minutes to recover.

Specifications
Brückenlegepanzer 68/88 armoured bridgelayer
Crew: 3
Weight:
  (with bridge) 47,000 kg
  (without bridge) 37,200 kg
Power-to-weight ratio: (with bridge) 14.04 hp/t (10.47 kW/t)
Length: (with bridge) 20.1 m
Width: (with bridge) 4 m
Height: (with bridge) 3.3 m
Ground clearance: 0.4 m
Track: 2.59 m
Track width: 520 mm
Length of track on ground: 4.22 m
Ground pressure: 0.98 kg/cm^2
Max speed: (road) 55 km/h
Range:
  (road) 300 km
  (cross-country) 160 km
Fuel capacity: 855 litres
Fording: 1.1 m
Gradient: 70%
Vertical obstacle: 0.7 m
Trench: 2 m
Engine: MTU MB 837 8-cylinder diesel developing 660 hp (492 kW) at 2,200 rpm
Transmission: semi-automatic with 6 forward and 6 reverse gears
Electrical system: 24 V
Batteries: 4 × 6 V, 360 Ah
Armament: 8 × 80 mm smoke grenade dischargers
Armour: 20-60 mm

Status
Production complete. In service with the Swiss Army. The Pz 68 MBT chassis on which this system is based on has now been phased out of service with the Swiss Army.

With the phase out of service of the locally designed and built Pz 61 and Pz 68 MBT's the only MBT deployed by the Swiss Army today is the German Leopard 2 MBT. Part of this fleet is being upgraded.

Contractor
RUAG Land Systems

Turkey

FNSS Savunma Sistemleri Mobile Floating Assault Bridge

Development
Early in 2007, following a competition, the Turkish company of FNSS Savunma Sistemleri was awarded a contract worth USD130.8 million from the Turkish Land Forces Command (TLFC) for the design, development and production of a new Mobile Floating Assault Bridge (MFAB).

Also competing for this TLFC MFAB contract was Otokar which offered a solution together with *Constructions Industrielles de la Mediterranee* (CNIM) of France.

Under the terms of this contract, which will run for a period of 69 months from early 2007, a total of 52 MFAB units will be delivered to the TLFC who at present do not have a system of this type. A total of four operational and one training MFAB sets will be delivered to the TLFC.

Description
Each operational MFAB set will consist of 12 8 × 8 amphibious units which when fully deployed and coupled together will have a total length of 150 m and will enable wet gaps of up to 620 m to be rapidly crossed with 52 bridges. Each MFAB unit will have a crew of three and both bridge and ramp units will be fielded.

Each unit MFAB will be fully amphibious while being propelled in the water by waterjets. The deck units will be traversed through 90° and the units shall be coupled together to form the bridge unit which will be held in position by the waterjets if there is a strong current.

The vehicles will be of welded aluminium construction with the powerpack consisting of a diesel engine coupled to a fully automatic transmission.

In addition to having 8 × 8 drive the chassis will also have 8 × 8 steering and be fitted with a central tyre pressure regulation system as standard.

Elements of the MFAB can be coupled together to form a ferry to transport vehicles and equipment across rivers and lakes.

The training version of the MFAB will have a total of four units and a total length of 50 m which is considered adequate for training purposes.

This system will be based on automotive components of the FNSS Savunma Sistemleri Pars family of wheeled Armoured Fighting Vehicles (AFV).

Pars is a complete family of 4 × 4 ,6 × 6, 8 × 8 and 10 × 10 wheeled armoured vehicles which all share a number of common components. MFAB will be the first Turkish production application for the Pars 8 × 8 wheeled armoured vehicles.

While development of the Pars family of wheeled combat vehicles was complete, as of late 2010, no production orders had been placed.

In April 2010 Malaysia announced that it was to order 257 AV8 (8 × 8) armoured personnel carriers and variants under the 10th Malaysian Plan of 2011 through to 2015.

This will be based on the Turkish Paris family of wheeled combat vehicles with the prime contractor being Deftech.

Amphibious Armoured Combat Earthmover (AACE)
It has been disclosed that the TLFC has awarded FNSS a contract for a total of 12 Amphibious Armoured Combat Earthmovers (AACE), with the first of these to be delivered in 2012. The contract covers one prototype vehicle and 11 production vehicles.

The company is also bidding to supply the TLFC with 71 armoured ammunition resupply vehicles. These will supply 155 mm ammunition (projectiles and charges) for TLFC 155 mm self-propelled artillery systems. Their proposal is based on the latest Armoured Combat Vehicle - Stretched design that has already been produced for the export market.

Specifications
Detailed specifications have not yet been released.

Status
Under development for Turkish Land Forces Command who have placed a contract for a total of 52 MFAB units.

Contractor
FNSS Savunma Sistemleri A/S

United Kingdom

BAE Systems Global Combat Systems TITAN Engineer Tank System (ETS)

Development
Following a competition, early in 2001 the then UK Defence Procurement Agency (DPA) awarded Vickers Defence Systems (which is today known as BAE Systems Global Combat Systems) a GBP250 million plus contract to supply the British Army with a new Engineer Tank System (ETS) which was previously called the Future Engineer Tank (FET).

In August 2000, the then Vickers Defence Systems were selected to be the preferred bidder in beating off rival bids from the then Alvis Vehicles and OBRUM/RO Defence.

The contract covered the supply of 66 ETS against the original requirement for 102 vehicles to replace the current in-service Armoured Vehicle Royal Engineer (AVRE) and Armoured Vehicle Launched Bridge (AVLB) systems, based on the now obsolete Chieftain MBT chassis.

Of the 66 vehicles, 33 are TROJAN ETS to replace the Chieftain AVRE and 33 are TITAN ETS to replace the Chieftain AVLB.

In addition to the 66 production vehicles, there are four prototype vehicles, two TITAN and two TROJAN, which were completed in early 2003. All development and production of the ETS was carried out at the BAE Systems Global Combat Systems facility at Newcastle-upon-Tyne.

Following extensive trials with two prototype vehicles, the TITAN AVLB member of the Engineer Tank System late in 2006 met its In Service Date (ISD) with a Full Operational Capacity (FOC) in 2008. First production vehicles were completed in 2005 with final deliveries in 2008.

When compared to the Chieftain based vehicles TITAN and TROJAN have a much higher level of protection and survivability and greater mobility which will allow them to keep up with other armoured vehicles in the battlegroup.

Since the contract was originally awarded there have been a number of changes with the most significant being the installation of the General Dynamics UK Bowman digital communications system and second the integration of an enhanced armour package as a result of operational experience in the Middle East.

The introduction of TITAN and TROJAN marked a number of firsts for the British Army, including the first vehicles to be developed for world wide deployment as they are fitted with a complete environmental control system, first production vehicles to be fitted with Bowman, first vehicles (TROJAN) with a remote controlled overhead weapon station, first purpose-built AVLB/breacher and first to be fitted for but not with a remote control capability for use in hazardous operations.

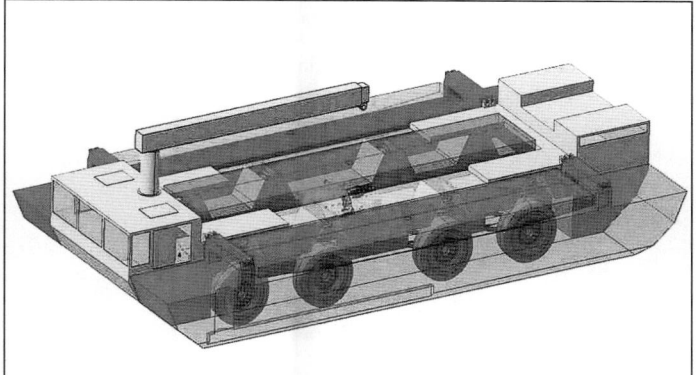

First computer generated drawing of the FNSS Mobile Floating Assault Bridge (MFAB) being developed for the Turkish Land Forces Command (FNSS) 1296068

TITAN AVLB carrying two number No 12 bridges and showing dozer/stabilising blade located at front of hull (Christopher F Foss) 1296069

TITAN AVLB in travelling configuration carrying No 10 scissors bridge
(Christopher F Foss)
1296070

TITAN AVLB deploying its No 10 scissors bridge over front of vehicle
(Patrick Allan/IHS Janes)
1198368

Production of the TROJAN and TITAN members of the Engineer Tank System has been completed and in June 2009 the Final Acceptance Build Standard (FABS) commenced at Newcastle-upon-Type.

The final FABS phase involves the return of all 66 production TITAN and TROJAN from the British Army for a series of upgrades to bring the fleet up to a common build standard.

Following completion of the upgrade work at Newcastle-upon-Tyne, FABS vehicles are then sent to the Defence Support Group (DSG) at Bovington for final refurbishment. After refurbishment and sign-off, they are finally sent back to the customer.

The complete FABS programme is scheduled to be completed by December 2011.

Description

The TITAN ETS AVLB is based on a much modified Challenger 2 MBT chassis with the crew compartment at the front and the diesel powerpack at the rear.

It has the same level of armour protection as the Challenger 2 MBT that provides a very high level of protection against direct fire weapons and it will have enhanced protection against mines.

The driver is seated at the front of the vehicle and is provided with a single-piece hatch cover and a day periscope, which can be rapidly replaced by a night vision devices.

The other two crew members, commander and bridge operator, are seated in the centre of the vehicle and each is provided with a hatch cover above their position that opens to the rear and periscopes.

TITAN can be fitted with a front-mounted hydraulic dozer blade, which can be replaced by a Pearson Engineering mine plough.

TITAN can launch the 26 m No 10 bridge in two minutes and using integral trestles and wedges can lay multiple combination bridges in depths of 5 m, and overbridge oil pipelines/and bridges. TITAN can also carry two 13.5 m No 12 bridges which are laid in only 90 seconds.

The bridges used on the TITAN are part of the Modular Bridging System, which is known as BR90, by the British Army. Full details of this are given in a separate entry in *Jane's Military Vehicles and Logistics*.

If required by the tactical situation, the TITAN bridge layer can also be fitted with a front-mounted Pearson Engineering dozer blade or track width mine plough.

Standard equipment on TITAN includes smoke grenade launchers, air conditioning, regenerative NBC system developed by Dominic Hunter, Bowman communications system and a full suite of day/night vision equipment.

TITAN is also fitted for, but not with, a remote control system. An auxiliary power unit is fitted as standard and this allows the main systems to be run with the main power pack switched off.

The power pack is mounted at the rear of the chassis and consists of a Perkins CV-12 diesel with digital electronic controls coupled to an improved David Brown Gear Systems TN54 transmission with six forward and two reverse gears. An APU is fitted based on a Perkins design, which provides 360 amps at an undisclosed voltage rating.

Variants

Joint Assault Bridge
The TITAN launch system consisting of the launch frame, pad, arm and hydraulics is used in the US Army/Marine Corps Joint Assault Bridge (JAB) which is covered in detail in a separate entry.

JAB is a modified General Dynamics Land Systems M1 Abrams series MBT chassis fitted with the launch mechanism of the TITAN and launches the current US Army/Marine Corps scissors type bridge over the front of the chassis.

Details of the Joint Assault Bridge are provided in a separate entry in *Jane's Military Vehicles and Logistics*.

Specifications

TITAN AVLB
Crew: 3
Armament: smoke grenade launchers
Training weight: 64,500 kg
Engine: Perkins Engines Company CV-12 8a developing 1,200 hp (895 kW)
Transmission: David Brown TN54, modified
Power-to-weight ratio: 18.6 hp/t (13.87 kW/t)
Length: 11.83 m
Width: 3.506 m
Height: 3.10 m
Max speed: (road) 56 km/h
Range: n/avail

Status

In addition to the two prototype TITAN AVLB, a total of 33 production vehicles have been built for the British Army with final deliveries in 2008.

BAE Systems Global Combat Systems is no longer marketing any Challenger 2 MBT based vehicles, including the TITAN and TROJAN.

Contractor

BAE Systems Global Combat Systems

BAE Systems Global Combat Systems Modular Bridging System - tank-launched bridges

Development

The Modular Bridging System (MBS) was originally developed by Thompson Defence Projects (part of the Industrial Power Group of Rolls-Royce plc) for the British Army's Bridging for the 1990s (BR90) programme.

It underwent an eight-year development programme and is a comprehensive bridging system covering tank launched or close support bridges (mechanised bridges) and line of communication or dry support bridges, together with dedicated logistic support vehicles.

In November 1993, the UK Ministry of Defence awarded a contract worth GBP140 million for the supply of production quantities of the BR90 system for the Royal Engineers.

BR90 is divided into four types of bridge: General Support Bridge; Close Support Bridge; Long Span Bridge; and Two Span Bridge.

The Close Support Bridges are launched by the Chieftain AVLB and supported by the Unipower 8 × 8 Tank Bridge Transporter. The latter are used for transporting, handling and launching dry support bridges.

Thompson Defence Projects was subsequently taken over by Vickers Defence Systems and then renamed Vickers Bridging.

Late in 2002 however, Vickers Defence Systems was purchased by Alvis PLC and Vickers Bridging was renamed Alvis Bridging Limited. At the same time, Vickers Defence Systems became Alvis Vickers Limited. Late in 2004, the company was taken over and renamed BAE Systems Land Systems. More recently this company has become BAE Systems Global Combat Systems.

British Army crew with current in service BR90 showing launching rail being extended for 32 m bridge (BAE Systems Global Combat Systems)
0577859

Two No 10 26 m close support bridges used in combination are crossed by a Warrior Observation Post Vehicle   0079530

Chieftain AVLB carrying two No 12 tank-launched bridges (Richard Stickland)   0121591

Key BR90 user requirements included a much more rapid deployment time and a significant reduction in manpower requirements. In British Army service, MBS is the replacement for the widely deployed Medium Girder Bridge (MGB) but it has now evolved into a complete bridge family which can meet a much wider range of operational requirements.

In British Army service, MBS is transported and launched from a UNIPOWER (8 × 8) high mobility truck chassis. In the end, the Royal Engineers took delivery of 176 bridges, 139 vehicles, 14 trestle sets and four pontoon sets as well as additional equipment to build longer span and two span bridges.

Production of the UNIPOWER series of high mobility 8 × 8 trucks has been completed and these are no longer marketed.

The only export contract for BR90 by late 2010 is for Malaysia and these systems were supplied integrated onto German MAN (8 × 8) high mobility cross-country trucks.

Description
All the BR90 bridges are built from a range of seven modular panels of advanced aluminium alloy fabrication. These are interchangeable through the various bridge types, to form two interconnecting trackways with a 4 m overall bridge width and a 1 m girder depth.

There are three basic Tank Launched Bridges (also known as Close Support or Assault Bridges): the No 10, No 11 and No 12.

The No 10 bridge is a single-fold scissoring bridge 26 m long and capable of spanning 24.5 m. A shorter bridge length can be achieved by the removal of two 4 m panels, reducing it to a 22 m bridge. It can also be fitted with an Assault Trestle to provide a 21 m trestle bridge. The No 10 bridge is constructed from 8 m ramp panels, 4 m panels and 2 m hinge panels. The folding mechanism uses scissoring parts which eliminate the need for hydraulics on the bridge, thus allowing the bridge to be launched on sites where longitudinal slopes would defeat horizontally launched bridges.

The No 11 bridge is built from four 8 m ramp panels and is a 16 m long, 14.5 m span up-and-over launched bridge.

The No 12, shortest of the Tank Launched Bridges, is 13.5 m long and capable of spanning 12 m. Its girder depth of 0.71 m enables two bridges, to be conveyed and launched by the Chieftain AVLB.

The two No 12 bridges with a unique launching system allow the AVLB to construct two bridges, without having to be resupplied, to cross two short gaps or, in combination, to cross a wider single gap, all without crew exposure.

Full decks and kerbs can be added to all BR90 bridges enabling the full range of military in-service vehicles to cross.

A small modification kit enables the existing Chieftain AVLB to convey and launch the new range of bridges from under armour, while still allowing existing in-service bridges to be carried and launched. Alternatively, any suitable armoured tracked or wheeled vehicle could be modified as a suitable launch platform.

One of the prototype ABLE (8 × 8) units crosses a 32 m general support bridge that it has just launched (BAE Systems Global Combat Systems)   1133712

Malaysian 52 m Axially Tensioned Long Span Bridge (ATLSB) deployed in position (BAE Systems Global Combat Systems)   1333646

All the bridges are designed and tested in accordance with the UK/US/D Trilateral Design and Test Code and are classified MLC 72 for both wheeled and tracked vehicles. They can all be crossed by fully laden tank transporters at MLC 105. Launching without crew exposure is possible with all bridges in three minutes and they can all be recovered in under five minutes from either end (except those fitted with a trestle).

To increase the length capability, combination bridges may be built using two or three of the above bridges, the first bridge being launched from the home bank with the far end supported on the base of the gap, a floating pier or a trestle. Gaps up to a nominal 60 m span and 5 m depth can be bridged in this way. Combination bridges are classified as MLC 70 for tracked vehicles.

A wheeled Tank Bridge Transporter (TBT), a suitably modified Unipower M Series 8 × 8 improved medium-mobility vehicle with an extended wheelbase, forms part of the system, its primary use being the rapid resupply of the AVLB. The TBT can carry all variants of the tank launched bridges and is equipped with mechanisms to load and offload them. An excellent cross-country performance and flexibility allow it to travel virtually anywhere tracked vehicles can go.

The TBT has a high degree of commonality with the vehicles used to launch and transport Dry Support Vehicles (see also entry in *Jane's Military Vehicles and Logics* under Tactical (non-floating) and line of communication bridges).

The company has proposed that the close support bridges associated with BR90 could be utilised as Airportable Low Profile Bridging with all the advantages of the BR90 system but at a lower rating of MLC 50 at 24 m. These bridges could be launched from suitable tank chassis or a trailer arrangement.

62 m two span
Two span bridges can be built up to 62 m in length and can be supplied with a specially designed pontoon pier.

Future developments
Upgrade packages cover 38, 44, 48 and 52 m bridges. The latter system uses a total of five 8 × 8 vehicles and can be assembled in less than 75 minutes. This provides a seamless gap crossing capability of 8 to 50 m.

The company is currently carrying out upgrade and refurbishment work on British Army MBS equipment at its Wolverhampton facility. This facility also stores some British Army MBS War Maintenance Reserve (WMR) stocks which are required to be deployed at very short notice. In the longer term it will move forward to 'contracting for availability'.

British Army BR90 Bridging Vehicle (8 × 8) upgraded for Afghanistan by BAE Systems Global Combat Systems with enhanced protection for the cab (BAE Systems)   1364008

This includes the introduction of a HUMS and an upgrade of the current Military Load Class 70 (Tracked) (MLC 70) to MLC 85 (T) to take account of the introduction of heavier vehicles into the British Army.

In the longer term (2012-2018) it is expected that the British Army will fund a Mid-Life Upgrade programme (or Capability Sustainment Programme as it is also referred to).

This could include the replacement of the existing chassis by a MAN (8 × 8) chassis which has now been introduced into the British Army as part of its Future Support Vehicle programme and the introduction of the Axially Tensioned Long Span Bridge (ATLSB) reinforcement system which is already in service with Malaysia.

Malaysian ATSLB
Late in 2004, BAE Systems Global Combat Systems supplied the first of its 52 m Axially Tensioned Long Span Bridges (ATLSB) to Malaysia.

ATLSB is a further development of the Bridging for the 90's (BR90) system first developed to meet the requirements of the UK's Royal Engineers.

BR90 was demonstrated at Defence Services Asia in 1998 (DSA 98) by a British Army team and in 2002 Kuantan based Amalgamated Metal Builders Sdn Bhd (AMB), the then Alvis Bridging's partner in Malaysia, successfully responded to a government request for bridging.

A contract, worth about GBP20 million, was placed with for three sets of the latest 52 mm ATLSB for the Royal Malaysian Army.

While the British Army BR90 systems are based on an Unipower (8 × 8) cross-country chassis, the Royal Malaysian Army systems are based on a German MAN (8 × 8) high mobility truck chassis.

It is understood that each of the Royal Malaysian Army 52 m ATLSB systems consists of a launcher vehicle and five trucks, which will enable gaps from 9 m to 50 m to be bridged.

System elements and bridges were manufactured at the BAE Systems Global Combat Systems facility in Wolverhampton and the launcher hampers were integrated onto the MAN (8 × 8) chassis at their facility at Telford.

As part of the contract, the then Alvis Bridging awarded a sub-contract to Aero-Composites Technologies Sdn Bhd (ACT) for the manufacture of the high technology composite launch rails for these systems. These were manufactured in Malaysia following successful production reliability testing of the first rails in the UK.

The new launch rail is constructed entirely of carbon fibre apart from the end couplings, fastenings and bipod and is about 60 per-cent of the weight of an equivalent aluminium alloy launch rail. The bridge is tensioned using recently developed amid synthetic fibre cables.

It is understood that the Royal Malaysian Army may have a requirement for further ATLSB systems in the future as their modernisation programme moves ahead and increasing numbers of heavier armoured vehicles enter their inventory.

Motorised Pontoon
In 2004 the capability of the system was further enhanced by the introduction into service of a motorised pontoon which is launched from standard British Army Leyland Demountable Rack Off-loading and Pick-up System (DROPS) (8 × 6) vehicles. This enables a bridge to be rapidly built between river banks that are over 60 m apart.

The UK MoD awarded the company a contract for the development, test and supply of two span bridge pontoons in 2000 and this was accepted for service following extensive user trials.

The pontoons motor into position in up to five knots of current and are then anchored to provide a floating support pier for 62 m length of bridge.

Further development of the pontoon system is now underway to enable equipment to be ferried across rivers.

Upgraded British Army protected BR90
In early 2010 the Royal Engineers deployed an upgraded BAE Systems, Global Combat Systems BR90 to Afghanistan which took part in the NATO Operation 'MOSHTARAK' in Helmand province.

A complete BR90 bridge system consisting of five uparmoured Unipower (8 × 8) cross-country vehicles, a 32 m bridge set and a 32 - 44 m span extension system were deployed.

The vehicles were upgraded by BAE Systems Global Combat Systems bridging facility at Wolverhampton under Urgent Operational Requirement (UOR) funding.

The cab was fitted with a protection package that provides protection from small arms fire and mine blast.

This was designed, developed and fitted in a seven week period, with the vehicles then being shipped to the Middle East with the last leg of the journey being air transport to Camp Bastion via a C-17.

This upgraded BR90 system was used to rapidly build a new bridge across the strategic stretch of the Nahr-e Bughra canal near the town of Shaheed. The 36 m bridge was deployed in about 90 minutes by the 12-man team.

Specifications
No 10 Tank Bridge
Length overall: 26 m
Ramp length: 6 m
Width overall: 4 m
Depth of section: 1 m
Max span: 24.5 m
Weight: 13,000 kg
Panels: 4 × 8 m ramp panels, 4 × 4 m panels, 2 × 2 m hinge panels

No 10 Trestle Bridge
Length overall: 21 m
Ramp length: 6 m
Width overall: 4 m
Depth of section: 1 m
Max span: 18 m
Weight: (with trestles) 13,000 kg
Panels: 2 × 8 m ramp panels, 4 × 4 m panels, 2 × 2 m hinge panels, 2 trestle adaptor panels, 2 assault trestles

No 11 Tank Bridge
Length overall: 16 m
Ramp length: 6 m
Width overall: 4 m
Depth of section: 1 m
Max span: 14.5 m
Weight: 7,000 kg
Panels: 4 × 8 m ramp panels

No 12 Tank Bridge
Length overall: 13.5 m
Ramp length: 5.25 m
Width overall: 4 m
Depth of section: 0.71 m
Max span: 12 m
Weight: 5,700 kg
Panels: 2 × 13.5 m trackways

Combination Bridge
Bridges: No 10 and trestle bridge, No 11 and No 12 bridges
Quantity: 2 or 3 bridges
Max span: 60 m
Max gap depth: 5 m

Status
Production as required. In service with Malaysia (8 × 8 only) and the UK (8 × 8 and tracked).

Contractor
BAE Systems Global Combat Systems

Vickers Chieftain AVLB

Development
The Chieftain Armoured Vehicle-Launched Bridge (AVLB) (FV4205) was developed as the replacement for the Centurion AVLB (FV4002) and the Centurion ARK (FV4016).

Development of the Chieftain AVLB began in 1962 but, owing to some necessary redesign, the first production vehicles were not delivered to the British Army until 1974.

Design work on the AVLB was carried out by the then Military Vehicles and Engineering Establishment, AP Precision Hydraulics and the Hydraulic Controls Department of Tubes (Birmingham).

The production total of Chieftain AVLBs for the British Army was 37, with a further 14 produced for Iran.

In recent years the prime contractor for the Chieftain AVLB has been Vickers Defence Systems at Newcastle-upon-Tyne.

Late in 2002 this company was purchased by Alvis PLC and the company was renamed Alvis Vickers Limited with sites at Leeds, Telford and Newcastle-upon-Tyne. Late in 2004, Alvis PLC was taken over by BAE Systems and the company was renamed BAE Systems Land Systems. More recently this company has been renamed BAE Systems Global Combat Systems.

Chieftain AVLB carrying No 8 tank bridge in travelling configuration
(Richard Stickland)

0069566

All British Army Chieftain AVLB have now been withdrawn from service and replaced by the BAE Systems Global Combat Systems TITAN AVLB. This is covered in a separate entry in *Jane's Military Vehicles and Logistics*.

Description

The hull of the AVLB is similar to that of the basic Chieftain MBT. The driver is seated at the front of the hull and is provided with a single-piece hatch cover and a single day periscope that can be replaced by a passive periscope for driving at night.

The commander and radio operator are behind the driver. The Leyland L60 engine and transmission are at the rear of the hull. The suspension is of the Horstmann type consisting of three bogies per side, each bogie with two sets of roadwheels and a set of three horizontal springs. The first and last roadwheel stations have a hydraulic shock-absorber. The drive sprocket is at the rear and the idler at the front, with three track-return rollers. The top half of the track is covered by armoured skirts, removable for maintenance. The Chieftain AVLB has an NBC system.

The Chieftain AVLB can utilise either a No 8 or a No 9 tank bridge, originally manufactured by the now Faun UK (previously Laird).

The No 8 bridge is carried folded and is launched over the front of the vehicle. The hull-mounted hydraulic pump, which is driven from a Power Take-Off (PTO) on the main engine, operates five cylinders arranged to launch the bridge in three manually sequenced stages. Once the clamps have been removed the launching can begin. The Stage 1 cylinders pivot the folded bridge about the forward part of the glacis casting. This operation is continued until the launching pad meets the ground or Stage 1 cylinders reach the end of their stroke, when the folded bridge will be at an angle of about 30° to the horizontal.

The Stage 2 cylinders then tilt the launching pad on the ground until approximately level. At this point the bridge is partly scissored by the rods connecting the central quadrant to the launching frame and is approximately vertical. Once the Stage 2 cylinders have reached the end of their strokes, the single Stage 3 cylinder is actuated, causing the bridge to scissor further until the far end reaches the required bank height. At this point the rods slacken and, on further lowering, the bridge becomes a rigid connection at its centre point. The rods are then free and can be detached using the remotely operated release mechanism, thus separating the rods from the launching structure.

The tank then reverses and the launching structure is removed from the bridge. The tank retracts all its cylinders and then either moves to the rear to pick up another bridge or crosses the bridge and picks up the bridge from the other end. The launch normally takes between three and five minutes, with recovery of the bridge taking about 10 minutes.

The bridge girders and launching structure are made of high-strength nickel-alloy maraging steel developed by the International Nickel Company. The deck and kerbing are of weldable aluminium alloy. The No 8 tank bridge is 24.4 m long and is made up of two tracks, each 1.62 m wide, with a 0.76 m centre gap between. Each track is divided into four parts, two toe pieces each 4.55 m long and two centre-pieces each 7.6 m long. A hinge is provided at each joint. The bridge has a maximum capacity of Class 60; Land Rovers and similar small vehicles can cross on a single track, allowing two-way traffic with vehicles of this size.

By hinging the 4.55 m long toes of the bridge and dropping them at will, it is possible to cater for a range of bank conditions. A bank-sensing device is incorporated in the ramp sections.

In order to facilitate crossing gaps that are wider than the standard No 8 bridge, an extension trestle was subsequently introduced. This trestle is fitted in place of the far bank end ramps on a standard No 8 bridge in such a fashion that the trestle is allowed to unfold and swing downwards as the bridge is fully extended. The trestle then supports the No 8 bridge to allow another AVLB to cross in order to lay a further bridge.

The No 9 bridge consists of two interconnected trackways 13.411 m long and 1.62 m wide, with a gap between them of 0.76 m. Total effective roadway width is 4.01 m. The bridge takes between three and five minutes to launch and can be recovered from either end. It is launched in three

stages: Stage 1 raises the bridge from the horizontal to an angle of 45°; Stage 2 raises it to the vertical; and Stage 3 lowers it to the horizontal. The launching arm is then disengaged, the vehicle is reversed away and the launching structure retracted.

Each Chieftain bridgelayer normally has one No 8 and one No 9 tank bridge, one carried on the vehicle and the other on a prime mover towing a semi-trailer.

Specifications

Chieftain AVLB with No 8 bridge
Crew: 3
Weight: 53,300 kg
Power-to-weight ratio: 13.70 hp/t (10.21 kW/t)
Length: 13.741 m
Width: 4.165 m
Height: 3.923 m
Ground clearance: 0.5 m
Track width: 610 mm
Length of track on ground: 4.8 m
Ground pressure: 0.9 kg/cm^2
Max speed: (road) 48 km/h
Range: 400 km
Fuel capacity: 950 litres
Fording: 1.066 m
Gradient: 60%
Vertical obstacle: 0.9 m
Trench: 3 m
Engine: Leyland L60, 2-stroke, compression-ignition, 12-cylinder vertically opposed multifuel developing 730 hp (544 kW) at 2,100 rpm
Transmission: David Brown Gear Systems TN12 with 6 forward and 2 reverse gears, plus emergency mechanical selection for second gear forward and low reverse
Electrical system: 28.5 V (24 V nominal)
Batteries: 4 × 12 V, 200 Ah
Armament: 1 or 2 × 7.62 mm L7A2 GPMGs

No 8 Tank Bridge
Overall length: 24.384 m
Centre-section length: 7.62 m
Ramp end length: 4.572 m
Overall width: 4.165 m
Roadway width: 4.012 m
Centre gap: 0.762 m
Depth of centre-section: 0.914 m
Max span:
    (firm banks) 22.86 m
    (soft banks) 22.25 m
Weight: 12,200 kg

No 9 Tank Bridge
Overall length: 13.411 m
Overall depth: 0.914 m
Overall width: 4.165 m
Max clear span: (firm bank) 12.192 m
Weight: 9,144 kg

Status

Production complete. In service with Iran. Production of the Chieftain AVLB was originally undertaken at the then Royal Ordnance Factory, Leeds. This was subsequently taken over by Vickers Defence Systems and shut down in late 1999.

Contractor

BAE Systems Global Combat Systems

Vickers Armoured Bridgelayer (VAB)

Development

Preliminary design work on the Vickers Defence Systems Armoured Bridgelayer (VAB) started during the late 1970s, to meet the requirement for a family of armoured support vehicles for the Vickers MBT which was being ordered in increasing numbers for the export market.

The first order for six VABs was placed by Nigeria in 1981. A further six were ordered in 1985.

In recent years, the prime contractor for the VAB has been Vickers Defence Systems at Newcastle-upon-Tyne.

Late in 2002 this company was purchased by Alvis PLC and the company was renamed Alvis Vickers Limited with sites at Leeds, Telford and Newcastle-upon-Tyne.

In 2004, Alvis PLC was purchased by BAE Systems and Alvis Vickers became BAE Systems Land Systems. The facility at Newcastle-upon-Tyne is now the UK's only production facility for armoured fighting vehicles.

Production of the Vickers Mk 3 MBT and its associated variants is now complete and it is no longer marketed.

Vickers is now part of BAE Systems Global Combat Systems.

Vickers Armoured Bridgelayer (VAB) in travelling configuration, but without skirts fitted (BAE Systems Global Combat Systems) 1164663

Description

The hull, automotive and running gear components of the VAB are based on the Vickers MBT with the hull structure divided into three main compartments. There is accommodation for a crew of three: the driver, radio operator and commander.

The forward compartment is divided into two sections by a panel on the right of the driver, who is seated on the centreline of the compartment. The panel provides a mounting face for some vehicle control units and behind it are the batteries and a stowage space.

The vehicle controls and the bridge control units are located within the driver's compartment. Three wide-angle day periscopes are provided for driving with the hatch closed. One of these periscopes can be replaced by a passive periscope for night driving. The driver's seat has provision for vertical and fore and aft adjustments. The maximum possible opening is provided between the centre and forward compartments. The driver, by dropping the seat backrest, can enter or leave position through the centre compartment, thus making a change of crew possible without opening up the vehicle.

The centre or crew compartment has seating for the commander and radio operator. The commander's seat is positioned directly under a rotating cupola fitted to the centre of the roof plate. Behind the commander and to his right is the radio operator and radio sets. Beneath the radio equipment are two batteries and space for personnel kit in the left-hand pannier space. The crew ventilation system is in the right-hand pannier space.

To the centre and left rear of the commander's seat are hydraulic pumps, filters, tank, valves and other components for operating the bridge launch equipment.

The rear compartment accommodates the power pack. The VAB may be fitted with a complete power pack that comprises a Detroit Diesel 12V-71T V-12 diesel engine, TN12 transmission and an associated cooling system. Panniers above each track contain bag-type fuel tanks. Lifting and towing eyes are welded to the hull front and rear.

Both batches of VABs for Nigeria are fitted with a conventional tank bridge. This bridge is 13.41 m long with a military load classification of 60/70. The bridge launching equipment is hydraulically-operated with the power provided by a pump driven from a Power Take-Off (PTO) from the main engine. The launching operation is in four stages:

• bridge securing and clamping devices released;
• bridge launched hydraulically;
• release of bridge from launching structure;
• vehicle reverses to withdraw clear of bridge.

To recover the bridge after use, the bridgelayer vehicle is aligned with the bridge so that the launching arm engages with the bridge lifting brackets. The hydraulic lifting mechanism then recovers the complete bridge on to the roof of the vehicle for reuse.

Specifications

Vickers Armoured Bridgelayer
Crew: 3
Weight: (with bridge) 43,910 kg
Power-to-weight ratio: 16.40 hp/t (12.23 kW/t)
Length: (with bridge) 13.7 m
Width: (with bridge) 4.16 m
Height: (with bridge) 3.25 m
Ground clearance: 0.432 m
Max range: 600 km
Fuel capacity: 1,000 litres
Fording: 1.1 m
Gradient: 60%
Side slope: 30%
Vertical obstacle: 0.914 m
Trench: 3 m
Engine: Detroit Diesel 12V-71T V-12 diesel developing 720 bhp (537 kW) at 2,500 rpm

Transmission: David Brown Gear Systems TN12 automatic
Clutch: centrifugal
Steering: Merritt regenerative
Electrical system: 24 V
Armament: 1 × 7.62 mm MG

Bridge
Length: (overall) 13.4 m
Width: 4.16 m
Classification: MLC 60/70

Status

Production complete. In service with the Nigerian Army (17). No longer marketed. The company continues to provide support to those users who have purchased the Vickers MBT and variants.

Contractor

BAE Systems Global Combat Systems

United States

General Dynamics/Krauss-Maffei Wegmann Wolverine Heavy Assault Bridge (HAB)

Development

The General Dynamics/Krauss-Maffei Wegmann Wolverine Heavy Assault Bridge (HAB) was the outcome of concept evaluation work by the US Army following on from the cancellation of the 'Bridging in the 1980s' programme in 1981.

The result of the evaluation was that a new HAB with a MLC 70 load classification would be required. A minimum gap-crossing capability of 30 m was initially specified.

A request for quotations was issued to industry and from the resultant designs, the US Army selected the submission from BMY (which is now BAE Systems US Combat Systems) with Israel Military Industries (IMI), Haifa Division, as a major subcontractor.

BMY was awarded a contract for the design and manufacture of one prototype HAB system in April 1983 and design approval was given in November 1984. Testing by the US government commenced in late 1988. However, during 1989, the US Army requested that all work on the project be stopped.

During late 1989, a US Army requirement for a new version of the HAB was issued, which was to have a total length of 26 m and be able to span a gap of up to 24 m. The bridge would include aluminium components in place of the original composite materials. It was to be so constructed that infantry would be able to walk across each deck.

BMY Combat Systems was awarded a contract to design and construct a new 26 m MLC 70 HAB, with IMI as a major subcontractor. The HAB, known as the HAB-26, was carried and launched from an M1 Abrams MBT chassis. Two launcher systems and bridges were completed and tested.

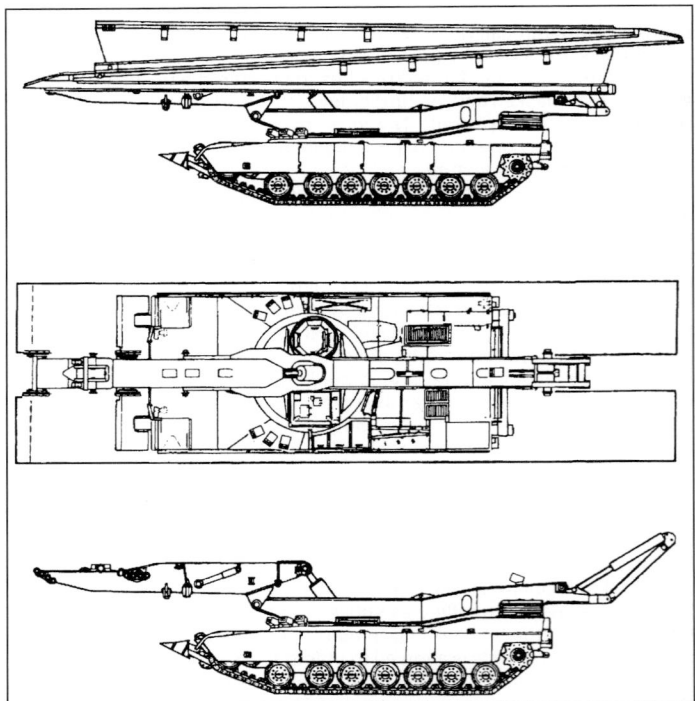

General arrangement drawing of General Dynamics/Krauss-Maffei Wegmann Wolverine Heavy Assault Bridge (HAB). The top two drawings include the bridge while the lower drawing shows system without bridge 0079534

General Dynamics/Krauss-Maffei Wegmann Wolverine heavy Assault Bridge with bridge extended over front of vehicle 0533531

General Dynamics/Krauss-Maffei Wegmann Wolverine Heavy Assault Bridge laying its bridge in position (GDLS) 0569070

In March 1990, General Dynamics, Land Systems Division, was also awarded a contract for a complete HAB based on the M1 MBT chassis. This HAB version used the German Krauss-Maffei Wegmann (previously Military Mobile Bridges) widely used LEGUAN bridge system, this covered in a separate entry in *Jane's Military Vehicles and Logistics*. Krauss-Maffei Wegmann was a subcontractor to General Dynamics Land Systems.

The General Dynamics/Krauss-Maffei Wegmann HAB contract involved two prototype demonstrators for the Fort Belvoir Research, Development and Engineering Center and was worth USD12.459 million. The contract called for the complete assembly and testing sequence to be completed by the end of October 1992.

In August 1992, it was announced that a third system was to be evaluated in connection with the HAB programme. Southwest Mobile Systems of St Louis, Missouri, was awarded a USD5,481,383 firm fixed-price contract to deliver and support two Chieftain AVLBs and two No 10 tank bridges.

The US Army conducted a comparative testing of the three systems from late 1992 and throughout 1993. In February 1994, it was announced that the US Army Tank Automotive Command had awarded General Dynamics Land Systems, prime contractor for the M1 MBT, a USD26.05 million, 39-month, engineering, manufacturing and development Phase II contract for the HAB, which included two prototypes. Up to six pilot vehicles were planned for a follow-on pre-Low Rate Initial Production (LRIP) phase.

In May 1998, the US Army Tank Automotive Command awarded General Dynamics, Land Systems Division, a USD106 million low rate production contract to manufacture 29 Wolverine HAB vehicles, the first for delivery in August 1999 and the last in December 2001.

The US Army subsequently cancelled the programme early in 2000 in order to fund other higher priority programmes.

At this time, General Dynamics Land Systems was building a total of 22 HABs. This comprised the original two prototypes, six pre-production vehicles and the first order of 14 under the Low Rate Initial Production (LRIP) contract award in May 1998.

The latter totalled 28 systems but the two final increments of 11 and 3 units were withheld. The 14 HABs ordered under the LRIP have been built and all were delivered to the US Army by the end of 2000.

In July 2000, General Dynamics Land Systems announced that the US Army had awarded the company a USD34.4 million contract for 10 HABs, thus re-starting the programme again.

These HABs were delivered at the rate of one per month from June 2001. In June 2001, the US Army Tank-automotive and Armaments Command awarded General Dynamics Land Systems a USD24.6 million contract for a further eight Wolverine HAB with options for a further nine vehicles.

Production of these eight vehicles commenced in March 2002 at the rate of one per month with first delivery taking place in January 2003. This contract represented the fourth increment of funding to the existing HAB multiyear contract and completes the order for 46 HAB under the LRIP plan.

In the end, the Wolverine HAB programme was cancelled by the US Army and the last of 43 units was delivered late in 2003.

In US Army service, the Wolverine Heavy Assault Bridge (HAB) will be supplemented by the new Joint Assault Bridge (JAB) that also uses the M1 chassis.

Details of the JAB are provided in a separate entry in *Jane's Military Vehicles and Logistics*.

Description

The General Dynamics/Krauss-Maffei Wegmann HAB uses the M1 Abrams chassis retaining over 85 per cent compatibility between the HAB chassis and the M1A2 Abrams MBT chassis.

The crew of two is provided with NBC protection, while fire protection is provided by an automatic three-zone extinguisher system.

The LEGUAN bridge involved has a length of 26 m and a load classification of Military Load Class 70/96 (MLC 70/96), allowing gaps up to 24 m wide to be crossed. Designed for a 5,000 MLC 70 crossings requirement, the bridge can be launched in less than 5 minutes and recovered in under 10 minutes.

The LEGUAN bridge consists of four interchangeable quarter sections with a flat ramp design, each 13 m long, 1.5 m wide and weighing 2,700 kg. Bolt-on cross members join the bridge sections and, when travelling, the bridge halves lie one on top of the other. A computer-controlled launch mechanism moves the bridge longitudinally by means of a gear and hydraulic actuators on roller guides.

The top bridge half is taken up by an arm at the front end and is supported by an auxiliary arm at the rear. The bridge can be laid with a traverse and longitudinal inclination of up to 10 per cent. Laying is carried out automatically with the crew monitoring the sequence from within the protection of the vehicle; redundant controls are provided at each crew station. No preparation of the crossing site is normally required.

The laying sequence commences with the Wolverine vehicle approaching the bank until the spade stabilisation system is close to the edge. The spade system was supplied by Caterpillar of Peoria, Illinois. The bridge halves are then coupled automatically by the launch mechanism.

The next step is for the bridge to be fully advanced by the gear drive supported by the roller carriages on the laying arm. At this stage the ramp tip is placed on the far bank. This removes the latch lever load from the rollers and the laying arm can then lower the bridge and separate from it. After the final stage the stabilising blade is retracted. The bridge is then ready for use.

The bridge is constructed of standard commercial grade aluminium alloy (Al-Zn-Mg, 94.5/4.5/1) and is designed to meet US Standards for the bridge life.

Power for the launch mechanism is provided by a 65 hp auxiliary power unit powered by a Volkswagen engine. There is a back-up pump on the main powerpack.

The Wolverine HAB chassis embodies the full M1A2 Abrams MBT Systems Enhancement Package (SEP) to enable it to operate 'full digital force' operational units.

Joint Assault Bridge

Details of this system also based on a M1A1 MBT chassis are given in a separate entry in *Jane's Military Vehicles and Logistics*.

Specifications

Wolverine Heavy Assault Bridge
Crew: 2
Bridge length: 26 m
Load capacity: MLC 70/96
Bridge weight: 10,750 kg
Weight: (complete) 63,503 kg
Power-to-weight ratio: 23.62 hp/t (17.61 kW/t)
Length:
(overall, with bridge) 13.4 m
(hull) 7.636 m
Width: (with bridge) 4 m
Height:
(with bridge) 3.95 m
(without bridge) 2.906 m
Ground clearance: 0.381 m
Length of track on ground: 2.845 m
Track width: 635 mm
Max speed: (governed) 72.4 km/h
Range: 354 km
Fording: (without kit) 1.219 m
Gradient: 60%
Vertical obstacle: 0.457 m
Trench: 2.13 m
Engine: Textron Lycoming AGT 1500 gas turbine developing 1,500 hp (1,119 kW) at 30,000 rpm
Transmission: Allison X-1100-3B automatic with 4 forward and 2 reverse gears
Electrical system: 24 V

Status
Production complete with a total of 43 units delivered to the US Army during late 2003.

Contractor
General Dynamics Land Systems
Krauss-Maffei Wegmann GmbH & Co KG

US Army/Marine Corps Joint Assault Bridge (JAB)

Development
In mid-2005 BAE Systems Global Combat Systems Newcastle-upon-Tyne facility supplied a modified TITAN launch system to the US Marine Corps for integration into a General Dynamics Land Systems M1A1 Main Battle Tank (MBT) chassis.

This is used to launch and recover the current US Marine Corps Military Load Class 60/70 steel scissors bridge that is today launched from an obsolete M60 tank chassis.

The first M1A1-based bridge layer demonstrator was completed in late 2006 with the conversion work carried out by the US Army Anniston Depot which has considerable experience in the overhaul and upgrade of armoured fighting vehicles, including the M1A1 MBT.

Following extensive trials with this prototype system in 2007, BAE Systems Global Combat Systems was awarded a contract worth USD9 million to integrate six of the JAB launchers on US Marine Corps M1A1 Abrams MBT chassis. These six units were preceded by a further two prototype systems that were completed in 2008.

The launcher system has been designed and developed by an engineering team based at Newcastle-upon-Tyne and Leeds with production being undertaken at Newcastle-upon-Tyne.

As of late 2010, the US Marine Corps requirements are for a total of 29 JAB, while the US Army requirement is for a total of 168 vehicles to support their Heavy Brigade Combat Teams.

Although BAE Systems Global Combat Systems has supplied a batch of JAB sub-systems, it is understood that the US DoD will now run a new JAB competition in 2011.

Details of the Joint Assault Bridge are provided in a separate entry in *Jane's Military Vehicles and Logistics*. The Joint Assault Bridge uses a surplus General Dynamics Land Systems M1 Abrams chassis.

Description
The launch system of the JAB is the same as the one used in the TITAN armoured vehicle launch bridge system that has now been deployed by the British Army and is covered in detail in a separate entry in *Jane's Military Vehicles and Logistics*. This consists of the launch frame, pad, arm and hydraulics.

The current US Marine Corps scissors bridge has a total length of 19.202 m and can be used to span a gap of up to 18.288 m with a maximum original design capacity of 54.4 tonnes.

Under contract to the UK's then Defence Procurement Agency (DPA), BAE Systems Global Combat Systems has built a total of 66 production Engineer Tank Systems (ETS) of which 33 are TITAN AVLB and 33 TROJAN breacher vehicles with first production vehicles being completed late in 2005 and final deliveries in 2008.

TITAN can launch the BAE Systems Global Combat Systems Modular Bridging System that is called BR90 by the British Army. This includes the No 10, 11 and 12 Tank Bridges plus other elements.

The No 10 bridge has an overall length of 26 m, No 11 bridge 16 m and No 12 bridge 13.5 m. Typically, a TITAN can carry one No 10 or two No 12 bridges which can be rapidly laid or retrieved under full armour protection. Full details of the BAE Systems Land Systems Modular Bridging System are given in a separate entry.

Joint Assault Bridge (JAB) on M1A1 chassis in travelling configuration (BAE Systems Global Combat Systems) 1296640

Joint Assault Bridge based on the M1A1 MBT launches a scissors bridge over the front of the chassis (US Army) 1340084

The introduction of the M1A1 JAB will assist the US Marine Corps in moving to a common heavy chassis.

Composite Joint Assault Bridge
The US Naval Facilities Engineering Command, Engineering Service Centre, was tasked by the Office of Naval Research (ONR) to develop the Composite Joint Assault Bridge (CJAB).

The CJAB will utilise Vacuum Assisted Resin Transfer Molding (VARTIM) technology.

This is a fabrication technology that draws resin under vacuum through a carbon fibre matrix reinforcement to form a new bridge deck, ramp and beam sections.

The weight of the new bridge will be reduced from 15 tonnes (US) to 13 tonnes (US) and modifications to the launching system will reduce the bridge launching time from three minutes to about two minutes.

In addition, the new CJAB will increase the bridge span from 59 ft (18 m) to 78 ft (24 m) and increase the load carrying capacity from 60 tonnes (US) to as much as 85 tonnes (US).

Status
First six production systems for US Marine Corps were ordered in 2007 for delivery in 2008. The General Dynamics Land Systems M1A1 Abrams chassis are taken from current stocks.

Contractor
BAE Systems Global Combat Systems

General Dynamics Land Systems M48 and M60 Armoured Vehicle Launched Bridges (AVLB)

Development
In the 1950s, the standard AVLB of the US Army was the General Dynamics Land Systems M48A2 AVLB. This was essentially an M48 tank with its turret removed and fitted with a launching system for a scissors bridge, designed by the US Army Engineer Research and Development Laboratories (now the Belvoir Research, Development and Engineering Center) at Fort Belvoir, Virginia.

Production of the M48 was completed in 1959 and from 1963 the chassis of the M60 MBT was used. The chassis of these two vehicles is almost identical, the major difference being the type of 12-cylinder petrol engine. The M48, M48A1 and M48A2 were all powered by a 12-cylinder petrol engine which developed between 810 and 825 hp at 2,800 rpm, while the M48A3 was powered by a now L3 Propulsion Systems (originally Teledyne Continental Motors) 12-cylinder diesel (AVDS-1790-2A) engine which developed 750 hp at 2,400 rpm, giving the vehicle an increased operational range.

In Fiscal Year 1978 the US Army requested USD20.9 million to convert 136 M48A1 and M48A2 tanks into M48A5 AVLBs. (These vehicles now have M60 AVLB launcher components and the AVDS-1790-2D diesel engine.)

NAPCO Inc of Hopkins, Minnesota, has provided complete AVLB system support including training, technical assistance, special tools packages, spare parts and technical manuals.

In US Army service the M48/M60 AVLBs replaced by the much more capable General Dynamics Land Systems Wolverine Heavy Assault Bridge (HAB) based on a modified M1 Abrams MBT chassis.

It was expected that the M48/M60 AVLB would be replaced on a one for one basis by the M1 based Wolverine HAB but this programme has now been cancelled and the last of 43 vehicles was completed by General Dynamics Land Systems in late 2003.

It is expected that the remaining US Army/Marine Corps M48/M60 AVLB will be replaced by the M1A1 based Joint Assault Bridge. The US Marine Corps placed its first order for six JAB on M1A1 Abrams MBT chassis in 2007. Details of the Joint Assault Bridge are provided in a separate entry in

The bridge takes three minutes to launch and can be recovered from either end. Recovery time is between 10 and 60 minutes depending on ground conditions. The bridge has an overall length of 19.202 m and can span a gap up to 18.288 m. Overall bridge width is 3.96 m, 3.81 m of which is usable roadway, with each trackway 1.486 m wide. Its maximum capacity is 54,431 kg.

Variants

M60 Razorback
The upgraded AVLB based on a M60 chassis with a new powerpack only reached the prototype stage.

Tandem AVLB
This system, developed by Israel Military Industries and based on a modified M48/M60 MBT chassis, is covered in another entry in *Jane's Military Vehicles and Logistics*.

Specifications

M60 AVLB
Crew: 2
Weight:
    (with bridge) 55,205 kg
    (without bridge) 41,730 kg
Power-to-weight ratio:
    (with bridge) 13.59 hp/t (10.13 kW/t)
    (without bridge) 17.97 hp/t (13.40 kW/t)
Length:
    (with bridge) 11.28 m
    (chassis) 8.648 m
Width:
    (with bridge) 4.002 m
    (chassis) 3.64 m
Height:
    (with bridge) 3.9 m
    (without bridge) 3.04 m
Ground clearance: 0.36 m
Track: 2.921 m
Track width: 711 mm
Length of track on ground: 4.235 m
Ground pressure: 0.92 kg/cm^2
Max speed: (road) 48.28 km/h
Range: 500 km
Fuel capacity: 1,420 litres
Fording: 1.219 m
Gradient: 30%
Vertical obstacle: 0.914 m
Trench: 2.59 m
Engine: L3 Combat Propulsion Systems AVDS-1790-2A or AVDS-1790-2D 12-cylinder diesel developing 750 bhp (559 kW) at 2,400 rpm
Transmission: Allison CD-850-6 with 2 forward and 1 reverse
Electrical system: 24 V
Batteries: 6 × 12 V, 100 Ah
Armament: nil

Armour
Hull front: 101-120 mm
Hull sides front: 76 mm
Hull sides and rear: 51 mm
Hull top: 57 mm
Hull floor: 12.7-63 mm
Hull rear: 44 mm

Status
Current users are known to be Israel, Pakistan (M48), Portugal, Singapore (12 M60), Spain, Taiwan and the US Army and Marine Corps. In US Army service this AVLB has been partly replaced by the Wolverine Heavy Assault Bridge (HAB) based on a modified M1 MBT chassis.

Contractor
General Dynamics Land Systems

M48 AVLB laying its scissors bridge over the front of the vehicle (US Army)
1044345

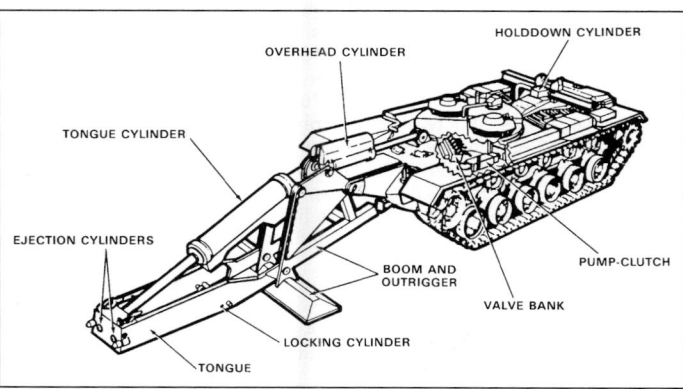

Drawing of M48 AVLB without its bridge
1133713

Jane's Military Vehicles and Logistics.
    The first user is the US Marine Corps who have a total requirement for 29 units with the total US Army requirement being for 168 units.

Description
The basic chassis of the M60 AVLB is almost identical to that of the M60 MBT, except that the driver is located aft of his MBT location and accommodation is made in the same area for the commander, since the MBT turret is removed in the AVLB configuration. The diesel engine and transmission are at the rear.

Early M48 AVLBs had two one-person turrets, each with a .50 (12.7 mm) M2 HB Browning machine gun, but these were later removed and replaced by two conventional hatch covers. The crew of two comprises the driver and commander.

The suspension is of the torsion bar type and consists either side of six dual rubber-tyred roadwheels with the idler at the front and the drive sprocket at the rear, with three track-return rollers. Hydraulic shock-absorbers are fitted at the first, second and sixth roadwheel stations.

The bridge weighs 13,380 kg and is made primarily of aluminium. It is carried folded and launched over the front of the vehicle hydraulically as follows: the AVLB is driven up to the obstacle and halted, the bridge is raised hydraulically into the vertical, unfolded and lowered into place and the launcher detached. The complete launch can be accomplished from under cover.

TACTICAL FLOATING BRIDGES AND FERRIES

China

Czech Republic

Type 79 and Type 79-A Ribbon Bridge

Development
The Type 79 Ribbon Bridge was developed from the Russian Federation PMP Heavy Folding Pontoon Bridge and the United States Ribbon Bridge. The construction, operating and other details are similar to those for the PMP, full details of which can be found elsewhere in this section.

Description
Figures supplied for the Type 79 Ribbon Bridge state that when a pontoon bridge is constructed across a river flowing at 2.5 m/s, a 50,000 kg capacity bridge 6.5 m wide and 312 m long can be erected. A 20,000 kg capacity bridge under similar circumstances can be 3.2 m wide and 527 m long. Construction of a floating bridge with a capacity of up to 110,000 kg takes 15 minutes.

Figures for the later Type 79-A Ribbon Bridge quote a capacity of 60,000 kg. The Type 79-A Ribbon Bridge is carried and launched from a Tiema XC2030 6 × 6 truck. One complete set of Type 79A Ribbon Bridge consists of 14 interior bays, 2 ramp bays, 5 motorboats (similar in configuration to Russian boats) and 21 refitted Tiema XC2030 trucks. The specification details of a single Type 79-A pontoon unit follow.

Specifications

Type 79 Ribbon Bridge - Single Pontoon
Weight: 7,200 kg
Length: 6.9 m
Width:
(folded) 3.202 m
(unfolded) 8.092 m
Bow height:
(folded) 2.236 m
(unfolded) 1.1 m
Roadway height: 740 mm

Status
In service with China. Believed to remain in production and offered for export.

Contractor
China Shipbuilding Trading Company Limited

Demonstration crossing of a People's Liberation Army (PLA) Type 79-A Ribbon Bridge (China Shipbuilding Trading Company Limited) 1128202

Type 79-A Ribbon Bridge section on a Tiema XC2200 (6 × 6) truck (China Shipbuilding Trading Company Limited) 1128201

Upgraded PMS folding pontoon bridge system

Development
With the accession of the Czech Republic to NATO it became necessary to upgrade (or modernise to utilise, the Czech term) the Czech Army's existing PMS folding pontoon bridge system, PMS being the Czech designation for the former Eastern Bloc PMP. During 1998 and 1999, a redesign programme was completed, followed by practical tests. Two distinct paths were followed. One was the upgrading of the standard PMS to have a MLC 70 load-carrying capacity and the second the introduction of a modified PMS with an inserted middle pontoon segment providing an increase in load-carrying capacity to MLC 80.

Involved in the development of the upgraded PMS, were the Czech Army and Ministry of Defence, including the Brno Military Academy and the Vyškov Military Research Institute.

Description
One of the main features of the upgraded PMS system is that all components are stored, transported and handled using a unified pontoon frame (the PR MO 2000 multipurpose transport frame), which extends to accommodate the new MO 2000 Veronika multipurpose bridging boat. Part of the upgraded PMS system is the PP MO 2000 multipurpose transport trailer which in addition to PMS components can also be used to carry various types of military container, including ISO 1C containers.

A complete upgraded PMS MLC 70 set comprises 32 mid-stream pontoon segments and two shore pontoon segments transported on TATRA T 815 VPR9 vehicles. Further details of this vehicle can be found in the Trucks section. The PMS MLC 70 set is completed by four MO 2000 bridging boats on PP MO 2000 transport trailers, four roadway laying trucks, four platform trucks, four trucks fitted with a BZT 815 dozer blade, plus eight ISO 1C containers carrying auxiliary equipment, tools and spare parts.

PMS folding pontoon bridge system components are constructed mainly of steel and the upgraded PMS can be assembled in running water with a maximum velocity of 2 m/s. Assembly in higher velocities is possible but within certain specified limitations.

TATRA T 815 VPR9 28.265 8 × 8.1R truck fitted with a PR MO 2000 multipurpose transport frame and carrying an upgraded PMS folding pontoon bridge centre section (Stefan Marx) 1128283

TATRA T 815 VPR9 28.265 8 × 8.1R truck fitted with a PR MO 2000 multipurpose transport frame and carrying an upgraded PMS folding pontoon bridge shore section (Stefan Marx) 1128284

Under development for use with both types of upgraded PMS is an unpowered boat to carry personnel and equipment. This will be used together with the MO 2000 Veronika bridging boat. Full details of the MO 2000 Veronika bridging boat can be found in the Bridging boats section.

Variants
Indian PMS
It became known in 2006 that pre-1990, Omnipol had delivered an unspecified quantity of PMS sets to India. It is understood that post-1990, further deliveries were to have occurred. These further deliveries, which did not take place, were to have consisted of two further sets from stock plus six sets from current production PMS; a transfer of production technology was also to occur. BEML of India is now producing PMS in India for the Indian Army. Available details of the Indian PMS can be found elsewhere in this section.

Specifications
PMS folding pontoon bridging system

	MLC 70	MLC 80
Max bridge length:	227 m	227 m
Width of roadway:	6.5 m	8.5 m
Carrying capacity of one midstream element:	20,000 kg	25,000 kg
Carrying capacity of one shore element:	10,000 kg	15,000 kg
Draft without load:	190 mm	190 mm
Draft with max load:	625 mm	654 mm
Deployment time:	50 min	50 min
Personnel:		
(assemblers)	68	68
(drivers)	34	34

Status
In service with the Czech Army. Previously supplied to India (see text). Available for export.

Marketing agency
Omnipol a.s.

France

CNIM Pont Flottant Motorisé Mle F1

Development
The Pont Flottant Motorisé Modèle F1 (PFM Mle F1) was developed by Constructions Navales et Industrielles de la Méditerranée, now Constructions Industrielles de la Méditerranée (then and now, CNIM), under contract to the Direction Technique des Armements Terrestres. It was tested in competition with a similar system developed by Creusot-Loire and compared to other equipment available in Western nations during 1979-1980. It was adopted by the French Army in early 1981.

Production of French Army PFM units commenced during February 1984, with the first deliveries to operational units starting at the end of 1985. In service the PFM is used in forward areas for tactical river crossings, while in rear areas it can be used to form line of communications bridges.

Description
The PFM Mle F1 may be employed as either a bridge or a raft/ferry. It can be used in rivers with a current of up to 3 m/s with MLC 70 loads. The equipment can be launched from banks up to 4 m high, used as a raft/ferry or bridge from banks 3 m high and recovered from banks 2 m high. The main advantages claimed for the PFM Mle F1 are that floating bridges and rafts/ferries can be assembled rapidly with minimum manpower and the main elements can be launched, driven and recovered without cranes, bridging boats or other ancillary equipment. Section assembly is eased by the use of pre-locking devices. The PFM Mle F1 is practically unsinkable as the various elements are filled with polyurethane foam or are partitioned.

The PFM Mle F1 consists of two major components, the centre section and the approach ramp. The centre section has locking elements at both ends, two wing tanks and two ballast tanks. The centre and wing units are constructed from light alloy, the ballast tanks from laminated GRP. Included in each ballast tank is a light alloy framework, which contains the outboard motor (75 hp). The approach ramps are also light alloy and their ends can be set hydraulically into various positions to suit the river bank height. The centre section and ramp are transported folded on a special semi-trailer towed by a 6 × 6 tractor truck. The resultant articulated unit normally has a 6 × 6 configuration but the trailer wheels can be hydraulically driven creating a 10 × 10 unit when crossing rough terrain. The semi-trailer is provided with power for unfolding, launching, recovery and refolding the section. The components are launched as follows: the

PFM Mle F1 across the river Rhine; length is 300 m (CNIM)

0589086

tractor reverses to the water's edge and the section is unfolded, the sliding frame is set back, hydraulic rams push up the forward end of the tilting frame and the section slides down into the water. A number of 10 m long sections are assembled in the water and the bridge is completed by adding the approach ramps. Each section is propelled in the water by two outboard motors and is fitted with a remote control box that allows one man to run its two outboard engines, thus reducing the crew.

To compliment the systems' standard TRM 10000 tractor truck, under a contract awarded in June 2006 Scania has supplied the French Army with 11 tractor units with fixed armoured cabs. These trucks were ordered as the cab of the TRM 10000 cannot be effectively armoured.

A team of 13 can assemble a MLC 70 raft in 20 minutes. Such a raft would consist of three centre sections and two approach ramps. A team of 28 can build a 100 m bridge within 45 minutes, although this time can be reduced to 15 minutes if there are no obstacles on the river side. This time reduction is due to the efficiency of the launch system, which makes it possible to carry out simultaneous launches from unprepared banks.

PFM Mle F1 sections can be launched from banks up to 4 m high, used as a raft or bridge from banks 3 m high and recovered from banks 2 m high. Any number of sections may be launched simultaneously from unprepared banks, speeding up the assembly process (CNIM)   0589088

From the rear, a French Army PFM Mle F1 centre section bridging unit on its dedicated semi-trailer. The tractor unit is a non-standard French Army Sisu E Tech 480 (Shaun C Connors)   1120446

PFM Mle F1 in use to evacuate animals during a flood (CNIM)   1431385

One option for use with this bridge is a ramp adapter kit that enables the bridge to be crossed by civilian vehicles with a short ground clearance.

Variants

BAC 20, BAC 60 and BAC 90 autonomous ferries
The BAC 20, BAC 60 and BAC 90 autonomous ferries are derived from the PFM Mle F1. They are constructed from PFM floating sections fitted with short ramps. Full details of the BAC 20, BAC 60 and BAC 90 autonomous ferries can be found elsewhere in this section.

PFM Short Integrated Ramps (SIR)
The PFM Short Integrated Ramps (SIR) is a variant of the PFM that allows for in-stride changing between assault raft and bridge mode. PFM SIR is in service with the Malaysian Army. Full details of the PFM SIR can be found elsewhere in this section.

Centralized OB engine control
With a view to achieving a significant saving in manpower to operate the PFM, CNIM has developed centralized control of the OB engines of each floating section.

Specifications
PFM Mle F1 - Main section
Weight: 10,500 kg
Length: 10 m
Width:
    (folded) 3.6 m
    (unfolded) 9.8 m
Track width: 4 m
Height:
    (folded) 2.1 m
    (unfolded) 730 mm
Draught: (unladen) 18 mm
Positive buoyancy: 42 t

PFM Mle F1 - Approach ramp
Weight: 7,500 kg
Length: 12 m
Track width: 4 m

Trailer and section with TRM 10 000 tractor
Weight: 31,000 kg
Length: 18 m
Width: 3.6 m
Height: 4 m
Ground clearance: 300 mm
Max road speed: 80 km/h
Max off-road speed: 10 km/h
Fording: 1.2 m

Status
In production. 3,400 m in service with the French Army, 1,100 m in service with the Swiss Army, and 1,100 m in production for the Italian Army.

Contractor
Constructions Industrielles de la Méditerranée (CNIM)

Enquiries to
CNIM Head Office

CNIM BAC 20, BAC 60 and BAC 90 autonomous ferries

Description
The Constructions Industrielles de la Méditerranée (CNIM) BAC 20, BAC 60 and BAC 90 autonomous ferries are intended for use in assault crossings by engineer units in infantry and armoured brigades. They can all carry wheeled or tracked vehicles and are derived directly from the Pont Flottant Motorisé (PFM) - full details of which can be found elsewhere in this section.

Launching of a CNIM BAC 20 autonomous ferry (CNIM)   0589098

The CNIM BAC 20 autonomous ferry is based on a single Pont Flottant Motorisé (PFM) floating section fitted with short ramps transported by a standard PFM semi-trailer (CNIM) 1186209

A CNIM BAC 20 loaded with one VAB and two P4 light vehicles (CNIM) 1186208

Ready-to-use time from arrival on site is seven minutes with a crew of six (three per transport vehicle) (CNIM) 0589109

The BAC 60 consists of two PFM floating sections, each of them fitted at one end with folding ramps (CNIM) 0589108

The BAC 90 consists of three PFM floating sections (CNIM) 1342294

retrieved by the PFM semi-trailer and its tractor truck crew. Ready-to-use time from arrival on site is seven minutes with a crew of nine (three per transport vehicle). When in water, propulsion is provided by six 75 hp (56 kW) outboard engines providing a maximum load dependant speed in calm water of 2.7 to 3.3 m/s. The BAC 90 is rated at MLC 90.

All versions can carry their own transport vehicle.

The BAC 20 ferry consists of a single PFM floating section with folding ramps fitted. It is transported, launched and retrieved by the PFM semi-trailer and its tractor truck crew of four. Ready-to-use time from arrival on site is less than five minutes and the ferry is ready to operate immediately after launching. When in the water, propulsion is provided by two 75 hp outboard engines, providing a maximum load dependant speed in calm water of 2.7 to 3.3 m/s. The BAC 20 is rated at MLC 20 or 30, dependant on current velocity.

The BAC 60 consists of two PFM floating sections each of them fitted at one end with folding ramps. Again, each section is transported, launched and retrieved by the PFM semi-trailer and its tractor truck crew. Ready-to-use time from arrival on site is seven minutes with a crew of six (three per transport vehicle). When in the water, propulsion is provided by four 75 hp outboard engines providing a maximum load dependant speed in calm water of 2.7 to 3.3 m/s. The BAC 60 is rated at MLC 50 or 60, dependant on current velocity.

The BAC 90 consists of three PFM floating sections, two short ramps with two hydraulic motor sets for operation, three dedicated semi-trailers and six outboard engines. Each section is transported, launched and

Specifications

CNIM BAC 20, BAC 60 and BAC 90 autonomous ferries

Model	BAC 20	BAC 60	BAC 90
Crew:	4	6	9
Weight:	15,900 kg	27,100 kg	37,600 kg
Length:			
(ramps folded)	11.6 m	21.6 m	31.6 m
(ramps unfolded)	17.4 m	27.4 m	37.4 m
(usable)	15 m	25 m	35 m
Width:			
(folded)	3.6 m	3.6 m	3.6 m
(unfolded)	9.8 m	9.8 m	9.8 m
Height:			
(folded)	2.1 m	2.1 m	2.1 m
(unfolded)	0.700 mm	0.700 mm	0.700 mm
Assembly time:	5 min	7 min	10 min
Special semi-trailer			
Weight: (laden)	23,900 kg	21,500 kg	21,500 kg
Length: (with TRM 10 000 tractor)	18 m	18 m	18 m
Width:			
(laden)	3.6 m	3.6 m	3.6 m
(unladen)	2.5 m	2.5 m	2.5 m
Height:	4 m	4 m	4 m
Speed:			
(road)	80 km/h	80 km/h	80 km/h
(off-road)	10 km/h	10 km/h	10 km/h

Status

BAC 90 in service with an undisclosed user.

Contractor

Constructions Industrielles de la Méditerranée (CNIM)

Enquiries to

CNIM Head Office

CNIM Pont Flottant Motorisé (PFM) Short Integrated Ramps (SIR)

Description

The PFM Short Integrated Ramps (SIR) is a variant of the Pont Flottant Motorisé (PFM) that allows for in-stride changes between assault raft and bridging configurations. Prior to launching the decision will be taken to launch individual sections with or without the detachable ramp section attached. If initially used in raft mode, when the tactical situation allows, rafts can detach from and leave their ramps on any suitable bank, then moving off to become standard bridge components.

A 100 m SIR unit consists of three standard PFM floating sections, two standard PFM access ramps and six PFM SIR floating sections fitted with a hydraulically operated short ramp. This set allows for the construction of three ferries or two 50 m bridges, or a single 100 m bridge with a crew of 28.

Each of the three ferries requires nine minutes to construct, has a load capacity of 90,000 kg and can operate in currents of up to 3 m/s unladen, this figure reducing to 2.2 m/s when laden. No bank preparation is required for bank heights of up to 1 m.

One of the 50 m bridges combines four PFM floating sections with the two standard PFM ramps, and measures 54 m end-to-end with a 1 m bank at both ends. The second bridge combines five PFM floating sections with SIR ramp units at both ends, and measures 57 m. The longest bridge possible with the 100 m SIR unit is made of nine sections and two standard PFM ramps, and dependant on configuration measures between 99 and 105 m end-to-end.

Specifications are broadly similar to the standard PFM, or a 'half BAC 60' for a floating PFM SIR section.

Status

Production as required. In service with the Malaysian Army.

Contractor

Constructions Industrielles de la Méditerranée (CNIM)

Enquiries to

CNIM Head Office

CNIM Pont Flottant Motorisé (PFM) Short Integrated Ramps (SIR) in ferry mode, having detached from and left the ramp section on-shore (CNIM)
0589121

CNIM Pont Flottant Motorisé (PFM) Short Integrated Ramps (SIR) (CNIM)
1431384

Nexter MLF light river crossing equipment

Description

The MLF light river crossing equipment (*Matériel Léger de Franchissement*), also known as the CASTOR light spanning equipment Type F2, was developed by the Etablissement Technique d'Angers and was adopted by the French Army in 1976.

The MLF can be used as a floating bridge; a raft or an individual flotation unit can be used as an assault or river boat. When being used as the latter, it can carry 32 personnel and is propelled in the water by paddles or an outboard motor.

The flotation units that are of light alloy construction, are made up of two flat-bottom boats assembled stern to stern by pins, having an assembled length of 9.8 m. The gunwales are capped by stiffeners that are attached to the boat by four locking pins. Each unit is also provided with handrails, outboard motor attachment and a floor.

The bridge deck comprises two tracks made up of deck components, steel assemblies, articulation units and ramp units. The central deck units fill the space between the tracks and are of reinforced plastic. The bridge decks are secured to the flotation units by the sets of tiltable pegs on the gunwale stiffeners. The bridge deck components are made of light alloy sections welded together and are provided with anti-skid strips. The deck bridge components are arranged in pairs, end to end and spaced 700 mm apart.

The articulated joints provide the connection between the bridge deck components located on the floating support and those acting on the ramp. Each articulation joint weighs 165 kg and is adjusted manually. The ramp units are of welded light alloy construction and assembled by means of pins. Each ramp weighs 50 kg and is provided with a steel contact edge. Each bridge deck unit can be fitted with a track guide in tubular light alloy, which is articulated on bosses welded to the outside of the bridge deck. The track guide can be retracted into a free space on the side of the bridge deck.

The French Army version of this system consists of four flotation units and three deck sections forming a loading length of 10.5 m with two ramp sections on each side. The resultant raft has a load capacity of MLC 16 in a river flow rate of 1.5 m/s. Propulsion is provided by two 40 hp outboard motors.

Rafts

Various types of raft of two, three, four, five or six flotation units can be assembled. A 4/3 type basic raft can be assembled by three teams of eight personnel in about 40 minutes. This raft can be carried on a Renault TRM 4000 4 × 4 4,000 kg truck, towing an SKD 3536 trailer carrying the eight flotation unit halves stacked one inside the other. The raft is either propelled in the water by outboard motors or pushed by a bridging boat. For example, a 4/3 raft would be propelled by two 40 hp outboard motors on the first and fourth flotation units.

Bridges

Two types of bridge can be built using the MLF system: the medium bridge composed of bridge deck units with flotation units under them and, the heavy-duty bridge with the flotation units positioned one alongside the other. The medium bridge (1/1) is 8.07 m long and will span a river 7 m wide, while the heavy-duty bridge has an overall length of 16.13 m and will span a river of 15 m.

Specifications

Individual flotation unit
Length: 4.9 m
Width: 1.75 m
Height: 750 mm
Weight:
   (without equipment) 160 kg
   (with floor and superstructure) 235 kg
   (with floor, superstructure and gunwale stiffeners) 250 kg

MLF light river crossing equipment flotation unit sections on a purpose-designed transport trailer. Joined stem to stern these units may also be used as an assault or river boat, carrying up to 32 personnel (Pierre Touzin)
1124705

Bridge decks
Length: 3.44 m
Width: 1 m
Depth: 260 mm
Weight: 205 kg

Raft and bridge load capacities in tons

Type of raft or bridge	Current speed		
	1.5 m/s	2 m/s	2.5 m/s
2/2 raft	6	-	-
3/3 raft	10	8	6
4/3 (basic) raft	16	13	10
6/4 raft	22	20	15
Medium-duty bridge	15	13	8
Heavy-duty bridge	22	20	16

Status
Production complete. Supplied to the armies of Brazil, France, Indonesia, Singapore and possibly others.

Contractor
Atelier de Construction de Tarbes (ATS), now part of Nexter (formerly Giat).

Enquiries to
Nexter

Germany

General Dynamics European Land Systems - Germany (GDELS-G) Bundeswehr Faltschwimmbrücke (FSB)

Development
In 1976, the West German Army decided to participate in the US Army's test and evaluation programme of the first production Ribbon Bridge, full details of which can be found elsewhere in this section. The trials were carried out in Germany between September 1976 and March 1977. Early in 1977, the West German Army decided to adopt the Ribbon Bridge System and subsequently undertook a redesign to meet European requirements and to enhance the overall technical design allowing production in Germany. Production by the then Eisenwerke Kaiserslautern GmbH (EWK) began in 1978 with first deliveries to the German Army in December of that year. Each of the German Army's 12 Division Combat Engineer Companies existing at that time had one complete set of 26 segments: 18 bridge segments and eight ramp elements. In Germany the system is known as the *Faltschwimmbrücke*, or FSB - Foldable Float Bridge.

The FSB has been supplied to 11 countries (including a steel version to the Egyptian Army). The total bridging length produced is over 11 km, involving a total of 1,693 bridging segments.

An order for FSB for the Australian Army was completed in 1989. The order was worth approximately AD15 million, with the bridges being partly manufactured in Australia by Transfield Construction Pty Limited (acquired by the John Holland Group in 2003) of New South Wales.

Due to the introduction of the latest generation of main battle tanks with a standard loading classification of MLC 70, EWK developed a FSB 2-MLC 70 version which is known as Improved Ribbon Bridge (IRB). Full details of the IRB can be found in this section. The IRB system remains interoperable with the standard MLC 60 pontoons of the FSB and the US Army's Standard Ribbon Bridge and can be transported on in-service

German Army FSB centre section being launched from a MAN 6 × 6 7,000 kg truck (Lkw 7t gl Brückentransporter) (Stefan Marx)   1128285

A German Army FSB ready for use (Stefan Marx)   1128286

trucks and manoeuvred by in-service bridge erection boats. The IRB has been ordered by the US Army and US Marine Corps has been used operationally in Iraq since early 2003.

The German Army has acquired a total of 25 Interior Bays and 11 Ramp Bays, and these have been in service since 2009.

General Dynamics Santa Bárbara Sistemas SA of Spain (GDSBS), a subsidiary of General Dynamics Corporation of Falls Church, Virginia, completed the acquisition of the assets of EWK on 31 October 2002. As of 1 November 2002 EWK was renamed General Dynamics Santa Bárbara Sistemas GmbH (GDSBS GmbH). The company is now known as General Dynamics European Land Systems - Germany GmbH (GDELS-G GmbH).

Description
The German version of the Ribbon Bridge, unlike the US model, is built to metric standards and incorporates a number of major improvements to suit German requirements, enhance reliability and ease maintenance, none of which affect its compatibility with the original US version.

The hydraulic system for raising the ramp bay to adjust to varying bank conditions has been modified and non-polluting hydraulic fluid introduced; on the original model, oil sometimes leaked out and water got in. Other improvements include: winch-operated approach ramps; changes to interior bays that prevent cables from getting crushed as the section folds; non-skid coating on roadways and walkways; and stops on the bridge sections to keep the bridging boats in place when the bridge is being used as a raft.

The Faltschwimmbrücke supplied to the German and Belgian armies is carried on the rear of a MAN 6 × 6 7,000 kg truck, designated the Lkw 7t gl Brückentransporter. The following next generation is known as the Faltschwimmbrücke Export, or FSB-E, supplied to the Australian, Belgian, Brazilian, Canadian, Nigerian, Portuguese, Singapore, Swedish and Turkish armies and carried on different trucks, usually an IVECO 6 × 6.

The now GDELS-G previously offered an all-steel version which is comparable/similar to the original PMP system. This version was originally developed for and is now in service with Egypt. The main differences between the steel and the aluminium versions can be seen in the specifications table.

Specifications

Faltschwimmbrücke - vehicle with folded unit
Cab seating: 1 + 2
Configuration: 6 × 6
Weight: (laden) 18,800 kg
Length: (overall) 10.4 m
Width: (overall) 3.33 m
Height: (overall) 3.9 m
Ground clearance: 415 mm
Wheelbase: 4.7 m + 1.4 m
Angle of approach/departure: 45°/31°
Max speed: 90 km/h
Range: 700 km
Max gradient: 50%
Fording: 1.2 m

Faltschwimmbrücke - bridge Section

	Aluminium	Steel
Weight:	5,450 kg	7,700 kg
Length:	6.7 m	6.7 m
Width unfolded:	8.18 m	8.02 m
Road width:	4.1 m	6.6 m

Faltschwimmbrücke - ramp section

	Aluminium	Steel
Weight:	5,660 kg	7,500 kg
Length:	5.6 m	5.5 m
Road width:	4.1 m	6.6 m

Status

Production as required. FSB supplied to the Australian, Belgian, Brazilian, Canadian, Egyptian (on IVECO Magirus 240-25 ANWM 6 × 6 trucks), German, Nigerian, Portuguese, Singapore, Swedish and Turkish (on IVECO Magirus 240-25 ANWM 6 × 6 trucks) armies. The IRB has been in service with the US Army since 2002, the USMC since 2008, and the German Army since 2009.

Contractor

General Dynamics European Land Systems - Germany GmbH (GDELS-G GmbH)

General Dynamics European Land Systems - Germany (GDELS-G) Improved Ribbon Bridge (IRB)

Development

Due to the introduction of the latest generation of main battle tanks with a standard loading classification of MLC 70 in 1998, the then Eisenwerke Kaiserslautern GmbH (EWK) began the development of a new MLC 70 rated Folding Float Bridge based on its 30 years of experience with the Bundeswehr Faltschwimmbrücke (FSB).

Testing of the Improved Ribbon Bridge (IRB) began in Germany in 1999 by German and US Army engineer units. In 2000 the US Army's Tank-automotive and Armaments Command (TACOM) placed an order worth DM80 million for 211 interior and 82 ramp bays. Twenty-four interior and 11 ramp bays were delivered for testing and field trials. These trials were completed in December 2002, with fielding of the first units in December 2002 and January 2003. Production was initially split 70/30 percent Germany/US, but has now returned 100 per cent to Germany.

In September 2007, a USD233 million multi-year requirement contract for additional Improved Ribbon Bridge (IRB) equipment was announced. The contract calls for a total of 541 interior bays and 218 ramp bays and annual production quantities will be subject to individual delivery orders.

As a member of the Improved Ribbon Bridge team AM General Corporation will provide spare parts, field service, and training support for the US Army's IRB from their Engineering and Product Development Centre at Livonia, Michigan.

The IRB has been successfully used during US Army operations in Iraq.

The German Army has acquired a total of 25 interior bays and 11 ramp bays, and these have been in service since 2009.

General Dynamics Santa Bárbara Sistemas SA of Spain (GDSBS), a subsidiary of General Dynamics Corporation of Falls Church, Virginia completed the acquisition of the assets of EWK on 31 October 2002. As of 1 November 2002 EWK was renamed General Dynamics Santa Bárbara Sistemas GmbH (GDSBS GmbH). The company is now known as General Dynamics European Land Systems - Germany GmbH (GDELS-G GmbH).

Description

The Improved Ribbon Bridge (IRB) is based on the design of the Faltschwimmbrücke (FSB) and, like the FSB, the IRB is built to metric standards. The IRB is fully interoperable with the FSB and US Army's Standard Ribbon Bridge (SRB), interoperability encompassing the mixing of bays, transport by in-service trucks and erection by in-service bridging boats. Full details of the FSB and SRB can be found elsewhere in this section.

Experience from use with the FSB and SRB has lead to numerous design improvements by GDSBS with the IRB. These include the use of a complete aluminium-based structure (FSB and SRB used a steel strongbar that proved vulnerable to corrosion); an improved folding and unfolding mechanism to avoid cable breakage; a longer ramp bay that can reach bank heights of 2.35 m; a wider useable roadway giving a total useable roadway width of 6.75 m for two-lane traffic for vehicles of up to MLC 20T/14W and a 4.5 m single-track roadway width for vehicles of up to MLC70T/96W; a new hydraulic system, a higher splash plate to prevent water flooding the roadway, and a NATO-tested non-skid surface. The IRB is useable in currents of up to 3.15 m/s.

In the US Army IRB bays are transported on the Oshkosh M1977 Common Bridge Transporter (CBT) based on the HEMTT (8 × 8) truck. Some units also still use the M821 (6 × 6) truck. Virtually any PLS capable truck with a minimum payload of 7.5 tonnes can be used as a means of transport, launch and retrieval.

For air transport, a complete interior or ramp bay may be transported by C-5, C-17, C-141 or A400M transport aircraft. A half interior or ramp bay may be transported by C-130 or C-160 transport aircraft; a CH-47 helicopter can transport a complete interior or ramp bay as an underslung load. IRB bays are readily transportable by rail flatcars or as open deck freight on any cargo vessel.

A five-bay ferry consisting of Standard Ribbon Bridge and Improved Ribbon Bridge bays (non-camouflaged) in use during a joint exercise by US and German army engineer units (GDELS-G)   0134398

An IRB (FSB-2) centre section (front), compared to a standard FSB section, rear - note the clearly visible higher splash plate that prevents water flooding the roadway (Stefan Marx)   1128287

Improved Ribbon Bridge (IRB) ramp bay being transported by an Oshkosh M1977 Common Bridge Transporter (CBT) (GDELS-G)   0134399

US Army 523 m Improved Ribbon Bridge (IRB) crossing the river Tigris near the city of Tikrit, Iraq (GDELS-G)   1139050

From the rear, an Improved Ribbon Bridge (IRB) ramp bay being transported by a German Army MAN 6 × 6 truck (Stefan Marx)   1128288

Specifications

Improved Ribbon Bridge (IRB)

	Interior bay	Ramp bay
Length:		
(total)	6.92 m	6.92 m
(useable)	6.705 m	6.7 m
Width:		
(folded)	3.3 m	3.199 m
(unfolded)	8.633 m	8.633 m
Weight: (total)	6,350 kg	6,350 kg
Height:		
(folded)	2.35 m	2.35 m
(unfolded)	1.304 m	1.304 m

Operations

	Bridge	Ferry
Immersion with MLC 70 crossing:	480 mm	640 mm
Max permissible water current:	3.15 m/s	3.15 m/s (MLC 70)
Useable roadway (bridge)/deck (ferry) width:		
(MLC 80T/96W)	4.5 m	4.5 m
(MLC20T/14W)	6.75 m (2-way traffic)	6.75 m
Construction time for 100 m bridge:	30-45 mins	n/app
Bridge bays required for 100 m bridge:	13 interior bays, 2 ramp bays	n/app
Boats required for ferry operations:	n/app	1 boat per 2-3 bays

Status

In production. In service with the German Army and the US Army (since 2002) and Marine Corps (since 2008). Twenty-four interior bays and 11 ramp bays were delivered for US Army testing and field trials, which were completed in December 2002. 211 interior bays and 83 ramp bays ordered by the US Army in 2000. First units fielded in December 2002 and January 2003. A further 541 interior bays and 218 ramp bays (with annual production quantities subject to individual delivery orders) were ordered by the US Army in September 2007. Has been deployed operationally in Iraq by the US Army.

Contractor

General Dynamics European Land Systems - Germany GmbH (GDELS-G GmbH)

FFB 2000

Development

Kraus-Maffei Wegmann (KMW) acquired the MAN AG industrial group's MAN Mobile Bridges (MMB) subsidiary in April 2005 for an undisclosed sum. MMB specialised in the design, manufacture and supply of military bridges worldwide including armoured vehicle launched bridges and floating bridges and the two companies had previously worked together for some years, especially on armoured vehicle launched bridges (AVLBs) based on the Leopard 1 and 2 chassis.

The *Faltschwimmbrücke* 2000 (FFB 2000 or Folding Float Bridge 2000) was developed jointly by the then KRUPP Fördertechnik GmbH (now ThyssenKrupp Fördertechnik GmbH) and the then MAN

A fully refurbished FFB float section photographed at BAE Systems Land Systems OMC Benoni facility in South Africa. BAE Systems Land Systems OMC are responsible for the in-service support of the SANDF's F2000 FFB, its transport trucks and associated bridging boats (Patrick Allen)   1110997

A MAN F2000 FFB ramp section undergoing refurbishment at BAE Systems Land Systems OMC Benoni facility; BAE Systems Land Systems OMC are responsible for the in-service support of the SANDF's FFB, its transport trucks and associated bridging boats (Patrick Allen)   1111037

Rear ³/₄ view of a FFB 2000 E (Enhanced) float section on a MAN Kat 1A1 (6 × 6) (Stefan Marx)   1121186

Gutehoffnungshütte AG, as a result of experience gained in the manufacture and use of the German version of the US Ribbon Bridge. The construction of the FFB 2000 followed extensive testing with models in the Research Institute for Inland Waterway Shipbuilding at Duisburg.

Description

The FFB 2000 can be used in water with stream velocities up to 3.5 m/s with a load of MLC 70, or up to MLC 80 in exceptional cases. It can be used in a similar fashion to the existing Ribbon Bridge and can be used for the construction of ferries and floating bridges. It is completely compatible with existing US and German Ribbon Bridges.

The FFB 2000 consists of inner and ramp sections with a new streamlined cross-section with 30° bows. Each inner and ramp section is folded into a 'W' shape for transport on an all-terrain 7,000 kg capacity truck. The sections unfold automatically as they are launched from the carrier truck. Once in the water, the sections can be assembled by a bridging boat into ferries or bridges. A ferry can be assembled in a modular fashion from two ramp sections and the necessary number of inner sections. The effective roadway width is 4.1 m (5.2 m for two-lane traffic up to MLC 16) with footpaths 2.2 m wide on either side of the road. The assembly time for a 100 m bridge can be as low as approximately 60 minutes and, up to 200 MLC 80 vehicles can cross the bridge every hour. A ferry consisting of two inner sections and two ramp sections can carry vehicles up to MLC 70 in stream velocities up to 3.5 m/s. To accommodate various bank conditions and heights, the ramp sections can be adjusted hydraulically to a height of approximately 2.2 m above water level. Minimum water depth for operations is 1.2 m. Each section has four crane lifting points for handling.

Advantages claimed for the FFB 2000 over similar equipment includes: improved floating stability due to the new cross-sectional shape; higher ferry capacity; the ability to cope with greater bank heights; flatter approach slope on to the bridge; improved bridge-crossing performance; continuous road panel; no heavy ramp plates; stronger overall construction; and improved handling in the water and at launch.

Specifications

FFB 2000
Weight:
  (inner section) 4,800 kg
  (ramp section) 5,200 kg
Effective length: 6.7 m
Width:
  (folded) 3.03 m
  (unfolded) 8.85 m
  (roadway) 4.1 m
  (walkways) 2 × 2.22 m
Height:
  (unfolded, bow) 1.27 m
  (unfolded, deck) 737 mm
  (folded) 2.35 m
  (road transport) 3.95 m
Material: AlMgSi

Status

Production as required. South Africa and Brazil are known to have received 'several hundred' metres of FFB approximately 14 years ago.

Contractor

Krauss-Maffei Wegmann GmbH & Co KG

LEGUAN ferry

Development

Kraus-Maffei Wegmann (KMW) acquired the MAN AG industrial group's MAN Mobile Bridges (MMB) subsidiary in April 2005 for an undisclosed sum. MMB specialised in the design, manufacture and supply of military bridges worldwide, including armoured vehicle launched bridges and floating bridges. The two companies had previously worked together for some years, especially on armoured vehicle launched bridges (AVLBs) based on the Leopard 1 and 2 chassis.

The LEGUAN ferry is based on a standard LEGUAN bridge which is provided with extra equipment so that it maybe used as a ferry. Full details of the LEGUAN bridgelayer and its normal operating sequence can be found in the Mechanised bridges section.

Description

The complete LEGUAN floating ferry consists of a modified LEGUAN bridge with ramps, a hydraulic system and pontoons with bridge saddles. To connect the ramp girder to a bridge, use is made of two openings in each LEGUAN bridge wheel tread girder. Normally these openings are closed by adapters held in place by plug-in strips and an interlocking system. Each adapter weighs 23 kg. When the bridge is used as a ferry, the openings are closed by the ramp connection systems that form the connection between the bridge on one side and the ramp girder and hydraulic system on the other. The units are 1.4 m wide and the ramp connection systems weigh 137 kg for each tread girder. All have the same anti-slip coating as the LEGUAN bridge.

Each ramp girder is 4.8 m long and can accommodate a difference in levels of approximately 1.32 m; which is a maximum gradient of 29 per cent (13°). One ramp girder weighs 620 kg. The hydraulic system is used as an adjusting element. The total weight of the hydraulic system for one ramp is 600 kg.

The pontoons used with the ferry are unsinkable aluminium alloy boats coupled at their bluff sterns to form a pontoon. The pontoons are connected to the LEGUAN bridge and are fixed to the lower chord sections of the outer sides of the wheel tread girders. Two sets of three pontoons are required for MLC 70 loads and three pontoons for loads up to MLC 27.

To lay the LEGUAN bridge across the pontoons, the laying procedure is much the same as for a normal LEGUAN bridge.

It is claimed that the LEGUAN ferry has good manoeuvrability and is well suited for use in shallow water.

MLC 70 LEGUAN ferry in use in Norway (KMW)   0007685

Two or more individual LEGUAN ferries can be joined together to form a floating bridge. The only additional equipment required for this capability is a coupling element for joining two ferry units together. In operation this coupling element is installed on one end of a ferry before the other ferry is moved in and attached to the coupling element. Coupling elements have been supplied to Norway.

A typical drive unit used with the LEGUAN ferry is a Schottel Pump Jet SPJ 20 driven by a KHD F 61 912 diesel engine which can be swivelled through 360°. When pontoons are stacked for storage or transport the drive unit is always in the top pontoon.

Specifications

Pontoons
Weight:
  (pontoon with drive) 2,055 kg
  (pontoon without drive) 1,185 kg
Length:
  (single pontoon) 8.8 m
  (double pontoon) 17.6 m
Width: 2.25 m
Height: 1.225 m

Ramps
Load capacity: MLC 60
Weight:
  (ramp with hydraulic system) 2,200 kg
Length: 4.8 m
Width: 1.97 m
Height: (overall) 645 mm

Status

Production as required. In service with Norway.

Contractor

Krauss-Maffei Wegmann GmbH & Co KGG

India

BEML PMS folding pontoon bridge system

Description

It became known in 2006 that pre-1990, Omnipol a.s. of the Czech Republic had delivered an unspecified quantity of PMS sets to India. It is understood that post-1990 further deliveries were to have occurred. These further deliveries, which did not take place, were to have consisted of two further sets from stock plus six sets from current production PMS; a transfer of production technology was also to occur.

India's then Bharat Earth Movers Limited (now BEML Ltd) announced in February 2006 that it would produce a local version of the PMP/PMS folding pontoon bridge system for the Indian Army and export market. The PMS is essentially the Czech version of the Russian Federation PMP. Full details of Omnipol's upgraded PMS can be found elsewhere in this section.

PMS sets have undergone extensive Indian Army trials including 1,000 passes by T-72 MBTs. Some minor local changes will be made to production systems but the Indian-produced PMS will remain compatible with the original Czech system.

BEML disclosed in February 2006 that an order for six complete systems had been received from the army and that these would be delivered at a rate of one per year from 2006.

In addition to the pontoon sections BEML will also supply the TATRA 8 × 8 transport and launcher vehicles, TATRA 8 × 8 trucks with a portable roadway system for use at bridging sites, TATRA 6 × 6 mobile cranes, and MO-634 bridging boats and SP-5 trailers.

The data provided in the accompanying Specifications table was supplied by BEML.

Specifications

	Midstream pontoon	Shore pontoon
Weight:	7,200 kg	7,700 kg
Length:	6.75 m	5.6 m
Width:		
(folded)	3.2 m	3.2 m
(open)	8.85 m	7.25 m
Height:		
(folded)	2.2 m	2.2 m
(open)	1.1 m	1 m

Status

In production (six sets ordered), entering service with the Indian Army. It is probable that this system is seen as the eventual successor to the earlier Bridge Assault Floating Heavy Class 50, currently in service with the Indian Army.

Contractor

BEML Ltd (formerly Bharat Earth Movers Limited).

Bridge Assault Floating Heavy Class 50T (Krupp Man)

Development

The Bridge Assault Floating Heavy Class 50T (Krupp Man) is an Indian-produced version of the German MAN Gutehoffnungshütte GmbH and Krupp Industrietechnik GmbH (now Man Technologie AG) Bridge, Pneumatic Float, Class 16/30/50 (sometimes referred to as the Light Metal Bridge).

This bridge is no longer in service with the German Army, having initially been supplemented by, and then replaced by, the Faltschwimmbrücke 2000 (FFB (Folding Float Bridge) 2000). It was also supplied to Indonesia.

It was disclosed during 2006 that India had, during around 2000, initially procured two complete PMS pontoon bridging sets from Omnipol a.s. of the Czech Republic and that BEML had recently received an order for six licence-produced sets of PMS from the Indian Army. It should be assumed that PMS will be the eventual successor to the Bridge Assault Floating Heavy Class 50T in Indian Army service. Available details of the Indian PMS project can be found elsewhere in this section.

Description

The bridge consists of an aluminium alloy superstructure supported on pneumatic polychloroprene-coated nylon fabric rubberised floats. The floats are inflated using an air compressor, and one end of each float is upturned and the other is fitted with a stern mount on which an outboard motor can be mounted. The deck balk and saddle beam assembly are also made of aluminium alloy and the connectors are made of steel. During bridge construction, two launching boats are employed.

This bridge is normally used for crossing water obstacles such as rivers and is capable of accepting MLC 50 (T) loads. Ferries of MLC 50 (T) class using a selection of bridge components can also be used.

Specifications

Max length: MLC 50 (T) 100 m
Roadway width: 4 m
Load class range: MLC 18, 24, 40, 50 (T), 70 (W)
Bank height:
  (max) 920 mm
  (min) 680 mm
Water current: 4 m/s
Min depth of water: (inshore float, laden) 1 m
Weight of float: 375 kg
Width of float: 3 m
Height of float:
  (at stern) 1.735 m
  (at bow) 1.735 m
Tube diameter: 1 m

Status

Production likely to be on an as required basis. In service with the Indian Army. Offered for export.

Contractor

Not known.

Enquiries to

Ordnance Factory Board

Israel

IMI Two-Tank Ferry Raft (2TFR)

Description

The Two-Tank Ferry Raft (2TFR) is intended for use as a ferry raft carrying one or two MBTs, or for connecting with one or more 2TFRs to form a floating bridge. On land the 2TFR is sufficiently mobile allowing it to be towed into position by the MBTs that will use it to cross water obstacles, while on roads the 2TFR may be towed by heavy trucks. Each 2TFR is an independent unit handled by a crew of three. A 33-man force with 11 2TFRs can bridge 300 m of water. Linking time for two 2TFR units is about five minutes.

The 2TFR consists of a floating loading platform, 21 m long and 5 m wide, with two side floats, each 21 m long and 1.6 m wide. The side floats are folded on to the loading platform during transit and are usually opened before reaching the operational area. At each end of the platform is a hinged loading ramp, 7.5 m long and 5 m wide, which is folded up on to the platform until the unit is launched. Both side floats and platform are filled with rigid polyurethane foam to ensure buoyancy in the event of battle damage.

The 2TFR is propelled by two identical power units that may be produced by Schottel of Germany or the former Stewart & Stevenson of the US (now BAE Systems). The two power units may be controlled from either of two control units, or from a remote-control unit that may be mounted anywhere on the 2TFR. The power units propel the raft in the water and raise and lower the side floats and loading ramps. Each power

A Two Tank Ferry Raft (2TFR) in use (Israel Military Industries)   1190258

On land, a Two Tank Ferry Raft (2TFR) being towed by an MBT (Shaun C Connors)   1340281

unit is connected to the propulsion unit by a 270° pivot for steering. The propeller shaft can be raised and lowered to suit varying water depths and in transit the whole propulsion unit can be angled upward and over for road clearance. On land the raft travels on a wheeled undercarriage with four pairs of wheels, each pair with its own suspension. The wheels are low pressure tyres and specially designed. Once waterborne the entire undercarriage can be uncoupled and dropped. A hydraulically operated tow boom, powered by either of the power units, is located on the stern of the raft and is self-uncoupling.

In use, the 2TFR is towed by a heavy truck to the nearest possible point of use by road. When the road is left, the 2TFR is hitched to a tank by the hydraulic boom on the stern of the raft and towed to the edge of the water obstacle. The MBT then pulls the raft round and pushes it into the water. The tow boom is uncoupled from the raft and drops off the MBT. The 2TFR can then proceed under its own power and the undercarriage can be separated from the raft. The loading ramps are extended and, once lowered, the raft can take on its load of two MBTs. The entire sequence, once the raft is in the water, takes under five minutes.

The wheels on the undercarriage may be fitted with high-speed brakes and for road towing the width of the 2TFR may be reduced to 4.25 m. For water use, the undercarriage can be supplied in a retractable form, in which state the wheels will extend only 500 mm. Propulsion hydrojets may be used in place of the normal propulsion units. Another option is that the 2TFR can be fitted with only one loading ramp, allowing the raft to be used as a one-direction raft with both propulsion units at the rear. A smaller version of the 2TFR can be produced which will carry only one tank. This unit will have a transit length of 17 m and a width of 4.45 m.

For maintenance, the power units can be removed and stored separately from the rest of the raft. Tank drivers need no special training to tow the 2TFR.

Specifications

Two-Tank Ferry Raft (2TFR)
Crew: 3
Length
  (transit) 21 m
  (water) 31 m
  (bridging formation) 27.5 m
Width
  (road) 4.25 m
  (water, side floats down) 8.25 m
  (loading platform width) 5 m

Height:
   (road) 5.1 m
   (water) 3.5 m
Weight
   (transit, less power units) 46,000 kg
   (ready for launch) 54,000 kg
   (waterborne) 48,000 kg
Towing speed
   (road) 60 km/h
   (tank-towed, off-road) 25 km/h
Uphill inclination angle: (tank-towed) 11°
Lateral inclination angle: (tank-towed) 15°
Turn radius: 20 m
Speed in water
   (unladen) 14 km/h
   (one tank) 11 km/h
   (two tanks) 9 km/h
Draught
   (unladen) 350 mm
   (one tank) 740 mm
   (two tanks) 1.2 m
Manoeuvrability: 360°
Operational time before refuelling: 12 h
Sea-going capability: ≤ Sea State 3
Bridging capability
   (resistance to current) ≤ 2.5 m/s
   (length) unlimited

Status
Production likely to be as required. In service with the Israeli Army.

Contractor
Israel Military Industries (IMI)

Japan

Heavy Floating Bridge

Description
In addition to the Light Foot Bridge and Light Gate Bridge (raft/ferry) and the heavier armoured vehicle-suitable Type 92 floating bridge (details of which can be found elsewhere in this section), the Japanese GSDF are also known to employ one other non-mechanised floating bridge system, the Heavy Floating Bridge (Jyu (Heavy) Fu (Floating) Kyo (Bridge)).

No specific information has been made available regarding the Heavy Floating Bridge, although it is known to be limited to light vehicle traffic, and most probably nothing heavier than a light truck or all-terrain vehicle.

Pneumatic float detail of the Heavy Floating Bridge (Mitsuhiro Kadota)

0587960

Public demonstration of the Heavy Floating Bridge (Mitsuhiro Kadota)

0587961

The Heavy Floating Bridge consists of a deck superstructure, most probably aluminium or similar light alloy, supported by pneumatic floats. No other details are known.

Status
Production likely to be on an as required basis. In service with the Japanese GSDF.

Contractor
Not known.

Light Foot Bridge

Description
The Japanese Light Foot Bridge (Kei (Light) To (Foot) Kyo (Bridge)) is similar to the old US M1938 footbridge. Major differences are that aluminium alloy is used instead of white pine for the float body and the duckboard stringer, with cedar wood substituted for pine in the transverse slats of the duckboard. The floats are filled with foam rubber to give increased buoyancy.

A bridge set, which is carried on two 2,500 kg trucks, consists of 36 parts and is sufficient to span 131.6 m. The duckboards measure 3.6 × 0.5 × 0.19 m (L × W × D), while the floats measure 3 × 0.28 × 0.415 m (L × W × H).

Crossing rates are 75 persons per minute (max) by day, 40 by night. Standard crossing rates are 38 personnel per minute (day), 20 by night. The maximum current in which the Light Foot Bridge can be used is 2.5 m/s.

Specifications
Light Foot Bridge

	Duckboards	Floats
Length:	3.6 m	3.0 m
Width:	0.5 m	0.28 m
Height:	0.19 m	0.415 m

Status
Production likely to be on an as required basis. In service with the Japanese GSDF.

Contractor
Nihon Aluminium Rolling Works Ltd

Demonstration build of a Light Foot Bridge (Mitsuhiro Kadota)

0587967

Light tactical raft

Description

The light tactical raft, known as the Kei Mon Kyo (Light (Kei) Gate (Mon) Bridge (Kyo)) is a raft-cum-ferry system similar to the US Bridge Floating: Raft Section, Light Tactical and is transported on 2,500 kg (6 × 6) trucks. It consists of Japanese folding assault boats which are joined stern to stern to form a pontoon. Either two bow sections or one bow and one stern section may be joined. Attached to the gunwales of the pontoons are dual plywood treadways forming the raft deck. Side rails are then placed along the inside edge of the treadways to stop vehicles being driven off.

Rafts of 9,000, 10,000 and 13,000 kg capacity can be assembled with three, four or five pontoons respectively. A three-pontoon raft is normally propelled by one 25 hp outboard motor and the four- and five-pontoon rafts are propelled by two outboard motors. Maximum speed of a loaded three-pontoon raft is 6.5 km/h.

Demonstration use of the Light Tactical Raft (Mitsuhiro Kadota)   0587969

Demonstration use of the Light Tactical Raft (Mitsuhiro Kadota)   0587970

Specifications

Light tactical raft

	Pontoon	Treadway
Weight:	269 kg	100 kg
Length:	7.7 m	2.5 m
Width:	1.5 m	900 mm
Depth:	650 mm	180 mm

Assembled raft

Raft Class	9 t	10 t	13 t
Number of pontoons:	3	4	5
Number of treadways	8	10	12
Overall length of deck:	9 m	12 m	15 m
Distance between pontoon centres:	2.5 m	2.5 m	2.5 m

Status

Production likely to be on as required basis. In service with the Japanese GSDF.

Contractor

Not known.

Type 92 floating bridge

Description

The Type 92 floating bridge (shiki (92) fu (floating) kyo (bridge)) entered service with the Japanese Ground Self-Defence Force (JGSDF) in 1992 and is reportedly capable of accepting MLC 60 (T) traffic, thereby allowing the latest Type 90 MBT to cross.

Very little firm information has been made available regarding the Type 92 floating bridge, however it is known that one full set spans 104 m and consists of the following: 14 sections - 12 centre sections and two end sections; seven bridging boats and two sets of truck-transported/deployed trackway. The complete set (boats and bridges sections) is carried on 21 6 × 6 trucks, the bridge section transport trucks weighing 22,200 kg and having dimensions of: 10.3 × 3 × 3.8 m (L × W × H).

Operating parameters include a maximum current of 2.5 m/s and a minimum water depth of 700 mm. Width is 4 m. It has not been stated, but it is probable that bridge sections can be used in conjunction with bridging boats to make rafts or ferries.

Status

Production likely to be on an as required basis. In service with the Japanese GSDF.

Type 92 Floating Bridge deployed and in use during a public demonstration/display (Mitsuhiro Kadota)   0587963

From the rear, a Type 92 Floating Bridge pontoon section on its dedicated Mitsubishi FW 419 series 6 × 6 transport truck (Mitsuhiro Kadota) 0587964

A Type 92 Floating Bridge pontoon section about to be launched from its dedicated Mitsubishi FW 419 series 6 × 6 transport truck (Mitsuhiro Kadota) 0587966

Contractor
Released information lists the following companies as manufacturers involved with the Type 92 floating bridge:
Hitachi, Hitachi Seisakusyo, Hitachi Shipyard (now Universal Shipyard) Hitachi Zosen (now Universal Shipbuilding Corporation), Kobe Seikosyo, Mitsubishi Jidosya, Mitsubishi Motorcar (now Mitsubishi Truck).

Netherlands

Damen FAC 540 floating bridges and ferries

Description
The Damen FAC 540 fast assault craft can be used in the construction of a floating footbridge or light ferries, for loads up to MLC 8. All the bridges and ferries are based on the use of the aluminium-hulled FAC 540, designed to carry a fully equipped infantry section of 12 personnel and two crew.

A tactical ferry raft for loads up to MLC 8 can be assembled using four FAC 540 boats joined stern to stern in a catamaran configuration. The same configuration can be used as a light tactical bridge. Each set of four FAC 540 boats is supplemented by a set comprising eight aluminium track units with a width of 762 mm for vehicles with single- or dual-rear tyres. The set also contains four aluminium track couplings and accessories, eight aluminium gunwale saddles to support the tracks, 12 nylon track fasteners to secure the tracks to the boats, six stainless steel pins to couple the tracks and four nylon rigging lines to raise or lower the hinged tracks. This type of raft can carry a 3,000 kg truck at speeds of 7 to 10 kt.

The same set can be used to assemble a trimaran ferry raft with a total of six FAC 540 boats joined stern to stern. This type of raft has a load capacity of MLC 8 'plus' and can carry vehicles up to 7.3 m long. A raft created using racks laid directly across three FAC 540 boats can have a capability of MLC 2. Both types of raft can travel at 10 to 15 kt.

Light tactical footbridges can be assembled using the same components as the ferry rafts but with special end ramps, anchor winches, heavy anchors and steel cables, and shore anchors. The FAC 540 boats may be joined stern to stern for MLC 8 bridges or used as single units to carry the single trackway.

When the FAC 540 boats are used as ferry rafts they can be powered by either a Johnson Workhorse 25 hp (19 kW) longshaft outboard motor with 22.7 litres of fuel or a Yamaha 40 hp (30 kW) longshaft model with 24 litres of fuel. The number of engines depends on the raft capacity; an MLC 8 raft requires two.

Damen FAC 540 fast assault craft in use in the light ferry role (Damen) 1340288

For rapid deployment forces and similar applications a Triple Raft Pack is available. This contains three FAC 540 boats together with wheel tracks, couplings, saddles and other components to form a light ferry raft. The pack can be towed on a light trailer or carried underslung by helicopter.

Specifications
FAC 540
Weight: 235 kg
Payload: 2,200 kg
Length: 5.4 m
Beam: 1.83 m
Draught: 620 mm
Max speed:
   (with 4 men) 25-30 kt
   (1,200 kg payload) 10-12 kt

Status
In service with the Royal Netherlands Marine Corps and the Corps of Engineers in Brunei and Malaysia. Also used by the International Red Cross in Nicaragua, the Ministry of Food and Agriculture in Ghana (supplied 2003), and the Port Autonome de Douala in Cameroon (2004).

Contractor
Damen Shipyards

Poland

PP-64 heavy folding pontoon bridge

Development
In 1964, following the success of the PMP heavy folding pontoon bridge, Poland started design work on a folding pontoon bridge. The initial prototype was finished in 1965, with first production units being completed the following year. In design, the PP-64 is different from the PMP and has a much faster construction rate.

Wojskowe Zaklady Inzynieryjne (Army Engineer Workshops) of Deblin, Poland, offers a complete GSP repair service as well as anti-corrosion treatments using up-to-date materials.

Description
The basic PP-64 pontoon bridge has a capacity of 40,000 kg, whereas the Russian PMP has a capacity of 60,000 kg. This, however, is not a great tactical disadvantage as the PP-64 can still handle T-54/T-55 and T-62 MBTs and can accommodate tanks such as the T-64 and T-72.

A PP-64 set consists of: 48 river pontoons carried on trucks; six shore pontoons carried on trucks; 12 ramps for ferries carried on trucks which also tow the KH-200 bridging boats; six KH-200 bridging boats; and one special connecting piece for use in joining PP-64 with PMP bridges.

Three types of bridge can be built: 40,000 kg (A), 40,000 kg (B) and 80,000 kg. The 40,000 kg (A) is single roadway type and is 186 m long, has a 4.35 m wide roadway, can take a 12,000 kg axle load and can be constructed in rivers with a maximum velocity of 1.2 m/s. A working party consists of 60 pontoon workers, 60 drivers, six powerboat operators and 10 NCOs. The 40,000 kg (B) is also a single roadway type and is 145 m long, 4.35 m wide, can take a 12,000 kg axle load and can be constructed in rivers with a maximum velocity of 2 m/s. A working party consists of 54 pontoon workers, 60 drivers, six powerboat operators and 10 NCOs. The 80,000 kg bridge is double width, 97 m long, has a roadway width of 8.7 m, can take a 12,000 kg axle load and be constructed in rivers with a maximum velocity of 3 m/s. The working party consists of 54 pontoon workers, 60 drivers, six powerboat operators and 10 NCOs.

The following ferries can be constructed with the basic PP-64 set: six 40,000 kg ferries 14.8 m long and 12.8 m wide, each with eight river pontoons, one shore pontoon and two ramps, a working party of 20

PP-64 heavy folding pontoon bridge in ferry configuration during a joint Polish/UK Exercise Ulan Eagle, held in Poland. The load is a British Army Challenger 1 MBT. To the right is a Polish Army KH-200 bridging boat (Shaun C Connors)
1124750

pontoon workers and three NCOs and two powerboats per ferry; or two large ferries 37 m long and 12.5 m wide, each with 20 river pontoons, two shore pontoons and four ramps, a working party of 30 pontoon workers and four NCOs and three powerboats per ferry.

PP-64 ferries can operate in rivers with a maximum velocity of 3 m/s.

The bridge is launched as follows: the truck backs up to the river and the pontoon, which is in two parts hinged in the middle, is unfolded and then launched. The pontoons are carried on the rear of a Star 660 M2 6 × 6 3,500 kg truck. PMP pontoons are much heavier and therefore have to be carried on a 7,000 or 7,500 kg 6 × 6 truck chassis. Bridging boats used with the PP-64 are the Russian Federation BMK-130 and the Polish KH-200.

According to some sources, maximum construction rate for a PP-64 bridge is over 25 m/min.

Specifications

PP-64 (single pontoon)
Weight: 1,000 kg
Length: 3.7 m
Width: 6.2 m
Depth: 850 mm

Status
In service with the Polish Army. Surplus stock available for export.

Contractor
Wojskowe Zaklady Inzynieryjne (WZINZ)

Romania

PR-60 heavy pontoon bridge

Description
The PR-60 was developed by Romania as a replacement for the Soviet-supplied TMP heavy pontoon bridge. It can also be used as a raft. The PR-60 is not of the folding type like the RFAS PMP and Polish PP-64 and is therefore slower to construct.

The PR-60 consists of enclosed shore and river pontoons, which are launched from the rear of a 4 × 4 4,000 kg truck by gravity. These are recovered by being lifted out of the water by a crane, as the truck has no recovery capability. Once launched, the pontoons are connected to form a continuous roadway. Both single- and double-lane bridges can be constructed, the latter with double pontoons.

A complete PR-60 pontoon set consists of 56 river pontoons and four shore pontoons. Each truck carries either one shore pontoon or two river pontoons resting on top of each other.

Specifications

Pontoon type	River	Shore
Weight:	1,200 kg	1,350 kg
Length:	6 m	6.2 m
Width:	2.4 m	4.2 m
Height/depth:	700 mm	700 mm
Bridge construction		
Bridge type	**40 t**	**60 t**
Width: (roadway)	3.8 m	7.6 m
Length:	142.8 m	80.4 m
Assembly time:	1 h	1.5 h
Number of pontoons:	50 (includes shore pontoons)	50 (includes shore pontoons)

Status
In service with the Romanian Army. Offered for export, new and surplus.

Agency
Romtechnica SA

Contractor
Romanian state factories.

Russian Federation

DPP-40 floating bridge equipment

Description
Reports have been made for at least ten years of a new floating bridge equipment known as the DPP-40. The DPP-40 uses inflatable pontoon supports and is capable of carrying light armoured vehicles. From what little information has become available, it would appear that the DPP-40 is used mainly by airborne formations, and possibly with a different designation.

This equipment does not appear to be offered for export at present.

Status
In service with the Russian Federation Armed Forces.

GSP heavy amphibious ferry

Description
The GSP (*Gusenichniy Samokhodniy Parom*), introduced in 1959, was the standard heavy amphibious ferry of the former Warsaw Pact armed forces. Numbers were used by the Egyptian Army during the crossing of the Suez Canal in October 1973.

A complete GSP ferry consists of two units, left and right. They enter the water separately and are then linked up. They are 'handed' and not interchangeable. Once linked together, the pontoon, which when travelling on land, is in the inverted position, is swung through 180° into the floating position. Each unit carries retractable trackways, which enable vehicles to be loaded or unloaded either side. The GSP can carry a maximum load of 52,000 kg. According to US reports, under favourable circumstances a tank is able to fire its main armament when loaded on the GSP.

The track suspension of the GSP is similar to that used on members of the PT-76 light amphibious tank family and consists of seven roadwheels with the idler at the front and the drive sprocket at the rear. There are no track-return rollers. The hull of the GSP is of lightweight welded steel, filled with plastic foam, both to increase its buoyancy and to reduce its vulnerability to damage by enemy fire. Before entering the water, a trim vane is erected at the front of the hull, although this was not fitted to early units. Each unit is propelled in the water by two propellers mounted in separate tunnels under the hull. As a direct result of user experience, the GSP has been modified in recent years. These modifications include an improved suspension, which has given the unit a higher ground clearance, a stronger hull and an improved cab for the crew at the front of the hull.

The GSP has two major disadvantages: GSPs cannot be joined together to form a floating bridge and the bank where the GSP unloads must be no higher than 500 mm with a minimum water depth of 1.2 m, otherwise the GSP will be damaged.

Belvneshpromservice of Belarus are one of a number of companies throughout the former Soviet Union now offering surplus Soviet-era equipment for export sale, in either 'as is' condition or refurbished and overhauled to customer requirements. In addition to the GSP heavy amphibious ferry, Belvneshpromservice offer a selection of other bridge and ferry related equipment including the PTS-M tracked amphibious

GSP heavy amphibious ferry (Shaun C Connors)
1340280

carrier, PMM-2 amphibious bridging and ferry system, PMP and PMP-M pontoon equipment sets, MTU-20 and MT-55A mechanised bridges and the TMM-3 heavy mechanised bridge.

Specifications

GSP - Half ferry unit
Crew: 3
Weight: 17,000 kg
Length: 12 m
Width: 3.24 m
Height: 3.2 m
Ground clearance: 350 mm
Track: 2.62 m
Track width: 360 mm
Length of track on ground: 4.83 m
Ground pressure: 0.52 kg/cm^2
Max speed: (road) 40 km/h
Range: (road) 300 km (estimate)
Fuel capacity: 370 litres
Fording: amphibious
Gradient: 45%
Vertical obstacle: 800 mm (estimate)
Trench: 3 m (estimate)
Engine: Model 8D6 6 cylinder water-cooled diesel developing 240 hp (179 kW) at 1,800 rpm

GSP - Full ferry
Weight: 34,000 kg
Length: 12 m
Width: 12.63 m
Draught:
 (laden) 1.5 m
 (unladen) 907 mm
Max water speed:
 (laden) 7.7 km/h
 (unladen) 10.8 km/h
Roadway width: 3.54 m
Roadway track: 1.66 m
Max payload: 52,000 kg

Status
Production complete. Known to have been supplied to Afghanistan (six - present status uncertain), Egypt, India (18), Iraq (present status uncertain), Israel, Nicaragua, Uganda, former Serbia and Montenegro and members of the former Warsaw Pact, including Poland. The GSP was known as the GSP-55 in the former East Germany.

Contractor
State factories.

NARM prefabricated floating road bridge

Description
The NARM prefabricated floating road bridge is intended for the crossing of medium and large rivers, providing a bridge with a load capacity of 60,000 kg and ferry crossings with capacities of 40,000, 60,000 and 90,000 kg.

A complete NARM set comprises 80 river units, eight end units, 48 transport semi-trailers and five containers for accessories and spares. Total weight of the bridge equipment is 250,000 kg

KAMAZ-43118 6 × 6 truck configured as a transporter for sections of the NARM prefabricated floating road bridge (James Kinnear)   1120471

The maximum bridge length using a single NARM set is 225 m, with a decking width of 6.8 m. A typical floating bridge could be assembled in two hours, using a workforce of 96 combat engineers, 48 truck drivers and four crane drivers.

Once the bridge is complete, tracked vehicles weighing up to 60,000 kg can cross at a speed of 30 km/h. For wheeled road trains weighing up to 90,000 kg the crossing speed is 25 km/h.

Status
Production likely to be on an as required basis. Offered for export.

Agency
Rosoboronexport

PMP and PMP-M heavy folding pontoon bridges

Development
The PMP (*Pomtommo Mostovoj Park*, or pontoon bridge set) was considered to be a major breakthrough in the design of floating bridges. The original bridge was a pre-1945 German Wehrmacht design taken up by the Soviet Union after the Second World War and developed into the all-steel PMP bridge. It was used successfully by Egyptian forces during the crossing of the Suez Canal in October 1973. Since the introduction of the PMP (or Ribbon Bridge as it is also known), and following examination of PMP bridge segments captured during the Arab-Israeli War, the US Army developed and produced a similar bridge system also called the Ribbon Bridge. The pontoons on the US system are made of aluminium rather than steel and are therefore considerably lighter: the US river pontoon weighs 5,440 kg while the Russian unit weighs 6,676 kg. The US shore pontoon weighs 5,310 kg while the Russian equivalent weighs 7,252 kg.

The then EWK of Germany developed the Faltschwimmbrücke (FSB) version of the Ribbon Bridge, full details of which can be found elsewhere in this section.

The PMP (Pomtommo Mostovoj Park, or pontoon bridge set) in use (Belvneshpromservice)   0589133

Ukrainian Army PMP pontoon bridge unit being transported on a KrAZ 255B 6 × 6 truck (James Kinnear)   0589055

PMP pontoon bridge unit on a KrAZ 255B 6 × 6 truck (Stefan Marx)   1128281

Ukrainian Army PMP pontoon bridge unit KrAZ 255B 6 × 6 transport truck, unladen (James Kinnear)   0589056

Slightly modified PMP-M pontoons are used with the PP-91 pontoon equipment set.

PMP bridges and components remain in service in the Czech Republic and Slovakia, where the system is known as the PMS. Czech and Slovak Army PMS components are carried on TATRA T 815 VPR9 28.2658x8.1R trucks. The PMS is marketed within the Czech Republic by Omnipol a.s. of Prague. Full details of updated versions of the PMS can be found elsewhere in this section.

A variant of the PMP is produced in China as the Type 79 Ribbon Bridge.

The Floating Bridge Set M71 (KPM-M71) produced in the former Yugoslavia is based on the PMP but differs in some details and dimensions.

Description

Each pontoon of the PMP is constructed of SKhL-4 steel and is in four major sections which are hinged together. These are carried in the folded position on the rear of a 6 × 6 or 8 × 8 truck. Initially the truck used was the Ukrainian KrAZ-214 6 × 6 7,000 kg truck chassis but this was later supplemented and eventually replaced by the more powerful KrAZ-255B 6 × 6 7,500 kg truck. This in turn will likely eventually be replaced by current generation heavy-trucks of Russian origin.

The pontoon is launched as follows: the travel locks on the pontoon are disengaged and the truck backs to the edge of the water; it brakes sharply and the pontoon slides over a roller system into the water where it almost immediately unfolds; six locking devices are activated stiffening the pontoon; the pontoons are then normally connected together on the near shore to form a continuous roadway which is swung into position by bridging boats. Once in position the bridge is ready for immediate use. The surface of the roadway is ribbed to prevent vehicles from skidding when crossing.

The pontoon is recovered as follows: the pontoon truck backs up to the water's edge and an integral jib is unfolded from the truck bed; two cables are strung from the winch, which is to the rear of the cab, through the jib pulley, around the pontoon retrieval guides and secured to the pontoon retrieval studs. The winch then simultaneously folds and lifts the pontoon on to the truck bed. The jib is folded back into the truck bed and the pontoon winched over the roller and secured.

The basic bridge has a capacity of 60,000 kg but it is also possible to build a half-width bridge of 20,000 kg capacity and of greater length. This is achieved by splitting the pontoons lengthwise once they are launched. Full-length pontoons are placed at intervals to give greater stability.

The PMP can also be used to construct ferries of varying sizes, the maximum having a capacity of 170 tonnes.

The Indian, Czech and Slovak armies use a TATRA 813 or 815 8 × 8 8,000 kg roadway truck in conjunction with the PMP (full details of which can be found in the Portable roadways section). They also have some of their TATRA 813 and 815 8 × 8 8,000 kg trucks fitted with a dozer blade for preparation of river banks before launching the pontoons. The PMP was used by East German forces to assist in the unloading of landing ships.

A complete PMP pontoon set consists of 32 river pontoons, four shore pontoons and 12 BMK-T (or BMK-130/BMK-130M or BMK-150/BMK-150M) bridging boats. A half set has 16 river and two shore pontoons.

There is also a PMP-M pontoon set. A complete PMP-M set comprises 32 river pontoons, four shore pontoons, 16 BMK-T, BMK-130M or BMK-150M bridging boats, two sets of loading equipment, two sets of crossing reconnaissance equipment, two sets of traffic control equipment, two sets of special equipment for winter crossings and four sets of portable roadway. The set is carried on 36 KrAZ-255B pontoon trucks, two KrAZ-255B roadway-laying trucks and 16 KrAZ-255B or ZIL-131 bridging boat carriers.

Belvneshpromservice of Belarus are one of a number of companies throughout the former Soviet Union now offering surplus Soviet-era equipment for export sale, in either 'as is' condition or refurbished and overhauled to customer requirements. In addition to PMP and PMP-M pontoon equipment sets, Belvneshpromservice offers a selection of other bridge and ferry related equipment including the GSP heavy amphibious ferry, PTS-M tracked amphibious carrier, PMM-2 amphibious bridging and ferry system, MTU-20 and MT-55A mechanised bridges and the TMM-3 heavy mechanised bridge.

Specifications

Bridge construction (PMP-M)

Type	20 t	60 t
Width: (roadway)	3.25 m	6.5 m
Length:		
(bridge, whole set)	382 m	227 m
(bridge, half set)	281 m	119 m
Working party:	72[1]	72[1]
Drivers:	36[1]	36[1]
Assembly time:	50 min[1]	30 min[1]

[1] Data is for whole set. Two additional shore pontoons are held in bridge set.

Number of whole pontoons Incl. shore

(whole set)	32	32
(half set)	18	18

The bridge can be constructed in water with a maximum velocity of 2 m/s

	River pontoon (open)	Shore pontoon (open)
Weight:	6,676 kg	7,252 kg
Length:	6.75 m	5.58 m
Width:		
(unfolded)	7.1 m	7.02-7.32 m
(folded)	3.21 m	3.3 m
Depth:	915 mm	730 mm

Ferry construction (PMP-M)

Type	40 t	60 t	80 t	120 t	130 t	170 t
Length:	13.5 m	20.25 m	27 m	40.5 m	46 m	59.5 m
Rafts per set:	16	10	8	5	4	4
Pontoons per raft:	2	3	4	6	6 + 1 shore	8 + 1 shore
Assembly time:	7 min	8 min	9 min	13-15 min	15-18 min	16-20 min
Working party:	4	6	8	12	14	18
Drivers:	2	3	4	6	7	9

Status

Production as required. In service with members of the former Warsaw Pact (except Poland, which uses the Polish-designed PP-64, and Romania, which uses the Romanian-designed PR-60). Also used by Afghanistan (15, status uncertain), China (Type 79), Egypt (some carried on German Magirus-Deutz 6 × 6 chassis), India (156, carried on TATRA 815 trucks), Iraq (status uncertain), Israel and Serbia and Montenegro. The PMP is known as the PMS in the Czech and Slovak armies.

It is intended that the PMP and PMP-M will be replaced in service by the PP-91 pontoon equipment set.

Contractor

Okskay Shipyard State Unitary Enterprise

PP-91 pontoon equipment set

Development
Designed by V Trefilov of the Scientific Research Institute, together with specialists from the 'Vympel' Central Design Bureau, the PP-91 pontoon equipment set is used to form bridge crossings and ferries of variable lengths and load capacities.

The original intention was that the PP-91 would replace the PMP and PMP-M pontoon bridge equipment currently in service.

Description
A complete PP-91 set comprises 16 BMK-225 bridge erection boats; 32 offshore units, four end sections, two containers with matting and four further containers for tools, accessories and auxiliary equipment. Also included in the set are water obstacle reconnaissance equipment, traffic control equipment, lifting tackle and special equipment to prepare crossing points during winter. The set is carried on 54 Ural-532361 trucks.

The offshore units are similar to PMP-M pontoons (full details of which can be found elsewhere in this section), consisting of two centre and two side hinge-connected pontoons. When deployed these units are 7.2 m long and 6.83 m wide. Connecting points at the end of each unit are used to join units to form ferries. On one of the end pontoons is a hinge-mounted deflector provided with connecting joints to connect with other offshore units to form double-width bridges.

The end sections consist of two centre, hinge-connected pontoons with two centre and two extreme ramps. Each section has connection points for offshore pontoons and the ramps have hydraulic lifting gear to lower the ramps on to the shore.

Each Ural 532361 pontoon truck has a special-purpose platform used to carry, load and unload all components of the set, apart from the bridge erection boats.

Specifications
PP-91

Load capacity:	60 t	90 t	120 t
Length: (of bridge in set)	268 m	165 m	141 m
Limiting conditions:			
(current velocity)	3 m/s	3 m/s	3 m/s
(swell scale)	2	2	3

Status
In production. In service with the Russian Federation Armed Forces. Offered for export and possibly supplied to India and the United Arab Emirates (UAE).

Contractor
Navashinsky Mashinostroitelny Zavod (NMZ) (Navashino Machinary Works)

Floating bridge erected from PP-91 pontoon equipment set (Navashino Machinary Works)   0007686

PPS heavy girder floating bridge

Description
The PPS heavy girder floating bridge, first observed in 1962, consists of large sectional pontoons and Warren-type truss girders with a full flushdeck roadway mounted on top. Each pontoon consists of a bow section, two centre sections and a stern power unit. Each section is carried on the rear of a ZIL-151 (6 × 6) 2,500 kg or similar truck. The pontoon is approximately 23 m long when assembled. The deck is about 380 mm below the gunwales, which support six rows of truss girders, with the top chords carrying I-beam stringers. Decking is laid on these I-beams to form a roadway about 6 m wide. The bridge has a maximum capacity of at least 60,000 kg.

Status
In service with the Russian Federation.

Contractor
Former state factories.

Serbia and Montenegro

Floating bridge set M71 (KPM-M71)

Description
The design of the floating bridge set M71, or KPM-M71, is based on the Russian Federation PMP heavy folding pontoon bridge. Each set is composed of 32 floating sections and four shore sections loaded on to 36 FAP 2026 BDS/AV-PMP (6 × 6) trucks equipped with special carrying platforms. A further two FAP 2026 BDS/AV-PMP trucks carry a set of bridge surfacing and anchor posts. The set is completed by up to 12 R-M88 bridging boats towed by FAP 2026 BDS/AVG trucks and, 12 C(H)A 70 aluminium boats with 40 hp outboard engines.

The KPM-M71 can be used to bridge water with a minimum depth of 400 mm at the shore and 400 to 800 mm under the floating sections if the bottom is flat. The maximum possible water velocity during use is 2 m/s. Vehicles driving over the bridge can attain a maximum speed of 20 km/h.

The KPM-M71 bridging set can be assembled to build a pontoon bridge with a 20,000 or 60,000 kg capacity. Ferries with payloads of 40,000; 60,000; 80,000; 110,000 or 150,000 kg can also be assembled. Bridge assembly time is given as 50 minutes while a ferry can be assembled in eight to 20 minutes, depending on the size.

When being driven on good roads, a complete KPM-M71 set can reach speeds of up to 60 km/h.

All bridge unit maintenance and minor repairs can be carried out using a set of tools, spare parts and materials supplied with each KPM-M71 set.

Specifications

Section	Floating	Shore
Length:	6.62 m	5.5 m
Width:		
(transport)	3.15 m	3.192 m
(floating)	8.03 m	7.186 m
(roadway)	6.5 m	6.5 m
Height:		
(transport)	2.22 m	2.2 m
(floating)	1.1 m	1.019 m
Weight of unit:	8,380 kg	8,730 kg
Weight with truck:	20,540 kg	20,890 kg

Status
In service with the former Yugoslav Army. Production as required. Offered for export sales.

Contractor
Yugoimport SDPR

Launching a floating section from a floating bridge set M71 (KPM-M71)   0511541

M-70 light pontoon bridge

Description
The M-70 is of local design and construction and can be used both as a light pontoon bridge and as a raft. Each pontoon consists of two aluminium half-pontoons joined together. The balk and decking are also of aluminium construction. The load of the bridge depends on the velocity of the stream. For example, a 12,000 kg bridge can be constructed in a stream with a maximum velocity of 2.5 m/s and a 16,000 kg bridge can be constructed in a stream with a maximum velocity of 2.1 m/s.

A raft normally consists of four complete pontoons (eight half-pontoons) and the balk from three bridge bays, with or without articulators. Again, the load depends on the velocity of the stream. Rafts of 12,000 kg can be constructed for use in streams with a maximum velocity of 2.5 m/s and 16,000 kg rafts can be constructed for use in streams with a maximum velocity of 2.1 m/s.

A complete M-70 light pontoon bridge set has a total of 60 half-pontoons plus deck balk and other ancillary equipment; the deck balk is carried in the rear of a TAM 4500 (4 × 4) 4,500 kg truck, which also tows a single-axle pole-type trailer carrying six half-pontoons inverted on top of each other.

Specifications

Pontoon
Weight: 295 kg
Length: 5.64 m
Width: 2.04 m
Depth: 860 mm

Bridge construction
Roadway width: 2.8 m
Length: 120 m
**Half-pontoons
  per support:** 2
Assembly time 45–60 min

Raft construction
Length: 9 m
Rafts per set: 7
Half-pontoons per raft: 8
Working party: 30 men
Assembly time: 15 min

Status
In service with the former Yugoslav Army. Production as required. Available for export.

Contractor
Yugoimport SDPR

Singapore

Floating Bridge System FBS 60

Description
The Floating Bridge System FBS 60 is intended for the construction of floating bridges and ferries and for ease of erection and speed of recovery. The complete FBS 60 consists of bridge sections, a bridge transporter, bridging boat (described as a push-pull tug boat) and a boat trailer or boat carriage. Full details of the associated bridging boat and its trailer or carriage can be found in the Bridging boats section.

An FBS 60 floating bridge consists of two types of section, inner and ramp. Both can be folded upwards for transport and will unfold automatically when launched into the water. The inner and ramp sections are made of aluminium and can be coupled together using pins to form floating bridges or rafts capable of carrying MLC 60 loads. Each section has four main assemblies, two outer pontoons and two inner pontoons. The inner pontoons form the roadway.

A typical FBS 60 floating raft, consisting of two inner sections with a ramp section at each end, is 27.2 m long and can be constructed by a team of 16 personnel. A normal FBS 60 kit consists of nine inner sections and four ramp sections. Using the nine inner sections and two of the ramp sections a floating bridge 74.1 m long can be constructed. If all the inner sections of two FBS 60 sets (that is, 18 inner sections) are combined with two ramp sections, a floating bridge 134.4 m long is formed.

The FBS 60 sections are normally carried on 6 × 6 7,000 kg bridge transporter trucks that are also used for the launching and retrieval of the sections. The complete length of a typical loaded bridge transporter truck is of the order of 10.8 m and height is around 4 m. Width overall is 3.4 m.

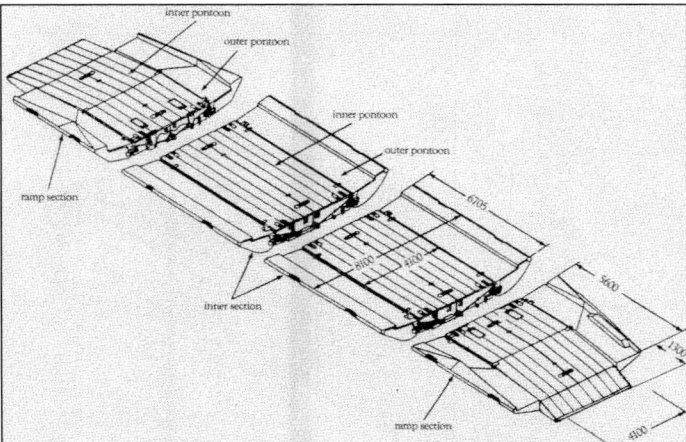

Inner and ramp bridge sections of the Floating Bridge System FBS 60 (Singapore Technologies Marine)   0511532

Specifications

FBS 60
(inner and ramp sections)
Weight: 5,500 kg
Width:
  (folded) 3.2 m
  (unfolded) 8.1 m
  (roadway) 4.1 m
Height: (unfolded) 1.1 m

Status
Available.

Contractor
Singapore Technologies Marine

Thailand

Aluminium pontoon raft

Description
This aluminium pontoon raft, described in sales brochures as a metal alloy flotation for raft building, is essentially similar to the now obsolete US M4T6 floating bridge. By combining 16 pontoons, each of which is basically an aluminium box structure supported by pneumatic floats, it is possible to carry MLC 55 loads, including tracked vehicles. Other loads can be accommodated, a typical example being a 155 mm M198 gun and its tractor vehicle with a combined weight of 25,000 kg. By combining pontoons in pairs it is possible to carry MLC 70 loads.

Specifications

Pontoon
Load capacity: (used in pairs) MLC 70
Weight: approx 500 kg
Length: 5.5 m
Width: 2.03 m
Height: 1.1 m

Status
Thought to be in service with the Royal Thai Army.

Contractor
Ministry of Defence

Aluminium pontoon raft in use by Royal Thai Army   0512459

United Kingdom

WFEL Limited Air Portable Ferry Bridge (APFB) Ferry

Development
To meet the increased mobility and flexibility demands being placed on its forces, the British Army issued a requirement for a new bridging system that could be utilised by light forces and that would (among other roles), on entering service replace the current Class 16 Air Portable Bridge, full details of which can be found elsewhere in this section.

The WFEL Limited Air Portable Ferry Bridge (APFB) was selected to meet the British Army's requirement and 11 sets have been delivered.

The Air Portable Ferry Bridge incorporates a ferry system that is classified at MLC 35 (T) and (W) and this is covered in detail in this entry. Full details of the dry gap crossing APFB Fly Forward , APFB Overbridge and APFB Reinforced can be found in the Tactical (non-floating) and lines of communication bridges section.

APFB Ferry pontoons stacked for transportation on a dedicated DROPS flatrack (WFEL Limited)   1047898

APFB Ferry pontoons being launched (WFEL Limited)   1047899

APFB Ferry transporting a Warrior Infantry Fighting Vehicle (IFV) (WFEL Limited)   1047907

Description
The WFEL Limited APFB is a deck type bridge of modular construction that is capable of being hand built by troops in a wide variety of climatic and operational scenarios. The overall design and construction of the APFB is based on that of the existing Single Storey Medium Girder Bridge (SSMGB). With the incorporation of relatively few new parts, existing MGB assets are given a new lease of life with extended capability. The complete system offers the following:

- MGB Ferry (MGB(F))
- Fly Forward MGB (FFMGB)
- Fly Forward Medium Girder Over Bridge (FFMGOB)
- Single Storey Reinforced MGB (SSRMGB).

APFB Ferry
In this role the APFB is a free ranging roll on/roll off ferry with an MLC rating of 35. It consists of a modular bridge, with hinged landing bays at each end, mounted across six pontoons. The bridge structure is secured on the pontoons by pier saddles. Two of the pontoons are fitted with diesel-powered propulsion units for manoeuvrability. These engines also power the hydraulics that are used to raise and lower the landing bays.

The APFB Ferry can be constructed with a maximum water speed of 2.5 m/s and has an operating speed of 3.5 m/s unladen and 2.5 m/s laden. The APFB Ferry can operate in 800 mm of water and each pontoon includes a self-bailing system that allows any water inside to drain away automatically. A pontoon walkway allows the crew to move freely when the ferry is carrying large loads.

The six pontoons required to construct the MLC 35 Ferry are carried on two dedicated DROPS flatracks with each carrying three pontoons. An integrated release system launches the pontoons sequentially into the water during construction once the flatrack is angled over a bank of up to 2.5 m in height.

The build crew for an APFB Ferry is 16; 14 soldiers plus two NCOs.

Status
In service with the British Army (11 sets).

Contractor
WFEL Ltd

Class 16 air-portable bridge
Development
The Class 16 air-portable bridge was designed by the then Military Engineering Establishment at Christchurch; now QinetiQ. Production and marketing of the bridge were undertaken by Laird (Anglesey) Limited (now FAUN Municipal Vehicles Ltd).

The British Army issued a requirement to replace their Class 16 bridges with the then titled Future Light Bridge, a bridging system to be used by airmobile and rapid deployment forces. It was stated the requirement was for 13 complete bridge/ferry sets. The WFEL Limited Air-Portable Ferry Bridge (APFB) was selected to meet this requirement and is now in service. A total of 11 bridges were delivered.

A number of surplus Class 16 bridges became available for sale through the UK MoD's disposal agents during 2004.

Description
The Class 16 air-portable bridge is constructed of a high-strength aluminium zinc-magnesium alloy and can be used as a clear span bridge up to 15.2 m in length, as a floating bridge of any length or as a powered raft with a maximum speed of 6 kt. All have a non-skid roadway 3.3 m wide when assembled.

The basic components of the Class 16 bridge are the deck boxes, ramps, articulator boxes, floats and the sponsons. These components are normally carried by a Land Rover-type vehicle, which would also tow a single-axle trailer. A Chinook helicopter can carry any component of the Class 16 bridge and a C-130 Hercules transport aircraft can carry all the components required to build a ferry.

The deck box combines the functions of bridge girders and cross girders and contributes buoyancy in floating applications. The top of the box forms the deck of the bridge. At either end of the bridge tapered ramps provide access. When being used as a floating bridge or raft, hydraulically operated articulator boxes are fitted between the deck boxes and the ramps to allow adjustment for varying heights. For floating bridges and rafts, pneumatic floats are fitted giving additional buoyancy and stability. When being used as a floating raft for powered raft operations, sponsons with integral turntable brackets are fitted at each corner of the raft, each sponson having a 30 kw (40 hp) outboard motor.

Clear span bridge
A 15.2 m clear span bridge is assembled from seven deck boxes and two pairs of ramps. Three Land Rover-type vehicles and trailers carry all the components for one 15.2 m clear span bridge. The bridge can be constructed and positioned by 16 personnel in approximately 20 minutes, using a special launching nose and rollers. A launching nose and three pairs of rollers are used for building and launching the bridge. One pair of rollers is subsequently used as a landing roller on the far bank. The angle of the launching nose can be altered by means of its built-in jack to allow for varying heights of the far bank. The far end of the bridge is lowered to the ground by operating a jack. One complete bridge can be carried underslung by a Chinook helicopter.

Floating bridge
A floating bridge 58 m long can be assembled from 40 deck boxes, two pairs of articulator boxes and two pairs of ramps and floats using a standard bridge set. Five Land Rover-type vehicles and trailers carry all the necessary components for a floating bridge. A team of 24 personnel takes 45 minutes to build the 58 m bridge and there is no limit to the length of floating bridge that can be built. The floating bridge is assembled in the same manner as the raft but the sponsons are omitted and floats fitted in their place.

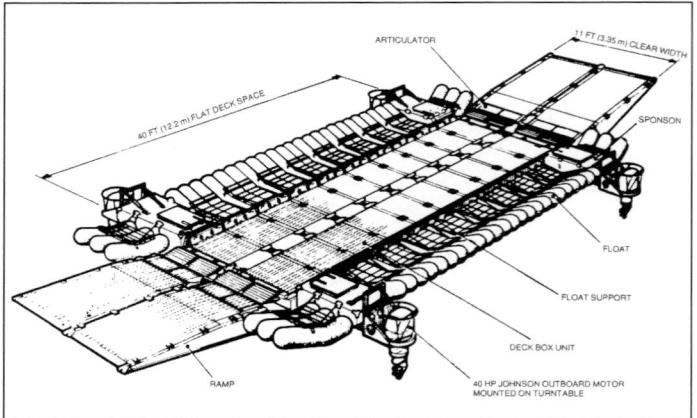

Outline drawing of a Class 16 air-portable bridge configured as a raft (FAUN Municipal Vehicles Ltd)   0511533

Powered raft

The standard raft has a 12.2 m level deck and is 22 m overall. It is assembled from 10 deck boxes, two pairs of articulator boxes, two pairs of ramps, floats and four sponsons with outboard motors. 20 Land Rover-type vehicles and trailers carry all the components necessary to build one standard powered raft. Building time is approximately 40 minutes with 24 personnel. The raft is constructed as follows: the ramps and articulators are assembled and launched in the water, deck boxes added, then the rear articulator and finally the rear ramps, the sponsons and outboard motors are fitted to the raft and the floats are fitted to the boxes. The floats are inflated from the transport vehicles' exhaust gases. Longer rafts may be built up to a maximum length of 28 m overall, with an 18.3 m level deck. These are powered by six outboard motors and have a total distributed load of 24,000 kg.

Specifications

Class 16 air-portable bridge

	Deck box	Ramp	Articulator box	Float and support frame	Sponson (with motor and accessories)
Length:	3.6 m	3.6 m	1.8 m	2 m	2 m
Width:	1.2 m	1.8 m	1.2 m	1.2 m	1.2 m
Height:	380 mm	380 mm	380 mm	750 mm	750 mm
Weight:	305 kg	346 kg	279 kg	23 kg	281 kg

Status

Production complete. Supplied to Australia (withdrawn July 2008 having exceeded LOT), Canada, Nigeria, the UK and possibly others (see text).

Contractor

FAUN Municipal Vehicles Ltd (formerly Laird (Anglesey) Limited)

Mabey Uniflote system

Development

The Mabey Bridge Limited (previously Mabey & Johnson) Uniflote was conceived in the late 1950s as a flotation system based on unit construction principles, in which identical flotation units can be assembled together to form rafts of various load-carrying capacities, as well as pontoon bridges.

The Uniflote has been supplied to numerous military forces for use as a floating bridge, ship-to-shore causeway, jetty and as vehicle and personnel rafts. It has also been widely used for civil purposes such as landing stages, roll-on roll-off terminals and temporary applications to carry land-based plant such as cranes, excavators and pile-driving equipment for marine works.

Description

The Mabey Uniflote was conceived as a flotation system based on unit construction principles, in which identical flotation units can be assembled together to form rafts of various load-carrying capacities, as well as pontoon bridges. All Uniflote equipment can be carried on standard military or commercial vehicles and if necessary can be skidded into the water. Assembly in the water is accomplished by a maximum of four personnel and the units are held together by locking pins inserted in the couplers.

The standard Uniflote is 5.283 m long, 2.438 m wide and 1.219 m deep. It is a structural steel-framed unit of all-welded construction with 4 mm skin-plates welded to the frame. Two internal watertight bulkheads are incorporated to provide three watertight compartments, each with a watertight hatch. Individual compartments in the flotation units can be flooded or emptied by compressed air. Under a load of 9,000 kg, each Uniflote maintains a freeboard in the region of 230 mm. Couplers are placed so that Uniflotes can be joined end to end, side to side and end to side. Steel gunwales are provided along the side of the Uniflote and are drilled allowing simple saddles to be fitted. The couplers allow for the transmission of loads throughout a Uniflote raft. Concentrated loads can

be applied to the gunwales through saddle attachments. Runners are attached to the bottom to assist in skidding operations on shore and four lifting shackles are fitted. The Uniflote is also available in a 1.828 m deep version.

The standard Uniflote has the deck set approximately 80 mm below gunwale level so that a replaceable timber deck may be fitted if required. This is fitted in the form of three pre-assembled mats (one centre and two outer sections) to each Uniflote. Each mat is designed so that it is retained laterally by the gunwales and is of such a thickness that it stands 50 mm above the gunwale level. Side rings enable Uniflotes to be craned from the shore to the water. Cross junction and side junction mats are also available. The special military version has an integral steel deck set level with the top of the gunwales over which traffic may drive direct.

Scow ends are designed to be attached to either end or side of the Uniflote and have identical end sections. They also have short lengths of gunwale to correspond with the gunwales in the Uniflote. The bottom plate slopes up at an angle of 30° and terminates in a reinforced nosing plate on which a bollard is mounted.

The ramp unit can be connected to the end or sides of the basic Uniflote by ramp connectors, which allow the ramp to articulate and gives access for shore loading over a wide variation in bank heights.

The various Interflote connectors available allow Uniflotes to be spaced apart, giving greater stability to floating platforms, where required, without the need for additional buoyancy.

A range of saddles is available to allow the secure fixing of winches and propulsion units. These saddles can be fitted over the following: a bow or stern unit, the junction between a bow or stern unit and a Uniflote, a Uniflote, the junction between two Uniflotes, or an outrigger (fitted to the side of a Uniflote). Other saddles are available for fixing Mabey panel bridging, and other ancillary equipment.

Specifications

Standard Uniflote (U4/1A)
Weight: 3,700 kg
Length: 5.283 m
Length: (coupler to coupler) 5.41 m
Width: 2.438 m
Height: (without gunwale) 1.219 m
Gunwale size: 76.2 × 76.2 mm

Bow Unit (female U4/3A, male U4/2A)
Weight: 843 kg
Length: 1.82 m
Width: 2.438 m
Height: 1.219 m

Ramp Unit (U4/5A)
Weight: 2,690 kg
Length: 5.28 m
Height: 1.219 m

Status

Production complete. Supplied to the armed forces of Belgium, Brazil and other undisclosed countries.

Contractor

Mabey Bridge Limited

MEXEFLOTE multipurpose pontoon and harbour equipment

Development

MEXEFLOTE, introduced into British Army service during the 1960s, is a multipurpose pontoon equipment designed specifically for marine applications.

Description

The MEXEFLOTE system is rated at MLC 60 and can be rapidly constructed as lighterage rafts, for use at sea and in harbours and can also be assembled as causeways, jetties and other floating structures. The equipment is based on the use of three steel pontoons: bow, centre and stern. These can be connected end to end and side to side to form rafts, causeways, jetties and floating platforms of any shape. The pontoons are of welded steel construction with flush sides. Built into the sides and ends of the pontoons are recessed slots into which the connectors are fitted. There is a 50 mm gap between pontoons.

The bow pontoon consists of a forward section, an aft section and a ramp. The forward section is hinged to the bottom edge of the box-shaped aft section and can articulate vertically to a maximum of 457 mm above the deck level and be lowered to a maximum of 380 mm below the surface of the aft section. The manually operated, demountable articulator is mounted in a recess in the aft section and is connected to the forward section by an articulator ram. The articulator has a safe working load of 81,280 kg. The pontoon ramp is hinged to the forward section and slides over the forward end of the aft section to bridge the gap between the sections.

Mabey Uniflote ferry in operation (Mabey Bridge Limited)   0007687

MEXEFLOTE

	Bow pontoon	Centre pontoon	Stern pontoon
Weight:	5,909 kg	4,654 kg	4,418 kg
Length:	7.92 m	6.1 m	6.1 m
Width:	2.44 m	2.44 m	2.44 m
Depth:	1.45 m	1.45 m	1.45 m

MEXEFLOTE in use transporting three FV 432 armoured vehicles ship to shore (Shaun C Connors)   0109510

A MEXEFLOTE off RFA Largs Bay delivering emergency rations and supplies in support of the international disaster relief effort in Haiti during 2010 (UK MoD)   1391258

MEXEFLOTE in position to load from a US Naval landing support vessel (Shaun C Connors)   0109509

The centre pontoon is a box-shaped unit with an internal lateral bulkhead dividing the interior into two watertight compartments. Each compartment has a hatch cover, air-line connector and a bilge discharge outlet fitted with nylon plugs set flush with the deck surface.

The stern pontoon is also a box-shaped unit with an internal lateral bulkhead dividing the interior into two watertight compartments. Each compartment has a hatch cover, air-line connector and a bilge discharge outlet fitted with nylon plugs set flush with the deck surface. The bottom edge of the stern pontoon is chamfered allowing the propeller and skeg of the propelling unit to be rotated through 360° when the unit is mounted at the stern of the pontoon. Propulsive power is provided by a pair of 75 hp Hydromaster six-cylinder diesel engines.

The pontoon connector is a rectangular unit weighing 73.94 kg, fits into any full-length connector slot of a pontoon and is used to join together pontoons side by side and end to end. Each connector has one fixed pin

and one movable pin at the bottom that can be raised or lowered by a handle in the top of the connector to make the bottom connection of adjoining pontoons. The top connection is made by passing a short bolt on each adjoining pontoon through a hole in the connector.

The pontoon link is a triangular box-shaped unit weighing 20.87 kg. This has short bolt holes through the top and a fixed pin at the bottom which fits through a hole in a jaw at the bottom of the short slot in the side of the bow pontoon forward section and in the end of the stern section.

MEXEFLOTE can be used in the following wave conditions:

Component	Wave height
Pontoons connected to form rafts, causeways and jetties	0.61 m
Operation of rafts, causeways and jetties	1.22 to 1.52 m
Survival of causeway, raft or jetty (unladen) at moorings	2.74 to 3.05 m
Survival of causeways or rafts (unladen) in tow	3.66 m

Rafts

The most common types of raft are:
- 20.22 × 7.42 m which can carry one Class 60 tank or three 4,000 kg trucks
- 38.4 × 7.42 m which can carry two Class 60 tanks or six 4,000 kg trucks
- 38.4 × 12.9 m (Maxi-MEXEFLOTE) which has a maximum capacity of 198,000 kg and can carry three Class 60 tanks or equivalent vehicles.

A Landing Ship Logistic, or similar ship, is capable of carrying one 38.4 × 7.42 m raft on each side or two 20.22 × 7.42 m rafts on each side. When approaching the beach these are released and can be used as rafts (with the addition of propulsion units) or connected end to end to form a causeway to the beach.

The MEXEFLOTE pontoons can easily be handled as they are compatible with ISO container storage and handling systems: the centre and bow pontoons conform to the 6.1 × 2.4 m container dimensions.

During late 1994, the British Army issued a requirement for the production of 50 MEXEFLOTE centre pontoons and in May 2001 invited tenders for the survey, repair and refurbishment of up to 60 MEXEFLOTE pontoon sections.

Specifications - See table above

Status
In service with the British Army and other unspecified armed forces.

Original
GEC Engineering (Accrington) Limited

WFEL Limited floating Medium Girder Bridge (MGB)

Description
Using the Medium Girder Bridge (MGB) pontoon (powered and/or unpowered), floating bridges can be constructed using MGB system components. Full details of the MGB can be found in the Tactical (non-floating) and line of communication bridges section. Single- or double-storey configurations can be constructed. The length of these bridges is limited only by the amount of equipment available.

The single-storey floating MGB is built in continuous construction from one site, allowing one bay of the bridge to be added every 30 seconds. Launching is simplified by the use of a winch cable across the gap, attached to the front of the bridge. This allows the bridge to be launched steadily throughout the assembly. Single-storey construction provides for load classes of up to MLC 60.

Double-storey floating construction allows long landing bays of up to 26.5 m and is suitable for higher bank heights (up to 5 m), difficult shore lines (such as marshy ground) or where there is a considerable rise and fall in the water level. Double-storey floating MGBs take longer to build than single storeys, but use fewer pontoons. Depending on the length of crossing, they may be multispan or continuous in form. Two spans are used for bridges between 31.1 and 51.5 m; three spans are used for bridges between 51.5 and 76 m. Over 76 m, construction proceeds as for the three span, except that intermediate pontoon piers are positioned at intervals in the centre section. This provides a very economical long floating bridge, which only requires span junction sets at the landing bays.

A three-span floating MGB under construction (WFEL Limited)   1128277

The marine grade aluminium pontoons used for floating MGBs are the same as those used for the MGB ferry, full details of which can be found elsewhere in this section.

Status
Production as required. Supplied to the armed forces of 38 nations.

Contractor
WFEL Limited

WFEL Limited Medium Girder Bridge (MGB) Powered Pontoon and Ferry

Description
The WFEL Limited (formally known as Williams Fairey Engineering Limited) Medium Girder Bridge (MGB) pontoon can be propelled by means of a Schottel Pump Jet (SPJ) driven by a Deutz air-cooled diesel engine. The engine assembly is mounted in a lightweight frame, secured to the floor by four clamps and can be rapidly removed for either maintenance or complete in-field replacement. The Schottel pump jet is mounted by clamps in the floor of the pontoon and can also be rapidly removed for servicing.

There are no protrusions on the underside of the pontoons, enabling the unit to operate in shallow or heavily obstructed water without problems of fouling. Steering is effected by rotating the jet outlet, which, with its 360° movement, provides the pontoon with a high level of manoeuvrability.

The powered pontoon has many uses including providing propulsion for MGB ferries, with four units on a MLC 70 and two each on MLC 27 and MLC 20 ferries. However, they can also be effectively used during the construction of floating bridges, providing a rapid means of placing piers.

Each pontoon is of open-top construction which allows stacking for transport and storage. The marine grade aluminium pontoons have sealed in-built buoyancy which alone provides adequate flotation for the ferry or bridge structure. They are self-draining and anchor winches are fitted as standard. Each pontoon has a (net) buoyancy of 12,000 kg at 300 mm freeboard. They can be stacked with four pontoons one inside the other to form a load 2.7 m high. Such a stack can be carried on a non-dedicated truck of the DROPS type which can be used to launch and recover the pontoons.

The MGB ferry is essentially a single-storey bridge connected to MGB pontoons to provide a range of ferries from MLC 20 upwards. The pontoons may be connected to form rafts by the use of raft saddles which pivot allowing the assembly to be stowed within the pontoon during transportation. The construction sequence is similar to that of a long single-storey MGB. The end of the bridge is supported on a roller beam and the first landing bay is completed by adding top panel bays followed by hinge panels. Further top panels are fitted and the girder boomed out to allow connection between the piers or rafts at the saddle or hinge panel position. The construction continues with further top panels up to the second pair of hinge panels and then completion of the second landing bay.

MGB ferry transporting a Foden IMMLC DROPS truck (WFEL Limited)
1128274

MGB ferry pontoon recovery by a Foden IMMLC DROPS truck
(WFEL Limited)   1128276

WFEL Limited currently markets a range of three ferry configurations: up to MLC 20, up to MLC 35 and up to 70. Other options up to MLC 100 are possible.

Specifications
MGB pontoon
Weight: (less power pack) approx 1,100 kg
Length: 7.96 m
Width: 2.6 m
Height: 1.17 m
Max current speed: (fully laden) up to 2.5 m/s (4.85 kts)
Available buoyancy: (net) 12,000 kg at 300 mm freeboard
Power pack: Deutz air-cooled diesel developing 75 hp (52 kW)
Water jet: Schottel pump-jet providing thrust through 360°

Status
Production as required. In service with three unspecified countries.

Contractor
WFEL Limited

United States

Aluminium floating footbridge

Description
The aluminium floating footbridge provides a standard means of rapidly crossing dismounted infantrymen in support of river crossing operations. It can be hand-erected and can safely be used in currents of up to 3.4 m/s, however capabilities are significantly reduced in currents over 2.4 m/s. A straight uniform reach is also desirable, the bridge being easily affected by eddies, cross-currents or river turbulence.

The aluminium floating footbridge consists of treadways, pontoons, handrail posts, ropes, holdfasts and approach posts. One bridge set contains 144 m of bridge in normal mode of assembly, weighs 4,105 kg and can be transported by two 2½ ton 6 × 6 trucks towing 2½ ton utility pole-type trailers. The complete bridge can also be carried in a C-130 Hercules transport aircraft and one half set of the footbridge can be delivered by parachute from a C-130 using two 2,721 kg bearing platforms.

The bridge is normally assembled using the successive bay method, but if the water is too deep for this method, the bridge is assembled in sections, which takes twice as long. The bridge can also be assembled on the shore, which requires a straight shore assembly area as long as the bridge, cleared to a width of 6.096 m. Finally the bridge can be assembled in the water or on steep banks. In this case, two skids are set in the water and inclined against the bank. This allows the bays or bridge sections to be launched into the water. In currents up to 2.4 m/s, the number of troops that can cross single file at two-pace intervals is as follows:

• Daylight: 75 personnel/min, single file, double time
• Moonlight: 40 personnel/min, single file, quick time
• Blackout: 25 personnel/min, single file, quick time.

If the current velocity is between 2.4 and 3.4 m/s, the crossing rates should be reduced by 20 per cent.

If required, the pontoons can also be used as paddle-propelled rafts. An expedient two-pontoon raft is formed, by lashing two pontoons side by side with one treadway placed across them. This will carry one wounded

Aluminium Floating Footbridge, designated Schützenschnellsteg or Schwimmsteg, of the German Army (Stefan Marx)   1121183

Specifications

Assembly time
(Trained and experienced troops assembling from stockpiled parts and including installation time of anchor cables and deadmen. Additional time should be allowed for assembly from trucks, possible anchorage difficulties or other delaying factors)
Day: 15 min plus 1 min per 4.572 m of bridge
Night: 20 min plus 1¼ min per 4.572 m of bridge (with illumination or moonlight)
Blackout: 30 min plus 2 min per 4.572 m of bridge

Maximum safe allowable deflection

Number of bays	Effective length of bridge	Max allowable deflection
4	13.716 m	50 mm
6	20.57 m	100 mm
8	27.43 m	152 mm
10	34.29 m	254 mm
12	41.148 m	381 mm
18	61.72 m	863 mm
24	82.29 m	1.549 m
36	123.44 m	3.479 m

Treadway
Weight: 38.1 kg
Length:
  (overall) 3.555 m
  (effective) 3.428 m
Width:
  (overall) 711 mm
  (walkway) 527 mm
Depth: 133 mm

Pontoon
Weight: 45.36 kg
Length: 4.267 m
Width: 609 mm
Depth: 367 mm (gunwale)
Weight: (complete bridge set) 4,105 kg

Status
In service with the US Army and other armed forces including Australia, Colombia, Germany[1] and South Korea. Has been licence-produced in Greece.

[1] The US Aluminium Floating Footbridge is used by German combat engineer battalions with the designation Schützenschnellsteg or Schwimmsteg; approximately 14 sets were reported to be in stock as of early 2005.

---

man and two paddlers, one in the bow and one in the stern. A three-pontoon expedient raft is formed, by lashing three pontoons side by side with one treadway placed across them and an additional treadway placed along each side of the centre treadway. This can carry four wounded men and four paddlers, two in the bow and two in the stern.

An expedient bridge 30.48 m long, which will take a Jeep-type vehicle and trailer, can be constructed from the components of one aluminium footbridge set. The treadways are blocked apart and lashed leaving an open space of 710 mm between them. The second bay, and succeeding alternate bays, are assembled with the two-pontoon bay downstream and the three-pontoon bay upstream. Handrail posts are installed only on the outer beam of each treadway. The bridge may not be used where the current exceeds 1.5 m/s.

Description of parts
The aluminium treadway consists of two parallel I-beams carrying traverse aluminium channels which support a corrugated aluminium sheet tread. The ends of the I-beam are fitted with spring-loaded connectors, male at one end and female at the other to provide connection between the treadways. This serves to distribute the load over several pontoons and provides a connection that does not require the insertion of separate connecting pins.

The pontoons are fabricated from sheet aluminium reinforced with light aluminium members. The pontoon has a false bottom 171 mm above its true bottom which provides a compartment filled with a light cellular plastic material. This renders the pontoon relatively unsinkable, even when subject to small arms fire or shell splinter damage. Each gunwale is fitted with two hooks which grip the outer bottom flanges of a treadway I-beam. Each pontoon has a hole 25 × 51 mm in the bow and stern just above the false bottom, making the pontoon self-bailing.

The aluminium handrail post is a 32 mm diameter tube mounted on an aluminium base and fitted at its top, with a cast aluminium attachment to receive a handrail rope. The handrail post weighs approximately 1.5 kg and is installed by inserting the base in a socket in the treadway and rotating the post 180° to lock it in position.

Each bridge set contains 12.7 mm diameter manila rope which is cut as required for handrail line, guy lines and bridle ties. There are two 183 m reels of 9.5 mm galvanised wire rope for use as anchor cables and guys for improvised cable towers. These are provided together with 20 wire rope clips, four holdfasts (each complete with nine pickets) and 16 approach posts.

Bridge Floating: Raft section, light tactical

Description
This bridge set has sufficient components for one four-pontoon reinforced raft, or 13.41 m of normal bridge. The same set is used in assembling a combination of floating bridges or rafts of various classes. One bridge set is carried by two 2½ ton 6 × 6 trucks, one of which tows a 2½ ton pole-type trailer that carries the eight half-pontoons stacked one on top of the other.

Two aluminium half-pontoons are joined stern to stern to form a complete pontoon. The deck panel is positioned and retained laterally by four retainer lugs on the pontoons. One end of each deck panel is male and the other female. Two deck filler panels are used to fill the space between one set of deck panels. These are normally retained in position by pintles, but provision is made for bolting the filler panels to the deck panels. Two types of ramp panel are provided, one to mate with the male end of a deck section and one with the female end. The articulating assembly is provided to permit variations in the end span abutment elevations in bridges and rafts from 1.041 m above the horizontal position of the deck to 482 mm below. It consists of male and female sections. A connecting pin and adjusting bar are used to join the two sections.

There are two sizes of kerb. The deck panel kerb is used on the normal bay of the superstructure and the short ramp kerb is used on the ramp and articulator panels. These are held in position by holding lugs that extend from the bottom of the kerb and bear directly on the underside of the top flange of the deck panel.

A raft normally consists of three bays of decking with ramps at each end on four complete pontoons. The loading space from kerb to kerb is 2.743 m and loading length is 8.992 m.

The bridge is rated as Class 11 in a current of 2.4 m/s and the four-pontoon three-bay raft as Class 12 in a current of up to 2.4 m/s. The light tactical bridge has loading space kerb to kerb of 2.743 m with the pontoons normally being spaced at 3.352 m centres. Reinforced bridges have the pontoons spaced at 2.4 m centres.

Each pontoon is provided with a fluked marine anchor and each raft set is issued with four outboard motor brackets. The outboard motors normally used are rated at 25 hp.

A six-pontoon, four-bay reinforced raft has a length of 21.336 m, a loading length of 12.192 m and a roadway width (kerb to kerb) of 3.352 m.

Ferry conversion set
Trail ferry method

A bicycle traveller allows the raft to move smoothly along a ferry cable. The ferry cable is stretched across the river and made fast. The bicycle traveller is attached to the cable so that its sheaves roll smoothly. The hauling line is attached to the grommet in the bicycle traveller and the manoeuvre lines to the snatch blocks which are attached to the sheave housing of the traveller. On the raft the hauling line is attached to the upstream end of the centre pontoon. The manoeuvre lines are attached to the gunwales of the outside pontoons. The ferry is operated by adjusting the manoeuvre lines so that the raft is at an angle to the stream current. The upstream end of the pontoon inclines towards the opposite shore. The current pushes against the upstream side of the pontoon and forces the raft across the river. As the pontoons are pushed into the current, the speed of the raft increases. This method may be used when the current exceeds 0.9 m/s.

The flying ferry works on a similar principle to the trail ferry except that the raft is held in the stream by an anchor well upstream from the crossing site. As the raft moves from shore to shore, it swings in an arc of a circle centred on the anchor. This ferry requires a maximum stream or river velocity of 1.2 m/s.

Specifications
Half pontoon
Weight: 295 kg
Length: 5.638 m
Width: 2.044 m
Depth: 863 mm

Deck panel
Weight: 256.28 kg
Length: 3.701 m
(effective) 3.352 m
Width: 1.066 m
Depth: 323 mm

Deck filler panel
Weight: 43 kg
Length: 1.647 m
Width: 787 mm
Height: 161 mm

Ramp panel
Weight:
(male) 149.9 kg
(female) 181 kg
Length:
(male) 2.438 m
(female) 2.136 m
Width: 1.066 m
Height: 323 mm

Articulating assembly
Weight: 290 kg
Length: 2.2 m
Width: 1.066 m
Height: 514 mm

Kerb
Weight:
(normal) 49.9 kg
(short) 9.07 kg
Length:
(normal) 3.295 m
(short) 865 mm

Construction time
4-pontoon, 3-bay raft: 30 min
5-pontoon, 5-bay raft: 35 min
6-pontoon, 4-bay raft: 45 min

Status
As of February 2001, a total of eight sets remained in the US Army's inventory. No training was being conducted and the future use of this equipment in river crossing operations was stated as uncertain. Remains in service with other armed forces including South Korea. Has been produced under licence in Greece.

Ribbon Bridge

Development
The Ribbon Bridge was developed by the Pacific Car and Foundry Company of Renton, Washington and the former US Army Mobility Equipment Research and Development (MERADCOM) Center (later the Belvoir Research, Development and Engineering Centre) at Fort Belvoir, Virginia and is based on the design of the Soviet PMP Ribbon Bridge. PMP segments captured by Israel during the 1973 Yom Kippur War were examined during the development of the Ribbon Bridge.

Development of the US bridge began in 1969 and the bridge was type classified as standard A in June 1972, less than three years after development started. The first production contract, worth USD10 million, was awarded to the Consolidated Diesel Electric Division of the CONDEC Corporation at Old Greenwich, Connecticut (later ConDiesel Mobile Equipment of Waterbury, Connecticut) and was for 250 interior bays, 50 ramp bays and 300 transporter trucks. The Ribbon Bridge system was first fielded by the US Army in Germany and South Korea in 1976. A US Army bridge company has 18 interior bays and 12 ramps.

A Fiscal Year 1984 request was for 585 interior bays and 257 ramp bays. The resultant contract was awarded to ConDiesel Mobile Equipment. Southwest Mobile Systems (later Systems & Electronics Inc (SEI), now DRS Sustainment Systems, Inc) was the only producer of the Ribbon Bridge between 1984 and 1993, during which period it completed two multi-year contracts with the US Army for over 500 systems. In July 1993, Precision Machining Inc, of Pensacola, Florida, was awarded a USD5 million firm fixed price contract for 67 Ribbon Bridge interior bays and 27 ramp bays. Work was completed by May 1995.

Description
The Ribbon Bridge has two main differences from the PMP: it is aluminium rather than steel and so weighs about a third less and the PMP uses torsion bars to help unfold the pontoons. This is effective in launching, but means that the torsion force must be overcome during retrieval, which results in longer retrieval times. In use the Ribbon Bridge augments and replaces the mobile assault bridging emplaced by the forward elements. It can be emplaced 10 times faster with a fifth of the personnel required to emplace standard floating bridges. The bridge can support 80,000 kg loads in currents up to 2.4 m/s and up to 110,000 kg when conditions are ideal.

The Ribbon Bridge consists of integral float-deck elements connected longitudinally to form a continuous floating roadway. There are two basic bridge elements, the interior bay and the ramp bay. The interior bay consists of the roadway pontoons and two bay pontoons joined by hinges and pins. During deployment, the bow and roadway pontoons automatically unfold in the water. The ramp bay unfolds in the same manner as the interior bay. Ramp bays also have the capability to adjust to river bank slopes up to 20° through the use of hydraulic cylinders.

The bays are carried folded on the rear of specially modified 5-ton 6 × 6 trucks, or other trucks of suitable capacity. Launching of bridge bays may be accomplished by one of three modes: free, controlled or high bank. In the free launch mode the truck is backed into the water. A minimum depth

US Ribbon Bridge ramp section on a M939A0 5-ton 6 × 6 truck
(Carl Schulze)   1340289

US Army Ribbon Bridge centre sections on M939A0 5-ton 6 × 6 trucks
(Carl Schulze)   1340290

US Army Ribbon Bridge assembled during an exercise in Europe
(Karl Schulze)   1340291

of 914 mm is required to free launch an interior bay (1.125 m for ramp bay) with a 10 per cent river bank slope. Water pressure and the pontoon hinging arrangement permit the bay to automatically unfold. The bridge assembly crew then lock the bay sections using a series of latches. Bays are joined together using a lock pin mechanism and a special T-wrench.

The bridge is normally assembled along the shore and the complete bridge is then swung across the river using bridge erection boats. Bridging boats are used to hold the bridge in position and in a current with a velocity of 2.5 m/s are normally positioned every 20 m. If the bridge is to remain in place for extended periods, overhead anchor cables may be employed. It can also be constructed using the method of successive bays or rafts. If required, individual bays can be emplaced by helicopter. The Ribbon Bridge can be constructed at the rate of 6.705 m/min over rivers with a current up to 2.4 m/s. The roadway itself is 4.089 m wide and there is a 1.219 m walkway on either side.

To retrieve a bridge bay, the transporter is backed into the water and the boom is raised to the vertical. The lifting cable runs from the winch over a sheave at the top of the boom and down to the bridge bay. The cable hook is attached to the roadway hinge pin and, when the cable is reeled in, one end of the bay is lifted out of the water until water pressure acting on the other end causes the bay to fold up. At this time, a series of latches automatically lock the bay in the folded position. The bay is then lowered into the aft tiedown locks at the back of the transporter, the boom is lowered and the bay is winched on to the transporter. The front locking pin is engaged and the vehicle is ready to drive away. Bridge sections are able to be launched or retrieved by one person but each transporter carries an assistant to speed up operations, especially during retrieval and to assist in assembling the bridge.

The bridge transporter was originally a dedicated vehicle of limited utility when not carrying bridge equipment. In order to overcome this shortcoming, a special pallet was developed which permits the transporter to haul up to 9,000 kg of cargo (4,500 kg across country). The pallet can be self-loaded or off-loaded while carrying up to 4,500 kg, a feature which lends itself to pre-palletised loads.

ROK Ribbon Bridge production
Ribbon Bridge components for the ROK armed forces are manufactured by Doosan Heavy Industries & Construction Co. Ltd. Released specification data indicates these are dimensional copies of US Ribbon Bridge components.

Doosan Heavy Industries & Construction Co. Ltd. was established in 1962 and is the ROK's largest general engineering company and in addition to military products is heavily involved in power plant, industrial plant and civil construction projects.

Specifications
Interior bay
Weight: 5,443 kg
Length:
(folded) 6.93 m
(unfolded) 6.93 m
Width:
(folded) 3.22 m
(unfolded) 8.13 m
Height:
(folded) 2.31 m
(at bow, unfolded) 1.12 m
(at roadway, unfolded) 1.09 m

Ramp bay
Weight: 5,307 kg
Length:
(folded) 5.79 m
(unfolded) 7.79 m
Width:
(folded) 3.2 m
(unfolded) 8.13 m
Height:
(folded) 2.31 m
(of roadway, unfolded) 736 mm
(of shore end, unfolded) 381 mm

Transporter loaded
Weight: 17,931 kg
Length: 9.6 m
Width: 3.43 m
Height: 3.91 m

Status
In service with the US Army (current purchases are the Improved Ribbon Bridge (IRB); see elsewhere in this section) and some other armed forces. Adopted by the German Army, Netherlands and South Korea. Manufactured in South Korea (see text).

Contractor
DRS Sustainment Systems, Inc
Doosan Heavy Industries & Construction Co Ltd

TACTICAL (NON-FLOATING) AND LINE OF COMMUNICATION BRIDGES

Australia

Transfield-MBK line of communication bridging system

Development
The Australian company, Transfield Construction, in association with design consultants McMillan, Britton and Kell of Sydney, New South Wales, designed a new line of communication bridging system for the Australian Army. The bridge, built at Transfield Construction's manufacturing plant at Seven Hills, Sydney, New South Wales, is of steel construction. Bridge construction and launching principles are similar to those of the Bailey Bridge. By using material handling equipment, component size and weight can be increased without jeopardising the speed and ease with which construction, launch and recovery can be accomplished. Thus individual sections can be heavier and are simpler and faster to put together than the equivalent Bailey-type bridge.

Testing was conducted by the School of Civil and Mining Engineering at the University of Sydney and full-scale user trials were conducted by the Australian Army School of Military Engineering. The Australian Army issued an initial contract for 32 bridging sets worth AUD7.5 million. The contract value was later increased to AUD11 million; production was completed during 1989.

Currently 10 sets of the Transfield line of communication bridge are understood to be in the Australian inventory, with a decision on the future of the system pending.

In 2003 the John Holland Group acquired Transfield Construction from Transfield Services.

Description
The bridge is two lanes wide with steel decking. The main load-carrying components comprise through-trusses each side, which are assembled from standard 5 m-long steel panels and chord reinforcements connected by pins. The arrangement of panels and reinforcement depends on the span and loading. Universal jackable end posts enable construction time to be shortened and launching rollers are adjustable for level and tilt. Each universal end post assembly incorporates a 1.5 m range jacking system. The deck units incorporate huck bolts to avoid distortion problems. The design loading is MLC 70 (single lane) or MLC 35 (twin lane).

The steel used in the bridge construction is Grade 350 to AS1250, with Grade 450 for panel diagonals. Pins are Grade 630 stainless steel and pin plates are Bisalloy 80 (Grade 690). All components are hot-dip galvanised to AS1650, ensuring optimum life in all environments, during both storage and deployment.

Status
In service with the Australian Army (see text).

Contractor
John Holland Group

Two 60 m spans assembled for launching over a dry river bed as part of a three-span bridge (John Holland Group)   1340293

Bulgaria

Prefabricated bridge modules

Description
These prefabricated bridge modules, used by the Bulgarian Army, are intended to be utilised with other rapid bridge-building equipment or else assembled on the remains of existing bridge structures. Each bridge module is 5 m long and can be used to assemble bridges up to 30 m long. For transport, the modules are carried two to a standard 5,000 kg or similar load capacity truck.

Once assembled, a complete bridge has a weight classification of MLC 60 for wheeled vehicles, MLC 80 for tracked vehicles and MLC 104 for vehicles such as loaded tank transporters. Once assembled, the modules can be arranged so that a track width of 4.2 m can carry single-lane traffic and a trackway 6.3 m wide can carry two-way traffic.

The linear weight per metre of bridge is 640 kg and the building rate is between 15 and 20 m/h.

Status
Understood to be in service with the Bulgarian Army. Offered for export sales.

Marketing agency
KINTEX

Czech Republic

MS-1 (SM-60) heavy panel bridge

Description
The MS-1 (SM-60) is a single-storey through-truss type bridge which in some respects resembles the Bailey Bridge. The MS-1, however, has truss members made of triangles placed back-to-back to form verticals while the Bailey Bridges are of the diamond-shaped pattern.

The bridge has a maximum capacity of 60,000 kg and a maximum clear span of 21 m. Its roadway is 4 m wide. Multispan bridges can be constructed with the aid of trestles. These have circular baseplates and can be adjusted for heights between 1.5 and 7 m. The bridge is assembled with the aid of cranes and is launched by the cantilever method. The heaviest part of the bridge weighs 3,150 kg. The bridge components are carried on standard TATRA 6 × 6 10,000 kg trucks or similar vehicles.

Status
Production complete. Supplied to the armies of the Czech Republic, Pakistan and Slovakia.

Contractor
Czech and Slovak state factories.

Germany

EADS Foldable Bridge

Development
A single 42 m dry support bridge prototype was developed by the now EADS Defence & Security (formerly Dornier/Eurobridge) in 1979, and was successfully tested with 15,000 crossings by MLC 70 Leopard 2 MBTs. During 1984, the Federal Procurement Office of the German Armed Forces awarded a contract to Dornier System GmbH, for the development and production of an operational prototype of a 40 m span Foldable Dry Support Bridge. Based on MAN trucks, the first Foldable Bridge set was handed over to the German Ministry of Defence proving ground in Koblenz in May 1987 for intensive tests.

A 40 m improved pre-series type bridge was also built and tested by the German Army starting in 1990 and obtained the certificate of suitability for German Army service.

In 1993 a 46 m upgrade of the improved 40 m demonstrator Dornier Foldable Bridge (DoFB) system was completed, based on Mercedes-Benz trucks.

In 1994, a contract was placed for the delivery of 10 bridge sets to the German Army, each set comprising one DoFB 40 m system and one DoFB 14 m system, and including two MAN 8 × 8 launching vehicles,

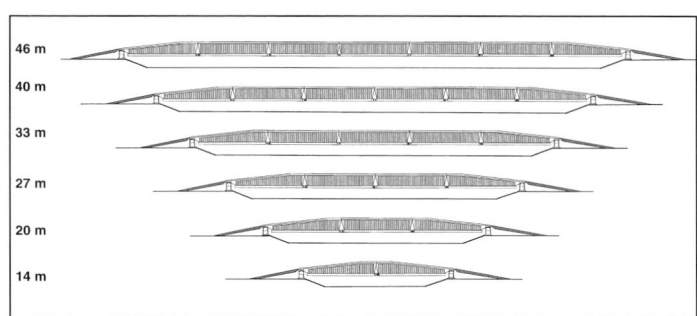

The modularity of the EADS Foldable Bridge makes various lengths of bridge possible (EADS)   0044074

A German Army Faltfestbrücke (FFB) being assembled (EADS)   0079381

A EADS Foldable Bridge bay unfolding automatically as it is lifted by a crane (EADS)   0044076

EADS Foldable Bridge of the Austrian Army under construction (EADS)   0547264

A German Army Faltfestbrücke (FFB) in use (EADS)   0593344

Austrian Army EADS Foldable Bridge components on a ÖAF transport truck (EADS)   0593337

Demonstration handling of EADS Foldable bridge components by the German Army (Michael Jerchel)   1124748

five MAN 8 × 8 transport trucks, plus logistic support and spares. The first of the 10 series production bridge sets was handed over to the German Army in June 1998. In German Army service, the bridge is known as the Faltfestbrücke (FFB).

The Foldable Bridge has been specified for near combat zone support tasks but it can also be used as a general support bridge during conflicts, out of area operations and disaster relief.

EADS Defence & Security is responsible for the worldwide marketing and sales, product/project management and product support of the DoFB. The company can also develop other mobile bridging equipment such as assault bridges, manually launched short trackway bridges, air-transportable bridges, trailer-launched bridges and special bridges to customer requirements.

Description

The main advantages claimed for the EADS Foldable Bridge (*Faltfestbrücke*) are: high mobility; easy transport due to compact folded bridge units during transport; limited bank space requirements (18 × 18 m); assembly without preparation and physical strain; a closed and obstacle free roadway surface over the entire width of 4.4 m with long ramps providing a high crossing capacity; ease of passage across the bridge for all types of vehicle; high transverse stiffness, and flexible spans from 14 up to 46 m, and with no cable reinforcement required even at the maximum span.

The EADS Foldable Bridge is a lightweight aluminium structure, transported on trucks with suitable rigs so that during transport the bridge bays do not exceed 2.75 m in width and 4 m in height. These dimensions allow the bridge to be carried on trains or transport aircraft. The bridge deck consists of sections folded parallel to the bridge axis and a supporting traversing beam with bank beams. The bridge has been designed for a nominal load of MLC 70 and a crossing speed of 25 km/h. The exceptional crossing load permitted is 110,000 kg. This is a German Army requirement to allow two Leopard 2 MBTs on a 2.5 m towbar, or a loaded tank transporter to cross the bridge.

The 40 m bridge can be assembled by a crew of six in less than 60 minutes without physical strain. On the launching vehicle chassis, a system frame is mounted that accommodates the hydraulic outriggers that stabilise the vehicle, the crane, and launching beam, as well as all electrical and hydraulic equipment including an Auxiliary Power Unit (APU). The hydraulic crane has a lifting capacity of 4,750 kg for a working radius of 7.7 m. It is equipped with a hoisting device for carrying the bridge bays and traversing beam sections. The bridge bays are so arranged that using the hoisting device, the bays will automatically unfold to full 4.4 m road width as they are lifted.

Austrian Army EADS Folding Bridge launching truck. In Austrian Army service the EADS Foldable bridge is known as the Brückenübersetzgerät (Brübs). The launching truck is an ÖAF badged MAN SX range truck (Stefan Marx)
1128279

On arrival at the bridging site the outrigger system of the launching vehicle is extended, the launching beam is placed into the launching position and after placing a traversing beam ramp section into position of the launching beam rail, a bank beam is attached. The traversing beam ramp with the bank beam attached is moved outwards. Then the first traversing beam inner section is positioned on the launching beam and coupled. The traversing beam sections are gradually moved outwards as more beam sections are coupled until the home bank traversing beam ramp is placed on to the launching vehicle and coupled. The traversing beam is then completely extended and the far bank beam is lowered on to the opposite bank. After fitting the home bank beam at the traversing beam ramp the gap is fully spanned and ready for the bridge assembly.

The launching vehicle remains in the position at the bank. The bridge assembly commences with the first bridge ramp bay being placed on to the traversing beam. While the crane lifts the bridge bays from the transport trucks, they unfold automatically by gravity. The launching beam is used to move the ramp bay along the traversing beam until a gear box with sprocket is engaged in the bridge bay for the movement towards the far bank. The ramp bay travels on top of the traversing beam allowing the first of the bridge interior bays to be placed into position and coupled using a snap ring mechanism on the top chord and a pin-joint mechanism on the lower chord (the latter can be operated manually or using a power tool). The coupled bridge bays are then advanced to the far bank and the process is repeated until the last interior bay is in position and the home bridge ramp bay is coupled. The bridge can then be lowered onto the bank beams, until the bridge ramp bay lower cords rest on the bank beam bearings. As a last step the access ramps are attached. The bridge is then ready for use.

In the majority of cases bank preparation will not be required. Slopes, soil strength and different bank heights up to 3 m are levelled out by the system.

The bridge is recovered in the reverse order. As the bridge bays are lifted by the crane hoisting device they fold automatically to transport width of 2.75 m.

In German Army service, a complete FFB includes 54 m of MLC 70 bridging equipment, two launching vehicles, five bridge transporters and a single 10,000 kg 8 × 8 truck. The Bundeswehr uses MAN 8 × 8 trucks for launch and logistic purposes, but 6 × 6 trucks can be used to carry the bridge components. The required payload for the four transport trucks is a maximum of 12,000 kg each. The launching vehicle payload with system frame, crane, launch beam hydraulics, electrical systems, auxiliary power unit and hydraulic outriggers, is approximately 17,500 kg. The system has been adapted to standard IVECO, MAN, Mercedes-Benz and ÖAF PLS-type trucks for different customers.

Bridge lengths that can be built include 13.9 m (two bays), 20.3 m (three bays), 26.7 m (four bays), 33.1 m (five bays), 39.5 m (six bays) and 45.9 m (seven bays). All bridges are constructed by the truck crews of five or six people only.

The useful life of a bridge is given as 20 years, 10,000 MLC 70 crossings or 3,000 launch-cycles. No log book recording is necessary as each individual bridge segment is provided with a powerless life monitoring system. Pedestrian walkways are also available for non-tactical use; these are in service with the Austrian Army.

Specifications

EADS Foldable Bridge
Length:
(modular bridge spans) 14 m up to 46 m in 6.4 m increments
(maximum gap) 45.2 m
(overall) 54 m
(inner section) 6.4 m
(ramp section) 7.1 m
(climbing ramp) 3.9 m
Load class: MLC 70
Transport width: 2.75 m

Road width: 4.4 m
Height: 1.26 m
Weight: (complete 46 m bridge) 30,000 kg
Launching time: 60 mins for DoFB 40 m, 75 mins for DoFB 46 m
Trucks: DoFB 46 m, 1 launching truck MLC 32, 5 transport trucks MLC 23

Status
Production as required. In service with Austria (6 × 40 m systems), Germany (10 × 40 m and 10 × 14 m systems), Singapore (46 m systems, numbers not disclosed), Spain (5 × 40 m and 2 × 14 m systems) and Slovenia (1 × 40 m system).

Contractor
EADS Defence & Security

EADS Light Bridge (DoLB)

Development
The EADS Defence and Security DoLB (Dornier Light Bridge) is a new, foldable, lightweight bridge designed for airborne, light and rapid reaction forces operating with medium helicopters, such as the CH-53.

EADS Defense and Security in Friedrichshafen, Germany began development of the DoLB as Eurobridge in 2002, qualified the bridge structure over the full-design life by static and dynamic testing in 2004 and demonstrated the DoLB, complete with its specialist trailers in 2005. The complete bridge structure is ready for delivery.

The German Army's tactical concept foresees the transport of the bridge by a minimum number of 2 CH-53 sorties, manual or mechanised launching of the bridge over gaps up to 20 m and crossings by vehicles up to MLC 12, all based on TRICODE conditions.

EADS Defence and Security is a division of the European Aeronautic Defence and Space company (EADS).

Until 2006 Eurobridge GmbH, previously known as Eurobridge Mobile Brücken GmbH, was a 100 per cent subsidiary of Dornier GmbH, which has since 2005 been merged to become EADS Deutschland GmbH.

Description
The EADS Defence and Security DoLB is a foldable, lightweight, aluminium alloy structure filled with carbon fibre roadway elements. The bridge consists of two parallel longitudinal lattice girders (foldable to reduce transport volume) with a hung-in trackway between. The main components are designed for common usage in a family of light and medium bridges. The upgrade to the medium bridge class is performed by means of structural add-ons.

All components for a standard 20 m bridge, with the possibility to construct two shorter bridges and including a manual launching device, are stored on three special trailers plus two pallets which are compatible with the payload area of the CH-53 helicopter. Ground transport is performed by lightweight trailers towed by a vehicle of the Mungo light vehicle class.

At the construction site all bridge components can be man-handled or transported by a special trolley. Four soldiers can assemble a standard bridge in less than 90 minutes, and without the aid of special tools. The heaviest single component weighs 160 kg.

The bridge can be emplaced by a simple launching system, by armoured vehicle, or as external load by helicopter. Modular spans from 4 m up to 20 m (upgradeable to 28 m) are available. The closed roadway width is 2.75 m. Load class is MLC 12/14, although this is upgradeable to MLC 40. Military service life of the DoLB is 20 years with 3,000 MLC 12 crossings and 1,000 launches/retrievals.

Demonstration crossing of 20 m span DoLB by a KMW Mungo light vehicle (EADS)
1174394

Specifications

EADS Light Bridge
Dimensions: (trailer) 4.5 × 1.85 × 1.6 m
Weight: <4,500 kg

Status

Ready for production.

Contractor

EADS Deutschland GmbH Defence & Security Systems

General Dynamics European Land Systems - Germany (GDELS-G) Infantry Assault Bridge

Description

The former EWK[1] Infantry Assault Bridge is issued as a bridge set comprising seven 4.43 m long bridge modules, a roller block, swimmer float, stretcher adapter, anchoring rope and a transport pallet. Total weight of one bridge set is 460.5 kg, or 875.5 kg when packed on the transport and protection pallet.

A bridge set (without transport pallet) can be carried by eight to ten soldiers. The main elements can be coupled in any order with a complete 30 m span assembled by eight personnel in about six minutes. The bridge will support loads of 135 kg with a distance between loads of 10 m. Crossing capacity is 40 soldiers in five minutes.

For free-launch operations, the entire bridge is assembled and pushed across a gap using the roller block. When bridging dry gaps, which exceed a clear span of 16 m, a further bridge set is used as a counterbalance. When bridging wet gaps wider than 16 m, the swimmer float is placed at the end of the assembled bridge and the bridge is pushed across. The bridge can be launched in currents up to 2.5 m/s. Multiple bridges can be assembled.
[1] General Dynamics Santa Bárbara Sistemas SA of Spain (GDSBS), a subsidiary of General Dynamics Corporation of Falls Church, Virginia completed the acquisition of the assets of Eisenwerke Kaiserslautern GmbH (EWK) on 31 October 2002. As of 1 November 2002, EWK was renamed General Dynamics Santa Bárbara Sistemas GmbH (GDSBS GmbH). The company is now known as General Dynamics European Land Systems - Germany GmbH (GDELS-G GmbH).

A British Army GDELS-G Infantry Assault Bridge as a free span bridge (GDELS-G)
1139049

A British Army GDELS-G Infantry Assault Bridge configured with a swimmer float for the crossing of wet gaps greater than 16 m (GDELS-G)
1139048

Status

Production as required. In service with the British (40 sets) and Irish armies.

Contractor

General Dynamics European Land Systems - Germany GmbH

KMW F bridge

Development

Kraus-Maffei Wegmann (KMW) acquired the MAN AG industrial group's MAN Mobile Bridges (MMB) subsidiary in April 2005 for an undisclosed sum. MMB specialised in the design, manufacture and supply of military bridges worldwide, including Armoured Vehicle Launched Bridges (AVLBs) and floating bridges and the two companies had previously worked together for some years, especially on armoured vehicle launched bridges based on the Leopard 1 and 2 chassis.

Description

The F bridge (F - Framework), is a bridge system consisting of standardised components for building single or two-lane bridges with a maximum span of 70 m in 3 m graduations. The bridges can be installed temporarily or permanently.

F bridge components are constructed of St 52 grade steel and are joined together by high-strength bolts. Steel or wood can be used for the deck materials. Constructed bridges can be dismantled at any time to be set up elsewhere in similar or different combinations. The usual method of installation is to roll the bridge into position using a launching nose and a short cantilever section at the rear to carry ballast. The launching nose and the cantilever section use the same type of components as the rest of the bridge. All elements of the F bridge system are of such a size that they can be handled by standard lifting tackle and carried on standard trucks.

A reinforced version, known as the FT bridge, is available for use as a railway bridge.

Specifications

F bridge

Bridge type	Single-lane	Two-lane
Deck width:	4 m	6.5 m
Free span:		
(single storey)	44 m	30 m
(double storey)	61 m	47 m
(three storey)	70 m	58 m

Status

Production as required. Believed to be in service in Myanmar (Burma) and Ghana.

Contractor

Krauss-Maffei Wegmann GmbH & Co KG

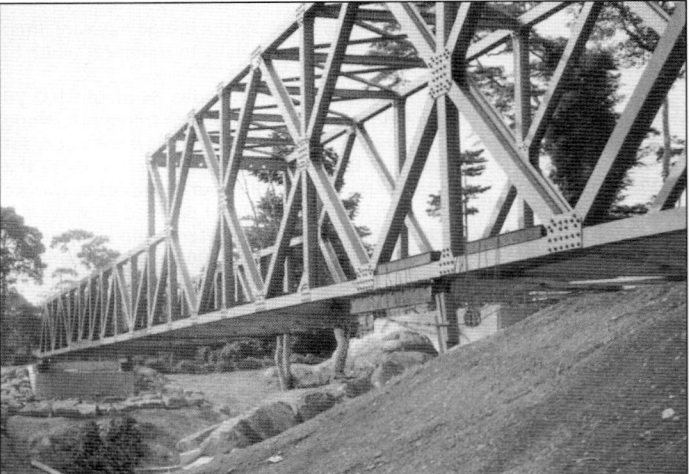

F bridge erected and ready for use (KMW)
1340292

KMW Short Trackway Bridge (STB)

Development

Kraus-Maffei Wegmann (KMW) acquired the MAN AG industrial group's MAN Mobile Bridges (MMB) subsidiary in April 2005 for an undisclosed sum. MMB specialised in the design, manufacture and supply of military bridges worldwide including armoured vehicle launched bridges (AVLBs) and floating bridges and the two companies had previously worked together for some years, especially on AVLBs based on the Leopard 1 and 2 chassis.

MMB Short Trackway Bridge MLC 30 sections, loaded for transport on the rear section of a Singapore Technologies Kinetics (STK) Bronco All Terrain Tracked Carrier (ATTC) (KMW) 0583270

Laying a MMB Short Trackway Bridge MLC 30 (KMW) 0583272

Preparing to lay the first trackway of a MMB Short Trackway Bridge MLC 30 (KMW) 0583269

A laid MMB Short Trackway Bridge MLC 30 with three trackway sections (KMW) 0583271

The Short Trackway Bridge (STB) was designed specifically to enable lighter weight vehicles to cross small gaps, ditches and gullies.

Description

The Short Trackway Bridge (STB) consists of identical trackways which are laid separately and then connected by detachable braces. Each trackway consists of one trackway girder with a fixed ramp, one hinged ramp and one connection bolt. The complete structure is constructed using extruded sections and sheets of a high-tensile aluminium alloy.

The Standard Bridge consists of one pair of trackways. It is 5.21 m long, can span gaps up to 4 m and can carry MLC 24 loads.

The Extended Bridge is 9.21 m long and can span gaps up to 8 m. This bridge is formed from two pairs of trackways joined by a connecting bolt and without any further reinforcement. This bridge can carry loads up to MLC 18 with a maximum crossing speed of 25 km/h.

On both bridges the distances between the trackways can be adjusted to intervals of 1, 1.2 or 1.4 m.

Standard and Extended Bridges can be vehicle launched and retrieved using a launching frame and a vehicle winch. The Standard Bridge can also be launched manually if bank conditions are suitable. Retrieval can be from either end of the bridge.

A single trackway weighs a maximum of 180 kg and can be carried by six personnel using integral carrying handles. Bridges can be transported on truck cargo areas or laterally attached to armoured vehicles such as M113 APCs.

Variants

MLC 30 Short Trackway Bridge

An improved MLC 30 version of the Short Trackway Bridge is in service with Singapore. The aluminium bridge sections are transported laterally on the rear section of a Singapore Technologies Kinetics (STK) All Terrain Tracked Carrier (ATTC), however the launching equipment can be adapted to suit other carrier vehicles.

In standard configuration, the MLC 30 Short Trackway Bridge can span gaps up to 4 m wide. An Extended Short Trackway Bridge can span gaps up to 8 m wide. Laid bridges may have either two or three trackways. Each trackway section weighs 125 kg and is man-portable.

Specifications - See table below

Status

Production as required. MLC 30 version in service with Singapore.

Contractor

Krauss-Maffei Wegmann GmbH & Co KG

Unit	Trackway	Standard Bridge	Extended Bridge
Weight:	180 kg	365 kg	730 kg
Length:	5.21 m	5.21 m	9.21 m
Max. span:	4 m	4 m	8 m
Track width:	600 mm	600 mm	600 mm
Width overall:	700 mm	700 mm	700 mm
Trackway height:	280 mm	280 mm	280 mm
Ramp slope:	1:4.5	1:4.5	1:4.5
Laying slope:	10%	10%	10%
Load class:	-	MLC 24	MLC 18

India

Manually Launched Assault Bridge (MLAB)

Development
The Manually Launched Assault Bridge (MLAB) was designed and developed by the Research and Development Establishment (Engineers) at Dighi, Pune. It is in service with the Indian Army as an assault bridge as well as a line of communication bridge and can be delivered in several bridging kit configurations to meet requirements.

Description
The MLAB is fabricated of a lightweight, high-strength weldable, self-ageing aluminium zinc-magnesium alloy capable of withstanding extremes of temperature and humidity. The heaviest component can be carried by a team of six personnel, while palletised loads can be configured for truck transport or for slinging under helicopters such as the Mil Mi-17. For vehicle transport, a standard 3-ton pallet is used.

The MLAB is a deck-type two-girder bridge system involving a fully modular, pin-jointed structure with inter-locking components, providing a 4 m-wide roadway. A standard double-storey bridge can bridge gaps up to 31 m (MLC 60). If longer gaps are encountered, this can be extended to 49 m using ancillary reinforcement equipment. If MLC 70 is required, shorter spans can be constructed.

A single-span MLAB is constructed using two parallel girders consisting of top panels, each 1.83 m long. With the addition of deck panels and bank-seat beams, bridges of MLC 60 at 9.8 m span and MLC 16 at 22 m span can be constructed.

By adding bottom panels to single-storey girders during construction, the girder depth is increased and strengthened to form a double-storey bridge, capable of carrying MLC 60 vehicles over a 31 m span or MLC 16 vehicles over a 49 m single span. A link reinforcement kit (LRK) can enhance the load carrying capacity to MLC 60 for a 49 m span.

Construction crew and times (MLC 60 bridge)

	9.8 m single storey	31 m double storey	49 m double storey with LRK
Crew:	10	30	40
Build time:	15 min	90 min	150 min

Status
Production as required. In service with the Indian Army.

Contractor
Ordnance Factory Ambajhari

Development agency
Research and Development Establishment (Engineers)

Israel

IMI RDB 11 to 62 m Rapid Deployment Bridge (RDB)

Description
Israel Military Industries Limited (IMI) has developed a lightweight, aluminium alloy 62 m modular Rapid Deployment Bridge (RDB). It can be transported by a fleet of 10 trucks and mechanically launched by a team of 12 personnel within 100 minutes. The RDB is capable of MLC 70 loads for tracked vehicles and MLC 96 loads for wheeled vehicles. The launching configuration uses the auxiliary bridge method. All launching operations are performed from the near side to the far bank. The RDB can bridge gaps of up to 60 m and has two trackways.

An early example of the Rapid Deployment Bridge
(Israel Military Industries)   1190256

Status
Exact operational status uncertain. A 34 m version is known to have been tested successfully by the Israeli Defence Forces.

Contractor
Israel Military Industries Limited (IMI)

IMI SPB36 sectional personnel bridge

Description
Intended for infantry use, the all aluminium SPB36 sectional personnel bridge is transported in nine 4 m sections and assembled on site by three personnel in 10 minutes. An earlier version was known as the SPB24 and used six 4 m sections. The bridge can be built to any length and as a floating bridge, for which floats and anchoring devices are required.

Each SPB36 section weighs 40 kg and is carried by two personnel using its retractable handles. When assembled, the bridge is 36 m long and can be launched across a gap by one person using a roller mounted on a small frame. The bridge has a handrail on each side and is only 980 mm wide. Stretchers can be carried across the bridge by placing them on a two-wheel bogie mounted on the handrails; the stretcher can then be pushed across the bridge by one person. When launching the bridge across water obstacles, a small pontoon can be fitted to the leading-edge. The SPB36 has been tested by the US Army.

It is possible to pack up to six bridge sections together with a launching pontoon for transport by truck or other vehicle, including a Jeep-towed two-wheel trailer platform.

Specifications
Weight: (each section) 40 kg
Length:
(complete bridge) 36 m
(section) 3.986 m
Width:
(overall) 980 mm
(walkway) 378 mm
Height: 750 mm

Dimensions packed
Length: 3.986 m
Width: 2.1 m
Height: 1.56 m
Crossing capacity:

Span	Personnel	Interval
36 m	3	17 m
32 m	3	17 m
28 m	4	11 m
24 m	6	4 m
20 m	9	2 m
16 m	10	1.5 m
8 m	close order formation	

Status
Operational status uncertain. Likely to be available for production.

Contractor
Israel Military Industries Limited (IMI)

Crossing an IMI SPB36 sectional personnel bridge
(Israel Military Industries Limited)   0007693

IMI TAB 12 AT 12 m, air-transportable Towed Assault Bridge (TAB)

Description
The IMI TAB 12 AT 12 m, air-transportable Towed Assault Bridge (TAB) is intended for bridging anti-tank ditches or other obstacles up to 10 m wide and can carry vehicles weighing up to 70,000 kg. The bridge was designed to be separated easily into two sections along its longitudinal axis for transport in a C-130 transport aircraft. It was also designed to absorb the loss of up to 50 per cent of its structural beams as well as its complete wheel and suspension system from mines or direct fire and still fulfil its MLC 70 mission.

IMI TAB 12 AT 12 m, air-transportable Towed Assault Bridge being pushed into position over a dry obstacle with front horns erected and pusher bar still connected to MBT (Israel Military Industries Limited)   1190257

The main body is constructed of four prestressed beams made of 2.2 mm steel plates. The upper surface consists of formed steel plates with anti-sliding elements. The front section is manufactured from steel bars which are extended to enable the bridge to reach the opposite bank of the obstacle when deployed for use.

The front section can be folded by operating a simple mechanism which is activated by the tank crew. Normally the bridge is towed into action by an M1 or M60 tank but many other types of tank can be used. The bridge is towed on four wheels on a single axle in the centre of the bridge. A coupling hook is also fitted for either towing the bridge or deploying the bridge when it is pushed across an obstacle.

In use, the bridge is towed to the obstacle with the bridge coupled to the rear of the tank. At the obstacle, the tank and bridge make a 180° turn ready for the bridge to be deployed in one of two possible ways. One is for the tank to reverse and push the bridge across the obstacle. For the other, the bridge can be uncoupled for the tank to make a further 180° turn and recouple the bridge to the front of the tank. This coupling operation is normally carried out some distance before the obstacle is reached. The bridge is then pushed across the obstacle. The bridge hitch is then disconnected from the tank using a mechanical device; early versions used a pyrotechnic disconnect.

The bridge is supplied with an adapter, which is bolted on to the tank's forward section, permitting connection with the bridge by means of the coupling hook.

Specifications
Weight: (total) 9840 kg
Length:
  (incl coupling hook and extensible front section) 19 m
  (bridge) 12 m   .
Width:
  (with siderails) 5 m
  (crossing) 4.2 m
Effective max height of obstacle: 2.5 m
Bridge classification: MLC 70

Status
Supplied to the Israeli Defence Forces and the US Marine Corps.

Contractor
Israel Military Industries Limited (IMI)

Italy

Drago modular mountain bridge

Description
Drago Engineering SpA were involved in the construction of light structures for over 40 years and produced a range of products including light modular bridges for use in mountain areas. The materials used for these modular mountain bridges are mainly light magnesium and aluminium alloys.

The modular mountain bridge could be constructed to accommodate three weight classes, MLC 5, 8 and 12. The bridges are built up from a number of 2.5 m span bays using tubular alloy components as the main structural elements. Deck baulks are added when the bridge structure is complete. The bridges can be constructed without recourse to special tools or equipment and it is possible to bring all the bridge components to the site using pack transport by animals or light vehicles. It is also possible to use many of the bridge components for other purposes such as the construction of aerial ropeway towers or observation towers and for the internal bracing of underground shelters and observation posts.

Specifications
Drago modular mountain bridge

Bridge class	5	8	12
Span of one bay:	2.5 m	2.5 m	2.5 m
Max span:	37.5 m	35 m	30 m
Width: (useful)	3.05 m	3.05 m	3.05 m
Height: (useful)	4.15 m	4.15 m	4.15 m

Bridge class	5	8	12
Length: (of longest element)	3.25 m	3.25 m	3.25 m
Weight:			
(heaviest element)	125 kg	125 kg	125 kg
(average weight/m)	470 kg	470 kg	470 kg
(bridge total weight)	19,700 kg	16,920 kg	14,000 kg
Useful deck surface:	114.37 m²	106.75 m²	91.5 m²

Status
Production complete. Believed to be in service with the Italian Army.

Contractor
Drago Engineering SpA

Japan

Bridge, Panel, Class 30

Description
The Bridge, Panel, Class 30, a modified version of the US M2 Bailey Bridge, was introduced in 1960. The main difference between the US and Japanese versions is that the Japanese components are smaller and lighter, facilitating handling and reducing transport requirements.

A typical example is the truss of the Japanese model which is 2.5 m long, 1.3 m high and weighs 222 kg compared with the US model which is 3.3 m long, 1.5 m high and weighs 262 kg. The Japanese bridge does, however, have a narrower roadway (3.4 m) and a smaller carrying capacity than the US M2 bridge. An MLC 30 bridge, which is assembled by a team of 40, is 25 m long and has a roadway width of 3.4 m.

The Bridge, Panel, Class 30 was originally manufactured by Kisha Seizo Kaisha Limited. This company was acquired by Kawasaki Heavy Industries in 1972.

Specifications
Truss panel
Weight: 222 kg
Length: 2.5 m
Width: 200 mm
Height: 1.3 m

Transoms
Weight: 241 kg
Length: 5 m
Width: 200 mm
Height: 250 mm

Stringers
Weight: 88 kg
Length: 2.5 m
Width: 0.6 m
Height: 100 mm

Status
Production likely to be on an as required basis. In service with the Japanese GSDF.

Contractor
Kawasaki Heavy Industries

Demonstration building of Bridge, Panel, Class 30 (Mitsuhiro Kadota)   0589868

Poland

DMS-65 heavy girder bridge

Description
The DMS-65 is basically a development of the Bailey panel bridge. It is normally built as a single-storey, through-truss road bridge, but can also be constructed as a deck-truss railway bridge. There are only five basic elements of the bridge which are carried in any suitable truck with a payload in excess of 2,500 kg. The DMS-65 can be assembled manually or with the aid of cranes and bridges of different lengths, with either single or multiple spans, can be built. The roadway consists of metal plates that can be covered with crushed stone.

Status
In service with the Polish Army.

Contractor
Polish state factories.

Bailey type panel bridges

Description
The British-designed Bailey Bridge was adopted by the US Army during the Second World War and the Soviet Union obtained some of these under the Lend-Lease programme. Some of these bridges may still be in service with former Warsaw Pact countries, together with local copies of the bridge. Poland is one of the countries that copied the Bailey Bridge with some minor modifications. This is distinguishable from the standard Bailey Bridge by the increased number of holes in the transom.

There are separate entries in this section for the Czech/Slovak MS-1 (SM-60) and the Polish DMS-65 panel bridges, both of which resemble the Bailey Bridge in some respects.

Status
In service with the Polish Army.

Contractor
Polish state factories.

Russian Federation

MVB rope-girder highway bridge

Description
This is a high-level bridge designed to span large water obstacles. The complete MVB bridge equipment set includes: five bridge frameworks, 42 m long; four intermediate piers, 10 m high; two bank piers, 5 m high; two ramps; one set of one-way footpath deck, 750 mm wide, plus all necessary installation equipment.

Specifications
MVB bridge
Capacity:
 (Tracked (T)) 80,000 kg
 (Wheeled (W)) 95,000 kg
Length: (less ramps) 210 m
Width: (decking) 4.5 m
Spans:
 (continuous bridge) 42 m
 (plate-girder bridge) 52.5 m
 (screw-pile bridge) 63 or 75.5 m
Underbridge clearance:
 (height) 10 m
 (width) 60 m
Weight of bridge equipment:
 (with rope system elements) 660 tonnes
 (without rope system elements) 635 tonnes

Status
In service with Russian Federation armed forces. Offered for export.

Contractor
Not known.

Agency
Rosoboronexport

PVM foot suspension bridge, LVM light suspension bridge and TVM heavy suspension bridge

Description
These suspension bridges were designed primarily for use in mountainous country and are normally transported by pack animals or, if the terrain is suitable, by motor transport.

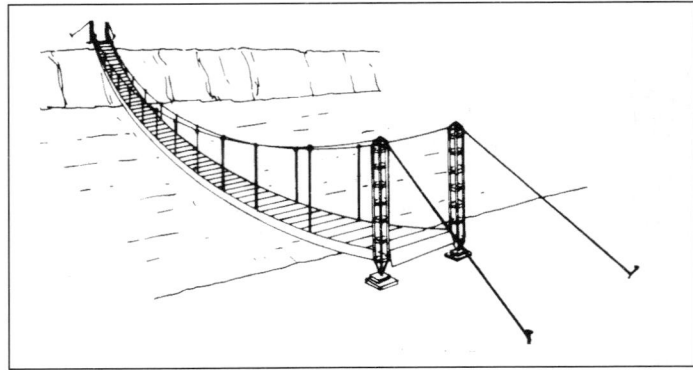

PVM foot suspension bridge   0511543

The PVM (pedestrian suspension footbridge) set contains sufficient components to construct either two bridges 60 m long and 700 mm wide, or a single bridge 120 m long and 700 mm wide. A team of 18 personnel can erect the former in two hours or the latter in three hours. The complete PVM bridge set weighs 4,360 kg and can be transported by 46 pack animals.

The LVM (light suspension bridge) set contains sufficient components to construct either two bridges 40 m long and 2 m wide or a single bridge 80 m long and 2 m wide. With a team of 27 personnel, the former can be erected in four hours and the latter in two hours. The complete LVM bridge set weighs 13,500 kg and can be transported by 160 pack animals, the maximum weight of each individual component not exceeding 50 kg. The LVM has a maximum-rated capacity of 2,000 kg, but the maximum axle load of any vehicle must not exceed 635 kg.

The TVM (heavy suspension bridge) is 60 m long and has a maximum rated capacity of 10,000 kg.

Status
In service with the Russian Federation Armed Forces.

Contractor
Former state factories.

Underwater bridge set

Description
This set consists of hollow pontoons carried on specially modified 6 × 6 3,500 kg trucks. The pontoons are estimated to be 8 to 8.5 m long and 3 to 3.5 m wide and are offloaded from the trucks by gravity (similar to the TPP and PMP pontoons). They are then assembled on the shoreline to form a ribbon bridge and brought into position by bridging boats. Bridge piers or pilings are then placed, after which the bridge is sunk into position by flooding the pontoons.

Status
In service with the Russian Federation Armed Forces.

Contractor
Former state factories.

SARM and SARM-M medium prefabricated road bridges

Description
The SARM and SARM-M medium prefabricated road bridges are sectional deck truss bridges made up of triangular and rectangular sections bolted together to support a roadway of steel deck panels. A single roadway bridge is 4.2 m wide with a capacity of 40,000 kg, while a dual roadway bridge has a capacity of 60,000 kg and is 7.2 m wide. Span lengths can be 18.6, 25.6 or 32.6 m.

A complete SARM or SARM-M bridge comprises three top-road frameworks with a rated span of 32.6 m and a width of 7.2 m, two piers 8.84 m high, erection equipment and transport accessories. Six 32.6 m bridges with a width of 4.2 m can be assembled and erected using a single SARM or SARM-M bridge equipment. Bridge components are carried on single-axle semi-trailers towed by any suitable 5,000 kg-rated tractor truck.

SARM and SARM-M bridges take a relatively long time to build compared with more recent tactical bridge designs. For example a 200 m bridge takes from 24 to 30 hours to construct. As the maximum weight of any individual component is only 4,400 kg, a 5,000 kg capacity crane is sufficient for construction of a SARM or SARM-M bridge. Other elements in the SARM/SARM-M bridge system could include USB-T or UZS pile drivers, crane trucks, gang saws and boats.

SARM medium prefabricated road bridge   0007695

Specifications

Bridge type	Single span	Two span
Load capacity:	40,000 kg	60,000 kg
Bridge length:		
(SARM)	200 m	100 m
(SARM-M)	252 m	143 m
Width:	4.2 m	7.2 m
Span variation step:	7 m	7 m
Pier height step:		
(SARM)	2 m	2 m
(SARM-M)	1 m	1 m
Weight of framework, 32.6 m:	31,600 kg	54,090 kg
Total weight of bridge equipment:		
(SARM)	252.21 tonnes	252.21 tonnes
(SARM-M)	350 tonnes	350 tonnes
Time to erect max		
length bridge:	24-30 h	24 h
(SARM)	24-30 h	24 h
(SARM-M)	up to 24 h	up to 20 h

Status
In service with the Russian Federation Armed Forces. Offered for export sales.

Contractor
Kashira Steel Structures Plant JSC

Agency
Rosoboronexport

BARM heavy prefabricated road bridge

Description
The BARM heavy prefabricated road bridge is used to repair or form high-level bridges on military standard roadways. A completed bridge has a load capacity of 60,000 kg, although special loads up to 90,000 kg can be accommodated.

The complete BARM equipment comprises two road frameworks with a rated span of 52.5 m and a width of 7 m, one intermediate pier structure 8.84 m high, installation equipment and transport accessories. The time required to install a BARM bridge is 24 hours.

BARM heavy prefabricated road bridge under construction (Ian Young)
0007694

Specifications
Load capacity: 60,000 kg (90,000 kg permissible)
Bridge length: 106 m
Max span: 52.5 m
Width: 7 m
Weight of framework, 52.5 m: 122.3 tonnes
Total weight of bridge equipment: 304.4 tonnes
Time to erect max length bridge: 24 h

Status
In service with the Russian Federation Armed Forces. Offered for export sales.

Contractor
Chelyabinsk Metal Structures Plant JSC

Agency
Rosoboronexport

MMP Small Span Bridge

Description
The MMP Small Span Bridge, sometimes referred to as the MMP Tactical Bridge, is intended for the rapid construction or repair of bridges over rivers up to 5 m deep and 180 m wide; total bridge length is 195 m. The MMP can also be used to create overbridges at road traffic intersections.

A complete MMP tactical bridge equipment comprises 18 prefabricated road frameworks with a rated span of 10 m and a width of 4.5 m, four ramps each 8 m long, two ramp sills, five intermediate piers Type 1 (from 4.5 to 6 m high), six intermediate piers Type 2 (from 3 to 4.5 m high), six intermediate piers Type 3 (from 1.5 to 3.5 m high) and installation equipment and accessories. Bridge components are carried on semi-trailers towed by KAMAZ-5410 series 6 × 4 tractor trucks or their current generation equivalent.

Once emplaced, the MMP has a load capacity of 60,000 kg, although special 80,000 kg tracked and 104 tonne wheeled loads can be accommodated with care. A bridge can be constructed at a rate of 20 m/h, with overbridges at a rate of 25 m/h.

Specifications
Load capacity: 60,000 kg (up to 104 tonnes permissible with care)
Bridge length: 195 m
Max span: 180 m
Bridge span variation step: 10 m
Width: 4.5 m
Height clearance: 6 m
Total weight of bridge equipment: 227 tonnes
Construction rate:
(bridge) 20 m/h
(overbridge) 25 m/h

Status
In service with the Russian Federation Armed Forces. Offered for export sales.

Agency
Rosoboronexport

REM-500 railway and road section bridge

Description
The REM-500 is a sectional railway bridge that can also be used as a road bridge with the addition of a wooden floor. It is employed over wide and shallow water barriers, closing breaches in railway lines and as approaches for floating bridges.

The bridge is composed of individual steel spans, 12.51 m long and weighing 10,700 kg, which rest on trestles that can be adjusted in height from 3 to 12.7 m and weigh between 5,000 and 7,000 kg. The trestles' feet are provided with large circular baseplates so that they will not sink into soft ground. The footers have an area of 7 m² and a ground pressure

REM-500 section bridge under construction   0511545

of 1.2 kg/cm². Both longitudinal and transverse bracing is provided where necessary. The bridge can be built across rivers with a maximum water depth of 7 m and a maximum water velocity of 1.2 m/s.

The bridge can have a single track of either European (1.435 m) or Russian Federation (1.524 m) standard gauge. The speed of a train crossing the bridge must not exceed 30 km/h, with a maximum axle load of 20,000 kg. The REM-500 can also be used in combination with floating railway bridges which use river barges as their floating supports. The bridge is constructed a span at a time, with each span and trestle positioned at once by an overhead gantry (called the SRK-2D) travelling along the completed spans.

Status
Supplied to Polish and Russian Federation Armed Forces.

Contractor
State factories.

Enquiries to
Rosoboronexport

Heavy barge bridges

Description
Former Warsaw Pact armies are known to have made wide use of heavy floating road and railway bridges, constructed from standard inland waterway barges of various capacities. Russian Federation forces would normally use standard 600 and 1,000 tonne barges suitably modified. These can be used to bridge a river in three different ways. The most common method is by placing the barges end to end with the vehicles crossing from one barge to another over the bows of the barge. A river 400 m wide would require seven 600 tonne standard barges that would take about 24 hours to position. Equipment required to position this bridge would include truck-mounted cranes, bulldozers, bracing equipment and three river tugboats, one with a 300 hp engine and two with 475 hp engines.

The second method is to connect the barges side by side with the barges resting in the direction of the current. Some of the barges used for this method have been provided with special supports which can carry an integral roadway.

The third method is to connect the barges side by side, but aligning them on a slant towards the current, with the vehicles crossing from one barge to another via the sides of the barges. The main disadvantages of these bridges are the length of time required to position the barges and the delay to other river traffic when the barges are in position.

These barges are also used for railway bridges, where the barges are used as pontoons. Finally, river barges have been used to construct heavy ferries pulled by tugboats.

This system was clearly conceived for use during the type of East/West conflict at one time anticipated across central Europe, therefore its use in current or anticipated scenarios is somewhat limited.

Status
Produced in most former Warsaw Pact countries using locally manufactured components. Known to be have been used in Hungary and the Russian Federation Armed Forces.

Contractor
State factories.

Singapore

Portable Assault Bridge PAB 15

Description
The Portable Assault Bridge PAB 15 was designed to be man-portable, carried by wheeled- or tracked-vehicles to bridge small gaps or other obstacles. It can carry loads up to 15,000 kg in any configuration.

The PAB 15 consists of two standard 4 m panels and one 2 m panel connector which can be coupled together to bridge gaps up to 10 m wide. For a complete PAB 15 the 2 m panel connector is placed in the centre of the two 4 m panels and a supporter unit is placed underneath. A 4 m panel can be used by itself to bridge small gaps. Two PAB 15 bridges are placed side by side to carry vehicles.

A complete PAB 15 bridge can be constructed by four personnel within 10 minutes.

Specifications
Panel:	4 m	2 m
Weight:	135 kg	62 kg
Length:	4.06 m	2.07 m
Width:	760 mm	760 mm
Height:	210 mm	210 mm

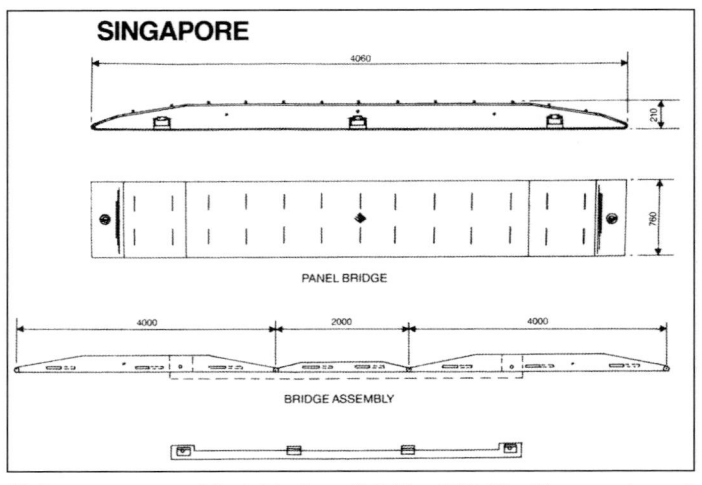

Main components of Portable Assault Bridge PAB 15 with supporter unit below (Singapore Technologies Marine)   0511553

Status
Production status uncertain.

Contractor
Singapore Technologies Marine

Sweden

Fast Bridge 48 (FB48) mobile bridge system

Development
The Fast Bridge 48 (FB48) is the result of co-operative research and development between the Swedish Defence Materiel Administration (FMV) and Kockums AB. This began in 1985, so a modern and efficient mobile bridge system for the Swedish Army could be designed. The bridge is constructed according to NATO standards and the 'Trilateral Design and Test Code for Military Bridging and Gap-crossing Equipment'. The design is patented. The FB48 has been thoroughly tested and approved by FMV throughout development and final design.

The first serial order for 10 FB48 (Kb 5) systems was placed with Kockums AB in October 1993; the order included an option for a further 10 to 20 systems.

The Fast Bridge family could be developed to include the following variants:
- FB56 - Emergency (and/or military) single-span 56 m MLC 50 bridge (now available)
- FB88 - Military double-span 88 mm MLC 70 bridge
- FB Multi - Military multispan MLC 100 bridge of unlimited length

In September 1996, Kockums AB, as one of two competing prime contractors, received an order from the US Army Tank-automotive and Armaments Command (TACOM) for the development of a Heavy Dry Support Bridge (HDSB). The HDSB contract was awarded to Williams Fairey Engineering Ltd, now WFEL Ltd. Full details of the WFEL Ltd HDSB (now designated as M18 HDSB) can be found elsewhere in this section.

Description
The FB48 is a combined tactical and line of communication bridge claimed to represent a new generation of dry support bridging and is primarily intended for the support of armoured and mechanised units. With a clear span of 46 m, the FB48 can take the load of all types of modern battle tank up to MLC 70.

The FB48 mobile bridge system consists of a 48 m long bridge with two additional 15 m ramps; the construction material is weight-optimised extra high tensile steel (1,100 MPa). Launching is carried out from one side and the bridge can be retrieved from either side of a gap.

A FB48 mobile bridge system emplaced and being crossed by a Leopard 2 MBT (Kockums AB)   1190259

A specially designed hydraulic launch unit, with a remotely-controlled crane, both powered by an integral air-cooled diesel engine with two separate hydraulic systems, is used to connect launching beam segments which are gradually extended over the gap to be bridged. When the beam reaches the other side, it is sustained on a nose support assembly ready for one launch crew member to cross to the opposite bank on a special trolley travelling along the beam. Bridge sections, ramps and other components are thereafter connected sequentially, using manually-operated push-pull rods and pushed out along the launching beam to complete the bridge. The total launch or retrieval time, day or night, is less than 75 minutes using a crew of seven personnel. The working area required for the operation measures 6 × 30 m (180 m²).

Maximum clear span, that is, between the innermost points of the supporting areas, is 46 m. A bridge length can vary from 24 to 48 m, made up of 8 m sections, so completed bridges may have lengths of 24, 32, 40 or 48 m. The usable trackway width is 4 m.

A single FB48 bridge section weighs 5,300 kg, measures 8 × 4 × 1.5 m and can be delivered fixed (4 m) or foldable (3 m).

The FB48 is designed to be transported on six standard non-specific trucks with a 12,000 to 14,000 kg payload capacity. Bridge length and load combinations are as shown in the table:

Bridge length:	56 m	48 m	40 m	32 m	24 m
Clear span:	54 m	46 m	38 m	30 m	22 m
Max load:	MLC 60/70	MLC 70	MLC 100	MLC 100	MLC 100

Specifications
Launch crew: 7
Max bridge length: 48 m
Max clear span: 46 m
Bridge section weight: 5,300 kg
Bridge section length: 6-8 m
Bridge section width: 3-4 m
Bridge section height: 1.5 m
Trackway width: 4 m
Max launch time: 75 min

Status
Production as required. In service with Swedish Armed Forces.

Contractor
Kockums AB Karlskronavarvet

United Kingdom

BAE Systems Modular Bridging System (MBS) - BR 90

Development
The BAE Systems Modular Bridging System (MBS), known as BR90 in the British Army, was originally developed by Thompson Defence Products (acquired by Rolls Royce in 1989 as part of its acquisition of Northern Engineering Industries Ltd), from 1995 Vickers Bridging, from October 2002 Alvis Bridging, and from September 2004, BAE Systems Land Systems (Bridging). It underwent an eight-year development programme following the production of concept demonstrators by the MoD UK bridging establishment at Christchurch.

In November 1993, MoD UK awarded a GBP140 million contract covering production for the British Army and the bridge systems started to enter service in 1996. The latest component, a motorised pontoon set, entered service in September 2004.

Following an international competition in September 2002 BAE Systems was awarded a GBP20 million contract to supply the Royal Malaysian Army with three sets of the latest generation 52 m MSB. All of these were delivered on schedule by January 2005 and have since been used in disaster relief operations in Malaysia. There is a total Malaysian requirement for up to 14 units.

The BAE Systems MBS is a comprehensive bridging system covering both tank-launched close support bridges and wheeled-vehicle launched general support bridges. The British Army BR90 system utilises a Unipower 8 × 8 high mobility wheeled chassis for general support bridge transport and launching. They also operate a variant for the transport of additional tank-launched close support bridges. The Malaysian Army systems will use a MAN 8 × 8 SX range chassis. BAE Systems has also carried out feasibility studies to integrate the MSB on a variety of other cross-country chassis including Kia, Mercedes-Benz and Oshkosh. Full details of the tank-launched BAE Systems MBS can be found in the Mechanised bridges section.

BAE Systems is currently carrying out upgrade and refurbishment work on British Army BR90 (MSB) equipment, at its Wolverhampton facility. In the longer term an upgrade is likely to take place of the current Military Load Class (MLC) 70 Tracked (T) to MLC 85 (T) to take account of the introduction of heavier vehicles into the British Army. Further in the future (2012-2018) it is expected that the British Army will fund a Mid-Life

Upgrade Programme (or Capability Sustainment Programme as it is also referred to) for BR90 that could include the replacement of the existing chassis, plus the introduction of the Axially Tensioned Long Span Bridge (ATLSB) reinforcement system which is already in service with Malaysia.

Description
The BAE Systems MBS is launched by the truck-mounted Automotive Bridge Launching Equipment (ABLE), with components transported to the bridging site on bridging vehicles. The ABLE consists of a truck-mounted crane and a launch mechanism. The launch is achieved by deploying a launch rail across the gap and lowering it on to the far bank. The bridge is assembled beneath the launch rail and winched across the gap. Due to the launch rails not being integral to the bridge structure they are recovered, thus allowing the ABLE to proceed to other bridge sites to carry out further launches. Recovery by ABLE can be carried out from either end of the bridge and ABLE can be used to recover any of the tank-launched bridges in the BAE Systems MBS.

The Bridging Vehicles (BVs) carry all the bridge components to the bridging site. They are fitted with truck-mounted cranes, which facilitate loading/unloading and assist in the launch of the bridge. The launch can be completed with only one crane operable, while the bridging vehicles can be used for carrying general cargo when not required for bridging purposes. The ABLE and BV are Improved Medium-Mobility Load Carriers (IMMLC) giving a good cross-country capability with 8 × 8 configuration, enabling them to reach most bridging sites accessed by AFVs. The vehicles have a high degree of commonality with each other and with the TBT used as part of the Tank Launched Bridge system (full details of which can be found in the Mechanised bridges section), although other vehicles could be used, such as the MAN SX range 8 × 8.

A British Army Bridge Set consists of 8 m ramp panels, 8 m panels, 4 m panels and 2 m panels to enable a bridge to be constructed from a minimum length of 16 m in 2 m increments up to 32 m. (Bridge sets can be produced to meet specific requirements.) The bridge is 4 m wide and, with in-fill deck units fitted, provides a continuous trackway over the width. A Bridge Set is carried on two BVs.

The 32 m General Support Bridge is launched, built and ready for trafficking within 30 minutes of arrival on site of the ABLE and bridging vehicles, including dressing with infill decks and kerbs which are added concurrently with recovery of the launching rail.

The latest addition to BR90 in British Army service is a motorised pontoon. Pontoons are transported on, launched from and recovered to, a special frame that can be carried by any standard DROPS vehicle. Use of these pontoons enables a bridge to be built rapidly between river banks over 60 m apart. The contract for the design, development, test and supply of the Two-Span Bridge Pontoons was placed in 2000 and the delivery and declaration of satisfactory in-service status followed intensive trials by

Work underway during a exercise launching of a 32 m General Support Bridge (Carl Schulze) 1296244

A 44 m Axially Tensioned Long Span Bridge (ATLSB) after launch and before recovery of the rail (BAE Systems Land Systems (Bridging)) 0101456

A 32 m General Support Bridge in place
(BAE Systems Land Systems (Bridging))   0101455

both BAE Systems Bridging and the British Army. In use the pontoons motor into position in up to 5 knots of current and are then anchored to provide a floating support pier for 62 m length of bridge. The pontoon is rated to take the weight of Challenger 2 with additional armour. The British Army has received four sets of pontoons in a contract valued at GBP9.6 million.

It is planned to develop the pontoon system into a ferry capable of transporting tanks across wider rivers or similar expanses of water.

Two Span Equipment options providing the flexibility for the bridge to be supported mid-span by an intermediate floating or fixed pier are also available for the export applications. An articulator panel and a rocking roller set provide both the support and change of angle at that support. The Long Span Equipment can also be used to reinforce one span of a two span bridge. The maximum Two Span Bridge length is 60 m with a fixed pier and 62 m with a floating pier. Two Span Equipment, including the necessary trackway to extend the bridge to 62 m, is carried on two extra BVs. Longer lengths and more spans are feasible for floating pier multispan bridges.

The Axially Tensioned Long Span Bridge (ATLSB) is formed by extending incrementally the GSB to 52 m using equipment which is deployed as part of the launch sequence. The ATLSB uses axially tensioned aramid fibre cables along its trackways so that a rigid, flat bridge can be built and trafficked. A 44 m ATLSB takes one hour from arrival on site, and 52 m takes 75 minutes.

The Malaysian Army order is for three sets of 52 m ATLSB. The composite launch rails for these will be developed and manufactured locally in Malaysia by CTRM Aero Composites.

Classification of the bridges is MLC 70 tracked and MLC 105 wheeled for all spans, including the 56 m Long Span Bridges. The bridges were designed using the US/UK/GE Trilateral Design and Test Code.

BAE Systems Land Systems (Bridging) has proposed that the bridges associated with MBS/BR90 could be configured as Airportable Low Profile Bridging having all the advantages of the MBS/BR90 but with a reduced load capacity, typically MLC 50 at 34 m. Launching and recovery methods could include existing MBS/BR90 systems but could be enlarged to include roller bed launching devices or even helicopter emplacement.

Specifications

32 m Bridge Set
Length overall: 32 m
Panels: 4 × 8 m ramp panels; 2 × 8 m panels; 3 × 4 m panels; 2 × 2 m panels
Ramp length: 6 m
Width overall: 4 m
Depth of section: 1 m
Max. span: 30 m
Weight: 18,900 kg
Launch/recovery times: 30 min/40 min
Dressing time: 10 min
Crew: 10

Long Span Equipment (current system capability)
Length overall: 44 m (using 32 m Bridge Set)
Extra panels: 16 m of panels; 2 × 4 m reinforcement panels; reinforcement anchorages; 2 additional launch rail panels
Width overall: 4 m
Depth of section: 1 m
Max. span: 42 m
Weight: (total, 44 m bridge) 31,093 kg
Launch/recovery times: 45 min/60 min
Dressing time: 15 min
Crew: 11

Axially Tensioned Long Span Bridges (ATLSB) equipment
Length overall: 44 m and 52 m (using 32 m Bridge Set)
Extra panels: 12 or 20 m of panels with additional launch rails; 2 × 4 m reinforcement panels; reinforcement anchorages; 2 additional launch rail panels
Width overall: 4 m
Depth of section: 1 m

Max. span: 42 or 50 m
Launch times: 60 min (44 m), 75 min (52 m)
Dressing time: 15 min
Crew: 12 (44 m), 14 (52 m)

Two Span Equipment
Length overall:
  (fixed pier) 60 m
  (floating pier) 62 m
Extra panels: extra 28 m of panels; 2 × 2 m articulator panels; 2 rocking rollers
Width overall: 4 m
Depth of section: 1 m
Max. span:
  (fixed pier) 58 m
  (floating pier) 60 m
Launch/recovery times: 60 min/90 min
Dressing time: 20 min
Crew: to be defined

Status
Production as required. Delivered to the British and Malaysian armies.

Contractor
BAE Systems Land & Armaments

BAE Systems Light Vehicle Bridging System (LVBS)

Development
BAE Systems developed the Light Vehicle Bridging System (LVBS) as a private venture and it was first shown publicly at Defence Vehicles Dynamics (DVD) in 2009.

The LVBS was developed to meet emerging user requirements, particularly those from current deployed operations that suggest an operational need for a lightweight easily transportable and deployable bridge. A key driving issue for this need, in Afghanistan for example, would be the numerous drainage and irrigation ditches that require crossing, the vast majority of these being less than 2.5 m wide.

Using existing limited infrastructure to cross such obstacles is predictable and can be hazardous. The use of an easily deployable bridge of the LVBS type not only reduces the hazard by reducing predictability, but also serves to enhance both strategic and tactical mobility.

Traditionally, bridging of all types would normally be positioned by combat engineers, but a major design factor of the LVBS was that it was intended to be carried and used by all personnel.

The LVBS could expand into a family of bridges, and during 2010 BAE Systems revealed details of two new light rapidly deployable bridges, the 3.3 m and 3.5 m Light Assault Bridges (LABs). Outline details of the LAB can be found elsewhere in this section.

Description
The Light Vehicle Bridging System (LVBS) is constructed from standard grade aluminium alloy and weighs 111 kg. Dimensions when laid are 3.5 × 2.25 m (L × W), giving it the ability to cross gaps of up to 2.5 m wide. The LVBS is capable of handling loads of up to 8,000 kg, at a maximum of 4,000 kg per axle.

The LVBS can be transported by truck, trailer or light vehicle, and dependent on space constraints can be transported either internally or externally. According to BAE Systems, the LVBS can be assembled by two people in less than five minutes, and disassembled in a similar period. In use, each bridge trackway is lowered into position and then joined by the cross bracing.

Status
Available.

Contractor
BAE Systems Land & Armaments

BAE Systems Light Assault Bridge (LAB)

Development
BAE Systems developed the Light Assault Bridge (LAB) as a private venture and it was first shown publicly at Defence Vehicles Dynamics (DVD) in 2010.

The LAB was developed to meet emerging user requirements, particularly those from current deployed operations that suggest the need for a lighter weight, easily transportable and deployable bridges. A key driving issue for this need, in Afghanistan for example, are the numerous drainage and irrigation ditches that require crossing, the vast majority of these less than 2.5 m wide.

Using existing limited infrastructure (which may not always have the capacity to handle larger/heavier vehicles) to cross such obstacles is predictable and can be hazardous. The use of an easily deployable bridge of the LAB type not only reduces the hazard by reducing predictability, but limits local infrastructure damage while enhancing both strategic and tactical mobility.

Traditionally, bridging of all types would normally be positioned by combat engineers, but a key factor of the LAB is that it has been designed to be carried and used by all personnel.

BAE Systems also offers the Light Vehicle Bridging System (LVBS), this of similar gap crossing capability to the LAB, but designed for lighter vehicles of the 8,000 kg class. Outline details of the LVBS can be found elsewhere in this section.

Description

The Light Assault Bridge (LAB) is constructed from standard grade aluminium alloy and weighs 200 kg. Dimensions when laid are 3.3 × 2.74 m (L × W), giving it the ability to cross gaps of up to 2.5 m wide. The LAB is capable of handling loads of up to 29,000 kg, allowing for wheeled heavy protected patrol vehicles of the MRAP-type to cross.

The LAB can be transported by truck, trailer or light vehicle, and dependent on space constraints can be transported either internally or externally. According to BAE Systems, the LAB can be assembled by four people in five to 10 minutes, and disassembled in a similar period. In use each bridge trackway is lowered into position and then joined by the cross bracing.

A 3.5 m length two-part version of the LAB is also available.

Status
Available.

Contractor
BAE Systems Land & Armaments

BAE Systems Land Systems (Bridging) Short Trackway Bridge

Description

The BAE Systems Land Systems (Bridging), previously Alvis, previously Vickers, Short Trackway Bridge has been developed to meet requirements for a lightweight portable bridge capable of being laid by manual means over short gaps. Designed to be carried by a variety of vehicles following minimal modification, the Short Trackway Bridge can be emplaced by a team of six in less than 15 minutes.

The MLC 30 Short Trackway Bridge is constructed using light alloy steels. The overall length is 5.2 m. As the bridge requires a minimum bank seat of 600 mm at each end, the maximum gap that can be spanned is 4 m. The bridge width is variable from 2.12 to 2.87 m in 150 mm increments, according to requirement. Optional kerbs can be added to the outside edges and in-fill decks can be fitted over the inter-trackway gap.

The heaviest bridge components weigh 140 kg, the total bridge weight being 700 kg.

Specifications
Load classification: MLC 30
Length overall: 5.2 m
Width overall: 2.12 to 2.87 m in 150 mm increments
Depth of section: max, 260 mm
Max span: 4 m
Weight: 700 kg

Status
Available.

Contractor
BAE Systems Land & Armaments

Bailey Bridge

Development
The Bailey Bridge was originally developed by Sir Donald Bailey, at the then Military Engineering Experimental Establishment at Christchurch and was widely used during the Second World War. In 1948, Thos Storey (Engineers) gained a licence from the National Research Development Corporation to manufacture and sell Bailey bridging components and equipment. In 1950 this licence was extended, granting exclusive rights to the patent, production and selling of the Bailey Bridge system. Thos Storey (Engineers) withdrew from bridging manufacture in 1994.

Description
The Bailey Bridge was designed as a universal unit-construction military bridging system, with the Bailey panel as its basic component. The great advantage of the system lies in its use of these standard interchangeable components, which, combined with the simplicity of design, enables it to be erected in a short time by unskilled labour under limited specialist supervision.

The Bailey panel, the basic component, is made of high-tensile steel. Panels can be connected together to form beams or columns. They are connected by panel pins and chord bolts to give a series of composite girders with varying strengths to meet loading conditions.

Using basic equipment, the maximum span is 61 m and the maximum military load is MLC 80. The bridge can be constructed in three widths, 3.28, 3.81 and 4.19 m. The bridge is normally constructed on rollers on one side of the gap and then launched into position using a skeleton, cantilever nose, which is detached after the bridge has crossed the gap.

Over the years, improvements have included a new steel decking which is quick and easy to erect, provides an anti-skid surface and, unlike the wooden deck, has a long life. This can be used with the standard, widened, extra wide or double width Bailey Bridges. Another development is the

The Royal Engineers constructing a triple-triple Bailey Bridge during a joint Polish/UK exercise Ulan Eagle in Poland (Shaun C Connors)   0589072

Launching of a triple-triple Bailey Bridge by the Royal Engineers during a joint Polish/UK exercise Ulan Eagle in Poland (Shaun C Connors)   1124749

Bailey panel, which provides an extra 40 per cent safe working shear load plus increased bending capacity and is completely interchangeable with the standard Bailey panel. Finally, a double width Bailey 7.23 m wide was developed to permit two-way traffic.

In 1991, a new decking system was introduced, comprising a main deck element, kerb units, transoms and fixings. The decking was designed in three weights: light, medium and heavy. Road widths are: standard, 3.285 m; single carriageway, 3.685 m; extra wide, 4.422 m; double wide, 7.37 m; and triple wide 11.055 m. New fixing systems make the decks easier and quicker to handle and install. The clamp design utilises a 'Halfen'-type channel system which allows deck elements to be placed in position with the hold-down bolts introduced afterwards. Normal installations require one bolt and clamp to hold down four deck units at the corners with outer edge corners needing only a single bolt and clamp. The units weigh between 309 and 339 kg.

In addition to being used as a road bridge, the Bailey Bridge has been widely used for other applications including rail and foot bridges, retractable lift bridges, derrick supports and mobile gantries.

Status
More modern designs have superseded the original Bailey Bridge concept and Bailey Bridges are currently being, or have been, replaced by some better-equipped armed forces. However, the Bailey Bridge (and its numerous copies) remains in service with numerous armed forces worldwide.

Contactor
The last manufacturer was Thos Storey (Engineers) who stopped manufacture in 1994.

Mabey Bailey and Panel bridging

Development
The Bailey Bridge was designed to take military traffic up to MLC 80 (T) standard and to cope with maximum single-axle loadings of 20,000 kg. Today, a bridge may have to be MLC 120 (W) to cope with the weight of a modern laden tank transporter should it need to cross. To meet such capacities the standard Bailey design would require extensive modifications.

Both Mabey Bridge Limited (previously Mabey & Johnson Ltd) and Thos Storey (Engineers) Ltd manufactured Bailey bridging for a number of years. They decided that improved Panel Bridge systems would be based on the Bailey concept, however they should also take advantage of modern developments in bridge design and steel technology.

A Bailey Bridge in use in Bosnia. Mabey Bridge Limited continues to supply Bailey and Panel Bridge components (Shaun C Connors)   0583257

Thos Storey (Engineers) Ltd subsequently initiated construction of the Acrow Panel Bridge, however the company withdrew from bridging manufacture in 1994. The intellectual property rights to the Acrow Panel Bridge now belong to Mabey Bridge Limited, which continues to supply components for the original Bailey Bridge, the improved M2 Bailey Bridge and the Acrow Panel Bridge. All three types remain in use with many armies worldwide. Complete bridges are no longer manufactured, Mabey Bridge Limited now promote its improved Compact 200 bridges and the Mabey Logistic Support Bridge for military applications.

Description
As with the Bailey Bridge, Panel Bridge decking can be either steel or timber, of varying load bearing strengths and in roadway widths of 3.43 m, 4.13 m, 4.84 m and 7.23 m, the widest of which gives two-lane traffic for standard equipment. Again, as with the Bailey, the Panel Bridge can be launched on rollers and constructed using unskilled labour and without a crane if necessary. All bridge components are designed to be readily transportable by standard military transport vehicles and bridges can be installed either for permanent use, or subsequently dismantled and stored for reuse when required.

Acrow panel equipment can be used more successfully than Bailey equipment to produce structures other than road bridges, for example rail bridges and gantries. In summary, the major advantages of the Panel Bridge over the Bailey design are improved bending-moment capacity; improved shear capacity; improved stability against buckling under load; increased efficiency of stress transfer; greater rigidity and stability overall; and a fatigue life approximately four times that of the standard Bailey Bridge.

Bridge widths

Roadway width	Type of bridge	Clearance between inner trusses
	Single traffic lane bridges	
3.43 m	standard Acrow Panel Bridge	3.76 m
4.13 m	extra wide Panel Bridge	4.78 m
4.85 m	ultra wide Panel Bridge	5.48 m
	Two traffic lane bridges	
7.23 m	double width Panel Bridge	7.6 m

Status
In service with numerous armed forces worldwide.

Contractor
Mabey Bridge Limited

Mabey Compact 200 Bridging System

Development
The Compact 200 Bridging System is marketed by Mabey Bridge Limited (previously Mabey & Johnson Ltd) primarily for aid and civil disaster relief application in non-conflict situations. The Compact 200 Bridging System is also widely used as a permanent bridge on rural roads around the world, in single- and two-lane configurations.

Spain has purchased Mabey Compact 200 bridging components and many Compact 200 bridges have been installed (by UK Armed Forces and others) to replace damaged or destroyed bridges throughout the Balkans, and more recently Afghanistan and Iraq. Many remain in place.

A 40 m Mabey Compact 200 MLC 80 bridge erected during 1996 by Hungarian engineers at Brčko in Bosnia. This bridge was replaced during 2000 by a permanent structure (Mabey Bridge Limited)   0100122

A 58 m Mabey Compact 200 TSHRH+ bridge at Perie in Bosnia. This bridge was launched by the Royal Engineers in March 1997, and de-launched by Romanian engineers in August 2002, to be replaced by a permanent structure (Shaun C Connors) 0552244

A US Army HMMWV crossing a 33 m Mabey Compact 200 DSHRH+++ bridge at Lendrum in Bosnia. This bridge was built and launched by the Royal Engineers in three days during September 1997 (Shaun C Connors) 0583256

Mabey Bridge Limited Logistic Support Bridge in use in Kosovo by the French Army (Shaun C Connors) 1185427

US Seabees erecting a 61 m Mabey Bridge Limited Logistic Support Bridge on the outskirts of Baghdad (Mabey Bridge Limited) 0595560

The Mabey Logistic Support Bridge is a Compact 200 bridge with components adapted for the military user making it more suitable for combat support or line of communications requirements. Full details of the Mabey Logistic Support Bridge can be found elsewhere in this section.

Mabey Bridge Limited also produce the Universal Bridging System which is used as a temporary or permanent civil structure. It is suited to two-lane highway configurations of spans and loadings beyond the capabilities of the Compact 200 or Logistic Support Bridge systems.

Description
The Mabey Bridge Limited Compact 200 Bridging System involves modular pre-engineered designs with supported clear spans of up to 61 m and up to MLC 110 (W) loading.

The Compact 200 Bridging System is easy to transport and can be assembled by hand if necessary. One or two roadway widths can be constructed.

When in position, Compact 200 bridges can be utilised for extended lengths of time, the main components being fully hot-dip galvanised and requiring less maintenance than comparable aluminium alloy bridges.

Status
In production. In service with Spain and used in Afghanistan and Iraq, and the Balkans by NATO. The bridge has been used in emergency situations in: Angola, Congo, Costa Rica, Ethiopia, Honduras, Indonesia (Asian Tsunami), Iraq, Lebanon, Nepal, Philippines, Sri Lanka (Asian Tsunami) and elsewhere.

Contractor
Mabey Bridge Limited

Mabey Logistic Support Bridge

Development
The Mabey Logistic Support Bridge is a further development of the Mabey Bridge Limited (previously Mabey & Johnson Ltd) Compact 200 Bridging System, this latest development being optimised for modern military use. The modular design of the Mabey Logistic Support Bridge provides a range of configurations that allows the bridge to be used throughout the support area, while also retaining the Mabey Compact 200's suitability for use in civil emergencies and other similar situations, where speed of deployment is vital.

Description
The Mabey Logistic Support Bridge can carry loads of up to Class 110 wheeled, Class 80 tracked and span gaps up to 61 m (200 ft), or more where the assembly of a multispan bridge is practicable.

For speed and simplicity, the number of different components used in the Mabey Logistic Support Bridge has been kept to a minimum and the bridge is normally built using available mechanical handling equipment. Where necessary it can be built by hand, and a 30 m bridge can be assembled and conventionally launched by 36 men in nine hours, depending on site conditions. Where cranes or materials handling equipment are available, the total number of man-hours to assemble a bridge is substantially reduced.

The bridge is generally constructed by the cantilever launch method without the need for any intermediate support. All connections are made on site using pins or bolts that are installed simply using hand tools, eliminating any requirement for pneumatic or electric powered equipment. All bridges are capable of being delaunched and when any deployment is complete the bridge can be fully dismantled for return to stock or for site relocation. If required, bridges can be left *in situ* as a permanent structure.

As with all Bailey-based variants, the Mabey Logistic Support Bridge system is made up of trusses of modular panels pinned end to end with transoms spanning between them, generally used to support a single extra-wide lane steel-decked roadway. However, a variety of different constructions can be achieved through the application of the general truss constructions and all main structural components are manufactured from high-quality steel, which is then hot-dip galvanised to prevent corrosion. A bridge requires minimal maintenance while in store or service and components are of rugged design and construction, but can be repaired in the field should they be damaged.

Decking is now supplied in steel as standard deck units are 1.05 × 3.05 m and are manufactured using robot welding technology to ensure accuracy. Deck units are manufactured to accommodate 1,000,000 cycles of loading and have a durbar finish that withstands both wheeled and tracked vehicles. Anti-skid coatings are also available for civilian traffic.

A ramp set is available for a variety of configurations, ranging from typically 13.5 to 18 m. Clearances and angles of approach have been calculated in order that all traffic, wheeled or tracked, can access the bridge. Stairs are available where ramp sets are used and 1 m wide footwalks can be attached in cantilever on one side of a standard bridge span.

The use of Mabey Uniflote or other pontoon systems further extends the application of the system to floating bridges, jetties, roll-on, roll-off (ro-ro) links and ferries. Full details of the Mabey Bridge Limited Uniflote System can be found in the Tactical floating bridges and ferries section.

Construction of a Mabey Bridge Limited Logistic Support Bridge
(Mabey Bridge Limited)   0583268

A Mabey Bridge Limited Logistic Support Bridge with a ramp system fitted,
that enables all traffic, including civilian, to use the bridge
(Mabey Bridge Limited)   0587658

Building time
(Logistic Support Bridge)

MLC	40 (T) and (W)	40 (T) and (W)	80 (T) and 110 (W)
Assembly method	hand	MHE	MHE
Span	30 m	30 m	39 m
Truss construction	SSHRH+++	SSHRH+++	DSHR2H+++
Manpower	36 men, 4 NCOs	18 men, 4 NCOs	22 men, 4 NCOs
Time to build	9 h	5 h	10 h
Approx recovery	14.5 h	7.5 h	15 h

Mechanical Handling Equipment (MHE) consists of two 25-tonne mobile cranes, plus one light or medium wheeled tractor. All times exclude all site setting out, levelling of rollers, assembly of ramps and fitting of any necessary footwalks.

Status
In production. The Mabey Logistic Support Bridge is in service with the British Army, Swiss Army, Slovenian Army as well as being in use with the French Army, Dutch Army and Swedish Army. It is also in service as the Spanish Army's Logistic Bridge, and is used and trained on by NATO as a Line of Communication Bridge (with emergency ramps) in Bosnia and Kosovo. The Mabey Logistic Support Bridge is currently in use in Afghanistan and Iraq, where a significant quantity of stock modules are held by the US Army and Marines.

Contractor
Mabey Bridge Limited

WFEL Limited Air Portable Ferry Bridge (APFB)

Development
To meet the increased mobility and flexibility demands being placed on its forces, the British Army issued a requirement for a new bridging system that could be utilised by light forces and that would (among other roles), on entering service, replace the current Class 16 Air Portable Bridge, full details of which can be found in the Tactical floating bridges and ferries section.

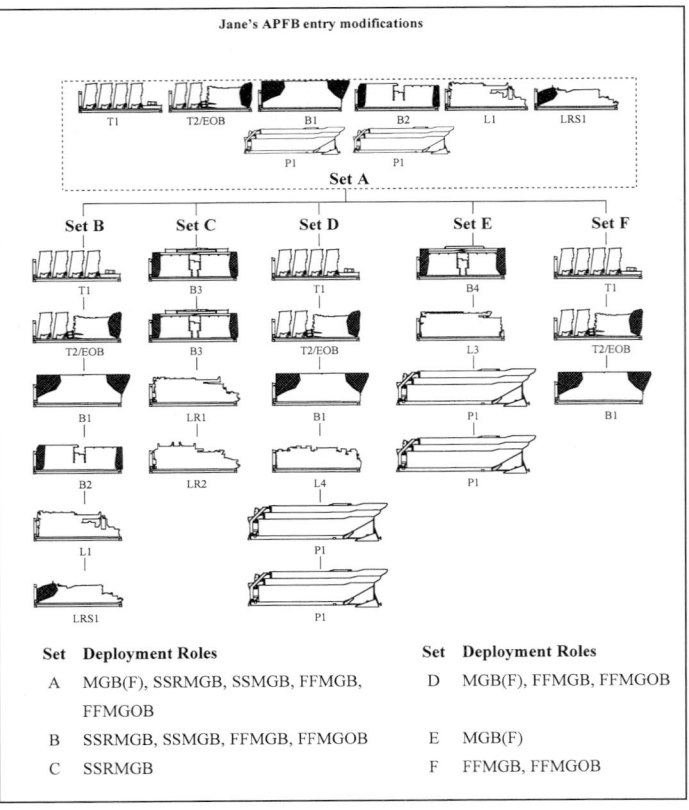

DROPS loads deployment roles (WFEL Ltd)   1190221

Set	Deployment Roles	Set	Deployment Roles
A	MGB(F), SSRMGB, SSMGB, FFMGB, FFMGOB	D	MGB(F), FFMGB, FFMGOB
B	SSRMGB, SSMGB, FFMGB, FFMGOB	E	MGB(F)
C	SSRMGB	F	FFMGB, FFMGOB

APFB Fly Forward (8-bay) being crossed by a Warrior Infantry Fighting Vehicle (WFEL Limited)   1047897

Unladen APFB trailer (WFEL Limited)   1047902

The WFEL Limited Air Portable Ferry Bridge (APFB) was selected to meet the British Army's requirement and 11 sets have been delivered.

The Air Portable Ferry Bridge has been developed as a complete bridging system that is capable of bridging both wet and dry gaps, can be used in over bridging roles and also incorporates a ferry system that is classified at MLC 35 (T) and (W). Full details of the APFB Ferry can be found in the Tactical floating bridges and ferries section.

The complete APFB system offers the following:
- APFB Fly Forward
- APFB Over Bridge
- APFB Reinforced
- APFB Ferry.

Unladen APFB trailer folded for transport (WFEL Limited)   1047901

A laden APFB trailer being transported underslung by Chinook helicopter (WFEL Limited)   1047903

A Leyland DROPS MMLC crossing an APFB Fly Forward (WFEL Limited)   1047904

Description

The WFEL Limited APFB is a deck type bridge of modular construction that is capable of being hand built by troops in a wide variety of climatic and operational scenarios. The overall design and construction of the APFB is based on that of the existing Single Storey Medium Girder Bridge (SSMGB). With the incorporation of relatively few new parts, existing MGB assets are given a new lease of life with extended capability.

The complete APFB system (Set A) is configured for storage and transportation using six standard and two dedicated pontoon DROPS flatracks. Each flatrack load can be transported using MMLC and IMMLC vehicles. Alternatively each load can be moved as an underslung load. While Set A provides all the necessary equipment to fulfil the full range of deployment roles, eight DROPS vehicles are required to move it. Should reconnaissance show that only certain deployment roles are required, the DROPS loads can be reconfigured to reduce the logistic requirement and five other configurations, as shown, are possible.

The deployment roles image illustrates the various DROPS loads deployment roles. The following abbreviations have been used: SS = Single-Storey: FF = Fly Forward: F = Ferry: R = Reinforced.

A Warrior Infantry Fighting Vehicle (IFV) crossing a 16-bay APFB Reinforced (WFEL Limited)   1047905

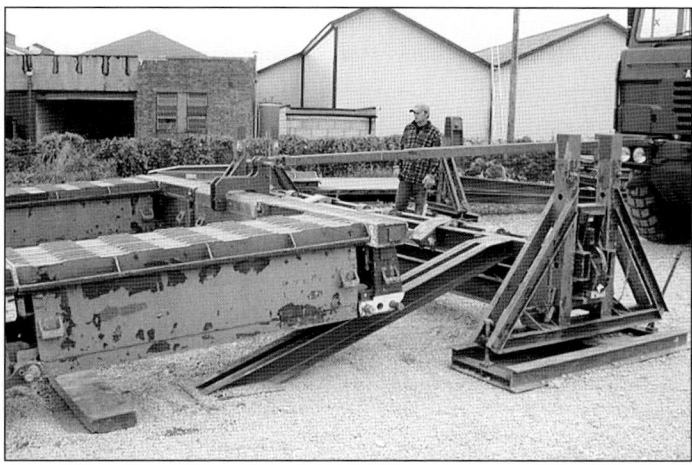

Deployment times for the APFB Reinforced have been reduced, compared to traditional building methods, by the introduction of bridge launching/recovery ramps and rollers (WFEL Limited)   1047906

APFB Fly Forward

The APFB Fly Forward spans gaps up to 14.5 m at MLC 35 and is optimised for use by light, fly forward and expeditionary forces.

In the Fly Forward role the bridge sections and launching equipment are transported on no more than six trailers, each towable by standard light vehicles. Four of the specially designed trailers, when folded, can be carried on a single DROPS flatrack.

All APFB Fly Forward components have been designed to be lightweight and fit into the available trailer space including a newly designed three-piece bankseat beam, two-piece roller beam and the approach ramps.

The APFB Fly Forward consists of two girders made up of top panels pinned end-to-end which are spaced and supported at each end of the bridge by bankseat beams. Approach ramps are fitted at each end followed by transverse deck units that fill the gap between the girders and, with kerbs added, a roadway of 4 m is created.

APFB Over Bridge

When traditional bridging infrastructure has been damaged or is no longer capable of carrying heavy traffic, an Over Bridge can be deployed allowing both civilian and military traffic to cross. The inclusion of wedges in key sections of the bridge ensures that the Over Bridge is raised sufficiently so as not to damage the existing bridge structure. As with the Fly Forward, the Over Bridge spans gaps of up to 14.5 m at MLC 35 and is optimised for deployment by light and fly forward units.

APFB Reinforced MGB

Introducing a Link Reinforcement Set to the APFB Fly Forward design allows its load capacity of MLC 35 to be maintained over gaps of up to 29.2 m. The Link Reinforcement Set consists of an adjustable kingpost with both anchor and tension links, which are used in addition to the standard reinforcement links, pins and tensioning assemblies taken from the Medium Girder Bridge (MGB).

The APFB Reinforced can be built while the reinforcement set is in contact with flowing water. By introducing bridge launch and recovery ramps and rollers deployment is also faster than traditional building methods.

APFB Reinforced also features a new modular fall arrest system that eliminates the risk of crew falling during construction. Operators wear safety harnesses attached by retractable lanyards to two lines suspended from each girder.

APFB Ferry

Full details of the APFB Ferry can be found in the Tactical floating bridges and ferries section.

Aid operations

In addition to operational military use, WFEL Limited is marketing the Air Portable Ferry Bridge as Disaster Relief Bridging for use on natural disaster relief and aid operations. The company states that any rapid response team could deploy the APFB from a centralised depot to anywhere in the world within 48 hours.

Specifications

Air Portable Ferry Bridge

	APFB Fly Forward	APFB Over Bridge	APFB Reinforced
Maximum gap:	14.5 m	14.5 m length (excluding ramps)	29.2 m
Width:	4 m	4 m	4 m
Load class:	MLC 35 (T) and (W)	MLC 35 (T) and (W)	MLC 35 (T) and (W)
Build crew:	13 (12 + 1 NCO)	13 (12 + 1 NCO)	25 (24 + 1 NCO)

Status

In service with the British Army (11 sets); deployed on current operations.

Contractor

WFEL Limited

WFEL Limited Axial Folding Bridge (AFB)

Development

The Axial Folding Bridge (AFB) was originally developed for the US Navy as a Lightweight Modular Multipurpose Spanning Assembly (LMMSA) for use in the support of amphibious operations. It was designed to provide a rapid means of crossing damaged sections of the US Navy's Elevated Causeway (ELCAS), providing a connection between ships and the causeway as well as for use during on-shore bridging operations.

The US Navy subsequently changed its requirements and only one example of the AFB was delivered. The AFB was further developed to become the M18 Dry Support Bridge (DSB) which is in current production for US Armed Forces.

The AFB is no longer actively marketed by WFEL Limited.

Variants

M18 Dry Support Bridge (DSB) (full details of which can be found elsewhere in this section).

Status

A single example of the AFB was delivered to the US Navy, no longer actively marketed.

Contractor

WFEL Limited

Launching an Axial Folding Bridge (AFB) using a roller frame and launching nose (WFEL Limited)   0007709

WFEL Limited M18 Dry Support Bridge (DSB)

Development

In September 1996, Williams Fairey Engineering Limited (now WFEL Limited), as one of two competing prime contractors, received a contract from the US Army Tank-automotive and Armaments Command (TACOM) for the development of a Heavy Dry Support Bridge (HDSB) based on the Axial Folding Bridge (AFB), full details of which can be found elsewhere in this section. The contract included the development of an automotive-based launcher for the HDSB and modifications to enhance the span load capacity of the existing AFB. For the HDSB requirement, the load carrying capacity of the basic 40 m AFB has been increased from MLC 70 to MLC 80 (T) and MLC 100 (W). In addition, the roadway width of the bridge has increased to 4.3 m.

Following the evaluation of prototypes, it was announced in June 2000 that TACOM had selected the Williams Fairey Engineering submission for the HDSB requirement. The initial contract was a five-year contract for 32 systems. The first system was scheduled for delivery for Product

Demonstration of the WFEL Dry Support Bridge (DSB) in South Korea (WFEL Limited)   1128261

Dry Support Bridge (DSB) in use in Iraq (WFEL Limited)   1128262

An Abrams MBT crossing a Dry Support Bridge (DSB) during a bridging demonstration (WFEL Limited)   1128263

Verification in November 2001, with initial operators testing and evaluation to be conducted at Fort Hood, Texas, from April 2002. The first unit was scheduled to be equipped in March 2003, but was equipped a month early in February 2003.

The equipment has subsequently been redesignated the M18 Dry Support Bridge (DSB).

In February 2005, WFEL was awarded a second five-year contract from TACOM for another 26 M18 Dry Support Bridges plus substantial options which will see the DSB remain in production for the foreseeable future. The total requirement could be for 130 systems.

In December 2006, WFEL completed a funded contract for TACOM to further develop the DSB from 40 to 46 m at a load class of MLC 80 (T). The contract included the design, manufacture and testing of the extended system, with the bridge proven in April 2006, following both working and proof-load tests, and the launching system in December 2006 following 1.5 times life fatigue testing.

System development continues with work on a floating version of the DSB underway.

Dry Support Bridge (DSB) launch vehicle (WFEL Limited)   1128264

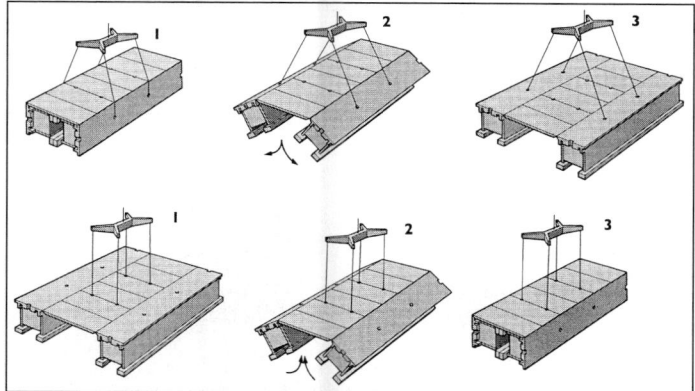

Diagrammatic sequence of how the modules of a Dry Support Bridge (DSB) fold and unfold (WFEL Limited)   0044083

Description

In general, the M18 DSB follows on from the AFB, brief details of which can be found elsewhere in this section. DSB modules are totally compatible with the DROPS and PLS load handling systems. Two DSB modules can be carried on a standard flatrack, and a complete 40 m bridge on four flatracks.

The DSB is transported as a palletised load by Oshkosh 8 × 8 HEMTTS and PLS trailers, or by service support units equipped with PLS trucks. The bridge transport HEMTTS are not bespoke for bridge carrying and may also be used as general purpose load handling vehicles. One bridge set consists of a launcher vehicle, six M1077 flat track loads of bridge components and one M1077 flat track load of launch beams. A 42 m MLC 80 (T)/100 (W) bridge, with a 40 m clear span, can be constructed and opened to traffic in less than 90 minutes by a crew of eight.

The development of the 46 m bridge system, which requires only two additional loads, increased spanning capabilities to 46 m at MLC 96 (W) while also enabling either two 30 m bridges or one 24 m and one 36 m bridge to be built through the incorporation of additional ramps.

The DSB launch vehicle was designed to meet US highway regulations and is therefore less than 4 m high, with a width of less than 3 m and a GVW of less than 40,000 kg. The launcher achieves its compact envelope through a unique fold and rotate system. With both the launching system and crane being demountable, the complete DSB system is transportable by C130 aircraft and is compliant with both GIC and AAR rail gauges.

The launcher is based on the Oshkosh M1075 (10 × 10) truck but may be re-engineered on to other manufacturer's chassis variants if required.

On arrival at site, the launching mechanism is unfolded to provide a stable and level platform for both launch beam and bridge deployment. The DSB launch system features an overhead launch beam which is sequentially built; using a crane mounted on the launch vehicle and boomed across the gap to support the bridge during construction. The Far Bank Support attached to the end of the launch beam is self-adjusting to accommodate the far bank ground conditions without the need for any soldier intervention. Bridge modules with decks and kerbs already attached, are assembled on the launcher and boomed across the wet or dry gap suspended under the launch beam. Upon completion, the bridge is lowered into its final position by a winch on the launcher. The launch beam is then recovered, the integral kerbs and bridge edge markers are deployed and lightweight approach ramps are fitted.

Specifications

Max span: 46 m
Span range and increments: up to 46 m in 6 m increments
Max load (MLC): 80 (T)/100 (W) at 40 m or 80 (T)/96 (W) at 46 m
Road width: 4.3 m
Bank heights: ±1:10 up to a max of 3 m
Bank slopes: 1 in 20

Crew: 8
Launch time: <90 min
Launch vehicle: 12 (L) × 2.98 (W) × 3.985 (H) m
Launch vehicle: (weight) 39,410 kg
Parallel module: (stowed) 5.95 (L) × 2.44 (W) × 1.1 (H) m
Parallel module: (deployed) 5.95 (L) × 4.3 (W) × 1.19 (H) m
Parallel module: (weight) 4,417 kg
Ramp module: (stowed) 5.95 (L) × 2.44 (W) × 1.1 (H) m
Ramp module: (deployed) 5.95 (L) × 4.3 (W) × 1.19 (H) m
Ramp module: (weight) 4,080 kg
End beam: 2.5 (L) × 0.375 (W) × 0.56 (H) m
End beam: (weight) 357 kg
Approach ramp: 4.09 (L) × 0.42 (W) × 0.19 (H) m
Approach ramp: (weight) 86 kg
Decking: integral
Kerbs: integral

Status

Entered US Army service in February 2003 and has been used in Iraq, Germany, South Korea and the US. Follow-on (second) production contract for a further 26 systems awarded in February 2005, with a total procurement objective being in the order of 130-150 systems.

Contractor

WFEL Limited

WFEL Limited Medium Girder Bridge (MGB)

Development

The Medium Girder Bridge (MGB) was designed and developed by the Military Vehicles and Engineering Establishment at Christchurch (MVEE(C)) (now QinetiQ) with production, marketing and further development undertaken by Williams Fairey Engineering Limited, now WFEL Limited. The MGB entered service with the British Army in 1971 and since then in excess of 500 units have been purchased by 38 customers worldwide.

The main advantages of the MGB can be summarised as follows: it is quickly and easily built by hand; little training is required; no site preparation or grillages are required; easily transported by road or air as palletised loads; of light and sturdy construction; has a multispan capability with span junction set; a portable pier set is available; can also be used as a ferry or floating bridge of unlimited length; has a load capacity of up to MLC 70 (T) or MLC 100 (W); and little maintenance is required.

Description

The MGB is a lightweight, easily transported bridging system which can be quickly erected by hand to provide a flexible and manoeuvrable bridging system covering the full range of military bridging requirements. The MGB has also been adopted by a number of governments for emergency bridging operations, following natural disasters.

Much of the success of the MGB lies in the material from which the components are manufactured. The then Royal Armament Research and Development Establishment (Christchurch) (RARDE(C)) developed a weldable alloy of aluminium, zinc and magnesium (DGFVE 232B)

MLC 70 Double-Storey MGB in use in Bosnia (WFEL Limited)   0007704

Training in the use and maintenance of the MGB (WFEL Limited)   1128267

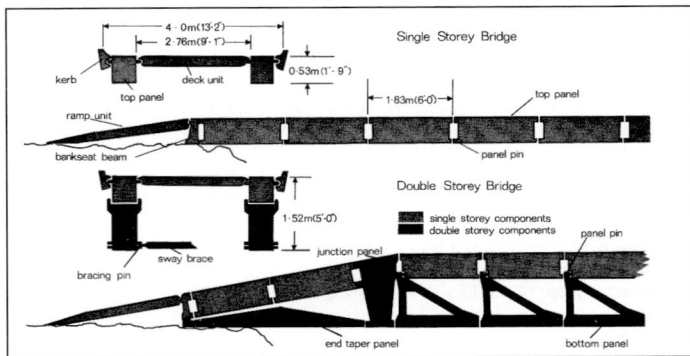

Main components of the MGB (WFEL Limited)   0511557

A Medium Girder Bridge with handrails and kerbs under construction (WFEL Limited)   1128269

Single-Storey MGB under construction in Oman during a British Army exercise (Ian Young)   1128273

An installed MGB with a reinforcement set fitted (WFEL Limited)   1128270

necessary to ensure both the strength and the lightness of the bridge. Seven major components are used in the basic bridge construction. Two of the parts require six personnel to lift; the other structural items require four. Deck units can be lifted by two.

The MGB is a two-girder, deck-type bridge in which the longitudinal girders with the deck units between, produce a 4 m wide roadway between the kerbs. Girders of top panels, joined at each end by a bank seat beam, form a shallow single-storey construction for heavy loads at short spans and lighter loads at longer lengths up to 22.6 m. A double-storey configuration using deeper girders of top and bottom panels, together with additional end-of-bridge components can be constructed for heavier loads over longer spans.

The MGB can be supported on unprepared and uneven ground without foundations. It is constructed on one roller beam for single-storey construction and on two roller beams 4.6 m apart in a building frame for double-storey construction. The ends of the roller beam can be adjusted in height within the building frame so that no levelling or other preparation of the ground is required.

All components of the MGB are transported in standard loads on a special pallet. When the vehicle and any trailer arrive at the bridge-building area, the pallet is attached to a stationary vehicle, or an alternative anchorage point and the towing vehicle is driven away pulling off the pallet, which falls on to the ground. Rubber buffers cushion the fall. A single 9.8 m bridge is transported on two pallet loads while a 31 m double-storey bridge is transported on 10 pallet loads. Any vehicle of suitable capacity may be used and special pallets for specific vehicles have been introduced.

Single-Span Bridging

The MGB can be built either in the single- or double-storey configuration. Single-span single-storey bridges can be used by MLC 70 vehicles at a length of 9.8 m and by lighter vehicles up to a maximum length of 22.6 m at MLC 16. Single-span double-storey bridges can be used by MLC 70 vehicles at lengths of up to 31 m and at increasing lengths for lower load classes, to a maximum length of 49.4 m at MLC 16.

The Single Storey MGB bridge is constructed using top panels that are pinned together to create two girders. These girders are then joined at each end by a bankseat beam to create a rigid framework. In the Double Storey MGB configuration, the girders are made up of top and bottom panels with junction panels and end taper panels forming the sloping end of the bridge. Ramp, deck and kerb units complete the construction in both configurations. Additional walkways are available if required.

Single-span bridges are launched using a centrally-mounted launching nose made up of 3 m sections. During launching, the bridge is supported on roller beams at the home bank and a roller at the far bank. Single-Storey MGB are launched using one roller beam, supported on base plates while

the Double-Storey uses two. Hydraulic jacks at each end of the roller beams lower the bridge onto each bank after construction. It is possible to launch Single-Storey MGBs over short gaps simply by pushing them off the near bank roller beam.

Reinforcement Set

This set extends the single-span capability of the MGB to MLC 60 at 49.4 m and MLC 70 at 45.7 m. It complements the capability of the MGB pier and span junction equipment as it can be used in terrain where deep valleys make it impractical to use piers. The set contains all the additional components required for use with normal double-storey bridge sets to construct a length of reinforced MLC 60 MGB from 32.9 to 49.4 m. More recent reinforcement sets provide a capability of MLC 70 at a span of 49.4 m. The set consists of reinforcing links 3.66 m long (with one pair of links 1.83 m long to provide the greatest range of spans). Links are connected to form a pair of chains, one beneath each bridge girder. Links are connected to bottom panels at the ends of the bridge by an anchorage assembly. The links are positioned 2 m below the bridge by reinforcing

A MACH MGB with reduced slope End of Bridge being crossed by a Challenger 1 MBT (WFEL Limited) 0007705

A Multispan MGB in place (WFEL Limited) 1128272

A MACH MGB under construction (WFEL Limited) 1128271

posts which enable the system to be tensioned towards a vertical position by Tirfor cable jacks. The reinforcing is added by an extra party of eight personnel while the bridge is being constructed by the normal team of 24 personnel.

The reinforcement set is in service with the British Army, US Army and Marine Corps and 16 other countries.

Reduced Slope End of Bridge
The standard slope of a Double-Storey MGB End of Bridge is 1:5. A reduced slope can be desirable when a bridge is being used in a line of communication role and thus by second echelon vehicles with longer wheelbases and lower ground clearances. For this purpose, an End of Bridge with a slope of 1:10 is available with an overall end of bridge length of 4.3 m, as opposed to the normal 3.1 m.

Span Junction Set
The basic Single-Span MGB can be given a multispan capability by the use of the MGB span junction set. This equipment enables bridges, typically up to 76 m, to be constructed at MLC 70 load capacity to be hand-built over most fixed or floating supports, existing or improvised.

The span junction set consists of span junction posts pinned to top and bottom panels. The span junction posts are themselves pinned together at the top and hinged by an articulator connected to the lower half of the span junction posts. A span junction link is fitted to join the bottom chords of the junction post to permit movement over rollers during launching. After launching, the junction link is removed to allow articulation of the junction posts. The other main component is the capsill. This is a beam to which

rocking rollers incorporating bridge bearings can be pinned. The capsill fitted with rocking rollers can be used on top of a pier to carry the bridge during launching or in the MGB adjustable roller beam support to form the heavy-duty Capsill Roller Beam (CRB) required when launching most multispan bridges.

Portable Pier Set
The Portable Pier Set provides the MGB with its own two-legged pier which can be assembled during the building of the bridge. The legs pass through housings at each end of a pier beam. The legs are constructed in 3 m sections and piers up to 12 m in height can be used in dry gaps and wet gaps with current speeds of up to 5.5 m/s.

The pier beam with housing, leg base section and one standard leg section at each end is preassembled and then pinned to the span junction post on the home bank and launched with the bridge. Once the bridge is in position, the adjustable braces are used to set the pier beam vertical before the legs are lowered and any additional leg sections are added. The pier components are also transportable on the standard MGB pallet, the heaviest component weighing 408 kg.

Multispan
Using the MGB portable pier set for multispan bridges, the piers can be launched with the bridge by temporarily placing the first pier in position as the next is brought up, then moving the piers successively by booming the bridge back and forward.

The span junction components allow double-storey floating bridges of any length to be constructed on virtually any type of floating support which has sufficient buoyancy.

The articulation provided by the span junction bay and the use of long landing bays, means that the MGB is the only modern military bridge equipment that can be used in a situation where bank heights range from 0 to 5 m. Even this range can be extended to 6 m if the MGB portable pier is used to form trestle bays.

Floating MGB/MGB Ferry/MGB Pontoon
Full details of this can be found in the Tactical floating bridges and ferries section.

MACH MGB
The Mechanically Aided Construction by Hand (MACH) was introduced to meet the reduced manning requirements of modern armed forces. With a minimal purchase of additional components, the normal MGB set can be held as part-assembled modules and constructed using a suitable crane or Crane Attachment Lorry-Mounted (CALM). The normal MGB team on an operational site can be reduced from 1 + 24 to 1 + 14 (optimum) or a minimum of 1 + 8.

Ski Jump for V/STOL Aircraft
The components of the MGB readily adapt to the Ski Jump profile when raised at one end. The ramp surface comprises three MGB single-storey girders supporting MGB deck units between them. Outrigger units provide a total ramp width of 10 m.

Rebuild Programme
US Army MGBs will remain in service for the foreseeable future. Following the introduction of the Dry Support Bridge (DSB) the US Army has formed Bridging Companies containing both MGB and DSB capabilities. Worn MGB sets can be returned to WFEL Limited in the UK for a complete refurbishment and rebuilding programme.

Specifications
Bridge parts

NATO stock number	Service designation	Unit weight
8714	Top panel	175 kg
8710	Bottom panel	197 kg
8713	Junction panel	182 kg
8611	End taper panel	272 kg
8687	Bankseat beam	258 kg
8723	Ramp unit	120 kg
8698	Deck unit	74 kg

Bridge lengths and load classification

Load class	Single-Storey		Double-Storey	
MLC	Bays	Span	2 ends + bays	Span
100 (W)	5	9.8 m	10	27.4 m
70 (T)	5	9.8 m	12	31.1 m
60	5	9.8 m	13	32.9 m
50	5	9.8 m	14	34.8 m
40	6	11.6 m	16	38.5 m
30	8	15.2 m	18	42 m
24	9	17.1 m	20	45.7 m
20	10	19.0 m	21	47.6 m
16	12	22.6 m	22	49.4 m

MGB configurations

Type	Length	Class	Building party	Building time	Transport in 4,000 kg pallet loads
Single-storey	9.8 m	70	9	15 min	2
	22 m	16	17	30 min	5
Double-storey	31 m	70	25	45 min	10
	49 m	16	25	1 h 20 min	16
2-span + pier	51 m	60	40	3 h	20
3-span + piers	76 m	60	40	6 h	27
Reinforcing kit					
Long Post	45.8 m	70	32	2 h	18
	49.4 m	60	32	2 h	18
Short Post	49.4 m	70	32	2 h	18
Single-storey floating bridge	any	60	32+	dependent on length	dependent on length
Double-storey floating bridge	any	70	40+	dependent on length	dependent on length

The load class (MLC) equates to a multi-axled wheeled vehicle of about the same weight in tonnes as the load class and, to a tracked vehicle of weight less than the load class (about six tonnes less for MLC 60). The exact load class of a vehicle depends on axle spacing, wheel loadings, track length and so on.

Span junction set

NATO stock number	Service designation	Unit weight
8159	Post span junction	260 kg
8157	Articulator, hydraulic	172 kg
8153	Capsill bridging	160 kg
8154	Roller assembly, rocker bearing	111 kg
8125	Beam, pier, half-section	445 kg
8123	Housing, pier leg	272 kg
8122	Pier leg, base section	162 kg
8121	Pier leg, standard section	208 kg
8119	Beam, grillage, pier	82 kg
8118	Sleeper pier	64 kg

Approximate weight of portable pier in bridge with length 12.2 m is 4,026 kg.

Status
In production. Supplied to Australia (LOT review increased LOT until 2018), Brunei, Canada, Denmark, Germany, Ghana, India, Iraq (present status uncertain), Ireland, Italy, Jordan, Kenya, South Korea, Malaysia, Morocco, Netherlands, New Zealand, Nigeria, Pakistan, Peru, Philippines, Singapore, South Africa, Sweden, Switzerland (Festbrücke 69), Tanzania, Thailand, UK, US (over 100 sets delivered to the US Army and Marine Corps), Venezuela and Zambia.

Contractor
WFEL Limited

United States

Acrow military bridges

Development
Acrow Corporation is a steel bridging company that has been trading for over 50 years. The company's prime business is the engineering, manufacturing and supply of prefabricated modular steel bridges for emergency, temporary detour, and permanent applications. The product line of steel bridges includes: Acrow Panel bridges; pedestrian bridges (modular or fixed length trusses); beam bridges (vehicle or pedestrian); movable bridges (vertical lift, bascule, retractable or swing); pipe bridges; falsework and formwork; Superprop shoring systems; heavy haul bridges; marine roll-on/roll-off ramps and railway bridges.

The Acrow Military Bridge is an adaptation of the Acrow 700XS Panel Bridging system.

A number of armed forces and governmental organisations have purchased or standardised on Acrow bridging, and these are known to include Australia, Canada, Colombia, Pakistan, United Nations (UN) and the US.

In 1995, the Canadian Department of National Defense adopted the Acrow Military Bridge as a replacement for its time-served Bailey bridges; 14 sets were purchased.

During 2004, the Australian Department of Defence standardised on the 700XS Panel bridge to meet their Land 139 fixed modular bridge requirement. The contract was signed in March 2004 and encompassed

Acrow 700XS Panel Bridge being assembled (Acrow)   0587591

Acrow 700XS Panel Bridge being assembled in Honduras by the USMC (Acrow)   0587597

the supply of 10 × 51 m Commercial-off-the-Shelf single-lane Fixed Modular Bridges (FMB), along with three two-lane upgrade kits, for delivery between September 2007 and May 2007. All have been upgraded to Military Load Classification (MLC) 80 Tracked and MLC100 Wheeled. The project is now effectively completed with the bridge successfully introduced into service.

During 2005, Acrow became the prime supplier of bridges to US Forces Korea, and between 2009 and 2012 the company will supply both dry and floating bridges to replace current in-service Bailey and other types of line of communication bridges.

Description
The Acrow Military Bridge uses mainly standard Acrow Panel Bridging system components, but with the introduction of certain custom components to enhance the systems' operational effectiveness as a rapidly deployed line of communication bridge for both military applications and disaster relief.

Military-specific modifications to the standard 700XS bridging system include allowing the use of pins, bolts, carrying bars, speciality tools, modular abutments and jacking pads and ramps. Hand construction is possible, steel or timber decking is available, deployment time is improved, and the use of sloped ramps to facilitate vehicle access from bearing seat elevation without the need for ballast walls.

The standard design criteria is for MLC60, although up to MLC110 is possible for spans of up to 76 m.

Bridges supplied to Australia to meet Land 139 (Enhanced Bridging: Phase 1 - Fixed Modular Bridge) are to replace Bailey bridges and each have a single span of 51.82 m and are complete with 10 m tall piers and other associated equipment.

Status

In production. In service with Australia, Bangladesh (via the UN), Canada, Columbia, Pakistan, United Nations (UN), the United States and possibly other undisclosed armed forces and governmental agencies.

Contractor

Acrow Corporation of America

M2 Bailey Bridge

Description

The M2 Bailey Bridge was developed by the US Army Research and Development Laboratories. It has been well proven both as a tactical and line of communication bridge and is capable of carrying heavy traffic loads. It is used for both temporary and permanent applications. In emergencies, it can be open to traffic in one to three days.

The M2 Bailey Bridge is an all-purpose prefabricated steel panel bridge designed for portability and speed of erection under adverse conditions. Optimum spans are 12.2 to 61 m. Width is 3.809 m between steel kerbs and 4.343 m between trusses. The components are manufactured in fixtures to ensure accuracy and interchangeability. The heaviest component weighs 281 kg.

The Bailey roadway is supported between two trusses or multiple-truss girders. It consists of longitudinal runner planks over transverse planks (chess) laid over steel stringers supported by floorbeams (transoms) which rest on and are clamped to truss bottom chords. Steel kerbs secure the chess to the stringers. The basic truss element is the panel that is 3.048 m long, 1.448 m deep and 165.1 mm wide. Pin-connected end to end, trusses of any length are formed. Where strength exceeding that of single trusses is needed, multiple-truss girders can be assembled with either two or three panels side by side in single-, double- or triple-storey heights. End ramps extend the deck 3.048 m on to the approach runway.

Bailey truss panels, end posts, transoms and ramps are of low-alloy high-tensile steel having a yield point of 3,515 kg/cm^2 and an ultimate strength of 4,921.7 kg/cm^2.

The cantilever method of erection is accomplished without falsework. The bridge is assembled on stationary rollers and then pushed or pulled across the gap. A skeleton-launching nose is assembled from standard bridge components and fixed to the leading end of the bridge. The nose precedes the leading end of the bridge while the bridge proper, acting as a counterweight, enables the nose to reach and land on rollers on the far bank. The bridge is then rolled into position, the nose is removed and the span is lowered on to its bearings. A 24.4 m double-truss bridge has been completed in less than 40 minutes in competitive trials.

There are approximately 15 major components in an average Bailey Bridge and about 50 components, fittings, accessories, special items and tools are available.

Bailey Bridges Inc now offers a two-lane upscaled version of the original M2 Bailey Bridge.

Specifications

Length of single span:
(min) 9.144 m
(max) 61 m
Width of roadway: 3.809 m

Status

Available. In service with the US Army (to be replaced) and numerous other armed forces.

Supplier

Bailey Bridges Inc

BRIDGING BOATS

Australia

Bridge Erection Propulsion Boat (BEPB)

Development
Australia's Defence Materiel Organisation (DMO) Project MINCS(L) 5.11 acquired 24 bridge erection and propulsion boats (BEPBs) and associated equipment for the Australian Army. The requirement was identified in 2000 and commenced in 2002 with an initial Request for Tender. The procurement was based on an open tender for the development of a trial/prototype platform, and at DMO discretion, the manufacture and production of the remaining 23 BEPBs to agreed specification.

At least two companies were shortlisted for the requirement (ADI - now Thales Australia - and Birdon Marine), with the contract awarded to Birdon Marine in April 2003. The two-stage contract included a prototype boat and transportation cradle with limited integrated logistics support package, followed by 23 boats, cradles, equipment, maintenance training and a three-year maintenance programme with the option to extend for the equipment procured.

Following trials of the prototype, a final design incorporating some modifications was developed through a number of contract change proposals. These amendments brought the contracted price to AUD15.6 million (initial contract price was AUD13.9 million). Deliveries were progressive, with the final boat introduced into service in August 2005. Each Australian Army Combat Engineer Regiment received five boats; the School of Military Engineering received five boats, with the remaining four boats being spare/rotational stock.

In service the BEPB replaced a fleet of boats that had been procured in 1969 and had reached the end of their viable service life.

Description
The Bridge Erection Propulsion Boat (BEPB) is based on the Bridge Erection Boat MB 3 (M-Boot 3), designed by Schottel and in service with the German and other armed forces. Full details of the MB 3 can be found elsewhere in this section.

The hull is lightweight aluminium and a forward-mounted semi-enclosed cabin provides the crew with weather protection.

The BEPB is powered by twin Cummins B5.9 water-cooled diesel engines, each operating a Schottel Pump-Jet for propulsion and manoeuvring. The switch from KHD (Deutz) air-cooled to Cummins water-cooled power units is the major change between the BEPB and the MB 3, these mounted centrally so that the operator has all-round access on the deck. There are a number of other smaller design changes that contribute to improved usability and operator safety, and generally upgrade the overall design of the boat.

The Schottel Pump-Jets used are the latest version of the SPJ 55 M, the SPJ 55 MR, developed by Schottel during 2002-03 and in conjunction with the German military. Compared with the earlier model, the SPJ 55 MR shows a 15 per cent increase in bollard pull.

The use of Pump-Jets fitted flush to the lower hull allows for operation of the BEPB in water 400 mm deep when fully laden and equipped.

Pump-Jet propulsion operates on the principle of a centrifugal pump. An impeller sucks in water from under the hull and forces it into a pump housing. The outlet nozzles are fitted in the bottom plate, making it possible for the jet to be installed in a flat-bottomed hull such as the BEPB. The Pump-Jet can be rotated through 360 degrees, providing full thrust in all directions and ensuring excellent manoeuvring performance, including the ability to rotate within the length of the craft.

The primary role of the BEPB is to build floating bridges and ferries.

Status
Production as required. In service with the Australian Army (24).

Contractor
Birdon Marine Pty Ltd

Australian Army Bridge Erection Propulsion Boat (BEPB)
(Australian DoD)   1186202

Belgium

Advanced Bridge Erection Boat (ABEB)

Description
In mid-1986, it was announced that a contract to supply FSB erection boats for the Belgian Army had been won by Meuse et Sambre SA, a member of the Belgian Shipbuilders Corporation NV. The boat involved was the Advanced Bridge Erection Boat (ABEB), which may also be used as a light tug, pusher, personnel or cargo transport, or as an assault craft.

The ABEB hull form has a moderate deep vee, a hard chine and spray deflection rails. The 7.76 m long hull form offers a high planing speed coupled with stability. The craft is configured such that flooding any one compartment will not affect the boat's ability to stay afloat and upright. A large working deck is provided aft and projects over the propulsion nozzles to provide them with protection. Draught is 530 mm.

The propulsion systems are placed amidships in two separate compartments. Should either one of these compartments flood, forcing an engine shutdown, the craft will still be able to operate at reduced power. The main engines are two Deutz BF 6 L 913 C air-cooled diesels with each engine coupled to a resiliently mounted Twin Disc MG 506 reverse/reduction gearbox unit. Two KaMeWa 32 S62/6 water-jet units are driven by a shaft from each gearbox unit via an SKF gear-type coupling. The water-jets were specially developed for the ABEB and are fitted with a six-bladed NAB impeller.

The twin water-jet units are widely spaced and are controlled by a single crew member using single levers. A hand hydraulic steering system is also incorporated for the nozzle direction control.

The ABEB can be carried on a special trailer but was designed to be carried on a MAN FSB carrier truck or a similarly equipped vehicle.

Specifications
ABEB
Length: 7.76 m
Beam: 3.23 m
Draught: 530 mm
Max speed: 52 km/h
Engines: 2 × Deutz BF 6 L 913 C air-cooled diesel engines, each developing 191 hp at 2,500 rpm
Fuel capacity: 400 litres
Endurance: (at full power) 5 h

Status
In service with the Belgian Army.

Contractor
Meuse et Sambre SA

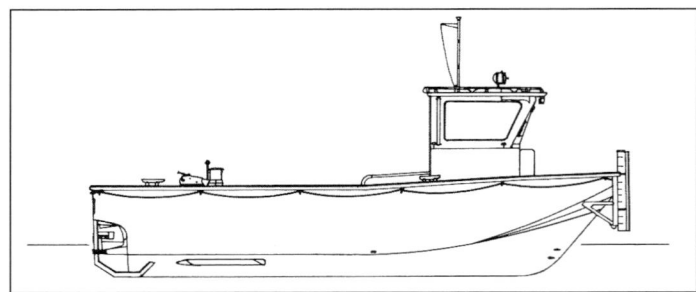

Advanced Bridge Erection Boat (ABEB)   0511562

Canada

Kamma & Blake Industries Bridge Boat Erection (BBE)

Development
Following introduction into service and 1989, Canadian forces received a total of 30 Model 27/4 Bridge Boat Erection (BBE) manufactured by the now defunct Versatech Products Inc of Burnaby, British Columbia.

Between 1997 and 1999 the Model 27/4 BBE was replaced by a new Bridge Boat Erection manufactured by Kamma & Blake Industries Ltd and developed in conjunction with the Canadian Department of National Defense.

Final in-service distribution was four BBEs to CFSME (Canadian Forces School of Engineering) and all regular force engineer regiments.

Kamma & Blake has also supplied the Canadian military with a number of Landing Craft/Work Boats, ranging from 24 to 36 ft.

Description

The hull of the BBE is constructed from welded aluminium. The boat is designed for a two-person crew. Propulsion is provided by twin STARPOWER STARDEC 300 V-8 diesel engines and twin WW357 water jets. The STARDEC 300 features electronic control and fault diagnostic. Additionally, the propulsion system can be run on land for ease of maintenance and launching. Static thrust is not less than 2273 kg forward and 1136 kg in reverse.

For use in the bridge erection role the BBE is fitted with two hydraulic rams complete with quick release hooks and bridge tensioning blocks for ease of securing bridging bays.

The BBE is designed to be carried, launched and recovered by trucks equipped to carry the Bridge Adaptor Pallet (BAP). In Canadian use this would be the Percheron Heavy Logistic Vehicle Wheeled (HLVW).

Specifications

BBE
Length: 7.58 m
Width: 3. 37 m
Draft: (full load) 500 mm
Weight:
    (total, including fuel and equipment) 6,200 kg
Engine: STARPOWER STARDEC 300 V-8 diesel
Max static thrust:
    (forward) 2,273 kg
    (reverse) 1,136 kg

Status

Production as required. In service with the Canadian Army (20 delivered 1997-99).

Contractor

Kamma & Blake Industries Ltd

Czech Republic

MO-108 and MO-111 bridging boats

The MO-108 and MO-111 are basically modifications of a Second World War German bridging boat and retain the German design of three rudders and a Kort nozzle, a metal ring guard which houses the screw. The MO-111 is transported on a large two-wheeled trailer called the SP-5. It is also known as the M-111 and the TATRA 111. The MO-111 was introduced in the 1950s and built at the CXD plant at Decin. The MO-108 is virtually identical to the MO-111 but is powered by a T-108, V-8 air-cooled diesel which develops 105 hp, giving the boat a lower performance than the MO-111 which is powered by a 170 hp V-12 air-cooled diesel.

The MO-108 and MO-111 were followed in service with the armies of the former Czechoslovakia by the MO-634. The data in the specifications table relates to the MO-634 and its dedicated SP-5 transport trailer.

Some examples of the MO-111 may remain in long-term storage and these are used with pontoon sets equipped with TATRA T813 transport trucks. The MO-634 remains in service and is used with pontoon sets equipped with TATRA T815 transport trucks. The MO-634 has also been supplied to India for use with PMS pontoon bridging sets licence-produced by BEML. The MO-634 is now understood to be licence produced in India by BEML.

Specifications

MO-634 and SP-5 dolly
Crew: 2
Weight: (max) 5,000 kg
Length: 8.07 m

Beam: 2.3 m
Draught: 960 mm
Max speed: 22 km/h
Pushing speed: 12 km/h
Engine: diesel developing 150 hp at 1,800 rpm
Gearbox: 1 forward and 1 reverse speed
Weight of dolly: 4,400 kg
Length of dolly: 9.66 m
Width of dolly: 2.65 m
Max towed speed on-road: 40 km/h
Max towed speed off-road: 6 km/h

Status

Production complete in the Czech and Slovak Republic, continues in India under licence by BEML. In service with the Czech, Slovak and Indian armies.

Contractor

Former Czech and Slovak state factories, BEML under licence in India.

MO 2000 Veronika multipurpose tug/tow boat

Description

The MO 2000 Veronika is described as a multipurpose tug/tow boat intended for the manoeuvring of separate or coupled pontoon bridge components during the deployment of pontoon or floating bridge assemblies. It can also be used in conjunction with diving operations, water-borne rescue work and the transport of cargo or personnel, or towing of other vessels or floating objects/devices.

The flat front of the boat is fitted with two pusher knees and coupling winches and the MO 2000 is quoted as being capable of pushing up to two PMS pontoon sections. A patented easily detachable tow hook mounted on the stern allows for towing. A ladder and holders for air cylinders are provided for diving operations.

The all-steel welded hull is 5 mm thick, sand-blasted and hot-dip galvanised for enhanced corrosion protection and longevity. The deck is covered in an anti-slip finish and hull split into separate watertight sections for the fuel tank, cargo, steering and control equipment, and engine room. An emergency shut-off valve is fitted between the engine and fuel tank for emergency use. A Volvo Penta FDC 3300 bilge pump powered by the 24 V electrical system is fitted and connected to each watertight compartment. A fire fighting system is also fitted.

Power is provided by two Volvo Penta D3-130EVC MC/DP S diesel engines with a total power output of 240 hp. Maximum speed is 15 km/h (8 kt) and the MO 2000 is designed to operate in temperatures from freezing water through to +50°C, and in wave heights of up to 2 m.

The MO 2000 is entering service with the Czech Army for use with the upgraded PMS folding pontoon bridge system, full details of which can be found in the Tactical floating bridges and ferries section. For use with PMS the MO 2000 is normally stored, transported and handled on a PR MO 2000 transport frame mounted on a TN 18 trailer, and known as the PP MO 2000 transport trailer. The MO 2000 can also be transported on a TATRA T 815 8 × 8 truck fitted with the PR MO 2000 transport frame or, if required, by any suitable flatbed truck or trailer of suitable capacity.

Specifications

MO 2000 Veronika
Weight: (without crew) 7,411 kg
Payload: 2,000 kg
Length: 7.130 m
Width: 3.02 m
Height: 3.355 m
Draught:
    (minimum) 635 mm
    (maximum) 1.055 m

MO-634 bridging boat and SP-5 dedicated transport and launch trailer/dolly (Stefan Marx)   1185420

The MO 2000 Veronika multipurpose tow/tug boat clearly showing the front end and two pusher knees (Omnipol a.s.)   0137707

Speed:
(maximum) 14.42 km/h
(with pontoons) 11.4 km/h
Engine: 2 × Volvo Penta D3-130EVC MC/DP S diesel developing 120 hp
(89 kW) each

Status
In production. In service with the Czech Army. Available for export.

Agency
Omnipol a.s.

France

Nexter F1 pontoon boat

Development
The F1 pontoon boat was designed to meet the requirements of the French
Army Corps of Engineers by the Etablissement Technique d'Angers
(ETAS), with production being undertaken by the Atelier de Construction
de Tarbes (ATS), now part of Nexter. The first prototype was built by the
ETAS with the second being built with the assistance of the ATS. The two
prototypes were followed by five pre-production boats completed in 1971.
A total of 135 production model F1 pontoon boats was built for the French
Army between 1972 and 1975.

The boat was designed to undertake a wide range of roles including the
pushing and pulling of pontoons, installation of protective nets, transport
of personnel and cargo, use as a platform for divers and other bridging and
mooring roles.

Description
The hull of the F1 pontoon boat is made of all-welded alloy (AG4MC) with
4.1 m³ of the boat filled with polyurethane foam to make it virtually
unsinkable. The boat consists of two sections, fore and aft. The fore section
contains the engine and crew compartment while the aft section contains
the two propellers, their protective frames and steering motor. This is
hinged to the main hull and can be swung upwards by two hydraulic joints
enabling the boat to be operated in very shallow water very close inshore.

The engine is mounted forward of the crew compartment and, transmits
power to a reduction gearbox with twin output shafts coupled via
electromagnetic clutches to two variable displacement hydraulic pumps.
Each pump feeds oil under pressure to a hydraulic motor mounted in a
submerged nacelle directly behind the propeller. Each propeller has four
blades and is 900 mm in diameter. The boat has no rudder as the
propellers, which are pod-mounted, can be traversed through 360°. The
boat has good rates of acceleration and deceleration.

The boat is provided with three bilge pumps with a capacity of 1,200
litres/h each. Hand-operated capstan winches with a 3,500 kg capacity are
mounted on either side of the hull and there is a towing post at the front of
the hull and a second towing post at the rear of the crew compartment. The
height of the rubber-clad bow fender post can be adjusted. There are two
white light searchlights (one movable and one fixed) with a range of 100 m
provided, together with two infra-red lights and a range of 50 m (one fixed
and one movable).

The F1 pontoon boat is normally carried in two sections, the bow section
is carried on the rear of a Berliet GBC 8 KT 6 × 6 4,000 kg truck (or Renault
GBC 180 6 × 6 5,000 kg truck as this type is known following rebuild under
a current refurbishment programme), which also tows a single-pole
2,500 kg trailer carrying the rear half of the boat. These are off-loaded by a
crane and assembled in the water. It takes three minutes to assemble the
two units.

Specifications
F1 pontoon boat
Crew: 2 or 3
Weight:
(forward section) 3,000 kg
(aft section) 1,800 kg
Length: 8.3 m
Beam: 2.49 m
Height above waterline: 1.3 m (excl lights)
Draught:
(max) 1.15 m
(min) 450 mm
Speed:
(maximum) 25 km/h
(carrying 3 crew plus 400 kg of cargo) 24.4 km/h
(pushing 4 pontoon floating bridge with a 40 t load) 9.36 km/h
Engine: Deutz F 10 L 413 V-10 air-cooled diesel developing 237 hp at
2,400 rpm
Electrical system: 24 V
Batteries: 4 × 6 V

Status
Production complete. In service with the French Army.

Contractor
Atelier de Construction de Tarbes (ATS)

Enquiries to
Nexter

Germany

Bridge Erection Boat Type MB 3

Development
The Bridge Erection Boat Type MB 3 (M-Boot 3) was designed by Schottel,
but manufacture was undertaken by the now General Dynamics European
Land Systems - Germany GmbH (GDELS-G GmbH), originally Eisenwerke
Kaiserslautern GmbH (EWK), as a subcontractor to Schottel.

Schottel continues to support marketing of M-Boots in co-operation with
boat manufacturers.

Description
The Bridge Erection Boat Type MB 3 (M-Boot 3) is used in the construction
of floating bridges and ferries. The hull is lightweight aluminium and a
basic windscreen and roof provide the operator with some degree of
protection from the elements.

The MB 3 is powered by twin air-cooled diesel engines, each operating a
Schottel Pump-Jet for propulsion and manoeuvring. The use of Pump-Jets
which are fitted flush to the lower hull allows for operation in water
450 mm deep when fully laden and equipped. Pump-Jet propulsion
operates on the principle of a centrifugal pump. An impeller sucks in water
from under the hull and forces it into a pump housing. The outlet nozzles
are fitted in the bottom plate, making it possible for the jet to be installed in
a flat-bottomed hull such as the MB 3. The Pump-Jet can be rotated
through 360 degrees, providing full thrust in all directions and ensuring
excellent manoeuvring performance, including the ability to rotate almost
on the spot.

Easily removable covers allow for maintenance work to be carried out on
the engines and pump jets from above, and with removing the units. The
boat can be carried and launched by either a standard bridging truck or its
own dedicated two-axle trailer.

Variant
The Australian Army's Bridge Erection Propulsion Boat (BEPB) supplied by
Birdon Marine and acquired under Project MINCS(L) 5.11 is based on the
Bridge Erection Boat Type MB 3. Full details of the BEPB can be found
elsewhere in this section.

Specifications
Bridge Erection Boat Type MB 3
Crew: 2
Weight: 5,000 kg
Length: 7 m
Beam: 3.26 m
Depth: 1.4 m
Max speed: >30 km/h
Engines: 2 × KHD BF 6 L913C exhaust turbocharged and charge air cooled,
air-cooled diesel units developing 178 hp (133 kW) each
Pump-jets: 2 × Schottel Type SPJ 55 M; 22 kN combined thrust

Status
In service with the German (140) and other undisclosed armies
(approximately 20). Locally developed variant in service with the
Australian Army (24).

Contractor
Schottel GmbH

Subcontractor
General Dynamics European Land Systems - Germany GmbH

Bridge Erection Boat Type MB 3 (Schottel)   1340287

General Dynamics European Land Systems (GDELS) TB2 Bridging Boat

Description
The General Dynamics European Land Systems - Germany GmbH (GDELS-G GmbH) TB2 bridging boat, known as the *Bugsierboot* or *M-boot*, is used in the construction of floating bridges and ferries. It has two adjustable pushing knees at the front, a windscreen that can be fitted with a removable canvas cover to give some degree of protection to the crew and is propelled in water by two propellers. The hull is aluminium and the built-in air compartments make it very difficult to sink. The boat is carried on and launched from a two-wheeled single-axle trailer, also produced by GDELS, formerly Eisenwerke Kaiserslautern GmbH (EWK).

GDSBS SA, Spain, a subsidiary of the General Dynamics Corporation of Falls Church, Virginia, completed the acquisition of the assets of EWK on 31 October 2002. As of 1 November 2002 EWK was renamed General Dynamics Santa Bárbara Sistemas GmbH (GDSBS GmbH) and is now known as General Dynamics European Land Systems - Germany GmbH (GDELS-G GmbH).

Specifications
TB2 Bridging Boat
Crew: 2
Weight: 4,200 kg
Length: 7.67 m
Beam: 2.7 m
Depth: (overall) 1.85 m
Max speed: 22.5 km/h
Engine: air-cooled diesel developing 250 hp

Trailer plus boat
Weight: 8,650 kg
Length: 9.8 m
Width: 2.48 m
Height: 3.25 m

Status
In service with the Brazilian, Egyptian, Nigerian and Turkish armies. A total of 117 boats have been produced.

Contractor
General Dynamics European Land Systems - Germany GmbH (GDELS-G GmbH).

GDELS TB2 Bridging Boat ready for use (GDELS)   0007710

GDELS TB2 Bridging Boat and single-axle transport trailer. The trailer is also produced by GDELS (GDELS)   0007711

Italy

SAI Ambrosini 121 Thruster bridging boat

Development
SAI Ambrosini was an Italian aircraft manufacturer established in Passignano sul Trasimeno, Italy in 1934 as the Società Aeronautica Italiana. During the 1960s the company ventured into boat-building.

SAI Ambrosini ceased to trade in 1992, although the brand/tradename is now used by T.A. Tecnologie d' Avanguardia, a manufacturer of timepieces.

Description
The SAI Ambrosini 121 Thruster bridging boat was designed to cope with loads involved in the assembly of Class 60 floating bridges on rivers and inland water obstacles. It entered service with the Italian Army in 1984.

The hull is constructed entirely from 2 and 2.5 mm thick AISI 316 L ribbed stainless steel sheets, reinforced with 4 mm flat ribs and spacers. The stern is 4 mm thick where the propulsion system is mounted. The cockpit, which is removable for major maintenance operations, is constructed from a single sheet of 5 mm thick aluminium alloy. The engine and propeller inspection hatches are also constructed from light alloy. All joints between differing materials are suitably insulated with plastic materials to prevent electrochemical corrosion. Unsinkability is guaranteed by three sealed compartments and appropriately placed closed-cell buoyancy material.

The SAI 121 is laid out with the steerage cockpit to the rear, the personnel/stores/working compartment forward, the two separated by the amidships located engine compartment.

The operator can lower the steerage cockpit windscreen for increased visibility when required. A bench-type seat for three persons is provided and the area can be covered with a canvas tilt during inclement weather conditions. The engine compartment houses two turbocharged diesel engines, each with a dry weight of 527 kg. Twin independent stainless steel fuel tanks are fitted. The forward-situated personnel/cargo compartment can accommodate up to four people or 500 kg of stores in addition to an anchor and accompanying 40 m of chain. This area also doubles up as a working area for bridge assemblers.

The bow is fitted with a pushing knee for nudging bridging components into place.

Specifications
Weight: (fully equipped) 4,450 kg
Max Load: 7 persons or 4 persons plus 500 kg of stores
Length: 7.45 m
Beam: 2.44 m
Max draught: 70 mm
Max speed: (calm water, no load) 25 km/h
Endurance: >6 h
Turning radius: 4 m
Fuel capacity: 274 litres
Engines: 2 × AIFO 8061 SM 5.5-litre 6-cylinder water-cooled (closed-circuit) turbocharged diesels developing 173 hp each at 2,950 rpm
Propulsion: Schottel SRP 50/50 steering traction screws traversing through 360°
Tow and thrust values:
 (forward) 2,400 kg
 (reverse) 1,200 kg
Electrical system: 24 V

Status
Production complete. In service with the Italian Army.

Contractor
SAI Ambrosini - Sociéta Aeronautica Italiana SpA (This company is no longer trading.)

SAI Ambrosini 126 multipurpose boat

Development
SAI Ambrosini was an Italian aircraft manufacturer established in Passignano sul Trasimeno, Italy in 1934 as the Società Aeronautica Italiana. During the 1960s the company ventured into boat-building.

SAI Ambrosini ceased to trade in 1992, although the brand/tradename is now used by T.A. Tecnologie d' Avanguardia, a manufacturer of timepieces.

Description
The SAI Ambrosini 126 multipurpose boat is intended for a variety of military roles but is equipped with a bluff bow enabling it to push heavy floating structures, such as bridging components in shallow waters. It is also suitable for towing similar equipment. The SAI Ambrosini 126 is powered by two inboard FIAT diesel engines each driving a Castoldi TD 318 hydrojet that can be traversed for a high level of manoeuvrability.

The hull of the SAI Ambrosini 126 was manufactured either in steel or in 5083 light alloy and was designed to render the vessel unsinkable. The cockpit is located well forward although other configurations were possible and it is possible to fit either a diving platform over the stern or carry stores or pallets behind the cockpit.

Specifications
Weight: 2,250 kg
Length: 7.5 m
Total width: 2.58 m
Draught: 450 mm
Max speed: 65 km/h
Endurance: 7 h at 37 km/h
Engines: 2 × FIAT AIFO 8061 SM06 diesels developing 170 hp each
Hydrojets: 2 × Castoldi TD 318

Status
Production figures/users not available.

Contractor
SAI Ambrosini - Socièta Aeronautica Italiana SpA (This company is no longer trading.)

SAI Ambrosini bridging boat

Development
SAI Ambrosini was an Italian aircraft manufacturer established in Passignano sul Trasimeno, Italy in 1934 as the Società Aeronautica Italiana. During the 1960s the company ventured into boat-building.

SAI Ambrosini ceased to trade in 1992, although the brand/tradename is now used by T.A. Tecnologie d' Avanguardia, a manufacturer of timepieces.

Description
This bridging boat was designed by SAI Ambrosini to meet the requirements of the Italian Army and entered service in 1974. The stainless steel hull is divided into six watertight compartments to guarantee buoyancy. The inboard-mounted engine is towards the front and the semi-enclosed cabin towards the rear.

Specifications
Crew: 2 or 3
Weight: 3,800 kg
Length: 7.5 m
Beam: 2.45 m
Height:
    (without cabin) 1.8 m
    (with cabin) 2.3 m
Draught: 700 mm
Max speed:
    (pushing or towing half MLC 60 raft in 1.75 m/s current) 3 km/h
    (unloaded, calm water) 25 km/h
Endurance: 6 h
Turning radius: 8.5 m
Engine: Deutz model SF 12 L 413 12-cylinder 16.96-litre air-cooled diesel developing 260 hp

Status
Production complete. In service with the Italian Army.

Contractor
SAI Ambrosini - Socièta Aeronautica Italiana SpA (This company is no longer trading.)

Japan

Japanese bridging boats

Description
The Japanese Ground Self-Defence Force uses an indigenously developed bridging boat with the Type 92 floating bridge and for other bridge/ferry-related tasks. The boat appears to be conventional in design and powered by a diesel engine. No technical data has been made available.

Japanese GSDF bridging boats (Mitsuhiro Kadota)   0587971

Status
Production likely to be on an as required basis. In service with the JGSDF.

Contractor
Not known.

Netherlands

Damen Bridge Support Boat 700

Description
The Damen Bridge Support Boat 700 (BSB 700) was designed specifically to operate with the Ribbon Bridge system. It has a high-tensile steel hull and one partly elevated deck with the engine located forward. The hull is divided into four watertight compartments accessible via flush deck-mounted hatches. All hatches and the mast are made of aluminium. Just aft of midships is an open cockpit with seating for a helmsman and all the controls.

A Damen BSB 700 on a Dutch Army Scania P124CB8x8HZ420 (8 × 8) truck fitted with a Multilift MSH 165SC load handling system and Bridge Adapter Pallet (BAP). 48 BAP adapted vehicles form part of the Wissel Laad Systeme (WLS) package (Shaun C Connors)   1128228

A Damen BSB 700 on a Dutch Army Scania P124CB8x8HZ420 (8 × 8) truck fitted with a Multilift MSH 165SC load handling system and Bridge Adapter Pallet (BAP). 48 BAP adapted vehicles form part of the Wissel Laad Systeme (WLS) package (Shaun C Connors)   1128227

Two Damen BSB 700s pushing an unladen Ribbon Bridge ferry (Damen)

0525474

Polish KH-200 bridging boat (Shaun C Connors)

0116248

Two Damen BSB 700s manoeuvring a laden Ribbon Bridge ferry (Damen)

0525475

Polish KH-200 bridging boat at speed (Shaun C Connors)

0536651

Power is derived from a single 246 hp air-cooled diesel engine which provides power for two hydraulic pumps driving two 560 mm diameter four-bladed propellers. The swivelling hydraulic propellers are also used for steering through 360°. The engine provides a static bollard pull of 2,600 kg and, for positioning bridge components in a water flow of around 9.3 km/h, the boat develops a thrust of 2,100 kg.

Standard equipment includes a helmsman seat in the cockpit, aluminium sun awning over the cockpit, polyethylene fender around the vessel (except the stern), two hand winches, two hoisting eyes, dismountable mast, hand bilge pump and an anchor and 30 m of line.

For ease of transport and launching, the Damen Bridge Support Boat 700 was designed to be carried on the DAF YGZ 2300 (6 × 6) 10,000 kg Ribbon Bridge launcher truck. From early 2006, this truck was replaced by the Scania P124CB8x8HZ420 (8 × 8) truck fitted with a Multilift MSH165SC load handling system and fitted with a Bridge Adapter Pallet (BAP), 48 of which were procured as part of the Wissel Laad Systemen (WLS) programme.

Specifications
Weight: 6,000 kg
Length overall: 7 m
Beam: 2.9 m
Depth: 1.35 m
Draught: 750 mm
Max speed: 16 km/h
Engine: Deutz BF 8L 513 air-cooled diesel developing 246 hp at 2,300 rpm

Status
Production complete. In service with the Royal Netherlands Army (58).

Contractor
Damen Shipyards

Poland

KH-200 bridging boat

Description
The KH-200 bridging boat was developed in the late 1960s and after four years of trials was approved for production in 1971. It has a hull of all-steel construction and a pusher knee mounted at the bow. The crew is seated in a cabin towards the bow, which has an open back. The engine is mounted to the rear of the crew and drives a single propeller at the rear. The KH-200 is used with the PP-64 heavy folding pontoon bridge and can also be used as a transport carrying up to 15 troops. The boat is transported on a large two-axle trailer, which weighs 2,800 kg unladen.

Specifications
KH-200 bridging boat
Crew: 2-3
Weight: 3,865 kg
Length: 8.14 m
Beam: 2.3 m
Draught: 720 mm
Max speed: 25 km/h
Endurance: 12.1 h
Towing power:
  (forward) 2,500 kg
  (reverse) 1,200 kg
Engine: Leyland UE 680 6-cylinder in-line water-cooled 4-stroke diesel developing 169 hp

Status
In service with the Polish Army.

Contractor
Polish state factories.

Russian Federation

BMK-130 and BMK-150 bridging boats

Description
BMK-130/BMK-130M
The hull of the BMK-130 is of steel construction and is divided into individual watertight compartments. Mounted each side of the hull is a strut and a wheel which assist in the launching and recovery of the boat. Once afloat, the wheels are folded up alongside the hull. The BMK-130M, introduced in the mid-1960s, has a modified hull and when afloat the wheels are swung forward and stowed in wells on either side of the hull. This reduces not only drag but also the chances of damage to the wheels when afloat. The launching sequence is as follows: the bow attachment is connected to the front bumper of the truck, the boat is pushed into the water stern first and once the boat is afloat it is disconnected from the truck and the wheels of the boat are swung forward and stowed in the wells.

The BMK-130 or BMK-130M can form part of the PMP and PMP-M pontoon equipment sets. The BMK-130M is the standard bridging boat used with the PP-91 pontoon equipment set.

A bridging boat based on the BMK-130M and known as the RPR M68 has been produced in the former Yugoslavia. Full details of this can be found elsewhere in this section.

BMK-130M bridging boat (Stefan Marx)   1185419

BMK-150/BMK-150M

Until the introduction of the BMK-T this was the most powerful bridging boat used by the Warsaw Pact. It has a hull of aluminium construction, is much lighter than the BMK-130 and BMK-130M and has two engines with separately controlled twin screws. Unlike the BMK-130 and BMK-130M, this boat is provided with a windscreen and a cover that can be erected in bad weather. The basic BMK-150 has wheels that fold up on the outside of the hull, while the later BMK-150M has wheel wells. The BMK-150 and BMK-150M can form part of the PMP and PMP-M pontoon equipment sets.

Specifications

Type	BMK-130M	BMK-150	BMK-150M
Crew:	2	2	2
Weight:	3,077 kg	2,500 kg	3,000 kg
Length:	7.85 m	8.2 m	7.4 m
Beam:	2.1 m	2.55 m	2.55 m
Depth:	1.5 m	2 m	n/a
Draught:	622 mm	660 mm	750 mm
Max speed:	19.5 km/h	22 km/h	22 km/h
Fuel capacity:	n/avail	300 litres	150 litres
Average consumption:	26.5 litres/h	n/avail	47 litres/h
Endurance:	12 h	7 h	6 h
Engine model:	YaAZ-204SP	M51-SPE-3.5(2)	M70 SPE-3.5(2)
Engine type:	diesel	petrol	diesel
Number of cylinders:	4	6	4
Hp:	100	62 × 2	62 × (2)
Cooling:	water	water	water
Towing power:			
(forward)	1,450 kg	1,500 kg	1,500 kg
(reverse)	800 kg	n/avail	n/avail

Status

Production likely to be on an as-required basis for the BMK-130M and BMK-150M only, which can form part of currently marketed pontoon equipment sets. In service with some members of the former Warsaw Pact.

Contractor

Former state factories.

BMK-T and BMK-225 bridging boats

Description

The BMK-T is believed to be the most powerful bridging boat in the Russian Federation armed forces inventories in quantity and is used with pontoon bridges such as the PMP and PMP-M. The boat is carried on the rear of a KrAZ-214 (6 × 6) 7,000 kg or KrAZ-255B (6 × 6) 7,500 kg truck chassis and is launched by gravity, often with its engine running ready for immediate use. The recovery technique is as follows: the truck is reversed into the water and a cable from the truck's winch is connected to the stern of the BMK-T. The boat is then pulled out of the water over runners at the rear of the truck until it is back in the travelling position.

The hull of the BMK-T is of the 'sled' design for greater stability and has four enclosed compartments. Even if two non-adjacent compartments are flooded, the boat will not sink. The crew cabin is towards the front of the boat and is fully enclosed. The engine compartment is to the rear of the crew cabin and is also fully enclosed, allowing the boat to operate in very rough water. It is moved through the water by two propellers at the stern, which have a maximum speed of 945 rpm. On encountering an obstacle during forward travel, the two propellers are lifted out of the water

BMK-T bridging boat being transported by a KrAZ-255B (6 × 6) 7,500 kg truck (James Kinear)   0589064

The BMK-225 is understood to have been developed (and possibly produced) by a member (or members) of the Concern of Medium and Small Tonnage Shipbuilding (KSMK) Joint-Stock Company (KSMK)   1190260

automatically by hinges at the stern. When in the travelling position, the propellers are swung through 180° so that they are on top of the boat. The BMK-T is highly manoeuvrable and can be steered equally well in reverse. All controls are electrical and if required the boat can be remote-controlled using a cable from a maximum distance of 30 m. A pusher knee is mounted at the bow, although the boat is also used for towing pontoons.

A new BMK-225 bridge erection boat has been seen, and while thought to be larger and more capable than the BMK-T, no technical details or other information for the BMK-225 have been officially released. The BMK-225 is understood to have been developed (and possibly produced) by a member (or members) of the Concern of Medium and Small Tonnage Shipbuilding (KSMK) Joint-Stock Company. KSMK comprises of the Yantar Shipyard (Kaliningrad); the Vympel Shipbuilding Plant (Rybinsk); JSC Interregional Investment Bank (MIB) (Moscow); the Amur Shipyard (Komsomolsk-on-Amur); the Kazan Electrotechnikal Plant JSC (Kazan), and the Khabarovsk Shipbuilding Plant (Khabarovsk).

Specifications

BMK-T
Crew: 2
Weight: 6000 kg
Length: 8.6 m
Beam: 2.7 m
Depth: 2.2 m
Draught: 750 mm
Max speed: 17 km/h
Fuel capacity: 300 litres
Fuel consumption: 20 litres/h
Endurance: 15-17 h
Towing power:
 (forward) 2000 kg
 (reverse) 750 kg
Engine: YaMZ 236 SP4 V-6 water-cooled diesel developing 130 hp at 2,100 rpm

KrAZ-255B with BMK-T Boat

Weight: 19100 kg
Length: 10.6 m
Width: 2.8 m
Height: 3.76 m

Status

BMK-T; production likely to be on an as-required basis by unspecified former state facilities, the BMK-T is in service with some former Warsaw Pact nations and is available with currently offered pontoon equipment sets. BMK-225; exact status uncertain (see text).

Contractor
(BMK-225)
Concern of Medium and Small Tonnage Shipbuilding (KSMK) Joint-Stock Company.

Serbia and Montenegro

RPR M68 bridging boat

Description
Described as a tug vessel, the RPR M68 bridging boat is based on the Russian Federation BMK-130M and is intended for pushing and towing floating bridges and ferries. It can also be used to carry personnel and cargo.

The RPR M68 has an all-steel hull and is equipped with travelling wheels that fold upwards into wheel wells when the boat is in the water; when the wheels are lowered the boat can be towed by a truck, and without the need for an intermediate trailer. Power is supplied by a single diesel engine located amidships and developing approximately 104 kW (140 hp).

A small cabin can be erected for the helmsman and a small mast carrying a floodlamp can also be provided.

Specifications
RPR M68
Crew: 2
Weight:
  (standard) 3,940 kg
  (full load) 4,220 kg
  (transport) 4,300 kg
Length: 7.88 m
Beam: 2.1 m
Draught: (mean) 640 mm
Max speed: (full load) 15.55 km/h
Engine: diesel developing approx 140 hp (104 kW)
Tractive force:
  (forward) 16.5 kN
  (astern) 8.25 kN

Status
In service with the former Yugoslav Army. Production as required. Available for export.

Contractor
Yugoimport SDPR

RPR M68 bridging boat (Yugoimport SDPR)   1340284

Singapore

FBS 60 bridging boat

Description
The FBS 60 bridging boat is an integral part of the Floating Bridge System FBS 60 (full details of which can be found in the Tactical floating bridges and ferries section) and is intended for manoeuvring FBS 60 bridge sections.

The craft is referred to as a push-pull tugboat and uses a single conventional screw propulsion system powered by a 250 hp engine. The boat is constructed of steel and is conventional in layout with the control position well forward and the engine located amidships. A pushing knee is fitted over the squared-off bows.

For road transport the awning over the control position can be lowered or removed. The boat can be carried on a special trailer towed behind a 6 × 6 7,000 kg bridge transporter vehicle. The trailer is 9.7 m long overall. As

an alternative, the boat may be carried on a special boat carriage by a bridge transporter vehicle. Using the boat carriage, launching and retrieval times are quicker than using the trailer. The boat carriage is 7 m long, 2.9 m wide and 2 m high. Weight is 1,400 kg.

Specifications
FBS 60 bridging boat
Length overall: 7.45 m
Length at waterline: 7 m
Beam: (moulded) 2.4 m
Depth: (moulded) 1.3 m
Max draught: (aft) 600 mm
Weight: 4,600 kg
Engine output: 250 hp
Bollard pull: 1,900 kg
Free running speed: 21.3 km/h (11.5 kt)

Status
Available.

Contractor
Singapore Technologies Marine

Slovakia

Czech and Slovak bridging boats

Description
The MO-108 and MO-111 are basically modifications of a Second World War German bridging boat and retain the German design of three rudders and a Kort nozzle, a metal ring-guard which houses the screw. The MO-111 is transported on a large two-wheeled trailer called the SP-5. It is also known as the M-111 and the TATRA 111. The MO-111 was introduced in the 1950s and built at the CXD plant at Decin. The MO-108 is virtually identical to the MO-111 but is powered by a T-108, V-8 air-cooled diesel which develops 105 hp, giving the boat a lower performance than the MO-111 which is powered by a 170 hp V-12 air-cooled diesel.

The MO-108 and MO-111 were followed in service with the armies of the former Czechoslovakia by the MO-634. The data in the specifications table relates to the MO-634 and its dedicated SP-5 transport trailer.

Some examples of the MO-111 may remain in long-term storage and these are used with pontoon sets equipped with TATRA T813 transport trucks. The MO-634 remains in service and is used with pontoon sets equipped with TATRA T815 transport trucks. The MO-634 has also been supplied to India for use with PMS pontoon bridging sets licence produced by BEML. The MO-634 is now understood to be licence produced in India by BEML.

Specifications
MO-634 and SP-5 dolly
Crew: 2
Max weight: 5,000 kg
Length: 8.07 m
Beam: 2.3 m
Draught: 960 mm
Max speed: 22 km/h
Pushing speed: 12 km/h
Engine model: diesel developing 150 hp at 1,800 rpm
Gearbox: 1 forward and 1 reverse speed
Weight of dolly: 4,400 kg
Length of dolly: 9.66 m
Width of dolly: 2.65 m
Max towed speed on-road: 40 km/h
Max towed speed off-road: 6 km/h
Tyres: 1,100 × 20, dual

MO-634 bridging boat and SP-5 dedicated transport and launch trailer/dolly (Stefan Marx)   1185420

Status

Production continues under licence in India by BEML. In service with the Czech, Slovak and Indian armies.

Contractor

Former state factories in the Czech and Slovak Republics, BEML in India.

United Kingdom

FBM Babcock Marine multirole Combat Support Boat (CSB)

Development

Based on a requirement issued by the UK Military Vehicles and Engineering Establishment at Christchurch (now QinetiQ, Christchurch), the Fairey company (now FBM Babcock Marine Limited) started development of the 8 m Combat Support Boat (CSB) in the Autumn of 1975, with the first prototype being delivered to the British Army for trials early in 1977. As a result of extensive trials by the British Army, a pre-production boat was ordered for further trials. It was delivered in May 1978. The boat was accepted for service with the British Army in February 1979 and an order placed for 56 boats the following year.

In 1983, the UK Ministry of Defence ordered a further 12 CSBs for the British Army to replace those lost during the Falklands War.

After extensive evaluation by the then US Army MERADCOM, the CSB was accepted under NATO Standardisation and Rationalisation arrangements and over 700 boats were delivered to the US Army, more than half of these having been license-produced in the US. The US Army and Marines refer to the CSB as the Bridge Erection Boat (BEB).

In response to a requirement from a South Korean customer, FBM developed a version of its CSB/BEB offering a drastic reduction in noise levels. The Stealth version of the CSB is in licensed production in South Korea.

In 1998, the British Army issued a requirement for a vessel to replace the CSB. This requirement was met by a Combat Support Boat produced by RTK Marine, full details of which can be found elsewhere in this section.

Opting to upgrade rather than replace, in August 2004 the US Army awarded FBM Babcock Marine Limited a contract to commence the overhaul and modernisation of their fleet of BEBs. The contract to upgrade the existing US Army BEBs of Mk1 and Mk2 specification to a new BEB Mk II S specification is being managed by FBM Babcock Marine Limited in conjunction with Silver Ships Inc. of Theodore, Alabama.

The work being performed under the modernisation program includes condition assessments, structural and coating overhauls, replacement of obsolete equipment including waterjets, marine diesel engines and control systems, and the development of a new Integrated Logistics Support (ILS) package. FBM Babcock Marine Limited has selected AM General LLC for the ILS contract which includes new technical manuals, parts breakdown books, operational manuals and training packages.

Description

Based on the Allday 8 m hull, the boat features a pusher bow and an aft-mounted capstan/tow hook. The mast and cabin top are both removable for low-profile operations and transport/stowage. The two self-draining cockpits are each designed to accommodate a standard 1,000 kg NATO pallet.

The CSB bridge erection boat is made of welded marine-grade aluminium alloy to give a lightweight yet strong boat. Based on a well-tried hull, the craft was designed to meet the requirements of the British Army for a boat to assist with bridging operations and other river and estuary support and assault duties. Ultra Dynamics water-jets enable the boat to be used in shallow water with twin 210 shp turbocharged marine diesels providing the power. Transport, launching and recovery is by special cradle on a Bridge Transporter Truck or by a towed off-road trailer.

Standard equipment includes: navigation and towing lights and a searchlight; fire extinguishers; windscreen wipers; bilge pumping system and heavy-duty fendering.

The batch of 12, ordered by the MoD during 1983, were fitted with 'winterisation' kits for operations at low temperatures. This kit included extra cable insulation, more powerful screen wipers, pump and engine heaters, defrosting equipment and personnel heaters.

Variants

In response to a requirement from a South Korean customer, FBM developed a version of its CSB Bridge Erection Boat offering a drastic reduction in noise levels. The noise level in the cab is reduced from 101 dBA to 84 dBA and the optimum speed for this reduced noise level is 13 km/h (7 kt). At this speed, the boat is inaudible at approximately 285 m with a background noise of 42 dBA approaching the listener and at 530 m when departing.

The twin Sabre Marine 212 diesel engine installation is enclosed by adding a glass fibre hood and transverse bulkheads, all lined with 32 mm black PVC-faced foam with a heavy polymeric barrier. Entry points for services through the bulkheads are sealed. Hull side panels and hatch covers are lined with 3 mm bitumen foil vibration-damping material.

A US Army BEB Mk II S; the contract to upgrade the existing US Army BEBs of Mk1 and Mk2 specification to the new BEB Mk II S specification is managed by FBM Babcock Marine Limited in conjunction with Silver Ships Inc. of Theodore, Alabama (FBM Babcock Marine Limited)   1173954

FBM Babcock Marine Bridge Erection Boats (BEBs) of the US Army at work (FBM Babcock Marine Limited)   0536763

Burgess 100 mm ADS through-adsorption type exhausts have replaced the side-shell water-injected units. The engines are installed on Metzeler Fluidastic rubber hydraulic resilient mounts. Extra cooling for the enclosed engine compartment is provided by two Jabsco 24 V electric fans.

Other changes introduced with the Stealth CSB involve the replacing of the original goal-post mast by a simple pole mast in front of the wheelhouse. The Stealth CSB prototype had rotatable nozzles fitted to the Dowty water-jets. These improve reversing and obviate icing problems.

The Stealth CSB has been in licensed production in South Korea with subcontractors Korea Tacoma Marine Industries (KTMI) since 1985. During 1992, FBM Support Services Limited was awarded a contract worth more than USD7 million for the supply of materials and technology transfer to KTMI. The initial contract involved the materials for 55 craft. It was anticipated that further contracts would result in the same number of sets being supplied each year until 1997 - material for a further 56 units was delivered during 1993, a further 55 during 1994 plus the same again in 1995. South Korea has thus become the largest single user of the CSB.

Specifications

Mk II S
Length:
(with pushing knee) 8.38 m
(waterline) 6.98 m
Beam over fenders: 2.49 m
Height:
(without cab) 1.98 m
(with cab) 2.79 m
Weight: (fully fitted out and fuelled) 4,500 kg
Maximum payload: 2,000 kg
Draught:
(fully fitted out and fuelled) 560 mm
(fully laden) 660 mm
Engines: twin Cummins 6 BT5.9M turbocharged 4-stroke marine diesels each continuously rated at 210 shp at 2,600 rpm
Propulsion units: twin Ultra 305 water-jets coupled to engines through Twin Disc MG5011SC reverse reduction gearbox
Max static forward thrust: 2,000 kg
Max static reverse thrust: 1,000 kg
Max speed:
(unladen) 44 km/h
(fully laden) 31 km/h
Fuel tank capacity: 227 litres

Status
In service with the engineer units of the Greek (18), Turkish and US (over 700 delivered) armies. The Stealth CSB is licence produced in South Korea.

Contractor
FBM Babcock Marine Limited

VT Halmatic Combat Support Boat

Development
During 1998, the British Army issued a requirement for a new Combat Support Boat (CSB) to replace its in-service FMB Marine CSBs. Tenders were issued in September 1998, with the production contract being issued to RTK Marine (now BVT Surface Fleet) which manufactured a pre-production prototype at its own expense. Two prototypes and dedicated trailers with a further 30 craft were delivered by the end of August 2001. There were options for a further eight craft. The CSBs are used by the Royal Engineers for a variety of combat tasks including bridge construction and support, as well as ferrying supplies and equipment The dedicated trailers were manufactured by Oldbury UK Limited.

Description
The CSB was designed to undertake a wide range of duties including bridging, tug boat, logistic supply and diving. The boat is capable of static thrusts up to 1,700 kg for tugging purposes and can transport 2,000 kg of

A British Army Combat Support Boat (CSB) on its dedicated transport/launch trailer. The CSB trailer was designed and manufactured by Oldbury Trailers (Patrick Allen)   1067519

cargo or 12 troops. The craft has an asymmetric catamaran hull form fitted with water-jets powered by twin 210 hp turbocharged marine diesel engines. The boat has a draught of 650 mm, allowing operation in very shallow water.

The hull of the CSB is made of glass fibre reinforced plastic and has a built-in foam buoyancy in excess of the craft's gross displacement, making the boat unsinkable. The hull requires the minimum of maintenance and can easily be repaired in operation. The deck has a non-slip bonded grit surface applied. Full peripheral fendering is provided at the gunwale and at the waterline. Drains for the removal of water from the well-deck are located at the engine bulkhead.

There is a pushing knee mounted at the bow and a towing post mounted aft. Standard equipment includes six warping bollards and four lifting points mounted on the gunwale rail, navigation lights, floodlight, klaxon, a rechargeable fire extinguisher and life rafts.

Optional equipment includes an illuminated helmsman's compass, deck gear, cargo lashing kit, de-mountable jib crane with a capacity of 100 kg and a four-wheel close-coupled boat trailer.

The CSB is built to Lloyds standards and meets the requirements of the MCA workboat code.

Status
Production as required. In service with the British Army.

Contractor
VT Halmatic Ltd

A British Army Combat Support Boat (CSB) at speed (VT Halmatic) 0121808

TRANSPORT EQUIPMENT

LIGHT VEHICLES

Austria

Steyr-Daimler-Puch Pinzgauer 710 (4 × 4) 1,000 kg and 712 (6 × 6) 1,500 kg vehicles 1971-1990

Development
The Pinzgauer 710 range of all-terrain vehicles was developed by Steyr-Daimler-Puch as the successor to the 700 AP Haflinger range of 4 × 4 vehicles. The first prototype of the Pinzgauer was completed in 1965 with first production models being completed in 1971. The vehicle was adopted by the Austrian Army in 1973. The 712 6 × 6 model was first shown in 1968 and entered production during 1971-1972. Production of the original petrol-powered models concluded in 1990, to be replaced by diesel-powered versions developed from 1983.

In July 2000 it was announced that all future Pinzgauer production would be carried out in the UK by Automotive Technik Limited (ATL). The Austrian production line built 30,000 vehicles for 24 countries over nearly 30 years.

In April 2005 it was announced that Stewart & Stevenson of tEhe US (then manufacturer of the Family of Medium Tactical Vehicles (FMTV)) had acquired ATL. Armor Holdings Inc announced in February 2006 it was to acquire Stewart & Stevenson. From May 2006, Automotive Technik Limited (ATL) became known as Pinzgauer Ltd. It was announced in August 2007 that Armor Holdings had been acquired by BAE Systems, Pinzgauer Ltd becoming BAE Systems Land Systems, Guildford.

BAE Systems announced early-2008 plans to discontinue the production of the Pinzgauer 1 vehicle and close its manufacturing facilities at Guildford and Fareham in the UK. A new Pinzgauer support business has been set up at the Guildford site, this continuing to support Pinzgauer fleets, primarily in the UK and New Zealand. Development of the Pinzgauer 2 vehicle was transitioned to the BAE Systems South Africa business, however, according to BAE Systems further analysis of the potential market (for Pinzgauer 2) revealed insufficient market interest to continue development.

Pinzgauer 712 M (6 × 6) 1,500 kg vehicle in service with the Austrian Army (Stefan Marx) 1128716

Description
Both the 710 (4 × 4) and 712 (6 × 6) models were available with two basic types of body, fully enclosed or with a military-type cargo body. The former has an all-steel fully enclosed body with two doors in each side and a single door at the rear and the military-type body has a single door each side for the driver and one passenger. The tops of the doors are removable and the windscreen can be folded forward onto the bonnet. The rear cargo area has removable bows and a tarpaulin cover and there are bench seats down each side of the rear body for eight personnel in the 710 (4 × 4) model and 12 in the 712 (6 × 6) model.

The chassis consists of a torsion-resistant central tube with independent swing axles incorporating the transfer box and axle drive. The engine is mounted towards the front of the vehicle and is coupled to a ZF manual gearbox, which transmits power via a propeller shaft to the transfer box, which also supports the hydraulically operated shifting clutch for the power transmission to the front axle. The drive shafts to the front and rear differentials are within the central tube chassis. The differentials have a hydraulically operated mechanical lock.

Optional equipment for the Pinzgauer included: antenna holder (middle and side), camouflage net holders, convoy lights, blackout blinds, divided windscreen, foldable table, jerrycan holders, rear mounting trays, rifle racks, mounting points for shovels, split battery system, rear towhook, and a 125-litre petrol tank.

Variants
Pinzgauer 716 (4 × 4) and 718 (6 × 6)
Full details of diesel-powered 716 (4 × 4) and 718 (6 × 6) models, and all subsequent diesel-powered models, can be found elsewhere in this section.

Ambulance (San-Pinzgauer)
Versions of both the 710 (4 × 4) and 712 (6 × 6) Pinzgauer were available with a fully enclosed rear body which can be fitted with air conditioning. In addition to the driver and one medical assistant, the vehicle in standard configuration, can carry four stretcher patients, or two stretcher and four seated patients, or six seated patients.

Ambulance version of the Pinzgauer 712 (6 × 6) 1,500 kg vehicle in service with Austrian Army (Stefan Marx) 1124724

Pinzgauer 710 M (4 × 4) 1,000 kg vehicle in service with Austrian Army (Stefan Marx) 1124723

Pinzgauer 712 M (6 × 6) 1,500 kg vehicle in service with the Royal Army of Oman (Richard Stickland) 0558998

Pinzgauer 712 (6 × 6) 1,500 kg vehicle in service with the Royal Army of Oman. This vehicle is fitted with a specialist shelter-type body
(Richard Stickland) 1047343

Anti-aircraft (712 Pinzgauer-FIA)

The Austrian Army fitted a number of 712 (6 × 6) Pinzgauers with 20 mm Oerlikon anti-aircraft cannon (2 cm IFlak 58) at the rear, with spare drum magazines stowed to the immediate rear of the driver's position. A single-axle trailer acted as storage for the crew's kit and extra ammunition.

Others

The basic military-type vehicles with cargo-type body are designated the 710 M (4 × 4) and 712 M (6 × 6), the radio vehicles the 710 K (4 × 4) and 712 K (6 × 6), the 6 × 6 firefighting vehicle the 712 FW, the 6 × 6 workshop vehicle the 712 W, and the flatbed version, used to carry the 20 mm cannon, is designated the 712 T.

In 1981 the 712 DK (6 × 6) was introduced; this had an enlarged four-door cab which extends to just over the second axle. Payload remained 1,500 kg.

Specifications

Configuration	710 (4 × 4)	712 (6 × 6)
Weight:		
(laden, soft top/hard top)	3,050/3,100 kg	3,900/4,100 kg
(unladen, soft top/hard top)	1,950/2,100 kg	2,350/2,600 kg
(max weight on front axle, laden)	1,500 kg	1,450 kg
(max weight on rear axle(s), laden)	1,550 kg	2,600 kg
(max load)	1,000 kg	1,500 kg
(towed load, on-road)	5,000 kg	5,000 kg
(towed load, off-road)	1,500 kg	1,800 kg
Load area:	2.25 × 1.592 m	3.03 × 1.592 m
Length:	4.175 m	4.955 m
Width:	1.76 m	1.76 m
Height:		
(overall)	2.045 m	2.045 m
(load area)	940 mm	940 mm
Ground clearance:	335 mm	335 mm
Track:	1.44 m	1.44 m
Wheelbase:	2.2 m	2 m + 980 mm
Angle of approach/departure:	45°/45°	45°/45°
Max speed:	110 km/h	100 km/h
Fuel capacity:	75 litres	75 litres
	(125 litres optional)	(125 litres optional)
Fuel consumption:		
(on-road)	17 litres/100 km	19 litres/100 km
(off-road)	6-10 litres/h	7-11 litres/h
Gradient: (laden)	100%	100%
Side slope:	88%	88%
Fording:	700 mm	700 mm
Engine:	Steyr 4-cylinder in-line air-cooled petrol developing 87 hp (65 kW) at 4,000 rpm	Steyr 4-cylinder in-line air-cooled petrol developing 87 hp (65 kW) at 4,000 rpm
Gearbox:	manual with 5 forward and 1 reverse gears	manual with 5 forward and 1 reverse gears
Clutch:	single dry plate	single dry plate
Transfer box:	2-speed	2-speed
Steering:	worm with roller	worm with roller

Configuration	710 (4 × 4)	712 (6 × 6)
Turning circle:	10.37 m	12.28 m
Suspension:	4 × 4: coil springs at all wheel stations. 6 × 6: coil springs, front; leaf springs and hydraulic shock-absorbers, rear	4 × 4: coil springs at all wheel stations. 6 × 6: coil springs, front; leaf springs and hydraulic shock-absorbers, rear
Tyres:	7.50 × 16	7.50 × 16
Brakes:	hydraulic, drums all-round	hydraulic, drums all-round
Electrical system:	24 V	24 V
Batteries:	2 × 12 V, 66 Ah	2 × 12 V, 66 Ah

Status

Production completed during 1990. Supplied to Austria, Ghana, Nigeria, Oman, Sudan, Switzerland (6,300 delivered from 1971 (4 × 4) and 1973 (6 × 6)), Tunisia, the former Yugoslavia and various other unspecified Middle Eastern and South American countries.

Contractor

Steyr-Daimler-Puch Fahrzeugtechnik AG & Co KG.

Enquiries to:

BAE Systems Land Systems, Guildford.

Pinzgauer (4 × 4) and (6 × 6) diesel-powered vehicles from 1985

Production of the original petrol-powered Pinzgauer 710 (4 × 4) and 712 (6 × 6) models concluded in 1990, to be replaced by a range of diesel-powered models first shown in 1985. Diesel-powered models were originally produced by Steyr-Daimler-Puch in Austria, but in July 2000 it was announced that all future production of the Pinzgauer would be carried out in the United Kingdom by Automotive Technik Limited (ATL). Full details of all diesel-powered Pinzgauer production can be found under the UK elsewhere in this section.

In April 2005, it was announced that Stewart & Stevenson of the US (then manufacturer of the Family of Medium Tactical Vehicles (FMTV)) had acquired ATL. Armor Holdings Inc announced in February 2006 it was to

Royal Air Force Pinzgauer 718 (6 × 6) configured as a Trauma Management Vehicle (Automotive Technik) 0547188

Royal Navy Pinzgauer 718 (6 × 6) configured as a bomb disposal vehicle (Automotive Technik) 1047352

acquire Stewart & Stevenson. From May 2006 Automotive Technik Ltd became known as Pinzgauer Ltd. It was announced in July 2007 that Armor Holdings had been acquired by BAE Systems.

BAE Systems announced plans in early-2008 to discontinue production of the Pinzgauer 1 vehicle and close its manufacturing facilities at Guildford and Fareham in the UK. A new Pinzgauer support business (originally at Guildford) has been established. This continues to support Pinzgauer fleets, primarily in the UK and New Zealand. Development of the Pinzgauer 2 vehicle was transitioned to the BAE Systems South Africa business, however, according to BAE Systems, further analysis of the potential market (for Pinzgauer 2) revealed insufficient market interest to continue development.

Contractor
Steyr-Daimler-Puch Fahrzeugtechnik AG & Co KG.

Enquiries to:
BAE Systems Land & Armaments, Newcastle-Upon-Tyne.

Australia

Land Rover 110 heavy-duty (6 × 6)

Development
During 1981, Leyland Australia (now Land Rover Australia) carried out market research that indicated a requirement for a heavy duty (6 × 6) derivative of the Land Rover Defender 110 with a payload of up to 3,000 kg and a rear chassis length of up to 3.3 m. Several alternative designs were investigated before a (6 × 6) version of the 110 was selected. A trials vehicle, produced by SMC Engineering (Bristol) Limited, in the United Kingdom, was sourced for evaluation. Once in Australia this vehicle was fitted with an Isuzu 3.9-litre diesel engine and the original coil springs at the rear were replaced by semi-elliptic leaf springs. Similar prototypes and pre-production vehicles were produced with Australian designed chassis, load-sharing rear suspension and innovative drive to the additional rear axle.

These vehicles were involved in the Australian Army's Project Perentie, which also involved Land Rover (4 × 4) vehicles. The first of 400 production vehicles was handed over to the Australian Army in March 1989 and the last during late 1998. The last batch of (6 × 6) vehicles delivered were 37 flatbed versions intended to carry the Parakeet satellite communications earth station.

The complete Project Perentie programme involved 3,800 (4 × 4) and (6 × 6) vehicles. A further 61 (4 × 4) and 250 (6 × 6) vehicles were sub-contracted to BAE Australia (now BAE Systems Australia Pty Ltd) as part of the Bushranger Phase 1 programme. In total, over 1,000 (6 × 6) vehicles were delivered to the Australian Army.

The Australian Department of Defence recently approved a dispensation for a GVW of 6,200 kg for a version of the (6 × 6).

With the exception of the Long Range Patrol Vehicle (LRPV) variant, used by Australia's Special Air Service Regiment (SASR) which it is understood will be replaced under Project Redfin, these vehicles will be replaced under the Australian Department of Defence's Defence Matériel Organisation's (DMO) multiphase project, Project Land 121; Project Overlander. Project Overlander details specific to the replacement of the Land Rover 110 heavy-duty (6 × 6) can be found in this entry, with a more detailed overview of Project Overlander to be found in the Mack RM6866RS truck entry.

Under the then Phase 3a of Land 121 it was announced early 2006 that three Requests for Tender (RfT), potentially worth up to AUD600 million had been issued. These RfTs involved superseding the high-readiness fleet of 1,400 medium, heavy and light vehicles, 1,300 trailers and 1,200 specialist modules.

Tenders involving medium/heavy vehicles were released to a shortlist of nine companies announced in December 2005 (the then ADI Limited, the then DaimlerChrysler Australia-Pacific, General Dynamics Land Systems-

Australian Army Land Rover 110 heavy duty (6 × 6) configured as an ambulance (Ron Fry) 0121284

Australia, MAN Nutzfahrzeuge, Mack Trucks Australia, Scania Australia, Stewart & Stevenson, the then Tenix Defence, Terex Corporation) and this was later cut to five compliant responses (ADI Limited (now Thales Australia), DaimlerChrysler Australia-Pacific (now Mercedes-Benz Australia-Pacific), MAN Nutzfahrzeuge, Mack Trucks Australia, Stewart & Stevenson (now BAE Systems Land Systems), while an open tender was issued for the light range of vehicles and modules.

The third RfT, involving trailers, was restricted to Australian-based manufacturers capable of supplying a proprietary trailer.

Each offer was required to include a through-life support component potentially extending for up to 30 years.

Late-2007, the now Mercedes-Benz Australia Pacific were announced as preferred tenderers for the light vehicle segment of the now Overlander Phase 3, then quoted as worth a total of USD2.65 billion. BAE Systems (medium/heavy), and Haulmark Trailers Australia (trailers) were also announced as preferred tenderers. It was announced in August 2008 that the medium/heavy segment of Land 121 would be re-tendered after BAE Systems proved unable to meet its contractual commitments.

In October 2008 it was disclosed that Mercedes-Benz Australia Pacific had been awarded a contract worth AUD350 million for the delivery of 1,200 Mercedes-Benz G-Class under the light vehicle segment of Phase 3. Six different configurations are involved, a (4 × 4) general-purpose station wagon; two (4 × 4) cargo variants; a (6 × 6) chassis-cab variant; a (6 × 6) dual cab variant; and a specialist surveillance and reconnaissance vehicle. Specific variants (ambulance and command post for example) will be fitted with specialist modules, these manufactured by G H Varley Pty Ltd. From November 2009 11 prototype G-Class were delivered for compliance and accepting testing within Australia from February 2010. Full production is scheduled to commence late-2010, with initial deliveries and first operational use scheduled for 2011. In service these G-Class will progressively replace many of the current 3,400 (approximately) Land Rover fleet.

In October 2008, the Australian government announced approval to commence planning for Phase 4 of Land 121. Phase 4 will replace the 1,300 Land Rovers not replaced under Phase 3 (light vehicle segment) with a fleet of protected light mobility vehicles.

As part of a plan to examine all options for Land 121 Phase 4, Australia announced that it would participate in the technology demonstration phase of the United States' Joint Light Tactical Vehicle (JLTV) programme. Additionally, Australia's Defence Matériel Organisation (DMO) issued a Request For Proposal (RFP) on 12 June 2009 for an AUD1.8 billion requirement for a light protected mobility vehicle (PMV-L) with at least 50 per cent of the production costs to occur in Australia.

Responses to the PMV-L RFP, which could see domestic manufacturers competing against the successful contender for the US Joint Light Tactical Vehicle (JLTV) programme, were due by 30 September 2009. The RFP,

Australian Army Land Rover 110 heavy duty (6 × 6) with workshop body (Gordon Arthur) 1340340

Australian Army Land Rover 110 heavy duty (6 × 6) (Gordon Arthur) 1340337

Long Range Patrol Vehicle (LRPV) variant of the Land Rover 110 heavy duty (6 × 6) operated by Australian Special Forces in Afghanistan. It is understood that under the approximate AUD350-450 million Project Redfin, Australia will acquire a new fleet of Special Operation Vehicles (SOVs) to replace the (6 × 6) Long Range Patrol Vehicle (LRPV) fleet (Cpl Ashley Roach)   0595296

One of a small number of crew-cab Land Rover 110 heavy duty (6 × 6) supplied to the Australian Army (Ron Fry)   0587631

to which there were 12 respondents, sought information on an Australian-manufactured option for Land 121 Phase 4, under which 1,300 new vehicles will provide an increased level of ballistic and blast protection over the Australian Defence Force's (ADF's) existing light assets.

In May 2010 it was disclosed that Force Protection Australasia, Thales Australia, and General Dynamics Land Systems Australia (GDLS-A) had been downselected for the PMV-L requirement, with each company awarded up to AUD9 million contracts for the development of two prototypes, expected to be ready for test within six months. Force Protection Australasia is offering a version of its Ocelot light protected patrol vehicle, Thales Australia is offering Hawkei, while GDLS-A is offering the latest Next Generation Eagle vehicle. These three designs will compete against those from the three prototype developers (BAE Systems/Navistar, General Dynamics/AM General and Lockheed Martin) already selected under the JLTV programme.

It is understood that neither the G-Class nor the PMV-L capability will replace the special forces Land Rover long range patrol vehicles, these being replaced under a separate and classified procurement program, Project Redfin. It was disclosed in late 2006 that the Special Air Service Regiment was to take delivery of around 30 new Special Operations Vehicles (SOVs) based on a Supacat platform. Full details of this vehicle can be found in the Special attack vehicles section.

Land 121 Phase 5 will provide the ADF with an estimated 2,000 unprotected Commercial-Off-The-Shelf (COTS) vehicles that will serve in the 'raise, train and sustain' functions, thereby replacing the remainder of the current fleet. First Pass Approval for this phase was expected in the last quarter of 2009, but this is understood to have slipped to around 2012.

The Land Rover (6 × 6) platform was also fitted with the Rover 3.5-litre V-8 petrol engine and marketed as part of the Land Rover range in the UK. No sales are known to have been made.

A small number of vehicles were supplied to Oman and Malawi and these vehicles are no longer in service. A variant was evaluated in Singapore and other countries known to have evaluated or considered the design are known to have included Canada and Papua New Guinea.

The Land Rover (6 × 6) has been further developed by Land Rover to meet emerging requirements for light vehicles with higher GVWs and increased payload capabilities. A concept vehicle was shown publicly for the first time at DVD 2007 in the UK. Available details of the vehicle can be found elsewhere in this section.

Description

The Land Rover 110 heavy duty (6 × 6) maintains some commonality with the basic (4 × 4) Land Rover Defender 110, although despite visual similarities no more than 30 per cent of the componentry is Land Rover sourced. The basic engine is an Isuzu 3.9-litre turbocharged diesel, although the standard Rover 3.5-litre V-8 petrol engine (no longer available), could be fitted if required. The cab and front end of the initial and civilian JRA vehicles were the same as the Defender 110 but the production military vehicles utilised a locally designed one-piece galvanised wider than standard cab with matching locally produced wider bonnet. Standard Defender 110 wings with a wider grille panel were utilised.

The chassis is a heavy duty rigid chassis frame fabricated from steel tubing and steel pressings with special anti-corrosion treatment on all surfaces. The spiral bevel front axle is an Australian designed uprated unit. The twin rear axles are Salisbury 8HA fully floating hypoid bevel gear axles with the centre axle differential offset to the right of the centre line and the rear axle differential offset to the left.

The rear tray on the basic vehicle carries a cargo/personnel carrier 3.2 m long and 2.082 m wide. It is normally covered by a heavy duty canvas canopy and inward or outward-facing seats can be provided for up to six

men each side. Various options were offered including a front-mounted Thomas T9000 M 4,000 kg recovery winch, a brush guard, a towing pintle, various stowage racks and tie-down points.

The standard electrical system is 12 V. Fitted-For-Radio (FFR) vehicles have a 24 V system with two 12 V batteries in a slide-out carrier under the left hand front corner of the rear body.

The initial contract covered seven derivatives: cargo; cargo with winch; air defence FFR with winch; ambulance FFR with winch; general repair with winch; electronics repair; and an armed Long Range Patrol Vehicle (LRPV) for the Australian SAS which carries on the rear a frame for a motor cycle. Other derivatives include a communications centre, a command post and a firefighting vehicle. A crew cab version was developed and supplied to the Australian Army in small numbers.

Additionally, a number of logistic vehicles were supplied to Malawi and Oman. A SWB Light Helicopter Transportable Vehicle (LHTV) was developed in prototype form as an artillery tractor for Singapore. This was not procured.

Modular rear bodies, such as those used for the electronics and general repair vehicles, can be unloaded and used as free-standing units if required. The sides of some shelters can open to increase working space. The bodies were produced by JAKAB Industries Pty Ltd of Tamworth, New South Wales.

Additional (6 × 6) vehicles produced under the Bushranger Phase 1 programme included an Interim Infantry Mobility Vehicle, an Assault Pioneer Vehicle, a Mortar Carrier and a Direct Fire Weapons Vehicle.

Specifications
Land Rover 110 heavy-duty (6 × 6)
Cab seating: 1 + 1 (up to 12 in rear)
Configuration: 6 × 6
Weight: (cargo/personnel FFR with winch)
  (unladen) 3,600 kg
  (laden) 5,600 kg (dispensation to 6,200 kg)
  (gross combination mass) 7,100 kg
Load area: 3.2 × 2.082 m
Length overall: 6.001 m
Width:
  (overall) 2.2 m
  (over mirrors) 2.43 m
Height:
  (cab, laden) 2.05 m
  (cab, unladen) 2.08 m
Ground clearance:
  (front) 235 mm
  (rear) 215 mm
Track: 1.698 m
Wheelbase: 3.04 m + 0.9 m
Angle of approach/departure:
(laden) 41°/30°
(unladen) 45°/33°
Max speed: 100 km/h
Range: (roads) 600 km
Fuel capacity: 2 × 65 litres
Max gradient: 60%
Engine: Isuzu 4BD1T 3.856-litre 4-cylinder in-line turbocharged water-cooled diesel developing 121 hp at 3,000 rpm
Gearbox: Land Rover LR95A manual with 4 forward and 1 reverse gears
Transfer box: 2-speed
Steering: Adwest variable ratio worm and peg with power-assistance
Suspension:
  (front) long travel coil springs with telescopic shock-absorbers
  (rear) dual rate semi-elliptic leaf springs linked via shackles to rubber-bushed load-sharing rocker beam
Tyres: 7.50 × 16, 10 ply
Brakes: dual vacuum/hydraulic
Electrical system: 12 V (24 V optional)

Battery:
 (standard) 1 × 12 V, 98 Ah
 (FFR) 2 × 12 V, 95 Ah
Alternator: 70 A

Status
Production complete. Supplied to Australia, Malawi and Oman.

Contractor
Land Rover Australia.

Brazil

ENGESA EE-12 (4 × 4) 500 kg light vehicle

Development
ENGESA was a private company with origins dating back to 1963. The company began by refurbishing old and time-served Brazilian Army vehicles. Ultimately the company would specialise in the defence (and agriculture) sector, specialising in the production of tactical military light vehicles and trucks, and armoured fighting vehicles. The bankruptcy of ENGESA was declared in October 1993.

Description
The EE-12 is a small four-seat vehicle of distinctive appearance. It has a conventional layout with the four-cylinder petrol or diesel engine at the front under a sloped bonnet and with separate seats for the driver and a passenger; a bench seat at the rear can accommodate a further two passengers. Normally the EE-12 is driven open with no weather protection for the occupants other than a forward-folding windscreen, but it is possible to fit a canvas tilt with roll-down blinds. There are no side doors other than canvas covers. A spare wheel is carried at the rear along with a jerrycan.

The overall construction of the EE-12 is very robust. The front and rear bumpers are equipped with towing shackles and a towing pintle is provided at the rear.

The EE-12 was available in a number of variations. One was as a carrier for a 7.62 or 12.7 mm machine gun, another for a 106 mm recoilless rifle. This carrier has an open rear with the jerrycan and spare wheel moved to the vehicle sides and the windscreen is split to allow the 106 mm gun barrel to protrude over the bonnet. A hardtop version also was available and was exported to Angola. Other variants included an anti-tank missile carrier, a radio communications vehicle and a front-line stretcher carrier.

Agrale Marruá
The Marruá light vehicle is produced by Agrale of Brazil and is similar in appearance and concept to the EE-12. It is understood the Marruá was designed/developed by some of the EE-12's original design team. The Marruá was specifically designed for the Brazilian Army and is now available in six primary versions: AM1/AM2 2.3 m WB four-seat soft-top, AM10/AM11 2.9 m WB five-seat soft-top, AM10/AM11 Rec 2.9 m WB four-seat reconnaissance with roll-cage and ring-mount, AM20/AM21 3.21 m WB logistics and cargo, AM20/AM21 3.21 m WB VCC - command-and-control, with in all cases the 1/2, 10/11 designations denoting Euro 2 or Euro 3 emissions compliant engines.

The Marruá is scheduled to replace the large number and variety of Jeep-type designs in service, with the first 100 being delivered for trials to the armed forces (Army and Marines); the Marines' version is designated AM2 MB TNE and the first 25 vehicles have been delivered. Commercial versions are also available. Full details of the Agrale Marruá can be found elsewhere in this section.

Specifications
Seating: 1 + 3
Configuration: 4 × 4 (selectable)
Weights:
 (laden) 2,160 kg
 (max load) 500 kg
 (towed load) 250 kg
Length: 3.57 m
Width: 1.77 m
Height:
 (overall) 1.9 m
 (windscreen down) 1.5 m
Ground clearance: 230 mm
Track: 1.454 m
Wheelbase: 2.16 m
Angle of approach/departure: 70°/50°
Max speed: (road) 110 km/h
Fuel capacity: 92 litres
Max gradient: 70%
Side slope: 30%
Fording: 600 mm
Engine: GM 151 2.47-litre, 4-cylinder in-line water-cooled petrol developing 85 hp (63 kW) at 4,400 rpm, or Perkins 2.8-litre, 4-cylinder in-line water-cooled diesel developing 70 hp (52 kW)
Transmission: Clark 240 V manual with 5 forward and 1 reverse gears
Transfer box: single speed
Steering: mechanical
Turning radius: 6 m
Suspension: coil springs and telescopic shock-absorbers, location by longitudinal and transverse control links; 250 mm wheel travel
Tyres: 7.50 × 16
Brakes: dual circuit, servo assisted; discs front, drums rear
Electrical system: 24 V
Batteries: 2 × 12 V, 63 Ah
Alternator: 40 A

Status
Production complete. Delivered to Angola (operational status uncertain) and possibly others.

Contractor
ENGESA Engenheiros Especializados SA.
(This company is no longer trading.)

Bernardini Xingu BT25 and BT50 (4 × 4) light vehicles

Development
The Bernardini Xingu BT25 and BT50 (4 × 4) light vehicles are Jeep-style vehicles and are based closely on the Toyota Bandeirante. The Toyota Bandeirante is a Toyota Landcruiser 40 Series that was built in Brazil by Toyota do Brasil Ltda (TDB) from the early 1960s until production ceased in 2001. Approximately 100,000 Bandeirantes were built in Brazil between 1961 and 2001. Toyota ceased production, in Japan, of the Landcruiser 40 Series in 1984.

Bernardini SA Indústria e Comércio ceased trading in 1992. It was reported in 2003 that a small number (models were not specified) of Bernardini light vehicles remained in service with Brazilian armed forces, and these are believed to remain in use.

Description
The Bernardini Xingu BT25 and BT50 (4 × 4) light vehicles are both are described as ½-tonne (500 kg) vehicles, the main difference between the two being the longer wheelbase of the BT50. Both vehicles are conventional in layout with the engine forward under a steel bonnet and seating for the driver and three passengers under an optional soft-top. Canvas screen doors are normally fitted. The BT50 can be used as a light

ENGESA EE-12 (4 × 4) 500 kg light vehicle (ENGESA)   1296282

Bernardini Xingu BT50 (4 × 4) light vehicle (Bernardini SA)   1296294

pick-up truck with the rear passenger bench seat removed. A protective grill for the radiator is fitted across the front of the vehicle and a spare wheel is usually carried at the rear on a small tailgate. A towing hitch is fitted under the tailgate. Floating axles are used front and rear.

In July 1990, the previously fitted OM-314 diesel engine was replaced on the production lines by an OM-364 unit delivering the same power output.

Variants of these vehicles included a ¾-tonne (750 kg) pick-up truck version of the BT50 with a canvas tilt carried over the bows and the spare wheel on the left- hand side in front of the cab door. A variant of the BT25 is used as a carrier for an M40A2 106 mm recoilless rifle - this version has a split front windscreen to accommodate the recoilless rifle barrel when travelling. Other variants of both models included communications vehicles with various radio fits.

Optional equipment on all models included a front-mounted 2,500 kg capacity winch, a folding aerial bracket and an extra spare wheel carrier. A light cargo trailer was also available.

Specifications
Cab seating: 1 + 3
Configuration: 4 × 4
Weight:
  (BT25) 1,600 kg
  (BT50) 1,700 kg
Length:
  (BT25) 3.93 m
  (BT50) 4.4 m
Width: 1.8 m
Height: 1.965 m
Ground clearance: 230 mm
Track:
  (front) 1.415 m
  (rear) 1.4 m
Wheelbase:
  (BT25) 2.285 m
  (BT50) 2.755 m
Max speed: 115 km/h
Range: 950 km
Max gradient: 60%
Side slope: 30%
Fording: 700 mm
Engine: OM-364 4-cylinder in-line water-cooled diesel developing 94 hp (70 kW) at 2,800 rpm
Gearbox: manual, 4 forward and 1 reverse gears; from 1993 all models have 5 forward and 1 reverse gears
Clutch: single dry plate
Transfer box: 2-speed
Steering: worm and roller; from 1993 all models have power steering
Turning radius:
  (BT25) 5.3 m
  (BT50) 6.3 m
Suspension: semi-elliptic leaf springs with double action hydraulic shock-absorbers
Tyres: 7.50 × 16
Brakes: dual circuit, hydraulic with vacuum auxiliary
Electrical system: 12 or 24 V
Batteries: 2 × 12 V, 60 Ah
Alternator: 35 A

Status
Production completed in 1992. Small numbers remain in service with Brazilian Armed Forces.

Contractor
Bernardini SA Indústria e Comércio
(This company is no longer trading)

ENGESA EE-34 (4 × 4) 750 kg light vehicle

Development
ENGESA was a private company with origins dating back to 1963. The company began by refurbishing old and time-served Brazilian Army vehicles. Ultimately the company would specialise in the defence (and agriculture) sector, specialising in the production of tactical military light vehicles and trucks, and armoured fighting vehicles. The bankruptcy of ENGESA was declared in October 1993.

The prototype ENGESA EE-34 (4 × 4) 750 kg light vehicle was completed in 1980 and production commenced in 1982. It was reported in 2003 that around 30 ENGESA EE-34 (4 × 4) light vehicles in command-and-control configuration remained in service with the Brazilian Army and Marines.

Description
The body of the EE-34 is made of pressed steel and the layout is conventional, with a cargo area at the rear. The standard form is a pick-up truck for general purpose load carrying with seating for the driver plus a bench seat for two passengers. Standard equipment included a windscreen that folds downwards onto the bonnet when not in use, vinyl doors, a removable vinyl top and a drop tailgate for loading stores. The maximum payload across country is 750 kg and 1,000 kg on roads.

ENGESA EE-34 (4 × 4) 750 kg light vehicle (ENGESA)   1340307

Variants included a light truck version, a command-and-control version and an ambulance with a pressed steel body. This has space for four stretchers or two stretchers plus three seated casualties or six seated casualties. The ambulance body is entered by two large rear doors.

Specifications
Cab seating: 1 + 2
Configuration: 4 × 4
Weight:
  (unladen) 2,500 kg
  (laden, road) 3,580 kg
  (laden, off-road) 3,330 kg
Max load:
  (on-road) 1,000 kg
  (off-road) 750 kg
Length: 5.32 m
Width: 2.04 m
Height:
  (tarpaulin) 2.2 m
  (cab top) 2 m
  (windscreen down) 1.493 m
Ground clearance: 230 mm
Track: 1.55 m
Wheelbase: 2.95 m
Angle of approach/departure: 42°/52°
Max speed: (road) 100 km/h
Range: 600 km
Max gradient: 60%
Max side slope: 30%
Engine: Perkins 4.236-litre 4-cylinder in-line water-cooled diesel developing 82 hp (61 kW) at 2,800 rpm
Gearbox: manual, 4 forward and 1 reverse gears
Clutch: single dry plate
Transfer box: mechanical, 2-speed
Steering: mechanical
Suspension: leaf springs and hydraulic shock-absorbers
Tyres: 7.50 × 16
Brakes:
  (main) hydraulic, discs front, drums rear
  (parking) drum, operating on transmission output shaft
Electrical system: 24 V

Status
Production completed in 1992. In service with the Brazilian armed forces (see text).

Contractor
ENGESA Engenheiros Especializados SA.
(This company is no longer trading.)

UAI M1-34 (4 × 4) 750 kg light vehicle

Description
The UAI M1-34 (4 × 4) 750 kg light vehicle is a conventional design powered by an 87 hp (65 kW) diesel engine coupled to a five-speed manual gearbox and two-speed transfer box. The cargo capacity for cross-country use is 750 kg plus a 1,000 kg trailer. On roads this cargo load can be increased to 1,000 kg, plus a towed load of 1,800 kg.

Manufacturer, Terex do Brasil SA ceased trading some time ago but it was reported, in 2003, that the vehicle remains in service with Brazilian Armed Forces, and with two anti-aircraft groups equipped with Bofors Defence 40 mm L/70 anti-aircraft guns.

UAI M1-34 (4 × 4) 750 kg light vehicle (Ian Young)   0511710

Status
Production complete. In service with Brazil (see text).

Contractor
Terex do Brasil SA.
(This company is no longer trading.)

Canada

Bombardier Iltis (4 × 4) 500 kg light vehicle

Development
In October 1981, Volkswagen AG of Germany agreed to cede and transfer to Bombardier Inc. of Canada the design and manufacturing technology of its Iltis (4 × 4) 500 kg light vehicle as used by the German Army. The agreement also granted to Bombardier the worldwide rights for the marketing, sale and distribution of the Iltis, as well as the rights to manufacture and market the civilian version. Bombardier also acquired the tooling equipment used in the manufacture of the Iltis.

Before this announcement, the Canadian Department of National Defense asked the company to submit a proposal, based on the Iltis, for the replacement of the existing utility (4 × 4) vehicles of the Canadian Forces. In November 1983, it was announced that the Canadian government had awarded a contract for 1,900 (later increased to 2,500) Iltis vehicles to the Logistic Equipment Division of Bombardier Inc. The contract included the supply of spare parts, manuals and training programmes for operators and maintainers and was valued at CAD68 million. Production for this contract began at the end of the second quarter of 1984 and was completed by the end of 1985. During 1984 an order for over 2,500 vehicles was placed for the Belgian Armed Forces (2,673 were delivered). Cameroon also received a never-quoted quantity of Bombardier-built Iltis vehicles, as did Oman. Production ceased in 1988.

The Canadian Department of National Defense has now completed the CAD241 million Light Utility Vehicle, Wheeled project, its focus to acquire a replacement for the Iltis fleet. Two differing types of vehicle are involved, with the Iltis fleet replacement understood to have been completed by early 2006.

In November 2002, the Canadian Department of National Defense announced its intention to award a CAD49.7 million contract to GM Defense for 861 Military Commercial-Off-The-Shelf (MilCOTS) trucks as the first stage of the replacement programme. Based on the GM Silverado LSSV series, 801 basic variants and 60 cable layers were initially ordered, with a contract option for an additional 200 basic variants subsequently being exercised. All 1,061 vehicles involved were delivered between November 2003 and November 2004.

In service, the LSSV is primarily used by reserve units within North America. Full details of the GM Defense Light Service Support Vehicle (LSSV) range can be found elsewhere in this section.

The Standard Military Pattern (SMP) part of the Light Utility Vehicle, Wheeled project (valued at USD130.4 million) was finally awarded to Mercedes-Benz in October 2003 for a vehicle based on the 2.85 m wheelbase G-Class with a maximum permissible GVW of 4,800 kg.

Canadian troops in Kabul, Afghanistan, took delivery of the first 60 vehicles between 5-13 March 2004, with all 802 vehicles and 160 Armour Protection System (APS) kits called for under the original contract delivered by December 2004. In July 2004 the Canadian Department of National Defence announced that it had exercised a CAD81 million contract option for an additional 357 vehicles and 20 protection kits. A further order for an additional 25 vehicles was subsequently placed, deliveries concluding in July 2006.

In service the SMP G-Class is used by both regular and reserve forces, and in addition to replacing the Iltis has also replaced Cougar Direct Fire Support Vehicles. Full details of the Mercedes-Benz G-Class can be found elsewhere in this section.

In August 2005, the Belgian Army awarded IVECO DVD of Italy a contract for 440 IVECO Light Armoured Tactical Vehicles (LATVs) plus 120 applique armoured protection kits, the contract including an option for a further 180

Bombardier-built Iltis (4 × 4) light vehicle of the Belgian Army
(Stefan Marx)   1047341

vehicles and 60 kits in two batches of 90 vehicles and 30 kits each. The LATV will part replace the Belgian Army's Iltis fleet, 931 of which remained in service as of February 2009. The original Belgian requirement, which specified a vehicle with an anti-personnel mine blast protected floorpan as standard plus add-on applique ballistic protection kits, called for 830 vehicles and 300 kits. It is expected that a militarised commercial pattern light vehicle will eventually be procured to make up the replacement shortfall.

Description
Originally a Volkswagen design, the Iltis uses components from the Volkswagen Polo and Audi Quattro vehicles. The all-steel body has a conventional layout with the engine at the front and the cargo area to the rear. The driver and front passenger have separate seats with seating for two more passengers to the rear. The rear seats can be folded down to increase the load-carrying area and the vehicle is provided with a folding hood, removable side flaps and a folding windscreen. The driver can select either a full 4 × 4 drive for cross-country or 4 × 2 for road drive, in which case the front axle is disengaged. An integral roll bar is provided.

The Iltis can be lifted by the UH-60 Black Hawk helicopter and has been tested for low-altitude parachute extraction from transport aircraft and for parachute dropping.

Optional extras for the Iltis included a turbocharged diesel engine, electric winch kit, rear pintle hook, three-door glass fibre hardtop and up to three radio equipment outlets. Also provided are weapon mounting systems for 7.62 mm and 0.50 inch/12.7 mm machine guns, the MK19 40 mm grenade launcher and Anti-Tank Guided Missile (ATGM) systems such as MILAN and TOW.

Variants of the basic Iltis include an ambulance, command vehicle, cable layer, communications vehicle and a version carrying artillery sound ranging equipment.

Specifications
Iltis (4 × 4)
Cab seating: 1 + 3
Configuration: 4 × 4
Weight:
  (laden) 2,050 kg
  (unladen) 1,550 kg
  (payload) 500 kg
  (towed load, braked) 2,000 kg
  (towed load, unbraked) 750 kg
Length: 3.887 m
Width: 1.52 m
Height: 1.837 m
Ground clearance: 225 mm
Track:
  (front) 1.23 m
  (rear) 1.26 m
Wheelbase: 2.017 m
Angle of approach/departure: 41°/32°
Max speed: 130 km/h
Fuel capacity: 85 litres
Range: 700 km
Max gradient: 77%
Fording: 600 mm
Engine: VW 183 1.7-litre 4-cylinder OHC water-cooled petrol developing 75 hp (56 kW) at 5,000 rpm
Gearbox: manual with 4 forward and 1 reverse gears plus a cross-country gear
Clutch: single dry plate
Steering: rack and pinion
Turning radius: 5.5 m
Suspension: overhead semi-elliptic leaf springs and double acting shock-absorbers
Tyres: 6.50 × R-16

Brakes:
(main) dual circuit, hydraulic, drums front and rear
(parking) mechanical
Electrical system: 24 V
Batteries: 2 × 12 V, 45 Ah

Status
Production complete. Some remain in service with Belgium (2,673 delivered, 931 in service as of February 2009; replacement underway), supplied to Cameroon's Armed Forces (status uncertain), replaced in the Canadian Army by early 2006, supplied to Oman (status uncertain).

Contractor
Bombardier Inc.
(Bombardier are no longer involved in this market sector.)

China

Beijing Automobile Works (BAW) BJ212, BJ212A, BJ2020S, BJ2020SA, BJ2020VB and BJ2022 light vehicles

Development
What is now the state-owned Beijing Automobile Works (BAW) was created in 1958 as the Beijing Automobile Works and as a military component manufacturer. In 1965 the BAW commenced production of the Beijing BJ212 light vehicle, this based on the Russian GAZ-69.

As a result of negotiations that commenced in 1979, in 1984 Beijing Jeep Corporation (BJC) was formed as a joint venture between Beijing Automobile Works and the then American Motors Corporation (AMC), to become China's first automotive joint venture. BJC was to manufacture the Jeep Cherokee for the Chinese market, although Cherokee technology would be used to enhance the BJ212.

In 1987 the remainder of BAW was merged with the Beijing Motorcycle Works to become Beijing United Automobile Manufacturing Co. (BAM). Both BAW and BAM would ultimately build BJ212 series vehicles.

Also in 1987, Chrysler bought AMC and assumed AMCs role as joint venture partner. In 1998 the newly formed DaimlerChrysler (now Chrysler LLC) took over 42.4 per cent of the stakes, while Beijing Auto Works held the remaining 57.6 per cent.

In 2001 BAM and its subsidiary Beijing Automotive Assembly (BAA) were reorganised into a new privately-owned concern known as Beijing Automobile Ltd Co.

In 2002 DaimlerChrysler and Beijing Automotive Industry (Group) Company (BAIC) announced details of a 30-year agreement that extended their joint venture until 2033.

In December, 2004 Beijing Jeep Corporation and the then DaimlerChrysler embarked on the construction of a new plant for local production of the Mercedes-Benz C- and E-class. This facility opened in September 2005, at which time production of Cherokee-based products ceased.

BJC was renamed Beijing Benz-DaimlerChrysler Automotive Co Ltd (BBDC) with DaimlerChrysler holding a 49 per cent stake in the joint venture, Beijing Automotive Industry Holding Co., Ltd (BAIHC) the majority 51%. Some sources state the joint venture was a 50-50 per cent arrangement.

In 2007, BAIHC acquired 33 per cent of BAW. At the same time the element of BBDC responsible for building the BJ2022 (the continuing

It became known in November 2005 that following at least a 200,000-mile test program including various road and weather conditions across China that the PLA GAD had selected the BJ2022 (commercial name Brave Warrior) as the PLA's next-generation 0.5-ton class vehicle (Dawei Xia)
1120495

Beijing BJ2020S (4 × 4) light vehicle of the People's Liberation Army (Beijing Jeep Corporation)
0114429

evolution of the BJ212 series) was separated from BBDC and reassigned to BAW. This increased BAIHC's share of BAW to 51 per cent, making it owner of BAW and returning it to state control. BAW currently builds the BJ2022 for the Chinese military. Following its restructure, Chrysler pulled out of the joint venture in early 2009.

In addition to the Beijing 2020 series (marketed commercially as the City Cruiser), the now Beijing Automobile Works has produced the Jeep Cherokee (XJ), Jeep Grand Cherokee, the Beijing Jeep Corporation (BJC) Cherokee (known locally as the Super Cherokee), and the Jeep Cherokee-based Jeep 2500/2700, the latter now marketed as Qishi by Beijing Automobile Works Co, Ltd (BAW).

Since batch production began in 1965/66, the BJ212/BJ2020 series has reportedly been exported to over 20 countries including Angola, Bangladesh, Cambodia, Colombia, Indonesia, Myanmar, Niger, North Korea, Philippines, Sudan, Zambia and others. Export figures are unknown.

The only figures to emerge in recent years suggest that in 2003 BJC exported 1,100 vehicles, the majority of which were BJ2020 series. Another report in 2000 indicated that 150 BJ2020SY were exported to 'an African country'. In all cases it is impossible to determine how many of these vehicles were destined for military/para-military purposes. One confirmed export of the military variant of the BJ2020 series is the November 2000 delivery of 96 right-hand drive BJ2020SJ (military variant) models to the Indonesian Army. According to one report, two right-hand drive BJ2020SJ vehicles completed a 10,000 km road test in Indonesia before a final purchase deal was reached. The 96 vehicles were the first part of a deal which included a total of 500 vehicles scheduled to be delivered by 2001.

It is known that an export deal for the series between the then BJC and Pakistan's AMC was signed in November 2003 to allow the Pakistani company to assemble the BJ2020VCR (local name, Zabardast) in a new plant located in the Economic Development District in Karachi. Assembly of the first 40 kits had been finished by the end of 2003, with an additional 150 kits imported in December 2003. It was expected that up to 1,000 kits would be imported from China during 2004. AMC (Adam Motor Co) is understood to be looking for export partners in Southern Asia and Africa.

According to reports in the Chinese media, the PLA General Armament Department (GAD) launched its next-generation 0.5-ton (although payload class is actually 500 kg) class high-mobility vehicle programme with an invitation for tenders in 1999 and that in cooperation with the then Beijing Jeep Corporation Ltd an agreement was signed on 4 September 2002 in Beijing for a vehicle that will be the eventual replacement for the BJ2020 series. It is understood there were ten contenders for this requirement.

It became known in November 2005 that following at least a 200,000-mile test program that the PLA GAD had selected the BJ2022JC (commercial name Brave Warrior) as the PLA's next-generation 0.5-ton class vehicle. Testing of prototype vehicles was conducted in the high-altitude conditions of Tibet, the high-latitude conditions of Heilongjiang province, the high-humidity conditions of Yunnan province and the dry conditions of Gansu province. The vehicle was also evaluated for airborne operations through air drops.

In an unusual public disclosure, the then Beijing Automobile Works (BAW) announced in August 2007 that the Chinese People's Liberation Army (PLA) was to buy 2,100 BJ2022JC 'Brave Warrior' light utility vehicles. Sources said that half would go to the Fujian military district, opposite Taiwan.

In May 2010 Chinese media reported that President Hu Jintao had agreed to donate 257 military vehicles, including 30 BJ2022, to the Cambodian Army. These vehicles have been delivered.

Description

Production of the basic BJ212 began in 1965/66. These light vehicles are similar in appearance (and based around) to the GAZ-69, the BJ212 seating five people and the BJ212A seating up to eight. The latter also has a slightly increased payload.

The BJ212A has no rear side door and has a conventional tarpaulin cover (if fitted), as opposed to the raised 'convertible' cover of the BJ212. A variant of the BJ212 is used to carry the NORINCO Type 75 105 mm recoilless rifle. This model can be identified by the split windscreen, provided to accommodate the length of the barrel.

Over 200,000 units of the BJ212 were produced by BAW between 1965 and 1983.

The BJ2020S and BJ2020SA were introduced by BJC in 1983 as successors to the twenty-year-old BJ212/A. Their military versions were known as BJ2020SJ and BJ2020SAJ. The BJ2020S featured a more powerful 85 hp petrol engine and a four-speed gear box. Beijing United Automobile Motorcycle Manufacturing Co. (BAM) also manufactured the BJ2020, including all weapon carrier variants.

In the early 2000s, BJC introduced the BJ2020V as a stop-gap before the BJ2020 replacement could be completed. The BJ2020V was based on the layout of the BJ2020S, but features the locally developed C498QA1 version of the 498 MPI engine as fitted on early Jeep Cherokee models. This could be made to meet EURO I emissions requirements if required. The BJ2020V series include the military variants BJ2020VJ (1 + 4 seating) and BJ2020VAJ (1 + 7 seating), as well as the civilian variants BJ2020VB and BJ2020VE (commercial name New City Cruiser).

All versions have an identical layout, with the engine at the front and the passenger or cargo compartment to the rear. Next to the driver is a seat for one passenger. On the BJ2020S a single bench seat accommodates three more passengers, while on the BJ2020SA, there are two bench seats along the sides for six passengers. The windscreen can be folded forward over the bonnet on both versions. The BJ2020SA has a rear tailgate that can be folded down for access allowing it to be used as a light utility vehicle.

The limited data currently available for the BJ2022 suggests two basic military versions are available, 1 + 4 (BJ2022JC) and 1 + 7 seat (BJ2022JLC) designs. Payloads are now given as 500 kg for the smaller vehicle, 750 kg for the larger vehicle. Motive power is provided by a 3.2-litre turbocharged and intercooled diesel engine developing 136 hp at 3,600 rpm and

Beijing BJ2020S (4 × 4) light vehicle of the People's Liberation Army (Beijing Jeep Corporation)
0567285

313 N.m torque at 2,000 rpm. Each of the two driven beam-type axles (4 × 4) are coil-sprung and fitted with locking differentials.

A civilian version of the BJ2022 is now available, this powered by either a 2.9-litre turbocharged diesel or 2.7-litre petrol engine.

Specifications

See table below

Status

The BJ range of light vehicles are in service with the People's Liberation Army, Bolivia, Chad, Indonesia, Pakistan, and other nations. Over 500,000 units have been produced. BJ2022 (commercial name Brave Warrior) now in production.

Contractor

Beijing Automobile Works (BAW)

Model	BJ2020S	BJ2020SA	BJ2020VB	BJ2020VE
Seating:	1 + 4	1 + 7	1 + 4	1 + 4
Configuration:	4 × 4	4 × 4	4 × 4	4 × 4
Weight:				
(laden)	2,005 kg	2,150 kg	1,945 kg	2,005 kg
(unladen)	1,550 kg	1,580 kg	1,520 kg	1,580 kg
(max load)	425 kg	600 kg	425 kg	425 kg
(towed load)	800 kg	800 kg	n/avail	n/avail
Length:	3.86 m	4.028 m	4.068 m	4.016 m
Width:	1.76 m	1.76 m	1.768 m	1.778 m
Height:				
(laden)	1.81 m	1.97 m	n/avail	1.942 m
(unladen)	1.99 m	2.1 m	1.99 m	n/avail
Wheelbase:	2.3 m	2.75 m	2.3 m	2.3 m
Track: (front and rear)	1.44 m	1.44 m	1.5 m	1.5 m
Ground clearance:	210 mm	210 mm	210 mm	210 mm
Max speed:	100 km/h	100 km/h	125 km/h	125 km/h
Gradient:				
(without trailer)	66%	66%	66%	60%[1]
(with trailer)	50%	50%	n/avail	n/avail
Fording:	500 mm	550 mm	n/avail	n/avail
Engine:	BN492 2.445-litre 4-cylinder in-line 4-stroke water-cooled petrol developing 75 hp (56 kW) at 3,800 rpm		C498QA1 2.5-litre 4-cylinder in-line 4-stroke water-cooled EFI (Electronic Fuel Injection) petrol developing 105 hp (78 kW) at 4,800 rpm. EURO I optional.	
Gearbox:	manual, 3 forward and 1 reverse, synchromesh on 2nd, 3rd		manual five-speed with synchromesh	
Clutch:		Single dry plate		
Transfer box:	2-speed	2-speed	2-speed	2-speed
Suspension:	longitudinal semi-elliptic leaf springs with hydraulic double acting telescopic shock-absorbers			
Steering:	recirculating ball		recirculating ball, power assisted	
Turning radius:	6 m	6 m	6 m	6 m
Brakes:	hydraulic, drums all-round	hydraulic, drums all-round	discs front, drums rear	discs front, drums rear
Tyres:	6.50R 16	6.50R 16	n/avail	215/80R 16
Electrical system:	12 V	12 V	12 V	12 V
Battery:	12 V, 54 Ah	12 V, 54 Ah	n/avail	n/avail

[1] Official literature quotes 60°. This is considered to be a printing error

Egypt

Egyptian Jeep production

Development
As part of the Arab Organisation of Industrialisation Plan, Egypt has manufactured a number of Jeep models under licence from the now Chrysler Group LLC.

The first production Egyptian Jeep vehicles were completed in 1977. Between 1977 and 1986, the Egyptian Army received a total of 11,776 Jeep CJ-6, CJ-7 and CJ-8 models with an average of 30 per cent local content. In total, approaching 14,000 Jeep vehicles were delivered during this time, these figures including 1,965 J-20 and AM-720 vehicles.

The Jeep YJ-L, sold commercially as the Wrangler, entered production in 1988 to 1989 with 350 units for the Kuwait Military Forces and 99 for the Egyptian Army. The last YJ-L vehicles were assembled for the Egyptian Army during 1998. Between 1988 and 1998, 3,199 Jeep YJ-Ls were delivered to the Egyptian Army.

The Jeep YJ-L differed from its predecessor by having an improved heavy-duty air flow system, larger 7.5 × 16 inch tyres, heavy-duty shock-absorbers and springs, and a payload of 750 kg.

The successor of the YJ-L model is the TJ-L model, and a prototype Jeep Wrangler TJ (2002 model-year) underwent an extensive five-month 15,000-mile (approximate) test period following which the Egyptian Armament Authorities signed off acceptance of the vehicle.

In mid-2003, it became known that the Egyptian military had ordered an initial 1,000 Jeep TJ-Ls, with production scheduled to run from August 2003 until January 2004. Production began in August 2003 and by November 2003, 350 vehicles had been delivered; deliveries concluded in March 2004. These vehicles were powered by a DaimlerChrysler petrol engine but the Egyptian Army specified a diesel engine for all future deliveries, and displayed at IDEX 2005 was a diesel-powered prototype, the selected engine being a VM Motori unit.

A further 1,250 vehicles were delivered between September 2005 and May 2006, and in September 2007 an additional 1,250 vehicles were ordered for delivery by year-end. The most recent known order was placed in December 2008 and called for a further 1,250 vehicles. Additional orders are anticipated.

Having not actively pursued them since the mid-1990s, the then DaimlerChrysler announced during 2005 that it was again looking seriously at militarised Jeep exports, with production (dependant on order size) likely to be CKD in Egypt or elsewhere. A number of countries were known to be considering military Jeep TJ-L models and a number of trials were carried out. Saudi Arabia carried out Summer trials of the TJ-L in July 2004, Angola and Oman purchased four examples each during 2004, Austria and South Africa received a single example each early 2005 and a number of West African countries are reported to have received vehicles from June 2005 onwards. An order from Iraq for 100 vehicles for a June 2005 delivery was placed earlier in 2005.

And while suitable for some requirements, general feedback from TJ-L trials indicated the need for air-conditioning, enhanced safety features including airbags and rollover protection, the potential for emissions and other legislative compliance, plus an increase in payload allowance. In answer to this feedback, the then DaimlerChrysler displayed a new Jeep Wrangler military concept vehicle AAD (South Africa) in 2006, and the military specific Jeep J8 was publicly displayed for the first time at DSEi (UK) in September 2007.

The Jeep J8 became available for production at the AAV plant late-2008, although dependent on order size, the now Chrysler Group LLC would likely give consideration to any requirement for either CKD or added local content, thus CKD production elsewhere remains a possibility.

The first known customer for the Jeep J8 was Poland, with a small number (around 10) of vehicles supplied to the Ministry of Interior during 2009. These were fitted with ballistic protection and may have been supplied to anti-terrorist units. Polish vehicles were manufactured in Egypt, with local content added by local Chrysler agent, Zeszuta.

Jeep TJ-L as supplied to Iraq during 2005 (Chrysler Group LLC)   1340315

It was disclosed in August 2009 that the now Chrysler Group LLC had appointed Jankel Group subsidiary Jeep Government and Military Sales (JGMS) as the worldwide distributor for the Jeep J8 for supply to government and military customers. From 2007 Chrysler had partnered with Jankel Armouring Limited of the UK to develop a range of modified Jeep J8 vehicles.

It is understood that a small number of Jeep J8 were ordered by the Jordanian Royal Guard mid-2010, these manufactured in Egypt and to be delivered through Jordan Light Vehicle Manufacturing (JLVM), a joint venture between KADDB and Jankel. These vehicles are understood to be powered by the non-standard HEMI 5.7-litre V8 petrol engine, long range fuel tanks and zoned armour protection.

In August 2010 it was disclosed that a small number of Jeep J8 in troop-carrying/cargo configuration had been supplied to Uruguayan peace-keeping troops through the US Army's TACOM for use in Haiti.

Full details of the Jeep J8 can be found elsewhere in this section.

Description
The Jeep YJ-L resembles the traditional Jeep in appearance. It is built on a 207 MPa yield strength (minimum) welded steel 100 × 63.5 mm ladder-frame chassis fitted with four cross members. Wheelbase is 2.931 m and the steel rear cargo box measures 1.6 × 1.403 × 0.417 m (L × W × H). Maximum payload is 900 kg. A number of body style variants are available including an eight-seat personnel carrier that seats two (driver plus one passenger) in the front of the vehicle, and six longitudinally on two inward-facing bench seats in the rear body.

Initial production vehicles are fitted with a DaimlerChrysler 3.958-litre six-cylinder petrol engine developing 181 hp. Later production vehicles are fitted with a VM Motori 2.8-litre four-cylinder diesel unit developing 120 hp.

Variants
Several variants of Egyptian-produced Jeep vehicles are in Egyptian Army use. They include versions of the CJ-7 used as Swingfire anti-tank missile launch vehicles (carrying four missiles) or Swingfire missile resupply vehicles (carrying 13 missiles). Other missile-carrying CJ-7s include versions for the SA-7 SAM and its Egyptian-produced version, the Sakr Eye.

Variants of the Jeep CJ-8 in Egyptian Army service include: 500 TOW anti-tank missile carriers delivered direct from the US, plus a number of TOW missile resupply vehicles; a refrigerated mobile blood bank with demountable electrical generators; 80 mm multiple rocket launcher

Prototype diesel-powered Jeep Wrangler TJ-L at IDEX 2005 (Patrick Allen)   0590731

Displayed at Eurosatory 2004, a pre-production Jeep TJ-L (Shaun C Connors)   1120449

carrier, full details of which can found in *Jane's Armour and Artillery*; mobile workshop; NBC reconnaissance vehicle; ambulance; communications vehicle; scatterable mine dispenser vehicle; and a command vehicle.

A border patrol unit based on the YJ-L was supplied to Kuwait, and fittings included a 0.50 inch/12.7 mm heavy machine gun mount, 24 V system, electronic land navigation system and an auxiliary fuel tank providing a total fuel capacity of 100 litres.

Specifications

Model	YJ-L	TJ-L
Configuration:	4 × 4	4 × 4
Weight:		
(kerb)	1,450 kg	1,520 kg (with ½ tank of fuel)
(weight distribution (front/rear axle))	n/avail	56%/44%
(GVW)	2,200 kg	2,418 kg
(weight distribution (front/rear axle))	n/avail	38%/62%
(max load)	750 kg	900 kg
(front axle load (laden/unladen))	n/avail	824/909 kg
(front axle rating)	n/avail	1,136 kg
(rear axle load (laden/unladen))	n/avail	641/1455 kg
(rear axle rating)	n/avail	1,591 kg
Length:	4.489 m	4.420 m
Width:	1.676 m	1.694 m
Height:		
(soft-top)	1.828 m	n/avail
(hard-top)	1.85 m	n/avail
(windscreen up)	n/avail	1.763
(windscreen down)	n/avail	1.410 m
Ground clearance:	230 mm	231 mm (under fuel tank skid plate at GVW)
Track:	1.473 m	1.483 m
Wheelbase:	2.627 m	2.931 m
Angle of approach/departure:	37°/30°	47°/34° (kerb weight)
Max speed:	n/avail	140 km/h
Fuel capacity:	76 litres	71.9 litres
Cruising range:	n/avail	>600 km (on-road), up to 500 km (off-road)
Max gradient: (laden)	n/avail	60% (subject to traction)
Max sideslope: (laden)	n/avail	20-45% (load dependant)
Engine:	MPI 4-litre 6-cylinder water-cooled petrol developing 180 hp (134 kW) at 4,500 rpm or MPI 2.5-litre 4-cylinder water-cooled petrol developing 117 hp (87 kW) at 5,250 rpm	VM Motori 2.8-litre 4-cylinder inline water-cooled diesel developing 120 hp (89 kW) at 3,800 rpm and 325 N.m torque at 2,000 rpm (current production); DaimlerChrysler Power Tech I-6 MPI 3.958-litre 6-cylinder in-line water-cooled petrol developing 181 hp (135 kW) at 4,600 rpm and 301 N.m torque at 2,800 rpm (initial production)
Gearbox:	manual with 5 forward and 1 reverse gears	New Venture Gear NV3550 manual with 5 forward and 1 reverse gears
Transfer box:	NP 231 2-speed	New Venture Gear NVG231 2-speed
Clutch:	n/avail	LUK single dry disc, (dia) 266.7 mm, hydraulic
Steering:	n/avail	Delphi Model 700, hydraulic power-assistance, recirculating ball, 14:1 reduction ratio
Turning radius:	n/avail	12.6 m
Suspension/axles:		
(front)	Dana Model 30 semi-floating axle with multileaf XHD springs mounted below, plus track and anti-roll bar	Dana Model M30 beam axle with Quadra Coil coil spring and hydraulic shock-absorber suspension
(rear)	Dana Model 44 (with Trac Lok) semi-floating with multileaf XHD springs mounted below; a track bar is utilised	Dana Model M44 beam axle with Trac Lok differential locking and Quadra Coil coil spring and hydraulic shock-absorber suspension
Tyres:	16 × 17.5 (sand-type)	Michelin LT215/85R 16 tubeless on ArvinMeritor 16 × 6 steel rims
Brakes:	discs front, drums rear	Bendix, discs front and rear
Electrical system:	12 V (24 V optional)	12/24 V (heavy-duty option)
Batteries:	n/avail	2 × 12 V (heavy-duty option)
Alternator:	n/avail	12/24 V, 100/150 A (heavy-duty option)

Status

Production of earlier models completed in 1999. These remain in service with Egypt (CJ and YJ), Kuwait (YJ), Oman (CJ), and possibly others. Production of model TJ-L commenced August 2003. TJ-L models are in production for, and service with, Egypt (see text), are in service with Iraq (100 delivered from June 2005), and have been supplied to Angola (four, 2004), Austria (one, 2005), Oman (four, 2004), South Africa (one, 2005) and a number of other undisclosed West African and Middle Eastern countries for evaluation.

Contractor

Arab American Vehicles Co (AAV)
Chrysler LLC

France

Renault Sherpa Light range of tactical vehicles

Development

Development of what is now known as the Sherpa Light range can be traced back to the United Arab Emirates (UAE) where, as part of an ongoing programme to find a locally produced alternative to the AM General HMMWV, development commenced in 1999.

The original vehicle was displayed publicly for the first time at IDEX 2003 where it was branded the Advanced Modular Vehicles (AMV) Al-Dhabi.

By IDEX 2005 the vehicle had migrated to the Renault stand and with the tentative designation of Sherpa 2.5. In December 2005 Renault Trucks Defense announced that it had acquired the full and sole rights to the design from AMV. The intention of this acquisition was to provide Renault Trucks Defense with a vehicle that could fill an identified gap within the company's product range between conventional (and currently out of

The latest version of the Sherpa Light APC, this shown for the first time at Eurosatory 2010 and featuring improved IED and mine blast protection, plus an assortment of other overall specification improvements (Shaun C Connors)   1391398

The Sherpa Light Carrier is a cargo/utility version that can be fitted with a short two-man or long four-man cab, this available unarmoured or armoured (to various levels). Maximum payload is around 4,500 kg and the rear body can be fitted with either a conventional cargo body or mount a shelter-type body including a standard 10 ft NATO shelter (Renault Trucks Defense)   1391410

The latest version of the Sherpa Light Scout, this shown for the first time at Eurosatory 2010 and featuring improved IED and mine blast protection, plus an assortment of other overall specification (Shaun C Connors)   1391407

fashion) Jeep-type light utility vehicles, and the then under-development 5,000 kg payload Sherpa Medium range of tactical trucks. Full details of the Sherpa Medium range of tactical trucks (including the Sherpa 5 and Sherpa 10) can be found in the Trucks section.

Throughout a four-/five-year period of developmental evolution a variety of designations and technical specifications for assorted Sherpa models were touted. By DSEi 2009 the available range had stabilised and the all-encompassing Sherpa Light designation had replaced the then current Sherpa 2 and Sherpa 3/3A designations; the A in 3A denoting armoured.

Renault's first sales for the Sherpa Light were announced during 2008, these for 35 then designated Sherpa 3 to NAMSA and 92 then designated Sherpa 3A Grand Volume to France's Gendarmerie. By early 2010 around 200 units in total had been ordered, these including a further 17 during 2009 for NATO use, four armoured Scout variants for NAMSA, and 33 then designated Sherpa 3 vehicles for use with France's Thales Syracuse III military satellite communications programme.

A Sherpa variant has been down-selected to meet the UK MoD's stalled OUVS (Large) requirement, and early 2009 Renault announced a teaming with Land Rover for current and emerging UK programs, this teaming possibly expanding to address international requirements in the future.

Description

The now designated Sherpa Light range began as a vehicle designed to replace the AM General HMMWV in a number of primarily Middle Eastern markets, and as such had some visual and dimensional similarities to the HMMWV at the early stages of development.

However, throughout its evolution the Sherpa Light has increased in areas of weights and dimensions, and from initial GVWs of 7,500 kg to 9,000 kg to the current 7,900 kg to 10,900 kg.

Most variants of the Sherpa Light are available with softskin or armoured cabs (ballistic and mine protection kits), the capability to accept armour without unacceptable performance degradation built in at design stage. The Sherpa Light Station Wagon, Sherpa Light APC and Sherpa Light HI are provided in armoured configuration as standard.

The Sherpa Light High Intensity, the most protected variant of Sherpa Light range (Shaun C Connors)   1391408

The Sherpa Light is based on a conventional chassis frame, and unlike many of its contemporaries which feature fully independent suspension set-ups, the Sherpa Light range feature beam axle and coil spring suspension, the differential bowls of the beam axles in-line and not offset to one another which is the norm in a two-axle all-wheel drive design.

All variants of the Sherpa Light share a common driveline to reduce maintenance and logistic costs. Motive power for the range is provided by a Renault MD-5 four-cylinder diesel engine developing 215 hp, this coupled to an Allison fully automatic transmission and Axletech two-speed transfer box.

A variety of cab and wheelbase options are available, with equipment options available for the range including right-hand drive, air-conditioning, a Central Tyre Inflation System (CTIS), run-flat inserts, electric winch front or rear, add-on armour, lighting protection and cable breaker, 300 A alternator, and an assortment of weapons and missions systems.

All versions of the Sherpa Light are fully air-transportable by C-130 Hercules transport aircraft.

Currently six primary versions of the Sherpa Light are available, these covering a wide variety of military and internal security needs. The basic configuration of the Sherpa Light would allow for further derivations to be developed in line with emerging user requirements. The six currently available primary versions of the Sherpa Light are listed below.

Variants

Sherpa Light Scout

The Sherpa Light Scout (previously designated Sherpa 2) is a four-door configuration that is optimised for reconnaissance/surveillance, patrol, convoy escort and command and control roles. Internal volume is 5.5 m^3 for the crew compartment, 3.5 m^3 for rear cargo compartment. A roof-mounted weapon can be installed if required. The Sherpa Light Scout is available unarmoured or armoured (to various levels) and has been ordered by NAMSA.

Sherpa Light Station Wagon

The Sherpa Light Station Wagon is a four-door four- or six-seat configuration that is fully armoured and optimised for protected patrol, command-and-control, or internal security and weapon system carrier roles. Internal volume is 7 m^3. A roof-mounted weapon can be installed if required.

At IDEX 2005 the vehicle that would evolve to become the Sherpa Light range had migrated to the Renault stand and with the tentative designation of Sherpa 2.5 (Shaun C Connors)   1391411

Model	Scout	Station Wagon	Carrier	APC	High Intensity
Seating:	4 to 5	4 to 6	2 to 4	10 (2 + 8)	4 to 6
Drive configuration:	4 × 4	4 × 4	4 × 4	4 × 4	4 × 4
Weight:					
(GVW)	7,900 to 10,400 kg	9,900 to 10,500 kg	7,700 or 9,600 kg	10,200 to 10,900 kg	10,500 kg
(payload)	1,350 to 3,850 kg (without armour)	1,750 to 2,350 kg (armoured)	3,500 or 4,500 kg	1,500 to 2,200 kg (armoured)	1,500 kg (armoured)
(GTW)	11,200 to 15,400 kg	13,400 to 15,500 kg	11,700 or 13,600 kg	13,700 to 15,900 kg	13,300 kg
Length:	5.43 m	5.43 m	wheelbase dependant	6 m	5.43 m
Width:	2.35 m	2.35 m	2.35 m	2.35 m	2.35 m
Height:	2.1 m	2.1 m	2.1 m (cab)	2.4 m	2.1 m
Ground clearance: (belly)	600 mm	600 mm	600 mm	600 mm	530 mm
Wheelbase:	3.54 m	3.54 m	4.1 to 4.5 m	3.79 m	3.54 m
Approach/departure angle:	n/avail	n/avail	n/avail	n/avail	n/avail
Max speed:	110 km/h	110 km/h	110 km/h	110 km/h	110 km/h
Range: (cruising)	1,000 km	1,000 km	1,000 km	1,000 km	1,000 km
Fuel capacity: (options)	165 litres	165 litres	165 litres	175 litres	165 litres
Max gradient:	60 to 100%	60%	60%	60%	60%
Max sideslope:	40%	40%	40%	40%	40%
Trench:	900 mm	900 mm	900 mm	900 mm	600 mm
Vertical step:	400 mm	400 mm	400 mm	400 mm	400 mm
Fording:					
(unprepared)	750 mm	750 mm	750 mm	750 mm	1.1 m
(prepared)	1.5 m	1.5 m	1.5 m	1.5 m	1.5 m
Engine:	Renault MD-5 EURO 5 emissions compliant 4-cylinder common rail injection water-cooled 4-stroke diesel developing 215 hp (158 kW) at 2,300 rpm and 800 N.m torque at 1,200 to 1,700 rpm. A EURO 3 option is available for certain markets				
Gearbox:	Allison S2500 fully automatic with 6 forward and 1 reverse gears				
Transfer box:	Axletech 2-speed				
Steering:	hydraluic power-assisted				
Tyres:	335/80R 20 or 13R 22.5				
Suspension:	beam axles, coil springs and hydraulic shock-absorbers, front and rear				
Brakes:	discs all round with ABS				
Electrical system:	12/24 V	12/24 V	12/24 V	12 V	12/24 V
Batteries:	n/avail	n/avail	n/avail	n/avail	4 × 12 V
Alternator:	100 A	100 A	100 A	100 A	100 A

Sherpa Light Carrier

The Sherpa Light Carrier (previously designated Sherpa 3) is a cargo/utility version that can be fitted with a short two-man or long four-man cab, this available unarmoured or armoured (to various levels). Maximum payload is around 4,500 kg and the rear body can be fitted with either a conventional cargo body or mount a shelter-type body including a standard 10 ft NATO shelter. A roof-mounted weapon can be installed if required. The Sherpa Light Carrier has been ordered by Thales for use with France's Thales Syracuse III military satellite communications programme (33) and NATO (17).

Sherpa Light APC

The Sherpa Light APC (previously designated Sherpa 3a) is a three-door configuration optimised for the transport of up to 10 troops or personnel. Internal volume is >10 m³. A roof-mounted weapon can be installed if required. France's Gendarmerie awarded Renault Trucks Defense a contract in 2008 for 92 Sherpa Light APC (then designated Sherpa 3 Grand Volume); delivery has been delayed due to budgetary constraints.

Sherpa Light Special Forces

The Sherpa Light Special Forces is optimised for long range patrol-type missions. Further details of the Sherpa Light Special Forces can be found in the Special attack vehicles section.

Sherpa Light High Intensity

The Sherpa Light High Intensity is the most protected variant of Sherpa Light range and offers high levels of protection from ballistic, mine and IED blast threats. Sherpa Light High Intensity is a four-door four/five-seat configuration optimised for combat missions such as offensive scouting, counterinsurgency roles or convoy escort. Internal volume is 5.5 m³ for the crew compartment, 3.5 m³ for rear cargo compartment. A roof-mounted remote controlled weapon station can be installed if required.

Specifications

See table above

Status

In production: Ordered by, or in use by, the French Army and Gendarmerie, NAMSA and NATO. See text for details.

Contractor

Renault Trucks Defense

Sovamag TC-10 (4 × 4) 1,100 kg multipurpose light vehicle

Development

The Sovamag concern (occasionally presented SOVAMAG) was acquired by Auverland (now Panhard General Defense) in 1989. Auverland's history traces back to the acquisition of Societe International de Matériel Industrial (SIMI), a Belin Group company, by Francois Servanin in 1984. SIMI produced the A2/SAMO, an evolution of the Cournil, a robust and functional light 4 × 4. Auverland continued the evolution of the A2/SAMO into the Auverland A3, full details of which can be found elsewhere in this section.

By the late 1980s Auverland was looking to expand its military business and primarily on the basis of French Ministry of Cooperation contracts for its TC-10 light vehicle, acquired the Sovamag concern in 1989. Following its acquisition of Sovamag, Auverland became known as Auverland-Sovamag, although this was generally disregarded in written references to the company. The Sovamag brand name was retained.

Wishing to capitalise on the success of the functional TC-10, by 1992 Auverland had begun development of the larger Sovamag TC-24, a 2,500 kg payload light truck. Development of the 5,000 kg payload TC-54 commenced in 2006. Full details of the TC-24 and TC-54 can be found in the Trucks section.

In July 2001, Auverland-Sovamag was acquired by (and recapitalised by) Société Nouvelle des Automobiles Auverland (SNAA). The name Auverland remained the one generally used when referring to the company. The TC-10 and TC-24 continued to be badged and marketed as Sovamag products.

Ministry of Cooperation contracts for the TC-10 continue and since 1990 more than 1,300 TC-10s have been produced. Nearly 900 have been supplied to the French Military of Cooperation. Details are sketchy, but TC-10s are known to have been supplied to a number of African countries, the most recent deliveries being 33 (30 soft-top, three ambulance) vehicles to the Central African Republic (CAR) during 2004 and three to Congo Brazzaville (Police) during 2006. The TC-10 is also in service with the Mauritanian Army, Auverland having secured a direct sale contract with Mauritanian Ministry of Defence in 1991 for 50 vehicles. Follow-on orders in 1993 (45); 1995 (60); 1997 (150) and 2000 (100) have brought the total supplied to 405 vehicles. Other disclosed users of the TC-10 include the French Air Force (300) and Army (68). The French Army vehicles (ordered in 1999 for a communications role) were upgraded with the fitting of new hard-tops during 2005.

Sovamag TC-10 (4 × 4) 1,100 kg multipurpose light vehicle of the French Army in Kosovo (Shaun C Connors)   1156027

In 1996, the Sovamag TC-10 SL appeared. This is basically similar to the TC-10 and is powered by the same engine but has a longer wheelbase. The French Air Force received 42 TC-10 SL for the transport of Mistral missiles.

It surprised many commentators, when in January 2005, it was announced that SNAA had acquired Panhard, builder of the Vehicule Blindé Leger (VBL), ERC Sagaie and other light armoured military vehicles. Panhard's parent company, the car manufacturer PSA Peugeot Citroen, is understood to have been open to offers for Panhard for a number of years, but the loss of the Petit Vehicle Protégé (PVP) contract to SNAA is understood to have been the catalyst in bringing disposal plans for France's oldest builder of light armoured military vehicles to the fore. Renault Trucks Defense, in conjunction with Thales was reportedly also interested in Panhard, and is understood to have made an offer. Details of SNAA's securing deal have not been disclosed, however the company is thought to have paid between EUR20-25 million for Panhard. Panhard vehicles have been bought by the armed forces of 45 countries and the company had net earnings of around EUR4 million on sales of EUR65 million in 2004. In 2008 the group sold 600 vehicles resulting in revenues of EUR90 million.

Early 2006, the SNAA became known as Panhard General Defense. The Auverland and Sovamag brand names have been retained, certainly in the short term, and production of these models continues at the now Panhard General Defense's Saint Germain Laval facilities.

It was disclosed mid-2006 that the Saudi Ministry Of Defence and Aviation (MODA), as part of a deal with NORINCO of China to supply PLZ-45 self-propelled howitzers, had specified in the awarded contract that wheeled logistic and tactical support vehicles for these SPGs be provided by Panhard General Defense. NORINCO subsequently awarded Panhard General Defense an order for the supply of 283 vehicles including 32 TC-10s in two basic configurations; station wagon and soft-top, both fitted out to transport seven or 10 men and fittings for a single or three tactical radios. The overall contract value was around EUR22 million and all vehicles were scheduled for delivery by mid-2008.

Saudi Arabia also operates the Auverland A3 light vehicle, around 50 of which were delivered during 2005, with an additional 84 A3L to be delivered as part of the previously mentioned MODA package of vehicles.

Description

The SOVAMAG TC-10 (4 × 4) 1,100 kg multipurpose vehicle has the general appearance of the US Jeep but is a larger vehicle and can carry a heavier (1,100 kg) payload. It has square functional military lines, features rectangular 120 × 60 mm chassis construction and galvanised body panels. Layout is entirely conventional, with the front-mounted engine and

Sovamag TC-10 SL (4 × 4) 1,500 kg multipurpose vehicle with 3.07 m wheelbase and soft-top body. This is one of 42 vehicles supplied to the French Air Force for the transport of (eight) Mistral missiles (Panhard General Defense)   0009620

Sovamag TC-10 SL of the French Air Force stripped down and with the front windscreen folded flat (Pierre Touzin)   1120401

radiator protected behind a substantial front bumper and a grille guard. This grille guard can be hinged forward to provide additional front stowage capacity. The forward-opening bonnet allows easy access to the engine and all maintenance and repairs can be carried out without the need for specialist tools.

There are seats for the driver and a front-seat passenger, while at the rear is the main cargo carrying area with a length of 2 m. This has a reinforced floor and bench seats for four people along each side. These seats can be folded up for access to three stowage compartments each side. A canvas roof carried on a removable light tubular steel frame provides overhead and side weather protection. In addition to carrying cargo or passengers, this area can be used to mount assorted light weapons. A hardtop version is also available, 68 examples of which have been supplied to the French Army. The SOVAMAG TC-10 is air-transportable.

The standard power plant is an IVECO 77 kW (103 hp) turbocharged diesel, although prior to April 1994 standard fit was a Peugeot XD3P 54 kW (72 hp) diesel. An IVECO five-speed gearbox and Auverland two-speed transfer box drive both leaf-sprung axles, the rear axle being fitted with a driver-activated differential lock for improved traction in difficult conditions. Standard equipment includes two 40-litre drinking water tanks and a jerrycan rack at the rear. A standard towing hook is also provided. The normal electrical system is 24 V.

A wide variety of options and configurations are available including left- and right-hand drive. Dual control driver training versions are also available. Van bodies, workshop bodies, 1,000-litre water tankers and firefighting vehicles are also manufactured. Armament options include 106 mm recoilless rifle, 20 mm Giat-type (now Nexter) 621 cannon, 0.5 in (12.7 mm) Heavy Machine Gun (HMG), and MILAN Anti-Tank Guided Weapon (ATGW), or air defence missile carriers. Front and pivot mounts for 5.56 and 7.62 mm machine guns and 40 mm Automatic Grenade Launchers (AGLs) can be fitted. Optional equipment fit can include front protection, fuel tank protection, gearbox and transfer box protection, radio and antenna fittings, and a front-mounted self-recovery winch.

In 1996, the SOVAMAG TC-10 SL appeared. This is basically similar to the TC-10 and is powered by the same engine but has a longer 3.07 m wheelbase, increasing the overall length to 4.85 m. This enables the vehicle to carry up to 12 personnel and their equipment or a payload of approximately 1,500 kg.

Specifications

TC-10
[TC-10 SL in square brackets where different]
Cab seating: 1 + 1 (8 in rear) [10]
Configuration: 4 × 4
Weight:
    (chassis cab) 1,900 kg [1,940 kg]
    (GVW) 3,000 kg [3,500 kg]
    (permissible front axle load) 1,200 kg
    (permissible rear axle load) 2,200 kg
    (payload) 1,100 kg [1,560 kg]
    (towed load, braked) 3,500 kg
    (towed load, unbraked) 750 kg
    (max GCW) 6,500 kg
Length: 4.45 m [4.9 m]
Width: (unladen) 1.654 m
Height: 2.12 m [2.15 m]
Ground clearance: (minimum) 240 mm [270 mm]
Track: (front and rear) 1.34 m
Wheelbase: 2.77 m [3.07 m]
Angle of approach/departure: 53°/44°
Max speed: 130 km/h
Range: 800 km
Fuel capacity: 100 litres
Gradient: 100%
Side slope: 88%
Fording: 600 mm

Engine: IVECO/SOFIM 2.8-litre 4-cylinder in-line turbocharged water-cooled 4-stroke diesel developing 77 kW (103 hp) at 3,600 rpm and 240 N.m torque at 1,900 rpm
Gearbox: IVECO 2826-5 manual with 5 forward and 1 reverse gears
Clutch: single dry plate
Transfer box: Auverland A80 2-speed
Steering: power-assisted
Turning radius: 6.5 m
Suspension: semi-elliptic leaf springs with double acting shock-absorbers, front and rear
Tyres: 7.50 × 16
Brakes: dual circuit, servo assisted hydraulic, discs front, drums rear
Electrical system: 24 V
Batteries: 2 × 12 V, 55 A

Status

In production. Supplied via the French Ministry of Cooperation to a number of undisclosed countries (approaching 900). Also in service with the French Air Force (342), French Army (68, 1999) and Mauritania Ministry of Defence (405, 1991-2000). Ordered for Saudi Arabia (see text).

Contractor

Panhard General Defense

LOHR Fardier FL 500 and FL 501 (4 × 4) 500 kg light vehicles

Development

These light air-portable vehicles were developed by SOFRAMAG (later LOHR, now SOFRAME) for use by airborne troops. The French Army received 300 vehicles, with other known users including Argentina, Spain and Tunisia. French Army vehicles were replaced some time ago by the Auverland (now Panhard General Defense) A3F fast attack vehicle, full details of which can be found in the *Special attack vehicles* section. Argentine vehicles remain in service, although the exact status of those supplied to Spain and Tunisia is now unclear and continued service in numbers is considered unlikely.

Description

The FL 500 has a chassis of welded tubular steel welded with the load area covered with aluminium sheeting. The driver is seated at the front of the vehicle on the left side and, if required, an inverted U-shaped safety bar can be fitted to the rear of the driver's position.

The engine is mounted transverse in the centre of the vehicle and connected to the front and rear axles by two Cardan-driven central transmission units with shock-absorbing guides. The light alloy-reinforced axles are mounted on cushioned rubber and the suspension arms consist of coil springs placed horizontally on each side of the chassis, in two suspension boxes.

Brakes are hydraulic discs on all wheels, with an independent parking brake for each rear wheel. A complete lighting system is installed, enabling the vehicle to be driven on roads.

The final production version was the FL 501 with a 36 hp engine fitted as standard. This allows loads of up to 800 kg to be towed.

The FL 500 was used for trials with the MILAN ATGW system and has been equipped with light machine guns. A light field ambulance version carrying two stacked stretchers has been observed. Alternative loads could include radios. The FL 500 and FL 501 can be used to tow 120 mm mortars.

LOHR Fardier light vehicle of the Argentine military
(Cesar Cruz Tantalean) 1296293

A C-130 or C-160 Transall transport aircraft can carry six FL 500s ready for air-dropping or 12 FL 500s for delivery as cargo. The SA 330 Puma helicopter can carry one FL 500 and one 120 mm mortar. The vehicle can carry a maximum load of 500 kg, including the driver and tow a trailer or weapon such as a 120 mm TDA mortar, weighing a maximum of 500 kg.

Specifications

FL 500 and FL 501
Seating: 1
Configuration: 4 × 4
Weight:
  (laden) 1,180 kg
  (unladen) 680 kg
  (max load) 500 kg
  (towed load, FL 500) 500 kg
  (towed load, FL 501) 800 kg
Load area: 1.93 m²
Length:
  (laden) 2.41 m
  (unladen) 2.375 m
Width: 1.5 m
Height:
  (steering wheel) 1.18 m
  (load area) 920 mm
Ground clearance:
  (laden) 200 mm
  (unladen) 260 mm
Track: 1.26 m
Wheelbase: 1.735 m
Angle of approach/departure: 90°/90°
Max speed: (road) 80 km/h
Range: (road) 200 km
Fuel capacity: 25 litres
Max gradient: 60%
Max side slope: 30%
Vertical obstacle: 200 mm
Fording: 400 mm
Engine:
  (FL 500) Citroën AK 2 flat twin petrol developing 29 hp at 6,750 rpm
  (FL 501) Citroën V06/630 flat twin, air-cooled petrol developing 36 hp at 5,500 rpm
Gearbox: Citroën manual with 4 forward and 1 reverse gears
Steering: rack and pinion
Turning radius: 4.8 m
Suspension: independent, with coil spring and hydraulic shock-absorber at each wheel station
Tyres: 165 × 15 mud + snow pattern
Brakes:
  (main) hydraulic discs
  (parking) handbrake on each rear wheel
Electrical system: 12 V
Battery: 1 × 12 V, 30 Ah
Alternator: 390 W

Status

Production complete. 300 delivered to France (no longer in service, see text), also delivered to Argentina (approximately 50 remain in service with the parachute brigade), Spain (parachute brigade) and Tunisia.

Contractor

SOFRAME

SOFRAME VLA Light Airmobile Vehicle

Development

The SOFRAME VLA *(Véhicule Léger Aéromobile)* was developed by the then LOHR Industrie in response to a requirement from the French Army for a light vehicle capable of being transported in or under an NH90 helicopter. Three prototypes were completed, with the second prototype undergoing French Army trials. The vehicle was not adopted by the French Army.

In February 1997, it was announced that the Royal Netherlands Army had ordered 180 VLAs to be built under licence in the Netherlands by SP Aerospace and Vehicle Systems of Geldrop. This company was declared bankrupt in August 2004.

Deliveries of three versions (general purpose, ambulance and anti-tank) of the VLA (Luchtmobiel Speciaal Voertuig (LSV) as the vehicle is known in service with the Royal Netherlands Army) commenced during the second quarter of 1998. In the Dutch inventory 159 examples were issued to 11 Airmobile Brigade (11 Luchtmobiele Brigade (AASLT)) RNLA, the remaining 20 to the Tactical Helicopter Group RNLAF.

Around 8,000 Dutch Armed Forces vehicles (including the LSV) are to be replaced under a programme, the Request For Information (RFI) for which was announced in June 2008. A revised RFI was announced in December 2008, although the programme has since been further delayed.

Description

The VLA is a 4 × 4 multipurpose light vehicle with a welded tube chassis and aluminium and polyester panel body; one or two roll bars can be incorporated. The engine is located in the centre of the chassis and is allied to an automatic transmission with an integral differential; all-wheel drive is permanent. The driver is seated far forward in a well with seating for one passenger on the right. The single-piece windscreen can be folded forward to lay on the vehicles' front panel when required. Behind the well is a small load platform over the engine compartment with a further cargo/passenger well at the rear; this can accommodate three passengers. The cargo well may be used to mount various weapons, such as a MILAN Anti-Tank Guided Weapon (ATGW) or a Machine Gun. An additional machine gun may be mounted in front of the passenger.

For air transport, a C-130 or C-160 transport aircraft can carry up to 10 VLAs stacked in pairs one above the other, or four vehicles on paradrop pallets. The VLA can be transported internally and externally (underslung) by helicopters such as the NH90 or CH-47D Chinook. For underslung transport, the VLA is provided with four lashing rings and stowage space for slings.

Optional equipment includes a winch, a tarpaulin to cover the load and rear areas and removable light modular armour. Proposed versions included an air defence variant carrying a light surface-to-air missile system, fire support vehicle with a 12.7 mm Heavy Machine Gun (HMG), field ambulance, light recovery version, light reconnaissance vehicle with radios, 120 mm mortar tractor, light load carrier towing a small trailer and a command version with an extendable canvas penthouse.

The proposed VLB 1000 and prototype VLB 2000 (*VLB - Véhicule Léger Blindé*) armoured airmobile light vehicles are essentially larger armoured variants of the VLA design.

Specifications

VLA
Seating: 2 + 4
Configuration: 4 × 4
Weight:
   (unladen) 1,350 kg
   (laden, combat) 2,250 kg
   (payload) 900 kg
   (towed load) 1,200 kg
   (GCW) 3,450 kg
Length: (overall) 3.36 m
Width: 1.72 m

Height:
   (body) 1.08 m
   (windscreen and roll bars folded) 1.32 m
   (roll bar, laden) 1.72 m
   (roll bar, unladen) 1.79 m
Ground clearance:
   (laden) 270 mm
   (unladen) 340 mm
Wheelbase: 1.965 m
Track: (front) 1.446 m
Angle of approach/departure: 40°/50°
Max speed: 80 km/h
Range: 700 km
Fuel capacity: 80 litres
Max gradient: 60%
Max side slope: 50%
Fording: 550 mm
Vertical obstacle: 350 mm
Engine: Peugeot XUD 9A 4-cylinder in-line 4-stroke water-cooled diesel developing 70 hp (52 kW)
Transmission: automatic with 4 forward and 1 reverse gears
Steering: rack bar
Turning radius: 5.5 m
Suspension: MacPherson strut front; torsion bar rear
Brakes: discs all-round
Tyres: 700R 16
Electrical system: 24 V
Batteries: 2 × 12 V, 70 Ah
Alternator: 65 A

Status

Production as required. In service with the Royal Netherlands Army (180 delivered); replacement programme running.

Contractor

SOFRAME

Panhard General Defense A3 (4 × 4) light vehicles

Development

The Panhard General Defense A3 (previously Auverland) can trace its origins back to the mid-1960s and the Cournil, a multipurpose vehicle designed for use both on and off the road. Over a period of 12 years, over 850 examples of the Cournil multipurpose 4 × 4 vehicle were produced and sold, and primarily to French farmers. In 1977 Bernard Cournil sold the licence for his design to Gervarm, a small tractor manufacturer and subsidiary of the Gevelot organisation. Around the same time, a licence was also sold to Portuguese manufacturer, Uniao Metalo Mecanica (UMM) of Lisbon.

The Cournil was a simple, robust and functional vehicle, with attributes that ensured military appeal and in 1977 the inevitable militarised variant was shown for the first time at the Satory Military Exhibition (now Eurosatory). The military Cournil was branded the SAMO, although very briefly appears to have been known as the Fennec.

Gervarm's association with the Cournil ended in March 1980 and from December 1980 the design was in the hands of Societe International de Materiel Industrial (SIMI). By November 1981 SIMI was owned by the Belin Group. The vehicle produced by SIMI had changed little in appearance from the original Cournil product, although there had been the inevitable mechanical upgrades/changes. During 1982 SIMI produced some 500 vehicles, with a projection for 1,200 during 1983, this figure including 230 military vehicles ordered by Zimbabwe. Claiming the delivered vehicles

SOFRAME VLA Light Airmobile Vehicle of the Royal Netherlands Army (Shaun C Connors)   1190233

From the rear, the ambulance version of the SOFRAME VLA Light Airmobile Vehicle (Shaun C Connors)   1190222

Front 3/4 view of the A3L 2.65 m wheelbase light vehicle sent to Bangladesh for trials during 2003 (Panhard General Defense)   1156179

Part of a batch of A3L 2.35 m wheelbase light vehicles supplied to Saudi Arabia during 2005 (Panhard General Defense)   1156169

A 2.25 m wheelbase A3 light vehicle mounting a MILAN ATGW (Panhard General Defense)   1156180

were not of the specification ordered, Zimbabwe paid only 50 per cent of its bill, ultimately leading to the near-bankrupt SIMI being acquired by French businessman Francois Servanin in August 1984.

Francois Servanin renamed the company Autoland although a dispute over the use of that name ensued, and the name Auverland was subsequently adopted. Auverland's production was initially based on two models, the Series A (later known as the A2) and the SC II. The Series A was a modified/updated Cournil, while the SC II was essentially the Cournil design.

Production in France of the A2/SAMO was completed in 1990, by which time it was reported to have been sold (military applications) to Burkina Faso, Burundi, Cameroon, Central African Republic, Chad, Congo, Ivory Coast, Madagascar, Zaire (now The Democratic Republic of the Congo), Zimbabwe and some other undisclosed countries. Production of the Cournil design, albeit substantially modified, continued in Portugal by UMM until 1993 for private customers, and until 1996 for military and utility service customers. UMM continues to offer spares support for the product. Full details of UMM-produced vehicles can be found elsewhere in this section.

Following the acquisition of SIMI, Auverland promptly commenced the development of a new light vehicle that would continue the Cournil tradition of simplicity and robustness. The new vehicle, the Auverland A3, was ready for commercial production by 1988. The first military/governmental order for the A3 came from France's Gendarmerie and was placed in 1988 and the first military order came in 1990 when France's DGA awarded a French Air Force contract. Since production commenced over 8,000 A3s have been produced with about 5,000 examples sold to French governmental organisations and armed forces, these including the French Air Force, Army and Navy, the Gendarmerie Mobile and Gendarmerie Nationale. The first known export customer for the A3 was the Indonesian Marine Corps which received 21 vehicles in 2000, and a further 21 vehicles in 2001.

By the late 1980s Auverland was looking to expand its military business and the company acquired the Sovamag concern in 1989. Sovamag (occasionally presented SOVAMAG) produced the TC-10 light vehicle (later complemented by the larger TC-24), full details of which can be found elsewhere in this section. In July 2001, Auverland-Sovamag

The 2.25 m wheelbase A3 light vehicle sent to Venezuela for trials with a 106 mm recoilless rifle during 2003 (Panhard General Defense)   1156181

(generally referred to as Auverland) were acquired by (and recapitalised by) Société Nouvelle des Automobiles Auverland (SNAA). The name Auverland remained the one generally used when referring to the company.

By late 2003 all commercial production of the Auverland A3 had ceased, the company opting to concentrate on military sales. In November 2003 it was announced that examples of an A3 for use with a 106 mm recoilless rifle would shortly be sent for trials in Bangladesh and Venezuela. The Bangladesh requirement (which technically still exists) called for 84 vehicles; Venezuela could ultimately require up to 600 vehicles. Trials in Saudi Arabia for a basic light utility vehicle during 2002-2003 resulted in an order for 50 vehicles and these were delivered during 2005.

It was disclosed mid-2006 that the Saudi Ministry Of Defence and Aviation (MODA), as part of a deal with NORINCO of China to supply PLZ-45 self-propelled howitzers, had specified in the awarded contract that wheeled logistic and tactical support vehicles for these SPGs be provided by Panhard General Defense. NORINCO subsequently awarded Panhard General Defense an order for the supply of 283 vehicles including 84 A3Ls in two basic configurations: station wagon and soft-top, each with seats for a crew of four (two fixed or foldable rear seats) and ready to receive one or two Panther VHF radios. Some vehicles will be fitted with a self-recovery winch. The overall contract value was around EUR22 million and all vehicles were scheduled for delivery by mid-2008. It is understood that delivery of the artillery system in question has yet to take place.

A single prototype example of a light armoured vehicle on the A3 chassis was produced. The type did not enter series production and while technically still available has been superseded by other designs in the Panhard General Defense product line-up.

It surprised many commentators when in January 2005 it was announced that SNAA had acquired Panhard, builder of the Vehicule Blindé Leger (VBL), ERC Sagaie and other light armoured military vehicles. Panhard's parent company, the car manufacturer PSA Peugeot Citroën, is understood to have been open to offers for Panhard for a number of years, but the loss of the Petit Vehicle Protégé (PVP) contract to SNAA is understood to have been the catalyst in bringing disposal plans for France's oldest builder of light armoured military vehicles to the fore. Renault Trucks Defense in conjunction with Thales were reportedly also interested in Panhard, and are understood to have made an offer. Details of SNAA's securing deal have not been disclosed, however the company is thought to have paid between EUR20-25 million for Panhard. Panhard vehicles have been bought by the armed forces of 45 countries and the company had net earnings of around EUR4 million on sales of EUR65 million in 2004. In 2008 the group sold 600 vehicles, resulting in revenues of EUR90 million.

Following the award of the PVP contract, Auverland further developed the PVP platform and at Eurosatory 2004 displayed a softskin variant of the design, the A4 Flexible Army Smart Transport (FAST), for the first time. The A4 FAST is essentially an enlarged next-generation A3 designed to meet many of the current and emerging light vehicle requirements, these calling for larger vehicles with increased payload and performance, plus the ability to accept appliqué protection from small arms fire and anti-personnel mines without payload or capability degradation. Full details of the A4 FAST can be found elsewhere in this section.

Early 2006, the SNAA became known as Panhard General Defense.

Description

The Panhard General Defense A3 is a small Jeep-type vehicle of conventional layout, having the engine at the front and seating for the driver and up to two passengers. A small area at the rear can be used to carry any payload, mounted equipment or additional passengers. The vehicle is constructed so that the body is isolated from the 100 × 50 × 3 mm rectangular box-section chassis.

The A3 is available in three wheelbase options, 2.25, 2.65 and 3 m, the two-door A3L base vehicle for the range being based on the 2.65 m wheelbase. This model has a 900 kg payload capacity. Four-door models

A3 (4 × 4) two-door light vehicle with soft-top as supplied to the Indonesian Marine Corps in 2000/2001 (Panhard General Defense)   0134166

(also based on the 2.65 m wheelbase) were originally marketed as the Auverland A4, but are now known as A3, four-door models. A wide variety of body styles and configurations are available for the A3 including hard-top, soft-top, crew-cab and pick-up truck. Cargo platform lengths may be 0.8, 1.4 or 1.9 m.

Specific variants include: The type A3MH intended for transport by helicopter, the type A3 'Gendarmerie' with a long wheelbase and hard-top, the type A3 produced for the French Air Force armed with a 7.62 mm machine gun, and the type A3-SL armed with a 12.7 mm machine gun or configured with two lateral benches for six passengers in the rear. There is also a type A3L armed with a 106 mm recoilless rifle or configured to carry MILAN or other Anti-Tank Guided Weapons (ATGW). The A3F is an armed fast attack/light strike variant of the A3 designed for use by airborne and light forces, and was first shown publicly in June 1994. Full details of this variant, which is used by the French Army, can be found in the Special attack vehicles section.

The standard power plant for current production A3s is a 92 hp (69 kW) Peugeot turbocharged diesel engine. This is coupled to a Peugeot 5F/1R gearbox and Auverland two-speed transfer box. Front and rear beam-type axles are sprung by long-travel coil springs, the rear axle being fitted with a limited slip differential for improved traction in difficult conditions. Options include left- or right-hand drive, a 24 V electrical system, and a front-mounted self-recovery winch.

Specifications

Type A3L
[data in square brackets relates to A3 four-door base model where different]
Cab seating: 1 + 3 [2 + 3]
Configuration: 4 × 4
Weight:
  (unladen) 1,400 kg [1,550 kg]
  (laden, GVW) 2,300 kg [2.500 kg]
  (max load) 900 kg [950 kg]
  (max front axle load) 890 kg [n/avail]
  (max rear axle load) 1,680 kg [n/avail]
  (towed load, unbraked) 605 kg [n/avail]
  (towed load, braked) 1,590 kg [n/avail]
  (maximum GCW (with braked towed load)) 3,890 kg [n/avail]
Length: 3.85 m [4.46 m]
Width: 1.54 m
Height: 1.7 m [1.76 m]
Ground clearance: 250 mm
Track: 1.342 m [n/avail]
Wheelbase: 2.65 m [2.65 m]
Angle of approach/departure: 50°/45° [departure: 35°]
Max speed: 130 km/h [125 km/h]
Range: 800 km [700 km]
Fuel capacity: 80 litres
Gradient: 100%
Side slope: 89%
Fording: 600 mm [580 mm]
Engine: Peugeot XUD9 TF 1.997-litre 4-cylinder in-line water-cooled turbocharged 4-stroke diesel developing 92 hp (69 kW) at 4,000 rpm and 196 N.m torque at 2,250 rpm; pre-1996 a naturally aspirated Peugeot XUD9 diesel developing 65 hp (48 kW) at 4,600 rpm was fitted
Gearbox: Peugeot BA 7/5 with 5 forward and 1 reverse gears; Peugeot BA 10/5 was an option
Clutch: single dry plate
Transfer box: Auverland A80 2-speed; full-time all-wheel drive
Steering: power-assisted
Turning radius: 5.5 m [5.5 m]
Axles: beam-type located longitudinally by leading (front axle) and trailing (rear axle) lower radius arms and laterally by an A-frame arrangement; limited slip rear differential

Suspension: long travel coil springs with internal hollow rubber bump stops, hydraulic shock-absorbers and anti-roll bars, front and rear
Tyres: 215/80R 16 or 7.00R 16
Brakes: dual-circuit, discs front, drums rear,
Electrical system: 12 V (24 V optional)
Battery: 1 × 12 V, 60 Ah

Status
Production as required. In service with Indonesia (Marine Corps, 42, 2000-2001), the French Air Force, Army and Navy, the French Gendarmerie Nationale and Gendarmerie Mobile (around 5,000), and Saudi Arabia (50, 2005; 84, 2007-2008). Trials vehicle delivered to Bangladesh (late 2003). Trials vehicle delivered to Venezuela (late 2003).

Contractor
Panhard General Defense

Panhard General Defense A4 FAST light vehicle

Development
The Panhard General Defense (previously Auverland) A4 Flexible Army Smart Transport (FAST) was first displayed at Eurosatory 2004. The A4 is essentially an enlarged next-generation A3 light vehicle that has been designed to meet many of the current and emerging light vehicle requirements, which call for larger vehicles with increased payload and performance, plus the ability to accept appliqué protection from small arms fire and anti-personnel mines without payload or capability degradation.

Full details of the A3, together with a history of the Auverland/Panhard General Defense company, can be found in the Panhard General Defense A3 entry elsewhere in this section.

The first use of the A4 platform (chassis and driveline) was for the Auverland Armoured Vehicle Light (AVL), the then Auverland's winning submission for the French Army's Petit Vehicle Protégé (PVP) requirement. Brief details of the A4 AVL can be found elsewhere in this section; full details of the A4 AVL/PVP can be found in *Jane's Armour and Artillery*.

It surprised many commentators when in January 2005 it was announced that Société Nouvelle des Automobiles Auverland (SNAA) had acquired Panhard, builder of the Véhicule Blindé Léger (VBL), ERC Sagaie and other light armoured military vehicles. Panhard's parent company, the car manufacturer PSA Peugeot Citroen, is understood to have been open to offers for Panhard for a number of years, but the loss of the Petit Vehicle Protégé contract to SNAA is understood to have been the catalyst in bringing disposal plans for France's oldest builder of light armoured military vehicles to the fore. Details of the deal have not been disclosed, however the company is thought to have paid between EUR20-25 million for Panhard.

Early in 2006, SNAA became known as Panhard General Defense.

Description
The A4 is a Jeep-type vehicle of conventional layout, having the engine at the front and seating for the driver and up to three passengers in conventional layout. When conventionally configured an area at the rear can be used to carry any payload, mounted equipment or additional passengers.

A full range of body options is available for the A4, and in addition to the conventional four-to-six seat troop carrying/cargo-type, variants including ambulance, armed reconnaissance/patrol (with or without protection), cargo/logistic and shelter carrier have been proposed by the company. The vehicle is based on a conventional box-section chassis of 120 × 60 and 140 × 60 mm dimensions, and the standard wheelbase is 3 m, but an extended 3.4 m wheelbase version is an option. The A4 was designed with an integral anti-personnel mine-blast protected floorpan and for the fitting of an appliqué protection kit, however full softskin variants are available if required.

Rear three-quarter view of the Panhard A4 FAST prototype as displayed at Eurosatory 2004 (Panhard General Defense)   1066934

Production standard Panhard General Defense PVP light protected vehicle deployed by French Army (Panhard General Defense)   1332778

The standard power plant is a 160 hp (119 kW) IVECO turbocharged diesel engine meeting EURO III emissions requirements. Alternative engines including those meeting EURO IV/V are available. A ZF automatic gearbox coupled to an Auverland-designed two-speed transfer box is standard, with a manual gearbox being a specified option.

Front and rear beam-type axles are sprung by long-travel coil springs, hydraulic shock-absorbers and anti-roll bars. The rear axle is fitted with a driver-controlled differential lock for improved traction in difficult conditions. ABS is standard.

Options include assorted protection kits, left- or right-hand drive, a front-mounted electric self-recovery winch, and a Central Tyre Inflation (CTI) system.

Variants

Auverland AVL

The Auverland Armoured Vehicle Light (AVL) was the first use of the chassis and running gear of the A4 FAST, and was developed specifically to meet the French Army's Petit Vehicle Protégé (PVP) requirement. In April 2001 the then Auverland responded to the PVP tender and in January 2002 was one of four companies awarded contracts for prototype vehicles. Those four companies were: Auverland, Panhard (teamed with the then DaimlerChrysler), SOFRAME (previously LOHR) and Vickers Defence Systems (now BAE Systems Global Combat Systems) of the UK. Each company was required to supply a single prototype vehicle, with trials commencing in September 2002.

Funding permitting, the French Army stated a requirement for up to 1,544 PVPs. The initial order PVP was expected to be for 312 vehicles, and the second for 232 vehicles, with five follow-on batches of 200 vehicles per batch. Deliveries would be spread over a seven-year period. Ultimately, the A4 was selected and an order worth EUR110 million was placed in late-2004 for 933 vehicles.

Two pre-production prototypes were delivered mid-2005. The first production batch consisted of 312 vehicles with first deliveries to the French Army being made early in 2008. Three additional PVP batches will consist of 232 (ordered), 200 (ordered) and 187 units, this bring the grand total up to 931 production units, plus the two pre-production units.

In service the PVP bridges a gap between the Panhard P4 and the Panhard Véhicule Blindé Léger (VBL) on security missions assigned to the French Army during peace keeping or restoring operations. The French Army will deploy two baseline variants of the PVP, infantry and command post with additional communications equipment. The former is expected to equip combat support and logistic support units while the command version will equip command cells for contract troops.

Front three-quarter view of the Panhard A4 FAST prototype as displayed at Eurosatory 2004 (Panhard General Defense)   1066342

The Ashok Leyland LSV is based on the chassis and automotives of the Panhard A4 (Ashok Leyland)   1296137

Ashok Leyland LSV

The Ashok Leyland Light Specialist Vehicle (LSV) is based on the chassis and automotives of the A4. The vehicle is one of a number of competitors for the Indian Army's Light Specialist Vehicle (LSV) requirement. The LSV Trials are understood to be complete, and the Army are understood to be preparing the report.

Specifications

A4 FAST

Cab seating: 1 + 1 + up to 4 in rear
Configuration: 4 × 4 (selectable)
Weight:
  (laden) 4,240 kg
  (unladen) 3,380 kg
  (payload) 860 kg
  (max front axle load) 2,400 kg
  (max rear axle load) 3,000 kg
Length: 4.272 m
Width: 1.97 m
Height: 1.95 m
Ground clearance: 312 mm
Wheelbase: 3 m
Angle of approach/departure: 76°/55°
Max speed: 120 km/h
Range: 800 km
Fuel capacity: 125 litres
Max gradient: 100%
Max side slope: 30%
Fording: (unprepared) 533 mm
Engine: IVECO EURO III emissions-compliant 2.8-litre 4-cylinder in-line turbocharged 4-stroke direct injection diesel, developing 160 hp (119 kW) at 3,600 rpm, and 320 N.m torque at 1,500 rpm; options available including EURO IV
Gearbox: ZF automatic; manual option
Transfer box: Auverland A80R 2-speed
Steering: Principe power-assisted
Turning radius: 6.25 m
Suspension: long-travel coil springs, hydraulic shock-absorbers and anti-roll bar, front and rear
Tyres: 255/100R 16 Michelin XZL (options available)
Brakes: discs all-round, ABS
Electrical system: 12/24 V split system

Status

Prototypes. Chassis and driveline used as the basis of the A4 AVL and Ashok Leyland LSV (see text).

Contractor

Panhard General Defense

Peugeot P4 (4 × 4) 750 kg light vehicle

Development

The standard light vehicle of the French military is the Peugeot P4, essentially a licence-built Mercedes-Benz G-Class - then G-Wagon. The P4 is often referred to as the VLTT (*Véhicule de Liaison Tout Terrain*).

To replace a fleet of Hotchkis 201 'jeeps' three manufacturers each submitted 12 vehicles to the French military for extensive trials; these were the Renault TRM 500 (4 × 4) 500 kg based on the Italian FIAT 1107 AD, the Citroën C 44 based on the German Volkswagen Iltis, and the G-Wagon-based Peugeot P4. Early in 1981 the French Army selected the Peugeot P4 and placed an order for a reported 15,000 vehicles.

French Army P4 (4 × 4) 750 kg light vehicle of the Gendarmerie in Kosovo (Shaun C Connors)   1186171

French Army P4 (4 × 4) 750 kg light vehicle in Kosovo (Shaun C Connors)   1156024

Mass production of the P4 by PSA Peugeot Citroën at Sochaux commenced early 1983, with the first 2,400 vehicles being fitted with petrol engines. PSA (Sochaux) produced 7,397 vehicles and from 1988 Panhard (Panhard's parent company at this time was PSA Peugeot Citroën) at Marolles en Hurepoix produced 6,103 vehicles bringing production totals to 13,500 vehicles. Of these, some 1,000 were supplied to the Gendarmerie, 150 to the Navy (Marines) and 200-300 to the Air Force.

A post-main production follow-on order for 30 vehicles for use with the Aspic air defence missile launcher was placed in 1994.

A total of 208 vehicles were exported throughout the production run (Chile, 23 (1991-92); Congo, 60; Gabon, 75; Ivory Coast, 20; Senegal, 10; Togo, 20). Some surplus French Army vehicles have subsequently been cascaded to other nations, although details of how many and to where remains sketchy.

As of June 2005 it was reported that 10,000 P4s remained in service with France's Armed Forces. Current estimates are that a replacement will be sought from around 2010-2012. It has been suggested that prior to full replacement an upgrade programme for the P4 will be initiated. Early information stated that the current 70 hp naturally aspirated diesel engine and four-speed manual gearbox would be replaced by a 140 hp turbocharged diesel engine and ZF automatic gearbox. This was revised during 2005 to an upgrade 'based around the engine', and around 3,000 vehicles would be upgraded from around 2007. In 2006 the now Panhard General Defense delivered a prototype of an upgraded P4 for trials. This vehicle is fitted with a 125 hp Steyr diesel engine coupled to an automatic gearbox.

While not an official replacement programme for the P4, the French military has received somewhere in the region of 1,700 Land Rover Defenders in various configurations since 2006. The current contract, valid for three years from February 2009, allows for the delivery of an unlimited quantity of vehicles. During 2009, approaching 550 examples were ordered.

In January 2005 it was announced that Société Nouvelle des Automobiles Auverland (SNAA) had acquired Panhard from PSA Peugeot Citroën. Panhard's parent company was understood to have been open to offers for Panhard for a number of years, but the loss of the Petit Vehicle Protégé (PVP) contract to SNAA is understood to have been the catalyst in bringing disposal plans for France's oldest builder of light armoured military vehicles to the fore. Renault Trucks Defence in conjunction with Thales were reportedly also interested in Panhard, and are understood to have made an offer. Details of SNAA's securing deal have not been disclosed, however the company is thought to have paid between EUR20

French Army Peugeot P4 (4 × 4) 750 kg light vehicle in Kosovo; the standard soft-top on this vehicle is folded back (Richard Stickland)   0121842

to 25 million for Panhard. Panhard vehicles have been bought by the armed forces of 45 countries and the company had net earnings of around EUR4 million on sales of EUR65 million in 2004. In 2008 the group sold 600 vehicles, resulting in revenues of EUR90 million.

Description
The layout of the P4 is conventional, with the engine at the front, driver and passenger immediately behind the engine and the cargo area at the rear, with a bench seat for two people down either side and an opening tailgate on which the spare wheel is mounted.

The front seats are adjustable and hinge forward to give access to the rear seats and the tool boxes beneath each of them. The driver and passengers are provided with seat belts. The bench seats in the rear can be folded down to enlarge the load-carrying area.

The chassis is formed from two parallel longitudinal beams with rectangular sections connected by five tubular transverse members. The rear axle is fitted with a hydraulically-controlled differential lock.

The sheet metal body is connected to the chassis with eight flexible mounts and has a removable roll-over bar and a folding windscreen of bonded safety glass. Fixtures, bumpers, inner bumper liners and the front portion are mounted to the body structure. For ease of replacement these are bolted on. The two cloth doors have translucent window panels and are removable. The rear troop/cargo area is covered by a tarpaulin of plastic-coated cloth, with translucent sides and rear windows, which folds to the rear and is easily removable.

The fuel tank is below the floor of the vehicle between the chassis beams. A fuel can is carried externally at the rear of the vehicle on the left side. The P4 is fitted with a towing eye at the front and a towbar at the rear with an electric trailer plug. The electrical system includes a park plug, lantern plug and a connection box for a two-way radio.

Optional equipment included: power-assisted steering, front locking differential, PTO front and rear, front-mounted electric winch, a 15-litre fuel can and various adapters for mounting machine guns and other weapons.

The basic vehicle is used by the French Army for a variety of roles, including one armed with twin F1 machine guns for use by scout teams and traffic control squads, while another is equipped with a MILAN ATGW launcher and four missiles and used by motorised infantry. An LWB model was also available with a drop tailgate, bows, tarpaulin cover and back-to-back seating for eight fully equipped soldiers at the rear. The P4 was demonstrated carrying an M40 series 106 mm recoilless rifle. Both the SWB and LWB versions are fitted with radios for use in the command role and fully enclosed van-type versions of both the LWB and SWB models are available. There is also a fully equipped workshop vehicle version and an ambulance, both LWB.

An armoured protection kit for the P4 has been produced by Panhard General Defense. It is proof against 7.62 mm ball rounds at 100 m and during 1996, 80 of these kits were supplied to the French military.

Front ¾ view of a French Army P4 (4 × 4) 750 kg light vehicle in Kosovo. This EOD team vehicle is fitted with an armoured protection kit produced by Panhard and during 1996, 80 of these kits were supplied to the French military (Shaun C Connors)   1156026

Prototype of Panhard's upgraded P4 (4 × 4) light vehicle (Panhard)   1296195

Specifications

Model	SWB	LWB
Configuration:	4 × 4	4 × 4
Weight:		
(laden (petrol/diesel))	2,565/2,645 kg	2,985/3,065 kg
(unladen (petrol/diesel))	1,815/1,895 kg	1,985/2,065 kg
Max load:	750 kg	750 kg
Length:	4.2 m	4.65 m
Width:		
(with antenna mount)	1.83 m	1.83 m
(less antenna mount)	1.7 m	1.7 m
Height:	1.9 m	1.9 m
Ground clearance:	240 mm	240 mm
Track:	1.4 m	1.4 m
Wheelbase:	2.4 m	2.85 m
Angle of approach/departure:	42°/37°	42°/37°
Fording:	500 mm	500 mm
Gradient: (laden (petrol/diesel))	73.5/55%	73.5/55%
Side slope: (laden)	30%	30%
Max speed: (petrol/diesel)	118/108 km/h	118/108 km/h
Fuel capacity:	75 litres	75 litres
Engine:	Peugeot 1.971-litre 4-cylinder water-cooled petrol developing 79 hp at 4,750 rpm or Peugeot 2.498-litre 4-cylinder in-line water-cooled 4-stroke diesel developing 70.5 hp at 4,500 rpm	
Gearbox:	manual, 4 forward and 1 reverse gears	
Clutch:	single dry disc with ball-bearing thrust mechanism	
Transfer box:	2-speed	2-speed
Steering:	rack and pinion with damper	
Turning radius:	5.5 m	6.45 m
Suspension:		
(front)	coil springs, anti-roll bar and double acting telescopic hydraulic shock-absorbers	
(rear)	coil springs and double acting telescopic hydraulic shock-absorbers	
Tyres:	700 RC 16 × C type L	700 RC 16 × C type L
Brakes:	hydraulic dual circuit, discs front, drums rear	
Electrical system:	24 V	24 V
Generator:	1,200 W	1,200 W

Status
Production complete. In service with the French Army (13,530 supplied (see text), 10,000 remained in service as of June 2005), Chile (23, 1991-1992), Congo (60), Ivory Coast (20), Gabon (75), Senegal (10), Togo (20) plus cascaded French Army surplus in undisclosed numbers to undisclosed recipients.

Contractor
Panhard General Defense

Germany

VW Iltis (4 × 4) 500 kg light vehicle

Development
In 1976, the Federal German Army issued a requirement for a (4 × 4) vehicle that could carry 500 kg of cargo both on roads and cross-country. Both Daimler-Benz and Volkswagen built prototypes for trials and in 1977 the Volkswagen Iltis was selected for production as the Lkw 0.5t tmil gl.

Production of the Iltis continued until December 1981 when the last of 8,800 vehicles was handed over to the German Armed Forces. Of this total, 8,470 went to the Army, 310 to the Luftwaffe and the remaining 20 to the Navy.

Production in Germany ceased in 1982, but in 1983 production of the Iltis was transferred to Bombardier of Canada. Full details of Canadian production can be found elsewhere in this section.

The Iltis has now been replaced in German military service by the Mercedes-Benz G-Class, with surplus Iltis vehicles having been supplied to a number of countries including Estonia (250 in 1997; 200 to the Defence Forces, 50 to the Border Guard), Latvia, Macedonia (300), Nicaragua (delivered 1983) and Niger. The French Army Berlin Brigade used approximately 50 vehicles between 1978-1991; these are probably no longer in service.

Status
Production complete. Phased out of German military service (approximately 8,800 supplied) with some vehicles having been transferred to other countries including Estonia (250), France (see text), Latvia, Macedonia (300), Nicaragua (delivered 1983) and Niger. In October 1981 the Canadian company Bombardier Inc. obtained a licence to produce the Iltis. Further details can be found elsewhere in this section.

Contractor
Volkswagenwerk AG

Ex-German Army Volkswagen Iltis 500 kg light vehicle now in service with the Army of Estonia (Stefan Marx)   1124728

Mercedes-Benz G-Class (4 × 4) light vehicle

Development
Development of the Mercedes-Benz G-Class can be traced back to at least 1972. The vehicle was originally developed with military markets in mind but was soon adapted as a response to trend towards All-Wheel Drive (AWD) vehicles for the leisure and commercial market. Mercedes-Benz had previously produced all-wheel drive light vehicles, but throughout post-war years manufactured nothing smaller than the Unimog. For this new lighter all-wheel drive venture the company opted to work in co-operation with Austria's Steyr-Daimler-Puch (SDP), a decision considered to have origins in SDP's Pinzgauer vehicle securing a lucrative Swiss Army contract in preference to Mercedes-Benz's Unimog around this time. The joint company, in which each had a 50 per cent share, was known as GeländeFahrzeug Gesellschaft (GFG).

Throughout the conception stage the idea of the G-Wagen was to develop a cross-country vehicle that would not only be present in the new civil all-wheel drive niche, but one that would be capable of addressing the needs of the military. To achieve both goals satisfactorily it was decided to give more design importance to practicality than aesthetics. It was also accepted from the outset of the project that for efficiency reasons as many components as possible would be supplied by the two partners, with chassis, engine, gearbox, transfer box, axles and steering coming from Mercedes-Benz, the body panels from SDP.

A number of names were considered for the new vehicle including H2 (Haflinger 2) but this was rejected for reasons of biased association with SDP, manufacturer of the Halfinger light 4 × 4. The chosen name G-Wagen (often Anglicised to G-Wagon) is short for the German word Geländewagen meaning all-terrain vehicle.

Latvian Army Mercedes-Benz G-Class in a long range patrol-type configuration photographed in Afghanistan during 2010 (Victor Barreira)
1391359

Norwegian Army Mercedes-Benz G-Class in a long range patrol-type configuration photographed during Exercise Cold Response 2010 (Carl Schulze)
1391199

Mercedes-Benz 270CDI (4 × 4) 2.85 m wheelbase light vehicles of the Danish Army (Martin Pagh)
1296144

Prototype of the Mercedes-Benz G-Class (6 × 6) in RHD Australian Army specification (Daimler)
1391031

The first wooden mock-up was made in April 1973; the first metal prototype appeared in 1974 and planning for the production facility at SDP's Graz plant in Austria commenced during 1975. At this stage it was anticipated the production life span of the G-Wagen would be no more than 10 years, with initial production targeted to be 9,000 units per year, sufficient to reach two per cent of the market. This was planned to increase to 11,000 units per year at a later stage, and it was anticipated that export sales would account for 96 per cent of production. Mercedes-Benz badging would be applied to 90 per cent of production, the remaining 10 per cent being badged Puch for SDP-favoured markets; these being Austria, Switzerland, the then Yugoslavia and other COMECON countries.

The German military were a targeted customer for the G-Wagen, and the Bundeswehr evaluated a prototype example as early as June 1973. It was widely anticipated that with the G-Wagen Mercedes-Benz would win the contract to replace the Bundeswehr's fleet of DKW Munga light vehicles. This did not happen, however, and in 1976 Volkswagen were awarded a contract for their Iltis, a cheaper vehicle and one that had some component commonality with the outgoing DKW Munga. When the Iltis itself required replacing, the G-Wagen was the chosen vehicle.

With Bundeswehr sales temporarily out of reach, the key decisive factor behind production start-up for the G-Wagen was the then Shah of Persia's mid-1970s order for 20,000 units for the then Iranian Imperial Army. Deliveries never occurred and following the start of production in February 1979, the first customers for the G-Wagen were the German Border Police and the Argentine Army. The Norwegian military followed soon after, and the continuing trend of customisation to suit user requirements began with an order from Indonesia.

During 1982 GFG was dissolved with Daimler-Benz taking full ownership of the product. The now Magna Steyr continues to manufacturer what was rebranded the Mercedes-Benz G-Class during 2002 for DaimlerChrysler; now Daimler. Mercedes-Benz is a brand of Daimler.

The 50,000th G-Class was produced during 1986, this figure reaching 100,000 by 1992, 130,000 by 1995, 185,000 by late-2005; by early-2009 this figure was approaching 200,000. In excess of 60,000 G-Class have been supplied to military users since production commenced. In addition to tactical military use, less utilitarian/militarised models of the G-Class are also widely used for assorted rear echelon roles. Governmental organisations, aid agencies and other similar bodies also use considerable numbers of G-Class light vehicles.

Throughout its production run, the G-Class, while remaining true to its original design concepts, has been continuously updated and a wide variety of engine, gearbox and body/chassis options have been produced. For designation purposes there have been only three series of vehicles, the former 460 series and the current 461 and 463 series. The 462 series is essentially a CKD 461 series built under licence by Hellenic Vehicle Industry S.A. (ELBO) in Greece from 1991.

In 1989 and in answer to emerging commercial trends for a more luxurious and car-like all-wheel drive product the 463 series was announced, this becoming available from March 1990. In 1991 the original 460 series was discontinued and in 1992, with traditional military, municipal and commercial users in mind, the 461 series was launched. The 461 series was essentially the 460 series revised and renamed. In excess of 90 per cent of 461 series manufactured have been supplied to military customers; the primary differences between 461 and 463 series are engines, gearboxes and trim.

Current military G-Class production (Greece CKD excluded) models were introduced from 2002, although from model year 2007 a new engine has been standard fit.

Mercedes-Benz has offered protected G-Class vehicles since around 1992. In view of recent global developments and the considerable rise in demand for discretely protected all-terrain vehicles Mercedes-Benz has increased the profile of protected G-Class. Further details of these vehicles can be found elsewhere in this entry.

Norwegian Army Mercedes-Benz (4 × 4) 3.428 m wheelbase light vehicle fitted with a crew cab (Shaun C Connors)
1186179

Mercedes-Benz 270CDI (4 × 4) 3.428 m wheelbase light vehicle of the Norwegian Army fitted with a specialist application shelter body (Shaun C Connors)   1186180

Mercedes-Benz (4 × 4) 2.4 m wheelbase light vehicle of the Danish Army in use in Kosovo by the Lithuanian Army (Shaun C Connors)   1185489

Mercedes-Benz 270CDI (4 × 4) 2.85 m wheelbase light vehicle of the Norwegian Army. This vehicle is fitted with protection (Shaun C Connors)   1186181

Mercedes-Benz (4 × 4) light vehicle in ambulance configuration of the Danish Army in Kosovo (Shaun C Connors)   1185490

To meet the trend for increasing payload, which may include armour, Mercedes-Benz has continually increased the GVW of the G-Class, and early 2007 officially disclosed that is was developing a heavier (6 × 6) variant. Initially for Australia's on-going Project Land 121 (Overlander), this (6 × 6) variant has a payload of up 3,000 kg. It was disclosed in October 2007 that Daimler had been selected as preferred tenderer for the unprotected lightweight and light vehicles segment of Overlander Phase 3.

In October 2008 it was disclosed that Daimler had been awarded a contract worth AUD350 million for the delivery of 1,100 Mercedes-Benz G-Class. Six different configurations are involved, a (4 × 4) general-purpose station wagon; two (4 × 4) cargo variants; a (6 × 6) chassis-cab variant; a (6 × 6) dual cab variant; and a specialist surveillance and reconnaissance vehicle. In service these G-Class will progressively replace a large percentage of the current Land Rover fleet.

Mercedes-Benz has never disclosed a comprehensive list of military G-Class sales, therefore details provided under Status should not be considered comprehensive. Known recent/current military sales include ongoing deliveries to the Bundeswehr, the armed forces of Hungary and

Mercedes-Benz (4 × 4) 2.85 m wheelbase light vehicle of the Danish Army in use in Kosovo (Shaun C Connors)   1185491

Norway, a recent framework contract with Danish Armed Forces and the supply of over 1,100 examples of a particularly specialised variant to the Canadian Department of National Defence (DND), full details of which can be found elsewhere in this entry.

Denmark operates a sizeable fleet of G-Class 240GD in 2.4 and 2.85 m wheelbase configurations (around 2,000 have been delivered although some have since been cast), plus smaller numbers of 290GD and 300GD models. Between 2003 and late-2008 around 450 of the recent G270CDI/G280 CDI models have been delivered under a five-year option contract that allows for up to 1,000 vehicles to be delivered.

During 2007 the Royal Netherlands Marines announced the purchase of 128 G280CDI models fitted with a roll-cage and weapon ring-mount.

Manufacturing contracts with Daimler AG have been renewed for the continued production of the Mercedes-Benz G-Class at Magna Steyr's facilities in Graz, Austria, until 2015.

Description
The layout of the base Mercedes-Benz (4 × 4) light vehicle is entirely conventional. The same chassis-frame design is used for all wheelbase variants, this using closed box-shaped side members in conjunction with tubular cross-members, providing high bending and torsional stiffness in a ladder-type frame to which the noise-insulated bodywork is attached by four rubber mountings. The frame and body panels are extensively corrosion protected and are also waxed and sealed.

The engine is front-mounted and is a Mercedes-Benz water-cooled unit. Since production commenced a number of diesel and petrol units have been fitted, many of which were never adopted by military users.

The first production models were known as the 460 series and were offered with an initial choice of three engines: a four-cylinder petrol unit developing 90 or 102 hp (model designation 230G), a four-cylinder diesel unit developing 72 hp (model designation 240GD) and a five-cylinder diesel unit developing 88 hp (model designation 300GD). Model 280G powered by a 155 hp six-cylinder petrol unit commenced production early 1981. All models were fitted with a four-speed manual gearbox and two-speed transfer box. Four-wheel drive and the rear axle differential lock were engageable on the move. A front axle differential lock was optional.

From 1981, a four-speed automatic transmission became optional for the 280G and 300GD models. Following the addition of petrol injection, in 1982 the 230G and 280G became the 230GE and 280GE; the 230G remaining available for certain markets. During 1983 a five-speed manual gearbox became optional for the 280GE and 300GD, and the four-speed

Mercedes-Benz (4 × 4) 2.85 m wheelbase light vehicle of the Danish Army in the locally converted escort configuration. Thirty examples were produced at the Danish Army's facilities in Hjoerring and were despatched to Iraq during July and August 2005 (Michael Wollertsen)   1185492

Commercially procured Mercedes-Benz (4 × 4) 2.85 m wheelbase light vehicle of the Swedish Army (Richard Stickland)   0121922

Mercedes-Benz (4 × 4) 2.85 m wheelbase light vehicle in four-door station wagon configuration of the Swiss Military Police. Modifications include a roof-rack, a light bar and a front-mounted antenna and self-recovery winch (Michael Jerchel)   1047606

Mercedes-Benz (4 × 4) 2.85 m wheelbase light vehicle in four-door station wagon configuration of the Swedish Army; note the circular roof hatch (Richard Stickland)   1047591

Mercedes-Benz (4 × 4) 2.85 m wheelbase light vehicle in two-door van-type (with windows) configuration of the Dutch Army (Richard Stickland)   1047595

The 461 series was essentially the 460 series revised and renamed. Engine options were the four-cylinder petrol unit developing 122 hp (model designation 230GE) and a new five-cylinder diesel unit developing 95 hp (model designation 290GD). The 230GE was discontinued in 1997 and from 1998 the 290GD became the 290GDT with the addition of a turbocharger. A five-speed manual gearbox became standard, a four-speed automatic becoming an option in 1998.

The 270CDI diesel engine developing 156 hp became the standard military engine option in 2002 and for the 07 model year this was replaced by the 280CDI diesel engine developing 184 hp and meeting EURO 4 emissions requirements. The recently introduced 300CDI is powered by essentially the same engine, but revised to meet EURO 5 emissions requirements. Other current engine options for the G-Class are a 224 hp diesel (G350CDI) or a 388 hp petrol (G500). A high-performance/high-specification model, the G55AMG powered by a 507 hp petrol unit, is also available. These engines are not available for tactical military applications.

Full-time four-wheel drive and driver-controlled front, rear and centre differential locks are now standard. Four-wheel drive remained selectable on the 461 series as did an optional front axle differential lock. Suspension on all models is by coil springs and telescopic shock-absorbers, with both axles located by a single transverse and two longitudinal control links. Disc brakes are now fitted as standard front and rear, although rear drums are optional for heavier weights. ABS is standard on vehicles.

A considerable variety of body options have been/are available for the G-Class. The 461 series was available in three wheelbases (2.4, 2.85 and 3.12 m) and seven factory-offered body versions. For military applications the most popular models have been a soft top in either 2.4 m (SWB) or 2.85 m (LWB) wheelbase configurations. Hard top, station wagon, van-type or pick-up-style bodies have also been produced. When so equipped, the SWB can seat up to eight, the LWB up to 10. A longer 3.12 m chassis was produced in chassis-cab form and various companies produced special bodies for this such as forward area ambulances, radio/command, communications or workshop. This wheelbase variant remained in production in Greece until 2004.

Current wheelbase options for the G-Class are 2.4 m (civil only), 2.85 m (civil and military) and 3.428 m (military only), the latter being the current chassis-cab option. Military models are currently offered with a 2.85 or 3.428 m wheelbase. Currently four factory-offered body versions are available; open vehicle with two side doors and a removable canvas top; station wagon with four doors and a tailgate; van with two doors and a closed body; chassis cab (3.428 m wheelbase only). The (6 × 6) G-Class has a wheelbase of 3.12 to 4.23 + 1.10 m.

automatic option was extended to the 230GE. During 1987 the 250GD powered by a five-cylinder diesel developing 84 hp and coupled to a five-speed manual gearbox became available. This replaced the earlier 240GD.

The 463 series was announced in 1989 and became available in 1990. That same year the 460 series was discontinued. The 463 series was aimed at the developing all-wheel drive niche within the upper to middle class passenger car market, and so-appointed is best described as suited to rear echelon duties, VIP transport and use by governmental organisations, aid agencies and other similar bodies. Aware of this and the continuing global market for a basic all-wheel drive light utility vehicle, Mercedes-Benz introduced the 461 series in 1992.

Mercedes-Benz (4 × 4) light vehicles of the Austrian Army (left), badged Puch, and German Army (right) badged Mercedes-Benz (Shaun C Connors) 1124769

At Eurosatory 2010 Mercedes-Benz disclosed the sale of an initial batch of around 45 LAPV 5.4 to the German Bundeswehr under the German Army's GFF1 requirement (Shaun C Connors) 1391356

Arctic Trucks are one of a number of companies that will modify conventional (4 × 4) light vehicles such as the G-Class for extreme off-road use. Arctic Trucks have supplied so-modified G-Class to at least two European armed forces (Shaun C Connors) 1296142

The LAPV 6.X retains the armoured body of the LAPV 1/LAPV 5.4, plus the 280CDI engine and matching gearbox, but is fitted with new lighter Unimog-style portal-type axles to give enhanced mobility and increase the overall GVW of the platform (Shaun C Connors) 1391357

An armoured protection kit proof against 7.62 mm ball rounds at 100 m has been produced for the G-Class in France by the now Panhard General Defense. It has been fitted to the Peugeot P4.

Variants

Peugeot P4
The French Army uses a licence-produced variant of the G-Class as its standard light vehicle; 13,500 were delivered between 1983 and 1992. Production was undertaken by the now Panhard General Defense. Full details of the Peugeot P4 can be found elsewhere in this section.

Panhard VPS special forces light vehicle
The Panhard VPS special forces light vehicle is based on the G270CDI G-Class. An initial order for 41 VPS was awarded to Panhard mid-2005, with a follow-on order for an additional 10 units. Full details of the Panhard VPS can be found in the Special attack vehicles section.

CKD production, Greece
Production of 462 series G-Class commenced in Greece by ELBO SA in 1991. 462 series G-Class are essentially 460/461 series G-Class supplied to Greece in Complete Knock-Down (CKD) form. In addition to Hellenic Armed Forces, ELBO also supplies vehicles to Cypriot armed forces and during 2004 supplied 20 vehicles to Albania. Full details of ELBO-produced G-Class can be found elsewhere in this section.

Contrary to some reports, the G-Class has not been assembled from CKD kits for the Turkish Army at the Mercedes-Benz plant in Aksaray, Turkey, but it could, as required.

Protected G-Class
Mercedes-Benz has offered factory-approved benign in appearance protected G-Class variants for over 15 years, however recent global developments have generated increased demand for protected light all-terrain vehicles for use by military, law-enforcement, aid and civil agencies. All G-Class models may be supplied direct from the factory either fitted with, or for but not with, all-round ballistic and blast protection.

To ensure maximum protection, throughout the assembly process ballistic protection panels are integrated into the bodyshell of the vehicle at points where an add-on appliqué-only kit could prove vulnerable.

Protection levels of up to VR7 are available.

Canada; Standard Military Pattern (SMP) Light Utility Vehicle Wheeled (LUVW)
Mercedes-Benz was awarded a contract to supply an initial 802 specialised variants of the G270CDI G-Class to the Canadian Army in October 2003. The contract covered the Standard Military Pattern (SMP) segment of the Light Utility Vehicle Wheeled (LUVW) programme to replace a fleet of Bombardier-built Iltis light vehicles, 2,500 of which were supplied between 1984-85.

This long-winded programme was first announced in 1995 as the Light Utility Vehicle (LUV) programme and the main bidders in a programme for (then) 2,300 light vehicles were AM General, Land Rover and Mercedes-Benz.

It was announced in November 2002 that the Canadian Department of National Defence was set to award a CAD49.7 million (USD31.8 million) contract to General Motors (GM) Defense for 861 Light Service Support Vehicle-based (LSSV) trucks to meet the Military Commercial-Off-The-Shelf (MilCOTS) segment of the LUV requirement. Full details of the GM LSSV can be found elsewhere in this section.

In late 2002 the Canadian Department of National Defence released a Request for Proposals (RfP) for up to 802 Standard Military Pattern (SMP) Light Utility Vehicles (LUVs) for use by deployable field force units. This especially demanding (technically) requirement called for a diesel engine, an automatic transmission, a 24 V electrical system, four doors, a hard top, seating for four troops, a payload capacity of 750 kg (including the crew), a sustainable speed of 100 km/h, a range of 400 km between refuelling stops, and the ability to tow an 850 kg payload trailer. An appliqué armour protection kit proof against 7.62 × 51 mm NATO ball ammunition, artillery fragments and 1 kg blast mine blast was also specified.

Three variants of SMP were required: basic; command and reconnaissance with a turret ring, and a military police variant. Five companies expressed an interest in bidding for the contract: AM General (HMMWV); Daimler-Benz (G-Class); the then General Motors Diesel Division (Bucher DURO); Land Rover (Defender 110 or 130), and Western Star (M1044).

The specifications originally called for a light truck that was in production and field-tested. That, however, would have excluded Canada's Western Star Trucks (now part of Daimler). Political considerations prevailed and developmental vehicles became acceptable. Ultimately only one company would bid, the then DaimlerChrysler.

Following contract award in October 2003, the first 60 SMP G-Class were delivered to Canadian forces operating in Afghanistan during March 2004. All 802 vehicles were delivered by year-end. A contract option bringing the total number of vehicles ordered to 1,159 was exercised during 2004, with deliveries running from 2005-06. A further order for an additional 25 vehicles was subsequently placed, deliveries concluding in July 2006.

The Canadian SMP G-Class is based on the 2.85 m wheelbase model and with a maximum permissible GVW of 4,800 kg.

G280 CDI Light Armoured Patrol Vehicle I (LAPV I)/LAPV 5.4

Germany's Federal Office of Defence Technology and Procurement (Bundesamt für Wehrtechnik und Beschaffung - BWB) is currently running the sizeable Armoured Command-and-Control Vehicle (Geschutzte Fuhrungs und Funktionsfahrzeug - GFF) programme. There are four elements to the GFF programme, the aim of which is to provide the German Army with wheeled vehicles better equipped to deal with current threats and operating environments than currently fielded vehicles.

	290GDT 2.4 m WB, soft top	G270CDI 2.85 m WB, soft top	G280CDI 2.85 m WB	G300CDI 2.85 m WB	G280CDI (6 × 6)
Configuration:	4 × 4 (selectable)	4 × 4 (full-time)	4 × 4 (full time)	4 × 4 (full time)	6 × 6 (full time)
Weight:					
(permissible front axle load)	1,200 kg	up to 2,200 kg	up to 2,200 kg	up to 2,200 kg	2,200 kg
(permissible rear axle load)	1,600 kg	up to 2,800 kg	up to 2,800 kg	up to 2,800 kg	2 × 2, 800 kg
(max load)	700 kg	up to 2,200 kg	up to 3,000 kg	up to 3,000 kg	up to 3,000 kg
(max towed load, braked)	2,800 kg	3,300 kg	3,300 kg	up to 3,140 kg	n/avail
(max towed load, unbraked)	750 kg	n/avail	n/avail	n/avail	n/avail
Length:	4.165 m	4.588 m	4.588 m	4.643 m	6.24 m
Width:	1.7 m	1.7 m	1.7 m	1.7 m	1.7 m
Height: (overall)	2.005 m	1.950 m	1.950 m	2.02 m	2.133 m
Ground clearance:	240 mm	220 mm	220 mm	213 to 245 mm	220 mm
Track:	1.425 m	1.475 m or 1.555 m	1.475 m or 1.555 m	1.475 m or 1.555 m	1.475 m or 1.555 m
Wheelbase:	2.4 m	2.850 m and 3.428 m	2.850 m and 3.428 m	2.850 m and 3.428 m	3.120 and 1.110 m
Angle of approach/departure:	39°/34°	39°/34°	45°/38°	44°/36° (chassis with cab)	45°/38°
Max road speed:	138 km/h (approx)	limited to 120 km/h (max 160 km/h)	limited to 120 km/h (max 160 km/h)	up to 160 km/h	120 km/h
Fuel capacity:	96 litres	96 litres	96 litres	96 litres	96 litres + 52 litres optional
Range:	n/avail	750 km, driver and conditions dependant	600-800 km, driver and conditions dependant	600-800 km, driver and conditions dependant	600-800 km, driver and conditions dependant
Max gradient: (at GVW)	80%	80%	80%	80%	n/avail
Side slope: (static)	56%	87%	87%	87%	n/avail
Fording: (unprepared)	600 mm	600 mm	600 mm	600 mm	600 mm
Engine:	OM 602 DE29LA 2.874 litre 5-cylinder in-line turbocharged and intercooled, water-cooled 4-stroke diesel developing 120 hp (89 kW) at 3,800 rpm	270CDI 2.685 litre 5-cylinder in-line turbocharged and intercooled, water-cooled common rail injection 4-stroke diesel developing 156 hp (116 kW) at 3,800 rpm and 370 N.m torque between 1,600-2,600 rpm	OM642DE30LA 2.987-litre V-6 turbocharged and intercooled, water-cooled common rail injection 4-stroke diesel developing 184 hp (137 kW) at 3,800 rpm and 400 N.m torque at 1,600-2,600 rpm	2.987-litre V-6 turbocharged and intercooled, water-cooled common rail injection 4-stroke diesel developing 181 hp (135 kW) at 3,800 rpm and 400 N.m torque at 1,600-2,600 rpm	OM642DE30LA 2.987-litre V-6 turbocharged and intercooled, water-cooled common rail injection 4-stroke diesel developing 181 hp (135 kW) at 3,800 rpm and 400 N.m torque at 1,600-2,600 rpm
Transmission:	W4A 028 UB 4-speed automatic	W5A 580 5-speed automatic with touchshift	W5A 580 5-speed automatic with touchshift	W5A 580 5-speed automatic with touchshift	W5A 580 5-speed automatic with touchshift
Transfer box:	VG 080 2-speed, part-time 4 × 4, selectable front-wheel drive	VG 150E-3W 2-speed full time 4 × 4 with lockable differential	VG 150E-3W 2-speed full time 4 × 4 with lockable differential	VG 150E-3W 2-speed full time 4 × 4 with lockable differential	VG 150E-3W 2-speed full time 4 × 4 with lockable differential
Steering:	LS 2 B power-assisted	LS 2 B power-assisted	LS 2 B power-assisted	LS 2 B power-assisted	LS 2 B power-assisted
Turning radius:	5.7 m	6.5 m	6.5 m	6.5 m	n/avail
Suspension:	coil springs and telescopic shock-absorbers, front and rear. All axles are located by 1 transverse and 2 longitudinal control links				
Tyres:	20.5R 16 (other sizes optional)	20.5R 16 (other sizes optional)	285/75R 16	225/75 R17.5 or 285/75 R16	285/75R 16
Brakes: (main)	hydraulic, dual circuit with vacuum booster, discs front, drums rear	hydraulic, dual circuit with vacuum booster, discs front, discs or drums rear, ABS standard	hydraulic, dual circuit with vacuum booster, discs front, discs or drums rear(s), ABS standard	hydraulic, dual circuit with vacuum booster, discs front, discs or drums rear(s), ABS standard	hydraulic, dual circuit with vacuum booster, discs front, discs or drums rear(s), ABS standard
Electrical system:	24 V	12/24 V (2 circuits, 2 alternators)	12/24 V (2 circuits, 2 alternators)	12/24 V (2 circuits, 2 alternators)	12/24 V (2 circuits, 2 alternators)
Batteries:	2 × 12 V, 60 Ah	3 × 12 V, 60 Ah (70 Ah optional)	3 × 12 V, 60 Ah (70 Ah optional)	3 × 12 V, 60 Ah (70 Ah optional)	3 × 12 V, 60 Ah (70 Ah optional)
Alternator:	28 V, 80A	28 V, 80A	28 V, 80A	28 V, 80A	28 V, 100A and 12 V, 180A

Once in service GFF vehicles will take over on deployed operations a number of roles currently performed by unarmoured or interim/makeshift armoured vehicles. Additionally they will undertake a number of roles currently developing on deployed operations, and for which Germany's (or any other) armed forces are not particularly well equipped.

To reduce procurement times the BWB stated a preference that proven designs should be offered to meet GFF requirements. In late-January 2006 the BWB disclosed it had awarded three contracts for single examples of a GFF Group 1 trials vehicle. Contracts were awarded to Krauss-Maffei Wegmann (KMW), Rheinmetall LandSysteme (RLS) and Volkswagen. Subsequent reports added the Achleitner Survivor (based on the Mercedes-Benz G-Class) to the list of vehicles being trialled, and at IDEX 2007 the now Daimler disclosed that it was offering the latest G-Class-based LAPV.

Developed in conjunction with Armoured Car Systems (ACS) of Germany, the Light Armoured Patrol Vehicle (LAPV) is based on 2.85 m wheelbase chassis and features a monocoque armoured shell that in standard configuration offers protection to STANAG Level 1 ballistic, DM 31 mine blast and side blast protection from 15 kg TNT at 2 m distance. GVW is 5,400 kg, payload is 900 kg with Level 2 ballistic protection. The front axle is rated at 2,200 kg, the rear at 3,400 kg.

The vehicle was initially designated Light Armoured Patrol Vehicle I (LAPV I), but is now known as the Light Armoured Patrol Vehicle 5.4 (LAPV 5.4), the 5.4 denoting a GVW of 5,400 kg.

A small number (thought to be around 10) of LAPV I/LAPV 5.4 were supplied to Germany's Armed Forces, with most of these understood to have been used/evaluated on operations in Afghanistan. At Eurosatory 2010 Mercedes-Benz disclosed the sale of an initial batch of around 45 LAPV 5.4 to the German Bundeswehr under the German Army's GFF1 requirement.

Light Armoured Patrol Vehicle 6.X (LAPV 6.X)
The LAPV 6.X retains the armoured body of the LAPV 1/LAPV 5.4, plus the 280CDI engine and matching gearbox, but is fitted with new lighter Unimog-style portal-type axles to give enhanced mobility and increase the overall GVW of the platform. Ground clearance increases to approximately 450 mm, unprepared fording depot is 1 m, and a Central Tyre Inflation System (CTIS) is fitted as standard.

The LAPV 6.X has a GVW of around 6,400 kg and a payload of up to 1,300 kg. Protection levels are enhanced over those of the LAPV 5.4, basic protection being Level 2 ballistic (Level 3 optional), with at least Level 2a blast protection with the optional mine deflector floor plate fitted.

Light Armoured Patrol Vehicle II (LAPV II)
Outline details of the Light Armoured Patrol Vehicle II (LAPV II), which at the time remained a project study, were released during 2008. The most significant change between LAPV II and LAPV I (aside from the use of a 3.428 m wheelbase chassis) is the fitting of higher capacity Unimog portal axles, these not only increasing GVW and potential payload capability, but improve off-road mobility. The first G-Class model fitted with Unimog portal axles was shown at IDEX 2005 by Rheinmetall. The LAPV II was first shown at Eurosatory 2008.

The then quoted GVW for LAPV II was 7,500 kg, giving a 2,600 kg payload when armoured to STANAG Level 2 ballistic and Level 2a mine blast. Optional Level 1 or 3 ballistic and Level 2b mine blast protection was quoted as available, with the corresponding effect on payload.

It was disclosed late-2008 that Daimler, offering the LAPV II, was one of seven companies that had been downselected for the UK MoD's Operational Utility Vehicle System (OUVS) small requirement. The company later disclosed it had withdrawn from the competition.

LAPV 7.X
The LAPV 7.X utilises the Unimog chassis concept, but mated to essentially a Mercedes-Benz G-Class engine and transmission. The LAPV 7.X, which was displayed publicly for the first time at Eurosatory 2010, uses near-standard G-Class front panels matched to a newly designed protected cabin and open rear cargo tray.

This LAPV 7.X, which was displayed publicly for the first time at Eurosatory 2010, uses near-standard G-Class front panels matched to a newly designed protected cabin and open rear cargo tray (Shaun C Connors)
1391358

GVW is around 7,500 kg, the chassis with engine weighs 2,800 kg, payload with Level 3 ballistic and 2b blast protection being around 1,500 kg.

Rheinmetall Landsysteme

Rheinmetall LandSysteme (RLS) has developed two specialised variants of the G-Class, the Light Infantry Vehicle (LIV) and Light Infantry Vehicle (Special Operations) (LIV (SO)), Serval.

The LIV was developed as a modular vehicle to meet the needs of special, expeditionary or deployable forces. The modular concept of the LIV is based around a common chassis with a frame-mounted quick-change system for various mission modules.

German Bundeswehr forces in Afghanistan evaluated eight prototypes of the LIV (plus eight prototypes of the Krauss-Maffei Wegmann Mungo) during 2003 to meet an urgent operational requirement for a 10-seat protected light transport vehicle for rapid reaction forces. These remain in use as MEDEVAC vehicles.

The RLS LIV (sometimes referred to as the Wolf ESK (Einsatzfahrzeug Spezialisierte Kräfte - vehicle for specialised forces) is based on the G-Class 270CDI with an extended 3.29 m wheelbase and GVW of up to 5,200 kg. The 10-seat body package is designed by Binz GmbH & Co. The driver, front seat passenger and the sides and rear of the open-topped troop compartment are protected from 7.62 mm rounds; a ballistically protected hard top is an option. Run-flat tyres are standard fit. Dimensions are 5.12 × 1.84 × 1.87-2.17 m (L × W × H). Unladen weight is 2,550 kg and maximum payload (including any mission module) is 2,650 kg.

The LIV(SO), now referred to as Serval, is in service with the German Bundeswehr's Special Forces, all 21 vehicles being delivered between January-June 2004. A small number of vehicles are understood to have been supplied to the Swiss Army. (Full details of the LIV(SO) can be found in the Special attack vehicles section.)

Specifications
See table on facing page

Status
In production. Supplied to Albania (20, license-produced in Greece, 2004), Algeria (90), Argentina (1,200, 900 remain in use), Australia (1,200 ordered 2008 see text), Austria (1,200), Bulgaria (deliveries ongoing, including G280 CDI), Canada (1,184 SMP LUVW G270CDI, 2004-2006), Croatia (approximately 300), Cyprus (Type 290 GD and 290GDT, license produced in Greece), Denmark (approximately >2,000, see text), Estonia, Finland (>175, deliveries ongoing), France (15,000, local production - see separate entry), Gabon, Germany (12,000 (including 280CDI) plus 870 for Federal German Border Guard and 200 for Federal German foreign aid, deliveries ongoing), Greece (approximately 11,000, local production), Guatemala (50), Hungary (more than 230, 2003-2009, deliveries ongoing), Ireland (no longer in service), Kuwait (400), Luxembourg (38), Malaysia (licence production from 2003), Mexico (>80, from 2008), Netherlands (3,195 ordered in mid-1990; 128 G280CDI ordered 2007), Norway (3,500 including 270CDI), NATO SHAPE (350), Poland (more than 130), Russia (usually State use), Serbia (badged Puch, deliveries inc. (200) 1984 and (approximately 150) 1998), Singapore (311), Slovenia, Slovakia, Sweden, Switzerland (5,300 + Serval), UAE (25 when Abu Dhabi), UNO (100), UK (captured Argentine vehicles used in Falkland Islands - status uncertain), US Army Europe (380), US Army (protected), US Marine Corps (157), former Yugoslavia (500), Zambia (50) and other undisclosed African countries (>50).

(Numbers given are usually those known to have been supplied, and numbers remaining in service will in some instances, differ.)

Contractor
Daimler AG

Mercedes-Benz Sprinter (4 × 4) utility vehicle

Development
The Sprinter van has been in commercial production since 1995, with second-generation models being introduced in 2006. All-wheel drive versions of current models were introduced in January 2007. Over 1.3 million Sprinter vans have been sold worldwide. The Volkswagen Crafter (also available with four-wheel drive) is essentially a re-badged Sprinter. In North America the Sprinter is badged Freightliner or Dodge.

The Mercedes-Benz Sprinter (4 × 4) utility vehicle is best described as suitable for operations in difficult road conditions, such as snow or ice, or on unsurfaced roads and light tracks. It is one of only a small number of civilian van-type vehicles available in a 4 × 4 drive configuration, and is also marketed by Mercedes-Benz for commercial applications.

Description
The (4 × 4) version of the Sprinter is essentially a civilian (4 × 2) van modified by the fitting of an all-wheel drive system. To give the required increase in under-body clearance, the front and rear axles are raised by 110 and 80 mm respectively, the front axle also being modified from its normal steer-only configuration.

The all-wheel drive components of the Sprinter add up to approximately 150 kg to the unladen weight of the vehicle, thus having a minimal affect on its payload capability. Under normal circumstances power is

Mercedes-Benz Sprinter (4 × 4) (Daimler)   1391030

distributed between the front and rear wheels at a 35/65 per cent ratio, however an electronic traction control system is fitted that works by applying braking force to any wheel that loses grip, thereby transferring power to those wheels that still have traction.

Aside from the all-wheel drive modification, military variants of the (4 × 4) Sprinter are essentially a base-trim level civilian vehicle supplied in military flat paint. Being based on an in-production civilian vehicle, throughout its production run the Mercedes-Benz Sprinter (4 × 4) has reflected the numerous minor design changes and specification upgrades associated with civilian van production.

At present two wheelbase variants (3.665 or 4.325 m) are offered. These can be supplied fitted with numerous types of body and cab including a double crew cab, a crewbus bodyshell with seating for up to 16, Luton van or estate-type bodies, working platforms mounting light cranes, hydraulic platforms or similar devices, a troop carrier/flatbed platform covered by a tarpaulin and bows, or a range of exchangeable bodies. Maximum payload (body and interior dependent) ranges from 1,000 to 2,700 kg, with the maximum allowable GVW being 5,000 kg.

Front axles are independently sprung and feature a stabiliser transverse leaf parabolic spring, the rear axle is sprung by parabolic leaf springs. Single or twin rear tyre options are available.

The current Sprinter is powered by a Mercedes-Benz OM 646 DELA 2.148-litre four-cylinder in-line common-rail water-cooled diesel engine or a OM 642 DELA 2.987-litre V6-cylinder common-rail water-cooled diesel. Power outputs range from 109 hp and 280 N.m torque and 184 hp and 400 N.m torque.

Gearbox options are either a Mercedes-Benz NSG 370-6 six-speed manual or a NAG W5A 380 five-speed automatic.

Mercedes-Benz Vito
The Mercedes-Benz Vito light van is available with a four-wheel drive system. The Mercedes-Benz Vito (4 × 4) has a similar four-wheel drive system to the Sprinter, but with limited clearances is best described as suitable for operations in difficult road conditions, such as snow or ice, or on damaged roads and light tracks.

Status
In production. In service with the Austrian, German, Swedish, Swiss (400) and possibly other undisclosed armed forces. The Swiss Army received 150 313 CDI and 250 413 CDI models between September 2000 and October 2001. The Austrian Army placed an order for around 132 313 CDI models with a 3.5 m wheelbase (to be fitted with various bodies) in 2002.

Contractor
Daimler AG

Greece

Hellenic Vehicle Industry G-Class licence-production

Development
The Mercedes-Benz (4 × 4) G-Class (previously known as the G-Wagen) has been licence-produced in Greece by Hellenic Vehicle Industry S.A. (ELBO) for a number of years. Designated 462 series by Mercedes-Benz, vehicles built by ELBO are essentially the 460/461 series supplied as Complete Knock-Down (CKD) kits from the G-Class manufacturing plant in Austria for local assembly. This involved the insertion of around 50 per cent local content and includes the frame, the majority of the body parts and the complete interior.

In excess of 11,000 G-Class have been licence-produced by ELBO to date. Some ELBO-produced vehicles have been supplied to Cyprus and during 2004 a small number (20) of vehicles were supplied to Albania. Cypriot versions differ slightly in specification, being right-hand drive.

ELBO will be obliged to switch over to the current G-Class drive train at some stage in the near future. Production of the 290GDT power plant, for supply to ELBO, was completed in Germany in 2003.

Type 290 GD (4 × 4) 2.4 m wheelbase light vehicle general purpose variant with soft top and fitted for radio (Shaun C Connors)   1185494

Type 290 GD (4 × 4) 3.12 m wheelbase light vehicle with a locally-produced general service style rear body tray which is usually used for troop transport (Shaun C Connors)   1185495

Full details of the Mercedes-Benz G-Class can be found elsewhere in this section.

Description
The first G-Class model to be assembled by ELBO was the 240GD. From 1990 the 290GD was produced, initially with a manual gearbox but later, for the 290GDT series an automatic gearbox became standard. ELBO-assembled G-Class for Hellenic Armed Forces are all supplied with front and rear axle differential locks as standard.

ELBO-assembled vehicles have been produced with either a 2.4 or 3.12 m wheelbase (3.12 m wheelbase until 2004), and in a number of versions, the base vehicle being a general purpose design with a removable soft top. Open-topped weapons carrier variants include a machine gun carrier with the machine gun mounted on a roll-over bar and anti-tank versions. These include a 106 mm M40 series recoilless rifle carrier with a split front windscreen and a blast screen over the bonnet and TOW or MILAN anti-tank missile carriers. A front-line ambulance version with a soft-top has also been produced.

All future production will be based on 2.85 or 3.4 m wheelbases.

Status
Production as required. In service with the Greek, Cypriot and Albanian (20, 2004) armed forces (approaching 11,000 in total).

Contractor
Hellenic Vehicle Industry SA

India

Maruti Gypsy (4 × 4) 600 kg light vehicle

Development
The Maruti Gypsy is essentially a Suzuki SJ Series SJ-413 light vehicle produced in India by the now Maruti Suzuki India Limited.

Maruti Suzuki India Limited is India's leading passenger car manufacturer with over a 45 per cent domestic market share. Maruti Suzuki India Limited was formed in 1982 when a Joint Venture (JV) agreement was signed between India's Maruti Udyog Limited and Japan's Suzuki Motor Corporation. The Maruti Gypsy was added to the then Maruti Udyog Limited's product portfolio in 1985.

Maruti Gypsy (4 × 4) light vehicle of the Indian Army (Gordon Arthur)
1391196

The Suzuki SJ Series has origins tracing back to the late-1960s. After acquiring the Hope Motor Company and its four-wheel drive HopeStar ON360 in 1968, Suzuki of Japan introduced its first four-wheel drive, the LJ10 in 1970. This model was followed by the LJ20 and LJ50 models, and in 1981 the Suzuki SJ Series was introduced. The JA Series was introduced in 1995, and in 1998 this was superseded by the revised JB Series. The JB Series remains in production. Depending on the market, the Suzuki SJ Series and later JA/JB series (or collectively Jimny) carries, or has carried, a number of names including Suzuki Samurai, Suzuki Sierra, Suzuki Potohar, Suzuki Caribbean, Suzuki Santana, Holden Drover and Mazda AZ Offroad.

The Indian Army has a sizeable fleet of Maruti Gypsy light vehicles, with the majority of recent light vehicles orders understood to have been for the Gypsy as opposed to Mahindra Jeep models.

Around 20,000 Maruti Gypsy light vehicles are currently understood to be in service with India's Armed and Paramilitary Forces.

Description

The Maruti Gypsy is based on the Suzuki SJ Series SJ-413 light vehicle. When first introduced to the Indian market in 1985, the Gypsy was powered by Suzuki's F10A four-cylinder 970 cc petrol engine that developed a modest 45 hp. Driveline was completed by a four-speed manual gearbox and two-speed transfer box. The vehicle carried the designation MG410 - Maruti Gypsy four-cylinder one-litre engine.

In 1993 Maruti introduced a revised model with a wider track, both front and rear track increasing by 90 mm. This version was designated MG410W, with the W denoting wide track.

In 1997 a revised model (designated MG413W and officially called the Gypsy King) was introduced, this fitted with a more powerful Suzuki G13BA four-cylinder 1.3-litre petrol engine developing 65 hp.

Visually the MG413W can be differentiated from the earlier MG410W by a pronounced bonnet bulge and a different grille design. In 2000, and for emissions reasons, Maruti introduced the G13BB petrol engine. A small number of other refinements were made at this time also.

The Gypsy is entirely conventional in design, the ladder frame chassis being sprung by leaf springs and shock-absorbers; the front beam-type axle is fitted with disc brakes, the rear with drums. ABS is not fitted.

The only body style available is two-door, with either a soft- or hard-top. An ambulance body option is also offered.

The Gypsy has been criticised in certain commercial automotive media for offering a relatively rough ride, having a utilitarian interior and generally lacking any overall refinement. However, it is this simple robust functionality which makes the Gypsy well-suited to the role of military light utility vehicle.

Specifications

Gypsy (4 × 4)
Cab seating: 1 + 1 (+ up to 4 in rear on bench seats)
Configuration: 4 × 4
Weight:
  (kerb, soft-top) 985 kg
  (kerb, hard-top) 1,050 kg
  (laden, soft-top) 1,585 kg
  (laden, hard-top) 1,650 kg
  (payload) 600 kg
Length: 4.01 m
Width: 1.54 m
Height:
  (soft-top) 1.875 m
  (hard-top) 1.845 m
Ground clearance: 210 mm
Track:
  (front) 1.3 m
  (rear) 1.31 m

Wheelbase: 2.375 m
Fuel capacity: 40 litres
Engine: Suzuki G13BB MPFI 1.298-litre 4-cylinder in-line water-cooled 16-valve multipoint fuel injection petrol developing 80 hp at 6,000 rpm and 103 N.m torque at 4,500 rpm
Gearbox: manual with 5 forward and 1 reverse gears
Transfer box: 2-speed
Steering: manual
Suspension: leaf spring and shock-absorber, front and rear
Tyres: 205/70R15
Brakes: discs front, drums rear; no ABS

Status

In production. In service with Indian Army (approximately 20,000) and India's Paramilitary Forces, the armed forces of Nepal and Sri Lanka, and other undisclosed countries.

Contractor

Maruti Suzuki India Limited

Mahindra (4 × 4) army model vehicles

Development

Mahindra & Mahindra Limited, part of the Mahindra Group, now the leading manufacturer of utility vehicles and tractors in India, first assembled imported Jeep kits. In October 1947 the first batch of 75 vehicles was imported in CKD form from the then Willys Overland Export Corporation of the US. The first vehicles were assembled in 1949. A phased local manufacture of the vehicle in co-operation with the then Kaiser Jeep Corporation was undertaken from 1954 onwards and was completed by 1968. A wide range of petrol and diesel utility vehicles is manufactured and well over one million vehicles have been sold worldwide; Mahindra & Mahindra Limited is a major supplier of light (4 × 4) vehicles to India's Armed Forces and of around 115,000 vehicles produced annually supplies between 1,200-1,500 to the military.

Exports commenced in 1968 and since then around 40,000 vehicles have been exported. From 1980, 25,000 units were delivered in knock-down form for assembly in Iran. Details of Mahindra's military export sales are limited. However, users of military products are known to include Afghanistan, Angola, Bangladesh, Congo, Ghana, Guyana, Nepal, Nigeria, Sierra Leone and Sri Lanka.

Mahindra MM series Jeep of the Indian Army (Gordon Arthur)   1391197

Mahindra MM 550XD (4 × 4) light vehicle (Mahindra & Mahindra)   0533627

The Mahindra field ambulance is based on the MM950XD single-cab 2.9 m wheelbase pick-up. The purpose-designed rear body has space for an attendant plus two lying and two sitting patients, or five sitting patients (Mahindra & Mahindra) 1156015

The Mahindra Striker is based on the Mahindra MM550XD with the doors and windscreen removed, and rear bodywork modified to provide space for ammunition, personal kit and 20 litres of water. A fixed central universal weapon mount can accommodate a single ATGW launcher (with four rounds carried), a 12.7 mm HMG or an AGL. A supplementary 7.62/5.56 mm LMG maybe mounted on the front scuttle panel (Mahindra & Mahindra) 1156016

The Mahindra Rakshak protected light vehicle (shown) is based on the MM775XD. Current models known as the Rakshak Plus are based on the Bolero (Mahindra & Mahindra) 1156017

The Mahindra Rapid Intervention Vehicle (RIV) was originally based on the Mahindra Utility (double cab) powered by a 55 hp direct injection diesel engine. The Rapid Intervention Vehicle is equipped to carry a crew of five plus 500 kg of equipment (Mahindra & Mahindra) 1156019

In 1979, the company entered into an agreement with Automobiles Peugeot of France to manufacture the XPD 4.90 diesel engine at its Igatpuri plant. Peugeot diesel engines were manufactured in the same plant from 1991 onwards.

Current military production is based around the MM550XD and MM540 (export variant) series of light vehicles which replaced the earlier CL 340 and CL 540 series of light vehicles in production in 1990.

The most recent Indian Army light utility vehicle orders have been split between Mahindra Defence Systems and Maruti (for the Gypsy, a copy of the Suzuki SJ 70), the bulk of recent orders being awarded to Maruti for the Gypsy. The Indian Army's fleet of approximately 39,000 light utility vehicles currently includes around 20,000 Maruti Gypsy and around 19,000 Mahindra vehicles.

An extensively revised MM550XD variant with a more powerful engine (around 90 hp) was being developed, although it was reported in 2005 that this project had been shelved and that a near new vehicle with increased payload and a EURO 3 emissions compliant common rail diesel engine was under development and would be launched around 2007. Some sources suggested that an order for around 3,500 vehicles would be placed during 2009.

The Indian Army is in the process of finalising a Joint Services Qualitative Requirements (JSQR) for an 800 kg load carrier, and while this does not read like a replacement requirement, the vehicle is at present the intended replacement for the Maruti Gypsy, Mahindra M550XD, and any remaining Jonga vehicles. The earlier (Army only) General Staff Qualitative Requirement (GSQR) suggested that vehicles like the Mahindra Scorpio/Bolero and Tata Grande were the target. Only a hard-top variant was required, the intended soft-top variant for which something like the Mahindra Scorpio Pick-Up single cab (as sold in South Africa) was suited, had been dropped. The RfP based on the GSQR was expected mid-2009, but the RfP now based on the revised JSQR is now not expected until 2010.

The current production version of the MM series is available featuring a regional emissions compliant engine and this is designated MM550XDB. A 4 × 2 version and other specialised versions of the MM series are also available. Specialist versions based on current Mahindra models and currently in production include a field ambulance, an armed reconnaissance/patrol light strike variant, a Rapid Intervention Vehicle (RIV) and the Rakshak Plus protected vehicle. Brief details of these variants can be found elsewhere in this entry.

The latest Mahindra models to enter production are the Scorpio and Bolero. The Bolero is a further development of the MM series for the commercial sector and is fitted with independent front suspension and revised front end styling. In 2004, it was disclosed that 80 Bolero and 40 MM550XD vehicles had been supplied to Afghanistan.

Scorpio has independent suspension all-round and is more SUV-like than previous Mahindra designs. The type is best described as being suited to rear echelon, command, control, communication, internal security duties, VIP transport, or for use by governmental, humanitarian or aid agencies. Scorpio has been supplied to India's Armed Forces for use on UN missions and to the armed forces of Djibouti and Sri Lanka. A protected variant of the Scorpio is also available and this has been supplied to India's State Police forces and exported to Sri Lanka.

Description
The CL series was available in 2.032 m and 2.286 m wheelbase versions and the MM series with at least three wheelbase options, the 2.426 m short wheelbase being the most numerous in military service. Like the CL series, the MM series comes with a variety of options for seating and body configurations.

The MM550XD/XDB is the base short wheelbase model with a soft-top and seating for seven plus the driver. Options for this model include reconnaissance/patrol vehicles, or the mounting of anti-tank missiles or a recoilless rifle. The current production model is designated MM550XDB and features an engine revised to meet Bharat Stage II emissions requirements and an increased 650 kg payload.

Standard military fittings throughout the range include: blackout lighting, radiator chaff screen, shovel and pick handle stowage, grip handles, dashlight switch, sign plates, speedometer seal, headlight brush guards, inspection socket, map reading lamp, fuel container holder and an oil can carrier.

The Mahindra Bolero is a further development of the MM series for the commercial sector and fitted with independent front suspension and revised front end styling. The Bolero is available to military and paramilitary users and has been supplied to Afghanistan
(Mahindra & Mahindra)   1156021

Variants

Field Ambulance
The Mahindra field ambulance based on the MM950XD single-cab 2.9 m wheelbase pick-up fitted with 7.50 × 16 sand-cum-highway tyres. The purpose-designed rear body has space for an attendant plus two lying and two sitting patients, or five sitting patients. Standard medical equipment includes a 220 V power supply, a defibrillator/ECG, a ventilator and a nebulizer.

Striker Armed Reconnaissance/Patrol Vehicle
The Mahindra Striker is a lightweight high-mobility combat vehicle based on the Mahindra MM550XD/XDB with the doors and windscreen removed, and rear bodywork modified to provide space for armament, ammunition, personal kit and 20 litres of water. The fixed central universal weapon mount can accommodate a single Anti-Tank Guided Weapon (ATGW) launcher (with four rounds carried), a 12.7 mm Heavy Machine Gun (HMG) or an Automatic Grenade Launcher (AGL). An additional 7.62/5.56 mm Light Machine Gun (LMG) can be mounted on the front scuttle panel. Other additional features include the fitting of 7.50 × 16-8 PR sand-cum-highway tyres and 2 × 20-litre fuel jerrycans to increase cruising range to 800 km on-road, 600 km off-road.

Rakshak/Rakshak Plus
This protected light vehicle was originally based on the MM775XD (Rakshak), and later on the Bolero (Rakshak Plus). Protection is provided for the six-man crew from a variety of threats ranging from 0.22 calibre up to 7.62 mm NATO ball. The lightweight composite armoured panels used are interchangeable between vehicles and are fitted with side and rear firing ports. A ballistic carpet for underbody protection from hand grenade blast is optional, as are runflat tyres and a roof-mounted LMG mount.

The Rakshak/Rakshak Plus is used by the Indian Army and Air Force, India's State Police and paramilitary forces, and the security forces of Guyana and Nepal.

Rapid Intervention Vehicle
The Rapid Intervention Vehicle (RIV) was original based on the Mahindra Utility (double cab) powered by a 55 hp direct injection diesel engine. Current models are based on the Bolero Camper powered by a turbocharged diesel engine developing 63 hp. The Rapid Intervention Vehicle is equipped to carry a crew of five plus 500 kg of equipment. Standard operational equipment includes riotous protection screens (full length fold-out for the two front doors), a light bar and Public Address (PA) system, drinking water and tea storage facility, generator, greater capacity protected fuel tank, tear gas launchers, a searchlight and side-running boards.

The Rapid Intervention Vehicle is in service with India's State Police and the security forces of Guyana.

Specifications
See table below

Status
In production. Mahindra's MM family and variants, Bolero and Scorpio, are in service with India's Armed Forces, paramilitary forces and State Police, plus the armed and/or security forces of a number of other nations including Afghanistan (40 MM550XD and 80 Bolero, 2004), Angola

Model	CL340	CL540	MM540	MM550XD
Seating:	1 + 3	1 + 5	1 + 5	1 + 6
Configuration:	4 × 4	4 × 4	4 × 4	4 × 4
Gross vehicle weight:	1,600 kg	1,770 kg	1,770 kg	2,280 kg (kerb weight: 1,700 kg)
Towing capacity:	1,000 kg	1,000 kg	1,000 kg	n/avail
Length:	3.39 m	3.78 m	3.81 m	3.86 m (incl. rear-mounted spare wheel)
Width:	1.65 m	1.65 m	1.78 m	1.65 m
Wheelbase:	2.032 m	2.31 m	2.426 m	2.43 m
Track: (with 7.00 × 15 tyres)	1.23 m	1.23 m	1.29 m	1.328 m
Max speed: (2.1 litre diesel)	105 km/h	105 km/h	105 km/h	n/avail
Fuel capacity:	40 litres	40 litres	60 litres	45 litres
Engine: (diesel)	2.1 litre	2.1 litre	2.5 litre	2.112-litre 4- cylinder in-line water-cooled naturally aspirated diesel developing 76 hp at 4,500 rpm and 121 N.m torque at 2,000 rpm
Transmission:	4-speed (1st gear non-synchromesh)	4-speed (1st gear non-synchromesh)	5-speed (all synchromesh)	4-speed with synchromesh on 2nd, 3rd and 4th (5 speed optional)
Clutch:	n/avail	n/avail	n/avail	single dry plate, 235 mm, mechanical
Transfer box:	2-speed	2-speed	2-speed	2-speed
Steering:	n/avail	n/avail	n/avail	recirculating ball
Turning radius:	5.3 m	5.86 m	6.34 m	5.4 m (wheelbase dependant)
Suspension:	semi-elliptic underslung leaf springs with double acting telescopic shock-absorbers			
Tyres:	6.00 × 16 or P235/75R 15 or P215R 15	215/75R 15	n/avail	n/avail
Brakes:				
(main)	hydraulic power-assisted, discs front, drums rear on MM 550 XD			
(parking)	mechanical on rear wheels			
Electrical system:	12 V	12 V	12 V	12 V
Battery:				
(diesel)	70 Ah	70 Ah	70 Ah	70 Ah
(petrol)	60 Ah	60 Ah	60 Ah	n/avail
Alternator:	65 A	65 A	65 A	65 A

(delivered early/mid-1990s), Argentina (Marines), Bangladesh (small number of model CL), Congo (delivered early/mid-1990s), Ghana, Guyana (Rakshak and RIV, security forces), Nepal (MM540, Rakshak, security forces), Nigeria (most recent known delivery 30-40 MM540, 2004), Sierra Leone (delivered early/mid 1990s) and Sri Lanka (regular deliveries).

Contractor
Mahindra Defence Systems

JONGA (4 × 4) 0.25 ton light vehicle

Development
The Jabalpur Ordnance aNd Gun-carriage Assembly (JONGA) is essentially the P60, an early generation Japanese Nissan Patrol (4 × 4) light vehicle, manufactured under licence at the now Vehicle Factory Jabalpur (VFJ).

VFJ was sanctioned in 1965 for the production of three non-fighting vehicles for the Indian military: the three ton Shaktiman truck, the one ton Carrier and 0.25 ton JONGA light vehicle. Production commenced at VFJ in 1969 and according to VFJ figures, a total of 209,448 of these three vehicle types were produced. The one ton Carrier is also based on a Nissan design, the Nissan D4W73. Production of the JONGA was completed in 1999. It was confirmed in 2003 that production of the Shaktiman had also ceased. Quantities of the Carrier and a reasonably large number of Shaktiman remain in Indian Army service. The JONGA was not adopted in such large numbers as the Carrier and Shaktiman, the Indian Army preferring Mahindra and Maruti light vehicles.

Description
The JONGA/Nissan Patrol is entirely conventional in design, however, the JONGA vehicle underwent numerous automotive changes during its production life. It was produced with a 145 hp four-litre petrol engine in place of an earlier 125 hp unit and was also available with a Perkins P4(V) diesel. The final standard engine was a four-litre Hino WO4D diesel developing 108 hp and introduced in 1996.

The JONGA was produced in both 4 × 4 and 4 × 2 versions, with the latter being mainly for commercial sales. Two wheelbase lengths were produced, 2.35 m and 2.8 m and there were three basic bodies. The 2.35 m wheelbase model could have either a three-door soft top or five-door hardtop, with seating for the driver and nine or 10 passengers respectively. The 2.8 m wheelbase model could have a five door hardtop with seating for the driver and up to 11 passengers. Other body variations included a pick-up and an ambulance. At one time the Indian Army used an open-backed version carrying SS-11 Anti-Tank Guided Weapons (ATGWs).

Optional equipment included a 2,000 kg self-recovery mechanically-driven winch and an extra fuel tank.

Specifications
JONGA (4 × 4)
(2.35 m WB, soft top)
Cab seating: 1 + 9
Configuration: 4 × 4
Weight:
 (GVW) 2,700 kg
 (max load) 500 to 700 kg
 (towed load) 2,000 kg
Length: 4.045 m
Width: 1.715 m
Height: 2.015 m
Ground clearance: 220 mm
Track:
 (front) 1.382 m
 (rear) 1.4 m
Wheelbase: 2.35 m

JONGA (4 × 4) 0.25 ton light vehicle (Roger Moor)   1340310

Max speed: 120 km/h
Fuel capacity: 80 litres
Max gradient: 60%
Engine: Hino WO4D 4.009-litre 4-cylinder in-line water-cooled direct injection 4-stroke diesel developing 108 hp (81 kW) at 3,200 rpm
Gearbox: manual, synchromesh with 3 forward and 1 reverse gears
Clutch: single dry plate
Transfer box: 2-speed
Steering: worm and roller
Turning radius: 5.3 m
Suspension: semi-elliptic leaf springs (4 front, 5 rear) with double acting telescopic shock-absorbers
Tyres: 7.00 × 16
Brakes: hydraulic, dual circuit
Electrical system: 12 V
Alternator: 35 A

Status
Production complete. Around 1,000 remain in service with the Indian Army. Also supplied to Mozambique and possibly others.

Contractor
Vehicle Factory Jabalpur

Carrier (4 × 4) 1 ton light truck

Development
The Carrier (4 × 4) 1 ton light truck is a Japanese Nissan D4W73 vehicle produced under licence in India. The first production units were completed at the now Vehicle Factory Jabalpur (VFJ) around 1969.

VFJ was sanctioned in 1965 for the production of three non-fighting vehicles for the Indian military: the 3 ton Shaktiman truck, the 1 ton Carrier and 0.25 ton JONGA light vehicles. Production at the factory commenced in 1969 and production of the Carrier was completed around 1990. Production of the JONGA, which is also based on a Nissan design (an early version of the Nissan Patrol) is also complete. It was confirmed in 2003 that production of the Shaktiman had also ceased. Quantities of the Carrier and a reasonably large number of Shaktiman remain in Indian Army service. The JONGA was not adopted in such large numbers as the Carrier and Shaktiman, the Indian Army preferring Mahindra and Maruti light vehicles.

Description
The Carrier is entirely conventional in design, the basic version being a general-purpose light utility truck with a hard-topped cab for two people and a cargo area covered by a canvas tilt over removable bows. The cab windscreen can be folded forwards on to the bonnet and some vehicles feature a square roof-hatch over the passenger seat. The cargo area has a drop tailgate and folding seats may be provided along the sides.

Some vehicles were fitted with a front-mounted winch. Variants included a desert operations vehicle with oversize sand tyres, field ambulance and a light fire tender.

Specifications
Carrier (4 × 4) 1 ton light truck
Cab seating: 1 + 1
Configuration: 4 × 4
Weight:
 (laden) 4,190 kg
 (unladen) 2,690 kg
Max load:
 (on-road) 1,500 kg
 (off-road) 750 kg
Length: 4.73 m
Width: 2.045 m
Height: (overall) 2.355 m
Ground clearance: (axles) 260 mm
Track: 1.6 m
Wheelbase: 2.8 m
Max speed: 95 km/h
Fuel capacity: 110 litres
Engine: 3.956-litre 6-cylinder in-line water-cooled petrol developing 145 hp (108 kW) at 3,800 rpm
Gearbox: manual, 4 forward and 1 reverse gears
Clutch: single dry plate
Transfer box: 2-speed
Suspension: semi-elliptic leaf springs, front and rear
Brakes: hydraulic
Electrical system: 12 V

Status
Production concluded during 1990. In service with the Indian Army, numbers reducing.

Contractor
Vehicle Factory Jabalpur

Tata Sumo (4 × 4) light vehicle

Development
The Tata Engineering & Locomotive Co Ltd (Telco) was established in 1945 to manufacturer steam locomotives and other engineering products, and in 1954 the company entered into a collaborative agreement with the then Daimler-Benz of Germany to manufacturer medium commercial vehicles. Heavy commercial vehicles (>16,000 kg GVW) followed in 1983, and in 1984 the Tata Sumo light utility vehicle was launched. The 100,000th Sumo was produced in 1987.

Tata Motors is the flagship of the Tata Group and is India's largest automobile company, with consolidated revenues of USD14 billion in 2008-2009. Over four million Tata vehicles are on the road in India, and Tata Motors is the largest commercial vehicle manufacturer and second largest passenger car manufacturer in the country. Additionally, the company is the world's fourth largest medium and heavy commercial truck manufacturer and second largest heavy bus manufacturer.

Since 1958 Tata Motors has supplied India's military and paramilitary forces with over 100,000 vehicles and in addition to ongoing domestic sales, currently exports around 450 to 500 military vehicles per year to (primarily) South East Asian and African armed forces.

In addition to the Tata Sumo, the most recent deliveries of light vehicles to India's military and paramilitary forces have included over 6,000 of the larger Tata SFC 407 light truck which entered commercial production in 1986. The type was quickly adopted by India's paramilitary forces as the standard medium troop carrying vehicle and deliveries to date have totalled around 6,000 to 7,000 vehicles. Deliveries continue at 800 to 900 per year and split 200-300/600 4 × 4/4 × 2. A protected version of the Tata SFC 407 is also in service. Full details of the Tata SFC 407 light truck can be found elsewhere in this section.

The Tata Sumo (4 × 4) light utility vehicle is currently in production for India's military and paramilitary forces. Around 200 examples per year of the Sumo in ambulance configuration are currently being delivered to the Indian Army, with a Mk 2 variant currently being evaluated. India's State Police operate around 3,000 examples of the Sumo (4 × 2) variant; deliveries continue at around 400 to 500 vehicles per year. Export customers for the Sumo are understood to have included Argentina, Bangladesh, Nepal, Spain and Sri Lanka.

An armoured version of the Sumo is available and small numbers are understood to have been produced.

Description
The Tata Sumo (4 × 4) light utility vehicle is entirely conventional in design and is based on a ladder-type cranked box-section 110 (max) × 60 mm frame with welded and bolted in cross members.

Tata Sumo (4 × 4) light vehicle protected variant displayed publicly for the first time at DefExpo 2006 (Shaun C Connors)   1156012

Tata Sumo (4 × 4) light vehicle ambulance variant (Tata)   1156013

In standard configuration the station wagon-type body is configured to seat nine; an individually seated driver plus two passengers on a bench seat in the front, three passengers on the bench seat immediately behind the driver/front passengers, and two passengers each on folding longitudinally mounted bench seats on the right- and left-hand side of the vehicle at the rear; maximum payload allowance for the Sumo in this configuration is 810 kg. The rear door mounts a spare wheel on a tubular frame. Motive power for the Tata Sumo is provided by a Tata 483 DL TC diesel engine which develops 115 hp (86 kW) and 190 N.m torque. This is coupled to a five-speed synchromesh manual gearbox and two-speed transfer box. Four-wheel drive is available in high and low range, two-wheel drive in high range only. The front steer-drive axle is independently sprung by torsion bars, hydraulic shock-absorbers and an anti-roll bar. Steering is power-assisted. The rear drive axle is sprung by semi-elliptic leaf springs, hydraulic shock absorbers and an anti-roll bar.

Variants
Tata Sumo (4 × 4) armoured
This six-seat (five plus driver) light armoured vehicle offers occupants protection against small arms fire and underbody hand grenade blast. Basic dimensions are 4.515 × 1.806 m (L × W) and a wheelbase of 2.435 m. GVW and payload figures are 3,120 and 500 kg, respectively.

Specifications
Cab seating: 1 + 9
Configuration: 4 × 4 (selectable)
Weight:
  (laden) 2,710 kg
  (unladen) 1,900 kg
  (payload) 810 kg
  (permissible front axle load, laden) 1,050 kg
  (permissible front axle load, unladen) 980 kg
  (permissible rear axle load, laden) 1,670 kg
  (permissible rear axle load, laden) 920 kg
  (towed load, unbraked) 750 kg
Length: 4.45 m
Width: 1.78 m
Height:
  (laden) 1.905 m
  (unladen) 160 mm
Ground clearance: 160 mm
Track:
  (front) 1.5 m
  (rear) 1.45 m
Wheelbase: 2.4 m
Angle of approach/departure: 40°/23°
Max speed: 115 km/h
Max range: 500 km
Fuel capacity: 65 litres
Max gradient: (at GVW) 65%
Max sideslope: 33%
Fording: 300 mm
Engine: Tata 483 DL TC 1.948-litre 4-cylinder inline turbocharged and intercooled water-cooled 4-stroke indirect injection diesel developing 115 hp (86 kW) at 4,300 rpm and 190 N.m torque at 2,000-3,000 rpm
Gearbox: Tata G-76-5/3.87 synchromesh with overdrive; 5 forward and 1 reverse gears
Transfer box: Tata 2-speed
Clutch: single dry plate, Ø228 mm
Steering: power-assisted
Turning radius:
  (kerb) 5.9 m
  (wall) 6.35 m
Suspension: double wishbone with torsion bar springs, hydraulic shock-absorbers and an anti-roll bar, front; semi-elliptic leaf springs, hydraulic shock absorbers and an anti-roll bar, rear
Tyres: 195R 15-8 PR
Brakes:
  (main) vacuum-assisted hydraulic, 271 mm discs front, 282 mm drums rear
  (parking) hand operated, cable, acting on rear drums only
Electrical system: 12 V
Batteries: 12 V, 70 Ah

Status
In production. Around 200 per year in ambulance configuration to the Indian Army. India's State Police operate around 3,000 examples of the (4 × 2) variant; deliveries continue at around 400 to 500 vehicles per year. An armoured variant is available and has been produced in small numbers. Export customers for the Sumo are understood to have included Argentina, Bangladesh, Nepal (>100), Spain and Sri Lanka (around 200).

Contractor
Tata Motors Limited

Tata SFC 407 (4 × 4) 1,000 kg light truck

Development

The Tata Engineering & Locomotive Co Ltd (Telco) was established in 1945 to manufacturer steam locomotives and other engineering products, and in 1954 the company entered into a collaborative agreement with the then Daimler-Benz of Germany to manufacturer medium commercial vehicles. Heavy commercial vehicles (>16,000 kg GVW) followed in 1983, and in 1986 Tata's first indigenously designed light commercial vehicle, the Tata SFC 407 was launched.

Tata Motors is the flagship of the Tata Group and is India's largest automobile company, with consolidated revenues of USD14 billion in 2008-2009. Over four million Tata vehicles are on the road in India, and Tata Motors is the largest commercial vehicle manufacturer and second largest passenger car manufacturer in the country. Additionally, the company is the world's fourth largest medium and heavy commercial truck manufacturer and second largest heavy bus manufacturer.

Since 1958 Tata Motors has supplied India's military and paramilitary forces with over 100,000 vehicles and in addition to ongoing domestic sales, currently exports around 450 to 500 military vehicles per year to (primarily) South East Asian and African armed forces.

In addition to the Tata SFC 407, the most recent deliveries of light vehicles to India's military and paramilitary forces have included quantities of the Tata Sumo, a (4 × 4) light utility vehicle of the Land Rover/Mercedes-Benz G-Class type. Around 200 examples per year of the Sumo in ambulance configuration are currently being delivered to the Indian Army. India's state Police operate around 3,000 examples of the Sumo (4 × 2) variant; deliveries continue at around 400 to 500 vehicles per year. Full details of the Tata Sumo (4 × 4) light vehicle can be found elsewhere in this section. The larger Tata SFC 407 light truck entered commercial production in 1986. The type was quickly adopted by India's paramilitary forces as the standard medium troop carrying vehicle and deliveries to date have totalled around 8,500-9,000 vehicles. The SFC 407 is also used by the Air Force and Navy. Deliveries continue at 800 to 900 per year and are split in a 1:2 ratio (4 × 4)/(4 × 2). A protected version of the Tata 407 is also in service.

Export sales figures for the SFC 407 totalled 3,797 as of May 2006 and customers are understood to have included Bangladesh, Nepal, Nigeria, Sri Lanka and South Africa. The official Tata model designation of the SFC 407 provides basic data for the type and can be broken down as follows: SFC – Semi-Forward Control; 4 – GVW tonnes (approximately rounded); 7 – engine power output hp × 10 (approximately).

Tata 407 (4 × 4) 1,000 kg light truck in standard soft-top troop carrying configuration (Tata Motors)
1156007

Protected variant of the Tata 407 (4 × 4) 1,000 kg light truck (Shaun C Connors)
1156009

Description

The Tata SFC 407 (4 × 4) 1,000 kg light truck is entirely conventional in design and is based on a 180 × 55 mm C-section chassis with riveted and bolted-in cross members. D-shackle style recovery/towing points are fitted at the front, a tow hook at the rear. The commercial semi-forward control cab seats three, a driver plus two others. The standard General Service (GS) style troop carrying body is fitted with steel drop sides, a single-piece drop tailgate, and a removable tarpaulin and bows. Wooden bench seats are provided for troop transport. A hard-top rear body is available. The payload rating of the Tata 407 is 1,000 kg.

Motive power for the Tata SFC 407 is provided by a Tata diesel engine, the current version of which meets Bharat Stage II emissions requirements. This is coupled to a five-speed synchromesh manual gearbox and two-speed synchromesh transfer box. Four-wheel drive is selectable. The front single reduction steer-drive axle is sprung by semi-elliptic leaf springs, hydraulic shock-absorbers and an anti-roll bar. Steering is manual. The rear single reduction drive axle is sprung by semi-elliptic leaf springs, hydraulic shock-absorbers and an anti-roll bar.

Specifications

SFC 407
(current production model)
Cab seating: 1 + 2
Configuration: 4 × 4
Weight:
　(laden) 3,800 kg
　(unladen) 2,800 kg
　(payload) 1,000 kg
　(permissible front axle load) 1,750 kg
　(permissible rear axle load) 2,200 kg
Length: 9.435 m
Width: (over body) 2.1 m
Height: (cab, unladen) 2.319 m
Ground clearance: (front and rear) 222 mm
Track: (front and rear) 1.648 m
Wheelbase: 3.075 m
Angle of approach/departure: 44°/21°
Max speed: (4 × 2) 96 km/h
Max range: 550 km
Fuel capacity: 90 litres
Max gradient: 48%
Max sideslope: 26%
Fording: 400 mm
Engine: Tata 497 SP 2.956-litre 4-cylinder in-line turbocharged water-cooled 4-stroke direct injection Bharat Stage II emissions compliant diesel developing 75 hp (56 kW) at 2,800 rpm and 225 N.m torque at 1,500-1,800 rpm
Gearbox: Tata GBS-18 synchromesh with 5 forward and 1 reverse gears
Transfer box: Tata 2-speed
Clutch: single dry plate (240 mm in diameter)
Steering: recirculating ball, manual
Turning radius:
　(kerb) 6.9 m
　(wall) 7.55 m
Suspension: semi-elliptic leaf springs, hydraulic shock-absorbers and anti-roll bar, front; semi-elliptic leaf springs, hydraulic shock absorbers and anti-roll bar, rear
Tyres: 7.5 × 16-16 PR
Brakes:
　(main) dual-circuit, vacuum assisted hydraulic, 304 mm drums front and rear
　(parking) hand operated, cable, acting on rear drums only (max hold at 20% gradient)
Electrical system: 12 V
Batteries: 12 V, 70 Ah
Alternator: 35 A

Status

In production. Around 8,500-9,000 delivered to India's Paramilitary Forces, Air Force and Navy. Current deliveries are at a rate of around 800 to 900 per year split one-third/two-thirds (4 × 4)/(4 × 2). Export figures for the SFC 407 totalled 3,797 as of May 2006 and customers are known to have included Bangladesh, Nepal, Nigeria, Sri Lanka and South Africa.

Contractor

Tata Motors Limited

Israel

M-240 Storm, M-242 Storm II and M-243 Storm III (4 × 4) MultiMission Vehicle (MMV)

Development

The original M-240 Storm (Sufa in Hebrew), later M-242 Storm II and current M-243 MultiMission Vehicles (MMVs) are designed to fulfil several military functions including general utility, patrol and reconnaissance, command and anti-tank missile carrier.

AIL M243 Storm III (armoured) for an undisclosed export customer (AIL)
1340316

AIL Storm III (armoured) (AIL) 1340319

AIL Storm III (AIL) 1340317

AIL M-240 Storm (4 × 4) of the Chilean Army (Cesar Cruz Tantalean) 1185482

AIL Storm III (AIL) 1340318

M-240 Storm (4 × 4) armoured version (AIL) 0098951

The Israel Defence Force (IDF) received around 5,000 M-240 Storm I between 1991 and 2006, from when deliveries of the Storm II commenced with an order for an initial 500 vehicles. The Storm III was announced during 2009, has now replaced all earlier models in production, and an initial IDF order is understood to have been placed.

The Storm is based on a Chrysler Jeep platform and components. The Storm I was based on a Chrysler Jeep YJ chassis, the Storm II was based on a Chrysler Jeep Wrangler TJL chassis, and the latest Storm III is based on the military Jeep J8 chassis.

Description

The following description is relevant to the current M-243 Storm III that, like its predecessors, has an overall length of approximately 4.4 m. However, the Storm III has an increased wheelbase of 2.94 m.

Designed to military specifications and with an enhanced payload of 1,053 kg, the Storm III is currently offered in a number of different versions, including a five-door commander's configuration with a 3,358 kg Gross

Vehicle Weight (GVW). The general purpose utility vehicle can be fitted with either a soft- or hard-top. Another version, designed for riot control, has a transparent polycarbonate roof and side panels, which protect the occupants against stones, splinters and general vandalism. A reconnaissance and patrol variant offers extra stowage of fuel, water and equipment and can be fitted with mountings for a machine gun or special equipment. A five door armoured variant, designed for peace-keeping missions, is also available. The armoured Storm III is designed for protection against 5.56 and 7.62 mm Ball or AP ammunition. It is already in service with the security forces of a central Asian country.

The Storm III is based on the automotive components of the Jeep J8 and as such is equipped with a 2.8-litre diesel engine coupled to a five-speed automatic transmission. The purpose-designed suspension system includes heavy duty coil springs, front, and heavy-duty leaf-springs, rear.

The Storm III comes equipped with an air-conditioning system and a Roll Over Protection Structure (ROPS). Optional equipment includes a radio antenna base, communications tray, container mounting and run-flat wheels. A right hand drive option is also available.

M-242 Storm II hard-top version (4 × 4) MultiMission Vehicle (MMV) (AIL)
1132845

Specifications

M-243 Storm III
Cab seating: 1 + 4
Configuration: 4 × 4
Payload: 1,053 kg
Length: 4.45 m
Width: 1.876 m
Height: (overall) 2.012 m
Ground clearance: (axles) 231/241 mm (front/rear)
Wheelbase: 2.946 m
Angle of approach/departure: 47°/34°
Max speed: 130 km/h
Fuel capacity: 85.2 litres
Fording: 762 mm
Engine: VM 2.766-litre 4-cylinder inline turbocharged water-cooled diesel developing 158 hp (118 kW) at 3,800 rpm and 400 N.m torque at 2,000 rpm
Transmission: automatic with 5 forward and 1 reverse gears
Transfer box: NVG 2-speed
Steering: power-assisted
Turning radius: 6.2 m
Axles: Dana 44 fully floating front, Dana 60 semi-floating rear
Suspension: coil springs and shock-absorbers, front; leaf springs and shock-absorbers, rear
Tyres: 265/70 R17
Brakes: dual circuit hydraulic, discs front and rear
Electrical system: 12 V
Batteries: 1 or 2 × 12 V, 60 Ah (100 Ah optional)
Alternator: 117 A

Status

Storm I, production complete; in service with the Israeli Defence Forces (IDF), Chile, Ecuador, El Salvador and possibly other undisclosed countries. Storm II, production complete; in service with Israeli Defence Forces (IDF) and possibly others. Storm III, in production; in service with Israeli Defence Forces (IDF) and others.

Contractor

Automotive Industries Limited (AIL)

Italy

Fresia F 18 (4 × 4) 550 kg mountain power truck

Development

The Fresia F 18 (4 × 4) 550 kg mountain power truck was developed to meet the requirements of Italian mountain troops (the Alpini) for a vehicle which could be used to transport equipment and stores over mountain roads and tracks. The prototype was completed in 1974 and, following extensive trials, a pre-production batch was delivered for operational trials with Italian mountain units in June 1978. The original vehicles were limited in load capacity to 200 kg but development increased the capacity to 400 kg and later 550 kg.

The F 18 mountain power truck never matched the mobility of the mules it replaced and was never a favourite of the Alpini. It is now rarely seen, although officially remains in service.

More recently, in the early 1980s the Pozza company produced a series of light special machines which were tested and acquired in limited numbers by the Army. Three models were produced, Alpenscooter, Alpenpara and Alpentre. The Alpenscooter was supplied to mountain infantry battalions which used it for scouting missions. The programme

Fresia F 18 (4 × 4) 550 kg mountain power truck (Fresia SpA)   1296194

was not logistically supported and although still officially in service, the Alpenscooter is understood to no longer be used. Both the Alpenpara and Alpentre were deployed within parachute infantry units however the logistic problems were similar to those of the previously mentioned Alpenscooter. Some examples are still used, although their operational usefulness is now considered doubtful.

Description

The Fresia F 18 is a small all-wheel drive vehicle with an automatic locking differential, wide track and 12.5 × 20 tubeless tyres to allow for operation in any surface condition. An open platform for the transportation of up to 550 kg of cargo is fitted. The vehicle can be steered by the operator when seated on the platform or when walking behind. The engine is mounted in the centre of the vehicle under the load area which has a folding handrail on the sides and rear. The transmission is hydrostatic and steering is power assisted on both axles. The hydrostatic drive allows for continuous speed regulation between 0 and 20 km/h. Each wheel has coil-spring independent suspension.

Specifications

Fresia F 18
Configuration: 4 × 4
Weight:
  (laden) 1,080 kg
  (unladen) 530 kg
  (max load) 550 kg
Length: (over load platform) 1.915 m
Width: 1.06 m
Height:
  (over steering wheel) 1 m
  (load platform) 750 mm
Ground clearance: 220 mm
Track: 710 mm
Wheelbase: 1.2 m
Max speed: 20 km/h
Fuel capacity: 40 litres
Max gradient: 70%
Max side slope: 30%
Engine: Briggs and Stratton Type 422400 694 cc 2-cylinder air-cooled petrol developing 18 hp (13 kW) at 3,600 rpm
Gearbox: hydrostatic closed circuit with variable displacement radial piston primary pump and 2 fixed displacement orbital hydraulic motors
Steering: hydraulic, power assisted on all 4 wheels
Turning radius: 2.15 m
Suspension: independent with coil springs for each axle and hydraulic shock-absorbers
Brakes:
  (main) operating on hydrostatic transmission
  (parking) disc brakes on drive line, hand-operated
Tyres: 12.5 × 20 tubeless
Electrical system: 12 V
Battery: 1 × 12 V, 45 Ah

Status

In limited service with Italian Army mountain units.

Contractor

Fresia SpA

Fresia F 25 (4 × 4) 1,000 kg airborne vehicle

Development

The Fresia F 25 (4 × 4) 1,000 kg airborne vehicle was specifically developed to meet the requirements of airborne units and was designed for high mobility, while retaining a useful personnel or cargo payload.

The 48 vehicles supplied to the Spanish Army were manufactured by Servicios y Protectos Avanzados (SPA) and in Spanish service are known as the SPA-15D Fox.

Description

The main structure of the Fresia F 25 is made of steel, the torsionally rigid chassis being of conventional open-channel construction. The load platform is made of aluminium and is attached directly to the chassis. The standard model has a central driving position with an additional fold-down seating position on either side of the driver. The rear load area has seating for an additional four passengers. These seats fold down under the loadbed when not in use. A demountable rollover safety bar is provided behind the driving position.

With a maximum of seven people (six plus driver), up to 400 kg of personal equipment or stores may be carried on the available 1.9 m² load area. With three people (two plus driver), up to 800 kg of personal equipment or stores may be carried on the available 3.6 m² load area. With just the driver the available load area increases to 4.6 m², typical loads including water desalination or communication equipment. As an option, two loading ramps can be carried and stored behind the driver's seat when not in use. A tarpaulin cover to protect the driver's area or the entire vehicle is a further option.

In addition to the standard troop carrying/cargo role, the Fresia F 25 can also mount the MILAN (or similar) Anti-Tank Guided Weapon (ATGW), a 12.7 mm heavy machine gun, a recoilless rifle, or be used to tow a light anti-aircraft weapon or 120 mm mortar. The maximum towed load on level ground is 1,500 kg. The laden vehicle is capable of climbing a 30 per cent gradient while towing 800 kg.

Motive power is provided by a Peugeot 1.9-litre four-cylinder turbocharged diesel engine mounted centrally between the axles and below the loadbed. Developing 92 hp this gives the fully laden vehicle a 32 hp/tonne power-to-weight ratio. A Chrysler three-speed automatic transmission is fitted and gives maximum speeds of 32 km/h in first gear, 55 km/h in second gear, 79 km/h in third gear, and 36 km/h in reverse. Fuel consumption of the unladen vehicle at 75 km/h on-road is 10 litres per km, giving a road range of 500 km from the 50-litre standard fuel tank. Off-road endurance for the unladen vehicle is between five and seven hours. A 20-litre supplementary fuel tank is an option to extend endurance.

Four-wheel drive is permanent, both front and rear axles being fitted with self-locking differentials. Suspension is fully independent and by variable rate coil springs and hydraulic shock-absorbers at each wheel station. Fitted with 16 in (406 mm) wheels and 7.50R 16 tyres, and with an approach angle of 50°, the Fresia F 25 is capable of surmounting a 350 mm vertical step. Michelin tyres are standard fit, these accepting the optional snow chains. A spare wheel is carried.

Disc brakes are fitted on all four wheels, the 130 cm² parking brake working on all wheels through the transmission and being capable of holding the fully laden vehicle on its maximum gradient. Rack and pinion steering is fitted.

Other options include a remotely controllable electrically-powered self-recovery winch rated at 3,600 kg and fitted with 24 m of 8 mm diameter cable.

Up to 10 vehicles can be stacked inside a C-130 or C-160 transport aircraft, the vehicle can also be transported underslung by helicopter, and may be para-dropped.

Specifications

Fresia F 25
Seating: 1 + up to 6
Configuration: 4 × 4
Weight:
  (unladen) 1,900 kg
  (GVW) 2,900 kg
  (max load) 1,000 kg
  (towed load, level ground) 1,500 kg
  (towed load, 30% gradient) 800 kg
Length: 3.32 m
Width: 1.94 m
Height:
  (loadbed, laden) 990 mm
  (roll bar) 1.95 m
Ground clearance:
  (laden) 290 mm
  (unladen) 330 mm
Track: (front/rear) 1.6 m
Wheelbase: 1.95 m
Angle of approach/departure: 50°/58°
Max speed: 79 km/h
Max range: (on-road) 500 km
Fuel capacity: 50 litres (optional 20 litres)

SPA Fox-15D (4 × 4) 1,000 kg light vehicle (SPA)   0009661

Max gradient:
  (laden) 60%
  (unladen) 100%
  (descent) 60%
Side slope: 30%
Fording: 500 mm
Engine: Peugeot XUD9TE/TF 1.905-litre 4-cylinder in-line air-cooled turbocharged indirect injection 4-stroke diesel developing 92 hp (69 kW) at 4,000 rpm and 196 N.m torque at 2,250 rpm
Gearbox: Chrysler automatic with 3 forward and 1 reverse gears
Steering: rack and pinion
Turning radius: (wall) 5 m
Suspension: fully independent with variable rate coil springs and hydraulic shock-absorbers at each wheel station
Tyres: 7.50R 16 Michelin
Brakes:
  (main) vacuum, independent control for front and rear axles, 254 mm diameter discs all-round
  (parking) mechanical, cable actuated working on transmission
Electrical system: 12 V
Batteries: 1 × 12 V, 88 Ah
Alternator: 50 A

Status

Production as required. In service with the Spanish Army's parachute brigade and other airborne units (48).

Contractor

Fresia SpA
Servicios y Protectos Avanzados SA (SPA) (Spanish Army vehicles)

Fiat Campagnola 1107 AD (4 × 4) 750 kg light vehicle

Development

The Fiat Campagnola 1107 AD (4 × 4) light vehicle has origins dating back to 1951, when it was first produced as the Fiat 1101; the military version was designated AR51. A much-revised version, the Fiat 1107 entered production in 1974 as the replacement for the earlier model. The main improvements included a more powerful engine, increased load-carrying capability and the option of a hardtop.

Production of the Fiat Campagnola effectively ceased during 1985, although small numbers were produced until 1987. The vehicle was also produced in the former Yugoslavia by Zastava.

In Italian military service the FIAT Campagnola is being replaced by the Land Rover Defender 90.

Description

The Fiat Campagnola was produced in hard- and soft-top versions and there was also a longer model, with an overall length of 4.025 m and with the same wheelbase, also in hard- and soft-top models. The longer model has bench seats for three passengers down either side behind the front seat rather than two as in the basic model.

Special equipment for operation in dusty and tropical zones includes: an air cleaner with centrifugal pre-cleaner; fuel filter between feed pump and carburettor; sealed type declutch thrust bearing; engine compartment front protection; and a low octane petrol engine with 7.5 compression ratio, developing 56 kW (75 hp).

The body is of all-steel construction and has two side doors and a tailgate. Seating is provided for three, including the driver, at the front and

Fiat Campagnola of the Italian Army (Richard Stickland)   1047344

four at the rear, two each side on bench-type seats. The canvas top and side curtains can be removed and the windscreen folded forward flat against the bonnet.

Standard equipment includes a spare wheel, heater, ventilating and defrosting system, pintle towing hook at the rear, towing eyes at the front, fire extinguisher, pick and shovel and additional fuel cans.

IVECO Campagnola

The Campagnola name was revived by Fiat Group company IVECO in 2008 for a 'luxury' version of the IVECO Massif light (4 × 4), the Massif an IVECO-branded version of the Santana PS-10. Military versions of the Santana and Massif are available, however, the Campagnola branded product is strictly commercial. Full details of the Santana PS-10 and the Santana/IVECO relationship can be found elsewhere in this section.

Specifications

Campagnola 1107 AD
(soft-top model [data in square brackets relates to hardtop where different])
Cab seating: 3 + 4 [3 + 6, LWB version]
Configuration: 4 × 4
Weight:
   (laden) 2,420 [2,490] kg
   (unladen) 1,670 [1,740] kg
   (max load) 750 kg
   (towed load, road) 1,300 kg
   (towed load, off road) 900 kg
Length: 3.775 [4.025] m
Width: 1.58 m
Height: 1.901 m
Ground clearance: 275 mm
Track:
   (front) 1.365 m
   (rear) 1.404 m
Wheelbase: 2.3 m
Angle of approach/departure: 44°/45° [44°/28°]
Max speed: (road) 120 km/h
Range: 400 km
Fuel capacity: 57 litres
Max gradient: (SWB) 100%
Max side slope: 40%
Fording: 700 mm
Engine: FIAT 4-cylinder inline petrol developing 80 hp (60 kW) at 4,600 rpm (other engine options were available including diesel)
Gearbox: manual with 5 forward and 1 reverse gears
Clutch: single dry plate
Transfer box: 2-speed
Steering: hour glass and roller
Turning radius: 5.4 m
Suspension: independent McPherson type with longitudinal torsion bar, single telescopic shock-absorbers at front and twin at rear
Tyres: 7.00 × 16 C
Brakes:
   (main) drum, hydraulically operated on all 4 wheels, dual circuit
   (parking) operates on rear drums
Electrical system: 24 V
Batteries: 2 × 12 V, 45 Ah
Generator: 26 A

Status

Production complete. In service with Italy (being replaced by the Land Rover Defender 90) and Tunisia (around 2,000 delivered). Produced at one time in the former Yugoslavia.

Contractor

Fiat

IVECO 40.10 WM (4 × 4) 1,500 kg light truck series

Development

The IVECO 40.10 WM (4 × 4) series of light trucks are an ongoing military derivative of the commercial IVECO Daily model and were developed via the interim 40 PM. The series designation is made up of nominal weights and nominal engine power outputs.

The original 40.10 prototypes were produced at IVECO's Brescia factory with the intention of providing a light truck for airborne and other similar formations. Production vehicles are manufactured at Bolzano. In its volume production forms (40.12 WM/40.13 WM) the vehicle has a payload of 1,500-2,100 kg and a maximum Gross Vehicle Weight (GVW) of up to 5,000 kg, making it ideally suited for many tactical roles as a troop and cargo carrier. It is suitable for mounting various forms of weapon including machine guns, anti-tank weapons and rocket launchers and can be used as a tractor for light artillery. The cargo bodied variant of the latest 40.15 (full designation M40E15WM) has a GVW of up 5,300 kg.

The 40.12 WM light truck, with a slightly more powerful (122 hp) EURO 2 emissions compliant engine, was the production successor of the original 40.10 WM. The 40.12 WM was itself succeeded by the 40.13 WM, powered by a EURO 3 emissions compliant engine developing 125 hp. The current 40.15 is powered by a more powerful current-generation EURO 3 emissions compliant engine, this developing 146 hp. A EURO 4 engine option became available in October 2006.

In October 1991, it was announced that the Canadian Forces had selected the IVECO 40.10 WM (4 × 4) light vehicle as the winner of a competition for the Light Support Vehicle Wheeled (LSVW) project. Production was by Western Star Trucks Inc with the final total manufactured being 2,815 in various forms. Full details of this vehicle can be found elsewhere in this section.

Militarised versions of the current commercial Daily are available, however, being a commercial product with all current concessions to ergonomics, legislation and so on, these models are best seen as occupying the middle ground between vehicle types such as the Volkswagen Sprinter and the 40.10 series.

Production of the 40.10 series continues, although for a number of years it has been suggested that a conclusion to production has been pending. To counter the potential gap in its product range any loss of the 40.10

IVECO 40.10 (4 × 4) series light truck of the Portuguese Army (Victor Barreira)   1391234

Nanjing NJ2045 High Mobility Vehicle in ambulance configuration (Gordon Arthur)   1391183

IVECO 40.10 WM (4 × 4) 1,500 kg light truck of the Italian Army at Tallil Air Base, Al Nasiriya, Southern Iraq; this vehicle is fitted with add-on small arms fire protection (Patrick Allen) 1033186

IVECO 40.10 WM (4 × 4) 1,500 kg light truck of the Italian Army in Kosovo (Richard Stickland) 1124755

IVECO 40.12 WM (4 × 4) 1,500 kg light truck of the Polish Army configured as an ambulance (Patrick Allen) 1120475

IVECO 40.10 WM (4 × 4) 1,500 kg light truck of the Spanish Army, configured as an ambulance (Richard Stickland) 0126589

China's Shaanxi Baoji Special Vehicles Company manufactures the ZFB05 series of (4 × 4) light armoured vehicles. These are based on the chassis and automotives of the NJ2046
(Shaanxi Baoji Special Vehicles Manufacturing Company) 1167709

at 103 hp, while for the 40.12 WM it is rated at 122 hp. For the EURO 3 compliant 40.13 WM it is rated at 125 hp. Power output of the latest EURO 3 compliant 40.15 WM is 146 hp. The transfer box is of the two ratio chain-type and is controlled by a single lever. The axles are of the single reduction type front and rear, both with locking differentials. Hydraulic power steering is standard. Left- and right-hand steering versions are available.

The standard truck can accommodate an S-250 container shelter at the rear and various other body configurations are possible. A van body is offered as is a four stretcher ambulance body. The same body may also be used as a command and communications centre and various weapons, including a 106 mm M40 series recoilless rifle, may be carried in the cargo area. The standard truck can be used to tow a 105 mm light artillery piece or a 120 mm mortar. Optional extras include a 2,400 kg capacity front winch. Two vehicles can be carried in a C-130 Hercules and a vehicle, stripped down, can be carried with an Otobreda 105 mm Pack Howitzer in an Alenia G222 transport aircraft.

Various special role bodies can be installed including a command post/mobile office, ambulance and light firefighting vehicle.

Chinese production

The IVECO 40.10 WM is licence built in China as the Nanjing NJ2045 and Nanjing NJ2046 High Mobility Vehicle by the Nanjing IVECO Motor Co (Naveco), a joint venture between the Nanjing Automobile Corporation and IVECO founded in 1996. In appearance and released specifications these two vehicles are very similar, the primary difference being ground clearance (260 mm (NJ2046), 235 mm (NJ2045)), this presumably brought about by wheel/tyre fitment. Both NJ2045 and NJ2046 are in service with the Chinese Armed Forces in numbers, the NJ2045 being the most numerous of the two. The NJ2045 is being deployed for personnel carrier and ambulance roles, while NJ2046 has been deployed for troop/paratrooper carrier, border security, special operations, and weapon carrier roles. Also the number of NJ2045 in service is higher than that of NJ2046.

One of the most important features of the NJ2046 is its capability to be transported and airdropped by a medium size transport aircraft such as Shaanxi Y-8. The first airdrop test took place in April 2002, when an NJ2046

series might cause, IVECO announced late-2007 that it was considering the development of a lighter, less-sophisticated and more cost-conscious version of its Light Multipurpose Vehicle (LMV), this new product combining the current LMV body with a Daily-derived chassis and driveline.

Description

The IVECO 40.10 WM series has a conventional layout, with the engine at the front and the cargo area to the rear. The semi-forward cab has seating for the driver and two passengers and is normally provided with a soft canvas top; a hard-top is optional. The all-steel cargo area has folding seats along each side facing inwards for 10 personnel. The tailgate folds downwards and when down the loading height is 980 mm. Wheelbase options are 2.8 and 3.2 m.

The bonnet may be removed for engine access and maintenance with routine maintenance operations designed to be kept to a minimum. The Model 8142 diesel engine is turbocharged and is a military version of a well-established commercial model. For the 40.10 WM the engine is rated

carried on a pallet was dropped from an altitude of 800 m using multiple parachutes and landed safely. Since then the vehicle has been spotted fielded by the PLA airborne force and special operations forces units.

China's Shaanxi Baoji Special Vehicles Company manufactures the ZFB05 series of (4 × 4) light armoured vehicles. These are based on the chassis and automotives of the NJ2046. It is understood that around a dozen vehicles have been deployed overseas by China as part of United Nations (UN) forces operating in Haiti and Lebanon. In addition to being marketed by the manufacturer, the ZFB05 has also been marketed by China North Industries Corporation (NORINCO). Export users of the type are understood to include Chad, Congo and Niger.

At Defendory 2008, Shaanxi Baoji Special Vehicles Company displayed a larger (6 × 6) version of the ZFB05, this designated ZFB08. Full details of the ZFB05 and ZFB08 can be found in *Jane's Armour and Artillery*.

Malaysian production

Since 2000, the IVECO 40.10/40.12 WM has been licence built in Malaysia by Deftech, part of the DRB Hicom group of companies. Ambulance bodied vehicles have been supplied, and numbers in service are thought to be around 25.

Specifications

	40.10 WM SWB cargo	40.13 WM SWB cargo	40.15 WM SWB cargo
Cab seating:	1 + 2 (10 in rear)	1 + 2 (10 in rear)	1 + 2 (10 in rear)
Configuration:	4 × 4	4 × 4	4 × 4
Weight:			
(laden)	4,450 kg	4,700 to 5,000 kg (with uprated suspension)	4,700 to 5,300 kg (with uprated suspension)
(unladen)	2,900 kg	2,900 kg	2,900 kg
(payload, max)	1,500 kg	up to 2,100 kg	up to 2,200 kg
(towed load, off-road)	1,500 kg	1,500 kg	1,500 kg
Load area:	2.075 × 1.8 m or 3 × 2 m	2.075 × 1.8 m or 3 × 2 m	2.075 × 1.8 m or 3 × 2 m
Length:	4.9 m	4.9 m	4.9 m
Width:	2 m	2 m	2 m
Height:			
(top of tilt)	2.4 m	2.4 m	2.4 m
(top of cab)	2.38 m	2.38 m	2.38 m
(load area)	980 mm	980 mm	980 mm
Ground clearance:	260 mm	260 mm	260 mm
Track:	1.67 m	1.67 m	1.67 m
Wheelbase:	2.8	2.8	2.8
Angle of approach/departure:	40°/40°	40°/40°	40°/40°
Max speed:	>100 km/h	>100 km/h	>100 km/h
Max gradient:	>60%	>60%	>60%
Side slope:	>30%	>30%	>30%
Range:	>500 km	>500 km	>500 km
Fuel capacity:	70 litres (90 litres, optional)	70 litres (90 litres, optional)	70 litres (90 litres, optional)
Fording:	700 mm	700 mm	700 mm
Engine:	IVECO 8142 2.5-litre 4-cylinder inline turbocharged water-cooled diesel developing 103 hp at 3,800 rpm	IVECO 8142 2.5-litre 4-cylinder inline turbocharged water-cooled diesel developing 125 hp at 3,800 rpm	IVECO F1C 3-litre 4-cylinder inline turbocharged water-cooled diesel developing 146 hp at 3,500 rpm and 300 N.m torque at 2,800 rpm
Gearbox:	manual with 5 forward and 1 reverse gears	manual with 5 forward and 1 reverse gears	manual with 5 forward and 1 reverse gears
Clutch:	single dry plate	single dry plate	single dry plate
Transfer box:	2-speed	2-speed	2-speed
Steering:	hydraulic power-assisted	hydraulic power-assisted	hydraulic power-assisted
Turning radius:	6 m	6 m	6 m
Suspension:	independent longitudinal torsion bars at front, leaf spring at rear, telescopic shock-absorbers front and rear	independent longitudinal torsion bars at front, leaf spring at rear, telescopic shock-absorbers front and rear	independent longitudinal torsion bars at front, leaf spring at rear, telescopic shock-absorbers front and rear
Tyres:	255/100R 16 (8.00R 16)	255/100R 16 (9.00R 16)	255/100R 16 (9.00R 16)
Brakes:			
(main)	split circuit, discs front, drums rear	split circuit, discs front, drums rear	split circuit, discs front, drums rear
(parking)	mechanical on rear wheels	mechanical on rear wheels	mechanical on rear wheels
Electrical system:	24 V	24 V	24 V
Batteries:	2 × 12 V, 55 Ah	2 × 12 V, 55 Ah	2 × 12 V, 55 Ah
Alternator:	28 V, 55 A	28 V, 55 A	28 V, 55 A

Status

In production. In service with Algeria (40.10), Bangladesh (not confirmed), Belgium (Gendarmerie), Brunei (>50), Canada (2,815 licence produced by Western Star Trucks Inc), China (see text), Egypt (>150), Italy (>1,400), Macedonia, Malaysia (est. 25), Pakistan (2,200), Poland (50, 40.12 ambulance; further delivery during 2007), Portugal, Spain (including some during 2007), UAE, Venezuela and other undisclosed countries; by late 2006 around 16,000 40.10 series vehicles had been produced, this figure including licence production agreements.

Contractor

IVECO SpA

IVECO M65E19WM Light Multirole Vehicle (LMV)

Development

IVECO's Defence Vehicles Division (DVD) designed and developed the Light Multirole Vehicle (LMV) as a private venture in response to emerging requirements for a (4 × 4) vehicle with a high payload, high levels of tactical mobility, and a high level of protection against mines. The LMV, also designated M65E19WM and previously referred to as the Light Multipurpose Vehicle (LMV), is the first European vehicle of its type to be built to a modular concept and with a mine-protected floorpan as standard, with any required ballistic or increased mine protection being installed during the production process or later as an in-service retro-fit, and not simply fitted as an expedient after-thought. The armouring system employed for the LMV was developed in conjunction with IBD-Deisenroth GmbH of Germany and is the same armouring system used for the dual role cab as fitted to the IVECO Multipurpose Medium Vehicle (MMV). With the base LMV, the overriding design aim is that of crew survivability at the expense of mechanicals.

By late 2002 IVECO had invested some EUR40 million (USD39.1 million) in the LMV programme and in addition to an original engineering development vehicle (PT0), which underwent a 10,000 km trial, the company was funding the construction of 10 prototype vehicles (PT01 to PT10).

In addition to successful mine blast testing carried out in Germany, prototype vehicles have undergone extensive trials with the Italian and British (PT05) armies, as well as by IVECO under a wide range of environmental conditions. By late 2002 some 100,000 km of trials had been clocked up, PT03 for example, having undergone 24,000 km of Italian Army trials. Extensive bench testing of subsystems such as chassis, power pack and suspension was also undertaken.

In total 11 LMV developmental vehicles were built, PT5 (the first of the second stage prototypes) being the vehicle trialed by the British Army. The final two development vehicles were completed late 2003, these being third stage prototypes that included changes made as a result of the British Army and IVECO's own ongoing trials programmes. These changes include an 80 mm higher roofline for improved crew comfort and safety; the trade-off for which is a slight reduction in stealth capability and the loss of an internal transport capability by CH-47 Chinook helicopter - all LMVs can be transported by CH-47 as an underslung load, with the proposed special operations version retaining an internal transport capability.

Other changes include the installation of a one-piece dashboard, a revised internal rollcage (for improved crew comfort and safety), and some minor chassis, drivetrain and suspension revisions, one of the latter being the use of a lighter and smaller lower front suspension link that allows for an increased 450 mm vertical step capability.

Late in 2003 the then Alvis Vickers (now BAE Systems Land Systems) was awarded a contract by the UK Defence Procurement Agency (DPA) for the supply of 401 Multirole Light Vehicles (MLVs) - to be named Panther late 2004 - to meet the operational requirement for a Future Command and Liaison Vehicle (FCLV). MLV/Panther is the UK naming of the Italian IVECO LMV.

It was announced in May 2009 that following successful trials with a small batch of vehicles in Oman and Afghanistan, the British Army had deployed its first batch of upgraded Panther Theatre Entry Standard (TES) command and liaison vehicles to Afghanistan (Shaun C Connors) 1340314

The 401 vehicles for the Command and Liaison Vehicle (CLV) requirement will be used in two configurations: 326 will be Group 2 and 75 Group 3. The Group 2 CLV will be fitted with a 7.62 mm Self-Defence Weapon (SDW), and a Surveillance and Target-Acquisition (STA) system. The Group 3 CLV will be fitted for but not with the SDW/STA.

Within UK Armed Forces there will be some 15 roles for the Panther Command and Liaison Vehicle (CLV), some of which will involve towing a trailer laden with additional equipment. While most vehicles will be used by the British Army, some will be used by the Royal Air Force Regiment. BAE Systems Land Systems' Newcastle-upon-Tyne facility completed the last of seven pre-series CLVs in June 2005. Due to now resolved issues that surfaced during trials, the Panther was not accepted for service with the British Army until mid-2008, by which time 217 of the 401 vehicles on order had been delivered and production was running at 20 vehicles per month. Production averaged 13 vehicles per month and final deliveries were in 2009.

The baseline LMV is provided to BAE Systems by IVECO's Defence Vehicles Division based in Bolzano, northern Italy.

Under a marketing accord signed in 2003, BAE Systems can sell the MLV to a number of countries in the Middle East and Far East, plus some other undisclosed countries. Mid-2005 it was disclosed that BAE Systems had placed an order for two vehicles for development and marketing purposes.

It was announced in May 2009 that following successful trials with a small batch of vehicles in Oman and Afghanistan, the British Army had deployed its first batch of upgraded Panther Theatre Entry Standard (TES) command and liaison vehicles to Afghanistan. It is understood that an initial 60 vehicles have been upgraded, and the final vehicles were delivered in September.

Late 2003 the Italian Army placed a contract for an initial batch of 66 LMVs (know locally as the VTLM - *Veicolo Tattico Leggero Multiruolo* (light multirole tactical vehicle)) for troop trials. This was followed by a further order for 1,150 vehicles for delivery over a five-year period, with the total requirement - funding permitting - for about 7,700 vehicles in the long term. Current Italian Army LMV orders total around 1,350.

The first two series-produced LMVs were delivered late 2004 to the Italian Army's test facilities in Montelibretti, near Rome, for final technical tests. Operational and logistic tests were completed during 2005. All 66 vehicles involved in the first order had been delivered by September 2006. This order included 30 baseline unarmoured (mine-protected floorpan only) vehicles that would mainly be used for training purposes. Seven of the 30 unarmoured vehicles had subsequently been fitted with armour kits. All vehicles involved in the second and subsequent add-on orders, will be supplied armoured.

The first six LMVs were deployed to Afghanistan in October 2006.

In addition to the Italian Army order, IVECO is understood to have received an order for six LMVs from the Italian Navy. These will be tested by the San Marco amphibious regiment

A longer 3.5 m wheelbase ambulance variant of the LMV has been ordered by the Italian Army in ambulance configuration (14 + prototype) which has a potential requirement for 50-60 vehicles of this type. Norway ordered (as part of a 35 vehicle package) two 3.5 m wheelbase variants. A small number of this model variant has also been ordered by Spain.

Other Italian Army LMV developments include a Spike Anti-Tank Guided Weapon (ATGW) platform and an NBC early detection vehicle. The Spike platform is understood to be entering service with a total requirement of 30-50 units. Late in 2009 it was announced that the Italian Army had awarded Oto Melara a contract valued at EUR18.8 million to supply 64 Hitrole Light Remote Control Weapon Stations (RCWS) for installation on LMV. Final deliveries under this contract will be made in 2011. The Hitrole Light RCWS supplied to the Italian Army will be capable of being armed with a 7.62 mm machine gun, 12.7 mm heavy machine gun or a 40 mm Automatic Grenade Launcher (AGL). Selex Galileo will provide the sensor package for the Hitrole Light RCWS which will include a TV camera, thermal imaging camera and a laser rangefinder.

An Italian Army LMV undergoing final pre-delivery checks at IVECO's Bolzano production facility (Shaun C Connors) 1169453

The LMV was one of a number of vehicles considered to meet Belgium's Light Protected Vehicle (LPV) requirement, the LPV being the intended replacement for the current - and increasingly difficult and expensive to maintain - Bombardier-built Volkswagen Iltis light vehicle, 2,673 of which were delivered between 1984-88. Tenders in the much-delayed LPV programme were finally submitted on October 13th 2004, with a decision anticipated during December 2004 and subsequent deliveries running through until 2008. At this time, the Belgian Army required 620 vehicles (originally 830), of which 180 (originally 300) were to be capable of being fitted with an appliqué armour kit. There were expected to be two contract options each for 90 vehicles and 30 armour kits. However, on December 24th 2004 it was announced that the procurement process had been halted. Bids were re-submitted mid-May 2005 and in July 2005 it was announced that IVECO had been awarded the contract to supply Belgium's Armed Forces with 440 LMVs and 120 appliqué protection kits. The awarded contract includes options for two batches of 90 vehicles and 30 protection kits. It is understood that under current Belgian Army plans this option will not now be exercised.

The first vehicles were delivered to the Belgian Army in September 2007, and from early 2008 these have been deployed overseas to Afghanistan, Chad, Kosovo and Southern Lebanon.

In May 2005, it was announced that following an agreement signed with IVECO's Defence Vehicles Division, Rheinmetall LandSysteme (RLS) of Germany would offer the LMV to meet a potential German Army requirement for an Armoured Command and Operations Vehicle (*Geschutzte Fuhrungs und Funktionsfahrzeug*, or GFF) programme. As of late 2010 no orders had been placed by Germany for the Caracal.

In March 2006 the Norwegian Army announced the selection of the LMV and placed an order for 25 LMVs, with an option for a further 47. The contract was worth approximately EUR8 million and the last of the contracted LMVs was delivered in April 2007. By late-2007 Norway was understood to have deployed around 20 vehicles on operations. Norway ordered a further 35 LMVs late-2007. These were not the previously mentioned contract option, and this was exercised in November 2008 (47 + 1). A further 63-vehicle option is now in place, and when this is exercised Norway will have a total fleet of 170 LMVs. All Norwegian LMVs are delivered armoured.

Late 2006 Croatia ordered 10 LMVs and these were delivered by the end of February 2007. These were supplied armoured and in order to meet urgent operational needs were promptly deployed on operations.

Spain placed an initial EURO14.4 million order for 40 LMVs late-2007. Deliveries commenced in December 2007 and were completed by March 2008. The Spanish order is understood to include a small number of LWB ambulance variants. A further 80 LMVs have since been ordered and delivered, with the total requirement standing at around 400 vehicles.

A longer 3.5 m wheelbase ambulance variant of the LMV has been ordered by the Italian Army in ambulance configuration (Shaun C Connors) 1296135

Front three-quarter view of an Italian Army LMV (Shaun C Connors) 1340302

Rear three-quarter view of an Italian Army LMV (Shaun C Connors) 1340301

In September 2008 the Spanish Army announced it would deploy a first batch of 17 LMVs to Afghanistan before the end of September. Originally the first of the batch of 40 vehicles ordered were due to start operating with Spanish troops on missions overseas by the second quarter of 2008. Delays were attributed by sources to Spanish-specific upgrades which included the provision of extra protection for the gunner. The Spanish LMV order was placed as a result of the Spanish MoD's acceleration and revision of a four-year old project to replace an ageing approx 750-vehicle BMR (*Blindado Medio de Rueda*) (6 × 6) light armoured vehicle fleet. The BMR being a <30-year old design not optimised for current operational scenarios. With a provisional budget of EURO320 million a total of 575 replacement vehicles (including around 400 LMV class vehicles) will be procured between late-2007 and 2013. Initially misrepresented by a variety of sources as an MRAP-type vehicle buy, it is now understood that after a six-month program to find a suitable vehicle that included an assessment of operational requirements by the deployed Spanish forces, the LMV was selected in preference to the KMW Dingo 2, MOWAG Eagle IV and URO VAMTAC.

In early 2008 the Czech MoD purchased four IVECO LMVs based on an urgent operational requirement for deployed operations without tender. Later in 2008 a further 15 LMVs were purchased, again without tender, their procurement based on fact that they four vehicles were already in service. Somewhere along this time frame an additional three LMVs to bring the total to 22; the purchase of the additional three LMVs was never announced. In late 2009 the Czech MoD announced it would procure a further 90 LMVs in a joint deal with Slovakia, which would procure 40 LMVs. When Czech deliveries are complete a total of 112 LMVs will be in service. Slovakia ordered an initial ten LMVs in July 2009.

It was announced in January 2009 that Austria had ordered 150 LMVs for delivery between 2009 and 2013, with the first 50 delivered to Austria by 2010. The basic vehicle parts will be produced in Italy, with final assembly taking place at Austrian EMPL Fahrzeugwerk.

It was announced in June 2009 that Slovakia had ordered 10 LMVs for delivery by the end of the year.

Description
The LMV utilises a conventional C-section chassis but with longitudinal reinforcements and tubular cross-members to give the required torsional rigidity. At present two wheelbase lengths are available, the standard 3.23 m and the extended 3.53 m, these giving overall lengths of 4.794 and 5.361 m respectively. The modular design of the LMV allows the base soft-skin vehicle to be readily configured to perform a wide variety of roles including command/reconnaissance or ATGW/heavy machine gun platform for the four- or five-seat cabin versions. Larger weapons systems such as air-defence missiles, shelter, box-type or even pick-up style bodies can be mounted behind a smaller two-seat cab.

The maximum gross weight of the design has grown throughout the production run and was originally set at 7,000-7,100 kg (model dependant) and with payload depending on model, wheelbase and any armour package fitted. Examples would be 2,500 kg for the 3.2 m wheelbase stealth version; 2,700 kg for the 3.5 m wheelbase short cab version; and depending on armour package, 1,200 to 2,000 kg for the 3.2 m wheelbase armoured crew carrier version.

To improve LMV's payload, IVECO initially developed two kits, these designated as IPK1 and IPK2. These kits, which can be incorporated at build stage, are based on vehicle net weight reduction and not GVW increasing measures. Using the basic 7,000 kg GVW vehicle as a reference point, IPK1 reduces net vehicle weight by 225 kg. The main components of IPK1 are a new lighter weight aluminium internal roll frame and smaller armoured glass windows. IPK1 was developed primarily to meet the evolving needs of existing customers, and to allow the installation of IED jammers or a remote weapon station on vehicles currently working at their specified GVW. IPK1 is understood to have been offered to Italy and Norway. Using the same 7,000 kg GVW reference specification, the more sophisticated IPK2 reduces net vehicle weight by 600 kg. To achieve these changes, some new lighter armour materials are included and lighter

aircraft-type suspended crew seats are installed. Development of IPK2 was complete by mid-2008. More recently, IVECO announced IPK3 which is quoted as allowing an additional 800 kg of payload at the baseline 7,000 kg GVW.

A GVW increase from the 7,100 kg maximum to 7,250 kg was anticipated during 2008, but to meet emerging requirements that call for greater payload and protection in the relatively small package of an LMV-sized vehicle, IVECO announced a GVW increase to 7,500 kg in June 2009. Austrian vehicles will be delivered with a near-7,500 kg GVW.

In addition to a 7,500 kg GVW option, from mid-2010 IVECO has offered a 3.53 m (LWB) LMV with an extended length crew compartment. This version also features an integral hard top in place of the roll cage, new seats and changed design of the transparent armour.

A special forces variant was also demonstrated during 2010. Further details of this variant can be found elsewhere in this section.

Motive power for all in production LMV models continues to be provided by an IVECO EURO 3 emissions compliant three-litre four-cylinder turbocharged and intercooled diesel engine developing 185 hp (138 kW). A power increase to accommodate the GVW increase is possible. A EURO 5 engine is available if required. A six-speed automatic gearbox is standard while a five-speed manual is an option. Four-wheel drive is full-time, and the two-speed transfer box is fitted with a lockable differential.

Independent suspension of the double A-arm type with coil springs and co-axial shock absorbers is fitted to all wheel stations. The single reduction differentials are connected to the vehicle chassis, each wheel having further epicyclic hub reduction gearing. Each axle has a driver-controlled cross-axle differential lock and is fitted with inboard air-over-hydraulic disc brakes, with an Anti-lock Braking System (ABS) that can be disengaged (for off-road operations). Standard tyres are 325/85R 16 Michelin XML.

In terms of performance, the LMV has a maximum speed of >130 km/h, a minimum speed of 4 km/h, a range of >500 km, and can climb >60% gradients and traverse >30% side slopes. It can surmount a 450 mm vertical step, operate throughout a –32°C to +49°C temperature range (without additional preparation), and ford to 850 mm without preparation, and to 1.5 m with minimal preparation.

As previously mentioned, the LMV was designed from the outset to offer a high level of mine protection as standard, and given that the majority of mine blasts are likely to be initiated by wheel pressure, the wheel stations are located well away from the crew cabin. As a result, should wheel pressure detonate a mine the explosion will vent upwards, damaging mechanical assemblies but leaving the crew cabin undamaged. A number of design features enhance this characteristic. The bonnet opens forward and is hinged to the chassis and not the crew cabin, while the rear compartment (on four/five-seat versions) is sacrificial, having been designed to detach and allow any explosion to vent.

In the event of the vehicle passing over and detonating an underbelly mine, a number of measures have been in-built to ensure crew survivability. Ground clearance has been maximised (401 to 473 mm dependent on version and floorpan armouring) and the floorpan has been given a gentle V-configuration to encourage any blast to vent outwards. The floorpan is made up of a 'sandwich' (two or three layers, dependent on protection levels required) that is designed to deform when impacted by the shockwave and absorb any residual blast energy that does not vent laterally. Large or heavy components and assemblies situated under the crew cabin could be forced through the floor by a mine blast and in order to avoid this, all such components have been relocated. The transfer box for example, is now situated in the rear compartment. To further enhance crew survivability the fuel tank is installed at the rear of the vehicle and the fuel filler cap is positioned as far away from the crew cabin as possible. The doors have been designed to a particularly fine tolerance to ensure they withstand the shockwave created by an explosion, and inside the air-conditioned crew cabin, a number of additional measures have been taken to reduce residual and secondary blast effects on the crew.

Nothing can be stowed under the crashworthy seats. These seats are not fixed directly to the vehicle floor in order to avoid direct transmission of the shockwave through the floor to the occupant. Lateral headrests are, and a suspension system can also be, fitted to the seats to further reduce any accelerative force on any occupant. Five-point quick-release safety belts are fitted as standard.

Specific protection levels are classified, however, it is understood that full Level 3 ballistic and Level 3a mine blast certification of LMV has been achieved, while classified IED blast protection enhancements have been developed and tested for the vehicle. To further enhance vehicle protection, IBD Deisenroth Engineering's Active Defense System (ADS) has been fitted to LMV for trials. It is understood that IVECO has an Italian Army order for 10 LMVs fitted with ADS. Details of the AMAP system remain highly classified.

As a candidate for a number of reconnaissance roles, the LMV has also been designed with stealth in mind. To reduce acoustic and thermal signatures, the exhaust manifolds and silencers are fitted within the chassis rails, and the engine turbocharger is located under the engine where maximum thermal shielding is provided. To further reduce the overall acoustic signature, noise emission levels meet EU standards and not the less restrictive military STANAGs. To help reduce detection by radar, particular attention has been paid to the design of all external body sections; the windows and door windows, for example, have been angled to provide the best level of radar reflectivity possible, while retaining all-round visibility.

Special Forces LMV

IVECO Defence Vehicles have built, using company funding, two prototypes of their LMV optimised for the Special Forces (SF) role. The SF version of the LMV is identical to the standard LMV below the middle of the vehicle but the upper part has been removed for enhanced all round situational awareness.

The bullet/splinter proof drivers windscreen has been retained and roll over protection is fitted as standard. On top of this is a ring mount on which various weapons can be mounted such as 7.62 mm or 12.7 mm machine gun or a 40 mm automatic grenade launcher.

The curb weight of the SF version is 4,200 kg, this allowing for a payload of over 3,000 kg. The unprotected area at the rear allows the vehicle to be adopted for specific mission related equipment or to carry additional fuel or supplies.

Seating arrangements are flexible and if required a seat facing the rear can also be provided with an associated weapon station to cover the rear arc.

Doors and the armoured glass in the windscreen provide a tunable level of ballistic protection and can be upgraded with add on armour packs.

The base SF LMV is fitted for but not with the anti-mine plate but this can be fitted if required.

While the first example of the SF LMV has the fixed anti-role bar, a collapsible roll bar has been developed which would allow the vehicle to fit inside of the CH-47 Chinook helicopter.

Specifications

	Standard cab - SWB	Standard cab - LWB	Short cab - SWB	Short cab - LWB	Long cab - SWB	Long cab- LWB
Configuration:	4 × 4	4 × 4	4 × 4	4 × 4	4 × 4	4 × 4
Weight:						
(GVW)	7,100 kg	7,500 kg	7,100 kg	7,500 kg	7,100 kg	7,500 kg
(kerb)	6,200 kg	6,300 kg	4,800 kg	4,900 kg	6,300 kg	6,600 kg
(max load with protection)	900 kg	1,200 kg	2,300 kg	2,600 kg	800 kg	900 kg
(max towed load)	3,500 kg	3,500 kg	3,500 kg	3,500 kg	3,500 kg	3,500 kg
Length:	4.794 m	4.794 m	5.31 m	5.31 m	5.31 m	5.31 m
Width:	2.2 m	2.2 m	2.2 m	2.2 m	2.2 m	2.2 m
Height:	2.05 m	2.05 m	2.05 m	2.05 m	2.121 m	2.121 m
Ground clearance: (under belly)	473 mm	473 mm	473 mm	473 mm	401 mm	401 mm
Track:	1.71 m	1.71 m	1.71 m	1.71 m	1.71 m	1.71 m
Wheelbase:	3.23 m	3.23 m	3.23 m	3.23 m	3.53 m	3.53 m
Angle of approach/departure:	54°/44°	54°/44°	54°/40°	54°/40°	47°/39°	47°/39°
Max road speed:	>110 km/h	>110 km/h	>110 km/h	>110 km/h	>110 km/h	>110 km/h
Max gradient:	>60%	>60%	>60%	>60%	>60%	>60%
Side slope:	>30%	>30%	>30%	>30%	>30%	>30%
Fording:						
(unprepared)	850 mm	850 mm	850 mm	850 mm	850 mm	850 mm
(prepared)	up to 1.5 m	up to 1.5 m	up to 1.5 m	up to 1.5 m	up to 1.5 m	up to 1.5 m

	Standard cab - SWB	Standard cab - LWB	Short cab - SWB	Short cab - LWB	Long cab - SWB	Long cab- LWB
Engine:	IVECO EURO 3 F1C 3-litre 4-cylinder inline variable geometry turbocharged and intercooled, water-cooled 4-stroke common rail diesel developing 138 kW (185 hp) at 3,700 rpm and 456 N.m torque at 1,800 rpm. EURO 5 engine available.					
Transmission:	ZF 6HP 26 automatic with 6 forward and 1 reverse gears; optional manual with 5 forward and 1 reverse gears					
Transfer box:	2-speed, full-time four-wheel drive					
Steering:	LS 2 B power-assisted					
Turning radius:	7.15 m	7.15 m	7.035 m	7.035 m	7.035 m	7.035 m
Suspension:	independent with coil springs and shock-absorbers at each wheel station					
Tyres:	325/85R 16 Michelin XML (optional 335/80R 20)					
Brakes:	air over hydraulic, inboard discs front and rear, disengageable ABS for off-road operations					
Electrical system:	24 V	24 V	24 V	24 V	24 V	24 V
Batteries:	2 × 12 V, 110 Ah	2 × 12 V, 110 Ah	2 × 12 V, 110 Ah	2 × 12 V, 110 Ah	2 × 12 V, 110 Ah	2 × 12 V, 110 Ah
Alternator:	24 V, 90 A	24 V, 90 A	24 V, 90 A	24 V, 90 A	24 V, 90 A	24 V, 90 A

Status

In production. Ordered by and/or in service with Belgium (440 + 180 total option), Croatia (10, 2007), Czech Republic (112 on order), Italy (Army and Navy approximately 1,350 (see text)), Norway (armoured, 25 + 35; 47 option (see text)), Slovakia (10), Spain (see text) and the UK (armoured, 401) to meet the Future Command and Liaison Vehicle (FCLV) requirement. Under evaluation by Germany (see text).

Contractor

IVECO SpA

Japan

Type 73 Small Truck

Development

In August 1998, after 45 years of continuous production, and after over 30 different models based on the Jeep CJ3B body style had been produced (during which time around 200,000 vehicles were produced, many of them for government use), Mitsubishi ceased production of Jeep-based vehicles.

Model J24A, designated the Type 73 Small Truck by the Japanese Ground Self-Defence Force (Army), was the final model supplied in quantity to the JGSDF, and considerable numbers remain in service with all branches of the Japanese military. However, the type is gradually being phased out of service, its replacement being a vehicle based on the Mitsubishi Pajero - also designated Type 73 Small Truck. No official details of the Pajero-based Type 73 Small Truck have been released, although some limited details are available, which as expected mirror those of the commercial base product, this also being known as the Montero or Shogun in certain markets.

Dimensions of the Type 73 Small Truck are regularly quoted as being: 4.14 m (L), 1.765 m (W), 1.97 m (H). Curb weight is quoted as 1,940 kg.

Mitsubishi Pajero-based Type 73 Small Truck of the JGSDF (Mitsuhiro Kadota) 1047621

Mitsubishi Pajero-based Type 73 Small Truck of the JGSDF
(Mitsuhiro Kadota)   1047622

Status

In production and service. There have been no known exports of this vehicle.

Contractor

Mitsubishi Motors Corporation

Mitsubishi (4 × 4) light vehicles 1953 to 1998

Description

In 1953, Mitsubishi obtained a licence from the then American Willys company to manufacture the Jeep in Japan for both civilian and military use. In August 1998, after 45 years of continuous production, and after over 30 different models based on the Jeep CJ3B body style had been produced (during which time around 200,000 vehicles were produced, many of them for government use), Mitsubishi ceased production of Jeep-based vehicles.

Variants included short, medium or long wheelbases, petrol or diesel engines (diesel only from the mid-1980s), left- or right-hand drive, and a variety of open or enclosed body options.

The original CJ3B-J3 model was joined by the CJ3B-J4 version in 1956. The CJ3B-J4C model was added to the range in 1958, and both J4 and J4C models were produced into the late 1960s, when they were replaced (for military applications) by the J54A. The J54A was, for many years, the standard ¼-tonne vehicle of the Japanese Self-Defence Force. It had essentially the same body as its predecessors but was fitted with a 2.7-litre 4DR5 diesel engine. This was coupled to a manual gearbox with three forward and one reverse gears, and a two-speed transfer box. Basic details of the J54A are: 3.33 m (L), 1.595 m (W), 1.85 m (H), 2.03 m wheelbase, 92 km/h maximum road speed and 6.00 × 16 tyres. Variants in service included an ambulance, anti-tank armed with a 106 mm Type 60 recoilless rifle and anti-tank armed with two KAM-3D (Type 64) wire-guided anti-tank missiles.

The J54A was replaced by the J24A, designated the Type 73 Small Truck by the Japanese Ground Self-Defence Force (Army). Considerable

Mitsubishi (4 × 4) CJ3B-based Jeep used by the Japanese Ground Self-Defence Force and fitted with optional soft-top weather protection
(Mitsuhiro Kadota)   1340313

Mitsubishi (4 × 4) CJ3B-based Jeep used by the Japanese Ground Self-Defence Force and fitted with a 106 mm recoilless rifle
(Mitsuhiro Kadota)   1047618

Mitsubishi (4 × 4) CJ3B-based Jeep used by the Japanese Ground Self-Defence Force towing a small single-axle trailer (Mitsuhiro Kadota) 1047619

numbers of J24A Mitsubishi Jeeps remain in service with all branches of the Japanese military, however the type is gradually being phased out of service, its replacement being a vehicle based on the Mitsubishi Pajero - also designated Type 73 Small Truck. Available data for the Pajero-based Type 73 Small Truck can be found elsewhere in this section.

Specifications

J24A
Seating: 1 + 1 + 4
Configuration: 4 × 4
Weight:
   (laden) 1,970 kg
   (unladen) 1,470 kg
   (max load) 480 kg
Length: 3.75 m
Width: 1.665 m
Height: 1.95 m
Ground clearance: 210 mm
Track: 1.296 m
Wheelbase: 2.225 m
Fuel capacity: 48 litres
Max speed: 100 km/h
Engine: Type 4DR5 2.7-litre 4-cylinder in-line water-cooled 4-stroke diesel developing 80 hp (60 kW) at 3,500 rpm
Gearbox: manual with 4 forward and 1 reverse gears
Clutch: single dry plate
Transfer box: 2-speed
Steering: recirculating ball
Turning radius: 5.8 m
Suspension: semi-elliptic leaf springs and hydraulic shock-absorbers
Tyres: 7.00 × 15
Brakes:
   (main) hydraulic
   (parking) mechanical
Electrical system: 24 V

Status

Production completed 1998, replacement in production and service (see text). In service with all branches of the Japanese Armed Forces. Supplied to Burma (Myanmar), Indonesia and Thailand.

Contractor

Mitsubishi Motors Corporation

Toyota Land Cruiser (4 × 4) series light vehicle

Description

What eventually became known as the Toyota Land Cruiser first appeared in 1950 as the Toyota Jeep Model BJ. This vehicle was based on the chassis of a one-tonne SB light truck and had a two-piece windscreen, a vertically ribbed front and an appearance not dissimilar to that of a conventional US-made Jeep. Production began in 1951 and in 1953 the vehicle was revised and officially named Land Cruiser, and more than 3.7 million Land Cruiser models have subsequently been sold. The Toyota Land Cruiser was originally intended for the civilian market, but throughout its production run the type has been adopted by numerous armed forces and for a wide variety of roles.

Land Cruiser models are identified by an alphanumeric code consisting of the engine series designation letter(s) and the frame designation number, the two separated by the letter J. For example, a two-door short wheelbase model with a 2F petrol engine would be model FJ40, the same vehicle with a B petrol engine, being the model BJ40.

The second-generation Land Cruiser, the 20 Series, was introduced in 1955. The 20 Series was replaced in 1960 by the 40 Series of which production continued until 1984 in Japan, although as the Bandeirante production continued in Brazil until 2001. The 40 Series is a two-door vehicle with a removable hard- or soft-top. The 45 Series is the long wheelbase version of the 40 Series. This was available with a pick-up body fitted with removable hard- or soft-top covers, or in hard- or soft-top configuration with seating for up to 11. Early 40 Series models had a three-speed gearbox, later examples a five-speed gearbox. Several engine types were fitted including the 3.8-litre six-cylinder F and the 4.2-litre 2F. Later production BJ40s were fitted with 3-litre B and 3.4-litre 3B four-cylinder engines. HJ models were fitted with the H and 2H six-cylinder diesel engines.

The 55, 60 and 62 Series have subsequently been produced, but the 70 Series followed the 40 Series into mass production and is the current Land Cruiser production model favoured by military and paramilitary users, although the Hilux pick-up/crew cab design is useful for non-tactical roles and, as regularly witnessed on news broadcasts, is a favoured ride for militants/rebel forces. US special forces uses the Tacoma (a US-specific Hilux) in Afghanistan.

The 70/71 series used a Short WheelBase (SWB) design, the 73/74 series a Medium WheelBase (MWB) and the 75/77 series a Long WheelBase (LWB). The 75/77 Series were replaced by the 78/79 series in 1999, but the overall design was retained. Most Land Cruiser 75s were produced in either a cab chassis pick up model or in a two-door troop carrier. These two body styles remain today as the exclusive models of the 78 and 79 Series Land Cruisers.

Toyota has continued to develop the Land Cruiser and 80, 90, 100 and 200 Series luxury models best described as suited to rear echelon, security or VIP transport duties have been produced. This example is in service with the Finnish Army (Carl Schulze) 1391200

Brazilian Army Military Police double-cab pick-up Toyota Bandeirante (4 × 4) in East Timor (Ron Fry) 0121283

Portuguese Army Toyota Land Cruiser (4 × 4) light vehicle in standard soft-top SWB configuration (Victor Barreira) 1391246

Arctic Trucks specialises in the conversion of (4 × 4) light vehicles including the Toyota Land Cruiser (Shaun C Connors) 1340311

Two-door station wagon variant of a Toyota Land Cruiser in service with the French Army (Shaun C Connors) 1340312

Pick-up variant of a Toyota Land Cruiser (4 × 4) light vehicle of the Swedish Army in Kosovo (Richard Stickland) 0121838

Land Cruiser 70 Series

Model	Regular wheelbase	Long wheelbase	Super long wheelbase
Configuration:	4 × 4	4 × 4	4 × 4
Weight:			
(laden)	2,295 kg	2,445 kg	3,035 kg
(unladen)	1,680 kg	1,740 kg	1,865 kg
(max load)	615 kg	705 kg	1,170 kg
Length:	3.915 m	4.275 m	4.955 m
Width:	1.665 m	1.665 m	1.665 m
Height:	1.955 m	1.96 m	2.03 m
Ground clearance:	210 mm	210 mm	225 mm
Track:			
(front)	1.415 m	1.415 m	1.415 m
(rear)	1.4 m	1.4 m	1.41 m
Wheelbase:	2.285 m	2.43 m	2.95 m
Fuel capacity:	85 litres	85 litres	85 litres
Engine:		6-cylinder in-line OHV petrol developing 135 hp at 3,600 rpm	
		6-cylinder in-line OHV diesel developing 103 hp at 3,500 rpm	
		4-cylinder in-line OHV petrol developing 90 hp at 3,500 rpm	
		4-cylinder in-line OHV diesel developing 80 hp at 3,600 rpm	
Gearbox:		all have manual, 4 forward and 1 reverse gears	
Clutch:	single dry plate	single dry plate	single dry plate
Transfer box:	2-speed	2-speed	2-speed
Steering:	recirculating ball	recirculating ball	recirculating ball
Turning radius:	5.3 m	5.5 m	6.5 m
Suspension: (front and rear)		semi-elliptic leaf springs with hydraulic double acting shock-absorbers at each wheel station	
Tyres:	7.00-15-6 PR	7.00-15-6 PR	7.50-16-8 PR
Brakes:			
(main)	hydraulic, all wheels	hydraulic, all wheels	hydraulic, all wheels
(parking)	mechanical	mechanical	mechanical
Electrical system:	12 V	12 V	12 V

70 Series Land Cruisers were produced in Venezuela (known locally as the Techo Duro) until 2008, and remain in production in Japan, but for export sales only and primarily to Africa, the Middle East, parts of the Indian sub-continent and a few other 'rugged' destinations as well as Australia and New Zealand. The current updated 70 Series began production in January 2007.

Pick-up models have been assembled from kits in Malaysia.

Toyota has continued to develop the Land Cruiser beyond the 70 Series for modern civilian markets and 80, 90, 100 and 200 Series luxury models have been produced, these carrying civilian brand names such as Land Cruiser Amazon. In general such models are best described as suited to rear echelon, security or VIP transport duties and companies such as Armor Holdings of the US produce add-on discreet armour protection packages designed to provide multihit protection against military assault rifles and grenade blasts for such models. However, the 80 Series Land Cruiser introduced in 1990 to address growing requirements for a 'luxury' off-roader is used by a number of armed forces. The last 80 Series (for most markets) was sold in 1997-98, but its (by modern standards) relatively basic chassis and suspension set-up ensured that - for certain markets - it continued in production in Colombia and Venezuela. The final 80 Series was built in Venezuela in 2008.

The 80 Series was replaced in mainstream production by the 100 Series in 1998, and while the 100 Series continued to evolve into a passenger car, there were still users who wished to drive it off-road. To meet these needs, such as in Australia and other rugged environments, Toyota created a Land Cruiser 105 series with a solid front axle and coil spring suspension. While officially the 105 series, it is often referred to as simply the base

model 100 Series or the 100 Series GX. What Toyota did was essentially place the 100 Series body and interior onto an older 80 Series frame and suspension. A number of Middle Eastern nations use 80/105 Series Land Cruisers, and some have been seen with a 12.7 mm Heavy Machine Gun (HMG) ring-mount in the roof. The 80 Series ceased production in 2007. The Toyota Land Cruiser was redesigned for 2008, the revised model known as the 200 Series. The 200 Series shares the platform and overall design of the Lexus LX.

Toyota Bandeirante

The first Toyota Bandeirantes were produced in Brazil in 1959 from Toyota Land Cruise 40 Series kits shipped out from Japan. By 1962 production was utilising parts manufactured in Brazil, and by 1968 no components were being imported from Japan. From 1962 until 1994 Mercedes-Benz diesel engines were used to power the Bandeirante. From 1994 until 2001 a Toyota 14B diesel engine was fitted.

Toyota do Brasil Ltda ceased production of the Bandeirante in November 2001 after over 40 years of continuous production during which time over 100,000 vehicles were produced. The Toyota Bandeirante was never officially adopted by Brazilian Armed Forces, however the Marines did (and still do) use small numbers of the Bandeirante/Land Cruiser-based Bernardini Xingu BT25 and BT50 light vehicles.

Multidrive Land Cruiser upgrades

MultiDrive Technology (MDT) is a 100 per cent Australian owned company located in Geelong, Victoria, Australia and is part of the Kinetic Group of Companies. Multidrive Technology offers a selection of Toyota Land Cruiser 78/79 series enhancements including uprated 4 × 4 and three-axle 6 × 4 and 6 × 6 models. The vehicles are fully compliant with the Australian Design Rules (ADR's) and have Australian Compliance Plate Approval.

Royal Army of Oman Toyota Land Cruiser (4 × 4) (Richard Stickland)
0533614

UAE Armed Forces Toyota Land Cruiser (4 × 4) (Richard Stickland)　1124763

MDT's 4 × 4 upgrades offer increased payload by increasing GVWs to 3,500 kg for the MDT 3500 or 3,700 kg for the MDT 3700, the latter model having a 200 mm chassis extension.

MDT's current range of three-axle vehicles have a GVW of 5,750 kg and are available in two wheelbase options. A Torque Manager power divider provides traction to the mid and rear wheels with no control input at all from the cabin. Suspension is a simple 100 per cent load sharing equaliser beam allowing wheel travel of 220 mm, and according to the company feels no different to a conventional 4 × 4 vehicle, and so requires no special driver training.

MDT Toyota Land Cruiser conversions have been supplied to a number of government, mining, military and firefighting customers. A 6 × 6 military conversion is understood to have undergone trials with the Ministry of Defence in Oman.

Specifications
See table on facing page

Status
In production (see text). In service with numerous armed forces worldwide, particularly those in the Middle East, South Africa and South America.

Contractor
Toyota Motor Corporation

Toyota Hilux (4 × 4) light vehicle

Development
The Toyota Hilux (4 × 4) light vehicle is one of a number of commercially available light (4 × 4) pick-up and/or crew-cab vehicles of an essentially similar design, and that are produced by a variety of manufacturers.

Similar vehicles produced by other Japanese motor manufacturers include the Mitsubishi Triton/L200 and the Nissan Frontier/Navara. Examples of similar vehicles produced by other motor manufacturers include the Chrysler-produced Dodge Ram and smaller Dodge Dakota, Ford F-Series, the General Motors-produced Chevrolet Silverado/GMC Sierra and Chevrolet S-10/GMC Sonoma, and the Mazda B-Series/Ford Ranger.

The Toyota Hilux first entered production in 1968 as a revised version of the second-generation Toyota Stout. A second-generation Hilux entered production in 1972, and with the introduction of the third-generation in 1979, four-wheel drive became available for the first time. Production of the seventh-generation Hilux commenced in 2005, at which time production in Japan ceased. The Hilux is currently produced in Argentina, Pakistan, South Africa and Thailand.

For a number of years, North American versions of the Hilux were given alternative names including the Toyota Tacoma. From 2005 the Toyota Tacoma, which remains visually similar to the Hilux, has been based on a current-generation Toyota Land Cruiser chassis.

The Toyota Hilux is not produced by Toyota as a military vehicle, however, considerable quantities of Hilux are in service with the military, paramilitary, law enforcement and armed irregular forces of many countries.

Military use of the Toyota Hilux by major NATO-grade or similarly capable armed forces is usually limited to crew-cab variants (as opposed to true pick-up variants) and in third line or rear echelon roles, although in certain instances vehicles are known to have been used by special forces and frontline/combat forces. The bulk of Toyota Hilux vehicles in frontline/combat use are generally employed by the less well equipped armies as well as irregular armed forces and assorted militias, primarily in Africa, but also in Asia and parts of the Americas.

Toyota Hilux (4 × 4) light vehicle of the Finnish Army photographed in Norway during Exercise Cold Response 2010 (Carl Schulze)   1391201

Toyota Hilux (4 × 4) light vehicle of Czech special forces in Afghanistan (Grzegorz Holdanowicz)   1391225

Toyota Hilux (4 × 4) light vehicle of Polish special forces (Grzegorz Holdanowicz)   1391226

Description
The Toyota Hilux is entirely conventional in design and is based on a box-section ladder-frame chassis. Early versions featured a two/three-seat single-row cab with an open pick-up body at the rear. Throughout the continuing production run, extended cabs, crew cabs and varying length pick-up bodies (with hard-top options) have been available.

Driveline options for the Hilux range have been extensive, with current market-dependant options, including both petrol and diesel engines, these ranging in size from a two-litre petrol unit available in Asia and South Africa only, to a four-litre petrol unit available in Australia, South Africa and the US. A version with a three-litre diesel unit is available in Asia, Australia, Europe, South Africa and South America. Current gearbox options include a five-speed manual, or a four- or five-speed automatic.

Suspension is currently independent torsion bar front, leaf springs rear, with disc brakes front and drums rear. Both two- and four-wheel drive versions of the Hilux remain available.

Technicals and the Toyota War
The Toyota Hilux (4 × 4) light vehicle and other similar vehicle types including the Toyota Land Cruiser 70 Series pick-up, the Mitsubishi Triton/L200, the Nissan Frontier/Navara and the Mazda B-Series/Ford Ranger are also occasionally referred to collectively as Technicals, an unofficial designation of undefined origins.

The term Technical usually refers to an improvised fighting vehicle, typically a civilian vehicle of the Hilux type that has been modified to provide an offensive capability. These vehicles usually mount in their rear tray or body a machine gun or guns, a light anti-aircraft gun, a recoilless rifle, or other support-type weapon.

Vehicles converted in this way are used legitimately by some developing world armed forces, however, the term Technical is predominantly applied to vehicles used by irregular forces such as African 'warlords' and other assorted militias.

The Toyota War is the name frequently given to the closing phase of the 1978-1987 Chadian-Libyan conflict. The name is derived from the large quantities of Toyota Hilux and 70 Series pick-up trucks used as Technicals to provide Chadian troops with mobility in Northern Chad and on the Libyan-Chadian border throughout 1987 as the conflict reached its conclusion.

Status
In production. In service with the numerous armed forces, and also large numbers of paramilitary and irregular forces.

Contractor
Toyota Motor Corporation

Mitsubishi L200 (4 × 4) light vehicle

Development
The Mitsubishi L200 (4 × 4) light vehicle is one of a number of commercially available light (4 × 4) pick-up and/or crew-cab vehicles of an essentially similar design, that are produced by a variety of manufacturers.

Similar vehicles produced by other Japanese motor manufacturers include the Nissan Frontier/Navara and the Toyota Hilux. Examples of similar vehicles produced by other motor manufacturers include the Chrysler-produced Dodge Ram and smaller Dodge Dakota, Ford F-Series, the General Motors-produced Chevrolet Silverado/GMC Sierra and Chevrolet S-10/GMC Sonoma, and the Mazda B-Series/Ford Ranger.

The Mitsubishi L200 first entered production in Japan during 1978 as the Forte, and from 1986 until recently was known as the Strada. The current name applied is Triton, however, for most export applications the vehicle is known as L200. Other export branding has been applied, names used including Rodeo, Storm Warrior, Colt Bakkie, while for the US market Dodge Ram 50, Plymouth Arrow Truck and Mighty Max have all been applied.

The fourth-generation L200 entered production in Thailand during 2005, and the L200 is currently assembled in Brazil, Japan, Philippines, South Africa and Thailand. The L200 is not produced by Mitsubishi as a military vehicle, however considerable quantities of L200 are in service with the military, paramilitary, law enforcement and armed irregular forces of many countries.

Military use of the Mitsubishi L200 by major NATO-grade or similarly capable armed forces is usually limited to crew-cab variants (as opposed to true pick-up variants) and in third line or rear echelon roles, although in certain instances vehicles are known to have been used by special forces and frontline/combat forces. The bulk of vehicles in frontline/combat use are generally employed by the less well equipped armies, as well as irregular armed forces and assorted militias, primarily in Africa, but also in Asia and parts of the Americas, with many such vehicles being fitted with light weapons installed ad-hoc on pedestal mounts in the rear body.

Description
The Mitsubishi L200 is entirely conventional in design and is based on a box-section ladder-frame chassis. Early versions featured a two/three-seat single-row cab with an open pick-up body at the rear. Throughout the continuing production run extended cabs, crew cabs and varying length pick-up bodies (with hard-top options) have been available.

Driveline options for the L200 range have been extensive, with current market-dependant options including both petrol and diesel engines. Axle and suspension set-up is currently independent front, beam axle and leaf springs rear. Both two- and four-wheel drive versions of the L200 remain available.

Mitsubishi L200 crew-cab of the Portuguese Army (Victor Barreira) 1391233

Mitsubishi L200 crew-cab of the Royal Brunei Land Forces
(Gordon Arthur)   1391232

Status
In production. In service with the numerous armed forces, and also large numbers of paramilitary and irregular forces.

Contractor
Mitsubishi Motors Corporation

Korea, South

Kia Motors KM410 series of light vehicles

Development
The Kia Motors KM410 series of light vehicles was the standard light vehicle of the South Korean Armed Forces until the 1997 introduction of the KM420 series, now generally known as the KM42 series.

KM410 (4 × 4) light vehicle (Gordon Arthur)   1340353

KM410 (4 × 4) light vehicle (Gordon Arthur)   1296192

KM410 (4 × 4) light vehicle (Gordon Arthur)   1296190

Model	KM410	KM410L	KM411	KM412	KM413	KM414	KM415
Purpose:	utility	long wheelbase utility	ambulance	TOW launcher carrier	TOW missile carrier	106 mm RR carrier	searchlight carrier
Cab seating:	1 + 3	1 + 5	1 + 1	1 + 3	1 + 1	1 + 3	1 + 1
Configuration:	4 × 4	4 × 4	4 × 4	4 × 4	4 × 4	4 × 4	4 × 4
Weight: (kerb)	1,180 kg	1,286 kg	1,380 kg	1,293 kg	1,290 kg	1,320 kg	1,290 kg
Weight: (GVW)	1,720 kg	1,786 kg	1,860 kg	1,880 kg	1,660 kg	1,969 kg	1,660 kg
Max load:	540 kg	620 kg	480 kg	587 kg	370 kg	649 kg	370 kg
Length:	3.35 m	3.925 m	3.841 m	3.405 m	3.276 m	3.301 m	3.276 m
Width:	1.475 m	1.675 m	1.68 m	1.85 m	1.85 m	1.734 m	1.85 m
Height:	1.705 m	1.946 m	1.946 m	1.705 m	1.73 m	1.705 m	1.73 m
Ground clearance:	210 mm	210 mm	233 mm	210 mm	210 mm	210 mm	210 mm
Track:	1.23 m	1.23 m	1.23 m	1.23 m	1.23 m	1.23 m	1.23 m
Wheelbase:	2.032 m	2.41 m	2.032 m	2.032 m	2.032 m	2.032 m	2.032 m
Angle of approach:	45°	45°	51°	45°	45°	45°	45°
Angle of departure:	30°	23°	19°	26°	30°	30°	19°
Max speed:	112 km/h	112 km/h	102 km/h	96 km/h	96 km/h	96 km/h	102 km/h
Range:	340 km	340 km	340 km	340 km	340 km	340 km	340 km
Fuel capacity:	45.5 litres	45.5 litres	45.5 litres	45.5 litres	45.5 litres	45.5 litres	45.5 litres
Gradient:	60%	60%	60%	60%	60%	60%	60%
Fording:	510 mm	510 mm	510 mm	510 mm	510 mm	510 mm	510 mm
Engine:	KG2000 1.985-litre 4-cylinder in-line OHV water-cooled petrol developing 70 hp at 4,000 rpm						
Gearbox:	manual with 4 forward and 1 reverse gears with synchromesh on all gears						
Clutch:	single dry plate						
Transfer box:	2 speed						
Steering:	ball and nut						
Turning radius:	5.06 m	6 m	5.06 m	5.06 m	5.06 m	5.06 m	5.06 m
Tyres:	6.00 × 16						
Brakes:	dual circuit, drums all-round						
Suspension: (front)	semi-elliptic leaf springs with hydraulic double-acting shock-absorbers						
(rear)	progressive semi-elliptic leaf springs with hydraulic double-acting shock-absorbers						
Electrical system:	24 V	24 V	24 V	24 V	24 V	24 V	24 V
Batteries:	2 × 12 V, 45 Ah	2 × 12 V, 45 Ah	2 × 12 V, 45 Ah	2 × 12 V, 45 Ah	2 × 12 V, 45 Ah	2 × 12 V, 45 Ah	2 × 12 V, 45 Ah
Alternator:	25 A	25 A	25 A	25 A	25 A	25 A	180 A

The KM410 series was developed in co-operation with the Agency of Defence Development (ADD) in Korea and, although similar in appearance to the Jeep CJ series (M38), there are many locally introduced changes to the original design.

Kia Motors was founded in 1944 as Kyongseong Precision, changing its name to Kia Industry Co Ltd in 1952. This changed in 1990 to Kia Motors Corporation, and in 1998 Hyundai Motor took control of the company.

Kia Motors is the sole provider of military vehicles to Korea's Armed Forces and has produced around 123,000 military vehicles in total. The total figure includes around 20,000 exported to over 20 countries over 30 years. Kia Motors currently supplies the armed forces of Korea with around 2,000 vehicles per year.

Description

The layout of the KM410 base vehicle is conventional, with the engine at the front and the driver and passenger/load-carrying area to the rear. The same engine is used throughout the series, a KG2000 1.985-litre four-cylinder OHV petrol engine developing 70 hp at 4,000 rpm.

The vehicles in the KM410 series are as follows:

- KM410 utility vehicle
- KM410L long-wheelbase version of KM410
- KM411 ambulance
- KM412 TOW anti-tank guided missile launcher carrier
- KM413 TOW anti-tank missile carrier
- KM414 106 mm M40 series recoilless rifle carrier
- KM415 23-inch/584 mm xenon searchlight carrier

All vehicles are based on a ladder frame chassis with 1.2 mm thick steel bodies. All models feature a front grille guard. A 24 V electrical system, with provision to carry radio equipment, is standard on all models.

Specifications

See table above

Status

Production complete. In service with the armed forces of South Korea but being replaced by the KM42 series. As of January 2009 it was understood the replacement programme was reaching its conclusion.

Contractor

Kia Motors Corporation

Kia Motors KM42 series ¼ ton (4 × 4) light utility vehicles

Development

The Kia Motors KM42 series ¼ ton utility vehicle was first announced in 1997 (as the KM420 series) and may be regarded as an updated version of the earlier KM410 series, full details of which can be found elsewhere in this section. The KM42 series is now the standard light utility vehicle of the South Korean Armed Forces and it is understood that by November 2004 the vast majority of earlier KM410 series and assorted other Nissan and Toyota designs had been replaced by the KM42 series in South Korea's inventory. By late 2007 six variants were disclosed as available, and figures made available in late 2006 stated that in excess of 23,000 vehicles had been produced, including small but officially undisclosed numbers for export sale.

Kia Motors KM42 series ¼ ton (4 × 4) KM420 light utility vehicle (Gordon Arthur)
1340352

Kia Motors KM42 series ¼ ton (4 × 4) KM420 light utility vehicle
(Gordon Arthur)   1296193

The only available export information states that 140 KM42 series vehicles were supplied to Indonesia in 2003, possibly as part of a larger vehicle package. A small number have been supplied to an undisclosed South American country, and a trials vehicle has been sent to Venezuela for trials mounting a 106 mm recoilless rifle.

Kia Motors was founded in 1944 as Kyomgseong Precision, changing its name to Kia Industry Co Ltd in 1952. This changed in 1990 to Kia Motors Corporation, and in 1998 Hyundai Motor took control of the company.

Kia Motors is the sole provider of military vehicles to Korea's Armed Forces and has produced around 123,000 military vehicles in total. The total figure includes around 20,000 exported to over 20 countries over 30 years. Kia Motors currently supplies the armed forces of Korea with around 2,000 vehicles per year.

Description

One of the main changes between the KM42 series and the earlier KM410 series involves a new two-litre petrol or diesel engine, the petrol unit providing almost double the previous available power (now 139 hp). The optional diesel unit is turbocharged and intercooled and develops 91 hp at 4,000 rpm. The engine is coupled to a five-speed manual transmission and a catalytic converter is provided to clean the exhaust. Power steering is fitted.

A ladder frame chassis similar to that on the KM410 series is retained and a roll bar is added for rollover protection. The chassis meets US Federal Motors Safety Standards (FMVSS) No 208.

The front wheels are provided with independent coil spring suspension. Transfers between two- and four-wheel drive can be accomplished at speeds of up to 60 km/h.

The KM420 can carry the driver and up to five passengers. Four of the passengers enter the rear via a steel door and are seated on individual fold-up padded seats, each with two-point seatbelts. The normal overall cover is a canvas soft-top. A grille guard is provided in front of the bonnet. On all but the KM424 106 mm recoilless rifle carrier, the spare wheel and tyre are mounted on the rear door.

Model	KM420 (utility)	KM424 (106 mm recoilless rifle carrier)[1]	KM426 (40 mm automatic grenade launcher carrier)[2]
Seating:	1 + 1 + 4	1 + 1 + 2	1 + 1 + 1
Configuration:	4 × 4 (selectable)	4 × 4 (selectable)	4 × 4 (selectable)
Weight:			
(laden, on-road)	2,110 kg	2,270 kg	2,140 kg
(laden, off-road)	1,930 kg	2,270 kg	2,140 kg
(kerb)	1,570 kg	1,590 kg	1,660 kg
(payload, on-road)	540 kg	680 kg	480 kg
(payload, off-road)	360 kg	680 kg	480 kg
Length:	4 m	3.9 m	4 m
Width:	1.745 m	1.93 m (inc. spare wheel)	1.745 m
Height:	1.915 m (soft top)	1.74 m (windscreen)	1.74 m (windscreen)
Ground clearance:	220 mm	220 mm	220 mm
Track: (front and rear)	1.47 m	1.47 m	1.47 m
Wheelbase:	2.36 m	2.36 m	2.36 m
Angle of approach/departure:	41°/32°	41°/32°	41°/32°
Max speed:	130 km/h	120 km/h	130 km/h
Cruising range:	480 km	480 km	480 km
Fuel capacity:	53 litres	53 litres	53 litres
Max gradient:	60%	60%	60%
Max sideslope:	40%	40%	40%
Fording:	510 mm	510 mm	510 mm
Engine:	FE DOHC 1.998-litre 4-cylinder in-line water-cooled petrol developing 139 hp at 6,000 rpm and 181 N.m torque at 4,000 rpm (standard), or 2-litre turbocharged and intercooled diesel developing 91 hp at 4,000 rpm (optional)	FE DOHC 1.998-litre 4-cylinder in-line water-cooled petrol developing 139 hp at 6,000 rpm and 181 N.m torque at 4,000 rpm (standard), or 2-litre turbocharged and intercooled diesel developing 91 hp at 4,000 rpm (optional)	FE DOHC 1.998-litre 4-cylinder in-line water-cooled petrol developing 139 hp at 6,000 rpm and 181 N.m torque at 4,000 rpm (standard), or 2-litre turbocharged and intercooled diesel developing 91 hp at 4,000 rpm (optional)
Gearbox:	synchromesh manual, with 5 forward and 1 reverse gears	synchromesh manual, with 5 forward and 1 reverse gears	synchromesh manual, with 5 forward and 1 reverse gears
Transfer box:	2-speed	2-speed	2-speed
Clutch:	single dry disc, hydraulic	single dry disc, hydraulic	single dry disc, hydraulic
Steering:	power-assisted	power-assisted	power-assisted
Turning radius:	5.2 m	5.2 m	5.2 m
Suspension:	double wishbone and coil springs, front; 4 bar link and coil springs, rear	double wishbone and coil springs, front; 4 bar link and coil springs, rear	double wishbone and coil springs, front; 4 bar link and coil springs, rear
Tyres:	235/75R 15 tubeless	235/75R 15 tubeless	235/75R 15 tubeless
Brakes:	discs, front; drums, rear	discs, front; drums, rear	discs, front; drums, rear
Electrical system:	24 V	24 V	24 V
Batteries:	2 × 12 V, 48 Ah	2 × 12 V, 48 Ah	2 × 12 V, 48 Ah
Alternator:	24 V, 45 A	24 V, 45 A	24 V, 45 A

[1] The spare wheel and tyre are mounted just ahead of and partially blocking the front passenger door. If the canvas door option is selected, the spare wheel can relocate to inside the rear body. The gunner and assistant gunner's seats are situated over the rear axle and fold up when not in use to provide more space for the gun crew.
[2] The 40 mm automatic grenade launcher can be mounted on a ring mount providing 360° rotation. Stowage space is provided in the rear body for three ammunition boxes, each containing 48 grenades. The operators seat has a two-point seatbelt and folds up when not in use.

Standard equipment on all KM42 series models includes: spare wheel and tyre; spare fuel car; shovel; axe; fire extinguisher; jack; warning triangle; toolkit, and manuals. Optional equipment includes electromagnetic shielding for electronic systems and a deep fording kit.

As of 2006 the following variants of the KM42 series base utility vehicle (the KM420) were stated to be in mass production:

- KM421 NBC reconnaissance vehicle (improvised)
- KM422 TOW anti-tank guided missile launcher carrier
- KM423 TOW anti-tank guided missile carrier
- KM424 106 mm M40 series recoilless rifle carrier
- KM426 K-4 40 mm automatic grenade launcher carrier

Specific details of the KM420 ¼ ton utility vehicle, KM424 106 mm recoilless rifle carrier and KM426 40 mm automatic grenade launcher carrier are included in the accompanying specifications table.

Specifications
See table on facing page

Status
In production. In service with the armed forces of Indonesia (140, 2003 - possibly more), South Korea (approximately 23,000), an undisclosed South American country and probably others.

Contractor
Kia Motors Corporation

Poland

Honker (4 × 4) light vehicle

Development
The first two prototypes of this vehicle were shown in 1980 and designated PW1 and PW2, respectively. They were manufactured at the Automotive Industrial Institute (PIMOT), Warsaw. The vehicle was introduced to the public in 1984 under the name Tarpan Honker. The primary purpose of the design was to replace UAZ vehicles in service with Polish Armed and Police forces.

Series production began at FSR Poznan in 1988. The first models had a 3.027 m wheelbase and the choice of three petrol engines. These were a 1.5-litre unit developing 75 hp, a 1.6-litre unit developing 82 hp, and an 86 hp unit shared with the FSO Polonez car. Diesel variants followed, these being fitted with naturally aspirated units developing 75 hp or turbocharged units developing 100 hp.

Numerous body styles were available, and while commercial variants were offered the majority of sales were for military or police applications. A prototype vehicle with a shorter 2.21 m wheelbase did not enter production.

In January 1996 production of the Honker was halted. In March 1996 Daewoo Motor Polska Lublin obtained the licence to produce the Honker and production resumed in July 1997 of a modernised design. Modernisation included the installation of an IVECO diesel engine, although aesthetically little changed. In 1994 the Honker 2324 was shown under the name Daewoo. In 1999 the new Honker II was shown. This featured a number of improvements including a revised suspension set-up.

Following Daewoo's well-publicised financial problems production of the current model, then designated Honker 2000, was undertaken by Polish engine-builder Andoria Motor in Lublin.

From January, 2004 a new Russian-American company, International Truck Alliance (Intrall) which was registered in the UK took over manufacturing rights for the Honker (and Lublin van). The '2000' was dropped from the designation during 2005. In the Spring of 2007 production of the Honker was again halted.

Polish Army Honker fitted with psyops equipment
(Grzegorz Holdanowicz) 1391360

Honker Skorpion-3 in Iraq (Grzegorz Holdanowicz) 1165197

In 2008 it was suggested that the Ukrainian company DP Naftogazbud Polior was to begin building the Honker again, but this did not happen. Also during 2008 Zaklad Produkcji Specjalnej (owned by Syndyk (trustee) of Intrall) was established to manufacture some 200 vehicles, but this did not happen either.

In 2009 the rights to the Honker were sold to DZT Tymińscy of Poland. It was disclosed in September 2010 that following an open tender, DZT Tymińscy had been awarded a contract to deliver 60 Honker 2000 Type 2N.

Figures available for total Honker deliveries often conflict, however the most recent available data is as follows for sales over the last decade, these including small numbers of commercial models: 1997:155; 1998: 232; 1999: 350; 2000: 200; 2001: 35; 2002: 140.

For 2003, it was envisaged that 215 Honker vehicles, including 31 in the Skorpion patrol variant for Iraqi operation, would be procured. In 2003 278 Honker off-roaders were completed, this figure including commercial models.

In September 2004 Poland's Ministry of National Defence (MND) awarded the Intrall Polska company a USD5.4 million contract to deliver 188 Honkers in eight different variants by the end of 2004. Total Honker production for 2004 was approximately 480 units, with - according to the company - around 90 per cent of these being delivered to the military.

Production during 2005 was 177 vehicles. The first export sale of the Honker was secured during 2005. An initial batch of 50 vehicles in two-stretcher ambulance configuration left Poland in May for Iraq and use by Iraq's Armed Forces. Iraq received a total of 100 ambulances, the second batch of 50 vehicles being dispatched around June 2005.

During 2006 approximately 245 vehicles were produced. Poland donated 10 Honker-based Skorpion 3 light armoured patrol vehicles to the Iraqi Army's 8th Division in June 2006.

During 2007 35 vehicles were produced.

For delivery during 2008 a further 99 vehicles were ordered at around USD40,000 each, plus an additional 22 vehicles for the ZWD-3 mobile command and communication stations. Delivery of these vehicles has not been confirmed.

The most recent Honker order was placed in September 2010 with current producer DZT Tymińscy.

An initial batch of 50 Honker light vehicles in two-stretcher ambulance configuration left Poland in May 2005 for Iraq and use by Iraq's Armed Forces (Grzegorz Holdanowicz) 1039710

Long wheelbase soft-top version of the Honker (4 × 4) light vehicle (early model) (Shaun C Connors) 0116262

Long wheelbase hard-top version of the Honker (4 × 4) light vehicle of the Polish Army (early model) (Shaun C Connors) 1120474

Description
The layout of all Honker light vehicles is conventional, with the engine forward, the driver and seating for one passenger next to him/her and a load area to the rear with a number of optional soft- or hard-tops and possible seating arrangements. The normal personnel carrier version has a soft-top and bench seats for up to eight personnel in the rear. Other rear area arrangements include seating for six or two personnel or an open 'pick-up' light utility cargo load platform. A chassis-cab variant can be fitted with assorted rear body types such as shelter/containers or an ambulance body.

Early Honkers were powered by a selection of petrol or diesel engines (including an IVECO unit) but from 1997 the Honker has been powered by Andoria diesel engines, the most recent fit being the 4CTi90-1BE turbocharged unit.

The Honker has undergone a number of face-lifts, some minor, in recent years. The most recent Honker features a number of design improvements to improve ride quality, performance and reduce engine emissions compared to earlier models. At present only a 2.827 m wheelbase option is offered.

Variants
During late 2003 the first prototype of the Honker Skorpion was shown and following extensive trials in Poland, in January 2004 commenced trials with the Polish contingent serving as part of the stabilisation force in Iraq.

The Lublin-based Andoria-Mot company developed the vehicle with the active involvement of the army's 4th Regional Technical Workshops (4 OWT) in Zurawica, following a request from the Polish Land Forces. The Skorpion is based on the Honker (4 × 4) utility variant and is powered by an Andoria 4C90 diesel engine developing 136 hp.

By December 2004 Polish forces in Iraq had received 40 of 50 Skorpion-3 armour kits for fitting to Honker all-terrain vehicles. The package can be installed in six hours in field workshops. The final model has steel armour plates on the sides of the vehicle while the bottom is protected by Lim-3 laminate. However, there are no bulletproof windows and there is no additional protection for the engine. The armour package increases the weight of the vehicle from 2,130 kg up to 2,575 kg and the number of people that can be carried is reduced from nine to five.

The vehicle is armed with the 7.62 mm machine gun that can be fitted with a PCS-5 night vision sight. The gunner is protected by a steel gunshield and a wire cutter installed above the vehicle's cab to cut steel cables stretched across the road.

Specifications
Cab seating: 2 + 2 + up to 8
Configuration: 4 × 4
Weights:
(GVW) 3,200-3,500 kg
(max load, front axle) 1,500 kg
(max load, rear axle) 2,200 kg
Length: 4.63 m
Width: 1.87 m
Height: (overall) 2.16 m
Ground clearance: (16-inch wheels) 220 mm
Wheelbase: 2.827 m
Track: (front/rear, 16-inch wheels) 1.635/1.630 m
Angle of approach/departure: (16-inch wheels) 40°/40°
Max speed: 110 km/h
Fuel capacity: 110 litres
Max gradient: 68%
Side slope: 42%
Fording: 800 mm
Engine: Andoria 4CTi90-1BE 2.417-litre 4-cylinder EURO 3 emissions compliant turbocharged water-cooled 4-stroke diesel developing 102 hp and 230 N.m torque at 2,000 rpm
Transmission: TS5-21 manual with 5 forward and 1 reverse gears
Transfer box: Borg Warner 2-speed
Steering: ZF power-assisted
Turning radius: 6.775 m (left), 6.75 m, right
Suspension: beam-type axles (lockable differential option on rear) with leaf springs and telescopic shock-absorbers, front and rear; anti-roll bar on rear axle
Tyres: 840-15 or 235/75R 15

Status
In production. Most recent order awarded to current producer DZT Tymińscy in September 2010 for 60 vehicles (see text for full details).

Contractor
DZT Tymińscy

Portugal

UMM (4 × 4) light vehicle

Development
The União Metalo Mecânica Limitada (UMM) light vehicle can trace its origins back to the mid-1960s and the Cournil, a multipurpose vehicle designed for use both on and off the road. Over a period of 12 years, in excess of 850 examples of the Cournil multipurpose (4 × 4) vehicle were produced and sold, primarily to French farmers. In 1977, Bernard Cournil sold the licence for his design to Gervarm, a small tractor manufacturer and subsidiary of the Gevelot organisation. Around the same time, a licence was also sold to Portuguese manufacturer UMM of Lisbon.

The Cournil was a simple, robust and functional vehicle, attributes that ensured military appeal and in 1977 the inevitable militarised variant was shown for the first time at the Satory Military Exhibition (now Eurosatory). The military Cournil was branded the SAMO, although very briefly appears to have been known as the Fennec.

Gervarm's association with the Cournil ended in March 1980 and from December 1980 the design was in the hands of Societe International de Matériel Industrial (SIMI). By November 1981, SIMI was owned by the Berlin Group. The vehicle produced by SIMI had changed little in appearance from the original Cournil product, although there had been the inevitable mechanical upgrades/changes. During 1982, SIMI produced some 500 vehicles, with a projection for 1,200 during 1983, this figure including 230 military vehicles ordered by Zimbabwe. Claiming the

UMM (4 × 4) light vehicle of the Portuguese Army (Victor Barreira) 1391026

delivered vehicles were not of the specification ordered Zimbabwe paid only 50 per cent of its bill, this ultimately leading to the near-bankrupt SIMI being acquired by French businessman Francois Servanin in August 1984.

Francois Servanin renamed the company Autoland, although a dispute over the use of that name ensued, and the name Auverland was subsequently adopted. Auverland's production was initially based on two models, the Series A (later known as the A2) and the SC II. The Series A was a modified/updated Cournil, while the SC II was essentially the Cournil design.

Production of the A2/SAMO in France was completed in 1990, by which time it was reported to have been sold (military applications) to Burkina Faso, Burundi, Cameroon, Central African Republic, Chad, Congo, Côte d'Ivoire (Ivory Coast), Madagascar, Zaire (now The Democratic Republic of the Congo), Zimbabwe and some other undisclosed countries.

Production of the Cournil design, albeit substantially modified, continued in Portugal by UMM and by the early 1980s UMM had embarked on an aggressive campaign to sell the design all over Europe. Between 1986-1988 there was a longer-wheelbase model, the Alter I, and then the improved Alter II. A further revitalised range was announced in 1991. UMM continued to offer the vehicle until 1993 for private customers, and until 1996 for military and utility service customers. The company still trades and until recently continued to offer spares support for the product, this now out-sourced to Europeças.

The A2/SAMO evolved into the Auverland A3, full details of which can be found elsewhere in this section.

Description

The UMM (4 × 4) light vehicle is built around a chassis formed from a 120 × 60 mm steel channel section 4 mm thick, which is reinforced by three cross-members. The body is formed from 2 mm steel plate welded to the chassis. The body layout is conventional, with the engine forward and the driver's position central. The rear of the body is an open platform on to which various types of body may be built. These range from a hard-top to various forms of soft-top. The driver's cab portion may be fitted with a canvas roof but may also accommodate a hard-top. The rear area may be configured for personnel seating in various layouts or left open for cargo carrying or for mounting various forms of light weapon or missiles.

The standard military version is powered by a 2.5-litre naturally aspirated Peugeot diesel engine that develops 76 hp, but a 110 hp turbocharged version of the same engine was available. Conventional beam-type axles are sprung by the combination of leaf springs and telescopic shock-absorbers. The rear axle is fitted as standard with a Trac-Loc limited slip differential.

Variants of the UMM were numerous and included an ambulance with a box body, mortar carrier, 106 mm M40 series recoilless rifle carrier and 7.62 and 12.7 mm machine gun carriers. Special missile-carrying variants included a version with a hardtop cab and a three-missile launcher for SS-11 anti-tank missiles, a MILAN or TOW anti-tank guided weapon launcher version and a special version with racks in the rear for ATLAS or Mistral surface-to-air missiles. Also produced were police versions and one variant carrying a hydraulic inspection platform.

A longer wheelbase (3.078 m) version of the UMM was also produced. This version has a maximum load capacity of 1,700 kg or up to 10 personnel in the rear.

The chassis cab model can carry standard NATO shelters.

The UMM can be para-dropped.

Specifications

UMM
(data in square brackets refer to long wheelbase version)
Cab seating: 2 + 6 [2 + 10 or 3 + 10]
Configuration: 4 × 4
Weight:
  (laden) 2,720 [3,470] kg
  (unladen) 1,610 [1,770] kg
  (max front axle load) 1,180 kg

UMM (4 × 4) light vehicle of the Portuguese Army (Victor Barreira) 1391027

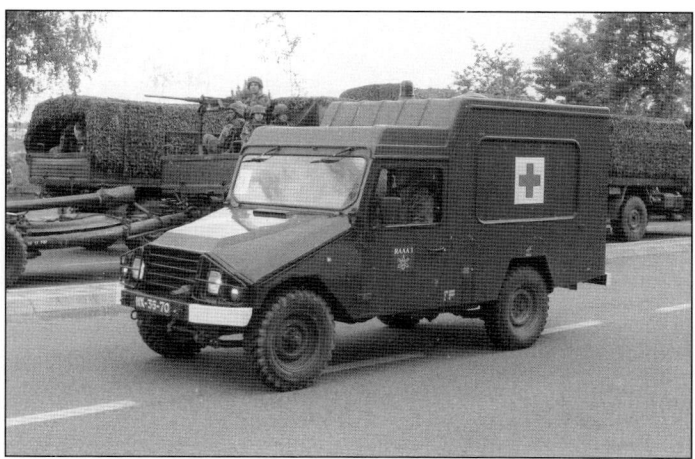

UMM (4 × 4) light vehicle of the Portuguese Army (Victor Barreira) 1391244

UMM (4 × 4) long wheelbase (3.078 m) light vehicle configured as a 12-seater troop transporter (UMM) 0079424

  (max rear axle load) 1,750 kg
  (max load, road) 1,110 [1,700] kg
  (towed load, trailer with brakes) 3,500 kg
  (towed load, trailer without brakes) 1,000 kg
Length: 4.139 [4.857] m
Width: 1.57 m
Height: 1.955 m
Ground clearance: 260 mm
Track: 1.342 m
Wheelbase: 2.56 [3.078] m
Angle of approach/departure: 48°/44° [48°/35°]
Max speed: 120 km/h (turbocharged version 140 km/h)
Fuel capacity: 60 litres (120 litres optional)
Max gradient: 45°
Fording: 600 mm
Engine: Peugeot 2.498-litre 4-cylinder in-line water-cooled diesel developing 76 hp at 4,500 rpm (naturally aspirated) or 110 hp at 4,150 rpm (turbocharged)
Gearbox: manual with 5 forward and 1 reverse gears
Clutch: single dry plate
Transfer box: 2-speed
Steering: worm and roller, power-assisted
Turning radius: 5.9 [6.5] m
Suspension: semi-elliptic leaf springs with double acting telescopic shock-absorbers, front and rear
Tyres: 7.00 × 16
Brakes: ventilated discs front and drums rear, servo-assisted, dual circuit
Electrical system: 12 or 24 V (FFR)
Battery: 1 × 12 V, 63 Ah
Alternator: 750 W [1,000 W]

Status

Production complete. Supplied to the armed forces of Angola, Cape Verde, Congo, Portugal and probably others.

Contractor

União Metalo Mecânica Limitada SA (UMM)

Romania

ARO 24 (4 × 4) 750 kg light vehicle

Development

Launched in 1971, the ARO 24 (4 × 4) 750 kg light vehicle was the successor to the earlier 1963-launched ARO M 461, this essentially being a Russian UAZ-69 fitted with a more powerful 70 hp engine. The ARO 24 was continually developed over four decades of production and as of 2001 an

ARO 243 (4 × 4) light utility vehicle with the rear soft-top removed (ARO)
0524728

estimated 70 per cent of vehicles of this class in Romanian military service were ARO 24 models. Longer wheelbase models, termed 'utility' models in company literature, have the designation ARO 32 (with reference to a 3.2 m wheelbase) but share common front body panels and driveline components.

The ARO 24 was joined in production in 1980 by the more commercially orientated ARO 10. In 1999 the ARO Super was launched, this being the combination of the platform and driveline of the ARO 24 with the bodywork of the ARO 10. Brief details of the ARO 10 can be found elsewhere in this entry.

For military applications the one-time likely successor to the ARO 24 series of vehicles was the ARO Dragon. The ARO Dragon was evaluated by Romanian Armed Forces. Full details of the ARO Dragon can be found elsewhere in this section.

ARO vehicles have reportedly been sold worldwide in Argentina, Brazil, China, Columbia, France, Germany, Italy, Peru, Russia and Spain and Venezuela, although details of military users outside of Romania have never been made available.

For a short period of time, Daihatsu-powered AROs were produced in Spain and Portugal under the brands Hisparo and Portaro, respectively.

In September 2003 Cross Lander USA acquired ARO's manufacturing facility located in Câmpulung, Romania, approximately 60 miles north of Bucharest. The facility was acquired from the Romanian government as part of its privatisation programme. The 8.5 million ft^2 complex employed up to 2,200 people, could produce up to 38,000 vehicles per year plus spare parts, and was constructed to produce only (4 × 4) vehicles. Since 1957 the plant has produced around 360,000 (4 × 4) vehicles, although during 2003 and 2004, respectively, only 661 and 303 vehicles were manufactured.

With a reported investment of USD32 million, Cross Lander set up a plant in Manaus, Amazonas in which production of the CL-244 and CL-330 pick-up reportedly started (a military variant of the CL-244 was also available) at the end of September 2002. In addition to local and other export market sales, the intention was to produce the Cross Lander 244X (a substantially revised model fitted with a Ford V-6 engine, an Eaton transmission and a number of other proprietary components) in Brazil for the US market. After some effort this project also failed and the Brazilian plant currently assembles Mahindra light vehicles.

ARO went into bankruptcy in June 2006. The company Amrom Automotive 2006 is understood to have purchased the company following bankruptcy, with plans to resume production of the ARO line of vehicles under the ARO name at the Câmpulung factory.

It was disclosed in 2009 that Auto Max Czech (AMC) was looking to restart production of ARO vehicles.

Description

The ARO 24 is entirely conventional in design, with the engine mounted longitudinally between the box-section chassis at the front, crew seating and any body following behind. As with all light utility vehicles the variety of bodies available for the ARO 24 was extensive and included soft- and hard-top pick-up and station wagon variants. As of 2001 three main models were offered: The ARO 243 with a two-door single cab and soft- or hard-top rear body; the ARO 244 four-door station wagon, and the ARO 246 four-door station wagon with a raised roof section over the rear seating/stowage area. These models all shared a common 2.35 m wheelbase but did vary in overall length. Maximum gross weight for all models was 2,515 kg, allowable payload varying from model-to-model, but being around 750 kg. Front axle maximum load was given as 955 kg, rear axle maximum load was given as 1,560 kg.

Model	ARO 243 2.35 m wheelbase two-door single cab	ARO 320 3.2 m wheelbase chassis-cab
Cab seating:	1 + up to 7	1 + 1
Configuration:	4 × 4	4 × 4
Weight:		
(max GVW)	2,515 kg	3,100 kg
(max load)	approx 750 kg	approx 750 kg
(towed load - with brakes)	2,300 kg	n/avail
(towed load - without brakes)	750 kg	n/avail
Length:	4.098 m	5.055 m
Width:	1.775 m	1.775 m
Height:	1.983 m	1.9 m
Ground clearance:	200 mm	190 mm
Track: (front/rear)	1.475/1,475 m	1.475/1.525 m
Wheelbase:	2.35 m	3.2 m
Angle of approach/departure:	43°/28°	41°/21°
Max speed:	120 km/h	110 km/h
Max gradient:	78%	56%
Engine:	ARO L 25 2.495-litre 4-cylinder in-line water-cooled carburettor-fed petrol engine requiring leaded fuel and developing 85 hp (63 kW) at 4,400 rpm and 160 N.m torque at 3,000 rpm. Options include the ARO TDX 28-02 (87 hp/65 kW), Andoria 4CT90-1ME (86 hp/64 kW) or Toyota 2L-T (89 hp/66 kW) turbocharged diesel engine, or the Toyota 2RZ-FE (140 hp/104 kW) naturally aspirated diesel engine	ARO L 25 2.495-litre 4-cylinder in-line water-cooled carburettor-fed petrol engine requiring leaded fuel and developing 85 hp (63 kW) at 4,400 rpm and 160 N.m torque at 3,000 rpm. Options include the ARO TDX 28-02 (87 hp/65 kW), Andoria 4CT90-1ME (86 hp/64 kW) or Toyota 2L-T (89 hp/66 kW) turbocharged diesel engine, or the Toyota 2RZ-FE (140 hp/104 kW) naturally aspirated diesel engine
Gearbox:	ARO manual with synchromesh and 4 forward and 1 reverse gears. Optional 5 forward and 1 reverse gears. Optional Toyota W56 with synchromesh and 5 forward and 1 reverse gears	ARO manual with synchromesh and 4 forward and 1 reverse gears. Optional 5 forward and 1 reverse gears. Optional Toyota W56 with synchromesh and 5 forward and 1 reverse gears
Transfer box:	ARO 2-speed constant mesh. Optional (in conjunction with Toyota W56 gearbox) Toyota VF 1A 2-speed	ARO 2-speed constant mesh. Optional (in conjunction with Toyota W56 gearbox) Toyota VF 1A 2-speed
Clutch:	single dry plate	single dry plate
Steering:	power-assisted	power-assisted
Suspension:	independent coil springs and telescopic shock-absorbers, front, leaf springs and telescopic shock-absorbers, rear	independent coil springs and telescopic shock-absorbers, front, leaf springs and telescopic shock-absorbers, rear
Tyres:	options including 6.50 × 16 and 235/75R 15	options including 6.50 × 16 and 235/75R 15
Brakes:	dual circuit, hydraulic, drums all-round	dual circuit, hydraulic, drums all-round
Electrical system:	12 V	12 V
Batteries:	66 Ah, 1 or 2 of	66 Ah, 1 or 2 of

ARO 323T (4 × 4) light utility vehicle fitted with a special-purpose rear body (ARO) 0524729

ARO 32 utility models have a 3.2 m wheelbase, the ARO 335 model having a longer 3.35 m wheelbase. Models available included the ARO 320 chassis-cab to which a pick-up or variety of box-type bodies could be fitted, the ARO 323 for special purpose bodies, and the ARO 324 four-door double-cab with a shorter load area. Maximum gross weight for all ARO 32 models was given as 3,100 kg, allowable payload varying from model-to-model, but being around 750 kg. Maximum axle weights varied according to model, the ARO 320 chassis-cab having maximum axle loadings of 1,300 kg, front, and 2,200 kg, rear. The ARO 335 having a maximum gross weight of 3,500 kg, and maximum axle loadings of 1,300 kg, front, 2,400 kg, rear.

An extensive choice of engines with capacities ranging from two to three litres was available throughout the ARO range, these having evolved over the years along with the base design. Some of the later options included a number of EURO 2 emissions compliant turbocharged or naturally aspirated diesel engines including Andoria (Polish), ARO, Peugeot and Toyota units, these varying in power outputs from 86 hp (Andoria 4CT90-1ME) to 140 hp (Toyota 2RZ FE). The majority of in-service vehicles are likely to be powered by the ARO L 25 four-cylinder petrol engine, the most recent version of which continued to be an option. A Toyota diesel unit for military applications has been evaluated.

Four- or five-speed gearboxes, including the Toyota all-synchronised W56, were available. The Toyota gearbox would be supplied in conjunction with a Toyota VF 1A (VF 2A in the ARO 335) two-speed transfer box. Four-wheel drive is selectable in all models. The majority of in-service vehicles are fitted with ARO four-speed main gearboxes and constant mesh two-speed transfer boxes.

Variants

ARO 10
The ARO 10, introduced in 1980, compared to the ARO 240 was a more commercially orientated design, however the basic characteristics of robust design and all-wheel drive made the type suitable for certain military or governmental applications.

Two wheelbase options were available, 2.4 and 2.65 m, and to these a wide variety of bodies could be fitted. Engine options included Dacia petrol (leaded), Daewoo petrol (unleaded), and Renault diesel, with power outputs of up to 105 hp.

Specifications
See table on facing page

Status
Production currently halted (see text). In service with Romanian and other undisclosed African and Middle Eastern armed forces.

Contractor
SC ARO SA (see text for the current status of this company)

ARO Dragon (4 × 4) light vehicle

Development
The ARO Dragon (4 × 4) light vehicle is a military-specific light utility vehicle designed by CESAR S.A. (Research, Design and Development Center).

The ARO Dragon has yet to enter series production, but has been evaluated by the Romanian Army. Three wheelbase options are known to have been proposed, these being designated Dragon I, II and III.

ARO vehicles have reportedly been sold worldwide in Argentina, Brazil, China, Columbia, France, Germany, Italy, Venezuela, Peru, Russia and Spain, although details of military users outside of Romania have never been made available.

ARO Dragon II (4 × 4) 2.6 m wheelbase light utility vehicle with optional hard-top rear body and side-mounted spare wheels (ARO) 0524726

ARO Dragon I (4 × 4) 2.35 m wheelbase light utility vehicle command variant (ARO) 0524727

In September 2003 Cross Lander USA acquired ARO's manufacturing facility located in Câmpulung, Romania, approximately 60 miles north of Bucharest. The facility was acquired from the Romanian government as part of its privatisation programme. The 8.5 million ft² complex employed up to 2,200 people, could produce up to 38,000 vehicles per year plus spare parts, and was constructed to produce only 4 × 4 vehicles. Since 1957 the plant has produced around 360,000 4 × 4s, although during 2003 and 2004, respectively, only 661 and 303 vehicles were manufactured.

With a reported investment of USD32 million, Cross Lander set up a plant in Manaus, Amazonas in which production of the CL-244 (a military variant of the CL-244 is available) and CL-330 pick-up started, at the end of September, 2002. In addition to local and other export market sales, the intention was to produce the Cross Lander 244X (a substantially revised model fitted with a Ford V-6 engine, an Eaton transmission and a number of other proprietary components) in Brazil for the US market. After some effort this project failed and the factory now produces Mahindra light vehicles.

ARO was declared bankrupt in June 2006. The company Amrom Automotive 2006 is understood to have purchased the company following bankruptcy, with plans to resume production of the ARO line of vehicles under the ARO name.

It was disclosed in 2009 that Auto Max Czech (AMC) of the Czech Republic hoped to restart production of ARO vehicles.

Description
The overall design of the ARO Dragon is entirely conventional, the engine being mounted longitudinally between the box-section chassis at the front, crew seating and anybody following behind.

The Dragon has been designed on a modular basis, using a common platform throughout the range and utilising standard and commercially available automotive components, many of which are shared with later ARO (4 × 4) light vehicles.

Dragon I
Dragon I is the most compact of the three vehicles proposed having a 2.35 m wheelbase. It can be configured as a soft-top command vehicle with additional seats and radio communication in the rear body, or as a combat vehicle mounting a 73 mm AG-9 recoilless rifle in an open rear body tray. When mounting the AG-9 (SPG-9 Kopye recoilless gun), four crew (three plus driver) are required, two travelling in the vehicle cab, two in the exposed rear body tray. The weapon may be used dismounted and 24 rounds of ammunition are carried stored in metal boxes. Full details of the SPG-9 Kopye recoilless gun can be found in *Jane's Infantry Weapons*.

For a lower profile on the battlefield, the Dragon I combat vehicle has a removable cab roof that acts as a camouflaging cover for the folding two-piece flat glass front windscreen, and door tops that fold out and down. Two spare wheels are mounted one on each side of the rear body tray. Options include a front-mounted, electrically-powered self-recovery winch and a portable 20 W radio set.

Dragon 1 could easily be configured for other roles suiting a compact light utility vehicle, but if armed would readily accept other light weapons including ATGWs and could be configured as a reconnaissance, fast attack or light strike vehicle armed with light and/or heavy machine guns.

Dragon II

The proposed Dragon II has a wheelbase of 2.6 m and is configured for the conventional light utility vehicle role, having side-mounted bench seats in the rear body for up to eight troops. The two-person cab has a single-piece flat glass windscreen, the passenger station being equipped with a portable 20 W radio. Soft- or hard-top rear bodies are available, both fitted with van-type twin rear doors, half-doors on the soft-top.

Two spare wheels may be carried and mounted either one on either side of the rear body tray, or one on the cab roof and one at the rear of the vehicle. Options include a front-mounted electrically powered self-recovery winch.

Dragon III

The proposed Dragon III has a 3.2 m wheelbase and can mount a conventional van-type rear body or a shelter/container such as a NATO-standard S-250-dimensioned tactical shelter weighing 500 kg. The S-250 tactical shelter is designed primarily for sensitive communication or electronic equipment, but other less specialised shelter/body types could also be fitted if required.

A single spare wheel is carried on the cab roof, and options include a front-mounted electrically powered self-recovery winch.

All three wheelbase lengths share a common driveline and all-steel front-end body panels. The single-piece bonnet, which incorporates the upper half of the front wings, tilts forward through approximately 90° to give full access to the engine compartment. There are some dimensional and performance differences between models and these are detailed in the accompanying specifications table.

Specifications
See table below

Status
Production of ARO vehicles is currently halted (see text). The ARO Dragon has been evaluated by the Romanian Army but production is now considered unlikely.

Contractor
SC ARO S.A.

Russian Federation

LuAZ-967M amphibious battlefield support vehicle

Development
This vehicle was developed in the 1960s and was first seen during trials with Russian troops based in the former East Germany during the latter part of that decade. It was generally deployed from 1976 and was originally used as a battlefield medical evacuation vehicle but was also used as a general light support vehicle. The LuAZ-967M uses some components of the LuAZ-969 (4 × 4) light vehicle, full details of which can be found elsewhere in this section.

More recently LuAZ has produced, in prototype form only, the 1901-Geolog, a three-axle 6 × 6 amphibian powered by a Lombardini diesel engine.

By 2005 LuAZ had become a major assembler of Lada designs, and new agreements with Hyundai and Kia saw the start of SKD assembly of their products by the end of 2005.

In 2009 the name of the Lutsk Automobile Plant was changed to become Public Joint Stock Company (PJSC) Automotive Company Bogdan Motors, the Bogdan Corporation founded in 2005 by the voluntary association of 20 legal entities.

Model	Dragon I	Dragon II	Dragon III
Cab seating:	1 + 1 (+ 2 in rear)	1 + 1 (+ up to 8 in rear)	1 + 1
Configuration:	4 × 4	4 × 4	4 × 4
Weight:			
(kerb)	2,050 kg	2,050 kg	1,915 kg
(max GVW)	2,560 kg	3,200 kg	3,415 kg
(towed load)	1,200 kg	1,200 kg	1,200 kg
Length:	4.05 m	4.455 m (including rear-mounted spare wheel)	5.13 m
Width:	2.235 m (over one side-mounted spare wheel each side)	1.720 m	1.815 m
Height:	1.95 m (cab roof)	2.14 m (cab roof-mounted spare wheel)	2.2 m (cab roof)
Ground clearance:	215 mm	215 mm	215 mm
Track: (front/rear)	1.475/1.475 m	1.475/1.475 m	1.475/1.475 m
Wheelbase:	2.35 m	2.68 m	3.2 m
Angle of approach/departure:	43°/29°	43°/29°	43°/29°
Max speed: (road)	120 km/h	120 km/h	115 km/h
Max gradient:	67%	67%	67%
Max sideslope:	56%	56%	56%
Engine:	ARO 2.66-litre 4-cylinder in-line water-cooled indirect injection turbocharged diesel engine developing 87 hp (65 kW) at 3,500 rpm and 191 N.m torque at 2,500 rpm	ARO 2.66-litre 4-cylinder in-line water-cooled indirect injection turbocharged diesel engine developing 87 hp (65 kW) at 3,500 rpm and 191 N.m torque at 2,500 rpm	ARO 2.66-litre 4-cylinder in-line water-cooled indirect injection turbocharged diesel engine developing 87 hp (65 kW) at 3,500 rpm and 191 N.m torque at 2,500 rpm
Gearbox:	manual with 5 forward and 1 reverse gears	manual with 5 forward and 1 reverse gears	manual with 5 forward and 1 reverse gears
Transfer box:	2-speed with selectable engagement of front axle for 4-wheel drive	2-speed with selectable engagement of front axle for 4-wheel drive	2-speed with selectable engagement of front axle for 4-wheel drive
Clutch:	single dry plate	single dry plate	single dry plate
Steering:	hydraulically-assisted, recirculating ball	hydraulically-assisted, recirculating ball	hydraulically-assisted, recirculating ball
Turning radius:	6.5 m	7.55 m	7.55 m
Suspension:	fully independent with coil springs and telescopic shock-absorbers, front; longitudinal leaf springs and telescopic shock-absorbers, rear	fully independent with coil springs and telescopic shock-absorbers, front; longitudinal leaf springs and telescopic shock-absorbers, rear	fully independent with coil springs and telescopic shock-absorbers, front; longitudinal leaf springs and telescopic shock-absorbers, rear
Brakes:	dual circuit, hydraulic, ventilated discs, front, drums, rear	dual circuit, hydraulic, ventilated discs, front, drums, rear	dual circuit, hydraulic, ventilated discs, front, drums, rear
Electrical system:	12 V	12 V	12 V
Batteries:	2 × 66 A	2 × 66 A	2 × 66 A

Description

The body of the LuAZ-967M is made of all-welded steel with the engine at the front. The driver sits immediately behind the windscreen which folds forward to reduce the overall height. His seat is on the centreline of the vehicle and can be folded down so that he can drive lying flat. The steering column and steering wheel can also be lowered.

As a battlefield medical evacuation vehicle, the LuAZ-967M has two folding seats for walking wounded as well as two stretchers, but its normal load is two patients plus the driver. It is fully amphibious, being propelled in the water by its wheels. A treadway is carried on each side of the vehicle for crossing trenches and other obstacles. There is a winch with a capacity of 200 kg and 100 m of cable mounted at the front of the vehicle; this winch may be used to winch in wounded personnel on a canvas mat.

The LuAZ-967M is also used by airborne forces as a light support vehicle and as a weapon carrier; in the latter role it has been observed carrying an AGS-17 automatic grenade launcher, the 9K111 Fagot anti-tank guided missile and an 82 mm B-10 recoilless rifle. A Ukrainian vehicle has been tested carrying two 82 mm mortars, these can be lowered to the ground from the vehicle for firing, but with their support carriages still connected to the vehicle for rapid deployment. An ammunition carrier version can carry up to 320 kg of small arms ammunition.

Specifications

LuAZ-967M
Seating: 1 + 2 or 3
Configuration: 4 × 4
Weight:
  (laden) 1,350 kg
  (unladen) 930 kg
  (max load) 420 kg
  (max towed load) 300 kg
Length: 3.682 m
Width: 1.74 m
Height: (inc. windscreen) 1.625 m
Ground clearance: 285 mm
Wheelbase: 1.8 m
Angle of approach/departure: 34°/36°
Max road speed: 75 km/h
Max water speed: 5-6 km/h
Range: 285 km
Fuel capacity: 34 litres
Fuel consumption: 9 litres/100 km at 40 km/h

Privately owned example of a LuAZ-967M amphibious battlefield support vehicle (Richard Stickland)
0079384

LuAZ-967M amphibious battlefield support vehicle of the Ukrainian Army. This vehicle (at a public demonstration) has entered the water with its hull bungs out, the front compartment is filling with water (hence the slightly nose-down configuration), and it would shortly lose buoyancy and sink (Hajo Renker)
0533602

Gradient: 58%
Fording: amphibious
Engine: MeMZ-967A 4-cylinder air-cooled petrol developing 37 hp (28 kW) at 4,300 rpm
Gearbox: manual, 4 forward and 1 reverse gears, plus cross-country gear
Turning radius: 5.8 m
Suspension: individual torsion bar
Electrical system: 12 V

Status

Production complete. In service with the armed forces of the Russian Federation and possibly others.

Contractor

PJSC Automobile Company Bogdan Motors

LuAZ-969, 1302 and 1301 series of (4 × 4) light vehicles

Development

In 1965, the Zaporozhe Motor Vehicle Plant developed a 250 kg vehicle, based on the ZAZ-966 passenger car, called the ZAZ-969, but it did not enter production. In the late 1960s the project was transferred to the Lutsk Machine Building Plant and the designation was changed from the ZAZ-969 to the LuMZ-969. Production finally began in 1972 under the designation LuAZ-969 as the plant name was changed from the Lutsk Machine Building Plant to the Lutsk Motor Vehicle Plant. The vehicle was intended primarily for civilian use, although it had military and paramilitary applications. The chassis of the LuAZ-969 light vehicle was also used as the basis for the LuAZ-967M amphibious battlefield medical evacuation vehicle, full details of which can be found elsewhere in this section.

The LuAZ Plant (*Lutskiy Automobilny Zavod*) was founded in 1967 and in the overall plan of Soviet production had the specific task of producing small jeep-like vehicles.

In 1979 production of the LuAZ-969A ceased and the type was replaced in production by the modified LuAZ-969M Volin. The LuAZ-969M was itself revised in the early 1990s and the designation changed to LuAZ-1302. A revised version of the LuAZ-1302 - designated LuAZ-1301 by a quirk of bureaucracy - was shown in 1994; a three-axle version was also shown. The LuAZ-1301 entered limited production in 2002.

The main activity of the former LuAZ concern today is the production under license of Lada, Hyundai and Kia models. The former LuAZ plant also now produces buses, coaches and trolley buses.

In 2009 the name of the Lutsk Automobile Plant was changed to become Public Joint Stock Company (PJSC) Automotive Company Bogdan Motors, the Bogdan Corporation founded in 2005 by the voluntary association of 20 legal entities.

Specifications

LuAZ-969
Cab seating: 1 + 1
Configuration: 4 × 4
Weight:
  (laden) 1,200 kg
  (unladen) 820 kg
  (front axle, unladen) 510 kg
  (rear axle, unladen) 310 kg
  (towed load) 300 kg
Length: 3.2 m
Width: 1.6 m
Height: 1.77 m
Ground clearance: 300 mm
Track: 1.32 m
Wheelbase: 1.8 m
Max speed: 75 km/h
Range: 400 km
Fuel capacity: 32 litres
Gradient: 58%
Fording: 450 mm
Engine: MeMZ-946 V-4 air-cooled petrol developing 27 hp (20 kW) at 4,000 rpm
Gearbox: manual with 4 forward and 1 reverse gears
Transfer box: 2-speed
Turning radius: 3 m
Suspension: torsion bar
Tyres: 5.90 × 13
Brakes:
  (main) hydraulic
  (parking) mechanical
Electrical system: 12 V

Status

Production complete. Current generation models in production for civilian applications.

Contractor

PJSC Automobile Company Bogdan Motors

UAZ-469/469B and 3151/Hunter series of (4 × 4) light vehicles

Development

The UAZ-469/469B and its successor series have been the standard Soviet (and now Russian) light utility vehicle since the UAZ-469/469B began to replace the GAZ-69 in service from 1972.

The GAZ-69/69A series had proven a reliable vehicle since its introduction in the early 1950s but the type had known design limitations, particularly the low engine power output and poor ground clearance, and by 1960 it was conceded that a new design was required. Originally it was intended to develop separate cargo and personnel variants (as with the existing GAZ-69/69A), but the requirement was changed to a single universal body type during the early design phase.

The first prototype of the new vehicle, designated UAZ-460, appeared in the Spring of 1960. Developed on the chassis of the GAZ-21 sedan car and fitted with that vehicle's four-cylinder 2.445-litre OverHead Valve (OHV) petrol engine and three-speed manual gearbox, the prototype was fitted with a larger cab than the GAZ-69 series and was clearly orientated towards personnel transport, having a small rear area for cargo. The UAZ-460 prototype was modified to become the UAZ-460B in 1963. Among many minor improvements, an uprated engine was fitted, the ultimate result being the production model UAZ-469B.

Although ready for production by 1965, production of the UAZ-469/469B would not commence until 1972 as the GAZ-69/69A had proven to be reliable in service and despite the previously mentioned shortcomings of the design, no immediate need was seen for a replacement. The primary difference between the UAZ-469 and UAZ-469B is ground clearance, this being 300 mm and 220 mm, respectively.

Preparation for production of the UAZ-469/469B began at the Ulyanovsk Plant (*Ulyanovsky Avtomobilny Zavod* (UAZ)) in 1969, production vehicles to utilise various components from the mid-1960s introduced range of UAZ-452 light trucks and vans. Production of the UAZ-469/469B continued until 1985, when the type was replaced by the essentially similar, but modernised, UAZ-3151 model series.

The UAZ-31512, the replacement for the UAZ-469, was introduced in 1986, the distinguishing feature being a single-piece front windscreen replacing the split screen of earlier models. The UAZ-31512, 31514 (hard top) and 3153 (long wheelbase hard top) have been discontinued and current production versions of the UAZ-3151 series became known as the UAZ Hunter from 2004 onwards, although more recently the designation UAZ-469 series has been reintroduced when referring to latest generation improved models.

During the early 1990s the UAZ-3172 appeared. Originally intended as the replacement for the UAZ-3151 series, the type has yet to enter series production, doubtless due to the current financial situation in the former Soviet Union.

Czech Army UAZ-31512 (4 × 4) light vehicle (Richard Stickland)   0533619

Since the mid-1990s UAZ has launched a selection of new-generation Sports Utility Vehicle-styled (SUV) designs. These models are best described as suited to rear echelon, command, control, communication, internal security duties, or use by governmental, humanitarian or aid organisations. From 2003 UAZ began a programme of revising vehicle designations from the earlier complex numbering system to a model name. The first renamed model was the SUV-styled UAZ-3162 which became known as the UAZ Simbir in the Spring of 2003. Sales of the Simbir were poor and in the Summer of 2005 a modernized Simbir, called Patriot was launched. The SUV-styled UAZ-3160 launched in 1997 was discontinued in 2005.

In mid-2004 the UAZ-2360, a 1,500 kg payload light (4 × 4) truck based on the Simbir platform was launched.

The most recent known sales of UAZ-3151/Hunter/469 series vehicles have included 250-300 vehicles supplied to Angola early 2002, while in February 2003 186 vehicles were delivered in kit-form to Uruguay for local assembly. In January 2004 1,000 vehicles were delivered to Afghanistan, possibly for use by UN personnel, with a further 600 vehicles scheduled for delivery in March 2004. Also in March 2004, Iraq received 421 vehicles (designation UAZ-31595-023 Hunter) originally ordered during Saddam's regime. It is understood the coalition paid the USD2.5 million bill. The Uruguayan and Angolan vehicles were fitted with Andoria diesel engines, a EURO 2 emissions compliant variant in the Uruguayan vehicles.

In 2003 it was announced that UAZ models would be assembled in Vietnam.

Description

The basic vehicle has an all-steel body with the engine at the front and the four-door crew compartment towards the rear, with a removable canvas top and windscreen that can be folded down flat against the bonnet. The tops of the doors can also be removed. There are two individual seats at the front, a seat for three people in the centre and two people can sit facing each other at the rear. Normal load (UAZ-469B) is two people plus 600 kg of cargo or seven people and 100 kg of cargo. A hard-top can be fitted if required.

Compared to the UAZ-469/469B the main improvements found in the UAZ-3151/Hunter and latest 469 models are an uprated engine, new suspension and improved ergonomics. The specifications table provides data for the UAZ-469B and the current Hunter.

Variants

Numerous variants of the UAZ-469/469B/3151/Hunter series of vehicles have been produced since production began in 1972, many of these being local adaptations by the wide variety of users of the type. Most recently a

UAZ-469 (4 × 4) light vehicle of the Slovakian Army's demining team in Afghanistan (Carl Schulze)   1391202

Ukrainian UAZ-469 (4 × 4) light vehicle (Richard Stickland)   0009458

UAZ-469 (4 × 4) light vehicle of the Ukrainian Army on ceremonial duties. Note the stowed hood and lack of door tops (James Kinnear)   0567860

UAZ-469 (4 × 4) light vehicle of the Latvian Army (Stefan Marx)   1124727

variety of armed variants (usually local adaptations) have been seen. Typical armaments include heavy machine guns, AGS-17 grenade launchers, and assorted anti-tank missiles. Iraqi Army UAZ-469s have been observed carrying four RPG-7 anti-tank rocket launchers on a post-type mounting in the rear area.

The UAZ 3151/Hunter/469 series continues to be available commercially, and currently in both soft or hardtop configurations, and in short and long wheelbases.

Specifications

Model	UAZ-469B	UAZ-31512/Hunter
Seating:	1 + 6	1 + 6
Configuration:	4 × 4	4 × 4
Weight:		
(unladen)	1,650 kg[1]	1,620 kg (petrol); 1,770 kg (diesel)
(laden)	2,290 kg	2,370 kg (petrol); 2,520 kg (diesel)
(payload)	695 kg	750 kg
(front axle, laden)	960 kg	n/avail
(rear axle, laden)	1,330 kg	n/avail
(towed load, braked)	2,000 kg	n/avail
(towed load, unbraked)	600 kg	n/avail
(GCW)	4,290 kg	n/avail
Length:	4.125 m	4.17 m
Width:	1.785 m	1.73 m
Height:	2.015 m	2.025 m
Ground clearance:	220 mm	210 mm
Track:	1.422 m	1.455 m
Wheelbase:	2.38 m	2.38 m
Angle of approach/departure:	52°/42°	48°/37°
Max speed:	100 km/h	130 km/h (petrol); 120 km/h (diesel)
Range:	620 km	n/avail
Fuel consumption:	n/avail	13.2 l/100 km (petrol); -10.1 l/100 km at 90 km/h
Fuel capacity:	78 litres	78 litres
Max gradient:	62%	69% (laden)
Max gradient at GCW:	40%	n/avail
Vertical obstacle:	450 mm	n/avail
Fording:	700 mm	500 mm
Engine:	ZMZ-451 MI 2.445-litre 4-cylinder in-line water-cooled petrol developing 75 hp at 4,000 rpm	ZMZ-409.10 2.7-litre 4-cylinder in-line water-cooled petrol injection developing 128 hp at 4,600 rpm and 218 N.m torque at 3,900 rpm; ZMZ-5413.10 2.2-litre 4-cylinder in-line water-cooled diesel developing 92 hp at 4,000 rpm and 230 N.m torque at 2,000 rpm

Model	UAZ-469B	UAZ-31512/Hunter
Gearbox:	manual, 4 forward and 1 reverse gears	manual, 5 forward and 1 reverse gears
Transfer box:	2-speed	2-speed
Turning radius:	6.5 m	n/avail
Tyres:	8.40 × 15	225/75R 16
Brakes:		
(main)	hydraulic, drums all round	hydraulic, discs front, drums rear
(parking)	mechanical	mechanical
Electrical system:	12 V	12 V

[1] Some sources state an unladen weight of 1,650 kg. Laden, axle and GCW weight are calculated at a GVW of 1,490 kg

Status

UAZ-469/469B production completed in 1985. Follow-on UAZ-3151/Hunter series introduced from 1986, with further revised/updated 469 introduced 2010. The UAZ-469/469B and UAZ-3151/Hunter series are in service with former members of the Warsaw Pact, including the Czech Republic and Slovakia, Hungary, Poland and the Russian Federation. Also exported to other countries including Angola, Afghanistan, Cuba, Egypt, Iran, Iraq, Syria and Uruguay.

Contractor

Ulyanovsky Avtomobilny Zavod OJSC

UAZ-3172 (4 × 4) light vehicle

Development

The UAZ-3172 (4 × 4) light vehicle may be regarded as a progressive update of the UAZ-3151 series, itself a follow-on from the UAZ-469 series. Full details of the UAZ-469 and UAZ-3151 series can be found elsewhere in this section. The UAZ-3172 first appeared in the early 1990s and was intended to be the replacement for the UAZ-3151 series. The vehicle has yet to enter series production, and it is now considered unlikely that it will.

Description

Compared to the earlier UAZ-469 and UAZ-3151 series, the UAZ-3172 is larger overall, being able to carry nine or 10 personnel (including the driver) or cargo loads weighing up to 1,000 kg. The overall layout and appearance remains much the same as the earlier vehicle and it appears that many components are shared, although the UAZ-3172 has a revised front end and grille.

The overall layout remains conventional, with the engine under a forward bonnet, the driving position central and the load or passenger carrying area at the rear. The vehicle body is all-metal with a removable canvas top over two safety bows. Five body doors are provided, one at the rear.

Power is provided by a UMZ-421.10 petrol engine developing 103 hp and coupled to a four-speed manual gearbox. There is an inter-axle locking differential. The suspension is of the rigid axle, coil spring type with hydraulic shock-absorbers.

The vehicle is intended to operate under extreme climatic conditions varying in temperature from –50 to +50°C, with relative humidities up to 98 per cent and at altitudes up to 4,500 m above sea level. Loads weighing up to 1,200 kg can be towed over all types of road and terrain.

Various types of light weapon, such as machine guns, can be mounted on the vehicle.

UAZ-3172, originally the replacement for the UAZ-469 and UAZ-3151 series of (4 × 4) light vehicles (James Kinnear)   0567861

Specifications

UAZ-3172
(provisional)
Cab seating: 1 + 8 or 9
Configuration: 4 × 4
Weight:
(laden) 2,950 kg
(unladen) 1,950 kg
(max payload) 1,000 kg
(towed load) 1,200 kg
(GCW) 4,150 kg
Length: 4.6 m
Width: 1.88 m
Height: 2.1 m
Ground clearance: 315 mm
Track: 1.46 m
Wheelbase: 2.7 m
Max speed: 115 km/h
Range: 650 km
Fuel capacity: 105 litres
Max gradient: 31°
Side slope: 20°
Fording: 1 m
Engine: UMZ-421.10 petrol developing 103 hp (77 kW)
Gearbox: manual with 4 forward and 1 reverse gears
Clutch: single dry plate
Transfer box: 2-speed
Turning radius: 7 m
Suspension: rigid axle, coil spring with hydraulic shock-absorbers
Tyres: I-288 275/8R 16
Electrical system: 12 V

Status

Believed to be ready for production (see text).

Contractor

Ulyanovsky Avtomobilny Zavod OJSC

UAZ-452 (4 × 4) series of 800 kg light vehicles

Development

The UAZ-452 (4 × 4) light vehicle entered production at the Ulyanovsk Plant (*Ulyanovsky Avtomobilny Zavod* (UAZ)) in 1966. Although intended primarily for civilian applications, the vehicle and its variants have been used in significant numbers by the military, especially as ambulances, light workshop and command vehicles.

The UAZ-452 was preceded by the UAZ-450 series of (4 × 4) vehicles which were in production from 1958 to 1966 and included the UAZ-450 (van), UAZ-450A (ambulance), UAZ-450B (bus) and the UAZ-450D (cargo truck). In 1962, a series of similar (4 × 2) vehicles, the UAZ-451 (van) and the UAZ-451D (cargo), entered production. These were replaced by the improved UAZ-451M in 1966. The UAZ-451DM is also a (4 × 2) vehicle.

Upgraded versions of the UAZ-452 series remain in production. These are essentially the same in appearance, but are generally improved and feature a revised selection of more powerful engines. The current models produced are listed as: UAZ-3303 flatbed truck; UAZ-3741 cargo van with all-metal body; UAZ-39625 special passenger van with cargo compartment at the front; UAZ-3909 special passenger van with cargo compartment at the rear; UAZ-39094 five-seat flatbed truck; UAZ-2206 11-seat minibus; UAZ-3962 ambulance.

Czech importer of UAZ vehicles, SIO plc, with a view to upgrading the Czech Army fleet of UAZ-452 vehicles, upgraded approximately 10 Czech Army UAZ-452 ambulances with the installation of a VM Motori VM 428 LTM supercharged diesel engine. These engines offer EURO 3 emissions compliance and approximately twice the fuel economy of the standard UAZ power plant. To address the issue of gearbox quality in the original gearboxes, a gearbox supplied by Praga Engineering has been subjected to trial testing for UAZ vehicles in Czech Army service, but at the time of writing - October 2010 - no decision regarding any upgrade programme is known. The approximately 140 UAZ-452 vehicles remaining in Czech Army service are scheduled for replacement by Land Rover vehicles.

Description

The base variant of the UAZ-452 series is the van, which because of the external similarities with a loaf of bread, became known as Буханка (loaf) in Russian.

In addition to the base variant, other variants of the vehicle include the UAZ-452A (ambulance carrying three seated patients plus three stretcher patients); UAZ-452D which as a two-door all-steel forward control type cab and a rear cargo area with drop sides and a drop tailgate; UAZ-452P (tractor truck); UAZ-452E (with shielded electrical system); UAZ-452DE (with shielded electrical system), and the UAZ-452V (10-seat bus).

The UAZ-452 is powered by a four-cylinder in-line water-cooled petrol engine developing 72 hp, this coupled to a four forward/one reverse gears gearbox and two-speed transfer box. The earlier UAZ-450 series was powered by a 65 hp petrol engine and had a gearbox with three forward and one reverse gears and a two-speed transfer box.

Czech Army UAZ-452A (4 × 4) 800 kg light ambulance vehicle
(Richard Stickland)   0079410

Upgraded versions of the UAZ-452 series remain in production. These are essentially the same in appearance, but are generally improved and feature a revised more powerful four-cylinder petrol engine with a power output of 112 hp (82 kW) at 4,000 rpm and 208 N.m torque at 3,000 rpm.

Specifications

UAZ-452 van
Cab seating: 1 + 1
Weight:
(laden) 2,520 kg
(unladen) 1,720 kg
(front axle weight, laden) 1,260 kg
(rear axle weight, laden) 1,410 kg
(max load) 800 kg
(towed load) 850 kg
Load area: 2.6 × 1.87 m
Length: 4.36 m
Width: 1.94 m
Height: 2.09 m
Ground clearance: 220 mm
Track: 1.442 m
Wheelbase: 2.3 m
Angle of approach/departure: 36°/30°
Max speed: 95 km/h
Range: 500 km
Fuel capacity: 56 + 30 litres
Fuel consumption: 13 litres/100 km
Gradient: 57%
Fording: 550 mm
Engine: ZMZ-451M1 4-cylinder in-line water-cooled petrol developing 72 hp (54 kW) at 4,000 rpm
Gearbox: manual with 4 forward and 1 reverse gears
Clutch: single dry disc
Transfer box: 2-speed
Turning radius: 6.6 m
Suspension: longitudinal semi-elliptic springs with hydraulic double-acting shock-absorbers on both axles
Tyres: 8.40 × 15
Brakes:
(main) hydraulic
(parking) mechanical
Electrical system: 12 V
Battery: 1 × STE-54EM
Generator: 250 W

Status

Production of updated commercial models continues. In service with former Warsaw Pact countries, Cambodia, Egypt and possibly others.

Contractor

Ulyanovsky Avtomobilny Zavod OJSC

South Africa

Jakkals (4 × 4) lightweight airborne vehicle

Development

The Jakkals (Jackal) lightweight airborne vehicle is a (4 × 4) utility vehicle that was designed specifically for use by airborne forces.

It was announced in October 2002 that the Crayford Gecko had been selected as the replacement for the Jakkals (4 × 4) lightweight airborne vehicle. Originally 100 vehicles and 200 trailers were required by the SANDF to replace the Jakkals, however, the production contract award was for 75 Geckos and 75 associated trailers. The final requirement called for 75 Geckos and 75 associated trailers, with all vehicles having been

Surplus SANDF Jakkals (4 × 4) lightweight airborne vehicles and their associated trailers have been offered for sale by South Africa's Defence Matériel Disposal (DMD), a division of ARMSCOR (Patrick Allen)   1037473

scheduled for delivery at the end of February 2003. It was announced in April 2003 that a further 31 vehicles and trailers had been ordered. Full details of the Gecko air-droppable rapid-deployment logistics vehicle can be found elsewhere in this section.

Surplus Jakkals lightweight airborne vehicles have been offered for sale by Defence Matériel Disposal (DMD), a division of ARMSCOR.

Description

The Jakkals lightweight airborne vehicle resembles a small jeep in appearance and is conventional in layout, with the engine at the front and the driver and single passenger in the centre; space behind the seats is very limited. It was assembled using the standard and commonly available vehicle components. Production was carried out by the now defunct Associated Automotive Distributors (Pty) Limited of Cape Town, South Africa.

The Jakkals has an impact-resistant glass fibre body that is quoted as being capable of withstanding an unlimited number of parachute drops. The vehicle would normally be used together with a small single-axle trailer. Weight of the vehicle and trailer together is 1,120 kg. Power is derived from a 1.6-litre petrol engine and a high- and low-range transmission with selectable 4 × 4 or 4 × 2 drive.

The vehicle carries a front-mounted hand-operated self-recovery winch and, a collapsible casualty evacuation stretcher, with securing straps, can be mounted over the passenger seat in less than one minute.

The dimensions of the Jakkals and its trailer are such, that two vehicles with trailers will fit on to a standard 8 × 9 ft (2.438 × 2.74 m) air supply pallet. Thus a cargo aircraft such as a C-130 can carry 10 units. For para-dropping, two 30.5 m or three 18.3 m parachutes are used for each pallet. The descent speed is typically 7 m/s. Once on the ground, the vehicle can be unpacked from its pallet and prepared for use by two people in 10 minutes.

The Jakkals was produced in four basic versions: a general purpose section vehicle carrying a 5.56 or 7.62 mm machine gun; an attack vehicle with dual 0.50 in/12.7 mm Browning M2 heavy machine guns; a mortar vehicle carrying an 81 or 120 mm mortar with ancillary equipment and first-line ammunition; and a stretcher vehicle for casualty evacuation. A Jakkals carrying a 106 mm M40 series recoilless rifle has been observed, as has another vehicle carrying a cluster of four FT5 light anti-tank weapon system tubes. The Jakkals can also be used as a stores carrier. Various adaptations of these basic variants are possible and any vehicle (other than the attack version) can be fitted with communications equipment and used as a command vehicle. A complete front line mobile medical centre has been produced using the Jakkals.

Specifications

Jakkals
Seating: 2
Configuration: 4 × 4
Weight:
  (tractor) 940 kg
  (trailer) 180 kg
Max load: (tractor) 350 kg
Towed load: 350 kg
Length: 2.408 m
Width:
  (tractor) 1.211 m
  (trailer) 1.191 m
Height:
  (packed, tractor) 963 mm
  (packed, trailer) 910 mm
  (operational) 1.23 m
Ground clearance: 19 mm
Track: 1.027 m
Wheelbase: 1.539 m
Angle of approach/departure: 45/44°
Range: 200 km
Fuel capacity: 60 litres

Engine: 1.6-litre 4-cylinder petrol developing 63 hp (47 kW) at 5,200 rpm
Gearbox: manual, synchromesh, with 4 forward and 1 reverse gears
Clutch: single dry plate
Transfer box: 2-speed
Turning circle: 9.74 m
Suspension: leaf springs front and rear with double-action shock-absorbers
Tyres: 670 × 14 6-ply
Brakes: discs front, self-adjusting drums rear

Status

Production complete. A replacement vehicle has been procured and surplus Jakkals are currently being offered for sale.

Enquiries to:

ARMSCOR (Defence Matériel Disposal (DMD))

Spain

EINSA Model MM-1 Multipurpose All-Terrain Vehicle (MATV)

Development

The EINSA Model MM-1 Multipurpose All-Terrain Vehicle (MATV) was developed as a lightweight (4 × 4) vehicle capable of being used as a personnel carrier, supplies carrier or light tractor. A further development of the Model MM-1 MATV is the Model MM-1A with an increased payload capacity of 1,200 kg. Full details of this can be found elsewhere in this section.

Both MATV models are in service in small numbers with Spain's Armed Forces.

Description

The Model MM-1 MATV is an open platform-type design and is powered by a water-cooled diesel engine mounted between the two drive axles. Three engine power outputs are quoted as available; 68, 74 and 90 hp. Drive is permanent (4 × 4), with central differential locking via a four-speed automatic gearbox with a torque converter and 'kick-down' load correcting. The front and rear axles are rigid, with ventilated disc brakes at the front and discs at the rear. Both axles have self-locking differentials. As an option the axles can be fitted with manually operated differential locking.

The load platform has two rows of nylon rollers, which permit the loading and unloading of palletised loads by the driver without additional assistance. The load platform also has a trap-door well which allows the vehicle to be used as a personnel carrier.

The vehicle is provided with a winch rated at 4,082 kg. This winch can be fitted at any one of five mounting points; front, rear, at each side, or on the load platform.

Up to 12 vehicles can be carried stacked in the hold of a C-130 transport aircraft and up to six vehicles can be para-dropped together, each with a load of 400 kg. Vehicles can also be underslung from helicopters.

A wide selection of optional accessories are available for the MM-1 MATV including the Model RR-1 1,000 kg off-road payload trailer.

The Model RR-1 trailer has an overall length of 2.9 m and weighs 520 kg unladen. The trailer is electrically powered and features two 750 mm length lifting forks which, when not in use, form part of the 1.33 × 1.78 m (L × W) load platform; load platform height is 900 to 950 mm. As a switch is operated, the load platform tilts backwards through 90° and the forks fold outwards ready to pick up the load. Once the load is on the forks the platform tilts forward to locate the load on the horizontal load platform. The trailer has its own integral hydraulic pump and motor unit powered by a 12 or 24 V electrical supply.

Suspension is by leaf springs and the trailer shares wheel and tyre size with its intended tow vehicle. The Model RR-1 trailer is suitable for a variety of missions and has four demountable posts to act as load

EINSA Model RR-1 trailer coupled to the MM-1 Multipurpose All-Terrain Vehicle (MATV) (EINSA)   0009957

EINSA Model MM-1 Multipurpose All-Terrain Vehicle (MATV) (EINSA)
0009461

EINSA Model MM-1A Multipurpose All-Terrain Vehicle (MATV) showing the 4,082 kg rated winch in the side-mounting position (EINSA) 0116888

EINSA Model MM-1A Multipurpose All-Terrain Vehicle (MATV) clearly showing the optional soft top weather protection and the nylon load-handling rollers on the loadbed (EINSA) 0116887

protection and a NATO tow bar with an inertia braking system. A standard towing pintle is located at the rear of the trailer to allow for the attachment of one or more additional trailers, thus increasing the overall load capacity of the train.

The EINSA Model RR-1A trailer is a dimensionally larger development of the Model RR-1 trailer and is intended primarily for use with the larger Model MM-1A MATV; either MATV can operate with either trailer.

Specifications

Model MM-1 MATV
Seating: 1 + up to 6 in rear
Configuration: 4 × 4
Weight:
  (on-road) 1,650 kg
  (load) 1,000 kg
  (towed load) ≤1,850 kg
Length: (air drop) 2.64 m
Width: 1.78 m
Height: (load platform, laden) 890 mm
Track: 1.48 m
Wheelbase: 1.88 m
Angle of approach/departure: 90°/60-90°
Max speed: 65-92 km/h according to engine
Gradient: (max load) 60%
Side slope: 40%
Fording: 450 mm
Engine: water-cooled 4-stroke diesel developing 61, 74 or 90 hp (51, 55 or 67 kW)
Gearbox: automatic with torque converter with 4 forward and 1 reverse gears
Brakes: ventilated disc front, disc rear

Status

Production as required. Small number in service with Spanish Armed Forces.

Contractor

Equipos Industriales de Manutención SA (EINSA)

EINSA Model MM-1A Multipurpose All-Terrain Vehicle (MATV)

Development

The EINSA Model MM-1A Multipurpose All-Terrain Vehicle (MATV) is a further development of the EINSA MM-1 Multipurpose All-Terrain Vehicle, full details of which can be found elsewhere in this section. The MATV utilises many of the proven components of the Model MM-1, but is described by the manufacturer as a new design with increased performance and capacity.

The MM-1A MATV is in service with the Spanish Army and Marines.

Description

The MM-1A MATV is designed to be capable of performing a variety of tasks including light tractor or personnel or supplies carrier. It is easily deployable and suitable for use by rapid reaction or other light forces. It can also be parachute-dropped or transported underslung from any suitable capacity helicopter. The vehicle is of open platform design with optional soft-top weather protection for the driver and front seat passenger. Motive power is provided by a water-cooled diesel engine mounted between the axles and beneath the load bed floor. Drive is full-time (4 × 4) and for improved traction in difficult conditions the four-speed automatic gearbox provides a locking centre differential, while

the drive axles feature self-locking cross-axle differentials. The front and rear rigid axles feature 300 mm diameter servo-assisted disc brakes and are sprung by the combination of telescopic shock-absorbers and coil springs.

The load platform measures 2.15 × 1.98 m and features a trap-door for feet/legs which allows the vehicle to be used as a personnel carrier. Equally spaced on the load platform are two rows of nylon rollers, which permit the loading and unloading of large or palletised loads by the driver without additional assistance. Maximum payload is 1,200 kg. A 4,082 kg rated winch is supplied as standard equipment and this can be mounted on the load platform or one of four other mounting points on the vehicle; front, rear or on either side.

Options available include a more powerful turbocharged diesel engine, manually controlled rear-axle steering in first or reverse gears and an electrically operated trailer, the Model RR-1A.

The Model RR-1A trailer is a dimensionally larger development of the Model RR-1 1,000 kg load-handling trailer which was designed for use with the MM-1 MATV; either MATV can operate with either trailer.

Both trailer models are electrically powered and feature two lifting forks which, when not in use, form part of the load platform. As a switch is operated, the load platform tilts backwards through 90° and the forks fold outwards ready to pick up the load. Once the load is on the forks the platform tilts forward to locate the load on the horizontal load platform. The trailer has its own integral hydraulic pump and motor unit powered by a 12 or 24 V electrical supply.

Both models have leaf spring suspension and share wheel and tyre sizes with their intended tow vehicle. They are suitable for a variety of missions and have four demountable posts to act as load protection and a NATO tow bar with an inertia braking system and a standard towing pintle is located at the rear. This allows the attachment of one or more additional trailers, thus increasing the overall load capacity of the train.

Specifications

Model MM-1A MATV
Seating: 1 + 1 (up to 6 in rear)
Configuration: 4 × 4
Weight:
  (unladen) 1,740 kg
  (payload) 1,200 kg
  (towed load) 2,000 kg
Length: 3.40 m
Width: 1.98 m
Height: (loadbed, unladen) 1.05 m
Ground clearance: 400 mm
Track: 1.575 m
Wheelbase: 2.47 m

Angle of approach/departure: 90/90°
Max road speed: 80 km/h
Gradient: (laden) 60%
Side slope: 40%
Fording: 700 mm
Engine: Peugeot XUD9A 1.9-litre 4-cylinder water-cooled indirect injection diesel developing 72 hp (54 kW) at 4,600 rpm and 122 N.m of torque at 2,000 rpm. (Optional turbocharged diesel developing 90 hp/67 kW)
Gearbox: ZF 4HP14 automatic with torque converter with 4 forward and 1 reverse gears
Steering: endless screw type, servo assisted
Turning radius: 13 m
Suspension: beam axles front and rear with coil springs and telescopic shock-absorbers
Tyres: 9.00R 16 Michelin XZL
Brakes: (main) dual circuit, servo assisted, discs front and rear

Status
Production as required. In service with the Spanish Marines (12) and Army (2).

Contractor
Equipos Industriales de Manutención SA (EINSA)

Santana Model 88 Militar (4 × 4) 500 kg light vehicle

Development
Metalurgica de Santa Ana (to become known as Santana, and later Santana Motor S.A.) began manufacturing licence-produced Land Rover (4 × 4) light vehicles in 1958, the company's association with Land Rover ending in 1985, although Santana-manufactured components were used in Land Rover models until the end of the 1980s.

The final Land Rover light vehicle designs produced by Santana for military use were the Model 88 Militar and Model 109 Militar designed in 1969. The first Santana Model 88 was produced in 1970 in a variety of military and civilian forms.

In 1986 Metalurgica de Santa Ana began manufacturing Suzuki light vehicles, and in 1991 Suzuki became the main shareholder of the renamed Santana Motor S.A. The Spanish Army had meanwhile procured a number of Nissan Patrol (4 × 4) pick-ups as a partial replacement for the Militar fleets. Militar 88 and 109 models remain in service with Spanish Armed Forces, however, a replacement programme is currently underway.

In 1995 the regional government of Andalusia took ownership of Santana Motor S.A. and the company again looked towards producing a functional, durable and affordable light (4 × 4) vehicle, suitable for both commercial and military-type applications. A mock-up vehicle was shown at the Seville Motor Show in 1999, after which development began in earnest and production of the PS-10 began in October 2002.

A replacement programme for Santana Model 88 and 109 Militar vehicles in service with Spanish Armed Forces began during 2003. Three vehicles were supplied for trials; the Land Rover Defender 110, Santana PS-10 and URO VAM TL. The Land Rover vehicle was excluded in the early stages of the programme for technical non-compliance, and mid-2004 it was announced that a contract for deliveries over five years had been awarded to Santana Motor for the PS-10. By early 2009 around 3,000 vehicles had been delivered, with a batch of 350 vehicles under delivery, and a final option of 300-400 additional vehicles available for order during 2009. Full details of the PS-10, Land Rover Defender range and VAM TL can be found elsewhere in this section.

Description
The Santana Model 88 Militar closely resembles the British air-portable 500 kg Land Rover (full details of which can be found elsewhere in this section). The chassis uses a stair-type construction with two parallel side members with welded cross-members. A galvanised anti-corrosive finish chassis was an option for vehicles to be used in a salt water environment. A 2.286-litre petrol engine was fitted, although a diesel engine was available if required. The front and rear axles both use the same differential, while the front axle half shafts have universal joints; the rear axle is fully floating. Front and rear suspension uses semi-elliptic springs combined with double action shock absorbers.

The driver and passenger to his right are provided with single seats. Up to four personnel can be carried in the rear and a soft- or hard-top may be fitted. A special deep wading version, capable of coping with water obstacles up to 1.9 m deep is available; this uses a depressurising system for the engine, gearbox and axles and all components are waterproofed.

Apart from the basic personnel and load (up to 500 kg) carried, the Model 88 Militar can be readily converted to a number of special purpose configurations and weapon carriers. The Model 88 Militar may also be para-dropped on a platform, which, together with the parachute and fittings, weighs 2,200 kg.

Variants
Communications version
This has a hard-top and the rear interior is fitted with a folding table for radio equipment or for use in the command role. The vehicle may be fitted with a 42 or 90 A alternator.

Santana Model 88 Militar (4 × 4) 500 kg light weight vehicle prepared for deep wading (Santana Motor) 0116264

106 mm recoilless rifle
The M40 series 106 mm recoilless rifle is loaded into the rear of the vehicle via short ramps and, once in position, the barrel may be pointed through the centre of a split windscreen that can be folded forwards over the bonnet. This version has a crew of four, the driver and three personnel, two of whom sit on squab seats at the rear on either side of the gun. Stowage is provided for eight rounds.

Machine gun carrier
A 7.62 mm machine gun is mounted on a pivot secured to the rear area floor. This mounting allows a full 360° traverse and a maximum elevation of 36°. A similar arrangement, which allows the mounting of a 0.50/12.7 mm Browning M2 HB machine gun limits maximum elevation to 30°.

MILAN
The Model 88 Militar can be configured to carry a MILAN ATGW launcher on a special rear-mounted pivot. The pivot allows a full 360° traverse and elevation and depression of 10°. Up to four missiles can be carried, one on the launcher itself and three in rear-mounted racks.

60 mm mortar
A 60 mm mortar is secured to the cargo area floor by a robust support plate. This allows firing through a full 360° arc.

Specifications
Model 88 Militar
Cab seating: 1 + 1 (up to 4 in rear)
Configuration: 4 × 4
Weight:
 (laden) 2,160 kg
 (unladen) 1,660 kg
 (payload) 500 kg
Length: 3.725 m
Width: 1.574 m
Height: (with hood) 1.905 m
Track: 1.309 m
Wheelbase: 2.235 m
Fuel capacity: 97 litres
Angle of approach/departure: 48°/32°
Engine: 2.286-litre 4-cylinder in-line water-cooled petrol developing 61 hp (45 kW) at 4,000 rpm or 2.286-litre 4-cylinder in-line water-cooled diesel developing 59 hp (44 kW) at 4,000 rpm
Gearbox: manual with 4 forward and 1 reverse gears
Clutch: hydraulic diaphragm and disc
Transfer box: 2-speed
Steering: worm and recirculating ball
Turning radius: 6.25 m
Suspension: semi-elliptic springs with double action telescopic shock-absorbers, front and rear
Tyres: 6.00 × 16
Brakes:
 (main) hydraulically-operated drums front and rear
 (parking) mechanical
Electrical system: 24 V
Batteries:
 (petrol) 2 × 12 V, 57 Ah
 (diesel) 2 × 12 V, 70 Ah
Alternator: 35 A (50 or 90 A optional)

Status
Production complete. In service with Spanish Armed Forces; replacement programme commenced during 2003. Supplied to some other nations including Egypt and Morocco; status uncertain.

Contractor
Santana Motor S.A.

Santana Model 109 Militar (4 × 4) light vehicle

Development

Metalurgica de Santa Ana (to become known as Santana, and later Santana Motor S.A.) began manufacturing licence-produced Land Rover (4 × 4) light vehicles in 1958, the company's association with Land Rover ending in 1985, although Santana-manufactured components were used in Land Rover models until the end of the 1980s.

The final Land Rover light vehicle designs produced by Santana for military use were the Model 88 Militar and Model 109 Militar.

In 1986 Metalurgica de Santa Ana began manufacturing Suzuki light vehicles, and in 1991 Suzuki became the main shareholder of the renamed Santana Motor S.A. The Spanish Army had meanwhile procured a number of Nissan Patrol (4 × 4) pick-ups as a partial replacement for the Militar fleets. Militar 88 and 109 models remain in service with Spanish Armed Forces, however, a replacement programme is currently underway.

In 1995 the regional government of Andalusia took ownership of Santana Motor S.A. and the company again looked towards producing a functional, durable and affordable light (4 × 4) vehicle suitable for both commercial and military-type applications. A mock-up vehicle was shown at the Seville Motor Show in 1999, after which development began in earnest and production of the PS-10 began in October 2002.

A replacement programme for Santana Model 88 and 109 Militar vehicles in service with Spanish Armed Forces began during 2003. Three vehicles were supplied for trials; the Land Rover Defender 110, Santana PS-10 and URO VAM TL. The Land Rover vehicle was excluded in the early stages of the programme for technical non-compliance, and mid-2004 it was announced that a contract for deliveries over five years had been awarded to Santana Motor for the PS-10. By early 2009 around 3,000 vehicles had been delivered, with 350 vehicles under delivery and a final option of 300-400 additional vehicles available for order during 2009. Full details of the PS-10, Land Rover Defender range and VAM TL can be found elsewhere in this section.

Description

The Santana Model 109 Militar bears a close resemblance to its British counterpart and is constructed along similar lines. Main differences occur with the engine, which may be either a locally produced 2.286-litre petrol or diesel engine or a 3.429-litre six-cylinder petrol or diesel engine. The basic model was produced in several versions and could be configured to meet a wide variety of requirements.

A deep-wading version of the Model 109 Militar was produced and was delivered to the Spanish Marines. The Model 109 Militar can also be prepared for parachute drops by lashing it to a special platform in a stripped-down state. The complete load of prepared vehicle, fixtures and platform weighs 2,800 kg.

Variants

Basic troop carrier

This is fitted with a soft-top but a hard-top version is available. The vehicle carries the driver and nine personnel and the rear area holds cargo or supplies. It is also possible to mount various weapons in the cargo area including machine guns, a 60 mm mortar and a MILAN ATGW launcher.

Communications

This version usually has a hard-top and is specially produced for the communications role with extra screening of components and wiring looms, a 90 A alternator, extra internal racking and stowage and an engine oil cooler. Of the five versions that have been produced, one has three long-range radios, another two ground-to-ground radio facilities. A further version acts as a 30-line telephone exchange, while a fourth version has three telex machines. The fifth version is a special ground-to-ground communications station.

Light recovery vehicle

This variant carries a light electrical crane in the cargo area. The crane winch can lift loads up to 1,000 kg while the jib can tow loads up to 750 kg if the towed vehicle uses only one axle and 2,040 kg if both axles are used.

Santana Model 109 Militar (4 × 4) light vehicle prepared for parachute dropping (Santana Motor) 0116269

Ambulance

This variant has an insulated ambulance body, capable of carrying either four stretcher cases or two stretcher cases and four seated casualties. Alternatively eight seated casualties can be accommodated. Two large access doors are provided at the rear and the interior is equipped with medical equipment stowage.

Specifications

Model 109 Militar
Cab seating: 1 + 1 (plus 6 in rear)
Configuration: 4 × 4
Weight:
  (laden) 3,150 kg
  (unladen) 1,890 kg
  (max load) 1,000 kg
Length: 4.546 m
Width: 1.574 m
Height: (with hood) 2.008 m
Track: 1.309 m
Wheelbase: 2.768 m
Fuel capacity: 114 litres
Angle of approach/departure: 52°/31°
Engine: 2.286-litre 4-cylinder in-line water-cooled petrol developing 61 hp (45 kW) at 4,000 rpm or 2.286-litre 4-cylinder in-line water-cooled diesel developing 59 hp (44 kW) at 4,000 rpm or 3.429-litre 6-cylinder in-line water-cooled petrol developing 95 hp (71 kW) at 4,000 rpm or 3.429-litre 6-cylinder in-line water-cooled diesel developing 92 hp (68 kW) at 4,000 rpm
Gearbox: manual with 4 forward and 1 reverse gears
Clutch: hydraulic diaphragm and disc
Transfer box: 2-speed
Steering: worm and recirculating ball
Turning radius: 6.25 m
Suspension: semi-elliptic springs with double acting telescopic shock-absorbers, front and rear
Tyres: 7.50 × 16
Brakes:
  (main) hydraulically operated drums front and rear
  (parking) mechanical
Electrical system: 24 V
Batteries:
  (petrol) 1 × 12 V, 57 Ah
  (diesel) 1 × 12 V, 70 Ah
Alternator: 35 A (50 or 90 A optional)

Status

Production complete. In service with the Spanish Armed Forces and some other nations including Egypt and Morocco. A programme to replace remaining Spanish Armed Forces vehicles commenced during 2003.

Contractor

Santana Motor S.A.

Santana PS-10/IVECO M30E18WM (4 × 4) light utility vehicle

Development

Metalurgica de Santa Ana (to become known as Santana) began manufacturing licence-produced Land Rover (4 × 4) light vehicles in 1958, the company's association with Land Rover ending in 1985, although Santana-manufactured components were used in Land Rover models until the end of the 1980s. The final Land Rover light vehicle designs produced by Santana for military use were the Model 88 Militar and Model 109 Militar designed in 1969.

In 1986 Metalurgica de Santa Ana began manufacturing Suzuki light vehicles, and in 1991 Suzuki became the main shareholder of the renamed Santana-Motor SA. The Spanish Army had meanwhile procured a number of Nissan Patrol (4 × 4) pick-ups as a partial replacement for the Militar fleets, although considerable numbers of Militar 88 and 109 models remained in service with Spanish armed forces in 2009.

In 1995 the regional government of Andalusia took ownership of Santana Motor SA and the company again looked towards producing a functional, durable and affordable light (4 × 4) vehicle suitable for both commercial and military-type applications. A mock-up vehicle was shown at the Seville Motor Show in 1999, after which development began in earnest and production of the PS-10 began in October 2002.

The first military sales of the PS-10 were to the Spanish Navy which received around 75 Station Wagons during 2003.

Late 2003 the PS-10 began trials to meet a Spanish Army requirement for troop-carrying vehicles. Other competitors included the VAMTAC VAM-TL and the Land Rover Defender 110. Land Rover was disqualified from the competition in its early stages, and it was announced mid 2004 the production contract had been awarded to Santana Motor for the PS-10.

It is understood the first batch of vehicles delivered to the Spanish Army was 750, and that by March 2008 approximately 3,000 vehicles had been delivered, with around 300-400 more on order. A final batch of vehicles

Santana PS-10 (4 × 4) 1,000 kg light vehicle at DVD 2004 and displayed in station wagon configuration (Patrick Allen) 1067585

was available for order during 2009. All Spanish vehicles are to broadly the same original PS-10 specification despite the introduction of the Massif/M30E18WM which has been progressively revised in a number of areas.

In May 2006 Santana and IVECO announced an agreement that outlined the general principles for potential long-term product development and collaboration in the field of light utility vehicles. The commercial IVECO Massif was announced in January 2007, this essentially a re-badged Santana PS-10. Further development continued and mid-2008 IVECO announced the M30E18WM, a militarised version of the Massif. Further details of the M30E18WM can be found elsewhere in this entry.

In September 2008 IVECO announced that it has signed an option (valid until 2010) to purchase Santana Motor, depending on the commercial success of Massif. No further announcement regarding this option has been made.

Description

The Santana PS-10/IVECO M30E18WM (4 × 4) light utility vehicle is based on a conventional all-steel box-section chassis with box-section cross-members. The rear full-width cross-member mounts a NATO towing pintle, two lashing eyes and on each end a retractable lifting eye for use when the vehicle is transported underslung by helicopter. At the front of the vehicle the more conventional one-piece C- or channel-section bumper is replaced by a tubular steel design that curves slightly at each end. Lifting eyes are fitted and a self-recovery winch may be bumper-mounted.

The body is located via a total of 14 chassis and chassis outrigger-mounted rubber blocks designed to reduce noise, vibration and suspension-induced stress. The body is constructed of aluminium panels on a steel framework, the rear load section from aluminium alloy. The one-piece ABS plastic front panel detaches for the forward removal of the engine.

The prototype military version was produced in soft-top format, although current options also include hardtop and station wagon designs (including armoured), a station wagon being the base commercial variant. A shorter wheelbase version was introduced mid-2008.

The removable soft-top that grafted over the driving compartment to form a roof on the prototype vehicle has been replaced by a truck cab with rear soft-top on production models for the Spanish Army. The rear compartment has side-mounted bench seats that seat a maximum of eight. These fold up when not required, the rear tray width being sufficient to accommodate a standard Euro pallet. The one-piece tailgate drops down for loading/entry and mounts the spare wheel and tyre.

Santana PS-10 (4 × 4) light vehicle in Spanish Army soft-top configuration, as displayed at DVD 2006 (Patrick Allen) 1183193

IVECO M30E18WM Light Utility Vehicle (LUV) (2.452 m wheelbase) (Shaun C Connors) 1333730

Motive power for Spanish military production is provided by an IVECO 8140.43 four-cylinder turbocharged common rail diesel engine customised for application. Available in either EURO 2 or EURO 3 versions, dependant on market requirements, the engine produces 106 hp and 250 N.m of torque (EURO 2) or 125 hp and 275 N.m of torque (EURO 3). This drives the rear, or all four wheels. The original updated Santana LT85 five-speed all-synchromesh manual gearbox fitted to prototypes and some early production models has been replaced in later production models by a ZF S5 31 five-speed manual unit, coupled to an updated Santana LT230 two-speed transfer box. Four-wheel drive can be selected/deselected on the move and four-wheel drive is available in both high and low ratios. For increased traction in difficult conditions a rear axle differential lock and front axle limited slip differential are optional.

Suspension is by the combination of leaf springs and telescopic shock-absorbers on both axles. Conventional multi-leaf or parabolic springs are available to suit individual requirements. The front axle has a maximum authorised loading of 1,175 kg (increased from 1,080 kg on early models), the rear a maximum authorised loading of 2,365 kg (uprated from 1,970 kg on early models). Maximum payload is 1,000 kg.

Disc brakes are fitted front and rear, solid on the rear axle, ventilated on the front axle. An Anti-lock Braking System (ABS) is optional. Parking braking is provided by a 220 mm diameter drum brake mounted at the rear of the transfer box. This will hold the fully laden vehicle on a 100 per cent slope. Steering is power assisted.

IVECO M30E18WM Light Utility Vehicle (LUV)

IVECO formally introduced the M30E18WM Light Utility Vehicle (LUV) mid-2008. The M30E18WM is a militarised variant of the commercially branded Massif and compared to Spanish military PS-10 production differs extensively in the areas of mechanical specification and performance.

The primary differences are in the driveline, the original IVECO 8140.43 EURO 2/EURO 3 engine and ZF S5 31 five-speed gearbox having been replaced by an IVECO F1C 2.998-litre EURO 4 engine that develops 176 hp at 3,500 rpm and 400 Nm torque at 1,250-3,000 rpm. This is coupled to a ZF S400 six-speed manual gearbox.

The original 2.768 m wheelbase model has been supplemented by shorter 2.452 m and longer 3.022 m wheelbase models. Kerb weight has reduced (by 150 kg; 2.768 m wheelbase) and IVECO has reduced the GVW rating of the vehicle from 3,300 kg to 3,050 kg, this giving a payload of 950 kg (2.452 m wheelbase), 900 kg (2.768 m wheelbase), 850 kg (3.022 m wheelbase). Towed load remains 3,000 kg.

Specifications

(PS-10 military)
Cab seating: 1 + 1 + up to 8 in rear
Configuration: 4 × 4
Weight:
    (unladen) 2,300 kg
    (laden) 3,300 kg
    (max load) 1,000 kg
    (towed load, without auxiliary brake) 750 kg
    (towed load, with auxiliary brake) 3,000 kg
Length: 4.675 m
Width: 1.75 m
Height: 2 m
Ground clearance: 200 mm
Track: (front and rear) 1.486 m
Wheelbase: 2.786 m
Angle of approach/departure: 50°/30°
Max speed: >140 km/h
Max range: 1,000 km
Fuel capacity: 100 litres
Max gradient: >60%
Side slope: (load dependant) up to 88%
Fording: 500 mm

Engine: IVECO 8140.43P EURO 3 2.8-litre 4-cylinder turbocharged and intercooled water-cooled common rail 4-stroke electronic fuel injection diesel developing 125 hp at 3,600 rpm and 275 N.m torque at 1,800, or EURO 2 with mechanical fuel injection and developing 106 hp and 250 N.m torque

Gearbox: (current) ZF S5 31 manual with five forward and one reverse gears

Transfer box: Santana LT230 2-speed

Clutch: double plate

Steering: hydraulically-assisted

Turning radius: 7.3 m

Suspension: leaf springs and telescopic shock-absorbers, front and rear. Multileaf or parabolic options

Tyres: 235/85R 16 Michelin XZL

Brakes:
(main) discs, solid rear, ventilated front. ABS optional
(parking) transmission drum, 220 mm

Electrical system: 12 or 24 V

Alternator: 90 A

Status

In production (Santana PS-10). In service with the Spanish Navy (75 approx), ordered by the Spanish Army mid-2004; approximately 3,500 (see text).

Contractor

Santana-Motor S.A.

URO VAM TL (4 × 4) light vehicle

Development

The URO VAM TL light vehicle, designed as a military vehicle, was first seen publicly during 2003. It was one of three light vehicles proposed to meet a Spanish Army requirement for troop-carrying vehicles. Other competitors included Land Rover and Santana Motor. Land Rover, offering a Defender 110, was disqualified from the competition in its early stages, and it was announced mid-2004 that an initial contract for deliveries over five years had been awarded to Santana Motor for the PS-10. Full details of the Land Rover Defender and Santana PS-10 can be found elsewhere in this section.

The VAM TL has subsequently been supplied to Angola, Ghana and Morocco. Angola received an initial delivery during 2003 and received a further 24 vehicles during 2008 in a package that included 24 URO VAMTAC and 150 URO F3-24.14 trucks. Ghana received a package of 30 URO vehicles during 2008, this made up of VAM-TL and VAMTAC. Morocco received an initial 100 examples during 2004, a further 200 examples during 2005, and placed an order during 2006 for around 50 ambulance variants. A further Moroccan order was disclosed early 2007, this calling for around 1,000 URO VAMTAC (HMMWV-like) light vehicles and around 800 other vehicles including additional quantities of URO VAM TL, around 250 URO light trucks, plus around 100 IVECO tractor units. Following some revision of the requirement (more VAMTAC and fewer VAM TL), it is understood that around 300 VAM TL were delivered, final deliveries under this contract being made around February 2009.

Commercial sales of the VAM TL have also been made.

The VAM TL 4.2 became available late 2006, the primary difference between this and the original VAM TL 2.2 version being powerplant. The bulk of sales have been for the original VAM TL 2.2 version.

Description

The VAM TL was designed for military applications, and as such features functional flat steel body panels, with maximum design consideration given to functionality and durability, the minimum to aesthetics.

VAM TL (4 × 4) light vehicle of standard soft-top configuration but with the soft-top removed, half-doors and a folded front windscreen (URO) 1156040

VAM TL (4 × 4) light vehicle in nine-seat, four-door extended hard-top configuration (URO)   1156039

The VAM TL is currently available in a single 3.1 m wheelbase that is available configured in two main forms, with a two-door, two-seat cab or with a four-door, six-seat crew-type cab. For each cab-type there are a number of soft- and hard-top rear body options which allow for up to nine (hard-top) or 10 (soft-top) persons (including the driver) to be carried. The two-door variant has 2.13 m of load space, the four-door variant has 1.255 m of loadspace. The two-door variant may be supplied in chassis-cab configuration, or with a soft-top cab, half-doors and a foldable front windscreen, this configuration allowing for assorted weapon mounts in the rear body.

The rigid box-section chassis features tubular crossmembers and mounts leaf-sprung beam-type axles. The rear axle is fitted as standard with a mechanically controlled differential lock, this is optional on the front axle.

Standard power plant of the initial 2.2 version is an IVECO EURO 3 emissions compliant diesel which is coupled to a ZF/IVECO five-speed manual gearbox and two-speed transfer box, the full-time all-wheel drive transfer box having a lockable centre differential. Fuel consumption is around 10 litres/h at 90 km/h.

Optional equipment for the VAM TL includes an electric front-mounted winch, alternators up to 180 A, an Anti-lock Braking System (ABS), various tyres, runflat inserts, a deep fording kit, coil spring suspension for the front axle, air-conditioning, and a selection of protection kits.

The VAM TL can be transported as in internal load by a CH-47 Chinook helicopter or C-130 Hercules transport aircraft.

VAM-TL 4.2

The VAM-TL 4.2, which became available late 2006, is a further development of the earlier VAM-TL 2.2. The primary differences between the two versions are a more powerful 145 hp engine and different six-speed gearbox in the VAM TL 4.2. The cooling system is revised for the new powerplant and the bonnet is slightly different in appearance. The VAM TL 4.2 has an increase in maximum permissible GVW to 4,000 kg.

Specifications

URO VAM TL 2.2 (4 × 4) light vehicle

Cab seating: 1 + 1 (up to 8 additional passengers dependant on configuration)

Configuration: 4 × 4 (full-time)

Weight:
(laden) 3,500 kg
(unladen) 2,300 kg
(payload) 1,110 kg
(front axle load) 1,600 kg
(rear axle load) 2,400 kg
(towed load, on-road) 1,200 kg
(GCW) 4,700 kg

Length: 4.65 m

Width: 1.95 m

Height: (cab roof) 1.95 m

Ground clearance: 410 mm

Track:
(front) 1.619 m
(rear) 1.619 m

Wheelbase: 3.1 m

Angle of approach/departure: 60°/40°

Max speed: 125 km/h

Max range: 900 km

Fuel capacity: 105 litres

Max gradient: >70%

Side slope: >40%

Fording:
(unprepared) 550 mm
(prepared, with optional kit) 1.5 m

Engine: IVECO EURO 3 emissions compliant 2.287-litre 4-cylinder in-line water-cooled 4-stroke common-rail diesel developing 116 hp (87 kW) and 270 N.m torque

Gearbox: ZF/IVECO Ecolite 5 S 270 manual with 5 forward and 1 reverse gears
Transfer box: 2-speed
Clutch: single dry disc
Steering: power-assisted
Turning radius: 6.8 m
Suspension: leaf springs, telescopic shock-absorbers and anti-roll bar, front; leaf springs, telescopic shock-absorbers, rear. Optional coil sprung front axle, rear axle shock-absorbers
Tyres: 265/75 R16 (options: 235/85 R16 or 275/70 R16)
Brakes: (main) dual circuit hydraulic, discs front and rear. ABS optional
Electrical system: 12/24 V
Batteries: 2 × 59 Ah
Alternator: 28 V, 65 Ah

Status
In production. In service with Angola, Ghana and Morocco (approx. 600); see text for further details.

Contractor
URO Vehiculos Especiales SA

An 8,000 kg GVW VAMTAC with various levels of protection up to STANAG Level 3 became available during 2010. This example was displayed at Eurosatory 2010 (Shaun C Connors)   1391368

URO VAMTAC (4 × 4) I3 and S3 high-mobility tactical vehicles

Development
The URO VAMTAC (4 × 4) high-mobility tactical vehicle was first shown publicly in mid-1998. It bears a visual resemblance to the US HMMWV, due to being designed to a similar specification and to meet a corresponding requirement from the Spanish Armed Forces for a multipurpose, air-portable, high mobility off-road vehicle with a viable payload capacity.

The VAMTAC (*Vehiculo de Alta Movilidad Tactico*) underwent extensive testing by the Spanish Ministry of Defence and a five-year contract with production running from 1998-2003 was subsequently awarded to URO Vehiculos Especiales SA.

Following a three-month trial period, in October 2005 the Spanish Ministry of Defence awarded URO a further contract for the VAMTAC. It is a five-year contract under which deliveries started late 2006, totals are dependant on the defence budget but could reach around 1,000 units, with purchases under this contract understood to be permissible until 2012.

The latest models feature a number of mechanical changes accompanied by designation changes; the former T3 model becoming the I3 and the former T5 model the S3. The bulk of vehicles to be procured under the latest Spanish Army contract will be S3 models.

Deliveries as of late-2009 totalled around 2,100 VAMTAC vehicles for the Spanish Armed Forces. Under the original 1998-2003 five-year contract, deliveries of approximately 1,200 vehicles were split 60/40 per cent T5/T3. Around 25 per cent of vehicles delivered under the original five-year contract have subsequently been fitted with an add-on ballistic protection kit. Around 900 vehicles had been delivered under the second five-year contract by late-2009, all of these the S3 variant. Around 30 per cent of vehicles delivered under the second five-year contract are delivered in protected configuration.

It was disclosed during 2005 that in a government-to-government deal, Portuguese Armed Forces were 'renting' over the short term a quantity of protected VAMTACs for use in Afghanistan, while an armouring solution for Portuguese Army HMMWVs was finalised. Logistic support for these VAMTACs was provided by Spanish forces.

As part of a package of vehicles totalling around 1,800, including around 250 URO trucks and around 300 URO VAM-TL light vehicles, Morocco received approximately 1,200 VAMTAC S3 variants between early 2007 and February 2009.

Malaysia announced a USD17.87 million contract with UROVESA's local partner Master-Defence (Malaysia) Sdn Bhd (MASDEF) in April 2008 that called for 60 VAMTAC vehicles configured as weapon carriers and 25 as self launching units-IGLA carriers; delivery ran over 11 months with final deliveries occurring early-2009. The contract included technical support for the in-country fabrication and installation of the vehicles' systems, together with an after sales service support element. In service it is understood these vehicles replaced Mercedes-Benz G-Class, and primarily on the basis of a higher combat payload.

VAMTAC deliveries have also been made to the Dominican Republic which received 60 vehicles (2000 (40); 2001 (20)), Ghana (30 protected; order including VAM-TL (2008)), and Angola (2003 and 24 during 2008) and Venezuela. Angola and Venezuela use the T5/S3 variants in Police roles.

During 2010 an 8,000 kg GVW version of the VAMTAC became available, this having optional protection levels of up to STANAG Level 3 ballistic and Level 2 mine blast. The basic armoured VAMTAC S3 has a GVW of 6,200 kg.

Description
The VAMTAC is available configured in three main forms, command/control, chassis-cab, and pick-up. Of these the chassis-cab and pick-up variants are available with one of three cab options: two-door; four-door; or a reduced size four-door version with smaller rear doors and consequently less cab space. The command/control variant is available only with four full size doors and has a 1.885 m cargo area that can covered with either a soft- or slightly sloping hard-top.

The chassis-cab versions have 2.11, 1.575 and 1.178 m of chassis space, respectively, between the cab rear wall and the rear chassis crossmember. This can be used to mount a wide variety of shelter-type or cargo bodies. The pick-up versions retain the lower rear body panels of the command/control variant, and on the two-person, two-door model, retain the lower half of the original rear doors.

The pick-up versions have 2.185, 1.625 and 1.285 m of available space respectively, for the addition of any hard-top or the mounting of any shelter-type structure or armament. Armament options can include machine guns, grenade launchers, TOW ATGW, an 81 mm mortar, a 106 mm M40 series recoilless rifle and light air defence missiles such as the Mistral system. The VAMTAC has been tested towing the then BAE Systems, RO Defence 105 mm Light Gun (the Spanish Armed Forces have 56 105/37 Light Guns). Open top models are also available and these can be fitted with rollover protection if required. Low profile variants with foldable front windscreens are also available.

As part of a package of vehicles totalling around 1,800 and including around 250 URO trucks and around 300 URO VAM-TL light vehicles, Morocco received approximately 1,200 VAMTAC S3 variants between early 2007 and February 2009 (UROVESA)   1391047

An 8,000 kg GVW VAMTAC with various levels of protection up to STANAG Level 3 became available during 2010 (UROVESA)   1391063

Displayed at Eurosatory 2006, this VAMTAC is fitted with an all-welded armoured steel body shell to the standard VAMTAC pattern (Shaun C Connors)   1156036

URO S3 VAMTAC (4 × 4) high mobility tactical vehicle fitted with an optional front-mounted winch (URO)   1128793

URO VAMTAC (4 × 4) 1,500 kg high-mobility tactical vehicle, two-door pick-up variant configured for the transport of up to 10 people (Shaun C Connors)   1120460

URO VAMTAC (4 × 4) 1,500 kg high mobility tactical vehicle, command/control variant mounting a TOW ATGW (URO)   0122733

The steel body can be easily removed from the chassis, and dependant on configuration is fixed at four or eight points. If required various levels of supplementary armour may be added. Around 25 per cent of the Spanish Army's initial contract deliveries have subsequently been fitted with an add-on ballistic protection kit, and 30 per cent of current deliveries are supplied in protected configuration.

Dependant on configuration the VAMTAC can transport up to 12 people (11 + driver); payload is dependant on variant and configuration but GVWs are currently 5,000 kg (model I3), 5,300 kg (model S3), and 5,800 kg for the heavy-duty version of the S3, the S3-HD.

The latest armoured versions of the S3 model are currently available with four varying levels of protection, these models having GVWs of either 6,200 or 8,000 kg.

A lightweight version of the VAMTAC with an aluminium body and soft-top and doors has been demonstrated.

The torsionally rigid chassis consists of two square section rails joined by what are termed as 'special structures'. A snowplough or light dozer blade can be installed on the front of the vehicle and it can mount a light crane.

The fully independent suspension set-up consists of coil springs and telescopic shock absorbers at each wheel station. The front axle is fitted with an anti-roll bar, this is optional for the rear. Double reduction portal axles (differential and hub) are fitted and four-wheel drive is permanent. Driver controlled differential locks are available for the transfer box and each axle giving full four-wheel lock-up when required. Some of the axle and suspension components are interchangeable, front and rear. Ventilated dual circuit disc brakes are fitted all-round, supplemented by an optional engine exhaust brake. On the I3 and S3 models Electronic Traction Control (ETC) works via the Anti-lock Braking System (ABS).

The original engine fit of the VAMTAC was a six-cylinder Steyr M16-TCA 3.2-litre in-line turbocharged and intercooled, water-cooled 4-stroke diesel unit developing 163 hp at 3,800 rpm. This was soon supplemented by an IVECO 2.8-litre 4-cylinder in-line turbocharged and intercooled, water-cooled 4-stroke diesel unit developing 140 hp. Those vehicles fitted with the Steyr unit are designated VAM T5, those with the IVECO unit as VAM T3. Approximately 60 per cent of 1,200 vehicles supplied to the Spanish Armed Forces under the original VAMTAC contract are of T5 designation and fitted with the Steyr engine option. This is coupled to an Allison AT 542 automatic with 4 forward and 1 reverse gears, plus Allison TC 275 torque converter and URO URM-15, two-speed transfer box. A five-speed ZF automatic gearbox was an option with this engine. These T5 vehicles are assigned what are termed tactical roles, the remaining (approximately) 40 per cent of T3 vehicles fitted the IVECO option are assigned logistic roles.

The IVECO engine option includes an IVECO 2826.5 manual gearbox with five forward and one reverse gears, coupled to a URO URM-15 two-speed transfer box. An automatic transmission was an option with this engine.

Fuel consumption with the 140 hp IVECO unit and manual gearbox improves from 15 litres/hr at 90 km/h with the Steyr/Allison combination, to 10 litres/hr at 90 km/h. Maximum speed reduces by 20 km/h to 110 km/h.

The later I3 and S3 models are powered by IVECO and Steyr diesel engines, respectively. The I3 (Logistic variant) is powered by an IVECO F1C unit developing 166 hp, while the S3 (Tactical variant) retains the Steyr M16-TCA engine but slightly revised and uprated to 188 hp, this now further uprated to 215 hp for all armoured versions. An Allison automatic transmission is now standard on both models. Fuel consumption is around 17 litres/km at 90 km/h for both engines.

Optional equipment for the VAMTAC includes an electrical 5,400 kg straight-pull winch, low-profile run-flat tyres, a Central Tyre Inflation (CTI) system, deep fording kit (up to 1.5 m), pneumatic trailer brake, sump and suspension guards, protection bars for the radiator grille, swing-out spare tyre carrier and/or jerrycan rack, and air conditioning.

URO VAMTAC (4 × 4) 1,500 kg high mobility tactical vehicle, four-door pick-up variant configured as a shelter carrier (URO)   0122732

The VAMTAC can be slung under a CH-47 Chinook helicopter or carried internally in a C-130 Hercules transport aircraft. It can be parachute-delivered from low altitude.

Specifications

Model	VAM T5 [data in square brackets relates to VAM T3 where different]	VAMTAC S3 [data in square brackets relates to VAMTAC I3 where different]
Cab seating:	1 + up to 9	1 + up to 9
Configuration:	4 × 4	4 × 4
Weight:		
(laden, GVW)	5,300 kg	5,000-5,300 kg (5,800 kg S3-HD) [5,000 kg]
(unladen, kerb)	3,000 to 3,500 kg (dependant on version)	3,000 to 3,500 kg (dependant on version)
(payload)	1,500 or 2,000 kg (dependant on suspension)	1,500 to 2,300 kg [up to 2,000 kg]
(weight on front axle)	2,200 kg	(rated) 2,500 kg
(weight on rear axle)	3,500 kg	(rated) 3,300 kg (3,600 kg on S3-HD)
(towed load, inertia brake)	3,500 kg	3,500 kg
(towed load, pneumatic brake)	4,000 kg	3,500 kg
Length:	4.845 m	4.845 m
Width:	2.189 m (over mirrors)	2.175 (body)
Height: (cab roof)	1.9 m	1.89 m
Ground clearance:	493 mm	493 mm
Track:	1.862 m	1.862 m
Wheelbase	3.385 m	3.385 m (5.55 m S3-HD)
Max speed:	130 km/h [110 km/h]	135 km/h [126 km/h]
Range: (road)	600 km	700 km
Fuel capacity:	110 litres	110 litres
Angle of approach/departure:		
(laden)	74°/47°	74°/47°
(unladen)	74°/52°	74°/52°
Gradient:	>70%	100%
Side slope:	>60%	50%
Fording:		
(without preparation)	750 mm	750 mm
(with preparation)	1.5 m	1.5 m
Engine:	Steyr M16-TCA 3.2-litre 6-cylinder in-line turbocharged and intercooled, water-cooled 4-stroke diesel developing 163 hp (122 kW) at 3,800 rpm [IVECO 2.8-litre 4-cylinder in-line turbocharged and intercooled, water-cooled 4-stroke diesel developing 140 hp (104 kW)]	Steyr M16-TCA-3 EURO 3 emissions compliant 3.2-litre 6-cylinder in-line turbocharged and intercooled, water-cooled 4-stroke diesel developing 188 hp (138 kW) and 410 N.m torque [IVECO F1C EURO 3 emissions compliant 2.998-litre 4-cylinder in-line turbocharged and intercooled, water-cooled 4-stroke Common Rail diesel developing 166 hp (124 kW) and 380 N.m torque]
Gearbox:	Allison AT 542 automatic with 4 forward and 1 reverse gears, plus Allison TC 275 torque converter; optional ZF automatic with 5 forward and 1 reverse gears [IVECO 2826.5 manual with 5 forward and 1 reverse gears; optional automatic plus torque converter]	Allison S1000 automatic with 5 forward and 1 reverse gears, plus Allison TC 210 torque converter with 3rd, 4th and 5th gear lock-up
Transfer box:	URO URM-15, 2-speed	URO URM-16, 2-speed
Clutch:	single dry plate (267 mm)	n/app
Steering:	power-assisted	C-300 power-assisted
Turning radius:	7.56 m	7.8 m (model dependant)
Suspension:	independent on each wheel with coil springs and telescopic shock-absorbers, anti-roll bar front, optional rear	independent on each wheel with coil springs and telescopic shock-absorbers; anti-roll bars optional front and rear; various spring rates available
Tyres:	37 × 12.5R 17.5	37 × 12.5R 17.5 (37 × 12.5R 16.5 optional)
Brakes:	dual-circuit, air, ventilated discs on all wheels	main: dual-circuit, air, ventilated discs on all wheels. ABS and ETC are standard. Parking: independent drum on transfer box
Electrical system:	12/24 V	12/24V
Batteries:	2 × 12 V, 70 Ah	2 × 12 V, 110 Ah
Alternator:	28 V, 80 A	28 V, 80 A [28 V 65 A]

Status

In production. In service with the Angola (Police; 2003 plus 24 S3 in 2008), Dominican Republic (60), Ghana (2008 (protected)), Malaysia (85), Morocco (est. 1,200 S3), Spain (approximately 1,800) and Venezuela (Police).

Contractor

URO Vehiculos Especiales SA

United Kingdom

EPS Springer and associated light vehicles

Development

Late 2008 and as the security situation in Afghanistan continued to deteriorate, the UK MoD recognised that it had an emerging requirement for a load carrying vehicle at the lower end of the weight and protection scale. This requirement called for a small and agile vehicle that could rapidly transport stores between helicopter landing/drop zones and Forward Operating Bases (FOBs), and included a payload requirement of around one tonne, that payload possibly palletised, and thereby ruling out anything of conventional ATV configuration.

Following competitive trails, in April 2009 the MoD awarded UK-based Enhanced Protection Systems (EPS) a GBP7 million contract for 78 Springer vehicles. The first of these were delivered within four months of contract award, with final deliveries made some six months later.

Springer is based on the Israeli-designed, US-built Tomcar all-terrain vehicle which has been available for around 30 years. Reportedly designed as a helicopter transportable light vehicle for the Israeli military, both civil and military versions of the continually evolving design are now widely available. The Tomcar also forms the basis of the G-NIUS Gardium, the first fully autonomous Unmanned Ground Vehicle (UGV) vehicle to be used operationally.

As a result of user feedback from British troops in Afghanistan EPS announced the uprated Springer 2 mid-2010, with some proposed Springer 2 revisions (including the wheels/tyres) capable of retro-fit to original production vehicles. Outline details and provisional Specifications of Springer 2 can be found elsewhere in this entry.

Description

The Springer is based on a current production Tomcar TM5. The base frame is considerably revised and while the original chassis is not strengthened, the overall protective rollcage is.

EPS Springer light vehicle of the British Army (Ian Young)   1391383

Rear three-quarter view of an EPS Springer light vehicle of the British Army (Ian Young)   1391384

EPS Springer 2. Note the larger equal sized wheels and tyres, this upgrade retrofittable to original Springer vehicles   1391385

EPS Whippet, a potential replacement design for ATVs and trailers   1391386

Dingo (originally AIL's Desert Raider) is the latest addition to the EPS vehicle portfolio   1391387

The rear loadbed, which tilts rearwards for automotives access, is modified and can carry up to one tonne including a standard NATO pallet, this loaded by the front-mounted 8,000 lb-rated electric winch and using the two side-mounted sand ladders as a ramp. The load tray on the front of the vehicle, which tilts forward for maintenance purposes, carries an additional 100 kg of stores, while the rack above the two crew members is used to mount an Electronic Counter Measures (ECM) package.

Blast protection was not considered a pressing need for this procurement (insurgents would have limited opportunities to lay mines or similar devices in anticipated areas of operations), or indeed practical for a vehicle that has an unladen weight of less than 1,000 kg. A degree of ballistic protection from the threat of rifle or sniper fire was, and composite material 'doors' that provide a classified level of ballistic protection are fitted.

The Lombardini naturally aspirated diesel engine is modified to run on military grade fuel, and in the process is adjusted to deliver a small increase in torque and around 3 hp more. The automatic V-belt CVT two-speed (high/low) transmission and oil-bathed chain-type final drives remain standard.

Other modifications carried out here in the UK by EPS include a complete re-wire. The four-wheel hydraulic disc brakes are revised, as are the front double wishbone dual coil over shock-absorber (343 mm travel) and rear trailing arm double wishbone dual coil over shock-absorber (334 mm travel) suspension set ups.

A spares package kit allows for the front-dimensioned spare wheel to fit a rear wheel station following a puncture.

When Springer is delivered to the UK MoD no more than 30 per cent of the original vehicle remains.

Springer 2

As a result of user feedback from British troops in Afghanistan EPS announced the uprated Springer 2 mid-2010.

Suggested revisions for Springer 2 include things as simple as moving some controls/switches and a gear shifting revision (to prevent accidental engagement of reverse), to more complicated things including an engine power upgrade of around 10 hp, a new starter motor and lighter yet more efficient radiator.

The key visual difference between the two versions is wheel and tyre fit. The original Springer has had some ground clearance issues in boulder and rock strewn Afghanistan, and to counter this Springer 2 has larger diameter equal-sized wheels and tyres. A further advantage here is that the new wheels are Commercial Off-The-Shelf (COTS).

Any production Springer 2 would be carried out by EPS in the UK and could be based on a further revised and wider frame, this mounting a wider body and re-styled front end.

Whippet

EPS also offers the Whippet. Whippet, which has some frame commonality with the proposed Springer 2, was designed and built by EPS in six weeks and in response to a UK MoD Urgent Operational Requirement (UOR) to potentially replace ATVs.

Whippet has a dry weight of 780 kg, a payload of 900 kg and its primary advantages over any ATV and trailer combination are that the operator is seated, thereby reducing operator fatigue considerably, while any payload is carried on a small loadbed.

Whippet remains at the prototype stage.

Pinscher

Pinscher was originally a competitor vehicle for the requirement awarded to the EPS Springer; it now forms part of the EPS product range in both (6 × 4) and (6 × 6) configurations. Pinscher has a dry weight of 995 kg and a cargo box payload of 1,500 kg.

Pinscher remains at the prototype stage.

Dingo

EPS further expanded its vehicle portfolio with the mid-2010 introduction of Dingo.

Dingo was designed in Israel, first appearing in 1997 as the Desert Raider Light Surveillance Vehicle (LSV). As far as is known, only four production vehicles were ever built, two for trials by the Israel Defence Force (IDF) and two for Uganda. The vehicle currently being demonstrated in the UK by EPS is the original prototype.

While the Dingo vehicle was initially designed as platform for a variety of patrol, reconnaissance and strike-type roles, EPS is as keen to demonstrate/highlight the unique suspension of the vehicle, and potentially as a retrofit and/or upgrade to a variety of lighter-weight Land Rover-class vehicles to enhance their off-road mobility.

Full details of the AIL Desert Raider can be found in the Special attack vehicles section.

Specifications

	Springer 1	Springer 2 (provisional)
Seating:	1 + 1	1 + 1
Configuration:	4 × 2	4 × 2
Weight:		
(unladen)	850 kg (1,300 kg armoured)	850 kg (1,300 kg armoured)
(GVW)	2,700 kg	2,700 kg
(payload)	1,400 kg (armoured)	1,400 kg (armoured)

	Springer 1	Springer 2 (provisional)
Length:	3.416 m	3.416 m
Width:	1.78 m	1.78 m
Height:	1.686 m	1.722 m
Ground clearance:	378 mm	406 mm
Track: (front and rear)	1.54 m/1.46 m	1.54 m
Wheelbase:	2.562 m	2.562 m
Angle of approach/departure:	84°/70°	86°/76°
Max speed:	64 km/h	64 km/h
Max range:	350 km	350 km
Fuel capacity:	54 litres	54 litres
Gradient: (at GVW)	34%	34%
Side slope:	>60%	>60%
Fording:	378 mm	406 mm
Engine:	Lombardini LDW 1404 4-cylinder 1.372-litre water-cooled 4-stroke diesel developing 38.2 hp	Lombardini LDW 1404 4-cylinder 1.372-litre water-cooled 4-stroke diesel developing approx. 48 hp
Gearbox/transmission:	automatic V-belt CVT with high/low ratios and locking differential	
Steering:	left-hand drive, rack and pinion steering	
Turning radius: (kerb)	9.4 m	9.4 m
Suspension:	double wishbone (front) with 343 mm travel, trailing arm (rear) with 334 mm travel, both with dual coil-over springs and gas/hydraulic shock-absorbers	
Tyres:	25/8/12 (F), 26/12/12 (R)	205/80/16 (F & R)
Brakes:	hydraulically operated discs all-round	
Electrical system:	12 V	12 V
Batteries:	12 V, 50 Ah	12 V, 50 Ah
Alternator:	12 V, 65 A	12 V, 65 A

Status
Springer in service with the UK MoD (78), Springer 2, Whippet, Pinscher and Dingo available.

Contractor
Enhanced Protection Systems (EPS) Ltd

Land Rover (4 × 4) range of vehicles

Development
Land Rover, the world's largest dedicated manufacturer of (4 × 4) vehicles, is now owned by India's Tata Motors Ltd, Tata acquiring Land Rover from previous owner the Ford Motor Company in 2008. Ford had acquired Land Rover from BMW mid-2000. Land Rover produces a full range of (4 × 4) vehicles that, in addition to the more common and recognisable light utility vehicle range, includes the Discovery, Range Rover, Range Rover Sport and Freelander models. The Discovery and Range Rover are best described as being better suited to rear echelon, command, control, communication, VIP transport or internal security duties, and full details of these can be found elsewhere in this section. The Range Rover Sport is a performance orientated (4 × 4) in the mould of the BMW X5 or Porsche

Land Rover Defender 110 hard-top and Land Rover Defender 130 vehicles of the US Air Force stationed in the UK (Shaun C Connors)   1120418

Cayenne (the latter being a Porsche badged/revised Volkswagen Touareg), while the Freelander/Freelander 2 has its off-road capability limited by lower clearances than a true off-road (4 × 4) and the lack of a two-speed transfer box. Consequently, use by governmental or military forces of the Range Rover Sport and Freelander/Freelander 2 would be limited.

Land Rover has been manufacturing (4 × 4) vehicles since 1948 and it has been estimated that of the two million plus Land Rover vehicles produced, 70 per cent remain in use. Around 200,000 vehicles a year are produced at the main Land Rover production facility at Solihull in the UK, 70 per cent of those for export. Land Rovers have been - or are - also assembled in Australia, Brazil, Congo (Democratic Republic), Kenya, Malaysia, Morocco, New Zealand, Nigeria, Pakistan, South Africa, Trinidad, Turkey, Zambia and Zimbabwe, with (as of 2009) Kenya, Malaysia, Pakistan, and Turkey being the most active.

Land Rover vehicles are currently estimated to be in service with more than 100 military and paramilitary forces worldwide and in a wide variety of roles ranging from ambulances to armed strike vehicles.

The basic design layout of the Land Rover (4 × 4) light utility vehicle has changed little throughout its near 60 years in production and while driveline and ergonomic improvements are ongoing, the box-section steel chassis still carries rigid beam axles and the functional bolt-on or riveted predominantly flat body panels are still constructed of corrosion-resistant aluminium. Possibly the most significant design change came with the introduction of coil spring suspension as part of a major improvement package in 1983. Prior to this, all Land Rover models had featured leaf spring suspension.

Production of the Land Rover began in 1948 with what is now universally known as the Series One model. This was followed by the Series II/IIA and III models, before the 1983 introduction of the coil sprung One-Ten model, this soon to be joined by the Ninety and then One-Two-Seven models. These vehicles evolved into the Defender 90, 110 and 130 models; in all cases the figures relating to nominal wheelbase lengths. As previously mentioned, Land Rovers have been put to numerous uses by various military users worldwide, with some purpose-development work and conversions being carried out in-house by Land Rover.

A small number of purpose-developed military models have entered quantity production, the most notable of these would be the Lightweight or Air-portable, the Forward Control (FC) 101, and the Defender XD (eXtra Duty) models. The FC 101 has now all but been retired from military service, the Lightweight continues in limited use worldwide and the British Armed Forces currently operate around 8,800 examples of the Defender XD model. The Netherlands Marines also use the Defender XD model. Full details of the Lightweight and Defender XD variants can be found elsewhere in this section.

In Bosnia (from left to right) a Land Rover Discovery, a military specification Land Rover Defender 110 hard-top and a commercial pattern (in military use) Land Rover 110 Station Wagon, all of the British Army (Shaun C Connors)   0121816

Depending on user, each model of military Land Rover would have been given its own specific military designation, so for ease of user reference the aforementioned Series and nominal wheelbase based designations will be used throughout all Land Rover entries in this section. For further ease of reference the main production of Land Rover (4 × 4) light utility vehicles will be split into two entries; 1948 to 1983 production, covering all leaf sprung variants; and 1983 to present, covering all coil sprung variants.

Status
In production. In service. Full details can be found elsewhere in this section.

Contractor
Land Rover

Land Rover (4 × 4) light vehicles 1948-1983

Development
After the end of the Second World War, the British government was compelled to ration steel to the motor industry in proportion to the value of its exports. This created serious difficulties for the Rover Company since its luxury cars were not proving to be exportable. It became obvious that the company would have to produce something that would have a world appeal and be outside the luxury class, a working vehicle that would attract buyers from agricultural and industrial markets of the world.

Early in 1947, a decision was made to build a new all-purpose cross-country vehicle, and by late 1947 prototypes of a (4 × 4) vehicle suitable for both agricultural and industrial applications had been built. Trials proved the concept and Rover introduced the Land Rover at the Amsterdam Motor Show in April 1948. Quantity production began at Land Rover's Solihull factory in July 1948.

The first model had a 2.032 m (80 in) wheelbase and was powered by a 1.6-litre petrol engine. The basic model was fitted with a canvas hood and this was followed late in 1948 by a fully enclosed estate model which could seat six plus the driver. The British government placed its first order for the Land Rover in 1949.

By 1950 over 24,000 Land Rovers had been built and in 1952 the 1.6-litre petrol engine was replaced by a two-litre petrol engine. In 1954 the original 2.032 m (80 in) wheelbase was increased to 2.184 m (86 in) and in 1955 a 2.717 m (107 in) model that could carry 750 kg joined the range. In 1956 the British Army adopted the Land Rover as its standard 1/4-tonne (4 × 4) vehicle and the 2.184 m (86 in) model gave way to the 2.23 m (88 in) and the 2.717 m (107 in) was replaced by the 2.768 m (109 in) model. In 1957 Land Rover offered a two-litre diesel engine to compliment the standard petrol engine.

In February 1958 the Series II Land Rover was introduced. This retained the 2.23 m (88 in) and 2.768 m (109 in) wheelbase configurations of the earlier model, but featured a larger, more powerful, 2.25-litre petrol engine. In September 1961 the Series IIA was introduced and the two-litre diesel engine option was replaced by a new 2.25-litre diesel engine option that produced an additional 11 hp and allowed for a 23 kg payload increase. By this time the Australian and Swiss armies had adopted the Land Rover as their standard light utility vehicle.

In 1962 the 1,000 kg Forward Control Land Rover was introduced and late in 1966 a 2.794 m (110 in) wheelbase model followed. This was powered by a six-cylinder petrol engine and capable of carrying 1,500 kg of cargo. Neither model was adopted in significant numbers for military applications.

From early 1967 a 2.6-litre six-cylinder petrol engine was offered for the 2.768 m (109 in) Land Rover. This was deleted in 1980 with the introduction of the 3.5-litre V-8 version.

Early in 1968, to comply with new legal requirements governing vehicle lighting in Netherlands, Belgium and Luxembourg, a headlight modification was introduced and for the first time the headlights were incorporated in the wings instead of the grille panel. In September 1968 the Air-portable and Forward Control (FC) 101 models came along. These were specifically for military use and were never officially sold

commercially. The Forward Control (FC) 101 has all but been withdrawn from military service, however the Air-portable remains in limited use and full details of this vehicle can be found elsewhere in this section.

In October 1971 the Series III model was introduced with a restyled grille, redesigned safety fascia, improved gearbox (having synchromesh on all forward gears for the first time) and other detailed modifications. Six-cylinder and V-8 petrol engine options were offered on the Series III throughout its production run, which continued on until 1985, despite production of its coil-sprung replacement beginning in 1983. The chassis of the Series III was also used as a basis for the Shorland armoured patrol vehicle and the SB401 armoured personnel carrier.

It is unlikely that any Series One models remain in military use, while any examples of Series II/IIA models will be ever-reducing in numbers. The Series III model remains in reasonably widespread service, though it decreases in numbers, being progressively replaced by more modern designs. The following brief description can be considered generic to Land Rover production from 1948 to 1983, while the specification table that follows is specific to the Series III.

Full details of the post-1983 production run of coil-sprung Land Rovers can be found elsewhere in this section.

Description
Throughout its production run the Land Rover (4 × 4) light utility vehicle has retained an all-welded steel box-section ladder-type chassis. The body is of predominantly flat aluminium panels with the steel bumpers, cappings and other vital components galvanised. The layout is conventional, with the engine at the front, driver and two passengers in the centre and the cargo area at the rear with a drop tailgate. The basic model has a galvanised steel hood frame and a full length hood. The front-mounted engine drives the rear or both axles (selectable) through a four-speed main gearbox and two-speed transfer box. Rigid beam axles are sprung by multi-leaf springs.

Specifications

	2.23 m (88 in) wheelbase	2.768 m (109 in) wheelbase
Seating:	1 + 2 in front (4 in rear)	1 + 2 in front (8 in rear)
Configuration:	4 × 4	4 × 4
Weight:		
(laden)	2,120 kg	2,600 kg
(unladen)	1,430 kg	1,750 kg
(max load)	690 kg	850 kg
Length:	3.65 m	4.56 m
Width:	1.68 m	1.68 m
Height:	1.97 m	1.98 m
Ground clearance:	200 mm	200 mm
Track:	1.33 m	1.33 m
Wheelbase:	2.23 m	2.768 m
Angle of approach/ departure:	46°/30°	45°/29°
Max speed: (road)	105 km/h	90 km/h
Range:	560 km	600 km
Fuel capacity:	45 litres	90 litres
Max gradient		
(high range)	39%	25%
(low range)	115% (subject to tyre adhesion)	58%
Fording:	500 mm	700 mm
Engine:	4-cylinder OHV in-line naturally aspirated water-cooled diesel developing 51 hp (38 kW) or 4-cylinder OHV in-line water-cooled petrol developing 69 hp (51 kW) at 4,000 rpm	
Gearbox:	manual with 4 forward and 1 reverse gears	manual with 4 forward and 1 reverse gears
Clutch:	single dry plate	single dry plate
Transfer box:	2-speed	2-speed
Steering:	recirculating ball	recirculating ball
Turning radius:	5.79 m	7.5 m
Suspension:	semi-elliptic springs front and rear with double acting telescopic shock-absorbers	
Tyres:	7.50 × 16	7.50 × 16
Brakes:		
(main)	tandem braking system, hydraulic, drums all-round	tandem braking system, servo-assisted, drums all-round
(parking)	drum, mechanical on transmission	drum, mechanical on transmission
Electrical system:	12 V (24 V optional)	12 V (24 V optional)

Series III 2.768 m (110 in) wheelbase Land Rovers of the UAE Army (Stefan Marx)   1124726

Status
Series One production concluded 1958; Series II/IIA production concluded 1971; Series III production concluded 1985. Reducing numbers remain in service with numerous armed forces worldwide.

Contractor
Land Rover

Land Rover (4 × 4) light vehicles 1983 - present

Development
Production of the Land Rover range of (4 × 4) light utility vehicles began in 1948 and prior to the introduction of the much-revised One-Ten model in 1983, all previous Land Rover models had featured leaf spring suspension. Full details of the pre-1983 leaf sprung range of Land Rover vehicles can be found elsewhere in this section.

Coil springs not only offered an improved on-road ride, but with increases in axle travel of 50 per cent (front) and 25 per cent (rear), coil sprung vehicles also had significantly improved off-highway mobility. To complete the coil sprung range of vehicles the One-Ten model was joined in production by the Ninety in 1984 and the One-Two-Seven in 1985, all three models taking their designations from their respective 110 in (2.79 m), 92.9 in (2.36 m) and 127 in (3.226 m) wheelbases. By 1985, and to compliment the new five-speed gearbox and full-time four-wheel drive system, engine choices were new 2.5-litre four-cylinder petrol or naturally aspirated diesel units, with a 3.5-litre V-8 petrol unit available as an option.

The first military sales of the new coil sprung range of Land Rovers were for 900 One-Ten models to an unspecified Asian customer and a considerably smaller number to the Royal Netherlands Marines, both in 1984. Considerable numbers of all wheelbases have subsequently been sold to numerous armed forces including those of the UK.

The Ninety and One Ten models are in service with British Armed Forces, in both soft- and hard-top configurations as Truck Utility Light (TUL) and Truck Utility Medium (TUM), and in both 12 and 24 V FFR (Fitted For Radio) versions. The longer One-Two-Seven model is more commonly used as a shelter carrier or fitted with an ambulance-type body. In August 1989 it was announced that 214 One-Two-Seven models were to be supplied to the Royal Air Force to support RAF Regiment Rapier surface-to-air missile squadrons. These were powered by the V-8 petrol engine, the then standard 2.5-litre naturally aspirated diesel engine being unable to provide sufficient power for the vehicles' intended role.

In September 1990, following the introduction of the new Land Rover Discovery, to help differentiate models the name Defender was adopted for the Ninety, One-Ten and One-Two-Seven models, becoming known as the Defender 90, 110 and 130. At the same time a further package of improvements were made. These included electrical system and cab ergonomic improvements, along with the choice of a more powerful version of the V-8 as the standard petrol engine. A 200 Tdi 2.5-litre four-cylinder direct injection turbocharged diesel engine was also introduced. It offered considerable improvements in power, torque and economy over the previous naturally aspirated and turbo-diesel units.

In 1993 disc brakes became standard all-round, and in 1995 the 300 Tdi engine and R380 five-speed gearbox were introduced. The 300 Tdi engine was replaced by the emissions compliant Td5 five-cylinder diesel engine during 1999, however the 300 Tdi engine remained available for certain markets and applications as Land Rover did not offer a tactical specification version of the Td5 engine. This however did not preclude Td5-powered vehicles from military use.

The 300 Tdi and Td5 engines were both phased out during 2006, and 2007 model year Land Rover Defenders are fitted with the Puma emissions compliant diesel engine coupled to a new six-speed manual gearbox. In

As displayed at Eurosatory 2010, a French Army Land Rover Defender 130 double-cab configured for the Psy Ops role (Shaun C Connors)   1391463

As displayed at Eurosatory 2010, a Land Rover Defender 110 Utility Station Wagon as supplied to NAMSA for an Operational Logistics Reconnaissance Team (OLRT) role (Shaun C Connors)   1391464

addition to a new engine and gearbox, 2007 model year Defenders also feature a wide range of other design improvements in what is the most significant package of improvements since the introduction of coil spring suspension in 1983.

By early 2003 Land Rover had streamlined production of the Defender and introduced a range of five Core Military Vehicles for production in the Land Rover factory at Solihull. All Core vehicles included a standard package of military features developed by Land Rover with their customers to comply with common NATO, STANAG and Mil standards. A range of special features was also available to special order to enhance the capabilities of the Core Military Vehicle.

The five Core Military Vehicle variants produced prior to the introduction of the 2007 model year Defender were: 90 Tdi 24 V GS soft-top; 110 Tdi 12 V GS soft- or hardtop; 110 Tdi 24 V GS soft- or hardtop; 110 Tdi 24 V FFR soft- or hardtop; 110 Td5 12 V GS soft- or hardtop. All 110 models were available in heavy duty configuration. All 90 models were fitted with the commercial heavy duty suspension package as standard.

Other military variants were available to special order, options including 130 inch wheelbase models, 90 inch wheelbase models with a 12 V electrical system, a hardtop or the Td5 engine. Station wagon-style bodies were a further option.

It is anticipated that broadly the same Core Military Vehicle variants and options will become available for the 2007 model year vehicle. Adoption of the Core Military Range, according to Land Rover, shortens order to delivery times considerably.

Since 1999, and in addition to the UK MoD, Land Rover Defender vehicles are known to have been supplied Built-Up (BU) to a wide variety of users worldwide. The Land Rover Defender is also available Knock-Down (KD) and since 2001 vehicles are known to have been supplied KD to a wide variety of users worldwide. Land Rover Defender vehicles are currently assembled from KD kits shipped from the UK in Kenya, Malaysia, Pakistan and Turkey (by Otokar), where further local adaptation to the base design often occurs during the build-up stage.

Land Rover quotes that over 70,000 Land Rover Defender vehicles are in service with armed forces around the world.

The following list while detailed, is not comprehensive as Land Rover is often unable to confirm exact sales figures for reasons of client confidentiality. However, since 1999 (Built-Up (BU)) and 2000 (Knock-Down (KD)) Land Rover Defender vehicles are known to have been supplied to:
- Brazil: c750 × 90 and 130 crew-cab for local conversion (Army) (KD)
- Brunei: 44 × 110 (incl 30 × 110 FFR, 2005) (BU)

Land Rover 110 station wagon of Poland's Operational Manoeuvre Reconnaissance Group (GROM). Poland's GROM is understood to operate 10 Land Rover Defender vehicles that were delivered during 2003-2004 (Grzegorz Holdanowicz)   1185459

Land Rover 110 soft top of Poland's Zandarmeria Wojskowa (ZW - Military Police) (Grzegorz Holdanowicz)   1185460

Land Rover 110 station wagon of the Finnish Army (Grzegorz Holdanowicz)   1185461

- Brunei: 25 FFR × 110 soft-top (2009) (BU)
- Chile: 208 in two batches (2009-2010) (BU)
- Czech Republic: around 600 (most of the early deliveries were commercial specification; later deliveries inc 45 × Core Military 300 Tdi 24 V hardtop, 2005; 24 Core Military 300 Tdi 24 V hardtop, 2006; 116 × 24 V GS (built late 06/early 07); 79 130 RDV converted by SVOS (BU)
- France: approx 200 (military, 2002-2006); 120 × 110 station wagon (Gendarmerie, 2002-2005) (there were some pre-2002 deliveries) (BU)
- France: around 1,700 delivered BU since 2006. The current contract, valid for three years from February 2009, allows for the delivery of an unlimited quantity of vehicles. During 2009 approaching 550 were ordered.
- Italy: 603 × 90 soft-top (Army, 2001), 12 × 90 RDV (Carabinieri, 2001), 301 × 90 soft-top (Army, 2002), 603 × 90 Core Military soft- top (Army, 2003), 334 × 90 (Army, 2005), 22 × 110 RDV (Carabinieri, 2005), 50 × 90 soft-top (Air Force, 2006), 184 × 90 station wagon (Air Force, 2006) (BU)
- Jordan: 1,500 × 110 civilian specification soft-top with NATO towing hook (BU)
- Kenya: 85 × 110 Core Military soft-top GS and FFR, 140 × 110 Core Military soft-top GS (70 each 12 V/24 V FFR, 2006) 140 × 110 Core Military soft-top GS (2007). Further orders anticipated (BU)
- Lebanon: commercial specification 110 (BU)
- Lithuania: 45 × 110 RDV-type (contract award 2005, deliveries over three years, prime contractor Ricardo Special Vehicles) (BU)
- Malaysia: 343 GS and 550 FFR, the latter being local conversions (KD)
- Mexico: 22 × 130 troop carriers (2010) (BU)
- NAMSA: >150 vehicles (2007-2009)
- Oman: c100 × 110 (BU)
- Pakistan: approx. 1,800 (1999-2000) (BU)
- Pakistan: 3,750 × 90 and 110 civilian spec for local conversion (Army, 2000-2005) (KD)
- Pakistan: 2,800 × 90/110/130 from 2006; around 1,000 supplied by January 2007. 1,100 Tdi, remainder 07 model year (KD) Pakistan's heavy industries Taxila produces the Mohafiz, a light armoured vehicle based on the Defender platform. By mid-2008 around 150 examples were in service with Pakistan's Police and para-military forces. Examples have been exported to Iraq (MoD Police)
- Pakistan: approx 800; delivery from late-2008 (further batch of around >200 vehicles anticipated from late-2010/early-2011)
- Paraguay: 58 × 130 double cab; delivery early-2011 (42 for troop transport, 12 for scouting role)
- Poland: more than 180 including some special forces and 138 × 110 (2005-2010) for the Zandarmeria Wojskowa (ZW - Military Police) (BU)
- South Africa: up to 100 per year, some exports inc Botswana (KD; BU from 2007)
- Trinidad: 40 × 110 FFR soft-top (2009) (BU)

Land Rover Defender 110 soft-top military specification (FFR) powered by a 300 Tdi turbocharged 2.5-litre four-cylinder diesel engine developing 111 hp. This vehicle was offered to meet a Spanish Army requirement (Shaun C Connors)   1120420

Land Rover Defender 110 soft-top military specification (FFR) powered by a 300 Tdi turbocharged 2.5-litre four-cylinder diesel engine developing 111 hp. This vehicle was offered to meet a Spanish Army requirement (Shaun C Connors)   1120419

- Turkey: c4,000 primarily 110 (Army and Gendarmerie) (KD)
- Venezuela: 25 × 90 hardtop, 23 × 110 civilian specification station wagon (Marines) (BU).

Turkey's Otokar received an order in April 2005 for around 400 Land Rover Defender-based ambulances for Iraq and in July 2005 it was confirmed that Otokar would also supply 573 Defender-based light APCs and 27 Defender tactical wheeled vehicles to Iraq; deliveries ran 2005-2006.

Description

In appearance, the Land Rover Defender is similar to earlier Land Rover models, but can be identified by a moulded injection grille and one-piece windscreen. The vehicle is based on a boxed section steel ladder frame chassis that is robot welded and has a centre section over 190 mm deep. 110 Heavy Duty models have a revised chassis. The detailed design of the chassis is such, that the fuel tank has added protection. A bolt-in cross-member facilitates removal of the gearbox and transfer box and the wiring looms are routed inside the chassis members for maximum protection. Many body panels are common across the range and all are constructed from corrosion resistant aluminium.

The increased track of the coil sprung models required the introduction of GRP deformable 'eyebrows' over the wheels and also led to a redesigned steering linkage that provided a reduced turning radius of 6.4 m. Coil spring suspension provides 180 mm of wheel travel at the front and 210 mm at the rear. Minimum ground clearance is 229 mm. Suspension movement at the front and rear is controlled by long-stroke hydraulic dampers. Heavy Duty models feature uprated suspension. On 90 models this is limited to heavier-duty rear springs. On 110 models, heavier-duty springs are fitted front and rear, the revised rear spring set-up including helper springs. Anti-roll bars are fitted front and rear. The Land Rover front beam-type axle is located by radius arms with a Panhard rod providing lateral location. 300 mm disc brakes have been fitted all round since 1993. The Salisbury axle, until recently fitted to the rear, has been replaced on the Core Military Vehicle (and beyond) by a Land Rover axle which offers improved ground clearance.

Until the 2007 model year Defender, the current-fit engine for the Defender range (for tactical military applications) was the 300 Tdi 2.5-litre four-cylinder direct injection turbocharged diesel, although since its 1983 introduction options for the coil-sprung range have included a 2.5-litre four-cylinder petrol, a 3.5-litre V-8 petrol, a 2.5-litre naturally aspirated diesel, a 2.5-litre turbo-diesel, and the 200 Tdi diesel. The 300 Tdi engine

Italian Army Land Rover Defender Core Military Vehicle 90 soft-top powered by a turbocharged 2.5-litre four-cylinder diesel engine developing 111 hp (Land Rover) 0569410

Displayed at IDET 2005, a Czech Army Land Rover Defender 130 complete with dedicated twin-axle trailer, both kitted out for the NBC detection role (Stefan Marx) 1124725

Jordanian Army Land Rover Defender 110 civilian specification soft-top powered by a turbocharged 2.5-litre four-cylinder diesel engine developing 111 hp (Land Rover) 0569409

meets up to EURO 2 emissions regulations if required and 24 V versions feature electromagnetic compatibility meeting MIL-STD 461. The Td5 engine meets EURO 3 emissions regulations. A 24 V inverter was available for the Td5 engine as an option.

For the 2007 model year and to meet EURO 4 emissions requirements, Land Rover introduced a 2.4-litre four-cylinder turbocharged diesel engine for the Defender. This has the same power rating as the outgoing Td5 unit (122 hp), but produces 35 per cent more torque. Two versions of this engine will be available, one meeting EURO 2 emissions requirements and optimised for lower grade fuels.

A fully suppressed 24 V version of the 2007 model year Defender was launched late-2009. This vehicle features a new electrical architecture with a dual 12 V/24 V power supply, replacing the 24 V system of the previous model. The total output is raised from 100 A to 280 A, enabling a significant increase in the amount of C4i equipment that can be operated. Two high-output 12 V glass mat, air-transportable military specification batteries are fitted, these now stowed under the rear floor, releasing extra space in rear body for equipment.

The transmission is permanent four-wheel drive with a five- or six-speed gearbox matched to a two-speed transfer box. This arrangement provides 10 or 12 forward and two reverse gears and the transfer box incorporates a lockable differential. The differential can be locked in both high and low ranges. The 2007 model year Defenders are fitted with a Getrag gearbox coupled to a Land Rover two-speed transfer box, the latter shared with the Land Rover Discovery 3. The 2007 model year vehicles also feature electronic traction control for the first time.

Pre-MY2011 production Land Rover Defenders can tow loads up to 4,000 kg and, depending on vehicle specifications, have payload capabilities of up 852 kg (90), 1,605 kg (110) and 1,600 kg (130). For MY2011 payload figures for EU customers will, as a result of the need to comply with N1 Masses and Dimensions legislation which determines where a load can be placed in the vehicle. Complying with this revision will result in changes to the rear axle limits and the Gross Vehicle Weight (GVW) of some Land Rover Defender derivatives.

An uprated Extra Heavy Duty Defender with a 4,500 kg GVW was scheduled to be available by mid-2009, although development work on this has now halted.

Standard military equipment for military variants includes: military front bumper with towing pintle, NATO two hook and 12 pin trailer socket, four JATE lashing/lifting towing rings fitted to chassis, load lashing cleats in the

Czech Army Land Rover Defender 110 Station Wagon in use as a military police vehicle (Richard Stickland) 0121846

rear body, jerrycan stowage in the body sides (110), two-piece removable doors with removable door tops and sliding windows, windscreen tiedown, Michelin 7.50 × 16 tyres on black rims, full length PVC hood with side windows (soft-top), side-hinged tailgate and swing-away spare wheel carrier (soft-top), rear seats for up to eight people (GS version).

Special order factory-approved options include roll-over protection for the crew, winch systems, winterisation, raised air intakes and rifle stowage. There are numerous non-factory approved options available for the range.

A variety of weapon system mounts have been developed by or in cooperation with Land Rover for the Defender 90 and 110. These include the MILAN ATGW, the LAU-97 70 mm multiple launch rocket system, and the M40 106 mm recoilless rifle. A wide range of body conversions have also been developed, primarily for the 110 version. These have included a special forces patrol vehicle, armoured patrol vehicle, mobile workshops, shelter vehicles, ambulances, fire tenders and armoured and discreetly armoured personnel carriers. The Defender 130 has also been developed into a number of variants including mobile workshops, shelter carrying vehicles and ambulances.

Variants

Defender XD

The Defender XD (eXtra Duty) was developed from the standard Defender model to meet a UK Ministry of Defence requirement to replace its Series III Land Rover fleet. It successfully completed UK Ministry of Defence trials and was selected for the British Armed Forces requirement in 1996. The only other user of the type are the Dutch Marines which received 71 vehicles. Full details of the Defender XD range can be found elsewhere in this section.

Special Operations Vehicle (SOV)

This vehicle was specifically designed to meet a US Army requirement for a rapid reaction, air-portable, all-terrain weapons platform for use by the Special Forces (75th Rangers regiment). Full details of the Defender SOV can be found in the Special attack vehicles section.

Rapid Deployment Vehicle (RDV)

This Defender RDV has been developed jointly with Ricardo Special Vehicles and builds on the experience of producing around 300 Weapons Mount Installation Kit (WMIK) for the UK MoD for fitting to the Defender XD 110. Full details of the Defender RDV can be found in the Special attack vehicles section.

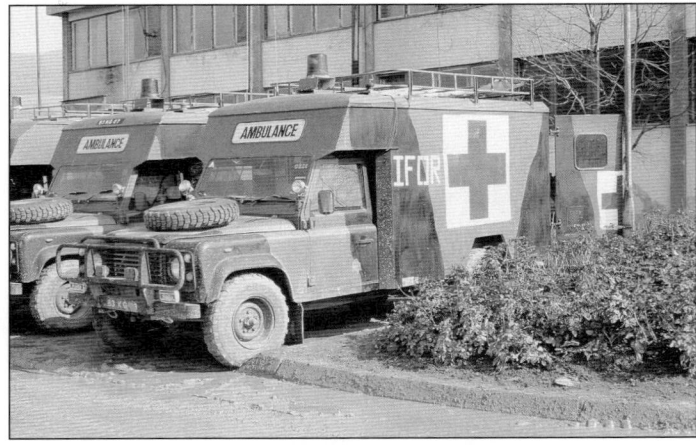

British Army Land Rover Defender One-Two-Seven/130 ambulance
(Shaun C Connors)   0121817

Czech Army Land Rover Defender 110 soft-top powered by a 300 Tdi
turbocharged four-cylinder diesel developing 111 hp (Richard Stickland)
                                                                0121849

Royal Air Force Land Rover Defender One-Two-Seven/130 Rapier tractor
powered by a V-8 petrol engine (Shaun C Connors)   0533608

Australian Army Land Rover Defender Td5 Station Wagon (Ron Fry)
                                                                0533611

British Army Land Rover Defender 110 hard-top powered by a naturally
aspirated 2.5-litre four-cylinder diesel engine developing 66 hp
(Shaun C Connors)   0121850

roles. A further 17 vehicles were delivered during 2004. Life of Type (LoT) for these vehicles is quoted as 10 years.

Project Perentie (and follow-on Land Rover buys) vehicles, which total around 3,400, will be replaced under the Australian Department of Defence's Defence Materiel Organisation's (DMO) multiphase project, Project Land 121; Project Overlander.

The now Mercedes-Benz Australia Pacific offering versions of the Mercedes-Benz G-Class were announced as preferred bidder for the light vehicle segment of Land 121's Phase 3 late-2007. A contract award worth AUD350 million was announced in October 2008, covering the delivery of 1,200 Mercedes-Benz G-Class to Australia's Armed Forces. Six different types of G-Wagon are to be acquired, these including a (4 × 4) general-purpose station wagon; two (4 × 4) cargo variants; a (6 × 6) chassis-cab variant; a (4 × 4) dual cab variant; and a specialist Surveillance and Reconnaissance Vehicle (SRV). Full details of the G-Class can be found elsewhere in this section.

Land 121's Phase 4 will replace the 1,300 Land Rovers not replaced under Phase 3 (light vehicle segment) with a fleet of protected light mobility vehicles.

Australian Land Rover 110

Land Rover 110s were produced in Australia by Land Rover Australia at their facility in Moorebank, New South Wales. An initial order for 2,500 (4 × 4) vehicles for the Australian Army was placed and the first vehicle was handed over in August 1987. The 1,000th vehicle was handed over in December 1988.

Australian (4 × 4) 110s are powered by an Isuzu 4BD1T 3.9 litre naturally aspirated diesel engine developing 98 hp at 3,000 rpm. The same engine, turbocharged, is used to power the Australian Land Rover 110 Heavy Duty (6 × 6) truck, full details of which can be found in the Trucks section.

Additional Land Rover (4 × 4) 110 vehicles were procured under the Bushranger Phase 1 programme. These were built by BAE Australia and brought the total procured by the Australian army to just over 3,000. This latest order included additional Fitted For Radio (FFR) vehicles and a new Surveillance Reconnaissance Vehicle (SRV) equipped with a light weapon gun ring in the rear and the ability to carry a swing arm weapon mount on the scuttle when the windscreen is removed and the vehicle is reduced to low profile.

During 2000 a small batch (33) of non-EMC Td5-powered Land Rover Defender vehicles were delivered to the Australian Army for semi-tactical

Land Rover Defender (6 × 6)

Land Rover displayed a (6 × 6) concept vehicle at DVD 2007. This vehicle was originally built to Australian Army Perentie specification but was actually one of a small number of the type exported to Oman. Four Omani examples were shipped back to the UK by Land Rover early 2007 and the best of these was stripped and fully refurbished by Ricardo Vehicle Engineering. The concept vehicle was fitted with a driveline (engine, gearbox, transfer box) from the current 2007 model year Land Rover Defender and originally featured a long range patrol vehicle-type body fitted with a rollcage/weapon ring-mount. For display at Eurosatory and DVD 2008 the demonstrator was configured as a utility truck, fitted with a demountable rear body plus a soft-top and cab doors.

The Defender (6 × 6) shares a common driveline with the standard 2007 model year Defender (with the addition of a third axle) for a high replacement parts commonality and similar driving characteristics. Some body panels are also shared, however, the (6 × 6) is wider by 190 mm and longer by 1.4 m. The (6 × 6) is designed for modular rear bodies and the chassis-cab payload in standard configuration is 3,000 kg. In heavy duty form payload will be around 4,000 kg.

Development of the Land Rover Defender (6 × 6) is currently halted.

Australian Army Land Rover Defender 110 GS (General Service) soft-top powered by an Isuzu 4BD1T 3.9-litre naturally aspirated four-cylinder diesel engine (Ron Fry) 0533610

Under Project Tithonus, a GBP10 million, three-year programme, the British Army was scheduled to refurbish around 3,500 of the 3,950 Defenders that remain in service (Shaun C Connors) 1333731

British Army refurbishment (Project Tithonus)

Some of the oldest Land Rovers in British Army service, the more than 20 year old pre-Defender XD (Wolf) naturally aspirated Defender fleet, were almost certain to have been replaced under the UK MoD's Operational Utility Vehicle System (OUVS) project. However, this replacement was delayed with the stalling of the OUVS programme and to remain a viable asset until OUVS (or any other programme) delivers a replacement, these vehicles required some attention.

To address this issue, it was disclosed in mid-2007 that under Project Tithonus, a GBP10 million, three-year program, that around 3,500 of the 3,950 Defenders that remained in service would be refurbished by ABRO (now Defence Support Group (DSG)). An initial 460 vehicles were upgraded between September 2007 and February 2008, and at the conclusion of the project in March 2010 around 1,230 vehicles had been completed.

The quite basic refurbishment requirement sees cavities wax-injected, the chassis undersealed, the vehicle repainted and 'Wolf' seating (including rear seatbelts) fitted. A rollcage designed by Ricardo Special Vehicles is fitted, but aside from some safety-related improvements (including brakes) the mechanical refurbishment was in most areas limited to Field Standard level.

Only 110 inch wheelbase models were refurbished under Project Tithonus, the smaller number of 90 inch wheelbase Defenders that remain in service will probably be cast, the 90 being too small for most current requirements.

Specifications
(Core Military Vehicle, pre-2007 model year)

	Defender 90	Defender 110	Defender 130
Seating:	1 + 1 (up to 4 in rear)	1 + 1 (up to 8 in rear)	up to 14
Configuration:	4 × 4	4 × 4	4 × 4
Weight:			
(laden)	2,550 kg	3,050 kg	3,500 kg
(laden, Heavy Duty)	/app	3,500 kg	n/app
(unladen)	1,698 kg	n/app	n/app
(unladen, soft-top)	/app	1,875 kg	n/app
(unladen, soft-top, Heavy Duty)	/app	1,885 kg	n/app
(unladen, hard-top)	/app	1,920 kg	n/app
(unladen, hard-top, Heavy Duty)	/app	1,930 kg	n/app
(front axle, rated)	1,200 kg	1,200 kg	n/app
(front axle, rated, Heavy Duty)	n/app	1,580 kg	n/app
(rear axle, rated)	1,500 kg	1,850 kg	n/app
(rear axle, rated, Heavy Duty)	n/app	2,200 kg	n/app
Max load:			
(soft-top)	852 kg	1,175 kg	n/app
(soft-top, Heavy Duty)	n/app	1,605 kg	n/app
(hardtop)	800 kg	1,130 kg	n/app
(hardtop, Heavy Duty)	n/app	1,570 kg	n/app
Towed load:			
(unbraked)	750 kg	750 kg	n/app
(with over-run brakes)	3,500 kg	3,500 kg	n/app
(4-wheel trailer with coupled braking)	4,000 kg	4,000 kg	4,000 kg
Length:	3.88 m	4.44 m	5.13 m
Width:	1.79 m	1.79 m	1.79 m
Height:	2.04 m	2.04 m	2.04 m
Ground clearance: (unladen)	229 mm	215 mm	215 mm
Track:	1.486 m	1.486 m	1.49 m
Wheelbase:	2.36 m	2.79 m	3.23 m
Angle of approach/departure: (unladen)	51°/53°	50°/34°	48°/35°
Fuel capacity:	54 litres	54 litres	54 litres
Max gradient: (unladen)	100%	100%	100%
Side slope: (unladen)	66%	66%	66%
Fording: (unprepared)	500 mm	500 mm	500 mm
Engine:	2.5-litre 4-cylinder in-line 300 Tdi turbocharged and intercooled, water-cooled 4-stroke mechanically-controlled direct injection diesel developing 111 hp (83 kW) at 4,000 rpm and 265 N.m torque at 1,800 rpm. Option: 2.5-litre 5-cylinder in-line Td5 turbocharged and intercooled, water-cooled 4-stroke electronically-controlled direct injection diesel developing 122 hp (91 kW) at 4,200 rpm and 300 N.m torque at 1,950 rpm		
Gearbox:	manual with 5 forward and 1 reverse gears	manual with 5 forward and 1 reverse gears	manual with 5 forward and 1 reverse gears
Clutch:	diaphragm spring	diaphragm spring	diaphragm spring
Transfer box:	2-speed	2-speed	2-speed
Steering:	power-assisted, recirculating ball	power-assisted, recirculating ball	power-assisted, recirculating ball
Turning radius:	6.15 m	6.4 m	7.54 m
Suspension:	beam axles front and rear with coil springs controlled by telescopic shock-absorbers		

Brakes:	dual servo-assisted, discs front and rear	dual servo-assisted, discs front and rear	dual line servo-assisted, discs front and rear
Electrical system:	24 V, 12 or 12/24 V options	12, 12/24 or 24 V	12, 12/24 or 24 V

Status

In production and service with numerous armed forces worldwide; earlier model in service with Australia (see text). In excess of 30,000 Land Rover Defender vehicles have been supplied to military users since 1996, an estimated 70,000 Land Rover Defender vehicles are in service worldwide (see text).

Contractor

Land Rover

Land Rover (4 × 4) Defender XD light vehicles

Development

The Land Rover Defender XD (eXtra Duty) range was developed by Land Rover to meet the UK MoD's requirement for a vehicle to replace its Truck Utility Light/Truck Utility Medium (TUL/TUM) fleets, made up predominantly of Series III Land Rover 2.768 m (109 in) and 2.23 m (88 in) air-portable vehicles. In 1991 the UK MoD issued industry with an Invitation To Tender (ITT) for the new TUL/TUM requirement, some 19 companies originally responding. Only three of those (IVECO Ford, Land Rover and Steyr Daimler Puch) eventually submitted bids, with only Land Rover being awarded a trials contract by the MoD.

Trials commenced in May 1993 with what were effectively the current Land Rover Defender 90 and 110 models fitted with disc brakes all-round and powered by the new 300 Tdi direct injection turbocharged diesel engine. Trials were suspended in September 1993 with the trials vehicles failing to achieve the required levels of reliability. Trials recommenced in September 1994, to conclude in May 1995 with the revised Defender XD (eXtra Duty) vehicles meeting the reliability requirement.

Running alongside the final stages of the TUL/TUM trials were the battlefield ambulance trials. The UK MoD had a requirement to replace a number of older Land Rover-based ambulances and to meet this requirement Land Rover offered a 3.226 m wheelbase (130 model) version of the revised Defender already involved in the TUL/TUM trials. IVECO Ford offered their 40.10 WM model, while Steyr Daimler Puch offered their Pinzgauer. Land Rover was awarded the 796 vehicle battlefield ambulance contract in 1996.

The total value of the two contract awards for Land Rover was in excess of GBP200 million; the contract award to Marshall Specialist Vehicles Ltd for the ambulance bodies was worth GBP15 million.

The first of 7,925 TUL/TUM vehicles ordered entered service with the UK MoD on 1 April 1997, production concluding in October 1998. Approximately 70 XD vehicles were also supplied to the Royal Netherlands Marines in 2000.

The Bowman tactical, secure voice and data communications system is currently being introduced into British Army service and while considerably more flexible than the Clansman system it replaces, it is also far heavier and bulkier. The introduction of Bowman created some issues with the softskin Land Rover fleet and all current Fitted For Radio (FFR) Wolf TUM (Truck Utility Medium; 110 in WB) vehicles underwent a suspension upgrade to accommodate Bowman. The standard Wolf TUM has a GVW of 3,350 kg. The suspension upgrade, known as Project Shoehorn, commenced in July 2005 and had concluded by mid-2007. Project Shoehorn sees the GVW figure increased from 3,350 kg to 3,500 kg, the required modification being the replacement of the rear anti-roll bar with a standard heavy-duty Defender chassis anti-roll bar, the type fitted to

Defender XD 90 (eXtra Duty) of the Military Police (Shaun C Connors)
0533612

Defender XD 110 (eXtra Duty) soft-top (Shaun C Connors)   1124746

the Pulse HS battlefield ambulance. With a GVW of 2,600 kg the FFR Wolf TUL (Truck Utility Light; 90 in WB) is incapable of accommodating the full Bowman fit for reasons of both payload and internal space, and will be fitted with a 'light' Bowman fit.

Project Shoehorn covered 3,446 vehicles (all FFR vehicles but including the WMIK fleet), plus 1,079 General Service (GS) TUM vehicles that had been converted from GS to FFR configuration by 31 March 2007, the GS to FFR conversion required to meet a shortfall of FFR configured vehicles on deployed operations. Additionally, the RAF exchanged 134 FFR TUM vehicles for the same number of GS vehicles with the army.

Recent deployed operations have also required a number of modifications to the Pulse ambulance fleet. From a revised future total fleet requirement figure that will see up to 190 surplus to requirement vehicles available for conversion to other roles, under Project Epione which commenced late-2003 and concluded during 2007, the remaining approximately 600 vehicles were scheduled for conversion from a four-

Land Rover Defender XD 110 (eXtra Duty) soft-top with current generation companion trailer (Shaun C Connors)   1391365

Winter Water variant of the Land Rover Defender XD 90 (eXtra Duty) soft-top operated by the UK Royal Marines. These vehicles can wade in 1.5 m of saltwater for six minutes following preparation; ambulance versions have a reduced 600 mm (+ 500 mm splash) saltwater capability as in around 1 m of water the vehicle becomes buoyant and it is not possible to flood the sterile interior of an ambulance for ballast (Shaun C Connors)   1120421

Defender XD 110 (eXtra Duty) Fitted For Radio (FFR) hardtop (Michael Jerchel) 1124745

Under Project Hebe it is proposed that around 200 surplus battlefield ambulances will be converted to a crew-cab utility vehicle configuration that, among other roles, may replace the Reynolds Boughton RB44 in the Mortar Section Role (Shaun C Connors) 1391364

A stripped (doors and top removed) Defender XD 110 (eXtra Duty) Fitted For Radio (FFR) of the RAF Regiment in Iraq. Note the wire cutter for crew protection from booby traps (Patrick Allen) 1023407

Defender XD 130 (eXtra Duty) battlefield ambulance. As of July 2005, 791 of the 796 delivered remained in service with British Armed Forces (Shaun C Connors) 0121819

stretcher configuration to a two-stretcher configuration that is equipped to carry more medical equipment. Other modifications were to include the installation of an uprated air-conditioning system for hot climates.

Project Epione was not fully realised and not all ambulances were converted. The current fleet now consists of temperate (421 plus 35 Winter/waterised), tropical (228) and desert (107) configurations.

Under Project Hebe it is proposed that around 200 surplus battlefield ambulances will be converted to a crew-cab utility vehicle configuration that, among other roles, may replace the now retired Reynolds Boughton RB44 in the Mortar Section Role. From around 2015 up to a total of 300 battlefield ambulances may become available for conversion.

The current Out of Service Date (OSD) for the XD TUL/TUM fleet has recently been revised from 2017 to 2030.

Description

The Land Rover Defender XD (eXtra Duty) was produced in the three standard Land Rover wheelbases of 2.36 m (XD 90), 2.79 m (XD 110) and 3.226 m (XD 130). The XD 90 and XD 110 models were produced in both soft- and hardtop configuration, and all with a 24 V electrical system. The XD 130 was only produced in ambulance configuration with a body designed and manufactured by Marshall Specialist Vehicles, and again fitted with a 24 V electrical system. Outwardly the appearance of the Defender XD range is not dissimilar to that of the Defender range, indeed there is considerable panel and component commonality between the two. However, the XD chassis frame has stronger cross-members and a new load bed, in some areas being up to six times the strength of comparable Defender models. In addition to strength, this originally (since increased further) allowed for a 20 per cent increase in payload. Springs and dampers are uprated and anti-roll bars are fitted front and rear on the XD 130, front only (pre-Project Shoehorn) on the XD 110. Axles have stronger 6 mm bowl casings as well as uprated half shafts and four pinion differentials. Power steering is fitted, as is enhanced steering protection. A new heavy-duty steel wheel was developed for use with the XD range. Body robustness improvements include a new radiator surround frame, reinforced front bulkhead, and on the TUL/TUM variants, reinforced cab top rails and sills, load floor lateral reinforcement, rear body reinforcement, a full roll cage and rear seat belt anchorage points.

The ambulance bodied version has a GVW of 3,800 kg and was originally procured configured to seat a medical attendant in the rear and in a four-stretcher configuration that could adapt from a four-stretcher

Defender XD 110 (eXtra Duty) R-Weapons Mount Installation Kit (RWMIK) (Shaun C Connors) 1391049

casualty configuration to either a two-stretcher and three-seated, or six-seated casualty configurations. Project Epione, covered elsewhere in this entry, details the current configuration changes.

The Defender XD range is powered by the Land Rover 300 Tdi 2.5-litre 4-cylinder turbocharged direct injection diesel that develops 111 hp at 4,000 rpm and peak torque of 265 N.m at 1,800 rpm, while returning an on-road fuel consumption 100 km per 9.5 litres of fuel at 90 km/h. Transmission is standard Land Rover R380 five-speed gearbox and two-speed transfer box with a lockable centre differential. Front axles are interchangeable across the range, with rear axles common on the XD 110 and XD 130 models. Suspension is by long travel coil springs and hydraulic telescopic shock-absorbers.

Variants

Weapons Mount Installation Kit (WMIK)

The WMIK was developed jointly between Land Rover and Ricardo Special Vehicles for the UK MoD and, following minimal preparation, can be fitted to any Defender XD 110 by four soldiers in under four hours. WMIK gives the vehicles a defensive/offensive capability by allowing the mounting and stable firing of heavy machine guns, grenade launchers or anti-armour missiles from a ring or pulpit mount attached to a full-length roll protection cage. A second, forward firing light machine is also fitted to the vehicle.

Sixteen Air Assault Brigades (and more recently others) currently operate around 250 so-converted vehicles, predominantly on operations in Afghanistan. Further deliveries are underway.

Following deployment to Afghanistan (primarily) and previously Iraq, a number of initiatives to further improve vehicle reliability and mobility plus increase the disposable payload of WMIK while providing the crew with a tactically acceptable level of protection, have been undertaken.

As covered elsewhere in this entry, it was announced mid-2005 that as part of the wider Project Shoehorn the GVW of the WMIK fleet would be increased from 3,350 to 3,500 kg. It was announced mid-2006 that to bolster the WMIK fleet 58, Defender XD vehicles would be converted to WMIK configuration under an Urgent Operational Requirement (UOR) contract by Ricardo Special Vehicles, and that 22 new-build WMIKs with a Ricardo-developed 4,100 kg GVW kit had been ordered from Ricardo Special Vehicles. These 80 vehicles (58 + 22) were collectively known as EWMIK. Further development of the WMIK enhancement package continued and from 2007 as part of a rolling upgrade programme the original 200 in-service WMIK fleet would be uprated to 4,100 kg GVW; upgraded vehicles are known as RWMIK. The primary differences between EWMIK and RWMIK are the latter having a more basic Bowman communications package fit, but an enhanced level of protection for the crew, this protection being built in and not an add-on as with EWMIK.

Late-2009 it was disclosed that the UK MoD was expected to order (as an Urgent Operational Requirement (UOR)) around 120-130 RWMIK+ from Ricardo Special Vehicles, and an initial order for around 70 vehicles was placed. Under this contract all remaining EWMIKs will be upgraded to RWMIK+ standard, the shortfall being the conversion of existing Land Rover Snatch platforms.

The RWMIK+ features a number of automotive improvements over RWMIK these including a power upgrade for the 300 Tdi engine, the fitting of a new ZF automatic gearbox (that has some commonality with the current Pinzgauer light vehicle fleet), a selection of ergonomic, protection, chassis and suspension upgrades, plus an increase in GVW to in excess of 4,500 kg.

It was also disclosed late-2009 that the existing RWMIK fleet (around 200) would be given an ergonomic and functionality upgrade based around some of the features of the RWMIK+.

Land Rover and Ricardo Special Vehicles further developed the WMIK and market the evolved product as the latest version of the Land Rover Defender Rapid Deployment Vehicle (RDV). Full details of this and the WMIK programme can be found in the Special attack vehicles section.

Winter Water

The Defender XD TUL/TUM contract required for the first time that vehicles be delivered with enhanced cold weather and wading abilities built in. Originally two programmes, these merged for practical and cost reasons and a total of 686 Winter Water Defender XD vehicles were delivered. The bulk of these are operated by the Royal Marines. These vehicles are modified to operate in temperatures as low as –49°C, and following a maximum of two hours preparation can wade in 1.5 m of saltwater for up to six minutes.

Specifications

	XD90	XD110	XD130 ambulance
Cab seating:	1 + 1 (6 in rear)	1 + 1 (8 in rear)	2 + patients
Configuration:	4 × 4	4 × 4	4 × 4
Weight:			
(GVW)	2,600 kg	3,344 kg (3,500 kg following Project Shoehorn)	3,800 kg
(max load)	600 kg	1,200 kg	1,200 kg
(towed load)	up to 4,000 kg	up to 4,000 kg	n/avail
Length:	3.84 m	4.55 m	5.19 m
Width:	1.79 m	1.79 m	2.09 m
Height:	2.03 m	2.08 m	2.57 m
Ground clearance:	240 mm	230 mm	200 mm
Track:			
(front)	1.52 m	1.52 m	1.52 m
(rear)	1.51 m	1.51 m	1.51 m
Wheelbase:	2.36 m	2.79 m	3.23 m
Fuel capacity:	55 litres	82 litres	n/avail
Fording:	600 mm (Winter Water, 1.5 m of saltwater for 6 mins following preparation)	600 mm (Winter Water, 1.5 m of saltwater for 6 mins following preparation)	600 mm (36 vehicles have a 600 mm saltwater (+ 500 mm splash) capability)

Engine:	300 Tdi 2.5-litre 4-cylinder in-line turbocharged water-cooled 4-stroke direct injection diesel developing 111 hp at 4,000 rpm	300 Tdi 2.5-litre 4-cylinder in-line turbocharged water-cooled 4-stroke direct injection diesel developing 111 hp at 4,000 rpm	300 Tdi 2.5-litre 4-cylinder in-line turbocharged water-cooled direct injection 4-stroke diesel developing 111 hp at 4,000 rpm
Gearbox:	manual, 5 forward and 1 reverse gears	manual, 5 forward and 1 reverse gears	manual, 5 forward and 1 reverse gears
Clutch:	diaphragm spring	diaphragm spring	diaphragm spring
Transfer box:	2-speed	2-speed	2-speed
Steering:	power-assisted, recirculating ball	power-assisted, recirculating ball	power-assisted, recirculating ball
Suspension:	coil springs and telescopic shock-absorbers, front and rear	coil springs and hydraulic telescopic shock-absorbers, front and rear	coil springs and hydraulic telescopic shock-absorbers, front and rear
Brakes:	dual line servo-assisted, discs front and rear	dual line servo-assisted, discs front and rear	dual line servo-assisted, discs front and rear
Electrical system:	24 V	24 V	24 V

Status

Production complete. In service with the British Army, 1411 XD 90, 6514 XD 110 and 796 XD 130 ambulances delivered (some lost to hostile action on deployment), and Royal Netherlands Marines (71, delivered around 2000).

Contractor

Land Rover

Land Rover (4 × 4) 564 kg air-portable light vehicle

Development

The Land Rover (4 × 4) 564 kg air-portable light vehicle was designed and developed by Rover in conjunction with the then Military Vehicles and Engineering Establishment (MVEE) to meet the special air-portable requirements of the British Army, Royal Air Force and Royal Marines. It was shown for the first time at the Commercial Motor Show at Earls Court in September 1968.

Production was phased out during 1985 and the Land Rover (4 × 4) 564 kg air-portable light vehicle is no longer in service with British Armed Forces, but limited numbers remain in service worldwide.

Description

The layout of the vehicle is similar to other Land Rovers, with the engine at the front, driver and two passengers in the centre and cargo area at the rear, with a drop tailgate and a bench seat down either side.

The engine, transmission, axles, suspension and brakes were from the commercial 2.23 m (88 in) Land Rover modified for military use.

The main feature of this vehicle is that the hood, body sides, doors, windscreen, bumpers and spare wheel can easily be removed to facilitate transport by aircraft or helicopter.

The basic model has a 12 V electrical system but a 24 V Fitted-For-Radio (FFR) version was available with the two batteries installed between the front seats in place of the third seat in the 12 V model.

Air-portable (4 × 4) 564 kg Land Rover of the Saudi Arabian National Guard (SANG). This vehicle is clearly used as a run-about (Rick Skipper) 0524811

Variants

Anti-tank

To meet the requirements of an undisclosed foreign army, Marshall of Cambridge (Engineering) Ltd (now Marshall Specialist Vehicles) designed a 106 mm Land Rover gun vehicle which entered service in 1977. This is the standard vehicle modified to mount a 106 mm M40 recoilless rifle in the rear of the vehicle. The design permits forward arc of fire of 180°. Seats for the crew of the weapon and stowage of 106 mm and 12.7 mm/0.50 in ranging machine gun ammunition are provided. A blast shield is fitted to the bonnet and a barrel clamp is fitted to the dashboard. Known users of this model included Saudi Arabia and Sudan.

Specifications

564 kg air-portable LV
Cab seating: 1 + 2
Configuration: 4 × 4
Weight:
   (laden) 2,020 kg
   (unladen) 1,386 kg
   (stripped down) 1,206 kg
   (max load) 564 kg
   (towed load) 1,130 kg
Load area: 1.14 × 1.40 m
Length: 3.65 m
Width: 1.52 m
Height:
   (overall) 1.95 m
   (reduced) 1.47 m
   (load area) 710 mm
Ground clearance: 210 mm
Track: 1.31 m
Wheelbase: 2.23 m
Angle of approach/departure: 49°/36° (58°/38° in stripped down form)
Max speed: (road) 105 km/h
Range: 600 km
Fuel capacity: 90 litres
Max gradient:
   (high) 39%
   (low) 115%
Fording: 500 mm
Engine: 2.286-litre 4-cylinder in-line OHV water-cooled petrol developing 70 hp (52 kW) at 4,000 rpm
Gearbox: manual with 4 forward and 1 reverse gears
Clutch: single dry plate
Transfer box: 2-speed
Steering: recirculating ball
Turning radius: 6.4 m
Suspension: semi-elliptic leaf springs and hydraulic shock-absorbers, front and rear
Tyres: 6.50 × 16 or 7.50 × 16
Brakes:
   (main) hydraulic dual line, servo-assisted, drums all-round
   (parking) drum, mechanical on transmission
Electrical system: 12 V (24 V optional)
Battery: 1 × 12 V

Status

Production complete. Believed to remain in service in limited numbers with Guyana, Hong Kong, Indonesia (812 delivered), Jamaica, Libya, Saudi Arabia, Sudan and possibly others.

Contractor

Land Rover

Land Rover Discovery (4 × 4) light vehicle

Development

The Land Rover Discovery (4 × 4) light vehicle was first announced in November 1989 as a three-door estate; a five-door version was introduced during 1990. The vehicle was designed to meet the requirements of customers requiring the ability to operate off-road, yet retain a degree of style for driving on roads. In terms of luxury and refinement, the vehicle sits between the Land Rover Defender and the Range Rover in the Land Rover product line up.

The Land Rover Discovery in standard form is best described as suited to rear echelon, command, control, communication, internal security duties, or use by governmental, humanitarian or aid organisations. The type was used extensively by armed forces in command and support roles during the 1990 to 1991 Gulf War and has subsequently been used in numbers for UN and peacekeeping roles, notably in the former Yugoslavia.

The base vehicle has proven suitable for conversion or adaptation and a number of companies worldwide offer conversions. Land Rover Special Vehicles offer a range of factory approved conversions including vehicles for police and paramilitary applications. A range of paramedic ambulances is also available in standard and extended wheelbase versions with medical and rescue equipment options.

Land Rover Discovery 3 of the German Bundeswehr (Land Rover) 1185457

The three-door model with van-type rear body, the Discovery Commercial, was available. The Discovery Commercial IEDD was specifically developed around this to meet the needs of Improvised Explosive Device Disposal (IEDD) teams. This variant has a body containing stowage racks for tools and equipment, including the remote-control Wheelbarrow Mark 8 and remote monitoring equipment.

The Discovery Series II was launched in October 1998, this being replaced by the all new Discovery 3 in 2004. The fourth-generation Discovery 4 was launched in 2009. These models, particularly the Discovery 3 and Discovery 4, feature a vast array of luxury and electronic equipment as standard, making them progressively less suited to operations in a tactical environment or one with low levels of support infrastructure.

Description

The Land Rover Discovery (4 × 4) light vehicle (Series I and Series II) is based on a box-section chassis to which exterior aluminium alloy body panels are fitted. Three- or five-door variants were standard, although no three-door or van-type bodies were available in the Series II or Discovery 3 range. The main distinguishing feature of the Series II range of was a slightly larger rear body and longer overhang; the Discovery 3 and Discovery 4 are both distinctly different from the earlier models, being far more aesthetically pleasing and less functional in appearance.

Throughout its production run the Land Rover Discovery has been fitted with a number of power plants, but the majority of Series I vehicles will be fitted with a variant of the Land Rover V-8 petrol or the Land Rover 200 or 300 Tdi four-cylinder diesel engines. Series II models will be fitted with either a four-litre version of the V-8 petrol or the five-cylinder Td5 diesel engine. Three engines have been offered in the Discovery 3: a Jaguar-derived 4.4-litre V-8 petrol, a Land Rover 2.7-litre V-6 diesel and, for some markets, a petrol 4.0 V-6. The Discovery 4 is offered with the choice of either a 2.7-litre of three-litre V6 diesel. Transmission for Series I and II models was a five-speed manual or a four-speed automatic gearbox and a two-speed transfer box, with permanent four-wheel drive and a lockable centre differential. Discovery 3 petrol models featured a six-speed automatic transmission, this optional in the diesel which features a six-speed manual transmission as standard. On Series I and II models beam axles are coupled to a long travel coil spring suspension all-round. Discovery 3 models have independent suspension, coil on the base model, air on all others. All Discovery 4 models have variable ride height air-suspension.

Data given in the accompanying specifications table relate to the Series II Discovery introduced in 1998, plus basic specifications for the armoured Discovery 3.

Variants

Range Rover Sport

The Range Rover Sport which became available from late-2005 is a performance orientated (4 × 4) Sports Utility Vehicle (SUV) in the mould of the BMW X5 and Porsche Cayenne, and while styling cues and name are certainly taken from the Range Rover product, the Range Rover Sport is actually based on the Land Rover Discovery 3 platform.

Finnish Army Land Rover Discovery (4 × 4) light vehicle operating in Kosovo (Richard Stickland) 1124761

As a performance orientated SUV, any use of the Range Rover Sport by governmental organisations or similar is likely to be limited.

Armoured Discovery 3 and Discovery 4
The armoured Discovery 3 was introduced in 2008. The vehicle is based on the standard Discovery 3 platform, uprated where required, and provides certified B6 ballistic and blast protection in accordance with European Standard EN1522.

Modifications to the standard vehicle include runflat tyres, Alcon six-pot aluminium brake callipers (front), four-pot (rear), uprated front and rear anti-roll bars/bushes and uprated front and rear dampers. Maximum speed is governed to 100 mph/160 kph and the engine can be modified to run at EURO 2 emission compliance levels on low grade fuel.

Armoured versions of the latest Discovery 4 will be available in the future.

Specifications

Model	Series II Discovery	Armoured Discovery 3
Cab seating:	1 + 4 (2 extra seats available)	1 + up to 4
Configuration:	4 × 4	4 × 4
Weight:		
(laden)	2,750-2,880 kg	4,050 kg
(unladen)	2,150-2,280 kg	3,550-3,635 kg
(towed load)	up to 3,500 kg when braked	n/app
Length:	4.705 m	4.848 m
Width: (over mirrors)	2.19 m	2.19 m
Height:	1.98 m	1.837 to 1.887 m
Ground clearance:	208 mm	to exhaust; 240 mm (running) to 310 mm (off-road)
Track:		
(front)	1.54 m	1.605 m
(rear)	1.56 m	1.605 m
Wheelbase:	2.54 m	2.885 m
Angle of approach/departure:	31°/25°	37°/30°
Max speed:		
(Td5 diesel)	157 km/h	n/app
(V-8 petrol)	170 km/h	n/app
(TDV6 diesel)	n/app	160 km/h
Fuel capacity:	93 litres	82.3 litres
Engine:	Land Rover Td5 2.5-litre 5-cylinder turbocharged water-cooled diesel developing 137 hp (102 kW) or Land Rover 4-litre V-8 water-cooled petrol developing 184 hp (137 kW)	Land Rover TDV6 2.7-litre V6 turbocharged water-cooled common rail diesel developing 190 hp (142 kW) at 1,4000 rpm and 440 N.m at 1,800 rpm with EURO 2 or EURO 4 options available
Gearbox:	manual, 5 forward and 1 reverse gears or automatic, 4 forward and 1 reverse gears	automatic with 6 forward and 1 reverse gears
Transfer box:	2-speed giving permanent 4-wheel drive with lockable centre differential	2-speed with computer controlled progressively locking centre differential
Steering:	recirculating ball with steering damper and power assistance	n/avail
Turning radius:	5.95 m	5.725 (wall)
Suspension:	coil springs, hydraulic shock-absorbers; axle location by radius arms	electronic air suspension
Brakes:		
(main)	hydraulic, dual circuit with servo assistance, discs front and rear	ventilated discs, front 317 mm, rear 325 mm; 4-channel ABS
(parking)	mechanical drum on transmission	n/avail
Electrical system:	12 V	12 V

Status
In production. In service with UK and other armed forces, and numerous governmental, humanitarian and aid organisations.

Contractor
Land Rover

Pinzgauer 716 (4 × 4) and 718 (6 × 6) vehicles 1985-2002

Development
Diesel-powered versions of the Pinzgauer (4 × 4) and (6 × 6) ranges were developed by Steyr-Daimler-Puch of Austria from 1983 onwards, and were first shown during 1985. Originally, the series was produced in Austria, in July 2000, and following a seven-year period of acting as the UK agent and importer for the Pinzgauer range, Automotive Technik Limited (ATL) of the UK assumed a licence to market worldwide and manufacture the Pinzgauer range.

In April 2005 it was announced that Stewart & Stevenson of the US (manufacturer of the Family of Medium Tactical Vehicles (FMTV)) had acquired ATL. Armor Holdings Inc announced in February 2006 it was to acquire Stewart & Stevenson. From May 2006 Automotive Technik Ltd became known as Pinzgauer Ltd. It was announced in August 2007 that Armor Holdings had been acquired by BAE Systems, Pinzgauer Ltd becoming BAE Systems Land Systems Guildford.

In January 2008 BAE Systems announced it planned to discontinue the production of the Pinzgauer 1 vehicle and close its manufacturing facilities at Guildford and Fareham. A support business (primarily for British and New Zealand Pinzgauer fleets) infrastructure was retained at the Guildford site, which has now been relocated to Telford. Development of the Pinzgauer 2 (announced in September 2007) was transitioned to BAE Systems Land Systems in South Africa, however, according to BAE Systems, further analysis of the potential market (for Pinzgauer 2) revealed insufficient market interest to continue development. Production of the armoured Vector (based on Pinzgauer 1) continued at BAE Systems Newcastle, UK facility.

Throughout their Austrian (1985 to 2000) and UK (2000 to 2002) production runs the 716 and 718 diesel-powered Pinzgauer ranges were continually revised and upgraded, however the standard model designations for the main production versions remained. These were:
- Pinzgauer 716 M
- Pinzgauer 716 MK
- Pinzgauer 716 K
- Pinzgauer 716 T
- Pinzgauer 718 M
- Pinzgauer 718 MK
- Pinzgauer 718 K
- Pinzgauer 718 T

A more detailed overview of each version is covered in the variants section of this entry.

The first diesel-powered Pinzgauer model is referred to as the Turbo D. In 1990 the Turbo D model was upgraded, the upgrade including an intercooler for the engine which resulted in more power. The upgraded model is referred to as the P93.

Pinzgauer 718M (6 × 6) Turbo D of the Thai Navy (Gordon Arthur)   1391194

Pinzgauer 718 M (6 × 6) of the Royal Army of Oman (Richard Stickland)
0558996

Pinzgauer 718 M (6 × 6) configured as a recovery vehicle for the Royal Army of Oman (BAE Systems)   0109498

Pinzgauer 718 M (6 × 6) of the Saudi Arabian National Guard (SANG) (Rick Skipper)   0524816

Pinzgauer 718 (6 × 6) of Saudi Arabian Armed Forces. The ambulance body is supplied by EMPL (Rick Skipper)   0524807

Pinzgauer Turbo D (6 × 6) licence built in Malaysia by DRB-HICOM Defence Technologies (T J Gander)   0109493

British Army Pinzgauer (4 × 4) GS Soft Top (Patrick Allen)   1194244

The first diesel-powered Pinzgauer vehicles to enter service with the UK MoD were delivered in 1995. In order to meet the UK's requirement further improvements to the P93 model were made, these including a payload increase. The resultant model became the standard production variant; it retained the P93 designation.

The British Army took delivery of an initial 394 Pinzgauer (4 × 4) vehicles. These were based on the 716 M model and designated Truck Utility Medium (Heavy Duty) (TUM(HD)) by the British Army. They were issued for service with Airmobile and Commando forces, some of them as artillery tractors for 105 mm Light Guns.

The British Army's original TUM(HD) fleet was made up of the following variants:
- GS Soft Top
- GS Soft Top with winch
- Waterproofed GS Soft Top
- Waterproofed Winterised GS Soft Top
- Waterproofed Winterised GS Soft Top with winch
- Waterproofed Winterised FFR Soft Top
- Waterproofed Winterised FFR Soft Top with winch
- FFR Hard Top
- FFR Hard Top with winch
- Waterproofed Winterised FFR Hard Top
- Waterproofed Winterised FFR Hard Top with winch (the fording ability of the waterproofed Pinzgauer is increased from the standard 700 mm of fresh water to 1.5 m of salt water).

The first part UK-produced Pinzgauer vehicles delivered to the UK MoD by the then Automotive Technik Limited were Trauma Management Vehicles (TMV); the TMV is based on the (6 × 6) 718 VAB model. Approximately 60 vehicles were involved in the order and these were delivered between 1998-2000. They were followed by the first of six vehicles based on the 718 HVB model and configured for a psychological operations (psyops) campaign in Afghanistan. The UOR for these was issued in November 2001, a contract was awarded in December 2001, and the first vehicle was delivered in April 2002. Also delivered under a UOR were the unspecified number of Sampling and Investigation of Biological Chemical and Radiological Agents (SIBCRA) vehicles delivered mid-2002. Around the same time a number of 718 MK TUM (HD) (6 × 6) vehicles were procured under a separate UOR for Explosive Ordnance Disposal (EOD) operations.

Automotive Technik also built a number of Pinzgauers for export. The first were an unspecified number of (6 × 6) recovery vehicles delivered to the Sultanate of Oman to support the Army's fleet of over 1,200 (mostly 6 × 6) Pinzgauers. Designed to carry a crew of four, these recovery vehicles are fitted with a rear-mounted electric hoist and front-mounted winch. Saudi Arabia also received at least 10 × 718 K model hard-top based command vehicles and 20 ambulance vehicles with prefabricated shelter-type bodies manufactured and installed by EMPL of Austria.

During 2002 the then Automotive Technik announced revised specification Pinzgauer models. These featured increased operational weights, performance and a EURO 3 emissions compliant Volkswagen five-cylinder diesel engine developing 130 hp. The final pre-EURO 3 Pinzgauers delivered were a quantity of TUM (HD) General Service (GS) vehicles supplied to the UK MoD under a UOR in early 2003.

In 2005 the designation X-treme Mobility (X-M) was announced following a minor specification revision centring on brakes and traction control.

The Pinzgauer 2 fitted with a EURO 4 compliant diesel engine was announced in September 2007. EURO 3 models were to remain available.

Full details of all post-2002 vehicles can be found elsewhere in this section.

Diesel-powered Pinzgauer models have been licence kit-produced in Malaysia by DRB-HICOM Defence Technologies Sdn Bhd (DEFTECH) in both (4 × 4) (HICOM Truck 1 ton (4 × 4)) and (6 × 6) (HICOM 2 ton (6 × 6)) forms.

Description

In appearance and general layout the (4 × 4) and (6 × 6) versions of the diesel-powered Pinzgauer models resemble the earlier petrol-powered models (full details of which can be found elsewhere in this section). The

Royal Air Force Pinzgauer (6 × 6) configured as a rapid intervention ambulance (T J Gander)   0100305

Pinzgauer 718 K (6 × 6) of the Austrian Army operating in the EOD role in Kosovo (Michael Jerchel)   1124744

main change was to a water-cooled and turbocharged six-cylinder diesel engine. Other changes included an increase in wheelbase on both the (4 × 4) and (6 × 6), plus a widening of the track. Disc brakes and power steering were introduced, changes were made to the driver's position instrument layout, and a larger fuel tank fitted to improve range. A five-speed manual gearbox remained standard, but on later models a four-speed automatic transmission became available as an option.

The (4 × 4) version has an automatic level control system acting on the rear axle. A pneumatic system is controlled by sensors that raise and lower the vehicle superstructure to suit the load being carried to maintain suspension travel.

Variants

Pinzgauer 716 M
(4 × 4) personnel carrier with canvas top carrying the driver and up to nine passengers.

Pinzgauer 716 MK
(4 × 4) cargo or personnel carrier with closed body carrying the driver and one front passenger, plus approximately 1,250 kg of payload or eight passengers in the rear compartment.

Pinzgauer 716 K
(4 × 4) command vehicle carrying the driver and one front passenger plus three seats in the rear compartment (seating for a further five passengers is an option).

Pinzgauer 716 T
(4 × 4) carrier for shelters and weapon systems carrying the driver, one passenger and approximately 1,300 kg of payload.

Pinzgauer 718 M
(6 × 6) personnel carrier with canvas top carrying the driver and up to 13 passengers.

Pinzgauer 718 MK
(6 × 6) cargo or personnel carrier with closed body carrying the driver and one front passenger plus approximately 1,700 kg of payload or 12 passengers in the rear compartment.

Pinzgauer 718 K
(6 × 6) command vehicle carrying the driver, one front passenger and three seats in the rear compartment (seating for seven more passengers is an option).

Pinzgauer 718 T
(6 × 6) carrier vehicle for shelters and weapon systems carrying the driver, one passenger and approximately 1,800 kg of payload.

Specifications
(The data in this table below, refers to British Army Pinzgauer 716 M 4 × 4 and Pinzgauer 718 M 6 × 6 models)

Status
Production now complete. Prior to 2002 Pinzgauer models were supplied to Angola, Australia, Austria, Croatia, Cyprus, France, Germany, Ghana, Jordan, Kenya, Malaysia, Nigeria, Oman (over 1,200), Pakistan, Papua New Guinea, Poland, Saudi Arabia, Seychelles, Sudan, Sweden, Switzerland, Thailand, Tunisia, UAE, UK (over 400 (4 × 4) and over 100 (6 × 6)), US, Venezuela, the former Yugoslavia and possibly other undisclosed countries. Licence-production occurred in Malaysia.

Contractor
Steyr-Daimler-Puch Fahrzeugtechnik AG & Co KG

Enquiries to:
BAE Systems Land & Armaments, Telford, UK.

Model	Pinzgauer 716 M	Pinzgauer 718 M
Configuration:	4 × 4	6 × 6
Weight:	2,350 kg (approx)	2,650 kg
GVW:	3,850 kg	4,850 kg
Max load:	1,400 kg	1,850 kg
Max towed load:	2,000 kg	2,000 kg
Length:	4.528 m	5.26 m
Width:	1.8 m	1.8 m
Height:	2.045 m	2.045 m
Ground clearance:	345 mm	335 mm
Track:	1.52 m	1.52 m
Wheelbase:	2.4 m	2.2 + 0.98 m
Angle of approach/departure:	40/45°	40/45°
Max speed:	122 km/h	112 km/h
Fuel capacity:	145 litres	145 litres
Gradient:	100%	84%
Side slope: (body/load dependant)	88%	88%
Fording:	700 mm	700 mm
Engine:	2.383-litre 6-cylinder in-line turbocharged and intercooled water-cooled 4-stroke diesel developing 115 hp at 4,350 rpm	
Transmission:	ZF S5 18/3 manual with 5 forward and 1 reverse gears or ZF 4HP 22 automatic with 4 forward and 1 reverse gears	
Transfer box:	2-speed	2-speed
Steering:	ZF Gemmer	ZF Gemmer
Turning radius:	5.75 m	6.5 m
Suspension:	coil springs front and rear (4 × 4); coil springs (front), parabolic leaf springs (rear) (6 × 6)	
Brakes:	dual circuit, power-assisted, discs all-round	
Electrical system:	24 V	24 V

Pinzgauer (4 × 4) and (6 × 6) vehicles 2003 onwards

Development

In July 2000 it was announced that Automotive Technik Limited (ATL) of Guildford had assumed a licence to market worldwide and manufacture the Pinzgauer range and that all future production would be carried out in the UK. Automotive Technik Limited (ATL) had previously (since 1993) been the UK agent and importer for Pinzgauer vehicles.

At Eurosatory 2002 the then Automotive Technik Limited displayed an early production example of an upgraded EURO 3 emissions compliant Pinzgauer model. EURO 3 models were developed in co-operation with Roush Technologies (now Revolve Technologies) and, compared with their immediate predecessors, feature increased payloads and GVW, plus improved performance. EURO 3 models are fitted with a Volkswagen diesel engine coupled to a ZF automatic transmission as standard.

By mid-2003 production of all pre-EURO 3 specification Pinzgauer models had ceased. Following the introduction of EURO 3 engines, Pinzgauer variant designations underwent some revision. These revisions included the dropping of the 716 and 718 nomenclature for the (4 × 4) and (6 × 6) variants, respectively, and the introduction of a more logical base model letter designation system. The revised designations are used throughout this entry although, for reference purposes, earlier designations accompany individual model descriptions or are used in text where appropriate.

The first order placed for the EURO 3 generation Pinzgauer model was from the UK Royal Navy for nine 718 HVB (6 × 6) models for use in the Explosive Ordnance Disposal (EOD) role. The contract was awarded late 2001, with deliveries scheduled to take place between 2002 and 2004. These vehicles are deployed (three at each) at the Royal Navy's Fleet Diving Units at Portsmouth, Plymouth and Faslane.

Deliveries of 20 Pinzgauer platforms involved in the UK's future Airborne STand-Off Radar (ASTOR) battlefield reconnaissance system. The six Tactical Ground Station (TGS) vehicles are based on the 718 T model (now P) and are fitted with specialist shelter bodies supplied by Marshall Specialist Vehicles were completed during 2002. Acquired under a GBP930 million (USD1.4 billion) contract, the ASTOR system had been expected to achieve an in-service date of around mid-2005. ASTOR was declared in service in December 2008.

In March 2003 the then Automotive Technik was awarded a GBP7 million (USD11 million) to supply approximately 100 718 M (6 × 6) (now GS) Truck Utility Medium - Heavy Duty (TUM (HD)) vehicles to carry the Army's High Velocity Missile (HVM) close air-defence weapon system. The Royal Artillery previously used 716 M (4 × 4) TUM (HD) Pinzgauer variants in this role. These were designed to operate with a single axle trailer as there is insufficient space inside the vehicle to transport all the required equipment. The larger (6 × 6) TUM (HD) can accommodate the complete package and has seats for a crew of four as well as carrying the tripod-based Lightweight Multiple Launcher, the Air Defence Alert Device, 10 HVM missiles plus logistics back-up. If required, the (6 × 6) vehicle can also be deployed with a trailer. Vehicles were scheduled to enter operational service in 2004, although not all are now used in the HVM role.

In July 2003, the UK's then Defence Procurement Agency (DPA) awarded the then Automotive Technik a contract worth more than GBP20 million to supply 360 Pinzgauer vehicles in TUM - Fitted For Radio (TUM (FFR)) configuration. This was the largest single contract won since production of the Pinzgauer range of vehicles transferred to the UK. The British Army TUM (FFR) is based on the Pinzgauer 716 MK (4 × 4) hard-top (now HT). The vehicles are used for the Army's General Dynamics UK Bowman radio communications system. The first 130 vehicles involved in the order had been delivered by late 2004, with the balance delivered during 2005. These vehicles are fitted with an Anti-lock Braking System (ABS), Electronic Traction Control (ETC) and Electronic Brake Distribution (EBD).

During mid-2003, the DPA also placed an order with Automotive Technik for approximately 40 (4 × 4) TUMs for use in the nuclear, biological and chemical defence role. Prior to this contract award, Automotive Technik had previously converted a number of in-service TUM (HD) vehicles under an Urgent Operational Requirement (UOR).

New Zealand issued a Request for Tender (RfT) in July 2002 for 321 Light Operational Vehicles (LOVs) to replace the reminder of its V8-powered Land Rover fleet. The selected vehicle was required to be capable of

About to be airlifted by a Royal Air Force HC2 Chinook helicopter, a Pinzgauer 6 × 6 C (718 K) command variant (Patrick Allen) 1183281

operating alongside the Army's 105 General Dynamics LAV III light armoured vehicles.

It was announced in April 2004 that New Zealand had signed a contract for the delivery of 188 Pinzgauers to meet the first part of the Army's LOV requirement. The first vehicles involved were delivered late 2004, with deliveries to be completed within 18 months. All vehicles involved are the EURO 3 (6 × 6) Pinzgauer and in the following configurations: 95 general service; 57 command-and-control; 13 special operations; 15 shelter and eight ambulance. The contract value was estimated at NZD52 million.

In May 2004 it was announced that the then ATL had been selected as preferred bidder for the second and final part of the LOV requirement, and in June the New Zealand government approved the purchase of a further 133 LOVs. This second order (bringing the total to 321) comprised 23 armoured and 42 unarmoured C2 variants and 37 armoured and 31 unarmoured weapons carrier variants. Deliveries were completed mid-2006. The total cost of the Pinzgauer LOV purchase has been confirmed at NZD93 million. The sole competitor for the Pinzgauer was the AM General HMMWV.

During 2005 the UK MoD ordered a further 15 Pinzgauer (6 × 6) C vehicles for use with the Airborne STand-Off Radar (ASTOR) battlefield reconnaissance system and 36 (6 × 6) C Bowman radio/command vehicles for the RAF. These two orders brought the total number of vehicles ordered by the UK MoD since 2002 to in excess of 600.

In April 2005, it was announced that Stewart & Stevenson of the US (then manufacturer of the Family of Medium Tactical Vehicles (FMTV)) had acquired ATL.

By late 2005, the revised X-treme Mobility (X-M) designation had been adopted for vehicles fitted with ABS, ETC and EBD. These features became standard production specification.

During 2006 armouring specialist S MacNeillie and Son Ltd was awarded a contract to supply 114 composite appliqué armour kits to the British Army for installation on unarmoured Pinzgauer (4 × 4) and (6 × 6) vehicles deployed overseas.

Armor Holdings Inc announced in February 2006 it was to acquire Stewart & Stevenson. From May 2006 Automotive Technik Ltd became known as Pinzgauer Ltd and some model designations were revised. It was announced on 1 August 2007 that Armor Holdings had been acquired by BAE Systems, Pinzgauer Ltd becoming part of BAE Systems Land Systems, now BAE Systems Land & Armaments.

Displayed at DVD 2005, rear three-quarter view of a Pinzgauer 718 K (now designated 718 C) (6 × 6) five-door hard-top ASTOR system vehicle of the British Army (Patrick Allen) 1146300

New Zealand Army Pinzgauer GS (718M) (Gordon Arthur) 1340328

Pinzgauer (4 × 4) and (6 × 6) vehicles

Model	4 × 4 (716) GS (M), GS HT (MK) and C (K)	6 × 6 (718) GS (M), GS HT (MK), C (K) and P (T)	6 × 6 (718) HVB	6 × 6 PPV	6 × 6 EP (Vector)
Configuration:	4 × 4	6 × 6	6 × 6	6 × 6	6 × 6
Weight: (GVW)	3,850 kg	5,000 kg	5,000 kg	6,300 kg	6,500 kg
Payload: (max)	1,400 kg	2,500 kg	2,500 kg	1,200 kg	1,400 kg
Axle loads:					
(front)	1,875 kg	1,875 kg	1,875 kg	2,400 kg	2,900 kg
(rear)	1,975 kg	1,900 kg per axle	1,900 kg per axle	1,900 kg per axle	1,900 kg per axle
Towed load:					
(recommended)	3,000 kg	2,000 kg	2,000 kg	1,000 kg	1,000 kg
(maximum)	5,000 kg	5,000 kg	5,000 kg	1,000 kg	1,000 kg
GCW: (maximum)	7,500 kg	7,500 kg	7,500 kg	7,500 kg	7,500 kg
Length:	4.528 m	5.308 m	2.44 m	5.31 m	5.5 m
Width:	1.8 m	1.8 m	2.06 m	1.8 m	1.8 m
Height:	2.045 m	2.045 m	2.44 m	2.045 m	2.06 m
Ground clearance:	360 mm	360 mm	360 mm	360 mm	360 mm
Track: (front and rear)	1.52 m	1.52 m	1.52 m	1.52 m	1.52 m
Wheelbase:	2.4 m	2.2 + 0.98 m	2.2 + 0.98 m	2.2 + 0.98 m	2.2 + 0.98 m
Angle of approach/ departure:	40°/45°	40°/45°	40°/45°	40°/45°	40°/45°
Max speed:	120 km/h	120 km/h	120 km/h	120 km/h	120 km/h
Max range: (145-litre tank)	800 km	800 km	800 km	800 km	800 km
Fuel capacity:	145 litres	145 litres[1]	145 litres	145 litres	145 litres
Max gradient: (laden)	100%	100%	100%	100%	100%
Max sideslope:	100%	100%	100%	100%	100%
Fording:	700 mm fresh water (unprepared). Up to 1.5 m salt water with preparation on certain models	700 mm fresh water (unprepared). Up to 1.5 m salt water with preparation on certain models	700 mm fresh water (unprepared). Up to 1.5 m salt water with preparation on certain models	700 mm fresh water (unprepared). Up to 1.5 m salt water with preparation on certain models	700 mm fresh water (unprepared). Up to 1.5 m salt water with preparation on certain models
Engine:	Volkswagen 2.46-litre 5-cylinder turbocharged and intercooled water cooled 4-stroke water-cooled diesel developing 130 hp at 4,500 rpm and 280 Nm torque between 1,400 and 2,400 rpm	Volkswagen 2.46-litre 5-cylinder turbocharged and intercooled water cooled 4-stroke water-cooled diesel developing 130 hp at 4,500 rpm and 280 Nm torque between 1,400 and 2,400 rpm	Volkswagen 2.46-litre 5-cylinder turbocharged and intercooled water cooled 4-stroke water-cooled diesel developing 130 hp at 4,500 rpm and 280 Nm torque between 1,400 and 2,400 rpm	Volkswagen 2.46-litre 5-cylinder turbocharged and intercooled water cooled 4-stroke water-cooled diesel developing 130 hp at 4,500 rpm and 280 Nm torque between 1,400 and 2,400 rpm	Volkswagen 2.46-litre 5-cylinder turbocharged and intercooled water cooled 4-stroke water-cooled diesel developing 130 hp at 4,500 rpm and 280 Nm torque between 1,400 and 2,400 rpm
Gearbox:	ZF 4-speed automatic	ZF 4-speed automatic	ZF 4-speed automatic	ZF 4-speed automatic	ZF 4-speed automatic
Transfer box:	ZF 2-speed, full synchromesh	ZF 2-speed, full synchromesh	ZF 2-speed, full synchromesh	ZF 2-speed, full synchromesh	ZF 2-speed, full synchromesh
Steering:	ZF Gemmer, power-assisted	ZF Gemmer, power-assisted	ZF Gemmer, power-assisted	ZF Gemmer, power-assisted	ZF Gemmer, power-assisted
Turning radius:	5.75 m	6.5 m	6.5 m	6.5 m	6.5 m
Suspension:					
(front)	coil springs, hollow rubber bump stops, hydraulic double-acting shock-absorbers	coil springs, hollow rubber bump stops, hydraulic double-acting shock-absorbers	coil springs, hollow rubber bump stops, hydraulic double-acting shock-absorbers	coil springs, hollow rubber bump stops, hydraulic double-acting shock-absorbers	coil springs, hollow rubber bump stops, hydraulic double-acting shock-absorbers
(rear)	coil springs, hollow rubber bump stops, hydraulic double-acting shock-absorbers with self-levelling (4 × 4); longitudinally-mounted rocking beam parabolic taper leaf springs, hollow rubber bump stops, hydraulic double-acting shock-absorbers (6 × 6)	coil springs, hollow rubber bump stops, hydraulic double-acting shock-absorbers with self-levelling (4 × 4); longitudinally-mounted rocking beam parabolic taper leaf springs, hollow rubber bump stops, hydraulic double-acting shock-absorbers (6 × 6)	coil springs, hollow rubber bump stops, hydraulic double-acting shock-absorbers with self-levelling (4 × 4); longitudinally-mounted rocking beam parabolic taper leaf springs, hollow rubber bump stops, hydraulic double-acting shock-absorbers (6 × 6)	coil springs, hollow rubber bump stops, hydraulic double-acting shock-absorbers with self-levelling (4 × 4); longitudinally-mounted rocking beam parabolic taper leaf springs, hollow rubber bump stops, hydraulic double-acting shock-absorbers (6 × 6)	coil springs, hollow rubber bump stops, hydraulic double-acting shock-absorbers with self-levelling (4 × 4); longitudinally-mounted rocking beam parabolic taper leaf springs, hollow rubber bump stops, hydraulic double-acting shock-absorbers (6 × 6)
Tyres:	285/75R 16 BF Goodrich Mud Terrain (M/T) or All Terrain (A/T) (specified, options available)	285/75R 16 BF Goodrich Mud Terrain (M/T) or All Terrain (A/T) (specified, options available)	285/75R 16 BF Goodrich Mud Terrain (M/T) or All Terrain (A/T) (specified, options available)	285/75R 16 BF Goodrich Mud Terrain (M/T) or All Terrain (A/T) (specified, options available)	285/75R 16 BF Goodrich Mud Terrain (M/T) or All Terrain (A/T) (specified, options available)

Model	4 × 4 (716) GS (M), GS HT (MK) and C (K)	6 × 6 (718) GS (M), GS HT (MK), C (K) and P (T)	6 × 6 (718) HVB	6 × 6 PPV	6 × 6 EP (Vector)
Brakes:					
(main)	vacuum assisted hydraulic, discs all-round, twin callipers on front axle; ABS now standard	vacuum assisted hydraulic, discs all-round, twin callipers on front axle; ABS now standard	vacuum assisted hydraulic, discs all-round, twin callipers on front axle; ABS now standard	vacuum assisted hydraulic, discs all-round, twin callipers on front axle; ABS now standard	vacuum assisted hydraulic, discs all-round, twin callipers on front axle; ABS now standard
(parking)	double disc mechanical on transmission	double disc mechanical on transmission	double disc mechanical on transmission	double disc mechanical on transmission	double disc mechanical on transmission
Electrical system:	24 V	24 V	24 V	24 V	24 V
Batteries:	2 × 12 V, 75 Ah	2 × 12 V, 75 Ah	2 × 12 V, 75 Ah	2 × 12 V, 75 Ah	2 × 12 V, 75 Ah
Alternator:	28 V, 100 A	28 V, 100 A	28 V, 100 A	28 V, 100 A	28 V, 100 A

[1] 120 litres for Pinzgauer 6 × 6 C (718 K)

In September 2007, BAE Systems announced the latest uprated Pinzgauer 2 models powered by a EURO 4 emissions compliant engine. EURO 3 models were scheduled to continue in production alongside the EURO 4 Pinzgauer 2.

The Description text and Specification table is specific to the EURO 3 Pinzgauer. Available details of Pinzgauer 2 models can be found elsewhere in this entry.

In January 2008 BAE Systems announced it planned to discontinue the production of the Pinzgauer 1 vehicle and close its manufacturing facilities at Guildford and Fareham. A support business (primarily for British and New Zealand Pinzgauer fleets) infrastructure was to be retained at the Guildford site (since being relocated to Telford). Development of the Pinzgauer 2 was transitioned to BAE Systems Land Systems in South Africa, however, according to BAE Systems, further analysis of the potential market (for Pinzgauer 2) revealed insufficient market interest to continue development.

Description
While weights, dimensions and performance figures have all changed, throughout its production run the Pinzgauer vehicle has changed little in overall appearance and remained based on a proven torsion-free central tube design with swinging half-axles.

EURO 3 Pinzgauers are powered by a Volkswagen 2.5-litre five-cylinder turbocharged diesel engine. This provides considerably more power and torque (particularly at low speeds) than the six-cylinder engine fitted to preceding (4 × 4) and (6 × 6) models. According to the manufacturer, EURO 3 powered models can accelerate from 0-80 km/h in 15 seconds and acceleration times when fully laden are comparable to those of preceding models when unladen. EURO 3 models are fitted as standard with a ZF four-speed automatic gearbox.

The twin crown wheel and pinion axle differentials form part of the central tube and provide both drive and suspension movement. A centre tube connects the front and rear (plus second and third on (6 × 6) models) differentials and houses the solid prop shafts, differential locks and all-wheel drive connections. Enclosed, these components are protected from terrain damage. The fully synchronised two-speed transfer box forms part of the centre tube system and is therefore also protected from possible terrain damage.

Range changes are possible on the move, and the cross-axle differential locks may also be engaged or disengaged on the move.

The independent hub-reduction portal-type swinging half-axles are sprung by coil springs front and rear, or on (6 × 6) models by rocking beam style parabolic taper-leaf springs shared longitudinally between the rear axle pairs. Telescopic double-acting shock absorbers are fitted all-round, and on (6 × 6) models rear air suspension options are available.

As standard the Pinzgauer is fitted with driver-controlled cross-axle differential locks and vacuum assisted hydraulic disc brakes on all axles; the front axle discs being of the twin calliper type. The double-disc mechanical transmission handbrake operates directly on the rear drive shaft and, with the differential locks engaged, effectively locks all axles and wheels.

From 2004 an Anti-lock Braking System (ABS), Electronic Traction Control (ETC) for use in marginal terrain, and Electronic Brake Distribution (EBD) became available, and later became standard fit on all models. The ETC system also engages when the vehicle is in rear-wheel drive mode only.

Power steering is standard, and the steering system remains operational without the power assistance.

Following extensive testing, ATL specified the BF Goodrich 285/75R 16M/T (Mud Terrain) as standard tyre equipment for the Pinzgauer, with the option of the A/T (All Terrain) version for applications where high road mileage were anticipated. Snow chains and run flat systems were available as options. Other equipment options included an engine pre-heater allowing the vehicle to operate at temperatures down to –46°C.

Base models
The Pinzgauer range consisted of five base models, all of these being (6 × 6) variants.

Pinzgauer (6 × 6) GS (718 M)
Soft-top with two side doors; roll over bar; drop-down windscreen; drop sides; 12 fold-down inward facing lateral seats; drop down tailgate; 145-litre fuel tank.

Pinzgauer (6 × 6) C (718 K)
Hard top five-door command with four side doors; three forward facing seats mid-vehicle; rear door; hard top; roll over bar; 120-litre fuel tank.

Pinzgauer (6 × 6) P (718 T)
Hard-top crew cab with a platform body with two side doors; roll over bar; two cab seats; 145-litre tank.

Pinzgauer (6 × 6) HVB
HVB high volume insulated box-body with two side doors; two container style rear doors; roll over bar; 145-litre tank.

Pinzgauer (6 × 6) WP
6 × 6 weapons platform for long range patrol, reconnaissance, or similar operations. Full details of weapons platform variants can be found in the Special attacks vehicles section.

Pinzgauer (6 × 6) Protected Patrol Vehicle (PPV) in service with the New Zealand Army in a command post role (Gordon Arthur)   1340331

The armoured Pinzgauer (EP) was developed in conjunction with then parent company, Armor Holdings. Named Vector, this vehicle was developed specifically to meet a UK MoD requirement for a Protected Patrol Vehicle (PPV) to supplement the lighter weight and more vulnerable Snatch Land Rover on overseas deployments (Shaun C Connors)   1340358

Universal Engineering Ltd has developed a single-axle 1,250 kg payload high-mobility trailer specifically for use with Pinzgauer light vehicles (Patrick Allen)   1326574

Pinzgauer (6 × 6) PPV

The Pinzgauer 6 × 6 Protected Patrol Vehicle (PPV) features an armoured body and floorpan developed by Pinzgauer in conjunction with S MacNeillie and Son Ltd. This variant is in service with the New Zealand Army in a command post role.

Pinzgauer (6 × 6) EP

The armoured Pinzgauer (EP) was developed in conjunction with then parent company, Armor Holdings. Named Vector, this vehicle was developed specifically to meet a UK MoD requirement for a Protected Patrol Vehicle (PPV) to supplement the lighter weight and more vulnerable Snatch Land Rover on overseas deployments.

Vector was developed and placed in quantity production in less than nine months. The first concept test bed (P1) was completed early 2006, this being followed by two prototype vehicles (P2 and P3) which were completed in June and July 2006.

Following a trials programme the first production vehicles were completed in December 2006. The initial UK order called for 62 vehicles consisting of the two prototypes and 60 production vehicles. A second order called for an additional 106 vehicles, all of which were expected to be delivered during 2007. A further 21 vehicles were ordered, these delivered during 2008. A further 20 Vector were manufactured for the UK MoD at BAE's Newcastle facility during 2009. According to BAE Systems, should further orders of sufficient quantity be received, production of Vector could be restarted.

Protection levels remain classified, however it is understood that the standard (6 × 6) Pinzgauer has been fitted with a new armoured floor, which supports an all-steel tubular frame with roll-over protection. The tubular frame also acts as the mounting point for a modular armour package. The troop compartment has two roof hatches and two doors.

The Vector PPV is fitted with General Dynamics' Bowman digital communications system.

Vector has the same mechanical layout as standard Pinzgauer EURO 3 production models.

All the above variants are C-130 Hercules transportable, without preparation. Tie-down points are provided and these may also be used for underslinging from helicopters of suitable capacity. With the rollcage dropped and windscreen folded the Pinzgauer WP is transportable internally by CH-47 Chinook helicopter. The Pinzgauer may also be para-dropped on a Medium Stressed Platform (MSP).

Other variants

Other specialist variants of the Pinzgauer have been produced, these including (4 × 4) models and fire and emergency service vehicles.

Displayed at DSEi 2003, a Pinzgauer 716 K (4 × 4) configured as the British Army's latest Truck Utility Medium (Heavy Duty) Fitted For Radio (TUM (HD) FFR) (Shaun C Connors)   0558995

During 2006 armouring specialist S MacNeillie and Son Ltd was awarded a contract to supply 114 composite appliqué armour kits to the British Army for installation on unarmoured Pinzgauer (4 × 4) and (6 × 6) vehicles deployed overseas (Patrick Allen)   1324444

Specifications

Pinzgauer 2

In September 2007 BAE Systems announced the introduction of a further revised Pinzgauer range, designated Pinzgauer 2. This latest vehicle, which was to compliment and not to replace earlier EURO 3 models, retains the proven torsion-free central tube design with swinging half-axles of the predecessors vehicle, but is larger, carries a greater payload, and is powered by a more powerful EURO 4 emissions compliant engine.

Pinzgauer 2 models are 140 mm wider and 190 mm taller (excluding WP variant) than their predecessors, and have a GVW of 7,000 kg. Each axle is rated at 3,000 kg, with independent air suspension fitted to the rear axles as standard.

Motive power is provided by a Steyr M16 six-cylinder 3.2-litre turbocharged water-cooled diesel engine developing 194 hp at 3,800 rpm and 410 N.m torque at 2,000 rpm. A six-speed ZF automatic gearbox coupled to a Pinzgauer designed two-speed transfer box is standard.

Other revisions include larger wheels and tyres, a revised nose, internal ergonomic changes and revised instrumentation. Additionally, all models will be fitted with a high-hardness steel floor and bulkhead as standard.

In January 2008 BAE Systems announced it planned to discontinue the production of the Pinzgauer 1 vehicle and close its manufacturing facilities at Guildford and Fareham. A support business (primarily for British and New Zealand Pinzgauer fleets) infrastructure has been retained at the Guildford site. Development of the Pinzgauer 2 was transitioned to BAE Systems Land Systems in South Africa, however, according to BAE Systems, further analysis of the potential market (for Pinzgauer 2) revealed insufficient market interest to continue development.

Universal Engineering Pinzgauer trailer

Universal Engineering Ltd has developed a single-axle 1,250 kg payload high-mobility trailer specifically for use with Pinzgauer light vehicles. For commonality with the prime mover this trailer features Pinzgauer wheels and tyres and to match the mobility levels of the towing vehicle, has the same wheel track and is fitted with independent swing arm coil spring suspension.

Status

See text for details. In service with New Zealand (321) and the UK - Army, Navy and Royal Air Force (more than 760, including Vector PPV).

Contractor

BAE Systems Land & Armaments, Telford, UK.

Range Rover (4 × 4) light vehicle

Development

The Range Rover, first announced in June 1970, quickly evolved from a vehicle with a utilitarian interior to one that combined cross-country mobility with the comfort and road performance of a high-speed saloon car. In terms of luxury and refinement it is top of the Land Rover range of (4 × 4) vehicles. In standard form all but the earliest of Range Rover models are best described as suited to rear echelon, command, control, communication, internal security duties, or for use by governmental, humanitarian or aid agencies. The base chassis of earlier models has proven suitable for conversion into ambulance, fire tender or similar style vehicles and a number of companies worldwide offer, or have offered, assorted conversions. A number of factory approved conversions by Land Rover Special Vehicles are also available and these have included (6 × 4)

A discretely armoured Range Rover displayed at IDEX 2003
(Shaun C Connors)
1124800

configurations equipped for use as fast response emergency units. More conventional (4 × 4) versions include police and rapid assault vehicles and discreetly armoured specifications for the transport of VIPs and personnel. The discreetly armoured specification features Level B6 ballistic protection, a specially developed heavy-duty suspension and a full range of security options.

The Range Rover has continually evolved throughout its production run. In approaching 40 years of production there have only been three all-new models, the first of these coming with the introduction of the 'new shape' Range Rover in 1994. At this time earlier production models became known as the Range Rover Classic. The current third-generation Range Rover, which for the first time features independent suspension, was announced late 2001. As part of a 2011 model year refresh the Range Rover received a minor external and interior face-lift, an upgraded four-wheel drive system, plus the introduction of a new 4.4-litre TDV8 diesel engine coupled to a ZF 8HP70 eight-speed automatic transmission.

The latest armoured Range Rover was unveiled during 2009, this based on the 2010 model year and having a GVW of 4,040 kg.

Description

Prior to the latest revisions all Range Rover models have been based on a rigid box-section steel chassis. The rubber-mounted steel body frame is clad in separate body panels, most of which are formed in lightweight, corrosion-resistant aluminium alloy. Numerous power plants have been fitted throughout the production run, but later options progressed the Rover V-8 petrol engine from 3.9- to 4.6-litres. Diesel engine options have included a Land Rover 2.5-litre four-cylinder turbocharged unit and a BMW 2.5-litre turbocharged and intercooled six-cylinder unit. Gearbox options have included a five-speed manual or a four-speed automatic, most current models being fitted with a six-speed automatic as standard.

Long-travel coil-spring suspension was supplemented and then replaced by an air-suspension system and being an in-production luxury motor car, the Range Rover has continuously received styling, trim and equipment level upgrades. The latest models are powered by either a five-litre V-8 petrol or a 3.6-litre TDV8 V-8 turbocharged diesel. All models now have all-round independent suspension and a vast array of electronic and luxury equipment fitted as standard.

The data given in the accompanying specification table relates to 1995 to 2000 Range Rover production models.

Variants

Range Rover Sport

The Range Rover Sport which became available from late-2005 is a performance orientated 4 × 4 Sports Utility Vehicle (SUV) in the mould of the BMW X5 and Porsche Cayenne, and while styling cues and name are certainly taken from the Range Rover product, the Range Rover Sport is actually based on the Land Rover Discovery 3 platform.

As a performance orientated SUV, any use of the Range Rover Sport by governmental organisations or similar is likely to be limited.

Specifications

Range Rover
Cab seating: 1 + 4
Configuration: 4 × 4
Weight:
  (2.5-litre diesel, manual, kerb) 2,115 kg
  (2.5-litre diesel, automatic, kerb) 2,130 kg
  (4-litre petrol, manual, kerb) 2,090 kg
  (4-litre petrol, automatic, kerb) 2,100 kg
  (4.6-litre petrol, auto, kerb) 2,220 kg
  (GVW, all models) 2,780 kg
  (max weight on front axle) 1,320 kg
  (max weight on rear axle) 1,840 kg
Length: 4.72 m

Width: 1.89 m
Height: 1.82 m
Ground clearance: 210 mm
Track:
  (front) 1.54 m
  (rear) 1.53 m
Wheelbase: 2.75 m
Angle of approach/departure: 38°/26°
Max speed:
  (4-litre petrol, manual) 190 km/h
  (4-litre petrol, automatic) 187 km/h
  (2.5-litre diesel, manual) 170 km/h
  (2.5-litre diesel, automatic) 162 km/h
  (4.6-litre petrol, automatic) 200 km/h
Fuel capacity:
  (petrol) 100 litres
  (diesel) 90 litres
Engine: Land Rover V-8 4-litre water-cooled petrol with fuel injection developing 190 hp (142 kW) at 4,750 rpm with catalyst or Land Rover V-8 4.6-litre water-cooled petrol with fuel injection developing 225 hp (167 kW) at 4,750 rpm with catalyst or BMW 2.5-litre 6-cylinder turbocharged and intercooled water-cooled indirect injection 4-stroke diesel developing 136 hp (101 kW) at 4,400 rpm
Gearbox:
  (manual) 5 forward and 1 reverse gears
  (automatic) 4 forward and 1 reverse gears
Clutch: (manual) single dry plate
Transfer box: 2-speed chain-driven with viscous control unit
Steering: power-assisted recirculating ball with safety column and steering damper
Turning radius: 5.95 m
Suspension: Electronic Air Suspension (EAS) with variable ride height. Air springs, composite radius arms, Panhard rod, anti-roll bar and dual-action telescopic hydraulic dampers
Brakes:
  (main) electronic 4-channel hydraulic power anti-lock braking system with outboard reverse ventilated discs, front; outboard solid discs, rear
  (parking) mechanical on transmission
Electrical system: 12 V

Status

In production. In service with a number of armed forces and governmental, humanitarian and aid organisations. The latest model of the Range Rover entered production late 2001.

Contractor

Land Rover

Supacat (6 × 6) light vehicle

Development

The Supacat (6 × 6) light vehicle, known as the All Terrain Mobile Platform (ATMP) by the British Army, was developed primarily as a marginal terrain vehicle, which retained a good hard surface performance. It is used in both military and civilian applications and has been in service with the British Army and RAF since 1984. Prime users are the airborne and air mobile brigades with others, such as Marines, making occasional training and more specific operational use.

The Supacat was first produced in 1982 and since then has been continuously developed to cater for increasing demands on its abilities. The most recently produced version is the Supacat Mk 3. Details and specifications given below relate to this model. As of October 2010 the Mk 4 remains under development, and improvements, should development progress, are likely to include a new emissions-compliant diesel engine.

In 1995, an agreement was established between Supacat Limited and Alvis Vehicles Limited (later Alvis Vickers Limited, now BAE Systems Land Systems) for Alvis to undertake the marketing and production of the

Supacat ATMP Mk 3 towing an SLLPT trailer and 105 mm light gun
(Supacat Limited)
0109519

Supacat All-Terrain Mobile Platform (ATMP) Mk 3 undergoing trials in Malaysia (Supacat Limited)   0096482

Supacat (6 × 6) vehicle for military markets; Supacat Limited retained the production and marketing rights for civilian applications. In June 2005 Supacat Limited regained sole marketing rights for the Supacat ATMP.

In August 1996, the UK Ministry of Defence announced a requirement for a further quantity of ATMPs and their associated SLLPT trailers. In March 1997, it became known that the GBP4 million-plus production contract for 86 ATMPs and 84 SLLPT trailers had been awarded to the then Alvis Vickers Limited (now BAE Systems Land Systems), although the contract was not formally announced until September 1999. First ATMP deliveries were made in late 2000, with first deliveries of the SLLPT trailer then scheduled for 2004. The final requirement called for 65 vehicles and 65 trailers; 55 trailers would eventually be delivered. Fifty-five vehicles were delivered to the Army, the remaining 10 to the Royal Marines.

The Supacat Mk 3 ATMP was deployed for the first time to Macedonia during Operation Essential Harvest, and has subsequently been deployed to Afghanistan and Iraq. Small numbers of vehicles have subsequently been cast.

A quantity of vehicles was delivered to the Canadian military during 1997. During 2002, six Supacat Mk 3s were delivered by the then Alvis Vickers to an undisclosed Asian export customer, later identified as Malaysia. This delivery was the first military export by the then Alvis Vickers of the Mk 3 version. A further order for a similar quantity of vehicles was subsequently received.

Description
The Supacat Mk 3 is a (6 × 6) low ground pressure vehicle running on 31 × 15.5 × 15 wide section low-pressure tyres. The vehicle is powered by a Volkswagen ADE 1900 turbocharged diesel engine coupled to a Volkswagen/Audi 01N automatic gearbox. Drive to the wheels is mechanical via a chain system with a single differential integral with the gearbox; traction control is via the handlebar brakes. Power-assisted steering is by handlebars which steer the front four wheels conventionally and also operate the brake steering as required. A conventional foot brake is also provided. Both foot and hand throttles are fitted.

The Supacat is capable of a speed of 64 km/h and has a limited amphibious capability. The Supacat is primarily an open vehicle but can be fitted with a variety of hard-, soft- or lightweight removable canopies. Load capacity was 1,000 kg but it is now rated to carry up to 1,600 kg in certain circumstances. It is possible to self-load a pallet using its Superwinch S9000 winch and ramps; the same ramps can be used for bridging and recovery.

The Supacat is designed to be a towing vehicle for trailers, light artillery pieces such as the 105 mm Light Gun and for vehicle recovery. Special trailers have been developed for use with the Supacat, including the Fork Lift Pallet Trailer (FLPT). Cranes can also be fitted.

The Supacat is fully air-portable. Schemes are approved for single, dual and quadruple vehicle underslung loads under suitable helicopters such as the Sea King (one), Black Hawk (two) and Chinook (four). Two Supacats can be driven into the Chinook and the vehicle is compatible with the EH 101. Supacat can be air-dropped and a number of schemes have been proved. These include two vehicles on one platform or one vehicle plus trailer or mixed stores. Supacats have been airlifted in a variety of aircraft such as the C-130 Hercules and trials have been carried out for the CASA 235. Vehicles can be stacked one on the other for air transport, using the vehicle's own equipment.

Supacats can be used for troop transport and as weapon platforms and carriers. Trials have been carried out with a number of weapons including 7.62 mm and 12.7 mm machine guns and the Euromissile MILAN Anti-Tank Guided Weapon (ATGW) system.

Supacats have been fitted with Palfinger PC 2400 lorry loaders with a lifting capacity of 590 kg at 4.2 m. These vehicles form part of the Canadian Disaster Assistance Relief Team (DART).

Supacats fitted with cranes are used for a variety of roles including the recovery of crashed aircraft for the UK Royal Air Force and others.

Specifications
Supacat Mk 3
Seating: 1 + 5
Configuration: 6 × 6
Weight:
  (maximum GVW) 2,650 kg (3,500 kg limited application)
  (unladen) 1,800-1,900 kg (spec dependant)
  (payload, maximum) 1,600 kg
  (towed load, ideal conditions) ≤2,400 kg (approx)
Load area: 1.445 × 1.87 m
Length: 3.44 m
Width: 2 m
Height:
  (roll bar) 1.87 m
  (cab) 2.01 m
  (folded down) 1.21 m
  (load platform) 940 mm
Ground clearance: 215 mm
Track: 1.601 m
Wheelbase: 923 mm + 923 mm
Angle of approach/departure: 57°/58°
Max speed: (road) 64 km/h
Fuel capacity: 63.6 litres
Max gradient: 100%
Side slope: 40°
Vertical obstacle: 500 mm
Fording: amphibious (limited capability)
Engine: VW ADE 1900 1.896-litre 4-cylinder in-line turbocharged water-cooled 4-stroke diesel developing 78 hp (58 kW) at 4,000 rpm
Gearbox: VW/Audi fully automatic 4-speed with park and reverse
Drive: twin helical reduction gearboxes to central axles and chain coupling to front and rear axles
Steering: combined power assisted Ackermann (1st and 2nd axles) and skid steer (all axles)
Brakes: hydraulic disc
Tyres: low pressure 31 × 15.5 × 15
Electrical system: 12 V (24 V optional)
Battery: 1 × 12 V, 65 Ah
Alternator: 65 A

Status
Production as required. The Supacat Mk 3 is in service with Canada, Malaysia, the UK (Army and Royal Marines) and possibly other undisclosed customers. Earlier models are known to be in service with Canada, Mexico and the US.

Contractor
Supacat Limited

United States

AM General High Mobility Multipurpose Wheeled Vehicle (HMMWV)

Development
The US Army released a draft specification for the development of a High Mobility Multipurpose Wheeled Vehicle (HMMWV) mid-1979. It wanted a vehicle that would fit into the 1¼ US ton category, but also wanted a vehicle that would be capable of considerably more duties than any previous standard truck. It wanted a weapons carrier-come-scout car like the Jeep and the M151 MUTT, combined with a light tactical battlefield truck, an ambulance and middleweight weapons carrier for anti-aircraft guns, a troop carrier and an artillery tractor, plus a vehicle that could perform utility functions. In meeting these requirements the new HMMWV would replace the M274 Mule (830 in service), M561 (troop)/M972 (ambulance) Gama Goat (11,000 in service), 80 per cent of the M151 MUTTs and selectively replace the M880 series. The remaining 20 per cent of the M151 fleet and the bulk of the M880s were to be replaced by the Commercial Utility Cargo Vehicle (CUCV). A small number of M151 MUTTs initially remained in service with the US Marines as these were internally transportable by CH-47 Chinook helicopter; the HMMWV is not. Large numbers of the CUCV fleet were subsequently replaced by HMMWVs.

Based on the draft specification issued by the US Army, AM General Corporation (now AM General LLC) designed and built a prototype HMMWV in the weapons carrier configuration. The first prototype was completed in August 1980 and was sent to the Nevada Automotive Test Center for extensive trials. By February 1981, the prototype had accumulated 21,000 km of instrumented and dynamic testing.

By February 1981 Tank-automotive and Armaments COMmand (TACOM) had finalised its specifications for the HMMWV programme and under the designation XM988 sent out invitations to some 61

Lithuanian Army M1035A2 HMMWV in soft top ambulance configuration (Grzegorz Holdanowicz) 1116252

Polish Army M1097A2 HMMWV. Between August and December 2004 Poland received 217 HMMWVs made up of 96 M1043A2, 60 M1025A2, 31 M1097A2, 18 M1045A2, 9 M1097A2 (shelter carriers) and 3 M1035A2 soft-top ambulances (Shaun C Connors) 1120482

manufacturers. Five responded with proposals and from these contracts were awarded to AM General, Chrysler Corporation and Teledyne Continental Motors for the design and construction of 11 prototype HMMWVs (six weapons carriers and five utility); these were delivered in May 1982.

Competitive testing followed and in March 1983, AM General was awarded a USD59.8 million contract by TACOM for 2,334 HMMWVs, which were then designated the M998 series to which the unofficial names Hummer and Humvee were soon applied, the HMMWV acronym proving unpronounceable. This was the first increment in a five-year contract for 54,973 vehicles worth approximately USD1.2 billion. Of these, approximately 39,000 were for the US Army and the remainder divided between the US Air Force, Navy and Marine Corps (initially 3,123). Initial Production Testing was carried out during late 1984, with production commencing at Mishawaka, Indiana, early in 1985. Contract options for a further 15,000 vehicles were exercised to bring the total production in mid-1991 to over 72,000 vehicles, including overseas sales.

In August 1989, the US Army awarded AM General a further multiyear contract worth approximately USD1 billion. The contract called for a further 33,331 vehicles until 1993, with two further option years. Production under the new contract began in January 1990 and production for the US Armed Forces continued until March 1995, by which time AM General had manufactured approximately 100,000 HMMWVs.

Production of the HMMWV continues and as of early 2011 over 270,000 examples had been produced; around 230,000 for the US government and in excess of 40,000 to over 50 foreign governments. By 2009, HMMWV production had peaked at 85 vehicles per day. Major export users of the HMMWV include Abu Dhabi, Afghanistan, Egypt, Iraq, Kuwait, Israel, Jordan, Mexico, Saudi Arabia and Taiwan. Current production models are the 2005-introduced ECV-based M1151, M1152 and M1165, and the 2008-introduced M1167 for US Armed Forces and some export customers. The A2 series and Expanded Capacity Vehicle (ECV) models remain available for export customers if required.

Full details of HMMWV model variants and other HMMWV developments can be found chronologically in the following entry's text.

US Army HMMWV contract (DAAE07-01-C-S001) was awarded to AM General during late 2000 and was for a further 2,962 examples of the A2 series, to be delivered during FY01. Worth USD191 million, the contract contained six single-year options running to FY07. At the time the contract was placed it was stated that the US Department of Defense (DoD) planned to purchase up to 31,474 vehicles. As of mid-2003 only 8,000 vehicles had

been ordered, however the subsequent Afghanistan/Iraq campaigns have seen a significant increase in HMMWV production with a number of contract amendments/options being exercised by the US government. During 2005/2006 these options included:

In March 2005 AM General was awarded a USD60 million contract modification for 814 M1152 and 31 M1151 HMMWVs with work expected to be completed by 31 March 2006.

In March 2005 AM General was awarded a USD5.3 million contract modification for 75 M1113 HMMWVs.

In June 2005 the US Army Tank-automotive and Armaments Command issued a pair of firm-fixed-price contract modifications for additional M1114 up-armoured HMMWVs. The total value of these contracts was USD216.4 million, with the then Armor Holdings receiving a USD95.6 million contract modification and AM General receiving a USD120.6 million contract modification; work was expected to be complete by November 2005.

In September 2005 the US Army Tank-automotive and Armaments Command issued a further three HMMWV contract modifications worth USD296.5 million, and covering over 3,000 vehicles for US and Iraqi armed forces. The first modification was valued at USD161.1 million and covered 1,000 M1151 and 280 M1152 HMMWVs for the US Army, and 713 up-armoured M1114 HMMWVs chassis for Iraqi Armed Forces. Work was expected to be complete by June 2006. The second contract modification was valued at USD106.6 million and covered M1114 and M1043A2 HMMWV chassis production; numbers were not specified. The third contract modification was for USD28.8 million and covered 1,302 up-armoured M1114 HMMWV chassis and a single M1043A2.

In March 2006 the US Army Tank-automotive and Armaments Command issued a trio of contract modifications to AM General for M1151 and M1152 HMMWVs. The awards totalled USD191.9 million (USD75.8 million M1152; USD9 million M1152 two-door; USD107.1 million M1151-P1). A further contract modification valued at USD56.2 million for M1152 two-door HMMWVs was also awarded to AM General in March 2006.

In August 2006 the US Army Tank-automotive and Armaments Command awarded AM General a USD 595.8 million contract modification for additional M1151A1 HMMWVs.

In September 2006 AM General received contract modifications valued at USD41.7 million for M1152A1 HMMWVs and USD88.6 million for M1151A1, M1152 and M1165 HMMWVs.

In November 2006 the US Army Tank-automotive and Armaments Command issued AM General contract modifications valued at USD571.5 million for M1151A1 HMMWVs and USD545.6 million for M1152A1 and M1165A1 HMMWVs.

In December 2006 the US Army Tank-automotive and Armaments Command issued AM General five contract modifications for additional HMMWVs including M1151A1, M1152A1 and M1165A1 models.

Contract amendments/options continued into 2007, and in January 2008 it was disclosed that negotiations to further extend HMMWV contract (DAAE07-01-C-S001) to around 2010 were taking place.

The US Army and US Marine Corps are understood to have ordered a total of 18,218 HMMWVs during 2008 for USD3.15 billion, these split 17,012 for the Army, 1,206 for the Marine Corps. These orders included:

In April 2008 it was disclosed that AM General had received a USD650.1 million firm-fixed price contract modification for 4,526 HMMWVs of various types. Production was expected to be complete by December 2009.

In May 2008 it was disclosed that AM General had received a USD522.4 million firm-fixed price contract modification for 3,216 HMMWVs. Production was expected to be complete by December 2009.

In September 2008 it was disclosed that AM General had received a USD745 million firm-fixed price contract modification for 4,853 HMMWVs. Production was expected to be complete by December 2009

The FY 2009 budget is understood to have called for 11,296 HMMWVs valued at around USD1.86 billion, and split 10,995 for the Army and 301 for the Marine Corps. By the conclusion of FY 2009 the following orders had been placed, these totalling around USD1.723 billion and covering the delivery of 11,677 HMMWVs.

Polish Army M1025A2 HMMWV. Between August and December 2004 Poland received 217 HMMWVs made up of 96 M1043A2, 60 M1025A2, 31 M1097A2, 18 M1045A2, 9 M1097A2 (shelter carriers) and 3 M1035A2 soft-top ambulances (Shaun C Connors) 1120481

Portuguese Army M1151w/B1 armour kit (Victor M S Barreira) 1391057

M1025 HMMWV of the Philippine Armed Forces in East Timor (Ron Fry)
1124775

In October 2008 it was disclosed that AM General had received a USD179.6 million firm-fixed price contract for HMMWVs. Work was expected to be complete by December 2009.

In November 2008 it was disclosed that AM General had received a USD100.4 million firm-fixed price contract for 853 HMMWVs. Work was expected to be complete by December 2009.

In December 2008 it was disclosed that AM General had received a USD17.2 million firm-fixed price contract for 146 HMMWVs and a USD252.2 million firm fixed price contract for 1,698 HMMWVs. Work was expected to be complete by December 2009.

In January 2009 it was disclosed that AM General had received a USD54.9 million firm-fixed price contract for HMMWVs. Work was expected to be complete by December 2009.

In February 2009 it was disclosed that AM General had received a USD510.8 million firm-fixed price contract for 3,401 HMMWVs. Work was expected to be complete by December 2009.

In April 2009 it was disclosed that AM General had received a USD14 million firm-fixed price contract for an additional 88 HMMWVs. Work was expected to be complete by December 2009.

In June 2009 it was disclosed that AM General had received a USD27.7 million firm-fixed price contract for 218 HMMWVs. Work was expected to be complete by December 2009.

In August 2009 it was disclosed that AM General had received a USD124.2 million firm-fixed price contract for 843 HMMWVs. Work was expected to be complete by December 2009.

In September 2009 it was disclosed that AM General had received a USD283 million firm-fixed price contract for 1,746 HMMWVs, a USD17.7 million firm-fixed price contract for 113 HMMWVs, a USD25.8 million firm-fixed price contract for 165 HMMWVs, a USD55.2 million firm-fixed price contract for 373 HMMWVs, and a USD60.1 million firm-fixed price contract for 335 HMMWVs. Work was expected to be complete by December 2009.

The FY 2010 request for HMMWVs is understood to be for 10,266 vehicles valued at USD1.75 billion, and split 10,214 for the Army and 54 for the Marine Corps.

In July 2010, AM General was awarded a new HMMWV production contract (W56HZV-10-C-0405), for the production of up to 8,995 HMMWVs. This contract is for a base year with two option years. The contract also provides for continuing HMMWV support such as service parts, supply chain management, training and field service.

The first award under contract W56HZV-10-C-0405 was announced on July 30 and is valued at USD618,974,038. This award covers vehicles for the Afghanistan police force and Afghanistan National Guard.

The second award under contract W56HZV-10-C-0405 was announced on December 15 and is valued at USD211,474,506. This award covers 1,263 HMMWVs of various models, with work scheduled for completion in June 2011. .

The US Army and Marines also have under contract a number of Recap and Reset programmes for service-worn HMMWVs. A TACOM-funded programme to find a replacement current-generation engine for the HMMWV has now been cancelled. (Further details of these programmes can be found elsewhere in this entry.)

In addition to US government and continuing sales to established customers, such as Mexico and Saudi Arabia, other known recent customers for the HMMWV (including donations) have included Afghanistan, Bulgaria, Chile, Croatia, Georgia, Hungary, Iraq, Kuwait, Latvia, Lithuania, Nepal, Peru, Poland, Portugal and Romania.

Afghanistan is understood to have received at least 5,000 HMMWVs by September 2009, and in July 2010 the previously mentioned further FMS award for 2,526 HMMWVs (with options) under contract W56HZV-10-C-0405 was announced. Deliveries under this award will continue until 2011, 2012 if all available options are exercised.

Bulgaria received 52 M1151/M1152 HMMWVs from 2007, and primarily for use in Afghanistan.

Chile is understood to have received around 100 M1114 HMMWVs between 2006 and 2007, and a further 50 vehicles were reportedly delivered during 2009.

Croatia is understood to have received a further 10 HMMWVs during 2010, bringing the total in service to around 80.

Georgia received 40 M1151 HMMWVs during 2010.

Hungary is expected to receive around 15 HMMWVs during 2010/2011.

Iraq is understood to currently operate at least 12,000 HMMWVs, however, only 700 of these have been delivered as new-build by AM General. In January 2008 a program to refurbish and transfer up-armoured HMMWVs to the government of Iraq commenced. More than 4,244 HMMWVs were scheduled for transfer by the end of 2008, numbers reaching more than 8,000 by the end of 2009. Prior to transfer vehicles receive a maintenance overhaul of brakes, belts and fluids before the appropriate paint scheme is applied, and quality assurance checks are conducted. The initial 13-month contract included an additional six month extension option. In July 2009 AECOM Government Services Inc. received a USD28.3 million cost-plus-fixed-fee contract for the maintenance and repair of the final 2,200 M1114 HMMWVs for transfer to the Iraqi Army. Work was expected to be completed by February 2010.

Latvia ordered 13 vehicles, these being a mix of M1043A2, M1113 and M1114. The final vehicle was scheduled for delivery in June 2005.

Lithuania, as part of a USD10.6 million US Foreign Military Funding (FMF) package, received a total of 69 HMMWVs (plus eight M1102 cargo trailers), 40 of the HMMWVs being up-armoured M1114s. A further 15 vehicles for use with the Stinger-based air-defence system and valued at USD1.6 million were ordered in October 2003, these being funded by Lithuania's defence budget. The complete Lithuanian package consists of 86 vehicles made up of: 13 × M1097A2, 10 × M1025A2, 5 × M1113, 3 × M1035A2 (all FMS, all delivered); 15 × M1097A2 (direct sale, all delivered) and 40 × M1114 (FMS, all delivered).

Nepal received 15 HMMWVs during 2010.

Peru is understood to have received around 50 M1151 HMMWVs during 2009.

Poland's Ministry of National Defence (MND) signed a Letter of Offer and Acceptance (LOA) with the US Defense Security Cooperation Agency (DSCA) in November 2003 to purchase a first batch of 217 HMMWVs with associated logistics and training packages. Funds for the USD23 million contract came from one of the US government's Foreign Military Financing (FMF) grants given to Poland during 2003. Between August and December 2004 Poland received 217 HMMWVs made up of 96 M1043A2, 60 M1025A2, 31 M1097A2, 18 M1045A2, 9 M1097A2 (shelter carriers) and 3 M1035A2 soft-top vehicles. The M1045A2 variants have been adopted to carry Rafael Armament Development Authority's Spike-LR long-range anti-tank guided missile launchers, the M1035A2 soft-top ambulances have been (during 2006) locally modified by AMZ Kutzo, and the M1097A2 shelter carriers have a locally developed shelter fitted. Poland's military had planned to order an additional 50-60 vehicles during 2006, and primarily for special forces use, but no orders were placed as no FMF funds were allocated. A batch of 12 M1152 HMMWVs were delivered during 2007–2008 as part of a package of equipment with two RQ-7B Shadow 200 UAVs.

Portugal has received a total of 51 HMMWVs, the most recent deliveries being 24 M1151 during 2008 and three M1165 during 2009.

Romania received six donated M1114 HMMWVs for use on deployed operations during 2006. A further 14 (8 + 6) M1113 HMMWVs were donated during 2007.

In 2002 it was disclosed that the first technology transfer involving the HMMWV had taken place. In 1999, Greece had disclosed the purchase of the HMMWV. It is understood that 70 vehicles in three configurations were procured - M1097 special operations and prime mover for artillery, and M1025 TOW/Missile Carrier for the Euromissile Milan ATGW. A further 98 up-armoured (Plasan Sasa armour) M1114GR vehicles (with an option for a further 98) were procured for use with the Russian-built Kornet E ATGW under Contract No. 26A/2002. These vehicles have 35 per cent local content and represent AM General's start-up programme for co-production of the HMMWV with ELBO. Mid-to-late 2002, a further 54 M1097-based vehicles are also understood to have been ordered for the Rheinmetall Defence

M1025A2 HMMWV armament carrier with winch and basic armour
(Peter Felstead)   0552260

Electronics ASRAD-Hellas surface-to-air missile system, these also having 35 per cent local content. In September 2003, the option under the initial contract (No. 26A/2002) has been exercised and an additional 98 up-armoured (Plasan Sasa armour) M1114GR were procured. In November 2003, Contract No. 042A/2003 was awarded for the procurement of 30 up-armoured (Plasan Sasa armour) M1118GR vehicles as carriers of the BORA A-550 battlefield surveillance radar (20 vehicles) and the Margot XXL electro-optic sensor (10 vehicles). In June 2005, the option under Contract No. 042A/2003 was exercised and an additional 30 up-armoured (Plasan Sasa armour) M1118GR vehicles were ordered; 20 vehicles as carriers of the BORA A-550 battlefield surveillance radar and 10 vehicles as carriers of Margot XXL electro-optic sensor.

By late 2005, Greece had received a total of 353 vehicles. The HMMWV represents a significant transfer of technology to ELBO (aluminium body, independent suspension and so forth) and local content will increase with any future programmes. ELBO will have the export rights to locally produced Kornet E and Rheinmetall Defence Electronics ASRAD-Hellas. In March 2006 a EUR73.5 million contract for the procurement of an additional 301 HMMWVs was awarded to ELBO. The contract covers the delivery of 165 vehicles as carriers of the 40 mm Heckler & Koch Grenade Machine Gun (GMG), 70 × M1116GR ambulances, 60 × M998 Field Maintenance Vehicles and six Special Operations Vehicles.

It had been known for some time that China's People's Liberation Army (PLA) were considering the acquisition of a HMMWV-like vehicle for use by ground and special forces and in February 2002, China's official military media disclosed details of a new (4 × 4) cross-country vehicle similar in appearance to the AM General HMMWV. The vehicle, initially called 'Zhanshen' (God of War), but later known as the SQF2040 Falcon, was developed by the Shenyang Aviation Company (SAC). This was joined later in the year by the very similar Dong Feng EQ2050. Both vehicles initially utilised Hummer H1 chassis supplied directly by AM General and in September 2004 AM General confirmed that it had supplied around two dozen chassis to China. China does not have a licence to manufacture the HMMWV, nor to export vehicles based on AM General-supplied chassis. The SAC SFQ2040 has an aluminium alloy body, the Dong Feng EQ2050 has a steel body.

Between 2004-2006, a total of 57 examples of the Dong Feng EQ2050 were delivered to the PLA for test and evaluation. These vehicles were tested in regions with some of the toughest weather and road conditions in China, including the Tibetan Plateau, Gobi desert, and the snow regions in the northeast Heilongjiang province, covering a total mileage of 1.03 million kilometres. According to Chinese media reports, the military version EQ2050 with 100 per cent Chinese-made parts passed the design finalisation trial by the PLA in December 2006.

USAF M1026A1 HMMWV at a US Air Force base in the UK
(Shaun C Connors)   0109512

SAC continues to promote SAC SFQ2040 and a version mounting a mobile air defence missile system developed jointly with NORINCO has been displayed. SAC emphasises the low cost of the SFQ2040, reported to be one third of the price of a US-made HMMWV.

The EQ2050 is generally identical to the HMMWV in appearance and size, but with re-designed headlights and grille. The vehicle is available in seven variants all sharing the same chassis, with four basic hull designs, soft-top, hard-top, truck, and van. Military variants are fitted with a license built Cummins EQB150-20 turbocharged diesel that can operate within a –41°C to +56°C temperature range and in up to 95 per cent humidity. The vehicle has a five-speed manual gear box and a two-speed transfer box.

The EQ2058 is the armoured version of the EQ2050. The vehicle appears to be fitted with basic protection, not unlike that fitted to early armament carrier variants of the AM General HMMWV.

In 2004, Santana of Spain considered an agreement with AM General to assemble/produce the HMMWV under licence in Spain should Santana Motor win a then pending Spanish MoD requirement for which the HMMWV could be offered. It is understood the agreement would have allowed the integration into Spanish-produced vehicles of locally fabricated or sourced components, and in addition to the Spanish military would have allowed Santana to offer the HMMWV for export sales, it is believed to other European and NATO countries. It became known late 2005 that this agreement had lapsed, the contract in question being awarded to UROVESA for further production of the HMMWV-like VAMTAC.

AM General has not officially disclosed HMMWV contract details for a number of years and the majority of HMMWV contract information is from third party sources.

Civilian consumer and industrial versions of the HMMWV are available. Production of civilian vehicles began in 1992 and an extensive dealer network was established in the US, as well as distributors in Canada, the Middle East, Asia and Europe. AM General designated civilian and commercial versions of the HMMWV as the HUMMER. In December 1999, AM General and General Motors Corporation finalised an agreement to jointly pursue product, marketing and distribution opportunities for HUMMER. Under the final agreement, GM acquired exclusive ownership of the HUMMER brand name worldwide and the original HUMMER was renamed the HUMMER H1.

For clarity, the HUMMER H1 is a civilian version of the HMMWV; the H1K is an industrial application version. The HUMMER H1/H1K is essentially the military vehicle, manufactured on the same production line in AM General's Military Assembly Plant, but adapted for civilian use. The military HMMWV is not sold to civilians by AM General, although some military surplus examples have become available. In 2004, GM sold 447 Hummer H1s. In 2005, GM sold 374 Hummer H1s. Production of consumer versions of the HUMMER H1 concluded in June 2006, with limited production of the industrial HUMMER H1K continuing.

The HUMMER H2, a 'next generation' civilian Sport Utility Vehicle (SUV), was designed by GM and inspired by the HMMWV. It was assembled by AM General in its Mishawaka, Indiana Commercial Assembly Plant, from parts supplied by GM, separate from the HMMWV/HUMMER H1 production line. The HUMMER H2 is not a military vehicle, was not designed to be a military vehicle, and there were never any plans to make it one. HUMMER H2s entered production in the spring of 2002 and were in dealers' showrooms by July 2002.

The HUMMER H3 was introduced mid-2005. The HUMMER H3 is a GM product, was manufactured by GM and shares its basic mechanical structure with Chevrolet and GMC mid-size pick-up trucks. The HUMMER H3 is not a military vehicle, was not designed to be a military vehicle, and there were never any plans to make it one.

GM had responsibility for marketing and distributing all civilian HUMMERs through about 300 GM franchised HUMMER dealers in 33 countries, over 170 of those in the US and Canada. During 2003 some 35,259 HUMMERS were sold, an 80 per cent increase on 2002; sales for 2004 were 29,345. During 2005, and thanks to the introduction of the H3, HUMMER sales nearly doubled globally to 61,000.

The economic downturn affected sales of the HUMMER, and in June 2008 GM announced the brand would be reviewed. On 1 June 2009 General Motors filed for Chapter 11 bankruptcy proceedings from which it emerged on 10 July 2009 in a reorganization in which a new entity acquired the most valuable assets. On 1 June 2009, as a part of the GM bankruptcy announcement, the company revealed that the HUMMER brand would be discontinued, the following day announcing that it would sell the brand to an undisclosed Chinese company, later identified as Sichuan Tengzhong Heavy Industrial Machinery Company. This deal did not materialise and late February 2010 GM announced it would begin dismantling the brand. AM General had not produced HUMMER H2 models for GM since February 2009, and the last HUMMER H3 left the production line in May 2010.

Light Service Support Vehicle (LSSV)

It was announced in April 2005 that AM General and General Motors had executed an agreement covering the development of a marketing arrangement through which AM General assumed marketing and sales responsibility for the GM-produced Light Service Support Vehicle (LSSV). AM General offered three LSSVs, all based on the Chevrolet Silverado 2500 HD and in either standard, extended or crew cab models, complete with a militarised cargo/troop carrier, as the baseline configuration or upgraded for off-road with an enhanced mobility package. Sales of the

LSSV range (which had previously included models based on the commercial Suburban and Tahoe models) in 2003 totalled approaching 1,700 units, primarily to US and international military organisations.

From FY07 the LSSV has no longer been offered by AM General as the 07 model year and beyond engine is not compatible with military JP8 fuel.

Full details of the LSSV can be found elsewhere in this section.

General Engine Products LLC
In 1999, AM General incorporated a wholly owned subsidiary, General Engine Products, Inc. and constructed a new plant in Franklin, Ohio to build the OPTIMIZER 6500 6.5-litre diesel engine. Production commenced mid-2000. General Motors no longer produces the 6.5-litre V-8 engine used in the HMMWV and the OPTIMIZER 6500 produced by General Engine Products is essentially an updated version of that engine. General Engine Products supplies service engines to General Motor's Service Parts Operation (SPO), and in addition to building engines for AM General's use in the HMMWV, produces engines for use in commercial, industrial and marine applications.

AM General Corporation became AM General LLC (Limited Liability Company) in April 2002.

General Transmission Products LLC
In 2008, General Transmission Products became the latest addition to AM General's subsidiaries. General Transmission Products produces the 4L80E transmission, formally manufactured by General Motors Powertrain. The 4L80E is produced to the Original Equipment Manufacturers (OEM) specifications.

Description
The HMMWV has either 1 + 1 or 2 + 2 seating (depending on the model) on each side of the drivetrain, which is in a midship position, allowing the front differential to be raised. This, together with the geared hubs, provides a ground clearance of up to 430 mm. The location of the crew on each side of the drive train also allows a low centre of gravity. The windscreen frame is strong enough to serve as a rollbar and support for various equipment kits. Other pillars also make the weapon station inherently strong and a steady location on which to mount a variety of weapons such as TOW, 7.62 and 12.7 mm machine guns and the MK19 40 mm automatic grenade launcher. At the rear the cargo bed is large enough to accommodate a S-250 or similar shelter without overhang; it also accommodates the Standard Integrated Command Post Systems (SICPS) shelter, with a 15 in (381 mm) overhang and all Mobile Subscriber Equipment (MSE) shelters.

To reduce life cycle and initial procurement costs, standard automotive components are used wherever possible, as in the engine, transmission, transfer box, brakes and steering.

The independent suspension, front and rear, gives good manoeuvrability, ease of handling and parts commonality. The geared hubs give up to 430 mm ground clearance (model/variant dependant) incorporating raised axles for a 1.92:1 torque output multiplication at the ground.

The suspended carrier front and rear axles are identical, have differentials and are mounted high-directly in the chassis frame. The front propeller shaft has double cardan joints and the rear propeller shaft has a single cardan joint which, according to AM General, give minimal motion, improved torque characteristics and higher reliability with resultant lower support costs. Vehicle handling is enhanced by the front stabiliser bar being attached to the lower control arms and pivot bracket reducing shock from the lower A-frame member to the chassis.

Acceleration of the A2 model HMMWV is such that it can move from a standstill to 48 km/h in 9.4 seconds and from a standstill to 80 km/h in 26.1 seconds.

Three HMMWVs can be carried in a C-130 Hercules transport aircraft, four in a C-130J-30, six in a C-141B and 15 in a C-5A Galaxy. Two may be underslung by CH-47 or CH-53 helicopters, one by UH-60. All models except the M997 ambulance may be deployed by Low Velocity Air-Drop (LVAD), but shelters must first be removed from shelter carrier models.

The first production series of HMMWV was known as the M998 series. A considerable number of variants were produced:
M998 Cargo/troop Carrier without winch
M1038 Cargo/troop Carrier with winch
M966 TOW Missile Carrier, basic armour, without winch
M1036 TOW Missile Carrier, basic armour, with winch
M1045 TOW Missile Carrier, supplemental armour, without winch
M1046 TOW Missile Carrier, supplemental armour, with winch
M1025 Armament Carrier, basic armour, without winch
M1026 Armament Carrier, basic armour, with winch
M1043 Armament Carrier, supplemental armour, without winch
M1044 Armament Carrier, supplemental armour, with winch
M997 Maxi-ambulance, four-litter, basic armour
M1035 Soft top Ambulance, two-litter
M1037 Shelter Carrier, without winch
M1042 Shelter Carrier, with winch.

In addition to the above, selected application kits are produced as follows:
Cargo/troop Carrier, soft top enclosure (two-door cab) for M998
Cargo/troop Carrier, soft top enclosure (four-door cab) for M998
Cargo/troop Carrier, soft top enclosure (two-door cab, troop seats) for M1038

The HMMWV has been adapted for use in a variety of surface-to-air missile launch vehicle roles. These have included the Boeing Avenger Pedestal-Mounted Stinger carrying eight Stinger surface-to-air missiles
(Peter Felstead)   0544602

M997A2 HMMWV Maxi-ambulances, four-litter, basic armour
(Peter Felstead)   0552254

Cargo/troop Carrier, soft top enclosure (two-door cab, troop/cargo) for M1038.
Cargo/troop Carrier, soft top enclosure (four-door cab, cargo) for M1038
Armament Carrier, basic armour with M60 7.62 mm machine gun for M1026
Armament Carrier, supplemental armour with M2 0.50/12.7 mm machine gun for M1044
Armament Carrier, supplemental armour with MK19 MOD3 grenade launcher for M1043
Retrofitable weapon station kit for the M998/M1038 (weight 114 kg).

In September 1992 AM General introduced the M1097 Heavy Hummer Variant (HHV). The M1097 HHV allowed for an increase in GVW to 4,536 kg and in the case of the M1097 cargo/troop carrier without winch, a payload increase to 1,996 kg. The M1097 chassis incorporated improved front and rear differentials, a new transfer box, new front and rear propshafts, an improved frame mounting for the steering gear, variable rate rear springs and new lower ball joints. The heavier chassis allowed the use of an up-armoured ballistic panel protection kit with 5.56 and 7.62 mm NATO ball protection and permitted the carriage of heavy weapons such as the then McDonnell Douglas Helicopter Systems (MDHS) 30 mm ASP-30 cannon and the then Giat Industries 20 and 30 mm cannon systems. Following the 1992 introduction of the M1097 HHV all M998 series HMMWV versions were available to be produced to this standard. The M1097 HHV was known as the Heavy Weapons Carrier or Heavy Armament Carrier.

M998A1 series
In late 1993, AM General began producing the M998A1 series of HMMWV for the US Army. All A1 models incorporate the M1097 HHV chassis components plus new front seats, an improved parking brake lever with safety release, a metal hood grill, improved slave receptacle, solid-state glow plug controller, modified rifle mounts and upgraded rear half-shafts. Using these common chassis components enhanced HMMWV standardisation across all models, leading to improvements in logistic support, training and fleet durability.

With the introduction of the A1 series the number of models was reduced to the following:
M998A1 Cargo/troop Carrier without winch

M1038A1 Cargo/troop Carrier without winch
M966A1 TOW Missile Carrier, basic armour, without winch
M1045A1 TOW Missile Carrier, supplemental armour, without winch
M1046A1 TOW Missile Carrier, supplemental armour, with winch
M1025A1 Armament Carrier, basic armour, without winch
M1026A1 Armament Carrier, basic armour, with winch
M1043A1 Armament Carrier, supplemental armour, without winch
M1044A1 Armament Carrier, supplemental armour, with winch
M997A1 Maxi-ambulance, four-litter, basic armour
M1035A1 Soft top ambulance, two-litter
M1097A1 Heavy Hummer Variant (HHV).

GVW for all A1 models, except the added M1097A1, increased by approximately 81 kg, although vehicle payloads and loads remained the same.

AM General offered a new front seat retrofit kit for the existing HMMWV fleet as part of the series production.

Production of the M998A1 series ceased in 1995.

M998A2 series

AM General started developing the M998A2 series of the HMMWV for the US Army in early 1993. US Army pilot vehicles were produced in mid-1995 and series production began in September 1995. The A2 series continues in limited production. In February 1996, a right-hand drive version was introduced.

Using the M1097A1 HHV as a baseline, the A2 series originally incorporated an EPA approved General Motors 6.5-litre naturally aspirated diesel engine developing 160 hp, with an electronically controlled four-speed transmission. From mid-2000 the OPTIMIZER 6500 6.5-litre diesel engine produced by General Engine Products (a wholly-owned subsidiary of AM General) has been fitted. Other A2 series enhancements designed to improve performance, vehicle maintenance and user comfort include increased payload, increased cargo bed tie-down capacity, improved heating and ventilation, new rear high-back seats, self-cancelling turn signals, an improved steering wheel and column, LED side marker lights, and revised transport tie-down provisions.

The M998A2 series consists of the following base variants:
M1097A2 base platform
M1097A2 Cargo/Troop Carrier/Prime Mover (replacing the M998A1)
M1097A2 Shelter Carrier
M1025A2 Armament/TOW Missile Carrier, basic armour
M1043A2 Armament Carrier, supplemental armour
M1045A2 TOW Missile Carrier, supplemental armour
M997A2 Maxi-ambulance, four-litter, basic armour
M1035A2 Soft top Ambulance, two-litter
M1123 Cargo/Troop Carrier, US Marines.

The M1097A2 is available either as a base platform, as a shelter carrier, as a cargo/troop carrier with optional hard top, or as a carrier/prime mover with optional hard top and troop seats.

All models are rated at 4,672 kg GVW, except the M997A2, which retains a 4,345 kg GVW.

As with all earlier series, a wide range of optional equipment is available for the M998A2 series. This can include: dual antenna mounts, winch, deep water fording kit, troops seats for up to eight, crew and cargo area canvas, arctic kit, countermine armour kit, hard top and doors, central tyre inflation system, desert filtration package, lightweight weapons station kit, driveline protection kit, spare tyre carrier, bulkhead spare tire kit, jerrycan carrier, brush and headlight guards, special paints, metric gauges, pedestal weapons mount and air conditioning.

The M1072A2 can officially mount the following armament: 5.56, 7.62 or 12.7 mm machine guns, GAU-19 12.7 mm 3-barrel Gatling gun, Giat 20 mm M621 cannon, McDonnell Douglas Helicopter Systems (MDHS) 30 mm ASP-30 cannon, MK 19 40 mm grenade launcher, M40A2 106 mm recoilless rifle (for export applications), Kornet E, Milan, TOW and TOW II anti-tank guided weapons. Many other weapons have been fitted to the HMMWV in local adaptations.

More recently, the US Army developed the Line-Of-Sight Anti-Tank (LOSAT) weapon system. This consists of the Kinetic Energy Missile (KEM) and its fire control system mounted on a modified M1113 ECV HMMWV. It was decided not to take LOSAT forward into production.

The HMMWV has also been adapted for use in a variety of surface-to-air missile launch vehicle roles. These have included the Boeing Avenger Pedestal-Mounted Stinger (PMS) carrying eight Stinger surface-to-air missiles. This became operational with the US Army in 1989-90 and by 2000 over 1,000 systems had been delivered. Taiwan also uses the system, having at least 74 launcher vehicles. The Avenger can also launch Mistral, Starburst and Starstreak missiles from other manufacturers. The Boeing/MBDA Guardian air defence system is a variant of the Avenger carrying Mistral missiles. This system is ready for production but as of late 2010 no orders had been placed. Full details of the Stinger and Avenger systems can be found in *Jane's Land-Based Air Defence*.

The Chung Shan Institute of Science and Technology (CSIST) Antelope is a ground-based low altitude Surface-to-Air Missile (SAM) system that uses the CSIST air-to-air Tien Chien (Sky Sword) 1 missile. For trials purposes the system was mounted on a HMMWV chassis. This consisted of four ready-to-fire missiles mounted on a pedestal. The production system, now in service with the Taiwan Air Force, is mounted on a 6,000 kg (4 × 4) truck. Full details of the Antelope system can be found in *Jane's Land-Based Air Defence*.

The US Army Aviation and Missile Command (AMCOM) Missile Research, Development and Engineering Centre (MRDEC) completed the prototype of a medium-range self-propelled air defence missile system based on the Raytheon Systems Company AIM-120 AMRAAM missile family and a modified HMMWV chassis. Originally known as Project 559 by AMCOM and the HUMRAAM by Raytheon Systems Company, the programme was not funded and there was no recognised requirement as such. The system today (January 2011) is known by two names: Surface Launched Advanced Medium Range Air-to-Air Missile (SL-AMRAAM), to the US Army; Complementary Low Altitude Weapon System (CLAWS), to the US Marine Corps. Low rate initial series production was announced in May 2009. Full details of CLAWS and SL-AMRAAM can be found in *Jane's Land-Based Air Defence*.

The HMMWV has also been used to mount a Multiple Launch Rocket System (MLRS). Under the designation AB19, Jordan's King Abdullah Design and Development Bureau (KADDB) has mounted twin China North Industries Corporation (NORINCO) 107 mm (12-round) Type 63 multiple rocket systems on the rear of a HMMWV, probably a M1097. Six systems were built and delivered by 2002 for use by Jordanian Special Operations Command deployed to Afghanistan. Full details of the Type 63 system can be found in *Jane's Armour and Artillery*.

The HMMWV chassis is used as the basis for the Swiss MOWAG Eagle armoured reconnaissance vehicle, while the Turkish Otokar Cobra armoured personnel carrier utilises HMMWV suspension and driveline. Initial details of an enhanced, high-protection Cobra based on the developmental ECV 2 were disclosed late-2007. Full details of these vehicles can be found in *Jane's Armour and Artillery*.

M1113 Expanded Capacity Vehicle (ECV)

AM General, under contract to the US Army, developed a HMMWV with a greater payload capacity known as the M1113 Expanded Capacity Vehicle, or ECV. The ECV provides the payload capacity allowing for larger and heavier communications shelters, improved armour protection level for scouts, military police, security police and explosive ordnance disposal platforms.

To meet the desired performance and mobility characteristics the ECV was originally powered by a General Motors 6.5-litre 190 hp turbocharged diesel engine coupled to a General Motors 4L80E four-speed automatic transmission. From mid-2000 the OPTIMIZER 6500 6.5-litre diesel engine produced by General Engine Products (a wholly-owned subsidiary of AM General) has been fitted. The ECV utilises modified differentials, improved half-shafts, a new exhaust system, improved brake and cooling systems, an improved suspension system, a modified steering system, upgraded wheels and a reinforced chassis frame.

The chassis of the M1113 ECV was used as the basis for the now abandoned Alvis Vehicles (now BAE Systems) Shadow Offensive Action Vehicle (OAV).

To meet an urgent requirement following the death of a number of soldiers operating in unarmoured HMMWVs in Somalia, the US Army began procurement of the XM1109 up-armoured Heavy HMMWV (UA-HHV) in mid-1993. Based on the M1079A1 HHV, the XM1109 provides the crew compartment with 360° 7.62 mm armour-piercing perimeter protection, as well as artillery airburst and underbody blast protection. The payload of the XM1109 is approximately 590 kg.

The XM1109 UA-HHV was replaced in production by the M1113 ECV-based M1114. The M1114 offers the same 1,016 kg payload and accepts all weapons used with the M1025/M1025A1 models which it replaced for many applications. The M1114 features a Central Tyre Inflation (CTI) system and air-conditioning, and has a kerb weight of 4,447 kg, giving a payload of 1,043 kg.

US Army pilot M1114 vehicles were produced in mid-1995. Production began in late 1995. The first overseas country to purchase the M1114 was Luxembourg. In June 1996, the US Army purchased 390 M1114s for operations in Bosnia, with orders for 738 vehicles (360 for the US Army and 378 for the US Air Force) and 245 (for the US Army) following. A total of 40 examples were ordered for the Qatari Police. The US Air Force issue a number of M1114 vehicles that differ in detail from the US Army model. Under the designation M1116 the type was specifically designed and tailored to the needs of the US Air Force. It features an expanded cargo area, armoured housing for the turret gun operator and increased interior heat and air circulation system. The US Air Force M1116 variant was designed to provide an improved capability for Civil Engineering (CE), Explosive Ordnance Disposal (EOD) and Security Forces (SF) personnel working in high threat environments.

Armour for the M1114/M1116 was manufactured by the former O'Gara-Hess & Eisenhardt Armoring Company of Fairfield, Ohio, now part of BAE Systems Land Systems. Prior to the introduction of the latest armoured HMMWV variants (M1151, M1152, M1165, M1167), and between 1993 and June 2006 the then Armor Holdings produced over 17,500 armoured HMMWVs (over 14,000 between 2003-2007), all but about 160 of the earliest models being models M1114 and M1116. Between 1996 and 2002 orders for armoured M1114/M1116 HMMWV variants averaged at less than 500 units per year. This figure doubled to 1,000 in 2003, had quadrupled to approaching 4,000 during 2004, and peaked at 32 units per day late in 2005. Production of the M1114/M1116 HMMWVs has now ceased in favour of the latest M1151, M1152, M1165, and from 2008 the M1167.

Additionally, between January 2004 and June 2006 the then Armor Holdings produced over 1,800 two- and four-door HArD (HMMWV Armored Demountable) protection kits for US Army HMMWVs. The USMC developed its own protection kit for HMMWVs, the MAK (Marine Armor Kit). The initial MAK requirement was for 3,100 kits but this was later increased to 5,550. Production of all 5,550 MAKs was scheduled for completion in December 2005.. Other companies, including Armor Works, offer protection kits for the HMMWV. Since a contract award in April 2004, Armor Works has supplied at least 1,500 HMMWV armour kits.

HMMWV add-on armour kits are also produced by Plasan Sasa of Israel, and Plasan-equipped vehicles are in service with Greece, Israel and Portugal.

AM General have attained ISO 9002 registration for the manufacture of all HMMWV variants.

HMMWV Frag Kits

As the Afghan/Iraqi conflicts developed so did the pressure for even more protection on the HMMWV. Increases in armouring efforts have been centred around the Frag (Fragmentation) Kits, these currently being fitted to M1114/M1116 and M1151, M1152, M1165 and M1167 variants. Frag Kits are constantly evolving, however weighing over 900 kg and with HMMWVs currently peaking at around 7,075 kg the limit has clearly been reached.

Frag Kit 1 is an aluminium overlay for the doors and rocker panel

Frag Kit 2 is front wheel arch armour

Frag Kit 3 is additional fuel tank protection (designated but not yet in production)

Frag Kit 4 is underbody mine blast protection (designated but not yet in production)

Frag Kit 5 is perimeter armour around the cab - primarily on the doors and fitting over the Frag Kit 1 (during 2006 the then Armor Holdings delivered over 14,000 Frag Kit 5s for US Army M1114 HMMWVs

Frag Kit 6 is additional side protection against Explosively Formed Penetrator (EFP) based attack

Frag Kit 7 includes roof appliqué armour and a gunner's turret overhead cover that combines overhead protection and transparent armoured glass to retain gunner awareness.

M1151, M1152, M1165 and M1167 HMMWVs

AM General announced the introduction of two new HMMWV models in June 2004. Designated M1151 and M1152, both models are based on a slightly modified M1114 Expanded Capacity Vehicle (ECV) chassis. The M1165 was introduced during 2006 for some variants previously covered by the M1152 designation, and late-2007 it was announced that from 2008 the M1167 variant would be available.

The M1151, M1152, M1165 and M1167 were designed from the outset to accept up-armouring kits, however unlike previous up-armoured HMMWVs such as the M1114 and M1116 which are produced in armoured configuration, these models are designed 'fitted for but not with' protection. Protection kits can be installed and removed from vehicles in the field, and using only basic tools. A two-part A- and B-kit armouring process is involved. The A-kit is the combination of some a limited amount of production line armouring together with a significant amount of armour installation attachments. Only armour for areas field personnel would find difficult to access, this including floorboard areas and behind the firewall, is added as part of the A-kit and this adds just over 300 kg to the base vehicle weight. The bulk of the armour, the B-kit, is installed in the field and on an as required basis. The use of add-on armour panels allows protection levels to be varied in accordance with threat, and has the additional benefit of allowing advances in armour technology to be adopted at any time

The M1152 started production in June 2005, with approximately 50 vehicles produced in the first month. Production of the M1151 was slated to begin in July 2005, with approximately 29 vehicles to be manufactured the first month. Between June 2005 and June 2006 the then Armor Holdings delivered over 2,000 kits for these latest HMMWV models.

The M1151 designation refers to the M1025/M1043 armament carrier body mated to the modified M1114 ECV chassis. The M1152 designation was originally applied to all other bodies mated to the modified M1114

M1114 HMMWV; armour for the M1114 is manufactured by O'Gara-Hess & Eisenhardt Armoring Company of Fairfield, Ohio, US (Peter Felstead)
0552253

ECV chassis. To reduce confusion with the wide coverage of the original M1152 designation, the M1165 designation was later introduced for all non-M1025/M1043 models with a four-passenger cab, leaving the M1152 designation for two-door, two-passenger models. The latest M1167 designation applies to TOW Missile Carrier variants.

To further cloud the designation issue, current M1151A1, M1152A1 and M1165A1 models have higher GVWs and payload than the initial A0 variants, and when fitted with the add-on-armour B-kit, vehicle designation changes to w/B1, w/B2 and w/B3, for the M1151/M1151A1, M1152/M1152A1 and M1165/M1165A1, respectively.

Production of standard A2 model HMMWVs continues, but within the US Army the M1151, M1152, M1165 and M1167 are replacing other models on an attrition basis.

One specialised variant of the M1152 available is fitted with the Ballistic Troop Enclosure Protection, an open-top ballistical protected rear body that fits a standard M1152 with no vehicle modification required. The enclosure can be fitted/removed in around 20 minutes, offers AP round protection and is fitted with four gunner positions.

Recap HMMWVs

Excluding the recent surge in orders, a large proportion of the HMMWV fleet was built in the first six years of the programme. The HMMWV was originally built with an expected service life of 15 years, and during FY00 the first vehicles reached the end of their anticipated service life, and by the end of FY01 the average HMMWV age was 10.8 years. At this time, funding levels were only for the acquisition of new vehicles.

A number of proposals to extend the viable service life and improve the reliability of the HMMWV fleet were considered, these including a proposal to return HMMWVs to a near zero miles/zero hours condition with a new driveline and other enhancements costing in the region of USD40,000 per vehicle; this proposal was projected to extend service life for an additional 21 years. Primarily for cost reasons, requirements were refined and in October 2004 a programme to recapitalise a total of 4,372 vehicles was approved. This programme would result in an extended service life of just 10 years.

By February 2009 the HMMWV Recap programme, which extends useful service life by 15 years, was averaging 800 vehicles per month. Figures released early 2010 stated that a total of 41,641 un-armoured HMMWVs had been Recap'd at Red River Army Depot (21,895), Letterkenny Army Depot (18,227), and the Maine Military Authority (1,519). The un-armoured Recap was scheduled to end FY10, with no projected future funding, due to the goal of 45,000 systems being reached. Recap'd HMMWVs under this programme are assigned an R1 designation for identification. Models

Without their armament, M1045A2 TOW-equipped HMMWVs of the Danish Army; a batch of 30 vehicles was supplied in 1999. A small number of these vehicles were converted to the fast attack vehicle role for use in the first stages of the Iraqi conflict during 2003. Doors and rear body panels were removed, and smoke dischargers, Infra-Red (IR) driving lights and a 12.7 mm Heavy Machine Gun (HMG) were added (Martin Pagh) 1124708

M1116 HMMWV of the US Air Force fitted with turret-mounted M82A1 Barrett rifle for use in the EOD role (Shaun C Connors) 0109515

As the Afghan/Iraqi conflicts developed so did the pressure for even more protection on the HMMWV. Increases in armouring efforts have been centred around the Frag (Fragmentation) Kits, these currently being fitted to M1114/M1116 and M1151, M1152, M1165 and M1167 variants. This M1151 is fitted with the latest Frag Kit 6 which was introduced in May 2009 (AM General)   1391058

eligible for Recap under this program were M998/A1, M1025/A1, M1026/A1, M1037, M1038/A1, M1097/A1, with all vehicles returning to service as either M1097R1 or M1025R1 models.

A Recap programme for armoured HMMWVs commenced with a Request For Information (RFI) to industry in January 2010. This programme is currently evolving, with contract award(s) anticipated during 2011..

The USMC Maintenance Center Albany began an Inspect and Repair Only As Necessary (IROAN) service for its HMMWV fleet in March 2007 and at a rate of around 80 vehicles per month.

The US Army has conducted a competition for a new, more capable HMMWV driveline including engine which could be inserted into both or either new and Recap HMMWVs upon selection. As part of this process, in May 2005 Ricardo Special Vehicles of the UK was awarded a USD4.5 million contract to supply seven vehicles for trials. These were delivered in October 2005 and were fitted with a 3.21-litre, six-cylinder EURO 3 emissions compliant Steyr M16 TCA turbocharged diesel engine developing 215 hp and 550 N.m torque, a 70 per cent power upgrade and a 40 per cent torque increase. The driveline upgrade included a GM 4L80-E transmission, a 242HD transfer box and a Ricardo developed cooling pack. This upgrade was trialed in the UAE during 2004 to meet a possible requirement to upgrade around 200 A0/A1 HMMWVs powered by the early 6.2-litre naturally aspirated engine. Also involved in the HMMWV re-power programme were AM General LLC and International Truck and Engine Corporation. Competitive testing commenced late-2005, although by mid-2006 the competition had been halted with no contract award.

A3 HMMWV

During late 2000 AM General were awarded a USD11.5 million contract to develop an A3 version of the HMMWV. Under this contract, AM General developed and delivered to the government 10 pilot vehicles of four different Army variants. Changes under consideration for the proposed A3 version included an improved electronically controlled engine, new transmission, anti-lock brakes, Central Tyre Inflation (CTI) system and

As the Afghan/Iraqi conflicts developed so did the pressure for even more protection on the HMMWV. Increases in armouring efforts have been centred around the Frag (Fragmentation) Kits, these currently being fitted to M1114/M1116 and M1151, M1152, M1165 and M1167 variants (Carl Schulze)   1391059

The M1151 is essentially the mating of a slightly modified M1114 chassis and M1025 body; the armouring is not fixed (AM General)   1128814

improved suspension. There will be no A3 HMMWV, the A2 and the A2-derived M1152 series will continue in production but with enhancements as required, some of these as a direct result of the A3 development programme.

HMMWV REV kit

The REV kit was developed by AM General as a private venture, with development commencing around 2005 and with some input from the earlier A3 HMMWV programme. The idea of the REV kit is to continuously upgrade and improve the performance and reliability of the HMMWV by the ongoing introduction or revised, uprated/upgraded or new components.

A number of improvements (REV Kit A, Group A) were introduced for US Army production vehicles from October 2007, with a further selection planned for introduction in April 2008. Improvements centre around an improved chassis (new higher-capacity construction), enhanced suspension (including springs, shock-absorbers, control arms and ball joints), improvements to the driveline, higher-capacity wheels and tyres, and improved engine cooling.

All of the initial REV Kit A, Group A improvement components are interchangeable with older components on current in-service vehicles. Vehicles without any REV Kit enhancements remain available for export sales.

Expanded Capacity Vehicle 2 (ECV 2)

It was disclosed late-2007 that the US Army had awarded AM General a contract for 15 next-generation Expanded Capacity Vehicle 2 (ECV 2) HMMWVs. The contract, which included an option for five additional vehicles, called for nine XM1211 (M1165 configuration) and six XM1213 (M1152 configuration). Vehicles were delivered from January 2008, with testing at the Aberdeen proving Ground expected to last for 14 months. A total of 25 ECV test vehicles were supplied to the government for testing.

It was the intention that the ECV 2 would form part of the next HMMWV contract , however, by mid-2009 the US Army had halted ECV trials as it was understood these were deemed non-competitive. AM General has continued ECV 2 development, and the type is understood to be ready for production on receipt of a suitably sized production start-up order. The US Army has a requirement for a protected battlefield ambulance; the ECV 2 is understood to be under consideration to meet this requirement.

Key features of the ECV 2 include: increased ground clearance; a removable parabolic-shaped blast-deflection plate under the crew compartment; a variable-height semi-active suspension system (which can be lowered for air transport); a raised internal floor to reduce transmission intrusion; and a raised roofline that gives greater usable volume for the crew. The ECV 2 will also feature improved fragment and

The M1151 and M1167 armament carriers will eventually replace all older HMMWV armament carriers (Carl Schulze)   1391056

Improvised Explosive Device (IED) protection and an uprated engine 250 hp GEP SCCS 400 turbocharged diesel engine coupled to an Allison 2550 six-speed automatic transmission with automatic traction control. Over the current equivalent HMMWV model, the ECV 2 has a 503 kg increase in usable payload (with add-on armour fitted) and, according to AM General, the estimated gross vehicle weight (GVW) is in the region of 7,250-7,700 kilograms.

Joint Light Tactical Vehicle (JLTV)

It was TACOM's original intention that the light component (Utility Vehicle (UV)) of the Future Tactical Truck System FTTS – the logistic support for the Future Combat System (FCS) – would eventually replace the HMMWV in the US Army's inventory, and possibly the USMC also. For a number of reasons this became unlikely, and in a more realistic approach the follow-on FTTS-MSV/UV Advanced Concept Technology Demonstrators (ACTDs), together with input from other efforts, were to be used to define requirements for future US Army trucks, including the HMMWV's intended successor, the Joint Light Tactical Vehicle (JLTV).

The Joint Light Tactical Vehicle (JLTV) programme is an ambitious joint US Army/USMC effort to design a family of vehicles that would incorporate the latest advances in armour protection, fuel efficiency and crew survivability. Throughout early-to-mid 2007 the Army and USMC had

been preparing to issue a formal request for JLTV proposals late-2007, but those plans were put on hold in September, with the request for proposals finally announced for the Technology Development (TD) phase of the JLTV program in February 2008. Industry proposals were due back no later than 7 April 2008, with contract awards then expected to follow in June or July. Following delays, three 27-month developmental contract awards, valued at around USD40 million each, were announced in October 2008, going to teams led by Lockheed Martin, General Dynamics and BAE Systems. BAE Systems partnered with Navistar International Corp for its contract; Lockheed Martin is paired with another BAE Systems unit (then known as Mobility & Protection Systems); and General Dynamics Land Systems has formed a joint venture known as General Tactical Vehicles with AM General.

By November 2008 the JLTV program had stalled following protests to the Government Accountability Office (GAO) from (initially) Northrop Grumman (teamed with Oshkosh), and later Textron (teamed with Boeing and Science Applications International Corporation). On 17 February 2009, the GAO denied the protests of Northrop Grumman and Textron Marine & Land Systems against the awards of the JLTV TD contracts.

Key deliverables under the 27-month JLTV TD phase included seven vehicles and four trailers representing the three mission role variants (infantry, general purpose and utility) comprising the JLTV Family of

Model	M1038A1	M1097A2	M1113 ECV
Cab seating:	1 + 1 (other models 1 + 3)	1 + 1	1 + 1 (other models 1 + 3)
Configuration:	4 × 4	4 × 4	4 × 4
Weight:			
(laden, GVW)	3,574 kg	4,672 kg	5,216 kg
(unladen, kerb)	2,544 kg	2,676 kg	2,903 kg
(max load)	1,077 kg	1,996 kg	n/avail
(max towed load)	1,542 kg	1,905 kg	2,041 kg
Length:	4.72 m	4.84 m	5 m
Width:	2.18 m	2.18 m	2.18 m
Height:	1.83 m	1.87 m	1.83 m
Ground clearance:	410 mm	430 mm	380 mm
Track:	1.82 m	1.82 m	1.82 m
Wheelbase:	3.3 m	3.3 m	3.3 m
Angle of approach/departure:	47°/45°	54°/38°	46°/41°
Max speed:	113 km/h	113 km/h	113 km/h
Range:	482 km	443 km	380 km
Fuel capacity:	94.6 litres	94.6 litres	94.6 litres
Max gradient:	60%	60%	60%
Side slope:	40%	40%	40%
Fording:			
(unprepared)	760 mm	760 mm	760 mm
(prepared)	1.52 m	1.52 m	1.52 m
Engine:	GM V-8 6.2-litre naturally aspirated water-cooled 4-stroke diesel developing 150 hp (112 kW) at 3,600 rpm	GM V-8 6.5-litre naturally aspirated water-cooled 4-stroke direct injection diesel developing 160 hp (119 kW) at 3,400 rpm and 393 N.m torque at 1,700 rpm. From mid-2000 the OPTIMIZER 6500 6.5-litre naturally aspirated water-cooled 4-stroke diesel engine produced by General Engine Products (a wholly-owned subsidiary of AM General) is being fitted. This engine also develops 160 hp (119 kW) at 3,400 rpm and 393 N.m torque at 1,700 rpm	GM 6.5-litre V-8 turbocharged water-cooled 4-stroke diesel developing 190 hp (142 kW) at 3,400 rpm and 515 N.m torque at 1,700 rpm. From mid-2000 the OPTIMIZER 6500 6.5-litre V-8 turbocharged water-cooled four-stroke diesel engine produced by General Engine Products (a wholly-owned subsidiary of AM General) is being fitted. This engine also produces 190 hp (142 kW) at 3,400 rpm and 515 N.m torque 1,700 rpm
Transmission:	automatic with 3 forward and 1 reverse gears	General Motors GM 4L80-E Turbo-Hydramatic automatic with 4 forward and 1 reverse gears	General Motors GM 4L80-E Turbo-Hydramatic automatic with 4 forward and 1 reverse gears
Transfer box:	2-speed, full-time 4-wheel drive	New Process NP242 2-speed, full-time four-wheel drive	New Process NP242 2-speed, full-time four-wheel drive
Suspension:	independent, double A-arm, coil spring	independent, double A-arm, coil springs and hydraulic shock-absorbers, front and rear	independent, double A-arm, coil springs and hydraulic shock-absorbers, front and rear
Steering:	power-assisted	power-assisted, 13/16:1 variable ratio	power-assisted, 13/16:1 variable ratio
Turning radius:	7.62 m	7.62 m	7.62 m
Brakes:			
(main)	hydraulic, discs front and rear	hydraulic, inboard discs all-round	hydraulic, inboard discs all-round
(parking)	N/A	manual working rear service brakes	manual working rear service brakes
Tyres:	37 × 12.50R 16.5 LT load range D	37 × 12.50R 16.5 LT, load range D, runflat inserts	37 × 12.50R 16.5 LT load range D, runflat inserts
Electrical system:	24 V	12/24 V waterproof	12/24 V waterproof
Batteries:	2 × 12 V	2 × 12 V	2 × 12 V
Alternator:	200 A	N/A	200 A

Vehicles; designs for each of 10 sub-configurations; and ballistic hulls and sample armour components for government testing. The design selection for the system development and demonstration phase could be made as early as mid-2011, with a contract for final production as early as 2013, according to a Congressional Research Service (CRS) report dated 28 August 2008. More recently, it has been stated that upon the completion of the TD phase, the services currently anticipate conducting another full and open competition with award of two contracts for further development and demonstration, with Milestone C decision in FY13 and full production and fielding anticipated in 2015.

Three categories of JLTV are to be developed. Category A requires a payload of 1,588 kg and will be configured as a general-purpose mobility vehicle. Category B will feature the most vehicles, with a payload of 1,814 kg for the USMC and 2,041 kg for the Army. It is to be configured in seven versions: Infantry Carrier Army, Infantry Carrier USMC, Reconnaissance, Command and Control, Heavy Guns Carrier, Close Combat Weapons Carrier, Utility and Ambulance. Category C will have payload of 2,313 kg and will be configured as a utility vehicle and an ambulance.

At an estimated fully equipped price of USD800,000 (base price of USD300,000), it is now unlikely that the JLTV will replace the legacy HMMWV fleet on a one-for-one basis.

XM1124 Hybrid Electric HMMWV

The XM1124 Hybrid Electric HMMWV is derived when the conventional mechanical driveline is removed from a conventional M1113 Expanded Capability Series HMMWV and replaced with a hybrid electric driveline. Compared to the conventional M1113, it is desired that any Hybrid-Electric HMMWV should, when compared to a conventionally powered HMMWV, have a higher top speed, faster acceleration, longer range, better fuel economy, increased payload capacity, and reduced emissions.

In 1998, the first prototypes of the Hybrid Electric HMMWV were shown. Developed by PEI Electronics Inc. of Huntsville, Alabama, as prime contractor for the US Army's Tank-Automotive and Armament Command (TACOM) and the Defense Advanced Research Projects Agency (DARPA) through a cost-shared programme.

In May 2001, AM General was awarded a USD3.6 million research and development contract for Phase 1 of the Hybrid Electric HMMWV Program. The contract (subsequently increased to USD8.6 million) called for the delivery of five prototype vehicles by May 2003. In July 2003, the US Army projected a requirement for 1,500 Hybrid Electric HMMWVs for scout/RSTA use, as well as 19,000 Hybrid Electric HMMWV shelter carriers. A sole source AMG-FFP contract was issued in July 2003 and a Design-CPFF contract was issued in December 2003.

FY04 and FY05 budgets funded continuation of the Hybrid Electric HMMWV programme. XM1124 vehicles went on to participate in the US Army's Tank Automotive Research, Development and Engineering Center's Air Assault Expeditionary Force Spiral B in 2005, Spiral C in 2006 and Spiral D in 2007.

Most recently, in November 2009 the US Army announced that it had awarded EnerDel Inc. a USD1.29 million contract to develop a battery system for the XM1124 HMMWV. EnerDel Inc. and the US Army's Tank Automotive Research, Development and Engineering Center (TARDEC) will be working together over the next 18 months to develop four hybrid HMMWV concepts.

Specifications
See table on facing page

Status
M998A2 series, ECV, M1151, M1152, M1165 and M1167 in production. ECV II, 25 prototypes produced. Earlier models are no longer in production.

In service with the US Army, Air Force, Navy and Marines - approx 154,000, 40 per cent of which are armoured). Also in service with Abu Dhabi (over 1,700), Afghanistan (>7,500), Algeria (approx. 80), Argentina (>50), Bahrain (277), Bolivia (30), Bulgaria (52), Canada (SF, small number), Chad (20), Chile (est. 150), China (chassis), Columbia (several hundred), Croatia, Czech Republic (26 + five, US loan for ISAF), Denmark (30, M1045A2 TOW - now converted to LRPV), Djibouti (18), Ecuador (est. 360), Egypt (est. 1,700), Georgia, Greece (654), Honduras (125), Hungary, Iraq (700 + est. 12,000 US surplus by early-2010), Israel (approx. 3,000), Japan (five), Jordan (700), Kuwait (est. 800), Latvia (13), Lithuania (86), Luxembourg (>69), Mexico (>3,500), Nepal (15), Oman (>150), Peru (est. 50), Philippines (440), Poland (229), Portugal (51), Romania (20), Qatar (40), Saudi Arabia (>4,629), Spain (est. 150), Switzerland (five), Taiwan (est. 5,500), Thailand (275), Tunisia (341), Turkey (two), UAE (several hundred) and Venezuela (small number). In some cases these figures relate to numbers delivered, in others to numbers thought to remain in service. In some cases, deliveries may be continuing, either regularly, or spasmodically.

The most recent official figures released by AM General date from August 1993. All updating from that date has been via third party sources. AM General will confirm that as of early 2011 over 270,000 HMMWVs had been produced. That figure includes over 230,000 for the US government, the remainder to over 50 foreign governments. Commercial HUMMER H1, H2 and H3 sales exceeded 75,000 during their production between 2003-2009.

Contractor
AM General LLC

General Motors Commercial Utility Cargo Vehicles (CUCV)

Development
Starting in 1981, a 14-month programme known as the 'Special Analysis of Wheeled Vehicle Requirements' (usually abbreviated to just 'WHEELS') was carried out by the then US Army Tank Automotive Command. Its objective was to find a commercial vehicle that could be easily procured for US Army use in areas where extreme environmental conditions would

Truck, Utility, Tactical ¾ ton, (4 × 4), M1009 of US Armed Forces stationed in Germany (Michael Jerchel)   1047626

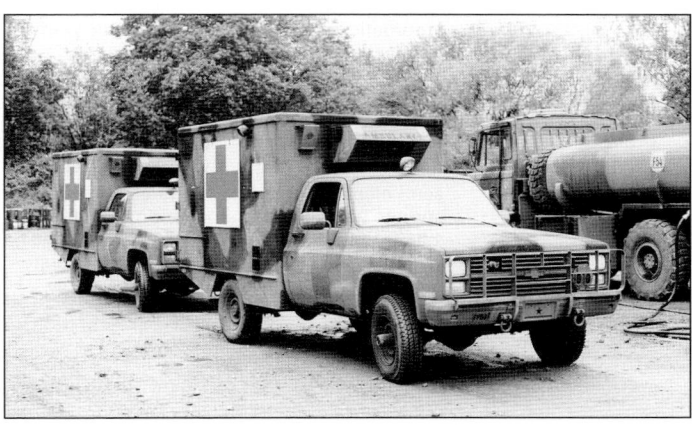

Truck, Ambulance, Tactical ¾ ton, (4 × 4), M1010 of US Armed Forces stationed in Germany (Michael Jerchel)   1047628

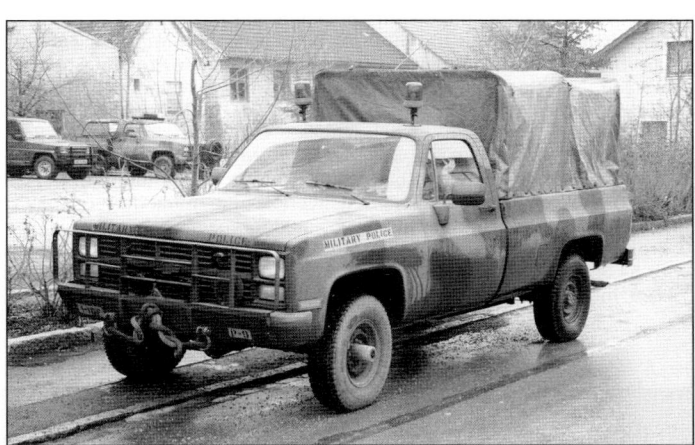

Truck, Cargo, Tactical ¾ ton, (4 × 4), M1008 of US Armed Forces stationed in Germany (Michael Jerchel)   1047627

Truck, Cargo, Tactical ¾ ton, (4 × 4) M1008 of the USAF stationed in Germany (Michael Jerchel)   1124737

General Motors Commercial Utility Cargo Vehicles (CUCV)

Type	A	B	C	D	E
Function:	utility	cargo	ambulance	truck	cargo, shelter carrier
Military designation:	M1009	M1008	M1010	M1031	M1028
GM model number:	K10516 Blazer	K30903 pick-up	K30903 chassis/cab	K30903 chassis/cab	K30903 pick-up
Cab seating:	1 + 1 + 3	3	1 + 1	3	3
Configuration:	4 × 4	4 × 4	4 × 4	4 × 4	4 × 4
Weight:					
(laden)	2,903 kg	3,992 kg	4,287 kg	4,334 kg	4,264 kg
Max payload:	544 kg	1,315 kg	943 kg	1,792 kg	1,633 kg
Length:	4.873 m	5.607 m	5.784 m	5.408 m	5.607 m
Width:	2.022 m	2.062 m	2.062 m	2.062 m	2.062 m
Height:					
(overall)	1.905 m	1.915 m	2.581 m	1.938 m	1.92 m
Track:					
(front)	1.485 m	1.488 m	1.488 m	1.488 m	1.488 m
(rear)	1.382 m	1.438 m	1.438 m	1.438 m	1.438 m
Wheelbase:	2.705 m	3.34 m	3.34 m	3.34 m	3.34 m
Fording:	508 mm	508 mm	508 mm	508 mm	508 mm
Engine:	General Motors 6.2-litre V-8 water-cooled 4-stroke diesel developing 135 hp (101 kW) at 3,600 rpm	General Motors 6.2-litre V-8 water-cooled 4-stroke diesel developing 135 hp (101 kW) at 3,600 rpm	General Motors 6.2-litre V-8 water-cooled 4-stroke diesel developing 135 hp (101 kW) at 3,600 rpm	General Motors 6.2-litre V-8 water-cooled 4-stroke diesel developing 135 hp (101 kW) at 3,600 rpm	General Motors 6.2-litre V-8 water-cooled 4-stroke diesel developing 135 hp (101 kW) at 3,600 rpm
Gearbox:	General Motors THM-400 3- speed automatic with 1 reverse	General Motors THM-400 3- speed automatic with 1 reverse	General Motors THM-400 3- speed automatic with 1 reverse	General Motors THM-400 3- speed automatic with 1 reverse	General Motors THM-400 3- speed automatic with 1 reverse
Transfer box:	2-speed	2-speed	2-speed	2-speed	2-speed
Suspension:					
(front)	tapered leaf springs with 1,021 kg capacity	tapered leaf springs with 1,021 kg capacity	tapered leaf springs with 1,021 kg capacity	tapered leaf springs with 1,021 kg capacity	tapered leaf springs with 1,021 kg capacity
(rear)	semi-elliptic multileaf springs with 850, 1,588, 1,588, 1,701, 1,701 kg capacity respectively	semi-elliptic multileaf springs with 850, 1,588, 1,588, 1,701, 1,701 kg capacity respectively	semi-elliptic multileaf springs with 850, 1,588, 1,588, 1,701, 1,701 kg capacity respectively	semi-elliptic multileaf springs with 850, 1,588, 1,588, 1,701, 1,701 kg capacity respectively	semi-elliptic multileaf springs with 850, 1,588, 1,588, 1,701, 1,701 kg capacity respectively
Tyres:	10.00 × 15	9.50 × 16.5	9.50 × 16.5	9.50 × 16.5	9.50 × 16.5
Electrical system:	28 V, 100 Ah	28 V, 100 Ah	28 V, 200 Ah	28 V, 100 Ah	28 V, 100 Ah

not be met and where expensive tactical-type vehicles were not necessary. The objective was to replace 20 per cent of the M151 Jeeps in use and the bulk of the M880 series of pick-up trucks. The vehicle type/types chosen would also be used by the US Air Force and Marine Corps.

During the programme the US Army purchased 26 commercial vehicles and subjected them to exhaustive tests at the Aberdeen Proving Grounds, Maryland. The final choice was a General Motors design, the Model K which is one of the GM C/K series, over nine million of which were produced.

In July 1982, a contract was awarded to General Motors worth USD689 million for a total of 53,248 vehicles known as the Commercial Utility Cargo Vehicles (CUCV). First deliveries were made in August 1983 and the initial production programme lasted three years.

Projected procurement was for 57,349 CUCVs for all the armed services with 54,087 for the US Army. Total production at the end of 1986 was 70,889, including FMS. Production ceased in 1987.

The US Marine Corps received 3,159 CUCVs of the following types: M1008 - 2,194; M1009 - 166; M1010 - 290; M1031 - 95; M1028 - 414.

Description
The CUCV fleet comprises the following five types of vehicle:
Type A, Truck, Utility, Tactical ¾ ton, (4 × 4), M1009
Type B, Truck, Cargo, Tactical 1¼ ton, (4 × 4), M1008
Type C, Truck, Ambulance, Tactical 1¼ ton, (4 × 4), M1010
Type D, Truck, Chassis, Tactical 1¼ ton, (4 × 4), M1031
Type E, Truck, Cargo, Shelter Carrier, Tactical 1¼ ton, (4 × 4), M1028.

All five types are based on a common power train, but utilise different body and/or chassis variations to fulfil a variety of purposes and have varying payloads to suit their role. All five types are powered by the same 6.2-litre diesel engine coupled to an automatic transmission and two-speed transfer box. Front and rear axles are the same for all types apart

Ex-US Armed Forces Truck, Utility, Tactical ¾ ton, (4 × 4), M1009 of the Latvian Army (Stefan Marx)   1124711

Truck, Cargo, Shelter Carrier, Tactical ¾ ton, (4 × 4), M1028 of US Armed Forces stationed in Germany (Michael Jerchel)   1047629

Ex-US Armed Forces Truck, Utility, Tactical ¾ ton, (4 × 4), M1008 of the Lithuanian Army (Shaun C Connors)   1391369

Truck, Chassis, Tactical ¾ ton, (4 × 4), M1031 fitted with a specialist tool carrying body of US Armed Forces stationed in Germany (Michael Jerchel)   1047630

Ex-US Armed Forces Truck, Utility, Tactical ¾ ton, (4 × 4), M1008 of the Latvian Army (Stefan Marx)   1124710

from the Type A. The same 28 V electrical system is used in all types apart from the Type C ambulance which has a system with doubled power.

The five types are all commercial models with the following alterations incorporated: blackout lights; camouflage paint (three colour, NATO); engine diagnostic connector assembly; military markings, including a removable red cross for the Type C ambulance; NBC warfare protection and kit provisions; rear pintle hook; slave-start capability; towing capability; weapon holders; and a winterisation kit to allow operations down to −46°C.

The Type C ambulance version has provision for four stretcher patients or eight seated casualties. An air-filter system is also provided along with air conditioning and extra lighting, including spotlights. The Type E cargo, shelter carrier is equipped with shelter tiedown brackets.

All five types are air-transportable.

Specifications
See table on facing page

Status
Production complete. There were 70,889 units delivered to all branches of the US Armed Forces. The total includes FMS to nations such as Columbia, Grenada, Honduras, Israel, Jamaica, Liberia (M1009), Mexico, Panama and Taiwan. Surplus US Army CUCVs are known to have been supplied to Estonia, Latvia and Lithuania.

Contractor
GM Defense

General Motors Commercial Utility Cargo Vehicles II (CUCV II)

Description
Following the completed production of the original CUCV range (full details of which can be found elsewhere in this section), General Motors (GM) Corporation, Military Vehicles Operation (now GM Defense), introduced a new range of economical tactical support vehicles known as the CUCV II. The CUCV II range followed the same general lines as the original CUCV range and similar basic General Motors commercial models were involved, but updated and revised. Production of the CUCV II range concluded in 2000, GM Defense introducing the further updated Light Service Support Vehicle (LSSV) range. From mid-2005 AM General LLC became responsible for sales and marketing of the LSSV range. Full details of the LSSV range can be found elsewhere in this section.

US Armed Forces did not field the CUCV II range, however around 800 were delivered through TACOM and GSA. Over 3,000 vehicles were supplied to Saudi Arabia in the early 1990s and other users in small numbers include (or included) Ecuador, Sweden, UK and Venezuela.

Description
The CUCV II range followed the same general lines as the original CUCV range and similar basic General Motors commercial models were involved, but updated and revised.

The base engine for the CUCV II range was a GM 6.5-litre V8 diesel developing 195 hp. Also available was a 5.7-litre petrol developing 255 hp or a 7.4-litre V8 petrol developing 290 hp. A further option was provided by a 6.5-litre diesel developing 150 hp. All engines could be coupled to General Motors automatic or manual transmissions.

The military standard options available for CUCV II varied from model to model, but included a 24 V electrical system, blackout lighting, a battery booster connector, a radiator brush guard, front and rear tiedowns, a trailer pintle hook and electrical connector, weapon racks and similar specialised items.

CUCV II Type A, Truck, Utility (GM Defense)   0044370

CUCV II Type B, Truck, Cargo (GM Defense)   0044371

CUCV II Type S (Suburban) Command/Personnel Carrier (GM Defense)   0044372

CUCV II truck series

Type	A	B	C	S
Function:	utility	carrier	ambulance	personnel carrier
GM model number:	K10516	K30903	K30903	K20906
Cab seating:	2 + 3	3 + 8	3 + 4	1 + 5
Configuration:	4 × 4	4 × 4	4 × 4	4 × 4
Weight: (GVW)	2,835 kg	4,172 kg	4,173 kg	3,900 kg
Payload:	475 kg	1,701 kg	907 kg	953 kg
Length:	4.902 m	5.669 m	5.9 m	n/avail
Width:	1.957 m	1.95 m	1.961 m	n/avail
Height: (overall)	1.869 m	1.93 m	2.713 m	1.836 m
Ground clearance:	229 mm	206 mm	206 mm	206 mm
Wheelbase:	2.832 m	3.34 m	3.34 m	3.34 m
Max speed:	88 km/h	88 km/h	88 km/h	88 km/h
Range:	400 km	400 km	400 km	400 km
Fording:	508 mm	508 mm	508 mm	508 mm
Engine:	GM 6.5-litre V-8 water-cooled 4-stroke diesel developing 195 hp (145 kW) at 3,400 rpm	GM 6.5-litre V-8 water-cooled 4-stroke diesel developing 195 hp (145 kW) at 3,400 rpm	GM 6.5-litre V-8 water-cooled 4-stroke diesel developing 195 hp (145 kW) at 3,400 rpm	GM 6.5-litre V-8 water-cooled 4-stroke diesel developing 195 hp (145 kW) at 3,400 rpm
Transmission:	GM THM 4L60E automatic with 4 forward and 1 reverse gears	GM THM 4L60E automatic with 4 forward and 1 reverse gears	GM THM 4L60E automatic with 4 forward and 1 reverse gears	GM THM 4L60E automatic with 4 forward and 1 reverse gears
Transfer box:	2-speed	2-speed	2-speed	2-speed
Suspension:				
(front)	independent heavy-duty torsion bar with shock-absorbers	independent heavy-duty torsion bar with shock-absorbers	independent heavy-duty torsion bar with shock-absorbers	independent heavy-duty torsion bar with shock-absorbers
(rear)	two-stage semi-elliptic leaf springs with shock-absorbers	two-stage semi-elliptic leaf springs with shock-absorbers	two-stage semi-elliptic leaf springs with shock-absorbers	two-stage semi-elliptic leaf springs with shock-absorbers
Tyres: (off road)	75R 16	75R 16E	75R 16E	75R 16E
Electrical system:	12/24 V	12/24 V	12/24 V	12/24 V

Available for fitment to the CUCV II series was a series of Military Equipment Packages. These packages could be added as optional extras or could be provided as standard according to model. The full listing of these packages is as follows:

ME01. 12/24 V power converter
ME02. Blackout lighting
ME03. NATO slave start
ME04. Front brush guard
ME05. Front tiedowns
ME06. Rear tiedowns
ME07. Towing pintle hook
ME08. Trailer light connection
ME09. M16 Rifle/M4 Carbine bracket
ME10. Transmission and axle vent filters
ME11. Government data plate
ME12. Cargo area troop seats
ME13. Cargo tiedowns
ME14. Cargo cover
ME15. Shelter tiedown kit
ME16. Shelter - communications
ME17. Ambulance body
ME25. Roof rack spare tyre
ME28. Winch, front mounted
ME32. On/off road mobility package
ME34C. Three-colour camouflage finish
ME40. Pioneer kit.

The CUCV II range consisted of six basic models:
Type A Utility based on the K10516 Yukon and generally similar to the original CUCV M1009
Type B Truck Cargo based on the K30903 Pick-up and generally similar to the original CUCV M1008
Type C Truck Ambulance based on the K30903 Chassis/cab and generally similar to the original CUCV M1010
Type E Shelter carrier based on the K30903 Pick-up and intended for demountable shelters
Type F Communications Shelter carrier based on the K30903 Pick-up
Type S Command Car (Suburban) based on the K20906 light truck and intended as a four-door personnel carrier.

Specifications
See table above

Status
Production complete. Supplied to Ecuador, Lithuania, Saudi Arabia (over 3,000), UK (small number, RAF), Venezuela and other undisclosed UN member countries.

Contractor
GM Defense

General Motors Light Service Support Vehicle (LSSV)

Description
Following the completion of production of the Commercial Utility Cargo Vehicles (CUCV) II range in 2000 GM Defense introduced a follow-on range of economical tactical support vehicles known as the Light Service Support Vehicle (LSSV) range. As with the earlier CUCV ranges, the LSSV range were essentially General Motors commercial products that after initial assembly in civilian configuration were subsequently militarised to levels required to suit their intended non-tactical role. The LSSV range was based on the then current Silverado pick-up and Suburban and Tahoe station wagon models.

As of January 1999, General Motors was on contract with the US Army's Tank-automotive and Armaments Command (TACOM) for a five-year supply of LSSVs to the US Air Force and Navy.

In November 2002 it was announced that the Canadian Department of National Defence was set to award a CAD49.7 million contract to General Motors Defense for 861 Military Commercial-Off-The-Shelf (MilCOTS) trucks, based on the GM Silverado Light Service Support Vehicle (LSSV) series. Two variants were involved, 801 basic variants (142 of which are fitted with lights and sirens for Military Police duties) and 60 cable layers. The basic variant has the GM designation GM K25743 and the cable layer has the GM designation GM K36053. Deliveries began in the second quarter of 2003, with the final vehicles delivered during early 2004. These vehicles are primarily for use by reserve units within North America. One non-standard option for these vehicles is the wiring and fittings for the Iris tactical communications system. A contract option for a further 200 vehicles was subsequently exercised.

GM Silverado pick-up based CUCV III Light Service Support Vehicle (LSSV), 1 ton (4 × 4). This vehicle is fitted with the optional front/rear-mounting self-recovery winch (GM Defense) 0552246

GM Tahoe-based CUCV III Light Service Support Vehicle (LSSV), half-ton (4 × 4), six-passenger (Command Tahoe) (GM Defense)   0552245

The MilCOTS contract was the first part of the CAD241 million Light Utility Vehicle Wheeled project to acquire a replacement for the Canadian Army's Bombardier-built Iltis vehicles.

It was announced in April 2005 that AM General and General Motors had executed an agreement covering the development of a marketing arrangement through which AM General would assume marketing and sales responsibility for the GM-produced Light Service Support Vehicle (LSSV). AM General offered three LSSVs, all based on the Chevrolet Silverado 2500 HD and in either standard, extended or crew cab models, complete with a militarised cargo/troop carrier, as the baseline configuration or upgraded for off-road with an enhanced mobility package. Sales of the LSSV range (which has previously included models based on the commercial Suburban and Tahoe models) in 2003 totalled approaching 1,700 units, primarily to US and international military organisations.

From FY07 onwards the LSSV was no longer offered by AM General. This was due to the engine in the 2007 year model being incompatible with the military fuel, JP8.

There were initially six main model-types in the LSSV range, with militarisation equipment fitted as standard throughout the range, consisting of: a front brush guard; front and rear tie-down shackles; rear towing pintle and trailer electrical connector; transmission, differentials and transfer box vent filters; protective Kevlar CV joint covers on the front axle; heavy-duty gas-filled shock absorbers; 12/24 V power converter; blackout lighting, NATO slave-start socket, M14/M16 weapons brackets and a government data plate. Optional military equipment available throughout the range consists of a remotely controllable winch; continuous output 5,000 W AC/DC generator, OnStar communications package, pioneer tool kit, and mil-spec removable seat covers.

Details of additional vehicle-specific military options can be found in the relevant sub-section.

Crew-cab cargo/troop carrier

The military designation of this model is Light Service Support Vehicle, 1 ton, 4 × 4. It has the General Motors truck model designation GM K25943HD and is a four-door crew-cab pick-up design with a 4.24 m wheelbase. The rear pick-up body is 2.479 m in length and may be covered with a glass fibre hard-top with locking side/rear access doors, or a tarpaulin under which troop seats may be fitted. The optional remotely-controllable winch is front- or rear-mounting and stores under the pick-up bed floor when not in use. Other model-specific military equipment options include run-flat tyres and a vehicle-mounted auxiliary 70 cfm at 150 psi air compressor.

On this model the front axle is rated at 2.045 kg, the rear axle at 2,765 kg. Underbody skid plates are fitted to the front differential, engine, transmission and transfer box.

As an option to the standard 6.6-litre 300 hp diesel engine and Allison 1000 Series automatic transmission, a Chevrolet six-litre V-8 water-cooled petrol developing 300 hp at 4,400 rpm and 488 N.m torque at 4,000 rpm, coupled to a 4L80E four-speed automatic transmission, may be fitted.

The Canadian Department of National Defence awarded GM Defense a CAD49.7 million contract for 861 Military commercial-Off-The-Shelf (MilCOTS) trucks, based on the GM Silverado Light Service Support Vehicle (LSSV) series. Two variants were involved, 801 basic variants (right) and 60 cable layers (left); a contract option was subsequently exercised that called for an additional 200 vehicles (GM Defense)   0552252

Cargo/troop carrier

As with the crew-cab cargo/troop carrier, the military designation of these models is Light Service Support Vehicle, 1 ton, 4 × 4. They share a 3.378 m wheelbase and have the General Motors truck model designations of GM K25903HD, and K25753HD for the extended cab. Optional military equipment and driveline options, axle ratings and underbody skid protection are identical to those of the crew-cab cargo/troop carrier model.

Ambulance

Two ambulance models were available, one with single rear wheels, the other with dual rear wheels. The military designation of both models is Truck Ambulance, 1 ton, 4 × 4. The dual rear-wheeled model has the General Motors designation GM K36003 chassis-cab, the single rear-wheeled model has the designation GM K25903 chassis-cab designation.

The maximum GVW of the single-wheeled model is 4,172 kg, with axle ratings of 2,182 kg (front) and 3,136 kg (rear). The dual-wheeled model has a maximum GVW of 5,455 kg and axle ratings of 2,182 kg (front) and 4,091 kg (rear). The optional remotely-controllable winch is front-mounting only.

The ambulance body including the two full-width rear doors is constructed of all-welded aluminium, the exterior panelling being 2.5 mm 50/52 H-32 aluminium, the floor panel being 3.1 mm thick. The roof, floor and sidewalls have 51 mm of glass fibre insulation. Air conditioning is standard. Internal arrangements will handle four litter patients or eight sitting patients, plus two attendants. The main difference between the two models is overall body width, and consequently available interior work and stowage space.

Specifications

See table on next page

Command Suburban

The military designation of this model is Light Service Support Vehicle, ¾ ton, 4 × 4, nine-passenger. It has the General Motors truck model designation GM K20906, Suburban, and is a four-door (plus two rear doors) design with three full-width bench-type seats and 3.92 m³ of cargo volume.

The optional remotely-controllable winch is front- or rear-mounting, the other model-specific military equipment option being run-flat tyres. On this model underbody skid plates are fitted to the front differential, engine and transfer box. The front axle is rated at 1,896 kg, the rear axle at 2,727 kg.

Command Tahoe

The military designation of this model is Light Service Support Vehicle, ½ ton, 4 × 4, six-passenger. It has the General Motors truck model designation GM K15706, four-door Tahoe, and is a four-door (plus two rear doors) design with two full-width bench-type seats - the rear of which folds - and 2.96 m³ of cargo volume.

GM Suburban based CUCV III Light Service Support Vehicle (LSSV), three-quarter-ton (4 × 4), nine-passenger (Command Suburban). This vehicle is fitted with the optional front/rear-mounting self-recovery winch (GM Defense)   0552247

The British Army uses the LSSV for escort and other duties at BATUS, Canada (GM Defense)   0552256

Function	Cargo/troop transport, crew-cab	Cargo/troop transport	Ambulance	Command, control and troop transport	command control and troop transport	Service vehicle
GM model number:	K25943HD	K25903HD K25753HD	K25903 chassis-cab K36003 chassis-cab	K20906	K15706	K36453 chassis-cab
Cab seating:	1 + 5	1 + 2	1 + 2	1 + 8	1 + 5	1 + 5
Configuration:	4 × 4	4 × 4	4 × 4	4 × 4	4 × 4	4 × 4
Weight:						
(max GVW)	4,172 kg	4,172 kg	(K25903) 4,172 kg (K36003) 5,455 kg	3,909 kg	3,136 kg	5,455 kg
(max load)	1,454 kg[1]	1,454 kg[1]	(K25903) 2.846 kg[2] (K36003) 1,773 kg[2]	1,181 kg[1]	696 kg[1]	2,590 kg[2]
Length:	6.503 m	5.639 m	n/avail	5.57 m	5.053 m	n/avail
Width:	2.023 m	1.994 m	(body) 2.413 m	2.002 m	2.004 m	n/avail
Height:	(cab) 1.943 m	(cab) 1.923 m	(body) 2.743 m	1.89 m	1.892 m	n/avail
Wheelbase:	4.24 m	3.378 m	(K25903) 3.383 m (K36003) 3.483 m	3.302 m	2.946 m	4.713 m
Fuel capacity:	114.5 litres	129 litres	(K25903) 114.5 litres (K36003) 134.7 litres	146 litres	98 litres	134.7 litres
Engine:	GM Duramax 6.6-litre V-8 water-cooled, turbocharged and intercooled common-rail direct-injection diesel developing 224 kW (300 hp) and 705 N.m torque at 1,800 rpm in models K25943HD K25903HD, K25753HD, and K25903, K36003 K36453 chassis-cabs (see main text for options); 6-litre V-8 water-cooled petrol developing 239 kW (320 hp) at 5,000 rpm and 488 N.m torque at 4,000 rpm in model K20906, and 4.8-litre V-8 water-cooled petrol developing 205 kW (275 hp) at 5,200 rpm and 393 N.m torque at 4,000 rpm in model K15706					
Transmission:	Allison 1000 Series automatic with 5 forward and 1 reverse gears in models K25943HD K25903HD, K25753HD, and K25903, K36003 K36453 chassis-cabs (see main text for options); GM automatic with 4 forward (plus overdrive and tow/haul switch) and 1 reverse gears in models K20906 and K15706					
Transfer box:	NVG 2 speed in models K25943HD K25903HD, K25753HD, and K25903, K36003 K36453 chassis-cabs; New Venture 246 2 speed in models K20906 and K15706					
Suspension:	independent torsion bar, plus gas-filled shock-absorbers and anti-roll bar, front, semi-elliptic leaf springs and gas-filled shock absorbers, rear					
Tyres:	245/75R 16 all models except (K36003) 215/85R 16, and (K36453) 235/85R 16					
Brakes:	discs front and rear, four-wheel Anti-lock Braking System (ABS)					
Electrical: system	12/24 V	12/24 V	12/24 V	12/24 V	12/24 V	12/24 V
Batteries:	2 ×12 V	2 × 12 V	2 × 12 V	2 × 12 V	2 × 12 V	2 × 12 V
Alternator:	105 A	105 A	2 of, 210 A total	130 A	130 A	1 ×12 V, 105 A 1 ×24 V, 130 A

[1] Estimate of payload and crew, varies with equipment levels
[2] Estimate of payload and crew without body

Ambulance

Model	GM K36003 chassis-cab with dual rear wheels	GM K25903 chassis-cab with single rear wheels
Body length:		
(overall)	2.845 m	2.845 m
(inside)	2.73 m	2.73 m
Body height:		
(overall)	2.743 m	2.743 m
(inside)	1.828 m	1.828 m
Body width:		
(overall)	2.413 m	2.057 m
(inside)	2.298 m	1.949 m

The optional remotely-controllable winch is front- or rear-mounting, the other model-specific military equipment option being run-flat tyres. On this model underbody skid plates are fitted to the front differential, engine, transfer box and fuel tank. The front axle is rated at 1,780 kg, the rear axle at 1,818 kg.

Service body
The military designation of this model is 4 × 4 Service Vehicle. It has the General Motors truck model designation GM K36453 chassis-cab, and is a two-door extended cab design with a fold-up second row bench seat and dual rear wheels. The rear chassis mounts a purpose-designed box-type maintenance body.

The optional remotely-controllable winch is front- or combined front- and rear-mounting, the other model-specific military equipment option being a deployable vehicle-mounted auxiliary 70 cmf at 150 psi air compressor. On this model underbody skid plates are fitted to the front differential, engine and transfer box. The front axle is rated at 2,042 kg, the rear axle at 3,910 kg.

Commercially Based Tactical Truck (Combatt) Tech Demonstrator
The Combatt Tech Demonstrator is an enhanced mobility truck based on the commercially available GM Silverado, but with militarisation above and beyond that available on the CUCV range of vehicles.

Key enhancements include raising the chassis by 152 mm for additional suspension travel and ground clearance, resulting in a minimum of 254 mm clearance (front) and 229 mm clearance (rear). Approach and departure angles increase to 43° and 34°, respectively. The Combatt Tech Demonstrator can climb a 60 per cent gradient, traverse a 30 per cent

sideslope, and ford to 0.762 m. Runflat 37 × 12.5R tyres are standard and the 17 inch (431.8 mm) aluminium wheel rims are fitted with beadlocks for low pressure operation, a Central Tyre Inflation (CTI) system with a rapid deflate feature as an option. To compliment this improved off-road mobility, additional underbody protection is fitted and both front and rear axles are fitted with limited-slip differentials.

Hybrid Electric LSSV
In January 2003 GM Defense, working in co-operation with TACOM, unveiled a parallel hybrid electric powered prototype based on the Silverado. The hybrid system selected uses a patented split power Continuously Variable Transmission (CVT) with integral electric motors and an energy storage system, to deliver power to the wheels. The lightweight nickel-metal hydride-based energy storage system weighs around a third less and is around half the size of lead-acid battery storage systems. The hybrid vehicle can produce up to 30 kW of exportable AC and DC electrical power.

The demonstrator is also fitted with a fuel cell Auxiliary Power Unit (APU). The 5 kW Proton Exchange Membrane (PEM) regenerative fuel cell system is capable of producing either electricity or pure water in power producing mode, or hydrogen and oxygen in electrolysis mode. As the vehicle is driven, the PEM electrolyser uses diesel engine provided electricity to electrolyse (break down) the water into hydrogen and oxygen, with the hydrogen stored for future use. Later, with the engine switched off, the stored hydrogen, together with oxygen from the air, is fed to the cell to produce electricity, returning the pure water as a by-product. This water, which can be consumed if required, is stored to repeat the cycle.

Specifications
See table on facing pages

Status
Production complete. In service with Canada (861 + 200), the UK (BATUS) and the US Air Force and Navy.

Contractor
AM General Corporation

Jeep AM 720 (4 × 4)

Description
The Jeep (now Chrysler LLC) AM 720 (4 × 4) 1,135 kg light truck is an updated version of the earlier AM 715, in that it resembles the general layout and appearance. The AM 720 is based on the commercial J-20 truck and was available with two main types of cargo body known as the Military Cargo Box or the Townside Cargo Box, with the latter intended mainly for the civilian market. Either can carry up to 13 personnel seated on folding benches and can be covered by a vinyl top resting on bows. The cab also has a vinyl top.

Numerous options were available for the AM 720, including various wheelbase lengths and left- or right-hand drive. An electric winch with a capacity of 2,832 kg can be fitted and a 24 V conversion kit is available.

This vehicle has been licence-produced in Egypt and full details of this can be found elsewhere in this section.

Specifications
AM 720
Cab seating: 1 + 2 (up to 13 in rear)
Configuration: 4 × 4
Weight:
 (unladen) 2,175 kg
 (laden) 3,814 kg
 (max load, off-road) 1,135 kg
 (max load, on-road) 1,639 kg
 (towed load) 3,629 kg
Length: 5.36 m
Width: 2.004 m
Height:
 (with cargo top) 2.286 m
 (cargo bed) 840 mm
Ground clearance: 208 mm
Track:
 (front) 1.626 m
 (rear) 1.661 m
Wheelbase: (standard) 3.322 m
Angle of approach/departure: 35°/21°
Fuel capacity: 69 litres
Fording: 457 mm
Engine: Model 258 CID 4.2-litre 6-cylinder OHV water-cooled developing 112 hp (84 kW) at 3,000 rpm, or 5.9-litre 8-cylinder water-cooled developing 144 hp (107 kW) at 3,200 rpm
Gearbox: manual with 4 forward and 1 reverse gears
Transfer box: 2-speed
Clutch: single dry disc
Steering: variable ratio power-assisted
Turning radius: 6.78 m
Suspension: longitudinal leaf springs with severe use shock-absorbers
Tyres: 9.50 × 16.5 or 9.00 × 16
Brakes: power, disc front; drum rear
Electrical system: 12 V (24 V optional)

Status
Production complete. Remains in widespread use; numbers reducing.

Contractor
Chrysler LLC

Jeep AM 720 (4 × 4) 1,135 kg light truck (Chrysler LLC)   0511830

Jeep Cherokee/Liberty and Grand Cherokee series of (4 × 4) light vehicles

Development
The Jeep Cherokee (SJ), in name, first became available in 1974, although this was essentially a slightly revised and sportier Jeep Wagoneer: a large truck-based four-door wagon with four-wheel drive that had been launched in the early 1960s and had changed little between then and the early 1970s. The 1984 launched Jeep Cherokee (XJ) shared only a name with its predecessor, being a smaller, more compact and modern design. Nearly 78,000 commercial Cherokees were sold in the first year of production. The XJ platform provided the mechanical basis for the MJ series Jeep Comanche pick-up. The Cherokee (XJ) was scheduled to be replaced by a new and larger model known as the XJC, however the ongoing popularity of the model ensured this did not occur and the intended replacement was named the Jeep Grand Cherokee when introduced in 1993. The Jeep Cherokee received a major mechanical/design face-lift in 1997, although visually the vehicles remained very similar. Production of the Jeep Cherokee concluded mid-2001.

The Jeep Cherokee (XJ) was replaced in the Jeep product lineup from 2002 by an entirely new design badged Jeep Liberty (KJ/KK). For most markets outside of North America and for marketing purposes the name Cherokee was retained for Liberty models. The Jeep Liberty received a complete redesign for the 2008 model year (KK) and now features a more boxy and traditional look.

The design origins of the Jeep Grand Cherokee date back to 1983, although production would not commence until 1993. Grand Cherokee ZJ models were manufactured from 1993 to 1998, these replaced in 1999 by the extensively redesigned Grand Cherokee WJ which remained in production until 2004. The then all new Jeep Grand Cherokee (WK) was introduced in 2005 and this remained in production until 2010. The next generation Jeep Grand Cherokee (WK2) went on sale in Summer 2010.

Jeep Cherokee/Liberty and Grand Cherokee models are essentially commercial designs that lend themselves to limited militarisation making them suited to certain military applications, these best being described as rear echelon, command, control, communication, internal security duties, or for use by governmental, humanitarian or aid agencies.

Various Cherokee models have been, or are, produced in China, including the XJ and WJ.

Specifications

Model	XJ Wagon (Cherokee)	XJ Truck (Comanche)
Cab seating:	1 + 4	1 + 2
Configuration:	4 × 4	4 × 4
Weight:		
(laden)	2,213 kg	2,464 kg
(unladen)	1,363 kg	1,464 kg
(max load)	750 kg	1,000 kg
(towed load)	2,268 kg	2,268 kg
Length:	4.2 m	4.928 m
Width:	1.79 m	1.822 m
Height: (hardtop)	1.63 m	1.666 m
Ground clearance:	210 mm	213 mm
Track:	1.473 m	1.473 m
Wheelbase:	2.576 m	3.033 m
Angle of approach/departure:	42°/32°	44°/27°
Fuel capacity:	76 litres	76 litres

UAE Army Chrysler Jeep Cherokee (Patrick Allen)   1138447

Model	XJ Wagon (Cherokee)	XJ Truck (Comanche)
Engine:	options throughout the production run were numerous and included a 2.5-litre 4-cylinder in-line water-cooled petrol developing 104 hp (78 kW) at 5,000 rpm, a 4-litre 6-cylinder water-cooled petrol developing 173 hp (129 hp) at 4,500 rpm and a 2.1-litre 4-cylinder turbocharged water-cooled diesel developing 85 hp (63 kW) at 3,750 rpm	options throughout the production run were numerous and included a 2.5-litre 4-cylinder in-line water-cooled petrol developing 104 hp (78 kW) at 5,000 rpm, a 4-litre 6-cylinder water-cooled petrol developing 173 hp (129 hp) at 4,500 rpm and a 2.1-litre 4-cylinder turbocharged water-cooled diesel developing 85 hp (63 kW) at 3,750 rpm
Gearbox:	manual with 4 forward and 1 reverse gears, automatic options	manual with 4 forward and 1 reverse gears, automatic options
Transfer box:	2-speed, New Venture NP-207 (until 1987) and NP-231 (from 1987) were standard for manual gearboxes	2-speed, New Venture NP-207 (until 1987) and NP-231 (from 1987) were standard for manual gearboxes
Clutch: (where applicable)	single dry plate	single dry plate
Steering:	recirculating ball (power steering optional)	recirculating ball (power steering optional)
Turning radius:	10.9 m	12 m
Suspension:	coil springs, front; semi elliptic leaf springs rear; all with hydraulic shock-absorbers	coil springs, front; semi elliptic leaf springs rear; all with hydraulic shock-absorbers
Brakes:	hydraulic dual circuit, discs front; drums rear (both power-assisted)	hydraulic dual circuit, discs front; drums rear (both power-assisted)
Electrical system:	12 V	12 V

Status

Production as either Jeep Liberty or Cherokee (market dependant) and Grand Cherokee continues. Examples of all models with limited militarisation in service with a number of armed forces.

Contractor

Chrysler LLC

Jeep CJ, YJ and TJ (4 × 4) series of light vehicles

Development

The original Jeep (general purpose) vehicle was developed and manufactured for the US Army by Willys-Overland. In 1953 Kaiser acquired Willys-Overland to form Kaiser Jeep, although the name Kaiser Jeep was not adopted until 1963. In 1970 American Motors Corporation (AMC) acquired Kaiser Jeep and created the Jeep Corporation subsidiary. AMC was itself acquired by Chrysler in 1987, with Chrysler then acquired by DaimlerBenz in 1998 to form DaimlerChrysler. In 2007 DaimlerChrysler announced the sale of 80.1 per cent of its stake in the Chrysler Group to Cerberus Capital Management for USD7.4 billion, and Chrysler Group then became Chrysler LLC. In April 2009 Daimler AG signed an agreement to give up its 19.9 per cent remaining stake in Chrysler LLC to Cerberus Capital Management, and almost immediately Chrysler LLC filed for Chapter 11 bankruptcy protection and announced a plan for a partnership with Fiat of Italy. Fiat will hold a 20 per cent stake in the now Chrysler Group LLC, with an option to increase this to 35 per cent, and eventually to 51 per cent.

The CJ series was introduced by Willys in 1945 as a follow-on from the ubiquitous WW II Jeep as the CJ-2A. As one of those facts that becomes clouded with the passing of time, CJ is generally believed to have originally stood for 'Civilian Jeep'. Following the CJ-2A were the CJ-3A and CJ-3B which were produced until 1968. A single CJ-4 prototype appeared in 1951, but the type did not enter production. The CJ-5 entered production in 1954 as a civilian version of the M38A1 military Jeep launched in 1952. Production of the CJ-5 concluded in 1983. Throughout its 30-year production run the CJ-5 was joined by the longer wheelbase CJ-6, which was to be superseded by the CJ-7 in 1976. Between 1981 and 1986 the longer wheelbase CJ-8 was also available.

The Jeep CJ-7 was replaced in production in 1987 by the YJ series, commercially known as Wrangler. The YJ series continued in production until 1995, to be replaced by the updated TJ series (also known commercially as Wrangler) that was available until 2006 when the new JK (Wrangler and four-door Wrangler Unlimited) were introduced.

Chrysler has had Jeep manufacturing or assembly licensees in Australia, China (Beijing Jeep Corporation), Egypt, India (by Mahindra & Mahindra), Indonesia, Mexico and Venezuela. Production of the YJ series

Commercial specification Jeep Wrangler YJ-L of Peru's special forces (Cesar Cruz Tantalean)   1185456

Commercial specification Jeep Wrangler YJ-L of Peru's Armed Forces (Cesar Cruz Tantalean)   1186167

Displayed at Eurosatory 2004, a pre-production military version of the Jeep TJ-L (the production replacement of the YJ-L) (Shaun C Connors)   1120451

for the Egyptian Army continued until 1999 by Arab American Vehicles Co (AAV), Egypt. Currently Chrysler supports production of the Jeep TJ-L series for the Egyptian Army, which commenced during 2003. Full details of Egyptian Jeep production together with details of the TJ-L series can be found elsewhere in this section.

The then DaimlerChrysler disclosed during 2004 that it was investigating the next potential version of the military Jeep and that following development and worldwide interest, diesel-powered Jeep TJ-L models had been supplied to a number of African, European and Middle Eastern countries for evaluation from 2004. And while suitable for some requirements, general feedback indicated the need for air-conditioning, enhanced safety features including airbags and rollover protection, the potential for emissions and other legislative compliance, plus an increase in payload allowance.

A concept of the new-generation military Jeep was first shown in September 2006. This concept was based on the 2007 model-year four-door Wrangler Unlimited and the company subsequently developed the J8 which is also based on the current long wheelbase Wrangler Unlimited, but with a number of enhancements and modifications. The Jeep J8 became available for production from early 2008 and full details of the vehicle can be found elsewhere in this section.

The description given relates to the Jeep YJ series, while the specification table covers the YJ and TJ-L series.

Description

The layout of the YJ series Jeep is conventional, with the engine at the front, individual seats for the driver and one passenger and folding transverse benches or two longitudinal seats in the rear. A vertically hinged tailgate provides access to the cargo area.

Automatic and manual four-speed and five-speed transmissions were available for the Jeep YJ series with a four-wheel drive system. A four-cylinder petrol engine is standard, a six-cylinder petrol engine being an option.

A wide range of optional and heavy-duty equipment was available including air conditioning, soft- or hard-tops, heavy-duty cooling, battery, tyres and suspension and power steering. The military versions of the Jeep YJ were available with additional equipment including military wrap springs, lifting eyes, tow hooks and pintle hook, a blackout lighting system, 24 V auxiliary power and severe-use oil, air and fuel filtration systems.

In the US, Cummins Military Systems proposed a retrofit programme for Jeep series vehicles in which the engine would be replaced by a Cummins B3.9-105 diesel engine developing 105 hp at 2,500 rpm. This would be coupled to a Chrysler A 727 automatic transmission to provide improved fuel economy, increased range and ease of maintenance.

Specifications

Jeep CJ, YJ and TJ (4 × 4) series of light vehicles

	YJ long wheelbase	TJ long wheelbase
Cab seating:	1 + 5	1 + up to 7 (6 in rear)
Configuration:	4 × 4	4 × 4
Weight:		
(laden)	2,200 kg	2,418 kg
(unladen)	1,471 kg	1,520 kg
(max load)	729 kg	900 kg
(towed load)	907 kg	n/avail
Length:	4.49 m	4.42 m
Width:	1.676 m	1.694 m
Height:		
(open body)	1.744 m	1.763 m
(soft-top)	1.828 m	n/avail
(hard-top)	1.785 m	n/avail
Ground clearance:	207 mm	231 mm
Track:	1.473 m	1.483 m
Wheelbase:	2.627 m	2.931 m
Angle of approach/departure:	32°/22°	34°/29°
Fuel capacity:	76 litres	71.9 litres
Range:	n/avail	>600 km on-road, up to 500 km off-road
Engine:	2.5-litre 4-cylinder inline water-cooled petrol developing 104 hp (78 kW) at 5,000 rpm or 4.2-litre 6-cylinder water-cooled petrol developing 112 hp (84 kW) at 3,000 rpm	VM Motori 2.8-litre 4-cylinder inline water-cooled diesel developing 120 hp (90 kW) at 3,800 rpm and 325 N.m torque at 2,000 rpm with unregulated emissions
Gearbox:	manual with 4 forward and 1 reverse gears	manual with 5 forward and 1 reverse gears
Transfer box:	2-speed	2-speed
Clutch:	single dry plate	single dry plate, hydraulic
Steering:	recirculating ball (power steering optional)	recirculating ball (power steering optional)
Turning radius:	10.9 m	12.6 m
Suspension:	semi-elliptic leaf springs with hydraulic shock-absorbers	quadra coil springs with gas-assisted shock-absorbers
Axles:	n/avail	Dana 30, front; Dana 44, rear
Brakes:	hydraulic dual circuit, discs front; drums rear (both power-assisted)	discs all-round, power-assisted
Electrical system:	12 V (24 V optional)	dual 12/24 V

Status

Production of Jeep YJ model complete, replaced in production by the TJ model and then the commercial JK model (see text).

Contractor

Chrysler Group LLC

Jeep J8 (4 × 4) light vehicle

Development

The original Jeep (general purpose) vehicle was developed and manufactured for the US Army by Willys-Overland. In 1953 Kaiser acquired Willys-Overland to form Kaiser Jeep, although the name Kaiser Jeep was not adopted until 1963. In 1970 American Motors Corporation (AMC) acquired Kaiser Jeep and created the Jeep Corporation subsidiary. AMC was itself acquired by Chrysler in 1987, Chrysler subsequently being acquired by Daimler-Benz in 1998 to form DaimlerChrysler. In May 2007 Daimler-Benz AG announced the sale of 80.1 per cent of the Chrysler Group to American equity firm Cerberus Capital Management LP. In April 2009, Daimler AG agreed to give up its remaining 19.9 per cent share of the then Chrysler LLC to Cerberus Capital Management. Almost immediately, Chrysler LLC filed for Chapter 11 bankruptcy protection and announced a plan for a partnership with Fiat of Italy. In June 2009 Chrysler LLC stated they were selling some assets and operations to the newly formed Chrysler Group LLC; Fiat will hold a 20 per cent stake in the new company, with an option to increase this to 35 per cent, and eventually to 51 per cent.

The Jeep J8 was first shown publicly at the DSEi show in the UK during September 2007. The design has origins in a diesel-powered variant of the Jeep TJ-L that was developed to meet the requirements of the Egyptian Army and following the delivery of an initial 1,000 petrol-powered TJ-Ls between August 2003 and March 2004.

The Egyptian Army has since ordered 3,750 diesel-powered Jeep TJ-Ls in three 1,250 batches, the third batch ordered in December 2008. Additional orders are anticipated.

All Egyptian Army Jeep TJ-Ls are CKD-produced with local content and adaptation at the Arab American Vehicles Co (AAV)/Chrysler LLC joint venture plant that was set up in Egypt during 1977. Full details of Egyptian Jeep production, and earlier CJ, TJ and YJ Jeeps can be found in separate entries elsewhere in this section.

With the exception of the ongoing Egyptian venture, Chrysler had not actively pursued military sales of the Jeep product since the mid-1990s. Following interest in the diesel-powered Jeep TJ-L, the company began to

Jeep J8 heavy duty hard-top personnel/cargo carrier (JGMS) 1391352

Jeep J8 standard 3- and 5-door variants (JGMS) 1391354

re-examine the potential market for military specific Jeep models and TJ-L models were subsequently supplied to a number of African, European and Middle Eastern countries for evaluation from 2004. While suitable for some requirements, general feedback indicated the need for air-conditioning, enhanced safety features including airbags and rollover protection, the potential for emissions and other legislative compliance, plus an increase in payload allowance.

Following the unveiling of a concept vehicle during 2006 that was based on the 2007 model-year four-door Wrangler Unlimited, the Jeep J8 (which is based on the current long wheelbase Wrangler Unlimited) was unveiled.

The Jeep J8 became available for production at the AAV plant late-2008, although dependent on order size, Chrysler Group LLC would likely give consideration to any requirement for either CKD or added local content, thus CKD production elsewhere is a possibility.

The first known customer for the Jeep J8 was Poland, with a small number (around 10) of vehicles supplied to the Ministry of Interior during 2009. These were fitted with ballistic protection and may have been supplied to anti-terrorist units. Polish vehicles were manufactured in Egypt, with local content added by local Chrysler agent, Zeszuta.

From 2007 Chrysler had partnered with Jankel Armouring Limited of the UK to develop a range of modified Jeep J8 vehicles. It was disclosed in August 2009 that the now Chrysler Group LLC had appointed Jankel Group subsidiary Jeep Government and Military Sales (JGMS) as the worldwide distributor for the Jeep J8 for supply to government and military customers.

It is understood that a small number of Jeep J8 were ordered by the Jordanian Royal Guard mid-2010, these manufactured in Egypt and to be delivered through Jordan Light Vehicle Manufacturing (JLVM), a joint venture between KADDB and Jankel. These vehicles are understood to be powered by the non-standard HEMI 5.7-litre V8 petrol engine, long range fuel tanks and zoned armour protection.

In August 2010 it was disclosed that a small number of Jeep J8 in troop-carrying/cargo configuration had been supplied to Uruguayan peace-keeping troops through the US Army's TACOM for use in Haiti.

Description

The Jeep J8 uses the current long wheelbase Jeep JK Wrangler Unlimited as a starting point and therefore remains entirely conventional in design. Two or four door bodies in left- or right-hand drive and a variety of soft- or hard-top configurations that seat from two to eight people are now available, as are specialist versions such as ambulance, overtly or discreetly armoured, or long-range or border patrol type configurations. Full details of long-range or border patrol type configurations can be found in the Special attack vehicles section.

Compared to the Wrangler Unlimited, the J8 features a reinforced chassis with uprated Dana 44 and Dana 60 axles to allow for a GVW of 3,364 kg, this giving a payload allowance of 1,164 kg (1,664 kg with PEK); towed load is up to 3,500 kg.

The standard coil spring rear suspension of commercial Jeep models is replaced by a heavier duty leaf spring set-up, while other modifications include a severe duty cooling package, new pressed steel wheels, heavy duty bumpers with a lift/tow capability, and enhanced wading and air filtration capabilities; the latter allowing for five hours operation in zero visibility sandstorm conditions.

Motive power for the J8 is provided by a EURO 4 or 5 capable (if required) VM Motori diesel engine developing 158 hp, and driving all four wheels (selectable 4WD) via a five-speed automatic transmission and 2-speed transfer case. From January 2011 Model Year 2011 versions will have a power increase to 194 hp and 460 N.m torque. The HEMI 5.7-litre V8 petrol engine is an option if required.

Armoured variants of the Jeep J8 utilise a hot-formed steel technology to create an external, non-parasitic protective shell that replaces the body with hot-formed ballistic steel shaped to the vehicle's precise contours. Conventional armouring methods rely on armoured steel components of various sizes welded beneath the original vehicle skin. According to the manufacturer, the advantages of hot-formed steel technology include lower kerb weight; reduced risk of penetration from faulty welds and joints; improved structural integrity; and lower acquisition and life cycle costs.

Jeep J8 armoured vehicle variants (discreet and military patrol) have been certified by Germany's Beschussamt test agency for BRV 2009 VR7 ballistic protection and ERV 2010 blast protection - floor, roof and side blast.

Specifications

Jeep J8 (4 × 4) 3- or 5-door light vehicle
Cab seating: 1 + up to 7 (6 in rear)
Configuration: 4 × 4 (selectable)
Weight:
(laden) 3,364 kg
(unladen) 2,200 kg
(max load) 1,164 kg (1,664 kg with Payload Enhancement Kit (PEK))
(towed load) 3,500 kg
(GCW) 6,864 kg
Length: 4.45 m
Width: 1.876 m
Height: 1.762 m
Ground clearance: 231 mm
Track: 1.610 m

Wheelbase: 2.946 m
Angle of approach/departure: 44°/40°
Fuel capacity: 85 litres
Range:
(on road) 860 km
(off road) up to 730 km
Max gradient: 100%
Max side slope: 80%
Fording: 762 mm
Engine: VM Motori Panther 2.8-litre 4-cylinder inline common rail water-cooled diesel developing 158 hp (118 kW) at 3,800 rpm and 400 N.m at 2,000 rpm. Unregulated emissions, but available to meet EURO 4 or 5 emissions requirements if desired. From January 2011 Model Year 2011 versions will have a power increase to 194 hp and 460 N.m torque
Gearbox: Chrysler 5-speed automatic with overdrive
Transfer box: 2-speed
Steering: recirculating ball, power-assisted
Turning radius: 6.2 m
Suspension: coil springs and shock-absorbers, front; leaf springs and shock-absorbers rear
Axles: Dana 44, front; Dana 60, rear
Tyres: 245/70 R17 BF Goodrich
Brakes: discs all round, power assisted, ABS standard
Electrical system: 12 V (dual 12/24 V optional) 180 A

Status

In production. In service with Jordan, Poland and Uruguay (see text).

Contractor

Chrysler LLC.

M151 (4 × 4) 362 kg light vehicle and variants

Development

In 1950, the Continental Army Command placed a requirement with the Ordnance Corps for a new ¼ ton vehicle. Research and development began that year at the Ordnance Tank Automotive Command. In 1951, the Ford Motor Company was awarded a development contract and the first prototypes were completed in 1952. A further batch was completed in 1954 under the designation XM151 and in 1956 the XM151E1 (of conventional steel construction) and the XM151E2 (of aluminium construction) were

M151 (4 × 4) ¼ ton light vehicle of the Royal Thai Army (Gordon Arthur)
1340320

M825 (4 × 4) ¼ ton light vehicle of the Philippine Marines armed with a 106 mm recoilless rifle (Gordon Arthur)
1296188

M151 (4 × 4) 362 kg light vehicle and variants

Model	M151	M151A1	M151A2	M718A1	M825
Cab seating:	1 + 3	1 + 3	1 + 3	1 + 1	1 + 3
Configuration:	4 × 4	4 × 4	4 × 4	4 × 4	4 × 4
Weight:					
(laden)	1,575 kg	1,633 kg	1,652 kg	1,656 kg	1,959 kg
(unladen)	1,012 kg	1,088 kg	1,107 kg	1,247 kg	1,174 kg
Weight on rear axle: (laden)	448 kg	481 kg	490 kg	626 kg	519 kg
Weight on front axle: (unladen)	574 kg	607 kg	618 kg	620 kg	655 kg
Max load:					
(on-road)	554 kg	544 kg	545 kg	409 kg	785 kg
(off-road)	362 kg	362 kg	363 kg	409 kg	785 kg
Towed load:					
(on-road)	970 kg	970 kg	970 kg	not authorised	not authorised
(off-road)	680 kg	680 kg	680 kg	not authorised	not authorised
Length:	3.352 m	3.371 m	3.371 m	3.631 m	3.645 m
Width:	1.58 m	1.634 m	1.633 m	1.819 m	1.943 m
Height:					
(overall)	1.803 m	1.803 m	1.803 m	1.94 m	1.621 m
(reduced)	1.332 m	1.332 m	1.333 m	1.313 m	1.346 m
Ground clearance:	260 mm	240 mm	240 mm	230 mm	210 mm
Track:	1.346 m	1.346 m	1.346 m	1.346 m	1.346 m
Wheelbase:	2.159 m	2.159 m	2.159 m	2.159 m	2.159 m
Angle of approach/departure:	66°/37°	65°/37°	66°/37°	67°/36°	62°/33°
Max speed:	106 km/h	104 km/h	90 km/h	90 km/h	80 km/h
Range:	482 km	482 km	482 km	442 km	483 km
Fuel capacity:	56 litres	56 litres	59.8 litres	59.8 litres	59.8 litres
Max gradient:	60%	60%	60%	60%	50%
Max side slope:	40%	40%	40%	40%	30%
Fording:					
(without preparation)	533 mm	533 mm	533 mm	533 mm	533 mm
(with preparation)	1.524 m	1.524 m	1.524 m	1.524 m	1.524 m
Engine:	L-142 4-cylinder in-line water-cooled OHV petrol developing 72 hp (54 kW) at 4,000 rpm	L-142 4-cylinder in-line water-cooled OHV petrol developing 72 hp (54 kW) at 4,000 rpm	L-142 4-cylinder in-line water-cooled OHV petrol developing 72 hp (54 kW) at 4,000 rpm	L-142 4-cylinder in-line water-cooled OHV petrol developing 72 hp (54 kW) at 4,000 rpm	L-142 4-cylinder in-line water-cooled OHV petrol developing 72 hp (54 kW) at 4,000 rpm
Gearbox:	manual with 4 forward and 1 reverse gears	manual with 4 forward and 1 reverse gears	manual with 4 forward and 1 reverse gears	manual with 4 forward and 1 reverse gears	manual with 4 forward and 1 reverse gears
Clutch:	single dry disc	single dry disc	single dry disc	single dry disc	single dry disc
Transfer box:	single speed, integral with transmission. Driver can select either 4 × 4 or 4 × 2 drive	single speed, integral with transmission. Driver can select either 4 × 4 or 4 × 2 drive	single speed, integral with transmission. Driver can select either 4 × 4 or 4 × 2 drive	single speed, integral with transmission. Driver can select either 4 × 4 or 4 × 2 drive	single speed, integral with transmission. Driver can select either 4 × 4 or 4 × 2 drive
Steering:	worm and double roller	worm and double roller	worm and double roller	worm and double roller	worm and double roller
Turning radius:	5.486 m	5.638 m	5.638 m	5.638 m	5.638 m
Suspension:	coil springs with hydraulic shock-absorbers	coil springs with hydraulic shock-absorbers	coil springs with hydraulic shock-absorbers	coil springs with hydraulic shock-absorbers	coil springs with hydraulic shock-absorbers
Tyres:	7.00 × 16	7.00 × 16	7.00 × 16	7.00 × 16	7.00 × 16
Brakes:					
(main)	hydraulic	hydraulic	hydraulic	hydraulic	hydraulic
(parking)	mechanical	mechanical	mechanical	mechanical	mechanical
Electrical system:	24 V	24 V	24 V	24 V	24 V
Battery:	1 × 2 HN	1 × 2 HN	1 × 2 HN	1 × 2 HN	1 × 2 HN

built and tested. The former was selected for production in 1959; Ford were awarded the first production contract and first production vehicles were completed in 1960 at Ford's Highland Park Plant. The M151 replaced the M38 (4 × 4) ¼ ton vehicle in service with the US Armed Forces. Later production contracts were awarded to the AM General Corporation. The Fiscal Year 1978 request was for only 3,880 vehicles at a cost of USD29.1 million. It was then stated that the engine of the vehicle no longer met emission standards and that this procurement would be the last for several years. Production ceased in 1985 only to start again in 1988 to supply vehicles for overseas sales to Pakistan and other nations.

Production of the M151 series has ceased in the US. All US Army and USMC M151 models have been replaced.

From 1994 onwards TRACE SA of Cascais, Portugal and São Paulo, Brazil, commenced the marketing of an M151A2 clone powered by a Renault J89-240 two-litre diesel engine and known as the TRACE Comando Mk 1.

Description

The body and chassis of the M151 are integral and are of all-welded construction. The layout of the vehicle is conventional, with the engine at the front and the crew area at the rear with a removable canvas top and side curtains and a windscreen that can be folded forward flat on the bonnet.

In 1964, the M151 was replaced in production by the M151A1 which had improved suspension, as the earlier model had a tendency to oversteer. The M151A2 followed in 1970 with modifications to the rear suspension, collapsible steering wheel, two-speed wipers and modified lighting. The M151A2LC has a gearbox with three forward and one reverse gears (other vehicles have four forward and one reverse gears) and two-speed transfer case (other vehicles have a single-speed transfer case). The vehicle also has a different suspension which consists of semi-elliptic springs and shock absorbers instead of the coil springs and telescopic shock absorbers fitted to other versions. There was no quantity production of this variant.

The basic vehicle can also be armed with a pintle-mounted 7.62 mm M60 or a 0.50/12.7 mm M2 HB Browning machine gun and were fitted with the TOW ATGW system.

Many kits are available including a front-mounted winch, heater, hard-top, 100 A alternator and a Xenon searchlight. The vehicle can ford to a depth of 533 mm without preparation and 1.524 m with the aid of a kit.

From October 1986, a programme was initiated to retrofit rollbars to about 11,000 M151 series vehicles. Most of the vehicles involved belonged to National Guard and Army Reserve units. A contract to provide kits for 6,000 vehicles was awarded to the Wright Automotive Corporation of Colorado Springs, Colorado in August 1987. The contract was worth just over USD4 million.

Variants

The M107 and M108 are communications vehicles with the radios installed in the rear of the vehicle. The passenger seat is rear facing enabling the radio operator to work his equipment.

The M718 and M718A1 are ambulance versions and have a crew of two, a driver and a medical attendant. This version can carry a stretcher and three seated patients, two stretcher and two seated patients or three stretcher patients.

The M825 is fitted with a M40 series 106 mm recoilless rifle mounted in the rear. This model was replaced in US Army service by the TOW ATGW, with kits available to convert the M825 to the M151A2 standard. However, during mid-1987 25 M151A2s were converted to M825 standard by TACOM in order to meet a requirement from Somalia.

Specifications

Status

Production complete. Supplied to over 100 countries including Argentina (200 remain), Bolivia, Chile (no longer in service), Congo (Democratic Republic), Ecuador (including M825; small number remain), Egypt, El Salvador, Gambia, Greece, Guatemala (200, 80 refurbished as of late 2003), Indonesia, Israel, Jamaica, Mexico (200-400 approx), Pakistan, Peru, Philippines, Portugal, Saudi Arabia, Senegal, Singapore (including M825), Somalia (M151 and M825), South Korea (141), Spain (Marines only), Thailand, Turkey, and Venezuela (including M825).

Contractor

AM General Corporation

R-1 Rescue All-Terrain Transport (RATT)

Development

The R-1 Rescue All-Terrain Transport (RATT) was developed by RACECO (now Flyer Defense LLC) as an emergency medical evacuation vehicle. The prototype contract was issued by the US Air Force Special Tactics Squadron in early 1991 with the prototype being delivered some six months later. After tests, a contract for a further 14 vehicles was placed in January 1992. These vehicles were delivered over the following two years.

Description

The R-1 chassis is built of aircraft-quality high-strength steel tubing, welded into a 'trussed bridge' structure. Secondary structures are made of high-strength aluminium alloys or aircraft-quality plastics. A thick aluminium alloy plate provides a smooth bottom skid plate for the entire length of the vehicle. The suspension employs multiple long-stroke shock-absorbers coupled with torsion and coil springs. Each wheel station has a tie-down strap reducing the overall vehicle height by approximately 100 mm for transport in some types of aircraft.

Various engines can be installed, although the in-service R-1s are powered by a rear-mounted 110 hp Type IV Porsche 914 petrol unit coupled to an automatic transmission with (4 × 4) drive and power steering. The wheels use run-flat tyres on the rear and smaller tyres at the front. A spare is carried under the rear platform to be used on any wheel station in an emergency. In addition the R-1 has an HMMWV bolt pattern allowing the use of HMMWV wheels as emergency spares.

Rear three-quarter view of the R-1 Rescue All-Terrain Transport (RATT) (Scott Gourley)   0533601

The R-1 can carry a crew of three (driver and two attendants) and six medical litters, with options for a further two litters. The litters are carried on folding racks on the side and rear of the vehicle with the central area available for the two medical attendants to treat casualties while on the move. An oxygen generator is provided to produce and distribute oxygen to all six patients and, each patient can be treated with plasma and medical equipment during transit. Lighting, navigation and communications equipment is provided for night operations.

Other equipment carried includes a removable 2,268 kg winch capable of operating to the front, sides or rear.

Specifications

R-1 RATT
Crew: 3 + 6 patients
Configuration: 4 × 4
Weight:
  (kerb) 1,270 kg
  (laden) 2,132 kg
  (max, gross) 2,631 kg
Length: 3.86 m
Width: 1.78 m
Height:
  (max) 1.93 m
  (compressed) 1.8 m
Ground clearance: 400 mm
Wheelbase: 2.667 m
Angle of approach/departure: 75°/60°
Max speed: 112 km/h
Range: 402 km
Fuel capacity: 75.7 litres
Fording: 760 mm
Gradient: 60%
Side slope: 60%
Vertical obstacle: 406 mm
Engine: Type IV Porsche 914 2.3-litre petrol developing 110 hp (82 kW)
Transmission: automatic, 3 forward and 1 reverse gears
Steering: Saginaw, power assisted
Suspension: A-arm with or without stage shock and spring, front; swing arm torsion bar with or without stage secondary spring, rear
Electrical system: 12 and 24 V

Status

Production as required. In service with the US Air Force (15).

Contractor

Flyer Defense LLC

SPECIAL ATTACK VEHICLES

China

NORINCO fast attack vehicle

Development
The China North Industries Corporation (NORINCO) fast attack vehicle was first announced in mid-2001. The vehicle has been fielded by airborne units of the People's Liberation Army (PLA) and despite disclosing the type being available for export sales, very little specific information has become available.

Description
The NORINCO fast attack vehicle appears to be of four-wheel drive (4 × 4) configuration with a rear-mounted engine and, in a central roll-over protected cage, seating for either four people, including the driver, or two people plus additional stores. The forward part of the vehicle carries a spare wheel and on/off-road tyre, and a front-mounted electric winch is provided for self-recovery operations.

The vehicle is 4 m long, 2.095 m wide and 2.21 m high, and combat weight is given as 1,950 kg. No further dimensional or driveline details have been released.

A wide range of weapon stations can be fitted and the example shown in released photographs is armed with a 7.62 mm machine gun on a swivel mount to the right of the driver's position and a Chinese 23 mm cannon installed in a circular mount on top of the roll-over protection system. The 23 mm cannon is fitted with a muzzle brake to reduce recoil forces so allowing it to be installed on light vehicles. The weapon can be traversed through a full 360° with elevation from −10° to +52° and the operator can select to fire single shots only or full automatic fire at the rate of 200 rpm or 400 rpm. The weapon is driven from a 24 V power source. Maximum effective range is 2,000 m. A total of 200 rounds of ready-to-use 23 mm ammunition is carried and, for increased accuracy, a day/night sighting system is installed above the weapon.

Status
Available for export. In service with the People's Liberation Army (PLA).

Contractor
China North Industries Corporation (NORINCO)

NORINCO fast attack vehicle armed with a roof-mounted 23 mm cannon and a pintle-mounted 7.62 mm machine gun (NORINCO) 0095611

France

Renault Sherpa Light Special Forces light vehicle

Development
The Sherpa Light Special Forces light vehicle is a variant of the Sherpa Light range. Currently six primary versions of the Sherpa Light are available, these covering a wide variety of military and internal security needs. Full details of the range can be found in the Light Vehicles section.

Development of what is now known as the Sherpa Light range can be traced back to the United Arab Emirates (UAE) where, as part of an ongoing programme to find a locally produced alternative to the AM General HMMWV, development commenced in 1999.

The original vehicle was displayed publicly for the first time at IDEX 2003 where it was branded the Advanced Modular Vehicles (AMV) Al-Dhabi.

By IDEX 2005 the vehicle had migrated to the Renault stand and with the tentative designation of Sherpa 2.5. In December 2005 Renault Trucks Defense announced that it had acquired the full and sole rights to the design from AMV. The intention of this acquisition was to provide Renault Trucks Defense with a vehicle that could fill an identified gap within the company's product range between conventional (and currently out of

The Sherpa Light Special Forces as displayed in the UK at DVD 2010 (Shaun C Connors) 1391409

fashion) Jeep-type light utility vehicles, and the then under-development 5,000 kg payload Sherpa Medium range of tactical trucks. Full details of the Sherpa Medium range of tactical trucks (including the Sherpa 5 and Sherpa 10) can be found in the Trucks section.

Throughout a four-/five-year period of developmental evolution a variety of designations and technical specifications for assorted Sherpa models were touted. By DSEi 2009 the available range had stabilised and the all-encompassing Sherpa Light designation had replaced the then current Sherpa 2 and Sherpa 3/3A designations; the A in 3A denoting armoured.

Renault's first sales for the Sherpa Light were announced during 2008, and by early 2010 around 200 units in total had been ordered.

A Sherpa variant has been down-selected to meet the UK MoD's stalled OUVS (Large) requirement, and early 2009 Renault announced a teaming with Land Rover for current and emerging UK programmes, this teaming possibly expanding to address international requirements in the future.

Description
The now designated Sherpa Light range began as a vehicle designed to replace the AM General HMMWV in a number of primarily Middle Eastern markets, and as such had some visual and dimensional similarities to the HMMWV at the early stages of development.

However, throughout its evolution the Sherpa Light has increased in areas of weights and dimensions, and from initial GVWs of 7,500 kg to 9,000 kg to the current 7,900 kg to 10,900 kg.

With a GVW of 9,600 kg the Sherpa Light Special Forces is one of the largest/heaviest vehicles in its class, both GVW and unladen weight exceeding those of some light trucks.

In keeping with all non-armoured (APC-style) variants of the Sherpa Light range, the Special Forces variant is available fitted with ballistic and mine protection kits, the norm for this being an armoured underside and protected sides and folding front windscreen. This capability to accept armour without unacceptable performance degradation is built in at design stage.

The Sherpa Light range is based on a conventional chassis frame, and unlike many of its contemporaries which feature fully independent suspension set-ups, the Sherpa Light range feature beam axle and coil spring suspension, the differential bowls of the beam axles in-line and not offset to one another which is the norm in a two-axle all-wheel drive design.

All variants of the Sherpa Light share a common driveline to reduce maintenance and logistic costs. Motive power for the range is provided by a Renault MD-5 four-cylinder diesel engine developing 215 hp, this coupled to an Allison fully automatic transmission and Axletech two-speed transfer box.

In standard configuration the Sherpa Light Special Forces seats five and the rear body accommodates a roll-over/ring mount for an assortment of light weapons. The overall layout of the vehicle is optimised for long range patrol-type missions.

The Special Forces variant of Sherpa Light can be fitted with a variety of weapons including 5.56, 7.62 and 12.7 mm machine guns. Configurations can be tailored to operator and/or role, with a typical configuration being a centrally-mounted 12.7 mm heavy machine gun, this supported by two rear pintle-mounted 7.62 mm machine guns and a single front-mounted 7.62 mm machine gun.

Equipment options available for the Special Forces variant, many of which are available across the Sherpa Light range, include right-hand drive, air-conditioning, a Central Tyre Inflation System (CTIS), run-flat inserts, electric winch front or rear, add-on armour, lighting protection, cable breaker and 300 A alternator.

The Sherpa Light Special Forces is fully air-transportable by C-130 Hercules transport aircraft.

Specifications

Model
Seating: 5
Drive configuration: 4 × 4
Weight:
  (GVW) 9,600 kg
  (payload) 2,600 kg
  (GTW) 13,600 kg
Length: wheelbase dependant
Width: 2.35 m
Height: 2.1 m
Ground clearance: (belly) 600 mm
Wheelbase: 3.55 to 4.1 m
Approach/departure angle: n/avail
Max speed: 120 km/h
Range: (cruising) 1,000 km
Fuel capacity: (options) 165 litres
Max gradient: 60%
Max sideslope: 40%
Trench: 600 mm
Vertical step: 500 mm
Fording:
  (unprepared) 750 mm
  (prepared) 1.5 m
Engine: Renault MD-5 EURO 5 emissions compliant 4-cylinder common rail injection water-cooled 4-stroke diesel developing 215 hp (158 kW) at 2,300 rpm and 800 N.m torque at 1,200 to 1,700 rpm. A EURO 3 option is available for certain markets
Gearbox: Allison S2500 fully automatic with 6 forward and 1 reverse gears
Transfer box: Axletech 2-speed
Steering: hydraulic power-assisted
Tyres: 335/80 R 20 or 13R 22.5
Suspension: beam axles, coil springs and hydraulic shock-absorbers, front and rear
Brakes: discs all round with ABS
Electrical system: 12/24 V
Batteries: n/avail
Alternator: 100 A

Status

Production as required. Sherpa Light range variants ordered by, or in use by, the French Army and Gendarmerie, NAMSA and NATO.

Contractor

Renault Trucks Defense

Panhard General Defense A3F (4 × 4) fast attack vehicle

Development

The Panhard General Defense (previously Auverland) A3F (4 × 4) fast attack vehicle was first shown publicly in June 1994, having been developed in response to a French Army requirement. During the second quarter of 1998, the French Army ordered an initial batch of 100 vehicles. Orders for two additional batches followed.

The first batch ordered involved 50 VAL and 50 VAC. The second batch ordered involved 56 VAL and 50 VAC. The third batch ordered involved a further 48 VAC, making a total number of both types of vehicle of 254 - 106 VAL and 148 VAC. Deliveries ran from January 1999 to December 2000. The vehicles are deployed with the French Army's 11th Airborne Division.

The first Auverland A3 (4 × 4) light vehicles were produced in 1988 by Auverland-SOVAMAG SA. In July 2001, Auverland-SOVAMAG SA were acquired by *Société Nouvelle des Automobiles Auverland* (SNAA).

In January 2005 it was announced that SNAA had acquired Panhard, builder of the *Vehicule Blindé Leger* (VBL), ERC Sagaie and other light armoured military vehicles. During early 2006, the SNAA became known as Panhard General Defense. The Auverland and Sovamag brand names have been retained, certainly in the short term, and production of these models continues on an as required basis at the now Panhard General Defense's Saint Germain Laval facilities.

In November 2003 it was announced that two A3F vehicles had been supplied to Sweden for trials for possible use with Sweden's to-be-acquired NH90 helicopters (Swedish military designation Hkp 14).

Description

The A3F is a development of the Auverland A3 (4 × 4) light vehicle (full details of which can be found in the Light vehicles section) modified with a coil spring suspension, revised rigid axles and drive shaft arrangement, and a frame superstructure. Optional equipment includes run-flat tyres and modular add-on armoured protection.

The VAL logistics version allows the loading of a 750 kg pallet with maximum dimensions of 1.2 × 1.2 × 1 m with loading assisted by a winch behind the two front seats; the cargo bed length behind the rear seat is 1.14 m. The VAC command version can carry a 5.56 or 7.62 mm machine gun on a front mounting. It also has a central mounting suitable for a 0.50 in/12.7 mm heavy machine gun, a Giat M 621 20 mm cannon, a 40 mm grenade launcher or a MILAN anti-tank missile launcher.

Auverland A3F (4 × 4) air mobile vehicle in VAC command vehicle form (Pierre Touzin)   1124701

Auverland A3F (4 × 4) air mobile vehicle in VAC command vehicle form prepared for transport by NH 90 helicopter (Auverland)   0558824

The dimensions of the A3F allow it to be carried inside the NH 90 helicopters ordered for the French Army and scheduled for delivery commencement in 2011. The A3F can also be dropped by parachute.

The French Army has tested a longer wheelbase version, the A3F SL.

Specifications

A3F
Seating: 1 + 2
Configuration: 4 × 4
Weight:
  (GVW) 2,510 kg
  (kerb) 1,350 kg
  (payload) 1,160 kg
Length: 3.4 m
Width: 1.58 m
Height:
  (overall) 1.9 m
  (roll bars folded) 1.4 m
Ground clearance: 255 mm
Wheelbase: 2.25 m
Angle of approach/departure: 50°/50°
Max speed: 130 km/h
Range: 700 km
Fuel capacity: 80 litres
Max gradient: 100%
Fording: (unprepared) 600 mm
Engine: Peugeot XUD 9TF 1.905-litre 4-cylinder in-line turbocharged water-cooled 4-stroke diesel developing 92 hp (69 kW) at 4,000 rpm
Gearbox: Peugeot with 5 forward and 1 reverse gears
Clutch: single dry plate
Transfer box: Auverland A-80 2-speed
Steering: power-assisted
Turning radius: 5 m
Suspension: coil springs with hydraulic shock-absorbers, front and rear
Tyres: 7.00 × 16 XZL
Brakes: servo-assisted; discs front, drums rear
Electrical system: 24 V

Status

Production as required. In service with the French Army (254), has been evaluated by the Swedish Army (two).

Contractor

Panhard General Defense

Panhard General Defense VPS special forces light vehicle

Development

Following tender responses in June/July 2004, the French Ministry of Defence (MoD) announced in mid-2005 that the Panhard VPS (*Le Véhicule Patrouille SAS*) had been selected to meet a requirement for a rapidly deployable vehicle capable of long-duration missions in extremes of climate. Delivery of the 41 vehicles involved in this requirement commenced in late 2006.

A further 10 vehicles have since been delivered to the French Army.

The VPS requirement is essentially a further incarnation of the earlier abandoned 63-vehicle VRI (*Véhicule Rapide d'Investigation*) requirement for which the G-Class-based Mechem BAT (in lightweight form) competed against buggy-based designs from Auverland (The Chenowth ASLV) and Flyer Defense.

Competing against Panhard for the revised VPS requirement was Société Nouvelle des Automobiles Auverland (SNAA) and Land Rover. SNAA proposed a variant of the A4 FAST, while Land Rover – in conjunction with Ricardo Special Vehicles – offered a version of the Defender 130 that was similar in configuration to the British Army's Defender 110-based Weapons Mount Installation Kit (WMIK).

The VPS requirement is understood to have called for a four-door, four-person vehicle with a payload of 1,100 kg. A mine-protected floorpan (DM 31) and mounting points (ring-mount) for a 12.7 mm heavy machine gun and a front-mount for a 7.62 mm light machine gun were required. A turbocharged diesel engine (with a 24 V electrical system) meeting performance criteria of a 120 km/h maximum speed and sufficient acceleration to cover 400 m from a standing start in 25 seconds was required. Other requirements include an 800 km range, a self-recovery winch, two spare wheels and blackout lighting. The base vehicle was required to have EU homologation.

In January 2005 it was announced that SNAA had acquired Panhard. In early 2006, SNAA became known as Panhard General Defense.

Description

The Panhard VPS as delivered to the French Army is based on the Mercedes-Benz 270 CDI G-Class, full details of which can be found in the Light vehicles section. The base vehicle is delivered direct to Panhard General Defence's Saint Germain Laval facilities as a running two-door (minus the doors) vehicle from Magna Steyr's Austrian production facility. All militarisation including painting and installation of the mine-blast protecting floorpan is carried out by Panhard at Saint Germain Laval. The basic crew of the VPS is two, driver (front left) and commander (front right), with the rear crew compartment configurable for payload or an additional one or two crew members. The two front doors are fabric covered, and the rear drop-down tailgate is steel. The volume of the open rear compartment is >3.5 m².

The VPS is designed to accept a 7.62 mm light machine gun on a front scuttle mount which is operated by the vehicle commander, and a 12.7 mm heavy machine gun in a ring-mount over the rear body. In addition to specified racking for ammunition and communication equipment, VPS is supplied as standard with a First Aid kit, 2 × 20-litre jerrycans, storage for 30 litres of food or water, two spare wheels, a shovel and pickaxe, and a 4,000 kg front bumper-mounted self-recovery winch. The floorpan is protected to Level 1 of STANAG 4569.

Alternative configurations to suit specific customer requirements are possible. The electrical system is split 12/24 V, the 12 V network serving primarily the engine, gearbox and management systems, the 24 V system primarily serving the starter, radios and external lighting. An air compressor is fitted in the engine compartment of the vehicle for the regulation of tyre pressures.

In addition to conventional road, rail or sea transport, VPS is transportable by C-160 Transall (two) and C-130 Hercules (two or three, variant dependant), and is supplied fitted with the necessary sling points to enable transport as an underslung load by helicopter.

Any future sales by Panhard General Defense would be on the current G-Class platform.

Specifications

VPS
Cab seating: 1 + 1 + up to 2 in rear
Configuration: 4 × 4 (full-time)
Weight:
  (unladen) 2,800 kg
  (laden) 4,000 kg
  (payload) 1,200 kg
Length: 4.87 m
Width: (over spare wheel) 2.21 m
Height: 2.5 m
Ground clearance: 360 mm
Track: 1.555 m
Wheelbase: 2.85 m
Max speed: 120 km/h
Range: 800 km
Fuel capacity: 96 litres
Max gradient: >60%
Max side slope: >30%
Fording: (unprepared) 500 mm
Engine: Mercedes-Benz OM612 DE27LA EURO 3 emissions compliant 2.685-litre 5-cylinder in-line turbocharged water-cooled 4-stroke diesel developing 156 hp (116 kW) at 2,600 rpm and 370 N.m torque at 2,600 rpm
Gearbox: Mercedes-Benz W5A 580 automatic with 5 forward and 1 reverse gears
Transfer box: Steyr VG-150 E-3W 2-speed
Steering: power-assisted
Turning radius: (wall) 7 m
Suspension: long-travel coil springs, hollow rubber helper springs and hydraulic shock-absorbers, front and rear
Tyres: 265/75R 16 BF Goodrich Mud Terrain (MT)
Brakes: dual circuit, hydraulic, discs front, drums rear. 3-channel ABS
Electrical system: 12/24 V split system
Batteries: 3 ×12 V (1 for 12 V network, 2 for 24 V network)
Alternator: 150 A/12 V × 1; 80 A/24 V × 1

Status

Production as required, 51 delivered to meet a French Army requirement (see text).

Contractor

Panhard General Defense

Panhard General Defense Véhicule d'Action dans la Profondeur (VAP)

Development

Panhard General Defense disclosed initial details of the *Véhicule d'Action dans la Profondeur* (VAP) in April 2006, with the vehicle being displayed publicly for the first time at Eurosatory 2006.

The VAP is a further development of the *Panhard Véhicule Blindé Léger* (VBL) (4 × 4) light scout vehicle, around 2,300 of which have been produced for France (>1,600) and at least 16 other nations since production commenced in 1990. The VAP has been developed by Panhard as a private venture to meet emerging requirements for a vehicle capable of undertaking special operations deep behind threat forces.

According to Panhard, typical roles of the VAP include reconnaissance and target designation, but its design is such that it can be fitted with a wide range of weapons and specialised equipment. Production can commence as soon as orders are placed. In January 2005 it was announced that *Société Nouvelle des Automobiles Auverland* (SNAA) had

Panhard VPS (special forces light vehicle) displayed at Eurosatory 2008 (Shaun C Connors)
1296141

Prototype VAP as displayed at Eurosatory 2006 (Shaun C Connors) 1185485

acquired Panhard. In early 2006, SNAA became known as Panhard General Defense.

Description
The VAP is based on the latest VBL Mk2 4 × 4 light scout vehicle, retaining the fully armour-protected floor and engine compartment of the base design. Full details of the VBL can be found in *Jane's Armour and Artillery*. The now open rear crew compartment of the VAP is provided with rollover protection which can be fitted with a ring-type mount for assorted weapons including light and heavy machine guns, an automatic grenade launcher or a 20 mm cannon.

The VAP also utilises the VBL Mk2 powerpack, this consisting of a 130 hp Steyr diesel engine coupled to a BVA transmission. This gives a maximum road speed of 120 km/h and an operating range of 700 km, with both of these figures being a significant improvement on the older VBL.

The VAP also has larger tyres for improved traction and cross-country mobility and a Central Tyre Inflation (CTI) system is fitted as standard.

Specifications
VAP
Cab seating: 1 + 1 + up to 2 in rear
Configuration: 4 × 4 (full-time)
Weight:
  (unladen) 2,500 kg
  (laden) 4,000 kg
  (payload) 1,500 kg
Length: 3.925 m
Width: 2 m
Height: 1.75 m
Ground clearance: 405 mm
Wheelbase: 2.7 m
Max speed: 120 km/h
Range: 700 km
Max gradient: >50%
Max side slope: 30%
Engine: Steyr M14VTI 2.1-litre turbocharged water-cooled 4-stroke diesel developing 130 hp (97 kW) and 285 N.m torque
Gearbox: ZF 4-speed automatic
Transfer box: 2-speed
Steering: power-assisted
Turning radius: 6 m
Suspension: independent, each wheel station rated at 1,500 kg
Tyres: 1100 × 16 Michelin XZL
Brakes: inboard discs all-round

Status
Ready for production.

Contractor
Panhard General Defense

Germany

Rheinmetall Landsysteme Light Infantry Vehicle for Special Operations (LIV (SO)), Serval

Development
Rheinmetall LandSysteme (RLS) has developed two specialised variants of the Mercedes-Benz G-Class light vehicle; the Light Infantry Vehicle (LIV) and the Light Infantry Vehicle for Special Operations (LIV (SO)), Serval. An overview of the LIV can be found elsewhere in this entry; full details of the Mercedes-Benz G-Class range can be found in the Light vehicles section.

The German Ministry of Defence awarded RLS a contract in March 2002 to develop the LIV (SO) on an 'immediate need basis', being given just 10 months to deliver the first example. All 21 vehicles ordered were delivered between January to June 2004 and the LIV (SO) is in service with the German Bundeswehr's special forces, and is known to have been used on deployed operations.

A small number of vehicles with some detail differences, including weapons fit, are understood to have been supplied to the Swiss Army during 2007. A variant of the LIV fitted with Mercedes-Benz Unimog portal axles has been developed and evaluated in the Middle East.

Rheinmetall AG and MAN Nutzfahrzeuge AG announced their respective intentions to form a joint wheeled military vehicles company in 2009. This alliance became a reality in January 2010 with the announcement of the founding of Rheinmetall MAN Military Vehicles (RMMV) GmbH. RMMV sees the merger of Rheinmetall's wheeled military vehicle activities with those of the military truck activities of MAN. Essentially this merger unites the complementary technological core competencies of MAN's automotive expertise in commercial-vehicle manufacture with Rheinmetall's technological know-how in the military land sector/systems field. The result is the creation of a new single-source provider for the entire range of armoured and unarmoured transport, command and role-specific wheeled vehicles.

German Army Rheinmetall Landsysteme Light Infantry Vehicle for Special Operations (LIV (SO)), Serval on deployed operations
(Rheinmetall Landsysteme GmbH)   1391228

Description
The LIV (SO) is based on the chassis and running gear of the Mercedes-Benz 270 CDI G-Class. The wheelbase and GVW rating of which are both increased from those of the standard vehicle for the LIV (SO) role. The current production G-Class is the 280 CDI.

The 270 CDI G-Class is powered by a EURO 3 emissions compliant 2.685-litre five-cylinder AVTUR, a low-grade fuel-tolerant diesel engine that develops 156 hp. This is coupled to a Mercedes-Benz five-speed Touchshift automatic transmission and two-speed transfer box. Mercedes-Benz beam axles are sprung by coil springs and damped by hydraulic shock-absorbers. Four-wheel drive is full-time, the transfer box and axles are fitted with driver actuated differential locks which may be engaged when the vehicle in motion.

For the LIV (SO) role, the base G-Class is delivered from Mercedes-Benz as a chassis with bodywork complete to the engine compartment rear bulkhead. The Rheinmetall-designed, Binz GmbH & Co produced rear body and frame are then fitted. The frame provides roll-over protection.

The underside of the LIV (SO) is protected against hand grenade blast and partial ballistic and hand grenade splinter protection body panels are an option. The engine compartment may also be armoured if required and the non-armoured front slide-out windscreen panels can be replaced with armoured glass. Underfloor armouring can be increased to counter anti-personnel mine blast if required.

For special forces and/or long range patrol-type roles the LIV (SO) is fitted for weapons, mounting an RLS WS609K weapon station that will ring-mount either a 12.7 mm Heavy Machine Gun (HMG) or a 40 mm Automatic Grenade Launcher (AGL). The LIV (SO) is also fitted with a front (passenger) mount and multiple rear mounts for 7.62 mm Light Machine Guns (LMGs).

Other features of the LIV (SO) include; a front- and rear-mounting detachable 9,000 kg-rated self-recovery winch, a brush guard, protected electrically-operated smoke discharger banks mounted at all four vehicle extremities, drop down flaps above the rear wheels for additional external stowage, a bonnet plate for tool stowage, a tyre inflation system, integrated spare wheels (one each side), and runflat inserts, with two-part wheel rims as an option. A single LIV (SO) complete with crew, and with the weapon station folded to lower the overall height, can be transported internally by CH-53G helicopter.

German Army Rheinmetall Landsysteme Light Infantry Vehicle for Special Operations (LIV (SO)), Serval on deployed operations
(Rheinmetall Landsysteme GmbH)   1391229

The Rheinmetall Landsysteme Light Infantry Vehicle (LIV) is based on the same extended wheelbase G-Class chassis as the LIV (SO)
(Rheinmetall Landsysteme GmbH)   1391231

Variants

Rheinmetall LandSysteme (RLS) Light Infantry Vehicle (LIV)

The RLS LIV was developed as a modular vehicle for expeditionary or special forces and is based around a chassis-cab platform on which various interchangeable mission-specific modules can be installed. The RLS LIV (sometimes referred to as the Wolf ESK (Einsatzfahrzeug Spezialisierte Kräfte - vehicle for specialised forces) is, like the LIV (SO), based on the 270 CDI G-Class with an extended 3.29 m wheelbase and GVW of up to 5,200 kg.

German Bundeswehr forces in Afghanistan evaluated eight prototypes of the LIV (plus eight prototypes of the Krauss-Maffei Wegmann (KMW) Mungo) during 2003 to meet an urgent operational requirement for a 10-seat protected light transport vehicle for rapid reaction forces. The KMW Mungo was selected to meet this requirement, however, the evaluated LIVs remain in use with German forces as MEDEVAC vehicles.

The 10-seat body package of the LIV is designed by Binz GmbH & Co. The driver, front seat passenger and the sides and rear of the open-topped troop compartment are protected from 7.62 mm ball ammunition; a ballistic-protected hard-top is also an option. Run-flat tyres are standard fit. Dimensions are 5.12 × 1.84 × 1.87-2.17 m (L × W × H). Unladen weight is 2,550 kg, and maximum payload (including any mission module) is 2,650 kg.

Specifications

LIV (SO)
Cab seating: 1 + up to 4
Configuration: 4 × 4
Weight:
  (unladen) 3,300 kg
  (laden) 5,200 kg
  (payload, max) 1,900 kg
  (towed load) 2,000 kg
  (GCW) 7,200 kg
Length: (incl. winch) 5.641 m
Width: (over body) 1.84 m
Height:
  (collapsed) 1.87 m
  (operating) 2.297 m
Ground clearance: 240 mm
Track: 1.55 m
Wheelbase: 3.29 m
Angle of approach/departure: n/avail
Max speed: (limited) 120 km/h
Max range: >500 km (up to 800 km with additional 54-litre long range tank)
Max gradient: 60%
Max side slope: (static) 30%
Fording: 600 mm
Engine: Mercedes-Benz DC 270 CDI EURO 3 emissions compliant 2.685-litre 5-cylinder in-line turbocharged and intercooled water-cooled common-rail diesel engine developing 156 hp (115 kW) at 3,800 rpm and 370 N.m torque between 1,600 and 2,600 rpm
Gearbox: Mercedes-Benz W5A 580 Touchshift automatic with 5 forward and 1 reverse gears
Transfer box: Mercedes-Benz VG 150E-3W 2-speed
Steering: LS-2B power-assisted
Turning radius: 6.25 m
Suspension: coil springs and telescopic shock-absorbers, front and rear
Tyres: 265/75 R16
Brakes: hydraulic, discs front, discs or drums rear, ABS standard
Electrical system: 12/24 V (2 circuits, 2 alternators)
Batteries: 3 × 12 V, 60 Ah
Alternator: 28 V, 80 A

Status

Production as required. In service with Germany (21) and Switzerland.

Contractor

Rheinmetall Landsysteme GmbH.

Israel

AIL Desert Raider (6 × 6) reconnaissance, surveillance and fast attack vehicle

Development

The Automotive Industries Limited (AIL) Desert Raider (6 × 6) reconnaissance, surveillance and fast attack vehicle, design designation M-626/G, is an air-portable, highly mobile surveillance and strike vehicle, capable of operating behind the front lines of a modern battlefield. It has undergone Israel Defence Force (IDF) Special Forces field trials and a small number (thought to be two) have been supplied to an unspecified customer, thought to be Uganda.

In 2010 EPS Technologies of the UK brought the original Desert Raider prototype to the UK, and dubbed Dingo sought to demonstrate/highlight the unique suspension of the vehicle, and potentially as a retro-fit and/or upgrade to a variety of lighter-weight Land Rover-class vehicles to enhance their off-road mobility.

Original AIL promotional photograph of the AIL Desert Raider (6 × 6) reconnaissance, surveillance and fast attack vehicle (AIL)   0079420

In 2010 EPS Technologies brought the original Desert Raider prototype to the UK, and dubbed Dingo sought to demonstrate/highlight the unique suspension of the vehicle, and potentially as a retro-fit and/or upgrade to a variety of lighter-weight Land Rover-class vehicles to enhance their off-road mobility (Shaun C Connors)   1391370

In 2010 EPS Technologies brought the original Desert Raider prototype to the UK, and dubbed Dingo sought to demonstrate/highlight the unique suspension of the vehicle, and potentially as a retro-fit and/or upgrade to a variety of lighter-weight Land Rover-class vehicles to enhance their off-road mobility (Shaun C Connors)   1391371

Description

The Desert Raider features a rear suspension that, it is claimed, combines the stability of a six-wheel vehicle with the mobility of a tracked vehicle. The 'tandem' rear suspension units with two wheel stations each side, is combined with coil springs and gas shock-absorbers giving a stroke of 600 mm. Full (6 × 6) drive involves an automatic computer-controlled gearbox, a differential lock and chains and sprockets to the tandem unit. The front suspension uses trapezoid arms with struts and adjustable coil springs giving a stroke of up to 400 mm.

The tubular space frame-type chassis has the power unit, a Chrysler 2.4-litre, four-cylinder water-cooled petrol engine, located at the rear. The driver is seated centrally towards the front, with seating for two passengers behind. Cargo space towards the rear is capable of carrying up to 1,200 kg or can be employed to accommodate two further passenger seats. Further stowage space is available over the engine covers. Folding roll bars are provided.

The Desert Raider can be carried internally by a CH-53 helicopter.

Design features include a low noise level and a low thermal signature.

Optional equipment includes a front or rear-mounted 4,000 kg winch, anchor points front and rear, a rear pintle hook, a spare wheel carrier, tie-down rings, two additional passenger seats and infra-red lighting.

Any further production would involve the integration of a current generation diesel-powered driveline.

Specifications

Desert Raider
Seating: 1 + 2 (+2 optional)
Configuration: 6 × 6
Weight:
 (kerb) 1,450 kg
 (GVW) 2,650 kg
 (payload) >1,200 kg
Length:
 (with spare wheel) 4.1 m
 (overall) 3.86 m
Width:
 (body) 1.95 m
 (wheels) 2 m
Height:
 (overall) 1.85 m
 (roll bars folded) 1.32 m
Ground clearance: 390 mm
Track:
 (front) 1.514 m
 (rear) 1.564 m
Wheelbase: 2.2 m + 900 mm
Angle of approach/departure: 75°/85°
Max speed: 110 km/h
Fuel capacity: 2 × 50 litres
Range: (operational) 500 km
Max gradient: 70%
Side slope: 70%
Fording: (without preparation) 700 mm
Vertical step: 600 mm
Engine: Chrysler 2.429-litre 4-cylinder in-line water-cooled fuel injected petrol developing 150 hp (112 kW) at 5,200 rpm
Transmission: Chrysler 41TE automatic with 4 forward and 1 reverse gears
Steering: power-assisted
Turning radius: 5.5 m
Suspension:
 (front) trapezoid arm type with struts, two gas shock-absorbers and adjustable coil springs, up to 400 mm stroke
 (rear) tandem, two wheels each side combined with coil springs and gas shock-absorbers, up to 600 mm stroke
Tyres: 235/75R 15
Brakes: power-assisted discs, front and rear
Electrical system: 12 V (24 V optional)
Battery: 2 × 12 V, 100 Ah
Alternator: 120 A

Status

Production as required. In addition to IDF trials it is believed that a small number were supplied to Uganda (see text).

Contractor

Automotive Industries Limited (AIL)

Jordan

Black Iris (4 × 2) and Desert Iris (4 × 4) light special forces vehicles

Development

The Black Iris (4 × 2) and Desert Iris (4 × 4) light special forces vehicles were developed by the King Abdullah II Design and Development Bureau (KADDB) working in association with SHP Motorsports of the United

Displaying its agility in the arena at IDEX 2005, a Desert Iris light special forces vehicle (Patrick Allen)   1138059

A Jordanian Special Operations Command Desert Iris at SOFEX 2004 complete with dedicated trailer (Patrick Allen)   1037323

A Jordanian Special Operations Command Desert Iris at SOFEX 2004 (Patrick Allen)   1037320

Kingdom. The vehicles were originally known by their KADDB project designation, AB3. Extensive prototype field trials were conducted in Jordan and South Africa from mid-1999 to mid-2001 and included deployment of some Black Iris vehicles with Jordanian forces on UN operations in Sierra Leone. Since then, the Jordanian Special Operations Command (SOCOM) has placed orders for initial quantities of the vehicle in both anti-tank and reconnaissance configurations. Further quantities of the (4 × 4) version have since been ordered by GHQ Jordan Armed Forces, these the replacement for M151 Jeeps.

It was reported in mid-2004 that KADDB had orders for 500 Desert Iris vehicles, 350 of these for Jordan's Armed Forces. The 150 export vehicles were for the UAE (at least 55) and Saudi Arabia. Libya ordered 25 of the earlier (4 × 2) Black Iris variants. By mid-2009 it was understood that around 600 Desert Iris vehicles had been built (none since late 2004), around 450 of these for Jordan's Armed Forces.

The vehicle was previously produced by Jordan Specialized Vehicle Manufacturing (JSVM), a joint venture between King Abdullah Design and Development Bureau (KADDB) and SHP Motorsport of the UK. JSVM has merged with Jordan Light Vehicle Manufacturing (JLVM), a joint venture between KADDB and the Jankel Group of the UK.

Civilian versions of the Iris are under development to address the tourist and recreational markets.

Desert Iris light special forces vehicles under construction at the KADDB main workshop (KADDB)   0556074

AB5 special forces vehicle configured for use by the Jordanian Ministry of Interior (JLVM)   0116897

Description
The Iris is based on a space frame chassis with the engine located at the front under a bonnet. The driver and passenger are seated centrally under roll-bar protection while a weapon mounting is located to the rear over a limited capacity cargo area. Various weapons options are available including 12.7 or 7.62 mm machine gun mounts, or interchangeable platforms for a TOW launcher or 106 mm recoilless rifle.

The standard Iris is capable of carrying up to four soldiers in combat order plus stores up to a maximum of 500 kg. Heavy duty versions can carry up to 750 kg.

Early vehicles were powered by a 2.4-litre diesel engine though this was later replaced with a 2.8-litre unit. Production vehicles are now powered by a 2.8-litre, four-cylinder in-line SOHC Toyota diesel engine, though the design of the engine compartment enables a range of both diesel and petrol engines to be fitted as required. In all cases the standard transmission is manual, although automatic transmissions are now available as an option.

Specifications
Desert Iris
Seating: 4
Configuration: 4 × 4
Payload: 500 kg (optional 750 kg)
Length: 4.25 m
Width: 1.9 m
Height: 1.75 m
Ground clearance: 350 mm
Wheelbase: 2.77 m
Max speed: (on-road) 120 km/h
Max range: 600 km on-road (400 km off-road)
Gradient: 60%
Side slope: 40%
Engine: 2.8-litre Toyota 4-cylinder in-line SOHC diesel developing 87 hp (65 kW) at 4,000 rpm and 185 N.m torque at 2,400 rpm (options available)
Gearbox: manual, 5 forward and 1 reverse gears (automatic optional)
Transfer box: 2-speed
Suspension: independent double wishbone with coil-over-shock (front); independent trailing arm with coil-over-shock (rear); 228 mm of suspension travel
Tyres: 265/75R 16 or 275/70R 16
Brakes:
  (main) dual circuit, discs front and rear
  (parking) mechanical, operating on rear wheels

Status
Production as required. In use by the Jordanian Armed forces including the Special Operations Command (SOCOM). Ordered by Libya (25 Black Iris), Saudi Arabia and UAE armed forces (at least 55).

Contractor
Jordan Light Vehicle Manufacturing (JLVM)

AB5 special forces vehicle

Development
The baseline AB5 special forces vehicle was launched at SOFEX 2000. The AB5 is intended for numerous tactical roles including fast attack, reconnaissance, border patrol and peacekeeping missions. The AB5 has been produced in a number of versions and the type has been deployed with Jordanian special forces on operations with the United Nations in Sierra Leone.

The AB5 has been supplied to Jordanian Special Operations Command (SOCOM) in unspecified numbers. A later version of the type has been supplied to the Ministry of Interior.

It was announced during 2006 that the AB5 had been superseded in the Jordan Light Vehicle Manufacturing (JLVM) product line-up by the Toyota Land Cruiser-based Al-Thalab (Fox) Long Range Patrol Vehicle (LRPV), full details of which can be found elsewhere in this section. JLVM is a joint venture between King Abdullah Design and Development Bureau (KADDB) and the Jankel Group of the UK.

Description
The AB5 special forces vehicle is built onto the chassis of a Land Rover Defender 110 and the baseline model, which was launched at SOFEX 2000, retains the Land Rover chassis, engine and driveline onto which is constructed a new body with tubular frame roll-over protection and a roof weapon ring installation for a 12.7 mm Heavy Machine Gun (HMG). There is also provision for a 7.62 mm M60 machine gun to be mounted on the front right-hand side for the front-seat passenger. The large load area is capable of carrying up to six soldiers in combat order or a maximum of 1,000 kg of stores. Other equipment for special forces operations includes a self-recovery winch, spare fuel container racks and smoke dischargers.

A later version of the type has been supplied to the Jordanian Ministry of Interior. This version has retained the Land Rover body, but features roll-over protection and weapons mounts derived from the Black Iris/Desert Iris programme. Full details of the Black Iris/Desert Iris light special forces vehicle can be found elsewhere in this section.

Specifications
AB5
Seating: 1 + 1 or 2 (+ 6)
Configuration: 4 × 4
Weight:
  (unladen) 3,050 kg
  (payload) 1,000 kg
Length: 4.5 m
Width: 2 m
Height: 1.94 m
Ground clearance: 200 mm
Wheelbase: 2.8 m
Angle of approach/departure: 60°/38°

AB5 special forces vehicles showing front-mounted self-recovery winch and smoke dischargers (JLVM)   0116895

Max speed: (on-road) 180 km/h
Max range: 600 km on-road (400 km off-road)
Engine: Rover 3.5-litre V8 water-cooled petrol developing 134 hp (100 kW)
Gearbox: Land Rover LT 85, manual with 5 forward and 1 reverse gears
Clutch: diaphragm spring
Transfer box: Land Rover LT85 2-speed, full-time four-wheel drive with lockable centre differential
Steering: manual, recirculating ball
Suspension: beam axles with coil springs and telescopic shock-absorbers, front and rear
Brakes:
 (main) direct-acting servo-assisted dual circuit. Discs front, drums rear
 (parking) transmission drum, cable-operated
Electrical systems: 12 V

Status
Production as required (on current generation platform). In use by the Jordanian Armed Forces, including the Special Operations Command (SOCOM), and the Jordanian Ministry of Interior.

Contractor
Jordan Light Vehicle Manufacturing (JLVM)

JLVM Al-Thalab (Fox) Long Range Patrol Vehicle (LRPV)

Development
Jordan Light Vehicle Manufacturing (JLVM) first disclosed details of the Al-Thalab (Fox) Long Range Patrol Vehicle (LRPV) in early 2004, and displayed a prototype/concept demonstrator of the design at the SOFEX 2004 exhibition in Amman, Jordan.

The Al-Thalab LRPV was designed primarily for internal security, reconnaissance and border patrol operations in arid and high-altitude areas of operation.

A Toyota chassis was selected as the base of the LRPV for its prevalence in anticipated areas of operation, plus its basic simplicity, ease of repair and ready availability of spare parts in remote areas where the vehicle might be expected to operate.

An important feature of the design is that the LRPV's automotive and mechanical components are of a standard and basic design, with minimal difficult-to-support electronic management systems.

An initial LRPV prototype based on a Land Rover platform was produced in 1999. The first order for the LRPV was announced in June 2004 when Jordan Light Vehicle Manufacturing confirmed that the Jordanian Armed Forces (JAF) had placed an order for 20-25 vehicles. By mid-2009 Jordan had received around 200 vehicles.

The first export order was for an initial 15 vehicles from an undisclosed African country (now known to have been Mauritania), this following shortly after the initial Jordanian order. Other export customers have included Brunei, Italy and Spain.

The vehicles for Mauritania were manufactured in the UK by Jankel and production was completed mid-2006. Production of the Jordanian (and other) vehicles was undertaken in Jordan.

The most recent known order for Al-Thalab was placed by Oman which received around 20 vehicles in 2010.

Jordan Light Vehicle Manufacturing LLC is a joint venture between King Abdullah Design and Development Bureau (KADDB) and the Jankel Group of the UK, and is located at the KHMW at Dulayl. Jankel has been building specialist protected vehicles for over 20 years and through this international collaboration with KADDB has helped develop a volume manufacturing facility in Jordan that is capable of constructing vehicles for both law enforcement and commercial applications, based on mass-produced commercial off-the-shelf chassis.

Description
The Al-Thalab Long Range Patrol Vehicle (LRPV) is based on a tropical specification 79 Series Toyota Land Cruiser with no major structural or mechanical changes. Full details of the Toyota Land Cruiser can be found

JLVM Al-Thalab (Fox) Long Range Patrol Vehicle (LRPV) (Jankel) 1186199

in the Light vehicles section. Motive power is provided by a six-cylinder diesel engine (naturally aspirated or turbocharged) coupled to a manual five-speed manual transmission. Compared to contemporary vehicles equipped with Euro III, IV or even V emissions-compliant electronic engine-management systems, the engine used in the LRPV features limited electronics and is fitted with an old-style mechanical fuel injection pump. This is not only better adapted to field maintenance on operations in remote areas where electronic diagnostic systems are unsupportable, but additionally will more readily cope with lower grade and/or JP8 fuels.

The modularity of the design allows for the LRPV to be adapted to different concepts of operation, but typically gives a range of 1,500 km carrying a crew of four, who can be supported in the field for 10 days without resupply.

To achieve an operational range of 1,500 km the baseline two 90-litre fuel tanks are supplemented by 20-litre jerrycans (which may also be used for water) stowed four on either side of the vehicle, plus two additional jerrycans in the rear of the vehicle, one of which is stowed beneath the cargo deck and beneath a footwell let into the deck.

Seating is variable in line with mission requirements, but the two crew normally carried in the rear have collapsible seats which may be removed to make room for two stretchers. The seats themselves are based on the ACS International ROPS (Roll-Over Protective Structure), a crash-proof seating system developed for truck-borne motorized infantry applications. This includes a safety harness, head restraint and a removable back cushion pad to allow the user to sit comfortably wearing belt equipment.

The LRPV can mount a full range of military communications equipment and has two antenna mounts fitted and 12V/24V plug-in jack points at the front and rear of the vehicle to support surveillance/communications systems.

Though not intended to be used as a dedicated weapons carrier, the LRPV can be equipped with front and rear weapon mounts. The main armament, up to and including a 12.7 mm heavy machine gun, is mounted on a rear-located ring-mount which can also support a 40 mm automatic grenade launcher. A front swing-arm mount can mount a 7.62 mm light machine gun.

Protection from the elements is provided by a demountable two-piece windscreen, plus a canopy which is designed to double as a lean-to shelter. The nominal operating temperature range is -15°/+55°C, but flexible hose extensions are provided to pipe hot air directly from the vehicle heater to personnel in the rear, inside their clothing if needed. The LRPV, fitted with a winch as well as a jack, carries strengthened sand channels that also serve as aids to crossing gaps of up to 2 m. Additional features can include a Vehicle Utility Ladder (VUL), part of Jankel's Urban Combat Access System (UCAS).

A single LRPV can be carried as an underslung load beneath a Puma helicopter, or three aboard a C-130 Hercules transport aircraft.

JLVM Al-Thalab (Fox) Long Range Patrol Vehicle (LRPV) (Jankel) 1116570

JLVM Al-Thalab (Fox) Long Range Patrol Vehicle (LRPV) (Jankel) 1186201

Specifications

JLVM Al-Thalab (Fox)
Cab seating: 1 + 1 + 2 in rear
Configuration: 4 × 4 (full-time)
Weight:
  (unladen) 2,471 kg
  (laden) 3,900 kg
  (payload) 1,329 kg
  (front axle load) 1,460 kg
  (rear axle load) 2,360 kg
  (towed load) 2,500 kg
Length: 5.6 m
Width: 1.895 m
Height: 1.905 m
Ground clearance:
  (front axle) 250 mm
  (rear axle) 240 mm
Track:
  (front) 1.435 m
  (rear) 1.420 m
Wheelbase: 3.180 m
Angle of approach/departure: 37°/28°
Max speed: 140 km/h
Max range: 1,500 km
Fuel capacity: 180 litres
Max gradient: >60%
Max side slope: 80%
Fording:
  (unprepared) 540 mm
  (prepared) 1.1 m
Engine: Toyota (1HZ) 4.164-litre 6-cylinder in-line naturally aspirated 4-stroke diesel developing 129 hp (96 kW) at 3,400 rpm; optional turbocharged variant developing 156 hp (116 kW) at 3,400 rpm
Gearbox: Toyota R151 manual with 5 forward and 1 reverse gears
Transfer box: 2-speed
Steering: power-assisted
Turning radius: 7.325 m
Suspension: coil springs front, leaf springs rear
Tyres: BF Goodrich All-Terrain T/A
Brakes: discs front, drums rear
Electrical system: 12 V
Batteries: 2 × 12 V, 80 Ah
Alternator: 70 A

Status

Production as required. In service with Brunei (six), Italy (two, evaluation), Jordan (approximately 200), Mauritania (15, 2006), Oman (21, 2010) and Spain (two, evaluation).

Contractor

Jankel Armouring Ltd
King Abdullah II Design and Development Bureau (KADDB)

Singapore

Singapore Technologies (ST) Kinetics Flyer and Spider light strike vehicles

Development

The Singapore Technologies (ST) Kinetics Spider Light Strike Vehicle (LSV) is an evolution of the earlier ST Kinetics Light Strike Vehicle, this vehicle having previously been marketed as the ST Kinetics Flyer Light Strike Vehicle.

The original Flyer vehicle was developed by the US HSMV Corporation, subsequently purchased by the Flyer Group. Production was carried out in Australia by ADI for a time before ST Kinetics obtained the full rights to the vehicle and developed the Flyer R-12D.

Promotional image of the ST Kinetics Spider LSV (ST Kinetics)   1128239

Official figures have never been released but it is understood that ADI supplied a single (possibly 2) Flyers to Indonesia, plus a total of 79 examples to Singapore, 29 being delivered in April 1998 with the first of the 50 follow-on vehicles being delivered in May 1990. The latest Spider LSV was displayed publicly for the first time at Asian Aerospace 2004 in Singapore, and differs in a number of areas from early designs.

The Flyer Group has evolved to become Flyer Defense LLC and as a subsidiary of The Marvin Group currently offers the Flyer Gen II platform.

Description

The ST Kinetics Flyer is powered by a rear-mounted two-litre 110 hp water-cooled turbocharged diesel engine coupled to a three-speed semi-automatic transmission. The space frame chassis is constructed of welded chrome-moly seamless tubing and a long travel suspension is employed to enable high-speed travel over rough terrain.

The roll-cage may be configured in a number of ways to accommodate various weapon installations. A typical weapon installation could be a 7.62 mm machine gun forward plus a pedestal mount for a missile launcher or a 40 mm automatic grenade launcher such as the 40AGL. Some vehicles in service with the Singapore defence forces carry a rear-mounted pedestal for two Spike Anti-Tank Guided Weapons (ATGW), with stowage for five missiles. Others have been seen with a combined 40 mm AGL and 7.62 mm machine gun mounting supplemented by a pintle-mounted 7.62 mm machine gun, while others have been seen mounting the MILAN ATGW. Singapore Armed Forces Flyers are equipped for right-hand drive.

While retaining the same basic design principles as the Flyer, the Spider LSV does differ in a number of key ways from its predecessor. Motive power is provided by a 130 hp VM Motori diesel engine (the original Spider and production Flyers were powered by 110 hp engines) which is certified up to EURO 3. Full-time four-wheel drive is retained. However the fully independent suspension and braking systems have been uprated.

The Spider is a six-seater (the Flyer seats a maximum of four) and this gives potential users greater flexibility to deploy the vehicle for a wider range of operations. The Flyer has a central driving position and a removable windscreen providing protection against the elements. The improved design of the Spider also offers a collapsible roll-cage frame that readily allows two vehicles to be stacked for rapid air deployment, enhancing the efficiency of air transportability by allowing more LSVs to be transported in a single operation. With this feature, it is now possible to accommodate six Spiders comfortably in a C-130 aircraft.

ST Kinetics light strike vehicle (ST Kinetics)   0569014

ST Kinetics Spider LSV displaying its mobility during the mobility display at IDEX 2005 (Patrick Allen)   0590721

A configurable tubular roll-cage system enables modification of the vehicle to suit a variety of missions that include attack, surveillance, reconnaissance, ambulance, emergency and combat support roles. The Spider may also be fitted with capsulised armour for protection against small arms of up to 7.62 mm. It may also be configured for unmanned operations.

Aside from a conventional power source, the Spider can also be fitted with a Motor Generator (MOGEN), a hybrid electric and motor unit. When operated on its electrical power, the MOGEN enables a vehicle to move in a silent (stealthy) mode. The MOGEN can also provide back-up power as an auxiliary power source.

Future Spider LSV designs will incorporate a patent-pending retractable wheel system. In operations, this offers the Spider a lower centre of gravity for improved stability and manoeuvrability at high speeds in off-road conditions. With the wheels fully retracted, the Spider takes on a more streamlined profile that allows it to be internally transported in narrow-body carriers such as the V-22 Osprey aircraft.

Specifications

	Flyer	Spider
Seating:	1 + 2 or 3	up to 6
Configuration:	4 × 4	4 × 4
Weight: (kerb)	1,400 kg	1,600 kg
Payload:	1,000 kg	1,200 kg
Length:	4.5 m	4.5 m
Width:	2.03 m	2.03 m
Height: (top of roll-cage)	1.9 m	1.9 m
Ground clearance:	400 mm	n/avail
Wheelbase:	2.85 m	2.85 m
Angle of approach/departure:	70°/40°	n/avail
Max speed:		
(on-road)	110 km/h	120 km/h
(off-road)	n/avail	80 km/h
Range:	525 km	700 km
Gradient: (dynamic)	60%	60%
Side slope:	50%	50%
Fording:	600 mm	n/avail
Vertical obstacle:	400 mm	400 mm
Engine:	2-litre turbocharged intercooled diesel developing 110 hp (82 kW) at 4,500 rpm	VM Motori 2.8-litre 4-cylinder in-line turbocharged water-cooled 4-stroke diesel developing 130 hp (97 kW) at 3,800 rpm and 410 N.m torque at 1,800 rpm
Transmission:	semi-automatic transaxle, 3 forward and 1 reverse gears	STK semi-automatic
Steering:	power-assisted	hydraulic power-assisted
Turning radius:	6.5 m	6.5 m
Suspension:	independent all-round	independent all-round, double wishbone with single shock-absorber, front; trailing arm with twin shock-absorbers, rear
Tyres:	35 12R 15	n/avail
Electrical system:	24 V	24 V
Batteries:	2 12 V, 52 Ah	n/avail
Alternator:	55 A (100 A optional)	n/avail

Status
Available. In service with Indonesia (see text) and Singapore (79).

Contractor
Singapore Technologies Kinetics

South Africa

BAE Systems Land Systems South Africa Wasp/Hornet Rapid Deployment Reconnaissance Vehicle (RDRV)

Development
The BAE Systems Land Systems South Africa (previously Alvis OMC, previously Vickers OMC) Wasp/Hornet Rapid Deployment Reconnaissance Vehicle (RDRV) was developed for use by special and airborne forces and was designed to be self-deployable by road or airlifted/dropped by helicopter or transport aircraft; a C-130B Hercules aircraft being capable of transporting four vehicles.

The Wasp (designated Hornet by the SANDF) was selected for the South African National Defence Force's (SANDF's) Ambition 1A requirement that called for an air-deployable mobility platform for use by special forces. The original requirement called for 40 vehicles, but in the request for tenders this was reduced to 25. Also competing for this requirement was the G-Wagon-based CSIR Defencetek BAT Mk 2 and (in the early stages of the programme) the Land Rover component-based MDB Taurus.

The original prototype was completed in September 2000 and following a Request For Proposals (RFP) issued by ARMSCOR in February 2001, the vehicle was evaluated between November 2001 and June 2002. The then Alvis OMC entered a tender process in August 2002 and the company was announced as Preferred Supplier in December 2002. The production contract was placed by ARMSCOR in July 2003 and included 25 vehicles, 50 interchangeable platforms (consisting of long range mortar platform, multiple rocket launcher platform, command, urban platform) and 25 weapon mounts.

Development of the vehicle in its delivered configuration commenced in July 2003 and a number of changes (detailed in the specifications below) were made to the prototype design. The first vehicle was delivered to ARMSCOR in June 2004, with production of all vehicles, platforms and weapon mounts completed in June 2005.

Description
In its basic configuration, the Wasp/Hornet provides three side-by-side seats in the front, the centre of these having dual (high/low) positions that enable the gunner to fire from a mounting on the windscreen frame. This would typically be a 7.62 mm machine gun, but the mounting will also accept a 12.7 mm heavy machine gun, a low-recoil 20 mm MG-151 type cannon, or a 40 mm automatic grenade launcher. The rear of the vehicle features a reconfigurable seat and the weapons pallet which can be fitted with light support weapons including a 60 mm mortar, a 107 mm multiple rocket launcher, or a pedestal mounted 20 mm cannon or 12.7 mm heavy machine gun. Other possible variants include an eight-seat troop carrier or a five-crew reconnaissance vehicle.

Maximum payload is 1,350 kg and the basic vehicle weight is 2,550 kg, giving a gross vehicle weight of 3,900 kg. This figure includes 60 litres of fuel, 60 litres of water and three-sided armoured protection for the engine, transmission, transfer box, fuel tank and batteries. Frontal ballistic protection is provided against 7.62 mm AP attack, while side protection is provided against 7.62 mm ball attack. The 38 mm armoured windscreen offers protection against 7.62 mm ball ammunition. Floor protection is provided against hand grenades detonated beneath the vehicle and anti-personnel mines detonated beneath the wheels. Additional protection is an option.

The Wasp/Hornet was originally powered by a VM Motori Detroit Diesel 2.5-litre four-cylinder turbocharged diesel developing 111 hp at 4,000 rpm and utilised a number of components from the RG-32 protected light vehicle. Production vehicles are powered by a more powerful VM Motori

Front three-quarter view on an early Land Systems OMC Wasp/Hornet Rapid Deployment and Reconnaissance Vehicle (RDRV) displayed at AAD 2004 (Patrick Allen)
1110656

Displayed at AAD 2010, an SANDF Wasp/Hornet Rapid Deployment and Reconnaissance Vehicle (RDRV) (Patrick Allen)   1431591

Detroit Diesel developing 134 hp. The engine is fitted as a 'powerpack' with a Chrysler four-speed automatic transmission (three-speed in prototype vehicles) with an integral chain-driven synchromesh two-speed transfer case for (4 × 4) operation.

Other changes in production vehicles include a 300 mm increase in overall length; 230 mm between the axles and 70 mm as a front bumper. The 100-litre fuel tank was replaced by a 60-litre tank and a number of aesthetic and ergonomic changes were also made. Additional 7.62 mm ball protection was added to the bonnet for engine protection.

Standard equipment on production vehicles includes tie-down and lifting hooks, attachment interfaces front and rear for the self-recovery winch, a 60-litre capacity stainless steel water tank, a manual tyre inflation system, bush-protected lighting, convoy lighting, 6 × 75 W bush-protected spot-lamps, 2 × bush-protected infra-red lights, plus a full set of tools and essential equipment.

Specifications

Wasp/Hornet RDRV
Cab seating: 1 + 7 (standard configuration) (1 + 5 in 60 mm mortar or 107 mm multiple rocket launcher configuration)
Configuration: 4 × 4
Weight:
  (unladen) 2,550 kg
  (laden) 3,900 kg
  (payload) 1,350 kg
  (towed load) 1,500 kg (in RDLV configuration)
Length: 3.598 m (in RDRV configuration)
Width: 2.26 m (in RDRV configuration)
Height: 1.97 m (to top of spare wheel, but dependant on user configuration)
Ground clearance: 243 mm
Track:
  (front) 1.865 m
  (rear) 1.865 m
Wheelbase: 2.53 m
Angle of approach/departure: 63°/74°
Max road speed: 116 km/h
Max range: (on road) 420 km at 80 km/h
Fuel capacity: 60 litres (plus optional 60 litres)
Max gradient: 60%
Side slope: 40%
Vertical obstacle: 300 mm
Fording: 600 mm
Engine: VM Motori Detroit Diesel 428L CRD 2.776-litre 4-cylinder in-line turbocharged and intercooled water-cooled 4-stroke direct injection diesel developing 134 hp (100 kW) at 3,800 rpm and 300 N.m torque at 1,800-2,600 rpm
Gearbox: Chrysler 45 RFE 4-speed automatic
Transfer box: Chrysler NVG 242 LHD 2-speed (chain driven)
Steering: Chrysler LS2A power-assisted re-circulating ball, left-hand drive
Turning radius: 5.5 m
Suspension: semi-elliptic leaf springs with double acting hydraulic shock-absorbers and progressive rubber bump stops, torsion bar fitted in conjunction with rear springs

Axles: Power Torque steer-drive, single reduction rigid rated at 1,850 kg, front; Daimler HLO/25-2.2 drive rated at 2,200 kg, rear
Tyres: 235/85R 16 BF Goodrich (runflat inserts; 50 km at 50 km/h, optional)
Brakes:
  (main) dual circuit, ventilated discs front, drums rear
  (parking) cable operated on rear drums
Electrical system: 12 V engine and starter; 24 V systems
Batteries: 2 × 12 V, 102 Ah
Alternator: 110 A

Status
In service with the SANDF (designated Hornet) (25).

Contractor
BAE Systems Land & Armaments, Global Tactical Systems, Land Systems OMC division

United Arab Emirates

ADCOM Hunter fast attack vehicle

Development
The ADCOM Hunter (previously known as the H2A) fast attack vehicle is described as a second-generation fast attack vehicle and has been developed by ADCOM Military Industries (previously known as ADCOM Trading Limited) of the UAE and initially for a long-standing UAE Armed Forces requirement believed to be for between 60 and 90 vehicles. As of mid-2010, no decision had been announced regarding this requirement, although it is known that extensive trials have been undertaken, the Singapore Technologies Kinetics (STK) Flyer being a known competitor.

The UAE requirement evolved during trials, the original requirement calling for a (4 × 2) petrol-powered dune buggy-type design.

It was stated in 2005 by the manufacturer that the Hunter had successfully completed Summer trials in Kuwait and the UAE.

In addition to local production, the Hunter is offered for export, being available in kit form or for local production if ordered in sufficient numbers. Available in a variety of configurations, the vehicle has been displayed prominently in an anti-armour harassment configuration; it is claimed to be able to strike at armour from ranges in excess of 5,000 m, its relative small size, stealthiness, speed and agility ensuring it remains difficult to locate and target.

Description
The main frame of the Hunter is constructed from 44.5 mm (1¾ in) mild steel tubing to facilitate rapid role changing and to allow for ease of repair with minimal facilities. Both front and rear suspension is of the fully independent coil-over-shock absorber design giving in excess of 250 mm of wheel travel and 410 mm of unobstructed underbody ground clearance. Power assisted steering and brakes are fitted, brakes being discs all-round. For the anti-armour/armour harassment role, extra-wide high flotation 35 × 17.5 × 15 tyres are fitted at 69 kPa (10 psi) and give a tyre footprint of 406 × 457 mm (0.186 m²) each.

In the armour harassment role, weapons fit consists of two 5.56 Minimi guns for self-protection, eight 66 mm smoke grenade launchers and a 12.7 mm Heavy Machine Gun (HMG) capable of air defence. Anti-tank missile armament is the Kornet-E. Laser guided maximum ranges of 5,500 m (day) and 3,500 m (night) are quoted and eight missile reloads can be carried. The weapons mounting system allows the HMG and missile launcher to be mounted together and used as required.

The most recent image of the ADCOM Hunter. The vehicle is painted in a midnight blue colour scheme for night operations
(ADCOM Military Industries)   1114585

ADCOM Hunter at speed in the main arena at IDEX 2003. Armament is the AEI Sharpshooter precision-fire version of the Giat (now Nexter) M621 20 mm cannon (Shaun C Connors)   0583282

At IDEX 2003, the Hunter was displayed armed with the AEI Sharpshooter precision-fire version of the Giat M621 20 mm cannon. As a result of trials, the version displayed at IDEX 2003 had been redesigned and the engine moved back 483 mm to reduce front overhang and improve mobility in sand dunes. Overall length of the vehicle reduces from 4.724 to 4.42 m, with spare wheel. The most recent image of the Hunter has it painted in a midnight blue colour scheme for night operations.

The latest version of the Hunter has a dry weight of 2,300 kg and a maximum gross weight of 3,500 kg. Motive power is provided by a Cummins 5.9-litre six-cylinder turbocharged diesel engine that develops 300 hp at 2,600 rpm, giving a power-to-weight ratio of 85.7 hp/tonne. The engine will run, with some loss in performance, on JP8.

Power to either the rear or both axles (selectable) is through a GM 4L80E four-speed (fourth is overdrive) automatic transmission (with manual override) and Borg Warner 4401 two-speed transfer box. Range and two- to four-wheel drive changes are possible on the move. Maximum sustained speed in high range is 150 km/h and 0-100 km/h can be achieved in 9.8 seconds. At 4.2 km per litre fuel consumption, the 136-litre capacity standard fuel tank gives a cruising range of 565 km. This increases to 900 km with the optional long-range fuel tank fitted. An earlier version was fitted with a larger 190-litre tank giving a cruising range of 800 km.

Other items of standard equipment include an on-board 827 kPa (120 psi) air compressor and reservoir, a 3,628 kg (8,000 lb) capacity self-recovery winch, and a GPS navigational system.

Specifications

Hunter fast attack vehicle
Cab seating: 1 + 3
Configuration: 4 × 2/4 (selectable)
Weight:
  (laden) 3,500 kg
  (unladen) 2,300 kg
  (payload) 1,200 kg
Length: (with rear-mounted spare wheel) 4.42 m
Width: 2.108 m
Height: weapons fit dependant
Ground clearance: 410 mm
Wheelbase: 3.124 m
Max speed: (standard tank) 140 km/h
Max range: 565 km
Fuel capacity: 135 litres
Max gradient: >60%
Side slope: >30%
Engine: Cummins 5.9-litre 6-cylinder in-line turbocharged and intercooled water-cooled 4-stroke diesel developing 300 hp (224 kW) at 2,600 rpm and 898 N.m torque at 1,600 rpm
Transmission: GM 4L80E 4-speed automatic; 4th gear being a 0.72 overdrive
Transfer box: Borg Warner 4401 2-speed
Steering: Saginaw, power assisted
Suspension: fully independent, coil-over-shock-absorber
Tyres: 35 × 17.5 × 15
Brakes: discs, front and rear
Electrical system: 24 V
Batteries: 2 × 12 V

Status
Ready for production. Completed Summer trials in Kuwait and the UAE.

Contractor
ADCOM Group, ADCOM Military Industries

United Kingdom

Land Rover Defender Special Operations Vehicle (SOV)

Development
The Land Rover Defender Special Operations Vehicle (SOV) was specifically designed to meet a US Army requirement for a rapid reaction, air-portable, all-terrain weapons platform to replace the M151-series 'gun-jeeps' then in use by the US Army's Special Forces (75th Ranger regiment). An initial order for 60 Ranger Special Operations Vehicle (RSOV) units was placed by the US Army late in 1992.

The RSOV has a projected service life of 20 years and in mid-2001 an upgrade programme to ensure continued tactical viability was initiated. Vehicles have been provided with improved suspension, wider tyres for improved ride stability, and the spare wheel has been relocated from the rear to the front of the vehicle.

In addition to their RSOV the US Rangers also operate small numbers (six) of Medical Special Operations Vehicles (MEDSOVs) and (six) MORTSOVs used by the mortar platoon.

Description
The RSOV is based on the Land Rover Defender 110 chassis and retains a high level of commonality with other Defender models, featuring the standard full-time four-wheel drive configuration and suspension, consisting of long travel coil springs front and rear combined with telescopic dampers, rear trailing links, a Panhard rod at the front and a centrally mounted 'A' bracket at the rear. A Land Rover 300 Tdi direct injection turbocharged and intercooled diesel engine was fitted, this driving through the standard Land Rover two-speed transfer box and five-speed gearbox. Steering and braking are also conventional Land Rover systems.

The basic RSOV configuration features either a Mk 19 40 mm grenade launcher or 12.7 mm (0.5 in) machine gun main weapon mounted on the frame rollbar over the rear of the vehicle, and secondary armament consisting of a front-passenger operated 7.62 mm machine gun. The RSOV is normally crewed by three, a driver, truck commander and top gunner, although depending on mission up to seven Rangers can be carried. All seating positions face outwards, and additional positions might include an anti-tank operator, radio telephone operator or a dismount team consisting of an M249 squad automatic weapon gunner, M203 gunner and rifleman. Racks and stowage bins located around the vehicle can be used to carry a 50 or 81 mm mortar and mounting and/or a Stinger missile launcher. Further stowage bins can carry mines or demolition equipment in addition to the crew's personal kit. Front impact protection and a front-mounted 3,180 kg winch are standard equipment.

The RSOV may be para-dropped and it can be carried inside a C-130 transport aircraft, or CH-47 and CH-53 helicopters. It may also be carried underslung by any suitable capacity medium-lift helicopter.

In addition to their RSOV the US Rangers also operate small numbers (six) of Medical Special Operations Vehicles (MEDSOVs) and (six) MORTSOVs used by the mortar platoon. The MEDSOVs have their weapons mounts replaced by fold-down racks capable of carrying six litter patients, while the MORTSOVs have their top gun mount replaced with stowage for 30 120 mm mortar rounds and additional mortar platoon equipment. In addition to this onboard capacity, the MORTSOV can be used to tow the platoon's 120 mm mortars.

Specifications
Crew: up to 7
Configuration: 4 × 4
Weight:
  (GVW) 3,515 kg
  (towed load, on road, full trailer brakes) 4,000 kg
  (towed load, off road) 1,000 kg
Length: 4.445 m
Width: 1.89 m
Height: (gun ring) 1.93 m
Ground clearance: 216 mm
Track: 1.486 m

A US Army RSOV in standard configuration and post upgrade (Ian C Young)   1296189

Wheelbase: 2.794 m
Engine: 2.5-litre 4-cylinder in-line direct injection turbocharged and intercooled water-cooled 4-stroke diesel developing 111 hp (83 kW) at 4,000 rpm
Gearbox: manual, 5 forward and 1 reverse gears
Clutch: diaphragm spring
Transfer box: LT 230T, 2 speed with differential lock
Steering: manual, recirculating ball
Turning radius: 6.4 m
Suspension: coil springs and telescopic hydraulic shock-absorbers, front and rear
Brakes: dual servo-assisted; discs front and rear
Tyres: 7.50 × 16
Electrical system: 12 V
Alternator: 65 A

Status
Production complete. In service with the US Rangers (60 delivered).

Contractor
Land Rover

Land Rover Defender Rapid Deployment Vehicle (RDV) and Weapons Mount Installation Kit (WMIK)

Development

Rapid Deployment Vehicle (RDV)
The original Land Rover Defender Rapid Deployment Vehicle (RDV) concept derives from the MultiRole Combat Vehicle (MRCV) concept introduced in 1993. The RDV was developed jointly by Land Rover and Ricardo Special Vehicles, with Ricardo primarily responsible for the vehicle conversion, roll-cage assembly and ring-mount design and development. The RDV is available on the military Defender 90 and 110 and gives vehicles a defensive/offensive capability by allowing the mounting of assorted light weapons. Full details of the Land Rover Defender range can be found in the Light vehicles section.

Around 200 examples of the RDV built on the Defender XD (eXtra Duty) 110 chassis were originally supplied to the British Army from 1999 and for use primarily by 16 Air Assault Brigade. An evolution of the first RDV designs, these vehicles are referred to by Land Rover, Ricardo and the UK MoD as WMIK, which stands for Weapons Mount Installation Kit.

The Dutch Marines received around 20 RDVs as part of a 71-vehicle package ordered in 2000. In 2001 the Italian Carabinieri received 12 RDVs based on the Core Military Defender 90. The Irish Army received six RDVs based on a Commercial Defender 110 HD platform prior to the 2004 delivery of their Ford F350-based Ricardo Rapid Deployment Vehicles (RDVs).

Following a competition that is understood to have included a Pinzgauer vehicle and the G-Class-based RLS LIV(SO), Lithuania awarded Ricardo Special Vehicles a contract late 2005 for 45 × Defender 110 RDV-type vehicles to be delivered over three years. These vehicles are two-door, four-seat, and feature a single rearward facing seat. They are powered by the Land Rover Td5 engine, and as there was no requirement for CH-47 transportability, are fitted with the standard soft-top height roll-cage.

To meet a French Army requirement for 41 RDV-type vehicles, Ricardo Special Vehicles developed a version of the RDV based on a Defender 130 chassis. This contract was awarded to Panhard for a design based on a G-Class platform.

Weapons Mount Installation Kit (WMIK)
The WMIK was developed jointly between Land Rover and Ricardo Special Vehicles for the UK MoD and, following minimal preparation, can be fitted to any Defender XD 110 by four soldiers in under four hours. WMIK gives

From 2007 and as part of a rolling upgrade programme the original 200 in-service WMIK fleet were uprated to 4,100 kg GVW by Ricardo Special Vehicles; upgraded vehicles are known as RWMIK (Shaun C Connors)
1304068

the vehicles a defensive/offensive capability by allowing the mounting and stable firing of heavy machine guns, grenade launchers or anti-armour missiles from a ring or pulpit mount attached to a full-length roll protection cage. A second, forward firing light machine is also fitted to the vehicle.

16 Air Assault Brigade (and more recently others) currently operate around 270 so-converted vehicles, predominantly on operations in Afghanistan. Following deployment to Afghanistan (primarily) and previously Iraq a number of initiatives to further improve vehicle reliability and mobility plus increase the disposable payload of WMIK, while providing the crew with a tactically acceptable level of protection have been undertaken.

As part of this process, it was announced mid-2005 that as part of the wider Project Shoehorn, the GVW of the WMIK fleet would be increased from 3,350 to 3,500 kg.

It was announced mid-2006 that to bolster the WMIK fleet 58 Land Rover Defender XD vehicles would be converted to WMIK configuration under an Urgent Operational Requirement (UOR) contract by Ricardo Special Vehicles, and that 22 'reconstituted' (new chassis) WMIKs with a Ricardo-developed 4,100 kg GVW kit had been ordered. These 80 vehicles (58 + 22) are collectively known as EWMIK and were for Afghanistan.

Further development of the WMIK enhancement package continued and from 2007 as part of a rolling upgrade programme the original 200 in-service WMIK fleet would be uprated to 4,100 kg GVW by Ricardo Special Vehicles; upgraded vehicles are known as RWMIK. The primary differences between EWMIK and RWMIK are the latter having a more basic Bowman communications package fit, but an enhanced level of protection for the crew, this protection being built in and not an add-on as with EWMIK.

Late-2009 it was disclosed that under the earlier RWMIK contract the MoD had placed an order with Ricardo for around 70 of the further enhanced RWMIK+. A second batch of 50 RWMIK+ were ordered early-2010, and a third and final batch of >60 are expected to be ordered shortly, with all deliveries to conclude by year-end. Under this latest award, all remaining EWMIKs (around 65) are being upgraded to RWMIK+ standard, the remainder of vehicles being created from the conversion of surplus Land Rover Snatch chassis.

The RWMIK+ features a number of automotive improvements over RWMIK, including a power upgrade to the 300 Tdi engine, the fitting of a new ZF automatic gearbox (that has commonality with the current Pinzgauer light vehicle fleet), a selection of ergonomic, protection, chassis and suspension upgrades, plus an increase in GVW to 4,700 kg.

Also disclosed late-2009, and as a further RWMIK contract amendment, was an ergonomic and functionality upgrade to the existing RWMIK fleet, this based around the front section of the higher roll-cage of RWMIK+.

New build 4,100 kg and 4,700 kg GVW vehicles are available, these based on current production Defender chassis.

Late-2009 it was disclosed that the UK MoD was expected to order (as an Urgent Operational Requirement (UOR)) a batch of RWMIK+ from Ricardo Special Vehicles (Shaun C Connors)
1391055

Land Rover Defender Rapid Deployment Vehicle (RDV) WMIK being prepared for underslung transport by an RAF Chinook HC2 helicopter. The vehicle belongs to the 1st Battalion, Argyll and Sutherland Highlanders, 16 Air Assault Brigade's air assault infantry battalion (Patrick Allen) 1111935

Land Rover Defender Rapid Deployment Vehicle (RDV) of the Italian Carabinieri. The Carabinieri has received 34 RDVs, 12 on the Core Military 90 chassis and 22 on the Core Military 110 chassis (Land Rover)　1128746

Land Rover Defender Rapid Deployment Vehicle (RDV) in two-door, four-person configuration with a full-height roll-cage as required to meet a Lithuanian requirement (Land Rover)　1185458

Description

Rapid Deployment Vehicle (RDV)

The Land Rover Defender Rapid Deployment Vehicle (RDV) was designed to be a versatile and highly mobile platform with powerful firepower capabilities. Performance and specifications are broadly in line with the military Land Rover product.

The distinctive RDV superstructure is comprised of a roll-over protection hoop and removable support structure constructed out of 44.5 mm (1.75 in) seamless tube. The hoop has been tested to withstand a fully-laden roll-over at 48 km/h. The support structure normally carries a 1.22 m inside diameter 360° traverse ring-mount, but this may be deleted in favour of a pedestal type mount if required. Options are available but standard floor space stowage is supplied for one 0.5 in (12.7 mm) M2 Heavy Machine Gun (HMG) and one 7.62 mm light machine gun. Seating is provided for driver and co-driver (commander), although optional rear seating is available for the normal third crew member; four-seat options are also available. Spare wheel(s) and spare barrel(s) for the HMG can be stowed attached to the support structure, for which an optional soft-top cover is available.

The unladen weight of the base RDV (on a 3,500 kg GVW platform) without the ring-mount is approximately 2,130 kg. Internal stowage is by the provision of flexible netting and straps and the standard RDV has an allowable maximum payload of approximately 1,370 kg. Various other options are available that allow the RDV to be configured in the field, to enhance its capabilities to suit a specific mission or role. These include a Crew Protection Weapon Post (CPWP) that mounts (left- or right-hand side) to the door hinge hard points in the A-post and provides an interface in front of the co-driver suitable for mounting a 7.62 mm light machine gun or 5.56 mm Minimi. Weight is 44 kg. The co-driver may also, for a 13 kg weight penalty, have a height-adjustable seat giving 150 mm travel. A side-hinged rear stowage pannier weighing 15 kg can be fitted in place of the rear tailgate. This has internal dimensions of 850 × 430 × 170 mm deep. A camouflage net stowage basket weighing 3 kg may be fitted to the bonnet and a wire cutter that affords crew protection (4 kg) may also be fitted. The optional soft-top weather protection canopy weighs approximately 10 kg.

Other options can include the fitting of self-recovery winches or an additional fuel tank, on certain models, that increases the standard approximate 500 miles range by an additional 400 miles. Protection from fragmentation grenades and AP mines can also be improved by the application of a composite armour system. The system consists of S2 glass and phenolic resin, weighs 175 kg and mouldings cover the dash panel, cab and load area floor. Run-flat tyres may also be fitted at an additional weight of 10 kg per wheel.

The standard RDV is fully air-portable, can be loaded either forward or reverse and without preparation, into a CH-47 helicopter. It may also be transported as an underslung load by CH-47 or CH-53 helicopters and is suitable for airdrop.

Ricardo Special Vehicles WMIK upgrades

Ricardo Special Vehicles has developed a number of capability upgrades for the base WMIK vehicle. The overall appearance of the vehicle remains the same, however, depending on upgrade package (4,100 or 4,700 kg) a considerable number of ergonomic, stowage, automotive and protection enhancements can be made.

As detailed elsewhere in this entry, all current in-service EWMIKs or RWMIKs were initially upgraded to a 4,100 kg GVW, with a further upgrade to 4,700 kg GVW involved in the RWMIK+ order.

New build 4,100 kg and 4,700 kg GVW vehicles are available, these based on current production Defender chassis.

Specifications for the RWMIK+ are included in the Specifications table.

Specifications

	Land Rover RDV	Ricardo Special Vehicles RWMIK+
Crew:	3 standard, 4 optional	4 plus upper gunner seat
Configuration:	4 × 4	4 × 4
Weight:		
(laden)	3,500 kg	4,700 kg
(unladen, without ring mount)	2,130 kg	approx 2,700 kg but dependant on equipment fit
(payload)	approx 1,370 kg	approx 2,000 kg
Length:	4.546 m	4.845 m
Width:	1.79 m	2.532 m; basic body 1.79 m
Height:	1.78 m	2.005 m (not including upper weapon when mounted)
Ground clearance:	230 mm	240 mm
Track:	1.486 m	1.486 m
Wheelbase:	2.794 m	2.794 m
Engine: (pre-2007 model year)	Land Rover 300 Tdi 2.5-litre 4-cylinder in-line turbocharged water-cooled 4-stroke direct injection (mechanical) diesel developing 111 hp at 4,000 rpm, or Land Rover Td5 2.5-litre 5-cylinder in-line turbocharged and intercooled water-cooled 4-stroke direct injection (electronically controlled) diesel developing 122 hp at 4,200 rpm and 300 N.m torque at 1,950 rpm	up-rated Land Rover 300 Tdi 2.8-litre 4-cylinder in-line turbocharged water-cooled 4-stroke direct injection (mechanical) diesel developing 127 hp (95 kW) at 3,500 rpm and 340 N.m torque at 1,800 rpm, current vehicles; Land Rover Durotorq 2.4-litre 4-cylinder in-line turbocharged water-cooled 4-stroke common rail direct injection diesel developing 134 hp (100 kW) at 3,500 rpm and 370 N.m torque at 1,750 rpm, new build vehicles
Gearbox:	manual with 5 forward and 1 reverse gears	ZF 4-speed automatic
Clutch:	diaphragm spring	n/app
Transfer box:	2-speed	2-speed
Steering:	worm and roller	worm and roller
Turning radius:	5.85 m	7.4 m
Suspension:	coil springs, telescopic hydraulic shock-absorbers and anti-roll bar, front; coil springs, helper springs, telescopic hydraulic shock-absorbers and anti-roll bar, rear	
Brakes:	dual servo assisted; discs all-round	hydraulic; discs all-round
Tyres:	7.50 × 16	LT265/75R 16
Electrical system:	12 or 24 V	24 V (12/24 V in new build)
Alternator: (pre-2007 model year)		
(Tdi 12 V)	65 A commercial unit	n/app
(Tdi 24 V)	1 or 2 50 A, 24 V, suppressed	n/app
(Td5 12 V)	120 A commercial unit	n/app
(RWMIK)	n/app	1 × 24 V, 55 A plus 1 × 24 V 130 A

Land Rover Defender Rapid Deployment Vehicle (RDV) WMIK ready for internal transport by RAF Chinook HC2 helicopter (Patrick Allen) 1111927

Status
Production as required. In service with the British Army on Defender XD 110 chassis (approximately 270 (see text)), Ireland (six), Italy ((12) Carabinieri, Core Military 90 chassis) and Lithuania (45) in four-seat configuration.

Contractor
Land Rover

Penman Trekker Extended Range Patrol Vehicle (ERPV)

Development
The Trekker Extended Range Patrol Vehicle (ERPV) designed by Penman Engineering Limited is based upon the Land Rover Defender 110 and 130 chassis and has evolved from the (6 × 6) Trekker conversion that has been in service since the mid-1980s. This latest evolution of the design has been developed in tandem with advances in Land Rover technology; the vehicle reflects the advantages of modern engine and transmission reliability and control, the use of standard Land Rover training and tools for in-country support and interoperability with other Land Rover fleets.

Full details of Land Rover 110 and 130 (4 × 4) vehicles can be found in the Light vehicles section; full details of Land Rover Australia (6 × 6) vehicles can be found in the Trucks section, and full details of Land Rover-produced special attack vehicles can be found elsewhere in this Special Attack Vehicles section.

Description
The Penman Trekker ERPV retains a very high level of commonality with Land Rover Defender models in terms of engine, transmission, transfer-box, front axle, rear axle, brakes, wheels, tyres, and suspension units, all of which are standard Land Rover parts. The chassis of the base Defender is extended, reinforced and a Penman middle drive-through axle added. The third axle is mounted using standard Land Rover parts and provides selectable four-wheel drive for on-road fuel economy, with six-wheel drive for enhanced off-road mobility. The vehicle is fitted with selectable transfer box differential and selectable axle differential locks on all axles. Six-wheel drive, transfer box differential and all three axle differentials can be selected by engaging one selector lever. The front differential lock may be omitted by use of a single switch.

The suspension uses long travel coil springs on all axles combined with telescopic shock-absorbers, rear trailing links and anti-roll bars at the front and rear. Power for the development vehicle was provided by five-cylinder Td5 turbocharged diesel engine, production of which ceased late-2006. Extended range is provided by using either a Land Rover supplementary fuel tank or by using dual purpose-built fuel tanks carrying significantly more fuel than standard. In either option standard Land Rover fuel pumping and filter equipment is used.

The ERPV is configured as an all-terrain long-range weapons platform and is equipped with a single rear weapons mount with 360° slew ring to accept a full suite of light, medium and heavy weapon systems. One commander's weapon station can accept a single light or medium weapon system for vehicle protection. Both weapon mounts are fitted to the roll-over structure for stability. The rear weapon mount is located centrally to the twin rear axles to maximise stability enabling accurate fire of heavy weapons at maximum ranges. Smoke grenade launchers can be fitted in any configuration as required.

The vehicle superstructure can be configured to suit customer preferences but will provide roll-over protection for all seated crew members and a canopy to provide weather protection whilst permitting use of both the commanders weapon station and the crew-served weapon. The design of the superstructure permits transport of the vehicle within C-130 aircraft and certain helicopters without dismantling.

Penman Trekker Extended Range Patrol Vehicle (ERPV) without armament and fitted with optional wide larger footprint tyres (Shaun C Connors) 0533628

The vehicle is available with a 12 V electrical system that is augmented with a 24 V system for radios and other electronic equipment. The ERPV is fitted with a battery monitoring system that protects essential systems from power drain and allows external slave start from 24 V systems through a NATO slave socket or similar. Specialist lighting systems including convoy isolation or Infra-Red (IR) systems can be fitted if required.

ERPV has standard NATO recovery points; two front and two rear, plus four dedicated hi-lift jacking points. A demountable 3,700 kg electric winch with ground anchor is provided. The winch may be fitted to the front or rear of the vehicle through the use of quick release fittings and military standard electrical connectors.

ERPV may be fitted with limited ballistic and mine protection to suit customer requirements.

Specifications
Trekker ERPV
Crew: 2 to 8
Configuration: 6 × 6
Weight: (GVW) 5,350 kg
Length: 5.6 m
Width: 1.85 m
Ground clearance: 210 mm
Track: 1.486 m
Wheelbase: 810 mm
Engine: (development vehicle) Td5 5-cylinder turbocharged water-cooled diesel developing 122 hp (91 kW) at 4,200 rpm
Gearbox: Land Rover manual with 5 forward and 1 reverse gears
Clutch: diaphragm spring
Transfer Box: 2-speed
Range: (terrain dependent) approximately 1,000 km
Steering: worm and roller
Turning radius: 7.5 m
Suspension: coil springs and hydraulic telescopic shock-absorbers, front and rear
Brakes: dual circuit, servo-assisted, discs all round
Tyres: 7.50 × 16 (other options available)
Electrical System: 12 V engine and vehicle systems, 24 V supplementary system for radios and other such equipment

Status
Available on a current generation platform. Earlier variant in service with the Bahrain Defence Force.

Contractor
Penman Engineering Limited

Pinzgauer Weapons Platform

Development
The Pinzgauer 710 (4 × 4) range of all-terrain vehicles was developed by Steyr-Daimler-Puch as the successor to the 700 AP Haflinger range of (4 × 4) vehicles. The first Pinzgauer prototype was completed in 1965 with first production models being completed in 1971. The 712 (6 × 6) model was first shown in 1968 and entered production during 1971-1972. Production of the original petrol-powered 710 and 712 models concluded in 1990, these progressively replaced by diesel-powered versions developed from 1983.

Diesel-powered models were originally produced by Steyr-Daimler-Puch in Austria and originally referred to as the Turbo D. In 1990 the Turbo D model was upgraded, the upgraded model referred to as the P93.

Displayed at DVD 2005, rear three quarter view of a Pinzgauer (6 × 6) Weapons Platform (WP) is similar to the 13 Special Operations variants involved in the 2004 award 321 vehicle contract for New Zealand's Armed Forces (Patrick Allen)   1146313

Displayed at DVD 2005, front three quarter view of a Pinzgauer (6 × 6) Weapons Platform (WP) is similar to the 13 Special Operations variants involved in the 2004 award 321 vehicle contract for New Zealand's Armed Forces (Patrick Allen)   1146312

In July 2000 it was announced that all future production of the Pinzgauer would be carried out in the United Kingdom by the then Automotive Technik Limited (ATL). During 2002 ATL announced significantly revised specification Pinzgauer models. These featured increased operational weights, performance and a EURO 3 emissions compliant engine.

Further technical enhancements such as ABS, ETC and EBD became available from 2005, so equipped vehicles carrying the X-treme Mobility (X-M) designation. ABS, ETC and EBD were included in the final standard production specification.

In April 2005 it was announced that Stewart & Stevenson of the US (manufacturer of the Family of Medium Tactical Vehicles (FMTV)) had acquired ATL. Armor Holdings Inc announced in February 2006 it was to acquire Stewart & Stevenson. From May 2006 Automotive Technik Limited (ATL) became known as Pinzgauer Ltd. It was announced as from 1 August 2007 that Armor Holdings had been acquired by BAE Systems.

The Pinzgauer II was announced in September 2007. This features further technical and performance enhancements, plus a new EURO 4 emissions compliant engine. EURO 3 models were to remain available.

Following the introduction of the Pinzgauer 2 during 2007 the 716 and 718 nomenclature was dropped.

In January 2008 BAE Systems announced it planned to discontinue the production of the Pinzgauer 1 vehicle and close its manufacturing facilities at Guildford and Fareham. A support business (primarily for British and New Zealand Pinzgauer fleets) infrastructure was retained at the Guildford site, this later relocated to Telford. Development of the Pinzgauer 2 was transitioned to BAE Systems Land Systems in South Africa, however, according to BAE Systems, further analysis of the potential market (for Pinzgauer 2) revealed insufficient market interest to continue development.

Throughout its production run the Pinzgauer vehicle in both (4 × 4) and (6 × 6) configurations has been available configured as a weapons platform under assorted designations, and in a variety of configurations. No official list of users of the type has ever been released by the company as users tend to be special operations forces. It is also possible that weapons platform-type vehicles formed part of larger orders. Additionally, in many instances in-theatre conversions of M/GS body types that can be limited to little more than a light machine gun on a weapon post will have been carried out, these often being confused with genuine factory produced variants.

This entry focuses on EURO 3 and the proposed Pinzgauer 2 (6 × 6) Weapons Platform (WP) variants. The only known recent sale of Pinzgauer weapons carrier variants is to New Zealand. It has been confirmed that as part of a two-tranch NZD93 million order for a total of 321 Pinzgauer vehicles that 13 special operations vehicles were delivered during 2005 as part of the first tranch.

Description

In appearance the final Pinzgauer weapon platform models closely resembled their predecessors, although over the years there were many automotive, performance and dimensional changes.

This descriptive text covers components common to both the September 2007 announced Pinzgauer 2 and its immediate EURO 3-powered predecessor models, and outlines the main revisions to the Pinzgauer 2. Further details of the Pinzgauer range of vehicles can be found in the Light vehicles section under Austria and the UK.

The Pinzgauer 2 was to feature a new engine, gearbox and transfer box, plus a revised suspension set-up for the heavier duty axles. Dimensionally it was to be wider than its immediate predecessor, and would have increased payload and GVW. Other Pinzgauer 2 revisions were to include larger wheels and tyres, a revised nose, internal ergonomic changes and revised instrumentation. Additionally, all models were to be fitted with a high-hardness steel floor and bulkhead as standard.

Weapons platform variants of all Pinzgauer models retain the torsion-resistant central chassis tube. Twin crown wheel and pinion axle differentials form part of the central tube and provide both drive and

suspension movement. A centre tube section connects the front to second and second to third differentials and houses the solid prop shafts, differential locks and all-wheel drive connections. Enclosed, these components are protected from terrain damage. The transfer box forms part of the centre tube system and is therefore also protected from possible terrain damage.

Range changes are possible on the move, and the standard cross-axle differential locks may also be engaged/disengaged on the move. An Electronic Traction Control (ETC) system (that also engages when the vehicle is in rear-wheel drive mode only) for use in marginal conditions became standard from 2005.

The Pinzgauer is fitted with vacuum-assisted hydraulic disc brakes on all axles, the front axle discs being of the twin calliper type. The double-disc mechanical transmission handbrake operates directly on the rear differential and, with the differential locks engaged, effectively locks all axles and wheels. From 2005 standard specification includes ABS and EBD.

Power steering is standard, and the steering system remains fully operational without the power assistance.

The accompanying Specifications table details the basic weights, dimensions and automotive set-up of both EURO 3 and proposed EURO 4 Pinzgauer 2 weapons platform models.

For the weapons platform role the standard cab and bodywork of the base Pinzgauer is extensively modified. The front windscreen can remain in drop-down configuration, or may be removed. Doors are removed, or half-doors can be fitted if required. Roll-over protection extends to form a 360° slew ring in the essentially open rear body for a variety of weapons including a 12.7 mm Heavy Machine Gun (HMG) or a 40 mm Automatic Grenade Launcher (AGL) (Mk19) and twin 7.62 or 5.56 mm Light Machine Guns (LMGs). The front passenger can be provided with a light machine gun on a swing-arm mount, additional swing arms can also be mounted on the rear of the vehicle. Various blast and fragmentation protection kits can be offered.

The rear body can be configured to suit a variety of roles and a number of seating and stowage options are available. A specified list of equipment options includes:
- first aid kit bracket
- provision for four jerrycans
- twin fuel tanks (2 × 200-litre)
- geared slew ring

Pinzgauer 2 Weapons Platform variant (BAE Systems)   1190255

- Universal Gun Mount (UMG) for Mk19 AGL, twin 7.62 mm GPMG, 12.7 mm HMG
- rear twin LMGs
- height adjustable commander's seat
- hot barrel clamps
- shell catchers
- ready ammunition stowage for rear gunner and commander
- GPS installation
- radio communication installation
- under floor protection
- IR driving lights (front and rear)
- tyre inflation compressor
- snow chains
- tyre runflat inserts
- smoke dischargers, front and/or rear
- demountable front self-recovery winch
- run flat wheel system
- provision for up to two spare wheels
- ROVIS crew intercom
- PTO on forward face of transfer case for additional electrical power (min 100 A) (Pinzgauer II only)
- engine pre-heater for operation at temperatures down to –46°C.

Specifications

Model	EURO 3	Pinzgauer 2 (EURO 4)
Seating:	2 + as required	2 + as required
Configuration:	6 × 6	6 × 6
Weights:		
(laden)	6,000 kg	7,000 kg
(unladen)	3,500 kg	3,000 kg
(payload max)	2,500 kg	4,000 kg
(front axle, rated load)	2,400 kg	3,000 kg
(rear axles, rated load)	1,900 kg (each)	3,000 kg (each)
(towed load)	1,500 kg	2,000 kg
(GCW)	7,500 kg	9,000 kg
Length:	5.308 m	5.308 m
Width:	1.8 m	1.9 m
Height: (CH-47 internal transport)	1.067 mm	1.067 mm
Ground clearance:	360 mm	360 mm
Track: (front and rear)	1.52 m	1.5 m
Wheelbase:	2.2 and 0.98 m	2.2 and 0.98 m
Angle of approach/departure:	40°/45°	40°/45°
Max speed:	110 km/h	120 km/h
Max range:	800 km	1,000 km
Fuel capacity (options):	200 litres	200 litres
Gradient:	100%	100%
Sideslope:	up to 100%	up to 100%
Fording:	700 mm fresh water (unprepared). Up to 1.5 m salt water with preparation	700 mm fresh water (unprepared). Up to 1.5 m salt water with preparation
Engine:	VW EURO 3 emissions compliant five cylinder inline 2.5-litre turbocharged water cooled 4-stroke diesel developing 107 hp at 3,800 rpm and 210 N.m torque at 3,000 rpm	Steyr M16 EURO 4 emissions compliant six cylinder inline 3.2-litre turbocharged water cooled 4-stroke diesel developing 194 hp at 3,800 rpm and 410 N.m torque at 2,000 rpm
Gearbox:	ZF HP22 4-speed automatic	ZF HP22 6-speed automatic
Transfer box:	ZF 2-speed automatic	Pinzgauer designed 2 speed
Steering:	ZF	ZF
Turning radius:	13 m	13 m
Suspension:	coil springs and shock-absorbers, front; parabolic taper leaf springs with shock absorbers, rear (option of air bags on rear axle)	coil springs and shock-absorbers, front; air bags, rear
Tyres:	285/75R 16 all terrain	325/60 R18 all terrain
Brakes:	twin calliper on front axle, single on rears	twin calliper on front axle, single on rears
Electrical system:	24 V	24 V
Batteries:	85 Ah	85 Ah
Alternator:	110 A	110 A

Certain weights, dimensions and performance figures may vary according to exact configuration

Status
Production complete (see text). In service with a number of countries. Recent known sales to New Zealand (EURO 3 model × 13 in 2006).

Contractor
BAE Systems Land Systems

Ricardo Special Reconnaissance Vehicle (SRV)

Development
The Special Reconnaissance Vehicle (SRV) is air-transportable by C-130 Hercules transport aircraft or CH-47 Chinook helicopter and is one of a number of developments of the Ricardo Rapid Deployment Vehicle (RDV) concept first applied to the Land Rover Defender platform. The SRV is a product of Ricardo Vehicle Engineering's experience in developing specialised wheeled vehicles and the development and production of weapon mounts for Land Rover (4 × 4) type vehicles for home and export.

Ricardo Vehicle Engineering selected the Ford F-350 Super Duty pick-up as the basis for the SRV as it met the potential user payload and performance requirements, as well as being a regular production vehicle and commercially available, delivering effective whole life costs and readily available off-the-shelf spare parts.

In September 2003, the Irish Defence Forces announced the award of the contract for the supply of the Special Reconnaissance Vehicle (SRV), for their worldwide peace keeping roles. The SRV has been in service since early 2004 and has been deployed to Liberia and Chad.

Description
The normal crew complement for the SRV is three, with the driver sitting at the front left and the vehicle commander sits to the right, with a third rearward-facing seat positioned in the rear for the gunner with the rest of the area free for payload.

The SRV is fitted with a further development of the Weapon Mount Installation Kit (WMIK) originally developed by Ricardo Vehicle Engineering for installation on Land Rover Defender (4 × 4) vehicles. A proven computer optimised rollover protection/weapons mount cage affords crew protection and incorporates a stable platform for the ring mount. SRV can be fitted with 5.56, 7.62 and 12.7 mm machine guns, a 40 mm automatic grenade launcher or a Euromissile MILAN anti-tank guided weapon. The weapon can traverse through a full 360° with lock at 15° intervals. Smoke grenade launchers are fitted front and rear.

The SRV can be fitted with a number of kits which have already been developed and built in production quantities for other applications. These include a Crew Protection Weapon Post for the vehicle commander that can be fitted with a 5.56 or 7.62 mm machine gun, height-adjustable seat for the crew commander, wire cutter and a selection of dedicated flexible stowage for weapons, fuel, ammunition, pioneer tools, camouflage systems, sand channels and other combat equipment.

A dismountable windshield and canopy system is provided along with covers for dashboard and weapons when in combat mode. Anti-reflection covers are included for lights, mirrors and the 5,440 kg rated winch incorporated into a heavy-duty front nudge bar and light guard assembly. Lightweight mesh seating can be provided all round.

The base vehicle has a 12 V electrical system with an additional 24 V system with separate tactical batteries for the communications systems which have been incorporated to the required EMC standards of MIL-STD

Rear three-quarter view of the prototype Ford F-350-based Ricardo Special Reconnaissance Vehicle (SRV) (Ricardo)
0567950

Front three-quarter view of the prototype Ford F-350-based Ricardo Special Reconnaissance Vehicle (SRV) (Ricardo)   0567951

461D. Dual alternators ensure the four on-board batteries support the other military electric's including black-out lighting, NATO tow socket, 24 V power sockets, hotbox, map reading lamp and NVG compatible instrument panel. A slave-start adapter, battery isolator, re-settable fuses and additional commander's odometer complete the system.

The ladder type steel frame chassis includes front/rear tie-downs and fuel tank, transfer box, engine/transmission, front and side protection skid guards. A NATO tow pintle and heavy-duty bumper are positioned at the rear. Motive power is provided by a V8 turbocharged diesel engine that works in unison with the transmission to help control vehicle speed when descending hills. The engine will run on NATO F-34 or JP-8 fuel. An automatic five-speed transmission and electronic shift-on-the-fly two-speed transfer box are standard. A tow/haul mode prevents unwanted gear search when towing on steep gradients. Mud-terrain tyres, with run-flat inserts, are fitted, and a limited slip rear axle differential improves traction in difficult conditions. Automatic deactivation of the ABS system can be catered for in 4 × 4 mode.

Technical training, support and literature are all available from Ricardo.

Specifications

Ricardo SRV
Seating: 2 front, 1 rear cargo area
Configuration: 4 × 4 (selectable)
Weight:
  (GVW) 4,490 kg
  (payload, approx.) 1,500 kg
  (max front axle load) 2,358 kg
  (max rear axle load) 3,098 kg
  (towed load) 5,670 kg
  (GCW) 9,072 kg
Length: 5.643 m
Width: 2.031 m
Height: 2.150 m (approx.), reduces to 1.910 m by folding the ROPS frame
Load area dimensions: 2.504 × 1.623 m (L × W)
Ground clearance: (under rear axle) 205 mm
Track:
  (front) 1.736 m
  (rear) 1.729 m
Wheelbase: 3.480 m
Angle of approach/departure: 30°/25° (approx.)
Max speed: 153 km/h
Fuel capacity: 143 litres
Max gradient: 60%
Fording: 600 mm
Engine: 6-litre turbocharged water-cooled 4-stroke diesel developing 325 hp (242 kW) at 3,300 rpm and 759 N.m torque at 2000 rpm
Gearbox: Ford TorqShift 5-speed automatic with overdrive
Transfer box: 2-speed
Clutch: torque converter
Steering: cross-tie linkage, Ford XR-50 power-assisted
Turning radius: (kerb) 7.687 m
Suspension:
  (front) heavy-duty single-stage constant rate leaf springs, gas shock-absorbers and anti-roll bar
  (rear) heavy-duty two-stage variable rate leaf springs and gas shock-absorbers
Tyres: LT265/75R 16, BF Goodrich Mud-Terrain
Brakes:
  (main) discs front and rear, diagonal split, dual piston pin-slider callipers with vacuum boost and 4-wheel (3-channel) ABS with auto disconnect in 4 × 4 mode available
  (parking) foot-operated, hand release. Cable-operated on drum in hat-type rear brake disc assemblies
Electrical system: 12 V vehicle, 24 V tactical
Batteries: 2 × 78 Ah vehicle, 2 × 100 Ah tactical
Alternator: dual 12 V, 130 A

Status
Production as required. In service with the Irish Army (12).

Contractor
Ricardo Vehicle Engineering

Supacat Surveillance and Reconnaissance Vehicle (SRV) and derivatives including Jackal

Development
The Supacat Surveillance and Reconnaissance Vehicle (SRV) is based on the Supacat High Mobility Transporter (HMT) 400 (4 × 4) platform and was originally designed to meet a then pending UK Ministry of Defence (MoD) requirement for an SRV. The design has since evolved considerably, the most recent variation being the Jackal range of vehicles currently being delivered to the British Army.

The first prototype of the HMT platform was introduced mid-1999, and by December 1999 two prototypes had been produced for extensive testing and demonstrations. It was disclosed in January 2001 that the UK's then Defence Procurement Agency (DPA) had opened up an international competition for the SRV requirement, also known as the Improved Medium Mobility Patrol Vehicle. In July 2001 it was announced that a Supacat HMT-based design had been selected to meet the SRV requirement.

Prior to the SRV requirement being issued, it is known that at least two vehicles were built in the UK and assessed for possible use by the SRV's intended user, the SAS. At this time the user was also looking for an Offensive Action Vehicle (OAV). The first of the two vehicles assessed was the Alvis Vehicles Shadow Light Strike Vehicle based on a (4 × 4) chassis designed by the then Reumech of South Africa. The second vehicle was also known as the Alvis Vehicles Shadow, but this was based on a shortened and narrowed AM General HMMWV M1113 Expanded Capacity Vehicle (ECV) chassis. Neither was accepted for a variety of reasons and when the SRV requirement, now fulfilled by the Supacat HMT was issued, it combined with the earlier OAV requirement.

Competitors for the UK MoD's SRV requirement are known to have included the then Automotive Technik Limited offering a (6 × 6) Pinzgauer, and Ricardo Special Vehicles offering a DURO-based (4 × 4) design.

Following contract award, there were a number of developmental difficulties with the SRV design and full rate production did not commence until 2003. Ultimately, 48 of the 65 vehicles initially ordered would be

Supacat Jackal 1 with armour package fitted at a UK demonstration (Shaun C Connors)   1391373

Supacat Jackal 1 without armour package at a UK demonstration (Shaun C Connors)   1391372

Supacat Jackal 2 during its initial public unveiling (Supacat)　1391108

Supacat Jackal 2a. The original vehicles, SRV, Jackal 1 and Jackal 2, all had an aluminium-skinned cab to which appliqué armour was fitted. The latest Jackal 2a features an all-steel armoured cab that according to the manufacturer offers an increase in protection levels for no increase in weight (Shaun C Connors)　1391375

manufactured by the then DML, Supacat's volume manufacturing partner. A further seven vehicles were subsequently ordered and delivered during 2006, these featuring a small number of design improvements over the original vehicles.

In 2004 the US Army placed an order with Supacat for an HMT-based patrol-type vehicle that was similar in configuration to the UK's SRV. A total of 47 vehicles, known as Marauder to the user were ordered, with 12 of these manufactured by Supacat and the remaining 35 by DML. Deliveries ran 2004-2005.

A further developed SRV-style HMT that has been redesigned to feature a new top hamper, upgraded automotives and an improved tubular chassis has also been produced by Supacat. Designated HMT4×4E (E – Extenda), this variant can be reconfigured from (4 × 4) to (6 × 6) configuration by the addition of a third axle module. Supacat supplied at least 15 HMT4×4E vehicles to the Danish Army in 2006/2007, plus at least two third axle modules for (6 × 6) configuration conversion.

In December 2006 Australia placed an order for 31 HMT4×4E vehicles (to be designated, Nary) under Phase 1A of JP 2097 Phase 1 - REDFIN (Enhancements to Special Operations Capability - Land Mobility Aspects). It was disclosed mid-2007 that for reasons of operational urgency the HMT4×4E procurement had been a sole-source acquisition, and that an Initial Operating Capability (IOC) of eight vehicles would be available by December 2007. This subsequently slipped to September 2008, with deliveries concluding early 2009. It has not been confirmed, but it is believed that a quantity of third axle modules are included in the Australian order, as was a protection kit.

In Australian Army service the HMT4×4E will replace the SASR's Land Rover (6 × 6) Perentie-based Long Range Patrol Vehicles (LRPV). These were delivered from 1987 onwards, with a planned Life Of Type (LOT) of 10 years. Deliveries of the 27 vehicles involved ran over five years, with some vehicles subsequently receiving an upgrade to extend their LOT to 15 years.

It was disclosed in June 2007 that for use in Afghanistan the UK MoD was to procure 130 SRV-style Supacat HMT 400 series vehicles under a Urgent Operational Requirement (UOR). With the exception of a blast and ballistic protection kit, these vehicles are very similar in configuration to the original SRV procurement, and are not HMT4×4E variants. The GBP30 million contract was awarded to the then DML in September 2007 and deliveries commenced in November 2007. The first vehicles were delivered to theatre in March 2008 and the 100th vehicle was produced in June 2008. In service the vehicle was initially known as Mobility Weapons Mount Installation Kit (MWMIK), but later became known as Jackal. The MWMIK/Jackal supplements (replaces for some missions) current Land Rover WMIK vehicles.

It was disclosed in June 2008 that as a contract modification the UK MoD would order an additional 72 Jackals with deliveries to conclude early 2009. A further 25 vehicles were ordered around the same time as an additional contract modification. Five of these vehicles, which were delivered during 2008, were configured as troop carriers (2 + 4 seats). A further 15 vehicles were then ordered as battle damage replacements. Production of these commenced in March 2009, with deliveries to be completed by mid-year.

In April 2009 the UK MoD announced the purchase of 119 enhanced Jackal 2 valued at around GBP30 million. Overall contract value was GBP74 million, this award including the supply of 76 HMT-based Coyote (6 × 6) vehicles to meet the Tactical Support Vehicle (Light) requirement.

For this contract award Supacat were prime contractor, being the overall design authority responsible for design, development, prototype, integration and overall programme management. Babcock Marine's Land Systems business took responsibility for detailed production planning, purchasing and manufacture at its facility in Devonport. A single project office, located at Supacat's Dunkeswell facility, oversaw the programme.

By early December 2009 around 100 Jackal 2 and 60 Coyote from this award had been delivered, and an undisclosed number of both vehicle types were in theatre. Deliveries under this award were completed by March 2010.

The most recent Jackal announcement was made in June 2010, when touted as part of the government's ongoing equipment support for operations in Afghanistan, the relevant minister announced an order for the delivery of more than 140 Supacat Jackal 2a long range patrol vehicles. The actual contract award had been made in early May and vehicles had been in production since February - at risk to the Supacat/Babcock alliance. This latest contract is valued at around GBP45 million, and at the time of the actual announcement it is understood that well over half the order had already been built.

The base design of the HMT (4 × 4) can be adapted for a variety of roles beyond SRV/LRPV-type applications and details of these can be found in the Trucks section.

The original HMT 400 was designed by Supacat Limited with funding provided by HMT Vehicles Limited. In January 2006 Lockheed Martin UK Holdings (a subsidiary of Lockheed Martin Corporation of the United States) acquired HMT Vehicles Limited and now licenses the suspension/axle technology that is the core of the HMT series design to Lockheed Martin Corporation.

Rear three-quarter view of the six-seat (4 + 2) Supacat Jackal variant (Supacat)　1391374

Supacat Tactical Support Vehicle (TSV) Light Coyote as first shown publicly at DVD 2009 (Shaun C Connors)　1391109

Danish Supacat HMT vehicles following delivery (Martin Pagh) 1391111

Lockheed Martin Corporation had previously licensed the technology from HMT Vehicles. Supacat of the UK was a licensee of the technology from HMT Vehicles, and remains a licensee of Lockheed Martin UK. Babcock Marine (formerly Devonport Management Limited (DML)) was granted a license for the manufacture of the Jackal 1 programme (now completed).

Description
The key feature of the Supacat HMT vehicle is its axle/suspension technology design and set up. This is based on variable ride height independent double wishbones front and rear with airbag suspension, the airbags and suspension carriers being located transverse and integral to the main chassis. The entire suspension package (hub brakes, springs, wishbones etc) is in an identical layout at each corner, thereby simplifying manufacture, reducing costs and easing repair/maintenance in the field.

Each wheel station has twin shock-absorbers and the suspension is self-levelling. Ride height is variable between a minimum (air out) of 180 mm and a maximum (load dependant) of 485 mm, with standard on- and off-road ride heights of 280 and 380 mm, respectively. At minimum and maximum heights an electronically controlled 10 km/h maximum speed restriction applies.

The spaceframe-type chassis of the HMT is constructed using an all-welded steel box section structure that can accept a selection of two or four person, open or closed cabs, and a selection of body options. The Extenda variant of the HMT can be configured as a (4 × 4) or (6 × 6) and has a detachable rear module, the fuel module. The fuel module is removed from the vehicle, the Extenda module is then either fitted or removed, and the fuel module refitted. The entire task can be accomplished in under two hours and using only hand tools. The Extenda module fully integrates with fuel, suspension, brake and electrical systems. The original SRV requirement for which the HMT 400 was designed, called for an off-road vehicle with a substantial payload, long range and superior cross-country mobility. Additionally, the vehicle had to fit inside a Chinook helicopter, with all of the limitations in height, width and weight that requirement implied. When dropped onto its bump-stops the SRV/Jackal is low enough to crawl up the rear ramp of a Chinook helicopter with around 12 mm to spare.

To help achieve the Chinook transport part of the initial requirement and to give good visibility over the terrain immediately ahead, the finalised design placed the driver and commander/navigator at the very front of the vehicle, inboard of the wheels and directly over the front axle. This broke with the tradition of a front-engined layout for vehicles of the SRV/LRPV-type and essentially dictated the unusual mid-engined design of the HMT. However, while the longitudinally mid-mounted engine offered ideal weight distribution and balance between the axles, it posed some significant packaging challenges for the passengers and drivetrain, and while solving the height issue, placing the crew inboard and directly over the front axle later caused some issues when developing a mine blast protection kit for the design became a priority.

The first SRVs delivered were unprotected in the traditional Long Range Patrol Vehicle (LRPV) style, however, the UK MWMIK UOR included a requirement for a modular up-armouring and blast-protection package that could be fitted to existing vehicles and to new-build UOR follow-ons. Following successful development of this package a contract was awarded to UK-based Jankel Armouring, the first 48 packages being delivered by April 2008. The classified package, which is thought to weigh in the region of 750 kg, is a mix of hard plate and spall liners, with considerable development time and design effort expended in the area of blast-attenuation measures.

Motive power for all but the most recent Jackal 2 (and Coyote TSV-L order) is provided by a Cummins 5.9-litre diesel engine developing 185 hp and coupled to a five-speed fully automatic transmission and two-speed transfer box. All wheels are driven and axles are fitted with Trac-lock limited slip differentials; full differential locking is not currently fitted. Tyres may be fitted with runflat inserts if required. A Central Tyre Inflation System (CTIS) is not currently fitted.

The major mechanical difference between the latest Jackal 2 (and Coyote) and all earlier HMT vehicles is the use of a 6.7-litre Cummins diesel engine, this replacing the original 5.9-litre version, not for any deficiencies, but rather because the legacy version is no longer in production. The 6.7-litre unit is currently rated at the same 185 hp and 700 N.m torque as the outgoing 5.9-litre unit, but can be tuned to produce considerably more power and torque if required. To meet operational requirements that include the possible use of low grade fuel, the use of JP-8 fuel, and non-reliance on fuel additives under normal operating conditions, the 6.7-litre unit (which relies on additive technology to meet current emissions requirements) is configured to the same EURO 3 emissions rating as the outgoing engine.

In addition to the new engine, the latest Jackal 2 (which is essentially now the production standard vehicle) features a number of additional improvements over the earlier Jackal 1 and other HMT-based SRV/LRPV variants.

A higher yield strength steel is used for the chassis, and Jackal 2 has an increase in GVW of 700 kg from 7,000 to 7,600 kg, 500 kg of this being increased payload allowance. To accommodate this increase in GVW the suspension has been uprated to accommodate up to 4,000 kg per axle, largely by the introduction of new, thicker wishbones.

In addition to a variety of improvements, many of which are simply based on operational experience and user feedback and will be retro-fitted to the Jackal 1, Jackal 2 includes a selection of new design modifications/changes, some of which have been taken from Australian/Danish vehicles. Where practical these will also be retro-fitted to Jackal 1 vehicles, an example here being an upgrade to twin callipers for the front disc brakes.

Further features include light-emitting diode-based rear lights instead of traditional electric bulb-based lamps, a shortened tailgate that eases access to the rear, more readily accessible fuel tank and engine air-filter, and improved rear stowage racks that fold out of the sides of the vehicle. A new power management system has been designed into Jackal 2, the proliferation of communications and jamming systems placing an ever-increasing demand on vehicle electrical systems.

Visually, compared to Jackal 1, Jackal 2 has a revised top hamper that is similar to the top hamper developed for Australian vehicles. The revised slightly higher top hamper, which allows for Chinook transport by dropping back on hinges, also allows for the fitting of an additional (fourth) blast protected seat in the rear, this replacing the basic non-blast protected jockey-type seat found in Jackal 1.

A design feature that was specified for the original Danish vehicles, mesh running-boards fitted each side, have proved useful and are now standard on the Jackal 2. As well as making it easier for crew members to enter and exit, the running boards can carry motorbikes and they enable the vehicles to rapidly extract or deliver extra dismounts, clinging on the side.

The two rear doors have been redesigned to open fully, and now mount spare wheels externally, this creating additional internal stowage space.

The most recent order places was for the further revised Jackal 2a. For Jackal 2a the armouring package has been revised in certain areas. The original vehicles, SRV, Jackal 1 and Jackal 2, all had an aluminium-skinned cab to which appliqué armour was fitted. The latest Jackal 2a features an all-steel armoured cab that according to the manufacturer offers an increase in protection levels for no increase in weight. Supacat is currently proposing a cab retrofit package for all Jackal and Coyote vehicles on deployed operations.

Variants
Tactical Support Vehicle (TSV) Light - Coyote
The UK Ministry of Defence (MoD) announced in November 2008 that it had selected the preferred bidders for the Tactical Support Vehicle (TSV) family. Following detailed contractual negotiations with individual manufacturers, award announcements for the TSV programme were made by the MoD in April 2009. Supacat received a GBP74 million contract that in addition to the further 119 Jackal patrol vehicles previously mentioned, called for 76 Coyote (TSV Light) valued at around GBP43 million.

Supacat Nary destined for Australia as shown discretely at DVD 2008 (Shaun C Connors) 1391110

The primary role of the TSV family will be support, as by mid-2008 it was becoming clear that the capacity of vehicles on deployed operations was not sufficient for the longer, extended missions that were being undertaken. TSV Light, Coyote (HMT 600), is a three-axle (6 × 6) version of the Jackal reconnaissance/patrol vehicle, and its primary role will be to support the Jackal on extended long range patrols, many of which now last for more than 24 hours. GVW of Coyote is around 10,500 kg, and payload with armour fitted is around 3,000 kg. Coyote, like Jackal, is being delivered through an alliance formed between Supacat as the prime contractor and Babcock Marine's land systems business as the manufacturer.

Specifications

	Jackal 1	Jackal 2/2a
Cab seating:	1 + 3	1 + 3
Configuration:	4 × 4	4 × 4
Weight:		
(laden)	7,000 kg	7,600 kg
(unladen with armour)	5,620 kg	5,760 kg
(payload with armour)	1,380 kg	1,840 kg
(front axle load)	3,500 kg	4,000 kg
(rear axle load)	3,500 kg	4,000 kg
(towed load)	750 kg	750 kg
(GTW)	7,750 kg	8,350 kg
Length:	5.44 m	5.79 m
Width:	2 m	2 m
Height:	1.89 - 2.45 m	1.89 - 2.45 m
Ground clearance:		
(max)	485 mm	485 mm
(min)	180 mm	180 mm
Track:	1.7 m	1.7 m
Wheelbase:	3 m	3 m
Angle of approach/departure:	40°/40°	40°/40°
Max speed:	120 km/h	120 km/h
Max range:	800 km	800 km
Fuel capacity:		
(main)	147 litres	147 litres
(auxiliary)	50 litres	50 litres
Max gradient:	60%	60%
Side slope:	40%	40%
Fording:	1 m	1 m
Engine:	Cummins B180 EURO 3 5.9-litre 6-cylinder turbocharged water-cooled 4-stroke diesel developing 185 hp (138 kW) at 2,500 rpm and 650 N.m torque at 1,500 rpm	Cummins EURO 3 6.7-litre 6-cylinder turbocharged water-cooled 4-stroke diesel developing 185 hp (138 kW) at 2,500 rpm and 650 N.m torque at 1,500 rpm
Gearbox:	Allison 2500 Series fully automatic with 5 forward and 1 reverse gears	Allison 2500 Series fully automatic with 5 forward and 1 reverse gears
Transfer box:	2-speed	2-speed
Steering:	Sheppard M-83 P2 power-assisted	Sheppard M-83 P2 power-assisted
Suspension:	independent double wishbone with air operated variable ride height and twin shock-absorbers per wheel station	independent double wishbone with air operated variable ride height and twin shock-absorbers per wheel station
Tyres:	335/80R 20 ZXL MPT TL	335/80R 20 ZXL MPT TL
Brakes:	air over hydraulic, outboard 360 mm diameter discs front and rear	air over hydraulic, outboard 360 mm diameter discs front and rear
Electrical system:	24 V	24 V
Batteries:	2 × 12 V, 50 Ah; 2 × 12 V, 50 Ah	2 × 12 V, 50 Ah; 2 × 12 V, 100 Ah
Alternator:	2 × 90 A	2 × 100 A

Specifications given in this table are for outline purposes only and may vary considerably according to variant, role and other factors.

Status
Approximately 740 vehicles in assorted SRV/LRPV configurations have been ordered by Australia, Denmark, UK (including 76 (6 × 6)) and the US; see text for full details.

Contractor
Supacat Limited

United States

Jeep J8 (4 x 4) long range and border patrol-type light vehicles

Development
The original Jeep (general purpose) vehicle was developed and manufactured for the US Army by Willys-Overland. In 1953 Kaiser acquired Willys-Overland to form Kaiser Jeep, although the name Kaiser Jeep was not adopted until 1963. In 1970 American Motors Corporation (AMC) acquired Kaiser Jeep and created the Jeep Corporation subsidiary. AMC was itself acquired by Chrysler in 1987, Chrysler subsequently being acquired by Daimler-Benz in 1998 to form DaimlerChrysler. In May 2007 Daimler-Benz AG announced the sale of 80.1 per cent of the Chrysler Group to American equity firm Cerberus Capital Management LP. In April 2009, Daimler AG agreed to give up its remaining 19.9 per cent share of the then Chrysler LLC to Cerberus Capital Management. Almost immediately, Chrysler LLC filed for Chapter 11 bankruptcy protection and announced a plan for a partnership Fiat of Italy. In June 2009 Chrysler LLC stated they were selling some assets and operations to the newly formed Chrysler Group LLC; Fiat will hold a 20 per cent stake in the new company, with an option to increase this to 35 per cent, and eventually to 51 per cent.

The Jeep J8 was first shown publicly at the DSEi show in the UK during September 2007. The design has origins in a diesel-powered variant of the Jeep TJ-L that was developed to meet the requirements of the Egyptian Army and following the delivery of an initial 1,000 petrol-powered TJ-Ls between August 2003 and March 2004.

The Egyptian Army has since ordered 3,750 diesel-powered Jeep TJ-Ls in three 1,250 batches, the third batch ordered in December 2008. Additional orders are anticipated.

All Egyptian Army Jeep TJ-Ls are CKD-produced with local content and adaptation at the Arab American Vehicles Co (AAV)/Chrysler LLC joint venture plant that was set up in Egypt during 1977. Full details of Egyptian Jeep production, and earlier CJ, TJ and YJ Jeeps can be found in separate entries elsewhere in the Light vehicles section.

With the exception of the ongoing Egyptian venture, Chrysler had not actively pursued military sales of the Jeep product since the mid-1990s. Following interest in the diesel-powered Jeep TJ-L, the company began to re-examine the potential market for military specific Jeep models and TJ-L models were subsequently supplied to a number of African, European and Middle Eastern countries for evaluation from 2004.

While suitable for some requirements, general feedback indicated the need for air-conditioning, enhanced safety features including airbags and rollover protection, the potential for emissions and other legislative compliance, plus an increase in payload allowance.

Following the unveiling of a concept vehicle during 2006 that was based on the 2007 model-year four-door Wrangler Unlimited, the Jeep J8 (which is based on the current long wheelbase Wrangler Unlimited) was unveiled.

The Jeep J8 became available for production at the AAV plant late-2008, although dependent on order size, the now Chrysler Group LLC would likely give consideration to any requirement for either CKD or added local content, thus CKD production elsewhere is a possibility.

Jeep J8 Light Patrol Vehicle (LPV)   1391353

Jeep J8 Light Patrol Vehicle (LPV) 1391351

It was disclosed in August 2009 that the now Chrysler Group LLC had appointed Jankel Group subsidiary Jeep Government and Military Sales (JGMS) as the worldwide distributor for the Jeep J8 for supply to government and military customers. From 2007 Chrysler had partnered with Jankel Armouring Limited of the UK to develop a range of modified Jeep J8 vehicles.

Description

The Jeep J8 uses the current long wheelbase Jeep JK Wrangler Unlimited as a starting point and therefore remains entirely conventional in design. In addition to conventional two or four door bodies in soft- or hard-top configurations that will seat from two to eight people, plus a selection of specialist versions such as ambulance or discreetly armoured designs, Jeep Government and Military Sales (JGMS) offers specialised long-range and border patrol type variants of the Jeep J8.

Compared to the Wrangler Unlimited, the J8 features a reinforced chassis with uprated Dana 44 and Dana 60 axles to allow for a GVW of up 3,864 kg. Both versions covered in this entry are fitted with the Payload Enhancement Kit (PEK), this giving a payload allowance of 1,264 kg for the Light Patrol Vehicle configuration and 1,160 kg for the Border Patrol Vehicle (BPV) configuration; in both cases towed load is up to 3,500 kg.

The standard coil spring rear suspension of commercial Jeep models is replaced by a heavier duty leaf spring set-up on the J8, while other modifications include a severe duty cooling package, new pressed steel wheels, heavy duty bumpers with a lift/tow capability, and enhanced wading and air filtration capabilities; the latter allowing for five hours operation in zero visibility sandstorm conditions.

Motive power for the J8 is provided by a EURO 4 or 5 capable (if required) VM Motori diesel engine developing 158 hp, and driving all four wheels (selectable 4WD) via a five-speed automatic transmission and two-speed transfer case. From January 2011 Model Year 2011 versions will have a power increase to 194 hp and 460 N.m torque. The HEMI 5.7-litre V8 petrol engine will remain an option if required.

Armoured variants of the J8 utilise a hot-formed steel technology to create an external, non-parasitic protective shell that replaces the body with hot-formed ballistic steel shaped to the vehicle's precise contours. Conventional armouring methods rely on armoured steel components of various sizes welded beneath the original vehicle skin. According to the manufacturer, the advantages of hot-formed steel technology include lower kerb weight; reduced risk of penetration from faulty welds and joints; improved structural integrity; and lower acquisition and life cycle costs.

Jeep J8 armoured vehicle variants (military patrol and discreet) have been certified by Germany's Beschussamt test agency for BRV 2009 VR7 ballistic protection and ERV 2010 blast protection - floor, roof and side blast.

Variants

Light Patrol Vehicle (LPV)

The Light Patrol Vehicle (LPV) variant is based on the three-door J8 platform with the roll-frame/weapon mount frame integrated into the vehicle chassis. The Payload Enhancement Kit (PEK) is standard on this variant, this giving an operational payload of 1,264 kg.

The front half-doors have removable upper sections and a fully removable soft-top is supplied.

The standard vehicle is fitted with a modular storage system, the rear traversing ring capable of mounting either a 7.62 mm Light Machine Gun (LMG), a 12.7 mm Heavy Machine Gun (HMG), or a 40 mm Automatic Grenade Launcher (AGL). Universal ammunition box holders are fitted. A front elevating commander's seat is equipped with a swing arm weapon mount.

The LPV is transportable by fixed wing aircraft and helicopter.

Optional equipment for the LPV variant can include recovery equipment (including winch and sand ladders), zoned armour, run-flat tyres, military blackout lighting, high-mounted snorkel, weapons mounts to suit customer requirements, long-range fuel tanks (156-litre/1,500 km range), 5.7-litre HEMI engine, communication fits, and other options as required.

Jeep J8 Border Patrol Vehicle (BPV) 1391355

Border Patrol Vehicle (BPV)

The Border Patrol Vehicle (BPV) variant is a five-door, four-seat platform designed for medium range patrol and surveillance missions. The tubular roll-frame/weapon mount frame is integrated into the vehicle chassis for enhanced occupant protection. The Payload Enhancement Kit (PEK) is standard on this variant, this giving an operational payload of 1,160 kg.

Half-doors are fitted and a fully removable soft-top is supplied.

The rear traversing ring is capable of mounting either a 7.62 mm Light Machine Gun (LMG), a 12.7 mm Heavy Machine Gun (HMG), or a 40 mm Automatic Grenade Launcher (AGL). Universal ammunition box holders are fitted. A front elevating commander's seat is equipped with a swing arm weapon mount; seats are of the lightweight military type.

Optional equipment for the BPV variant can include recovery equipment (including winch and sand ladders), zoned armour, run-flat tyres, military blackout lighting, high-mounted snorkel, weapons mounts to suit customer requirements, long-range fuel tanks (156-litre/1,500 km range), 5.7-litre HEMI engine, communication fits, and other options as required.

Specifications

	Light Patrol vehicle (LPV)	Border Patrol Vehicle (BPV)
Cab Seating:	1 + 2	1 + 3
Configuration:	4 × 4 (selectable)	4 × 4 (selectable)
Weight:		
(laden)	3,864 kg	3,864 kg
(unladen)	2,600 kg	2,704 kg
(max load)	1,264 kg	1,160 kg
(towed load)	3,500 kg	3,500 kg
(GCW)	7,364 kg	7,364 kg
Length:	4.45 m	4.45 m
Width:	1.876 m	1.876 m
Height:	1.762 m	1.762 m
Ground clearance:	231 mm	231 mm
Track:	1.610 m	1.610 m
Wheelbase:	2.946 m	2.946 m
Angle of approach/departure:	44°/40°	44°/40°
Fuel capacity:	85 litres	85 litres
Range:		
(on road)	860 km	860 km
(off road)	up to 730 km	up to 730 km
Max gradient:	100%	100%
Max side slope:	80%	80%
Fording:	762 mm	762 mm
Engine:	VM Motori Panther 2.8-litre 4-cylinder inline common rail water-cooled diesel developing 158 hp at 3,800 rpm and 400 N.m at 2,000 rpm. Unregulated emissions, but available to meet EURO 4 or 5 requirements if desired. From January 2011 Model Year 2011 versions will have a power increase to 194 hp and 460 N.m torque	
Gearbox:	Chrysler 5-speed automatic with overdrive	
Transfer box:	2-speed	2- speed
Steering:	recirculating ball, power-assisted	
Turning radius:	6.2 m	6.2 m
Suspension:	coil springs and shock-absorbers, front; leaf springs and shock-absorbers rear	

	Light Patrol vehicle (LPV)	Border Patrol Vehicle (BPV)
Axles:	Dana 44, front; Dana 60, rear	
Tyres:	245/70 R17 BF Goodrich	
Brakes:	discs all round, power assisted, ABS standard	
Electrical system:	12 V (dual 12/24 V optional) 180 A	

Status
In production. The Jeep J8 is in service with Jordan, Poland and Uruguay.

Contractor
Chrysler and JGMS.

Chenowth Advanced Light Strike Vehicle (ALSV)

Development
In October 1996 Chenowth unveiled a development model of the Advanced Light Strike Vehicle (ALSV), described as a third-generation high-performance surveillance, light strike and reconnaissance vehicle and the successor to Chenowth Light Strike Vehicle (LSV), full details of which can be found elsewhere in this section.

In March 1997 the ALSV was exhibited in Abu Dhabi, after which it went to Jordan to undergo trials and evaluation for possible procurement by the Jordanian Army. A second ALSV was procured by the UAE armed forces and delivered in April 1997 for trials and evaluations by Special Forces.

ALSVs are understood to have been operated by US Navy SEALS and the Marine Corps during Desert Storm, and more recently US Navy SEAL teams are reported to have used them in Afghanistan and Iraq. According to Chenowth, other Central American, NATO and Middle Eastern countries operate the ALSV.

Description
The ALSV has seating for a crew of two, three or four protected by a tubular rollbar upper frame hamper. It features a main weapon station with a full 360° traverse at the rear. The station can mount either a 12.7 mm M2 heavy machine gun or a 40 mm MK 19 automatic grenade launcher. Light machine guns and man-portable anti-tank weapons can also be carried. Remote-control and stabilised weapon platforms are possible, as are integral and configurable light armour and various stowage arrangements.

The ALSV has full 4 × 4 drive and is powered by a 140 hp water-cooled diesel engine; a petrol engine version is also available. Extensive use is made of commercial-off-the-shelf components.

The ALSV can be carried internally by CH-47 and CH-53 helicopters. Two may be carried by a C-130 Hercules for para-dropping, or three as cargo.

Specifications
Chenowth ALSV
Seating: 1 + up to 3
Configuration: 4 × 4
Weight:
  (laden) 2,450 kg
  (kerb) 1,350 kg
  (payload) 1,100 kg
Length: 4.25 m
Width: 2.11 m
Height: 1.9 m
Ground clearance: 380 mm
Wheelbase: 2.85 m
Max speed:
  (on-road) 130 km/h
  (off-road) 110 km/h
Range: 500 km
Gradient: >60%

Chenowth Advanced Light Strike Vehicle (ALSV) (T J Gander)   0044186

Side slope: >40%
Engine: 2.5-litre 5-cylinder water-cooled diesel developing 140 hp; a petrol engine is available
Gearbox: manual, 5 forward and 1 reverse gears
Suspension: independent
Steering: rack and pinion
Electrical system: 12 V (24 V optional)

Status
Production as required. Understood to be in use by US and other unspecified armed forces.

Contractor
Chenowth Racing Products, Inc.

Chenowth Light Strike Vehicle (LSV)

Development
The Chenowth Light Strike Vehicle (LSV) is a development of Chenowth's original off-road racing vehicle, which combines low weight, high speed and good cross-country mobility and manoeuvrability. The original military model was the two-seat Fast Attack Vehicle (FAV) produced during the early-1980s from which three- and six-seat Desert Patrol Vehicle (DPV) configurations were further developed.

The first delivery to US Armed Forces was for 180 vehicles. During Operation Desert Shield/Storm US FAV and DPV models were operated by US and UK special forces and by the US Marines.

By mid-2002 the DPV fleet was in storage awaiting a decision on retention in storage or disposal. Following the 11 September 2001 terrorist attacks six DPVs (four in three-seat configuration, two in three-seat configuration) were withdrawn from storage for refurbishment, upgrade and immediate deployment to Afghanistan. Vehicles were subsequently deployed to Iraq.

Description
The LSV/FAV/DPV chassis is an open high-strength 4130 chrome-moly tubular frame with an integral chrome-moly steel roll-cage. Other safety features include a racing type fuel cell, which is explosion resistant, and run-flat capable rims on all four tyres. The standard engine, a 125 hp petrol unit, is air-cooled and rear-mounted. Maximum speed is 97 km/h, acceleration from 0-45 km/h taking four seconds.

Upgraded and refurbished Chenowth Desert Patrol Vehicle (DPV) prior to deployment to Afghanistan (Scott Gourley)   0567864

Upgraded and refurbished Chenowth Desert Patrol Vehicle (DPV) prior to deployment to Afghanistan (Scott Gourley)   0567865

Just forward of and above the engine, the gunner/vehicle commander has the capability to fire forward and to the rear on a swivel seat. The assistant driver, the lower gunner, rides in the right-hand seat. All positions have suspension-type bucket seats fitted with retaining straps.

Weapons can include two 7.62 mm machine guns, mounted fore and aft, together with one 0.50 in (12.7 mm) M2 machine gun or a 40 mm MK 19 automatic grenade launcher. The LSV can also carry a TOW 2 anti-tank guided missile launcher, a 30 mm ASP-30 cannon, an AT-4 anti-tank rocket launcher or the Stinger Surface-to-Air Missile (SAM). Light armour may be added as required, as can special stowage configurations.

The LSV/DPV can be carried internally by CH-47 and CH-53 helicopters. Two may be carried by a C-130 Hercules for para-dropping, or three as cargo.

Prior to deployment to Afghanistan, and in addition to standard post-long-term storage refurbishment, suspension systems were upgraded, electrical wiring systems were replaced, an Internal Communications System (ICS) was added, and the 2.16-litre petrol engines of the three-seat variants were replaced by 2.332-litre petrol engines. The six-seat variant is powered by a 2.6-litre petrol engine. In the longer term a single 2.6-litre engine upgrade for all vehicles was a possibility.

Specifications

Chenowth LSV
Seating: 1 + 2
Configuration: 4 × 2
Weight:
   (laden) 1,660 kg
   (kerb) 960 kg
   (payload) 700 kg

Length: 4.08 m
Width: 2.11 m
Height: 2.01 m
Ground clearance: 410 mm
Wheelbase: 2.84 m
Angle of approach/departure: 81°/48°
Max speed: 97 km/h
Range: 500 km
Gradient: 75%
Side slope: >45%
Engine: 2.16-, 2.332- or 2.6-litre (see text) air-cooled petrol, the 2.16-litre developing 125 hp (93 kW)
Gearbox: manual, 4 forward and 1 reverse gears
Suspension: independent
Steering: rack and pinion
Electrical system: 12 V (24 V optional)

Status

Production as required. Supplied to the US Navy, Marine Corps and Army (two-man FAV), plus a number of undisclosed Central American, Middle Eastern and NATO countries with users thought to include Greece, Mexico, Oman, Portugal and Spain.

Contractor

Chenowth Racing Products, Inc

TRUCKS

Australia

Mack Model RM6866RS (6 × 6) truck

Development

The Mack Model RM6866RS (6 × 6) truck was produced in Australia by Mack Trucks Australia Pty Limited as the Truck, Cargo, Heavy, MC3. It is a version of the basic US Mack 'R' series. Three prototypes were produced (in Australia) in 1978. After evaluation, an order was placed in 1981 for 906 units. These were all delivered by the end of 1986. In 1988, a further 19 units were built and delivered, bringing the total to 925.

During 1993 a contract to upgrade 541 of these trucks was awarded to Mack Trucks Australia Pty Limited. The contract, worth AUD8.77 million, involved the replacement of mechanical suspension units with an SA441W air suspension system and was scheduled to take two years.

In 1994 an extension to the contract was issued to cover the remainder of the Australian Army's Mack fleet, together with modifications on Cargo/Cargo with Winch variants to fit container twist locks. Between 1994 and April 1996, 288 cargo variants were fitted with eight container twist locks to enable the transport of a 20 ft ISO container or one, two or three 6 ft containers. This work was carried out around Australia in Mack

Truck, cargo, heavy, MC3 carrying mobile hospital shelter/containers (Barry Marriott)   0009605

branches and dealers. Also in 1994, four dump truck variants were converted to Truck, Tanker, Fuel variants under the Bushranger project. This work was carried out in Brisbane.

Between 1999 and 2000, 185 Cargo, Army Tractor/Medium Gun and Cargo, Crane variants had the Abbey CTM 3000 hydraulic crane removed and replaced with Hiab 090-3 cranes.

The Heavy Recovery Vehicle MC3 is a Mack Model RM6866RS (6 × 6) truck chassis that has undergone major modifications. The HRV entered operational service with the Australian Army in April 2005 and replaced the earlier Truck, wrecker, heavy, MC3.

Under Phase 2a of the Australian Department of Defence's Defence Matériel Organisation (DMO) multiphase project, Project Land 121; Project Overlander a project to reduce the in-cab noise of the Mack Model RM6866RS was undertaken. By mid-2008 all the required noise reduction kits (cabin insulation and air-conditioning kits) had been delivered and approximately 400 vehicles had been modified before a minor design defect in the air-conditioning halted progress. Work towards correcting the defect was scheduled, with installation of the remaining kits to follow.

Also under Phase 2a of Land 121 a contract to modify the Mack gun tractor fleet with twist locks was signed in December 2006. The modification programme commenced in May 2007 and was scheduled for completion by the end of 2008.

Phase 2a of Land 121 addressed capability shortfalls within the current field vehicle and trailer fleet that are a result of significant occupational health and safety issues. Phase 2A was an 'umbrella project' for six separate sub-projects.

The Mack Model RM6866RS fleet will be replaced under Project Land 121.

It was announced in December 2005 that Land 121 tenders involving medium/heavy vehicles and modules (known as the MHC segment) had been released to a shortlist of nine companies, these being the then ADI Limited, the then DaimlerChrysler Australia-Pacific, General Dynamics Land Systems-Australia, MAN Nutzfahrzeuge, Mack Trucks Australia, Scania Australia, the then Stewart & Stevenson, the then Tenix Defence, and Terex Corporation.

By early 2006 three Requests For Tender (RFT) worth up to AUD600 million and covering Phase 3a of Land 121 had been issued. These initial Land 121 Phase 3a RFTs involved superseding the ADF's high-readiness fleet of 1,400 medium, heavy and light vehicles, 1,300 trailers and 1,200 specialist modules. Land 121 Phase 3b, the replacement of the remaining bulk of the fleet, was to follow on from Phase 3a.

With the second pass approval of Land 121, Phases 3a and 3b ceased to exist as independent phases. Phase 3a became Phase 3, Phase 3b became Phase 5, and Land 121 Phase 4 emerged. With the second pass approval of

Truck, cargo, heavy, MC3 with standard cargo/troop carrying body and tarpaulin (Ron Fry)   1124780

Truck, cargo, heavy, with crane (Abbey CTM 3000-1), MC3 with shortened cargo/troop carrying body and tarpaulin (Ron Fry)   1047346

Truck, cargo, heavy, MC3 with winch, laden with timber and coupled to a 20-tonne plant trailer (Ron Fry)   0121280

Truck, wrecker, heavy, MC3 fitted with Holmes recovery gear (Ron Fry)
1047347

Truck, cargo, army tractor/Medium gun, heavy, MC3 ammunition
(Gordon Arthur)
1340342

The layout of the vehicle is conventional, with the engine located at the front under a prominent bonneted cab and the cargo area to the rear. The front axle is a Kelsey Hayes SDA 18B (Fabco) rated at 8,165 kg. The tandem rear axle unit is a Mack SA441W bogie rated at 20,000 kg.

The cab has seating for the driver and one passenger while the cargo area can have seating for 26 fully equipped troops. Various types of trailer can be towed.

Power is provided by an 11-litre Mack EM6-285 Maxidyne turbocharged diesel engine coupled to a five-speed Maxitorque gearbox.

The standard winch carried is an Ateco 24L with a maximum pull of 10,575 kg and 60 m of cable.

The data in the specifications table refers to the basic cargo vehicle.

Variants

Truck, cargo, heavy, with crane, MC3
On this variant, an Abbey CTM 3000-1 hydraulic crane is mounted directly behind the cab. The crane has a maximum lift capacity of 3,400 kg at 1.8 m. Power for the crane's hydraulic system is provided by a Powauto AH23BR11 Power Take-Off (PTO) on the transfer box. The cargo area is 5.016 m long and 2.39 m wide with seating reduced to 22 fully equipped troops. Twistlocks for containers have not been retrofitted on this variant and some vehicles have had the original Abbey crane replaced by a Hiab crane. The with-crane MC3 variant weighs 12,810 kg unladen.

Truck, wrecker, heavy, MC3
On this variant, which has been upgraded, the cargo area was originally replaced by a Holmes A750 recovery rig with a maximum towing lift of 7,800 kg. The vehicle also had a 10,500 kg recovery winch provided with 100 m of cable. This variant weighed 16,000 kg unladen.

Heavy Recovery Vehicle, MC3
The RM6866RS Heavy Recovery Vehicle was developed by Mack Trucks Australia (MTA) to meet the operational requirements of the Australian Army, who ordered a total of 64 units. The HRV entered operational service with the Australian Army in April 2005.

Prior to the introduction of the Heavy Recovery Vehicle, MC3, off-road heavy recovery had previously been provided to deployed forces through the Truck Wrecker, Heavy, MC3 (TWH) fitted with the Holmes 750 twin boom recovery system. Due to mechanical failure of the recovery module and the associated operational restrictions and other health and safety

Side view of the Mack RM6866RS Heavy Recovery Vehicle (HRV)
(Mack Trucks)
1156190

Land 121 the total quantity required under the new standalone Phase 3 requirement increased to 2,090 vehicles, 1,506 of these armoured. The total value of Land 121 Phase 3 reached around AUD3.3 billion.

Late-2007, BAE Systems (medium/heavy), the now Mercedes-Benz Australia Pacific Pty Ltd (light), and Haulmark Trailers Australia (trailers) were announced as preferred tenderers for Phase 3 of Land 121, the quoted value of which was USD2.65 billion. Land 121 Phase 3 was to acquire approximately 2,400 Family of Medium Tactical Vehicles (FMTVs) from BAE Systems (which by this stage was producer of the FMTV), 3,000 trailers of different sizes from Haulmark Trailers and 1,000 Mercedes-Benz G-Class (4×4) and (6×6) utility vehicles from Mercedes-Benz Australia Pacific.

It was announced in October 2008 that the medium/heavy segment of Land 121 Phase 3 (for which BAE Systems was preferred bidder) would be halted and a new process commenced as a result of technical risks eventuating with the FMTVs during the testing phase, and the DoD identifying the need for higher levels of blast and ballistic protection as a consequence of deployed operations.

Conditions of tender for the first stage of the revised tender process were released in December 2008. The first stage consisted of six months of comparative evaluation testing of a total of 24 vehicles of various types submitted by four bidders. The four bidders are understood to have submitted the following vehicle types; BAE Systems – FMTV and Scania; Mercedes-Benz Australia Pacific - Unimog, Zetros and Actros; MAN – TG, HX and SX ranges; Thales – Bushmaster derivative and Oshkosh MTVR derivatives.

It was disclosed in February 2010 that comparative evaluation testing had been completed and that a down-select to Mercedes-Benz, MAN and Thales had been made. An Offer Definition and Refinement Process (ODRP) had commenced and from that a final preferred bidder (or bidders) will be announced late-2011.

Land 121 Phase 5 will provide the ADF with an estimated 2,000 unprotected Commercial-Off-The-Shelf (COTS) vehicles that will serve in the 'raise, train and sustain' functions. First Pass Approval for this phase was expected in the last quarter of 2009, but this is now understood to have slipped to around 2012.

Description
The basic vehicle is the Truck, cargo, heavy, MC3 which may be fitted with a winch. It is classified as an MLC 22 8,000 kg capacity vehicle and many components and subassemblies are produced in Australia. The cargo body is a Mack design built by Walsh Engineering of Toowoomba, Queensland, and the EDE alternator is produced by the Ordnance Factory at Maribyrnong, Victoria.

From the rear and showing the lift/tow recovery equipment, the Mack RM6866RS Heavy Recovery Vehicle (HRV) (Mack Trucks)
1156189

Truck, dump, heavy, MC3 (Gordon Arthur)　　　1340334

limitations that have been in place since 1995, this recovery system was not providing the intended service needed for the conduct of recovery tasks, route and battlefield clearance and rescue of deployed forces.

The Heavy Recovery Vehicle MC3 is a Mack Model RM6866RS (6 × 6) truck chassis that has undergone major modifications from the standard Mack RM6866RS chassis, for use in the specialised recovery role and to increase its overall capability in the field. The primary role of the HRV is to recover heavy and medium trucks, ASLAV, Bushmaster, M113 and a variety of heavy commercial support vehicles, and within the designed mobility parameters of those vehicle variants.

The engine power output has been uprated from 285 to 320 hp; the maximum torque range is now from 1,600 rpm. The transmission has been upgraded to an Eaton Fuller RTXF-14710B unit which gives a wider operating range for the loads required to be towed. The major difference is the range change within the transmission to give five speeds in low range and five more speeds in high range.

The R model cab has been modified substantially. The rear cab wall has been removed and a crew cab has been fixed to the rear allowing the carriage of the recovered crew (two) people along with their webbing. The complete cab set-up is mounted on an air suspended sub-frame.

A new integrated recovery unit has been mounted to the rear of the vehicle. The new unit consists of Material Handling Equipment (MHE), two retrieval winches with fairlead systems, a lift/towing system, and stowage facilities for recovery stores, equipment, and for crew personal weapons and kit.

The two aluminium locker assemblies, one on either side of the vehicle, each comprise of four key-lockable CES lockers and one key-lockable locker containing winch and lift/tow control panels. The lift/tow system consists of three hydraulic rams, one for lifting and two for alignment of the crossbar and to assist with lifting.

The MHE is a Palfinger PK9501 crane, which can be operated by both manual and remote controls. The crane has a maximum lifting capacity of 5,700 kg, an outreach of 5.8 m and a slewing angle of 210°. The crane is fitted with the Paltronic 50 overload protection device. To provide a more stable platform when operating the crane, two hydraulically controlled stabiliser legs are lowered to the ground, one on either side of the cab rear.

The unit is fitted with two Sepson 63.02-009 winches which are hydraulically driven, drum-type, two-speed, constant force winches. The capacity in auto mode is 13,000 kg constant force on all layers, and in manual mode 13,000 kg on the bottom layer, reducing to 9,000 kg on the top layer. There are four rope layers. The ropes used are Casar 17 mm IWRC, Grade G1960, 98 m in length.

The walkways on top of the recovery body have a reduced slip coating on the lockers, and a non-slip fold up and removable aluminium walkway between the lockers. A reduced slip coating has also been applied to the bonnet area. The spare tyre is located on top of the rear section of the recovery body and is removed by using the Palfinger crane. A closed circuit TV monitor is fitted to the dash, with two cameras fitted at the rear of the body to enable the driver to see the casualty vehicle when reversing for hook up and whilst travelling.

A tamper-proof speed limiter is fitted to the vehicle to set the speed to 100 km/h. The original two fuel tank set-up have been replaced by a single larger fuel tank located between the chassis rails, under the walkway. The fuel tank holds 498 litres.

Truck, cargo, army tractor/medium gun, heavy, MC3 ammunition

This variant is used to tow the Australian Army's 155 mm M198 howitzers and may also be used to carry ammunition. A collapsible crew shelter for the gun crew is provided behind the driving cab; it may be removed to provide more ammunition carrying capacity. The cargo area is replaced by a flatbed platform divided by an Abbey CTM 3000-2 ammunition-handling hydraulic crane. The crane has a maximum lift capacity of 2,000 kg at 3.053 m and a full 360° traverse. Some vehicles have had the original Abbey crane replaced by a Hiab crane. Power for the hydraulic system is provided by a Powauto AH23BR11 Power Take-Off (PTO) on the transfer case. A winch is fitted. This variant weighs 13,180 kg unladen. Under Phase

Truck, tank, water, heavy, MC3 (Ron Fry)　　　1047349

2a of Land 121 a contract to modify the Mack gun tractor fleet with twist locks was signed in December 2006. The modification program commenced in May 2007 and was scheduled for completion by the end of 2008.

Mixer, concrete, truck-mounted, heavy, MC3

This variant carries a Fowlerex Rheem Model 5 KH mixer produced at Bulimba in Queensland. The hydraulically driven mixer has a capacity of 5.5 m^3, and is used in association with a 204-litre water tank. This variant uses a ZF Model PK1400 gearbox and has an unladen weight of 13,700 kg.

Truck, dump, heavy, MC3

On this variant the cargo area is replaced by an 8 m^3 capacity dump body produced by Hockney Alcan of Rocklea, Queensland. It is possible to arrange troop seating inside the dump body and up to 18 fully equipped troops can be carried. A winch may be fitted. In addition, this vehicle can tow plant trailers carrying dozers and other construction equipment. This variant weighs 11,520 kg unladen.

Truck, tank, fuel, heavy, MC3

For the refuelling role this variant carries a three-compartment tank produced by Holmwood Industries of Rochedale, Queensland. The tank has a capacity of 11,380 litres and the vehicle also carries the associated electrical and refuelling equipment, such as four hose reels. This variant is 9.475 m long and weighs 12,160 kg unladen.

Truck, tank, water, heavy, MC3

Mounting an aluminium three-compartment water tank with a highway operation capacity of 9,240 litres, this variant also carries a spray bar, two hose reels, a 60 m hose and three dispensing cocks. This variant is 9.474 m long and weighs 11,800 kg unladen.

Distributor, bituminous substance, tank type, truck-mounted, heavy, MC3

This variant differs from the others in the Australian Mack range in having a 6 × 4 drive configuration. The steel tank has aluminium lagging and a highway operations capacity of 7,740 litres. A spray bar is provided along with two tar burner tubes. This variant is 10.194 m long and weighs 13,960 kg unladen.

Truck, bridge recovery, heavy, MC3

This variant is equipped to launch and recover Ribbon Bridge sections and carries a Techlaunch ARK221 roll-on hook loader that can also be used to load a cargo tray when the Ribbon Bridge is not required. The loader is produced by Techmark Australia and manufactured in Melbourne, Victoria. It has a capacity of 6,000 kg. The cargo tray is 5.8 m long and 2.5 m wide.

When carrying a Ribbon Bridge section this variant is 10.3 m long. When carrying the cargo tray the length is 10.5 m. The unladen weight is 14,800 kg.

Truck, tank, fuel, heavy, MC3 (Gordon Arthur)　　　1391377

Specifications

Truck, cargo, heavy, MC3
Cab seating: 1 + 1
Configuration: 6 × 6
Weight:
   (front axle, unladen) 5,070 kg
   (rear axle, unladen) 6,510 kg
   (total, unladen) 11,570 kg
Load area: 5.714 × 2.39 m
Length: 9.6 m
Width: 2.5 m
Height:
   (laden) 3.125 m
   (unladen) 3.155 m
Ground clearance:
   (laden) 280 mm
   (unladen) 318 mm
Track:
   (front) 1.911 m
   (rear) 1.81 m
Wheelbase: 4.765 m + 1.4 m
Angle of approach/departure: (laden) 31.5°/30.5°
Range: (first-class roads) 550 to 590 km
Fuel capacity: 265 litres
Max gradient: 50%
Side slope: 50%
Fording: 800 mm
Engine: Mack EM6-285 Maxidyne 11-litre 6-cylinder inline turbocharged and intercooled water-cooled diesel developing 283 hp (211 kW) at 2,100 rpm
Gearbox: Maxitorque with 5 forward and 1 reverse gears
Transfer box: 2-speed
Clutch: Spicer twin dry plate
Steering: Sheppard Model 592, integrated power-assistance
Turning radius: 12.1 m
Suspension: air, Neway ARDST2446
Tyres: 12.00 × 20
Brakes:
   (main) dual circuit, air, drums all-round
   (parking) spring on rear axles
   (trailer) dual circuit, air
Electrical system: 24 V
Batteries: 2 × 12 V, 61 Ah
Alternator: 140 A

Status

In service with the Australian Army (925 produced). Replacement programme running (see text).

Contractor

Mack Trucks Australia Pty Ltd.

Austria

Steyr trucks

Development

The now MAN Nutzfahrzeuge Österreich AG can trace its origins back to 1864 as a manufacturer of arms. The company produced its first truck in 1922. Following a number of mergers, the truck-making division of Steyr-Daimler-Puch AG (Steyr Nutzfahrzeuge AG) was in a loss-making situation when, in January 1990, MAN Nutzfahrzeuge AG of Germany acquired an 85 per cent share of the truck-building activities of Steyr Nutzfahrzeuge

A Steyr-badged Steyr Medium Tactical Truck of the Thai Navy
(Gordon Arthur)   1391192

OAF-badged MAN SX range high mobility tactical truck mounting the Thales RAC-3D low-level air-defence radar system (Stefan Marx)   1128715

AG. In 1993 MAN exercised their option to acquire the remaining 15 per cent share of the business. Steyr Nutzfahrzeuge AG became known as MAN Steyr AG during 2002 and during 2005 as MAN Nutzfahrzeuge Österreich AG.

Following a lengthy period of consolidation and reorganisation, by 2002 the MAN tactical truck ranges (the FX, LX and SX) were assembled by MAN Sonderfahrzeuge AG (now MAN Nutzfahrzeuge Österreich AG) at the former Österreich Automobilfabrik ÖAF-Gräf und Stift AG plant in Vienna, MAN having acquired truck-maker ÖAF in 1936. The LX range was phased out of production during 2004 and the FX range during 2005. Both ranges have been replaced by the HX range of tactical trucks. Some components for the MAN tactical truck ranges, such as the torsionally rigid chassis frame of the SX range, and the MAN modular military cab fitted to all X range trucks, were manufactured at the Star truck plant in Poland. They are now manufactured in Austria. Star Sp. z.o.o. was acquired by MAN Nutzfahrzeuge AG in December 1999.

As part of the consolidation and reorganisation process, by the late 1990s, Steyr's 17 M (4 × 4) and 24 M (6 × 6) ranges of heavy military trucks had been phased out of production, to be replaced by militarised versions of the MAN F2000 heavy range of commercial trucks; HX range trucks for certain applications. Militarised F2000 models were also produced at the former Österreich Automobilfabrik ÖAF-Gräf und Stift AG plant. The F2000 range was replaced in production during 2004 by equivalent models based on the heavier models of the current MAN TGA range. Details of the Steyr 17 M (4 × 4) and 24 M (6 × 6) ranges, the MAN F2000 range and current TGA range can be found elsewhere in this section.

Steyr's (4 × 4) Medium Tactical Truck range was also phased out of production during the late 1990s in favour of MAN designs; in this instance militarised versions of the MAN L2000 and M2000 ranges of light and medium two-axle commercial trucks. The Steyr Medium Tactical Truck range and the MAN L2000 and M2000 ranges are visually similar as they share versions of the same Steyr-designed cab. All L2000 and M2000 trucks (including commercial production) trucks were assembled at the former Steyr plant in Steyr, near Vienna.

MAN introduced the TGL and TGM range of two-axle commercial trucks during 2005 to replace the L2000 and M2000 ranges. Militarised versions of the TGL and TGM became available during 2006, with the Austrian Army being the launch customer. By mid-2007 all militarised L2000 and M2000

Steyr 12 M 18 (4 × 4) 5, 000 kg truck of the Austrian Army operating in Kosovo in the EOD role. Austria ordered around 2,000 Steyr 12M 18 trucks from 1985 as a partial replacement for the Steyr 680 fleet
(Michael Jerchel)   1124742

OAF-badged MAN F2000 range (FE460) truck of the Austrian Air Force (Stefan Marx) 1128733

OAF-badged MAN F2000 range (19.403) truck of the Austrian Air Force (Stefan Marx) 1185448

models will have been replaced in production in Austria by equivalent models from the TGL and TGM ranges. Production of L2000 and M2000 models has shifted to India where production continues and primarily for local and Asian markets by Man Force Trucks Pvt. Ltd (MFTL), a joint venture company between Force Motors (formerly Bajaj Tempo) and MAN Nutzfahrzeuge AG.

Dependant on market, essentially the same model from either the tactical ranges or militarised commercial ranges of trucks may now be marketed and branded as either MAN or Steyr (or for the Austrian market only, as ÖAF), although the emphasis is placed heavily on the MAN brand. For the purpose of clarification, the models included in this section as Steyr trucks will either be Steyr-specific models produced prior to the final consolidation of the MAN/Steyr ranges during 2000, or will be tactical (LX, FX, HX or SX) or militarised (TGA, TGL, TGM, F2000, L2000 or M2000) models supplied branded as a Steyr or ÖAF product. Where the same model is known to have also been supplied branded MAN, this will be noted in the entry text.

Taking the Steyr 32 M 40 model as an example, the designations of all Steyr-branded trucks can be broken down as follows: the 32 denotes nominal Gross Vehicle Weight (GVW), the M denotes military (S denotes commercial) and the 40 denotes nominal engine horsepower (400 hp).

Certain MAN/Steyr models have been supplied to ELBO of Greece in Semi Knock Down (SKD) configuration for final assembly and inclusion of local content. The most recent models supplied include the 14 M 22 (4 × 4) and the 33 M 41 (6 × 6). Full details of these, and previously supplied models, can be found else wherein this section.

In January 2010 it was announced that Rheinmetall's wheeled military vehicle activities would merge with the military activities of MAN with the founding of Rheinmetall MAN Military Vehicles GmbH (RMMV). Essentially this merger units the complimentary technological core competencies of MAN's automotive expertise in commercial vehicle manufacture with Rheinmetall's technological know-how in the military land sector/systems field. The result is the creation of a new single source provider for the entire range of armoured and unarmoured transport, command and role-specific wheeled vehicles. Under the terms of the agreement, Rheinmetall will have a stake of 51 per cent and MAN 49 per cent in the new company.

Status
In production.
Enquiries to: RMMV GmbH; MAN Nutzfahrzeuge Österreich AG

Steyr 18 M 28 (4 × 4) truck

Development
The Steyr 18 M 28 (4 × 4) truck is a militarised example of the MAN M2000 range of commercial trucks. Full details of the relationship between the current MAN and Steyr military truck ranges can be found in the Steyr trucks or MAN trucks entries elsewhere in this section but in brief: In January 1990 MAN Nutzfahrzeuge AG of Germany acquired an 85 per cent share of the truck-building activities of Austria's Steyr Nutzfahrzeuge AG. In 1993 MAN exercised their option to acquire the remaining 15 per cent share of the business. Steyr Nutzfahrzeuge AG became known as MAN Steyr AG during 2002 and is now known as MAN Nutzfahrzeuge Österreichische AG.

As part of a reorganisation and consolidation process, by the late 1990s Steyr's (4 × 4) Medium Tactical Truck range had been phased out of production and replaced by militarised examples of the MAN L2000 and M2000 ranges of light and medium two-axle commercial trucks. All L2000 and M2000 trucks (including all commercial variants) were assembled at the former Steyr plant in Steyr, near Vienna.

MAN introduced the TGL and TGM range of two-axle commercial trucks during 2005 to replace the L2000 and M2000 ranges. Militarised versions of the TGL and TGM became available during 2006, with the Austrian Army being the launch customer. By mid-2007 all militarised L2000 and M2000 models will have been replaced in production in Austria by equivalent models from the TGL and TGM ranges. Production of L2000 and M2000 models has shifted to India where production continues and primarily for local and Asian markets by MAN Force Trucks Pvt. Ltd (MFTL), a joint venture company between Force Motors (formerly Bajaj Tempo) and MAN Nutzfahrzeuge AG.

In January 2010 it was announced that Rheinmetall's wheeled military vehicle activities would merge with the military activities of MAN with the founding of Rheinmetall MAN Military Vehicles GmbH (RMMV). Essentially this merger units the complimentary technological core competencies of MAN's automotive expertise in commercial vehicle manufacture with Rheinmetall's technological know-how in the military land sector/systems field. The result is the creation of a new single source provider for the entire range of armoured and unarmoured transport, command and role-specific wheeled vehicles. Under the terms of the agreement, Rheinmetall will have a stake of 51 per cent and MAN 49 per cent in the new company.

Description
The Steyr 18 M 28 (18 - nominal GVW in tonnes; M - military; 28 - nominal hp (280)) is entirely conventional in design. Its tiltable, all-steel, forward control cab is common throughout the MAN L2000 and M2000 ranges of commercial trucks. Normal configuration is left-hand drive and with seating for the driver and a single passenger. Right-hand drive, a passenger's bench seat, a full-size roof hatch, air-conditioning, an auxiliary heater, radio preparation and a self-recovery winch are some of the extensive equipment options that were available. The standard compact cab may be replaced by an optional medium-length cab 300 mm deeper. A version optimised for tropical climates was also available.

The conventional C-section chassis has riveted- and bolted-in tubular cross-members and mounts beam axles sprung by parabolic leaf springs with shock-absorbers and an anti-roll bar. Single or dual rear wheels were available, and with wheelbase options of 3.6, 3.9 or 4.5 m. The rear drive axle is rated at 9,000 kg and fitted with a differential lock as standard. Full-time four-wheel drive and a differential lock for the 7,500 kg rated front steer-drive axle were optional. An Anti-lock Braking System (ABS) with off-road logic was a further option. The service braking system is supplemented by a compressed air actuated engine brake.

Motive power is provided by a MAN six-cylinder 280 hp turbocharged diesel engine coupled to an Eaton 8209 nine-speed manual gearbox and G1000/2 transfer box. Driveline options included a ZF 16 S 109 16-speed manual gearbox, a fully automatic gearbox, or a Steyr VG 750 transfer box with Automatic Drivetrain Management (ADM).

Steyr 18 M 28 truck; over 100 of these are in service with Saudi Arabia's National Guard (SANG) (MAN Nutzfahrzeuge Österreichische AG) 0044265

The Steyr 18 M 28 would normally be configured as a drop side cargo truck, but the chassis is capable of accepting a variety of alternatives including a light recovery hamper, shelter or workshop type bodies, or fuel or water tanks. The standard drop side cargo body may be covered by a tarpaulin over bows and the platform is also suitable for mounting weapons such as light air defence guns.

The normal military payload of the 18 M 28 is quoted as approximately 8,000 kg. However, the chassis-cab carrying capacity (which is cab type and wheelbase dependant) is a maximum of 10,385 kg with single rear wheels, 12,115 kg with dual rear wheels, and in both cases with the compact cab and a 3.6 m wheelbase. For all variants, the maximum gross vehicle weight is 16,000 kg; Gross Train Weight (GTW) is 24,000/30,000 kg on-/off-road.

The Steyr 18 M 26 is essentially the same vehicle with identical GVW/GTW but with the engine downrated by 20 hp to a maximum of 260 hp at 2,300 rpm, and with a resultant 10 N.m drop in peak toque to 1,000 N.m between 1,350 and 1,700 rpm.

Specifications

18 M 28
(3.9 m wheelbase, medium cab and single rear wheels)
Cab seating: 1 + 1 or 2
Configuration: 4 × 4
Weight:
  (chassis-cab) 5,700 kg
  (GVW) 16,000 kg
  (chassis-cab payload) 10,300 kg
  (towed load, on-road) 14,000 kg
  (GTW, on-road) 30,000 kg
  (towed load, off-road) 8,000 kg
  (GTW, off-road) 24,000 kg
Length: (overall) 6.3 m
Width:
  (cab) 2.2 m
  (rear wheels) 2.4 m
  (overall) 2.49 m
Height:
  (cab, laden) 2.893 m
  (cab, unladen) 2.99 m
Ground clearance:
  (front axle) 372 mm
  (rear axle) 365 mm
Track:
  (front) 2.08 m
  (rear) 2.03 m
Wheelbase: 3.9 m
Angle of approach/departure: 38°/32°
Max speed: (road) 90 km/h
Fuel capacity: 150 litres
Gradient: >60%
Sideslope: 30% (approx.)
Fording: up to 750 mm
Engine: MAN Type D0826LFL EURO 2 6.871-litre 6-cylinder in-line exhaust gas turbocharged and intercooled, water-cooled direct injection 4-stroke diesel developing 280 hp (209 kW) at 2,400 rpm and 1,100 N.m torque between 1,200 and 1,700 rpm
Gearbox: Eaton 8209 manual with 9 forward and 1 reverse gears (options available)
Transfer box: MAN G1000/2 2-speed (options available)
Clutch: single dry plate
Steering: ZF, power- assisted
Turning radius: 8.5 m
Suspension: parabolic leaf springs with telescopic shock-absorbers and anti-roll bar, front and rear
Tyres: 365/85R 20
Brakes: dual circuit, air, drums all-round. ABS optional
Electrical system: 24 V
Batteries: 2 × 12 V, 88 Ah
Alternator: 28 V, 35 A

Status

Production complete. Replaced from mid-2007 by equivalent model from the MAN TGL/TGM range. In service with Saudi Arabia (>100).

Contractor

RMMV GmbH
MAN Nutzfahrzeuge Österreichische AG

Steyr 14 M 22 (4 × 4) truck

Development

The Steyr 14 M 22 (4 × 4) truck is a militarised example of the MAN M2000 range of commercial trucks. Full details of the relationship between the current MAN and Steyr military truck ranges can be found in the Steyr trucks or MAN trucks entries elsewhere in this section but in brief: In January 1990 MAN Nutzfahrzeuge AG of Germany acquired an 85 per cent share of the truck-building activities of Austria's Steyr Nutzfahrzeuge AG.

Steyr 14 M 22 (4 × 4) truck with dual rear tyres (left), Steyr 14 M 22 (4 × 4) truck with single tyres (right) (MAN Nutzfahrzeuge Österreichische AG)
0547187

In 1993 MAN exercised their option to acquire the remaining 15 per cent share of the business. Steyr Nutzfahrzeuge AG became known as MAN Steyr AG during 2002 and is now known as MAN Nutzfahrzeuge Österreichische AG.

As part of a reorganisation and consolidation process, by the late 1990s Steyr's (4 × 4) Medium Tactical Truck range had been phased out of production and replaced by militarised examples of the MAN L2000 and M2000 ranges of light and medium two-axle commercial trucks. All L2000 and M2000 trucks (including all commercial variants) were assembled at the former Steyr plant in Steyr, near Vienna.

MAN introduced the TGL and TGM range of two-axle commercial trucks during 2005 to replace the L2000 and M2000 ranges. Militarised versions of the TGL and TGM became available during 2006, with the Austrian Army being the launch customer. By mid-2007 all militarised L2000 and M2000 models had been replaced in production in Austria by equivalent models from the TGL and TGM ranges. Production of L2000 and M2000 models shifted to India where production continues and primarily for local and Asian markets by Man Force Trucks Pvt Ltd (MFTL), a joint venture company between Force Motors (formerly Bajaj Tempo) and MAN Nutzfahrzeuge AG.

In January 2010 it was announced that Rheinmetall's wheeled military vehicle activities would merge with the military activities of MAN with the founding of Rheinmetall MAN Military Vehicles GmbH (RMMV). Essentially this merger units the complimentary technological core competencies of MAN's automotive expertise in commercial vehicle manufacture with Rheinmetall's technological know-how in the military land sector/systems field. The result is the creation of a new single source provider for the entire range of armoured and unarmoured transport, command and role-specific wheeled vehicles. Under the terms of the agreement, Rheinmetall will have a stake of 51 per cent and MAN 49 per cent in the new company.

Description

The Steyr 14 M 22 (14 - nominal GVW in tonnes; M - military; 22 - nominal hp (220)) is entirely conventional in design. Its tiltable, all-steel, forward control cab is common throughout the MAN L2000 and M2000 ranges of commercial trucks. Normal configuration is left-hand drive, with seating for the driver and a single passenger. Right-hand drive, a passenger's bench seat, a full-size roof hatch, air-conditioning, an auxiliary heater, radio preparation and a self-recovery winch are some of the extensive equipment options that were available. The standard compact cab may be replaced by an optional medium-length cab 300 mm deeper. A version optimised for tropical climates was also available.

The conventional C-section chassis has riveted and bolted-in tubular cross-members and mounts beam axles sprung by parabolic leaf springs with shock-absorbers and an anti-roll bar. Single or dual rear wheels were available. Wheelbase options of 3.2, 3.6, 3.9 or 4.2 m were available. The rear drive axle is rated at 9,000 kg and fitted with a differential lock as standard. Full-time four-wheel drive and a differential lock for the 5,000 kg rated front steer-drive axle were optional. An Anti-lock Braking System (ABS) with off-road logic was a further option. The service braking system is supplemented by a compressed air actuated engine brake.

Motive power is provided by a MAN six-cylinder 220 hp turbocharged diesel engine coupled to a selection of gearboxes that included an automatic or a range of manual gearboxes, such as a ZF 6 S 850 six-speed, a ZF 16 S 109 16-speed with splitter, or an Eaton 8309 nine-speed, all further coupled to a Steyr G1000/2 two-speed transfer box or a Steyr VG750 transfer box with Automatic Drivetrain Management (ADM).

The Steyr 14 M 22 is normally configured as a drop side cargo truck, but the chassis is capable of accepting a variety of alternatives including a light recovery hamper, shelter or workshop type bodies, or fuel or water tanks. The standard drop side cargo body may be covered by a tarpaulin over bows and the platform is also suitable for mounting weapons such as light air defence guns.

The normal military payload is quoted as approximately 5,000 kg. However, the chassis-cab carrying capacity (which is dependant on a number of factors) is a maximum of 7,985 kg with single rear wheels, 8,190 kg with dual rear wheels, and in both cases with the compact cab and a 3.2 m wheelbase. For all variants, the gross vehicle weight is 13,500 kg.

The Steyr 14 M 22 with single rear wheels is in service with Venezuela designated the MAN 14.224 and, with dual rear wheels, with the Hellenic Armed Forces designated the ELBO 14 ME 22. Previously MAN Nutzfahrzeuge Österreich AG had supplied ELBO with the Steyr 14 M 14, for which production is now complete. Like its predecessor, the 14 M 22 was delivered to ELBO in Semi Knock Down (SKD) form for final assembly and insertion of local content.

Specifications

14 M 22
(with 3.9 m wheelbase, compact cab and single rear wheels)
Cab seating: 1 + 1 or 2
Configuration: 4 × 4
Weight:
  (chassis cab) 5,540 kg
  (GVW) 13,500 kg
  (payload on chassis cab) 7,960 kg
  (towed load) 10,500 kg
  (GTW) 24,000 kg
Length overall: 6.3 m
Width:
  (cab) 2.2 m
  (rear wheels) 2.4 m
  (overall) 2.49 m
Height:
  (cab, laden) 2.864 m
  (cab, unladen) 2.932 m
Ground clearance:
  (front axle) 372 mm
  (rear axle) 365 mm
Wheelbase: 3.9 m
Max speed: (road) 88 km/h
Fuel capacity: 150 litres
Gradient: >60%
Sideslope: approx. 30%
Fording: up to 750 mm
Engine: MAN Type D0826LFL EURO 2 6.871-litre 6-cylinder in-line exhaust gas turbocharged and intercooled, water-cooled direct injection 4-stroke diesel developing 220 hp (164 kW) at 2,400 rpm and 825 N.m torque between 1,400 and 1,700 rpm
Gearbox: ZF 6 S 850 manual with 6 forward and 1 reverse gears (options available)
Transfer box: MAN G1000/2 2-speed (options available)
Clutch: single dry plate
Steering: power assisted, ZF 8095
Turning radius: 8.5 m
Suspension: parabolic leaf springs with telescopic shock-absorbers and anti-roll bar, front and rear
Tyres: 365/85R 20
Brakes: dual circuit, air, drums all-round. ABS optional
Electrical system: 24 V
Batteries: 2 × 12 V, 88 Ah
Alternator: 28 V, 35 A

Status

Production complete, replaced from around mid 2007 (see text). In service with Burundi (14, 2001), China, Pakistan (40, 2002), Venezuela (as MAN 14.224, approximately 450) and Zimbabwe (59, 2001) and possibly others. Supplied to Greece SKD as the ELBO 14 ME 22 (approximately 80 delivered).

Contractor

RMMV GmbH
MAN Nutzfahrzeuge Österreichische AG

Steyr 10 M 22 (4 × 4) truck

Development

The Steyr 10 M 22 (4 × 4) truck is a militarised example of the MAN M2000 range of commercial trucks. Full details of the relationship between the current MAN and Steyr military truck ranges can be found in the Steyr trucks or MAN trucks entries elsewhere in this section but in brief: In January 1990 MAN Nutzfahrzeuge AG of Germany acquired an 85 per cent share of the truck-building activities of Austria's Steyr Nutzfahrzeuge AG. In 1993 MAN exercised their option to acquire the remaining 15 per cent share of the business. Steyr Nutzfahrzeuge AG became known as MAN Steyr AG during 2002 and is now known as MAN Nutzfahrzeuge Österreichische AG.

MAN 10.224 LAEC (4 × 4) truck of the Portuguese Army, this also available badged Steyr 10 M 22 (Victor M.S. Barreira) 1391028

As part of a reorganisation and consolidation process, by the late 1990s Steyr's (4 × 4) Medium Tactical Truck range had been phased out of production and replaced by militarised examples of the MAN L2000 and M2000 ranges of light and medium two-axle commercial trucks. All L2000 and M2000 trucks (including all commercial variants) were assembled at the former Steyr plant in Steyr, near Vienna.

MAN introduced the TGL and TGM range of two-axle commercial trucks during 2005 to replace the L2000 and M2000 ranges. Militarised versions of the TGL and TGM became available during 2006, with the Austrian Army being the launch customer. By mid-2007 all militarised L2000 and M2000 models will have been replaced in production in Austria by equivalent models from the TGL and TGM ranges. Production of L2000 and M2000 models shifted to India where production continues and primarily for local and Asian markets by Man Force Trucks Pvt. Ltd. (MFTL), a joint venture company between Force Motors (formerly Bajaj Tempo) and MAN Nutzfahrzeuge AG.

In January 2010 it was announced that Rheinmetall's wheeled military vehicle activities would merge with the military activities of MAN with the founding of Rheinmetall MAN Military Vehicles GmbH (RMMV). Essentially this merger units the complimentary technological core competencies of MAN's automotive expertise in commercial vehicle manufacture with Rheinmetall's technological know-how in the military land sector/systems field. The result is the creation of a new single source provider for the entire range of armoured and unarmoured transport, command and role-specific wheeled vehicles. Under the terms of the agreement, Rheinmetall will have a stake of 51 per cent and MAN 49 per cent in the new company.

Description

The Steyr 10 M 22 (10 - nominal GVW in tonnes; M - military; 22 - nominal hp (220)) is entirely conventional in design. Its tiltable, all-steel, forward control cab is common throughout the MAN L2000 and M2000 ranges of commercial trucks. Normal configuration is left-hand drive and with seating for the driver and a single passenger. Right-hand drive, a passenger's bench seat, a full-size roof hatch, air conditioning, an auxiliary heater, radio preparation and a self-recovery winch are some of the extensive equipment options that were available. The standard compact cab could be replaced by an optional medium-length cab 300 mm deeper. A version optimised for tropical climates was also available.

The conventional C-section chassis has riveted- and bolted-in tubular cross-members and mounts beam axles sprung by parabolic leaf springs with shock-absorbers and an anti-roll bar. Single or dual rear wheels were available. Wheelbase options of 2.91, 3.26 or 3.56 m were available, 2.91 m with the shorter compact cab only. The rear drive axle is rated at 5,500 kg and fitted with a differential lock as standard. Full-time four-wheel drive and a differential lock for the 4,500 kg rated front steer-drive axle were optional. An Anti-lock Brake System (ABS) with off-road logic was a further option. The service braking system is supplemented by a compressed air actuated engine brake.

Motive power is provided by a MAN six-cylinder 220 hp turbocharged diesel engine coupled to a ZF 6 S 850 six-speed manual gearbox and G1000/2 transfer box. A Steyr VG 750 transfer box with Automatic Drivetrain Management (ADM) could be fitted.

The Steyr 10 M 22 would normally be configured as a drop side cargo truck, but the chassis is capable of accepting a variety of alternatives including a light recovery hamper, shelter or workshop type bodies, or fuel or water tanks. The standard drop side cargo body may be covered by a tarpaulin over bows and the platform is also suitable for mounting weapons such as light air defence guns.

Carrying capacity of the chassis cab is dependant on a number of factors including cab type and wheelbase, but with single rear wheels fitted the maximum carrying capacity is 5,615 kg, this being the 2.91 m wheelbase variant fitted with a compact cab. For all variants, the Gross Vehicle Weight (GVW) is 10,000 kg; Gross Train Weight (GTW) is 24,000 kg.

Specifications

10 M 22
(3.26 m wheelbase, compact cab and single rear wheels)
Cab seating: 1 + 1 or 2
Configuration: 4 × 4
Weight:
  (chassis cab) 4,385 kg
  (GVW) 10,000 kg
  (max load capacity) 5,615 kg
  (towed load, road) 14,000 kg
  (GTW) 24,000 kg
Length overall: 5.717 m
Width:
  (cab) 2.2 m
  (rear wheels) 2.268 m
  (overall) 2.295 m
Height:
  (cab, laden) 2.791 m
  (cab, unladen) 2.858 m
Ground clearance:
  (front axle) 354 mm
  (rear axle) 348 mm
Track: (front/rear) 1.906 m/1.906 m
Wheelbase: 3.26 m
Max speed: (road) 88 km/h
Fuel capacity: 150 litres
Gradient: >60%
Side slope: 30% (approx.)
Fording: ≤750 mm
Engine: MAN Type D0826LFL EURO 2 6.871-litre 6-cylinder in-line exhaust gas turbocharged and intercooled water-cooled direct injection 4-stroke diesel developing 220 hp (164 kW) at 2,400 rpm and 825 N.m torque between 1,400 and 1,700 rpm
Gearbox: ZF 6 S 850 manual, 6 forward and 1 reverse gears
Transfer box: MAN G1000/2 2-speed (options available)
Clutch: single dry plate
Steering: power-assisted, ZF
Turning radius: 7 m
Suspension: parabolic leaf springs with telescopic shock-absorbers and anti-roll bar, front and rear
Tyres: 365/80R 20
Brakes: dual circuit, air, drums all-round. ABS optional
Electrical system: 24 V
Batteries: 2 × 12 V, 88 Ah
Alternator: 28 V, 35 A

Status

Production complete. Replaced in production from around mid-2007 (see text). In service with Portugal (40 approximately, as MAN 10.224 LAEC), UAE (20 approximately, as MAN 10.224 LAEC), Zimbabwe (105) and possibly others.

Contractor

RMMV GmbH
MAN Nutzfahrzeuge Österreichische AG

Steyr 12 S 22 (4 × 2) driver training vehicle

Development

The Austrian Army procured 51 examples of the Steyr 12 S 22 (4 × 2) during 2000, for use in the driver training role. The Steyr 12 S 22 is based on the Steyr/MAN M2000 range of commercial trucks. Full details of the relationship between the MAN and Steyr brands can be found in the Steyr trucks entry elsewhere in this section, but in brief: In January 1990, MAN Nutzfahrzeuge AG of Germany acquired an 85 per cent share of the truck-building activities of Steyr Nutzfahrzeuge AG. In 1993 MAN exercised their option to acquire the remaining 15 per cent share of the business. Steyr Nutzfahrzeuge AG became known as MAN Steyr AG during 2002 and during 2005 as MAN Nutzfahrzeuge Österreich AG.

MAN introduced the TGL and TGM models in 2005 to replace the L2000 and M2000 ranges, with military TGL and TGM variants available from 2006.

In January 2010 it was announced that Rheinmetall's wheeled military vehicle activities would merge with the military activities of MAN with the founding of Rheinmetall MAN Military Vehicles GmbH (RMMV). Essentially this merger units the complimentary technological core competencies of MAN's automotive expertise in commercial vehicle manufacture with Rheinmetall's technological know-how in the military land sector/systems field. The result is the creation of a new single source provider for the entire range of armoured and unarmoured transport, command and role-specific wheeled vehicles. Under the terms of the agreement, Rheinmetall will have a stake of 51 per cent and MAN 49 per cent in the new company.

Description

The Steyr 12 S 22 offers the benefit of a high degree of commonality with other Steyr/MAN L2000, M2000 and F2000 range based trucks in current Austrian Army service, but without the technicalities, complexities and

Steyr 12 S 22 (4 × 2) driver training vehicle of the Austrian Army
(MAN Nutzfahrzeuge Österreichische AG)   0567283

associated running costs of an all-wheel drive tactical military truck. As with all Steyr L2000, M2000 and F2000 range trucks, the designation denotes: 12 - permissible gross weight in tonnes, S (commercial design), 22 - nominal engine power output (220 hp).

The enlarged L2000/M2000 range cab seats six, five trainees plus an instructor, and is fitted with a full set of dual controls for the instructor; steering wheel connected by mechanical chain-drive, plus a full set of foot pedals. Three doors are fitted, a single door on the drivers' side (left-hand), an additional passenger door on the right-hand side giving access to the rear four seating positions.

Specifications

12 S 22
Cab seating: 1 + 5
Configuration: 4 × 2
Weight:
  (GVW) 12,000 kg
  (max front axle load) 4,450 kg
  (max rear axle load) 8,500 kg
Width: 2.5 m
Wheelbase: 4.575 m
Engine: MAN Type D0836LFL EURO 3 6-cylinder in-line turbocharged water-cooled 4-stroke diesel developing 220 hp (164 kW)
Gearbox: Eaton 8309 manual with 9 forward and 1 reverse gears. Dual-control clutch system fitted
Steering: power-assisted, ZF. Dual-control system fitted
Suspension: parabolic leaf springs with telescopic shock-absorbers and anti-roll bar, front; airbags, rear
Tyres: 245/75R 17.5
Brakes: dual circuit, air. Dual-control system fitted
Electrical system: 24 V

Status

Production complete. Any current production would be based on the current TGL/TGM equivalent commercial model. In service with the Austrian Army (51).

Contractor

RMMV GmbH
MAN Nutzfahrzeuge Österreichische AG

Steyr 17 M range of (4 × 4) 7,000 kg trucks

Development

The Steyr 17 M (17 - nominal GVW in tonnes; M - military) (4 × 4) 7,000 kg series of cargo trucks share many common components with the Steyr 24 M (6 × 6) 12,000 kg series of trucks. The 17 M series are extensively militarised commercial designs and were available in a variety of similar versions, all with power outputs ranging from 280 to 320 hp, payloads of around 7,000 kg and GVWs of around 16,000 kg.

In January 1990 MAN Nutzfahrzeuge AG of Germany acquired an 85 per cent share of the truck-building activities of Austria's Steyr Nutzfahrzeuge AG. In 1993 MAN exercised their option to acquire the remaining 15 per cent share of the business. Steyr Nutzfahrzeuge AG became known as MAN Steyr AG during 2002 and is now known as MAN Nutzfahrzeuge Österreichische AG.

As part of the reorganisation and consolidation process, by the late 1990s production of the 17 M and 24 M series had concluded with Switzerland one of the last known customers receiving 250 (17 M) and 60 (24 M) examples during 1997-1998. It is understood that various versions of this series of trucks continue to be produced in China as part of the Hongyan heavy-duty truck range manufactured at the Sichuan Truck Plant, Chongqing.

Steyr 17 M 29 7,000 kg truck (MAN Nutzfahrzeuge Österreichische AG)
1128718

The 17 M series of heavy military trucks was superseded by militarised versions of the MAN F2000 heavy range of commercial trucks. The F2000 range was replaced in production during 2004 by equivalent models based on the heavier models of the current MAN TGA range. Details of the MAN F2000 and TGA ranges can be found elsewhere in this section.

Full details of the relationship between MAN and Steyr can be found in the Steyr trucks or MAN trucks entries elsewhere in this section.

In January 2010 it was announced that Rheinmetall's wheeled military vehicle activities would merge with the military activities of MAN with the founding of Rheinmetall MAN Military Vehicles GmbH (RMMV). Essentially this merger units the complimentary technological core competencies of MAN's automotive expertise in commercial vehicle manufacture with Rheinmetall's technological know-how in the military land sector/systems field. The result is the creation of a new single source provider for the entire range of armoured and unarmoured transport, command and role-specific wheeled vehicles. Under the terms of the agreement, Rheinmetall will have a stake of 51 per cent and MAN 49 per cent in the new company.

Description

The Steyr 17 M (4 × 4) 7,000 kg series of trucks are entirely conventional in design. The forward control cab is of all-steel construction and can be tilted forward at an angle of 70° to allow access to the engine and transmission for maintenance purposes. The driver's suspension seat is adjustable and the cab can be fitted with a single or twin passenger seat. The cab has two doors, observation/machine gun hatch in the roof, heater and a fresh air ventilator.

The chassis consists of a low-distortion parallel ladder frame with bolted tubular cross members. Leaf spring suspension and beam-type axles are employed.

The standard rear cargo area is provided with removable bows, tarpaulin cover, drop tailgate and, down the centre, collapsible seats for 20 fully-equipped troops. Seat benches, bows and the tarpaulin cover can be stowed behind the headboard.

Optional equipment included a winch with a capacity of 10,000 kg and 60 m of cable; alternative engines and transmissions were also available.

The Steyr 17 M has been produced in airfield crash tender form.

Specifications

17 M 29
Cab seating: 1 + 1 or 2
Configuration: 4 × 4
Weight:
(laden) 17,000 kg
(unladen, approx.) 10,000 kg
(weight on front axle, laden) 7,000 kg
(weight on front axle, laden) 10,000 kg
(max load) 7,000 kg
(towed load, on-road) ≤11,500 kg
(towed load, off-road) 10,000 kg
Load area: 5 × 2.43 m
Length: 7.73 m
Width: 2.5 m
Height: (cab platform) 3.246 m
Ground clearance: 370 mm
Track: 2.072 m
Wheelbase: 4.2 m
Angle of approach/departure: 31°/36°
Max speed: (road) 95 km/h
Range: 700 km
Fuel capacity: 320 litres (400 litres optional)
Gradient: (low range) >80%
Sideslope: 30%
Fording: 800 mm (1 m optional)
Engine: Steyr model WD 615.73, 9.726-litre 6-cylinder in-line turbocharged and intercooled water-cooled direct injection 4-stroke diesel developing 287 hp (214 kW) at 2,200 rpm and 1,175 N.m torque at 1,300 rpm

Gearbox: ZF 9 S 109 GP manual with 9 (8 + crawler) forward and 1 reverse gears
Clutch: single dry plate, 420 mm diameter (optional ZF WSK 400 hydraulic torque converter)
Transfer box: Steyr VG 1200 2-speed
Steering: ZF, hydraulic
Turning radius: 9.8 m
Suspension: semi-elliptic springs with telescopic shock-absorbers, front and rear
Tyres: 14.00R × 20
Brakes:
(main) dual circuit, air, drums all-round
(parking) spring energy, air-operated
Electrical system: 24 V
Batteries: 2 × 12 V, 135 Ah

Status

Production complete in Austria. Supplied to numerous countries including Egypt, Ghana, Indonesia (>200), Saudi Arabia and Switzerland (>250). License production continues in China.

Contractor

RMMV GmbH
MAN Nutzfahrzeuge Österreichische AG

Steyr 24 M (6 × 6) 12,000 kg truck series

Development

The Steyr 24 M (24 - nominal GVW in tonnes; M - military) (6 × 6) 12,000 kg series of cargo trucks share many common components with the Steyr 17 M (4 × 4) 7,000 kg series of trucks. The 24 M series are extensively militarised commercial designs and were available in a variety of similar versions, all with power outputs of around 320 hp, payloads of around 12,000 kg and GVWs of around 24,000 kg.

A more powerful 26 M 42 (42 - nominal hp (420)) version for trials in the United Arab Emirates (UAE) and fitted with a Load Handling System (LHS), and a much revised tractor truck version (37 M 42) were also produced.

The Steyr 24 M 32 040/6 × 6 M variant was produced to participate in the Canadian Heavy Logistic Vehicle Wheeled (HLVW) programme. During 1988 the Canadian Department of National Defence ordered 1,200 units to be assembled in Canada by UTDC Inc of Kingston, Ontario. Full details of this vehicle, known as the Percheron, can be found elsewhere in this section.

A military firefighting version of the 24 M series was produced by Hellenic Vehicle Industry SA (ELBO) in Greece. It carries a 5,500-litre water tank and a 700-litre foam tank.

In January 1990 MAN Nutzfahrzeuge AG of Germany acquired an 85 per cent share of the truck-building activities of Austria's Steyr Nutzfahrzeuge AG. In 1993 MAN exercised their option to acquire the remaining 15 per cent share of the business. Steyr Nutzfahrzeuge AG became known as MAN Steyr AG during 2002 and is now known as MAN Nutzfahrzeuge Österreichische AG.

As part of the reorganisation and consolidation process, by the late 1990s production of the 24 M and lighter 17 M series had concluded with Switzerland one of the last known customers receiving 60 (24 M) and 250 (17 M) examples during 1997-1998. It is understood that various versions of this series of trucks continue to be produced in China as part of the Hongyan heavy-duty truck range manufactured at the Sichuan Truck Plant, Chongqing.

The 24 M series of heavy military trucks was superseded by militarised versions of the MAN F2000 heavy range of commercial trucks; in some instances by examples of the FX tactical range. The F2000 range was replaced in production during 2004 by equivalent models based on the heavier models of the current MAN TGA range; the FX range was replaced by the HX range during 2005. Details of the MAN F2000, TGA, FX and HX ranges can be found elsewhere in this section.

Steyr 24 M 32 (6 × 6) 12,000 kg truck (MAN)
1128722

Full details of the relationship between MAN and Steyr can be found in the Steyr trucks or MAN trucks entries elsewhere in this section.

In January 2010 it was announced that Rheinmetall's wheeled military vehicle activities would merge with the military activities of MAN with the founding of Rheinmetall MAN Military Vehicles GmbH (RMMV). Essentially this merger units the complimentary technological core competencies of MAN's automotive expertise in commercial vehicle manufacture with Rheinmetall's technological know-how in the military land sector/systems field. The result is the creation of a new single source provider for the entire range of armoured and unarmoured transport, command and role-specific wheeled vehicles. Under the terms of the agreement, Rheinmetall will have a stake of 51 per cent and MAN 49 per cent in the new company.

Description

The Steyr 24 M (6 × 6) 12,000 kg series of trucks are entirely conventional in design. The forward control cab is of all-steel construction and can be tilted forward at an angle of 70° to allow access to the engine and transmission for maintenance purposes. The driver's suspension seat is adjustable and the cab can be fitted with a single or twin passenger seat. The cab has two doors, observation/machine gun hatch in the roof, heater and a fresh air ventilator.

The chassis consists of a low-distortion parallel ladder frame with bolted tubular cross members. Leaf spring suspension and beam-type axles are employed, the rear two axles are sprung independently. Differential locks are provided for the transfer box and rear axles.

The standard rear cargo area is provided with removable bows, tarpaulin cover, drop tailgate and collapsible seats for 26 troops down the centre. Seat benches, bows and the tarpaulin cover can be stowed behind the headboard.

Optional equipment included a materials handling crane, air-conditioning, modifications for severe off-road operation, and a winch with a capacity of 10,000 kg and 60 m of cable.

Specifications

Steyr 24 M 32
Cab seating: 1 + 1 (or 1 + 2)
Configuration: 6 × 6
Weight:
  (laden, max) 24,000 kg
  (unladen, approx.) 12,000 kg
  (towed load, on/off-road) 15,000 kg
Load area: 6.2 × 2.43 m
Length: 8.92 m
Width: 2.5 m
Height: (cab platform) 3.246 m
Ground clearance: 370 mm
Track: (front) 2.072 m
Wheelbase: 4 m + 1.4 m
Angle of approach/departure: 31°/36°
Max speed: (road) 95 km/h
Range: (approx.) 700 km
Fuel capacity: 400 litres
Max gradient: >80%
Sideslope: 30%
Fording: 800 mm (1 m optional)
Engine: Steyr model WD 815.78, 9.7-litre 6-cylinder in-line turbocharged, boosted air intercooled, water-cooled 4-stroke diesel developing 320 hp (239 kW) at 2,200 rpm and 1,265 N.m torque at 1,300 rpm
Gearbox: ZF 5 S 111 GP manual with 9 forward (8 + 1 crawler) and 1 reverse gears
Clutch: single dry plate, 420 mm diameter, mechanically operated with assistance of compressed air. Optional ZF WSK 400 hydraulic torque converter
Transfer box: Steyr VG1200 2-speed, full-time all-wheel drive with lockable centre differential
Steering: ZF Type 8046, hydraulic
Turning radius: 10.45 m
Suspension: semi-elliptic leaf springs with telescopic shock-absorbers, front and rear; rear axles are sprung independently
Tyres: 14.00R × 20
Brakes:
  (main) dual circuit, air, drums all-round
  (parking) spring energy, air operated operating on rear wheels
Electrical system: 24 V
Batteries: 2 × 12 V, 135 Ah

Status

Austrian, Canadian and Greek SKD/CKD production complete; production is believed to continue in China (see text). In service with numerous countries including Canada, Cyprus, Egypt, Hong Kong (delivered from China), Saudi Arabia and Switzerland (60).

Contractor

RMMV GmbH
MAN Nutzfahrzeuge Österreichische AG

ÖAF Type 20.320 (6 × 6) 10,000 kg truck

Development

The ÖAF Type 20.320 (6 × 6) 10,000 kg truck is a modified version of the German MAN 7,000 kg Kat A1 truck built by the then Österreichische Automobilfabrik ÖAF-Gräf und Stift AG in Vienna, Austria. Modifications included the replacement of the Klockner-Humbolt-Deutz (KHD) engine by a MAN unit, installation of a hydraulic crane and provision for mounting a light machine gun on the roof of the cab. The initial order was for 350 trucks, the first of which was handed over in 1975. Some are employed as Oerlikon Contraves 35 mm GDF series light air defence gun and associated air defence radar tractors.

ÖAF became a subsidiary of MAN in 1936 and in 1970 merged with Gräf und Stift. Following the completion of a period of considerable reorganisation after MAN's acquisition of Star (Poland) in 1998 and Steyr (Austria) in 1993, the former ÖAF plant became known as MAN Sonderfahrzeuge AG (later MAN Nutzfahrzeuge Österreichische AG) and assembles the MAN HX and SX (previously FX and LX, replaced during 2003-2005 by HX) tactical truck ranges, together with the MAN TGA (previously F2000, replaced during 2004 by TGA) heavy commercial truck range. Dependant on market, these trucks may be branded MAN or Steyr, or ÖAF for the Austrian market only. Full details of the relationship between the current MAN and Steyr military truck ranges can be found in the Steyr trucks or MAN trucks entries elsewhere in this section.

In January 2010 it was announced that Rheinmetall's wheeled military vehicle activities would merge with the military activities of MAN with the founding of Rheinmetall MAN Military Vehicles GmbH (RMMV). Essentially this merger units the complimentary technological core competencies of MAN's automotive expertise in commercial vehicle manufacture with Rheinmetall's technological know-how in the military land sector/systems field. The result is the creation of a new single source provider for the entire range of armoured and unarmoured transport, command and role-specific wheeled vehicles. Under the terms of the agreement, Rheinmetall will have a stake of 51 per cent and MAN 49 per cent in the new company.

Description

The chassis of the ÖAF Type 20.320 (6 × 6) 10,000 kg truck is constructed from welded longitudinal box-section strengthened by tubular cross members. An auxiliary frame to the rear of the cab carries the loading crane.

The cab is made of welded sheet steel and is mounted on the chassis by rubber supports. It is divided into two compartments, crew at the front and engine at the rear. Forward-opening doors are fitted left and right and there are seats for three people which can be arranged to provide two couchettes. The centre seat has a 180° vertical movement and serves as a step for the machine gun slew-ring mounted on the roof. The roof has a sliding hatch. The spare wheel is housed in the upper part of the engine compartment and there is a small hoist provided to raise and lower it. The battery box is on the right side of the engine compartment.

The base for the body comprises seven sheet steel cross members bolted firmly to the chassis, the floor of which is 40 mm tongue-and-groove pine. The side and tailboards consist of 25 mm hollow-section aluminium. The front is 1.5 m high and the sides and rear boards 700 mm high. The side boards are divided and removable seats for eight men are fitted to the floor either to the front or rear. If required, a second similar seat-group can be fitted. With only one eight-seater in place there is a load area for 72 ammunition boxes on the floor. The three adjustable bows support the canvas tarpaulin which has windows towards the top.

The vehicle is radio suppressed and a junction for an external current supply is provided. An Eberspeicher independent diesel-driven warm air heating unit is fitted as standard. Mounted to the rear of the cab is a Palfinger PK 7500 loading crane with a capacity of 7,000 kg; this model is known as the Type 20.230/G1. The Type 20.230/G3 uses an alternative Palfinger 17 t/m crane.

The last production version of the Type 20.230 was the Type 20.320/G2 which has a centrally mounted winch with a 7,500 kg capacity front and rear.

ÖAF Type 20.320 (6 × 6) 10,000 kg truck of the Austrian Army (Stefan Marx)
1124719

The ÖAF 20.320/G5 is a special NBC decontamination vehicle carrying special-to-role equipment.

Specifications
ÖAF Type 20.320
Cab seating: 1 + 2
Configuration: 6 × 6
Weight:
(laden, off-road) 22,000 kg
(unladen with crane and winch) 12,500 kg
(max load, off-road) 10,000 kg
Length: 8.85 m
Width: 2.5 m
Height:
(tarpaulin cover) 3.34 m
(cab) 3 m
Ground clearance: 415 mm
Track: 2.07 m
Wheelbase: 3.8 m + 1.4 m
Angle of approach/departure: 42°/38°
Max road speed: 84 km/h
Max range: 700 km
Fuel capacity: 500 litres
Gradient: 60%
Fording: 800 mm
Engine: MAN D 2538 MTX V8 water-cooled 4-stroke diesel developing 320 hp (237 kW) at 2,500 rpm
Gearbox: hydraulic torque converter with lock-up clutch (foot-operated), 6-speed gearbox (6 forward and 1 reverse gears) and 3-axle transfer box with differential lock between front and rear axle drive
Steering: recirculating ball with hydraulic assistance
Turning circle: 19.5 m
Suspension: progressively acting coil springs and hydraulic shock-absorbers
Tyres: 14.00R × 20
Brakes:
(main) air/hydraulic
(parking) mechanical
Electrical system: 24 V

Status
Production complete. In service with the Austrian Army.

Contractor
RMMV GmbH
MAN Nutzfahrzeuge Österreichische AG

Steyr 680 M (4 × 4) and 680 M3 (6 × 6) trucks

Development
The Steyr 680 M is a (4 × 4) cargo truck designed to carry a maximum of 2,500 kg of cargo across country, or 4,500 kg on roads. The Steyr 680 M3 is a (6 × 6) cargo truck designed to carry a maximum of 3,500 kg of cargo across country, or 5,500 kg on roads and is a direct development of the Steyr 680 M, sharing a number of common components including cab and cargo body.

In 1972 Steyr built a production facility in Greece for the manufacture of the 680 M (as the 680 MH) and 680 M3 (as the 680 MH) for the Hellenic Armed Forces, with the bulk of production occurring between 1975 and 1980. Production concluded in 1985, by which time the Greek government had taken ownership of the former Steyr Hellas SA facility. Vehicles produced by Steyr Hellas SA included up to 55 per cent local content.

Steyr 680 M (4 × 4) of the Austrian Army with a standard cargo/troop carrying body (Stefan Marx) 1128717

Steyr 680 M (4 × 4) of the Austrian Army mounting a horse box body (Stefan Marx) 1124721

Steyr 680 M3 (6 × 6) medical vehicle of the Austrian Army (Stefan Marx) 1124720

As of early 2003 an estimated 8,500 Steyr 680 vehicles remained in service with Hellenic Armed Forces with the manufacture and supply of all spare parts for these being undertaken by the Hellenic Vehicle Industry SA (Elliniki Viomikhania Okhimaton - ELBO).

In a statement dated May 2002 the then Minister of National Defence, A Tsohatzopoulos spoke of the award of a contract for the refurbishment of 581 early 680 MH-680 MH3 trucks. This contract was not placed and these trucks have not been refurbished. The intention was for the refurbished vehicles to remain in service alongside later deliveries until the projected bulk fleet replacement began around 2006-2009. The requirement to replace the 680 fleet remains.

Throughout its production run the Steyr 680 was also known to be supplied to Algeria, Austria, Indonesia, Nigeria and Switzerland. Between 1,500 and 2,000 examples are believed to remain in service in Algeria. The Austrian Army ordered 2,000 Steyr 12 M 18 (4 × 4) trucks from 1985 as a partial replacement for their 680 fleet, but as of late 2004 continued to operate around 1,000 680 M and 1,200 680 M3 models. The Swiss Army received around 1,800 680 M models with single rear wheels between 1968 and 1974, a considerable number of these remaining in service.

Description
The forward control all-steel cab seats two and is fixed, being non-tiltable. An observation hatch, heater and fresh air ventilator are standard equipment. Cargo variants are the norm, these being provided with a tarpaulin cover over removable bows, a drop tailgate and collapsible troop seats for up to 20 men along the centreline. The load area measures 4.06 × 2.2 m (L × W).

A 4,500 kg capacity winch with 90 m of 13 mm cable is standard on the 680 M and was fitted to the majority of 680 M3s. Some of the 680 M3 vehicles have a self-loading hydraulic crane mounted behind the cab and some of the Swiss Army 680 M vehicles have a shortened load area and a hydraulic crane mounted on the rear of the chassis.

Dump truck (680 M3 only) and fuel/water tanker variants have been produced, and both models can mount a variety of shelter or box-type bodies.

Specifications

Model	Steyr 680 M (4 × 4)	Steyr 680 M3 (6 × 6)
Cab seating:	1 + 1	1 + 1
Configuration:	4 × 4	6 × 6
Weight:		
(laden, on-road)	11,000 kg	12,000 kg
(laden, off-road)	8,500 kg	10,000 kg

Model	Steyr 680 M (4 × 4)	Steyr 680 M3 (6 × 6)
(unladen)	5,830 kg (inc winch)	6,500 kg
(towed load, on-road)	8,000 kg	4,000 kg
(towed load, off-road)	4,500 kg	4,000 kg
Length:	6.57 m	6.73 m
Width:	2.4 m	2.4 m
Height:		
(cab)	2.63 m	2.63 m
(tarpaulin)	2.85 m	2.85 m
(load bed)	1.16 m	1.16 m
Ground clearance:	300 mm	300 mm
Track:		
(front)	1.81 m	1.81 m
(rear)	1.67 (twin rear wheels)	1.72 m
Wheelbase:	3.7 m	2.76 + 1.2 m
Angle of approach/departure:	28°/28°	28°/32°
Max speed: (road)	80 km/h	80 km/h
Range:	450 km	500 km
Fuel capacity:	160 litres	180 litres
Gradient:	60% (low range at 10,000 kg)	99% (low range at 10,500 kg)
Fording:	800 mm	800 mm
Engine:	Steyr WD 610.23 6-cylinder in-line water-cooled direct injection 4-stroke diesel developing 132 hp (98 kW) at 2,800 rpm	Steyr WD 610.74 6-cylinder in-line supercharged water-cooled direct injection 4-stroke diesel developing 165 hp (123 kW) at 2,800 rpm
Gearbox:	manual with 5 forward and 1 reverse gears	manual with 5 forward and 1 reverse gears
Transfer box:	2-speed	2-speed
Clutch:	single dry plate	single dry plate
Steering:	ZF, hydraulic	ZF, hydraulic
Turning radius:	7.25 m	7.25 m
Suspension:	semi-elliptic leaf springs, front and rear	semi-elliptic leaf springs and telescopic shock-absorbers, front; inverted semi-elliptic leaf springs with reversible spring hangers positioned in middle of rear axles
Tyres:	9.00 × 20	9.00 × 20
Brakes:		
(main)	air-assisted hydraulic	air-assisted hydraulic
(parking)	mechanical	mechanical
Electrical system:	24 V	24 V
Batteries:	2 × 12 V, 110 Ah	2 × 12 V, 110 Ah

Status

Production completed mid-1980s. Supplied to Algeria, Austria, Greece, Indonesia, Nigeria and Switzerland (see text for available details).

Contractor

RMMV GmbH
MAN Nutzfahrzeuge Österreichische AG
Hellenic Vehicle Industry SA

Brazil

ENGESA EE-15 (4 × 4) 1,500 kg truck

Development

The EE-15 (4 × 4) 1,500 kg truck was designed by ENGESA for both civil and military use.

ENGESA was a private company with origins dating back to 1963. The company began by refurbishing old and time-served Brazilian Army vehicles. Ultimately the company would specialise in the production of tactical military light vehicles and trucks, and armoured fighting vehicles. The bankruptcy of ENGESA was declared in October 1993.

ENGESA EE-15 (4 × 4) 1,500 kg truck (ENGESA) 1185454

Description

The EE-15 (4 × 4) 1,500 kg truck has a chassis is of high-tensile steel with cross-members riveted into position. A rear towing hook and four lifting eyes are fitted. The cab has a vinyl top and doors, fold-down windscreen with wipers, adjustable seat for the driver and a seat for two passengers. The standard all-steel cargo body has a tailgate, bows and a tarpaulin cover.

A wide range of optional equipment was available including a body with tilting troop seats, a power take-off and engine starting pilot for cold areas.

ENGESA supplied the EE-15 with other types of body including ambulance, crash tender and van.

Specifications

EE-15
Cab seating: 1 + 2
Configuration: 4 × 4
Weight:
  (laden, road) 7,050 kg
  (laden, off-road) 5,550 kg
  (unladen) 4,050 kg
  (max load, on-road) 3,000 kg
  (max load, off-road) 1,500 kg
  (max towed load) 1,500 kg
  (GCW) 8,550 kg
Length: 5.65 m
Width: 2.25 m
Height:
  (cab) 2.4 m
  (tarpaulin) 2.5 m
Ground clearance: 270 mm
Track: 1.71 m
Wheelbase: 3.3 m
Angle of approach/departure: 42°/35°
Max speed: (road) 80 km/h
Range: 600 km
Fuel capacity: 136 litres
Max gradient: (laden, off-road) 60%
Max side slope: 30%
Fording: 900 mm
Vertical obstacle: 400 mm
Engine: Mercedes-Benz OM-352 5.7-litre 6-cylinder in-line water-cooled 4-stroke diesel developing 130 hp (97 kW) at 2,800 rpm
Gearbox: Mercedes-Benz G-3-60 manual with 5 forward and 1 reverse gears
Transfer box: ENGESA mechanical, 2-speed with constant mesh helical gears, optional front or rear left side PTO
Clutch: single dry disc
Suspension: semi-elliptic leaf springs and double acting hydraulic shock-absorbers, front and rear
Steering: mechanical
Turning radius: 8 m
Tyres: 9.00 × 20-12PR
Brakes:
  (main) air/hydraulic, drums front and rear
  (parking) mechanical acting on transfer box
Electrical system: 24 V
Batteries: 2 × 12 V, 95 Ah

Status

Production complete. Supplied to Angola, Bolivia, Brazil (500 remaining in service), Chile (withdrawn), Colombia, Gabon and other undisclosed countries.

Contractor

ENGESA Engenheiros Especializados S.A.
(This company is no longer trading)

ENGESA EE-25 (6 × 6) 2,500 kg truck

Development
The EE-25 (6 × 6) truck was developed by ENGESA for both civil and military applications.

ENGESA was a private company with origins dating back to 1963. The company began by refurbishing old and time-served Brazilian Army vehicles. Ultimately the company would specialise in the defence (and agriculture) sector, specialising in the production of tactical military light vehicles and trucks, and armoured fighting vehicles. The bankruptcy of ENGESA was declared in October 1993.

Description
The layout of the ENGESA EE-25 (6 × 6) 2,500 kg truck is conventional, with the engine at the front, cab in the centre and the cargo area at the rear. The cab has a vinyl top and doors, fold-down windscreen with wipers, adjustable seat for the driver, and a single seat for two passengers. The all-steel body has a tailgate, bows and a tarpaulin cover. The chassis is of high-tensile steel with cross-members riveted into position; a rear towhook is provided.

With the award of a contract to supply EE-25 trucks to Angola, some modifications to the vehicle were introduced. The main changes were a strengthened chassis and a new body and cab. The engine and transmission remained the same but an air cleaner was introduced to the right-hand side of the bonnet. A 24 V electrical system was incorporated. Vehicles delivered to Angola had a brushguard over the front.

Optional equipment included: a 6 t/m capacity hydraulic crane; a centre or rear-located winch with a 7,500 kg capacity and two drums with 80 m of 16 mm diameter cable; a Power Take-Off (PTO); and an engine start pilot for cold areas. A (4 × 4) model of the EE-25 was also available.

The basic chassis could be used for a variety of roles including ambulance, crash tender, dump truck (4 × 4), recovery, tanker (fuel or water), lubrication vehicle, van (for example, command or workshop) and NBC decontamination truck (4 × 4).

Specifications

EE-25 (6 × 6) model
Cab seating: 1 + 2
Configuration: 6 × 6
Weight:
(laden, road) 12,100 kg
(laden, off-road) 9,600 kg
(unladen) 7,100 kg
(max load, on-road) 5,000 kg
(max load, off-road) 2,500 kg
Length: 6.99 m
Width: 2.25 m
Height:
(cab) 2.5 m
(tarpaulin) 3.1 m
Ground clearance: (axles) 270 mm
Track: 1.78 m
Wheelbase: (front axle to centre of rear axle) 4.2 m
Angle of approach/departure: 46°/50°
Max speed: (road) 80 km/h
Range: 700 km
Fuel capacity: 200 litres
Max gradient: 60%
Max side slope: 30%
Fording: 900 mm
Vertical obstacle: 600 mm
Engine: Mercedes-Benz OM-352A 5.7-litre 6-cylinder in-line water-cooled 4-stroke diesel developing 156 hp (116 kW) at 2,800 rpm
Gearbox: manual with 5 forward and 1 reverse gears
Clutch: single dry disc
Transfer box: ENGESA 2-speed
Steering: hydraulic
Turning radius: 9.5 m

Suspension: semi-elliptic springs with double acting hydraulic shock-absorbers, front; semi-elliptic springs, rear. The rear axle is of the ENGESA Boomerang type with walking beams
Tyres: 11.00 × 20-14 PR
Brakes:
(main) air/hydraulic, drums all-round
(parking) mechanical acting on transfer box
Electrical system: 24 V

Status
Production complete. Supplied to Angola, Bolivia (597 delivered), Brazil (>250 remain in service), Chile (withdrawn), Colombia, Ecuador (24 remain), Gabon, Libya and other undisclosed countries.

Contractor
ENGESA Engenheiros Especializados S.A.
(This company is no longer trading)

ENGESA EE-50 (6 × 6) 5,000 kg truck

Development
The ENGESA EE-50 (6 × 6) 5,000 kg truck was designed to meet the requirements of the Brazilian Army. Following trials with prototypes, it was selected to become the standard 5,000 kg truck of the Brazilian Army in the 1980s. First production vehicles were completed during late 1980.

ENGESA was a private company with origins dating back to 1963. The company began by refurbishing old and time-served Brazilian Army vehicles. Ultimately the company would specialise in the defence (and agriculture) sector, specialising in the production of tactical military light vehicles and trucks, and armoured fighting vehicles. The bankruptcy of ENGESA was declared in October 1993.

Description
The chassis of the ENGESA EE-50 (6 × 6) 5,000 kg truck is made of riveted steel rails and cross-members. The all-steel forward control cab can be tilted forward to allow access to the engine. The windscreen is in two parts, left and right, both hinged at the top and with a windscreen wiper.

The all-steel rear cargo area is provided with lateral tilting troop seats, drop tailgate, removable bows and a tarpaulin cover. Optional equipment included an engine-starting pilot for cold weather and a fire detection and extinguishing system.

The EE-50 could be supplied with a number of types of body including an ambulance, van, fuel tanker, light recovery, water tanker, fire tender and mobile workshop.

Specifications

EE-50
Cab seating: 1 + 1
Configuration: 6 × 6
Weight:
(laden, road) 22,000 kg
(unladen, off-road) 17,000 kg
(unladen) 12,000 kg
(max load, on-road) 10,000 kg
(max load, off-road) 5,000 kg
(max towed load) 6,000 kg
Length: 7.85 m
Width: 2.6 m
Height:
(cab hatch) 3.025 m
(tarpaulin cover) 3.5 m
Ground clearance: 305 mm
Track: 2.1 m
Wheelbase: 4.5 m
Angle of approach/departure: 40°/50°
Max speed: 80 km/h
Range: 700 km

Brazilian Navy ENGESA EE-25 (Cesar Cruz Tantalean)   1185453

ENGESA EE-50 (6 × 6) 5,000 kg truck (ENGESA)   0511749

Fuel capacity: 300 litres
Max gradient: 60%
Max side slope: 30%
Fording: 1.4 m
Vertical obstacle: 600 mm
Engine: Scania D11 6-cylinder in-line water-cooled 4-stroke diesel developing 202 hp (150 kW) at 2,100 rpm
Gearbox: manual with 5 forward and 1 reverse gears
Clutch: single dry plate
Transfer box: mechanical, 2-speed
Suspension:
 (front) leaf springs, front wheels driven by hypoid angular transmission and bevel differential gears
 (rear) leaf springs, ENGESA Boomerang articulated axle with hypoid angular transmission, bevel differential gears and side walking beams with helical gears
Steering: integral hydraulic
Tyres: 14.00 × 20-18PR
Brakes:
 (main) air, drums all-round
 (parking) air, on transfer box output shaft
Electrical system: 24 V

Status

Production complete. Supplied to Angola, Brazil (numbers delivered and status uncertain), and at least one other undisclosed country.

Contractor

ENGESA Engenheiros Especializados S.A.
(This company is no longer trading)

Canada

Bombardier 2½ ton (6 × 6) Medium Logistic Vehicle Wheeled (MLVW)

Development

In 1981 Bombardier Inc was awarded a contract to supply 2,765 license-produced AM General M35 series 2½ ton trucks to replace the Canadian armed forces ageing 2½ ton truck fleet. Deliveries of these, the Medium Logistic Vehicle Wheeled (MLVW), commenced in 1982. The MLVW is also known as the M35 CDN. A total of 2,769 vehicles were delivered.

Following completion of the Canadian order, Bombardier Inc marketed the MLVW in certain other markets but no export sales of the type were made. Bombardier's former Logistic Equipment Division no longer trades and in 2000 and following a withdrawal from service due to corrosion of the wheel assemblies, rectification work on the MLVW fleet and its associated 2,542 trailers was carried out by Western Star Trucks of Kelowna. This work was completed by the Autumn of 2001. Western Star is part of Daimler AG.

When the MLVW entered service in 1982 its projected service life was 15 years. Mid-2006 the Canadian DoD confirmed that a project to acquire new medium-sized trucks (called a Medium Support Vehicle System (MSVS)) for the Canadian Forces and the Reserves was in the initial stages of the procurement process.

The subsequently released MSVS Request For Proposal (RFP) was split to include two vehicle purchases, Militarised Commercial-Off-The-Shelf (MilCOTS) and Standard Military Pattern (SMP).

In January 2009 it was disclosed that Navistar Defense LLC had been awarded the CAD274 million MilCOTS segment of the MSVS requirement, Navistar's primary in-country partner for this award being DEW Engineering. Deliveries of 1,300 trucks in six primary variants commenced in July 2009, and by March 2010 approximately 600 vehicles had been delivered, with final deliveries then scheduled for Autumn 2010. Full details of Navistar's MSVS offering and the full Navistar range of military vehicles can be found elsewhere in this section.

Draft technical specifications for the SMP truck segment of the MSVS requirement first appeared in October 2007, with deliveries then slated to commence in 2008. Extensive delays have ensued and following the eventual issue of a draft Resulting Contract in October 2009, the MSVS SMP RFP is anticipated late-2010/early-2011. The SMP requirement currently calls for up to 1,500 trucks, 150 armour protection systems and 300 companion trailers.

Description

The MLVW is based on the AM General M35 series 2½ ton (6 × 6) truck, full details of which can be found elsewhere in this section. The Bombardier-produced MLVW claimed over 1,500 improvements compared to the standard M35 series, the most significant of which were as follows:

- A Detroit Diesel 8.2-litre V-6 four-stroke diesel engine to replace the petrol unit found in contemporary US M35 series at the time
- An Allison MT-643 4F/1R automatic transmission with lock-up in third and fourth gears
- A new power-assisted steering system
- An improved rear suspension system that allows a greater flexibility when crossing obstacles
- The use of 11.00R 20 super single tyres on all axles
- An improved tyre tread design compared to the traditional bar grip style tread fitted to contemporary US M35 series
- The incorporation of an Explosafe fuel tank
- An insulated cab with improved heating
- An improved dual circuit air-over-hydraulic braking system.

Three variants of the MLVW were produced: the M35 CDN, the M36 CDN and the M36C CDN. Unlike the US M35 series, the longer wheelbase M36 vehicles do not have a longer cargo/troop body, the additional behind-cab space being used to mount storage bins or specialist equipment. The standard cargo/troop body measures 3.73 × 2.24 m (L × W). All three models were available with or without front-mounted winches. Production totals were as follows:

- M35 CDN: 618 w/winch, 1,832 wo/winch
- M36 CDN: 66 w/winch, 72 wo/winch
- M36C CDN: 119 w/winch, 62 wo/winch.

An add-on protection kit has been developed for the MLVW. The Canadian Forces (CF) introduced Add-on Armour (AoA) in the mid-1990s for soft-skin vehicles serving in Bosnia-Herzegovina. The armour was of a composite design fabricated by DEW Engineering, providing both ballistic and mine blast protection. Since then, over 600 AoA kits have been produced for legacy CF vehicles including the MLVW. With regard to AoA, Canadian Army policy is that local installations, or in-theatre modifications are not permitted.

Specifications

M35 CDN
(unless stated)
Cab seating: 1 + 2
Weight:
 (GVW, road, M35 CDN) 11,320 kg
 (GVW, road, M36 CDN) 11,650 kg
 (GVW, road, M36C CDN) 11,190 kg
 (unladen, road, M35 CDN) 6,320 kg
 (unladen, road, M36 CDN) 6,650 kg
 (unladen, road, M36C CDN) 7,780 kg
 (GVW, off-road, M35 CDN) 8,590 kg
 (GVW, off-road, M36 CDN) 8,920 kg
 (GVW, off-road, M36C CDN) 8,920 kg

Canadian Army Medium Logistic Vehicle Wheeled (MLVW)
(Canadian DND)   1391376

Canadian Army Medium Logistic Vehicle Wheeled (MLVW) photographed in the former Yugoslavia. The vehicle is in the standard troop/cargo carrying configuration and towing a single-axle water bowser trailer
(Richard Stickland)   1047350

(GCW, road, M35 CDN) 15,856 kg
(GCW, road, M36 CDN) 16,186 kg
(GCW, road, M36C CDN) 15,726 kg
(GCW, off-road, M35 CDN) 11,310 kg
(GCW, off-road, M36 CDN) 11,640 kg
(GCW, off-road, M36C CDN) 11,640 kg
(rated payload, road, M35 CDN) 5,000 kg
(rated payload, road, M36 CDN) 5,000 kg
(rated payload, road, M36C CDN) 3,410 kg
(rated payload, off-road, M35 CDN) 2,270 kg
(rated payload, off-road, M36 CDN) 2,270 kg
(rated payload, off-road, M36C CDN) 1,140 kg
(towed load, road) 4,536 kg
(towed load, off-road) 2,720 kg
Length: 6.172 m
Width: 2.483 m
Height:
(unladen) 3.188 m
(load bed) 850 mm
Ground clearance: 320 mm
Track:
(front) 1.7 m
(rear) 1.7 m
Wheelbase: 3.912 + 1.219 m
Max speed: 90 km/h
Max range:
(laden) 480 km
(unladen) 536 km
Fuel capacity: 177 litres
Max gradient: 60%
Engine: Detroit Diesel 4087-7101 8.2-litre V-6 water-cooled 4-stroke diesel developing 165 hp (123 kW) at 3,000 rpm
Gearbox: Allison MT-643 automatic with 4 forward and 1 reverse gears
Transfer box: 2-speed
Steering: power assisted recirculating ball
Suspension: semi-elliptic leaf springs all-round
Tyres: 11.00R 20
Brakes:
(main) dual circuit, air-over-hydraulic, drums all-round
(parking) mechanical
Electrical system: 24 V
Batteries: 4
Alternator: 60 A

Status
Production complete. In service with the Canadian Armed Forces (2,769 delivered). A replacement programme is currently underway running (see text).

Contractor
Bombardier Inc, Logistic Equipment Division

Percheron (6 × 6) 10,000 kg truck Heavy Logistic Vehicle Wheeled (HLVW)

Development
In March 1988, the Canadian Department of National Defence (DND) signed a contract with UTDC Inc of Kingston, Ontario to produce the Heavy Logistic Vehicle Wheeled (HLVW) for the Canadian Forces. Production was completed in November 1991 after 1,212 units had been delivered. Eighty-nine dedicated two-axle dolly-type trailers were also procured. According to the Canadian DND the Percheron entered service from 1992.

The UTDC submission was an Austrian vehicle, the Steyr 1491.6 × 6 M; full details of which can be found elsewhere in this section. The HLVW is based on the Steyr 1491.310/040/6 × 6 M and in Canadian service is known as the Percheron.

An add-on protection kit has been developed for the HLVW. The Canadian Forces (CF) introduced Add-on Armour (AoA) in the mid-1990s for soft-skin vehicles serving in Bosnia-Herzegovina. The armour was of a composite design fabricated by DEW Engineering, providing both ballistic and mine blast protection. Since then, over 600 AoA kits have been produced for legacy CF vehicles including the HLVW. With regard to AoA, Canadian Army policy is that local installations, or in-theatre modifications are not permitted.

For operations in Afghanistan, the Canadian Department of Defense disclosed in mid-2007 that it had awarded the then DaimlerChrysler AG an approx. CAD87 million contract for 82 Mercedes-Benz Actros (8 × 8) Armored Heavy Support Vehicle System (AHSVS) trucks for use on deployed operations. Deliveries were scheduled to commence late 2007, with final deliveries scheduled for March 2008.

With the exception of 15 vehicles retained in Canada for training purposes, the AHSVS fleet is used by Canadian Forces deployed on operations in Afghanistan where they have replaced Steyr-based Heavy Logistics Vehicle Wheeled (HLVW) trucks that are now considered unsuitable for a variety of reasons, such as the inability to accept the required level of blast and ballistic protection.

A further 13 AHSVS have since been ordered as a contract option.

Percheron (6 × 6) 10,000 kg truck Heavy Logistic Vehicle Wheeled (HLVW) Heavy Mobile Repair Team (HMRT) variant in Afghanistan (Carl Schulze)
1391203

The Canadian DND's Logistics Vehicle Modernization project, which includes light and heavy support vehicles (which include the HLVW), is currently in the identification phase. The Army project staff are currently identifying the capabilities of the current fleet and what requirements will be needed for the future combat logistics support vehicles.

Description
The Percheron differs from the original Steyr vehicle in several respects. These include a camouflage net storage space behind the cab, cold weather start capability to allow starting at –40°C, brush guard, cargo bay walkway and a radio installation kit.

Originally there were eight variants of the basic Percheron, produced in the following numbers:
- Basic cargo - 276
- Basic cargo with winch - 147
- Basic cargo with winch and crane - 388
- Recovery - 124
- Tractor - 46
- Dumper - 25
- Bridge transport/flatrack system - 176
- Heavy Mobile Repair Team - 18.

The three cargo variants are essentially similar and have drop sides and a rear tailgate. The version with the material-handling crane has its cargo area reduced in length from 6 to 5 m.

The recovery variant is a combination of the Vulcan recovery unit and the Pitman PK 19000 material-handling crane, forming an integrated system. The Vulcan recovery unit consists of a heavy-duty hydraulic lift and carry system at the rear together with two stabilising and anchoring legs. There is also a recovery winch with a capacity of 25,000 kg. A special bogie-type suspension is used with this variant.

The dumper has a three-way tipper body with a capacity of 8,500 kg.

The tractor can tow loads of up to 25,000 kg with a 12,000 kg fifth-wheel capacity. The rear suspension is of the bogie type.

The bridge transporter is used to carry Ribbon Bridge components and is equipped with a modified Multilift Mark 4 (now designated MPH 165) Load-Handling System (LHS) carrying a Bridge Adaptor Pallet (BAP) weighing 1,600 kg. This system can also be used to carry cargo flatracks.

The Heavy Mobile Repair Team (HMRT) vehicle is used to provide forward maintenance support for the Canadian Forces' Leopard C1 MBT and M109 155 mm self-propelled howitzer units. A Pitman PK 19000

Basic cargo version of the Heavy Logistic Vehicle Wheeled (HLVW), the Percheron (Shaun C Connors)
0121829

material-handling crane is mounted at the rear. This crane has a lifting capacity of 19,000 kg and can lift a Leopard C1 engine pack. The HMRT can carry major assemblies and also carries a workshop area.

The Canadian Department of National Defense currently lists 11 variants of the HLVW: cargo, cargo with material handling crane, recovery, tractor, bridge transporter/flatrack, Heavy Mobile Repair Team, refueller 10,000 litres, air-refueller 7,000 litres, pallet loading system 16,000 kg, water tanker 8,500 litres.

Specifications
Percheron HLVW
Cab seating: 1 + 2
Configuration: 6 × 6
Weight:
  (laden) 22,000 kg
  (unladen) 9,700 kg
  (max load, without winch) 10,000 kg
  (max load, with winch) 9,600 kg
Length: 9.12 m
Width: 2.5 m
Height: (cab roof) 3.025 m
Ground clearance: 370 mm
Track: 2.072 m
Wheelbase: 4 m + 1.4 m
Angle of approach/departure: 31°/35°
Max speed: 95 km/h
Range:
  (laden) 550 km
  (unladen) 700 km
Fuel capacity: 400 litres
Max gradient: 100%
Fording: 800 mm
Engine: Steyr model WD 615.98 m 9.7-litre 6-cylinder in-line turbocharged and intercooled water-cooled 4-stroke direct injection diesel developing 306 hp (228 kW) at 2,300 rpm
Transmission: ZF WSK 400 +4 S 150 GP hydrodynamic torque converter with single dry disc, synchromesh gearbox with 8 forward and 1 reverse gears
Transfer box: Steyr VG1200 2-speed
Steering: hydraulic power assisted, ZF 80 46
Turning radius: 10.5 m
Suspension: semi-elliptic leaf springs with double acting hydraulic shock-absorbers
Tyres: 1400R 20
Brakes:
  (main) dual circuit, air, drums all-round
  (parking) spring-loaded on both rear axles
Electrical system: 24 V
Batteries: 4 × 12 V, 100 Ah

Status
Production complete. In service with Canadian Armed Forces (1,212 delivered).

Contractor
UTDC Inc
(This company is no longer trading.)

Western Star M 1500 1,500 kg (4 × 4) Light Support Vehicle Wheeled (LSVW)

Development
In March 1992, Western Star Trucks Inc of Kelowna, British Columbia, was awarded the contract (valued in 1993 at CAD250 million) for a new Light Support Vehicle Wheeled (LSVW) to replace Chevrolet 1¼ ton (4 × 4) vehicles then in service. The competitor for this contract was the Mercedes-Benz Unimog, Germany's Mercedes-Benz being partnered with Freightliner for the competition.

Following Canadian trials covering 250,000 km, LSVW fielding started in March 1994 and by October 1995 2,815 Western Star M 1500 (4 × 4) LSVW vehicles in 46 different configurations had been delivered, along with a full Logistics Support Analysis (LSA) and Integrated Logistic Support (ILS) deliverables.

Western Star Trucks Inc. were acquired by the now Daimler AG subsidiary, Freightliner LLC, in July 2000. Western Star's Kelowna truck plant and headquarters closed in September 2002, with production transferring to Freightliner's production plant in Portland, Oregon. From 2007 Freightliner LLC has been known as Daimler Trucks North America LLC; the Freightliner brand is retained.

The LSVW has not been offered for purchase for a number of years.

The Canadian DND's Logistics Vehicle Modernization project, which includes light and heavy support vehicles (which include the LSVW), is currently in the identification phase. The Army project staff are currently identifying the capabilities of the current fleet and what requirements will be needed for the future combat logistics support vehicles.

Description
The Western Star M 1500 LSVW is based on the IVECO 40.10 WM, modified to incorporate a higher power engine, a longer wheelbase and an automatic transmission. The LSVW is a high-mobility 1,500 kg payload vehicle powered by a 2.5-litre turbocharged and intercooled IVECO FIAT diesel engine producing 116 hp, coupled to a four-speed automatic transmission and a Borg Warner transfer box delivering power to the front and rear axles. A front independent suspension coupled with leaf springs at the rear provide good ground clearance and mobility with a full payload.

The semi-forward control hardtop cab can have two- or three-man configurations and is provided with three seatbelt anchor points and a centralised electrical system.

The M 1500 LSVW met all Canadian Motor Vehicle Safety Standards at the time of its production. As the standard operating temperature range is −40 to +49°C, all vehicles are equipped with a fuel-fired coolant heater mounted in the On-Vehicle Equipment (OVE) module, located behind the cab. All bodies are attached to the frame through six flexible mounts and can be heated via a heat exchanger mounted in the on-vehicle equipment that facilitates rapid body interchange. A soft-top cab is also available and has been provided. The three basic body variations are cargo, a multipurpose van body and utility, upon which are based troop carriers, an ambulance, a communications vehicle, a cable layer, shelter carriers, mobile workshops and other bodies. The LSVW can be fitted with a mid-mounted front-pull winch.

An add-on protection kit has been developed for the LSVW. The Canadian Forces (CF) introduced Add-on Armour (AoA) in the mid-1990s for soft-skin vehicles serving in Bosnia-Herzegovina. The armour was of a composite design fabricated by DEW Engineering, providing both ballistic and mine blast protection. Since then, over 600 AoA kits have been produced for legacy CF vehicles including the LSVW. With regard to AoA, Canadian Army policy is that local installations, or in-theatre modifications are not permitted.

Specifications
M 1500 LSVW
Cab seating: 1 + 1 or 2
Configuration: 4 × 4
Weight:
  (GVW) 5,250 kg
  (payload) 1,500 kg
  (towed load) 1,650 kg
Length: (overall) 5.61 m
Width: (overall) 2.01 m

Western Star M 1500 1,500 kg (4 × 4) Light Support Vehicle Wheeled (LSVW) with shelter-type rear body (Richard Stickland)   1047351

Western Star M 1500 1,500 kg (4 × 4) Light Support Vehicle Wheeled (LSVW) with a DEW Engineering-supplied Add-on Armour (AoA) kit fitted (Richard Stickland)   0009608

Height:
   (overall) 2.579 m
   (cab) 2.2 m
Ground clearance: 280 mm
Track: 1.67 m
Wheelbase: 3.2 m
Angle of approach/departure: 40°/30°
Fuel capacity: (per tank) 90 litres
Max speed: (road) 100 km/h
Gradient: 60%
Fording: (unprepared) 700 mm
Engine: IVECO FIAT 8142-47-1811 2.5-litre turbocharged and intercooled water-cooled 4-stroke diesel developing 116 hp (87 kW) at 2,200 rpm
Transmission: ZF 4HP 220 automatic with torque converter giving 4 forward and 1 reverse gears
Transfer box: Borg Warner 2-speed
Suspension: independent; front, leaf springs, rear
Tyres: Michelin 9.00 × 16
Electrical system: 24 V
Alternator: 110 A

Status
Production complete. In service with Canadian Armed Forces.

Contractor
The original contractor was Western Star Trucks Inc., now no longer trading (see text)

Enquiries to
Daimler Trucks North America LLC

Western Star M4866S (6 × 6) Heavy Engineering Support Vehicle (HESV)

Development
The Western Star M4866S (6 × 6) Heavy Engineering Support Vehicle (HESV) is a high-mobility (6 × 6) truck with a payload of 15,000 kg and a Gross Combination Weight (GCW) of 63,500 kg - on-road. It is derived from the 4800 model series, having similar bonnet, cab and engine installation arrangements, but has a sleeper/storage compartment option provided immediately behind the cab. The wheelbase is increased to 6.3 m, and the frame features heavy-duty deep double-channel rails with oversized cross-members and an extreme duty rear air suspension subframe.

Fifty-four of these vehicles were delivered to the Canadian Department of National Defense in 1996/97 and fielded in three variant configurations: a Pallet Loading System (PLS) with multirole capability (demountable rear tipping 6.8 to 10.2 m³ dump module, 20 ft/6.096 m ISO container transporter, Ribbon Bridge bay carrier/launcher, NATO flatrack carrier including self-containing modules such as a radar station, fuel/water bowser/pump unit and so on); a dedicated three-way tipping 7.2 to 10.3 m³ dump body with removable sides for dual use as a general purpose cargo carrier; and a tractor for fifth wheel semi-trailer or pintle hook trailer operations.

A further 11 vehicles were delivered during 2000-2002, and between 2002-2004 a further 30 vehicles based on the successor M4900SA chassis were delivered.

Western Star Trucks Inc. were acquired by the now Daimler AG subsidiary, Freightliner LLC, in July 2000. Western Star's Kelowna truck plant and headquarters closed in September 2002, with production transferring to Freightliner's production plant in Portland, Oregon. From 2007 Freightliner LLC has been known as Daimler Trucks North America LLC; the Freightliner brand is retained.

Western Star M4866S (6 × 6) Heavy Engineering Support Vehicle (HESV) with PLS flatrack (Western Star)   0009611

Western Star M4866S (6 × 6) Heavy Engineering Support Vehicle (HESV) with demountable dump module (Western Star)   0009612

Description
The cab is air suspended on the chassis frame and the driver and co-driver seats are of the high-back air ride type to reduce crew fatigue and stress during prolonged off-road operations.

Motive power is provided by a Caterpillar C12 full electronic control 12-litre, 410 hp turbocharged diesel with a three-stage Jacobs brake. This drives through an Allison HD4560P five-speed automatic transmission and Fabco two-speed transfer box with air-shift high/low/neutral selection.

The drive train features driver-select full locking Meritor axles with a rear tandem inter-axle differential lock. The front steer-drive axle is rated at 9,525 kg and sprung by the combination of semi-elliptic leaf springs and heavy duty double acting shock-absorbers, the rear single reduction drive axle pair is rated at 20,865 kg and sprung by a Neway AD246 air suspension system with instant response self-levelling ride height control valves and heavy duty double acting shock-absorbers. The airbrake system incorporates a four-channel Wabco ABS, electronically interfaced to the engine and transmission.

The vehicle is fully rated from −40 to +40°C with automatic cold start ether injection, a 40,000 BTU diesel-fired coolant heater, a thermostatically controlled in-tank fuel heater, cab air conditioning, and severe duty engine, transmission and transfer case cooling packages. The engine, transmission and ABS all feature onboard diagnostics with a common ProLink interface for stored data download, programming, fault code interrogation, and real-time datalink.

Post-production options include ballistic and mine protection kits, and a Central Tyre Inflation (CTI) system.

Specifications
M4866S HESV
Cab seating: 1 + 1
Configuration: 6 × 6
Weight:
   (kerb) 15,360 kg
   (GVW) 30,418 kg
   (GCW) 63,500 kg
Length: 10.05 m
Width: (with 395/85R 20 tyres) 2.59 m
Height:
   (overall, unladen) 3.29 m
   (laden with 8 ft 6 in ISO container) 4.25 m
   (5th wheel) 1.37 m
Track: 2.591 m
Wheelbase: 6.3 m
Max speed: 108 km/h
Range: (cruising) 700 km
Fuel capacity: 454 litres
Gradient:
   (at GVW) 60%
   (at GCW) 30%
Fording: (unprepared) 800 mm
Engine: Caterpillar C12 12- litre 6-cylinder in-line full electronic control turbocharged water-cooled 4-stroke diesel developing 410 hp (306 kW) at 1,800 rpm and 1,967 N.m torque at 1,300 rpm
Transmission: Allison HD 4560P electronic automatic with 5 forward and 1 reverse gears
Transfer case: Fabco 270, 2-speed
Steering: hydraulically assisted, dual gear
Turning radius: 13.4 m
Suspension: semi-elliptic leaf springs with heavy duty double-acting shock-absorbers, front; Neway AD246 air suspension system with instant response self-levelling ride height control valves and heavy duty double-acting shock-absorbers, rear
Tyres: standard, 395/85R 20
Brakes: dual circuit, air, ABS (4-channel)
Electrical system: 24 V (12 V optional)
Alternator: 110 Ah

Status
Production of current model as required. In service with the Canadian Department of National Defense.

Contractor
The original contractor was Western Star Trucks Inc., no longer trading (see text)

Enquiries to
Daimler Trucks North America LLC

China

Jiefang CA-30 (6 × 6) 2,500 kg truck

Development
The Jiefang CA-30 (6 × 6) 2,500 kg truck entered production at the First Automobile Works, Changchun, in 1959, with serial production commencing in 1964. The CA-30 which was based on the Russian Zil-157 was the standard vehicle in its class in the People's Liberation Army, however, the type has been superseded by the Dong Feng EQ240/245 series, full details of which can be found elsewhere in this section.

Production of the CA-30 ceased in 1986, although the type remained in widespread use with the PLA into the early 1990s. By 2003 it was reported that only small numbers, primarily in shelter configuration, remained in service.

Description
Being based on the Russian Zil-157, the CA-30 is very similar to this vehicle in overall appearance, but does have a slightly different cab, with the headlamps sometimes in the mudguards rather than mounted externally as on the ZiL-157.

The layout of the vehicle is conventional, with the engine at the front, two-door fully enclosed cab in the centre and at the rear the cargo area, which consists of a wooden platform with sides, bench seats down each side which can be folded up when the vehicle is carrying cargo, and a drop tailgate. If required, the vehicle can be fitted with bows and a tarpaulin cover.

In addition to a troop carrying/cargo role, the CA-30 has been used for a number of military roles including that of tanker, dump truck, crane and artillery tractor. Additionally, this type has been used as the chassis for a number of weapon systems including multiple 122 mm rocket launchers, an example of which would be the Type 74 Minelaying Rocket System.

Specifications
Cab seating: 1 + 2
Configuration: 6 × 6
Weight:
(laden, road) 9,950 kg
(laden, off-road) 7,950 kg
(unladen) 5,450 kg
(on front axle, unladen) 2,360 kg
(on rear bogie, unladen) 3,090 kg
(max load, on-road) 4,500 kg
(max load, off-road) 2,500 kg
(towed load, off-road) 3,600 kg
Load area: 3.57 × 1.8 m
Length: 6.684 m
Width: 2.315 m
Height: (cab) 2.36 m
Ground clearance: 305 mm
Track: (front and rear) 1.752 m

Jiefang CA-30 (6 × 6) 2,500 kg truck with winch and with box body for use in command post role (Christopher F Foss) 0511750

Wheelbase: (first axle to centre of rear bogie) 4.785 m
Max speed: (road) 65 km/h
Range: 680 km
Fuel capacity: 150 litres
Max gradient: 30%
Fording: 850 mm
Engine: Chieh'Fang 120 6-cylinder water-cooled petrol developing 95 hp (71 kW) at 2,800 rpm
Gearbox: manual with 5 forward and 1 reverse gears
Transfer box: 2-speed
Clutch: single dry plate
Turning radius: 12.1 m
Suspension: leaf springs on all axles
Tyres: 12.00 × 18
Brakes:
(main) air, drums all-round
(parking) mechanical
Electrical system: 12 V

Status
Production complete. Small numbers remain in service with the People's Liberation Army (PLA). Possibly exported.

Contractor
First Automobile Works

Enquiries to
China First Automobile Group Import and Export Corporation (CFAGIEC)

Chongqing Tiema Automobile Corporation/Baotou Bei Ben Heavy Duty Truck Co. Ltd. (North-Benz) ranges of trucks

Development
China produces similar ranges of trucks based on Mercedes-Benz technology and components at two different facilities. These trucks are produced by Chongqing Tiema Industries Corporation and Baotou Bei Ben Heavy Duty Truck Co. Ltd.

These trucks have been promoted for export by NORINCO, this concern being one of seven joint owners of the current Baotou Bei Ben Heavy Duty Truck Co. Ltd.

As with many things Chinese, the history and evolution of these trucks is somewhat cloudy in places and these two manufacturing operations are now understood to have connections.

Chongqing Tiema Industries Corporation (originally Chongqing-based 256 Factory) began development of the TMSC2030 (later renamed Tiema XC2030) heavy duty 8,000 kg truck in the early 1980s. The XC2030 design is based on the Mercedes-Benz 2026 (6 × 6) truck, China having imported some examples of this truck in the late 1970s for military and oil industry uses.

Negotiations between China and Mercedes-Benz for localisation of the product are understood to have lasted for a number of years, but ultimately proved fruitless. As an alternative solution, China decided to copy the truck by reverse-engineering it. The first prototype rolled out in 1982, with volume production commencing in 1986, at around 2,000 trucks per year.

It is understood that the XC2030 is powered by a Deutz air-cooled diesel engine coupled to a ZF manual gearbox with nine forward and one reverse gears. Maximum laden weight is 20,000 kg, this giving an on-road payload of 9,000 kg, an off-road payload of 8,000 kg.

In 2003, Chongqing Tiema was 'acquired' by Baotou North-Benz (now Baotou Bei Ben) Heavy Duty Truck Co. Ltd.

The now Baotou Bei Ben Heavy Duty Truck Co. Ltd. was formed as a joint venture between the then Daimler-Benz and Inner Mongolia First Machinery Group Corporation (FIRMACO) in 1988. The company has been producing a range of heavy and special-purpose trucks under the North-Benz brand since 1995, using the Mercedes-Benz truck technology transferred under the joint venture agreement.

Tiema XC2030) heavy duty 8,000 kg truck 1391093

Tiema XC2030) heavy duty 8,000 kg truck 1391100

Early variants of the North-Benz truck are understood to have relied on some German-made parts, however, following the end of the co-production agreement with the then DaimlerChrysler in 2003, Baotou Bei Ben continued to build the truck with 100 per cent Chinese-made parts.

Baotou Bei Ben has been producing the North-Benz series military trucks in the (4 × 4) (6 × 6) and (8 × 8) configurations, offering payload capacities from 5-tonnes to around 15-tonnes. The truck manufacturing facility in Baotou reportedly has the capacity to build over 6,000 trucks per annum, however, the annual production rate is understood to be much lower.

The Chongqing Tiema/Baotou Bei Ben product is used by the PLA primarily as an artillery tractor and engineering equipment transport. Export sales of Chongqing Tiema products have been made to Indonesia, Pakistan, Sri-Lanka and Thailand, although it is not confirmed these involved trucks for military applications. No military export sales of Baotou Bei Ben products are known of.

Status
In production. In service with the PLA and other undisclosed countries that may include Indonesia, Pakistan, Sri-Lanka and Thailand.

Contractor
Baotou Bei Ben Heavy-Duty Truck Co Ltd
Chongqing Tiema Industries Corporation

Dong Feng EQ2061E (4 × 4) 1,500 kg truck

Development
The Dong Feng (export name Aeolus) EQ2061E (4 × 4) 1,500 kg truck is the latest model in the EQ2081E (6 × 6) range, full details of which can be found elsewhere in this section.

The Dong Feng Motor Corporation was originally known as the Second Automobile Works. The Second Automobile Works was established in the early 1970s by relocating part of the facilities and technicians of the First Automobile Works (FAW) to the rural area in the Hubei Province. Dong Feng is now one of China's largest automotive manufacturers.

Description
Compared to the EQ2081E (6 × 6) truck the main changes are the removal of the rear axle, plus alterations to the transfer box gear ratios and to the rear suspension. The engine continues to be the same EQ6100-1B petrol unit as that on the EQ2081E. The EQ2061E is a right-hand drive vehicle intended for operations in mountainous areas and over rough roads and tracks.

Layout is conventional, with the engine forward, the steel cab seating the driver and two passengers, and the load area to the rear. The cargo body has a steel and wood floor, steel side racks and a tailgate. Optional extras include a power take-off and a 4,500 kg winch mounted behind the front bumper.

Specifications
Cab seating: 1 + 2
Configuration: 4 × 4
Weight:
  (laden, road) 6,350 kg
  (laden, off-road) 6,100 kg
  (unladen) 4,390 kg
  (max load, on-road) 1,750 kg
  (max load, off-road) 1,500 kg
  (towed load) 1,500 kg
Load area: 2.6 × 2.18 m
Length: 5.662 m
Width: 2.4 m

Dong Feng EQ2061E (4 × 4) 1,500 kg truck (Dong Feng) 0009613

Height:
  (cab, unladen) 2.4 m
  (tarpaulin) 2.996 m
Ground clearance: 286 mm
Track: 1.774 m
Wheelbase: 3.4 m
Angle of approach/departure: 45°/44°
Max speed: 88 km/h
Gradient:
  (1,500 kg payload) 60%
  (2,000 kg payload) >40%
Fording: 850 mm
Trench: 700 mm
Ditch crossing: 400 mm
Engine: EQ6100-1B 6-cylinder OHV in-line water-cooled petrol developing 135 hp (101 kW) at 3,000 rpm and 353 N.m torque at 1,300 rpm
Gearbox: manual with 5 forward and 1 reverse gears
Transfer box: 2-speed
Clutch: single dry disc (325 mm)
Turning radius: 7.5 m
Tyres: 11.00 × 18
Brakes: air, split circuit, drums front and rear

Status
In production. In service with Thailand, probably the People's Liberation Army (PLA) and possibly other undisclosed countries.

Contractor
Dong Feng Motor Industry

Enquiries to
Dong Feng Motor Industry Import & Export Corporation (DFMIEC)

Dong Feng EQ2080E (6 × 6) 2,500 kg truck series

Development
The Dong Feng (export name Aeolus) EQ2080E (6 × 6) 2,500 kg series truck are a diesel-powered variant of the earlier Dong Feng EQ240 (later known as the EQ2081) series of trucks that first entered service with the PLA in 1974. The EQ240 was Dong Feng's first product.

The designation of the EQ240 series changed to EQ2081 in the 1990s with the introduction of the new motor vehicle designation system.

The Dong Feng EQ2080/2081, together with the larger but visually similar EQ2100, are currently one of the most numerous troop carrying/cargo truck in service with the PLA. The EQ2080/2081 is the 2,500 kg class chassis for workshop shelters in service with the air force and navy.

According to the manufacturer, the EQ2080 is intended for operations in mountainous areas and over rough roads and tracks.

The Dong Feng EQ2080E appears to be referred to as the EQ2082E by some sources.

The EQ2082E6D is an improved model introduced in 2000 and powered by a Cummins 6BT5.9 5.9-litre turbocharged diesel engine.

To replace a selection of US-built M35 series and Russian-built Ural 375 trucks, Peru received in excess of 400 trucks from Dong Feng between 1995-1998 carrying the designation EQ2082E. Another 200 EQ2080/EQ2081 trucks are reported to have been delivered during 2005.

The Dong Feng Motor Corporation was originally known as the Second Automobile Works. The Second Automobile Works was established in the early 1970s by relocating part of the facilities and technicians of the First Automobile Works (FAW) to the rural area in the Hubei Province. Dong Feng is now one of China's largest automotive manufacturers.

Description
The layout of the EQ2080E is entirely conventional, with the engine forward, the steel cab seating the driver and two passengers, and the load area to the rear. A conventional C-section chassis is used, with beam-type axles sprung by leaf spring suspension.

Dong Feng EQ2080E4D (6 × 6) 2,500 kg truck (Dong Feng) 0116268

The standard cargo body of the EQ2080E has a steel and wood floor, steel side racks and a tailgate. Body options are stated to include dump, tanker and crane. Optional equipment includes a power take-off and a 4,500 kg winch mounted behind the front bumper.

Variants

EQ2081
The EQ2081 is the design on which the diesel-powered EQ2080 series is based on. The EQ2081 series (originally known as the EQ240 series) are powered by a selection of petrol engines. The EQ2080 (previously known as the EQ240) is fitted with an EQ6100 petrol engine, while the improved EQ2081E, which was introduced in the 1990s, is fitted with an EQ6100-1B petrol engine. Full details of the EQ2081 series can be found elsewhere in this section.

EQ245/EQ2100/EQ2100E6D
The now EQ2100 series is a 3,500 kg payload class troop carrying/cargo truck, slightly larger than, but visually similar to, the EQ2081 series. Full details of the EQ2100 series can be found elsewhere in this section.

EQ2061E
The EQ2061E is a 1,500 kg (4 × 4) payload class troop carrying/cargo truck derived from the EQ2081. Full details of the EQ2061E can be found elsewhere in this section.

Specifications

EQ2080E
Cab seating: 1 + 2
Configuration: 6 × 6
Weight:
(laden, road) 9,300 kg
(laden, off-road) 7,800 kg
(unladen, without winch) 5,090 kg
(unladen, with winch) 5,310 kg
(max load, on-road) 4,000 kg
(max load, off-road) 2,500 kg
(towed load) 2,500 kg
Load area: 3.545 × 2.18 m
Length:
(with winch) 6.53 m
(without winch) 6.34 m
Width: 2.41 m
Height:
(cab, unladen) 2.4 m
(tarpaulin) 3.016 m
Ground clearance: 286 mm
Track: 1.774 m
Wheelbase:
(front axle to centre of rear bogie) 3.19 m
(between rear axles) 1.1 m
Angle of approach (with winch)/departure: 31.5°(45°)/44°
Fuel capacity: 145 litres
Max speed: 80 km/h
Gradient: 60%
Fording: 850 mm
Engine: Cummins 6BT5.9 5.9-litre 6-cylinder OHV in-line water cooled 4-stroke diesel developing 130 hp (97 kW) at 2,800 rpm and 382 N.m torque at 1,300 rpm
Gearbox: manual with 5 forward and 1 reverse gears
Transfer box: 2-speed
Clutch: single dry disc (325 mm)
Turning radius: 8.2 m
Suspension: semi-elliptic leaf springs all-round
Tyres: 11.00 × 18
Brakes: air, split system, drums all-round

Status
In production. In service with the People's Liberation Army (PLA), Peru (>400, see text), Thailand (235) and possibly others.

Contractor
Dong Feng Motor Industry

Enquiries to
Dong Feng Motor Industry Import & Export Corporation (DFMIEC)

Dong Feng EQ240/EQ2081 (6 × 6) 2,500 kg truck series

Development
The Dong Feng (export name Aeolus) EQ2081 (6 × 6) 2,500 kg series truck first entered service in 1974 as the Dong Feng EQ240 and was Dong Feng's first product. Early models were reported to suffer from serious quality problems, but these were subsequently solved and the type was praised by the PLA during the 1979 China-Vietnam border conflict.

The designation of the EQ240 changed to EQ2081 in the 1990s with the introduction of the new motor vehicle designation system.

The original EQ240 was continually updated and a number of more recent technologies have been inserted into the design since the 1980s. The EQ2081E which is powered by an improved engine was subsequently introduced.

The Dong Feng EQ2081, together with the larger but visually similar EQ2100, are currently one of the most numerous troop carrying/cargo truck in service with the PLA. The EQ2081 is the 2,500 kg class chassis for workshop shelters in service with the air force and navy.

The Dong Feng Motor Corporation was originally known as the Second Automobile Works. The Second Automobile Works was established in the early 1970s by relocating part of the facilities and technicians of the First Automobile Works (FAW) to the rural area in the Hubei Province. Dong Feng is now one of China's largest automotive manufacturers.

Description
According to the manufacturer, the EQ2081 is intended for operations in mountainous areas and over rough roads and tracks.

The original EQ240 was powered by EQ6100/6105 petrol engines, the EQ2081E which is powered by an improved EQ6100-1B petrol engine was subsequently introduced.

The layout of the vehicle is entirely conventional, with the engine forward, the steel cab seating the driver and two passengers, and the load area to the rear. The standard cargo body has a steel and wood floor, steel side racks and a tailgate. Body options are stated to include dump truck, tanker and crane. Optional equipment includes a power take-off and a 4,500 kg winch mounted behind the front bumper.

Variants

EQ2080E
The EQ2080E is essentially the EQ2081 design powered by a Cummins 6BT5.9 5.88-litre diesel unit. Some sources appear to refer to the EQ2080E as the EQ2082E6D. Full details of the EQ2080E can be found elsewhere in this section.

EQ245/EQ2100/EQ2100E6D
The now EQ2100 series is a 3,500 kg payload class troop carrying/cargo truck, slightly larger than, but visually similar to, the now EQ2080 series. Full details of the EQ2100 series can be found elsewhere in this section.

EQ2061E
The EQ2061E is a 1,500 kg (4 × 4) payload class troop carrying/cargo truck derived from the EQ2081. Full details of the EQ2061E can be found elsewhere in this section.

Specifications

EQ240/EQ2081
Cab seating: 1 + 2
Configuration: 6 × 6
Weight:
(laden, road) 9,010 kg
(laden, off-road) 8,510 kg
(unladen, with winch) 5,230 kg
(unladen, without winch) 5,010 kg
(max load, on-road) 4,000 kg
(max load, off-road) 2,500 kg
(towed load) 2,500 kg
Length: 6.34 m
Width: 2.41 m
Height: (tarpaulin) 2.996 m
Ground clearance: 285 mm
Wheelbase:
(front axle to centre of rear bogie) 3.74 m
(between rear axles) 1.1 m
Angle of approach (with winch)/departure: 31.5°(45°)/44°
Max speed: 80 km/h
Gradient: 60%
Vertical obstacle: 555 mm
Trench: 1.6 m
Fording: 850 mm

Engine: various (see text)
Gearbox: manual with 5 forward and 1 reverse gears
Transfer box: 2-speed
Clutch: single dry disc (325 mm)
Turning radius: 8.2 m
Suspension: semi-elliptic leaf springs all-round
Tyres: 11.00 × 18
Brakes: air, split system, drums all-round

Status
In production.

Contractor
Dong Feng Motor Industry

Enquiries to
Dong Feng Motor Industry Import & Export Corporation (DFMIEC)

Dong Feng EQ2102 (6 × 6) 3,500 kg truck

Development
The Dong Feng (export name Aeolus) EQ2102 (6 × 6) 3,500 kg truck is a second-generation high-mobility vehicle primarily employed by the People's Liberation Army for the transport of troops and cargo. The type entered service in the mid-1990s to replace a number of designs that had been in service since before the 1980s.

The Dong Feng Motor Corporation was originally known as the Second Automobile Works. The Second Automobile Works was established in the early 1970s by relocating part of the facilities and technicians of the First Automobile Works (FAW) to the rural area in the Hubei Province. Dong Feng is now one of China's largest automotive manufacturers.

Description
Layout of the EQ2102 is entirely conventional, with the engine forward, the steel forward control cab having seating for the driver and four passengers, and the load area to the rear. A conventional C-section chassis is used, with beam-type axles sprung by leaf spring suspension.

The standard cargo body has a steel and wood floor and steel side racks. The cargo bed can be fitted with optional bench seats for troop transport. The standard EQ2102 has a five-man (four-door) cab, the EQ2102G has a three-man (two-door) cab and a longer cargo bed.

Body options are stated to include a long wheelbase chassis, dump truck, tanker and crane. Box-type or shelter bodies may also be fitted, either mounting directly to the chassis locating on the cargo bed.

Specifications
EQ2102G
Cab seating: 1 + 4
Configuration: 6 × 6
Weight:
  (laden, road) 12,120 kg
  (laden, off-road) 10,620 kg
  (kerb) 7,120 kg
  (max load, road) 5,000 kg
  (max load, off-road) 3,500 kg
Length: 7.495 m
Width: 2.47 m
Height:
  (cab) 2.74 m
  (tarpaulin) 3.24 m
Ground clearance: 305 mm
Track:
  (front) 1.876 m
  (rear) 1.87 m

Dong Feng EQ2102 (6 × 6) 3,500 kg truck (Gordon Arthur)　　1391184

Wheelbase:
  (front axle to centre of rear bogies) 4.1 m
  (between rear axles) 1.25 m
Angle of approach/departure: 35°/34°
Max speed: 90 km/h
Max gradient: 60%
Fording: 1 m
Engine: Cummins 6BT5.9 5.88-litre 6-cylinder in-line turbocharged water-cooled 4-stroke diesel developing 158 hp (118 kW) at 2,800 rpm and 546 N.m torque at 1,700 rpm
Gearbox: manual with 5 forward and 1 reverse gears
Clutch: single dry disc (350 mm)
Transfer box: 2-speed
Steering: power-assisted
Turning radius: 9.4 m
Suspension: semi-elliptic leaf springs all-round
Tyres: 12.5R 20
Brakes:
  (main) air, slit system, drums all-round
  (parking) expanding, acting on transfer box output shaft

Status
In production. In service with the People's Liberation Army (PLA) and offered for export.

Contractor
Dong Feng Motor Industry

Enquiries to
Dong Feng Motor Industry Import & Export Corporation (DFMIEC)

Dong Feng EQ2100 (6 × 6) 3,500 kg truck series

Development
The Dong Feng (export name Aeolus) EQ2100 (6 × 6) 3,500 kg series truck is a 3,500 kg payload class troop carrying/cargo truck, slightly larger than, but visually similar to, the EQ2080 series from which it derives. Formerly known as the EQ245, the designation changed to EQ2100 in the 1990s with the introduction of the new motor vehicle designation system.

The latest model is known as the EQ2100E6D (EQ2100E6DY with right-hand drive and power-assisted steering) and is powered by a Cummins 6BT5.9 5.88-litre turbocharged diesel engine. The earlier EQ2100E was powered by an EQ6105-1 petrol engine.

This vehicle is also used for commercial purposes such as geological and oil exploration, and may also carry various forms of technical service vehicle bodies.

The Dong Feng Motor Corporation was originally known as the Second Automobile Works. The Second Automobile Works was established in the early 1970s by relocating part of the facilities and technicians of the First Automobile Works (FAW) to the rural area in the Hubei Province. Dong Feng is now one of China's largest automotive manufacturers.

Dong Feng EQ2102 (6 × 6) 3,500 kg truck (Dong Feng)　　0009614

Dong Feng EQ2100E6D (6 × 6) 3,500 kg truck (Dong Feng)　　0009615

Description

The layout of the EQ2100 is entirely conventional, with the engine forward, the steel cab seating the driver and two passengers, and the load area to the rear. A conventional C-section chassis is used, with beam-type axles sprung by leaf spring suspension.

The standard cargo body of the EQ2100 has a steel and wood floor, steel side racks and a tailgate. There is provision for towing a trailer weighing up to 4,500 kg. A self-recovery winch may be fitted.

Specifications

EQ2100
Cab seating: 1 + 2
Configuration: 6 × 6
Weight:
   (laden, road) 11,500 kg
   (laden, off-road) 10,000 kg
   (unladen, with winch) 6,290 kg
   (unladen, without winch) 6090 kg
   (max load, on-road) 5,000 kg
   (max load, off-road) 3,500 kg
   (towed load) 4,500 kg
Length:
   (with winch) 6.996
   (without winch) 6.844 m
Width: 2.4 m
Height:
   (cab, unladen) 2.462 m
   (tarpaulin) 3.302 m
Ground clearance: 305 mm
Track:
   (front) 1.876 m
   (rear) 1.87 m
Wheelbase:
   (front axle to centre of rear bogies) 3.4 m
   (between rear axles) 1.25 m
Angle of approach (with winch)/departure: 34° (44.5°)/45°
Max speed: 85 km/h
Fuel capacity: 145 litres
Gradient: 60%
Fording: 900 mm
Engine: Cummins 6BT5.9 5.88-litre 6-cylinder in-line OHV turbocharged water-cooled 4-stroke diesel developing 158 hp (118 kW) at 2,600 rpm and 559 N.m torque at 1,400 rpm
Gearbox: manual with 5 forward and 1 reverse gears
Transfer box: 2-speed
Clutch: single dry disc (350 mm)
Steering: recirculating ball, power-assistance optional
Turning radius: 9.3 m
Suspension: semi-elliptic leaf springs all-round
Tyres: 12.00 × 20
Brakes:
   (main) air, split system, drums all-round. Supplementary engine exhaust brake
   (parking) expanding, acting on transfer box output shaft

Status

In production. In service with the People's Liberation Army (PLA) and offered for export.

Contractor

Dong Feng Motor Industry

Enquiries to

Dong Feng Motor Industry Import & Export Corporation (DFMIEC)

Dong Feng EQ1093F6D (4 × 4) 5,000 kg truck

Development

The Dong Feng (export name Aeolus) EQ1093F6D (4 × 4) 5,000 kg truck is similar in appearance to a wide variety of Dong Feng commercial (4 × 2) trucks, the most common of which is the EQ1112 series.

The Dong Feng Motor Corporation was originally known as the Second Automobile Works. The Second Automobile Works was established in the early 1970s by relocating part of the facilities and technicians of the First Automobile Works (FAW) to the rural area in the Hubei Province. Dong Feng is now one of China's largest automotive manufacturers.

Description

Layout of the EQ1093F6D is entirely conventional. A bonneted design, the Cummins diesel engine sits forward of the three-seat steel cab (driver and two passengers), with a load area to the rear. The riveted pressed steel chassis is of conventional C-section design. The beam-type axles are sprung by leaf springs, front and rear, and are rated at 2,800 kg (front) and 7,500 kg (rear).

The cargo body has a steel and wood floor, steel side racks and a tailgate. Internal dimensions are 4.052 × 2.294 × 0.55 m (L × W × H). Options include left- or right-hand drive.

Dong Feng EQ1093F6D (4 × 4) 5,000 kg truck (Dong Feng)   0567866

Compared to purpose-designed military vehicles such as the EQ2061E, the EQ1093F6D has a far higher payload rating (5,000 kg compared to 1,500 kg), yet at 4,505 kg has a kerb weight of only 115 kg greater. However, the off-road mobility of the EQ1093F6D would not be comparable with that of the EQ2016E (or similar), as the EQ1093F6D has a conventional driveline, comprising a five-speed manual gearbox coupled to a single-speed transfer box. It therefore lacks the low ratio gears necessary when operating off-road in difficult terrain.

Specifications

EQ1093F6D
Cab seating: 1 + 2
Configuration: 4 × 4
Weight:
   (GVW) 9,715 kg
   (unladen) 4,505 kg
   (front axle weight, unladen) 1,078 kg
   (rear axle weight, unladen) 3,427 kg
   (payload) 5,000 kg
Length: 6.91 m
Width: 2.47 m
Height: 2.46 m
Ground clearance: 260 mm
Wheelbase: 3.95 m
Angle of approach/departure: 42.5°/26°
Max speed: 94 km/h
Fuel capacity: 160 litres
Gradient: 55%
Vertical obstacle: 400 mm
Trench: 700 mm
Fording: n/avail
Engine: Cummins 6BT5.9 5.88-litre 6-cylinder in-line turbocharged water-cooled direct injection 4-stroke diesel developing 158 hp (118 kW) at 2,600 rpm and 558 N.m torque at 1,700 rpm
Gearbox: manual with 5 forward and 1 reverse gears
Transfer box: single-speed
Clutch: single dry disc (350 mm)
Turning radius: 8 m
Suspension: semi-elliptic leaf springs and hydraulic shock-absorbers, front; semi-elliptic leaf springs with auxiliary helper springs, rear
Tyres: 9.00 × 20PR 14, 7 of (including 1 spare)
Brakes:
   (main) air, split system, drums all-round. Supplementary engine exhaust brake
   (parking) mechanical acting on transfer box
Electrical system: 24 V
Batteries: 2 × 12 V, 100 Ah
Alternator: 28 V, 45 A

Status

In production.

Contractor

Dong Feng Motor Industry

Enquiries to

Dong Feng Motor Industry Import & Export Corporation (DFMIEC)

Hongyan CQ 261 (6 × 6) 8,250 kg truck

Development

The CQ 261 (6 × 6) 8,250 kg truck can trace its design origins back to the early 1960s when Berliet GBU and GCH trucks were imported into China. Licence production in China followed and in 1977 the CQ 261 appeared.

An (8 × 8) version is used to carry the components of the Type 79 Ribbon Bridge.

CQ 261 (6 × 6) 8,250 kg truck towing Type 66 152 mm Gun-Howitzer 0511754

Similar vehicles are the Shaanqi SX2150 (previously known as the Yan'An SX 250) (6 × 6) truck and the SX 161 (6 × 4) truck. The Yan'An QD 360 is a (6 × 4) dump truck variant of the SX 161. Full details of the SX2150 can be found elsewhere in this section.

Description
The Hongyan CQ 261 bears an overall resemblance to the Berliet GBU original, but features many minor changes to suit local production methods. The large forward control cab has a distinctive radiator grille and seating for at least two passengers in addition to the driver; some cabs are also fitted with a roof hatch. At least two forms of passenger door have been seen, with later models having 'straight line' doors in place of the earlier sloping rear edge. The cargo area to the rear has steel drop sides and a tailgate and towing hook are provided. Bench seats can be fitted along each side of the cargo area. A canvas tilt can be fitted.

A tractor version of this vehicle is known as the CQ 261Q25 and is fitted with a Model 614OZ engine developing 250 hp. There is also a long wheelbase tractor truck known as the CQ 261C25 and an (8 × 4) crane truck known as the CQ 40D.

Specifications
Hongyan CQ 261 (6 × 6) 8,250 kg truck
Cab seating: 1 + 2 or 3
Configuration: 6 × 6
Weight:
  (laden, on-road) 26,460 kg
  (laden, off-road) 22,460 kg
  (max load, on-road) 12,260 kg
  (max load, off-road) 8,266 kg
Length: 7.947 m
Width: 2.5 m
Height: (top of cab) 3 m
Wheelbase: 4.93 m
Max speed: 61 km/h
Engine: Chongfa Model 6150 14.78-litre 6-cylinder water-cooled 4-stroke diesel developing 200 hp (149 kW)
Gearbox: manual with 5 forward and 1 reverse gears
Clutch: single dry plate
Transfer box: 2-speed
Brakes: dual circuit, air

Status
Production is thought to have been completed. In service with the People's Liberation Army.

Contractor
Si Chuan Special Motor Vehicle Plant

Jiefang CA-10 (4 × 2) Liberation 3,540 kg truck

Development
The CA-10 (4 × 2) Liberation 3,540 kg truck entered production at the First Automobile Works at Changchun in July 1956. It is based on the pattern of the Russian ZIL-150 (4 × 2) 3,500 kg truck. Although it has a limited cross-country capability and was primarily produced for commercial purposes, it was used in some numbers as a cargo carrier and as a prime mover for light artillery. Compared with the original it has a less efficient engine and a lack of climbing power.

Over one million CA-10s of all types had been produced by the beginning of 1983.

By the mid-1980s the First Automobile Works had commenced production of the CA-141 (later CA-1091) series of trucks, the replacement for the CA-10 and CA-30 series. It was reported late-2003 that small numbers of the CA-10 remain in service with the PLA, mainly in air force and communications units.

Description
The layout of the vehicle is entirely conventional, with the engine at the front, two-door fully enclosed cab in the centre and the cargo area at the rear with drop sides and a drop tailgate. Both left- and right-hand drive models were produced, and variants are known to have included a tractor truck, firefighting vehicles, tankers, crane carriers and dump trucks. Various wheelbase lengths have been produced. The QH-140 truck, produced at the Qinghai plant, was a special variant for use at high altitudes. It was produced in petrol- and diesel-engined forms.

Jiefang CA-10B (4 × 2) Liberation 3,540 kg truck (Ian Young)　　0511751

The initial CA-10 was followed by the CA-10B in 1960. The CA-10BX, with a higher compression ratio, maximum speed and power output, appeared in September 1980. It also had changes to the camshaft, carburettor, fuel pump, oil sump, radiator, clutch, starter motor and electrical system, all of which went some way to overcoming earlier technical drawbacks.

The CA-10C appeared in January 1982 and is rated at 4,500 kg. The CA-10CJ is fitted with a 100 hp engine and the CA-10CT with a 110 hp engine. The CA-15 has a 5.55-litre 115 hp engine.

Specifications
Cab seating: 1 + 1
Configuration: 4 × 2
Weight:
  (laden, road) 7,375 kg
  (unladen) 3,840 kg
  (on front axle, unladen) 1,735 kg
  (on rear axle, unladen) 2,100 kg
  (max load, road) 3,540 kg
Load area: 3.54 × 2.26 m
Length: 6.502 m
Width: 2.29 m
Height: 2.33 m
Ground clearance: 270 mm
Track:
  (front) 1.69 m
  (rear) 1.74 m
Wheelbase: 3.98 m
Angle of approach/departure: 40°/24°
Max speed: 80 km/h
Range: 415 km
Fuel capacity: 158 litres
Max gradient: 37%
Engine: CA-10 6-cylinder in-line water-cooled petrol developing 95 hp (71 kW) at 2,800 rpm
Gearbox: manual with 5 forward and 1 reverse gears
Clutch: single dry plate
Turning radius: 9 m
Suspension: semi-elliptic leaf springs and hydraulic shock-absorbers, front; semi-elliptic leaf springs with overload springs, rear
Tyres: 9.00 × 20
Brakes:
  (main) air
  (parking) mechanical
Electrical system: 12 V
Batteries: 2 × 6 V

Status
Production complete. Small numbers remain in service with the People's Liberation Army. Replaced from 1987 onwards by the CA-141 (later CA-1091) series of trucks.

Contractor
First Automobile Works

Enquiries to
China First Automobile Group Import and Export Corporation (CFAGIEC)

Jiefang CA-1091 (C-141) 5,000 kg trucks

Development
The Jiefang CA-1091 (C-141) series of trucks are the successors to the Jiefang CA-10 truck series, full details of which can be found elsewhere in this section. There are currently four main models in production, the commercial CA-1091K2 and CA-1091K2Y, and the military CA-1091K2E2 and CA-1091K2YE2. The military versions are known as 5T Diesel Military

Jiefang CA-1091 series 5,000 kg 5T Diesel Military High Rack Truck (Jeifang)　　　0511752

High Rack Trucks. The CA-3101K2 and CA-3101K2Y are essentially a commercial dump truck variant, and the CA-1092 a cab-over-engine version. It is understood that all models share essentially the same driveline.

The Jiefang CA1091 series of trucks have been exported (sometimes in KD form) to around 20 countries and regions including: Bolivia, Indonesia, Korea, Myanmar, Saudi Arabia, South Africa, Tanzania, Thailand, United Arab Emirates, and Uganda. The China First Automotive Group Import and Export Corporation (CFAGIEC), a subsidiary under the direct jurisdiction of the China First Automotive Group Corporation (CFAGC), has also established assembly plants in South Africa and Tanzania.

Description

The Jiefang CA-1091 series are entirely conventional in design and are based on a C-section chassis of riveted pressed longitudinal beams with eight cross members. Towing hooks are provided at the front and rear. The all-steel cab has seating for the driver and two passengers. The one-piece bonnet (hood) can be tilted forward 50° for engine access. Optional equipment for the cab includes defrosting equipment.

The cargo body uses mixed steel and timber construction and is fitted with side racks. A tailboard is provided along with a ladder for access and a rainproof tarpaulin. The dump body has a maximum tip angle of 54°.

Specifications

Cab seating: 1 + 2
Configuration: 4 × 2
Weight:
　(CA-1091K2/1091K2Y, kerb) 4,350 kg
　(CA-3101K2/3101K2Y, kerb) 5,140 kg
　(CA-1091K2E2/1091K2YE2, kerb) 4,560 kg
　(CA-1091K2/1091K2Y, GVW) 9,545 kg
　(CA-3101K2/3101K2Y, GVW) 10,335 kg
　(CA-1091K2E2/1091K2YE2, GVW) 9,755 kg
Max load: 5,000 kg
Load area: (not dump body) 4.2 × 2.3 m
Width:
　(CA-1091K2/1091K2Y) 2.476 m
　(CA-3101K2/3101K2Y) 2.39 m
　(CA-1091K2E2/1091K2YE2) 2.484 m
Height:
　(CA-1091K2/1091K2Y) 2.435 m
　(CA-3101K2/3101K2Y) 2.46 m
　(CA-1091K2E2/1091K2YE2) 3.02 m
Ground clearance: (min) 265 mm
Track:
　(front) 1.8 m
　(rear) 1.74 m
Wheelbase: 4.5 m
Angle of approach/departure:
　(CA-1091K2/1091K2Y) 28°/19°
　(CA-3101K2/3101K2Y) 30°/36°
　(CA-1091K2E2/1091K2YE2) 30°/36°
Max speed:
　(CA-1091K2/1091K2Y) 86 km/h
　(CA-3101K2/3101K2Y) 86 km/h
　(CA-1091K2E2/1091K2YE2) 90 km/h
Fuel consumption: 18 litres per 100 km
Max Gradient: 28%
Engine: Model CA-6110Z5A2-2 6.842-litre 6-cylinder in-line turbocharged water-cooled direct injection 4-stroke diesel developing 168 hp (125 kW) at 2,900 rpm and 392 N.m torque between 1,800 and 2,000 rpm
Gearbox: manual with 6 forward and 1 reverse gears
Transfer box: single-speed
Clutch: DS330, single dry plate
Steering: recirculating ball
Turning radius: 8.2 m
Suspension: semi-elliptic leaf springs and double acting hydraulic shock-absorbers, front; semi-elliptic leaf springs with auxiliary springs, rear
Tyres: 9.00 × 20 or 9.00R 20
Brakes:
　(main) air, split circuit, drums all-round
　(parking) mechanical
Electrical system: 24 V

Status

In production. In service with the People's Liberation Army (PLA).

Contractor

First Automobile Works

Enquiries to

China First Automotive Group Import and Export Corporation (CFAGIEC)

Shaanxi SX2150/SX2150K 5,000 kg (6 × 6) truck

Development

The Shaanxi SX2150 (previously known as Yan'an SX250) 5,000 kg (6 × 6) truck was introduced by the Xi'an-based Shaanxi Automobile Works (now Shaanxi Automobile Group Co Ltd) in 1968.

The SX2150 was China's first heavy (6 × 6) cross-country military truck. The design was originally based on the chassis of the Soviet Ural-375, this mated to a cab and cargo bed based on those of the French Berliet GBU 15.

The SX2150 entered service with the PLA in 1974 and mainly in artillery and heavy equipment transport roles. More recently the SX2150 has been used primarily as the chassis for weapons systems and workshop shelters.

The latest version of the Shaanxi SX2150, designated SX2150K, uses Steyr technology and in addition to a driveline upgrade that includes a Steyr diesel engine and Fuller manual gearbox, features a Steyr pattern cab. Shaanxi Automobile Group Co Ltd signed a co-production/licence agreement with Steyr of Austria in the 1980s.

The Shaanxi SX2150K 5,000 kg (6 × 6) is similar in appearance to the Shaanxi SX2190 7,000 kg (6 × 6) truck, this also developed using Steyr technology. Full details of the SX2190 7,000 kg (6 × 6) truck can be found elsewhere in this section.

A 5,000 kg payload (4 × 4) variant of the SX2150K (designated SX2151) that also features the Steyr pattern cab has been developed; this model was exported to Kenya during 2005.

Shaanxi Automobile Group Co Ltd has an annual production output of 30,000 heavy-duty automobiles, 20,000 medium trucks, 1,500 buses and 50,000 heavy-duty truck axles.

Shaanxi Automobile Group Co Ltd owns 11 subsidiaries and holding companies. In 2003 the company signed a strategic cooperation agreement with MAN of Germany.

Shaanxi Automobile Group Co Ltd has exported products to more than 30 countries.

Description

The Shaanxi SX2150/SX2150K truck is of entirely conventional design. The forward control all-steel Berliet-derived cab of the earlier models has four doors, the front pair opening in so-called suicide door style (hinges to the rear). This cab has seating for at least four.

On cargo versions of all variants the rear cargo body is provided with a drop tailgate and sides, and removable bows with canvas cover.

Early versions of the SX2150 were powered by an indigenous water-cooled diesel coupled to a five-speed manual gearbox. Later variants (SX2150K) are fitted with a Steyr WD615.71 turbocharged diesel coupled to a Fuller nine-speed manual gearbox. Suspension is by conventional leaf springs.

Specifications

SX2150K
Cab seating: 1 + 3
Configuration: 6 × 6
Weight:
　(laden, off-road) 14,490 kg
　(laden, on-road) 19,490 kg
　(unladen) 9,490 kg
　(payload, off-road) 5,000 kg
　(payload, on-road) 10,000 kg
　(towed load) 6,500 kg
Length: 7.12 m
Width: 2.52 m

Shaanxi SX2150 5,000 kg (6 × 6) truck (Gordon Arthur)　　　1391068

Height: 3.05 m
Ground clearance: 385 mm
Track: 2.08 m
Wheelbase: 3.125 + 1.35 m
Max speed: 70 km/h
Fuel capacity: 280 litres
Max gradient: 58%
Fording: 1.2 m
Engine: Steyr WD615.71 6-cylinder in-line turbocharged water-cooled 4-stroke diesel developing 256 hp (191 hp) at 2,600 rpm
Gearbox: Fuller RT11509C manual with 9 forward and 1 reverse gears
Transfer box: n/avail
Clutch: n/avail
Steering: power-assisted
Turning radius: 9 m
Suspension: leaf springs all-round
Tyres: 1300 × 20 (16-ply)
Brakes: drums all-round
Electrical system: 24 V

Status

In production (SX2150K). In service with the People's Liberation Army (PLA) and possibly other undisclosed countries. A 5,000 kg payload (4 × 4) variant (SX2151) is in service with Kenya (see text).

Contractor

Shaanxi Automobile Group Co Ltd

Shaanxi SX2190 7,000 kg (6 × 6) truck

Development

The Shaanxi SX2190 7,000 kg (6 × 6) truck was developed using technology from Austrian Steyr designs. A co-production/licensing agreement having been signed by the now Shaanxi Automobile Group Co Ltd with Austria in the 1980s.

The SX2190 truck is understood to have entered PLA service in the 1990s to replace ageing Huanghe JN252 and Hongyan CQ261 trucks. The SX2190 is primarily deployed as an artillery tractor or by engineering troops in the Heavy Equipment Transport (HET) role.

As well as the standard version, the SX2190 is also available in a range of variants, these including the SX2190BQ (short cab), SX2190D (with winch), SX2190E (long wheelbase), and SX4260 (tractor/semi-trailer).

Steyr technology was also used by the Shaanxi Automobile Group Co Ltd to update the Shaanxi SX2150 5,000 kg (6 × 6) truck. The resultant version - the SX2150K - featuring the same Steyr pattern cab as the SX2190, and therefore looking very similar to the slightly larger SX2190. Full details of the SX2150 5,000 kg (6 × 6) truck can be found elsewhere in this section. A (4 × 4) 5,000 kg payload variant of the SX2150K, designated SX2151, was developed and this was successfully exported to Kenya in 2005.

Shaanxi Automobile Group Co Ltd has an annual production output of 30,000 heavy-duty automobiles, 20,000 medium trucks, 1,500 buses and 50,000 heavy-duty truck axles.

Shaanxi Automobile Group Co Ltd owns 11 subsidiaries and holding companies. In 2003 the company signed a strategic cooperation agreement with MAN of Germany.

Shaanxi Automobile Group Co Ltd has exported products to more than 30 countries.

Description

The Shaanxi SX2190 truck is of entirely conventional design. The forward control, all-steel, Steyr pattern cab has two doors and seats four; two with a single bunk option. A single spare wheel is mounted vertically behind the crew cab.

Shaanxi SX2190 7,000 kg (6 × 6) truck of the PLA (Gordon Arthur) 1391191

The rear cargo body is provided with a drop tailgate and sides, and removable bows with canvas cover. A front and rear pull 10,000 kg hydraulic winch is optional.

Motive power is provided a Steyr WD615.50 diesel, this coupled to a Fuller RT11609 nine-speed gearbox. Suspension is by conventional leaf springs.

Specifications

SX2190
Cab seating: 1 + 1 or 1 + 3
Configuration: 6 × 6
Weight:
 (laden, off-road) 18,500 kg
 (laden, on-road) 22,500 kg
 (unladen) 11,500 kg
 (payload, off-road) 7,000 kg
 (payload, on-road) 10,000 kg
 (towed load) 10,000 kg
Length: 7.994 m
Width: 2.55 m
Height: 2.67 m
Ground clearance: 385 mm
Track: 2.072 m
Wheelbase: 3.375 + 1.4 m
Max speed: 80 km/h
Fuel capacity: 400 litres
Max gradient: 60%
Fording: 1.2 m
Engine: Steyr WD615.50 9.762-litre 6-cylinder in-line turbocharged water-cooled 4-stroke diesel developing 276 hp (206 kW) at 2,400 rpm
Gearbox: Fuller RT11609 manual with 9 forward and 2 reverse gears
Transfer box: n/avail
Steering: power-assisted
Suspension: leaf springs all-round
Tyres: 15.5 × 20 (18-ply)
Brakes: drums all-round
Electrical system: 24 V

Status

In production. In service with the People's Liberation Army (PLA) and possibly other undisclosed countries. A (4 × 4) variant with a 5,000 kg payload has been exported to Kenya (see text).

Contractor

Shaanxi Automobile Group Co Ltd

Wanshan WS21050 (14 × 12) heavy-duty off-road vehicle

Development

The Wanshan WS21050 (14 × 12) heavy-duty off-road vehicle is manufactured by the Wanshan Special Vehicle Co. Ltd, this being one of 26 subsidiaries of China Sanjiang Space Group (CSSG). China Sanjiang Space Group is a large state-owned enterprise group under the direct control of China Aerospace Science and Industry Corporation (CASIC). From its formation in 1969, CSSG has specialised in missile and space technology.

The company manufactured its first heavy-duty off-road vehicle in 1980. Wanshan military truck chassis are predominantly used as launchers, transporters or support role vehicles for military missile and multiple launch rocket systems.

Following a display in 2001 during which China's Second Artillery Force (SAF) displayed their newly-equipped Dong Feng-31 intercontinental ballistic missiles (ICBMs) on a new (12 × 12) chassis, a source from the Minsk Wheeled Tractor Plant (MZKT) in the now Belarus disclosed that a joint working group had been established between MZKT and China to help Beijing design and build a wheeled vehicle for use with the Dong Feng-31 ICBM and other missile systems.

The source emphasised that the technology transferred to China was civil-based, however, the differences between MZKT civil and military products is not believed to be significant.

Wanshan Special Vehicle Co. Ltd has since used the transferred technology to develop a wide range of specialist heavy-duty chassis, these having from three to the seven axles of the WS21050.

Available details of some other WS heavy-duty off-road vehicle chassis can be found elsewhere in this section.

Wanshan Special Vehicle Co. Ltd also produces military vehicles not based on MZKT technology. Available details of some of these vehicles can be found elsewhere in this section.

The main competitor to the Wanshan WS series of heavy-duty off-road vehicles is the TAS series of heavy-duty trucks developed by the Taian Special Vehicle Plant. The TAS series is an indigenous Chinese design, but this may also have benefited from some former Soviet Union technology.

Description

The WS21050 is clearly based on MZKT technology and features a torsionally rigid chassis and torsion-bar independent-wheel suspension. The wide footprint tyres can be fitted with a central tyre inflation system that allows for pressures to be varied between 0.3 and 0.44 MPa.

Wanshan WS21050 (14 × 12) heavy-duty off-road vehicle (Wanshan)
1391083

Wanshan WS2180 (6 × 6) truck (Wanshan)   1391089

Released data is more comprehensive than for most WS range vehicles, and includes details of main driveline components that are not of indigenous Chinese, or former Soviet Union development.

Released images of the WS21050 show the vehicle with either a two-door or larger four-door cab.

Specifications

WS21050
Cab seating: n/avail
Configuration: 14 × 12
Weight:
  (kerb) 40,000 kg
  (laden) 105,000 kg
  (payload) 65,000 kg
Length: 19.4 m
Width: 3.35 m
Height: 3.0 m
Ground clearance: 400 mm
Track: 2.7 m
Wheelbase: 2.05 + 2.4 + 3.5 + 2.05 + 2.05 + 2.05 m
Angle of approach/departure: 14°/24°
Max speed: 50 km/h
Max range: (highway) 500 km
Fuel capacity: n/avail
Fuel consumption: 160 litres/100 km
Max gradient: 25%
Fording: 1.2 m
Trench crossing: 2.5 m
Engine: Deutz BF12L513C 19.144-litre V-12 turbocharged air-cooled 4-stroke diesel developing 517 hp (386 kW) and 1,900 N.m torque
Gearbox: ZF 8S221 manual with 8 forward and 1 reverse gears, plus WSK400 torque converter
Transfer box: 2-speed with differential lock
Steering: power-assisted on axles 1, 2, 3, 6 and 7; emergency steering back-up
Turning radius: 19 m
Suspension: independent torsion bar
Tyres: 1600 × 600-685 with CTI
Brakes: drums all-round, air-over-hydraulic or full dual-circuit air options, supplementary engine exhaust brake and hydraulic retarder
Electrical system: 24 V

Status
Production status uncertain. Probably in service with the People's Liberation Army (PLA).

Contractor
Wanshan Special Vehicle Co. Ltd

Wanshan WS2180 (6 × 6) truck

Development
The Wanshan WS2180 (6 × 6) truck is manufactured by the Wanshan Special Vehicle Co. Ltd, this being one of 26 subsidiaries of China Sanjiang Space Group (CSSG). China Sanjiang Space Group is a large state-owned enterprise group under the direct control of China Aerospace Science and Industry Corporation (CASIC). From its formation in 1969, CSSG has specialised in missile and space technology.

The company manufactured its first heavy-duty off-road vehicle in 1980 and following a display in 2001 during which China's Second Artillery Force (SAF) displayed their newly-equipped Dong Feng-31 intercontinental ballistic missiles (ICBMs) on a new (12 × 12) chassis, a source from the Minsk Wheeled Tractor Plant (MZKT) in the now Belarus disclosed that a joint working group had been established between MZKT and China to help Beijing design and build a wheeled vehicle for use with the Dong Feng-31 ICBM and other missile systems.

The source emphasised that the technology transferred to China was civil-based, however, the differences between MZKT civil and military products is not believed to be significant.

Wanshan Special Vehicle Co. Ltd has since used the transferred technology to develop a wide range of specialist heavy-duty chassis, these having from three to seven axles, and predominantly used as launchers, transporters or support role vehicles for military missile and multiple launch rocket systems.

Available details of some of these chassis can be found elsewhere in this section.

Wanshan Special Vehicle Co. Ltd also produces military vehicles not based on MZKT technology, and the WS2180 appears to be one of these. The WS2180 is usually shown configured as a conventional troop carrying/cargo General Service (GS) truck. The bonneted WS2180 bears some considerable visual resemblance to the Oshkosh Medium Tactical Vehicle Replacement (MTVR), and while the overall length and wheelbase of the two designs are not the same, both designs do feature fully independent coil spring suspension.

There is no known licensing or technology transfer agreement between Wanshan Special Vehicle Co. Ltd and Oshkosh.

Available details of some other Wanshan Special Vehicle Co. Ltd vehicles not based on MZKT technology, and including the WS2250 which resembles the Oshkosh Heavy Expanded Mobility Tactical Truck (HEMTT), can be found elsewhere in this section.

The main competitor to the Wanshan WS series of heavy-duty off-road vehicles is the TAS series of heavy-duty trucks developed by the Taian Special Vehicle Plant. The TAS series is an indigenous Chinese design, but this may also have benefited from some former Soviet Union technology.

Description
Released data for the WS2180 is more comprehensive than for most WS range vehicles, and includes some limited details of main driveline components.

Unlike some other Wanshan Special Vehicle Co. Ltd designs the WS2180 is clearly not based on MZKT technology, the overall design of the vehicle being more like a conventional troop or load carrying General Service (GS) truck than a specialist role MZKT technology derived chassis.

The WS2180 is a conventional bonneted design, the entire front end (cab and bonnet) bearing considerable visual resemblance to the Oshkosh MTVR. A torsionally stiff chassis is employed as suspension is by fully independent coil springs on each axle; first to second axle wheelbase is 3.95 m, the equivalent wheelbase of the Oshkosh MTVR is 4.674 m.

Specifications

WS2180
Cab seating: n/avail
Configuration: 6 × 6
Weight:
  (kerb) 11,000 kg
  (payload, on-road) 14,000 kg
  (payload, off-road) 7,000 kg
  (laden, on-road) 25,000 kg
  (laden, off-road) 15,000 kg
Length: 8.05 m
Width: 2.5 m
Height: 3.09 m
Ground clearance: 410 mm
Track: 2.032 m
Wheelbase: 3.95 + 1.45 m
Max speed: 105 km/h
Max range: (highway) 600 km
Fuel capacity: n/avail
Max gradient: 60%
Fording: 1.2 m
Trench crossing: 700 mm
Vertical obstacle: 550 mm
Engine: 6-cylinder in-line turbocharged and intercooled water-cooled 4-stroke diesel developing 346 hp (258 kW) and 1,450 N.m torque
Gearbox: manual with 9 forward and 1 reverse gears
Transfer box: 2-speed with differential lock

Steering: power-assisted on front axle
Turning radius: 11 m
Suspension: fully independent coil spring on all axles
Tyres: 1600R 20 with CTI (0.3 to 0.65 MPa)
Brakes: drums all-round, ABS fitted
Electrical system: 24 V

Status
Production status uncertain. Offered for export.

Contractor
Wanshan Special Vehicle Co. Ltd.

Wanshan WS2250 (8 × 8) truck

Development
The Wanshan WS2250 (8 × 8) truck is manufactured by the Wanshan Special Vehicle Co. Ltd, this being one of 26 subsidiaries of China Sanjiang Space Group (CSSG). China Sanjiang Space Group is a large state-owned enterprise group under the direct control of China Aerospace Science and Industry Corporation (CASIC). From its formation in 1969, CSSG has specialised in missile and space technology.

The company manufactured its first heavy-duty off-road vehicle in 1980 and following a display in 2001, during which China's Second Artillery Force (SAF) displayed their newly-equipped Dong Feng-31 intercontinental ballistic missiles (ICBMs) on a new (12 × 12) chassis, a source from the Minsk Wheeled Tractor Plant (MZKT) in the now Belarus disclosed that a joint working group had been established between MZKT and China to help Beijing design and build a wheeled vehicle for use with the Dong Feng-31 ICBM and other missile systems.

The source emphasised that the technology transferred to China was civil-based, however, the differences between MZKT civil and military products is not believed to be significant.

Wanshan Special Vehicle Co. Ltd has since used the transferred technology to develop a wide range of specialist heavy-duty chassis, these having from three to seven axles, and predominantly used as launchers, transporters or support role vehicles for military missile and multiple launch rocket systems.

Available details of some of these chassis can be found elsewhere in this section.

Wanshan Special Vehicle Co. Ltd also produces military vehicles not based on MZKT technology, and the WS2250 appears to be one of these. The WS2250 is usually shown configured as a conventional cargo truck with dropside-type body. The WS2250 bears some considerable visual resemblance to the Oshkosh Heavy Expanded Mobility Tactical Truck (HEMTT), some promotional imagery of the WS2250 clearly featuring a 'photo-shopped' HEMTT cab. The overall length, wheelbase and suspension of the two designs are not the same. There is no known licensing or technology transfer arrangement between Wanshan Special Vehicle Co. Ltd and Oshkosh.

Available details of some other Wanshan Special Vehicle Co. Ltd vehicles that are not based on MZKT technology, and including the WS2180 which resembles the Oshkosh Medium Tactical vehicle Replacement (MTVR), can be found elsewhere in this section.

The main competitor to the Wanshan WS series of heavy-duty off-road vehicles is the TAS series of heavy-duty trucks developed by the Taian Special Vehicle Plant. The TAS series is an indigenous Chinese design, but this may also have benefited from some former Soviet Union technology.

Description
Released data for the WS2250 is more comprehensive than for most WS range vehicles, and includes some limited details of main driveline components.

Unlike some other Wanshan Special Vehicle Co. Ltd designs the WS2250 is clearly not based on MZKT technology. For example, suspension while independent is not of the torsion bar type. Additionally, the trademark

wide low pressure tyres of MZKT designs are not used, these replaced by more conventional 20-inch rims and Western standard 1600R 20 radial ply tyres. Further, the overall design of the WS2250 is more like a conventional heavy cargo truck than a specialist role MZKT technology derived chassis.

The WS2250 is a conventional cab-before-engine design (the engine and cooling pack mounted on the chassis rails behind the cab), the entire front end bearing considerable visual resemblance to the Oshkosh HEMTT. As previously mentioned, visual likeness aside, key weights and dimensions of the two designs are not mirrored. For example, the WS2250 has a wheelbase of 1.75 + 3.65 + 1.45 m, the equivalent wheelbase of the Oshkosh HEMTT is 1.524 + 5.334 + 1.524 m.

Specifications
WS2250
Cab seating: n/avail
Configuration: 8 × 8
Weight:
  (kerb) 15,000 kg
  (payload, on-road) 16,000 kg
  (payload, off-road) 10,000 kg
  (laden, on-road) 31,000 kg
  (laden, off-road) 25,000 kg
Length: 10.1 m
Width: 2.5 m
Height: 2.58 m
Ground clearance: 410 mm
Track: 2.032 m
Wheelbase: 1.75 + 3.65 + 1.45 m
Max speed: 105 km/h
Max range: (highway) 600 km
Fuel capacity: n/avail
Fuel consumption: 60 litres/100 km
Max gradient: 60%
Fording: 1.2 m
Trench crossing: 1.8 m
Vertical obstacle: 550 mm
Engine: 6-cylinder in-line turbocharged and intercooled water-cooled 4-stroke diesel developing 433 hp (323 kW) and 1,920 N.m torque
Gearbox: fully automatic
Transfer box: 2-speed with differential lock
Steering: power-assisted on front two axles
Turning radius: 13.5 m
Suspension: fully independent coil spring on all axles
Tyres: 1600R 20 with CTI (0.3 to 0.65 MPa)
Brakes: drums all-round
Electrical system: 24 V

Status
Production status uncertain. Offered for export.

Contractor
Wanshan Special Vehicle Co. Ltd.

Wanshan WS2300 (6 × 6) heavy-duty off-road vehicle

Development
The Wanshan WS2300 (6 × 6) heavy-duty off-road vehicle is manufactured by the Wanshan Special Vehicle Co. Ltd, this being one of 26 subsidiaries of China Sanjiang Space Group (CSSG). China Sanjiang Space Group is a large state-owned enterprise group under the direct control of China Aerospace Science and Industry Corporation (CASIC). From its formation in 1969, CSSG has specialised in missile and space technology.

The company manufactured its first heavy-duty off-road vehicle in 1980. Wanshan military truck chassis are predominantly used as launchers, transporters or support role vehicles for military missile and multiple launch rocket systems.

Following a display in 2001 during which China's Second Artillery Force (SAF) displayed their newly-equipped Dong Feng-31 intercontinental ballistic missiles (ICBMs) on a new (12 × 12) chassis, a source from the Minsk Wheeled Tractor Plant (MZKT) in the now Belarus, disclosed that a joint working group had been established between MZKT and China to help Beijing design and build a wheeled vehicle for use with the Dong Feng-31 ICBM and other missile systems.

The source emphasised that the technology transferred to China was civil-based, however, the differences between MZKT civil and military products is not believed to be significant.

Wanshan Special Vehicle Co. Ltd has since used the transferred technology to develop a wide range of specialist heavy-duty chassis, these having from three to seven axles. Available details of some of these chassis can be found elsewhere in this section.

Wanshan Special Vehicle Co. Ltd also produces military vehicles not based on MZKT technology. Available details of some of these vehicles can be found elsewhere in this section.

The main competitor to the Wanshan WS series of heavy-duty off-road vehicles is the TAS series of heavy-duty trucks developed by the Taian Special Vehicle Plant. The TAS series is an indigenous Chinese design, but this may also have benefited from some former Soviet Union technology.

Wanshan WS2250 (8 × 8) truck (Wanshan)   1391091

Wanshan WS2300 (6 × 6) heavy-duty off-road vehicle (Wanshan) 1391071

Description

Beyond some basic weights and dimensions, very little information specific to the WS2300 has been released by the manufacturer. The vehicle is, however, clearly based on MZKT technology and features a torsionally rigid chassis and torsion bar independent wheel suspension. The wide footprint tyres can be fitted with a central tyre inflation system that allows for pressures to be varied between 0.1 and 0.38 MPa.

The four door cab-over-engine configuration allows for the seating of two or four crew.

With the exception of the weights and dimensions included in the Specifications table, no other details, including engine or other driveline component details, have been released.

Specifications
WS2300
Cab seating: 1 + 1 or 1 + 3
Configuration: 6 × 6
Weight:
  (kerb) 15,000 kg
  (laden) 30,000 kg
Length: 10.045 m
Width: 3.05 m
Height: 2.97 m
Ground clearance: 400 mm
Track: 2.375 m
Wheelbase: 4.2 + 2.2 m
Max speed: 85 km/h
Max range: (highway) 650 km
Fuel capacity: n/avail
Fuel consumption: 56 litres/100 km
Max gradient: 60%
Fording: 1.2 m
Engine: n/avail
Gearbox: n/avail
Transfer box: n/avail
Clutch: n/avail
Steering: power-assisted on front axle
Turning radius: 13 m
Suspension: independent torsion bar
Tyres: n/avail
Brakes: drums all-round
Electrical system: 24 V

Status

In production. In service with the People's Liberation Army (PLA), and possibly other undisclosed countries.

Contractor

Wanshan Special Vehicle Co. Ltd

Wanshan WS2400 (8 × 8) heavy-duty off-road vehicle

Development

The Wanshan WS2400 (8 × 8) heavy-duty off-road vehicle is manufactured by the Wanshan Special Vehicle Co. Ltd, this being one of 26 subsidiaries of China Sanjiang Space Group (CSSG). China Sanjiang Space Group is a large state-owned enterprise group under the direct control of China Aerospace Science and Industry Corporation (CASIC). From its formation in 1969, CSSG has specialised in missile and space technology.

The company manufactured its first heavy-duty off-road vehicle in 1980. Wanshan military truck chassis are predominantly used as launchers, transporters or support role vehicles for military missile and multiple launch rocket systems.

WS2400 (8 × 8) heavy-duty off-road vehicle (Gordon Arthur) 1391075

Following a display in 2001 during which China's Second Artillery Force (SAF) displayed their newly-equipped Dong Feng-31 intercontinental ballistic missiles (ICBMs) on a new (12 × 12) chassis, a source from the Minsk Wheeled Tractor Plant (MZKT) in the now Belarus disclosed that a joint working group had been established between MZKT and China to help Beijing design and build a wheeled vehicle for use with the Dong Feng-31 ICBM and other missile systems.

The source emphasised that the technology transferred to China was civil-based, however, the differences between MZKT civil and military products is not believed to be significant.

The Wanshan WS2400 is believed to be based on the MZKT/MAZ-543, the two vehicles having identical wheelbases and many other weight and dimensional similarities.

One known use of the WS2400 chassis is in the Transporter-Erector-Launcher (TEL) and support roles for the CSSG DF-11 short range ballistic missile. The WS2400 chassis is also used in the TEL and support roles with the HQ-9/FT-2000 surface-to-air Anti-Radiation Missile (ARM) system.

Since the initial transfer of MZKT technology Wanshan Special Vehicle Co. Ltd has developed a wide range of specialist heavy-duty chassis, these having from three to seven axles.

Available details of some of these chassis can be found elsewhere in this section.

Wanshan Special Vehicle Co. Ltd also produces military vehicles not based on MZKT technology. Available details of some of these vehicles can be found elsewhere in this section.

The main competitor to the Wanshan WS series is the TAS series of heavy-duty trucks developed by the Taian Special Vehicle Plant. The TAS series is an indigenous Chinese design, but this may also have benefited from some former Soviet Union technology.

Description

Beyond some basic weights and dimensions, very little information specific to the WS2400 has been released by the manufacturer. The vehicle is, however, clearly based on MZKT technology, and obviously the MAZ-543. The WS2400 features a torsionally rigid chassis and torsion bar independent wheel suspension, the wide footprint tyres can be fitted with a central tyre inflation system that allows for pressures to be varied between 0.1 and 0.38 MPa.

The four door cab-over-engine configuration has seating for two or four crew. Photographs suggest that a number of cosmetic changes have been applied to the cab throughout its production run.

With the exception of the weights and dimensions included in the Specifications table, no other details, including engine or other driveline component details, have been released.

Specifications
WS2400
Cab seating: 1 + 1 or 1 + 3
Configuration: 8 × 8
Weight:
  (kerb) 18,730 kg
  (laden) 41,000 kg
Length: 11.065 m
Width: 3.05
Height: 2.97 m
Ground clearance: 400 mm
Track: 2.375 m
Wheelbase: 2.2 + 3.3 + 2.2 m
Angle of approach/departure: 28°/36°
Max speed: 80 km/h
Max range: (highway) 650 km
Fuel capacity: n/avail
Fuel consumption: 68 litres/100 km
Max gradient: 60%
Fording: 1.2 m
Engine: n/avail
Gearbox: n/avail
Transfer box: n/avail
Steering: power-assisted on front two axles
Turning radius: 14.5 m
Suspension: independent torsion bar

Tyres: n/avail
Brakes: drums all-round
Electrical system: 24 V

Status
In production. In service with the People's Liberation Army (PLA), and probably other undisclosed countries that may include Pakistan and Iran.

Contractor
Wanshan Special Vehicle Co. Ltd

Wanshan WS2500 (10 × 8/10 × 10) heavy-duty off-road vehicle

Development
The Wanshan WS2500 (10 × 8/10 × 10) heavy-duty off-road vehicle is manufactured by the Wanshan Special Vehicle Co. Ltd, this being one of 26 subsidiaries of China Sanjiang Space Group (CSSG). China Sanjiang Space Group is a large state-owned enterprise group under the direct control of China Aerospace Science and Industry Corporation (CASIC). From its formation in 1969, CSSG has specialised in missile and space technology.

The company manufactured its first heavy-duty off-road vehicle in 1980. Wanshan military truck chassis are predominantly used as launchers, transporters or support role vehicles for military missile and multiple launch rocket systems.

Following a display in 2001 during which China's Second Artillery Force (SAF) displayed their newly-equipped Dong Feng-31 intercontinental ballistic missiles (ICBMs) on a new (12 × 12) chassis, a source from the Minsk Wheeled Tractor Plant (MZKT) in the now Belarus disclosed that a joint working group had been established between MZKT and China to help Beijing design and build a wheeled vehicle for use with the Dong Feng-31 ICBM and other missile systems.

The source emphasised that the technology transferred to China was civil-based, however, the differences between MZKT civil and military products is not believed to be significant.

Wanshan Special Vehicle Co. Ltd has since used the transferred technology to develop a wide range of specialist heavy-duty chassis, these having from three to seven axles. One believed use of the WS2500 chassis is in the Transporter-Erector-Launcher (TEL) role for the Dong Feng-21C Intermediate Range Ballistic Missile (IRMB).

The WS2500 is similar in appearance to the WS2600, this also having a five-axle configuration. The WS2500 has a lower GVW, at 56,000 kg this some 9,000 kg lower than that of the WS2600. The overall length and second-to-third axle wheelbase of the WS2500 are slightly less than those of the WS2600. The cab is located further forward on the WS2600, and as a direct result of this approach angle reduces to 18 degrees.

Available details of some other WS heavy-duty off-road vehicle chassis (including the WS2600) can be found elsewhere in this section.

Wanshan Special Vehicle Co. Ltd also produces military vehicles not based on MZKT technology. Available details of some of these vehicles can be found elsewhere in this section.

The main competitor to the Wanshan WS series of heavy-duty off-road vehicles is the TAS series of heavy-duty trucks developed by the Taian Special Vehicle Plant. The TAS series is an indigenous Chinese design, but this may also have benefited from some former Soviet Union technology.

Description
Beyond some basic weights and dimensions, very little information specific to the WS2500 has been released by the manufacturer. The vehicle is, however, clearly based on MZKT technology and features a torsionally rigid chassis and torsion bar independent wheel suspension. The wide footprint tyres can be fitted with a central tyre inflation system that allows for pressures to be varied between 0.1 and 0.38 MPa. The WS2500 appears to be available with either a two-door or four-door cab.

The (10 × 8/10 × 10) designation of the WS2500 appears to refer to the fact that both (10 × 8) and (10 × 10) drive options are available.

Wanshan WS2500 (10 × 8) heavy-duty off-road vehicle (Gordon Arthur)
1391080

With the exception of the weights and dimensions included in the Specifications table (which are for a four-door cab variant), no other details, including engine or other driveline component details, have been released.

Specifications
WS2500
Cab seating: 1 + 1 or 1 + 3
Configuration: 10 × 8/10 × 10
Weight:
  (kerb) 21,300 kg
  (laden) 56,000 kg
Length: 15.45 m
Width: 3.05 m
Height: 2.97 m
Ground clearance: 400 mm
Track: 2.375 m
Wheelbase: 2.2 + 4.6 + 2.2 + 2.2 m
Angle of approach/departure: 27°/35°
Max speed: 75 km/h
Max range: (highway) 650 km
Fuel capacity: n/avail
Max gradient: 40%
Fording: 1.2 m
Engine: n/avail
Gearbox: n/avail
Transfer box: n/avail
Clutch: n/avail
Steering: power-assisted on front and rear axle pairs
Turning radius: 15 m
Suspension: independent torsion bar
Tyres: n/avail
Brakes: drums all-round
Electrical system: 24 V

Status
In production. In service with the People's Liberation Army (PLA), and possibly other undisclosed countries.

Contractor
Wanshan Special Vehicle Co. Ltd

Wanshan WS2600 (10 × 8) heavy-duty off-road vehicle

Development
The Wanshan WS2600 (10 × 8) heavy-duty off-road vehicle is manufactured by the Wanshan Special Vehicle Co. Ltd, this being one of 26 subsidiaries of China Sanjiang Space Group (CSSG). China Sanjiang Space Group is a large state-owned enterprise group under the direct control of China Aerospace Science and Industry Corporation (CASIC). From its formation in 1969, CSSG has specialised in missile and space technology.

The company manufactured its first heavy-duty off-road vehicle in 1980. Wanshan military truck chassis are predominantly used as launchers, transporters or support role vehicles for military missile and multiple launch rocket systems.

Following a display in 2001 during which China's Second Artillery Force (SAF) displayed their newly-equipped Dong Feng-31 intercontinental ballistic missiles (ICBMs) on a new (12 × 12) chassis, a source from the Minsk Wheeled Tractor Plant (MZKT) in the now Belarus disclosed that a joint working group had been established between MZKT and China to help Beijing design and build a wheeled vehicle for use with the Dong Feng-31 ICBM and other missile systems.

The source emphasised that the technology transferred to China was civil-based, however, the differences between MZKT civil and military products is not believed to be significant.

Wanshan Special Vehicle Co. Ltd has since used the transferred technology to develop a wide range of specialist heavy-duty chassis, these having from three to seven axles.

The WS2600 is similar in appearance to the WS2500, this also having a five-axle configuration. The WS2600 has a greater GVW, at 65,000 kg this some 9,000 kg greater than that of the WS2500. The overall length and second-to-third axle wheelbase of the WS2600 are slightly greater than those of the WS2500. The cab is located further forward on the WS2600, and as a direct result of this approach angle reduces to 18 degree.

Available details of some other WS heavy-duty off-road vehicle chassis (including the WS2500) can be found elsewhere in this section.

Wanshan Special Vehicle Co. Ltd also produces military vehicles not based on MZKT technology. Available details of some of these vehicles can be found elsewhere in this section.

The main competitor to the Wanshan WS series of heavy-duty off-road vehicles is the TAS series of heavy-duty trucks developed by the Taian Special Vehicle Plant. The TAS series is an indigenous Chinese design, but this may also have benefited from some former Soviet Union technology.

WS2600 (10 × 8) heavy-duty off-road vehicle (Wanshan)   1391078

Wanshan WS2900 (12 × 12) heavy-duty off-road vehicle (Wanshan) 1391081

Description

The WS2600 is clearly based on MZKT technology and features a torsionally rigid chassis and torsion bar independent wheel suspension. The wide footprint tyres can be fitted with a central tyre inflation system that allows for pressures to be varied between 0.25 and 0.47 MPa.

Released data is more comprehensive than for most WS range vehicles, and includes details of main driveline components that are not of indigenous Chinese, or former Soviet Union development.

Specifications

WS2600
Cab seating: n/avail
Configuration: 10 × 10 (the 4th axle appears undriven)
Weight:
  (kerb) 22,500 kg
  (laden) 65,000 kg
  (payload) 42,500 kg
Length: 16.35 m
Width: 3.05 m
Height: 2.82 m
Ground clearance: 400 mm
Track: 2.375 m
Wheelbase: 2.2 + 4.65 + 2.05 + 2.05 m
Angle of approach/departure: 18°/25°
Max speed: 70 km/h
Max range: (highway) 650 km
Fuel capacity: n/avail
Fuel consumption: 100 litres/100 km
Max gradient: 40%
Fording: 1.2 m
Trench crossing: 2.5 m
Vertical obstacle: 400 mm
Engine: Deutz BF12L513C 19.144-litre V-12 turbocharged air-cooled 4-stroke diesel developing 544 hp (406 kW) and 2,040 N.m torque
Gearbox: ZF 6HP902 fully automatic with 6 forward and 1 reverse gears
Transfer box: 2-speed with differential lock
Steering: power-assisted on front and rear axle pairs; emergency steering back-up
Turning radius: 15 m
Suspension: independent torsion bar
Tyres: 1500 × 600-635 with CTI
Brakes: drums all-round, air-over-hydraulic or full dual-circuit air options, supplementary engine exhaust brake and hydrodynamic retarder
Electrical system: 24 V

Status

Production status uncertain. Probably in service with the People's Liberation Army (PLA).

Contractor

Wanshan Special Vehicle Co. Ltd

Wanshan WS2900 (12 × 12) heavy-duty off-road vehicle

Development

The Wanshan WS2900 (12 × 12) heavy-duty off-road vehicle is manufactured by the Wanshan Special Vehicle Co. Ltd, this being one of 26 subsidiaries of China Sanjiang Space Group (CSSG). China Sanjiang Space Group is a large state-owned enterprise group under the direct control of China Aerospace Science and Industry Corporation (CASIC). From its formation in 1969, CSSG has specialised in missile and space technology.

The company manufactured its first heavy-duty off-road vehicle in 1980. Wanshan military truck chassis are predominantly used as launchers, transporters or support role vehicles for military missile and multiple launch rocket systems.

Following a display in 2001 during which China's Second Artillery Force (SAF) displayed their newly-equipped Dong Feng-31 intercontinental ballistic missiles (ICBMs) on a new (12 × 12) chassis, a source from the Minsk Wheeled Tractor Plant (MZKT) in the now Belarus disclosed that a joint working group had been established between MZKT and China to help Beijing design and build a wheeled vehicle for use with the Dong Feng-31 ICBM and other missile systems.

The source emphasised that the technology transferred to China was civil-based, however, the differences between MZKT civil and military products is not believed to be significant.

The chassis in question could be the Wanshan WS2900, and Wanshan Special Vehicle Co. Ltd has since used the transferred technology to develop a wide range of specialist heavy-duty chassis, these having from three to seven axles. Available details of some of these chassis can be found elsewhere in this section.

Wanshan Special Vehicle Co. Ltd also produces military vehicles not based on MZKT technology. Available details of some of these vehicles can be found elsewhere in this section.

The main competitor to the Wanshan WS series of heavy-duty off-road vehicles is the TAS series of heavy-duty trucks developed by the Taian Special Vehicle Plant. The TAS series is an indigenous Chinese design, but this may also have benefited from some former Soviet Union technology.

Description

Beyond some basic weights and dimensions, very little information specific to the WS2900 has been released by the manufacturer. The vehicle is, however, clearly based on MZKT technology and features a torsionally rigid chassis and torsion bar independent wheel suspension. The wide footprint tyres can be fitted with a central tyre inflation system that allows for pressures to be varied between 0.1 and 0.38 MPa.

With the exception of the weights and dimensions included in the Specifications table, no other details, including engine or other driveline component details, have been released.

Specifications

WS2900
Cab seating: 1 + 1 or 1 + 3
Configuration: 12 × 12
Weight:
  (kerb) 34,000 kg
  (laden) 90,000 kg
Length: 17.53 m
Width: 3.35 m
Height: 3.04 m
Ground clearance: 400 mm
Track: 2.7 m
Wheelbase: 2.05 + 2.4 + 3.5 + 2.7 + 2.7 m
Angle of approach/departure: 26°/27°
Max speed: (highway) 60 km/h
Max range: 650 km
Fuel capacity: n/avail
Fuel consumption: 150 litres/100 km
Max gradient: 30%
Fording: 1.2 m
Engine: n/avail
Gearbox: n/avail
Transfer box: n/avail
Clutch: n/avail
Steering: power-assisted on front and rear axle pairs
Turning radius: 17 m
Suspension: independent torsion bar
Tyres: n/avail
Brakes: drums all-round
Electrical system: 24 V

Status
In production. In service with the People's Liberation Army (PLA).

Contractor
Wanshan Special Vehicle Co. Ltd

Wanshan WS5251 (6 × 6) truck

Development
The Wanshan WS5251 (6 × 6) truck is manufactured by the Wanshan Special Vehicle Co. Ltd, this being one of 26 subsidiaries of China Sanjiang Space Group (CSSG). China Sanjiang Space Group is a large state-owned enterprise group under the direct control of China Aerospace Science and Industry Corporation (CASIC). From its formation in 1969, CSSG has specialised in missile and space technology.

The company manufactured its first heavy-duty off-road vehicle in 1980. Wanshan military truck chassis are predominantly used as launchers, transporters or support role vehicles for military missile and multiple launch rocket systems.

Following a display in 2001 during which China's Second Artillery Force (SAF) displayed their newly-equipped Dong Feng-31 intercontinental ballistic missiles (ICBMs) on a new (12 × 12) chassis, a source from the Minsk Wheeled Tractor Plant (MZKT) in the now Belarus disclosed that a joint working group had been established between MZKT and China to help Beijing design and build a wheeled vehicle for use with the Dong Feng-31 ICBM and other missile systems.

The source emphasised that the technology transferred to China was civil-based, however, the differences between MZKT civil and military products is not believed to be significant.

Wanshan Special Vehicle Co. Ltd has since used the transferred technology to develop a wide range of specialist heavy-duty chassis, these having from three to seven axles. Available details of some of these chassis can be found elsewhere in this section.

Wanshan Special Vehicle Co. Ltd also produces military vehicles not based on MZKT technology, and the WS5251 appears to be one of these, the WS5251 based on a conventional chassis and featuring beam-type axles and leaf spring suspension, not the torsionally rigid chassis and fully independent torsion bar-type suspension of MZKT-derived designs.

Available details of some other Wanshan Special Vehicle Co. Ltd vehicles not based on MZKT technology can be found elsewhere in this section.

The main competitor to the Wanshan WS series of heavy-duty off-road vehicles is the TAS series of heavy-duty trucks developed by the Taian Special Vehicle Plant. The TAS series is an indigenous Chinese design, but this may also have benefited from some former Soviet Union technology.

Description
Beyond some basic weights and dimensions, very little information specific to the WS5251 has been released by the manufacturer. However, unlike some other Wanshan Special Vehicle Co. Ltd designs the vehicle is clearly not based on MZKT technology, featuring a conventional chassis and leaf spring suspension.

The four door cab, which seats six, appears to provide ballistic and probably limited blast protection in standard configuration.

With the exception of the weights and dimensions included in the Specifications table, no other details, including engine or other driveline component details, have been released.

Specifications
WS5251
Cab seating: 6
Configuration: 6 × 6
Weight:
  (kerb) 11,490 kg
  (laden) 25,000 kg
Length: 7.3 m
Width: 2.5 m
Height: 2.95 m
Ground clearance: 380 mm
Track: 2.056 m
Wheelbase: 2.9 + 1.45 m
Max speed: 90 km/h
Max range: (highway) 600 km
Fuel consumption: 40 litres/100 km
Fuel capacity: n/avail
Max gradient: 58%
Fording: 1.2 m
Engine: n/avail
Gearbox: n/avail
Transfer box: n/avail
Clutch: n/avail
Steering: power-assisted on front axle
Turning radius: 10 m
Suspension: leaf springs, inverted on rear bogie
Tyres: n/avail
Brakes: drums all-round
Electrical system: 24 V

Wanshan WS5251 (6 × 6) truck (Wanshan)   1391085

Status
Probably in service with the People's Liberation Army (PLA).

Contractor
Wanshan Special Vehicle Co. Ltd.

Wanshan WS5252 (6 × 6) truck

Development
The Wanshan WS5252 (6 × 6) truck is manufactured by the Wanshan Special Vehicle Co. Ltd, this being one of 26 subsidiaries of China Sanjiang Space Group (CSSG). China Sanjiang Space Group is a large state-owned enterprise group under the direct control of China Aerospace Science and Industry Corporation (CASIC). From its formation in 1969, CSSG has specialised in missile and space technology.

The company manufactured its first heavy-duty off-road vehicle in 1980. Wanshan military truck chassis are predominantly used as launchers, transporters or support role vehicles for military missile and multiple launch rocket systems. The WS5252 chassis, known as the SH-1, is used to mount NORINCO 155 mm/52 calibre artillery.

Following a display in 2001 during which China's Second Artillery Force (SAF) displayed their newly-equipped Dong Feng-31 Inter-Continental Ballistic Missiles (ICBMs) on a new (12 × 12) chassis, a source from the Minsk Wheeled Tractor Plant (MZKT) in the now Belarus disclosed that a joint working group had been established between MZKT and China to help Beijing design and build a wheeled vehicle for use with the Dong Feng-31 ICBM and other missile systems.

The source emphasised that the technology transferred to China was civil-based, however, the differences between MZKT civil and military products is not believed to be significant.

Wanshan Special Vehicle Co. Ltd has since used the transferred technology to develop a wide range of specialist heavy-duty chassis, these having from three to seven axles. Available details of some of these chassis can be found elsewhere in this section.

Wanshan Special Vehicle Co. Ltd also produces military vehicles not based on MZKT technology, and the WS5252 appears to be one of these, the WS5252 based on a conventional chassis and featuring beam-type axles and leaf spring suspension (certainly on the rear bogie), not the torsionally rigid chassis and fully independent torsion bar-type suspension of MZKT-derived designs.

Available details of some other Wanshan Special Vehicle Co. Ltd vehicles not based on MZKT technology can be found elsewhere in this section.

Wanshan WS5255 (6 × 6) truck (Wanshan)   1391087

The main competitor to the Wanshan WS series of heavy-duty off-road vehicles is the TAS series of heavy-duty trucks developed by the Taian Special Vehicle Plant. The TAS series is an indigenous Chinese design, but this may also have benefited from some former Soviet Union technology.

Description
Beyond some basic weights and dimensions, very little information specific to the WS5252 has been released by the manufacturer. However, unlike some other Wanshan Special Vehicle Co. Ltd designs the vehicle is clearly not based on MZKT technology, featuring a conventional chassis and leaf spring suspension on the rear bogie, and possibly on the front steer-drive axle also.

The four-door bonneted cab, which seats six, provides ballistic and probably limited blast protection in standard configuration.

With the exception of the weights and dimensions included in the Specifications table, no other details, including engine or other driveline component details, have been released.

The NORINCO SH1 155 mm/52 calibre self propelled howitzer is known to be based on the WS5252. The SH1 self-propelled howitzer was developed by NORINCO from 2002 for the export market. The system was first shown publicly in 2007, and it is understood that Pakistan received around 90 examples. Some sources are suggesting the SH1 may enter service with the PLA in the near future.

Specifications
WS5252
Cab seating: 6
Configuration: 6 × 6
Weight:
  (kerb) 10,000 kg
  (laden) 22,000 kg
Length: 7.4 m
Width: 2.5 m
Height: 2.6 m
Ground clearance: 380 mm
Track: 2.056 m
Wheelbase: 3.45 + 1.45 m
Max speed: (highway) 90 km/h
Max range: (highway) 600 km
Fuel capacity: n/avail
Fuel consumption: 36 litres/100 km
Max gradient: 58%
Fording: n/avail
Engine: n/avail
Gearbox: n/avail
Transfer box: n/avail
Clutch: n/avail
Steering: power-assisted on front axle
Turning radius: 10 m
Suspension: leaf springs, inverted on rear bogie
Tyres: n/avail
Brakes: drums all-round
Electrical system: 24 V

Status
In production. In service with Pakistan and probably in service with the People's Liberation Army (PLA).

Contractor
Wanshan Special Vehicle Co. Ltd

Czech Republic

Praga V3S (6 × 6) 3,000 kg truck

Development
The Praga V3S was developed in the early 1950s, entering production in 1952. Initial production was undertaken by Praga but in 1964 this was transferred to Avia as Praga began to concentrate on automotive components. In September 2006 Ashok Leyland of India announced it had signed a framework agreement to acquire the Truck Business Unit of Avia a.s., this company now known as Avia Ashok Leyland Motors (AALM).

Both Czech and Slovak armed forces still operate sizeable fleets of the Praga V3S, primarily for second-line and rear area duties despite the design being technically obsolete and increasingly difficult and expensive to maintain. Slovakia has begun the replacement of its Praga V3S fleet with a new indigenously produced (4 × 4) truck, the TANAX a.s. (previously TATRA Sipox) AKTIS. Full details of the TANAX AKTIS can be found elsewhere in this section. An attempt in the late 1990s to replace the Czech V3S fleet stalled after the selected manufacturer, Roudnické strojírny a slévárny a.s. (ROSS), went bankrupt after producing just 21 ROSS R210 trucks between 1997-99.

It was disclosed at IDET 2003, that following extended negotiations TATRA had acquired full rights to the ROSS 210 design, and that in conjunction with Renault Trucks of France would offer the Czech MoD an upgraded design then designated TATRA R210.12VV6×6M to replace the Praga V3S fleet.

Praga V3S (6 × 6) 3,000 kg truck fitted with an office-type rear body (Stefan Marx)   1185415

Praga V3S (6 × 6) 3,000 kg trucks fitted with a troop carrying/cargo bodies (James C O'Halloran)   0120081

Specialist ARS-12M NBC decontamination apparatus carrier variant of the Praga V3S truck (Stefan Marx)   1185416

It was reported in March 2003 there would be a tender for 583 medium trucks (6,000 kg) worth CZK1.7 billion to replace the Praga V3S. It was unclear if this would be an open [international] tender as the Czech government had the option to procure the TATRA design as a strategic procurement, thereby avoiding any legal obligation to issue a tender.

It was disclosed mid-2006 that deliveries of TATRA medium trucks were to have commenced in the second half of 2006, but had been delayed by a CZK5 billion cut in the Czech defence budget. It was announced in September 2006 the Czech government had bowed to pressure from the Czech Ministry of Defence (MoD) and motioned to release nearly CZK600 million (USD26.9 million) from the state budget to allow for procurement of these trucks for the Czech Army.

In December 2006, it was announced that following budgetary driven delays, the Czech Republic Ministry of Defence (MoD) had finally signed a USD124 million contract with TATRA for 556 TATRA T 810 - 1ROR26 13 177 6 × 6.1R (6 × 6) medium trucks to be delivered between mid-2007 and 2009. The contract award includes options for a further 247 trucks in six specialised variants.

Full details of the TATRA T 810-1ROR26 13 177 6×6.1R truck can be found elsewhere in this section.

Praga V3S (6 × 6) 3,000 kg truck fitted with an office-type rear body
(Richard Stickland)   0116903

Description

The layout of the Praga V3S is conventional, with the engine under a distinctive attenuated bonnet at the front, the two-man cab in the centre and the cargo area at the rear. There is provision for stowing fuel containers behind the front bumper. The two-door cab is of all-steel construction. There is a circular observation hatch in the right side of the roof. The windscreen is of the split type and both parts can be opened horizontally for increased vision. The rear cargo area has a tarpaulin cover and removable bows, which can be stowed to the rear of the cab when not required. Some V3S trucks have a winch with a 3,500 kg capacity.

Variants include: a crane truck, hopper-type dump truck (V3S-K), various shop/van models (including some with an A-frame mounted at the front of the vehicle), tanker (special), 3,000-litre capacity tanker (V3S-C), ARS-12M NBC decontamination apparatus carrier, and tractor truck (V3S-A). The chassis was also used to mount the 130 mm (32-round) M51 multiple rocket system, full details of which can be found in *Jane's Armour and Artillery*.

A (4 × 2) model of the Praga V3S was built under the designation S5T.

Specifications

Praga V3S
Cab seating: 1 + 1
Configuration: 6 × 6
Weight:
   (unladen) 5,350 kg
   (laden, road) 10,650 kg
   (laden, track) 8,650 kg
   (laden, off-road) 8,350 kg
   (payload, road) 5,300 kg
   (payload, tracks) 3,300 kg
   (payload, off-road) 3,000 kg
   (towed load, road) 5,500 kg
   (towed load, off-road) 3,100 kg
Length: 6.91 m
Width: 2.31 m
Height:
   (cab) 2.51 m
   (tarpaulin) 2.92 m
Ground clearance: 400 mm
Track:
   (front) 1.87 m
   (rear) 1.755 m
Wheelbase: 3.58 m + 1.12 m
Angle of approach/departure: 72°/32°
Max speed: 62 km/h
Range: 500 km
Fuel capacity: 120 litres
Fuel consumption: 27 litres/100 km
Max gradient: 60%
Fording: 800 mm
Engine: TATRA T-912 in-line air-cooled diesel developing 98 hp (73 kW) at 2,100 rpm (late production vehicles have TATRA T-912-2 developing 110 hp (82 kW) at 2,200 rpm, which is also installed in the Praga S5T2 truck)
Gearbox: manual with 4 forward and 2 reverse gears
Clutch: single dry plate
Transfer box: 2-speed
Turning radius: 10.5 m
Suspension: semi-elliptic leaf springs, front and rear
Tyres: 8.25 × 20
Brakes:
   (main) hydraulic, air assisted
   (parking) mechanical
Electrical system: 12 V

Status

Production complete. In service with the Czech (1,612 remaining as of early 2009) and Slovak (845 remaining as of early 2009) armed forces, other former Warsaw Pact countries, and some countries in the Middle East. Replacement underway in the Czech Republic and Slovakia.

Contractor

Avia a.s.

ROSS R210 (6 × 6) truck

Development

The Roudnické strojírny a slévárny a.s. (ROSS) R210 was developed in the late 1990s as the intended successor of the Praga V3S (6 × 6) 3,000 kg truck in Czech military service. The replacement programme stalled after Roudnické strojírny a slévárny a.s. became bankrupt, after producing just 21 vehicles between 1997 and 1999. Full details of the Praga V3S (6 × 6) 3,000 kg truck can be found elsewhere in this section.

It was disclosed at IDET 2003, that following extended negotiations TATRA had acquired full rights to the ROSS 210 design, and that in conjunction with Renault Trucks of France would offer the Czech MoD an upgraded design then designated TATRA R210.12VV6 × 6M to replace the Praga V3S fleet.

It was reported in March 2003 that there would be a tender for 583 medium trucks (6,000 kg) worth CZK1.7 billion to replace the Praga V3S. It was unclear if this would be an open (international) tender as the Czech government had the option to procure the TATRA design as a strategic procurement, thereby avoiding any legal obligation to issue a tender.

It was disclosed mid-2006 that deliveries of TATRA medium trucks were to have commenced in the second half of 2006, but had been delayed by a CZK5 billion cut in the Czech defence budget. It was announced in September 2006 the Czech government had bowed to pressure from the Czech Ministry of Defence (MoD) and motioned to release nearly CZK600 million (USD26.9 million) from the state budget to allow for procurement of these trucks for the Czech Army.

It was announced in December-2006 that following budgetary driven delays the Czech Republic Ministry of Defence (MoD) had finally signed a USD124 million contract with TATRA for 556 TATRA T 810-1ROR26 13 177 6 × 6.1R (6 × 6) medium trucks to be delivered between mid-2007 and 2009. The contract award includes options for a further 247 trucks in six specialised variants.

Full details of the TATRA T 810-1ROR26 13 177 6 × 6.1R truck can be found elsewhere in this section.

Description

The ROSS R210 is of conventional design, being based on a ladder frame chassis fitted with beam-type axles. A Renault commercial cab is fitted. Motive power is provided by a Renault diesel engine, this coupled to an Eaton gearbox, Rockwell (now ArvinMeritor) transfer box and driving through Praga portal axles.

Status

Production complete. In service with the Czech Army (bridging units) (14).

Contractor

TATRA, a.s.

ROSS R210 (6 × 6) truck of the Czech Army; only 21 examples were delivered (James C O'Halloran)   0120079

TATRA FORCE family (10 × 10) and (12 × 12) multi-axle chassis

Development

The TATRA T 815-6 FORCE family (previously designated T 816 FORCE family) of tactical trucks was introduced by TATRA in 1996 as the continued evolution of the T 815 series first introduced in 1983. Full details of the T 815, the 1998-introduced T 815 ARMAX families, and the 2004-introduced T 815-7 tactical range (with a military-specific cab) can be found elsewhere in this section.

TATRA T815-6MWR8T 45 324 12 × 12.1R FORCE family (12 × 12) multi-axle chassis of the Indian Army mounting a PJ-10 Brahmos (Gordon Arthur)
1391185

TATRA T 815-6MWR8T 39 324 10×10.1R FORCE family (10 × 10) multi-axle chassis (TATRA a.s.)
1185469

The T 815 ARMAX family are based around commercially available designs, militarised as required, and are constructed to comply with all relevant legislation including emissions, noise and axle loadings, although in a number of cases vehicle payload capabilities exceed allowable peacetime maximums. The T 815-6 FORCE family are purpose designed no-compromise trucks for tactical military applications and are fitted with a range of water-cooled engines all producing over 400 hp.

TATRA, a.s. became a Joint Stock Company in 1992. In November 2001, it was announced that the Czech government had approved the purchase of a 92 per cent stake in TATRA, a. s. by SDC International of the US. Following a brief period of difficult-to-follow ownership reorganisation, in September 2003 it was announced that Terex Corporation of the US had acquired 70.51 per cent of TATRA shares. Vectra (a London-based Indian-owned company) owned 21.11 per cent of shares, the remaining 8.38 per cent being privately owned. The company became known as TATRA, a. s., a Terex company, with products continuing to be branded TATRA.

In October 2006 it was announced that Terex Corporation had sold its 81 per cent holding of TATRA, a.s. to a consortium of Czech and US investors. The Czech registered Blue River s.r.o. consortium is made up of Belgium-based KBC Private Equity, Vectra Ltd, a US investor, plus Meadow Hill. Vectra Ltd - a construction equipment, bus and truck maker - folded its existing 11.1 per cent stake into Blue River. Blue River s.r.o. is now known as TATRA Holdings.

Description

The overall layout of the TATRA T 815-6ZVR8T 43 400 10×10.1R, T 815-6MWR8T 39 324 10×10.1R (10 × 10) and T 815-6MWR8T 45 324 12×12.1R (12 × 12) multi-axle chassis follows closely that of earlier and more conventional TATRA truck designs. The torsionally rigid tubular backbone-type chassis is retained, as is the swinging half-axle independent wheel suspension system. Using an (8 × 8) chassis as a starting point, the wheelbase between the second and third axles has been increased and the additional rear axles have been added by the modular use of TATRA's swinging half-axles and tubular backbone chassis components.

The (10 × 10) chassis have the front steer-drive axles sprung by the combination of leaf springs and telescopic shock-absorbers, the leaf springs being shared longitudinally between the axle pair. The third and fourth drive axle pairing are sprung by TATRA's combination suspension system that uses the commercial name KING FRAME. The so-called heavy version of this combination suspension system is fitted. This combines airbags and leaf springs, the airbag units being mounted above the backbone tube to protect from impact or damage while operating off-road, the leaf springs being shared longitudinally between the axle pair. The fifth and rearmost steer-drive axle uses the so-called light version of system. This combines airbags with internal coil springs and telescopic shock-absorbers on each half-axle, the airbag units again being mounted above the backbone tube. The (12 × 12) chassis is fitted with the more conventional TATRA leaf spring set-up, but complemented by rubber limiters, with the front and rear steer-drive axle pairings also having telescopic shock-absorbers.

A further derivative of TATRA's airbag suspension set-up is used on the latest TATRA T815-7 series of tactical trucks, full details of which can be found elsewhere in this section.

Motive power for T 815-6ZVR8T 43 400 10×10.1R is provided by a Deutz 15.87-litre V-8 water-cooled four-stroke diesel developing 544 hp, while the T 815-6MWR8T 39 324 10×10.1R as well as the T 815-6MWR8T 45 324 12×12.1R are powered by a Cummins ISM 10.82-litre in-line 6-cylinder water-cooled four-stroke diesel, developing 440 hp. On all chassis the hub reduction axles are driven via a Twin Disc torque converter and fully automatic transmission. The model 8-FLW-1754-1 torque converter is fitted with a lock-up clutch and two Power Take-Off's (PTO's). The fully automatic TD61-1175 (T 815-6ZVR8T 43 400 10×10.1R only) or TD61-1177

transmission is integrated into the backbone tube thus eliminating the need for a separate transfer box. Six forward and one reverse gears are available and there is a lockable front/rear torque divider. A 'limp home' facility is also provided. The drive to the rear two axles on the T 815-6MWR8T 45 324 12×12.1R is disengageable for on-road use.

Dual circuit drum brakes are fitted all-round the T 815-6MWR8T 39 324 10×10.1R and T 815-6MWR8T 45 324 12×12.1R being fitted with an Anti-lock Braking System (ABS) with manual disconnect for off-road driving conditions. An engine exhaust brake is fitted to supplement the main braking system. For improved traction off-road driver-controlled longitudinal and cross-axle differential locks are fitted, and a semi-automatic Central Tyre Inflation (CTI) system is standard. Bead locks to enable extreme low-pressure operation are standard on the T 815-6MWR8T 39 324 10×10.1R and the T 815-6MWR8T 45 324 12×12.1R, an option on the T 815-6ZVR8T 43 400 10×10.1R. 1600R 20 tyres are standard fit and all chassis can surmount 600 mm vertical obstacle and cross a 2 m trench. Without additional preparation the T 815-6MWR8T 39 324 10×10.1R and T 815-6MWR8T 45 324 12×12.1R chassis can operate throughout a –30 to +50°C temperature range, to +55°C for the TATRA T 815-6ZVR8T 43 400 10×10.1R chassis.

The all-steel two-door cab is of conventional design and features a curved single piece windscreen and a single roof hatch. Two full-size seats are standard, with an occasional/emergency seat fixed to the central engine cover. The cab tilts forward hydraulically for maintenance purposes. An air-conditioning system, an independent diesel-fuelled cab heater and an NBC protection set for the crew are standard equipment.

TATRA has developed a C-130 transportable variant of this cab. This can be reduced for air-transport by two people in around 40 minutes; nine bolts are involved. Larger four-door or crew-type cabs with bunks or additional seating are available.

As chassis-cabs these multi-axle designs are capable of accepting a wide variety of bodies including bridging, radar or missile system related. The maximum quoted payloads are T 815-6ZVR8T 43 400 10×10.1R (25,100 kg), T 815-6MWR8T 39 324 10×10.1R (22,000 kg) and T 815-6MWR8T 45 324 12×12.1R (26,560 kg). TATRA are unable to comment this particular subject for contractual confidentiality reasons, however it is known that multi-axle FORCE family chassis are being supplied to India for use with the Russian Splav 300 mm BM 9A52 (12-round) Smerch Multiple Rocket System (MRS) (10 × 10), and the PJ-10 Brahmos, an Indian version of the original Russian 3M55 Onyx supersonic surface-to-surface missile that can be fired from land, surface ships, submarines and aircraft (12 × 12). At the time of writing (November 2010), it was understood that around 100 chassis are involved, the (10 × 10) chassis being the most predominant.

TATRA T 815-6ZVR8T 43 400 10×10.1R FORCE family (10 × 10) multi-axle chassis (TATRA a.s.)
0524792

Model	T 815-6ZVR8T 43 400 10×10.1	T 815-6MWR8T 39 324 10×10.1R	T 815-6MWR8T 45 324 12×12.1
Cab seating:	1 + 1 (+1 occasional)	1 + 1 (+1 occasional)	1 + 1 (+1 occasional)
Configuration:	10 × 10	10 × 10	12 × 12
Weight:			
(unladen)	17,900 kg	16,890 kg	18,440 kg
(laden)	43,000 kg	39,000 kg	45,000 kg
(payload)	25,100 kg	22,000 kg	26,560 kg
Length: (chassis-cab)	11.54 m	13.9 m	14.03 m
Width:	2.5 m	2.5 m	2.5 m
Height:	3.14 m (max)	3.1 m	3.15 m (max)
Ground clearance:	410 mm	390 mm	390 mm
Wheel track:			
(front)	2.034 m	2.074 (and rearmost axles)	2.074 m
(rear)	2.05 m	2.014 (3rd and 4th)	2.074 m
Wheelbase:	1.65 + 3.82 + 1.45 + 2.1 m	1.65 + 5 + 1.45 + 2.1 m	1.65 + 5 + 1.45 + 2.11 + 1.65 m
Angle of approach:	39°	39°	39°
Max speed:	90 km/h	82 km/h	81 km/h
Cruising range:	850 km	600 km	500 km
Fuel capacity:	840 litres	570 litres	570 litres
Gradient:	70%	80%	85%
Sideslope: (chassis-cab)	57%	66.6%	57%
Fording:	1.25 m	1.25 M	1.25 m
Engine:	Deutz BF8M 1015C 15.874-litre V-8 turbocharged and charge-air-cooled water-cooled direct injection diesel developing 544 hp (406 kW) at 2,100 rpm and 2,600 N.m torque between 1,200 and 1,400 rpm	Cummins ISM 440E 10.823-litre 6-cylinder in-line turbocharged and charge-air-cooled water-cooled direct injection diesel developing 440 hp (328 kW) at 1,800 rpm and 2,100 N.m torque at 1,200 rpm	Cummins ISM 440E 10.823-litre 6-cylinder in-line turbocharged and charge-air-cooled water-cooled direct injection diesel developing 440 hp (328 kW) at 1,800 rpm and 2,100 N.m torque at 1,200 rpm
Transmission:	Twin Disc TD61-1175 automatic with 6 forward and 1 reverse gears, plus Twin Disc 8-FLW-1754-1 torque converter with lock-up clutch	Twin Disc TD61-1177 automatic with 6 forward and 1 reverse gears, plus Twin Disc 8-FLW-1754-1 torque converter with lock-up clutch	Twin Disc TD61-1177 automatic with 6 forward and 1 reverse gears, plus Twin Disc 8-FLW-1754-1 torque converter with lock-up clutch
Steering:	power assisted on 1st, 2nd and 5th axles, two independent circuits with emergency steering pump	power assisted on 1st, 2nd and 5th axles, two independent circuits with emergency steering pump	power assisted on 1st, 2nd, 5th and 6th axles, two independent circuits with emergency steering pump
Turning radius: (kerb)	15 m	17.1 m	17.1 m
Suspension:			
(front axle pair)	leaf springs, shared longitudinally between the axle pair, and telescopic-shock absorbers (see text for details)	leaf springs, shared longitudinally between the axle pair, and telescopic-shock absorbers (see text for details)	leaf springs, rubber limiters and telescopic shock-absorbers (see text for details)
(rear axles)	airbags and leaf springs on the third and fourth axles, airbags with internal coil springs plus telescopic shock-absorbers on the fifth axle (see text for details)	airbags and leaf springs on the third and fourth axles, airbags with internal coil springs plus telescopic shock-absorbers on the fifth axle (see text for details)	leaf springs and rubber limiters on third and fourth axles, leaf springs, rubber limiters and telescopic shock-absorbers on fifth and sixth axles (see text for details)
Tyres:	1600R 20	1600R 20	1600R 20
Brakes:	dual circuit, air, drums all-round	dual circuit, air, drums all-round	dual circuit, air, drums all-round
Electrical system:	24 V	24 V	24 V
Batteries:	2 × 12 V, 165 Ah	2 × 12 V, 165 Ah	2 × 12 V, 180 Ah
Alternator:	28 V, 80 A	28 V, 70 A	28 V, 70 A

It is understood that the bulk of Indian (10 × 10) deliveries are Deutz-powered, however an additional two chassis with a longer wheelbase and powered by a Cummins diesel engine have been supplied for trials, possibly with an indigenously developed UAV.

A detailed overview of the T 815 FORCE family can be found elsewhere in this section.

Specifications
See table above

Status
In production for India, around 100 (predominantly (10 × 10)) delivered from 2003 onwards.

Contractor
TATRA a.s.

TATRA T 810-1ROR26 13 177 6 × 6.1R (6 × 6) truck

Development
The TATRA T 810-1ROR26 13 177 6 × 6.1R (6 × 6) truck is expected to be the eventual replacement for the Praga V3S (6 × 6) 3,000 kg truck in Czech military service.

The ROSS (Roudnické strojírny a slévárny a.s.) R210 (details of which can be found elsewhere in this section) was developed in the late 1990s as the intended successor of the Praga V3S but the replacement programme

stalled after Roudnické strojírny a slévárny a.s. became bankrupt, after producing just 21 vehicles between 1997 and 1999. The ROSS R210 used a Renault commercial cab and Renault diesel engine. It was disclosed at IDET 2003, that following extended negotiations TATRA had acquired full

Production standard TATRA T 810-1ROR26 13 177 6 × 6.1R (6 × 6) truck with a standard troop-carrying/cargo-type body fitted (TATRA a.s.) 1391041

TATRA T 810-1ROR26 13 177 6 × 6.1R (6 × 6) truck in standard troop-carrying/cargo configuration but fitted with an armoured cab
(TATRA a.s.)   1391378

rights to the ROSS 210 design, and that in conjunction with Renault Trucks of France would offer the Czech MoD an upgraded design then designated TATRA R210.12VV6 × 6M to replace the Praga V3S fleet.

TATRA proposed the upgraded vehicle would use a new cab (from the current Renault Midlum commercial range), be fitted with a more powerful Renault EURO 3 emissions compliant diesel engine coupled to an integrated Praga gearbox/transfer box. The original Praga axles would be redesigned and upgraded to improve braking performance and incorporate an anti-lock braking system (ABS). A prototype vehicle was built.

It was reported in March 2003 there would be a tender for 583 medium trucks (6,000 kg) worth CZK7 billion to replace the Praga V3S, however it remained unclear if there was to be an open international tender as the Czech government was free to opt to procure the TATRA design as a strategic procurement, avoiding any legal obligation to issue a tender.

It was disclosed mid-2006 that deliveries of TATRA medium trucks were to have commenced in the second half of 2006, but had been delayed by a CZK5 billion cut in the Czech defence budget. It was announced in September 2006 the Czech government had bowed to pressure from the Czech Ministry of Defence (MoD) and motioned to release nearly CZK600 million (USD26.9 million) from the state budget to allow for procurement of these trucks for the Czech Army. It was announced in December 2006 that following budgetary driven delays, the Czech Republic's Ministry of Defence (MoD) had finally signed a USD124 million contract with TATRA for 556 TATRA T 810 - 1ROR26 13 177 6 × 6.1R (6 × 6) medium trucks to be delivered between mid-2007 and 2009. The contract award includes options for a further 247 trucks in six specialised variants.

By October 2009 all 556 trucks had been delivered, 530 in flatbed configuration and 26 in specialised configurations.

TATRA has indicated that a (4 × 4) variant of the T810 will be developed. The current (4 × 4) chassis offered by TATRA have payload ratings of 5,000 to 8,000 kg and chassis-cab weights of around 8,000 kg. The introduction of lighter (4 × 4) and (6 × 6) designs (with payloads ranging from 3,500 to 6,000 kg) will effectively bridge a gap in the current TATRA product range. Full details of the TATRA range of trucks can be found elsewhere in this section.

Description

The overall layout of the TATRA T 810-1ROR26 13 177 6 × 6.1R (6 × 6) truck is different to that of earlier TATRA truck designs in that TATRA's trademark torsionally rigid tubular backbone-type chassis and swinging half-axle independent wheel suspension system is replaced by a conventional ladder-type C-section chassis and portal beam axles.

The front Praga steer-drive portal hub-reduction axle is fitted with a cross-axle differential lock and is sprung by the combination of coil springs and telescopic shock-absorbers. The rear Praga drive portal hub-reduction axles are fitted with a longitudinal and cross axle differential locks and are sprung by leaf springs.

The conventional chassis has bolted and riveted in cross-members and in addition to the standard troop-carrying/cargo-type body is capable of mounting shelters/containers, recovery hampers or tanker bodies. A front or rear pull winch with 60 m of rope and rated at 78 kN is fitted.

Motive power is provided by a Renault Dxi7 four-stroke water-cooled diesel engine developing 237 hp. This drives the rear four - or all six wheels - via a ZF manual gearbox with six forward and one reverse gears and a two-speed transfer box. The main gearbox is provided with synchromesh on all but reverse gear and a PTO for winch output. For on-road use drive to the front axle can be disconnected. For improved traction off-road driver-controlled longitudinal and cross-axle differential locks are fitted and a central tyre inflation (CTI) system is standard. With an approach angle of 37° the vehicle can surmount a 600 mm vertical obstacle. A trench 900 mm wide can be crossed. Without additional preparation the vehicle can operate throughout a –32 to +44°C temperature range.

Power-assisted steering is standard, as is an anti-lock braking system (ABS). Dual circuit drum brakes are fitted all-round, supplemented by an engine exhaust brake. The standard all-steel two-door cab is supplied by Renault and is the design currently fitted to the Midlum commercial range of trucks. An armoured floor protecting the three cab occupants is fitted. An armoured cab developed by SVOS is available and around ten vehicles are understood to have been fitted with cab.

Specifications

T 810-1ROR26 13 177
Cab seating: 1 + 2
Configuration: 6 × 6
Weight:
　(unladen) 8,500 kg
　(laden) 13,000 kg
　(payload) 4,500 kg
　(towed load) 12,000 kg
　(GCW) 25,000 kg
Length: (chassis-cab) 7.365 m
Width: 2.55 m
Height: (ring mount) 3.32 m
Ground clearance: 430 mm
Wheelbase: 3.15 + 1.2 m
Angle of approach/departure: 37°/38°
Max speed: 106 km/h
Max range: (cruising) 800 km
Fuel capacity: 320 litres
Gradient: 100%
Sideslope: 40%
Fording: 1.2 m
Engine: Renault Dxi7 7.1-litre 6-cylinder in-line turbocharged and charge-air-cooled, water-cooled direct injection 4-stroke EURO 3 diesel developing 237 hp (177 kW) at 2,300 rpm and 920 N.m torque at 1,200-1,600 rpm
Gearbox: ZF 6S 1000 TO manual with 6 forward and 1 reverse gears
Transfer box: ZF/Steyr VG750 2-speed with front axle disconnect, PTO output for winch
Clutch: SAE2, 395 mm diameter, single dry plate
Steering: power-assisted
Suspension: coil springs and telescopic shock-absorbers, front; leaf springs, rear
Tyres: 365/80 R20
Brakes: dual circuit, air, drums front and rear, supplementary engine exhaust brake, ABS fitted
Electrical system: 24 V
Batteries: 2 × 12 V, 170 Ah
Alternator: 28 V, 100 A

Status

Production as required. In service with the Czech Army (see text).

Contractor

TATRA a.s.

TATRA T 815 ARMAX family of trucks

Development

The TATRA T 815 ARMAX family of trucks was introduced by TATRA in 1998 to join the earlier TERRN°1 and T 815-6 FORCE (originally designated T 816 FORCE) families of trucks, all of which are the continued evolution of the T 815 series first introduced in 1983. Full details of the T 815, the T 815-6 FORCE families, and the 2004-introduced T 815-7 tactical range (with military-specific cab) can be found elsewhere in this section.

The TERRN°1 family comprises essentially commercial designs, but are suitable for certain military applications. The T 815-6 FORCE family are purpose designed no-compromise trucks for tactical military applications and as such are fitted with a range of high-powered water-cooled engines all producing over 400 hp. The T 815 ARMAX family are based around commercially available designs, militarised as required, and are constructed to comply (when required) with all relevant legislation including emissions, noise and axle loadings, although in many cases vehicle payload capabilities exceed allowable peacetime maximums.

ARMAX range trucks are understood to be in service with the armed forces of the Czech Republic, India, Malaysia and Slovakia, with the Czech Republic being by far the biggest user.

The most recent stated intention of the Czech government was that it intended to procure 633 ARMAX range trucks for delivery between 2003-08 and for an overall contract value given as CZK6 billion (USD206 million) including bodies and superstructures. Under this contract around 80 vehicles in a mix of (4 × 4) and (6 × 6) chassis were delivered during 2004, with a further 128 delivered during 2005. During 2006 143 vehicles were scheduled for delivery, including some (8 × 8) chassis fitted with Hiab Load Handling Systems (LHS). Deliveries of LHS-equipped vehicles (which retain the old style T 815 series cab) commenced in March 2006, with 170 vehicles of this type to be delivered over a two-year period. Further specific delivery details are currently unavailable.

ACHR-90M chemical decontamination body on a TATRA ARMAX (6 × 6) chassis (Stefan Marx)   1185466

TATRA ARMAX family (6 × 6) truck fitted with a conventional troop carrying/cargo-type body (TATRA a.s.)   0122773

TATRA, a.s. became a Joint Stock Company in 1992. In November 2001, it was announced that the Czech government had approved the purchase of a 92 per cent stake in TATRA a.s. by SDC International of the US. Following a brief period of difficult-to-follow ownership reorganisation, in September 2003 it was announced that Terex Corporation of the US had acquired 70.51 per cent of TATRA shares. Vectra (a London-based Indian-owned company) owned 21.11 per cent of shares, the remaining 8.38 per cent being privately owned. The company became known as TATRA a. s., a Terex company, with products continuing to be branded TATRA.

In October 2006 it was announced that Terex Corporation had sold its 81 per cent holding of TATRA, a.s. to a consortium of Czech and US investors. The Czech registered Blue River s.r.o. consortium (now TATRA Holdings) is made up of Belgium-based KBC Private Equity, Vectra Ltd, a US investor, plus Meadow Hill. Vectra Ltd - a construction equipment, bus and truck maker - folded its existing 11.1 per cent stake into Blue River.

Description

The overall layout of the T 815 ARMAX family follows closely that of earlier TATRA truck designs. The torsionally rigid tubular backbone-type chassis is retained, as is the swinging half-axle independent wheel suspension system. The front steer-drive axle on both (4 × 4) and (6 × 6) designs is sprung by the combination of torsion bars and telescopic shock-absorbers. The front steer-drive axles on (8 × 8) designs are sprung by leaf springs and telescopic shock-absorbers. The rear drive axle(s) are now sprung by TATRA's combination suspension that uses the commercial name KING FRAME. The light version of this combination suspension system uses airbags with internal coil springs and telescopic shock-absorbers on each half-axle, the airbag units being mounted above the backbone tube to protect from impact or damage while operating off-road. Maximum individual axle loadings for the light version are 11,500 kg. The heavy version (available on (6 × 6) chassis) of this combination suspension system combines the use of airbags on the individual half-axles with leaf springs shared longitudinally between the rear axle pair. Although in excess of peacetime legislation in many countries, the heavy version allows for individual axle loadings of 15,000 kg.

A further derivative of the airbag suspension set-up is used on the latest TATRA T815-7 series of tactical trucks, full details of which can be found elsewhere in this section.

For on-road use drive to the front axle can be disconnected. For improved traction off-road driver-controlled longitudinal and cross-axle differential locks are fitted, and on all single-tyred models a semi-automatic Central Tyre Inflation (CTI) system is standard. Bead locks are an option for extreme low-pressure operation. 1400R 20 tyres are standard fit although 1200R 20 tyres on dual rear wheels are available on models requiring a higher payload capability such as the T815-260R24 33 255 6×6.2, fitted with the Multilift Mark 4 Load Handling System (LHS). This model has a maximum Gross Vehicle Weight (GVW) of 33,000 kg and with a slightly different designation and reduced 28,700 kg GVW was originally marketed as part of the TERRN°1 family. Vehicles fitted with 1200R 20 tyres and dual rear wheels are usually classified by TATRA as medium mobility. With an approach angle of 37°, all models fitted with 1400R 20 tyres can surmount a 500 mm vertical obstacle and cross a 900 mm trench. Without additional preparation, the T 815 ARMAX family is designed to operate throughout a –30 to +40°C temperature range.

The T 815 ARMAX family is powered by the EURO 2 (EURO 3 on request) emissions compliant TATRA 12.7-litre V-8 four-stroke air-cooled diesel engines, producing between 308 and 408 hp. Water-cooling is an option, with power outputs ranging from 265 to 350 hp. Main gearbox is model-dependant but is usually a TATRA 10 TS 160 manual with 10 forward and two reverse gears, and synchromesh on all but reverse and first gears. A two-speed transfer box is standard, a single-speed transfer box being an option. Power assisted steering is standard, drum brakes are fitted all-round, supplemented by an engine exhaust brake. An Anti-lock Braking System (ABS) is an option.

The standard all-steel two-door cab is of conventional design and features a single roof hatch. Larger cabs with additional stowage, crew or berthing space, or four doors are options. Two full-size seats are standard,

with an occasional/emergency seat fixed to the central engine cover. A curved single piece or four-piece split windscreen can be fitted. The cab tilts forward hydraulically for maintenance purposes and an independent fuel-powered cab heater and air-conditioning are options. To meet a potential IDF requirement, TATRA developed a version of the standard cab that splits at waist level for C-130 air-transport. This process takes two people less than 40 mins; nine bolts are involved.

In addition to the standard troop carrying/cargo-type body with drop sides, bows and a tarpaulin cover, the ARMAX chassis can be fitted with a wide variety of bodies, the torsionally rigid TATRA backbone chassis making the ARMAX, and other TATRA truck families, particularly well suited to the transport of shelters or containers.

At present the ARMAX (4 × 4) is available with a wheelbase of 3.7, 4.09 or 4.5 m, the 1400R 20 single-tyred ARMAX (6 × 6) with a 3.44 or 4.09 +1.45 m wheelbase, with varying chassis lengths. A tractor truck version of the 6 × 6 with a 3.7 + 1.45 m wheelbase, 1200R 24 tyres and dual rear wheels and carrying the designation T815-29 ON3T 38 300 6×6.2R/371 has been supplied to Slovakia in small numbers. Having a gross combination weight of 75,000 kg, full details of this model (and an earlier derivative of it) can be found in the *Heavy equipment transporters* section.

The following are T 815 ARMAX models were available as of November 2009. Full details of certain models can be found elsewhere in this section:

- T 815-25RR45/50T: 7,200 kg payload (on chassis-cab), 16,500 kg GVW, 32,500 kg GTW, 308 hp
- T 815-26OR45/451: 8,600 kg payload (on chassis-cab), 17,000 kg GVW, 41,000 kg GTW, 342 hp
- T 815-26WR45/10T: 9,200 kg payload (on chassis-cab), 17,000 kg GVW, 41,000 kg GTW, 342 hp
- T 815-26WR45/11T: 9,200 kg payload (on chassis-cab), 17,000 kg GVW, 41,000 kg GTW, 342 hp
- T 815-26WR45/12T: 8,400 kg payload (on chassis-cab), 17,000 kg GVW, 41,000 kg GTW, 342 hp
- T 815-26WR45/13T: 8,700 kg payload (on chassis-cab), 17,000 kg GVW, 41,000 kg GTW, 342 hp
- T 815-26WR 45/14T: 9,200 kg payload (on chassis-cab), 17,000 kg GVW, 41,000 kg GTW, 342 hp
- T 815-26MR25/31T: 16,000 kg payload (on chassis-cab), 26,000 kg GVW, 48,000 kg GTW, 342 hp
- T 815-26WR25/10T: 16,000 kg payload (on chassis-cab), 26,000 kg GVW, 48,000 kg GTW, 342 hp
- T 815-26WV25/10T: 14,500 kg payload (on chassis-cab), 26,000 kg GVW, 48,000 kg GTW, 342 hp
- T 815-26OR84/269: 20,400 kg payload (on chassis-cab), 34,000 kg GVW, 55,000 kg GTW, 342 hp
- T 815-27OR84/261: 17,000 kg payload (on chassis-cab), 41,000 kg GVW, 60,500 kg GTW, 402 hp

Status

In production. T 815 ARMAX family trucks are in service with Czech, Indian, Malaysian and Slovak armed forces.

Contractor

TATRA, a.s.

TATRA T 815-6 FORCE family of tactical trucks

Development

The TATRA T 815-6 FORCE family of tactical trucks (previously designated T 816 FORCE family) was introduced by TATRA in 1996 and are the continued evolution of the T 815 series first introduced in 1983. Full details of the T 815, the 1998-introduced T 815 ARMAX families and 2004-introduced T 815-7 tactical range (with a military specific cab) can be found elsewhere in this section.

TATRA T 815-6MWV27 26 298 6×6.1R FORCE family 26,000 kg GVW (6 × 6) truck fitted with the light version of TATRA's combination suspension system on the rear axles (TATRA a.s.)   0122774

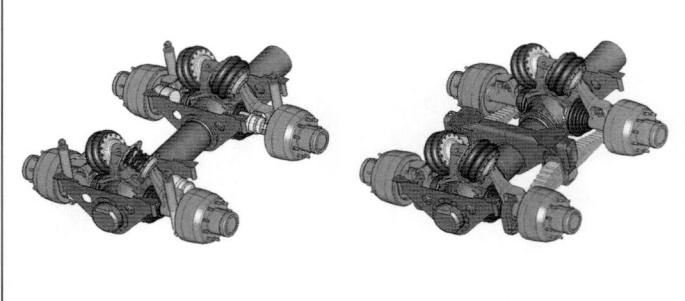

TATRA's combination suspension system for rear-axle pairs is known commercially as KING FRAME. The light version (left) uses airbags with internal coil springs and telescopic shock absorbers on each half-axle, the airbag units being mounted above the backbone tube to protect from impact or damage while operating off-road. Maximum individual axle loadings for the light version are 11,500 kg. The heavy version (right) of this combination suspension system combines the use of airbags on the individual half-axles with leaf springs shared longitudinally between axle pairs. Maximum individual axle loadings for the heavy version are 15,000 kg (TATRA a.s.)   0524775

The T 815 ARMAX family is based around commercially available designs, militarised as required, and the trucks are constructed to comply with all relevant legislation including emissions, noise and axle loadings, although in a number of cases vehicle payload capabilities exceed allowable peacetime maximums. The T 815-6 FORCE family comprises purpose-designed, no-compromise trucks for tactical military applications which are fitted with a range of water-cooled engines all producing over 400 hp. The strengths of such a no-compromise military design make the FORCE family particularly suitable for certain markets as well as some civilian applications, such as mining or construction, where some aspects of truck design legislation are not applicable.

TATRA, a.s. became a Joint Stock Company in 1992. In November 2001, it was announced that the Czech government had approved the purchase of a 92 per cent stake in TATRA a.s. by SDC International of the US. Following a brief period of difficult-to-follow ownership reorganisation, in September 2003 it was announced that Terex Corporation of the US had acquired 70.51 per cent of TATRA shares. Vectra (a London-based Indian-owned company) owned 21.11 per cent of shares, the remaining 8.38 per cent being privately owned. The company became known as TATRA, a. s., a Terex company, with products continuing to be branded TATRA.

In October 2006 it was announced that Terex Corporation had sold its 81 per cent holding of TATRA a.s. to a consortium of Czech and US investors. The Czech registered Blue River s.r.o. (now TATRA Holdings) consortium is made up of Belgium-based KBC Private Equity, Vectra Ltd, a US investor, plus Meadow Hill. Vectra Ltd - a construction equipment, bus and truck maker - folded its existing 11.1 per cent stake into Blue River.

Description

The overall layout of the T 815-6 FORCE family follows closely that of earlier TATRA truck designs. The torsionally rigid tubular backbone-type chassis is retained, as is the swinging half-axle independent wheel suspension system. The front steer-drive axle on the 6 × 6 design is sprung by the combination of torsion bars and telescopic shock-absorbers, the front steer-drive axle pairs on the 8 × 8 design by the combination of telescopic shock-absorbers and leaf springs shared longitudinally. The rear drive axles can be sprung by the conventional TATRA set-up of leaf springs shared longitudinally by axle pairs, or by TATRA's combination suspension that uses the commercial name KING FRAME. The so-called light version of this combination suspension system uses airbags with internal coil springs and telescopic shock-absorbers on each half-axle, the airbag units being mounted above the backbone tube to protect from impact or damage while operating off-road. Maximum individual axle loadings for the light version are 11,500 kg. The heavy version of this combination suspension system combines the use of airbags on the individual half-axles with leaf springs shared longitudinally between axle pairs. Although in excess of peacetime legislation in many countries, the heavy version allows for individual axle loadings of 15,000 kg.

A further derivative of the airbag suspension set-up is used on the latest TATRA T815-7 series of tactical trucks, full details of which can be found elsewhere in this section.

FORCE family chassis are also available in (10 × 10) and (12 × 12) configurations, these effectively being the modular addition of swinging half-axle assemblies and backbone tube sections. Full details of these multi-axle chassis can be found elsewhere in this section.

Power assisted steering is standard and all-wheel drive is permanent on chassis with up to six axles. For improved traction off-road driver-controlled longitudinal and cross-axle differential locks are fitted, and a semi-automatic Central Tyre Inflation (CTI) system is standard. A fully automatic CTI system with four terrain settings, flat detection and run-flat function is an option. Bead locks are a further option for extreme low-pressure operation. 1600R 20 tyres are standard fit and with an approach angle of 37° all models can surmount a 600 mm vertical obstacle. The (6 × 6) chassis can cross a 1 m trench, while those chassis designs with twin front axles can cross a 2 m trench. Without additional preparation the T 815-6 FORCE family is designed to operate throughout a –30 to +50°C temperature range, some models up to +55°C.

The T 815-6 FORCE family is offered with high power output water-cooled engine options that would usually be Caterpillar or Cummins. Hub-reduction gearing and automatic transmissions are standard, usually Twin Disc units and with six or 10 forward gears. Power Take-Off (PTO) facilities are standard. Drum brakes are fitted all-round, supplemented by an engine exhaust brake.

The standard all-steel two-door cab is of conventional design and features a single roof hatch. Larger cabs with additional stowage, crew or berthing space, or four doors are options. Two full-size seats are standard, with an occasional/emergency seat fixed to the central engine cover. A curved single piece or four-piece split windscreen can be fitted. The cab tilts forward hydraulically for maintenance purposes and an independent fuel-powered cab heater and air-conditioning are options. To meet a potential IDF requirement, TATRA developed a version of the standard cab that splits at waist level for C-130 air-transport. This process takes two people less than 40 minutes; nine bolts are involved.

In addition to the standard troop carrying/cargo-type body with drop sides and tailgate, bows and a tarpaulin cover, the FORCE chassis can be fitted with a wide variety of bodies, the torsionally rigid TATRA backbone chassis making the FORCE, and other TATRA truck families, particularly well suited to the transport of shelters or containers. Fuel and water tanks, a recovery hamper and a Multilift Mark 4 (now designated MPH 165) Load Handling System (LHS) have been fitted to T 815-6 FORCE chassis.

Additional options available include a winch with 50 m of cable and a rear pull capacity of 90 kN. A front underbody protection guard, a long-range fuel tank with 420 litres capacity and an NBC protection set for the crew.

Full details of certain models from the T 815 FORCE family can be found elsewhere in this section.

Variants

The American Truck Company (ATC) was selected mid 2003 as preferred bidder to supply the Ministry of Defence of Israel (IMOD) with approximately 315 Medium Tactical Trucks (MTTs) plus associated support. In January 2004 it was announced that the American Truck Company (ATC) had been awarded and entered into a contract with the US Army Tank-armaments and Automotive Command (TACOM) to supply IMOD with 302 Medium Tactical Trucks and associated logistics support.

The selected truck is a TATRA T 815-6MWV27 26 298 6×6.1R FORCE model.

These trucks were supplied to Israel by the United States under the US Foreign Military Sales (FMS) programme. The initial value of the order is approximately USD54 million before options. IMOD also has options to purchase an additional 243 trucks for value in excess of USD40 million. The announcement followed the conclusion of a two-year competition between ATC and other US truck manufacturers Oshkosh (MTVR) and Stewart and Stevenson (FMTV) that included extended testing of vehicles and an evaluation of after-market support capabilities.

The procurement includes a combination of cargo trucks (some with material handling cranes) that have replaced ageing M35 series trucks. Contract work commenced mid-2004 and was scheduled for completion by June 2008. By late-2006 TATRA had delivered all 302 trucks. A contract option for 10 additional trucks was exercised during 2008.

Status

In production. In service with Israel (via ATC, see text). In service with India (multi-axle chassis, see text).

Contractor

TATRA a.s.

TATRA T 815-7 tactical truck family

Development

Development of the TATRA T 815-7 series of trucks commenced in 2004. The T 815-7 series combine some mechanical features of the earlier T 815 ARMAX family and T 815-6 FORCE families of trucks with a purpose-designed tactical applications flat-panelled cab. The T 815-6 FORCE family (originally designated T 816 FORCE) of tactical trucks was introduced by TATRA in 1996. The T 815 ARMAX family was introduced in 1998. While visually similar (sharing the same commercial pattern cab) the ARMAX and FORCE families differs in that the T 815 ARMAX family is constructed to comply with all relevant legislation including emissions, noise and axle loadings and so on, while the FORCE family is not.

The T 815-7 series is available with varying levels of legislative compliance, tailored to suit individual user requirements. Early T 815-7 models (6 × 6) and (8 × 8) were offered to South Africa to meet the Project Vistula requirement, and to the USMC (10 × 10) to meet the LVSR requirement.

T 815-7 models have been supplied to the armed forces of the Czech Republic, India and Slovakia.

TATRA, a.s. became a Joint Stock Company in 1992. In November 2001, it was announced that the Czech government had approved the purchase of a 92 per cent stake in TATRA a.s. by SDC International of the US. Following a brief period of difficult-to-follow ownership reorganisation, in September 2003 it was announced that Terex Corporation of the US had acquired 70.51 per cent of TATRA shares. Vectra (a London-based Indian-owned company) owning 21.11 per cent of shares, the remaining 8.38 per cent being privately owned. The company became known as TATRA, a. s., a Terex company, with products continuing to be branded TATRA.

Late-2006 Terex Corporation announced it had sold its 81 per cent share of TATRA, a.s. to the Czech-based Blue River s.r.o. (now TATRA Holdings), a consortium of Czech and US investors that included Vectra Ltd, Vectra folding its existing 11.1 per cent stake into Blue River.

Description

The overall mechanical layout of the TATRA T 815-7 truck series follows closely that of earlier TATRA truck designs. The torsionally rigid tubular backbone-type chassis is retained, as is the swinging half-axle independent wheel suspension system. The suspension is however revised, and a 3-D frame is now formed by connecting the backbone tube with a conventional ladder frame via cross-members. Air bellows-type

height adjustable (+90/-105 mm) suspension units are located between the half-axles and ladder frame, these supplemented at each wheel station by hydraulic shock-absorbers, and where required, anti-roll bars for axle pairs. This design revision further improving vehicle mobility in a difficult terrain, while increasing stability during cornering and at higher road speeds.

Motive power for the T 815-7 series may be provided by either a TATRA air-cooled or a Cummins water-cooled unit. TATRA's T3-928 V-8 engine can be supplied to meet EURO 2, 3 or 4 emissions requirements, and all without an electronically controlled injection system. Water-cooled Cummins engine options can be EURO 3 or 4 emissions compliant, but are electronically controlled.

TATRA hub reduction axles are permanently driven via a TATRA 10- or 14-speed manual gearbox as standard, although options include a ZF manual gearbox or Twin Disc or Allison fully automatic transmission. Full-time all-wheel drive with or without a torque divider is standard, as is

TATRA T 815-790R99 38 300 8×8.1R (8 × 8) high mobility heavy duty chassis-cab as supplied to the Czech Army in bridgelayer configuration (TATRA a.s.) 1391046

TATRA T 815-790R39 29 300 6×6.1R (6 × 6) high mobility heavy duty universal container carrier as supplied to the Slovak Army (TATRA a.s.) 1391380

TATRA T 815-790R99 38 300 8×8.1R (8 × 8) high mobility heavy duty cargo/troop carrier as supplied to the Slovak Army (TATRA a.s.) 1391381

TATRA T 815-77RR89 38 300 8×8.1R (8 × 8) high mobility heavy duty crane, a single example of which has been supplied to the Indian Army (TATRA a.s.) 1391044

TATRA T 815-780R59 19 270 4×4.1R (4 × 4) high mobility heavy duty 5,300-litre tanker as supplied to the Slovak Army (TATRA a.s.) 1391379

a disengageable front axle(s). Rear axles are also disengageable on (10 × 10) or (12 × 12) variants. Dual circuit drum brakes with ABS are fitted all-round, supplemented by an engine exhaust brake.

For improved traction off-road driver-controlled longitudinal and cross-axle differential locks are fitted. A manually operated Central Tyre Inflation (CTI) system is standard, while a fully automatic system with four terrain settings, flat detection and run-flat function is an option. Bead locks are a further option for extreme low-pressure operation. 1400 or 1600R 20 Michelin XZL tyres are standard fit, but options are available. Without additional preparation the T 815-7 series can operate throughout a –32 to +49°C temperature range.

TATRA has developed a new cab for the T 815-7 series, and one that meets current requirements in areas of C-130 transportability and ballistic protection. In connection with height-adjustable air-suspension the basic T 815 series is air-transportable by C-130 Hercules aircraft. The cab has also been designed to accept appliqué protection kits of up to STANAG Level 2. Two standard versions of cab are available, the standard two-door or an extended two-door with bunk.

Variants

Currently available T815-7 range variants include the following:
T 815-7L0R59 19 257 4×4.1R (4 × 4) high mobility heavy duty cargo/troop carrier
T 815-780R59 19 270 4×4.1R (4 × 4) high mobility heavy duty universal container carrier
T 815-780R59 19 270 4×4.1R (4 × 4) high mobility heavy duty 5,300-litre tanker
T 815-7APR59 19 240 4×4.1R (4 × 4) high mobility heavy duty chassis
T 815-79PR39 29 300 4×4.1R (4 × 4) high mobility heavy duty chassis
T 815-790R39 29 300 6×6.1R (6 × 6) high mobility heavy duty universal container carrier
T 815-790R99 38 300 8×8.1R (8 × 8) high mobility heavy duty universal container carrier
T 815-790R99 38 300 8×8.1R (8 × 8) high mobility heavy duty cargo/troop carrier
T 815-790R99 38 300 8×8.1R (8 × 8) high mobility heavy duty chassis-cab with load handling system
T 815-790R99 38 300 8×8.1R (8 × 8) high mobility heavy duty 18,000-litre fuel tanker
T 815-77RR*9 38 300 8×8.1R (8 × 8) high mobility heavy duty crane

Specifications

	T 815-780R59 19 270 4×4.1R	T 815-79OR39 29 300 6×6.1R	T 815-790R99 38 300 8×8.1R
Variant:	high mobility heavy duty universal container carrier	high mobility heavy duty universal container carrier	high mobility heavy duty cargo/troop carrier
Cab seating:	1 + 1 (+1 occasional centre seat)		
Configuration:	4 × 4 (selectable)	6 × 6 (selectable)	8 × 8
Weight:			
(unladen)	10,870 kg (w/armoured cab)	13,100 kg	16,900 kg (w/armoured cab)
(GVW, max)	19,000 kg	29,000 kg	38,000 kg
(payload, max)	8,130 kg	15,900 kg	21,000 kg
(towed load, max)	20,000 kg	n/avail	n/avail
(GCW)	39,000 kg	n/avail	n/avail
Length: (chassis-cab)	7.53 mm	9.345 m	9.445 m
Width:	2.5 m	2.5 m	2.5 m
Height:	2.765 m (over cab)	2.7 m (over cab)	2.775 m (over cab)
Ground clearance: (adjustable)	380 mm	380 mm	410 mm
Track: (front and rear)	2.072 m	2.072 m	2.072 m
Wheelbase:	4.09 m	4.09 + 1.45 m	1.95 + 2.86 + 1.45 m
Angle of approach/departure:	45°/32°	42°/25°	45°/41°
Max speed: (road)	115 km/h	105 km/h	110 km/h
Max range: (cruising)	1,200 km	900 km	750 km
Fuel capacity:	220 litres (320 and 420 litres optional)	420 litres	420 litres
Gradient: (at GVW)	100%	90%	60%

	T 815-780R59 19 270 4×4.1R	T 815-79OR39 29 300 6×6.1R	T 815-790R99 38 300 8×8.1R
Variant:	high mobility heavy duty universal container carrier	high mobility heavy duty universal container carrier	high mobility heavy duty cargo/troop carrier
Side slope:	45%	45%	45%
Fording:	1.5 m	1.5 m	1.5 m
Engine:	TATRA T3C-928.90 12.667-litre V8-cylinder turbocharged and charge-air-cooled direct injection 4-stroke EURO 3 diesel developing 362 hp (270 kW) at 1,800 rpm and 1,850 N.m torque at 1,000 rpm	TATRA T3C-928.90 12.667-litre V8-cylinder turbocharged and charge-air-cooled direct injection 4-stroke EURO 3 diesel developing 402 hp (300 kW) at 1,800 rpm and 2,100 N.m torque at 1,000 rpm	TATRA T3C-928.90 12.667-litre V8-cylinder turbocharged and charge-air-cooled direct injection 4-stroke EURO 3 diesel developing 402 hp (300 kW) at 1,800 rpm and 2,100 N.m torque at 1,000 rpm
Gearbox/ Transmission:	TATRA 14 TS 210L manual with 14 forward and 2 reverse gears (synchromesh on all but 1st and reverse gears)	TATRA 14 TS 210L manual with 14 forward and 2 reverse gears (synchromesh on all but 1st and reverse gears); PTO output	TATRA 14 TS 210L manual with 14 forward and 2 reverse gears (synchromesh on all but 1st and reverse gears); PTO output
Transfer box:	TATRA 2.30 TRS 0.8/1.9 2-speed	TATRA 2.30 TRS (1.85/0.8) 2-speed with PTO output	TATRA 2.30 TRS (1.85/0.8) 2-speed
Steering:	Left-hand drive, integrated power-assisted		
Turning radius: (kerb)	8 m, ±500 mm	10.25 m, ±500 mm	12 m, ±500 mm
Suspension:			
(front)	airbags plus telescopic shock-absorbers	airbags plus telescopic shock-absorbers	airbags plus telescopic shock-absorbers and anti-roll bars
(rear)	airbags plus telescopic shock-absorbers and anti-roll bar	airbags plus telescopic shock-absorbers and anti-roll bars	airbags plus telescopic shock-absorbers and anti-roll bars
Tyres:	1600R 20	1400R 20	1600R 20
Brakes:	dual circuit, air, drums all-round. ABS fitted. Supplementary engine exhaust brake		
Electrical system:	24 V	24 V	24 V
Batteries:	2 × 12 V, 170 Ah	2 × 12 V, 170 Ah	2 × 12 V, 170 Ah
Alternator:	28 V, 80 A	28 V, 80 A	28 V, 80 A

Status
In production. In service with the Czech Republic, India and Slovakia.

Contractor
TATRA a.s.

TATRA/Navistar heavy truck joint venture

Development
TATRA and Navistar announced a joint venture/strategic partnership in October 2009, the aim of which was to develop a new range of heavy trucks that combined the relevant engineering, technology, through life support and marketing/commercial strengths of the two companies. Initial requirements that could be targeted as a result of this alliance could be Canada and the Standard Military Pattern (SMP) segment of the Medium Support Vehicles System (MSVS) requirement, and South Africa's Vistula requirement.

The first two vehicles developed as part of the TATRA/Navistar alliance were announced at Eurosatory 2010, the ATX6 and ATX8.

Full details of TATRA and the T 815-7 range (the base design for the ATX6 and ATX8) and Navistar and the company's range of military vehicles can be found elsewhere in this section.

Description
The ATX6 (6 × 6) and ATX8 (8 × 8) are based on TATRA T 815-7 designs, the primary production differences being that their standard TATRA engines and transmissions have been replaced.

Development of the TATRA T 815-7 series of trucks commenced in 2004. The T 815-7 series combine some mechanical features of the 1998-introduced T 815 ARMAX family and 1996-introduced T 815-6 FORCE families of trucks, but with a purpose-designed tactical application flat-panelled cab replacing the commercial design fitted to the ARMAX and FORCE families.

TATRA and Navistar announced a joint venture/strategic partnership in October 2009 and the first two vehicles developed as part of this alliance were announced at Eurosatory 2010, the ATX6 (shown) and ATX8 (TATRA/Navistar) 1364374

The overall mechanical layout of the TATRA T 815-7 truck series follows closely that of earlier TATRA truck designs. The torsionally rigid tubular backbone-type chassis is retained, as is the swinging half-axle independent wheel suspension system. The suspension is however revised, and a 3D frame is now formed by connecting the backbone tube with a conventional ladder frame via cross-members. Air bellows-type height adjustable (+90/–105 mm) suspension units are located between the half-axles and ladder frame, these supplemented at each wheel station by hydraulic shock-absorbers, and where required, anti-roll bars for axle pairs. This design revision further improving vehicle mobility in a difficult terrain, while increasing stability during cornering and at higher road speeds.

Motive power for the ATX6 and ATX8 is provided by Navistar's MaxxForce D 12.4 emissions compliant diesel engine, this replacing the T 815-7 family's standard TATRA T3-928 V-8 engine. An Allison 4500SP fully automatic transmission replaces the standard TATRA manual gearbox; TATRA's two-speed transfer box is retained.

Full-time all-wheel drive with or without a torque divider is standard, as is a disengageable front axle(s). Dual circuit drum brakes with ABS are fitted all-round, supplemented by an engine exhaust brake.

For improved traction off-road driver-controlled longitudinal and cross-axle differential locks are fitted. A Central Tyre Inflation (CTI) system is standard, with bead locks an option for extreme low-pressure operation. 1600R 20 Michelin XZL tyres are standard fit, but options are available. Without additional preparation the ATX6 and ATX8 can operate throughout a –32°C to +49°C temperature range.

The standard T 815-7 series cab (which is retained) has been designed to accept appliqué protection kits of up to STANAG Level 2. The ATX6 and ATX8 are also available with an interchangeable armoured cab, this providing Level 3/4 protection. Two standard versions of cab are available, the standard two-door or an extended two-door with bunk.

In connection with height-adjustable air-suspension the ATX6 and ATX8 (in chassis-cab configuration) are air-transportable by C-130 Hercules aircraft.

Specifications

	ATX6 Universal Container Carrier	ATX8 Cargo Carrier With Crane
Seating:	1 + 1	1 + 1
Configuration:	6 × 6	8 × 8
Weight:		
(unladen)	12,100 kg	16,900 kg (w/armoured cab)
(GVW, max)	29,000 kg	38,000 kg
(payload, max)	16,900 kg	21,000 kg
Length: (chassis-cab)	9.485 m	9.75 m
Width:	2.5 m	2.5 m
Height:	2.735 m (over cab)	2.765 m (over cab)
Ground clearance: (adjustable)	410 mm	410 mm
Track: (front and rear)	2.072 m	2.072 m
Wheelbase:	4.09 m	1.95 + 3.25 + 1.45 m
Angle of approach/departure:	42°/25°	45°/39°
Max speed: (road)	117 km/h	115 km/h
Max range: (cruising)	1,000 km	1,100 km
Fuel capacity:	420 litres	570 litres
Gradient: (at GVW)	80%	55%
Side slope:	45%	45%
Fording:	1.5 m	1.5 m

	ATX6 Universal Container Carrier	ATX8 Cargo Carrier With Crane
Engine:	Navistar emissions compliant 12.4-litre 6-cylinder in-line turbocharged and charge-air-cooled, water-cooled direct injection 4-stroke diesel developing 450 hp (335 kW) at 1,700 rpm and 1,972 N.m torque at 1,000 rpm	
Gearbox/transmission:	Allison 4500SP with 6 forward and 1 reverse gears	
Transfer box:	TATRA 2.30 TRK 0.9/2.4 2-speed	
Steering:	left- or right-hand drive, power-assisted	
Turning radius: (kerb)	10.75 m, ±500 mm	13 m, ±500 mm
Suspension:	air, drums all-round. ABS standard. Supplementary engine exhaust brake	
(front)	airbags plus telescopic shock-absorbers and anti-roll bar	
(rear)	airbags plus telescopic shock-absorbers and anti-roll bar	
Tyres:	1600R 20	1600R 20
Brakes:	dual-circuit, air, drums all-round. ABS fitted. Supplementary engine exhaust brake	
Electrical systems:	24 V	24 V
Batteries:	4 × 12 V, 220 Ah	2 × 12 V, 170 Ah
Alternator:	28 V, 260 A	28 V, 80 A

Status
Ready for production (T815-7 models in production and service).

Contractor
TATRA AS
Navistar Defense LLC

TATRA T 815-26WR25 26 255 6 × 6.1 ARMAX family (6 × 6) chassis-cab truck

Development
The TATRA T815-26WR25 26 255 6 × 6.1 chassis-cab truck is a member of the T 815 ARMAX family of (4 × 4) and (6 × 6) trucks and is designed primarily for the transport of shelters and containers, particularly those housing sensitive electronic equipment. The T 815 ARMAX family of trucks was introduced by TATRA in 1998 to join the earlier TERRN°1 and T 815-6 Force (originally designated T 816 FORCE) families of trucks, all of which are the continued evolution of the T 815 series first introduced in 1983. Full details of the T 815 and T 815-6 FORCE families can be found elsewhere in this section.

The TERRN°1 family is essentially commercial in design, but is suitable for certain military applications. The T 815-6 FORCE family is purpose designed, no-compromise trucks for tactical military applications and as such, are fitted with a range of water-cooled engines all producing over 400 hp. The T 815 ARMAX family are based around commercially available designs, militarised as required, and are constructed to comply with all relevant legislation (when required) including emissions, noise and axle loadings, although in many cases vehicle payload capabilities exceed allowable peacetime maximums.

TATRA, a.s. became a Joint Stock Company in 1992. In November 2001, it was announced that the Czech government had approved the purchase of a 92 per cent stake in TATRA a.s. by SDC International of the US. Following a brief period of difficult-to-follow ownership reorganisation, in September 2003 it was announced that Terex Corporation of the US had acquired 70.51 per cent of TATRA shares. Vectra (a London-based Indian-owned company) owned 21.11 per cent of shares, the remaining 8.38 per cent being privately owned. The company became known as TATRA a.s. a Terex company, with products continuing to be branded TATRA.

In October 2006 it was announced that Terex Corporation had sold its 81 per cent holding of TATRA a.s. to a consortium of Czech and US investors. The Czech registered Blue River s.r.o. (now TATRA Holdings) consortium is made up of Belgium-based KBC Private Equity, Vectra Ltd, a US investor, plus Meadow Hill. Vectra Ltd - a construction equipment, bus and truck maker - folded its existing 11.1 per cent stake into Blue River.

Description
The overall layout of the TATRA T 815-26WR25 26 255 6 × 6.1 chassis-cab truck follows closely that of earlier TATRA truck designs. The torsionally rigid tubular backbone-type chassis is retained and to it are located the mounting and support points for the selected shelter or container. The chassis load capacity is 16,000 kg. Also retained is the swinging half-axle independent wheel suspension system. The front steer-drive axle is sprung by the combination of torsion bars and telescopic shock-absorbers, while the rear drive axles are sprung by TATRA's combination suspension that uses the commercial name King Frame. The so-called light version of this combination suspension system is fitted. This uses airbags with internal coil springs and telescopic shock-absorbers on each half-axle, the airbag units being mounted above the backbone tube to protect from impact or damage while operating off-road. Maximum individual axle loadings for the light version are 11,500 kg.

TATRA T 815-26WR25 26 255 6 × 6.1 ARMAX family (6 × 6) chassis-cab truck (TATRA a.s.)   0524777

Motive power is provided by a EURO 2 (EURO 3 on request) emissions compliant TATRA 12.7-litre V-8 four-stroke air-cooled diesel engine developing 347 hp. This drives the rear four - or all six wheels - via a TATRA 10 TS 160 manual gearbox with 10 forward and two reverse gears and a TATRA two-speed transfer box. The main gearbox is provided with synchromesh on all but reverse and first gears. For on-road use drive to the front axle can be disconnected.

For improved traction off-road driver-controlled longitudinal and cross-axle differential locks are fitted as is a driver-controlled Central Tyre Inflation (CTI) system. Bead locks are an option for extreme low-pressure operation. With an approach angle of 37° the vehicle can surmount a 500 mm vertical obstacle. A trench 900 mm wide can be crossed. Without additional preparation the vehicle can operate throughout a –30 to +40°C temperature range.

Power-assisted steering is standard, as is a dual circuit Anti-lock Braking System (ABS). Drum brakes are fitted front and rear, supplemented by an engine exhaust brake.

The standard all-steel two-door cab is of conventional design and features a single roof hatch; a larger cab with additional stowage, crew or berthing space is an option. Two full-size seats are standard, with an occasional/emergency seat fixed to the central engine cover; the seating arrangements are such that they can be converted in to a berth. A curved single-piece or four-piece split windscreen can be fitted. The cab tilts forward hydraulically for maintenance purposes and in addition to engine-provided in-cab heating, an independent diesel-powered cab heater is fitted; air-conditioning is an option.

To meet a potential IDF requirement, TATRA developed a version of the standard cab that splits at waist level for C-130 air-transport. This process takes two people less than 40 minutes; nine bolts are involved. Larger four-door or crew-type cabs with additional seating or bunks are also available for ARMAX family trucks.

At present a 3.44 + 1.45 m wheelbase is standard for 1400R 20 single-tyred ARMAX 6 × 6 trucks, these being available with varying chassis lengths. The T 815-26WR25 26 255 6 × 6.1 has an overall chassis length of 8.625 m. Chassis with 1200R 20 tyres and dual rear wheels are available.

A detailed overview of the T 815 ARMAX family can be found elsewhere in this section.

Specifications

T 815-26WR25 26 255 6 × 6.1 ARMAX
Cab seating: 1 + 1 (+1 occasional)
Configuration: 6 × 6
Weight:
    (unladen, chassis-cab) 10,000 kg
    (laden) 26,000 kg
    (payload, on chassis-cab) 16,000 kg
    (towed load) 20,000 kg
    (GCW) 46,000 kg
Length: (chassis) 8.625 m
Width: 2.5 m
Height:
    (behind-cab exhaust stack) 3.19 m
Ground clearance: 360 mm
Wheel track:
    (front) 2.034 m
    (rear) 2.050 m
Wheelbase: 3.44 + 1.45 m
Angle of approach/departure: 37°/23°
Max speed: (road) limited to 85 km/h
Max range: (cruising) 1,000 km
Fuel capacity: 420 litres
Gradient: 75% (45% at GCW of 43,200 kg)
Side slope: 45%
Fording: 1.2 m

Engine: TATRA T3B-928.60 EURO 2 12.667-litre V-8-cylinder turbocharged and charge-air-cooled, air-cooled direct injection 4-stroke diesel developing 347 hp (259 kW) at 1,800 rpm and 1,570 N.m torque at 1,200 rpm. EURO 3 option available
Gearbox: TATRA 10 TS 160 manual with semi-automatic split giving 10 forward and 2 reverse gears. Synchromesh on all except first and reverse gears
Transfer box: TATRA 2.30 TRK 1.6/2.6 2-speed with front axle disconnect
Clutch: single dry plate, (dia) 430 mm
Steering: power assisted
Turning radius: 10.5 m
Suspension:
    (front) torsion bars and telescopic shock-absorbers
    (rear) airbags with internal coil springs and telescopic shock-absorbers (see text for details)
Tyres: 1400R 20
Brakes: dual circuit, air, drums all-round, ABS. Supplementary engine exhaust brake
Electrical system: 24 V
Batteries: 2 × 12 V, 165 Ah
Alternator: 28 V, 55 A

Status

In production. In service with the Czech Army. T 815 ARMAX family trucks are also in service with Indian, Malaysian and Slovak armed forces.

Contractor

TATRA a.s.

TATRA T815-26WR45 17 255 4 × 4.1 ARMAX family (4 × 4) chassis-cab truck

Development

The TATRA T 815-26WR45 17 255 4 × 4.1 chassis-cab truck is a member of the T 815 ARMAX family of (4 × 4) and (6 × 6) trucks and is designed primarily for the transport of shelters and containers, particularly those housing sensitive electronic equipment. The T 815 ARMAX family of trucks was introduced by TATRA in 1998 to join the earlier TERRN°1 and T 815-6 Force (originally designated T 816 Force) families of trucks, all of which are the continued evolution of the T 815 series first introduced in 1983. Full details of the T 815 and T 815-6 Force families can be found elsewhere in this section.

The TERRN°1 family is essentially commercial in its designs, but is suitable for certain military applications. The T 815-6 Force family comprises purpose-designed, no-compromise trucks for tactical military applications and, as such, are fitted with a range of water-cooled engines, all producing over 400 hp. The T 815 ARMAX family is based around commercially available designs, militarised as required, and is constructed to comply with all relevant legislation (when required) including emissions, noise and axle loadings, although in many cases vehicle payload capabilities exceed allowable peacetime maximums.

TATRA, a.s. became a Joint Stock Company in 1992. In November 2001, it was announced that the Czech government had approved the purchase of a 92 per cent stake in TATRA, a.s. by SDC International of the US. Following a brief period of difficult-to-follow ownership reorganisation, in September 2003 it was announced that Terex Corporation of the US had acquired 70.51 per cent of TATRA shares. Vectra (a London-based Indian-owned company) owned 21.11 per cent of shares, the remaining 8.38 per cent being privately owned. The company became known as TATRA, a.s., a Terex company, with products continuing to be branded TATRA.

In October 2006 it was announced that Terex Corporation had sold its 81 per cent holding of TATRA a.s. to a consortium of Czech and US investors. The Czech registered Blue River s.r.o. (now TATRA Holdings) consortium is made up of Belgium-based KBC Private Equity, Vectra Ltd, a US investor, plus Meadow Hill. Vectra Ltd - a construction equipment, bus and truck maker - folded its existing 11.1 per cent stake into Blue River.

4.09 m wheelbase version of the TATRA T815-26WR45 17 255 4 × 4.1 ARMAX family (4 × 4) chassis-cab truck (TATRA, a.s.)   0524776

TATRA T815-26WR45 17 255 4 × 4.1 ARMAX family (4 × 4) chassis-cab truck of the Czech Army fitted with a shelter-type rear body (Stefan Marx) 1185467

Description

The overall layout of the TATRA T815-26WR45 17 255 4 × 4.1 chassis-cab truck follows closely that of earlier TATRA truck designs. The torsionally rigid tubular backbone-type chassis is retained and to it are located the mounting and support points for the selected shelter or container. The chassis load capacity is 9,200 kg. Also retained is the swinging half-axle independent wheel suspension system. The front steer-drive axle is sprung by the combination of torsion bars and telescopic shock-absorbers, while the rear drive axle is sprung by TATRA's combination suspension that uses the commercial name King Frame. The so-called light version of this combination suspension system is fitted. This uses airbags with internal coil springs and telescopic shock-absorbers on each half-axle, the airbag units being mounted above the backbone tube to protect from impact or damage while operating off-road. Maximum individual axle loadings for the light version are 11,500 kg.

Motive power is provided by a EURO 2 (EURO 3 on request) emissions compliant TATRA 12.7-litre V-8 four-stroke air-cooled diesel engine developing 347 hp. This drives the rear only, or all four wheels, via a TATRA 10 TS 160 manual gearbox with 10 forward and two reverse gears and a TATRA two-speed transfer box. The main gearbox is provided with synchromesh on all but reverse and first gears. For on-road use drive to the front axle can be disconnected.

For improved traction off-road driver-controlled longitudinal and cross-axle differential locks are fitted as is a Central Tyre Inflation (CTI) system. Bead locks are an option for extreme low-pressure operation. With an approach angle of 37° the vehicle can surmount a 500 mm vertical obstacle. A trench 900 mm wide can be crossed. Without additional preparation the vehicle can operate throughout a −30 to +40°C temperature range.

Power-assisted steering is standard, as is an Anti-lock Braking System (ABS). Dual circuit drum brakes are fitted front and rear, supplemented by an engine exhaust brake.

The standard all-steel two-door cab is of conventional design and features a single roof hatch; a larger cab with additional stowage, crew or berthing space is an option. Two full-size seats are standard, with an occasional/emergency seat fixed to the central engine cover; the seating arrangements are such that they can be converted in to a berth. A curved single piece or four-piece split windscreen can be fitted. The cab tilts forward hydraulically for maintenance purposes and an independent fuel-powered cab heater is optional.

To meet a potential IDF requirement, TATRA developed a version of this cab that splits at waist level for C-130 air-transport. This process takes two people less than 40 minutes; nine bolts are involved. Larger four-door or crew-type cabs with additional seating or bunks are also available for ARMAX family trucks.

Three wheelbase lengths are available, 3.7, 4.09 or 4.5 m, these affecting the overall vehicle length, departure angle and turning radius accordingly. Figures given in the specification table relate to the 4.09 m wheelbase, overall length, departure angle and turning radius of the 3.7 and 4.5 m wheelbases being 6.61 m, 37° and 9.5 m, and 7.41 m, 31° and 11.5 m, respectively.

A detailed overview of the T 815 ARMAX family can be found elsewhere in this section.

Specifications

T815-26WR45 17 255 4×4.1 ARMAX
Cab seating: 1 + 1 (+1 occasional)
Configuration: 4 × 4
Weight:
(chassis-cab) 7,800 kg
(GVW) 17,000 kg
(payload, on chassis-cab) 9,200 kg
(towed load) 24,000 kg
(GCW) 41,000 kg
Length: 7 m
Width: 2.5 m

Height: (cab roof) 2.99 m
Ground clearance: 360 mm
Wheel track:
(front) 2.034 m
(rear) 2.050 m
Wheelbase: 4.09 m
Angle of approach/departure: 37°/37°
Max speed: (road) 105 km/h (limited to 85 km/h)
Max range: (cruising) 1,000 km
Fuel capacity: 320 litres
Gradient: 100%
Side slope: 45%
Fording: 1.2 m
Engine: TATRA T3B-928.60 EURO 2 12.667-litre V-8-cylinder turbocharged and charge-air-cooled, air-cooled direct injection 4-stroke diesel developing 347 hp (259 kW) at 1,800 rpm and 1,570 N.m torque at 1,200 rpm. EURO 3 option available
Gearbox: TATRA 10 TS 160 manual with semi-automatic split giving 10 forward and 2 reverse gears. Synchromesh on all except first and reverse gears
Transfer box: TATRA 2.30 TRK 1.6/2.6 2-speed with front axle disconnect
Clutch: single dry plate, (dia) 430 mm
Steering: power assisted
Turning radius: 10.5 m
Suspension:
(front) torsion bars and telescopic shock-absorbers
(rear) airbags with internal coil springs and telescopic shock-absorbers
(see text for details)
Tyres: 1400R 20
Brakes: dual circuit air with ABS, drums front and rear. Supplementary engine exhaust brake
Electrical system: 24 V
Batteries: 2 × 12 V, 165 Ah
Alternator: 24 V, 55 A

Status

In production. In service with the Czech Army. T 815 ARMAX family trucks are also in service with Indian, Malaysian and Slovak armed forces.

Contractor

TATRA, a.s.

TATRA T 815-26WV25 26 255 6 × 6.1 ARMAX family (6 × 6) cargo truck

Development

The TATRA T 815-26WV25 26 255 6×6.1 truck is a member of the T 815 ARMAX family of (4 × 4) and (6 × 6) trucks. The T 815 ARMAX family of trucks was introduced by TATRA in 1998 to join the earlier TERRN°1 and T 815-6 FORCE (originally designated T816 FORCE) families of trucks, all of which are the continued evolution of the T 815 series first introduced in 1983. Full details of the T 815 and T 815-6 FORCE families can be found elsewhere in this section.

The TERRN°1 family is essentially commercial in its designs, but is suitable for certain military applications. The T 815-6 FORCE family comprises purpose-designed, no-compromise trucks for tactical military applications and, as such, they are fitted with a range of water-cooled engines all producing over 400 hp. The T 815 ARMAX family are based around commercially available designs, militarised as required, and are constructed to comply with all relevant legislation (when required) including emissions, noise and axle loadings, although in many cases vehicle payload capabilities exceed allowable peacetime maximums.

TATRA, a.s. became a Joint Stock Company in 1992. In November 2001, it was announced that the Czech government had approved the purchase of a 92 per cent stake in TATRA, a.s. by SDC International of the US. Following a brief period of difficult-to-follow ownership reorganisation, in September 2003 it was announced that Terex Corporation of the US had acquired 70.51 per cent of TATRA shares. Vectra (a London-based Indian-owned company) owned 21.11 per cent of shares, the remaining 8.38 per cent being privately owned. The company became known as TATRA, a.s., a Terex company, with products continuing to be branded TATRA.

In October 2006 it was announced that Terex Corporation had sold its 81 per cent holding of TATRA, a.s. to a consortium of Czech and US investors. The Czech registered Blue River s.r.o. (now TATRA Holdings) consortium is made up of Belgium-based KBC Private Equity, Vectra Ltd, a US investor, plus Meadow Hill. Vectra Ltd - a construction equipment, bus and truck maker - folded its existing 11.1 per cent stake into Blue River.

Description

The overall layout of the TATRA T 815-26WV25 26 255 6×6.1 truck follows closely that of earlier TATRA truck designs. The torsionally rigid tubular backbone-type chassis is retained, as is the swinging half-axle independent wheel suspension system. The front steer-drive axle is sprung by the combination of torsion bars and telescopic shock-absorbers, while the rear drive axles are sprung by TATRA's combination suspension that uses the commercial name KING FRAME. The so-called light version of this combination suspension system is fitted. This uses

TATRA T815-26WV25 26 255 6 × 6.1 ARMAX family (6 × 6) 14,700 kg truck (TATRA, a.s.)   1185470

airbags with internal coil springs and telescopic shock-absorbers on each half-axle, the airbag units being mounted above the backbone tube to protect from impact or damage while operating off-road. Maximum individual axle loadings for the light version are 11,500 kg.

Motive power is provided by a EURO 2 (EURO 3 on request) emissions compliant TATRA 12.7-litre V-8 four-stroke air-cooled diesel engine developing 347 hp. This drives the rear four - or all six wheels - via a TATRA 10 TS 160 manual gearbox with 10 forward and two reverse gears and a TATRA two-speed transfer box. The main gearbox is provided with synchromesh on all but reverse and first gears. For on-road use drive to the front axle can be disconnected.

For improved traction off-road driver-controlled longitudinal and cross-axle differential locks are fitted as is a driver-controlled Central Tyre Inflation (CTI) system. Bead locks are an option for extreme low-pressure operation. With an approach angle of 37° the vehicle can surmount a 500 mm vertical obstacle. A trench 900 mm wide can be crossed. Without additional preparation the vehicle can operate throughout a –30 to +40°C temperature range.

Power-assisted steering is standard, as is an Anti-lock Braking System (ABS). Dual circuit drum brakes are fitted all-round, supplemented by an engine exhaust brake.

The standard all-steel two-door cab is of conventional design and features a single roof hatch; a larger cab with additional stowage, crew or berthing space is an option. Two full-size seats are standard, with an occasional/emergency seat fixed to the central engine cover; the seating arrangements are such that they can be converted in to a berth. A curved single piece or four-piece split windscreen can be fitted. The cab tilts forward hydraulically for maintenance purposes and an independent fuel-powered cab heater and air-conditioning are options.

To meet a potential IDF requirement, TATRA developed a version of the standard cab that splits at waist level for C-130 air-transport. This process takes two people less than 40 minutess; nine bolts are involved. Larger four-door or crew-type cabs with additional seating or bunks are also available.

The rear cargo body is fitted with a treated non-slip plywood floor and has a steel frame and removable drop sides and tailgate. Tilting bench seats for troop transport are an option and a tarpaulin cover supported by bows may be fitted. Dimensions of the rear body are 5 × 2.5 m (L × W). A payload of up to 14,700 kg may be carried.

At present a 3.44 + 1.45 m wheelbase is standard for 1400R 20 single-tyred ARMAX (6 × 6) trucks, these being available with varying chassis lengths. Chassis with 1200R 20 tyres and dual rear wheels are available.

A detailed overview of the T 815 ARMAX family can be found elsewhere in this section.

Specifications

T 815-26WV25 26 255 6 × 6.1 ARMAX
Cab seating: 1 + 1 (+1 occasional)
Configuration: 6 × 6
Weight:
(unladen, chassis-cab) 11,300 kg
(laden) 26,000 kg
(payload, on chassis-cab) 14,700 kg
(towed load) 17,200 kg
(GCW) 43,200 kg
Length: 7.88 m
Width: 2.5 m
Height:
(cab roof) 2.99 m
(body sides) 3.54 m
Ground clearance: 360 mm
Wheel track:
(front) 2.034 m
(rear) 2.050 m
Wheelbase: 3.44 + 1.45 m

Angle of approach/departure: 37°/38°
Max speed: (road) 105 km/h
Max range: (cruising) 1,000 km
Fuel capacity: 420 litres
Gradient: 75%
(laden, solo) 75%
(43,200 kg GCW) 45%
Fording: 1.2 m
Engine: TATRA T3B-928.60 EURO 2 12.667-litre V-8-cylinder turbocharged and charge-air-cooled air-cooled direct injection 4-stroke diesel developing 347 hp (259 kW) at 1,800 rpm and 1,570 N.m torque at 1,200 rpm. EURO 3 option available
Gearbox: TATRA 10 TS 160 manual with semi-automatic split giving 10 forward and 2 reverse gears. Synchromesh on all except first and reverse gears
Transfer box: TATRA 2.30 TRK 1.6/2.6 2-speed, with front axle disconnect
Clutch: single dry plate, (dia) 430 mm
Steering: power assisted
Turning radius: 10.5 m
Suspension:
(front) torsion bars and telescopic shock-absorbers
(rear) airbags with internal coil springs and telescopic shock-absorbers
(see text for details)
Tyres: 1400R 20
Brakes: dual circuit air with ABS, drums front and rear. Supplementary engine exhaust brake
Electrical system: 24 V
Batteries: 2 × 12 V, 165 Ah
Alternator: 28 V, 55 A

Status
In production. In service with the Czech Army. T815 ARMAX family trucks are also in service with Indian, Malaysian and Slovak armed forces.

Contractor
TATRA, a.s.

TATRA T 815-26OR24 33 255 6 × 6.2 ARMAX family (6 × 6) truck

Development
The TATRA T 815-26OR24 33 255 6 × 6.2 (6 × 6) truck is a member of the T 815 ARMAX family of (4 × 4) and (6 × 6) trucks. The T 815 ARMAX family of trucks was introduced by TATRA in 1998 to join the earlier TERRN°1 and T 815-6 FORCE (originally designated T 816 FORCE) families of trucks, all of which are the continued evolution of the T 815 series first introduced in 1983. Full details of the T 815 and T 815-6 FORCE families can be found elsewhere in this section.

The TERRN°1 family are essentially commercial designs, but are suitable for certain military applications. The T 815-6 FORCE family are purpose designed no-compromise trucks for tactical military applications and as such are fitted with a range of water-cooled engines all producing over 400 hp. The T 815 ARMAX family are based around commercially available designs, militarised as required, and are constructed to comply with all relevant legislation (when required) including emissions, noise and axle loadings, although in many cases vehicle payload capabilities exceed allowable peacetime maximums.

TATRA, a.s. became a Joint Stock Company in 1992. In November 2001, it was announced that the Czech government had approved the purchase of a 92 per cent stake in TATRA, a.s. by SDC International of the US. Following a brief period of difficult-to-follow ownership reorganisation, in September 2003 it was announced that Terex Corporation of the US had acquired 70.51 per cent of TATRA shares. Vectra (a London-based Indian-owned company) owned 21.11 per cent of shares, the remaining 8.38 per cent being privately owned. The company became known as TATRA, a.s. a Terex company, with products continuing to be branded TATRA.

In October 2006, it was announced that Terex Corporation had sold its 81 per cent holding of TATRA, a.s. to a consortium of Czech and US investors. The Czech registered Blue River s.r.o. (now TATRA Holdings) consortium is made up of Belgium-based KBC Private Equity, Vectra Ltd, a US investor, plus Meadow Hill. Vectra Ltd - a construction equipment, bus and truck maker - folded its existing 11.1 per cent stake into Blue River.

Description
The TATRA T 815-26OR25 31 255 6 × 6.2 (6 × 6) truck is fitted with a Multilift Mark 4 (now known as the MPH 165) load handling system, but the overall layout of the vehicle follows closely that of earlier TATRA truck designs. The torsionally rigid tubular backbone-type chassis is retained, as is the swinging half-axle independent wheel suspension system. The usual 1400R 20 single tyres of the TATRA T 815 ARMAX range are however replaced by smaller 1200R 20 tyres, with dual wheels on the rear two axles. Compared to single tyres, the dual wheel/tyre arrangement on the rear axles allows for an increase in axle loadings, while allowing the vehicle laden with a standard 1C ISO container to remain under 4 m in height. The compromise for this type of wheel/tyre arrangement is a reduction in off-road mobility, TATRA describing the vehicle as a medium mobility

TATRA T815-26OR24 33 255 6 × 6.2 (6 × 6) truck fitted with a Multilift Mark 4 (now designated MPH 165) Load Handling System (LHS) (TATRA, a.s.)
0524781

chassis, using the term high mobility for vehicles fitted with 1400R 20 single tyres.

The front steer-drive axle is sprung by the combination of torsion bars and telescopic shock-absorbers, while the rear drive axle is sprung by TATRA's combination suspension that uses the commercial name King Frame. The so-called light version of this combination suspension system is fitted. This uses airbags with internal coil springs and telescopic shock-absorbers on each half-axle, the airbag units being mounted above the backbone tube to protect from impact or damage while operating off-road. Maximum individual axle loadings for the light version are 11,500 kg.

Motive power is provided by a EURO 2 (EURO 3 on request) emissions compliant TATRA 12.7-litre V-8 four-stroke air-cooled diesel engine developing 347 hp. This drives the rear two - or all three axles - via a TATRA manual gearbox with 10 forward and two reverse gears and a TATRA two-speed transfer box. The main gearbox is provided with synchromesh on all but reverse and first gears. For on-road use drive to the front axle can be disconnected, decreasing fuel consumption while reducing component wear. For improved traction off-road driver-controlled longitudinal and cross-axle differential locks are fitted.

Power assisted steering is standard, as is an anti-lock braking system. Dual circuit drum brakes are fitted all-round, supplemented by an engine exhaust brake. Without additional preparation the vehicle can operate throughout a −30 to +40°C temperature range.

The standard all-steel two-door cab is of conventional design and features a single roof hatch. Two full-size seats are standard, with an occasional/emergency seat fixed to the central engine cover; the seating arrangements are such that they can be converted in to a berth. A curved single piece or four-piece split windscreen can be fitted. The cab tilts forward hydraulically for maintenance purposes. An independent fuel-powered cab heater is standard, air-conditioning is an option.

To meet a potential IDF requirement, TATRA developed a version of this cab that splits at waist level for C-130 air-transport. This process takes two people less than 40 minutes; nine bolts are involved. Larger four-door or crew-type cabs with additional seating or bunks are available for ARMAX family trucks.

The Multilift Load Handling System (LHS) fitted is essentially the system fitted to the British Army's DROPS fleet and is therefore fully interoperable with this and the US Army's PLS system. Any standard flatracks, or with the use of an intermediate Container Handling Unit (CHU), ISO 1C or 1CC containers can be handled. Loading action time is given as 25 seconds, unloading action time as 33 seconds. The maximum permissible payload of the vehicle is 19,300 kg, the maximum transportable within current legislation is 12,300 kg. Full details of Multilift load handling systems and the Multilift CHU can be found in the Materials handling equipment section.

A detailed overview of the T815 ARMAX family can be found elsewhere in this section.

Specifications

T 815-26OR24 33 255 6 × 6.2 ARMAX
Cab seating: 1 + 1 (+1 occasional)
Configuration: 6 × 6
Weight:
  (unladen) 13,700 kg
  (laden, design) 33,000 kg
  (laden, within legislation) 26,000 kg
  (payload, design) 19,300 kg
  (payload, within legislation) 12,300 kg
  (towed load) 18,900 kg
  (GCW) 51,900 kg
Length: 9 m
Width: 2.5 m
Height:
  (cab roof) 2.94 m
  (ISO 1C container) 3.96 m
Ground clearance: 290 mm

Track:
  (front) 1.994 m
  (rear) 1.774 m
Wheelbase: 4.09 + 1.32 m
Angle of approach/departure: 33°/34°
Max speed: (road) 95 km/h
Max range: (cruising) 600 km
Fuel capacity: 320 litres
Gradient: (at GVW) 61%
Engine: TATRA T3B-928.60 EURO 2 12.667-litre V-8-cylinder turbocharged and charge-air-cooled water-cooled 4-stroke direct injection diesel developing 347 hp (259 kW) at 1,800 rpm and 1,570 N.m torque at 1,200 rpm. EURO 3 option available
Gearbox: TATRA 10 TS 160 manual with semi-automatic split giving 10 forward and 2 reverse gears. Synchromesh on all except first and reverse gears
Transfer box: TATRA 2.30 TRK 1.6/2.6 2-speed with front axle disconnect
Clutch: single dry plate, (dia) 430 mm
Steering: power assisted
Turning radius: (kerb) 11 m
Suspension:
  (front) torsion bars and telescopic shock-absorbers
  (rear) airbags with internal coil springs and telescopic shock-absorbers
(see text for details)
Tyres: 1200R 20
Brakes: dual circuit air with ABS, drums front and rear, supplementary engine exhaust brake
Electrical system: 24 V
Batteries: 2 × 12 V, 165 Ah
Alternator: 28 V, 55 A

Status

Production as required. T 815 ARMAX family trucks are in service with the Czech, Indian and Slovakian armed forces.

Contractor

TATRA, a.s.

TATRA T 815-26OR84 34 255 8 × 8.1 ARMAX family (8 × 8) cargo truck

Development

The TATRA T 815-26OR84 34 255 8 × 8.1 truck is a member of the T 815 ARMAX family. The T 815 ARMAX family of trucks was introduced by TATRA in 1998 to join the earlier TERRN°1 and T 815-6 FORCE families (originally designated T 816 FORCE) of trucks, all of which are the continued evolution of the T 815 series first introduced in 1983. Full details of the T 815 and T 815-6 FORCE families can be found elsewhere in this section.

The TERRN°1 family is essentially commercial in its designs, but is suitable for certain military applications. The T 815-6 FORCE family comprises purpose-designed, no-compromise trucks for tactical military applications and, as such, they are fitted with a range of water-cooled engines all producing over 400 hp. The T 815 ARMAX family are based around commercially available designs, militarised as required, and are constructed to comply with all relevant legislation (when required) including emissions, noise and axle loadings, although in many cases vehicle payload capabilities exceed allowable peacetime maximums.

TATRA, a.s. became a Joint Stock Company in 1992. In November 2001, it was announced that the Czech government had approved the purchase of a 92 per cent stake in TATRA, a.s. by SDC International of the US. Following a brief period of difficult-to-follow ownership reorganisation, in September 2003 it was announced that Terex Corporation of the US had acquired 70.51 per cent of TATRA shares. Vectra (a London-based Indian-owned company) owns 21.11 per cent of shares, the remaining 8.38 per cent being privately owned. The company became known as TATRA, a.s., a Terex company, with products continuing to be branded TATRA.

In October 2006 it was announced that Terex Corporation had sold its 81 per cent holding of TATRA, a.s. to a consortium of Czech and US investors. The Czech registered Blue River s.r.o. (now TATRA Holdings) consortium is made up of Belgium-based KBC Private Equity, Vectra Ltd, a US investor, plus Meadow Hill. Vectra Ltd - a construction equipment, bus and truck maker - folded its existing 11.1 per cent stake into Blue River.

Description

The overall layout of the TATRA T 815-26OR84 34 255 8 × 8.1 truck follows closely that of earlier TATRA truck designs. The torsionally rigid tubular backbone-type chassis is retained, as is the swinging half-axle independent wheel suspension system. The front steer-drive axles are sprung by the combination of leaf springs and telescopic shock-absorbers, while the rear drive axles are sprung by TATRA's combination suspension that uses the commercial name KING FRAME. The so-called light version of this combination suspension system is fitted. This uses airbags with internal coil springs and telescopic shock-absorbers on each half-axle, the airbag units being mounted above the backbone tube to protect from impact or damage while operating off-road. Maximum individual axle loadings for the light version are 11,500 kg.

TATRA T 815-26OR84 34 255 8 × 8.1 ARMAX family (8 × 8) 20,400 kg truck with conventional cargo/troop-carrying body (TATRA, a.s.) 1185474

Motive power is provided by a EURO 2 (EURO 3 on request) emissions compliant TATRA 12.7-litre V-8 four-stroke air-cooled diesel engine developing 342 hp. This drives the rear four - or all eight wheels - via a TATRA 14 TS 180T manual gearbox with 14 forward and two reverse gears and a TATRA two-speed transfer box. The main gearbox is provided with synchromesh on all but reverse and first gears. For on-road use drive to the front axles can be disconnected.

For improved traction off-road driver-controlled longitudinal and cross-axle differential locks are fitted. With an approach angle of 37° the vehicle can surmount a 500 mm vertical obstacle. A trench 1.9 m wide can be crossed. Without additional preparation the vehicle can operate throughout a –30 to +40°C temperature range.

Power assisted steering is standard, as is an Anti-lock Braking System (ABS). Dual circuit drum brakes are fitted all-round, supplemented by an engine exhaust brake.

The standard all-steel two-door cab is of conventional design and features a single roof hatch. Larger cabs with additional stowage, crew or berthing space, or four doors are an option for the ARMAX range. Two full-size seats are standard, with an occasional/emergency seat fixed to the central engine cover; the seating arrangements are such that they can be converted in to a berth. A curved single piece or four-piece split windscreen can be fitted. The cab tilts forward hydraulically for maintenance purposes and an independent fuel-powered cab heater and air-conditioning are options. TATRA developed a version of the standard cab that splits at waist level for C-130 air-transport. This process takes two people less than 40 minutes; nine bolts are involved.

The rear cargo body is fitted with a treated non-slip plywood floor and has a steel frame and removable drop sides and tailgate. Tilting bench seats for troop transport are an option, and a tarpaulin cover supported by bows may be fitted. Dimensions of the rear body are 5.92 × 2.55 m (L × W).

Specifications

T 815-26OR84 34 255 8 × 8.1 ARMAX
Cab seating: 1 + 1 (+1 occasional)
Configuration: 8 × 8
Weight:
    (unladen, chassis-cab) 13,600 kg
    (laden) 34,000 kg
    (payload, on chassis-cab) 20,400 kg
    (towed load) 20,000 kg
    (GCW) 54,000 kg
Length: 8.59 m
Width: 2.55 m
Height: (exhaust, unladen) 3.33 m
Ground clearance: 370 mm
Wheel track:
    (front) 2.034 m
    (rear) 2.050 m
Wheelbase: 1.65 + 2.6 + 1.45 m
Angle of approach/departure: 37°/39°
Max speed: (road, limited) 85 km/h
Max range: (cruising) 1,000 km
Fuel capacity: 320 litres
Gradient:
    (at GVW) 58%
    (at GCW) 30%
Fording: 1.2 m
Engine: TATRA T3B-928.60 EURO 2 12.667-litre V-8 turbocharged and charge-air-cooled, air-cooled direct injection 4-stroke diesel developing 342 hp (255 kW) at 1,800 rpm and 1,570 N.m torque at 1,200 rpm. EURO 3 option available
Gearbox: TATRA 14 TS 180T manual with semi-automatic split giving 14 forward and 2 reverse gears. Synchromesh on all except first and reverse gears
Transfer box: TATRA 2.30 TRS 2.9/1.24 2-speed with front axle disconnect
Clutch: single dry plate, (dia) 430 mm

Steering: power-assisted, dual circuit with emergency steering pump
Suspension:
    (front) leaf springs and telescopic shock-absorbers
    (rear) airbags with internal coil springs and telescopic shock-absorbers (see text for details)
Tyres: 1400R 20
Brakes: dual circuit, air, drums front and rear. ABS fitted
Electrical system: 24 V
Batteries: 2 × 12 V, 180 Ah
Alternator: 28 V, 55 A

Status
In Production. In service with Slovakia. T 815 ARMAX family trucks are also in service with Czech, Indian and Malaysian armed forces.

Contractor
TATRA, a.s.

TATRA T 815-27OR84 41 300 8 × 8.2 ARMAX family (8 × 8) chassis-cab with LHS

Development
The TATRA T 815-27OR84 41 300 8 ×8.2 truck is a member of the T 815 ARMAX family. The T 815 ARMAX family of trucks was introduced by TATRA in 1998 to join the earlier TERRN°1 and T 815-6 FORCE families (originally designated T 816 FORCE) of trucks, all of which are the continued evolution of the T 815 series first introduced in 1983. Full details of the T 815 and T 815-6 FORCE families can be found elsewhere in this section.

The TERRN°1 family is essentially commercial in its designs, but is suitable for certain military applications. The T 815-6 FORCE family comprises purpose-designed, no-compromise trucks for tactical military applications and, as such, they are fitted with a range of water-cooled engines all producing over 400 hp. The T 815 ARMAX family are based around commercially available designs, militarised as required, and are constructed to comply with all relevant legislation (when required) including emissions, noise and axle loadings, although in many cases vehicle payload capabilities exceed allowable peacetime maximums.

TATRA, a.s. became a Joint Stock Company in 1992. In November 2001, it was announced that the Czech government had approved the purchase of a 92 per cent stake in TATRA, a.s. by SDC International of the US. Following a brief period of difficult-to-follow ownership reorganisation, in September 2003 it was announced that Terex Corporation of the US had acquired 70.51 per cent of TATRA shares. Vectra (a London-based Indian-owned company) owns 21.11 per cent of shares, the remaining 8.38 per cent being privately owned. The company became known as TATRA, a.s., a Terex company, with products continuing to be branded TATRA.

In October 2006 it was announced that Terex Corporation had sold its 81 per cent holding of TATRA, a.s. to a consortium of Czech and US investors. The Czech registered Blue River s.r.o. (now TATRA Holdings) consortium is made up of Belgium-based KBC Private Equity, Vectra Ltd, a US investor, plus Meadow Hill. Vectra Ltd - a construction equipment, bus and truck maker - folded its existing 11.1 per cent stake into Blue River.

Description
The overall layout of the TATRA T 815-27OR84 41 300 8 × 8.2 truck follows closely that of earlier TATRA truck designs. The torsionally rigid tubular backbone-type chassis is retained, as is the swinging half-axle independent wheel suspension system. The front steer-drive axles are sprung by the combination of leaf springs and telescopic shock-absorbers, while the rear drive axles are sprung by TATRA's combination suspension that uses the commercial name KING FRAME. The heavy version of this combination suspension system is fitted. This uses airbags with internal coil springs in combination with leaf springs on each half-axle, the airbag units being mounted above the backbone tube to protect from impact or damage while operating off-road. Maximum individual axle loadings for the heavy version are 15,000 kg.

T 815-27OR84 41 300 8 × 8.2 ARMAX family (8 × 8) 26,000 kg truck fitted with a Multilift Load Handling System (LHS) (TATRA, a.s.) 1185412

Motive power is provided by a EURO 2 (EURO 3 on request) emissions compliant TATRA 12.7-litre V-8 four-stroke air-cooled diesel engine developing 402 hp. This drives the rear four - or all eight wheels - via a TATRA 14 TS 180T manual gearbox with 14 forward and two reverse gears and a TATRA two-speed transfer box. The main gearbox is provided with synchromesh on all but reverse and first gears. For on-road use drive to the front axles can be disconnected.

For improved traction off-road driver-controlled longitudinal and cross-axle differential locks are fitted. With an approach angle of 31° the vehicle can surmount a 400 mm vertical obstacle. A trench 1.9 m wide can be crossed. Without additional preparation the vehicle can operate throughout a –30 to +40°C temperature range.

Power assisted steering is standard, as is an Anti-lock Braking System (ABS). Dual circuit drum brakes are fitted all-round, supplemented by an engine exhaust brake.

The standard all-steel two-door cab is of conventional design and features a single roof hatch. Larger cabs with additional stowage, crew or berthing space, or four doors are an option for the ARMAX range. Two full-size seats are standard, with an occasional/emergency seat fixed to the central engine cover; the seating arrangements are such that they can be converted in to a berth. A curved single piece or four-piece split windscreen can be fitted. The cab tilts forward hydraulically for maintenance purposes and an independent fuel-powered cab heater and air-conditioning are options. TATRA developed a version of the standard cab that splits at waist level for C-130 air-transport. This process takes two people less than 40 mins; nine bolts are involved.

The T 815-27OR84 41 300 8×8.2 is fitted with a Multilift MPH 165 (previously designated Mark 4) Load Handling System (LHS). When fitted with a container handling unit the T 815-27OR84 41 300 8 × 8.2 is capable of transporting a standard ISO 1C container at under 4 m overall height.

Specifications

T 815-27OR84 41 300 8 × 8.2 ARMAX
Cab seating: 1 + 1 (+1 occasional)
Configuration: 8 × 8
Weight:
(unladen, chassis-cab) 15,000 kg
(laden) 41,000 kg
(payload, on chassis-cab) 26,000 kg
(payload, legal) 17,000 kg
(towed load) 19,500 kg
(GCW) 60,500 kg
Length: 8.59 m
(chassis-cab) 8.533 m
(with 20 ft ISO container) 9.066 m
Width: 2.55 m
Height:
(exhaust) 3.33 m
(with ISO 1C container) 3.98 m
Ground clearance: 275 mm
Track:
(front) 1.994 m
(rear) 1.774 m
Wheelbase: 1.65 + 2.6 + 1.45 m
Angle of approach/departure: 31°/33°
Max speed: 95 km/h
Max range: (cruising) 650 km
Fuel capacity: 320 litres
Gradient: 51%
Fording: 800 mm
Engine: TATRA T3B-928.70 EURO 2 12.667-litre V-8 turbocharged and charge-air-cooled, air-cooled direct injection 4-stroke diesel developing 402 hp (300 kW) at 1,800 rpm and 1,830 N.m torque at 1,200 rpm. EURO 3 option available
Gearbox: TATRA 14 TS 180T manual with semi-automatic split giving 14 forward and 2 reverse gears. Synchromesh on all except first and reverse gears
Transfer box: TATRA 2.30 TRS 2.9/1.24 2-speed with front axle disconnect
Clutch: single dry plate, (dia) 430 mm
Steering: power-assisted, dual circuit with emergency steering pump
Turning radius: (kerb) 11 m
Suspension:
(front) leaf springs and telescopic shock-absorbers
(rear) airbags with internal coil springs and telescopic shock-absorbers
(see text for details)
Tyres: 1300R 22.5
Brakes: dual circuit, air, drums front and rear. Supplementary engine exhaust brake. ABS fitted
Electrical system: 24 V
Batteries: 2 × 12 V, 180 Ah
Alternator: 28 V, 55 A

Status
In service with Slovakia. T 815 ARMAX family trucks are also in service with Czech, Indian and Malaysian armed forces.

Contractor
TATRA, a.s.

TATRA T 815-6MOR87 33 324 8 × 8.1R FORCE family (8 × 8) 12,500-litre fuel tanker truck

Development
The TATRA T 815-6 FORCE (originally designated T 816 FORCE) family of tactical trucks was introduced by TATRA in 1996 and is the continued evolution of the T 815 series first introduced in 1983. Full details of the T 815 and 1998-introduced T 815 ARMAX families, and the 2004-introduced T 815-7 tactical range (with military-specific cab), can be found elsewhere in this section.

The T 815 ARMAX family is based around commercially available designs, militarised as required, and has been constructed to comply with all relevant legislation (when required) including emissions, noise and axle loadings, although in a number of cases, vehicle payload capabilities exceed allowable peacetime maximums. The T 815-6 FORCE family comprises purpose-designed, no-compromise trucks for tactical military applications, which are fitted with a range of water-cooled engines, all producing over 400 hp. The strengths of such a no-compromise military design make the FORCE family particularly suitable for certain markets as well as some civilian applications, such as mining or construction, where some aspects of truck design legislation are not applicable.

TATRA, a.s. became a Joint Stock Company in 1992. In November 2001, it was announced that the Czech government had approved the purchase of a 92 per cent stake in TATRA, a.s. by SDC International of the US. Following a brief period of difficult-to-follow ownership reorganisation, in September 2003 it was announced that Terex Corporation of the US had acquired 70.51 per cent of TATRA shares. Vectra (a London-based Indian-owned company) owns 21.11 per cent of shares, the remaining 8.38 per cent being privately owned. The company became known as TATRA, a. s., a Terex company, with products continuing to be branded TATRA.

In October 2006 it was announced that Terex Corporation had sold its 81 per cent holding of TATRA, a.s. to a consortium of Czech and US investors. The Czech registered Blue River s.r.o. (now TATRA Holdings) consortium is made up of Belgium-based KBC Private Equity, Vectra Ltd, a US investor, plus Meadow Hill. Vectra Ltd - a construction equipment, bus and truck maker - folded its existing 11.1 per cent stake into Blue River.

Description
The overall layout of the TATRA T 815-6MOR87 33 324 8 × 8.1R truck follows closely that of earlier TATRA truck designs. The torsionally rigid tubular backbone-type chassis is retained, as is the swinging half-axle independent wheel suspension system. The front steer-drive axles are sprung by the combination of torsion bars and telescopic shock-absorbers, the rear drive axles sprung by TATRA's combination suspension that uses the commercial name KING FRAME. The so-called light version of this combination suspension system is fitted. This uses airbags with internal coil springs and telescopic shock-absorbers on each half-axle, the airbag units being mounted above the backbone tube to protect from impact or damage while operating off-road. Maximum individual axle loadings for the light version are 11,500 kg.

Motive power is provided by a Cummins 10.8-litre six-cylinder four-stroke water-cooled diesel developing 440 hp. All four hub reduction axles are permanently driven via a Twin Disc torque converter and fully automatic transmission. The torque converter is fitted with a lock-up clutch and two Power Take-Offs (PTOs). The fully automatic transmission is integrated into the backbone tube thus eliminating the need for a separate transfer box. Six forward and one reverse gears are available and there is a lockable front/rear torque divider. A 'limp home' facility is also provided. Dual circuit drum brakes are fitted all-round, supplemented by an engine exhaust brake.

For improved traction off-road driver-controlled longitudinal and cross-axle differential locks and a semi-automatic tyre inflation system are fitted. A fully automatic Central Tyre Inflation (CTI) system with four terrain settings, flat detection and run-flat function is an option. Bead locks are a further option for extreme low-pressure operation. 1600R 20 tyres are

TATRA T815-6MOR87 33 324 8 × 8.1R FORCE family (8 × 8) 12,500-litre fuel tanker truck (TATRA, a.s.) 1185473

standard fit and with an approach angle of 41° a 600 mm vertical obstacle can be surmounted. A 2 m trench can be crossed. Without additional preparation the T 815-6MOR87 33 324 8 × 8.1R can operate throughout a −30 to +50°C temperature range, this increases to +55°C for some models in the FORCE family.

The standard all-steel two-door cab is of conventional design and features a single roof hatch; a larger cab with additional stowage, crew or berthing space is an option. Two full-size seats are standard, with an occasional/emergency seat fixed to the central engine cover. A curved single piece or four-piece split windscreen can be fitted. The cab tilts forward hydraulically for maintenance purposes and an independent fuel-powered cab heater and air-conditioning are options. TATRA has developed a version of the standard cab that splits at waist level for C-130 air-transport. This process takes two people less than 40 mins; nine bolts are involved. A NATO-standard towing pintle is fitted, as is a NATO slave start connector. Additional options available include a front underbody protection guard and a long-range fuel tank with 420-litre capacity.

The base chassis will readily accept a wide variety of bodies and roles.

The two-chamber fuel tanker body is constructed of stainless steel and has a capacity of 12,500 litres and meets EU requirements for international road transport of hazardous material – ADR Class 3. A two-line delivery system has a capacity of 300 litres per line per minute.

A detailed overview of the T 815-6 FORCE family can be found elsewhere in this section.

Specifications

T 815-6MOR87 33 324
Cab seating: 1 + 1 (+1 occasional)
Configuration: 8 × 8
Weight:
(unladen, chassis-cab) 13,400 kg
(laden) 33,000 kg
(payload, on chassis-cab) 19,600 kg
(towed load) 25,000 kg
(GCW) 58,000 kg
Length: (chassis) 9.01 m
Width: 2.55 m
Height: (exhaust) 3.295 m
Ground clearance: 390 mm
Track: (front/rear) 2.074 m
Wheelbase: 1.65 + 2.97 + 1.45 m
Angle of approach/departure: 41°/38°
Max speed: (road) 110 km/h
Max range: (cruising) 600 km
Fuel capacity: 320 litres
Gradient: 100%
Side slope: 45%
Fording: 1.25 m
Engine: Cummins ISM 440E EURO 3 emissions compliant 10.8-litre 6-cylinder in-line turbocharged and charge-air-cooled, water-cooled direct injection 4-stroke diesel developing 440 hp (328 kW) at 1,800 rpm and 2,100 N.m torque at 1,200 rpm
Transmission: Twin Disc TD61-1177 automatic with 6 forward and 1 reverse gears, plus Twin Disc 8-FLW-1754 torque converter with lock-up clutch and twin PTOs
Steering: power-assisted
Turning radius:
(kerb) 12.5 m
(wall) 13.35 m
Suspension:
(front) leaf springs and telescopic shock-absorbers
(rear) airbags with internal coil springs and telescopic shock-absorbers (see text for details)
Tyres: 1600R 20
Brakes: dual circuit, air, drums all-round
Electrical system: 24 V
Batteries: 2 × 12 V, 180 Ah
Alternator: 28 V, 70 A

Status

Production as required. FORCE family trucks are in service with Israel (via American Truck Company) and India.

Contractor

TATRA, a.s.

TATRA T 815-6MWV27 26 298 6×6.1R FORCE family (6 × 6) 12,600 kg truck

Development

The TATRA T 815-6 FORCE family (originally designated T 816 FORCE family) of tactical trucks was introduced by TATRA in 1996 and is the continued evolution of the T 815 series first introduced in 1983. Full details of the T 815 and 1998-introduced T 815 ARMAX families can be found elsewhere in this section. The T 815 ARMAX family is based around commercially available designs, militarised as required, and has been

TATRA T 815-6MWV27 26 298 6×6.1R FORCE family (6 × 6) 12,600 kg cargo truck as displayed at IDET 2005 (Stefan Marx)   1185472

constructed to comply with all relevant legislation (when required) including emissions, noise and axle loadings, although in a number of cases, vehicle payload capabilities exceed allowable peacetime maximums. The T 815-6 FORCE family comprises purpose-designed, no-compromise trucks for tactical military applications, which are fitted with a range of water-cooled engines, all producing over 400 hp. The strengths of such a no-compromise military design make the FORCE family particularly suitable for certain markets as well as some civilian applications, such as mining or construction, where some aspects of truck design legislation are not applicable.

The American Truck Company (ATC) was selected mid-2003 as preferred bidder to supply the Ministry of Defence of Israel (IMOD) with an estimated 315 Medium Tactical Trucks (MTTs) plus associated support. In January 2004 it was announced the American Truck Company had been awarded and entered into a contract with the US Army Tank-armaments and Automotive Command (TACOM) to supply the Ministry of Defense of Israel (IMOD) with 302 Medium Tactical Trucks and associated logistics support.

The model selected by Israel is the T 815-6MWV27 26 298 6×6.1R. These trucks are being supplied to Israel by the United States under the US Foreign Military Sales (FMS) programme. The initial value of the order is approximately USD54 million before options. IMOD also has options to purchase an additional 243 trucks valued at in excess of USD40 million. The announcement followed the conclusion of a two-year competition between ATC and other US truck manufacturers Oshkosh (MTVR) and Stewart and Stevenson (FMTV) that included extended testing of vehicles and an evaluation of after-market support capabilities.

The procurement includes a combination of cargo trucks (some with material handling cranes) that will replace ageing M35 series trucks. Contract work commenced mid-2004 and was scheduled for completion by June 2008. By late 2006 TATRA had supplied all 302 trucks. A contract option for an additional 10 trucks was exercised during 2008.

TATRA, a.s. became a Joint Stock Company in 1997. In November 2001, it was announced that the Czech government had approved the purchase of a 92 per cent stake in TATRA by SDC International of the US. Following a brief period of difficult-to-follow ownership reorganisation, in September 2003 it was announced that Terex Corporation of the US had acquired 70.51 per cent of TATRA shares. Vectra (a London-based Indian-owned company) owned 21.11 per cent of shares, the remaining 8.38 per cent being privately owned. The company became known as TATRA, a.s., a Terex company, with products continuing to be branded TATRA.

In October 2006 it was announced that Terex Corporation had sold its 81 per cent holding of TATRA, a.s. to a consortium of Czech and US investors. The Czech registered Blue River s.r.o. (now TATRA Holdings) consortium is made up of Belgium-based KBC Private Equity, Vectra Ltd, a US investor, plus Meadow Hill. Vectra Ltd - a construction equipment, bus and truck maker - folded its existing 11.1 per cent stake into Blue River.

Terex Corporation was a two-thirds owner of the American Truck Company (ATC).

Description

The overall layout of the TATRA T 815-6MWV27 26 298 6×6.1R cargo truck follows closely that of earlier TATRA truck designs. The torsionally rigid tubular backbone-type chassis is retained, as is the swinging half-axle independent wheel suspension system. The front steer-drive axle is sprung by the combination of torsion bars and telescopic shock-absorbers, the rear drive axles sprung by TATRA's combination suspension that uses the commercial name KING FRAME. The so-called light version of this combination suspension system is fitted. This uses airbags with internal coil springs and telescopic shock-absorbers on each half-axle, the airbag units being mounted above the backbone tube to protect from impact or damage while operating off-road. Maximum individual axle loadings for the light version are 11,500 kg.

Motive power is provided by a Cummins 10.8-litre six-cylinder four-stroke water-cooled diesel developing 400 hp. All three hub reduction axles are permanently driven via a Twin Disc torque converter and fully

TATRA T 815-6MWV27 26 298 6×6.1R FORCE family (6 × 6) 12,600 kg cargo truck (TATRA, a.s.)　0524774

automatic transmission. The torque converter is fitted with a lock-up clutch and two Power Take-Off's (PTO's). The fully automatic transmission is integrated into the backbone tube thus eliminating the need for a separate transfer box. Six forward and one reverse gears are available and there is a lockable front/rear torque divider. A 'limp home' facility is also provided. Dual circuit drum brakes are fitted all-round, supplemented by an engine exhaust brake.

For improved traction off-road driver-controlled longitudinal and cross-axle differential locks are fitted, and a semi-automatic Central Tyre Inflation (CTI) system is standard. A fully automatic CTI system with four terrain settings, flat detection and run-flat function is an option. Bead locks are a further option for extreme low-pressure operation. 1600R 20 tyres are standard fit and with an approach angle of 39° a 600 mm vertical obstacle can be surmounted. A 1 m trench can be crossed. Without additional preparation the T 815-6MWV27 26 298 6×6.1R can operate throughout a –30 to +50°C temperature range, this increases to +55°C for some models in the FORCE family.

The standard all-steel two-door cab is of conventional design and features a single roof hatch. Larger cabs with additional stowage, crew or berthing space, or four doors are options. Two full-size seats are standard, with an occasional/emergency seat fixed to the central engine cover. A curved single piece or four-piece split windscreen can be fitted. The cab tilts forward hydraulically for maintenance purposes and an independent fuel-powered cab heater and air-conditioning are options.

To meet a potential requirement of the IDF TATRA developed a version of the standard cab that splits at waist level for C-130 air-transport. This process takes two people less than 40 minutes; nine bolts are involved.

The troop carrying/cargo-type body is fitted with two-section steel drop sides and a single-section tailgate and comes complete with bows over which a tarpaulin cover can be fitted. The load area measures 6.145 × 2.47 m (L × W) and can transport a single 20 ft ISO container or 26 seated troops. The maximum payload is 12,600 kg, reducing to 11,600 kg to retain what TATRA define as 'high mobility'. Between the single spare wheel, mounted directly behind the cab, and the cargo body a hydraulic materials handling crane with a capacity of 1,000 kg at 7 m may be mounted. A NATO-standard towing pintle is fitted, as is a NATO slave start connector.

Additional options available include a winch with 50 m of cable and a rear pull capacity of 90 kN. A front underbody protection guard and a long-range fuel tank with 420 litres capacity.

A detailed overview of the T 815 FORCE family can be found elsewhere in this section.

Specifications

T 815-6MWV27 26 298 6×6.1R FORCE
Cab seating: 1 + 1 (+1 occasional)
Configuration: 6 × 6
Weight:
　(unladen) 13,400 kg
　(laden, on/off-road) 26,000 kg
　(laden, high mobility) 25,000 kg
　(payload, on/off-road) 12,600 kg
　(payload, high mobility) 11,600 kg
　(towed load) 25,000 kg
　(GCW) 51,000 kg
Length: 9.06 m
Width: 2.55 m
Height:
　(cab roof) 3.07 m
　(crane, stowed) 3.17 m
　(tarpaulin) 3.61 m
Ground clearance: 390 mm
Wheel track:
　(front) 2.034 m
　(rear) 2.054 m
Wheelbase: 4.09 + 1.45 m
Angle of approach/departure: 39°/34°
Max speed: (road) 110 km/h
Max range: (cruising) 600 km

Fuel capacity: 420 litres
Gradient: 100%
Side slope: 45%
Fording: 1.25 m
Engine: Cummins ISM 400 10.8-litre 6-cylinder in-line turbocharged and charge-air-cooled, water-cooled direct injection 4-stroke diesel developing 298 kW (400 hp) at 1,800 rpm and 1,966 N.m torque at 1,200 rpm
Transmission: Twin Disc TD61-1177 automatic with 6 forward and 1 reverse gears, plus Twin Disc 8-FLW-1750 torque converter with lock-up clutch and twin PTO's
Steering: power assisted
Turning radius:
　(kerb) 12.5 m
　(wall) 13.35 m
Suspension:
　(front) torsion bars and telescopic shock-absorbers
　(rear) airbags with internal coil springs and telescopic shock-absorbers
(see text for details)
Tyres: 1600R 20
Brakes: dual circuit, air, drums all-round
Electrical system: 24 V
Batteries: 2 × 12 V, 165 A/h
Alternator: 28 V, 70 A

Status
In production. In service with Israel.

Contractor
TATRA, a.s.

TATRA 813 (6 × 6) and (8 × 8) trucks

Development
The TATRA 813 series of trucks, also known as the Kolos series, was developed in the former Czechoslovakia in the early 1960s with the first (8 × 8) production vehicles being completed in 1967. The vehicle is related to the OT-64 (8 × 8) amphibious armoured personnel carrier.

Small numbers of the TATRA 813 (8 × 8) are still used by the Czech Republic and Slovakia armies as a cargo/personnel carrier, for towing heavy artillery up to 152 mm in calibre, and for towing trailers carrying engineer equipment and MBTs. The type was first supplemented by the follow-on TATRA T 815 series and is now in the final stages of replacement by the current TATRA T 815 ARMAX family and T 815-7 models, full details of which can be found elsewhere in this section.

VOP 025 of Novy Jicín in the Czech Republic offers a complete overhaul and repair service for TATRA 813 trucks and offers refurbished vehicles in a virtually as-new condition.

In November 2001, it was announced that the Czech government had approved the purchase of a 92 per cent stake in TATRA, a.s. by SDC International of the US. Following a brief period of difficult-to-follow ownership reorganisation, in September 2003 it was announced that Terex Corporation of the US had acquired 70.51 per cent of TATRA shares. Vectra (a London-based Indian-owned company) owned 21.11 per cent of shares, the remaining 8.38 per cent being privately owned. The company became known as TATRA, a.s., a Terex company, with products continuing to be branded TATRA.

In October 2006 it was announced that Terex Corporation had sold its 81 per cent holding of TATRA, a.s. to a consortium of Czech and US investors. The Czech registered Blue River s.r.o. (now TATRA Holdings) consortium is made up of Belgium-based KBC Private Equity, Vectra Ltd, a US investor, plus Meadow Hill. Vectra Ltd - a construction equipment, bus and truck maker - folded its existing 11.1 per cent stake into Blue River.

TATRA 813 (8 × 8) truck of the Czech Army fitted with a dozer blade mounting the AM-50 (Automoblin Most 50) scissors bridge (Richard Stickland)　1124759

TATRA 813 (8 × 8) truck of the Czech Army (Stefan Marx)   1185476

Description

The TATRA 813 series of trucks are designed around TATRA's torsionally rigid tubular backbone-style chassis made up of the axle differentials joined by rigid tubular load-bearing sections, to which a through-frame for supporting the cab and any superstructure are located. Swinging half-axles are sprung by longitudinally located leaf springs shared between axle pairs. This set-up allows for individual axle movement. The front two steer-drive axles on (8 × 8) models are also fitted with telescopic shock-absorbers. On (6 × 6) models the single front axle is sprung by the combination of torsion bars and telescopic shock-absorbers.

The standard cargo truck version has an all-steel forward control cab, which usually has one or two circular observation hatches in the roof. The cab is pressurised and is provided with an effective ventilation system and individual masks for each member of the crew. The engine is in the centre of the cab at the front, with the transmission to the rear of the cab, under the cargo area. The rear cargo area has all-steel drop sides and a drop tailgate, removable seats, and can be equipped with bows and a tarpaulin cover if required.

All military versions are fitted with a Central Tyre Inflation (CTI) system and a 22,000 kg capacity winch. The vehicle is sometimes fitted with the BZ-T hydraulically operated dozer blade at the front; a snow plough can also be fitted.

A late production model was the TATRA 813-12 powered by a 310 hp multifuel engine.

Variants

The basic chassis (8 × 8) has been used for a variety of roles including carrying and launching PMP heavy floating pontoon bridge units (these vehicles are often fitted with the BZ-T hydraulically operated dozer blade) and for carrying and laying the truck-mounted AM-50 scissors bridge, full details of which can be found in the Mechanised Bridges section. There is also a special roadway laying version which is used with the PMP system, full details of which can be found in the Portable Roadways section.

The TATRA 813 (road prime mover) is the basic truck with the rear cargo area replaced with ballast. There is also a (6 × 6) cargo truck version with a multifuel engine, designated the TATRA 813-8.

The TATRA 813 (8 × 8) chassis was used as the basis for the RM-70 122 mm (40 round) multiple rocket system with a fully armoured cab with 40 rockets in the ready to launch position and another 40 rockets ready to reload the launcher. Full details of this model can be found in *Jane's Armour and Artillery*. These are often fitted with the BZ-T hydraulically operated dozer blade for clearing obstacles and preparing fire positions.

There are two prime movers for civil use, the TATRA 4-813 T-3 (6 × 6) and the TATRA 4-813 T-2 (4 × 4), which can tow a trailer weighing up to 65,000 kg. These do not have the CTI system as fitted to military versions. At least three dump truck models were produced, the TATRA 813 S1 (6 × 6), TATRA 813 S3 (6 × 6) and the TATRA 813 S1 (8 × 8). These models also lack the CTI system. Crane versions were also produced for both civil and military use.

Specifications

TATRA 813
Cab seating: 1 + 6
Configuration: 8 × 8
Weight:
 (unladen) 13,800 kg
 (laden) 22,000 kg
 (laden weight on 1st and 2nd axles) 5,150 kg
 (laden weight on 3rd and 4th axles) 5,850 kg
 (max load) 8,200 kg
 (towed load, road) 100,000 kg
Length: 8.8 m
Width: 2.5 m
Height:
 (cab) 2.69 m
 (tarpaulin) 3.355 m
Ground clearance: 425 mm

Track: (front/rear) 2.03 m/2.03 m
Wheelbase: 1.65 m + 2.2 m + 1.45 m
Max speed: (road) 80 km/h
Range: (road) 1,250 km
Fuel capacity: 520 litres
Max gradient: 65%
Trench: 1.4 m
Vertical obstacle: 600 mm
Fording: 1.4 m
Engine: TATRA T-930-3 V-12 air-cooled 4-stroke diesel developing 250 hp (186 kW) at 2,000 rpm
Gearbox: dual range 5-speed plus overdrive providing a total of 20 forward and 4 reverse gears
Steering: power assisted
Tyres: 15.00 × 21
Brakes:
 (main) air, drums front and rear
 (parking) mechanical
Electrical system: 24 V

Status

Production complete. In service with the Czech Republic, India, Slovakia and possibly others in small numbers.

Contractor

TATRA, a.s.

TATRA T 815 (8 × 8) truck series

Development

TATRA can trace its origins back to Austria and 1850 and the company produced its first truck in 1898. As a result of the First World War the part of Austria TATRA originated from became part of the then Czechoslovakia. TATRA's unique tubular backbone-style frame was introduced in 1923.

The TATRA T 815 series of (8 × 8) trucks replaced the earlier TATRA 813 series in production in the former Czechoslovakia in 1983 and for a while the name of Kolos was applied to both. By 1989 the original (8 × 8) and (6 × 6) versions of the TATRA T 815 had been joined by a (4 × 4) version. The TATRA T 815 series has been produced for both military and civil use and in a variety of forms including platform trucks, ballast tractors and special versions. Over time the T 815 has been developed in to the commercial TERRN°1 family and military T 815 ARMAX, T 815-6 FORCE (originally designated T 816 FORCE) and T 815-7 families. Full details of the T 815 (6 × 6) and (4 × 4) models and the T 815 ARMAX, T 815-6 FORCE and T 815-7 families can be found elsewhere in this section.

Vojenského Opravárenského Podniku, š.p (VOP 025) of Nový Jičín, Czech Republic, offers a complete repair and overhaul service for time-expired TATRA trucks, including the TATRA T 815 (8 × 8) series and associated vehicles.

TATRA became a Joint Stock Company in 1992. In November 2001, it was announced that the Czech government had approved the purchase of a 92 per cent stake in TATRA, a.s. by SDC International of the US. Following a brief period of difficult-to-follow ownership reorganisation, in September 2003 it was announced that Terex Corporation of the US had acquired 70.51 per cent of TATRA shares. Vectra (a London-based Indian-owned company) owned 21.11 per cent of shares, the remaining 8.38 per cent being privately owned. The company became known as TATRA, a.s., a Terex company, with products continuing to be branded TATRA.

In October 2006 it was announced that Terex Corporation had sold its 81 per cent holding of TATRA, a.s. to a consortium of Czech and US investors. The Czech registered Blue River s.r.o. (now TATRA Holdings) consortium is made up of Belgium-based KBC Private Equity, Vectra Ltd, a US investor, plus Meadow Hill. Vectra Ltd - a construction equipment, bus and truck maker - folded its existing 11.1 per cent stake into Blue River.

Description

The TATRA T 815 (8 × 8) series followed the same general lines as the earlier TATRA 813 but there were many overall improvements. Two basic military versions of the T 815 (8 × 8) were produced. One is the T 815 VVN 26.265 8 × 8.1R, described as an off-road truck, having a two-door cab. The second, the TATRA T 815 VT 26.265 8 × 8.1R is described as a special heavy road tractor and has a four-door cab and a correspondingly shorter (5.35 m as opposed to 6.25 m) load area. The load capacity for the T 815 VVN is 12,000 kg off-road, or a towed load of 20,000 kg off-road (65,000 kg on hard roads). For the T 815 VT the figures are 10,000 kg or a towed load of 25,000 kg (100,000 kg on hard roads).

Both types of cab are all-metal, have a roof hatch, and unlike those of the earlier 813 series, can be tilted forward for maintenance purposes. The VVN two-door cab has seating for a driver and three passengers, with provision for an occasional berth. The four-door VT cab has seating for the driver and five passengers, with provision for an occasional berth slung above the front seats. Both types of cab have a multifuel heater. They are also equipped with a collective NBC protection system that connects to individual masks, in addition to an air filtering and ventilation system.

The torsionally rigid chassis is of frameless construction with the load-bearing area consisting of axle differentials interconnected by load-bearing tubes. Mounted on the cross members is a through-frame to

BEML-produced TATRA T815 (8 × 8) mounting the Pinaka 12 × 214 mm MultiBarrel Rocket System (MBRS) (Shaun C Connors) 1156187

which the cab, engine and clutch, steering box, winch, truck platform and front and rear bumpers (together with the trailer coupling) are all fitted. The load-carrying platform is mounted on the frame behind the cab and is fitted with a fixed head, drop sides and a hinged tailgate. Side board extensions can be converted into benches for carrying troops. A tarpaulin over sliding bows can be used to cover the load-carrying area.

The swinging half-axles are fitted with hub reduction gearing to reduce driveline stress and increase the vehicle's tractive effort. Individual axle movement is possible and suspension is by leaf springs shared longitudinally between axle pairs, the front steer-drive axle pair being fitted with telescopic shock-absorbers. All wheels are permanently driven and for uniform driving torque division, between the individual axle pairs a torque divider is inserted in the power train. There is also a system of inter- and cross-axle differential locks giving full eight-wheel drive when required.

With the exception of first and reverse gears, all gears in the 10-speed gearbox are provided with block synchromesh. There is also an auxiliary two-speed gearbox directly coupled to the gearbox with power take-off for winch drive.

The winch has a capacity of 12,000 kg on all models and is supplied with 83 m of cable.

All (8 × 8) models are equipped to carry the ŠSP 1000 arrow-type snow plough and can accommodate the BZ-T 815 dozer blade.

Variants

TATRA T 815 VVN 26.265 8 × 8.1R
Platform off-road truck - see text; carrier for ALS-M airfield lighting set.

TATRA T 815 VT 26.265 8 × 8.1R
Heavy off-road tractor - see main text.

TATRA T 815 VTV 26.265 8 × 8.1R
Carrier for PMS bridge roadway components.

TATRA T 815 VPR9 28.265 8 × 8.1R
Bridging equipment carrier for PMS (Ribbon) bridge ramp and pontoons; chassis for 122 mm RM-70 and 70/85 multiple rocket system, with armoured cab; carrier for SB-4H pile-driver system.

TATRA T 815 VP13 32.265 8 × 8.1R
Truck chassis adaptable to carry specialised bodies; carrier for ST-T 815 NBC decontamination system. Full details of which can be found in *Jane's Nuclear Biological and Chemical Defence*.

TATRA T 815 (8 × 8) truck series of the Slovakian Army's demining team in Afghanistan (Carl Schulze) 1391204

TATRA T 815-27ET96 28 300 8×8.1R truck as produced by BEML for the Indian Army (Tatra, a.s.) 1185465

TATRA T 815 VP14 32.265 8 × 8.1R
UP-82 command shelter carrier with armoured cab and permanent dozer blade; chassis for VZ-92 minelaying system and support/reload vehicle, both with armoured cabs.

TATRA T 815 VP19 32.265 8 × 8.1R
Carrier for AM-50B bridge components; carrier for Tamara passive radar reconnaissance system aerial.

TATRA T 815 VP31 29.265 8 × 8.1R
Chassis for 152 mm self-propelled gun-howitzer DANA; chassis for 152 mm self-propelled gun-howitzer Ondava; chassis for 155 mm self-propelled gun-howitzer Zuzana; chassis for Strop air defence system.

AV-15
Heavy recovery vehicle.

AV-20
Heavy recovery vehicle.

TATRA T 815 260R81 36.255 8 × 8.2
Chassis to carry Multilift Mark 4 (now known as the MPH165) 16,500 kg capacity load handling system; gross vehicle weight up to 32,000 kg.

BEML Limited
The TATRA T 815 series of trucks continues to be produced in India by BEML Limited. Following the formation of the Czech Republic and Slovakia in 1993, the former Czechoslovakian TATRA concern became two entities, TATRA a.s. in the Czech Republic and TATRA Sipox a.s. (now Tanax) in Slovakia. The latter set up a wholly-owned subsidiary TATRA Sipox (UK) Ltd in 1994-95 to address overseas markets, including India.

Between 1987-2005, BEML supplied 5,300 TATRA vehicles to the Indian Army. Figures released during 2009 suggested that a total of 10,500 (est.) TATRA T815 range trucks had been delivered to the Indian Army in, primarily, (6 × 6) and (8 × 8) configurations. At DefExpo 2006 BEML announced that manufacture of a (4 × 4) light recovery vehicle in collaboration with TATRA Sipox and based on the TATRA T 815-25RR45 17 230 4 × 4.1 chassis was to commence.

Deliveries commenced during 2003 of current generation TATRA (10 × 10) and (12 × 12) chassis for specialist applications.

India's Research & Development Establishment (Engrs) at Pune has developed an armoured protection kit for the cab of the TATRA T815 series of trucks. An example (fitted to an (8 × 8) chassis) was displayed at DefExpo 2006 (Shaun C Connors) 1156186

BEML states 42 per cent indigenisation in (6 × 6) production, 44 per cent in (8 × 8) (set to increase to 58 per cent). Indian-specific roles for BEML-produced TATRA T 815 (8 × 8) trucks include carrier for part of the Indra radar system, and carrier and launch vehicle for various Indian missile, bridging and portable roadway systems. BEML also offers a heavy recovery vehicle based on the TATRA T 815 (8 × 8) chassis; this vehicle has a 15,000 kg capacity recovery crane and a 15,000 kg capacity winch.

BEML-produced TATRA T815 series trucks are now fitted with EURO 2 emissions compliant engines. Two main models known to be in production.

T 815-27ET96 28 300 8 × 8.1R

This chassis-cab is fitted with a six-seat crew-type cab and is primarily used by the Indian Army as a tank and heavy equipment transporter in conjunction with a BEML-supplied dolly-type multi-axle 20,000 or 50,000 kg trailer. This chassis is also used as the transporter/layer for the Pavement Laying Truck (locally produced derivative of the Czech truck-mounted roadway laying system) used in conjunction with BEML-produced PMS pontoon bridging systems. GVW of the T 815-27ET96 28 300 8 × 8.1R is 28,000 kg. Motive power is provided by a 402 hp (300 kW) EURO 2 (Bharat Stage 2) emissions compliant TATRA T3B-928.70 V-8 diesel engine and the T 815-27ET96 28 300 8 × 8.1R is essentially the current generation variant of an earlier model that was powered by a non-emissions compliant V-12 TATRA diesel developing 355 hp

T 815-27ER96 28 300 8 × 8.1R

This chassis-cab is fitted with a the same engine as the T 815-27ET96 28 300 8 × 8.1R and is again essentially the current generation variant of an earlier model powered by a non-emissions compliant V-12 TATRA diesel developing 355 hp. GVW is 28,000 kg. In addition to troop transport and assorted radar/command-type bodies, specific uses for the TATRA T 815-27ER96 28 300 8 × 8.1R have been stated as the transporter/layer of the Sarvatra truck-mounted bridging system, the mounting vehicle for the 30 m telescopic mobile mast used with the radar systems, the pontoon vehicle for the indigenous PMS pontoon bridge system entering Indian Army service, and the launcher and support vehicle base for the Pinaka (sometimes called Pinacha) MultiBarrel Rocket System (MBRS). A longer wheelbase model, the T 815-27ER96 30 300 8 × 8.1R 4150, with a GVW of 30,000 kg is also available. This is for various ground support applications of IGMP, India's Integrated Guided Missile Project, plus other roles such as a launching platform for Project Nishant Unmanned Aerial Vehicles (UAVs), a mounting vehicle for special radar, and a launching vehicle for special multi-span bridges.

BEML states that the new EURO 2 models were launched in India during 2006-2007 and with 22 per cent indigenisation for (4 × 4) production, 35 per cent indigenisation for (6 × 6) production (set to increase to 45 per cent), and 33 per cent indigenisation for (8 × 8) production (set to increase to 44 per cent).

India's Research & Development Establishment (Engrs) at Pune has developed an armoured protection kit for the cab of the TATRA T815 series of trucks. An example (fitted to an 8 × 8 chassis) was displayed at DefExpo 2006.

Specifications

T 815-27ER96 28 300 8× 8.1R
(T 815-27ET96 28 300 8×8.1R in square brackets where different)
Cab seating: 1 + 3 (two standard and two 'emergency' seats) [1 + 5]
Configuration: 8 × 8
Weight:
(chassis-cab) 13,100 kg [13,800 kg]
(laden) 28,000 kg
(payload on chassis-cab) 14,900 kg [14,300 kg]
(towed load, off-road) 16,000 kg [25,000 kg]
(towed load, on-road) 65,000 kg [100,000 kg]
Length: (chassis-cab) 9.28 m [9.34 m]
Width: 2.5 m
Height:
(overall) 3.69 m
(cab roof beacon) 3.197 m [3.197 m]
Ground clearance: 395 mm
Track:
(front) 2.044 m
(rear) 1.988 m
Wheelbase: 1.65 m + 2.97 m + 1.45 m
Angle of approach/departure: 31°/50°
Max speed: (road) 86 km/h
Cruising range: 1,000 km
Fuel capacity: 400 litres
Gradient: 100%
Side slope: 45%
Trench: 2 m
Vertical obstacle: 600 mm
Fording: 1.2 m
Engine: TATRA T3B-928 .70 12.7-litre V-8 turbocharged and charge air-cooled, air-cooled direct injection 4-stroke diesel developing 402 hp at 1,800 rpm and 1,830 N.m torque at 1,200 rpm
Gearbox: TATRA 10 TS 180 manual with 10 forward and 2 reverse gears
Transfer box: TATRA 2.30 TRK 1.1/1.8 2-speed
Clutch: single dry plate, 430 mm in diameter

Steering: worm and roller, power-assisted
Suspension:
(front) leaf springs, telescopic shock-absorbers
(rear) leaf springs
Turning radius: (kerb) 15.5 m
Tyres: 15.00 × 21
Brakes: dual circuit, air, drums front and rear, supplementary engine exhaust brake
Electrical system: 24 V
Batteries: 2 × 12 V, 180 Ah
Alternator: 28 V, 55 A

Status

Replaced in production in the Czech Republic by the TERRN°1, T 815 ARMAX, T 815 FORCE and T 815-7 families. Licence production continues in India by BEML (see text). In service with the armed forces of the Czech Republic, India, Saudi Arabia (possibly), Slovakia and others.

Contractor

TATRA, a.s.
Bharat Earth Movers Limited (BEML)

TATRA T 816 G3 LIWA (8 × 8) truck series

Development

Although these trucks outwardly resemble the T 815 series of (8 × 8) trucks they differs in many automotive respects, the original TATRA T 816 G3 LIWA having been developed to meet the specific requirements of the United Arab Emirates (UAE), and using a number of driveline components of western origin. Following extensive trials held in July/August 1995, in February 1996 it was announced that the UAE had awarded TATRA a USD180 million contract for 1,100 of these trucks in various configurations, including cargo/troop carriers, and fuel and water tankers, the tanks for the latter being provided by VSS of the Slovak Republic. Deliveries were carried out between 1996 and 1997.

With improvements the T 816 G3 LIWA design remains available as part of the current T 815-6 FORCE family (originally designated T 816 FORCE) of tactical trucks introduced by TATRA in 1996. Along with the TERRN°1 (commercial), T 815-7 (tactical) and T 815 ARMAX (militarised) families of trucks, the T 815-6 FORCE family are the continued evolution of the T 815 series first introduced in 1983. Full details of the T 815, T 815-7, T 815 ARMAX and T 815-6 FORCE families can be found elsewhere in this section.

TATRA, a.s. became a Joint Stock Company in 1992. In November 2001, it was announced that the Czech government had approved the purchase of a 92 per cent stake in TATRA by SDC International of the US. Following a brief period of difficult-to-follow ownership reorganisation, in September 2003 it was announced that Terex Corporation of the US had acquired 70.51 per cent of TATRA shares. Vectra (a London-based Indian-owned company) owned 21.11 per cent of shares, the remaining 8.38 per cent being privately owned. The company became known as TATRA, a. s., a Terex company, with products continuing to be branded TATRA.

In October 2006 it was announced that Terex Corporation had sold its 81 per cent holding of TATRA, a.s. to a consortium of Czech and US investors. The Czech registered Blue River s.r.o. (now TATRA Holdings) consortium is made up of Belgium-based KBC Private Equity, Vectra Ltd, a US investor, plus Meadow Hill. Vectra Ltd - a construction equipment, bus and truck maker - folded its existing 11.1 per cent stake into Blue River.

Description

The overall layout of the TATRA T 816 G3 LIWA truck follows closely that of the other (8 × 8) models of the TATRA family. It retains the torsionally rigid tubular backbone-style chassis and, on vehicles delivered to the UAE, the conventional leaf sprung suspension for the swinging half-axles.

TATRA T 816 6ZVV86/31 cargo/troop carrying truck to United Arab Emirates (UAE) specification (T J Gander)

0100338

Model	T 816-6ZVV86324008×8.1R/31 (cargo/troop)	T 816-6ZVR86304008×8.1R/31 (fuel tanker)	T 816-6ZVR86304008×8.1R/30 (water tanker)
Cab seating:	1 + 1 (+ 1 occasional)	1 + 1 (+ 1 occasional)	1 + 1 (+ 1 occasional)
Configuration:	8 × 8	8 × 8	8 × 8
Weight:			
(unladen)	15,700 kg	17,640 kg	16,600 kg
(laden)	32,000 kg 36,000 kg (see text) 29,400 kg (high mobility)	28,140 kg (off-road)	28,600 kg (off-road)
(payload)	16,300 kg 20,300 kg (see text) 13,700 kg (high mobility)	10,500 kg (off-road)	12,000 kg (off-road)
(towed load)	65,000 kg (on-road) 25,000 kg (off-road) 15,000 kg (sand)	65,000 kg (on-road) 25,000 kg (off-road) 15,000 kg (sand)	65,000 kg (on-road) 25,000 kg (off-road) 15,000 kg (sand)
Load area:	5.49 × 2.5 m	n/app	n/app
Length:	8.9 m	9.25 m	9.25 m
Width:	2.6 m	2.5 m	2.5 m
Height:	3.14 m (air intake)	3.14 m (air intake) 3.27 m (tank steps)	3.14 m (air intake)
Ground clearance:	410 mm	410 mm	410 mm
Track:			
(front)	2.04 m	2.04 m	2.04 m
(rear)	1.99 m	1.99 m	1.99 m
Wheelbase:	1.65 + 2.97 + 1.45 m	1.65 + 2.97 + 1.45 m	1.65 + 2.97 + 1.45 m
Angle of approach/departure:	37°/44°	37°/37°	37°/37°
Max speed:	115 km/h	115 km/h	115 km/h
Max range: (road, cruising)	800 km	800 km	800 km
Fuel capacity:	580 litres	580 litres	580 litres
Max gradient:	100%	100%	100%
Sideslope:	57%	57%	57%
Fording:	1.25 m	1.25 m	1.25 m
Engine:	Deutz BF8M 1015C 15.87-litre V-8 turbocharged and charge-air-cooled, water-cooled direct injection 4-stroke diesel developing 544 hp (406 kW) at 2,100 rpm and 2,650 N.m torque between 1,200 and 1,400 rpm		
Gearbox:	Twin Disc TD61-1175 8 automatic with 6 forward and 1 reverse gears, plus Twin Disc FLW 1754 1 torque converter with lock-up clutch and 2 PTO's. Lockable front/rear torque divider and limp-home facility		
Steering:	power assisted	power assisted	power assisted
Turning radius:	13.5 m	13.5 m	13.5 m
Suspension:	swinging half-axles with independent wheel suspension provided by leaf springs shared between axle pairs, front and rear. Telescopic shock-absorbers, front axle pair only		
Tyres:	1600R 20 (Michelin XZL)	1600R 20 (Michelin XZL)	1600R 20 (Michelin XZL)
Brakes:	dual circuit, air, drums front and rear	dual circuit, air, drums front and rear	dual circuit, air, drums front and rear
Electrical system:	24 V	24 V	24 V
Batteries:	2 ×12 V, 165 Ah	2 ×12 V, 165 Ah	2 ×12 V, 165 Ah
Alternator:	55 A	55 A	55 A

A two-door all-steel forward-control cab with a four-piece windscreen is provided, with the cab tilting forward hydraulically for maintenance purposes. Adjustable sprung seats are provided for the driver and passenger, with an additional supplementary third-person seat provided on the engine cover for occasional use.

Motive power is provided by a Deutz water-cooled diesel developing 544 hp and 2,650 N.m torque. Maximum speed is 115 km/h. The engine is coupled to a Twin Disc six-speed automatic gearbox and torque converter integrated into the chassis backbone tube, thus eliminating the need for a separate transfer box. Hub reduction gearing is employed.

Cooling systems for the transmission oil, water, charge air and fuel are provided from Langerer and Reich of Germany. Dual circuit drum brakes are fitted all round, with supplementary braking provided by an engine exhaust brake. Tyres are 1600R 20, the more standardised 20 inch wheel rims replacing 21 inch rims fitted to most earlier single-tyred TATRA vehicles.

To improve mobility under desert conditions, a semi-automatic Central Tyre Inflation (CTI) system produced by TATRA is provided. This allows the driver to adjust tyre pressures to suit the terrain being crossed, from the driving position and while on the move. Hutchinson bead locks are an option for extreme low-pressure operations. With an approach angle of 37° the T 816 can surmount a 600 mm vertical step, and with a wheelbase measurement of 1.65 + 2.97 + 1.45 m can cross a 2 m trench. Driver operated differential locks are provided on/between all axles, giving full (8 × 8) drive when required.

The standard cargo/troop carrying vehicle is fitted with a 13.7 m³ body produced by TATRA and is designated T 816-6ZVV86 32 400 8 × 8.1R/31. Curb weight of the standard vehicle is 15,700 kg and, with optional rims and leaf springs, maximum load capacity and GVW are 20,300 and 36,000 kg, respectively. Without the aforementioned optional rims and leaf

TATRA T 816-6ZVV86 28 400 8×8.1R/30 cargo truck with rear-mounted crane (TATRA, a.s.)   0524784

TATRA T 816-6ZVR86 30 400 8×8.1R/30 12,000-litre water tanker (TATRA, a.s.)   0524790

*TATRA T 816-6ZVR86 30 400 8×8.1R/31 12,500-litre fuel tanker
(TATRA, a.s.)*   0524787

springs maximum load capacity and GVW drops to 16,300 and 32,000 kg, respectively. To retain the level of mobility defined as 'high-mobility' maximum load capacity and GVW are 13,700 and 29,400 kg, respectively.

The standard cargo/troop carrying body has a steel frame, aluminium drop sides and a floor made of water-resistant plywood with an anti-slip surface. A canvas cover and bows can be provided. Tanks on the fuel and water variants are produced by VSS of the Slovak Republic. Rear-mounted loading cranes are provided by Fassi of Italy. A winch can be fitted if required.

Variants

TATRA T 816-686 28 400 8×8.1R/30 Cargo Truck with Crane
This variant (UAE designation T 816-6ZVV86/30) retains the standard 13.7 m^3 cargo/troop carrying body produced by TATRA, but mounts a Fassi crane on the rear of the chassis. The crane has a maximum capacity of 2,945 kg at 2.3 m and increases the overall length of the vehicle from 8.9 to 9.37 m, reducing the departure angle from 44° to 37°. Curb weight of this variant is 16,900 kg and, with optional rims and leaf springs, maximum load capacity and GVW are 19,100 and 36,000 kg, respectively. Without the aforementioned optional rims and leaf springs maximum load capacity and GVW drops to 13,900 and 30,800 kg, respectively. To retain the level of mobility defined as 'high-mobility' maximum load capacity and GVW are 11,100 and 28,000 kg, respectively. Maximum towed loads are 65,000 kg on-road, 25,000 kg off-road, and 15,000 kg in sandy conditions.

TATRA T 816-6ZVV86 32 400 8×8.1R/31 Cargo Truck
Full details of this variant (UAE designation T 816 6ZVV86/31) can be found in the specifications table.

TATRA T 816-6ZVR86 30 400 8×8.1R/31 12,500-litre Fuel Tanker
Full details of this variant (UAE designation T 816 6ZVR86/31) can be found in the specifications table.

TATRA T 816-6ZVR86 30 400 8×8.1R/30 12,000-litre Water Tanker
Full details of this variant (UAE designation T 816 6ZVR86/30) can be found in the specifications table.

TATRA T 816-6ZVR86 35 400 8×8.1R/33.
Can be provided with a Container Handling Unit (CHU).

TATRA T 816-6ZVR86 36 400 8×8.1R/32
This variant is fitted with the Multilift Mark 4 Load Handling System (LHS). Chassis for various superstructures. Load capacity 21,800 kg (max).

TATRA T 816-6ZVP8T 44 400 8×8.1R. Heavy recovery truck
Also known as the RV-20 SAS. Full details of this vehicle can be found in the Recovery vehicles section.

Specifications
See table on page 329

Status
Current generation models available. In service with the United Arab Emirates (UAE) Armed Forces (1,100 delivered).

Contractor
TATRA, a.s.

TATRA T 815 (6 × 6) truck series

Development
TATRA can trace its origins back to Austria and 1850 and the company produced its first truck in 1898. As a result of the First World War the part of Austria TATRA originated from became part of the then Czechoslovakia. TATRA's unique tubular backbone-style frame was introduced in 1923.

The TATRA T 815 (6 × 6) truck series entered production in 1983 alongside the (8 × 8) series, full details of which can be found elsewhere in this section. Many of the major assemblies and components of the (6 × 6) series are interchangeable with the (8 × 8), and the (4 × 4) series of vehicles which had entered production by 1989.

The TATRA T 815 series has been produced for both military and civil use and in a variety of forms including platform trucks, ballast tractors and special versions. Over time the T 815 has been developed in to the commercial TERRN°1 family and military T 815 ARMAX, T 815-6 FORCE (originally designated T 816 FORCE) and T-815-7 families. Full details of the T 815 ARMAX, T 815-6 FORCE and T 815-7 families can be found elsewhere in this section.

Vojenského Opravárenského Podniku, š.p (VOP 025) of Nový Jičín, Czech Republic, offers a complete repair and overhaul service for time-expired TATRA trucks, including the T 815 6 × 6 series and associated vehicles.

TATRA became a Joint Stock Company in 1992. In November 2001, it was announced that the Czech government had approved the purchase of a 92 per cent stake in TATRA, a.s. by SDC International of the US. Following a brief period of difficult-to-follow ownership reorganisation, in September 2003 it was announced that Terex Corporation of the US had acquired 70.51 per cent of TATRA shares. Vectra (a London-based Indian-owned company) owned 21.11 per cent of shares, the remaining 8.38 per cent being privately owned. The company became known as TATRA, a. s., a Terex company, with products continuing to be branded TATRA.

In October 2006 it was announced that Terex Corporation had sold its 81 per cent holding of TATRA, a.s. to a consortium of Czech and US investors. The Czech registered Blue River s.r.o. (now TATRA Holdings) consortium is made up of Belgium-based KBC Private Equity, Vectra Ltd, a US investor, plus Meadow Hill. Vectra Ltd - a construction equipment, bus and truck maker - folded its existing 11.1 per cent stake into Blue River.

Description
The overall layout and construction of the TATRA T 815 (6 × 6) variants follows the same general lines as those of the (8 × 8) vehicles. The front axle suspension does differ, using a torsion bar and shock-absorber set up as opposed to a leaf spring and shock-absorber set-up on (8 × 8) vehicles.

The main military (6 × 6) version is the TATRA T 815 VVN 20.235 6×6.1R, which uses the same two-door all-metal cab as the (8 × 8) VVN model. The load capacity of the T 815 VVN 6 × 6 is 8,000 kg off-road, where it can also tow up to 16,000 kg. Maximum towed load (on hard roads) is 65,000 kg.

A BEML-produced TATRA T 815 26RR36 22 225 6×6.1R (6 × 6) Field Artillery Tractor (FAT). By March 2006 an order for 160 examples of this variant to join 50 previously delivered had been completed (Shaun C Connors)
                                                      1156188

TATRA T 815-26RR36 22 255 6×6.1R as currently produced in India by BEML (TATRA, a.s.)   1185463

Czech Army TATRA T 815 VW 20.235 6×6.IR truck in Kosovo
(Richard Stickland) 0116912

Czech Army TATRA T 815 (6 × 6) fitted with a tanker body
(Richard Stickland) 1124758

Variants

TATRA T 815 VP21 VV 26.230 6×6.1R. Platform off-road truck, powered by TATRA T3B-928-10 V-8 engine developing 313 hp; GVW 25,000 kg

TATRA T 815 VP21 WV 25.230 6×6.1R. Platform off-road truck for export applications

TATRA T 815 VP11 20.235 6×6.1R. Tanker using truck chassis

TATRA T 815 VP12 28.235 6×6.1R. Special body carrier with disengageable front axle and Central Tyre Inflation (CTI) system; carrier for V-24 universal drilling machine; carrier for UDS-114a hydraulic shovel

TATRA T 815 VP33 24.235 6×6.1R. Special body carrier; carrier for ACHR-90 NBC decontamination system

TATRA T 815 VPR8 20.235 6×6.1R. Special body carrier with weight up to 10,650 kg; derivative of T 815 VVN 20.235 6×6.1R

TATRA T 815 VNT 28.235 6×6.1R. Semi-trailer tractor

TATRA T 815 PR2 22.235 6×6.1. ISO container carrier with self-loading equipment

TATRA T 815 PR4 28.208 6×6.1. Bridge component carrier

TATRA T 815 VPR8 20.235 6×6.1R. Carrier for VOSK antenna; carrier for ALS-M airfield lighting set

TATRA T 815 VP21 21.265 6×6.1R. Chassis for TATRApan armoured personnel carrier; chassis for VESPRA mobile command post

TATRA T 815 S1 6×6. 10,700 kg rear-tipping dump truck

TATRA T 815 S3 6×6. 10,700 kg three-way tipping dump truck

SONDA. Multipurpose environmental monitoring vehicle

AD-20T and AD 20.2. Crane trucks

AD-28. 28,000 kg maximum lift capacity crane truck with low-slung forward control cab and longer wheelbase (3.95 m + 1.32 m)

APZ-94. Decontamination vehicle for liquid spill situations

AV-14. Multipurpose crane truck

AVS. Medium recovery vehicle with traversing crane

CAN-03. 16,000-litre tanker for flammable liquids

CAP-6. 5,830-litre forward area refuelling tanker (fibreglass tank)

CAPL-16. 15,550-litre aircraft refuelling vehicle (three compartment fibreglass tank)

CA-18. 17,500-litre equipment/aircraft fuel tanker (three compartment fibreglass tank)

CAS-32. Rapid intervention fire tender

CNPL-45. Tractor truck for towing fuel semi-trailers

CAHD-15. Ground equipment refuelling tanker

CKV-7. 7,000-litre ISO 1C dimensioned drinking water tanker

PHA-32. Foam firefighting truck

RBS 15 missile carrier. Coastal defence system in service with Croatia

TATRA T 815-2. Commercial model; models include a tractor truck and a 37-seater bus.

Some of the above were fitted with 12.00 × 20 tyres and dual rear wheels.

BEML Limited (formerly Bharat Earth Movers Ltd)

The TATRA T815 series of trucks continues to be produced in India by BEML. Following the formation of the Czech Republic and Slovakia in 1993, the former Czechoslovakian TATRA concern became two entities, TATRA,

Czech Army TATRA T 815 (Richard Stickland) 0116911

Czech Army TATRA T 815 (6 × 6) truck fitted with UDS-114a shovel/excavation equipment (Richard Stickland) 0116913

TATRA T 815 (6 × 6) AD20.2 crane truck (Richard Stickland) 0524762

a.s. in the Czech Republic and TATRA Sipox a.s. (now Tanax) in Slovakia. The latter set up an wholly-owned subsidiary TATRA Sipox (UK) Ltd in 1994-95 to address overseas markets, including India.

Between 1987-2005, BEML supplied 5,300 TATRA vehicles to the Indian Army. Figures released during 2009 suggested that a total of 10,500 (est.) TATRA T815 range trucks had been delivered to the Indian Army in, primarily, (6 × 6) and (8 × 8) configurations. At DefExpo 2006 BEML announced that manufacture of a (4 × 4) light recovery vehicle in collaboration with TATRA Sipox and based on the TATRA T 815-25RR45 17 230 4 × 4.1 chassis was to commence.

Deliveries commenced during 2003 of current generation TATRA (10 × 10) and (12 × 12) chassis for specialist applications.

BEML states 42 per cent indigenisation in (6 × 6) production, 44 per cent in (8 × 8).

BEML-produced TATRA T815 series trucks are now fitted with EURO 2 emissions compliant engines. The current General Service (GS) (6 × 6) model is the TATRA T815 26RR36 22 255 6 × 6.1R. Earlier generation (6 × 6) models are powered by versions of the T3-930 V-12 multifuel engine developing 315 hp.

The T 815-26RR36 22 255 6×6.1R is provided by a 342 hp EURO 2 (Bharat Stage 2) emissions compliant TATRA T3B-928.60 V-8 diesel engine and the (6 × 6) is essentially the current generation variant of an earlier model that was powered by a non-emission compliant V-12 TATRA diesel developing 315 hp. GVW is 21,500 kg. In addition to troop transport as a High Mobility Vehicle (company designation), other applications for the T 815-26RR36 22 255 6×6.1R have been stated as Field Artillery Tractor (FAT), ammunition limber, Crash Fire Tender (CFT) and carrier vehicle for short span mounted bridging system.

BEML states that the new EURO 2 models launched in India during 2006-2007 have 22 percent indigenisation (4 × 4), 35 per cent indigenisation (6 × 6) (set to increase to 45 per cent), and 33 per cent (8 × 8) (set to increase to 44 per cent).

India's Research & Development Establishment (Engrs) at Pune has developed an armoured cab for the TATRA T815 series of trucks. An example (fitted to an (8 × 8) chassis) was displayed at DefExpo 2006.

Specifications

T 815-26RR36 22.255 6 × 6.1R
Cab seating: 1 + 3 (2 full-size seat, one emergency centre seat)
Configuration: 6 × 6
Weight:
  (unladen, chassis-cab) 11,000 kg
  (laden) 21,500 kg
  (front axle weigh, laden) 7,000 kg
  (rear axle weight, laden) 2 × 7,250 kg
  (payload on chassis-cab) 10,500 kg
  (towed load, off-road) 16,000 kg
  (towed load, on-road) 65,000 kg
Length: (chassis-cab) 8.394 m
Width: 2.5 m
Height: (cab roof) 3.01 m
Ground clearance: 410 mm
Track:
  (front) 2.044 m
  (rear) 1.988 m
Wheelbase: 3.27 m +1.45 m
Angle of approach/departure: 30°/33°
Max speed: (road) 90 km/h
Cruising range: 1,000 km
Fuel capacity: 400 litres
Gradient: (at GVW) 100%
Trench: 900 mm
Vertical obstacle: 600 mm
Fording: 1.4 m
Engine: TATRA T3B 928-60 V-8-cylinder EURO 2 emissions compliant turbocharged and charge air cooled air-cooled direct injection 4-stroke diesel developing 342 hp (255 kW) at 1,800 rpm and 1,570 N.m torque at 1,200 rpm
Gearbox: TATRA 10 TS 140 manual with 10 forward and 2 reverse gears
Transfer box: TATRA 2.30 TRK 1.1/1.8 2-speed; disengageable front axle
Clutch: single dry plate, (diameter) 430 mm
Steering: RH-drive, worm and roller, power assisted
Turning radius: (kerb) 10 m
Suspension:
  (front) torsion bars and shock-absorbers
  (rear) leaf springs
Tyres: 15.00 × 21
Brakes: dual circuit air, drums front and rear, supplementary engine exhaust brake
Electrical system: 24 V
Batteries: 2 × 12 V, 180 Ah
Alternator: 28 V, 55 A

Status

Replaced in production in the Czech Republic by the TERRN°1, T 815 ARMAX, T 815 FORCE and T 815-7 ranges. Production continues in India by BEML (see text). In service with the armed forces of Croatia, the Czech Republic, India, Slovakia and others.

Contractor

TATRA, a.s.
BEML Limited

TATRA T 815 (4 × 4) truck series

Development

TATRA can trace its origins back to Austria and 1850 and the company produced its first truck in 1898. As a result of the First World War the part of Austria TATRA originated from became part of the then Czechoslovakia. TATRA's unique tubular backbone-style frame was introduced in 1923.

The TATRA T 815 (4 × 4) truck series entered production in 1989 to complement the earlier (6 × 6) and (8 × 8) series of T 815 vehicles. Some design details of the T 815 (4 × 4) series were adapted from the TATRA T 815 4 × 4 VE commercial truck series that entered production in 1983. The (4 × 4) series follows the same general layout and construction lines of the larger (6 × 6) and (8 × 8) T 815 vehicles, also introduced in 1983, and shares many of their major assemblies and components, including the all-metal, two-door cab. Full details of the T 815 (6 × 6) and (8 × 8) series can be found elsewhere in this section.

The TATRA T 815 series has been produced for both military and civil use and in a wide variety of forms including platform trucks, ballast tractors and special versions. Vojenského Opravárenského Podniku, š.p (VOP 025) of Nový Jičín, Czech Republic offer a complete repair and overhaul service for time-expired TATRA trucks.

TATRA T 815-25RR45 17 230 4 × 4.1 chassis-cab fitted with a EURO 2 emissions compliant engine, and as currently available in India produced by BEML Ltd (TATRA, a.s.)   1185475

Over time the T 815 has been developed in to the commercial TERRN°1 family and military T 815 Armax, T 815-6 Force (originally designated T 816 Force) and T815-7 families. Full details of the T 815 Armax, T 815-6 Force and T 815-7 families can be found elsewhere in this section.

TATRA became a Joint Stock Company in 1992. In November 2001, it was announced that the Czech government had approved the purchase of a 92 per cent stake in TATRA, a.s. by SDC International of the US. Following a brief period of difficult-to-follow ownership reorganisation, in September 2003 it was announced that Terex Corporation of the US had acquired 70.51 per cent of TATRA shares. Vectra (a London-based Indian-owned company) owned 21.11 per cent of shares, the remaining 8.38 per cent being privately owned. The company became known as TATRA, a. s., a Terex company, with products continuing to be branded TATRA.

In October 2006 it was announced that Terex Corporation had sold its 81 per cent holding of TATRA, a.s. to a consortium of Czech and US investors. The Czech registered Blue River s.r.o. (now TATRA Holdings) consortium is made up of Belgium-based KBC Private Equity, Vectra Ltd, a US investor, plus Meadow Hill. Vectra Ltd - a construction equipment, bus and truck maker - folded its existing 11.1 per cent stake into Blue River.

Description

The basic model of TATRA T 815 (4 × 4) series is the TATRA T 815 VV 15.170 4 × 4.1. This has a nominal load capacity of 5,800 kg and can tow trailers weighing up to a maximum of 16,000 kg on hard roads. The cargo area can be configured to carry 20 passengers but can also be arranged to carry ZSK shop/van bodies that can be fitted out to perform a number of control, communication, workshop or office roles.

Variants

TATRA T 815 61VV41 15.200 4 × 4.1. Cargo off-road truck powered by a turbocharged TATRA diesel engine.
  TATRA T 815 23VV41. Cargo truck with armoured cab. GVW 16,100 kg.
  TATRA T 815 23VR41. Chassis for various superstructures.
  TATRA T 815 VV 15.170 4 × 4.1. Platform off-road truck.
  TATRA T 815 VPS 15.170 4 × 4.1. Special body carrier; carrier for PDZ-2/TA tank and automotive equipment mobile workshop; carrier for SOJKA drone reconnaissance system launch and control system.
  TATRA T 815 VPK 15.170 4 × 4.1. Special body carrier; carrier for PD-OA mobile workshop for accumulators; carrier for PD-2ES series of mobile electrical workshops; carrier for PDZ-2T series of mobile armoury and light engineering workshops.
  TA-4. Firefighting technical support truck.
  TATRA T 815 4 × 4 VE. Commercial model.
  POP-2. Mobile casualty station formed by containerised box body and completed by a further body on a two-axle trailer.

BEML Limited (formerly Bharat Earth Movers Ltd)

The TATRA T 815 series of trucks continues to be produced in India by BEML Limited. Following the formation of the Czech Republic and Slovakia in 1993, the former Czechoslovakian TATRA concern became two entities, TATRA a.s. in the Czech Republic and TATRA Sipox a.s. (now Tanax) in Slovakia. The latter set up an wholly-owned subsidiary TATRA Sipox (UK) Ltd in 1994-95 to address overseas markets, including India.

Between 1987-2005, BEML supplied 5,300 TATRA vehicles to the Indian Army. Figures released during 2009 suggested that a total of 10,500 (est.) TATRA T815 range trucks had been delivered to the Indian Army in, primarily, (6 × 6) and (8 × 8) configurations. At DefExpo 2006 BEML announced that manufacture of a (4 × 4) light recovery vehicle in collaboration with TATRA Sipox and based on the TATRA T 815-25RR45 17 230 4 × 4.1 chassis was to commence.

Deliveries commenced during 2003 of current generation TATRA (10 × 10) and (12 × 12) chassis for specialist applications.

BEML states 42 per cent indigenisation in (6 × 6) production, 44 per cent in (8 × 8).

Czech Army TATRA T815 (4 × 4) truck fitted with a specialist shelter-type rear body (Stefan Marx)
1185462

Czech Army TATRA T815 (4 × 4) cargo trucks operating in Kosovo (Richard Stickland)
0524764

BEML-produced TATRA T 815 series trucks are now fitted with EURO 2 emissions compliant engines and the current T 815 (4 × 4) High Mobility Vehicle/General Service (GS) model produced by BEML is the TATRA T815-25RR45 17 230 4 × 4.1; specifications for this vehicle can be found in the Specifications table. An earlier EURO 1 emissions complaint version of this vehicle is powered by a TATRA T3B-928-10 engine.

BEML states that the new EURO 2 models launched in India during 2006-2007 have 22 per cent indigenisation in the (4 × 4) product, 35 per cent indigenisation in the (6 × 6) product (set to increase to 45 per cent), and 33 per cent in the (8 × 8) product (set to increase to 44 per cent).

India's Research & Development Establishment (Engrs) at Pune has developed an armoured cab for the TATRA T815 series of trucks. An example fitted to an (8 × 8) chassis was displayed at DefExpo 2006.

Specifications

T 815 25RR45 17 230 4 × 4.1 General Service (GS) truck
Cab seating: 1 + 2 (two full-size seats, one 'emergency' centre seat)
Configuration: 4 × 4 (selectable)
Weight:
 (kerb) 9,300 kg
 (GVW) 16,500 kg
 (payload) 7,200 kg
 (towed load) 16,000 kg
 (GCW) 32,500 kg
 (front axle, unladen) 5,780 kg
 (rear axle, unladen) 5,780 kg 3,520 kg
 (front axle, laden) 8,000 kg
 (rear axle, laden) 8,500 kg
Length: (overall) 7.380 m
Width: 2.55 m
Height:
 (cab) 3.06 m
 (tarpaulin of GS body) 3.69 m
Ground clearance: 374 mm
Track: (front and rear) 2.032 m
Wheelbase: 4.09 m
Angle of approach/departure: 38°/42°
Max speed: (road) 80 km/h
Cruising range: 1,000 km
Fuel capacity: 320 litres
Gradient: (GCW) 100%
Side slope: 45%
Trench: 900 mm
Vertical obstacle: 500 mm

Fording: 1.4 m
Engine: TATRA T3B-928.50 12.67-litre V-8-cylinder turbocharged EURO 2 emissions complaint air-cooled direct injection 4-stroke diesel developing 308 hp (230 kW) at 2,000 rpm and 1,400 N.m torque at 1,200 rpm
Gearbox: TATRA 10 TS 140 manual with 10 forward and 2 reverse gears
Transfer box: TATRA 1.30 TR 2.25 single-speed with front axle disconnect
Steering: RH-drive, worm and roller, power-assisted
Turning radius: 9.5 m
Suspension:
 (front) swinging half-axles with torsion bars and telescopic shock-absorbers
 (rear) swinging half-axles with air bags with internal coil springs and telescopic shock-absorbers
Tyres: 1,500 × 21
Brakes: dual circuit air, drums front and rear, supplementary engine exhaust brake
Electrical system: 24 V
Batteries: 2 × 12 V, 180 Ah
Alternator: 28 V, 55 A

Status
Replaced in production in the Czech Republic by the TERRN°1, T 815 Armax, T 815 Force and T 815-7 ranges. Production continues in India by BEML (see text). In service with the armed forces of the Czech Republic, India, Slovakia and others.

Contractor
TATRA, a.s.
BEML Limited

TATRA 148 (4 × 4) and (6 × 6) trucks

Development
TATRA can trace its origins back to Austria and 1850 and the company produced its first truck in 1898. As a result of the First World War the part of Austria TATRA originated from became part of the then Czechoslovakia. TATRA's unique tubular backbone-style tubular chassis frame was introduced in 1923.

The TATRA 148 range of trucks was introduced in 1972 as the replacement for the TATRA 138 series. The 148 range are similar in appearance to the earlier vehicles but are fitted with more powerful 12.6-litre engines and have an increased payload. A further development of the TATRA 148, the TATRA 157, was also built. Approaching 114,000 TATRA 148 trucks had been produced when production was completed in 1982, almost 64,000 of these being exported to 43 different countries. The replacement model of the 148 was the TATRA T 815 series, full details of which can be found elsewhere in this section.

TATRA 148 is the designation for the basic cargo model. This has a conventional layout, with the engine at the front, all-steel two-door cab and the cargo area at the rear with a drop tailgate, bows and a tarpaulin cover. Vehicles fitted with a winch have the suffix N, for example TATRA 148 N.

TATRA became a Joint Stock Company in 1992. In November 2001, it was announced that the Czech government had approved the purchase of a 92 per cent stake in TATRA, a.s. by SDC International of the US. Following a brief period of difficult-to-follow ownership reorganisation, in September 2003 it was announced that Terex Corporation of the US had acquired 70.51 per cent of TATRA shares. Vectra (a London-based Indian-owned company) owned 21.11 per cent of shares, the remaining 8.38 per cent being privately owned. The company became known as TATRA, a. s., a Terex company, with products continuing to be branded TATRA.

Dump trucks on the T 148 chassis have included the TATRA 148 S1 (6 × 6), TATRA 148 S3 (6 × 6), TATRA 148 S3 CH-HMH (6 × 6), TATRA JMH ((6 × 6), single-seater cab on left side), TATRA TMCH (forward control type cab, (6 × 6)) and the TATRA 148 S3 CH-JMH (4 × 4); this is a Czech Army TATRA 148 S1 (6 × 6) (Stefan Marx)
1185477

Czech Army TATRA TTt (4 × 4) tractor truck and office body-style rear semi-trailer (Richard Stickland)   1124757

TATRA 148 (6 × 6) truck of the Slovakian Army fitted with UDS-114a shovel/excavation equipment (Stefan Marx)   1124718

In October 2006 it was announced that Terex Corporation had sold its 81 per cent holding of TATRA, a.s. to a consortium of Czech and US investors. The Czech registered Blue River s.r.o. (now TATRA Holdings) consortium is made up of Belgium-based KBC Private Equity, Vectra Ltd, a US investor, plus Meadow Hill. Vectra Ltd - a construction equipment, bus and truck maker - folded its existing 11.1 per cent stake into Blue River.

Variants
The TZ-74 decontamination vehicle is based on the chassis of the TATRA 148 (6 × 6) truck chassis. Full details can be found in *Jane's Nuclear, Biological and Chemical Defence*.

The CAS 32 is a specialist fire appliance with a 6,000 litre water tank and a 600 litre foam tank.

A hydraulic servicing/inspection platform carrier was produced between 1975 and 1979.

Dump trucks included the TATRA 148 S1 (6 × 6), TATRA 148 S3 (6 × 6), TATRA 148 S3 CH-HMH (6 × 6), TATRA JMH (6 × 6, single-seater cab on left side), TATRA TMCH (forward control type cab, 6 × 6) and the TATRA 148 S3 CH-JMH (4 × 4).

Tractor trucks included the TATRA 148 NTt (6 × 6), TATRA 148 NTPt (6 × 6), TATRA NTPst (6 × 6), TATRA NTt (4 × 4) and TATRA TTt (4 × 4).

VOP 0025 of Nový Jičín in the Czech Republic offers a complete repair and overhaul service to produce the following TATRA 148 models virtually as new:

T 148 VNM: 13,000 kg payload cargo truck (seated capacity on bench seats, 40) capable of towing trailers up to 20,000 kg

T 148 VVN: 12,000 kg payload truck (8,000 kg off-road) capable of towing trailers up to 30,000 kg on roads (10,000 kg off-road)

T 148 CL: uses T 148 PP 36 VN 6 × 6 chassis to carry a 11 m³ steel fuel tank. GVW is 22,800 kg

T 148 CAPL 15: as T 148 CL but with a 15 m³ tank for the transport of assorted fuels. The tank is made of fibreglass composite with epoxy-coated inner surfaces; the pumping unit is engine driven. The CAPL 17 is designed for a maximum on-road weight of 23,850 kg

T 148 CAPL 17: as T 148 CL but with a 17 m³ tank for use with vehicle or aircraft fuels. The pumping unit is engine driven and allows for fuel and de-fuel operations. Climatic operational range is –30°C to +50°C. The CAPL 17 is designed for a maximum on-road weight of 24,500 kg and a maximum off-road weight of 22,000 kg

T 148 AM-369: concrete carrier/mixer with chassis load capacity of 16,740 kg

T 148 S1: 15,340 kg payload tipper truck with a rock-type dump body

T 148 S3: 15,200 kg payload three-sided tipper truck. Towed load on-road is 38,000 kg

TATRA T 148 CAPL 17 fuel tanker fitted with a 17 m³ tank for the fuelling/de-fuelling of vehicles and aircraft (Stefan Marx)   1185478

T 148 HARA 60 Klanice: flatbed truck fitted with HARA 60 hydraulic grab crane located between the driver's cabin and the cargo platform. This variant is used for the transport and handling of trees/logs and has a payload of 12,000 kg on-road, 9,800 kg off-road. The design of the chassis and other technical parameters are identical with the T 148 HARA 60 VNM

T 148 HARA 60 VNM: cargo truck with HARA 60 hydraulic grab crane

T 148 CAS 32: is a specialist fire fighting vehicle for use at airports or at other similar high risk environments. The rear body features a water tank, a foam agent tank, a pump with a drive, and foam-making equipment. The vehicle can be used for immediate intervention with foam or water but may also use water from an external supply. After mounting a sprinkling bar it can also be used as a decontaminating or sprinkling vehicle.

Specifications
TATRA 148
Cab seating: 1 + 2
Configuration: 6 × 6 (front axle disengages for road use)
Weight:
(unladen) 11,060 kg
(laden) 25,640 kg
(max load, on-road) 14,580 kg
(towed load, on-road) 13,580 kg
Length: 9.0 m
Width: 2.5 m
Height: 2.44 m
Ground clearance: 290 mm
Track:
(front) 1.966 m
(rear) 1.77 m
Wheelbase: 4.8 m + 1.32 m
Max speed: 71 km/h
Fuel capacity: 200 litres
Fording: 1.4 m
Engine: TATRA T 2-928 12.667-litre V-8 air-cooled 4-stroke diesel developing 212 hp (158 kW) at 2,000 rpm
Gearbox: TATRA manual with 5 forward and 1 reverse gears; synchromesh on 2nd to 5th gears
Transfer box: TATRA 2-speed with lockable differential
Clutch: twin dry plate, hydraulic with air-booster
Steering: worm and roller, power assisted with mechanical back-up
Suspension: independent swinging half-axles sprung by leaf springs
Tyres: 11.00 × 20
Brakes: drums all-round, service (air), emergency and parking (mechanical) circuits
Electrical system: 24 V

Status
Production complete. In service in reducing numbers with the armed forces of the Czech Republic and Slovakia. Supplied to other undisclosed users.

Contractor
TATRA, a.s.

Egypt

Egyptian truck production

Description
Three main types of truck have previously been licence produced in Egypt. The first was a licence-manufactured version of the Jeep (DaimlerChrysler) AM 720 1,135 kg light vehicle (full details of which can be found elsewhere in this section), which was produced by the Arab American Vehicles (AAV) Company at Horreia, Heliopolis. About 40 to 45 per cent of the vehicle is local content and the AM 720 was produced in various forms, such as troop carrier, ambulance, mobile workshop (with a ¼-tonne trailer) and communications shelter carrier. Another locally

Egyptian Army United Nations NASR 3,350 kg (4 × 4) truck deployed in East Timor (Ron Fry)   0536762

produced Jeep product was the J-20, which was produced in pick-up form for a variety of civil and military roles. About 20 per cent of the J-20 is local content. Military production of the J-20 and AM-720 models concluded in 1987, and between 1986-1987 it is understood that 1,965 J-20 and AM-720 vehicles were delivered.

AAV also produced CJ-7, CJ-8 and YJ-L Jeeps, and recently began production of the latest TJ-L model. Full details of these models can be found in the Lightweight vehicles section.

The third vehicle is a locally produced version of the Magirus-Deutz (now IVECO) Mercur, known as the NASR. This is a 4 × 4 vehicle, the German origins of which date back to the 1950s. It was produced in several forms including a basic troop and cargo carrier with a 3,350 kg payload, a mobile surgery and at least two types of NBC decontamination vehicle. The mobile surgery has an air conditioned office-type body with its own 4 kW electrical generator, a clean water supply system and enough medical equipment and supplies (including a refrigerated blood bank) to remain in the field for 3.3 days. When in position, two penthouse tents can be erected each side of the vehicle or separately to provide extra working space. Each tent measures 4 × 4 m on each side and is 2.4 m high. The NASR was produced under the auspices of the Egyptian Ministry of Defence Vehicles Department.

It was reported recently (although not confirmed officially) that Egyptian Armed Forces operate 246 types of wheeled vehicles, the oldest of which is 55 years old.

Specifications

NASR
Cab seating: 1 + 1 or 2
Configuration: 4 × 4
Weight:
  (unladen) 3,800 kg
  (laden) 7,150 kg
  (max lcad) 3,350 kg
Length: 7.2 m
Width: 2.4 m
Ground clearance: 315 mm
Wheelbase: 4.2 m
Fuel capacity: 150 litres
Engine: NASR 112 H6 air-cooled diesel developing 112 hp (82 kW) at 2,300 rpm (licence-produced version of the Deutz F 6 L 614)
Gearbox: ZF 35 AK5 manual with 5 forward and 1 reverse gears
Clutch: single dry plate
Transfer box: 2-speed
Turning radius: 9 m
Suspension: semi-elliptic leaf springs with auxiliary springs on the rear axle and shock-absorbers on the front axle
Tyres: 20.00 × 10

Status
All the above are in service with the Egyptian Armed Forces.

Finland

Sisu A2045 (4 × 4) 5,000 kg Military Logistic Wheeled Vehicle

Development
Sisu was founded in 1931, and the company is currently privately owned by a group of Finnish investors that acquired it from KONE Corporation in 2004. The Finnish state sold its majority shareholding in Sisu to Partek in 1997, KONE Corporation acquiring Sisu as part of its acquisition of Partek in 2002.

Sisu A2045 (4 × 4) 5,000 kg Military Logistic Wheeled Vehicle (Sisu) 1391434

Sisu produced its first 12 trucks in 1932, with the company's foray into the military sector beginning in 1938 with a prototype of an armoured military vehicle. It would, however, be 1962 before Sisu manufactured its first prototype (4 × 4) off-road truck, this in collaboration with the Finnish Defence Forces. Sisu has since manufactured a wide range of trucks for the Finnish military.

Sisu signed a partnership agreement with France's Renault in 1997, this including the purchase of cabs, engines, axles, and the sale of Renault commercial vehicles in Finland. This arrangement essentially evolved into a Sisu-Volvo deal, when the Swedish company gained control of Renault Trucks in 2000.

In mid-2010, Sisu announced that it had concluded an arrangement with Daimler for the supply of Mercedes-Benz heavy truck components, including engines. This arrangement replaces the Renault/Volvo joint venture.

During 2011 Sisu expects to build around 150 to 200 Mercedes-Benz component based trucks, this increasing to an annual output of around 400 units. Vehicles produced will use engines, cabs and transmissions from Daimler, but with Sisu axles and an in-house chassis. An Eaton Fuller manual gearbox will be among the specified options.

The Finnish Army currently has a fleet of around 2,400 Sisu trucks of assorted types in service, this figure including somewhere in the region of 1,700 all-wheel drive types, the most numerous of these being the SA-150 (4 × 4), E11T (6 × 6), SA-181 (4 × 4), SA-130 (4 × 4) and SA-241 (6 × 6).

The most recent Finnish Army procurements of Sisu trucks include the announcement made just prior to Eurosatory 2008 that the Finnish government had awarded Sisu a EUR29 million contract for 234 Sisu A2045 (4 × 4) trucks split 215 Class/Type 1 (eight-12-tonne) and 19 Class/Type 2 (12-14-tonne). Deliveries commenced in December 2009, and in service these trucks will replace assorted Sisu (4 × 4) trucks. The award includes options for an additional 240 trucks, split 200 Class/Type 1 and 40 Class/Type 2, these available until 2013.

In May 2009 it was announced that as part of a package of orders valued at EUR61 million for 142 trucks in total that Sisu would deliver an additional 42 Sisu A2045 (4 × 4) trucks.

Description
The Sisu A2045 (4 × 4) is entirely conventional in design, is based on the chassis and automotives of a militarised MAN TGM range truck, and is constructed using predominantly standard MAN, Sisu or third party supplier commercial components to reduce operating costs and maintenance demands.

The A2045 is fitted with a purpose-designed Sisu cab and the height of unladen vehicle does not exceed 2.7 m, thus enabling transport by C-130 Hercules transport aircraft.

Motive power is provided by a MAN turbocharged diesel engine, this coupled to a ZF automated gearbox. All axles are MAN components, the front being a VP-06 unit, the rear a HP-0728. Full-time four-wheel drive is provided and both axles are fitted with cross-axle differential locks.

Differences between Class/Type 1 and Class/Type 2 vehicles are limited to some differences in chassis frame, axles and suspension. Cargo bodies on Class/Type 1 vehicles are equipped with rails for troop safety seats. Cargo bodies on Class/Type 2 vehicles are not equipped with rails and are slightly longer (5 m vs. 4.1 m). Some Class/Type 2 vehicles are fitted with an open cargo bed and materials handling crane, the remainder with enclosed cargo body and tailgate lifter.

Options can include 14.00R 20 tyres, tyres chains, and a 56 kN front-mounted winch that can be controlled from the cab.

Specifications
Sisu A2045
Cab seating: 1 + 2
Configuration: 4 × 4
Weight:
  (laden) 12,000 kg
  (chassis-cab with winch) 6,000 kg
  (max load) 5,000 kg
  (towed load) n/avail

Length: (chassis) 6.45 m
Width: 2.44 m
Height: (cab roof) 2.65 m
Ground clearance: (axles) 370 mm
Wheelbase: 3.25 m
Track: (rear) 1.98 m
Angle of approach: 35°
Max speed: 105 km/h
Range: >800 km
Fuel capacity: 300 litres
Gradient: >60%
Side slope: 60%
Fording: 750 mm
Engine: MAN DO836LFL63 6.87-litre 6-cylinder EURO 5 emissions compliant in-line turbocharged and air-to-air intercooled water-cooled 4-stroke diesel developing 250 hp (186 kW) at 2,300 rpm and 1,000 N.m torque at 1,200-1,750 rpm
Gearbox: ZF 12AS 1210 OD MAN Tipmatic automated gearbox
Transfer box: MAN G102
Steering: power-assisted
Suspension: parabolic twin leaf springs and hydraulic shock-absorbers, front; ECAS air-suspension and shock-absorbers, rear
Tyres: 365/80R 20
Brakes: dual circuit, air
Electrical system: 24 V
Batteries: 2 × 12 V
Alternator: 110 A

Status

In production, deliveries commenced December 2009 (see text).

Contractor

Sisu Defence Oy

Sisu E11T-6 × 6/415 + 140 15,000 kg High Mobility Tactical Vehicle (HMTV)

Development

Sisu was founded in 1931, and the company is currently privately owned by a group of Finnish investors that acquired it from KONE Corporation in 2004. The Finnish state sold its majority shareholding in Sisu to Partek in 1997, KONE Corporation acquiring Sisu as part of its acquisition of Partek in 2002.

Sisu produced its first 12 trucks in 1932, with the company's foray into the military sector beginning in 1938 with a prototype of an armoured military vehicle. It would, however, be 1962 before Sisu manufactured its first prototype (4 × 4) off-road truck, this in collaboration with the Finnish Defence Forces. Sisu has since manufactured a wide range of trucks for the Finnish military.

Sisu signed a partnership agreement with France's Renault in 1997, this including the purchase of cabs, engines, axles, and the sale of Renault commercial vehicles in Finland. This arrangement essentially evolved into a Sisu-Volvo deal, when the Swedish company gained control of Renault Trucks in 2000.

Sisu E11T-6 × 6/415+140 15,000 kg High Mobility Tactical Vehicle (HMTV) of the Finnish Army photographed in Norway during Exercise Cold Response 2010 (Carl Schulze)   1391205

Mid 2010 Sisu announced that it had concluded an arrangement with Daimler for the supply of Mercedes-Benz heavy truck components, including engines. This arrangement replaces the Renault/Volvo joint venture.

During 2011 Sisu expects to build around 150 to 200 Mercedes-Benz component based trucks, this increasing to an annual output of around 400 units. Vehicles produced will use engines, cabs and transmissions from Daimler, but with Sisu axles and an in-house chassis. An Eaton Fuller manual gearbox will be among the specified options.

The Finnish Army currently has a fleet of around 2,400 Sisu trucks of assorted types in service, this figure including somewhere in the region of 1,700 all-wheel drive types, the most numerous of these being the SA-150 (4 × 4), E11T (6 × 6), SA-181 (4 × 4), SA-130 (4 × 4) and SA-241 (6 × 6).

The Sisu E11T-6 × 6/415 + 140 15,000 kg High Mobility Tactical Vehicle (HMTV) was designed and developed in co-operation with the Finnish Defence Forces, the objective being to produce a vehicle combining excellent on and off road mobility with a large payload capacity under extreme conditions. It was the first model in the Sisu Off-Road series intended for a wide variety of civil and military defence applications. An (8 × 8) version, designated the E11T-8 × 8/1850 + 3750 + 1400 19,700 kg High Mobility Vehicle (HMV), has subsequently also been produced. Full details of this can be found elsewhere in this section.

The first example of the E11T-6 × 6 HMTV was shown in May 1998. Series production commenced during September 1998. A total of 71 vehicles were delivered to the Finnish Defence Forces during 1998 plus a further 25 during the Spring of 1999. Totals delivered as of December 2009 were in excess of 200.

In April 2003 Sisu announced it had developed the E12T-6 × 6 High Mobility Tactical Vehicle (HMTV) for certain markets.

Description

The Sisu E11T-6 × 6/415 + 140 15,000 kg HMTV is entirely conventional in design and constructed using standard Sisu or third party supplier commercial components to reduce operating costs and maintenance demands.

Sisu E11T-6 × 6/415 + 140 15,000 kg High Mobility Tactical Vehicles (HMTV) of the Finnish Defence Forces (Sisu)   0109497

Sisu E11T-6 × 6/415 + 140 15,000 kg High Mobility Tactical Vehicle (HMTV) chassis-cab demonstrating axle travel (Sisu)   0536758

The C-section ladder-type chassis is constructed from high-tensile steel 8 mm thick and is 460 mm deep under the load area; 300 mm deep under the cab. Tubular cross-members are bolted in. Critical components such as the electrical, fuel and pneumatic systems, are located in protected areas within the purpose-designed chassis.

The all-steel Premium model two-seat sleeper-type cab is supplied by Renault and militarised by Sisu. Four-point coil spring suspension is fitted. The cab tilts forward hydraulically for maintenance purposes. Cab options include a third-person seat and option of a third seat and an armour kit proof against small arms fire.

Motive power for Finnish Army vehicles is provided by a 405 hp Cummins engine and Allison automatic gearbox. The E11T-6 × 6/415 + 140 was originally offered with a choice of two 11-litre Cummins diesel engines (380 or 405 hp), these coupled to either an Eaton manual or Allison automatic transmission. Any current production would feature current generation automotive components.

All axles are Sisu components, the front steer-drive being a Sisu FSDP-09-S unit rated at 7,500 kg, the rear drive axles being Sisu FRMP-10-S (first) and FRDP-10-S (second) units rated at a combined 20,000 kg. Full-time six-wheel drive is provided and all axles are fitted with cross-axle differential locks. The transfer box and rear tandem axles are fitted with locking longitudinal differentials.

A variety of bodies can be accommodated, the base model having a flatbed cargo area with a tailgate and drop sides, all covered by a tilt over bows.

Among a range of options are 16.00R 20 tyres, fuel tanks up to 500 litres total capacity, ADR equipment, a hydraulic 10,000 kg winch that can be controlled from the cab and directed to the front or rear, and an emergency hydraulic steering circuit should the main circuit fail.

Variants

Sisu E12T-6 × 6/415 + 140 15,000 kg HMTV

The Sisu E12T-6 × 6 HMTV is essentially a Sisu E11T-6 × 6 HMTV fitted with a Deutz diesel engine.

The engine selected is a Deutz model BF6M 1015 12-litre six-cylinder in-line water-cooled four-stroke unit developing 450 hp at 1,900 rpm and 2,050 N.m torque at 1,200 rpm. This is coupled to an Allison HD 4560P automatic gearbox, an option on the E11T-6 × 6.

Any changes in unladen weight will be minimal; there is a 10 km/h increase in maximum speed, and there are performance enhancements appropriate to the additional 70 or 45 hp available.

Sisu offers the same Deutz engine option for the E11T-8 × 8 HMTV.

Specifications

E11T-6 × 6/4150 + 1400
Cab seating: 1 + 1 or 2
Configuration: 6 × 6
Weight:
  (chassis with winch) 10,500 kg
  (GVW) 26,000 kg
  (max load) 15,500 kg
Length: (chassis) 8.65 m
Width: 2.55 m
Height:
  (laden, cab roof) 3.1 m
  (unladen, cab roof) 3.16 m
Ground clearance: (axles) 380 mm
Wheelbase: 4.15 m + 1.4 m
Angle of approach/departure: 43°/28°
Max speed: 115 km/h
Fuel capacity: 250 litres

Engine: Cummins M405E 11-litre 6-cylinder in-line turbocharged water-cooled 4-stroke diesel developing 405 hp (302 kW) at 1,900 rpm and 2,000 N.m torque at 1,200 rpm
Transmission: Allison HD 4560P 6-speed automatic
Transfer box: Steyr VG 2000/300 2-speed
Steering: ball and nut, power assisted
Turning radius: (outer) 9.85 m
Suspension:
  (front) parabolic leaf springs, 290 mm travel
  (rear) parabolic leaf springs and hydraulic shock-absorbers supported by V-links and reaction rods, 270 mm travel
Tyres: 14.00R 20 (16.00 R 20 option)
Brakes:
  (main) dual circuit, air, drums all-round, 4-channel ABS. Supplementary engine exhaust brake
  (parking) spring brakes on rear tandem
Electrical system: 24 V
Batteries: 2 × 12 V, 180 Ah
Alternator: 80 A (100 A option)

Status

Production as required. In service with the Finnish Defence Forces (around 200).

Contractor

Oy Sisu Auto Ab.

Sisu E11T-8 × 8/1850 + 3750 + 1400 19,700 kg High Mobility Tactical Vehicle (HMTV)

Development

Sisu was founded in 1931, and the company is currently privately owned by a group of Finnish investors that acquired it from KONE Corporation in 2004. The Finnish state sold its majority shareholding in Sisu to Partek in 1997, KONE Corporation acquiring Sisu as part of its acquisition of Partek in 2002.

Sisu produced its first 12 trucks in 1932, with the company's foray into the military sector beginning in 1938 with a prototype of an armoured military vehicle. It would, however, be 1962 before Sisu manufactured its first prototype (4 × 4) off-road truck, this in collaboration with the Finnish Defence Forces. Sisu has since manufactured a wide range of trucks for the Finnish military.

Sisu signed a partnership agreement with France's Renault in 1997, this including the purchase of cabs, engines, axles, and the sale of Renault commercial vehicles in Finland. This arrangement essentially evolved into a Sisu-Volvo deal, when the Swedish company gained control of Renault Trucks in 2000.

In mid-2010 Sisu announced that it had concluded an arrangement with Daimler for the supply of Mercedes-Benz heavy truck components, including engines. This arrangement replaces the Renault/Volvo joint venture.

During 2011 Sisu expects to build around 150 to 200 Mercedes-Benz component based trucks, this increasing to an annual output of around 400 units. Vehicles produced will use engines, cabs and transmissions from Daimler, but with Sisu axles and an in-house Sisu chassis. A manual Eaton Fuller gearbox will be an offered option.

The Finnish Army currently has a fleet of around 2,400 Sisu trucks of assorted types in service, this figure including somewhere in the region of 1,700 all-wheel drive types, the most numerous of these being the SA-150 (4 × 4), E11T (6 × 6), SA-181 (4 × 4), SA-130 (4 × 4) and SA-241 (6 × 6).

The Sisu E11T-8 × 8/1850 + 3750 + 1400 19,700 kg High Mobility Tactical Vehicle (HMTV) was designed and developed in co-operation with the Finnish Defence Forces, the objective being to produce an off-road vehicle combining excellent on- and off-road mobility with a large payload capacity under extreme conditions. It may be regarded as the (8 × 8) equivalent of the Sisu E11T-6 × 6/415 +140 HMTV, full details of which can be found elsewhere in this section.

It was announced in March 2001 that Sisu Auto Ab had been contracted by the Finnish Defence Forces to supply 27 E-11T-8 × 8 vehicles by the end of 2001. These vehicles were fitted with a Multilift (now Hiab) hooklift Load Handling System (LHS) integrated into the chassis. Details of multilift load handling systems can be found in the Materials handling equipment section.

Sisu Auto Ab also announced in March 2001 that international marketing of the E-11T-8 × 8 was to commence. In April 2003 it was announced Sisu had developed the E12T-8 × 8 HMTV for certain markets.

It was disclosed in 2006 that Finnish Defence Forces had ordered a further 16 LHS-equipped E11T-8 × 8 HMTVs. These vehicles differ from the earlier delivery in that the automatic gearbox has been replaced by a ZF 16S 221 16-speed manual, the manual option allowing for more finite speed control when manoeuvring in Finland's many wooded areas.

By early-2007 around 70 Sisu E11T-8 × 8/1850 + 3750 + 1400 had been ordered.

Description

The Sisu E11T-8 × 8/1850 + 3750 + 1400 19,700 kg HMTV is entirely conventional in design and constructed using standard Sisu or third party supplier commercial components to reduce operating costs and maintenance demands.

Sisu E11T-8 × 8/1850 + 3750 + 1400 19,700 kg High Mobility Tactical Vehicle (HMTV) fitted with a Multilift Load Handling System (LHS). The front axle suspension travel of the vehicle is such that unchecked the tyres foul the corners of the transported container (Shaun C Connors)   1120455

Sisu E11T-8 × 8/1850 + 3750 + 1400 19,700 kg High Mobility Tactical Vehicle (HMTV) fitted with a Multilift Load Handling System (LHS)
(Shaun C Connors)   1120454

The C-section ladder-type chassis is constructed from high-tensile steel 10 mm thick and is 460 mm deep under the load area; 300 mm deep under the cab. Tubular cross-members are bolted in. Critical components such as the electrical, fuel and pneumatic systems, are located in protected areas within the purpose-designed chassis.

Sisu's E-series of trucks feature a purpose-designed military/off-road chassis and as such allow for a load handling system to be integrated within the chassis rails, and not on them as with the vast majority of other designs. In addition to lowering the vehicle's overall centre of gravity, this integration of the LHS also allows for a 4 m overall height with standard ISO container requirement to be met without the mobility compromise of smaller wheels/tyres and limited axle articulation.

The all-steel Premium model two-seat sleeper-type cab is supplied by Renault and militarised by Sisu. Four-point coil spring suspension is fitted. The cab tilts forward hydraulically for maintenance purposes. Cab options include a third-person seat and an armour kit proof against small arms fire.

Motive power is provided by an 11-litre Cummins diesel engine connected to either a seven-speed automatic transmission or a 16-speed manual. All axles are Sisu components, the front steer-drive being a Sisu FSDP-09-S unit rated at 7,500 kg, the second steer-drive being a Sisu FSMP-09-S unit rated at 7,500 kg, the rear drive axles being Sisu FRMP-10-S (first) and FRDP-10-S (second) units rated at a combined 20,000 kg. Full-time eight-wheel drive is provided and all axles are fitted with cross-axle differential locks. The transfer box and individual axle pairs are fitted with locking longitudinal differentials.

A wide variety of bodies can be accommodated, Finnish Army models having been fitted with a Multilift (Hiab) LHS.

Among a range of options are 16.00R 20 tyres, fuel tanks up to 500 litres total capacity, ADR equipment, a hydraulic 10,000 kg winch that can be controlled from the cab and directed to the front or rear, and an emergency hydraulic steering circuit should the main circuit fail.

Variants

Sisu E12T-8 × 8/185 + 372 + 145 HMTV
The Sisu E12T-8 × 8 HMTV is essentially a Sisu E11T-8 × 8 HMTV fitted with a Deutz diesel engine.

The engine selected is a Deutz model BF6M 1015 12-litre 6-cylinder in-line water-cooled four-stroke unit developing 450 hp at 1,900 rpm and 2,050 N.m torque at 1,200 rpm. The E12-8 × 8 HMTV retains the original ZF/Steyr automatic transmission of the E11T-8 × 8 HMTV.

Any changes in unladen weight will be minimal; there has been a 10 km/h increase in maximum speed and there are performance enhancements appropriate to the additional 40 hp available.

Sisu E11T-8 × 8/1850 + 3750 + 1400 19,700 kg High Mobility Vehicle fitted with a Multilift Load Handling System (LHS) (Sisu)   0558820

Sisu has introduced the same Deutz engine option for the E11T-6 × 6 HMTV.

Specifications

Sisu E11T-8 × 8/1850 + 3750 + 1400
Cab seating: 1 + 1 or 2
Configuration: 8 × 8
Weight:
   (chassis with winch) 12,500 kg
   (GVW) 32,000 kg
   (max load) 19,700 kg
Length: (chassis) 8.57 m
Width: 2.55 m
Height:
   (laden, cab roof) 3.1 m
   (unladen, cab roof) 3.16 m
Ground clearance: (axles) 380 mm
Wheelbase: 1.85 + 3.75 + 1.4 m
Track: (rear) 2.18 m
Angle of approach: 43°
Max speed: 110 km/h
Engine: Cummins 11-litre 6-cylinder in-line turbocharged water-cooled 4-stroke diesel developing 410 hp (306 kW) at 1,900 rpm
Transmission: ZF 7HP 900 automatic with 7 forward and 1 reverse gears and integral retarder; optional ZF 16 S 221 16-speed manual
Transfer box: Steyr VG 2000/300 2-speed
Steering: power assisted, dual circuit with primary pump engine driven, secondary wheel-driven pump on transfer box
Turning radius: 12 m (approx)
Suspension:
   (front axle pair) three-leaf parabolic springs and shock-absorbers, 320 mm travel
   (rear axle pair) progressive parabolic leaf springs and shock-absorbers, 310 mm travel
Tyres: 14.00R 20 (16.00R 20 option)
Brakes:
   (main) dual circuit, air, drums all-round, 4-channel ABS. Supplementary engine exhaust brake and gearbox retarder
   (parking) spring brakes on rear tandem
Electrical system: 24 V
Batteries: 2 × 12 V, 180 Ah
Alternator: 80 A (100 A option)

Status
Production as required. Around 70 delivered to the Finnish Defence Forces (2001-2006).

Contractor
Oy Sisu Auto Ab

Sisu ETP range of high mobility tactical trucks

Development
Sisu was founded in 1931, and the company is currently privately owned by a group of Finnish investors that acquired it from KONE Corporation in 2004. The Finnish state sold its majority shareholding in Sisu to Partek in 1997, KONE Corporation acquiring Sisu as part of its acquisition of Partek in 2002.

Sisu produced its first 12 trucks in 1932, with the company's foray into the military sector beginning in 1938 with a prototype of an armoured military vehicle. It would, however, be 1962 before Sisu manufactured its

Sisu E13TP (8 × 8) LHS variant of the Lithuanian Army (Shaun C Connors)   1391129

Sisu E13TP (8 × 8) LHS variant of the Lithuanian Army (Shaun C Connors)   1391130

Sisu E15TP bridgelayer of the Finnish Army (Sisu)   1344544

Sisu E13TP (8 × 8) Recovery variant of the Lithuanian Army (Shaun C Connors)   1391131

first prototype (4 × 4) off-road truck, this in collaboration with the Finnish Defence Forces. Sisu has since manufactured a wide range of trucks for the Finnish military.

Sisu signed a partnership agreement with France's Renault in 1997, this including the purchase of cabs, engines, axles, and the sale of Renault commercial vehicles in Finland. This arrangement essentially evolved into a Sisu-Volvo deal, when the Swedish company gained control of Renault Trucks in 2000.

Mid 2010 Sisu announced that it had concluded an arrangement with Daimler for the supply of Mercedes-Benz heavy truck components, including engines. This arrangement replaces the Renault/Volvo joint venture.

During 2011 Sisu expects to build around 150 to 200 Mercedes-Benz component based trucks, this increasing to an annual output of around 400 units. Vehicles produced will use engines, cabs and transmissions from Daimler, but with Sisu axles and an in-house chassis. An Eaton Fuller manual gearbox will be among the specified options.

The Finnish Army currently has a fleet of around 2,400 Sisu trucks of assorted types in service, this figure including somewhere in the region of 1,700 all-wheel drive types.

While under state ownership Sisu's military sales focused on local requirements, however since privatised export markets have been explored and in April 2002 Renault Trucks was awarded a contract to supply the French Army with 110 (60 plus an option of 50) Sisu E-Tech 480 (6 × 4) heavy equipment transporters. Full details of these vehicles can be found n the Heavy equipment transporters section.

In April 2003, Sisu announced it had developed the E12T for certain markets. The E12T is essentially the E11T fitted with an alternative driveline.

In December 2005, Lithuania awarded Sisu a contract valued at around EUR20 million for an undisclosed number of E13TP trucks, with an additional approximately EUR10 million option for additional vehicles.

The procurement process commenced in late 2003, with an initial tender for around 120 vehicles with Level 3 ballistic and mine protection issued in early 2005. A revised tender, which included a Level 2 protection requirement, was issued in late 2005. Around eight European and US truck manufacturers were initially involved in the tender process with sources suggesting that, in addition to Sisu, proposals from MAN and IVECO were eventually shortlisted.

Numbers involved have not been officially released although some sources have suggested that around 50 vehicles are involved in the original order. Deliveries commenced during June 2007 and were concluded by mid 2009.

All vehicles involved in the Lithuanian order are (8 × 8). The majority of these 16,000 kg payload trucks are fitted with a C-130-transportable Multilift MIH-165-SCA integrated Load Handling System (LHS).

Sisu E15TP bridgelayer of the Finnish Army (10 × 10) (Sisu)   1344543

A small quantity of the Lithuanian order were recovery vehicles. These have a design GVW of 36,000 kg and are rated to recover wheeled and tracked vehicles up to 30,000 kg in weight. Recovery equipment includes a Hiab materials handling crane and EMPL-supplied recovery hamper. The main recovery winch has a capacity of 30,000 kg and a 50 m rope; the front-mounted self-recovery winch has a capacity of 15,000 kg and a 25 m rope.

At Eurosatory 2006, Sisu displayed a five-axle (10 × 10) ETP chassis, and at the same time formerly announced details of a full family of trucks sharing the armoured cab concept developed for the Lithuanian vehicles. This family included (4 × 4), (6 × 6), (8 × 8) and (10 × 10) chassis. Finnish Armed Forces have since ordered ETP range trucks in (6 × 6), (8 × 8) and (10 × 10) configurations.

Nine E15TP (10 × 10) chassis were delivered 2006-2008, these having a GVW of 44,000 kg and configured as dedicated bridge transporter/layer platforms. The bridge is launched horizontally over the rear of the chassis, and to provide a more stable launch platform, two hydraulic stabilisers are lowered to the ground at the rear of the chassis before launching commences. Bridges and laying equipment are furnished by Krauss-Maffei Wegmann (KMW).

In May 2009 it was announced that Sisu had been awarded a contract valued at €36 million and calling for 60 E13TP (8 × 8) trucks. 20 of these will be fitted with up-armoured cabs, the remainder will be fitted with the standard Sisu mine blast protected cab. A further ordered followed, this valued at approximately €25 million and calling for 86 trucks, 30 of these Sisu E13TP (8 × 8) with LHS and 14 E13TP (8 × 8) with STS. The remaining 42 vehicles are Sisu A2045 (4 × 4) general support trucks.

Model	E13TP (6 × 6)	E13TP (8 × 8)	E15TP bridgelayer (10 × 10)
Cab seating:	1 + 1 (optional 6-seat crew-type cab)	1 + 1	1 + 1
Configuration:	6 × 6	8 × 8	10 × 10
Weight:			
(unladen, chassis-cab)	12,000 kg	15,000 kg (with winch)	19,000 kg
(payload, on chassis-cab)	16,000 kg	21,000 kg	24,000 kg
(GVW)	28,000 kg	36,000 kg	44,000 kg
Length:			
(chassis-cab)	10.1 m	10.22 m	11.57 m
Width:			
(chassis-cab)	2.55 m	2.55 m	2.55 m
Ground clearance:(axle)	380 mm	380 mm	380 mm
Wheelbase:	4.85 + 1.4 m	1.55 + 4.05 + 1.4 m	1.85 + 3.15 + 1.45 + 1.52 m
Track:			
(front)	2.18 m	2.18 m	2.18 m
(rear)	2.18 m	2.18 m	2.18 m
Angle of approach:	35°/35°	35°	18°
Max speed:	105 km/h	105 km/h	90 km/h
Range: (at 60 km/h)	>800 km	>800 km	>400 km
Fuel capacity:	500 litres	500 litres	350 litres
Max gradient:	60%	60%	60%
Max sideslope:	>30%	>30%	25% (with bridge) >30% (without bridge)
Vertical obstacle:	450 mm	450 mm	450 mm
Fording:			
(unprepared)	900 mm	900 mm	1 m
Engine:	Caterpillar C13-445 Euro IV emissions compliant 12.5-litre 6-cylinder in-line turbocharged and air-to-air intercooled 4-stroke water-cooled diesel developing 445 hp (332 kW) and 2,270 N.m torque at 1,200 rpm		Caterpillar C15-550 Euro IV emissions compliant litre 6-cylinder in-line turbocharged and air-to-air intercooled 4-stroke water-cooled diesel developing 550 hp (410 kW) at 1,900 rpm and 2,508 N.m torque at 1,200-1,500 rpm
Transmission:	Allison HD4500SP with 6 forward and 1 reverse gears	Allison HD4500SP with 6 forward and 1 reverse gears	Allison HD4076SP with 7 forward and 1 reverse gears
Torque converter:	TC531	TC531	TC542
Transfer box:	Steyr VG 2000/300 2 speed	Steyr VG 2000/300 2 speed	Steyr VG2700 2 speed
Steering:	power assisted (dual-circuit)	power assisted (dual circuit)	power assisted, 1st, 2nd and 5th axles (dual circuit)
Turning radius:	11. 5 m	14 m	11.5 m
Suspension:	3-leaf parabolic springs and shock-absorbers, front (both axles on 8 × 8); 3-leaf parabolic bogie springs and shock-absorbers, rear		3-leaf parabolic springs and shock-absorbers 1st, 2nd and 5th axles, 3-leaf parabolic bogie springs and shock-absorbers on tandem
Tyres:	14.00R 20	14.00R 20	14.00R 20
Brakes: (main)	dual-circuit air, drums all round. ABS fitted (all models)		
Electrical system:	24 V	24 V	24 V
Batteries:	2 × 220 Ah	2 × 220 Ah	2 × 220 Ah
Alternator:	80 A	80 A	80 A
A (4 × 4) variant has been proposed, but has yet to enter production.			

Description

The full range of ETP trucks come as standard with an integrated mine blast shield and an all-steel cab that in base configuration provides protection from shell splinters and fragments. The mine blast shield provides STANAG Level 2a protection as standard, and optionally Level 2b, 3a or 3b, although this will increase to include Level 4a and 4b options in the future. Cab protection is achieved by the replacement of doors and windscreen, and the internal addition of either steel or titanium-based composite panels 30 mm thick. The fitting/removal of the armour kit which weighs 1,600 kg takes two men eight hours. The standard cab seats two and comes complete with a circular roof hatch to which a light weapon ring-mount may be attached. A larger six-person crew-type cab is an option on all chassis.

ETP range chassis are formed from 460 to 330 mm × 10 mm high-grade steel, although this can vary depending upon design requirements. Each chassis is designed for purpose and so has no surplus-to-requirement pre-drilled holes or fixings.

On LHS variants the LHS assembly also sits within, and not on/above the chassis frame rails. This, according to the manufacturer, is a unique feature of the Sisu design and offers a number of advantages over other similar designs. Aside from reducing the centre of gravity, even when fitted with 14.00R 20 single off-road tyres and with 320 to 310 mm (front/rear) of suspension travel, the Sisu vehicle fits within the all important 4 m height envelope when laden with a standard ISO 1CC container.

All current members of the ETP family are powered by Caterpillar engines which operate at current emissions levels without the tactical burden of fuel additives. Radiators are located immediately behind the cab and out of the fouling zone.

Allison automatic transmissions and Steyr two-speed transfer boxes are standard; all axles are Sisu beam-type sprung by leaf springs. All axles are fitted with driver-controlled pneumatically operated differential locks and all tyres are capable of accepting snow chains. Steering angle of the Sisu beam-type steer-drive axles is up 41°.

Sisu E15TP bridgelayer of the Finnish Army (Sisu)   1344545

A Central Tyre Inflation System (CTIS) and runflat inserts are available as options. Standard climatic operational range without additional modifications is -39°C to +49°C.

All models are fitted with a front-mounted self-recovery winch rated at 15,000 kg. Design life at an anticipated annual mileage of 20,000 km (8,000 km on-road, 12,000 km off-road) is 20 years.

Specifications
See table on facing page

Status
In production. In service with Finland and Lithuania.

Contractor
Sisu Defence Oy

Sisu range of trucks

Development
Sisu was founded in 1931, and the company is currently privately owned by a group of Finnish investors that acquired it from KONE Corporation in 2004. The Finnish state sold its majority shareholding in Sisu to Partek in 1997, KONE Corporation acquiring Sisu as part of its acquisition of Partek in 2002.

Sisu produced its first 12 trucks in 1932, with the company's foray into the military sector beginning in 1938 with a prototype of an armoured military vehicle. It would, however, be 1962 before Sisu manufactured its first prototype (4 × 4) off-road truck, this in collaboration with the Finnish Defence Forces. Sisu has since manufactured a wide range of trucks for the Finnish military.

Sisu signed a partnership agreement with France's Renault in 1997, this including the purchase of cabs, engines, axles, and the sale of Renault commercial vehicles in Finland. This arrangement essentially evolved into a Sisu-Volvo deal, when the Swedish company gained control of Renault Trucks in 2000.

Mid 2010 Sisu announced that it had concluded an arrangement with Daimler for the supply of Mercedes-Benz heavy truck components, including engines. This arrangement replaces the Renault/Volvo joint venture.

During 2011 Sisu expects to build around 150 to 200 Mercedes-Benz componemt based trucks, this increasing to an annual output of around 400 units. Vehicles produced will use engines, cabs and transmissions from Daimler, but with Sisu axles and an in-house chassis. An Eaton Fuller manual gearbox will be among the specified options.

The Finnish Army currently has a fleet of around 2,400 Sisu trucks of assorted types in service, this figure including somewhere in the region of 1,700 all-wheel drive types, the most numerous of these being the SA-150 (4 × 4), E11T (6 × 6), SA-181 (4 × 4), SA-130 (4 × 4) and SA-241 (6 × 6).

The most recent Finnish Army procurements of Sisu trucks include the announcement made just prior to Eurosatory 2008 that the Finnish government had awarded Sisu a EUR29 million contract for 232 Sisu A2045 (4 × 4) trucks, the award including options for an additional 240 trucks. Deliveries will take place between 2009-2011, and in service these trucks will replace an assortment of older Sisu (4 × 4) models.

Additionally, in May 2009 it was announced that Sisu had been awarded a contract valued at €36 million and calling for 60 E13TP (8 × 8) trucks. 20 of these will be fitted with up-armoured cabs, the remainder will be fitted with the standard Sisu mine blast protected cab. A further ordered followed, this valued at approximately €25 million and calling for 86 trucks, 30 of these Sisu E13TP (8 × 8) with LHS and 14 E13TP (8 × 8) with STS. The remaining 42 vehicles are Sisu A2045 (4 × 4) general support trucks.

Sisu SA-240 CKH 6 × 6 /3740+1440 (6 × 6) truck (Sisu)   1391128

Sisu SA-150 (4 × 4) 6,500 kg truck of the Finnish Army (Peter Felstead)
0558829

While under state ownership Sisu's military sales focused on local requirements, however since privatised export markets have been explored and in April 2002 Renault Trucks was awarded a contract to supply the French Army with 110 (60 plus an option of 50) Sisu E-Tech 480 (6 × 4) heavy equipment transporters. Full details of these vehicles can be found in the Heavy equipment transporters section.

In April 2003, Sisu announced it had developed the E12T for certain markets. The E12T is essentially the E11T fitted with an alternative driveline.

In December 2005, Lithuania awarded Sisu a contract valued at around EUR20 million for an undisclosed number of E13TP trucks, with an additional approximately EUR10 million option for additional vehicles.

Description
With a small number of exceptions (none of which remain in Finnish military service), the Sisu range of trucks are all entirely conventional in design, being built around a C-section ladder-frame chassis. Some of these chassis are purpose-designed for military roles, while others are based around Sisu commercial products. However, it should be noted that Sisu commercial chassis are specifically designed for role and should be described as severe- and/or heavy-duty chassis. Cabs could be either a Sisu military-specific design, a Sisu produced commercial pattern, or from 1997 a Renault-sourced commercial pattern cab. Both cab-over-engine and bonneted configurations have been produced and remain in service. It should be noted that the most recent Sisu A2045 (4 × 4) is essentially a MAN TGM model fitted with a purpose-designed Sisu cab.

Motive power for Sisu military trucks can be provided by a variety of engines, with Valmet and then Cummins being the preferred suppliers from the early 1980s until the privatisation of Sisu in 1997, from when a wider variety of options appeared. Currently Caterpillar or Cummins are the preferred choice for Sisu military vehicles, although options including Deutz are available.

Suspension is predominantly by leaf springs, with all drive axles being Sisu-produced units. Non all-wheel drive trucks often have lift axles.

A brief overview of a small number of legacy fleet Sisu all-wheel drive military trucks in service with Finland's armed forces follows. Full details of the current Sisu EIIT 15,000 kg (6 × 6), Sisu EIIT 19,750 kg (8 × 8), Sisu ETP range, and Sisu A2045 (4 × 4) can be found elsewhere in this section.

Sisu SA-130
The SA-130 (4 × 4) 6,500 kg all-terrain truck is the medium-heavy model in the SA series of all-terrain trucks developed by Sisu Defence for the Finnish Army during the late 1970s and early 1980s. The SA-130 is an all-terrain truck primarily designed to tow medium and heavy artillery while having a good cargo carrying and hauling capacity. The visually similar SA-150 is fitted with a more powerful Valmet diesel engine. The Specifications table includes details of the Sisu SA-130 and SA-150. Both models remain in service with Finland's Armed Forces.

Sisu SA-150
The design of the SA-150 (4 × 4) 6,500 kg truck began during the second half of 1978 with the first prototype being completed in February 1980. Following successful trials the vehicle was adopted by the Finnish Army and first production vehicles were completed in October 1980. The vehicle was designed primarily to tow artillery but is suitable for a wide range of other military applications. The visually similar SA-130 is fitted with a less powerful Valmet diesel engine. The Specifications table includes details of the Sisu SA-150 and SA-130. Both models remain in service with Finland's Armed Forces.

Sisu SA-240
The Sisu SA-240 (6 × 6) 10,000 kg all-terrain truck is a straightforward derivation of the SA-130. The overall construction and many components are the same or similar, and are carried over from the SA-130; these

	Sisu SA-130	Sisu SA-150	Sisu SA-240	Sisu SA-241
Cab seating:	1 + 2	1 + 2	1 + 2	1 + 2
Configuration:	4 × 4	4 × 4	6 × 6	6 × 6
Weight:				
(laden)	14,000 kg	14,000 kg	20,000 kg	22,000 kg
(unladen)	7,500 kg	7,600 kg	9,950 kg	10,000 kg
(max front axle load)	7,000 kg	7,000 kg	n/avail	7,500 kg
(max rear axle load, each)	8,000 kg	8,000 kg	n/avail	8,000 kg
(max load, off-road)	6,500 kg	6,400 kg	10,000 kg	12,000 kg
(towed load)	10,000 kg	n/avail	n/avail	15,000 kg
Length:	6.75 m	6.76 m	7.8 m	7.8 m
Width:	2.58 m	2.48 m	2.48 m	2.48 m
Height:				
(cab)	2.9 m	2.9 m	2.13 m	2.13 m
(tarpaulin)	3.1 m	3.1 m	3.13 m	3.3 m
(load area)	1.5 m	1.5 m	n/avail	n/avail
Ground clearance: (axles)	400 mm	400 mm	400 mm	400 mm
Wheelbase:	3.85 m	3.85 m	3.74 + 1.44	3.74 + 1.44
Track:	2.18 m	2 m	2.01 m	2.01 m
Angle of approach/departure:	43°/40°	42°/39°	38°/54°	38°/54°
Max speed:	100 km/h	100 km/h	95 km/h	95 km/h
Range:	800 km	800 km	n/avail	600 km
Fuel capacity:	225 litres	225 litres	200 litres	250 litres
Fording:	1 m	1 m	1 m	1 m
Engine:	Valmet 620 DSI 6-cylinder in-line water-cooled diesel developing 175 hp (130 kW) until 1994; Valmet 620 DS 6-cylinder in-line turbocharged water-cooled diesel developing 180 hp (134 kW) at 2,500 rpm	Valmet 611 CSBA 6-cylinder in-line water-cooled diesel developing 204 hp at 2,500 rpm and 695 N.m torque at 1,500 rpm	Cummins L 10 6-cylinder in-line turbocharged and intercooled water-cooled 4-stroke diesel developing 330 hp (246 kW) at 2,200 rpm and 1,068 N.m torque at 1,400 rpm	Cummins LTA 10-330 6-cylinder in-line turbocharged and intercooled water-cooled 4-stroke diesel developing 340 hp (254 kW) at 2,200 rpm
Gearbox:	ZF S6-66 manual with 6 forward and 1 reverse gears	ZF manual with 6 forward and 1 reverse gears	ZF manual with 8 forward and 1 reverse gears; plus torque convertor	ZF 4S-150 with 8 forward and 1 reverse gears; plus torque convertor
Transfer box:	2-speed	2-speed	single-speed	single-speed
Steering:	power-assisted	power-assisted	power-assisted	power-assisted
Turning radius:	8.2 m	8.2 m	n/avail	n/avail
Suspension:	parabolic leaf springs and hydraulic shock-absorbers, front and rear	parabolic leaf springs and hydraulic shock-absorbers, front; parabolic leaf springs, rear	parabolic twin leaf springs and hydraulic shock-absorbers	parabolic twin leaf springs and hydraulic shock-absorbers
Tyres:	14.00R 20	14.00R 20	14.00R 20	14.00R 20
Brakes:				
(main)	dual circuit, air operated	dual circuit, air operated	dual circuit, air operated	dual circuit, air operated
(parking)	spring operated, controlled by compressed air, operating on rear wheels	spring operated, controlled by compressed air, operating on rear wheels	spring operated, controlled by compressed air, operating on rear wheels	spring operated, controlled by compressed air, operating on rear wheels
Electrical system:	24 V	24 V	24 V	24 V
Batteries:	2 × 12 V, 150 Ah	n/avail	n/avail	2 × 12 V, 150 Ah

include the chassis and cab. The SA-240 is powered by a Cummins diesel engine, and the driveline includes a torque converter. Primary role for the SA-240 is heavy artillery tractor, although variants include a longer wheelbase version, one version of which mounts the RBS-15AK anti-ship missile. The visually similar SA-241 is fitted with a slightly more powerful Cummins diesel engine and is rated at 12,000 kg payload. The Specifications table includes details of the Sisu SA-240 and SA-241. Both models remain in service with Finland's Armed Forces.

Sisu SA-241
The Sisu SA-241 (6 × 6) 12,000 kg all-terrain truck is a straightforward derivation of the SA-150. The overall construction and many components are the same or similar, and are carried over from the SA-150; these include the chassis and cab. The SA-241 is powered by a Cummins diesel engine, and the driveline includes a torque converter. Primary role for the SA-241 is heavy artillery tractor. The visually similar SA-240 is fitted with a slightly less powerful Cummins diesel engine and is rated at 10,000 kg payload. The Specifications table includes details of the Sisu SA-241 and SA-240. Both models remain in service with Finland's Armed Forces.

Specifications
See table above

Status
Production of current models continues. In service with Finnish Armed Forces and the Lithuanian Army.

Contractor
Oy Sisu Auto Ab.

France

Renault Sherpa range of tactical trucks

Development
Following the completion of production of the TRM 10000 (6 × 6) 10,000 kg tactical truck for the French Army in 1999, and prior to the 2004 introduction of the Sherpa tactical range, Renault Trucks Defence military truck offerings had been based around militarised versions of the company's Kerax heavy commercial product range.

Many commentators believe the recent trend towards rapid deployment and global long-term peace-keeping/enforcing-type operations, often in hostile environments with minimal support infrastructure, have combined to highlight inherent weaknesses in using what are essentially commercial trucks on operations where a purpose-designed or military specific product should really be used. These and other factors, in particular the considerable interest being shown in the GBC 180 and its capabilities, encouraged Renault Trucks Defence to undertake a number of market studies, the aim of which was to assess the potential world market for a truck of the GBC 180 type.

The GBC 180 is not a new-build truck, but Renault's designation for a refurbished/upgraded Berliet GBC 8KT 4,000 kg payload (6 × 6) truck. The GBC 8KT was originally designed for use in Africa and other similar harsh operating environments; over 19,000 were produced. In 1997, and in an industrial partnership with the French Army, Renault Trucks Defense began the refurbishment/upgrade of 5,620 time-served French Army examples. The GBC 8KT/180 refurbishment/upgrade process includes a full stripdown and overhaul, plus the installation of a new cab, engine and

Displayed at Eurosatory 2004, a Sherpa 5 (crew-type cab) with a standard troop carrying/cargo-type body fitted (Shaun C Connors)   1128796

It was disclosed mid 2005 that Renault Trucks Defense had been awarded a contract by Giat Industries for 72 examples of the Sherpa 5. These will be used as the platform for the C-130 Hercules transportable CAmion Equipé d'un Systéme d'ARtillerie (CAESAR) 155 mm/52-calibre self-propelled artillery system, for which Giat was awarded a EUR300 million contract in December 2004 (Shaun C Connors)   1391133

gearbox. This refurbishment/upgrade is now also available to other users of the GBC 8KT; around 2,000 examples were exported to a number of countries.

Full details of the Berliet GBC 8KT and Renault GBC 180 can be found elsewhere in this section.

At the earliest stages of the Sherpa range development programme the yet to be named Sherpa 5 was likely to be a new-build GBC 180. However, it soon became clear a vehicle with further increased capability was required to meet emerging market trends and the current configuration of the base Sherpa range truck evolved. Compared to the GBC 180 the Sherpa 5 has a greater payload (6,000 kg (currently 7,300 kg) opposed to 5,000 kg) and lower ground pressure, has an emissions compliant engine (EURO 3 or 5) that develops around 30 per cent more hp and torque and is consequently faster and more mobile, with 20 and 33 per cent improvements in gradeability and sideslope capability, respectively, being prime examples of the latter.

The Sherpa 5 can also comply fully with current EU legislation and is therefore available (with limited modifications) to governmental/commercial users who require a severe duty all-terrain truck.

Early in the Sherpa 5 development process the decision to develop a larger (approximately 10,000 kg payload) version was taken and the Sherpa 10 was developed. The Sherpa 10 is essentially a current generation TRM 9000/10000. The larger capacity Sherpa 15 and Sherpa 20 chassis were subsequently developed, and the full range (Sherpa 5, 10, 15 and 20) was first displayed publicly by Renault Trucks Defence at Eurosatory 2004. Renault subsequently introduced the Sherpa Light (originally designated Sherpa 2 and Sherpa 3 (4 × 4)). This is an HMMWV-type design and not a load carrying vehicle as such, and will therefore not be covered in this entry.

At Eurosatory 2008 Renault Trucks Defence announced an MRAP-class design based on a Sherpa 10 chassis. Outline details of this vehicle can be found elsewhere in this entry.

By early 2009 Renault had ceased promotion of the Sherpa 15 and 20, and for uniformity the Sherpa 5 and Sherpa 10 models, while retaining their separate denominations, were both categorised as Sherpa Medium models.

By mid-2010 Renault had disclosed the availability of (4 × 4) versions of the Sherpa 5 and Sherpa 10.

The cab and a number of other components for the Sherpa family are manufactured in Turkey.

It was disclosed mid-2005 that Renault Trucks Defense had been awarded a contract by Giat Industries for 72 examples of the Sherpa 5. These will be used as the platform for the C-130 Hercules transportable CAmion Equipé d'un Systéme d'ARtillerie (CAESAR) 155 mm/52-calibre

self-propelled artillery system, for which Giat was awarded a EUR300 million contract in December 2004. Renault delivered a development chassis late 2005, and by mid-2010 60 examples had been delivered; all systems are due to be delivered by 2011. The first CAESAR examples were deployed to Afghanistan in August 2009.

The first example of CAESAR (a concept demonstrator) was completed by Giat as a private venture in 1994. The system was subsequently demonstrated in Asia, the Middle East and the US. France first trialled the system in 1998 and ordered five systems in late 2000; these were delivered during 2003. All previous examples of CAESAR have utilised a Unimog (6 × 6) chassis; Mercedes-Benz currently does not offer a (6 × 6) Unimog. The French Army subsequently ordered 77 CAESAR (72 on a hybrid Sherpa 5/Sherpa 10 chassis), and the first example was officially handed over to the DGA late-July; by mid-2010 60 examples had been delivered. The first CAESAR examples were deployed to Afghanistan in August 2009. France's current spending plans indicate that 141 CAESAR systems are required, with the remaining 64 likely to be ordered in 2013 for delivery between 2015 and 2020.

The first export sale of CAESAR was announced in April 2007 and was an order for six units (on a Sherpa chassis) from Thailand. The 100 (estimate) CAESAR ordered by Saudi Arabia from July 2007 will be mounted on a converted Unimog U5000 (4 × 4) chassis, the conversion to (6 × 6) being carried out under contract to SOFRAME. Full details of CAESAR can be found in *Jane's Armour and Artillery*.

A French Army Sherpa 5 truck order was disclosed at Eurosatory 2008. This was placed early 2008 and calls for 200 Sherpa 5 ammunition limbers. 121 of these will be fitted with armoured cabs (ordered in 2 batches, 31 (2008) and 90 (2009)).

Renault was founded in 1898 to build cars, and built its first truck in 1903. In 1955 and through the merger of Renault, Latil and Somua, Saviem was created and by 1965 the Renault name was no longer used on heavy trucks. In 1974 Saviem and Berliet were joined to make one truck business. Following Saviem's reorganisation into Renault Vehicles Industriels (subsequently Renault V.I.) in 1978, by 1980 the names Berliet and Saviem had been dropped and the Renault name reinstated for trucks. In 1981 Renault V.I. acquired Chrysler's former truck business in the UK plus Chrysler Espana, builders of Spanish Dodge trucks; these had been owned by Peugeot since 1978. Renault completed its acquisition of the Mack brand in 1990, and in 2001 became part of the Volvo Group. In the 2002 the international name of the company was changed to Renault Trucks and Renault Trucks Defence was formed.

Description

Being a bonneted design, the Sherpa range of trucks is visually similar to the Renault C series of heavy bonneted trucks, production of which concluded in the late 1990s. The Sherpa family are not related to the C series and are a completely new design that leverage off Renault's considerable experience with the GBC 8KT refurbishment/upgrade, plus the earlier production of tactical military trucks such as the TRM 10000, TRM 9000, and ongoing involvement with armoured vehicles such as the VAB (*Véhicule l'Avant Blindé*) and the VBCI (*Véhicule Blindé de Combat d'Infanterie*). The Sherpa 5 and 10 are based on a purpose-designed chassis, the no longer promoted Sherpa 15 and 20 were based on chassis from the heavier elements of Renault's commercial Kerax heavy truck range which was first introduced during 1997. Early Sherpa 10 prototypes were based on a Kerax range chassis.

The Sherpa 5 chassis has a boxed-section front end with flitch plates inserted towards the rear of the chassis for increased stiffness and durability; sidemember sections measure 230 × 90 × 8 mm; the Sherpa 10 chassis is essentially an enlarged version of the Sherpa 5 chassis. The chassis used as the basis for CAESAR is further reinforced to withstand firing recoil forces. All chassis are available with or without a retractable

Displayed at Eurosatory 2004, a Sherpa 5 (short cab) in chassis-cab configuration (Shaun C Connors)   1128795

	Sherpa 5 (6 × 6) [(4 × 4) in square brackets where different]	**Sherpa 10 (6 × 6) [(4 × 4) in square brackets where different]**
Cab seating:	1 + 2	1 + 2
Configuration:	6 × 6 [4 × 4]	6 × 6 [4 × 4]
Weight:		
(laden)	15,000 kg [14,000 kg]	20,500 kg [18,000 kg]
(payload)	7,300 kg [6,700 kg]	12,000 kg [10,200 kg
(GVW)	23,000 kg [22,000 kg]	32,500 kg [30,000 kg]
Length:	wheelbase dependent	wheelbase dependent
Width: (cab)	2.5 m	2.5 m
Height: (cab, unladen)	2.775 m	2.964 m
Ground clearance: (centre)	520 mm	490 mm
Track:		
(front)	1.999 m	2.047 m
(rear)	1.999 m	2.047 m
Wheelbase:	4.00 to 4.5 m + 1.35 m [4.75 m]	4.5 to 5.85 m+ 1.35 m [4.75 m]
Angle of approach/departure:	44.5°/45° [n/avail]	45°/45° [n/avail]
Max/min speed:	90/<4 km/h	90/<4 km/h
Cruising range:	850 km	850 km
Fuel capacity:	200 litres	310 litres
Max gradient: (GVW)	60%	60%
Max sideslope: (GVW)	30%	30%
Vertical step:	500 mm	500 mm
Trench:	900 mm	900 mm
Fording:	1.2 m	1.2 m
Engine:	Renault MD-7 7.14-litre EURO 5 6-cylinder in-line exhaust turbocharged and air-to-air intercooled, water-cooled common rail injection 4-stroke diesel developing 265 hp (195 kW) at 2,300 rpm and 1,010 N.m torque between 1,200-1,700 rpm, or 295 hp (217 kW) at 2,300 rpm and 1,071 N.m torque between 1,200-1,700 rpm (Sherpa 5); 340 hp (247 kW) at 2,300 rpm and 1,306 N.m torque between 1,200-1,700 rpm (Sherpa 10). For certain markets earlier generation EURO 3 emissions compliant Renault engines may be available All engines can be adapted to run on F36, F54 and F34 fuels	
Gearbox:	ZF 6S 1000 manual with 6 forward and 1 reverse gears, Sherpa 5; ZF 9S 1310 with 8 forward and 1 reverse gears, Sherpa 10; optional ZF 6HP 502 automatic with 6 forward and 1 reverse gears, Sherpa 5 and 10. Optional gearbox-mounted PTO on all models	
Transfer box:	Steyr VG750 2-speed, Sherpa 5; Steyr VG1600 2-speed, Sherpa 10	
Clutch:	single dry plate, 395 mm in diameter	single dry plate, 395 mm in diameter
Steering:	power-assisted, single circuit, single pump	power-assisted, single circuit, single pump
Suspension:	double parabolic leaf springs, telescopic shock-absorbers and anti-roll bar, front; reinforced parabolic leaf springs and anti-roll bar, rear	
Tyres:	Sherpa 5: 13R 22.5 or 395/85R 20. Sherpa 10: 395/85R 20	
Brakes:		
(main)	dual circuit air, discs all-round; supplementary pneumatically-operated exhaust brake (optional additional engine brake), ABS fitted. Options include a 60% hill brake and front towing couplings	
(parking)	pneumatically-controlled spring actuators	pneumatically-controlled spring actuators
Electrical system:	24 V, electromagnetic compatibility to MIL STD 461, optional GAM EG 13	
Alternator:	100 A	100 A

rear under-run guard, a front-mounted self-recovery winch, tie-down rings for air-transport and a variety of recovery/towing attachments. The all-steel front bumper is independent of the chassis.

The cab used for the Sherpa range of trucks is a further development of the cab fitted to the GBC 180. A bonneted non-commercial cab design was selected by Renault for a number of reasons. Compared to a dimensionally comparable Cab-Over-Engine (COE) design, a bonneted cab will allow an overall height reduction of around 160 mm and an increase in useable internal volume, further it improves collision safety by providing a minimum of 1.3 m between the driver and the front of the vehicle. The approximately 1 m increase in vehicle overall length brought about by the use of a bonnet is seldom an issue in a military environment and more than compensated for by improvements in engine access for both service and large-scale maintenance; the bonnet tilts forward 70°. A bonneted design will offer important interior ergonomic improvements, plus with its set-forward first axle, a considerable ride improvement over a similarly specified COE design. Additionally, a set-forward front axle provides a limited degree of inherent protection in the event of mine blast.

Three basic versions of the Sherpa cab are available, short, torpedo, or long. The standard short cab seats two or three (dependent on requirement), the long cab having the option of either five seats or three seats plus bunking. The torpedo cab is a half-cab with a collapsible fabric soft-top and this design is popular with users in hot climates that do not wish for the complexities of an air-conditioning system. Torpedo cabbed vehicles are transportable by C-130 Hercules aircraft.

Military considerations include the interior being primarily steel or washable plastic/vinyl, a hand throttle, manually operated door windows, a circular roof hatch with the option for a roof-mounted 7.62 mm machine gun in a ring-type mount, plus a hermetically sealed instrument panel for the torpedo cabbed version. There is 80 per cent component commonality between all cabs, and all are fixed to the chassis via four point reinforced suspension mounts.

Renault has developed an optional interchangeable armoured short or long cabin for the Sherpa family, the Sherpa 5 version allowing for C-130 Hercules transport following some preparation. Standard protection is to STANAG Level 2, although Level 3 with additional add-on protection is

Renault Trucks Defense offers an MRAP-type design on the Sherpa 10 chassis (Shaun C Connors) 1391397

The Renault GBC 180 is a refurbished/upgraded Berliet GBC 8KT and interest in this joint Renault/French Army programme was a catalyst in the development of the Sherpa range of tactical trucks (Shaun C Connors)

1128794

available. For the CAESAR application an armoured cab is fitted. There is 80 per cent component commonality between all armoured cabs.

The Sherpa truck range, with payloads ranging from around 7,000 to 12,000 kg, is intended to cover the light to medium spectrum of tactical military load carrying requirements and the eventual number of model variations produced will likely be well into double figures. As of November 2010 Renault had outlined the two base models of the Sherpa family, the Sherpa 5 and Sherpa 10, and released outline specifications for these. It should be noted however that a considerable number of detail variations from the two models will be available, with up to four wheelbase, three cab and both two- or three-axle configurations so far outlined. Some of these variations may result in designation changes/amendments.

There was no 4 × 4 chassis in the Sherpa range when initially announced, Renault opting for a three axle configuration for the Sherpa 5 to ensure the design had a genuine high mobility performance. The bulk of competing designs in the 6,000/7,000 kg payload class are 4 × 4 chassis and most feature a COE design. Compared to a comparable 4 × 4 COE design the 6 × 6 configuration of the Sherpa 5 offers around a 25 per cent reduction in vertical loads and around a 35 per cent reduction in horizontal loads to driver and cargo.

Compared to a 6 × 6 chassis, a comparable payload/driveline 4 × 4 chassis will cost less to procure and, with less componentry, will on paper be slightly less expensive to operate. In other areas, axle loading, weight distribution, additional load capacity for cab armouring, ground pressure, approach, departure and ramp breakover angles and so on, a 6 × 6 chassis is the better option.

To cater for those users/markets that either do not require or are unable to procure a 6 × 6 chassis, by mid-2010 Renault had made 4 × 4 versions of the Sherpa 5 and Sherpa 10 available, these essentially the 6 × 6 chassis with the second axle removed.

Power for the Sherpa range of trucks is provided by the latest generation AB Volvo Group turbocharged common rail injection EURO 5 emissions compliant water-cooled diesel engines. For certain markets earlier generation Renault engines may be available as an option.

Climatic operational range is –20 to +50°C (–32°C with the optional engine cold starting kit) for all the range.

To ensure that weight constraints brought about by a C-130 transportability requirement for CAESAR are met, this Sherpa 5 variant has a different, lighter, engine to the standard Sherpa 5, being powered by a dXi 5 4.761-litre four-cylinder engine developing 215 hp at 2,300 rpm and 800 N.m. torque at 1,200 rpm.

All Sherpa models will have manual or automatic gearbox options. The Sherpa 5 is fitted with a ZF six-speed manual, the Sherpa 10 with a nine-speed manual, and in both cases coupled to a Steyr two-speed transfer box. Automatic option is a ZF unit; a gearbox-mounted PTO is an option for all models.

Driveline of the Sherpa range is completed by either AxleTech or Renault double-reduction beam-type axles. In standard configuration all models feature a disengageable front axle for road use, full-time all-wheel drive with a torque dividing lockable centre differential being an option.

Front steer-drive axles are sprung by a combination of parabolic leaf springs, hydraulic telescopic shock-absorbers and an anti-roll bar. Rear axle(s) are sprung by parabolic leaf springs and anti-roll bars. All axles are fitted with driver-controlled cross-axle differential locks; there are longitudinal differential locks between the rear axle pair and the transfer box on 6 × 6 chassis. All models are available with beadlocks and a tyre runflat option. A Central Tyre Inflation (CTI) system is available. Standard tyre size for the Sherpa 5 is 13R 22.5, the standard tyre size for the Sherpa 10 is 395/85R 20.

Sherpa Medium MRAP

At Eurosatory 2008 Renault Trucks Defense announced a Mine Resistant Ambush Protected (MRAP) category vehicle based on a Sherpa 10 chassis fitted with a fully armoured body that is claimed to provide a high level of protection against small-arms fire, mines and IEDs.

The V-shaped armoured body mounts to the standard truck chassis and seats up to 12 personnel and their equipment; internal volume is 15 m³.

The Sherpa Medium MRAP has a GVW of 20,000 kg and a payload of 4,000 kg.

Specifications

In certain instances technically permissible maximum GVW and GCW may exceed those legally allowed in peacetime. See table on facing page.

Status

Sherpa 5 ordered by the French Army (see text); chassis to be supplied to Nexter for CAESAR deliveries to France and Thailand (see text).

Contractor

Renault Trucks Defense

Renault B110 Turbo (4 × 4) light vehicle

Development

The Renault B110 Turbo (4 × 4) light vehicle is the military version of the Renault Messenger commercial van. The vehicle, which is no longer in production, was available configured for a variety of roles ranging from a 2,285 kg light truck to a military ambulance.

Two chassis versions were produced, the B110-35D and B110-45D, these differing in their gross vehicle weight capacities, with the B110-45D having the greater capacity.

In April 1994, 300 units were ordered for the French Gendarmerie. In 1993, 170 examples of a (4 × 2) version were ordered for the French Gendarmerie.

The Renault B110 Turbo has been replaced in the Renault product line up by similar versions of current-production light commercial vans.

Description

The B110 Turbo uses a flat frame chassis with parallel channel side members treated with corrosion protection. The vehicle uses a steel monocoque semi-forward control cab that seats the driver and two passengers on a separate bench seat.

As a light tactical truck the cargo area can be covered by a fabric tilt on removable bows; payload of this version was quoted as approximately 1,600 kg. The van-bodied version could be supplied with or without side-opening doors. For the ambulance version the bodywork alterations are carried out by subcontractors. The ambulance body carries six stretchers or six seated patients. Entrance to the ambulance section is normally through two large doors at the rear but there is a side door on the right-hand side of the body.

Optional equipment available included: an airlift kit, making the vehicle suitable for transport in the C-130, C-160 or similar aircraft; right-hand drive; a removable towing bracket for mounting front or rear, and a removable electric winch.

A Sherpa 5 (short cab) with a standard troop carrying/cargo-type body fitted (Shaun C Connors)

1128797

Renault B110 Turbo (4 × 4) light vehicle of the French Gendarmerie (Shaun C Connors)

1190216

Specifications

Fourgon van model
Cab seating: 1 + 2
Configuration: 4 × 4
Weight:
  (chassis cab) 2,775 kg
  (GVW, B110-35D) 3,500 kg
  (GVW, B110-45D) 4,500 kg
  (max load, B110-35D) 725 kg
  (max load, B110-45D) 1,725 kg
Length: 5.652 m
Width: (over cab) 2.06 m
Height: (van body, unladen) 3.06 m
Ground clearance: (laden) 287 mm
Track:
  (front) 1.714 m
  (rear) 1.703 m
Wheelbase: 3.26 m
Angle of approach/departure: 52°/28°
Max speed: 105 km/h
Fuel capacity: 67 litres
Range: 620 km
Engine: Type 8140.27 IDS 2.5-litre 4-cylinder in-line turbocharged water-cooled 4-stroke diesel developing 106 hp (78 kW) at 3,800 rpm
Gearbox: Type S 5-24 manual synchromesh with 5 forward and 1 reverse gears
Clutch: single dry plate
Transfer box: Type 100 2-speed
Steering: worm and screw with hydraulic power assisted
Suspension: leaf springs, hydraulic shock-absorbers and anti-roll bars, front and rear
Tyres: 9.00R × 16 H
Brakes:
  (main) dual circuit, hydraulic vacuum assisted, discs front, drums rear,
  (parking) mechanical on rear axle
Electrical system: 12 V
Batteries: 1 × 12 V, 90 Ah
Alternator: 70 A

Status

Production complete. Military versions of current generation similar vehicles are now available.

Contractor

Renault Trucks Defense

Renault TRM 1200 (4 × 4) 1,200 kg truck

Development

The Renault TRM 1200 was previously known as the Saviem TP3 and was in production at Renault's Blainville factory from 1969. By mid-1981 some 9,200 had been produced, of which 4,000 were for the French Army and 4,000 for overseas military sales.

Description

The Renault TRM 1200 is based on standard commercial components and can carry 12 fully equipped men or 1,200 kg of cargo.

The chassis consists of cold-drawn steel side members with the cross-members welded into position. The vehicle was delivered with a two-door all-steel fully enclosed cab, or a cab with a tarpaulin roof, removable door tops and a windscreen which folds forward onto the bonnet when not required. The rear cargo area has removable drop sides, a drop tailgate, removable bows and a tarpaulin cover. Removable seats can be installed down the centre of the vehicle (back to back) or along each side of the vehicle.

Optional equipment included: a 72 hp petrol engine; a winch with a capacity of 2,000 kg; a 120-litre fuel tank in place of the standard 70-litre fuel tank; 7- and 12-pin outlet sockets; 10.50 × 20 tyres and a fire extinguisher.

Variants included: an ambulance capable of carrying six stretcher patients or 12 seated patients, which is in service with the French Army; command post (supplied to the French police); dump truck; fire-fighting vehicle; and a light recovery vehicle.

Specifications

TRM 1200
Cab seating: 1 + 1
Configuration: 4 × 4
Weight:
  (laden) 3,950 kg
  (unladen) 2,620 kg
  (max load, off-road) 1,330 kg
  (max towed load) 1,000 kg
Load area: 3.025 × 1.85 m
Length: 5.005 m
Width: 1.996 m

Height:
  (cab) 2.4 m
  (tarpaulin) 2.594 m
  (load area) 1.094 m
Ground clearance: 270 mm
Track: 1.641 m
Wheelbase: 2.64 m
Angle of approach/departure: 31°/40°
Max speed: 95.5 km/h
Range: 600 km
Fuel capacity: 70 litres
Max gradient: 58.9%
Fording: 500 mm
Engine: Renault 712 4-cylinder 4-stroke water-cooled diesel developing 72 hp (53 kW) at 3,200 rpm
Gearbox: Renault 321-4 manual with 4 forward and 1 reverse gears
Transfer box: Renault 433 2-speed
Clutch: single dry disc
Steering: cam and roller
Turning radius: 8.25 m
Suspension: leaf springs with Evidgom pads and hydraulic shock-absorbers
Tyres: 9.00 × 16
Brakes:
  (main) hydraulic
  (parking) mechanical
Electrical system: 24 V
Batteries: 2 × 12 V, 96 Ah

Status

Production complete. Supplied to Algeria, France, Morocco and other undisclosed countries.

Contractor

Renault Trucks Defense

SUMB (4 × 4) 1,500 kg MH 600 BS truck

Development

The Simca-Unic Marmon-Bocquet (SUMB) 1,500 kg model MH 600 BS truck was developed in the late 1950s by M Bocquet, who was president of Marmon-Herrington which subsequently became Marmon-Bocquet. Series production was undertaken from 1964 and although production ceased some time ago, it remains in service with the French Army.

Description

The engine and cab of the SUMB are at the front with the cargo area at the rear. The cab has two doors and a canvas top mounted on an articulated frame, which enables the top to be folded to the rear to reduce the vehicle's overall height. The windscreen can be folded forward onto the bonnet. The rear cargo area has a drop tailgate, bows and a removable tarpaulin cover. A bench seat can be fitted down the centre of the rear cargo area when the truck is carrying passengers. A locking differential is fitted to the rear axle. Some versions have a front-mounted winch with 60 m of cable.

A long wheelbase model of this vehicle, known as the SUMB (4 × 4) 3,000 kg truck, was produced from 1971 with the same engine, transmission and cab as the 1,500 kg version.

Variants include a fuel servicing vehicle and a light digger with a Poclain light shovel mounted to the rear of the cab. The SUMB is also used to carry communication shelters.

SUMB Upgrade

Renault Trucks Defense has upgraded 1,000 SUMB (4 × 4) 1,500 kg trucks for the French Army. The upgrade involves the replacement of the existing petrol engine with the same Type 720 SPC diesel developing 115 hp as

SUMB (4 × 4) 1,500 kg truck (Pierre Touzin)   0100353

used in the Renault TRM 2000 truck, along with the transmission from the TRM 2000. Other upgrade changes include electrical components, also from the TRM 2000, and the braking system was updated to meet then current EC legislation.

Specifications

SUMB MH 600 BS
[Data in square brackets applies to the 3,000 kg truck where it differs from the 1,500 kg model]
Cab seating: 1 + 1
Configuration: 4 × 4
Weight:
   (laden) 5,300 [7,420] kg
   (unladen) 3,670 [4,220] kg
   (max load) 1,500 [3,000] kg
   (towed load) 2,000 kg
Load area: 2.95 × 1.97 [4.4 × 2.29] m
Length: 5.195 [6.55] m
Width: 2.305 [2.41] m
Height:
   (cab) 2.27 m
   (tarpaulin) 2.88 [2.97] m
Ground clearance: 330 [380] mm
Track: 1.704 m
Wheelbase: 2.9 [4.1] m
Angle of approach/departure: 43°/42°
Max speed: (road) 85 [82] km/h
Range: 550 km
Fuel capacity: 130 litres
Fuel consumption: 30-32 litres/100 km
Max gradient: 60 [50]%
Max side slope: 30%
Fording:
   (without preparation) 800 mm
   (with preparation) 1.2 m
Engine: 8-cylinder petrol developing 100 hp (74 kW) at 3,000 rpm [6-cylinder diesel developing 100 hp (74 kW) at 3,000 rpm]
Gearbox: manual with 4 forward and 1 reverse gears
Transfer box: 2-speed
Clutch: single dry plate
Turning radius: 7.5 [11.5] m
Suspension: coil springs and hydraulic shock-absorbers
Tyres: 10.00 × 20 [12.50 × 20]
Brakes:
   (main) hydraulic
   (parking) mechanical
Electrical system: 24 V
Batteries: 2 × 12 V

Status
In service with the French Army. Upgrade programme complete.

Contractor
FFSA
(This concern is no longer trading)

Enquiries to
Renault Trucks Defense

Renault TRM 2000 (4 × 4) 2,000 kg truck

Development
Following a competition for a new 2,000 kg truck in which five vehicles were tested by the French Army, it was announced in March 1981 that the High Mobility version of the Renault TRM 2000 (4 × 4) 2,000 kg truck had been selected. The French Army then had a requirement for some 12,000 vehicles, with first production vehicles completed at Renault's Blainville facility during 1983. The first 2,000 examples were delivered to signal units in the three French Army corps to carry RITA communications equipment. Production is now complete.

Since April 2008, Renault Trucks Defence has operated a 10-year Maintenance in Operational Conditions (MOC) contract with the French Army for tactical trucks. This EUR484 million contract covers 2,530 TRM 2000, plus 3,200 GBC 180, 805 TRM 10000, and 2,000 VTL.

Description
The Renault TRM 2000 was available in two versions, Standard and High Mobility. The main difference between the two is that the Standard has a ground clearance under the axle of 302 mm as opposed to 425 mm for the High Mobility version.

The chassis consists of C-section side members (180 × 70 × 4 mm) with the cross-members riveted and bolted together. A towing bracket and a protective skid plate are provided at the front with a 5,000 kg rated towing hook at the rear.

The forward control cab is of all-steel construction but may have a tarpaulin cover, and is mounted onto the chassis at three points with elastic pads and two shock-absorbers at the rear. The cab tilts forward and

A High Mobility version of the Renault TRM 2000 (4 × 4) 2,000 kg truck mounting an air defence cannon, almost certainly a 20 mm Tarasque 53 T2 anti-aircraft cannon (Pierre Touzin) 1047633

A High Mobility version of the Renault TRM 2000 (4 × 4) 2,000 kg truck carrying a shelter. This truck is assigned to NATO Eurocorps (Stefan Marx) 1047636

A High Mobility version of the Renault TRM 2000 (4 × 4) 2,000 kg truck fitted with a standard cargo/troop carrying drop side body with tarpaulin. This truck is fitted with a winch (Pierre Touzin) 1047632

is provided with a torsion bar tilting mechanism with double lock and warning indicator lamp, toughened glass windscreen, fully wind-down door windows, rear quarter lights, two-man passenger seat and an adjustable driver's seat. To the rear of the cab is a spare wheel rack. In the cab roof a Creusot-Loire Industrie STR TA rail-mounted rotary support is fitted to a hatch. This mounting can accommodate a 7.62 mm machine gun and is a standard fitting.

The cargo area is provided with drop sides and rear, bows and a tarpaulin cover. If required, seats can be fitted down the centre of the vehicle to carry 12 fully equipped troops (for example six down each side facing outwards).

Optional equipment included a front-mounted winch with a capacity of 2,500 kg and a pioneer tool holder.

Variants included: a fully enclosed ambulance; command post with shelter-mounted RITA system; forward air control; 2,000-litre fuel tanker; missile carrier; prime mover for heavy mortars, prime mover or carrier (mounted on the cargo bed) for the 20 mm Tarasque 53 T2 anti-aircraft cannon; recovery vehicle; water tanker; a field ambulance carrying six casualties; and a workshop vehicle.

A High Mobility version of the Renault TRM 2000 (4 × 4) 2,000 kg truck towing a single axle cargo trailer. This truck is not fitted with the optional front-mounted winch (Pierre Touzin)
0100355

Sovamag TC-24 (4 × 4) 2,500 kg multipurpose vehicle (Shaun C Connors)
0536750

Specifications

TRM 2000
Cab seating: 1 + 2 (up to 12 in rear)
Configuration: 4 × 4
Weight:
    (laden) 6,300 kg
    (unladen) 3,980 kg
    (max load) 2,320 kg
    (towed load) 2,000 kg
Length: 5.02 m
Width: 2.2 m
Height: (cab) 2.713 m
Ground clearance:
    (axles) 425 mm
    (centre of vehicle) 604 mm
Track: (front and rear) 1.8 m
Wheelbase: 2.7 m
Angle of approach/departure: 42°/48°
Maximum road speed: 89 km/h
Range: 1,000 km
Fuel capacity: 130 litres
Max gradient:
    (1st gear, high range) 35%
    (1st gear, low range) 50%
Max side slope: 30%
Fording: 900 mm
Engine: Type 720S 4-cylinder inline turbo compressor supercharged 4-stroke diesel developing 115 hp (85 kW) at 3,000 rpm
Gearbox: S 5-24/3, 5 forward and 1 reverse gears
Clutch: single dry plate
Transfer box: 2-speed
Steering: ball race, hydraulic
Turning radius: 7 m
Suspension: semi-elliptic leaf springs front and rear, with Evidgom pads, hydraulic telescopic shock-absorbers and anti-roll bar on the rear axle
Tyres: 12.50 × 20
Brakes:
    (main) dual circuit, air, with load equaliser on rear circuit
    (parking) mechanical
Electrical system: 24 V
Batteries: 2 × 12 V, 6TN, 125 Ah

Status

Production complete. In service with the French Army and Gendarmerie. Also supplied to other armed forces including Morocco (190), Namibia (50) and Qatar (10).

Contractor

Renault Trucks Defense

Sovamag TC 24 (4 × 4) 2,500 kg multipurpose vehicle

Development

The Sovamag concern (occasionally presented SOVAMAG) was acquired by Auverland (now Panhard General Defense) in 1989. Auverland's history traces back to the acquisition of Societe International de Matériel Industrial (SIMI), a Belin Group company, by Francois Servanin in 1984. SIMI produced the A2/SAMO, an evolution of the Cournil, a robust and functional light 4 × 4. Auverland continued the evolution of the A2/SAMO into the Auverland A3, full details of which can be found elsewhere in this section.

By the late 1980s Auverland was looking to expand its military business and primarily on the basis of French Ministry of Co-operation contracts for its TC-10 1,100 kg multipurpose light vehicle, the company acquired the Sovamag concern in 1989. Full details of the TC-10 can be found in the Light vehicles section.

Following its acquisition of Sovamag, Auverland became known as Auverland-Sovamag although this was generally disregarded in written references to the company. The Sovamag brand name was retained. Wishing to capitalise on the success of the functional TC-10, by 1992 Auverland had begun development of the larger Sovamag TC-24.

In July 2001, Auverland-Sovamag were acquired by (and recapitalised by) Société Nouvelle des Automobiles Auverland (SNAA). The name Auverland remained the one generally used when referring to the company. The TC-10 and TC-24 continued to be badged and marketed as Sovamag products.

The TC-24 has been supplied to a number of nations via the French Ministry of Foreign Affairs, and usually in small numbers. The following Ministry of Foreign Affairs figures have been released: Benin (two), Central African Republic (CAR) (47, most recently 20 during 2005 and five during 2006), Congo Brazzaville (five), Côte d'Ivoire (one), Gabon (two), Guinea (two), Senegal (one). Additionally, the TC-24 has been evaluated by Bangladesh Armed Forces in the gun tractor role and at the time of writing (November 2010) a decision and possibly contract award remained pending. The TC-24 has also been evaluated in Mauritania (2003) and Morocco. Two examples were shipped to China for examination/evaluation by NORINCO with a view to licence production. This project did not progress.

A single prototype example of a light armoured vehicle on the TC-24 chassis was produced. The type did not enter series production and while technically still available has been superseded by other designs in the Panhard General Defense product line-up.

It surprised many commentators when in January 2005 it was announced that SNAA had acquired Panhard, builder of the Vehicule Blindé Leger (VBL), ERC Sagaie and other light armoured military vehicles. Panhard's parent company, the car manufacturer PSA Peugeot Citroen, is understood to have been open to offers for Panhard for a number of years, but the loss of the Petit Vehicle Protégé (PVP) contract to SNAA is understood to have been the catalyst in bringing disposal plans for France's oldest builder of light armoured military vehicles to the fore. Renault Trucks Defense in conjunction with Thales were reportedly also interested in Panhard, and are understood to have made an offer. Details of SNAA's securing deal have not been disclosed, however the company is thought to have paid between EUR20 million and EUR25 million for Panhard. Panhard vehicles have been bought by the armed forces of 45 countries and the company had net earnings of around EUR4 million on sales of EUR65 million in 2004. In 2008 the group sold 600 vehicles, resulting in revenues of EUR90 million.

Early 2006, the SNAA became known as Panhard General Defense.

It was disclosed mid-2006 that the Saudi Ministry Of Defence and Aviation (MODA), as part of a deal with NORINCO of China to supply PLZ-45 self-propelled howitzers, had specified in the awarded contract that wheeled logistic and tactical support vehicles for these SPGs be provided by Panhard General Defense. NORINCO subsequently awarded Panhard General Defense an order for the supply of 283 vehicles, including 34 TC-24s in two basic configurations; soft top (some for personnel transport - 2 + 12) and water/fuel carrier. The Saudi order includes 133 of the under-development five-tonne payload TC-54. The overall contract value was around EUR22 million and all vehicles were to be delivered by mid-2008. It is understood that delivery of the artillery system in question has yet to take place.

Saudi Arabia also operates the Auverland A3 light vehicle, around 50 of which were delivered during 2005.

Sovamag TC-24 (4 × 4) 2,500 kg multipurpose vehicle
(Panhard General Defense) 0009622

Description

The Sovamag TC-24 (4 × 4) 2,500 kg multipurpose vehicle is based on a C-section 150 × 70 mm chassis with a galvanised sheet-steel body. Compared to the TC-10 it has an increased payload capacity that allows shelter/container-type bodies to be carried. Proposed applications for the base chassis have included a firefighting vehicle, tanker and an armoured personnel carrier version, the TC-24 Blindé. Right-hand drive and driver training models are available. Also available is the Sovamag TC-24 SL. This is similar to the TC 24 and is powered by the same engine but has a longer 4.4 m wheelbase. A lightened variant (total weight 3,500 kg) of the TC-24 has a nominal payload of 1,070 kg.

In standard configuration the Jeep-type steel cab of the TC-24 has seating for a driver and one or two passengers, while the cargo body - in wide-body format - can be provided with seating for up to 18 passengers on folding bench seats. In addition to carrying troops or cargo this area can be used to mount assorted light weapons. Proposed weapon installations have included the 106 mm M40 series recoilless rifle, 20 mm cannon and MILAN anti-tank or Mistral air defence missiles.

Specifications

SOVAMAG TC 24
[Data in square brackets relate to TC-24 SL where different]
Cab seating: 1 + 2 (up to 18 in rear) [24]
Configuration: 4 × 4 (selectable)
Weight:
  (GVW) 5,000 kg
  (unladen) 2,430 kg [2,500 kg]
  (permissible front axle load) 2,200 kg
  (permissible rear axle load) 3,200 kg
  (payload) 2,570 kg [2,500 kg]
  (towed load, braked) 3,500 kg
  (towed load, unbraked) 750 kg
  (max GCW) 8,500 kg
Length: (chassis cab) 5.15 m [6.15 m]
Length: (overall) 5.47 m
Width: 1.974 m
Height: (cab) 2.27 m [2.35 m]
Ground clearance: (minimum) 280 mm
Wheelbase: 3.6 m [4.4 m]
Track: (front and rear) 1.7 m
Angle of approach/departure: 65°/45°
Max speed: 110 km/h
Range: (cruising) 800 km
Fuel capacity: 2 × 80 litres
Gradient: 100%
Side slope: 66%
Fording: 900 mm
Engine: IVECO/SOFIM 2.8-litre 4-cylinder in-line turbocharged water-cooled 4-stroke diesel developing 122 hp (91 kW) at 3,600 rpm and 285 N.m torque at 1,800 rpm
Gearbox: IVECO 2826-5 manual with 5 forward and 1 reverse gears
Transfer box: New Venture Type 241 2-speed
Steering: power-assisted
Turning radius: 7 m
axles: beam-type, limited slip differential in rear axle
Suspension: semi-elliptic leaf springs plus helper pneumatics, with double acting shock-absorbers, front and rear
Tyres: 9.00 × 16
Brakes: dual circuit, servo-assisted hydraulic, discs front, drums rear
Electrical system: 24 V

Status

Production as required. Supplied via the French Ministry of Foreign Affairs to Benin (two), Central African Republic (CAR) (47, most recently 20 during 2005 and five during 2006), Congo Brazzaville (five), Côte d'Ivoire (one), Gabon (two), Guinea (two), Senegal (one). Evaluated by Bangladesh,

China, Mauritania and Morocco (see text). Ordered by Saudi Arabia (see text).

Contractor
Panhard General Defense

ACMAT Light Tactical Vehicle (ALTV)

Development

The ACMAT Light Tactical Vehicle (ALTV) was first shown publicly at Eurosatory 2008. The ACMAT LTV is a 3,500 kg GVW light utility vehicle stated to be built to the same levels of durability as the ACMAT VLRA (*Véhicule de Liaison, de Reconnaissance et d'Appui*), full details of which can be found in the Trucks section.

The ACMAT story began in 1948 when, for use in harsh operating environments, the company's founder started a business improving the durability/reliability of mass-produced trucks. The original VLRA was introduced in 1965 and has its origins in the VCOM (Overseas Combat Vehicle), this modified to become the VLRA.

Since the mid-1960s around 12,000 VLRA have been produced by Ateliers de Construction Mécanique de l'Atlantique (ACMAT) and have been supplied to at least 48 countries on five continents, company figures quoting 93 per cent of ACMAT sales as export.

The ACMAT factory at Saint Nazaire was established in 1965 and has the capacity to manufacture up to 1,200 vehicles of all types every year.

It was announced during 2006 that Renault Trucks had acquired ACMAT. The company had been in financial difficulty and looking for a buyer for some time, and during 2004 a bid by Malaysian company Pesaka Astana was defeated in the French courts. Following its acquisition of the company, Renault stated an intention to maintain the ACMAT brand along with its product range, and to continue the company's programme of research and development at its Saint-Nazaire facility.

As previously mentioned, in 2008 a revitalised ACMAT announced the Light Tactical Vehicle (LTV). At the same time the company announced the VLRA 2 (originally presented as VLRB).

This VLRA 2 is ACMAT's recognition that the original VLRA needs to evolve in line with consumer requirements, including emissions and legislative compliance, if the company is to secure volume sales. However, clearly aware of its traditional customer base and their probable requirement for a vehicle of this type, ACMAT also offers a EURO 2 version of the vehicle with a far simpler non-electronically controlled engine.

Full details of the VLRA 2 can be found in the Trucks section.

ACMAT Light Tactical Vehicles (ALTVs) (ACMAT) 1407649

ACMAT Light Tactical Vehicle (ALTV) displayed at Eurosatory 2008
(ACMAT) 1391125

ACMAT Light Tactical Vehicle (ALTV) in long range patrol-type configuration (Shaun C Connors) 1391404

Description

The layout of the ACMAT LTV is entirely conventional, with the engine at the front, cab in the centre, and cargo area at the rear.

The ALTV is based on the strengthened chassis and modified running gear of an ACMAT Group African market light utility/pick-up worldwide platform. The conventional or crew-cab sections of the base design are retained, however, the bonnet and rear cargo areas are replaced by far more utilitarian flat-panelled ACMAT-designed replacements.

The ALTV is powered by a EURO 4 emissions compliant diesel engine, however, a far simpler EURO 1 emissions compliant engine is available for certain markets. A six-speed manual or five-speed automatic gearbox is fitted, this coupled to a two-speed transfer box.

Special equipment fitted as standard can include long-range fuel tanks to allow up to 1,600 km of travel, and a 50-litre water tank. Standard equipment includes four 20-litre jerrycans for additional fuel or water.

A wide range of additional equipment can be specified for the ALTV, this including a winch, runflat inserts for the tyres, ballistic protection kits, and assorted weapon mounts.

A protected version of the ALTV was displayed publicly for the first time at Eurosatory 2010.

Specifications

ALTV
Cab seating: dependant on configuration; up to 1 + 9
Configuration: 4 × 4
Weight:
  (kerb) 2,100 kg
  (laden) 3,500 kg
  (payload) 1,400 kg
  (GCW) 5,800 kg
Length: 5.3 m
Width: 1.9 m
Height: (cab) 1.77 m
Ground clearance: 260 mm
Track: 1.57 m
Wheelbase: 3.2 m
Angle of approach/departure: 35°/30°
Max speed: 170 km/h
Max range: 800-1,600 km
Fuel capacity: 80-160 litres
Max gradient: 80%
Side slope: 100%
Fording: 500 mm
Ditch crossing: 600 mm
Vertical obstacle: 350 mm
Engine: 2.5-litre 4-cylinder in-line turbocharged and intercooled water-cooled 4-stroke diesel developing 190 hp (140 kW) at 4,000 rpm and 450 N.m torque at 2,000 rpm
Gearbox: manual with 6 forward and 1 reverse gears, or fully automatic with 5 forward and 1 reverse gears
Transfer box: 2-speed with differential lock
Steering: power-assisted
Turning radius: 6.65 m
Suspension: independent double wishbone with coil-over-shock-absorber, front; leaf spring and shock-absorber, rear
Tyres: 245/75 R16
Brakes: ventilated discs front, drums rear; ABS fitted
Electrical system: 12/24 V

Status

In production. In service with undisclosed users.

Contractor

Ateliers de Constructions Mécaniques de l'Atlantique (ACMAT)

ACMAT VLRA (4 × 4) vehicles

Development

The ACMAT story began in 1948 when the company's founder started a business improving the durability/reliability of mass-produced trucks, for use in harsh operating environments. The ACMAT VLRA (*Véhicule de Liaison, de Reconnaissance et d'Appui*) was introduced in 1965 and has its origins in the VCOM (Overseas Combat Vehicle), 193 of which were supplied to the French Foreign Legion in Djibouti by ACMAT's predecessor (ALM) between 1963-1964. The VCOM design was modified to become the VLRA and ACMAT (*Ateliers de Construction Mécanique de l'Atlantique*) was established. The VLRA and its variants have been adopted by the French Army and many other countries throughout the world, many of these in Africa and other harsh operating environments. The design is also used for a variety of civil applications, for example by oil companies. Since production commenced, around 12,000 VLRA have been produced.

The ACMAT factory at Saint Nazaire, which was established in 1965, has the capacity to manufacture up to 1,200 vehicles of all types every year.

The base vehicle in the ACMAT range is the VLRA (4 × 4), of which over 80 assorted models have been available, including armoured versions, tactical, logistic and specialised variants such as ambulances. ACMAT vehicles have been supplied to at least 48 countries on five continents, company figures quoting 93 per cent of ACMAT sales as export.

In 1998, and in response to pending European requirements, ACMAT began development of the VLRB (armoured liaison and reconnaissance vehicle) based on the VLRA chassis, but with an emissions compliant engine, a fully automatic transmission, and an Anti-lock Braking System (ABS). In keeping with the ACMAT philosophy of modularity and interchangeability of components, this updated VLRB driveline (TCM 4 20) was designed to be fully transposable into any VLRA variant. Full details of the VLRB can be found in *Jane's Armour and Artillery*.

It was announced during 2006 that Renault Trucks had acquired ACMAT. The company had been in financial difficulty and looking for a buyer for some time, and during 2004 a bid by Malaysian company Pesaka Astana was defeated in the French courts. Following its acquisition of the company, Renault stated an intention to maintain the ACMAT brand along with its product range, and to continue the company's programme of research and development at its Saint-Nazaire facility.

In 2008 ACMAT announced the VLRA 2, the continued development of the ACMAT VLRA concept. Brief details of the VLRA 2 can be found elsewhere in this entry, with full details available elsewhere in this section.

In 2008 ACMAT also announced the ACMAT Light Tactical Vehicle (ALTV), a 3,500 kg GVW light utility vehicle which according to the manufacturer is built to the same levels of durability as the ACMAT VLRA. Full details of the ACMAT ALTV can be found in the Light vehicles section.

Description

The layout of the ACMAT VLRA (4 × 4) is conventional, with the engine at the front, cab in the centre and cargo area at the rear. The cab has a windscreen which can be folded forward onto the bonnet and a removable nylon canvas roof and side doors. A so-called 'European cab' (metal door and fabric top) and an all-metal cab are available. The spare wheel is mounted to the left of the driver's position, or in the rear cargo space. The cargo area at the rear has a drop tailgate, removable bows and nylon canvas covers. Seats can be fitted down the sides or centre of the cargo area for carrying personnel.

A primary strength of the ACMAT design is the continued interchangeability/commonality of components, examples here being axles, transfer case and engine.

With regard to the engine, a few early VLRA were built with a six-cylinder Ford petrol engine, but from around 1965 essentially the same (albeit evolving) Perkins diesel engine has been fitted. From around 1965 and until 1980/1981 the standard engine was the Perkins 6354.0 four-cylinder diesel developing 120 hp. By 1981 this had been replaced by an evolution of that engine, the 6354.4 which developed 135 hp. When Perkins stopped

Time-served ACMAT VLRA (4 × 4) trucks of the French Army have been returning to the ACMAT facility for a refurbishment since 2006 (Shaun C Connors) 1391119

production of the 6354.4, ACMAT bought up all the remaining stock, although by 2004 VLRA were being produced and fitted with the closest possible alternative, a Perkins Phazer 1 unit developing 145 hp (4 × 4), 160 hp (6 × 6) or 215 hp (tractor units). French Army VLRA had been fitted with the Phazer 1 engine from 1993. The TCM 4 20 (VLRB) driveline variant mentioned earlier became available for users of the VLRA who required emissions compliance, however this option has now been superseded by the introduction of the VLRA 2.

Special equipment fitted as standard to most variants includes long-range fuel tanks to allow up to 1,600 km of travel or 34 hours of cross-country operation, and a 200-litre water tank. Standard equipment also includes four jerrycans, two sand channels, twin-dry and oil-based air filtration equipment and a six-bladed 500 mm fan driven by twin fanbelts, as well as a specially designed water radiator. A heavy-duty all-welded steel chassis, gearbox and suspension are also employed. The transfer box and axles are of ACMAT design.

All vehicles are suppressed to the second degree (NATO standard) and a 3,000 kg winch can be fitted to the front of the vehicle if required. A 6,000 kg towing hook is standard and a multiposition version is also available for the artillery-towing role. Full EC lighting equipment is available if required, as is power-assisted steering. All VLRA vehicles can be produced in left- or right-hand drive forms.

The basic vehicle can be armed with a 5.56 or 7.62 mm machine gun, which is pedestal-mounted, and a 12.7 mm machine gun ring-mounted above the passenger's seat if required. Various types of weapon can be carried on the rear cargo area.

It is important to note the high degree of commonality of wearing parts throughout the entire range of ACMAT vehicles. Not only is the same engine used in every ACMAT VLRA vehicle (see above), but a commonality level of over 80 per cent exists across the entire range of ACMAT VLRA (4 × 4) and (6 × 6) chassis and cabs. While detailed items are the subject of continued research and development, the overall dimensions of the major components do not change. Thus, ACMAT is able to guarantee the availability of exchange components for the life-span of the vehicle.

Variants

VLRA variants
(Currently available)
TPK 4.20 VCT
Seven-seat command and communications vehicle. GVW is 6,500 kg, payload is up to 1,700 kg.

TPK 4.15 STL
12-seat multirole troop carrier. The flat rear platform measures 2.5 m × 2.1 m (L × W) with tilting and demountable side panels, and can be used to carry 10 passengers, cargo or a special purpose frame. The reinforced floor can accept a weapon support mounting. GVW is 6,500 kg, payload is up to 1,700 kg. Wheelbase is 3.3 m.

TPK 4.20 STL
14-seat multirole troop carrier. The flat rear platform measures 2.9 m × 2.1 m (L × W) with tilting and demountable side panels, and can be used to carry 12 passengers, cargo or a special purpose frame. The reinforced floor can accept a weapon support mounting. GVW is 7,500 kg, payload is up to 2,500 kg. Wheelbase is 3.6 m.

TPK 4.25 STL
16-seat multirole troop carrier. The flat rear platform measures 3.3 m × 2.1 m (L × W) with tilting and demountable side panels, and can be used to carry four passengers, cargo or a special purpose frame. The reinforced floor can accept a weapon support mounting. GVW is 6,500 kg, payload is up to 1,500 kg. Wheelbase is 3.3 m.

TPK 4.21 STL
11-seat double-cab multipurpose vehicle. The flat rear platform measures 1.65 m × 2.1 m (L × W) with tilting and demountable side panels, and can be used to carry 16 passengers, cargo or a special purpose frame. The reinforced floor can accept a weapon support mounting. GVW is 8,500 kg, payload is up to 3,000 kg. Wheelbase is 3.9 m.

ACMAT VLRA (4 × 4) of the French Army (Shaun C Connors) 1391120

ACMAT VLRA (4 × 4) of the French Army (Shaun C Connors) 1391123

TPK 4.25 SH
Load and shelter carrier. The flat rear platform measures 3.4 × 2.1 m (L × W) with twistlocks for carrying a SH 285A shelter. A 6 kVA generator set and spare wheel is carried on the reinforced front part of the platform. GVW is 8,500 kg, payload is up to 3,200 kg. Wheelbase is 3.9 m.

TPK 4.25 SCC/SCE
2,500-litre tanker for water (SCC) or fuel (SCE). GVW is 8,500 kg. Wheelbase is 3.9 m.

TPK 4.31 STL
15-seat double-cab multipurpose vehicle. The flat rear platform measures 2.5 m × 2.1 m (L × W) with tilting and demountable side panels, and can be used to carry eight passengers cargo or a special purpose frame. The reinforced floor can accept a weapon support mounting. GVW is 9,400 kg, payload is up to 3,400 kg. Wheelbase is 4.3 m.

TPK 4.36 STL
18-seat multipurpose vehicle. The flat rear platform measures 3.91 m × 2.1 m (L × W) with tilting and demountable side panels, and can be used to carry 16 passengers, cargo or a special purpose frame. The reinforced floor can accept a weapon support mounting. GVW is 9,400 kg, payload is up to 3,400 kg. Wheelbase is 4.3 m.

TPK 4.36 SH
Shelter carrier. The flat rear platform measures 4.01 m × 2.1 m (L × W) with twistlocks for carrying a SH 285A shelter. Up to 3 × 6 kVA generator sets and spare wheel can be carried on the reinforced front part of the platform. GVW is 9,400 kg, payload is up to 3,500 kg. Wheelbase is 4.3 m.

TPK 4.20 SL7
Light recovery vehicle. Provided with special tools and equipment together with an overhead gantry for light recovery tasks. GVW is 7,500 kg, payload is up to 1,500 kg. Wheelbase is 3.6 m.

TPK 4.36 SCM
Loading and material handling vehicle. This variant has a hydraulic crane located behind the cab. The crane arm has a full 360° traverse and can lift 900 kg at 6 m. GVW is 9,400 kg, payload is up to 2,500 kg. Wheelbase is 4.3 m.

TPK 4.25 PCR
Radio communication van. Body measures 3.31 m × 2.02 m × 1.675 m (L × W × H). Air conditioning is provided. GVW is 8,500 kg, payload is up to 2,500 kg. Wheelbase is 3.9 m.

TPK 4.25 SAM
Ambulance. Equipped to carry up to four casualties in a body measuring 3.31 × 2.02 × 1.675 m (L × W × H). Air conditioning is provided. GVW is 7,500 kg, payload is up to 1,500 kg. Wheelbase is 3.9 m.

New-build ACMAT VLRA (4 × 4) at the ACMAT facility (Shaun C Connors) 1391121

One of 50 time-served ACMAT VLRA (4 × 4) ambulances of the French Army at the ACMAT facility for a refurbishment. These vehicles received a new rear body and a 210 mm chassis extension (Shaun C Connors) 1391122

TPK 4.30 F

Multirole van. Maintenance and general mechanical repair, maintenance and repair of small arms, stores van, command post and so on. GVW is 9,400 kg, payload is up to 3,000 kg. Wheelbase is 4.3 m.

ACMAT trailers

ACMAT produces a range of two- and four-wheel trailers, with payloads of up to 6,000 kg and that have similar build quality to the VLRA product. These trailers are designed for maximum possible compatibility with the ACMAT range of vehicles and throughout the range, suspension systems, wheels, tyres, hubs (and bearings), braking and electrical systems are all shared with the ACMAT VLRA range of trucks.

VLRA 2

VLRA 2 (originally presented as VLRB) was first shown publicly at Eurosatory 2008 and is ACMAT's recognition that the original VLRA needs to evolve in line with consumer requirements, including emissions and legislative compliance, if the company is to continue to secure volume sales. However, clearly aware of its traditional customer base and their probable requirement for a vehicle of this type, ACMAT also offers a EURO 2 version of the vehicle with a far simpler non-electronically controlled engine.

The VLRA 2 in standard configuration has the same 3.3 m wheelbase as the original VLRA, but with an increased GVW of 8,000 kg (VLRA - 6,500 kg), this increasing to 10,500 kg (9,400 kg - VLRA) for the longest 4.3 m wheelbase models. The new vehicle strives to retain as much of the VLRA's durability/longevity as possible and while some of the original purpose-designed ACMAT driveline components (gearbox, and axles) will no longer be used, the basic vehicle retains many of the VLRA's best-known attributes, these including simple flat-panelled bodywork and an all-welded box-section heavy-duty chassis frame. The VLRA of course remains very much the traditional ACMAT product and the company has clearly stated that it has no plans to stop production of the type, or indeed even sideline it.

Full details of the VLRA 2 can be found elsewhere in this section.

Other variants
(Not currently available)
TPK 4.33 SB

Cross-country bus. The body can be configured as a personnel carrier, a mobile command post or as a casualty carrier.

ACMAT VLRA 2 displayed publicly for the first time at Eurosatory 2008 (Shaun C Connors) 1296125

TPK 4.32 SB

Cross-country bus. Available in two chassis lengths. The short version can carry up to 28 passengers and the long version up to 34. Air conditioning can be provided.

TPK 4.20 PMB

81 mm mortar carrier. The mortar can be fired from on board the vehicle.

TPK 4.20 SM3

Light reconnaissance and support vehicle. This parachute deployable and air transportable (4 × 4) troop-carrying vehicle has the capacity for 17 fully equipped soldiers in the rear cargo body together with a spare wheel housing. It can be adapted to carry a wide range of weapons. Payload up to 2,500 kg.

TPK 4.15 SM3

Patrol vehicle for special forces. This parachutable, air transportable (4 × 4) troop/cargo carrier has a carrying capacity of 15 fully equipped soldiers or 1,500 kg of cargo. An operating range of 900 km is available, and a 100-litre drinking water tank is standard. Virtually all wearing parts are identical to the TPK 4.20 SM3. This vehicle can be delivered by the Low Altitude Parachute Extraction System (LAPES).

TPK 4.15 FSP

Weapons carrier for special forces. Essentially the same as the TPK 4.15 SM3 but with provision to act as a light weapon carrier, typically a MILAN ATGW.

TPK 4.15 LRM

Multiple rocket-launcher vehicle. This vehicle mounts a 40-tube launcher for the Belgian LAU-97 multiple rocket system with a range of 8,000 m. Weight of this variant with the launcher loaded is 5,650 kg.

TPK 4.25 F

Workshop body vehicle. The workshop bodies will vary according to role. Payload up to 3,500 kg, according to type.

TPK 4.25 STL

Tanker with CSE 285 SCC frame. Can carry 2,500 litres of fuel or water.

TPK 4.20 BL

Light armoured vehicle. Multipurpose personnel carrier with internal space for up to 10 personnel.

TPK/TGM 4.20 FFM

Forest firefighting vehicle with 2,000-litre tank.

TPK/TGM 4.31 FFM

Forest firefighting vehicle with 2,000-litre tank and six-seat cab.

TPK/TGM 4.31 FPTL

Light fire pump water tender.

TPK 4.21 SM3

Double cabin patrol vehicle. The double cabin which has four doors and cab seating for the driver and five personnel. There is seating for a further 12 in the rear which is identical to the rear cargo area of the ACMAT TPK 4.15 SM3. The all-metal cab has roll-over bars incorporated and a heavy duty air conditioner is optional.

Specifications
TPK 4.20 VCT command and communication vehicle (current)
Cab seating: 1 +1
Configuration: 4 × 4
Weights:
    (laden) 6,500 kg
    (unladen) 4,800 kg
    (max load) 1,700 kg
    (max towed load) 3,500 kg
Length: 5.36 m
Width: 2.07 m
Height: (overall) 2.22 m
Ground clearance: 500 mm
Track:
    (front) 1.76 m
    (rear) 1.66 m
Wheelbase: 3.3 m
Angle of approach/departure: 43°/41°
Max road speed: 100 km/h
Range: 700 km
Fuel capacity: 210 litres
Max gradient: (laden) 65%
Fording: 900 mm
Engine: Perkins Phazer 1 6-cylinder in-line water-cooled 4-stroke diesel developing 145 hp (110 kW) at 2,600 rpm and 460 N.m torque at 1,450 rpm
Transfer box: ALM ACMAT 2-speed
Gearbox: manual with 4 forward and 1 reverse gears
Clutch: single dry plate (330 mm)
Steering: worm and nut

Turning radius: n/avail
Suspension: leaf springs and heavy duty double action hydraulic shock-absorbers, front and rear
Tyres: 335/80R 20
Brakes:
  (main) air/hydraulic
  (parking) mechanical
Electrical system: 24 V
Batteries: 2 × 12 V, 100 Ah

Status

In production. ACMAT vehicles have been supplied to at least 48 countries worldwide. Current known users include Bangladesh (approximately 10, ambulance), Benin, Burkina Faso, Cameroon, Chad, Côte d'Ivoire, Cyprus (Army, >120), Democratic Republic of Congo (including 20 from August 2004), Djibouti, France, Gabon, Gambia, Ireland, Libya (600 delivered, all types), Morocco (including 600 from 2008), Senegal, Somalia, Sweden, Togo, UK (10, specialist role) and Zimbabwe (50).

Contractor

ACMAT (*Ateliers de Construction Mécanique de l'Atlantique*) (now part of Renault Trucks Defense)

ACMAT VLRA (6 × 6) vehicles

Development

The ACMAT story began in 1948 when, for use in harsh operating environments, the company's founder started a business improving the durability/reliability of mass-produced trucks. The VLRA *(Véhicule de Liaison, de Reconnaissance et d'Appui)* was introduced in 1965 and has its origins in the VCOM (Overseas Combat Vehicle), 193 of which were supplied to the French Foreign Legion in Djibouti by ACMAT's predecessor (ALM) between 1963-1964. The VCOM design was modified to become the VLRA and Ateliers de Construction Mécanique de l'Atlantique (ACMAT) was established. Since production commenced around 12,000 VLRA have been produced, and the vehicle and its variants have been adopted by the French Army and many other countries throughout the world, many of these in Africa and other harsh operating environments. The design is also used for a variety of civil applications, for example by oil companies.

The base vehicle in the ACMAT range is the VLRA (4 × 4), of which over 80 assorted models have been available, including armoured versions, tactical, logistic and specialised variants such as ambulances. The ACMAT factory at Saint-Nazaire was established in 1965 and has the capacity to manufacture up to 1,200 vehicles of all types every year, and VLRA (6 × 6) vehicles may be regarded as versions of the VLRA (4 × 4) range enhanced by the addition of an extra axle at the rear.

ACMAT vehicles have been supplied to at least 48 countries on five continents, company figures quoting 93 per cent of ACMAT sales as export.

In 1998, and in response to pending European requirements, ACMAT began development of the VLRB (armoured liaison and reconnaissance vehicle) based on the VLRA chassis, but with an emissions compliant engine, a fully automatic transmission, and an Anti-lock Braking System (ABS). In keeping with the ACMAT philosophy of modularity and interchangeability of components, this updated VLRB driveline (TCM 4 20) was designed to be fully transposable in to any VLRA variant. Full details of the VLRB can be found in *Jane's Armour and Artillery.*

It was announced during 2006 that Renault Trucks had acquired ACMAT. The company had been in financial difficulty and looking for a buyer for some time, and during 2004 a bid by Malaysian company Pesaka Astana was defeated in the French courts. Following its acquisition of the company, Renault stated an intention to maintain the ACMAT brand along with its product range, and to continue the company's programme of research and development at its Saint-Nazaire facility.

In 2008 ACMAT announced the VLRA 2, the continued development of the ACMAT VLRA concept. Brief details of the VLRA 2 can be found elsewhere in this entry, with full details available elsewhere in this section.

In 2008 ACMAT also announced the ACMAT Light Tactical Vehicle (ALTV), a 3,500 kg GVW light utility vehicle built to the same levels of durability as the ACMAT VLRA. Full details of the ACMAT ALTV can be found in the Light vehicles section.

Description

The layout of the ACMAT VLRA 6 × 6 is conventional, with the engine at the front, cab in the centre and cargo/load area at the rear. The cab has a windscreen which can be folded forward onto the bonnet and a removable nylon canvas roof and side doors. A so-called 'European cab' (metal door and fabric top) and an all-metal cab are available. The spare wheel is mounted to the left of the driver's position, or in the rear cargo space. The cargo area at the rear has a drop tailgate, removable bows and nylon canvas covers. Seats can be fitted down the sides or centre of the cargo area for carrying personnel.

A primary strength of the ACMAT design is the continued interchangeability/commonality of components, examples here being axles, transfer case and engine.

With regard to the engine, a few early VLRA were built with a six-cylinder Ford petrol engine, but from around 1965 essentially the same (albeit evolving) Perkins diesel engine has been fitted. From around 1965 and

ACMAT VLRA (6 × 6) (Shaun C Connors)   1391124

until 1980/1981 the standard engine was the Perkins 6354.0 four-cylinder diesel developing 120 hp. By 1981 this had been replaced by an evolution of that engine, the 6354.4 which developed 135 hp. When Perkins stopped production of the 6354.4, ACMAT bought up all the remaining stock, although by 2004 VLRA were being produced and fitted with the closest possible alternative, a Perkins Phazer 1 unit developing 145 hp (4 × 4), 160 hp (6 × 6) or 215 hp (tractor units). French Army VLRA had been fitted with the Phazer 1 engine from 1993. The TCM 4 20 (VLRB) driveline variant mentioned earlier became available for users of the VLRA who required emissions compliance, however this option has now been superseded by the introduction of the VLRA 2.

Special equipment fitted as standard to most variants includes two 180- or 210-litre fuel tanks to allow up to 1,600 km of travel or 34 hours of cross-country operation, and a 200-litre water tank. Standard equipment also includes jerrycans, sand channels, twin-dry and oil-based air filtration equipment and a six-bladed 500 mm fan driven by twin fanbelts, as well as a specially designed water radiator. A heavy duty all-welded steel chassis, gearbox and suspension are also employed. The transfer box and axles are of ACMAT design.

All vehicles are suppressed to the second degree (NATO standard) and a winch can be fitted to the front of the vehicle if required. A 6,000 kg towing hook is standard. Full EU lighting equipment is available. All ACMAT VLRA (6 × 6) vehicles can be produced in left- or right-hand drive forms.

The basic vehicle can be armed with a 5.56 or 7.62 mm machine gun, which is pedestal-mounted, and a 12.7 mm machine gun ring-mounted above the passenger's seat if required. Various types of weapon can be carried on the rear cargo area.

There are currently nine base variants in the ACMAT (6 × 6) range.

Variants

VLRA 2

VLRA 2 (originally presented as VLRB) was first shown publicly at Eurosatory 2008. It is ACMAT's evolution of the original VLRA. Clearly aware of its traditional customer base and their probable requirement for a vehicle of this type, ACMAT also offers a EURO 2 version of the vehicle with a far simpler non-electronically controlled engine.

The VLRA 2 in standard configuration has the same 3.3 m wheelbase as the original VLRA, but with an increased GVW of 8,000 kg (VLRA – 6,500 kg), this increasing to 10,500 kg (9,400 kg – VLRA) for the longest 4.3 m wheelbase models. The new vehicle strives to retain as much of the VLRA's durability/longevity as possible and while some of the original purpose-designed ACMAT driveline components (gearbox, and axles) will no longer be used, the basic vehicle retains many of the VLRA's best-known attributes, these including simple flat-panelled bodywork and an all-welded box-section heavy-duty chassis frame. The VLRA of course remains very much the traditional ACMAT product and the company has clearly stated that it has no plans to stop production of the type, or indeed even sideline it.

The VLRA 2 has only been shown in (4 × 4) configuration, however, it would be logical to assume that to meet any pending requirement a (6 × 6) configuration could be produced.

Full details of the VLRA 2 can be found elsewhere in this section.

VLRA (6 × 6) variants
(Currently available)

TPK 6.40 STL

18-seat multipurpose troop carrier. The 3.91 m × 2.4 m (L × W) cargo area has hinged removable side panels and can carry up to 16 personnel. GVW is 12,000 kg, payload up to 4,900 kg. Wheelbase is 4.1 m.

TPK 6.40 SH

Shelter carrier vehicle. Platform measures 4.01 m × 2.4 m (L × W). GVW is 12,000 kg, payload up to 5,200 kg. Wheelbase is 4.1 m.

TPK 6.50 SH

Shelter carrier vehicle. This variant can carry an AT 15 or ATM 15 shelter. Platform measures 5 m × 2.4 m. GVW is 12,000 kg, payload up to 5,000 kg. Wheelbase is 4.5 m.

TPK 6.40 SCC/SCE
4,500-litre tanker for water (SCC) or fuel (SCE). GVW is 12,000 kg. Wheelbase is 4.10 m.

TPK 6.41 STL
19-seat double-cab multipurpose vehicle. The flat rear platform measures 4.9 m × 2.4 m (L × W) with tilting and demountable side panels, and can be used to carry 20 passengers cargo or a special purpose frame. The reinforced floor can accept a weapon support mounting. GVW is 12,000 kg, payload is up to 4,500 kg. Wheelbase is 4.5 m.

TPK 6.50 STL
22-seat multipurpose vehicle. The flat rear platform measures 3.26 × 2.4 m (L × W) with tilting and demountable side panels, and can be used to carry 14 passengers cargo or a special purpose frame. The reinforced floor can accept a weapon support mounting. GVW is 12,000 kg, payload is up to 4,500 kg. Wheelbase is 4.35 m.

TPK 6.35 SL7
Breakdown vehicle with recovery gantry. GVW is 12,000 kg, GCW is 22,000 kg. Wheelbase is 3.85 m.

TPK 6.40 WRT
Recovery vehicle. This 5,000 kg capacity variant has a hydraulic crane located behind the cab. The crane arm can lift 20 t/m, and 5,000 kg at 4 m radius. Kerb weight is 12,000 kg, GCW is 22,000 kg. Wheelbase is 4.1 m.

TPK 6.35 TSR
Tractor truck. This variant can have a two- or four-door cab and weighs 6,000 kg unladen; total (GCW) weight is 22,000 kg. The engine is uprated to 210 hp and fuel capacity is reduced to two 155-litre tanks so the operating range is 800 km. One possible semi-trailer for this vehicle is the ACMAT SR 490 with brakes, axles and suspension interchangeable with the VLRA 6 × 6 range. The semi-trailer platform can accommodate a 6.096 m/20 ft ISO shelter.

TPK 6.50 APL
This variant is fitted with a Load Handling System (LHS) of the DROPS/PLS-type. GVW is 12,000 kg, GCW is 22,000 kg. Wheelbase is 4.05 m.

ACMAT trailers
ACMAT produces a range of two- and four-wheel trailers, with payloads of up to 6,000 kg and that have similar build quality to the VLRA product. These trailers are designed for maximum possible compatibility with the ACMAT range of vehicles and throughout the range, suspension systems, wheels, tyres, hubs (and bearings), braking and electrical systems are all shared with the ACMAT VLRA range of trucks.

VLRA (6 × 6) variants
(Not currently available)
TPK 6.40 SM3
Personnel carrier for up to 18 passengers or cargo carrier for loads up to 5,000-5,600 kg. The vehicle can also be configured as a weapons carrier. The side panels are fixed.

TPK 6.41 GBS
Tipper. Equipped with rear tipper body and a loading and handling crane with a capacity of 7.2 tonnes at 1 m.

TPK 6.50 BL/CTL
Vehicle with armoured cab. Fitted with a cargo body or can carry up to 10 troops under armoured protection.

TPK 6.40 CSD
NBC decontamination vehicle. This variant has a rear deck with foldable and extending rear and side panels to provide 750 mm wide walkways around the rear area. The rear area carries a motor pump, a 3,000-litre tank and stowage for decontamination equipment and chemicals. Also carried is a diesel-powered UMTH 1000 II hydraulic unit to provide steam and hot water under pressure.

TPK 6.41 VPC
Weapon carrier with six-seat double cab. The rear platform can accommodate a twin 20 mm air defence gun; the weapon can be fired from the platform.

TPK 6.41 SH/STL
Shelter carrier vehicle. The flat rear platform can carry an ATM 15 or AT 15 shelter for the Horizon or Samantha radar systems.

TPK 6.40 SC
Tanker vehicle. Provided with 4,500-litre tank for fuel or water.

TPK 6.35 FFL
Forest firefighting vehicle. Provided with 3,500-litre tanker body.

TPK 6.41 FFL
Forest firefighting vehicle. Provided with 3,500-litre tanker body and six-seat cab.

TPK 6.35 TSR 3 EC
Tractor truck with four-door extended cab produced for use with the ROLAND air defence missile system.

TPK 6.35/SR 475
Tractor truck with ACMAT SR 475 8,000-litre tanker semi-trailer.

TPK 6.35 TSR/SR 475 FFGC
Configured as firefighting tanker vehicle/semi-trailer combination with 8,500-litre tanker semi-trailer.

Specifications
TPK 6.40 STL (current)
Cab seating: 1 + 1
Configuration: 6 × 6
Weight:
　(laden) 12,000 kg
　(unladen) 7,100 kg
　(max load) 4,900 kg
　(max towed load) 10,000 kg
Load area: 3.91 × 2.4 m
Length: 6.91 m
Width: 2.4 m
Height: (overall) 2.72 m
Ground clearance: 480 mm
Track:
　(front) 1.76 m
　(rear) 1.8 m
Wheelbase: 4.1 m
Angle of approach/departure: 44°/41°
Max road speed: 85 km/h
Range: 1,200 km
Fuel capacity: 2 × 210 litres
Max gradient: 55%
Side slope: 30%
Fording: 900 mm
Engine: Perkins Phazer 1 6-cylinder in-line water-cooled 4-stroke diesel developing 160 hp (120 kW) at 2,600 rpm and 520 N.m torque at 1,600 rpm
Gearbox: manual with 5 forward and 1 reverse gears
Clutch: single dry plate (356 mm)
Transfer box: 2-speed
Steering: hydraulic power-assisted
Turning radius: n/avail
Suspension: leaf springs and heavy-duty double action hydraulic shock-absorbers
Tyres: 335/80R 20
Brakes:
　(main) air/hydraulic
　(parking) mechanical
Electrical system: 24 V
Batteries: 2 × 12 V, 100 Ah

Status
In production. In service with the French Armed Forces and numerous other countries.

Contractor
ACMAT (*Ateliers de Construction Mécanique de l'Atlantique*) (now part of Renault Trucks Defense)

ACMAT VLRA 2

Development
The ACMAT VLRA 2 is essentially the continued evolution of the ACMAT VLRA, full details of which can be found elsewhere in this section.
　The ACMAT story began in 1948 when, for use in harsh operating environments, the company's founder started a business improving the

ACMAT VLRA 2 displayed publicly for the first time at Eurosatory 2008 (Shaun C Connors)
1296125

ACMAT VLRA 2 (Shaun C Connors) 1391405

durability/reliability of mass-produced trucks. The original VLRA (*Véhicule de Liaison, de Reconnaissance et d'Appui*) was introduced in 1965 and has its origins in the VCOM (Overseas Combat Vehicle), 193 of which were supplied to the French Foreign Legion in Djibouti by ACMAT's predecessor (ALM) between 1963-1964. The VCOM design was modified to become the VLRA and Ateliers de Constructions Mécaniques de l'Atlantique (ACMAT) was established.

Since the mid-1960s around 12,000 VLRA have been produced and supplied to at least 48 countries on five continents, company figures quoting 93 per cent of ACMAT sales as export.

The ACMAT factory at Saint Nazaire was established in 1965 and has the capacity to manufacture up to 1,200 vehicles of all types every year.

It was announced during 2006 that Renault Trucks had acquired ACMAT. The company had been in financial difficulty and looking for a buyer for some time, and during 2004 a bid by Malaysian company Pesaka Astana was defeated in the French courts. Following its acquisition of the company, Renault stated an intention to maintain the ACMAT brand along with its product range, and to continue the company's programme of research and development at its Saint-Nazaire facility.

VLRA 2 (originally presented as VLRB and VLRA EURO 5) was first shown publicly at Eurosatory 2008 and is ACMAT's recognition that the original VLRA needs to evolve in line with consumer requirements, including emissions and legislative compliance, if the company is to secure volume sales. However, clearly aware of its traditional customer base and their probable requirement for a vehicle of this type, ACMAT also offers a EURO 2 version of the vehicle with a far simpler non-electronically controlled engine.

In 2008 ACMAT also announced the Light Tactical Vehicle (LTV), a 3,500 kg GVW light utility vehicle that according to the company is built to the same levels of durability as the ACMAT VLRA. Full details of the ACMAT LTV can be found in the Light vehicles section.

An armoured version of the VLRA 2 was displayed publicly for the first time at Eurosatory 2010.

Description

The layout of the ACMAT VLRA 2 follows that of the standard VLRA and is entirely conventional, with the engine at the front, cab in the centre, and cargo area at the rear. The cab has a windscreen which can be folded forward onto the bonnet and can either be of all-metal construction, have metal doors and a fabric top, or have a removable nylon canvas roof and side doors.

The multirole rear flatbed can be configured to carry water or fuel tanks, shelters or containers, recovery equipment, or be fitted with a conventional dropside body for a cargo/troop-carrying role. When used in the troop carrying role at least 14 personnel can be carried on bench seats in the rear of the vehicle, an additional three in the cab.

An armoured version of the VLRA 2 was displayed publicly for the first time at Eurosatory 2010 (Shaun C Connors) 1391389

The VLRA 2 is powered by a Volvo Group EURO 5 emissions compliant diesel engine, however, a far simpler non-electronic EURO 2 emissions compliant engine is available for certain markets. A six-speed ZF manual or five-speed automatic gearbox is coupled to a new ACMAT two-speed transfer box.

Special equipment, fitted as standard, includes long-range fuel tanks to allow 1,400 km of travel, and a 180-litre water tank. Standard equipment includes four 20-litre jerrycans for additional fuel or water.

A heavy-duty all-welded steel chassis is employed, the required strength being built in and achieved without reinforcement. Beam-type axles (with differential locks) are sprung by parabolic multi-leaf springs.

A wide range of additional equipment can be specified, this including a winch, a Central Tyre Inflation System (CTIS), runflat inserts for the tyres, ballistic and blast protection kits, and assorted weapon mounts.

Specifications

VLRA 2
Cab seating: 1 + 2 (up to 14 in rear)
Configuration: 4 × 4
Weight:
  (kerb) 6,000 kg
  (laden) 8,000-10,000 kg
  (payload) 2,000-4,500 kg
Length: 5.5-6.5 m
Width: 2.2 m
Height: 2.2 m
Ground clearance: 350 mm
Track: 1.83 m
Wheelbase: 3.3-4.3 m
Angle of approach/departure: 46°/45°
Max speed: 110 km/h
Max range: 1,400 km
Fuel capacity: 2 × 180 litres
Max gradient: 65%
Side slope: 30%
Fording: 1 m
Ditch crossing: 800 mm
Vertical obstacle: 500 mm
Engine: Volvo Group 5-litre 6-cylinder in-line turbocharged water-cooled 4-stroke diesel developing 190 hp (140 kW) at 2,300 rpm and 680 N.m torque at 1,200 rpm
Gearbox: ZF manual with 6 forward and 1 reverse gears, or fully automatic with 5 forward and 1 reverse gears
Transfer box: ACMAT 2-speed with differential lock
Steering: power-assisted
Turning radius: 7.25 m
Suspension: parabolic multi-leaf springs and shock-absorbers
Tyres: 365/80R 20 Michelin XZL (CTIS and runflat options)
Brakes: discs all-round, air-over-hydraulic, ABS can be disabled
Electrical system: 24 V

Status

In production. In service with undisclosed users.

Contractor

ACMAT (*Ateliers de Construction Mécanique de l'Atlantique*) (now part of Renault Trucks Defense)

ACMAT VLA (4 × 4) ALM WPK 4.40 STL and SH 5,000 kg trucks

Development

A prototype of the ACMAT VLA (4 × 4) ALM WPK 4.40 5,000 kg truck was first shown in 1992 as a (4 × 4) version of the ACMAT WPK (8 × 8) vehicle, full details of which can be found elsewhere in this section. The vehicle was produced as a private venture and forms part of the ACMAT Medium Tactical Vehicle (MTV) family, being described as a logistics transport vehicle.

It was announced during 2006 that Renault Trucks had acquired ACMAT. The company had been in financial difficulty and looking for a buyer for some time, and during 2004 a bid by Malaysian company Pesaka Astana was defeated in the French courts. Following its acquisition of the company, Renault stated an intention to maintain the ACMAT brand along with its product range, and to continue the company's programme of research and development at its Saint-Nazaire facility.

Description

The WPK 4.40 has a semi-forward control steel cab with a hard- or soft-top and seats for the driver and one passenger. A 12.7 mm machine gun can be mounted on the roof over the passenger's seat and the one-piece windscreen can be folded forward or dismounted. To the rear of the cab is the multipurpose cargo body with drop sides, drop tailgate, removable bows and a tarpaulin cover.

Two variants are currently available although it can be assumed that the range of models could expand as required. Current models are the WPK 4.40 SH shelter carrier and the WPK 4.40 STL multipurpose vehicle. Both

ACMAT MTV (4 × 4) WPK 4.40 SH/STL 4,000 kg logistic vehicle (ACMAT)
0044290

ACMAT VLA (6 × 6) ALM WPK 6.65 APL 7,500 kg forward logistic support vehicle fitted with a Marrel AL 10,000 DM Ampliroll load handling system (Shaun C Connors)
0536749

are basically similar, and both are air transportable by C-130 and C-160 transport aircraft. The rear area can be configured to carry 20 troops, ammunition pallets or other stores. The WPK 4.40 SH can be configured to carry a shelter or container.

Standard equipment includes a 24 V electrical system and one or two fuel tanks to provide a range of up to 1,300 km. A 170-litre water tank is mounted between the body and the chassis.

Specifications
Cab seating: 1 + 1 (up to 20 in rear)
Configuration: 4 × 4
Weight:
　(laden, STL version) 11,000 kg
　(unladen, STL version) 6,000 kg
　(laden, SH version) 11,000 kg
　(unladen, SH version) 5,500 kg
　(max load, STL version) 5,000 kg
　(max load, SH version) 5,500 kg
　(towed load) 8,000 kg
Load area: 5.19 × 2.4 m
Length: 6.645 m
Width: 2.4 m
Height: (unladen) 2.895 m
Ground clearance: 510 mm
Wheelbase: 3.9 m
Track: 1.95 m
Angle of approach/departure: 35°/30°
Max speed:
　(high range) 100 km/h
　(low range) 50 km/h
Fuel capacity: 1 or 2 × 210 litres
Range: up to 1,300 km
Gradient: (laden) 65%
Side slope: 30%
Fording: 1 m
Engine: Perkins 6-cylinder turbocharged and water-cooled diesel developing 180 hp (132 kW) at 2,600 rpm. Perkins Phazer 1 developing 210 hp (154 kW) at 2,600 rpm from 2005
Transmission: Type S 6.65 with 6 forward and 1 reverse gears
Transfer box: ALM/ACMAT Type AL450 2-speed
Steering: hydraulic power-assisted
Suspension: semi-elliptic 80 mm wide leaf springs and heavy duty telescopic shock-absorbers
Brakes: air/hydraulic (EU standard)
Tyres: 375/70R 20
Electrical system: 24 V
Batteries: 2 × 12 V, 100 Ah

Status
Production as required. In service with the French Army (40).

Contractor
ACMAT (*Ateliers de Construction Mécanique de l'Atlantique*) (now part of Renault Trucks Defense)

ACMAT VLA (6 × 6) ALM WPK 6.65 STL, SH and APL 7,500 kg trucks

Development
A prototype of the ACMAT VLA (6 × 6) ALM WPK 6.65 7,500 kg truck was first shown in mid-1994 as a (6 × 6) version of the ACMAT WPK (8 × 8), full details of which can be found elsewhere in this section. The vehicle was produced as a private venture and forms part of the ACMAT Medium Tactical Vehicle (MTV) family, being described as a forward logistics support vehicle.

It was announced during 2006 that Renault Trucks had acquired ACMAT. The company had been in financial difficulty and looking for a buyer for some time, and during 2004 a bid by Malaysian company Pesaka Astana

was defeated in the French courts. Following the acquisition of the company, Renault stated an intention to maintain the ACMAT brand along with its product range, and to continue the company's programme of research and development at its Saint-Nazaire facility.

Description
The WPK 6.65 has a semi-forward control steel cab with a hard- or soft-top and seats for the driver and one passenger. A 12.7 mm machine gun can be mounted on the roof over the passenger's seat and the one-piece windscreen can be folded forward or dismounted. To the rear of the cab is the multipurpose cargo body with drop sides, drop tailgate, removable bows and a tarpaulin cover.

Three variants are currently available although it can be assumed that the range of models could expand as required. The STL and SH models mirror similar models in the WPK (4 × 4) and (8 × 8) ranges, the WPK 6.55 STL being a multipurpose carrier and the WPK 6.65 SH being a dedicated shelter carrier. Both are basically similar, and both are air transportable by C-130 and C-160 transport aircraft. The rear area of the STL variant can be configured to carry a 4.57 m/15 ft shelter, ammunition pallets or other stores. The SH variant can be configured to carry a 6.096 m/20 ft shelter or ISO container weighing up to 6,000 kg.

The third model, the WPK 6.65 APL, is fitted with a Marrel AL 10,000 DM Ampliroll load handling system.

Standard equipment for all models includes a 24 V electrical system and two fuel tanks to provide a range of 1,000 km. A 170-litre water tank is mounted between the body and the chassis.

Specifications
Cab seating: 1 + 1
Configuration: 6 × 6
Weight:
　(laden, STL variant) 16,000 kg
　(unladen, STL variant) 8,500 kg
　(laden, SH variant) 16,000 kg
　(unladen, SH variant) 8,000 kg
　(laden, APL variant) 16,000 kg
　(unladen, APL variant) 8,000 kg
　(max load, STL variant) 7,500 kg
　(max load, SH variant) 8,000 kg
　(max load, APL variant) 8,000 kg
　(towed load) 8,000 kg
Length: 7.445 m
Width: (unladen) 2.4 m
Height: 2.895 m
Ground clearance: 510 mm
Wheelbase: 4.2 m
Track: 1.95 m

ACMAT VLA (6 × 6) ALM WPK 6.65 SH 7,500 kg forward logistic support vehicle (ACMAT)
0044291

Angle of approach/departure: 35°/30°
Max speed:
  (high range) 100 km/h
  (low range) 50 km/h
Fuel capacity: 365 litres: 210 litres (LH-side tank), 135 litres (RH-side tank)
Range: 1,000 km
Gradient: (laden) 55%
Side slope: 30%
Fording: 1 m
Engine: Perkins Phazer 1 6-cylinder turbocharged and water-cooled diesel developing 210 hp (154 kW) at 2,600 rpm
Transmission: Type S 6.65 with 6 forward and 1 reverse gears
Transfer box: ALM/ACMAT Type AL450 2-speed
Steering: hydraulic power-assisted
Suspension: semi-elliptic springs with heavy duty telescopic shock-absorbers, front, inverted leaf springs with reaction rods, rear
Brakes: air/hydraulic (EU standard)
Tyres: 375/70R 20
Electrical system: 24 V
Batteries: 2 × 12 V, 100 Ah

Status

Production as required. A single vehicle has been supplied to the French Army.

Contractor

ACMAT (*Ateliers de Construction Mécanique de l'Atlantique*) (now part of Renault Trucks Defense)

ACMAT VLA (8 × 8) ALM WPK 8,000 kg logistic vehicles

Development

The ACMAT VLA (8 × 8) ALM WPK 8,000 kg logistic vehicle was first shown in 1987 and was primarily designed to be a front-line carrier for various forms of communications and radar shelters and containers. The vehicle was designed to a French Army requirement and is air transportable.

These vehicles acted as the base model for ACMAT's Medium Tactical Vehicle (MTV) family, the (4 × 4) model first being shown in 1992, a (6 × 6) model following in 1994.

It was announced during 2006 that Renault Trucks had acquired ACMAT. The company had been in financial difficulty and looking for a buyer for some time, and during 2004 a bid by Malaysian company Pesaka Astana was defeated in the French courts. Following its acquisition of the company, Renault stated an intention to maintain the ACMAT brand along with its product range, and to continue the company's programme of research and development at its Saint-Nazaire facility.

Description

The ACMAT VLA (8 × 8) ALM WPK chassis has a full (8 × 8) drive configuration with both front axles being of the steer-drive type. As with all other vehicles in the ACMAT range, a high degree of component commonality has been maintained, with many components of the (8 × 8) vehicle being the same as those used with the ACMAT (4 × 4) and (6 × 6) VLRA and WPK models. The main visual change on the (8 × 8), apart from the two twin-axle groupings, is to the cab, which is a semi-forward control design. The cab may be either soft- or metal-topped with the dismountable windscreen folding forward on both types. The metal-topped version has provision for a 12.7 mm machine gun ring mounting over a roof hatch.

Under the rear carrier platform is provision for a spare wheel, side storage lockers and a locker at the rear for a shelter access ladder housing. Towing hooks are provided front and rear. A toolkit is provided.

Data has been released for four variants, although it may be assumed that these could be joined by others as required. The WPK 8.70 STL is a multipurpose carrier, the WPK 8.70 SH and WPK 8.75 SH are dedicated shelter carriers, and all three are basically similar with the WPK 8.75 SH having a 980 mm longer overall length. The rear area of the STL variant can be configured to carry 24 people on centre-line mounted outward facing bench seats, a 4.57 m/15 ft shelter or container, ammunition pallets or other stores. The 8.70 SH variant is configured to carry a 4.57 m/15 ft shelter or container, the 8.75 SH variant to carry a 6.096 m/20 ft ISO shelter or container.

The WPK 8.70 APL variant is configured to carry a Marrel 100 NB Ampliroll load handling system.

A single side-mounted 210-litre fuel tank is standard on all variants, with the STL variant having a second (opposite) side-mounted 210-litre tank. The SH and STL variants have an under-platform 170-litre tank used for water on the STL, or additional fuel or water on the SH variant.

Specifications
Cab seating: 1 + 1
Configuration: 8 × 8
Weight:
  (laden, STL variant) 18,000 kg
  (unladen, STL variant) 8,000 kg
  (laden, 8.70 SH variant) 14,000 kg
  (unladen, 8.70 SH variant) 7,000 kg
  (laden, 8.75 SH variant) 14,000 kg
  (unladen, 8.75 SH variant) 7,000 kg
  (laden, APL variant) 14,000 kg
  (unladen, APL variant) 8,000 kg
  (max load, STL variant) 10,000 kg
  (max load, 8.70 SH variant) 7,000 kg
  (max load, 8.75 SH variant) 7,000 kg
  (max load, APL variant) 6,000 kg
Length:
  (STL variant) 7.5 m
  (8.70 SH variant) 7.5 m
  (8.75 SH variant) 8.74 m
  (APL variant, with flatrack) 7.25 m
Width: 2.4 m
Height: (cab roof, unladen) 2.725 m
Ground clearance: 300 mm
Track: 1.95 m
Wheelbase: 1.22 m + 3.75 m (8.75 SH, variant 4.6 m) + 1.22 m
Angle of approach/departure: (STL variant) 35°/33°
Max speed:
  (high range) 100 km/h
  (low range) 50 km/h
Range:
  (STL variant) 1,000 km
  (8.70 SH variant with 380 litres) 800 km
  (8.75 SH variant with 380 litres) 800 km
  (APL variant) 500 km
Fuel capacity:
  (STL variant) 2 × 210 litres
  (8.70 SH variant) 210 litres + 170 litres optional
  (8.75 SH variant) 210 litres + 170 litres optional
  (APL variant) 210 litres
Max gradient: (laden) 55%
Side slope: 30%
Fording: 1 m
Engine: Perkins Phazer 1 6-cylinder turbocharged and water-cooled diesel developing 210 hp (154 kW) at 2,900 rpm
Gearbox: Type S 6.65 manual with 6 forward and 1 reverse gears
Clutch: single dry plate (356 mm (14 inch))
Transfer box: ALM ACMAT type AL 450 2 speed
Steering: hydraulic power-assisted
Suspension: slide-mounted inverted leaf springs front and rear with radius arms mounted on silent blocks; telescopic shock-absorbers, front only
Tyres: 375/70R 20
Brakes: air/hydraulic (EEC standard)
Electrical system: 24 V
Batteries: 2 × 12 V, 100 Ah

Status

Production as required. In service with France and Morocco.

Contractor

ACMAT (*Ateliers de Construction Mécanique de l'Atlantique*) (now part of Renault Trucks Defense)

ACMAT VLA 8.75 SH (8 × 8) of the Moroccan Army (Shaun C Connors)
1296168

Renault TRM 4000 (4 × 4) 4,000 kg truck

Development

The Renault TRM 4000 (4 × 4) 4,000 kg truck was selected to be the standard vehicle in its class in the French Army which, in the early 1970s, stated that it then had a requirement for 15,000 vehicles of this type. Production commenced at Renault's Blainville facility in 1973. At the end of 1987 the French Army's adjusted total requirement was 7,500. Production is complete and while the type remains in French Army service, numbers are reducing.

Renault TRM 4000 (4 × 4) 4,000 kg truck. The adjustable tarpaulin is at standard height (Pierre Touzin) 1120403

Renault TRM 4000 (4 × 4) 4,000 kg truck (Shaun C Connors) 1190212

Description

The Renault TRM 4000 (4 × 4) 4,000 kg truck is essentially a commercial vehicle (the Saviem SM8) modified to meet the requirements of the French Army and uses proven commercial components, including cab, engine, transmission, chassis and axles.

The basic model has single rear wheels and a payload of 4,000 kg but there is also a model with dual rear wheels and a payload of 5,800 kg. The chassis consists of longitudinal side members with the cross-members welded into position. The two-door cab (type 812) is of all-steel construction and is of the forward control type. It can be tilted forward to an angle of 50° to allow access to the engine and was available delivered with an observation hatch in the roof. The rear cargo area has drop sides, drop tailgate, removable bows and a tarpaulin cover, and removable seats can be installed down the centre or sides of the vehicle.

Optional equipment included long-range fuel tanks, different tyres, 4,500 kg capacity winch, twin rear wheels, differential lock, additional seat in the cab, exhaust retarder, 24 V electrical system, blackout lights, 12-pin current outlet inspection socket on the dashboard and a cab which can be split at door level to reduce overall height for air transport.

Variants included: a Crotale missile carrier vehicle complete with hydraulic crane, a crane truck, a dump truck, firefighting vehicles, a light recovery vehicle, a 5,000-litre tanker/refueller (Decauville), a radar carrier, a van/command vehicle and a water tanker.

Specifications

Renault TRM 4000
Cab seating: 1 + 1
Configuration: 4 × 4
Weight:
  (laden, road) 11,200 kg
  (laden, off-road) 10,000 kg
  (unladen) 5,680 kg
  (max load, road) 5,340 kg
  (max load, off-road) 4,320 kg
  (towed load) 6,000 kg
Load area: 4.48 × 2.296 m
Length: 6.538 m
Width: 2.47 m
Height:
  (cab) 2.75 m
  (tarpaulin) 3.26 m
  (loadbed) 1.26 m
Ground clearance: 280 mm

Track:
  (front) 1.836 m
  (rear) 2.018 m
Wheelbase: 3.85 m
Angle of approach/departure: 37°/39°
Max speed: (road) 87 km/h
Range: 700 km
Fuel capacity: 150 litres
Max gradient: 50%
Max side slope: 30%
Fording: 900 mm
Engine: Renault model 797 6-cylinder water-cooled 4-stroke diesel developing 133 hp (99 kW) at 2,900 rpm
Gearbox: ET 301 manual with 5 forward and 1 reverse gears
Clutch: single dry plate
Transfer box: G 300 2-speed
Steering: cam and roller with hydraulic power assistance
Turning radius: 10 m
Suspension: leaf springs with Evidgom pads, hydraulic shock-absorbers
Tyres: 12.00 × 20
Brakes:
  (main) dual circuit, air, drums all-round
  (parking) mechanical
Electrical system: 24 V
Batteries: 2 × 12 V, 95 Ah
Alternator: 25/30 A

Status

Production complete. In service with the French Army and other undisclosed countries.

Contractor

Renault Trucks Defense

Berliet GBC 8 KT (6 × 6) 4,000 kg truck

Development

In the 1950s, Berliet developed a (6 × 6) truck for use in North Africa called the Gazelle. With modifications, it was subsequently adopted by the French Army in the late 1950s and, by the time production had been completed, over 19,000 trucks had been built, 17,000 of these for the French Army.

In May 1997 it was announced that 2,800 French Army GBC 8 KT trucks were to be upgraded to Renault GBC 180 standard. The programme now calls for 5,620 GBC 8 KT trucks to be upgraded, all but a handful of which had been completed by October 2010. Full details of the GBC 180 can be found elsewhere in this section.

Description

The layout of the Berliet GBC 8 KT is conventional, with the engine at the front, cab in the centre and cargo area at the rear. The two-door cab has a removable top, there are removable door tops and the windscreen can be folded forward onto the bonnet. The rear cargo area is provided with a drop tailgate with an integral step, removable side boards, bows and a tarpaulin cover. The height of the bows can be adjusted for road or rail transport and bench-type seats can be fitted down the centre of the vehicle if required. Optional equipment included a Pan-Bonnier winch with a capacity of between 5,000 and 7,000 kg and drop sides for the rear cargo area. The KT series is powered by a multi-fuel engine while the MT series is powered by a diesel which develops 125 hp at 2,100 rpm.

Variants

In addition to variants listed below, other variants include; a firefighting vehicle, a 5,000-litre fuel tanker, a mobile compressor, and a number of communications and command post vehicles carrying container/shelters.

Berliet GBC 8 KT (6 × 6) 4,000 kg truck carrying Trailor field refuelling equipment. The normal tarpaulin cover has been removed
(Shaun C Connors) 1190218

Small numbers of Berliet GBC 8 KT (4 × 4) version were built for the Portuguese Army under the designation GBC 8 (4 × 4) (Victor Barreira)
1391245

Berliet GBC 8 KT (6 × 6) 4,000 kg truck fitted with a snowplough and carrying road gritting equipment (Shaun C Connors)
1190217

Renault GBC 180 (6 × 6) 5,000 kg truck
Full details of this vehicle can be found in a separate entry in this section.

Long wheelbase
This is 8.32 m long, 2.4 m wide and 3.23 m high unladen; the wheelbase is 3.71 m + 1.28 m and empty weight of the vehicle is 9,400 kg.

(4 × 4) version
Small numbers of a (4 × 4) version were built for the Portuguese Army under the designation of GBC 8 (4 × 4).

Recovery vehicles
Details of these can be found in the entry for the Berliet TBC 8 KT (6 × 6) wrecker in the Recovery vehicles section.

Berliet GBC 8 KT (6 × 6) 4,000 kg truck with office-type rear body (Pierre Touzin)
1047635

Long wheelbase version of the Berliet GBC 8 KT (6 × 6) 4,000 kg truck (Shaun C Connors)
1190219

Berliet GBC 8 KT (6 × 6) 4,000 kg truck with standard troop carrying/cargo body (Pierre Touzin)
1047634

Tipper
Sometimes known as the GBC 8 KT Genie, this can carry 4 m³ of soil. Laden weight is 12,500 kg and principal dimensions are: length 7.175 m; width 2.4 m; height 2.845 m; length inside tipper body 3.8 m; and width inside tipper body 2.3 m.

Field Refueller
Outwardly resembling a standard cargo vehicle with a tarpaulin, this variant carries a fuel tank and equipment supplied by Trailor (later General Trailers) for the field refuelling role.

Tractor truck
This has an overall length of 6.521 m, width of 2.4 m and a height (reduced) of 2 m.

Specifications
GBC 8 KT
Cab seating: 1 + 2
Configuration: 6 × 6
Weight:
  (laden) 12,370 kg
  (unladen) 8,370 kg
  (weight on front axle, unladen) 4,180 kg
  (weight on rear bogie, unladen) 4,190 kg
  (max load, off-road) 4,000 kg
Load area: 4.36 × 2.35 m
Length: 7.28 m
Width: 2.4 m
Height:
  (cab) 2.7 m
  (tarpaulin) 3.3 m
Ground clearance: (axles) 280 mm
Track: 1.86 m
Wheelbase: 3.31 m + 1.28 m
Angle of approach/departure: 45°/45°
Max speed: 80 km/h
Range: 800 km
Fuel capacity: 200 litres
Max gradient: 50%
Fording: 1.2 m
Engine: Berliet MK 520 5-cylinder OHV water-cooled multifuel developing 125 hp (93 kW) at 2,100 rpm
Gearbox: Berliet BDSL 13 manual with 6 forward and 1 reverse gears
Transfer box: 2-speed
Clutch: single dry plate
Steering: worm gear and nut, servo-assisted
Turning radius: 10.5 m
Suspension:
  (front) semi-elliptic springs and hydraulic shock-absorbers
  (rear) leaf springs on oscillating pivot

Tyres: 12.00 × 20
Brakes:
  (main) air
  (parking) mechanical
Electrical system: 24 V
Batteries: 4 × 12 V, 100 Ah

Status
Production complete. Supplied to Algeria, Austria, China, France, Iraq, Morocco and Portugal.

Contractor
Berliet is now part of Renault Trucks Defense

Renault GBC 180 (6 × 6) 5,000 kg truck

Description
Renault Trucks Defense is undertaking a major upgrade of the Berliet GBC 8 KT (6 × 6) 4,000 kg truck for the French Army, to produce a virtually new vehicle with a much extended life and greatly improved on- and off-road performance. Full details of the GBC 8 KT can be found elsewhere in this section. The upgraded vehicle is known as the Renault GBC 180 (6 × 6) 5,000 kg truck to the French Army.

The initial programme called for the upgrading of 2,800 trucks, an initial batch of 800 followed by two optional batches of 1,000 each. The programme commenced during the latter part of 1997 and at a rate of 90 vehicles per month. Deliveries under the initial contract have now been completed, and from a grand total of around 5,620 contracted vehicles most of these had been completed by November 2010.

Only the more numerous shorter 3.31 m wheelbase variant of the GBC 8KT was upgraded, and excluding the added ADR configuration, these are returned to service in the following versions: standard cab with flatbed body; standard cab with flatbed body and winch; standard cab with General Service (GS) body; standard cab with General Service (GS) body and winch; torpedo (soft-top/collapsible) cab with flatbed body; torpedo (soft-top/collapsible) cab with flatbed body and winch; torpedo (soft-top/collapsible) cab with General Service (GS) body; torpedo (soft-top/collapsible) cab with General Service (GS) body and winch; standard cab with Hiab materials handling crane; standard cab with maintenance-type rear body; torpedo (soft-top/collapsible) cab with tanker body (only around 50 of these have been done).

Programme work is being carried out at the Renault facility at Limoges in an industrial partnership with the French Army establishment at Neuvy Pailloux. The programme is supervised by the French Army's Service des Programmes d'Armement Terrestres (SPART) and involves a joint testing and trials programme.

Service-worn GBC 8 KT trucks are stripped to the bare chassis at Neuvy Pailloux, and following a complete rebuild with all new moving parts for the original axle casings and transfer box, plus new suspension components (all to the original specification) the fully refurbished and reinforced rolling chassis is then shipped to Limoges. At Limoges the cab, body and major driveline components are added. The new steel and glass-fibre cab is based on the original GBC 8 KT cab design and is available in desert-type (torpedo) with a soft-top, this allowing for air transportable by C-130 or C-160 aircraft. This cab will also accept a 12.7 mm weapon mounting. An appliqué protection kit is available for the standard cab.

Automotive upgrades centre around the replacement of the existing Berliet multifuel engine with a EURO 2 emissions compliant Renault MIDR 06.02.26 turbocharged and boost air intercooled diesel developing 175 hp at 2,500 rpm and 575 N.m torque at 1,400 rpm. This engine is the same as that fitted to the Renault TRM 180 and 200 series of trucks. The new engine is coupled to an Eaton 4106 OD gearbox providing six forward and one reverse gears and further coupled to a new HWT 2030 two-speed transfer box. TRW power steering is provided and the entire lighting and electrical

Renault GBC 180 (6 × 6) 5,000 kg truck mounting a shelter/container (Pierre Touzin)   1047639

system is updated to full 24 V standard - components from the Renault TRM 2000 and TRM 10 000 are involved. New wheel rims and tubeless tyres are fitted and the braking system is revised to meet the latest EU directives.

The rebuilt vehicle then returns to Neuvy Pailloux for final painting and French Army checks before a return to service as a GBC 180.

Rebuilt vehicles have a maximum speed of 88 km/h (an increase of 8 km/h), retain a cruising range of 800 km, gradeability and sideslope capabilities of 50 per cent and 30 per cent respectively, and a fording depth of 1.2 m. Climatic operational range (including engine starting) is −20 to +45°C. Payload is increased to 5,000 kg (an increase of 1,000 kg), and towed loads are quoted as 6,000 kg on-road, and up to 4,000 kg off-road.

Based on experience gained with the GBC 8 KT upgrade programme and an analysis of current global requirements for tactical trucks, at Eurosatory 2004 Renault Trucks officially released details of the Sherpa range of tactical trucks, the smallest of which - the Sherpa 5 - is essentially a new-build and revised GBC 180. Full details of the Sherpa range can be found elsewhere in this section.

Status
Refurbishment/upgrade programme; deliveries to the French Army are currently underway.

Contractor
Renault Trucks Defense

Renault TRM 180 and TRM 200 (4 × 4) truck series

Development
The Renault TRM 180 and TRM 200 (4 × 4) truck series, referred to as the militarised civilian range, was developed from the earlier Renault TRM 150.11 (4 × 4) truck primarily to meet the military requirements of less technically advanced nations for a maintainable logistic vehicle with a reasonable degree of cross-country mobility. Many of the components used on the vehicles are of commercial origin.

Bangladesh ordered 275 TRM 180.11 trucks in July 1996 with a follow-on order for a further 200 anticipated. It is not thought this option was exercised. The French Army ordered approximately 150 TRM 200-13 trucks, including a tanker version.

Description
Two base versions of each model were offered, these being the TRM 180.11 and 180.13, and the TRM 200.11 and 200.13. The first figure denotes approximate engine power output, the second an approximate GVW. Described as the four- and eight-tonne ranges, with chassis cabs weighing from 5,370 to 5,600 kg, payloads (including body) ranged from 6,010 to 7,900 kg.

Renault GBC 180 (6 × 6) 5,000 kg truck fitted with a standard cargo/troop carrying dropside body (Shaun C Connors)   1391050

Renault TRM 200.13 (4 × 4) truck (Ian Young)   0056337

Renault TRM 200.13 (4 × 4) flat bed truck carrying Samantha communications system shelter (Pierre Touzin)   0056391

The same engine, a Renault MIDR.06.02.26 six-cylinder unit, was common across the range. In early versions this met EURO 1 emissions regulations, in later versions EURO 2. Power outputs also varied slightly. A speed limiter is fitted.

Three mobility level options were offered across the range, these being defined by the location of the air cleaner, spare wheel holder and battery box. The Cross-Country 'T' version featured the air cleaner above the chassis, the spare wheel holder located behind the cab, and the battery box on the left-hand side within the wheelbase. Fording depth for this version was 1 m. The Track 'P' version featured the air cleaner above the chassis, with the spare wheel holder and battery box located between the wheelbase, left and right-and side, respectively. Fording depth for this version was 1 m. The Off-Road 'C' version featured the air cleaner under the chassis, with the spare wheel holder and battery box located between the wheelbase, left and right-and side, respectively. Fording depth for this version was 750 mm.

The three-seat forward control cab is similar to that used on the Renault TRM 2000, full details of which can be found elsewhere in this section. The all-steel cab can be tilted forward 52° for engine and transmission access. The standard hard-topped cab may be fitted with a roof hatch for access to a light machine gun mounting. As an alternative, the cab was available produced in 'torpedo' form with a canvas top or a removable hardtop. On the latter the windscreen can be folded forward onto the bonnet. With all cab types the driver is provided with an adjustable seat, a fixed bench seat being provided for the two passengers. Left- or right-hand drive options were available.

The conventional channel section chassis is formed from beams measuring 234 × 70 × 7 mm and is fitted with towing/recovery points front and rear. The TRM 180.11 is fitted with the type 3MRDIS double reduction steer-drive front axle; all other models are fitted with a type 4MRDIA double reduction steer-drive front axle. In all cases suspension is by semi-elliptic leaf springs with rubber bump stops and telescopic shock-absorbers. An anti-roll bar became optional on the TRM 200 range. All models are fitted with a type P941A double reduction rear drive axle. Suspension on the TRM 180.11 and 200.11 is by semi-elliptic leaf springs with rubber bump stops and telescopic shock-absorbers. The TRM 180.13 and 200.13 are fitted with additional helper springs in place of telescopic shock-absorbers. All models are fitted with an anti-roll bar. Front and rear axles are fitted with air-actuated driver-controlled differential locks. The two-speed transfer box is fitted with an air-actuated driver-controlled longitudinal differential lock

The vehicles are equipped with a multipurpose platform suitable for a variety of military roles including cargo or troop carrier (16 to 20 man), shelter carrier (10 or 20 ft ISO), recovery vehicle, water or fuel carrier, or weapon carrier. Depending on the location of the mobility level defining ancillaries, this gives overall lengths ranging from 6.52-6.88 m

Various options were available on request. These included: a Power Take-Off (PTO) from the gearbox or transfer box; a fuel pre-heater; an additional 235-litre fuel tank or spare wheel holder; a removable front-mounted electric or hydraulic winch; a chassis-mounted hydraulic winch (not 'C' version); tyre bead locks for low-pressure operation; Class A interference suppression. A kit was available to convert a truck into a light recovery vehicle.

Specifications

TRM 180 and TRM 200

Model	TRM 180.11	TRM 180.13	TRM 200.11	TRM 200.13
Cab seating:	1 + 2	1 + 2	1 + 2	1 + 2
Configuration:	4 × 4	4 × 4	4 × 4	4 × 4
Weight:				
(GVW)	11,500	13,500	11,500	13,500
(chassis-cab)	5,370 kg	5,600 kg	5,490 kg	5,600 kg

Model	TRM 180.11	TRM 180.13	TRM 200.11	TRM 200.13
(payload, with platform body)	5,230 kg	7,000 kg	5,110 kg	7,000 kg
(permissible front axle load)	5,000 kg	6,000 kg	5,000 kg	6,000 kg
(permissible rear axle load)	7,000 kg	8,500 kg	7,000 kg	8,500 kg
(GCW)	17,000 kg	19,000 kg	17,000 kg	19,000 kg
Length: (with platform body)	6.52 m (C version) to 6.88 m (T version)			
Width:				
(cab)	2.365 m	2.365 m	2.365 m	2.365 m
(rear tyres)	2.37 m	2.37 m	2.37 m	2.37 m
Height (top of cab, unladen)	2.895 m	2.921 m	2.921 m	2.921 m
Ground clearance:				
(spare wheel)	316 mm	316 mm	316 mm	316 mm
(front axle, laden)	374 mm	362 mm	362 mm	362 mm
Track:				
(front)	1.896 m	1.96 m	1.96 m	1.96 m
(rear)	2 m	2 m	2 m	2 m
Wheelbase:	3.85 m	3.85 m	3.85 m	3.85 m
Angle of approach/departure:	39°/40°	39°/40°	39°/40°	39°/40°
Max speed: (restricted)	85 km/h	85 km/h	85 km/h	85 km/h
Range:	950 km	950 km	900 km	900 km
Fuel capacity:	single 235 litre tank plus 2 or 3 20-litre jerrycans. Optional additional 235-litre tank			
Gradient: (stop, hold and restart)	50%	50%	50%	50%
Max side slope:	30%	30%	30%	30%
Fording:	750 mm-1 m (see text)			
Engine:	MIDR.06.02.26 EURO 1/2 6.18-litre 6-cylinder in-line turbocharged and intercooled water-cooled 4-stroke direct injection diesel developing between (model/emissions dependant) 175 and 209 hp (131 and 156 kW) at 2,500 rpm and peak torque of between (model/emissions dependant) 575 and 655 N.m			
Gearbox:	Renault 41.060D manual with 6 forward and 1 reverse gears. Automatic option on some versions			
Transfer box:	Renault T600R 2-speed with lockable longitudinal differential			
Clutch:	350 DR 11500 single dry plate, hydraulic			
Steering:	screw and nut and recirculating ball, power assisted			
Suspension:	leaf springs, rubber bump stops, shock-absorbers and anti-roll bar. See text for details			
Tyres:	365/85R 20 Michelin XZL (options were available)			
Brakes:				
(main)	dual circuit, air, drums front and rear			
(parking)	manual brake valve acting on rear wheel spring cylinders			
Electrical system:	24 V	24 V	24 V	24 V
Batteries:	2 × 12 V, 125 Ah, type 6 TN B			
Alternator:	55 A	55 A	55 A	55 A

Status

Production complete. TRM 180.11 in service with Bangladesh (see text). TRM 200-13 in service with French Armed Forces (approximately 150).

Contractor

Renault Trucks Defense

Renault TRM 9000 (6 × 6) 9,000 kg truck

Development

The Renault TRM 9000 (6 × 6) truck (formerly known as the Berliet GBD) uses many components, such as the cab, gearbox, transfer case and steering, of the earlier TRM 6000 (4 × 4) 6,000 kg truck.

Production was undertaken at Vénissieux. First production vehicles were completed in 1975. The largest orders came from Algeria (500) and Morocco (1,500). Production is now complete.

Further development of the TRM 9000 resulted in the TRM 10 000 (6 × 6) truck adopted by the French Army. Full details of the TRM 10 000 can be found elsewhere in this section.

Description

The two-door forward control cab has a removable canvas roof, removable side screens and a windscreen that can be folded forward against the bonnet if required. The rear cargo area is fitted with drop sides and a drop tailgate, removable bows and a canvas cover. If required, seats can be fitted in the rear. Optional equipment included: a four-door, six- or seven-seat cab; fully enclosed two- or four-door cab; a winch with a capacity of 3,500/4,500 kg and 60 m of cable; different tyres; dual wheels on the rear axles; an additional 200-litre fuel tank; and an exhaust brake.

Variants include: an artillery tractor able to tow 155 mm artillery weapons as well as carrying a gun crew and ammunition; a command/radio vehicle fitted with a container on the rear which could be fitted with communications equipment; a 6,000-litre water or fuel tanker; and a tipper with a two-man cab. The chassis has been used to mount Exocet or Otomat (for Egypt) anti-shipping missiles, as an RPV launching vehicle, and for supporting the Shahine anti-aircraft system supplied to Saudi Arabia; 38 vehicles were supplied to Saudi Arabia for this role. A recovery version known as the TRM 9000 CLD is fitted with a four-door cab. A tractor variant can tow a semi-trailer weighing a maximum of 27,000 kg; unladen weight is 15,000 kg.

Specifications

TRM 9000
Cab seating: 1 + 1
Configuration: 6 × 6
Weight:
    (laden) 20,000 kg
    (unladen) 11,000 kg
    (max load, off-road) 9,000 kg
    (max towed load) 10,000 kg
Length: 9.87 m
Width: 2.48 m
Height: (cab) 3.066 m
Ground clearance: 382 mm
Track:
    (front) 1.971 m
    (rear) 1.886 m
Wheelbase: 3.8 m + 1.4 m
Angle of approach/departure: 45°/50°
Max speed: 82 km/h
Range: 800 km
Fuel capacity: 200 litres
Max gradient: 45%
Max side slope: 30%
Fording: 1 m
Engine: Renault MIDS 06-20-30 6-cylinder turbocharged water-cooled 4-stroke diesel developing 228 hp (170 kW) at 2,200 rpm
Gearbox: BDS manual with 6 forward and 1 reverse gears
Transfer box: BT 20 2-speed
Clutch: air-assisted
Steering: power-assisted
Turning radius: 11 m
Suspension:
    (front) leaf springs with auxiliary springs and 2 mechanical buffer stops, telescopic shock-absorbers
    (rear) balanced by leaf springs and 4 mechanical buffer stops

Renault TRM 9000 wrecker in action at IDEX 2009's mobility demonstration (Shaun C Connors)   1296223

Tyres: 14.00 × 20
Brakes:
    (main) air, drums all-round
    (parking) mechanical
Electrical system: 24 V
Batteries: 4 × 6TN, 190 Ah

Status

Production complete. Supplied to a number of armed forces including Algeria (500), Egypt (50), Morocco (1,500), Saudi Arabia (38) and the UAE. This vehicle was not adopted by the French Army.

Contractor

Renault Trucks Defense

Berliet GBU 15 (6 × 6) 6,000 kg truck

Development

In the 1950s, the Rochet-Schneider company developed a (6 × 6) truck called the T-6. This concern was subsequently taken over by the Berliet Company and production of the vehicle, called the GBU 15, began in 1959. Production is complete and its replacement in the French Army is the Renault TRM 10 000 (6 × 6) 10,000 kg truck.

Description

The forward control cab has four doors, removable canvas top and side screens and the windscreen can be folded down onto the front of the cab if not required. The rear cargo area is provided with a drop tailgate, removable sides, removable bows and a canvas cover.

Mounted at the rear of the vehicle is a winch with a capacity of 8,000 kg. The engine is the multifuel type and will run on a variety of fuels including petrol, paraffin, JP4, gas-oil, light fuel and mineral or vegetable oils in the lower power ranges. The rear wheel train consists of two tandem axles operating with a flexible progressive air-driven differential device. This ensures drive, even when two wheels on one side of the vehicle are not in contact with the ground, or have lost traction.

Variants included an artillery tractor used to tow French Army 155 mm Model 1950 howitzers and a tractor, designated the TBU 15, with an unladen weight of 13,500 kg; it can tow a semi-trailer carrying a maximum weight of 22,000 kg. A wrecker variant is called the TBU 15 CLD; full details of which can be found in the Recovery vehicles section. There are also tanker and tipper variants.

Chinese production

In 1968, China's Shaanxi Automobile Works (now Shaanxi Heavy-duty Automobile Group Co., Ltd) introduced China's first (6 × 6) 5,000 kg military cross-country military truck the Yan'an SX250 (current designation SX2150). This truck was based on the chassis design of the Soviet Ural-375 and the cab/cargo-bed designs of the Berliet GBU 15. Batch production of the truck was delayed for six years due to poor reliability and other technical problems with the initial design, the modified SX250 entering batch production in 1974. It has been fielded by the PLA in significant numbers since then.

The SX2150K is a second-generation variant of the SX2150 and is upgraded with Austrian Steyr truck technologies, including the WD615.71 turbo-charged diesel engine and Fuller RT11509C gearbox. Early SX2150K models retain the original Berliet-based cab, while later models (SX2150KS) feature a more modern Steyr-based design.

Specifications

Cab seating: 1 + 3
Configuration: 6 × 6
Weight:
    (laden, road) 24,500 kg
    (laden, off-road) 20,500 kg
    (unladen) 14,500 kg
    (max load, on-road) 10,000 kg
    (max load, off-road) 6,000 kg
    (max towed load) 15,000 kg
Length: 7.974 m
Width: 2.5 m
Height:
    (cab) 3 m
    (tarpaulin) 3.25 m
Track: 2.04 m
Wheelbase: 3.48 m + 1.45 m
Angle of approach/departure: 45°/45°
Max speed: 75 km/h
Range: 800 km
Fuel capacity: 400 litres
Max gradient: 60%
Fording: 1 m
Engine: Berliet 6-cylinder water-cooled 4-stroke multifuel developing 214 hp (157 kW) at 1,800 rpm
Gearbox: manual with 5 forward and 1 reverse gears
Transfer box: 2-speed
Clutch: dry

Berliet GBU 15 (6 × 6) 6,000 kg flatbed truck (T J Gander)   0044296

Steering: screw and nut, power assisted
Turning radius: 9.2 m
Suspension: longitudinal springs
Tyres: 14.00 × 20
Brakes:
  (main) air, 3 circuits; front, rear and trailer
  (parking) operates on rear wheels only
  (emergency) pneumatic handbrake operates on rear wheels
Electrical system: 24 V

Status
Production complete. Supplied to Belgium (withdrawn from service), China (see text), France (limited numbers may remain) and the United Arab Emirates (status uncertain).

Contractor
Berliet is now part of Renault Trucks Defense

Renault TRM 10000 (6 × 6) 10,000 kg truck

Development
The Renault TRM 10000 (6 × 6) 10,000 kg truck was developed from the Renault TRM 9000 (6 × 6) 9,000 kg truck. The main differences between the TRM 9000 and the TRM 10000 are that the latter has a longer wheelbase, a more powerful engine and a different transmission.

The TRM 10000 (6 × 6) 10,000 kg truck was selected by the French Army to be its standard truck in this class; the initial requirement called for 5,000 vehicles. Pre-production manufacture commenced at Renault's Blainville factory in 1985. Production of the first full production batch of 178 vehicles commenced during mid-1987 and later the same year an order for a further 759 vehicles was placed. By 1994 an increased 29,000 kg GVW weight variant was available.

Production of the TRM 10000 ceased during 1999. In total 2,500 vehicles were delivered to the French Army with a further 200 vehicles being exported. There were 26 specific versions based on five main types of chassis: 23,000/29,000 kg GVW cargo; artillery tractor; Load Handling System (LHS); Pont Flottant Motorisé (PFM) tractor truck; recovery. Details of the cargo, artillery tractor, LHS and PFM variants can be found elsewhere in this section; full details of the recovery variant can be found in the Recovery vehicles section.

Currently Renault Trucks offers two ranges of military trucks. The first are based on the Kerax range of heavy duty commercial vehicles introduced in 1997, the second are the Sherpa range of tactical trucks shown for the first time at Eurosatory 2004. An overview of the Kerax and Sherpa ranges can be found elsewhere in this section.

Renault TRM 10000 (6 × 6) 10,000 kg cargo truck (Shaun C Connors) 1185502

Renault TRM 10000 (6 × 6) 10,000 kg cargo truck with all body sides and tarpaulin removed (Pierre Touzin)   1047675

Since April 2008, Renault Trucks Defence has operated a 10-year Maintenance in Operational Conditions (MOC) contract with the French Army for tactical trucks. This EUR484 million contract covers 805 TRM 10000, plus 3,200 GBC 180, 2,530 TRM 2000, and 2,000 VTL.

Description
The basic TRM 10000 cargo variant was produced in two versions, the first having a GVW of 23,000 kg, the second a GVW of 29,000 kg. The standard soft-top forward control cab is provided with a nylon tarpaulin cover over retractable roof bows; the main windscreen folds forward and down through 180°. The cab seats two, the driver on an adjustable suspended seat, and can be tilted forward for maintenance. A full range of heating, defrosting and ventilation equipment is fitted as standard. The artillery tractor and PFM tractor truck variants are fitted as standard with a larger four-door cab.

The conventional 302 × 85 × 8 mm channel-section chassis has cross-members bolted and riveted into position. The front bumper is provided with a front towing shackle, and impact buffers and shackles are provided front and rear. The rear towing hook is rated at 20,000 kg; 10,000 kg on the artillery tractor and PFM tractor truck.

The front steer-drive axle was originally the double reduction type PA721 on all models. Suspension is by semi-elliptic leaf springs (main and equalizer), mechanical bump stops and telescopic shock absorbers. An anti-roll bar was optional. A late option was the 9,500 kg-rated type 941C front axle. This axle allowed for the installation of an Anti-lock Braking System (ABS). The rear double drive bogie is type PMR2021 on the 23,000 kg GVW chassis, and the type PMR2141 on the 29,000 kg GVW chassis. Suspension is by semi-elliptic leaf springs, mechanical bump stops, and twin anti-roll bars on all models with the exception of the artillery tractor; this has a single anti-roll bar. The rear axles are fitted with inter- and cross-axle differential locks.

Various equipment options were available on request. These included: a 12.7 mm HMG race on the optional hard-top cab roof; two extra seats or a single bunk in the two-door cabs; four-door five- or eight-seat cabs; sand-type tyres; 12.00R 20 tyres with dual wheels on the rear bogie; winches for all but the artillery tractor which was fitted with a centre-mounted 8,000 kg capacity winch as standard. Optional winches could (model dependent) be either front-mounted or located centrally between the chassis rails.

Variants
TRM 10000 PTAC 23,000 kg GVW chassis
The 23,000 kg GVW chassis was available in two (first to second axle) wheelbase variants: 4.3 and 5.2 m, and in three overall lengths: 9.076, 9.276 or 10.366 m, with respective 6.18, 6.38 and 7.5 m load areas. In standard troop carrying/cargo configuration the rear cargo area is

Renault TRM 10000 (6 × 6) 10,000 kg truck modified to carry and launch CL289 remotely-piloted vehicle (Pierre Touzin)   0056328

TRM 10000

Variant	23,000 kg GVW	29,000 kg GVW	Artillery tractor	LHS	PFM tractor truck
Configuration:	6 × 6	6 × 6	6 × 6	6 × 6	6 × 6
Weight:					
(GVW)	23,000 kg	29,000 kg	23,000 kg	29,000 kg (now 31,000 kg)	23,000 kg
(chassis cab)	10,290 kg	11,010 kg	n/avail	13,540 kg (with LHS)	12,040 kg
(payload, inc. body)	12,710 kg	17,990 kg	n/avail	13,000 kg	10,960 kg
(permissible front axle load)[1]	7,500 kg	7,500 kg	7,500 kg	7,500 kg	7,500 kg
(permissible rear bogie load)	17,000 kg	21,600 kg	17,000 kg	21,600 kg	17,000 kg
(towed load)	10,000 kg	19,000 kg	12,000 kg	n/avail	38,000 kg GTW
(GCW)	33,000 kg	48,000 kg	35,000 kg	n/avail	38,000 kg GTW
Length: (chassis)	9.076/9.276/10.366 m	9.276/10.366 m	9.046 m	8.023 m	7.336 m
Width: (cab)	2.48 m	2.48 m	2.48 m	2.48 m	2.48 m
Height: (unladen, cab roof)	3.11 m	3.11 m	3.07 m	n/avail	3.02 m
Ground clearance: (under axle, laden)	382 mm	382 mm	382 mm	360 mm	297 mm
Track: (front)	2.004 m	2.004 m	n/avail	2.015 (rear)	2.004 m
Wheelbase:	4.3/5.2 m	4.3/5.2 m	4.3 m	4.3 m	4.3 m
Angle of approach/departure:	42°/27, 28, 32° (rear overhang dependant)	42°/27, 28° (rear overhand dependant)	42°/33°	42°/65° (without flatrack)	42°/n/app
Max speed:	89 km/h	88 km/h	n/avail	88 km/h	89 km/h
Fuel capacity:	2 × 250 litre tanks chassis-mounted between axles 1 and 2, one right-hand side, one left-hand side				
Max gradient: (laden)	44%	>50%	n/avail	>50%	30%
Side slope:	30%	30%	n/avail	30%	20%
Fording: (without preparation)	1.2 m	1.2 m	1.2 m	1.2 m	1.2 m
Engine:	Renault MIDS.06.20.45 9.839 litre 6-cylinder in-line exhaust turbocharged water-cooled 4-stroke direct injection diesel developing 264 hp (194 kW) at 2,200 rpm; turbocharged and intercooled for 29,000 kg GVW applications, and developing 326 hp (240 kW) at 2,000 rpm and 1,200 N.m torque at 1,200 rpm				
Gearbox:	Renault B9 manual with 9 forward and 1 reverse gears. Artillery tractor only - ZF 6HP 500 automatic				
Transfer box:	A 800 3 D 2-speed with locking power divider differential. Artillery tractor only - VG-500 2-speed				
Clutch:	430 DOT 2400, hydropneumatic	430 DPT 23000, single plate, hydropneumatic	n/app	430 DPT 23000, single plate, hydropneumatic	430 DPT 2400, hydropneumatic
Steering:	type 8046, power-assisted				
Turning radius: (4.3 m wheelbase)	11.25 m	11.25 m	11.25 m	11.25 m	11.10 m
Suspension:	semi-elliptic leaf springs, all round (see text for details)				
Tyres: (standard)	14.00R 20 all-round except 29,000 kg GVW chassis: 14.00R 20 (front and spare), 475/80R 20 (rear)				
Brakes:					
(main)	air, dual circuit, drums all-round. Engine exhaust brake on 23,000 kg GVW chassis				
(parking)	air, manually operated, locking on rear wheels				
Electrical system:	24 V	24 V	24 V	24 V	24 V
Batteries:	4 × 12 V, 125 Ah, type 6 TN	4 × 12 V, 125 Ah, type 6 TN B	4 × 12 V, 125 Ah, type 6 TN	4 × 12 V, 125 Ah, type 6 TN B	4 × 12 V, 125 Ah, type 6 TN
Alternator:	50 A	50 A	50 A	50 A	50 A

[1] This can be uprated to 9,500 kg with the type 941C axle fitted

provided with removable sides and tailgate, bows and a tarpaulin cover, and can be fitted with removable seats for 24 fully equipped troops. With the sides and rear removed, the TRM 10000 can carry standard 20 ft ISO containers. Superstructure dependent, the TRM 10,000 is air transportable by C-130 and C-160 transport aircraft.

TRM 10000 PTAC 29,000 kg GVW chassis
By 1994 the 29,000 kg GVW chassis had been introduced. This was first shown in 1990 equipped with a Marrel load-handling system, full details of which can be found elsewhere in this entry. Further development of the uprated chassis resulted in a fuel tank carrier intended for field refuelling of Leclerc MBT and combat helicopter units. Another truck version acts as the

carrier for the ASTER launching unit together with its firing command and control systems - it is understood that 150 units were involved in this requirement. The uprated chassis allowed for the fitting of a small arms fire protected cab.

The 29,000 kg GVW chassis was available in two (first to second axle) wheelbase variants: 4.3 and 5.2 m, and in two overall lengths: 9.276 or 10.366 m, with respective 6.38 and 7.5 m load areas. Superstructure dependent, the TRM 10,000 is air-transportable by C-130 and C-160 transport aircraft.

TRM 10000 artillery tractor
The TRM 10000 artillery tractor variant is capable of towing artillery weighing between 8,000-12,000 kg and was developed specifically to tow and serve the French Army's Giat Industries 155 mm towed gun TR and

Renault TRM 10000 (6 × 6) 10,000 kg truck fitted with a materials handling crane (Shaun C Connors)
1185505

Renault TRM 10000 T (6 × 6) tractor truck towing a semi-trailer carrying a PFM Mle F1 centre section bridging unit (Pierre Touzin)
0536760

Artillery tractor variant of the Renault TRM 10000 (6 × 6) 10,000 kg truck. The crew-type cab and materials handling crane are clearly visible (Pierre Touzin) 1047676

Artillery tractor variant of the Renault TRM 10000 (6 × 6) 10,000 kg truck. The crew-type cab has been folded; the weapons mount is now clearly visible (Pierre Touzin) 1047677

Artillery tractor variant of the Renault TRM 10000 (6 × 6) 10,000 kg truck (Pierre Touzin) 1047678

remaining 155 mm howitzer Model 50. 150 examples of this variant were delivered to the French Army.

The vehicle has a 4.3 m (first to second axle) wheelbase, an overall length of 9.046 m and a cargo bed length of 5.41 m. The purpose-designed platform body transports 48 rounds of ammunition plus associated camouflage and support equipment for the gun and tractor. A three-tonne/m hydraulic crane and six/eight-tonne centrally-mounted hydraulic self-recovery winch are fitted. The four-door crew-type cab has seating for the gun crew of eight.

The artillery tractor is the only TRM 10000 model to be fitted with an automatic transmission as standard.

TRM 10000 PM
In 1990 Renault demonstrated a TRM 10000 equipped with a Marrel load-handling system capable of handling a 13,000 kg capacity flatrack. This version had a GVW 29,000 kg, now 31,000 kg, and was adopted by the French Army. A total of 792 vehicles were ordered for delivery over a four-year period; 700 vehicles were delivered.

TRM 10000 T
The TRM 10000 T is provided with a fifth wheel to tow semi-trailers carrying PFM floating bridging and pontoon units. Four-hundred and fifty examples of this variant were delivered.

TRM 10000 CLD recovery
Full details of this vehicle can be found in the recovery vehicles section.

Specifications
See table on facing page

Renault TRM 10000 PM (6 × 6) 10,000 kg truck. This example is fitted with a Marrel Load Handling System (LHS) and has a GVW of 31,000 kg (Shaun C Connors) 1185504

This Renault TRM 10000 (6 × 6) 10,000 kg wrecker variant is fitted with basic pouch/blanket-type ballistic protection, the folding cab style adopted for the TRM 10000 being unable to support the additional weight of anything more comprehensive (Shaun C Connors) 1185503

Renault TRM 10000 (6 × 6) 10,000 kg truck of the French Air Force. The payload is the Aladin radar system (Pierre Touzin) 1120408

Status
Production complete. In service with the French Army (2,500) including 500 cargo, 150 artillery tractor, 450 PFM tractor trucks, 700 LHS and 250 recovery vehicles. A total of 200 vehicles were exported to Cyprus, Greece, Saudi Arabia (67) and other Middle Eastern countries.

Contractor
Renault Trucks Defense

Renault G 290 (6 × 4) VTL transport vehicle

Development
In January 1988, the French Army awarded a contract worth FFr3,500 million for 3,500 Renault G 290.26 (6 × 4) trucks, 3,500 Bennes Marrel (now Marrel) Ampliroll 155NB load handling systems, 2,500 LOHR (now SOFRAME) RM19 trailers, 12,000 20 ft/6.096 m platforms and 100 tilt-type semi-trailers. The order was completed by December 1993 and the combined logistic package is known as the VTL (*Véhicule de Transport Logistique*).

A total of 2,050 examples of a revised version of the truck component, the G 340, have also been delivered to the French Army.

Renault VTL (6 × 4) transport vehicle fitted with a Marrel Ampliroll 155NB Load Handling System (LHS) (Shaun C Connors)   1340304

Side view of a Renault VTL (6 × 4) VTL transport vehicle, clearly visible is the Marrel Load Handling System (LHS) (Pierre Touzin)   1120410

The VTL package is used by about 40 transport regiments and various other Army units.

Since April 2008, Renault Trucks Defence has operated a 10-year Maintenance in Operational Conditions (MOC) contract with the French Army for tactical trucks. This EUR484 million contract covers around 8,500 trucks including 2,000 VTL.

The VTL package is due for replacement under France's current major vehicle replacement programme, PPT. PPT, for which the initial RfQ was originally issued in August 2004, is also expected to undertake some of the roles currently performed by Renault TRM 10000 (6 × 6) truck. The programme subsequently stalled, to re-emerge in January 2010. At the time of writing (November 2010) an award or similar announcement was pending. Further details of the PPT programme can be found elsewhere in this entry.

Description
The Renault G 290.26 is a logistic transport vehicle fitted with a hydraulic loading system produced by Bennes Marrel (now Marrel). The system is capable of loading and unloading platforms carrying loads of up to 16,000 kg. Loading time is 38 seconds and unloading 34 seconds. The system can withstand misaligned loads of up to 10° either side. Apart from the usual cargo-carrying platforms the system can be used with tanker and tipper bodies.

The Renault G 290.26 vehicle can carry a maximum load of 18,000 kg. It is powered by a Type MIDR 06-20-45 turbocharged diesel developing 291 hp at 2,100 rpm and has a Type B9 gearbox with nine forward and one reverse gears. The cab has seating for the driver and two passengers. Gross vehicle weight is 26,000 kg.

One version of the Renault G 290.26 is used as a carrier and layer for the MOBI-MAT tactical deployable mobility matting.

Porteur Polyvalente Terrestre (PPT)
Porteur Polyvalente Terrestre (PPT) is the replacement programme for the VTL package. The initial RfQ for PPT was issued in 2004 and is understood to have called for around 2,500 trucks (mainly (8 × 8), but also some (8 × 4) and (6 × 6)), 50 per cent of which were to be fitted with a DROPS/PLS-type Load Handling System (LHS). In addition to replacing VTL, it was suggested at this early stage that PPT would also undertake some of the roles currently performed by the Renault TRM 10000 (6 × 6) truck. The stated in-service date at this time was 2008 and PPT was to be based on a commercially available design. However, the technical specifications were complex, and while not impossible to achieve, compliance would have had unacceptable cost implications for the programme. Hence, the tender (to which Renault Trucks Defense is understood to have been the only respondent) was withdrawn.

Renault VTL (6 × 4) transport vehicle and its associated LOHR (now SOFRAME) trailer transporting a containerised/palletised load (Pierre Touzin)   1047673

Unladen Renault VTL (6 × 4) transport vehicle and its associated LOHR (now SOFRAME) trailer (Shaun C Connors)   1391390

A further PPT tender was announced in November 2007, this split into two main component parts; the logistic vehicles (which includes basic trucks – including dump trucks – and trailers), and repair/recovery vehicles.

Basic STANAG Level 1 ballistic protection was required for the armoured cabs. Some sources suggested at the time this may increase.

The quantities stated for PPT at this time were 2,200 vehicles, spilt 2,050 logistic trucks and 150 repair/recovery trucks, with tender submission due during March 2007. A revised figure of 2,400 vehicles was quoted in February 2008, this calling for 2,250 logistic trucks (1,650 of which were to be equipped with a LHS) and 150 repair/recovery trucks. A total of 550 trailers were required. With a significant downsizing of France's Armed Forces pending at the time it was believed by some at this stage that the PPT requirement would eventually reduce to a maximum of 1,800 vehicles.

Information current as of July 2009 suggested that PPT would call for an (8 × 4) truck, with an (8 × 8) recovery component, and that the requirement would slip further, with an interim buy for deployed operations. Repair/recovery variants are an integral part of the PPT requirement as the French Army's current repair/recovery assets would be unsuitable for the PPT recovery role for a number of reasons including mobility, capacity, legislative compliance, age and crew protection issues.

PPT re-emerged in January 2010 with an initial UOR requirement for 150 trucks with LHS and armoured cabs and more than 40 trailers, the latter not confirmed. Responses were due by March 2010, with an award expected later in 2010. Follow-on additional batches and options of 2,400 trucks and 550 trailers can be ordered/delivered between 2012-2017.

Rear three-quarter view of a Renault VTL (6 × 4) VTL transport vehicle, clearly visible is the Marrel Load Handling System (LHS) (Shaun C Connors)   1391391

The 2,350 trucks are currently expected to be split 1,650 with LHS, 500 with fixed platforms in three configurations (standard, with tilt, with crane), 100 dump trucks and 150 recovery vehicles, with some trucks fitted with armoured cabs.

No preference for an (8 × 4) or (8 × 8) chassis has been stated by the DGA.

Status
Production complete. In service with French Armed Forces.

Contractor
Renault Trucks Defense
Marrel SA

Renault CBH range of bonneted trucks

Development
Renault's commercial C range of bonneted trucks was sold mainly outside of Europe, European commercial legislation not favouring a bonneted design.

Commercial considerations are not a major consideration for military users, and a number of essentially similar bonneted Renault designs (varying primarily in engine power outputs and operating weights) are also employed by French Armed Forces in small numbers, including heavy tractor trucks.

The CBH 385 is one C range model adopted by the French Military. It mounts a 18,000-litre fuel tanker, and in the usual French military style the tank is tarpaulin covered. Between 1995-1997 some 60 of these vehicles were procured with accompanying 18,000-litre trailers, also covered by tarpaulin. The 18,000-litre tank body is designed for the bulk transport and transfer of fuel (to smaller tankers or fuel bladders) and is not capable of refuelling individual items of equipment.

Other C range models employed by the French Army include the CBH 340 long wheelbase cargo truck, CBH 320 (6 × 4) dump truck fitted with a heavy-duty rock-type dump body, and the CBH 280 (6 × 4) dump truck fitted with a conventional dump body with tailboard. As engineering assets the dump truck models can tow plant trailers such as the ACTM two-axle low-bed plant trailer, this trailer capable of transporting loads such as a Caterpillar D6 bulldozer. These dump trucks can be fitted with snowploughs for snow clearing work.

The French Army also uses a C range heavy tractor truck (designated TRM 340.34T), full details of which can be found in the Heavy equipment transporters section.

Commercial production of these bonneted models is now complete, replaced in production by militarised versions of the commercial KERAX range of trucks. An overview of the KERAX range can be found elsewhere in this section.

In Kosovo, a French Army CBH 280 (6 × 4) dump truck fitted with a conventional dump body with tailboard (Shaun C Connors) 1185499

In Kosovo, a French Army CBH 320 (6 × 4) dump truck fitted with a heavy-duty rock-type dump body (Shaun C Connors) 1185498

The CBH 385 is one C range model adopted by the French Military. It mounts an 18,000-litre fuel tanker, and in the usual French military style the tank is tarpaulin covered (Shaun C Connors) 1185501

Renault CBH 340 long wheelbase cargo truck (Stefan Marx) 1296117

Description
The Renault C range has a semi-forward control cab with an adjustable seat for the driver and a bench seat for two passengers. The cab is constructed of high-stress steel and is provided with air conditioning and standard instruments. For maintenance the cab can be tilted forward to an angle of 70°.

The chassis is constructed from high-strength steel C-section members with section dimensions of 356 × 100 × 8 mm. Chassis cross-members are bolted to the webs of the side members while the integral front bumper is fitted with a towing block; various types of towing hook can be fitted. Renault axles are fitted, and usually double reduction and with differential locks.

Optional equipment included various spare wheel carriers, reinforced rear cross members for towing trailers weighing up to 75,000 kg, enlarged or extra fuel tanks, power take-offs from the gearbox and accessories such as a fully sprung driving seat.

Status
Production complete. In service with French Army and other unspecified armed forces.

Contractor
Renault Trucks Defense

Renault Kerax range of trucks

Development
Renault was founded as Renault Frères to build cars in 1898, the company building its first truck in 1903. Renault was nationalised in 1945 and in 1955 SAVIEM (*Société Anonyme de Véhicules Industriels et d'Equipements Mécaniques*) was formed by the merger of Renault, Latil, Somua and Floriat. In 1975 SAVIEM acquired the Berliet truck business from Citroen. Renault Véhicules Industriels (RVI) was established in 1977 and acquired Chrysler Espana and Chrysler's former UK truck business in 1981. In 2000 it was announced that Mack of the US had become a wholly owned subsidiary of Renault Véhicules Industriels (RVI). In January 2001 Renault Trucks was acquired by Volvo AB of Sweden.

Renault's Kerax range was introduced commercially in 1997, and by January 2007 in excess of 55,000 had been produced. As of December 2009 the French Army were known to have ordered in excess of 400 vehicles in five types including (4 × 4) rigid and tractor truck configurations, (6 × 6) rigid and (8 × 4) (recovery and dump) configurations, with a recent order being for 141 vehicles to be delivered by 2010 as part of the Aster missile air-defence system.

The only other current known users of the Kerax range of military trucks are Bangladesh, Belgium, Chad, Egypt, Morocco and Thailand. Bangladesh operates a small number of (6 × 6) chassis alongside its CBH

Kerax (8 × 8) fitted with a Palfinger (Guima) load handling system and interchangeable armoured cab (Shaun C Connors) 1391127

An (8 × 8) chassis was added to the Kerax range during 2006 and first displayed publicly at Eurosatory in June 2006 (Shaun C Connors) 1190213

vehicles and 202 TRM 180s, the Belgian Army operates 27 (8 × 4) heavy recovery vehicles similarly specified to vehicles in service with the French Army, Chad ordered two batches of trucks (one in 2008, the other in 2009) totalling around 120, the bulk of these being Kerax, Morocco received two Kerax tractor trucks for specialist logistic support duties, and Thailand operates eight Kerax tractor trucks in a fleet of around 100 Renault trucks. Additionally, at Eurosatory 2008 Renault disclosed the sale of around 80 Kerax ((4 × 4), (6 × 6) and (8 × 8)) to NAMSA (NATO). Most recently (in 2010) it was disclosed that Egypt had ordered a batch of approximately 30 Kerax (6 × 6) trucks.

Based on an in-production range of commercial trucks, the Renault Kerax range of military trucks is likely to reflect many minor design changes and specification upgrades associated with civilian truck production.

Description

The Renault Kerax range of trucks for military logistic applications are based on the Kerax range of heavy-duty civilian trucks, militarised to varying degrees to suit specific operator requirements. The Kerax range initially replaced all earlier military vehicles produced by Renault, however, it is now supplemented by the Sherpa range of purpose-designed tactical military trucks. Renault also offers mildly militarised versions of its other commercial truck ranges, the Midlum, Premium and Magnum.

The layout and design of the Kerax range is entirely conventional, cabs and the majority of driveline components shared with the Kerax civilian range of trucks, with all components being commercially available and proven. Prior to the availability of the EURO 4/5 DXi 11 (power outputs ranging from 380 to 460 hp) engine option from October 2006, all Kerax models were supplied as standard meeting EURO 3 emissions requirements and were fitted with the same Renault MIDR 06 23 56 11.1-litre six-cylinder in-line turbocharged common rail four-stroke diesel engine in versions with power outputs ranging from 265 to 412 hp. A EURO 3 option remains available for certain markets.

Gearbox options are currently a ZF 16-speed manual coupled to a single or two-speed transfer box, a fully automatic transmission or Renault's Optidriver automated gearbox.

Two-, three- or four-axle chassis are available and in a variety of drive configurations, with single or dual wheels on the rear axles. Longitudinal and cross-axle differential locks are available, for/between all drive axles and all-wheel drive variants, feature full-time all-wheel drive. All axles are Renault units.

Standard models in the (4 × 4) range have wheelbase options from 3.495 to 5.495 m with a GVW of up to 18,000 kg. Engine power outputs are 380 hp, 420 hp, or 460 hp.

Renault Kerax (8 × 4) dump truck of the French Army. The three-axle dolly-type trailer is a Nicolas design (Shaun C Connors) 1120456

Renault Kerax (6 × 6) truck of the French Army fitted with a behind-cab materials handling crane (Pierre Touzin) 1391392

Standard models in the (6 × 6) range have 3.495 and 4.995 m first to second axle wheelbase options and a GVW of up to 25,000 kg. Engine power outputs are 380 hp, 420 hp, or 460 hp.

In 2006 the existing (8 × 4) chassis was joined by an (8 × 8). Current wheelbase options for these four-axle chassis are 5.35 and 5.65 m (8 × 8) and 5.99 m for the (8 × 4). Engine power output is 460 hp @ EURO 5; 450 hp @ EURO 4 in the recovery variant. A heavy tractor truck variant with a GCW of 120,000 kg was added to the range in 2010. Outline details of the heavy tractor truck variant can be found in the Heavy equipment transporters section.

Three chassis ratings are available for the Kerax range; light, medium and heavy. Chassis is of conventional C-section design and on all models the chassis may be fitted with a variety of bodies (which according to wheelbase and payload capacity) can include dropside (with front- or rear-mounted materials handling crane), box-body, tanker, dump, recovery hamper, or DROPS/PLS load handling systems. Two- or three-axle tractor truck versions are also available.

The two-door forward-control all-steel cab can be based around either civilian day or sleeper cabs and will accept add-on protection panels. Alternatively the entire cab can be removed in half a day and be replaced by a purpose-designed four-seat armoured cab that offers protection from 7.62 mm ammunition fired at 100 m. Options for this cab include additional panels providing protection up to 12.7 mm ammunition, protection from anti-personnel and blast-effect mines, an NBC protection

Renault Kerax (6 × 6) truck of the French Army fitted with a behind-cab materials handling crane (Pierre Touzin) 1391394

Renault Kerax (8 × 4) truck of the French Army (Pierre Touzin)   1391395

Renault Kerax tractor truck of the French Army (Pierre Touzin)   1391393

kit, air conditioning, and a weapon mount on the roof for up to a 12.7 mm machine gun. Also available is an air-transportable cab that, like the armoured cab, can be fitted to all Kerax models. Essentially, the same as the production cab, the air-transportable cab has been redesigned to include removable and folding elements that enable C-130 transport, as well as transport on rail flat wagons. The hardtop roof and upper section of the rear-wall panel lift away in one piece, as do the upper sections of the doors. The main windscreen is fixed on hinges and folds forward through approximately 180° to lock in position for transport.

Other Renault commercial vehicles
Renault also produces the Midlum light commercial range which is available in all-wheel drive configuration, the Premium medium-weight commercial (which also includes the heavier-duty Premium Lander), and the Magnum tractor truck. The Midlum is available with a reasonable degree of militarisation, the Premium and Magnum less so.

Status
In production. In service with Bangladesh, Belgium, Chad, Egypt, France, Morocco, Thailand and NATO (NAMSA) (see text).

Contractor
Renault Trucks Defense

Germany

MAN trucks

Development
Maschinenfabrik Augsburg Nürnberg (MAN) of Germany began truck building in 1920, previously the company had built Saurer trucks under licence and had pioneered the first diesel engine in close cooperation with Dr Rudolf Diesel. MAN acquired truck-maker Österreich AutomobilFabrik (ÖAF) of Austria in 1936; in the early 1970s ÖAF absorbed Gräf und Stift Automobilfabrik AG. By 1971 MAN had completed its acquisition of Büssing Automobilwerke AG.

More recently, the now MAN Nutzfahrzeuge AG acquired an 85 per cent share of the truck-building activities of Austria's Steyr Nutzfahrzeuge AG in January 1990, and in 1993 the company exercised its option to acquire the remaining 15 per cent share of the business. Steyr Nutzfahrzeuge AG became known as MAN Steyr AG during 2002 and during 2005 as MAN Nutzfahrzeuge Österreich AG.

Following a lengthy period of consolidation and reorganisation, by 2002 the MAN tactical truck ranges (the FX, LX and SX) were assembled by MAN Sonderfahrzeuge AG (now MAN Nutzfahrzeuge Österreich AG) at the former Österreich Automobilfabrik ÖAF-Gräf und Stift AG plant in Vienna.

The LX range was phased out of production during 2004 and the FX range during 2005. Both ranges have been replaced by the HX range of tactical trucks. Some components for the MAN tactical truck ranges, such

A MAN M2000 range (4 × 4) truck, model 16.284 LAE (16 - 16 tonnes GVW; 284 - engine hp; L - L/M 2000 range; A - all-wheel drive; E - single wheels) (Shaun C Connors)   0544856

as the torsionally rigid chassis frame of the SX range, and the MAN modular military cab fitted to all X range trucks, were manufactured at the Star truck plant in Poland, they are now manufactured in Austria. Star Sp. z.o.o. was acquired by MAN Nutzfahrzeuge AG in December 1999.

As part of the consolidation and reorganisation process, by the late 1990s, Steyr's 17 M (4 × 4) and 24 M (6 × 6) ranges of heavy military trucks had been phased out of production, to be replaced by militarised versions of the MAN F2000 heavy range of commercial trucks; HX range trucks for certain applications. Militarised F2000 models were also produced at the former Österreich Automobilfabrik ÖAF-Gräf und Stift AG plant. The F2000 range was replaced in production during 2004 by equivalent models based on the heavier models of the MAN TGA range. Details of the Steyr 17 M (4 × 4) and 24 M (6 × 6) ranges, the MAN F2000 range and TGA range can be found elsewhere in this section.

Steyr's (4 × 4) Medium Tactical Truck range was also phased out of production during the late 1990s in favour of MAN designs, in this instance militarised versions of the MAN L2000 and M2000 ranges of light and medium two-axle commercial trucks. The Steyr Medium Tactical Truck range and the MAN L2000 and M2000 ranges are visually similar as they

A MAN TGM range (4 × 4) truck (MAN)   1190247

A MAN F2000 range (6 × 6) truck, model 33.464 DFAE (33 - tonnes GVW; 464 - engine hp; D - three axle, heavy range; F - cab-over engine; A - all-wheel drive; E - single wheels) (Shaun C Connors)   1047651

A MAN TGA range (6 × 6) truck. TGA (and TGL/TGM) range designations denote: TGA (range); 26 (GVW, tonnes); 310 (power output, hp); 6 × 6 (configuration); BB (suspension, leaf front/leaf rear) (Shaun C Connors)   1185449

A MAN SX range truck. Designations for MAN SX (and HX) truck ranges have recently been simplified and now denote SX/HX (range); 32 (GVW, tonnes); 440 (engine power output, hp); 8 × 8 (configuration). Additionally, and to further simplify identification, each HX/SX range truck now has its own specific designation, in the case of model SX 32.440 8 × 8 this being SX 45 (MAN)   0536659

share versions of the same Steyr-designed cab. All L2000 and M2000 trucks (including commercial production) trucks were assembled at the former Steyr plant in Steyr, near Vienna.

MAN introduced the TGL and TGM range of two-axle commercial trucks during 2005 to replace the L2000 and M2000 ranges. Militarised versions of the TGL and TGM became available during 2006, with the Austrian Army being the launch customer. By mid-2007 all militarised L2000 and M2000 models had been replaced in production in Austria by equivalent models from the TGL and TGM ranges. Production of L2000 and M2000 models will shift to India where production will continue and primarily for local and Asian markets by Man Force Trucks Pvt. Ltd. (MFTL), a joint venture company between Force Motors (formerly Bajaj Tempo) and MAN Nutzfahrzeuge AG.

Dependant on market, essentially the same model from either the tactical ranges or militarised commercial ranges of trucks may now be marketed and branded as either MAN or Steyr, or for the Austrian market only, as ÖAF. For the purpose of clarification, the models included in this section as MAN trucks will either be MAN-specific models produced prior to the final consolidation of the MAN/Steyr ranges during 2000, or will be tactical (LX, FX, HX or SX) or militarised (TGA, F2000, L2000 or M2000) models supplied branded as MAN. Where the same model is known to have also been supplied branded Steyr or ÖAF, this will be noted in the entry text.

Throughout 2006 MAN revised and simplified the designation of its military truck ranges. Prior to this and taking the model 25.413 DFAEG as an example, the designation can be broken down as follows: 25 denotes nominal Gross Vehicle Weight (GVW) in tonnes, while 413 denotes engine horsepower. The complex lettering designations (of which there were other less frequently applied examples) denote: D - three-axle, heavy range; F - Cab-Over-Engine (COE); A - all-wheel drive; E - single wheels; G - high-mobility. Taking current model TGA 26.310 6 × 6 BB as an example, the revised basic designations now denote: TGA (range); 26 (GVW, tonnes); 310 (power output, hp); 6 × 6 (configuration); BB (suspension, leaf front/leaf rear). HX and SX range models have a similar designation system (minus suspension type), but HX/SX range identification is further simplified as each specific model has its own model number, in the case of HX 32.440 8 × 8 this being HX77.

In addition to five plants in Germany, two in Austria and Poland, MAN has production facilities in South Africa (Johannesburg) and Turkey (Ankara), and in 2000 the company acquired British truck maker ERF from Western Star of Canada (now owned by Freightliner LLC). MAN also has a 51 per cent stake in the Minsk Automobil Zavod (MAZ) company of Minsk, Belarus.

Certain MAN/Steyr models have been supplied to ELBO of Greece in Semi KnockDown (SKD) configuration for final assembly and inclusion of local content. The most recent models supplied include the 14 M 22 (4 × 4) and the 33 M 41 (6 × 6). Full details of these, and previously supplied models, can be found elsewhere in this section.

MAN military trucks are assembled CKD in Hungary by RÁBA, and have been built under licence in Romania.

MAN Nutzfahrzeuge AG and Rheinmetall AG announced their respective intentions to form a joint wheeled military vehicles company in 2009. This alliance became a reality in January 2010 with the announcement of the founding of Rheinmetall MAN Military Vehicles (RMMV) GmbH. RMMV sees the merger of Rheinmetall's wheeled military vehicle activities with those of the military truck activities of MAN. Essentially this merger unites the complementary technological core competencies of MAN's automotive expertise in commercial-vehicle manufacture with Rheinmetall's technological know-how in the military land sector/systems field. The result is the creation of a new single-source provider for the entire range of armoured and unarmoured transport, command and role-specific wheeled vehicles. Throughout all entries MAN and/or RMMV designations and references are made to suit context.

Status
In production. In service worldwide (refer to specific entries for details).

Contractor
Rheinmetall MAN Military Vehicles (RMMV)

MAN L2000 and M2000 ranges of trucks

Development
MAN L2000 and M2000 trucks are essentially MAN commercial designs militarised to suit individual customer requirements. Some L2000 military models were produced, however production focused on the heavier M2000 range and by 2004 L2000 models were available as special build only.

MAN L2000 and M2000 trucks were assembled at the MAN Nutzfahrzeuge Österreich AG (formerly Steyr Nutzfahrzeuge AG) plant in Steyr, Austria, and for certain markets may have been branded as Steyr. Full details of the relationship between the current MAN and Steyr military truck ranges can be found in the MAN trucks or Steyr trucks entries elsewhere in this section. Full details of specific models from the L2000 and M2000 ranges can also be found elsewhere in this section.

MAN introduced the TGL and TGM range of two-axle commercial trucks during 2005 in order to replace progressively the L2000 and M2000 ranges. Militarised versions of the TGL and TGM became available during 2006, with the Austrian Army being the launch customer. By mid-2007 all militarised L2000 and M2000 models had been replaced in production in Austria by equivalent models from the TGL and TGM ranges. Full details of TGL and TGM ranges can be found elsewhere in this section.

Production of L2000 and M2000 models shifted to India, where production continues and primarily for local and Asian markets by Man Force Trucks Pvt. Ltd. (MFTL), a joint venture company between Force Motors (formerly Bajaj Tempo) and MAN Nutzfahrzeuge AG.

The final known major orders for M2000 range trucks were placed by Oman and Sudan. Oman received around 600 model LE18.280 4 × 4 BB, while Sudan placed an order for 2,700 model LE16.220 4 × 4 BB early-2006, with deliveries running until mid-2007.

MAN Nutzfahrzeuge AG and Rheinmetall AG announced their respective intentions to form a joint wheeled military vehicles company in 2009. This alliance became a reality in January 2010 with the announcement of the

MAN M2000 range truck demonstrating a combination of suspension travel and chassis twist. L2000 and M2000 range trucks are sprung by the combination of parabolic leaf springs, complemented by shock-absorbers and anti-roll bars on both axles (Shaun C Connors)   0547182

MAN 10.224 LAEK (4×4) L2000 range truck of the Portuguese Army (Victor Barreira)   1168553

MAN 18.280 4x4 BE (4 × 4) 18,000 kg GVW truck from the M2000 range; the revised designation system introduced from 2005 denoting: 18 - nominal GVW in tonnes; 280 - nominal engine hp; 4 × 4 - drive configuration; BB - leaf springs front and rear. This example, displayed at IDEX 2005, was destined for the UAE Navy (Shaun C Connors)   1128723

founding of Rheinmetall MAN Military Vehicles (RMMV) GmbH. RMMV sees the merger of Rheinmetall's wheeled military vehicle activities with those of the military truck activities of MAN. Essentially this merger unites the complementary technological core competencies of MAN's automotive expertise in commercial-vehicle manufacture with Rheinmetall's technological know-how in the military land sector/systems field. The result is the creation of a new single-source provider for the entire range of armoured and unarmoured transport, command and role-specific wheeled vehicles. Throughout this entry MAN and/or RMMV designations and references are made to suit context.

Description
Possible variations and configurations for the L2000 and M2000 ranges were extensive and militarisation packages included a tropical kit, a fording capability, blackout lighting, NATO trailer coupling, EMC protection, rifle brackets in the cab, a circular roof hatch for observation and/or weapon mounting, and a cab protection system. Dual rear wheels/tyres were available, as was a conventional (4 × 2) driveline. For most military applications single wheels/tyres and a (4 × 4) driveline were standard. Automatic Drivetrain Management (ADM), an Anti-lock Braking System (ABS) and automatic Central Tyre Inflation (CTI) were further options.

MAN L2000 and M2000 trucks are entirely conventional in design, based on a C-section ladder-frame chassis mounting a common all-steel forward-control cab. The cab tilts forward for engine access and can be supplied in compact, medium length or double-cab sizes. A variety of body types could be fitted, and in addition to the standard troop carrying/cargo-type body can include fuel or water tankers, shelter/box-type bodies or light recovery hampers.

The final M2000 range had GVWs ranging from 10,000 to 18,000 kg. The base model carries the LE10.180 4 × 4 BB (10 - 10 tonnes GVW; 180 - 180 hp; four-wheel drive; leaf springs front and rear) designation, and when fitted with a 220 hp engine the designation becomes LE10.220 4 × 4 BB. The heavier LE14 and LE18 models were both available with 220, 245 or 285 hp engine options.

MAN EURO 3 turbocharged diesel engines were fitted across the range, with EURO 2 emissions versions remaining an option for certain markets. Gearbox options across the range included Eaton manual and Allison automatic. Suspension is by conventional leaf springs, complemented by shock-absorbers and anti-roll bars.

Status
Some L2000 military models were produced, however production focused on the heavier M2000 range. In service (badged either MAN or Steyr) with a number of countries particularly in Asia, the Middle East and South America including Austria, Belgium, Burundi, China, Denmark, Greece (SKD), Kuwait, Oman (approx 600 model 18.284 LAEC (LE18.280 4x4 BB)), Pakistan, Portugal, Qatar, Saudi Arabia, Singapore, Spain, Sudan (2,700 LE16.220 ordered early 2006), Thailand, UAE, Venezuela and Zimbabwe.

Contractor
Rheinmetall MAN Military Vehicles (RMMV)

MAN F2000 range of (6 × 6) and (8 × 8) trucks

Development
MAN F2000 trucks are essentially MAN commercial designs militarised to suit individual customer requirements. The F2000 range entered production in 1992 as the successor to the earlier F90 range. Militarised MAN F2000 trucks were assembled by the now MAN Nutzfahrzeuge Österreichische AG (previously MAN Sonderfahrzeuge AG) at the former Österreichische Automobilfabrik ÖAF-Gräf und Stift AG plant in Vienna, and for certain markets were branded Steyr or (Austria only) ÖAF. Full

MAN 27.314 DFAEC (6 × 6) F2000 range truck of the Danish Army mounting Arthur artillery locating radar (Martin Pagh)   1128720

MAN 32.464 VFAEC (8 × 8) truck of the UAE Army (Shaun C Connors)
1128735

MAN 41.464 VFAEC (8 × 8) F2000 range truck fitted with a water tanker rear body; this example has the larger crew-type cab (Shaun C Connors) 1047646

MAN 27.314 DFAEC (6 × 6) F2000 range truck of the Danish Army; around 250 27.314 DFAEC trucks in four main versions were delivered to the Danish Army between 2001-2004 (Martin Pagh)   1185451

details of the relationship between the current MAN and Steyr military truck ranges can be found in the MAN trucks or Steyr trucks entries elsewhere in this section. Briefly, in January 1990 MAN Nutzfahrzeuge AG of Germany acquired an 85 per cent share of the truck-building activities of Austria's Steyr Nutzfahrzeuge AG. In 1993 MAN exercised their option to acquire the remaining 15 per cent share of the business. Steyr Nutzfahrzeuge AG became known as MAN Steyr AG during 2002 and is now known as MAN Nutzfahrzeuge Österreichische AG.

Production of the F2000 range concluded during 2004. The F2000 range was initially replaced by equivalent models from the MAN TGA range of trucks (full details of which can be found elsewhere in this section). However, from 2007 the TGA range was replaced for mainstream European commercial markets by TGS and TGX models. TGA WorldWide models continue to be available for certain markets. These vehicles are manufactured in Poland and are fitted with EURO 2 or EURO 3 engines. The F2000 chassis also served as the base for the MAN FX range of tactical trucks. The FX range was phased out of production during 2005, to be replaced by the TGA-based HX tactical truck range. Full details of the HX range can be found elsewhere in this section.

Final known sizeable deliveries of militarised F2000 models were made to the UAE and Saudi Arabia. The UAE received around 100 F2000 (6 × 6) and 300 (8 × 8) trucks prior to 2003, and Saudi Arabia received around 140 33.464 DFA (6 × 6) trucks between 2001-2003. Other post-2001 deliveries of F2000 range trucks have included those to Algeria, Denmark, Greece (for SKD), Oman, Qatar and Zimbabwe.

MAN Nutzfahrzeuge AG and Rheinmetall AG announced their respective intentions to form a joint wheeled military vehicles company in 2009. This alliance became a reality in January 2010 with the announcement of the founding of Rheinmetall MAN Military Vehicles (RMMV) GmbH. RMMV sees the merger of Rheinmetall's wheeled military vehicle activities with those of the military truck activities of MAN. Essentially this merger unites the complementary technological core competencies of MAN's automotive expertise in commercial-vehicle manufacture with Rheinmetall's technological know-how in the military land sector/systems field. The result is the creation of a new single-source provider for the entire range of armoured and unarmoured transport, command and role-specific wheeled vehicles. Throughout this entry MAN and/or RMMV designations and references are made to suit context.

Description

Possible variations and configurations for the F2000 range were extensive and militarisation packages have included a fording capability, blackout lighting, NATO trailer coupling, EMC protection, rifle brackets in the cab, a

circular roof hatch for observation and/or weapon mounting, and a cab protection system. Dual rear wheels/tyres were available, as was a conventional (6 × 4) or (8 × 4) driveline. For most military applications single wheels/tyres and an all-wheel drive driveline were standard. Automatic Drivetrain Management (ADM), an Anti-lock Braking System (ABS) and automatic Central Tyre Inflation (CTI) were further options. These option have been carried through to militarised TGA models.

Final primary options for F2000 militarised (6 × 6) chassis included four chassis with 27,000 kg GVWs and carrying capacities of up to 16,500 kg, and four chassis with 33,000 kg GVWs and carrying capacities of up to 22,300 kg. The same engine options were available for both GVW chassis which were MAN turbocharged diesel engines developing 360 hp (EURO 2), 370 hp (EURO 1), 410 hp (EURO 2), 420 hp (EURO 1) or 460 hp (EURO 3).

Final primary options for F2000 militarised (8 × 8) chassis included three chassis with 32,000 kg GVWs and carrying capacities of up to 19,900 kg, and three chassis with 37,000 kg GVWs and carrying capacities of up to 24,300 kg. For certain markets GVWs of up to 41,000 kg were permissible. The same engine options were available for all GVW chassis which were MAN turbocharged diesel engines developing 410 hp (EURO 1 or 2), 420 hp (EURO 1) or 460 hp (EURO 2 or 3).

One of two MAN 41.372 VAFE (8 × 8) F2000 range heavy recovery trucks delivered to the Danish Army in 1994 (Shaun C Connors)   1391446

MAN F2000 range trucks are of conventional design, being based on a C-section low distortion ladder frame chassis with riveted cross-members. The three-seat forward-control commercially derived cab is of all-steel construction and tilts forward 70° to allow access to the engine and transmission. The driver has a suspended seat and single or twin passenger seats can be fitted. The cab is fully enclosed and a circular roof hatch is fitted. If required, a light machine gun can be mounted. Cab options are available.

Motive power (final options) is provided by a choice of MAN 2866 or 2876 (460 hp) series diesel engines coupled to a 16 speed ZF manual gearbox. A ZF hydraulic torque converter is an option to the conventional clutch, a further option being a fully automatic ZF gearbox.

Conventional beam axles and leaf spring suspension is employed, the rear axles being fitted with cross-axle differential locks as standard. A differential lock was optional on the front axle(s).

The standard rear troop carrying/cargo body is covered by tarpaulin and removable bows and is fitted with removable drop sides and tailgate, and has collapsible troop seats down the body centreline. The bench seats, tarpaulin and bows may be stowed behind the headboard when not required. Other body/superstructure options are available, the most popular options being recovery or tanker (fuel or water).

Specifications

	MAN 33.464 (6 × 6) truck	MAN 41.464 (8 × 8) truck
Cab seating:	1 + 2	1 + 2
Configuration:	6 × 6	8 × 8
Weight:		
(laden, GVW)	33,000 kg	37,000 kg (41,000 kg option)
(chassis-cab)	9,850 kg	12,200 kg
(chassis carrying capacity)	22,000 kg	24,300 kg (@ 37,000 kg GVW)
(front axle(s) max load)	7,500 kg	7,500 kg (each)
(rear axles max load)	13,000 kg (each)	13,000 kg (each)
(towed load)	7,000 kg	23,000 kg (@ 37,000 kg GVW)
(GTW)	40,000 kg	60,000 kg
Length: (chassis cab)	9.1 m	8.22 m
Width:	2.5 m	2.5 m
Height: (top of cab)		
(laden)	3.218 m	3.229 m
(unladen)	3.293 m	3.319 m
Ground clearance: (minimum)	353 mm	353 mm
Track: (front)	2.072 m	2.072 m
Wheelbase:	4.075 +1.4 m	1.5 + 3.175 + 1.4 m
Angle of approach/departure:	38°/38°	28°/40°
Max speed: (road, with limiter)	88 km/h	88 km/h
Fuel capacity:	300 litres	300 litres
Max gradient:	60%	60%
Max sideslope:	30%	30%
Engine:	33.464 - MAN D2876LF03 (EURO 3) or D2876LF02 (EURO 2) 11.967-litre 6-cylinder in-line turbocharged water-cooled direct injection diesel developing 460 hp (338 kW) between 1,700 and 1,900 rpm and 2,100 N.m torque between 900-1,300 rpm.	

	MAN 33.464 (6 × 6) truck	MAN 41.464 (8 × 8) truck
Gearbox:	ZF 16S 151 manual with 16 forward and 1 reverse gears. Options included ZF hydraulic torque converter in combination with ZF all-synchromesh manual gearbox, or fully automatic ZF gearbox	
Clutch:	single dry plate	single dry plate
Transfer box:	MAN VG 1700 single speed, 2-speed optional	
Steering:	ZF 8098, power-assisted	ZF 8098, power-assisted
Turning radius: (kerb)	9.55 m	13 m
Suspension:	leaf springs with rubber stops; asymmetrical reinforced springs with telescopic shock-absorbers and anti-roll bar, front axles; slide shackle springs, rear axles	
Tyres:	525/65R 20.5	525/65R 20.5
Brakes: (main)	dual circuit, air, drums all-round	dual circuit, air, drums all-round
Electrical system:	24 V	24 V
Batteries:	2 × 12 V, 170 Ah	2 × 12 V, 170 Ah
Alternator:	28 V, 35 A	28 V, 35 A, 55

Status

Production completed during 2004 and replaced by equivalent models from the MAN TGA range (see text). In service (branded either MAN, Steyr or ÖAF) with numerous countries including Algeria, Austria, Denmark (1995-2004, inc. approx 250 27.314 DFAEC 2001-2004), Greece (supplied as Steyr for SKD assembly by ELBO), Oman, Qatar, Saudi Arabia (33.464 DFA (6 × 6) (140) 2001-2003), UAE (approx 300 inc 41.464 (8 × 8) (74) 2001-2003; 33.464 (6 × 6) (32) 2003; 33.423 (10) 2003), and Zimbabwe (33.373 (seven) 2001).

Contractor

Rheinmetall MAN Military Vehicles (RMMV)

IFA L60 LA/PVB (4 × 4) 5,000 kg trucks

Development

IFA L60 LA/PVB (4 × 4) trucks are of East German origin, placed in production to supersede the earlier W50 series. The vehicle was produced for commercial as well as military purposes with the first examples appearing during 1986. Approximately 591,500 IFA W50 and L60 trucks were produced and exported to 49 countries between 1966 and 1991.

IFA Automobilwerk Ludwigsfelde was taken over by the now Daimler in 1990 and shortly after that, production switched to Mercedes-Benz light trucks and vans. IFA Gesellschaft für Internationalen Fahrzeughandel mbH is the successor of the former IFA Automobilwerk Ludwigsfelde and this company is responsible for the worldwide supply of original spare parts and components for IFA W50 and IFA L60 trucks.

Description

The L60 follows the same overall design layout as the earlier W50 but has a slightly different forward control cab (which can be tilted forward for engine access), revised cab interior, more powerful engine with improved fuel consumption, new transmission and a revised chassis. The chassis uses a torsionally soft ladder frame and can accommodate a variety of types of body. The standard cargo body uses an all-steel platform covered by a tarpaulin stretched over bows with side benches along the side boards to accommodate passengers.

Most variants are fitted with a 50 kN winch with 60 m of cable.

From 2001 at least 55 MAN 35.464 (8 × 8) F2000 range trucks were delivered to the Danish Army (Shaun C Connors) 1391447

IFA L60 LA of the German Army (Stefan Marx) 1128725

IFA W50 of the Lithuanian Army mounting a specialist medical body
(Stefan Marx)   1128726

Variants
L60 AP-N: standard 4 × 4 cargo truck
L60 APB-N: short wheelbase (3.26 m) 4 × 4 cargo truck with 5,500 kg payload; no winch
L60 AC-N: LAK and LAP shelter carrier (4 × 4)
L60 APB: standard 4 × 4 cargo truck with double wheels on rear axle to increase payload to 5,600 kg; no winch
L60 AP: 4 × 2 cargo truck
L60: 4 × 2 tractor truck
L60 N: 4 × 4 maintenance truck
L60 DSK-N: 4 × 4 tipper truck
L60 AIKB: 4 × 2 insulated shelter carrier
L60 ANKB: 4 × 4 or 4 × 2 shelter carrier
L60 AKKB: 4 × 2 shelter carrier
L60 ADK100-N: 4 × 4 crane truck

Specifications
L60 AP-N
Cab seating: 1 + 2
Configuration: 4 × 4
Weight:
    (laden) 12,000 kg
    (unladen) 7,000 kg
    (payload, road) 5,000 kg
    (front axle load) 4,700 kg
    (rear axle load) 7,500 kg
    (towed load, road) 12,000 kg
    (GCW, road) 24,000 kg
Length: 7.13 m
Width: 2.95 m
Height: 3.375 m
Track:
    (front) 2 m
    (rear) 1.97 m
Wheelbase: 3.816 m
Angle of approach/departure: 33°/32°
Max speed: 100 km/h
Fuel consumption: 28 litres/100 km
Fuel capacity: 180 litres
Max gradient: 55%
Fording: 1.2 m
Vertical obstacle: 400 mm
Trench: 750 mm
Engine: Model 6-VD-13 13.5/12 SRF 6-cylinder in-line water-cooled 4-stroke diesel developing 173 hp (129 kW) at 2,300 rpm
Gearbox: manual, synchronised, with 8 forward, 1 reverse and 1 crawler gears or manual with 5 forward and 1 reverse gears
Clutch: with hydropneumatic assistance
Transfer box: 2-speed, lockable
Steering: hydraulic power-assisted
Turning radius: 8.75 m
Brakes: dual circuit, combined air/hydraulic
Tyres: 18.00 × 20
Electrical system: 24 V
Alternator: 840 W

Status
Production complete. The IFA W50 and L60 have been supplied to the armed forces of various nations including Albania, Cambodia, Estonia, Germany (small numbers may remain), Greece (vehicles donated by Germany), Hungary, Iraq (status uncertain), Latvia and Lithuania (vehicles donated by Germany).

Contractor
VEB IFA-Automobilwerke (now Daimler)

Mercedes-Benz Unimog (4 × 4) series 1946-2001

Development
The Unimog (*Universal Motor Gerät*, or universal power-plant) was originally designed in 1946, primarily for industrial and agricultural use. Production commenced in 1948 and by 1994 over 300,000 Unimogs had been produced in a wide variety of models for both civilian and military use.

Current production models replaced the earlier U1550 L and U2150 L (4 × 4) and U2450 L (6 × 6) in production from August 2002 (U3000 and U4000), with the U5000 entering production mid-2003.

To coincide with the introduction of the U3000 and U4000 models, Unimog production moved from Gaggenau to a new facility at Wörth, Germany. Full details of the U3000, U4000 and U5000 models can be found elsewhere in this section.

Unimogs have been licence-produced in Argentina, Australia, Indonesia, South Africa and Turkey.

Description
The layout of all vehicles in the Unimog series is basically the same, with the engine and cab at the front and the cargo area at the rear. Most military models have a two-door cab with a hard or soft-top, and on some models

Mercedes-Benz Unimog U1700L of the Australian Army in Afghanistan; this example is fitted with a replacement Valir Armoured Cab
(Carl Schulze)   1391208

Mercedes-Benz Unimog U1700L of the Australian Army in Afghanistan; note the add-on-armour package (Carl Schulze)   1391207

Mercedes-Benz Unimog U2450L (6 × 6) 7,000 kg truck chassis configured as a Medium Recovery Vehicle for the Australian Army (Ron Fry) 0121282

Model	U1300L	U1550L	U2150L/38	U2450L
Cab seating:	1 + 2 (standard)	1 + 2 (standard)	1 + 2 (standard)	1 + 2 (standard)
Configuration:	4 × 4	4 × 4	4 × 4	6 × 6
Weight:				
(laden)	7,500 kg	8,500 kg	12,500 kg (options up to 14,000 kg)	17,000 kg
(unladen, approx)	5,000 kg	5,000 kg	7,000 kg	8,100 kg
(max load, standard)	3,000 kg	3,000 kg	5,000 kg	7,000 kg
(front axle load)	4,000 kg	4,000 kg	5300 kg	5,300 kg
(rear axle load)	4,000 kg	4,000 kg (4,600 kg optional)	7,200 kg	6,000 kg (per axle)
(GTW, braked trailer)	10,500 kg	11,200 kg (12,750 kg optional)	13,000 kg	12,000 kg
(GTW, unbraked trailer)	1,500 kg	2,100 kg (reduces to 1,500 kg with 12,750 kg braked trailer option)	1,500 kg	not available
Load area:	3.15 × 2.2 m	3.15 × 2.2 m or 3.8 × 2.2 m	4.25 × 2.38 m	5.2 × 2.43 m
Length:	5.55 m	5.54 or 6.4 m	6.67 m	7.58 m
Width:	2.3 m	2.3 m	2.5 m	2.5 m
Height:				
(cab)	2.63 m	2.63 m	2.83 m	2.8 m
(canvas cover)	2.8 m	2.8 m	3.095 m	3.3 m
Ground clearance:	440 mm	440 mm	500 mm	480 mm
Track:	1.86 m	1.86 m	1.92 m	1.87 m
Wheelbase:	3.25 m	3.25 or 3.7 m	3.85 m	3.9 m + 1.4 m
Angle of approach/departure:	46°/51°	40°/47°	48°/36°	47°/49°
Max speed: (road)	85 km/h	85 km/h	85 km/h	95 km/h
Fuel capacity:	160 litres	160 litres	160 litres	165 litres (220 litres optional)
Gradient:	80%	80%	80%	80%
Side slope:	88%	88%	88%	88%
Fording:	1.2 m	1.2 m	1.3 m	1.3 m
Engine:	OM 352 5.675-litre 6-cylinder inline water-cooled direct injection 4-stroke diesel developing 130 hp (97 kW) at 2,800 rpm and 363 N.m torque at 1,800 rpm (U1300L); OM 366 A EURO II 5.958-litre 6-cylinder in-line exhaust gas turbocharged with charge air cooling water-cooled 4-stroke diesel developing 163 (122), 211 (157) or 240 hp (179 kW) at 2,400 rpm and peak torque of 580, 780 or 850 N.m (U1550L); 211 hp (211 kW) at 2,400 rpm and 780 N.m torque between 1,300 and 1,400 rpm or 240 hp at 2,600 rpm and 850 N.m torque between 1,200 and 1,400 rpm (U2150L/38); 240 hp (179 kW) at 2,600 rpm and 760 N.m torque between 1,400 and 1,600 rpm (U2450L)			
Gearbox:	UG 3/40 synchromesh manual with 8 forward and 8 reverse gears	UG 3/65 synchromesh manual with 8 forward and 8 reverse gears.		
Clutch:	single dry plate	single dry plate (330 mm)	single dry plate (360 mm)	single dry plate (360 mm)
Steering:	hydraulic power-assisted	hydraulic power-assisted	hydraulic power-assisted, LS 6E (LS 7 optional)	hydraulic power-assisted, LS 6E (LS 7F optional)
Turning radius:	7 m	7.2 or 7.9 m	8.1 m	9.9 m
Tyres:	12.5R 20	12.5R 20 (14.5R 20 optional)	13R 22.5 (options included 13R 20 Pilote XL, 365/85 XZL, 365/80R 20, 395/80R 20 or 455/70R 24)	14.5R 20 (options included 365/85R 20, 14.5R 24, 455/70R 24)
Brakes:	dual circuit, hydraulic with compressed air booster, discs all-round	dual circuit, air, discs all-round, ABS optional	dual circuit, air, discs all-round, ABS optional	
Electrical system:	12 or 24 V	24 V	24 V	24 V
Batteries:	1 × 120 Ah (12 V), 2 × 125 Ah (24 V)	2 × 12 V, 70 Ah	2 × 12 V, 70 Ah	2 × 12 V, 125 Ah
Alternator:	n/avail	55 A	55 A	55 A

the windscreen folds forward onto the bonnet. The rear cargo area is usually fitted with a drop tailgate, drop sides, removable bows and a tarpaulin cover, although box and shelter-type bodies are regularly installed on the torque resistant chassis. A wide range of optional equipment is available for the Unimog including a fully enclosed two- or four-door cab, generator, front-mounted pump, snow ploughs/blowers, sweepers, cranes and winches.

Mercedes-Benz Unimog U1700L (4 × 4) truck of the New Zealand Army (Gordon Arthur) 1340329

Mercedes-Benz Unimog U1300L (4 × 4) truck of the New Zealand Army (Gordon Arthur) 1340330

Mercedes-Benz Unimog U1350L (4 × 4) 3,000 kg truck fitted with a specialist shelter-type body of the Belgian Army (Stefan Marx)   1047650

Mercedes-Benz Unimog U1700L (4 × 4) truck of the Australian Army fitted with a cargo/troop carrying dropside body. This vehicle is fitted with a crew-type cab (Ron Fry)   1124777

Mercedes-Benz Unimog U1700L (4 × 4) truck of the Australian Army fitted with a dump body. The dump body may be fitted with bench seats an a tarpaulin cover if required (Ron Fry)   1124776

The Unimog vehicle is well known for its excellent cross-country capabilities and all recent vehicles are fitted with a differential lock on both the front and rear coil-sprung axles. Portal beam-type axles are employed for greater under-axle ground clearance.

There are numerous military users of the Unimog family, with many early models remaining in service around the world. One example of the longevity of the base design is the refurbishment programme undertaken by the New Zealand Army. In July 2001 the last of 429 U1700L Unimogs purchased from civilian sources between 1982 and 1986 completed a refurbishment programme that was expected to give a 10-year life extension to the fleet.

The Specifications table provides data for a selection of the more recent Unimog models.

Specifications
See table on page 475

Status
Supplied to Algeria, Angola, Australia (including U2450 6 × 6), Belgium (1,512 U1350 L), Brazil (including U2450 6 × 6), Chile, Denmark, Egypt (inc 200 U1600, 100 with trenchcutter, 100 with backhoe and front-end loader),

Mercedes-Benz Unimog U1300L (4 × 4) 3,000 kg truck and associated trailer of the German Army (Stefan Marx)   1047649

France, Germany, Indonesia, Iraq, Kenya, Kuwait, Libya, Morocco, Mozambique, Netherlands, New Zealand, Nigeria, Pakistan, Peru, Portugal, Saudi Arabia, Singapore, South Africa, Syria, Tanzania, Tunisia, Turkey, United Arab Emirates, UK (Army and Royal Air Force), US and possibly others.

Unimogs have been licence-produced in Argentina, Australia, Indonesia, South Africa and Turkey.

Contractor
Daimler AG

IVECO-Magirus 75-13 AWM (4 × 4) 2,500 kg and 110-16/110-17 (4 × 4) 5,000 kg trucks

Development
Like many older companies the now IVECO-Magirus (part of the IVECO group) can trace its origins back a number of years and through a number of mergers, acquisitions and so on. A more detailed overview of the company history, can be found in the IVECO-Magirus 160-23 ANWM/232 D 16 AL (6 × 6) 7,000 kg truck and associated model entries elsewhere in this section. Briefly, in January 1975, the then KHD commercial vehicles division (Magirus-Deutz Motoren AG) was integrated into IVECO (which is an abbreviation for Industrial VEhicle COrporation). Five unhappy years later, KHD sold its IVECO stock to its parent company Fiat, leaving behind the Magirus name and production plant at Ulm, but regaining its independence as an engine manufacturer. By the mid-1980s, the IVECO brand name had officially replaced any mention of Magirus in the IVECO line-up.

The vehicles covered in this entry, are a based commercial range production which ceased during 1994. Throughout their production run, in addition to the numerous production changes associated with the commercial product, the range of trucks covered in this entry, can also be seen in various reference sources referred to as Magirus-Deutz, IVECO-Magirus, Magirus, or on rare occasions just IVECO. To further muddle the identification issue, some time after the formation of IVECO, the alpha-numeric designation of models was changed to bring it in line with other IVECO products. Not only did this change revise the meanings of any letters used in the designation, but numerically it changed the presentation of the GVW/engine rating information and also reversed its sequencing.

IVECO-Magirus 75-13 AWM (4 × 4) 2,500 kg truck with portal axles and single rear wheels/tyres (IVECO-Magirus)   1185435

Danish Army IVECO-Magirus 110-16 AWM (4 × 4) 5,000 kg truck with single rear wheels/tyres; the vehicle beside it (partly shown) is an IVECO Trakker (Shaun C Connors) 1391417

When taking the 75-13 AWM/130 M 7 FAL model as an example, its post-IVECO 75-13 AWM designation denotes: 75 - GVW tonnes (rounded ÷10); 13- engine hp (rounded ×10); A - air-cooled; W - all-wheel drive; M - military, while its pre-IVECO Magirus-Deutz 130 M 7 FAL designation denotes: 130 - engine hp; M - Magirus; 7 - GVW tonnes (rounded); F - forward control cabin; - A - alrad (all-wheel drive); L - Lkw (truck chassis).

Known users of this range of trucks include Denmark, Egypt, Germany, Greece, Sudan and Tunisia.

Description

All models in this range are essentially commercial designs, but militarised as required. All are based on a conventional Cab-Over-Engine (COE) ladder-type chassis. The all-steel cab is of the tilt type. Motive power is provided by a selection of Deutz air-cooled diesel engines, either naturally aspirated or turbocharged. Manual gearboxes and a two-speed transfer box are standard. The beam-type axles are sprung by leaf springs, with single or dual wheel/tyre options available for rear axle(s).

IVECO-Magirus 75-13 AWM (4 × 4) 2,500 kg truck

The IVECO-Magirus 75-13 AWM (4 × 4) 2,500 kg truck was previously known as the 130 M 7 FAL. Two versions of this truck were produced, one with conventional banjo axles and dual rear wheels/tyres, the other with double reduction portal-type axles and single rear wheels/tyres. Both versions can transport up to 12 troops in a conventional troop carrying/cargo-type body, a shelter/container or a 2,500 kg payload.

The German Army was a major user of the 75-13 AWM. Denmark (and others) have received surplus German Army vehicles. Other confirmed users of the 75-13 AWM are Egypt, Sudan and Tunisia.

IVECO-Magirus 110-16/110-17 AWM (4 × 4) 5,000 kg truck

The IVECO-Magirus 110-16/110-17 AWM (4 × 4) 5,000 kg truck was previously known as the 168 M 11FAL. The post-IVECO designation for this model was originally 110-16 but this was later revised to 110-17, the latter designation more closely reflecting the 168 hp engine power output.

These trucks were available in (4 × 2) or (4 × 4) configuration, the latter having the option of single or dual rear wheels/tyres. Two wheelbase lengths were available, 3.6 or 4.2 m.

The German (designated 110-17 AWM) and Danish (most designated 110-16 AWM) armies are major users of the type, with other known users including Greece (German Army surplus) and Tunisia. Some German Army surplus examples designated as 110-17 have been supplied to the Danish Army.

The 75-13 AWM and 110-16/110-17 AWM were the main models supplied for military use although other models from this range of trucks have been supplied for military use, albeit in small numbers. Other models supplied are known to have included the 90 M 6 FL, 80-13 AM and 232 D 20 FAL, all of which were supplied to the Danish Army.

German Army IVECO-Magirus 110-17 AWM (4 × 4) 5,000 kg truck with dual rear wheels/tyres (Stefan Marx) 1047679

Specifications

Model	75-13 AWM (portal axles)	110-16/110-17 AWM (twin-wheeled (4 × 4))
Cab seating:	1 + 2	1 + 2
Configuration:	4 × 4	4 × 4
Weight:		
(laden)	7,500 kg	11,800 kg
(unladen)	4,900 kg	6,400 kg
(max load)	2,600 kg	5,400 kg
(towed load)	7,500 kg	11,800 kg
Length:	5.51 m	7.1 m
Width:	2.4 m	2.466 m
Height:		
(cab)	2.835 m	2.835 m
(tarpaulin)	3.24 m	3.25 m
(load area)	1.44 m	1.49 m
Ground clearance:	440 mm	264 mm
Track:	1.852 m	1.92/1.724 m front/rear
Wheelbase:	3.1 m	3.6 m
Angle of approach/departure:	39°/50°	35°/24°
Max speed:	83 km/h	80 km/h
Range:	900 km	600 km
Fuel capacity:	130 litres	130 litres
Gradient:	>60%	>60%
Side slope:	30%	30%
Fording:	800 mm (optional 1.2 m)	800 mm (optional 1.2 m)
Engine:	Deutz Diesel F 6 L 913 6.128-litre 6-cylinder naturally aspirated air-cooled 4-stroke diesel developing 130 hp (97 kW) at 2,500 rpm and 353 N.m torque at 1,600 rpm	Deutz Diesel BF 6 L 913 6.128-litre 6-cylinder turbocharged air-cooled 4-stroke diesel developing 168 hp (125 kW) at 2,650 rpm and 520 N.m torque at 1,600 rpm
Gearbox:	manual, 5 forward and 1 reverse gears	manual, 6 forward and 1 reverse gears
Clutch:	single dry disc	single dry disc
Transfer box:	2-speed	2-speed
Steering:	ball and nut, assisted	ball and nut, assisted
Turning radius:	7.1 m	7.9 m
Suspension:	semi-elliptic leaf springs with hydraulic shock-absorbers, front and rear (rear anti-roll bar optional)	
Tyres:	12.5R × 20	10R 22.5
Brakes:		
(main)	dual circuit, air over hydraulic, drums all-round (exhaust brake optional)	dual circuit, air over hydraulic, drums all-round
(parking)	mechanical on rear wheels	mechanical on rear wheels
Electrical system:	24 V	24 V
Batteries:	2 × 12 V, 100 Ah	2 × 12 V, 100 Ah
Alternator:	28 V, 35 A	28 V, 35 A

Status

Production complete. Various models in service with Egypt, Denmark, Germany, Greece, Sudan, Tunisia and other undisclosed countries in smaller numbers (see text).

Contractor

IVECO-Magirus AG

IVECO-Magirus 160-23 ANWM/232 D 16 AL (6 × 6) 7,000 kg truck and associated models

Development

Like many older companies, the now IVECO-Magirus (part of the IVECO group) can trace its origins back a number of years and through a number of mergers, acquisitions and so on. IVECO-Magirus has its origins in a fire brigade and accessories equipment company set up in Ulm by Conrad Dietrich Magirus in 1861. This company launched its first truck, the three-tonne payload 3C, in 1917 and supplied its first trucks to the German Army in 1918. In 1936 Magirus AG was effectively taken over by Humboldt-Deutz-Motoren AG of Cologne.

IVECO-Magirus 90-13 ANWM/130 D 9 AL (4 × 4) 4,000 kg truck
(IVECO-Magirus)   1185432

IVECO-Magirus 160-23 ANWM/232D16AL (6 × 6) 7,000 kg truck of the Portuguese Army (Victor Barreira)   1391243

Humboldt-Deutz-Motoren was the result of a 1930 merger between Humboldt AG and Deutz-Motoren AG. Humboldt AG which arose in 1871 from a machinery factory that had been set up in 1865 while Deutz-Motoren AG dated back to 1864 when it was founded as N A Otto & Cie, the world's oldest engine manufacturer and inventor of the four-stroke engine.

In 1938 and because of a financial linking with Klockner-Werke AG, Humboldt-Deutz-Motoren became Klockner Humboldt-Deutz - usually abbreviated to KHD. KHD is today perhaps best-known for its air-cooled diesel engine range which was introduced shortly after WW2. Magirus-Deutz would become the main adopted name for KHD's truck production in post-war years (although some models were still badged Deutz) and by 1964 the company had dropped the previously popular planet names (Jupiter, Mercury, Saturn, Uranus and so on) in favour of an alpha-numeric designation system.

In 1974 Magirus-Deutz Motoren AG was founded as a separate company and as part of a co-operation agreement in the field of commercial vehicles between Klockner-Humboldt-Deutz AG of Germany and Fiat of Italy. In January 1975 the KHD commercial vehicles division (Magirus-Deutz Motoren AG) was integrated into IVECO (which is an abbreviation for Industrial VEhicle COrporation) but five unhappy years later KHD would sell its IVECO stock to Fiat, leaving behind the Magirus name and production plant at Ulm, but regaining its independence as an engine manufacturer. By the mid-1980s, the IVECO brand name had replaced any mention of Magirus in the IVECO line-up, and in 1997 Klockner Humboldt-Deutz changed its name to Deutz AG.

The IVECO-Magirus bonneted trucks covered in this entry were produced commercially from 1971 until 1998. They differed visually from earlier generation Magirus-Deutz bonneted models such as the Jupiter and Uranus in that the cab and bonnet was no longer curved or rounded in any way, it being far more angular and functional in appearance. There was no direct replacement for this range of trucks in the IVECO line-up.

As heavy duty models, these trucks were intended primarily for commercial use in quarries and on construction sites, and some 10,000 commercial examples were sold to Russia in 1974 for work on a trans-Siberian railway project. However, a truck of this type is also clearly well-suited to military applications and as a result, several thousand examples were sold to a number of armed forces, the majority of sales being to African or Middle Eastern nations.

By the early 1970s, Germany had opted for MAN tactical truck designs, and with most other European countries having an indigenous truck manufacturing capability at this time, there was little European military opportunity for the then Magirus-Deutz with this range.

A comprehensive list of users has never been made available by IVECO-Magirus, however it is known that in addition to small quantities supplied to a number of other users including Egypt, Peru, Turkey and the United Arab Emirates (UAE), Algeria, Sudan and Tunisia had also received large quantities. Several thousand examples of two models from this range were also licence-produced in South Africa as the SAMIL 50 and SAMIL 100. Full details of the SAMIL range can be found elsewhere in this section.

Algeria is known to have received around 6,000 160-23 ANWM models, the final batch of this model produced being 1,000 vehicles for Algeria; deliveries were completed during 1985. Around 4,000 of Algeria's 160-23 ANWM fleet are thought to remain in service and prior to 2007, in co-operation with IVECO-Magirus, around 1,000 examples had been refurbished/rebuilt. A further 300 vehicles had been completed by the end of 2010.. Algeria has also received quantities of the 200-23 ANWM and the 210-32 ANWM, and during 1982-1983 some 600 (6 × 6) 400M33 AS heavy tank transporter tractor trucks fitted with twin Rotzler winches. A further 99 400M33 AS vehicles with the revised IVECO-style 330-40 ANWTM designation were delivered during 1985.

Tunisia received around 600 160-23 ANWM, of which around 500 are thought to remain in service. A rebuild programme began in 1996 and late-2010 it was confirmed this had concluded with around 450 examples rebuilt. Tunisia also received quantities of the 90-13 ANWM, 120-19 ANWM, 260-23 ANWM (tippers) and 330-32 ANWTM (6 × 6) tractor trucks for use in the tank transport role.

Tunisia also received small numbers of 75-13 AWM 2,500 kg payload (4 × 4) and 110-16 AWM 5,000 kg payload (4 × 4) trucks, these trucks being of the Cab-Over-Engine (COE) type and powered by 130 hp naturally aspirated (75-13) and 168 hp turbocharged (110-16) versions of the Deutz F 6 L 913 6.128-litre 6-cylinder air-cooled engine as used in the bonneted range. Full details of these and other similar IVECO-Magirus COE models can be found elsewhere in this section.

Sudan is understood to have received examples of the 90-13 ANWM, 120-19 ANWM, 160-23 ANWM, 260-23 ANWM (tippers) and some 330-32 ANWTM (6 × 6) tractor trucks for use in the tank transport role. One further user of these trucks in the tank transport role is Peru which operates an undisclosed number of 310M32 ANWTM models. Full details of the heavy equipment transporters can be found in the Heavy equipment transporters section.

The only known European military user of this range was the UK which received 91 330-25 ANWM models fitted with a heated (via the engine exhaust) dump body assembled in UK by EDBRO. Eight of these vehicles, which were replaced in service by the Foden Medium Dump Truck (MDT), were modified to operate at temperatures down to –40°C.

Description
The range of trucks covered in this entry can, in various reference sources, be seen referred to as Magirus-Deutz, IVECO-Magirus, Magirus, or on rare occasions just IVECO. To further confuse identification issues, some time after the formation of IVECO the alpha-numeric designation of models was changed to bring it in line with other IVECO products. Not only did this change revise the meanings of any letters used in the designation, but numerically it not only changed the presentation of the GVW/engine rating information, it also reversed its sequencing.

Taking model 160-23 ANWM/232 D 16 AL as an example its post-IVECO 160-23 ANWM designation denotes: 160 - GVW tonnes (rounded ±10); 23 - engine hp (rounded ×10); A - air-cooled; N - bonneted; W - all-wheel drive; M - military, while its pre-IVECO Magirus-Deutz 232 D 16 AL designation denotes: 232 - engine hp; D - Deutz engine; 16 - GVW tonnes (rounded); A – alrad (all-wheel drive); L - Lkw (truck chassis). AK and AS designations were also used, these denoting tipper (K - kipper) and tractor (S - Sattelzugmaschine).

A number of different military models were produced in (4 × 4) and (6 × 6) drive configurations, the latter including heavy tractor trucks for the tank transport role. All models were essentially similar in their base design and were built on a conventional C-section ladder-type chassis. Axles were either single or double reduction and sprung by leaf springs, inverted on the rear bogies of (6 × 6) chassis. Manual gearboxes (six speed on virtually all but heavy tractor trucks) were coupled to a two speed transfer box.

A selection of Deutz air-cooled diesel engines were used across the range, these including the 6.128-litre F 6 L 913 with six cylinders, the 11.310-litre F 8 L 413, 12.763-litre F 8 L 413 F or 13.382-litre F 8 L 513 with eight cylinders, and the 15.953-litre F 10 L 413 F with 10 cylinders. For most applications, these engines were naturally aspirated, but where a turbocharger was fitted the engine designation was prefixed by the letter B, for example the F 6 L 913 became the BF 6 L 913 when fitted with a turbocharger.

The main visual difference between the models in chassis-cab form was the bonnet while three bonnets of differing length available could accommodate either the six-, eight,- or 10-cylinder engines. Final production models (of which no military sales are known) were manufactured in Italy (Bolzano) and fitted with the longer bonnet and IVECO six cylinder in-line water-cooled engines. Production shifted to Italy when the Ulm production plant began to manufacture the IVECO Euro range of trucks in 1992.

Models produced in (4 × 4) configuration, included the 4,000 kg payload 90-13 ANWM and 90-14 ANWM, the main difference between these two models being the more powerful (150 hp and 109 N.m torque) turbocharged version of the BF 6 L 913 engine fitted to the latter. One other

(4× 4) model was the 5,000 kg payload 120-19 ANWM, and it was on this model on which the South African SAMIL (which is an abbreviation for South African MILitary) 50 was based.

Rigid chassis (6 × 6) models produced, included the 7,000 kg payload 160-23 ANWM, 8,000 kg payload 160-25 ANWM, 10,000 kg payload 200-23 ANWM and 210-32 ANWM (on which the South African SAMIL 100 is based), and 12,000 kg payload 240-25 ANWM and 240-32 ANWM. By far the most popular military model was the 7,000 kg payload 160-23 ANWM. Tractor truck models produced, included the 310-32 ANTWM, 330-32 ANTWM and 330-40 ANWTM, the T in the designation denoting tractor.

Specifications

Model	90-13 ANWM/130 D 9 AL (4 × 4) [90-14 where different]	(160-23 ANWM/232 D 16 AL (6 × 6)
Cab seating:	1 + 2 (up to 16 in rear)	1 + 2 (up to 18 in rear)
Configuration:	4 × 4	6 × 6
Weight:		
(laden)	10,100 kg	16,400 kg
(unladen)	6,100 kg	9,400 kg
(max load)	4,000 kg	7,000 kg
(towed load)	5,000 kg	12,000 kg
Length:	7.195 m	8.55 m
Width:	2.5 m	2.5 m
Height:		
(air intake)	2.97 m	2.99 m
(tarpaulin)	3.2 m	3.365 m
(load area)	1.4 m	1.565 m
Ground clearance:	310 mm	370 mm
Track:		
(front)	1.97 m	2.005 m
(rear)	1.902 m	2.048 m
Wheelbase:	4.2 m	4.2 m + 1.38 m
Angle of approach/ departure:	42°/31°	38°/38°
Max speed:	82 km/h	80 km/h
Range:	900 km [850 km]	700 km
Fuel capacity:	130 litres	200 litres (optional 300 litres or 300 litres plus 200 litres)
Max gradient:	43% [60%]	>60%
Side slope:	30%	30%
Fording:	800 mm (optional 1.2 m)	800 mm (optional 1.2 m)
Engine:	Deutz Diesel F 6L 913 6.128-litre 6-cylinder naturally aspirated air-cooled diesel developing 130 hp (97 kW) at 2,500 rpm and 353 N.m torque at 1,600 rpm. Deutz Diesel BF 6L 913 6.128-litre 6-cylinder turbocharged air-cooled diesel developing 145 hp (108 kW) at 2,500 rpm and 462 N.m torque at 1,800 rpm	Deutz Diesel F 8 L 413 11.31-litre V8 naturally aspirated air-cooled diesel developing 232 hp (174 kW) at 2,650 rpm and 676 N.m torque at 1,500 rpm
Gearbox:	manual with 6 forward and 1 reverse gears	manual with 6 forward and 1 reverse gears
Clutch:	single dry disc	single dry disc
Transfer box:	2-speed, lockable centre differential	2-speed, lockable centre differential
Steering:	ball and nut, assisted	ball and nut, assisted
Turning radius:	9.9 m	10.4 m
Suspension:		
(front)	leaf springs with hydraulic telescopic shock-absorbers	single flexibility leaf springs with hydraulic telescopic shock-absorbers
(rear)	leaf springs with hydraulic telescopic shock-absorbers	inverted single flexibility leaf springs
Tyres:	13.00 × 20	14.00 × 20
Brakes:		
(main)	dual circuit, drums all-round	dual circuit (supplementary engine exhaust brake), drums all-round
(parking)	mechanical on rear wheels	mechanical on rear wheels

Model	90-13 ANWM/130 D 9 AL (4 × 4) [90-14 where different]	(160-23 ANWM/232 D 16 AL (6 × 6)
Electrical system:	24 V	24 V
Batteries:	2 × 12 V, 100 Ah	2 × 12 V, 100 Ah
Alternator:	28 V, 35 A	28 V, 35 A

Status

Production complete. In service with (or supplied to) Algeria, Egypt, Peru, Portugal, Sudan, Tunisia, Turkey, UAE, UK and other undisclosed countries (see text for details).

Contractor

IVECO-Magirus AG

Mercedes-Benz Zetros family of tactical trucks

Prior to the public debut of the serial production vehicles just prior to Eurosatory 2008, throughout their development process the Zetros family of tactical trucks were known as the S2000 family.

Over recent years the number of long-term peacekeeping/enforcing style deployments undertaken by the world's military have increased considerably. Such deployments have seen the life cycles of logistic vehicles accelerate considerably. Military trucks are now required to operate globally during prolonged low intensity operations, plus there is an emerging trend for full manufacturer-supplied service support, further reducing the logistic support and cost burdens of modern armies.

Mercedes-Benz identified a possible need for a new generation of adaptable and affordable military support vehicles to replace the often ageing and unsuitable fleets that are becoming ever more expensive to maintain on such deployments. As a result, the company implemented a number of studies to examine emerging truck needs, following which it assessed how it could best meet those needs.

It soon became apparent there was an emerging capability gap within the then current Mercedes-Benz military vehicle product line: the G-Class (4 × 4) light utility vehicle, the Unimog (4 × 4) high mobility family and militarised versions of the commercial families. To plug this gap the company took the decision to develop a new family of off-road vehicles, the Zetros family.

Mercedes-Benz Zetros 1833A (4 × 4) in Bulgarian Army configuration (Daimler) 1391429

Mercedes-Benz Zetros 1833A (4 × 4) during trials for Australia's Land 121 Project Overlander. At the time of writing (December 2010) no contractual decision regarding Overlander had been announced (Daimler) 1391430

Zetros family

Model	1833A (4 × 4)	2733A (6 × 6)
Cab seating:	3 (individual seating)	3 (individual seating)
Weight:		
(laden)	18,000 kg	27,000 kg
(unladen, chassis-cab)	8,100 kg	10,500 kg
(payload, on chassis-cab)	4,000-6,000 kg	7,000-10,000 kg
(max front axle load)	7,500 kg (9,000 kg optional)	7,500 kg (9,000 kg optional)
(max. rear axle load)	9,000 kg (tyre size dependant)	2 × 9,000 kg (tyre size dependant)
Load area dimensions: (L × W)	5.1 × 2.55 m	6.2 × 2.55 m
Wheelbase:	4.8 m	4.75 + 1.45 m
Approach angle:	34°	34°
Speed: (at 75% max rpm)	89 km/h	89 km/h
Fuel capacity:	300 litres	300 litres
Fording:	800 mm standard (1.2 m option)	800 mm standard (1.2 m option)
Engine: (options available)	OM926 LA 6-cylinder in-line turbocharged water-cooled 4-stroke EURO 5 emissions compliant diesel developing 326 hp (240 kW) and 1,300 N.m torque at 1,200-1,600 rpm (EURO 3 option)	
Gearbox:	manual, 9 forward (8 plus crawler) and 1 reverse gears; optional Allison automatic	
Transfer box:	VG1700-3W/1.6	VG1700-3W/1.6
Clutch:	GF 395	GF 395
Steering:	LS 8, power-assisted	LS 8, power-assisted
Turning radius:	10.3 m	11.4 m
Suspension:	multileaf parabolic steel springs on all axles	multileaf parabolic steel springs on all axles
Axles: (standard)	AL 7/52 DS-9, front; HL 7/52 DS-13, rear	AL 7/52 DS-9, front; HL 7/52 DS-13, rears
Tyres: (options available)	1400R 20	1400R 20
Brakes:	dual circuit, air, drums all-round. Supplementary combined engine and exhaust brake. ABS with off road cut-out function fitted	
Electrical system:	24 V	24 V

Lessons learned working with the Bundeswehr on earlier military vehicle projects were carried into the development process of Zetros, a fourth generation truck family, but the first designed from the outset with an intention to offer cost effective military support vehicles with the essential capability for world-wide supportability during operations and deployment. The Zetros was also designed for commercial applications such as operations in open cast mines and on disaster relief operations, and as such was designed to be suitable for operations in countries with little or no infrastructure.

Mercedes-Benz Zetros 2733A (6 × 6) fitted with an exchangeable armoured cab developed by Mercedes-Benz and LMT of South Africa (Daimler)
1391433

Mercedes-Benz Zetros 2733A (6 × 6); note the high degree of chassis twist (Daimler)
1391432

Development began with the then DaimlerChrysler's (now Daimler) International Government Business department undertaking two market surveys on military customers' requirements.

A survey into the potential market for military trucks over the 2002 to 2015 time frame revealed that a number of armed forces would be looking to replace ageing fleets, with the bulk of these requirements being for trucks with payloads of 6,000 kg and over. The second survey considered the capability that potential military customers required from their future fleet. The survey identified that 80 per cent of customers researched were seeking to replace their existing truck fleets with tactical off-road vehicles rather than militarised commercial designs vehicles. In particular, customers rated tactical and strategic mobility, active and passive protection and operations under extreme climatic conditions as high priorities. Commercial operating costs, durability and standards of reliability and maintainability were equally as desirable.

Mercedes-Benz concluded that the desired levels of military tactical mobility could be achieved at an affordable price by using a 'parts box' approach to commercial drive train components, however strategic mobility and crew protection requirements could not be achieved using the latest generation of commercial cabs.

Large, high-volume commercial truck cabs do not fit the C-130 Hercules transport aircraft envelope, primarily by reason of height. Similarly, height poses problems when transport by rail is required. After evaluation of a number of concepts Mercedes-Benz concluded that C-130 compatibility could not be achieved using a commercially based Cab-Over-Engine (COE) design if ergonomic and internal space criteria were to be met, and when consideration to other requirements including protection were examined the decision was taken to recommend the development of a new modular cab for the Zetros family.

The option of some form of crew protection is now virtually a prerequisite on support (B) vehicles, and the Zetros cab was designed to be fitted with armoured protection from the outset, and without

Mercedes-Benz Zetros 1833A (4 × 4) fitted with an exchangeable armoured cab developed by Mercedes-Benz and LMT of South Africa (Daimler)
1391431

Mercedes-Benz Zetros family (4 × 4) prototype. At this point in time the vehicle was known by the designation S2000 (Daimler) 0569396

Mercedes-Benz Zetros family (6 × 6) prototype fitted with a standard dropside troop-carrying cargo-type rear body, as displayed at DVD 2004. At this point in time the vehicle was known by the designation S2000 (Patrick Allen) 1067473

compromising other design criteria. The initial option chosen was one of a 'fit as required' benign in appearance internal appliqué kit. This concept was developed to meet a German Army requirement and subsequently fitted to Mercedes-Benz trucks of the Norwegian and German armies during 1995.

As threat levels on deployed operations have escalated, so have protection requirements, and together with LMT of South Africa Mercedes-Benz has now developed a fully armoured exchange cab solution that meets current protection requirements. The chassis and cab design of the Zetros range allows for the armouring of the passenger compartment together with mine blast, without overloading the front axle.

Free from engine intrusion, the cab is insulated from engine noise and offers a three-seat environment. In terms of size and ergonomics the Zetros cab has been designed to be operated by 5th percentile female up to 95th percentile male. The cabin interior design is based on components and controls from the Axor/Atego commercial truck ranges, thus ensuring that legislative and ergonomic criteria are met while also providing the reliability advantages of proven components.

The standard military cab accommodates three seated (complete with full kit) and has sufficient space for military communications equipment.

The Zetros family comprises (4 × 4) and (6 × 6) bonneted variants. For maintainability, the clamshell bonnet opens wide to provide access to the engine and front axle. An (8 × 8) chassis was proposed during the development process but according to Mercedes-Benz this is no longer under consideration.

Zetros is built around a C-section chassis frame that is used as the basis for Actros all wheel drive commercial construction variants. These have laden weights of up to 41,000 kg and use chassis frames constructed from 9.5 mm thick steel in place of the 7 mm or 8 mm steel for on-road use. In addition to providing a mounting for the enlarged cooling system, the only new component required for Zetros is a reinforced chassis front end to mount snow ploughs or meet the military requirement for suspended towing.

With the exception of the automatic gearbox option, all major driveline components used throughout the Zetros range are Daimler designed, developed and manufactured items.

An in-line multivalve six-cylinder turbocharged and intercooled diesel engine was selected to power the Zetros family. This engine has been developed progressively over a number of years and meets current emission standards. This engine was selected as a Daimler 'world engine' as these are deployed around the globe in numerous arduous duty applications, on- and off-highway, with support available from any of Mercedes-Benz's 5,000-plus dealerships.

The selected engine is from the 900 Series, these having been in production since 1995 and currently fitted to all Mercedes-Benz light and medium trucks, including the Unimog. They are also fitted in tracked construction vehicles, ski slope maintenance vehicles, mobile cranes and other off-highway vehicles.

Manual or automatic gearbox options are available. Manual option is a Mercedes-Benz nine-speed unit. Allison provide the automatic units. The selected gearbox is coupled to a two-speed Mercedes-Benz transfer box.

All Zetros variants are sprung by multileaf parabolic steel springs on all axles. The 6 × 6 is fitted with a fully articulated twin rear axle bogie. All axles are fitted with shock-absorbers and anti-roll bars as required. Axles are of the heavy-duty planetary hub reduction type as supplied by Mercedes-Benz to third party truck and military vehicle manufacturers. All axles are fitted with pneumatically operated differential locks to further enhance off road performance.

The Zetros family uses the Mercedes-Benz heavy-duty variable ratio recirculating ball power steering system, of which over 250,000 units have been supplied since 1995. In common with all Mercedes-Benz off-road trucks the Zetros family is fitted with a dual circuit air pressure 'S' cam drum braking system supplemented by a combined engine and exhaust brake. The service brake system is fitted with and Advanced Braking System (ABS) with an off-road cut-out function and a load-sensing valve on the rear axles to optimise braking power under different load conditions. Fitted as standard are 14.00R 20 high profile off-road tyres. A Central Tyre Inflation (CTI) system and tyres with a run-flat capability may be fitted as options to enhance mobility in extremely soft conditions or following a puncture.

All Zetros variants are capable of unprepared fording to a depth of 800 mm, with 1.2 and 1.5 m options. The off-road tactical mobility for the Zetros family in standard configuration is equivalent to Improved Medium Mobility as defined by Defence Standard 23-6.

To ensure a global operating capability, the Zetros family has been designed to operate through a –32°C to +49°C temperature range. Winterised variants can operate down to –45°C without compromising hot climate operations.

The first (4 × 4) prototype was shown publicly in June 2000. The first (6 × 6) prototype was shown publicly in July 2003. Serial production Zetros models were first shown publicly in June 2008, at which time sales to Bulgaria and Germany were disclosed.

Specifications
See table on facing page

Status
In production. Supplied to Bulgaria (as part of a multivehicle/multiyear contract) and Germany (prototypes).

Contractor
Daimler AG

Mercedes-Benz Vario (4 × 4) light truck

Development
The Mercedes-Benz Vario was originally launched in 1986 as the T2, only gaining the Vario designation following a facelift in 1996. In reality, the Vario's bodyshell has remained little-changed over nearly 25 years of production.

The military Vario is essentially the commercial product fitted with a four-wheel drive system and adapted for military applications.

There are currently three Vario models available for military applications, the 813 DA, 816 DA and 818 DA, the primary difference between models being engine power output.

Description
The Mercedes-Benz Vario (4 × 4) light truck is produced with two possible wheelbases. The standard wheelbase is 3.7 m while a longer version has a 4.25 m wheelbase. A shorter version with a 3.15 m wheelbase has also been produced.

All models are based on a parallel monoframe chassis and have an enclosed commercial-type steel semi-forward control cab for the driver and two passengers. An enlarged crew cab is an option. The load area to the rear can be configured as a pick-up (with provision for a tarpaulin and removable bows), or mount a shelter- or box-type body. Further options include a tipping rear body, while a panel van model can have either a standard or high roof.

Motive power is provided by a Mercedes-Benz four-cylinder diesel engine with power output varying by model, this driving the front 3,000 kg-rated axle and rear 5,600 kg-rated axle via a six-speed gearbox and two-speed transfer box.

Specifications
Mercedes-Benz Vario
3.7 m wheelbase version
Cab seating: 1 + 2
Configuration: 4 × 4
Weight:
(laden, GVW) 7,490 kg
(unladen) 3,340 kg
(payload rating) 2,500 to 4,200 kg
Length: 6.28 m
Width: 2.24 m
Height: (cab) 2.505 m

Norwegian Army ambulance variant of the Mercedes-Benz Vario (4 × 4) light truck (Carl Schulze) 1391206

Mercedes-Benz Vario (4 × 4) light truck fitted with a crew cab and container body (Daimler) 0100326

Ground clearance: 237 mm
Track:
  (front) 1.861 m
  (rear) 1.64 m
Wheelbase: 3.7 m
Angle of approach/departure: 39°/22°
Max speed: 113 km/h
Fuel capacity: 70 litres
Gradient: 73%
Engine: Mercedes-Benz OM 904 LA 4.25-litre 4-cylinder in line turbocharged and intercooled, water-cooled 4-stroke EURO 4 diesel developing 129 hp (95 kW) and 500 N.m torque (model 813DA), 156 hp (115 kW) and 600 N.m torque (model 816DA) and 177 hp (130 kW) and 675 N.m torque (model 818DA)
Transmission: G56 6-speed
Clutch: MF 362 single dry disc
Transfer box: Mercedes-Benz VG550-3W/1.67 2-speed
Steering: Mercedes-Benz LS 4 power-assisted
Turning radius: (approx.) 7.35 m
Brakes: internally ventilated discs, front and rear
Tyres: 9.5R 17.5 or 215/75R 17.5
Electrical system: 24 V
Batteries: 2 × 12 V, 66 Ah
Alternator: 80 A

Status
In production. In service with Chile, Germany, Norway and other undisclosed countries.

Contractor
Daimler AG

Mercedes-Benz Unimog U3000, U4000 and U5000

Development
The Unimog (Universal Motor Gerät, or universal power-plant) was originally designed in 1946, primarily for industrial and agricultural use. Production commenced in 1948 and by 1994 over 300,000 Unimogs had been produced in a wide variety of models for both civilian and military use.

Current production standard (EURO 5 engine) Mercedes-Benz Unimog U5000 (Daimler) 1391424

Mercedes-Benz Unimog U5000 fitted with an armoured cab supplied by Ressenig of Austria (Daimler) 1391425

Mercedes-Benz U4000 Unimog with crew-cab and with a standard NATO shelter in the cargo body (Daimler) 1391427

Current production models for military applications are the U4000 and U5000, these replacing the earlier U1550 L and U2150 L (4 × 4) and U2450 L (6 × 6). The U3000, which was the lightest of the latest Unimog range, is no longer offered. To coincide with the introduction of the first current models (U3000 and U4000), Unimog production moved from Gaggenau to a new facility at Wörth, Germany. Production of the U5000 commenced mid-2003. Full details of earlier Unimog models can be found elsewhere in this section.

Mercedes-Benz also currently produces the Unimog U300, U400 and U500. These are described as implement carriers by the company and while retaining many established Unimog traits, the range-specific panoramic-type cab and driveline choice makes these models better-suited to civilian use. Also available is the U20. The U20 is the smallest Unimog and is based on a shortened U300 frame and features a cab from the Brazilian Accelo light truck (Caminhões Leves) series.

As with previous generations of Unimog, the base chassis and driveline of the latest U4000 and U5000 models is adaptable for a number of other roles, in particular that of light armoured vehicles. The Unimog U5000 is the base of the Doosan Infracore Defense Products BG Barracuda APC, the Krauss-Maffei Wegmann (KMW) All-Protected Vehicle (APV), the Nexter

Displayed at Eurosatory, a Unimog U5000 3,600-litre aircraft refueller (Shaun C Connors) 1296149

Mercedes-Benz Unimog U5000 of the Lithuanian Army. The tanker body and single axle trailer are supplied by EMPL of Austria (Shaun C Connors) 1296171

Demonstrated at DVD 2005, a Mercedes-Benz Unimog U5000 with standard troop-carrying cargo body and an optional front-mounted self-recovery winch (Patrick Allen) 1146255

On the basis of experiences gained with the KMW Dingo, other similar platforms, and developing vehicle requirement, at Eurosatory 2010 Mercedes-Benz unveiled the FGA 14.5 Special Chassis. The FGA 14.5 chassis essentially takes the strengths of the proven Unimog concept and expands upon it to deliver a product optimised for the needs of modern armed forces, plus other users that require something more than an adapted commercial vehicle chassis (Shaun C Connors) 1391426

Aravis, the Rheinmetall Landsysteme Condor APC, and the Tenix (now BAE Systems) S600 Internal Security Vehicle. Outline details of these vehicles can be found elsewhere in this entry. Full details of these vehicles can be found in *Jane's Armour and Artillery.*

Description

The overall layout of the latest generation Unimog remains the same as that of earlier models, that being conventional with the engine and cab at the front and the standard troop carrying/cargo body at the rear; both mounted on a chassis with integrated mounting areas for maximum flexibility. Any significant visual differences in the current models are limited to a grille that was reshaped to accommodate the radiator that comes with the now optional EURO 3 emissions compliant engines. EURO 5 emissions compliant engines are now standard. In addition to new engines, the latest generation Unimogs are also fitted with a Mercedes-Benz Electronic Pneumatic Shift (EPS) gearbox for the first time. Compared to a manual gearbox, this reduces both driver fatigue and driveline stresses, particularly when operating off-road for extended periods.

The standard cab is an all-steel tiltable two-door model that seats two or three (two-passenger bench seat optional). A roof hatch is standard; the backrest of the passengers' seat tilting forward to form a standing platform. Hydraulic suspension for driver and single passenger seats is an option, as is air-conditioning. A seven-seat crew-type cab is a further option. Left- or right-drive versions of all models are available.

An exchangeable armoured cab has been developed for the Unimog by Mercedes-Benz in conjunction with Ressenig of Austria.

The cab mounts to the chassis via three bearing mounting points. The chassis is a C-section torque-resistant ladder-type design with tubular cross-members. Tow and/or recovery points can be fitted front and rear. Platforms, box-type bodies and flats for shelters are mounted on the chassis by means of a torsion-free sub-frame. The standard troop carrying/cargo-type body can seat up to 16.

Early U3000 and U4000 Unimogs were powered by the OM 904 LA engine, the larger U5000 being powered by the OM 924 LA, a bored and stroked version of the OM 904 LA. Motive power for the current U4000 and U5000 Unimogs is now provided by a EURO 5 version of these engines; EURO 3 options remain available. For the first time in the Unimog range engines are coupled to a Mercedes-Benz eight-speed EPS gearbox. A further eight working gears are optional, as is fully automatic shifting. A two-speed transfer box is integrated within the gearbox and all aggregates are sealed against dust, sludge and water. In the event of an electronics failure, some gears may be engaged pneumatically via an emergency switch.

To allow for the fixing of accessories such as engineering attachments, winch, snow plough, dozer blade or crane, a single circuit hydraulic system with two quick-release couplings front and rear, a maximum working pressure of 240 bar and a circuit capacity of 60 l/min is optional, as is a 2,200 or 3,600 rpm (at an engine speed of 2,200 rpm) Power Take-Off (PTO).

The Unimog is well known for its excellent cross-country capabilities. This results mainly from the combination of portal beam-type hub-reduction axles, long-travel coil springs and differential locks that can be engaged/disengaged pneumatically while on the move, without touching the clutch. A Central Tyre Inflation (CTI) system that allows the driver to adjust tyre pressure on the move to suit prevailing ground conditions is an option. A selection of tyre sizes and tread types are available.

Variants

FGA 14.5 Special Chassis

The Unimog chassis has been used as the basis for a variety of light armoured vehicles for many years, most recently the likes of Germany's Krauss-Maffei Wegmann (KMW) have used an enhanced Unimog U5000 chassis for the Dingo 2 All-Protected Vehicle (APV), 700 of which have been ordered by the German and other armies since 2005.

On the basis of experiences gained with the KMW Dingo, other similar platforms, and developing vehicle requirement, at Eurosatory 2010 Mercedes-Benz unveiled the FGA 14.5 Special Chassis. The FGA 14.5 chassis essentially takes the strengths of the proven Unimog concept and expands upon it to deliver a product optimised for the needs of modern armed forces, plus other users that require something more than an adapted commercial vehicle chassis.

With a 6,000 kg net weight the FGA 14.5 chassis features an optimised-for-role OM926LA six cylinder diesel engine developing 306 hp (225 kW), this equipped with new generators that develop up to 335 A. The standard Unimog transmission remains available, this supplemented by a fully automatic six-speed transmission.

The cranked chassis, portal axles and long-travel coil-spring suspension concept of the Unimog is retained to deliver a vehicle with similar mobility characteristics.

Mercedes-Benz suggests that a full range of similar chassis, these ranging from a light (4 × 4) with a GVW of around 7,500 kg, through to a (6 × 6) with a GVW of around 18,000 kg, could ultimately become available.

Dingo 2 All-Protected Vehicle (APV) as displayed at Eurosatory 2008; the Dingo 2 is based on the Unimog U5000 chassis (Shaun C Connors) 1296148

In mid-2010 Krauss-Maffei Wegmann (KMW) completed company trials of the Unimog U5000-based Dingo 2 (6 × 6) Armoured Recovery Vehicle (ARV). Mercedes-Benz does not offer a (6 × 6) variant of the Unimog (Shaun C Connors) 1391428

Light armoured vehicles on the Unimog chassis

The Krauss-Maffei Wegmann (KMW) Dingo 2 is based on the Unimog U5000 chassis; the earlier Dingo 1 was based on the Unimog U1550L chassis. The Dingo is a small-arms fire and mine blast protected light armoured vehicle.

The first Dingo 2 demonstrator was completed by Krauss-Maffei Wegmann (KMW) in 2003 with a total of three pre-production vehicles following, two long wheelbases (LWB) (3.85 m) and one short wheelbase (SWB) (3.25 m). These were funded by the BWB and one additional vehicle was funded by Krauss-Maffei Wegmann and Mercedes-Benz for presentations. Two of the LWB vehicles underwent a six-month trial from November 2003 through to May 2004 by a joint evaluation team consisting of the user and the manufacturer, which involved extensive road and cross-country trials as well as maintenance.

Dingo 2 was accepted for service early in 2004 and the German Army has ordered an initial batch of 52 vehicles with the first of these delivered in late 2004. In mid-2006 the German Parliament gave the green light for the procurement of an additional 149 Dingo 2 APVs worth EUR109 million for the German Army. Of this order, the first 15 were to meet an Urgent Operational Requirement (UOR) and were delivered in 2006, with the remaining following in 2007. In July 2008 it was announced that the German Army had placed an order for an additional 50 Dingo 2 patrol and backup vehicles and four Dingo 2 battle damage repair vehicles. In March 2010 the German BWB awarded KMW a contract for a batch of 44 Dingo 2 optimised for the battle repair role. These and an additional batch of 41 Dingo 2 in baseline configuration (ordered in April 2010) were delivered by late-2010.

The German Army has selected the Dingo 2 as the platform for a mast-mounted battlefield surveillance role. Two prototype vehicles have been completed, these expected to be followed by a further 78 production vehicles.

The Dingo 2 is a potential candidate for the German Army GFF Class 3 requirement, which is for a vehicle with a gross weight of between 10,000 and 13,000 kg and has a minimum payload of 2,000 kg.

In mid-2010 KMW completed company trials of the Dingo 2 (6 × 6) Armoured Recovery Vehicle (ARV) which was shown publicly for the first time at Eurosatory 2010. Mercedes-Benz does not offer a (6 × 6) variant of the Unimog.

In September 2004 Austria placed a contract for 20 Dingo 2 APVs, which were delivered from late 2004 through to 2005. Austria became the launch customer for an enhanced Dingo 2 by placing an order for a total of 15 vehicles in specialist configurations.

Rheinmetall MAN Military Vehicles (RMMV) (previously Rheinmetall Landsysteme) produces the Condor 2 APC which is based on the Unimog U5000 chassis (Rheinmetall Landsysteme) 0590333

In early 2005 Belgium placed a contract with KMW covering the supply of 220 Dingo 2 APVs with an option of an additional 132 units. The Dingo 2 was selected by Belgium following a competition to meet a Belgian Army requirement for a MultiPurpose Protected Vehicle (MPPV). One vehicle was due to be delivered to Belgium late in 2005, with series production vehicles to be delivered between 2006 and 2011.

In March 2008 Luxembourg selected the Dingo 2 as the basis for its Protected Reconnaissance Vehicle (PRV) requirement and placed an order for 48 vehicles. Prime contractor for the overall Luxembourg PRV requirement is Thales France.

The Czech Republic purchased a batch of four Dingo vehicles in early 2008. These are the same build standard as German Army vehicles. An additional 15 vehicles were subsequently ordered and delivered late-2008.

The Dingo 2 is one of seven vehicles downselected for the UK MoD's delayed Operational Utility Vehicle System (OUVS) small requirement.

France's Nexter displayed the Unimog U5000-based Aravis for the first time at Eurosatory 2008. It was announced in May 2009 that the French defence procurement agency (Délégation Générale pour l'Armement - DGA) had ordered 15 Aravis from Nexter. The total value of the contract, including vehicles, turrets and support, is EUR20 million. The first four vehicles were to be delivered in late 2009, enabling training to start prior to overseas deployment. The remaining 11 were to be delivered in the first quarter of 2010 and were declared operational in Afghanistan in November 2010, and in support of mine and IED clearance and neutralisation operations.

The Tenix Defence (now BAE Systems Australia) S600 Internal Security Vehicle (ISV) is also based on the Unimog U5000 chassis. First-generation S600 vehicles were based on earlier Unimog U1550L or U2150L chassis. The U5000-based S600 can carry a maximum of 14 people including commander and driver with specialised versions including a 3,000-litre water cannon and another fitted with a Mobile Adjustable Ramp System (MARS) for use in terrorist, hostage or other emergency situations. U5000-based S600 ISVs have been supplied to Singapore (two, 2005).

The now Rheinmetall MAN Military Vehicles (RMMV) produces the Condor APC, over 600 of which have been built. The latest Condor 2 vehicles, of which eight were recently delivered to the Kuwait National Guard, are based on the Unimog U5000 chassis.

South Korea's Doosan Infracore Defense Products BG (previously Daewoo Heavy Industries & Machinery Ltd) produces the Barracuda APC. This is almost identical to the German Rheinmetall Landsysteme TM 170, which was built in large numbers for the home and export markets, including a batch for South Korea. The Barracuda is based on the Unimog U5000 chassis and it is understood that in addition to the home market, export sales have been made to Indonesia (44) and Iraq (12).

Specifications

Model	U3000	U4000	U5000
Cab seating:	1 + 1 or 2	1 + 1 or 2	1 + 1 or 2
Configuration:	4 × 4	4 × 4	4 × 4
Weight:			
(unladen, chassis)	4,100-4,600 kg	4,100-4,600 kg	4,800-5,300 kg
(laden, standard model)	7,500 kg	8,500 kg	12,500 kg
(max load, front axle)	4,500 kg	4,000 kg	5,500 kg
(max load, rear axle)	4,400 kg	4,600 kg	7,500 kg
Length:	(3.25 m wheelbase)	(3.25 m wheelbase)	(3.25 m wheelbase)
(chassis cab)	5.12 m	5.12 m	5.12 m
(with body)	5.41 m	5.41 m	5.41 m

Model	U3000	U4000	U5000
(body)	3.25 m	3.25 m	3.25 m
Length:	(3.85 m wheelbase)	(3.85 m wheelbase)	(3.85 m wheelbase)
(chassis cab)	5.72 m	5.72 m	5.72 m
(with body)	6.01 m	6.01 m	6.01 m
(body)	4.1 m	4.1 m	4.1 m
Width:	2.3 m	2.3 m	2.3 m
Height: (unladen, standard tyres)			
(cab)	2.72 m	2.72 m	2.83 m
(chassis, front)	960 mm	960 mm	1,060 mm
(chassis, rear)	1.13 m	1.13 m	1.16 m
Ground clearance: (unladen, standard tyres)	440 mm	440 mm	480 mm
Track:	1.927 m	1.927 m	1.927 m
Wheelbase:	3.25 or 3.85 m	3.25 or 3.85 m	3.25 or 3.85 m
Angle of approach/ departure:	46°/51°	46°/51°	48°/54°
Max speed: (limited)	102 km/h	102 km/h	110 km/h
Fuel capacity:	160 litres	160 litres	160 litres
Fording:	800 mm standard, 1.2 m optional with kit		
Engine: (current)	OM 924 LA 4.8-litre 4-cylinder in-line EURO 5 (EURO 3 option) emissions complaint turbocharged and intercooled, water-cooled direct injection 4-stroke diesel developing 177 hp (130 kW) at 2,200 rpm and 810 N.m torque at 1,200-1,600 rpm (U4000); OM 924 LA 4.8-litre 4-cylinder in-line EURO 5 (EURO 3 option) emissions complaint turbocharged and intercooled, water-cooled direct injection 4-stroke diesel developing 218 hp (160 kW) at 2,200 rpm and 810 N.m torque at 1,200-1,600 rpm (U5000)		
Gearbox:	Mercedes-Benz Electrical-Pneumatic Shifting (EPS) with integrated transfer box and pneumatically engaging four-wheel drive; optional fully automatic shifting. 8 forward and 6 reverse gears with synchronised forward/reverse shifting; additional 8 forward and 6 reverse working gears optional. A fully automatic shift is an option. Emergency pneumatic gear select		
Transfer box:	MB 2-speed, integrated with gearbox		
Steering:	hydraulic power-assisted, ZF 8095. Left- or right-hand drive options		
Turning radius:	7.25 m	7.25 or 8.25 m	8.25 m
Axles:	beam-type portal with hub reduction gearing and differential lock; retained by Panhard rods and torque tubes		
Suspension:	coil springs, telescopic shock-absorbers and anti-roll bar, front and rear		
Tyres:			
(standard)	12.5R 20	12.5R 20	14.5R 20
(optional)	335/80R 20, 365/80R 20, 405/70R 20	335/80R 20, 365/80R 20, 405/70R 20	335/80R 20, 365/85R 20, 405/70R 24
Brakes:	air, dual circuit, discs all-round. 4-channel disengageable ABS. Air-actuated 2-stage engine exhaust brake		
Electrical system:	24 V	24 V	24 V
Batteries:	2 × 12 V, 66 Ah, 2 × 12 V 125 Ah (option)		
Alternator:	28 V, 80 A, 28 V, 100 Ah (option)		

Status

In production. In service with Algeria (75, 2008), Austria, Brazil, Bulgaria, Cyprus (40, 2006), Egypt, Finland, France (30, 2007/2008 (refueller)), Germany, Hungary (100 delivered 2003-2004, deliveries continue), Lithuania, Mexico (164, 2009/2010), Saudi Arabia (6 × 6 conversion), Thailand, Turkey (40, 2005), and possibly others. In most cases these figures are from third party sources, Mercedes-Benz unable to comment officially on Unimog military sales for reasons of confidentiality.

Contractor

Daimler AG

Mercedes-Benz LA1113 and LA911B (4 × 4) 4,500 kg trucks

Description

The Mercedes-Benz LA1113 and LA911B (4 × 4) 4,500 kg trucks are essentially the same truck, that later LA911B having a slightly different cab. These trucks were in production for a number of years and remain in widespread military (and civilian) use, particularly in Africa and Asia.

Final production LA911B trucks were available in two wheelbase lengths, 3.6 m and 4.2 m. The layout of all models is conventional, with the engine forward under a distinctive curved bonnet, and the cab is all steel. The cab has seating for the driver and two passengers with the passenger's bench seat folding down to provide access to the roof hatch. The standard cargo area can be used to seat up to 24 personnel and can be covered by a tarpaulin. A spare wheel is carried under the load area. Various other types of body were fitted to these trucks and known to remain in service are ambulance, workshop, light recovery and firefighting bodies. On all models the electrical system is splashproof and to NATO standard, with an external plug socket.

Variants

Botswana Defence Force (BDF) refurbishment

One particular example of the longevity of these models would be the recent refurbishment of around 100 Mercedes-Benz LA1113 trucks by the Botswana Defence Force (BDF).

The aim of the project was to recondition around 100 Mercedes-Benz LA1113 trucks that were procured by the BDF between 1982 and 1986, and with a mileage of around 150,000 km.

The project was carried out in cooperation with the now Daimler (previously DaimlerChrysler), the German government and Ministry of Defence; the BDF contributing 30 per cent of the cost of each truck's refurbishment, the German government the balance. The German

Mercedes Benz LA 1113 of the Botswana Defence Force (BDF), post-refurbishment (Daimler) 1047682

Mercedes-Benz LA911B (4 × 4) 4,500 kg truck (Daimler) 1391029

Mercedes-Benz LA911B (4 × 4) 4,500 kg truck of the UAE Army
(Shaun C Connors)   0567957

Mercedes-Benz LA911B (4 × 4) 4,500 kg truck (in water tanker
configuration) of UAE Armed Forces (Shaun C Connors)   1124799

Ministry of Defence contributed EUR4 million, plus provided the technical skills necessary to ensure the success of the project. Under Phase 1 of the project, the first refurbishment started in November 1996 and by June 1998, a total of 50 vehicles had been returned to service.

Phase 2 of the project commenced in 2001 and was again partly financed by the German government (EUR3 million). The 100th vehicle was completed in July 2002. Refurbishment is intended to extend vehicle life by at least seven to 10 years.

Specifications

LA1113
Cab seating: 1 + 2
Configuration: 4 × 4
Weight:
   (laden) 10,000 kg
   (unladen) 5,500 kg
   (max load) 4,500 kg
   (front axle load) 4,000 kg
   (rear axle load) 6,400 kg
   (towed load) 11,000 kg
   (GCW) 21,600 kg
Length:
   (3.6 m WB) 5.98 m
   (4.2 m WB) 6.9 m
Width: 2.46 m
Height:
   (cab) 2.71 m
   (tarpaulin) 3.13 m
Ground clearance: 340 mm
Track: 1.97 m
Wheelbase: 3.6 m or 4.2 m
Angle of approach/departure: 37°/46°
Max speed: 84 km/h
Fuel capacity: 135 litres
Gradient:
   (GVW) 68%
   (GCW) 26%
Fording: 900 mm
Engine: Mercedes-Benz OM 352 5.675-litre 6-cylinder in-line water-cooled 4-stroke diesel developing 130 hp (97 kW) at 2,000 rpm and 363 N.m torque at 2,000 rpm; optional Mercedes-Benz OM 352A 5.675-litre 6-cylinder in-line turbocharged water-cooled 4-stroke diesel developing 168 hp (125 kW) at 2,000 rpm

Gearbox: Mercedes-Benz G3/50-5/8.5 manual with 5 forward and 1 reverse gears
Clutch: single dry disc
Transfer box: Mercedes-Benz VG500-3W/1.6 2-speed
Steering: recirculating ball (power steering optional)
Turning radius: 8.1 m
Tyres: 12.00R × 20
Brakes: single circuit hydraulic, compressed air-assisted
Electrical system: 24 V
Batteries: 2 × 12 V, 100 Ah
Alternator: 55 A

Status
Production complete. Remains in military service, particularly in Africa and Asia.

Contractor
Daimler AG

Mercedes-Benz Model 1017 (4 × 2) and Model 1017A (4 × 4) 5,000 kg trucks

Development
These two vehicles were developed by Mercedes-Benz to meet the requirements of the German Army for standard commercial vehicles for second-line duties that utilised the maximum possible number of COTS (Commercial Off The Shelf) components, and with only necessary minor modifications to make them suitable for military use. Adaptations included a modified electrical system, a torsion free platform with stowage boxes and adequate structure plus mounting points for van bodies, additional stowage space on the rear wall of the cab for military equipment and installation of an observation hatch in the roof of the cab.

The original contract called for 22,000 vehicles but this was subsequently reduced by 7,000 vehicles to involve other manufacturers in the programme. Final deliveries of the Mercedes-Benz 1017 and 1017A to the German military would total around 15,300 trucks, with final deliveries being made in 1987. The main difference between the two models are the four-wheel drive and larger tyres of the latter. Around 95 per cent of deliveries were 1017A, with the bulk of vehicles being fitted with a standard troop carrying/cargo-type rear body that can be fitted with a tarpaulin and bows if required. These trucks are being replaced by IVECO, MAN and Mercedes-Benz models supplied to the German military by BwFuhrparkService, a private sector company. Of those that remain in

Mercedes-Benz 1017A (4 × 4) of the Slovenian Army (Stefan Marx)   1296152

Mercedes-Benz 1017A (4 × 4) 5,000 kg truck of the German Army. This variant is used for the transport of field generators (Stefan Marx)   1047644

Mercedes-Benz 1017A (4 × 4) 5,000 kg truck of the Portuguese Army
(Victor Barreira) 1391241

Mercedes-Benz 1017A (4 × 4) 5,000 kg truck of the German Army. This variant is used for the transport of mules (Stefan Marx) 1047642

service, many are now used for the transport/mounting of shelters/cabins and generators or other similar sized mobile equipment. A small number of specialised variants including around 100 tipper trucks and fire-fighting vehicles were also produced.

Other users of the MB 1017 included Belgium, the Netherlands, Portugal, Switzerland, and some were also used by the US military in Europe. Surplus German Army vehicles have been cascaded to other users.

Description
The layouts of both vehicles are identical, with the forward control cabs at the front and the cargo areas at the rear.

The parallel ladder chassis is bend-resistant but flexible; the side members are the fish belly type in that the height of the web is tailored to the load acting on the chassis at the respective point. Open hat section cross-members, cold-riveted to the frame, provide the desired torsional elasticity. With this design the chassis adapts to the surface of the road or track and imposes little stress on the material.

The all-steel forward control cab is noise and temperature insulated and the front rests on two rubber-bushed pivot bearings and its rear end on two vibration-damped spring struts.

The heating system keeps the internal temperature between –4 and +25°C and the cab has a ventilation system incorporating a blower. Adjustable air inlets ensure air distribution and window defrosting.

The load carrying platform has a wooden bed with sectional steel seam and is provided with lashing eyelets for pallets and supplies, plus countersunk anchors for the centre seat benches for the transport of troops. The top edges of the drop type wooden side boards are covered by U-sections and side racks are installed for troop transport. The tarpaulin can be removed and the bows, which are adjustable for height, can be removed and stowed away. The truck can be loaded from the sides, even with the bows installed.

Specifications

Model	1017	1017A
Cab seating:	1 + 1 (1 + 2 optional)	1 + 1 (1 + 2 optional)
Configuration:	4 × 2	4 × 4
Weight:		
(laden)	11,700 kg	12,200 kg
(unladen)	6,250 kg	6,800 kg
(max load)	5,450 kg	5,400 kg

Model	1017	1017A
(max towed load)	12,800 kg	12,300 kg
Length:	7.19 m	7.19 m
Width:	2.47 m	2.47 m
Height:		
(cab, laden)	2.665 m	2.843 m
(cab, unladen)	2.7 m	2.88 m
(load area, unladen)	1.425 m	1.525 m
Load area dimensions:	5 × 2.38 m	5 × 2.38 m
Ground clearance:	267 mm	267 or 288 mm; variant dependant
Track: (front)	1.923 m	2.055 m
Wheelbase:	3.6 m	3.6 m
Angle of approach/departure:	23°/20°	30°/23°
Max speed:	87 km/h	81 km/h
Range:	730 km	695 km
Fuel capacity:	135 litres	135 litres
Fuel consumption:	18.5 litres/100 km	19.4 litres/100 km
Gradient:		
(road)	45%	46%
(off-road)	n/avail	80%
Fording:	500 mm	500 mm
Engine:	OM 352A 6-cylinder turbocharged water-cooled 4-stroke direct injection diesel developing 172 hp (128 kW) at 2,800 rpm	
Clutch:	hydraulically operated	hydraulically operated
Transfer box:	none	2-speed
Steering:	hydraulic	hydraulic
Turning radius:	7.4 m	8.75 m
Suspension: (front and rear)	leaf springs, telescopic shock-absorbers and torsion bar stabilisers, rear axle has secondary leaf spring,	
Tyres:	8R 22.5	10R 22.5
Brakes:		
(main)	dual circuit, hydraulic with air-assistance, drums all-round	dual circuit, hydraulic with air-assistance, drums all-round
(parking)	spring loaded	spring loaded
(exhaust brake)	standard	standard
Electrical system:	24 V	24 V
Batteries:	2 × 12 V	2 × 12 V

Status
Production complete. Supplied to Belgium, Germany, Netherlands, Portugal, Slovenia (ex-German Army), Switzerland and the US military and some other undisclosed NATO countries.

Contractor
Daimler AG.

MAN-Volkswagen Type 8.136 FAE, 9.136 FAE, 8.150 FAE and 9.150 FAE (4 × 4) 3,000 kg light trucks

Development
These light trucks, originally the Type 8.136 FAE and 9.136 FAE and later the Type 8.150 FAE and 9.150 FAE (8/9 - nominal GVW in tonnes; 136/150 - engine hp), were developed jointly by MAN and Volkswagen and first shown during Spring 1983.

In late 1984, the Danish Army ordered more than 725 of the Type 8.136 FAE version, at a reported cost of DKK45 million, for delivery between 1985 and 1989; by late 1990, 989 examples had been delivered with an outstanding option for a further 60. These trucks were the direct replacement for the Unimog 416.

As of late 2005 it was reported that 893 Type 8.136 FAE remained in service with the Danish Army (55 of these a HMF-TL3000-K1 materials handling crane); 14 with the Air Force and four with the Navy.

In September 2005, Denmark's Army Material Command announced the donation of 100 surplus-to-requirement Type 8.136 light trucks to Iraq. Valued at DKK10 million, the complete package included training and spares worth DKK1 million.

In 1987, MAN received an order from the British Army for 42 Type 9.136 FAE vehicles. In early 1988 the engine rating was increased to 150 hp and the British Army ordered 15 units of the new model Type 9.150 FAE. By the end of September 1990 100 units had been delivered. Denmark's armed forces also operate the Type 8.150 FAE, with (as of late 2005) 81 examples in service with the Army, five with the Air Force and nine with the Navy.

MAN-Volkswagen Type 8.136 FAE 3,000 kg truck of the Danish Army in Kosovo with a shelter-type rear body (Shaun C Connors) 1296179

MAN-Volkswagen Type 8.136 FAE 3,000 kg truck of the Danish Army in Kosovo fitted with a standard troop carrying/cargo-type body and tarpaulin (Shaun C Connors) 1296180

A 3.5 m wheelbase version of these trucks has been licence-produced in Hungary by the RÁBA Works Truck and Tractor Factory at Gyor. This model is known as the RÁBA H9.114-4.4 and is powered by a MAN D0828GF01 diesel developing 155 hp at 2,700 rpm.

Description

These trucks are of conventional layout, with all-steel forward control cabs. Seating is provided inside the cab for the driver and one or two passengers and there is space for a spare wheel and tool stowage behind the cab. The cab tilts forward for full engine access. Various body options are available, including standard dropside troop/cargo or a variety of shelter/box bodies up to a maximum weight of 3,785 kg (8.150 FAE) or 5,195 kg (9.150 FAE) for the 3.1 m wheelbase variant.

The conventional C-section chassis has riveted cross-members and the two rigid beam axles are sprung by semi-elliptic leaf springs and telescopic shock-absorbers, front and rear. Maximum axle loadings are 3,700 kg (front), 4,000/5,700 kg (rear), models 8.150 FAE/9.150 FAE, respectively. Four wheel drive is permanent and a rear axle and inter-axle differential lock are standard. Hub-reduction axles allow for increased ground clearance. 9.00R 20 or 10.00R 20 single tyres are standard but 12.5R 20 single tyres, a rear axle anti-roll bar and an anti-lock braking system were options on the later 8.150 FAE and 9.150 FAE models. A self-recovery winch is located behind the rear axle with the cable leading through rollers mounted on the front bumper.

The vehicles for the Danish order are fitted with external engine starting, stowage over the cab, movable running boards and chassis shackles for use when carried on rail cars; and the alternator and fan have been moved to allow fording through water obstacles of 1 m depth.

Specifications

(Type 8.150 FAE; data for 9.150 FAE in square brackets where different)
Cab seating: 1 + 1 or 2
Configuration: 4 × 4
Weight:
  (laden) 7,490 [8,990] kg
  (chassis cab, 3.1 m WB) 3,580 [3,670] kg
  (chassis cab, 3.5 m WB) 3,620 [3,710] kg
  (max chassis load 3.1 m WB) 3,785 [5,195] kg
  (max chassis load 3.5 m WB) 3,745 [5,155] kg
  (towed load) 9,150 [8,010] kg
  (GCW) 17,000 kg
Length: 5.92 m
Width: 2.245 m

Height:
  (laden, top of cab) 2.65 m
  (unladen, top of cab) 2.68 [2.7] m
Ground clearance: 325 [340] mm
Track: 1.8 m
Wheelbase: 3.1 or 3.5 m
Angle of approach/departure: 35°/36°
Max speed:
  (10.00R 20 tyres) 95 km/h
  (9.00R 20 tyres) 92 km/h
Fuel capacity: 100 litres
Max gradient: (at GVW) 60% (with special sump), (at GCW) 38.8 [37.4]% (with 6.44 axle ratio)
Fording: (prepared) 1 m
Engine: D0826 6.87-litre 6-cylinder in-line water-cooled direct injection diesel developing 150 hp (112 kW) at 2,700 rpm
Gearbox: VW7 with 5 forward and 1 reverse gears
Transfer box: MAN G300, 2-speed
Clutch: single dry disc
Steering: ZF Type 8036, hydraulic-assist
Turning circle: 15.5 m
Suspension: semi-elliptic leaf springs with double acting hydraulic shock-absorbers, front and rear
Tyres: 9.00R 20, 10.00R 20 or 12.5R 20
Brakes:
  (main) dual circuit, air
  (parking) mechanical on rear wheels
Electrical system: 24 V

Status

Production complete. Supplied to the Danish (some cascaded to Iraq) and British armies. Licence-produced in Hungary.

Contractor

Rheinmetall MAN Military Vehicles (RMMV)

MAN HX tactical range of trucks

Development

In addition to militarised versions of its extensive commercial range, full details of which can be found elsewhere in this section, MAN also produces a selection of tactical military trucks. These are collectively referred to as the X range.

Development of the X range begins with the Kat 1/KAT 1 (Category 1) high mobility trucks, deliveries of which commenced in 1976; the usual abbreviation for Category 1 vehicles is Kat or KAT 1, although this is sometimes presented as Cat or CAT 1. The Kat 1 range are purpose designed trucks that meet the most stringent of military tactical requirements and have been the subject of continued evolution by MAN, current models carrying the SX range designation.

To compliment the high mobility SX range MAN also produces/has produced the FX, HX and LX tactical truck ranges. As the FX, HX and LX ranges share MAN's modular military cab, to the untrained eye these are often confused with the Kat 1/SX range; there are in fact quite a number of application/capability defining differences between the ranges.

The SX range of tactical trucks are the most mobile of MAN's truck ranges and were purpose-designed to be capable of maintaining pace with tracked combat vehicles across any terrain. They are based around a purpose-designed box-section torsionally rigid (non-flexing) chassis frame design that mounts beam axles sprung by long-travel coil springs. Engines and cooling packs are located behind the cab; all SX range trucks are air-transportable by C-130 Hercules.

The LX range of tactical trucks was introduced in 1988. Compared to the SX range these were designed as a lighter weight, highly mobile and C-130-transportable range of trucks and are based on modified chassis

MAN HX60 (4 × 4) truck of the British Army (Carl Schulze) 1391209

A Project Fortress MAN HX60 (Shaun C Connors)   1391150

A small number of the UK MoD's HX and SX models will be supplied with 7,000-litre tanks for use as Unit Support Tankers (USTs). USTs will operate forward of the Oshkosh Wheeled Tanker and will replace the current Unit Bulk Refuelling Equipment (UBRE) system. UBRE consists of two or three (vehicle dependent) 2,100-litre tanks and pumping equipment mounted on either a flatbed 4,000 kg (two) or 8,000 kg (three) truck. The UBRE concept is more complex than a dedicated tanker but was designed to be interchangeable between trucks if required. However, even before the issue of legislative compliance of a standard cargo truck transporting fuel came along, UBRE units seldom moved from the modified vehicles they were originally mounted on, and so the concept itself - although theoretically sound - slowly became redundant (Shaun C Connors) 1296185

from MAN's M2000 medium weight commercial range. LX range trucks have a conventionally positioned engine, the cooling pack is however located behind the cab. MAN's small block engines are fitted to reduce overall height.

Two- and three-axle LX chassis were available, with carrying capacities ranging from 3,500 to 10,000 kg. For enhanced off-road mobility three-axle LX chassis have the rear axle pair sprung individually by leaf springs.

The FX range of tactical trucks were introduced in 1990 and being optimised for heavy gross vehicle and combination weights, were initially based on chassis from MAN's F90 heavy commercial range, production of which ran from 1986-1992. From 1992 onwards FX range trucks were based on the F2000 heavy commercial range. Most FX range trucks have a conventionally positioned engine. The cooling pack, and for certain applications (heavy tractor trucks for example) the engine, is located behind the cab.

MAN confirmed development of the HX tactical range of trucks at Defence Vehicles Dynamics (DVD) 2003 and first publicly displayed an HX tactical range truck at DSEi 2003. The company subsequently confirmed the HX range will be developed to cover the payload and mobility (both tactical and strategic) areas covered by both the FX and LX ranges. The LX range was superseded during 2004, the FX range during 2005. To cover the weight range encompassed by the LX and FX ranges, the HX range will utilise a wide range of chassis and driveline components, including both small and big block engines, and the eventual number of models will be well into double figures.

By 2002, following a lengthy period of consolidation and reorganisation, assembly of the MAN FX, LX and SX tactical truck ranges had been transferred to the former Österreichische Automobilfabrik ÖAF-Gräf und Stift AG plant in Vienna, briefly renamed MAN Sonderfahrzeuge AG but now known as MAN Österreichische AG. MAN acquired truck-maker ÖAF in 1936. Some components for the MAN tactical truck ranges, such as the torsionally rigid chassis frame of the SX range, and the MAN modular military cab fitted to all ranges, were manufactured at the Star truck plant in Poland, they are now manufactured in Austria. Star was acquired by MAN in 1999.

Dependent on market, essentially the same model from the MAN X range of tactical trucks may now be marketed and branded as either MAN or Steyr, or for the Austrian market only, as ÖAF. MAN Nutzfahrzeuge AG

acquired an 85 per cent share of the truck-building activities of Austria's Steyr Nutzfahrzeuge AG in January 1990, and in 1993 the company exercised its option to acquire the remaining 15 per cent share of the business. Steyr Nutzfahrzeuge AG became known as MAN Steyr AG during 2002 and during 2005 as MAN Österreichische AG. Further details of the relationship between current MAN and Steyr truck ranges, can be found in the MAN trucks or Steyr trucks entries elsewhere in this section.

MAN Nutzfahrzeuge AG and Rheinmetall AG announced their respective intentions to form a joint wheeled military vehicles company in 2009. This alliance became a reality in January 2010 with the announcement of the founding of Rheinmetall MAN Military Vehicles (RMMV) GmbH. RMMV sees the merger of Rheinmetall's wheeled military vehicle activities with those of the military truck activities of MAN. Essentially this merger unites the complementary technological core competencies of MAN's automotive expertise in commercial-vehicle manufacture with Rheinmetall's technological know-how in the military land sector/systems field. The result is the creation of a new single-source provider for the entire range of armoured and unarmoured transport, command and role-specific wheeled vehicles. Throughout all entries MAN and/or RMMV designations and references are made to suit context.

UK Support Vehicle contract (5,165 vehicles + 2,077 option)

It was announced in October 2004 that the UK Defence Procurement Agency (DPA) had selected the MAN ERF UK Ltd proposal for the UK armed forces' Support Vehicle requirement; a contract award followed in March 2005. MAN acquired UK truck-maker ERF from Western Star of Canada (now owned by DaimlerChrysler) during 2000.

The Support Vehicle contract is expected to be worth GBP1.3 billion (USD1.97 billion). The base contract award covered 5,165 vehicles and 69 recovery trailers with the first vehicles entering service in June 2007. Production is expected to continue to 2013 and the contract includes a major support package. The order covered 4,851 cargo trucks and 314 recovery vehicles (now 288), which will replace a range of Bedford, Leyland and Foden vehicles. The contract also includes 1,098 appliqué protection kits.

MAN disclosed at DVD 2006 that after considering a number of options including the possible refurbishment of current DAF four-tonne trucks, the UK MoD had exercised its maximum possible option under the SV contract by ordering an additional of 2,077 vehicles. Delivery totals including the 2,077 option were 7,285 including 69 recovery trailers and a revised figure of 288 recovery vehicles. First Support Vehicle deliveries were made to the British Army in early 2007 with the first cargo versions meeting their In-Service Date (ISD) of June 2007. By early 2011, around 5,000 vehicles had been delivered to the UK MoD, and examples had been deployed to both Afghanistan and Iraq. By late 2010 the total number of Support Vehicles (including trailers) and derivatives contracted to the MoD was 7,479.

The SV contract calls for two model ranges to be delivered to the MoD, SX Improved Medium Mobility (IMM) and HX Medium Mobility (MM), with a >90 per cent quantity bias towards HX models. Three HX models are involved, the 330 hp 6,000 kg payload HX60 (HX 18.330 4 × 4 BB) (4 × 4) cargo truck which forms the bulk of the fleet, the 440 hp 9,000 kg payload HX58 (HX 26.440 6 × 6 BB) (6 × 6) cargo truck (and Unit Support Tanker (UST)) and 440 hp 15,000 kg payload HX77 (HX 32.440 8 × 8 BB) (8 × 8) cargo truck. The contract option covers 2,009 HX60 and 68 HX77.

The two (6 × 6) improved medium mobility vehicles and the two (8 × 8) recovery vehicles are based on SX chassis.

Also competing for this contract was Mercedes-Benz, Oshkosh Truck and Stewart & Stevenson. The Support Vehicle bids were submitted three times with the final bids submitted in October 2003. The contract was originally worth GBP1.4 billion and covered the supply of a maximum of 8,620 vehicles. At one time the DPA was looking at a Private Finance Initiative (PFI) solution but this was subsequently abandoned in favour of a direct acquisition.

Export sales

It was announced late 2005 that as an extension of a current framework contract MAN would supply Denmark's armed forces with 123 HX range trucks. The complete order calls for 20 SX range trucks and 123 HX range trucks, the majority of the HX models being HX77, the remainder being HX58. The majority of the order will be fitted with a Load Handling System (LHS) and with the exception of the seven HX58 and three HX77 trucks destined for the Danish Air Force, all of the Army's 113 HX77 trucks will be fitted for but not with an appliqué protection kit. A small number of vehicles were delivered late-2006, with the bulk of deliveries following during 2007/2008. The total Danish order for HX range trucks now totals around 200, 113 HX77 fitted with a load handling system, 83 HX77 in conventional cargo/tanker truck configurations, and around five HX58 in cargo configuration to the Danish Air Force.

As part of multiyear contract awarded to RABA of Hungary that (mid-2006) called for up to around 4,350 trucks between 2005-2018 and includes the locally produced RABA H-14 (4 × 4) and RABA H-25 (6 × 6) trucks, Hungary will receive up to 150 HX77 trucks, with 45 delivered between 2005-2009 (CKD since 2007). RABA H-14 and H-25 trucks, of which production commenced in 2004, are fitted with MAN engines and use the MAN modular military cab.

MAN Türkiye A.S. produces military MAN models, current production being based on a local adaptation of the MAN F2000 chassis combined

HX77 of the Danish Army (Shaun C Connors)　1296182

Displayed at DVD 2006, this HX77 is to South African spec, the only significant difference between this and UK MoD spec HX77s is the addition of a central tyre inflation system and a fully automatic gearbox opposed to the automated gearbox (automatic changing - two pedals - but retaining a conventional clutch in the driveline) of UK vehicles (Patrick Allen)　1183129

with the F96 cab, the previous generation modular military cab. It is expected that Turkish production will shift to CKD HX (and SX) models in the near future.

UK MoD Urgent Operational Requirements (UORs)

Details of a number of Urgent Operational Requirements to enhance the capabilities of the Support Vehicle fleet were disclosed by the UK MoD during 2008.

Project Fortress (run by the General Support Vehicle (GSV) Integrated Project Team (IPT)) covered the upgrade of 280 vehicles, with the main emphasis on crew survivability. By late 2008 42 had been deployed to Afghanistan and 36 to Iraq, with a further 36 to Afghanistan by mid-2009. All of the 280 vehicles involved are equipped with electronic and enhanced electronic countermeasures equipment in an effort to neutralise Improvised Explosive Devices (IEDs). The forward control cab is fitted with appliqué passive armour to classified ballistic and blast protection levels. The cab's front and sides have been fitted with bar armour to neutralise High Explosive Anti-Tank (HEAT) warhead-equipped Rocket-Propelled Grenades (RPGs) before they impact the main armour. Mounted on the roof of the cab is a Protected Weapon Station (PWS) fitted with a 7.62 mm General-Purpose Machine Gun (GPMG).

Additionally, all UOR SVs are fitted with Infra-Red (IR) headlights, rear-position lights and night-vision devices. Run flat tyres are standard and all are finished in desert camouflage paint. All vehicles are being fitted with the General Dynamics UK Bowman VHF and HP clip-in digital communications equipment and vehicle intercom. All production MAN SVs are fitted with a roof-mounted air-conditioning system as standard. Vehicle types upgraded under the UOR are: the 6,000 kg (4 × 4) cargo light; the 9,000 kg (6 × 6) cargo medium; the 15,000 kg (8 × 8) cargo heavy; the 7,000-litre Unit Support Tanker (UST) (6 × 6); the Enhanced Palletised Load System (EPLS) (8 × 8); the 9,000 kg cargo medium (6 × 6); and the recovery vehicle (8 × 8).

The Enhanced Palletised Load System EPLS is another UOR, this procured under Project Barricade. This EPLS vehicle supplements/replaces the currently deployed Leyland DAF Medium Mobility Load Carrier (MMLC) and Foden Improved Medium Mobility Load Carrier (IMMLC) Demountable Rack Off-loading and Pick-up System (DROPS). Under Project Barricade around 90 standard HX77 15,000 kg payload (8 × 8) cargo trucks were initially converted to a Load Handling System (LHS) configuration, complete with integral container handling unit. Flatrack payload of the EPLS is 13,500 kg.

Under Project Barricade around 90 standard HX77 15,000 kg payload (8 × 8) cargo trucks have been converted to a load handling system configuration, complete with integral container handling unit (Shaun C Connors)　1391151

An additional 87 (56 + 31) EPLS trucks have since been procured outside of the Support Vehicle contract, the 31 vehicles a training fleet. Additionally, in excess of 300 Support Vehicles (including the 56 new-build EPLS) are currently being upgrading to the latest Theatre Entry Standard (TES), with around two-thirds of the required work being carried out in-theatre.

The UK MoD will also receive an additional 107 HX60 (4 × 4) 6,000 kg cargo trucks. These are being supplied by MAN under contract with BAE Systems as carrier vehicles for the Falcon Area Communications Systems, the original platform choice (Supacat) unable to accommodate evolving requirements that included a cab armouring solution.

In summary, the total number of Support Vehicles (including trailers) and derivatives contracted to the MoD to date is 7,479. Additionally, two UK specification Support Vehicle recovery variant (and trailers) will be delivered to the Irish Army during 2010-2011.

Description

The HX range of trucks are essentially the continuance of the earlier FX and LX range concept; the combination of commercial driveline and chassis with a modular military-specific cab. The HX range are based on chassis and driveline components from the heavier elements of MAN's commercial TGA heavy truck range which was first introduced during 2000. MAN describes the HX range as medium mobility trucks, however there is no international standard by which mobility levels are measured, allowing considerable ambiguity and leading to the occasional ambitious claim by manufacturers. There are vehicles available described as high mobility by their manufacturers that are clearly less mobile, both tactically and strategically, than the MAN HX range of trucks.

The HX range of trucks are fitted with the latest version of MAN's modular military cab. This is 290 mm deeper than it's immediate predecessor and has more than 600 litres of gross stowage space in the rear, sufficient for radio equipment and the full kit of three soldiers. The air-sprung vinyl-covered seats for driver and passenger are fitted with integral seatbelts that prevent uncomfortable and potentially dangerous belt-locking on rough terrain. For severe off-road terrain the seats' suspension can be locked. The centre seat has a lap belt and the steel-backed backrest folds down to form a platform step for access to the roof hatch. The roof is reinforced to take the weight of two soldiers and the recoil forces of a 12.7 mm (0.5 in) HMG in a ring-mount.

Two types of modular detachable hard top roof are available; a standard flat roof or a version with extended height for the optional air-conditioning equipment, plus an NBC filtration system for the over-pressured cab if required. A blast-proof vertical split-windscreen is fitted as standard and a riot protection kit is available. An appliqué protection kit has been developed for this cab in conjunction with Ressenig of Austria. This cab is interchangeable between HX60, HX58 and HX77 models. Known as the Modular Integrated Cab (MIC), it affords protection from Level 1 blast and Level 2 ballistic, according to STANAG 4569. Weight of the kit is around 1,300 kg and the hard-top is removable for air-transport if required.

The interior of the walk-through cab is primarily steel or washable plastic/vinyl, the bulk of the instrumentation package having been taken from MAN's TGA commercial range as this being deemed more practical and cost-effective than the purpose-designed instrumentation of earlier cabs. Where required, controls and/or layout have been revised to accommodate combat or arctic clothing.

Chassis with twin front axles can also be fitted with the Integrated Armour Cabin (IAC), originally developed in conjunction with Krauss-Maffei Wegmann (KMW) for the SX range of trucks.

The engine is positioned conventionally - longitudinally between the chassis rails to give a Cab-Over-Engine (COE) configuration; the cooling pack is located transversely at the rear of the cab. This location offers protection from damage and blockage of the radiator with mud etc when operating off-road. It also allows for a larger volume radiator to be used,

Model	HX60 (HX 18.330 4 × 4 BB)	HX58 (HX 26.440 6 × 6 BB)	HX77 (HX 32.440 8 × 8 BB)
Configuration:	4 × 4	6 × 6	8 × 8
Cab seating:	1 + 2	1 + 2	1 + 2
Weight:			
(permissible GVW, single tyres)	18,000 kg	25,000 kg	32,000 kg
(unladen, chassis-cab)	7,950 kg	11,800 kg	13,500 kg
(chassis carrying capacity)	10,000 kg	13,000 kg	18,500 kg
(permissible GCW)	n/app	n/app	n/app
(permissible GTW)	33,000 kg	44,000 kg	44,000 kg
Overall length: (chassis cab)	7.71 m	8.866 m	10.336 m
Width: (cab)	2.55 m	2.55 m	2.55 m
Height: (top of cab, unladen)	2.934 m	3.325 m	3.308 m
Ground clearance: (front/rear)	428/428 mm	428/386 mm	420/386 mm
Wheelbase:	4.5 m	4 + 1.5 m	1.8 + 3.875 + 1.5 m
Angle of approach/departure:	40°/35°	40°/38°	40°/43°
Max speed: (limited)	88 km/h	88 km/h	88 km/h
Max gradient:	60%	60%	60%
Max sideslope:	40%	40%	40%
Fuel capacity:	400 litres	400 litres	400 litres
Fording:			
(unprepared)	750 mm	750 mm	750 mm
(prepared)	1.5 m	1.5 m	1.5 m
Engine:	MAN small block D0836 LFG EURO 4 6.871-litre six-cylinder inline turbocharged and intercooled, water-cooled EURO 4 common rail injection diesel developing 326 hp (243 kW) between 1,500-1,900 rpm and 1,250 N.m torque between 1,200-1,800 rpm, HX60 (HX 18.330 4 × 4 BB); D2066 LF 10.518-litre EURO IV six-cylinder inline turbocharged and intercooled, water-cooled common rail injection diesel developing 440 hp (328 kW) at 1,900 rpm and 2,100 N.m torque between 1,000-1,400 rpm, HX58 (HX 26.440 6 × 6 BB) and HX77 (HX 32.440 8 × 8 BB)		
Gearbox:	ZF 12 AS 1210 (HX60) or ZF 12 AS 2301 OD (HX58 and HX77) AS-Tronic automatic constant mesh gearbox (branded TipMatic in MAN's commercial product line) with 12 forward and 2 reverse gears		
Transfer box:	MAN G102 two-speed with engageable front axle(s) drive	MAN G172 two-speed with engageable front axle(s) drive	MAN G172 two-speed with engageable front axle(s) drive
Steering:	ZF 8098, hydraulic power-assistance		
Turning radius: (kerb)	9.5 m	9.55 m	12.6 m
Axles:			
(front, all models)	MAN VP-09 with planetary hub-reduction gearing and differential lock, 9,000 kg rating		
(2nd, 8 × 8 only)	MAN VPD-09 with planetary hub-reduction gearing and differential lock, 9,000 kg rating		
(rear, HX 18.330 4 × 4 BB)	MAN HP 1333-E with planetary hub-reduction gearing and differential lock, 13,000 kg rating		
(rear bogie, 6 × 6 and 8 × 8)	MAN HPD-1372-E (front), MAN HP-1342-E (rear) with planetary hub-reduction gearing and differential lock, 13,000 kg rating		
Suspension:	front axle(s): parabolic leaf springs with progressively acting rubber assistors and hydraulic telescopic shock-absorbers: rear axle (HX60); parabolic leaf springs with progressively acting rubber assistors and hydraulic telescopic shock-absorbers: rear axles (HX58/HX77); inverted multi-leaf trapezoidal springs with radius rods and anti-roll bar on second rear axle		
Tyres:	1400R 20 (1600R 20 option) Michelin XZL, run flat inserts and CTI optional		
Brakes: (main)	dual circuit, air, drums on all axles, Electronic Brake System (EBS) with ABS with off-road logic included supplemented by air-actuated exhaust brake with additional Exhaust Valve Brake system		
Electrical system:	24 V, three-phase		
Batteries:	4 × 12V, 100 Ah NATO batteries		
Alternator:	28 V, 110 Ah		

which enhances hot-climate operating capability. Modern electronically-controlled engines reduce their power output as operating temperatures increase. The use of a larger rear-mounted radiator allows HX range trucks to operate at full power and GVW, in temperatures of +49°C for prolonged periods.

Aside from the modular military cab, location of the cooling pack and a small number of military specific ancillary items and modifications (including all external compartments being watertight for an optional 1.5 m fording depth), MAN has strived for maximum commonality with the TGA commercial product, the aim being to reduce (compared to the SX range) both procurement and life costs. The compromise, as there must always be in engineering, is a lower level of high speed off-road mobility than the SX range.

As previously mentioned, The HX range will eventually cover the payload and mobility (both tactical and strategic) areas covered by both the FX and LX ranges, and to achieve this will utilise a wide range of driveline components, including both small and big block engines. The eventual number of variants will be well into double figures, those powered by small block engines being C-130-transportable. Preparation for C-130 transport is limited to lowering the spare wheel and removing the roof hard top. There is no requirement to clamp springs, partially deflate tyres or fold down the cab.

As of December 2009 MAN had provided full details of three rigid chassis HX models and a single four-axle tractor truck. HX60, HX58 and HX77 rigid chassis models will be supplied to Denmark, Hungary and the UK, and full details of these models can be found in the specifications table below. Details of the HX81 heavy tractor truck can be found in the Heavy equipment transporters section.

Taking the HX60 (HX 18.330 4 × 4 BB) rigid chassis as an example, in all instances MAN designations denote: HX - model range; 18 - GVW (can be limited by tyre choice); 330 - engine power output (326 hp); 4 × 4 - drive configuration (4 × 4); BB - suspension type (leaf springs front and rear). In the case of tractor trucks an additional S (BBS) denotes tractor truck configuration.

Power for HX range trucks is provided by the latest generation MAN turbocharged and intercooled common rail injection EURO 4 emissions compliant water-cooled diesel engines in both small and big block configurations. All current HX range trucks are fitted with a 12F/2R ZF AS-Tronic automatic constant mesh gearbox (branded TipMatic in MAN's commercial product line) coupled to a new generation MAN two-speed transfer box. For high mobility requirements, the powershift-type automatic transmission as fitted to the SX range is the preferred choice because it gives faster almost stepless gear shifts while virtually eliminating breaks in traction during shifting. A powershift-type transmission comes with a purchase and through life cost premium, and for a medium mobility application an automatic constant mesh-type transmission (which allows shorts breaks in drive during shifting as a conventional clutch is employed in the drivetrain) is the current preferred choice.

Driveline of the HX range is completed by MAN's latest 'single tyre specific' hub-reduction axles. With the exception of the heavy tractor trucks which are full-time all-wheel drive for traction and torque distribution reasons, all models have disengageable front axle(s) drive for on-road use, thereby reducing component wear. Axle ratings are 9,000 kg for front axles, 10,000 kg for single wheel rear axle(s). Various torque ratings (which dictate the towed load, hence GTW) are also available. The standard front axle rating for a truck (commercial or military) has traditionally been 7,500 kg. The 9,000 kg front axle was introduced by MAN to take into account the additional weight of cab armouring which now constitutes an almost standard requirement. MAN has developed a small arms fire and mine blast protected appliqué armour kit for the HX range and at the production stage vehicles can be fitted for, but not with, this kit. Earlier generation Kat 1/SX range chassis of the German and Austrian armed forces have previously been fitted with cab armouring kits supplied by Krauss-Maffei Wegmann (KMW).

Front steer-drive axles (including the 2nd axle on (8 × 8) chassis) are sprung by a combination of parabolic leaf springs with progressively acting rubber assistors and hydraulic telescopic shock absorbers. Rear axles are sprung by inverted multi-leaf trapezoidal springs with radius rods and an anti-roll bar. A conventional rear bogie set-up is employed for (6 × 6) and (8 × 8) chassis. All axles are fitted with driver-controlled cross-axle differential locks; there are longitudinal differential locks in rear (and front on (8 × 8) chassis) axle pairs and the transfer box. A Central Tyre Inflation (CTI) system and run-flat inserts are options. The standard 1400R 20 tyres may be replaced by 1600R 20 tyres if required.

The HX61, of which only outline details have been released, will be a high mobility class, lighter weight air-transportable (6 × 6) model. Motive power will be provided by a small block engine, allowing the C-130 envelope to be met. This model will be fitted with lower torque rated, lighter in weight rear axles. It will also be fitted with an independent rear axle suspension set-up with axles individually sprung by semi-elliptic leaf springs. This set-up provides considerably higher mobility and ride quality than conventional bogie-type set-ups for this load class of truck.

Specifications
See table on page 491

Status
Replaced the earlier LX range during 2004 and the FX range during 2005. Ordered by Denmark, Hungary, Ireland and the UK (see text).

Contractor
Rheinmetall MAN Military Vehicles (RMMV)

Mercedes-Benz 1114A and 1117A (4 × 4) 4,500 kg trucks

Development
The Mercedes-Benz 1114A and 1117A (4 × 4) 4,500 kg trucks are two-axle, cross-country trucks designed for the transport of personnel or supplies and as a tractor for light artillery. Both are militarised examples of the Mercedes-Benz commercial Light Class (LK) which was available from 1984; the Light Class was also known as the LN2 range. With GVWs and power outputs ranging from 6,500 to 13,000 kg and 90 to 204 hp, LK models overlapped slightly the heavier Mercedes-Benz ranges of the time, the NG and SK.

The Atego which entered commercial production in 1998 was the replacement for the LK, final European deliveries of the LK series being 60 1117A models to the Irish Army between 2000 and 2002. To supplement the Atego and heavier Actros ranges the mid-weight Axor (4 × 4) was introduced from 2001.

Description
The Mercedes-Benz 1114A and 1117A have forward control cabs with seating for the driver and two passengers. The LK range standard cab can be tilted forward to an angle of 55° for engine and other maintenance. Day-to-day engine checks can be carried out via a flap in the cab front. Cab heating and ventilation systems are provided.

A permanent 4 × 4 drive configuration is provided, the drive axles fitted with differential locks for enhanced traction in difficult conditions. All major drive components are protected against splash water and mud, allowing a fording depth of between 500 mm and 1 m.

Mercedes-Benz 1117A (4 × 4) 4,000 kg truck (Mercedes-Benz)   1128748

The cargo body, when fitted, has drop sides and a drop tailgate and may be protected by a cover and tilt. Purpose-built bodies were available for a number of applications and these included fuel and water tankers, recovery vehicles, ISO container carriers and shelter-type bodies for mobile offices and workshops.

Optional equipment included a wading kit to allow for fording up to a depth of 1.2 m.

Specifications
Cab seating: 1 + 2
Configuration: 4 × 4
Weight:
(laden, GVW) 11,000 kg
(unladen, kerb) 6,900 kg
(max payload) 4,000 kg
(front axle load) 4,700 kg
(rear axle load) 7,000 kg
(GCW) 21,000 kg
Load area: 4.5 × 2.35 m
Length: 6.98 m
Width: 2.48 m
Height:
(top of cab hatch) 2.830 m
(tarpaulin) 3.255 m
(load area) 1.37 m
Ground clearance: 314 mm
Track: 2.066 m
Wheelbase: 3.64 m
Angle of approach/departure: 30°/42°
Max speed: (1117A) 98 km/h
Fuel capacity: 200 litres
Max gradient:
(high range) 40%
(low range) 80%
(high range, GCW with trailer) 19%
(low range, GCW with trailer) 35%
Fording: 800 mm (1 m optional)
Engine: (1117A) Mercedes-Benz OM 366A 5.959-litre 6-cylinder in-line turbocharged water-cooled 4-stroke diesel developing 170 hp (127 kW) at 2,600 rpm and 560 N.m torque at 1,500 rpm
Gearbox: Mercedes-Benz G 4/65-6/9.0 synchromesh manual with 6 forward and 1 reverse gears
Clutch: single dry disc
Transfer box: Mercedes-Benz VG500-3W with differential lock, 2-speed
Steering: Mercedes-Benz LS 5 F, power-assisted
Turning radius: 7.95 m
Tyres: 1200R 20 or 14.75/80R 20
Brakes: dual circuit compressed air with Automatic Load-dependent Brake (ALB) pressure control, plus exhaust brake
Electrical system: 24 V
Batteries: 2 × 12 V, 88 Ah

Status
Production complete, these and similar models were supplied to a number of undisclosed countries.

Contractor
Daimler AG

MAN 630 Series (4 × 4) 5,000 kg trucks

Development
The MAN 630 Series, together with the MB LG 315/46, was the standard 5,000 kg truck of the German Army until the introduction of the follow-on generation of MAN high mobility tactical trucks, full details of which can be found elsewhere in this section.

From around 1958 approximately 20,000 vehicles were supplied to the German Federal Armed Forces, the bulk of these being either troop carrying/cargo variants with a dropside body and removable tarpaulin, or vehicles fitted with an office-type rear body.

The bulk of the German Army's MAN 630 fleet were replaced by MAN Kat 1 designs, with many ex-German Army vehicles passing into commercial hands. A large number of surplus German Army vehicles were passed on to the Turkish Army.

The 630 L2AE model was assembled in Belgium by Ets Hocké and known as the L2AE-B. These trucks have now been replaced.

MAN Nutzfahrzeuge AG and Rheinmetall AG announced their respective intentions to form a joint wheeled military vehicles company in 2009. This alliance became a reality in January 2010 with the announcement of the founding of Rheinmetall MAN Military Vehicles (RMMV) GmbH. RMMV sees the merger of Rheinmetall's wheeled military vehicle activities with those of the military truck activities of MAN. Essentially this merger unites the complementary technological core competencies of MAN's automotive expertise in commercial-vehicle manufacture with Rheinmetall's technological know-how in the military land sector/systems field. The result is the creation of a new single-source provider for the

MAN 630 L2AE (4 × 4) 5,000 kg truck (Stefan Marx) 0567958

entire range of armoured and unarmoured transport, command and role-specific wheeled vehicles. Throughout this entry MAN and/or RMMV designations are references are made to suit context.

Description

The layout of the 630 Series is entirely conventional, with the engine and cab at the front and the cargo area at the rear. The cab has a removable canvas top, windscreen which can be folded forward onto the bonnet and a single door on each side, the tops of which can be removed. The all-steel rear cargo area has a drop tailgate, removable bows and a tarpaulin cover. Some vehicles are fitted with a front-mounted winch.

The 630 Series was produced in two basic models, the MAN 630 L2A with dual rear wheels and the MAN 630 L2AE with single rear wheels.

A number of specific variants were produced, German Army variants including a carrier platform for the Pershing 1A, drone carrier for the Canadian AN/USD-501 reconnaissance system; an ambulance for up to four stretcher patients, decontamination vehicle called the TER-Kfz; field kitchen; radar vehicle for AN/TPS-1E system; tanker with two fuel tanks in the rear and dispensing equipment; tipper with a short wheelbase and either single or dual wheels at the rear; tractor with a wheelbase of 4.1 m and dual rear wheels.

Specifications

[Data in square brackets relates to L2AE where different from the L2A]
Cab seating: 1 + 1
Configuration: 4 × 4
Weight:
 (laden) 13,000 [13,200] kg
 (unladen) 7,515 [7,980] kg
Load area: 5 × 2.35 m
Length: 7.9 [7.73] m
Width: 2.5 m
Height: (tarpaulin) 2.845 [2.98] m
Ground clearance: 350 [400] mm
Track:
 (front) 1.92 [2.51] m
 (rear) 1.76 [2.51] m
Wheelbase: 4.6 m
Angle of approach/departure: 32°/45°
Max speed: (road) 66 km/h
Range: 440 km
Fuel capacity: 110 litres
Fuel consumption: 25 litres/100 km
Max gradient: 60%
Fording: 850 mm
Engine: MAN Model D1246 MV3A/W 6-cylinder in-line water-cooled multifuel developing 130 hp (97 kW) at 2,000 rpm
Gearbox: manual with 6 forward and 1 reverse gears
Transfer box: 2-speed
Turning radius: 9.75 m
Suspension: semi-elliptic leaf springs with hydraulic shock-absorbers
Tyres: 11.00 × 20 [14.00 × 20]
Brakes:
 (main) air, drums front and rear
 (parking) mechanical
Electrical system: 24 V
Batteries: 2 × 12 V, 100 Ah

Status

Production complete. Supplied to Belgium (assembled in Belgium by Ets Hocké and known as the L2AE-B), Germany, India, Turkey (German Army surplus) and possibly some nations in Central and South America, these thought to include El Salvador.

Contractor

Rheinmetall MAN Military Vehicles (RMMV).

Mercedes-Benz 2028A (6 × 6) 10,000 kg truck and variants

Development

The Mercedes-Benz 2028A (6 × 6) 10,000 kg cross-country truck is a militarised example of the Mercedes-Benz New Generation (NG) truck range, introduced commercially in 1973 and as the successor to the earlier LP range. The 2028A is a model from the revised NG80 range (New Generation 1980; introduced in 1980), this itself being superseded by the visually similar NG80DLO (NG80 with an upgraded driveline) before being supplemented by, later replaced by, the all new but visually quite similar SK range which was introduced commercially in 1988. The Actros range introduced commercially in 1996 was the replacement for the SK range. The Axor range, introduced from 2001, provided a new medium-weight commercial option between the Actros and lighter 1998-introduced Atego. Full details of the SK, Actros and Axor ranges can be found elsewhere in this section.

The Mercedes-Benz 2028A was initially described as a 9,000 kg payload truck; this later being revised to a 10,000 kg payload and with no increase in an unladen weight figure of approx. 11,200 kg.

The Mercedes-Benz 2628A was an uprated 2028A, having a greater (12,000 kg) payload. The 2628A was not produced in the same numbers as the 2028A, the latter being adopted by a number of undisclosed armed forces, particularly in the Middle East and Asia. The Mercedes-Benz 1628A is essentially a (4 × 4) 7,000 kg payload version of the 2028A; small numbers were produced. Mercedes-Benz also offered the 1217CA and 1222A, both 5,500 kg payload (4 × 4) NG-series trucks.

Tractor truck versions of the NG/NG80 range were produced and details of these can be found in the Heavy equipment transporters section.

Description

The cab of the 2028A (6 × 6) 10,000 kg truck has seating for the driver and two passengers. The centre seat has a folding backrest to allow clear access to the roof-mounted hatch, which is provided with a rail grip. A medium length cab was available which had extra space for crew equipment while a crew-type cab had space for up to seven occupants. The cab type can be tilted forward for engine access to an angle of 65°. For normal day-to-day maintenance, access flaps are provided. Behind the cab there is spare wheel stowage and on the front of the cab the headlights and radiator grille are protected by heavy-duty tubular guards.

All the undersides and major drive components could be fully waterproofed for a fording depth of 1.2 m without preparation and the air intake pipe is routed upwards over the cab roof side. The load area has 500 mm high drop sides and tailgate, and is provided with lash-down points and a canvas tilt. A towing hook for trailers or artillery is provided at the rear. Optional equipment included a hydraulic 10,000 kg winch with

Mercedes-Benz 1222A (4 × 4) 5,500 kg payload NG-series truck (Victor Barreira) 1391247

Mercedes-Benz 2028A (6 × 6) 10,000 kg truck of UAE Armed Forces fitted with an office-type rear body (Stefan Marx) 1296156

Mercedes-Benz 2028A (6 × 6) 10,000 kg truck with standard cargo body and canvas tilt; the 12,000 kg payload 2628A is visually identical to the 2028A (Daimler) 1128749

cable control to the front or rear. Various box and cab bodies were produced, and the model was suitable for use as a tanker, fire tender or command and communication vehicle.

The standard single-tyred version was available with a Central Tyre Inflation (CTI) system as an optional extra.

Specifications

2028A
[10,000 kg payload]
Cab seating: 1 + 2 or up to 6
Configuration: 6 × 6
Weight:
  (laden) 22,000 kg
  (unladen) approx 11,300 kg
  (payload) 10,000 kg
  (front axle load) 7,500 kg
  (rear axle load) 2 × 8,000 kg
  (GCW) 40 000 kg
Length: 8.3 m
Width: 2.495 m
Height:
  (cab) 3.09 m
  (canvas cover) 3.5 m
Load area: 5.5 × 2.35 m
Ground clearance: 427 mm
Track: 2.07 m
Wheelbase: 3.8 m + 1.45 m
Angle of approach/departure: 35°/46°
Max speed: 93 km/h
Fuel capacity: 300 litres
Gradient: 80%
Fording: (optional) 1.2 m
Engine: Mercedes-Benz OM 422 14.618-litre V-8 water-cooled 4-stroke diesel developing 280 hp (209 kW) at 2,300 rpm and 1,040 N.m torque at 1,200 rpm
Transmission: ZF 5S 111 GP fully synchronised manual with 9 forward (8 plus crawler) and 1 reverse gears; optional ZF S6 90 6-speed, with torque converter on early models
Transfer box: Mercedes-Benz VG1400/3W-1.4
Clutch: GF420 single dry plate
Turning radius: 10.15 m (approx.)
Tyres: 14.00R 20
Brakes: dual circuit, air, drums all-round
Electrical system: 24 V
Batteries: 2 × 12 V, 115 Ah
Alternator: 55 A

Status
Production complete. Supplied to a number of countries including Pakistan, Portugal and the United Arab Emirates (UAE).

Contractor
Daimler AG

MAN 14.240 FAEG (4 × 4) 6,000 kg and 20.280 DFAEG (6 × 6) 10,000 kg trucks

Development
MAN developed the Category III vehicles basing them on the Category I (Kat 1) vehicles developed for the German Army. Production of these models ceased during 1989.

MAN Nutzfahrzeuge AG and Rheinmetall AG announced their respective intentions to form a joint wheeled military vehicles company in 2009. This alliance became a reality in January 2010 with the announcement of the founding of Rheinmetall MAN Military Vehicles (RMMV) GmbH. RMMV sees the merger of Rheinmetall's wheeled military vehicle activities with those of the military truck activities of MAN. Essentially this merger unites the complementary technological core competencies of MAN's automotive expertise in commercial-vehicle manufacture with Rheinmetall's technological know-how in the military land sector/systems field. The result is the creation of a new single-source provider for the entire range of armoured and unarmoured transport, command and role-specific wheeled vehicles. Throughout this entry MAN and/or RMMV designations are references are made to suit context.

Description
MAN Category III vehicles use the same suspension and drive train technology as the Category I vehicles, torsionally stiff chassis, coil springs, axles with planetary gear hub reduction, but use MAN engines (at a time when Kat 1 trucks used KHD engines), commercial tilt cabs and allow a high payload; 6,000 kg for the 14.240 FAEG (4 × 4) and 10,000 kg for the 20.280 DFAEG (6 × 6).

The chassis consists of hollow section longitudinal members welded with tubular cross members. The cab is a MAN two-door all-steel forward control type which can be tilted forward to allow access to the engine for maintenance purposes. The rear cargo area has a steel subframe, aluminium drop sides with two side walls and one tailgate, fixed corner stakes in the front, insertable stakes in the middle and rear, pinewood floor, removable bows and a tarpaulin cover.

Specifications

Model	14.240 FAEG	20.280 DFAEG
Configuration:	4 × 4	6 × 6
Weight:		
(laden)	14,350 kg	20,300 kg
(unladen)	8,350 kg	10,300 kg
(payload)	6,000 kg	10,000 kg
Load area:	5 × 2.44 m	6.1 × 2.44 m
Length:	7.85 m	8.95 m
Width:	2.49 m	2.49 m
Height: (cab)	3.01 m	3.01 m
Wheelbase:	4.5 m	4 m + 1.4 m
Angle of approach/departure:	40°/43°	40°/40°
Max road speed:	80 km/h	80 km/h
Fuel capacity:	310 litres	310 litres
Max gradient:	limit of tyre adhesion	limit of tyre adhesion
Fording:	1 m	1 m
Engine:	MAN D2566 6-cylinder in-line water-cooled 4-stroke diesel developing 240 hp (177 kW) at 2,200 rpm	
Gearbox:	manual with 6 forward and 1 reverse gears	
Clutch:	torque converter	torque converter
Transfer box:	MAN G 801 2-speed with differential lock	
Tyres:	14.00 × 20	14.00 × 20
Brakes:	dual circuit, air over hydraulic with spring-loaded auxiliary brake and starting auxiliary brake (climbing brake), supplementary engine exhaust brake	
Steering:	ZF re-circulating ball hydro-steering	
Suspension:	progressive coil springs and hydraulic telescopic shock-absorbers	
Electrical system:	24 V	24 V
Batteries:	2 × 12 V, 110 Ah	2 × 12 V, 110 Ah

MAN Cat III 20.268 DFAEG (6 × 6) of the Peruvian Army in use as a field artillery tractor. In Peruvian service the vehicle is known as the MAN M20/280DF (Cesar Cruz Tantalean) 1296181

Status

Production complete. Supplied to Algeria, Ireland (36 delivered), Oman, Peru (165 delivered, >100 remained in service as of late-2008), Singapore, Venezuela and possibly others.

Contractor

Rheinmetall MAN Military Vehicles (RMMV).

MAN 16.284 LAERC (4 × 4) truck

Development

The MAN 16.284 (4 × 4) truck forms part of the MAN L2000 and M2000 militarised commercial ranges, a full overview of which can be found elsewhere in this section.

MAN introduced the TGL and TGM range of two-axle commercial trucks during 2005 to replace the L2000 and M2000 ranges. Militarised versions of the TGL and TGM became available during 2006, with the Austrian Army being the launch customer. By mid-2007 all militarised L2000 and M2000 models had been replaced in production in Austria by equivalent models from the TGL and TGM ranges. The TGM designation for a model with equivalent GVW and engine power output to the 16.284 LAERC would be 16.280 4x4 BB.

Production of L2000 and M2000 models has shifted to India where production continues and primarily for local and Asian markets by Man Force Trucks Pvt. Ltd. (MFTL), a joint venture company between Force Motors (formerly Bajaj Tempo) and MAN Nutzfahrzeuge AG.

MAN Nutzfahrzeuge AG and Rheinmetall AG announced their respective intentions to form a joint wheeled military vehicles company in 2009. This alliance became a reality in January 2010 with the announcement of the founding of Rheinmetall MAN Military Vehicles (RMMV) GmbH. RMMV sees the merger of Rheinmetall's wheeled military vehicle activities with those of the military truck activities of MAN. Essentially this merger unites the complementary technological core competencies of MAN's automotive expertise in commercial-vehicle manufacture with Rheinmetall's technological know-how in the military land sector/systems field. The result is the creation of a new single-source provider for the entire range of armoured and unarmoured transport, command and role-specific wheeled vehicles. Throughout this entry MAN and/or RMMV designations are references are made to suit context.

Description

The MAN 16.284 LAERC (16 - nominal GVW in tonnes; 284 - nominal engine power output pre-tropicalisation (280 hp); L - L/M 2000 model; A - all-wheel drive; E - single rear tyres; R - right-hand drive; C - chassis-cab) is entirely conventional in design and is based on a C-section low-torsion ladder-frame chassis with riveted and bolted cross members. Recovery, towing and pusher points are fitted front and rear. The insulated all-steel cab seats three and tilts forward hydraulically for engine access. The backrest of the co-drivers seat can be folded forward to create a standing platform for access to the circular roof hatch. The roof is reinforced to take the weight of two persons. Air conditioning and an 82 dB(A) noise reduction package are included in the cab specification, as is a front-mounted brush guard and a window in the cab rear wall.

The standard platform body is fitted with two-piece steel drop sides and a single-piece drop tailgate, and a removable tarpaulin and bows. Fitted with the compact cab there is a maximum of 5.4 m (including a 400 mm permissible overhang) available for the body. A materials handling crane can be mounted between the cab and any body. The 16.284 LAERC has a maximum GVW of 16,000 kg, and at a chassis-cab weight of 5,600 kg this gives a carrying capacity of 10,400 kg, including any superstructure.

MAN 16.284 LAERC (4 × 4) 16,000 kg GVW truck of the Singapore armed forces. This variant is fitted with a materials handling crane between the compact cab and drop side body, and has a number of options including a tropics package, a fuel prefilter and separator for areas where low-grade fuel is a probability, a front-mounted brush guard and front/rear mounted pusher plates. The cab is air-conditioned and noise-insulated to 82 dB(A), the roof has a circular hatch and is reinforced (Shaun C Connors) 0129766

Motive power is provided by a EURO 2 emissions compliant MAN 6.87-litre six-cylinder turbocharged diesel engine developing 267 hp, giving a power-to-weight ratio of 16.69 hp/ton at maximum GVW. An engine cold start device is fitted and the cooling system has been revised for operations in areas of high ambient temperatures.

Axles are of the hub reduction type and driven via an Allison MD 3560P six-speed automatic transmission coupled to a VG 750 two-speed transfer box. An Automatic Drivetrain Management (ADM) system is fitted. This automatically selects four-wheel drive by engaging the front axle and locks the transfer box and individual axle differentials as required, giving full four-wheel lock-up when required. It should be noted that ADM does not work as a traction control system through the anti-lock braking system (ABS).

The front 7,500 kg-capacity steer-drive axle is sprung by the combination of parabolic leaf springs, telescopic shock-absorbers and an anti-roll bar, the rear 9,000 kg-capacity drive axle by the combination of parabolic leaf springs, telescopic shock-absorbers and an anti-roll bar. Steering is power-assisted.

Tyres are 1400R 20 Michelin XZL and a Syegon automatic central tyre inflation (CTI) system with four pressure presettings for road, off-road, sand and emergency, is fitted. Drum brakes are fitted front and rear, the anti-lock braking system (ABS) having an off-road setting.

Specifications

(The Description text and Specification table data is specific to the MAN 16.284 LAERC model supplied to Singapore)
Cab seating: 1 + 2
Configuration: 4 × 4
Weight:
  (laden) 16,000 kg
  (unladen, chassis-cab) 5,600 kg
  (payload, chassis-cab) 10,400 kg
  (towed load, off-road 8,000 kg
  (GCW, off-road) 24,000 kg
Length: (chassis-cab) 7.5 m
Width: 2.49 m
Wheelbase: 4.17 m
Max speed: 100 km/h with limiter restricting to 60 or 100 km/h
Fuel capacity: 300 litres
Max gradient: (laden, without trailer) >60%, dependant on available traction
Max side slope: (approx) 30%
Fording: 800 mm
Engine: MAN D0836LFL EURO 2 6.871 litre 6-cylinder in-line exhaust gas turbocharged and intercooled, water-cooled 4-stroke direct injection diesel developing 267 hp (196 kW) at 2,400 rpm and 1,045 Nm torque between 1,200 and 1,750 rpm
Gearbox: Allison MD 3560P automatic with 6 forward and 1 reverse gears
Transfer box: VG 750 2-speed (high/low) with Automatic Drivetrain Management (ADM) (see text)
Steering: ZF Type 8095, power-assisted
Turning radius: (wall) 9.5 m
Suspension: parabolic leaf springs, telescopic shock-absorbers and anti-roll bar, front and rear
Tyres: 1400R 20
Brakes: air, drums front and rear, ABS with off-road setting
Electrical system: 24 V
Batteries: 2 × 12 V, 145 Ah
Alternator: 28 V, 55 A

Status

See text for production details. In service with Singapore armed forces (approximately 1,200 delivered around 2002).

Contractor

Rheinmetall MAN Military Vehicles (RMMV).

MAN (4 × 4), (6 × 6) and (8 × 8) Category 1 (Kat 1) high-mobility tactical trucks

Development

In the late 1950s and early 1960s the West German Technical Office for Armament and Military Purchases drew up requirements for a new range (or second generation) of vehicles for the army. Covering all weight classes and mobility levels, the Bundeswehr's second generation requirement originally called for some 62,000 vehicles (of all classes including cars and buses) including 4-tonne (4 × 4), 7-tonne (6 × 6) and 10-tonne (8 × 8) trucks, (4 × 4) and (6 × 6) armoured amphibious load carriers and an (8 × 8) amphibious reconnaissance vehicle.

To meet development and production demands, a joint venture led by MAN and including Klockner-Humboldt-Deutz (KHD), Rheinstahl-Henschel, Krupp (which later dropped out) and Bussing (acquired by MAN in 1971) was set up. The first prototype vehicles were shown at the end of the 1960s, and a further two prototype series were developed before the first genuine pre-production vehicles were designed and built.

Along the development trail it became clear that the highly technical vehicles as originally specified would simply not be affordable, so many of the more ambitious wish list-type features were dropped; truck numbers

MAN Kat 1 5,000 kg (4 × 4) cargo truck of the German Bundeswehr. When fitted with a winch the Bundeswehr designation for this vehicle is Type 461 LKW 5t mil gl MW Pritsche, without a winch the designation is Type 451 LKW 5t mil gl Pritsche (Stefan Marx)   1128745

MAN Kat 1 Type 461/451 LKW 5t mil gl MSA 5,000 kg (4 × 4) cargo truck of the German Bundeswehr fitted with a protection kit manufactured by Krauss-Maffei Wegmann (KMW). Around 140 of these were supplied (Michael Jerchel)   1128744

MAN Kat I Type 464 LKW 10t mil gl MW Pritsche Kran 10,000 kg (8 × 8) cargo truck of the German Bundeswehr fitted with a self-recovery winch and body-mounted materials handling crane (Stefan Marx)   1128742

were also reduced to 18,000. In 1972 the amphibious specification and the requirement that the vehicles should be powered by an air-cooled multifuel engine were dropped. In 1975 the 4-tonne rating was uprated to 5-tonne and at the same time this models' rear cargo platform was lengthened and the wheelbase was increased from 4.3 to 4.5 m. Armoured vehicles evolved to become a separate development.

MAN's current SX range of trucks has its design origins in the original Category 1 category of trucks, the most mobile of eight truck classes required and purpose-designed from the outset to be capable of maintaining pace with combat vehicles across any terrain.

MAN Nutzfahrzeuge AG and Rheinmetall AG announced their respective intentions to form a joint wheeled military vehicles company in 2009. This alliance became a reality in January 2010 with the announcement of the founding of Rheinmetall MAN Military Vehicles (RMMV) GmbH. RMMV sees the merger of Rheinmetall's wheeled military vehicle activities with those of the military truck activities of MAN. Essentially this merger unites the complementary technological core competencies of MAN's automotive expertise in commercial-vehicle manufacture with Rheinmetall's technological know-how in the military land sector/systems field. The result is the creation of a new single-source provider for the entire range of armoured and unarmoured transport, command and

MAN Kat I LKW 10t mil gl 10,000 kg (8 × 8) cargo truck of the German Bundeswehr. This example could be fitted with a self-recovery winch and materials handling crane, the tarpaulin cover making recognition difficult (Michael Jerchel)   1128741

MAN Kat 1 A1 LKW 7t mil gl A1.1 AMA-RiFu 7,000 kg (6 × 6) truck mounting a Dornier 34 m radio antenna mast (Stefan Marx)   1128739

role-specific wheeled vehicles. Throughout this entry MAN and/or RMMV designations and references are made to suit context.

Category I

In December 1975, MAN was awarded a contract to build 8,385 (4 × 4), (6 × 6) and (8 × 8) Category 1 vehicles at a cost of DM1,400 million; this production total was further reduced to 7,925 in 1979.

The usual abbreviation for Category 1 vehicles is Kat or Kat 1, although this is sometimes presented as Cat or CAT 1.

The (8 × 8) version was the first Kat 1 model to enter production and first deliveries were made in 1976. Deliveries of a (6 × 6) tipper and the (4 × 4) cargo truck began in 1977. Deliveries of the (6 × 6) cargo truck began in January 1979; final deliveries were made in 1981. By 1983, 8,617 vehicles of all Kat 1 configurations had been delivered to the West German armed forces. By the end of 1986, 411 examples had been delivered to the Austrian Army and 82 to the Belgian Army.

This complete range of Kat 1 vehicles, which was produced at MAN's Watenstedt plant, was designed specifically for cross-country operations and to keep up with mechanised forces operating across country. The Bundeswehr designation for the 5,000 kg (4 × 4) and 7,000 kg (6 × 6) Kat 1 cargo without winches is LKW 5t (or 7t) mil gl Pritsche, with winch this becomes LKW 5t (or 7t, or 10t in the case of the 10,000 kg (8 × 8)) mil gl MW Pritsche.

The Bundeswehr received a total of seven Kat 1 5,000 kg (4 × 4) variants, 14 Kat 1 7,000 kg (6 × 6) variants, and 9 Kat 1 (8 × 8) 10,000 kg variants.

Many components of the Kat 1 range, such as axles, engines and gearboxes, were commercially available components so that spare parts could be easily obtained; MAN (as RMMV) continues to support in full the Kat 1 range.

Category II

The next generation was the Category II (or Kat II/Cat II) version which was developed at the request of and in close co-operation with the US armed forces. By the end of 1986, 534 of these trucks had been delivered to the US armed forces, 157 to France and 42 to Canada.

Category III

In a parallel development the so-called Category III (or Kat III/Cat III) vehicles were developed. These are similar to the Category I vehicles but are fitted with a cab from the MAN civilian truck range, modified for military use. A total of 1,594 Category III trucks were delivered to Algeria (280), Ireland, Oman (95), Peru (165), Singapore (104), Venezuela (405) and possibly others.

Model	Kat I A1 (4 × 4)	Kat I A1 (6 × 6)	Kat I A1 (8 × 8)	Kat I A1 (8 × 8) (2.9 m width)
Cab seating	1 + 2	1 + 2	1 + 2	1 + 2
Configuration	4 × 4	6 × 6	8 × 8	8 × 8
Weight				
(laden)	16,000 kg	26,000 kg	32,000 kg	32,000 kg
(unladen)	9,500 kg	11,300 kg	13,400 kg	12,800 kg
(chassis carrying capacity)	7,500 kg	13,500 kg	20,000 kg	20,000 kg
Load area	5.1 × 2.44 m	6.2 × 2.44 m	7.2 × 2.44 m	7.2 × 2.44 m
Length	8.17 m	9.27 m	10.27 m	10.27 m
Width	2.5 m	2.5 m	2.5 m	2.9 m
Height				
(cab)	2.64 + 0.29 m	2.64 + 0.29 m	2.64 + 0.29 m	2.64 + 0.29 m
(load area)	1.54 m	1.54 m	1.54 m	1.54 m
Ground clearance	410 mm	410 mm	410 mm	410 mm
Track	2.07 m	2.07 m	2.07 m	2.47 m
Wheelbase	4.5 m	4.5 m + 1.5 m	1.93 m + 3.57 m + 1.5 m	
Angle of approach/departure	34°/39°	34°/39°	34°/39°	34°/39°
Max cruising speed (road)	90 km/h	90 km/h	90 km/h	90 km/h
Fuel capacity	400 litres	400 litres	400 litres	400 litres
Max gradient	limit of tyre adhesion	limit of tyre adhesion	limit of tyre adhesion	limit of tyre adhesion
Fording	1.2 m	1.2 m	1.2 m	1.2 m
Engine	KHD V-configuration air-cooled diesel engines, naturally aspirated or supercharged with charge-air cooling, developing 256–320 hp (188-235 kW) (optional MAN V-configuration water-cooled diesel engines, naturally aspirated or turbocharged			
Gearbox	range of ZF synchronised gearboxes with between 9 and 16 forward gears; with or without integrated transfer box,			
Clutch	mechanical or hydraulic converter with lock-up clutch			
Steering	recirculating ball hydro-steering type:			
	ZF 8046	ZF 8046	ZF 8096, dual circuit	
Turning radius	9.65 m	10.6 m	13.7 m	13.8 m
Suspension	progressively acting coil springs	progressively acting coil springs	progressively acting coil springs	progressively acting coil springs
Tyres	1400R 20 (optional 1600R 20)	1400R 20 (optional 1600R 20)	1400R 20 (optional 1600R 20)	1400R 20 (optional 1600R 20)
Brakes	dual circuit, air, drums all-round	dual circuit, air, drums all-round	dual circuit, air, drums all-round	dual circuit, air, drums all-round
Electrical system	24 V	24 V	24 V	24 V
Batteries	2 × 12 V, 170 Ah (optional 4 × 12 V, 100 Ah)	2 × 12 V, 170 Ah (optional 4 × 12 V, 100 Ah)	2 × 12 V, 170 Ah (optional 4 × 12 V, 100 Ah)	2 × 12 V, 170 Ah (optional 4 × 12 V, 100 Ah)

Category I A1

In April 1985, MAN presented the first of the revised Category I A1 models to the German Federal Office for Military Technology and Procurement (BWB) and to the Test Centre 41 facility. It was planned that there would be 35 test vehicles of all configurations, including an extra-wide (8 × 8) version for the Patriot and Roland systems. Production of the new category vehicles began in 1987.

The Category I A1 generation was a development of the Category I with improved performance on and off road due to higher power output engines and an improved design of chassis and cab. Category 1 A1 included a new (as a direct replacement for the earlier Kat 1 10,000 kg) 15,000 kg (8 × 8) weight class. This model was designed with a chassis carrying capacity of up to 16,000 kg, and by using 13,000 kg rated axles, up to 25,000 kg.

From 1988 the Bundeswehr ordered 1,100 Cat 1A1 models.

Planned changes introduced on the Category I A1 vehicles included the following:

- A hand-tiltable cab, for better access to the engine which can then be removed or installed in about 30 minutes as opposed to the previous 10 hours
- A rearrangement of components so that the cab no longer has to be tilted for routine checks
- A fully integrated anti-corrosion treatment package for extreme climate conditions and operational use for more than 20 years
- A paint finish that fulfils all military requirements including camouflage pattern, infra-red reflection and NBC decontamination needs
- Extended use of more commercial components to reduce costs
- All vehicles able to use 1600R × 20 radial-ply tyres
- A removable cab roof to assist rail and air transport
- Logistic commonality with earlier vehicles would be maintained

The layout of all the basic vehicles is almost identical. All vehicles are fitted with a hydraulically tiltable uniform three-man cab specifically designed for military purposes. The plastic roof can support the weight of a man and is fitted with an observation hatch; it can be removed for air transport. A low-torsion frame is used together with coil springs and

MAN Kat 1 Type 462/452 LKW 7t mil gl MW Pritsche/Pritsche (with/without winch) 7,000 kg (6 × 6) cargo truck of the German Bundeswehr fitted with standard drop side body and tarpaulin (Shaun C Connors) 0121833

Swedish Army MAN Kat 1 A1 (8 × 8) truck mounting Giraffe agile multibeam (AMB) air defence search radar (Stefan Marx) 1185511

telescopic shock-absorbers. Most vehicles are fitted with a Rotzler self-recovery winch. All attachments, such as stowage compartments and canister brackets, are fastened to the frame so that different bodies and platforms can be fitted.

Category 1 A1.1
Category 1 A1 models developed from 1988 carry the Cat 1 A1.1 designation. Cat 1A1 models used some commercial components from MAN's F90 range of heavy commercial trucks introduced in 1986, but retained KHD air-cooled V-8 diesel engines. The later Cat 1A1.1 models were developed between 1988-1991 and were based on components from MAN's F2000 range of heavy commercial trucks introduced in 1992. The MAN designation of SX range became prevalent around this time. From 1993 the Bundeswehr ordered around 500 MAN Category 1 A1.1 trucks.

MAN FX, LX and SX ranges
In 1989 MAN introduced the LX range of high mobility trucks. The LX range is based on experience gained with extended production of earlier high mobility tactical trucks, but is of lighter construction and based around a conventional C-section ladder-frame chassis sprung by leaf springs. The LX range was subsequently joined by the FX and SX ranges. The FX range are essentially chassis from the MAN F2000 heavy-duty commercial range but fitted with the MAN modular military cab plus other military features as required. The SX range may be regarded as the successor range to the Cat 1 AI models, production of which is now complete. Full details of the FX, LX and SX ranges can be found elsewhere in this section.

Airfield crash tenders
A range of high performance airfield crash tenders were produced on the Category 1 A1 extra-wide (2.9 m) chassis, and continue to be produced on the successor SX range 2.9 m wide chassis.

German Bundeswehr's GTF programme
The Bundeswehr's MAN Kat 1 tactical truck fleet are currently scheduled for replacement, these to be replaced under the GTF programme. GTF will procure a range of 2,000, 5,000, 9,000 and 15,000 kg protected trucks, with vehicles provided by IVECO, MAN (RMMV) and Mercedes-Benz currently being evaluated. When first muted back in late-1980s it was suggested that 33,000 replacement trucks would be required under GTF. The project has since been fully re-evaluated at least three times and the current projection is for 2,500 trucks of all classes, with the possibility this figure will reduce still further.

Figures released in 2008 stated that around 6,500 Kat 1 trucks remained in service.

Specifications
See table on page 497

Status
Production complete. In service with numerous armed forces, worldwide.

Contractor
Rheinmetall MAN Military Vehicles (RMMV).

MAN FX, LX and SX ranges of tactical trucks

Development
In addition to militarised versions of its extensive commercial range, full details of which can be found elsewhere in this section, MAN also produces a selection of tactical military trucks. These are collectively referred to as the X range.

Development of the X range begins with the Category 1 high mobility trucks, deliveries of which commenced in 1976. The usual abbreviation for Category 1 vehicles is Kat or KAT 1, although this is sometimes presented as Cat or CAT 1. The Kat 1 range are purpose designed trucks that meet the most stringent of military tactical requirements and have been the subject of continued evolution by MAN, current models carrying the SX range designation. Full details of the Kat 1 range and all other pre-SX range high mobility trucks can be found in a separate entry elsewhere in this section.

To compliment the high mobility SX range MAN also produces/has produced the FX, HX and LX tactical truck ranges. As the FX, HX and LX ranges share MAN's modular military cab, to the untrained eye these are often confused with the Kat 1/SX range; there are in fact quite a number of application/capability defining differences between the ranges.

The LX tactical range was introduced in 1988 and was based on a modified chassis from MAN's M2000 medium weight commercial range. The LX was designed as a lighter weight, highly mobile and C-130-transportable vehicle. The FX tactical range was introduced in 1990 and being optimised for heavier gross vehicle and combination weights was based on chassis from MAN's heavy commercial range. The LX range was superseded by the HX range during 2004, the FX range was superseded by the HX range during 2005. Full details of the HX range can be found in a separate entry elsewhere in this section.

By 2002, following a lengthy period of consolidation and reorganisation, assembly of the MAN FX, LX and SX tactical truck ranges had been transferred to the former Österreich Automobilfabrik ÖAF-Gräf und Stift AG plant in Vienna, briefly renamed MAN Sonderfahrzeuge AG but now

Bundeswehr MAN FX range tactical truck in (4 × 4) tractor truck configuration (Michael Jerchel)   1047596

known as MAN Österreich AG. MAN acquired truck-maker ÖAF in 1936. Some components for the MAN tactical truck ranges, such as the torsionally rigid chassis frame of the SX range, and the MAN modular military cab fitted to all ranges, were manufactured at the Star Trucks plant in Poland, they are now manufactured in Austria. Star Sp. z.o.o. was acquired by MAN in 1999.

Dependant on market, essentially the same model from the MAN X range of tactical trucks may now be marketed and branded as either MAN or Steyr, or for the Austrian market only, as ÖAF. MAN Nutzfahrzeuge AG acquired an 85 per cent share of the truck-building activities of Austria's Steyr Nutzfahrzeuge AG in January 1990, and in 1993 the company exercised its option to acquire the remaining 15 per cent share of the business. Steyr Nutzfahrzeuge AG became known as MAN Steyr AG during 2002 and during 2005 as MAN Österreich AG. Further details of the relationship between current MAN and Steyr truck ranges can be found in the MAN trucks or Steyr trucks entries elsewhere in this section.

MAN Nutzfahrzeuge AG and Rheinmetall AG announced their respective intentions to form a joint wheeled military vehicles company in 2009. This alliance became a reality in January 2010 with the announcement of the founding of Rheinmetall MAN Military Vehicles (RMMV) GmbH. RMMV sees the merger of Rheinmetall's wheeled military vehicle activities with those of the military truck activities of MAN. Essentially this merger unites the complementary technological core competencies of MAN's automotive expertise in commercial-vehicle manufacture with Rheinmetall's technological know-how in the military land sector/systems field. The result is the creation of a new single-source provider for the

MAN SX44 (6 × 6) cargo truck of the British Army (Shaun C Connors)   1296187

Oman armed forces MAN LX range tactical truck (R Stickland)   1047607

MAN SX45 (8 × 8) recovery vehicle of the British Army fitted with additional armour, electronic countermeasures equipment and a protected weapon station (Shaun C Connors)   1296120

entire range of armoured and unarmoured transport, command and role-specific wheeled vehicles. Throughout this entry MAN and/or RMMV designations and references are made to suit context.

UK Support Vehicle contract (5,165 vehicles + options)

It was announced in October 2004 that the UK Defence Procurement Agency (DPA) had selected the MAN ERF UK Ltd proposal for the UK armed forces' Support Vehicle requirement; a contract award followed in March 2005. MAN acquired UK truck-maker ERF from Western Star of Canada (now owned by Daimler) during 2000.

The Support Vehicle contract is expected to be worth GBP1.3 billion. The base contract award covered 5,165 vehicles (inc 314 recovery) and 69 recovery trailers, with first vehicles entering service in June 2007. Production is expected to continue to 2013 and the contract includes a major support package. The order covers 4,851 cargo trucks and 288 recovery vehicles (reduced from 314), which will replace a range of Bedford, Leyland and Foden vehicles. The contract also included 1,089 applique protection kits.

MAN disclosed at DVD 2006 that after considering a number of options including the possible refurbishment of current DAF 4-tonne trucks, that the UK MoD had exercised its maximum possible option under the SV contract, ordering an additional 2,077 vehicles.

The SV contract calls for two model ranges to be delivered to the MoD, SX Improved Medium Mobility (IMM) and HX Medium Mobility (MM), with an over 90 per cent quantity bias towards HX models.

The two (6 × 6) improved medium mobility vehicles required, cargo and tanker, are based on the SX44 high-mobility chassis; the (8 × 8) recovery vehicle is based on the SX45 high-mobility chassis. The medium mobility vehicles are based on MAN HX range chassis. The contract option covers HX models only.

Following some additional purchases, the total number of Support Vehicles (including trailers) and derivatives contracted to the MoD to date is 7,479, with around 5,000 of these delivered by December 2010.

Also competing for the Support Vehicle contract was Mercedes-Benz, Oshkosh Truck and Stewart & Stevenson. The Support Vehicle bids were submitted three times with the final bids submitted in October 2003. The contract was originally worth GBP1.4 billion and covered the supply of a maximum of 8,620 vehicles. At one time the DPA was looking at a Private Finance Initiative (PFI) solution but this was subsequently abandoned in favour of a direct acquisition.

Description

SX range of tactical trucks

The MAN SX range of tactical trucks (occasionally previously presented as SX 2000) has a design origin in the original Kat 1 category (German Bundeswehr designation) of trucks, the most mobile of the Bundeswehr's truck classes and purpose-designed to be capable of maintaining pace with tracked combat vehicles across any terrain. The first of 8,618 Kat 1 trucks was handed over to the German Bundeswehr in 1976, the last in 1983. From 1988 the Bundeswehr ordered 1,100 of the follow-on evolved Kat 1A1 models, and from 1993 ordered around 500 of the follow-on and further evolved Category 1A1.1 models.

All Kat 1/SX models are fitted with MAN's purpose-designed modular military cab and share the concept of a purpose-designed box-section torsionally rigid (non-flexing) chassis frame design that mounts beam axles sprung by long-travel coil springs. Early models (Kat 1/Kat 1A1) were powered by KHD air-cooled diesel engines as these were deemed to be essential at the time, being less susceptible to damage from small arms fire and shell splinters. This requirement was later found to be largely irrelevant and as development progressed the use of commercial components (water-cooled engine, gearbox, axles and so on) from MAN's heavy commercial truck ranges increased, firstly from the F90 range introduced in 1986 and later (Kat 1A1.1 models) from the F2000 range introduced in 1992. It was around this time the MAN designation of SX range became prevalent.

In conjunction with Krauss-Maffei Wegmann (KMW), MAN has developed a Level 3 ballistic and anti-tank mine blast-protected cab for its SX (8 × 8) chassis. With the space cab attachment removed, the vehicle retains a rail and C-130 transport capability (Shaun C Connors)   0572373

Full details of the Kat 1-Kat 1A1.1 models can be found in a separate entry elsewhere in this section.

Model evolution continues and the latest models are fitted with current driveline components, including MAN's latest generation engine line-up taken from the TGA commercial range.

The modular military cab fitted to SX range trucks is a continuing development of the cab fitted to the original Kat 1 vehicles. The latest version is 290 mm deeper than it's immediate predecessor and has more than 600 litres of gross stowage space in the rear, sufficient for radio equipment and the full kit of three soldiers. The air-sprung vinyl-covered seats for driver and passenger are fitted with integral seatbelts that prevent uncomfortable and potentially dangerous belt-locking on rough terrain. For severe off-road terrain the seats' suspension can be locked. The centre seat has a lap belt and the steel-backed backrest folds down to form a platform step for access to the roof hatch. The roof is reinforced to take the weight of two soldiers and the recoil forces of a 12.7 mm (0.5 in) HMG in a ring-mount.

Danish Army MAN SX range (8 × 8) Multi fitted with a Level 3 ballistic and mine blast-protected cab developed jointly by MAN and Krauss-Maffei Wegmann (KMW) (Martin Pagh)   1296119

Model	SX 25.440 6 × 6 (SX 44)	SX 32.440 8 × 8 (SX 45) with 1400R 20 tyres	SX 32.440 Multi 2 (SX 45) with 1400R 20 tyres	SX 32.440 Multi 2 IAC 3/3 (SX 45)
Cab seating:	1 + 2	1 + 2	1 + 2	1 + 2
Configuration:	8 × 8	8 × 8	8 × 8	8 × 8
Weight:				
(laden, GVW)	25,000 kg	32,000 kg	32,000 kg	38,000 kg (technically permissible)
(unladen, chassis-cab)	10,950 kg	13,500 kg	17,000 kg (chassis-cab with LHS)	ca. 21,300 kg (chassis-IAC with LHS and container handling system)
(chassis carrying capacity)	14,000 kg	18,500 kg	15,000 kg	ca. 16,700 kg (technically permissible)
(permissible front axle load)	9,000 kg	9,000 kg (each)	9,000 kg (each)	9,000 kg
(permissible rear axle load)	13,000 kg (each)	13,000 kg (each)	13,000 kg (each)	13,000 kg (each)
(max GCW)	40,000 kg	40,000 kg	40,000 kg	58,000 kg (technically permissible)
Length	9.2.85 m (chassis, inc tow hitch)	10.465 m (chassis, inc tow hitch)	10.3 m	10.3 m
Width(across cab)	2.55 m	2.55 m	2.55 m	2.55 m
Height				
(top of spare wheel, unladen)	2.899 m	2.913 m	2.937 m	2.937 m
(top of spare wheel, laden)	2.882 m	2.886 m	2.902 m	2.902 m
(chassis, unladen)	1.265 m	1.265 m	1.265 m	1.265 m
(chassis, laden)	1.195 m	1.195 m	1.195 m	1.195 m
Ground clearance:				
(front)	430 mm	430 mm	430 mm	430 mm
(rear)	430 mm	390 mm	390 mm	430 mm
Track:	2.47 m	2.47 m	2.47 m	2.47 m
Wheelbase	4.54 + 1.5 m	1.93 + 3.86 + 1.5 m	1.93 + 3.86 + 1.5 m	1.93 + 3.86 + 1.5 m
Angle of approach/departure	40°/35°	40°/35°	40°/35°	40°/35°
Max speed	88 km/h (limited)	88 km/h (limited)	88 km/h (limited)	88 km/h (limited)
Fuel capacity	1 × 400 litres	1 × 400 litres	1 × 400 litres	1 × 400 litres
Range	approx 800 km	approx 800 km	approx 800 km	approx 800 km
Gradient	>60%	60%	60%	60%
Sideslope:	40%	40%	40%	40%
Fording:				
(unprepared)	1.2 m	1.2 m	1.2 m	1.2 m
(prepared)	1.5 m	1.5 m	1.5 m	1.5 m
Engine	MAN D2066 LFG EURO 4 10.518-litre 6-cylinder inline turbocharged and intercooled, water-cooled common rail injection 4-stroke diesel developing 440 hp (324 kW) at 1,900 rpm and 2,100 Nm torque between 1,000-1,400 rpm			
Transmission:	ZF 6HP 902 Powershift automatic with 6 forward and 1 reverse gears			
Transfer box:	(6 × 6) - ZF G 172 2-speed, full-time all-wheel drive, inter-axle differential lock; (8 × 8) -ZF VG 1600 2-speed, full-time all-wheel drive, inter-axle differential lock.			
Steering:	ZF 8099, hydraulic power-assisted			
Turning radius:				
(kerb)	9.85 m	13.25 m	13.25 m	13.25 m
(wall)	10.75 m	14.3 m	14.3 m	14.3 m
Axles:				
(front)	MAN VP-09-G with hub-reduction gearing and differential lock, 9,000 kg rating	MAN VP-09-G/VPD-09-G with hub-reduction gearing and differential lock, 2 × 9,000 kg rating	MAN VP-09-G/VPD-09-G with hub-reduction gearing and differential lock, 2 × 9,000 kg rating	MAN VP-09-G/VPD-09-G with hub-reduction gearing and differential lock, 2 × 9,000 kg rating
(rear)	MAN HPD 1372-G/HP-1342-G with hub-reduction gearing and differential lock, 2 × 13,000 kg rating. Axle location by links and wishbones	MAN HPD-1372-G/HPD-1342-G with hub-reduction gearing and differential lock, 2 × 13,000 kg rating. Axle location by links and wishbones	MAN HPD-1372-G/HPD-1342-G with hub-reduction gearing and differential lock, 2 × 13,000 kg rating. Axle location by links and wishbones	MAN HPD-1372-G/HPD-1342-G with hub-reduction gearing and differential lock, 2 × 13,000 kg rating. Axle location by links and wishbones
Suspension:	progressively acting coil springs with large-displacement shock absorbers on front axle, double shock- absorbers with additional springs on rear axle pair			

Model	SX 25.440 6 × 6 (SX 44)	SX 32.440 8 × 8 (SX 45) with 1400R 20 tyres	SX 32.440 Multi 2 (SX 45) with 1400R 20 tyres	SX 32.440 Multi 2 IAC 3/3 (SX 45)
Tyres:	1400R 20; optional 1600R 20 or 395/85R 20	1400R 20; optional 1600R 20 or 395/85R 20	1400R 20; optional 395/85R 20	395/85R 20 with runflat inserts
Brakes:				
(main)	dual circuit, air, drums all-round. MAN EBS (Electronic Brake System) with ABS with off-road logic supplemented by air actuated exhaust brake with additional Exhaust Valve Brake system; integral retarder in gearbox			
(parking)	mechanical on rear wheels	mechanical on rear wheels	mechanical on rear wheels	mechanical on rear wheels
Electrical system:	24 V, 3-phase	24 V, 3-phase	24 V, 3-phase	24 V, 3-phase
Batteries:	4 × 12 V, 100 Ah NATO type	4 × 12 V, 100 Ah NATO type	4 × 12 V, 100 Ah NATO type	4 × 12 V, 100 Ah NATO type
Alternator:	28.5 V, 120 A	28.5 V, 120 A	28.5 V, 120 A	28.5 V, 120 A

Two types of modular detachable hard top roof are available, a standard flat roof or a version with extended height for the optional air-conditioning equipment, plus an NBC filtration system for the over-pressured cab if required.

The interior of the walk-through cab is primarily steel or washable plastic/vinyl, the bulk of the instrumentation package having been taken from MAN's TGA commercial range as this being deemed more practical and cost-effective than the purpose-designed instrumentation of earlier models. Where required controls and/or layout have been revised to accommodate combat or arctic clothing.

The engine and cooling pack are located transversally at the rear of the cab. This location offers protection from damage and blockage of the radiator with mud etc when operating off-road. It also allows for a larger volume radiator to be used, this enhancing hot-climate operating capability. Modern electronically-controlled engines reduce their power output as operating temperatures increase. The use of a larger rear-mounted radiator allows SX range trucks to operate at full power, at full GVW, in temperatures of +49°C for prolonged periods. A rear-mounted engine and cooling pack also ensures all standard width SX range trucks (subject to rear body fit) are air-transportable by C-130 Hercules aircraft, even with 1600R 20 tyres fitted. A 2.9 m wide SX chassis is available for certain applications.

Preparation for C-130 transport is limited to lowering the spare wheel and removing the roof hard top. There is no requirement to clamp springs, partially deflate tyres or fold down the cab.

Motive power for the current SX range is provided by MAN's exhaust turbocharged and intercooled 6-cylinder common rail diesel engines coupled to a ZF Powershift automatic transmission and MAN two-speed transfer box, with shift-controlling software developed by MAN. Separate and condition-specific shifting programmes are set for high (on-road) and low (off-road) ranges. Manual gear selection is available when required.

Drum brakes are fitted all-round, these utilising MAN's EBS (Electronic Brake System) which is fully integrated into the vehicles' CAN structure. The ABS system features MAN-specified off-road logic so does not require disconnection when operating off-road. Selecting 'off-road' mode activates an ABS mode with adapted anti-lock responses, essential on loose or slippery ground where a standard ABS will not provide a satisfactory brake performance. With the off-road mode selected the ABS system will automatically revert to conventional mode during periods where speeds reach or exceed 40 km/h. To assist during prolonged or steep descents there is an integral gearbox retarder, plus a three-stage driver-controlled exhaust brake.

All current SX range models are fitted with MAN's latest beam-type hub-reduction axles fitted as standard with driver-controlled cross- and inter-axle differential locks. All rear drive axles have full-width casings and have been designed from the outset to accept single wheels/tyres and not being axles originally designed for twin wheels. Standard tyres are

MAN's SX range of trucks (originally known as Category 1 range) were designed from the outset for high levels of strategic and tactical mobility, and have proven readily adaptable to modern doctrines, having, amongst other features, a purpose-designed cab that enables C-130 and rail transport, and also readily accepts appliqué armour kits
(Shaun C Connors) 0572375

Michelin XZL 1400R 20 or 1600R 20, although options including 24R 21 rear tyres for heavy recovery variants are available. Hydropneumatic suspension is a further option, as is a central tyre inflation (CTI) system.

Individual axle ratings for all SX range models are 9,000 kg, front, and 13,000 kg, rear. The 9,000 kg rating for the front axle(s) (traditionally front truck axles, commercial and military, have been rated at around 7,500 kg) is to accommodate an increasing number of requirements worldwide that call for vehicles capable of accepting a ballistic and anti-personnel mine protection kit.

MAN's modular military cab readily accepts protection kits and at the production stage can be fitted for, but not with, an appliqué armour kit. During the 1990s Krauss-Maffei Wegmann (KMW) supplied the Bundeswehr with around 140 appliqué armour kits for Kat 1 trucks deployed on global peacekeeping-style operations. A current generation kit has been developed in conjunction with Ressenig of Austria and is known as the Modular Integrated Cab (MAC). The MAC affords protection from Level 1 blast and Level 2 ballistic, according to Stanag 4569. Weight of the kit is around 1,300 kg and the hard-top is removable for air-transport if required.

Following experiences in the Balkans the German Bundeswehr raised their mine protection requirements, and in conjunction with KMW MAN has developed a protected cab for the SX (8 × 8) chassis that offers Level 3 protection from both small arms fire and anti-tank mine blast. To achieve Level 3 mine blast protection an all-steel armoured cab option was adopted in preference to an appliqué kit. The cab retains a tilt ability for maintenance purposes, and following the removal of the space cab attachment (which contains the air-conditioner, NBC equipment and gun pod cradle) the base vehicle fits the STANAG rail transport envelope and is C-130 transportable. The all-steel Integrated Armour Cabin (IAC) is currently available on SX range (8 × 8) chassis only (for axle weight reasons) but is expected to become available for SX (6 × 6) and HX (6 × 6) and (8 × 8) models. The IAC cab on SX (8 × 8) chassis has been adopted by Austria (24, delivery from early 2007), Denmark (20 (+ option of 10, delivery from 2007), Norway (6) and Germany (157).

Since production commenced, over 12,000 Kat 1/SX range trucks have been supplied to over 60 countries (sometimes in small numbers). The latest SX range has been supplied to, is currently being supplied to, or has been ordered by a number of countries including Austria (8 × 8), Denmark (30, (8 × 8)), Germany ((6 × 6), (8 × 8)), Greece (6 × 6), Lithuania (3, (8 × 8)), Luxembourg, Malaysia (8 × 8), Norway (approx 45, (8 × 8)), Sweden (approx 25, (8 × 8)) and the UK ((6 × 6), (8 × 8)).

Current SX range production is based on two base chassis/driveline variants, the SX44 (SX 25.440 6 × 6) and SX45 (SX 32.440 8 × 8). Taking the SX45 (SX 32.440 8 × 8) as an example, in all instances MAN designations denote: SX - model range; 32- GVW (can be limited by tyre choice or legislation); 440 - engine power output; 8 × 8 - drive configuration (8 × 8).

LX range of tactical trucks
The MAN LX range of tactical trucks (occasionally presented as LX 2000) was introduced in 1988. Compared to the SX range which is based on a purpose-designed torsionally stiff chassis, the LX range was designed as a lighter weight, highly mobile and C-130-transportable range of trucks and are based on modified chassis from MAN's M2000 medium weight commercial range. Two- and three-axle LX chassis were available, with carrying capacities ranging from 3,500 to 10,000 kg.

All LX range trucks are fitted with MAN's modular military cab but have a conventionally positioned engine. The cooling pack is located behind the cab. MAN's small block engines were fitted to reduce overall height.

Three-axle LX chassis have the rear axle pair sprung individually by leaf springs. While more complex than the more common bogie-type set-up in which inverted leaf springs are shared longitudinally by the axle pair, individual axle suspension offers improved off-road mobility.

LX range trucks are known to have been procured by Greece (badged Steyr), Luxembourg and Oman (400-500, 1992 onwards).

Commercial production of the M2000 range on which the LX range were based continued in Europe until early 2007, although from late 2004 the LX range was replaced by the TGA-based HX range.

FX range of tactical trucks
The MAN FX range of tactical trucks (occasionally presented as FX 2000) was introduced in 1990 and being optimised for heavy gross vehicle and combination weights, were initially based on chassis from MAN's F90

heavy commercial range, production of which ran from 1986-1992. From 1992 onwards FX range trucks were based on the F2000 heavy commercial range. From late 2005 HX range trucks replaced FX range trucks.

All FX range trucks are fitted with MAN's modular military cab and most have a conventionally positioned engine. The cooling pack, and for certain applications (heavy tractor trucks for example) the engine, is located behind the cab.

FX range trucks are known to have been procured by Germany, Greece, Spain (Air Force, FCR) and Turkey. Vehicles produced in Turkey are manufactured by MAN Türkiye A.S.

Specifications
See table on pages 500 and 501

Status
SX range in production. LX range replaced in production during 2004 by the HX range, FX range replaced in production by HX range during 2005 (see text).

Contractor
Rheinmetall MAN Military Vehicles (RMMV)

Mercedes-Benz 2628A (6 × 6) 12,000 kg truck

Development
The Mercedes-Benz 2628A (6 × 6) 12,000 kg cross-country truck is a militarised example of the Mercedes-Benz New Generation (NG) truck range, introduced commercially in 1973 and as the successor to the earlier LP range. The 2628A is a model from the revised NG80 range (New Generation 1980; introduced in 1980), this itself being superseded by the visually similar NG80DLO (NG80 with an upgraded driveline) before being supplemented by, and later replaced by, the all new but visually quite similar SK range which was introduced commercially in 1988. The Actros range introduced commercially in 1996 was the replacement for the SK range. The mid-weight Axor was introduced to supplement the Actros and lighter weight Atego in 2001. Full details of the SK, Actros and Axor ranges can be found elsewhere in this section.

The Mercedes-Benz 2628A is essentially an uprated Mercedes-Benz 2028A. The 2628A was not produced in the same numbers as the 2028A, the latter being adopted by a number of undisclosed armed forces, particularly in the Middle East and Asia. The Mercedes-Benz 1628A is essentially a (4 × 4) 7,000 kg payload version of the 2028A; small numbers were produced. Around the same time, Mercedes-Benz also offered the 1217CA and 1222A, both 5,500 kg payload (4 × 4) NG-series trucks.

Tractor truck versions of the NG/NG80 range were produced and details of these can be found in the Heavy equipment transporters section.

The 2628A was licence produced by TECTRAN in Brazil, where it was fitted with an armoured cab and assorted bodies for the AVIBRAS ASTROS II multiple rocket system. Later ASTROS chassis were Actros-based.

Description
The cab of the 2628A (6 × 6) 10,000 kg truck has seating for the driver and two passengers. The centre seat has a folding backrest to allow clear access to the roof-mounted hatch, which is provided with a rail grip. A medium length cab was available which had extra space for crew equipment while a crew-type cab had space for up to seven occupants. The cab can be tilted forward for engine access to an angle of 65°. For normal

The 2628AS (A - all-wheel drive; S - tractor truck) is a 38,000 kg GCW-rated (65,000 kg option) tractor truck variant of the 2628A 12,000 kg cargo truck (Daimler) 1128755

Mercedes-Benz 2628A (6 × 6) 12,000 kg truck with standard troop carrying/cargo-type body (Daimler) 1128750

day-to-day maintenance, access flaps are provided. Behind the cab there is spare wheel stowage and on the front of the cab the headlights and radiator grille are protected by heavy-duty tubular guards.

All the undersides and major drive components can be fully waterproofed for an optional fording depth of 1.2 m without preparation and the engine air intake pipe is routed upwards over the cab roof side. The load area has 500 mm high drop sides and tailgate, and is provided with lash-down points and a canvas tilt. A towing hook for trailers or artillery is provided at the rear. Optional equipment included a hydraulic 10,000 kg winch with cable control to the front or rear; the standard single-tyred version was available with a Central Tyre Inflation (CTI) system as an optional extra.

Various box and cab bodies were produced, and the model was suitable for use as a tanker, fire tender or command and communication vehicle. A version was produced as a heavy recovery vehicle carrying a Marrel MH 45 or Hägglunds Moelv recovery hamper.

Variants

Mercedes-Benz 2634A
The Mercedes-Benz 2634A is externally identical to the 2628A but is powered by an OM 422A turbocharged V-8 diesel developing 340 hp at 2,100 rpm. Maximum speed is 89 km/h.

The 2628AS was a (6 × 6) tractor truck intended to tow engineer equipment on a semi-trailer with a gross combination weight of 38,000 kg, 65,000 kg with reinforcements.

Specifications
Cab seating: 1 + 2 or up to 6
Configuration: 6 × 6
Weight:
    (laden) 24,000 kg
    (unladen) approx 11,300 kg
    (payload) approx 12,000 kg
    (weight on front axle) 7,500 kg
    (weight on rear axle) 2 × 9,000 kg
    (GCW) 40,000 kg
Length: 8.3 m
Width: 2.495 m
Height:
    (cab) 3.09 m
    (tarpaulin) 3.5 m
Load area: 5.5 × 2.35 m
Ground clearance: 427 mm
Track: 2.07 m
Wheelbase: 3.8 m + 1.45 m
Angle of approach/departure: 35°/46°
Max speed: 93 km/h
Fuel capacity: 300 litres
Gradient:
    (high range) 66%
    (low range) >80%
    (with trailer, GCW 40,000 kg, high range) 34%
    (with trailer, GCW 40,000 kg, low range) 66%
Fording: 1.2 m
Engine: Mercedes-Benz OM 422 14.618-litre V-8 water-cooled direct injection diesel developing 280 hp (209 kW) at 2,300 rpm

Transmission: ZF 5S 111 G fully synchronised with 9 forward (8 plus crawler) and 1 reverse gears: optional ZF S6 90 6-speed with torque converter on early models
Transfer box: VG1400 2-speed
Clutch: GF420 single dry disc
Turning radius: approx 10.15 m
Brakes: dual circuit, air, drums all-round
Tyres: 14.00R × 20
Electrical system: 24 V
Batteries: 2 × 12 V, 115 Ah
Alternator: 55 A

Status
Production complete, supplied to a number of undisclosed countries.

Contractor
Daimler AG

Mercedes-Benz SK range of trucks

Development
The Mercedes-Benz SK range of trucks are militarised examples of the Mercedes-Benz SK range introduced commercially in 1988. The SK range initially supplemented the earlier and later replaced the earlier and visually similar New Generation (NG) truck range, introduced commercially in 1973 and as the successor to the earlier LP range. The Actros range introduced commercially in 1996 was the replacement for the SK range. The mid-weight Axor was introduced from 2001 to supplement the Actros and lighter weight Atego. Full details of the NG range (models 2028 and 2628) and Axor and Actros ranges can be found elsewhere in this section.

The SK family consisted of the following:
- 2638, (6 × 4), wheelbase 4.5 m + 1.35 m
- 2638A, (6 × 6), wheelbase 4.1 m + 1.35 m
- 2638S, (6 × 4), wheelbase 3.2 m + 1.35 m
- 2638AS, (6 × 6), wheelbase 3.5 m + 1.35 m
- 2638K, (6 × 4), wheelbase 3.2 or 3.5 m + 1.35 m
- 2638AK, (6 × 6), wheelbase 3.5 or 3.85 m + 1.35 m

A - all-wheel drive; K - tipper; S - tractor truck.

Description
The cab of the SK (6 × 6) series of trucks has seating for the driver and two passengers. The centre seat has a folding backrest to allow clear access to the roof-mounted hatch. A medium length cab was available which had extra space for crew equipment while a crew-type cab had space for up to seven occupants. The cab type can be tilted forward for engine access. A Krauss-Maffei Wegmann (KMW) armouring system was available for this vehicle.

Mercedes-Benz 2638A SK range (6 × 6) trucks of a Middle Eastern Army; note the purpose-designed single axle trailers and front-mounted winch on the first vehicle (Ian Young) 1128752

Mercedes-Benz 2638A SK range (6 × 6) trucks in tanker configuration of a Middle Eastern Army (Ian Young) 1128753

Mercedes-Benz 2638AS SK range (6 × 6) tractor truck of the German Bundeswehr in Kosovo; this vehicle is fitted with a small arms fire protection kit supplied by Krauss-Maffei Wegmann (KMW) (Michael Jerchel) 1128751

The vehicle is based on a ladder frame chassis with a high load-bearing capacity, bending resistance and torsional flexibility. A cargo body was standard although numerous other types of body could be fitted, including tankers or load handling systems.

Specifications
2638A (6 × 6) 14,000 kg truck
Cab seating: 1 + 2 (crew-type cab options available)
Configuration: 6 × 6
Weight:
    (laden) 26,000 kg
    (max payload) approx 14,000 kg
    (max front axle load) 7,500 kg
    (max rear axle load) 2 × 13,000 kg
Length: (chassis) 8.84 m
Width: 2.49 m
Height: (cab roof) 3.32 m
Ground clearance: 347 mm
Track:
    (front) 1.99 m
    (rear) 1.804 m
Wheelbase: 4.1 m + 1.35 m
Max speed: 94 km/h
Fuel capacity: 300 litres
Engine: Mercedes-Benz OM 402 LA EURO I 12.763-litre V-8 turbocharged and intercooled, water-cooled direct injection 4-stroke diesel developing 381 hp (284 kW) at 1,900 rpm
Transmission: Mercedes-Benz G180-16/11.9 manual with 16 forward and 2 reverse gears
Clutch: single dry disc
Transfer box: VG2400 2-speed
Turning radius: 9.5 m
Brakes: dual circuit, air, drums all-round
Tyres: 12.00R 22.5; options available including 1400R 20
Electrical system: 24 V
Batteries: 2 × 12 V, 165 Ah
Alternator: 55 A

Status
Production complete, in service with a number of undisclosed armed forces.

Contractor
Daimler AG

Mercedes-Benz Actros range of trucks

Description
The Mercedes-Benz Actros range of trucks for military applications are based on the most recent range of Mercedes-Benz Actros civilian trucks, but militarised to varying degrees to suit specific operator requirements. Layout and design are entirely conventional and the range utilises only commercially available and proven driveline components.

Power is provided by Mercedes-Benz V6 or V8 EURO 4 emissions compliant diesel engines with power outputs ranging from 320 to 510 hp. Engines meeting EURO 2, 3 or 5 emissions requirements are available for certain territories. Throughout the range gearbox options include the Telligent gearshift system with clutch (electronic selection, pneumatic shifting) or the Telligent fully automatic gearshift system without clutch. Two, three or four-axle chassis are available and in a variety of drive configurations and with single or dual wheels on the rear axles. Payload ratings range from 6,000 to 18,000 kg.

With the exception of the Actros 8 × 8, which is available with hydro-pneumatic or air suspension as an option, all axles are leaf-sprung with driven axles featuring planetary hub reduction gearing and driver-controlled differential locks. Anti-lock Brakes (ABS), a Central Tyre Inflation (CTI) system and a self-recovery winch are included as options.

Wheelbase options currently range between 3.6 m on (4 × 4) and (6 × 6) chassis to 4.8 m on (8 × 8) chassis. The standard C-section chassis can be fitted with a variety of bodies including drop side, box-body, tanker, dump,

recovery hamper and DROPS/PLS load handling systems. Tractor truck versions are also available and full details of those tractor trucks having a GCW of greater than 65,000 kg can be found in the Heavy equipment transporters section.

The two-door forward-control all-steel tilt-cab can be specified based around either a civilian two/three-person day-cab or the larger sleeper-cab, which can be supplied with or without bunks. Options can include enhanced heating and air-conditioning systems, an observation hatch in the roof, or a high-roof version of the sleeper cab.

A benign in appearance replacement armoured cab has been developed for the Actros. This was developed by Daimler in conjunction with Land Mobility Technologies (LMT) of South Africa, and is available in three configurations; day cab, mid-size and crew-type. A version of the mid-size version of this cab is fitted to the Actros vehicles supplied to Canada under the Armored Heavy Support Vehicle System (AHSVS) requirement, further details of which can be found elsewhere in this entry.

Being based on an in-production range of commercial trucks, throughout their production, the Mercedes-Benz Actros range of military trucks are likely to reflect the many minor design changes and specification upgrades associated with civilian truck production.

The (6 × 6) range of Mercedes-Benz Actros trucks currently consists of seven vehicles with wheelbases ranging from 3.6 to 4.5 m. Engine power outputs range from 320 to 510 hp. All seven models have a payload of up to 12,000 kg (Daimler)   1391418

Mercedes-Benz Actros (6 × 6) truck (in water tanker configuration) of UAE Armed Forces (Shaun C Connors)   1124798

Mercedes-Benz Actros 4151 (8 × 8) during trials for Australia's Land 121, Project Overlander. At the time of writing (December 2010), no contractual announcement regarding Overlander had been made (Daimler)   1391435

Mercedes-Benz Actros model 2031A (4 × 4) truck configured as a tanker and fitted with dual rear wheels (Daimler)   0121913

Mercedes-Benz Actros (8 × 8) configured for German Army trials (Daimler)   1391419

Mercedes-Benz Actros (6 × 4) tractor truck (Daimler)   0121916

Actros (4 × 4)

The (4 × 4) range of Mercedes-Benz Actros trucks currently consists of 11 vehicles with wheelbases of 3.6, 3.9 or 4.5 m and payload options of 6,000 or 7,000 kg. Engine power outputs range from 320 to 510 hp.

Models 1832A, 1836A, 1841A, 1844A and 1846A are available with a 3.6 or 3.9 m wheelbase and are powered by a V6 engine developing 320 hp (1832A), 360 hp (1836A), 408 hp (1841A), 435 hp (1844A) or 456 hp (1846A). Model 1851A is available with a 3.9 m wheelbase and is powered by a V8 diesel developing 510 hp. All of these models have a 6,000 kg payload.

Models 2032A, 2036A, 2041A, 2044A and 2048A are available with a 3.9 m wheelbase, models 2032A and 2036A also available with a 4.5 m wheelbase. All are powered by a V6 engine developing 320 hp (2032A), 360 hp (2036A), 408 hp (2041A), 435 hp (2044A) or 476 hp (2048A). All of these models have a 7,000 kg payload.

Actros two-axle models are also available in a (4 × 2) drive configuration, and with single or dual tyres on the rear axle. Tractor truck variants are also available.

Mercedes-Benz Actros (6 × 6) truck fitted with dual rear wheels and a behind-cab materials handling crane and standard cargo body (Daimler)
0121914

Mercedes-Benz Actros model 3340A (6 × 6) truck fitted optional front impact protection and configured to transport standard 20 ft ISO containers (Daimler)
0121915

Mercedes-Benz Actros (8 × 8) truck fitted with dual rear wheels and a special purpose body (Daimler)
0121917

From 2001, and in order to cover the specific 5,000- to 7,000 kg payload/GVW segment with a truck better suited to the requirements of some users (including the German Army), Mercedes-Benz introduced militarised variants of the mid-weight Axor commercial model to supplement the lightest Actros (4 × 4) models and the heaviest Atego models. Full details of the Atego and Axor ranges can be found elsewhere in this section.

Actros (6 × 6)

The (6 × 6) range of Mercedes-Benz Actros trucks currently consists of seven vehicles with wheelbases ranging from 3.6 to 4.5 m. Engine power outputs range from 320 to 510 hp. All seven models have a payload of up to 12,000 kg. Models 3332A (320 hp), 3336A (360 hp), 3341A (408 hp), 3344A (435 hp), 3346A (456 hp) and 3348A (476 hp) have wheelbase options of 3.6, 3.9, 4.2 and 4.5 m and are powered by a V6 engine. Model 3351A (510 hp) has a 3.6 m wheelbase and is powered by a V8 engine. Engines of higher power output are available on request.

Actros three-axle models are also available in (6 × 4) and (6 × 2) drive configurations, and with single or dual tyres on the rear axles. Tractor truck variants are also available.

Actros (8 × 8)

The (8 × 8) range of Mercedes-Benz Actros trucks currently consists of five vehicles with a 4.8 m wheelbase and payload capacity of up to 18,000 kg. Models 4141A (408 hp), 4144A (435 hp), 4146A (456 hp) and 4148A (476 hp) are powered by a V6 engine, while model 4151 (510 hp) is powered by a V8 diesel. Engines of higher power outputs are available on request.

Actros models are also available in an (8 × 4) drive configuration, and with single or dual tyres on the rear axles. A model with hydro-pneumatic suspension that allows the transport of an 8 ft 6 in ISO container on a vehicle fitted with a load handling system, without exceeding 4 m overall height, is available. Air suspension is also an option on the rear bogie. Tractor trucks are also available.

Canadian Armored Heavy Support Vehicle System (AHSVS)

The Canadian Department of Defense disclosed mid-2007 that it had awarded the then DaimlerChrysler AG an approximately CAD87 million contract for 82 Mercedes-Benz Actros (8 × 8) Armored Heavy Support Vehicle System Trucks (AHSVS) for use on deployed operations.

Following a Request for Proposal (RfP) that was issued to industry during January 2007, responses from three potential contractors (DaimlerChrysler, MAN and Sisu) were received and the contract award, which includes an option for an additional 26, was made during March 2007. Deliveries were scheduled to commence late 2007, with final deliveries scheduled for March 2008.

With the exception of 15 vehicles retained in Canada for training purposes, the AHSVS fleet is used by Canadian Forces deployed on operations in Afghanistan where they have replaced Steyr-based Heavy Logistics Vehicle Wheeled (HLVW) trucks that were procured in the late 1980s, and are now considered unsuitable for a variety of reasons, such as the inability to accept the required level of blast and ballistic protection. AHSVS consists of four main variants:

- 25 cargo with material handling crane (inc. eight gun tractors for the M777 howitzer)
- 40 Palletized Loading System (PLS) with container handling unit variant vehicles (10 petroleum, oils, and lubricants variants and five water variants)
- five recovery variant vehicles
- 12 heavy tank transporter tractor variant vehicles.

All AHSVS vehicles are fitted a medium-sized version of a benign in appearance armoured cab family designed by Daimler in conjunction with Land Mobility Technologies (LMT) of South Africa.

The Canadian Department of Defense disclosed mid-2007 that it had awarded the then DaimlerChrysler AG an approximately CAD87 million contract for 82 Mercedes-Benz Actros (8 × 8) Armored Heavy Support Vehicle System Trucks (AHSVS) for use on deployed operations. Shown in Afghanistan is one of 40 Palletized Loading System (PLS) with container handling unit variant vehicles (Carl Schulze)
1391420

The Canadian Department of Defense disclosed mid-2007 that it had awarded the then DaimlerChrysler AG an approximately CAD87 million contract for 82 Mercedes-Benz Actros (8 × 8) Armored Heavy Support Vehicle System Trucks (AHSVS) for use on deployed operations. Shown in Afghanistan and complete with companion trailer is one of 40 Palletized Loading System (PLS) with container handling unit variant vehicles (Carl Schulze)   1391421

All AHSVS vehicles feature full-time (8 × 8) drive and are powered by V8 diesel engines developing in excess of 500 hp and meeting EURO 3 emissions requirements (not the current EURO 5) on account of operational considerations – mainly fuel quality. All vehicles are fitted with a 16-speed automated (with manual option) gearbox and two-speed transfer box, and in order to cope with the combined weights of around 120,000 kg, the tractor truck variant driveline features a torque converter.

Bodies including recovery hampers, will be provided by EMPL of Austria, with PLS and materials handling equipment sub-contracted to Hiab (Multilift). Semi-trailers used with the tractor truck variants are King GTS 110/7 manufactured in Germany by DOLL.

A total of 13 AHSVS vehicles have been acquired under the contract option. The 13 vehicles were made up of three variants: four cargo, six heavy mobile repair team and three flat deck recovery system. Three DOLL 35,000 kg recovery trailers were also ordered under the option, specifically the flat deck recovery system option. Also ordered as a contract option were four protected troop transport pods from Daimler's sub contractor, Land Mobility Technologies (LMT).

Status
In volume production. In service with numerous armed forces in Asia, Europe and the Middle East including those of Algeria, Australia (Air Force), Botswana, Bulgaria, Canada, Chile, Gabon, Germany, Kuwait, Pakistan (400, 2006), Poland, Portugal, Qatar, Saudi Arabia (30, 2007), Singapore (8 × 8), Slovenia, Taiwan, Turkey, UAE, Venezuela, Yemen (est. 200, 2006-2010), and the UK. For contractual reasons, in many cases Daimler cannot make official comment on military sales of Actros and many of the above figures are unconfirmed and from third party sources.

Contractor
Daimler AG

Mercedes-Benz Atego range of trucks

Development
The Mercedes-Benz Atego range of two-axle trucks for military applications, are based on the most recent range of Mercedes-Benz Atego civilian trucks, but are militarised to suit specific operator requirements.

The Atego range, while suitable for military applications, are designed to be of lighter construction, have less powerful engines and a higher payload to GVW ratio than any comparable truck in the heavier-duty Actros range. To better meet the GVW/payload requirements previously covered by lighter Actros models and heavier Atego models, from 2001, Mercedes-Benz introduced militarised versions of the mid-weight Axor. Full details of the Axor range can be found elsewhere in this section.

Being based on an in-production range of commercial trucks, throughout their production run by the Mercedes-Benz Atego range of military trucks, are likely to reflect the many minor design changes and specification upgrades associated with civilian truck production.

Description
Layout and design of the Mercedes-Benz Atego range is entirely conventional and utilises only commercially available and proven driveline components, these militarised to suit specific operator requirements.

Power for all Atego models is provided by Mercedes-Benz EURO 4 emissions compliant four- and six-cylinder in-line turbocharged and intercooled diesel engines with power outputs ranging from 177 to 286 hp. Engines meeting EURO 2, 3 or 5 emissions requirements are available if required. The Telligent gearshift system (electronic selection, pneumatic shifting) is an option for the heavier Atego models, as is the new Telligent fully automatic shifting.

Atego (and the slightly heavier Axor) are currently being procured by BwFuhrparkService GMBH, the private sector company that is contracted to provide non-tactical transport services to Germany's Bundeswehr (Shaun C Connors)   1391033

Mercedes-Benz 1017A Atego (4 × 4) truck of the Gabon Army fitted with an EMPL-supplied dropside troop-carrying cargo-type body (EMPL)   1186191

Both (4 × 4) and (4 × 2) drive configurations are available, and with single or dual wheels on the rear axles. Payload ratings range from 3,000 to 5,000 kg, depending on vehicle execution and options, and all axles are leaf-sprung with driven axles featuring planetary hub reduction gearing and driver-controlled differential locks. An anti-lock braking system (ABS) is standard, while a central tyre inflation (CTI) system and self-recovery winch are options. The standard C-section chassis can be fitted with a variety of bodies including drop side, box-body, tanker, dump or light recovery hamper.

The two-door forward-control all-steel tilt-cab can be specified based around either a civilian three-person day-cab or the larger sleeper-cab, which can be supplied with or without bunks. Options can include enhanced heating and air-conditioning systems, an observation hatch in the roof, or a high-roof version of the sleeper cab.

There are currently seven base (4 × 4) models in the Atego range of military vehicles. Models 1018A and 1024A have a wheelbase of 3.26 m and engine power outputs are 177 hp (1018) and 238 hp (1024). Models 1318A, 1324A, 1524A, 1526A and 1529A have wheelbase options of 3.26 and 3.56 m. Engine power outputs are 177 hp (1318A), 238 hp (1324A/1524A), 256 hp (1526A) and 286 hp (1529A).

Status
In volume production. In service with numerous armed forces in Asia, Europe and the Middle East, including: Argentina, Bulgaria, Cameroon, Finland, Gabon, Germany, Netherlands, Taiwan, Turkey, and the UK. For contractual reasons, in many cases Daimler cannot make official comment on military sales of Atego and many of the above figures are unconfirmed and from third party sources.

Contractor
Daimler AG

Mercedes-Benz Axor range of trucks

Development
The Mercedes-Benz Axor range of two-axle trucks for military applications, are based on the most recent range of Mercedes-Benz Axor civilian trucks. The Axor range, while suitable for military applications, are designed to be of lighter construction, have less powerful engines and a higher payload to GVW ratio than any comparable truck in the heavier-duty Actros range. The Axor range was introduced commercially in 2001 to better meet the GVW/payload requirements previously covered by lighter Actros models and heavier Atego models. Full details of the Atego and Actros ranges can be found elsewhere in this section.

Axor (and the lighter Atego) are currently being procured by BwFuhrparkService GMBH, the private sector company that is contracted to provide non-tactical transport services to Germany's Bundeswehr (Daimler) 1391423

Axor (and the lighter Atego) are currently being procured by BwFuhrparkService GMBH, the private sector company that is contracted to provide non-tactical transport services to Germany's Bundeswehr (Daimler) 1391422

Being based on an in-production range of commercial trucks, throughout their production run by the Mercedes-Benz Axor range of military trucks, are likely to reflect the many minor design changes and specification upgrades associated with civilian truck production.

Description

Layout and design of the Mercedes-Benz Axor range of trucks is entirely conventional and utilises only commercially available and proven driveline components, these can be militarised as required to suit specific user requirements.

Power for all Axor models is provided by Mercedes-Benz EURO 4 emissions compliant four- and six-cylinder in-line turbocharged and intercooled diesel engines with power outputs ranging from 238 to 326 hp. Engines meeting EURO 2, 3 or 5 emissions requirements are available if required. The Telligent gearshift system (electronic selection, pneumatic shifting) is an option for the heavier Axor models, as is the new Telligent fully automatic shifting.

Both (4 × 4) and (4 × 2) drive configurations are available, and with single or dual wheels on the rear axles. Payload ratings range from 5,000 to 7,000 kg, depending on vehicle execution and options, and all axles are leaf-sprung with driven axles featuring planetary hub reduction gearing and driver-controlled differential locks. An Anti-lock Braking System (ABS) is standard, while a Central Tyre Inflation (CTI) system and self-recovery winch are options. The standard C-section chassis can be fitted with a variety of bodies including drop side, box-body, tanker, dump or light recovery hamper.

The two-door forward-control all-steel tilt-cab can be specified based around either a civilian three-person day-cab or the larger sleepercab, which can be supplied with or without bunks.

Options can include enhanced heating and air conditioning systems, an observation hatch in the roof, or a highroof version of the sleeper cab.

There are currently four base (4 × 4) models in the Axor range of military vehicles. Models 1824A and 1826A have wheelbase options of 3.6 and 3.9 m and engine power outputs of 238 hp (1824A) and 256 hp (1826A). Models 1829A and 1833A have wheelbase options of 3.6, 3.9, 4.2 and 4.5 m and engine power outputs of 286 hp (1829A) and 326 hp (1833A).

Status

In volume production. In service with German Armed Forces.

Contractor

Daimler AG

Greece

ELBO 14 ME 22

Development

The ELBO 14 ME 22 4 × 4 truck is a Steyr 14 M 22 truck supplied to ELBO in SKD (semi knock down) form for final assembly and insertion of local content. The Steyr 14 M 22 is a militarised example of the MAN M2000 range of commercial trucks and readers are referred to the Steyr Trucks entry elsewhere in this section for full details of the relationship between the current MAN (RMMV) and Steyr military truck ranges.

The ELBO 14 ME 22 is essentially the follow-on model for the ELBO 14 ME 14 (Steyr 14 M 14) and around 850 examples of which are in service with Hellenic and Cypriot armed forces. Full details of the ELBO 14 ME 14 can be found elsewhere in this section.

Final deliveries of L/M2000 series based trucks to the Greek Army were completed in 2004, when 31 vehicles were delivered. L and M2000 series trucks have been replaced in the current MAN (RMMV) product range by TGL and TGM models.

Description

A full description of the Steyr 14 M 22, which was available with a number of options including cab style and wheelbase, can be found elsewhere in this section. In brief, the vehicle is entirely conventional in design, the forward control all-steel cab being mounted on a conventional C-section chassis fitted with beam-type axles and leaf spring suspension.

Motive power is provided by a EURO II emissions compliant MAN turbocharged diesel engine. Driveline options fitted to the Greek vehicles include a differential lock in the front axle (a rear axle differential lock is standard equipment), a ZF 16S 109 16 speed (with splitter) gearbox, and an anti-lock braking system (ABS) with off-road logic. Eight vehicles supplied for use with the Patriot missile system are fitted with the Steyr VG 750 two-speed transfer box with ADM (Automatic Drivetrain Management), an automatic traction control system.

The base vehicle chassis, in a selection of wheelbases, was supplied to ELBO who were responsible for the installation of a number of body types including fuel and water tankers, box- and shelter-type bodies and the standard drop side cargo/troop carrying body, the latter being designed and manufactured by ELBO.

Specifications

14 M 22
(3.6/3.9 m wheelbase and compact cab)
Cab seating: 1 + 1 or 2
Configuration: 4 × 4
Weight:
(chassis cab) 5,400 kg (approx)
(GVW) 13,500 kg
(chassis load capacity) ≤8,100 kg
(towed load) 10,500 kg
(GTW) 24,000 kg
(max load on front axle) 5,000 kg
(max load on rear axle) 9,000 kg
Length overall: 6.0/6.3 m
Width:
(cab) 2.2 m
(rear wheels) 2.4 m
(overall) 2.49 m
Height:
(cab, unladen) 2.932
(cab, laden) 2.864 m
Ground clearance:
(front axle) 372 mm
(rear axle) 365 mm

ELBO 14 ME 22 (4 × 4) truck with dual tyres. The ELBO 14 ME 22 is a license produced SKD version (with added local content) of the Steyr 14 M 22 (RMMV) 0547200

Wheelbase: 3.9/3.6 m
Max speed: (road) 85 km/h (with speed limiter)
Fuel capacity: 150 litres
Gradient: >60%
Sideslope: 30% (approx.)
Fording: ≤750 mm
Engine: MAN Type D 0826LFL EURO II 6.871-litre 6-cylinder in-line exhaust gas turbocharged and intercooled direct injection water-cooled 4-stroke diesel developing 220 hp (164 kW) at 2,400 rpm and 825 N.m torque between 1,400 and 1,700 rpm
Gearbox: ZF 16S 109 16-speed manual with splitter
Transfer box: G 1000/2 2-speed or VG 750 with ADM (see text)
Steering: power-assisted, ZF 8095
Turning radius: 8.5 m
Suspension: parabolic leaf springs with telescopic shock-absorbers and anti-roll bar, front and rear
Tyres: 10R 22.5, dual rear (standard), 365/85R 20 single tyres (optional)
Brakes: dual circuit, air, drums all-round. ABS with off-road logic
Electrical system: 24 V
Batteries: 2 × 12 V, 88 Ah
Alternator: 28 V, 35 A

Status

Production complete; replaced by equivalent TGL/TGM series models. In service with Greece (approx 80 delivered).

Contractor

Hellenic Vehicle Industry SA

ELBO 14 ME 14 (4 × 4) 8,000 kg truck

Description

The ELBO 14 ME 14 (4 × 4) 8,000 kg truck was produced in Greece under licence from the then Steyr Nutzfahrzeuge AG of Austria.

The ELBO 14 ME 14 4 × 4 truck is a Steyr 14 M 14 truck supplied to ELBO in SKD (semi knock down) form for final assembly and insertion of local content. The Steyr 14 M 14 is a militarised example of the MAN M2000 range of commercial trucks and readers are referred to the Steyr Trucks entry elsewhere in this section for full details of the relationship between the current MAN (RMMV) and Steyr military truck ranges.

The ELBO 14 ME 14 is essentially the predecessor model of the ELBO 14 ME 22 (Steyr 14 M 22), full details of which can be found elsewhere in this section.

Around 850 ELBO 14 M 14 trucks were delivered to the Hellenic and Cypriot armed forces. Much smaller numbers of the 14 M 22 were delivered from 2002. Final deliveries of L/M2000 series based trucks to the Greek Army occurred in 2004, when 31 vehicles were delivered. L and M2000 series trucks have been replaced in the current MAN product range by TGL and TGM models.

Description

The overall layout of the 14 ME 14 closely follows that of the Steyr 14 M 14 original, and thus involves a forward control tiltable cab and the superstructure area to the rear. There are some minor changes from the original to suit Greek requirements. The cab has seating for the driver and one passenger.

Body options produced in Greece include an 8,000 kg general cargo version with steel sides and tailgate with folding benches, all covered with removable bows and a tarpaulin cover. Other bodies include a 5,000 litre fuel or water tanker, 5,000 litre water-foam firefighting body, 8 m³ refuse body, 6,000 kg sewage treatment body, 8,000 kg container carrier, mobile workshops and so on.

Options included a right-hand drive version, a 5,000 kg capacity hydraulic winch with front or rear pull, driver training cab and a two-passenger cab seat.

ELBO 14 M 14 (4 × 4) 8,000 kg truck of the Hellenic Army
(Shaun C Connors)   1296176

Specifications

ELBO 14 ME 14
Cab seating: 1 + 1 or 1 + 2
Configuration: 4 × 4
Weight:
   (unladen, general cargo body) 6,000 kg
   (GVW) 14,000 kg
   (max front axle load) 5,000 kg
   (max rear axle load) 9,200 kg
   (max load) 8,000 kg
   (towed load, on-road) 10,000 kg
   (towed load, off-road) 5,000 kg
Load area: 3.99 × 2.28 m
Length:
   (with general cargo body) 6.56 m
   (chassis) 6.261 m
Width: 2.4 m
Height: 3.15 m
Ground clearance: 280 mm
Track:
   (front) 1.879 m
   (rear) 1.721 m
Wheelbase: 3.7 m
Angle of approach/departure: 40°/37°
Max speed: 80 km/h
Range: 800 km
Fuel capacity: 200 litres
Max gradient:
   (without trailer) 54%
   (with trailer) 40%
Side slope: 30°
Fording: 800 mm
Engine: ELBO/Steyr WD 612.91 6.595-litre 6-cylinder in-line water-cooled direct injection 4-stroke diesel developing 136 hp (101 kW) at 2,400 rpm
Gearbox: ZF S6/36, 6 forward and 1 reverse gears
Clutch: single dry plate
Transfer box: Steyr VG 450, 2-speed
Steering: ZF 8043, power-assisted
Turning radius: 7.6 m
Suspension: semi-elliptic leaf springs front and rear with telescopic shock-absorbers at front
Tyres: 9.00 × 20
Brakes:
   (main) dual-circuit hydropneumatic
   (parking) spring-actuated, air operated
Electrical system: 12 or 24 V
Batteries: 2 × 12 V, 110 Ah

Status

Production complete. In service with the Greek armed forces (approx 850).

Contractor

Hellenic Vehicle Industry SA

ELBO 26 S 28 P38 (6 × 6) 20,000 kg general cargo train

Development

The chassis for the ELBO 26 S 28 P38 (6 × 6) truck was produced in Greece under licence from the then Steyr Nutzfahrzeuge AG of Austria. The ELBO 26 S 28, of which around 250 examples were produced, was replaced in production by the Steyr 33 M 41. Initial deliveries of the MAN TGA based Steyr 33 M 41 were made during 2002. Further TGA based heavy trucks were delivered to the Hellenic Army during 2004 (14), 2005 (24) and 2007 (12).

Description

Layout of the ELBO 26 S 28 (6 × 6) truck is conventional with a forward control tiltable cab and the general cargo body to the rear. The general cargo body is all steel with three hinged side doors along each side, a tailgate, removable bows and a tarpaulin cover. The cab has seating for the driver and a co-driver. Various bodies other than the general cargo can be fitted.

The trailer and the general cargo bodies were developed and produced in Greece.

Options included a 9,000 kg capacity hydraulic winch with a front or rear pull and a second co-driver's seat.

Variants

ELBO 26 S 28 K35 (6 × 6) 8 m³ dump truck

This vehicle chassis is closely allied to the general cargo truck described above but is fitted with a rear-tipping 8 m³ dump body. Other bodies, such as a 10,000 kg general cargo body, can be fitted to this chassis.

ELBO 26 S 31 S38 (6 × 6) tractor truck

Full details of the ELBO 26 S 31 S 38 tractor truck can be found in the Heavy equipment transporters section.

Specifications
ELBO 26 S 28 P38
Cab seating: 1 + 1 or 1 + 2
Configuration: 6 × 6
Weight:
  (unladen, general cargo body) 13,000 kg
  (laden) 32,000 kg
  (max front axle load) 6,500 kg
  (max rear axle load) 13,000 kg (each axle)
  (towed load, on-road) 12,000 kg
  (towed load, off-road) 6,000 kg
  (GTW) 38,000 kg
Load area: 4.6 × 2.3 m
Length: (general cargo train) 17 m
Width: 2.5 m
Height: 3.13 m
Ground clearance: 300 mm
Track:
  (front) 1.958 m
  (rear) 1.8 m
Wheelbase: 3.8 m + 1.35 m
Angle of approach/departure: 30°/40°
Max speed: 80 km/h
Range: 500 km
Fuel capacity: 400 litres
Max gradient:
  (without trailer) 70%
  (with trailer) 60%
Side slope: 30°
Fording: 800 mm
Engine: Steyr WD 615.73 9.73-litre 6-cylinder in-line turbocharged and intercooled water-cooled 4-stroke direct injection diesel developing 278 hp (207 kW) at 2,200 rpm
Gearbox: ZF 5S111GP with 8 forward plus 1 crawler and 1 reverse gears
Clutch: single dry plate
Transfer box: Steyr VG 1200, 2-speed
Steering: ZF 8043, power-assisted
Turning radius: 9.3 m
Suspension:
  (front) semi-elliptic reinforced leaf springs with telescopic shock-absorbers
  (rear) semi-elliptic reinforced reversed leaf springs with torsion bars
Tyres: 12.00 R 20
Brakes:
  (main) dual-circuit air
  (parking) spring-actuated, air operated
Electrical system: 24 V
Batteries: 2 × 12 V, 143 Ah

Status
Production complete. In service with the Greek (and possibly Cypriot) armed forces (approx 250).

Contractor
Hellenic Vehicle Industry SA

Hungary

Csepel D-562 (4 × 2), D-564 (4 × 4), D-566 (6 × 6) and D-566.02 (6 × 6) trucks

Development
The Csepel D-566 (6 × 6) cargo truck appeared in 1970 and entered production the following year. The D-562 (4 × 2) and D-564 (4 × 4) vehicles were introduced in 1972, with first production vehicles being completed in 1974.

Csepel ceased production of military vehicles in 1995 and in May 2001 was reported to be in liquidation.

Description
The Csepel D-566 (6 × 6) cargo truck has a two-door all-steel forward control cab, with the cargo area at the rear with a drop tailgate, bows and tarpaulin cover. A central tyre pressure regulation system is fitted as standard. Variants of the D-566 include a recovery vehicle and a shop/van.

The D-566.02 is identical to the D-566 but has a 7,000 kg capacity winch with 60 m of cable.

The D-562 (4 × 2) and D-564 (4 × 4) vehicles also have a two-door all-steel forward control cab, with the cargo area at the rear with a drop tailgate, drop sides, a tarpaulin cover and bows. Both are provided with a central tyre pressure regulation system. A dump truck model was produced.

Specifications

Model	D-562	D-564	D-566
Configuration:	4 × 2	4 × 4	6 × 6
Weight:			
(unladen)	5,200 kg	5,400 kg	9,500 kg
(laden, off-road)	9,200 kg	9,400 kg	14,500 kg
(payload, road)	5,000 kg	5,000 kg	8,000 kg
(payload, off-road)	4,000 kg	4,000 kg	5,000 kg
(towed load, road)	n/avail	n/avail	10,000 kg
(towed load, off-road)	n/avail	n/avail	5,000 kg
Length:	6.43 m	6.43 m	7.18 m
Width:	2.5 m	2.5 m	2.5 m
Height:	2.67 m	2.67 m	2.74 m
Ground clearance:	n/avail	n/avail	465 mm
Track:	2 m	2 m	2.05 m
Wheelbase:	3.7 m	3.7 m	2.9 m + 1.4 m
Max speed:	87.9 km/h	87.9 km/h	80 km/h
Range:	n/avail	n/avail	800 km
Fording:	n/avail	n/avail	1.4 m
Engine model:	D-614.33	D-614.33	RÁBA-MAN
Engine type:	D-614.33 6-cylinder water-cooled 4-stroke diesel developing 145 hp (108 kW) at 2,300 rpm (D-562 and D-564); RABA-MAN 2156 HM6-01 6-cylinder water-cooled 4-stroke diesel developing 200 hp (149 kW) at 2,200 rpm (D-566)		
Gearbox:	n/avail	n/avail	manual, 6 forward and 1 reverse gears
Transfer box:	n/app	n/avail	2-speed
Tyres:	16.5 × 19.5	16.5 × 19.5	14.00 × 20
Turning circle:	n/avail	n/avail	19 m
Electrical system:	24 V	24 V	24 V
Batteries:	n/avail	n/avail	2 × 120 Ah
Generator:	n/avail	n/avail	750 W

Status
The D-566 and numerous other Cseple models were supplied to the Hungarian Army. A replacement programme is underway.

Contractor
Csepel Automotive Works

India

Ashok Leyland (4 × 4) Topchi Field Artillery Tractor (FAT)

Development
Ashok Leyland, India's second largest producer of commercial vehicles, can trace its origins back to 1948 when, as Ashok Motors, the company began assembly of Austin cars in Madras; Chennai since 1996.

The company commenced assembly of Leyland trucks in 1950, and in 1954 Leyland Motors took a stake in the company and the name Ashok Leyland was adopted. Production was centred around assorted Leyland models, many of which were obsolete in the UK. The company was the first to introduce articulated vehicles, double decker buses and multi-axle vehicles into India. In 1987 the Hinduja Group gained a controlling interest in Ashok Leyland and its associate companies when it acquired the UK-based Land Rover Leyland International Holdings (LRLIH) Ltd, jointly with IVECO. IVECO, through its share in LRLIH, had an indirect 15 per cent share of Ashok Leyland. Since July 2006 the Hinduja Group has been the 100 per cent holder of LRLIH.

In September 2006 Ashok Leyland announced it had signed a framework agreement to acquire the Truck Business Unit of Avia a.s. in Prague. Avia manufactures the D Line trucks in the 6,000 to 9,000 kg GVW range and has marketing footprints in Europe. The acquisition covers the facility at the heart of the Czech capital, with an annual production capacity of 20,000 vehicles, which is supported by a state-of-the-art cataphoretic paint shop and R&D facilities. The newly acquired company has been named Avia Ashok Leyland Motors s.r.o.

Prototype example of the Ashok Leyland Topchi (4 × 4) Field Artillery Tractor, 261 examples of which were ordered by the Indian Army in 2005 (Ashok Leyland)   1156004

In 2007, the company announced a joint venture with Nissan (Renault Nissan Group).

Ashok Leyland has an annual production capacity of 105,000 vehicles and 87,000 diesel engines. Turnover was USD1.4 billion in 2008-2009, sales including 54,431 medium and heavy vehicles.

Ashok Leyland supplied the Indian Army with 1,000 General Service (GS) role Leyland Hippos in the 1970s but the company's first tactical military vehicle to be adopted by the Indian Army was the 5,000 kg payload Stallion 4 × 4. Since 1994 around 58,000 Stallions have been delivered to the Indian Army, all but 350 of these being the current Stallion Mk III. Deliveries continue at around 3,000-5,000 vehicles per year. Ashok Leyland has a Transfer of Technology agreement with the Ordnance Factory Board of the Ministry of Defence for assembling Stallion vehicles at the Vehicle Factory Jabalpur (VFJ).

Ashok Leyland originally developed the Topchi (4 × 4) Field Artillery Tractor (FAT) in the late 1980s to meet an Indian Army requirement. The vehicle was approved by the Indian Army, however the first order, for 261 vehicles, was not placed by the Indian Army until 2005; deliveries ran 2005-2006.

As part of a USD139 million order from Honduras announced in January 2009, Ashok Leyland supplied a quantity of Topchi (4 × 4) to the Honduras Armed Forces (HAF).

Ashok Leyland commenced an active export campaign for its military products during 2004. In addition to the Topchi FAT, the company also offers the in-production Stallion, the commercially-based Comet (4 × 4) which has been delivered to Sri Lanka, the Stallion (6 × 6) (previously referred to as the High Mobility Vehicle (HMV)), and a larger (6 × 6) FAT and variants. Full details of these vehicles can be found elsewhere in this section.

According to Ashok Leyland, the African, Asian, Latin American and some Middle Eastern countries are seen as target markets for the company's current product range. In addition to Honduras, small numbers of Ashok Leyland military trucks have been sold to Ecuador, Iraq (via the US Army) and Thailand.

Description
The Ashok Leyland Topchi (4 × 4) FAT is entirely conventional in design and is based on a 228 × 76 × 6.3 mm C-section chassis with bolted in cross members and recovery and/or towing points fitted front and rear. A chassis-mounted hydraulic self-recovery winch rated at 5,000 kg single line pull is fitted. The purpose-designed all-steel tiltable cab is based on Ashok Leyland's C45 Front End Structure cab and features a two-part flat glass windscreen, a roof hatch, and may be fitted with air-conditioning if required. Seating for two including the driver is provided. The gun crew of six occupy a dedicated section of the rear cargo body. Communication between the driver and crew cabins is possible. A 100-litre capacity potable water tank is carried. The cargo body is fitted with steel drop sides and a single-piece drop tailgate and measures 4.19 × 2.5 m (L × W). The entire rear body is covered by a tarpaulin. Payload is 3,000 kg.

In service the Topchi FAT is used with the Indian Army's 105 mm light gun of which around 500 are currently thought to be operational.

The base chassis of the FAT is designed to be capable of accepting a wide variety of other light-duty (3,000 kg class) body types. Motive power is provided by an uprated version of the Ashok Leyland L62N Mk II diesel engine which develops 157 hp at 2,400 rpm and 587 N.m torque at 1,350 rpm. This is coupled to a six-speed ZF gearbox licence-produced by Ashok Leyland and a two-speed transfer box with selectable front axle drive. The front steer-drive axle is sprung by the combination of progressive semi-elliptic leaf springs and telescopic shock-absorbers. Steering is hydraulically power-assisted. The rear drive axle is fitted with a driver controlled differential lock and is sprung by progressive semi-elliptic leaf springs and telescopic shock-absorbers. The FAT was developed to meet or exceed the operating requirements of the Indian Army and is capable of operation at altitudes of up to 15,000 ft and at temperatures ranging from –30°C to +55°C.

Specifications
Cab seating: 1 + 1
Configuration: 4 × 4 (selectable)
Weight:
(laden) 10,140 kg
(unladen) 7,140 kg
(payload) 3,000 kg
(front axle load) 4,550 kg
(rear axle load) 5,590 kg
(towed load off-road) 5,000 kg
(GCW) 15,140 kg
Length: 6.362 m
Width: 2.5 m
Height: (cab) 2.95 m
Ground clearance: 305 mm
Track:
(front) 2.03 m
(rear) 2.06 m
Wheelbase: 3.607 m
Angle of approach/departure: 35°/35°
Max speed: 85 km/h
Max range: 1,375 km
Fuel capacity: 250 litres
Max gradient: 66%
Side slope: 78%
Fording: 760 mm
Engine: Ashok Leyland AL 402 6-cylinder in-line water-cooled direct injection 4-stroke diesel developing 157 hp (115 kW) at 2,400 rpm and 587 N.m torque at 1,350 rpm
Gearbox: licence-produced ZF 6S 36 with 6 forward and 1 reverse gears
Transfer box: Ashok Leyland 2-speed, selectable four-wheel drive
Clutch: single dry plate, Ø353 mm
Steering: power assisted
Turning radius: 7.75 m
Suspension: parabolic leaf springs and telescopic shock-absorbers, front; inverted semi-elliptic leaf springs and telescopic shock-absorbers, rear
Tyres: 12.00 × 20-18 PR
Brakes: dual-circuit, air, drums all-round
Electrical system: 24 V
Batteries: 2 × 12 V, 110 Ah
Alternator: 24 V, 45 A

Status
Production as required. In service with Honduras and the Indian Army (261 delivered 2005-2006).

Contractor
Ashok Leyland

Ashok Leyland (6 × 6) Field Artillery Tractor (FAT)

Development
Ashok Leyland, India's second largest producer of commercial vehicles, can trace its origins back to 1948 when, as Ashok Motors, the company began assembly of Austin cars in Madras; Chennai since 1996.

The company commenced assembly of Leyland trucks in 1950, and in 1954 Leyland Motors took a stake in the company and the name Ashok Leyland was adopted. Production was centred around assorted Leyland models, many of which were obsolete in the UK. Ashok Leyland introduced articulated vehicles, double-decker buses and multi-axle vehicles into India. In 1987 the Hinduja Group gained a controlling interest in Ashok Leyland and its associate companies when it acquired the UK-based Land Rover Leyland International Holdings (LRLIH) Ltd, jointly with IVECO. IVECO, through its share in LRLIH, had an indirect 15 per cent share of Ashok Leyland. Since July 2006, the Hinduja Group has been the 100 per cent holder of LRLIH.

The original Field Artillery Tractor (FAT) prototype (Ashok Leyland) 1156093

In September 2006 Ashok Leyland announced it had signed a framework agreement to acquire the Truck Business Unit of Avia a.s. in Prague. Avia manufactures the D Line trucks in the 6,000 to 9,000 kg GVW range and has marketing footprints in Europe. The acquisition covers the facility at the heart of the Czech capital, with an annual production capacity of 20,000 vehicles, which is supported by a state-of-the-art cataphoretic paint shop and R&D facilities. The newly acquired company has been named Avia Ashok Leyland Motors s.r.o.

In 2007, the company announced a joint venture with Nissan (Renault Nissan Group).

Ashok Leyland has an annual production capacity of 105,000 vehicles and 87,000 diesel engines. Turnover was USD1.4 billion in 2008-2009, sales including 54,431 medium and heavy vehicles.

Ashok Leyland supplied the Indian Army with 1,000 General Service (GS) role Leyland Hippos in the 1970s but the company's first tactical military vehicle to be adopted by the Indian Army was the 5,000 kg payload Stallion (4 × 4). Since 1994 around 58,000 Stallions have been delivered to the Indian Army, all but 350 of these being the current Stallion Mk III. Deliveries continue at around 3,000-5,000 vehicles per year. Ashok Leyland has a Transfer of Technology agreement with the Ordnance Factory Board of the Ministry of Defence for assembling Stallion vehicles at the Vehicle Factory Jabalpur (VFJ).

Ashok Leyland originally developed the Field Artillery Tractor (FAT) in the late 1990s to meet a then current Indian Army requirement. The original vehicle was evaluated (with Volvo, BEML and possibly other types) by the Indian Army, but with a move towards heavier guns the General Staff Qualitative Requirements (GSQR) has changed and a Request for Proposal (RfP) to meet this revised requirement (now known as Common Gun Tower (CGT)) is currently anticipated. The revised requirement is expected to be for about 4,000 vehicles to tow a selection of new and upgraded 155 mm artillery pieces. Development of the current Ashok Leyland FAT began during 2005. Other bidders for the ongoing FAT requirement could include BEML (TATRA design), MAN (Force Motors), Tata and Volvo. BEML is the current supplier of heavy tactical vehicles, including artillery tractors, to the Indian Army.

Since its introduction, the Ashok Leyland FAT has been further developed into a High Mobility Vehicle (HMV) with an 8,000/10,000 kg (on-/off-road) payload, and a MultiBarrel Rocket Launcher (MBRL) platform. The Indian Army is understood to have a requirement for an initial 100 chassis of the MBRL type on which it will mount Russian BM-21 GRAD type Multiple Rocket Launchers (MRLs). Compared to the current FAT, these latest variants feature revised wheelbases (4.3 m MBRL/4.66 m HMV), have role-adjusted laden/unladen weights and feature different gearbox options, the MBRL including an Allison 3200SP fully automatic transmission as standard.

Ashok Leyland commenced an active export campaign for its military products during 2004. In addition to the FAT (and later variants), the company also offers the in-production Stallion, the commercially-based Comet (4 × 4) which has been supplied to Sri-Lanka, the Topchi 3,000 kg (4 × 4) FAT which has been supplied to the Indian Army, and the (6 × 6) Stallion (initially referred to as the High Mobility Vehicle (HMV)). Full details of these vehicles can be found elsewhere in this section.

According to Ashok Leyland, the African, Asian, Latin American and some Middle Eastern countries are seen as target markets for the company's current product range. Small numbers of Ashok Leyland military trucks have been sold to Ecuador, Honduras, Iraq (via the US Army) and Thailand.

Description

The Ashok Leyland FAT is entirely conventional in design and is based on a 306 × 85 × 8 mm C-section chassis with bolted in cross members and recovery and/or towing points fitted front and rear. A chassis-mounted hydraulic winch rated at 16,000 kg single line pull and which may be used for self-recovery purposes if required, is optional. The purpose-designed all-steel tiltable cab features a two-part flat glass windscreen, a roof hatch, and may be fitted with air-conditioning if required. The gun crew occupy a separate chassis-mounted enclosed cabin. Communication between the driver and crew cabins is possible. A 150-litre capacity potable water tank is standard equipment.

The cargo section of the body is fitted with steel drop sides and a single-piece drop tailgate and measures 4 × 2.5 m × 800 mm (L × W × H). A 2.7 t/m capacity hydraulic crane mounted between the crew cabin and rear body for ammunition handling is optional.

The base chassis of the FAT is designed to be capable of accepting a wide variety of other heavy-duty body types.

Motive power is provided by an Ashok Leyland N Series diesel engine developing 360 hp and 1,400 N.m torque. An eight-speed ZF manual gearbox is coupled to a single-speed transfer box. The front hub-reduction steer-drive Axle Tech axle is permanently engaged and is sprung by the combination of parabolic leaf springs and telescopic shock-absorbers. Steering is hydraulically power-assisted. The rear drive tandem bogie is sprung by inverted semi-elliptic leaf springs. The Axle Tech hub-reduction axles are fitted with driver-controlled inter- and cross-axle differential locks. A Central Tyre Inflation (CTI) system is optional.

The FAT was developed to meet or exceed the operating requirements of the Indian Army and is capable of operation at altitudes of up to 15,000 ft and at temperatures ranging from –30°C to +55°C.

Motive power for the previous prototype was provided by a Caterpillar C-12 diesel engine developing 430 hp and 2,101 N.m torque, this coupled

Prototype of the Ashok Leyland Field Artillery Tractor (FAT) as displayed at DefExpo 2006 (Shaun C Connors) 1156172

to a seven-speed Allison automatic gearbox and ZF Steyr single-speed transfer box. The original prototype featured slightly different bodywork and was powered by a 345 hp IVECO engine coupled to an eight-speed manual gearbox with torque converter.

Specifications

Cab seating: 1 + 1
Configuration: 6 × 6
Weight:
  (laden) 21,402 kg
  (unladen) 13,752 kg
  (payload) 10,000 kg
  (front axle load, laden) 6,335 kg
  (rear axle load, laden) 15,067 kg
Length: 8.435 m
Width: 2.5 m
Height: (cab/crew cab) 3/3.1 m
Ground clearance: 400 mm
Track:
  (front) 2.054 m
  (rear) 2.02 m
Wheelbase: 4.66 m
Angle of approach/departure: 35°/35°
Max speed: (tyre restricted) 86.5 km/h
Max range: (highway, solo) 1,000 km
Fuel capacity: 500 litres
Max gradient:
  (solo) 60%
  (with gun) 44%
Side slope: 60%
Fording: 800 mm
Engine: Ashok Leyland N Series EURO 3 emissions compliant diesel developing 360 hp (265 kW) at 2,200 rpm and 1,400 N.m torque at 1,300 rpm
Gearbox: ZF 8S 151 manual with 7 forward and 1 reverse gears
Transfer box: single-speed
Clutch: 430 mm dia
Steering: power assisted
Turning radius: 11.5 m
Suspension: parabolic leaf springs and telescopic shock-absorbers, front; inverted semi-elliptic leaf springs, rear
Tyres: 16.00R 20 (14.00R 20, optional)
Brakes: dual-circuit, air, drums all-round
Electrical system: 24 V
Batteries: 2 × 12 V, 150 Ah
Alternator: 100 A

Status

Prototype. An earlier prototype has been evaluated by the Indian Army.

Contractor

Ashok Leyland

Ashok Leyland Azad Super 2,500 kg (4 × 4) light truck

Development

Ashok Leyland, India's second largest producer of commercial vehicles, can trace its origins back to 1948 when, as Ashok Motors, the company began assembly of Austin cars in Madras; Chennai since 1996.

The company commenced assembly of Leyland trucks in 1950, and in 1954 Leyland Motors took a stake in the company and the name Ashok Leyland was adopted. Production was centred around assorted Leyland

Prototype of the Ashok Leyland Azad Super 2,500 kg (4 × 4) light truck
(Ashok Leyland)   1156005

models, many of which were obsolete in the UK. The company was the first to introduce articulated vehicles, double decker buses and multi-axle vehicles into India. In 1987 the Hinduja Group gained a controlling interest in Ashok Leyland and its associate companies when it acquired the UK-based Land Rover Leyland International Holdings (LRLIH) Ltd, jointly with IVECO. IVECO, through its share in LRLIH, had an indirect 15 per cent share of Ashok Leyland. Since July 2006, the Hinduja Group has been the 100 per cent holder of LRLIH.

In September 2006 Ashok Leyland announced it had signed a framework agreement to acquire the Truck Business Unit of Avia a.s. in Prague. Avia manufactures the D Line trucks in the 6,000 to 9,000 kg GVW range and has marketing footprints in Europe. The acquisition covers the facility at the heart of the Czech capital, with an annual production capacity of 20,000 vehicles, which is supported by a state-of-the-art cataphoretic paint shop and R&D facilities. The newly acquired company has been named Avia Ashok Leyland Motors s.r.o.

In 2007, the company announced a joint venture with Nissan (Renault Nissan Group).

Ashok Leyland has an annual production capacity of 105,000 vehicles and 87,000 diesel engines. Turnover was USD1.4 billion in 2008-2009, sales including 54,431 medium and heavy vehicles.

Ashok Leyland supplied the Indian Army with 1,000 General Service (GS) role Leyland Hippos in the 1970s but the company's first tactical military vehicle to be adopted by the Indian Army was the 5,000 kg payload Stallion 4 × 4. Since 1994 around 58,000 Stallions have been delivered to the Indian Army, all but 350 of these being the current Stallion Mk III. Deliveries continue at around 3,000-5,000 vehicles per year. Ashok Leyland has a Transfer of Technology agreement with the Ordnance Factory Board of the Ministry of Defence for assembling Stallion vehicles at the Vehicle Factory Jabalpur (VFJ).

The Ashok Leyland Azad Super was developed by the company in the early 1990s to meet the Indian Army's requirement for a new General Service (GS) role light truck with a 2,500 kg payload. Following trials the Azad Super was approved for Indian Army use, however on pricing the order was given to Tata Motors for the LPTA 713 TC. The Tata LPTA 713 TC is assembled CKD at the Vehicle Factory Jalbapur (VFJ) and since 1999 at least 23,000 examples have been produced for the Indian Army; production continues. Full details of the Tata LPTA 713 TC can be found elsewhere in this section. Also competing for the 2,500 kg GS requirement was a Swaraj Mazda design, some hundreds of which have been supplied to non-field force Indian Army units.

Ashok Leyland commenced an active export campaign for its military products during 2004. In addition to the in-production Stallion, the commercially-based Comet 4 × 4 which was supplied to Sri Lanka and the Topchi 3,000 kg (4 × 4) Field Artillery Truck (FAT) which is in service with the Indian Army, the company has also introduced a heavier (6 × 6) FAT (and later variants) and the Stallion (6 × 6). Details of these vehicles can be found elsewhere in this section. A current generation Azad Super is currently under development.

According to Ashok Leyland, the African, Asian, Latin American and some Middle Eastern countries are seen as target markets for the company's current product range. Small numbers of Ashok Leyland military trucks have been sold to Ecuador, Honduras, Iraq (via the US Army) and Thailand.

Description
The Ashok Leyland Azad Super is entirely conventional in design and is based on a 185 × 65 × 6 mm C-section chassis with bolted in cross members and recovery and/or towing points fitted front and rear. The two-person all-steel tiltable cab is similar to that of the Stallion and is an enlarged version of the old IVECO Ford Cargo cab, this still being fitted to a number of Ashok Leyland's commercial designs.

The standard troop carrying/cargo-type platform body is fitted with steel drop sides, a single-piece drop tailgate, and a removable tarpaulin and

bows. The body measures 3.45 × 2.205 m (L × W). Wooden/steel bench seats may be provided for troop transport. The base chassis is designed to be capable of accepting a wide variety of light-duty body types.

Motive power is provided by an Ashok Leyland W06E naturally aspirated water-cooled diesel engine developing 122 hp at 2,400 rpm and 375 N.m torque at 1,600 rpm. A six-speed synchromesh ZF manual gearbox licence-produced by Ashok Leyland is coupled to an Ashok Leyland two-speed transfer box. The front steer-drive axle is disengageable for on-road driving and is sprung by the combination of semi-elliptic leaf springs and telescopic shock-absorbers. Steering is hydraulically power assisted. The rear drive axle is sprung by the combination of semi-elliptic leaf springs and telescopic shock-absorbers. The Azad Super was developed to meet or exceed the operating requirements of the Indian Army and is capable of operation at altitudes of up to 15,000 ft and at temperatures ranging from –30°C to +55°C.

Specifications
Cab seating: 1 + 1
Configuration 4 × 4
Weight:
  (laden) 7,990 kg
  (unladen) 5,490 kg
  (payload) 2,500 kg
  (front axle load) 3,285 kg
  (rear axle load) 4,705 kg
Length: 6.05 m
Width: 2.5 m
Height: 2.97 m
Ground clearance: 375 mm
Track:
  (front) 1.855 m
  (rear) 1.855 m
Wheelbase: 3.4 m
Angle of approach/departure: 45°/45°
Max speed: 85 km/h
Max range: 675 km
Fuel capacity: 150 litres
Max gradient: 67%
Side slope: 56%
Fording: 760 mm
Engine: Ashok Leyland (Hino derived) W06D 6.65-litre 6-cylinder in-line naturally aspirated water-cooled 4-stroke diesel developing 122 hp (90 kW) at 2,400 rpm and 375 N.m torque at 1,600 rpm
Gearbox: licence-produced ZF 6S-36 with 6 forward and 1 reverse gears
Transfer box: Ashok Leyland 2-speed, disengageable front axle drive
Clutch: single dry plate, Ø353 mm
Steering: power assisted
Turning radius: 8 m
Suspension: semi-elliptic leaf springs and telescopic shock-absorbers, front and rear
Tyres: 12.00 × 20-18 PR
Brakes: dual circuit, air, drums all-round
Electrical system: 24 V
Batteries: 2 × 12 V, 110 Ah
Alternator: 55 A, 24 V

Status
Prototype produced. Has been evaluated and approved by the Indian Army. New-generation design currently being developed.

Contractor
Ashok Leyland

Ashok Leyland Comet (4 × 4) 10,000 kg truck

Development
Ashok Leyland, India's second largest producer of commercial vehicles, can trace its origins back to 1948 when, as Ashok Motors, the company began assembly of Austin cars in Madras; Chennai since 1996.

The company commenced assembly of Leyland trucks in 1950, and in 1954 Leyland Motors took a stake in the company and the name Ashok Leyland was adopted. Production was centred around assorted Leyland models, many of which were obsolete in the UK. The company was the first to introduce articulated vehicles, double decker buses and multi-axle vehicles into India. In 1987 the Hinduja Group gained a controlling interest in Ashok Leyland and its associate companies when it acquired the UK-based Land Rover Leyland International Holdings (LRLIH) Ltd, jointly with IVECO. IVECO, through its share in LRLIH, had an indirect 15 per cent share of Ashok Leyland. Since July 2006, the Hinduja Group has been the 100 per cent holder of LRLIH.

In September 2006 Ashok Leyland announced it had signed a framework agreement to acquire the Truck Business Unit of Avia a.s. in Prague. Avia manufactures the D Line trucks in the 6,000 to 9,000 kg GVW range and has marketing footprints in Europe. The acquisition covers the facility at the heart of the Czech capital, with an annual production capacity of 20,000 vehicles, which is supported by a state-of-the-art cataphoretic paint shop and R&D facilities. The newly acquired company has been named Avia Ashok Leyland Motors s.r.o.

In 2007, the company announced a joint venture with Nissan (Renault Nissan Group).

Ashok Leyland has an annual production capacity of 105,000 vehicles and 87,000 diesel engines. Turnover was USD1.4 billion in 2008-2009, sales including 54,431 medium and heavy vehicles.

Ashok Leyland supplied the Indian Army with 1,000 General Service (GS) role Leyland Hippos in the 1970s but the company's first tactical military vehicle to be adopted by the Indian Army was the 5,000 kg payload Stallion (4 × 4). Since 1994 around 58,000 Stallions have been delivered to the Indian Army, all but 350 of these being the current Stallion Mk III. Deliveries continue at around 3,000-5,000 vehicles per year. Ashok Leyland has a Transfer of Technology agreement with the Ordnance Factory Board of the Ministry of Defence for assembling Stallion vehicles at the Vehicle Factory Jabalpur (VFJ).

The Ashok Leyland Comet (4 × 4) is a militarised development of the commercial Ashok Leyland Comet (4 × 2) which has been in production in various guises for a number of years. The militarised (4 × 4) version was developed to meet the General Service (GS) role needs of the Sri Lankan Army and during 2004 around 200 vehicles were ordered and delivered.

Ashok Leyland commenced an active export campaign for its military products during 2004 and in addition to the Comet (4 × 4), the Stallion (4 × 4) and Topchi 3,000 kg (4 × 4) Field Artillery Tractor (FAT) which are in service with the Indian Army, the company has also introduced a heavier (6 × 6) FAT (and later variants) and the Stallion (6 × 6). Details of these vehicles can be found elsewhere in this section. According to Ashok Leyland, the African, Asian, Latin American and some Middle Eastern countries are seen as target markets for the company's current product range. Small numbers of Ashok Leyland military trucks have been sold to Ecuador, Honduras, Iraq (via the US Army) and Thailand.

Description

The Ashok Leyland Comet (4 × 4) 10,000 kg truck is based on the commercial Comet model with some limited militarisation (including blackout lights) to suit the requirements of the Sri Lankan Army.

The Ashok Leyland Comet is entirely conventional in design and is based on a 228.6 × 76.2 × 6.3 mm C-section chassis with bolted in cross members. Basic recovery points are fitted to the all-steel bumper at the front of the vehicle, a towing point is fitted at the rear. The two-person all-steel tiltable cab is essentially the Comet commercial cab.

The standard troop carrying/cargo-type platform body is fitted with steel drop sides, a single-piece drop tailgate, and a removable tarpaulin and bows. The body measures 5.2 × 2.5 m (L × W). Wooden/steel bench seats may be provided for troop transport. The base chassis is designed to be capable of accepting a wide variety of medium-duty body types.

Motive power is provided by an Ashok Leyland diesel engine developing 113 hp and coupled to a five-speed constant mesh gearbox. The front steer-drive axle is disengageable for on-road driving and is sprung by the combination of semi-elliptic leaf springs and telescopic shock-absorbers. Steering is hydraulically power assisted. The rear drive axle is sprung by the combination of semi-elliptic leaf springs and telescopic shock-absorbers.

Specifications

Cab seating: 1 + 1
Configuration 4 × 4
Weight:
(laden) 15,660 kg
(unladen) 5,335 kg
(payload) 10,000 kg
(front axle load) 5,460 kg
(rear axle load) 10,200 kg
Length: 7.315 m
Width: 2.5 m
Height: 2.860 m
Ground clearance: 238 mm

Ashok Leyland Comet (4 × 4) of the Sri Lankan Army (Ashok Leyland)
1156092

Track:
(front) 1.979 m
(rear) 1.816 m
Wheelbase: 4.2 m
Angle of approach/departure: 30°/25°
Max speed: 75 km/h
Max range: 680 km
Fuel capacity: 160 litres
Max gradient: 66%
Fording: 640 mm
Engine: Ashok Leyland 6-cylinder in-line water-cooled 4-stroke diesel developing 113 hp (83 kW) at 2,400 rpm
Gearbox: constant mesh with 5 forward and 1 reverse gears
Transfer box: Ashok Leyland 2-speed, selectable 4 × 4 drive
Clutch: single dry plate, Ø353 mm
Steering: power assisted
Turning radius: 8.525 m
Suspension: semi-elliptic leaf springs with helper springs (rear axle only) and telescopic shock-absorbers, front and rear
Tyres: 9.00 × 20-14 PR, twin at rear
Brakes: dual-circuit, air, drums all-round
Electrical system: 24 V
Batteries: 2 × 12 V, 110 Ah
Alternator: 55 A, 24 V

Status

Production as required. Supplied to Sri Lanka (200 in 2004).

Contractor

Ashok Leyland

Ashok Leyland Stallion (6 × 6)

Development

Ashok Leyland, India's second largest producer of commercial vehicles, can trace its origins back to 1948 when, as Ashok Motors, the company began assembly of Austin cars in Madras; Chennai since 1996.

The company commenced assembly of Leyland trucks in 1950, and in 1954 Leyland Motors took a stake in the company and the name Ashok Leyland was adopted. Production was centred around assorted Leyland models, many of which were obsolete in the UK. The company was the first to introduce articulated vehicles, doubledecker buses and multi-axle vehicles into India. In 1987 the Hinduja Group gained a controlling interest in Ashok Leyland and its associate companies when it acquired the UK-based Land Rover Leyland International Holdings (LRLIH) Ltd, jointly with IVECO. IVECO, through its share in LRLIH, had an indirect 15 per cent share of Ashok Leyland. Since July 2006, the Hinduja Group has been the 100 per cent holder of LRLIH.

In September 2006 Ashok Leyland announced it had signed a framework agreement to acquire the Truck Business Unit of Avia a.s. in Prague. Avia manufactures the D Line trucks in the 6,000 to 9,000 kg GVW range and has marketing footprints in Europe. The acquisition covers the facility at the heart of the Czech capital, with an annual production capacity of 20,000 vehicles, which is supported by a state-of-the-art cataphoretic paint shop and R&D facilities. The newly acquired company has been named Avia Ashok Leyland Motors s.r.o.

In 2007, the company announced a joint venture with Nissan (Renault Nissan Group).

Ashok Leyland supplied the Indian Army with 1,000 General Service (GS) role Leyland Hippos in the 1970s but the company's first tactical military vehicle to be adopted by the Indian Army was the 5,000 kg payload Stallion (4 × 4). The Stallion (6 × 6) was introduced in 2004, shown publicly for the first time at IDEX 2005, and was originally known as the High Mobility Vehicle (HMV).

The Mk I Stallion (4 × 4) produced in 1989/90 was a prototype, the first production model being the Stallion Mk II. Between 1994-1996 some 330 Mk II Stallions were delivered to the Indian Army. These were manufactured at Ashok Leyland's Hosur facility.

The Mk III Stallion was introduced in 1996. The first 3,200 Stallion Mk IIIs were produced at Ashok Leyland's Chennai facility and during the first two years of production. In 1998, Stallion production shifted to the state-owned Vehicle Factory Jalbapur (VFJ). Some specialist military variants, commercial and all export Stallion vehicles are still manufactured by Ashok Leyland at Hosur.

VFJ was established in 1969/70 for the production of three non-fighting vehicles for the Indian military; the three-tonne Shaktiman truck, the one-tonne Carrier and 0.25-tonne Jonga light vehicles. It was confirmed in 2003 that production of the Shaktiman had ceased, the last known order being for 3,000 trucks delivered between 1993-1996. As of 2009 it was believed that around 7,000 Shaktiman trucks remained in service with the Indian Army.

The one-tonne Carrier and 0.25-tonne Jonga are both based on Nissan designs, the Carrier on the Nissan D4W73 and the Jonga on the Nissan Patrol. Production of these models was completed around 1987 (Jonga) and 1990 (Carrier).

Ashok Leyland Stallion (6 × 6), as the High Mobility Vehicle (HMV), was displayed publicly for the first time at IDEX 2005 (Shaun C Connors)

1156003

Full details of the Shaktiman and Carrier can be found elsewhere in this section. With production of these older designs complete, the political decision was taken to move production of the Stallion to VFJ, Ashok Leyland supplying a combination of SKD/CKD kits to the factory. VFJ also currently CKD-produces the Tata LPTA 713 TC (4 × 4) 2,500 kg light truck, essentially the replacement for the Carrier. Full details of the Tata LPTA 713 TC can be found elsewhere in this section.

Since production of the Mk III Stallion commenced in 1996 the Indian Army has received around 58,000 vehicles, at least 55,000 of these being the standard troop carrying/cargo variant, although the Indian Army converts some to other roles post delivery. Production of the Stallion continues at around 3,000-5,000 units per year and it is envisaged the type will eventually replace the bulk of the remaining Shaktiman trucks in Indian Army service.

Ashok Leyland announced in February 2006 that it had been awarded a contract to supply the Indian Army with 872 Potable Water Bowsers on the Stallion Mk III chassis. The contract, which includes spares, is valued at INR2.3 billion. These vehicles were manufactured by Ashok Leyland with production scheduled for completion by January 2007. Ashok Leyland also manufactured a Light Recovery Vehicle based on the Stallion Mk III chassis; around 1,500 have been delivered.

As previously mentioned, the Ashok Leyland Stallion (6 × 6) was originally known as the High Mobility Vehicle (HMV), the type being a 5,000 kg payload class vehicle that is designed for desert and difficult underfoot conditions, and for use where the performance of a Stallion-type (4 × 4) design is not adequate.

The Stallion (6 × 6) has completed formal trials for an Indian Army requirement for an undisclosed (but likely to be around 5,000) quantity of vehicles. Competitors for this requirement, for which a procurement decision was anticipated during 2006 but has yet to materialise, are Tata and Bharat Earth Movers Limited (BEML).

An initial 10 Stallion (6 × 6) trucks were delivered to the Royal Thai Navy during 2008 for use in a gun tractor role, and during 2009 a further 63 vehicles were ordered, these split 48 rated at 2,500 kg payload and 15 rated at 5,000 kg payload.

Ashok Leyland commenced an active export campaign for its military products during 2004. In addition to the Stallion (6 × 6), the Stallion (4 × 4), the commercially-based Comet (4 × 4) which has been supplied to Sri Lanka and the Topchi 3,000 kg (4 × 4) Field Artillery Tractor (FAT) which is in service with the Indian Army, the company has also recently introduced a heavier (6 × 6) FAT and variants. Details of these vehicles can be found elsewhere in this section.

According to Ashok Leyland, the African, Asian, Latin American and some Middle Eastern countries are seen as target markets for the company's current product range. In addition to Thailand, recent sales of small numbers of Ashok Leyland military trucks have been made to Ecuador, Honduras and Iraq (via the US Army).

Description

The Ashok Leyland Stallion (6 × 6) is entirely conventional in design and is based on a 228 × 76 × 6 mm C-section chassis with nine bolted in cross members and recovery and/or towing points fitted front and rear. A chassis-mounted hydraulic self-recovery winch is optional. The two-person all-steel tiltable cab is common to the Stallion and is an enlarged version of the old IVECO Ford Cargo cab, this still being fitted to a number of Ashok Leyland's commercial designs.

The standard troop-carrying/cargo-type platform body is fitted with steel drop sides, a single-piece drop tailgate, and a removable tarpaulin and bows. The body measures 5.2 m × 2.5 m × 550 mm (L × W × H). Wooden/steel bench seats may be provided for troop transport.

The base chassis is designed to be capable of accepting a wide variety of body types and a heavy recovery vehicle equipped with crane and winch has been prototyped.

Motive power is provided by either an Ashok Leyland H Series diesel engine developing 180 hp (132 kW) and 590 N.m torque for the 2,500 kg rated variant, or an Ashok Leyland J Series diesel engine developing 260 hp (191 kW) and 745 N.m torque for the 5,000 kg rated variant These meets EURO II emissions levels but are available to meet EURO III emissions levels if required. Other engine options, including Cummins, to suit individual market requirements are available. A six-speed ZF manual gearbox licence-produced by Ashok Leyland is coupled to a Steyr two-speed transfer box. The front steer-drive axle is disengageable for on-road driving and is sprung by the combination of semi-elliptic leaf springs and telescopic shock-absorbers. Steering is hydraulically power-assisted. The rear drive axles are sprung by leaf springs and are fitted with driver-controlled inter- and cross-axle differential locks.

Motive power for Royal Thai Navy vehicles is provided by an Ashok Leyland J08 CTI turbocharged and intercooled diesel engine developing 260 hp and 745 N.m torque.

The HMV was developed to meet or exceed the operating requirements of the Indian Army and is capable of operation at altitudes of up to 15,000 ft and at temperatures ranging from –30°C to +55°C.

The Stallion (6 × 6) is available with 2,500, 5,000 or 8,000 kg payload ratings.

Variants

HMV Heavy Recovery Vehicle (HRV)

The Heavy Recovery Vehicle (HRV) variant of the Stallion (6 × 6) has been produced in prototype form and was first displayed at India's DefExpo 2006. The hydraulic recovery equipment consists of a crane with a maximum lift capacity (with outriggers deployed) of 12,000 kg at 2.5 m radius (10,000 kg at 3 m radius). Maximum boom length is 7.5 m, maximum lift radius is 6 m. A recovery winch with a maximum single line pull of 16,000 kg is mounted on the rotating platform. A self-recovery winch is also fitted.

Specifications

Stallion (6 × 6)

	2,500 kg payload rating	5,000 kg payload rating
Cab seating:	1 + 1	1 + 1
Configuration:	6 × 6	6 × 6
Weight:		
(laden)	11,900 kg	14,515 kg
(unladen)	9,400 kg	9,515 kg
(payload)	2,500 kg	5,000 kg

Ashok Leyland Stallion (6 × 6) (Ashok Leyland)   1156094

Ashok Leyland Stallion (6 × 6) Heavy Recovery Vehicle (HRV) as displayed at DefExpo 2006 (Shaun C Connors)   1156001

	2,500 kg payload rating	**5,000 kg payload rating**
(front axle load, laden)	4,797 kg	4,685 kg
(rear axles load, laden)	7,103 kg	9,830 kg
(front axle load, unladen)	4,383 kg	4,275 kg
(rear axles load, unladen)	5,017 kg	5,240 kg
Length:	8.054 m	8.054 m
Width:	2.5 m	2.5 m
Height: (cab)	3 m	3 m
Ground clearance:	330 mm	330 mm
Track:		
(front)	2.03 m	2.03 m
(rear)	2.05 m	2.05 m
Wheelbase:	4.267 m	4.267 m
Angle of approach/departure:	30°/30°	30°/30°
Max speed:	93 km/h	93 km/h
Max range: (road)	1,000 km	1,000 km
Fuel capacity:	350 litres (2 × 175)	350 litres (2 × 175)
Max gradient:	47%	47%
Fording:	760 mm	760 mm
Engine:	Ashok Leyland H series water-cooled 4-stroke EURO II emissions compliant diesel developing 180 hp (132 kW) at 2,400 rpm and 590 N.m torque at 1,440 rpm; EURO III option available	Ashok Leyland J series water-cooled 4-stroke EURO II emissions compliant diesel developing 260 hp (191 kW) at 2,500 rpm and 745 N.m torque at 1,500 rpm; EURO III option available
Gearbox:	licence-produced ZF S6 36 with 6 forward and 1 reverse gears	licence-produced ZF S6850 with 6 forward and 1 reverse gears
Transfer box:	2-speed, disengageable front axle drive	2-speed, disengageable front axle drive
Clutch:	single dry plate, Ø380 mm	single dry plate, Ø380 mm
Steering:	power assisted	power assisted
Turning radius:	10.5 m	10.5 m
Suspension:	semi-elliptic leaf springs and, on front axle only, telescopic shock-absorbers	semi-elliptic leaf springs and, on front axle only, telescopic shock-absorbers
Tyres:	1,400 × 20 18PR	1,400 × 20 18PR
Brakes:	dual-circuit, air, drums all-round	dual-circuit, air, drums all-round
Electrical system:	24 V	24 V
Batteries:	2 × 12 V, 130 Ah	2 × 12 V, 130 Ah
Alternator:	55 A	100 A

Status
Production as required. Has been evaluated by the Indian Army (procurement decision pending, see text). In service with Thailand (73).

Contractor
Ashok Leyland

Ashok Leyland Stallion Mk III 7,500/5,000 kg (4 × 4) truck

Development
Ashok Leyland, India's second largest producer of commercial vehicles, can trace its origins back to 1948 when, as Ashok Motors, the company began assembly of Austin cars in Madras; Chennai since 1996.

The company commenced assembly of Leyland trucks in 1950, and in 1954, Leyland Motors took a stake in the company and the name Ashok Leyland was adopted. Production was centred around assorted Leyland models, many of which were obsolete in the UK. The company was the first to introduce articulated vehicles, doubledecker buses and multi-axle vehicles into India. In 1987 the Hinduja Group gained a controlling interest in Ashok Leyland and its associate companies when it acquired the UK-

Ashok Leyland Stallion Mk III (4 × 4) 5,000 kg truck (Ashok Leyland) 1156002

based Land Rover Leyland International Holdings (LRLIH) Ltd, jointly with IVECO. IVECO, through its share in LRLIH, had an indirect 15 per cent share of Ashok Leyland. Since July 2006, the Hinduja Group has been the 100 per cent holder of LRLIH.

In September 2006 Ashok Leyland announced it had signed a framework agreement to acquire the Truck Business Unit of Avia a.s. in Prague. Avia manufactures the D Line trucks in the 6,000 to 9,000 kg GVW range and has marketing footprints in Europe. The acquisition covers the facility at the heart of the Czech capital, with an annual production capacity of 20,000 vehicles, which is supported by a state-of-the-art cataphoretic paint shop and R&D facilities. The newly acquired company has been named Avia Ashok Leyland Motors s.r.o.

In 2007, the company announced a joint venture with Nissan (Renault Nissan Group).

Ashok Leyland has an annual production capacity of 105,000 vehicles and 87,000 diesel engines. Turnover was USD1.4 billion in 2008-2009, sales including 54,431 medium and heavy vehicles.

Ashok Leyland supplied the Indian Army with 1,000 General Service (GS) role Leyland Hippos in the 1970s but the company's first tactical military vehicle to be adopted by the Indian Army was the Stallion.

The Mk I Stallion produced in 1989/90 was a prototype, the first production model being the Stallion Mk II. Between 1994-1996 some 330 Mk II Stallions were delivered to the Indian Army. These were manufactured at Ashok Leyland's Hosur facility.

The Mk III Stallion was introduced in 1996. The first 3,200 Stallion Mk IIIs were produced at Ashok Leyland's Chennai facility and during the first two years of production. In 1998, Stallion production shifted to the state-owned Vehicle Factory Jalbapur (VFJ). Some specialist military variants, commercial and all export Stallion vehicles are still manufactured by Ashok Leyland at Hosur.

VFJ was established in 1969/70 for the production of three non-fighting vehicles for the Indian military; the three-tonne Shaktiman truck, the one-tonne Carrier and 0.25-tonne Jonga light vehicles. It was confirmed in 2003 that production of the Shaktiman had ceased, the last known order being for 3,000 trucks delivered between 1993-1996. As of 2009 it was believed that around 7,000 Shaktiman trucks remained in service with the Indian Army.

The one-tonne Carrier and 0.25-tonne Jonga are both based on Nissan designs, the Carrier on the Nissan D4W73 and the Jonga on the Nissan Patrol. Production of these models was completed around 1987 (Jonga) and 1990 (Carrier).

Full details of the Shaktiman and Carrier can be found elsewhere in this section. With production of these older designs complete, the political decision was taken to move production of the Stallion to VFJ, Ashok

Ashok Leyland Stallion Mk III 7,500/5,000 kg (4 × 4) truck of the Indian Army (Gordon Arthur) 1391187

Ashok Leyland Stallion Mk IV (4 × 4) 5,000 kg truck (Ashok Leyland) 1156098

Ashok Leyland Stallion Mk III (4 × 4) 5,000-litre water bowser as currently in production for the Indian Army (Ashok Leyland)   1156095

Ashok Leyland Stallion Mk III (4 × 4) 5,000 kg truck Light Recovery Vehicle (LRV) variant as currently in production for the Indian Army (Ashok Leyland)   1156096

Leyland supplying a combination of SKD/CKD kits to the factory. VFJ also currently CKD-produces the Tata LPTA 713 TC (4 × 4) 2,500 kg light truck, essentially the replacement for the Carrier. Full details of the Tata LPTA 713 TC can be found elsewhere in this section.

Since production of the Mk III Stallion commenced in 1996 the Indian Army has received around 58,000 vehicles, at least 55,000 of these being the standard troop carrying/cargo variant, although the Indian Army converts some to other roles post delivery. Production of the Stallion continues at around 3,000-5,000 units per year and it is envisaged the type will eventually replace the bulk of the remaining Shaktiman trucks in Indian Army service.

Ashok Leyland announced in February 2006 that it had been awarded a contract to supply the Indian Army with 872 Potable Water Bowsers on the Stallion Mk III chassis. The contract, which includes spares, is valued at INR2.3 billion. These vehicles were manufactured by Ashok Leyland with production scheduled for completion by January 2007. Ashok Leyland also manufactured a Light Recovery Vehicle based on the Stallion Mk III chassis; around 1,500 have been delivered.

Following the successful introduction into Indian military service of the Stallion, Ashok Leyland commenced an active export campaign for its military products during 2004. In addition to the in-production Stallion, the commercially-based Comet 4 × 4 which was supplied to Sri Lanka and the Topchi 3,000 kg (4 × 4) Field Artillery Truck (FAT) which is in service with the Indian Army, the company has also introduced a heavier (6 × 6) FAT (and later variants) and the Stallion (6 × 6). Details of these vehicles can be found elsewhere in this section.

According to Ashok Leyland, the African, Asian, Latin American and some Middle Eastern countries are seen as target markets for the company's current product range. Small numbers of Ashok Leyland military trucks have been sold to Ecuador, Honduras, Iraq (via the US Army) and Thailand.

During 2010 an armoured version of the Stallion was announced, this featuring a protected cab and rear troop compartment. Compared to the standard Stallion Mk III of the Indian Army, engine power output is reduced slightly, some weights are slightly different, the greatest here being a 3,500 kg (opposed to 5,000 kg) payload.

Description

The Ashok Leyland Stallion Mk III (4 × 4) truck is entirely conventional in design, albeit a design optimised for use in harsh environments where support infrastructure may be limited. The vehicle is based on a 229 × 76 × 6.35 mm C-section chassis with bolted in cross members and recovery and/or towing points fitted front and rear. A 5,000 kg rated chassis-

mounted hydraulic self-recovery winch is optional. The two-person all-steel tiltable sleeper-type cab is an enlarged version of the old IVECO Ford Cargo cab, this still being fitted to a number of Ashok Leyland's commercial designs.

The standard troop carrying/cargo-type platform body is fitted with steel drop sides, a single-piece drop tailgate, and a removable tarpaulin and bows. The body measures 4.7 × 2.5 m × 550 mm (L × W × H). Wooden bench seats may be provided for troop transport. A torsion-free body is optional. The Stallion Mk III is dual-payload rated, 7,500 kg on-road, 5,000 kg off-road. The base chassis is designed to be capable of accepting a wide variety of body types and shelter/container, tanker and recovery types have all been produced. Commercial 4 × 4 and versions with a 4 × 2 driveline are also available.

Motive power is provided by an Ashok Leyland Hino-derived W06 DTI turbocharged and intercooled diesel engine developing 160 hp and 490 N.m torque. This meets EURO II emissions levels but is available to meet EURO I emissions levels if required. Other engine options, including Cummins, to suit individual market requirements are available.

A six-speed ZF manual gearbox licence-produced by Ashok Leyland is coupled to an Ashok Leyland two-speed transfer box. An automatic transmission is optional. The front steer-drive axle is disengageable for on-road driving and is sprung by the combination of semi-elliptic leaf springs and telescopic shock-absorbers. Steering is hydraulically power-assisted. The rear drive axle is sprung by semi-elliptic leaf springs and telescopic shock-absorbers and is fitted with a driver-controlled cross-axle differential lock.

The Stallion was developed to meet the specific requirements of the Indian Army and is capable of operation at altitudes of up to 15,000 ft and at temperatures ranging from –30°C to +55°C.

Variants

Stallion Mk II
The main difference between the Stallion Mk II and Stallion Mk III is the cab. The Mk II was fitted with a locally-produced cab fabricated from sheet steel. The Mk III uses an enlarged version of the old IVECO Ford Cargo cab. Mechanically the Mk II and Mk III are very similar, the engine being revised to meet EURO II emissions in the Mk III.

Stallion Mk III Light Recovery Vehicle (LRV)
The recovery equipment package fitted to the Stallion LRV was initially designed and developed on a Tata 1210D LPT chassis and was offered to the Indian Army in 1995. The Indian Army subsequently expressed a preference for the equipment to be mounted on the Stallion chassis, the standard vehicle of this weight class in the Indian Army. The Stallion-mounted version was, following trials, approved in December 1998.

The Stallion Mk III LRV is a basic recovery asset and has been designed for the recovery and unditching of military 'B' vehicles with a payload of up to 7,500 kg. It is capable of rigid or suspended towing of wheeled vehicles of the same load class. The twin boom crane is rated at 4,500 kg, the winch (which may also be used for self-recovery) is rated at 7,000 kg. Tyres are 14.00R 20. Around 1,500 vehicles had been delivered to the Indian Army by early-2009.

Full details of the Ashok Leyland Stallion LRV can be found in the Wheeled recovery vehicles section.

Stallion Mk III Potable Water Bowser
Ashok Leyland announced in February 2006 that it had been awarded a contract to manufacture and supply the Indian Army with 872 potable water bowsers on the Stallion Mk III chassis. The contract, which includes spares, is valued at INR2.3 billion. Delivery commenced in March 2006 and was scheduled for completion by January 2007. The 5,000-litre capacity tank is manufactured from SS 316 stainless steel and is dual-skinned, a layer of insulating polyurethane foam separating the two skins; a non-

Ashok Leyland Stallion Truck Fire-Fighting (TFF) (4 × 2) which is based on the Ashok Leyland Stallion Mk III (4 × 4) 5,000 kg truck (Ashok Leyland)

1156097

insulated version is also available. The tank is elliptical in design to give the lowest possible centre of gravity for the truck and is fitted with longitudinal and transverse baffles to minimise the effects of surge.

Stallion Mk III (4 × 2) Fire-Fighting Vehicle

A 4 × 2 multipurpose fire-fighting variant of the Stallion Mk III, the Truck Fire-Fighting (TFF) Large Mk IV, is also in production at Ashok Leyland's Chennai facility. The first delivery consisted of 260 vehicles, with a further 349 to be delivered by March 2007. The water tank has a 3,200-litre capacity, the foam tank a 425-litre capacity. Pumping rate is 2,250 litres/min at 7 bar. The extended crew cab seats five.

Stallion Mk IV

The Mk IV Stallion was displayed publicly for the first time at IDEX 2005. The Mk IV Stallion is essentially the Mk III but further optimised for desert-type environments. The standard 160 hp engine has been uprated to 180 hp and the gearbox has been uprated accordingly to cope with higher torque loads. Longer span leaf springs improve ride and handling and the cab features an improved three-point suspension system. Left- or right-hand drive options are available. Air-conditioning may be fitted. Standard tyre size is 355/90 × 20-18 PR.

A further updated Stallion Mk IV was disclosed in 2010, this featuring a EURO III emissions compliant engine. Details of the Stallion Mk IV are included in the Specifications table elsewhere in this entry.

Yak 5,000 kg (4 × 4) truck

The Yak 5,000 kg (4 × 4) truck is essentially a much-enhanced Stallion Mk III and was developed specifically to meet the possible requirements of an Asian customer. No order was received. The Yak is powered by an IVECO 8060.25 diesel engine developing 177 hp, and coupled to an Allison MD 3560P four-speed automatic gearbox and Steyr two-speed transfer box.

Stallion (6 × 6)

The Stallion (6 × 6) was introduced in 2004, shown publicly for the first time at IDEX 2005, and was originally known as the High Mobility Vehicle (HMV). The Stallion (6 × 6) is a 5,000 kg payload class vehicle that is designed for desert and difficult underfoot conditions, and for use where the performance of a Stallion-type (4 × 4) design is not adequate.

The Stallion (6 × 6) has completed formal trials for an Indian Army requirement for an undisclosed (but likely to be around 5,000) quantity of vehicles. Competitors for this requirement, for which a procurement decision was anticipated during 2006 but has yet to materialise, are Tata and Bharat Earth Movers Limited (BEML).

An initial 10 Stallion (6 × 6) trucks were delivered to the Royal Thai Navy during 2008 for use in a gun tractor role, and during 2009 a further 63 vehicles were ordered, these split 48 rated at 2,500 kg payload and 15 rated at 5,000 kg payload.

Full details of the Stallion (6 × 6) can be found elsewhere in this section.

Specifications

	Stallion Mk III	Stallion Mk IV; EURO III version in [square brackets] where different
Cab seating:	1 + 1	1 + 1
Configuration:	4 × 4 (selectable)	4 × 4 (selectable)
Weight:		
(laden, 5,000 kg payload)	12,200 kg	12,250 kg
(laden, 7,500 kg payload)	14,700 kg	14,750 kg
(unladen)	7,200 kg	7,250 kg
(payload)	5,000/7,500 kg	5,000/7,500 kg
(front axle load, 5,000 kg payload)	5,770 kg	5,630 kg [5,785 kg]
(rear axle load, 5,000 kg payload)	6,430 kg	6,620 kg [6,465 kg]
(front axle load, 7,500 kg payload)	6,490 kg	n/avail
(rear axle load, 7,500 kg payload)	8,210 kg	n/avail
(towed load, off-road)	10,000 kg	n/avail
(GCW)	22,200/24,700 kg	n/avail
Length:	7.32 m	7.39 m
Width:	2.5 m	2.5 m
Height: (unladen)	2.985 m	2.96 m
Ground clearance:	305 mm	305 mm
Track:		
(front)	2.03 m	2.03 m
(rear)	2.06 m	2.06 m
Wheelbase:	4.5 m	4.5 m
Angle of approach/departure:	35°/35°	35°/35°
Max speed:	84 km/h	85 km/h
Max range:		
(on-road)	1,440 km	1,440 km
(off-road)	960 km	960 km
Fuel capacity:	320 litres (2 × 160)	320 litres (2 × 160)
Max gradient: (5,000 kg payload)	47%	47%
Side slope:	n/avail	n/avail
Fording:	760 mm	760 mm
Engine:	Ashok Leyland W06 DTI 5.8-litre 6-cylinder in-line turbocharged and intercooled water-cooled 4-stroke EURO II (EURO I option) diesel developing 160 hp at 2,400 rpm and 490 N.m torque at 1,600 rpm	Ashok Leyland H Series turbocharged and intercooled water-cooled 4-stroke EURO II diesel developing 180 hp (132 kW) at 2,400 rpm and 598 N.m torque at 1,600 rpm [EURO III diesel developing 184 hp (135 kW) at 2,400 rpm and 660 N.m torque at 1,600-1,800 rpm]
Gearbox:	licence-produced ZF S6 36 with 6 forward and 1 reverse gears. Optional automatic	licence-produced ZF S6 36 Mk II with 6 forward and 1 reverse gears. Optional automatic [ZF S5 36 OD]
Transfer box:	Ashok Leyland 2-speed, selectable four-wheel drive	Ashok Leyland 2-speed, selectable four-wheel drive
Clutch:	single dry plate, diameter 353 mm	single dry plate, diameter 380 mm
Steering:	HFB-64/8043, power assisted	power assisted
Turning radius:	9.25 m	10.5 m
Suspension:	semi-elliptic leaf springs and telescopic shock-absorbers, front and rear	semi-elliptic leaf springs and telescopic shock-absorbers, front and rear
Tyres:	12.00 × 20-18 PR	355/90 × 20
Brakes:	dual-circuit, air, drums front and rear	dual-circuit, air, drums front and rear
Electrical system:	24 V	24 V
Batteries:	2 × 12 V, 110 Ah	2 × 12 V, 130 Ah
Alternator:	55 A, 24 V	55 A, 24 V

Status

Stallion Mk I, prototype only. Stallion Mk II, production complete, 330 delivered to the Indian Army 1994-1996. Stallion MK III, approaching 59,000 delivered to the Indian Army by December 2009, production continues at around 3,000-5,000 units per year (see text). Stallion Mk IV, available. Stallion (6 × 6) delivered to Thailand.

Contractor

Ashok Leyland

Shaktiman (4 × 4) 4,000 kg truck

Development
The first Shaktiman rolled off the production line at the now Vehicle Factory Jabalpur (VFJ) in June 1959. The Shaktiman was based on a MAN design and was initially assembled from components supplied by Germany, but as production built up an increasing number of the components were supplied by Indian companies. The final significant order for the Shaktiman from the Indian Army was for 3,000 vehicles. This order was placed in 1993, with deliveries completed around 1996. It was confirmed in 2003 that production of the Shaktiman had ceased, however it is technically possible to resume production in the unlikely event of significant export orders being received. In total, around 75,000 examples were produced for the Indian Army, with around 7,000 of these confirmed as remaining in 2009.

VFJ also produced the Carrier (4 × 4) 1 ton light truck and the 0.25 ton JONGA light vehicle. These were both based on Nissan designs and production of both types is now complete. According to released figures, in total, VFJ produced 209,448 Shaktiman, Carrier and JONGA vehicles.

The Ashok Leyland Stallion 5,000/7,500 kg (4 × 4) truck, of which around 57,000 examples have so far been built (most from CKD kits at the Vehicle Factory Jabalpur (VFJ)), will be the eventual replacement for the Shaktiman in the Army's inventory. Full details of the Ashok Leyland Stallion can be found elsewhere in this section.

Description
The Shaktiman 4,000 kg (4 × 4) truck which is entirely conventional in design is similar to the German MAN 415 L1 AR truck, the main visual difference between the German and Indian vehicle being that the latter has dual rather than single rear wheels.

The Shaktiman is in Indian military service in both 4 × 4 and 4 × 2 versions and in both hard- and soft-top form. Variants in use include a 4,000 litre fuel tanker body version, a light recovery version, a version capable of carrying shelter bodies, such as a radio relay or similar communications equipment, and an artillery tractor version with a separate crew shelter behind the driver's cab. This version is used to tow Indian Ordnance Factories 105 mm Light Field Guns, is fitted with a winch and has a GVW of 8,350 kg. A version with a deeper chassis frame, a heavy-duty suspension and larger tyres for a GVW of 11,000 kg is also understood to have been produced.

Specifications
Shaktiman
Cab seating: 1 + 2
Configuration: 4 × 4 or 4 × 2
Weight:
  (laden) 9,020 kg
  (unladen) 5,075 kg
  (rated payload) 3,000 kg
  (max front axle load) 3,300 kg
  (max rear axle load) 6,600 kg
  (GCW) 18,000 kg
Load area dimensions: 4.45 × 2.25 m
Length: 6.825 m
Width: 2.4 m
Height:
  (overall, laden) 2.48 m
  (load area) 1.13 m
Ground clearance: 308 mm
Track:
  (front) 1.824 m
  (rear) 1.632 m
Wheelbase: 4.2 m
Max speed: 72 km/h
Fuel capacity: 300 litres (2 × 150 litres)

Gradient:
  (laden) 67%
  (GCW) 33%
Engine: D 0026 M 8 A 5.88-litre 6-cylinder in-line water-cooled 4-stroke direct injection diesel developing 110 hp (81 kW) at 2,500 rpm
Gearbox: AK5-35 constant mesh manual with 5 forward and 1 reverse gears
Clutch: single dry plate, diameter 280 mm
Transfer box: 2-speed, lockable centre differential
Steering: heavy duty roller
Turning radius: 8.6 m
Suspension: semi-elliptic leaf springs, front and rear
Tyres: 8.25 × 20, 12 ply
Brakes:
  (main) hydropneumatic, front, pneumatic, rear, drums all-round
  (parking) mechanical
Electrical system: 12 V with 24 V starter
Batteries: 2 × 12 V, 92 Ah
Alternator: 40 A

Status
Production complete (see text). In service with India (approximately 7,000 remain), Bangladesh and possibly others in small numbers.

Contractor
Ordnance Factory Board

Tata LPTA 713 TC (4 × 4) 2,500 kg light truck

Development
The Tata Engineering & Locomotive Co Ltd (Telco) was established in 1945 to manufacture steam locomotives and other engineering products. In 1954 the company entered into a collaborative agreement with the then Daimler-Benz of Germany to manufacture medium commercial vehicles. The first heavy commercial vehicle (>16,000 kg GVW) was produced by Tata in 1983. The joint venture agreement with the now Daimler ended in 2001. In 1993 Tata entered into a joint venture with the Cummins Engine Co Inc to produce the Cummins B-series engine in India and in 2004 Tata announced that it had completed the acquisition of Daewoo Commercial Vehicle Company Limited (DWCV), Korea, a significant milestone for the company.

In 2005, Tata Motors acquired a 21 per cent stake in the Spanish bus and coach manufacturer, Hispano Carrocera. In 2007, Tata formed a joint venture with Marcopolo of Brazil and introduced low-floor in the Indian market. In 2008, Tata acquired British Jaguar Land Rover (JLR). In 2010, Tata acquired an 80 per cent stake in Italy-based design and engineering company Trilix. Tata Motors has R&D centres in South Korea, Spain and the UK.

Tata Motors is the flagship of the Tata Group and is India's largest automobile company, with revenues of USD8.5 billion in 2009. Over 5.9 million Tata vehicles are estimated to be on the road in India, and Tata Motors is the largest commercial vehicle manufacturer and second largest passenger car manufacturer in the country. Additionally, the company is the world's fourth largest medium and heavy commercial truck manufacturer and second largest heavy bus manufacturer.

Since 1958 Tata Motors has supplied India's military and paramilitary forces with over 100,000 vehicles and in addition to ongoing domestic sales, currently exports around 450 to 500 military vehicles per year to (primarily) South East Asian and African armed forces.

The most recent light vehicle and truck deliveries to India's military and paramilitary forces have included:
- Tata Sumo (4 × 4) light vehicle of which around 200 examples per year in Ambulance configuration are currently being delivered to the Indian Army. India's state Police operate in excess of 3,000 examples of the 4 × 2 variant; deliveries continue at around 400 to 500 vehicles per year. Full details of the Tata Sumo (4 × 4) light vehicle can be found in the Light vehicles section.
- Tata SFC 407 (4 × 4) 1,000 kg light truck/medium troop carrier of which 8,500 to 9,000 examples have so far been delivered to India's paramilitary forces at around 800 to 900 per year, these split 200-300/600 4 × 4/4 × 2. Full details of the Tata SFC 407 (4 × 4) 1,000 kg light truck can be found in the Light vehicles section.
- Tata SD 1015 TC (4 × 4) FAT (Field Artillery Tractor) of which around 2,000 were delivered between 1999-2004 to the Army and paramilitary forces. Full details of the Tata SD 1015 TC (4 × 4) can be found elsewhere in this section.
- Tata SA 1212 TC (4 × 4) troop and load carrier of which around 6,000 were delivered. The Tata LPTA 1413 (4 × 4) troop and load carrier will be the production replacement of the SA 1212 TC and the type is currently under evaluation by India's paramilitary forces. Full details of the Tata SA 1212 TC and Tata LPTA 1413 (4 × 4) trucks can be found elsewhere in this section.
- Tata SA 1613 (4 × 2) troop and load carrier. Essentially a civilian vehicle fitted with a military troop carrying/cargo-type body with bench seats, a removable tarpaulin and bows.
- Tata SA 1615 (4 × 2) Line Of Communication (LOC) logistic truck of which around 600 examples (at 200 per year) have been delivered between 2003 and 2006; deliveries continue.

Shaktiman (4 × 4) 4,000 kg truck of the Indian Army (Gordon Arthur) 1391190

4-stretcher ambulance variant of the Tata LPTA 713 TC (4 × 4) 2,500 kg light truck (Tata Motors)
1156010

Tata LPTA 713 TC (4 × 4) 2,500 kg light truck of the Indian Army (Shaun C Connors)
1156170

- Tata LPTA 1623 (6 × 6) of which around 70 examples were ordered during 2009 by BEL as mounting vehicles for Indian Air Force radar.
- Tata LPTA 713 TC (4 × 4) 2,500 kg light truck.

The Tata LPTA 713 TC (4 × 4) 2,500 kg light truck entered production in 1999 as part of the Indian Army's type rationalisation process. The contract was awarded to Tata Motors Ltd following evaluation of the LPTA 713 TC, the Ashok Leyland Azad Super and a Swarej Mazda design. Production of the LPTA 713 TC is carried out at the state-owned Vehicle Factory Jalbapur (VFJ).

VFJ was established in 1969/70 for the production of three non-fighting vehicles for the Indian military; the 3 ton Shaktiman MAN-based truck, the 1 ton Nissan-based Carrier and 0.25 ton Nissan-based Jonga light vehicles. Production of all these models was completed between 1987 and 1993.

Full details of the Shaktiman can be found elsewhere in this section. With production of these older designs complete, the political decision was taken to move production of the LPTA 713 to VFJ, Tata supplying CKD kits to the factory. VFJ also currently CKD-produces the Ashok Leyland Stallion (the successor to the Shaktiman) 5,000 kg truck. Full details of the Ashok Leyland Stallion can be found elsewhere in this section.

Since production of the LPTA 713 commenced in 1999 around 23,000 examples have been supplied to the Indian Army; production continues. In addition to the standard General Service (GS) troop carrying body around 400 examples of a four-stretcher field ambulance and 600 2,000 litre water tanker variants have been delivered. The LPTA 713 TC has also been supplied to Afghanistan, Nepal, Sri-Lanka and some undisclosed African countries.

The official Tata model designation of this vehicle provides basic data for the type and can be broken down as follows: LP – abbreviation of the German terms for fully forward control; T- Truck; A- All-wheel drive; 7 – GVW tonnes (approx. rounded); 13 – engine power output hp × 10 (approx. rounded); TC – engine type (Tata Cummins).

Description

The Tata LPTA 713 TC (4 × 4) 2,500 kg light truck is entirely conventional in design and is based on a C-section chassis with bolted in cross members and recovery and/or towing points fitted front and rear. The two-person all-steel tiltable cab is fitted with a roof hatch. The standard General Service (GS) style troop carrying/cargo-type platform body is fitted with steel drop sides, a single-piece drop tailgate, and a removable tarpaulin and bows. Wooden bench seats are provided for troop transport. The payload rating of the LPTA is 2,500 kg.

The base chassis is designed to be capable of accepting a wide variety of body types and in addition to ambulance and water bowser variants already in production, an armoured troop carrier variant of the LPTA 713

was displayed publicly for the first time at DefExpo 2006. Further details of this variant can be found elsewhere in this entry. Motive power for the LPTA 713 is provided by a Tata Cummins turbocharged diesel engine that meets EURO I emissions levels and develops 125 hp and 400 N.m torque. A five-speed synchromesh manual gearbox is coupled to a two-speed constant transfer box. The front steer-drive axle can be disengaged for on-road driving and is sprung by semi-elliptic leaf springs. Steering is hydraulically power-assisted. The rear drive axle is sprung by semi-elliptic leaf springs.

Variants

Tata LPTA 713 2,500 kg light truck/armoured
The armoured troop carrier variant of the LPTA 713 has a GVW of 8,150 kg and a payload of 800 kg (9 + driver at 80 kg per person). The all-steel armour and ballistic glass offers protection against 7.62 mm ball ammunition and double HE 36 underbody hand grenade blast. Overall dimensions are 6.24 × 2.26 × 3.225 m (L × W × H). Options include runflat tyres. Early 2009 it was disclosed that a pilot order for 37 vehicles had been received.

Specifications

Tata LPTA 713 TC
Cab seating: 1 + 1
Configuration: 4 × 4 (selectable)
Weight:
    (laden) 7,650 kg
    (unladen) 5,150 kg
    (payload) 2,500 kg
    (front axle load) 3,750 kg
    (rear axle load) 4,000 kg
    (towed load) 5,000 kg
    (GCW) 12,650 kg
Length: 5.746 m
Width: 2.16 m
Height: (cab) 2.85 m
Ground clearance: 245 mm
Track:
    (front) 1.81 m
    (rear) 1.824 m
Wheelbase: 3.225 m
Angle of approach/departure: 35°/45°
Max speed:
    (4 × 2) 82 km/h
    (4 × 4) 54 km/h
Max range: 800 km
Fuel capacity: 200 litres
Max gradient: 70%
Max sideslope: 30%
Fording: 650 mm
Engine: Tata Cummins 6BT EURO I emissions compliant 5.883-litre 6-cylinder in-line turbocharged water-cooled direct injection 4-stroke diesel developing 125 hp (93 kW) at 2,500 rpm and 400 N.m torque at 1,400-1,700 rpm
Gearbox: GBS-40 with 5 forward (synchromesh) and 1 (constant mesh) reverse gears
Transfer box: 2-speed constant mesh, selectable four-wheel drive
Clutch: single dry plate, diameter 310 mm
Steering: hydraulically power-assisted
Turning radius: 7.15 m
Suspension: semi-elliptic leaf springs front and rear
Tyres: 1,200 × 20-18 PR
Brakes: dual circuit, air, drums front and rear
Electrical system: 12 V
Batteries: 12 V, 180 Ah
Alternator: 135 A

Status

In production. Over 23,000 delivered to the Indian Army between 1999 and 2009, production continues. As of May 2006 around 353 vehicles had been exported to Afghanistan, Nepal, Sri-Lanka and some undisclosed African countries.

Contractor

Tata Motors Limited

Tata SD 1015 TC (4 × 4) Field Artillery Tractor

Development

The Tata Engineering & Locomotive Co Ltd (Telco) was established in 1945 to manufacture steam locomotives and other engineering products. In 1954 the company entered into a collaborative agreement with the then Daimler-Benz of Germany to manufacture medium commercial vehicles. The first heavy commercial vehicle (>16,000 kg GVW) was produced by Tata in 1983. The joint venture agreement with the now Daimler ended in 2001. In 1993 Tata entered into a joint venture with the Cummins Engine Co

Tata SD 1015 TC (4 × 4) Field Artillery Tractor (FAT) of the Indian Army
(Tata Motors)   1156088

Inc to produce the Cummins B-series engine in India and in 2004 Tata announced that it had completed the acquisition of Daewoo Commercial Vehicle Company Limited (DWCV), Korea, a significant milestone for the company.

In 2005, Tata Motors acquired a 21 per cent stake in the Spanish bus and coach manufacturer, Hispano Carrocera. In 2007, Tata formed a joint venture with Marcopolo of Brazil and introduced low-floor in the Indian market. In 2008, Tata acquired British Jaguar Land Rover (JLR). In 2010, Tata acquired an 80 per cent stake in Italy-based design and engineering company Trilix. Tata Motors has R&D centres in South Korea, Spain and the UK.

Tata Motors is the flagship of the Tata Group and is India's largest automobile company, with revenues of USD8.5 billion in 2009. Over 5.9 million Tata vehicles are estimated to be on the road in India, and Tata Motors is the largest commercial vehicle manufacturer and second largest passenger car manufacturer in the country. Additionally, the company is the world's fourth largest medium and heavy commercial truck manufacturer and second largest heavy bus manufacturer.

Since 1958 Tata Motors has supplied India's military and paramilitary forces with over 100,000 vehicles and in addition to ongoing domestic sales, currently exports around 450 to 500 military vehicles per year to (primarily) South East Asian and African armed forces.

The most recent light vehicle and truck deliveries to India's military and paramilitary forces have included:

- Tata Sumo (4 × 4) light vehicle of which around 200 examples per year in Ambulance configuration are currently being delivered to the Indian Army. India's state Police operate around 2,500 to 3,000 examples of the 4 × 2 variant; deliveries continue at around 400 to 500 vehicles per year. Full details of the Tata Sumo (4 × 4) light vehicle can be found in the Light vehicles section.
- Tata SFC 407 (4 × 4) 1,000 kg light truck/medium troop carrier of which 8,500 to 9,000 examples have so far been delivered to India's paramilitary forces at around 800 to 900 per year, these split 200-300/600 4 × 4/4 × 2. Full details of the Tata SFC 407 (4 × 4) 1,000 kg light truck can be found in the Light vehicles section.
- Tata LPTA 713 TC (4 × 4) 2,500 kg light truck of which around 23,000 have been supplied since the commencement of its production in 1999. Full details of the Tata LPTA 713 (4 × 4) can be found elsewhere in this section.
- Tata SD 1212 TC (4 × 4) troop carrier of which over 6,000 were delivered to the Indian Army between 1999 and 2006. Full details of the Tata SD 1212 TC (4 × 4) can be found elsewhere in this section.
- Tata SA 1613 (4 × 2) troop and load carrier. Essentially a civilian vehicle fitted with a military troop carrying/cargo-type body with bench seats, a removable tarpaulin and bows.
- Tata SA 1615 (4 × 2) Line Of Communication (LOC) logistic truck of which around 600 examples (at 200 per year) have been delivered between 2003 and 2006; deliveries continue.
- Tata LPTA 1623 (6 × 6) of which around 70 examples were ordered during 2009 by BEL as mounting vehicles for Indian Air Force radar.
- Tata SD 1015 TC (4 × 4) FAT (Field Artillery Tractor).

The Tata SD 1015 TC (4 × 4) FAT (Field Artillery Tractor) is used by the Indian Army in the gun tractor role. Approximately 2,000 vehicles have been delivered to the Indian Army since 1999, with some sources quoting as many as 5,000 examples delivered. Other users of the SD 1015 are known to include Afghanistan, Malawi, Sri Lanka and Kuwait.

The Tata SD 1015 TC remains in production and available, however future Indian Army gun tractor requirements will likely be met by a larger (6 × 6) vehicle such as the Tata LPTA 1623 TC or Ashok Leyland High Mobility Vehicle (HMV).

The official Tata model designation of this vehicle provides basic data for the type and can be broken down as follows: S – cab, Semi-forward control; D – Desert application, single rear wheels/tyres; 10 – GVW tonnes (approx rounded); 15 – engine power output hp × 10 (approx rounded); TC – engine type (Tata Cummins).

Description

The Tata SD 1015 TC (4 × 4) FAT is entirely conventional in design and is based on a 223 (max) × 60 mm C-section chassis with bolted and riveted in cross members. Tow and recovery points in the form of two D-type shackles and a central towing hook are fitted to the front bumper, a swivel-type tow hook is fitted at the rear. A 5,000 kg maximum line pull winch 60 m of 16 mm diameter cable is fitted. This may be used for front or rearward pulls.

The standard Tata all-steel bonneted cab seat three (two plus driver) and is fitted with a roof hatch.

The rear platform body is all-steel and fitted with steel drop sides, a single-piece drop tailgate, and a removable tarpaulin and bows. A separate 1.2 m deep crew cabin for the gun crew of six is provided within the body, this leaving approximately 2.98 m of storage space within the 4.2 m body. Basic communication in the form of a buzzer is provided between the crew cabin and vehicle cab. Platform height (unladen) is 1.36 m and the standard interior height of the body is 1.6 m, although this is adjustable within a 1.43 to 1.83 m range. A 100 litre capacity potable water tank is standard equipment. Motive power for the SD 1015 is provided by a Tata Cummins turbocharged diesel engine. At least 1,500 of the vehicles delivered will be fitted with the EURO I emissions compliant version of this engine, the remainder with the later EURO II emissions compliant version. The current engine develops 145 hp and 499 N.m torque. For most commercial applications (and when fitted to the SA 1212 TC) Tata rate the 6BT engine at around 125 hp, the increase in power output considered necessary for the gun tractor role. A cold start pilot is fitted to facilitate cold weather/high-altitude starting.

A six-speed manual gearbox with side-mounted Power Take-Off (PTO) rated at 40 hp for the winch is coupled to a two-speed constant transfer box which provides 4 × 2 drive in high range, 4 × 4 drive in low range. The front Tata FA-104 steer-drive axle is sprung by semi-elliptic leaf springs and hydraulic shock-absorbers. Steering is power-assisted. The rear Tata RA-107 single reduction drive axle is fitted with a driver-actuated differential lock and is sprung by semi-elliptic leaf springs and hydraulic shock-absorbers.

Specifications

Tata SD 1015 TC

Cab seating: 1 + 2 (gun crew of 6 in rear)
Configuration: 4 × 4 (selectable)
Weight:
  (max permissible laden) 10,350 kg
  (unladen) 6,440 kg
  (payload) 3,910 kg
  (permissible front axle load) 3,820 kg
  (permissible rear axle load) 6,530 kg
  (with body) 6.455 m
Width:(max) 2.43 m
Height:
  (laden) 2.96 m
  (adjustable) 2.79-3.19 m
Ground clearance: 300 mm
Track:
  (front) 2.034 m
  (rear) 2.014 m
Wheelbase: 3.625 m
Angle of approach/departure: 28°/31°
Max recommended speeds: (4 × 2, on-road, prepared track, off-road) 82/48/15 km/h
Max range: 700 km
Fuel capacity: 225 litres
Max gradient:
  (4 × 2) 36%
  (4 × 4) 53%
Max sideslope: 42%
Fording: 600 mm
Engine: Tata Cummins 6BTAA 5.9-20 5.883-litre 6-cylinder in-line turbocharged and intercooled water-cooled 4-stroke direct injection EURO II emissions compliant diesel developing 145 hp (108 kW) at 2,500 rpm and 499 N.m torque at 1,600 rpm
Gearbox: Tata G-600 with 6 forward and 1 reverse gears, synchromesh on all forward gears, constant mesh on reverse. Side-mounted PTO with safety interlock to prevent engine starting while engaged. 765 rpm at max engine speed, rated at 40 hp (30 kW) (constant)
Transfer box: Tata 2-speed constant mesh
Clutch: single dry plate, Ø352 mm
Steering: power-assisted
Turning radius: (kerb) 8.5 m
Suspension: semi-elliptic 70 mm ×1.45 m leaf springs and hydraulic shock-absorbers, front; 80 mm × 1.6 m (main) and 1.1 m (auxiliary) semi-elliptic leaf springs and hydraulic shock-absorbers, rear
Tyres: 1200 × 20-18 PR sand/highway pattern (cross-country pattern, optional)
Brakes:
  (main) dual-circuit, air-over-hydraulic, 414 mm drums front, 412 mm drums rear. Pneumatically operated engine exhaust brake interlinked with the service (main) brake
  (parking) spring actuated acting on rear drums only

Electrical system: 12 V
Battery: 12 V, 180 Ah
Alternator: 55 A

Status

Production as required (see text). Around 2,000 delivered to the Indian Army between 1999 and 2004; 400 in production for 2009 delivery. Some sources quote as many as 5,000 examples delivered. As of May 2006 around 519 vehicles had been exported, known users including Afghanistan, Kuwait, Malawi and Sri Lanka.

Contractor

Tata Motors Limited

Tata SA 1212 TC (4 × 4) 4,000 kg truck

Development

The Tata Engineering & Locomotive Co Ltd (Telco) was established in 1945 to manufacture steam locomotives and other engineering products. In 1954 the company entered into a collaborative agreement with the then Daimler-Benz of Germany to manufacture medium commercial vehicles. The first heavy commercial vehicle (>16,000 kg GVW) was produced by Tata in 1983. The joint venture agreement with the now Daimler ended in 2001. In 1993 Tata entered into a joint venture with the Cummins Engine Co Inc to produce the Cummins B-series engine in India and in 2004 Tata announced that it had completed the acquisition of Daewoo Commercial Vehicle Company Limited (DWCV), Korea, a significant milestone for the company.

In 2005, Tata Motors acquired a 21 per cent stake in the Spanish bus and coach manufacturer, Hispano Carrocera. In 2007, Tata formed a joint venture with Marcopolo of Brazil and introduced low-floor in the Indian market. In 2008, Tata acquired British Jaguar Land Rover (JLR). In 2010, Tata acquired an 80 per cent stake in Italy-based design and engineering company Trilix. Tata Motors has R&D centres in South Korea, Spain and the UK.

Tata Motors is the flagship of the Tata Group and is India's largest automobile company, with revenues of USD8.5 billion in 2009. Over 5.9 million Tata vehicles are estimated to be on the road in India, and Tata Motors is the largest commercial vehicle manufacturer and second largest passenger car manufacturer in the country. Additionally, the company is the world's fourth largest medium and heavy commercial truck manufacturer and second largest heavy bus manufacturer.

Since 1958 Tata Motors has supplied India's military and paramilitary forces with over 100,000 vehicles and in addition to ongoing domestic sales, currently exports around 450 to 500 military vehicles per year to (primarily) South East Asian and African armed forces.

The most recent light vehicle and truck deliveries to India's military and paramilitary forces have included:

- Tata Sumo (4 × 4) light vehicle of which around 200 examples per year in Ambulance configuration are currently being delivered to the Indian Army. India's state Police operate around 2,500 to 3,000 examples of the 4 × 2 variant; deliveries continue at around 400 to 500 vehicles per year. Full details of the Tata Sumo (4 × 4) light vehicle can be found in the Light vehicles section.
- Tata SFC 407 (4 × 4) 1,000 kg light truck/medium troop carrier of which 8,500 to 9,000 examples have so far been delivered to India's paramilitary forces at around 800 to 900 per year, these split 200-300/600 4 × 4/4 × 2. Full details of the Tata SFC 407 (4 × 4) 1,000 kg light truck can be found in the Light vehicles section.
- Tata LPTA 713 TC (4 × 4) 2,500 kg light truck of which around 23,000 have been supplied since production commenced in 1999. Full details of the Tata LPTA 713 (4 × 4) can be found elsewhere in this section.
- Tata SD 1015 TC (4 × 4) Field Artillery Tractor (FAT) of which around 2,000 were delivered between 1999 and 2004 to India's Army and paramilitary forces. Full details of the Tata SD 1015 TC (4 × 4) can be found elsewhere in this section.

Tata SA 1212 TC (4 × 4) troop carrying/cargo truck of the Indian Army (Shaun C Connors) 1156090

- Tata SA 1613 (4 × 2) troop and load carrier. Essentially a civilian vehicle fitted with a military troop carrying/cargo-type body with bench seats, a removable tarpaulin and bows.
- Tata SA 1615 (4 × 2) Line Of Communication (LOC) logistic truck of which around 600 examples (at 200 per year) have been delivered between 2003 and 2006; deliveries continue.
- Tata LPTA 1623 (6 × 6) of which around 70 examples were ordered during 2009 by BEL as mounting vehicles for Indian Air Force radar.
- Tata SA 1212 TC (4 × 4) troop and load carrier.

The Tata SA 1212 TC (4 × 4) 6,500 kg troop carrying/cargo truck is used by India's Paramilitary forces primarily in the troop carrying role, although 6,000 litre water bowser variants have also been produced. Approximately 6,000 vehicles were delivered to the Indian Army over about 12 years. Other users of the SA 1212 TC are known to include Bhutan, Kuwait, Saudi Arabia, Sri Lanka and Zambia.

The official Tata model designation of this vehicle provides basic data for the type and can be broken down as follows:

- S - cab, Semi-forward control
- A - All-wheel drive
- 12 - GVW tonnes (approx. rounded)
- 12 - engine power output hp × 10 (approx. rounded)
- TC - engine type (Tata Cummins).

Description

The Tata SA 1212 TC (4 × 4) 6,500 kg truck is entirely conventional in design and is based on a 223 (max) × 60 mm C-section chassis with bolted and riveted in cross members. Recovery points are fitted with the front bumper and the chassis rear cross member may be fitted with a towing hook. The bonneted all-steel cab is a Tata design and seats three, driver plus two.

The standard General Service (GS) style troop carrying/cargo-type platform body is fitted with steel drop sides, a single-piece drop tailgate, and a removable tarpaulin and bows. Wooden bench seats are provided for troop transport.

The base chassis could be adapted to handle a variety of body types and in addition to the standard troop carrying/cargo variant, the Indian army also operates a 6,000-litre capacity water bowser variant.

Motive power for the SA 1212 is provided by a Tata Cummins turbocharged diesel engine. The final 500 examples supplied to the Indian Army meet EURO II emissions requirements, the 1,200 delivered prior to those meet EURO I emissions requirements. The current engine develops 125 hp and 410 N.m torque. A five-speed manual gearbox is coupled to a two-speed constant transfer box which provides 4 × 2 drive in high range, 4 × 4 drive in low range. The front Tata FA-104 steer-drive axle is sprung by semi-elliptic leaf springs and hydraulic shock-absorbers. Steering is manual. The rear Tata RA-108RR drive axle is sprung by semi-elliptic leaf springs; hydraulic shock-absorbers are optional.

Specifications

Tata SA 1212 TC

Cab seating:	1 + 2
Configuration:	4 × 4 (selectable)
Weight:	
(max permissible laden)	12,180 kg
(chassis-cab)	4,510 kg
(payload incl. body on chassis-cab)	7,670 kg
(permissible front axle load)	4,060 kg
(permissible rear axle load)	8,120 kg
Length: (chassis)	6.97 m
Width: (max)	2.43 m
Height:	2.613 m
Ground clearance:	249 mm
Track:	
(front)	1.988 m
(rear)	1.809 m
Wheelbase:	4.225 m
Angel of approach/departure:	35°/30°
Max recommended speed: (4 × 2)	75 km/h
Max range:	700 km
Fuel capacity:	225 litres
Max gradient:	42%
Max sideslope:	42%
Fording:	550 mm
Engine:	Tata Cummins 6BTAA 5.9 5.883-litre 6-cylinder in-line turbocharged and intercooled water-cooled 4-stroke direct injection EURO II emissions compliant diesel developing 125 hp (92 kW) at 2,500 rpm and 410 N.m torque at 1,400-1,700 rpm

Gearbox:	Tata GBS-40 with 5 forward and 1 reverse gears, synchromesh on all forward gears, constant mesh on reverse
Transfer box:	Tata 2-speed constant mesh
Clutch:	single dry plate, diameter 330 mm
Steering:	mechanical, manual, power-assisted option
Turning radius:	
(kerb)	8.8 m
(wall)	9.55 m
Suspension:	semi-elliptic 1.45 m span leaf springs and hydraulic shock-absorbers, front; 1.6 m (main) and 1.1 m (auxiliary) span semi-elliptic leaf springs, rear. Optional hydraulic shock-absorbers on rear axle
Tyres:	9.00 × 20-12 PR, single front, dual-rear
Brakes:	
(main)	dual-circuit, air-over-hydraulic, 414 mm drums front, 412 mm drums rear, supplementary pneumatically operated engine exhaust brake interlinked with the service (main) brake
(parking)	spring actuated acting on rear drums only
Electrical system:	12 V
Battery:	12 V, 150 Ah (180 Ah optional)
Alternator:	55 A

Status

Production complete. Over 6,000 delivered between 1999 and 2006, with around 4,000 to 4,500 thought to remain in service as of mid-2006. A total of 302 vehicles are known to have been exported with users known to include Bhutan, Kuwait, Saudi Arabia, Sri Lanka and Zambia.

Contractor

Tata Motors Limited

Tata LPTA 1413 (4 × 4) 5,000 kg General Service (GS) truck

Development

The Tata Engineering & Locomotive Co Ltd (Telco) was established in 1945 to manufacture steam locomotives and other engineering products. In 1954 the company entered into a collaborative agreement with the then Daimler-Benz of Germany to manufacture medium commercial vehicles. The first heavy commercial vehicle (>16,000 kg GVW) was produced by Tata in 1983. The joint venture agreement with the now Daimler ended in 2001. In 1993 Tata entered into a joint venture with the Cummins Engine Co Inc to produce the Cummins B-series engine in India and in 2004 Tata announced that it had completed the acquisition of Daewoo Commercial Vehicle Company Limited (DWCV), Korea, a significant milestone for the company.

In 2005, Tata Motors acquired a 21 per cent stake in the Spanish bus and coach manufacturer, Hispano Carrocera. In 2007, Tata formed a joint venture with Marcopolo of Brazil and introduced low-floor in the Indian market. In 2008, Tata acquired British Jaguar Land Rover (JLR). In 2010, Tata acquired an 80 per cent stake in Italy-based design and engineering company Trilix. Tata Motors has R&D centres in South Korea, Spain and the UK.

Tata Motors is the flagship of the Tata Group and is India's largest automobile company, with revenues of USD8.5 billion in 2009. Over 5.9 million Tata vehicles are estimated to be on the road in India, and Tata Motors is the largest commercial vehicle manufacturer and second largest passenger car manufacturer in the country. Additionally, the company is the world's fourth largest medium and heavy commercial truck manufacturer and second largest heavy bus manufacturer.

Since 1958 Tata Motors has supplied India's military and paramilitary forces with over 100,000 vehicles and in addition to ongoing domestic sales, currently exports around 450-500 military vehicles per year to (primarily) South East Asian and African armed forces.

The most recent light vehicle and truck deliveries to India's military and para-military forces have included:

- Tata Sumo (4 × 4) light vehicle of which around 200 examples per year in Ambulance configuration are currently being delivered to the Indian Army. India's state Police operate around 2,500 to 3,000 examples of the 4 × 2 variant; deliveries continue at around 400 to 500 vehicles per year. Full details of the Tata Sumo (4 × 4) light vehicle can be found in the Light vehicles section.
- Tata SFC 407 (4 × 4) 1,000 kg light truck/medium troop carrier of which 8,500 to 9,000 examples have so far been delivered to India's paramilitary forces at around 800 to 900 per year, these split 200-300/600 4 × 4/4 × 2. Full details of the Tata SFC 407 (4 × 4) 1,000 kg light truck can be found in the Light vehicles section.

Tata LPTA 1413 (4 × 4) 5,000 kg General Service (GS) truck as displayed at DefExpo 2006 and fitted with a hard-top rear troop carrying body (Shaun C Connors)   1156014

- Tata LPTA 713 TC (4 × 4) 2,500 kg light truck of which around 23,000 have been supplied since production commenced in 1999. Full details of the Tata LPTA 713 (4 × 4) can be found elsewhere in this section.
- Tata SD 1015 TC (4 × 4) Field Artillery Tractor (FAT) of which around 2,000 were delivered between 1999-2004 to India's Army and paramilitary forces. Full details of the Tata SD 1015 TC (4 × 4) can be found elsewhere in this section.
- Tata SA 1212 TC (4 × 4) troop and load carrier of which over 6,000 were delivered to the Indian Army.
- Tata SA 1613 (4 × 2) troop and load carrier. Essentially, a civilian vehicle fitted with a military troop carrying/cargo-type body with bench seats, a removable tarpaulin and bows.
- Tata SA 1615 (4 × 2) Line Of Communication (LOC) logistic truck of which around 600 examples (at 200 per year) have been delivered between 2003 and 2006; deliveries continue.
- Tata LPTA 1623 (6 × 6) of which around 70 examples were ordered during 2009 by BEL as mounting vehicles for Indian Air Force radar.

The Tata LPTA 1413 (4 × 4) 5,000 kg General Service (GS) truck is the replacement within the Tata range for the current SA 1212 TC troop carrying/cargo truck. The LPTA 1413 is currently under evaluation by the India's paramilitary forces. The official Tata model designation of this vehicle provides basic data for the type and can be broken down as follows: LP – abbreviation of the German terms for fully forward control; T- Truck; A- All-wheel drive; 14– GVW tonnes (approx rounded); 13 – engine power output hp × 10 (approx rounded).

Specifications

Tata LPTA 1413

Cab seating: 1 + 4 (22 in rear)
Configuration: 4 × 4 (selectable)
Weight:
  (max permissible laden) 14,260 kg
  (payload) 7,800 kg
  (permissible front axle load) 4,060 kg
  (permissible rear axle load) 10,200 kg
Length: 8.1 m
Width: 2.325 m
Height: 2.7 m
Ground clearance: 311 mm
Track:
  (front) 1.81 m
  (rear) 1.809 m
Wheelbase: 4.2 m
Angle of approach/departure: 20°/27°
Max speed: 75 km/h
Max range: 750 km
Fuel capacity: 250 litres
Max gradient: 42 %
Max sideslope: 42%
Fording: 650 mm
Engine: Tata Cummins 6BT 5.9 5.883-litre 6-cylinder in-line turbocharged and intercooled water-cooled 4-stroke direct injection EURO II emissions compliant diesel developing 125 hp (93 kW) at 2,500 rpm and 410 N.m torque at 1,400-1,700 rpm

Gearbox: Tata GBS-40 with 5 forward and 1 reverse gears, synchromesh on all forward gears, constant mesh on reverse
Transfer box: Tata 2-speed constant mesh
Clutch: single dry plate, Ø330 mm
Steering: power-assisted
Turning radius: (kerb) 8.8 mm
Suspension: semi-elliptic leaf springs and hydraulic shock-absorbers, front; semi-elliptic leaf springs and hydraulic shock-absorbers, rear
Tyres: 10.00 × 20 – 16PR
Brakes:
(main) dual-circuit, air-over-hydraulic, drums front and rear. Supplementary pneumatically operated engine exhaust brake interlinked with the service (main) brake
(parking) spring-actuated acting on rear drums only
Electrical system: 12 V
Batteries: 150 Ah
Alternator: 65 A

Status
Production as required. Understood to be under evaluation by India's paramilitary forces.

Contractor
Tata Motors Limited.

Tata LPTA 1623 TC (6 × 6) 5,000 kg truck

Development
The Tata Engineering & Locomotive Co Ltd (Telco) was established in 1945 to manufacture steam locomotives and other engineering products. In 1954 the company entered into a collaborative agreement with the then Daimler-Benz of Germany to manufacture medium commercial vehicles. The first heavy commercial vehicle (>16,000 kg GVW) was produced by Tata in 1983. The joint venture agreement with the now Daimler ended in 2001. In 1993 Tata entered into a joint venture with the Cummins Engine Co Inc to produce the Cummins B-series engine in India and in 2004 Tata announced that it had completed the acquisition of Daewoo Commercial Vehicle Company Limited (DWCV), Korea, a significant milestone for the company.

In 2005, Tata Motors acquired a 21 per cent stake in the Spanish bus and coach manufacturer, Hispano Carrocera. In 2007, Tata formed a joint venture with Marcopolo of Brazil and introduced low-floor in the Indian market. In 2008, Tata acquired British Jaguar Land Rover (JLR). In 2010, Tata acquired an 80 per cent stake in Italy-based design and engineering company Trilix. Tata Motors has R&D centres in South Korea, Spain and the UK.

Tata Motors is the flagship of the Tata Group and is India's largest automobile company, with revenues of USD8.5 billion in 2009. Over 5.9 million Tata vehicles are estimated to be on the road in India, and Tata Motors is the largest commercial vehicle manufacturer and second largest passenger car manufacturer in the country. Additionally, the company is the world's fourth largest medium and heavy commercial truck manufacturer and second largest heavy bus manufacturer.

Since 1958 Tata Motors has supplied India's military and paramilitary forces with over 100,000 vehicles and in addition to ongoing domestic sales, currently exports around 450 to 500 military vehicles per year to (primarily) South East Asian and African armed forces.

The most recent light vehicle and truck deliveries to India's military and paramilitary forces have included:
- Tata Sumo (4 × 4) light vehicle of which around 200 examples per year in Ambulance configuration are currently being delivered to the Indian Army. India's state Police operate around 2,500 to 3,000 examples of the 4 × 2 variant; deliveries continue at around 400 to 500 vehicles per year. Full details of the Tata Sumo (4 × 4) light vehicle can be found in the Light vehicles section.
- Tata SFC 407 (4 × 4) 1,000 kg light truck/medium troop carrier of which 8,500 to 9,000 examples have so far been delivered to India's paramilitary forces at around 800 to 900 per year, these split 200-300/600 4 × 4/4 × 2. Full details of the Tata SFC 407 (4 × 4) 1,000 kg light truck can be found in the Light vehicles section.
- Tata LPTA 713 TC (4 × 4) 2,500 kg light truck of which around 23,000 have been supplied since production commenced in 1999. Full details of the Tata LPTA 713 (4 × 4) can be found elsewhere in this section.
- Tata SD 1015 TC (4 × 4) Field Artillery Tractor (FAT) of which around 2,000 were delivered between 1999-2004 to India's Army and paramilitary forces. Full details of the Tata SD 1015 TC (4 × 4) can be found elsewhere in this section.
- Tata SA 1212 TC (4 × 4) troop and load carrier of which over 6,000 were delivered. The Tata LPTA 1413 (4 × 4) 5,000 kg General Service (GS) truck is the replacement within the Tata range for the SA 1212 and is essentially an updated SA 1212 with some driveline revisions and a new forward control-type cab. The LPTA 1413 is currently under evaluation by the India's paramilitary forces. Full details of the Tata SA 1212 TC and Tata LPTA 1413 can be found elsewhere in this section.
- Tata SA 1613 (4 × 2) troop and load carrier. Essentially a civilian vehicle fitted with a military troop carrying/cargo-type body with bench seats, a removable tarpaulin and bows.

An early prototype of the Tata LPTA 1623 (6 × 6) truck (Tata Motors) 1156011

- Tata SA 1615 (4 × 2) Line Of Communication (LOC) logistic truck of which around 600 examples (at 200 per year) have been delivered 2003-2006; deliveries continue.

It was disclosed early in 2009 that BEL had ordered around 70 Tata LPTA 1623 TC trucks and that these trucks would be used to mount Indian Air Force radar.

The official Tata model designation of the LPTA 1623 provides basic data for the type and can be broken down as follows: LP – abbreviation of the German terms for fully forward control; T – Truck; A – All-wheel drive; 16 – GVW tonnes (approx. rounded); 23 – engine power output hp × 10 (approx. rounded).

Specifications
Tata LPTA 1623 TC
(provisional)
Cab seating: 1 + 2
Configuration: 6 × 6
Weight:
(max permissible laden, on-road) 16,300 kg
(max permissible laden, off-road) 13,800 kg
(unladen) 8,800 kg
(payload, on-road) 7,500 kg
(payload, off-road) 5,000 kg
(permissible front axle load, on-road) 4,500 kg
(permissible rear tandem load, on-road) 11,800 kg
(permissible front axle load, off-road) 4,000 kg
(permissible rear tandem load, off-road) 9,800 kg
Length: 8.67 m
Width: (max) 2.44 m
Height:
(laden) 3.05 m
(unladen) 3.7 m
Ground clearance: 390 mm
Track:
(front) 1.965 m
(rear) 2.106 m
Wheelbase: 4.235 m
Angle of approach/departure: 34°/25°
Max speed: 84 km/h
Max range: 750 km
Fuel capacity: 400 litres
Max gradient: 56%
Max sideslope: 50%
Fording: 860 mm
Engine: Tata Cummins 6BT 5.9 5.883-litre 6-cylinder in-line turbocharged and intercooled water-cooled 4-stroke direct injection EURO II emissions compliant diesel developing 235 hp (175 kW) at 2,500 rpm and 800 N.m torque at 1,500 rpm
Gearbox: Tata with 9 forward (8 + crawler) and 1 reverse gears, synchromesh on all forward gears, constant mesh on reverse. PTO (power take off fitted)
Transfer box: 2-speed
Clutch: single dry plate, Ø352 mm
Steering: power-assisted
Turning radius: (kerb) 9.5 m
Suspension: 70 mm × 1.68 m span semi-elliptic leaf springs and hydraulic shock-absorbers, front; 80 mm × 1.29 m span semi-elliptic leaf springs, rear
Tyres: 1400R 20-18 PR
Brakes:
(main) dual-circuit, air, 420 mm drums all-round
(parking) spring-actuated parking brake acting on rear wheels
Electrical system: 12 V
Batteries: 12 V, 180 Ah
Alternator: 65 A

Status
In production; 70 vehicles ordered early 2009.

Contractor
Tata Motors Limited

Israel

M-462 Abir (4 x 4) multipurpose tactical vehicle

Development
The M-462 Abir (4 x 4) multipurpose tactical vehicle was designed and developed using the considerable experience gained by Automotive Industries Limited (AIL) during its involvement with the earlier M-325 Commandcar series of 4 x 4 trucks. The M-325 Commandcar remained in production until 1997 and the type remains in service with a number of countries, particularly those in Central and South America. The M-462 Abir was first introduced in 1987 and is essentially the continuing evolution of the Commandcar.

The all-new Abir II, brief details of which can be found elsewhere in this entry, was disclosed by AIL during 2010.

The M-462 Abir remains available, and between 1987 and 2008 it is understood that over 2,600 examples were produced. Of that figure some 1,400 were supplied to the IDF, with export customers understood to have included Chile, Colombia, and Peru.

Description
The M-462 Abir is essentially the continuing evolution of the earlier M-325 Commandcar, but includes many new features to improve crew comfort, the smoothness of the ride and enhance all-round visibility.

The Abir continues to use primarily US-sourced automotives, but whereas the Commandcar was powered by an inefficient Chrysler 3.687-litre six cylinder petrol engine developing 100 hp, and featured a Chrysler four-speed manual gearbox (and New Process two-speed transfer box), the Abir is powered by a GM 6.5-litre six cylinder diesel developing 170 hp, this coupled to a fully automatic three-speed transmission and two-speed transfer case.

The standard version of the Abir can have a canvas top to the cab and a canvas tilt over the cargo area, this seating up to 12 passengers. The cab doors are also canvas and can be readily removed. Metal doors are available as an option, together with a hardtop cabin cover and air conditioning. Also available as options are various armoured protection kits or complete bodies providing protection against projectiles up to 7.62 mm armour-piercing.

Versions of the Abir include the following: multipurpose cargo and personnel carrier; patrol and reconnaissance vehicle; police duties vehicle; weapon carrier (including mortars); light weapon tractor; communication shelter carrier; ambulance; mine-shielded patrol vehicle; and water or fuel tanker. There are also fire tender versions. The Model W-1000 is a special forest firefighting vehicle. One model of the Abir was modified to carry a 106 mm M40 series recoilless rifle to meet a potential export requirement.

Variants

Abir II
The Abir II was disclosed by AIL during 2010. The Abir II, which features a purpose-designed rear body tray, is based on the commercially available Dodge Ram 4500. It is understood that ultimately a variety of body styles

M-462 Abir (4 x 4) multipurpose tactical vehicles of the Peruvian Army (Cesar Cruz Tantalean)   1391453

M-325 Commandcar of the Peruvian Army. The M-325 Commandcar was the predecessor of the M-462 Abir (Cesar Cruz Tantalean)   1391455

The Dodge RAM-based Abir II was announced by AIL during 2010 (AIL)
1391454

M-462 Abir (4 x 4) multipurpose tactical vehicles (AIL)   1341800

will be available, including armoured. AIL is understood to have received an initial governmental order for the Abir II and is already actively marketing the vehicle in the company's traditional export markets.

The Abir II has a GVW of 5,800 kg, a payload of 1,700 kg and is powered by a Cummins 6.7-litre six cylinder diesel engine developing 305 hp at 2,900 rpm.

Specifications
M-462 Abir
Cab seating: 1 + 2
Configuration: 4 × 4
Weight: (laden) 4,700 kg
Max load: 1,890 kg
Length: 5.25 m
Width: 2.06 m
Height: 2.35 m
Ground clearance: 400 mm
Wheelbase: 3.2 m
Track: 1.715 m
Angle of approach/departure: 52°/30°
Max speed: 110 km/h
Range: 600 km
Fuel capacity: 144 litres
Max gradient: 78%
Side slope: 70%
Vertical obstacle: 450 mm
Fording: 760 mm
Engine: GM 6.5-litre water-cooled 4-stroke diesel developing 170 hp (127 kW) at 3,400 rpm
Transmission: automatic with 3 forward and 1 reverse gears
Transfer box: NP 205 2-speed
Steering: integral power steering
Turning radius: 7.1 m
Suspension:
    (front) semi-elliptic multileaf plus shock-absorbers
    (rear) semi-elliptic multileaf plus shock-absorbers
Tyres: 9.00 × 16
Brakes: dual circuit hydraulic; hydro/booster power; self-aligning drums, rear, discs, front
Electrical system: 24 V
Batteries: 2 × 12 V, 100 Ah
Alternator: 60 A (100 A optional)

Status
Production as required (over 2,400 produced). In service with Chile, Colombia (approximately 300), Israel (>1,400 delivered), Peru (approximately 200) and possibly other undisclosed nations.

Contractor
Automotive Industries Limited (AIL)

Italy

IVECO Cargo range of trucks

Development

IVECO (which stands for Industrial Vehicle Corporation) came into being on 1 January 1975 when a joint company between Italy's Fiat and Germany's Magirus-Deutz (the truck making division of Klockner Humboldt Deutz) was set-up to cooperate on development and manufacturer, the aim being that IVECO would be better able to compete with the then European market leaders Daimler-Benz and Volvo. The collaboration lasted only five years, with KHD pulling out of IVECO to regain its independence as an engine manufacturer. In 1986 IVECO merged with Ford's UK truck division, and four years later acquired Spain's Pegaso (ENASA), which included the acquisition of Seddon Atkinson. In 1992 IVECO acquired International Trucks Australia.

IVECO's extensive range of trucks for military logistic applications is based on the company's range of civilian trucks, militarised to varying degrees to suit specific operator requirements. The current range consists of the EuroCargo medium range of rigid chassis and the Trakker (EuroTrakker prior to a 2004 face-lift) heavy off-road range of tractor trucks and rigid chassis. The earlier EuroTech heavy on-road range of tractor trucks and rigid chassis, and the EuroStar heavy on-road range of tractor trucks have been replaced by the Stralis range.

The EuroTech, EuroStar and Stralis heavy on-road ranges are best described as suited to third-line road-haul logistical support roles and are only available in conventional (4 × 2), (6 × 2) or (6 × 4) drive configurations. For most military logistic applications variants of the heavier duty Trakker/EuroTrakker range are better suited.

Militarised (4 × 4) EuroCargo variants are known to be in service with the Algerian, Croatian, Egyptian, German (ordered mid-2006), Irish, Italian, Macedonian, Saudi Arabian, Slovenian, Tanzanian and UK (RAF and Navy) armed forces.

While not an exhaustive list, recent deliveries of EuroCargo/Cargo trucks are known to have included 86 (4 × 4) vehicles to the Slovenian Army during 2002, and 20 (4 × 4) vehicles delivered to the Irish Army in February 2003. Also in 2003 (January), IVECO announced that it had been selected to meet the logistic vehicle component of the Hungarian MoD's ongoing and then estimated 10,000-vehicle requirement; this has reduced in number substantially. EuroCargo models were to make up an unspecified percentage of the then estimated 5,000 logistic vehicles to be delivered

In July 2006 it was announced that following a competitive tender BwFuhrparkService (a service provider to the German Army) had ordered 320 IVECO Cargo trucks, split approximately 50/50 between model 140E24W (shown) and model 100E21W. Further orders have followed (Patrick Allen)   1183067

IVECO Cargo ML140E18W (4 × 4) with standard drop side cargo/troop body of the Irish Army (Shaun C Connors)   0556039

In July 2006 it was announced that following a competitive tender BwFuhrparkService (a service provider to the German Army) had ordered 320 Cargo trucks, split approximately 50/50 between model 140E24W and model 100E21W (shown). Further orders have followed (IVECO)   1185445

over a 15-year period. Following two years of complex legal wrangling, the part of the tender related to logistic vehicles (by this stage reduced to 1,500 vehicles) was cancelled.

Other recent deliveries of the EuroCargo have included around 100 vehicles (Cargo and Trakker) delivered to Croatia during 2005, and in July 2006 it was announced that following a competitive tender, BwFuhrparkService (a service provider to the German Army) had ordered 320 Cargo trucks, split approximately 50/50 between model 140E24W (5,000 kg payload, 4.15 m WB) and model 100E21W (2,000 kg payload). A further 200 of the same variants were ordered during 2008.

Around 300 vehicles (EuroCargo and Trakker) were delivered to Saudi Arabia during 2006-2007, with a further 500 ordered for late-2007/early-2008. An unspecified quantity of vehicles were delivered to Algeria during 2006-2007, and 126 assorted IVECO vehicles (including EuroCargo) were delivered to Tanzania during 2007, with a similar quantity to follow from a EUR65 million order during 2008.

There is also a level IV armoured bus based on the EuroCargo (4 × 2) driveline, that is the A120E23 Crocodile.

The IVECO EuroCargo range is based on an in-production range of commercial trucks and throughout their production run they are likely to reflect the many minor design changes and specification upgrades associated with civilian truck production. The range was significantly revised during 2003, revisions including a cab and some driveline upgrades.

Within the IVECO truck range, the EuroCargo range of militarised civilian trucks is complemented by the heavier IVECO Trakker range of militarised civilian heavy-duty trucks covering the 19,000 kg to 41,000 kg GVW range, and the purpose-designed IVECO/ASTRA range of high-mobility tactical trucks with payloads ranging from 7,000 to 17,500 kg. The purpose-designed IVECO Multipurpose Medium Vehicle (MMV) range of high-mobility (4 × 4) tactical trucks with payloads ranging from 4,000 to 6,900 kg are also available. Full details of these vehicles can be found elsewhere in this section.

Description

The militarised EuroCargo, the commercial version of which was originally added to the IVECO range in 1991, is the lightest component of IVECO's militarised truck range and its layout and design are entirely conventional. Cabs and driveline components are shared with the EuroCargo civilian range of trucks and are all commercially available and proven. Engine power outputs from the two base turbocharged EURO 4 or 5 emissions compliant diesel engines are 140, 160 and 180 hp for the four-cylinder unit, and 220, 250, 280 and 300 hp for the six-cylinder unit. EURO 3 and EURO 2 emissions compliant engines (EURO 2 with mechanical fuel injection) are available for certain territories. Gearbox options include a ZF six-speed automated unit, an Allison fully automatic unit in certain models, and five-, six- or nine-speed ZF manual gearboxes.

The EuroCargo is available in (4 × 2) or (4 × 4) configuration and with single or dual wheels on the rear axles. Longitudinal and cross-axle differential locks are standard for/between all drive axles and all-wheel drive variants feature full-time all-wheel drive and an IVECO two-speed transfer box. An Anti-lock Braking System (ABS) and either central or external tyre inflation systems are optional. All axles are leaf-sprung, multileaf standard, semi-elliptic optional.

The conventional C-section chassis can be fitted with a variety of bodies which (according to wheelbase and payload capacity) can include drop side (with front or rear-mounted materials handling crane), box-body, tanker, medium recovery hamper. A chassis-mounted self-recovery winch with front and rear pull is optional. Payload ratings are dependant on specification, with GVWs ranging from 6,000 to 16,000 kg.

The two-door forward-control all-steel cab seats three (including driver). Options can include add-on armoured protection from small arms fire in varying levels up to 7.62 mm AP, air-conditioning and a roof-hatch with/without integral machine gun ring-mount.

Specifications

	ML110EW	ML150EW	ML140E18W (Irish Army)
Cab seating:	1 + 1 (1 + 2 optional)	1 + 1 (1 + 2 optional)	1 + 2
Configuration:	4 × 4	4 × 4	4 × 4
Weight:			
(laden, GVW)	11,500-12,000 kg	15,000-15,500 kg	14,000 kg
(unladen, kerb)	5,500-5,900 kg	5,800-6,300 kg	5,620 kg
(body and payload)	n/avail	n/avail	8,380 kg
(GCW)	21,000 kg	26,000 kg	28,000 kg
Length: (chassis-cab)	wheelbase dependant	wheelbase dependant	6.68 m
Width:	2.49 m	2.49 m	2.49 m
Height:	2.972 m	3.014 m	3.06 m
Ground clearance:	351 mm (365/80R 20 tyres)	392 mm (395/85R 20 tyres)	n/avail
Track:	n/avail	n/avail	n/avail
Wheelbase:	3.69, 3.915 or 4.15 m	3.69, 3.915 or 4.15 m	3.915 m
Angle of approach/departure:	wheelbase and wheel/tyre dependant	wheelbase and wheel/tyre dependant	n/avail
Max speed:	>90 km/h	>90 km/h	up to 90 km/h
Max range:	n/avail	n/avail	n/avail
Fuel capacity:	n/avail	n/avail	185 litres
Max gradient:	60%	60%	60%
Side slope:	30%	30%	30%
Fording:	700 mm	700 mm	700 mm
Engine:	IVECO Cursor developing 217 hp (160 kW) or 251 hp (185 kW)	IVECO Cursor developing 251 hp (185 kW) or 279 hp (205 kW)	IVECO TECTOR 5.88-litre EURO 3 emissions compliant 6-cylinder in-line turbocharged water-cooled common rail direct injection diesel developing 183 hp at 2,700 rpm and 570 N.m torque at 1,200-2,100 rpm
Gearbox:	ZF/IVECO 6 S 800 manual with 6 forward and 1 reverse gears	ZF/IVECO 6 S 1000 manual with 6 forward and 1 reverse gears	IVECO 2856 manual with 6 forward and 1 reverse gears
Transfer box:	IVECO TC 850 2-speed	IVECO TC 850 2-speed	IVECO TC700 2-speed, full-time all-wheel drive split 33% front, 67% rear; centre differential lock
Steering:	power-assisted	power-assisted	power-assisted
Turning radius:	wheelbase dependant	wheelbase dependant	8.5 m
Suspension:	multileaf springs with telescopic shock-absorbers and anti-roll bars, front and rear		
Tyres: (options available)	365/80R 20	395/85R 20	14.00R 20
Axles:	beam type	beam type	beam type with differential lock as standard, model 5956 (design rated at 5,000 kg) front; model 451046 (design rated at 9,500 kg), rear
Brakes:			
(main)	dual circuit air, drums all-round. ABS standard	dual circuit air, drums all-round. ABS standard	dual circuit air, drums all-round. Supplementary engine exhaust brake. ABS standard
(parking)	spring-loaded on rear wheels		

	ML110EW	ML150EW	ML140E18W (Irish Army)
Electrical system:	24 V	24 V	24 V
Batteries:	n/avail	n/avail	2 × 110 Ah
Alternator:	n/avail	n/avail	70 A

Status

(4 × 4 variant)

In production. In service (see text for details) with Algeria, Croatia, Egypt, Germany (230 ordered mid-2006; 200 ordered 2008), Ireland (20, 2003), Italy, Macedonia, Saudi Arabia, Slovenia (86, 2002), Tanzania, UK (RAF, 1998) and other undisclosed countries.

Contractor

IVECO SpA

IVECO Trakker/EuroTrakker range of trucks

Description

IVECO's extensive range of trucks for military logistic applications are based on the company's range of civilian trucks, militarised to varying degrees to suit specific operator requirements. The range consists of the EuroCargo) medium range of rigid chassis and the Trakker heavy off-road range of tractor trucks and rigid chassis, the name Trakker having been adopted following a 2004 revision of the EuroTrakker range. The EuroTech heavy on-road range of tractor trucks and rigid chassis and the EuroStar heavy on-road range of tractor trucks have been superseded by models from the Stralis range.

The EuroTech, EuroStar and Stralis heavy on-road ranges are best described as suited to third-line road-haul logistic support roles and are only available in conventional (4 × 2), (6 × 2) or (6 × 4) drive configurations. For most military logistic applications variants of the heavier duty Trakker/EuroTrakker range are better suited.

The Trakker is the heaviest component of IVECO's commercial range and its layout and design are entirely conventional. Cabs and driveline components are shared with the Trakker civilian range of heavy-duty trucks and are all commercially available and proven. Engine power outputs for military versions of the Trakker range from 310 hp from the EURO 5 emissions compliant Cursor-8 engine, up to 500 hp from the EURO 5 emissions compliant Cursor-13 engine. All Cursor engines have been

German Army IVECO Trakker AT-N410T45W (8 × 8) chassis mounting the Kärcher TEP 90 decontamination system and fitted with a Krauss-Maffei Wegmann (KMW) all-steel armoured cab (Shaun C Connors) 1296121

IVECO Trakker AT-N410T45W (8 × 8) chassis fitted with a load handling system and winch displayed at DVD 2008 (Shaun C Connors) 1296122

A Belgian Army MP410E44H (8 × 4) chassis fitted with a TAM load handling system; note the riotous behaviour protection kit (Shaun C Connors)
1185442

German Army IVECO Trakker AT440T44TP (6 × 4) tractor truck, 52 of which were delivered during 2005-2006 (Shaun C Connors)
1185443

Photographed in Kosovo, an IVECO EuroTrakker (8 × 8) fuel tanker of the German Army. This example is fitted with a mine-blast- and 7.62 mm AP-protected cab (Michael Jerchel)
1124741

Danish Army IVECO EuroTrakker MP260E37W (6 × 6) truck fitted with add-on armour in Afghanistan (Patrick Allen)
1209113

Danish Army IVECO EuroTrakker MP410E42W (8 × 8) truck fitted with a Multilift (Hiab) Load Handling System (LHS), 21 of which were delivered from 1999 (Shaun C Connors)
1185439

Swiss Army IVECO EuroTrakker MP260E44W (6 × 6) truck fitted with a Multilift (now Hiab) Load Handling System (LHS) and Container Handling Unit (CHU) shown cross-loading a container between truck and trailer (IVECO DVD)
0121899

provided with variable geometry turbine and injector pumps, to exploit the maximum engine performance. EURO 4 engines became standard in October 2006, however EURO 3 emissions compliant engines remain available, as do EURO 2 engines (with mechanical fuel injection) for certain territories. Higher power output engines are available in some instances to meet specialist requirements. Throughout the Trakker range gearbox options primarily consist of ZF units, from traditional manual gearboxes such as the 16S 151 and 16S 221, through to the ZF EuroTronic family which utilises a conventional gearbox, coupled to an electronic gear auto-selection lever. For maintenance and support purposes, fleet management software can be integrated into the onboard Computerised Diagnostic System (CDS).

Two, three or four-axle chassis are available and in a variety of drive configurations and with single or dual wheels on the rear axles. Longitudinal and cross-axle differential locks are available for/between all drive axles and all-wheel drive variants feature full-time all-wheel drive and an IVECO two-speed transfer box. Automatic Driveline Management (ADM), an Anti-lock Braking System (ABS) and either central or external tyre inflation systems are optional.

GVWs range from a maximum of 19,000 kg on a two-axle chassis to a maximum of 41,000 kg on a four-axle chassis. All axles are leaf-sprung, with air-suspension an option on certain models. Wheelbase options currently range from 3.8 m on a two-axle chassis, to a 5.65 m wheelbase on a four-axle chassis. The conventional C-section chassis is available in two thicknesses, 7.7 and 10 mm, and can be fitted with a variety of bodies which, according to wheelbase and payload capacity, can include drop side (with front or rear-mounted materials handling crane), box-body, tanker, dump, recovery hamper, DROPS/PLS load handling systems. Specialised shelter/container bodies can be fitted and the chassis is designed to be capable of mounting drilling platforms or other specialised engineer equipment. Tractor truck versions are available and full details of those tractor trucks having a GCW in excess of 65,000 kg can be found in the Heavy equipment transporters section.

The standard two-door forward-control all-steel cab is available based around either the civilian day or sleeper cab models. The smaller cab seats up to three (including driver), while the larger cab comes with the option of additional stowage space, a bench seat or up to two bunks. Options can include air-conditioning, a roof-hatch with/without integral machine gun ring-mount and add-on armoured protection.

Model	AT190TWM	AT380TWM	AT410TWM
Cab seating:	1 + 1 (1 + 2 optional); 2 + 2 in armoured cab option		
Configuration:	4 × 4	6 × 6	8 × 8
Weight:			
(laden)	18,000-19,000 kg	26,000-29,000 kg (33,000 kg with twin rear wheels/tyres)	38,000 kg (41,000 kg with twin rear wheels/tyres)
(unladen, with armoured cab - approx)	9,800-10,600 kg	12,900-13,800 kg	15,100-16,200 kg
(unladen - approx)	7,500-8,400 kg	10,200-11,500 kg	12,100-12,700 kg
(GCW)	40,000-44,000 kg	40,000-44,000 kg (50,000 kg with twin rear wheels/tyres)	56,000-70,000 kg
Length:	wheelbase dependent		
Width:	2. 55 m		
Height: (cab roof)	3.15 m (365/85R 20 tyres)		
Ground clearance:	380 mm (365/85R 20 tyres)		
Track:			
(front)	axle, wheel/tyre dependent		
(rear)	axle, wheel/tyre dependent		
Wheelbase:	3.8, 4.2, 4.5, 4.7 m (4.7 m unarmoured cab only)	3.5, 3.82, 4.2, 4.5 + 1.39 m	1.875/2.875 + 3.325-3.775 + 1.4 m
Angle of approach/departure:	wheelbase, wheel/tyre dependent		
Max speed:	>90 km/h		
Max range:	driveline, fuel capacity dependent		
Fuel capacity:	400 litres max	500 litres max	500 litres max
Max gradient:	60%	60%	60%
Side slope:	30%	30%	30%
Fording:	800 mm	800 mm	800 mm
Engine:	up to a EURO 5 compliant; 360 hp (265 kW), 410 (301 kW) or 450 hp (332 kW) at EURO 5	up to a EURO 5 compliant 450 hp (332 kW) or 500 hp (368 kW)	up to a EURO 5 compliant 450 hp (332 kW) or 500 hp (368 kW)
Gearbox:	AT190TWM: ZF 12 AS 1930 TD 16-speed manual or ZF 12 AS 2330 TO EuroTronic 16-speed automated; AT380TWM and AT410TWM: ZF 12 AS 2330 TO EuroTronic 16-speed automated		
Transfer box:	Steyr VG2000/300 2-speed		
Steering:	servo-assisted		
Turning radius:	wheelbase dependent		
Suspension:	semi-elliptic, parabolic leaf springs; optional air on rear axle(s)		
Tyres:	365/85R 20; options		
Brakes:			
(main)	drums, front and rear (ABS)		
(parking)	spring-loaded on rear wheels		
Electrical system:	24 V	24 V	24 V
Batteries:	up to 220 Ah	up to 220 Ah	up to 220 Ah

IVECO offers a small arms fire and mine blast protection kit for the Trakker range cab and announced mid-2006 that is was developing an interchangeable all-steel armoured cab for the Trakker range in conjunction with Germany's Krauss-Maffei Wegmann (KMW). An earlier proposal to offer the Trakker chassis fitted with the Dual Role Cab as currently fitted to the IVECO Multipurpose Medium Vehicle (MMV) has been shelved. Full details of the MMV and Dual Role Cab can be found elsewhere in this section.

Militarised Trakker/EuroTrakker variants are known to be in service (sometimes in unspecified numbers) with Algeria, Argentina, Belgium, Croatia, Denmark, Egypt, Germany, Italy, Malaysia, Oman, Poland, Portugal, Saudi Arabia, Slovenia, Spain, Switzerland, Tanzania, Tunisia and the UK.

Like those of most manufacturers, IVECO's designations are initially somewhat confusing but once understood reveal quite a lot about the vehicle in question. Taking the MP340E44W as an example the first two digits (MP) denote cab type (current cab types are AD, AT and AS); the following three figures (340) are nominal GVW/GCW × 10 (34,000 kg); the E denotes Euro range truck (this is now T in the case of Trakker); the following two figures (44) denote nominal engine power output divided by 10 (440 hp); the W denotes all-wheel drive. Additionally, WT denotes all-wheel drive tractor truck, HT denotes 4 × 2/6 × 4 truck tractor, H denotes 4 × 2/6 × 4/8 × 4; HB denotes 8 × 4 heavy chassis designed for 'B' Betonmischer; concrete mixer; P denotes rear air suspension; FP denotes air suspension on all axles.

The largest single military customer for the Trakker/EuroTrakker range to date are the Swiss Armed Forces who currently operate around 750 Euro range trucks. In 1998, a six-month competitive trials programme between IVECO, MAN and Mercedes-Benz began with each manufacturer supplying three prototype vehicles, two configured as (4 × 4), the other as a 6 × 6. A further six months of trials between IVECO and Mercedes-Benz followed before IVECO were awarded an initial contract for EuroTrakker MP190E35W/P (4 × 4) and MP260E44W (6 × 6) vehicles to be delivered over a two-year period.

The (4 × 4) vehicles have a payload of 9,000 kg, a GVW of 18,000 kg and a driveline consisting of an IVECO Cursor-8 7.79-litre six-cylinder in-line diesel developing 350 hp, coupled to a ZF 12 AS 12-speed EuroTronic

automated gearbox. The (6 × 6) vehicles are fitted with a Multilift (now Hiab) Load Handling System (LHS) and have a payload of 11,000 kg, a GVW of 26,000 kg and a driveline consisting of an IVECO Cursor-13 12.9-litre six-cylinder in-line diesel developing 440 hp, coupled to a ZF 16 AS 16-speed EuroTronic automated gearbox. A GPS navigation system and Automatic Driveline Management (ADM) is standard.

In late 2002, the Swiss government placed a follow-on order for 150 (4 × 4), (6 × 6) and (8 × 8) EuroTrakker range vehicles for delivery during 2003. The (4 × 4) and (6 × 6) chassis are fitted with dual rear wheels and tyres, the (8 × 8) are fitted with larger single wheels and tyres. Trakker deliveries under this award included models MP190E44W (4 × 4), 260E48W (6 × 6), MP440E43T (6 × 4) tractor truck, MP260E44W/P (6 × 6) and MP260E54W (6 × 6).

A third Swiss requirement was announced in January 2006, and a contract was awarded to IVECO during 2007, the contract calling for up to 357 vehicles. Deliveries commenced during 2007, with the bulk of the small number of vehicles ordered under this award delivered 2009-2010.

A further Swiss award to IVECO was announced in December 2010. This award, valued at EURO125 million, calls for up to 925 Trakker vehicles in various configurations.

One other large user of the EuroTrakker range are the Danish Army. Model types in service with the Danish Army include the MP190E37WT (4 × 4) 3; MP380E42W (6 × 6) 10; MP260E37H (6 × 4) 27; MP410E42W (8 × 8) 40, with the majority of the Danish Army vehicles (approaching 350 delivered) being model MP260E37W (6 × 6) (including some tractor trucks (WT)). In addition to cargo bodies with cranes, specific Danish Army variants include fuel tankers and specialised shelter vehicles for DALLADS, the Danish Army's missile air defence system. Tractor trucks (6 × 6) mounting a 7,500 kg capacity materials handling crane between the cab and fifth wheel and (4 × 4) tractor trucks for towing semi-trailers mounting Hammar container sideloaders and are also in service.

The Danish Army also use the IVECO EuroTrakker in the heavy equipment transporter role and full details of these vehicles can be found in the Heavy equipment transporters section.

Over recent years IVECO has supplied a number of EuroTrakker range vehicles to Germany's armed forces, including a wide selection of fuel vehicles. An example here would be the 52 Trakker AT-N440T45T/P (6 × 4) tractor units with 32,000-litre semi-trailers delivered during 2005-2006.

From around 1996 IVECO delivered an initial 86 MP340E42W (8 × 8) 18,000-litre fuel tankers, these powered by an IVECO 8210 engine. 24 of this original delivery were fitted with a benign in appearance 7.62 mm AP and mine blast protected cab developed by KMW. The intention was these kits would be removed after about two years and the cabs refurbished as required; they remain on the vehicles and in service. During 2006, and following the 2002 delivery of a next-generation MP340E44W (8 × 8) non-armoured cab prototype, IVECO delivered a further nine vehicles, these fitted with the updated Cursor-13 engine, EuroTronic 2 automated gearbox and ADM; all are fitted with KMW-supplied armour kits of the type fitted to the initial delivery.

To meet the current needs of the German and other armed forces, KMW and IVECO have jointly developed an all-steel interchangeable armoured cab for the Trakker range. It was disclosed mid-2006 that an order for 72 Trakker (8 × 8) AT-N410T45W chassis fitted with the all-steel interchangeable cab had been placed by the German Army. These vehicles will be equipped to carry the Kärcher TEP 90 decontamination system. A further order for 37 Trakker chassis fitted with the all-steel interchangeable cab and fuel tanker bodies have also been placed. Deliveries under both contract awards commenced in 2008.

The Swiss Army will receive a small number of Trakker chassis fitted with the all-steel interchangeable cab. The British Army has also received a small number of Trakker chassis fitted with the all-steel interchangeable cab, details of which can be found elsewhere in this entry.

In March 2006 deliveries to the Belgian Army of EuroTrakker MP410E44H (8 × 4) chassis were completed. In December 2002 following a competitive tender including bids by DAF, Mercedes-Benz, Renault, Scania and Volvo, IVECO was awarded a contract valued in the region of EUR25 million to supply the Belgian Army with EuroTrakker chassis fitted with a TAM load-handling system; deliveries commenced early 2004. These vehicles are fitted with a EURO 3 IVECO Cursor-13 turbocharged diesel engine developing 440 hp and coupled to an IVECO EuroTronic 2 automated gearbox. IVECO has previously supplied 24 EuroTrakker MP410E37H (8 × 4) chassis to the Belgian Army. These vehicles are fitted with a Multilift TSH230 load handling system and are known as Container Load Trucks (CLTs), having been procured specifically for use with 20 ft ISO containers. The latest vehicles, known as Autonomous Load Carriers (ALCs), are capable of handling all NATO-standard flatracks, including the cross-loading of trailers.

Between 2005-2008 Belgium also received 400 (120, 2005; 120, 2006; 100, 2007; 60, 2008 and 350 applique armour kits supplied by IBD-Deisenroth) M250.45WM 8,000 kg payload (6 × 6) trucks. These were ordered in December 2003. The M250.45WM combines Trakker range driveline components with chassis and cab from the IVECO/ASTRA tactical range. For fleet commonality the Belgian M250.45WM is fitted with the same commercial driveline fitted to the MP410E44H EuroTrakkers ordered during 2003.

In January 2003 IVECO announced that it had been selected to meet the logistic vehicle component of the Hungarian MoD's ongoing and then estimated 10,000-vehicle requirement; this has reduced in number substantially. Trakker models were to make up an unspecified percentage of the then estimated 5,000 logistic vehicles to be delivered over a 15-year period. Following two years of complex legal wrangling the part of the tender related to logistic vehicles (by this stage reduced to 1,500 vehicles) has been cancelled.

Saudi Arabia received around 300 assorted IVECO trucks (including Trakker) during 2006-2007, with a follow-on order for around 500 trucks placed during 2007 for delivery during 2007-2008.

Tanzania placed a EURO65 million contract with IVECO during 2006 for up to 800 assorted IVECO vehicles and spares support. During 2007 126 assorted vehicles were delivered under this contract, with a similar figure expected for 2008. Final deliveries under this award were made during 2009.

The Malaysian Army received two C-130 transportable EuroTrakker (8 × 4) vehicles fitted with a foldable front windscreen and soft-top half-cab, and during 2002 ordered an undisclosed quantity (thought to be around 50 including a contract option) of EuroTrakker MP720E52WT (6 × 6) tractor trucks for the tank transporter role; 28 vehicles were delivered 2003-2004 and these are used with a locally designed and built semi-trailer. Poland also uses the EuroTrakker in a tank/heavy equipment transporter role, as does Algeria and Argentina. Available details of these vehicles can be found in the Heavy equipment transporters section.

One other known user of the EuroTrakker is the British Army which received two (6 × 6) EuroTrakker chassis during 2001. These were for use by the Royal Engineers, have been fitted with EADECO well-drilling equipment, and replaced a small number of earlier Scammell-based designs.

As part of its 16-year Private Finance Iniative (PFI) undertaking for the UK MoD's C-vehicle fleet, ALC placed an order in November 2008 for 206 Trakker (6 × 6) chassis to replace an assortment of engineer vehicles including the Volvo Self-Loading Dump Truck (SLDT), Foden Medium Dump Truck (MDT) and EADECO well-drilling equipment vehicles. The requirement was revised and ultimately called for a total of 182 Trakker range trucks. The bulk of the fleet are tippers (63 Medium Dump Truck/71 Self-Loading Dump Truck), with the remainder split between Truck-Mounted Loader (TML) and small quantities of drilling rigs and flush capping system platforms. Outside of this PFI procurement, IVECO will

also supply the MoD direct with 15 (including a trials vehicle) (8 × 8) Trakker SLDTs fitted with the KMW armoured cab.

Being based on an in-production range of commercial trucks, throughout their production run the IVECO Trakker range of military trucks are likely to reflect the many minor design changes and specification upgrades associated with civilian truck production. A major range revision occurred during 2004, this including the use of a new cab from the Stralis range of trucks.

Within the IVECO truck range the Trakker heavy range of militarised civilian trucks is complemented by the similar IVECO Cargo medium range of trucks with 10,000 to 14,000 kg GVWs and the purpose-designed IVECO/ASTRA range of high-mobility tactical trucks with payloads ranging from 7,000 to 17,500 kg. The purpose-designed IVECO Multipurpose Medium Vehicle (MMV) range of high-mobility (4 × 4) tactical trucks with payloads ranging from 4,000 to 6,900 kg is also available. Full details of these vehicles can be found elsewhere in this section.

Specifications
See table on facing page

Status
In service (see text for details) with Algeria, Argentina, Belgium, Croatia, Denmark, Egypt, Germany, Italy, Malaysia, Oman, Poland, Portugal, Saudi Arabia, Slovenia, Spain, Switzerland, Tanzania, Tunisia, UK and other undisclosed countries.

Contractor
IVECO SpA

IVECO 75-14 WM (4 × 4) 2,500-3,000 kg cargo truck

Development
This IVECO 75-14 WM (4 × 4) 2,500-3,000 kg cargo truck is an improvement of the 75 PM 13 (4 × 4) 2,000 kg truck and 90 PM 16 (4 × 4) 4,000 kg truck, these designated ACL/75 and ACM-80 by the Italian Army. The two vehicles have a high degree of standardisation.

The standard dropside cargo body variant was delivered to the Italian Army, and a small number of similar vehicles were ordered by Somalia.

Description
The chassis of the IVECO 75-14 WM (4 × 4) 2,500-3,000 kg cargo truck consists of longitudinal members to which the cross members are cold-riveted. The cab is all steel and is of the forward control type. It can be tilted forward 55° to allow access to the engine. A circular observation hatch is provided in the roof of the cab on the passenger side. The rear cargo area has drop sides and a drop tailgate and, if required, bows and a tarpaulin cover can be installed.

Optional equipment included a front- or rear-mounted winch with a capacity of 4,000 kg and an air-operated lockable front differential.

Various body options were made available but only the standard dropside cargo body variant was delivered to the Italian Army.

Specifications
75.14 WM
Cab seating: 1 + 1 (up to 12 in rear)
Configuration: 4 × 4
Weight:
(laden) 7,750-8,250 kg
(unladen) 5,250 kg
(max load) 2,500-3,000 kg
(towed load) 4,000 kg
Load area: 3.01 × 2.195 m

IVECO 75.14 (4 × 4) 2,500 kg truck (IVECO) 1391025

Length: 5.178 m
Width: 2.3 m
Height:
   (cab) 2.646 m
   (tarpaulin) 2.96 m
   (load area) 1.4 m
Ground clearance: 445 mm
Track: 1.852 m
Wheelbase: 2.75 m
Angle of approach/departure: 45°/45°
Max speed: >80 km/h
Range: >500 km
Fuel capacity: 155 litres
Max gradient: >60%
Max side slope: 30%
Fording: 700 mm
Engine: Model 8060.05 5.861-litre 6-cylinder water-cooled direct injection 4-stroke diesel developing 139 hp (104 kW) at 3,000 rpm
Gearbox: manual with 5 forward and 1 reverse gears
Clutch: single dry plate
Transfer box: 2-speed
Steering: recirculating ball with hydraulic servo
Turning radius: 6 m
Suspension: leaf springs (dual at rear) with hydraulic telescopic shock-absorbers
Tyres: 12.5 × 20
Brakes:
   (main) air-hydraulic, drums all-round with separate circuits
   (parking) on rear wheels
Electrical system: 24 V
Batteries: 2 × 12 V, 110 Ah
Alternator: 28 V, 30 A

Status
Production complete. In service with the Italian Army. Also supplied to Somalia.

Contractor
IVECO SpA.

IVECO 90.17 WM (4 × 4) 4,000 kg cargo truck

Development
The IVECO 90.17 WM (4 × 4) 4,000 kg truck is an improvement of the earlier, and similar, 90 PM 16 (4 × 4) 4,000 kg truck and the 75 PM 13 and 75 PM 14 families.

Production concluded during 2002, with Pakistan taking delivery of the last vehicles produced.

Description
The chassis of the IVECO 90.17 WM (4 × 4) 4,000 kg truck consists of longitudinal members to which the cross members are cold-riveted. The forward control cab is all steel and can be tilted forwards to an angle of 55° to allow access to the engine. There is a circular observation hatch in the roof of the cab on the right side. The rear cargo area has drop sides and a drop tailgate and if required bows and a tarpaulin cover can be installed.

Optional equipment included a front- or rear-mounted winch with a capacity of 4,000 kg, an air-operated lockable front differential and 14.5 R 20 tyres.

Variants produced include a light recovery vehicle (full details of which can be found in the Recovery vehicles section), tanker, mobile workshop, light artillery tractor and a firefighting vehicle.

IVECO 90.17 WM (4 × 4) 4,000 kg cargo truck of the Portuguese Army
(Victor Barreira)   1391248

Italian Army IVECO 90.17 WM (4 × 4) 4,000 kg cargo truck (R Stickland)
0126597

Specifications
90.17 WM
Cab seating: 1 + 1 (up to 18 in rear)
Configuration: 4 × 4
Weight:
   (laden) 9,740 kg
   (unladen) 5,740 kg
   (max load, off-road) 4,000 kg
   (towed load, off-road) 4,000 kg
Load area: 4.365 × 2.3 m
Length: 6.358 m
Width: 2.3 m
Height:
   (cab) 2.68 m
   (tarpaulin) 3.18 m
   (load area) 1.4 m
Ground clearance: 476 mm
Track: 1.852 m
Wheelbase: 3.7 m
Angle of approach/departure: 45°/35°
Max speed: >80 km/h
Range: >500 km
Fuel capacity: 155 litres
Max gradient: >60%
Side slope: >30%
Fording: 700 mm
Engine: Model 8060.25 5.861-litre 6-cylinder supercharged water-cooled direct injection 4-stroke diesel developing 170 hp (125 kW) at 3,000 rpm
Gearbox: manual with 5 forward and 1 reverse gears
Clutch: single dry plate
Transfer box: 2-speed
Steering: recirculating ball with hydraulic servo
Turning radius: 7.5 m
Suspension: leaf springs (dual at rear) with hydraulic telescopic shock-absorbers
Tyres: 14.5R 20
Brakes:
   (main) air-hydraulic on all wheels with separate circuits, drums all-round
   (parking) on rear wheels
Electrical system: 24 V
Batteries: 2 × 12 V, 110 Ah

Status
Production concluded during 2002. In service with Italy, Pakistan, Portugal, Singapore (approximately 3,000 delivered, including 90.16), Somalia (100 delivered) and other undisclosed countries.

Contractor
IVECO SpA

IVECO M135E24WM (4 × 4) Multipurpose Medium Vehicle (MMV)

Development
The first example of the IVECO Multipurpose Medium Vehicle (MMV) was shown publicly during mid-2000. The Multipurpose Medium Vehicle range was designed by IVECO with input from the Italian Army, the intention being to produce a highly adaptable, high-mobility, medium-weight truck, specifically designed to meet current and perceived operational scenarios. The resultant design has high tactical and strategic mobility, is air-transportable by C-130 aircraft without preparation, but continues to benefit from the use of commercially proven components. The current M135E24WM model is available in three possible wheelbase lengths

IVECO M135E24WM	3.7 m wheelbase	4 m wheelbase	4.6 m wheelbase
Cab seating:	1 + 2	1 + 2	1 + 2
Configuration:	4 × 4	4 × 4	4 × 4
Weight:			
(laden, GVW)	13,500 kg	13,500 kg	13,500 kg
(unladen, kerb)	5,880 kg	5,900 kg	6,000 kg
(payload, on chassis-cab, kerb)	7,620 kg	7,600 kg	7,500 kg
(towed load)	6,000 kg (or a vehicle of the same class over short distances)		
Load area:	3.5 × 2.3 m	4.3 × 2.3 m	5.2 × 2.3 m
Length:	6.056 m	6.472 m	7.305 m
Width:	2.5 m	2.5 m	2.5 m
Height: (cab roof)	2.69 m	2.69 m	2.69 m
Ground clearance: (under belly)	500 mm	500 mm	500 mm
Wheelbase:	3.7 m	4 m	4 6 m
Angle of approach/departure:	46°/45°	46°/38°	46°/32°
Max speed:	>90km/h	>90 km/h	>90 km/h
Range:	>800 km	>800 km	>800 km
Gradient:	>60%	>60%	>60%
Side slope:	>30%	>30%	>30%
Vertical step:	500 mm	500 mm	500 mm
Fording: (with/without preparation)	850 mm/1.2 m	850 mm/1.2 m	850 mm/1.2 m
Engine:	IVECO NEF 5.9-litre 6-cylinder inline turbocharged and intercooled, water-cooled 4-stroke common rail direct-injection diesel developing 240 hp (179 kW) at 2,700 rpm and 812 N.m torque at 1,250 rpm		
Gearbox:	IVECO manual with 6 forward and 1 reverse gears, or Allison MD 3060 automatic with 5 forward and 1 reverse gears		
Transfer box:	IVECO TC 850 with full-time four-wheel drive and lockable longitudinal differential		
Clutch:	single dry plate, 380 mm diameter		
Steering:	hydraulic power-assisted, recirculating ball type		
Turning radius:	7.57 m	8.1 m	9.14 m
Suspension:	semi-elliptic leaf springs (single flexibility), anti-deflection rubber pads and double-effect telescopic hydraulic shock-absorbers (front), semi-elliptic leaf springs (double flexibility) with auxiliary springs and end-stroke rubber pads (rear)		
Tyres:	365/85R 20	365/85R 20	365/85R 20
Brakes:			
(main)	air over hydraulic, independent split circuits, discs (front), drums (rear), supplemented by an engine exhaust brake		
(parking)	mechanical, operating on rear wheels		
Electrical system:	24 V	24 V	24 V
Batteries:	2 × 125 Ah	2 × 125 Ah	2 × 125 Ah
Alternator:	90 A	90 A	90 A

although provisional specifications for essentially similar variants fitted with lower (210 hp) and higher (270 hp) power output versions of the common IVECO EURO 3 emissions compliant diesel engine have been made available. A EURO 4 engine became available in October 2006, this followed by a EURO 5 engine if required.

The MMV is fitted as standard with the IVECO Dual Role Cab. This cab was developed in conjunction with Deisenroth GmbH of Germany and was designed from the outset to allow unrestricted air-transportability by C-130 aircraft, while providing variable levels of crew protection by the modular use of exchangeable amour panels that locate inside the cab structure, with little or no alteration to the vehicle's profile.

The armouring concept employed for the Dual Role Cab is also employed on the IVECO Light Multirole Vehicle (LMV). Full details of the IVECO LMV can be found in the Light Vehicles section.

Prototype IVECO M135E24WM (4 × 4) Multipurpose Medium Vehicle (MMV) as displayed at DVD 2005 (Patrick Allen)   1146171

Description

The IVECO M135E24WM (4 × 4) Multipurpose Medium Vehicle (MMV) is of conventional design, although dimensions such as ground clearance ensure the vehicle has a high level of tactical mobility, a fact further augmented by the high power to weight ratios involved. The design is based on a conventional C-section ladder-type chassis, reinforced and fitted with tubular cross-members. At present 3.7, 4 or 4.6 m chassis length options are available. Recovery and/or towing points are fitted front and rear, and a front-mounted 5,000 kg capacity self-recovery winch is an option.

Vehicles so far displayed have been fitted with a standard general service type drop side body with tarpaulin cover and bows, the loadbed area measuring (wheelbase dependant) 3.5, 4.3 or 5.2 × 2.3 m (L × W). Doubtless the base chassis is capable of accepting a variety of other bodies including fuel/water tankers and assorted box or shelter-type bodies suitable for command, control, or communication roles, or less technical designs for use as workshop or engineering facilities.

The small quantity of vehicles delivered to date are powered by a EURO 3 emissions compliant IVECO NEF 5.9-litre six-cylinder turbocharged diesel developing 240 hp, giving the fully laden vehicle a power-to-weight ratio of 17.7 hp/ton. Maximum road speed is >90 km/h, minimum speed is approximately 4.5 km/h and at two thirds of maximum speed road range is >800 km. A single 200-litre capacity fuel tank is located on the chassis RH-side. With an auxiliary heater fitted the climatic operational range meets STANAG 2895, C1 to A1 (−32°C to +49°C).

A six-speed IVECO all-synchromesh gearbox coupled to an IVECO TC850 two-speed transfer box with lockable centre differential, giving a total of 12 forward and two reverse gears, is standard. An Allison MD 3060 five-speed automatic gearbox coupled to the same transfer box is an option.

Four-wheel drive is full-time, with both IVECO hub-reduction portal-type axles being fitted with sensors for off-road ABS. They are also fitted for but not with an optional Central Tyre Inflation (CTI) system. A driver-actuated differential lock is standard in the rear axle, optional in the front axle. The front steer-drive axle is rated at 6,500 kg and is sprung by the combination of semi-elliptic leaf springs (single flexibility), anti-deflection rubber pads and double-effect telescopic hydraulic shock-absorbers. The rear drive axle is rated at 8,000 kg and is sprung by the combination of semi-elliptic leaf springs (double flexibility) with auxiliary springs and end-stroke rubber pads. Parabolic springs are available as an option.

The front axle is fitted with 405 mm disc brakes with twin 60 mm callipers, the rear axle is fitted with 410 × 130 mm drum brakes. The service braking system is supplemented by an engine exhaust brake.

Steering is power-assisted. Standard fit tyres are 365/85R 20 Michelin XZL pattern, although options include 1400R 20 and 395/85R 20 tyres. Runflat tyres (to Finabel 20A5) are a further option. A single spare wheel/tyre is carried, mounted between the cab and rear body.

The MMV is fitted with the IVECO Dual Role Cab, so called because a vehicle fitted with it can fulfil both a conventional unprotected role during training and low-risk operations, and a protected role, with variable levels of protection on the same basic structure, for higher-risk, higher-intensity operations. The Dual Role cab was developed in conjunction with IBD-Deisenroth GmbH of Germany.

Unlike more conventional protection solutions that opt for either substituting the original cab with an armoured replacement, or the use of appliqué panels mounted on the original cab shell, the Dual Role cab adopts a 'skin' concept.

Ballistic protection is afforded by the combination of a demountable armoured glass windscreen and drop-in armour packs that are inserted between the inner and outer-skin of the cab, or in the case of doors, replacement units. This system allows the operator to change protection levels to suit the threat environment, and with the added benefit of minimal alterations to the vehicle's inherent benign profile. This approach not only allows flexibility in the protection system used, but allows upgrades in armour technology to be readily incorporated.

At present three levels of protection are available, offering protection from 7.62 mm NATO ball at 30 m and 155 mm burst at approximately 100 m, to protection from 7.62 mm AP at 30 m and 155 mm burst at approximately 60 m. In addition to ballistic protection, countermine protection can also provided through the use of a Kevlar 'carpet'. This will provide protection up to STANAG 4569 Annex B Level 1 against hand grenades, unexploded artillery bomblets and other small anti-personnel explosive devices anywhere under the vehicle.

In addition to protection provided by the armour arrays previously described, other measures to ensure crew survivability have been included in the cab design from the outset. These include the provision of suspended (not floor-mounted) seats fitted with a five-point harness, the elimination of loose stowage in the cab and the use of crashworthy materials in the construction of the cab.

Despite the measures taken to enhance crew survivability, the MMV cab was designed to show little evidence of these in its configuration. The basic cab is a two-door forward control design with structural components made entirely of steel. The cab tilts forward for engine maintenance and full access to the engine is maintained at all levels of armour protection. The driver's seat is fully adjustable, the two in-line passenger seats are fixed and the central passenger seat has a foldable backrest to give access to the roof hatch and the optional weapon ring that can mount a light (up to 7.62 mm) machine gun. Left- or right-hand drive, and air-conditioning are options.

Specifications
See table on page 531

Status
Production as required. A small quantity (<10) ordered by the Italian Air Force early 2005.

Contractor
IVECO SpA

IVECO (Fiat) 6605 (6 × 6) series

Development
In the 1960s, IVECO (as Fiat) built a light artillery tractor (6 × 6) called the Model 6606 (TL65) and a medium artillery tractor (6 × 6) called the Model 6605 (TM65). The TM65 (TM standing for *Trattore Medio*) was powered by a petrol engine; further development resulted in the diesel-engined TM69 which was adopted by the Italian Army. The base model of the range is the 6605 TM and this was used for towing artillery such as the 155 mm FH-70.

Vehicles supplied to the Italian Army were withdrawn from service from around 2004 and replaced by an ASTRA tactical range truck. The exact status of vehicles supplied to Iraq, Libya and Somalia is unknown.

Model	6605 TM	6605 FH	6605 A
Cab seating:	1 + 11	1 + 11	1 + 1
Configuration:	6 × 6	6 × 6	6 × 6
Weight:			
(unladen)	11,800 kg	12,600 kg	12,000 kg
(laden)	17,000 kg	19,220 kg	20,500 kg
(max load)	5,000 kg	6,620 kg	8,500 kg
(towed load)	15,000 kg	15,000 kg	15,000 kg
Length:	7.33 m	7.33 m	7.33 m
Width:	2.5 m	2.5 m	2.5 m
Height:			
(cab)	2.92 m	2.92 m	2.78 m
(tarpaulin)	2.87 m	2.78 m	3.08 m
(load area)	1.533 m	1.533 m	1.522 m
Ground clearance:	363 mm	363 mm	363 mm
Track:	2.072 m	2.072 m	2.072 m
Wheelbase:	3.217 m + 1.365 m	3.217 m + 1.365 m	3.217 m + 1.365 m
Angle of approach/departure:	45°/40°	45°/40°	45°/40°
Max speed: (road)	80 km/h	80 km/h	80 km/h
Range:	700 km	700 km	700 km
Fuel capacity:	360 litres	360 litres	360 litres
Max gradient:	60%	60%	60%
Max side slope:	20%	20%	20%
Fording:	1.5 m	1.5 m	1.5 m
Engine:	Model 8212.02.500 6-cylinder in-line water-cooled 4-stroke diesel developing 260 hp (194 kW) at 2,200 rpm		
Gearbox:	manual with 8 forward and 2 reverse gears		
Clutch:	twin dry plate	twin dry plate	twin dry plate
Transfer box:	2-speed	2-speed	2-speed
Steering:	ZF hydraulic, assisted	ZF hydraulic, assisted	ZF hydraulic, assisted
Turning radius:	8 m	8 m	8 m
Suspension:			
(front)	2 semi-elliptic constant rate leaf springs with double acting hydraulic shock-absorbers		
(rear)	rocker and torque arms with 2 constant-rate leaf springs		
Tyres:	14.00 × 20	14.00 × 20	14.00 × 20
Brakes:			
(main)	dual circuit, air, drums all-round		
(parking)	drum, hand operated, mounted on transfer rear output shaft		
Electrical system:	24 V	24 V	24 V
Batteries:	4 × 12 V, 90 Ah	4 × 12 V, 90 Ah	4 × 12 V, 90 Ah

Description

The chassis is of the ladder type with two longitudinal pressed steel channels, to which are riveted the cross members, brackets and spring supports. The forward control cab is all steel and has a removable canvas top and side screens and a windscreen which can be folded flat against the bonnet. A cab heater and ventilator are standard on all versions. The space to the rear of the cab and body, houses the spare wheel, two water and two fuel containers, tyre chain locker and the exhaust pipe.

The rear cargo area is all steel with a wood-lined floor. The sides consist of two boards, the front a drop type and the rear fixed. The drop tailgate is fitted with integral steps and is removable. The rear cargo area is covered by removable bows and a tarpaulin cover. When not required the bows can be stowed under the central area of the body. The cargo space is divided into three compartments by removable partitions: the first is used for stowing the charges, the second for the projectiles and the rear for stores and the tarpaulin cover.

The transmission consists of a set of gears mounted on four shafts (input, primary, layshaft and reverse). Shifting from each gear is controlled by a lever through a pneumatic servo. Shifting from the high to the low range, or vice versa, is by an electropneumatic control with a preselector switch, interlocked with the clutch pedal. The transfer box is mechanical and consists of helical constant mesh gears mounted on three shafts (input, intermediate and output) of which the input shaft carries the dog clutch with a lockable divider differential distributing power to front and rear axles.

Mounted at the rear of the vehicle is a worm type winch with a capacity of 10,000 kg which can be used to the front or rear of the truck and has 60 m of 18 mm diameter cable.

The 6605FH is almost identical to the 6605 TM but has a shorter rear cargo area as a hydraulic crane is mounted between the cab and the cargo area for unloading pallets of ammunition. The prototype was completed in 1974 with first production vehicles completed in 1976.

The model 6605A is the truck version and has a two-man cab with the cargo area at the rear with tiltable troop seats down each side, drop tailgate with integral steps, removable bows and a tarpaulin cover. The prototype was completed in 1974 and first production vehicles in 1976.

A recovery version, the 6605 AG, was also produced and full details can be found in the Recovery Vehicles section.

Specifications

See table on facing page

Status

Withdrawn from Italian Army service, replaced by an artillery tractor variant of the IVECO tactical range of trucks. Also supplied to Iraq (200 supplied 1984/85, status uncertain), Libya and Somalia. Somalia received 10 6605 TM, 200 6605 A, 12 10,500-litre fuel tankers, 10 recovery vehicles, four command posts, five aircraft refuellers and 50 8,000-litre water tankers.

Contractor

IVECO SpA

IVECO 230.35 WM (6 × 6) 10,000 kg artillery truck/tractor

Development

The IVECO 230.35 WM (6 × 6) 10,000 kg artillery truck/tractor is an updated version of the former 230 PM 35.

In addition to Italy's armed forces, the only other known customer for this model was Abu Dhabi which took an initial 70 vehicles during 1987/88, with a further 43 delivered during 1992.

Description

The IVECO 230.35 WM (6 × 6) 10,000 kg artillery truck/tractor has a forward control cab for the driver and two passengers. The cab has a canvas roof that can be easily removed and can tilt forward for engine and transmission access. The cargo area is covered with a tarpaulin resting on bows. The tailgate and side boards are all tiltable and removable and there are folding benches for 22 personnel. A spare wheel holder is located between the cab and the cargo body.

IVECO 230.35 WM (6 × 6) 10,000 kg artillery truck/tractor (IVECO)   0512237

Options included a 10,000 kg hydraulic winch, sand tyres, hardtop cab with observation hatch, power take-off on the gearbox, brake couplings for towing, spare wheel holder with a tyre-handling crane, towing hook, 900 kg material-handling crane and a jib for handling artillery trail legs.

The IVECO 230.35 WM could be produced in an artillery tractor version with the cargo body divided into two sections. One section is used to carry a gun crew of 10 personnel, while the other section is used to carry ammunition and other supplies up to a weight of 8,500 kg. The crew compartment can be made removable if required. The tractor could tow artillery pieces of up to 15,000 kg.

Other variants of this vehicle include a recovery vehicle (full details of which can be found in the Recovery vehicles section), tanker, mobile workshop, mobile hospital, logistics vehicle carrying a pallet-loading system and a missile system carrier.

Specifications

Cab seating: 1 + 2 (up to 22 in rear)
Configuration: 6 × 6
Weight:
  (GVW) 23,000 kg
  (kerb) 13,000 kg
  (max load) 10,000 kg
  (towed load) 15,000 kg
Load area: 5.05 × 2.35 m
Length: 7.762 m
Width: 2.5 m
Height:
  (cab) 3.05 m
  (tarpaulin) 3.43 m
  (load area) 1.58 m
Ground clearance: 360 mm
Track:
  (front) 2.027 m
  (rear) 2.032 m
Wheelbase: 3.3 m + 1.38 m
Angle of approach/departure: 42°/40°
Max speed: > 80 km/h
Range: > 600 km
Fuel capacity: 300 litres
Max gradient: 60%
Side slope: 30%
Fording: 1.2 m
Engine: 8280.02 17.174 litre V-8 water-cooled 4-stroke diesel developing 352 hp (259 kW) at 2,400 rpm
Gearbox: ZF 4 S 150 GPA with 8 forward and 1 reverse gears
Transmission: torque converter
Transfer box: electro-pneumatically lockable
Steering: recirculating ball, power-assisted
Turning radius: 9.5 m
Suspension:
  (front) single flexibility leaf springs with hydraulic shock-absorbers
  (rear) single flexibility leaf springs, reversed, fully articulated
Tyres: 14.00 × 20
Brakes: air operated, drums all-round
Electrical system: 24 V
Batteries: 2 × 12 V, 143 Ah
Generator: 650 W

Status

Production complete. In service with Abu Dhabi (113 delivered in 2 batches).

Contractor

IVECO SpA.

IVECO (ASTRA) tactical truck range

Development

IVECO's Defence Vehicles (IVECO DV) produces a wide range of vehicles, with vehicles on offer with GVWs of around 3,500 kg for the lightest (4 × 4), through to a GCW of 130,000 kg for the heaviest tank transporter.

The lightest vehicle in the IVECO range is the Land Rover-like M30E18WM Light Utility Vehicle (LUV) which has a GVW of 3,050 kg. The LUV was officially introduced into the IVECO range during 2008. IVECO also offers the Fiat Daily-based M40.13WM (4 × 4) light vehicle. Originally designated as 40.10, then 40.12, then 40.13 and now 40.15 with the still current EURO 3 engine , this vehicle was designed to fill a gap between jeep-type vehicles and light trucks. Payload for the 40.15, is up to 2,200 kg for models with uprated suspension. Full details of the M30E18WM and 40.10 range can be found in the Light vehicles section.

For payloads of 4,000 kg or above, IVECO offers militarised versions of its commercial truck ranges. For all-wheel drive variants these are based on either the EuroCargo medium range of rigid chassis or Trakker (previously known as EuroTrakker) heavy off-road (off-road in the commercial construction/quarry environment sense) range of tractor trucks and rigid chassis. For most military logistic applications variants of the heavier duty Trakker range, militarised as required, are best suited. For less demanding roles, militarised versions of the lighter two- and three-axle EuroCargo range are available.

A logistic family SMH88.45 (8 × 4) fitted with a Multilift Mark 4 (now known as the MPH165) Load Handling System (LHS) license-produced in Italy by ISOLI SpA (Shaun C Connors) 1047598

This specialised gun tractor variant of the tactical family M250.40WM (SM 66.40) has replaced the aged IVECO 6605TM with Italian Army FH70 155 mm towed artillery batteries. The six-seat gun crew compartment is fitted with air-sprung seats and air-conditioning. Bunks for three are carried under the cargo body which carries four 1,385 kg ammunition pallets handled by a 10-tonne/m crane (Shaun C Connors) 1047600

All tactical family M320.42/45WMs supplied to the Irish (excluding the one recovery vehicle), Italian and Spanish armies have been fitted with a Multilift Load Handling System (LHS). Italian and Spanish vehicles are fitted with the Mark 4 system (now known as the MPH165) license-produced in Italy by ISOLI SpA. Irish Army vehicles are fitted with Multilift-produced systems, four with Mark 4 and 18 with the C-130-transportable Mark 5 (now known as the MPH165A) system (Shaun C Connors) 1047601

Just off the production line, this tactical family M170.31WM (SM 44.31) has yet to receive its Italian Army camouflage finish (Shaun C Connors) 1047599

A logistic family SMH66.45 fitted with a standard dropside cargo body. Because of their high payload ratings many logistic range chassis supplied to the Italian Army have been fitted with dump or other construction-related bodies (Shaun C Connors) 1047597

A logistic family SMH66.45 fitted with a concrete pump-mixer. Because of their high payload ratings many logistic range chassis supplied to the Italian Army have been fitted with construction-related bodies (IVECO) 1128297

Militarised commercial designs suit the operating needs of many armed forces and can be suited to a wide variety of military and/or peacekeeping/enforcing type roles, depending on a number of factors including the base chassis in use and degree of militarisation. For certain applications, a purpose-designed tactical truck is better suited and in order to meet such requirements, IVECO offers a full range of tactical vehicles. These are designed for purpose and while utilising commercially available driveline components, they offer far higher levels of strategic and tactical mobility than any other commercially based design.

The IVECO tactical range of trucks are produced by ASTRA Veicoli Industriali SpA. Astra was formed in 1946 in Cagliari as a refurbisher of military vehicles and the name ASTRA is taken from Azienda Sarda TRasformazione Autoveicoli. In 1951 the company transferred its headquarters to its current 135,200 m² site (43,500 m² of which is covered) in Piacenza. In 1986 IVECO bought the company. ASTRA military truck production is branded IVECO for export applications while the ASTRA name is retained for the domestic market only as this is a leading brand in Italy. For the Spanish market, ASTRA-produced military trucks are branded IVECO-Pegaso. For the purpose of clarity and continuity the brand name IVECO and IVECO designations will be used throughout this entry.

However, where appropriate, any ASTRA designations will also be provided.

The IVECO tactical range can be split in to two families, these being referred to by the company as the tactical family and the logistic family. Deliveries of the tactical family commenced during 1996; deliveries of the logistic family commenced during 2003. The differences between these two families of trucks are outlined elsewhere in this entry.

A number of export sales of tactical range trucks have been made, however the Italian Army remain the main user of the type. Current available figures show that between 1996 and mid-2005, Italian Armed Forces received around 800 tactical family models, and between 2003 and mid-2005, around 275 logistic family were delivered. Production and delivery of all models continues at around 150 vehicles per year.

Tactical range export customers include Denmark, Ireland, Spain and the UK, with Spain being by far the largest customer. Denmark procured five M320.42WM tactical family chassis fitted with a specialist crane (30-tonnes at 3.8 m). Full details of the M 320.42 mobile crane variant can be found in the Recovery vehicles section. Ireland procured 23 M320.42WM chassis - 22 fitted with a hooklift-type load handling system and one fitted with EKA recovery equipment. The Irish LHS vehicles are fitted with

Two roof options are available for IVECO's tactical cab. The standard roof is shown on a logistic family vehicle, the lower roof for C-130 transportability is shown on a tactical family vehicle (Shaun C Connors)
1047603

In December 2003 the Belgian MoD awarded IVECO a contract for 400 (plus an option of 379) 8,000 kg payload tactical range (6 × 6) trucks complete with 350 appliqué armour kits developed in conjunction with IBD Deisenroth of Germany. These trucks combine components from the tactical and logistic families (Shaun C Connors)
1156101

systems supplied by Multilift. The first four vehicles delivered (1998) are fitted with the Mark 4 system (now designated MPH165: MPH - Military Pivoting Hooklift; 165 - 16,500 kg handling capacity), as fitted to the British Army DROPS fleet. All subsequent vehicles (1999 - 2000) are fitted with a modified version of the Mark 4 system on which the hookarm folds for C-130 air-transport. Full details of Multilift load handling systems can be found in the Materials handling equipment section. The British Army received three M150.30WM tactical family chassis fitted with specialist well-drilling equipment. Spain has received approximately 1,000 tactical range trucks since 2003. At least 50 of these are an M320.42/M320.45 chassis fitted with LHS, however, the bulk of deliveries are M250.37WM/M250.40WM chassis fitted with a variety of bodies including cargo, dump, water and fuel tankers, recovery and LHS. Around 100 vehicles were delivered to Spain during 2007, fitted for but not with an applique protection kit similar in configuration and specification to ASTRA-cabbed vehicles delivered to the Belgian Army (further details of this can be found elsewhere in this entry), with around 100 additional vehicles (20 fitted for but not with) ordered during 2008. Deliveries continue including around 20 'fitted for but not with' during 2009 and 2010.

As a builder of specialist trucks in relatively small numbers, ASTRA can meet the individual requirements of individual customers with relative ease, without the unacceptable levels of disruption which such requirements would create on lines of mass-production of commercial trucks. This enables IVECO DV to tailor the tactical range, to meet a wide range of requirements, examples of this flexibility being the Italian Army's latest tank and light equipment transporters, and the model M250.45WM involved in a recent contract placed by Belgium. Details of the M1100.50WTM and ASTRA SMH66.45 can be found in the Heavy equipment transporters section.

In December 2003 the Belgian MoD awarded IVECO a contract for 400 (plus an option of 379) 8,000 kg payload tactical range (6 × 6) trucks complete with 350 appliqué armour kits developed in conjunction with IBD Deisenroth of Germany. These trucks combine components from the tactical and logistic families. The standard IVECO export designation for a tactical range 25-tonne GVW/450 hp chassis (M250.45WM) is applied. For fleet commonality, the Belgian M250.45WM is fitted with the same commercial driveline fitted to the 150 LHS-equipped (8 × 4) MP410E44H EuroTrakkers ordered by the Belgian Army during 2003. Deliveries of these were completed during 2006. This consists of a Cursor 13 engine rated at 450 hp coupled to IVECO's EuroTronic automatic gearbox. Deliveries to the Belgian Army of the M250.45WM began during 2005 (120) and continued until 2008 (120, 2006; 120, 2007; 40, 2008). The contract option involves flatbed variants only, not GS (General Service) variants, and does not include additional ballistic protection kits.

In addition to the tactical truck range, IVECO also produces (at its Bolzano facility) the HMMWV-like M65E19WM Light Multirole Vehicle (LMV) and the Multipurpose Medium Vehicle (MMV) range of high-mobility (4 × 4) tactical trucks. Full details of both the LMV can be found in the Light vehicles section, full details of the MMV can be found elsewhere in this section.

IVECO is part of the Fiat Group. IVECO came into being following the partnering of Fiat's truck-building activities with Germany's Magirus-Deutz, the truck manufacturing division of KHD (*Klockner Humboldt Deutz*). In the early 1970s, Fiat had a virtual monopoly in its home market, commanding around 80 per cent of truck sales. It had absorbed most of the major Italian truck manufacturers over the years (including OM and Lancia), and owned Unic of France, but needed to increase its share of the world market if it were to survive. Hence, the January 1975 merger with KHD. IVECO stands for Industrial VEhicle COrporation.

After five years KHD pulled out of IVECO, but IVECO retained the Magirus name. By the mid-1980s, the IVECO brand name had replaced all others.

IVECO M320.42 WM (8 × 8) 15,000 kg tactical family truck of the Irish Army fitted with a Multilift Mark 4 (now known as the MPH165) Load Handling System (LHS) (Keith Bendell)
0109507

In 1986, IVECO and Ford's UK truck division merged to form IVECO Ford Truck Ltd, and four years later IVECO added Spain's Pegaso (ENASA) to its ranks. This acquisition saw IVECO becoming parent to Seddon Atkinson of the UK which became part of the ENASA in 1983 when International Harvester sold off its European truck interests. Seddon Atkinson-badged trucks are now built in Spain.

In 1992 IVECO acquired International Trucks Australia Ltd.

Description

In keeping with most manufacturers, IVECO has a model designation system, a basic knowledge of which will greatly assist understanding of product ranges. There are exceptions, but in general the tactical range designations follow the following pattern: taking model M320.45WM as an example: M - Military (used for export only); 320 - GVW in tonnes (320 - 32-tonnes; 45 - engine power output (45 - 450 hp); W - all-wheel drive; M - multipurpose. This designation is then completed by either tactical or logistic, depending on family. When branded ASTRA designations are different, the same truck for the domestic market would be the ASTRA SM88.45. The tactical family are Standard Military (SM); 88 - drive type (88 - 8 × 8); 45 - engine power output (45 - 450 hp). Three additional letters can follow which define (in order) wheelbase, gearbox type and brake type. The logistic range are known as Standard Military Heavy (SMH).

Tactical family models commenced delivery to the Italian Army during 1996. The tactical family consists of three main models, original deliveries of which were fitted with EURO 2 emissions compliant diesel engines. From early 2003 more powerful EURO 3 emissions compliant engines have been fitted, resulting in family-wide designation changes. From late 2008 EURO 5 emissions compliant engines have been fitted (with some designation changes) and deliveries of these are currently running alongside EURO 3 deliveries. EURO 4 engines became available in October 2006 (without designation changes) but were not fitted to production vehicles.

The (4 × 4) chassis of this range was originally designated M150.30WM when fitted with a EURO 2 engine. The EURO 3 engine option version (which remains available) is designated M170.31WM. The latest EURO 5 version is designated M170.33WM.

The (6 × 6) chassis of this range was originally designated M250.37WM when fitted with a EURO 2 engine. The EURO 3 engine option version (which remains available) was originally designated M250.40WM, but is also currently available with a EURO 3 version of the latest EURO 5 engine and in this configuration is designated M250.45WM. The latest EURO 5 versions are designated M250.41WM or M250.45WM.

The specifications provided in the following tables are for vehicles produced prior to the introduction of EURO 5 emissions compliant engine options

Tactical family model (ASTRA designation in brackets)	M170.31WM (SM44.31)	M250.40WM (SM66.40)	M320.45WM (SM88.45)
Configuration:	4 × 4	6 × 6	8 × 8
Cab seating:	1 + 3	1 + 3	1 + 3
Weight:			
(GVW)	17,000 kg	25,000 kg	32,000 kg
(chassis-cab)	8,350 kg	10,410 kg	12,150 kg (17,000 kg with LHS)
(payload on chassis-cab)	8,650 kg	14,590 kg	19,850 kg (15,000 kg with LHS)
(payload, troop/cargo body fitted)	7,000 kg	12,000 kg	17,000 kg
(towed load)	20,000 kg	20,000 kg	20,000 kg
Overall length: (chassis cab)	6.45/7.275/7.875 m	7.69/8.142/8.592 m	9.34/10.145 m
Width:	2.5 m	2.5 m	2.5 m
Height: (standard (with ring-mount) cab/low-height cab, all unladen)	2.87 (3.035)/2.767 m	2.87 (3.035)/2.767 m	2.87 (3.035)/2.767 m
Ground clearance: (under axle)	435 mm	435 mm	435 mm
Track:	2.062 m	2.062 m	2.062 m
Wheelbase:	3.5/4.2/4.8 m	3.3/3.75/4.2 m	1.955 + 2.995 or 3.595 + 1.45 m
Angle of approach/departure:	45°/43°	45°/45°	45°/35°
Max speed:	>90 km/h	>90 km/h	>90 km/h
Max gradient:	>60%	>60%	>60%
Fording: (unprepared/prepared)	850 mm unprepared, optional 1.2 m with limited preparation		
Engine:	Cursor 8 7.8-litre (M170.31WM) or Cursor 13 12.91-litre (M250.40WM and M320.45WM) in-line EURO 3 (EURO 4 available from October 2006) turbocharged water-cooled 4-stroke diesel developing 310 hp (231 kW) between 1,950-2,400 rpm and 1,115 N.m torque between 1,100-1,950 rpm (M170.31WM), 400 hp (298 kW) at 2,100 rpm and 2000 N.m torque at 1,100 rpm (M250.40WM) and 450 hp (336 kW) 2,100 rpm and 2,000 N.m torque at 1,100 rpm (M320.45WM)		
Transmission:	ZF 5HP 502 Powershift automatic with 5 forward and 1 reverse gears, option: ZF 16S 109 16-speed manual	ZF 6HP 902 Powershift automatic with 6 forward and 1 reverse gears, option: ZF 16S 221 16-speed manual and ZF WSK 400 torque converter	
Transfer box:	IVECO 2-speed	IVECO 2-speed	IVECO 2-speed
Steering:	power assisted, ZF Servocom type 8098		power assisted, ZF Servocom type 8099, dual circuit with auxiliary cylinder and 3 pumps (2 on engine, 1 on transmission)
Turning radius:	7.25 m (3.5 m WB) 8.47 m (4.2 m WB) 9.52 m (4.8 m WB)	8.16 m (3.3 m WB) 8.95 m (3.75 m WB) 9.74 m (4.2 m WB)	10.45 m (2.995 m WB) 11.45 m (3.595 m WB
Suspension:	semi-elliptic leaf springs, anti-roll bar, shock-absorbers and bumpers, front (and rear on (4 × 4)); inverted semi-elliptic leaf springs with centre pin and slider connections to axles, 4 lower reaction rods and 2 upper reaction triangles, rear on (6 × 6) and (8 × 8)		
Tyres:	1400R 20 Michelin XZL, CTI and runflat inserts optional		
Brakes:			
(main)	air, dual circuit, discs all-round. ABS standard		
(parking)	mechanical on rear axle(s)		
Electrical system:	24 V	24 V	24 V
Batteries:	4 × 12 V, 110 Ah	4 × 12 V, 110 Ah	4 × 12 V, 110 Ah
Alternator:	90 A	90 A	90 A

The (8 × 8) chassis of this range was originally designated M320.42WM when fitted with a EURO 2 engine. The EURO 3 engine option version (which remains available) is designated M320.45WM. The latest EURO 5 version remains designated M320.45WM.

Payloads for this range, with a standard cargo body fitted, are 7,000, 12,000 and 17,000 kg, respectively.

Logistic family models commenced delivery to the Italian Army during 2003 and from the outset were fitted with EURO 3 emissions compliant diesel engines. From late 2008 EURO 5 emissions compliant engines have been fitted and deliveries of these are currently running alongside EURO 3 deliveries.

IVECO's logistic family is made up of four main models, all of which have GV- and GTWs that exceed EU legislation. The M200.31WM is a (4 × 4); the M330.45WM is a (6 × 6); the (M400.45WM) is available as either an (8 × 8) or (8 × 8). Payloads with a standard cargo body fitted are 9,500, and up to 25,000 and 32,000 kg, respectively.

Variations to the base models of both ranges are available, an example here would be a specialist SMH range (4 × 4) tractor unit (for a cement batching plant semi-trailer) that is fitted with an SMH range (6 × 6) driveline.

Prior to the 2003 introduction of the logistic family, militarised versions of ASTRA's then commercial range of HD6 trucks were produced. To meet the changing demands of Italian (and other) armed forces, particularly for ever-increasing levels of tactical and strategic mobility, upon the introduction of the HD7 commercial range (now HD8 with the latest IVECO Cursor range engines) the decision was taken to develop and offer the logistic family for applications where previously HD range models would have been offered.

Visually, the only significant difference between the tactical and logistic families is tyre size and the use of dual rear wheels for the latter. Standard tyre size for the tactical family is 14.00R 20, standard tyre size for the logistic family is 12.00R 20. Both families share IVECO's tactical flat-panelled GRP cab, a cab designed from the outset to meet military requirements. The driver and front-seat passenger are provided with air-sprung seats separated by an engine tunnel down the centreline of the cab. While lacking the interior space of a commercially derived contemporary, the use of this cab ensures both families are rail transportable on a standard rail flatcar (without preparation) and air-transportable by C-130 Hercules aircraft, with minimal preparation and the optional low-roof cab. Added benefits of a flat-panelled cab are ease of field-repair, concealment and camouflage, and such a cab is more adaptable to the now almost essential appliqué armour kit.

Both families also share a similar purpose-designed C-section 8 mm thick chassis which is constructed from special high yield strength 530 N/mm² steel (450 N/mm² is the commercial norm) that is imported from Sweden for all ASTRA trucks. This steel, plus the careful design of the chassis contribute to enabling the high levels of twist (torsion) and flex (bending moment) required by a military off-road vehicle, without any associated stress or damage.

The vast majority of driveline components for both families are commercially proven and taken from the Trakker range of commercial trucks. The main differences are the use of higher payload rated axles for the logistic family, plus considerably higher levels of militarisation for tactical family components brought about by requirements such as MIL-STD 461C for EMC, a standard 850 mm fording depth (1.2 m with minimal further modifications) and a climatic operational range of −32°C/+49°C.

Logistic family model (ASTRA designation in brackets)	M170.31WM (SMH 44.31)	M250.40/45WM (SMH 66.40/45)	M320.45WM (SMH 84/88.45)
Configuration:	4 × 4	6 × 6	8 × 4 and 8 × 8
Cab seating:	1 + 3	1 + 3	1 + 3
Weight:			
(GVW)	≤20,000 kg	≤38,000 kg	≤48,000 kg
(payload, troop/cargo body fitted)	≤9,500 kg	≤25,000 kg	≤32,000 kg
(towed load)	≤29,000 kg	≤34,000 kg	≤24,000 kg
Overall length: (chassis cab)	6.695, 7.395 or 7.995 m	8.48, 8.88, or 9.18 m	10.23 m
Width:	2.5 m	2.5 m	2.5 m
Ground clearance: (under axle)	310 mm	310 mm	310 mm
Wheelbase:	3.5, 4.2 or 4.8 m	3.85, 4.25 or 4.5 m	1.955 + 3.645 + 1.4 m
Angle of approach/departure:	39°/30°	39°/30°	39°/30°
Max speed:	>85 km/h	>85 km/h	>85 km/h
Max gradient:	>60%	>60%	>60%
Fording: (unprepared/prepared)	850 mm unprepared		
Engine:	Cursor 8 7.8-litre (M170.31WM) or Cursor 13 12.91-litre (M250.40/45WM and M320.45WM) in-line Euro III (Euro IV available from October 2006) turbocharged water-cooled 4-stroke diesel developing 310 hp (231 kW) between 1,950-2,400 rpm and 1,115 N.m torque between 1,100-1,950 rpm (M170.31WM), 400/450 hp (298/336 kW) at 2,100 rpm and 2,000 N.m torque at 1,100 rpm (M250.40/45WM) and 450 hp (336 kW) at 2,100 rpm and 2,000 N.m torque at 1,100 rpm (M320.45WM)		
Transmission:	ZF 5HP 502 Powershift automatic with 5 forward and 1 reverse gears	ZF 6HP 902 Powershift automatic with 6 forward and 1 reverse gears	
Transfer box:	IVECO 2-speed	IVECO 2-speed	IVECO 2-speed
Steering:	power assisted, ZF Servocom type 8098	power assisted, ZF Servocom type 8099, dual circuit with auxiliary cylinder and 3 pumps (2 on engine, 1 on transmission)	
Suspension:	parabolic leaf springs, anti-roll bar, shock-absorbers and bump stops, front (and rear on (4 × 4)); inverted parabolic leaf springs with centre pin and slider connections to axles, 4 lower reaction rods and 2 upper reaction rods, rear on (6 × 6) and (8 × 8)		
Tyres:	1200R 20 (options available)		
Brakes:			
(main)	air, dual circuit, drums all-round. ABS standard		
(parking)	mechanical on rear axle(s)		
Electrical system:	24 V	24 V	24 V
Batteries:	4 × 12 V, 110 Ah	4 × 12 V, 110 Ah	4 × 12 V, 110 Ah
Alternator:	90 A	90 A	90 A

IVECO's Cursor 8 7.8-litre ((4 × 4) chassis only) or Cursor 13 12.9-litre electronically controlled turbocharged and intercooled six-cylinder diesel engines are used throughout the range. Compared to the EURO 2, 8210 units replaced at EURO 3 these engines reduced emissions by an average of 30 per cent while providing seven per cent more power and five per cent more torque. EURO 4 versions of these engines became available in October 2006 but were not fitted to production vehicles. From late 2008 EURO 5 emissions compliant engines have been fitted and deliveries of these are currently running alongside EURO 3 deliveries. Engines fitted to tactical family vehicles feature a number of modifications including a revised sump (oil flow on gradients), waterproof alternator and starter motor, and to ensure EMC and fording requirements can be achieved, the engine's ECUs are relocated to a shielded and sealed compartment behind the cab.

Tactical family trucks are fitted as standard with a ZF Powershift automatic transmission and IVECO 32180 (now TC1800 or TC2200) two-speed transfer box. The (4 × 4) M170.31WM and M170.33WM are fitted with the 5HP502 five-speed unit, while the (6 × 6) M250.40WM, M250.41WM and M250.45WM, and the (8 × 8) M320.45WM are fitted with the 6HP902 six-speed unit. The earlier EURO 2 M150.30WM was fitted with the 5HP500 unit, while the earlier M250.37WM and M320.42WM were fitted with the 6HP900 unit. All M320.42WM and the initial M320.45MW models supplied to the Italian Army have however been fitted with the then optional ZF 16S 221 16-speed manual gearbox coupled to a WSK 400 torque converter and IVECO two-speed transfer box. The automatic option was subsequently adopted by the Italian Army and the first M320M.45WM fitted with a 6HP902 'box was completed in February 2004. The current option to the ZF fully automatic transmission is the 16-speed ZF 16 AS 2330 TO (M170.31WM and M170.33WM) or ZF16 AS 2601 OD (M250.40WM, M250.41WM, M250.45WM, M320.45WM) automated gearbox.

Logistic family trucks, chassis dependant, are fitted with either an automatic (4 × 4) or manual plus torque converter (6 × 6/8 × 4/8) gearbox.

One of the original main defining differences between the two tactical range families was suspension, axles and brakes. The logistic range are sprung by parabolic leaf springs (inverted on rear bogies), with anti-roll bars and shock-absorbers fitted as required. The tactical family were originally sprung by semi-elliptic leaf springs (inverted on rear bogies), with anti-roll bars and shock-absorbers fitted as required. Parabolic leaf springs were introduced as standard for the the tactical family along with the introduction of EURO 5 engines and a small number of other detail changes.

All drive axles are of the hub-reduction type and taken from the Trakker range of commercial trucks. All front axles are rated at 8,500 kg for the tactical family, 9,000 kg for the logistic family. Rear axles are rated at 10,500 kg each for the tactical family; 17,500 kg each for the logistic family to meet their increased payload requirements.

Logistic family axles are equipped with drum brakes (with ABS), tactical family models are equipped with disc brakes (with ABS). Disc brakes were selected for the tactical family because of their better self-cleaning performance when off-road. A Central Tyre Inflation (CTI) system that allows the driver to adjust tyre pressures to suit prevailing ground conditions is available for tactical family models. An external system is available for logistic family models, the dual rear wheel set-up not suited to a conventional CTIS set-up.

IVECO quotes 66 per cent commonality of major components across the tactical family, with 81 per cent commonality between (4 × 4) and (6 × 6) chassis, 75 per cent commonality between (6 × 6) and (8 × 8) chassis, and 64 per cent commonality between (4 × 4) and (8 × 8) chassis.

In conjunction with IBD Deisenroth of Germany, IVECO has developed an appliqué ballistic and mine protection kit for the tactical family. This benign-in-appearance kit features a replacement front panel, doors and windscreen, with all other panels mounting internally and to the stainless steel framework of the standard cab.

It is understood that a small number of Italian Army tactical family trucks (around 40) are fitted with an appliqué protection kit developed in conjunction with Plasan Sasa of Israel.

Specifications
See table above and on facing page

Status
In production. IVECO tactical range trucks (tactical family) are in service with Denmark, Ireland, Italy (production and deliveries continue), Spain (deliveries continue), and the UK (M150.30WM, 3; to be replaced during 2011).

IVECO tactical range trucks (logistic family) are in service with Italy (production and deliveries continue). The M250.45WM ordered by Belgium (400 + optional 379) combines features of both the tactical and logistic families.

Contractor
IVECO SpA
Astra Veicoli Industriali SpA

ASTRA HD series (6 × 6) trucks

Development
ASTRA Veicoli Industriali S.p.A. was formed in 1946 in Cagliari as a refurbisher of military vehicles and the name ASTRA is taken from Azienda Sarda Trasformazione Autoveicoli. In 1951 the company transferred its headquarters to its current 135,200 m² site (43,500 ² of which is covered) in Piacenza, Italy. In 1986 IVECO acquired the company.

In 1994, ASTRA introduced a range of (6 × 6) trucks known as the HD series to replace the earlier ASTRA 300 series. Military variants were produced and supplied to Algeria, Italy and possibly other armed forces and included the ASTRA HD 66.45/5S - C-IMT tractor truck (full details of which can be found elsewhere in this section) and the ASTRA 66.45 TIM tractor truck (full details of which can be found in the Heavy equipment transporters section).

From mid 2003 the HD series have no longer been offered for military applications. To meet the changing demands of Italian (and other) armed forces, particularly for ever-increasing levels of tactical and strategic mobility, and upon the introduction of the HD7 commercial range, the decision was taken to develop and offer the ASTRA/IVECO logistic family for applications where previously HD range models would have been offered.

Visually the logistic family is very similar to ASTRA/IVECO's established tactical family. The only significant visual difference between the two families of trucks being tyre size and the use of dual rear wheels for the latter. Full details of both families, branded ASTRA for the domestic market, and IVECO for the export market, can be found elsewhere in this section.

Description
The ASTRA HD (6 × 6) chassis was offered in a variety of wheelbase lengths (3.5 m + 1.4 m; 3.8 m + 1.4 m; and 4.1 m + 1.4 m) and with a variety of engine fits (345, 370, 420, 440 and 520 hp). Single and double cabs were available, as were numerous other customer-specific features such as tyre size and power take-off facilities.

Current HD series models are the HD8, these available in a variety of drive configurations from 4 × 2 to 8 × 8 and fitted with a revised cab and options of EURO 3 or EURO 5 emissions compliant engines. The HHD8 (Heavy Heavy Duty), fitted with EURO 3 engine options, are also available, these having GVWs of up to 150,000 kg.

Specifications

HD 66.45
Cab seating: 1 + 2
Configuration: 6 × 6
Weight:
   (GVW) 33,000 kg
   (unladen) 10,435 kg
Length: 7.735 m
Width: 2.5 m
Height: (overall) 3.405 m
Ground clearance: 310 mm
Track:
   (front) 2.02 m
   (rear) 1.825 m
Wheelbase: 3.5 m + 1.4 m, 3.8 m + 1.4 m or 4.1 m + 1.4 m
Max road speed: 80 km/h
Fuel capacity: 300 litres
Max. gradient: 60%
Engine: IVECO 8280 TCA 17.17-litre V-8 turbo intercooled water-cooled 4-stroke diesel developing 440 hp (328 kW) at 1,900 rpm
Gearbox: ZF 16 S 221 with 16 forward and 2 reverse gears
Clutch: single dry disc
Transfer box: 2-speed
Steering: ZF Servocom Type 8098
Turning circle: 17.3 m

Suspension:
   (front) semi-elliptic springs with shock-absorbers, torsion bar and bumpers
   (rear) reinforced oscillating springs with pivot system
Tyres: 12.00 × 20
Brakes:
   (main) air, drums all-round
   (parking) mechanical on rear axles
Electrical system: 24 V
Batteries: 4 × 12 V, 110 Ah
Alternator: 80 A

Status
Production complete (see text). In service with the Italian Army.

Contractor
ASTRA Veicoli Industriali SpA
IVECO Spa

ASTRA HD6 84.45 (8 × 4 × 4) logistic transport truck

Development
Formed in 1946 in Cagliari as a refurbisher of military vehicles, ASTRA Veicoli Industriali S.p.A. took its name from Azienda Sarda Trasformazione Autoveicoli. In 1951 the company transferred its headquarters to its current 135,200 m² (43,500 m² of which is covered) in Piacenza, Italy. In 1986 IVECO acquired the company.

In 1994, ASTRA introduced a range of (6 × 6) trucks known as the HD series to replace the earlier ASTRA 300 series. The ASTRA HD6 84.45 (8 × 4 × 4) logistic transport truck was derived from the HD6 range to meet Italian Army specifications for the STL logistic transport system.

The HD series have not been offered for military applications since 2003. To meet the changing demands of Italian (and other) armed forces, particularly for ever-increasing levels of tactical and strategic mobility, and upon the introduction of the HD7 commercial range, the decision was taken to develop and offer the ASTRA/IVECO logistic family for applications where previously HD range models would have been offered.

Visually, the logistic family is very similar to ASTRA/IVECO's established tactical family, the only significant visual difference between the two families of trucks being tyre size and the use of dual rear wheels for the latter. (Full details of both families, branded ASTRA for the domestic market, and IVECO for the export market, can be found elsewhere in this section.)

Description
The HD6 84.45 logistic transport truck is fitted with a Multilift (now Hiab) Mark 4 Load Handling System (LHS) provided by Isoli. Full details of this equipment can be found in the Materials handling equipment section. The HD6 84.45 can carry loads up to 15,000 kg and these can be lowered to the ground in 33 seconds or retrieved in 25 seconds. The system is cross-operational with other load handling systems in use with NATO and other nations such as the British Army's DROPS and US Army's PLS systems, and can handle 6.096 m (20 ft) ISO standard platforms or ISO 1C standard containers.

Motive power is provided by a 440 hp diesel coupled to a 16-speed gearbox. The front two non-driven axles steer.

Current HD series models are the HD8, these available in a variety of drive configurations from 4 × 2 to 8 × 8 and fitted with a revised cab and options of EURO 3 or EURO 5 emissions compliant engines. The HHD8 (Heavy Heavy Duty), fitted with EURO 3 engine options, are also available, these having GVWS of up to 150,000 kg.

ASTRA SM 66.45M (6 × 6) dump truck (ASTRA)   0512505

ASTRA HD6 84.45 (8 × 4) logistic transport truck (Chris Bowler)   0109514

Specifications
Cab seating: 1 + 1
Configuration: 8 × 4 × 4
Weights:
 (laden 31,200 kg
 (GVW) 32,000 kg
 (unladen) 16,200 kg
 (payload, incl flatrack) 15,000 kg
Length: 8.97 m
Width: 2.5 m
Height: (cab) 3.36 m
Ground clearance: 310 mm
Track:
 (front) 2.03 m
 (rear) 1.825 m
Wheelbase: 1.76 m + 3.24 m + 1.4 m
Max road speed: 82 km/h
Range: 600 km
Fuel capacity: 300 litres
Max gradient: 50%
Engine: IVECO 8280 TCA 17.17-litre V-8 turbocharged and intercooled water-cooled 4 stroke diesel developing 440 hp (328 kW) at 1,900 rpm
Gearbox: ZF 16 S 221 with 16 forward and 2 reverse gears
Clutch: single dry disc
Steering: ZF Servocom 8099
Turning radius: 10.3 m
Suspension:
 (front) semi-elliptic springs with shock-absorbers, torsion bar and bumpers
 (rear) reinforced oscillating springs with pivot system
Tyres: 12.00R 20
Brakes:
 (main) air, drums all-round
 (parking) mechanical on rear axles
Electrical system: 24 V
Batteries: 4 × 12 V, 110 Ah
Alternator: 80 A

Status
Production complete (see text). In service with the Italian Army.

Contractor
ASTRA Veicoli Industriali SpA
IVECO SpA

ASTRA HD 66.45/5S - C-IMT (6 × 6) tractor truck

Development
ASTRA Veicoli Industriali S.p.A. was formed in 1946 in Cagliari as a refurbisher of military vehicles and the name 'ASTRA' is taken from Azienda Sarda Trasformazione Autoveicoli. In 1951 the company transferred its headquarters to its current 135,200 m² site (43,500 m² of which is covered) in Piacenza, Italy. In 1986 IVECO acquired the company.

In 1994, ASTRA introduced a range of (6 × 6) trucks known as the HD series to replace the earlier ASTRA 300 series. The ASTRA HD 66.45/5S - C-IMT (6 × 6) tractor truck is derived from the ASTRA HD series.

From mid-2003 the HD series have no longer been offered for military applications. To meet the changing demands of Italian (and other) armed forces, particularly for ever-increasing levels of tactical and strategic mobility, and upon the introduction of the HD7 commercial range, the decision was taken to develop and offer the ASTRA/IVECO logistic family

Rear three-quarter view of an ASTRA HD 66.45/5S - C-IMT (6 × 6) tractor truck at the ASTRA facility in Piacenza (Shaun C Connors) 1391415

Front three-quarter view of an ASTRA HD 66.45/5S - C-IMT (6 × 6) tractor truck at the ASTRA facility in Piacenza (Shaun C Connors) 1391414

for applications where previously HD range models would have been offered.

Visually similar to ASTRA/IVECO's established tactical family, the logistic family has a different tyre size and the uses dual rear wheels. (Full details of both families, branded ASTRA for the domestic market, IVECO for the export market, can be found elsewhere in this section.)

Description
The ASTRA HD 66.45/5S - C-IMT (6 × 6) tractor truck is derived from the ASTRA HD series and modified to render it suitable for towing a special semi-trailer used to carry and launch CNIM PFM pontoon bridge components. The modifications included placing a torque converter between the engine and gearbox, a four-door five-passenger cab with a hydraulic tilting system, a hydraulic system to launch and recover the bridge and to power the motors on the semi-trailer wheels, a winch for self-recovery and a fifth wheel.

Current HD series models are the HD8, these available in a variety of drive configurations from 4 × 2 to 8 × 8 and fitted with a revised cab and options of EURO 3 or EURO 5 emissions compliant engines. The HHD8 (Heavy Heavy Duty), fitted with EURO 3 engine options, are also available, these having GVWS of up to 150,000 kg.

Specifications
Cab seating: 1 + 4
Configuration: 6 × 6
Weight: (empty, with hydraulic system and winch) 13,500 kg
Load on 5th wheel: 7,000 kg
Length: 8.035 m
Width: 2.5 m
Height: 3.31 m
Ground clearance: 370 mm
Track:
 (front) 2.053 m
 (rear) 2.117 m
Wheelbase: 4.1 m + 1.4 m
Max road speed:
 (possible) 103 km/h
 (with limiter) 85 km/h
Fuel capacity: 300 litres
Engine: IVECO 8280 TCA 17.17 litre V-8 turbocharged and intercooled water-cooled 4-stroke diesel developing 440 hp (328 kW) at 1,900 rpm
Gearbox: ZF WSK 400.90 torque converter plus ZF 16 S 221 manual gearbox with 16 forward and 2 reverse gears
Transfer box: 2-speed
Steering: ZF Servocom Type 8098
Turning radius: 11.3 m
Suspension:
 (front) semi-elliptic springs with shock-absorbers, torsion bar and bumpers
 (rear) reinforced oscillating springs with pivot system and torsion bar
Tyres: 14.00 × 20
Brakes:
 (main) air, drums all-round
 (parking) mechanical on rear axles
Electrical system: 24 V
Batteries: 4 × 12 V, 110 Ah
Alternator: 80 A

Status
Production complete (see text). In service with the Italian Army.

Contractor
ASTRA Veicoli Industriali SpA.
IVECO Spa.

Japan

Kohkidohsha 1,500 kg (4 × 4) high-mobility vehicle

Development
The term *Kohkidohsha* translates as high-mobility vehicle. It is a 4 × 4, 1,500 kg vehicle developed as a possible replacement for many existing Type 73 2,000 kg and Isuzu 2,500 kg trucks currently in Japanese Ground Self-Defence Force service.

It was disclosed after the vehicle had entered production that the Kohkidohsha high mobility vehicle was manufactured by Toyota and that the design was based around components of the Toyota Mega Cruiser civilian off-road vehicle that was available commercially between 1995-2002.

Description
The Kohkidohsha 1,500 kg (4 × 4) high-mobility vehicle visually resembles the US M998 HMMWV series

The Kohkidohsha can carry at least four people including the driver. Power is derived from a 4-litre water-cooled 150 hp diesel coupled to an automatic transmission and there is permanent four-wheel drive. Steering is power assisted on all four wheels and independent suspension is provided, also on all four wheels.

Specifications
Kohkidohsha 1,500 kg (4 × 4) high-mobility vehicle
Cab seating: 1 + 3
Configuration: 4 × 4
Weight: approx 2,440 kg
Max load: approx 1,500 kg
Length: 4.91 m
Width: 2.15 m
Height: 2.09 m
Ground clearance: 400 mm
Wheelbase: 3.4 m
Angle of approach/departure: 73°/51°
Max speed: 100 km/h
Engine: 4-litre water-cooled diesel developing 150 hp (110 kW)
Transmission: automatic
Transfer box: permanent 4-wheel drive

Kohkidohsha 1,500 kg (4 × 4) high-mobility vehicle in standard light utility soft top configuration (Gordon Arthur)   1340324

Kohkidohsha 1,500 kg (4 × 4) high-mobility vehicle configured as a shelter carrier (Mitsuhiro Kadota)   1047616

Steering: power assisted on all 4 wheels
Suspension: independent
Tyres: run-flat

Status
In service with the Japanese Ground Self-Defence Force.

Type 73 (4 × 4) 2,000 kg truck

Development
The Type 73 (4 × 4) 2,000 kg truck was standardised in 1973 as the successor to Nissan and Toyota (4 × 4) 750 kg trucks in service since the 1950s. The Type 73 is a militarised version of the Toyota WB500 light truck, manufactured by Hino Motors.

It is understood that in many roles the Type 73 is scheduled for replacement by the Kohkidohsha 1,500 kg (4 × 4) high-mobility vehicle, available details of which can be found elsewhere in this section.

Description
The Type 73 has an over-engine cab with a steel back and sides up to seat-top height and steel doors with glass windows. The single-piece windscreen can be folded forwards. The roof is a single-piece waterproof

Type 73 (4 × 4) 2,000 kg truck (Gordon Arthur)   1340323

Type 73 (4 × 4) 2,000 kg truck in ambulance configuration (Gordon Arthur)   1340322

Type 73 (4 × 4) 2,000 kg truck (Mitsuhiro Kadota)   1047617

tarpaulin that can be fixed in place by removable braces. With the tarpaulin in place a high-capacity heater-blower-defroster system can be used. Seats for the driver and one passenger are provided, each with space for kit stowage behind.

The cargo body is all steel but has wooden side stakes and rails that are held in place by latches and unfold to serve as benches. The tailgate has a built-in step that will unfold when a ring on each side is pulled. A heavy canvas tilt and braces can be used to cover the cargo area which is 3 m long and 1.95 m wide.

Standard equipment includes a rear fender, tool box, canvas tilt and spare tyre and carrier. Optional equipment includes a winch (front-mounted), a power take-off and a tropical cooling system.

An ambulance version with a fully enclosed cab and rear body has been produced. The truck version has been used to carry mortars.

Specifications

Type 73 (4 × 4) 2,000 kg truck
Cab seating: 1 + 1
Configuration: 4 × 4
Weight:
  (unladen) 3,195 kg
  (gross weight, on-road) 5,355 kg
  (gross weight, off-road) 4,855 kg
Max load:
  (on-road) 2,000 kg
  (off-road) 1,500 kg
Front axle load: 2,325 kg (on road, laden)
Rear axle load: 3,030 kg (on road, laden)
Length: 5.36 m
Width: 2.09 m
Height: 2.49 m
Ground clearance: 280 mm
Wheelbase: 2.9 m
Track:
  (front) 1.61 m
  (rear) 1.635 m
Angle of approach/departure: 37°/32°
Max speed: 87 km/h
Fuel capacity: 115 litres
Max gradient: 60%
Fording: 800 mm
Engine: Hino DQ100 4.3-litre water-cooled diesel developing 95 hp (70 kW) at 3,000 rpm
Gearbox: 5 forward and 1 reverse gears
Transfer box: 2 speed
Clutch: single dry disc
Steering: recirculating ball
Turning radius: 6.4 m
Suspension: semi-elliptic leaf springs with shock-absorbers
Tyres: 8.25 × 20
Brakes: hydraulic with vacuum servo
Electrical system: 24 V
Batteries: 2 × 12 V, 100 Ah
Generator: 400 W

Status
Production likely to be on an as required basis. In service with the Japanese Ground Self-Defence Force.

Contractor
Toyota Motor Corporation

Isuzu SKW (6 × 6) 3,500 kg truck series

Description
The SKW (6 × 6) 3,500 kg truck was developed by Isuzu from the late 1960s to replace the range of 2,500 kg (6 × 6) trucks then used by the Japanese Self-Defence Forces. After trials and modifications it was standardised in 1973 as the Type 73 large truck series and since then it has been produced in large numbers for the JGSDF.

The first model was the SKW440 but since then many improvements have been made to the engine, axles, cab and so on. The latest model is the SKW475.

The forward control cab has a windscreen that can be folded forward onto the bonnet and a removable canvas top. The basic cargo body is all steel and has a drop tailgate, bench troop seats down either side, removable bows and a tarpaulin cover. This basic model can carry 3,500 kg of cargo across country or 6,000 kg on roads.

There are two basic models, one with single-tyred rear wheels (cargo, tanker and so on) and the other with dual-tyred rear wheels (dump and light wrecker).

A 5,500 kg capacity winch can be mounted on the front of the vehicle.

Variants
Models with single rear wheels
Truck, Cargo with winch (SKW475M 6 × 6)
This is the base model of the cargo series and can carry 3,500 kg of cargo across country and 6,000 kg on roads. The base version can be used to carry shelters and has been used to carry radar systems and surface-to-air missile systems (such as the Tan SAM). When fitted with the optional winch the designation changes to SKW475MW. There is a version with a longer wheelbase, this is designated the SKW525M and has a slightly increased GVW and reduced on-road payload.

Tanker, Utility (SKW475MV 6 × 6)
This tanker has a maximum payload of 5,100 kg of fuel.

Tanker, Water (SKW475MV 6 × 6)
Carries a tank for 5,000 litres of water.

Models with dual rear wheels
Truck, Dump (SKW475MD 6 × 6)
This has an all-steel rear tipping body with an on-road payload of 5,000 kg. It can also be used to carry cargo.

Isuzu SKW475MD (6 × 6) 3,500 kg truck (Mitsihiro Kadota)

1340351

Model	SKW475M	SKW475MW	SKW475MV	SKW475MV	SKW475MV	SKW475MD	SKW464MR	SKW525M
Type	Cargo truck	Cargo truck (W/W)	Tanker (utility)	Water tanker	Crane	Dump truck	Light wrecker	Cargo truck (long)
Cab seating	1 + 1 (or 2)	1 + 1 (or 2)	1 + 1 (or 2)	1 + 1 (or 2)	1 + 1 (or 2)	1 + 1 (or 2)	1 + 1 (or 2)	1 + 1 (or 2)
Configuration	6 × 6	6 × 6	6 × 6	6 × 6	6 × 6	6 × 6	6 × 6	6 × 6
Weights								
(unladen)	8,570 kg	9,000 kg	9,490 kg	9,500 kg	9,460 kg	10,200 kg	14,220 kg	8,860 kg
(laden, road)	14,730 kg	15,160 kg	14,750 kg	14,660 kg	14,620 kg	15,360 kg	14,380 kg	14,020 kg
(laden, cross-country)	11,230 kg	11,660 kg	n/avail	n/avail	12,120 kg	12,860 kg	n/avail	11.520 kg
(max load, road)	6,000 kg	6,000 kg	5,100 kg	5,000 kg	5,000 kg	5,000 kg	-	5,000 kg
(max load, cross-country)	3,500 kg	3,500 kg	n/avail	n/avail	3,500 kg	3,500 kg	-	3,500 kg
(towed load, road)	6,000 kg	6,000 kg	6,000 kg	6,000 kg	6,000 kg	6,000 kg	6,000 kg	6,000 kg
(towed load, cross-country)	4,000 kg	4,000 kg	4,000 kg	4,000 kg	4,000 kg	4,000 kg	4,000 kg	4,000 kg
Length	7.15 m	7.41 m	7.31 m	6.93 m	7.6 m	7.29 m	7.810 m	8.25 m
Width	2.485 m	2.485 m	2.485 m	2.485 m	2.485 m	2.485 m	2.490 m	2.485 m
Height	3.15 m	3.15 m	2.865 m	2.865 m	3.395 m	3.395 m	3.060 m	3.18 m
Ground clearance	330 mm	330 mm	330 mm	330 mm	330 mm	330 mm	330 mm	330 mm
Track								
(front)	1.97 m	1.97 m	1.97 m	1.97 m	1.97 m	1.97 m	1.84 m	1.97 m
(rear)	1.97 m	1.97 m	1.97 m	1.97 m	1.97 m	1.84 m	n/avail	1.97
Wheelbase	3.395 m + 1.31 m	3.395 m + 1.31 m	3.395 m + 1.31 m	3.395 m + 1.31 m	3.395 m + 1.31 m	3.395 m + 1.31 m	3.395 m + 1.31 m	3.895 m + 1.31 m
Max road speed	105 km/h	105 km/h	105 km/h	105 km/h	105 km/h	105 km/h	95 km/h	105 km/h
Range	500 km	500 km	500 km	500 km	500 km	500 km	500 km	500 km
Fording	800 mm	800 mm	800 mm	800 mm	800 mm	800 mm	800 mm	800 mm
Turning radius	9.2 m	9.2 m	9.2 m	9.2 m	9.2 m	9.2 m	9.4 m	9.2 m
Fuel capacity	190 litres	190 litres	190 litres	190 litres	190 litres	190 litres	170 litres	190 litres
Engine	Isuzu 8PE1 V-8 water-cooled diesel developing 286 hp (210 kW) at 2,300 rpm (250 hp (184 kW) at 2,200 rpm in the preceding SKW464 model)							
Gearbox	Allison MD automatic with six forward and one reverse gears. The preceding SKW464 model had a manual gearbox with 5 forward and 1 reverse gears							
Clutch	single dry plate							
Transfer box	2 speed with lockable planetary inter-axle differential							
Steering	power	power	power	power	power	power	power	power
Brakes	air/hydraulic							
Suspension	semi-elliptic leaf springs and hydraulic shock-absorbers, front, semi-elliptic leaf springs, rear							
Electrical system	24 V	24 V	24 V	24 V	24 V	24 V	24 V	24 V
Tyres	11.00R 20	11.00R 20	11.00R 20	11.00R 20	11.00R 20	11.00R 20	11.00R 20	11.00R 20

Truck, Wrecker, Light (SKW464MR 6 × 6)
Full details of the SKW464MR can be found in the Recovery vehicles section. No equivalent variant of the current SKW475 model has been produced and for comparative purposes specifications of this model, some of which are common throughout the SKW464 model range, are included in the SKW475 specifications table that follows.

Isuzu SKW475MD (6 × 6) 3,500 kg dump truck (Mitsuhiro Kadota) 1340349

Specifications
See table above

Status
In production. In service with the Japanese Self-Defence Force.

Contractor
Isuzu Motors Limited

Mitsubishi FW419 Type 74 (6 × 6) trucks and derivatives

Description
The Mitsubishi FW419 series of 6 × 6 trucks was introduced in 1987 when it replaced the FW415 series in production. The FW419 series is known as the Type 74.

There have been numerous detail changes to the FW419 range of trucks throughout the production run and following recent changes it is understood that the designation for the ongoing development of this range of trucks is simply 7-tonne Truck. It is also understood that the latest modifications see a non-commercial chassis used as the basis of the 7-tonne Truck.

Mitsubishi Fuso Truck and Bus Corporation has a confidentiality agreement with the Japanese Ministry of Defence which precludes comment on military products.

Model	FW419L3	FW419LD	FW419LD1	FW419M	FW419M1
Role	truck	truck	truck	drop	recovery
	w/winch		w/winch	side	
Cab seating	1 + 2	1 + 2	1 + 2	1 + 2	1 + 2
Configuration	6 × 6	6 × 6	6 × 6	6 × 6	6 × 6
Weight					
(unladen)	13,340 kg	11,490 kg	12,210 kg	10,990 kg	18,780 kg
(laden)	19,860 kg	18,730 kg	19,450 kg	18,230 kg	19,020 kg
Max load (off road)	5,800 kg	7,000 kg	7,000 kg	7,000 kg	-
Length	8.59 m	8.135 m	8.135 m	9.245 m	9.32 m
Width	2.49 m	2.49 m	2.49 m	2.49 m	2.49 m
Height	3.65 m	3.1 m	3.1 m	3.06 m	3.18 m
Wheelbase	3.855 m +	3.855 m +	3.855 m +	4.125 m +	4.125 m +
	1.3 m	1.3 m	1.3 m	1.3 m	1.3 m
Max road speed	95 km/h	95 km/h	95 km/h	95 km/h	95 km/h
Engine	Mitsubishi Model 8DC11-1A diesel developing 355 hp (261 kW) at 2,200 rpm				

Variants

FW419L drop-side heavy-duty truck
This is the base model of the FW419 series and has a conventional heavy duty rear cargo deck with provision for a canvas tilt. When not in use the folded tilt supports are stowed forward. The cargo area has a tailgate at the rear and a spare wheel is stowed in the space between the cab rear and the front of the cargo area.

Mitsubishi Type 74 heavy duty truck (Gordon Arthur)　　　　1340345

Mitsubishi Type 74 heavy duty truck (Gordon Arthur)　　　　1340343

Mitsubishi Type 74 heavy duty truck (Gordon Arthur)　　　　1340344

FW419L3 drop side heavy duty truck with winch
This is a version of the FW419L with a 10,000 kg capacity rear-mounted winch and a 2,000 kg crane. It can be used as an artillery tractor for light weapons.

FW419LD heavy duty truck
The FW419LD heavy duty truck has an all-steel heavy duty dump body with a cab protector. It is provided with a centrally mounted winch with the controls on each side of the cargo area between the body and the cab rear.

FW419LD1 heavy duty truck
This is a version of the FW419LD with a 6,000 kg rear winch.

FW419M drop side truck
The length of the cargo area is 6.71 m.

FW419M1 recovery vehicle
Full details of this vehicle can be found in the Recovery vehicles section.

Prime Mover Medium
This is a tractor vehicle used to tow 155 mm FH-70 howitzers and is equipped with a 10,000 kg crane to handle ammunition stowed on a shortened cargo area.

Specifications
See table above

Status
Production as required. In service with the Japanese Ground Self-Defence Force.

Contractor
Mitsubishi Motors Corporation

Jordan

NIMR/Tiger SAS 4 × 4 and 6 × 6 High Mobility Tactical Vehicles (HMTV)

Development
The NIMR High Mobility Tactical Vehicle/Tiger SAS High Mobility Tactical Vehicle (HMTV) was announced in late 2000 as a joint venture between Jordan's King Abdullah II Design and Development Bureau (KADDB) and Bin Jabr Enterprises of the United Arab Emirates (UAE). It was described as a multipurpose vehicle intended to address the requirements for replacement of existing 4 × 4 light tactical vehicles, primarily in the Middle East and Asia. High levels of design consideration had been given to low acquisition and running costs, and the maximum possible use of Commercial-Off-The-Shelf (COTS) components was made to enable global logistic support. When announced it carried the KADDB project designation of AB17. NIMR is the Arabic equivalent of Tiger.

At IDEX 2001 a prototype vehicle was publicly displayed for the first time and Jordan's Prince Faisal Bin Al Hussein was reported to have signed a contract worth around USD45 million for the co-production in Jordan of 1,500 vehicles, although some sources stated 1,700 vehicles. A dedicated production facility was to be set up at Duleil, Jordan, and production was then expected to commence late 2002.

The original AB17 was designed in the Russian Federation by GAZ and throughout a long, troubled and cloudy gestation period a number of automotive design house-style companies in countries such as Austria (not confirmed), Australia and South Africa are known to have had involvement in proposed redesigns/re-engineering of the original vehicle. GAZ is no longer involved in the project and subsequently introduced the GAZ-2975 series (now designated GAZ-2330 series), relatively small numbers of which have been supplied to the Russian Army.

Displayed at IDEX 2009, a NIMR/Tiger in double cabin cargo configuration
(Shaun C Connors)
1391010

Displayed at IDEX 2009, a NIMR/Tiger in open top LRPV-type configuration
(Shaun C Connors)
1391011

*Displayed at IDEX 2009, a NIMR/Tiger 6 × 6 in multipurpose cargo
configuration* (Shaun C Connors)
1391013

*The NIMR II, shown for the first time at IDEX 2007, is a development of the
baseline 4 × 4 NIMR* (Patrick Allen)
1311308

*Displayed at IDEX 2007, a baseline NIMR/Tiger SAS High Mobility Tactical
Vehicle (HMTV)* (Patrick Allen)
1322374

*Displaying its mobility at IDEX 2005, an early NIMR/Tiger SAS High
Mobility Tactical Vehicle (HMTV) in two-door pick-up-type configuration*
(Patrick Allen)
1138115

It was announced at IDEX 2005 that Advanced Industries of Arabia (AIA), an 80/20 per cent share co-operative venture between Bin Jabr Group and KADDB, had been awarded a USD41 million contract to supply UAE Armed Forces with 500 examples of the NIMR HMTV in four variants over 18 months; deliveries were scheduled to begin in June 2005. It was suggested the UAE order could increase to 5,000 vehicles. The Bin Jabr Group also announced at IDEX 2005 that it had signed a joint venture agreement with India's Vectra Group for the manufacture of NIMR vehicles to meet Indian market requirements. It was understood the NIMR would be offered to meet a then anticipated Indian Army requirement for unarmoured (1,500 kg payload) and armoured (900 kg payload) HMMWV-type light vehicles. The General Staff Qualitative Requirement (GSQR) for these vehicles - reportedly some 12,000 unarmoured and 2,000 armoured vehicles - was issued mid-2005 but by October 2005 the programme had been halted. A revised requirement was subsequently announced.

A 5,000 kg payload 6 × 6 variant of the NIMR was displayed publicly for the first time at IDEX 2005.

Advanced Industries of Arabia, a subsidiary of the UAE's Bin Jabr Group (BJG), unveiled the NIMR II, essentially the ongoing development of the 2000-unveiled AB-17, at IDEX 2007. The NIMR II is available in 4 × 4 and 6 × 6 configurations and features all-round ballistic and blast protection.

At that time the BJG stated that it had sold 500 baseline variants of its NIMR HMTV to the UAE Armed Forces.

At IDEX 2009 BJG stated that 150-200 of the previously mentioned 500 vehicle order had been delivered, and that a contract for (6 × 6) shelter carrier vehicles (in a Joint venture (JV) with Germany's Zeppelin) had been signed. According to BJG officials around 1,000 NIMR were on contract (or delivered) as of early-2009, with an additional 1,000 as contract options. These figures include at least 120 NIMR in softskin (LRPV) and armoured mix delivered to Libya during 2008, and may include a further 500 (approximately) vehicles for Libya.

Bin Jabr Group sources have stated that KADDB has had no involvement with NIMR since 2005.

From the side, a four-door, four-seat pick-up-type variant of the NIMR/Tiger SAS High Mobility Tactical Vehicle (HMTV) as displayed in 2005. Note the twin spare wheels mounted at the rear of the vehicle (Patrick Allen)
1138101

Front three-quarter view of the 6 × 6 variant of the NIMR/Tiger SAS High Mobility Tactical Vehicle (HMTV as displayed at IDEX 2005) (Patrick Allen)
1138103

Description

The NIMR/Tiger 4 × 4 has so far been displayed in five basic body configurations. These are a four-door, four-seat station wagon-type body, a four-docr, four-seat pick-up-style with a limited-space rear cargo area, a two-door, two-seat pick-up, and a four-door open top long range patrol-type body. These variants are all fitted with baseline protection. A fully armoured 4 × 4 that can be armed with an assortment of weapons including air defence and anti-tank missiles is also available, this designated NIMR II. The 6 × 6 has been displayed with a two-door, two-seat cab and configured as shelter carrier or cargo vehicle, or with the rear platform mounting a multiple launch rocket system. A fully armoured 6 × 6 troop carrier has also been displayed.

Early technical specifications for the NIMR/Tiger quoted motive power provided by a Cummins 5.9-litre diesel engine developing 190 hp and couple to a four-speed (five-speed optional) automatic transmission. This was later revised to the same engine but rated at 225 hp and coupled to a Allison LTC 1000 five-speed automatic transmission. Further specification revisions retained the Allison LTC 1000 transmission, but were coupled to a 6.3-litre MTU diesel engine developing 280 hp. The current specifications return to a Cummins engine, the 5.9-litre ISBe 250 developing 250 hp or the 6.7-litre ISBe 300 developing 300 hp, and coupled to the Allison LTC 1000 transmission in 4 × 4 models and to the Allison MD3060 in 6 × 6 models.

A custom-made cooling pack optimised for desert/hot climate operations is fitted, the climatic operational range of the vehicle being quoted as −25°C/+55°C at 90 per cent humidity.

Fully independent suspension is fitted and the three-piece split-type 20-inch wheel rims are fitted with 335/80R 20 Michelin tyres as standard. A Central Tyre Inflation (CTI) system that allows the driver to adjust tyre pressures to suit the terrain being crossed is standard equipment. Bead locks for low pressure operation or run flat inserts may be fitted. Each axle is fitted with a driver-controlled air-operated differential lock. There is a driver-controlled differential lock in the transfer box.

The baseline NIMR/Tiger vehicle is provided with protection against anti-personnel mine blast and small arms fire (excluding the roof and bonnet). Variants offering protection to at least STANAG Level 2a/2b mine blast and Level 3 ballistic protection are also available. NBC, FFR preparation, ABS, GPS and air-conditioning are further options, as is a 'softskin' version with an aluminium body.

All NIMR models are easily transportable by C-130 and C-160 transport aircraft; the 4 × 4 may also be transported as an underslung load by a CH-53 helicopter.

Specifications

NIMR/Tiger SAS

Model:	Single cabin cargo	Double cabin cargo	Open top LRPV	6 × 6 cargo
Cab seating:	2 (+ up to 6 depending on role)	4 (+ up to 4 depending on role)	4 (+ up to 2 depending on role)	2 (+ up to 10 depending on role)
Configuration:	4 × 4	4 × 4	4 × 4	6 × 6
Weight:				
(laden)	9,250 kg	8,750 kg	8,250 kg	12,800 kg
(unladen)	5,750 kg	6,250 kg	5,750 kg	7,800 kg
(max payload)	3,500 kg	2,500 kg	2,500 kg	5,000 kg
Length:	4.9 m	5.5 m	4.9 m	6.75 m
Width:	2.2 m	2.2 m	2.2 m	2.2 m
Height:	2.05 m	2.05 m	2.05 m	2.05 m
Ground clearance:	450 mm	450 mm	450 mm	430 mm
Track:	1.84 m	1.84 m	1.84 m	1.84 m
Angle of approach/departure:	51°/51°	51°/51°	51°/51°	51°/51°
Max road speed:	135 km/h	135 km/h	135 km/h	135 km/h
Cruising range: (on-road)	700 km	700 km	700 km	700 km
Fuel capacity:	175 litres	175 litres	175 litres	200 litres
Gradient:	60%	60%	60%	60%
Vertical obstacle:	500 mm	500 mm	500 mm	500 mm
Fording: (unprepared)	1.2 m	1.2 m	1.2 m	1.2 m
Engine:	Cummins ISBe 250 5.9-litre 6-cylinder in-line turbocharged water-cooled 4-stroke diesel developing 250 hp (186 kW) and 750 N.m torque	Cummins ISBe 300 6.7-litre 6-cylinder in-line turbocharged water-cooled 4-stroke diesel developing 300 hp (224 kW) and 1,100 N.m torque	Cummins ISBe 250 5.9-litre 6-cylinder in-line turbocharged water-cooled 4-stroke diesel developing 250 hp (186 kW) and 750 N.m torque	Cummins ISBe 300 6.7-litre 6-cylinder in-line turbocharged water-cooled 4-stroke diesel developing 300 hp (224 kW) and 1,100 N.m torque
Gearbox:	Allison LCT 1000 5-speed automatic	Allison LCT 1000 5-speed automatic	Allison LCT 1000 5-speed automatic	Allison MD 3060 5-speed automatic
Transfer box:	2-speed with air-operated longitudinal differential lock	2-speed with air-operated longitudinal differential lock	2-speed with air-operated longitudinal differential lock	2-speed with air-operated longitudinal differential lock
Steering:	ZF hydraulic power-assisted	ZF hydraulic power-assisted	ZF hydraulic power-assisted	ZF hydraulic power-assisted
Axles:	hub-reduction gearing, air-operated differential locks			
Turning radius:	7.25 m	7.25 m	7.25 m	7.25 m
Suspension:	fully independent, double wishbone coil spring type with torsion bar and shock-absorbers; anti-roll bars front and rear			
Tyres:	335/80R 20 Michelin XZL with beadlocks or run flat inserts and a CTI system			
Brakes:	dual circuit, air-over-hydraulic, discs all-round. Optional ABS	dual circuit, air-over-hydraulic, discs all-round. Optional ABS	dual circuit, air-over-hydraulic, discs all-round. Optional ABS	dual circuit, air-over-hydraulic, discs all-round. Optional ABS
Electrical system:	24 V	24 V	24 V	24 V

Status
In production. Supplied to Libya and the UAE (see text).

Contractor
Advanced Industries of Arabia

Korea, South

KM45 (4 × 4) 1¼ ton truck series

Development
The Kia Motors KM45 series (or 450 series as they are sometimes referred) of 4 × 4 trucks are similar in appearance to the US M715/AM 715 1¼ ton trucks, but differ in a number of areas including mechanical systems.

Kia Motors was founded in 1944 as Kyongseong Precision, changing its name to Kia Industry Co Ltd in 1952. This changed in 1990 to Kia Motors Corporation, and in 1998 Hyundai Motor took control of the company.

Kia Motors traditionally makes little or no official comment regarding military vehicle sales, however, it is known that in addition to Korea's Armed Forces the KM45 series is used by the Philippines and Thailand. The Philippines received around 650 vehicles between 2007-2009, and Thailand received approximately 200 vehicles around 2006/2007. An estimated 500 Korean Army KM45 series vehicles have been fitted with a basic protection kit.

Kia Motors is the sole provider of military vehicles to Korea's Armed Forces. Around 50,000 Kia vehicles are currently in service, with around 2,000 new/replacement vehicles delivered each year. Kia Motors has produced around 123,000 military vehicles, this figure including 20,000 vehicles exported to 20 countries over 30 years.

Description
The Kia Motors KM45 series (or 450 series as they are sometimes referred) of 4 × 4 trucks are similar in appearance to the US M715/AM 715 1¼ ton trucks but are fitted with MZBA1 diesel engines and a revised power train.

The base model of the series is the KM450 (also designated the K311) light cargo truck. The driver's cab has a canvas top and seats are provided for the driver and one passenger. The cargo area at the rear can be covered

KM451 (4 × 4) field ambulance. Note the concealment of all unit/tactical markings (Gordon Arthur)   1340362

KM450 (4 × 4) 1¼ ton cargo truck. Note the concealment of all unit/tactical markings (Gordon Arthur)   1340363

by a canvas tilt and side boards are usually fitted. Bench seats can be fitted to carry six passengers along each side. There is a drop tailgate at the rear. The cargo area dimensions are 2,345 × 1,626 mm and items up to 4 m³ in volume or a maximum 1,350 kg can be carried.

Other models currently produced are:
- KM451 (K312) field ambulance with a fully enclosed van body and two outward-opening doors at the rear. This model has been updated to feature a wider 'luton-type' rear body and a new, more powerful, engine
- KM452 (K313) shop van with a box-panel body
- KM453 (K316) mobile NBC reconnaissance vehicle equipped with NBC agent detection, analysis and monitoring equipment carried inside a box body with smooth lines to assist NBC decontamination measures
- (K314) telecommunications network shop van
- (K315) surveillance decoding shop van
- Artillery fire-control shop van (not yet designated)
- Explosive ordnance shop van (not yet designated).

KM452 (4 × 4) shop van (Gordon Arthur)   1340364

Upgraded version of the KM451 ambulance variant as displayed at IDEX 2003. Note the more capacious luton-type rear body which replaces the box-type body (joined to the cab by a soft top) on the original version (Shaun C Connors)   0567959

KM452 (4 × 4) shop van (Gordon Arthur)   1340365

Model	KM450 (K311)	KM451 (K312)	KM452 (K313)	KM453 (K316)
Role:	cargo truck	ambulance (upgraded variant from 2003)	shop van	NBC reconnaissance
Cab seating:	1 + 1	1 + 1	1 + 1	1 + 1
Configuration:	4 × 4	4 × 4	4 × 4	4 × 4
Weight:				
(kerb)	2,550 kg	3,820 kg	3,550 kg	4,195 kg
(GVW, off road)	3,700 kg	4.900 kg	4,470 kg	4,595 kg
(payload, off road)	1,150 kg	1,080 kg	920 kg	400 kg
Length:	5,328 m	5,719 m	5,732 m	5.460 m
Width:	2.008 m	2.18 m	2.008 m	2.182 m
Height:	2.37 m	2.75 m	2.555 m	3.395 m
Ground clearance:	254 mm	254 mm	254 mm	233 mm
Wheelbase:	3.2 m	3.2 m	3.2 m	3.2 m
Angle of approach/departure:	45°/25°	45°/23°	30°/23°	45°/25°
Max speed:	96 km/h	110 km/h	96 km/h	80 km/h
Range:	450 km	770 km	450 km	600 km
Fuel capacity:	106 litres	106 litres	106 litres	106 litres
Max gradient:	60%	60%	60%	60%
Fording:	760 mm	760 mm	760 mm	510 mm
Engine:	MZBA1 4.052-litre 6-cylinder water-cooled diesel developing 115 hp (85 kW) at 3,600 rpm; upgraded ambulance variant from 2003: d4DA 3.907-litre 4-cylinder in-line diesel developing 140 hp (103 kW) at 2,900 rpm and 373 N.m torque at 1,600 rpm			
Gearbox:	manual, 5 forward and 1 reverse gears			
Transfer case:	2-speed	2-speed	2-speed	2-speed
Steering:	power-assisted	power-assisted	power-assisted	ball and nut
Turning radius:	8.5 m	8.5 m	8.5 m	8.5 m
Suspension:	front and rear; semi-elliptic leaf spring with hydraulic shock-absorbers			
Tyres:	9.00 × 16 × 10	9.00 × 16 × 10	9.00 × 16 × 10	37 × 12.5 × 16.5
Electric system:	24 V	24 V	24 V	24 V
Batteries:	2 × 12 V, 80 Ah	2 × 12 V, 100 Ah	2 × 12 V, 80 Ah	2 × 12 V, 80 Ah
Alternator:	45 A	24 V, 100 A	45 A	200 Ah

Specifications
See table above

Status
In production. In service with the armed forces of South Korea, Philippines, Thailand and possibly others.

Contractor
Kia Motors Corporation

KM25 (6 × 6) 2½ ton truck series

Development
Kia Motors was founded in 1944 as Kyongseong Precision, changing its name to Kia Industry Co Ltd in 1952. This changed in 1990 to Kia Motors Corporation, and in 1998 Hyundai Motor took control of the company.

Kia is the sole provider of military vehicles to Korea's Armed Forces and has produced around 123,000 military vehicles in total (that figure including around 20,000 exported to over 20 countries over 30 years), and currently supplies the armed forces of Korea with around 2,000 vehicles per year.

Description
The Kia Motors KM25 series (or the KM250 series as they are sometimes referred) of 2½ ton (6 × 6) trucks closely follow the appearance of the US M44A2 truck and are fitted with MAN diesel engines and locally produced power trains; the recent KM250A has a revised engine installation.

The KM25 series is currently produced in the following forms:
- KM250 (K511) cargo truck
- KM251 (K517) LWB cargo truck
- KM254 NBC decontamination truck. (This version is no longer in production)
- KM255 (K513) fuel tanker with 4,540-litre stainless steel tank body and field refuelling equipment
- KM256 (K515) water tanker with 3,780-litre stainless steel tank body
- KM258 (K512) shop van for field workshops and similar applications.
- KM259 (KM9) decontamination apparatus truck
- (K516) surveillance and decoding shop van
- Artillery fire-control shop van (not yet designated)
- Water purification shop van (not yet designated)
- Explosive ordnance disposal shop van (not yet designated).

The KM250A cargo truck is a later addition to the range. The main differences between this and earlier versions is the installation of a KK-74 diesel engine which develops 183 hp and wider single tyres on all axles.

A 4,500 kg capacity winch equipped with 61 m of cable is optional for all models. Both left- and right-hand drive models are available.

Kia KM255 (6 × 6) tanker (Gordon Arthur) 1340354

Kia KM250 (6 × 6) 2½ ton truck (Gordon Arthur) 1340355

Model	KM250 (K511)	KM251 (K517)	KM255 (K513)	KM256 (K515)	KM258 (K512)
Role:	cargo	LWB cargo	fuel tanker	water tanker	shop van
Cab seating:	1 + 2	1 + 2	1 + 2	1 + 2	1 + 2
Configuration:	6 × 6	6 × 6	6 × 6	6 × 6	6 × 6
Weight:					
(kerb)	6,200 kg	7,000 kg	6,872 kg	6,042 kg	8,070 kg
(GVW, off road)	8,450 kg	9,430 kg	8,461 kg	7,932 kg	9,010 kg
(max load, off road)	2.250 kg	2,430 kg	2,270 litres	1,890 litres	940 kg
Length:	6.712 m	8.38 m	6.68 m	6.68 m	6.807 m
Width:	2.438 m	2.438 m	2.438 m	2.438 m	2.489 m
Height: (overall)	2.845 m	2.845 m	2.467 m	2.467 m	3.302 m
Ground clearance:	278 mm	278 mm	278 mm	278 mm	278 mm
Track:					
(front)	1.721 m	1.721 m	1.721 m	1.721 m	1.721 m
(rear)	1.728 m	1.728 m	1.728 m	1.728 m	1.728 m
Wheelbase:	3.911 m	4.826 m	3.911 m	3.911 m	3.911 m
Angle of approach/departure:	47°/40°	47°/24°	47°/40°	48°/40°	47°/40°
Max speed:	89 km/h	80 km/h	80 km/h	85 km/h	85 km/h
Range:	560 km	560 km	483 km	483 km	483 km
Fuel capacity:	200 litres	200 litres	200 litres	200 litres	200 litres
Max gradient:	60%	60%	60%	60%	60%
Fording:	762 mm	762 mm	762 mm	762 mm	762 mm
Engine:	MAN DO846M 7.225-litre 6-cylinder water-cooled diesel developing 160 hp (118 kW) at 2,500 rpm				
Gearbox:	manual, synchromesh with 5 forward and 1 reverse gears				
Transfer box:	2-speed	2-speed	2-speed	2-speed	2-speed
Steering:	power-assisted	power-assisted	power-assisted	power-assisted	power-assisted
Turning radius:	10.4 m	12.7 m	10.4 m	10.4 m	10.4 m
Suspension:					
(front)	semi-elliptic leaf springs with shock-absorber				
(rear)	semi-elliptic inverted leaf springs				
Tyres:	9.00 × 20	9.00 × 20	9.00 × 20	9.00 × 20	9.00 × 20
Electrical system:	24 V	24 V	24 V	24 V	24 V
Batteries:	2 × 12 V, 80 Ah	2 × 12 V, 80 Ah	2 × 12 V, 80 Ah	2 × 12 V, 80 Ah	2 × 12 V, 80 Ah
Alternator:	60 Ah	60 Ah	60 Ah	60 Ah	60 Ah

Specifications

KM250A cargo truck
Cab seating: 1 + 2
Configuration: 6 × 6
Weight:
(kerb) 6,200 kg
(GVW, off road) 8,540 kg
(max load, off road) 2,250 kg
Length: 6.72 m
Width: 2.44 m
Height:
(top of tilt) 2.845 m
(top of cab) 2.467 m
Ground clearance: 270 mm
Track:
(front) 1.813 m
(rear) 1.81 m
Wheelbase: 3.912 m
Angle of approach/departure: 46°/40°
Max speed: 90 km/h
Range: 600 km

Fuel capacity: 200 litres
Max gradient: 60%
Fording: 760 mm
Engine: KK-74 7.412-litre 6-cylinder in-line water-cooled diesel developing 183 hp (135 kW) at 2,900 rpm
Gearbox: manual, synchromesh, with 5 forward and 1 reverse gears
Clutch: single dry plate
Transfer box: 2-speed
Steering: power-assisted
Turning radius: 10.5 m
Suspension:
(front) semi-elliptic leaf springs with shock-absorbers
(rear) semi-elliptic inverted leaf springs
Tyres: 12.5R 20 TL
Brakes:
(main) air over hydraulic, internal expanding
(parking) dual grip mounted on transfer case
Electrical system: 24 V
Batteries: 2 × 12 V, 80 Ah
Alternator: 80 A

Kia KM258 (6 × 6) 2½ ton shop van truck (Gordon Arthur) 1340357

Kia KM250 (6 × 6) 2½ ton truck (Gordon Arthur) 1340356

KM250A (6 × 6) 2½ ton cargo truck (Kia Motors) 0059704

KM500 (6 × 6) 5 ton cargo truck (Gordon Arthur) 1340361

Status
In production. In service with the armed forces of South Korea.

Contractor
Kia Motors Corporation

KM50 (6 × 6) 5 ton truck series

Development
The KM50 series (or KM250 series as they are sometimes known) of 5 ton (6 × 6) trucks are similar in appearance to the US M809 truck chassis, but differ in a number of areas including various mechanical systems.

Kia Motors was founded in 1944 as Kyongseong Precision, changing its name to Kia Industry Co Ltd in 1952. This changed in 1990 to Kia Motors Corporation, and in 1998 Hyundai Motor took control of the company.

Kia Motors is the sole provider of military vehicles to Korea's Armed Forces. Around 50,000 Kia vehicles are currently in service, with around 2,000 new/replacement vehicles delivered each year. Kia Motors has produced around 123,000 military vehicles, this figure including 20,000 vehicles exported to 20 countries over 30 years.

Description
The KM50 series (or KM250 series as they are sometimes known) of 5 ton (6 × 6) trucks are similar in appearance to the US M809 truck chassis but are fitted with MAN 10.35 litre diesel engines and locally produced power trains. The KM50 series is currently produced in nine forms:
- KM500 (K711) cargo truck
- KM501 (K713) dump truck
- KM502 (K712) wrecker (see entry in the Recovery vehicles section)
- KM503 (K715) tractor truck
- KM504 (K716) expandable van
- KM505 (K720) LWB cargo
- KM506 (K2280) Ribbon bridge carrier
- (K717) spare parts shop van
- Multiple rocket launcher carrier (not yet designated).

The KM500A cargo truck is the latest addition to the range with the main change being the installation of a more powerful 11-litre diesel engine, wider single tyres on all axles and a revised electrical system.

A 9,070 kg capacity winch with 61 m of cable is optional on all models.

Model	KM500 (K711)	KM501 (K713)	KM503 (K715)	KM504 (K716)	KM505 (K720)
Role:	cargo	dump truck	tractor truck	expandable van	LWB cargo
Cab seating:	1 + 2	1 + 2	1 + 2	1 + 2	1 + 2
Configuration:	6 × 6	6 × 6	6 × 6	6 × 6	6 × 6
Weight:					
(kerb)	9.722 kg	10.548 kg	9,200 kg	12,477 kg	10,780 kg
(GVW, off road)	14,257 kg	15,083 kg	15,950 kg	19,281 kg	27,787 kg
(max load, off road)	4,535 kg	4,535 kg	6,750 kg	6,804 kg	4,530 kg
Length:	7.652 m	6.935 m	6.719 m	9.144 m	9.584 m
Width:	2.477 m	2.477 m	2.477 m	2.489 m	2.477 m
Height:	2.946 m	2.832 m	2.68 m	3.467 m	2.946 m
Ground clearance:	270 mm	270 mm	270 mm	270 mm	267 mm
Track:					
(front)	1.88 m	1.88 m	1.88 m	1.88 m	1.88 m
(rear)	1.829 m	1.829 m	1.829 m	1.829 m	1.829 m
Wheelbase:	4.547 m	4.242 m	4.242 m	5.461 m	5.461 m
Max speed:	85 km/h	85 km/h	85 km/h	84 km/h	80 km/h
Fuel capacity:	295 litres	416 litres	416 litres	295 litres	295 litres
Range:	563 km	772 km	563 km	563 km	560 km
Max gradient:	60%	60%	60%	60%	60%
Fording:	760 mm	760 mm	760 mm	760 mm	762 mm
Engine:	MAN D2156 HM 10.35-litre 6-cylinder in line water-cooled diesel developing 236 hp (173 kW) at 2,200 rpm				
Gearbox:	manual with 5 forward and 1 reverse gears				
Clutch:	single dry plate	single dry plate	single dry plate	single dry plate	single dry plate
Transfer case:	2-speed	2-speed	2-speed	2-speed	2-speed
Steering:	power-assisted	power-assisted	power-assisted	power-assisted	power-assisted
Turning radius:	12.75 m	11.7 m	11.7 m	14.5 m	14.7 m
Suspension:					
(front)	semi-elliptic leaf springs with shock-absorber				
(rear)	semi-elliptic inverted leaf springs				
Tyres:	11.00 × 20	11.00 × 20	11.00 × 20	11.00 × 20	11.00 × 20
Electrical system:	24 V	24 V	24 V	24 V	24 V
Batteries:	2 × 12 V, 160 Ah	2 × 12 V, 160 Ah	2 × 12 V, 160 Ah	2 × 12 V, 160 Ah	2 × 12 V, 160 Ah
Alternator:	60 A	60 A	60 A	60 A	60 A

KM505 (6 × 6) 5 ton LWB cargo truck (Gordon Arthur)   1340360

Specifications

KM500A cargo truck
Cab seating: 1 + 2
Configuration: 6 × 6
Weight:
(kerb) 9,440 kg
(GVW, off road) 13,975 kg
(max load, off-road) 4,535 kg
Length:
(without winch) 7.67 m
(with winch) 8.045 m
Width: 2.48 m
Height: 2.95 m
Ground clearance: 270 mm
Track: (front/rear) 1.974 m
Wheelbase: 4.547 m
Angle of approach/departure: 44°/38°
Max speed: 90 km/h
Range: 600 km
Fuel capacity: 295 litres
Max gradient: 60%
Fording: 760 mm
Engine: 6D22Ci 11-litre 6-cylinder water-cooled diesel developing 270 hp (198 kW) at 2,200 rpm
Gearbox: manual, 5 forward and 1 reverse gears
Clutch: single dry plate
Transfer box: 2-speed
Steering: integral power-assisted
Turning radius: 12.75 m
Suspension:
(front) semi-elliptic leaf springs with shock-absorbers
(rear) semi-elliptic inverted leaf springs
Tyres: 395/85R 20 TL
Brakes:
(main) air over hydraulic, internally expanding
(parking) dual grip mounted on transfer case
Electrical system: 24 V
Batteries: 2 × 12 V, 160 Ah
Alternator: 60 A

Status

In production. In service with the armed forces of South Korea and possibly others.

Contractor

Kia Motors Corporation

Malaysia

Hicom Handalan (4 × 4) 3,000 kg truck

Development

First unveiled in April 1996, the Hicom Handalan (4 × 4) 3,000 kg truck (originally known as the Hicom FSS 32G) was developed in close collaboration with the Malaysian Army and Isuzu Motors Limited of Japan. It is basically an Isuzu light truck supplied in KD form and assembled in Malaysia, with the addition of some local content, by the now DRB-HICOM Defence Technologies Sdn Bhd (DEFTECH).

Following trials which lasted six months, a contract worth more than MYR10 million (USD4 million) was awarded for the initial supply of 60 units to the Malaysian Army. It was anticipated that the Malaysian Army would procure a further 3,000-4,000 units in total and by mid-2003 around 1,870 units (1,800 cargo, 70 shelter carrier) had been delivered.

Hicom Handalan I (4 × 4) 3,000 kg truck (T J Gander)   0044305

In early-2003 a revised model, the Handalan II, with a more powerful engine and based on a current-generation Isuzu chassis, was introduced. By mid-2003 around 240 Handalan II in GS configuration had been delivered with 150 more projected by year-end. Current projections are that around 1,000 more vehicles will be required to meet the needs of Malaysia's Armed Forces. Up to 250 vehicles are required by civil authorities for fire and rescue duties. The most recent disclosed deliveries were for 87 cargo trucks, 50 delivered during 2007 and 37 during 2008.

Handalan trucks are known to have carried out trials in the Philippines and interest is understood to have been shown by Bangladesh, Brunei and Pakistan. It was disclosed in 2007 that 69 Hicom Handalan II 3,000 kg (4 × 4) trucks were supplied to Brunei during 2005.

Description

The Hicom Handalan (4 × 4) 3,000 kg truck is based on a ladder chassis frame with channel sections with fully floating axles front and rear (FD 039 split at front, RO 65 banjo at the rear). The suspension employs semi-elliptic steel alloy leaf springs with hydraulic double-acting telescopic shock-absorbers front and rear. Power-assisted steering is provided.

The forward control cab has seating for the driver and two passengers. Special attention is provided to supplying cooling air to the cab interior. A circular roof hatch is provided. The standard body is a cargo platform which may be covered by a canvas tilt over bows. A full 24 V electrical system is provided with a trailer socket provided close to the towing hook at the rear.

Standard equipment includes a rotary pintle hook at the rear, two tie-down hooks at the front, a bull bar, tyre inflator and hose, tool kits, fire extinguisher and two rifle racks. Optional equipment includes an air conditioning system, automatic lubrication system and a vehicle monitoring system.

Apart from the general service cargo vehicle version of the Handalan, the Malaysian Army also operates a self-loading version equipped with a hydraulic crane capable of lifting 1,550 kg at the maximum extension of 5.1 m, a model with storage bins on the load area and a shelter carrier.

Specifications

Handalan I
(Handalan II in square brackets where known to be different)
Cab seating: 1 + 2
Configuration: 4 × 4
Weight:
(laden) 8,980 kg [10,000 kg]
(unladen) 5,800 kg [4,200 kg, quoted as kerb weight] (approx)
(max load, on-road) 3,000 kg [4,800 kg]
(max load, off-road) 3,000 kg
(towed load) 3,000 kg [4,500 kg]
Length: 6.935 m [6.84 m]
Width: 2.4 m
Height:
(cab roof) 2.72 m
(top of tarpaulin) 3.23 m [3.5 m]
Ground clearance: 295 mm [280 mm]
Track: (front and rear) 1.945 m
Wheelbase: 3.8 m
Angle of approach/departure: 33°/32° [40°/32°]
Max speed: (road) 105 km/h [95 km/h]
Fuel capacity: 140 litres
Max gradient: (at GVW) 93%
Side slope: 30%
Fording: 800 mm
Engine: DRB (Isuzu) 6HE1 7.127-litre 6-cylinder in line water-cooled diesel developing 180 hp (134 kW) at 3,000 rpm [HICOM 6HH1 (Isuzu) EURO I 8.226-litre 6-cylinder in-line water-cooled direct injection 4-stroke diesel developing 195 hp (145 kW) at 2,850 rpm and 500 N.m torque at 1,700 rpm]

Gearbox: MGB 5A manual, 5 forward and 1 reverse gears [Allison AT545 automatic, 4 forward and 1 reverse gears; now Allison 2500 SP]
Clutch: single dry plate
Transfer box: 2-speed
Steering: recirculating ball, power-assisted
Turning radius: 8.5 m
Suspension: semi-elliptic steel leaf springs with telescopic shock-absorbers, front and rear
Tyres: 11.00R 20 14PR [11.00R 20 16PR]
Brakes: air over hydraulic, dual circuit with ABS
Electrical system: 24 V
Batteries: 2 × 12 V, 65 Ah
Alternator: 24 V/40 A

Status

Handalan I, production complete. Approximately 1,870 delivered; 1,800 GS, 70 shelter 13 recovery, two GS with crane (Navy). Handalan II in production. Sixty-nine were delivered to Brunei during 2005.

Contractor

DRB-HICOM Defence Technologies Sdn Bhd (DEFTECH)

Netherlands

DAF YA 4442 DNT (4 × 4) 4,000 kg truck

Development

In December 1985, the Netherlands Ministry of Defence (MoD) ordered 5,125 DAF YA 4442 DNT (4 × 4) 4,000 kg trucks. After verification trials, production commenced in mid-1988 and continued until 1994.

The DAF YA 4442 DNT was produced in three main forms: the YA 4442 DNT is a general-purpose cargo vehicle, the YAL 4442 DNT is a general-purpose cargo vehicle with a driver training cab, and the YAK 4442 DNT is a cargo vehicle with a HIAB loading crane. The YAM 4442 is a sub-variant of the YA 4442 produced for the Dutch Marines.

The YF 4442 DNT 'Refueller' was developed by DAF for the Royal Netherlands Army and carries a 4,000-litre fuel tank and pump unit. A total of 395 were ordered with the last delivered in December 1994.

These vehicles are currently scheduled to be replaced under the Dutch Defence Wide Replacement Programme of Wheeled Vehicles. This programme, the initial RfI for which traces back to mid-2008, stalled following the analysis of submissions made by industry following a second RfI from late-2008. It is understood that the Dutch MoD is of the opinion that it cannot procure the quantities or quality of vehicles required within the allocated budget. As a result of this, a reassessment of the requirement is currently underway.

Approximately some 8,000 vehicles ranging from Light Strike Vehicles (LSVs) to 10,000 kg (6 × 6) trucks are scheduled for replacement, with any contract award now not likely until at least 2012.

Description

The DAF YA 4442 DNT is similar in appearance to the DAF YA 4440, full details of which can be found elsewhere in this section. The YA 4442 DNT has a revised radiator grille and the common commercially derived four-person F 218 tilt cab front has revised protection. The reinforced cab roof allows the installation of a ring mount for a light machine gun. The frame which supports this ring is bolted directly to the cab roof over the manhole cover. The cab may be tilted forward to allow access to the engine for maintenance.

DAF YAD 4442 DNT 4,000 kg truck (Richard Stickland)   0056348

DAF YAS 4442 DNT 4,000 kg truck carrying communications shelter (Richard Stickland)   0056342

The torsionally stiff rear cargo platform has bows, tarpaulin cover, side boards and a tailgate, all of which can be removed to enable the truck to carry containers or pallets, if required. When used for troop transport, seating in the form of six removable drop-down benches is provided for 18.

Motive power is provided by a DAF DNT 620 six-cylinder turbocharged diesel engine that replaces the DAF DT 615 diesel engine of the YA 4440. Power is transmitted to the rear DAF model 2235V and front (selectable) DAF model 1635 axles via a ZF six-speed fully synchronised gearbox (replacing the five-speed gearbox of the YA 4440) and two-speed transfer box. Dual or single rear wheels may be fitted; the rear axle is fitted with a limited slip differential.

The truck is fitted with air brakes, with the parking brake acting on the front axle, an exhaust brake and a trailer brake. The electrical system is splashproof and radio suppressed. Compared to the YA 4440, changes were also made to the electrical and brake systems.

Climatic operational range is –32°C to +45°C.

Specifications

YA 4442 DNT
Cab seating: 1 + up to 3 (up to 18 in rear)
Configuration: 4 × 4 (selectable)
Weight:
   (laden) 11,750 kg
   (unladen) 7,620 kg
   (payload on/off-road) 4,000 kg
   (max front axle load) 6,000 kg
   (max rear axle load) 6,750 kg
   (towed load on/off-road) 6,000 kg
   (GCW) 17,750 kg
Length: 7.3 m
Width: 2.47 m
Height: 3.42 m
Ground clearance: 290 mm
Track:
   (front) 1.9 m
   (rear) 1.8 m
Wheelbase: 4.05 m
Angle of approach/departure: 36°/30°
Max continuous speed: 93 km/h
Range: 500 km (approx)
Fuel capacity: 200 litres
Max gradient: 50%
Side slope: 30%
Fording: 900 mm

DAF YF 4442 DNT fitted with a 4,000-litre capacity fuel tank and pump unit (Shaun C Connors)   0121830

Engine: DAF DNT 6.242 litre 6-cylinder in-line turbocharged water-cooled direct injection 4-stroke diesel developing 172 hp (126 kW) at 2,600 rpm and 535 N.m torque at 1,700 rpm
Gearbox: ZF S6-36 synchromesh with 6 forward and 1 reverse gears
Clutch: single dry plate (ϕ 350 mm)
Transfer box: Steyr VG 450 2-speed
Steering: power assisted, ZF 8043
Turning radius: 9.8 m (approx)
Suspension: semi-elliptic leaf springs with double-acting shock-absorbers, front and rear
Tyres: 13R 22.5
Brakes: dual circuit, air, drums all-round. Supplementary exhaust brake
Electrical system: 24 V
Batteries: 2 × 12 V, 125 Ah
Alternator: 95 A

Status
Production complete. In service with the Netherlands Armed Forces (5,125 delivered), replacement programme running.

Contractor
DAF Trucks NV

DAF YA 4440 (4 × 4) 4,000 kg truck

Development
The YA 4440 (4 × 4) 4,000 kg medium-mobility vehicle was developed by DAF to meet the requirements of the Royal Netherlands Army. The first five prototypes were handed over to the Army for trials late in 1974. Late in 1976 the Royal Netherlands Army placed an order for 4,000 vehicles for delivery between 1977 and 1980. Late in 1977 a further order for 2,500 vehicles was placed, with final deliveries made in mid-1983. The YA 4440 is based on proven commercial components and shared many common components with the DAF YA 2442 (4 × 4) 2 ton truck (this was developed to prototype stage but not placed in production), including the cab, engine, transfer case and transmission. It was designed to carry 4,000 kg of cargo both on roads and across country and to tow a trailer with a maximum weight of 6,000 kg.

DAF delivered 17 examples of the YAK 4440 for trials fitted with a hydraulic crane for rapid unloading of ammunition and cargo. These have the same chassis as the basic YA 4440, but to accommodate the crane which is located immediately behind the cab, they have a shorter cargo body which has no bows or tarpaulin cover. Of the 17 units, eight had a PESCI (P445G) crane and nine a Hiab (850S) crane. Following trials with these prototype vehicles, the Royal Netherlands Army placed an order for 200 units fitted with the Hiab crane.

Final production figures for YA 4440 series trucks supplied to the Netherlands Ministry of Defence are 7,612 vehicles. Not all of these remain in service; an undisclosed number having been cast, some subsequently made available for resale through surplus military equipment dealers.

In February 1984 it was announced that Portugal had ordered 300 YA 4440 trucks following tests with four vehicles. The order was stated to be worth G26 million; 35 per cent of the value of the vehicles was offset by assembling the vehicles in Portugal and using some Portuguese components. Starting in July 1984 the first vehicles were assembled in Portugal by EVICAR of Setubal. The order was completed by the end of January 1985.

The Netherlands government transferred 279 YA 4440 trucks to Botswana in 1995, possibly followed by a further 81 vehicles. 90 YA 4440 and 10 YAK 4440 vehicles have also been passed on to Nigeria. During 2004 the Netherlands Ministry of Defence (MoD) sold 50 DAF YA-4440 4 × 4 trucks to L Jackson & Co (a surplus military equipment dealer) in the UK for transfer to Angola. This sale followed an earlier batch of 100 trucks of this type sent to Angola during 2003.

An early example of the DAF YA 4440 (4 × 4) 4,000 kg truck of the Dutch Army (DAF Trucks)   1156066

DAF YA 4440 (4 × 4) 4,000 kg truck of the Portuguese Army (Victor Barreira)   1391236

It was announced in January 2002 that RDM Technology BV was to supply Jordan's Armed Forces with 18 MOBile ArTillery (MOBAT) 105 mm truck-mounted howitzers with an option for an additional 20 systems. The truck platform involved was surplus to requirement Dutch Army DAF YA 4440s.

All remaining DAF YA 4440 trucks are currently scheduled to be replaced under the Dutch Defence Wide Replacement Programme of Wheeled Vehicles. This programme, the initial RFI for which traces back to mid-2008, stalled following the analysis of submissions made by industry following a second RfI from late-2008. It is understood that the Dutch MoD is of the opinion that it cannot procure the quantities or quality of vehicles required within the allocated budget. As a result of this, a reassessment of the requirement is currently underway.

Approximately some 8,000 vehicles ranging from Light Strike Vehicles (LSVs) to 10,000 kg (6 × 6) trucks are scheduled for replacement, with any contract award now not likely until at least 2012.

Description
The four-person all-steel cab of the YA 4440 is of the forward control type and derived from the commercial DAF F218 cab. It can be tilted forward to allow access to the engine for maintenance. The reinforced cab roof allows the installation of a ring mount for a light machine gun. The frame which supports this ring is bolted directly to the cab roof over the manhole cover.

The torsionally stiff rear cargo platform has bows, tarpaulin cover, side boards and a tailgate, all of which can be removed to enable the truck to carry containers or pallets, if required. When used for troop transport, seating in the form of six removable drop-down benches is provided for 18.

Motive power is provided by a DAF DT 615 diesel engine. Power is transmitted to the DAF model 2235V front and model 1635 rear beam-type axles via a ZF five-speed manual gearbox and ZF two-speed transfer box.

The YA 4440 is fitted with air brakes, with the parking brake acting on the front axle, an exhaust brake and a trailer brake. The electrical system is splashproof and radio suppressed. Climatic operational range is –32 to +45°C, and when required an external pre-heater can be fitted to the engine cooling system for starting in extreme cold.

Optional equipment included: an hydraulic crane to the rear of the cab with a capacity of 7,000 kg; stabilisers on each side of the chassis for when the hydraulic crane is being used; automatic transmission; two-man passenger seat in place of the standard one-man seat; and a manually operated crane with a 1,000 kg capacity.

The YAL 4440 is used for training drivers and has a tilt cab with seats for the driver under instruction, an instructor and two student drivers. In total, 375 of these vehicles were built for the Royal Netherlands Army.

Specifications
YA 4440
Cab seating: 1 + up to 3 (up to 18 in rear)
Configuration: 4 × 4
Weight:
    (laden) 11,000 kg
    (unladen) 7,000 kg
    (payload) 4,000 kg
    (front axle, permissible) 6,000 kg
    (rear axle, permissible) 7,400 kg
    (towed load) 6,000 kg
    (GCW) 17,000 kg
Length: 7.19 m
Width: 2.44 m
Height:
    (tarpaulin) 3.42 m
    (load area) 1.43 m
Ground clearance: 300 mm

Track: 1.91 m
Wheelbase: 4.05 m
Angle of approach/departure: 36°/30°
Max speed: (road) 80 km/h
Range: 500 km
Max gradient:
  (without trailer) 50%
  (with 4,000 kg trailer) 20%
Side slope: 30%
Fording: 900 mm
Engine: DAF DT 615 6.17-litre 6-cylinder in-line turbocharged direct injection water-cooled 4-stroke diesel developing 153 hp (112 kW) at 2,400 rpm and 505 N.m torque at 1,600 rpm
Gearbox: ZF S5-35/2 synchromesh with 5 forward and 1 reverse gears
Clutch: hydraulic, single dry disc (diameter 350 mm)
Transfer box: ZF VG 250/2 2 speed
Steering: hydraulic power-assisted, ZF 8042
Turning radius: 9 m
Suspension: 8-leaf 1.54 m semi-elliptic springs with double-acting hydraulic shock-absorbers, front; 10-leaf 1.54 m semi-elliptic springs with double-acting hydraulic shock-absorbers, rear
Tyres: 12.00R 20
Brakes:
  (main) dual circuit, air (plus exhaust brake), drums all-round
  (parking) mechanical, also holding brake
Electrical system: 24 V
Batteries: 2 × 12 V, 100 Ah
Alternator: 85 Ah

Status

Production complete. Three-hundred delivered to Portugal, 7,612 delivered to the Royal Netherlands Army and Navy (replacement programme running), of which 279 (and possibly a further 81) have been passed to Botswana, 100 to Nigeria and 100 (2003) and 50 (2004) to Angola. Surplus vehicles used as the base for the RDM MOBAT 105 mm truck-mounted howitzer (see text).

Contractor

DAF Trucks NV

DAF YA 5444 DNT (4 × 4) 5,000 kg truck

Development

The DAF YA 5444 DNT (4 × 4) 5,000 kg truck is a further development of the DAF YA 4442 4,000 kg series (full details of which can be found elsewhere in this section), designed for logistic roles, such as a carrier for generator sets, fuel tanks, munitions, shelters. First deliveries went to the Royal Netherlands Air Force.

These vehicles are currently scheduled to be replaced under the Dutch Defence Wide Replacement Programme of Wheeled Vehicles. This programme, the initial RfI for which traces back to mid-2008, stalled following the analysis of submissions made by industry following a second RfI from late-2008. It is understood that the Dutch MoD is of the opinion that it cannot procure the quantities or quality of vehicles required within the allocated budget. As a result of this, a reassessment of the requirement is currently underway.

Approximately some 8,000 vehicles ranging from Light Strike Vehicles (LSVs) to 10,000 kg (6 × 6) trucks are scheduled for replacement, with any contract award now not likely until at least 2012.

Description

The three-person all-steel cab of the YA 5444 is of the forward-control type and derived from the commercial DAF F218 cab. It can be tilted forward to allow access to the engine for maintenance. The reinforced cab roof allows the installation of a ring mount for a light machine gun. The frame which supports this ring is bolted directly to the cab roof over the manhole cover.

The rear cargo platform has bows, tarpaulin cover, side boards and a tailgate, all of which can be removed to enable the truck to carry containers or pallets, if required.

DAF YA 5444 DNT (4 × 4) 5,000 kg trucks (Richard Stickland) 0100360

Motive power is provided by a DAF DNT diesel engine. Power is transmitted to the DAF model 2235V front and model 1635 rear beam-type axles via a ZF six-speed manual gearbox and Steyr two-speed transfer box.

The YA 5444 is fitted with air brakes, with the parking brake acting on the rear axle. The electrical system is splashproof and radio suppressed.

Specifications

Cab seating: 1 + 2
Configuration: 4 × 4 (selectable)
Weight:
  (laden) 13,600 kg
  (unladen) 8,400 kg
  (payload) 5,000 kg
  (front axle, permissible) 6,000 kg
  (rear axle, permissible) 8,000 kg
  (towed load, on-road) 7,000 kg
  (GCW) 20,500 kg
Length: 8.2 m
Width: 2.5 m
Height: (cab) 3 m
Ground clearance: 260 mm
Track:
  (front) 1.9 m
  (rear) 1.8 m
Wheelbase: 4.05 m
Angle of approach/departure: 36°/20°
Max speed: 95 km/h
Range: 500 km (approx)
Fuel capacity: 200 litres
Max gradient: (with/without trailer) 30%/50%
Side slope: (static) 30%
Fording: 900 mm
Engine: DAF DNT 6.242 litre 6-cylinder in-line turbocharged water-cooled direct injection 4-stroke diesel developing 172 hp (126 kW) at 2,600 rpm and 585 N.m torque at 1,700 rpm
Gearbox: ZF S6-36 with 6 forward and 1 reverse gears
Clutch: single dry plate (∅ 350 mm)
Transfer box: Steyr VG 450 2-speed
Steering: power assisted, ZF 8043
Turning radius: 9.8 m (approx)
Suspension: 8-leaf 1.54 m semi-elliptic leaf springs and telescopic hydraulic double acting shock-absorbers front; 20-leaf 1.54 m semi-elliptic leaf springs and telescopic hydraulic double acting shock-absorbers, rear
Tyres: 10.00R 20
Brakes:
  (main) dual circuit, air, drums all-round
  (parking) spring cylinders on rear axle
Electrical system: 24 V
Batteries: 2 × 12 V, 125 Ah
Alternator: 95 A

Status

Production complete. In service with the Dutch Armed Forces; replacement programme running.

Contractor

DAF Trucks NV

DAF YA 5441 and YA 5442 (4 × 4) 5,000 kg trucks

Development

The DAF YA 5441 (4 × 4) 5,000 kg truck was designed to carry 5,000 kg of cargo both on and off roads. It was developed from a standard commercial design and uses many components of the YA 4440 (4 × 4) 4,000 kg truck in service with the Royal Netherlands Army and Navy. A second production series with slight modifications is known as the YA 5442.

Royal Netherlands Air Force DAF YAK 5442 fitted with Hiab 2027 AVL 20 t/m hydraulic crane over the rear axle (DAF Trucks) 1156068

DAF YA 5442 DT (4 × 4) 5,000 kg truck (DAF Trucks)   1156067

These vehicles are currently scheduled to be replaced under the Dutch Defence Wide Replacement Programme of Wheeled Vehicles. This programme, the initial RfI for which traces back to mid-2008, stalled following the analysis of submissions made by industry following a second RfI from late-2008. It is understood that the Dutch MoD is of the opinion that it cannot procure the quantities or quality of vehicles required within the allocated budget. As a result of this, a reassessment of the requirement is currently underway.

Approximately some 8,000 vehicles ranging from Light Strike Vehicles (LSVs) to 10,000 kg (6 × 6) trucks are scheduled for replacement, with any contract award now not likely until at least 2012.

Description

The two-person all-steel cab of the YA 5441 and YA 5442 trucks is of the forward-control type and is derived from the commercial DAF F218 cab. It normally seats two, but an optional centre third seat could be fitted. The cab tilts forward to allow access to the engine for maintenance. The roof is reinforced and allows for the installation of a ring mount for a light machine gun. The frame which supports this ring is bolted directly to the cab roof over a manhole cover.

The torsionally stiff rear cargo platform has bows, tarpaulin cover, side boards and a tailgate, all of which can be removed to enable the truck to carry containers or pallets if required.

Motive power is provided by a DAF DT 615 diesel engine. Power is transmitted to the DAF model 2235V front and model 1635 rear beam-type axles via a ZF five-speed manual gearbox and ZF two-speed transfer box.

The YA 5441 and YA 5442 are fitted with air brakes, with the parking brake acting on the rear axle, an exhaust brake and a trailer brake. The electrical system is splashproof and radio suppressed. Climatic operational range is −32° to +45°C, and when required an external pre-heater can be fitted to the engine cooling system for starting in extreme cold.

Model	YA 5441	YA 5442
Cab seating:	1 + 1 or 2	1 + 1 or 2
Configuration:	4 × 4	4 × 4
Weight:		
(laden)	12,290 kg	12,600 kg
(unladen)	7,290 kg	7,300 kg
(payload)	5,000 kg	5,000 kg
(front axle, permissible)	4,900 kg	4,800 kg
(rear axle, permissible)	8,100 kg	8,100 kg
(towed load)	4,000 kg	4,000 kg
(GCW)	16,290 kg	16,600 kg
Length:	7.54 m	7.54 m
Width:	2.47 m	2.44 m
Height:		
(overall)	2.96 m	2.96 m
(load area)	1.3 m	1.28 m
Ground clearance:		
(axle)	265 mm	265 mm
(chassis)	450 mm	450 mm
Track:		
(front)	1.938 m	1.93 m
(rear)	1.729 m	1.8 m
Wheelbase:	3.85 m	3.85 m
Angle of approach/departure:	32°/23°	32°/24°
Max speed:	80 km/h	80 km/h
Range:	500 km	500 km
Fuel capacity:	200 litres	200 litres
Max gradient:		
(without trailer)	59%	60%
(with trailer)	38%	40%
Side slope:	30%	30%
Fording:	600 mm	600 mm
Engine:	DAF model DT 615 6.17-litre 6-cylinder in-line turbocharged water-cooled direct injection 4-stroke diesel developing 153 hp (112 kW) at 2,400 rpm and 505 N.m torque at 1,600 rpm	
Gearbox:	ZF S5-35/2 manual with 5 forward and 1 reverse gears	
Clutch:	single dry plate (φ 350 mm)	single dry plate (φ 350 mm
Transfer box:	ZF VG250/2 2-speed	ZF VG250/2 2-speed
Steering:	power assisted, ZF 8065	power assisted, ZF 8065
Suspension:	8-leaf 1.4 m semi-elliptic leaf springs with double acting telescopic shock-absorbers, front; 8 + 2-leaf 1.4 m semi-elliptic leaf springs, plus 6 + 1 950 mm auxiliary leaf springs and double acting telescopic shock-absorbers, rear	
Tyres:	10.00R 20	10.00 R 20
Brakes:		
(main)	dual circuit, air, drums all-round	dual circuit, air, drums all-round
(parking)	spring-brake cylinders on rear axle	
Electrical system:	24 V	24 V
Batteries:	2 × 12 V, 100 Ah	2 × 12 V, 100 Ah
Alternator:	28 V, 35 A	28 V, 35 A

A version with a naturally aspirated DAF DH825 diesel engine was offered but not produced.

Variants

YAK 5442

The YAK 5442 was produced during 1984 for the Royal Netherlands Air Force (16) and is a crane truck mounting a Hiab Type 2027 AVL 20 t/m hydraulic crane over the rear axle. Telescopic outrigger legs on the ends of sliding jibs are provided at each corner of the cargo body area. Some vehicles have 8,000 kg recovery winches.

Specifications

See table on facing page

Status

Production complete. Supplied to the Royal Netherlands Air Force (195 delivered); replacement programme running.

Contractor

DAF Trucks NV

DAF YAV 2300 DHTD (4 × 4) 7,000 kg truck

Development

The DAF YAV 2300 DHTD (4 × 4) 7,000 kg truck was derived from the YAZ 2300 (6 × 6) 10,000 kg series, full details of which can be found elsewhere in this section. It was designed to meet military specifications using components from DAF's commercial vehicle range.

In 1984 the Netherlands Ministry of Defence placed an order, on behalf of NATO, for 85 of these trucks. These vehicles are used to carry shelters and electronic equipment.

Description

The two-person all-steel cab of the YAV 2300 DHTD is of the forward-control type and derived from the commercial DAF F218 cab. It can be tilted forward to allow access to the engine for maintenance. The reinforced cab roof allows the installation of a ring mount for a light machine gun. The frame which supports this ring is bolted directly to the cab roof over the manhole cover.

The chassis is of ladder-type construction that is partially bolted and partially riveted with two C-section 280 × 75 × 7.5 mm longitudinal members with C-section 265 × 65 × 5 mm reinforcements, joined by C-section and tubular cross-members. The torsionally stiff rear cargo platform mounts to the chassis at four points and has side boards and a tailgate, all of which can be removed to enable the truck to carry shelters and containers when required.

Motive power is provided by a DAF DHTD 825 diesel engine. Power is transmitted to the Kirkstall SD 65-11-1S front and DAF model 2699 rear beam-type hub-reduction axles via a ZF eight-speed manual gearbox, ZF two-speed transfer box and torque convertor. The rear axle is fitted with a differential lock.

The YAV 2300 DHTD is fitted with air brakes, with the parking brake acting on the rear axle, an exhaust brake and a trailer brake. The electrical system is splashproof and radio suppressed. Climatic operational range is –32°C to +45°C.

Specifications

Cab seating: 1 + 1 or 2
Configuration: 4 × 4
Weight:
(laden) 15,500 kg
(laden, max permissible) 20,000 kg
(unladen) 10,200 kg
(payload) 7,000 kg (5,300 kg off-road)
(front axle load, permissible) 7,000 kg
(rear axle load, permissible) 13,000 kg
(GCW) 35,000 kg
Length: 7.82 m
Width: 2.46 m
Height: (overall) 3.1 m
Load area: 5 × 2.35 m
Ground clearance: 320 mm
Track:
(front) 1.98 m
(rear) 1.82 m
Wheelbase: 4.5 m
Angle of approach/departure (laden): 30°/30°
Max speed: 89 km/h
Range: 600 km
Fuel capacity: 300 litres
Max gradient:
(with trailer) >35%
(without trailer) >60%
Side slope: 35%
Fording: 900 mm
Engine: DAF DHTD 825 Mil. 8.25-litre 6-cylinder in-line turbocharged water-cooled direct injection 4-stroke diesel developing 213 hp (157 kW) at 2,400 rpm and 690 N.m torque at 1,600 rpm

DAF YAV 2300 DHTD (4 × 4) 7,000 kg truck transporting an electronics-type shelter (DAF Trucks)
1156073

Torque converter: ZF WSK 400/25
Gearbox: ZF 5S-111 GPA with 8 forward and 1 reverse gears
Steering: hydraulic power assisted, ZF 8046
Min turning radius: 11 m
Suspension:
(front) DAF trapezium with adjustable KONI hydraulic telescopic double acting shock-absorbers
(rear) DAF trapezium with auxiliary spring and adjustable KONI hydraulic telescopic double acting shock absorbers
Tyres: 13R 22.5K (14.75/80R 20 optional)
Brakes:
(main) dual circuit, air, drums all-round. Supplementary exhaust retarder
(parking) spring-brake cylinders on rear axle
Electrical system: 24 V
Batteries: 4 × 12 V, 125 Ah
Alternator: 28 V, 35 A

Status

Production complete. Delivered to NATO.

Contractor

DAF Trucks NV

DAF YAZ 2300 (6 × 6) 10,000 kg truck

Development

Mid-1981, following trials with a number of prototypes, the Netherlands Ministry of Defence placed an order with DAF Trucks worth ANG236.5 million for a family of new 10,000 kg (6 × 6) trucks in order to replace the then DAF YA 616 6,000 kg (6 × 6) trucks. The YA 2300 series is based on the commercial 2300 range and is powered by a DAF DHS 825 250 hp diesel.

Delivery of the first batch commenced in mid-1983 and was completed during 1985. In 1988 the Netherlands MoD ordered a further batch of over 1,400 YA 2300 series vehicles. Total deliveries of this series of vehicles was 1,500.

These vehicles are currently scheduled to be replaced under the Dutch Defence Wide Replacement Programme of Wheeled Vehicles. This programme, the initial RfI for which traces back to mid-2008, stalled following the analysis of submissions made by industry following a second RfI from late-2008. It is understood that the Dutch MoD is of the opinion that it cannot procure the quantities or quality of vehicles required within the allocated budget. As a result of this, a reassessment of the requirement is currently underway.

Approximately some 8,000 vehicles ranging from Light Strike Vehicles (LSVs) to 10,000 kg (6 × 6) trucks are scheduled for replacement, with any contract award now not likely until at least 2012.

Description

The YAZ 2300 (6 × 6) general cargo truck may be taken as being typical of the other vehicles in the series. It has a chassis designed as a common ladder-type platform and comprises two C-section frame rails with C-section and tubular cross-members. The longitudinal C-sections are strengthened over their full length.

The fully enclosed two-door all-steel cab was developed from the civilian F218 type and can be tilted forward to an angle of 60° allowing access to the engine for maintenance. The cab has a large capacity heating and ventilation system and thermal and sound insulation. The driver's and co-driver's seats are adjustable, with the third seat with foot rest being mounted against the cab rear wall. The reinforced roof cab roof, in the cargo model only, is fitted with an observation hatch on which can be mounted a light machine gun.

Model	YAZ 2300 Truck	YKZ 2300 Tipper	YHZ 2300 Tractor	YGZ 2300 Bridging
Cab seating:	1 + 2	1 + 2	1 + 2	1 + 2
Configuration:	6 × 6	6 × 6	6 × 6	6 × 6
Weight:				
(laden)	27,500 kg	27,500 kg	25,500 kg	20,150 kg
(unladen)	13,500 kg (with crane)	13,500 kg	12,500 kg	13,700 kg
(front axle load, permissible)	7,500 kg	7,500 kg	7,500 kg	7,500 kg
(rear axle load, permissible)	20,000 kg	20,000 kg	18,000 kg	20,000 kg
(GCW)	40,000 kg	40,000 kg	40,000 kg	4,000 kg
Length:	9.55 m	8.03 m	7.74 m	8.75 m
Width:	2.49 m	2.49 m	2.49 m	3.45 m
Height: (overall)	3.59 m	3.54 m	3.59 m	4 m
(load area)	1.5 m	1.5 m	1.63 m	1.55 m
Ground clearance:	320 mm	320 mm	320 mm	320 mm
Track:				
(front)	1.98 m	1.98 m	2.05 m	2.05 m
(rear)	1.82 m	1.82 m	2.01 m	2.1 m
Wheelbase:	4.85 m	4.45 m	4.45 m	5.35 m
Angle of approach/departure:	30°/20°	30°/30°	30°/32°	30°/20°
Max speed:	88 km/h	88 km/h	88 km/h	88 km/h
Range: (minimum)	600 km	600 km	600 km	600 km
Fuel capacity:	300 litres	300 litres	300 litres	300 litres
Max gradient:	50%	50%	50%	50%
Side slope:	30%	30%	30%	30%
Fording:	750 mm	750 mm	750 mm	750 mm
Engine:	DAF DHS 825 8.25 litre 6-cylinder in-line turbocharged water-cooled direct injection, 4-stroke diesel developing 250 hp (184 kW) at 2,400 rpm and 915 N.m torque at 1,500 rpm			
Torque converter:	ZF WSK 400/1	ZF WSK 400/1	ZF WSK 400/1	ZF WSK 400/1
Gearbox:	ZF 5S-110 GPA with 8 forward and 1 reverse gears. Transfer box is a ZF A 600/3D with lockable differential and is an integral part of the gearbox			
Steering:	hydraulic power-assisted, ZF 8046,			
Turning radius:	11.2 m	11 m	11 m	12 m
Suspension:				
(front)	semi-elliptic leaf springs and hydraulic telescopic double action shock-absorbers			
(rear)	inverted semi elliptic leaf springs			
Tyres:	13R 22.5	13R 22.5	14.75R 20	14.75/80R 20
Brakes:				
(main)	dual circuit, air, drums all-round. Supplementary engine exhaust brake			
(parking)	spring brake	spring brake	spring brake	spring brake
Electrical system:	24 V	24 V	24 V	24 V
Batteries:	2 × 12 V, 125 Ah	2 × 12 V, 125 Ah	2 × 12 V, 125 Ah	2 × 12 V, 125 Ah
Alternator:	55 A	55 A	55 A	55 A

The rear cargo area is of aluminium construction and is provided with removable drop sides and a drop tailgate. To the rear of the cab is a hydraulic crane for unloading cargo but, before this is used, stabilisers are lowered to the ground either side of the vehicle to the rear of the cab.

The front axle is a Kirkstall DS 65, the rear bogie is a DAF 2699 T fitted with lockable longitudinal and cross-axle differentials.

Standard equipment includes: a seven- and 12-pole trailer connector; slave connector; trouble light connector at front and rear; standard commercial traffic lighting and blackout lighting to NATO specifications. At the front is a push/pull NATO pin and at the rear is a 24,000 kg towing hook.

Variants

YFZ 2300 Tanker
Carries a 12,000 litre fuel tank for field refuelling.

DAF Trucks YKZ 2300 tipper variant. This model has a maximum payload of 14,000 kg and a kerb weight of 13,500 kg (Shaun C Connors) 1156077

DAF Trucks YWZ 3300 recovery vehicle (full details of which can be found in the Recovery vehicles section) on which the recovery hamper has been removed and replaced by a Technamics container Load Handling System (LHS). This conversion was carried out by the Dutch MoD and did not involve DAF Trucks (Shaun C Connors) 0121827

DAF Trucks YAC 2300. This model has provision for carrying standard ISO containers; max payload is 12,260 kg (Shaun C Connors)   1156075

DAF Trucks YAZ 2300 (6 × 6) 10,000 kg cargo truck with materials handling crane (Shaun C Connors)   1156076

200YAC 2300 Container Carrier
Has provision for carrying standard ISO containers. Max payload 12,260 kg.

YTV 2300 Tractor
4 × 4 tractor truck for semi-trailers.

YWZ 2300 MOGOS
Carries a load handling system to transport, load and unload the Mobiel Geneeskindig Operatiekamer Systeem (MOGOS) containerised mobile medical unit.

YAZ 2300 Snow Fighting Vehicle
This is a special snow clearing vehicle used by the Royal Netherlands Air Force for clearing airfield runways. It is equipped with a de-icing fluid tank, pumping gear and swing-out spray bars. It is possible to fit a snow plough on the front.

YKZ 2300 Tipper
This was developed as the replacement for the DAF YK 616 three-way tipper. It has a maximum payload of 14,000 kg and a kerb weight of 13,500 kg.

YHZ 2300 Artillery Tractor
This variant was ordered by the Netherlands Ministry of Defence and production of 78 commenced in 1987. It is used to tow 155 mm M114 and M114/39 howitzers and has seating for 12 personnel and two 12-round racks for ammunition.

YGZ 2300 Bridging Vehicle
This variant is designed to carry and launch Ribbon Bridge units using a DAF Special Products system in place of the normal cargo body. The system can also be used to carry and launch rolls of trackway.

YAZ 2301 Truck
Although described as a general cargo truck, the YAZ 2301 (6 × 6) is used to carry container/shelters associated with the Patriot tactical air defence system.

YTZ 2301 Truck Tractor
This is used to tow the Patriot tactical air defence system missile launcher.

Specifications
See table on facing page

Status
In service with the Royal Netherlands Army, Marines and Air Force (Patriot) (1,500 supplied); replacement programme running.

Contractor
DAF Trucks NV

Pakistan

Yasoob 3,000 kg (4 × 4) and 6,000 kg (6 × 6) trucks

Development
The decision to proceed with the development of a family of military and commercial trucks was taken by the Pakistan government in July 1989. The first two prototypes of the resultant military truck, named Yasoob after the fastest horse of the Prophet, were handed over to the Pakistan Army for trials during 1990. These vehicles had 40 per cent local content, which increased when full production commenced. Components for all major vehicle units, such as the engine, transmission, axles and transfer, were manufactured under licence (with provision for buy-back arrangements). The first production unit was delivered to the Pakistan Army in 1994.

Development of a Yasoob 4 × 4 Mark II model was completed. This model had a forward control cab manufactured by the then Leyland Trucks Limited of the UK. Apart from the standard cargo body, recovery, tanker, mobile workshop and long wheelbase versions were scheduled.

As of 1999 Trans Mobile Limited (manufacturers of the Yasoob range) were understood to have ceased trading. No production figures for the Yasoob range were officially released, however it is understood that around 450 (6 × 6) and 250 (4 × 4) models were delivered between 1993-95.

Description
The Yasoob (4 × 4) 3,000 kg and (6 × 6) 6,000 kg trucks were designed as all-purpose vehicles intended for general logistic purposes, the 6,000 kg truck also capable of towing artillery. The standard models were cargo/troop carrying (3,000 kg) or cargo (6,000 kg), and in both cases layout was entirely conventional.

Commercial versions of the Yasoob were to have GVWs of 14,000 to 24,000 kg.

Specifications
Standard 6 × 6 cargo version
Cab seating: 1 + 2
Configuration: 6 × 6
Weight:
  (laden, front axle) 6,500 kg
  (laden, rear bogie) 15,000 kg
  (total) 21,500 kg
  (max load, road) 12,000 kg
  (max load, cross-country) 6,000 kg
  (towed load) 10,000 kg
Length: 7.73 m
Width: 2.5 m
Height:
  (unladen, overall) 3.1 m
  (reduced) 2.75 m
Ground clearance: 335 mm

Yasoob (6 × 6) 6,000 kg truck with hydraulic load handling crane (Trans Mobile Limited)   0512507

Track:
(front) 2.063 m
(rear) 2.112 m
Wheelbase: 4.6 m + 1.4 m
Angle of approach/departure: 40°/35°
Max speed with towed load:
(road) 80 km/h
(off-road) 50 km/h
Range: (cruising) 550 km
Fuel capacity: 270 litres
Gradient: (with towed load) 60%
Fording: 750 mm
Engine: 8.3-litre 6-cylinder direct injection 4-stroke diesel developing 240 hp (179 kW) at 2,400 rpm
Gearbox: manual with 9 forward and 2 reverse gears
Clutch: twin dry plate
Transfer box: 2-speed
Steering: power assisted, ZF 8097
Turning radius: 12.75 m
Suspension: semi-elliptic 8 leaf springs, front; inverted semi-elliptic 13 leaf springs, rear
Tyres: 13.00R 20
Brakes:
(main) air
(parking) spring/air
Electrical system: 24 V
Batteries: 2 × 12 V, 150 Ah
Alternator: 150 A

Standard 4 × 4 cargo version
Cab seating: 1 + 2
Configuration: 4 × 4
Weight:
(GVW, road) 10,400 kg
(GVW, of-road) 9,400 kg
(max load, road) 4,000 kg
(max load, off-road) 3,000 kg
(towed load) 3,000 kg
Length: 6.895 m
Width: 2.5 m
Height:
(unladen, overall) 3.23 m
(top of cab) 2.925 m
Ground clearance: 515 mm
Track:
(front) 2.082 m
(rear) 2.096 m
Wheelbase: 3.9 m
Angle of approach/departure: 40°/40°
Max speed: 94 km/h
Range: (cruising) 900 km
Gradient: 75%
Fording: 800 mm
Engine: Cummins 6BTA 5.9/180 5.88-litre 6-cylinder direct injection diesel developing 180 hp (134 kW) at 2,500 rpm
Gearbox: Eaton 4106 manual with 6 forward and 1 reverse gears
Clutch: 13/330-1DLB dry plate
Transfer box: VG 450 2-speed
Steering: power-assisted, TAS 55
Turning radius: 7.9 m
Suspension: semi-elliptic leaf springs with telescopic shock-absorbers, front and rear
Tyres: 11.00 × 20
Brakes:
(main) dual circuit, air
(parking) spring/air
Electrical system: 24 V
Batteries: 2 × 12 V, 100 Ah
Alternator: 45 A

Status
Production complete. In service with the Pakistan's Armed Forces (see text).

Contractor
Trans Mobile Limited (This company is no longer trading.)

Poland

Star 944 (4 × 4) 3,000 kg truck

Development
The Star 944 (4 × 4) 3,000 kg truck was first shown in 1999 along with the larger Star 1466 (6 × 6) 6,000 kg truck. The Star 944 was the successor of the earlier Star 744 (4 × 4) 4,000 kg truck, itself essentially a (4 × 4) evolution of

A Polish Army Star 944 (4 × 4) 3,000 kg truck as displayed at MSPO 2005. The body-mounted shelter contains elements of the Krokus broadband tactical communication system under development for the Polish Army (Patrick Allen/IHS Jane's)   1149168

the Star 266 (6 × 6) 3,500 kg truck. The Star 744 did not enter volume production, the Star 944 being the series production successor of the earlier Star 244 (5,000 kg) truck. The Star 1466 was the series production successor of the Star 266.

The first four Star 944 trucks were delivered to Polish Armed Forces for trials during the autumn of 2000, and while then current Polish procurement plans called for 797 examples to be delivered between 2001-2006, only 35 vehicles (at a cost of USD57,000 each) were delivered during 2001, 86 during 2002, and 71 (plus some additional vehicles purchased by WZL for mounting specialist communication equipment; Star delivered 120 trucks in total during 2003) during 2003. Production concluded during 2007, by which time 650 Star 944 trucks had been delivered.

Full details of the Star 66/660, 266 and 1466 trucks can be found elsewhere in this section.

The then Zaklady Starachowickie Star SA was acquired by MAN of Germany in 2000.

Description
The Star 944 is of conventional design, being based on a C-section ladder frame chassis with a front-mounted forward-control two-person all-steel cab based on the MAN L2000 commercial design. The cab is fully enclosed, has a single roof hatch, a flat single-piece windscreen and tilts forward engine access. Three variants of cab may be fitted: Type K, the standard fit, is a two-person cab based on the commercial day-cab design; type M is based on a commercial sleeper-type cab and retains a bunk, while the Type DK is a four-door six-person crew cab design.

The Star 944 is designed for operations in relative humidity up to 98 per cent and in dry/dusty environments of up to 1.5 g/cm³. Climatic operational range is –30°C to +50°C, and with preparation the vehicle can ford to 1.2 m.

Motive power is provided by a MAN DO824LFL09 four-cylinder diesel engine developing 155 hp. This is coupled to a six-speed ZF manual gearbox and MAN two-speed transfer box. Four-wheel drive is permanent and both axles are fitted with differential locks. Conventional MAN beam axles and leaf spring suspension is employed.

The standard troop carrying/cargo body is covered by tarpaulin and removable bows and is fitted with removable drop sides and tailgate, and may have folding troop seats along the side boards. In conjunction with

Star 944 (4 × 4) 3,000 kg truck fitted with the standard type K cab and drop side troop carrying/cargo body (Greg Holdanowicz)   0525603

the standard type K cab, internal dimensions of the body are 4.5 × 2.44 × 1.74 m (L × W × H), sufficient for 10 Euro-standard pallets. The base chassis is suitable for a variety of other bodies/superstructures, up to a permissible maximum of 9,700 kg.

A winch of 5,400 kg capacity with 38 m of cable is fitted as standard.

Specifications
Cab seating: 1 + 1
Configuration: 4 × 4
Weight:
  (chassis-cab) 4,400 kg
  (max load, on-road) 4,000 kg
  (max load, off-road) 3,000 kg
  (GVW, on-road) 9,700 kg
  (GVW, off-road) 8,700 kg
  (towed load) 4,500 kg
Load area:
  (with type K cab) 4.5 × 2.44 × 1.74 m
  (with type DK cab) 3.5 × 2.44 × 1.74 m
Length:
  (chassis-cab) 6.22 m
  (with standard troop carrying/cargo body) 6.64 m
Width: 2.49 m
Height:
  (cab, unladen) 2.83 m
  (cab, laden) 2.88 m
  (tarpaulin) 3.085 m
Ground clearance: 380 mm
Track:
  (front) n/avail
  (rear) n/avail
Wheelbase: 3.725 m
Angle of approach/departure: 39°/41°
Max speed: (road) 90 km/h
Range: 650 km
Fording:
  (unprepared) 800 mm
  (prepared) 1.2 m
Engine: MAN DO824LFL09 EURO II 4.58-litre 4-cylinder in-line water-cooled turbocharged and intercooled direct injection diesel developing 155 hp (116 kW) at 2,400 rpm and 580 N.m torque at 1,600 rpm
Gearbox: ZF S6-45 manual with 6 forward and 1 reverse gears
Clutch: single dry plate
Transfer box: MAN G1000 2-speed
Steering: power assisted, ZF 8095
Turning radius: n/avail
Suspension: semi-elliptic leaf springs, front and rear
Tyres: 1200 × 20
Brakes:
  (main) dual circuit air, with ABS
  (parking) mechanical
Electrical system: 24 V
Batteries: 2 × 12 V, 120 Ah
Alternator: 28 V, 55 A

Status
Production complete. In service with Polish Armed Forces. 650 delivered between 2001-2007.

Contractor
Star Trucks Sp. z o.o

Enquiries to:
Rheinmetall MAN Military Vehicles (RMMV)

Star 66, 660M1 and 660M2 (6 × 6) 2,500 kg trucks

Development
The Star 66 (6 × 6) 2,500 kg truck was developed simultaneously with the (4 × 4) Star 44, the Star 44 not entering series production. The first Star 66 models were produced by the then national Fabryka Samochodów Ciezarowych (FSC) truck factory in Starachowice during 1958, production continuing until 1964 - with minor improvements.

The improved Star 660M1 was launched in 1965. In addition to numerous details changes, this featured 1200 × 18 tyres, replacing earlier 1100 × 20 tyres, a new braking system and cross-axle differential locks for the rear bogie. The further-improved Star 660M2 followed in 1968, this model having an all-steel cargo/troop carrying rear body, a shielded and waterproofed wiring and ignition system, and the ability to wade water obstacles of up to 1.8 m depth.

The eventual production successor of the Star 66/660 series of trucks was the Star 266 which entered production in 1973. Full details of the Star 266 can be found elsewhere in this section.

Production of the Star 660M2 concluded in 1985, although the type remains in service with Polish armed forces in numerous specialist roles. In co-operation with IVECO, Wojskowe Zaklady Mechaniczne (WZM) of Siemianowice Slaskie has developed an upgrade package for Star

Star 660M2 (6 × 6) ZSH-6S 11,000 kg capacity crane truck
(Greg Holdanowicz)   0525602

660M1/M2 trucks. The proposed cost to upgrade these trucks to Star 660M3 standard would be approximately 25 per cent of that of a new vehicle. The upgrade would involve the fitting of a new four-cylinder IVECO 165 hp diesel engine, a 24 V electrical system and a suspended seat for the driver.

Commercial variants of the Star 66/660 series were produced. The only other known military customer for the Star 66 was the then North Vietnam.

The then Zaklady Starachowickie Star SA was acquired by MAN of Germany in 2000.

Description
The Star 66/660 series of trucks are of conventional design, being based on a C-section ladder frame chassis with a front-mounted forward-control two-person cab. The cab features a removable canvas-type roof and side windows, the two-piece flat windscreen folding forward when required. Crew-cab variants were also produced.

The Star 66 was powered by a S47 six-cylinder petrol engine, the 660M1 by a S474 six-cylinder petrol engine, the 660M2 by a S47E3W watertight and radio-suppressed six-cylinder petrol engine, all of 4.68 litre displacement. A five-speed manual gearbox and two-speed transfer box are fitted, with front-wheel drive being selectable when required. Suspension is by beam axles and leaf springs, the rear bogie arrangement not being dissimilar to that used on WW2-vintage GMC CCKW (6 × 6) trucks.

A 5,900 kg capacity drum winch with 50 m of cable is fitted as standard.

Specifications
(Star 660M2 cargo/troop carrying configuration)
Cab seating: 1 + 1
Configuration: 6 × 6
Weight:
  (kerb) 5,700 kg
  (GVW on-road) 9,700 kg
  (GVW off-road) 8,200 kg
  (towed load, on-road) 4,400 kg
  (towed load, off-road) 3,500 kg
Length: 6.97 m
Width: 2.42 m
Ground clearance: 285 mm
Track: (front) 1.804 m
Wheelbase: 2.858 + 1.2 m
Angle of approach/departure: 33°/30°
Max speed: (road) 73 km/h
Fuel capacity: 2 × 150 litres
Range: (roads) 800 km
Max gradient: 77%
Fording: 1.8 m
Engine: S47E3W 4.68-litre 6-cylinder in-line water-cooled overhead valve petrol developing 105 hp (78 kW) at 3,000 rpm and peak torque at 1,600 rpm
Gearbox: manual with 5 forward and 1 reverse gears
Clutch: single dry plate
Transfer box: 2-speed
Steering: manual
Turning radius: 10 m
Suspension: semi-elliptic leaf springs, inverted on the rear bogie
Tyres: 1200 × 18
Brakes:
  (main) hydraulic with air assistance, drums all-round,
  (parking) mechanical
Electrical system: 12 V
Batteries: 136 Ah

Status
Production complete. Remains in service with Polish Armed Forces in specialised roles.

Contractor
Star Trucks Sp. z o.o.

Enquiries to:
Rheinmetall MAN Military Vehicles (RMMV)

Star 266 (6 × 6) 3,500 kg truck

Development
The Star 266 3,500 kg truck was the production replacement for the older Star 66/660 2,500 kg range of 6 × 6 trucks, numerous examples of which continue in service with Polish Armed Forces. The major improvements of the Star 266 over the earlier Star 66/660 vehicles are its increased load-carrying capability, more powerful engine, all-steel fully enclosed two-seat cab and larger tyres. Full details of the Star 66/660 can be found elsewhere in this section.

The first prototype Star 266 was completed in 1971 and production began in 1976. Production was concluded in July 2000 and following the acquisition of the then Zaklady Starachowickie Star SA by MAN of Germany. The MAN-influenced Star 1466 Star (6 × 6) 6,000 kg truck first shown in 1999, is the successor of the Star 266. Full details of the Star 1466 can be found elsewhere in this section.

Star Trucks has developed the Star 266M (MAN) upgrade package for the considerable numbers of ageing but little-used Star 266 trucks remaining in the Polish military inventory. At around USD25,000 this upgrade package includes the same MAN-derived cab as fitted to the Star 1466, while the original Star 359M engine will be replaced by a MAN EURO 2 emissions compliant engine. During 2001 some 10 vehicles were upgraded, the estimate for 2002 was 70 vehicles. Figures for 2003-2004 are not currently available. During 2005, 42 vehicles were upgraded. The current figure is quoted as a total of approximately 120 vehicles which have been upgraded.

This upgrade package could become available to other users of the Star 266, these including Angola, Lithuania and Yemen. Yemen was the last export customer for the Star 266 having ordered 550 vehicles in a number of variants. A contract valued at USD20 million was placed in February 1999, with deliveries beginning in August 1999. When production of the Star 266 concluded in July 2000, 400 of the 550 vehicles had been delivered.

Star 266 (6 × 6) 3,500 kg truck mounting ZU-23-2 AA gun
(Greg Holdanowicz)   0525604

Star 266 (6 × 6) 3,500 kg truck fitted with an office-type rear body
(Richard Stickland)   1124754

Star 266 (6 × 6) 3,500 kg truck with standard dropside cargo/troop body
(Richard Stickland)   0121825

Star 266 (6 × 6) 3,500 kg truck fitted with an expandible van-type body
(Richard Stickland)   0121824

Description
The Star 266 is of conventional design, being based on a C-section ladder frame chassis with a front-mounted forward-control two-person all-steel cab. The cab is fully enclosed and has two circular roof hatches fitted. The two-piece flat windscreen is hinged at the top and opens outwards for additional ventilation. Both seats are fixed, a sprung seat being an option for the driver. A folding bunk is mounted behind the front seat positions.

The Star 266 is designed for operations throughout a −40°C to +50°C temperature range, in relative humidity up to 98 per cent and in dry/dusty environments of up to 1.5 g/m³. Fording depth is 1.8 m. To help achieve this a waterproof starter and batteries are standard equipment. The electrical system is described as 'water resistant'.

Motive power is provided by a Star six-cylinder diesel engine developing 147 hp. This is coupled to a five-speed license-built ZF manual gearbox and two-speed transfer box. Front axle drive is selectable and there is a driver-controlled longitudinal differential lock between the second and third axles. Conventional beam axles and leaf spring suspension is employed. A 6,000 kg capacity winch with 50 m of cable is provided.

The standard troop carrying/cargo body is covered by tarpaulin and removable bows and is fitted with removable drop sides and tailgate, and may have folding troop seats along the side boards. Other body/superstructure variants are available and include workshop bodies, a communication shelter body, fuel or water tanker, hydraulic crane carrier and a mobile medical centre.

Star 266 (6 × 6) 3,500 kg truck fitted with a 360° excavator rear body for engineering work (Richard Stickland)   1124753

Star 266 (6 × 6) 3,500 kg truck of the Polish Army fitted with an office-type rear body (Shaun C Connors) 1120479

The following special bodies have been produced for the Star 266, although not all may remain in service:

SARNA II: van body configured as workshop, command post, ambulance, mobile dressing station, laundry, bakery or canteen
786: sealed container body for electronic equipment
DSRT-0081: 8,000 kg lift capacity mobile crane
DSR-0101: 10,000 kg lift capacity mobile crane
WUS-3: mobile cleaning station for heavy equipment
A3-578: fuel tanker
A3-579.2: fuel tanker
A3-522: fuel tanker
A3-531: fuel dispenser station
A3-518: NBC decontamination station for personnel and equipment; also used for firefighting
Platform truck component carrier for the PP-64 folding pontoon bridge
A 6 × 6 tractor truck variant was also produced.

Specifications

Star 266
Cab seating: 1 + 1
Configuration: 6 × 6
Weight:
  (chassis-cab) 5,895 kg
  (max front axle load, on-road) 4,000 kg
  max front axle load, off-road) 3,850 kg
  max rear bogie load, on-road) 8,350 kg
  (max rear bogie load, off-road) 7,000 kg
  (GVW, on-road) 12,350 kg
  (GVW, off-road) 10,850 kg
  (towed load) 4,000 kg
Load area: 3.9 × 2.2 m
Length: (chassis) 6.68 m
Width: 2.5 m
Height: (cab) 2.69 m
Ground clearance: 325 mm
Track:
  (front) 1.97 m
  (rear) 2.004 m
Wheelbase: 2.99 m + 1.25 m
Angle of approach/departure: 37°/42.5°
Max speed: (road) 90 km/h
Fuel capacity: 2 × 150 litres
Range: 800 km
Max gradient: 78%
Side slope: 56%
Fording: 1.8 m
Engine: Star 359M R6 6.842-litre 6-cylinder in-line water-cooled, 4-stroke diesel developing 147 hp (110 kW) at 2,100 rpm
Gearbox: ZF S5-45 manual with 5 forward and 1 reverse gears
Clutch: single dry plate
Transfer box: 2-speed
Steering: ZF 8060 with hydraulic servo
Turning radius: 8.5 m
Suspension: semi-elliptic leaf springs with double-acting hydraulic shock-absorbers
Tyres: 1200 × 20
Brakes:
  (main) dual circuit, hydraulic
  (parking) mechanical
Electrical system: 24 V
Batteries: 2 × 12 V, 165 Ah
Alternator: 24 V, 30 A

Status

Production complete. In addition to Polish Armed Forces Star 266 trucks have been supplied to, and may remain in service in, Afghanistan, Angola, Lithuania, Myanmar (Burma, crane-trucks), and Yemen (400 delivered 1999/2000).

Contractor

Star Trucks Sp. z o.o.

Enquiries to:

Rheinmetall MAN Military Vehicles (RMMV)

Star 1466 (6 × 6) 6,000 kg truck

Development

The Star 1466 (6 × 6) 6,000 kg truck was first shown in 1999 along with the smaller Star 944 (4 × 4) 3,000 kg truck. The Star 1466 was the successor of the earlier Star 266 (6 × 6) 3,500 kg truck. Had funding permitted, the Star 1466 was likely to replace the Star 266, along with the remaining examples of the earlier Star 66/660 (6 × 6) 2,500 kg trucks, in Polish military service. Production of the Star 1466 is now complete. A Polish Army project to procure a new (6 × 6) truck of this class was put on hold with the Polish defence cuts announced early-2009. Full details of the Star 66/660, 266 and 944 trucks can be found elsewhere in this section.

The then Zaklady Starachowickie Star SA was acquired by MAN of Germany in 2000.

Description

The Star 1466 is of conventional design, being based on a C-section ladder frame chassis with a front-mounted forward-control two-person all-steel cab based on the MAN L2000 commercial design. The cab is fully enclosed, has a single roof hatch, a flat single-piece windscreen and tilts forward engine access. Three variants of cab may be fitted: Type K is a two-person cab based on a commercial day-type cab; type M is a two-person plus bunk cab based on a commercial sleeper-type cab, while the type DK is a four-door six-person crew cab design. The type DK cab is fitted to the chassis involved in the Huta Stalowa Wola (HSW) upgraded BM-21 multiple rocket launcher, full details of which can be found in *Jane's Armour and Artillery*.

The Star 1466 is designed for operations in relative humidity up to 98 per cent and in dry/dusty environments of up to 1.5 g/m³. Climatic operational range is –30°C to +50°C, and the vehicle can ford to 1.2 m.

Motive power is provided by a MAN DO826LFLG15 six-cylinder diesel engine developing 220 hp. This is coupled to a six-speed ZF manual gearbox and MAN two-speed transfer box. A Power Take Off (PTO) point was optional. Conventional MAN beam axles and leaf spring suspension is employed, each axle being fitted with a differential lock. A 6,000 kg single-line pull winch with 100 m of cable was fitted as standard.

The standard troop carrying/cargo body is covered by tarpaulin and removable bows and is fitted with removable drop sides and tailgate, and may have folding troop seats along the side boards. In conjunction with the standard type M cab, internal dimensions of the body are 4.4 × 2.44 × 1.74 m (L × W × H), sufficient for 10 Euro-standard pallets. A materials handling crane with a working radius of 6 m may be fitted between the cab and body. For this version body dimensions are 3.44 × 2.44 × 1.74 m (L × W × H), sufficient for eight Euro-standard pallets.

The base chassis was suitable for a wide variety of other bodies/superstructures, up to a permissible maximum of 14,000 kg. One proposed role for the Star 1466 was that of ammunition limber for the 155 mm Krab self-propelled howitzer.

Star 1466 (6 × 6) 6,000 kg truck fitted with the DK cab and mounting an upgraded Huta Stalowa Wola (HSW) BM-21 multiple rocket launcher system (Shaun C Connors) 1120477

Specifications
Cab seating: 1 + 1
Configuration: 6 × 6
Weight:
(max load) 6,000 kg
(GVW) 14,000 kg
(towed load) 8,500 kg
Load area:
(with type M cab) 4.4 × 2.44 × 1.74 m
(with type M cab and materials handling crane) 3.5 × 2.44 × 1.74 m
Length:
(chassis-cab) 7.2 m
(with standard troop carrying/cargo body) 7.4 m
Width: 2.49 m
Height: (cab) 3.3 m
Ground clearance: 350 mm
Wheelbase: 4 + 1.37 m
Angle of approach/departure: 35°/40°
Max speed: (road) 86 km/h
Range: 650 km
Fording: 1.2 m
Engine: MAN DO826LFLG15 EURO II 6.87-litre 6-cylinder water-cooled direct injection turbocharged and intercooled diesel developing 220 hp (162 kW) at 2,400 rpm and 820 N.m torque at 1,500 rpm
Gearbox: ZF S6-850 manual with 6 forward and 1 reverse gears
Clutch: single dry plate
Transfer box: MAN G1000 2-speed
Steering: power assisted, ZF 8095
Suspension: semi-elliptic leaf springs, front and rear
Tyres: 1400 × 20
Brakes:
(main) dual circuit air, with ABS
(parking) mechanical
Electrical system: 24 V
Batteries: 2 × 12 V, 170 Ah
Alternator: 28 V, 55 A

Status
Production complete. In service with Polish Armed Forces. Twenty-four delivered during 2001 as chassis for upgraded BM-21 MLRS; five delivered during 2003, four as carriers for ELNIT systems, one, a prototype logistics carrier for the Loara SPAAG.

Contractor
Star Trucks Sp. z o.o.

Enquiries to
Rheinmetall MAN Military Vehicles (RMMV)

Star 244 (4 × 4) 5,000 kg truck

Development
The Star 244 (4 × 4) 5,000 kg truck series was developed from the (4 × 2) Star 200 series. The proposed replacement for the Star 244 was the Star 744 (4 × 4) 3,000 kg truck. The Star 744 was subsequently replaced by the MAN-influenced Star 944 (4 × 4) 3,000/4,000 kg truck first displayed in 1999. Full details of the Star 944 can be found elsewhere in this section. Small numbers of Star 744 trucks are believed to have entered service with Polish armed forces and a small number of Star 742, a (4 × 2) variant, were supplied to the Polish Air Force as carriers of LUZES ground Auxiliary Power Units (APU).

MAN acquired the then Zaklady Starachowickie STAR SA in 2000.

Star 244 (4 × 4) 5,000 kg truck fitted with shelter-type rear body (Richard Stickland) 0121823

With essentially the same engine and a similar but shorter cab than the Star 266 (6 × 6), the Star 744 (4 × 4) 3,000 kg truck was the intended replacement for the Star 244. It never entered series production, being superseded by the MAN-influenced Star 944 (4 × 4) 3,000/4,000 kg truck (Star) 0044311

Description
The Star 244 (4 × 4) 5,000 kg truck series differs from the earlier Star 200 series mainly by the addition of front-axle drive and a reduction gear. The Type 359 6.842-litre diesel engine was retained. The forward control all-steel cab was developed in association with Chausson of France.

Variants of the basic Star 244 are the Star 244RS, produced primarily for agricultural purposes; the A244 adapted to carry various forms of cross-country bodies; the P244L (wheelbase 3.9 m) for mounting fire truck bodies; and the 3W244 (wheelbase 3 m) for tipper bodies.

The proposed replacement for the Star 244, the Star 744 (4 × 4) 3,000 kg truck fitted with a shorter but essentially similar cab to the Star 266 (6 × 6) 3,500 kg truck, and powered by the same (but updated) Star T359E R6 6.842-litre six-cylinder 147 hp diesel engine.

Specifications
Star 244
Configuration: 4 × 4
Weight:
(unladen) 5,500 kg
(max load) 5,000 kg
(towed load) 8,500 kg
Length: 6.34 m
Width: 2.46 m
Height: (cab) 2.59 m
Ground clearance: 280 mm
Track:
(front) 1.9 m
(rear) 1.8 m
Wheelbase: 3.4 m
Angle of approach/departure: 40°/27°
Engine: S-359 6.842 litre 6-cylinder water-cooled diesel developing 150 hp (110 kW) at 2,800 rpm
Gearbox: S5-45 manual with 5 forward and 1 reverse gears
Transfer box: 2-speed
Clutch: single dry plate
Steering: ZF 8060 with hydraulic servo
Tyres: 8.25 × 20
Electrical system: 24 V
Batteries: 2 × 12 V, 135 Ah
Alternator: 30 A

Status
Production complete. The Star 244 remains in service with Polish Armed Forces, but is due for replacement.

Contractor
Star Trucks Sp. z o.o.

Enquiries to:
Rheinmetall MAN Military Vehicles (RMMV)

Romania

ROMAN 33.360 DFA (6 × 6) truck

Development
The ROMAN 33.360 DFA (6 × 6) truck is available with one of two cab designs and is available in a variety of body configurations. It has been supplied to the Malaysian Army.

ROMAN 33.360 DFA (6 × 6) logistic support truck fitted with a Multilift (Hiab) MPH165 load handling system and Container Handling Unit (CHU) (ROMAN SA) 1323555

Roman SA is a Romanian truck manufacturer that was established after World War II on the foundation of the old ROMLOC automotive factory built in 1921. The plant was named Steagul Rosu (the Red Flag) and in 1954 the first batch of SR 101 trucks (a Russian ZIS-150 clone) was produced.

In 1971 an agreement for the licence build of MAN products was reached. Since 1990 DAC has been the special trucks division of ROMAN trucks.

It was announced during 2003 that Pesaka Astana of Malaysia had acquired a 94.27 per cent stake in ROMAN SA, including a 100 per cent takeover of two of ROMAN SA's subsidiaries which control the assembly plant and axle parts manufacturing facilities. The takeover did not involve any liabilities or debts of ROMAN SA.

After one week Pesaka Astana gave up its share of ROMAN SA to SC PRO ROMAN SA, Brasov. From 2004, the current privatised company began trading. Between 1995 and early 2007, ROMAN SA supplied around 1,300 assorted trucks to the Romanian Army and around 200 to the Malaysian Army (1995-2003), the latter under the AMDAC name and in conjunction with Pesaka Astana. In support of operations in Iraq, the company has also received at least 13 contracts from TACOM for 15 different types of truck for the civilian and logistic support of the Iraqi Army.

Following privatisation in 2004 the company decided to use ROMAN as the primary brand name. ROMAN designations are based around the same system as earlier DAC/AMDAC designations and define approximate GVW (tonnes) and approximate engine power output (hp), with the additional lettering defining a variety of things including cab type, drive configuration, wheel/tyre fit, body/chassis type.

Description

The chassis frame of the 33.360 DFA is a conventional channel section design with riveted or bolted cross members. The base chassis is capable of accepting a wide variety of bodies including cargo, 10,000-litre fuel or water tankers or a recovery hamper. Fifth wheel tractor truck variants are also available.

Full time all-wheel drive is provided, conventional beam-type axles and leaf spring suspension being employed. The front steer-drive axle is fitted with single wheels/tyres, the rear drive axles with dual wheels/tyres. An Anti-lock Braking System (ABS) is fitted as standard.

Motive power is a MAN 12-litre water-cooled diesel engine developing 360 hp. The engine is capable of operation with NATO F34/F54 fuels and is coupled to a 16-speed manual gearbox and two-speed transfer box. An automatic transmission is optional. A single 310-litre capacity fuel tank is chassis mounted, a 410-litre capacity tank is optional.

ROMAN 33.360 DFA 10,000-litre fuel tanker of the Malaysian Army (ROMAN SA) 1186159

ROMAN 33.360 DFA (6 × 6) truck fitted with a 10,000-litre fuel tanker (ROMAN SA) 0113046

Two cabs are available for this chassis, both all steel two-door, two or four-seat designs that are fitted thought the ROMAN military truck range in various configurations. One is based on a MAN commercial design and features a curved single-piece main windscreen, the other is a flat-panelled cab fabricated with a two-piece flat windscreen.

Both cabs tilt forward hydraulically for engine maintenance and checks and are fitted with a high-performance heating and ventilation system. An observation hatch is fitted in the cab roof for the passenger.

Climatic operational range is –33°C to +52°C. The vehicle is rail transportable.

Specifications

ROMAN 33.360 DFA
Cab seating: 1 + 1
Configuration: 6 × 6
Weight:
  (laden) 33,000 kg
  (unladen) 13,000 kg
  (payload) 20,000 kg
  (towed load) 20,000 kg
  (GTW) 50,000 kg
Length: 9.187 m
Width: 2.5 m
Height: 2.95 m
Ground clearance: (rear) 330 mm
Angle of approach/departure: 25°/25°
Max speed: 100 km/h
Fuel capacity: 310 litres (optional 410 litres)
Max gradient: 44%
Side slope: 33%
Fording: 800 mm
Engine: MAN 12-litre 6-cylinder inline water-cooled diesel developing 360 hp (265 kW)
Gearbox: manual with 16 forward and 2 reverse gears
Transfer box: 2-speed
Steering: hydraulic power-assisted,
Turning radius: (kerb) 11.75 m
Suspension:
  (front) semi-elliptic leaf springs, telescopic shock-absorbers and anti-roll bar
  (rear bogie) semi-elliptic leaf springs, inverted
Tyres: 315/80R 22.5
Brakes: dual circuit, pneumatic, drums all-round
Electrical system: 24 V

Status

Production as required. Supplied to the Malaysian Army.

Contractor

ROMAN SA

ROMAN 33.360 DFA (6 × 6) tractor truck

Description

The ROMAN 33.360 DFA (6 × 6) tractor truck is a development of the ROMAN 33.360 DFA (6 × 6) truck, full details of which can be found elsewhere in this section. The vehicle is available with one of two cab designs and has been supplied to the Malaysian Army for use with a two axle low bed semi-trailer for the transport of light armoured vehicles and similar equipment.

Roman SA is a Romanian truck manufacturer that was established after World War II on the foundation of the old ROMLOC automotive factory built in 1921. The plant was named Steagul Rosu (the Red Flag) and in 1954 the first batch of SR 101 trucks (a Russian ZIS-150 clone) was produced.

In 1971 an agreement for the licence build of MAN products was reached. Since 1990 DAC has been the special trucks division of ROMAN trucks.

It was announced during 2003 that Pesaka Astana of Malaysia had acquired a 94.27 per cent stake in ROMAN SA, including a 100 per cent takeover of the two ROMAN SA's subsidiaries which control the assembly plant and axle parts manufacturing facilities. The takeover did not involve any liabilities or debts of ROMAN SA. After one week Pesaka Astana give up its share of ROMAN SA to SC PRO ROMAN SA, Brasov. The current privatised company began trading in 2004.

Between 1995 and early 2007, ROMAN SA supplied around 1,300 assorted trucks to the Romanian Army and about 200 assorted trucks to the Malaysian Army (1995-2003) under the AMDAC name and in conjunction with Pesaka Astana. In support of operations in Iraq, the company has received at least 13 contracts from TACOM for 15 different types of truck for civilian and logistic support of the Iraqi Army.

Following privatisation in 2004 the decision was taken to use ROMAN as the primary brand name. ROMAN designations are based around the same system as earlier DAC/AMDAC designations and define approximate GVW (tonnes) and approximate engine power output (hp), with the additional lettering defining a variety of things including cab type, drive configuration, wheel/tyre fit, body/chassis type.

Description
The chassis frame of the 33.360 DFA is of conventional channel section design with riveted or bolted cross members. For the tractor truck role a 3½ inch (87 mm) JOST fifth wheel is fitted. A TH 10 winch with 50 m of rope is optional.

Full time all-wheel drive is provided, conventional beam type axles and leaf spring suspension being employed. The front steer drive axle is fitted with single wheels/tyres, the rear drive axles with dual wheels/tyres. Anti-lock brakes (ABS) are fitted as standard. Motive power is provided by a MAN 12-litre water-cooled diesel engine developing 360 hp. The engine is capable of operation with NATO F34/F54 fuels and is coupled to a 16-speed manual gearbox and two speed transfer box. An automatic transmission is optional. A single 410-litre capacity fuel tank is chassis mounted.

Two cabs are available for this chassis, both all steel two door, two or four-seat designs that are fitted thought the ROMAN military truck range in various configurations. One is based on a MAN commercial cab and features a curved single-piece main windscreen, the other is a flat panelled cab fabricated with a two piece flat panelled windscreen. Both cabs tilt forward hydraulically for engine maintenance and checks and are fitted with a high-performance heating and ventilation system. An observation hatch is fitted in the cab roof for the passenger.

Climatic operational range is –33°C to +52°C.

Specifications
ROMAN 33.360 DFA
Cab seating: 1 + 1
Configuration: 6 × 6
Weight:
(unladen, tractor) 10,000 kg
(GVW, tractor) 33,000 kg
(payload, trailer) 35,000 kg
(GCW, tractor) 50,000 kg
Length: (overall) 17.5 m
Width: 2.5 m
Height: 3.15 m
Ground clearance: 330 mm
Angle of approach/departure: 20°/20°
Max speed: 100 km/h
Max gradient: 33%
Fuel capacity: 410 litres
Fording: 500 mm
Side slope: 22%
Engine: MAN 12-litre 6 cylinder inline water-cooled diesel developing 360 hp (265 kW)
Gearbox: manual with 16 forward and 2 reverse gears
Transfer box: 2-speed
Steering: hydraulic power assisted
Turning radius: (kerb) 11.75 m
Suspension: semi-elliptic leaf springs, telescopic shock-absorbers and anti-roll bar, front; semi-elliptic leaf springs, inverted, rear bogie
Tyres: 315/80R 22.5
Brakes: dual circuit, air, drums all-round
Electrical system: 24 V

Status
Production as required. In service with Malaysia.

Contractor
ROMAN SA

ROMAN 33.360 DFAS (6 × 6) tractor truck

Development
The ROMAN 33.360 DFAS (6 × 6) tractor truck is a development of the ROMAN 33.360 DFA (6 × 6) truck, full details of which can be found elsewhere in this section. The vehicle is available with one of two cab designs and has been supplied to the Malaysian Army.

ROMAN SA is a Romanian truck manufacturer that was established after World War II on the foundation of the old ROMLOC automotive factory built in 1921. The plant was named Steagul Rosu (the Red Flag) and in 1954 the first batch of SR 101 trucks (a Russian ZIS-150 clone) was produced.

In 1971 an agreement for the licence build of MAN products was reached. Since 1990 DAC has been the special trucks division of ROMAN trucks.

It was announced in 2003 that Pesaka Astana of Malaysia had acquired a 94.27 per cent stake in ROMAN SA, including a 100 per cent take over of two ROMAN SA's subsidiaries which control the assembly plant and axle parts manufacturing facilities. The takeover did not involve any liabilities or debts of ROMAN SA. After one week Pesaka Astana gave up its share of ROMAN SA to SC PRO ROMAN SA, Brasov. The current privatised company began trading in 2004.

Between 1995 and early 2007 ROMAN SA supplied around 1,300 assorted trucks to the Romanian Army and around 200 assorted trucks to the Malaysian Army (1995-2003) under the AMDAC name and in conjunction with Pesaka Astana. In support of operations in Iraq the company has also received at least 13 contracts from TACOM for 15 different types of trucks for civilian and logistic support of the Iraqi Army.

Following privatisation in 2004 the decision was taken to use ROMAN as the primary brand name. ROMAN designations are based on the same system as earlier DAC/AMDAC designations and define approximate GVW (tonnes) and approximate engine power output (hp), with the additional lettering defining a variety of things including cab type, drive configuration, wheel/tyre fit, body/chassis type and so on.

Description
The chassis frame of the 33.360 DFAS is of conventional channel section design with riveted or bolted cross-members. Full-time all-wheel drive is provided, conventional beam-type axles and leaf spring suspension is used. The front steer-drive axle is fitted with single wheels/tyres, the rear drive axles with dual wheels/tyres. Anti-lock brakes (ABS) are fitted as standard.

Motive power is by a MAN 12-litre water-cooled diesel engine developing 360 hp. The engine is capable of operation with NATO F34/F54 fuels and is coupled to a 16-speed manual gearbox and two-speed transfer box. An automatic transmission is optional. A single 310-litre capacity fuel tank is chassis mounted. Two cabs are available for this chassis, both all-steel two-door, two or four-seat designs which are fitted thought the ROMAN military truck range in various configurations. One is based on a MAN commercial cab and features a curved single-piece main windscreen, the other is a flat-panelled cab made with a two-piece flat-panelled windscreen. Both cabs tilt forward hydraulically for engine maintenance and checks and are fitted with a high-performance heating and ventilation system. An observation hatch is fitted in the cab roof for the passenger.

Climatic operational range is –33°C to +52°C.

Specifications
ROMAN 33.360 DFAS
Cab seating: 1 + 1
Configuration: 6 × 6
Weight:
(unladen, tractor) 10,000 kg
(payload, including trailer) 30,000 kg
(GCW, tractor) 40,500 kg
Length: (overall) 16.4 m
Width: 2.5 m
Height: 3.35 m
Ground clearance: 320 mm
Angle of approach/departure: 20°/20°

The ROMAN 33.360 DFAS (6 × 6) tractor truck is in service with the Malaysian Army (ROMAN SA)   1186158

Max speed: 100 km/h
Max gradient: 33%
Fuel capacity: 310 litres
Fording: 500 mm
Side slope: 22%
Engine: MAN 12-litre 6 cylinder in-line water-cooled diesel developing 360 hp (265 kW) manual with 16 forward and 2 reverse gears
Gearbox: manual with 16 forward and 2 reverse gears
Transfer box: 2-speed
Steering: hydraulic power assisted
Suspension: semi-elliptic leaf springs, telescopic shock-absorbers and anti-roll bar, front; semi-elliptic leaf springs, inverted, rear bogie
Tyres: 315/80R 22.5
Brakes: dual circuit, air, drums all-round
Electrical system: 24 V
Turning radius: (kerb) 9.1 m

Status

Production as required. In service with Malaysia (with 20,000-litre fuel and water tanker semi-trailers); a light equipment transporter variant is also available.

Contractor

ROMAN SA

ROMAN 10.150 FAE (4 × 4) 4,000 kg truck

Development

The ROMAN 10.150 (4 × 4) truck is a derivative of the earlier and visually similar DAC 8.120 FAE, DAC 8.130 FAE and DAC 8.140 FAE trucks, this later model features a more powerful engine and having an increased GVW and payload capacity.

ROMAN SA is a Romanian truck manufacturer that was established after World War II on the foundation of the old ROMLOC automotive factory built in 1921. The plant was named Steagul Rosu (the Red Flag) and in 1954 the first batch of SR 101 trucks (a Russian ZIS-150 clone) was produced.

In 1971 an agreement for the licence build of MAN products was reached. Since 1990 DAC has been the special trucks division of ROMAN trucks.

It was announced during 2003 that Pesaka Astana of Malaysia had acquired a 94.27 per cent stake in ROMAN SA, including a 100 per cent takeover of two of ROMAN SA's subsidiaries which control the assembly plant and axle parts manufacturing facilities. The takeover did not involve any liabilities or debts of ROMAN SA. After one week Pesaka Astana give up its share of ROMAN SA to SC PRO ROMAN SA, Brasov. From 2004 the current privatised company began trading.

Between 1995 and early 2007, ROMAN SA supplied around 1,300 assorted trucks to the Romanian Army and around 200 assorted trucks to the Malaysian Army (1995-2003), the latter under the AMDAC name and in conjunction with Pesaka Astana. In support of operations in Iraq the company has also received at least 13 contracts from TACOM for 15 different types of trucks for civilian and logistic support of the Iraqi Army.

Following privatisation in 2004 the decision was taken to use ROMAN as the primary brand name. ROMAN designations are based around the same system as earlier DAC/AMDAC designations and define approximate GVW (tonnes) and approximate engine power output (hp), with the additional lettering defining a variety of things including cab type, drive configuration, wheel/tyre fit, body/chassis type.

Description

The chassis frame of the ROMAN 10.150 FAE is a conventional channel section design with riveted or bolted cross-members. A 6,000 kg capacity hydraulic self-recovery winch is standard.

Full time all-wheel drive is provided, conventional beam-type axles and leaf spring suspension being employed. The front steer-drive axle and rear drive axle are fitted with single wheels/tyres. Anti-lock Breaking Systems (ABS) are fitted as standard.

Motive power is provided by a MAN 4.58-litre EURO 3 emissions compliant water-cooled diesel developing 150 hp. The engine is capable of operation with NATO F34/F54 fuels and is coupled to a five-speed manual gearbox and two-speed transfer box. An automatic transmission is optional. A single 220-litre capacity fuel tank is chassis mounted.

The earlier 8.120 FAE is powered by a ROMAN 798-05 six cylinder 5.491-litre non-emissions compliant diesel engine developing 120 hp, the 8.130 FAE is powered by a type 392 L4 DTI four cylinder 3.92-litre EURO 1 emissions compliant diesel engine developing 130 hp, the 8.140 FAE is powered by a Steyr WD 612.02 six cylinder 6.595-litre non-emissions compliant diesel engine developing 140 hp, all coupled to a five speed manual gearbox and two speed transfer box. All three models have a GVW of 8,500 kg.

The all steel flat-panelled cab of the 8.140 FAE is fitted with a two piece flat glass windscreen and is standard throughout the ROMAN military truck range in various configurations.

The cab tilts forward hydraulically for engine maintenance and checks and is fitted with a high-performance heating and ventilation system. An observation hatch is fitted in the cab roof for the passenger.

Climatic operational range is –33°C to +52°C.

The rear troop carrying/cargo area has a steel platform and is equipped with drop sides and tailgate. Side-mounted lateral folding benches provide seating for 20 personnel. A tarpaulin and bows are provided for protection from the elements. The vehicle is transportable by rail. Essentially the same chassis cab is used with 3,000-litre capacity fuel and water tankers.

Specifications

ROMAN 10.150 FAE
Cab seating: 1 + 1
Configuration: 4 × 4
Weight:
  (laden) 10,000 kg
  (unladen) 6,000 kg
  (payload) 4,000 kg
  (towed load, on-road) 3,500 kg
  (towed load, off-road) 2,500 kg
  (GVW, on road) 13,500 kg
  (GVW, off-road) 12,500 kg
Length: 7.1 m
Width: 2.2 m
Height: 2.82 m
Ground clearance: (rear) 320 mm
Angle of approach/departure: (tractor) 30°/30°
Max speed: 90 km/h
Max gradient: 44%
Fuel capacity: 310 litres
Side slope: 33%
Engine: MAN 4.58-litre EURO 3 emissions compliant 4-cylinder in-line water-cooled diesel developing 150 hp (110 kW)
Gearbox: manual with 5 forward and one reverse gears
Transfer box: 2-speed
Steering: hydraulic power assisted
Turning radius: (kerb) 7.7 m
Suspension: semi-elliptic leaf springs, front and rear
Brakes: dual circuit, air, drums all round; ABS fitted
Electrical system: 24 V

Status

Available.

Contractor

ROMAN SA

ROMAN 15.220 DFAEG (6 × 6) 5,000 kg high mobility truck

Development

The ROMAN 15.220 (6 × 6) high mobility truck is a derivative of the earlier DAC 15.215 DFAEG and DAC 15.240 DFAEG trucks, this latest model features a more emissions complaint engine and a number of ergonomic improvements to the cab and troop carrying/cargo body.

The DAC 15.215 was at one time known as the DAC 665T.

Roman SA is a Romanian truck manufacturer that was established after World War II on the foundation of the old ROMLOC automotive factory built in 1921. The plant was named Steagul Rosu (the Red Flag) and in 1954 the first batch of SR 101 trucks (a Russian ZIS-150 clone) was produced.

In 1971 an agreement for the licence build of MAN products was reached. Since 1990 DAC has been the special trucks division of ROMAN trucks.

It was announced during 2003 that Pesaka Astana of Malaysia had acquired a 94.27 per cent stake in ROMAN SA, including a 100 per cent takeover of two of ROMAN SA's subsidiaries which control the assembly

The earlier DAC 15.215 DFAEG (6 × 6) 5,000 kg truck is visually similar to the ROMAN 15.220 DFAEG (6 × 6) 5,000 kg truck (ROMAN) 0044315

ROMAN 15.220 DFAEG (6 × 6) 5,000 kg truck in standard cargo/troop carrying configuration (ROMAN)   1323547

ROMAN 15.220 DFAEG (6 × 6) 5,000 kg truck mounting the locally produced Aruncator de Projectile Reactive (APR-40) multiple rocket launcher (ROMAN)   1186155

ROMAN DFAEG (6 × 6) 5,000 kg truck upper air sounding station variant (ROMAN)   1186156

The 15.220 DFAEG (6 × 6) 5,000 kg truck designated MITC is used as a resupply vehicle for the Aruncator de Projectile Reactive (APR-40) multiple rocket launcher (ROMAN)   1186154

ROMAN 15.220 DFAEG (6 × 6) 5,000 kg truck fitted with a 5,000-litre capacity fuel tanker body (ROMAN)   1186153

ROMAN 15.220 DFAEG (6 × 6) 5,000 kg truck fitted with a 5,000-litre capacity water tanker body (ROMAN)   1186152

plant and axle parts manufacturing facilities. The takeover did not involve any liabilities or debts of ROMAN SA. After one week, Pesaka Astana gave up its share of ROMAN SA to SC PRO ROMAN SA, Brasov. From 2004 the current privatised company began trading.

Between 1995 and early 2007 ROMAN SA supplied around 1,300 assorted trucks to the Romanian Army and around 200 assorted trucks to the Malaysian Army (1995-2003) under the AMDAC name and in conjunction with Pesaka Astana. In support of operations in Iraq the company has also received at least 13 contracts from TACOM for 15 different types of trucks for civilian and logistic support of the Iraqi Army.

Following privatisation in 2004 a decision was taken to use ROMAN as the primary brand name. ROMAN designations are based around the same system as earlier DAC/AMDAC designations and define approximate GVW (tonnes) and approximate engine power output (hp), with the additional lettering defining a variety of things including cab type, drive configuration, wheel/tyre fit, body/chassis type.

Description
The chassis frame of the ROMAN 15.220 DFAEG has a conventional channel section design with riveted or bolted cross members. A 10,000 kg capacity hydraulic self-recovery winch is standard. Towing, air and

electrical connections are NATO standard. Full time all-wheel drive is provided, conventional beam type axles and leaf spring suspension are used. The front steer drive axle and rear drive axles are fitted with single wheels/tyres, the tyres being of directional cross-country tread pattern. An Anti-lock Braking System (ABS) is fitted as standard.

Motive power is provided by MAN 6.87-litre water-cooled diesel developing 220 hp. The engine is EURO 3 emissions compliant, capable of operation with NATO F34/F54 fuels and is coupled to a six speed manual gearbox and two speed transfer box. An automatic transmission is optional. Two 310-litre capacity fuel tanks are chassis mounted. The earlier DAC 15.215 DFAEG was powered by a non-emissions compliant D2156 HMN six cylinder diesel engine developing 215 hp, and the DAC 15.240 DFAEG by a EURO 2 emissions compliant Deutz BF6M 1013 six cylinder diesel engine developing 236 hp.

The all steel flat-panelled cab is fitted with a two-piece flat glass windscreen and is standard throughout the ROMAN military truck range in various configurations. The cab tilts forward hydraulically for engine maintenance and checks and is fitted with a high performance heating and ventilation system. An observation hatch is fitted in the cab roof for the passenger.

Climatic operational range is –33°C to +52°C.
The rear troop carrying/cargo area has a steel platform and is equipped with drop sides and tailgate. Side-mounted lateral folding benches provide seating for 20 personnel. A tarpaulin and bows are provided for protection from the elements. The vehicle is transportable by rail.

The basic chassis cab of the 15.220 DFAEG and earlier 15.215 DFAEG and 15.240 DFAEG models is or has been used as the basis for a number of variants including 5,000-litre water and fuel tankers, pontoon transporters, mobile cranes and some specialist shelter/box-type body applications including an upper air sounding station. One further specialist variant mounts a locally produced 122 mm calibre, 40 round multiple rocket launching system designated APR-40 (*Aruncator de Projectile Reactive*), or 40 APRA 122 FMC for the latest version. The mounting vehicle (APR-40) carries a crew of up to five and weighs 17,250 kg laden.

The resupply vehicle is designated MITC and carries two launcher reload modules and a rear mounted MH 90 crane. The crane has a maximum lift capacity of 6,000 kg at minimum reach, and 2,000 kg at maximum reach. Maximum lift height is 6 m. The resupply vehicle weighs 16,440 kg laden and can tow a RM-13 four wheeled two axle trailer carrying a further 80 × 122 mm rockets in four 20 round racks. Total weight of a fully laden trailer is 11,530 kg.

Full details of the APR-40 system can be found in *Jane's Armour and Artillery*.

Specifications

ROMAN 15.220 DFAEG
Cab seating: 1 + 3
Configuration: 6 × 6
Weight:
  (laden) 15,600 kg
  (unladen) 10,600 kg
  (payload) 5,000 kg
  (towed load, on-road) 10,000 kg
  (towed load, off-road) 5,000 kg
  (GCW, on-road) 25,600 kg
  (GCW, off-road) 20,600 kg
Length: 7.96 m
Width: 2.5 m
Height: 2.85 m
Ground clearance: (rear) 430 mm
Angle of approach/departure: 38°/35°
Max speed: 85 km/h
Fuel capacity: 2 × 310 litres
Max gradient: 66%
Side slope: 44%
Engine: MAN 6.87-litre EURO 3 emissions compliant 6-cylinder water-cooled diesel developing 220 hp (162 kW)
Gearbox: manual with 6 forward and one reverse gears; automatic option
Transfer box: 2-speed
Steering: hydraulic power assisted
Turning radius: (kerb) 10.6 m
Suspension: semi-elliptic leaf springs, inverted at rear
Brakes: dual circuit, air, drums all-round. ABS fitted
Electrical system: 24 V

Status
In service with some former Warsaw Pact countries (15.215 DFRAEG) and Romania (15.215 DFAEG, 15.240 DFAEG - 26 delivered 2003-2005).

Contractor
ROMAN SA

ROMAN 16.220 FA (4 × 4) 7,500 kg truck

Development
The ROMAN 16.220 FA (4 × 4) 7,500 kg payload truck is a derivative of the earlier DAC 16.215 FA and DAC 16.240 FA trucks, this latest model features a more emissions complaint engine and a number of ergonomic improvements to the cab and troop carrying/cargo body.

ROMAN SA is a Romanian truck manufacturer that was established after World War II on the foundation of the old ROMLOC automotive factory built in 1921. The plant was named Steagul Rosu (the Red Flag) and in 1954 the first batch of SR 101 trucks (a Russian ZIS-150 clone) was produced.

In 1971 an agreement for the licence build of MAN products was reached. Since 1990 DAC has been the special trucks division of ROMAN trucks.

The ROMAN 16.220 FA is also available configured as a 6,000-litre capacity water tanker (ROMAN)   1186151

The earlier DAC 16.240 FA (and DAC 16.215 FA) are visually similar to the ROMAN 16.220 FA, differing primarily in engine and gearbox (ROMAN)
0113049

It was announced during 2003, that Pesaka Astana of Malaysia had acquired a 94.27 per cent stake in ROMAN SA, including a 100 per cent takeover of two of ROMAN SA's subsidiaries which control the assembly plant and axle parts manufacturing facilities. The takeover did not involve any liabilities or debts of ROMAN SA. After one week Pesaka Astana gave up its share of ROMAN SA to SC PRO ROMAN SA, Brasov. From 2004 the current privatised company began trading. Between 1995 and early 2007 ROMAN SA supplied around 1,300 assorted trucks to the Romanian Army and around 200 assorted trucks to the Malaysian Army (1995-2003) under the AMDAC name and in conjunction with Pesaka Astana. In support of operations in Iraq, the company has also received at least 13 contracts from TACOM for 15 different types of trucks for civilian and logistic support of the Iraqi Army.

Following privatisation in 2004, a decision was taken to use ROMAN as the primary brand name. ROMAN designations are based around the same system as earlier DAC/AMDAC designations and define approximate GVW (tonnes) and approximate engine power output (hp), with the additional lettering defining a variety of things including cab type, drive configuration, wheel/tyre fit, body/chassis type.

Description
The chassis frame of the ROMAN 16.220 FA is a conventional channel section design with riveted or bolted cross members. A 10,000 kg capacity hydraulic self-recovery winch is standard. All towing ancillaries are to NATO compatible.

Full time all-wheel drive is provided, conventional beam-type axles and leaf spring suspension are used. The front steer-drive axle is fitted with single wheels/tyres, the rear drive axle with dual wheels/tyres. An Anti-lock Braking System (ABS) is fitted as standard. Motive power is provided by MAN 6.87-litre water-cooled diesel developing 220 hp. This engine is EURO 3 emissions compliant, capable of operation with NATO F34/F54 fuels and is coupled to a six speed manual gearbox and two speed transfer box. An automatic transmission is optional. A single 220 litre capacity fuel tank is chassis mounted.

The earlier DAC 16.215 FA is powered by a non-emissions compliant D2156 six-cylinder diesel engine developing 215 hp and coupled to a 10 speed manual gearbox. The earlier DAC 16.240 FA is powered by a EURO 2 emissions compliant Deutz BF 6M 1013 six-cylinder diesel engine developing 236 hp and coupled to a five-speed manual gearbox and two speed transfer box.

The all steel flat-panelled cab of the 16.220 FA is fitted with a two-piece flat glass windscreen and is standard throughout the ROMAN military truck range in various configurations.

The cab tilts forward hydraulically for engine maintenance and checks and is fitted with a high-performance heating and ventilation system. An observation hatch is fitted in the cab roof for the passenger.

The ROMAN 16.220 FA is also available configured as a 6,000-litre capacity fuel tanker (ROMAN)   1186172

ROMAN 16.220 FA (4 × 4) 7,500 kg truck (ROMAN)   1323549

Climatic operational range is –33°C to +52°C.

The rear troop carrying/cargo area has a steel platform and is equipped with drop sides and tailgate. Side and centre mounted folding benches provide seating for 33 personnel. A tarpaulin and bows are provided for protection from the elements. The vehicle is transportable by rail.

The basic chassis cab of the 16.220 FA (and earlier models) is/was also available configured as a 6,000-litre capacity water or fuel tanker.

Specifications

ROMAN 16.220 FA
Cab seating: 1 + 1
Configuration: 4 × 4
Weight:
   (laden) 15,500 kg
   (unladen) 8,000 kg
   (payload) 7,500 kg
   (towed load) 10,000 kg
   (GCW) 25,500 kg
Length: 8.795 m
Width: 2.5 m
Height: 2.8 m
Ground clearance: (rear) 330 mm
Angle of approach/departure: 30°/21°
Max speed: 90 km/h
Fuel capacity: 220 litres
Max gradient: 44%
Side slope: 33%
Engine: MAN 6.87-litre EURO 3 emissions compliant 6 cylinder inline water-cooled diesel developing 220 hp (162 kW)
Gearbox: manual with 6 forward and one reverse gears; automatic option
Transfer box: 2-speed
Steering: hydraulic power assisted
Turning radius: (kerb) 10 m
Suspension: semi-elliptic leaf springs
Brakes: dual circuit, air, drums all-round. ABS fitted
Electrical system: 24 V

Status
In service with the some former Warsaw Pact countries (16.215 FA) and Romania (16.215 FA - 825 delivered 1985-1994, 16.240 FA).

Contractor
ROMAN SA

ROMAN 16.310 FAEG (4 × 4) 6,000 kg high mobility truck

Development
The ROMAN 16.310 FAEG (4 × 4) 6,000 kg payload high-mobility truck is a derivative of the earlier DAC 17.280 FAE, the main improvement in this latest model being a more powerful, more emissions complaint MAN diesel engine.

The ROMAN 16.310 FAEG (4 × 4) 6,000 kg high mobility truck has been supplied to Malaysia.

ROMAN SA is a Romanian truck manufacturer that was established after World War II on the foundation of the old ROMLOC automotive factory built in 1921. The plant was named Steagul Rosu (the Red Flag) and in 1954 the first batch of SR 101 trucks (a Russian ZIS-150 clone) was produced.

In 1971 an agreement for the licence build of MAN products was reached. Since 1990 DAC has been the special trucks division of ROMAN trucks.

It was announced during 2003 that Pesaka Astana of Malaysia had acquired a 94.27 per cent stake in ROMAN SA, including a 100 per cent takeover of two of ROMAN SA's subsidiaries which control the assembly plant and axle parts manufacturing facilities. The takeover did not involve any liabilities or debts of ROMAN SA. After one week, Pesaka Astana gave up its share of ROMAN SA to SC PRO ROMAN SA, Brasov. From 2004 the current privatised company began trading.

ROMAN 16.310 FAEG (4 × 4) 6,000 kg high mobility truck of the Malaysian Army with a mobile workshop body (ROMAN)   1186173

Between 1995 and early 2007 ROMAN SA supplied around 1,300 assorted trucks to the Romanian Army and around 200 assorted trucks to the Malaysian Army (1995-2003) under the AMDAC name and in conjunction with Pesaka Astana. In support of operations in Iraq the company has also received at least 13 contracts from TACOM for 15 different types of trucks for civilian and logistic support of the Iraqi Army.

Following privatisation in 2004 a decision was taken to use ROMAN as the primary brand name. ROMAN designations are based around the same system as earlier DAC/AMDAC designations and define approximate GVW (tonnes) and approximate engine power output (hp), with the additional lettering defining a variety of things including cab type, drive configuration, wheel/tyre fit, body/chassis type.

Description
The chassis frame of the ROMAN 16.310 FAEG is a conventional channel section design with riveted or bolted cross members. A 10,000 kg capacity hydraulic self-recovery winch is standard.

Full time all-wheel drive is provided, conventional beam-type axles and leaf spring suspension being employed. The front steer-drive and rear drive axle are fitted with single wheels/tyres and a Central Tyre Inflation (CTI) system which allows the driver to adjust tyres pressures to suit prevailing ground conditions, from the cab. An Anti-lock Braking System (ABS) is fitted as standard.

Motive power is provided by MAN 12-litre water-cooled diesel engine developing 310 hp. This engine is EURO 3 emissions compliant, capable of operation with NATO F34/F54 fuels and is coupled to a 16 speed manual gearbox and two speed transfer box. An automatic transmission is optional. A single 310 litre capacity fuel tank is chassis mounted.

The forward control all steel flat-panelled cab is a MAN design now fitted as standard throughout the ROMAN military truck range in various configurations with two to six seats, and two or four doors. A flat panelled all steel cab with a two piece flat glass windscreen (also fitted to certain ROMAN military models) is an option for this chassis. The cab tilts forward hydraulically for engine maintenance and checks and is fitted with a high-performance heating and ventilation system. An observation hatch is fitted in the cab roof for the passenger.

Climatic operational range is –33°C to +52°C.

The rear troop carrying/cargo area has a steel platform and is equipped with drop sides and tailgate. Folding benches provide seating for 22 personnel. A tarpaulin and bows are provided for protection from the elements. The vehicle is transportable by rail. The basic chassis cab of the 16.310 FAEG has also been produced configured as 6,000-litre capacity water and fuel tankers, and a mobile workshop.

ROMAN 16.310 FAEG (4 × 4) 6,000 kg high mobility truck of the Malaysian Army (ROMAN)   1323550

Specifications

ROMAN 16.310 FAEG
Cab seating: 1 + 1
Configuration: 4 × 4 (full time)
Weight:
  (laden) 16,000 kg
  (unladen) 10,000 kg
  (payload) 6,000 kg
  (towed load, on road) 10,000 kg
  (towed load, off road) 5,000 kg
  (GCW, on road) 26,000 kg
  (GCW, off road) 21,000 kg
Length: 8 m
Width: 2.5 m
Height: 3 m
Ground clearance: (rear) 400 mm
Angle of approach/departure: 30°/30°
Max speed: 90 km/h
Fuel capacity: 310 litres
Max gradient: 66%
Side slope: 44%
Engine: MAN 12-litre EURO 3 emissions compliant 6-cylinder in-line water-cooled diesel developing 310 hp (228 kW)
Gearbox: manual with 16 forward and 2 reverse gears; automatic option
Transfer box: 2-speed
Steering: hydraulic power-assisted
Turning radius: (kerb) 8.8 m
Suspension: semi-elliptic leaf springs
Brakes: dual circuit, air, drums all round. ABS fitted
Electrical system: 24 V

Status

Production as required. Supplied to Malaysia.

Contractor

ROMAN SA

ROMAN 26.360 DFAEG (6 × 6) truck

Development

The ROMAN 26.360 DFAEG (6 × 6) truck is a specialist application military vehicle that is suitable for a variety of roles. It has been produced as an artillery tractor/limber and mobile crane for the Malaysian Army. It forms the prototype of the launcher and resupply vehicles for the LAROM 160 Multiple Artillery Rocket System, a joint development between Aerostar of Romania and Israel Military Industries (IMI), and is the base chassis for the Soltam Systems developed ATROM 155 mm/52-calibre self-propelled artillery system. Full details of the LAROM 160 Multiple Artillery Rocket System and ATROM 155 mm/52-calibre self-propelled artillery system (ATROM is essentially the Israeli Soltam Systems Autonomous Truck Mounted-Howitzer System (ATMOS) mounted on the 26.360 DFAEG chassis) can be found in *Jane's Armour and Artillery*.

ROMAN SA is a Romanian truck manufacturer that was established after World War II on the foundation of the old ROMLOC automotive factory built in 1921. The plant was named Steagul Rosu (the Red Flag) and in 1954 the first batch of SR 101 trucks (a Russian ZIS-150 clone) was produced.

In 1971 an agreement for the licence build of MAN products was reached. Since 1990 DAC has been the special trucks division of ROMAN trucks.

It was announced during 2003 that Pesaka Astana of Malaysia had acquired a 94.27 per cent stake in ROMAN SA, including a 100 per cent takeover of two of ROMAN SA's subsidiaries which control the assembly plant and axle parts manufacturing facilities. The takeover did not involve any liabilities or debts of ROMAN SA. After one week Pesaka Astana gave up its share of ROMAN SA to SC PRO ROMAN SA, Brasov. From 2004 the current privatised company began trading.

Between 1995 and early 2007, ROMAN SA supplied around 1,300 assorted trucks to the Romanian Army and around 200 assorted trucks to the Malaysian Army (1995-2003) under the AMDAC name and in

The ROMAN 26.360 DFAEG (6 × 6) truck is in production as an artillery tractor/limber for the Malaysian Army (ROMAN)   1323552

The ROMAN 26.360 DFAEG (6 × 6) is the base chassis for the Soltam Systems developed ATROM 155 mm/52-calibre self-propelled artillery system (ROMAN)   1186174

conjunction with Pesaka Astana. In support of operations in Iraq the company has also received at least 13 contracts from TACOM for 15 different types of trucks for civilian and logistic support of the Iraqi Army.

Following privatisation in 2004 the decision was taken to use ROMAN as the primary brand name. ROMAN designations are based on the same system as earlier DAC/AMDAC designations and define approximate GVW (tonnes) and approximate engine power output (hp), with the additional lettering defining a variety of things including cab type, drive configuration, wheel/tyre fit, body/chassis type.

Description

The chassis frame of the ROMAN 26.360 DFAEG is of conventional channel section design with riveted or bolted cross members. A 10,000 kg capacity hydraulic self-recovery winch is standard.

Full time all-wheel drive is provided, conventional beam type axles and leaf spring suspension being employed. The front steer-drive and rear drive axles are fitted with single wheels/tyres and a Central Tyre Inflation (CTI) system that allows the driver to adjust tyres pressures to suit prevailing ground conditions, from the cab. An Anti-lock Braking System (ABS) is fitted as standard.

Motive power is provided by MAN 2866 LF 24 12-litre six cylinder water-cooled diesel developing 360 hp. This engine is capable of operation with NATO F34/F54 fuels and is coupled to a 16-speed manual gearbox and two speed transfer box. An automatic transmission is optional. A single 310-litre capacity fuel tank is chassis-mounted, a 410-litre capacity tank is optional.

The forward control all steel flat-panelled cab is a MAN design now fitted as standard throughout the ROMAN military truck range in various configurations with two to six seats, and two or four doors. A flat panelled all steel cab with a two piece flat glass windscreen (also fitted to certain ROMAN military models) is an option for this chassis. The cab tilts forward hydraulically for engine maintenance and checks and is fitted with a high-performance heating and ventilation system. An observation hatch is fitted in the cab roof for the passenger.

Climatic operational range is –33°C to +52°C.

Specifications

ROMAN 26.360 DFAEG
Cab seating: 1 + 1
Configuration: 4 × 4 (full time)
Weight:
  (laden) 26,000 kg
  (payload on chassis cab) 15,000 kg
Length: 8.895 m
Width: 2.5 m
Height: 2.7 m
Ground clearance: 400 mm
Angle of approach/departure: 30°/25°
Max speed: 90 km/h
Fuel capacity: 310 litres (optional 410 litres)
Max gradient: 56%
Side slope: 33%
Engine: MAN 2866 LF 24 12-litre 6-cylinder in-line water-cooled diesel developing 360 hp (265 kW)
Gearbox: manual with 16 forward and 2 reverse gears; automatic option
Transfer box: 2-speed
Steering: hydraulic power assisted
Turning radius: (kerb) 11.8 m
Suspension: semi-elliptic leaf springs
Brakes: dual circuit, air, drums all round. ABS fitted
Electrical system: 24 V

Status

Production as required. Supplied to Malaysia (>40) and Romania (12 delivered 2006-2008).

Contractor

ROMAN SA

Russian Federation

BAZ-5937 and BAZ-5939 (6 × 6) special purpose vehicles and current models

Development

BAZ stands for Bryansk Auto Zavod (Bryansk Auto/Automobile Plant). The plant was originally established in 1958 to initially manufacture ZIL-designed heavy trucks for the Soviet Union and its allies and to date has developed around 95 different chassis.

In addition to military roles, current generation BAZ special chassis are in use for a variety of specialist roles in the hydrocarbons and associated industries, and as chassis for the mounting of mobile cranes.

An outline of current primary models can be found elsewhere in this entry.

Description

The BAZ-5937 and BAZ-5939 are basically similar (6 × 6) special purpose vehicles that are amphibious and highly mobile. The vehicles have many uses and are employed as carriers for components of the SA-8a and SA-8b 'Gecko' surface-to-air missile systems and the SS-21 'Scarab' surface-to-surface missile system. The BAZ-5937 is used for the SA-8a and SA-8b 'Gecko' transporter/erector/launcher and radar systems and for the SA-8 transport and reloading vehicle; the BAZ-5939 is used as the basis for the SS-21 'Scarab' launcher and reloading vehicles. The BAZ-5937 has its engine located just in front of the rear wheels, while the SS-21 versions of the BAZ-5939 have the engine located between the first and second set of wheels. Many components are interchangeable between the two vehicles.

The two vehicles are similar and often referred to as the BAZ-5937/39. Both use a long boat-shaped hull with the driver/operators' cab set forward in front of the load-bearing area. The cab has room for three occupants with one occupant seated in a semi-prone position behind the driver. The cab is equipped with an NBC protection system with the air filtration unit inside the cab over the left front wheel. A diesel heater is provided, with the heater blower coupled to the air filtration system.

The load area is constructed from welded steel plating with supports for strength and stabilisation. A door is used for access to the engine and generator area. Both vehicles use a type 5020B six-cylinder, four-stroke, water-cooled diesel engine rated at 290 hp. The air intake system uses a two-stage filter; the air can be heated in the Winter. The primary starter system uses air pressure with a back-up electrical starter. Fuel is carried in a 320-litre tank mounted in front of the left rear wheel.

The five-speed automatic transmission can be operated manually during amphibious operations. There is a two-stage hydraulic system. Final drive is transmitted to all six roadwheels independently. For lubrication there is a dry sump oil injection system with pumps, a centrifugal filter and a cooling system. The engine cooling system is similar to that used on the BMP ICV, using injection cooling. The pump involved is combined with the oil pump. A diesel pre-warmer for the engine is provided by routeing the exhaust pipe through the oil and hydraulic fluid reservoirs.

BAZ-6402 (6 × 6) tractor trucks with semi-trailers mounting the S-400 anti-aircraft missile system (BZKT)   1391457

The BAZ-5937 is used for the SA-8a and SA-8b 'Gecko' transporter/erector/launcher and radar systems and for the SA-8 transport and reloading vehicle (Ian C Young)   1391456

BAZ-5939 special purpose vehicle (T J Gander)   0511758

Both vehicles are provided with power steering and brakes. The brakes are a two-part system with the first part controlling the right front, left middle and right rear wheels; the second part controls the left front, right middle and left rear wheels. A two-drum emergency brake system is provided.

A 24 V electrical system is provided and the lighting system is similar to that used on the Ural-4320 (6 × 6) 4,500 kg truck. The BAZ-5937 carries a 50 kW generator driven by a gas turbine along with a back-up 35 kW generator powered by the transmission. Both generators can be used to provide power for the various weapon systems carried. An R-123 radio and an R-124 intercom are carried.

For amphibious operations the BAZ-5937/39 is powered by two water-jets located in the rear. Maximum speed in water is 8 km/h. In the water, steering is effected by a rudder and the cab is protected by a raised baffle plate; the driver and co-driver use special vision devices.

Current range

Most recently a new range of special purpose chassis has been produced by the Bryansk Motor Vehicle Plant. Many of these, which may be in use for military roles, have been adopted for use in the hydrocarbons industry or as chassis for the mounting of mobile cranes. Current models include the BAZ-69095 (6 × 6) chassis, BAZ-8026 (6 × 6) chassis for mobile cranes, BAZ-69098 (8 × 8) chassis, BAZ-690902 (8 × 8) chassis, BAZ-69096 (10 × 8) chassis, BAZ-69099 (12 × 12) chassis, BAZ-64022 (6 × 6) tractor truck, and BAZ-6403 (8 × 8) chassis. All are of conventional design and fitted with a three-seat forward-control-type cab behind which is located a transversally mounted YaMZ diesel engine. This latest range are non-amphibious.

Specifications

BAZ-5937
Cab seating: 1 + 4
Configuration: 6 × 6
Weight:
   (basic configuration) 11,400 kg
   (max load) 7,280 kg
Length: 9.165 m
Width: 2.782 m
Height: 1.948 m
Ground clearance: 430 mm
Track: 2.275 m
Wheelbase: 2.8 m + 2.6 m

BAZ-5937 special purpose vehicle (T J Gander)   0511759

Max speed:
  (land) 70 km/h
  (water) 8 km/h
Fuel capacity: 320 litres
Fuel consumption: 50 litres/100 km
Range: 760 km
Max gradient: 60%
Side slope: 44%
Fording: amphibious
Engine: 5D20B-300 V-6 four-stroke diesel developing 300 hp
Gearbox: 5 forward and 1 reverse gears
Clutch: hydraulically-operated twin dry disc
Transfer case: 2-speed
Suspension: independent torsion bar with hydraulic shock-absorbers
Turning radius: 12 m
Tyres: 12.00 × 500-508 ID-P284
Electrical system: 24 V
Batteries: 4 × 6 V 6ST-190

Status

BAZ-5937 (SA-8) supplied to Algeria, Angola, Czech Republic, Guinea-Bissau, Hungary, India, Iraq[1], Jordan, Kuwait, Libya, Poland, Russian Federation, Slovakia, Syria and the former Yugoslavia.

BAZ-5939 (SA-21) supplied to the Czech Republic, Russian Federation, Slovakia and Syria.

[1] Continued serviceability is questionable.

Contractor

Bryansk Motor Vehicle Plant JSC

Marketing agency

Rosoboronexport

GAZ-3937 (4 × 4) high mobility vehicle

Development

The GAZ-3937 series of (4 × 4) high mobility vehicles, also referred to as the Vodnik, was first seen in 1995. The original vehicle was called the GAZ-47 which was produced in wheeled (GAZ-4701) and tracked (GAZ-4707) versions but it was decided to concentrate on the wheeled version. As far as it is known, no variants of the Vodnik have entered service with the Russian Army so far. The Vodnik family is now being offered on the export market. In late 2006 it was revealed that Uruguay had placed an order for 48 units. As far as it is known this is the first export order for the GAZ-3937 Vodnik series of light armoured vehicle. These have all been delivered and are now in service.

Description

The GAZ-3937 is of modular construction, consisting of three main modules, the chassis, body and cabin. The chassis uses components from the Russian BRDM-2 (4 × 4) and BTR-80 (8 × 8) series of armoured vehicles. A wide range of mission-specific modules can be fitted to the GAZ-3937 (some reports say up to 26). The front module is for the driver and single crew member and has been seen configured with a conventional style cab or with as a half-cab in which the co-driver sits behind the driver. Conventional forward-opening side doors are fitted, but the half-cab version has a single large square roof hatch, while the conventional cab version has two smaller circular roof hatches that open to the rear. The engine is set back and to the right of the driver and is contained within the front module which is hermetically sealed and can be lightly armoured.

The rear module, when used in the personnel carrier role, can seat up to eight people and has been seen configured with a tarpaulin and bows, although a lightly armoured module offering protection from small arms fire and shell splinters is more common. The module used in the APC role

Prototype example of the GAZ-3937 Vodnik (4 × 4) high mobility vehicle
(Jim Kinnear)   0037355

Prototype example of the GAZ-3937 Vodnik (4 × 4) high mobility vehicle
(Jim Kinnear)   0037351

has a slightly raised roofline and for rapid deployment has two hatches either side, plus two large doors at the rear. Firing ports are also provided. The rear module space has been seen occupied by a conventional tactical shelter. One of the most recent GAZ-3937 variants displayed has mounted the turreted Phoenix air-defence system.

The GAZ 3937 has been designed to operate in outdoor temperatures ranging from −40°C to +50°C, in a wind speed of up to 30 m/s and at altitudes of up to 4,500 m. It is fully amphibious being propelled at up to 4 km/h in the water by its wheels and standard equipment includes power-steering on the front axle and a Central Tyre Inflation (CTI) system that allows the driver to adjust the tyre-pressure to suite the terrain being crossed.

Specifications

GAZ-3937
Crew: up to 11
Configuration: 4 × 4
Weight:
  (GVW) 6,900 kg
  (payload) 1,500-2,500 kg
Length: 7.74 m
Width: 2.625 m
Height: rear module dependant
Ground clearance: 475 mm
Wheelbase: 3.05 m
Max speed:
  (road) 112 km/h
  (water) 4-5 km/h
Range: (road) 1,000 km
Max gradient: 66%
Engine: GAZ-5423 6.23-litre 6-cylinder in-line turbocharged diesel developing 175 hp (129 kW)
Gearbox: manual, 5-speed
Suspension: independent, torsion bar
Steering: power assisted

Status

Production as required. In service with Uruguay (48).

Contractor

Arzamas Machinery Plant

GAZ medium truck series

Development

The GAZ Group is Russia's largest automotive manufacturer of light commercial vehicles, trucks, buses, cars, diesel engines, power-train components and road construction equipment. The current GAZ Group was established in 2005 with the restructuring of the then RusPromAuto's production assets. GAZ, as an automobile manufacturer, started in 1929 and the first vehicle rolled off the production line in 1932.

The GAZ medium truck series was developed during the early 1990s to be the eventual commercial and military replacement for the GAZ-66 truck series, but delays intervened to the extent that the vehicle was not marketed internationally until 1999. The base model of the series is the GAZ-3307, a (4 × 2) chassis with dual rear wheels.

By July 2004, two distinct ranges of trucks, Sadko and Zemlyak, were being marketed. The Sadko are a 2,000 kg payload series, the Zemlyak are a 4,000 kg payload series.

Description

The layout of the GAZ medium truck series is entirely conventional, the main visible change from the earlier GAZ-66 series being the introduction of a bonnet. The design of the vehicle is stated to be modular to assist maintenance and spare part supply.

GAZ-3308 Sadko (4 × 4) 2,000 kg truck (GAZ)   0056387

GAZ-3308 Sadko (4 × 4) 2,000 kg truck of the Russian Armed Forces
(James Kinnear)   1120457

All models are fitted as standard with conventional cargo-type rear bodies, the primary visual difference being larger single wheels and tyres (1200R 18) on the Sadko series, smaller (with dual rear) wheels and tyres (8.25R 20) on the Zemlyak series.

The current Sadko production models are the GAZ-3308, GAZ-33081 and GAZ-33082, and the current Zemlyak production models are the GAZ-33085 and GAZ-33086.

The GAZ-3308 is powered by either a ZMZ-513 4.25-litre or ZMZ-5233 4.67-litre petrol engine developing (respectively) 116 and 122 hp; the GAZ-33081 is powered by either a MMZD-245.7 or MMZD-245.7E2 turbocharged diesel engine both developing 117 hp; the GAZ-33082 is powered by a GAZ-562 3.2-litre turbocharged diesel engine developing 150 hp, this being a licence-produced Steyr engine.

The GAZ-33085 is powered by a ZMZ-5233 4.67-litre petrol engine; the GAZ-33086 is powered by the MMZD-245.7 4.75-litre turbocharged diesel engine developing 117 hp.

Four- or five-speed synchromesh manual gearboxes and two-speed transfer boxes are fitted across both ranges. Limited slip differentials are fitted to the leaf sprung drive axles, with a central tyre pressure regulation system being a standard feature for military versions.

It is anticipated that the number of available models will increase with time as the GAZ-66 series is gradually supplemented and then replaced. The GAZ-3308 Sadko series are best suited to military applications and the specifications table below refers to this series.

Specifications

GAZ-3308 Sadko
Cab seating: 1 + 1
Configuration: 4 × 4
Weight:
(laden) 5,950 kg
(unladen) 3,710 kg
(max load) 2,000 kg
Length: 6.25 m
Width: 2.34 m
Height: (cab roof) 2.52 m
Ground clearance: 315 mm
Track:
(front) 1.82 m
(rear) 1.77 m
Wheelbase: 3.77 m
Max speed: (road) 90 km/h (ZMZ-513 engine and 4-speed gearbox option);
95 km/h (ZMZ-5233 engine and 5-speed gearbox option)
Range: 910 km at 60 km/h (ZMZ-513 engine and 4-speed gearbox option);
950 km at 60 km/h (ZMZ-5233 engine and 5-speed gearbox option)

GAZ-3308 Sadko (4 × 4) 2,000 kg truck (James Kinnear)   1120458

GAZ-3308 Sadko (4 × 4) 2,000 kg truck fitted with a VSZ-3308 airfield water/alcohol refueller rear body (James Kinnear)   1120459

Fuel capacity: 210 litres (2 × 105-litre tanks)
Fording: 800 mm to 1 m
Engine: ZMZ-513 4.25-litre V-8 water-cooled carburettor petrol developing 116 hp (85 kW) at 3,200 rpm and 271 N m torque at 2,250 rpm, or ZMZ-5233 4.67-litre V-8 water-cooled carburettor petrol developing 122 hp (90 kW) at 3,200 rpm and 299 N m torque at 2,250 rpm
Gearbox: manual, 4 forward and 1 reverse gears (ZMZ-513 engine option); manual, 5 forward and 1 reverse gears (ZMZ-5233 engine option)
Transfer box: 2-speed, with PTO
Clutch: single dry plate, hydraulic assist
Steering: recirculating ball, power assisted
Turning radius: 11 m
Suspension: leaf springs and telescopic hydraulic shock-absorbers, front and rear
Tyres: 1200R 18
Brakes: drums all round
Electrical system: 24 V

Status
In production. Offered for export sales. In service with the armed forces of Iraq, the Russian Federation, and other undisclosed users.

Contractor
Gorky Automobile Plant (GAZ Joint Stock Company)

GAZ-66 (4 × 4) 2,000 kg trucks

Development
The GAZ-66 (4 × 4) 2,000 kg truck was the replacement for the GAZ-63. Following prototypes produced in 1962, the GAZ-66 entered production at the Gorky Automobile Plant in 1964. Production of the GAZ-66 concluded in 1999 and the type is being supplemented, and it is anticipated that it will eventually be replaced, by the GAZ-3308 Sadko range of trucks (full details of which can be found elsewhere in this section). Given the numbers of GAZ-66 in service, full replacement may not take place for some time. The GAZ-66 is also used for a wide variety of civilian roles.

Description
The two-door all-steel forward control cab hinges forward to allow access to the engine for maintenance. The all-steel rear cargo body has fixed sides and a drop tailgate. The vehicle can be fitted with five bows and a tarpaulin

cover if required. Standard equipment includes a cab heater and an engine pre-heater as the vehicle is intended for use over a temperature range of −50°C to +50°C. Many vehicles have a winch.

All vehicles built since 1968 have a Central Tyre Inflation (CTI) system fitted as standard. The final production model is the turbo diesel powered GAZ-66-40, sometimes presented as GAZ-6640, and this model is designed to operate at altitudes of up to 4,500 m above sea level.

Variants
GAZ-66-02: with crane
GAZ-66-04: with shielded electrical system
GAZ-66-05: with shielded electrical system and crane
GAZ-66-01: with tyre pressure regulation system (also known as GAZ-66-51)
GAZ-66-02: with tyre pressure regulation system and winch
GAZ-66-03: with shielded electrical system
GAZ-66-04: with shielded electrical system and tyre pressure regulation system
GAZ-66-05: with shielded electrical system, tyre pressure regulation system and winch
GAZ-66-40: final production model; the data in the Specifications table relates to this model
GAZ-66-51: with tyre pressure regulation system and tropical equipment
GAZ-66-52: with winch and tropical equipment
GAZ-66-54: with shielded electrical system and tropical equipment
GAZ-66-55: with shielded electrical system, winch and tropical equipment
GAZ-66A: with tyre pressure regulation system and winch
GAZ-66E: with shielded electrical system
GAZ-66P: tractor truck, not placed in production
GAZ-66B: for airborne forces, with collapsible canvas cab, removable doors and windscreen, telescopic steering wheel and tie-down points for parachute dropping
DDA-53C: NBC decontamination vehicle
AVTs-1.7: 1,700 litre water tanker, built at Dalmatovo Molmashstroy plant
MZ-66: motor oil supply vehicle (820 litres).

Shop/van for command, communications and other roles (weight loaded 5,800 kg).

Multiple Rocket Launcher: the GAZ-66B is used as a carrier for a lightweight 12-tube version of the BM-21 known as the BM-21V Grad-P. For details of the BM-21 system refer to *Jane's Armour and Artillery*.

Specifications
GAZ-66-40
Cab seating: 1 + 1 (up to 21 in rear)
Configuration: 4 × 4
Weight:
  (unladen) 4,090 kg
  (laden) 6,810 kg
  (max load) 2,300 kg
  (towed load) 2,000 kg
Load area: 3.313 × 2.05 m
Length: (office body) 5.65 m
Width: (office body) 2.4 m
Height:
  (cab) 2.49 m
  (tarpaulin) 2.52 m
  (office body) 3.25 m
Ground clearance: (axles) 315 mm
Track: 1.8 m
Wheelbase: 3.3 m
Angle of approach/departure: 42°/32°
Max speed: (road) 90 km/h
Range: 1,400 km
Fuel capacity: 210 litres (2 × 105-litre tanks)
Max gradient: 67%
Side slope: 44%
Fording: 1.2 m
Engine: GAZ-5441 4-cylinder in-line air-cooled turbocharged diesel developing 123 hp (90 kW)

GAZ-66 (4 × 4) 2,000 kg truck of the Lithuanian Army (Stefan Marx) 1047625

GAZ-66 (4 × 4) 2,000 kg truck of the former East German Army with an office-type rear body (Stefan Marx)　1124715

Gearbox: manual with 5 forward and 1 reverse gears
Clutch: single dry plate, hydraulic assist
Transfer box: 2-speed, with PTO
Steering: globoid worm with 3-collar roller and hydraulic booster
Turning radius: 9.45 m
Suspension: longitudinal semi-elliptic springs and hydraulic double-acting shock-absorbers
Tyres: 12.00R 18 KI-115
Brakes:
  (main) hydraulic
  (parking) mechanical operating on transmission
Electrical system: 24 V

Status
Production complete. In service with former Warsaw Pact countries plus many others, including Angola, Cambodia, Cuba, Egypt, Finland, Iran, Iraq (status uncertain), Lithuania and Syria.

Contractor
Gorky Automobile Plant (GAZ Joint Stock Company)

KAMAZ range of trucks

Development
Construction work on the Kama Automobile Plant (occasionally presented Kamsky Automobile Plant) on the banks of the River Kama near the city of Naberezhnye Chelny began in December 1969. When conceived, the plant was designed to have seven production areas covering in the region of 40 square miles, and was to encompass virtually the full production cycle for a new range of heavy trucks. Facilities were to include an engine plant, pressing, casting and forging facilities, and upon reaching full capacity the plant was calculated to be capable of producing 150,000 vehicles and 250,000 diesel engines each year.

Initial studies regarding the proposed new heavy truck family confirmed that improving road infrastructure in the former Soviet Union throughout the 1960s would allow for a Cab-Over-Engine (COE) configuration to be adopted, although to ensure mobility on all categories of roads and in all climatic conditions, a maximum 6,000 kg axle load for these 8,000 kg payload trucks (that would be capable of towing an 8,000 kg trailer) was deemed essential, as was a power-to-weight ratio of 8 hp/tonne.

In the Spring of 1968 the Russian government tasked Zil (Zavod Imeni Likhacheva) to create a new family of heavy diesel trucks, the long-term aim of this new project being to deliver a standardised three-axle heavy chassis-cab design powered by a diesel engine, and that would encompass a full range of models including dump trucks and tractor trucks. In the Spring of 1969 the Russian government instructed what is now the Yaroslavl Diesel Engine Plant to develop a suitable power plant for this new range of trucks.

By May 1969 the prototype of what was designated Zil-170 (but would become the KAMAZ-5320) was under test, and over a two or three year period more than 50 prototype vehicles would be produced. Bench testing of the first engines and gearboxes also commenced during 1969.

Following successful operational testing of Zil-170 three axle (6 × 4) trucks, Zil-170T tractors and Zil-170S construction trucks, by late-1972, and with testing continuing across Russia, prototypes and documentation had been submitted to KAMAZ. The first five KAMAZ-5320 trucks left the production line in February 1976, with other models including tractor trucks and construction chassis following. By June 1979 the 100,000 KAMAZ truck had been produced, and by July 1999 the production complex had manufactured 1.6 million vehicles and 2.16 million diesel engines; this figure increasing to around 1.8 million trucks by January 2007, and 2.5 million diesel engines by February 2008.

KAMAZ-43118 (6 × 6) (OJSC KAMAZ)   1109536

KAMAZ-63502 (8 × 8), a 6,000 kg axle load derivative of the Mustang family KAMAZ-6350 (8 × 8) (OJSC KAMAZ)   1109537

KAMAZ trucks are reportedly in use in around 90 countries, with approximately 25 per cent of current production exported. The current KAMAZ truck range is made up of around 30 basic models, that with specified modifications make somewhere in the region of around 300 variants available.

Although designed for commercial purposes the KAMAZ-5350 and its derivatives were quickly adopted by the armed forces of the former Soviet Union for a wide variety of roles.

KAMAZ introduced its first all-wheel drive truck in 1981, the (4 × 4) KAMAZ-4310, this soon followed by the (6 × 6) 43101. These initial offerings were followed from 1991 by a family of three trucks based on the KAMAZ-43114 (6 × 6) and including the KAMAZ-4326 (4 × 4) and KAMAZ-431184 (6 × 6). These were later joined by the KAMAZ-44108 (6 × 6) tractor truck and KAMAZ-43261 (4 × 4). Current production standard KAMAZ-4326/43261, 43114, 43118 and 44108 remain available to both military and commercial users, these known as dual purpose/dual role trucks in the former Soviet Union.

The 10-seat KAMAZ-43269 wheeled armoured vehicle introduced in 2007 is the first vehicle of its type to be produced by KAMAZ, and is based on the chassis and driveline of the KAMAZ-4326 truck.

For more demanding military applications, in the early 1990s KAMAZ commenced development of the Mustang family of trucks, this initially consisting of the KAMAZ-4350 (4 × 4), the KAMAZ-5350 (6 × 6), and

KAMAZ-65224 (6 × 6) shown publicly for the first time at IDEX 2005. The KAMAZ-65224 is a single wheel variant of the KAMAZ-5244 and is based on the 20,000 kg payload heavy KAMAZ-6520 (6 × 4) (Patrick Allen) 1138072

KAMAZ-43501 (4 × 4), a derivative of the Mustang family KAMAZ-4350 (4 × 4) which has a shorter chassis and a reduced payload (Jim Kinnear) 1169348

An early KAMAZ-5411 (6 × 4) rear tipper truck (T J Gander)   0109488

KAMAZ-6350 (8 × 8). The Mustang family covers broadly the same range of payloads as the earlier 43114 family, however, their design does feature considerably more militarisation than previously produced KAMAZ dual purpose trucks, it including a chassis better-suited to the transport and mounting of military shelter-type bodies. The Mustang family of trucks began entering service with Russia's armed forces in 2003 and are available only to military customers.

The Mustang family has evolved considerably since its development commenced, with each original vehicle now having derivatives. The KAMAZ-4350 has been developed into the KAMAZ-43502 which has an increased payload, and also the KAMAZ-43501 which has a shorter chassis and a reduced payload. The KAMAZ-5350 has been developed into the KAMAZ-53501 which has a lengthened wheelbase and increase in payload. The KAMAZ-53504 is a tractor truck variant of the KAMAZ-5350. The (8 × 8) KAMAZ-6350 has been developed into the KAMAZ-63501 and KAMAZ-63502, and the KAMAZ-6450 tractor truck.

KAMAZ also offers military customers a range of heavier-rated dual purpose trucks, these based on the 20,000 kg payload (6 × 4) KAMAZ-6520. The KAMAZ-6522 is essentially an all-wheel drive version of the KAMAZ-6520, the KAMAZ-65224 a further derivative that has single wheels/tyres all-round to replace the twin rears on the KAMAZ-6522. The KAMAZ-6560 is a four-axle all-wheel drive derivative of the KAMAZ-6522/65224.

KAMAZ also offers a range of heavy all-wheel drive tractor trucks derived from the base KAMAZ-6520, these currently including the (6 × 6) KAMAZ-65225 with a GCW of 59.3-tonnes, the (6 × 6) KAMAZ-65226 with a GCW of 97-tonnes, and the (8 × 8) KAMAZ-65228 with a GCW of 120-tonnes.

The (4 × 4) KAMAZ-4911 Extreme is based on an extensively modified KAMAZ-6520 chassis. The KAMAZ-4911 Extreme has been in production since 2002 and is essentially the serial production version of KAMAZ's record eight times Dakar Rally winning trucks. The 15,600 kg KAMAZ-4911 is powered by a 730 hp V8 diesel, has a tyre-limited maximum speed of 165 km/h, and can accelerate from a standing start to 100 km/h in 16 seconds.

KAMAZ has never officially disclosed details of military sales, although known users of KAMAZ military trucks are known to include Russia, the independent states that once formed part of the Soviet Union, most former Warsaw Pact countries, some Middle Eastern countries, some countries in the Americas, some Asian and African countries, and a small number of 'Western' countries such as Greece that have limited numbers of trucks, usually in support roles for Russian-supplied missile, rocket, radar or similar complex systems. KAMAZ trucks are also used by, and have been supplied through, the United Nations (UN).

Model	KAMAZ-4326	KAMAZ-43114	KAMAZ-43118	KAMAZ-43502	KAMAZ-63501	KAMAZ-65224
Type:	cargo truck	cargo truck	cargo truck	cargo truck	cargo truck	cargo truck
Cab seating:	1 + 2	1 + 2	1 + 2	1 + 2	1 + 2	1 + 2
Configuration:	4 × 4	6 × 6	6 × 6	4 × 4	8 × 8	6 × 6
Weight:						
(unladen)	8,090 kg	9,335 kg	10,500 kg	8,200 kg	12,750 kg	12,150 kg
(laden)	11,600 kg	15,420 kg	20,650 kg	12,700 kg	26,900 kg	26,350 kg
(payload)	3,210 kg	5,785 kg	10,000 kg	4,500 kg	14,000 kg	14,000 kg
(front axle(s) load, laden)	5,600 kg	5,490 kg	5,600 kg	5,400 kg	11,200 kg	7,500 kg
(rear axle/bogie load, laden)	6,000 kg	9,930 kg	15,200 kg	7,300 kg	15,700 kg	18,850 kg
(GTW)	16,600 kg	22,920 kg	32,650 kg	19,700 kg	37,900 kg	38,350 kg
Length:	7.94 m	7.94 m	8.645 m	7.95 m	9.61 m	8.96 m
Width:	2.5 m	2.5 m	2.5 m	2.5 m	2.5 m	2.5 m
Height: (cab)	2.94 m	2.94 m	3.035 m	3.035 m	3.03 m	3.225 m
Ground clearance:	380 mm	380 mm	380 mm	380 mm	380 mm	410 mm
Track:	2.01 m	2.01 m	2.05 m	2.05 m	2.01 m	2.09 m
Wheelbase:	4.2 m	3.34 + 1.32 m	3.69 + 1.32 m	4.18 m	1.94 + 3.34 + 1.32 m	4.2 + 1.44 m
Angle of approach/departure:	33°/27°	33°/35°	32°/18°	33°/27°	33°/35°	38°/33°
Max speed:	90 km/h	90 km/h	90 km/h	n/avail	85 km/h	90 km/h
Fuel capacity:	n/avail	n/avail	n/avail	n/avail	n/avail	n/avail
Gradient:	60%	60%	60%	60%	60%	60%
Fording:						
(unprepared)	800 mm	1.5 m	1.5 m	1.5 m	1.5 m	1.5 m
(prepared - 15 mins prep)	1.5 m	1.75 m	1.75 m	1.75 m	1.75 m	1.75 m
Engine:	KAMAZ-740.11.240 EURO 1 emissions complaint 10.85-litre V8 water-cooled turbocharged 4-stroke diesel developing 240 hp (179 kW) at 2,200 rpm; KAMAZ-740.31.240 EURO 2 option developing 240 hp (179 kW)	KAMAZ-740.13.260 EURO 1 emissions complaint 10.85-litre V8 water-cooled turbocharged 4-stroke diesel developing 260 hp (194 kW) at 2,200 rpm; KAMAZ-740.31.240 EURO 2 option developing 240 hp (179 kW) at 2,200 rpm	KAMAZ-740.13.260 EURO 1 emissions complaint 10.85-litre V8 water-cooled turbocharged 4-stroke diesel developing 260 hp (194 kW) at 2,200 rpm; KAMAZ-740.30.260 EURO 2 option developing 260 hp (194 kW) at 2,200 rpm	KAMAZ-740.30.260 EURO 2 emissions complaint 10.85-litre V8 water-cooled turbocharged 4-stroke diesel developing 260 hp (194 kW) at 2,200 rpm	KAMAZ-740.50.360 EURO 2 emissions complaint 11.76-litre V8 water-cooled turbocharged 4-stroke diesel developing 360 hp (268 kW) at 2,200 rpm	KAMAZ-740.50.360 EURO 2 emissions complaint 11.76-litre V8 water-cooled turbocharged 4-stroke diesel developing 360 hp (268 kW) at 2,200 rpm
Clutch:	twin dry plate, Model 142	twin dry plate, Model 17	twin dry plate, Model 17	n/avail	ZF SACHS MFZ-430 single dry plate	ZF SACHS MFZ-430 single dry plate
Gearbox:	KAMAZ-142 with 5 forward and 1 reverse gears	KAMAZ-142 with 5 forward and 1 reverse gears	KAMAZ-154 with 10 forward and 1 reverse gears	KAMAZ-154 with 10 forward and 1 reverse gears	ZF 16S151 with 16 forward gears	ZF 16S151 with 16 forward gears
Transfer box:	KAMAZ-43114 2-speed	KAMAZ-43114 2-speed	KAMAZ-65111 2-speed	KAMAZ-65111 2-speed	Steyr VG2000/300 2-speed	Steyr VG2000/300 2-speed
Steering:	power assisted	power assisted	power assisted	power assisted	power assisted	power assisted
Turning radius:	11.3 m	11.3 m	11.5 m	n/avail	n/avail	n/avail
Suspension:	leaf springs and telescopic shock-absorbers, front; leaf springs, rear	leaf springs and telescopic shock-absorbers, front; leaf springs and anti-roll bar, rear	leaf springs and telescopic shock-absorbers, front; leaf springs and anti-roll bar, rear	leaf springs and telescopic shock-absorbers, front; leaf springs, rear	leaf springs and telescopic shock-absorbers, front; leaf springs and anti-roll bar, rear	leaf springs and telescopic shock-absorbers, front; leaf springs and anti-roll bar, rear
Tyres:	Kama 425/85R 21	Kama 425/85R 21	Kama 425/85R 21	Kama 425/85R 21	Kama 425/85R 21	Michelin 1600R 20 XZL
Brakes:	air, drums all round	air, drums all round	air, drums all round	air, drums all round	air, drums all round	air, drums all round
Electrical system:	24 V	24 V	24 V	24 V	24 V	24 V
Batteries:	2 × 12 V, 190 Ah	2 × 12 V, 190 Ah	2 × 12 V, 190 Ah	2 × 12 V, 190 Ah	2 × 12 V, 190 Ah	n/avail
Alternator:	28 V	28 V	28 V	28 V	28 V	n/avail

Description

All KAMAZ trucks are entirely conventional in design and are essentially the continuing evolution of a well-proven base design. They are built around a ladder frame C-section chassis, this mounting leaf sprung beam axles, with telescopic shock-absorbers and anti-roll bars as required.

To ensure a suitable level of mobility on Russia's still developing road network, the initial development concept called for the new range of KAMAZ trucks to have maximum axle loads of 6,000 kg per axle, and at a desired payload of 8,000 kg. Over time Russia's road network improved and payload requirements increased, and axle loadings of 8,000 kg, and later 10,000 to 13,000 kg have been introduced on certain models. A mobility-driven 10,000 kg limit that is only approached on rear bogies of fully laden vehicles, has remained for military models.

Commercially KAMAZ has developed trucks with cabs sourced from both Sisu and DAF, however, the bulk of production, and all military offerings, still feature the continuing development of the original KAMAZ-5320 cab. This forward-tilting all-steel cab seats two or three, the third seat being an 'occasional' centre seat that doubles up as a standing platform for the roof cupola. An extended cab that allows for a sleeping berth or additional stowage space is usually fitted to military models. KAMAZ offers internal or externally fitting small arms fire protection kits for this cab.

Motive power for the vast majority of KAMAZ trucks is provided by current versions of KAMAZ's original 10.85-litre V8 KAMAZ-740 unit. This, like the chassis/cab, has been continuously developed and now produces up to 260 hp and meets up to EURO 2 emissions requirements. An 11.76-

An early KAMAZ 43101 (6 × 6) cargo truck of the Ukraine Army fitted with a standard drop side military body (Shaun C Connors)   0109504

litre version of this engine is now fitted to some heavier trucks, this capable of developing up to 400 hp and meeting up to EURO 3 emissions requirements. The KAMAZ-740 engine is equipped with a pre-heater for extreme cold weather (below –25°C) starting as standard.

The two heaviest tractor trucks in the current KAMAZ range, the KAMAZ-65226 and KAMAZ-65228, are offered with a 544 hp 15.87-litre Deutz BF8M1015C V8 and 600 hp 15-litre six-cylinder Cummins ISX 600, respectively. During the late 1980s/early 1990s, KAMAZ previously offered Cummins engines in its commercial trucks (in conjunction with a Sisu cab), and in 2006 announced a licensing agreement with Cummins for the production of 140-275 hp B Series engines. The B-Series powers the KAMAZ-4308 5,500 kg payload medium weight truck introduced commercially by KAMAZ during 2003/2004.

KAMAZ military trucks have traditionally been fitted with KAMAZ manual five- or 10-speed gearboxes, these coupled to a KAMAZ two-speed transfer box which has the facility to accept a power-Take-Off (PTO). Some of the latest Mustang family are offered with ZF manual gearboxes and Steyr two-speed transfer boxes, as are some of the most recent heavier military/dual purpose trucks. Other recent models are offered with fully automatic ZF transmissions coupled to Steyr two-speed transfer boxes.

With the exception of heaviest tractor trucks that are fitted with dual rear wheels and tyres, the standard tyre fit for all single-wheeled KAMAZ military trucks has traditionally been 425/85R 21 Kama radials, these fitted with a Central Tyre Inflation (CTI) system as standard. More recently, certain KAMAZ models have been offered with 1600R 20 Michelin XZL tyres.

The design operating parameters for KAMAZ military trucks when fitted with KAMAZ driveline components and Kama tyres are a climatic operational range of between –40°C and +50°C, relative humidity up to 98 per cent at +25°C, dust content in the air of up 1.5 g/m³, wind speeds of up 20 m/sec, and at altitudes of up to 4,500 m above sea level. Fording depth is up to 1.75 m (with 15 minutes preparation), a vertical obstacle of up to 500 mm can be surmounted, a 60 per cent slope can be climbed, and dependent on wheel configuration, a trench of up to 1.7 m can be crossed. A chassis-mounted self-recovery winch with 80 m of cable and front/rear pull is optional on most military models.

Specifications
See table on page 575

Status
In production. In service with numerous armed forces worldwide (see text).

Contractor
Open Joint Stock Company KAMAZ

MAZ-543 (8 × 8) trucks

Development
The independent Minsk Wheeled Tractor Plant (MWKT, Cyrillic MZKT) was established in 1991 from a special-purpose wheeled tractor division of the Minsk Automobile Plant (MAZ). MAZ, in which MAN of Germany now has a controlling interest, continues to manufacture commercial and conventionally-styled military trucks with up to three axles, while the Minsk Wheeled Tractor Plant concentrates on speciality multi-axle chassis for military and specialised commercial uses

For a number of years military vehicles produced at Minsk were based on the (8 × 8) MAZ-543 truck and MAZ-537 tractor trucks (full details of which can be found in the Heavy equipment transporters section), and while these remain in production, in recent years the company has expanded its range of products somewhat. Some products, including the MAZ-543 series, retain the former MAZ designation but other current products now use the MWKT/MZKT name.

MAZ-543M (8 × 8) truck chassis as part of the S-300V (NATO SA-12a Gladiator/SA-12b Giant) multichannel all-weather Anti-Tactical Ballistic Missile (ATBM) and Surface-to-Air Missile (SAM) system (Stefan Marx)   1047641

MAZ-543M (8 × 8) truck chassis used as the basis for the Splav 300 mm BM 9A52 Smerch multiple rocket system (Stefan Marx)   1047640

Description
The MAZ-543 (8 × 8) truck uses many automotive components of the MAZ-537 (8 × 8) tractor truck, including a similar engine. It was seen in public for the first time in November 1965.

The MAZ-543 is a four-axle (8 × 8) truck chassis designed for off-road use, with steerable wheels on the front two axles. The basic chassis has a nominal load capacity of 20,000 kg and can be used for many special applications apart from as a cargo or load carrier.

The MAZ-543 series is powered by a 525 hp D12A-525A 38.88-litre V-12 diesel engine located between two separate two-man cabs. There is a hydromechanical transmission with a torque converter and three-speed planetary gearbox. The drive axles have central reduction gears with self-locking differentials, semi-axle Cardan joints and constant velocity universal joints in the steerable wheel linkages, plus planetary wheel reduction gears. The wide-profile tyres have a tyre inflation system. The suspension features independent torsion bar stations with double acting telescopic type shock-absorbers.

Variants
Military (8 × 8) variants of the MAZ-543 produced at Minsk include the following models:

MAZ-543A
On this model the nominal load capacity is increased to 22,000 kg. The engine is located further forward, resulting in one of the two cabs having seating for only one person. GVW is 43,300 kg and axle loading is increased to 11,300 kg.

MAZ-543M
With this model the engine is moved to the front of the vehicle, resulting in a single two-man cab on the left-hand side. This allows a further increase in load capacity to 22,600 kg. This model is used to carry multiple rocket systems and associated loads.

MAZ-7313
This model is a cargo carrier with a load capacity of 21,000 kg in a conventional flatbed cargo body.

MAZ-73132
On this tractor truck model the chassis is shortened to 10.815 m and the wheelbase to 2.2 m + 2.65 m + 1.7 m. GVW is 45,150 kg and axle load 12,500 kg.

Other models
Variants of the MAZ-543 are used to carry and launch the 'Scud A' (SS-1b), 9P117M 'Scud B' (SS-1c) and 'Scaleboard' (SS-12) surface-to-surface missiles. The Scud launchers are known as the MAZ-543LTM or MAZ-7310LTM Uragan (Hurricane), or Kashalot (Sperm Whale); the vehicle is 12 m long, and, with the missile, weighs 29,000 kg. A version with single

MAZ-543M (8 × 8) truck chassis (MZKT)   0044323

forward cab is used to carry the SSC-3 coastal defence missile system. Other missile-related variants include the fire-control vehicle, Trailer-Erector-Launcher (TEL) and other units for the SA-10b 'Grumble' surface-to-air system. The 300 mm BM 9A52 Smerch 12-round multiple launch rocket system is based on the MAZ-543M and there is also an associated reload vehicle, the 9T234-2. Many vehicles carry control centre, workshop, accommodation and office bodies for various weapon systems in addition to launch vehicles.

MAZ-543 variants are used to carry components of a mobile 130 mm A-222 BEREG coastal artillery system. Other mobile coastal defence systems involving the MAZ-543 include the Raduga Rubezh-A (boundary) SSC-3 Styx coastal defence missile, and the Granit Central Institute Bal (whale) SSC-6 coastal defence missile system. Offered for export as the Bal-E, this latter system is not believed to have entered production as of 2004.

There is also a MTP-A4 technical support vehicle based on a MAZ-543 chassis variant, the KZKT-74281, with a shortened wheelbase. This carries a heavy recovery winch and some repair equipment. It can tow disabled vehicles weighing up to 45,000 kg over hard roads.

Other MAZ-543 variants include an aircraft crash and fire tender, a heavy crane carrier and a tanker with a full-width forward control cab.

Chinese variants

Sources indicated during 2003 that the Minsk Wheeled Tractor Plant had provided assistance to China's Sanjiang Special Vehicle Technology Centre for the development of a Chinese versions of the MAZ-543 for, initially, the TEL for the Dong Feng-II short range ballistic missile.

A wide range of vehicles that appear to leverage MAZ-543 technology are now produced in China. Details of these can be found elsewhere in this section.

Specifications

MAZ-543M
Cab seating: 1 + 1
Configuration: 8 × 8
Weight:
  (GVW) 43,300 kg
  (kerb) 21.300 kg
  (max load, nominal) 22,600 kg
Length: (chassis) 11.465 m
Width: 3.07 m
Height: (top of cab) 2.9 m
Ground clearance: 400 mm
Track: (front and rear) 2.375 m
Wheelbase: 2.2 m + 3.3 m + 2.2 m
Angle of approach/departure: 28°/35°
Max speed: 63 km/h
Fuel capacity: 550 litres
Range: 1,525 km
Max gradient: 57%
Side slope: 44%
Vertical obstacle: 780 mm
Trench: 3.38 m
Fording: 1.3 m
Engine: D12A-525A 38.88-litre V-12 water-cooled diesel developing 525 hp (395 kW) at 2,100 rpm
Transmission: hydromechanical with lockable torque converter and 3-speed planetary gearbox with gearshift; 1 reverse gear
Transfer box: 2-speed
Turning radius: 13.5 m
Suspension: independent torsion bar with double acting hydraulic telescopic shock-absorbers
Brakes: air/hydraulic, drums all-round
Tyres: 15.00 × 600-635 Vi-77
Electrical system: 24 V
Batteries: 4 × 6 V 6ST-190

Status

Production as required. In service with former Warsaw Pact countries, Iraq (status uncertain) and the former Yugoslavia.

Contractor

Minsk Wheeled Tractor Plant.

MZKT range of heavy trucks

Development

The independent Minsk Wheeled Tractor Plant (MWKT, Cyrillic МЗКТ, English conversion MZKT) was established in 1991 from a special-purpose wheeled tractor division of the Minsk Automobile Plant (MAZ). MAZ, in which MAN of Germany now has a controlling interest, continues to manufacture commercial and conventionally-styled military trucks with up to three axles. What became the Minsk Wheeled Tractor Plant had previously specialised in the production heavy vehicles for mobile missile systems and similar and continues to concentrate on speciality multi-axle chassis, but the new concern has diversified into heavy construction plant and multiwheel drive configurations for tasks such as oil drilling and exploration or construction applications.

The 'Volat' series of commercial multi-axle chassis utilise various components originally intended for military purposes, but normally have mechanical transmissions in place of the hydromechanical equivalents used by military vehicles; they also have lower powered engines. They nearly all have commercial pattern forward control cabs.

Chassis for specialist military applications are still produced, some of these now having just two or three axles.

Description

The commercial and military 'Volat' families include the following models, not all of which are in current production, and many of which are likely to have undergone some form of continued development and possible designation amendments/changes:

MZKT-543 and MZKT-543M chassis-cabs

There is a separate entry in this section for the MZKT-543 series of military trucks.

MZKT-7301

This 8 × 8 cargo truck with conventional dropside cargo body and rear-mounted KMU-90 materials handling crane was introduced in 2007. Specifications for the MZKT-7301, which is of conventional cab-over-engine (COE) configuration, can be found in the Specifications table elsewhere in this entry.

MZKT-73011

This 8 × 8 chassis is fitted with a DROPS/PLS-type MPR-2 Load Handling System (LHS) and was introduced in 2007. Specifications for the MZKT-73011, which is of conventional cab-over-engine (COE) configuration, can be found in the Specifications table elsewhere in this entry.

MZKT-7301 8 × 8 cargo truck fitted with a rear-mounted KMU-90 materials handling crane (MZKT)   1346048

MZKT-73011 8 × 8 fitted with a DROPS/PLS-type MPR-2 load handling system (MZKT)   1346047

(MZKT) MAZ-79191 (12 × 12/10) 55,150 kg heavy special vehicle chassis (MZKT) 0044324

MZKT-7930

This 8 × 8 load carrier was designed in 1992 and is primarily a military vehicle, the base chassis suitable for a variety of roles including bridge transportation/laying, shelter transport and missile system mounting. GVW is 45,200 kg and chassis load capacity is 24,200 kg. Power is provided by a YaMZ-846 diesel developing 500 hp and coupled to a YaMZ-202-04 hydromechanical gearbox.

MZKT-79306

This 8 × 8 load carrier was designed in 1996 and is primarily a military vehicle, the base chassis suitable for a variety of roles including bridge transportation/laying, shelter transport and missile system mounting. GVW is 45,000 kg and chassis load capacity is 24,000 kg. The primary differences between the MZKT-79306 and the MZKT-7903 are engine and gearbox, the former (which is an export version of the latter) being powered by a Deutz BF8M1015C diesel developing 544 hp, this coupled to an Allison HD4560P fully automatic transmission.

MZKT-79098

There is a separate entry in this section for the MZKT-79098 cargo truck.

MZKT-8021

This 6 × 6 chassis was designed in 1999 to accommodate the Pechora-2 anti-aircraft missile system. GVW is 32,000 kg and chassis load capacity is 18,500 kg. Power is provided by a YaMZ-75117.10 diesel developing 400 hp, this coupled to an Allison HD4560P fully automatic gearbox.

MZKT-80211

This 6 × 6 chassis was designed in 2001 to accommodate the fire-control radar for the Pechora-2 anti-aircraft missile system. GVW is 32,000 kg and chassis load capacity is 18,500 kg. Power is provided by a YaMZ-75117.10 diesel developing 400 hp, this coupled to an Allison HD4560P fully automatic gearbox.

MZKT-8022

This 4 × 4 chassis was designed in 2001 to accommodate the command post for the Pechora-2 anti-aircraft missile system. GVW is 16,000 kg and chassis load capacity is 6,000 kg. Power is provided by a YaMZ-236 diesel developing 250 hp, this coupled to an Allison MD3560P fully automatic gearbox.

MZKT-79092

8 × 8 load carrier with a 24,000 kg load capacity and GVW of 43,500 kg. Power is provided by a YaMZ-8424.10 or YaMZ-8424.10-03 diesel, this coupled to a YaMZ-202-04 hydromechanical gearbox.

MZKT-65151

8 × 4 dump truck with a 25,000 kg load capacity and a GVW of 41,000 kg. Power is provided by a YaMZ-7511.10 diesel engine, this coupled to a MZKT-65151 mechanical gearbox.

MZKT-652511-011

6 × 6 bonneted dump truck with a 19,500 kg load capacity and a GVW of 36,000 kg. Power is provided by a YaMZ-7511.10 diesel engine, this coupled to a MZKT-65151 mechanical gearbox.

MZKT-75165

8 × 8 dump truck with a 24,500 kg load capacity and a GVW of 47,000 kg. Power is provided by a YaMZ-8424.10 diesel engine, this coupled to a YaMZ-202-04 mechanical gearbox.

MZKT-7402

8 × 8 ballast truck tractor with a ballast payload of 21,500 kg and a GVW of 40,000 kg. Power is provided by a YaMZ-7513.10 diesel engine, this coupled to a YaMZ-239 mechanical gearbox.

MZKT-742952 + 93783

8 × 8 tractor truck with a GCW of 95,000 kg. Normally used with MZKT-93783 semi-trailer. Power is provided by a Daimler (Mercedes-Benz) OM502LA diesel developing 544 hp, this coupled to an Allison HD4560PR fully automatic gearbox.

MZKT-74296 + 93782

8 × 8 tractor truck with a GCW of 105,700 kg. Normally used with MZKT-93782 semi-trailer. Power is provided by a Deutz BF8M1015C diesel developing 544 hp, this coupled to an Allison HD4560PR fully automatic gearbox.

MZKT 8022 4 × 4, the chassis for the Pechora-2 command post (MZKT)
1391005

MZKT 8022 4 × 4, the chassis for the Pechora-2 command post (MZKT)
1391006

MZKT 8021 6 × 6 chassis for the Pechora-2 anti-aircraft missile system (MZKT)
1391007

MZKT 8021 6 × 6 chassis for the Pechora-2 anti-aircraft missile system (MZKT)
1391008

MZKT 80211 6 × 6 chassis for the Pechora-2 anti-aircraft missile system (MZKT)
1391009

MZKT-7429 + 9378
8 × 8 tractor truck with a GCW of 88,000 kg. Normally used with MZKT-9378 semi-trailer. Power is provided by a YaMZ-8424.10-03 diesel developing 470 hp, this coupled to a YaMZ-202-04 hydromechanical gearbox.

MZKT-742953 + 99943
8 × 8 tractor truck with a GCW of 125,000 kg. Normally used with MZKT-99943 semi-trailer. Power is provided by a YaMZ-8401.10-14 diesel developing 650 hp, this coupled to a MZKT hydromechanical gearbox.

MZKT-74131 + 99867
8 × 8 tractor truck with a GCW of 124,000 kg. Normally used with MZKT-99867 semi-trailer. Power is provided by a Daimler (Mercedes-Benz) OM444LA diesel developing 680 hp, this coupled to an Allison M6610AR fully automatic gearbox.

MZKT-74171
6 × 6 bonneted tractor truck with GVW of 36,500 kg and a maximum fifth wheel loading of 22,500 kg. Power is provided by a YaMZ-7511 diesel developing 400 hp, this coupled to a YaMZ-239 hydromechanical gearbox.

MZKT-7401
8 × 8 tractor truck with GVW of 43,800 kg and a maximum fifth wheel loading of 27,000 kg. Power is provided by a YaMZ-7511 diesel developing 400 hp, this coupled to a MZKT-65151 mechanical gearbox.

MZKT-74173
6 × 6 tractor truck with GVW of 35,300 kg and a maximum fifth wheel loading of 21,000 kg. Power is provided by a YaMZ-7511 diesel developing 400 hp, this coupled to a MZKT-65151 mechanical gearbox.

MZKT-74132
8 × 8 ballast truck tractor with a ballast payload of 15,000 kg and a GVW of 42,400 kg. Power is provided by a YaMZ-8401.10-04 diesel engine, this coupled to a MZKT hydromechanical gearbox.

MZKT-692374-010/110
8 × 4 tractor trucks with GVW of 40,000/38,000 kg and maximum fifth wheel loadings of 27,000/25,000 kg. Power is provided by a YaMZ-7513.10 diesel developing 420 hp, this coupled to a YaMZ-239 hydromechanical gearbox.

MZKT-79091
8 × 8 chassis with GVW of 43,500 kg and a maximum payload of 24,000 kg. Power is provided by a YaMZ-8424.10 (or 8424.10-03) diesel developing 425 (or 470) hp, this coupled to a YaMZ-202-04 hydromechanical gearbox.

MZKT-79092
8 × 8 chassis with GVW of 43,500 kg and a maximum payload of 19,500 kg. Power is provided by a YaMZ-8424.10 (or 8424.10-03) diesel developing 425 (or 470) hp, this coupled to a YaMZ-202-04 hydromechanical gearbox.

MZKT-69234
8 × 4 chassis with GVW of 41,000 kg and a maximum payload of 24,800 kg. Power is provided by a YaMZ-238E2 diesel developing 330 hp, this coupled to a YaMZ-238M hydromechanical gearbox.

MZKT-692382
8 × 4 chassis with GVW of 41,000 kg and a maximum payload of 27,400 kg. Power is provided by a YaMZ-7513.10 diesel developing 420 hp, this coupled to a YaMZ-239 hydromechanical gearbox.

MZKT-79081
8 × 8 chassis for mobile crane applications with GVW of 58,000 kg and a maximum payload of 28,000 kg. Power is provided by a Deutz BF6M1015CPO diesel developing 449 hp, this coupled to a ZF 16S181 (SG) automatic gearbox. All four axles steer.

MZKT-790986
8 × 8 chassis fitted with a recovery hamper. Full details of this vehicle can be found in the Recovery vehicles section.

MZKT-79069-010 + 90011
8 × 8 tractor trucks with GCW of 80,000/106,300 kg. Normally used with MZKT-90011 extendable semi-trailer for oilfield/gas pipe transport. Power is provided by a YaMZ-8424.10 diesel developing 470 hp, this coupled to a MZKT-202 hydromechanical gearbox.

MZKT-692371
8 × 4 chassis with GVW of 41,000 kg and a maximum payload of 29,000 kg. Power is provided by a YaMZ-7511.10 diesel developing 400 hp, this coupled to a MZKT-65151 mechanical gearbox.

MZKT-65271
8 × 8 chassis with GVW of 46,000 kg and a maximum payload of 29,500 kg. Power is provided by a YaMZ-7511.10 diesel developing 400 hp, this coupled to a MZKT-65151 mechanical gearbox.

MZKT-652511-2010
6 × 6 bonneted chassis with GVW of 36,000 kg and a maximum payload of 22,760 kg. Power is provided by a YaMZ-7511.10 diesel developing 400 hp, this coupled to a MZKT-65151 mechanical gearbox.

MZKT-65274
6 × 6 chassis with GVW of 36,000 kg and a maximum payload of 22,850 kg. Power is provided by a YaMZ-7511 diesel developing 400 hp, this coupled to a MZKT-65151 mechanical gearbox.

MZKT-652513
6 × 6 chassis with GVW of 29,200 kg and a maximum payload of 14,650 kg. Power is provided by a YaMZ-7511.10 diesel developing 400 hp.

MZKT-7001
10 × 10 (3 + 2 axles) chassis on which the front two axles steer. GVW is 69,000 kg, and maximum payload is 21,000 kg. Power is provided by a YaMZ-7511 diesel developing 400 hp, this coupled to a YaMZ-202.11 or MZKT-79081 mechanical gearbox.

MZKT-7004

10 × 8 (2 + 3 axles) chassis on which the front two axles steer. GVW is 59,000 kg, and maximum payload is 40,000 kg. Power is provided by a Caterpillar C-15 diesel developing 482 hp, this coupled to an Allison 4700 fully automatic gearbox.

MZKT-7003

12 × 10 chassis on which the front three and rear two axles steer. GVW is 90,000 kg, and maximum payload is 55,150 kg. Power is provided by a YaMZ-8401.10-14 diesel developing 650 hp, this coupled to a hydromechanical gearbox.

MZKT-79191

12 × 12 chassis on which the front three axles steer. GVW is 52,000 kg, and maximum payload is 44,000 kg. Power is provided by a Caterpillar C-15 diesel, this coupled to an Allison HD4700 fully automatic gearbox.

MZKT-79092

8 × 8 chassis with GVW of 44,150 kg and a maximum payload of 22,150 kg. Power is provided by a YaMZ-8424.10 diesel developing 425 hp, this coupled to a YaMZ-202.04 hydromechanical gearbox.

MZKT-79097

8 × 8 chassis with GVW of 46,900 kg and a maximum payload of 21,000 kg. Power is provided by a YaMZ-238424.10 diesel developing 470 hp, this coupled to a YaMZ-202.04 hydromechanical gearbox.

ATZ-20-237

This is a specialist fuel tanker and dedicated dolly-type trailer. GVW of the truck/combination are 33,340/61,390 kg. Power is provided by a YaMZ-7511.10 diesel developing 400 hp, this coupled to a MZKT-65151 hydromechanical gearbox.

Specifications

Model	MZKT-7301	MZKT-73011
Cab seating:	1 + 3	1 + 3
Configuration:	8 × 8	8 × 8
Weight:		
(GVW)	42,000 kg	38,000 kg
(kerb, chassis-cab)	17,700 kg	17,700 kg
(payload)	24,000 kg	20,000 kg
(permissible front axle load)	8,500 kg (per axle)	7,500 kg (per axle)
(permissible rear axle load)	12,500 kg (per axle)	11,250 kg (per axle)
Track: (front/rear)	2.078/2.064 m	2.075/2.095 m
Wheelbase:	1.83 + 3.24 + 1.4 m	1.83 + 3.24 + 1.4 m
Max speed:	85 km/h	75 km/h
Fuel capacity:	350 litres	350 litres
Engine:	YaMZ-7511.10 V8 turbocharged and intercooled water-cooled 4-stroke diesel with direct fuel injection developing 400 hp (298 kW) at 1,900 rpm and 1,715 N.m torque at 1,100-1,300 rpm	YaMZ-7511.10 V8 turbocharged and intercooled water-cooled 4-stroke diesel with direct fuel injection developing 400 hp (298 kW) at 1,900 rpm and 1,715 N.m torque at 1,100-1,300 rpm
Gearbox:	MZKT-65151 with 9 forward and 1 reverse gears	MZKT-65151 with 9 forward and 1 reverse gears
Clutch:	YaMZ-184 double dry plate	YaMZ-184 double dry plate
Transfer box:	2-speed with locking inter-bogie differential	2-speed with locking inter-bogie differential
Steering:	hydraulic, power-assisted	hydraulic, power-assisted
Suspension:	leaf springs and hydraulic shock-absorbers, front; inverted bogie-type leaf springs, rear	leaf springs and hydraulic shock-absorbers, front; inverted bogie-type leaf springs, rear
Brakes:	dual-circuit air/hydraulic, drums all-round	dual-circuit air/hydraulic, drums all-round
Tyres:	445/65R 22.5 with CTI	445/65R 22.5 with CTI
Electrical system:	24 V	24 V
Batteries:	2 × 12 V, 190 Ah	2 × 12 V, 190 Ah

Status
See text.

Contractor
Minsk Wheel Tractor Plant (MZKT)

Ural-375D (6 × 6) 4,000 kg truck

Development

The now Ural Automobile Works of Miass is the largest company in Russia that specialises in the manufacture of all-terrain trucks. The Ural Automobile Works JSC was set up in 1941 on the site of the evacuated workshops of the Moscow Automobile Works (ZIS). In 2001, Ural Automobile Works JSC became part of the GAZ Group. The GAZ Group is Russia's largest automotive manufacture of light commercial vehicles, trucks, buses, cars, diesel engines, power-train components and road construction equipment. The GAZ Group was established in 2005 with the restructuring of RusPromAuto's production assets and currently comprises 18 automotive and machine building producers in Russia. In 2008 GAZ Group sales volume totalled around USD4.7 billion.

The first model of the Ural-375 entered production in 1961. The second model was the Ural-375A which was standardised as the Ural-375D. The Ural-377 (6 × 4) truck uses many components of the Ural-375.

The layout of the vehicle is conventional, with the engine at the front, fully enclosed two-door all-steel three-person cab in the centre and the cargo area at the rear with hinged bench-type seats, removable bows and a tarpaulin cover and drop tailgate. Standard equipment includes a cab heater, an engine preheater and a Central Tyre Inflation (CTI) system.

In 1973, a Ural-375D was tested with a new diesel engine and with further design revisions this model entered production as the Ural-4320 (6 × 6) 4,500 kg truck. Full details of the Ural 4320 range of trucks can be found elsewhere in this section.

Production of the Ural-375D ceased in 1977.

Description

The first model of the Ural-375 had an open cab with a canvas top and a stake-type rear cargo body. The second model, the Ural-375A, featured a number of automotive improvements as well as a fully enclosed all-steel cab.

The layout of the vehicle is conventional, with the engine at the front, fully enclosed two-door all-steel three-person cab in the centre and the cargo area at the rear with hinged bench-type seats, removable bows and a tarpaulin cover and drop tailgate. Standard equipment includes a cab heater, an engine preheater and a Central Tyre Inflation (CTI) system.

In 1973, a Ural-375D was tested with a YaMZ-740 V-8 water-cooled diesel engine developing 210 hp and used in the KamAZ range of 6 × 4 trucks. With further design revisions this model entered production as the Ural-4320 (6 × 6) 4,500 kg truck.

Variants

Ural-375DK-1: Ural-375 adapted for operations in northern Russian Federation states
Ural-375K: Ural-375 adapted for operations in northern Russian Federation states
Ural-375L: timber truck
Ural-375N: cargo truck with drop sides
Ural-375S: tractor truck for towing semi-trailers
Ural-375Yu: designed for use in the tropics
ATs 5-375: 5,000-litre fuel tank truck
ATsM 4-375: fuel tank truck
TZ 5-375: 5,000-litre fuel service truck which also tows a PTs 4-754 trailer with another 4,200 litres of fuel. This unit is provided with three 3 m hoses, a 15 m dispensing hose and a 9 m pressure hose
TMS-65: truck-mounted decontamination apparatus used for the rapid decontamination of vehicles and equipment. Full details can be found in *Jane's NBC Protection Equipment*
ATsG-5-375: 5,000-litre fuel tanker, equipped with four SRGS-70 3 m and four SRGS-32 3 m metal hoses
ATMZ-4.5-375: fuel lubricant truck (4,500 litres), equipped with six dispensing hoses
ATO-40: workshop body truck
APA-5: aircraft starting and refuelling truck
AC-40: fire engine
Crane truck: the crane model is fitted with an 8 T 210 crane on the rear
Shop/van: the basic chassis is used to mount a wide range of van-type bodies for command, communications and other roles
Recovery vehicle: designated the KET-L. Full details of which can be found in the Recovery vehicles section

Polish Army Ural 375D towing a trailer laden with a KH-200 bridging boat (Greg Holdanowicz)
1391461

Multiple Rocket Launcher: the Ural-375D is used to mount the BM-21 (40-round) 122 mm multiple rocket system. Full details can be found in *Jane's Armour and Artillery*
RMT-35M: electrical testing laboratory
Pontoon-carrying vehicle
SA-4 'Ganef' transporter-loader (TZM)

Specifications
Cab seating: 1 + 2
Configuration: 6 × 6
Weight:
  (unladen, with winch) 8,400 kg
  (laden, road) 13,200 kg
  (weight on front axle, laden) 3,900 kg
  (weight on rear axles, laden) 4,650 kg (each)
  (max load, road) 4,800 kg
  (max load, cross-country) 4,000 kg
  (towed load, road) 10,000 kg
  (towed load, dirt road) 5,000 kg
Load area: 3.9 × 2.43 m
Length: 7.35 m
Width: 2.69 m
Height:
  (cab) 2.68 m
  (tarpaulin) 2.98 m
  (load area) 1.42 m
Ground clearance: 400 mm
Track: 2 m
Wheelbase: 3.5 m + 1.4 m
Angle of approach/departure: 44°/40°
Max speed: (road) 75 km/h
Range: 570 km
Fuel capacity: 360 litres
Max gradient: 65%
Vertical obstacle: 800 mm
Trench: 700 mm
Fording:
  (without preparation) 1 m
  (with preparation) 1.5 m
Engine: ZIL-375 7-litre V-8 water-cooled petrol developing 180 hp (132 kW) at 3,200 rpm
Gearbox: manual with 5 forward and 1 reverse gears
Clutch: twin dry discs
Transfer box: 2-speed
Steering: double-thread worm, hydraulic booster
Turning radius: 10.5 m
Suspension:
  (front) longitudinal semi-elliptic springs with hydraulic shock-absorbers (all interchangeable with same units on the MAZ-500)
  (rear) bogie with longitudinal semi-elliptic springs
Tyres: 14.00 × 20
Brakes:
  (main) air/hydraulic
  (parking) mechanical

Electrical system: 12 V
Battery: 1 × 6-STEN-140M
Generator: G51

Status
Production complete. In service with the Russian Federation and other former Warsaw Pact countries and some Middle Eastern nations.

Contractor
Ural Automobile Plant 1.

Ural-432067 (4 × 4) truck

Development
The now Ural Automobile Works of Miass is the largest company in Russia that specialises in the manufacture of all-terrain trucks. The Ural Automobile Works JSC was set up in 1941 on the site of the evacuated workshops of the Moscow Automobile Works (ZIS). In 2001 Ural Automobile Works JSC became part of the GAZ Group. The GAZ Group is Russia's largest automotive manufacture of light commercial vehicles, trucks, buses, cars, diesel engines, power-train components and road construction equipment. The GAZ Group was established in 2005 with the restructuring of RusPromAuto's production assets and currently comprises 18 automotive and machine building producers in Russia. In 2008 GAZ Group sales volume totalled around USD4.7 billion.

Ural has developed a 4 × 4 variant of the Ural-4320 series of 6 × 6 trucks, and primarily for potential export sales, the single rear axle and reduction in unladen weight is a more attractive and less expensive option than the 6 × 6 model in some market areas. Full details of the 4320 series can be found elsewhere in this section.

Current 4 × 4 models are designated as 432067.

Description
The Ural-432067 carries over the same cab together with some of the mechanical attributes of the Ural-4320, although a YaMZ-236M2 diesel engine rated at 180 hp is standard. The standard all-steel cargo body is a revised design with a tailgate and removable bows and tilt; there is provision for seating up to 24 personnel.

Maximum payload (dependent on variant) ranges from 3,000 to 4,200 kg. Maximum towed load is 7,000 kg. The central tyre inflation of the 6 × 6 model is also provided.

A number of variants of the 432067 are available.

Variants
Ural-432067 platform truck with sides
The base cargo/troop carrying version of the Ural-432067 range has a kerb weight of 7,650 kg and a payload of 4,200 kg, bringing GVW up to 12,075 kg. A winch rated at 10,000-11,000 kg with 60 m rope is an option.

Ural-432067 platform truck with sides for training
This version of the Ural-432067 is visually and dimensionally similar to the Ural-432067, differing primarily in payload and GVW. Kerb weight is 7,500 kg and payload is 3,000 kg, giving a GVW of 10,800 kg. A winch rated at 10,000-11,000 kg with 60 m rope is an option.

	Ural-432067	Ural-432067 (training)	Ural-432067-0551
Cab seating:	1 + 2 (up to 24 in rear)	1 + 2 (up to 24 in rear)	1 + 2
Configuration:	4 × 4	4 × 4	4 × 4
Weight:			
(laden)	12,075 kg	10,800 kg	12,150 kg
(unladen)	7,650 kg	7,500 kg	8,400 kg
(payload)	4,200 kg	3,000 kg	3,500 kg
(front axle load at GVW)	4,670 kg	4,800 kg	4,625 kg
(rear axle load at GVW)	7,405 kg	6,000 kg	7,525 kg
(towed load)	7,000 kg	7,000 kg	7,000 kg
Length:	7.746 m	7.746 m	7.776 m
Width:	2.550 m	2.550 m	2.462 m
Height:	2.765 m	2.805 m	2.78 m
Body: (internal)	3.9 × 2.462 m	3.9 × 2.462 m	3.5 × 2.462 m
Fuel capacity:	210 + 60 litres	210 + 60 litres	210 litres
Max speed:	80 km/h	80 km/h	80 km/h
Max gradient:	60%	60%	60%
Ground clearance:	360 mm	400 mm	360 mm
Fording:	1.2 m	1.2 m	1.2 m
Engine:	YaMZ-236M2 V6 water-cooled 4-stroke diesel developing 180 hp (132 kW) at 2,100 rpm and 667 N.m torque at 1,250 to 1,450 rpm		
Gearbox:	manual with 5 forward and 1 reverse gears		
Transfer box:	2-speed	2-speed	2-speed
Turning radius: (wall)	11.4 m	11.4 m	11.4 m
Tyres:	1200 × 500-508	1400 × 20	1200 × 500-508

Ural-432067-0551

The Ural-432067-0551 has a six-seat, four-door crew-type cab and a shorter rear cargo body of the conventional drop-side type. Payload is 3,500 kg.

Specifications

See table on page 581

Status

In production. In service with the armed forces of the Russian Federation and possibly other undisclosed countries.

Contractor

Ural Automobile Works JSC.

Ural-4320 (6 × 6) truck series

Development

The now Ural Automobile Works of Miass is the largest company in Russia that specialises in the manufacture of all-terrain trucks. The Ural Automobile Works JSC was set up in 1941 on the site of the evacuated workshops of the Moscow Automobile Works (ZIS). In 2001 Ural Automobile Works JSC became part of the GAZ Group. The GAZ Group is Russia's largest automotive manufacture of light commercial vehicles, trucks, buses, cars, diesel engines, power-train components and road construction equipment. The GAZ Group was established in 2005 with the restructuring of RusPromAuto's production assets and currently comprises 18 automotive and machine building producers in Russia. In 2008 GAZ Group sales volume totalled around USD4.7 billion.

Ural produces a full range of two-, three-, four- and five-axle trucks for military applications in both bonneted and Cab-Over-Engine (COE) configurations, all engineered specifically to cope with the terrain and climatic extremes associated with certain parts of Russia and elsewhere.

The Ural-4320 (6 × 6) and other associated truck series covered in this entry are essentially an ongoing diesel-engined development of the Ural-375D; development of this started in 1972 and the first production examples of which were produced in 1978. The main change in the outward appearance of the Ural-4320 series compared to the earlier Ural-375D is that the radiator shell has been lengthened in front to accommodate the longer diesel engine. Other major improvements for these early Ural-4320 series trucks compared to the Ural-375D related to the fuel, cooling, exhaust and electrical systems, which were all redesigned. Modifications were also made to the chassis, clutch, front suspension and other assemblies. Safety alterations included individual brake control links, an auxiliary engine brake and some warning devices. Inside the cab, alterations were made to the instrument layout and to the driver's seat. A more powerful heater was installed and changes were made to the layout of the steering wheel and other controls. The batteries were relocated from the cab.

The base Ural-4320 range chassis is currently designated the Ural-432007; a number of variants with assorted payload ratings are available on this chassis. Many, including the standard Ural-432007-31, the 432007-10 and Ural-432007-30 are based on a dimensionally identical 3.525 m wheelbase chassis. The Ural-432007-31 is used as the base for a number of specific variants including the MTP-A2.1 wrecker truck, TEA wrecker truck and the KTL light wheeled wrecker.

Chassis with longer wheelbases but that follow the same basic lines, and are also essentially the further development of the 4320 series, are also currently available and include the Ural-4320-0311-31, Ural-4320-0911-30, Ural-432007-0919-30 and Ural-432007-1912-30. Outline specifications for some of these models can be found in the Specifications table. Details of a selection of current specific variants can be found elsewhere in this entry. The earlier mass-produced Ural-375D (6 × 6) petrol-engined truck, plus current two-axle (4 × 4) and four- and five-axle (8 × 8) and (10 × 10) Ural trucks are covered in separate entries elsewhere in this section.

Ural-4320 series trucks have been supplied to a wide variety of countries with around 90 per cent of all trucks produced delivered to armed forces of the former Soviet Union. Ural has never provided a full list of export sales, however recent export sales are understood to have been made to Argentina, Chile, Mexico, Syria and Uruguay, while vehicles are understood to have recently been evaluated in a number of countries including Columbia, Guatemala and Venezuela.

Description

The layout of the Ural-4320 series is entirely conventional. The C-section chassis uses beam-type axle and leaf spring suspension and mounts a bonneted cab, with a selection of cab types including armoured or larger crew-types fitted with additional seating or bunks available. A wide variety of body types may be fitted to these trucks and depending on chassis and other specifications, these may include basic troop carrying/cargo-type bodies, workshop/engineering or specialist command/control-type bodies, fuel or water tankers, construction or plant equipment including cranes, excavators and dump bodies, weapon systems including multiple launch rocket systems and specialist fire appliance bodies. Fifth wheel tractor trucks are also produced.

Polish military Ural-4320 (6 × 6) 4,500 kg truck mounting an MUR-20 ELectronic INTeligence ((ELNIT) shelter-type body (Greg Holdanowicz)
1391462

The Ural 4320 series is continually revised, the current base model being the Ural-432007-31. This and the vast majority of current production models are fitted as standard with the YaMZ-238M2 V8 engine developing 240 hp. Specified engine options include the V6 YaMZ-236NE2 developing 230 hp and the V6 YaMZ-236M2 developing 180 hp. Ural-4320 trucks have been supplied fitted with Caterpillar diesel engines.

The original diesel engine fitted to the Ural 4320 was the YaMZ-740.10-20, produced at the Kama Motor Vehicle Plant, Naberezhyne Chelny. This is a 10.85-litre, eight-cylinder naturally aspirated engine developing 210 hp at 2,600 rpm. The YaMZ-740 engine is some 280 kg heavier than the ZIL-375 petrol engine of the Ural-375D it replaced. This increase in weight leads to some revision of axle loadings. The front axle assumes 4,350 kg of the total weight instead of 3,865 kg; the rear axle assumes 9,075 kg instead of 9,335 kg. This revision improves the traction of the Ural-4320 over soft ground. Using typical Russian Federation figures the YaMZ-740 engine (compared to the ZIL-375 unit it replaced) produces 16 per cent more power at 19 per cent fewer rpm and fitting this engine enabled the payload of early 4320 series models to be increased by 500 kg to 4,500 kg. Maximum speed increased to 85 km/h while fuel consumption decreased by 30 per cent. Maintenance requirements reduced by 10.8 per cent.

A five-speed manual gearbox coupled to a two-speed transfer box is standard in all Ural-4320 trucks, and in addition to a longitudinal differential lock, current models are fitted with cross-axle differential locks on the rear bogie.

Ural-4320 series trucks are designed for operation at altitudes of up to 4,500 m and in ambient temperatures ranging from –50 to +50°C. Single KAMA tyres, usually with a directional tread pattern, are standard fit. A Central Tyre Inflation (CTI) system that allows the driver to adjust tyre pressure from the cab to suit prevailing terrain conditions is available for all models. Mobility parameters include the ability to operate in virgin snow of up to 1 m in depth, cross ditches (model dependant) up to 1.2 m wide, climb a 550 mm vertical obstacle, a 31° gradient and a 20° sideslope (body dependant). All models are capable of wading to 1.75 m with preparation.

Specified options include an independent cab heater, an automatic pre-heater/heater, protection kits, 10,000 or 11,000 kg capacity winches, assorted cab refinements, larger cabs, additional cold climate preparation, anti-lock brakes, a reinforced auxiliary Power Take-Off (PTO), and a supplementary fuel tank.

A wide variety of body types/variants of the Ural-4320 series have been produced and outline details of a selection of current variants can be found below.

Ural-4320-10 (6 × 6) 4,500 kg truck (Ural Automobile Works JSC) 0056421

MTP-A1.1 variant of the Ural-4320 of the Ukrainian Army
(Shaun C Connors)   0109503

Variants

MRS-AM.1 mobile repair and fitting workshop
The MRS-AM.1 mobile repair and fitting workshop is based on the Ural-432037-31 chassis and is designed for the maintenance and repair of assorted vehicles under field conditions. The ventilated and filtered rear body is fitted with assorted engineering equipment and has three work stations. Additional work stations may be set up under cover. Overall dimensions are (L × W × H) 8.55 × 2.5 × 3.43 m; GVW is 13,795 kg.

PARM mobile repair workshop
The PARM mobile repair workshop is based on the Ural-432037-31 chassis and is designed for diagnostics, maintenance and the routine repair of assorted vehicles under field conditions. The ventilated and filtered rear body which is similar to that of the MRS-AM.1 mobile repair and fitting workshop is fitted with assorted engineering equipment including a lathe, drill and grinder and has four work stations. Overall dimensions are (L × W × H) 8.5 × 2.5 × 3.8 m; GVW is 13,410 kg.

MZA-M2.1 repair of storage batteries workshop truck
The MZA-M2.1 repair of storage batteries workshop truck is based on the Ural-432037-31 chassis and is designed for maintenance and repair of storage batteries. Overall dimensions are (L × W × H) 8.3 × 2.5 × 3.44 m; GVW is 13,900 kg.

Ural-432007-0311-31
The Ural-432007-0311-31 has a slightly longer (3.8 m) wheelbase and chassis than the standard Ural-432007-31. Kerb weight of the Ural-432007-0311-31 is 9,260 kg, giving a maximum payload allowance of 7,000 kg.

MTP-A2.1 wrecker (recovery) truck
The MTP-A2.1 wrecker (recovery) truck is based on the Ural-432007-31 chassis. Full details of the MTP-A2.1 can be found in the Recovery vehicles section.

TEA wrecker (recovery) truck with PK-10000 hydraulic crane
The TEA wrecker (recovery) truck is based on the Ural-432007-31 chassis. Depending on method employed for towing, casualty vehicles of up to 15,500 kg can be recovered.

KTL light wheeled wrecker (recovery) truck
The KTL light wheeled wrecker (recovery) truck is based on the Ural-432007-31 chassis. Depending on method employed for towing, casualty vehicles of up to 15,500 kg can be recovered. The KTL light wheeled wrecker is similar to the TEA wrecker (recovery) truck with PK-10000 hydraulic crane, the former not being fitted with a hydraulic materials handling crane.

URAL-4320 (6 × 6) truck of the Russian Army mounting a Splav 122 mm BM-21 (40-round) Multiple Rocket Launcher (MRL, full details of which can be found in Jane's Armour and Artillery) (Stefan Marx)   1124713

URAL-4320 (6 × 6) truck in standard troop-carrying/cargo configuration of the former East German Army (Stefan Marx)   1124714

Ural-44202-41 tractor truck
The Ural-44202-41 is a fifth wheel tractor truck designed for towing assorted semi-trailers of up to 19,100 kg on- and off-road including a selection of low semi-trailer tankers that include the ChMZAP-99859C and ChMZAP-9907.1 (15,000 litres) PPTs-9631 (16,000 litres) and the PPTs 967441 (18,500 litres). Maximum GVW is 16,815 kg, maximum fifth wheel load is 8,100 kg. Maximum road speed is 85 km/h.

Ural-4320-0710-31
The Ural-4320-0710-31 is essentially the earlier Ural-4320-31 cargo/troop carrying variant fitted with a KDZ armour package consisting of cab armour protection and an armoured box/container in the rear body that transports 24 fully armed troops while providing protection from small arms fire and blast fragments. A single rear door is fitted to the container, as are individual weapon ports for the crew. GVW of the Ural-4320-0710-31 is 15,470 kg, giving a payload allowance of 3,500 kg.

Ural-432009-31
The Ural-432009-31 is essentially the Ural-4320-31 cargo/troop carrying variant fitted with a Ural designed replacement armoured cab and armoured engine compartment, protection extending to the main fuel tank and battery box. GVW of the Ural-432009-31 is 15,350 kg, giving a payload allowance of 5,500 kg. An earlier version of the Ural-432009-31 was designated Ural-4320B.

Other Ural-4320 series armour packages
A number of various armour packages have been developed for the Ural-4320 series of trucks. Some of the earliest kits were provided as field fitted kits by the Muromteplovoz plant and for use in Afghanistan. These were followed by a selection of purpose designed modifications, the most current of which would (in addition to those mentioned above) include the Zvezda B kit produced by Spetztechnika. The Zvezda B features cab and engine compartment armouring, together with an armoured box/container in the rear body that accommodates 19 fully armed troops.

Ural-432007-0911-30
The Ural-432007-0911-30 is a heavier-duty, longer wheelbase version of the Ural-432007-10. It is fitted with a conventional troop carrying/cargo-type body and has a GVW of 20,550 kg, giving a payload allowance of 10,00000 kg. Maximum towed load is 12,000 kg.

Ural-432007-0919-30
The Ural-432007-0919-30 is a heavier-duty, longer wheelbase version of the Ural-432007-10. It is fitted with a conventional troop carrying/cargo-type body and has a GVW of 20,550 kg, giving a payload allowance of 10,000 kg. Maximum towed load is 12,000 kg.

Ural-432007-1912-30
The Ural-432007-1912-30 is a heavier-duty, longer wheelbase version of the Ural-432007-10. It is fitted with a conventional troop carrying/cargo-type body, but with a hydraulic materials handling crane between the cab and body. GVW is 20,930 kg, payload is 9,000 kg.

Ural-432007-10
Compared to the base model Ural-432007-31, the Ural-432007-10 has a kerb weight of 8,375 kg and a maximum permissible payload of 6,000 kg; maximum payload of the Ural-432007-31 is 6,500 kg. Maximum road speed is 75 km/h.

Ural-432007-30
Compared to the base model Ural-432007-31, the Ural-432007-30 has a kerb weight of 9,160 kg and a maximum permissible payload of 10,000 kg; maximum payload of the Ural-432007-31 is 6,500 kg. Maximum road speed is 78 km/h.

Ural-432007-41
The Ural-432007-41 is essentially the Ural-432007-10 fitted with a YaMZ-236NE2 V6 turbocharged diesel engine that develops 230 hp (169 kW) at 2,100 rpm and 880 N.m torque at 1,100 to 1,300 rpm. Dimensions are identical, payload is identical at 6,000 kg, there being a small number of specification changes and minor differences in unladen weight etc.

Model	Ural-432007-31 truck	Ural-432007-30 truck	Ural-432007-0911-30 truck
Cab seating:	1 + 2	1 + 2	1 + 2
Configuration:	6 × 6	6 × 6	6 × 6
Weight: (kerb)	8,750 kg	9,160 kg	10,250 kg
GVW:	15,550 kg	19,460 kg	20,550 kg
Payload:	6,500 kg	10,000 kg	10,000 kg
Towed load:	11,500 kg	11.500 kg	12,000 kg
Length:	7.739 m	7.739 m	9.530 m
Width:	2.55 m	2.55 m	2.55 m
Height:	2.805 m	2.805 m	2.740 m
Body, dimensions: (internal; L × W)	3.9 × 2.462 m	3.9 × 2.462 m	5.66 × 2.462 m
Max speed:	82 km/h	78 km/h	78 km/h
Range: (cruising)	1,080 km		
Fuel capacity:	300 + 60 litres	300 + 60 litres	300 + 60 litres
Gradient:	60%	50%	n/avail
Fording:	1.2 m	1.2 m	1.2 m
Engine:	YaMZ-238M2 V8 water-cooled 4-stroke diesel developing 240 hp (176 kW) at 2,100 rpm and 883 N.m torque at 1,250 to 1,450 rpm		
Gearbox:	manual with 5 forward and 1 reverse gears	manual with 5 forward and 1 reverse gears	manual with 5 forward and 1 reverse gears
Transfer box:	2-speed with locking inter-axle differential	2-speed with locking inter-axle differential	2-speed with locking inter-axle differential
Clutch:	twin dry disc	twin dry disc	twin dry disc
Turning radius:	11.4 m	11.4 m	14 m
Electrical system:	24 V	24 V	24 V

Refuelling trucks
The Ural-chassis has traditionally been used as the basis for a selection of refuelling trucks. These include the ATZ-12, ATZ-10, ATZ-9, ATZ-7.5 and ATZ-6.5. In all instances the designations refer to capacity.

Tanker trucks
The Ural-chassis has traditionally been used as the basis for a selection of tanker trucks for the transport and temporary storage of light petroleum products. These include the ATs-12, ATs-10, ATs-9, ATs-7.5 and ATs-6.5. In all instances the designations refer to capacity.

TZA-10 aircraft refuelling truck
The Ural-4320 chassis is used as the basis of the TZA-10 aircraft fuelling vehicle. The TZA-10 has a capacity of 10,700 litres and is designed for the fuelling of aircraft with either fuel or fuel mixed with anti-icing fluids, and at air temperatures between −40 and +40°C.

Crane trucks
The Ural-chassis has traditionally been used as the basis for a selection of crane trucks. These include the KS-35714, KS-55722-1, KS-35719-3-02, KS-45719-3A, Ivanovets KS-45717-1, Ulyanovets MKT-25.5 and KS-55713-3K.

Other wheel configurations
Also currently produced by Ural are the Ural-432067 and Ural-532301 series of trucks. The Ural-432067 is a 4 × 4 derivative of the 4320 series and is powered by the V6 180 hp YaMZ-236M2 engine, while the Ural-532301 series of trucks are a forward control (Cab-Over-Engine (COE)) range of 8 × 8 chassis. A 10 × 10 chassis designated 692431-10 is also available. Details of these ranges of trucks can be found elsewhere in this section.

Specifications
See table above

Status
In production. In service with the armed forces of the Russian Federation and others.

Contractor
Ural Automobile Works JSC

Marketing agency
Rosoboronexport

Ural-532301 (8 × 8) 10,000 kg truck and variants

Development
The now Ural Automobile Works of Miass is the largest company in Russia that specialises in the manufacture of all-terrain trucks. The Ural Automobile Works JSC was set up in 1941 on the site of the evacuated workshops of the Moscow Automobile Works (ZIS). In 2001 Ural Automobile Works JSC became part of the GAZ Group. The GAZ Group is Russia's largest automotive manufacture of light commercial vehicles, trucks, buses, cars, diesel engines, power-train components and road construction equipment. The GAZ Group was established in 2005 with the restructuring of RusPromAuto's production assets and currently comprises 18 automotive and machine building producers in Russia. In 2008 GAZ Group sales volume totalled around USD4.7 billion.

Prior to the break-up of the former Soviet Union, Soviet military manufacturers specialised in certain categories of military vehicle production with Ural in the medium-weight truck category and the Ural-4320 series of 6 × 6 trucks. Since the break-up of the former Soviet Union and with MAZ and KrAZ heavy truck production being based in Belarus and Ukraine, respectively, the emphasis has changed and in common with most Russian manufacturers, Ural is now producing vehicles in all weight classes.

Ural production remains concentrated on the 6 × 6 4320 series chassis, but in addition to lighter 4 × 4 trucks the company also now offers heavier 6 × 6 chassis as well as larger 8 × 8 and 10 × 10 chassis.

Description
The Ural-532301 (8 × 8) 10,000 kg truck can be used for transporting supplies or personnel and may be used as the basis for mounting weapons or various combat systems including the Pantsir-S1 ADM system. The base model of the range is currently designated Ural-532301 and this has a rated payload of 10,000 kg; GVW is 22,260 kg and towed load is 12,000 kg.

The Ural-532301 is entirely conventional in design, although unlike the majority of Ural models it is of Cab-Over-Engine (COE) and not bonneted configuration.

The standard engine of the Ural-532301 is the YaMZ-238B V8 300 hp turbocharged diesel, although the YaMZ-7601 unit developing 300 hp is an option.

The gearbox is a four-speed unit with splitter, which is coupled to a two-speed transfer box and provides 16 forward gears. Inter-axle, and on the rear axles, cross-axle, differential locks are provided.

Maximum gradient climbable is 58 per cent and the Ural-532301 can ford to a depth of 1.2 m. Ditch crossing is 1.2 m. Maximum road speed is 82 km/h.

A 10,000-11,000 kg capacity winch with 60 m of cable is an option.

Ural-532301 (8 × 8) 10,000 kg truck (James Kinnear)   1391101

Variants

Ural-532303 with armoured cab
The Ural-53203 is essentially the Ural-532301 fitted with an all-steel small arms fire protected cab. Payload reduces to 9,500 kg.

Ural-542301 tractor truck
The Ural-542301 is essentially a tractor truck version of the Ural-532301. The tractor unit has an unladen weight of 11,530 kg. Rated fifth wheel load is 10,000 kg and towed load is 28,000 kg. Maximum road speed is reduced to 80 km/h.

USB-T-53236
The USB-T-53236 Pile-Driving truck is based on the Ural-532361-1010 chassis.

Ural-692341-10 (10 × 10) chassis-cab
The Ural-692341 is essentially a lengthened Ural-532301 chassis fitted with an additional steering rear axle. The chassis-cab kerb weight is 13,100 kg and payload on the chassis-cab is 23,500 kg. Motive power is provided by a YaMZ-7601.10 turbocharged diesel developing 300 hp. This is coupled to a YaMZ-2391 nine-speed gearbox. A 10 × 8 chassis-cab with a 24,000 kg payload on the chassis-cab is also available.

Status
In production. In service with the armed forces of the Russian Federation and possibly others.

Contractor
Ural Automobile Works JSC

ZIL-157 (6 × 6) 2,500 kg truck

Development
The ZIL-157 (6 × 6) truck replaced the ZIL-151 (6 × 6) truck in production from 1958 and in 1961, the improved ZIL-157K entered production, to be replaced in 1966 by the more powerful ZIL-131 (6 × 6) 3,500 kg truck. In appearance the ZIL-157 is very similar to the ZIL-151 but has a slightly different cab (also fitted to late production ZIL-151s) and single instead of dual rear wheels.

Description
The layout of the ZIL-157 is conventional, with the engine at the front, two-door fully enclosed cab in the centre and the cargo area at the rear. The latter consists of a wooden platform with sides, bench seats down each side, these can be folded up when the vehicle is carrying cargo and a drop tailgate. If required, the vehicle can be fitted with bows and a tarpaulin cover. Standard equipment includes a cab heater, an engine pre-heater and many vehicles also have a winch.

Variants
ZIL-157V and ZIL-157KV: tractor trucks for towing semi-trailers (for example carrying SA-2, FROG-3, FROG-4 or FROG-5 missiles)
ZIL-157KG: with shielded electrical system
ZIL-157KE: temperate climate export model of ZIL-157K
ZIL-157KYu: tropical climate export model of ZIL-157K
ZIL-157GT: tropical climate export model of ZIL-157K with shielded electrical system
ZIL-157KYe: ZIL-157K chassis for special bodies
ZIL-157KYel: ZIL-157KYe chassis with high-output generator

ZIL-157K (6 × 6) 2,500 kg truck of the Czech Army mounting P-15 Tropa (NATO reporting name Flat Face A) radar   1391460

ZIL-157K (6 × 6) 2,500 kg truck with shielded box body containing R-140 communications equipment (Stefan Marx)   0512387

ZIL-157KYeG: ZIL-157KG chassis with shielded electrical system
ZIL-157YeGT: ZIL-157KYeG chassis, tropical climate export model
ZIL-157KYeGT: ZIL-157KYeG chassis, tropical climate export model (chassis has features of the ZIL-157KYu)
ZIL-157YeT: ZIL-157KYe chassis, tropical climate export model (chassis contains features of ZIL-157KYu)
ARS-12U: decontamination vehicle
AGV-3M and AGW-3M: decontamination stations
ATsM-4-157K: 4,000-litre fuel truck (also on ZIL-157 chassis)
ATZ-3-157K and ATZ-3, 8-157K: fuel service trucks
ATsMM-4-157K: 4,000-litre oil tank truck
AVTs 28-157: 2,800-litre water tanker
CAS 16: Czech fire engine

Carrying pontoons and other bridging equipment
  Crane truck
  Carrying KMM treadway bridge system (details of this version are given in the Mechanised bridges section)
  VMZ-ZIL-157K: water and oil service truck which carries 1,400 litres of water and 700 litres of oil, equipped with a heater system which maintains the temperature of the water at between +15°C and +90°C and the oil at +80°C.

Specifications
ZIL-157
Cab seating: 1 + 1
Configuration: 6 × 6
Weight:
  (laden, with winch) 8,450 kg
  (unladen, with winch) 5,800 kg
  (max load, road) 4,500 kg
  (max load, off-road) 2,500 kg
  (towed load, dirt road) 3,600 kg
  (towed load, off-road) 2,500 kg
  (towed load, roads) 3,600 kg
Load area: 3.57 × 2.09 m
Length: (with winch) 6.922 m
Width: 2.315 m
Height:
  (cab) 2.36 m
  (tarpaulin) 2.915 m
  (load area) 1.388 m
Ground clearance: 310 mm
Track:
  (front) 1.755 m
  (rear) 1.75 m
Wheelbase: 3.655 m + 1.12 m
Angle of approach/departure: 33°/43°
Max speed: (road) 65 km/h
Range: 460 km
Fuel capacity: 150 litres
Max gradient: 53%
Fording: 850 mm
Engine: ZIL-157K 5.55-litre 6-cylinder water-cooled petrol developing 109 hp (80 kW) at 2,800 rpm
Gearbox: manual with 5 forward and 1 reverse gears
Transfer box: 2-speed
Clutch: single dry plate
Steering: cone worm with 3-ridge roller
Turning radius: 11.2 m
Suspension:
  (front) longitudinal semi-elliptic springs with hydraulic double acting shock-absorbers
  (rear) bogie with semi-elliptic leaf springs
Tyres: 12.00 × 18

Brakes:
(main) air
(parking) mechanical
Electrical system: 12 V
Batteries: 2 × ST-84

Status

Production complete. In service in declining numbers with former Warsaw Pact countries and other armed forces.

Contractor

ZIL Auto Plant

ZIL-131 (6 × 6) 3,500 kg truck

Development

The ZIL-131 (6 × 6) truck entered production in December 1966 as the replacement for the earlier ZIL-157 (6 × 6) 2,500 kg truck and uses many components of the ZIL-133 (6 × 4) truck. Production of the ZIL-131N ceased in 1995 with the introduction of the Zil-433420 range of (6 × 6) trucks.

Description

The layout of the Zil-131 is conventional, with the engine at the front, fully enclosed two-door all-steel cab in the centre and the cargo area at the rear, consisting of a wooden platform with metal fittings and a hinged tailgate. The platform has recesses for the bows and hinged bench seats are provided down either side of the platform.

Main improvements of the Zil-131 over the earlier ZIL-157 can be summarised as increased load-carrying capacity, more powerful engine, power steering, shorter wheelbase, waterproof ignition and the central tyre pressure regulation system. The front axle is engaged automatically when the driver selects first gear and the driver can also engage the front axle manually when in second gear. The vehicle is used for transporting cargo or personnel and as a prime mover for towing artillery such as the 122 mm D-30 howitzer.

The ZIL-131 has a central tyre pressure regulation system and a 4,500 kg capacity winch. Standard equipment includes a cab heater and an engine preheater.

Variants

ZIL-131A: this is a truck with a standard ignition system rather than the shielded ignition system as fitted on the standard ZIL-131
ZIL-131D: dump truck
ZIL-131V: for towing semi-trailers
ZIL-131PM: fire engine
ZIL-137: tractor truck for towing a two-axle powered trailer (the complete unit then becomes a 10 × 10); also used to tow SA-6 'Gainful' SAMs on a single-axle trailer
ARS-14: decontamination vehicle
ATs 4, 2-131: 4,200 litre fuel tank truck
ATs 4, 2-131: 4,100 litre fuel tank truck
ATs 4, 3-131: 4,400 litre fuel tank truck
ATZ 3, 8-131: 4,300 litre fuel service truck
ATZ 4, 3-131: 4,300 litre fuel service truck
AVTs 28-131: 2,800 litre water tanker
PBU 50M: German well drilling plant.

Shop/van

Various models are in service including bakery, maintenance and a field kitchen.

MA-41

This is a combined fuel, lubricant and water service vehicle. It carries 1,700 litres of diesel, 340 litres of petrol, two 170 litre tanks of oil and 700 litres of water. Both the diesel and water tanks are heated as this unit is used in very cold climates.

ZIL-131 (6 × 6) truck carrying workshop body (Ian C. Young)   0009651

ZIL-131 (6 × 6) 3,500 kg truck (Stefan Marx)   1047638

SA-6 'Gainful' SAM Resupply Vehicle

Three missiles are carried in a triangular formation with the warhead sections projecting over the roof of the cab. A foldable crane is mounted at the rear of the truck to facilitate reloading of the SA-6 tracked launcher vehicle.

SA-3 'Goa' SAM Resupply Vehicle

Two missiles are carried adjacent to each other on a rail system with the warhead sections projecting over the roof of the cab. The SA-3 launcher is reloaded by backing the vehicle in line with the twin launcher rails, connecting up the resupply rails and then winching the missiles onto the launcher rails.

Multiple Rocket Launcher

A number of ZIL-131 trucks have been fitted with the 140 mm BM-14-16 multiple rocket system normally carried on the rear of a ZIL-151 (6 × 6) truck chassis and the 122 mm BM-21 multiple rocket system. Full details of these can be found in *Jane's Armour and Artillery.*

Specifications

ZIL-131
Cab seating: 1 + 2
Configuration: 6 × 6
Weight:
(laden, off-road) 10,425 kg
(unladen, with winch) 6,700 kg
(weight on front axle, laden) 3,360 kg
(weight on rear axle, laden) 7,065 kg
(max load, on-road) 5,000 kg
(max load, off-road) 3,500 kg
(towed load, road) 6,500 kg
(towed load, dirt road) 4,000 kg
Load area: 3.6 × 2.32 m
Length:
(without winch) 6.9 m
(with winch) 7.04 m
Width: 2.5 m
Height:
(cab) 2.48 m
(tarpaulin) 2.975 m
(load area) 1.43 m
Ground clearance: 330 mm
Track: (front and rear) 1.82 m
Wheelbase: 3.35 m + 1.25 m
Angle of approach/departure: 36°/40°
Max speed: (road) 80 km/h
Range: 645 km
Fuel capacity: 340 litres
Max gradient: 58%
Fording: 1.4 m
Engine: ZIL-131 6 litre V-8 water-cooled petrol developing 150 hp (110 kW) at 3,200 rpm
Gearbox: manual with 5 forward and 1 reverse gears
Transfer box: 2-speed
Clutch: single dry plate
Steering: screw and nut with hydraulic booster
Turning radius: 10.1 m
Suspension:
(front) longitudinal semi-elliptic springs with double acting hydraulic shock-absorbers
(rear) equaliser arm on longitudinal semi-elliptic springs
Tyres: 12.00 × 20 ND
Brakes:
(main) air
(parking) mechanical
Electrical system: 12 V
Battery: 1 × 6 ST 78

Contractor
Zil Auto Plant

ZIL-130 (4 × 2) 4,500 kg truck

Development
The ZIL-130 (4 × 2) truck entered production in late 1964 as the replacement for the older ZIL-164 (4 × 2) truck. Despite its age the ZIL-130 continues to serve on as a general utility vehicle and in a wide range of military and commercial variants (see following), some of which may no longer be in service. The ZIL-130 formed the basis for the ZIL-131 (6 × 6) and ZIL-133 (6 × 4) trucks.

Description
The layout of the ZIL-130 is conventional, with the engine at the front, a two-door fully enclosed sheet-steel cab in the centre and the cargo area at the rear with drop sides and tailgate.

The closest equivalents in the current Zil trucks range are the Zil-433360 (petrol) which has a GVW of 11,000 kg, or the Zil-432930E (diesel) which has a GVW of 9,790 kg.

Variants
ZIL-130A1: cargo truck capable of pulling trailers
ZIL-130D1: chassis for ZIL-MMZ-555 dump truck with 3.3 m wheelbase
ZIL-130D2: dump truck chassis
ZIL-130D1E: ZIL-MMZ-555 dump truck chassis, temperate climate export model
ZIL-130D1T: export model of ZIL-130D1E for tropical climates
ZIL-130G: long cargo bed (length 4.686 m) with 4.5 m wheelbase
ZIL-130GE: temperate climate export model of ZIL-130G
ZIL-130GT: tropical climate export model of ZIL-130G
ZIL-130S: for use in northern RFAS
ZIL-130T: temperate climate export model
ZIL-1361: export model with Perkins diesel engine
ZIL-1361G: long wheelbase export model with Perkins diesel engine
ZIL-1361D1: dump truck chassis with Perkins diesel engine
ZIL-130V1: tractor truck with 3.3 m wheelbase
ZIL-130V1T: tropical climate export model of ZIL-130V1
ZIL-130Ye: ZIL-130 with shielded electrical system
ZIL-130YeT: tropical climate export model of ZIL-130Ye
ZIL-130YeE: temperate climate export model of ZIL-130Ye
ZIL-MMZ-554: agricultural dump truck
ZIL-MMZ-555: agricultural dump truck
ATs 4,2-130: 4,200-litre fuel tanker
ATs 3,8-130: 3,800-litre fuel servicing truck
AVTs 2,8-130: 2,800-litre water tanker
DDA-53B: NBC decontamination vehicle
PAZS-3152: mobile fuelling unit
PSG-160: POL transfer pump unit
Shop-van: for various applications
Crane truck.

Specifications
ZIL-130 with radio body
Cab seating: 1 + 2
Configuration: 4 × 2
Weight:
  (laden) 9,000 kg
  (unladen) 4,500 kg
  (weight on front axle, laden) 2,575 kg
  (weight on rear axle, laden) 6,950 kg
  (max load) 4,500 kg
  (towed load) 6,400 kg
Width: 2.5 m
Height:
  (cab) 2.35 m
  (tarpaulin) 3.5 m
  (load area) 1.43 m
Ground clearance: 0.275 m
Track:
  (front) 1.8 m
  (rear) 1.79 m
Wheelbase: 3.8 m
Angle of approach/departure: 38°/27°
Max speed: (road) 85 km/h
Range: 500 km
Fuel capacity: 150 litres
Max gradient: 36%
Fording: 700 mm
Engine: ZIL-130 6-litre V-8 water-cooled petrol developing 170 hp (127 kW) at 3,600 rpm
Gearbox: manual with 5 forward and 1 reverse gears

ZIL-130 (4 × 2) 4,500 kg truck of the former East German Army (Stefan Marx) 1047637

Clutch: single dry plate
Steering: screw and nut with hydraulic booster
Turning radius: 8 m
Suspension:
  (front) longitudinal semi-elliptic springs with hydraulic telescopic 2-way shock-absorbers
  (rear) semi-elliptic springs and check springs
Tyres: 9.00 × 20
Brakes:
  (main) air
  (parking) mechanical
Electrical system: 12 V
Battery: 1 × 6-ST 78EMSZ
Generator: 350 W

Status
Production complete. In service with the armed forces of the Russian Federation and others.

Contractor
Zil Auto Plant

ZIL-135 Series (8 × 8) trucks

Development
Automobile Plant ZIL was established in 1916. Today, the plant primarily manufactures 3,000 to 8,000 kg capacity trucks, vans, buses and limousines. Zil also manufactures a variety of specialised vehicles and equipment, these including ambulances, firefighting vehicles, road sweeping vehicles, dump and cross-country (4 × 4) and (6 × 6) trucks. Trucks produced include the Zil-443420 series of 3,750 kg payload (6 × 6) trucks, these being the military successor of the earlier Zil-131 series of 3,500 kg payload (6 × 6) trucks, production of which concluded in 1995.

The ZIL-135 series of (8 × 8) trucks was introduced during the 1960s. The original design and development was carried out at the Likhachev Motor Vehicle Plant near Moscow, but production was carried out at the Bryansk Automobile Works, for which reason the range is sometimes known as the BAZ-135L4 (the cargo truck version is also known as the ZIL-135L4). These trucks are widely used by members of the former Warsaw Pact for both military and civil applications. Production of these models ceased some time ago.

Description
The ZIL-135 is powered by two petrol engines, each of which drives the four wheels on one side of the vehicle. Steering is by the front and rear wheels only and these wheels are carried on axles with torsion bar suspension. The two central axles are fixed (un-sprung) and a central tyre pressure regulation system is fitted. The fully enclosed forward control cab has two doors, one on each side. When being used for missile launching roles the windscreen is fitted with covers to protect it from blast and flying debris when the missile is launched.

Variants
9M21 Transporter/Launcher Vehicle
This carries and launches the FROG-7 (9M21 Luna M R-75) surface-to-surface tactical rocket system. Mounted on the right side of the vehicle is a hydraulic crane for reloading purposes. Stabiliser jacks are lowered to the ground before the missile is launched to provide a more stable firing platform.

9T29 Resupply Vehicle
This carries three FROG-7 rockets.

Sepal Transporter/Launcher Vehicle
This has a large cylindrical container which acts as the launcher for the Sepal cruise missile. This version has a different cab from the other members of this series and two stabiliser jacks are lowered to the ground either side before the missile is launched.

ZIL-135 (8 × 8) truck configured as launch vehicle for BM-22 Uragan 220 mm multiple rocket system (Ian C Young)   0056419

BM-22 Multiple Rocket System

The ZIL-135 series chassis is also used for the 9P140 220 mm Uragan (BM-22) 16-round multiple rocket launcher and its associated 9T452 transloader. For details see *Jane's Armour and Artillery.*

ZIL-135 Convoy Escort Vehicle

Reports from Afghanistan mentioned the use of an improvised convoy escort vehicle formed by mounting a ZU-23 twin 23 mm cannon on the rear of a ZIL-135 truck. Some form of armour was provided for the gun crew.

BAZ-135L4 Cargo Truck

This was produced at the Bryansk Plant and is used for carrying cargo. The rear cargo area is provided with a drop tailgate. Also referred to as ZIL-135L4.

ZIL-135 Tractor Truck

As far as is known, this is only used for civilian roles, primarily for carrying long lengths of pipe used in constructing pipelines.

Specifications

BAZ-135L4 cargo truck
Cab seating: 1 + 2
Configuration: 8 × 8
Weight:
   (laden) 19,000 kg
   (unladen) 9,000 kg
   (max load) 10,000 kg
   (towed load, road) 20,000 kg
   (towed load, off-road) 18,000 kg
Length: 9.27 m
Width: 2.8 m
Height: 2.53 m
Ground clearance: (axles) 580 mm
Track: 2.3 m
Wheelbase: 2.415 m + 1.5 m + 2.415 m
Max speed: 70 km/h
Range: 500 km
Fuel capacity: 768 litres
Fuel consumption: 160 litres/100 km
Max gradient: 57%
Vertical obstacle: 685 mm
Trench: 2.63 m
Fording: 580 mm
Engines: 2 × ZIL-375 7-litre V-8 water-cooled petrol each developing 180 hp (132 kW) at 3,200 rpm
Gearbox: hydromechanical
Steering: power-assisted, 1st and 4th axles
Turning radius: 12.5 m
Suspension: 1st and 4th axles have torsion bars, 2nd and 3rd axles are fixed and un-sprung
Tyres: 16.00 × 20
Brakes: (main) hydraulic, air-assisted
Electrical system: 24 V

Status

Supplied to Afghanistan[1,] (Uragan), Algeria (FROG-7), Angola (FROG-7), Bulgaria (FROG-7), Cuba (FROG-7), Czech Republic, Egypt (FROG-7), Hungary (FROG-7), Iraq[1] (FROG-7), North Korea (FROG-7), Kuwait (FROG-7), Libya (FROG-7), Poland (FROG-7), Russian Federation, Romania (FROG-7), Slovakia, Syria (Uragan and FROG-7), Yemen (FROG-7) and the former Yugoslavia.
[1] Recent developments in these countries must make the continued serviceability of these systems debatable

Contractor

Bryansk Motor Vehicle Plant JSC

Serbia and Montenegro

FAP 1118 BS/AV (4 x 4) truck

Development

In 1953 FAP (Korporacija a.d. Pribo) introduced its first heavy-duty vehicles following the acquisition of a license to produce vehicles under the then Saurer-Werke brand. In 1959 the company had in place machining and vehicle assembling lines with a production capacity of 3,600 vehicles per year. In 1975 a licence agreement with the now Daimler commenced. This was extended to heavier trucks in 1978, with developments including the FAP 2026 BDS/6x6 (6 × 6) truck. In 1983 the FAP 2632 BDS/8x8 (8 × 8) truck was introduced. By 1987 the FAP production facility had a capacity of 15,000 vehicles per year.

The FAP 1118 BS/AV was developed specifically for the now Serbian Army; following the breakup of Yugoslavia in the 1990s, Serbia once again became an independent state in 2006, following the Montenegrin independence referendum.

Description

The FAP 1118 BS/AV (4 × 4) is entirely conventional in design, being based on a channel section chassis with beam-type axles and leaf spring suspension. A central tyre inflation system is fitted; tyres are 13R 22.5 and the drive axles are fitted with driver-controlled differential locks. A chassis-mounted 7,000 kg capacity winch is fitted as standard. The two-door all-steel cab which tilts forward 62° for maintenance is of the forward control type, and is based on a Mercedes-Benz pattern.

Specifications

FAP 1118 BS/AV
Cab seating: 1 + 1 (up to 16 in cargo area)
Configuration: 4 × 4
Weight:
   (laden) 11,400 kg
   (unladen) 7,400 kg
   (max load) 4,000 kg
   (towed load) 4,800 kg
   (front axle, laden) 5,500 kg
   (rear axle, laden) 5,900 kg
Load area dimensions: (L × W) 4 × 2.4 m
Length: 6.41 m
Width: 2.5 m
Height: (top of cab) 3.232 m
Wheelbase: 3.6 m
Angle of approach/departure: 30°/34°
Max speed: 80 km/h
Range: 600 km
Max gradient: 73%
Max sideslope: 30%
Ditch crossing: 700 mm
Vertical step: 500 mm
Fording: 1 m
Engine: R-4 (OM 904 LA) EURO 3 emissions compliant 4.25-litre 6-cylinder turbocharged and intercooled water-cooled 4-stroke diesel developing 174 hp (128 kW) and 675 N.m torque at 1,200-1,600 rpm
Gearbox: FAP 6MS 80 with 6 forward and 1 reverse gears; originally FAP 5MS 60 with 5 forward and 1 reverse gears
Clutch: GF 395 single dry plate; originally GF 380 single dry plate
Transfer box: 2-speed
Steering: PPT 8042 hydraulic, ball and joint
Turning radius: 9 m
Suspension: leaf springs with additional rubber springs and telescopic shock-absorbers, front; leaf springs, rear
Tyres: 13R 22.5
Brakes:
   (main) dual circuit, air, drums all-round
   (parking) mechanical with air actuation

FAP 1118 BS/AV (4 x 4) truck (FAP)   1340274

Electrical system: 24 V
Batteries: 2 × 12 V, 110 Ah

Status
In service with Serbia. Available for export.

Contractor
FAP Korporacija a.d.

Enquiries to
Yugoimport SDPR

FAP 2026 BS/AV (6 × 6) truck series

Development
In 1953 FAP (*Korporacija a.d. Pribo*) introduced its first heavy-duty vehicles following the acquisition of a license to produce vehicles under the then Saurer-Werke brand. In 1959 the company had in place machining and vehicle assembling lines with a production capacity of 3,600 vehicles per year. In 1975 a licence agreement with the now Daimler commenced. This was extended to heavier trucks in 1978, with developments including the FAP 2026 BDS/6×6 (6 × 6) truck. In 1983 the FAP 2632 BDS/8×8 (8 × 8) truck was introduced. By 1987 the FAP production facility had a capacity of 15,000 vehicles per year.

The FAP 2026 (6 × 6) was developed specifically for the now Serbian Army; following the breakup of Yugoslavia in the 1990s, Serbia once again became an independent state in 2006, following the Montenegrin independence referendum. The FAP 2028 is a further development of the FAP 2026 BS/AV (6 × 6) truck. The current model is designated FAP 2228. The FAP 2026 and subsequent follow-on models are designed for the transport of general cargo, but may be used as an artillery tractor or a mounting platform for assorted weapons including the 128 mm (32-round) M-77 Oganj multiple rocket system. Details of the Oganj multiple rocket system can be found in *Jane's Armour and Artillery*.

FAP 2026 BS/AV (FAP Korporacija a.d)   1340271

The latest FAP 2228 BS/AV prototype (FAP Korporacija a.d)   1391465

Description
The FAP 2026 BS/AV (6 × 6) is entirely conventional in design, being based on a channel section chassis with beam-type axles and leaf spring suspension. A central tyre inflation system is fitted; tyres are 1500 × 21 and the drive axles are fitted with driver-controlled differential locks. Climatic operational range is −30°C to +50°C. A chassis-mounted 10,000 kg hydraulic winch is fitted as standard. The two-door all-steel cab which tilts forward 62° for maintenance is of the forward control type, and is based on a Mercedes-Benz pattern.

The main differences between the original FAP 2026 BS/AV (which was produced in considerable numbers for the armies of the former Yugoslavia) and the later FAP 2028/2228 are engine and gearbox. The earlier FAP 2026 was produced powered by a 256 hp V8 diesel engine built under licence from the former British Leyland. This is coupled to a 6MA-80 six-speed gearbox and two-speed transfer box. Later 2028 and 2228 models are fitted with a Mercedes-Benz engine coupled to a ZF gearbox and ZF/Steyr two-speed transfer box. Weights, dimensions and performance of all models is broadly similar.

Specifications
FAP 2026 BS/AV

	FAP 2026 BS/AV	**FAP 2028/FAP 2228 BS/AV**
Cab seating:	1 + 1 (up to 20 in cargo area)	1 + 1 (up to 20 in cargo area)
Configuration:	6 × 6	6 × 6
Weight:		
(laden)	21,000 kg	22,000 kg
(unladen)	11,000 kg	n/avail
(max weight on front axle, laden)	6,000 kg	6,000 kg
(max weight on rear axles, laden)	15,000 kg	16,000 kg
(max load)	10,000 kg	6,000 kg on-road, 10,000 kg off-road
Max towed load:	7,200 kg	n/avail
Max winch capacity:	10,000 kg	10,000 kg
Load area:	4.53 × 2.342 m	4.53 × 2.342 m
Length:	7.72 m	7.72 m
Width:	2.49 m	2.49 m
Height: (top of cab)	3.1 m	3.1 m
Wheelbase:	3.4 + 1.4 m	3.4 + 1.4 m
Track:	2.02 m	n/avail
Angle of approach/departure:	40°/40°	40°/40°
Max speed:	80 km/h	80 km/h
Fuel consumption:	33 litres/100 km	n/avail
Range:	600 km	600 km
Max gradient:		
(less trailer)	60%	60%
(with trailer)	40%	40%
Fording:	1.2 m	1 m, 1.2 m splash
Engine:	V-8 direct injection water-cooled 4-stroke diesel developing 256 hp (188 kW) at 2,500 rpm and 834 N.m torque at 1,400 rpm	Mercedes-Benz OM 906 LA EURO 3 emissions compliant 6.37-litre water-cooled 4-stroke diesel developing 279 hp (205 kW) at 2,200 rpm and 1,100 N.m torque at 1,200-1,600 rpm
Gearbox:	6MS-80 with 6 forward and 1 reverse gears	ZF 9S 109 with 9 forward and 1 reverse gears
Clutch:	single dry plate	MF 395 single dry plate
Transfer box:	2-speed	ZF/Steyr VG1600/396 2-speed
Steering:	hydraulic, ball and joint	PPT 5045 hydraulic, ball and joint
Turning radius:	11 m	11 m
Suspension:	leaf springs with additional rubber springs and telescopic shock-absorbers	leaf springs with additional rubber springs and telescopic shock-absorbers

	FAP 2026 BS/AV	**FAP 2028/FAP 2228 BS/AV**
Tyres:	15.00 × 21 with CTI	15.00 × 21 with CTI
Brakes:		
(main)	dual circuit, air, drums all-round	dual circuit, air, drums all-round. ABS fitted
(parking)	mechanical, air actuated	mechanical, air actuated
Electrical system:	24 V	24 V
Batteries:	2 × 12 V, 143 Ah	2 × 12 V, 143 Ah

Status
FAP 2026; in service with armies of the former Yugoslav Army. Exported to Saudi Arabia and possibly other undisclosed countries. FAP 2228; in service with the Serbian Army, available for export.

Contractor
FAP Korporacija a.d.

Enquiries to
Yugoimport SDPR

FAP 2832 BS/AV (8 × 8) 9,000 kg truck

Development
In 1953 FAP (Korporacija a.d. Pribo) introduced its first heavy-duty vehicles following the acquisition of a license to produce vehicles under the then Saurer-Werke brand. In 1959 the company had in place machining and vehicle assembling lines with a production capacity of 3,600 vehicles per year. In 1975 a licence agreement with the now Daimler commenced. This was extended to heavier trucks in 1978, with developments including the FAP 2026 BDS/6x6 (6 × 6) truck. In 1983 the FAP 2632 BDS/8x8 (8 × 8) truck was introduced. By 1987 the FAP production facility had a capacity of 15,000 vehicles per year.

The FAP 2832 BS/AV (8 × 8) 9,000 kg truck is the (8 × 8) equivalent of the FAP (6 × 6) series of trucks, full details of which can be found elsewhere in this section.

The FAP 3232 BDST/AV is a tractor truck version of the FAP 2832. Full details of the FAP 3232 can be found in the Heavy equipment transporters section.

Current or future production of the FAP 2832 BS/AV (8 × 8) 9,000 kg truck would involve the use of current generation driveline components and would result in a designation change. A revised prototype designated FAP 3240 BS/AV is expected during 2011.

Description
The FAP 2832 BS/AV (8 × 8) is entirely conventional in design, being based on a channel section chassis with beam-type axles and leaf spring suspension. A central tyre inflation system is fitted; tyres are 1500 × 21 and the drive axles are fitted with driver-controlled longitudinal and cross-axle differential locks. Climatic operational range is -30°C to +55°C. A chassis-mounted 10,000 kg hydraulic winch is fitted as standard. The two-door all-steel cab which tilts forward 62° for maintenance is of the forward control type, and is based on a Mercedes-Benz pattern.

The FAP 2832 BS/AV can be used to tow artillery weighing up to 11,000 kg and can carry a maximum load of 14,000 kg on roads, reducing to 9,000 kg off-road.

FAP 3240 BS/AV prototype
A prototype of the latest FAP 3240 BS/AV (8 × 8) 10,000 kg truck is anticipated during 2011. Outline specifications give an unladen weight of 16,000 kg, payloads of 14,000 and 10,000 kg (on- and off-road), and GVWs of 32,000 and 26,000 kg (on- and off-road). Wheelbase will be 1.6 + 3.2 +

1.4 m. Motive power will be provided by a Euro 3 emissions compliant Mercedes-Benz OM 457 LA 12-litre six-cylinder diesel developing 401 hp (295 kW), this coupled to a ZF 16 S 221 16-speed manual gearbox.

Specifications
FAP 2832 BS/AV
Cab seating: 1 + 1
Configuration: 8 × 8
Weight:
  (laden, road) 30,000 kg
  (laden, off-road) 25,000 kg
  (unladen) 16,000 kg
  (max load, road) 14,000 kg
  (max load, off-road) 9,000 kg
  (towed load) 11,000 kg
Length: 9.02 m
Width: 2.5 m
Height: (top of canvas tilt) 3.319 m
Ground clearance: 380 mm
Track: 2.02 m
Wheelbase: 1.5 + 3.2 + 1.4 m
Angle of approach/departure: 41°/45°
Range: 600 km
Max gradient: 32%
Fording: 1.2 m (+ 300 mm splash)
Engine: Mercedes-Benz OM 403 15.95-litre V-10 4-stroke water-cooled diesel developing 320 hp (235 kW)
Gearbox: manual with 8 forward and 1 reverse gears
Clutch: WSK 400 torque convertor
Transfer box: 2-speed
Steering: hydraulic, ball and joint
Turning radius: 13 m
Suspension: parabolic leaf springs
Tyres: 15.00 × 21 T-101
Brakes:
  (main) dual circuit, air, drums all-round, supplementary engine exhaust brake
  (parking) mechanical with air actuation
Electrical system: 24 V
Batteries: 2 × 12 V, 210 Ah

Status
In service with armies of the former Yugoslav Army. Production as required; revised prototype anticipated during 2011. Available for export.

Contractor
FAP Korporacija a.d.

Enquiries to
Yugoimport SDPR

Slovakia

TANAX AKTIS 4 × 4.1R (4 × 4) 4,500 kg truck

Development
The TANAX (previously Tatra Sipox) AKTIS 4×4.1R (4 × 4) 4,500 kg truck was developed as the potential replacement for a large number of Slovak (previously Czechoslovakian) armed forces medium weight military trucks. These include small numbers of Ural-375D (6 × 6) 4,000 kg, ZIL-157 (6 × 6) 2,500 kg, ZIL-131 (6 × 6) 3,500 kg and KAMAZ trucks, but are predominantly Praga V3S (6 × 6) 3,000 kg trucks. All of these designs are

FAP 2832 BS/AV (8 × 8) 9,000 kg truck (FAP)   1340273

One of the first AKTIS 4×4.1R (4 × 4) 3,500 kg trucks supplied to the Slovak Army (TANAX a.s.)   0524752

Chassis-cab of the AKTIS 4×4.1R (4 × 4) 3,500 kg truck showing clearly the MAN-Steyr parentage of the cab (TANAX a.s.)   0524753

TANAX AKTIS 4×4.1R (4 × 4) 3,500 kg truck chassis fitted with an AD 10 crane with a maximum lift capacity of 10,000 kg at 2.5 m (TANAX a.s.)
0524756

now technically obsolete and are becoming increasingly difficult and expensive to maintain. They also fail to meet the vast majority of current applicable European legislation, thereby restricting their use in certain European countries.

The Slovak government decided that any replacement programme would be carried out by Slovak industry, thereby ensuring cost-effective through-life support for the selected vehicle (or vehicles), while also helping to invigorate Slovakia's automotive industry. Comparative testing of a number of vehicle designs began in 1995.

Throughout 1995-96 four 4 × 4 vehicle types were assessed at Vojensky Technicky a Skusobny Ustav, VTSU (Military Technical and Testing Unit), Zahorie. These were Austria's Steyr 12 M 21, Germany's Mercedes-Benz 1117A and Unimog 1550L/38, and Slovakia's Sipox Corso. On the basis of test results submitted by VAB Sipox (later Tatra Sipox a.s.) the decision was taken that working in conjunction with Austria's Steyr (now MAN), the then Tatra Sipox (now TANAX) would develop a vehicle based on the Steyr 12 M 21 design.

Steyr would supply the cab, engine and gearbox, leaving the then Tatra Sipox to design, develop and manufacture the chassis, axles, additional transmission components and chassis ancillaries. Final production would take place in Slovakia. Six prototypes, four platform trucks and two box body/shelter carriers, were tested between 1997 and 2000 at VTSU Zahorie, the Slovak military facility at Nitra and on the vehicle test track at TATRA's Koprivnica facility in the Czech Republic. The prototype vehicles met all the Slovak Army's tactical and technical requirements and the type was first shown publicly at IDEE 2000. On 5 October 2000, it was announced the AKTIS would be adopted by the Slovak Army.

An initial thirty-five vehicles were supplied to the Slovak Army during 2001. Eighteen of these were made available to Slovak troops serving on UN duties in Cyprus, East Timor and Eritrea, with KFOR in Kosovo, and most recently with the Sloval contingent in Iraq. By 2009 around 120 vehicles had been delivered, with deliveries scheduled to continue.

Development of the AKTIS was financed by the Ministry of Economy and Manufacturing. Tactical and technical requirements and the trials programme were managed by the Slovak Army.

The now TANAX was previously part of the TATRA organisation and in 1990 the factory separated from the former Czech state enterprise TATRA Koprivnice, and the independent state enterprise VAB šp Bánovce nad

Bebravou was formed. In 1993 the company concluded its privatisation and the major share holder became the SIPOX. In November 2002 the then Tatra Sipox became TANAX, (joint stock company), Bánovce nad Bebravou. The principal share holders of TANAX a.s. are Vectra Limited, UK and TB TRADE a.s. (joint stock company), Bánovce nad Bebravou, each having a 50 per cent stake in the company.

Description

The MAN supplied cab is taken from the MAN M2000 range of trucks, this the replacement for the earlier cab originally fitted to the Steyr 12 M 21. An all-steel design, the sound-proofed and insulated cab tilts forward for engine access and the roof is fitted with a central hatch and mount for a light machine gun. Internal fittings include two sprung seats with an additional third-person occasional/emergency seat. All occupants have seat belts. The front windscreen is heated, the rear view mirrors are heated and remotely controlled, and internal noise levels are below 82 dB(A). Air conditioning is optional.

A total of 17 different body types are presently available and can be fitted to the AKTIS. In addition to the standard platform body these include assorted box- or shelter-type bodies suitable for command, control, or communication roles, or less technical designs for use as workshop or engineering facilities. Various tanker bodies, a fire appliance or a crane or light recovery hamper are other possible options. Brief details of these variants can be found here.

The standard platform body has a removable tarpaulin cover and bows, a removable steel tailgate, drop sides and corner/centre posts. The tailgate has integral steps and the drop side-mounted wooden bench seats are collapsible. A headboard mounted light is standard and an independent diesel-powered hot air heater is an option. The loadbed is floored with plywood. If required a powered tailgate or chassis-mounted hydraulic crane can be fitted.

The standard AKTIS chassis-cab weighs 5,400 kg. With a maximum permissible Gross Vehicle Weight (GVW) of 11,000 kg for the military version, this allows a maximum of 5,600 kg for superstructure and payload, giving the standard drop side platform truck a payload of 4,500 kg. The AKTIS may also be rated at 12,000 kg GVW. Including trailer, the gross combination weight of both versions is 21,000 kg. This gives a maximum towed (braked) load of 10,000 kg on-road.

The AKTIS is powered by the option of EURO 2 or EURO 3 emissions compliant MAN 6.8-litre six-cylinder turbocharged diesel engines developing 220 hp, giving the fully laden vehicle a power-to-weight ratio of 20 hp/tonne. Maximum road speed is 100 km/h for the military variant, minimum speed is 2 km/h. At 75 km/h and maximum GVW fuel consumption does not exceed 24 litres per 100 km. A single 180 litre capacity fuel tank is mounted on the right-hand side of the chassis. In standard configuration the engine is equipped to start at temperatures down to −30°C. The climatic operational range stretches from −30 to +50°C.

A nine-speed ZF 9S 109 all-synchromesh gearbox is coupled to a TANAX three-shaft two-speed transfer box with lockable longitudinal differential, giving a total of 18 forward and two reverse gears. There is a Power Take Off (PTO) facility on the transfer box. This can be used to drive a winch or hydraulic pump for any fitted crane or other materials handling equipment. A single-speed transfer box is fitted to the faster Police variant.

Two- or four-wheel drive are selectable, with both TANAX-designed hub reduction axles being fitted with cross-axle differential locks. The front and rear axle are sprung by a combination of parabolic leaf springs and hydraulic shock-absorbers, the rear axle only having an anti-roll bar fitted. Steering is power-assisted. A variety of cross-country tyre types can be fitted to the 20 inch wheel rims, including all-terrain, sand or snow bias, or directional 'traction' types. The AKTIS can cross a 700 mm trench and climb a 400 mm vertical step.

Drum brakes are fitted all-round, with uprated discs being fitted to the front axle of the faster Police variant. An Anti-lock Braking System (ABS) that can be disconnected for off-road use is standard. The pneumatic dual

AKTIS 4×4.1R (4 × 4) 3,500 kg truck chassis mounting a 5 m³ capacity ISO 1DX water tank and integral pumping equipment (TANAX a.s.)   0524757

circuit braking system is compatible with trailers fitted with either single or dual circuit brakes, and in the case of older unbraked trailers, a separate connector can be fitted. The maximum towed load for an unbraked trailer is 3,500 kg.

Variants

AKTIS 4 × 4.1R PV
The AKTIS 4 × 4.1R PV is the military chassis variant.

AKTIS 4 × 4.1R VV
The AKTIS 4 × 4.1R VV is the military platform truck variant.

AKTIS 4 × 4.1R SV
The AKTIS 4 × 4.1R SV variant is fitted with an air-tight superstructure SKS.

AKTIS 4 × 4.1R CV
The AKTIS 4 × 4.1R CV is a fuel tanker variant.

AKTIS 4 × 4.1R ML
The AKTIS 4 × 4.1R ML is a container carrier variant.

AKTIS 4 × 4.1R IS
The AKTIS 4 × 4.1R IS is an ISO container carrier variant.

AKTIS 4 × 4.1R PP
The AKTIS 4 × 4.1R PP variant is fitted with a police chassis.

AKTIS 4 × 4.1R VP
The AKTIS 4 × 4.1R VP is a police platform truck variant.

AKTIS 4 × 4.1R SP
The AKTIS 4 × 4.1R SP is fitted with a police superstructure.

AKTIS 4 × 4.1R PH
The AKTIS 4 × 4.1R PH is the fire chassis variant.

AKTIS 4 × 4.1R VH
A fire appliance body has been demonstrated. This has a capacity of 2,400 litres of water and 200 litres of foam and weighs 9,150 kg, 12,000 kg loaded with water and foam. Dimensions are 7 × 2.55 × 3.25 m (L × W × H)

Police variant of the AKTIS 4×4.1R (4 × 4) 3,500 kg truck, designated AKTIS 4×4.1R SP (TANAX a.s.)   0524754

TANAX AKTIS 4x4.1R (4 × 4) 3,500 kg truck of a Slovakian Army deployable medical facility (Stefan Marx)   1124712

Fire appliance variant of the AKTIS 4x4.1R (4 × 4) 3,500 kg truck, designated AKTIS 4x4.1R VH (TANAX a.s.)   0524755

and the vehicle can climb a 38 per cent gradient, fully laden, and has a static sideslope angle of 30° (66 per cent). An enlarged four-door cab is fitted for the five-person (four + driver) crew.

AKTIS 4 × 4.1R with AD 10 crane
The base chassis has also been fitted with an AD 10 crane with a lifting capacity of 10,000 kg at 2.5 m. Maximum lift height is 12.5 m, 15.7 m with the optional jib extension fitted. Dimensions are 7.756 × 2.5 × 3.82 m (L × W × H), width increasing to between 3.3 and 3.77 m with the stabilisers deployed. Maximum road speed for this variant is restricted to 60 km/h. A 5,000 kg trailer may be towed.

AKTIS 4 × 4.1R with ISO 1DX water tank
Also available is the base AKTIS chassis fitted with an ISO 1DX water tank complete with pumping equipment. The tank unit weighs 1,100 kg, empty, measures 2.99 × 2.42 × 1.6 m (L × W × H) and has a capacity of 5 m weighing approximately 5,000 kg (water), giving a total weight (container and payload) of 6,100 kg ±5 per cent. The integral pump can deliver up to 4.5 m³/hr at a maximum pressure of 0.53 mPa and withdraw water from a maximum depth of 40 m. Temperature of the medium pumped can be within a 0 to +40°C temperature range, the ambient temperature up to +55°.

Specifications

AKTIS 4x4.1R
(military platform truck variant unless stated)
Cab seating: 1 + 1 (+ 1 occasional)
Configuration: 4 × 4
Weight:
    (laden, military platform) 11,000 kg
    (laden, ISO) 12,000 kg
    (chassis-cab, unladen) 5,400 kg
    (total load, with any superstructure) 5,600 kg
    (payload, platform truck, on-road) 4,500 kg
    (towed load, braked, on-road) 10,000 kg
    (towed load, braked, off-road) 3,500 kg
    (towed load, unbraked) 3,500 kg
    (GCW) 21,000 kg
Length: 6.910 m
Width: 2.55 m
Height:
    (cab) 2.93 m
    (tarpaulin) 3.31 m
Ground clearance: 348 mm
Track:
    (front) 2.03 m
    (rear) 2.06 m
Wheelbase:
    (standard) 3.8 m
    (option) 3.5 m
Angle of approach/departure: 40°/28°
Max speed:
    (military) 100 km/h
    (Police) 120 km/h
Range: >700 km
Fuel capacity: 180 litres
Max gradient: 60%
Max sideslope: 44%
Fording: 800 mm
Engine: MAN D 0826 LFL 10 EURO 2 or MAN D 0836 LFL 02 EURO 3, 6.817-litre 6-cylinder in-line turbocharged water-cooled 4-stroke diesel developing 220 hp (164 kW) at 2,400 rpm and 820 N.m torque at 1,400 rpm
Gearbox: ZF 9S 109 manual, 9 forward and 1 reverse gears
Clutch: MFZ 395 single dry plate (395 mm)

Transfer box: TANAX three-shaft, 2-speed with lockable centre differential
A single-speed transfer box is fitted to the Police variant
Steering: power-assisted
Turning radius:
(3.8 m wheelbase) 7.6 m
Suspension: parabolic leaf springs and hydraulic shock-absorbers, front and rear. Anti-roll bar, rear axle only
Tyres: options include 365/80R 20 and 14.5R 20
Brakes: disengageable ABS fitted, drums, front and rear (military), discs front, drums rear (Police)
Electrical system: 24 V
Batteries: 2 × 12 V, 135 Ah
Alternator: 28 V, 80 A

Status
In production (see text). In service with the Slovak Army and Police forces.

Contractor
TANAX a.s.

Slovenia

TAM 110 T7 BV (4 × 4) 1,500/2,500 kg truck

Development
The foundation of the now Tovarna Vozil Maribor company was an aircraft component factory built during 1942 to meet the needs of the German war industry. At the conclusion of WWII the factory commenced production of commercial vehicles carrying the TAM brand name.

Following the break-up of the former Yugoslavia, the company was reorganised into a group of M.P.P. companies, among them M.P.P. Vozila (vehicles), M.P.P. Razvoj (development) and M.P.P. DUF. In June 2001 these three companies merged to become Torvarna Vozil Maribor.

In addition to the production of mini and midi buses, the company currently offers the 182 T10 (4 × 4) truck and is the only official supplier of original spare parts for TAM military vehicles, such as the TAM 110 T7 BV 1,500/2,500 kg truck.

The TAM 110 T7 BV was developed specifically to meet the requirements of the former Yugoslav Army, using the design of the German Magirus-Deutz 130T7FAL as a basis (which did not enter production). It is the (4 × 4) component of two basically similar vehicles, the other being the TAM 150 T11 BV 6 × 6 vehicle, full details of which can be found elsewhere in this section.

The TAM 110 T7 BV has been referred to as the TAM 1500.

Description
The two-door all-steel forward control cab has a reinforced PVC material roof which can be removed, as can the side windows. The cab has seating for two and can be tipped forward to an angle of 55° for engine access. The windscreen can be tipped forward over the bonnet if required. Two forms of cab heating are available. The cargo body is of all-steel construction and has two collapsible benches fitted to each side to seat 12 personnel. The cargo area has a capacity of 3.31 m³ and is 3.02 × 2.12 m (L × W) and the single-section drop sides are 0.64 m high. A tarpaulin may be fitted over removable bows. A towing hook is provided at the rear under the downward-opening tailgate.

Motive power is provided by a TAM F4 L413 R 5.88-litre air-cooled diesel engine mounted forward under the cab. This has a fuel consumption of 16 to 21 litres per 100 km and develops 110 hp (some sources state 115 hp). This engine is a version of the TAM 413 engine that was produced in the former Yugoslavia under licence from Klockner-Humboldt-Deutz (KHD).

Mounted forward under the cab is a 2,500 kg capacity winch that can be used to the front or rear. Special equipment carried on the vehicle includes equipment for the winch, pioneer tools and an NBC kit. The vehicle is fitted with radio interference protection and space is provided for the fitment of an infra-red device for the driver. A central tyre inflation (CTI) system is fitted, allowing the driver to vary tyre pressures between 10 and 51 psi (0.7 and 3.5 bar) to suit prevailing terrain while driving. Climatic operational range of the vehicle is –30 to +40°C.

A signals vehicle variant houses its signals equipment in a removable container, weighing 2,165 kg, that can be lifted off the vehicle using four (one at each corner) telescopic support legs. The container has external dimensions of 3.43 × 2.34 × 1.8 m (L × W × H), the polyurethane foam insulated panelling giving internal dimensions of 2.87 × 2.12 × 1.68 m. The container is equipped with two slide-out AB-2-230 generating sets mounted in the front cabin and accessible through external doors. Operation 'closed down' with these doors closed and the generator stowed is possible. Up to 1,000 kg of additional equipment may be installed, the maximum permissible weight of the vehicle being 6,700 kg.

An ambulance variant has a box-body and can carry up to four stretchers and associated medical equipment. Total weight is 6,400 kg.

Specifications
TAM 110 T7 BV truck
Cab seating: 1 + 1 (up to 12 in rear)
Configuration: 4 × 4
Weight:
(unladen) 4,500 kg
(GVW, on-road) 7,000 kg
(GVW, off-road) 6,000 kg
(max load, on-road) 2,500 kg
(max load, off-road) 1,500 kg
(towed load) 1,800 kg
(GCW, on-road) 8,800 kg
(GCW, off-road) 7,800 kg
Load area: 3.02 × 2.12 m
Length: 4.85 m
Width: 2.275 m
Height: (top of cab) 2.47 m
Ground clearance: 300 mm
Wheelbase: 2.85 m
Angle of approach/departure: 49°/45°
Max speed:
(on-road) 90 km/h
(off-road) 49 km/h
Fuel capacity: 100 litres
Max gradient:
(without trailer) 67%
(with trailer) 44.5%
Fording: 1 m
Engine: TAM (KHD) F 4 L 413 R 5.88-litre 4-cylinder in-line air-cooled direct injection diesel developing 115 hp (85 kW) at 2,650 rpm and 358 Nm torque at 1,400 rpm.
Gearbox: ZF 5-35S with 5 forward and 1 reverse gears
Clutch: GF 310 K hydraulic with single dry plate
Transfer box: R 28 NP 2-speed
Steering: hydraulic, ZF 8038
Turning radius: 6.5 m
Suspension: leaf springs with rubber buffers and telescopic shock-absorbers
Tyres: 12.00 × 18PR 8
Brakes:
(main) dual circuit air-hydraulic, drums all-round
(parking) mechanical with air servo-assisted on rear wheels
Electrical system: 24 V
Batteries: 2 × 12 V, 110 Ah

Status
Production complete. In service with the former Yugoslav Army and other nations once part of the former Yugoslavia.

Contractor
Tovarna Vozil Maribor d.o.o.

TAM 110 T7 BV (4 × 4) of the Bosnian Serb Army confiscated by SFOR (Richard Stickland)   1047342

TAM 150 T11 BV (6 × 6) 3,000/5,000 kg truck

Development
The foundation of the now Tovarna Vozil Maribor company was an aircraft component factory built during 1942 to meet the needs of the German war industry. At the conclusion of WWII, the factory commenced production of commercial vehicles carrying the TAM brand name.

Following the break-up of the former Yugoslavia, the company was reorganised into a group of M.P.P. companies, among them M.P.P. Vozila (vehicles), M.P.P. Razvoj (development) and M.P.P. DUF. In June 2001 these three companies merged to become Torvarna Vozil Maribor.

In addition to the production of mini and midi buses, the company currently offers the 182 T10 (4 × 4) truck and is the only official supplier of original spare parts for TAM military vehicles, such as the TAM 150 T11 BV 1,500/2,500 kg truck.

The TAM 150 T11 BV can be considered an enlarged version of the TAM 110 T7 BV (4 × 4) that was developed specifically to meet the requirements of the former Yugoslav Army. Full details of the TAM 110 T7 BV can be found elsewhere in this section.

Description

The TAM 150 TII uses the same cab and has a generally similar layout to the TAM 110 T7 BV, but it uses a V6 diesel engine and not an in-line four-cylinder unit.

The two-door all-steel forward control cab has a reinforced PVC material roof which can be removed, as can the side windows. The cab has seating for two and can be tipped forward 55° for engine access. The windscreen may be folded forward over the bonnet if required.

A central tyre inflation (CTI) system is fitted, allowing the driver to vary tyre pressures between 10 and 51 psi (0.7 and 3.5 bar) to suit prevailing terrain while driving. Climatic operational range of the vehicle is −30 to +50°C.

Croatian Army TAM 150 T11 BV (6 × 6) 3,000/5,000 kg truck carrying NBC decontamination equipment (T J Gander)   0056426

TAM 150 T11 BV (6 × 6) 3,000/5,000 kg cargo truck
(Tovarna Vozil Maribor d.o.o .)   0524751

TAM 150 T11 BV (6 × 6) 3,000/5,000 kg cargo truck fitted with a shelter-type body (Siete Meeter)   0583248

Motive power is provided by a TAM F 6L 413 F 9.57-litre V6 air-cooled diesel engine mounted forward under the cab. This has a fuel consumption of 24 to 30 litres per 100 km. The engine was built under licence from Klockner-Humboldt-Deutz (KHD) of Germany.

The rear cargo body is of all-steel construction and has a 4.4 m³ capacity, measuring 4.17 × 2.12 m (L × W). The two-piece drop sides are 500 mm high. Collapsible benches are fitted along each side to seat 18 personnel. A downward-opening single-piece tailgate is provided. A tarpaulin may be fitted over removable bows.

A 5,000 kg capacity winch with 88 m of 13 mm steel cable may be fitted under the cargo body rear for use in self-recovery operations, in either direction. Power for the winch is supplied via a reduction gear and a power take-off for tools may be fitted.

A rear-mounted hook may be used to tow a trailer or light artillery piece such as an anti-tank gun, up to 5,000 kg in weight, on-road, up to 3,600 kg in weight, off-road. A version of the TAM 150 T11 BV carrying NBC decontamination equipment was produced and may be utilised as a water tanker.

Specifications

TAM 150 T11 BV
Cab seating: 1 + 1 (up to 18 in rear)
Configuration: 6 × 6
Weight:
    (unladen) 6,200 kg
    (GVW, on-road) 11,200 kg
    (GVW, off-road) 9,260 kg
    (max load, on-road) 5,000 kg
    (max load, off-road) 3,000 kg
    (towed load, on-road) 5,000 kg
    (towed load, off-road) 3,600 kg
    (GCW, on-road) 16,200 kg
    (GCW, off-road) 12,860 kg
Load area: 4.17 × 2.12 m
Length: 6.55 m
Width: 2.275 m
Height:
    (tarpaulin) 2.82 m
    (cab) 2.42 m
Ground clearance: 305 mm
Wheelbase: 3.1 + 1.2 m
Track: 1.86 m
Angle of approach/departure: 48/40°
Max speed:
    (on-road) 94.7 km/h
    (off-road) 55.2 km/h
Fuel capacity: 150 litres
Max gradient:
    (without trailer) 71%
    (with trailer) 43%
Fording: 1 m
Engine: TAM (KHD) F 6 L 413 F 9.572 litre V6 air-cooled 4-stroke direct injection diesel developing 154 hp (113 kW) at 2,650 rpm and 515 N.m torque at 1,400 rpm
Gearbox: ZF 5-35S with 5 forward and 1 reverse gears
Clutch: G 350 KR single dry plate
Transfer box: R 28 NP 2-speed
Steering: ZF 8038, hydraulic
Turning radius: 7.85 m
Suspension: leaf springs with rubber buffers and telescopic shock-absorbers, additional front rubber springs
Tyres: 12.00 × 18PR 10
Brakes:
    (main) dual circuit air-hydraulic, drums all-round
    (parking) mechanical, air-servo assisted on rear wheels
Electrical system: 24 V
Batteries: 2 × 12 V, 143 Ah

Status

Production complete. In service with the former Yugoslav Army and other nations once part of the former Yugoslavia, including Croatia.

Contractor

Tovarna Vozil Maribor d.o.o.

TAM 162 T9 and TAM 182 T10 (4 × 4) trucks

Development

The foundation of the now Tovarna Vozil Maribor company was an aircraft component factory built during 1942 to meet the needs of the German war industry. At the conclusion of WWII the factory commenced production of commercial vehicles carrying the TAM brand name.

Following the break-up of the former Yugoslavia the company was reorganised into a group of M.P.P. companies, among them M.P.P. Vozila (vehicles), M.P.P. Razvoj (development) and M.P.P. DUF. In June 2001 these three companies merged to become Torvarna Vozil Maribor.

TAM 182 T10 (4 × 4) 4,000 kg truck (TVM)   1035159

In addition to the production of coaches, mini and midi buses, the company currently offers a (4 × 4) chassis and the 182 T10 (4 × 4) truck. Additionally, the company is the only official supplier of original spare parts for TAM military vehicles.

The TAM 162 T9 (4 × 4) 3,500 kg light truck was announced between 2000 and 2001 and was developed to meet a Slovenian Army requirement that initially called for approximately 100 trucks with possible further future options. This contract was awarded to IVECO for a version of the EuroCargo range and no series production of the TAM 162 T9 was undertaken. The TAM 182 T10 is the successor model and is essentially an updated TAM 162 T9 fitted with a more powerful EURO 3 emissions compliant engine and other associated automotive improvements. No serial production of the TAM 182 T10 has been undertaken.

Status
Pre-production only. No serial production.

Contractor
Tovarna Vozil Maribor d.o.o.

TAM 4500/5000/5500/6500 trucks

Development
The foundation of the now Tovarna Vozil Maribor company was an aircraft component factory built during 1942 to meet the needs of the German war industry. At the conclusion of WWII the factory commenced production of commercial vehicles carrying the TAM brand name.

Following the break-up of the former Yugoslavia the company was reorganised into a group of M.P.P. companies, among them M.P.P. Vozila (vehicles), M.P.P. Razvoj (development) and M.P.P. DUF. In June 2001 these three companies merged to become Torvarna Vozil Maribor.

In addition to the production of mini and midi buses, the company currently offers the 182 T10 (4 × 4) truck and is the only official supplier of original spare parts for TAM military vehicles such as the TAM 4500 series.

The TAM 4500 series of trucks was manufactured in the former Yugoslavia under licence from Magirus-Deutz.

Description
The TAM 4500 is powered by an F 4 L 514 four-cylinder air-cooled diesel developing 85 hp, giving the vehicle a maximum road speed of 75 km/h. Payload on roads is 4,500 kg. The layout of the vehicle is conventional, with the engine at the front, a fully enclosed two-door all-steel cab in the centre and the cargo area at the rear with drop sides and a drop tailgate. Suffixes are used to designate different versions: B for forward control, D for (4 × 4) drive and K for dump truck. The TAM 4500D is the (4 × 4) model used by the former Yugoslav Army and is similar in layout to the civil version but has a different rear cargo area with a drop tailgate. Bench seats can be installed if required. The forward control version is the TAM 4500B and the dump truck version is the 4500K.

The TAM 5000 is powered by the same engine as the TAM 4500 and was available in two versions: (4 × 2) (TAM 5000) and (4 × 4) (TAM 5000DV). The DV version was developed specifically for the former Yugoslav Army and has a central tyre inflation (CTI) system. A dump truck model is designated the TAM 5000K (4 × 2).

The TAM 5500 is powered by a F 4 L 614 V-6 air-cooled diesel engine, developing 85 hp and giving the vehicle a maximum road speed of 85 km/h. Payload is 5,000 kg. The dump truck model is the TAM 5500DK (4 × 4) and there is also a tractor truck model.

The largest model in the range is the TAM 6500, which can carry 6,500 kg and, there is also a dump truck model.

Production of TAM 4500/5000/5500 and 6500 range trucks ceased some time ago. Full details of the follow-on TAM 110 T7 BV (4 × 4) and TAM 150 T11 BV (6 × 6) models can be found elsewhere in this section.

TAM 4500D cargo truck (Richard Stickland)   0056384

Specifications
(TAM 5000DV)
Configuration: 4 × 4
Weight:
  (unladen) 4,500 kg
  (max load) 5,000 kg
  (max GCW, road) 9,500 kg
Length: 6.75 m
Width: 2.19 m
Height: (cab) 2.75 m
Wheelbase: 4.2 m
Engine: F 4 4-cylinder air-cooled diesel developing 85 hp (62 kW) at 2,300 rpm
Tyres: 12.00 × 18

Status
Production complete. In service with the former Yugoslav Army and other nations once part of the former Yugoslavia; numbers reducing.

Contractor
Tovarna Vozil Maribor d.o.o.

South Africa

SAMIL 20 Mark 2 (4 × 4) 2,000 kg truck

Development
SAMIL trucks were originally manufactured by TruckMakers (Pty) Ltd. This company is no longer trading and in-service support of the SAMIL range of trucks is now carried out by BAE Systems Land Systems South Africa OMC, formerly Alvis South Africa (Pty) Limited, formerly Vickers OMC (Pty) Limited.

Development of the SAMIL 20 Mark 2 (4 × 4) 2,000 kg truck began in 1981, with the vehicle being unveiled in 1985. The SAMIL 20 Mark 2 retains the overall configuration and general appearance of the earlier SAMIL 20 Mark 1 from which it was developed, but the basic specification was altered.

Approximately 3,500 SAMIL 20s remain in SANDF service and a project to replace these is likely to be announced during 2011.

Quantities of surplus SANDF SAMIL 20 trucks have recently started to become available and a number of manufacturers offer these for sale to military or commercial customers, and in a variety of conditions including fully refurbished.

Description
The SAMIL 20 is based on the Magirus-Deutz 130 FAL. The 130 FAL lost out in a German Army competition to the Unimog and never entered production with a Magirus-Deutz badge. However, in addition to the SAMIL 20, it forms the basis of the Slovenian TAM 110 T7.

The SAMIL 20 is of conventional design, being based on a single-piece ladder frame chassis with bolted in cross members. Axles are of the portal type, giving 460 mm ground clearance. Motive power in the SAMIL Mark 1 was provided by a Deutz air-cooled diesel coupled to a 6F/1R manual gearbox and two-speed transfer box.

The SAMIL 20 Mark 2 retained the overall configuration and general appearance of the earlier SAMIL 20 Mark 1 from which it was developed, but the basic specification was altered. The most significant change was that the engine became a South African manufactured ADE 352N (Atlantis Diesel Engines) water-cooled diesel weighing 420 kg and corresponding alterations to the gearbox and transfer box ratios were introduced. The forward control cab became a fully enclosed hard cab. The fuel tank is high-density polyethylene and the associated piping systems are made of a nylon-based material. These changes, along with other new locally produced components such as propshafts, mean that over 90 per cent of the vehicle contains local content.

A fully refurbished SAMIL 20 Mark 2 (4 × 4) truck (Patrick Allen)   1110960

Variants

Protected transport
This version has the driver's cab protected against mine blast and small arms fire by an angled arrangement of armoured plates around the cab and engine. The cargo area is slightly reduced in size from the normal version.

Bulldog
This is a completely armoured personnel and load carrier originally based on the SAMIL 20 Mark 1. There is a centrally placed cab for the driver. The rear carrying area is enclosed by folding armour plates round the sides. The open top may be covered by a canvas cover.

Protected troop carrier (Rhino)
This version has a fully armoured body with a two-person front cab and protection for 10 personnel in the rear. Rear access is by two outward-opening armoured doors and 13 firing ports are provided on the sides and rear. Armoured glass windows and vision ports are provided. The rear passengers normally face inwards.

Valkiri rocket launcher
The SAMIL 20 Mark 1 was originally used for the vehicle component of the production version of the Valkiri multiple artillery rocket system. The SAMIL 20 can be used as the launcher vehicle as well as the meteorological vehicle associated with the system (early versions of the Valkiri system used Unimog light trucks). When in use as the launch vehicle the SAMIL 20 carries 24 launching tubes and when covered with a canvas tilt it is virtually identical to the standard SAMIL 20 truck. Full details of the Valkiri system can be found in *Jane's Armour and Artillery 1999-2000*.

Light repair workshop
On this version of the SAMIL 20 the rear area is occupied by a cabin constructed from glass fibre panels reinforced by steel strips and brackets. The rear and sides are flaps that fold upwards for access to the body interior and when raised act as partial weather protection. The interior contains racks for repair equipment.

The Hunter LSV is a radical conversion of the SAMIL 20 2,000 kg truck, 3,500 of which remain in South African National Defence Force service (Patrick Allen)   1431529

A fully refurbished SAMIL 20 Mark 1 (4 × 4) truck. Surplus SANDF SAMIL trucks are now available through a number of outlets including ARMSCOR's Defence Matériel Disposal (DMD) division (Patrick Allen)   1037586

Container body carrier
When the SAMIL 20 is used as a container body carrier, the container is fixed directly on to the chassis frame and can then carry a payload of up to 2,000 kg. The containers may also be used as mobile offices, control or command posts, radio and other equipment.

OTT Hunter Light Strike Vehicle (LSV)
At South Africa Aerospace and Defence 2010, OTT (Offroad Truck and Trailer) technologies unveiled the Hunter Light Strike Vehicle (LSV), this based on surplus remanufactured SAMIL 20 chassis.

The Hunter LSV has a GVW of 7,700 kg and a payload of 2,000 kg. Armament depends on customer requirement but would typically include a heavy weapon system such as a ring-mounted 12.7 mm (.50 calibre) or 14.5 mm heavy machine gun, or a 40 mm automatic grenade launcher, backed up with up to three pintle-mounted 5.56 mm or 7.62 mm light machine guns. Pods of smoke grenade launchers can also be installed at the front of the vehicle.

Standard equipment includes roll-over protection, bush guards at the front of the vehicle, a wire cutter and 40-litre water containers. As well as the LSV version, the vehicle can be configured for a number of specialised roles, such as a command post or, with suitable modification, a weapons carrier which could include a turntable-mounted 60 mm mortar at the rear.

A batch of Hunter LSVs are understood to have been delivered to an undisclosed export customer late-2010.

Specifications
SAMIL 20 Mark 2
Cab seating: 1 + 1
Configuration: 4 × 4
Weight:
   (laden) 7,700 kg
   (chassis-cab) 4,830 kg
   (payload) 2,870 kg
   (front axle rated load) 3,700 kg
   (rear axle rated load) 4,000 kg
   (towed load) 1,360 kg
Length: (chassis-cab) 5.692 m
Width: 2.438 m
Height: (highest point; air-cleaner) 2.82 m
Ground clearance: 470 mm
Track: (front and rear) 1.852 m
Wheelbase: 2.9 m
Angle of approach/departure: 40/45°
Max speed: (road) 97 km/h
Range: 800 km
Fuel capacity: 200 litres
Max gradient: (GVW) 70%
Fording: 1.2 m at 5 km/h
Engine: ADE 352N 5.675-litre 6-cylinder in-line water-cooled 4-stroke direct injection diesel developing 106 hp (79 kW) at 2,800 rpm and 375 N.m torque at 1,500 rpm
Gearbox: ZF S6-35/2 manual with 5 forward and 1 reverse gears
Transfer box: ZF Z65 2-speed, pneumatic
Clutch: single dry plate
Steering: ZF ball and nut, power-assisted
Turning radius: 7.275 m
Suspension:
   (front) semi-elliptic leaf springs with telescopic shock-absorbers
   (rear) semi-elliptic leaf springs with telescopic shock-absorbers and anti-roll bar
Tyres: 14.5 × 20PR 12-ply

Brakes: dual circuit, air assisted hydraulic with spring brakes on rear axle and engine-mounted exhaust retarder
Electrical system: 24 V
Batteries: 2 × 12 V, 118 Ah

Status
In service with South African National Defence Forces and Mozambique. Surplus SANDF vehicles are now available.

Contractor
TruckMakers (Pty) Ltd
(This concern is no longer trading.)

Enquiries to
Armscor (for ex-SANDF stock disposal)
BAE Systems Land Systems OMC (spares and support)

Fully refurbished SAMIL 50 Mark 1 (4 × 4) truck (Patrick Allen)   1110954

SAMIL 50 (4 × 4) 5,000 kg truck

Description
The SAMIL 50 (4 × 4) 5,000 kg truck is based on the Magirus (now IVECO) 192D12AL but with a reinforced (deeper) chassis and suspension. Two models were produced, the SAMIL 50 Mk 1 and SAMIL 50 Mk 2. Development of the SAMIL 50 Mk 2 began in 1981 with the first examples being shown in 1985. The Mk 2 was developed from the earlier Mk 1 and retains its general configuration. However the basic specification was altered with the most significant alteration being the politically-driven inclusion of a South African produced ADE (Atlantis Diesel Engines) 409N diesel engine weighing 675 kg. The new engine is housed under an enlarged bonnet in front of a locally produced cab. The front axle was upgraded for increased durability and the transmission was modified accordingly. Other changes included the two 200 litre fuel tanks manufactured using high-density polyethylene and the associated piping made from a nylon-based material. These changes mean the local content of the vehicle totalled over 90 per cent.

The SAMIL 50 Mark 2 retains the personnel and general cargo body of the SAMIL Mark 1, with removable bench seating for 32 personnel. It can also be readily converted to carry containers/shelters.

SAMIL trucks were originally manufactured by TruckMakers (Pty) Ltd. The company is no longer trading and in-service support of the SAMIL range of trucks is now carried out by BAE Systems Land Systems South Africa OMC, formerly Alvis South Africa (Pty) Limited, formerly Vickers OMC (Pty) Limited.

The SANDF has just over 5,000 SAMIL 50s to replace and these will be replaced under Project Vistula, an overview of which can be found elsewhere in this entry

Quantities of surplus SANDF SAMIL 50 trucks have recently started to become available and a number of manufacturers offer these for sale to military or commercial customers, and in a variety of conditions including fully refurbished.

Project Vistula
As of early-2009 ARMSCOR, the South African Defence Acquisition Agency, was set to relaunch Project Vistula, the project to acquire a new family of tactical logistic vehicles after nearly three and a half years delay over allegations of impropriety. The new Request for Offers (RfO) for Project Vistula was expected sometime around November 2009, albeit for a modified acquisition that included 5,000 kg payload (4 × 4) trucks. The preferred bidder was likely to be announced by mid-2010, with (following contract award) deliveries under various orders running from 2012 to 2017. Further slippage occurred and an RFO is now expected in mid 2011, with an equivalent knock-on to other dates within the previous acquisition timeline.

SAMIL 50 MK 1 (4 × 4) truck (Ian C Young)   1391024

The original Vistula requirement was for a fleet of 946 (6 × 6) and 796 (8 × 8) trucks (over 1,000 of which were to be fitted with a DROPS/PLS hooklift system) to replace the SAMIL 100 10,000 kg (6 × 6) fleet. Trucks acquired under the revised procurement will now replace the SAMIL 100 (6 × 6) and SAMIL 50 (4 × 4) truck fleets (plus any remaining SAKOM/SAMAG trucks), all of which began entering service in the 1970s. The SAMIL 20 (4 × 4) fleet will be replaced under a separate programme. The revised Vistula requirement is expected to call for approximately 1,800 (4 × 4), 400 (6 × 6) and 2,600 (8 × 8) trucks.

Around 15,500 SAMILs were originally delivered and current fleets number approximately just under 3,000 SAMIL 100s, just over 5,000 SAMIL 50s and approximately 3,500 SAMIL 20s. By the end of production in 1992, no fewer than 16,864 SAMIL, SACOM and SAMAG vehicles had been built by the now defunct Truckmakers and delivered to the SANDF.

Variants
Recovery Vehicle
Full details of this vehicle can be found in the Recovery vehicles section.

Protected transport
The is the same vehicle as the basic SAMIL 50 but provided with a mine-protected armoured cab and engine cover; only small numbers (10-20) were produced. An armoured ambulance was developed but this did not enter production.

Telecommunications workshop
This version has a glass fibre superstructure to house work tables and drawers for telecommunications repair requirements. Small windows are provided in the sides with burglar proofing bonded to the superstructure. An air conditioner is standard. Access to the rear door is by a ladder extending to the roof.

Battery charging vehicle
This has a box-type body with side and rear panels hinging upwards if required. Inside there are two sets of battery charging equipment each capable of charging 18 batteries arranged on a bench.

Mobile welding workshop
This follows the same general lines as the battery charging vehicle but encloses a fully equipped welding workshop.

Water tanker
The superstructure of this variant consists of a 4,500 litre water tank fitted with a tropical roof. There are five taps each side of the tank from which water can be drawn. At the rear is a single draw-off point and a spray bar for sprinkling. Two sections of armoured hose 75 mm in diameter and 4 m long are stored in boxes alongside the tank. These hoses can be quickly coupled to the rear draw-off point. A water pump capable of passing 500 litres/min for filling or disposal is driven by a power take-off from the gearbox.

Fuel tanker
This variant has an oval-section mild-steel fuel tanker body with a capacity of 5,000 litres. The tank has a tropical roof cover and three manholes on the top. A 400 litres/min fuel pump is provided and a meter and control platform is situated at the tank rear. Four delivery lines for can filling are provided.

Mobile pantry
On this SAMIL 50 variant the superstructure box body is formed from rigid sandwich sections of foamed polyurethane contained in seamless glass fibre skins with reinforcing members. Internally there are two compartments, with the forward section refrigerated and the rear for the stowage of canned and non-perishable goods. Each section has shelves. The front section is equipped with stainless steel trays while the rear section is equipped with bins and baskets for handling and stowage purposes. The temperature can be controlled between −20 and +20°C in the front compartment.

Container shower

The SAMIL 50 can carry a specially developed 4.5 m container shower for use by personnel in field locations. Showers can be provided for eight personnel at one time with each of the shower heads being individually operated. The container is mounted on twist-locks and equipped with three liquid gas draw-off water heaters, a petrol engine driven self-priming pumping plant and liquid draw-off gas cylinders mounted outside the front panel. The water-heating compartment is provided with fire protection using an automatic roof-mounted fire extinguisher. Internal lighting is provided by a 12 V battery charged by the pump engine. The shower container is non-stackable and can only be lifted by a forklift.

Specifications

SAMIL 50
Cab seating: 1 + 1
Configuration: 4 × 4
Weight:
    (laden) 12,400 kg
    (chassis-cab) 6,600 kg
    (body and payload allowance; max) 8,500 kg
    (GVW; max) 15,000 kg
    (towed load) 6,000 kg
Length: 7.78 m
Width: 2.5 m
Height: 2.955 m
Ground clearance: 355 mm
Track:
    (front) 1.985 m
    (rear) 2.03 m
Wheelbase: 4.9 m
Angle of approach/departure: 32/37°
Max speed: 85 km/h
Range: 1,000 km
Fuel capacity: 400 litres (200 + 200 litres)
Max gradient: 60%
Fording: 1.2 m
Engine: ADE 409N 9.51-litre 5-cylinder in-line water-cooled direct injection 4-stroke diesel developing 165 hp (123 kW) at 2,200 rpm and 674 N.m torque at 1,300 rpm
Gearbox: ZF S6-65 manual, 6 forward and 1 reverse gears
Transfer box: ZF Z65 2-speed
Clutch: single dry plate
Steering: ZF 8065 ball and nut, power assisted
Turning radius: 11.5 m
Suspension: semi-elliptic leaf springs and hydraulic telescopic shock-absorbers, anti-roll bar on rear axle
Tyres: 14.00 × 20 PR 18-ply
Brakes: dual circuit, air with spring brakes on rear axle plus exhaust retarder
Electrical system: 24 V
Batteries: 2 × 12 V, 118 Ah

Status

In service with South African National Defence Force (SANDF), replacement pending. Surplus SANDF SAMIL trucks are believed to have been supplied to the Angola, Democratic Republic of Congo, Ghana, Jordan (small quantity), Mozambique, Namibia, possibly Sudan, Tanzania, Zambia (possibly) and Zimbabwe.

Contractor

TruckMakers (Pty) Ltd
(This concern is no longer trading.)

Enquiries to

ARMSCOR (for ex-SANDF stock disposal)
BAE Systems Land Systems OMC (spares and support)

SAMIL 100 (6 × 6) 10,000 kg trucks

Description

The SAMIL 100 (6 × 6) 10,000 kg truck is based on the Magirus (now IVECO) 210-32 ANWM with some reinforcement to the chassis and suspension. It shares some components with the smaller SAMIL 50, the cab being one example. Unlike the SAMIL 20 and SAMIL 50, no ADE-powered Mk 2 model entered production; a prototype was produced.

The basic SAMIL 100 is a cargo truck. The rear body is constructed of pressed steel to form a sturdy unit and fixed to the chassis by spring-loaded mountings for flexibility in off-road conditions. The floor is of 5 mm flat sheet metal with supporting cross members fitted with drop-out twist locks to transport containers (one 6 m, two 3 m or four 1.5 m). The drop sides and tailgate are bottom-hinged to fold down and are detachable. On the mine-protected versions, expanded metal extensions are side-hinged to the support pillar and swing open by removing two pins either side or can be detached by removing all four pins. All support pillars can fold down and are detachable. A 6 t/m elephant trunk-type crane is mounted between the driver's cab and rear body for cargo handling. This crane is fully power-controlled through an arc of 360° and is capable of lifting 1,200 kg at a jib length of 5 m.

A fully refurbished SANDF surplus SAMIL 100 (6 × 6) 10,000 kg truck (Patrick Allen)   1037581

SAMIL trucks were originally manufactured by TruckMakers (Pty) Ltd. The company is no longer trading and in-service support of the SAMIL range of trucks is now carried out by BAE Systems Land Systems South Africa OMV, formerly Alvis South Africa (Pty) Limited, formerly Vickers OMC (Pty) Limited.

There are approximately just under 3,000 SAMIL 100s remaining in SANDF service, and these will be replaced under Project Vistula, full details of which can be found elsewhere in this entry.

Quantities of surplus SANDF SAMIL 100 trucks have recently started to become available and a number of manufacturers offer these for sale to military or commercial customers, and in a variety of conditions including fully refurbished.

Project Vistula

As of early-2009 ARMSCOR, the South African Defence Acquisition Agency, was set to relaunch Project Vistula, the project to acquire a new family of tactical logistic vehicles after nearly three and a half years delay over allegations of impropriety. The new Request for Offers (RfO) for Project Vistula was expected sometime around November 2009, albeit for a modified acquisition that included 5,000 kg payload (4 × 4) trucks. The preferred bidder was likely to be announced by mid-2010, with (following contract award) deliveries under various orders running from 2012 to 2017. Further slippage occurred and an RFO is now expected in mid 2011, with an equivalent knock-on to other dates within the previous acquisition timeline.

The original Vistula requirement was for a fleet of 946 (6 × 6) and 796 (8 × 8) trucks (over 1,000 of which were to be fitted with a DROPS/PLS hooklift system) to replace the SAMIL 100 10,000 kg (6 × 6) fleet. Trucks acquired under the revised procurement will now replace the SAMIL 100 (6 × 6) and SAMIL 50 (4 × 4) truck fleets (plus any remaining SAKOM/SAMAG trucks), all of which began entering service in the 1970s. The SAMIL 20 (4 × 4) fleet will be replaced under a separate programme. The revised Vistula requirement is expected to call for approximately 1,800 (4 × 4), 400 (6 × 6) and 2,600 (8 × 8) trucks.

Around 15,500 SAMILs were originally delivered and current fleets number approximately just under 3,000 SAMIL 100s, just over 5,000 SAMIL 50s and approximately 3,500 SAMIL 20s. By the end of production in 1992, no fewer than 16,864 SAMIL, SACOM and SAMAG vehicles had been built by the now defunct Truckmakers and delivered to the SANDF.

Variants

Protected transport

This is the same vehicle as the basic SAMIL 100 but is fitted with a mine-protected armoured cab and engine cover.

SAMIL 100 (6 × 6) 10,000 kg truck configured as Valkiri MKII multiple artillery rocket system (MARS) (ARMSCOR)   0500906

Armoured personnel carrier

This version of the SAMIL 100 has a fully mine-protected cab and engine cover and the rear is fully enclosed in an armoured hull. Seating is provided internally and there are five bullet-resistant vision windows on each side.

Tipper

This is a conventional tipper truck with a 7.5 m³ capacity body and dual-tire rear wheels.

Water tanker

This follows the same general lines as the SAMIL 50 water tanker but the tank capacity on the SAMIL 100 is 9,100 litres. A water pump with a rate of 910 litres/min is provided. The oval-section stainless steel tank has a manhole on the top and internal baffles. Spray devices are fitted at the rear and all controls are situated between the cab and the tank.

Fuel tanker

The tank for this variant is subdivided into two baffled compartments and has a capacity of 13,000 litres. Each compartment has its own sump drain and manhole on the top. A 64 mm diameter hose is used to fill containers directly from the tank and four smaller hoses can be used to fill cans. All controls are on the left-hand side of the tank.

Artillery tractor

Developed to tow the 155 mm G5 howitzer, the SAMIL 100 artillery tractor has a superstructure consisting of a crew compartment, cargo drop side body, elephant trunk-type crane and a 10,000 kg winch. The crew compartment provides seating for seven crew members and storage space for their personal equipment. A 150 litre hydraulic oil tank is situated under the rearward-facing seats and a 200 litre water tank is located under the forward-facing seats. An observation hatch is fitted centrally in the roof with provision for mounting a machine gun. The cargo drop-side body, immediately behind the crew compartment, consists of built-in storage for 60 propellant charges and winching equipment. On top of these compartments storage is provided for 15 projectile pallets, each weighing 189 kg. A canvas cover is provided to cover the cargo body and ground pegs are supplied to allow the cover to be used as a ground shelter. A 360° traverse crane is mounted behind the rear cargo area with an 800 kg lift at a jib length of 3.5 m. It is used mainly to handle the projectile pallets. The hydraulic drag winch located at the rear between the longitudinal chassis members has a 10,000 kg capacity on the first layer with the cable routed front or rear.

SANDF SAMIL 100 (6 × 6) 10,000 kg truck (Patrick Allen) 1110610

SANDF SAMIL 100 (6 × 6) 10,000 kg bridging truck with armoured cab. This example is being refurbished by BAE Systems Land Systems South Africa OMC (Patrick Allen) 1111051

Canteen

The canteen box body has a load capability of 8,500 kg and consists of front and rear compartments manufactured from glass fibre and polyurethane sandwich-constructed panels. A cooling unit is provided on the front panel of the front compartment which is used for storing cooled products. The rear compartment is fitted with a food warmer, microwave oven, till, mini-safe, counter, shelves, potato chip dispenser, bulk storage compartment, roof lights, ventilation fans and a trickle charger. A service platform and a power plant are fitted and stored under the body.

Cargo panel body

Designed mainly for the transport of perishable products, the panel body has a maximum load of 9,700 kg. The body is manufactured from glass fibre and polyurethane sandwich-constructed panels. The interior is equipped with lashing eyes and roof lights. There are two rear doors and one side door.

Mobile beer cooler

This box-bodied variant of the basic SAMIL 100 can carry 500 cases (4,140 litres) of cooled beer; each case holds 24 cans. The body is manufactured from glass fibre and polyurethane constructed panels. A cooling unit is fitted to the front panel. Roof lights and two rows of four racks each are fitted to the interior to hold the beer cases. A ladder and a platform are provided on the outside to assist in servicing the cooling unit.

Medical provisions carrier

A number of SAMIL 100 trucks have been converted to carry medical and associated provisions in a compartmented body with sides that fold up to provide shelter when the vehicle is at a medical location. More shelter can be provided by erecting wide screens and the mine-proof bonnet can accommodate a folding tent for the crew.

Recovery vehicles

The SAMIL 100 was also available in a recovery variant. Details of this and other SAMIL-based recovery vehicles can be found in the Recovery vehicles section.

Valkiri Mk II

The SAMIL 100 chassis was adapted to act as a carrier for a 40-round version of the Valkiri Mk II 127 mm multiple artillery rocket system (MARS), also known as Bateleur. The chassis used for this version has its front axle capacity increased from 6,500 to 7,500 kg and extra fuel tanks are provided. Combat weight of the system is 21,500 kg and length travelling is 8.53 m. A mine-proof cab is provided for the five-personnel crew. Full details of this system can be found in *Jane's Armour and Artillery*.

Zumlac

The SAMIL 100 chassis with an armoured mine-proof cab has been adapted to carry the Zumlac 23 mm air defence gun system.

Specifications

SAMIL 100 truck
(base model)
Cab seating: 1 + 1
Configuration: 6 × 6
Weight
  (GVW, max) 26,500 kg
  (chassis-cab) 8,940 kg
  (payload and body, max) 17,560 kg
  (towed load) 14,000 kg
Length: 10.943 m
Width: 2.5 m
Height: 3.02 m
Ground clearance: (front axle) 355 mm
Track: (front) 2.002 m
Wheelbase: 5.25 + 1.38 m
Angle of approach/departure: 30/30°
Max speed: (road) 87 km/h
Range: 800 km
Fuel capacity: 400 litres
Max gradient: (GVW) 50%
Fording: 1.2 m at 5 km/h
Engine: Deutz F10L413F 15.95-litre V10 air-cooled diesel developing 268 hp (200 kW) at 2,500 rpm and 1,020 N.m torque at 1,500 rpm
Gearbox: ZF S6-90 manual, 6 forward and 1 reverse gears
Transfer box: ZF Z90 2-speed
Clutch: single dry plate
Steering: ZF 8043 power-assisted, ball and nut
Turning radius: 11.9 m
Suspension: leaf springs and telescopic hydraulic shock-absorbers
Tyres: 14.00 × 20 16-ply
Brakes: dual-circuit air, drums all round; supplementary engine exhaust brake
Electrical system: 24 V
Batteries: 2 × 12 V, 120 Ah

Status

In service with the South African National Defence Force (SANDF). Surplus SAMIL trucks are understood to have been supplied to Angola, Democratic Republic of Congo (DRC), Ghana, Jordan (small number), Mozambique, Namibia, Sudan (possibly), Zambia (possibly), Zimbabwe and some other undisclosed Middle Eastern countries.

Contractor
TruckMakers (Pty) Ltd
(This concern is no longer trading.)

Enquiries to
ARMSCOR (surplus ex-SANDF for disposal)
Alvis South Africa (Pty) Limited (spares and support)

South African Aljaba applications

Description
Following the adoption by the South African National Defence Force
(SANDF) of the Kynos Aljaba (8 × 8) truck tractor under the name Cavallo,
the Kynos Aljaba chassis was adapted for several other applications with
the SANDF, details of which can be found elsewhere in this entry. Full
details of the Kynos Aljaba can be found in the Heavy equipment
transporters section. All South African vehicles have ballistic and mine-
protected cabs.

It was announced in November 2003 that Group SPA (Servicios Y
Proyectos Avanzados) had acquired the assets, technology and contracts
of Kynos S.A.

Cavallo truck tractor
Full details can be found in the Heavy equipment transporter section.

Kameelperd gunnery control vehicle
The Kameelperd (Giraffe) gunnery control vehicle acts as a battery
command post for self- propelled air defence gun batteries. It carries a 6 m
ISO standard sub-frame on which is mounted a 60 kW range surveillance
radar and its 13 m extending antenna arm. The Kameelperd is 10.64 m
long and has a wheelbase of 1.524 m + 5 m + 1.524 m.

Zebra maintenance and repair vehicle
The Zebra is a front line maintenance and repair vehicle for mobile forces
and carries three ISO modules and a 28,000 kg/m folding crane with a
reach of 8.2 m. One of the modules is a 3 m ISO container containing
workshop tools. One of the two 1.5 m ISO modules containers a
compressor, generator, welding set, steam washer and other equipment.
The third module carries special tools and spares. The Zebra is 11.84 m
long and has a wheelbase of 1.524 m + 5.8 m + 1.524 m.

The Skimmel is intended to recover heavy armoured vehicles
(Shaun C Connors)   1296218

*Following the adoption by the South African National Defence Force
(SANDF) of the Kynos Aljaba (8 × 8) truck tractor under the name Cavallo
(shown), the Kynos Aljaba chassis was adapted for several other
applications with the SANDF (Shaun C Connors)*   1296219

The Zebra is a front line maintenance and repair vehicle for mobile forces
(Shaun C Connors)   1296220

Bridgelayer
This variant is as yet unnamed, has yet to appear in prototype form and
most probably will not. The bridge involved is the LEGUAN MLC 70 26 or
42 m bridge. The vehicle has a wheelbase of 1.524 m + 5 m + 1.524 m and
is 13.297 m long when carrying a bridge.

Skimmel heavy recovery vehicle
Intended to recover heavy armoured vehicles, the Skimmel is provided
with a radial tow arm system with a max lift capacity of 188 kN m (12,000
kgf.m) with a reach from 750 mm to 1.6 m above normal ground level.
Maximum casualty vehicle mass is 48,000 kg. Also carried is a 196 kN
(20,000 kgf) capacity main winch, a 500 kg auxiliary winch and a 74.5 kN.m
(7,600 kgf.m) folding crane with a reach of 4 m. The Skimmel is 10.132 m
long and has a wheelbase of 1.524 m + 5 m + 1.524 m.

Ammunition and cargo carrier
Produced in prototype form in late 1996 this ammunition and cargo carrier
was developed for the front line support of 155 mm G5 and G6 artillery
batteries, carrying ammunition and other supplies in up to four 1.5 m ISO
standard containers on a flat bed cargo area. Also carried is a 209 kN.m
(21,135 kgf.m) folding crane with a maximum reach of 9.25 m. The vehicle
is 11.84 m long and has a wheelbase of 1.524 m + 5.8 m + 1.524 m.

Status
Production as required. In service with South African National Defence
Force (SANDF) (72).

Contractor
FAF Engineering

Spain

Santana S-2000 Militar (4 × 4) light truck

Description
The first forward control vehicle developed by Metalurgica de Santa Ana
(to become known as Santana) was the Model 1300, first produced in
1967 in both petrol- and diesel-engined versions. From this evolved the
S-2000, produced in both military and civil versions. The Model Militar has
a payload of 2,000 kg and was produced in several forms for military use.

In its basic form as a troop carrier, the S-2000 has a forward control cab
for the driver and passenger and seating for up to 12 personnel in the rear.
In the rear area the troops are seated along two outward-facing bench
seats down the centre line of the body. The body sides and tailgate can be
quickly folded down for easy access and the rear area can be covered by a
non-flammable canvas tilt carried on bows. The cab roof may have a hatch
and provision for a light machine gun mounting.

The chassis has a stair-type construction with two parallel side-
members and seven cross-members welded into position. All the chassis
members are rectangular in cross-section and are painted once finished; if
required a special galvanised finish is applied for use in a saline
environment. A six-cylinder 3.5-litre petrol engine was standard fit, but a
diesel engine could be fitted as an option.

Several versions of the S-2000 exist and the model can be converted for
a number of roles.

In 1991 Suzuki became the main shareholder of the renamed Santana-
Motor S.A. In 1995 the regional government of Andalicia took ownership of
Santana-Motor S.A.

Variants

Command post
This version uses a van body with sliding rear windows and wide rear
doors with a concealed rear step. The body is made from duraluminium
sheet with insulating panels and fibre panels for the interior. The normal

Basic troop-carrying version of S-2000 (4 × 4) light truck (Santana) 0511823

command interior includes a table, two swivelling seats, document cabinet, lamps, two portable fans and a fire extinguisher. Electrical equipment can be powered by a 42 or 90 A alternator or two auxiliary batteries. An office version was produced.

Communications version
This version also uses a van body but can contain various radio communication installations.

Mobile workshop
On this version the items of workshop equipment are contained in a series of lockers situated each side of the vehicle rear. The centre area of the rear body is used for equipment stowage and there are lighting masts carried over the lockers. Equipment provided includes a generating set powered from a power take-off and capable of delivering 15 kW, compressor, welding equipment and electrical, pneumatic and manual tools. One side of the body rear folds down to form a workbench, complete with a vice. A 500 kg crane is also supplied.

Tanker
This version has a rear-mounted tank body that can be used to carry 1,600 litres of fuel or water. The tank is 2.2 m long and 800 mm high and the equipment will vary according to the liquid carried.

Generating set
This carries a 15 kW generator powered from a power take-off on the vehicle. This equipment is used mainly for lighting purposes and carries up to four strings of lamps or 1,000 W halogen lamps together with all the necessary leads and components.

Container carrier
This version is used for the carriage of S-250 and other container/shelters.
A fire tender was also produced.

Specifications
Santana S-2000 Militar light truck
Cab seating: 1 + 1 (up to 12 in rear)
Configuration: 4 × 4
Weight:
  (unladen) 2,360 kg
  (laden) 4,360 kg
  (max load) 2,000 kg
Length: 4.949 m
Width: 1.96 m
Height: 2.235 m
Ground clearance: 270 mm
Track:
  (front) 1.461 m
  (rear) 1.486 m

Flatbed version of S-2000 (4 × 4) light truck carrying S-250 container/shelter (Santana) 0511824

Wheelbase: 2.565 m
Angle of approach/departure: 37°/34°
Fuel capacity: 157 litres
Engine: 3.429 litre 6-cylinder in-line water-cooled petrol developing 100 hp (73.5 kW) at 4,000 rpm
Gearbox: manual with 4 forward and 1 reverse gears
Clutch: diaphragm and disc, hydraulic
Transfer box: 2-speed
Steering: worm and recirculating ball with power-assistance
Turning radius: 6.75 m
Suspension: semi-elliptic underslung springs with double-acting shock-absorbers
Tyres: 9.00 × 16
Brakes: hydraulic drum, front and rear, dual circuit
Electrical system: 24 V
Batteries:
  (petrol) 2 × 12 V, 57 Ah
  (diesel) 2 × 12 V, 120 Ah
Alternator: 35 A (50 or 90 A optional)

Status
Production complete. In service with the Spanish armed forces (numbers reducing) and some other undisclosed nations.

Contractor
Santana-Motor S.A.

URO M3 (MT) and MA3 (MAT) (4 × 4) trucks

Development
As a result of trials held between April and late June 1983, a new 2,000 kg nominal payload (4 × 4) tactical truck was introduced to the Spanish armed forces. The only company to submit a vehicle for the competition was URO Vehiculos Especiales S.A., formed in 1981. This company produced a truck prototype and a 10 vehicle preproduction series. The first order for the Spanish Army was placed in October 1984, with further orders following in 1990 and 1997. Since 1984 URO has been the sole supplier of trucks in this weight class to the Spanish armed forces and the type has been in uninterrupted production since that date. Approaching 1,000 vehicles had been delivered by July 2002. Commercial and military production continues.

The initial model delivered to the Spanish armed forces was the 115 PM between 1984 and 1989, this being fitted with a 115 hp Perkins Military diesel engine. The model MT-149 AT was delivered between 1990 and 1995, deliveries of the model MAT-18.16 commencing in 1997; the specifications table provides data for this model. The most recent production models are fitted with IVECO turbocharged diesel engines meeting EURO 3 emissions requirements, following the introduction of which some model designation changes occurred. The former MT range became the M3, and the former MAT range (A denoting automatic transmission) became the MA3.

In addition to Spanish armed forces other users of the URO range of trucks include Headquarters NATO EUROCORPS (42), Angola (150 model F3-24.14 - Police), Cameroon (75 models MT 15.14 and MT 18.14), Dominican Republic (100+ models MT 15.14, MT 18.14 and MT 18.16) and Morocco (100 model 18.14 plus 250 model M3-21.14, 2007-2009), with all these deliveries having been made since 1996. Uruguay received 100 examples of an earlier model in 1994.

The URO range has been continually developed since production commenced in 1984 and while the base-design principles have remained constant, there have been a number of minor componentry and designation changes. The current range of URO military models which are each available in a variety of wheel/tyre, wheelbase and chassis length configuration is as follows:
- M3-21.14, 210 hp, GVW 14,000 kg
- M3-21.16, 210 hp, GVW 16,000 kg
- M3-24.14, 240 hp, GVW 14,000 kg (the specifications table provides data for this model)
- M3-27.14, 270 hp, GVW 14,000 kg
- M3-28.18, 275 hp, GVW 18,000 kg (EU legislative version of M3-28.20)
- M3-28.20, 275 hp, GVW 20,000 kg

  F (F3) would denote a civil version.

Description
URO M3 and MA3 series trucks are built on a weldable steel C-section chassis with four cross members designed to combine strength and rotational flexibility. The chassis is arranged to allow fixtures such as spring brackets to be bolted on and removed as required, these and other components being of modular design. Towing hooks and other equipment including self-recovery winches can be mounted front and rear. The chassis is attached to the engine and cab at only three points to allow maximum chassis torsion.

The two- or three-seat all-metal forward control cab can be tilted forward to an angle of 48° or 56° for engine and gearbox access. Day-to-day maintenance is done via a liftable front cover. The cab structure uses steel

URO MAT-23.14 5,000 kg payload (4 × 4) tactical truck demonstrating axle articulation (URO) 0122731

URO M3-24.14 14,000 kg GVW (4 × 4) truck (Shaun C Connors) 1120461

tube for the frame and GRP panels are fitted for thermal and acoustic insulation. Crew cabs for six or nine passengers are available, as is air conditioning. A soft-top, 'torpedo' style cab is a further option.

Motive power for current models is provided by a EURO 3 emissions compliant IVECO 5.9-litre six-cylinder diesel engine developing up to 275 hp, dependant on model. A manual gearbox is standard but an automatic option is available, and for certain specialised applications a Clark Powershift gearbox and torque converter are optional. Models previously designated MT are usually fitted with an IVECO manual gearbox with six or nine forward and one reverse gears, models previously designated MAT are fitted with an Allison four-speed automatic gearbox and torque converter. The current manual gearbox option is nine-speed IVECO unit. A URO-designed UR-50 two-speed transfer box with lockable centre differential remains standard. A power take off (PTO) may be fitted. The U-40 two-speed transfer box featuring disengageable front-wheel drive may be fitted. Additional PTO points are an option, as are crawler gears allowing for speeds down to 75 m/hr, or 310 m/h at 1,000 rpm. With additional crawler gears, increasing gear options to 24 forward and four reverse, up to 150,000 kg can be moved on tarmac, up to 900,000 kg on rails.

Conventional beam-type axles and leaf spring suspension is employed, the URO-designed axles being of the double reduction, differential and wheel, type. Both axles are fitted with driver-controlled differential locks. Front axle suspension is by the combination of parabolic leaf springs and telescopic shock absorbers, an anti-roll bar being an option. Rear axle suspension is by semi-elliptic leaf springs, with a helper spring, plus an anti-roll bar. Telescopic shock-absorbers are an option. A wide variety of spring types and ratings are available.

Numerous tyre size options are available, and dual rear wheels may be fitted.

14,000 kg GVW models are available in a choice of four wheelbases, 3.2, 3.5, 3.8 and 4.5 m, and with a rear chassis overhang of 1.12 m as standard, 1.498 m optional. 18,000 kg GVW models are available in 3.6, 4, 4.5 and 5 m wheelbases, and with a rear chassis overhang 1.13 as standard, 2 m optional. A wide variety of body options are available, these including a conventional drop side body with optional tarpaulin and bows, water or fuel tankers, light recovery hampers, fire tenders, dump bodies, and numerous shelter-type bodies (fixed or demountable) for roles including ambulance (four-stretcher), radio communication or workshop. The chassis can also accept a snow plough or snow blower. A materials handling crane may be located between the cab and any rear body.

The URO is also produced commercially.

Specifications

Model	MT-18.16	M3-24.14
Cab seating:	1 + 1	1 + 1
Configuration:	4 × 4	4 × 4
Weight:		
(kerb, chassis-cab)	4,680 kg	4,750 kg
(max, front axle)	7,000 kg	7,000 kg
(max, rear axle)	9,750 kg	9,750 kg
(GVW)	16,000 kg	16,000 kg
(payload, nominal)	2,000 kg	2,000 kg
Length:		
(chassis, 3.2 m wheelbase)	5.959 m	5.630 m
(chassis, 4 m/4.5 m wheelbase)	7.159 m	6.930 m
Width:	2.271 m	2.020 m
Height: (cab)	2.66 m	2.76 m
Ground clearance:	384 mm	384 mm
Track:	1.583 m	1.583 m
Wheelbase	3.2 m, 3.5 m, 3.8 m or 4 m	3.2 m, 3.5 m, 3.8 m or 4.5 m
Max speed:	100 km/h	100 km/h
Range: (road)	up to 550 km	up to 550 km
Fuel capacity:	130 or 200 litres	130 or 200 litres
Angle of approach/departure:	44°/60°	44°/60°
Gradient:	100%	100%
Side slope:	40%	40%
Fording:	800 mm	800 mm
Engine:	IVECO 8060.45B 5.861-litre 6-cylinder in-line water-cooled turbocharged and intercooled diesel developing 177 hp (132 kW)	IVECO 6-cylinder in-line water-cooled turbocharged and intercooled diesel developing 177 hp (132 kW)
Gearbox:		
(manual)	IVECO 2870.9 manual with 9 forward and 1 reverse gears	IVECO manual with 9 forward and 1 reverse gears
(automatic option)	Allison automatic with 4 forward and 1 reverse gears, plus torque converter	Allison automatic with 4 forward and 1 reverse gears, plus torque converter
Transfer box:	URO U-50, 2-speed	URO U-50, 2-speed
Clutch:	single dry disc	single dry disc
Steering:	C-500 power-assisted	C-500 power-assisted
Turning radius:	8.2 to 9.85 m	8.2 to 9.85 m
Suspension:	leaf springs and telescopic shock-absorbers, front, leaf springs (plus helper) and anti-roll bar, rear	leaf springs and telescopic shock-absorbers, front, leaf springs (plus helper) and anti-roll bar, rear
Tyres:	10.00R 20 (other options)	13.00R 20 (other options)
Brakes:	dual circuit air, drums front and rear	dual circuit air, drums front and rear
Electrical system:	24 V	24 V
Batteries:	2 × 12 V, 110 Ah	2 × 12 V, 145 Ah
Alternator:	35 A	70 A

Status

Various models in production. In service with Headquarters NATO EUROCORPS (42) and the armed forces of Angola (150, Police), Cameroon (75 - 50 × MAT 15.14; 25 × MT 18.14), Dominican Republic (100+ including 40 × MT 15.14 and 27 × MT 18.16), Morocco (100 + 250)), Spain (approx. 1,000), Uruguay (100), and other undisclosed nations.

Contractor

URO Vehiculos Especiales SA

Pegaso 3045 to 7226 series of (4 × 4) cargo trucks

Development

This series of trucks began with the introduction of the Pegaso 3045 in the late 1960s, early 1970s. The Pegaso 3045 was powered by a Pegaso Leyland Comet diesel engine (Leyland of the UK were involved with this company at this time) developing either 125 or 135 hp. The Pegaso 3045G was a variant fitted with a six-cylinder DAF petrol engine developing 125 hp at 3,500 rpm.

The follow-on Pegaso 3046 truck series were developed primarily as export/commercial models and were a direct evolution of the earlier and visually similar Pegaso 3045, and by the early 1980s the 3046 series had superceded the earlier 3045 series in production. The first widely available 3046 model was the 3046/50 which had a nominal payload of 3,000 kg. This was replaced by the Pegaso 3046/10, with a nominal payload of 5,000 kg; this model was sold to Egypt. The first contract to export 2,650 Pegaso 3046/10 trucks to Egypt was signed in November 1980. In July 1981 a contract was signed for a further 5,000 trucks and a contract for another 4,000 trucks was subsequently awarded. More than 4,000 units were supplied to the Spanish Army and a further 1,000 units were delivered to Morocco, Peru and Somalia.

Evolution of the type continued to the Model 7217, production of which commenced in 1987 with 200 units delivered to the Spanish Armed Forces. The Model 7217 is fitted with a Pegaso 10.17-litre naturally aspirated diesel engine developing 170 hp at 2,100 rpm. The follow-on Model 7222 is powered by a IVECO-Pegaso 10.52-litre turbocharged diesel engine developing 210 hp at 2,100 rpm.

The latest model in this series is the Model 7226. This is effectively a complete current-generation EuroTrakker/Trakker driveline supplied by parent company IVECO, and on to which the Pegaso soft-top cab is fitted.

A similar series of 6 × 6 chassis was also produced. Full details of these can be found elsewhere in this section.

Pegaso, as ENASA (Empresa Nacional de Autocamiones), was absorbed into the IVECO Group in September 1990 to become IVECO Pegaso SA.

Description

The layout of all models in this series is essentially similar. The two-man cab is situated well forward over the engine and has a soft top which can be removed if required. The two-piece windscreen can fold forward over the short bonnet to reduce the vehicle height. In front of the bonnet a large steel frame provides protection for the radiator grille and headlamps which are set into the bodywork. At the rear, the normal load-carrying body is an open cargo/personnel area that can be used to carry 5,000 kg (Model 7217) or 6,000 kg (Model 7227) of stores on-road, 4,000 kg (Model 7217 and 7227) off-road, or 20 personnel on bench seats situated along each side. A canvas tilt can be fitted. A spare wheel is carried under the load area on the left-hand side; the corresponding area on the right is occupied by the fuel tank. On some versions the spare wheel is carried behind the cab.

Pegaso Model 7217 (4 × 4) 4,000 kg cargo truck of the Spanish Army in Kosovo (Richard Stickland)
0126588

Pegaso model 3046/10 (4 × 4) 4,000 kg cargo truck of the Peruvian Marines (Cesar Cruz Tantalean)
1156041

Optional equipment for these models has included: a metal roof for the cab, fording kit, power take-off on the gearbox and a 4,500 kg capacity front winch. Versions other than the cargo/personnel type include: a tanker, recovery vehicle with a swivelling crane, ambulance, communications post vehicle, mobile workshop, refrigerated cold storage vehicle and a command post. Various weapons can be fitted.

Specifications

Model 3046
(data for models 7217/7222 in square brackets where applicable)
Cab seating: 1 + 1 (20 in rear)
Configuration: 4 × 4
Weight:
   (laden, on road) 12,200 [13,250/13,800] kg
   (laden, off road) 10,200 [11,250/11,800] kg
   (unladen) 7,200 [7,250/7,800] kg
   (payload, on road) 5,000 kg [6,000 kg (Model 7222)]
   (payload, off road) 3,000 kg [4,000] kg
   (towed load, on road) 7,500 kg [n/avail]
   (towed load, off road) 4,500 kg
Length: 6.085 [7.1] m
Width:
   (cab) 2.4 m
   (over rear axle) 2.406 m
Height: (cab) 2.765 [2.755] m
Ground clearance: 340 [320] mm
Track: 1.96 m
Wheelbase: 3.7 [4.14] m
Angle of approach/departure: 49°/49° [49°/36°]
Max speed: 89 [90/100] km/h
Range: 900 km
Fuel capacity: 350 litres
Max gradient: 70%
Side slope: 30%
Engine: Pegaso Model 9100/42, 10.17-litre 6-cylinder in-line, 4-stroke diesel developing 170 hp (127 kW) at 2,100 rpm [Pegaso 10.17-litre 6-cylinder in-line, naturally aspirated, water-cooled, 4-stroke diesel developing 170 hp (127 kW) at 2,100 rpm and 632 N.m torque at 1,300 rpm/IVECO-Pegaso 10.52-litre 6-cylinder in-line turbocharged water-cooled 4-stroke diesel developing 210 hp (157 kW) at 2,100 rpm and 932 N.m torque at 1,300 rpm
Gearbox: Pegaso Model 8256.10 manual with 6 forward and 1 reverse gears [Pegaso synchronised with 6 forward and 1 reverse gears/Pegaso synchronised with 6 forward and 1 reverse gears]
Clutch: Model 8500.01 single dry disc
Transfer box: Pegaso pneumatic 2-speed [IVECO 2-speed]
Steering: block, servo-hydraulic
Turning radius: 9.5 [11.3] m
Suspension: semi-elliptic leaf springs and hydraulic shock-absorbers, front and rear
Tyres: 13.00 × 20 or 14.00 × 20
Brakes: dual circuit, air
Electrical system: 24 V
Batteries: 2 × 12 V, 110 Ah
Alternator: 840 W

Status

Production as required (Model 7226). Other models supplied to Egypt (approx. 10,500), Morocco, Peru, Somalia and the Spanish Armed Forces.

Contractor

IVECO Pegaso SA

Pegaso models 3050, 3055 and 7323 (6 × 6) 6,000 kg trucks

Development

Shortly after the introduction of the Pegaso 3045 series of (4 × 4) trucks in the late 1960s, early 1970s, the larger (6 × 6), 10,000 kg payload Pegaso 3050 truck was introduced. This was followed in the early 1980s by the enhanced Pegaso 3055, and in March 1982 it was announced that the Pegaso 3055 was to be the standard 6,000 kg off-road truck chassis for all three Spanish armed services.

The Pegaso 3055 was produced in the following versions: medium truck; medium fuel tanker; medium water tanker; heavy crane; medium tipper truck; firefighting vehicle; tractor; van body for workshops, stores, refrigerated bodies and so on. A tractor truck for use as a heavy equipment transporter was also produced. The type has also been used as an artillery tractor, and the base chassis acts as the resupply and mounting vehicle for the 14 Teruel artillery rocket launcher systems (full details of which can be found in *Jane's Armour and Artillery*) supplied to the Spanish Army.

The final production version in this series was the longer wheelbase Model 7323. The Model 7323 replaced the Model 3055 in production in 1987 (the prototype was completed in 1986) and during 1987 and 1988 more than 1,000 units were delivered to Morocco. The Model 7323 was produced as an artillery tractor, fuel or water tanker, recovery vehicle with a crane, mobile workshop, ambulance, firefighting vehicle, tipper and as a multiple rocket launcher carrier.

Pegaso Model 3050 (6 × 6) 6,000 kg truck of the Peruvian Marines
(Cesar Cruz Tantalean)   1156043

Other known users of models 3050, 3055 and 7323 are Peru and Somalia.
Pegaso, as ENASA (Empresa Nacional de Autocamiones), was absorbed into the IVECO Group in September 1990.

Description
The cab of the 6 × 6 models is the same as that used on the 4 × 4 models. It has a canvas hood as standard with an optional metal top. The cab has seating for the driver and one passenger and, if required, the hood can be removed and the windscreen folded forward over the short bonnet. The main load-carrying area is at the rear and on the standard cargo/personnel body there is bench seating for 30.

The original Model 3050 was powered by a 170 hp diesel engine. The follow-on Model 3055 could have either a 200 or 220 hp diesel engine, with the latter selected for use with the Spanish Armed Forces. The final model in this series, the Model 7323, is powered by a Pegaso 225 hp naturally aspirated diesel engine.

Optional extras for the series included: a hardtop cab, power take-off, run-flat tyres and a 4,500 or 6,000 kg capacity winch.

Specifications
Model 3055
(data in square brackets relates to the model 7323 where different)
Cab seating: 1 + 1 (up to 30 in rear)
Configuration: 6 × 6
Weight:
   (laden, on road) 19,000 [19,700] kg
   (laden, off road) 15,000 [15,700] kg
   (unladen) 9,000 [9,700] kg
   (payload, on road) 10,000 kg
   (payload, off-road) 6,000 kg
   (towed load, on road) 14,500 kg
   (towed load, off-road) 7,500 kg
Length:
   (chassis-cab) 6.956 [7.483] m
   (overall) 8.5 m
Width:
   (cab) 2.4 m
   (rear wheels) 2.406 m
Height: (cab) 2.71 [2.8] m
Ground clearance: 340 [320] mm
Track: 1.96 [1.93] m
Wheelbase: 3.245 m + 1.484 m [3.7 m + 1.484 m]
Angle of approach/departure: 49°/36°
Max speed: 80 [90] km/h
Range: 550 km
Fuel capacity: 350 litres [360 litres - 200, 400 and 560 litres optional]
Max gradient: 70% [60%]
Side slope: 30%

Pegaso Model 7323 (6 × 6) 6,000 kg truck of the Spanish Army in the former Yugoslavia (Shaun C Connors)   0536753

Fording: 1.3 m [1.9 m with preparation]
Engine: Pegaso model 9220/10 10.518-litre 6-cylinder in-line turbocharged water-cooled 4-stroke diesel developing 200 hp (149 kW) (220 hp (164 kW) optional) at 2,000 rpm and 803 N.m torque at 1,350 rpm [Pegaso 10.52-litre 6-cylinder naturally aspirated diesel developing 225 hp (168 kW) at 2,000 rpm]
Gearbox: Pegaso/ZF Model 8256.10.09 manual with 6 forward and 1 reverse gears [ZF with 6 forward and 1 reverse gears]
Transfer box: Pegaso [ZF] 2-speed
Clutch: Model 8500.01 single dry disc
Steering: recirculating ball, power-assisted
Turning radius: 10.5 [11.1] m
Suspension:
   (front) semi-elliptic leaf springs and telescopic shock-absorbers
   (rear) inverted semi-elliptic leaf springs
Tyres: 13.00 × 20 or 14.00 × 20
Brakes: dual circuit, air
Electrical system: 24 V
Batteries: 2 × 12 V, 105 Ah
Alternator: 840 [1,300] W

Status
Production complete. In service with Peruvian, Somalian and Spanish Armed Forces, and possibly others. Model 7323 in service with the Spanish and Moroccan Armed Forces, and possibly others.

Contractor
IVECO Pegaso SA

Sweden

Volvo 4140 series of (4 × 4) and (6 × 6) cross-country vehicles

Development
In the early 1960s, the Swedish Army Materiel Department drew up its requirements for a new generation of tactical vehicles for the 1970s and 1980s. In 1966, Volvo were awarded the development contract for the Class 1 and 2 vehicles in the 1,000 to 2,500 kg range and Saab-Scania the contract for the heavier Class 3 and 4 vehicles, subsequently known as the Scania SBA (4 × 4) and SBAT (6 × 6).

Primary requirements were: a high power-to-weight ratio; forward control cab; good angle of approach and departure; high ground clearance; tough suspension; chassis which could be adapted to accept a wide variety of bodies; commercial components to be used wherever possible; ease of repair and maintenance; low training requirement; and a minimum total service life cost.

During the development stage it was decided to increase the payload of the Volvo (4 × 4) model to 2,000 kg and the (6 × 6) model to 2,500 kg. An (8 × 8) version was developed to the prototype stage but was not placed in production.

Description
(4 × 4) 4140/4141 (or C303)
The first prototypes completed in 1966 were powered by a B-20 (94 hp) engine, which was subsequently replaced by the more powerful B-30 (145 hp) engine. First deliveries were made to the Swedish Army in 1974.

Two basic models were built, the 4140 cargo and the 4141 fully enclosed, or hardtop. Both have a two-door fully enclosed cab which can be split above the waist line. The cargo model has an all-steel rear cargo area with a drop tailgate, removable bows and a tarpaulin cover. The hardtop model has a fully enclosed steel rear body with an aluminium roof and a large door at the rear and a door in each side.

All-wheel drive is engaged by a press-button when in high range, and automatically when low range is selected. Both front and rear axles have

Volvo 4143 (6 × 6) armed with a light machine gun (Volvo)   0056315

Volvo 4140 series

Model	C303 hard top	C304 chassis and cab	C306 chassis and cab
Cab seating:	1 + 6	1 + 1	1 + 1
Configuration:	4 × 4	4 × 4	6 × 6
Weight:			
(unladen)	2,250 kg	1,940 kg	2,400 kg
(laden)	3,450 kg	3,900 kg	5,500 kg
Weight on front axle:			
(laden)	1,650 kg	1,800 kg	1,000 kg
Weight on rear axles:			
(laden)	1,800 kg	2,100 kg	1,800 kg
Max load:	1,200 kg	1,960 kg (incl body)	3,100 kg (incl body)
Towed load:	2,500 kg	2,500 kg	2,500 kg
Load area:	2.25 × 1.8 m	n/a	n/a
Length:	4.25 m	4.28 m	5.735 m
Width:	1.9 m	1.87 m	1.88 m
Height:			
(cab)	2.13 m	2.13 m	2.13 m
(load area)	830 mm	n/app	n/app
Ground clearance:	386 mm	386 mm	386 mm
Track:	1.54 m	1.54 m	1.54 m
Wheelbase:	2.3 m	2.53 m	2.72 m + 1.05 m
Angle of approach/departure:	45°/45°	45°/45°	45°/40°
Max speed:			
(road)	120 km/h	100 km/h	90 km/h
Fuel capacity:	83 litres	125 litres	150 litres
Max gradient:	100%	100%	100%
Max side slope:	40%	40%	40%
Fording:			
(without preparation)	700 mm	700 mm	700 mm
Engine:	Volvo B-30 6-cylinder in-line OHV petrol developing 125 hp (92 kW) at 4,250 rpm		
Gearbox:	manual, with 4 forward and 1 reverse gears		
Clutch:	single dry plate	single dry plate	single dry plate
Transfer box:	2-speed	2-speed	2-speed
Steering:	cam and roller type		
Turning radius:	5.77 m	5.73 m	8.25 m
Tyres:	8.90 × 16	8.90 × 16	8.90 × 16
Electrical system:	12 V	12 V	12 V
Battery:	1 × 12 V, 60 Ah	1 × 12 V, 60 Ah	1 × 12 V, 60 Ah

vacuum-operated mechanical differential locks which can be engaged separately or together. The chassis consists of box-section side members with tubular cross members welded into position. The chassis is torsionally stiff to avoid stressing the superstructure.

The front suspension consists of underslung semi-elliptic leaf springs carried in rubber mountings, hollow-rubber springs and double-acting telescopic shock-absorbers. The rear suspension consists of overslung semi-elliptic leaf springs carried in rubber mountings, hollow-rubber springs and double-acting telescopic shock-absorbers. The main brakes are vacuum-hydraulic drum-type, dual circuit, with one vacuum cylinder per circuit.

The handbrake is mechanical and acts on the propeller shaft. Optional equipment included: an air conditioning system; electric engine heater; electric compressor with 10 m of hose for pumping tyres; PTO; protective wooden floor ribs; roof ventilator; tow hook; trailer electrical socket; Webasto engine and passenger area heater; and a 2,200/3,000 kg capacity winch. The basic model is fitted with a thermostatically controlled heater, defroster system and a two-speed blower in the cab, with a heater and two-speed blower for the rear compartment.

The C304 (4 × 4) version is almost identical to the C303 but has a wheelbase of 2.53 m.

(6 × 6) 4143 (or C306)
The (6 × 6) model is based on the (4 × 4) model and has the same engine, gearbox, transfer box and cab. The vehicle was fitted with a variety of bodies including cargo, fully enclosed and ambulance. The cargo model has drop sides, drop tailgate, removable bows and a tarpaulin cover. The fully enclosed body version has a large door in the rear and a door in each side and can be used for a variety of roles including radio/command.

The front suspension consists of underslung semi-elliptic leaf springs, hollow-rubber springs and double-acting telescopic shock absorbers. The rear suspension is of the double cantilever type with parabolic springs with progressively acting hollow-rubber springs and double-acting telescopic shock absorbers. The main brakes are of the vacuum-hydraulic drum-type, with the mechanical parking brake operating on the transfer box output shaft. Optional equipment was similar to that available for the (4 × 4) version.

Specifications
See table above

Status
Production complete. In service with the Swedish Armed Forces (numbers reducing) and Malaysia (4 × 4) and (6 × 6).

Contractor
Volvo Truck Corporation

Volvo 4141 (4 × 4) fully enclosed version (T J Gander)   0511826

Scania SBA 111 4,500 kg (4 × 4) and SBAT 111S 6,000 kg (6 × 6) trucks

Development
In the early 1960s, the Swedish Army Materiel Department drew up its requirements for a new generation of tactical vehicles for the 1970s and 1980s. Volvo was awarded the contract for the lighter Class 1 and 2 vehicles and Scania the contracts for the heavier Class 3 (4 × 4) and Class 4 (6 × 6) vehicles.

Scania started design work in 1966 and received its first development contract in 1968. Primary requirements of the Swedish Army were for a vehicle which would be easy to handle and maintain, use proved and standardised commercial components wherever possible, be reliable, have a low repair cost and finally have a low total service life cost. The first prototypes were completed early in 1971 with the second series of prototypes being completed late in 1972. The Swedish Army placed its first production order in 1974 for 2,000 vehicles (both (4 × 4) and (6 × 6)) at a total cost of SEK225 million for delivery between 1976 and 1979. In 1977 a further 258 vehicles were ordered for the Swedish Air Force and Navy. A total of 2,500 vehicles were delivered to the Swedish Army. Production was completed in 1989.

A modified version of the SBAT was produced for the Indian Army to tow Bofors 155 mm FH-77B howitzers.

Description
The layout of both vehicles is almost identical, the only major differences being in their engines and configurations. The components of both vehicles are 90 per cent interchangeable.

The chassis consists of two longitudinal C-section members with the cross-members riveted into position. The two-door forward control cab is all steel and has a hatch in the right side of the roof. The driver's windscreen is hinged at the top and can be opened upward for improved visibility. The cab can be tilted forward to an angle of 55° with the aid of a double-acting hydraulic pump. The grille on the front of the cab opens upwards to allow access to the oil dipstick, oil filter and oil tank for daily checks.

The engines of the two vehicles differ only in that the SBAT (6 × 6) has a turbocharger. The engine is fitted with a special fuel pump which allows the engine to continue running when inclined at an angle of 35°.

The gearbox is of the automatic split type in which two-thirds of the power is always transmitted mechanically. The gearbox consists of the automatic gearbox, distributor gearbox and a torque converter. The main gearbox has six speeds, three hydraulic and three mechanical. The transfer box has one ratio for cross-country operations and another for road operations.

All axles on both trucks are identical and each axle has a central bevel gear, hub reduction gears and a differential lock.

The rear platform is torsionally rigid and the basic cargo models have removable drop sides and a drop tailgate.

Both vehicles have an 8,000 kg capacity winch mounted on the right side of the chassis, driven by a PTO on the transfer box and operated by a switch on the dashboard and a winch brake control in front of the steering wheel. The winch can be used to the front or rear of the vehicle.

Cold weather equipment includes: an engine heater, battery heater, fuel preheater, starting pilot and connections for starting cables.

Ex-Swedish Army SBAT 111S (now of the Latvian Army) mounting the Giraffe radar system in travelling mode (Stefan Marx)   1296115

Variants
SBA (4 × 4)
This basic model was designed for carrying cargo although some were delivered to the Swedish Army with a 1,500 kg hydraulic crane at the rear for unloading. Some have been fitted with bows, canvas cover and bench seats down each side for carrying passengers; others have a small hardtop crew shelter.

SBAT (6 × 6)
The basic model was designed for carrying cargo but other variants include a version with a 5,500 kg hydraulic crane mounted to the rear of the cab, which is used for ammunition resupply for the Bofors 155 mm FH-77 howitzer and the 120 mm KARIN towed coast defence gun. The FH-77 and KARIN are towed by an SBAT truck fitted with a fully enclosed cabin for the crew of 10 at the forward end of the platform. Mounted at the rear of the vehicle is a 1,500 kg hydraulic crane. A (6 × 6) recovery vehicle was built to the prototype stage but was not ordered by the Swedish Army. The (6 × 6) version is used to carry the Giraffe radar system used in conjunction with the Bofors RBS 70 and RBS 90 SAM systems. In March 1989, the Swedish Defence Materiel Administration ordered 83 of these vehicles.

Scania SBA 111 series

Model	SBA 111	SBAT 111S
Cab seating:	1 + 2	1 + 2
Configuration:	4 × 4	6 × 6
Weight:		
(unladen)	9,150 kg	11,650 kg
(laden, off-road)	13,700 kg	20,650 kg
(max load, off-road)	4,500 kg	6,000 kg
(max load, on-road)	6,000 kg	9,000 kg
(towed load)	6,000 kg	12,000 kg
Load area:	4.2 × 2.35 m	4.75 × 2.35 m
Length:	6.75 m	7.78 m
Width:	2.48 m	2.48 m
Height:		
(cab)	2.9 m	2.9 m
(load area)	1.472 m	1.472 m
Ground clearance:	400 mm	420 mm
Track:	2.02 m	2.02 m
Wheelbase:	4 m	3.55 m + 1.48 m
Angle of approach/departure:	45°/40°	45°/40°
Max speed:	85 km/h	85 km/h
Range: (road)	600 km	550 km
Fuel capacity:	167 litres	167 litres
Max gradient:	60%	60%
Max side slope:	40%	40%
Fording:	800 mm	800 mm
Engine:	Scania D11 6-cylinder diesel developing 202 hp (148 kW) at 2,200 rpm (4 × 4); Scania DS11 6-cylinder turbocharged diesel developing 296 hp (218 kW) 2,200 rpm (6 × 6)	
Steering:	hydraulic	hydraulic
Turning radius:	9 m	10.3 m
Suspension:	semi-elliptic springs with double acting hydraulic shock-absorbers	
Tyres:	14.00 × 20	14.00 × 20
Brakes:	dual circuit, air. Hand, spring type operating on front and rear wheels	
Electrical system:	24 V	24 V

Ex-Swedish Army SBAT 111S (now of the Latvian Army) in position with the Giraffe radar system fully extended (Stefan Marx)   1296242

Scania 3 Series (6 × 4) tractor truck of the Thai Navy (Gordon Arthur)   1391193

Scania R420 (6 × 6) of the Irish Army. Full details of specific in-service models from the Scania 4 Series and P, G and R Series ranges can be found elsewhere in this section (Scania)   1391054

Crash rescue vehicles

Following trials with two prototype bodies, the Swedish armed forces ordered 47 crash rescue vehicles for delivery in 1979. They have a laden weight of 16,000 kg and are fitted with both firefighting and crash rescue equipment.

Snow-clearing vehicle

This version is based on the chassis of the SBA (4 × 4) truck and used by the Swedish Air Force for clearing snow from airfield runways; 45 of these vehicles were ordered at a cost of SEK12 million. When being driven forward on the road the vehicle is driven from the normal driver's position, but when clearing snow it is driven in reverse from the second cab which faces the rear. Maximum speed when clearing snow is 30 km/h. Steering during snow-clearing operations is by a duplicated hydrostatic steering system which acts on the ordinary steering mechanism of the vehicle. The snow-clearing equipment fitted is a Rolba 1500S, which is of the cut and sling type and has a capacity of 30 to 35,000 kg of snow/min.

Specifications

Status

Production complete. In service with Finland (1), India (660 SBATs ordered in 1986) Sweden (numbers reducing) and other countries that have received surplus Swedish vehicles including Latvia.

Contractor

Scania CV AB

Scania range of trucks

Description

Scania's range of trucks for defence applications are based on the modular use of components from the company's range of heavy commercial models, allowing for a wide variety of specific operator requirements to be met.

The current P, G and R Series became available from 2004 and these progressively replaced the earlier 4 Series which had replaced the earlier 3 Series in production during 1996. As of January 2005, the 4 Series was only produced in South America and sold to the South American, Asian and African markets. Production of the 4 Series concluded during 2007. The P, G and R Series are visually similar to the 4 Series models they succeed and

Scania P93 MK 4×4Z (4 × 4) 5,000 kg 3 Series truck of the Norwegian Army (Shaun C Connors)   1391052

should be considered a revision of the 4 Series (albeit a significant revision), and not a wholly new product range. The denomination of 5 Series was not adopted for marketing reasons.

Being based on a range of commercial trucks, throughout their production run Scania's P, G and R Series-based trucks for defence applications (as did the earlier 4 and 3 Series) will reflect the many minor design changes and specification upgrades associated with civilian truck production.

As of January 2011 the Scania range of P, G and R Series heavy trucks had a Gross Vehicle Weight (GVW) range from 16,000 kg to 48,000 kg, and a Gross Combination Weight (GCW) range from 30,000 kg to 150,000 kg, although the maximum GCW may be increased to 250,000 kg with special specifications and conditions. Motive power is provided by four basic Scania turbocharged and intercooled water-cooled four-stroke diesel engines: a nine-litre five-cylinder unit developing 230, 270, 280, 310 or 320 hp; a 12-litre six-cylinder unit developing 340, 380, 420 or 480 hp; a 13-litre six-cylinder unit developing 360, 400, 440 or 480 hp, and a 16-litre V-8 unit developing 500, 560, 580, 620 or 730 hp. All engines meet EURO 4 or EURO 5 emissions requirements and utilise either EGR or SCR emissions technology. EURO 3 engines remain available on request.

Scania P113 HK (8 × 6) 3 Series truck with Multilift Mk 4 (now known as the MPH165) load handling system of the Norwegian Army
(Shaun C Connors)   1391053

Scania P113HK8×6HZ (8 × 6) 3 Series carrier/launch truck for 4 land-based Saab RBS-15 anti-ship missiles (Martin Pagh)   1129973

Driveline options include 8- and 12-speed manual gearboxes with a conventional clutch and with or without crawler gears or range splitters. A two-speed transfer box is an option on models with a driven front axle. The majority of manual gearboxes are available with Scania's Opticruise automated gear changing system and/or a retarder. Various automatic gearbox options are also available in combination with engines of up to 420 hp. For heavy-duty combinations with a GCW above 150,000 kg, a gearbox with torque converter is available. Single or double reduction drive axles complete the drivetrain.

Different chassis frame strength classes are available, with several axle configurations in each class. There is also a wide range of forward control cab options (including four-door) of two major types, P (low-mounted), G (mid-mounted) and R (high-mounted). The bonneted (T) option was phased out of production during 2005. Chassis-mounted anti-tank mine protection is available and has been supplied to Norway and Sweden. Fourth generation protection for cabs against small arms fire, artillery shell fragments and the effects of IED explosions is also now available. Earlier generations of this protection was supplied to the Netherlands (third-generation), Norway (second-generation) and Sweden (first- and second-generation).

Scania 4-series dump truck of the Portuguese Army (Victor Barreira)
                                                       1391240

Scania P113 HK (8 × 6) 3 Series truck with Multilift Mk 4 (now known as the MPH165) load handling system as produced for Norwegian Army
(Scania)   0056444

Norwegian Army Scania P93 MK 4×4-8T (4 × 4) 3 Series truck with dropside body and mechanical tail-lift (Richard Stickland)   0126613

Vehicle designation, as with most other truck manufacturers, is complex but informative when understood. For example, the designation P420CB8×8EHZ denotes - (P - cab type) low forward control; (420 - engine power output) 420 hp; (C - transport type) construction; (B - chassis adaptation) rigid; (8 × 8 - wheel configuration) four-axle truck, all wheels driven; (E - duty class) extra heavy duty; (H - chassis height) high chassis; (Z - suspension) leaf springs all-round.

Scania has delivered a large number of special vehicles both to military and civilian customers. Among the former are the Norwegian armed forces, which ordered 1,700 Scania vehicles of different types in 1986 at a cost of SKR750 million. These included the P93 M (4 × 4), P113 H (6 × 6) and the R143EK (6 × 6) tank transporter. Vehicles were delivered as chassis from Scania with bodies fitted by Norsk Scania A/S in Norway. Deliveries continued until August 1995. The Norwegian Army also operates the Scania P113 HK 8 × 6/4 with a Multilift Mk 4 load handling system (now known as the Multilift MPH165 system). This model has a GVW of 34,000 kg and is powered by a DS11 75 six-cylinder turbocharged diesel developing 310 hp at 2,000 rpm. In 2003 Scania was awarded a contract to supply ballistic and AT mine protection for approximately 50 cabs to Norway for use on earlier delivered vehicles used on international operations.

In total 255 Scania T113 HK (6 × 6) trucks plus spare parts were ordered by the Brazilian ENGESA concern. It received locally produced vehicles from Scania's Brazilian subsidiary, provided them with new coachwork and delivered them to Angola. The order was worth SKR120 million. ENGESA is no longer trading.

Swedish Army Scania P113 HK (6 × 6) 3 Series truck with Mulitilift HL26 load handling system (Scania)   1129984

Model	P93 MK 4×4Z	P93 MK 4×4-8T	P93 HK 4×4 + 2/S42	P113 HK (6×6)
Purpose:	truck	truck	bridge carrier	truck
Cab seating:	1 + 2	1 + 2	1 + 2	1 + 2
Configuration:	4 × 4	4 × 4	6 × 4	6 × 6
Weight:				
(unladen)	9,300 kg	9,500 kg	13,360 kg	13,400 kg
(max load)	5,000 kg	8,000 kg	11,140 kg	11,540 kg
Length:	7.15 m	8.56 m	8.41 m	7.6 m
Width:	2.48 m	2.48 m	3.4 m	2.66 m
Height:	3.3 m	3.28 m	3.34 m	3.4 m
Ground clearance:				
(front)	410 mm	400 mm	400 mm	400 mm
(rear)	410 mm	335 mm	285 mm	335 mm
Track:				
(front)	2.02 m	2.03 m	2.03 m	2.03 m
(rear)	2.02 m	2.03 m	1.83 m	2.03 m
Wheelbase:	4 m	4.6 m	4.6 m + 1.315 m	3.55 m + 1.35 m
Angle of approach/departure:	34°/41°	33°/23°	n/avail	n/avail
Max speed:	90 km/h	105 km/h	90 km/h	90 km/h
Engine:	Scania DS9 water-cooled 4-stroke developing 252 hp (188 kW) at 2,200 rpm	Scania DS9 water-cooled 4-stroke developing 252 hp (188 kW) at 2,200 rpm	Scania DS9 water-cooled 4-stroke developing 252 hp (188 kW) at 2,200 rpm	Scania DS11 water-cooled diesel developing 310 hp (230 kW) at 2,000 rpm
Gearbox:	manual, 5 speed	manual, 5 speed	manual, 5 speed	manual, 10 speed
Tyres:	14.00 × 20	14.00 × 20	13 × 22.5 or 12.00 × 20	14.00 × 20

The largest single user of Scania trucks is the Swedish Armed Forces. Scania had an option contract with the Swedish Defence Matériel Administration (FMV) that allowed for unlimited orders to be placed from 2000 until 2005. Deliveries of the 4 Series under the previously mentioned now concluded option contract have included at least 60 P124CB6×6NZ360 trucks fitted with a Multilift HL26 load handling system (as a follow-on to deliveries of the similar Scania P113HK (6 × 6) truck), at least 12 P124CB8×6/4NZ360 (8 × 6) trucks (also fitted with Multilift HL26 load handling system), 138 P124CB(6×6HZ420 (6 × 6) trucks fitted with a Multilift LHS26.50 load handling system, 66 P124CB8×8HZ420 (8 × 8) trucks with armoured cabs (including mine protection) and a Multilift LHS26.50 load handling system, 35 P124CB6×6 trucks fitted with a Quick Lock mounting system, an additional 28 P124GB6×2NZ420 (6 × 2) multipurpose airbase vehicles for the Swedish Air Force, and undisclosed numbers of P124CB6×6HZ (6 × 6) four-door crew cab platform trucks for the Swedish Coastal Artillery, and P124CB6×6HZ recovery vehicles for the Army.

Other recent sales of the 4 Series range include T-cab (6 × 4) heavy tractor trucks with 530 hp V-8 engines to Belgium (26 (150,000 kg GCW)), France (12 (124,000 kg GCW)) and Sweden (31 (150,000 kg GCW)), 13 P114CB 4 × 4 vehicles with dump bodies to Portugal, and 81 P114CB4×4HZ340 (4 × 4) trucks worth AUD13.5 million to the Australian DoD between July and December 2002; a small number of additional vehicles (12 + 11) were subsequently delivered during 2003/2004.

In an USD88 million contract announced in September 2002, Scania supplied 242 R114CB6×6HZ340 (6 × 6) 10 m³ fuel tankers to the French Army. Two pre-series vehicles were completed during November 2003 with deliveries of the 242 vehicles completed in September 2005. In service these new tankers will primarily be used with Leclerc regiments, the current TRM 10000-based Leclerc refueller being re-roled to replace ageing Berliet GBC 8KT refuellers in assorted other roles. In 2006 Scania received an order for 10 additional fuel tankers, these on R340CB6×6HHZ chassis.

It was announced in October 2003 that Scania, in the company's largest export sale deal of 4 Series defence vehicles, had been selected to supply 548 R124CB8×8HZ420 (8 × 8) trucks fitted with the Multilift TSH 230 (now known as the MSH165SC) Load Handling System (LHS) trucks and seven container side loaders from Hammar Maskin AB on the same chassis to the Netherlands Armed Forces. The deal also includes 262 ballistic protection kits from Åkers Krutbruk Protection AB. These kits will be retrofitted on demand. The project is worth up to EUR172.5 million (USD201.9 million), and to secure it Scania defeated a competing offer from Mercedes-Benz of Germany (Actros (8 × 8) chassis fitted with a Marrel (France) load handling system). Vehicles were assembled at Scania's Dutch subsidiary, Scania Nederland BV and are to have an operational lifetime of at least 13 years, based on an annual mileage of 30,000 km.

During 2005 the Scania distributor in the Netherlands, Scania Beers, secured an award for the global repair and maintenance of these vehicles during their service lives.

In 2003 Scania was awarded a contract to supply 30 and mount 26 anti-tank mine protection kits on previously delivered Swedish Army P124CB6×6 trucks. Scania was also awarded a contract to develop anti-mine protection kits - offering a higher level of anti-tank mine blast protection than earlier delivered kits.

In July 2004 it was announced the Irish Defence Forces had selected a Scania (8 × 8) truck to meet an Irish Army requirement for a minimum of 10 Load Handling System-equipped (LHS) trucks. The contract was then extended for the supply of 15 Scania R124CB8×8 HZ420 trucks and awarded to local Scania dealer, Westward Scania. With the exception of an

Allison automatic transmission which replaces the Scania Opticruise automated gear changing system, these trucks have similar specifications to the Dutch R124CB8×8HZ420 vehicle and were delivered to the Irish Army late 2004/early 2005. Assembly was carried out by Scania Nederland BV at Zwolle. The fitted Multilift MPH165SC LHS features an integral Container Handling Unit (CHU) and its stowage.

In October 2004 Scania announced the sale of 45 4 Series trucks to the Finnish Army, bringing the total of trucks purchased by Finnish defence forces during 2004 to 50 (45, Army; three, Air Force; two, Navy); This contract includes Scania R164CB8×4 HETs to be used in heavy haulage and a selection on non all-wheel drive chassis. Between 2000-2004, 131 trucks have been delivered with contract options allowing for the purchase of a further 40 trucks per year during 2005 and 2006. Trucks delivered under the option contracts included Scania R500LB8×4HHZ (8 × 4) and Scania R500LB6×4HHZ (6 × 4) with commercial LHS.

In 2006 Scania received an order for R420LA4×2HNB (4 × 2) tractor trucks for fuel tankers from Swedish defence forces.

In 2007 Scania received orders from the Finnish defence forces for nine P380CB4×4HHZ (4 × 4) crewcab chassis for fire fighting vehicles, 16 P380CB6×6HHZ (6 × 6) crewcab chassis for decontamination vehicles, four P380CB6×6HHZ (6 × 6) crewcab chassis for rescue vehicles, and 9 R480CB8×2MSZ (8 × 2) fuel tankers. Between 1999 and 2007 Finnish defence forces ordered a total of 219 assorted vehicles from Scania.

Scania announced at Eurosatory 2008 that series deliveries to the French Army of 150 (6 × 6) P340 tippers with Marrel 8 m³ bodies, 11 (6 × 6) P340 12,000-litre water tankers with Rivard bodies and 23 interchangeable armoured cabs supplied by Centigon would run from September 2008 until January 2009. Following a competition that is understood to have included Renault (and possibly others), this contract was awarded in December 2006. Pre-series vehicles were delivered in the autumn of 2007 for testing which was completed in February 2008. To meet urgent operational needs some 22 tipper chassis had cargo flatbeds fitted instead of tipper bodies by the French Army. The current French Army logistic truck in this category is the TRM 10000, the cab of which cannot be armoured. Scania has also supplied the French Army with 11 R420 tractor units with fixed armoured cabs. This contract was awarded in June 2006 and these trucks have been delivered and in service are used with the CNIM PFM Mle F1 floating bridge and ferry system. Again, these trucks were ordered as the standard French Army truck in this class, the TRM 10000, cannot be armoured.

Details of other then recent Scania defence orders were also disclosed during 2008. An Algerian order covering four (6 × 6) recovery vehicles was disclosed at Eurosatory 2008 with the vehicles in transit at that time. Following an initial order for 15 LHS trucks for delivery during 2005-2006, the Irish Army more recently ordered 36 (6 × 6) R420 and two (8 × 4) trucks that were delivered 2007-2008. Irish deliveries did not include a protection kit requirement. The Irish Army also received during 2008, 10 (4 × 2) Scania vehicles for EOD use. These are understood to have been fitted with protected rear bodies supplied by Penman Engineering.

As part of a larger award announced late-June 2008 that also included 232 Sisu (4 × 4) trucks, Scania was awarded a contract for 21 (8 × 8) trucks with commercial LHS by Finnish Armed Forces; the award includes an option for an additional four vehicles. Later in 2008 Scania also received an order for a total of 91 road going trucks with an option for >100 additional trucks.

Most recently, during 2010, Scania released details of an order from Sweden's Defence Matériel Administration (FMV) for 88 logistic vehicles. The order, which forms part of a framework purchasing agreement that includes Volvo and has run from 2006, calls for 80 G400 (6 × 2) chassis fitted with a JOAB hooklift system, four of which will be fitted with four-seat crewcabs for driver training, and eight P400 (8 × 2) chassis with crane and platform bodywork. These vehicles are essentially commercial specification and will mainly be used for road haul work within Sweden. For the first time in a deal with the Swedish FMV these vehicles will be fitted with Scania's Communicator 200 on-board data collector for remote follow-up of vehicle and driver via a web portal. This is also the first time a repair and maintenance contract has been signed with the FMV, this including access to the Scania sales and service network throughout Sweden. Deliveries are scheduled for early 2011.

Scania also announced details of an order from the NATO Maintenance and Supply Agency (NAMSA) for the supply of 31 G480 (8 × 8) trucks to the Luxembourg Army. The vehicles are primarily destined for use on peacekeeping missions and 13 will be fitted with a ballistic protection kit, 28 will be fitted with hooklift system and three with a recovery hamper supplied by EMPL of Austria. Deliveries are scheduled for 2011.

It was also disclosed during 2010 that Scania, as a sub-contractor to local prime contractor HEMA ENDUSTRI A.S., would supply the Turkish Army with 45 R480CB6×6 (6 × 6) heavy equipment transporter tractor trucks for use with a locally supplied semi-trailer. Two tractor units are understood to have been supplied for pre-series testing.

Full details of specific in-service models from the Scania 4 Series range can be found elsewhere in this section. The data provided in the table below may be taken as typical for only a small portion of the earlier Scania 3 Series range, relating specifically to vehicles supplied to Norway.

Specifications
See table on page 609

Status
Production of the 3 Series was completed during 1996 and superseded by the 4 Series. From 2004 the 4 Series was replaced in production by the P, G and R Series. The bonneted T Series was phased out of production during 2005. Scania 3 Series trucks are in service with numerous armed forces including Greece, Norway and Sweden, the 4 Series are in service with Australia, Belgium, Denmark, Finland, France, Ireland, Netherlands (555 units), Portugal, Sweden and possibly other undisclosed countries. The latest P, G and R Series are in service with Finland, France, Ireland and Sweden.

Contractor
Scania CV AB

Scania P114CB4×4HZ 340 (4 × 4) truck

Development
Following a competitive tender involving Mack, MAN, Mercedes-Benz, TATRA and Volvo, Scania were awarded a AU$13.5 million contract to deliver 81 Scania P114CB4×4HZ 340 (4 × 4) 4-series trucks to the Australian DoD between July and December 2002. They were purchased as additional vehicles and as such did not directly replace any in-service trucks. Two additional purchases followed, these for 12 vehicles in 2003 and 11 during 2004. Projected service life is up to 10 years.

As with all Scania trucks for defence applications, the P114CB4×4HZ 340 is based around the company's commercial trucks and the modular use of components from these. As with all Scania 4-series model designations, P denotes cab-type (non-sleeper), 11 denotes nominal engine cubic capacity and 4 denotes the Scania 4-series of trucks.

The Scania 4-series all wheel drive range was released in January 1996 as part of the Construction segment C-Class of trucks, with 11 and 12 litre engine options. It was originally available in 4 × 4 and 6 × 6 configurations, with an 8 × 8 version being released in June 2000.

Scania P114CB4×4HZ 340 (4 × 4) cargo variant (Scania Australia Pty Ltd)
0536764

Scania P114CB4x4HZ340 (4 × 4) cargo variant with materials handling crane (Scania Australia Pty Ltd)
1128250

Scania P114CB4×4HZ 340 (4 × 4) tipper variant (Scania Australia Pty Ltd)
0567941

The current Scania P and R series became available throughout 2004 and these progressively replaced the earlier 4-series, which had replaced the earlier 3-series in production during 1996. By January 2005 the 4-series was only produced in South America for South American, Asian and African markets. Production of the 4-series concluded during 2007.

Description
The Scania P114CB4×4HZ 340 (4 × 4) truck supplied to the Australian defence forces was delivered in four variants, the 81 original vehicles supplied consisting of: 67 cargo, eight cargo with crane, four water tanker, and two tipper. The bulk of these vehicles (75) are operated by the Army, with the two tippers and four water tankers being operated by the Air Force.

All models are fitted with a Scania CP14 two-door safety non-sleeper forward control cab. The cab accommodates a driver and two passengers, and is fitted with Steyr weapon mount brackets. The fitted cruise control was not a tender requirement, but is standard equipment with the Scania DC11.01 engine. The CD player was carried over from the commercial cab to enhance the driver environment, as while these vehicles are suitable for off-road deployment, they will primarily be used on highways over extended distances.

Motive power is provided by a Scania 11-litre six-cylinder turbocharged diesel engine developing 340 hp. This drives through a Scania 12-speed gearbox and Steyr GTD 800 two-speed transfer box to provide constant four-wheel drive. The front axle is a Scania RP731 spiral hub reduction unit, the rear axle is a Scania RP832 spiral hub reduction unit.

The cargo variant is fitted with a 5.5 m drop side body, tarpaulin and a Ringfeeder towing attachment. It has a kerb weight of 8,245 kg and can be loaded to a gross vehicle weight (GVW) of 20,100 kg and a gross combination weight (GCW) of 70,000 kg, although peacetime load restrictions reduce both from that technically permitted. The cargo variant with crane is fitted with a 4.7 m drop side body, a Ferrari 550 A1 truck-mounted crane, a tarpaulin and a Ringfeeder towing attachment. The tanker version is fitted with a 6,000 litre stainless steel tank body, hose reels, and a Vickers 26M hydraulic motor coupled to a GAAM MK300 two stage pump. The tipper variant is fitted with a 5 m³ Bisalloy tipping body, and a Ringfeeder towing attachment.

All variants are fitted with a heavy duty aluminium bull bar to protect against animal strike and that incorporates recovery and lifting hooks into the base.

Specifications
Cab seating: 1 + 2
Configuration: 4 × 4
Weight:
    (max GVW) 20,100 kg
    (legal GVW on-road (Australia)) 15,000 kg
    (max GCW) 70,000 kg
    (legal GCW on-road (Australia)) 42,500 kg
Length: approx 7.8 m
Width: 2.5 m

Height: 3.15 m
Ground clearance:
(front, 11R 22.5 tyres) 380 mm
(rear, 11R 22.5 tyres) 470 mm
Track:
(front) 2.09 m
(rear) 1.83 m
Wheel base: 4100 + 2150 m rear overhang
Angle of approach/departure: 29°/24°
Fuel capacity: 400 litres
Max gradient: 47.4%
Max sideslope: not tested
Fording: 750 mm
Engine: Scania DC11.01 EURO 2 emissions compliant 11-litre 6-cylinder in-line turbocharged water-cooled 4-stroke diesel developing 340 hp (250 hp) at 1,800 rpm and 1,600 N.m torque between 1,100 and 1,400 rpm
Gearbox: Scania GRS890 with 12 forward gears
Transfer box: Steyr GTD 800 2-speed
Clutch: Scania K 432 15, 430 mm
Steering: power assisted, Ross TAS 85
Turning radius:
(kerb) 7.58 m
(wall) 8.56 m
Tyres: 11R 22.5
Brakes: dual circuit, air, drums all-round. ABS
Electrical system: 24 V
Batteries: 2 × 12 V, 170 Ah
Alternator: 65 A

Status

Production complete. Replaced in production by equivalent model from the 2004-introduced P and R series of trucks. In service with the Australian Army (see text).

Contractor

Scania CV AB

Scania P124CB6×6NZ360 (6 × 6) truck

Development

The first 60 examples of the Scania P124CB6×6NZ360 (6 × 6) 4-series truck equipped with Multilift HL26.52 Load Handling Systems (LHS) were delivered to the Swedish Army during 1997. These deliveries were a continuation from an earlier series of similar vehicles based on the previous Scania 3-series chassis.

A number of similar vehicles designated Scania P124CB6×6HZ360 were delivered during 1998. These had CP31 four-door forward control cabs and 14.00R 20 tyres.

In 2003 Scania was awarded a contract to supply 35 P124CB6x6 4-series trucks fitted with the Quick Lock body mounting system. Scania also supplied a number of bodies plus 80 system flatracks for the transportation of 20 ft ISO containers. A similar contract (for 30 vehicles) was awarded to Volvo at the same time.

During 2003 Scania was also awarded a contract to supply 30 and mount 26 anti-tank mine kits to previously delivered P124CB6×6 trucks. A contract to develop, supply and mount 12 anti-tank mine kits offering a higher level of protection than any of those previously delivered was also awarded. These kits will also be mounted on previously delivered P124CB6×6 trucks.

The current Scania G, P and R series trucks became available from 2004 and these progressively replaced the earlier 4-series which had replaced the earlier 3-series in production during 1996. As of January 2006, the 4-series was only produced in South America for South American, Asian and African markets. Production of the 4-series concluded during 2007.

Swedish Army Scania P124CB6×6HZ360 (6 × 6) truck fitted with the CP31 four-door crew cab (Scania) 0536765

Description

The Scania P124CB6×6NZ360 (6 × 6) truck has a Scania CP14 two-door safety sleeper forward control cab (without beds). The cab can accommodate the driver and two passengers, with provision for carrying their personal equipment. An optional crew cab can seat the driver and a further six passengers.

With the Multilift H26.52 load handling system the vehicle has a kerb weight of 13,860 kg and can be loaded to a Gross Vehicle Weight (GVW) of 34,000 kg and a Gross Combination Weight (GCW) of 70,000 kg. Peacetime load restrictions reduce the GVW (and GCW) from that technically permitted. The LHS has a lifting capacity of 19,000 kg and, with a suitable body, a tipping capacity of 20,000 kg.

The front axle is a Scania AMD900/RP731, with the rear axles being Scania AD1500/RBP832 units.

A Stepson H70PS self-recovery winch, deployable to the front or rear, is located on the right-hand side. The winch has a capacity of 70,000 kg and is equipped with 50 m of 14 mm diameter cable. Other equipment includes a connector for engine heating, heat exchanger, blow torch, electric engine heater, 24 V emergency connector for starting the truck or another truck or armoured vehicle and snow chains.

Specifications

Scania P124CB6×6NZ360 truck
Cab seating: 1 + 2 (CP31 crew cab 1 + 6)
Configuration: 6 × 6
Weight:
(kerb, with LHS) 13,860 kg
(GVW) 34,000 kg
(GCW) 70,000 kg
Length: approx 9.04 m
Width: 2.6 m
Height: 3.4 m
Ground clearance:
(front, with 14.00R 20 tyres) 400 mm
(rear, with 14.00R 20 tyres) 350 mm
Track:
(front) 2.08 m
(rear) 2.03 m
Wheelbase: 4.65 m + 1.445 m
Angle of approach: 23°
Fuel capacity: 350 litres
Engine: Scania DSC1202 EURO II 6-cylinder in-line turbocharged water-cooled 4-stroke diesel developing 360 hp (265 kW) between 1,600 and 1,900 rpm
Gearbox: Scania GR900 with 8 forward road gears and 1 crawler gear
Transfer case: Steyr GTD 900, 2-speed
Turning radius: 10.7 m
Tyres: 315/80R 22.5
Brakes: dual circuit, air, drums all-round, ABS fitted
Electrical system: 24 V
Batteries: 2 × 12 V, 170 Ah
Alternator: 90 A

Status

Production complete. Replaced in production by equivalent model from the G, P and R series of trucks. In service with the Swedish Army and Navy.

Contractor

Scania CV AB

Scania P124CB8×6/4NZ360 (8 × 6) truck

Development

The first 12 examples of the Scania P124CB8x6/4NZ360 (8 × 6) 4-series truck equipped with Multilift HL26.52 Load Handling Systems (LHS) were delivered to the Swedish Army during 1997. These deliveries were a continuation from an earlier series of similar vehicles based on the previous Scania 3-series chassis.

The current Scania G, P and R series trucks became available from 2004 and these progressively replaced the earlier 4-series which had replaced the earlier 3-series in production during 1996. As of January 2006, the 4-series was only produced in South America for South American, Asian and African markets. Production of the 4-series concluded during 2007.

Description

The Scania P124CB8x6/4NZ360 (8 × 6) truck has a Scania CP19 two-door safety sleeper forward control cab (without beds). The cab can accommodate the driver and two passengers, with provision for carrying their personal equipment.

With the Multilift H26.52 load handling system the vehicle has a kerb weight of 15,500 kg and can be loaded to a Gross Vehicle Weight (GVW) of 40,500 kg and a Gross Combination Weight (GCW) of 70,000 kg. Peacetime load restrictions reduce the GCW (and GVW) from that technically permitted. The LHS has a lifting capacity of 19,000 kg and, with a suitable body, a tipping capacity of 20,000 kg.

The front axle is a Scania AMD900/RP731, with the rear axles being Scania AA1500/RBP832 units.

Scania P124CB8x6/4NZ360 (8 × 6) truck with Multilift H26.52 load handling system carrying a Hägglunds Pbv 392 APC (Scania)   0044332

A Stepson H70PS self-recovery winch, deployable to the front or rear, is located on the right-hand side. The winch has a capacity of 7,000 kg and is equipped with 50 m of 14 mm diameter cable. Other equipment includes a connector for engine heating, heat exchanger, blow torch, electric engine heater, 24 V emergency connector for starting the truck or another truck/armoured vehicle and snow chains.

Specifications

Scania P124CB8×6/4NZ360 truck
Cab seating: 1 + 2
Configuration: 8 × 6
Weight:
(kerb, with LHS) 15,500 kg
(GVW) 40,500 kg
(GCW) 70,000 kg
Length: approx 9.29 m
Width: 2.6 m
Height: 3.4 m
Ground clearance:
(front, with 14.00R 20 tyres) 400 mm
(rear, with 14.00R 20 tyres) 350 mm
Track:
(front) 2.08 m
(rear) 2.03 m
Wheelbase: 4.955 m + 1.445 m
Fuel capacity: 400 litres
Engine: Scania DSC1202 EURO II 6-cylinder in-line water-cooled 4-stroke diesel developing 360 hp (265 kW) between 1,600 and 1,900 rpm
Gearbox: Scania GR900 with 8 forward road gears and 1 crawler gear
Transfer case: Steyr GTD 900, 2-speed
Turning radius: 11.3 m
Tyres: 315/80R 22.5 (10 + 1), 295/60R 22.5 (2)
Brakes: dual circuit, air, ABS fitted
Electrical system: 24 V
Batteries: 2 × 12 V, 170 Ah
Alternator: 90 A

Status

Production complete. Replaced in production by equivalent model from the G, P and R series of trucks. In service with the Swedish Army.

Contractor

Scania CV AB

Scania P124CB8x8HZ420 (8 × 8) truck

Development

The Scania P124CB8x8HZ420 (8 × 8) 4-series truck is based around Scania's commercial trucks and the modular use of components from these. The P124CB8x8HZ420 chassis was first publicly displayed at Eurosatory 2000 and makes use of only three component parts not normally found within the Scania parts range. As with all Scania 4-series model designations, P denotes cab-type, 12 denotes nominal engine cubic capacity and 4 denotes the Scania 4-series of trucks.

The first customer for the Scania P124CB8x8HZ420 (8 × 8) truck were the Swedish armed forces who took delivery of 66 vehicles during 2001. These were fitted with armoured cabs offering crew protection from 7.62 AP small arms fire and anti-tank mine blast. The first 57 vehicles were fitted with the Multilift LHS 261 load handling system (LHS), the following nine vehicles being fitted with a Quick-Lock system.

In December 2001, Scania handed over two R124CB8x8HZ420 (8 × 8) trucks equipped with the Multilift TSH 230 (now designated MSH165SC) load handling system (LHS) to the Royal Netherlands Army for around 12 months of competitive trials for the supply of between 791 and 1,530 vehicles to all three armed forces.

Scania's P124CB8x8HZ420 (8 × 8) 4-series truck is based around Scania's commercial trucks and the modular use of components from these. The Dutch Army have received 555 examples (2005/2006), the Swedish 66 (2001) and the Irish 15 (2004/2005). The are slight specification variances between the three deliveries, these are detailed in the entry text (Scania)   1128245

The particularly stringent requirements of the Royal Netherlands armed forces called for a legislatively compliant LHS-equipped off-road capable vehicle that could handle and carry a standard 20 ft ISO container at an overall height below 4 m (8 ft 6 in).

It was announced in October 2003 that Scania had been selected to supply 555 trucks to the Netherlands armed forces under a project worth up to EUR185 million. Scania defeated a competing offer from Mercedes-Benz of Germany (Actros (8 × 8) chassis fitted with a Marrel (France) load handling system) and produced the vehicles at its Dutch subsidiary, Scania Nederland BV. These trucks are to have an operational lifetime of at least 13½ years, based on an annual mileage of 30,000 km.

The reduction in number of trucks to be procured is the result of a reduction in the Netherlands' ambition level in terms of military capabilities, and the resulting restructuring of the armed forces.

The Scania P124CB8x8HZ420 trucks were the first purchase for, and form the basis of, the Wissel Laad Systemen (WLS) programme. WLS, launched in 1996, was designed to meet the changing needs of the Dutch defence forces and is based on witnessed experience of the British and US Army's combat proven DROPS (Demountable Rack Off-loading and Pick-up System) and PLS (Palletized Load System) on deployed operations. Now fully implemented, WLS represents a step-change in Dutch logistic and engineer support thinking. The first WLS-equipped Dutch Army units were ready for deployment from early 2006 and following procurement of additional equipment, including trailers, flatracks, container handlers and ISO-dimensioned fuel and water racks under the WLS2 (Overig (other)) programme, full implementation of WLS was scheduled for mid-2007. The overall budget for the programme was EUR 226 million.

WLS is tri-service and replaced a large part of the current fleet of DAF Trucks-supplied 4,000/5,000 kg (4 × 4) and 10,000 kg (6 × 6) vehicles.

The Royal Netherlands armed forces order covered 548 Scania P124CB8x8HZ420 trucks equipped with the Multilift TSH230 load handling system (LHS) trucks, plus seven container side loaders from Hammar Maskin AB on the same chassis. The seven examples fitted with Hammar Maskin container sideloaders are for the Royal Netherlands Air Force (RNAF). Of the 548 LHS-equipped trucks, 145 are fitted with Hiab materials handling cranes and 355 with stowable container handling units (CHUs), cranes and CHUs being interchangeable units. Forty-eight trucks are adapted to carry Bridge Adapter Pallets (BAPs) for use with the Ribbon Bridge system and a small number of marines' vehicles will be kitted out for deep (1.5 m) wading. All 555 trucks will be fitted for, but not with, ballistic protection, the order including 262 cab appliquè armour kits supplied by Åkers Krutbruk Protection AB.

The particularly stringent requirements of the Royal Netherlands armed forces called for a legislatively compliant LHS-equipped off-road capable vehicle that could handle and carry a standard 20 ft ISO container at an overall height below 4 m (8 ft 6 in) (Scania)   1128241

7 of the 555 Scania P124CB8x8HZ420 (8 × 8) trucks delivered to the Royal Netherlands armed forces between September 2005-October 2006 were fitted with Hammar sideloaders. These vehicles were for the Royal Netherlands Air Force (RNAF) (Shaun C Connors) 1128248

Of the 548 LHS-equipped Scania P124CB8x8HZ420 (8 × 8) trucks delivered to the Royal Netherlands armed forces between September 2005-October 2006, 48 are adapted to carry Bridge Adapter Pallets (BAPs) for use with the Ribbon Bridge system (Shaun C Connors) 1128247

Of the 548 LHS-equipped Scania P124CB8x8HZ420 (8 × 8) trucks delivered to the Royal Netherlands armed forces between September 2005-October 2006, 355 are fitted with stowable container handling units (CHUs) and 145 with Hiab materials handling cranes; the cranes and CHUs are interchangeable units (Scania) 1128244

Of the 548 LHS-equipped Scania P124CB8x8HZ420 (8 × 8) trucks delivered to the Royal Netherlands armed forces between September 2005-October 2006, 145 are fitted with Hiab materials handling cranes and 355 with stowable container handling units (CHUs); the cranes and CHUs are interchangeable units (Scania) 1128243

During mid-2004 the Dutch defence forces decided to outsource the repair and maintenance of their Scania R124CB8x8HZ420 trucks for the planned lifetime of these vehicles. A Request For Quotations concerning this was announced 3Q05, the award going to Scania's Netherlands distributor, Scania Beers.

In July 2004 it was announced the Irish Defence Forces had selected a Scania (8 × 8) truck to meet an Irish Army requirement for a minimum of ten load handling system-equipped trucks. The contract for the supply of 15 Scania R124CB8x8 HZ420 trucks was awarded to local Scania dealer, Westward Scania. The trucks involved have similar specification to the Dutch R124CB8x8HZ420 vehicles and were delivered to the Irish Army late 2004/early 2005. Assembly was carried out by Scania Nederland at Zwolle. The fitted MPH165SC (previously designated Mk 4) LHS is manufactured by Multilift and features an integral container handling unit (CHU) and its stowage.

Description

The Scania P124CB8x8HZ420 (8 × 8) truck supplied to the Swedish defence forces is fitted with a Scania CP19 two-door safety sleeper forward control cab with two bunks. The cab accommodates a driver and one passenger, with provision for carrying their personal equipment. With the armoured cab and LHS fitted, the vehicle has a kerb weight of 17,825 kg and can be loaded to a gross vehicle weight (GVW) of 41,000 kg and a gross combination weight (GCW) of 70,000 kg, although peacetime load restrictions reduce both from that technically permitted.

Motive power is provided by a Scania EURO III emissions compliant 12-litre six-cylinder turbocharged diesel engine developing 420 hp. This drives all four axles (8 × 8) through a Scania nine-speed gearbox and Steyr GTD 901 two-speed transfer box. The first axle is a Scania AMD900/RP731 unit, the second a Scania AMD900/RBP731. The rear bogie axles are Scania AD1500/RBP832 units.

A Sepson H70PS self-recovery winch, deployable to the front or rear, is located on the right-hand side. The winch has a capacity of 7,000 kg and is equipped with 50 m of 14 mm diameter cable. Other standard equipment includes a connector for engine heating, heat exchanger, blowtorch, electric engine heater, 24 V Interstart socket (for emergency starting of the truck or another truck or armoured vehicle), and snow chains.

Examples supplied to the Royal Netherlands Army are fitted with a Scania CR19 two-door safety sleeper forward control cab. The cab has an interchangeable interior that allows for either the driver, one passenger and two bunks, or the driver and four passengers without bunks. Both configurations allow adequate provision for personal equipment. The cab is prepared for later mounting of ballistic and anti-personnel mine protection.

With ballistic and anti-personnel mine protection and a Multilift MPH165SC load handling system fitted, the vehicle can carry a 16,500 kg load and can be loaded to a gross vehicle weight (GVW) of 36,000 kg and a gross combination weight (GCW) of 70,000 kg although peacetime load restrictions reduce both from that technically permitted.

Driveline of the Netherlands vehicles is essentially similar to the earlier-delivered Swedish vehicles, the exceptions being the fitting of a Steyr GT 901 two-speed transfer box and the use of Scania AD1101P/RBP735 axles for the rear bogie.

The vehicles supplied to the Irish Army are fitted with a Scania CP19 two-door safety sleeper forward control cab with two bunks. These cabs are not prepared for ballistic protection. The driveline is essentially similar to Royal Netherlands vehicles, the exception being the use of a Scania GA852R fully automatic gearbox.

Specifications

Cab seating: 1 + 1, 1 + 2 or 1 + 4
Configuration: 8 × 8
Weight:
(Kerb, with Multilift LHS 261, Sepson H70PS and armouring) 17,825 kg
(GVW) 41,000 kg (Sweden), 36,000 kg (Netherlands/Ireland)
(GCW) 70,000 kg
Length: approximately 9.4 m
Width: 2.6 m
Height:
(CP19 cab) 3.4 m
(CR19 cab) 3.55 m
Ground clearance:
(Sweden) (AD1500/RBP832 rear axles and 365/85R 20 tyres) 290 mm
(Netherlands) (AD1101P/RBP735 rear axles and 315/80R 20 tyres) 350 mm
(Ireland) (AD1101P/RBP735 rear axles and 1400R 20 tyres) 400 mm
Track:
(front) 2.08 m
(rear) 2.03 m

Wheel base:
(Sweden) 5.100 + 1.445 m
(Netherlands/Ireland) 5.550 + 1.355 m
Angle of approach:
(Sweden) 30°
(Netherlands) 37°
(Ireland) 40°
Max speed: 85 km/h (limited)
Fuel capacity:
(Sweden) 300 litres
(Netherlands/Ireland) 2 × 200 litres
Engine: Scania DSC1201 EURO III 12-litre 6-cylinder in-line turbocharged water-cooled 4-stroke diesel developing 420 hp (309 kW) between 1,600 and 1,900 rpm
Gearbox: Scania GRS890R with 8 forward road gears and 1 crawler gear
(Sweden) Scania GRS890R with 9 forward gears (8 road plus crawler) and 1 reverse gear
(Netherlands) Scania GRS890R Opticruise automated with 9 forward (8 road plus crawler) and 1 reverse gears
(Ireland) Scania GA852R 6-speed fully automatic with hydraulic torque convertor
Transfer box:
(Sweden) Steyr GTD 901 2-speed
(Netherlands/Ireland) Steyr GT 901 2-speed
Steering: Scania, power-assisted
Suspension: three-leaf parabolic leaf springs and anti-roll bar, front; four-leaf parabolic leaf springs, rear bogie
Tyres:
(Sweden) 365/85R 20 or 315/80R 22.5
(Netherlands) 385/65R 22.5 (front steer-drive axles, axles rated at 9,000 kg), 315/80R 22.5 (rear drive axles)
(Ireland) 1400R 20
Brakes: dual-circuit air, ABS, drums all-round, supplementary engine exhaust brake
Electrical system: 24 V
Batteries:
(Sweden) 2 × 12 V, 170 Ah
(Netherlands) n/avail
(Ireland) 2 × 12 V, 175 Ah
Alternator:
(Sweden/Ireland) 90 A
(Netherlands) 2 × 90 A

Status
In service with the Irish (15, 2004/2005), Netherlands (555 delivered September 2005-October 2006) and Swedish (66, 2001) armies. The 4-series of trucks (from 2004) were replaced in Scania's product range by the revised and updated P, R and G series of trucks, full details of which can be found in the Scania range of trucks entry elsewhere in this section.

Contractor
Scania CV AB

Scania P124GB6×2NZ360 (6 × 2) truck

Development
The first 12 examples of the Scania P124GB6×2NZ360 (6 × 2) 4-series truck equipped with Multilift HL26.52 Load Handling Systems (LHS) were delivered to the Swedish Air Force during 1998. Designated a multipurpose airbase vehicle, these deliveries were a continuation from an earlier series of similar vehicles based on the previous Scania 3-series chassis. A further 14 vehicles were delivered in 2000, with a further 14 delivered in 2001.

The current Scania G, P and R series trucks became available throughout 2004 and these progressively replaced the earlier 4-series which had replaced the earlier 3-series in production during 1996. As of January 2006, the 4-series was only available produced in South America and for South American, Asian and African markets. Production of the 4-series concluded during 2007.

Description
The Scania P124GB6x2NZ360 (6 × 2) truck has a Scania CP14 two-door safety sleeper forward control cab (without beds). The cab can accommodate the driver and one passenger, with provision for carrying personal equipment.

With the Multilift H26.52 load handling system the vehicle has a kerb weight of 13,800 kg and can be loaded to a Gross Vehicle Weight (GVW) of 29,000 kg and a Gross Combination Weight (GCW) of 50,000 kg. Peacetime load restrictions reduce the GCW (and GVW) from that technically permitted. The LHS has a lifting capacity of 19,000 kg and, with a suitable body, a tipping capacity of 20,000 kg. Bodies employed in the multipurpose airbase vehicle role include a runway sweeper, heavy load carrier, tipper, de-icing, and a general cargo body.

The first batch of vehicles delivered were fitted with an Allison automatic transmission as the vehicle was required to be capable of operating with a snowplough attachment. Subsequent testing by the Swedish Air Force demonstrated it was possible to carry out ploughing operations with the Scania Opticruise gearbox. This was fitted to subsequent deliveries.

Scania P124GB6×2NZ360 (6 × 2) multipurpose airbase vehicle configured for gritting/de-icing operations (Scania)   0536766

In automatic mode the Scania Opticruise gearbox works as an automatic gearbox, the clutch only being required to pull away.

The front axle is a Scania AMD 920, with the rear unit being a Scania bogie AD100/RP832. The vehicle is equipped with a Robson drive on the rear bogie for increased traction in slippery surface conditions.

Specifications
Scania P124GB6x2NZ360 truck
Cab seating: 1 + 1
Configuration: 6 × 2
Weight:
(kerb, with LHS) 13,800 kg
(GVW) 29,000 kg
(GCW) 50,000 kg
Length: approx 8.9 m
Width: 2.6 m
Height: 2.9 m
Ground clearance:
(front, with 385/65 R 22.5 tyres) 250 mm
(rear, with 295/80 R 22.5 tyres) 230 mm
Track:
(front) 2.12 m
(rear) 1.83 m
Wheelbase: 4.7 m + 1.315 m
Fuel capacity: 500 litres
Engine: Scania DSC1202 EURO II 6-cylinder in-line turbocharged water-cooled 4-stroke diesel developing 360 hp (265 kW) between 1,600 and 1,900 rpm
Gearbox: Allison GA852R automatic (initial deliveries) Scania Opticruise (subsequent deliveries)
Turning radius: 10.1 m
Tyres:
(front) 385/65R 22.5
(rear) 295/80R 22.5
Brakes: dual circuit, air, ABS fitted
Electrical system: 24 V

Status
Production complete. Replaced in production by equivalent model from the 2004-introduced G, P and R series of trucks. In service with the Swedish Air Force.

Contractor
Scania CV AB

Volvo FL/FL6 (4 × 4) trucks

Development
The Volvo FL6 (4 × 4) truck is a militarised version of a commercial design and was designed and developed in Sweden, but produced at the Volvo Europa Truck plant at Ghent, in Belgium. Militarised FL6 trucks are used by Swedish Armed Forces.

Commercial production of the FL6 continues for certain markets, and Volvo continues to offer militarised versions as a special build. An all new Volvo FL was launched for other markets in 2006.

Description
The Volvo FL6 has a tilting forward control, all-steel crash-resistant cab available with various optional layouts and equipment fits. A crew cab with seating for five or six is also available. Special models include a version for airborne operations, a desert version and a mobile communications shelter.

The conventional C-section chassis is available in various wheelbase lengths varying from 3.7 to 4.6 m, and with a 3,000 to 9,020 kg payload capacities. Engine power outputs vary from engines 180 to 250 hp. Engine dependant six- or nine-speed manual gearboxes are standard fit, with the

Desertised version of the Volvo FL6 (4 × 4) truck (Stefan Marx) 1128255

Prototype Volvo FL12 (8 × 8) high mobility vehicle fitted with a load handling system and transporting a UNITEAM 3 in 1 container (Volvo) 0524739

option of a four- or five-speed automatic. Suspension is by tapered leaf springs with double-acting telescopic shock-absorbers, front and rear. Front and rear axles are fitted with a cross-axle differential lock, and a longitudinal differential lock is fitted to the two-speed transfer box. Power take-off (PTO) is optional.

Commercially produced FL6 trucks have GVWs ranging from 7,500 to 26,000 kg and are available with two or three axles; options including two-axle tractor trucks. For three axle military applications heavier designs from the Volvo FM/FMX ranges are better suited.

Specifications

Volvo FL6
Cab seating: 1 + 1 or 1 + 2
Configuration: 4 × 4
Weight:
(kerb) 4,890 kg
(front axle) 3,480 kg
(rear axle) 1,500 kg
(max payload) 9,020 kg
(towed load) 7,000 kg
Length: (chassis) wheelbase dependent
Width: (over cab) 2.368 m
Height: (cab, unladen) 2.826 m
Wheelbase: 3.7 m to 4.6 m
Angle of approach/departure: 36°/38°
Fuel capacity: 200 litres
Engine: (current) Volvo D6B180 6-cylinder in-line water-cooled turbocharged direct injection 4-stroke diesel developing 180 hp (132 kW) at 2,400 rpm and 575 N.m torque between 1,400-1,800 rpm or Volvo D6B220 6-cylinder in-line water-cooled turbocharged and intercooled 4-stroke direct injection diesel developing 220 hp (162 kW) at 2,400 rpm and 700 N.m torque between 1,400-1,800 rpm or Volvo D6B250 6-cylinder in-line water-cooled turbocharged and intercooled 4-stroke direct injection diesel developing 250 hp (184 kW) at 2,400 rpm and 825 N m torque between 1,400-1,800 rpm
Gearbox: (current) 6- or 9-speed manual, 4- or 5-speed automatic option
Clutch: single dry plate (torque convertor with automatic option)
Transfer box: 2-speed
Steering: ball and nut, power assisted
Turning radius: wheelbase dependent
Suspension: tapered leaf springs with telescopic double acting shock-absorbers, front and rear
Tyres: 12.00R 20 18PR all-terrain (other options available)
Brakes: dual circuit, air
Electrical system: 24 V
Batteries: 2 × 12 V, 160 Ah
Alternator: 55 A

Status

In service with the Swedish Armed Forces. Available as special build with current generation components.

Contractor

Volvo Truck Corporation
Volvo Europa Trucks

Volvo FL10 and FL12 trucks

Development

Military variants of the Volvo FL10 and FL12 trucks were based on the extensive range of Volvo FL10 and FL12 commercial trucks. These have now been replaced in production by the FM range, this recently joined by the heavier duty FMX.

Volvo FL12 (6 × 6) Self-Loading Dump Truck (SLDT) of the British Army in Kosovo (Richard Stickland) 0524738

Volvo FL12 (6 × 6) truck with load handling system (Volvo) 0056352

Description

All FL10 and FL12 models utilise an all-welded, forward control, steel crash-resistant cab produced with various seating arrangements, including a five/six-passenger crew cab and optional roof hatches or other openings.

A wide variety of drive configurations were available, the base FL10 and FL12 vehicles being built in (4 × 4) and (6 × 6) configurations although (4 × 2), (6 × 2), (6 × 4), (8 × 2) and (8 × 4) options were available. Engine power options varied from 320 to 420 hp and there was a choice of manual or automatic gearboxes, driven axles with or without hub reduction and differential locks between the wheels or axles.

Both models were suitable for a variety of applications including tractors, cargo vehicles or tankers when fitted with the appropriate superstructure.

FL10 and FL12 models are powered by 10- and 12-litre engines respectively - all engines being six-cylinder, in-line, turbocharged and intercooled. Gross vehicle design weights ranged from 20,000 kg in the (4 × 4) configuration to 40,000 kg for the (8 × 4) configuration. Gross combination weights ranged from 44,000 kg to 150,000 kg enabling FL12 tractor trucks to be employed in the tank transporter role if required.

Typical (6 × 6) applications were as a carrier for a Load Handling System (LHS) or as a dump truck. The UK MoD (Royal Engineers) received 144 of these in the role of Self Loading Dump Truck (SLDT). Of these, 17 were equipped with riotous protection kits for use in Northern Ireland. UK MoD vehicles are powered by a D12A340 diesel developing 340 hp at 1,700 to 1,800 rpm.

An FL12 (8 × 8) prototype high mobility load carrier was built, this fitted with a load handling system and having a payload of 15,000 kg. This version was fitted with Timoney independent suspension and was powered by a Volvo D12A420 diesel developing 420 hp. There was no series production of this variant.

Specifications

FL12 self-loading dumptruck
Cab seating: 1 + 1 or 2
Configuration: 6 × 6
Weight:
   (chassis) 10,170 kg
   (on front axle) 7,500 kg
   (on rear bogie) 26,000 kg
   (GVW) 33,500 kg
   (max load, body and payload, road) 23,330 kg
Length: (chassis) 7.52 m
Width: (cab) 2.49 m
Height: (cab roof, unladen) 3.065 m
Ground clearance: 300 mm
Track:
   (front) 2 m
   (rear) 1.95 m
Wheelbase: (front axle to first drive axle) 3.75 m
Angle of approach/departure: 27°/45°
Fuel capacity: 200, 300 or 400 litres
Engine: Volvo D12A340 EURO II emissions compliant 12.1-litre 6-cylinder in-line water-cooled turbocharged and intercooled direct injection 4-stroke diesel developing 340 hp (254 kW) at 1,700-1,800 rpm
Gearbox: Volvo R1700 manual 8-speed with crawler and one reverse gears
Transfer box: Volvo FD7 single-speed
Steering: ball and nut, power assisted
Turning radius: 8.9 m
Suspension:
   (front) leaf springs with shock-absorbers
   (rear) leaf springs with shock-absorbers and anti-roll bar
Tyres: 315/80R 22.5
Brakes: air-actuated dual circuit drum-type
Electrical system: 24 V
Batteries: 170 or 220 Ah
Alternator: 55 or 80 A

Status

Production complete. Replaced by the FM9, FM12 (now designated FM) and FMX ranges. In service with the Swedish Army (approximately 200), British Army (PFI replacement underway) and with the UN in the former Yugoslavia.

Contractor

Volvo Truck Corporation

Volvo N10 and N12 ranges of trucks

Development

The Volvo N10 and N12 ranges of trucks were designed as heavy-duty commercial vehicles and, as such, proved ideally suited for military applications. They were superseded in production by the NL10 and NL12 models with uprated drivelines, the NL10 and NL12 models themselves being replaced in production in 1998 by the current NH range of trucks. No all-wheel drive NH models are known to have been produced or adopted for tactical military roles.

Description

The Volvo N10 and N12 ranges of trucks were produced in both two- and three-axle configurations but three-axle versions are the only ones known to have been adopted for military use, and in (6 × 2), (6 × 4) and (6 × 6) drive configurations. The N10 and N12 designation refers to engine capacities, the N10 using a 9.61-litre engine, the N12 using a 12.1-litre engine.

Belgian Army Volvo N10 (6 × 6) truck in dump truck configuration; note the twin rear wheels (Stefan Marx)
1047669

Belgian Army Volvo N10 (6 × 4) truck with standard cargo body; the tarpaulin and bows have been removed from this vehicle (Stefan Marx)
1047671

Belgian Army Volvo N10 (6 × 4) truck with cargo body and crane (Christopher F Foss)
1047670

The layout of the N10/N12 is conventional, with the engine located forward under a squared-off bonnet, the cab having seating for the driver and at least one passenger and with the cargo area to the rear. Some cargo vehicles are fitted with a handling crane just behind the cab and the all-steel cargo body has drop sides and a tailgate. Tanker, tipper, LHS and recovery variants were also produced. Three wheelbase lengths were available, 4.835, 5.235, and 5.635 m and these were available with various chassis lengths. Gross vehicle weights varied between 26,500 and 33,500 kg for the (6 × 6) models.

A tractor truck variant of the N12 model with a 4.2 m wheelbase is in service with the Swedish Army in the heavy equipment transporter role. Full details of this vehicle can be found in the Heavy equipment transporters section.

Belgium adopted the N10, with local production being carried out in Belgium by Hocké at Alsemberg. A total of 1,221 units were procured. 721 of these were (6 × 4), the remainder (6 × 6). Deliveries included 683 examples configured as cargo trucks; 78 with enclosed bodies for offices, maintenance and so on; 133 tipper bodies; 40 examples fitted with the Marrel Amplirol load handling system (LHS); 145 recovery vehicles, and 20 with bodies for the medical services. Manumat cranes fitted to Belgian vehicles have a capacity of 1,100 kg and a reach of 5.6 m. As of February 2009, 1,054 N10 trucks remained in service with the Belgian Army.

Belgian Army Volvo N10 (6 × 6) truck in recovery configuration (Stefan Marx)
1047668

One of 80 Volvo N10 (6 × 2) fuel tankers supplied to the Swedish Air Force (Richard Stickland)
0524737

Volvo NL12 (6 × 6) truck fitted with a Load Handling System (LHS) (Stefan Marx)
1128256

In December 2002 it was announced the Belgian Army had awarded IVECO a contract valued in the region of EURO 25 million to supply 150 EuroTrakker range trucks fitted with TAM load handling systems (LHS) (full details of the EuroTrakker range can be found elsewhere in this section). Deliveries commenced early 2004 and as these trucks entered service many of the N10 fleet were re-roled, replacing an ageing fleet of MAN 11.136 HA 5,000 kg MAN (4 × 4) trucks, 512 of which remained in service as of February 2009.

Specifications
N10 6 × 6
Cab seating: 1 + 1 or 2
Configuration: 6 × 6
Weight: (basic chassis, 5.235 m wheelbase) 9,155 kg
Max payload: (incl superstructure) 17,345 kg
Length: (chassis) 7.992 m
Width: (overall) 2.4 m
Height: (cab) 3.02 m
Wheelbase: 5.235 m
Fuel capacity: 300 litres
Engine: 9.6-litre 6-cylinder in-line water-cooled turbocharged and intercooled 4-stroke diesel developing 275 hp (202 kW) at 2,200 rpm
Gearbox: R1400, 8 forward (plus crawler) and 2 reverse gears
Clutch: KFD214A twin dry plate
Transfer box: FD6 2-speed
Steering: ball and nut, power assisted
Suspension: leaf springs and hydraulic shock absorbers, front and rear
Tyres: 12.00R 20, 14.00R 20 or 12.00R 24
Brakes: dual circuit air
Electrical system: 24 V

Status
Production complete. N10 (6 × 4) and (6 × 6) in service with the Belgian Army (1,221 delivered, 1,054 in February 2009). N10 (6 × 2) in service with the Swedish Air Force (80 delivered).

Contractor
Volvo Truck Corporation

Volvo NL10 (4 × 4) and NL12 (6 × 6) trucks

Development
The Volvo NL10 (4 × 4) and NL12 (6 × 6) trucks were the successors to the Volvo N10 and N12 trucks and follow the same general layout, differing primarily in a revised driveline. Full details of the N10 and N12 trucks can be found elsewhere in this section. Production of the NL10 and NL12 models was completed in Sweden during 1993, and during 1998 in Australia and Brazil. The NL10 and NL12 models were replaced in production by the NH range. No all-wheel drive NH models are known to have been produced or adopted for tactical military roles.

Description
As with other Volvo trucks, components such as engines, gearboxes, axles, cabs and most chassis parts for the NL10 and NL12 ranges were designed and produced in-house by Volvo. NL range trucks were available with a wide range of optional equipment for different military roles. Various types of suspension, differing rear axle ratios with single or hub reduction, differential locks, crew cabs and various wheelbase lengths were also offered. (4 × 2), (6 × 2) and (6 × 4) drive configurations were also available.

A 10,000 kg desert transporter version was developed. This, in common with other NL10/12 (6 × 6) trucks, was capable of accepting a load handling system (LHS). This version had an on-road payload of 16,000 kg.

Specifications
Cab seating: 1 + 1 or 2
Configuration:
   (NL10) 4 × 4
   (NL12) 6 × 6
Weight:
   (NL10) 6,880-6,920 kg
   (NL12) 9,000-9,150 kg
Max payload: (inc superstructure)
   (NL10) 12,770-12,820 kg
   (NL12) 23,700 kg
Length: (chassis only)
   (NL10) 6.952-8.292 m
   (NL12) 7.962-9.662 m
Width: (overall) 2.4 m
Height: (cab) 3.02 m
Wheelbase: 4.3-5.1 m
Fuel capacity: 300 to 600 litres
Engine:
   (NL10) Volvo 9.6-litre 6-cylinder in-line water-cooled turbocharged and intercooled 4-stroke diesel developing between 275 and 320 hp (202 and 235 kW)
   (NL12) Volvo 12-litre 6-cylinder in-line water-cooled turbocharged and intercooled 4-stroke diesel developing between 329 and 405 hp (242 and 298 kW)
Gearbox:
   (NL10) R1400 range and SR1400 range, 8 forward (plus crawler) and 2 reverse gears
   (NL12) R1700 range and SR1700 range, 8 forward (plus crawler) and 2 reverse gears
Clutch: KFD 117C single dry plate
Transfer box: Volvo FD7 2-speed
Steering: ball and nut, power assisted
Suspension: leaf springs and hydraulic shock-absorbers, front and rear
Tyres: 12.00R 20, 14.00R 20 or 12.00R 24
Brakes: dual circuit, air, drums all-round
Electrical system: 24 V

Status
Production complete. Volvo has never disclosed any details relating to the sale of militarised NL10/NL12 trucks, however some essentially commercial specification examples are known to have been procured for military use by armed forces in South/Central America.

Contractor
Volvo Truck Corporation

Volvo BM A25C (6 × 6) truck

Description
The Volvo BM A25C (6 × 6) truck is one of a series of similar Volvo commercial machines built on an articulated chassis to provide a payload of about 19,000 kg while operating over rough terrain. By far the most common commercial application for these machines is that of dump truck; Volvo's product range being known as articulated haulers. Frame-steer or articulated dump trucks are other well-used descriptions of the type. The current generation of Volvo articulated haulers carry the E designation - A25E for example.

The Swedish Army use the BM A25C as a multipurpose carrier fitted with a HIAB 8801/3 hydraulic crane and use the vehicle to support Swedish Army 155 mm self-propelled gun batteries; it could be readily adapted to other similar heavy-duty roles.

Volvo BM A25C of the Swedish Army fitted with a Multilift Load Handling System (LHS) (Carl Schulze)   1391210

From the rear, a Volvo BM A25C of the Swedish Army fitted with a Multilift Load Handling System (LHS) (Carl Schulze)   1391227

Due to the articulated chassis, the front section and cab can turn to an angle of 45° either side and independently of the rear cargo area. The Volvo BM two-seat cab is Roll-Over and Falling Object Protected (ROPS and FOPS) and mounted on rubber pads. A seven-litre Volvo turbocharged and intercooled diesel provides 255 hp and is connected to a five-speed fully automatic gearbox with a torque converter and integrated hydraulic retarder. A Volvo drop-box has a power take-off and differential lock providing full six-wheel drive with the possibility of 100 per cent differential locking on all axles.

The front axle is suspended on a three-point suspension while the Volvo rear bogie permits individual oscillation between the axles but is not sprung.

If required, Volvo articulated haulers can be equipped with a Multilift Load Handling System (LHS). The type has also been fitted with a number of weapons systems for trials and evaluation purposes. For these roles the chassis has been modified with a fully armoured NBC-protected cab that can accommodate up to a six-man crew. Armoured protection extends to the engine compartment.

Weapons mounted on the chassis for trials include the upper part of the now BAE Systems Bofors (formerly Bofors Defence, then part of United Defense of the US) 120 mm KARIN/CD 80 mobile coast defence gun and the now BAE Systems Bofors 40 mm L/70 anti-aircraft gun system, the latter being called the TRIDON. Neither system progressed beyond prototype stage.

Production standard Archer fitted with armoured cab and a Lemur Remote Weapon Station (RWS). Archer is based on a Volvo A30E chassis (BAE Systems)   1391467

Volvo BM A25C (6 × 6) truck of the Swedish Army fitted with container handling equipment, unladen (Richard Stickland)   0126598

In January 2009 it was announced that Sweden's FMV had awarded BAE Systems a USD70 million contract to complete development of the FH-77 BD L52 Archer self propelled artillery system, this contract including a production option covering the supply of 48 systems. The FH-77 BD L52 self propelled artillery system is based on a Volvo A30E chassis. Work on the first automotive prototype of what would eventually mature to become Archer began in 1992.

Specifications

BM A25C
Cab seating: 1 + 1
Configuration: 6 × 6
Weight:
    (front axle, laden) 11,500 kg
    (rear axles, laden) 28,770 kg
    (GVW) 40,270 kg
    (payload, off-road) 19,000 kg
Load area: 6.42 × 3 m
Length: 11.7 m
Width: (overall) 3.1 m
Height:
    (cab) 3.24 m
    (crane) 3.91 m
Ground clearance: 465 mm
Track: 2.15 m
Wheelbase: 5.165 m + 1.8 m
Max speed: 52 or 63 km/h
Fuel capacity: 280 or 360 litres
Fording: 1 m
Engine: Volvo 7 litre 6-cylinder in-line water-cooled turbocharged and intercooled 4-stroke diesel developing 255 hp (187 kW)
Transmission: ZF 5 HP 500 automatic with 5 forward and 1 reverse gears, plus torque converter
Transfer box: Volvo FL652 2-speed
Steering: hydromechanical, power assisted
Suspension:
    (front) 3 point axle suspension
    (rear) unsprung Volvo bogie with individual axle movement
Tyres: 23.5R 25
Brakes: dual circuit air
Electrical system: 24 V

Status
Current model in production. In service with the Swedish Army (see text for details).

Contractor
Volvo Construction Equipment

Volvo FM/FMX ranges of trucks

Development
The Volvo FM range of trucks was introduced in 1998 as the FM7, FM10 and FM12, these replacing the earlier generation FL7, FL10 and FL12. FM denotes Forward control Medium height cab, with the associated numbers indicating engine capacity in litres.

First generation FM range trucks (FM7, FM10 and FM12) were available from 1998 until 2001. In 2001 the FM range underwent a major revision. The current generation of FM trucks was introduced in 2005 and from this time engine capacity is no longer indicated in model denomination.

Of all Volvo commercial truck ranges the weight classes covered, engine power outputs and overall design traits of the FM range ensure these are by far the most popular Volvo product with military users. The most

Volvo FM12 (6 × 6) truck (Volvo) 1128251

In addition to the FM range, Volvo also offers the FL6, FL, FE, FH, VHD/VN and VM ranges. This FH12 (6 × 4) is used by the Indian Army in a ballast tractor role with the AGNI III IRBM (Gordon Arthur) 1391186

Volvo FM12 (6 × 6) truck chassis cab (Volvo) 1128252

Volvo FM12 (6 × 6) truck of the Swedish Army fitted with a Multilift L26.50 Load Handling System (LHS) (Volvo) 0059690

Volvo FM12 (6 × 6) truck (Volvo) 1128253

Cab armouring system for the Volvo FM range of trucks (Volvo) 0059686

popular model for military applications has been the heavier-duty FM12. With the exception of some earlier generation models and an FM12 prototype in 8 × 8 configuration with independent suspension, Volvo trucks for military applications are now mildly militarised commercial products.

As with all Volvo models, the majority of the major components used in the FM range, including engines, transmissions, cabs and chassis frames, are designed and manufactured in-house.

During 2010 Volvo introduced the heavier duty FM-based FMX, this targeted at heavy duty on-/off-road commercial applications.

The most recent Swedish Army FM12 range procurements have included 40 FM12 6 × 6 chassis for use with the EWK FSB ribbon bridge system. These were delivered in December 2002.

In March 2003 and following the 2002 delivery of a prototype, Volvo was awarded the contract to supply three 6 × 2 aircraft de-icing units to the Swedish Air Force. These vehicles were required to meet international legislation and are capable of global deployment in support of Swedish peacekeeping/humanitarian operations. The bodies were supplied by Kiitokori of Finland.

In April 2003 Volvo was awarded a contract for 30 FM12 6 × 6 trucks fitted with a container handling solution from Swedish body builder Laxa.

In March 2004 Volvo was awarded a contract to supply 16 (30 including options) Fire Crash Tenders to the Swedish Air Force. The specification is based around the FM12 6 × 6 fitted with a crew-cab and bodywork furnished by Autokaross Rescue System AB (ARS) of Sweden. The prototype was delivered in May 2005 with deliveries scheduled to run until June 2007.

Early 2005 Volvo was awarded a contract for four 40-passenger all-terrain transports. These vehicles are based on the chassis and driveline of a Volvo FM9 4 × 4 truck and on which the conventional cab is essentially extended backwards to form bus-type coachwork.

Poland's Armed Forces use a small number of locally procured Volvo FM12 6 × 6 chassis fitted with a Multilift load handling system for specialist applications.

Volvo FM12 (6 × 6) truck of the Swedish Army fitted with a Multilift L26.50 Load Handling System (LHS) and configured for the cargo role (Volvo)
0059689

Early 2005 Volvo was awarded a contract for four 40-passenger all-terrain transports. These vehicles are based on the chassis and driveline of a Volvo FM9 4 × 4 truck and on which the conventional cab is essentially extended backwards to form bus-type coachwork (Volvo)
1391048

Description

With the exception of the high mobility FM12 8 × 8 designed in cooperation with Timoney Technology of Ireland and fitted with Timoney independent suspension, all military FM range trucks are based on the standard commercial FM range chassis, militarised as required, but without extensive modification. Two, three or four-axle chassis, in varying lengths, are available, and in a wide variety of drive configurations. Like the earlier FL ranges, the FM utilises an all-steel safety cab in day, sleeper, high-roof Globetrotter and crew cab configurations.

Volvo has developed a cab armouring system for the FM which, by way of an appliquè kit attached to built-in fixing points, allows the standard cab to be fully protected within a short space of time. Depending on cab type and protection levels required, the total weight of the add-on armour will be approximately 1,500 to 1,600 kg. Loading on the original cab structure is limited to approximately 1,100 kg, the rear wall of the cab being fixed to the chassis frame. The optional mine protection is also designed for fixing directly to the chassis frame.

The base engines used throughout the FM range are currently the Volvo D11C, Volvo D13B and Volvo D13C. The D11C is a 10.8-litre unit with power output options of 330, 370, 410 and 450 hp, the D13B is a 12.7-litre unit with power outputs of 360, 400 or 440 hp, and the D13C a 12.8-litre unit with power output options of 380, 420, 460 and 500 hp. All are six-cylinder in-line units and meet current EURO emission requirements.

Transmission options include nine- and 14-speed (with or without overdrive) manual gearboxes, Volvo's I-shift (automated gear change), or six-speed Powertronic fully automatic gearboxes. Single- or hub-reduction drive axles are available. Air suspension is becoming standard for commercial vehicles, although for most military applications the optional leaf or parabolic spring suspension remains the preferred choice.

The FM model range is suitable for a variety of military applications, these including tractor trucks, cargo/LHS vehicles, recovery and tankers. Military all-wheel drive versions of the FM range are equipped to meet NATO specification requirements with front/rear towing facilities, recovery points, blackout lighting and inter-vehicle start sockets and so on. Waterproofing for deep salt-water wading and winterisation for operation in extreme cold is also possible.

Other Volvo ranges

Volvo also offers the FL6, FL, FE, FH, VHD/VN and VM ranges of trucks.

Volvo FM12 (6 × 2) truck of the Swedish Air Force; the specialist de-icing bodies were supplied by Kiitokori of Finland (Volvo)
1128254

The FL6 and associated FL (introduced 2006) are Volvo's smallest truck ranges. The FL6, which has been produced in all-wheel drive versions, is now only available in selected markets. An overview of the FL/FL6 ranges can be found elsewhere in this section.

The Volvo FE is a medium duty truck and was introduced in 2006 to replace the earlier FL7. The FE is available in rigid chassis or tractor truck variants and shares engine and gearboxes with the Volvo FL.

The FH range was introduced in 1993 as the FH12 and FH16 and production continues, FH denoting Forward control High cab, with the associated numbers indicating engine capacity in litres. FH range trucks are predominantly used for tractor truck roles, with military use (outside of 'third line' logistic support roles) predominantly as heavy equipment transporters. An overview of the FH range can be found in the Heavy equipment transporters section.

The VHD/VN ranges are bonneted designs and only available in Canada, Mexico and the US.

The Volvo VM, available as a rigid chassis or tractor truck, is produced in Brazil for regional markets.

Specifications

FM12 6 × 6
(Swedish Army)
Cab seating: 1 + 2
Configuration: 6 × 6
Weight:
  (laden, permissible GVW) 35,000 kg
  (unladen) 12,560 kg
  (payload) 22,440 kg (13,440 kg at legal 26,000 kg GVW)
  (front axle load) 9,000 kg
  (rear axle load) 26,000 kg
  (towed load) 34,000 kg
  (GCW) 60,000 kg
Length: 8.78 m
Width: 2.55 m
Height: 3.3 m
Ground clearance: 370 mm
Track:
  (front) 2.11 m
  (rear) 1.81 m
Wheelbase: 4.6 m
Angle of approach/departure: 27°/35°
Max speed: 95 km/h
Range: 1,100 km
Fuel capacity: 410 litres
Max gradient: 38%
Max sideslope: 30%
Fording:
  (unprepared 750 mm
  (prepared) 1.3 m
Engine: Volvo D12D420 12-litre 6-cylinder in-line water-cooled turbocharged and intercooled 4-stroke diesel developing 420 hp (309 kW) and 2,000 N.m torque at 1,050-1,450 rpm
Gearbox: Volvo VT 2014 manual with splitter giving 14 forward gears (12 + 2 crawler)
Clutch: CD40B twin dry plate, 400 mm diameter
Transfer box: Volvo single-speed
Steering: recirculating ball and nut
Turning radius: 9.56 m
Suspension: multileaf with rubber assistors and shock-absorbers, front; multileaf, anti-roll bar and shock-absorbers, rear
Tyres: 385/65R 22.5, front; 315/80R 22.5, rear
Brakes: dual circuit, air, drums all-round, Anti-lock Braking System (ABS)
Electrical system: 24 V (to ADR standard)
Batteries: 2 × 12 V, 225 Ah
Alternator: 80 Ah

Status

In production in Sweden. In service with Kuwait, Poland and Sweden.

Contractor

Volvo Truck Corporation

Volvo FM12 (8 × 8) truck

Development
The Volvo FM12 (8 × 8) truck is a high-mobility, all-wheel-drive, multipurpose vehicle, and was designed in co-operation with Timoney Technology of Ireland. Full details of the Volvo FM truck range and an overview of other Volvo truck ranges can be found elsewhere in this section.

Description
The Volvo FM12 8 × 8 high-mobility truck has been designed primarily for military applications but remains compliant with all relevant civilian legislation. For improved mobility the design features a torsionally rigid box-section chassis and Timoney independent suspension on all axles. Suspension units are common to all axles and are a double wishbone with coil spring and shock-absorber design. Load rating is 9,000 kg per axle, although this can be increased to 10,000 kg. Any axle can be adapted from drive to steer-drive configuration, giving the option of all-wheel steer for improved manoeuvrability.

The FM12 is based on the standard Volvo FM12 range and uses the standard Volvo forward control tilt cab together with standard Volvo driveline components. The prototype vehicle is fitted with a Volvo 12-litre 420 hp turbocharged diesel engine and Powertronic automatic transmission.

Specifications
FM12
Cab seating: 1 + 1 or 2
Configuration: 8 × 8
Weight:
  (design GVW) 40,000 kg
  (front axles, each) 10,000 kg
  (rear axles, each) 10,000 kg
  (max load, approx body + payload) 25,000 kg
Length: 8.995 m
Width: 2.5 m
Height: 3.2 m
Ground clearance: 0.452 m
Track: (front/rear) 2.08 m (approx)
Wheelbase: various
Fuel capacity: 300 litres
Engine: Volvo D12C420 EURO 2 emissions compliant 12.1-litre 6-cylinder in-line water-cooled turbocharged and intercooled direct-injection 4-stroke diesel developing 420 hp (313 kW) at 1,800 rpm and peak torque of 2,000 N.m between 1,100 and 1,300 rpm
Gearbox: Volvo VT1906PT Powertronic fully automatic 6-speed
Transfer box: Steyr VG 2001/396 single-speed
Steering: ball and nut, power assisted
Turning circle: wheelbase dependent
Suspension:
  (front) fully independent coil and wishbone with shock-absorbers
  (rear) fully independent coil and wishbone with shock-absorbers (option for hydrastruts with variable ride height)
Tyres: 395/85R 22.5 Michelin XZL
Brakes: air actuated dual circuit discs located outboard, option of drums or inboard discs
Electrical system: 24 V
Batteries: 2 × 12 V, 220 Ah
Alternator: 80 Ah

Status
Prototype. May be available as special build on current generation chassis.

Contractor
Volvo Truck Corporation

Volvo FM12 (8 × 8) high-mobility truck in chassis-cab configuration (Volvo)   0059700

Switzerland

MOWAG DURO (4 × 4) and (6 × 6) range of military vehicles

Development
Development of the DURO began in the 1980s. It was one of more than 15 vehicles involved in trials to replace the Swiss Army's ageing light vehicle fleet, and following over 750,000 km of trials in Switzerland and elsewhere, an initial order for 2,000 vehicles was placed with Bucher Industries Bucher Automotive Division in 1993. Deliveries began during 1994, continuing until 1999. A second batch of 1,000 vehicles was subsequently ordered. Production of these concluded during 2001. Swiss Army vehicles are now designated DURO I and are powered by a VM Motori diesel engine. 3,007 vehicles were delivered in total.

DURO stands for *Dauerhaft, Unabhängig, Robust, Oekonomisch* - Durable, Self-reliant, Robust, Economic, or more simply, DUrable and RObust.

An Austrian-Swiss consortium consisting of Bucher-Guyer and Steyr-Daimler-Puch Spezialfahrzeug of Austria was set up to offer the DURO in selected markets. A result from this co-operation was the sale of 150 vehicles, in 4 × 4 configuration, to the Venezuelan Ministry of Defence for use by the Venezuelan National Guard. Valued at USD18.1 million, deliveries took place during 2001. A further 150 4 × 4 vehicles were subsequently ordered for use by the Venezuelan Army. Deliveries of this batch concluded late 2002, and by mid 2003 Venezuela had received a total of 358 DURO vehicles, all of these being DURO I.

Between 2000 and 2002, South Africa and Singapore procured the DURO for use a fire vehicles. South Africa received 14 vehicles, Singapore 61.

In November 2002 Bucher Industries announced plans to sell the DURO All-Terrain Transport Vehicle Unit to MOWAG Motorwagenfabrik AG (now MOWAG GmbH; MOWAG is a General Dynamics company). The sale was completed early 2003.

The DURO chassis, in 6 × 6 configuration, was selected by the then Nortel Networks (now Cogent Defence and Security Networks Ltd) as the platform for the Cormorant communication system for the British Army. Eighty three chassis are involved and all mount a shelter-type body supplied by Marshall Specialist Vehicles and can tow a dedicated trailer manufactured by Penman Engineering. A follow-on order for an additional 35 vehicles fitted with a Penman Engineering-supplied cargo-type body and a Hiab materials handling crane for Cormorant system 'loose stowage' items were ordered during 2005. By June 2006 these had been delivered.

The British Army's Cormorant requirement DUROs features a EURO III emissions compliant Cummins ISB 5.9 litre diesel engine coupled to an uprated transmission. This version of the DURO was also available in both 4 × 4 wheelbase variants and is known as the DURO II; MOWAG no longer offers the DURO IIL (L - long wheelbase).

Bucher (now MOWAG) DURO I 4 × 4 truck of the Venezuelan National Guard (MOWAG)   0095044

Demonstrated at DVD 2005, a MOWAG DURO II (6 × 6) fitted with a standard troop-carrying body (Patrick Allen)   1067509

Rear three-quarter view of a DURO II (6 × 6) Project Cormorant vehicle of
the British Army, as displayed at DVD 2005 (Patrick Allen)   1146264

Front three-quarter view of a DURO II (6 × 6) Project Cormorant vehicle of
the British Army, as displayed at DVD 2005 (Patrick Allen)   1146263

Front three-quarter view of a DURO II (6 × 6) Project Cormorant loose
stowage vehicle of the British Army, as displayed at DVD 2005
(Shaun C Connors)   1156034

Eight DURO I 6 × 6 vehicles were fitted with specialist EOD bodies
removed from surplus Leyland chassis to meet a UK MoD UOR (Urgent
Operational Requirement) for EOD vehicles for deployment to Iraq during
the second Gulf War. A further four DURO II 6 × 6 chassis for EOD use and
fitted with a riotous protection kit were delivered early 2004.

Between 2000 and 2003 Malaysia received 57 DURO I 6 × 6 chassis.
These were supplied as chassis-cabs with local content in the form of
bodies being manufactured and fitted by DRB-HICOM. These were the last
DURO I models produced; MOWAG no longer offers the DURO I.

It was announced mid 2005 that MOWAG had signed a licensing
agreement with DRB-HICOM for the production of the DURO II in Malaysia.
Mid 2009 it was disclosed this agreement had expired.

In December 2003 the Irish Army received six DURO II 6 × 6 chassis fitted
with EOD bodies manufactured by Penman Engineering of the UK. Three
of these chassis have blast-proof rear bodies and armoured cabs.

Demonstrated at DVD (Defence Vehicles Dynamics) 2006, a MOWAG
DURO II (4 × 4) fitted with a standard troop-carrying body
(Shaun C Connors)   1156033

Displayed at DVD 2006, a Project Citizen DURO III EOD vehicle
(Shaun C Connors)   1156035

MOWAG announced the DURO III in 2003. The DURO III was initially only
available in 6 × 6 configuration and was designed from the outset with a
small arms fire and anti-personnel mine protected cab. Unarmoured
versions of the DURO III became available and have also been produced. In
June 2006 MOWAG announced the introduction of a DURO III 4 × 4 chassis.

In February 2004 two pre-production DURO III 6 × 6 chassis were
delivered to the UK MoD for various trials including the Reacher
programme (part of Skynet 5), for which the DURO III was selected. The
Reacher programme prime contractor procured the 48 DURO III chassis
required.

During 2005 a further 18 DURO III chassis-cabs were delivered to the UK
MoD, with eight of these being for EOD use and fitted with protection kits;
in service these vehicles replaced the earlier procured DURO I EOD
vehicles. It was disclosed mid-2006 that to meet operational requirements
14 of these 18 chassis had, under UOR Project Citizen, been fitted with blast
protection for EOD use on deployed operations.

It was disclosed in June 2006 that under UOR Project Teller the UK MoD
would procure 18 DURO III 4 × 4 chassis for EOD use by the Royal
Engineers. These vehicles have been fitted with protected cabs and bodies
supplied by Penman Engineering and were scheduled for delivery during
November 2006. Initial deployment commenced during June 2007.

It was also disclosed during June 2006 that MOWAG would supply six
DURO III (P) in 6 × 6 configuration to the Swiss Army. These vehicles will be
fitted with a MOWAG-developed small arms fire and blast protection kit
and were scheduled for delivery between November 2006 and January
2007.

It was disclosed in January 2007 that MOWAG had been awarded a
CHF32.26 million (USD26.5 million) contract by the Danish Army Materiel
Command (DAMC) for 29 DURO III (P) Protected in 6 × 6 configuration and
configured in an Armoured Ambulance Vehicle (AAV) configuration. The
first vehicles were delivered from the Swiss production line in October
2007 to meet an urgent operational requirement (UOR).

During 2008 it was disclosed that an additional four DURO III 6× 6 had
been procured by the UK MoD for an undisclosed user. These vehicles are
for a communications role and are fitted with Penman-supplied rear
bodies.

In February 2009 it was disclosed that the Swiss Army was to order 220
DURO IIIP 6 × 6 armoured personnel carriers under the Army's Geschütztes
Mannschaftstransportfahrzeug (GMTF) requirement, and 12 nuclear,
biological, chemical (NBC) laboratory DURO IIIP versions, all for delivery
between 2010 and 2012.

Displayed at DVD 2007, a British Army Project Teller vehicle based on the DURO III 4 × 4 chassis (Shaun C Connors) 1190245

In February 2009 it was disclosed that the Swiss Army was to order 220 DURO IIIP 6 × 6 armoured personnel carriers under the Army's Geschütztes Mannschaftstransportfahrzeug (GMTF) requirement (MOWAG) 1332654

Description

MOWAG DURO (4 × 4) and (6 × 6) vehicles are constructed using a low-slung, torsion-resistant steel box-section ladder-type chassis with tubular cross-members. All vehicles use a forward control cab of pressed aluminium construction with reinforced plastic panels. The cab sits on shock absorbing rubber mounts and tilts forward for access to the engine. There is seating for the driver and a co-driver with space for an extra third person seat. Wide-vision windows are provided for all cab occupants, a padded instrument panel is standard and options include air-conditioning. Roll-over protection constructed of pressed aluminium is located between the cab and the rear body. This is wide enough to allow for the location of a single spare wheel and tyre complete with raise/lower device between the cab and load area. The spare wheel is accessed by tilting the cab forward. Armoured cabs and rear bodies are available.

Over 30 different bodies using a standard platform base can be mounted on the rear chassis of the DURO in its basic form, and as delivered to the Swiss Army. These bodies are interchangeable and in addition to being swapped by crane, can be swapped using four purpose-designed lifting/support legs. In addition to the standard canvas-topped troop carrying/cargo body a wide variety of glass fibre reinforced plastic (GRP) shelter or box-type designs suitable for various command, control and communication roles are available. Ambulance, UAV launcher and fire/rescue variants of the DURO are also produced, as are armoured variants. Basic details of armoured DURO variants including the Eagle IV and Rheinmetall Landsysteme Yak can be found elsewhere in this entry; full details can be found in *Jane's Armour and Artillery*.

Dependant on wheelbase, the standard troop carrying/cargo variant of the DURO can transport four to six standard pallets or 14 to 18 fully equipped troops. Depending on model, a trailer of up to 5,000 kg may be towed by any variant.

The DURO I is powered by a EURO II emissions compliant 4.2-litre six-cylinder turbocharged diesel developing 160 hp. This is coupled to a Mercedes-Benz or Allison automatic gearbox with four forward and one reverse gears. The DURO II is powered by a EURO III emissions compliant Cummins 5.9-litre six-cylinder turbocharged diesel engine developing 185 hp. This is coupled to an uprated Allison 1000 Series automatic gearbox with five forward and one reverse gears.

DURO I was available in three wheelbase models, 4 × 4S (short), 4 × 4L (long) and 6 × 6; DURO II was initially available in the same three options, however the DURO II 4 × 4L is now no longer marketed. Within each production option, wheelbase measurements and some other dimensions and performance figures differ model to model. In general the more powerful DURO II versions are slightly larger, and weigh and carry more.

For example: The DURO I 4 × 4 Sin chassis-cab configuration weighs 2,830 kg and has a payload of 2,970 kg, the DURO II 4 × 4S in the same configuration weighs 3,750 kg and has a payload of 3,050 kg.

To accommodate its specific shelter the UK's Project Cormorant DURO IIs, while retaining the same wheelbase as the standard DURO II 6 × 6, have a slightly longer chassis and consequent reduced angle of departure.

The DURO III is powered by the same Cummins 5.9-litre diesel engine as the DURO II but uprated to 245 hp for the DURO III. From mid-2006 all DURO IIIs produced have been prepared to meet EURO IV emissions requirements, but operate at the current EURO III levels. During 2006 the EMC characteristics of the engine were further improved and a 300 Ah water proofed alternator fitted as standard. Transmission of the DURO III was initially an Allison 2000 Series automatic, but from mid-2006 a military-specific Allison 2500 SP Series unit has been fitted. In protected configuration (DURO IIIP) the DURO III in shelter configuration weighs 10,000 kg, has a payload of approximately 3,000 kg, and a combat weight of 13,000 kg. This increased to a GVW of 13,500 kg for the DURO-based Yak from October 2006. Larger 335/80R 20 tyres are fitted to all DURO III models.

The DURO is permanent all-wheel drive (4 × 4 or 6 × 6 dependant on configuration) and each axle is fitted with a Torsen self-locking cross-axle differential. The MOWAG two-speed synchromesh transfer box is fitted with a Torsen self-locking longitudinal differential. The De-Dion tubular axles are fitted with hub reduction gearing and for increased lateral stability and to ensure wheel geometry remains stable under braking conditions, a patented stabiliser system is located on the outside of each chassis rail between the front and rear.

The front axle is sprung by a coil spring, gas pressure damper and Cellasto supplementary spring on each side. The rear (4 × 4), or second (6 × 6) axle, is sprung by two coil springs, a single gas-pressure damper and Cellasto supplementary springs on each side. The rearmost axle on the 6 × 6 DURO is sprung by a coil spring, gas pressure damper and Cellasto supplementary spring on each side. The dual circuit hydraulic braking system works on ventilated inboard disc brakes on all axles; DURO III and EAGLE IV operate with the same system but air-over-hydraulic. Anti lock brakes (ABS) were an option on the DURO I but are fitted as standard to the DURO II and III. The ball and nut steering system is power-assisted. Left- or right-hand drive models are available. A central tyre inflation (CTI) system is an option.

Variants

Yak Armoured Multi-Role Vehicle

The Yak Armoured Multi-Role Vehicle is based on the DURO III 6 × 6 chassis and was developed as a private venture by Rheinmetall Landsysteme (RLS) of Germany.

Rheinmetall Landsysteme builds the armoured cab, which is then sent to MOWAG in Switzerland who integrate the cab with its chassis. The latter is then sent to Kassel where Rheinmetall Landsysteme integrate the rear specialised armoured body or mission module and then deliver the complete vehicle to the Germany Army.

During 2005 and under an Immediate Operational Requirement contract the German Bundeswehr ordered a total of 30 Yak vehicles made up of ambulance (12), Explosive Ordnance Disposal (EOD) (10), military police (4) and support vehicles for the LUNA unmanned aerial vehicle (4). Some of these were deployed immediately to Afghanistan as part of the German contribution to the International Security Assistance Force (ISAF). Under a contract awarded in October 2005, a further 100 YAK vehicles in personnel carrier configuration will be delivered to the German Army from October 2006. These will have a GVW of 13,400 kg; the initial 30 vehicles were rated at 12,000 kg GVW by MOWAG. A further seven specialised configuration vehicles have since been ordered, bringing order totals to 137.

The forward control cab of the Yak has seats for the commander (right) and driver (left) and provides the occupants with protection from small arms fire and shell splinters. The one-piece windscreen is electrically heated, as are the electrically adjustable rear view mirrors. There is an

Yak Armoured Multi-Role Vehicle of the German Army in Afghanistan (Rheinmetall Landsysteme) 1333584

emergency hatch in the roof and to allow access to the power pack the cab can be tilted forwards using a hydraulic device. The standard armour package provides protection against projectile attack to STANAG 4569 Level 1 (7.62 mm × 51 NATO ball) and Level 2 (7.62 mm × 39 armour piercing) and partial protection against Level 3 (7.62 mm × 54 armour piercing). Mine protection is also to STANAG 4569 Level 1 (hand grenades and anti-personnel mines, including the DM 31 splinter mine). Higher levels of protection are available to meet users' specific operational requirements.

Mounted to the immediate rear of the cab is the auxiliary power unit (APU) and air-conditioning units, which serve both the front and rear units. This provides power for heating, air-conditioning and additional electrical power. Also mounted to the rear of the cab are mission-critical components such as the fuel system, brake units, batteries, cooling system and electronics.

The rear body consists of a steel frame and steel floor, to which panels of ceramic armour are attached, with entry via two rearward opening doors. Payload depends on the rear mission module but can be between 2,000

Model	DURO I 4 × 4S	DURO II 4 × 4S	DURO I 4 × 4L	DURO I 6 × 6	DURO II 6 × 6	DURO III 4 × 4	DURO III 6 × 6 (IIIP in brackets where different)
Cab seating:	1 + 1 or 2	1 + 1 or 2	1 + 1 or 2	1 + 1 or 2	1 + 1 or 2	1 + 1 or 2	1 + 1 or 2
Configuration:	4 × 4	4 × 4	4 × 4	6 × 6	6 × 6	4 × 4	6 × 6
Weight:							
(laden, GVW)	5,800 kg	6,800 kg	6,000 kg	7,000 kg	8,600 kg	9,000 kg	12,000 kg (13,000 kg)
(unladen, chassis-cab)	2,830 kg	3,750 kg	2,890 kg	3,325 kg	4,400 kg	4,800 kg	5,700 kg (7,000 kg)
(payload)	2,970 kg	3,050 kg	3,100 kg	3,675 kg	4,200 kg	4,200 kg	6,300 kg (6,000 kg)
(towed load)	3,500 kg, increasing to 5,000 kg with air-braked trailer	3,500 kg, increasing to 5,000 kg with air-braked trailer	3,500 kg, increasing to 5,000 kg with air-braked trailer	3,500 kg, increasing to 5,000 kg with air-braked trailer	3,500 kg, increasing to 5,000 kg with air-braked trailer	3,500 kg, increasing to 5,000 kg with air-braked trailer	3,500 kg, increasing to 5,000 kg with air-braked trailer
Load area inside length:	3 m	3. m	3.76 m	4.15 m	4.16 m	3.2 m	4.175 m
Length:	5.07 m	5.2 m	6 m	6.22 m	6.6 m	5.5 m	6.53 m (6.7 m)
Width:	1.96 m	1.99 m	1.96 m	1.96 m	1.99 m	2.16 m	2.16 m
Height: (unladen)	2.6 m	2.6 m	2.6 m	2.6 m	2.6 m	2.6 m	2.6 m
Ground clearance:	360 mm	360 mm	360 mm	360 mm	360 mm	400 mm	400 mm
Track:	1.68 m	1.71 m	1.68 m	1.68 m	1.71 m	1.82 m	1.82 m
Wheelbase:	3.23 m	3.53 m	3.88 m	3.23 m + 1.15 m	3.53 m + 1.15 m	3.53 m	3.53 + 1.2 m
Angle of approach/departure:	47°/36°	47°/47°	47°/32°	47°/36°	47°/47°	45°/40°	45°/47° (43°/40°)
Max speed: (high range)	110 km/h	110 km/h	110 km/h	110 km/h	110 km/h	100 km/h	100 km/h
Max range:	550 km	550 km	550 km	500 km	500 km	650 km	600 km
Fuel capacity:	120 litres	120 litres	120 litres	120 litres	120 litres	180 litres	180 litres
Max gradient:	80%	>70%	80%	80%	>70%	>60%	>60%
Side slope:	40%	40%	40%	40%	40%	40%	40%
Fording:	800 mm	800 mm	800 mm	800 mm	800 mm	800 mm	800 mm
Engine:							
(DURO I)	VM EURO II 4.162-litre 6-cylinder inline exhaust gas turbocharged and intercooled, water-cooled electronically controlled direct injection diesel developing 150/160 hp (112/119 kW) at 4,000/3,000 rpm						
(DURO II)	Cummins ISBe 185 EURO III 5.883-litre 6-cylinder inline turbocharged water-cooled common rail direct injection diesel developing 185 hp (138 kW) at 2,500 rpm and 700 N.m torque between 1,200 and 1,700 rpm						
(DURO III)	Cummins ISBe EURO III 5.88- litre 6-cylinder inline turbocharged water-cooled common rail direct injection diesel developing 245 hp (183 kW) at 2,500 rpm and 750 N.m torque between 1,100 and 2,300 rpm						
Transmission:							
(DURO I)	Mercedes-Benz W4A 028 or Allison 542/545 with torque converter and 4 forward and 1 reverse gears						
(DURO II)	Allison 1000 Series with torque converter lock-up and 5 forward and 1 reverse gears						
(DURO III)	Allison 2000 Series with torque converter lock-up and 5 forward and 1 reverse gears						
(DURO III - from mid-2006)	Allison 2500 SP Series with torque converter lock-up and 5 forward and 1 reverse gears						
Transfer box:	Bucher 2-speed	MOWAG 2 S 22 2-speed	Bucher 2-speed	Bucher 2-speed	MOWAG 2 S 22 2-speed	MOWAG 2 S 22 2-speed	MOWAG 2 S 22 2-speed
Steering:	ZF Servocom 8090, power-assisted	ZF Servocom 8095, power-assisted	ZF Servocom 8090, power-assisted	ZF Servocom 8090, power-assisted	ZF Servocom 8095, power-assisted	ZF Servocom 8095, power-assisted	ZF Servocom 8095, power-assisted
Turning radius:	6.25 m	6.75 m	7.25 m	7 m	7.25 m	8.25 m	8.75 m
Suspension:	coil spring with gas pressure shock absorber and Cellasto supplementary springs, MOWAG roll stabiliser between front and rear (4 × 4) and front and second (6 × 6) axles						
Tyres:	275/80R 20	275/80R 20	275/80R 20	275/80R 20	275/80R 20	335/80R 20	335/80R 20
Brakes:	dual circuit hydraulic for DURO I and II, dual circuit air-over-hydraulic for DURO III, ventilated inboard discs on all axles. Anti lock braking system standard on EURO III models, optional on EURO II models						
Electrical system:	24 V	24 V	24 V	24 V	24 V	24 V	24 V
Batteries:	80 Ah	80 Ah	80 Ah	80 Ah	80 Ah	100 Ah	100 Ah
Alternator:	35 or 100 A	100 A	35 or 100 A	35 or 100 A	100 A	300 A	100 A (300 A from mid-2006)

Yak Armoured Multi-Role Vehicle if the German military in military police role and armed with a roof-mounted 40 mm automatic grenade launcher (Rheinmetall) 1167833

In Danish Army configuration, a MOWAG Eagle IV (BAE Systems) 1191290

and 5,500 kg according to the manufacturer. The design of the Yak is such that it is possible to change rear mission modules to meet specific operational requirements and when used in the armoured personnel carrier role, a maximum of 12 troops can be carried and these are seated six down either side facing inwards. The rear modules may also be used as standalone units.

Some variants of the Yak also tow a trailer, for example the EOD model used by the German Army has a trailer that carries the remote-controlled EOD system, as does the LUNA UAV model.

The German Army has a possible requirement for around 1,000 vehicles of the Yak type.

MOWAG Eagle IV

MOWAG announced in 2003 that it would use the DURO II as the platform for the MOWAG Eagle IV light armoured vehicle and by mid-2005 a total of three prototypes/pre-production vehicles had been built. Almost 500 Eagle I, II and III versions have been produced by MOWAG for home and export markets. The Eagle I, II and III are based on the AM General HMMWV platform.

In December 2005, following an international competition, the Danish Army Material Command (DAMC) ordered the MOWAG Eagle IV to meet its requirements for a five-person Armoured Patrol Vehicle (APV). Deliveries of the 90 vehicles involved commenced in October 2006 and were completed in December 2007. It was disclosed in June 2006 that Denmark's Eagle IVs would be on the heavier DURO III platform, and not the DURO II as shown.

Following competitive trials between the Eagle IV and the Rheinmetall Landsysteme (RLS) Caracal, the former was selected by the German Army to meet the Protected Command and Function vehicle (GFF) Group 2 requirement, and in mid 2008 a contract was placed for an initial 25 vehicles to meet an Urgent Operational Requirement (UOR). The first of these were handed over in mid-November 2008. In late 2008 the German Bundesamt fur Wehrtechnik und Beschaffung (BWB) awarded MOWAG a contract for an additional 173 vehicles. Further orders followed and included an order placed in December 2010 the total currently stands at 473. Further options, if exercised, could increase the total buy to at least 672 units.

Other variants

Earlier uses of the DURO chassis have included: Italian company ARIS SpA developed their VAT tactical vehicle using the DURO I 4 × 4 chassis as a basis. General Motors Defense Limited (then Diesel Division General Motors (DDGM)) selected the DURO I 4 × 4 as the base for their Brute light armoured vehicle. Neither type entered series production. Ricardo Vehicle Engineering of the UK, in conjunction with the then UK agent and importer for the DURO, Jack Allen Limited, developed the DURO RDV (Rapid Deployment Vehicle) for a specific UK MoD requirement, for which HMT Supacat Limited were the successful bidder. There has been no further development of DURO RDV.

Specifications
See table on facing page

Status
In production. In service with Denmark (29 DURO III (P)) deliveries from late 2007), Germany (30 (DURO III 6 × 6 (RLS Yak)) 2003-2005; 107 ordered for delivery from October 2006), Ireland (6, EOD (DURO II 6 × 6) 2003), Malaysia (57 (DURO I 6 × 6) 2000-2003), Singapore (61, 2000-2002), South Africa (14, 2000-2002), Switzerland (3,007 (DURO I 4 × 4) 1994-2002; 7 (DURO III 6 × 6) 2006-2007 delivery; 232 (DURO IIIP 6 × 6) 2010-2012 delivery, UK (around 220 ordered in total (DURO II 6 × 6, DUROIII 4 × 4 and 6 × 6)), UAE (2, 1999) and Venezuela (approx. 358 (DURO I 4 × 4) 2001-2003).

Contractor
MOWAG GmbH

Saurer 6 DM (4 × 4) 6,000 kg and 10 DM (6 × 6) 10,000 kg trucks

Development
During the late 1970s, Adolph Saurer Limited started the development of a new family of 6,000 and 10,000 kg trucks to meet the requirements of the Swiss Army. The first prototypes, the D250MF (4 × 4) and D3000MF (6 × 6) were completed in 1978. They were subsequently redesignated the 6 DM (4 × 4) and 10 DM (6 × 6). By late 1981 the vehicles had been tested by the

Saurer 6 DM and 10 DM trucks

Model	6 DM	10 DM
Configuration:	4 × 4	6 × 6
Weight:		
(unladen)	10,000 kg	12,000 kg
(laden)	16,000 kg	22,000 kg
(max load)	6,000 kg	10,000 kg
Length:	7.705 m	8.905 m
Width:	2.5 m	2.5 m
Height: (cab)	3.335 m	3.46 m
Ground clearance:	380 mm	380 mm
Wheelbase:	4.35 m	4 m + 1.4 m
Track:	2.1 m	2.1 m
Angle of approach/departure:	40°/40°	40°/40°
Fuel capacity:	300 litres	300 litres
Fording:	1.15 m	1.15 m
Engine:	Saurer D4KT 12 L 6-cylinder in-line turbocharged 4-stroke diesel developing 250 hp (184 kW) at 2,200 rpm	
Gearbox:	ZF S 690 with torque converter, retarder and splitter group	
Transfer box:	ZF A 800 3D electropneumatically lockable	
Turning radius:	8.75 m	9.75 m
Axles:	Saurer with lockable bevel gear differential	
Tyres:	14.00 × 20	14.00 × 20
Brakes: (main)	dual circuit, air	dual circuit, air
Electrical system:	24 V	24 V

Saurer 10 DM (6 × 6) 10,000 kg truck (Swiss MoD)   1391472

BMC EFE 185-09 B (4 × 4) 2,500 kg Tactical Wheeled Vehicle (TWV)
(BMC Sanayi ve Ticaret AS)   1391468

Swiss Army and production commenced soon after. Production ceased in February 1986. Deliveries totalled 550 6 DM without winch, 250 with a Rotzler TR 080/2 winch; 200 10 DM without winch, 100 with a Rotzler TR 080/2 winch, and 100 10 DM chassis to mount a Gottwald 360° crane.

In the early 1980s Adolph Saurer Limited formed a joint organisation called NAW (Nutzfahrzeuggeselschaft Arbon & Wetzikon). In 1982 Daimler-Benz (now Daimler) acquired a major shareholding in NAW and soon took full control.

Description
Both vehicles share many common components, including the engine. Both have a two-door fully enclosed all-steel forward control cab with a circular observation hatch in the roof. The rear cargo area is provided with removable drop sides and a drop tailgate, removable bows and a tarpaulin cover.

The chassis is semi-flexible having independent leaf spring suspension with telescopic dampers, all axles are fitted with differential locks. On both vehicles the front and rear axles are interchangeable.

Specifications
See table on page 625

Status
In service with the Swiss Armed Forces.

Contractor
Adolph Saurer Limited
(This facility has closed.)

Turkey

BMC EFE 185-09 B (4 × 4) 2,500 kg Tactical Wheeled Vehicle (TWV)

Development
BMC Sanayi ve Ticaret AS has produced a number of all-wheel-drive trucks since the company was originally established in 1964. Until 2008 these came exclusively from the in-production Fatih range, production of which commenced in 1986 after BMC signed a license agreement to manufacture Cummins engines.

Fatih range models presently available include the 150-09, 170-13, 200-13, 200-15 and 220-18. These are all (4 × 4) designs, and in all cases the designations follow the standard BMC practice and reflect engine horsepower and Gross Vehicle Weight (GVW).

Models 215-09 (2,500 kg) and 235-16 (5,000 kg), which are both (4 × 4) configuration, were the first BMC all-wheel drive models to be selected by Turkey's armed Forces. Export sales have also been made, and both models remain in production and service.

A (6 × 6) model, the BMC 380-26, was also produced and it is currently in service with Turkey's Armed Forces.

During 2008 BMC launched an entirely new series of military vehicles, the (4 × 4) EFE 185-09B (2,500 kg), the (4 × 4) 235-16P (5,000 kg) and (6 × 6) 380-26P (10,000 kg).

The EFE 185-09B is of bonneted configuration, while the 235-16P and 380-26P are Cab-Over-Engine (COE). Full details of the 235-16 P and 380-26 P (6 × 6), for which orders have been received, can be found elsewhere in this section.

BMC refers to these vehicles and previous generation military trucks as Tactical Wheeled Vehicles (TWVs).

Since 1989 BMC Sanayi ve Ticaret AS has been wholly owned by Cukurova Holding of Turkey.

Description
The BMC 185-09 B (4 × 4) 2,500 kg truck is an entirely new design. Construction is based on a conventional C-section chassis with C-profile flitch plates inserted for reinforcement where required. Recovery and/or towing points are fitted front and rear, a NATO standard pintle being fitted at the rear. A front-mounted electric self-recovery winch is an option.

A new bonneted configuration three-seat all-steel tilt-type cab is fitted. Options for this include rifle racks, a single circular roof hatch, and a roof-mounted weapon mount.

The standard troop carrying/cargo platform-type body is fitted with single-piece steel drop sides and a tailgate, and a removable tarpaulin with bows. This body measures 2.4 × 2.5 m (L × W) and wooden bench seats are provided for troop transport. A wide variety of other body types may be fitted to base chassis.

Motive power is provided by a EURO 3 emissions compliant Cummins diesel engine, this developing 185 hp and giving the fully laden vehicle a 19.5 hp/tonne power-to-weight ratio. An engine cold start kit is fitted and the cooling system has been adapted for tactical applications.

Driveline is completed by a ZF six-speed all synchromesh gearbox coupled to an Axletech two-speed transfer box with selectable two- or four-wheel drive. Options include full time four-wheel drive, a power take off from either the gearbox of transfer box, or a fully automatic transmission.

For improved ground clearance Axletech hub reduction portal axles are fitted. The front steer-drive axle is a model 4814 SFW rated at 5,000 kg capacity and sprung by the combination of coil springs, telescopic shock-absorbers and an anti-roll bar, the rear drive axle is a model 4824 SFW rated at 6,000 kg capacity and sprung by the combination of coil springs, telescopic shock-absorbers and an anti-roll bar. Both are fitted with driver-controlled pneumatically operated cross-axle differential locks. An automatic traction control system is an option. Steering is power assisted.

Single 335/80R 20 tyres are standard. A Central Tyre Inflation System (CTIS) can be fitted. Drum brakes are fitted front and rear, supplemented by an engine exhaust brake. An Anti-lock Braking System (ABS) can be fitted.

Specifications
BMC EFE 185-09 B
Cab seating: 1 + 2
Configuration: 4 × 4
Weight:
(laden) 10,050 kg
(unladen; troop carrier body) 7,280 kg
(payload) 2,520 kg
(front axle load, max GVW) 4,630 kg
(rear axle load max GVW) 5,170 kg
(towed load) 2,500 kg
(GCW) 12,500 kg
Length: 5.79 m
Width: 2.53 m
Height: (cab) 2.74 m
Ground clearance: 420 mm
Track:
(front) 2.01 m
(rear) 1.99 m
Wheelbase: 3.25 m
Angle of approach/departure: 42°/52°
Max speed: 100 km/h
Max range: 1,000 km
Fuel capacity: 230 litres
Max gradient: (laden) 70%
Side slope: (static) 47%
Fording:
(unprepared) 800 mm
(prepared) 1.2 m

Engine: Cummins ISB 4.5 E3 EURO 3 emissions compliant 4.5-litre 4-cylinder in-line water-cooled turbocharged and intercooled 4-stroke diesel developing 185 hp (136 kW) at 2,500 rpm and 650 N.m torque at 1,700 rpm
Gearbox: Allison 2500SP fully automatic with 5 forward and 1 reverse gears
Transfer box: Axletech BT600 2-speed (high/low) with selectable all-wheel drive
Steering: power-assisted, HEMA 8098
Turning radius: (wall) n/avail
Suspension: semi-elliptic leaf springs, telescopic shock-absorbers and anti-roll bar, front and rear
Tyres: 335/80R 20
Brakes: air actuated, drums front and rear, ABS optional
Electrical system: 24 V
Batteries: 2 × 12 V, 125 Ah
Alternator: 90 A

Status

An order for 700 vehicles has been received from Turkey's Armed Forces. Former models in service with the armed forces of Azerbaijan, Bangladesh (24), Bosnia and Herzegovina, Georgia (approx 20), Kyrgyzstan, Macedonia (approx 20) and Turkey (approx 500).

Contractor

BMC Sanayi ve Ticaret AS

BMC 215-09 (4 × 4) 2,500 kg Wheeled Tactical Vehicle (WTV)

Development

BMC Sanayi ve Ticaret AS has produced a number of all-wheel drive trucks since the company was originally established in 1964 in partnership with the then British Motors Corporation (BMC) of the UK. Until the introduction during 2008 of the latest models, these have previously come from the in-production Fatih range, production of which commenced in 1986 after BMC signed a license agreement to manufacture Cummins engines. Fatih range models presently available include the 150-09, 170-13, 200-13, 200-15 and 220-18 models. These are all 4 × 4 designs and in all cases the designations follow the standard BMC practice and reflect engine horsepower (hp) and gross vehicle weight (GVW). The most recent 4 × 4 models, the 215-09 and 235-16, were the first all-wheel drive models to have been selected by Turkish and allied countries' armed forces, and both models remain in current production and service. A 6 × 6, the BMC 380-26, is also produced. Full details of the BMC 235-16 (4 × 4) and BMC 380-26 can be found elsewhere in this section.

The most recent BMC military models (available from 2008) are the ERE 185-09 B (4 × 4), 235-16 P (4 × 4) and BMC 380-26 P (6 × 6). The ERE 185-09 B is the replacement for the 215-09. Full details of the EFE 185-09 B, and 235-16 P (4 × 4) and BMC 380-26 P (6 × 6) models, can be found elsewhere in this section. BMC refers to these and previous military range trucks as Wheeled Tactical Vehicles (WTVs).

Since 1989 BMC Sanayi ve Ticaret A.S. has been wholly owned by Cukurova Holding of Turkey.

Description

The BMC 215-09 (4 × 4) 2,500 kg WTV is entirely conventional in design and is based on a C-section chassis with L-profile flitch plates inserted for reinforcement, where required. Recovery and/or towing points are fitted front and rear, a NATO standard pintle being fitted at the rear. A front-mounted electrical or hydraulically driven self-recovery winch is an option. The three-person all-steel tilt-cab is based on the Leyland Redline G cab, as fitted to the Fatih range of trucks. Modifications can include rifle racks and a single circular roof hatch, for which a weapon mount is optional.

The standard platform body is fitted with single-piece steel drop sides and tailgate, and a removable tarpaulin and bows. The body measures 3.5 × 2.48 m (L × W). Wooden bench seats are provided for troop transport. A wide variety of body types may be fitted to base chassis, up to a maximum weight (including any superstructure) of 2,500 kg. Kerb weight of the vehicle is 6,500 kg, giving axle weights of 3,700 and 2,800 kg. These increase to 4,300 and 4,700 kg at the maximum 9,000 kg GVW.

Motive power is provided by a EURO II emissions compliant Cummins B215 5.88-litre six-cylinder turbocharged diesel engine developing 215 hp, giving the fully laden vehicle a 23.8 hp/tonne power-to-weight ratio. An engine cold start kit is fitted and the cooling system has been revised for tactical applications.

A ZF 6S 850 six-speed all synchromesh gearbox is coupled to a Axletech BT600 two-speed transfer box with selectable two or four-wheel drive. Full time four-wheel drive is an option. A power take off from either the gearbox or transfer box is an option. For improved ground clearance Axletech hub reduction portal axles are fitted. The front steer-drive axle is a model 4814 SFW rated at 5,000 kg capacity and sprung by the combination of semi-elliptic leaf springs, telescopic shock absorbers and an anti-roll bar, the rear drive axle a model 4824 SFW rated at 6,000 kg capacity and sprung by the combination of semi-elliptic leaf springs, telescopic shock absorbers and an anti-roll bar. Both are fitted with driver-controlled pneumatically operated cross-axle differential locks. An automatic traction control system is an option. Steering is power assisted.

BMC 215-09 (4 × 4) 2,500 kg truck with standard drop side troop carrying/cargo body (BMC Sanayi ve Ticaret AS)   1171395

Single 335/80R 20 tyres are standard. A Central Tyre Inflation (CTI) system can be fitted. Drum brakes are fitted front and rear, supplemented by an engine exhaust brake. An Anti-lock Braking System (ABS) can be fitted.

Specifications

BMC 215-09
Cab seating: 1 + 2
Configuration: 4 × 4
Weight:
  (unladen, kerb) 6,500 kg
  (laden, max) 9,000 kg
  (payload) 2,500 kg
  (towed load) 2,500 kg
  (GCW) 11,500 kg
Length: 5.72 m
Width: 2.48 m
Height:
  (cab) 2.89 m
  (tarpaulin) 3.15 m
Ground clearance: 400 mm
Track:
  (front) 2 m
  (rear) 2 m
Wheelbase: 3.86 m
Angle of approach/departure: 35°/49°
Max geared speed: 95 km/h
Max range: (cruising) 1,000 km
Fuel capacity: 230 litres
Max gradient: (laden) 70%
Max side slope: (static) 47%
Fording:
  (unprepared) 700 mm
  (prepared) 1.2 m
Engine: Cummins B215 EURO 2 5.88-litre 6-cylinder in-line water-cooled turbocharged and intercooled 4-stroke diesel developing 215 hp (160 kW) at 2,500 rpm and 700 N.m torque at 1,500 rpm
Gearbox: ZF 6S 850 manual with 6 forward and 1 reverse gears
Clutch: single dry plate (355 mm diameter)
Transfer box: Axletech BT600 2-speed (high/low) with selectable 4 × 2 or 4 × 4 drive plus neutral
Steering: power assisted, ZF 8043
Turning radius: (wall) 7.4 m
Suspension: semi-elliptic leaf springs, telescopic shock-absorbers and anti-roll bar, front and rear
Tyres: 335/80R 20
Brakes: air, drums front and rear, ABS optional
Electrical system: 24 V
Batteries: 2 × 12 V, 150 Ah
Alternator: 55 A

Status

Production as required. In service with the armed forces of Azerbaijan (approx 80), Bosnia and Herzegovina, Georgia (30), Macedonia (approx 10) and Turkey (approx 200). Has been tested and approved in the UAE.

Contractor

BMC Sanayi ve Ticaret AS

BMC 235-16 (4 × 4) 5,000 kg Wheeled Tactical Vehicle (WTV)

Development

BMC Sanayi ve Ticaret AS has produced a number of all-wheel drive trucks since the company was originally established in 1964 in partnership with the then British Motors Corporation (BMC) of the UK. Until the introduction during 2008 of the latest models, these have previously come from the in-production Fatih range. Production of the range commenced in 1986 after BMC signed a license agreement to manufacture Cummins engines. Fatih range models presently available include the 150-09, 170-13, 200-13, 200-15 and 220-18 models. These are all 4 × 4 designs and in all cases the designations follow the standard BMC practice and reflect engine horsepower (hp) and Gross Vehicle Weight (GVW).

The most recent Fatih range 4 × 4 models, the 215-09 and 235-16, were the first all-wheel drive models to have been selected by Turkish and allied countries' armed forces, both models remain in current production and service. A 6 × 6, the 380-26, is also produced. Full details of the 215-09 (4 × 4) and 380-26 can be found elsewhere in this section.

The most recent BMC military models (available since 2008) are the EFE 185-09 B (4 × 4), 235-16 P (4 × 4) and 380-26 P (6 × 6). The 235-16 P is the replacement for the 235-16. Full details of the and 235-16 P (4 × 4), and EFE 185-09 B (4 × 4) and 380-26 P (6 × 6) models, can be found elsewhere in this section. BMC refers to these and previous military range trucks as Wheeled Tactical Vehicles (WTVs).

Since 1989 BMC Sanayi ve Ticaret AS has been wholly owned by Cukurova Holding of Turkey.

Description

The BMC 235-16 (4 × 4) 5,000 kg WTV is entirely conventional in design and is based on a C-section chassis with L-profile flitch plates inserted for reinforcement where required. Recovery and/or towing points are fitted front and rear, a NATO standard pintle being fitted at the rear. A front-mounted electrical or hydraulically driven self-recovery winch is an option. The three-person all-steel tilt-cab is based on the Leyland Redline G cab, as fitted to the Fatih range of trucks. Modifications can include rifle racks and a single circular roof hatch, for which a weapon mount is optional.

The standard platform body is fitted with two-piece steel drop sides and a single-piece drop tailgate, and a removable tarpaulin and bows. The body measures 4.63 × 2.5 m (L × W). Wooden bench seats are provided for troop transport. The BMC 235-16 has a tactical payload rating of 5,000 kg, but with a maximum possible payload of 8,550 kg (including superstructure), the type is capable of accepting a variety of body options and performing a variety of roles. Chassis-cab weight is 7,450 kg, giving axle weights of 4,200 and 3,250 kg. These increase to 7,100 and 8,900 kg at the maximum 16,000 kg GVW.

BMC 235-16 (4 × 4) 5,000 kg truck (BMC Sanayi ve Ticaret AS)   1326960

BMC 235-16 (4 × 4) 5,000 kg truck, mobile repair workshop variant (BMC Sanayi ve Ticaret AS)   1326959

BMC 235-16 (4 × 4) 5,000 kg truck with standard dropside troop carrying/cargo body (Shaun C Connors)   1120463

Motive power is provided by a EURO 2 emissions compliant Cummins 5.88-litre six-cylinder turbocharged diesel engine developing 235 hp, giving a power-to-weight ratio of 18.89 hp/tonne at 5,000 kg payload, and 14.7 hp/tonne at maximum GVW. An engine cold start kit is fitted and the cooling system has been revised for tactical applications.

A ZF 9S 75 nine-speed all synchromesh gearbox is coupled to a Axletech BT600 two-speed transfer box with selectable two- or four-wheel drive, although full time four-wheel drive is an option. A longitudinal driver-controlled pneumatically operated differential lock is fitted. A power take off from either the gearbox of transfer box is an option. The front steer-drive axle is a Axletech 4314 SFW unit rated at 7,500 kg capacity and sprung by the combination of semi-elliptic leaf springs, telescopic shock absorbers and an anti-roll bar, the rear drive axle a Axletech 4424 SFW unit rated at 11,000 kg capacity and sprung by the combination of semi-elliptic leaf springs, telescopic shock absorbers and an anti-roll bar. Both are fitted with driver-controlled pneumatically operated cross-axle differential locks. An automatic traction control system is an option. Steering is power assisted.

Single 1400R 20 tyres are standard, dual wheels and tyres on the rear drive axle are an option. A Central Tyre Inflation (CTI) system can be fitted. Drum brakes are fitted front and rear, supplemented by an engine exhaust brake. An Anti-lock Braking System (ABS) can be fitted.

Variants

BMC 215-13 (4 × 4) 5,000 kg truck
The BMC 215-13 (4 × 4) 5,000 kg truck is a right-hand drive variant of the BMC 235-16. It is powered by the same Cummins B215 EURO II 5.88-litre six-cylinder in-line water-cooled turbocharged and intercooled four-stroke diesel engine as the BMC 215-09 (4 × 4) 2,500 kg truck, but is right-hand drive and has a longer wheelbase. The GVW is 13,000 kg, giving a payload (including any superstructure) of 6,400 kg.

Specifications

BMC 235-16
Cab seating: 1 + 2
Configuration: 4 × 4
Weight:
    (unladen) 7,450 kg
    (laden, max) 16,000 kg
    (load, max) 8,550 kg
    (towed load) 5,000 kg
    (GCW) 21,000 kg
Length: 6.84 m
Width: 2.5 m
Height: (cab) 2.99 m
Ground clearance: 400 mm
Track:
    (front) 2.02 m
    (rear) 2.02 m
Wheelbase: 3.86 m
Angle of approach/departure: 37°/38°
Max geared speed: 100 km/h
Max range: (cruising) 1,000 km
Fuel capacity: 300 litres
Max gradient: (laden) 60%
Max side slope: (static) 47%
Fording:
    (unprepared) 800 mm
    (prepared) 1.2 m
Engine: Cummins B235 EURO 2 5.88-litre 6-cylinder in-line water-cooled turbocharged and intercooled 4-stroke diesel developing 235 hp (175 kW) at 2,500 rpm and 800 N.m torque at 1,500 rpm
Gearbox: ZF 9S 75 manual with 9 forward and 1 reverse gears
Clutch: single dry plate (diameter 355 mm)
Transfer box: (wall) Axletech BT600 2 speed (high/low) with selectable 4 × 2 or 4 × 4 drive plus neutral

Steering: power-assisted, ZF 8098
Turning radius: 9.35 m
Suspension: semi-elliptic leaf springs, telescopic shock-absorbers and anti-roll bar, front and rear
Tyres: 1400R 20
Brakes: air actuated, drums front and rear, ABS optional
Electrical system: 24 V
Batteries: 2 × 12 V, 150 Ah
Alternator: 55 A

Status
Production as required. In service with the armed forces of Azerbaijan, Bangladesh (24 with 5,000-litre water tankers), Bosnia-Herzegovina, Georgia (approx 20), Kyrgyzstan, Macedonia (approx 20) and Turkey (approx 500). Has been trialed/tested in Malaysia, Pakistan, Sudan, Tanzania and the UAE.

Contractor
BMC Sanayi ve Ticaret AS

BMC 235-16 P (4 × 4) 5,000 kg Tactical Wheeled Vehicle (TWV)

Development
BMC Sanayi ve Ticaret AS has produced a number of all-wheel drive trucks since the company was originally established in 1964. Until 2008 these came exclusively from the in-production Fatih range, production of which commenced in 1986 after BMC signed a license agreement to manufacture Cummins engines.

Fatih range models presently available include the 150-09, 170-13, 200-13, 200-15 and 220-18. These are all (4 × 4) designs, and in all cases the designations follow the standard BMC practice and reflect engine horsepower and Gross Vehicle Weight (GVW).

Models 215-09 (2,500 kg) and 235-16 (5,000 kg), which are both (4 × 4) configuration, were the first BMC all-wheel drive models to be selected by Turkey's Armed Forces. Export sales have also been made, and both models remain in production and service.

A (6 × 6) model, the BMC 380-26, was also produced and it is currently in service with Turkey's Armed Forces.

During 2008 BMC launched an entirely new series of military vehicles, the (4 × 4) EFE 185-09 B (2,500 kg), the (4 × 4) 235-16 P (5,000 kg) and (6 × 6) 380-26 P (10,000 kg).

The EFE 185-09 B is of bonneted configuration, while the 235-16 P and 380-26 P are Cab-Over-Engine (COE). Full details of the 185-09 B (4 × 4) and 380-26 P (6 × 6) can be found elsewhere in this section.

BMC refers to these vehicles and previous generation military trucks as Tactical Wheeled Vehicles (TWVs).

Since 1989 BMC Sanayi ve Ticaret AS has been wholly owned by Cukurova Holding of Turkey.

Description
The BMC 235-16 P (4 × 4) 5,000 kg truck is an entirely new design. Construction is based on a conventional C-section chassis with C-profile flitch plates inserted for reinforcement where required. Recovery and/or towing points are fitted front and rear, a NATO standard pintle being fitted at the rear. A front-mounted hydraulically operated self-recovery winch is an option.

The three-person all-steel tilt-cab is based on the cab fitted to the Professional commercial range of trucks, with militarisation options including rifle racks, a single circular roof hatch, and a roof-mounted weapon mount.

The standard troop carrying/cargo platform-type body is fitted with two-piece steel drop sides and a tailgate, and a removable tarpaulin with bows. This body measures 4.66 × 2.5 m (L × W) and wooden bench seats are provided for troop transport. The BMC 235-16 P has a tactical payload

rating of 5,000 kg, although maximum possible payload (including superstructure) is 9,000 kg (including superstructure). A wide variety of other body types may be fitted to base chassis.

Motive power is provided by a EURO 2 emissions compliant Cummins diesel engine developing 235 hp and giving a power-to-weight ratio of 20.6 hp/tonne at 5,000 kg payload, and 16.7 hp/tonne at maximum GVW. An engine cold start kit is fitted and the cooling system has been adapted for tactical applications.

Driveline is completed by an Allison six-speed fully automatic transmission (or an optional ZF nine-speed all synchromesh gearbox) coupled to an Axletech two-speed transfer box with selectable two- or four-wheel drive, although full time four-wheel drive is an option. A longitudinal driver-controlled pneumatically operated differential lock is fitted. A power take off from either the gearbox or transfer box is an option. The front steer-drive axle is an Axletech 4414 SFW unit rated at 7,000 kg capacity and sprung by the combination of semi-elliptic leaf springs, telescopic shock-absorbers and an anti-roll bar, the rear drive axle a Axletech 4424 SFW unit rated at 9,500 kg capacity and sprung by the combination of semi-elliptic leaf springs, telescopic shock-absorbers and an anti-roll bar. Both are fitted with driver-controlled pneumatically operated cross-axle differential locks. An automatic traction control system is an option. Steering is power assisted.

Single 1400R 20 tyres are standard, dual wheels and tyres on the rear drive axle are an option. A Central Tyre Inflation System (CTIS) can be fitted. Drum brakes are fitted front and rear, supplemented by an engine exhaust brake. An anti-lock braking system (ABS) can be fitted.

Specifications

BMC 235-16 P
Cab seating: 1 + 2 (selectable)
Configuration: 4 × 4
Weight:
  (unladen) 7,000 kg
  (laden) 16,000 kg
  (payload) 9,000 kg
  (front axle load, max GVW) 7,000 kg
  (rear axle load, max GVW) 9,000 kg
  (towed load) 5,000 kg
  (GCW) 20,100 kg
Length: 7.31 m
Width: 2.5 m
Height: (cab) 3.15 m
Ground clearance: 400 mm
Track:
  (front) 2 m
  (rear) 2 m
Wheelbase: 4.2 m
Angle of approach/departure: 35°/35°
Max speed: 100 km/h
Max range: 1,000 km
Fuel capacity: 300 litres
Max gradient: (laden) 60%
Side slope: (static) 47%
Fording:
  (unprepared) 800 mm
  (prepared) 1.2 m
Engine: Cummins B235 EURO 2 emissions compliant 5.88-litre 6-cylinder in-line water-cooled turbocharged and intercooled 4-stroke diesel developing 235 hp (175 kW) at 2,500 rpm and 800 N.m torque at 1,500 rpm
Gearbox: Allison 3500 SP automatic transmission with 6 forward and 1 reverse gears; optional ZF 9S 75 manual with 9 forward and 1 reverse gears
Transfer box: Axletech BT600 2 speed (high/low) with selectable all-wheel drive
Clutch: single dry plate (380 mm diameter)
Steering: power-assisted, ZF 8043
Turning radius: (wall) 9.35 m
Suspension: semi-elliptic leaf springs, telescopic shock-absorbers and anti-roll bar, front and rear
Tyres: 1400R 20
Brakes: air actuated, drums front and rear, ABS optional
Electrical system: 24 V
Batteries: 2 × 12 V, 150 Ah
Alternator: 55 A

Status
Four-hundred supplied to Turkey's Armed Forces during 2010. Former models in service with the armed forces of Azerbaijan, Bangladesh (24), Bosnia and Herzegovina, Georgia (approx 20), Kyrgyzstan, Macedonia (approx 20) and Turkey (approx 500).

Contractor
BMC Sanayi ve Ticaret AS

BMC 235-16 P (4 × 4) 5,000 kg Tactical Wheeled Vehicle (TWV) (BMC)
1391470

BMC 380-26 (6 × 6) 10,000 kg Tactical Wheeled Vehicle (TWV)

Development

BMC Sanayi ve Ticaret AS has produced a number of all-wheel drive trucks since the company was originally established in 1964 in partnership with the then British Motors Corporation (BMC) of the UK. Until the introduction during 2008 of the latest models, these have previously come from the in-production Fatih range, production of which commenced in 1986 after BMC signed a license agreement to manufacture Cummins engines. Fatih range models presently available include the 150-09, 170-13, 200-13, 200-15 and 220-18 models. These are all 4 × 4 designs and in all cases the designations follow the standard BMC practice and reflect engine horsepower (hp) and Gross Vehicle Weight (GVW). The most recent Fatih range 4 × 4 models, the 215-09 and 235-16, were the first all-wheel drive models to have been selected by Turkish and allied countries' armed forces, and both models remain in current production and service.

The BMC 380-26 (6 × 6) is essentially an elongated 4 × 4 chassis with the necessary driveline upgrades to accommodate the increases in both unladen and laden weights, and was developed as a private venture by BMC.

The most recent BMC military models (available from 2008) are the 185-09 B (4 × 4), 235-16 P (4 × 4) and 380-26 P (6 × 6). The 380-26 P is the replacement for the 380-26. Full details of the 380-26 P (6 × 6), and 185-09 B (4 × 4) and 235-16 P (4 × 4) models, can be found elsewhere in this section. BMC refers to these and previous military range trucks as Wheeled Tactical Vehicles (WTVs).

Since 1989 BMC Sanayi ve Ticaret AS has been wholly owned by Cukurova Holding of Turkey.

Description

The BMC 380-26 (6 × 6) 10,000 kg TWV is entirely conventional in design and is based on a C-section chassis with C-section flitch plates inserted for reinforcement where required. Recovery and/or towing points can be fitted front and rear as required, as can a front-mounted self-recovery winch. The three-person all-steel tilt-cab is based on the Leyland Redline G cab, as fitted to the Fatih range of trucks. Modifications can include rifle racks and a single circular roof hatch for which a weapon mount is optional.

A platform body fitted with two-piece steel drop sides, a single-piece tailgate, wooden bench seats and a removable tarpaulin and bows would be the standard body option. The BMC 380-26 has a tactical payload rating of 10,000 kg, but with a maximum possible payload (including superstructure) of 15,500 kg, the type is capable of accepting a variety of body options and performing a variety of roles. Chassis-cab weight is 10,500 kg, giving axle weights of 6,300 kg on the front axle, 4,200 kg on the rear bogie. These increase to 9,500 and 16,500 kg at the maximum 26,000 kg GVW.

Motive power is provided by a EURO 3 emissions compliant Cummins 10.8-litre six-cylinder turbocharged diesel engine developing 385 hp, giving a power-to-weight ratio of 18.8 hp/tonne at 10,000 kg payload, and 14.8 hp/tonne at maximum GVW. A ZF 16S 151 16 speed all synchromesh gearbox is coupled to a ZF VG 1600 transfer box giving permanent all-wheel drive. A longitudinal driver-controlled pneumatically operated differential lock is fitted. A torque convertor option is available.

The front steer-drive hub reduction axle is an Axletech 4514 SFW unit rated at 10,000 kg capacity and sprung by the combination of semi-elliptic leaf springs, telescopic shock absorbers and an anti-roll bar, the tandem rear drive hub reduction axles are Meritor 4524 SFW units rated at 11,000 kg capacity each and sprung by inverted leaf springs. All are fitted with driver-controlled pneumatically operated cross-axle differential locks. An automatic traction control system is an option. Steering is power assisted.

Single 1400R 20 tyres are standard, and run-flat inserts and a Central Tyre Inflation (CTI) system are options. Drum brakes are fitted front and rear, and an Anti-lock Braking System (ABS) is an option.

BMC 380-26 (6 × 6) 10,000 kg truck (BMC)   1171397

Specifications

BMC 380-26
Cab seating: 1 + 2
Configuration: 6 × 6
Weight:
  (unladen) 10,500 kg
  (laden, max) 26,000 kg
  (load, max) 15,500 kg
  (towed load) 10,000 kg
  (GCW) 36,000 kg
Length: (overall) 7.67 m
Width: 2.5 m
Height: (overall) 2.95 m
Ground clearance: 400 mm
Track:
  (front) 2 m
  (rear) 2 m
Wheelbase: 3.86 + 1.35 m
Angle of approach/departure: 35°/38°
Max geared speed: 100 km/h
Range: 1,000 km
Fuel capacity: 450 litres
Max gradient: 60% (laden)
Max sideslope: 56% (static)
Fording: 1 m
Engine: Cummins ISM 385 E30 EURO 3 10.8-litre 6-cylinder in-line water-cooled turbocharged and intercooled diesel developing 287 kW (385 hp) at 1,900 rpm and 1,825 N.m torque at 1,200 rpm
Gearbox: ZF 16S 151 manual, 16 forward and 2 reverse gears
Clutch: single dry plate, (dia) 430 mm
Transfer box: ZF VG 1600, full time all-wheel drive
Steering: power-assisted, ZF 8098
Turning radius: (wall) 11.35 m
Suspension: semi-elliptic leaf springs, telescopic shock-absorbers and anti-roll bar, front; inverted leaf springs, rear
Tyres: 1400R 20
Brakes: air actuated, drums all-round, ABS optional
Electrical system: 24 V
Batteries: 2 × 12 V, 150 Ah
Alternator: 55 A

Status

Small number in service with the Turkish Army. Has been tested in Pakistan and Turkey.

Contractor

BMC Sanayi ve Ticaret AS

BMC 380-26 P (6 × 6) 10,000 kg Tactical Wheeled Vehicle (TWV)

Development

BMC Sanayi ve Ticaret AS has produced a number of all-wheel drive trucks since the company was originally established in 1964. Until 2008 these came exclusively from the in-production Fatih range, production of which commenced in 1986 after BMC signed a license agreement to manufacture Cummins engines.

Fatih range models presently available include the 150-09, 170-13, 200-13, 200-15 and 220-18 models. These are all (4 × 4) designs, and in all cases the designations follow the standard BMC practice and reflect engine horsepower and Gross Vehicle Weight (GVW).

Models 215-09 (2,500 kg) and 235-16 (5,000 kg), which are both (4 × 4) configuration, were the first BMC all-wheel drive models to be selected by Turkey's Armed Forces. Export sales have also been made, and both models remain in production and service.

A (6 × 6) model, the BMC 380-26, was also produced and it is currently in service with Turkey's Armed Forces.

During 2008 BMC launched an entirely new series of military vehicles, the (4 × 4) EFE 185-09 B (2,500 kg), the (4 × 4) 235-16 P (5,000 kg) and (6 × 6) 380-26 P (10,000 kg).

The EFE 185-09 B is of bonneted configuration, while the 235-16 P and 380-26 P are Cab-Over-Engine (COE). Full details of the EFE 185-09 B (4 × 4) and 235-16 P (4 × 4) can be found elsewhere in this section.

BMC refers to these vehicles and previous generation military trucks as Tactical Wheeled Vehicles (TWVs).

Since 1989 BMC Sanayi ve Ticaret AS has been wholly owned by Cukurova Holding of Turkey.

Description

The BMC 380-26 P (6 × 6) 10,000 kg truck is an entirely new design. Construction is based on a conventional C-section chassis with C-profile flitch plates inserted for reinforcement where required. Recovery and/or towing points are fitted front and rear, a NATO standard pintle being fitted at the rear. A front-mounted hydraulically operated self-recovery winch is an option.

BMC 380-26 P (6 × 6) 10,000 kg Tactical Wheeled Vehicle (TWV) (BMC Sanayi ve Ticaret AS)   1391471

The three-person all-steel tilt-cab is based on the cab fitted to the Professional commercial range of trucks, with militarisation options including rifle racks, a single circular roof hatch, and a roof-mounted weapon mount.

The standard troop carrying/cargo platform-type body is fitted with two-piece steel drop sides and a tailgate, removable tarpaulin with bows and wooden bench seats. The BMC 380-26 P has a tactical payload rating of 10,000 kg, although maximum possible payload (including superstructure) is 15,200 kg. A wide variety of other body types may be fitted to base chassis.

Motive power is provided by a EURO 3 emissions compliant Cummins diesel engine developing 380 hp and giving a power-to-weight ratio of 18.8 hp/tonne at 10,000 kg payload, and 14.6 hp/tonne at maximum GVW. An engine cold start kit is fitted and the cooling system has been adapted for tactical applications.

Driveline is completed by an Allison 4500SP fully automatic transmission or a ZF 16-speed all synchromesh gearbox coupled to a ZF two-speed transfer box giving full-time all-wheel drive. A longitudinal driver-controlled pneumatically operated differential lock is fitted. A torque convertor option is available. The front steer-drive hub-reduction axle is an Axletech 4514 SFW unit rated at 7,500 kg capacity and sprung by the combination of semi-elliptic leaf springs, telescopic shock-absorbers and an anti-roll bar, the tandem rear drive hub reduction axles are Axletech 4524 SFW and TFW units rated at 9,500 kg capacity each and sprung by inverted leaf springs. All are fitted with driver-controlled pneumatically operated cross-axle differential locks. An automatic traction control system is an option. Steering is power assisted.

Single 1400R 20 tyres are standard, and run-flat inserts and a Central Tyre Inflation System (CTIS) are options. Drum brakes are fitted front and rear, and an Anti-lock Braking System (ABS) is an option.

Chassis-cab weight is 10,800 kg, giving axle weights of 5,900 kg on the front axle and 4,900 kg on the rear bogie. These increase to 7,500 and 18,500 kg at the maximum 26,000 kg GVW.

Specifications

BMC 380-26 P
Cab seating: 1 + 2
Configuration: 6 × 6
Weight:
  (unladen, chassis-cab) 10,800 kg
  (laden) 26,000 kg
  (payload) 15,200 kg
  (front axle load, chassis-cab) 5,900 kg
  (rear bogie load, chassis-cab) 4,900 kg
  (front axle load, GVW) 7,500 kg
  (rear bogie load, GVW) 18,500 kg
  (towed load) 10,000 kg
  (GCW) 36,000 kg
Length: 8.15 m
Width: 2.5 m
Height: 3.19 m
Ground clearance: 400 mm

Track:
  (front) 2.06 m
  (rear) 2.06 m
Wheelbase: 4 + 1.35 m
Angle of approach/departure: 35°/45°
Max speed: 95 km/h
Max range: 1,000 km
Fuel capacity: 450 litres
Max gradient: (laden) 60%
Side slope: (static) 47%
Fording: 1 m
Engine: Cummins ISM 380 E20 EURO II emissions compliant 10.8-litre 6-cylinder in-line water-cooled turbocharged and intercooled diesel developing 380 hp (280 kW) at 1,900 rpm and 1,825 N.m torque at 1,200 rpm
Gearbox: Allison 4500 SP automatic transmission with 6 forward and 1 reverse gears; optional ZF 16S 1820 TO manual with 16 forward and 2 reverse gears
Transfer box: ZF VG 2000, full time all-wheel drive
Clutch: (with manual gearbox option) single dry plate (430 mm diameter)
Steering: power-assisted, ZF 8098
Turning radius: (wall) 11.35 m
Suspension: semi-elliptic leaf springs, telescopic shock-absorbers and anti-roll bar, front; inverted leaf springs, rear
Tyres: 1400R 20
Brakes: air actuated, drums all-round, ABS optional
Electrical system: 24 V
Batteries: 2 × 12 V, 180 Ah
Alternator: 70 A

Status
Ready for serial production upon order.

Contractor
BMC Sanayi ve Ticaret AS

MANAS 16.230 FAEG (4 × 4) 7,500 kg and 26.372 DFAEG (6 × 6) 14,500 kg trucks

Description
These heavy-duty trucks were originally developed by MAN Nutzfahrzeuge AG to meet requirements for front line logistic supply vehicles capable of crossing rough terrain. The two vehicles share many components, with the main difference between the two, apart from the differing drive configurations, being the engines. The 16.230 FAEG (4 × 4) vehicle is fitted with a MAN D 0826 LF 08 6.87-litre turbocharged diesel developing 230 hp at 2,400 rpm. The 26.372 DFAEG (6 × 6) has an 11.97-litre turbocharged diesel, the MAN D 2866 LF 15, developing 370 hp at 2,000 rpm.

MANAS 16.230 FAEG and 26.372 DFAEG trucks

Model	16.230 FAEG	26.372 DFAEG
Cab seating:	1 + 2	1 + 2
Configuration:	4 × 4	6 × 6
Weight:		
(chassis)	7,450 kg	9,770 kg
(GVW)	16,000 kg	25,000 kg
(max load)	8,550 kg	16,230 kg
Length:	7.45 m	7.65 m
Width:	2.48 m	2.48 m
Height: (top of cab)	approx 2.935 m	3.055 m
Ground clearance:	455 mm	455 mm
Wheelbase:	4.2 m	3.575 m + 1.4 m
Angle of approach/departure:	38°/35°	40°/37°
Max speed:	84 km/h	83 km/h
Fuel capacity:	300 litres	300 litres
Max gradient:	60%	60%
Fording:	1 m	1.2 m
Engine:	MAN D 0826 LF 08 6.87-litre in-line turbocharged water-cooled 4-stroke diesel developing 230 hp (169 kW) at 2,400 rpm	MAN D 2866 LF 15 11.97-litre in-line turbocharged water-cooled 4-stroke diesel developing 370 hp (272 kW) at 2,000 rpm
Gearbox:	manual with 9 forward and 1 reverse gears	manual with 16 forward and 2 reverse gears
Transfer box:	G1000, 2-speed	G1700, 2-speed
Clutch:	Single dry plate	single dry plate
Steering:	power assisted, ZF 8098	power assisted, ZF 8098
Tyres:	14.00R 20	14.00R 20
Brakes:	dual circuit, air, drums all-round	dual circuit, air, drums all-round
Electrical system:	24 V	24 V
Batteries:	2 × 12 V, 150 Ah	2 × 12 V, 180 Ah
Alternator:	55 A	55 A

The two vehicles share the same all-steel MAN cab with seating for the driver and two passengers. A roof hatch is provided. The cab can be tilted forward for maintenance. The chassis has longitudinal members of pressed C-section made of high-quality steel. Cross-members are fixed to the main members by rivets or bolts. There is a tow pin at the front and a NATO-type tow hook at the rear; electrical and brake circuits are provided for trailers. A cable winch is located in the centre of the vehicle between the frame members. It has a 5,000 kg pull capacity to the front and 10,000 kg to the rear. The winch has 60 m of cable.

The body is steel with a canvas cover. Swing-open side and rear walls are provided. A tool box and steps are provided at the rear and there is stowage for extra fuel canisters. A swing-out spare wheel carrier is located behind the cab.

Specifications
See table above

Status
Production complete, replaced by current generation models including 10.163 LAEC, 16.220 FAEX and 26.372 DFAEX.

Contractor
MAN Türkiye A.Ş

Ukraine

KrAZ-255B and 255B (B1) (6 × 6) 7,500 kg trucks

Development
The KrAZ-255B (6 × 6) 7,500 kg truck entered in production in 1965, with full series production commencing in 1967. The KrAZ-255B was the direct replacement of the earlier serially produced KrAZ-214 7,000 kg (6 × 6) truck. The KrAZ-255B (B1) was a later model that featured a revised braking system.

The KrAZ-255B had some visual similarities with the earlier KrAZ-214 but had a more powerful engine, a V-8 four-stroke diesel developing 240 hp to replace the six-cylinder two-stroke 205 hp unit of the KrAZ-214. Other design improvements included a hydraulic steering booster replacing the pneumatic booster of the KrAZ-214, and the standard 1400 × 20 tyres of the KrAZ-214 were replaced by new wide section pressure adjustable tires with a centralised tire inflation system controlled by the driver directly from cab. In 1976 the KrAZ-255B was equipped with a new dual-circuit braking system that replaced an earlier single circuit system, and such vehicles were given the revised KrAZ-255B (B1) model designation.

Many of the roles previously undertaken by the KrAZ-214 were transferred to the KrAZ-255B when it entered series production, these

including carrying and laying the TMM treadway bridge; carrying and launching the PMP heavy floating pontoon bridge; carrying and launching the BMK-T bridging boat; mounting of assorted engineer/construction equipment and cranes including the USM pile driving set, the E-305 BV crane shovel, and the EDV-4421 excavator; assorted tankers including the ATsM 7-255B 7,000 litre fuel tanker towing the PTsM 8925 5,800 litre trailer. The Heavy Mechanised Bridge (HMB) was developed specifically for use with the KrAZ-255B.

The KrAZ-255B (B1) could also tow a variety of trailers including artillery pieces up to 30,000 kg on roads or prepared tracks, and off-road weighing up to 10,000 kg.

Of basic design and being simple to maintain and operate, from 1968 the KrAZ-255B was supplied to the armed forces of numerous Warsaw Pact countries and others in Africa/North Africa (including Egypt), Latin America and South-East Asia. When production of the KrAZ-255B (B1) concluded in 1993 the type had reportedly been supplied for military use in 57 countries.

The KrAZ-255B (B1) was supplemented and then replaced in production by the KrAZ-260, full details of which can be found elsewhere in this section. Only small numbers of the KrAZ-260 had entered service with the Soviet Army prior to the break-up of the country and large numbers of the earlier 255B and B1 models remain in service, however these have been more quickly replaced in the Ukraine.

The now KrAZ (Kremenchug Automobile Plant) had previously produced bridges, later harvesters, and in 1958 was established as a heavy duty truck manufacturer. Nowadays KrAZ is a recognised producer of simple-to-maintain, rugged trucks for military, agriculture and heavy industry applications. Once employing 19,000 people and using a capacity to produce 30,000 trucks per year, KrAZ has produced around 800,000 trucks and these have been sold to 57 countries around the world. The plant currently employs around 7,000 people.

KrAZ-255B (6 × 6) 7,500 kg truck configured as transporter/laying vehicle for the TMM-3 truck mounted scissors bridge (Shaun C Connors) 0059685

KrAZ-255B (6 × 6) 7,500 kg truck (James Kinnear) 0567940

The company established an assembly production operation in Vietnam during 2003.

Description

Layout of the KrAZ-255B (6 × 6) 7,500 kg truck is entirely conventional. Of bonneted design, the three-seat cabin is wood framed and covered with sheet steel. The split front (two piece) flat windscreen opens outwards for increased ventilation.

The C-section chassis frame consists of side-members made from hot-rolled steel. The standard rear body is of the troop carrying/cargo type with dropsides and tailgate and is normally fitted with wooden bench-type seats and a tarpaulin cover.

Motive power is provided by a naturally aspirated diesel engine fitted as standard with an engine start pre-heater for use in temperatures below −20°C. The KrAZ-255B (and (B1)) and KrAZ-255V (and V1)) are intended for operation at temperatures ranging from +45°C to −45°C in temperate climate conditions. From 1972 production of versions for tropical (T) climates and temperatures up to +50°C were introduced, such models having a revised KrAZ-255BT or VT (T - Tropical) designation.

On all models all three axles are leaf sprung and are driven, with front axle engagement being mechanical and controlled from the cab. A five-speed manual gearbox and two-speed transfer box are fitted. The transfer box consists of two units joined together, the main unit housing the double-reduction gear with gear ratios of 1.23 and 2.28. The additional unit features two output shafts for rear axle drive and the inter-axle locking differential. An air operated braking system is fitted, with drums on all axles. The parking brake is of the transmission drum type.

Variants

In addition to the uses/variants on the base chassis previously covered, a number of specialised variants of the KrAZ-255B were also produced. The KrAZ-255 (V1) fifth-wheel tractor is based on the KrAZ-255B (B1) and can tow semi-trailers weighing up to 26,000 kg on roads, or 18,000 kg across country. Also based on the KrAZ-255B (B1) is the KrAZ-255L (L1) (6 × 6) timber truck tractor with a load carrying capacity of 8,000 kg. The KrAZ-255L (L1) timber truck tractor forms a road train when used in conjunction with the TMZ-9383 two-axle timber trailer; GVW of the road train is 39,000 kg.

The Kremenchug Automobile Plant also manufactured the KrAZ-256B (B1), a 6 × 4 dump truck with a load carrying capacity of 12,000 kg, the KrAZ-257B (B1) 6 × 4 platform truck and chassis with a load carrying capacity of 12,000 kg, and the KrAZ-258 (B1) 6 × 6 fifth-wheel tractor truck with a load carrying capacity of 12,000 kg and the ability to tow assorted semi-trailers of up to 30,000 kg.

Specifications

KrAZ-255B
Cab seating: 1 + 2
Configuration: 6 × 6
Weight:
  (laden, off-road) 19,750 kg
  (unladen) 11,950 kg
  (weight on front axle, laden) 5,600 kg
  (weight on rear axles, laden) 14,150 kg
  (max load) 7,500 kg
  (towed load, on-road) 30,000 kg
  (towed load, off-road) 10,000 kg
Load area: 4.56 × 2.5 m
Length: 8.645 m
Width: 2.75 m
Height:
  (cab) 2.94 m
  (tarpaulin) 3.17 m
  (load area) 1.65 m
Ground clearance: 360 mm
Track: (front and rear) 2.16 m
Wheelbase: 4.6 m + 1.4 m

Angle of approach/departure: 48°/32°
Max speed: 70 km/h
Range: 490 km
Fuel capacity: 330 litres
Max gradient: >60%
Vertical obstacle: 600 mm
Trench: 680 mm
Fording: 1 m
Engine: YaMZ-238 14.86-litre V-8 water-cooled 4-stroke diesel developing 240 hp (179 kW) at 2,100 rpm
Gearbox: manual, 5 forward and 1 reverse gears
Clutch: twin dry disc
Transfer box: 2-speed with inter-axle differential lock
Steering: screw and nut with roller ball, hydraulic booster
Turning radius: 14.5 m
Suspension:
  (front) longitudinal semi-elliptic springs with telescopic double acting shock-absorbers
  (rear) equaliser type on 2 longitudinal semi-elliptical springs
Tyres: 1300 × 530-533
Brakes:
  (main) air
  (parking) mechanical
Electrical system: 24 V
Batteries: 2 × 6-TST-165EMS
Generator: 500 W

Status

Production completed in 1993. Supplied to a reported 57 armed forces including those of the Russian Federation, other former Warsaw Pact countries and numerous unspecified countries in Africa/North Africa (including Egypt), Latin America, South-East Asia and elsewhere.

Contractor

Foreign Trade Firm KrAZ JSC

KrAZ-260 (6 × 6) 9,000 kg truck and variants

Development

The KrAZ-214 7,000 kg (6 × 6) truck was replaced in production by the KrAZ-255B in 1967, with the (B1) variant of the KrAZ-255B remaining in production until 1993. The KrAZ-260 (6 × 6) 9,000 kg truck was designed on the instructions of the then Ministry of Defence of the USSR and in 1979 entered production in parallel with the KrAZ-255B (B1), and as the intended eventual replacement of the earlier vehicle.

The KrAZ-260 was first seen in public participating in the Moscow military parade and towing the 2A36 152 mm nuclear-capable gun.

The KrAZ-260 was the base vehicle for a family of high mobility trucks, this family comprising the KrAZ-260 chassis and the 260G long wheelbase chassis (both rated at 10,000 kg payload), and the KrAZ-260B tractor truck rated at 9,500 kg payload. Around 80 specific variants of the KrAZ-260 were produced, including those for commercial use in the timber, oil, gas and other severe service industries.

A number of commercial designs based on the KrAZ-260 and fitted with dual rear wheels and tyres were also produced, main models including the KrAZ-64372 timber truck, the KrAZ-6443 tractor truck, and the KrAZ-65032 dump truck.

In 1999 the revised KrAZ-6322 truck replaced the KrAZ-260 in production. The KrAZ-6322 family included the KrAZ-63221 long wheelbase chassis rated at 11,000 kg payload and the KrAZ-6446 tractor truck rated at 10,000 kg payload.

In addition to the armed forces of the former Soviet Union, KrAZ-260 family vehicles have been supplied to a number of countries including India, Egypt, India, Iraq and Pakistan.

KrAZ-260 (6 × 6) 9,000 kg truck (KrAZ) 0114376

KrAZ-260V (6 × 6) 9,000 tractor truck (KrAZ)   0114375

The now KrAZ (Kremenchug Automobile Plant) had previously produced bridges, later harvesters, and in 1958 was established as a heavy duty truck manufacturer. Nowadays KrAZ is a recognised producer of simple-to-maintain, rugged trucks for military, agriculture and heavy industry applications. Once employing 19,000 people and using a capacity to produce 30,000 trucks per year, KrAZ has produced around 800,000 trucks and these have been sold to 57 countries around the world. The plant currently employs around 7,000 people.

The company established an assembly production operation in Vietnam during 2003.

Description

Despite visual similarities to the earlier KrAZ-255B, the KrAZ-260 truck while retaining the basic design principles and robust simplistic design of the earlier model, was a newly designed vehicle and carried only the pressure adjustable wide section tyres over from the earlier design.

A bonneted design, the KrAZ-260 is equipped with a three-seat sheet metal cab that compared to earlier KrAZ cabs features a greater internal volume and revised windscreen, the main two-piece flat glass screen now being supplemented by two smaller quarter light-style side screens. Following its adoption for the KrAZ-260, this cab was subsequently fitted to all KrAZ models.

Motive power is provided by a YaMZ-238L multifuel engine manufactured by the Yaroslavskiy Motor Plant, JSC. KrAZ-260 trucks are intended to be operated in temperate, tropical and cold climates and at temperature extremes ranging from +50°C to –50°C. A cold start device for temperatures lower than –20ºC is standard equipment.

The conventional C-section chassis is construction from hot rolled steel and is fitted with towing/recovery points front and rear. All three beam-type leaf-sprung axles are driven via an eight-speed manual gearbox and three-shaft two-speed transfer box with ratios of 1.013 and 1.31. The transfer box is fitted with a PTO for the 12,000 kg self-recovery winch. The rear axles are fitted with driver-controlled cross-axle differential locks.

1300 × 530 × 533 tubed wide section pressure adjustable tyres are fitted, pressure settings of 1 to 4 atm being controlled by the driver from the cab, and while on the move (1 atm = 14.696 psi).

The standard body for the KrAZ-260 was of the troop carrying/cargo-type fitted with a removable tarpaulin and bows, plus drop-down bench seats. A considerable number of bridging, construction and engineering style bodies were fitted to the KrAZ-260, many of these being further developments of similar systems fitted to the earlier KrAZ-255B chassis and designed to take advantage of the greater carrying capacity of the KrAZ-260 chassis.

The KrAZ-260 is rated to tow trailers of up to 30,000 kg on hard roads or prepared tracks, and up to 10,000 kg off-road.

Variants

KrAZ-260V

A 6 × 6 tractor truck version with a fifth wheel for towing semi-trailers is known as the KrAZ-260V. It replaced the earlier KrAZ-255V1 and KrAZ-258B1 tractors in production. Maximum fifth wheel load is 9,500 kg and the full weight of a towed semi-trailer is 27,500 kg.

One application for this vehicle is as a tractor for various components, including the erector/launcher and missile resupply trailer, of the SA-10a 'Grumble' surface-to-air missile system (full details of which can be found in *Jane's Land-based Air Defence*).

KrAZ-260G

A multipurpose chassis with the wheelbase lengthened to 5 m + 1.4 m.

KrAZ-250

This is a 6 × 4 variant with twin-tyred rear wheels and an on-road load capacity of 16,575 kg and can pull trailers of up to 20,000 kg. Wheelbase is 4.88 m + 1.4 m. As well as being used for cargo bodies this chassis was also fitted with a wide variety of civil construction/engineering-type bodies including cranes, mixers and assorted equipment specific to the oil and gas industries.

KrAZ-5444

A 4 × 2 truck tractor with a maximum fifth wheel load of 9,400 kg and a towed semi-trailer maximum weight of 32,000 kg. Wheelbase is 4.7 m. Twin rear wheels are fitted.

KrAZ-6443

A 6 × 6 tractor truck intended for towing semi-trailers weighing up to 48,000 kg. Power output is 318 hp.

KrAZ-64431

A 6 × 4 tractor truck primarily for commercial use. Maximum towed weight is 32,700 kg. The KrAZ-64431 has a sleeper-style cab and the turbocharged V-8 diesel develops 330 hp.

KrAZ-6444

A 6 × 4 tractor truck primarily for commercial use. Maximum towed weight is 32,000 kg. Power output is 240 hp.

KrAZ-6510

A 6 × 4 dump truck with an 8 m³ tipper body carrying loads up to 13,500 kg. GVW is 26,400 kg. Power output is 240 hp.

KrAZ-65032

A 6 × 6 dump truck with a 12 m³ tipper body carrying loads up to 18,000 kg. GVW is 31,250 kg. Power output is 330 hp.

KrAZ-6322

A 6 × 6 truck that is essentially a modernised/upgraded KrAZ-260. Maximum permissible payload is 10,000 kg, GVW is 23,000 kg. This truck forms a large part of a package of vehicles supplied to Iraq.

Specifications

KrAZ-260
Cab seating: 1 + 2
Configuration: 6 × 6
Weight:
  (unladen with driver and fuel) 12,300 kg
  (laden) 21,600 kg
  (weight on front axle, laden) 6,500 kg
  (weight on rear axles, laden) 15,100 kg
  (max load) 9,000 kg
  (towed load, on-road) 30,000 kg
  (towed load, off-road) 10,000 kg
Load area: 5 × 2.52 m
Length: 9.006 m
Width: 2.724 m
Height: (top of tilt) 3.26 m
Ground clearance: 370 mm
Track:
  (front and rear) 2.16 m
Wheelbase: 4.6 m + 1.4 m
Angle of approach/departure: (loaded) 35°/26°
Max speed: 80 km/h
Range: (road, cruising) 930 km
Fuel capacity: 2 × 165 litres + 1 × 45 litres
Max gradient: 58%
Side slope: 36%
Vertical obstacle: 500 mm
Trench: 650 mm
Fording: 1.2 m
Engine: YaMZ-238L (or YaMZ-238BL) 14.86-litre V-8 turbocharged water-cooled 4-stroke diesel developing 300 hp (224 kW) at 2,100 rpm
Gearbox: manual, synchronised, with 8 forward and 2 reverse gears
Clutch: twin dry discs
Transfer box: 2-speed with asymmetric differential
Steering: worm and nut
Turning radius: 13 m
Suspension:
  (front) semi-elliptic leaf springs with telescopic double action shock-absorbers
  (rear) inverted semi-elliptic leaf springs
Tyres: 1300 × 530-533
Brakes:
  (main) dual circuit, air, drums all round. Supplementary engine exhaust brake
  (parking) mechanical, drum on transmission
Electrical system: 24 V
Batteries: 2 × 12 V, 190 Ah, 6ST-190
Generator: 1000 W

Status

Production complete, replaced by revised model (see text). In addition to the armed forces of the former USSR KrAZ-260 trucks have been supplied to Egypt, India, Iraq, Pakistan and others.

Contractor

Foreign Trade Firm KrAZ JSC

KrAZ-6322 10,000 kg (6 × 6) truck and variants

Development
The KrAZ-214 7,000 kg (6 × 6) truck was replaced in production by the KrAZ-255B in 1967, with the (B1) variant of the KrAZ-255B remaining in production until 1993. The KrAZ-260 (6 × 6) 9,000 kg truck was designed on the instructions of the then Ministry of Defence of the USSR and in 1979 entered production in parallel with the KrAZ-255B (B1), and was the intended eventual replacement of the earlier vehicle. In 2001 the revised KrAZ-6322 truck replaced the KrAZ-260 in production. The KrAZ-6322 family includes the KrAZ-63221 long wheelbase chassis and the KrAZ-6446 tractor truck.

The KrAZ-6322 truck forms a significant part of a package of vehicles and equipment ordered for Iraq mid-2004, and is also understood to be in service with the armed forces of Angola, Egypt, India, Indonesia (UN), Nigeria (Police), Ukraine and Yemen.

The now KrAZ (Kremenchug Automobile Plant) had previously produced bridges, later harvesters, and in 1958 was established as a heavy duty truck manufacturer. Nowadays KrAZ is a recognised producer of simple-to-maintain, rugged trucks for military, agriculture and heavy industry applications. Once employing 19,000 people and using a capacity to produce 30,000 trucks per year, KrAZ has produced around 800,000 trucks and these have been sold to 57 countries around the world. The plant currently employs around 7,000 people.

The company established an assembly production operation in Vietnam during 2003.

Description
The KrAZ-6322 10,000 kg (6 × 6) truck is representative of the traditional design of KrAZ vehicles. It is based on a 300 × 9.5 mm C-section ladder frame chassis made of 30B-1 steel with stamped cross-members. Recovery and/or towing points are fitted front and rear, a mechanical self-recovery winch is an option. The three-person all-steel bonneted cab is standard across the KrAZ range and is very similar to that of the earlier KrAZ-260 truck, and features a two-piece flat glass windscreen.

The standard troop carrying/cargo-type platform body is fitted with steel drop sides, a single-piece drop tailgate, and a removable tarpaulin and bows. The body measures 5 × 2.52 m × 360 mm (L × W × H) internally. Wooden bench seats may be provided for troop transport. The KrAZ-6322 with standard dropside troop carrying/cargo-type body has a tactical payload rating of 10,100 kg, but the maximum permissible load with 1350 × 550-533 tyres is 12,000 kg.

The base chassis is designed to be capable of accepting a wide variety of body types and the overall width of the KrAZ-6322 is 2.72 m.

Motive power is provided by the range standard YaMZ 238D turbocharged diesel engine developing 330 hp, and produced at the Yaroslavl Motor Plant. To meet EURO II emissions levels if required the YaMZ 238DE2 engine may be fitted. Other engine options, including Cummins, Deutz, Volvo or others to suit individual market requirements are available. An engine cold start pre-heater and additional cab heater are available as options. The climatic operational range of the KrAZ-6322 is –45 to +50°C.

An eight-speed manual gearbox coupled to a two-speed transfer box with an inter-axle differential lock is fitted. The front steer-drive axle is sprung by the combination of semi-elliptic leaf springs and telescopic shock-absorbers. The rear drive axles are sprung by inverted semi-elliptic leaf springs. Axles are double reduction and fitted with driver-controlled cross-axle differential locks. Steering is hydraulically power assisted.

Single wide footprint 1300 × 530-533 tyres are standard, although 1350 × 550-553 with a higher payload rating are an option. A Central Tyre Inflation (CTI) system can be fitted. Drum brakes are fitted front and rear, supplemented by an engine exhaust brake. The parking park is of the drum type, mechanically operated and located on the transfer box output shaft.

KrAZ-6322-56. This model has been supplied to Iraq
(Foreign Trade Firm KrAZ JSC) 1391016

KrAZ-6133KE (Foreign Trade Firm KrAZ JSC) 1391015

KrAZ-5133BE (Foreign Trade Firm KrAZ JSC) 1391017

Variants
Unless otherwise stated all variants are powered by the standard YAMZ 238D 14.86-litre V-8 water-cooled turbocharged diesel engine developing 330 hp at 2,100 rpm and 1,225 N.m torque between 1,200-1,400 rpm, and coupled to an eight-speed manual gearbox and two-speed transfer box.

KrAZ-6133KE
This is intended for engineering equipment and recovery crew transportation, and features a purpose-designed 29-seat bus-type rear body based on the long wheelbase chassis of the KrAZ-63221. The body may be fitted out in a variety of role-specific ways. The KrAZ-5133KE follows the same general lines but is mounted on the smaller KrAZ-5133BE (4 × 4) chassis and seats 22.

KrAZ-6322-056
This variant of the KrAZ-6322 is intended for recovery work and is equipped with a variety of specialist equipment, including an 8 kW capacity diesel generator set, an air compressor, oxyacetylene equipment, a full set of tools and a behind-cab M150 materials handling crane rated at 12 t/m, and with a maximum reach of 8.6 m. This variant has been supplied to Iraq.

KrAZ-5133BE
This is a 4 × 4 variant of the KrAZ-6322. Specifications for the KrAZ-5133BE can be found in the accompanying Specifications table.

KrAZ-6333PE (Foreign Trade Firm KrAZ JSC) 1391018

KrAZ-6446 (Foreign Trade Firm KrAZ JSC)   1391023

KrAZ-6333PE
This model is fitted with a specialist body for the transport of tracked vehicles. The flatbed-type body is fitted with rear ramps and a 12,000 kg capacity winch with 35 m of cable. Kerb weight is 13,500 kg and GVW is 33,500 kg, giving a payload allowance of 20,000 kg. Tyres (twin on the rear bogie) are 1200R 20.

KrAZ-63221-044
This is a chassis-cab with a 5 + 1.4 m wheelbase and overall length of 10 m, giving 6.32 m of chassis for the mounting of specialist type bodies. Kerb weight is 13,500 kg and GVW is 31,200 kg, giving a payload allowance (on the chassis-cab) of 20,400 kg. Tyres (twin on the rear bogie) are 1200R 20 and overall width is 2.5 m.

KrAZ-65032-061
This is a 4.08 + 1.4 m wheelbase 12 m³ capacity dump truck variant with an unladen weight of 13,800 kg and a payload of 13,100 kg. Tyres are 1350 × 550-533 and overall width is 2.72 m.

KrAZ-65032-043
This is a 4.08 + 1.4 m wheelbase 12 m³ capacity dump variant with an unladen weight of 13,200 kg and a payload of 18,000 kg. Tyres (twin on the rear bogie) are 1200R 20 and overall width is 2.5 m.

KrAZ-65032
This is a 4.08 + 1.4 m wheelbase 10.5 m³ capacity dump variant with an unladen weight of 13,200 kg and a payload of 15,000 kg. Tyres (twin on the rear bogie) are 1200R 20 and overall width is 2.5 m.

KrAZ-6446
This is essentially a fifth wheel tractor truck variant of the KrAZ-6322. The fully articulating fifth wheel coupling has a maximum vertical load rating of 12,600 kg; a Jost or George Fisher fifth wheel coupling is an option.

	KrAZ-6322 platform truck	KrAZ-5133BE platform truck	KrAZ-6446 tractor truck
Cab seating:	1 + 2	1 + 2	1 + 2
Configuration:	6 × 6	4 × 4	4 × 4
Weight:			
(laden)	23,000 kg	16,300 kg	23,000 kg
(unladen)	12,700 kg	11,000 kg	11,400 kg
(payload)	10,100 kg	5,100 kg	12,000 kg
(front axle load, laden)	7,000 kg	7,200 kg	7,000 kg
(rear axle(s) load, laden)	8,000 kg	9,100 kg	16,000 kg
(front axle load, unladen)	6,100 kg	6,200 kg	6,000 kg
(rear axle(s) load, unladen)	3,300 kg	4,800 kg	5,400 kg
(towed load, on-road)	30,000 kg	10,000 kg	34,000 kg
(towed load, off-road)	10,000 kg	7,000 kg	23,000 kg
(towed load, aircraft etc.)	75,000 kg	30,000 kg	n/app
(GCW, on-road)	53,000 kg	26,300 kg	45,400 kg
(GCW, off-road)	33,000 kg	23,300 kg	34,400 kg
Length:	8.98 m	7.9 m	8.1 m
Width:	2.72 m	2.72 m	2.72 m
Height: (cab roof, unladen)	3.1 m	3.15 m	3.1 m
Load area:	5 × 2.52 m	4.55 m × 2.52 m	n/app
Ground clearance:	370 mm	400 mm	370 mm
Track: (front and rear)	2.16 m	2.16 m	2.16 m
Wheelbase:	4.6 + 1.4 m	5 m	4.6 + 1.4 m
Angle of approach/departure: (unladen)	38°/30°	40°/36°	38° (approach)
Max speed:	80 km/h	80 km/h	80 km/h
Fuel capacity:	2 × 250 litres	350 litres	2 × 250 litres
Max gradient:	58%	58%	18% (at GCW)
Fording:	1.2 m	1.2 m	1.2 m
Engine:	YaMZ 238D 14.86-litre V8 turbocharged water-cooled direct injection 4-stroke diesel engine developing 330 hp (246 kW) at 2,100 rpm and 1.225 kN.m torque at 1,200-1,400 rpm; EURO 2 option (YaMZ-238DE2) developing 330 hp (246 kW) at 2,100 rpm and 1.274 kN.m torque at 1,100-1,300 rpm		
Gearbox:	manual with 8 forward and 1 reverse gears	manual with 8 forward and 1 reverse gears	manual with 8 forward and 1 reverse gears
Transfer box:	2-speed	2-speed	2-speed
Clutch:	twin dry disc	twin dry disc	single dry disc
Steering:	mechanical with hydraulic booster; right-hand drive optional	mechanical with hydraulic booster; right-hand drive optional	mechanical with hydraulic booster; right-hand drive optional
Turning radius:	13.5 m	13 m	13.5 m
Suspension:	semi-elliptic leaf springs and hydraulic shock-absorbers, front, inverted semi-elliptic leaf springs, rear bogie (KrAZ-6322 and KrAZ-6446); semi-elliptic leaf springs and hydraulic shock-absorbers, front and rear (KrAZ-5133BE)		
Tyres:	1350 × 550-533	1350 × 550-533	530/70R 21
Brakes:			
(main)	dual circuit, air, drums on all axles; supplementary engine exhaust brake	dual circuit, air, drums on all axles; supplementary engine exhaust brake	dual circuit, air, drums on all axles; supplementary engine exhaust brake
(parking)	mechanically operated drum-type transmission brake on transfer box output shaft	mechanically operated drum-type transmission brake on transfer box output shaft	mechanically operated drum-type transmission brake on transfer box output shaft
Electrical system:	24 V	24 V	24 V

KrAZ-7140H6 (Foreign Trade Firm KrAZ JSC)　　1391020

Maximum towed loads are 23,000 kg off-road, 34,000 kg on metal covered roads. Full specifications for the KrAZ-6446 can be found in the accompanying Specifications table.

KrAZ-7140H6

This is a four-axle chassis with a single front axle and a tridem rear. The chassis is designed for the mounting of specialist equipment and has a load carrying capacity of 24,500 kg; GVW is 37,600 kg. Motive power is provided by a YaMZ 7511.10 developing 400 hp.

KrAZ-6443

This is a (6 × 4) fifth wheel tractor truck variant with a 4.08 + 1.4 m wheelbase. The fully articulating fifth wheel coupling has a maximum vertical load rating of 17,000 kg; a Jost or George Fisher fifth wheel coupling is an option. Maximum towed load is 48,000 kg.

KrAZ-6135B6 Heavy Military Vehicle

The KrAZ-6135B6 Heavy Military Vehicle is designed to transport both conventional loads and 20 ft ISO containers. Motive power is provided by a EURO 3 emissions compliant Deutz TSD2015VO6 diesel engine developing 350 hp, this coupled to an Allison automatic transmission. Gearing is set up to provide sustainable maximum and minimum speeds of 100 and 4 km/h, respectively. Front axle drive can be disengaged for prolonged road use, thus reducing both fuel consumption and driveline wear.

KrAZ Raptor Heavy Armoured Vehicle

The KrAZ Raptor Heavy Armoured Vehicle is based on the chassis of the KrAZ-6322. The armoured rear body and cab provide crew and up to 20 passengers with ballistic and blast protection. The armoured rear module has side and rear windows that allow good situational awareness for the occupants. Firing ports located side and rear together with hatches allow for fire to be returned in combat situations. The vehicle is climate-controlled and an intercom system connects the driver and rear compartment occupants.

In addition to conventional troop transport, the Raptor can also be used as a medical evacuation vehicle or for the transport of high-value cargo.

Other models

The current range of KrAZ vehicles consists of 25 base models with in excess of 150 modifications/variants of two-, three- and four-axle chassis available. These may be fitted with 240, 330 or 400 hp YaMZ diesel engines coupled to an eight-speed gearbox. Options include Cummins, Deutz or Volvo engines, Allison automatic transmission, and Michelin 1600R 20 or JSC Belshina tyres for an overall width of 2.5 m. All KrAZ trucks are designed for use in areas with limited support infrastructure, and are suited for use on unsurfaced roads.

Specifications

See table on facing page

Status

In production. Current KrAZ models are understood to be in service in Angola, Egypt, India, Indonesia (UN), Iraq (around 2,000 models approximately, 1,600 model 6322 and 6322-056 (6 × 6)), Nigeria, Ukraine and Yemen.

Contractor

Foreign Trade Firm KrAZ JSC

United Kingdom

JCB High Mobility Fastrac (4 × 4) general support tractor

Development

The JCB High Mobility Fastrac (HMF) is a militarised variant of a fully suspended tractor capable of fast travel, both on and off road. It offerers road speeds of up to 88 km/h, this without degrading the machines

JCB Fastrac (4 × 4) General Support Tractor of the RAF towing a Chinook helicopter (Patrick Allen)　　1209341

JCB Fastrac (4 × 4) General Support Tractor of the RAF (Patrick Allen)　　1209343

performance as a tractor, or when operating off-road. The UK Royal Air Force (RAF) received 26 JCB Fastrac tractors in 1989, primarily to tow Harrier vertical/short take-off and landing jets in and out of their hides. The majority of these remain in service performing a wide variety of airfield support roles. Some of these RAF machines have been winterised to allow for operations at temperatures down to –35°C. Within the RAF these vehicles are known as the General Support Tractor. JCB continues to offer the High Mobility Fastrac for military applications.

Description

The current commercial Fastrac range consists of eight machines with engine power outputs ranging from 159 to 260 hp.

All Fastracs are fitted with an anti-lock braking system and where permitted are capable of operating on-road at GTWs of up to 24,000 kg at greater than 88 km/h; faster than any other comparable machine. When militarised the mid-mounted two-person cab of the Fastrac range can be fitted with riot protection. The vehicle can also be configured for air transportation by C-130 and other suitable aircraft.

Assorted implements can be front- and/or rear-mounted with the Fastrac having a hydraulic system typical of a well-specified farm tractor. Both front- and rear-mounted Power Take-Off (PTO) points are available. A small load area is located behind the cab, this has a carrying capacity of

JCB Fastrac (4 × 4) General Support Tractor of the RAF (Patrick Allen)　　1032824

1,000 kg and can be used for transport, mounting or storage purposes. In an airfield support role the Fastrac can be used as a winch vehicle, snow plough, snow blower, salt spreader, de-icer, armament tower and other assorted roles.

Technology and components developed by JCB for the Fastrac range have been used by the company to develop military-specific materials handling and plant, with examples such as the convoy speed-capable HMRTF and the High Mobility Engineer Excavator (HMEE). Full details of these machines can be found in their respective sections.

Status
In commercial production. Supplied to the UK Royal Air Force as the General Support Tractor (26).

Contractor
JCB Defence Products

JCB High Mobility Utility Vehicle (HMUV)

Development
In addition to supplying what are essentially commercial-off-the-shelf products, JCB will design, develop and carry out militarisation of their commercial products to meet specific military requirements. Additionally, the company is one of few within the construction equipment sector which will undertake the design, development and manufacture of military specific equipment. Examples of these are the High Mobility Rough Terrain Forklift (HMRTF), the High Mobility Engineering Excavator (HMEE), and most recently the High Mobility Variable Reach Truck (HMVRT) and High Mobility Utility Vehicle (HMUV).

All of these machines leverage off JCB's considerable industry experience, combined in varying degrees, with elements of JCB's proven Fastrac technology. The JCB Fastrac is the world's only fully suspended tractor and is capable of speeds in excess of 88 km/h on-road.

The HMRTF (previously designated JCB 523M) was developed to meet a particularly demanding UK MoD requirement, and while utilising JCB's Fastrac experience in both design and construction, is a purpose designed high-speed materials handler. It is not based on the Fastrac platform. Full details of the HMRTF can be found in the Materials handling equipment section.

The JCB High Mobility Engineering Excavator (HMEE) was the first true example of JCB's Fastrac-based high mobility family. Development of the HMEE commenced in 2002 and in September 2005 JCB was awarded a US Army contract by TACOM . Full details of the HMEE can be found in the Field fortifications and related emplacements section.

Based on experiences with the HMEE and a company analysis of emerging military requirements for high-speed, high-mobility construction and handling equipment, in June 2006 JCB demonstrated a fully functional prototype of the High Mobility Variable Reach Truck (HMVRT). The HMVRT is a HMEE-based telescopic handler that is optimised for work with 20 ft ISO containers. Development work of the HMVRT is currently halted.

Also during June 2006, JCB previewed a concept stage prototype of the High Mobility Utility Vehicle (HMUV). The HMUV is based on Fastrac technology and HMEE/HMVRT components for fleet commonality and logistic footprint reduction and has been developed around the military requirement for a four-tonne payload vehicle with high levels of tactical and strategic mobility for use in a close support role; it is an entirely new type of vehicle for JCB. The HMUV, for EU Construction and Use regulations, is classed as a Large Goods Vehicle (LGV) and not agricultural or construction equipment.

Proposed specialised roles for the HMUV in its current configuration include utility vehicle, cargo carrier, tactical shelter carrier, artillery limber and a long range patrol type, special operations vehicle.

As of the present date (December 2010), development of the HMUV is currently halted.

Description
For maximum logistic support and training commonality, as previously mentioned the HMUV is based on JCB Fastrac technology and components, and shares a number of these with the HMEE and HMVRT.

The HMUV concept vehicle is powered by a Cummins ISBe 4 250 6.7-litre six-litre EURO IV emissions compliant turbocharged and water-cooled diesel engine which develops 247 hp, gives the laden HMUV a power-to-weight ratio of 20 hp/tonne; conventional load-carrying vehicles have on average a 10 hp/tonne power-to-weight ratio. The engine is positioned longitudinally, and centrally between the drive axles, is a refined (to meet the more stringent emissions levels for trucks) version of the QSB 02 engine fitted to the HMEE. All current Fastrac models are powered by Cummins engines. Production HMUVs could be fitted with a variety of diesel engines, including non current emissions compliant mechanically controlled engines, to suit individual user requirements.

A JCB Powershift automatic transmission allows for a maximum road speed of 100 to 110 km/h. A Power Take-Off (PTO) and hydraulic power for hand-held attachments is optional.

JCB beam-type axles are fitted, four-wheel drive is selectable. JCB soft engage differential locks allow for differential locking while on the move. Dual circuit outboard disc brakes and ABS are fitted as standard.

JCB HMUV as displayed at DVD 2006 (Patrick Allen)   1183078

Suspension is HMEE-derived and is height adjustable, having one setting for normal use, and a second that enables the C-130 Hercules transport height limit to be met. Standard tyre size is 445/70R 24, runflat inserts are an option.

The HMUV has been designed with a standard no preparation required 1.5 m wading capability and is capable of operating in temperatures of up to +50°C in standard configuration. Cold weather limits will be determined by kits yet to be developed but will meet or exceed NATO standards. Ground pressure, Maximum Mean Pressure (MMP), of the current 4 × 4 vehicle is 450 to 600 kPa, minimum ground clearance is 300 mm, maximum gradability (subject to tyre adhesion) is 100 per cent (45°), and turning radius (kerb-to-kerb) is 9.5 m.

The overall dimensions of the HMUV are a length (including spare wheel) of 5.632 m, a width of 2.415 m, a minimum height of 2.616 m and a maximum height of 3.0 m; wheelbase and track are 2.926 and 1.535 m, respectively.

The current two or three-seat cab has the carrying capacity to be armoured. The HMUV has a 4,000 kg payload and the dropside load bed measuring 2.595 × 2.355 m (L × W) will accommodate four standard NATO pallets. A full air-brake and electrical connection system allows the HMUV to tow a braked load of up to four tonnes.

Status
Prototype stage. Development currently halted.

Contractor
JCB Defence Products

Seddon Atkinson Strato (6 × 4) tractors

Description
The Seddon Atkinson Strato T3 24.38C (6 × 4) tractor was a military development of a commercial prime mover. Three variants of the type would eventually be procured by the UK Ministry of Defence, but only one type was initially ordered, as part of a large vehicle contract awarded to Seddon Atkinson Vehicles in 1992. That contract was for 'white fleet' (non-combat) tractors for all three armed services and made up primarily of (4 × 2) tractors for the Royal Navy and Royal Air Force and (6 × 4) tractors for the Army.

Shortly after the contract award, Seddon Atkinson Vehicles were requested to adapt the existing (6 × 4) design to enable it to act as a prime moving tractor unit for assorted loads, including the Warrior Infantry Fighting Vehicle (IFV) and a variety of Royal Engineer plant and equipment

Seddon Atkinson Strato (6 × 4) light 'A' tractor and Trailmaster trailer laden with a Coles 315M Medium Field Crane (Shaun C Connors)   1124793

Seddon Atkinson Strato (6 × 4) tractor in bulk fuel configuration with the Royal Air Force (Shaun C Connors) 0059688

up to a maximum weight of 44,000 kg. The contract was subsequently amended so that 20 of the originally ordered (6 × 4)s remained to original specification, the unspecified remainder being redesignated as 'green fleet' Light 'A' tractors which replaced the bulk of the Scammell Crusader (6 × 4) 35-tonne tractor fleet.

Seddon Atkinson Vehicles were also requested to develop an ADR (carriage of dangerous substances by road) compliant variant of the tractor to be used as prime mover for a bulk fuel semi-trailer with a capacity of 32,000 litres. Some 14 of the 20 white fleet (6 × 4) tractors were subsequently converted to the bulk fuel specification.

All the tractors were supplied and manufactured to the then latest EC regulations and were certified for use throughout Europe.

In April 2002 it was announced that future production of Seddon Atkinson trucks would be carried out at the former Pegaso plant in Spain, Pegaso and Seddon Atkinson both being part of the IVECO Group. Only sales, service and support activities remain in the UK.

Variants

White fleet (6 × 4) tractor
This was originally specified to give the Army an environmentally friendly and legislative compliant (6 × 4) tractor for general haulage throughout Europe. Both LHD and RHD types were produced with twin bunks in a forward control sleeper-cab supported on steel spring suspension for driver comfort. The tractor was designed to operate at the 1992 maximum GTW of 38,000 kg and future projected increases up to 46,000 kg.

Green fleet (6 × 4) tractor (bulk fuel)
This variant was almost identical in specification to the white fleet tractor, but with the addition of IRR green paint finish, DEF STAN recovery eyes, tow hooks and ADR (Petroleum Regulations) certification.

Hydraulic pumping gear was fitted for loading and discharging the fuel cargo and the installation was designed to be adaptable and capable of discharging fuel quickly in bulk, or in sufficiently small amounts to refuel light vehicles such as the Land Rover.

The General Support Tanker (GST) requirement involved the replacement of the current Seddon Atkinson-fronted GST with approximately 50 new vehicles that were planned to enter service in approximately 2012-2013. GST was originally part of the Wheeled Tanker programme but was subsequently removed to become a project in its own right. Further evolution of the programme followed and as the Combined Articulated Vehicle Programme (CAVP) this requirement, plus the LET replacement requirement (outlined elsewhere in this entry), plus a possibly RAF vehicle buy, remains current as of late 2010. It is expected that the 2010 Strategic Defence and Security Review (SDSR) will impact on the CAVP programme.

Green fleet (6 × 4) (light 'A' tractor)
This variant was the greatest departure from the original design. The maximum GTW for operation was increased from 38,000 kg to 68,000 kg. To cope with the extra loading, items including axles, tyres, gearbox, chassis frame, the fifth wheel and its mountings were all uprated, increasing the tractor unit's GVW from 8,260 kg to 10,200 kg. The standard rear air suspension was replaced by a more durable and heavy duty rubber-spring bogie type. An EKA recovery winch to assist in loading was located behind the cab. This has a static line pull of 11,000 kg.

These Seddon Atkinson tractor trucks were originally supplied for use with Trailmaster three-axle stepframe lowloader trailers procured at the same time. Trailmaster ceased trading shortly after delivery and in-service support for these trailers was supplied by King Trailers. Due to ongoing problems with these trailers, a buy of replacement trailers was made from 2004. Following a competitive tender, Dutch company Broshuis BV supplied 99 trailers. In service these new trailers, which have a limited off-highway capability, are towed by the existing Seddon Atkinson (6 × 4) tractor trucks and are able to carry a maximum load of 44,000 kg.

The now Combined Articulated Vehicle Programme (CAVP) has been rumbling on for a number of years and is essentially the evolution of the programme to replace the current Seddon Atkinson-fronted light 'A' tractor, the Light Equipment Transporter (LET) fleet. The most recent developments here have included the January 2009 disclosure that FLET (F – Future) had been cancelled for reassessment, and following submissions by MAN (a Support Vehicle HX derivative) and Oshkosh (a Wheeled Tanker derivative). It is understood that the Oshkosh proposal was preferred by the MoD.

In September 2009 the MoD announced that Frazer-Nash Consultancy had been appointed to oversee the CAVP programme, which at the time was expected to call for a common tractor unit in a requirement that in addition to FLET included a replacement for the 32,500-litre General Support Tanker (GST) for the RAF, plus a small number of specialist transporters for the RAF.

As an interim expedient, a small number of Oshkosh Wheeled Tanker tractors have been converted to the LET role for use on deployed operations.

As of late 2010 no further movement of CAVP had been disclosed, and it is expected that the 2010 Strategic Defence and Security Review (SDSR) will impact on this programme.

Specifications

	White fleet	Bulk fuel	Light 'A'
Model:	24.38C	24.38C	24.38C
Cab seating:	1 + 1	1 + 1	1 + 1
Configuration:	6 × 4	6 × 4	6 × 4
Weights:			
(tractor weight)	8,260 kg	9,100 kg	10,200 kg
(design GVW)	24,000 kg	24,000 kg	24,000 kg
(design GTW)	46,000 kg	46,000 kg	46,000 kg
(STOGO GVW, occasional)	26,000 kg	26,000 kg	30,000 kg
(STOGO GVW, constant)	n/a	n/a	30,000 kg
(STOGO GTW, occasional)	65,000 kg	65,000 kg	68,000 kg
(STOGO GTW, constant)	n/a	n/a	68,000 kg
Length:	6,391 mm	6,698 mm	6,748 mm
Width:	2,500 mm	2,500 mm	2,500 mm
Height:			
(overall)	3,300 mm	3,080 mm	3,338 mm
(5th wheel)	1,200 mm	1,200 mm	1,550 mm
Track:			
(front)	2,016 mm	2,016 mm	2,016 mm
(rear)	1,844 mm	1,844 mm	1,844 mm
Wheelbase: (outer axles	4,000 mm	4,000 mm	4,050 mm
Max speed: (geared)	107 k/h	106 k/h	106 k/h
Range:	950 km	950 km	680 km
Fuel capacity:	425 litres	425 litres	425 litres
Max gradient: (at 46,000 kg)	35.5 %	35.5 %	35.5 %
Engine:	Cummins N380 14-litre 6-cylinder in-line air-to-air charged-cooled water-cooled 4-stroke diesel developing 380 hp (279 kW) at 1,900 rpm and 1,728 N.m torque at 1,200 rpm		
Gearbox:	Eaton TS12612 direct top, 12 speed constant mesh	Eaton TS12612 direct top, 12 speed constant mesh	Eaton TS13612 direct top, 12 speed constant mesh
Clutch:	twin plate ceramic faced	twin plate ceramic faced	twin plate ceramic faced
Suspension:	steel spring front, air spring bogie	steel spring front, air spring bogie	steel spring front, rubber spring bogie
Axles:			
(front)	'I' section forged beam	'I' section forged beam	'I' section forged beam
(rear)	Rockwell (ArvinMeritor) RT44-153 double drive, single reduction	Rockwell (ArvinMeritor) RT44-153 double drive, single reduction	Rockwell (ArvinMeritor) RT52-153 drive, single reduction
Turning radius:	6.725 m	6.725 m	6.75 m
Tyres:	275/70R 22.5	275/70R 22.5	295/80R 22.5
Brakes:	dual circuit, air 'S' cam brakes assemblies, auto brake adjusters, Anti-lock Braking System (ABS), 2 line trailer braking system, 3 line trailer compatible		
Electrical system:	24 V double pole	24 V double pole	24 V double pole
Batteries:	2 × 210 Ah	2 × 210 Ah	2 × 210 Ah

Status
Production complete. In service with the British Army and Royal Air Force.

Contractor
Seddon Atkinson Vehicles Ltd.

Reynolds Boughton RB-44 (4 × 4) truck

Development
The RB-44 was developed as a private venture by the Boughton Group and was originally called the RB-510. In addition to its use as a cargo, troop or shelter carrier, it can be used for a variety of other roles, such as towing a 105 mm artillery piece or the MBDA Rapier SAM system and its associated radar.

The RB-44 Mark 2 was one of the two final contenders for the British Army's 2-tonne Truck Utility Heavy (TUH) requirement. During mid-1988 it was announced that the RB-44 had been selected as the successful contender. The production order was for 846 vehicles. The first examples entered service with the British Army during 1992 and production was completed in 1993. In-service problems were experienced resulting in a lengthy correction programme.

The RB-44 was one of a number of vehicle types scheduled for replacement and/or upgrade under the UK MoD's stalled Operational Utility Vehicle System (OUVS) programme.

It was confirmed late 2010 that by October 2010 the last RB-44s had been withdrawn from British Army service.

Description
The Reynolds Boughton RB-44 (4 × 4) truck has a ladder-type bolted chassis, which can be fitted with various types of body. A three-seat semi-forward control pressed-steel cab is standard, but an extended crew cab conversion was available for carrying extra personnel and equipment. Three wheelbase lengths were available: 3.226 m, 3.68 m and 4.06 m.

The standard production engine was a Perkins Phaser 110MT diesel but options were available. A Boughton designed and manufactured two-speed transfer box incorporating six- and eight-stud SAE power take-offs capable of between 30 and 90 hp is fitted and the transfer box provides a permanent 4 × 4 drive configuration incorporating a differential lock.

Conventional semi-elliptic leaf springs are used for the suspension, fitted with double-acting telescopic shock-absorbers. Vacuum assisted brakes, with a dual servo split system are fitted front and rear. The front and rear axles have hypo gearing with a ratio of 4.1:1. The front axle's rated capacity is 2,500 kg, with 2,800 kg for the rear.

RB-44 TUH variants for the British Army included general service cargo FFR, soft- and hard-top and truck container body variants.

Reynolds Boughton undertook the private venture development of ambulance, command and administration and recovery vehicle variants. No sales of these are known to have been made.

Specifications
RB-44 (4 × 4) truck
Cab seating: 1 + 2 (up to 12 in rear)
Configuration: 4 × 4
Weight:
  (laden) 5,300 kg
  (kerb, basic wheelbase chassis) 3,000 kg
  (max load) 2,250 kg
  (towed load) 2,200 kg
Length:
  (3.226 m wheelbase) 5.06 m
  (3.68 m wheelbase) 5.65 m
  (4.06 m wheelbase) 6.03 m
Width: 2.1 m
Height: (cab top, laden) 2.348 m
Ground clearance: 255 mm
Wheelbase: 3.226 m, 3.68 m or 4.06 m
Track: (front and rear) 1.789 m
Angle of approach/departure: 45°/40°
Max speed: 109 km/h
Gradient: 60%
Side slope: 73%
Fording: 750 mm

Engine: Perkins Phaser 110MT 4-cylinder in-line water-cooled direct injection 4-stroke diesel developing 109 hp (81 kW) at 2,800 rpm
Gearbox: Spicer T5-250 manual with 5 forward and 1 reverse gears or Chrysler A727 Torqueflite automatic with 3 forward and 1 reverse gears
Clutch: single plate, hydraulic
Transfer case: Boughton 2-speed
Steering: hydraulic power assisted, ZF
Turning radius: (3.226 m wheelbase) 7.4 m
Suspension: heavy duty leaf springs with AEON rubber assisters and double-acting shock-absorbers, front and rear
Tyres: 9.00 × 16 or 11.00 × 16
Brakes: dual line, hydraulic servo assisted, drums all-round
Electrical system: 12 V or 12 V with 24 V FFR
Alternator: (12 V) 65 A

Status
Production complete. Withdrawn from British Army service; 846 delivered.

Contractor
Reynolds Boughton Limited

Reynolds Boughton 4 × 4 and 6 × 6 all-wheel drive chassis

Description
Reynolds Boughton Limited has produced over 450 of these all-wheel drive chassis, predominantly for the airfield crash tender role, but is offering the base chassis designs as options for a variety of special purpose body applications requiring high performance, high mobility and low ground pressure. Three chassis are currently available; the Barracuda 4, Barracuda 6, and Marlin. Reynolds Boughton offer these supplied fully fitted and functioning for subsequent body integration.

Status
In production. Over 450 produced.

Contractor
Reynolds Boughton Limited.

Supacat HMT high mobility transporter and variants

Development
The Supacat HMT 400 (4 × 4) was designed by Supacat Limited with funding provided by HMT Vehicles Limited. In January 2006 Lockheed Martin UK Holdings (a subsidiary of Lockheed Martin Corporation of the United States) acquired HMT Vehicles Limited and now licenses the suspension/axle technology that is the core of the HMT series design to Lockheed Martin Corporation. Lockheed Martin Corporation had previously licensed the technology from HMT Vehicles. Supacat of the UK was a licensee of the technology from HMT Vehicles, and remains a licensee of Lockheed Martin UK. Babcock Marine (formerly Devonport Management Limited (DML)) was granted a license for the manufacture of the Jackal 1 programme (now completed).

The original HMT 400 (4 × 4) was designed to meet a pending UK Ministry of Defence (MoD) requirement for a Surveillance and Reconnaissance Vehicle (SRV) and the first prototype HMT was introduced mid-1999. By December 1999 two prototypes had been produced for extensive testing and demonstrations. It was disclosed in January 2001 that the UK's then Defence Procurement Agency (DPA) had opened up an international competition for the SRV requirement, also known as the Improved Medium Mobility Patrol Vehicle. In July 2001 it was announced that the Supacat HMT design had been selected to meet the SRV requirement.

Prior to the SRV requirement being issued, it is known that at least two vehicles were built in the UK and assessed for possible use by the SRV's intended user, the SAS. At this time the user was also looking for an Offensive Action Vehicle (OAV). Neither was accepted for a variety of reasons, and when the SRV requirement now fulfilled by the Supacat HMT was issued, it combined the earlier OAV requirement.

Competitors for the SRV requirement are known to have included the then Automotive Technik Limited offering a (6 × 6) Pinzgauer, and Ricardo Special Vehicles offering a DURO-based (4 × 4) design.

Following contract award, there were a number of developmental difficulties with the SRV design and full rate production did not commence until 2003. Ultimately, 48 of the 65 vehicles initially ordered would be manufactured by the then DML, Supacat's volume manufacturing partner. A further seven vehicles were subsequently ordered and delivered during 2006, these featuring a small number of design improvements over the original vehicles.

In 2004 the US Army placed an order with Supacat for an HMT-based patrol-type vehicle that was similar in configuration to the UK's SRV. Forty-seven vehicles, known as Marauder to the user were ordered, with 12 of these manufactured by Supacat and the remaining 35 by DML. Deliveries ran 2004-2005.

Reynolds Boughton RB-44 (4 × 4) General Service (GS) troop/cargo carrying soft top as displayed at DVD 2006 (Shaun C Connors)   1185507

Supacat Coyote Tactical Support Vehicle (TSV) Light as first shown publicly at DVD 2009 (Shaun C Connors) 1391103

Lockheed Martin continues to develop vehicles based around the HMT's suspension technology and one of these developments, the AVA, is shortlisted for the heavy segment of the UK's ever-changing Operational Utility Vehicle System (OUVS) requirement (Shaun C Connors) 1391104

Supacat Jackal 1 with armour package fitted at a UK demonstration (Shaun C Connors) 1391373

In May 2006 it was announced that Lockheed Martin had been selected by the USMC to build four LightWeight Prime Mover (LWPM) prototypes. The LWPM is based on Supacat's HMT suspension technology (Lockheed Martin UK) 1391106

A further developed SRV-style HMT that has been redesigned to feature a new top hamper, upgraded automotives and an improved tubular chassis has also been produced by Supacat. Designated HMT4x4E (E – Extenda), this variant can be reconfigured from (4 × 4) to (6 × 6) configuration by the addition of a third axle module. Supacat supplied at least 15 HMT4x4E vehicles to the Danish Army in 2006/2007, including two in (6 × 6) configuration.

In December 2006 Australia placed an order for 31 HMT4x4E vehicles (to be designated Nary) under Phase 1A of JP 2097 Phase 1 - REDFIN (Enhancements to Special Operations Capability - Land Mobility Aspects). It was disclosed mid-2007 that for reasons of operational urgency the HMT4x4E procurement had been a sole-source acquisition, and that an Initial Operating Capability (IOC) of eight vehicles would be available by December 2007. This subsequently slipped to September 2008, with deliveries concluding early 2009. It has not been confirmed, but it is believed that a quantity of (6 × 6) vehicles are included in the Australian order, as was a protection kit.

In Australian Army service the HMT4x4E will replace the SASR's Land Rover (6 × 6) Perentie-based Long Range Patrol Vehicles (LRPV). These were delivered from 1987 onwards with a planned Life Of Type (LOT) of 10 years. Deliveries of the 27 vehicles involved ran over five years, with some vehicles subsequently receiving an upgrade to extend their LOT to 15 years.

It was disclosed in June 2007 that for use in Afghanistan the UK MoD was to procure 130 SRV-style Supacat HMT 400 series vehicles under an Urgent Operational Requirement (UOR). With the exception of a blast and ballistic protection kit, these vehicles are very similar in configuration to the original SRV procurement, and are not HMT4x4E variants. The GBP30 million contract was awarded to the then DML in September 2007 and deliveries commenced in November 2007. The first vehicles were delivered to theatre in March 2008 and the 100th vehicle was produced in June 2008. In service the vehicle was initially known as MWMIK, which stands for Mobility Weapons Mount Installation Kit, but later became known as Jackal. The MWMIK/Jackal supplements (replaces for some missions) current Land Rover WMIK vehicles.

It was disclosed in June 2008 that as a contract modification the UK MoD would order an additional 72 Jackals for delivery by January 2009. A further 25 vehicles were ordered around the same time as an additional contract modification. Five of these vehicles, which were delivered during 2008, were configured as troop carriers (2 + 4 seats). A further 15 vehicles were then ordered as battle damage replacements. Production of these commenced in March 2009, with deliveries to be completed by mid-year.

In April 2009 the UK MoD announced the purchase of 119 enhanced Jackal 2 valued at around GBP30 million. Overall contract value was GBP74 million, this award including the supply of 76 HMT-based Coyote (6 × 6) vehicles to meet the Tactical Support Vehicle (Light) requirement.

For this latest contract award Supacat are prime contractor, being the overall design authority responsible for design, development, prototype, integration and overall programme management. Babcock Marine's Land Systems business will take responsibility for detailed production planning, purchasing and manufacture at its facility in Devonport. A single project office, located at Supacat's Dunkeswell facility, will oversee the programme.

By early December 2009 around 100 Jackal 2 and 60 Coyote from this award had been delivered, and an undisclosed number of both vehicle types were in theatre. Deliveries under this award were completed by March 2010.

The most recent Jackal announcement was made in June 2010, when touted as part of the government's ongoing equipment support for operations in Afghanistan, the relevant minister announced an order for the delivery of more than 140 Supacat Jackal 2a long range patrol vehicles. The actual contract award had been made in early May and vehicles had been in production since February - at risk to the Supacat/Babcock alliance. This latest contract is valued at around GBP45 million, and at the time of the actual announcement it is understood that well over half the order had already been built.

The base design of the HMT (4 × 4) can be adapted for a variety of roles beyond SRV/LRPV-type applications and cargo/shelter-mounting models have been developed for trials. In addition to the HMT4x4E previously mentioned, a fixed three-axle version of the HMT concept was proposed from the outset of the development programme for a selection of higher payload requirements. For trials purposes an early prototype (4 × 4) was fitted with an extra unpowered third axle, converting the vehicle into a (6 × 4). Further three-axle (6 × 6) prototypes followed, and by January 2004 Supacat had produced a number of (6 × 6) prototypes (one with a three/four person crew-type cab) and the HMT 600 design had been selected for, or was under consideration as the platform for a selection of specialist applications.

In August 2003 it was announced that a Lockheed Martin UK-led team had been selected by the UK MoD as preferred supplier for Project Soothsayer, the next-generation battlefield electronic warfare system for

Prototype of Supacat HMT (4 × 4) high-mobility load carrier (Supacat)
0109518

Prototype of Supacat HMT (4 × 4) high-mobility load carrier configured as a shelter carrier (Supacat)
0109517

Lockheed Martin continues to develop vehicles based around the HMT's suspension technology. This is one of those developments, the AVA 1 (Shaun C Connors)
1391105

Supacat HMT (6 × 6) high mobility load carrier prototype as displayed at DVD 2005 (Patrick Allen)
1146576

the British Army and Royal Marines to enter service from 2008. The HMT 600 platform was manufactured by Babcock Marine (formerly DML) and all 35 vehicles ordered had been produced by late-2008. Despite the successful delivery of the base platforms, the Soothsayer project was cancelled mid-2009.

In September 2004 it was disclosed that HMT Vehicles and Supacat had signed an agreement with Lockheed Martin of the United States to market the Supacat HMT range of (4 × 4) and (6 × 6) vehicles for the North American market and for other countries covered by the US Foreign Military Sales (FMS) programme.

The US Marine Corps (USMC) Systems Command announced late-2004 that it was seeking a commercial tactical wheeled vehicle, running on JP-8 fuel, to act as a Light Weight Prime Mover (LWPM). The vehicle was required to meet two primary requirements: external transport beneath the MV-22 tiltrotor, requiring a weight of less than 4,500 kg; and the ability to tow the heavier (more than 4,500 kg) M777 LW155 howitzer. Internal transport within the CH-53E heavy-lift helicopter was desired. Earlier analyses, a market survey and a capability assessment indicated that no US-developed vehicle would be suitable as the LWPM. The USMC therefore conducted a Foreign Comparative Test of suitable contenders that included the Supacat HMT. Other contenders are understood to have been the then Automotive Technik Ltd (UK), Krauss-Maffei Wegmann (Germany) and MOWAG (Switzerland). In May 2006 it was announced that Lockheed Martin had been selected by the USMC to build four LightWeight Prime Mover (LWPM) prototypes. These were delivered to the USMC during December 2006/January 2007 for a production qualification test and an operational field user's evaluation. The USD2.1 million contract includes an option for a further 120 vehicles, worth around USD30 million. During 2007 the LWPM programme was cancelled by the USMC.

Lockheed Martin continues to develop vehicles based around the HMT's suspension technology and one of these developments, the AVA, is shortlisted for the UK's ever-changing Operational Utility Vehicle System (OUVS) requirement.

In August 2003, the UK Defence Procurement Agency (DPA) awarded a GBP6 million contract to then INSYS (now Lockheed Martin UK) to design, build and test a system demonstrator for the Lightweight Mobile Artillery System Rocket (LIMAWS (R)) for the British Army. The system was expected to enter service in 2007 and Supacat was to provide the 24 (6 × 4) platforms required. It was confirmed in May 2008 that the LIMAWS (R) project had been cancelled.

An (8 × 6) Supacat vehicle (HMT 800) was the base for the BAE Systems Land Systems portee version of its M777 155 mm/39-cal lightweight howitzer, one of two candidates for the UK MoD's Lightweight Mobile Artillery Weapon System Gun (LIMAWS (G)) programme. Development commenced early 2004 and around 45 systems were required. It was confirmed in September 2007 that LIMAWS (G) had been cancelled.

In October 2007 it was confirmed that Falcon, the UK MoD's battlefield communication network that is due to enter service in 2010, would now be mounted on a MAN ERF 6,000 kg truck, the original Supacat HMT 600 not having the stretch potential to accommodate the recently added requirement for an armoured cab.

The Supacat HMT 600 is the chosen ground station platform for the UK MoD's Watchkeeper Unmanned Air Vehicle (UAV) project currently scheduled to enter service in 2010.

The UK Ministry of Defence (MoD) announced in November 2008 that it had selected the preferred bidders for the Tactical Support Vehicle (TSV) family. Following detailed contractual negotiations with individual manufacturers, award announcements for the TSV programme were made by the MoD in April 2009. Supacat received a GBP74 million contract that in addition to the further 119 Jackal patrol vehicles previously mentioned, called for 76 Coyote (TSV Light) valued at around GBP43 million. The primary role of the TSV family will be support, as by mid-2008 it was becoming clear that the capacity of vehicles on deployed operations was not sufficient for the longer, extended missions that were being undertaken. TSV Light, Coyote, is a three-axle (6 × 6) version of the Jackal reconnaissance/patrol vehicle, and its primary role will be to support the Jackal on extended long range patrols, many of which now last for more than 24 hours. GVW of Coyote is around 10,500 kg, and payload with armour fitted is around 3,000 kg. Coyote, like Jackal, is being delivered through an alliance formed between Supacat as the prime contractor and Babcock Marine's Land Systems business as the manufacturer.

Description

The key feature of the Supacat HMT vehicle is its axle/suspension technology design and set up. This is based on variable ride height independent double wishbones front and rear with airbag suspension, the airbags and suspension carriers being located transverse and integral to the main chassis. The entire suspension package (hub brakes, springs, wishbones etc) is in an identical layout at each corner, thereby simplifying manufacture, reducing costs and easing repair/maintenance in the field.

Each wheel station has twin shock-absorbers and the suspension is self-levelling. Ride height is variable between a minimum (air out) of 180 mm and a maximum (load dependant) of 485 mm, with standard on- and off-road ride heights of 280 and 380 mm, respectively. At minimum and maximum heights an electronically controlled 10 km/h maximum speed restriction applies.

Supacat HMT (6 × 4) high mobility load carrier Light Mobile Artillery Weapon System (Rocket) (LIMAWS (R)). Displayed publicly for the first time at DVD 2005, LIMAWS (R) is a system that was to complement LIMAWS (G) (G -Gun) within the ranks of the UK's Royal Artillery. Both systems have been cancelled (Patrick Allen/IHS Jane's) 1146355

An (8 × 6) Supacat vehicle (HMT 800) was the base for the BAE Systems portee version of its M777 155 mm/39-calibre lightweight howitzer, one of two candidates for the UK MoD's Lightweight Mobile Artillery Weapon System Gun (LIMAWS (G)) programme. Development commenced early 2004 and around 45 systems were required. It was confirmed in September 2007 that LIMAWS(G) had been cancelled (Shaun C Connors) 1391107

The spaceframe-type chassis of the HMT is constructed using an all-welded steel box section structure that can accept a selection of two or four person, open or closed cabs, and a selection of body options. The Extenda variant of the HMT can be configured as a (4 × 4) or (6 × 6) and has a detachable rear module, the fuel module. The fuel module is removed from the vehicle, the Extenda module is then either fitted or removed, and the fuel module refitted. The entire task can be accomplished in under two hours and using only hand tools. The Extenda module fully integrates with fuel, suspension, brake and electrical systems.

As previously mentioned, the HMT design has its origins in a special forces vehicle programme from the late 1990s. This requirement called for an off-road vehicle with a substantial payload, long range and superior cross-country mobility. Additionally, the vehicle had to fit inside a Chinook helicopter, with all of the limitations in height, width and weight that requirement implied.

To give good visibility over the terrain immediately ahead the finalised design placed the driver and commander/navigator at the very front of the vehicle. This broke with the tradition of a front-engined layout for vehicles of the SRV/LRPV-type and essentially dictated the unusual mid-engined design of the HMT. However, while the longitudinally mid-mounted engine offered ideal weight distribution and balance between the axles, it posed some significant packaging challenges for the passengers and drivetrain.

Motive power for all but the most recent Jackal 2 and Coyote orders is provided by a Cummins 5.9-litre diesel engine developing 185 hp and coupled to a five-speed fully automatic transmission and two-speed transfer box. All wheels are driven, although versions of the HMT with non-driven axles have been produced. Axles are fitted with Trac-lock limited slip differentials; full differential locking is not currently fitted. Tyres may be fitted with runflat inserts if required. A Central Tyre Inflation System (CTIS) is not currently fitted.

The major mechanical difference between the latest Jackal 2 (and Coyote) and all earlier HMT vehicles is the use of a 6.7-litre Cummins diesel engine, this replacing the original 5.9-litre version, not for any deficiencies, but rather because the legacy version is no longer in production. The 6.7-litre unit is currently rated at the same 185 hp and 700 N.m torque as the outgoing 5.9-litre unit, but can be tuned to produce considerably more power and torque if required. To meet operational requirements that

include the possible use of low grade fuel, the use of JP-8 fuel, and non-reliance on fuel additives under normal operating conditions, the 6.7-litre unit (which relies on additive technology to meet current emissions requirements) is configured to the same EURO 3 emissions rating as the outgoing engine.

In addition to the new engine, the latest Jackal 2 (which is essentially now the production standard vehicle) features a number of additional improvements over the earlier Jackal 1 and other HMT-based SRV/LRPV variants.

A higher yield strength steel is used for the chassis, and Jackal 2 has an increase in GVW of 700 kg from 7,000 to 7,600 kg, 500 kg of this being increased payload allowance. To accommodate this increase in GVW the suspension has been uprated to accommodate up to 4,000 kg per axle, largely by the introduction of new, thicker wishbones.

SRV/LRPV/Jackal variants

Beyond the 35 (6 × 6) Soothsayer vehicles manufactured during 2008 all >600 production HMTs ordered from Babcock/Supacat to date have been in SRV/LRPV-type configurations, the vast majority of these in (4 × 4) configuration. Available details of these vehicles can be found in the Special attack vehicles section. The Specifications table in this entry includes details of the Jackal 1.

Specifications

	Jackal 1	HMT 600	Extenda
Cab seating:	up to 4 (any rear seating as required)	up to 4 (any rear seating as required)	up to 4 (any rear seating as required)
Configuration:	4 × 4	6 × 6	4 × 4/6 × 6
Weight:			
(laden)	7,000 kg	10,500 kg	7,600/10,500 kg
(unladen with armour)	5,620 kg	6,730 kg	5,760/6,730 kg
(payload with armour)	1,380 kg	3,000 kg	1,500/3,000 kg
(towed load)	750 kg	750 kg	750 kg
(GTW)	7,750 kg	11,250 kg	8,350/11,250 kg
(rated front axle(s) load)	3,500 kg	4,000 kg	4,000 kg
(rated rear axle(s) load)	3,500 kg	4,000 kg	4,000 kg
Length:	5.44 m	7.04	5.79/7.04 m
Width:	2.05 m	2.05 m	2.05 m
Height:	1.89-2.45 m	1.89-2.45 m	1.89-2.45 m
Ground clearance:			
(max)	485 mm	485 mm	485 mm
(min)	180 mm	180 mm	180 mm
Wheelbase:	3 m	3 + 1.25 m	3 m/3 + 1.25 m
Track:	1.7 m	1.7 m	1.7 m
Angle of approach/departure:	40°/40°	40°/40°	40°/40°
Max speed:	120 km/h	120 km/h	120 km/h
Range:	800 km	800 km	800 km
Fuel capacity:	147 litres (main), 50 litres (auxiliary)	147 litres (main), 50 litres (auxiliary)	147 litres (main), 50 litres (auxiliary)
Gradient:	60%	60%	60%
Side slope:	40%	40%	40%
Fording:	1 m	1 m	1 m
Engine:	Cummins B180 EURO 3 5.9-litre 6-cylinder turbocharged water-cooled 4-stroke diesel developing 185 hp (136 kW) at 2,500 rpm and 650 N.m torque at 1,500 rpm; current production is Cummins EURO 3 6.7-litre 6-cylinder turbocharged water-cooled 4-stroke diesel developing 185 hp (136 kW) at 2,500 rpm and 650 N.m torque at 1,500 rpm		
Gearbox:	Allison 2500 Series fully automatic with 5 forward and 1 reverse gears		
Transfer case:	2-speed	2-speed	2-speed
Steering:	Sheppard M-83 P2 power-assisted	Sheppard M-83 P2 power-assisted	Sheppard M-83 P2 power-assisted
Suspension:	independent double wishbone with air operated variable ride height and twin shock-absorbers per wheel station		

	Jackal 1	HMT 600	Extenda
Tyres:	335/80R 20 ZXL MPT TL	335/80R 20 ZXL MPT TL	335/80R 20 ZXL MPT TL
Brakes:	air over hydraulic, outboard 360 mm diameter discs front and rear		
Electrical system:	24 V	24 V	24 V
Batteries:	2 × 2 × 12 V, 50 Ah	2 × 12 V, 50 Ah + 2 × 12 V, 100 Ah	2 × 12 V, 50 Ah + 2 × 12 V, 100 Ah
Alternator:	2 × 90 A	2 × 100 A	2 × 100 A

Specifications given in this table are for outline purposes only and may vary considerably according to variant, role and other factors.

Status
In production. Approximately 800 vehicles including prototypes and around 740 in various SRV/LRPV configurations have been supplied to Australia, Denmark, UK and the US; see text for full details.

Contractor
Supacat Limited

Leyland Trucks (4 × 4) 4,000/5,000 kg truck

Development
Originally rated at 4,000 kg payload, this vehicle was developed by Leyland Trucks under the project number T 244 to participate in the British Army's 4-tonne truck replacement contest along with Volvo (GB) Limited and Bedford. In December 1987, eight prototypes were handed over to the MoD to take part in a series of technical trials. The result of the contest was that, in June 1989, Leyland Trucks was awarded a contract worth GBP155 million for 5,350 vehicles over a five-year period. That contract was completed in April 1995 after some 4,200 vehicles had been delivered. Follow-on orders to the UK MoD and others have followed, bringing production totals to approximately 4,500 vehicles.

Production was based at the Leyland Trucks Assembly Plant in Lancashire using largely British-sourced components. The first six production vehicles were handed over for acceptance in July 1990, with deliveries to the MoD commencing in early August 1990.

These trucks are normally referred to as Leyland but occasionally DAF or Leyland DAF, with most vehicles being badged Leyland DAF. Truck maker Leyland was sold by the UK government to DAF Trucks of Holland in 1987, UK product subsequently being marketed as Leyland DAF. In 1993 DAF collapsed, the subsequent rescue package not including the UK part of the operation, which following a management buy-out returned to UK ownership. The then Leyland Trucks was sold to Paccar of the US in 1998, two years after Paccar had acquired DAF. Paccar also owns the now defunct Foden Trucks.

During 1995 a payload option of 5,000 kg was introduced; a small number of British Army vehicles subsequently being uprated.

The Leyland 4,000/5,000 kg truck is one of a number of types to be replaced by the UK Defence Procurement Agency's (DPA) Support Vehicle (SV) programme, the preferred bidder for which (MAN ERF UK Ltd) was announced in October 2004, with a contract valued at GBP1.1 billion (now quoted as GBP1.3 billion) awarded to MAN ERF UK Ltd in March 2005. Also competing for the Support Vehicle contract was Mercedes-Benz, Oshkosh Truck and Stewart & Stevenson. The Support Vehicle bids were submitted three times with the final bids submitted in October 2003. The contract was originally worth GBP1.4 billion and covered the supply of a maximum of 8,620 vehicles. At one time the DPA was looking at a Private Finance Initiative (PFI) solution but this was subsequently abandoned in favour of a direct acquisition.

The Support Vehicle contract award covered 5,165 vehicles and 69 recovery trailers, plus an option for an additional 2,077 vehicles that was exercised during 2006. The first vehicles were delivered in June 2007 and

Leyland Trucks (4 × 4) 4,000 kg truck of the Malaysian Armed Forces fitted with a tanker body supplied by Reynolds Boughton Limited (Shaun C Connors) 0116906

production is expected to continue until 2013. The contract includes a major support package. The base order covered 4,851 cargo trucks and 314 (reduced to 288) recovery vehicles, the option cargo trucks only.

By early 2011 around 5,000 Support Vehicles of all types had been delivered, with vehicles deployed to Afghanistan and Iraq. Full details of the Support Vehicle requirement can be found elsewhere in this section.

An earlier proposed Invitation To Tender (ITT) for the refurbishment of the Leyland 4,000/5,000 kg truck fleet did not occur.

Description
The vehicle is conventional in layout and design and some key components used are shared with the commercial 45 Series light truck. The T 244 uses the sleeper cab version of the C44 forward control cab, which has room for the driver, two passengers and stowage for their full kit. As an alternative, the space provided may be used for driver training (the driver plus four personnel) or radio communications equipment.

The cab roof is reinforced to take the weight of two personnel and has a roof hatch and provision for a machine gun installation over an observer's platform inside the cab. For maintenance the cab can be hydraulically tilted forward 50°.

The vehicle is powered by a Leyland 313 turbocharged diesel engine coupled to a transmission using a five-speed, all-synchromesh gearbox. There is permanent (4 × 4) drive. The front axle has a rating of 5,000 kg, with an offset bowl to reduce overall cab height. The rear axle has a rating of 7,500 kg.

Fitments include: front and rear end rotating tow hooks, lugs for suspended or supported recovery, helicopter lift points and an infra-red reflective paint finish. The vehicle can be transported by C-130 Hercules transport aircraft, or underslung by CH-47 Chinook helicopter.

The body is produced and fitted by Edbro Limited and has a fixed flat platform and bulkhead with provision for interchangeable drop sides, tailboard, superstructure and tarpaulin. The flat platform can be used to carry various forms of military equipment including containers, seats, fuel pods, NATO pallets, Class 30 trackway and Medium Girder Bridge (MGB) sections. A vehicle carrying a 'mini DROPS' load handling system was developed as a concept exploration vehicle.

Options included: left- or right-hand drive, winch, hydraulic crane, tipping body, tankers, specialist-vehicles for refuelling operations, snowplough/gritters or a chassis and cab-only arrangement. The crane has a capacity of 6.5 t/m while the winch (produced by Reynolds Boughton) has a capacity of 5,500 kg front and rear and is provided with 75 m of cable.

It was disclosed during 2006 that Permali had supplied 16 add-on armour kits for Leyland 4,000 kg trucks deployed on operations in Afghanistan and Iraq.

Side view of a Leyland Trucks (4 × 4) 4,000 kg truck of the British Army fitted with the Simon Gloster SaroUnit Bulk Refuelling Equipment (UBRE) field refuelling system (Shaun C Connors) 0547270

Leyland Trucks (4 × 4) 4,000 kg truck of the Irish Defence Force in GS (general service) configuration (Shaun C Connors) 1047665

It was disclosed during 2006 that Permali had supplied 16 add-on armour kits for Leyland 4,000 kg trucks deployed on operations in Afghanistan and Iraq (Shaun C Connors)   1185508

Leyland Trucks (4 × 4) 4, 000 kg truck of the British Army in General Service (GS) configuration (Shaun C Connors)   1124796

Specifications

Leyland Trucks 4,000/5,000 kg truck
Cab seating: 1 + 2
Configuration: 4 × 4
Weight:
(laden) 10,800 kg
(unladen) 6,010 kg
(unladen w/winch) 6,720
(GCW) 16,260 kg
(towed load, on/off-road) 5,460 kg
Length: 6.65 m
Width: 2.49 m
Height: 3.43 m
Platform height: (unladen) 1.41 m
Ground clearance: 320 mm
Track: (front and rear) 2.1 m
Wheelbase: 3.95 m
Angle of approach/departure: 41°/38°
Max speed: 89 km/h
Range: 500 km (approx)
Fuel capacity: 135 litres
Max gradient, restart: (fully laden, with trailer) 33%
Side slope: (static) 73%
Fording: 750 mm
Engine: Leyland 313 5.9-litre 6-cylinder in-line turbocharged water-cooled 4-stroke direct injection diesel developing 145 hp (108 kW) at 2,600 rpm and 497 N.m torque at 1,550 rpm
Gearbox: Turner T5-350 synchromesh with 5 forward and 1 reverse gears
Transfer box: Getrag 304 2-speed, 33%/67% torque split front/rear, differential lock
Clutch: servo assisted self-adjusting single dry plate (ϕ 330 mm)
Steering: power-assisted, ZF 8045
Turning radius: 9 m
Suspension:
(front) twin taper-leaf springs with telescopic hydraulic double-acting shock-absorbers and progressive rubber bump-stops
(rear) three taper-leaf dual- rated springs with telescopic hydraulic double-acting shock-absorbers and progressive rubber bump-stops
Tyres: 12.00R 20

Brakes:
(main) Girling dual circuit, air, drums all-round
(parking) spring actuators on all wheels
Electrical system: 24 V
Batteries: 2 × 12 V, 95 Ah
Alternator: 40 A

Status

Production complete (Leyland Trucks currently offers no all-wheel drive vehicles). In service with the British Army, Navy and Royal Air Force, the Irish Defence Force (52, 1997-1999), the UN and the armed forces of Brunei (41), Indonesia (14 delivered), Kenya (approximately 50, 2000/2001) and Malaysia (40, status uncertain).

Contractor

Leyland Trucks

Bedford MT series (4 × 4) and (6 × 6) trucks

Development

The Bedford MT range includes the follow-on generation of the current in-service M-Type (4 × 4) trucks, full details of which can be found elsewhere in this section.

The simplistic and functional overall design of the MT range made the type particularly appealing to African, Asian and Middle Eastern customers, and while a complete list of military and governmental sales has never been made available, some of the final known sales of the MT range included: January 1995, a rolling contract to supply over 100 (4 × 4) and (6 × 6) logistic vehicles to the Botswana Defence Force; February 1995, 15 Bedford (4 × 4) fire appliances to the Cypriot fire service; March 1995, eight Bedford (6 × 6) bridge building vehicles to the Royal Thai Army; June 1995, 25 × 4,000 kg GS (4 × 4) trucks and six (6 × 6) DROPS/PLS light tank transporters to the Indonesian MoD; December 1995, a rolling contract to supply 50 vehicles (4 × 4) to Abu Dhabi.

Bedford Trucks was acquired by Marshall SPV Limited in October 1992; production moved to Cambridge where the Marshall Group's aerospace and vehicle facilities are based. In January 1994, Marshall SPV Limited acquired the Bedford name and parts business from General Motors. The production of all Bedford trucks had ceased by March 1999 when the Bedford parts business, product designs and some of the assets of the Bedford trucks range were acquired by ERF Limited. It was announced in October 2002 that the Amethyst Group Logistics Division had been

Bedford MT (4 × 4) chassis-cab, possibly destined for Abu Dhabi (Shaun C Connors)   0536895

Bedford MT range (4 × 4) truck (Marshall Specialist Vehicles)   0059699

appointed to run the Bedford Genuine Parts business. In a parallel move Automotive Group Limited (AGL) acquired the design and marketing rights to Bedford Genuine Parts from ERF. AGL is the ultimate parent company of Amethyst Group Logistics Division. The supply of parts also includes the contracted support of the UK MOD's fleet of Bedford vehicles, primarily MK/MJ (4 × 4) and TM (4 × 4) and (6 × 6).

Description

Bedford MT (4 × 4) Range

The Bedford MT (4 × 4) range includes the follow-on generation of the current in-service M-Type (4 × 4) trucks, full details of which can be found elsewhere in this section. All 16 standard models made available as part of the MT (4 × 4) range are of conventional layout and design with a forward control cab on a flat-topped C-section ladder-type chassis frame capable of accommodating a wide range of bodies.

The cab is all-steel with hydraulic tilting for easy engine access having hinged panels for day-to-day checks. A reinforced cab roof, able to take the weight of two personnel, has a hatch with hip ring and cover for access to a mounting for a light machine gun. There is internal stowage for personal kit, rifles and other equipment. Power steering and engines from the Perkins range give enhanced off-road mobility with increased payloads compared to earlier M-Type models.

Numerous equipment options were available including Cummins engines as power options for each model, different axle options (Rockwell all-round), power take-off (front and rear), extreme climate modifications for the engine, and different wheel and tyre sizes.

With specialised bodies and equipment the Bedford MT range was suitable for a multitude of military requirements including the transport of ammunition, fuel or water, NATO pallets, containers, shelters and troops, as well as general cargo.

Bedford MT series

	MT12-14/16/18	MT15-16/18	MT17-21	MT19-21	MT24-21	MT26-30
Cab seating:	1 + 1 or 1 + 2	1 + 1 or 1 + 2	1 + 1 or 1 + 2	1 + 1 or 1 + 2	1 + 1 or 1 + 2	1 + 1 or 1 + 2
Configuration:	4 × 4	4 × 4	4 × 4	4 × 4	6 × 6	6 × 6
Weight:						
(laden)	12,000 kg	14,750 kg	17,000 kg	19,000 kg	24,000 kg	26,000 kg
(unladen)	4,760 kg	4,900 kg	5,026 kg	5,026 kg	7,286 kg	7,586 kg
(payload; max)	6,000 kg	8,000 kg	10,000 kg	12,000 kg	14,500 kg	17,000 kg
(front axle, design)	4,750 kg	4,750 kg	7,000 kg	7,000 kg	7,000 kg	7,000 kg
(rear axle, design)	7,620 kg	10,000 kg	10,500 kg	13,000 kg	20,000 kg	20,000 kg
(GTW)	17,100 kg	19,750 kg	24,000 kg	24,000 kg	n/avail	32,000 kg
Length: (chassis)	6.53/6.87 m	6.53/6.87 m	6.60/6.95 m	6.6 m	9.36 m	8.87 m
Width:	2.48 m	2.48 m	2.48 m	2.49 m	2.47 m	2.47 m
Height: (top of cab)	2.63 m	2.7 m	2.7 m	2.59 m	2.72 m	2.72 m
Track: (front)	2.09 m	2.09 m	2.07 m	1.93 m	2.02 m	2.02 m
Track: (rear)	2.05 m	2.05 m	2.09 m	1.82 m	2.08 m	2.08 m
Wheelbase:	3.94/4.24 m	3.94/4.24 m	4.01/4.24 m	4.01 m	5.01/5.4 m	5.01 m
Angle of approach/departure:	44°/39°	44°/39°	46°/41°	46°/41°	44°/38°	44°/38°
Max speed:	87 km/h (12-14) 104 km/h (12-16/18)	104 km/h	105 km/h	105 km/h	86 km/h	104 km/h
Fuel capacity:	109 litres	209 litres	209 litres	209 litres	209 litres	209 litres
Restart gradability:	49% (12-14) 46% (12-16) 52% (12-18)	37% (15-16) 42% (15-18)	39%	35%	45%	72%
Engine:	Perkins Phaser 6-cylinder 135 hp (96 kW) (12-14) 160 hp (118 kW) turbocharged (12-16) 180 hp (132 kW) turbocharged and intercooled (12-18)	Perkins Phaser 6-cylinder 160 hp (118 kW) turbocharged (15-16) 180 hp (132 kW) turbocharged and intercooled (15-18)	Perkins Phaser 6-cylinder 210 hp (154 kW) wastegated, turbocharged and intercooled	Perkins Phaser 6-cylinder 210 hp (154 kW) wastegated, turbocharged and intercooled	Perkins Phaser 6-cylinder 210 hp (154 kW) wastegated and turbocharged	Perkins Peregrine 6-cylinder 300 hp 220 kW) turbocharged and air-to-air intercooled
Gearbox:	Spicer T5-350/4 5-speed (12-14) Spicer T5-400 5-speed (12-16/18)	Spicer T5-4292 5-speed	Eaton 4106B 6-speed	Eaton 5206B 6-speed	Eaton 6109 9-speed	Fuller RT-11609A 9-speed
Clutch - air assisted:	Borg & Beck organic (12-14) Lipe 13-330 cerametallic (12-16/18)	Lipe 13-330 cerametallic	Lipe 14-1DLB cerametallic	Lipe 14-1DLB cerametallic	Lipe 14-1DLB cerametallic	Lipe 14 in twin plate
Transfer box:	Bedford 2-speed	Bedford 2-speed	Rockwell SVI 2-speed	Rockwell SVI 2-speed	Steyr VG1600/300 2-speed	Steyr VG1600/300 2-speed
Steering:	power assisted, recirculating ball type	power assisted, recirculating ball type	power assisted, recirculating ball type	power assisted, recirculating ball type	power assisted, recirculating ball type	power assisted, recirculating ball type
Turning radius (kerb):	9 m	9 m	9.65 m	9.65 m	10.75 m	10.75 m
Front suspension:	8-leaf semi-elliptic		8-leaf semi-elliptic	8-leaf semi-elliptic	2-leaf tapered semi-elliptic	2-leaf tapered semi-elliptic
Rear suspension:	9-leaf semi-elliptic taper leaf helper	9-leaf semi-elliptic taper leaf helper	9-leaf semi-elliptic taper leaf helper	9-leaf semi-elliptic taper leaf helper	Hendrickson Norde HN460 rubber	Hendrickson Norde HN460 rubber
Tyres:	12.00R 20 (single rears)	14.75/80R 20 (single rears)	14.75/80R 20 (single rears)	12.00R 20 (dual rears)	12.00R 20 (dual rears)	12.00R 20 (dual rears)
Brakes:	full air	air/hydraulic	full air	full air	full air	full air
Electrical system:	24 V	24 V	24 V	24 V	24 V	24 V
Batteries:	2 × 12 V 90 Ah	2 × 12 V 90 Ah	2 × 12 V 90 Ah	2 × 12 V 90 Ah	2 × 12 V 90 Ah	2 × 12 V 90 Ah
Alternator:	55 A	55 A	55 A	55 A	55 A	55 A

Bedford MT (6 × 6)

The Bedford MT (6 × 6) trucks are a development of the MT (4 × 4) and extend the payload capabilities up to 21,000 kg. Power was originally provided by either Perkins Phaser 210 hp engines or the 300 hp Peregrine engines, with Cummins engines becoming an option on later-produced models.

With specialised bodies and equipment options the Bedford MT (6 × 6) range was suitable for a wide variety of applications, including recovery units, PLS/DROPS load handling systems, ammunition carrier, water/fuel tankers, refuellers, firefighting vehicles and tipper/dumpers.

Specifications

See table on facing page

Status

Production complete. In service with armed forces in Africa, the Middle East and Southeast Asia (see text) and on behalf of NATO.

Contractor

Marshall Specialist Vehicles Ltd

Enquiries to

Amethyst Group

Bedford MK/MJ (4 × 4) 4,000 kg trucks

Development

In the early 1960s, the British Army issued a requirement for a (4 × 4) 4,000 kg (nominal payload) truck to replace the then current Bedford RL. To meet this requirement Austin submitted the FJ (FV 13701), Commer the CB (FV 13901) and Vauxhall the RK (FV 13801). After comparative trials the Vauxhall model, based on its civilian TK (4 × 2) truck, was selected and standardised as the Truck Cargo (Bedford MK 4 tonne (4 × 4)).

As from April 1981, Bedford changed the designation of the MK to MJ as the K multi-fuel engine was superseded by the J diesel engine. The designation MK is an abbreviated form of the alpha designation MKP2BMO, MJ being MJP2BMO. B becomes W for winch variants.

In mid-1982, a GBP46 million order was announced for new MJP trucks fitted with a new 5.42-litre turbocharged diesel engine designated the 5.4/105TD. This series of trucks incorporated a number of minor modifications to take advantage of the new engine's power and production of the new model commenced in September 1982.

Bedford MJP (4 × 4) 4,000 kg general service (GS) truck with standard dropside cargo/troop-carrying body and tarpaulin and winch (Shaun C Connors)   1124738

A late production Bedford MJP (4 × 4) 4,000 kg general service truck with AWD Bedford badging (Shaun C Connors)   0536898

Bedford M type (4 × 4) 4,000 kg truck of UAE armed forces fitted with Reynolds Boughton recovery equipment (Richard Stickland)   1047666

Production totals for M-series vehicles, including both military and civilian models, stood at 48,318 in December 1988 with a further 200 being built between 1989 and 1992, when production ceased in favour of the MT series (full details of which will be found elsewhere in this section).

In October 1992 Marshall SPV Limited acquired the product designs and some of the assets of AWD/Bedford Ltd. Production of all Bedford Trucks had ceased by March 1999 when the Bedford parts business, product designs and some of the assets of the Bedford Trucks range were acquired by ERF Ltd. It was announced in October 2002 that the Amethyst Group Logistics Division had been appointed to run the Bedford Genuine Parts business. In a parallel move Automotive Group Limited (AGL) acquired the design and marketing rights to Bedford Genuine Parts from ERF. AGL is the ultimate parent company of Amethyst Group Logistics Division. The supply of parts also includes the contracted support of the UK MOD's fleet of Bedford vehicles.

Between financial year 1995-96 and financial year 2006-07 a total of 3,441 Bedford MJ vehicles were refurbished to at least Field Standard by the UK MoD.

All M-series Bedford trucks in British Army service are scheduled for replacement under the Support Vehicle (SV) programme. In May 2001 there were still 6,415 in service, by May 2005 this figure had reduced to 5,002 and by May 2006 it had further reduced to 4,660.

Following a lengthy procurement process that can be traced back to the Future Cargo Vehicle (FCV) requirement (1998) and the Future Wheeled Recovery Vehicle (FWRV) requirement (1999). The Support Vehicle contract was finally awarded to MAN ERF UK Ltd in March 2005. From those shortlisted, following the Support Vehicle's January 2001 Invitation To Tender (ITT), only four companies would eventually participate in the

Bedford M type (4 × 4) 4,000 kg truck fitted with a Permali protection kit (Shaun C Connors)   1185487

Bedford MK (4 × 4) 4,000 kg truck fitted with bulk refuelling equipment
(Shaun C Connors)   0059695

Bedford MJP (4 × 4) 4,000 kg truck Crane Lorry Mounted variant fitted with
a two-ton materials handling crane between the cab and repositioned
standard length drop side body (Shaun C Connors)   0536896

Bedford MJP (4 × 4) 4,000 kg truck with specialist communications
equipment body (Shaun C Connors)   0059696

bid process: MAN ERF UK Ltd; Mercedes-Benz; Oshkosh; Stewart &
Stevenson. Both Volvo and Leyland withdrew from the competition prior
to the June 2002 bid submission date. Throughout the process the four
companies submitted bids three times with final bids in October 2003.

The initial Support Vehicle contract award covered 4,851 cargo trucks,
314 recovery vehicles (now 288) and 69 recovery trailers. At mid-2006 the
UK MoD exercised its maximum possible contract option by ordering an
additional 2,077 vehicles. The requirement was originally to supply up to a
maximum of 8,620 vehicles.

The first of the 7,285 (inc. 69 recovery trailers) vehicles involved in the
Support Vehicle requirement entered service during June 2007, with
deliveries scheduled to run until 2013. By mid early 2011 around 5,000
vehicles of all weight categories and configurations had been delivered,
and vehicles had been deployed to Afghanistan and Iraq. Full details of the
Support Vehicle award can be found elsewhere in this section.

Description
The ladder type chassis has six cross members, two of 'alligator jaw'
design. The all-steel two-door forward control cab has a circular
observation hatch in the roof. Access to the engine for maintenance is via
the top-hinged panels on the rear quarters of the cab at either side. The cab
rear panel, between the driver's and passenger's seats, is removable for
engine access.

The all-steel rear cargo area has drop sides and a drop tailgate, which
can be removed to provide a platform for the carriage of containers,
pallets, or the Simon Gloster Saro demountable fuel pod. Removable
bows and a tarpaulin cover are fitted as standard. A materials handling
crane can be fitted for unloading. Detachable outward-facing seats can be

Bedford MJP (4 × 4) 4,000 kg truck fitted with a snowplough
(Shaun C Connors)   0536897

fitted in the centre of the cargo area for carrying passengers. The body of
the MJP is manufactured by Marshall of Cambridge (Engineering) Limited
(now Marshall Specialist Vehicles).

The standard MJP2 has a 3.962 m wheelbase, but a model with a
wheelbase of 3.505 m was also available (MOR1). Power is provided by a
5.42-litre diesel engine in turbocharged or naturally aspirated form.

The basic models of the M-type are designated the FV 13801/FV 13802
or, when fitted with a winch, the FV 13803/FV 13804. The winch has a
capacity of 5,080 kg and 76 m of cable. Provision is made for a PTO to be
driven from either the front or rear of the transfer box casing. In addition,
a standard six-stud SAE PTO facing is fitted to the side of the gearbox. The
MJP has single rear wheels with either 12.00 × 20 or 13.00 × 20 tyres, but
dual rear wheels with 9.00 × 20 tyres can be fitted. Standard equipment
includes a heater and defroster and stowage racks for small arms.

It was disclosed mid-2006 that during late-2005, and in conjunction with
Israel's Plasan Sasa, Permali had been awarded a contract to provide 86
protection kits for Bedford 4-tonne trucks on deployed operations.

Variants
Drone carrier, dump truck, refueller, mineproof cab (conversion work
carried out by Reynolds Boughton), portable roadway laying vehicle and
with special bodies. The Royal Air Force uses the M-type for roles
including carrying bombs and munitions supporting Harrier V/STOL
aircraft.

Specifications
Model MK
Cab seating: 1 + 1
Configuration: 4 × 4
Weight:
   (laden, on road) 11,180 kg
   (laden, off road) 9,650 kg
   (unladen) 5,129 kg
   (weight on front axle, max load) 4,060 kg
   (weight on rear axle, max load) 7,620 kg
   (max load, single rear wheels) 6,060 kg
   (towed load) 4,570 kg
Load area: 4.28 × 2.01 m
Length: 6.579 m
Width: 2.489 m
Height:
   (cab) 2.501 m
   (tarpaulin) 3.404 m
Ground clearance: 343 mm
Track:
   (front) 2.05 m
   (rear) 2.03 m
Wheelbase: 3.962 m
Angle of approach/departure: 41°/38°
Max speed: (road) 77 km/h
Range: 560 km
Fuel capacity: 155 litres
Max. gradient: 49%
Fording: 762 mm
Engine: Bedford 5.42-litre 6-cylinder in-line naturally aspirated water-
cooled 4-stroke diesel developing 98 hp (73 kW) at 2,600 rpm
Gearbox: manual with 4 forward and 1 reverse gears
Clutch: single dry plate
Transfer box: 2-speed
Steering: semi-irreversible worm and sector
Turning radius: 9 m
Suspension: semi-elliptic springs with telescopic hydraulic double action
shock-absorbers
Tyres: 12.00 × 20, 13.00 × 20, or 9.00 × 20
Brakes:
   (main) air/hydraulic
   (parking) mechanical
Electrical system: 24 V
Batteries: 2 × 12 V, 128 Ah

Status
Production complete. Supplied to Bangladesh, Belgium, Brunei, Indonesia, Ireland, Kenya, Netherlands, Turkey (300), Uganda, United Arab Emirates, UK and other undisclosed countries.

Contractor
Main production was carried out by Bedford Trucks at Dunstable

Enquiries to:
Amethyst Group

Bedford TM 4-4 (4 × 4) 8,000 kg truck

Development
In the early 1970s, the British Army issued a requirement for a new (4 × 4) 8,000 kg (nominal payload) cargo truck as a part of its Medium Mobility Vehicle Programme. To meet this requirement prototypes were built by Foden, Leyland and Bedford. After comparative trials, in September 1977, Bedford was awarded a contract worth almost GBP40 million for 2,099 of its model Bedford TM 4-4. Production began in September 1980 and first vehicles were delivered to the British Army in April 1981.

In October 1992, Marshall SPV Limited acquired the product designs and some of the assets of AWD Limited. The production of all Bedford trucks had ceased by March 1999 when the Bedford parts business, product designs and some of the assets of the Bedford Trucks range were acquired by ERF Ltd. It was announced in October 2002 that the Amethyst Group Logistics Division had been appointed to run the Bedford Genuine Parts business. In a parallel move Automotive Group Limited (AGL) acquired the design and marketing rights to Bedford Genuine Parts from ERF. AGL is the ultimate parent company of Amethyst Group Logistics Division. The supply of parts also includes the contracted support of the UK MOD's fleet, which at the time numbered more than 9,000 Bedford vehicles.

A refurbishment programme intended to prolong the service life of the TM 4-4 commenced during 1995. The work, carried out by the Army Base Repair Organisation (ABRO) workshops at Catterick, Colchester and Stirling, involved complete strip-down, overhaul and examination with defective parts replaced. Existing tyres were replaced with new Michelin XZLs. Between financial year 1995-96 and financial year 1999-00 a total of 1,308 Bedford TM 4-4 vehicles were refurbished.

All Bedford TM 4-4 trucks in British Army service are scheduled for replacement under the Support Vehicle (SV) programme. Some 1,460 Bedford TM 4-4 trucks remained in service with the British Army in April 2005 and, by May 2007, there were at least 1,199 units still in service.

Following a lengthy procurement process that began as a possible Private Finance Initiative (PFI) procurement that can be traced back to the Future Cargo Vehicle (FCV) requirement (1998) and the Future Wheeled Recovery Vehicle (FWRV) requirement (1999), the Support Vehicle contract was finally awarded to MAN ERF UK Ltd in March 2005. From those shortlisted following the Support Vehicle's January 2001 Invitation To Tender (ITT), only four companies eventually participated in the bid process: MAN ERF UK Ltd; Mercedes-Benz; Oshkosh; Stewart & Stevenson. Both Volvo and Leyland withdrew from the competition prior to the June 2002 bid submission date. Throughout the process, the four bidders would be required to submit bids three times, with the final bids submitted in October 2003.

The initial Support Vehicle contract award covered 4,851 cargo trucks, 314 recovery vehicles (now 288) and 69 recovery trailers. It was disclosed in mid-2006 that the UK MoD had exercised its maximum possible contract option, ordering an additional 2,077 vehicles. The requirement originally called for the supply of up to 8,620 vehicles.

The first of the 7,285 vehicles (inc. 69 trailers) involved in the Support Vehicle requirement entered service during June 2007, with deliveries scheduled to run until 2013. By early 2011 around 5,000 vehicles of all

Bedford TM 4-4 (4 × 4) 8,000 kg truck (CALM - Crane Lorry Mounted) operating in Afghanistan (Patrick Allen)   1209305

weight categories and configurations had been delivered, and around vehicles had been deployed to Afghanistan and Iraq. Full details of the Support Vehicle award can be found elsewhere in this section.

Description
The basic cargo model is designated the WNV3NPO and has a GVW of 17,000 kg and a GTW of 25,000 kg.

The TM 4-4 has a ladder-type chassis with 450 N/mm² yield structural steel channel-section side members and constant depth and section throughout, with special rear cross-members for drawbar trailer operations. The full width heavy duty front bumper is bolted to the first chassis cross-member. Front towing pintle and brake pipeline couplings for trailer brake operations and vehicle recovery are incorporated.

The front axle is a Kirkstall fully floating, single-speed, spiral bevel with 3.857:1 hub reduction with overall axle ratio of 5.887:1. The rear axle is also a Kirkstall fully floating, single-speed, spiral bevel with 3.857:1 hub reduction and air-actuated differential lock. Overall axle ratio is 5.887:1.

The all-steel two-door forward control cab has an observation hatch in the roof. The cab can be tilted forwards hydraulically through 60° locking in a number of intermediate positions. The hinged front grille provides access to the engine for checking oil and other services such as heater and steering systems. The water level can be checked in the expansion tank at the rear of the cab and fuses can be changed from inside. Standard equipment includes an inter-vehicle starting system, heater and ventilation system and a spare wheel carrier and spare wheel.

The cargo body was built and mounted on to the chassis by Marshall of Cambridge (Engineering) Limited. It is steel with a wooden floor, removable drop sides and tailboard, lashing shackles for NATO pallets and longitudinal folding bench seats for personnel. An alternative platform body was available with headboard only. Twistlock attachments or lashing hooks for securing containers are also fitted.

The central roof-mounted hip ring has a glass fibre reinforced cover which is stowed on the rear of the cab when removed. The gunner's platform is centrally mounted in the cab, for use with the hip ring. The roof is reinforced to withstand the load of a light machine gun and two personnel.

The standard vehicle is equipped with a 24 V electrical system, an exhaust system and fire screening which complied with then current UK petroleum-carrying regulations.

Power is transmitted from the engine to the gearbox and then to the transfer case which provides drive to the front and rear hub reduction axles.

The following optional equipment was available for the Bedford TM 4-4: exhaust brake, cab painted in NATO IRR green, Ringfeeder drawbar coupling, flitch plates, NATO batteries, cab roof front marker lights, dry charged batteries (for CKD purposes), reverse lamps, rear fog guard lamps, tachograph, steering column lock and electric stop control, mid-mounted winch, ATLAS hydraulic crane, inertia reel seat belts for driver and passenger, multileaf springs, transfer box differential, transfer box with PTO adapter, transfer box with differential and PTO adapter and military-type cargo body.

It was disclosed during 2006 that NP Aerospace had supplied 13 protection kits for Bedford 8- and 16-tonne trucks deployed on operations.

Variants

TM 4-4 with tipper body
These have the Bedford designation of WNV6NPO + RPO 585, a wheelbase of 3.883 m, GVW of 16,300 kg and GTW of 24,300 kg. The Edbro military tipper body has a capacity of 6.5 m³. The body can be tipped to an angle of 54° and is of all-steel construction with a three-stage front end ram. The tailgate is hinged at the top and bottom with hydraulic drive via the main gearbox PTO.

TM 4-4 with Atlas self-loading crane
Over 700 of these were delivered to the British armed forces and have the Bedford designation of WNV3NPO + RPO 355. Mounted to the cab rear is an ATLAS self-loading crane controlled by the operator standing at the hip

Bedford TM 4-4 (4 × 4) 8,000 kg truck (Shaun C Connors)   0059692

ring position. In service they are known as Crane Lorry Mounted (CALM). The hydraulic crane is driven via the main gearbox PTO and has a slew angle of 193° and the following capabilities: 3,650 kg lift at 2.02 m reach, 2,140 kg lift at 3.46 m reach and 1,700 kg lift at 4.32 m reach.

TM 4-4 with winch

These are fitted with a mid-mounted winch with a capacity of 8,000 kg powered from a transfer box from a PTO. The cable is 75 m long and has a minimum speed of 4.5 m/min and a maximum speed of 23 m/min. The controls are air-operated with fair leads and pulleys for front and rear winching capability, band-type winch brake and safety overload cutout. The Bedford designation for this model is WNV3NPO + RPO 414.

TM 6-6 (6 × 6) 14,000 kg truck

The Bedford TM 6-6 (6 × 6) 14,000 kg truck was developed from the Bedford TM 4-4 (4 × 4) 8,000 kg truck and in response to a British Army General Staff Requirement for a cost-effective (6 × 6) vehicle with the same 14,000 kg payload as the TM 4-4 and trailer combination (such as 10 standard NATO pallets). Full details of the TM 6-6 can be found elsewhere in this section.

Specifications

Model TM 4-4
Cab seating: 1 + 1
Configuration: 4 × 4
Weight:
(laden) 17,000 kg
(unladen) 8,300 kg
(max load) 8,000 kg
(towed load) 10,000 kg
(GCW) 27,000 kg
Length: 6.623 m
Width: 2.476 m
Height:
(cab) 2.997 m
(tarpaulin) 3.454 m
Ground clearance:
(axles) 352 mm
(mid-wheelbase) 470 mm
Track:
(front) 2.02 m
(rear) 2.08 m
Wheelbase: 4.325 m
Angle of approach/departure: 41°/38°
Max road speed: 93 km/h
Max range: 500 km
Fuel capacity: 155 litres
Gradient: 55%
Side slope: (unladen) 43°
Fording: 750 mm
Engine: Bedford 8.2/205 TD 8.2-litre 6-cylinder in-line turbocharged water-cooled direct injection 4-stroke diesel developing 206 hp (154 kW) at 2,500 rpm
Gearbox: Spicer T6-47026 manual with 6 forward and 1 reverse gears
Clutch: twin dry plate
Transfer box: Rockwell T226-133, 2-speed
Steering: recirculating ball with integral power-assistance
Suspension: semi-elliptic taper leaf springs with hydraulic double acting telescopic shock-absorbers, front and rear
Tyres: 15.50/80R 20 XZL (original fitment Michelin XL)
Brakes:
(main) air
(parking) air released spring brakes
Electrical system: 24 V

Status

Production complete. Supplied to Bahrain, Oman, United Arab Emirates, the UK and possibly others.

Contractor

Main production was carried out by Bedford Trucks at Dunstable

Enquiries to:
Amethyst Group

Bedford TM 6-6 (6 × 6) 14,000 kg truck

Development

The Bedford TM 6-6 (6 × 6) 14,000 kg truck was developed from the Bedford TM 4-4 (4 × 4) 8,000 kg truck (full details of which will be found elsewhere in this section). It was in response to a British Army General Staff Requirement for a cost-effective (6 × 6) vehicle with the same 14,000 kg payload as the TM 4-4 and trailer combination (such as 10 standard NATO pallets). The TM 6-6 uses many of the same components as the TM 4-4 and the first pretest prototype was completed in November 1981. A further four prototypes were built during 1983 and another eight MoD validation vehicles were built during 1984 for trials at the then RARDE Chertsey and user trials that extended into 1985. Volume production commenced in September 1986 with initial MoD contracts for 1,045 vehicles.

Bedford TM 6-6 (6 × 6) 14,000 kg truck, Crane Lorry Mounted (CALM) variant (Shaun C Connors) 0536900

In October 1992, Marshall SPV Limited acquired the product designs and some of the assets of AWD Ltd. The production of all Bedford trucks had ceased by March 1999 when the Bedford parts business, product designs and some of the assets of the Bedford Trucks range were acquired by ERF Ltd. It was announced in October 2002 that the Amethyst Group Logistics Division had been appointed to run the Bedford Genuine Parts business. In a parallel move Automotive Group Limited (AGL) acquired the design and marketing rights to Bedford Genuine Parts from ERF. AGL is the ultimate parent company of Amethyst Group Logistics Division. The supply of parts also includes the contracted support of the UK MOD's fleet of Bedford vehicles.

All remaining Bedford TM 6-6 trucks in British Army service are scheduled for replacement under the Support Vehicle (SV) programme. Some 900 Bedford TM 6-6 trucks remained in service with the British Army in April 2005, and by May 2007 there were still at least 753 examples in service.

Following a lengthy procurement process that began as a possible Private Finance Initiative (PFI) procurement which can be traced back to the Future Cargo Vehicle (FCV) requirement (1998) and the Future Wheeled Recovery Vehicle (FWRV) requirement (1999), the Support Vehicle contract was finally awarded to MAN ERF UK Ltd in March 2005. From those shortlisted following the Support Vehicle's January 2001 Invitation To Tender (ITT), only four companies eventually participated in the bid process: MAN ERF UK Ltd; Mercedes-Benz; Oshkosh; Stewart & Stevenson. Both Volvo and Leyland withdrew from the competition prior to the June 2002 bid submission date. Throughout the process, the four bidders were required to submit bids three times, with the final bids submitted in October 2003.

The initial Support Vehicle contract award covered 4,851 cargo trucks, 314 recovery vehicles (now 288) and 69 recovery trailers. It was disclosed mid-2006 that the UK MoD had exercised its maximum possible contract option, ordering an additional 2,077 vehicles. The requirement originally called for the supply of up to 8,620 vehicles.

The first of the 7,285 vehicles (nc, 69 trailers) involved in the Support Vehicle requirement entered service during June 2007, with deliveries scheduled to run until 2013. By early 2010 around 5,000 vehicles of all weight categories and configurations had been delivered, and vehicles had been deployed to Afghanistan and Iraq. Full details of the Support Vehicle award can be found elsewhere in this section.

Description

The cabs of the TM 4-4 and TM 6-6 are identical, with the roof having a central hip ring with a detachable cover. The interior layout is also the same as the TM 4-4 except for modifications to controls associated with

British Army Bedford TM 6-6 (6 × 6) trucks fitted with the standard dropside troop carrying/cargo-type body (Shaun C Connors) 1120464

permanent six-wheel drive and the revised transmission. The roof is reinforced to take the weight of a machine gun and two personnel. Provision is made for stowage of a rifle at each end of the instrument panel. By using a hydraulic pump the cab can be tilted forward 62° allowing engine maintenance. The engine is the same as that used with the TM 4-4 but the TM 6-6 has an exhaust brake operated from a foot pedal. Features common to both vehicles include the cooling system, exhaust, front axle and suspension, steering wheel and tyres. The electrical and braking systems are modified to suit the (6 × 6) configuration.

Features of the TM 6-6 designed for ease of operation include the synchronising engagement of the transfer box for on-the-move ratio changes. This provides more effective use of the transfer box combining the advantages of the wider gear ratio spread with the advantages of a range change.

A six-link rear bogie suspension provides equalised axle loading on wide wheel centres for optimum traction and large axle articulation through maintenance-free rubber bushed links for good axle control. Tapered-leaf chevron-profile springs provide high durability with weight savings over multileaf designs.

Three versions of the TM 6-6 were produced. The load-carrier with a standard cargo body that was manufactured by Edbro Limited. This is a basic flatbed with body sides, tailboard, and tarpaulin cover. An alternative cargo-bodied version has a centrally mounted hydraulic winch produced by FW Engineering Limited. This can be used for the recovery of loads up to 10,000 kg front and rear. A third variant is a platform body version equipped with an ATLAS crane capable of lifting 1,400 kg at a radius of 6.55 m. In service this variant is known as the Crane Lorry Mounted (CALM). The crane, with controls immediately behind the cab, is only operable when the stabiliser legs are extended. All versions are fitted with a towing pintle, lashing and lifting eyes.

It was disclosed during 2006 that NP Aerospace had supplied 13 protection kits for Bedford 8- and 16-tonne trucks deployed on operations.

Specifications

Model TM 6-6
Cab seating: 1 + 1
Configuration: 6 × 6
Weight:
(laden) 24,390 kg
(unladen) 8,682 kg
(max load) 14,000 kg (uprated to 16,000 kg in 1988)
Length: 8.59 m
Width: 2.47 m
Height: (cab) 3.04 m
Ground clearance: (axle) 350 mm
Track:
(front) 2.02 m
(rear) 2.08 m
Wheelbase: (mean) 5 m
Max speed: (road) 89.7 km/h
Fuel capacity: 227 litres
Range: 500 km
Side slope: 62%
Fording: 750 mm
Engine: Bedford 8.2/205TD 8.195-litre 6-cylinder in-line turbocharged water-cooled direct-injection 4-stroke diesel developing 206 hp (153 kW) at 2,500 rpm
Gearbox: ZF S6-80 manual with 6 forward and 1 reverse gears
Transfer box: Kirkstall AGB 42 2-speed with synchronised shift
Clutch: twin dry plate
Steering: recirculating ball, power-assisted
Turning circle: 21.5 m
Suspension:
(front) semi-elliptic taper leaf springs with telescopic shock-absorbers
(rear) six-leaf bogie-type with chevron-profile springs and telescopic shock-absorbers
Tyres: 15.50/80R × 20
Electrical system: 24 V

Status

Production complete. In service with the British Army and possibly others in small numbers.

Contractor

Main production was carried out by Bedford Trucks at Dunstable

Enquiries to:
Amethyst Group

Bedford TM 30-30 and TM 30-43 (6 × 6) trucks

Description

The Bedford TM 30-30 and TM 30-43 (6 × 6) trucks were derived from the TM 6-6 truck (full details of which will be found elsewhere in this section) and were developed specifically for military off-road operations.

ERF Limited acquired the Bedford parts business, product designs and some of the assets of the Bedford Trucks range in March 1999. Production of all models has ceased. It was announced in October 2002 that the

Bedford TM (6 × 6) water tanker in service with Abu Dhabi Armed Forces
(Shaun C Connors)　0567955

Amethyst Group Logistics Division had been appointed to run the Bedford Genuine Parts business. In a parallel move Automotive Group Limited (AGL) acquired the design and marketing rights to Bedford Genuine Parts from ERF. AGL is the ultimate parent company of Amethyst Group Logistics Division.

Description

The layout of the TM 30-30 and TM 30-43 is conventional, with a forward control cab. Power from a 300 hp Caterpillar 10.5-litre (TM 30-30) or 14.6-litre (TM 30-43) turbocharged and after-cooled diesel is transmitted to the front and rear Kirkstall hub reduction axles via a synchromesh gearbox and single-speed transfer box on the TM 30-30 and an Allison automatic gearbox and two-speed transfer box on the TM 30-43. This driveline, plus cross- and inter-axle differential locks on the rear bogie, provides the tractive effort required to tow guns or trailers weighing up to 20,000 kg in off-road conditions.

The vehicles met then-current fuel and explosives carrying requirements and with specialised bodies could be used for the carriage of ammunition, fuel or water and the loading and unloading of palletised equipment.

Specifications

TM 30-30 and TM 30-43 Model Trucks
Cab seating: 1 + 1
Configuration: 6 × 6
Weight:
(design weight, front axle) 8,000 kg
(design weight, rear bogie) 22,000 kg
(GVW) 30,000 kg
(body and payload capacity) 20,700 kg (approx)
Length: (chassis)
(TM 30-30) 8.91 m
(TM 30-43) 10.27 m
Width: (over tyres)
(TM 30-30) 2.47 m
(TM 30-43) 2.6 m
Height: (cab)
(TM 30-30) 3.1 m
(TM 30-43) 3.23 m
Ground clearance: 420 mm
Track:
(front) 2 m
(rear) 2.1 m
Wheelbase: (TM 30-30/TM 30-43)
(centre of front axle to centre of rear bogie) 5 m/5.5 m
(between centres of rear axles) 1.61 m/1.42 m
Angle of approach/departure: 38°/30°
Max speed:
(TM 30-30) 90 km/h
(TM 30-43) 96 km/h
Fuel capacity: 2 × 340 litres
Gradient:
(TM 30-30) 50%
(TM 30-43 high ratio) 42%
(TM 30-43 low ratio) 86%
Engine:
(TM 30-30) Caterpillar 3306B ATAAC 10.487-litre 6-cylinder in-line turbocharged water-cooled 4-stroke diesel developing 300 hp (224 kW) at 2,100 rpm
(TM 30-43) Caterpillar 3406B ATAAC 14.6-litre turbocharged water-cooled 4-stroke diesel
Gearbox:
(TM 30-30) ZF synchromesh range change splitter giving 16 forward and 2 reverse gears
(TM 30-43) Allison CL(B) T754 automatic with TC 496 torque converter

Transfer box:
(TM 30-30) ZF A800 permanent 6 × 6 drive with lockable inter-axle differential
(TM 30-43) 6KN Kirkstall AGB 7000 Mark II pneumatically controlled from cab
Steering: recirculating ball, power assisted
Suspension: leaf springs and hydraulic shock-absorbers, front and rear
Tyres: 1600R 20
Brakes: air
Electrical system: 24 V
Batteries: 2 × 12 V, 120 Ah

Status
Production complete. These and similar Bedford range trucks are in service with UAE and possibly other undisclosed users.

Contractor
Main production was carried out by Bedford Trucks at Dunstable

Enquiries to
Amethyst Group

Foden Trucks (6 × 6) Medium Dump Truck (MDT)

Development
The Foden Trucks (6 × 6) Medium Dump Truck (MDT) was developed to meet a UK MoD requirement for a vehicle to replace the current Royal Engineers IVECO-based MDT. Based on the A36R model from the Alpha commercial range, and in preference to a Volvo design, Foden was awarded a contract for 55 vehicles in December 2000. Production commenced in late 2001, with deliveries scheduled for completion by February 2003. A small number of vehicles were delivered with winterisation and deep wading kits fitted. The original MDT requirement was believed to have been nearer to 188 vehicles, but with the Royal Engineers equipment being the subject of a possible (since awarded) Private Finance Initiative (PFI) contract, numbers were reduced.

The then Fodens Ltd was acquired by Paccar of the US in 1980 and assembly of the MDT was at the Leyland Assembly Plant, Lancashire, UK; Leyland Trucks was acquired by Paccar in 1988. Production of all Foden branded trucks concluded in July 2006.

The Foden MDT, along with a selection of other dump trucks and truck-based specialist engineering vehicles are currently being replaced under an early-2009 182-vehicle (originally 206 vehicles) PFI award to ALC. The award includes the supply of 63 Medium Dump trucks on an IVECO Trakker AD380T45W (6 × 6) chassis.

Description
A (6 × 6) configuration, the Foden MDT is basically a civilian sleeper-cab design, modified for military use. The all-steel cab is mounted on heavy-duty four-point suspension and is finished in infra-red reflective paint. Operating controls remain standard, with the addition of military blackout lighting, and the bunk has been removed for added stowage. Standard military features include recovery eyes, towing pintles, a wading capability, NATO Interstart socket and NATO trailer socket.

The 273 × 89 × 95 mm C-section chassis frame has been reinforced for military applications with a 6.4 mm thick insert/flitch. A high articulation suspension set up features two Sisu FR2P-22-S hub reduction axles at the rear, suspended by a two-spring bogie rated at 26,000 kg. Front axle is a Sisu FRDP-10-S hub reduction steer-drive unit fitted with taper leaf springs and rated at 9,000 kg. All axles are fitted with driver-controlled cross-axle differential locks.

Motive power is provided by a Cummins ISM380E Celect EURO 3 emissions compliant turbocharged diesel developing 380 hp. This drives all three axles through a Eaton RTSO 17312 12-speed synchromesh gearbox and Steyr VG1600/300 two-speed transfer box with differential lock-up.

The heavy-duty 10 m³ steel 'rock' type tip-body is fitted with a scow end and tailgate. The tip-body was designed, and was fitted, by Roelofs of the Netherlands. The Edbro DK14 tipping gear which features a power-down facility on the last stage of the ram, was also fitted in the Netherlands.

Foden Trucks proposed the base MDT chassis would also be suitable for military construction (dump body), recovery or palletised load handling applications. No sales were made.

Specifications
Foden Trucks MDT
Cab seating: 1 + 2
Configuration: 6 × 6
Weight:
(max GVW) 31,000 kg
(max GTW) 45,000 kg
(towed load) 14,000 kg
Width: 2.5 m
Wheelbase: 4.525 m
Angle of approach/departure: 36°/47°
Fording: 750 mm
Engine: Cummins ISM380E Celect EURO 3 6-cylinder in-line turbocharged water-cooled 4-stroke diesel developing 380 hp (283 kW)
Gearbox: Eaton RTSO 17312 12-speed synchromesh
Transfer box: Steyr VG1600/300 two-speed
Steering: power-assisted
Turning radius: 8.8 m
Suspension:
(front) taper leaf springs
(rear) Foden FS26 two-spring 8 rod rear bogie
Tyres: 395/85R 20 Michelin XZL
Brakes:
(main) dual-circuit air, drums all-round
(parking) mechanical, rear bogie
Electrical system: 24 V

Status
Production complete. Supplied to the British Army (55 delivered); deliveries of replacement vehicle underway (see text).

Contractor
Foden Trucks

Foden (8 × 6) DROPS IMMLC logistic support truck

Development
The then Fodens Ltd was acquired by US truck manufacturer Paccar in 1980, Foden Trucks being the name adopted by the UK operation in 1983. Production of Foden branded trucks concluded in July 2006. The final Foden-branded trucks were built at the Leyland Trucks plant in Lancashire, Leyland having been acquired by Paccar in 1998.

Competing against Leyland for the British Army's Demountable Rack Off-loading and Pick-up System (DROPS) programme, Foden Trucks developed two logistic support trucks for evaluation. Termed the Medium Mobility Load Carrier (MMLC) and Improved Medium Mobility Load Carrier (IMMLC) they completed concept field trials and the IMMLC was selected for production which following some developmental delays commenced in January 1994. Over 400 vehicles were involved in the GBP75 million four-year contract. In service the main intended role for the Foden DROPS vehicles was the supply of ammunition flatracks to the Royal Artillery's 155 mm AS90 batteries. In service the vehicles are actually used for a wider range of roles.

A slightly modified IMMLC chassis is used as the carrier vehicle for the Royal Artillery's COBRA counter-battery radar system.

Foden Trucks (6 × 6) Medium Dump Truck (MDT) (Shaun C Connors)

1120438

Reynolds Boughton DROPS/PLS pallet trailer (Shaun C Connors)   0567956

Foden (8 × 6) DROPS IMMLC logistic support truck with a full load of AS90 artillery ammunition (Shaun C Connors) 0536905

The MMLC part of the DROPS contract was awarded to Leyland. Full details of the Leyland Medium Mobility Load Carrier (MMLC) can be found elsewhere in this section.

In June 1999 it was announced that all in-service DROPS vehicles would be equipped with Anti-lock Braking Systems (ABS) with Leyland Trucks as prime contractor and supported by Foden Trucks, Reynolds Boughton and King Trailers in support of their respective associated DROPS equipment. By October 2001, the ABS upgrade programme had been completed.

During 2007 a programme to refurbish (initially) 50 per cent of the Foden IMMLC fleet was expected to be announced. This did not happen, but may do so in the future given the tempo of operations in Afghanistan and previously, Iraq.

The Heavy Load and Distribution Capability (HLDC) was planned to replace the current British Army DROPS fleet, load handling systems and flatracks, plus address any heavy load distribution capability shortfalls. The HLDC project was superseded by the Non Articulated Vehicle Programme (NAVP), although as of late 2010 little progress had been made with this programme, the DROPS replacement likely to be affected by the 2010 Strategic Defence and Security Review (SDSR).

It was disclosed mid-2005 by NP Aerospace that the company was supplying protection kits for Foden IMMLC DROPS vehicles. The original requirement (confirmed mid-2006) for these approximately 250 kg kits was for 53 kits.

To support ongoing operations in Afghanistan and Iraq and to provide vehicle crews with a higher level of protection, as part of the Project Fortress Urgent Operational Requirement (UOR), the UK MoD disclosed that 90 of the 15-tonne MAN HX77 (8 × 8) Support Vehicle fleet cargo variant (currently entering service) would be converted from conventional cargo trucks to Enhanced Palletised Load System (EPLS) configuration. These replace a proportion of the current Foden IMMLC and Leyland MMLC DROPS vehicles on deployed operations. Full details of the Support Vehicle contract award can be found elsewhere in this section. It was disclosed in September 2009 that a further 56 vehicles were to be converted, a further 31 (training fleet) subsequently added to that total.

Description

The Foden (8 × 6) DROPS IMMLC logistic support truck uses a 10,000 kg capacity forward steer-drive axle, a second steer only axle also of 10,000 kg capacity, and 20,000 kg double drive rear bogie, all manufactured by the then GKN. Motive power is provided by a Perkins (Rolls Royce) Eagle 350 MX diesel engine coupled to a ZF Ecomat 6HP 600 fully automatic six-speed transmission. The load handling system is the Multilift (now Hiab) Mark 4 (full details of which can be found in the Materials handling equipment section) using flatracks manufactured by Marshall of Cambridge that can carry up to 15,000 kg of palletised military stores.

The vehicle can tow, load and offload a custom-built drawbar trailer incorporating ISO twistlocks and designed to carry standard 20 ft containers or flatracks.

The IMMLC is built to a width of 2.9 m and is fitted with 20.5R × 25 tyres. Wheelbase is 5.06 m and turning circle 22.4 m. Operational gross vehicle weight is 32,960 kg.

Reynolds Boughton DROPS/PLS pallet trailer

The British Army procured the Reynolds Boughton DROPS/PLS pallet trailer for use with the Foden IMMLC DROPS vehicle. The trailer is a drawbar two-axle close-coupled type of skeletal construction designed specifically for the transportation of ISO-configured flatracks and their loads. In addition to the Foden prime mover it may be towed by any suitable capacity truck, ideally one fitted with a DROPS/PLS type load handling system as utilising the prime movers load handling system, the flatrack can be transferred to and from the trailer with the trailer coupled to the vehicle.

The trailer is fitted with Ridewell Dynaflex suspension and is fitted with 16.5 × 22.5 385-65R 22.5 single tyres. The braking system was upgraded during 2000-2001 to incorporate an Anti-lock Braking System (ABS).

Status

Production complete. The Foden IMMLC DROPS truck is in service with the British Army (404 delivered); the Reynolds Boughton DROPS/PLS pallet trailer is in service with the British and other undisclosed armed forces.

Contractor

Foden Trucks, a division of Paccar UK Limited
Reynolds Boughton Limited

Scammell Crusader (6 × 4) tractors

Description

The Scammell Crusader (6 × 4) tractor is basically a standard civilian vehicle adapted to meet British military requirements. Two basic military models were produced, a 35,000 and a 20,000 kg payload tractor. The 20,000 kg payload version had a smaller two-man cab and a limited number of design differences including a nine-speed gearbox and was the first variant to be withdrawn from service.

The two-door forward control pressed steel cab has two individual seats at the front (one for the driver and one for a passenger) and, in the 35,000 kg payload tractor, two seats at the rear. The rear seats convert to bunks. The cab is mounted on the chassis by two rubber-bushed trunnion mountings at the front and two coil springs with integral telescopic dampers at the rear. Mounted to the rear of the cab is a Plummett capstan Model CA80 winch with 120 m of 16 mm cable which has a maximum capacity of 8,000 kg at a speed of 27.5 m/min. The winch can be used either to the front or rear and is fitted with an overload warning bell.

In August 1996, the British Army had 20 Crusader tractors and their associated Crane Fruehauf Royal Engineers (RE) plant trailers overhauled to prolong their effective service life. A second batch of 24 tractor/trailer combinations were overhauled to a higher In Depth Repair (IDR) standard during 1998.

Until recently the Scammell Crusader remained in British Army service to supplement a shortfall in numbers of the more recently procured Seddon Atkinson TC24.38C tractor and Trailmaster 35-tonne stepframe trailer (full details of which can be found elsewhere in this section), but by late 2008 all remaining examples of the Scammell Crusader had been withdrawn from service

Late in 1977 the British Army ordered 130 Scammell Crusader (6 × 4) recovery vehicles. Details of these vehicles can be found in the Recovery vehicles section.

Specifications

(35,000 kg tractor)
Cab seating: 1 + 3
Configuration: 6 × 4
Weight: (empty) 11,095 kg
Towed load: 35,000 kg
Length: 6.66 m
Width: 2.502 m
Height:
  (overall) 3.3 m
  (5th wheel) 1.549 m
Track:
  (front) 2.05 m
  (rear) 1.845 m
Wheelbase: (1st axle to centre of rear bogie) 3.962 m
Max speed: (road) 65 km/h
Range: 500 km
Fuel capacity: 455 litres
Max gradient: (stop and restart) 20.9%
Engine: Rolls-Royce Eagle 305 Mk III turbocharged water-cooled 4-stroke diesel developing 305 hp at 2,100 rpm
Gearbox: manual, 15 forward and 3 reverse gears

Scammell Crusader (6 × 4) 35,000 kg tractor truck (Shaun C Connors)
0109613

Clutch: twin dry plate
Steering: ball and nut, power-assisted
Turning radius: 9.5 m
Suspension:
(front) longitudinal semi-elliptic springs pivoted front with slipper rear ends and telescopic shock absorbers
(rear) fully articulated, inverted longitudinal semi elliptic springs, trunnion-mounted at centre with slipper rear ends
Tyres: 11.00 × 20
Brakes: air on all axles incorporating 3-line brake system, drums all-round
Electrical system: 24 V
Batteries: 4 × 12 V, 100 Ah

Status
Production complete. Withdrawn from service by late-2008.

Contractor
Scammell Motors

Enquires to:
BAE Systems Land Systems UK

Unipower M Series (8 × 8) BR90 bridging system TBT and ABLE variants

Development
The Unipower M Series of 8 × 8 designs was promoted as a new generation of specialist heavy logistic vehicles designed without compromise for demanding military applications. As a high-mobility load carrier the design had a payload capacity of up to 20,000 kg and capability to follow tracked vehicles over the most difficult terrain. The first of 129 examples of the BR90 bridging variant of the M Series entered service with the British Army in 1997.

The only other sales of the M Series (excluding a number of (6 × 6) tractor trucks to Oman) were for two prototype Beach Landing Transporters to the French Army in 1999, and a single (possibly two, one in kit form) six-axle prototype to the Indian Army during 1996/97, the latter understood to be under consideration for use in the TEL (transporter/erector/launcher) role, most likely for Brahmos which was subsequently mounted on a TATRA chassis.

Alvis Vehicles (Alvis was acquired by BAE Systems in 2004) acquired Unipower in 1994 and by 2000 had effectively ceased active marketing of the M Series and was looking to divest the assets of the former Unipower.

It was disclosed during 2008 that French company MPI had produced under licence 10 (possibly 12) additional Beach Landing Transporter vehicles, with cabs supplied from the UK by Penman Engineering.

Any future production of the M Series is considered unlikely, the only possibility being that of bridge transport vehicles for future sales of the BAE Systems Land Systems (Bridging) Advanced Modular Bridging System (AMBS), AMBS essentially being an updated and revised for export variant of the British Army's BR90.

Description
The BR90 bridging variant of the Unipower M Series (8 × 8) high-mobility load carrier was supplied to the British Army in two variants, the Tank Bridge Transporter (TBT) and Automatic Bridge Laying Equipment (ABLE), both being powered by an 11-litre 400 hp Cummins diesel engine coupled to a ZF fully automatic transmission that provides constant drive to all four axles. The four GKN drive axles have cross- and inter-axle differential locks and have similar design ratings to spread the load evenly from front to rear. Taper leaf springs are fitted to the front two axles and the rear suspension is a centrally pivoted spring pack providing equal axle loading over uneven ground. Standard tyres were Michelin 24R 21 XL, but are now Michelin 24R 21 XZL.

Unipower M Series (8 × 8) BR90 Tank Bridge Transporter (TBT) of the British Army (Shaun C Connors)   0536903

The engine-behind-cab configuration ensures that there is no engine intrusion into the cab, maximising cab space for personnel and their equipment. The cab is low, facilitating rapid entry and exit and ease of camouflage. The M Series has an unprepared wading depth in excess of 1 m.

As part of an Urgent Operational Requirement (UOR) for operations in Afghanistan, BAE Systems uparmoured five Unipower M Series BR90 bridging vehicles at its bridging facility in Wolverhampton. The cabs were fitted with a package that provides protection from small-arms fire and mine blast. This was designed, developed and fitted in a seven-week period.

Specifications
Unipower M Series (8 × 8) BR90 bridging system
Cab seating: 1 + 2
Configuration: 8 × 8
Weight:
(front axle pair) 9,500 kg
(rear axle pair) 10,000 kg
(kerb) 15,600 kg
(GVW) 39,000 kg
(body and payload) 23,000 kg
Length: 10.7 m
Width: 3 m
Height: 2.8 m
Ground clearance: 330 mm
Track: 2.8 m
Wheelbase: 6.4 m
Max speed: (laden) 84 km/h
Fuel capacity: 450 litres
Range: 1,000 km
Gradient: (restart, laden) 35%
Fording: > 1 m
Engine: Cummins M11-T405E 11-litre 6-cylinder in-line turbocharged and aftercooled water-cooled 4-stroke diesel developing 400 hp (294 kW) at 1,900 rpm
Transmission: ZF 6HP 900 fully automatic providing 6 forward and 1 reverse gears plus torque converter
Transfer box: ZF single-speed
Steering: power-assisted, ZF 8098
Suspension:
(front) two slipper-ended semi-elliptic parabolic springs per axle
(rear) two fully articulating semi-elliptic multileaf springs trunnion-mounted on bearings

Unipower M Series (8 × 8) BR90 Tank Bridge Transporter (TBT) of the British Army (Shaun C Connors)   0121822

Unipower M Series (8 × 8) BR90 Tank Bridge Transporter (TBT) of the British Army (Shaun C Connors)   0121821

As part of an Urgent Operational Requirement (UOR) for operations in Afghanistan, BAE Systems uparmoured five Unipower M Series BR90 bridging vehicles at its bridging facility in Wolverhampton. The cabs were fitted with a package that provides protection from small-arms fire and mine blast. This was designed, developed and fitted in a seven-week period (BAE Systems)   1364008

Brakes: dual circuit, air, drums all-round
Tyres: 24R 21
Electrical system: 24 V
Batteries: 2 × 12 V, 150 Ah
Alternator: 90 A

Status

Production considered complete. BR90 Tank Bridge Transporter (TBT) and Automatic Bridge Laying Equipment (ABLE) versions in service with the British Army (129). Beach Landing Transporter prototypes (two) delivered to the French Army (1999) with a further 10 (possibly 12) delivered 2008, and one (possibly 2) six-axle chassis delivered to India 1996/97.

Contractor

BAE Systems Land Systems UK

Leyland Trucks (8 × 6) DROPS logistic support vehicle

Development

Two Leyland Trucks logistic support vehicles, a (6 × 6) and an (8 × 6), were developed as part of the British Army's Demountable Rack Off-loading and Pick-up System (DROPS) programme. The (8 × 6) version was selected in late 1986 as the DROPS Medium-Mobility Load Carrier (MMLC). Under a contract worth GBP150 million, 1,522 units were ordered in April 1989. The first vehicle came off the production line in November 1989 and the first examples entered British Army service in early 1990. The contract was completed in March 1994. Regular repeat orders were placed by the British Army and small numbers are in service with other armed forces. Total production figures totalled 1,650.

These trucks are referred to as Leyland, however they are badged Leyland-DAF although the bulk of the design and development work was carried out by Scammell Motors of Watford, the then Scammell Lorries becoming part of the Leyland empire in 1955 but continuing to produce a range of specialist and heavy duty trucks with a reasonable degree of autonomy. Leyland was sold by the UK government to DAF Trucks of Holland in 1987. In 1993 DAF collapsed, the subsequent rescue package not including the UK part of the operation, which following a management buy-out returned to UK ownership. The then Leyland Trucks was sold to Paccar of the US in 1998, two years after Paccar had acquired DAF. Paccar also owns Foden Trucks.

Leyland Trucks (8 × 6) DROPS logistic support vehicle
(Shaun C Connors)   0109608

Leyland Trucks (8 × 6) DROPS logistic support vehicle in Afghanistan
(Patrick Allen)   1209304

Leyland DROPS vehicles have been used on active service with the UN in the former Yugoslavia where some have been lost to hostile actions, in both UK and Malaysian armed forces hands. They have also been deployed by UK forces to Afghanistan and Iraq during both Gulf Wars. From a maximum figure of 1,612 vehicles, prior to the current Afghan and recent Iraqi deployments the British Army fielded around 1,600 vehicles.

All vehicles have undergone an extensive In Depth Repair programme at Army Base Repair Organisation (ABRO) workshops at Warminster and Catterick, with the last vehicle completed mid-2006.

In June 1999 it was announced that all in-service Leyland Truck logistic support vehicles would be equipped with Anti-lock Braking Systems (ABS). The work was carried out by Leyland Trucks who acted as prime contractor for similar refurbishment work undertaken by Foden, Reynolds Boughton and King Trailers in support of other DROPS equipment. By October 2001, the ABS upgrade programme had been completed.

In addition to the ABS upgrade some 40 vehicles used by the Royal Marines were also upgraded from their standard 750 mm fresh water wading capability to a 1.5 m salt water capability.

The Heavy Load and Distribution Capability (HLDC) was planned to replace the current British Army DROPS fleet, load handling systems and flat racks, plus address any heavy load distribution capability shortfalls. The HLDC project was superseded by the Non Articulated Vehicle Programme (NAVP), although as of late 2010 little progress had been made with this programme, the DROPS replacement likely to be affected by the 2010 Strategic Defence and Security Review (SDSR).

Some MMLC DROPS vehicles operating in the former Yugoslavia were modified for the installation of appliqué armour panels around the cab and windscreen, although these are not known to have been fitted. For use on operations in Afghanistan and Iraq, it was disclosed mid-2005 by NP Aerospace that the company was supplying protection kits for Leyland MMLC vehicles. The original requirement (confirmed mid-2006) called for 93 of these approx 250 kg kits. The possible purchase of around 90 fully armoured cabs for the Leyland DROPS vehicle was announced mid-2006. This option was not pursued and to support ongoing operations in Afghanistan and Iraq and to provide vehicle crews with a higher level of protection, as part of the Project Fortress Urgent Operational Requirement (UOR), the UK MoD disclosed that 90 of the 15-tonne MAN HX77 (8 × 8) Support Vehicle fleet cargo variant (currently entering service) would be converted from conventional cargo trucks to Enhanced Palletised Load System (EPLS) configuration. These replaced some of the current Leyland MMLC (and Foden IMMLC) DROPS vehicles on deployed operations. It was disclosed in September 2009 that a further 56 EPLS trucks would be converted, a further 31 (training fleet) subsequently added to that total. Full details of the Support Vehicle contract award can be found elsewhere in this section.

Leyland Trucks (8 × 6) DROPS logistic support vehicle fitted out for snow clearance and gritting work (Shaun C Connors)   0536904

Leyland Trucks (8 × 6) DROPS logistic support vehicle (Patrick Allen)
1067432

Leyland Trucks (8 × 6) DROPS logistic support vehicle (unladen) during off-road driver training prior to overseas deployment (Shaun C Connors)
1124794

Description

The Leyland Trucks (8 × 6) logistic support vehicle can carry a 15,000 kg payload with a mobility equivalent to Medium Mobility Load Class (MMLC). It uses a forward control S26 cab with seating for the driver and a second crew member, with space for their kit. A hatch with a machine gun mounting is located in the roof and the cab roof can take the weight of two personnel.

Motive power is provided by a Perkins (Rolls Royce) Eagle 350LM six-cylinder turbocharged four-stroke diesel, developing 350 hp. The transmission uses a six-speed fully automatic ZF 6 HP 600 gearbox with a lockable torque converter. Drive to the first, third and fourth axles is via a single-speed auxiliary gearbox. Kirkstall axles are fitted.

The vehicle is fitted with the Multilift (now Hiab) Mark 4 load handling system (full details of which can be found in the Materials handling equipment section). Also included in the British Army's DROPS package were 24 flatracks configured as Rail Transfer Equipment (RTE). These can be transported by any DROPS vehicle.

Specifications

Leyland Trucks (8 × 6) DROPS logistic support vehicle
Cab seating: 1 + 1 or 2
Configuration: 8 × 6
Weight:
  (laden) 32,000 kg
  (unladen) 14,038 kg
  (max load) 15,000 kg (plus flatrack)
  (towed load) 20,000 kg
  (GCW) 52,000 kg
Length: 9.11 m
Width: 2.5 m
Height: 3.18 m
Ground clearance: 290 mm
Track: 1.99 m
Wheelbase: 5.54 m
Angle of approach/departure: 34°/38°
Max speed: 75 km/h
Range: 500 km
Fuel capacity: 272 litres
Max gradient: 61%
Fording: 750 mm

Engine: Perkins Eagle 350LM 12.17-litre 6-cylinder in-line turbocharged water-cooled 4-stroke diesel developing 350 hp (261 kW) at 2,100 rpm and 1,600 N.m torque at 1,100 rpm
Gearbox: ZF 6 HP 600 with 6 forward and 1 reverse gears
Clutch: lockable torque converter
Transfer box: Leyland single speed
Steering: power assisted, ZF 8098
Turning radius: 12.5 m
Suspension: taper leaf springs, telescopic shock-absorbers and an anti-roll bar (second axle only), front axle pair; inverted taper leaf springs, rear bogie pair
Tyres: 18R 22.5 Michelin XL (now Michelin XZL)
Brakes:
  (main) dual circuit; air, drums all-round. Wabco D series 1 × 6 channel ABS now installed
  (parking) spring on 3 axles
Electrical system: 24 V
Batteries: 4 × 6TN
Alternator: 100 A

Status

Production complete. In service with the British Army; supplied to Indonesian and Malaysian forces, initially for UN operations.

Contractor

Leyland Trucks

United States

GM Commercial Enhanced-Mobility Medium-Duty Truck (CEMMV)

Development

The GM Commercial Enhanced-Mobility Medium-Duty Truck (CEMMV) has the General Motors Corporation truck model number GMC C7H042. It is a (4 × 4) vehicle using various components of commercial origin.

Production of the first-generation CEMMV concluded during 2001, with a follow-on range of Medium (4 × 4) and Heavy (6 × 6) Duty Service Support vehicles (MDSSV/HDSSV) launched during 2002. These have been supplied to Mexico.

Description

The GM Commercial Enhanced-Mobility Medium-Duty Truck (CEMMV) is a (4 × 4) vehicle that uses various components of commercial origin. The cab and bonnet are adaptations of commercial components, as is much of the other bodywork. Seating for the two-door cab is a three-passenger bench seat, although bucket seats, with suspension under the driver's seat, were available as options. The tapered leaf and multileaf suspension is strengthened and heavy-duty shock-absorbers added.

The original 6.6-litre Caterpillar 3116 diesel engine was replaced by a 7.2-litre Caterpillar 3126B providing 230 hp, this similar to the unit fitted to A1 series FMTV trucks. This is coupled to an Allison five-speed automatic transmission and a two-speed transfer case. All terrain tyres are provided for off-road traction.

The standard military pattern cargo body can be fitted with troop seats and there is also a cargo cover. Tie-down shackles are provided front and rear, while a platform body can be provided for loads such as shelters or containers. Other equipment included an Eaton Central Tyre Inflation (CTI) system with four pressure settings selected from within the cab and a 4,990 kg capacity self-recovery winch mounted centrally. A fully swivelling towing pintle is fitted along with NATO 7- and 12-pin sockets. A spare wheel is located behind the cab together with a crane handling system. A brush guard is positioned in front of the radiator grille.

Optional equipment included dual 189-litre fuel tanks, cab air conditioning, an adjustable tilt steering wheel and dual-circuit power steering.

4 × 4 version of GM CEMMV (GM Defense)
0512406

Variants

6 × 6 CEMMV

The (6 × 6) CEMMV is essentially a lengthened version of the (4 × 4) CEMMV and has the GM truck model number GMC C7H064. It has a payload, with body and crew, of 6,165 kg and a GVW of 15,873 kg. Towed load capacity is up to 6,804 kg. Wheelbase is 5.004 m.

Specifications

GM Commercial Enhanced-Mobility Medium-Duty Truck (CEMMV)
Cab seating: 1 + 2
Configuration: 4 × 4
Weight:
(GVW) 10,431 kg
(max load, inc body and crew) 4,989 kg
(towed load) 4,536 kg
Load area: 3.6 × 2.4 m
Wheelbase: 4.902 m
Fuel capacity: 189 litres
Engine: Caterpillar 3126B 7.2-litre 6-cylinder in-line water-cooled 4-stroke diesel developing 230 hp (169 kW) at 2,200 rpm
Transmission: Allison MD 3050P automatic with 5 forward and 1 reverse gears
Transfer box: Fabco TC-38 2-speed
Steering: power assisted
Suspension: multileaf (front), tapered spring (rear), with heavy-duty shock-absorbers
Tyres: 395/85R 20G SBR
Brakes: air, drums all-round
Electrical system: 12/24 V
Batteries: 3 × 12 V
Alternator: 100 A

Status

Production complete. In service with undisclosed countries, possibly including Egypt. Follow-on models, the MDSSV and HDSSV have been supplied to Mexico.

Contractor

GM Defense

Family of Medium Tactical Vehicles (FMTV)

Development

By the early 1980s, the US Army's Vietnam-era M44 series 2.5 ton (2,267 kg) trucks were showing their age, and while the 5 ton (4,535 kg) M939 series remained in production, earlier generation M54 and M809 series 5 ton trucks were also becoming outdated. Additionally, during President Reagan's first four-year term, the size of the US Army increased by 22-23 per cent, and consequently its need for trucks followed suit.

The origins of the Family of Medium Tactical Vehicles (FMTV) can be traced to a 1983-issued US Army TRAining and DOctrine Command (TRADOC), an issued requirements document for a Medium Tactical Truck (MTT) regarding the intended 2.5 ton truck replacement. This requirement

FMTV M1083A1P2 of the US Army in Afghanistan (Carl Schulze) 1391211

5 ton M1082 FMTVs fitted with Low Signature Armored Cabs (LSAC) (Carl Schulze) 1391140

was quickly quashed for technical reasons, and in July 1984, a programme to look at a future 5 ton truck procurement to replace the then 2.5 and 5 ton trucks began.

On the basis of a successful argument that this procurement should in fact be for both 2.5 and 5 ton trucks, FMTV formally began as a programme in October 1984. The winning 'family' argument was based on cost analysis: It had been estimated that at the proposed 45/55 per cent 2.5/5 ton split, on a one-for-one basis, an all 5 ton procurement would cost an additional USD1 billion (unit production costs of a (6 × 6) 5 ton truck being 18 per cent more than that of a (4 × 4) 2.5 ton truck), and have an ongoing life cycle premiums of over 18 per cent per year for every 5 ton truck performing the role of a 2.5 ton truck. Additionally, military trucks of the medium weight class had traditionally 'cubed out' before reaching any payload limit and the cubic capacity of a 5 ton truck's standard 14 ft (4.267 m) load body is only 6 per cent greater than that of a 2.5 ton truck's 12 ft (3.658 m) load body.

In 1Q1988 the official Request For Proposals (RFP) for the FMTV was issued, the long list of respondents for what was then expected to be a USD20 billion, 120,000 truck purchase over three five-year contracts including European bidders IVECO and MAN. In October 1988, the US Army's TACOM (now Tank automotive and Armaments COMmand) announced that contracts for Phase 1 of the FMTV programme had been awarded to Stewart & Stevenson, the Tactical Truck Corporation (a 50/50 joint venture between General Motors Military Vehicles and the BMY Wheeled Vehicle Division of the HARSCO Corporation), and Teledyne Continental Motors. All three contracts for 15 prototype vehicles each, were to be completed by January 1989.

Following budgetary and other delays, the first five-year FMTV contract was awarded to Stewart & Stevenson (now BAE Systems Global Tactical Systems) in October 1991. However, since FMTVs conception things had changed somewhat, the US Army was entering a period of major contraction (around 40 per cent in numbers), and consequently funding had become a major issue. In fact such were the budgetary issues, that at one point during 1994 consideration was given to cancellation of the FMTV programme.

Production under the initial FMTV contract was expected to total 20,000 vehicles over the five year contract, but this was reduced in the contract award to 10,843 vehicles valued at USD1.2 billion, and over what would be extended to seven contract years. Some options were added to the first contract, resulting in a total of 11,197 vehicles when deliveries concluded in January 1999.

Actual fielding of the first FMTVs began in January 1996 at Fort Bragg, North Carolina. On entering service, the original intention was that FMTV would replace current 2.5 and 5 ton trucks in units sets. This did not happen, as in a budget driven move, around 75 per cent of the first contract deliveries were the cheaper 2.5 ton variants.

FMTV M1088A1R of the US Army in Afghanistan and fitted with a Low Signature Armored Cab (LSAC) (Carl Schulze) 1391212

2.5 ton M1078 FMTV fitted with Low Signature Armored Cab (LSAC)
(Carl Schulze)   1391148

DRS Technical Services convoy escort gun truck showing the slatted armour cage mounted on top of the steel armour plates protecting the cargo bed, and the additional pintle mounts for anti-ambush suppressive fire weapons (Patrick Allen)   0578925

During the first production contract, development work and later testing began on an upgraded FMTV, the main improvements of which were an uprated engine (1998 EPA compliant) and transmission, and the introduction of Anti-lock Braking System (ABS) and Interactive Electronic Technical Manuals (IETMs). The FMTV IETM assists vehicle repair by the rapid and accurate diagnosis of problems. FMTV manuals on three CDs are loaded by an operator onto the hard drive of a laptop computer and the computer is plugged into the vehicle's diagnostic port. The IETM reads any error codes from the electronic control modules for the engine, transmission, Central Tyre Inflation (CTI) system and ABS. The IETM database then automatically leads maintenance personnel through the correct repair procedures and notes the necessary spare parts.

The second multiyear production contract for the FMTV was awarded to Stewart & Stevenson in October 1998 and called for 8,000 FMTV trucks (designated FMTV A1) and 1,500 FMTV trailers. Production was expected to continue until 2003; the initial contract value was USD1.4 billion. Actual total quantities under this second five-year production contract, after exercised options, were 11,491 trucks and 2,292 trailers, delivered between September 1999 and October 2004. Fielding of FMTV A1 vehicles began in July 2000 at Fort Carson, Colorado.

In 2000, Stewart & Stevenson received option orders from the US National Guard, US Air Force and US Air National Guard for 5 ton tractor and 2.5 ton cargo trucks valued at an additional USD38.3 million, while successfully completing an intensive driveline upgrade program on approximately 9,000 FMTVs throughout the world. In early 2001, Stewart & Stevenson received a USD36.9 million contract option award for 242 vehicles for the US Army Reserve and National Guard.

In April 2001 the US Army awarded Stewart & Stevenson and the then Oshkosh Truck Corporation contracts valued at USD4.4 and USD5.6 million, respectively, for Phase 1 of the FMTV A1 Competitive Rebuy (CR) programme, essentially the third FMTV production contract. US Army requirements called for a 2004 Environmental Protection Agency (EPA) compliant diesel engine, plus bidders were free to propose ways of further reducing life cycle costs, further improve OR rates and further increase fleet commonality.

The US Army exercised its second production option valued at USD396 million in late 2002, for 2,880 additional FMTVs.

In April 2003, Stewart & Stevenson was awarded the follow-on A1 Competitive Rebuy production contract for the FMTV, estimated at USD2 billion, for 11,000 vehicles over five contract years, with an option for 12,000 additional vehicles, all to be designated FMTV A1R trucks and trailers. Production under the FMTV A1R contract began in the last quarter of 2004. Further details of the FMTV A1R can be found elsewhere in this entry.

In March 2003, Stewart & Stevenson received its second services contract from Lear Siegler Services Inc. to upgrade approximately 883 FMTV M1088 tractors (USD6 million), after successfully completing the upgrade of 1,100 M1088 tractors in the field. Also in 2003, the US Army exercised a USD32.8 million contract option for an additional 279 FMTV trucks, followed by a further option for 40 additional FMTV trucks for the Army National Guard and the Air Force.

By July 2003, Stewart & Stevenson had been awarded contracts valued at more than USD80 million for 44 HIgh Mobility Artillery Rocket System (HIMARS) launcher chassis, 104 HIMARS resupply vehicles and 104 HIMARS resupply trailers. Stewart & Stevenson first delivered a special prototype FMTV chassis to Lockheed Martin Missiles and Fire-Control in 1997, these to serve as a weapons platform for the HIMARS. Development of the platform and weapon system continued for a number of years, and finally early HIMARS prototypes were deployed in Operation Iraqi Freedom.

In 2004, the US Army exercised FMTV contract options valued at USD261.8 million for an additional 3,083 FMTVs consisting of M1078A1 LMTV cargo, M1079A1 LMTV vans, M1085A1 long cargo, M1086A1 long cargo with MHE, M1088A1 tractors, M1089A1 wreckers, and added the new model XM1148 8,000 kg-rated Load Handling System (LHS) with companion trailer.

To meet emerging threats in Iraq and elsewhere, Stewart & Stevenson developed the Low Signature Armored Cab (LSAC) as an exchange replacement for the standard FMTV cab. Between 2004-2006 Stewart & Stevenson received contract awards of USD172 million in total for the test and manufacture 2,060 LSAC cabs, and late-2007 it was disclosed that an additional 600-1,000 LSACs were required. Originally initiated in April 2003, by late-2008 total LSAC contract value was worth USD3.6 billion. Full details of the LSAC cab and other FMTV armouring solutions can be found elsewhere in this entry.

During 2004, Stewart & Stevenson also received contracts to reset over 1,000 FMTVs (and other US Army tactical vehicles) returned from Iraq (USD19.3 million), a USD7 million contract award to repair/reset 200 FMTV A0 and A1 vehicles, and a USD14 million contract award for the manufacture of an additional 748 FMTV trailers.

In 2005, Stewart & Stevenson received a number of contract and option awards totalling USD983 million for FMTV trucks and trailers.

In the first quarter of 2006, the US Army called up USD362 million worth of options in vehicles. In May 2006, Stewart & Stevenson was acquired by Armor Holdings Inc. for USD755 million. Also in May 2006, options were exercised by the US Army for an additional USD295 million. These were followed by another set of options in August for USD22 million. Option and call up awards for 2006 totalled USD691 million as of November 2006. In September 2006, TACOM awarded USD24.7 million contract to Stewart & Stevenson for FMTV reset, partnering with the Red River Army Depot for a two-year remanufacture contract.

Further FMTV contract options were exercised throughout 2007, and by late-2007 about 32 FMTVs per day were being produced at the Sealy, Texas production facility. In August 2007, Armor Holdings was acquired by BAE Systems for USD4.5 billion (unless historical and until the FMTV confirmed contract award in February 2010 to Oshkosh Defense, all references to the FMTV from this point forward in this entry will be as the BAE Systems FMTV). By January 2008, in excess of 47,000 FMTVs and trailers had been produced, with production expected to peak at 45 FMTVs per day during FY 2009.

In April 2008 BAE Systems announced that it had been awarded a USD43.6 million contract for 730 Long Term Armor Strategy (LTAS) FMTV cargo vehicles, these designated FMTVA1P2. Full details of the LTAS armouring package can be found elsewhere in this entry, but in brief: LTAS is based around the A and B kit principles, this allowing for vehicles to be armoured as required, and with the add-on appliqué package adaptable to prevailing threats and upgradeable as new armouring technologies emerge. The A-Kit, which includes a new cab, modifies the FMTV to allow the addition of armour; the B Kit being the armour itself. The initial production contract called for 730 LTAS A-Kit configured vehicles, with a follow-on modification (announced at the same time) calling for an additional 103 A-Kit configured vehicles, resulting in a total of 833 A-Kit

There are two FMTV variants, the 2.5 ton LMTV and the 5 ton MTV
(Shaun C Connors)   1155671

Extensively modified Stewart & Stevenson 2.5 ton LMTV as used by US special forces (Scott R Gourley) 0558999

BAE Systems FMTV 10 ton dump prototype during testing (Stewart & Stevenson) 0559000

vehicles. Deliveries commenced in August 2008 and were scheduled to be completed by November 2008. An order for 761 B-Kits worth up to USD45 million followed in July 2008.

In May 2008 BAE Systems announced that it had been awarded a USD54 million contract modification to manufacture approximately 370 FMTVs in various configurations, including dump trucks, cargo trucks, wreckers, and trailers. Approximately 100 of the FMTVs involved in this contract modification were of the LTAS configuration.

The third FMTV production contract (the competitive rebuy contract awarded in April 2003) officially ran until mid-2008, and by which time the US Army could have received a maximum of around 46,000 trucks and trailers from a stated requirement for 83,000 trucks of the FMTV weight class. All other current US Army contracts for tactical wheeled vehicle platforms were scheduled to conclude during a 2006-2008 time-frame, leaving the US Army a potentially sizeable procurement gap between 2006/2008 and 2011, 2011 generally being accepted as the earliest any entirely new design that may have resulted from the Future Truck System-Manoeuvre Sustainment Vehicle (FTTS-MSV) and FTTS-Utility Vehicle (UV) Advanced Concept Technology Demonstration (ACTD) efforts could reach service.

The Family of Heavy Tactical Vehicles (FHTV) contract with Oshkosh Defense was extended (and then renewed as FHTV 3) by the US Army. The FMTV contract was also extended, and it was proposed that a one-year (with a single year option) bridging contract for the FMTV would commence from October 2008, with this followed by a further FMTV re-buy competition.

In June 2008 it was disclosed that BAE Systems had been awarded a bridging contract for the supply of up to 10,000 FMTVs or trailers, this worth up to USD2.2 billion, with USD1.65 billion of funding agreed at the time of the announcement. The contract included a one-year option for the procurement of 10,000 additional vehicles. Deliveries of the base contract were expected to be complete by February 2010, with deliveries of the included option to be complete by November 2010.

In November 2008 BAE Systems announced that it had been awarded a USD1.6 billion contract to build another 10,000 FMTVs and trailers for delivery during 2009 and 2010. This contract award brought the total award value for FMTVs in 2008 to USD3.7 billion. The latest award calls for vehicles manufactured in LTAS configuration and variants to be built will include cargo trucks, wreckers, expansible vans, shop vans, tractors, load handling systems, High Mobility Artillery Rocket System support vehicles and Low Velocity Air Drop (LVAD) configured trucks. Deliveries of this option segment will be completed by November 2010, by which time in excess of 59,000 FMTVs and trailers will have been manufactured.

The US Army's original intention was that the FTTS (the logistic support for the Future Combat System (FCS)) with just two variants would eventually replace virtually all of the current tactical wheeled vehicle fleet. In a more realistic approach, the follow-on FTTS-MSV/UV ACTDs (with input from other efforts) continues to be used 'to define requirements' for future US Army trucks.

After having received a draft Request For Proposals (RfP) in October 2008, BAE Systems, Navistar Defense and Oshkosh Defense each announced in May 2009, they had submitted proposals to the US Army's Tank-Automotive and Armaments Command (TACOM) Life Cycle Management Command for the Family of Medium Tactical Vehicles (FMTV) A1P2 competitive rebuy programme.

Oshkosh Defense announced in late August 2009 that it had been awarded the FMTV A1P2 rebuy production contract. The FMTV A1P2 rebuy is a five-year 'build-to-print' requirements-type award that allows the US government to order from zero up to 12,415 trucks and 10,926 trailers. The award, which includes support services and engineering through to calendar year 2014, was worth USD3.023 billion (value at award date) if all options are exercised.

Shortly after the announcement award it was disclosed that the first FMTV A1P2 contract delivery order, valued at around USD281 million for a total of 2,568 trucks and trailers, had been placed. Delivery of test platforms was scheduled for mid-2010, these to be followed by production deliveries later in the year.

In early September 2009, BAE Systems filed an initial award protest with the US Government Accountability Office (GAO), and then two subsequent supplemental protests thereafter. Navistar, the other losing bidder, also filed a protest.

The GAO announced on December 14, 2009, that some elements of the protests had been upheld. Specifically, the Government's evaluation of Oshkosh facilities was brought into question along with whether a re-evaluation may change the proposed schedule. On February 12 2010 the US Army announced that it had re-evaluated the contract award decision for the FMTV in line with the GAO recommendations, confirming in that announcement the award remained with Oshkosh. Oshkosh states that it utilised its own resources to 'lean forward' before its original contract award was affirmed by the Army on February 12, 2010, and so that original production/delivery deadlines could be achieved. Available details of FMTV contract awards and delivery orders to Oshkosh Defense can be found elsewhere in this entry.

Some FMTV variants were excluded from the rebuy competition, those excluded include specialist FMTV variants such as HIMARS, Patriot, MEADS and LVAD, plus all the armoured cabs developed by BAE Systems including the Low Signature Armored Cab (LSAC), over 4,000 of which are in-service, the Individual Crew Protection (ICP) cab fitted to current HIMARS and the base LTAS cab, over 9,000 of which have been produced to date for the A1P2 variant. All Oshkosh FMTV vehicles will include the company's own Long-Term Armor Strategy (LTAS)-compliant armour solution.

BAE Systems will continue development and marketing of the FMTV for export, and while not guaranteed, will probably be called upon to continue deliveries of the specialist variants not covered by the rebuy award.

At DSEi 2009 BAE Systems unveiled the FMTV General Tactical Vehicle (GTV), a EURO 5 emissions-compliant European-optimised FMTV that is currently being touted for at least one European country's requirement.

According to BAE Systems, the FMTV has proven itself over 608 million km of use to be the US Army's most reliable logistic vehicle by some considerable margin, with current models having demonstrated, at 17,143 miles (27,583 km) Mean Miles Between Hardware Mission Failures (MMBHMF) almost six times the originally required rate, together with an Operational Readiness (OR) rate >eight per cent greater than desired. The US Army's Cost and Operational Effectiveness Analysis (COEA) for the FMTV estimated an average peacetime mileage of 2,200 miles per year. Current average mileages on Operation Iraqi Freedom (OIF) are around 16,000-19,000 km per year, with some M1088 tractors and 'gun trucks' peaking at 48,000 km. From a pre-OIF peak of over 98 per cent OR rate, FMTVs were returning (mid-2006) 95 per cent OR, 94 per cent in south-west Asia. Mid-2006, the US Army had around more than 6,000/300 FMTVs deployed on operations in Iraq-Kuwait/Afghanistan.

In addition to the US military, export sales of the FMTV have been made. Pre-2003, around 300 FMTVs were exported to Greece and New Zealand (M1089), Taiwan, Thailand and Saudi Arabia (around 100 Patriot support vehicles). More recently, a small number of FMTV-LHS with LSAC cabs are

M1184 8,000 kg LHS FMTVs (Shaun C Connors) 1155673

BAE Systems 2.5 ton (4 × 4) LMTV in M1078A1R standard cargo truck form
(Shaun C Connors)   1296165

understood to have been supplied to the Canadian forces operating in Afghanistan and following around 100 primarily M1085 cargo trucks supplied via Foreign Military Sale (FMS) to Jordan in two batches, a third Jordanian FMS order valued at USD6 million (and bringing the total Jordanian order value to USD16 million) was announced in April 2008.

In October 2007, BAE Systems was named as the preferred bidder for the 2,400 medium/heavy component of Australia's Land 121 (Project Overlander), this calling for a selection of (4 × 4), (6 × 6) and (8 × 8) platforms, all of which were to be based on FMTV designs. In August 2008 the decision to re-tender the medium and heavy truck segment of Land 121 was announced by the Australian Department of Defence (DoD). The DoD cited a testing and risk mitigation process that identified the need for higher levels of vehicle protection as the reason for the re-tender.

Conditions of tender for the first stage of the revised tender process were released in December 2008. The first stage consisted of Comparative Evaluation Testing (CET) which was to lead to down selection to two vehicle types, this expected to occur in early 2010, with the final bidder announcement then expected in July 2011. The four competitors for this segment of Land 121 were BAE Systems (offer including Scania heavy trucks), MAN, Mercedes-Benz and Thales. It was disclosed in February 2010 that a down-select to Mercedes-Benz, MAN and Thales had been made.

Oshkosh Defense FMTV contract awards and delivery orders

Oshkosh Defense announced in late August 2009 that it had been awarded the FMTV A1P2 rebuy production contract. Following protests filed by the losing bidders (BAE Systems and Navistar), some elements of which were upheld by the US Government Accountability Office (GAO), the US Army confirmed in February 2010 that following a re-evaluation of the FMTV award in line with GAO recommendations that the award remained with Oshkosh Defense.

The FMTV A1P2 rebuy is a five-year 'build-to-print' requirements-type award that allows the US government to order from zero up to an estimated 12,400 trucks and 10,900 trailers. The award, which includes support services and engineering, could be worth approximately USD3 billion if all options are exercised. The formal completion date of the contract is March 31 2012.

Shortly after the August 2009 contract award announcement it was disclosed that the first FMTV A1P2 contract delivery order, valued at around USD281 million for a total of 2,568 trucks and trailers, had been placed. Delivery of test platforms under this award was scheduled for mid-2010, these to be followed by production deliveries later in the year.

Oshkosh announced in May 2010 that it had received a delivery order valued at USD410.1 million from the US Army's TACOM Life Cycle Management Command (LCMC) for the production and delivery of 2,230 Family of Medium Tactical Vehicles (FMTV) trucks and 404 FMTV trailers for the US Army. This award is for deliveries scheduled between March and December 2011. Prior to this award Oshkosh had received orders valued at more than USD690 million for 5,209 FMTV trucks and trailers under the five-year FMTV requirements-type contract.

Also during May 2010 the first FMTVs were delivered for performance and durability testing, with deliveries scheduled to commence in October 2010.

Oshkosh announced two FMTV awards in July 2010, a USD30.9 million award for 167 Family of Medium Tactical Vehicles (FMTV) trucks, 37 armour B-kits, and 119 FMTV trailers, and a USD105.6 million award for 621 FMTV trucks and 43 FMTV trailers. These brought total FMTV and trailer orders to 6,159.

Oshkosh announced in August 2010 that it had received an award valued at more than USD180 million for 1,288 FMTV trucks and trailers. Three truck and two trailer variants are covered by the order which is destined for the National Guard and Reserve.

Oshkosh announced in September 2010 that it had received a USD260.1 million award for 2,060 FMTV trucks, that order including more than 1,300 trucks in eight different variants and approaching 700 FMTV trailers.

Oshkosh announced in November 2010 that it had received a USD797.9 million award for 4,183 Family of Medium Tactical Vehicles (FMTV) trucks and 590 FMTV trailers. Deliveries under this award are scheduled to begin in September 2011, and finish in August 2012.

Based on announced contract details to date, by November 2010 the current rebuy programme has issued delivery orders valued at USD2.1 billion, these calling for 13,239 trucks, 1,156 trailers, and 37 armour B-Kits.

Oshkosh announced in December 2010 that it had received awards valued at USD513.3 million for more than 2,050 Family of Medium Tactical Vehicles (FMTV) trucks and more than 1,650 FMTV trailers. All deliveries under this award are destined for US Army National Guard units and will run from November 2011 until May 2013.

These latest awards bring FMTV delivery order totals to at least 13,210 trucks and 4,800 trailers, with award totals currently in excess of USD2.6 billion.

Description

The 2.5 ton (4 × 4) FMTV is designated as the Light Medium Tactical Vehicle (LMTV), while the 5 ton (6 × 6) is designated the Medium Tactical Vehicle (MTV).

The FMTV is based on the Austrian Steyr 12 M 18 (4 × 4) truck, but substantially modified to meet US Army requirements that included a minimum 50 per cent US content. The original 15 FMTV prototypes were assembled in Austria and while based on the 12 M 18 chassis-cab, were fitted with a number of US-supplied/specification components including a Caterpillar diesel engine, Allison automatic transmission and Meritor axles.

The original Steyr product had been fully 'Americanised' prior to production commencing. Even so, the design has never remained static and to further increase reliability/OR rates, user friendliness and so on, detailed refinements/upgrades have continued throughout FMTVs production run. All evolutionary upgrades are made with due consideration to interoperability and commonality, with the vast majority of these being retro-fitable if required. A current non-LSAC/LTAS FMTV may look much like one from 1991, but all that remains of the original are a small number of pressed steel cab panels still sourced from Austria. The LTAS FMTV features a new cab and other enhancements including upgraded axles and braking system, however, there remains 85 per cent commonality between the LMTV and MTV base cargo chassis.

In moves to enhance production techniques, with the exception of driveline assemblies, 70 per cent of FMTV machine parts and weldments by value and part number were manufactured on-site by BAE Systems.

In a move away from US Army tradition, a cab-over-engine (COE) design was selected for the FMTV as while the US Army did not specify this configuration, given the Cold War situation prevailing at the time it had indicated that overall length for shipboard transport was a consideration. All three bidders subsequently proposed COE designs, and on a model-for-model basis the FMTV is around 1 m shorter than its bonneted predecessors while retaining the essential C-130 transport capability. Subject to load dimensions, all original FMTV variants are C-130 transportable at GVW and all models are capable of being transported, when underslung, by helicopter as all are fitted with a sliding outrigger system. Low Altitude Parachute Extraction System (LAPES), later revised to Low Velocity Air Drop (LVAD) variants of A0 production LMTV (M1081 cargo) and MTV (M1093 cargo and M1094 dump) variants were produced.

The non LSAC/LTAS stamped commercial pattern panel steel cab of the FMTV has sufficient space for three soldiers plus kit, and features a roof strengthened to accommodate a ring mount for assorted weapons up to a 12.7 mm HMG and purpose-designed non-commercial waterproof instrumentation and control panels. Current operational scenarios have lead to an increasing emphasis being placed on crew protection and BAE Systems developed the Low Signature Armored Cab (LSAC) and Long Term Armor Strategy (LTAS) cabs for all variants of the FMTV. The LTAS cab essentially became standard fit for all FMTVs from late-2008, with the designation A1P1 applied to LSAC-fitted FMTVs. Full details of FMTV armouring solutions can be found elsewhere in this entry.

BAE Systems 5 ton (6 × 6) MTV in M1083A1 standard cargo truck form
(Stewart & Stevenson)   0009691

FMTV is built around a conventional bolted/huck-bolted cold-formed C-section chassis with bolted-in tubular cross-members. The high-grade 758 Mpa steel used, is specified to combine chassis flex with tensile strength and is sourced from Sweden. Both chassis and cab feature extensive corrosion protection and the FMTV was the first truck to pass the US Army's 22-year accelerated corrosion test. All steel parts are rustproofed by an electrodepositing (E-coat) primer process prior to the Chemical Agent Resistant Coating (CARC) top coat and camouflage application. Additionally, all cab panels are double-side galvanised (prior to E-coat) and all floor and side panels (to window height) are polyurethane coated (post-CARC).

Current FMTVs are powered by a Caterpillar C7 six-cylinder 7.2-litre turbocharged diesel engine developing 275 hp (LMTV) or 330 hp (MTV), earlier versions of essentially the same engine being fitted to A0/A1 models. The current Allison MD 3070 automatic seven-speed transmission has also evolved with the FMTV. An integral single-speed transfer box provides full-time all-wheel drive with a front/rear 30/70 per cent (on-road) or 50/50 per cent (off-road) torque split. Radial steel-belted tyres are used with a Central Tyre Inflation (CTI) system. This system has settings for roads, cross-country, air transport, sand/mud/snow and emergency. The controls for the CTI system are mounted in the cab.

All models are fitted with Meritor beam axles sprung by a combination of parabolic tapered leaf springs (inverted on the MTV rear bogie), telescopic shock-absorbers, and an anti-roll bar for the rear axle/bogie; maximum suspension travel is 254 mm. Both versions utilise a Meritor Model R-611 Type 1 front axle. The LMTV rear axle is a Rockwell Model R-611 Type 2; those for the MTV are a Type 3 and a Type 4. The wrecker and tractor truck versions of the MTV have the Type 5 and Type 6 rear axles.

For the A1R contract, Stewart & Stevenson eliminated the lighter capacity MTV axle sets, all current production MTVs having the higher capacity front-rear and rear-rear axles fitted.

Following the introduction of the LSAC, a front suspension upgrade of heavier-duty coil-over shock-absorbers was introduced, and from late-2006, a block upgrade option of a heavier-duty front axle rated at 8,618 kg became available. Uprated axles form part of the LTAS package.

LMTV variants can be fitted with a DP-10J winch with a 4,990 kg line pull. MTV variants use a DP-515 winch with a 7,031 kg line pull.

Cargo versions of the FMTV without a dedicated crane may be fitted with an optional electrical loading/unloading crane capable of lifting 680 kg at 1.8 m.

FMTV model numbers and applications (production and pending) are as follows:
M1078A0/A1/A1R - LMTV Standard Cargo
M1079A0/A1/A1R - LMTV Van
M1080A0/A1/A1R - LMTV Chassis (3.9 m)
M1081A0 - LMTV Cargo-airdrop LVAD
M1082A1/A1R - LMTV Trailer
M1083A0/A1/A1R - MTV Standard Cargo
M1084A0/A1/A1R - MTV Cargo with Crane
M1085A0/A1/A1R - MTV Long Wheelbase Cargo
M1086A0/A1/A1R - MTV Long Wheelbase Cargo with Crane
M1087A1R - MTV Expansible Van
M1088A0/A1/A1R - MTV Tractor Truck
M1089A0/A1/A1R - MTV Wrecker
M1090A0/A1 - MTV Dump
M1091 - MTV 1,500 gallon Fuel Tanker
M1092A0/A1/A1R - MTV Chassis (4.1 m)
M1093A0 - MTV Cargo-airdrop LVAD
M1094A0 - MTV Dump-airdrop LVAD
M1095A1/A1R - MTV Trailer
M1096A0/A1/A1R - MTV Long Wheelbase (4.5 m) Chassis
M1084A1/A1R Truck, Cargo, Resupply Vehicle (HIMARS)
M1140A1/A1R HIMARS, launcher chassis
M1147A1R Trailer, FMTV Load Handling System
M1148A1R Load Handling System, eight metric tonnes
M1157A1R 10 ton dump
XM1160 10 ton MEADS air defence chassis (5.5 m wheelbase)
Mongoose Mobile Launcher Chassis (MLC) (cancelled).

There were originally 17 FMTV variants, four 3.9 m wheelbase LMTVs and 13 MTVs with (model dependant) a 4.1, 4.3, 5.3 or 5.5 m wheelbase. In addition to ongoing block upgrades and development work regarding the evolution of the base FMTV to meet part or all of the US Army's future needs and since the original contract award, the now BAE Systems added four variants to the FMTV family. Production of the M1140 HIMARS launcher and M1084 HIMARS resupply vehicle began in 2003, production of the M1148 Load Handling System (LHS) commenced in June 2005, while the latest addition to the FMTV family, the M1157 10 ton (9,070 kg) dump, entered full rate production late 2006.

The primary difference between the M1084 and M1084 (HIMARS) is that on the latter a Hiab materials handling crane replaces the Grove material handling crane of the former. A Hiab crane is now standard for all M1084 models.

Current production FMTVs (and late BAE Systems production) for the US Army are designated A1P2, for example the previous M1083A0/A1/A1R is now designated M1083A1P2.

FMTV trailers

Two cargo trailers are being manufactured as components of the Family of Medium Tactical Vehicles (FMTV). Fielding began with US Army units in August 2001.

The lightest is the M1082 for use with the LMTV cargo truck and has a matching payload of 2,268 kg, thereby doubling the carrying capacity of the LMTV cargo truck. The second trailer is the M1095 for use with the MTV cargo truck, which has a matching payload of 4,536 kg, thereby doubling the carrying capacity of the MTV cargo truck. Both trailers share many components, including the Meritor axles (one on the M1082 and two on the M1095), an anti-lock airbrake system, a 12/24 V electrical system with blackout lights, tiedown points, and integral sling bars. Both trailers also use the same dropsides, tailgate and 395/80R 20 tyres. A cargo cover with bows is optional, as is a tyre-inflation system.

The main variable between the two trailers is the size of the steel cargo bodies, which duplicate those of the appropriate towing vehicle. Both have removable drop sides with storage rails for these once removed. An access ladder is provided at the rear of both trailers.

Mid-2002 BAE Systems awarded the Tactical Vehicle Systems division of Stewart & Stevenson a USD3.3 million contract to design, build and test 16 Mobile Launcher Chassis (MLC) for the Mongoose minefield clearance system. The Mongoose system was terminated prior to type classification and is not being procured.

Variants

The FMTV chassis is currently being, or has been, utilised for a number of trials/developmental programmes; these programmes include:

Tilt Bed Carrier: The FMTV was selected as the platform to demonstrate that an XM777 155 mm howitzer and prime mover could, for the first time, be deployed in the same C-130 aircraft.

HHV: The FMTV Hybrid Hydraulic Vehicle (HHV) was selected as the test platform for the development of a hybrid hydraulic propulsion system. The US Army's Tank Automotive Research Development and Engineering Centre (TARDEC) evaluated a FMTV fitted with a hybrid hydraulic drive system supplied by Permo-Drive of Australia.

Flex-Frame: In conjunction with Multidrive of the UK, the FMTV has been used to build an (8 × 8) powered trailer C-130 air-transportable vehicle with a 15,000 kg payload capacity.

HIMARS: The FMTV is the platform for the US Army's latest artillery system, High Mobility Artillery Rocket System (HIMARS), a C-130 transportable package.

HREE: The FMTV has been selected as the test platform for the development of a Height Reducible Electronics Enclosure (HREE) capable of high-cube capacity, but being C-130 air-transportable without enclosure removal.

Hybrid Electric FMTV

Stewart & Stevenson produced five hybrid electric FMTVs, each tailored for a specific application. The first was a series hybrid in conjunction with Lockheed Martin and the National Automotive Centre (NAC) - a part of the Army's Tank-automotive and Armaments Command (TACOM). The second, a second-generation series hybrid was a joint effort by Stewart & Stevenson Tactical Vehicle Systems, LP; BAE Systems Controls, and the National Automotive Center. In September 2003 it was announced this second hybrid electric FMTV had completed three months and 5,000 miles of testing at Aberdeen Proving Grounds, Maryland. The propulsion system was evaluated in a 4,000-mile durability test after characterisation testing of more than 1,000 miles. The vehicle used BAE systems' HybriDrive propulsion system, this integrating a diesel-powered traction generator with two electric motors and an energy storage unit.

In a series hybrid the diesel engine turns the generator, the generator powering the electric motors, there being no mechanical transmission linking engine speed to road wheel speed.

The dual-function capability of the engine/generator powerpack allows a hybrid electric FMTV to furnish up to 200 kW of continuous power to service mobile or stationary battlefield electrical requirements. This on-

BAE Systems 5 ton (6 × 6) MTV in M1088A1R tractor truck form (Shaun C Connors)   1296162

LMTV series

Model	M1078A1R	M1079A1R	M1080A1R	M1081
Type:	standard cargo	van	chassis	cargo-airdrop (LVAD)
Cab seating:	1 + 2	1 + 2	1 + 2	1 + 2
Configuration:	4 × 4	4 × 4	4 × 4	4 × 4
Weight:				
(unladen, kerb)	7,978 kg	8,875 kg	6,021 kg	7,954 kg
(max load, not inc kits)	2,268 kg	2,268 kg	on request	2,268 kg
(towed load)	5,443 kg	5,443 kg	5,443 kg	5,443 kg
Length:	6.42 m	6.64 m	6.4 m	6.42 m
Width:	2.44 m	2.44 m	2.44 m	2.44 m
Height:				
(overall)	2.845 m	3.529 m	2.845 m	2.845 m
(programme transport)	2.68 m	2.68 m	2.68 m	2.68 m
Ground clearance: (laden)	559 mm	559 mm	559 mm	559 mm
Wheelbase:	3.9 m	3.9 m	3.9 m	3.9 m
Angle of approach/departure:	40°/40°	40°/40°	40°/40°	40°/40°
Max speed:	94 km/h	94 km/h	94 km/h	94 km/h
Range: (max, laden)	645 km	645 km	645 km	645 km
Max gradient:	60%	60%	60%	60%
Fording:				
(with preparation)	1.524 m	1.524 m	1.524 m	1.524 m
(without preparation)	914 mm	914 mm	914 mm	914 mm
Engine:	Caterpillar C73126 7.2-litre 6-cylinder inline turbocharged and aftercooled, water-cooled 4-stroke diesel developing 275 hp (205 kW) at 2,400 rpm and 1,107 N.m torque at 1,600 rpm			
Transmission:	Allison MD 3070PT automatic 7-speed			
Transfer case:	Allison single-speed integral to transmission with planetary inter-axle differential (lockable)			
Steering:	power	power	power	power
Turning radius:	8.5 m	8.5 m	8.5 m	8.5 m
Suspension:				
(front)	parabolic tapered leaf springs with hydraulic shock-absorber; coil-over-shock-absorbers from late-2005			
(rear)	parabolic tapered leaf springs with hydraulic shock-absorbers and anti-roll bar			
Tyres:	395/85R 20 XML	395/85R 20 XML	395/85R 20 XML	395/85R 20 XML
Brakes:	dual circuit, 4 channel air, drums all-round. Supplemental air-actuated driver-controlled engine exhaust brake. ABS fitted			
Electrical system:	12/24 V	12/24 V	12/24 V	12/24 V
Alternator:	100 A; optional 200 A	100 A; optional 200 A	100 A; optional 200 A	100 A; optional 200 A

board power generation capability can eliminate the need for a separate towed generator for some systems and reduces the number of different pieces of equipment that need to be deployed. Use of an optional inverter and power distribution panel enables the hybrid electric FMTV to power almost anything when and where needed. Examples include mobile requirements such as radar systems, communication shelters, missile/weapons systems such as HIMARS, hospitals and field kitchens. The optional inverter also can use the energy of the high-capacity HEV traction battery pack to considerably extend weapon or support system 'silent watch' capabilities. The HEV incorporates a sealed electrical motor and generator (liquid-cooled), which gives it fording capability.

The third hybrid electric FMTV was developed by Stewart & Stevenson in conjunction with Allison and is a parallel hybrid. In a parallel hybrid both the diesel engine and electric motor can provide propulsion power, both being connected directly to the transmission, so the vehicle is capable of operating either mechanically, electrically, or both. Stewart & Stevenson,

in partnership with Lockheed Martin, built a US MEADS Hybrid Electric Launcher Concept (Air Defense Launcher), with the Allison parallel hybrid drive as propulsion. Testing was performed at the Stewart & Stevenson test facility in Sealy, Texas.

In 2004, Stewart & Stevenson built a fourth hybrid electric vehicle, teaming with Lockheed Martin, DRS Technologies, Moog, and Armour Holdings to produce a hybrid electric High Mobility Artillery Rocket System (HIMARS) vehicle. This hybrid HIMARS was designed as a parallel hybrid drive, where the standard transmission was replaced with a transmission/generator, which drives the wheels mechanically but also generates electrical power to charge a battery bank. This electrical storage allows silent watch capabilities, where all target acquisition and communication gear, turret positioning, and air-conditioning systems can run completely on battery power while the weapon system is 100 per cent operational.

In 2005, Stewart & Stevenson built a fifth hybrid electric vehicle, again teaming with Lockheed Martin and utilizing an ISE series hybrid drive on an upgraded hybrid HIMARS.

BAE Systems 5 ton (6 × 6) MTV in M1084A1R cargo truck with crane. The primary difference between the M1084 and M1084 (HIMARS) is that on the latter a Hiab materials handling crane replaces the Grove material handling crane of the former. A Hiab crane is now standard for all M1084A1R models (Shaun C Connors)   1296164

BAE Systems 5 ton (6 × 6) MTV in M1089A1R wrecker form (Shaun C Connors)   1296161

BAE Systems 5 ton (6 × 6) MTV in M1087A1R Expansible Van form
(Shaun C Connors) 1296163

BAE Systems 5 ton (6 × 6) MTV in M1090A1 dump truck form
(Stewart & Stevenson) 0044375

M1148 A1 9 ton (8,000 kg) FMTV-LHS

The FMTV-LHS load handling system variant is based on a modified 5.3 m wheelbase FMTV 5 ton cargo chassis on which flitch plates are added to the channel-section chassis for additional strength. The M1148 is fitted with a Hiab (Multilift) load handling system rated at 8,000 kg and that is part-integrated between the FMTVs chassis rails. The M1148 retains its C-130 air-transportability complete with LHS (unladen) and associated container handling frame. The part-integration of the LHS enables the vehicle to have a 4 m clearance when laden with a standard 20 × 8 × 8 ft ISO container. When laden with a 8 ft 6 in ISO container, the vehicle is just outside the 4 m height limit.

Trials of the M1148 commenced in April 2003 and were completed in June 2004, with production commencing in June 2005. First Unit Equipped (FUE) occurred during 2007. The system has been selected to transport US Army Combat Support Hospitals and will fulfil an initial requirement for in excess of 400 trucks and equal capacity companion trailers.

In addition to ISO containers, the M1148 is fully compatible with all standard US Army flatracks - M1, M3 and M1077. An equal capacity companion trailer is available and features articulated (dolly-type) steering, is fitted with ABS and air ride suspension and can be cross-loaded/unloaded by the towing M1148.

The unladen FMTV-LHS weighs 11,263 kg, and has a GVW of 19,305 kg.

The 8,000 kg payload chassis is available in the full range of FMTV configurations.

M1157 A1 10 ton MTV dump

To meet a US Army increased payload requirement for the FMTV M1090 dump variant, Stewart & Stevenson partnered with the Project Manager, Medium Tactical Vehicles (PM-MTV), the National Automotive Centre (NAC), Keweenaw Research Centre (KRC), Crysteel KFG Inc., and GS Engineering to develop the FMTV dump chassis into a 10 ton (9,070 kg) payload capacity design. Trials were completed in the third quarter of 2003 with production starting late-2006.

In April 2009, BAE Systems announced it had been awarded a contract modification from the US Army worth USD64.1 million to produce 500 FMTV 10 ton dump trucks in LTAS configuration.

Modifications to the base 5 ton MTV M1090 chassis include the addition of flitch plates to the channel-section chassis. The strengthened chassis is fitted with a Crysteel 7.65 m³ (approx) dump body and twin-ram under-floor tipping gear. The vehicle retains its C-130 air-transportability.

The unladen M1157 A1 weighs 11,939 kg, and has a payload of 9,072 kg.

The 10 ton payload chassis is available in the full range of FMTV configurations.

11 ton FMTV A1

Stewart & Stevenson developed an 11 ton FMTV A1 demonstrator to demonstrate the growth potential of the FMTV family and C4ISR integration potential, via technology insertions, while retaining maximum commonality with the current FMTV fleet.

Based on a modified 5 ton MTV chassis, modifications to demonstrate payload growth potential included the addition of flitch plates to the channel-section chassis. Larger 14.00R 20 tyres were fitted.

Kerb weight of the 11 ton FMTV A1 is approximately 10,884 kg (12 tonnes), giving a payload to weight ratio of approaching 1:1. The vehicle is C-130 deployable with in excess of 6,349 kg (seven tonnes) of payload.

11 ton FMTV A1 tilt bed carrier

Following on from the 11 ton FMTV A1 Stewart & Stevenson developed a second 11 ton FMTV, this later vehicle fitted with a tilt-type bed to meet a FTTS requirement for a transport vehicle with the ability to load/unload a C-130 transport aircraft with a standard ISO container.

13 ton MTTD

This vehicle was first displayed at the Association of the United States Army (AUSA) annual convention in Washington DC in October 2003.

Working with the US Army Tank Automotive Research, Development and Engineering Center's (TARDEC) National Automotive Center (NAC), and in conjunction with a variety of companies, the then Stewart & Stevenson, developed an advanced technology 13 ton (11,791 kg) (6 × 6) Medium Tactical Truck Demonstrator (MTTD).

The MTTD incorporated many of the key technologies and capabilities that the Army envisioned for its future trucks, including cab and vehicle sub-systems addressing increased crew protection, improved C-130 interoperability, serviceability and ease of use, independently suspended wheels and active suspension, advanced braking systems, embedded DriverTech IETM web-centric diagnostic system, and others.

Base of the MTTD is a modified FMTV (6 × 6) chassis, this uprated to a capacity of 13 tons (11,791 kg) and fitted with a state-of-the-art three-man cab. The MTTD is all wheel drive and steer, and includes independent suspension in combination with active Davis struts. Loading and unloading tasks are handled by the material-handling crane, mounted behind the cab, and a sliding cargo bed with integral winch. The MTTD comes complete with both active and passive weapons systems, capable of stand-off detection and destruction of Rocket Propelled Grenades (RPGs), and add-on armour. The MTTD is C-130 transportable with approximately a 50 per cent payload.

The futuristic looking cab provides a fully integrated self-sustaining environment with the ability to provide protection for a three-man crew. The cab forward design aids in mine blast protection and the angled flat panel exterior allows for easy up-armouring. Within the cab are two identical driver control modules, one on each side, with multiple flat panel displays. In addition to standard vehicular monitoring information, to include advanced diagnostics and prognostics, these panels are also connected to infrared and video cameras mounted for forward and rear views around the vehicle. Satellite connections provide GPS, situational awareness, and real time communication capabilities. Each of these control modules can also remotely operate the crane, the tilt bed, or the weapon system module mounted on top of the cab, and serve as a backup to each other should one be damaged. The middle seat in the cab can be fully reclined to allow one soldier to sleep, allowing for rotational shifts on long missions.

The Integrated Weapons Module, mounted on top of the cab, makes use of both existing and developing technologies for active and passive defence. The package includes a machine gun, smoke protection, laser warning detection, active protection against RPGs and similar weapons, and the ability to release UAVs for reconnaissance. The weapons module is operated and reloaded from within the cab, and is modular in design such that it can be interchanged with other weapon modules in the case of changes to the threat environment level.

The articulating crane is forward mounted on the cargo bed, allowing the 6.4 m reach to access material anywhere around the vehicle, including in front of the cab. The crane can be provided with a standard hook lift, or a forklift end that facilitates movement of pallets, and can be operated from beside the truck or from within the cab.

The tilt bed with winch assists in loading and unloading directly from a cargo aircraft as the bed can be extended and lowered to meet the deck height of the aircraft. The deck of the tilt bed is covered with a roller system, allowing rotation or manipulation of the cargo to facilitate cargo handling, and a winch on the top of the bed controls the movement of the load on to or off of the bed during loading. The tilt bed operation can also be controlled from within the cab if necessary in a threatening environment.

For enhanced mobility the MTTD is fitted with fully independent suspension on all three axles, and has all wheel steer, making it a 6 × 6 × 6 designation. Available options for the driver are to select either co-ordinated or crab steer for greatest manoeuvrability. An active suspension system via Davis struts enables high cross country speeds, a smooth ride, and an adjustable ride height with up to 330 mm of vertical wheel travel, controllable from within the cab. A Central Tyre Inflation (CTI) system is fitted. The wheels are forged aluminium to save weight.

Other current technologies installed on the MTTD vehicle include the electronically controlled vehicle thermal management system, which eliminates all standard mechanically driven cooling and circulation pumps and fans on the engine and transmission, greatly reducing parasitic loads. Replacing them is a thermal management system, which monitors and

5 ton MTV series

Model	M1083A1R	M1084A1R	M1085A1R	M1086A1R	M1087A1R	M1088A1R	M1089A1R
Type:	standard cargo	cargo/crane	LWB cargo	LWB cargo/crane	expansible van	tractor	wrecker
Cab seating:	1 + 2	1 + 2	1 + 2	1 + 2	1 + 2	1 + 2	1 + 2
Configuration:	6 × 6	6 × 6	6 × 6	6 × 6	6 × 6	6 × 6	6 × 6
Weight:							
(unladen, kerb)	9,606 kg	11,254 kg	10,287 kg	11,755 kg	16,908 kg	9,151 kg	15,732 kg
(payload, not inc kits)	4,536 kg	4,536 kg	4,536 kg	4,536 kg	2,268 kg	11,340 kg[1]	4,990 kg[2]
(towed load)	9,526 kg	9,526 kg	9,526 kg	9,526 kg	9,526 kg	27,216 kg	16,330 kg
Length:	6.96 m	7.78 m	8.861 m	9.683 m	9.927 m	7.14 m	9.305 m
Width:	2.44 m	2.44 m	2.44 m	2.44 m	2.44 m	2.44 m	2.44 m
Height:							
(overall)	2.845 m	2.845 m	2.845 m	2.845 m	3.730 m	2.845 m	2.845 m
(air transport)	2.680 m	2.680 m	2.680 m	2.680 m	n/app	2.680 m	2.680 m
Ground clearance: (laden)	559 mm	559 mm	559 mm	559 mm	559 mm	559 mm	559 mm
Wheelbase:	4.1 m	4.5 m	4.5 m	5.5 m	5.5 m	4.1 m	5.3 m
Angle of approach/departure:	40°/60°	40°/36°	40°/20°	40°/21°	40°/17°	40°/44°	40°/40°
Max speed:	94 km/h	94 km/h	94 km/h	94 km/h	94 km/h	94 km/h	94 km/h
Range: (max, laden)	>483 km	>483 km	>483 km	>483 km	>483 km	>483 km	>483 km
Max gradient:	60%	60%	60%	60%	60%	60%	60%
Fording:							
(with kit)	1.524 m	1.524 m	1.524 m	1.524 m	1.524 m	1.524 m	1.524 m
(without kit)	914 mm	914 mm	914 mm	914 mm	914 mm	914 mm	914 mm
Engine:	Caterpillar C73136 7.2-litre 6-cylinder inline turbocharged and aftercooled, water-cooled 4-stroke diesel developing 330 hp (246 kW) at 2,400 rpm and 1,153 N.m torque at 1,600 rpm						
Transmission:	Allison MD 3070PT automatic 7-speed						
Transfer case:	Allison single-speed integral to transmission with planetary inter-axle differential (lockable)						
Steering:	power	power	power	power	power	power	power
Turning radius:	9.35 m	11 m	11 m	12.95 m	12.95 m	9.35 m	12.95 m
Suspension:							
(front)	parabolic tapered leaf springs with hydraulic shock-absorbers; coil-over-shock-absorbers from late-2005						
(rear)	tandem axles with parabolic tapered leaf springs, hydraulic shock-absorbers and anti-roll bar						
Tyres:	395/85R 20 XML	395/85R 20 XML	395/85R 20 XML	395/85R 20 XML	395/85R 20 XML	395/85R 20 XML	395/85R 20 XML
Brakes:	dual circuit, 4 channel air, drums all-round. Supplemental air-actuated driver-controlled engine exhaust brake. ABS fitted						
Electrical system:	12/24 V	12/24 V	12/24 V	12/24 V	12/24 V	12/24 V	12/24 V
Alternator:	100 A; optional 200 A	100 A; optional 200 A	100 A; optional 200 A	100 A; optional 200 A	100 A; optional 200 A	100 A; optional 200 A	100 A; optional 200 A

[1] Towed 5th wheel load
[2] Maximum load on lift and tow stinger

satisfies the vehicles' cooling requirements, while reducing energy consumption, providing faster vehicle warm-up, precise component thermal control and extended ambient operational capability. The thermal management system can also be adapted to provide modified thermal signature capability.

The MTTD was built in the then Stewart & Stevenson engineering prototype facilities in Sterling Heights, Michigan by a dedicated team of engineers and technicians. Stewart & Stevenson (Sterling Heights and Sealy, Texas) and the National Automotive Center (NAC) took the lead, and assistance and equipment was furnished by a broad spectrum of automotive and defence related companies.

13 ton FMTV

The 13 ton FMTV is essentially the follow-on from the earlier 11 ton FMTV. This vehicle is fitted with an LSAC cab and configured as a LHS with container handling capability This 13 ton demonstrator included a 30 kW exportable power generation capability, and a digitised multiplex wiring solution to demonstrate expanded diagnostic and added prognostics systems, plus an ability to install on an as required basis complex 'plug and play' electronically driven systems. An ABS-controlled stability and traction control system was also fitted, and it was proposed at the time that this system could be offered as a future FMTV block upgrade, as could an active or semi-active suspension system.

Both active and semi-active, and independent suspension solutions were assessed by BAE Systems, however with regard to an independent option, the sustained view is that the present set-up offers the best compromise of cost, performance and reliability.

FMTV (8 × 8) platforms

An (8 × 8) 13 ton FMTV, that in addition to a LHS has a materials handling crane, was completed late-2006, as was an (8 × 8) FMTV with a 16,500 kg payload. The latter of these was clearly targeted at Australia's Land 121

(Project Overlander) requirement. Land 121, for which BAE Systems was announced as preferred bidder in October 2007 with a selection of designs based on the FMTV platform, requires 2,400 medium and heavy vehicles including two (8 × 8) platforms, a 16,500 kg LHS vehicle and a recovery vehicle. In August 2008 the decision to re-tender the medium and heavy truck segment of Land 121 was announced by the Australian Department of Defence (DoD), the DoD citing a testing and risk mitigation process that identified the need for higher levels of vehicle protection as the reason for the re-tender.

BAE Systems 2.5 ton (4 × 4) LMTV in M1079A1R van form (Shaun C Connors)

1296166

5 ton MTV series
(continued)

Model	M1090A1R	M1091A1R	M1092A1R	M1093R	M1094R	M1096A1R
Type:	dump	1,500 gallon (US) fuel tanker	chassis	cargo-airdrop (LVAD)	dump-airdrop (LVAD)	chassis 4.5 m
Cab seating	1 + 2	1 + 2	1 + 2	1 + 2	1 + 2	1 + 2
Configuration:	6 × 6	6 × 6	6 × 6	6 × 6	6 × 6	6 × 6
Weight:						
(unladen, kerb)	10.580 kg	11,065 kg	7,616 kg	9,498 kg	10,641 kg	7,863 kg
(payload, not inc. kits)	4,536 kg	4,797 kg (fuel)	on request	4,536 kg	4,536 kg	on request
(towed load)	9,526 kg	n/avail	9,526 kg	9,526 kg	9,526 kg	9,526 kg
Length:	7.226 m	8.054 m	6.935 m	6.935 m	7.182 m	8.86 m
Width:	2.438 m	2.438 m	2.438 m	2.438 m	2.438 m	2.438 m
Height:						
(overall)	3.03 m	2.845 m	2.845 m	2.845 m	2.845 m	2.845 m
(air transport)	2.680 m	2.680 m	2.680 m	2.680 m	2.680 m	2.680 m
Ground clearance: (laden)	559 mm	559 mm	559 mm	559 mm	559 mm	559 mm
Wheelbase:	4.1 m	4.5 m	4.1 m	4.1 m	4.1 m	4.5 m
Angle of approach/departure:	40°/44°	40°/40°	40°/60°	40°/60°	40°/44°	40°/20°
Max speed:	94 km/h	94 km/h	94 km/h	94 km/h	94 km/h	94 km/h
Range: (max, laden)	>483 km	>483 km	>483 km	>483 km	>483 km	>483 km
Max gradient	60%	60%	60%	60%	60%	60%
Fording:						
(with kit)	1.524 m	1.524 m	1.524 m	1.524 m	1.524 m	1.524 m
(without kit)	914 mm	914 mm	914 mm	914 mm	914 mm	914 mm
Engine:	Caterpillar C73126 7.2-litre 6-cylinder inline turbocharged and aftercooled, water-cooled 4-stroke diesel developing 330 hp (246 kW) at 2,400 rpm and 1,153 N.m torque at 1,600 rpm					
Transmission:	Allison MD 3070PT automatic 7-speed					
Transfer box:	Allison single-speed integral to transmission with planetary inter-axle differential (lockable)					
Steering:	power	power	power	power	power	power
Turning radius:	9.35 m	11 m	9.35 m	9.35 m	9.35 m	11 m
Suspension:						
(front)	parabolic tapered lead springs with hydraulic shock-absorbers; coil-over-shock-absorbers from late-2005					
(rear)	tandem axles with parabolic tapered lead springs, hydraulic shock-absorbers and anti-roll bar					
Tyres:	395/85R 20 XML	395/85R 20 XML	395/85R 20 XML	395/85R 20 XML	395/85R 20 XML	395/85R 20 XML
Brakes:	dual circuit, 4 channel air, drums all-round. Supplemental air-actuated driver-controlled engine exhaust brake. ABS fitted					
Electrical system:	12/24 V	12/24 V	12/24 V	12/24 V	12/24 V	12/24 V
Alternator:	100 A; optional 200 A	100 A; optional 200 A	100 A: optional 200 A	100 A; optional 200 A	100 A; optional 200 A	100 A; optional 200 A

Also on (8 × 8) chassis are the two FTTS-MSV ACTDs built under a USD10 million contract awarded to Stewart & Stevenson late-2005. Complete with an independently mobile three-axle trailer, these 13 ton-rated trucks are fitted with a multi-functional crane-come-LHS that can be programmed to operate as crane, forklift or LHS, together with host of other current and cutting edge technologies including a LTAS cab, fully independent air-suspension, and a hybrid power output boost from 450 to 620 hp.

LMTV

As part of continuing LMTV development work, a bonneted LMTV Utility Variant complete with an armoured cab was shown by the now BAE Systems at AUSA 2006. With its 3,000 kg payload, this vehicle is clearly targeted at roles now out-growing HMMWV-type designs.

An LMTV fitted with a hydrostatic drive system commenced testing late-2006 at Aberdeen Proving Ground. To meet the wide range of power and torque demands in a vehicle of the FMTVs type, the vehicle is fitted with three (small, medium and large) commercial hydraulic motors. The primary object of this exercise was a fuel saving demonstration, this expected to be in the region of 30 per cent, and a requirement of the then current FTTS programme.

Other recent LMTV developments include a fully armoured LMTV on which the LSAC cab is extended rearwards into a troop-carrying body. This design was offered to the US Army for the Iraqi Light Armoured Vehicle (ILAV) requirement.

FMTV A1R

In April 2001 the US Army awarded Stewart & Stevenson Tactical Vehicle Systems and Oshkosh Truck Corporation contracts valued at USD4.4 and USD5.6 million, respectively, for the Evaluation Phase (Phase 1) of the Family of Medium Tactical Vehicles A1 Competitive Rebuy (FMTV A1 CR) programme for the next FMTV production contract. The US Army required a new 2004 Environmental Protection Agency (EPA) compliant diesel engine, and bidders were free to propose ways of further reducing FMTV life cycle costs and improve the current 98 per cent operational readiness state and increase the current 85 per cent commonality across the fleet.

Each bidder was provided with eight government furnished FMTV A1 models on which to integrate engines and carry out modifications. Following trials on these vehicles undertaken by the US Army, in April 2003 Stewart & Stevenson was awarded the Family of Medium Tactical Vehicles A1 Competitive Rebuy (FMTV A1 CR) production contract.

The FMTV A1 CR programme has a potential value in excess USD2 billion and includes production that could reach nearly 11,000 trucks and trailers over five years, with an option for 12,000 additional vehicles. Production of the FMTV A1 CR (designated FMTV A1R) commenced in the third quarter of 2004. A total of 21,149 FMTVs and trailers were built under the FMTVA1R contract award.

Stewart & Stevenson proposed a number of enhancements to the FMTV A1R, not all of which were adopted by the US Army. Major adopted improvements include a new Caterpillar C7 EPA 2004 compliant diesel engine. This features the same power and torque curves as the FMTV A1 Caterpillar 3126 engine. The cooling system has been uprated to take into account the increased heat rejection from the Caterpillar C7 engine. The uprated cooling system is suitable for use with FMTVs rated up to 10,000 kg. Transmission cooling has also been uprated.

All FMTV A1R models feature the heavier duty axle sets and brakes as fitted to A1 recovery and tractor truck models.

Other enhancements include improved three-point suspension for the cab; tail lights now incorporated into the rear cargo bed (similar to FMTV trailers); conversion of wire harnesses from MIL spec to SAE; improvements to in-cab stowage; introduction of a stamped steel grille and stronger front bumper. A number of user enhancements have been made to the cab.

Caiman Mine Protected Ambush Protected (MRAP) vehicle and derivatives

The Caiman MRAP vehicle is based on the MTV A1R platform. With a bonneted configuration, the Caiman retains the basic chassis and automotive set-up of the MTV for commonality, but for crew protection is fitted with a V-hulled armoured body specifically designed to counter current and emerging threats on deployed operations.

Prototype (8 × 8) 16,500 kg LHS for Australia's Land 121 requirement
(BAE Systems)   1296295

Following an initial award for four trials and evaluation vehicles, the USMC placed an initial order with the then Armor Holdings for 1,170 Caiman MRAP vehicles in July 2007. The order was valued at USD518 million including support and called for 1,158 Category 1 (Cat 1) vehicles and 12 Category 2 (Cat 2) vehicles. In December 2007, the USMC placed a follow-on order valued at USD448 million for an additional 668 Caiman Cat 1 MRAP vehicles. Also in December 2007 six Caiman MRAP II vehicles ordered through BAE Systems Ground Systems, the prime contractor for the MRAP 2 requirement. In March 2008 an order for an additional 1,024 Caiman Category 1 vehicles worth USD715 million was placed bringing the total order book for the now BAE Systems Mobility and Protection Systems Caiman to 2,868. By mid-June 2008 some 1,470 vehicles had been produced, with production of all 2,868 vehicles ordered completed during November 2008.

Caiman is currently achieving a sustained operational readiness rate average of 95 per cent on deployed operations.

Various other designs from a selection of other manufacturers have also been ordered by the USMC to meet the MRAP requirement.

BAE Systems unveiled the Caiman Light (CLT) at the 2008 Association of the United States Army Annual Meeting & Exposition in Washington. Caiman Light is a five-man (4 × 4) version of the (6 × 6) Caiman MRAP and offers protection comparable to the 17,000 kg Caiman at around two-thirds the weight.

BAE Systems unveiled the Caiman MultiTerrain Vehicle (MTV) at AUSA Winter in 2010. Caiman MTV is a modified version of the base Caiman that features a revised driveline, new chassis and upgraded fully independent suspension.

The MTV, which is available in three versions - troop carrier, ambulance, command and control, can accommodate a 10-man crew for troop transport missions or a four litter setup with attendant when equipment for medical missions. The basic MTV design is fitted with a high-capacity HVAC (heating, ventilating and air conditioning) temperature control system to safeguard passengers and sensitive computer systems from hot or cold weather.

Mechanically the redesigned MTV features a wider 2.578 m track and Arvin Meritor fully independent suspension that features dual-rate coil springs and hydraulic shock-absorbers at each wheel station. Motive power is provided by a Caterpillar C9 six-cylinder diesel engine that develops 450 hp and peak torque of 1,849 N.m, this coupled to a Caterpillar CX28 automatic/select six-speed transmission. This set up, which delivers more power and torque, replaces the Caterpillar C7 diesel engine and Allison 3700SP transmission that legacy Caiman MRAPs shared with the FMTV fleet.

The FMTV-based Caiman Mine Resistant Ambush Protected (MRAP)
vehicle has been ordered by the USMC (BAE Systems)   1296160

M1095 cargo trailer for MTV. The lighter M1082 LMTV trailer is similar in
appearance but has a single and not twin axles (Stewart & Stevenson)
                                                                 0009961

According to BAE Systems, the MTV is available as new build or as a recapitalisation of existing Caiman MRAPs.

It was disclosed in August 2010 that the US government was to award BAE Systems a USD629 million order under a previous contract to deliver 1,700 Caiman MTVs. The award, announced by BAE Systems in September 2010, will have new rolling chassis produced in Sealy, Texas from November 2010, with the bulk of the final integration completed in Kuwait. Work under this award is expected to be completed by the end of December 2011.

FMTV cab armouring solutions
Working in partnership to meet the US Army's transformation requirements for greater crew protection and vehicle survivability, the then Stewart & Stevenson and O'Gara-Hess & Eisenhardt Armoring Company (OHE), a subsidiary of Armor Holdings, Inc., designed a ballistically protected cab for the HIMARS in 2001. This cab, called the Crew Protected Cab, offered Foreign Object Debris (FOD) protection, flash protection during launch, featured a cab overpressurisation system for NBC protection, and retained C-130 air-transportability. Designs followed for an Enhanced Crew Protected Cab, and later an Armor Protected Cab, each adding more ballistic capability against direct fire, artillery burst and mines.

Current operational scenarios have lead to an increasing emphasis being placed on crew protection and the now BAE Systems has developed the Low Signature Armored Cab (LSAC) for all variants of the FMTV. In contrast with the FMTV up-armouring kits of three-dimensional armour plates that began fielding during 2004, the air-conditioned LSAC design replaces the standard FMTV cab (with which it shares internals) in a remove and replace operation that can be accomplished by two individuals in approximately four hours. Alternatively, the LSAC can be fully integrated on the FMTV production line. Compared to add-on appliqué armour kits the LSAC is stated to offer around 50 per cent greater ballistic protection and a 40 per cent weight saving. Specific LSAC ballistic protection levels include cab and glass direct-fire protection of NATO STANAG 4569 Level 2 and mine protection exceeding NATO STANAG 4569 2a to 3a.

The bulk of the initial 2,060 LSACs produced were delivered during 2004/2005. Late-2007 it was disclosed that an additional 600-1,000 LSACs were required, and following an LSAC award in July 2008 total LSAC contract value was quoted as USD134.2 million.

In 2005, Stewart & Stevenson introduced the LSAC-H (H - HIgh Mobility Artillery Rocket System (HIMARS)). This lighter cab is designed to accept the bulk of its protection as appliqué panels so that front axle imposed load limits for C-130 transportability can be met. Fitted to current production HIMARS as standard, this cab will be retro-fitted to previously delivered HIMARS, these having a lightweight Foreign Object Debris-protected (FOD) cab. In December 2008 BAE Systems announced it had been awarded a USD6.26 million contract by Lockheed Martin to manufacture 26 Increased Crew Protection (ICP) cabs for the HIMARS. The contract also includes 26 cab up-armour appliqué kits. The ICP cabs and appliqué kits will replace unarmoured cabs on US Army and USMC HIMARS vehicles. The ICP cab has more than 40 enhancements from previous cab designs, these enhancements including: improved crew survivability, hatch and door ergonomics, cab entry and exit, pressurization and water entry sealing. In addition, composite materials were used to meet mission essential transportability requirements.

In November 2009, BAE Systems announced a USD13.97 million contract from the Army Aviation and Missile Life Cycle Management Command (AMCOM) for 64 ICP cab upgrade kits for HIMARS. The contract also includes 65 cab up-armour appliqué kits and spares. The ICP cabs and appliqué kits will replace unarmoured cabs on Army and Marine Corps HIMARS vehicles, and will be produced by October 2010. Also in November 2009, BAE Systems announced a USD23.75 million award from TACOM to manufacture 65 M1140A1 Launcher Chassis, which include the ICP cab for HIMARS. The contract also includes 65 cab up-armour appliqué kits. The launcher chassis vehicles and ICP cabs will be delivered to the Army and Marine Corps by December 2010.

BAE Systems announced in November 2010 that it had been awarded a USD16.3 million contract for an additional 44 HIMARS vehicles, these vehicles to be equipped with BAE Systems' Increased Crew Protection

(ICP) cab. Deliveries will be completed by December 2011. This order followed an earlier order placed in June 2010 for 63 HIMARS vehicles and protection kits, this valued at USD24 million.

To meet the US Army's current Long Term Armor Strategy (LTAS) A+B kit policy for armoured cabs, BAE Systems developed the LTAS cab for the FMTV. The first order for LTAS-cabbed FMTVs was placed in April 2008, was valued at USD43.6 million and called for 730 LTAS FMTV cargo vehicles, these designated FMTVA1P2. The initial production contract called for 730 LTAS A-Kit configured vehicles, with a follow-on modification (announced at the same time) calling for an additional 103 A-Kit configured vehicles, resulting in a total of 833 A-Kit vehicles. Deliveries commenced in August 2008 and were scheduled to be completed by November 2008. An order for 761 B-Kits worth up to USD45 million followed in July 2008. A further 100 LTAS-cabbed FMTVs formed part of a USD54 million FMTV order placed in May 2008.

In November 2008 BAE Systems announced that it had been awarded a USD1.6 billion contract to build another 10,000 FMTVs and trailers for delivery during 2009 and 2010, this award calling for all vehicles to be manufactured in LTAS configuration. Variants (designated FMTV A1P2) to be built will include cargo trucks, wreckers, expansible vans, shop vans, tractors, load handling systems, HIMARS support vehicles and Low Velocity Air Drop (LVAD) configured trucks.

In February 2009, BAE Systems announced it had been awarded a contract to supply more than 5,100 LTAS armour kits for LTAS configured FMTVs. The contract was worth up to USD190 million.

BAE Systems states that it has produced over 9,000 LTAS cabs for the FMTVA1P2 variant.

All Oshkosh FMTV vehicles will include the company's own Long-Term Armor Strategy (LTAS)-compliant armour solution.

LTAS is based around the A and B kit principles, this allowing for vehicles to be armoured as required, and with the add-on appliqué package adaptable to prevailing threats and upgradeable as new armouring technologies emerge. The A-Kit, which includes a new cab, modifies the FMTV to allow the addition of armour; the B-Kit being the armour itself.

DRS Technical Services FMTV protection kit

To meet an urgent need for armoured protection kits for FMTV family trucks operating in Iraq, over a 13 month period the then Radian Inc., in association with the US Army Program Executive Office Combat Support and Combat Service Support (PEO CS&CSS), developed an add-on protection kit for all currently deployed FMTV variants. The Armor Protection Kit effort was started in April 2003, when the now DRS Technical Services was asked to redesign the initial effort conducted by the government. The prototype kits and developmental testing were completed in August 2003, with the award to finalise the design and provide operational test kits following in October 2003. Operational testing was completed in December 2003.

In March 2004 DRS Technical Services announced that it had been awarded by the US Army's Tank-automotive and Armaments Command (TACOM) a USD16.3 million contract to provide 272 armour protection kits for the FMTV. A total of 1,862 FMTV armour kits are understood to have been produced in total.

The DRS Technical Services kit includes ballistic-protection panels installed on standard FMTV cabs, incorporating armoured glass and high-hardness steel, whose low carbon content is said to minimise spalling in the event of shaped-charge attack. The armoured doors include special ports for presenting documents or passes at checkpoints. Other elements of the kit include a floor plate, reinforced leaf springs, an uprated lift cylinder to tilt the cab, a protected battery box, a protected blower motor for the cabin air-conditioning unit, and a HMWWV-type lightweight ring-mount in the cab roof for up to a 12.7 mm machine gun.

At the 2004 Association of the US Army (AUSA) exhibition held in Washington, DC, the then Radian Inc displayed its latest 'gun truck' kit, which has been proposed as an ad hoc convoy-protection vehicle based on the FMTV. In addition to the ballistic-protection cab, this exploits a cargo-protection kit incorporating steel armour side and bottom plates, augmented along the sides and rear with a 'birdcage' of slatted armour to detonate shaped-charge warheads. Three pintle mounts with protective shields for 7.62 mm machine guns are added along each side of the truck, with another in the rear for an additional 12.7 mm machine gun. In troop-carrying mode, modified seating can be supplied, with passengers sitting back to back along the vehicle centreline.

Specifications

See tables on pages 662, 664 and 665

Status

In series production for US Armed Forces (see text). Export sales to Canada (2006, M1148 + LSAC - unconfirmed) and Jordan (2006, M1089A1 (10) and M1085A1 (45); 2007, M1085A1 (45); further order in 2008). Prior to 2003 around 300 FMTVs were exported to Greece (M1089, 10-20), New Zealand (M1089), Saudi Arabia (approximately 100 Patriot support vehicles), Taiwan (1996) and Thailand (1996, 20-60 cargo).

Contractor

BAE Systems Land & Armaments, Global Tactical Systems

Navistar Defense (International) range of military vehicles

Development

The now Navistar Defense can trace its history back to 1831 when Cyrus Hall McCormick invented a machine for reaping grain. In 1902, McCormick Harvesting merged with four other agriculture machinery manufacturers to form International Harvester. International Harvester became a leading manufacturer of agricultural and construction machinery, but following years of financial losses the company sold off many primary businesses and from 1986 (renamed Navistar International Corporation) focused on diesel truck and engine production. Navistar International Corporation is now America's largest manufacturer of medium- and heavy-duty diesel trucks.

The now Navistar Defense first undertook military business during World War One, when production was adapted to military vehicle manufacturing. When America entered World War Two, the company was again called upon to shift its focus to military vehicle production, for both America and its allies. In addition to supplying agricultural equipment, International - which had been producing trucks since 1907 - supplied allied forces with a wide range of commercially based trucks, and even turned production to its own versions of a the ubiquitous half-track and 'Deuce-and-a-half' (Jimmy) 2½-ton 6 × 6 truck.

Post-WW2 International avoided high-risk military business, however, in the wake of a period of wider commercial decline, International Military and Government LLC was born late-2003, its aim to boost Navistar's profit by securing a slice of the potentially lucrative military market that was developing around ongoing operations in Afghanistan and Iraq. Since receiving its first sizeable contracts in 2005 the now Navistar Defense had by early 2011 racked up approximately USD7.8 billion in sales covering an

Cargo variant Afghan Family Medium Tactical Vehicles (AFMTVs) of the Afghan Army (Carl Schulze) 1391218

International 5000 Series (now PayStar) heavy equipment transporter and four-axle Loadcraft semi-trailer of the Iraqi Army (Navistar) 1391180

Canadian Army MSVS MilCOTS truck pre-deliver (Navistar) 1391177

Cargo variant of the 7000MV-based Afghan Family of Medium Tactical Vehicles (AFMTV) (Navistar) 1391178

In April 2009 the UK MoD placed an order for 262 Husky Tactical Support Vehicles (TSV), these based on a much-modified International MXT chassis, this based on a DuraStar/4000 Series medium duty truck platform (Shaun C Connors) 1391182

estimated 29,000 vehicles. International Military and Government LLC received its first sizeable military order early 2005, this from civilian contractor KBR, Inc. (previously Kellog Brown and Root) and calling for up to 2,000 5000MV heavy line haul tractor units (with armoured cabs) for use in Iraq; 578 vehicles were delivered under this contract.

Further orders followed, and in March 2005 International was awarded a contract valued at up to USD467 million by the US Army's Tank Automotive and Armaments Command (TACOM) for 2,781 7000MV (6 × 6) Afghan Family of Medium Tactical Vehicles (AFMTVs) in cargo, tanker (fuel and water), and recovery variants. In total, 2,916 vehicles were delivered under this contract, 1,963 to Afghanistan, 910 to Iraq and 43 to Yemen.

A follow-on USD1.28 billion AFMTV contract was awarded to Navistar Defense in May 2008, this calling for up to 7,072 additional vehicles. A further 505 trucks were ordered late-2009 (bringing contract totals to 7,577), with final deliveries due by December 2010. A further order was placed in May 2010, this valued at USD191 and calling for an additional 629 vehicles (bringing contract totals to 8,206), deliveries of which commenced in October 2010. As part of a selection of delivery orders announced in September 2010 a further 248 vehicles were ordered under the May 2008 award, this bringing current totals under that award to 8,452. Deliveries under this latest award are due to commence in December 2010.

International Military and Government LLC (now Navistar Defense LLC) received its first sizeable military order early 2005, this from civilian contractor KBR, Inc. and calling for up to 2,000 5000MV heavy line haul tractor units with armoured cabs (Navistar) 1391179

Other assorted TACOM orders for the Iraqi/Afghan reconstruction efforts have called for somewhere in the region of 1,400 vehicles, including an order to Navistar's school bus subsidiary valued at USD31.6 million for 289 buses. One order called for 40 International 5000 Series (now PayStar) heavy equipment transporters complete with four-axle semi-trailers provided by Loadcraft for the Iraqi Ministry of Defense. These tractor units leveraged Navistar's June 2008 announced strategic-alliance relationship with Caterpillar, being powered by a Caterpillar diesel engine.

Navistar received its first order that will see trucks supplied directly for use by US forces in October 2010. This award, valued at USD18.9 million, was placed by the Naval Facilities Engineering Command (NAVFAC) and calls for 38 International 5000MV Heavy Truck Tractors (HTTs) that will support Navy Seabee transportation needs. Production of these vehicles will commence early 2012. Spare parts and training services are included in the contract which includes three option periods for additional vehicle orders.

International's first direct sale military export success was a USD250 million five-year contract awarded in April 2005 to a local partner San Yang International Company Ltd in Taiwan for up to 5,000 7000 Series (now WorkStar) 2,500 kg (4 × 4) trucks. Delivery of the 4,791 trucks ordered was completed by the end of 2008, with an additional 59 trucks ordered during 2009. In February 2008 International Military and Government LLC were combined to become Navistar Defense LLC.

Navistar Defense secured a further sizeable export when Canada's Medium Support Vehicle System MSVS requirement reached a semi-conclusion with a USD231 million award for 1,300 MILitarised Commercial Off-The-Shelf (MilCOTS) trucks based on the WorkStar platform. Under the terms of the contract disclosed in January 2009, Navistar will deliver a total of 1,300 trucks in six primary variants and these will be serviced and maintained by Navistar's 93 Canadian dealerships. Deliveries are currently underway, with over 1,000 trucks delivered by October 2010.

For Canada's MSVS Standard Military Pattern (SMP) segment, which should be announced during 2011, Navistar will exercise the option to leverage its October 2009 announced strategic alliance with Czech tactical truck maker TATRA.

Navistar's most recent military truck export order was placed by Israel, which ordered 114 WorkStar-based medium tactical vehicles in January 2010. Navistar has previously supplied Israel's Armed Forces with just under 200 non-tactical trucks.

Navistar also produces armoured vehicles, and as these are based on an in-production truck chassis, outline details of these vehicles can be found elsewhere in this entry.

International MaxxPro Dash DXM fitted with fully independent coil spring suspension (Navistar) 1391181

Navistar unveiled the high-mobility Medium Tactical Vehicle (MTV) at the Modern Day Marine Exposition in September 2010 (Navistar) 1390123

Medium Tactical Vehicle (MTV)

Navistar unveiled the high-mobility Medium Tactical Vehicle (MTV) at the Modern Day Marine Exposition in September 2010. Based on the International 7000MV platform, the most significant difference between the 7000MV and the MTV is the DXM independent suspension of the latter, this replacing the conventional beam axle and leaf spring set up of the 7000MV.

Description

Navistar's military truck offerings are all based on militarised versions of the company's commercial truck platforms, these branded International to both commercial and military customers.

The current International commercial product line-up consists of the CityStar and DuraStar medium duty, PayStar and WorkStar severe duty, and TranStar, ProStar, LoneStar and 9000 Series heavy-duty ranges. The CityStar is the lightest weight-range truck and is the only Cab-Vver-Engine (COE) product in the Navistar range. The TranStar, ProStar, LoneStar and 9000 Series are all tractor truck ranges.

With the exception of some heavy tractor trucks, the vast majority of Navistar's military offerings are based on the WorkStar range, with certain models based on a lighter weight DuraStar/4000 Series chassis.

All International trucks are entirely conventional in design and are based on a ladder-frame C-section chassis. Throughout the various product ranges a wide variety of axle configurations, overall dimensions and GVWs are available.

Most models are offered with one of a selection of Navistar's MaxxForce range of diesel engines, power outputs for these ranging from 220 to 300 hp for the smallest 6.4-litre V8 MaxxForce 7, to 410 to 475 hp for the largest 12.4-litre six-cylinder MaxxForce 13. Certain models are available with Caterpillar or Cummins engine options, and for certain applications earlier generation engines remain available.

Gearboxes, axles, suspension and other driveline aggregates are all sourced from a variety of third party suppliers including; Allison, Dana Spicer, Fuller and Meritor.

Cab armouring solutions are available, and in addition to the KBR requirement which featured armoured cabs, a small number of trucks fitted with armoured cabs have been supplied to a Central American country. Navistar also offers purpose-designed armoured vehicles built on its commercial product range chassis; outline details of these vehicles follows.

Navistar (International) armoured vehicles

Possibly the best known of Navistar's armoured vehicle offerings would the MaxxPro Mine Resistant Ambush Protected (MRAP) family.

In 2006 the US Department of Defense (DoD) embarked on the MRAP vehicle programme as a reaction to the increasing numbers of IED (improvised explosive device) attacks in Iraq. Navistar are the current leader in the US MRAP program supply stakes, having received orders for 8,014 vehicles in total, orders split 2,975 MaxxPro, 2,247 of the heavier and even better protected MaxxPro Plus, 2,447 of the lighter and more agile MaxxPro Dash, and 250 wrecker variants ordered in November 2010. The overall total increases to 8,109 of 95 FMS MaxxPro dash are included. All MaxxPro Dash will be fitted with Navistar's DXM independent suspension, either during production (most recent orders) or in-theatre (previous orders).

Model	7000MV (AFMTV) cargo	7000MV (AFMTV) water/POL tanker	7000MV (AFMTV) wrecker	5000MV tractor unit (KBR)	MaxxPro Dash DXM MRAP	Husky TSV
Seating:	n/avail	n/avail	n/avail	sleeper configuration	2-man crew plus 4 to 6	2-man crew plus 2
Configuration:	6 × 6	6 × 6	6 × 6	6 × 4	4 × 4	4 × 4
Weight:						
(laden)	24,489 kg	24,489 kg	24,843 kg	31,745 kg (GVWR)	22,221 kg	n/avail
(kerb)	11,120 kg	12,753 kg	17,732 kg	13,812 kg	16,906 kg	n/avail
(payload)					>4,535 kg	n/avail
(front axle - rating)	6,349 kg (14,000 lbs)	6,349 kg (14,000 lbs)	7,256 kg (16,000 lbs)	8,183 kg (18,000 lbs)	n/avail	n/avail
(rear axle(s) - rating)	18,140 kg (40,000 lbs)	18,140 kg (40,000 lbs)	18,140 kg (40,000 lbs)	23,582 kg (52,000 lbs)	n/avail	n/avail
Length:	9.6 m	9.6 m	9.65 m	8.79 m	6.44 m	6.12 m
Width:	2.59 m	2.59 m	2.59 m	2.64 m	2.60 m	2.44 m
Height:	3.15 m	3.15 m	3.05 m	3.54 m	2.92 m	2.59 m
Ground clearance:	n/avail	n/avail	n/avail	n/avail	368 mm	n/avail
Wheelbase:	5.45 m	5.45 m	6.55 m	2.58 m	3.7 m	383.5-12.6ft
Angle of approach/departure:	n/avail	n/avail	n/avail	n/avail	58°/46-48°	n/avail
Fuel capacity:	265 litres	265 litres	265 litres	2 × 379 litres	n/avail	n/avail
Max gradient:	60%	60%	60%	n/avail	60%	n/avail
Max sideslope:	30%	30%	30%	n/avail	30%	n/avail
Fording:	762 mm	762 mm	762 mm	762 mm	1 m (unprepared)	n/avail
Engine:	MaxxForce DT530 8.7-litre 6-cylinder in-line turbocharged water-cooled 4-stroke diesel developing 285 hp (209 kW) and 1,083 N.m torque			Caterpillar C-13 12.5-litre 6-cylinder in-line turbocharged and water-cooled 4-stroke diesel developing 445 hp (327 kW) and 2,235 N.m torque	MaxxForce EPA 1998 D9.316 9.3-litre 6-cylinder in-line turbocharged and water-cooled 4-stroke diesel developing 355 hp (261 kW) at 2,200 rpm and 1,612 N.m torque at 1,250 rpm	MaxxForce D6 6-litre V-8 turbocharged water-cooled 4-stroke diesel developing 340 hp (250 kW)
Gearbox:	Fuller manual with 6 forward and 1 reverse gears			Fuller manual with 18 forward gears	Allison 3200 fully automatic with 5 forward and 1 reverse gears	Allison 2500SP fully automatic with 5 forward and 1 reverse gears
Transfer box:		Meritor 2-speed		n/app	2-speed	2-speed
Steering:	Sheppard	Sheppard	Sheppard	Sheppard	Sheppard	power
Tyres:	Goodyear 12R 22.5	Goodyear 12R 22.5	Goodyear 12R 22.5	Goodyear 315/80R 22.5	Michelin 1600R 20 XZL	Michelin 395/85R 20 with runflat inserts
Suspension:	leaf springs front and rear, inverted at rear				fully independent coil springs front and rear	adjustable height independent air suspension
Brakes:	air (ABS)	air (ABS)	air (ABS)	air (ABS)	air (ABS)	air (ABS)
Electrical system:	12/24 V	12/24 V	12/24 V	12/24 V	12/24 V	12/24 V
Batteries:	n/avail	n/avail	n/avail	n/avail	4 × 12 V	n/avail
Alternator:	n/avail	n/avail	n/avail	n/avail	570 A	n/avail

Highlighting the capability of the organisation, MaxxPro production peaked at around 500 units per month during 2008/2009. All MaxxPro models are based on modified WorkStar chassis.

In April 2009 the UK MoD placed an order for 262 Husky Tactical Support Vehicles (TSV), these based on a much-modified International MXT chassis, this based on a DuraStar/4000 Series medium duty truck platform. In September 2010 Navistar announced that it had received a second delivery order valued at USD56 million from the UK MoD for an additional 89 Husky TSV utility variants. Deliveries commenced at the end of October 2010, to conclude early 2011.

Navistar (teamed with BAE Systems) remains one of three competitors vying for the US Army's Joint Light Tactical Vehicle (JLTV) production contract, the JLTV the intended replacement for the AM General HMMWV, with at least 60,000 JLTVs valued at USD40 billion potentially required.

Specifications
See table on page 669

Status
In production. In service with Afghanistan, Canada, Iraq, Israel, Taiwan, Yemen and other undisclosed countries. Armoured vehicles based on International truck chassis are in service with Singapore, the UK, US and at least five FMS-supplied users.

Contractor
Navistar Defense LLC

Navistar/TATRA heavy truck joint venture

Development
Navistar and TATRA announced a joint venture/strategic partnership in October 2009, the aim of which was to develop a new range of heavy trucks that combined the relevant engineering, technology, through life support and marketing/commercial strengths of the two companies.

The first two vehicles developed as part of this alliance were announced at Eurosatory 2010, the ATX6 and ATX8.

Full details of Navistar and TATRA and these companies' respective ranges of vehicles (including the T 815-7 range on which the ATX6 and ATX8 are based) can be found elsewhere in this section.

Status
Ready for production.

Contractor
Navistar Defense LLC
TATRA AS

Navistar and TATRA announced a joint venture/strategic partnership in October 2009 and the first two vehicles developed as part of this alliance were announced at Eurosatory 2010, the ATX6 (shown) and ATX8 (Navistar/TATRA) 1391382

M35/M44A2 (6 × 6) 2½ ton cargo truck series

Development
In the late 1940s, Reo and the Truck and Bus Division of General Motors Corporation, each developed a new 2½ ton (6 × 6) truck for the US Army to replace wartime vehicles. Reo was awarded the initial production contract for 5,000 vehicles and delivered the first vehicle in 1950. Originally it was to have been only an interim solution pending large-scale production of the General Motors design, but as soon as the Korean War broke out it was apparent that Reo alone could not meet the requirements of the Army so the General Motors models were placed in immediate production. They were the M135 with single rear wheels and the M211 with dual rear wheels,

M35/M44A2 (6 × 6) 2½ ton cargo truck series M49 fuel tanker variant of the Portuguese Army (Victor Barreira) 1391242

M35A2 2½ ton (6 × 6) cargo/personnel truck of the Thai Navy (Gordon Arthur) 1391195

but they were phased out of production after the end of the Korean War in favour of the Reo design which was also built by Studebaker and was commonly known as the Eager Beaver.

The first vehicles were powered by a Reo (Model OA-331) or Continental (COA-331) petrol engine which developed 146 hp at 3,400 rpm, but later models with the suffix A1 (for example M35A1) were powered by a Continental LDS 427-2 multifuel engine. Later models (for example M35A2) have the LD 465-1 multifuel engine which develops 140 hp (gross) at 2,600 rpm; this engine was manufactured by the Hercules Engine Company.

In 1964, the Kaiser Jeep Corporation bought the Studebaker facilities in South Bend, Indiana and was awarded contracts to build both 2½ ton (6 × 6) and 5 ton (6 × 6) trucks for the US Army.

In 1967, Kaiser Jeep formed the Defense and Government Products Division to handle its government contracts, but in 1970 Kaiser Jeep was acquired by American Motors and the Defense and Government Products Division was named the General Products Division of the Jeep Corporation. In 1971 it was renamed the AM General Corporation (now AM General LLC), then a wholly-owned subsidiary of American Motors Corporation.

By early 1980, AM General had produced over 150,000 M35/M44 series 6 × 6 trucks. A product-improved prototype, designated the M963 series, was developed by the company under contract to the US Army but it did not enter production.

The M963 series was powered by a Caterpillar Model 3208 V-8 diesel developing 210 hp coupled to an Allison MT643 four-speed automatic transmission. New axles gave the vehicle a wider track and larger tyres improved soft soil mobility, allowing single instead of the usual dual rear wheels to be fitted. Other improvements included redesigned suspension, brakes and steering, a forward-tilting bonnet for easier maintenance and a wider cab for three people with a spring-mounted seat for the driver.

In September 1988, it was announced that AM General would discontinue medium and heavy truck production to concentrate on production of the HMMWV series, the final AM General deliveries of M44A2s being the 399 ordered for delivery by October 1988. The South Bend plant closed in late 1989.

In October 1990, it was announced that the Southeastern Equipment Company Inc of Augusta, Georgia, had been awarded a USD10,908,791 contract to rebuild 285 M35A2C trucks.

The US Army's 2½ ton Extended Service Programme (ESP) was designed to provide M35/M44A2 vehicles that reduced operational and service costs, while offering enhanced performance and improved user safety. The programme concluded in April 1999 after 1,845 vehicles had been fielded because of withdrawal of program funding. Under the ESP program, existing M35/M44A2 cargo trucks were completely disassembled and reusable parts were reworked as required. New trucks were then reassembled to better-than-new configuration on a production line using a combination of the reworked parts and a significant number of new parts and components. New components in ESP vehicles include a Caterpillar 3116 diesel engine (meeting 1993 EPA emission standards), an Allison 1545 automatic transmission, a new cooling system, reworked axles and transfer box, a new electronically controlled Central Tyre Inflation (CTI) system, single radial-ply tyres, air assisted steering, an improved independent circuit air/hydraulic brake system, three-point seat belts, a new ergonomically designed driver's seat, electric windscreen wipers and washer, and an improved heater and defroster system. ESP vehicles carry the designation M35A3.

The US Army currently plans to have withdrawn all remaining M35 variants in service by the end of FY11.

Description

In the 1950s there were two basic models in this series: the M34 with single rear wheels and the M35 with dual rear wheels. The former still remains in service, especially in Central/South America.

The layout of the basic cargo model is conventional, with the engine at the front; two-door cab in the centre with a windscreen that can be folded forward on to the bonnet and a removable canvas top; and the cargo area at the rear with a drop tailgate, removable bows, tarpaulin cover and troop seats down either side.

A wide range of kits was available including A-frame, alcohol evaporator, arctic, cargo body closure (arctic), central troop seats, electric brakes, fording, hardtop for cab, hoist and rail for installation in rear of vehicle for carrying out minor repair work, ring mount for machine gun

Model:	M35A2	M36A2	M49A2C	M50A3	M109A3	M342A2
Type:	cargo	cargo	fuel	water	Van	dump
Cab seating:	1 + 2	1 + 2	1 + 2	1 + 2	1 + 2	1 + 2
Configuration:	6 × 6	6 × 6	6 × 6	6 × 6	6 × 6	6 × 6
Weight:						
(unladen)	5,900 kg	6,900 kg	6,500 kg	6,644 kg	6,800 kg	6,800 kg
(laden, road)	10,400 kg	11,500 kg	10,100 kg	10,408 kg	10,200 kg	11,300 kg
Weight on front axle:						
(laden)	2,700 kg	3,200 kg	2,700 kg	2,880 kg	3,000 kg	3,100 kg
Weight on rear axle:						
(laden)	7,700 kg	8,300 kg	7,400 kg	7,528 kg	7,100 kg	8,300 kg
Max load:						
(road)	4,535 kg	4,535 kg	4,542 litres	3,785 litres	3,401 kg	4,535 kg
(cross-country)	2,268 kg	2,268 kg	2,271 litres	1,893 litres	2,268 kg	2,268 kg
Towed load:						
(road)	4,535 kg	4,535 kg	4,535 kg	4,535 kg	3,628 kg	4,535 kg
(off-road)	2,721 kg	2,721 kg	2,721 kg	2,721 kg	2,721 kg	2,721 kg
Load area:	3.7 × 2.2 m	5.3 × 2.2 m	n/avail	n/avail	n/avail	3.3 × 1.9 m
Length:						
(without winch)	6.7 m	8.4 m	6.7 m	6.7 m	6.8 m	6.6 m
Width:	2.4 m	2.4 m	2.4 m	2.4 m	2.4 m	2.4 m
Height:						
(reduced)	2.1 m	2.1 m	2.3 m	2.4 m	3.3 m	2.1 m
(overall)	2.9 m	3.2 m	2.6 m	2.6 m	3.3 m	2.7 m
(load area)	1.32 m	1.4 m	n/avail	n/avail	1.3 m	1.3 m
Ground clearance:						
(axles)	280 mm	208 mm	280 mm	280 mm	280 mm	280 mm
Track:						
(front/rear)	1.721/1.778 m	1.721/1.778 m	1.721/1.778 m	1.721/1.778 m	1.721/1.778 m	1.721/1.778 m
Wheelbase:	3.912 m	4.826 m	3.912 m	3.912 m	3.912 m	3.912 m
Angle of approach/departure:	47°/40°	47°/24°	47°/40°	47°/40°	47°/40°	47°/70°
Max speed:						
(road)	90 km/h	90 km/h	90 km/h	90 km/h	90 km/h	90 km/h
Range:	480 km	480 km	480 km	480 km	480 km	480 km
Fuel capacity:	189 litres	189 litres	189 litres	189 litres	189 litres	189 litres
Max gradient:	60%	60%	60%	60%	60%	60%
Fording:						
(without preparation)	760 mm	760 mm	760 mm	760 mm	760 mm	760 mm
(with preparation)	1.98 m	1.98 m	1.98 m	1.98 m	1.52 m	1.83 m
Engine:	LDT-465-1C 6 cylinder in-line water-cooled multifuel diesel developing 140 hp (103 kW) at 2,600 rpm					
Gearbox:	manual with 5 forward and 1 reverse gears					
Clutch:	single dry plate					
Transfer box:	2-speed	2-speed	2-speed	2-speed	2-speed	2-speed
Steering:	cam and twin lever type					
Turning radius:	11 m	13.7 m	11 m	11 m	11 m	11 m
Suspension:						
(front/rear)	semi-elliptic leaf springs/semi-elliptic leaf springs, inverted					
Tyres:	9.00 × 20	9.00 × 20	9.00 × 20	9.00 × 20	9.00 × 20	9.00 × 20
Brakes:						
(main)	air over hydraulic	air over hydraulic	air over hydraulic	air over hydraulic	air over hydraulic	air over hydraulic
(parking)	internal/external	internal/external	internal/external	internal/external	internal/external	internal/external
Electrical system:	24 V	24 V	24 V	24 V	24 V	24 V
Batteries:	2	2	2	2	2	2

USAF M35A2 2½ ton (6 × 6) cargo/personnel truck (Shaun C Connors)
0109513

over cab, hot water personnel heater, fuel-burning personnel heater, power plant heater, slave cable and a thermal barrier. Many vehicles are fitted with a 4,536 kg capacity winch that can be used to the front or rear of the vehicle and has 61 m of 13 mm diameter cable with two speeds forward and one speed in reverse.

Variants

Models with single rear wheels
M34: cargo truck with an empty weight of 5,332 kg, chassis designated M44
M47: dump truck with an empty weight of 6,100 kg, chassis designated M57
Truck, maintenance: earth-boring machine and pole setter V18A/MTQ, chassis M44
Truck, maintenance: telephone construction and maintenance V17A/MTQ, chassis M44.

Models with dual rear wheels
M35: this is the basic member of the series and is based on the M45 chassis; the final production model was designated the M35A2. The M35A2C (chassis M46A2C) is almost identical but has drop sides. Both drop sides and tailgate of this model are interchangeable with those of the M54A2C (5 ton) truck
M36: this cargo truck is the long wheelbase version of the M35 and its chassis is designated the M36. Final production model was the M36A2
M48: tractor truck for towing semi-trailers, chassis designation M45
M49: fuel tanker, final model the M49A2C (chassis M45A2), has an all-steel tank which holds 4,542 litres of fuel for road travel or 2,271 litres of fuel for cross-country travel. Fuel can be dispensed by gravity or pumped under pressure at a maximum rate of 303 litres/min and the pump can also be used to refill the tank. The tanker can be fitted with bows and a tarpaulin cover to make detection more difficult
M50: water tanker, final model the M50A3, has an aluminium tank which holds 3,785 litres of water for road travel or 1,893 litres of water for cross-country travel. Water can be dispensed by gravity or pumped under pressure at a maximum rate of 303 litres/min and the pump can also be used to refill the tank. The tanker can be fitted with bows and a tarpaulin cover to make detection more difficult
M59: dump truck, chassis designation M58
M60: light wrecker, full details of which can be found in the Recovery vehicles section
M108: wrecker, full details of which can be found in the Recovery vehicles section

M35A2 2½ ton (6 × 6) cargo/personnel truck of the Philippine Marines (Gordon Arthur)
1340346

M109A3 shop van variant of the M35 series of the US Army's SFOR contingent in the former Yugoslavia (Ian Young)
1124736

M35A3 ESP (Extended Service Program)/ 2½ ton (6 × 6) cargo truck of US armed forces in former Yugoslavia towing an M105 series 1½ ton trailer (Michael Jerchel)
1047656

M109: shop van, chassis designated M45, final production model the M109A3, has a fully enclosed rear body and is used for a variety of roles such as workshop and maintenance
M132: medical van
M185: repair van, M45 chassis; late models were M185A3
M275: tractor truck for towing semi-trailers weighing up to 16,329 kg on-road and up to 7,712 kg off-road. Late production model was M275A2
M292: shop van with extensible sides
M342: dump truck, final production model was the M342A2 (chassis M45A2G) which can carry 1.9 m³ of soil
M756A2: pipeline maintenance truck (chassis M45A2), fitted with rear winch, PTO and rear- or side-mounted A-frame, removable cargo rack and sides
M763: telephone maintenance truck
M764: truck, maintenance, earth-boring machine and pole setter, equipped with rear winch, PTO, boring machine. Pole setting is accomplished using derrick tube of boring machine and rear winch.

Bombardier Medium Logistic Vehicle Wheeled (MLVW) M35 CDN
In 1981 Bombardier Inc of Canada was awarded a contract to supply 2,765 license-produced AM General M35 series 2½ ton trucks to replace the Canadian armed forces ageing 2½ ton truck fleet. As the Medium Logistic Vehicle Wheeled (MLVW), deliveries commenced in 1982. The MLVW is also known as the M35 CDN. A total of 2,769 vehicles were delivered.

When the MLVW entered service its projected service life was 15 years. These vehicles are currently being replaced. Full details of the MLVW can be found elsewhere in this section.

Specifications
See table on page 671

Status
Production complete. In service with the armed forces of the US (numbers reducing; withdrawal scheduled for completion by the end of FY11) and numerous other countries including Afghanistan (US surplus), Argentina, Bolivia, Brazil, Canada (2,769 delivered circa 1982 as the MLVW), Chad, Chile (majority replaced), Ecuador (US surplus), El Salvador, Greece, Guatemala, Haiti, Honduras, Israel, Djibouti, Jordan, South Korea, Lebanon, Liberia, Morocco (some US surplus), Pakistan, Panama, Peru, Philippines, Saudi Arabia, Senegal, Somalia, Spain (over 2,000 of which were re-engined), Sudan, Taiwan, Thailand, Turkey, Venezuela (some being refurbished) and the then named Zaïre (now known as the Democratic Republic of Congo). An undisclosed number were supplied to the People's Republic of China.

Contractor
AM General LLC

M809 (6 × 6) 5 ton Cargo Truck Series

Development
The M809 series of (6 × 6) 5 ton cargo trucks is similar to the older M54 series but was fitted with a diesel engine in place of the multifuel engine by the then AM General Corporation (now AM General LLC) under a product engineering development and test programme.

AM General Corporation started production of the M809 series in 1970 and by the middle of 1980 had completed some 38,000 vehicles. Further development of the M809 series by AM General, under an engineering contract with the US Army, resulted in the much improved M939 series of which production commenced in 1982. Full details of the M939 series can be found elsewhere in this section.

In September 1988, it was announced that AM General would be withdrawing from the production of medium and heavy vehicles and their South Bend plant closed in late 1989.

US Army figures released late-2007 state that 6,405 M809 series trucks remained in service at that time, and that none had been deployed on OEF/OIF.

The US Army's current plans are that all remaining M809 series trucks will be divested by the end of FY15.

Description
The chassis of the M809 series consists of two rail-type beams with six reinforced cross-members. Both front and rear axles are of the hypoid, single-speed, double-reduction type. The vehicle layout is conventional, with the engine at the front; two-door cab in the centre with a windscreen which can be folded flat against the bonnet and a removable canvas top; and the cargo area at the rear. The basic cargo model has an all-steel rear cargo body with drop sides, removable bows, tarpaulin cover and troop seats down either side which enable 18 fully equipped troops to be carried.

There are three basic chassis in the series: the M809 (used for the M813, M813A1, M816 and M815), the M810 (used for the M817 and M818) and the M811/M812 (used for the M814, M819, M820 and M821). A variety of kits are available for the range including: A-frame, airbrake, closure hardtop, deep water fording, level wind device, slave receptacle, thermal barrier, water personnel heater, winterisation personnel heater kit and a winterisation power plant kit. All models except the M820 can be fitted with a winch at the front.

M809 series vehicles can be fitted with the Enhanced Mobility System (EMS) for increased mobility over sand, mud and snow.

Variants
M813 (Cargo Truck, 5 ton, 6 × 6)
This is the basic cargo model and can carry 4,535 kg of cargo off-road and 9,070 kg on road. The foldable seats enable 26 fully equipped troops to be carried.

M809 series truck of US Armed Forces in the former Yugoslavia; the vehicle immediately behind the M809 in the line up is a M939 series, the follow-on series (Michael Jerchel) 1047658

M809 series truck of US Armed Forces in the former Yugoslavia; armament is a 40 mm Automatic Grenade Launcher (AGL) (Michael Jerchel) 1047657

M809 series truck of US Armed Forces (Michael Jerchel) 1047659

M54 series (the predecessor of the M809 series) dump truck of the Maltese Army (Michael Jerchel) 1124735

M813A1 (Drop side, Cargo Truck, 5 ton, 6 × 6)
This is similar to the M813 but has drop sides as well as a drop tailgate.

M814 (Long Cargo Truck, 5 ton, 6 × 6)
This is the long wheelbase model and was available with removable bows and a tarpaulin cover.

M815 (Bolster Truck, 5 ton, 6 × 6)
This has the M809 chassis and can carry a maximum load of 4,536 kg off-road or 9,072 kg on-road. Towed load is identical to the M813 cargo truck.

M816 (Wrecker, Truck, 5 ton, 6 × 6)
Full details of this vehicle can be found in the Recovery vehicles section.

M817 (Dump Truck, 5 ton, 6 × 6)
This has an all-steel 3.8 m³ capacity rear dump body which can be fitted with bows and a tarpaulin cover.

M818 (Tractor, Truck, 5 ton, 6 × 6)
This has both a fifth wheel and a pintle tow hook and can tow semi-trailers weighing up to 17,025 kg off-road or 24,970 kg on-road.

M819 (Tractor, Wrecker, 5 ton, 6 × 6)
Full details of this vehicle can be found in the Recovery vehicles section.

M809 series M817 dump truck of US Armed Forces in the former Yugoslavia (Michael Jerchel) 1047660

M820 (Van, Expansible, Truck, 5 ton, 6 × 6)
This is provided with a fully enclosed body at the rear which is 2.1 m wide and 1.9 m high in its normal position. When static, the sides of the van are extended either side and the interior is then 4.2 m wide. Access to the body is via steps at the rear.

M821 (Bridge Transport, 5 ton, 6 × 6)
This is used to carry bridging components and is based on the M812 chassis.

Ribbon Bridge Carrier and Launching Vehicle
An M809 chassis is used to carry and launch the Ribbon Bridge system as well as carrying and launching a bridge erection boat.

Specifications See table below
(These specifications relate to a vehicle without a winch, with the exception of the M817 which is fitted with a winch as standard equipment.

All other vehicles, except M820, can be fitted with a front-mounted winch. When fitted with a front-mounted winch the vehicles have an angle of approach of 34°)

Status
Production complete. In service with the armed forces of the US; supplied to numerous other countries including Afghanistan (US surplus), Democratic Republic of the Congo (the then Zaire), El Salvador, Honduras, Iraq, Jamaica, Jordan, South Korea, Lebanon, Liberia, Pakistan, Panama, Philippines, Portugal, Saudi Arabia, Senegal, Somalia, Spain, Sudan, Taiwan, Thailand and Venezuela. An undisclosed number were supplied to the People's Republic of China.

Contractor
AM General LLC

Designation	M813	M813A1	M814	M817	M818	M820
Type:	cargo	cargo	cargo (LWB)	dump	tractor	van
Cab seating:	1 + 2	1 + 2	1 + 2	1 + 2	1 + 2	1 + 2
Configuration:	6 × 6	6 × 6	6 × 6	6 × 6	6 × 6	6 × 6
Weight:						
(unladen)	9,733 kg	10,043 kg	11,297 kg	10,776 kg	9,202 kg	12,474 kg
(laden, road)	18,985 kg	18,993 kg	20,549 kg	20,028 kg	20,349 kg	29,459 kg
(front axle, laden)	5,015 kg	5,016 kg	5,326 kg	4,981 kg	4,950 kg	4,936 kg
(rear axles, laden)	13,969 kg	13,976 kg	15,223 kg	15,047 kg	15,399 kg	14,523 kg
(max load, on-road)	9,070 kg	9,070 kg	9,070 kg	9,070 kg	n/a	6,803 kg
(max load, off-road)	4,535 kg	4,535 kg	4,535 kg	4,535 kg	n/a	2,268 kg
(towed load, on-road)	13,620 kg	13,620 kg	13,620 kg	13,620 kg	24,943 kg	13,620 kg
(towed load, off-road)	6,802 kg	6,802 kg	6,802 kg	6,802 kg	17,007 kg	6,802 kg
Load area:	4.3 × 2.2 m	4.3 × 2.2 m	6.2 × 2.2 m	3.2 × 2.1 m	n/a	5.2 × 2.1 m
Length:	7.652 m	7.652 m	9.609 m	6.86 m	6.71 m	9.144 m
Width:	2.464 m	2.464 m	2.464 m	2.464 m	2.464 m	2.483 m
Height:						
(overall)	2.946 m	2.946 m	2.946 m	2.946 m	2.946 m	3.467 m
(reduced)	2.172 m	2.172 m	2.172 m	2.832 m	2.172 m	3.467 m
(load area)	1.4 m	1.4 m	1.4 m	n/avail	n/avail	n/avail
Ground clearance: (axles)	295 mm	295 mm	295 mm	295 mm	295 mm	295 mm
Track : (front/rear)	1.88/1.829 m	1.88/1.829 m	1.88/1.829 m	1.9/1.829 m	1.9/1.829 m	1.9/1.829 m
Wheelbase:	3.86 m + 1.371 m	3.86 m + 1.371 m	4.775 m + 1.371 m	3.55 m + 1.371 m	3.55 m + 1.371 m	4.775 m + 1.371 m
Angle of approach/departure:	46°/35°	46°/35°	46°/23.5°	34°/69°	45°/69°	46°/24°
Max speed: (road)	84 km/h	84 km/h	84 km/h	84 km/h	84 km/h	84 km/h
Range:	563 km	563 km	563 km	772 km	563 km	563 km
Fuel capacity:	295 litres	295 litres	295 litres	295 litres	295 litres	295 litres
Max gradient:						
(without towed load)	67%	67%	61%	61%	60%	65%
(with towed load)	42%	42%	38%	31%	42%	41%
Max side slope: (off-road	20%	20%	20%	20%	20%	20%
Fording:						
(without preparation)	760 mm	760 mm	760 mm	760 mm	760 mm	760 mm
(with preparation)	1.98 m	1.98 m	1.98 m	1.98 m	1.98 m	1.98 m
Engine:	Cummins NHC-250 14-litre 6-cylinder in-line water-cooled 4-stroke diesel developing 240 hp (179 kW) at 2,100 rpm					
Gearbox:	manual with 5 forward and 1 reverse gears					
Clutch:	single dry plate	single dry plate	single dry plate	single dry plate	single dry plate	single dry plate
Transfer box:	2-speed	2-speed	2-speed	2-speed	2-speed	2-speed
Steering:	power-assisted	power-assisted	power-assisted	power-assisted	power-assisted	power-assisted
Turning radius:	12.75 m	12.75 m	14.3 m	12.75 m	12.75 m	14.53 m
Suspension: (front/rear)	semi-elliptic leaf springs/semi-elliptic leaf springs, inverted					
Tyres:	11.00 × 20	11.00 × 20	11.00 × 20	11.00 × 20	11.00 × 20	11.00 × 20
Brakes:	main, air over hydraulic; parking, dual grip on transfer case					
Electrical system:	24 V	24 V	24 V	24 V	24 V	24 V
Batteries:	4	4	4	4	4	4

M915 series of trucks

Development

One of the recommendations of the 'WHEELS' study was that the US Army should use commercial trucks wherever practicable. In January 1977, the US Army's then Automotive Material Readiness Command (TARCOM) issued a request for technical proposals for a series of heavy trucks ranging from 22,680 to 34,019 kg Gross Vehicle Weight (GVW). The army subsequently received technical proposals from six truck manufacturers: AM General Corporation, Four Wheel Drive (FWD) Corporation, General Motors Truck and Coach, International Harvester Corporation, Kenworth Truck Corporation and White Autocar Corporation.

The six manufacturers that responded to the original request qualified to offer priced bids under the second step of the procurement. Bids were opened in June 1977, with AM General Corporation the lowest at USD252.8 million for the requirement of 5,507 trucks. In June 1977, a contract was awarded to AM General for 5,507 trucks and in addition the government had the right to exercise options on an additional 5,507 trucks, giving a potential of 11,014 units. The contract was for four years with the first test vehicles (M915 Line Haul Tractor) delivered early 1978.

The US government did not exercise its option on the additional 5,507 trucks, but in September 1981, awarded AM General a contract for 2,511 M915A1 (6 × 4) tractor trucks, which was later completed.

The contract also required complete after-market support of the M915 including spare-part provisions and a full complement of maintenance and service publications, as well as the training of army instructors. The army received warranty covering defects in design, materials and workmanship for a period of 15 months or for 19,312 km. In addition, the army received 'free time' up to six months, for new vehicles stored in depots.

The AM General M915 Series was based on the Centaur series of trucks built by the Crane Carrier Company of Tulsa, Oklahoma and consisted of the M915/M915A1, M916, M917, M918, M919 and M920. A licence agreement between AM General and Crane Carrier gave AM General the rights to manufacture and sell vehicles to the US government. Later production versions of the M915 Series were the M915A2, M916A1/A2 and the M917A1, followed by the M915A3, M916A3 and M917A2 dump truck models; these versions being produced by Freightliner LLC, previously the Freightliner Corporation. A total of 1,857 M915 Series vehicles were produced under a contract awarded to Freightliner in September 1988, a five-year programme for 583 vehicles (with options) followed in December 1995, and in September 2000 a seven year contract (DAAE07-00-D-S022) valued at just under USD400 million was awarded for the supply approximately 3,400 vehicles, plus training, logistics support and interactive electronic technical manuals. Production began in 2001 of M915A3 and M916A3 Line Haul Tractors and M917A2 dump trucks, with the M915A5 entering production in 2010. This contract was subject to three one-year extensions, these running 8 September 2007 to 7 September 2008, 8 September 2008 to 7 September 2009 and 8 September 2009 to 7 September 2010. It is understood that a single-source two-year follow-on contract is to be awarded early 2011. By late 2010 just over 10,000 M915 series trucks had been ordered under contract DAEE07-00-D-S022.

It is understood that the proposed M915 series rebuy is currently on indefinite hold.

Freightliner LLC markets the M915 Series worldwide as the Freightliner Military Truck Range and examples have been sold to the Philippines. The Philippine order consisted of four M916A1 tractor trucks, four M917A1 dump trucks and 10 M916-based wreckers. Full details of the wrecker variant can be found in the Recovery vehicles section.

Rigid chassis variants of the M915A3 in flatbed and septic tank variants have also been produced for the US military.

Freightliner proposed to the US Army a Load Handling System (LHS), consisting of a truck and trailer combination in 2005. The truck is a 6 × 4 with a pusher lift axle.

Several armouring companies have developed a small arms fire, mine blast and Improvised Explosive Device (IED) protection kits for the M915 family of trucks. Over 3,000 kits are reported to have been supplied to US armed forces, primarily for operations in Iraq. Vehicles fitted with this protection kit require a front axle/suspension upgrade. Israel's Plasan Sasa is one company that has developed a protection kit for the M915A2, A3 and A4 series of trucks and at least 1,300 kits have been supplied to US Armed Forces. Kits have also been supplied by Radian Inc (now DRS Technologies) and Armor Works. Radian supplied 305 kits for M915 and M915A1 variants under a USD7.1 million contract awarded in December 2004, while mid-2005 Armor Works received a USD18 million contract to supply 500 kits for M915 series trucks.

The M915A5, further details of which can be found elsewhere in this entry, features a new cab for which BAE Systems has developed and supplied a new protection package that meets the A-Kit/B-kit requirements of the US Army's Long Term Armor Strategy (LTAS).

Description

Throughout their production run the M915 Series has been based on commercial vehicles with the minimum of modifications to make them suitable for military use, such as forest green paint, rear-mounted pintle hooks, front and rear tow hooks and blackout lights. There were originally three basic chassis, (6 × 4) for road use and (6 × 6) and (8 × 6) for both road and cross-country use. Freightliner LLC has only produced (6 × 4) or (6 × 6) chassis.

AM General-produced M915 series tractor truck fitted with an appliqué protection kit (Carl Schulze)   1304070

AM General-produced M915 series tractor truck fitted with an appliqué protection kit (Carl Schulze)   1304073

The layout of all vehicles is similar, with the engine at the front, two-door fully enclosed cab in the centre and the fifth wheel or body at the rear. AM General produced vehicles had an all-steel cab, while Freightliner produced vehicles (with the exception of the M915A5) have cabs manufactured using aluminium and sheet-moulded compounds for enhanced corrosion resistance.

M915, (tractor, truck, 14-ton, (6 × 4))

This is powered by a Cummins Model NTC 400 six-cylinder diesel which develops 400 hp (gross) at 2,100 rpm, coupled to a Caterpillar semi-automatic gearbox with 16 forward and two reverse gears. The suspension consists of Rockwell Asymmetrical leaf pin and shackle, front, and Hendrickson RTE 380 walking beam, rear.

The M915 is used primarily for the long distance movement of containers and normally tows the 34-ton (US) M872 semi-trailer. It replaced the 5-ton military series tractors and certain commercial tractors used in moving cargo from the port of embarkation to the division rear boundary.

M915A1, (tractor, truck, 14-ton, (6 × 4))

In September 1981, AM General Corporation was awarded a contract by the US Army Tank Automotive Command for 2,511 M915A1 (6 × 4) tractor trucks. This contract was worth USD130 million with a 100 per cent option for an additional 2,511 units. Production began at the company's South Bend plant in January 1983 and continued for 18 months.

The M915A1 is similar to the earlier M915 except that it has an Allison HT 754 CR automatic transmission with five forward and one reverse gears.

Specifications

See tables on pages 676 and 677

M915A1, (tractor, truck, 14-ton, (6 × 4))
(similar to the M915 except for the following details)
Length: 6.489 m
Width: 2.438 m
Height: 2.984 m
Fording: 616 mm
Road speed: (max) 91.7 km/h
Speed on 3% gradient: 45 km/h
Gradient: (max) 18.4%
Fuel capacity: 446 litres

M915A2, (tractor, truck, 14-ton, (6 × 4))
The M915A2 was manufactured by Freightliner LLC (then the Freightliner Corporation) and is a (6 × 4) tractor truck powered by a Detroit Diesel DDE 12.7-litre diesel developing 400 hp at 2,100 rpm, coupled to an Allison HT-740 automatic transmission. Weight empty is 8,481 kg and the M915A2 is 7 m long, 2.49 m wide and 3.02 m high overall. Wheelbase is 4.12 m.

AM General-produced M915 series

Designation	M915	M916	M917	M920
Type:	tractor	tractor	dump truck	tractor
Cab seating:	1 + 2	1 + 2	1 + 2	1 + 2
Configuration:	6 × 4	6 × 6	8 × 6	8 × 6
Weight:				
(unladen)	8,446 kg	11,327 kg	14,768 kg	12,414 kg
(laden)	22,213 kg	29,629 kg	33,070 kg	30,716 kg
(weight on front axle, laden)	5,443 kg	6,543 kg	3,775 kg	3,864 kg
(weight on rear axles, laden)	17,236 kg	23,036 kg	33,070 kg	30,716 kg
(GCW)	47,627 kg	57,153 kg	n/a	61,235 kg
Length:	6.49 m	7.48 m	8.9 m	8.11 m
Width:	2.49 m	2.49 m	2.49 m	2.49 m
Height:				
(cab)	2.93 m	3.25 m	3.25 m	3.25 m
(overall)	3.61 m	3.61 m	3.61 m	3.61 m
Ground clearance:	254 mm	305 mm	305 mm	295 mm
Track: (front/rear)	1.99/1.82 m	1.98/1.85 m	1.98/1.85 m	1.98/1.85 m
Wheelbase: (excluding pusher axle)	4.24 + 1.32 m	4.72 + 1.42 m	4.876 + 1.42 m	4.876 + 1.46 m
Angle of approach:	38°	42°	41°	42°
Max speed:				
(road)	107 km/h	103 km/h	107 km/h	103 km/h
(3.9% gradient)	40.2 km/h	40.2 km/h	40.2 km/h	40.2 km/h
Fuel capacity:	416 litres	416 litres	416 litres	416 litres
Fording:	501 mm	730 mm	610 mm	610 mm
Steering:		Ross integral power system		
Turning radius:	8.15 m	12.2 m	13.65 m	13.65 m
Tyres:	10.0 × 20	11.0 × 24	11.0 × 24	11.0 × 24
Electrical system: (24 V optional)	12 V	12 V	12 V	12 V
Batteries:	4 × 12 V	4 × 12 V	4 × 12 V	4 × 12 V

The first M915A2 contract was awarded to Freightliner on 20 September 1988 and was for 385 units. With options, deliveries totalled 848 units, the first vehicles being delivered in May 1989 and the first production vehicles entering the US Army's inventory in November 1990. Further A2 models were involved in the five-year USD106 million contract awarded to Freightliner LLC in December 1995 for 583 various M915 series vehicles.

M915A3, (tractor truck, 14-ton (6 × 4))

This Freightliner (6 × 4) tractor truck is part of contract (DAAE07-00-D-S022) awarded to Freightliner LLC in September 2000 for approximately 3,400 M915 Series vehicles. The M915A3 is powered by a Series 60 Detroit Diesel DDEC IV 12.7-litre diesel that develops 430 hp at 2,100 rpm. Transmission is an Allison Generation IV 4500SP automatic giving six forward and one reverse gears. The front Arvin-Meritor FG941 axle is rated at 6,623 kg and sprung by taper leaf springs (rated at 6,350 kg). The twin rear Arvin-Meritor RT40-145 axle bogie is rated at 18,144 kg, fitted with Trac-Tech no-spin differentials for improved traction on slippery surfaces and is sprung by Freightliner TufTrac suspension. Michelin tyres are provided on all axles, with 12R 22.5 (16 ply) XZE on the front axle and 11R 22.5 (14 ply) XZE on the rear axles. Suspension seats for driver and passenger, an air conditioning system, anti-lock brakes (ABS) and an Eaton VORAD collision warning system are standard equipment.

Production of M915A3 tractor trucks began in 2001.

Freightliner-produced M915A3 tractor truck fitted with an add-on armour kit and coupled to an M872 semi-trailer (Carl Schulze) 1391217

M915A3 LHS/T (load handling system with trailer (6 × 4))

In 2005 Freightliner introduced to the US Army the M915A3 LHS/T, a Load Handling System (LHS) consisting of a (6 × 4) truck (with third lift axle) and a combination trailer. The M915A3 LHS/T is powered by a Series 60 Detroit Diesel DDEC IV 12.7-litre diesel that develops 430 hp at 2,100 rpm. Transmission is an Allison Generation IV 4500SP automatic, giving six forward and one reverse gears. The front Arvin-Meritor FL-941 axle is rated at 8,165 kg and sprung by taper leaf springs. The twin rear Arvin-Meritor RT46-164P axle bogie is rated at 20,866 kg, fitted with Trac-Tech no-spin differentials for improved traction on slippery surfaces and is sprung by Freightliner Airliner rear suspension. Michelin 315/80R 22.5 (20 ply) XZY-2 tyres are provided on all axles. Suspension seats for driver and passenger, an air conditioning system, anti-lock brakes (ABS) and an Eaton VORAD collision warning system are standard equipment. The load handling system is a Hiab Multilift Mk 4 (now designated MPH 165) system with a Hiab Multilift Stowable Container Handling Unit (CHU). The combination trailer is provided by Columbia Body Manufacturing of Clackamas, Oregon, US. The load, transfer, transport, and unload total payload capacity is 18,597 kg. The system is capable of handling ISO standard 20 ft containers, flatracks, and CROPs. Three Freightliner M915A3 LHS/T combination vehicles have been evaluated by the US Army.

M915A4

During 1997, the then US Army Tank-Automotive Command (TACOM) announced a requirement for 2,150 'Glider' modification kits to update existing M915 series trucks in service with the regular army, the US Army Reserve and the National Guard.

The kit involves the retention of the existing reconditioned engine but allied with an Allison automatic transmission, an Anti-lock Braking System (ABS), a virtually new cab with state-of-the-art equipment including an air conditioning system, plus numerous other updating measures ensuring the vehicle will be able to remain in service for some years to come. The cost of the upgrade, per truck, is approximately 50 per cent of the cost of acquiring a new vehicle.

The designation M915A4 has been applied to the updated vehicles. Both Freightliner and Mack Trucks offered packages to suit the requirement. This programme was due to conclude in 2003. In August 2004 it was announced the US Army's TACOM intended to acquire on a sole source basis 1,500 further M915 Glider Kits from Freightliner LLC. This acquisition is the final buyout of M915 FOV Glider Kits and modified the M915 Family of Vehicles Contract DAAE07-00-D-S022.

M915A5

In August 2009 the US Army's Tank-automotive and Armaments Command awarded Daimler Trucks North America LLC (DTNA) a contract for the production of 1,780 enhanced M915A5 line haul tractors. The

Freightliner-produced M915 family of vehicles series

Designation	M915A3	M916A3	M917A2	M915A3 LHS/T
Type:	tractor	tractor	dump truck	Load Handling System (LHS)
Cab seating:	1 + 1	1 + 1	1 + 1	1 + 1
Configuration:	6 × 4	6 × 6	6 × 6	6 × 4 (with third lift axle)
Weight:				
(kerb)	8,473 kg	12,202 kg	13,880 kg	33,385 kg
(GCW)	47,628 kg	58,968 kg	30,845 kg	55,611 kg
(on front axle, laden)	6,350 kg	8,392 kg	8,392 kg	8,165 kg
(on rear axle, laden)	18,144 kg	23,587 kg	23,587 kg	20,866 kg
(on lift axle, laden)	n/app	n/app	n/app	5,988 kg
Length:	7 m	7.37 m	7.65 m	10.22 m
Width:	2.49 m	2.59 m	2.59 m	2.49 m
Height:				
(cab)	2.79 m	2.98 m	n/avail	2.79 m
(overall)	3.02 m	3.25 m	3.15 m	n/avail
Ground clearance:	230 mm	230 mm	230 mm	230 mm
Track:				
(front)	2.029 m	2.05 m	2.05 m	n/avail
(rear)	1.843 m	1.84 m	1.84 m	n/avail
Wheelbase:	4.11 m	4.55 m	4.66 m	6.4 m
Angle of approach:	25.9°	37.4°	37.4/58.1°	n/avail
Max speed:				
(road)	104.6 km/h	107.8 km/h (limited to 80.5 km/h)	109.4 km/h (limited to 80.5 km/h)	n/avail
(3% gradient)	46.7 km/h	40.2 km/h	67.6 km/h	n/avail
(20% gradient)	8 km/h	6.4 km/h	8 km/h	n/avail
Cruising range:	800 km	(at 48.2 km/h and 59,020 kg GCW) 772 km	(at 48.2 km/h and 30,845 kg GVW) 885 km	n/avail
Fuel capacity:	379 litres	379 litres	379 litres	n/avail
Fording:	510 mm	510 mm	510 mm	n/avail
Engine:	Detroit Diesel Series 60 DDEC IV 6-cylinder water-cooled 4-stroke diesel developing 430 hp (316 kW) and 1,966 N.m torque			
Transmission:	Allison Generation IV 4500SP automatic with 6 forward and 1 reverse gears	Allison Generation IV 4700SP automatic with 7 forward and 1 reverse gears	Allison Generation IV 4700SP automatic with 7 forward and 1 reverse gears	Allison Generation IV 4700SP automatic with 7 forward and 1 reverse gears
Transfer box:	n/avail	Meritor T-2119 single speed	Meritor T-2119 single speed	Meritor T-2119 single speed
Steering:	Ross power assisted	Ross power assisted	Ross power assisted	Ross power assisted
Turning radius: (wall)	7.87 m	11.78 m	n/avail	n/avail
Suspension:	taper leaf springs, front, Freightliner TufTrac, rear	taper leaf springs, front, Freightliner TufTrac, rear	taper leaf springs, front, Freightliner TufTrac, rear	taper leaf springs, front, Freightliner TufTrac, rear
Tyres:	Michelin XZE 12 R22.5 (16 ply) front; Michelin XZE 11R 22.5 (14 ply) rear	Michelin XZY-3 425/65R 22.5 (20 ply) front; Michelin XDY-3 315/80R 22.5 (20 ply) rear	Michelin XZY-3 425/65R 22.5 (20 ply) front; Michelin XZY-3 315/80R 22.5 (20 ply) rear	Michelin XZY-2 315/80R 22.5 (20 ply) front and rear
Brakes: (main)	air/mechanical, WABCO 4-channel ABS	air/mechanical, WABCO 4-channel ABS	air/mechanical, WABCO 4-channel ABS	air/mechanical, WABCO 4-channel ABS
Electrical system:	dual 12/24 V	dual 12/24 V	dual 12/24 V	dual 12/24 V
Batteries:	4 × 12 V	4 × 12 V	4 × 12 V	4 × 12 V
Alternator:	140 A	140 A	140 A	140 A

M915A5 entered production in January 2010 and by early 2011 2,166 vehicles (including options) were on contract.

The M915A5 represents a block upgrade from the previous M915A3 model, the major change being the use of a Long Term Armor Strategy (LTAS) compliant A-kit/B-kit system. The armouring solution was developed by BAE Systems Security and Survivability.

The M915A5 also features a new larger cab, this based on the Western Star 4900 commercial pattern cab. Compared to the M915A3 cab, this cab is 250 mm wider and extends 865 mm behind the driver and passenger seat.

The M915A5 is powered by a Series 60 Detroit Diesel 12.7-litre diesel that develops 500 hp. Transmission is an Allison 4500SP automatic giving six forward and one reverse gears. The front Arvin-Meritor -FG941 axle is rated at 9,072 kg and sprung by taper leaf springs. The twin rear axle bogie is rated at 20,866 kg, fitted with Trac-Tech no-spin differentials for improved traction on slippery surfaces and is sprung by Freightliner

M915A5 tractor truck without the add-on armour B-kit
(Daimler Trucks North America)   1391473

M915A5 tractor truck with the add-on armour B-kit fitted (BAE Systems)
                                                 1391474

TufTrac suspension. Michelin XZU-S 315/80R22.5 20 tyres are provided on all axles. Suspension seats for driver and passenger, an air conditioning system, anti-lock brakes (ABS) and an Eaton VORAD collision warning system are standard equipment.

M916, (tractor, truck, 20-ton, (6 × 6))

This replaced the M123 (6 × 6) tractor and has the same engine and transmission as the M915, but is fitted with an Oshkosh F-U29 transfer case. Suspension is the same as fitted to the M915, with differential lock-ups on the driven front axle as well as the common rear bogie. Mounted behind the cab is a hydraulic winch with a capacity of 20,250 kg.

The M916 (and subsequent A1 to A3 models) is used by units throughout the world as the prime mover for the M172A1 low-bed trailer to transport heavy construction equipment within the theatre of operations. It also operates efficiently hauling the M870 40 ton low-bed semi-trailer when fully loaded; however, a 6 in (152 mm) fifth-wheel spacer must be used for compatibility with the M870 king-pin height.

M916A1/A2, (tractor truck, 20-ton, (6 × 6))

The M916A1/A2 was manufactured by Freightliner LLC and is a (6 × 6) tractor truck powered by a Detroit Diesel DDE 12.7-litre diesel developing 400 hp at 2,100 rpm. This is coupled to an Allison HT-740 automatic transmission and Oshkosh two-speed transfer case. Weight empty is 12,594 kg. Length is 7.35 m, width 2.49 m and the height is 3.24 m overall. Wheelbase is 4.41 m.

The M916A1 contract was awarded to Freightliner in September 1988, for 393 vehicles. The first deliveries were made in May 1989 and the first production vehicles entered the US Army's inventory in November 1990. Total M916A1 deliveries made under this contact amounted to 1,009 vehicles. Further A2 models were involved in the five year USD106 million contract awarded to Freightliner LLC in December 1995 for 583 various M915 Series vehicles. The differences between A1 and A2 configuration were minimal and as a result the types are often referred to jointly as M916A1/A2.

M916A3 (tractor truck, 20-ton (6 × 6))

This M916A3 (6 × 6) tractor truck is part of contract (DAAE07-00-D-S022) awarded to Freightliner LLC in September 2000 for approximately 3,400 M915 Series vehicles. The M916A3 is powered by a Series 60 Detroit Diesel DDEC IV 12.7-litre diesel that develops 430 hp at 2,100 rpm. This drives all three axles (front axle selectable) through an Allison Generation IV 4700SP seven-speed automatic transmission and Meritor T-2119 single-speed transfer case. The front Axle-Tech 4414SFW steer-drive axle is rated at 8,392 kg and sprung by taper leaf springs. The twin rear Arvin-Meritor RT52-160P axle bogie is rated at 23,587 kg, fitted with Trac-Tech no-spin differentials for improved traction on slippery surfaces and is sprung by

With the base truck retaining its temperate camouflage scheme the installed ballistic protection kit on this Freightliner M916A3 tractor truck is clearly visible (Carl Schulze)   1304072

Freightliner-produced M916A3 tractor truck fitted with an appliqué protection kit (Carl Schulze)   1304069

M917A2 (6 × 6) dump truck produced by Freightliner LLC (Michael Jerchel)   0583283

M917 (8 × 6) 20-ton dump truck produced by AM General (Pierre Touzin)   0511838

Freightliner TufTrac suspension. Michelin tyres are provided on all axles, with 425/65R 22.5 (20 ply) XZY-3 on the front axle and 315/80R 22.5 (20 ply) XDY-3 on the rear axles. A DP model 53324 winch rated at 20,412 kg is mounted behind the cab. Standard equipment includes air conditioning, suspension seats for driver and passenger, anti-lock brakes (ABS), an Eaton VORAD collision warning system, and an Eaton Central Tyre Inflation (CTI) system to further improve soft ground mobility.

M917 (dump truck 20-ton (8 × 6)), M917A1, M917A2, (dump truck 18.5-ton (6 × 6))

The M917 has a rear tipping dump body by Fruehauf that has a heaped capacity of 10.7 m³. It uses the same engine, gearbox, transfer box and suspension as the M916. The M917 range are used for earthmoving and construction projects, augmenting current fleets of 20 ton dump trucks and in some selected units having replaced 5-ton dump trucks.

Freightliner manufactured the M917A1 model, an unspecified number of which were involved in the December 1995 M915 Series contract award. The M917A2 is is part of contract (DAAE07-00-D-S022) awarded to Freightliner LLC in September 2000 for approximately 3,400 M915 Series vehicles. The M917A2 has a Crysteel 18.5-ton 11.1 m³ payload capacity dump body and is powered by the same Series 60 Detroit Diesel DDEC IV 12.7-litre diesel used in the M915A3 and M916A3 models, sharing driveline components with the M916A3. Michelin tyres are provided on all axles, with 425/65R 22.5 (20 ply) XZY-3 on the front axle and 315/80R 22.5 (20 ply) XZY-3 on the rear axles. An Eaton Central Tyre Inflation (CTI) system is fitted to further improve soft ground mobility. Suspension seats for driver and passenger, an air conditioning system and anti-lock brakes (ABS) are standard equipment.

M918, (bituminous distributor, (6 × 6))

This has a bituminous spreader on the rear manufactured by E D Etnyre and Company of Oregon. Engine, transmission, transfer box and suspension are the same as for the M916.

The M918 is used for distributing liquid bitumen for road and airfield construction and is provided with a hydrostatically driven bituminous pump.

The M918 is not supported by Freightliner as part of the M915 family of vehicles contract DAAE07-00-D-S022.

M919, (concrete mobile, 8 cu yd, (8 × 6))

This has a concrete mixer to the rear manufactured by the National Concrete Machinery Company of Lancaster, Pennsylvania. The engine, transmission, transfer box and suspension are the same as in the M916. It can transport dry concrete ingredients and water, mix the ingredients in

AM-General-produced M920 tractor truck 20-ton (8 × 6) (Carl Schulze)
1304071

various increments and proportions and pour the mixed concrete. The M919 is charged with dry ingredients by aggregate bins or scoop loaders and discharges into mixed concrete handling equipment. This vehicle can also be used as a central mix plant, where large amounts of concrete are required at a single location.

The engine, transmission, transfer box and suspension are carried over from the M916 model. The second axle is of the pusher type, which can be raised if required, usually when unladen or when crossing rough ground. The M919 weighs 15,971 kg empty, 32,056 kg fully loaded.

The M919A1 (6 × 6) version was produced by Freightliner LLC.

The M919 is not supported by Freightliner as part of the M915 family of vehicles contract DAAE07-00-D-S022.

M920, (tractor truck, 20-ton, (8 × 6))

The M920 (8 × 6) tractor truck is used to haul semi-trailers and has a (6 × 6) driveline and suspension set-up carried over from the M916 model. The undriven extra second axle is of the pusher type which can be raised if required, usually when the tractor is running solo or unladen, or when additional weight, usually for traction, is required by the drive axles. The M920, together with the M916, replaces the M123 and is used to haul the M870 semi-trailer.

The M920 is not supported by Freightliner as part of the M915 family of vehicles contract DAAE07-00-D-S022.

Contractor

AM General Corporation
Freightliner LLC

M939 (6 × 6) 5 ton cargo truck

Development

When the M809 was type classified it was intended that a product-improvement programme would be carried out in the areas of transmission, transfer box and brakes. Extensive testing of the M809 series during 1970 had demonstrated that product improvements in these three areas would be most beneficial. The programme was shelved when the US Army withdrew from Vietnam but was reinstituted in 1975.

In October 1979, the M939 (6 × 6) 5 ton cargo truck was type classified for inclusion in US Army field units. In April 1981, the then AM General Corporation (now AM General LLC) was awarded a contract for 11,394 M939 trucks, later increased to 22,789, by the then US Army Tank Automotive Command (TACOM). The total value of the five-year contract eventually reached USD1.6 billion. Production began in the first half of

M939A2 (6 × 6) 5-ton cargo truck with cab armour (Carl Schulze)   1296118

1982 at AM General's plant at South Bend, Indiana. Production under this five-year contract was completed in September 1986, but production was extended until April 1987 by the award of a further contract. Production by AM General Corporation ceased in late 1989, when the company withdrew from the medium and heavy truck markets and their South Bend plant closed.

During the mid-1980s, the basic M939 design was upgraded to the M939A1. This version was equipped with 14.00R 20 'Super Single' tyres with a single tyre replacing the dual biased-ply tyres on the rear axles. Only a limited number of M939A1s were produced. The M939 series became available for export during late-1983.

In May 1986 ARVECO, a joint venture between BMY Corporation and the General Automotive Corporation, won a contract to produce 15,218 M939A2 vehicles over a five-year period. The initial one-year contract was for 2,046 vehicles at a cost of USD145 million, while the full five-year contract was expected to be worth USD1 billion. Following the contract award, BMY acquired the General Automotive Corporation's portion of ARVECO. HARSCO renamed this wholly owned organisation BMY-Wheeled Vehicles Division and began deliveries from its new truck plant in Marysville, Ohio, in early 1987. By late 1990, the base contract quantity was fixed at 17,092 vehicles, with production extending into 1993 following orders from the US government that included FMS quantities for Saudi Arabia.

HARSCO ceased direct management involvement in the defence business in 1994 when it transferred the BMY Combat Systems Division into United Defense LP, a joint venture with the FMC Corporation. In 1997 HARSCO exited the defence industry by selling all of its interests in United Defense.

As of early 2011 around 22,000 M939 series trucks remained in US Army service, with the active/reserve forces split around 50/50 per cent. It is anticipated that the last M939 series trucks will remain in service until around 2022.

Description

The M939 is essentially the existing M809 series but improved in three major areas: transmission, transfer box and brake system.

The M809's manual transmission and transfer box were under capacity and mismatched to the engine/axle ratio and performance requirements. The M939 has a fully automatic transmission that eliminates the problems of engine overspeeding (rpm too high) or labouring in many gear ratio selections. It also requires less driver training, reduces fuel consumption, is more reliable/durable, lessens driver fatigue and improves safety.

M939 series (6 × 6) 5-ton cargo truck model M934A2/M935A2 expansible van (Gordon Arthur)
1340332

M939 series (6 × 6) 5-ton cargo truck model M936A2: wrecker with winch (Gordon Arthur)
1340333

Model	M923A2	M925A2	M927A2	M928A2	M929A2	M930A2
Type:	cargo	cargo	LWB cargo	LWB cargo	dump	dump
Winch:	no	yes	no	yes	no	yes
Cab seating:	1 + 2	1 + 2	1 + 2	1 + 2	1 + 2	1 + 2
Configuration:	6 × 6	6 × 6	6 × 6	6 × 6	6 × 6	6 × 6
Weight:						
(kerb)	9,494 kg	9,993 kg	10,791 kg	11,290 kg	10,805 kg	11,304 kg
(GVW)	14,030 kg	14,529 kg	15,327 kg	15,826 kg	15,340 kg	15,840 kg
Payload:	4,536 kg	4,536 kg	4,536 kg	4,536 kg	4,536 kg	4,536 kg
Towed load:	6,804 kg	6,804 kg	6,804 kg	6,804 kg	6,804 kg	6,804 kg
Length:	7.887 m	8.433 m	9.792 m	10.363 m	6.934 m	7.48 m
Width:	2.474 m	2.474 m	2.474 m	2.474 m	2.474 m	2.474 m
Height:						
(overall)	3.073 m	3.073 m	3.063 m	3.063 m	3.175 m	3.175 m
(reduced)	2.385 m	2.385 m	2.375 m	2.375 m	2.375 m	2.375 m
Track:						
(front)	1.98 m	1.98 m	1.98 m	1.98 m	1.98 m	1.98 m
(rear)	2.065 m	2.065 m	2.065 m	2.065 m	2.065 m	2.065 m
Wheelbase:	4.547 m	4.547 m	5.461 m	5.461 m	4.242 m	4.242 m
Ground clearance:	330 mm	330 mm	330 mm	330 mm	330 mm	330 mm
Fording:						
(normal)	760 mm	760 mm	760 mm	760 mm	760 mm	760 mm
(with kit)	1.98 m	1.98 m	1.98 m	1.98 m	1.98 m	1.98 m
Engine:	Cummins 6CTA8.3 8.3 litre 6-cylinder in-line turbocharged and aftercooled water-cooled diesel developing 240 hp (176 kW) at 2,100 rpm					
Gearbox:	Allison MT654CR 5-speed automatic					
Transfer box:	2- speed with high ratio 0.732:1, low ratio 1.790:1					
Steering:	Sheppard power assisted					
Suspension:	leaf springs front and rear					
Tyres:	14.00R 20					
Electrical system:	24 V	24 V	24 V	24 V	24 V	24 V
Alternator:	60 A	60 A	60 A	60 A	60 A	60 A

The M939 transfer box is pressure lubricated, not splash-lubricated as on the M809 series, and the M939's transfer box can shift between high and low ratios while the vehicle is moving. The driver now controls the engagement of the front wheels for (6 × 6) drive with an air system, eliminating a mechanical sprag clutch of the M809 which frequently failed.

The M809 is fitted with manually adjusted air-over-hydraulic brakes, the M939 is fitted with full airbrakes that are self-adjusting and backed by fail-safe mechanical spring brakes. Tests demonstrated that the full airbrakes on the M939 have four times the brake shoe life of those on the M809.

The front-mounted winch is hydraulically driven and stops when overloaded and restarts when the overload is removed. The older mechanically driven winches used on the M809 require shear-pin replacement when similarly overloaded.

The M939 bonnet and bumpers tilt forward so maintenance can be carried out from the ground, whereas even opening the M809's bonnet necessitates climbing on to the bumpers.

Flat tyres are replaced using a boom just behind the cab. The cab holds three personnel, the M809 only two.

The M939 was the first truck built with special connectors for use with the US Army's diagnostic equipment (STE/ICE). This encourages the use of test equipment, reduces maintenance time and eliminates incorrect replacements based on poor diagnosis. The M939 was also the first tactical truck to meet Surgeon General standards for noise in the cab, even with the windows open. This was achieved by relocating intake/exhaust ports behind the cab.

The upgraded M939A2, produced by BMY-Wheeled Vehicles Division (BMY-WVD) incorporates an Eaton Central Tyre Inflation (CTI) system integrated with 14.00R 20 'Super Single' radial tyres. The engine is changed to a Cummins 6CTA8.3 8.3 litre six-cylinder water-cooled diesel developing 240 hp at 2,100 rpm, providing an increase in range to 830 km. Due to the lighter engine the kerb weight is reduced. Modifications were also made to the cooling system.

Variants
M939 variants are as follows:
M923: drop side cargo
M924: cargo; equivalent to M814
M925: drop side cargo with winch
M926: cargo with winch
M927: long wheelbase cargo
M928: long wheelbase cargo with winch
M929: dump truck; equivalent to M817
M930: dump truck with winch
M931: tractor
M932: tractor with winch
M933: tractor wrecker with winch

M939 series (6 × 6) 5-ton cargo truck model M923A2 (Peter Felstead)
0552257

M939 series (6 × 6) 5-ton cargo truck with winch model M925A0 as produced by AM General (Peter Felstead)
0552259

Model	M931A2	M932A2	M934A2	M935A2	M936A2
Type:	tractor	tractor	exp van	exp van	wrecker
Winch:	no	yes	no	no	yes
Cab seating:	1 + 2	1 + 2	1 + 2	1 + 2	1 + 2
Configuration:	6 × 6	6 × 6	6 × 6	6 × 6	6 × 6
Weight:					
(kerb)	9,024 kg	9,523 kg	12,717 kg	13,624 kg	16,724 kg
(GVW)	26,034 kg	26,533 kg	14,985 kg	15,892 kg	19,918 kg
Payload:	6,804 kg[1]	6,804 kg[1]	2,268 kg	2,268 kg	3,175 kg
Towed load:	6,804 kg[2]	6,804 kg[2]	6,804 kg	6,804 kg	9,072 kg
Length:	6.718 m	7.264 m	9.21 m	9.55 m	9.195 m
Width:	2.474 m	2.474 m	2.489 m	2.489 m	2.474 m
Height:					
(overall)	3.078 m	3.078 m	3.614 m	3.609 m	3.048 m
(reduced)	2.39 m	2.39 m	3.614 m	3.609 m	2.756 m
Track:					
(front)	1.98 m	1.98 m	1.98 m	1.98 m	1.98 m
(rear)	2.065 m	2.065 m	2.065 m	2.065 m	2.065 m
Wheelbase:	4.242 m	4.242 m	5.461 m	5.461 m	5.547 m
Ground clearance:	333 mm	333 mm	333 mm	333 mm	333 mm
Fording:					
(normal)	760 mm	760 mm	760 mm	760 mm	760 mm
(with kit)	1.98 m	1.98 m	1.98 m	1.98 m	1.98 m
Engine:	Cummins 6CTA8.3 8.3 litre 6-cylinder in-line turbocharged and aftercooled water-cooled diesel developing 240 hp (176 kW) at 2,100 rpm				
Gearbox:	Allison MT654CR 5-speed automatic				
Transfer box:	2-speed with high ratio 0.732:1, low ratio 1.790:1				
Steering:	Sheppard power assisted				
Suspension:	leaf springs front and rear				
Tyres:	14.00R 20				
Electrical system:	24 V	24 V	24 V	24 V	24 V
Alternator:	60 A	60 A	60 A	60 A	60 A

[1] on 5th wheel
[2] pintle

M934: expansible body
M935: expansible van body
M936: wrecker with winch
M939: chassis with or without winch
M939: chassis with winch
M940: chassis with winch
M941: chassis without winch
M941: chassis with winch
M942: long wheelbase chassis with or without winch
M943: long wheelbase chassis with winch
M944: long wheelbase chassis
M945: long wheelbase chassis with winch.
M939A2 production models are as follows:
M923A2: drop side cargo without winch
M925A2: drop side cargo with winch
M927A2: long wheelbase cargo without winch
M928A2: long wheelbase cargo with winch
M929A2: dump truck without winch
M930A2: dump truck with winch
M931A2: tractor truck without winch
M932A2: tractor truck with winch
M934A2: expansible van without winch

M935A2: expansible van with hydraulic tailgate
M936A2: wrecker with winch
M942A2: chassis with or without winch
M944A2: chassis without winch
M945A2: chassis with winch.

Also produced were 7,570-litre water and fuel tankers and a cargo truck with a loading/unloading crane.

The following kits are available for the M939 and M939A2 series of trucks: airbrake, automatic chemical alarm, deep water fording, bow and tarpaulin cover, electric brake, engine coolant heater, front and rear lifting points, fuel burning heater, hardtop closure, radiator and hood cover and rifle racks. M939A2 series cargo and dump trucks fitted with a winch can also be fitted with a front-mounted A-frame kit. This can be fitted in the field and has a lifting capacity of up to 1,362 kg.

M939 OEF/OIF armouring solutions
Although not great in numbers, 165 armour kits were developed for the M939 series during operations in Bosnia and these still existed in Army warehouses when the need for protection became apparent on Operation Enduring Freedom/Operation Iraqi Freedom. As an early expedient measure an upgrade to this kit (enhanced side blast protection in particular) was first looked at by the US Army. Following this, the US

M932A2 (6 × 6) tractor truck and trailer of US Armed Forces operating in the former Yugoslavia (Michael Jerchel) 1047662

M939 series (6 × 6) 5-ton cargo truck model M925A0 (Richard Stickland) 1124752

Army's Tank-Automotive Research, Development and Engineering Center (TARDEC) developed a prototype design of a new M939 armour kit, and highlighting the difficulties of providing an armour solution for something clearly never designed to be armoured, despite it's relatively straightforward shape, the prototype cab required more than 300 drawings and consisted of 260 individual components.

Available figures show the M939 5 ton truck armouring effort included manufacturing armouring kits for 3,000 trucks at six army facilities. Production began in December 2004 and was completed in July 2005. Once produced, production kits were shipped to installation sites in the United States, Middle East, and Europe, where they were installed onto trucks by military or contractor personnel

The M-939 series armouring requirement was met by the Ground Systems Industrial Enterprise (GSIE), an Army organisation of depots and other facilities. GSIE comprised Anniston Army Depot, Red River Army Depot, Sierra Army Depot, Rock Island Arsenal, Watervliet Arsenal, the Lima Tank Plant (a government-owned, contractor-operated facility), and a business centre staff located at Rock Island Arsenal. GSIE's objective was to operate as a single business unit, efficiently using the industrial capabilities of each installation while simultaneously transforming those capabilities to meet the needs of Army forces.

Specifications
See tables on pages 680 and 681

Status
Production of all models complete. In service with the US Army, Egypt, Saudi Arabia and other undisclosed countries. Late-2007 28,268 M939 series trucks were in service with the US Army; current figures (late 2010) suggest around 22,000 now remain.

Contractor
AM General LLC
HARSCO BMY-Wheeled Vehicles Division (see text)

Oshkosh M977 Heavy Expanded Mobility Tactical Truck (HEMTT) and M989A1 Heavy Expanded Mobility Ammunition Trailer (HEMAT)

Development
In May 1981, and following the evaluation of proposals submitted by AM General, MAN, Pacific Car & Foundry (PACCAR) and Oshkosh Truck Corporation, the US Army Tank Automotive COMmand (now Tank-automotive and Armaments COMmand; then and now TACOM) awarded an initial five-year contract valued at USD251.13 million to Oshkosh Truck Corporation for production of the 10 ton (9,070 kg) 8 × 8 Heavy Expanded Mobility Tactical Truck (HEMTT). The first prototype HEMTT was completed in December 1981, pre-production examples followed during March 1982, with the first production vehicles produced in September 1982. Under the initial contract the US Army was to receive 250 vehicles valued at USD31.73 million during the first contract year, with a total of 2,140 vehicles to be delivered over the five contract years. The contract included production options for up to an additional 5,351 vehicles, bringing production totals to 7,490 vehicles. The bulk of the available contract options were exercised.

A follow-on (second) HEMTT contract was awarded to Oshkosh Truck Corporation in April 1987. This contract called for a base quantity of 1,403 vehicles, with options for an additional 1,684 vehicles; all contract options were exercised. A supplemental agreement added a further 1,449 vehicles (plus an option for 363 vehicles) to the second HEMTT contract in April 1989; the contract option was exercised. By mid-1994 and with the award of a third HEMTT production contract, over 14,000 HEMTTS had been produced. The third production contract concluded with a total of 744 vehicles built, 329 for the US Army and 415 for FMS customers. The fourth HEMTT production contract was awarded in August 1995. This contract was valued at USD33.6 million, and extended HEMTT production through September 2001.

The Family of Heavy Tactical Vehicles (FHTV) contract was awarded to Oshkosh Truck by the US Army in March 2001 and covered the production period 03/2001 until mid-FY06. In addition to the HEMTT (both new and re-manufacture), the then FHTV contract covered the M1070 HET (deliveries complete), M1074 and M1075 Palletized Load System (PLS) trucks and M1076 PLS trailers. FHTV called for up to 5,398 trucks and 1,100 trailers (including options) and was valued at in excess of USD1 billion (including options).

To meet the ongoing needs of the US Army, the FHTV contract was extended and renegotiated, and in February 2007, Oshkosh Truck announced it had been awarded a USD878 million contract to continue production of the Family of Heavy Tactical Vehicles. The follow-on FHTV contract (FHTV 2) covered new production of HEMTTs (including A4 variants from mid-2008) and Palletized Load System (PLS) vehicles and PLS trailers, and under the contract, Oshkosh were contracted to deliver 1,857 new vehicles and 2,599 new trailers. In addition to new vehicle production, the contract also called for the re-manufacture of 1,130 HEMTTs under the Recapitalization (RECAP) programme.

In March 2008 Oshkosh Defense announced it had received a contract modification from the US Army to the current family of heavy tactical vehicles (FHTV 2) contract, ordering the manufacture of 1,084 HEMTTs in A4 configuration. This contract modification raised the total of HEMTT A4s under contract to 1,745, for a total contract modification of more than USD321 million. An original contract modification was awarded on February 1, 2008, while the second modification designated the vehicle models to be manufactured as HEMTT A4s. Production of product-improved HEMTT A2s continued until production of the HEMTT A4 commenced in July 2008. The exception here being the M1977 which remains at A2 configuration for fleet commonality reasons. The final major improvements to the HEMTT A2 were a fully air conditioned cab and cab structural changes that makes installation of add-on-armour in the field quicker and easier.

In June 2008 Oshkosh Defense announced it had received a USD120 million FHTV 2 contract modification for HEMTT A4 vehicles from the US Army Tank Automotive and Armaments Command (TACOM). With this addition, HEMTT A4 production totalled 1,978 vehicles at USD658 million, and brought the current FHTV contract total value to more than USD2 billion. This contract modification added 233 HEMTT A4 vehicles to the fleet, with variants produced under this contract including the recovery vehicle, fuel service vehicle and Load Handling System (LHS) vehicle.

In October 2008 Oshkosh Defense announced that it had been awarded the Family of Heavy Tactical Vehicles 3 (FHTV 3) contract by the US Army's TACOM. Under this three-year contract more than 6,000 upgraded vehicles and trailers can be delivered. The FHTV 3 contract will be awarded in increments and covers not only the HEMTT A4 but also A1 models of the PLS and HET, and both new and Recap'd vehicles. All three FHTV 3 families will be Long Term Armor Strategy (LTAS) compliant and come off the assembly line fitted with upgraded suspensions and integral composite (A-kit) armour. They also will be ready to receive an add-on (B-kit) armour appliqué.

The first FHTV 3 order was valued at USD1.2 billion and delivery commenced in November 2008. By late 2009 around 11,500 HEMTT A4s (new build and Recap) had been ordered under the FHTV 2 and 3 contracts.

During 2010 a further >1,000 (new build and Recap) HEMTT A4s were ordered under the FHTV 3 contract. The bulk of the disclosed orders were for new-build vehicles (around 950), these variants of the base M977 cargo and including wreckers, tankers, tractor trucks and LHS and specialist cargo/handling variants. A small quantity (20) of M983A2 LET were ordered during 2010, and the first orders for A4 variants of the M977 Electrical Power Plant (EPP) and Large Repair Parts Transporter (LRPT), and M985 Guided Missile Transporter (GMT) were disclosed.

FMS sales of A4 HEMMTs to Egypt and the United Arab Emirates (UAE) were also disclosed during March 2010.

The Egypt sale was valued at USD29 million and is understood to have called for 75 M978A4 tankers. The UAE sale was valued at USD11.9 million and forms part of the UAE's Patriot Advanced Capability (PAC-3) purchase. The award covers Patriot tractor, wrecker and Guided Missile Transporter (GMT), with production and deliveries occurring during July-September 2011.

As of early 2011, in excess of 22,000 HEMTTs of all variants had been produced, the bulk of these supplied to US Armed Forces. In addition to the US military, the HEMTT has been supplied to a number of other countries, particularly those in the Middle East. Oshkosh does not traditionally disclose export details for the HEMTT beyond a figure of around 1,100 vehicles, however it is known that users of the HEMTT include: Egypt (including A4), Greece (28; 24 M985 cargo and four M984A1 recovery for use with MLRS and Patriot), Israel, Jordan, Korea, Oman, Qatar, Saudi Arabia, Taiwan, Turkey (including M997 and M984A2 - 42, 2005; 36, 2006), and the UAE (including A4). Commercial variants have also been sold.

The base vehicle of the HEMTT range is the M977 cargo truck. Production commenced with the following other variants available: M978 fuel/water tanker, M983 tractor truck, M984 wrecker, M985 cargo truck. As part of the HEMTT overhaul/rebuild programme two additional models were introduced, the M1120 Load Handling System (LHS) and M1977 Common Bridge Transporter (CBT). All current generation models have the A4 suffix. Only the M984 wrecker was produced in A1 configuration and this resulting in the change of recovery crane and retrieval system. The A3 suffix is applied to developmental hybrid drive HEMTTs. Further details of all HEMTT variants can be found elsewhere in this entry.

Development of the HEMTT A2 which became available from April 2002, commenced in 2000 and modifications adopted for the A2 HEMTT have their origins in the proposed HEMTT Extended Service Program (ESP).

Late 1998, two HEMTT vehicles (a M978 tanker and a M984 wrecker) incorporating proposed ESP features commenced testing. In addition to a number of other differences that included air-suspension, two different power trains were involved in the tests. The M984A1 wrecker was fitted with an electronically controlled next generation (DDEC III) version of the Detroit Diesel 8V92TA engine fitted to the original HEMTT, but coupled to a new Allison HD 4560P six-speed transmission. The M978 tanker was fitted with a Detroit Diesel Series 60 14-litre diesel developing 500 hp and coupled to an Allison HD 4070P seven-speed transmission.

HEMTT A4 was developed to meet the requirement for an improved power pack and the ability to accept heavier cab armour and be compliant with the US Army's Long Term Armour Strategy (LTAS) of A and B kit armouring.

Following extensive service, and since an initial USD10.1 million contract award in September 2005 for 123 vehicles (with a 100 per cent option), Oshkosh Truck had (by December 2007) Reset/Recap'd 4,526 service-worn HEMTTs under a number of contracts. Under the earliest contracts and with the exception of certain safety-related items, vehicles were returned to original build standard; i.e.: A0 to A0. Under the next generation of contracts all vehicles were returned to new build standard (originally A2, introduced in April 2002), and returned to service in zero miles/zero hours condition, and with a full new vehicle warranty. Cost to the US DoD per vehicle is around 75 per cent of new build. To differentiate between new and rebuilt vehicles, rebuilt vehicles have the A2R designation. Under all but the most recent contracts Reset vehicles were returned to original build standard, while Recap vehicles were returned to new build standard. Only A2 models were Reset, any A0 or A1 vehicles returned to Oshkosh Truck, unless beyond economical repair, were automatically Recap'd.

The A4 build standard has now been introduced into the Recap programme and in September 2008 Oshkosh Defense announced it had been awarded a contract valued at more than USD82.6 million to Recap 292 HEMTT A4s. HEMTT A0 and HEMTT A2 variants will be returned to Oshkosh, stripped to the chassis frame rails and completely rebuilt to meet the specifications of the new HEMTT A4.

Oshkosh also refurbishes service worn HEMTTs under the US Army's Theatre Provided Equipment Refurbishment (TPER) contract award. In mid-February 2007 the US Army awarded Oshkosh an initial contract for TPER of 319 FHTV units under a four-year indefinite delivery/indefinite quantity contract. Work was performed in Oshkosh's facility in Jahra, Kuwait. The award covered PLS, HEMTT and HET vehicles, as well as HET trailers. Under the most recent award, by May 2011 in excess of 1,600 trucks and trailers will have been refurbished and returned to service.

Description

M977 Heavy Expanded Mobility Tactical Truck (HEMTT)

The HEMTT was developed from the outset as a tactical truck, but to minimise procurement and life cycle costs featured extensive use of militarised-as-required commercial automotive components, these including a standard diesel engine and automatic transmission. Some of the components used in the original HEMTT are common with the original LVS (8 × 8) vehicles which remain in use by the US Marine Corps, and full details of which can be found elsewhere in this section.

With the exception of the M984 wrecker variant (254 × 89 × 9.5 mm, front; 356 × 89 × 9.5 mm, rear), on all HEMTT variants the chassis is formed of 257 × 89 × 9.5 mm heat-treated carbon manganese steel with a yield strength of 758 MPa. Bolted construction with Grade 8 bolts is used throughout. The chassis is provided with heavy-duty front bumper and skid plate, external hydraulic connection (not on tractor trucks), service and emergency airbrake connection, slave start connection and trailer electrical connector. A centrally mounted self-recovery winch with a bare drum capacity of 9,072 kg is an option; around 20 per cent of production has a winch fitted.

The two-person, two-door forward control cab is of heavy-duty welded steel construction with corrosion-resistant skins. Standard equipment for A2 variants includes air-suspension seats for the driver and passenger, four-point seat belts, variable speed electric windscreen wipers and electric and air horns. The spare tyre and wheel assembly mounted behind the cab is provided with a davit to assist in lowering it to the ground.

An add-on armour kit for use in the former Yugoslavia in the 90s was originally developed for the HEMTT series by Simula Inc. (acquired by Armour Holdings in 2003 and now BAE Systems) and 186 examples were produced but not issued. These were subsequently taken out of storage during 2004 and were used in Iraq. BAE Systems subsequently developed a next-generation armour kit for the HEMTT A0-A2/PLS A0 cab and has supplied around 3,600 kits to the US Army. Current US Army requirements for HEMTT A0/A2 protection kits had been met by late-2006.

In November 2008, Oshkosh Defense announced it had been awarded a contract for more than 660 armour B-kits for the HEMTT A4 cab. A further contract for an additional 1,700 armour B-kits followed in January 2009.

The most recently disclosed B-kit award was announced in May 2010, was valued at USD8 million and called for a further 90 kits.

HEMTT A0 and A1 models are powered by a Detroit Diesel 8V92TA V-8 two-stroke diesel developing 445 hp. HEMTT A2 models are powered by the DDECIV version of this engine. HEMTT A4 models are powered by a Caterpillar C-15 developing 500 hp. HEMTT A0 and A1 models are fitted with a Allison HT 740D 4F/1R automatic gearbox, torque converter and Oshkosh 55000 two-speed transfer box with front tandem disconnect. HEMTT A2 variants are fitted with a Allison HD 4560P 6F/1R automatic gearbox. HEMTT A4 models are fitted with a Allison 4500 SP 5F/1R automatic gearbox.

The front tandem axles on all HEMTTs (including A4) are Oshkosh 46K single-reduction units with a 32° front turning angle, single cardan joint, closed-type steering ends and a driver-controlled differential lock, the rear tandem axles are Dana (formerly Eaton) single reduction units; these vary according to model. Suspension for A0-A2 models is provided by Hendrickson leaf springs with equalising beams. Vertical axle travel is 250 mm, front and rear. A4 models are fitted with air suspension.

A variety of cross-country tyre types can be fitted to the 20 inch wheel rims including all-terrain, sand or snow bias, or directional 'traction' types. HEMTT A0 and A1 models were fitted as standard with Michelin XL 1600R 20 tyres. This tyre has been superseded by the Michelin XZL and this is

Oshkosh M977A2 (8 × 8) HEMTT cargo truck (Shaun C Connors)   1128761

standard fit for the HEMTT A2 and A4. Drum brakes (419 × 127 mm, front; 419 × 178 mm, rear) are fitted all-round.

An overview of the major changes to A4 HEMTT variants can be found elsewhere in this entry.

Variants

M977A0, A2 and A4

The M977 cargo truck variant is the base member of the HEMTT family. The current model is the M977A4; there was no M977A1. Three variants of the M977 are available, the basic M977A0/A2/A4 cargo truck, the M977A0/A2/A4 Electrical Power Plant (EPP) and the M977A0/A2/A4 Large Repairs Parts Transporter (LRPT).

The basic M977 cargo truck and M977 LRPT variant are fitted with a light-duty Grove materials handling crane mounted at the rear of the chassis and after the 5.486 m inside length dropside cargo body. The crane is rated at 1,134 kg at 5.79 m. The M977 LRPT is used as a Patriot air-defence missile system support vehicle and is essentially a M977 cargo truck variant with some storage box differences and additional slings for lifting operations.

The M977 Electrical Power Plant (EPP) has an extended cargo body (6.041 m inside length) with fold down side panels that can be secured in the horizontal position and used as a walking platform. There is no material handling crane on the EPP which is used to hold and transport generators for the Patriot air-defence missile system.

All three M977 variants are available with or without a 9,072 kg bare drum capacity self-recovery winch.

Approximately 5,000 M977 cargo, 50 M977 EPP and 10 M977 LRPT units had been produced by January 2008.

The vast majority of M977 cargo trucks returned to Oshkosh Truck for Reset/Recap have been converted to either M1120 Load Handling System (LHS) trucks or M1977 Common Bridge Transporter (CBT) trucks. Around 10 M977 cargo trucks have been converted (50/50) into M977 EPP and M977 LRPT variants. During 2006 approximately 150 M977 cargo trucks were rebuilt as M977 cargo trucks.

The first disclosed order for M977A4 EPP and LRPT variants was announced in February 2010, the >USD5 million award calling for more than 15 vehicles in total.

M978A0, A2 and A4

The M978 variant is a 9,500 litre capacity tanker. The current model is the M978A4; there was no M978A1. The M978A0 was produced in both potable water (approximately 18) and fuel servicing truck variants, the A2 and A4 models have only been produced in the fuel servicing truck variant.

Oshkosh M978A2 (8 × 8) HEMTT 9,500-litre tanker; this is a fuel tanker, only a small number of potable water tankers have been produced (Shaun C Connors)   1128760

Oshkosh M978 (8 × 8) HEMTT 9,500-litre tanker; this is a fuel tanker destined for the Israeli Armed Forces (Shaun C Connors)   0126578

Fuel servicing is provided through two hand lines (1.5 inch (38 mm) diameter by 60 feet (18.29 m) long) capable of flow rates to 80 US gallons per minute using automotive type nozzles. Bulk fuel discharge to a flow rate of up to 300 US gallons per minute is through a single point nozzle. Fuel is filtered by the use of a filter separator.

A 9,072 kg bare drum capacity self-recovery winch is an option.

To reduce the risk of fire during fuel transport a self-sealing coating that seals punctures from small arms fire or other small high-velocity objects can be applied to the fuel tank. In a USD5 million award disclosed during May 2010, Oshkosh continued work that commenced in September 2009 by applying this coating to a further >300 new-build and recapitalised M978A4 HEMTTs.

M983A0, A2 and A4

The M983 Patriot tractor is a tractor truck model for use with the Patriot air-defence missile system. The rear tandem consists of Eaton (now Dana) DS-480 axles and Hendrickson RT340 suspension; Holland AD-246 air on the A4 model. There was no A1 model. A 9,072 kg bare drum capacity self-recovery winch is an option.

The M983A2 Light Equipment Transporter (LET) is intended primarily for engineer applications. The LET has a fifth wheel load rating of 18,144 kg and a Gross Combination Weight (GCW) of 61,290 kg. To assist with loading/unloading operations a 20,440 kg capacity drum winch is mounted

A new-build M983A2 tractor truck (Shaun C Connors)   1128780

The M983 Light Equipment Transporter (LET) is a development of the M983 Patriot tractor (Oshkosh Truck)   1128781

The M983 Patriot tractor is a tractor truck model for use with the Patriot air-defence missile system; this is probably an M983A0 (Oshkosh Truck)   1128770

between the cab and fifth wheel. During 2007, some 13 new build LETs were produced. Additionally, between late-2007 and April 2008, Oshkosh Truck Recap'd 39 M938 Patriot tractors as M938A2 LETs.

The first M983A4 LETs were ordered in December 2009. Under a USD56 million delivery order from the US Army Oshkosh will deliver more than 200 M983 HEMTT A4 LETs by September 2010. This award brought the US Army's total FHTV 3 contract awards to more than USD3.2 billion.

M984A0, A1, A2 and A4

The M984 wrecker is the only HEMTT variant to have been produced in A1 configuration, and this resulting in the change of recovery crane and retrieval system between A0 and A1 configurations. The current model is the M984A4 and this is fitted with a 27,240 kg capacity two-speed recovery winch, a rear-mounted 11,340 kg capacity vehicle retrieval system, and a 6,350 kg at 2.74 m capacity Grove materials handling crane. A 9,072 kg bare drum capacity self-recovery winch is fitted as standard on the M984. Full details of the M984 wrecker can be found in the Recovery vehicles section.

M985A0, A2 and A4

The M985 is available in two variants, M985 cargo and M985E1 Guided Missile Transporter (GMT). The current models are A4; there were no A1 models.

The M985 is available in two variants, M985 cargo and M985E1 Guided Missile Transporter (GMT). The M985E1 GMT was developed specifically for use with the Patriot air-defence system. This is easily distinguishable by the rear-mounted materials handling crane. This example is fitted with the optional winch (Shaun C Connors)   1128778

From the rear, a M984 wrecker. Full details of the M984 wrecker can be found in the Recovery vehicles section (Shaun C Connors)   1128779

The M1120 HEMTT LHS variant was initially introduced as part of the HEMTT overhaul/rebuild programme during which returned M977 cargo trucks have their cargo bodies and materials handling cranes removed, to be replaced by a load handling system (Shaun C Connors)   1128777

Oshkosh M1120 (8 × 8) HEMTT-LHS fitted with Multilift MPH165-LHS (previously designated Mark 5) LHS (Shaun C Connors)   0126577

BAE Systems (previously Armour Holdings) developed an armour kit for the HEMTT A0-A2/PLS cab and supplied around 3,600 kits to the US Army (Armor Holdings)   1190249

The M1977(8 × 8) HEMTT CBT is a further development of the M1120 LHS, and in common with the M1120 LHS was initially introduced as part of the HEMTT overhaul/rebuild programme (Oshkosh Truck)   1128776

The M985 cargo variant was developed to support the Multiple Launch Rocket System (MLRS) with a M989A1 HEMAT trailer, but may also used to transport Patriot missiles. The M985 cargo is similar to M977 cargo truck but has MLRS pod feet restraints in the floor of the cargo body and the rear-mounted Grove materials handling crane is heavier duty, being rated at 2,449 kg at 5.029 m. Around 2,700 M985 cargo variants had been produced as of January 2006; there was no M985 production during 2007 or 2008.

The first disclosed order for M985A4 GMT models was announced in March 2010, these as part of a USD11.9 million FMS order for the UAE. The UAE order forms part of the UAE's Patriot Advanced Capability (PAC-3) purchase and covers Patriot tractor, wrecker and Guided Missile Transporter (GMT), with production and deliveries occurring during July-September 2011.

The M985E1A2 Guided Missile Transporter (GMT) was developed specifically for use with the Patriot air-defence system. This has a rear-mounted Hiab 8108/2 materials handling crane rated at 2,449 kg at 5.029 m and 2,041 kg at 6.096 m.

The M985 cargo and GMT are rated at 9,798 kg payload and compared to the base M977 HEMTT, the chassis assembly, rear axles, rear suspension and cargo body and all have higher ratings. Around 45 M985 GMT variants had been produced as of January 2006; there was no M985E1 production during 2007 or 2008.

The M985 is available with or without a 9,072 kg bare drum capacity self-recovery winch.

M1120A2 and A4

The M1120 HEMTT Load Handling System (LHS) variant was initially introduced as part of the HEMTT overhaul/rebuild programme during which returned M977 cargo trucks have their cargo bodies and materials handling cranes removed, to be replaced by a Multilift Mark 5 (now designated MPH165-LHS) load handling system, as fitted to the Oshkosh PLS truck. Other modifications include an upgrade of the rear suspension.

The first rebuilt M1120 was produced late 1999, with new build M1120A2 examples (now A4) available from February 2004. The M1120 is interoperable with the M1076 PLS trailer.

M1977A0 and A2

The M1977 HEMTT Common Bridge Transporter (CBT) is a further development of the M1120 LHS, and in common with the M1120 LHS was initially introduced as part of the HEMTT overhaul/rebuild programme. For the M1977 variant, and in addition to the LHS and rear suspension

upgrade, a winch and other additional systems modifications to enable the launch/recovery of Ribbon Bridge sections and bridging boats are carried out.

The first rebuilt M1977 was produced late 1997, with new build M1977A2 examples available from July 2001. For fleet commonality reasons all current build M1977 CBTs are to A2 configuration.

Oshkosh Defense announced in December 2008 that under a FHTV 3 contract modification award valued at approximately USD5 million approximately 30 CBT A0 variants of the HEMTT would be Recap'd to the current A2 configuration.

THAAD Missile Launcher

The HEMTT-based Terminal (formerly Theatre) High Altitude Area Defense (THAAD) missile launcher is similar to the earlier 10 × 10 PLS-based THAAD. The HEMTT A2 THAAD missile launcher uses the HEMTT chassis for weight reduction to allow air transport by C-130 Hercules. A total of seven HEMTT THAAD launchers had been delivered by November 2007, with a further eight to follow.

Outline specifications for the HEMTT THAAD give a GVW of around 32,500 kg. Automotive changes compared to the base HEMTT include an extended wheelbase, uprated rear axles and the use of air suspension for the rear tandem.

The HEMTT-based THAAD missile launcher is similar to the earlier 10 × 10 PLS-based THAAD but uses the HEMTT chassis for weight reduction to allow air transport by C-130 Hercules (Oshkosh Truck)   1128775

HEMTT Tactical Fire Fighting Truck (TFFT) (Oshkosh Truck)   1156184

HEMTT A3 (Oshkosh Truck)   1156185

HEMTT M1142 Tactical Fire Fighting Truck (TFFT) and HEWATT M1158 Water Tender

The HEMTT M1142 Tactical Fire Fighting Truck (TFFT) contract was awarded to Pierce Manufacturing (Oshkosh Truck Corporation Company) with Oshkosh Truck Corporation as a subcontractor to Pierce.

The HEMTT TFFT is a multi-purpose vehicle, designed to cover aircraft rescue, fuel storage protection, and structural and wildland firefighting and rescue. The TFFT is based on an the HEMTT M977A2 chassis with the heavier duty M1120 LHS HEMTT variant rear suspension.

The first TFFT was delivered to the US Army reserve in September 2002, this contract eventually covering the delivery of 43 vehicles. A further 95 vehicles have been ordered since then, with deliveries continuing through September 2009.

Following successful evaluation of four prototype vehicles during 2007, in August 2007 Pierce Manufacturing was awarded a five-year USD4.5 million contract by the US Army for the production of 10 HEMTT-based Water Tender (HEWATT) vehicles, with deliveries commencing during 2008. The most recent order (placed in March 2009) for 21 additional vehicles brings the total HEWATTS under contract to 68. A total of 119 vehicles worth an estimated USD56 million can be ordered.

Designation	M977A2	M978A2	M983A2 [LET]	M984A2	M985A2 [GMT]	M1120A2 LHS	M1977A2 CBT
Type:	cargo	tanker	Patriot tractor	wrecker	cargo	load handling system	load handling system, Ribbon Bridge
Cab seating:	1 + 1	1 + 1	1 + 1	1 + 1	1 + 1	1 + 1	1 + 1
Configuration:	8 × 8	8 × 8	8 × 8	8 × 8	8 × 8	8 × 8	8 × 8
Weight:							
(laden)	28,123 kg	28,123 kg	n/avail	43,091 kg	30,844 kg	29,938 kg	29,938 kg
(unladen)	17,600 kg	17,300 kg	14,605 [16,327] kg	23,088 kg	17,985 [19,459] kg	16,103 kg	16,782 kg
(GCW)	45,360 kg	45,360 kg	45,360 [61,236] kg	70,308 kg	45,360 kg	46,721 kg	45,360 kg
Length:	10.173 m	10.173 m	8.903 m	9.957 m	10.173 [10.846] m	10.173 m	10.173 m
Width:	2.438 m	2.438 m	2.438 m	2.438 m	2.438 m	2.438 m	2.438 m
Height:							
(cab)	2.565 m	2.565 m	2.565 m	2.565 m	2.565 m	2.565 m	2.565 m
(spare wheel)	2.845 m	2.845 m	2.845 m	2.845 m	2.845 m [3.708 m over crane]	2.845 m	2.845 m
Wheelbase:	1.524 + 5.334 + 1.524 m	1.524 + 5.334 + 1.524 m	1.524 + 4.597 + 1.542 m	1.524 + 4.851 + 1.524 m	1.524 + 5.334 + 1.524 m	1.524 + 5.334 + 1.524 m	1.524 + 5.334 + 1.524 m
Angle of approach/departure:	43°/45°	43°/45°	43°/66°	43°/n/avail	43°/45° [43°/26°]	43°/45°	43°/45°
Max speed:	100 km/h	100 km/h	100 km/h	100 km/h	100 km/h	100 km/h	100 km/h
Gradient:	60%	60%	60%	60% (tractor)	60%	60%	60%
Range:	644 km	644 km	644 km	644 km	644 km	644 km	644 km
Fuel capacity:	587 litres	587 litres	587 litres	587 litres	587 litres	587 litres	587 litres
Engine:	A0 and A1 models: Detroit Diesel 8V92TA V-8 12.1-litre diesel developing 445 hp (332 kW) at 2,100 rpm and maximum torque of 1,695 N.m; A2 models have the electronically-controlled DDEC IV version of the 8V92TA engine						
Gearbox:	A0 and A1 models: Allison HT 740D automatic with torque converter, 4 forward and 1 reverse gears; A2 models: Allison HD 4560P automatic with torque converter, 6 forward and 1 reverse gears						
Transfer box:	Oshkosh 55000, 2-speed						
Steering:	power-assisted on front tandem						
Suspension tandems:	front: Hendrickson RT340 with equalising beam, all models; rear: Hendrickson RT340 with equalising beams, M977 (all variants), M978, M1120 and M1977 (rated at 16,330 kg on M1120 and M1977); Hendrickson RT520 with equalising beams, M983 (both variants); Hendrickson RT650 with equalising beams, M984; Hendrickson RT380 with equalising beams, M985 (both variants). 250 mm vertical axle travel on front and rear tandems						
Axles:	front: Oshkosh single-reduction 46K, all models; rear: Dana (previously Eaton) single-reduction DS480, M977 (all variants), M978, M985 (both variants), M1120 and M1977; Dana (previously Eaton) single-reduction DS580, M983 (both variants); Dana (previously Eaton) single-reduction DS650, M984						
Tyres:	1600R × 20, original standard fit was Michelin XL, current standard fit is Michelin XZL						
Brakes:							
(main)	dual circuit, air-operated S-cam, drums all-round						
(parking)	spring brakes acting on 3rd and 4th axles						
Electrical system:	24 V	24 V	24 V	24 V	24 V	24 V	24 V
Batteries:	4 × 12 V	4 × 12 V	4 × 12 V	4 × 12 V	4 × 12 V	4 × 12 V	4 × 12 V

The M1158 HEWATT is designed to support the TFFT while providing supplementary fire suppression capabilities. Each HEWATT is each equipped with a 2,500 US gallon integrated water tank, 500 US gallons per minute single-stage pump, 50 US gallon foam cell and 250 US gallons per minute front bumper mounted turret/monitor. The HEWATT is based on the M985A2 HEMTT chassis.

Hybrid electric (ProPulse) and HEMTT A3 variants

In August 2001 Oshkosh Truck Corporation announced it had been selected as an industry partner for hybrid-electric technology applications for military vehicles. The selection was made by the National Automotive Center (NAC) and included directions to integrate the Oshkosh ProPulse hybrid-electric system into an Oshkosh HEMTT as part of a subcontract from Southwest Research Institute (SwRI), an independent research and development organisation. SwRI was the prime contractor to the US Army's TACOM on this project, and Oshkosh a major subcontractor to SwRI. The program manager for heavy tactical vehicles at TACOM provided the vehicle to be equipped with the ProPulse system.

In February 2002 Oshkosh Truck demonstrated the ProPulse HEMTT (the first heavy-payload defence truck with an electric hybrid drive) at the Association of the United States Army (AUSA) Winter Symposium. The ProPulse system consists of a diesel engine, running at a constant speed, which turns a generator that powers electric motors at each differential.

In February 2003, Oshkosh Truck announced the Department of Defense, through the National Automotive Center and US Army's TACOM, had awarded the company USD500,000 in research grants for Oshkosh's development of a ready-for-production version of its ProPulse technology in military vehicles. In February 2005, Oshkosh Truck announced it had developed the next generation of its HEMTT for the US Army. Known as the HEMTT A3, this third-generation design features a number of advanced technologies such as hybrid-electric drive, an enhanced Load Handling System (LHS) and independent suspension to improve performance and enhance the US Army's deployability and mobility.

Oshkosh unveiled the HEMTT A3 at the Association of the US Army Winter Exposition in Fort Lauderdale. The HEMTT A3 is the first production-ready tactical defence vehicle to feature a diesel-electric drive system. The fitted ProPulse system design uses a modular series-hybrid arrangement to simplify the transmission of power to the wheels. The diesel engine powers an electric generator, which provides direct power to the wheels, eliminating the torque converter, automatic transmission, transfer box and drive shafts. A dedicated motor controlled from its own power converters drives each axle independently.

ProPulse technology, it is claimed, can increase fuel economy by up to 40 percent over conventional power trains. The diesel engine is optimised to run at the most efficient speed based on power demand, and transient loads to the engine are eliminated using stored energy. This eliminates the inefficiency associated with changing rpm levels during acceleration and deceleration, and also reduces emissions. During stopping operations, the electric motors operate as generators, and energy is stored for use during the next acceleration. Other stated advantages of the system include the system acting as an on-board generator, providing enough electricity (up to 200 kW of AC power) to power a small airfield, hospital or military command centre. Since the system uses no batteries, they never need to be replaced, and the amount of fuel needed to supply ProPulse-equipped trucks will be less; at one stage it was costing USD400 a gallon to deliver fuel to forces in Afghanistan.

The HEMTT A3 was developed under a research and development grant from the Department of Defense, through the Heavy Tactical Vehicle Program Office and TACOM. The vehicle underwent 10,000 miles of contractor directed testing at Nevada Automotive Test Centre in mid-2007 with continuous development of software and hardware as test results were received. By early 2008, the vehicle was at Aberdeen Test Center undergoing testing on its hybrid-electric/export power capabilities, and was scheduled for additional endurance testing.

In December 2008 Oshkosh Defense announced it had been awarded a contract modification for continuing research and development of the HEMTT A3. Valued at USD9.4 million, the contract modification includes additional improvements to the current HEMTT A3 technology demonstrator to provide an operationally complete and fully equipped vehicle for the US Army. The vehicle's engine horsepower will be uprated and it will incorporate a US Army Long-Term Armour Strategy (LTAS) compliant integral lightweight composite armour (A-kit) and add-on lightweight composite armour appliqué (B-kit) to improve crew protection. The contract modification also will result in the production of two new HEMTT A3 vehicles, one of which will be provided to the US Army for a 20,000-mile durability test at its Aberdeen Test Center. The second vehicle will be used for performance-capability testing of the HEMTT A3 against current HEMTT A2/A4 production vehicles.

HEMTT A4

The HEMTT A4 was developed to meet US Army requirements for a vehicle with a more modern power pack, improved crew protection and compatibility with the Long Term Armour Strategy (LTAS). US Army trials commenced in June 2006, and the initial HEMTT A4 was placed in October 2007. The initial USD207 contract million called for 526 vehicles in a variety of configurations. The A4 HEMTT entered production in July 2008.

The HEMTT A4 is powered by a 500 hp Caterpillar C-15 EPA 2004 compliant engine that peaks at 515 hp and provides up to 70 hp more than the Detroit Diesel 8V92TA engine of the HEMTT A2 it replaces. This is coupled to a 600 hp-rated Allison 4500P five-speed automatic transmission, and uprated Oshkosh 55,000 two-speed transfer box. The conventional leaf spring suspension of the HEMTT A2 has been replaced by air suspension on the HEMTT A4.

The other main differences between the A2 and A4 models are cab-related. While visually similar, the HEMTT A4 is fitted with the slightly larger current PLS A1 cab. This cab complies with the US Army's LTAS requirements of an A- and B-kit armouring philosophy. Additionally, it comes as standard with integrated floor armour, an integrated mount a for a machine gun and gunner protection kit, and air-conditioning.

lp;qUS Customs Service HEMTT

The US Customs Service operates a small number of HEMTTs which have been specially modified to act as mobile winch and anchor vehicles for aerostats (non-motorised blimps) equipped with General Electric radar. The vehicles are located along the US-Mexican border to counter drug-smuggling activities. Each vehicle carries a cable drum and winch gear to allow an aerostat to operate at heights up to 4,570 m.

M989A1 Heavy Expanded Mobility Ammunition Trailer (HEMAT)

The M989A1 Heavy Expanded Mobility Ammunition Trailer (HEMAT - originally the XM989) is a primary trailer for use with the HEMTT and is intended for the carrying of Multiple Launch Rocket System (MLRS) rocket pods although other applications include transporting ammunition pallets as well as fuel bladders and pods.

A contract was awarded in FY82 for 400 trailers but this contract was suspended in 1985, following the discovery of a stability problem after 353 trailers had been delivered. In 1986, the US Army solicited bids for a new multiyear production phase. Bids were submitted by the Southwest Mobile Systems Corporation (later Systems & Electronics Inc. (SEI), now DRS Sustainment Systems Inc.), Teledyne Continental Motors, Landoll and Prototype Development. In 1987, the then Southwest Mobile Systems Corporation was awarded a four-year contract for 1,046 M989A1 HEMAT trailers with a 50 per cent option. Testing of the first article units was carried out during 1989. Contract deliveries commenced during 1990.

Following a further production contract issued in March 2000, production of the M989A1 started again during late 2000. Changes introduced for the new production batch included new radial tyres, revised lighting, extra corrosion resistance and improved storage box protection.

The most recent contract was awarded in September 2005. Under this five-year Indefinite Delivery/Indefinite Quantity (ID/IQ) contract up to 583 trailers valued at USD40 million could be delivered between award and October 2009. The initial order under the contract was valued at USD4.8 million and called for 61 M981A1 HEMATs. The most recent award under this contract was announced in September 2008 and is valued at USD42 million, and called for in excess of 670 additional M989A1 Heavy Expanded Mobility Ammunition Trailers (HEMATs).

On 26 January 2006 DRS Technologies Inc. announced that it had completed its acquisition of Engineered Support Systems, Inc. In the transaction, a wholly-owned subsidiary of DRS was merged with Engineered Support Systems (ESSI), forming DRS's third operating segment – the Sustainment Systems & Services Group.

The HEMAT is a two-axle trailer with the front axle featuring an Ackerman steering design; the rear axle is stationary. The brakes are air-actuated while the air suspension is designed for on- and off-road mobility; the suspension is automatically self-adjusting with self-levelling control. Mission profile is 50 per cent primary roads, 50 per cent cross-country. The trailer meets all the requirements for a 0.55 g lateral stability.

The treated hardwood deck is surrounded by 22 tiedown rings, evenly spaced for securing MLRS pods and other payloads up to 10,000 kg. The HEMAT is normally towed by the M985 HEMTT but can be towed by other military or commercial tractors as well as the M270 MLRS launch vehicle. The HEMAT can be air-transported, unloaded, in a C-130 Hercules transport aircraft, or in a loaded state by C-17 and C-5 aircraft. It can also be carried, loaded, by a CH-47D Chinook helicopter.

It has been proposed that the M989A1 could be used to carry a 9,463 litre fuel tank for field refuelling. It could also be used for the road transportation of customised shelters. The M989A1 was proposed as a candidate for the MTVR trailer for the US Marine Corps.

Specifications See table at bottom of previous page
M989A1 HEMAT
Weight:
(gross) 14,932 kg
(kerb) 4,932 kg
(max payload) 10,000 kg
Length: 7.85 m
Width:
(cargo area) 2.44 m
(wheels) 2.5 m
Height: 1.45 m
Cargo area: 4.47 × 2.44 m
Ground clearance:
(bottom of axles) 370 mm
(trailer structure) 550 mm
Wheelbase: 5.94 m
Gradient: 40%
Side slope: 30%
Brakes: air
Suspension: air ride

Status

HEMTT: In production. In service with US Armed Forces (more than 22,000 delivered, deliveries continue) and others; as of January 2011 around 1,100 vehicles have been exported (see text). Commercial variants have also been sold.

HEMAT: Production as required, in service with the US Army (around 2,900 produced).

Contractor

Oshkosh Truck Corporation
DRS Sustainment Systems Inc.

Oshkosh (6 × 6) Medium Tactical Vehicle Replacement (MTVR) and trailers

Development

The Oshkosh Defense (previously Oshkosh Truck Corporation) MTVR has its design origins in two US military programmes, the 5 ton Tactical Truck Replacement (5TTR) for the US Army, and the Medium Tactical Vehicle Replacement (MTVR) for the US Marines. The aim of these programmes was to upgrade, refurbish and prolong the effective service life of around 3,400 US Army M923 series 5 ton 6 × 6 trucks, and 8,100 US Marines M809 and M939 series 5 ton 6 × 6 trucks.

In 1996, both the then Oshkosh Truck and the then AM General Corporation (now AM General LLC) were awarded prototype and development contracts for both the 5TTR and MTVR programmes, however, the US Army's 5TTR programme was terminated early for financial reasons. The MTVR programme continued and at this stage it remained the intention of the Marines' not to replace with new vehicles but to upgrade their aging M809 and M939 fleets from 5 ton (4,536 kg) into dual-rated 7.1 ton (6,441 kg) off-road, 15 ton (13,608 kg) on-road capacity trucks. In addition to an 80 per cent more powerful approximate 425 hp engine, anti-lock brakes and a traction control system, the biggest single improvement planned for the programme was the fitting of fully independent coil-sprung suspension.

With only the bonnet, cab and loadbed of the original vehicles proving salvageable - and these all requiring structural enhancements to meet the revised payload and off-road performance requirements, plus extensive anti-corrosion treatments to meet the Marines' requirement for a 22-year service life from their upgraded vehicles - it soon became clear to Oshkosh that a new-build option would be a far more cost-effective route to take and development of the Oshkosh MTVR commenced.

In February 1999 the US Department of Defense (DoD) awarded Oshkosh Truck a multi-year production contract with the first 20 of 5,666 vehicles scheduled for delivery by the end of 1999. The initial contract potential called for up to 8,168 MTVRs (including options for 2,502) in four variants over five programme years. Deliveries under the initial contract concluded during August 2005 following the delivery of 6,931 vehicles, 6,393 to the USMC and 538 to the Navy (Seabees). The first MTVRs were fielded by the USMC in July 2001.

The four variants initially covered by the first production contract are as follows:

MK23 - standard cargo truck, 4.674 m wheelbase
MK25 - standard cargo truck with winch, 4.674 m wheelbase
MK27 - extended cargo truck, 5.486 m wheelbase
MK28 - extended cargo truck with winch, 5.486 m wheelbase.

These were followed by three additional variants:

MK29 - dump truck without winch, 4.674 m wheelbase
MK30 - dump truck with winch, 4.674 m wheelbase
MK36 - wrecker, 5.486 m wheelbase.

A follow-on FY05-FY10 MTVR production contract was awarded to Oshkosh in July 2004. Production under this Requirements-type contract which initially only covered potential FMS, plus the continuing requirements of the US Navy, commenced in March 2005. The US Navy and USMC combined will now receive in excess of 2,000 vehicles under this contract.

The 10,000th MTVR was completed on 16th of May 2008.

The US Navy currently has under contract the following MTVR variants: MK25, MK28, MK28C, MK30, MK31 and MK36. The most recent MTVR variant to enter production is the MK31 Medium Equipment Transporter (MET) tractor truck which following user evaluation, entered production for the Seebees early 2005; up to 460 are required. From late 2005, the USMC also received MK31 METs. Full details of the MK31 MET can be found in the Heavy equipment transporter section.

The US Navy also has a requirement to replace a fleet of assorted Special Purpose Vehicle (SPV) types based on a mix of tactical and commercial truck chassis. These include: water distributor, 2,000 US gallon; fuel, 1,500 US gallon; field service; asphalt distributor; earth auger. The US Navy's intention is to replace this fleet with a new MTVR variant, the MK28C. Interchangeable Commercial-Off-The-Shelf (COTS) - or modified COTS - bodies will be procured and then fitted to MK28C chassis as field circumstances dictate. As of late 2005, it was projected that a total of 66 water distributor, 52 fuel (increased to 2,000 US gallon capacity), 58 field service, 24 asphalt distributor and 42 earth auger bodies would be procured during FY05-FY10.

Current production MTVR (2008) fitted with a Plasan Sasa developed Armor Protection Kit (APK) (Shaun C Connors)   1296271

Under a separate contract, Oshkosh commenced production in July 2004 of a further MTVR variant, the MK37. Based on the MK27 and fitted with a rear-mounted Hiab materials handling crane rated at 2,500 kg at 6.1 m maximum reach, the MK37 has been designed as a resupply vehicle for the US Marines HIgh Mobility Artillery Rocket System (HIMARS). The contract covers around 80 vehicles and a similar number of associated trailers. The trailer, designated as MK38, is based on a modified Oshkosh MTVR trailer. Full details of MTVR trailers can be found elsewhere in this entry.

The most recent announced MTVR (vehicle) delivery award was disclosed in January 2010 and called for in excess of 90 vehicles, primarily cargo variants but including small quantities of wrecker, tractor truck and dump variants. The award, valued at USD31.5 million, also included an armour-related component. Deliveries were scheduled for completion late-2010.

Prototype and developmental MTVR variants have also been produced. These variants have included 6 × 6 and 8 × 8 chassis fitted with a Multilift (now Hiab) Load Handling System (LHS). Two each off 6 × 6 and 8 × 8 LHS prototypes have been built. The 6 × 6 chassis are 9/14 ton (8,165/12,701 kg) on-/off-road rated, while the two 8 × 8 prototypes are rated at 16.5 US tonnes (14,967 kg) and 15,000 kg payload. Both 8 × 8 chassis are fitted with a tridem rear axle layout, the rear axles (of which axles three and four steer) sprung hydraulically. On the 16.5 ton version, which has an overall length (with flatrack) of 10.211 m, the tridem rear bogie individual wheelbases are a uniform 1.435 m. On the 15,000 kg version, which has an overall length (with flatrack) of 11.135 m, the tridem rear bogie wheelbases are 1.968 m (2nd to 3rd) and 1.473 m (3rd to 4th).

Other MTVR variants including two 4 × 4 variants have been developed and are available. The 4 × 4 Short Bed Cargo Truck has an overall length of 6.774 m, and with a GVW of 15,629 kg can carry (without armour) 4,536 kg off-road, around 1,800 kg less than the 6 × 6. The 4 × 4 Lightweight Cargo Truck has an overall length of 7.48 m, has an unladen weight of 9,072 kg and has a payload of 5,000 kg without armour. The Short Bed Cargo Truck has a high degree of commonality with the 6 x 6 MTVR and is targeted at the USMC, while the Lightweight 4 × 4 is aimed at the opposite end of the payload/capability scale, this MTVR variant being fitted with beam-type axles and a simpler leaf spring (front) and airbag (rear) suspension set-up for markets where the sophistication of an independent set-up is not-required.

Also available is a four-door crew cab MTVR. This shares the same 5.486 wheelbase has the MK27/MK28 extended cargo truck, but behind the crew cab has the cargo body of the standard 4.674 m wheelbase MK24/MK24

Current production (2008) Oshkosh (6 × 6) Medium Tactical Vehicle Replacement (MTVR) in standard cargo truck configuration (Shaun C Connors)   1296270

cargo truck fitted. The four-door crew cab variant has an overall length of 8.788 m, a GVW rating of 28,213 kg and has an unladen weight of 14,968/15,422 kg (without/with winch).

A European-friendly forward control (with the engine mounted behind the cab) variant of the MTVR, designated as Z Series, has also been built.

In conjunction with Pierce Manufacturing (an Oshkosh Corporation Company), Oshkosh has developed the MTVR MK23/25-based Hawk Extreme, a wildland firefighting water tender. This product has been sold commercially.

In July 2005, Oshkosh was awarded a five-month contract from the Office of Naval Research for the first phase of a four-phase project to develop an MTVR with a 60 kW on-board power generating capability. Phase IV of the programme called for a vehicle to be ready for test in FY08. Following tests at Aberdeen Proving Ground in May 2008, Oshkosh demonstrated a modified MTVR equipped with enough exportable electrical energy to produce 21 kW of power-on-the-move for mobile command post shelters, communications and weapons systems. Stationary, the vehicle produces 120 kW of military-grade power.

Following on from these On-Board Vehicle Power (OBVP) technology development efforts between Oshkosh and the Office of Naval Research, in July 2010, Oshkosh announced that it had been awarded a contract by the US Marine Corps Systems Command (MARCORSYSCOM) to supply OBVP kits for military testing. Contract value is in excess of USD8 million.

The OBVP kits will be installed on Marine Corps MTVR standard and extended MTVR cargo trucks for government evaluation and testing. The installation is expected to be completed in January 2012 and the evaluation and testing is expected to begin in March 2012. The MTVR with OBVP will provide 120 kW of exportable military-grade power while stationary, and 21 kW of military-grade power while on the move. Oshkosh also will provide the training and sustainment support required during government testing.

In July 2009 Oshkosh was awarded two further contracts from the Office of Naval Research, the aims of which are to help advance diesel-electric and hybrid-electric drive technologies to improve fuel efficiency and on-board power capabilities. Work on both contracts is scheduled to run until 2011.

Oshkosh Truck was awarded a contract by the USMC to re-manufacture 27 MTVRs in 2005. Under the terms of this contract, these trucks were to be returned to as new configuration and with a full new vehicle warranty. A further 26 MTVRs have since been re-manufactured, the last of these completed early-2007.

Together with a selection of industry partners, Oshkosh has developed the MTVR-based TerraMax, an autonomous vehicle equipped with an extensive array of sensors, cameras and navigational computers. TerraMax competed in the 2004 (175 miles), 2005 (150 miles), 2006 (132 miles) and 2007 (one of 11 finalists) DARPA Grand Challenge, a Pentagon-sponsored autonomous vehicle race designed to spur robotic development for military ground vehicle applications. Oshkosh Defense has the long-term goal of providing driverless support vehicles for the US military.

In January 2009 Oshkosh announced a Cooperative Research and Development Agreement (CRADA) with the US Army's Tank and Automotive Research, Development and Engineering Center (TARDEC) to refine technology for the operation of unmanned ground vehicles in convoy missions in real-world environments. The CRADA calls for a three-year collaboration between the Army and Oshkosh to integrate a Convoy Active Safety Technology (CAST) surrogate system onto Oshkosh's unmanned TerraMax vehicle. The objective is to create a lead vehicle that can navigate and operate in missions, while communicating route information to another unmanned follower vehicle. The vehicles must be able to operate near-autonomous in a safe manner among people, animals, vehicles and other obstacles at operational speeds and in tactical environments.

Export sales

The MTVR has been demonstrated to a number of potential export customers and in March 2003 the UK MoD became the first export customer for the type when Oshkosh Truck was awarded the Wheeled

From the rear and showing the rear-pull winch, an Oshkosh MK28 (6 × 6) Medium Tactical Vehicle Replacement (MTVR) in extended cargo truck (with winch) configuration; without winch the designation is MK27
(Shaun C Connors)   1128702

Oshkosh MK29 (6 × 6) Medium Tactical Vehicle Replacement (MTVR) in dump truck configuration; with a winch fitted the designation is MK30. The Crysteel Manufacturing dump body measures (internally) 4.16 × 2.15 × .56 m (L × W × H) and has a struck capacity of 4.97 m³
(Shaun C Connors)   1128704

Tanker contract. Valued at approximately GBP160 million (USD250 million) for initial vehicle acquisition and support over 15 years, the Wheeled Tanker requirement called for 218 × 20,000-litre Close Support Tankers (CSTs) (fuel); 82 × 15,000-litre Tactical Aircraft Refuellers (TARs) and 48 × 18,000-litre CSTs (water); a contract option for an additional nine CST (water) has been exercised. An articulated combination, the tractor truck is a modified MK23 MTVR with a wheelbase shortened by 330 mm (13 in) and the cab extended by 660 mm (24 in). Automotive changes include the Caterpillar C-12 six-cylinder diesel uprated from 425 to 445 hp and upgraded to meet EURO III emissions regulations. The 7F/1R Allison HD 4070P automatic transmission of the standard MTVR is replaced by a 6F/1R 'wide ratio' Allison HD 4560P unit. Wheeled Tanker deliveries commenced in February 2005 and were completed in November 2006. Full details of the 20,000-litre Close Support Tankers (CSTs) (fuel) and 15,000-litre Tactical Aircraft Refuellers (TARs) can be found in the Bulk fuel transportation and storage section. Full details of the 18,000-litre CSTs (water) can be found in the Water supplies section.

Oshkosh Truck proposed a family of seven MTVR-based designs to meet the UK MoD's Support Vehicle requirement. MAN was awarded this contract in March 2005.

Greece has received a total of 73 MTVRs to date, with an initial 18 MK27 chassis delivered to ELBO (Hellenic Vehicle Industry) during 2004. A further 15 MK27 chassis were delivered during 2005, and during October 2006 a further 40 MK27 chassis were delivered. Initial deliveries (2004/2005) are fitted with medium recovery equipment supplied by Eyal of Israel, while the October 2006 delivery are fitted out as ammunition transporter vehicles to operate alongside the Hellenic Army's Leopard MBTs.

The MTVR is a purpose-designed tactical truck and as such comes with a price premium compared to militarised commercial designs and while this can be recouped in terms of longevity and through life operating costs, not all armed forces can afford the initial outlay for such a truck. To address this issue, mid 2005 Oshkosh Truck announced the Medium Tactical Truck (MTT). The combination of selected MTVR components (including the chassis) together with components from other Oshkosh military and severe duty commercial products has enabled a vehicle to be developed that offers many of the attributes/capabilities of the MTVR, but at a price far closer to that of a militarised commercial design. An initial 30 MTTs were delivered to Egypt from 2007.

Description

Unless specifically stated, this descriptive text refers to the MTVR variants used by the USMC.

All versions of the Oshkosh (6 × 6) Medium Tactical Vehicle Replacement (MTVR) are based on the same 6 × 6 drive configuration with the engine under a forward non-corroding and weight-saving fibreglass bonnet. The three-seat cab is of welded aluminium extrusion construction with adhesive bonded aluminium skins. The aluminium hinged windscreen, roof, side-walls, door frames and rear wall can be folded down to reduce overall height to 2.489 m. From mid-2007, production vehicles are armour-ready and have air-conditioning, revised cab mounts and upgraded cab suspension.

The chassis frame of the MTVR is constructed using bolted/huck-bolted formed channel (248 × 76 × 9.7 mm) made of heat-treated carbon manganese steel with a yield strength of 758 MPa. Both chassis and cab feature extensive corrosion protection as the US Marines required the MTVR to have sufficient corrosion protection to ensure an effective service life of 22 years.

With the exception of the UK's Wheeled Tanker variants and proposed 4 × 4 variants, all MTVRs are powered by a Caterpillar C-12, Advanced Diesel Engine Management (ADEM) III 11.9-litre six-cylinder inline turbocharged, water-cooled four-stroke diesel that develops a maximum 425 hp at 1,800 rpm and 2,101 N.m of torque at 1,200 rpm. Engine cooling is

Oshkosh MK31 (6 × 6) Medium Tactical Vehicle Replacement (MTVR) tractor trucks (Shaun C Connors) 1296269

provided by 8.006 cm² radiator and 813 mm diameter nine-blade fan. Power output of the engine is automatically reduced by around 20 per cent when the Central Tyre Inflation (CTI) system is set at 0 to 1,814 kg (two tonnes) payload, 425 hp being considered unnecessary for the 12,500-14,000 kg (approximately) unladen MTVR. This power reduction not only reduces fuel consumption and driveline stresses, but has the benefit of giving laden an unladen trucks broadly the same response characteristics. Maximum sustainable speed on paved roads is 105 km/h, cruising range (model dependant) is up to 483 km. A three-stage (two, four or six cylinder) manually selected, automatically applied engine compression brake is fitted to assist the braking system.

The engine is coupled to an Allison HD 4070P automatic 7F/1R transmission, TC-541 torque converter and an Oshkosh 30000 Series single-speed transfer box. The combination of torque converter and an extra low ratio (7.63:1) first gear allows for a single-speed transfer box to replace the more complex two-speed unit more commonly associated with off-road vehicles. Full-time all-wheel drive is employed and under highway driving conditions the torque split is 32 per cent front, 68 per cent rear.

For suspension the MTVR uses Oshkosh TAK-4 independent suspension, this utilising a coil spring and upper and lower control arms at wheel position. This system provides each front wheel with a total vertical travel of 406 mm and a travel of 325 mm on the rear axles. The front axle is rated at 7,257 kg, the second at 10,659 kg, the third at 11,567 kg. The MK36 wrecker and MK31 tractor variants have Hendrickson hydraulic suspension on the rear axles. Full details of the MK36 MTVR wrecker variant can be found in the Recovery vehicles section. In trials MTVR demonstrated an ability to cover rough ground at more than twice the speed of a conventionally sprung vehicle, and (at comparable speeds) with a significant reduction in the amount of damaging energy transmitted into the vehicle chassis, bodywork, mechanicals and driver. This reduction in transmitted energy being a major factor in increasing the all-important longevity of components and reduction of driver fatigue.

MTVR is fitted with 1600R 20 Michelin XZL super singles tyres. With the exception of the MK36 wrecker variant, no spare wheel and tyre is carried, the loss of its 463 kg being critical in keeping the unladen weight of the base MK23 MTVR below the 12,700 kg maximum for underslung transport by CH-53 helicopter. Compensating for no spare wheel is a runflat setting option on the CTI system. A CTI system allows the driver to adjust tyre pressures to suit both payload and terrain conditions, from the driving seat. In an emergency the MTVR system can be directed to continuously inflate one tyre only. The 508 × 254 mm two-piece bolt-together steel wheel rims are fitted with beadlocks for extreme low-pressure operations

Oshkosh MK27 chassis of the Hellenic Army fitted with recovery equipment supplied by Eyal of Israel (Shaun C Connors) 1190251

Two 9/14 ton (8,165/12,701 kg) on/off-road rated 6 × 6 Load Handling System (LHS) MTVR prototypes with a 6.02 m wheelbase have been produced. A single 15 ton (14,969 kg) 8 × 8 with a tridem rear bogie, hydraulic rear suspension and steered third and fourth axles has also been produced (Shaun C Connors) 1067541

and tyres will remain seated at pressures down to 10 psi. In the event that any one tyre should fail totally, a limp-home facility allows for a second axle suspension unit to be raised and secured, its wheel then rolled and fitted in the position of the damaged tyre.

The CTI system has three payload and four terrain settings. The three payload settings being; 0 to 1,814 kg (two tonnes), 1,814 to 6,441 kg (7.1 tonnes) and 6,441 to 13,608 kg (15 tonnes); MTVR following the usual US practice of being dual payload rated, 6,441 kg (7.1 tonnes) off-road, 13,608 kg (15 tonnes) on primary or secondary roads. The four terrain settings are; highway, cross-country, mud/sand/snow, and emergency. At the highway setting an Automatic Traction Control (ATC) system operates via the anti-lock brakes (ABS), applying braking force to any wheel detected as slipping, thus allowing torque to transfer to the non rotating opposite wheel. From cross-country through to emergency settings the ABS operates in off-road mode and the ATC is automatically disconnected and differential locks are automatically engaged in stages up to full cross and inter-axle lock-up in the emergency setting. The driver retains full control over these systems and at any time may disconnect the ATC or manually engage the differential locks in three stages; transfer box, rear inter-axle and full cross axle locks.

To assist with repairs and diagnosis the On Board Diagnostic System (OBDS) features an information display screen and fault indicators from the engine, transmission, ABS, ATC and CTI. It also has a laptop interface that allows access to the full MTVR database for in-the-field maintenance, diagnostics and repair.

At its maximum 6,441 kg (7.1 ton) off-road payload MTVR was required by the US Marines to climb, hold (for two minutes) and then restart on a 60 per cent gradient. The Marines requirement also specified an ability to traverse a 40 per cent sideslope carrying 6,441 kg and an ability to surmount a 610 mm vertical step and ford 1.52 m of water. MTVR has a climatic operational range of between –32° (with kits from –46°) and +52°C.

All four MTVR cargo body models have removable tailgates and dropsides. The load area for the MK23 and MK25 is 4.3 m long and the MK27 and MK28 is 6.1 m long. The flatbeds can accommodate ISO compatible loads such as containers and shelters. A cargo covering kit is supplied with every cargo truck to provide covering for the cargo area. Front and rear towing eyes are provided along with a tow hook together with electrical and air brake connectors. The S20K self-recovery winch fitted to the MK25, MK28 and MK30 has a 9,072 kg capacity to the rear only. The MTVR is air-transportable in C-5, C-17, C-130 and C-141 aircraft as well as the CH-53 helicopter, although the latter is limited to the MK23 and as an underslung load only. Optional equipment includes an arctic kit for the engine, cargo and personnel arctic kit, a machine gun mounting kit, NBC alarm and decontamination apparatus mounting kits, a pioneer tool kit, tow bar adapter kit, a S-280 shelter access platform kit and a S-280 shelter tie-down kit.

Protection kit and associated upgrades

Oshkosh now promotes the current MTVR armour packages as the MTVR Armor Systems (MAS).

The current Standard MAS with Survivability Upgrade (MAS-SU) kit is available for MK23, MK25, MK27, MK29, MK30, Mk31 and MK37 MTVRs, respective kits designated AMK23 through to AMK37. A specialist variant designated AMK36 is available for the MK36 wrecker. The Reducible Height MAS (MAS-RH) is available for the same MTVR variants as the standard MAS-SU.

Three specific Troop Carrier options are available. The 10 ft (2.54 m) Troop Carrier seats eight fully-equipped troops, is useable on the 4 × 4 MTVR, FMTV and M939 series. Laden weight (including troops) is 3,990 kg. The 14 ft (3.56 m) Troop Carrier seats 12 fully-equipped troops and is useable on the MTVR. Laden weight (including troops) is 5,714 kg. The 20 ft (5.08 m) Troop Carrier seats 20 fully-equipped troops, is useable on the LVSR, PLS and HEMTT LHS, mounting on a standard 20 ft flatrack. Laden weight (including troops) is 9,070 kg.

A UK Wheeled Tanker tractor truck fitted a small arms fire and mine blast protection kit developed by Plasan Sasa in co-operation with Permali Gloucester of the UK (Shaun C Connors) 1296272

Initial development of an MTVR protection kit began in 2003, and following a redesign to address the current increased threat requirement, particularly that posed by Improvised Explosive Devices (IEDs), an initial production contract was awarded late 2004.

Under a contract valued at USD100 million, Israeli armour solutions manufacturer Plasan Sasa (as a subcontractor for the then Armor Holdings of the US) supplied between April and December 2005 some 920 baseline appliqué Armor Protection Kits (APKs) for the MTVR MK23, MK25, MK27, MK28 cab and wheel arch sections, plus 460 modular armoured rear troop-carrier compartments. The cab and troop carrier kits, while complimentary, are separate units and can be installed as such.

The APK, which uses a composite metal armour solution to provide protection to no less than STANAG level 2, offers protection to both vehicle and crew from IEDs, mine blast and other assorted other threats. Installation of the APK requires a vehicle front axle and cab suspension mount upgrade, plus a revision to the cab roof gun mount. Air-conditioning is also fitted.

A follow-on contract for the supply of additional APKs for the same MTVR variants was awarded late 2005. Also valued at USD100 million, this follow-on contract called for the supply of 930 appliqué kits for the MTVR cab and wheel arch sections and 465 modular armoured rear troop-carrier compartments. Deliveries were scheduled to begin early 2006, with full deployment due to be complete by the end of that year.

More recently, two additional APK orders were placed early and mid 2007, these calling for a further 238 and 55 kits, respectively. These kits were for MK29 dump, MK31 tractor truck and MK36 wrecker variants. There are some minor differences in the MK36 wrecker kit.

A reducible height armour package has been developed for the MTVR and this became available from early 2008. In August 2008 the company announced an initial contract award, valued at USD11.7 million, to install height reducible armour kits on MVTRs. An award for 200 kits was made in September 2008, and in October 2008 Oshkosh Defense announced that it had been awarded a contract valued at more than USD180 million for more than 1,500 height reducible armour kits for MTVRs. Further smaller orders have followed, these including a >USD10 million 400-kit award in April 2009 (this including some standard wrecker kits), and a 300-vehicle award in January 2010.

In April 2010 Oshkosh announced it had received an award from the USMC valued at more than USD44 million (but not to exceed USD89 million) for in excess of 5,750 armour/protection-related upgrade kits for the MTVR. Under this award Oshkosh was contracted to deliver in excess of 950 weapons mount kits that allow the installation of motorised Marine Corps Transparent Armor Gun Shields (MCTAGS), these replacing the gunner protection kits on up-armoured vehicles. Oshkosh was also contracted to supply 2,000 door-upgrade kits to support MTVR non-reducible-height armour kits used on trucks that were armoured during 2005-2007. These kits make the doors common with those on MTVRs using the reducible-height armour kits, which Oshkosh began producing in 2008. Additionally, Oshkosh was contracted to deliver MTVR Troop Carrier upgrades. This upgrade included 800 dual-ladder kits, this kit installed in place of single ladders for improved ingress and egress, as well as more than more than 1,000 seatbelt kits to support the Troop Carrier's occupants and more than 1,000 lift-point kits for improved transportability. Work under this award was scheduled for completion in September 2010.

Plasan Sasa, in co-operation with Permali Gloucester of the UK, has also developed a small arms fire and mine blast protection kit for the UK MoD's MTVR-fronted Wheeled Tanker fleet. Fitted vehicles have been deployed by the British Army to Afghanistan and Iraq.

Bull Mine Resistant Ambush Protected Vehicle (MRAP)

In October 2007 Ideal Innovations Inc., Oshkosh Truck Corporation, and Ceradyne Inc. announced that they had delivered Category I and Category II Mine Resistant Ambush Protected (MRAP) II vehicles (known as the Bull) to the US Army Aberdeen Test Centre for further service evaluation. Bull is based on the MTVR.

In December 2007, and following the elimination of proposals by manufacturers including Force Protection (upgraded Cougar), GDLS (upgraded RG-31), Navistar (upgraded MaxxPro) and PVI (upgraded Golan), the USMC awarded two companies, BAE Systems and Ideal Innovations contracts to develop MRAP II vehicles. Each company was contracted to supply six prototypes in MRAP Category I configuration.

By January 2010 no orders for MRAP II vehicles had been placed, and none were expected.

MTVR trailers

The original Medium Tactical Vehicle Replacement (MTVR) trailer was designed and developed by Oshkosh Truck to provide a matching trailer for the MTVR truck. Current in-service trailers are unable to match the performance and mobility of the MTVR.

Two MTVR trailers in cargo configuration formed part of a prototype contract awarded to Oshkosh Truck in July 1999. The two prototype MTVR trailers were manufactured and tested between May 2000 and March 2001. These trailers were subsequently converted into prototype resupply trailers for the Lockheed Martin Missiles and Fire-Control HIgh Mobility Artillery Rocket System (HIMARS). They retain around 90 per cent commonality with the cargo trailer.

Under a contract awarded in August 2001, Oshkosh Truck manufactured six HIMARS resupply systems, a system consisting of an MTVR truck and accompanying trailer. Under a separate contract, production commenced in July 2004 of around 80 MTVR MK37 HIMARS resupply variants and their associated trailers. The US Army is also procuring HIMARS. Full details of the HIMARS system can be found in *Jane's Armour and Artillery*.

In June 2005 the US Marine Corps System Command (MARCORSYSCOM) awarded the Choctaw Manufacturing and Developing Corporation (CMDC) a USD1.9 million Small Business Sole Source design and development contract for the Medium Tactical Vehicle Replacement (MTVR) Trailer (MTVR-Trailer). In service. The MTVR-Trailer will replace the M149 water tank (Water Bull) trailer, M353 general purpose trailer, and the M105 cargo trailer.

During 2006 CMDC delivered six prototype MTVR-Trailers, two each in cargo, general purpose and water configuration, to the Nevada Automotive Test Center (NATC) for performance testing. In March 2009 a contract was placed for 724 trailers valued at up to USD56.5 million (including options).

The Oshkosh-produced MTVR HIMARS trailer is a two-axle trailer with turntable steering. The trailer has lower profile tyres than its intended towing vehicle to meet stringent lateral stability requirements, but truck and trailer share a common 20-inch wheel rim that allows for interchangeability if circumstances dictate. The spare wheel carrier at the front of the trailer is capable of handling two wheels in any combination for either the trailer (395/85R 20) or MTVR towing vehicle (16.00R 20).

Self-levelling air-ride suspension provides 241 mm of total wheel travel and maintains a consistent cargo deck height independent of payload. Anti-lock brakes (ABS) and an electronically controlled Central Tyre Inflation (CTI) system with on- and off-road settings are standard equipment. An air-assisted drawbar lift is fitted, and the turntable steering has an automatic locking feature to aid in reversing operations. The trailer is air-transportable by C-130 aircraft and is fitted with hard lift points for handling by crane.

Numerous parts of the Oshkosh design are common to the MTVR range of cargo trucks. These include the ISO bed configuration (MTVR MK23 and MK25), bow and tarpaulin kit, removable tailgate and drop sides, and wheels. The headboard is removable.

The Oshkosh MTVR trailer is capable of carrying 5,624 kg of payload while being towed either on or off-road by the MTVR. The payload of the HIMARS variant is two HIMARS rocket pods.

Choctaw Manufacturing and Developing Corporation's MTVR-Trailers share a common chassis that feature an independent wheel suspension system.

Two MTVR trailers in cargo configuration formed part of a prototype contract awarded to Oshkosh Truck in July 1999. These prototypes were subsequently converted into prototype resupply trailers for the Lockheed Martin Missiles and Fire Control HIgh Mobility Artillery Rocket System (HIMARS). Under a contract awarded in August 2001, Oshkosh Truck manufactured six HIMARS resupply systems. Under a separate contract, production commenced in July 2004 of around 80 MTVR MK37 HIMARS resupply variants and their associated trailers (Shaun C Connors) 1128714

Model	MK23	MK25	MK27	MK28	MK29	MK30	MK37
Cab seating:	1 +2	1 + 2	1 + 2	1 + 2	1 +2	1 + 2	1 + 2
Configuration:	6 × 6	6 × 6	6 × 6	6 × 6	6 × 6	6 × 6	6 × 6
Weight:							
(kerb)	12,610 kg	13,013 kg	13,688 kg	14,093 kg	13,982 kg	14,290 kg	15,451 kg
(GVW)	26,218 kg	26,621 kg	27,296 kg	27,700 kg	26,308 kg	26,308 kg	27,700
(payload - primary and secondary roads)	13,608 kg	13,608 kg	13,608 kg	13,608 kg	12,701 kg	12,701 kg	12,247 kg
(payload, all-terrain)	6,441 kg	6,441 kg	6,441 kg	6,441 kg	5,534 kg	5,534 kg	5,080 kg
(towed load)	9,980 kg	9,980 kg	9,980 kg	9,980 kg	9,980 kg	9,980 kg	9,980 kg
Length:	7.998 m	7,998 m	9.817 m	9,817 m	8.052 m	8.052 m	9.136 m
Width:	2.49 m	2.49 m	2.49 m	2.49 m	2.49 m	2.49 m	2.49 m
Height: (top of cab)	3.185 m	3.185 m	3.172 m	3.172 m	3.163 m	3.163 m	3.108 m
Track:	2.052 m	2.052 m	2.052 m	2.052 m	2.052 m	2.052 m	2.052 m
Wheelbase:	4.674 m	4.674 m	5.486 m	5.486 m	4.674 m	4.674 m	5.486
Angle of approach/departure:	50°/36°	50°/36°	50°/20°	50°/20°	50°/36°	50°/36°	50°/28°
Max speed: (road)	105 km/h	105 km/h	105 km/h	105 km/h	105 km/h	105 km/h	105 km/h
Range: (road)	483 km	483 km	483 km	483 km	483 km	483 km	483 km
Fuel capacity:	295 litres	295 litres	295 litres	295 litres	295 litres	295 litres	295 litres
Gradient: (CCGVW)	60%	60%	60%	60%	60%	60%	60%
Side slope: (CCGVW)	40%	40%	40%	40%	40%	40%	40%
Fording: (without preparation)	1.524 m	1.524 m	1.524 m	1.524 m	1.524 m	1.524 m	1.524 m
Engine:	Caterpillar C-12 ADEM (Advanced Diesel Engine Management) III 11.9-litre 6-cylinder inline turbocharged and water-cooled 4-stroke diesel developing 425 hp (317 kW) at 1,800 rpm and 2,101 N.m torque at 1,200 rpm						
Transmission:	Allison HD 4070P with 7 forward and 1 reverse gears; TC-541 torque converter, second gear start						
Transfer box:	Oshkosh 30000 single-speed with torque proportioning differential and manual differential lock						
Steering:	Shepard power-assisted with booster and separate fluid reservoir						
Turning radius: (wall to wall)	13 m	13 m	14.54 m	14.94 m	13 m	13 m	14.94 m
Suspension:	Oshkosh TAK-4 independent suspension, coil spring upper/lower control arms; anti-roll bar on second and third axles. Front axle rated at 7,257 kg, second at 10,659 kg, third at 11,567 kg						
Tyres:	1600R 20 Michelin XZL with CTI system						
Brakes:	dual circuit, air, drums on all axles (Meritor 410 × 180 mm, front; Eaton 419 × 178 mm, rear). ABS with off-road programme. Supplementary three-stage (2-, 4- or 6-cylinder) manually selected, automatically applied engine compression brake						
Electrical system:	24 V	24 V	24 V	24 V	24 V	24 V	24 V
Batteries:	2 × 12 V	2 × 12 V	2 × 12 V	2 × 12 V	2 × 12 V	2 × 12 V	2 × 12 V
Alternator:	150 A	150 A	150 A	150 A	150 A	150 A	150 A

Specifications See table above

Oshkosh HIMARS MTVR trailer

Weight:
(gross) 9,979 kg
(kerb) 4,354 kg
(max payload) 5,624 kg

Length:
(inc drawbar) 7.996 m
(loadbed) 4.062 m

Width: 2.43 m

Height:
(overall - top of headboard) 2.075 m
(cargo bed, loaded) 1.36 m

Cargo area: (L × W) 4.06 m × 2.34 m

Ground clearance: 420 mm

Track: 2.06 m

Wheelbase: 3.97 m

Gradient: 60%

Side Slope: 30%

Fording: (without preparation) 1.524 m

Axles/suspension: Dana Spicer axles, air suspension

Tyres: 395/85R 20 Michelin XML

Brakes: air, drums (419 × 178 mm) front and rear. Haldex ABS fitted

Electrical: 24 V

Status
MTVR: Supplied to Greece (73, 2004–2006), the UK (Wheeled Tanker tractor truck, 357 (including option)), the US Marine Corps and Navy (see text for details).

Trailers: Oshkosh - Prototypes produced and tested in cargo variants; HIMARS resupply variant in production (approximately 80). CMDC: MTVR-Trailer design and development contract awarded June 2005, deliveries of test examples during 2006, 724-unit production award in March 2009.

Contractor
Oshkosh Truck Corporation
Choctaw Manufacturing and Development Corporation (CMDC)

Oshkosh MK48 Series Logistic Vehicle System (LVS)

Development

The United States Marine Corps (USMC) Logistic Vehicle System (LVS) has its origins in an ambitious project started well over 40 years ago by Lockheed. As one of several projects in the company's long range business plan for diversification into technological areas outside of the aerospace field, in the early 1960s Lockheed began an intensive study of the requirements and current limitations of military combat vehicles. A feasibility study was conducted to determine the possibility of designing a vehicle that would result in at least 2 to 1 improvement in military vehicle performance. In February 1965 the Twister project was established in-house by Lockheed as a company-funded programme, and within nine months the first test bed was completed.

The US Army became interested, and Lockheed was awarded a USD1.9 million contract in 1969 for three Twister vehicles, two test beds (one amphibious) and an armoured version, the latter being designated XM808. Twister was a twin-bodied, twin-engined, eight-wheel, all-wheel

Oshkosh MK48/14 logistics platform truck (Oshkosh Defense)   1128790

Details of MK family programmes

LVS production totals	MK48	MK14	MK15	MK16	MK17	total
First programme year (1984):	139	92	14	9	27	
Second programme year (1985):	148	58	14	34	42	
Third programme year (1986):	354	176	26	68	84	
Fourth programme year (1987):	360	110	23	138	87	
Fifth programme year (1988):	432	408				
Programme totals:	1,433	844	77	277	240	2,871
Options:	14	14				
	14	14	4		1	
	66	66				
	155	511	16		8	
Option totals:	249	605	20		9	883
Overall initial contract award total:	1,682	1,449	97	277	249	3,754

drive design and despite performing exceptionally well in mobility trials, the maintenance and cost implications of such a complex design set-up soon became apparent and as a project, Twister was cancelled.

Based on their experience with Twister, Lockheed built two prototypes of a larger, more truck-like version called the Dragon Wagon, and these were extensively tested. A short production run of 15 vehicles followed, and during 1978 Lockheed announced the company was investigating the possibilities of licensing the programme to an outside company for further production.

In May 1979, the then Oshkosh Truck Corporation and Lockheed Missile and Space Company announced they had begun a joint effort to produce the Dragon Wagon. Oshkosh officials were credited at the time with indicating the team would initially concentrate on military programmes such as the US Army's Heavy Expanded Mobility Tactical Truck (HEMTT). Around 1978, and prior to the Oshkosh/Lockheed announcement, it had been reported that a Dragon Wagon (known as Model 901M by Lockheed) was one of three vehicles being tested by the US Army as potential replacements for the GOER family of vehicles, the other contenders being MAN and Paccar. The GOER family would eventually be replaced by the Oshkosh HEMTT (full details of which can be found elsewhere in this section), the first contract for which would be placed in 1981.

In December 1980 the USMC awarded Oshkosh a contract worth USD500,000 for two Model D-3858 Dragon Wagon trucks, which were delivered early in 1981. At the time it was reported that following the successful completion of trials the Marine Corps would place orders for around 600 of a 12½-ton version, and 800 of a 22-ton version.

By this stage the commercial-looking cab of early Dragon Wagons had been replaced with the 'trademark' Oshkosh angular flat-panelled two-person cab, and the design had been designated the DA Series by

Oshkosh MK48/16 tractor truck (Oshkosh Defense)　　　1128787

Oshkosh MK48/17 cargo truck with Material Handling Crane (MHC) in service with the USMC (Oshkosh Defense)　　　1128788

Oshkosh. Unlike the earlier Twister on which the central joint allowed pitch, roll and yaw movement, on the Dragon Wagon this was limited to roll and yaw. Articulated steering on the Dragon Wagon was complemented by front axle steering.

A further two prototype vehicles were delivered in 1982, and, as a result of extended user trials, a contract was placed in September 1983 for the MK48 Logistic Vehicle System (LVS). This was a five-year contract valued at USD245 million and production totals (including exercised options) would reach 3,754 LVS modules.

Contract award details.

MK14/MK18 conversion contract award (Reynolds Boughton):	320
1994 MK14/MK18A1 conversion contract award:	164
1994 MK14/MK18A1 conversion contract option:	55
1994 MK14/MK18A1 conversion contract total (Oshkosh):	219
1995 contract award:	149
1995 contract award exercised options:	45
1995 contract award total:	194

By the late 1980s the USMC was formulating a requirement to convert a quantity of standard MK14 cargo modules into MK18 tilt bed type load handling system modules. The contract was awarded to Reynolds Boughton and by late 1992, 320 units had been ordered. In addition to conventional cargo, the MK18 module is capable of handling (loading/unloading) and transporting a 20 ft ISO container, a Ribbon Bridge section or a Combat Support Boat (CSB) in its cradle.

In 1994 Oshkosh was awarded a contract valued at USD9.7 million to convert 164 standard MK14 cargo modules to load handling system equipped modules. These were designated MK48/18A1. The contract included a 100 per cent option clause; final deliveries under the contract would total 219.

In August 1995, Oshkosh was awarded a further contract for a base quantity of 149 LVS modules, with an option for 64 additional units. Final deliveries under this contract would be 194 units. The contract value was quoted as USD21.7 million. The main vehicle differences between the two contract awards was corrosion prevention measures, although on MK15 (recovery) and MK17 (cargo with crane) modules, on the second contract the original Wajax crane was replaced by a Grove crane.

One major change to the LVS since its introduction into service has been the requirement to armour cabs brought about primarily by operations in Afghanistan and Iraq. Information regarding US Army/USMC armouring efforts is now classified, but prior to these restrictions the following information regarding LVS armouring was made available by the USMC.

The LVS armouring requirement was initially addressed in two phases. The first phase, to armour 204 vehicles, was validated in January 2004. The first phase of armouring used interim armour, which included Kevlar/ceramic panels, 3/16-inch High-Hardness Steel (HHS) doors, and ballistic blankets. This solution offered limited protection against IEDs and the improved requirement met in the second phase, to armour 221 trucks (including re-armouring the 204 trucks fitted with interim armour), was established in April 2004.

The second phase of armouring employed add-on armour which offered better protection against IEDs as it included a higher grade steel, ballistic glass, and additional protection for the underbody, tailgate, roof, and other components. As of January 2006, USMC fielding data revealed that 235 LVS trucks operating outside forward bases in CENTCOM's area of responsibility in Iraq had add-on armour.

On entering service, LVS was originally projected to have a 20-year service life, this including a projected rebuild, which did not take place. The additional weight of armour, together with increased usage in harsh operating conditions, will clearly have impacted on the serviceability and availability of LVS. Since the invasion of Iraq (later Afghanistan), a number

Model	MK48/14	MK48/15	MK48/16	MK48/17	MK48/18A1
Type:	logistics platform	wrecker (recovery)	tractor truck	cargo with crane	LHS
Cab seating:	1 + 1	1 + 1	1 + 1	1 + 1	1 + 1
Configuration:	8 × 8	8 × 8	8 × 8	8 × 8	8 × 8
Weight:					
(unladen)	18,597 kg	23,133 kg	18,597 kg	21,769 kg	20,454 kg
(payload, on-road)	20,412 kg	9,072 kg[1]	20,866 kg[2]	18,144 kg	20,045 kg
(payload, off-road)	11,340 kg	n/a	n/a	9,072 kg	11,337 kg
(GCW, on-road)	68,040 kg	69,840 kg	85,277 kg	69,840 kg	69,840 kg
(GCW off-road)	47,628 kg	47,628 kg	47,628 kg	47,628 kg	47,628 kg
Length:	11.582 m	11.278 m	10.09 m	11.582 m	11.5 m[3]
Width:	2.438 m	2.438 m	2.438 m	2.438 m	2.566 m[4]
Height: (cab)	2.591 m	2.591 m	2.591 m	2.591 m	2.591 m
Track:	2.007 m	2.007 m	2.007 m	2.007 m	2.007 m
Wheelbase:	1.524 + 6.579 + 1.524	1.524 + 6.579 + 1.524	1.524 + 5.817 + 1.524	1.524 + 6.579 + 1.524	1.524 + 6.579 +1.524
Angle of approach/departure:	45°/45°	45°/48°	45°/65°	45°/40°	45°/40°
Max speed: (road)	84 km/h	84 km/h	84 km/h	84 km/h	84 km/h
Range: (cruising)	483 km	483 km	483 km	483 km	483 km
Fuel capacity:	2 × 284 litres	2 × 284 litres	2 × 284 litres	2 × 284 litres	2 × 284 litres
Gradient:	60%	60%	60%	60%	60%
Side slope:	30%	30%	30%	30%	30%
Fording:	1.524 m	1.524 m	1.524 m	1.524 m	1.524 m
Engine:	Detroit Diesel 8V92TA V-8 12.1-litre water-cooled 2-stroke diesel developing 445 hp (332 kW) at 2,100 rpm and peak torque of 1,695 N.m				
Gearbox:	Allison HT 740D 4-speed automatic with torque converter				
Transfer box:	Oshkosh 2-speed				
Steering:	hydraulic powered yaw steering, power-assisted on front axle				
Turning radius:	11.7 m	11.7 m	10.4 m	11.7 m	11.7 m
Suspension:	3 × 102 mm leaf springs with steel saddle and six torque rods, front; 3 × 127 mm leaf springs with steel saddle and six torque rods, rear; 356 mm of vertical wheel travel front and rear				
Axles:	Oshkosh 23K (wide track) steer-drive with single reduction with cross- and inter-axle differential lock and 15° steering angle, 1st; Eaton (now Dana) RS381 (wide track) single reduction with differential lock, 2nd; Eaton (now Dana) DS580 (wide track) single reduction with differential lock, 3rd and 4th (inter-axle differential lock on 3rd axle)				
Brakes:	dual circuit, air, drums all-round				
Tyres:	1600R × 21	1600R × 21	1600R × 21	1600R × 21	1600R × 21
Electrical system:	24 V	24 V	24 V	24 V	24 V
Batteries:	4 × 12 V	4 × 12 V	4 × 12 V	4 × 12 V	4 × 12 V
Alternator:	24 V, 62 A	24 V, 62 A	24 V, 62 A	24 V, 62 A	24 V, 62 A

[1] Towed load 14,515 kg
[2] Load on 5th wheel
[3] Variable according to load
[4] 3.25 m when configured for bridging

of LVS trucks have been through (and will continue to go through) a selection of USMC initiated refurbishment programmes to maintain their reliability and availability until fully replaced by the Logistic Vehicle System Replacement (LVSR).

The LVSR programme (full details of which can be found elsewhere in this section) will replace the current MK48 Logistic Vehicle System (LVS) fleet. The LVSR will increase mobility, maintainability, and reliability for the heavy fleet, while increasing off-road payload. Three LVSR variants will replace the current five LVS variants. The first LVSR cargo variant production vehicle was fielded to Afghanistan in September 2009.

Description
The MK48 Series truck is comprised of two separate chassis modules that are coupled together by a centre articulation joint to form an integral (8 × 8) vehicle. The centre joint allows roll and yaw movement, the latter giving 64° of powered steering motion. This is coordinated with 15° of steering lock on the front steer-drive axle to give the MK48 Series a 30 per cent shorter turning radius than a conventionally steered truck of the same wheelbase/length.

The articulated joint also provides 6° of roll capability (left or right) between the front and rear modules, and when coupled with the taper leaf spring suspension set-up that provides 356 mm wheel travel, enables all wheels to keep in contact with the ground in most off-road scenarios.

The front axle is an Oshkosh 23K (wide track) steer-drive single reduction unit with cross- and inter-axle differential locks. The second axle is an Eaton (now Dana) RS381 (wide track) single reduction unit with differential lock; the third and fourth axles are Eaton DS580 (wide track) single reduction units with differential locks. Drum bakes are fitted all round. Tyres are 1600R 21.

The chassis frame is constructed of C-section T1 grade steel with a yield strength of 689 Mpa. The front chassis section is 257 × 76.2 × 9.5 mm, the rear is 314 × 96 × 9.5 mm. Welded and bolted construction with Grade 8 bolts is used throughout.

The front module is essentially the cab and powerpack. Motive power is provided by a Detroit Diesel 8V92TA 12.06-litre V-8 two-stroke diesel developing 445 hp at 2,100 rpm and a maximum 1,695 N.m of torque.

The powerpack is completed by an Allison HT740D four-speed automatic transmission and Oshkosh two-speed transfer box.

The rear body/module can be disconnected and another body/module of a different type connected in 30 minutes, and with hand tools only. The front and rear modules when disconnected fit the standard 20 ft ISO container envelope. Four body modules were included in the original purchase, these being designated as follows:
- MK14 - logistics platform truck
- MK15 - recovery vehicle
- MK16 - tractor truck
- MK17 - cargo truck with materials handling crane.

The MK14 logistics platform uses an aluminium flat deck with standard container lashing points. Deck length is 6.096 m. The early 1990s contract award to Reynolds Boughton called for the conversion of existing MK14

The LVSR will replace the current MK48 Logistic Vehicle System (LVS) fleet with three variants. The first LVSR cargo variant production vehicle was fielded to Afghanistan in September 2009 (Shaun C Connors) 1296266

Oshkosh MK48/16 tractor truck in service with the USMC; the combination of M88 APV payload and M747 semi-trailer would exceed the rated GCW of the MK48/16 by around 7,000 kg (Oshkosh Defense)   1128786

The first test bed for the LVSR add-on armour kit seen at Oshkosh's Wisconsin facility (Shaun C Connors)   1296268

Oshkosh MK48/15 recovery vehicle (Oshkosh Defense)   1128785

modules into MK18 modules. The MK18 tilt bed type module can handle bridging, bridging boats and ISO containers. Conversion of the equipment to a conventional flatbed body requires the insertion of metal floor panels which, when in position, make some of the hydraulic functions inoperable. The 1994 contract awarded to Oshkosh called for the conversion of existing MK14 rear modules into MK18A1 modules. The conversion involved the installation of a US Army Palletized Load System (PLS) load handling system together with some additional features. These additional features included a winch and an integral Container Lift Kit (CLK). The MK18A1 module can handle bridging, bridging boats, flatracks and ISO containers without them being flatrack mounted first.

The MK15 recovery module is equipped with a recovery crane that has a maximum lift capacity of 18,700 kg and a recovery winch with a capacity of 27,216 kg.

The MK16 module is fitted with a fully oscillating fifth wheel and a 27,216 kg capacity recovery winch.

The MK17 module is fitted with a dropside cargo body and 18,650 kg capacity materials handling crane mounted at the rear.

Specifications
See tables on pages 693 and 694

Status
Production complete, replacement programme running (see text). In service with the US Marine Corps.

Contractor
Oshkosh Defense

Oshkosh Logistic Vehicle System Replacement (LVSR)

Development
The MK48 Logistic Vehicle System (LVS), full details of which can be found elsewhere in this section, entered service with the USMC from 1985, and in May 2006 the USMC announced that the now Oshkosh Defense had been awarded an initial order under a five year (one year with four option years) Indefinite Delivery/Indefinite Quantity (ID/IQ) contract for the LVS replacement vehicle, the LVSR - Logistic Vehicle System Replacement.

The project to replace the LVS has origins back in the late 1990s, and as a precursor to the formal replacement programme Oshkosh was one of a number of manufacturers that cooperated with the USMC under a research and development effort to build and evaluate an Advanced Technology Demonstrator (ATD).

The ATD was built at the Nevada Automotive Test Centre (NATC) and focused on the fabrication and testing of the ATD as well as Logistics Vehicle System (LVS) Modification Demonstrators (LVS-MDs), which integrated commercially proven state-of-the-industry automotive components and technologies to provide improved performance, improved Reliability, Availability, Maintainability (RAM), and Durability (RAM-D), and to ensure life cycle supportability.

Proof of concept testing demonstrated the feasibility of such integration efforts. A concurrent vehicle dynamics M&S effort was also conducted to provide an acquisition and life cycle management tool to assist vehicle design, modifications, and upgrades in later stages of the acquisition.

In April 2001, Logistics Management Institute (LMI) completed their final report for the 'Analysis of Alternatives (AoA) for the USMC Logistics Vehicle System Replacement (LVSR)'. This report was the final task of a multiple month effort to help determine the best way to maintain the USMC heavy fleet. Five alternatives were fully considered:
- Inspect and Replace Only As Necessary (IROAN) the LVS
- rebuild the LVS
- re-manufacture the LVS to a higher standard
- rebuy a vehicle similar to the LVSR Technology Demonstrator
- research and develop an entirely new vehicle.

The results of the effectiveness and life cycle cost analyses indicated that the best alternative for the Marine Corps to pursue for replacement of the LVS was to rebuy a vehicle similar to the LVSR Technology Demonstrator.

Around the same time the USMC stated that any LVS replacement (yet to be designated LVSR) would need to be in production by 2005-2006 if it were to avoid a funding clash with the Corps' other main procurement projects, the Advanced Amphibious Assault Vehicle (now known as the Expeditionary Fighting Vehicle) and the V-22 Osprey tilt rotor aircraft. It was also suggested that 2,000-3,000 vehicles might be required. The LVSR Request for Information (RfI) had been expected in May 2000. An industry day was held late-2001, and a formal solicitation to industry was eventually released early 2003, having been further delayed from an expected April-2002. By this stage the number of vehicles required had reduced to around 1,200.

The then Oshkosh Truck Corporation announced in March 2004 that the US Marine Corps had awarded the company a Phase I System Development and Demonstration Contract to supply three Logistic Vehicle System Replacement (LVSR) trucks. Under this contract, which was the first phase of a two-part acquisition competition valued at (in March 2004) up to USD783 million for up to 1,581 vehicles (initially 1,022 vehicles), the three trucks were to be delivered to the Marines for extensive endurance and performance testing within 12 months.

One of the two LVSR wrecker variants that formed part of the initial LVSR order (Shaun C Connors)   1296267

Designation	MKR18	MKR15	MKR16
Type:	cargo	wrecker	tractor
Cab seating:	2	2	2
Configuration:	10 × 10	10 × 10	10 × 10
Weight:			
(laden)	44,929 kg	30,526 kg	45,813 kg
(unladen)	24,517 kg	25,990 kg	22,680 kg
(payload)	20,412 kg	4,536 kg	23,133 kg
(towed load)	24,040 kg	44,929 kg	56,699 kg
(GCW)	68,969 kg	75,455 kg	79,379 kg
Length:	10.98 m	11.60 m	10.41 m
Width:	2.49 m	2.46 m	2.49 m
Height:			
(cab)	2.59 m	2.59 m	2.59 m
(with 20 ft ISO container)	4.11 m	n/app	a/app
Wheelbase (2nd to 3rd axle; front tandem to rear tridem):	5.67 m	5.42 m	5.42 m
Angle of approach/departure:	39°/57°	39°/41°	39°/61°
Max speed:	105 km/h	105 km/h	105 km/h
Gradient:	60%	60%	60%
Sideslope:	30%	30%	30%
Range:	483 km	483 km	483 km
Fuel capacity:	628 litres	628 litres	628 litres
Engine:	CAT C15 15.2-litre 6-cylinder in-line turbocharged, water-cooled 4-stroke diesel developing 600 hp (447 kW) at 1,800 rpm and 2,508 N.m torque at 1,200 rpm		
Transmission:	Allison 4700SP with 7 forward and 1 reverse gears		
Transfer box:	Oshkosh 35000 single-speed		
Steering:	power-assisted, axles one, two, four and five steer		
Turning radius:	24.9 m (wall to wall)		
Suspension:	Oshkosh TAK-4 independent. Front axles rated at 7,666 kg; rear axles rated at 10,478 kg (cargo), 11,566 kg (wrecker/tractor truck)		
Tyres:	16.00R 20	16.00R 20	16.00R 20
Brakes:			
(main)	drums all-round, air operated		
Electrical system:	24 V	24 V	24 V
Batteries:	4 × 6TMF	4 × 6TMF	4 × 6TMF
Alternator:	260 A	260 A	260 A

Oshkosh was one of two companies selected for the Phase I evaluation contract, the other being American Truck Company (ATC) with a TATRA-based design. Competition for the Phase II production award (scheduled for March 2006) was limited to those companies that successfully completed Phase I evaluation. Phase I testing, along with the Phase II proposal, was to determine the single supplier of the LVSR.

Phase 1 testing was completed during 2005 and in late-May 2006 the USMC awarded the LVSR Phase II contract to Oshkosh Truck Corporation. ATC had supplied three LVSR prototypes for Pre-Production Qualification Testing (PPQT) but due to technical and schedule problems these were unable to complete PPQT.

Under the terms of a USD28.01 million initial order issued on 31st May 2006, Oshkosh was to supply 22 cargo, two wrecker (recovery) and tractor LVSR variants to the USMC, plus assorted spares, support and training services.

The first LVSR began testing at the Aberdeen Proving Ground in June 2007, and this was scheduled to conclude by June 2008. The full rate production decision for the LVSR cargo variant (now designated MKR18) was expected around November 2008. Tractor and wrecker prototype vehicles began testing in November 2007 and April 2008 respectively. An additional 123 cargo variants which completed Low Rate Initial Production (LRIP) quantities were subsequently ordered under option year two of the production contract bringing the total ordered to 145; deliveries of all 145 vehicles was completed by April 2009.

In January 2009, Oshkosh announced an LVSR contract order valued at USD176 million. This called for more than 425 LVSR, add-on armour kits (>170) and weapon mounts (>270). This award transition LVSR from LRIP into full-rate production.

LVSR fielding began in April 2009 for user trials and testing. The first LVSR cargo variant production vehicle was delivered in June 2009, and the first vehicle was fielded to Afghanistan in September 2009.

By January 2010 a total of 875 LVSRs were under contract, with production scheduled to run until October 2010.

In February 2010 Oshkosh announced an LVSR delivery award valued at in excess of USD158 million for in excess of 400 LVSRs, the bulk of the order (385) MKR18 cargo variants, the remainder MKR16 tractor trucks. This delivery order extended LVSR production and delivery into July 2011.

In December 2010 Oshkosh announced an LVSR delivery award valued at in around USD50 million for in excess of 100 LVSR MKR18 cargo variants and 120 enhanced protection kits. Production of the vehicles is scheduled to begin in August 2011 and be completed in April 2012.

By January 2011 a total of approaching 1,400 LVSRs were under contract, with production scheduled to run until at least April 2012.

The five year Indefinite-Delivery/Indefinite-Quantity (ID/IQ) LVSR contract is worth a potential USD740.22 million overall and will see Oshkosh supply a maximum of 1,322 cargo vehicles, 105 wreckers and 272 tractor variants.

The LVSR has been designed to complement the USMC Oshkosh MTVR fleet with both types sharing some common parts and similar maintenance training. Once deployed the LVSR is intended to increase mobility, maintainability, and reliability for the USMC heavy fleet while increasing off-road payload. Among other improvements, the LVSR will incorporate increased crew survivability and simplified maintenance.

Description

Unlike the original LVS which articulated around a central joint, the LVSR is based on a conventional C-section rigid chassis. The articulated design did have manoeuvrability benefits, however, the trade-off for this was stability issues in certain circumstances. To achieve the required turning circle, axles one, two, four and five of the LVSR steer. For enhanced reliability and simplified maintenance, the rear two axles are steered mechanically and not electronically.

Suspension is fully independent all-round, and by coil springs on the front two axles, hydraulic on the rear three. Tyres are 1600R 20 Michelin XZL and these are fitted with a central tyre inflation system that allows the driver to adjust tyre pressures to suit prevailing ground conditions. In the event of a puncture the CTI system also allows for air to be diverted to the punctured tyre. No spare is carried. Suspension, axles, wheels and tyres are common with the USMC MTVR.

The two-seat cab fitted to the LVSR is similar in appearance to the trademark Oshkosh angular cab fitted to LVS, Heavy Expanded Mobility Tactical Truck (HEMTT) and Palletized Load System (PLS), but is in fact a second-generation version of that cab. This cab is slightly larger than the original cab, but more importantly in today's operational scenarios, was designed from the outset to accept add-on armour. The add-on armour kit for LVSR was developed and is currently being supplied by Plasan Sasa of Israel. Plasan Sasa was awarded a contract mid-2006 for 12 LVSR armour kits for testing. Up to 635 kits may be required.

LVSR is powered by a 15.2-litre Caterpillar C15 six-cylinder in-line turbocharged, water-cooled four-stroke diesel developing 600 hp. This is coupled to a seven-speed Allison automatic gearbox and Oshkosh single-speed transfer box. Maximum road speed is 65 mph.

The MKR18 LVSR cargo variant measures 10.98 × 2.49 × 2.59 m (L × W × H) and has a kerb weight of 24,517 kg. Gross Vehicle Weight (GVW) is 44,929 kg, giving a payload of 20,412 kg that includes items such as the integral Container Handling Unit (CHU) and flatracks. The load handling

Oshkosh LVSR. One of many specialist loads for the LVSR is the Combat Support Boat in its purpose-designed cradle (Shaun C Connors)   1296266

From the rear, a rebuilt Oshkosh (10 × 10) M1074 PLS truck fitted with a materials handling crane between the LHS hook arm and engine; without crane the designation is M1075 (Shaun C Connors)   1128773

system fitted to the LVSR cargo variant is essentially the same system fitted to Oshkosh M1074/M1075 PLS and M1120 HEMTT, these systems being a licence-produced and revised version of the Multilift Mark 4 (now designated MPH165) system fitted to the British Army's De-mountable Rack Off-loading and Pick-up System (DROPS).

The requirement for an LVSR companion trailer is currently being addressed by the Marine Corps and may be also be provided by Oshkosh. The M1076 which is already in service with the US Army as the companion trailer for the Oshkosh M1074/M1075 PLS has been favourably evaluated by the Marine Corps for use with the LVSR. In May 2009 it was announced that the Marine Corps would receive an initial 30 M1076 PLST for use with the LVSR.

Specifications
See table on facing page

Status
In production for the USMC.

Contractor
Oshkosh Defense

Oshkosh (10 × 10) Palletized Load System (PLS)

Development
The then US Army Tank Automotive Command awarded prototype contracts to three contractors for prototype Palletized Load System (PLS) vehicles in January 1989. Each of the three firms involved delivered nine trucks, six trailers and 30 flatracks. Prototype hardware testing began in September 1989. The three firms involved in the programme were Oshkosh Truck Corporation, the PACCAR Government Group and General Motors, Military Vehicle Operations.

In September 1990, Oshkosh Truck Corporation was awarded a five-year USD860 million contract for 2,626 PLS trucks, 1,050 M1076 PLS trailers and 11,030 M1077 PLS flatracks. Further details of PLS flatracks and the PLS trailer (a licence-produced LOHR/Soframe design) can be found elsewhere in this entry. The initial PLS contract included annual 100 per cent options raising the contract value to approximately UDSD1.1 billion. Production commenced in 1992 and under the original PLS contract Oshkosh Truck Corporation produced 2,905 PLS trucks and 1,534 trailers between 1992

and 1997. One half (1,400) of the original contract trucks are equipped with a Grove material handling crane with a capacity of 1,769 kg at 12.1 m and are designated the M1074; trucks without the material handling crane are designated the M1075.

Under an additional add on contract from 1997 to 2001, Oshkosh Truck Corporation produced 595 PLS trucks and 800 trailers, bringing the PLS fleet to 3,500 trucks and 2,334 trailers. In March 2001, Oshkosh Truck was awarded the Family of Heavy Tactical Vehicles (FHTV) contract that included provision for up to 740 PLS trucks and 1,060 trailers. The FHTV contract was originally extended to mid-FY06, and following further extension, a new USD878 million contract that enabled Oshkosh Truck to continue producing PLS for the FHTV requirement was awarded in February 2007. Under the FHTV 2 contract, Oshkosh Truck was required to deliver a total of 1,857 new vehicles and 2,599 new trailers.

In October 2008 Oshkosh Defense announced it had been awarded the Family of Heavy Tactical Vehicles 3 (FHTV 3) contract by the US Army. The three-year FHTV 3 will add more than 6,000 upgraded vehicles to the US Army's FHTV fleet. The FHTV 3 programme will be awarded in increments, the first order being valued at USD1.2 billion, with deliveries commencing in November 2008. FHTV covers deliveries of Heavy Expanded Mobility Tactical Truck (HEMTT), Palletized Load System (PLS) and PLS trailers (PLST), and Heavy Equipment Transporter (HET). As part of the contract, Oshkosh Defense will supply the US Army with the next-generation HEMTT, the HEMTT A4, and A1 models of the PLS and HET. These new next-generation vehicles will feature increased horsepower and performance features due to powertrain and suspension upgrades. In addition, all three vehicle families will be Long Term Armor Strategy (LTAS) compliant and come off the assembly line fitted with upgraded suspensions and integral composite (A-kit) armour. They also will be ready to receive an add-on (B-kit) armour appliqué.

By mid-2009 Oshkosh had produced almost 6,000 PLSs (including initial small quantities of PLS A1), and by late 2009 had received orders for around 11,500 PLS trailers. PLS trailers are also used with the Oshkosh HEMTT and LVSR.

In January 2010 Oshkosh announced that it had received an FHTV 3 contract delivery award order valued at in excess of USD290 million for in excess of 725 PLS A1 trucks. Production was scheduled to commence in April 2010 and be completed in September 2011.

In June 2010 Oshkosh announced that it had received an FHTV 3 contract delivery award for in excess of 530 PLS trailers. PLS trailer production will commence in June 2011 and be completed in October 2011.

In October 2010 Oshkosh announced that it had received an FHTV 3 contract delivery award order valued at in excess of USD459 million for in excess of 1,050 PLS A1 trucks. This award included around 150 HEMTT A4 trucks and deliveries are expected to be complete by August 2012.

Mirroring the British Army which initially procured the similar DROPS for ammunition resupply, the US Army initially purchased PLS for the same, and as with the British Army the US military were not slow to realise

Oshkosh (10 × 10) M1075 PLS truck mounting an M5 Engineer Mission Module - Concrete Mobile Mixer (EMM-CMM) and towing an M1076 PLS trailer mounting a M6 Engineer Mission Module - Dump Body (EMM-DB) (Oshkosh Truck)   0126580

A new-build Oshkosh (10 × 10) M1075 PLS truck fitted with a Container Handling Unit (CHU); normal flatrack handling operations are capable with the CHU stowed - as shown (Oshkosh Truck)   1128771

the flexibility and force multiplication capability of a DROPS/PLS-style system. Consequently PLS was soon in demand for a myriad of other roles, many not requiring the capabilities of a five-axle (10 × 10) platform. The lighter and more cost effective LHS-equipped (8 × 8) HEMTT-based M1120, introduced into US Army service in 1999, is now the more popular choice for most of the US Army's LHS applications, however a number of additional PLS applications remain under development.

Most recently a PLS version optimised for the transport and handling of Heavy Dry Support Bridge (HDSB) components entered service. Another recent development has been the Engineer Mission Module (EMM), further details of which can be found elsewhere in this section.

Since the award of two separate contracts during 2004, Oshkosh (in addition to HEMTTS and HETs) has rebuilt/overhauled service-worn PLS trucks to new-build standard. The completed vehicles are returned to service in zero miles/zero hours condition and with a new vehicle warranty. Under the second contract, for which first deliveries were made in March 2005, PLS trailers have also been covered.

Oshkosh is also refurbishing PLS (and other vehicles) through the Theatre-Provided Equipment Refurbishment (TPER) programme. The most recent TPER award announced by Oshkosh was in December 2010 and covered HEMTT and HET trucks, plus M1000 HET semi-trailers – these not originally produced by Oshkosh. By late 2010 Oshkosh had refurbished approaching 1,500 heavy vehicles at the company's facility in Kuwait.

Description
The Oshkosh PLS is based on a C-section chassis formed of 356 × 89 × 9.5 mm SAE 1027 modified heat-treated carbon manganese steel with a yield strength of 758 Mpa. Bolted construction with Grade 8 bolts is used throughout. The chassis is provided with heavy-duty front bumper and skid plate. A dp Manufacturing PLS-22K self-recovery winch with a capacity of 9,072 kg is an option.

The two-person, two-door forward control cab is a development of the Oshkosh M977 HEMTT cab and is of heavy-duty welded steel construction with corrosion-resistant skins. Standard equipment currently includes suspension seats and four-point seat belts for the driver and passenger. The PLS A1 has a visually similar but slightly larger revised cab.

A spare tyre and wheel assembly is mounted behind the cab on A0 variants, and is provided with a davit to assist in lowering it to the ground. On A1 variants the spare wheel and tyre is located on the right-hand side of the vehicle, on the top of the engine/cooling compartments.

An add-on armour kit has been developed for the M1074/M1075 (and M977 HEMTT which uses essentially the same cab) by Armor Holdings Inc. and by mid-2006 the company had supplied around 3,600 kits for PLS/HEMTT, meeting the US Army's current armouring requirement for

Oshkosh (10 × 10) PLS truck fitted with the Oshkosh Container Handling Unit (CHU) (Oshkosh Truck)   0533624

Oshkosh (10 × 10) M1075 PLS truck mounting a M6 Engineer Mission Module - Dump Body (EMM-DB). The EMM-DB is manufactured by Crysteel Manufacturing (Oshkosh Truck)   1128792

Oshkosh (10 × 10) M1075 PLS truck mounting a Forward Repair System (FRS). Full details of the FRS can be found in the Recovery vehicles section (Oshkosh Truck)   1128791

these types. PLS A1 variants are Long Term Armor Strategy (LTAS) compliant and are manufactured with the base armour kit fitted as standard, this known as the 'A-kit'. The more substantial add-on 'B-kit' is fitted as required.

PLS A0 was initially powered by a Detroit Diesel 8V92TA V-8 two-stroke turbocharged diesel developing 500 hp, with later production examples having the DDECIV electronically-controlled version of this engine. Prior to October 2005 all PLS A0 were fitted with an Allison CLT-755 ATEC 5F/1R automatic gearbox, torque converter and Oshkosh 55000 two-speed transfer box. Post October 2005 an Allison HD-4500 Generation 4 six-speed automatic was fitted. The current A1 variants are fitted with Caterpillar C-15 four-stroke diesel developing 600 hp, this coupled to an Allison six-speed automatic transmission and Oshkosh two-speed transfer case.

PLS is unusual in that it is a five-axle truck, with two front and three rear axles. On A0 variants the front tandem is leaf-sprung and consists of two rigid steer-drive axles, on A1 variants the front two axles are independently sprung using Oshkosh's TAK-4 fully independent coil spring suspension. On all variants the rear tridem unit consists of a single air-sprung drive axle (3rd axle) and a leaf-sprung tandem (4th and 5th axles) on which the rearmost axle contra-steers.

A five-axle (10 × 10) configuration provides optimum turning capability and good weight distribution between all axles providing mobility and capability above the desired level of the US Army specification. Competing PLS designs were both four-axle (8 × 8s), the Paccar offering having a single front axle and rear tridem, the General Motors offering being an Americanised MAN Kat 1 (8 × 8).

The PLS truck is capable of transporting 16.5 tonnes (14,965 kg) of flatrack-mounted cargo and can tow a PLS trailer loaded with the same payload.

The PLS truck/trailer design includes an integral self-load/unload capability using the PLS flatrack. Oshkosh selected the Multilift Mark 5 load handling lift system (now designated MPH165-LHS by Multilift/Hiab) and license produce the system for the PLS and HEMTT contracts. A single operator can load or unload a laden flatrack in less than one minute without leaving the cab.

PLS trucks and trailers are air-transportable in C-5A and C-17 cargo aircraft and can be carried in C-141 aircraft with preparation.

Variants
(Plus ancillaries)

PLS A1
Under the Family of Heavy Tactical Vehicles 3 (FHTV 3) contract awarded to Oshkosh Defense in October 2008 the PLS A1 variant becomes available. The primary differences between the original A0 variant and the A1 variant are replacement of the original Detroit Diesel engine with a more powerful Caterpillar CAT C15 that develops 600 hp (100 hp more than the current engine), uprated suspension and new cab that is compliant with the US Army's Long Term Armor Strategy (LTAS).

The first PLS A1 trucks were delivered to the US Army in August 2010.

M1120 HEMTT LHS
The M1120 HEMTT Load Handling System (LHS) is essentially an HEMTT (8 × 8) fitted with the same load handling system as a PLS truck. The M1120 HEMTT variant was initially introduced as part of the HEMTT overhaul/rebuild programme during which returned M977 HEMTT cargo trucks have their cargo bodies and materials handling cranes removed, to be replaced by a Multilift Mark 5 (now designated MPH165-LHS) load handling system. The first rebuild M1120 was produced late 1999, with new build M1120A2 examples available from February 2004.

Compared to the M1074/M1075, the M1120 has a reduced payload of around 9,977 kg, but in the majority of PLS cases this is adequate and therefore the more cost-effective LHS option. The M1120 is interoperable with the all PLS flatracks, the CHU and the M1076 PLS trailer.

PLS/R recovery vehicle
Oshkosh displayed a prototype of a specialised recovery variant of the PLS, the PLS/R (R - recovery), in February 2008. The PLS/R is designed with a towing and recovery device to operate in a tactical environment and

Oshkosh (10 × 10) PLS truck mounting a 2,500 US gallon (9,463-litre) fuel flatrack that forms part of the under-development Load handling system Modular Fuel Farm (LMFF) (Oshkosh Truck)   0126579

recover and evacuate vehicles without causing additional damage to the suspension and axles of heavily armoured wheeled vehicles. The vehicle is fitted with dual 11,340 kg pull winches, an Iowa Mold Tooling Inc. crane and a Tru-Hitch recovery system. The Tru-Hitch recovery system which is in service with the US and British armies can flat-tow, lift-tow and overturn stuck or disabled vehicles without causing any additional damage.

Forward Repair System (FRS)
A Forward Repair System (FRS), previously designated as FRS-H (H - Heavy), prototype was produced based on the Oshkosh PLS (10 × 10) chassis. Production of the FRS, which is also transportable by M1120 LHS, is by the US Army's Rock Island Army depot. Full details of the FRS can be found in the Recovery vehicles section.

Flatracks
The M1077 and M1077A1 General Purpose A-frame flatracks are sideless flatracks used to transport pallets of ammunition and other classes of supplies. M1077 flatracks are 6.058 m long, 2.438 m wide and 1.5915 m high over the A-frame; there is no current production of this type of flatrack.

On the ISO-compatible Palletized Flatrack (IPF) Type M1 there are two end walls, one incorporating the A-frame. Both walls can fold down inwardly for stacking when empty. The dimensions of the IPF are the same as for the M1077, apart from the end walls which have a height of 2.083 m; there is no current production of this type of flatrack.

Currently in production is the M3 Container Roll-in/Out Platform (CROP), a flatrack which fits inside a 20 ft ISO container. The US Army plans to procure up to 12,000 CROPs. The current supplier of the CROP is SUMMA Technologies (now AAR SUMMA Technologies) that was awarded a five-year Indefinite Delivery/Indefinite Quantity (IDIQ) contract in 2005.

Container Handling Unit (CHU) and Enhanced Container Handling Unit (E-CHU)
The Oshkosh-produced Container Handling Unit (CHU) is an add-on kit suitable for both PLS and the M1120 HEMTT LHS that allows for the loading/unloading and transport of standard ISO containers without the need for an intermediate flatrack. M1075 PLS trucks can have an integral CHU stowage facility between the LHS hook arm and engine. CHUs were procured as part of the original Family of Heavy Tactical Vehicles (FHTV) contract.

The current Enhanced Container Handling Unit (E-CHU) is manufactured by GT Machining & Fabricating Ltd in Canada. By September 2010 over 1,000 E-CHUs had been produced.

Universal Power Interface Kit (UPIK)
The Universal Power Interface Kit (UPIK) can be installed on M1075/M1075A1 vehicles equipped with a 200 A alternator and without the optional self-recovery winch. The UPIK provides pneumatic, hydraulic and electrical power to flatrack-based systems such as the Engineer Mission Modules (EMM).

M1076 PLS trailer
The SOFRAME RM 22 PLM load handling trailer was selected as the M1076 trailer component of the US Army's Palletized Loading System. The RM 22/M1076 is a three-axle dolly-type trailer. It uses a mainframe assembled using electric welding, with a secondary frame supporting the front axle on a turning table and the drawbar; a steering lock allows the steering to be fixed when required. Two axles are provided at the rear and braking is on all three axles. Flatracks can be on- and off-loaded from the trailer by the prime mover's load handling system.

The M1076 PLS trailer is also used with the Oshkosh HEMTT and LVSR.

Engineer Mission Modules (EMM)
Engineer Mission Module (EMM) components are flatrack-based and designed to be used on the UPIK-equipped M1075 PLS truck. Three EMMs were procured under the initial Family of Heavy Tactical Vehicles (FHTV) contract, the M4 Bituminous Distributor (EMM-BD), the M5 Concrete Mobile Mixer (EMM-CMM), and the M6 Dump Body (EMM-DB).

The M4 Bituminous Distributor (EMM-BD) provides the capability to spread measured amounts of bituminous material for road preparation, repair, and other engineer applications. The unit has a 2,800 US gallon capacity and a laden weight of 15,757 kg. It is transportable but not operable by/on the M1074 PLS truck and M1076 PLS trailer. The M4 EMM-BD is manufactured by E.D. Etnyre.

The M5 Concrete Mobile Mixer (EMM-CMM) transports raw concrete materials, mixes concrete as needed, and emplaces the mixed concrete. The unit is self-powered and can be used on the PLS truck or trailer (mobile mode) or on the ground (standalone mode). Its bins store enough material for five cubic yards of mixed concrete in mobile mode and eight cubic yards in standalone mode. The M5 EMM-CMM is manufactured by Cementech, Inc.

The M6 Dump Body (EMM-DB) transports and spreads engineering construction material such as rocks, gravel, sand, and soil. The unit has a 9.2 to 10.7 m³ capacity by volume, 11,791 kg by weight. It is powered by the PLS truck, and can be operated on the truck or trailer. The M6 EMM-DB is manufactured by Crysteel Manufacturing.

Water distributor and modular fuel farm modules have also been produced.

Specifications

Model	M1074/M1075A0	M1074/M1075A1
Cab seating:	1 + 1	1 + 1
Configuration:	10 × 10	10 × 10
Weight:		
(laden, GVW)	39,916 kg	41,050 kg
(unladen, kerb, with crane and flatrack)	24,948 kg	23,814 kg
(unladen, kerb, without crane, with flatrack)	22,680 kg	26,082 kg
(max flatrack payload)	14,969 kg (M1074)	14,969 kg (M1074)
(GCW)	62,378 kg	63,503 kg
Length:		
(chassis)	10.693 m	10.796 m
(with flatrack)	11.201 m	n/avail
(vehicle and trailer, max)	18.936 m	n/avail
Width:	2.438 m	2.483 m
Height:		
(LHS hook)	3,251 m	3.287 m
(cab)	2.616 m	2.637 m
(flatrack bed)	1.803 m	1.742 m (laden)
Ground clearance:	400 mm	n/avail
Track:	1.925 m	1.925 m
Wheelbase:	1.524 m (1st to 2nd axle); 5.69 m (2nd to 4th axles); 1.499 m (3rd to 4th axles); 1.524 m (4th to 5th axle)	1.473 m (1st to 2nd axle); 6.461 m (2nd to 4th axles); 1.499 m (3rd to 4th axles); 1.524 m (4th to 5th axle)
Angle of approach/departure:	42°/61°	n/avail
Max speed: (GCW, on-road)	92 km/h	100 km/h
Range: (cruising)	804 km	n/avail
Fuel capacity:	700 litres	379 litres
Max gradient: (laden)	60%	60%
Fording:	1.219 m	1.219 m

Front three-quarter view of an Oshkosh-produced M1076 PLS trailer; note the location of the spare wheel (Shaun C Connors)   1128211

Model	M1074/M1075A0	M1074/M1075A1
Engine:	Detroit Diesel Model 8V92TA 12.01-litre V-8 turbocharged and aftercooled, water-cooled 2-stroke diesel developing 500 hp (373 kW) at 2,100 rpm and 1,993 N.m torque at 1,200 rpm; current production A0 vehicles have the DDECIV version of this engine	Caterpillar C-15 14.6-litre 6-cylinder in-line turbocharged water-cooled 4-stroke diesel developing 600 hp (447 kW)
Transmission:	Allison HD-4560 Generation 4 automatic with six forward and one reverse gears (from October 2005); Allison CLT-755 ATEC automatic with five forward and one reverse gears (pre October 2005); TC-496 torque convertor	Allison 6-speed automatic
Transfer box:	Oshkosh 55000 Series two-speed, full-time all-wheel drive with 30/70 front/rear torque split and driver-controlled differential lock	Oshkosh 2-speed
Steering:	power-assisted front tandem co-ordinated with power-assisted rear axle steer	power-assisted front two axles co-ordinated with power-assisted rear axle steer
Turning radius: (wall)	36.5 m	n/avail
Suspension:	Hendrickson walking beam front (RT340) and rear (RT400), Hendrickson-Turner air ride suspension on mid-axle (3rd)	Oshkosh TAK-4 fully independent coil on axles 1 and 2, Hendrickson walking beam on axles 4 and 5, rearHendrickson-Turner air ride suspension on mid-axle (3rd)

Model	M1074/M1075A0	M1074/M1075A1
Axles:	Rockwell SVI 5MR with planetary hub-reduction and individual differential locks	AxleTech
Tyres:	1600R 20 Michelin with Central Tyre Inflation (CTI) system; options available	1600R 20 Michelin with Central Tyre Inflation (CTI) system; options available
Brakes:		
(main)	dual circuit, air, drums all-round	dual circuit, air, drums all-round
(parking)	spring brake mounted on rear tridem axles	spring brake mounted on rear tridem axles
Electrical system:	12/24 V	24 V
Batteries:	4 × 12 V	n/avail
Alternator:	200 A	260 A

M1076 PLS trailer
Weight:
  (kerb) 7,484 kg
  (gross) 22,463 kg
  (max payload inc flatrack) 14,969 kg
Length: 8.316 m
Width: 2.431 m
Height:
  (overall) 2.941 m
  (flatbed) 1.801 m
Ground clearance: 460 mm
Track: 2.04 m
Wheelbase: 3.793 m
Max road speed: 90 km/h
Side slope: 30%
Tyres: (original fit) 1300R 20 Michelin XL

Status
Production commenced in early 1992 for the US Army (see text for details).

Contractor
Oshkosh Truck Corporation

HEAVY EQUIPMENT TRANSPORTERS

Introduction

This section covers fifth-wheel tractor truck prime movers, which are used principally for towing semi-trailers carrying main battle tanks (MBTs) or other heavy indivisible loads. Many standard military trucks are also produced as fifth wheel tractor trucks, these being used for towing semi-trailers carrying cargo or light armoured and construction vehicles. The GTW (gross train weight) used in this section to differentiate between heavy equipment transporter and fifth wheel tractor trucks is, broadly (as there can be a number of influencing factors) a 35,000 kg payload on the semi-trailer. Further, some armed forces (India for example) employ platform body (non fifth wheel) trucks (the TATRA 815 series in the case of India) coupled to drawbar or dolly-type trailers for the transport of tanks and other heavy armour. Details of such vehicles can be found in the Trucks section.

Austria

Steyr 33 M 41 (6 × 6) tractor truck

Development

The Steyr 33 M 41 (6 × 6) tractor truck is a militarised example of the MAN heavy duty F2000 commercial range of trucks and readers are referred to the Steyr trucks or MAN trucks entries in the Trucks section for full details of the relationship between the current MAN and Steyr military truck ranges but in brief: In January 1990 MAN Nutzfahrzeuge AG of Germany acquired an 85 per cent share of the truck-building activities of Austria's Steyr Nutzfahrzeuge AG. In 1993 MAN exercised their option to acquire the remaining 15 per cent share of the business. Steyr Nutzfahrzeuge AG became known as MAN Steyr AG during 2002 and is now known as MAN Nutzfahrzeuge Österreichische AG.

The Steyr 33 M 41 was selected by the Hellenic Army as the replacement vehicle for the earlier Steyr 26 S 28 rigid and Steyr 26 S 31 tractor truck designs of which production concluded during the late 1990s. The Steyr 33 M 41 was supplied in tractor truck and rigid configuration, and like its predecessor, vehicles supplied to the Hellenic armed forces included a degree of local content courtesy of Hellenic Vehicle Industry SA (ELBO).

As with all MAN F2000 range based trucks with Steyr branding the designation denotes: 33 - permissible gross weight in tonnes, M (military), 41 - nominal engine power output (410 hp). In tractor truck configuration the Steyr 33 M 41 is capable of operating at combination weights of up to 100,000 kg.

The MAN F2000 range was replaced in production during 2004 by equivalent models based on the heavier models of the current MAN TGA range.

MAN Nutzfahrzeuge AG and Rheinmetall AG announced their respective intentions to form a joint wheeled military vehicles company in 2009. This alliance became a reality in January 2010 with the announcement of the founding of Rheinmetall MAN Military Vehicles (RMMV) GmbH. RMMV sees the merger of Rheinmetall's wheeled military vehicle activities with those of the military truck activities of MAN. Essentially this merger unites the complementary technological core competencies of MAN's automotive expertise in commercial-vehicle manufacture with Rheinmetall's technological know-how in the military land sector/systems field. The result is the creation of a new single-source provider for the entire range of armoured and unarmoured transport, command and role-specific wheeled vehicles. Throughout all entries MAN and/or RMMV designations and references are made to suit context.

A Steyr 33 M 41 (6 × 6) tractor truck of the Hellenic Army
(Periklis Zorzovolis)   1128732

Description

The Steyr 33 M 41 is entirely conventional in design, its tiltable, all-steel, forward control cab being common throughout the MAN F2000 range of commercial trucks. Three cab types were available, short haul, long haul or large capacity. The large capacity cab is fitted with air suspension, four-point coil spring suspension being fitted to the long haul and short haul cabs. Normal configuration is left-hand drive and with seating for the driver and a single passenger. Right-hand drive, a centre passenger seat and various stowage/bunking arrangements in the larger cabs were options. A full size roof-hatch, additional passenger door glazing, air-conditioning, an auxiliary heater and radio preparation and are some of the extensive cab equipment/fittings options that were available. A version optimised for tropical climates was also available.

The conventional C-section chassis has riveted- and bolted-in tubular cross members and mounts hub-reduction beam axles sprung by parabolic leaf springs. Two wheelbases were available. Standard tyre equipment is 13R 22.5 tyres, a single spare being carried. Tyre options were available.

As with all heavy equipment tractor trucks, equipment and driveline options were extensive but in standard configuration the Steyr 33 M 41 will be fitted with a front steer-drive axle rated at 7,500 kg and twin rear drive axles rated at 13,000 kg per axle. Drive to the front axle is engaged when required, options including permanent all-wheel drive and a differential lock. The rear axles are fitted as standard with cross-axle and an inter-axle differential lock. Various axle ratios were available. An Anti-lock Braking System is fitted as standard, but could be omitted if required.

Motive power is provided by a MAN six-cylinder 410 hp turbocharged diesel engine coupled to a ZF 16 S 181 16-speed manual gearbox and Steyr G1700/2 two-speed transfer box. Gearbox options included an Eaton TRSO 12316 16-speed manual with or without a Voith retarder. Transfer box options included the Steyr VG 1700/1 single speed without an off-road gear or the Steyr VG 2500/2 two-speed transfer box. A single dry plate hydraulically-actuated and air assisted clutch was fitted as standard. Various Power Take-Offs (PTO) could be fitted.

Specifications

(3.5 m first to second axle wheelbase, 13R 22.5 tyres and short haul cab. Long haul and large capacity cabs, respectively, in square brackets where different. Any additional figures in italics relating to 3.825 m first to second axle wheelbase where different)

Steyr 33 M 41

Cab seating: 1 + 1 or 1 + 2, plus various bunking options
Configuration: 6 × 6
Weight:
 (chassis cab) 9,310 kg, *9,335 kg* [9,415 kg, *9,470 kg*; 9,455 kg, *9,510 kg*]
 (chassis carrying capacity) 23,690 kg, *23,665 kg* [23,585 kg, *23,530 kg*; 23,545 kg, *23,490 kg*]
 (permissible gross weight) 33,000 kg
 (permissible trailer load) 27,000 kg
 (permissible gross train weight (GTW)) 60,000 kg, *100,000 kg*
 (permissible front axle load) 7,500 kg
 (permissible rear axle load) 13,000 kg each, 26,000 kg total
Length: 7.472 m, *7.797 m*
Width:
 (across cab) 2.28 m [2.44 m, large capacity cab only]
 (rear wheels) 2.472 m
 (overall) 2.49 m
Height:
 (cab, laden) 3.174 m [3.274 m, long haul and large capacity cabs]
 (cab, unladen) 3.256 m [3.356 m, long haul and large capacity cabs]
 (chassis, laden) 1.086 m
 (chassis, unladen) 1.186 m
Wheelbase: 3.5 m + 1.4 or 3.825 + 1.4 m
Max speed: (road) 88 km/h (limiter fitted, other limiters available)
Fuel capacity: 300 litre tank on RH-side (200 or 400 litre options available)
Gradient: (without trailer) >60%
Sideslope: (without trailer) approx 30%
Engine: MAN type D2866LF EURO II 11.967-litre 6-cylinder in-line exhaust gas turbocharged and intercooled, water-cooled direct injection 4-stroke diesel developing 410 hp (301 kW) between 1,700 and 1,900 rpm and 1,850 N.m torque between 900 and 1,300 rpm.
Gearbox: ZF 16 S 181 with 16 forward and 2 reverse gears (see text for options)
Clutch: single dry plate
Transfer box: G 1700/2 2-speed (see text for options)
Steering: ZF, power-assisted
Suspension: parabolic leaf springs with telescopic shock-absorbers and anti-roll bar, front; slide shackle springs with anti-roll bar, rear
Brakes: dual circuit, air, drums all-round with supplementary exhaust brake. ABS as standard
Electrical system: 24 V
Batteries: 2 × 12 V, 140 Ah, optional 2 × 12 V, 180 Ah
Alternator: 28 V, 55 A, optional 28 V 80 A

Status

Production complete. In service with Greece as the ELBO 33 ME 41 (36 plus one wrecker)

Contractor

RMMV
MAN Nutzfahrzeuge Österreichische AG

Steyr 1491.330.S34 (6 × 6) and 3891 (6 × 6) tractor trucks

Development

The Steyr 1491.330.S34 (6 × 6) tractor truck is based on a heavy-duty all-wheel drive commercial vehicle adapted to meet military requirements. It was designed to pull semi- trailers on roads and prepared surfaces up to a Gross Combination Weight (GCW) of 85,000 kg. Most of the components used on this tractor truck are identical to those used on the Steyr 1491 M (6 × 6) series of trucks. At the time of their replacement in the Steyr product range by the MAN F2000 range of trucks the Steyr 1491 M (6 × 6) series of trucks had evolved a generation and were designated the 24 M series of trucks for most applications.

Readers are referred to the Steyr trucks entry in the Trucks section for full details of the relationship between the current MAN and Steyr military truck ranges but in brief: In January 1990 MAN Nutzfahrzeuge AG of Germany acquired an 85 per cent share of the truck-building activities of Austria's Steyr Nutzfahrzeuge AG. In 1993 MAN exercised their option to acquire the remaining 15 per cent share of the business. Steyr Nutzfahrzeuge AG became known as MAN Steyr AG during 2002 and is now known as MAN Nutzfahrzeuge Österreichische AG.

Around 50 examples of the 1491.330.S34 (6 × 6) tractor truck were supplied to Nigeria in the mid-to-late 1980s. A version fitted with 14.00R 20 MPT tyres, single at the front and dual on the rear axles, was produced. This is known as the Steyr 3891/6 × 6 and around 40 examples were delivered to Saudi Arabia during the mid-to-late 1980s.

MAN Nutzfahrzeuge AG and Rheinmetall AG announced their respective intentions to form a joint wheeled military vehicles company in 2009. This alliance became a reality in January 2010 with the announcement of the founding of Rheinmetall MAN Military Vehicles (RMMV) GmbH. RMMV sees the merger of Rheinmetall's wheeled military vehicle activities with those of the military truck activities of MAN. Essentially this merger unites the complementary technological core competencies of MAN's automotive expertise in commercial-vehicle manufacture with Rheinmetall's technological know-how in the military land sector/systems field. The result is the creation of a new single-source provider for the entire range of armoured and unarmoured transport, command and role-specific wheeled vehicles. Throughout all entries MAN and/or RMMV designations and references are made to suit context.

Description

The Steyr 1491.330.S34 (6 × 6) tractor truck is entirely conventional in design. The forward control cab is all steel, has seating for the driver and two passengers and may be tilted forward 70° for engine access. An observation hatch in the roof is standard and a machine gun may be mounted on the roof. The chassis frame is of the parallel ladder type with an integrated subframe for the winch and the fifth wheel. There are two hydraulic winches, each with a pulling capacity of 20,000 kg and are mounted behind the cab for loading and offloading. The vehicle is fully transportable by rail and can be used with all conventional semi-trailers.

Specifications

Steyr 1491.330.S34
Cab seating: 1 + 2
Configuration: 6 × 6
Weight:
  (kerb) 13,000 kg
  (5th wheel) 21,000 kg
  (GCW) 85,000 kg
Length: 7.051 m
Width: 2.462 m
Height: 3.14 m
Ground clearance: 314 mm
Wheelbase: 3.4 m + 1.35 m
Max speed: 60 km/h
Fuel capacity: 380 litres
Max gradient: (85,000 kg GCW) 25%
Engine: Steyr Model WD 815.74 V-8 turbocharged water-cooled direct injection 4-stroke diesel developing 340 hp (250 kW) at 2,200 rpm
Gearbox: ZF 5 S 111 GP manual, synchronised with eight speeds plus one crawler forward and one reverse
Transfer box: Steyr VG 1200 two-speed
Steering: ZF Type 8046, hydraulic power-assisted
Turning radius: 9 m
Suspension: semi-elliptic leaf springs with shock-absorbers, front, two swivel springs, rear
Tyres: 12.00R × 20 (14.00R 20 MPT optional)
Brakes:
  (main) dual circuit, air, drums all-round
  (trailer) two-line, air
  (parking) spring energy brake cylinder, air-operated
Electrical system: 24 V
Batteries: 2 × 12 V, 135 Ah

Status

Production complete. Steyr 1491.330.S34 in service with Nigeria (approx. 50, mid-to-late 1980s); Steyr 3891/6×6 in service with Saudi Arabia (approx. 40, mid-to-late 1980s).

Contractor

RMMV
MAN Nutzfahrzeuge Österreichische AG

Steyr 1491.830.S34 (6 × 6) tractor truck (Rotzler)   1185450

Around 40 examples of Steyr 3891/6×6 were delivered to Saudi Arabia during the mid-to-late 1980s (MAN)   1128731

Steyr 40 M 60 6 × 6 tractor truck

Development

The Steyr 40 M 60 (40 - nominal GVW in tonnes; M - military; 60 - nominal hp (600)) 6 × 6 truck is a Steyr-branded member of the MAN FX tactical truck range and is in service with the Hellenic Army. As the MAN 40.633 DFAETX, essentially the same vehicle in service with UAE Armed Forces. Details of the MAN 40.633 DFAETX can be found elsewhere in this section.

Full details of the relationship between the current MAN and Steyr military truck ranges can be found in the Steyr trucks or MAN trucks entries in the Trucks section but in brief: In January 1990 MAN Nutzfahrzeuge AG of Germany acquired an 85 per cent share of the truck-building activities of Austria's Steyr Nutzfahrzeuge AG. In 1993 MAN exercised their option to acquire the remaining 15 per cent share of the business. Steyr Nutzfahrzeuge AG became known as MAN Steyr AG during 2002 and is now known as MAN Nutzfahrzeuge Österreichische AG.

An initial 30 Steyr 40 M 60 tractor trucks were supplied to the Hellenic Army, with an option for a further 36 vehicles being exercised during 2002. Deliveries of this second batch commenced in April 2003, with completion in October 2003. Limited local content was added by Hellenic Vehicle Industry SA (ELBO). In service with the Hellenic Army the Steyr 40 M 60 has supplemented/part-replaced a fleet of 71 Oshkosh M911 tractor trucks supplied during 1991/92 (full details of the Oshkosh M911 can be found elsewhere in this section), and is coupled to a Nik Kioleides NK1000-76 four-axle semi-trailer. One of the main loads for this combination will be the Hellenic Army's Leopard 2 MBT (and variants) fleet currently on order. Full details of the NK1000-76 semi-trailer can be found elsewhere in this entry.

Steyr 40 M 60 (6 × 6) tractor truck coupled a Nik Kioleides NK1000-76 four-axle semi-trailer (MAN Nutzfahrzeuge Österreichische AG)   0100375

MAN's FX range of tactical trucks were phased out of production during 2005 and have been replaced by the HX range of tactical trucks. Full details of the HX range of tactical trucks can be found in the Trucks sections; details of the HX range heavy tractor trucks can be found elsewhere in this section.

MAN Nutzfahrzeuge AG and Rheinmetall AG announced their respective intentions to form a joint wheeled military vehicles company in 2009. This alliance became a reality in January 2010 with the announcement of the founding of Rheinmetall MAN Military Vehicles (RMMV) GmbH. RMMV sees the merger of Rheinmetall's wheeled military vehicle activities with those of the military truck activities of MAN. Essentially this merger unites the complementary technological core competencies of MAN's automotive expertise in commercial-vehicle manufacture with Rheinmetall's technological know-how in the military land sector/systems field. The result is the creation of a new single-source provider for the entire range of armoured and unarmoured transport, command and role-specific wheeled vehicles. Throughout all entries MAN and/or RMMV designations and references are made to suit context.

Description

The MAN FX range of tactical trucks is based on the MAN F2000 range of heavy commercial trucks but militarised as required and fitted with the MAN modular military cab. The C-section chassis is manufactured from high-strength fine-grain steel with riveted and bolted-in cross-members and is fitted with four towing eyes and a recovery pintle, front and rear, for towing and recovery operations. A 3.5 inch (89 mm) oscillating fifth wheel is fitted. The all-steel modular military cab features a full-size observation hatch, is air conditioned and extended to accommodate a bench seat for a tank crew of four.

Motive power is provided by a MAN D2840LF 10-cylinder (in V configuration) that, for this application, meets EURO II emissions regulations. Engine cooling is by twin hydrostatically-driven fans and two heavy-duty radiator systems mounted in a protected area on top of the chassis and behind the cab. An oil coolant heat exchanger is provided for the torque converter.

Permanent drive is transmitted to all three axles via a ZF torque converter with automatically controlled lock-up clutch and built-in primary retarder, a ZF 8-speed (with splitter) double H pattern gearbox giving 16 forward and two reverse gears, and a Steyr two-speed transfer box with lockable longitudinal differential and power take off for the emergency steering pump.

With 24R 21 tyres the maximum permissible load on the front model VA9-0950 steer-drive axle is 9,500 kg, the maximum permissible load on each model H/HD 9-16120 rear drive axle is 13,500 kg. All axles feature planetary final drives in the wheel hubs, and cross-axle differential locks. The front-axle differential lock automatically disengages when approximately 30 km/h is reached. Conventional leaf spring suspension is employed.

Maximum road speed is limited to 85 km/h, the calculated maximum speed being 128 km/h. At 110,000 kg GCW in first gear, low range, the maximum gradient climbable (subject to surface adhesion) is 33 per cent. An Anti-lock Braking System (ABS) is fitted. Two spare wheels are carried.

Specifications

Steyr 40 M 60
(with 24R 21 tyres)
Cab seating: 1 + 2 + 4 tank crew
Configuration: 6 × 6
Weight:
  (tractor, GVW) 38,000 kg
  (tractor, chassis-cab) 17,050 kg
  (max permissible towed load) 72,000 kg
  (max permissible GCW) 110,000 kg
  (5th wheel load) 21,000 kg
Length: 8.329 m

Width:
  (cab) 2.44 m
  (rear wheels) 2.9 m
Height:
  (cab, laden) 3.569 m
  (cab, unladen) 3.6 m
  (5th wheel, laden) 1.695 m
  (5th wheel, unladen) 1.795 m
Ground clearance:
  (front) 481 mm
  (rear) 435 mm
Wheelbase: 4.025 m + 1.5 m
Max speed: (road, limited) 85 km/h
Min speed: 3 km/h
Fuel capacity: 820 litres (1 × 600 litre [LH side], 1 × 220 litres [RH side])
Gradient: (110,000 kg GCW) 21% in high range, 33% in low range
Sideslope: 30%
Fording: 850 mm
Engine: MAN type D2840LF EURO II 18.27-litre V-10 exhaust gas turbocharged and intercooled, water-cooled direct injection 4-stroke diesel developing 600 hp (447 kW) at 1,900 rpm and 2,700 N.m torque between 1,100 and 1,450 rpm
Gearbox: ZF 16 S 251 manual with 16 forward and 2 reverse gears and ZF WSK 440 torque converter
Transfer box: Steyr G2500 2-speed
Steering: ZF Servocom, power-assisted,
Turning radius: 11.8 m
Suspension:
  (front) progressive acting semi-elliptic leaf springs with rubber stops, telescopic shock-absorbers and anti-roll bar
  (rear) slide shackle springs with anti-roll bar
Tyres: 24R 21
Brakes: dual circuit, air, drums all-round, ABS and twin air dryer
Electrical system: 24 V
Batteries: 2 × 12 V, 180 Ah
Alternator: 28 V, 55A

NK 1000-76T semi-trailer

The primary semi-trailer used with the Steyr 40 M 60 tractor truck in Hellenic Army service is the NK 1000-76T. The prototype of this semi-trailer was shown for the first time at the Defendory '98 exhibition in Greece. It is stated as being compatible with all European and US tractor trucks.

The chassis frame of the NK 1000-76T is composed of longitudinal beams and vertical mounting brackets. It consists of one main central beam 600 mm in depth, with two supporting beams on which the suspension is mounted. ST 52-3 steel is used throughout. Eight four-wheeled swivelling half-width axles in four rows, giving a total of 32 wheels provide suspension. Each half-width axle is rated at 13 tonnes and is capable of 10° of longitudinal oscillation. All but the first axle row steer by a hydraulically actuated mechanical linkage regulated by the movement of the fifth wheel, a set-up that gives an outside turning radius of 12.5 m and an inside turning radius of 6.5 m, allowing an intersection in 8 m wide roads to be negotiated in one pass. A dual line Anti-lock Braking System (ABS) is fitted.

Powered by either battery or an optional 6 hp diesel Auxiliary Power Unit (APU), a system of hydraulics allows for loadbed height adjustment of +378 to –181 mm. For reduced tyre wear when operating unladen the first or first and second axle rows can be lifted, and any individual axle may be lifted if disabled, or rotated to facilitate tyre replacement when required. Hydraulic power is also provided for the 2.6 × 1 m (L × W) loading ramps. These are fitted with anti-slip bars at 300 mm spacing and give a loading angle of 15° on level ground. Using tractor-mounted winches the trailer is fully equipped to load/unload disabled MBTs. The front Jost-supplied manual/hydraulic independently operating landing legs have a static support load of 60,000 kg, the rear hydraulic leg pair having a static support load of 80,000 kg.

The king-pin is a 89 mm (3½ inch) Jost unit mounted on a heavy-duty hydraulic steering assembly. Loadbed flooring is 10/12 mm thick chequer-plate steel. Two fixed front chocks, two adjustable rear chocks, a set of securing chains and 14 fixing points located to accommodate assorted armoured vehicle or MBT loads are provided. In addition to a single MBT, the use of a purpose-designed pair of ramps will allow the trailer to transport two infantry fighting vehicles such as the BMP-1.

Specifications

NK 1000-76T
Weight:
  (unladen) 27,000 kg
  (operational payload) 76,000 kg
  (at reduced speeds) 100,000 kg
Length:
  (overall, ramps raised) 14.55 m
  (overall, ramps lowered) 16.9
  (deck) 10.18 m
Width: 3.7 m
Height:
  (loadbed, laden) 1.13 m
  (king-pin, laden) 1.625 m

Ground clearance:
(laden to chassis) 530 mm
Wheelbase: 1.6 + 1.6 + 1.7 m
Max speed: (76,000 kg payload)
(road) 80 km/h
(prepared tracks) 40 km/h
(off-road) 15 km/h
Tyres: 235/75R 17.5 (32 + 2 trailer-mounted spares)
Electrical system: 24 V

Status
Tractor truck: Production complete. Replaced by equivalent model from the HX range of tactical trucks. In service with the Hellenic Army (66). Semi-trailer: Production as required. In service with the Hellenic Army (120; 70 (30 + a 35 option) + 55, all delivered 2000-05).

Contractor
RMMV
MAN Nutzfahrzeuge Österreichische AG
Nik Kioleides SA

Canada

Western Star 6900XD series tank transporter

Description
The Western Star 6900XD series tank transporter is a development of Western Star's heavy-duty off-road vehicle series. The layout is conventional with the engine in front of the galvanised all-steel cab. The standard cab provides seating for the driver and two passengers. Additional accommodation for four passengers is available if required.

Power is provided by the option of a Caterpillar or Detroit turbocharged diesel engine with approximate power outputs of 625 and 515 hp (459 and 378 kW), respectively. These are coupled to an Eaton/Fuller manual or optional Twin Disc automatic transmission.

The front Meritor, Dana Spicer or Sisu axles are rated at between 9,060 and 12,684 kg, the rear Meritor or Sisu tandems are rated at between 20,838 and 49,830 kg. The dual channel chassis frame is constructed from high tensile 758 MPa yield strength steel and has a wheelbase of 4.35 m on the standard (6 × 6) chassis. Options include suspension types and rating, winches and a ballistic and mine protection kit. The 6900 series is also available in (8 × 8) configuration, and can be supplied as a rigid chassis or tractor truck.

Western Star Trucks Inc. was acquired by the now Daimler subsidiary, Freightliner LLC, in July 2000. Western Star's Kelowna truck plant and headquarters closed late 2002, with production transferring to Freightliner's Oregon production plant.

Specifications
Western Star 6900XD
Cab seating: 1 + 2 or 1 + 5
Configuration: 6 × 6 (options of 8 × 8 or 10 × 10)
Weight: (payload) up to 100,000 kg
Wheelbase: (standard) 4.35 m
Max speed: 81 km/h
Range: (cruising) 1,000 km
Engine: options - see text
Transmission: options - see text
Transfer box: single or 2-speed
Tyres: (standard) 24R 21
Brakes: dual circuit, air, drums all-round. ABS standard
Electrical system: 24 V (12 V optional)

Status
Available. A demonstrator of an earlier variant has been produced and is known to have been trialled in Kuwait.

Contractor
Western Star Trucks Inc
(This facility closed late 2002.)

Enquiries to
Freightliner LLC
Western Star Trucks

Western Star M4866S Medium Equipment Transporter

Development
The Western Star M4866S (6 × 6) Medium Equipment Transporter is the fifth-wheel tractor-truck variant of the Western Star M4866S High Mobility Engineering Vehicle (HMEV), of which an initial 54 examples were delivered to the Canadian Department of National Defense in 1996/97 in three versions. As a tractor truck the M4866S has a gross combination weight of 63,500 kg.

The M4866S is derived from the 4800 model series, having similar hood, cab and engine installation arrangements, but has a sleeper/storage compartment option provided immediately behind the cab. The wheelbase is increased to 6.2 m, and the frame features heavy-duty deep double-channel rails with oversized cross-members and an extreme duty rear air suspension subframe.

The 4900SA is the current Western Star series of trucks for military applications. These are available in a wide variety styles and with a number of aggregate options.

Western Star Trucks Inc. were acquired by the now Daimler's subsidiary, Freightliner LLC, in July 2000. Western Star's Kelowna truck plant and headquarters closed in September 2002, with production transferring to Freightliner's Oregon production plant.

Description
The cab of the M4866S is air-suspended on the chassis frame, is fitted with air conditioning and the driver and co-driver seats are of the high-back air ride type.

Motive power is provided by a Caterpillar C12 full electronic control 12-litre, 410 hp turbocharged diesel with a three-stage Jacobs brake. This drives through an Allison HD4560P five-speed automatic transmission and Fabco two-speed transfer box. The front steer-drive axle is rated at 9,525 kg and sprung by the combination of semi-elliptic leaf springs and heavy-duty, double-acting shock absorbers, the rear single reduction drive axle pair are fitted with differential locks and is rated at 20,865 kg. Suspension is by a Neway AD246 air suspension system with instant response self-levelling ride height control valves and heavy-duty, double-acting shock-absorbers. The airbrake system incorporates a four-channel Wabco ABS, electronically interfaced to the engine and transmission.

The vehicle is fully rated from –40 to +40°C with automatic cold start ether injection, a 11.7 kW (40,000 BTU/h) diesel-fired coolant heater, a thermostatically controlled in-tank fuel heater, and severe duty engine, transmission and transfer case cooling packages. The engine, transmission and ABS all feature onboard diagnostics with a common ProLink interface for stored data download, programming, fault code interrogation, and real-time datalink.

Specifications
Western Star M4866S
Cab seating: 1 + 1
Configuration: 6 × 6
Weight:
(GVW) 30,000 kg
(GCW) 63,500 kg
Width: (with 395/85R 20 tyres) 2.59 m
Height: (5th wheel) 1.37 m
Track: 2.59 m
Wheelbase: 6.207 m
Max speed: 108 km/h
Range: (cruising) 700 km
Fuel capacity: 454 litres
Gradient:
(at GVW) 60%
(at GCW) 30%
Fording: (unprepared) 800 mm
Engine: Caterpillar C12 12-litre 6-cylinder in-line full electronic control turbocharged water-cooled 4-stroke diesel developing 410 hp (301 kW) at 1,800 rpm and 1,967 N.m torque at 1,300 rpm
Transmission: Allison HD 4560P electronic automatic with 5 forward and 1 reverse gears
Transfer case: Fabco 270, 2-speed
Steering: hydraulic assist, dual gear
Turning radius: 13.4 m
Suspension:
(front) semi-elliptic leaf springs with heavy duty double acting shock-absorbers
(rear) Neway AD246 air suspension system with instant response self-levelling ride height control valves and heavy duty double acting shock-absorbers
Tyres: 395/85R 20
Brakes: dual circuit, air, ABS (4-channel)
Electrical system: 24 V (12 V optional)
Alternator: 110 Ah

Status
Replaced in production by the revised 4900SA series. In service with Bangladesh.

Contractor
Western Star Trucks Inc
(This facility closed in September 2002.)

Enquiries to
Freightliner LLC
Western Star Trucks

China

Hanyang HY 4390 (8 × 8) tractor truck

Description
The HY 4390 (8 × 8) tractor truck is used for the moving of heavy loads carried on a semi-trailer and uses a standard fifth wheel (88.9 mm) carried between the third and fourth axles at the rear. The cab is of the forward control type with seating for a driver and one passenger. There is room behind the seats for a bunk or seating for four passengers. The cab can be tilted forward for maintenance access to the engine and other components.

Specifications
HY 4390 (8 × 8)
Cab seating: 1 + 5
Configuration: 8 × 8
Weight:
  (unladen) 15,000 kg
  (max GVW) 39,000 kg
  (5th wheel load) 24,000 kg
  (GCW) 80,000 kg
Length: 9.1 m
Width: 2.75 m
Height:
  (top of cab) 2.95 m
  (fifth wheel) 1.5 m
Ground clearance: 290 mm
Wheelbase: 1.45 m + 3.5 m + 1.45 m
Track:
  (front) 2.19 m
  (front) 2.084 m
Max speed: 64 km/h
Max gradient: 40%
Engine: Deutz BF12L413FC developing 500 hp (368 kW) at 2,500 rpm and 165 N.m torque at 1,800 rpm
Gearbox: ZF 4S 150G 8/8 14 - 1
Clutch: ZF WSK 400
Turning radius: 12 m
Tyres: 12.00 × 20
Electrical system: 24 V

Status
Production status uncertain. In service with the People's Liberation Army (PLA).

Contractor
Hanyang Special Auto Works

Hanyang HY 4390 (8 × 8) tractor truck (Hanyang Special Auto Works)
1391014

PLA Type 82 HET

Description
Development of the Type 82 Heavy Equipment Transporter (HET) began in the late 1970s. The Type 82 HET is used by the PLA for the road transport of main battle tanks and other tracked armoured vehicles and consists of the Hanyang Special Vehicle Works HY 473 (6 × 6) tractor truck coupled to the HY 962 three-axle semi-trailer. The HY 473 tractor truck adopted some technologies of the Tiema XC2200 military truck, including the air-cooled diesel engine and gearbox. A number of variants of the HY 473 have been developed for various purposes, including Transporter-Erector-Launcher (TEL) vehicles for the DF-21 Intermediate Range Ballistic Missile (IRBM) and DF-31 InterContinental Ballistic Missile (ICBM) systems. Derivatives of the truck are also available in (4 × 4) and (8 × 8) configurations.

The HY 472 and HY 473A are essentially similar vehicles intended mainly for commercial use.

Hanyang HY 473 (6 × 6) tractor truck with HY 962 tank transporter semi-trailer (Hanyang Special Auto Works)   0044364

Hanyang HY 473 (6 × 6) tractor truck (Hanyang Special Auto Works) 0044365

Specifications
PLA Type 82 HET
Cab seating: 1 + 4 to 6
Configuration: 6 × 6
Weight:
  (tractor truck) 12,500 kg
  (5th wheel loading) 19,500 kg
  (payload, trailer) 50,000 kg
  (GCW, tractor truck and trailer, unladen) 32,000 kg
  (GCW, laden) 91,000 kg
Length: 7.345 m
Width: 2.58 m
Height:
  (cab, laden) 2.95 m
  (5th wheel) 1.45 m
Ground clearance: 340 mm
Wheelbase: 3.5 m + 1.5 m
Track:
  (front) 2.05 m
  (rear) 1.92 m
Max speed: 64 km/h
Gradient: (with laden semi-trailer) 22%
Engine: NORINCO/KHD F 12 L 413F diesel developing 355 hp (261 kW) at 2,500 rpm
Gearbox: ZF 5S 111GPA with 9 forward and 1 reverse gears
Transfer box: ZF A800/3D
Turning radius: 10 m
Tyres: 12.00 × 20
Electrical system: 24 V

Status
Production as required. In service with the People's Liberation Army (PLA).

Contractor
Hanyang Special Auto Works.

Czech Republic

TATRA T 815-29ON3T 38 300 6 × 6.2R/371 (6 × 6) ARMAX family tractor truck

Development
The TATRA T 815-29ON3T 38 300 6 × 6.2R/371 and earlier T 815-24EN34 33 270 6 × 6.2 (6 × 6) tractor trucks are members of the T 815 Armax family of 4 × 4 and 6 × 6 trucks and are designed for hauling assorted semi-trailers up to a maximum GCW of 75,000 kg. This allows these vehicles to move most military equipment, with the exception of the heavier Main Battle Tanks (MBTs). The T 815 Armax family of trucks was introduced by TATRA in 1998 to join the earlier TERRN°1 and T 815-6 Force families (originally designated T 816 Force) of trucks, all of which are the continued evolution of the T 815 series first introduced in 1983. Full details of the T 815 and T 815-6 Force families can be found in the Trucks section. The members of

TATRA T 815-29ON3T 38 300 6 × 6.2R/371 (6 × 6) Armax family tractor truck (TATRA, a.s.)

1185471

the TERRN°1 family are essentially commercial designs, but are suitable for certain military applications. The vehicles in T 815-6 Force family are purpose designed no-compromise heavy-duty trucks for tactical military applications.

The T 815 Armax family are based around commercially available designs, militarised as required, and are constructed to comply with all relevant legislation including emissions, noise and axle loadings, although in many cases vehicle payload capabilities exceed allowable peacetime maximums.

TATRA, a.s. became a Joint Stock Company in 1992. In November 2001, it was announced that the Czech government had approved the purchase of a 92 per cent stake in TATRA, a.s. by SDC International of the US. Following a brief period of difficult-to-follow ownership reorganisation, in September 2003 it was announced that Terex Corporation of the US had acquired 71.5 per cent of TATRA shares. Vectra (a London-based Indian-owned company) owned 21.11 per cent of shares, the remaining 8.38 per cent being privately owned. The company became known as Terex-TATRA, with products continuing to be branded TATRA.

In October 2006 it was announced that Terex Corporation had sold its 81 per cent holding of TATRA, a.s. to a consortium of Czech and US investors. The Czech registered Blue River s.r.o. consortium is made up of Belgium-based KBC Private Equity, Vectra Ltd, a US investor, plus Meadow Hill. Vectra Ltd - a construction equipment, bus and truck maker - folded its existing 11.1 per cent stake into Blue River. Blue River is expected to change its name to TATRA Holdings.

The Description section and Specifications table relate specifically to the TATRA T 815-29ON3T 38 300 6×6.2R/371.

Description

The overall layout of the TATRA T 815-29ON3T 38 300 6 × 6.2R/371 (6 × 6) tractor truck follows closely that of earlier TATRA truck designs, in that it retains the torsionally rigid tubular backbone-type chassis and the swinging half-axle independent wheel suspension system. The front steer-drive axle is sprung by the combination of torsion bars and telescopic shock-absorbers, while the rear drive axle is sprung by TATRA's combination suspension that uses the commercial name King Frame. The so-called heavy version of this combination suspension system is fitted. This uses airbags in combination with leaf springs. Each swinging half-axle has an airbag unit mounted above the backbone tube to protect from impact or damage while operating off-road. The leaf springs are shared longitudinally between axle pairs and allow for individual axle movement. Design-maximum individual axle loadings for the heavy version are 15,000 kg.

Motive power is provided by a EURO 3 emissions compliant TATRA 12.7-litre V-8 four-stroke air-cooled diesel engine developing 402 hp. The rear two - or all three axles - are driven via a TATRA 14 TS 210L manual gearbox with 14 forward and two reverse gears and a TATRA 2.30 TRS 1.85 (0.8) two-speed transfer box. The main gearbox is provided with synchromesh on all but reverse and first gears. For on-road use drive to the front axle can be disconnected, decreasing fuel consumption while reducing component wear. For improved traction on difficult surfaces driver-controlled longitudinal and cross-axle differential locks on all axles are fitted.

Power-assisted steering is standard, and dual circuit drum brakes are fitted all-round, supplemented by an engine exhaust brake.

The standard all-steel crew-type two-door cab is of conventional design and features a single roof hatch. Two full-size seats and a single bunk are provided. A curved single-piece or four-piece split windscreen can be fitted. The cab tilts forward hydraulically for maintenance purposes and an independent fuel-powered cab heater, air-conditioning and an NBC set for the crew are options.

To meet a potential IDF requirement, TATRA developed a version of the standard cab that splits at waist level for C-130 air-transport. This process takes two people less than 40 minutes; nine bolts are involved.

A Jost 3.5 inch (89 mm) oscillating fifth wheel is standard, a 2 inch (51 mm) fifth wheel being an option. Other options include winches.

Specifications

T 815-29ON3T 38 300
Cab seating: 1 + 1 + bunk
Configuration: 6 × 6
Weight:
 (tractor, unladen) 11,700 kg
 (front axle, max permissible load) 8,000 kg
 (rear axles, max permissible load) 15,000 kg (each)
 (tractor, GVW) 38,000 kg
 (fifth wheel load) 26,000 kg
 (GC W) 75,000 kg
Length: 7.565 m
Width: 2.5 m
Height: (cab roof) 2.99 m
Track:
 (front) 1.994 m
 (rear) 1.774 m
Wheelbase: 3.7 + 1.45 m
Max speed: (with limiter) 85 km/h
Fuel capacity: 2 × 320 litres
Gradient: (at max GCW) 37.8%
Engine: TATRA T3C-928.90 12.667-litre EURO 3 emissions compliant V-8-cylinder turbocharged and charge-air-cooled, air-cooled direct injection diesel developing 402 hp (300 kW) at 1,800 rpm and 2,100 N.m torque at 1,200 rpm
Gearbox: TATRA 14 TS 210L manual with semi-automatic split giving 14 forward and 2 reverse gears. Synchromesh on all except first and reverse gears
Transfer box: TATRA 2.30TRS1.85 (0.8), 2-speed with front axle disconnect
Clutch: single dry plate, (dia) 430 mm
Steering: power assisted
Turning radius: (kerb) 10.5 m
Suspension:
 (front) torsion bars and telescopic shock-absorbers
 (rear) airbags and leaf springs
Tyres: 1200R 24
Brakes: dual circuit, air, drums front and rear. Supplementary engine exhaust brake. ABS fitted
Electrical system: 24 V
Batteries: 2 × 12 V, 180 Ah
Alternator: 28 V, 80 A

Status

In service with Slovakia. T 815 Armax family trucks are in service with Czech, Indian, Malaysian and Slovak armed forces.

Contractor

TATRA, a.s

TATRA T 816-6VWN9T 43.610 8×8.1R (8 × 8) FORCE family tractor truck

Development

The TATRA T 816-6VWN9T 43.610 8×8.1R (8 × 8) tractor truck was developed in 1997 for towing very heavy tank transporter semi-trailers in off-road and hot ambient conditions. It now forms the heaviest component of the TATRA FORCE family of heavy-duty tactical trucks (now designated T 815-6 FORCE family) and shares some components with the TATRA T 816 LIWA vehicles, full details of which can be found in the Trucks section. The TATRA T 815-6 FORCE family of tactical trucks was introduced by TATRA in 1996, and are the continued evolution of the T 815 series first introduced in 1983.

The TATRA T 816-6VWN9T 43.610 8×8.1R (8 × 8) tractor truck has been tested in the Middle East.

TATRA became a Joint Stock Company in 1992. In November 2001 it was announced that SDC International of the US had been given Czech Republic governmental approval to purchase a 92 per cent stake of TATRA, a.s. Following a brief period of difficult-to-follow ownership reorganisation, in September 2003 it was announced that Terex Corporation of the US had acquired 71.5 per cent of TATRA shares. Vectra (a London-based Indian-owned company) owned 21.11 per cent of shares, the remaining 8.38 per cent being privately owned. The company became known as Terex-TATRA, with products continuing to be branded TATRA.

In October 2006 it was announced that Terex Corporation had sold its 81 per cent holding of TATRA, a.s. to a consortium of Czech and US investors. The Czech registered Blue River s.r.o. consortium is made up of Belgium-based KBC Private Equity, Vectra Ltd, a US investor, plus Meadow Hill. Vectra Ltd - a construction equipment, bus and truck maker - folded its existing 11.1 per cent stake into Blue River. Blue River is expected to change its name to TATRA Holdings.

Description

The TATRA T 816-6VWN9T 43.610 8 × 8.1R tractor truck is designed to haul semi-trailers bearing tanks, other armoured vehicles or other heavy vehicles to a maximum weight of 74,000 kg, both on roads and over rough terrain in regions with high ambient temperatures, high air humidity and in dusty environments. Maximum GCW is 115,000 kg.

TATRA T 816-6VWN9T 43 610 8×8.1R (8 × 8) FORCE family tractor truck coupled to a five-axle semi-trailer (TATRA, a.s.) 0524794

The overall layout of the vehicle follows closely that of earlier TATRA truck designs. The torsionally rigid tubular backbone-type frameless chassis is retained, as is the swinging half-axle independent wheel suspension system. The front steer-drive axles are sprung by the combination of telescopic shock-absorbers plus longitudinally located leaf springs shared between axles pairs, the rear drive axles by TATRA's combination suspension that uses the commercial name KING FRAME. The heavy version of this combination suspension system is fitted. This uses airbags in combination with leaf springs. The airbag units are mounted above the backbone tube to protect from impact or damage while operating off-road, the leaf springs shared longitudinally between axle pairs. Individual half-axle movement is possible. Maximum individual axle loadings for the heavy version are 15,000 kg.

Motive power is provided by a MTU V-12 turbocharged four-stroke water-cooled diesel developing 818 hp. All four hub reduction axles are permanently driven via a Twin Disc torque converter and fully automatic transmission. The torque converter is fitted with a lock-up clutch and two Power Take Off's (PTO's). The fully automatic transmission is integrated into the backbone tube, protecting it from impact damage and eliminating the need for a separate transfer box. Ten forward gears are available and there is a lockable front/rear torque divider. A 'limp home' facility is also provided.

Dual circuit drum brakes are fitted all-round, supplemented by an engine exhaust brake. Options include an Anti-lock Braking System (ABS), a Konstant Drossel engine brake and a hydrodynamic retarder between the engine and transmission.

For improved traction off-road driver-controlled longitudinal and cross-axle differential locks are fitted, and a driver-controlled Central Tyre Inflation (CTI) system is standard. An electronic CTI system is optional. Bead locks for extreme low-pressure operation, in soft sand for example, are standard. With an approach angle of 37° the tractor truck can surmount a 600 mm vertical obstacle. A 2 m trench can be crossed.

The all-steel forward control cab features a four-piece windscreen and has four doors for access to eight (seven plus driver) internal seats. It can be tilted forward for maintenance purposes. Two hatches are provided in the roof and air-conditioning can be fitted.

Two 275 kN Rotzler winches are provided for loading. These are driven hydraulically from the torque converter PTO. Each winch has 70 m of 26 mm diameter cable. A 20 kN auxiliary winch with 150 m of 8 mm cable is optional.

Specifications

T 816-6VWN9T 43.610 8×8.1R (8 × 8) FORCE
Cab seating: 1 + 7
Configuration: 8 × 8
Weight:
  (unladen) 20,500 kg
  (fifth wheel load) 23,000 kg
  (GVW) 43,800 kg
  (GCW) 115,000 kg
  (max load on front axles, each) 8,000 kg
  (max load on rear axles, each) 15,000 kg
Length: 9.02 m
Width: 2.78 m
Height: (exhaust) 3.51 m
Ground clearance: 400 mm
Wheelbase: 1.65 m + 3.1 m + 1.45 m
Wheel track:
  (front) 2.042 m
  (rear) 2.155 m
Angle of approach/departure: 37°/60°
Max speed: 85 km/h
Range: (road) 1,000 km
Fuel capacity: 1,200 litres (2 × 600 litres)
Max gradient: 32%
Side slope: 35%

Fording: 1.25 m
Engine: MTU 12V 183 TD22 21.93-litre V-12 turbocharged charge-air-cooled, water-cooled 4-stroke diesel developing 818 hp (610 kW) at 2,100 rpm and 3,100 N.m torque at 1,400 rpm
Transmission: Twin Disc (TD) 101-3600 electronically controlled automatic with 10 forward gears; plus Twin Disc 8FLW-1854-1 torque converter with lock-up clutch
Steering: power assisted
Turning radius: (kerb) 14 m
Suspension:
  (front) leaf springs and telescopic shock-absorbers
  (rear) air bags and leaf springs (see text for details)
Tyres:
  (front) 1600R 20 with bead locks
  (rear) 24R 20.5 or 24R 21 with bead locks
Brakes: dual circuit, air, drums all-round
Batteries: 2 × 12 V, 180 Ah
Alternator: 28 V, 80 A

Status
Current generation model available.

Contractor
TATRA, a.s.

TATRA T 815-29ON9T 42 300 8 × 8.1R (8 × 8) ARMAX family tractor truck

Development
The TATRA T 815-29ON9T 42 300 8 × 8.1 (8 × 8) tractor truck is a member of the T 815 ARMAX family of trucks and is designed for hauling assorted semi-trailers up to a maximum GCW of 90,000 kg. This allows the vehicle to move most military equipment, with the exception of the heaviest Main Battle Tanks (MBTs). The T 815 ARMAX family of trucks was introduced by TATRA in 1998 to join the earlier TERRN°1 and T 815-6 FORCE (initially designated T 816 FORCE) families of trucks, all of which are the continued evolution of the T 815 series first introduced in 1983. Full details of the T 815 and T 815-6 FORCE families can be found in the Trucks section. The members of the TERRN°1 family are essentially commercial designs, but are suitable for certain military applications. The vehicles in the T 815-6 FORCE family are purpose designed no-compromise heavy-duty trucks for tactical military applications.

The T 815 ARMAX family are based around commercially available designs, militarised as required, and are constructed to comply with all relevant legislation (when required) including emissions, noise and axle loadings, although in many cases vehicle payload capabilities exceed allowable peacetime maximums.

TATRA, a.s. became a Joint Stock Company in 1992. In November 2001, it was announced that the Czech government had approved the purchase of a 92 per cent stake in TATRA, a.s. by SDC International of the US. Following a brief period of difficult-to-follow ownership reorganisation, in September 2003 it was announced that Terex Corporation of the US had acquired 71.5 per cent of TATRA shares. Vectra (a London-based Indian-owned company) owns 21.11 per cent of shares, the remaining 8.38 per cent being privately owned. The company became known as TATRA, a.s., a Terex company, with products continuing to be branded TATRA.

In October 2006 it was announced that Terex Corporation had sold its 81 per cent holding of TATRA, a.s. to a consortium of Czech and US investors. The Czech registered Blue River s.r.o. (now TATRA Holdings) consortium is made up of Belgium-based KBC Private Equity, Vectra Ltd, a US investor, plus Meadow Hill. Vectra Ltd - a construction equipment, bus and truck maker - folded its existing 11.1 per cent stake into Blue River.

TATRA T 815-29ON9T 42 300 8 × 8.1R (8 × 8) ARMAX family tractor truck (TATRA, a.s.) 1185413

Description

The overall layout of the TATRA T 815-29ON9T 42 300 8 × 8.1R (8 × 8) tractor truck follows closely that of earlier TATRA truck designs, in that it retains the torsionally rigid tubular backbone-type chassis and the swinging half-axle independent wheel suspension system. The front steer-drive axles are sprung by the combination of leaf springs and telescopic shock-absorbers, while the rear drive axles are sprung by TATRA's combination suspension that uses the commercial name KING FRAME. The so-called heavy version of this combination suspension system is fitted. This uses airbags in combination with leaf springs. Each swinging half-axle has an airbag unit mounted above the backbone tube to protect from impact or damage while operating off-road. The leaf springs are shared longitudinally between axle pairs and allow for individual axle movement. Design-maximum individual axle loadings for the heavy version are 15,000 kg.

Motive power is provided by a EURO 3 emissions compliant TATRA 12.7-litre V-8 four-stroke air-cooled diesel engine developing 402 hp. The rear two (or all four axles) are driven through a TATRA 14 TS 210L manual gearbox with 14 forward and two reverse gears and a TATRA 2.30 TRS 1.85 (0.8) two-speed transfer box. The main gearbox is provided with synchromesh on all but reverse and first gears. For on-road use drive to the front axles can be disconnected, decreasing fuel consumption while reducing component wear. For improved traction on difficult surfaces driver-controlled longitudinal and cross-axle differential locks on all axles are fitted.

Power assisted steering is standard, and dual circuit drum brakes with ABS are fitted all-round, supplemented by an engine exhaust brake.

The standard all-steel two-door cab is of conventional design and features a single roof hatch. Seating is provided for two with a single bunk in the rear. A curved single-piece or four-piece split windscreen can be fitted. The cab tilts forward hydraulically for maintenance purposes and an independent fuel-powered cab heater and air-conditioning are fitted.

A 3.5 inch (89 mm) or 2 inch (51 mm) oscillating 5th wheel may be fitted.

Specifications

T 815-29ON9T 42 300 8 × 8.1R
Cab seating: 1 + 1 + bunk
Configuration: 8 × 8
Weight:
  (tractor, kerb) 14,250 kg
  (fifth wheel load) 27,500 kg
  (tractor, GVW) 42,000 kg
  (GCW) 90,000 kg
  (front axles, max permissible load) 8,000 kg each
  (rear axles, max permissible load) 13,000 kg each (tyre limited)
Length: 8.14 m
Width: 2.5 m
Height: (exhaust) 3.288 m
Track:
  (front) 2.074 m
  (rear) 2.018 m
Wheelbase: 1.65 + 2.6 + 1.45 m
Max speed: (limited) 85 km/h
Fuel capacity: 2 × 320 litres
Gradient: (at GCW): 27.8%
Engine: TATRA T3B-928.90 EURO 3 emissions complaint 12.667-litre V-8 turbocharged and charge-air-cooled, air-cooled direct injection 4-stroke diesel developing 402 hp (300 kW) at 1,800 rpm and 2,100 N.m torque at 1,000 rpm
Gearbox: TATRA 14 TS 210L manual with semi-automatic split giving 14 forward and 2 reverse gears. Synchromesh on all except first and reverse gears
Transfer box: TATRA 2.30 TRS 1.85 (0.8) 2-speed with front axle disconnect
Clutch: single dry plate, (dia) 430 mm
Steering: power-assisted
Turning radius: (kerb) 13 m
Suspension:
  (front) leaf springs and telescopic shock-absorbers
  (rear) airbags and leaf springs (see text for details)
Tyres: 1600R 20
Brakes: dual circuit, air, drums front and rear. Supplementary engine exhaust brake. ABS fitted
Electrical system: 24 V
Batteries: 2 × 12 V, 180 Ah
Alternator: 28 V, 80 A

Status

Available. T 815 ARMAX family trucks are in service with Czech, Indian, Malaysian and Slovak armed forces.

Contractor

TATRA, a.s.

Finland

Sisu E-Tech 480 (6 × 4) heavy equipment tractor

Development

Sisu was founded in 1931, and the company is currently privately owned by a group of Finnish investors that acquired it from KONE Corporation in 2004. The Finnish state sold its majority shareholding in Sisu to Partek in 1997, KONE Corporation acquiring Sisu as part of its acquisition of Partek in 2002.

Sisu produced its first 12 trucks in 1932, with the company's foray into the military sector beginning in 1938 with a prototype of an armoured military vehicle. It would, however, be 1962 before Sisu manufactured its first prototype (4 × 4) off-road truck, this in collaboration with the Finnish Defence Forces. Sisu has since manufactured a wide range of trucks for the Finnish military.

Sisu signed a partnership agreement with France's Renault in 1997, this including the purchase of cabs, engines, axles, and the sale of Renault commercial vehicles in Finland. This arrangement essentially evolved into a Sisu-Volvo deal, when the Swedish company gained control of Renault Trucks in 2000.

In mid-2010 Sisu announced that it had concluded an arrangement with Daimler for the supply of Mercedes-Benz heavy truck components, including engines. This arrangement replaces the Renault/Volvo joint venture.

During 2011 Sisu expects to build around 150 to 200 Mercedes-Benz component based trucks, this increasing to an annual output of around 400 units. Vehicles produced will use engines, cabs and transmissions from Daimler, but with Sisu axles and an in-house Sisu chassis. A manual Eaton Fuller gearbox will be an offered option.

The Sisu E-Tech 480 (6 × 4) heavy equipment tractor is based on a commercial Sisu design and was developed in conjunction with Renault Trucks to meet a French Army requirement for a heavy equipment transporter for the road transport of heavy loads. It was announced in April 2002 that following an international tender Renault Trucks had been awarded the contract to supply the French Army with 110 (60 plus an option of 50) Sisu E-Tech 480 (6 × 4) heavy equipment transporters. These vehicles were manufactured at Sisu's Karjaa plant in Finland. Deliveries to the French Army commenced in 2005 at a rate of eight vehicles per month. A possible follow-on contract award for an additional 34 vehicles had not been awarded by late-2010.

The original French Army requirement called for a GCW of 85,000 kg, this later increasing to a GCW of 120,000 kg. In service the Sisu E-Tech 480 is used in the tank and heavy equipment transport role for which it is normally coupled to a multi-axle trailer procured under a separate contract.

First production example of the Sisu E-Tech 480 (6 × 4) heavy equipment tractor (Renault)　　0558827

Sisu E-Tech 480 (6 × 4) heavy equipment tractor coupled to a two-axle semi-trailer (Pierre Touzin)　　1391004

Sisu E-Tech 480 (6 × 4) heavy equipment tractor fitted with interchangeable armoured cab (Sisu)   0558828

The Sisu E-Tech 480 has replaced the French Army's Renault TRM 700-100 tractor truck in roles where 700 hp and all-wheel drive are not deemed necessary. Full details of the TRM 700-100 tractor truck can be found elsewhere in this section.

Description

The Sisu E-Tech 480 (6 × 4) tractor truck is entirely conventional in design and is a militarised and uprated commercial tractor truck. The ladder-type channel-section chassis is constructed from 8 mm high-tensile steel, is 300 mm deep and fitted with 4 mm thick, 284 mm deep flitch plates for reinforcement. Tubular cross-members are bolted in. The two front-mounted towing eyes conform to STANAG 4019.

The all-steel Premium Route model sleeper-type cab is supplied by Renault and modified and militarised by Sisu. Seating is for two, with the lower of the twin bunks doubling up as additional seating for two. All seating positions are provided with seat belts. The cab tilts forward for engine access. Air conditioning is standard. Fitting for radio is an option. Modifications include racks for two assault rifles, a 6 kg powder fire extinguisher and a 2.5 kg decontamination bottle.

Renault supplied 20 armoured cabs for these vehicles. These armoured cabs are fully interchangeable with the standard cab in approximately four hours and offer ballistic protection up to STANAG 4569 Level 3. With the armoured cab fitted, the standard front 13R 22.5 tyres are replaced by 425/65R 22.5 tyres with runflat inserts, and the standard rear 13R 22.5 tyres by 12R 20 tyres, also with runflat inserts.

A double oscillating 3½ in (89 mm) fifth wheel with ±17° of longitudinal and ±7° transverse movement is fitted. The E-Tech 480 has a chassis weight of 10,530 kg and a payload of 24,470 kg. The spare wheel is located behind the cab. As an option twin SAMIIA type BI TREUIL 18,000 kg capacity winches may be chassis-mounted between the cab rear wall and fifth wheel assembly.

Motive power is provided by a EURO III emissions compliant Mack 11.93-litre six-cylinder turbocharged diesel engine driving the rear bogie (6 × 4) via a ZF 16-speed manual gearbox. A ZF intarder provides up to 420 kW of braking power. The rear 17,000 kg-rated Renault PMA1845B drive axles are sprung by leaf springs. Drum brakes are fitted. Cross- and inter-axle differential locks are fitted for increased traction on loose or slippery surfaces.

The front 10,000 kg-rated Sisu FSND-10-P steer-axle is sprung by the combination of parabolic leaf springs and telescopic shock-absorbers. Disc brakes are fitted. Steering is power-assisted.

Standard tyres are 13R 22.5 tubeless, with Michelin or Goodyear being specified options. All tractor and semi-trailer tyres can be inflated by an onboard air compressor in less than 40 minutes.

Climatic operational range is −20°C to +40°C; an engine pre-heater is optional.

Specifications

Sisu E-Tech 480
Cab seating: 1 + 1 + 2
Configuration: 6 × 4
Weight:
  (permissible GVW) 35,000 kg
  (chassis-cab) 10,530 kg
  (max load, chassis payload) 24,470 kg
  (max permissible front axle load) 10,000 kg (tyre limited to 8,000 kg with 13.00R 22.5 tyres)
  (max permissible rear axle load) 34,000 kg (bogie rating)
  (GCW, permissible) 120,000 kg
Length: 7.43 m
Width: 2.55 m
Height:
  (cab, laden) 3.22 m
  (cab, unladen) 3.32 m

Track:
  (front) 2.023 m
  (rear) 1.810 m
Max speed: (level surface, +20°C, below 1,000 m altitude) 89 km/h
  (2% gradient) 55 km/h
  (5% gradient) 27 km/h
  (9% gradient) 16 km/h
Max range: 1,200 km at 45 km/h average on level ground
Fuel capacity: 2 × 365 litres
Max gradient: (stop and restart) 25%
Engine: Mack MIDR.06.24.65 EUP 11.93-litre 6-cylinder in-line turbocharged water-cooled 4-stroke Electronic Unit Pump (EUP) injection diesel engine developing 480 hp (358 kW) at 1,900 rpm and 2,250 N.m torque from 1,100 to 1,400 rpm
Gearbox: ZF Ecosplit 16 S 221 OD 16-speed manual gearbox with intarder
Steering: TRW type TAS-85, engine-driven hydraulic power-assisted
Turning radius:
  (kerb) 7.389 m
  (wall) 8.184 m
Suspension:
  (front axle) 4-leaf parabolic springs and telescopic shock-absorbers
  (rear bogie) type PMR3045 9-leaf
Tyres: 13.00R 22.5, tubeless. 425/65R 20 (front axle), 12.00R 20 (rear bogie), with optional armoured cab fitted
Brakes:
  (main) 4-circuit, air, discs, front, drums, rear, ABS
  (parking) spring brake cylinders on all axles. 16% gradient, up or down, at GCW
Electrical system: 24 V
Batteries: 2 × 12 V, 180 Ah, type 6 TN B
Alternator: 28 V/80 Ah

Status

Production of current model as required. Delivered to the French Army (110).

Contractor

Oy Sisu Auto Ab

France

Renault R 390 (6 × 4) tractor truck

Development

The R 390 (6 × 4) tractor truck is a standard commercial vehicle adapted to meet military requirements. It was adopted by the French Army for road use and is primarily used in conjunction with the Nicolas STA 43 semi-trailer.

The French Army uses a similar version of the Renault R 390 (6 × 4) tractor truck for towing semi-trailers carrying fuel and other supplies.

A later (6 × 4) tractor version known as the R385ti using Renault's 12-litre six-cylinder in-line turbocharged and aftercooled MIDR 063540 engine was produced and customers included the Royal Thai Army which purchased 66 units.

Description

The chassis of the R390 (6 × 4) tractor truck consists of two C-section side members with five cross-members welded and riveted into position. The vehicle is fitted with a model KB 2480 cab which is of the two-door forward control type and has seats for the driver, two passengers and two bunks at the rear of the cab. The cab is heated and soundproofed and can be tilted forward to an angle of 70° to allow maintenance work on the engine.

Renault R390 (6 × 4) tractor truck of the French Army coupled to a Nicolas STA 45 semi-trailer (Pierre Touzin)   1047654

Optional equipment included a hydraulic winch with a capacity of 15,000 kg and 90 m of cable, dividing curtain, elbow rests, heating system, fog lamps, tachograph, radio equipment, blackout lights, searchlight, flashing light, combined air/electric cables and an anti-freeze device for the brake circuit.

The R 390 (6 × 4) tractor truck is primarily used in conjunction with the Nicolas STA 43 semi-trailer, but can be used with other semi-trailers carrying MBTs up to a maximum weight of 55,000 kg.

Specifications
Cab seating: 1 + 4
Configuration: 6 × 4
Weight:
    (laden) 34,500 kg
    (unladen) 10,300 kg
    (front axle, laden) 6,500 kg
    (front axle, unladen) 5,300 kg
    (rear bogie, laden) 28,000 kg
    (rear bogie, unladen) 5,000 kg
Max weight on 5th wheel: 24,000 kg
Length: 6.53 m
Width: 2.49 m
Height: 3 m
Ground clearance: 303 mm
Track:
    (front) 2.028 m
    (rear) 1.825 m
Wheelbase: 2.95 m + 1.35 m
Angle of approach/departure: 22°/45°
Max speed: 66 km/h
Range: 800 km
Fuel capacity: 650 litres
Max gradient: (70,600 kg GVW) 15%
Fording: 700 mm
Engine: Renault model MIVR 08-35-30 8-cylinder supercharged water-cooled diesel developing 390 hp (287 kW) at 2,100 rpm
Gearbox: Renault B 9 with 18 forward and 2 reverse gears
Steering: 8065 hydraulic power-assisted
Turning radius: 8.5 m
Suspension:
    (front) leaf springs and shock-absorbers
    (rear) torsion bar stabiliser
Tyres: 13 × 22.5
Brakes: pneumatic
Electrical system: 24 V
Batteries: 4 × 12 V, 200 Ah

Status
Production complete, replaced by equivalent models from the Renault Kerax range. In service with the French Army; similar models used by others including Thailand (66).

Contractor
Renault Trucks Defense

Renault TRM 340.34 T (6 × 6) tractor truck

Development
Renault's commercial C range of bonneted trucks was sold mainly outside of Europe, European commercial legislation not favouring a bonneted design. Commercial considerations are not a major consideration for military users, and a number of essentially similar bonneted Renault designs (varying primarily in engine power outputs and operating weights) are also employed by French Armed Forces in small numbers, including heavy tractor trucks, designated TRM 340.34T.

French Army TRM 340.34 T tractor truck (Shaun C Connors)   1340272

Commercial production of all heavy bonneted models is now complete, replaced in production by militarised versions of the commercial KERAX range of trucks. An overview of the KERAX range can be found elsewhere in this section.

Description
The TRM 340.34 was designed for towing semi-trailers both on roads and across country up to a maximum weight of 65,000 kg. The chassis consists of C-section side members with the cross-members bolted into position. The layout of the vehicle is conventional, with the engine at the front, cab in the centre and fifth wheel at the rear. The rear bogie has both cross- and inter-axle differential locks.

Optional equipment included a heating system and a sleeper cab with one bunk. The engine could have a preheating system, a heavy-duty air filter and a vertical exhaust. A power take-off was an option on the transfer case and the chassis will accept an 89 mm (3.5 in) fifth-wheel coupling with single or double oscillation. Electrical equipment can include an interference suppressor and blackout lighting. Further options included twin 15,000 kg hydraulic winches.

Specifications
TRM 340.34 T
Cab seating: 1 + 2
Configuration: 6 × 6
Weight:
    (laden) 34,000 kg
    (max GCW, on road) 100,000 kg
    (unladen) 9,905 kg
    front axle, (laden) 7,500 kg
    (front axle, unladen) 5,049 kg
    rear bogie, (laden) 27,000 kg
    (rear bogie, unladen) 4,856 kg
    (max weight on 5th wheel) 14,500 kg
Length: 7.78 m
Width: 2.49 m
Height:
    (cab) 3.005 m
    (5th wheel bracket) 1.365 m
Ground clearance: 312 mm
Track:
    (front) 1.91 m
    (rear) 1.825 m
Wheelbase: 3.9 m + 1.35 m
Angle of approach: 28°
Max speed: 82 km/h
Range: 700 km
Fuel capacity: 250 litres
Gradient: (towing fully laden semi-trailer) 18%
Side slope: 30%
Fording: 850 mm
Engine: Renault MIDR 06-35-40 6-cylinder turbocharged intercooled 4-stroke diesel developing 336 hp (251 kW) at 1,900 rpm
Gearbox: Type B9 with 8 forward and 1 reverse gears
Transfer box: Type VG 1200, 2-speed
Steering: Type 8046
Turning radius: 10.8 m
Suspension:
    (front) semi-elliptic springs with rubber bump stops and double acting hydraulic shock-absorbers
    (rear) trunnion suspension using semi-elliptic leaf springs with axle torque rods
Tyres: 12.00R 20
Brakes: air, drums all round
Electrical system: 24 V
Batteries: 2 × 12 V, 143 Ah

Status
In service with the French Army. Production complete, replaced by equivalent models from the Renault Kerax range.

Contractor
Renault Trucks Defense

Renault TRM 700-100 (6 × 6) tractor truck and SOFRAME SRPB 60 tank transport semi-trailer

Development
The Renault TRM 700-100 (6 × 6) tractor truck was first shown at the 1987 Satory exhibition (now Eurosatory) and was designed as a tactical tank transporter for the Leclerc MBT. In December 1993, following a Europe-wide competitive tender, the French Army contract for an initial order for 179 of these vehicles was placed with Renault VI, with a second order for 121 vehicles being anticipated at the time. This did not follow and production of the TRM 700-100 is now complete. The Renault TRM 700-100

Renault TRM 700-100 (6 × 6) tractor truck coupled to a SOFRAME SRPB 60 six-axle semi-trailer laden with a GIAT Leclerc MBT (Pierre Touzin)   0121836

Renault TRM 700-100 (6 × 6) tractor truck coupled to a SOFRAME SRPB 60 six-axle semi-trailer (Pierre Touzin)   1120412

SOFRAME SRPB 60 six-axle semi-trailer (Pierre Touzin)   1391002

is used with the SOFRAME SRPB 60 (Semi-Remorque Porte Blindés 60 tonnes) tank transporter semi-trailer which was designed and developed to meet a French Ministry of Defence requirement for the on-road transport of the Leclerc MBT.

To supplement the Renault TRM 700-100 in many of its peacetime tank transport roles - where all-wheel drive and 700 hp is not deemed necessary - the French Army placed an order with Renault Trucks during 2002 for the delivery of 110 Sisu E-Tech 480 (6 × 4) tractor trucks. These are normally used in conjunction with semi-trailers procured under a separate contract. Full details of the Sisu E-Tech 480 can be found elsewhere in this section.

Description

The Renault TRM 700-100 (6 × 6) tractor truck is based on a conventional channel section ladder-type chassis with dimensions of 302 × 85 × 8 mm. Internal reinforcing channel side members are fitted and a central recovery/towing point and two shackle brackets are fitted to the front all-steel bumper. A 3.5 inch (89 mm) double oscillation fifth wheel is fitted.

The forward control, hard-topped, four-door cab is similar to that used on the Renault TRM 10 000 (6 × 6) 10,000 kg truck (full details of which can be found in the Trucks section) but enlarged to carry the driver and four passengers. The driver and three passengers have suspended seats, the fifth seat is fixed and folds out to form a sleeping berth. The cab tilts forward hydraulically for engine access.

The TRM 700-100 is powered by a Renault E9 V-8 turbocharged diesel engine developing 700 hp, giving a fully laden combination a power-to-weight ratio of 6.6 hp/tonne. Maximum road speed is 80 km/h and the

minimum sustainable speed on a 20 per cent gradient is 3 km/h. The vehicle is designed to be capable of maintaining an average speed of 50 km/h over distances exceeding 800 km.

Driveline consists of a Type WR torque converter, with lock-up clutch and integrated Power Take-Off (PTO) units coupled to a Type PS 226 six-speed automatic gearbox. The transfer box is integrated into the gearbox and permanently distributes drive to all three axles via a mechanically locking torque divider at a ratio of: 25 per cent to the front axle and 75 per cent to the rear tandem unit.

Renault double reduction axles are fitted, the rear Type PMR 3045 tandem unit being fitted with cross and longitudinal differential locks. Differential locking was an option in the front Type PA 945 axle. Without semi-trailer the axle loadings of the unladen tractor truck are 8,400 kg on the front axle and 8,400 kg on the rear tandem unit. Maximum axle loadings are 10,000 kg on the front axle, 30,000 kg on the rear tandem unit. Steering is power assisted, the dual circuit system being fitted with three pumps. All terrain tyres are fitted to the 20 inch wheel rims.

Drum brakes are fitted all-round. The pneumatic dual circuit braking system is fitted with a load sensing valve on the rear tandem axle unit. An anti-lock braking system (ABS) is fitted.

Specifications

TRM 700-100
Cab seating: 1 + 4
Configuration: 6 × 6
Weight:
  (kerb) 16,800 kg
  (GVW) 39,000 kg
  (GCW) 106,000 kg
Towed load: 90,000 kg
Max load on front axle: 10,000 kg
Max load on rear axles: 30,000 kg
Max load on 5th wheel: 23,000 kg
Length: 8.110 m
Width: (overall) 2.9 m
Height: (unladen) 3.283 m
Ground clearance: (rear axle, loaded) 341 mm
Wheelbase: 4.325 m + 1.35 m
Track:
  (front) 2.12 m
  (rear) 2.03 m
Angle of approach: 42°
Max speed: 80 km/h
Fuel capacity: 1,000 litres (2 × 500 litres)
Range: 850 km
Max gradient: 20%
Engine: RVI Type E9 16.4-litre V-8 turbocharged and intercooled direct injection water-cooled 4-stroke diesel developing 700 hp (515 kW) at 2,500 rpm
Transmission: Type PS 226 automatic with 6 forward gears and 1 reverse gear; Type WR hydraulic torque converter with lock-up clutch and hydraulic retarder
Transfer box: single-speed
Steering: hydraulic power-assisted, type 8099
Turning radius: 14 m
Suspension:
  (front) semi-elliptic leaf springs with auxiliary equaliser spring and hydraulic telescopic shock-absorbers
  (rear) inverted semi-elliptic leaf springs, oscillating swivels and reaction rods
Tyres: 385/95 × T4 TL 1646
Brakes: dual circuit, air, drums all-round, ABS
Electrical system: 24 V
Batteries: 4 × 12 V 6 TN B, 125 Ah
Alternator: 50 A

SOFRAME SRPB 60 tank transport semi-trailer

The SOFRAME SRPB 60 (Semi-Remorque Porte Blindés 60 tonnes) tank transporter semi-trailer was designed and developed to meet a French Ministry of Defence requirement for the on-road transport of the Leclerc MBT. It is also capable of transporting the Ariete, Challenger 2, Leopard 2, M1A2 Abrams and all other current generation MBTs and other heavy vehicles over long distances and at speeds up to 85 km/h. In addition to France, which operates 120 examples, the SRPB 60 semi-trailer has also been supplied to the Belgian Army (as the SMC 60 6/3D-B), the Italian Army, and the Polish Army (as the SMC 60 6/3D-P).

The SOFRAME SRPB 60 semi-trailer has six axles. The front three axles are fixed while the rear three are steerable, being automatically controlled by the tractor-trailer angle. In total there are 24 road wheels; tyres are 265/70R 19.5. Overall trailer length is 15.22 m, platform length is 10.94 m, and overall width is 3.35 m.

The stated maximum payload of the trailer is 70,000 kg, unladen weight being 19,500 kg. At 85 km/h the maximum on-road payload of the trailer is 65,360 kg, at a maximum speed of 60 km/h this increases to 69,800 kg.

For suspension, two hydraulic cylinders are fitted on each axle. Each cylinder is fitted with accumulators, which have a hydraulic circuit on each side. These connect the six cylinders to equalise the load. A central lubrication system is provided. Dual circuit air brakes meet EU regulations.

The gooseneck is articulated, actuated by a hydraulic cylinder. It adjusts the height of the deck together with the hydraulic suspension to maintain the load deck horizontal. Two gooseneck options are available, a short one for three-axle tractors and a longer version for four-axle tractors.

The two loading ramps are hydraulically operated for one-man operation. Standard equipment includes pulleys and cable guide rollers for loading and unloading. A 24 V electrical power pack is mounted on the gooseneck to provide power for all the hydraulic operations on the semi-trailer. Two spare road wheels are carried.

Status
Renault TRM 700-100 (6 × 6) tractor truck; production complete, in service with the French Army (179). SOFRAME SRPB 60 tank transport semi-trailer; production as required, in service with Belgium, France (120), Italy (28) and Poland.

Contractor
Renault Trucks Defense

Germany

IVECO-Magirus 330-32 ANWTM/320 D 34 AS (6 × 6) tractor truck and associated models

Development
This range of heavy equipment transporters were produced by IVECO-Magirus (now part of the IVECO group). Like many older companies the now IVECO-Magirus can trace its origins back a number of years and through a number of mergers, acquisitions and so on. A historical overview of the company, which has its origins in a fire brigade and accessories equipment company set up in Ulm by Conrad Dietrich Magirus in 1861, can be found in the IVECO-Magirus 160-23 ANWM/232 D 16 AL (6 × 6) 7,000 kg truck and associated models entry in the Trucks section.

The bonneted range of commercial trucks on which these heavy equipment transporters are based were in commercial production from 1971 until 1998. As heavy trucks intended primarily for commercial use in quarries and on construction sites they proved well-suited to military applications and several thousand examples, including a selection of heavy equipment transporters, were supplied to a number of armed forces, primarily in Africa and the Middle East.

A comprehensive list of users of this range of trucks has never been made available by IVECO-Magirus, however, the biggest customers for the base range of these trucks were Algeria, Sudan and Tunisia.

IVECO-Magirus 330-32 ANWTM heavy tractor truck. This model is known to be in service with Sudan and Tunisia (IVECO-Magirus)   1185434

Designated Magirus 310M32AS, this vehicle is in service with the Peruvian Army (Cesar Cruz Tantalean)   1047614

Among at least 7,000 assorted models supplied to Algeria was a batch of some 600 400M33AS (6 × 6) heavy tractor trucks fitted with twin Rotzler winches. These were supplied during 1982-1983. A further 99 400M33AS vehicles with the revised IVECO-style 330-40 ANWTM designation were delivered during 1985. Most recently (2002-2006) Algeria has received 146 IVECO MP720E44WT (6 × 6) EuroTrakker range tractor trucks for use in the tank transport role; full details of these can be found elsewhere in this section.

Among an assortment of models from this range of trucks, Tunisia received a quantity of 330-32 ANWTM (6 × 6) heavy tractor trucks for use in the tank transport role. Sudan is also understood to have received some 330-32 ANWTM (6 × 6) heavy tractor trucks for use in the tank transport role.

One further known user of these trucks in the tank transport role is Peru which operates an undisclosed number (at least 70 as of early-2009) of 310-32 ANWTM (6 × 6) models, this model being powered by a naturally aspirated version of the 15.953-litre BF 10 L 513 10-cylinder air-cooled engine fitted to the 330-40 ANWTM model.

Description
The range of trucks covered in this entry can, in various reference sources, be seen referred to as Magirus-Deutz, IVECO-Magirus, Magirus or on rare occasions just IVECO. To further muddle the identification issue, some time after the formation of IVECO the alpha-numeric designation of models was changed to bring it in line with other IVECO products. Not only did this change revise the meanings of any letters used in the designation, but numerically it not only changed the presentation of the GVW/engine rating information, it also reversed its sequencing.

When taking the 330-32 ANWTM/320 D 34 AS model as an example its post-IVECO 330-32 ANWTM designation denotes: 330 - GVW tonnes (rounded ÷ 10); 32 - engine hp (rounded ×10); A - air-cooled; N - bonneted; W - all-wheel drive; T - tractor; M - military, while its pre-IVECO Magirus-Deutz 320 D 34 AS designation denotes: 232 - engine hp; D - Deutz engine; 34 - GVW tonnes (rounded); A - alrad (all-wheel drive); S - tractor (S - Sattelzugmaschine).

A number of different military models were produced or proposed in (6 × 4) and (6 × 6) drive configurations, although all models were essentially similar in their base design and were built on a conventional C-section ladder-type chassis with a double articulated fifth wheel located over the rear axles. Axles were double reduction and sprung by leaf springs, inverted on the rear bogies. Manual gearboxes (usually ZF 8-speed) were coupled to a 2-speed transfer box, some models having a conventional clutch, others a torque convertor.

The standard engine was a Deutz F 10 L 513 15.953-litre 10-cylinder air-cooled unit which could be either naturally aspirated or turbocharged. Where a turbocharger was fitted the engine designation was prefixed by the letter B.

Optional twin hydraulic 20,000 kg recovery winches were fitted to some models. Other standard options included a cab roof hatch, a blackout lighting system and a twin-compartment crew cab. The 330-40 ANWTM could be fitted with special tyres for use over sandy terrain - single 14.00R 20 at the front and single 24-20.5 at the rear.

There was no direct replacement for this range of trucks in the IVECO line-up.

Specifications
IVECO-Magirus 330-32 ANWTM/320

Model	330-40 ANWTM	330-32 ANWTM
Cab seating:	1 + 2	1 + 2
Configuration:	6 × 6	6 × 6
Weight:		
(kerb)	14,200 kg	12,000 kg
(on 5th wheel)	21,500 kg	21,000 kg
(GVW)	35,700 kg	33,000 kg
(GCW)	up to 87,000 kg	up to 83,000 kg

Model	330-40 ANWTM	330-32 ANWTM
Length:	7.86 m	7.86 m
Width:		
(over cab)	2.5 m	2.5 m
(over rear wheels)	2.802 m	2.802 m
Height: (top of air intake)	2.965 m	2.965 m
Ground clearance:	372 mm	372 mm
Track:		
(front)	2.002 m	2.002 m
(rear)	2.802 m	2.802 m
Wheelbase:	4 m + 1.45 m	4 m + 1.45 m
Angle of approach/departure:	30°/54°	30°/54°
Max speed:	84 km/h	63 km/h
Range:	800 km	500 km
Fuel capacity: (standard)	400 + 300 litres	300 litres
Max gradient:	63%	>35%
Side slope:	20%	20%
Fording:	800 mm	800 mm
Engine:	Deutz Diesel BF 10 L 513 15.953-litre 10-cylinder turbocharged air-cooled 4-stroke diesel developing 415 hp (305 kW) at 2,300 rpm	Deutz Diesel F 10 L 513 15.953-litre 10-cylinder naturally aspirated air-cooled 4-stroke diesel developing 320 hp (235 kW) at 2,500 rpm and 1,020 N.m torque at 1,500 rpm
Gearbox:	ZF 4 S-150 GP manual, 8 forward and 1 reverse gears	ZF 4 S-150 GP manual, 8 forward and 1 reverse gears
Transfer box:	2-speed	2-speed
Clutch:	WSK 400 torque converter	single dry plate
Steering:	ball and nut, power assisted	ball and nut, power assisted
Turning radius:	9.8 m	9.8 m
Suspension:		
(front)	semi-elliptic leaf springs, hydraulic shock-absorbers	semi-elliptic leaf springs, hydraulic shock-absorbers
(rear)	inverted semi-elliptic leaf springs	inverted semi-elliptic leaf springs
Tyres:	14.00R 20, twin at rear	14.00R 20, twin at rear
Brakes:		
(main)	drum, air on all wheels plus exhaust retarder	drum, air on all wheels plus exhaust retarder
(parking)	mechanical on rear wheels	mechanical on rear wheels
Electrical system:	24 V	24 V
Batteries:	2 × 12 V, 100 Ah	2 × 12 V, 100 Ah
Alternator:	28 V, 35 A	28 V, 35 A

Status

Production complete. In service with Algeria (330-40 ANWTM/400M33AS (699)), Peru (310M32AS), Sudan (330-32 ANWTM), Tunisia (330-32 ANWTM) and possibly other undisclosed countries.

Contractor

IVECO-Magirus AG

MAN 40.633 DFAETX (6 × 6) tank transporter

Development

The MAN 40.633 DFAETX 6 × 6 truck is a member of the MAN FX tactical truck range and is in service with the UAE Army. As the Steyr 40 M 60, essentially the same vehicle in service with the Hellenic Army. Details of the Steyr 40 M 60 can be found elsewhere in this section. Full details of the relationship between the current MAN and Steyr military truck ranges can be found in the Steyr trucks or MAN trucks entries in the Trucks section but in brief: In January 1990 MAN Nutzfahrzeuge AG of Germany acquired an 85 per cent share of the truck-building activities of Austria's Steyr Nutzfahrzeuge AG. In 1993 MAN exercised their option to acquire the remaining 15 per cent share of the business. Steyr Nutzfahrzeuge AG became known as MAN Steyr AG during 2002 and is now known as MAN Nutzfahrzeuge Österreichische AG.

Rear three-quarter view of a MAN 40.633 DFAETX (6 × 6) tractor truck of UAE Armed Forces displayed at IDEX 2005 (Patrick Allen)   1137936

MAN 40.633 DFAETX (6 × 6) tractor truck and Crossmobil STU5-70 semi-trailer of UAE Armed Forces seen at IDEX 2005 (Shaun C Connors)   1120465

MAN Nutzfahrzeuge AG and Rheinmetall AG announced their respective intentions to form a joint wheeled military vehicles company in 2009. This alliance became a reality in January 2010 with the announcement of the founding of Rheinmetall MAN Military Vehicles (RMMV) GmbH. RMMV sees the merger of Rheinmetall's wheeled military vehicle activities with those of the military truck activities of MAN. Essentially this merger unites the complementary technological core competencies of MAN's automotive expertise in commercial-vehicle manufacture with Rheinmetall's technological know-how in the military land sector/systems field. The result is the creation of a new single-source provider for the entire range of armoured and unarmoured transport, command and role-specific wheeled vehicles. Throughout all entries MAN and/or RMMV designations and references are made to suit context.

Approximately 30 MAN 40.633 DFAETX (6 × 6) tank transporters have been supplied to UAE Armed Forces coupled to a Crossmobil STU5-70 five-axle semi-trailer.

MAN's FX range of tactical trucks were phased out of production during 2005, to be replaced by the HX range of tactical trucks. Full details of the HX range of tactical trucks can be found in the Trucks sections; outline details of HX range heavy tractor trucks can be found elsewhere in this section.

Description

The MAN FX range of tactical trucks is based on the MAN F2000 range of heavy commercial trucks, but militarised as required and fitted with the MAN modular military cab. The C-section chassis is manufactured from high-strength fine-grain steel with riveted and bolted-in cross members and is fitted with four towing eyes and a recovery pintle, front and rear, for towing and recovery operations. A 3½ in (89 mm) oscillating fifth wheel is fitted. The all-steel modular military cab features a full-size observation hatch, is air-conditioned and extended to accommodate a bench seat for a tank crew of four.

Motive power is provided by a MAN D2840LF 10-cylinder (in V configuration) that if required (with some reduction in power output) can meet EURO II emissions regulations. Engine cooling is by twin hydrostatically-driven cooling fans and two heavy-duty radiator systems mounted in a protected area on top of the chassis and behind the cab. An oil coolant heat exchanger is provided for the torque converter.

Permanent drive is transmitted to all three axles via a ZF torque converter with automatically controlled lock-up clutch and built-in primary retarder, a ZF eight-speed (with splitter) double H pattern gearbox giving 16 forward and two reverse gears, and a Steyr two-speed transfer box with lockable longitudinal differential and power take-off for the emergency steering pump.

The optional Central Tyre Inflation (CTI) system is fitted to the UAE vehicles. Wide high-flotation 24R 21 single tyres are fitted to all axles, the maximum permissible load on the front model VA9-0950 steer-drive axle being 9,500 kg, the maximum permissible load on each model H/HD 9-16120 rear drive axle being 14,500 kg. 14.00R 20 tyres (dual on rear axles) are an option. All axles feature planetary final drives in the wheel hubs, and cross-axle differential locks. The front axle differential lock automatically disengages when approximately 30 km/h is reached. Conventional leaf spring suspension is employed.

Maximum road speed is limited to 88 km/h, the calculated maximum speed being 128 km/h. At 110,000 kg GCW in first gear, high range, the maximum gradient climbable (subject to surface adhesion) is 21 per cent. At 110,000 kg GCW in first gear, low range, this increases (subject to surface adhesion) to 33 per cent. An Anti-lock Braking System (ABS) is fitted. Two spare wheels are carried.

Specifications

MAN 40.633 DFAETX
Cab seating: 1 + 2 + 4 tank crew
Configuration: 6 × 6
Weight:
  (tractor, GVW) 38,000 kg
  (tractor, chassis-cab) 17,050 kg
  (max permissible GCW) 180,000 kg
  (5th wheel load) 21,000 kg
Length: 8.329 m
Width:
  (cab) 2.44 m
  (rear wheels) 2.9 m
Height:
  (cab, laden) 3.569 m
  (cab, unladen) 3.6 m
  (5th wheel, laden) 1.695 m
  (5th wheel, unladen) 1.795 m
Ground clearance:
  (front) 481 mm
  (rear) 435 mm
Wheelbase: 4.025 m + 1.5 m
Max speed: (road, limited) 88 km/h
Min speed: 3 km/h
Fuel capacity: 820 litres 1 × 600-litre (LH side), 1 × 220 litres (RH side)
Gradient: up to 40% without trailer
Sideslope: 30%
Fording: 850 mm
Engine: MAN type D2840LF 18.27-litre V-10 exhaust gas turbocharged and intercooled, water-cooled direct injection diesel developing 630 hp (463 kW) between 1,700 and 2,100 rpm and 2,830 N.m torque between 1,100 and 1,450 rpm
Gearbox: ZF 16S 251 manual with 16 forward and 2 reverse gears and ZF WSK 440 torque converter
Transfer box: Steyr G 2500, 2 speed
Steering: ZF Servocom power assisted
Turning radius: 11.8 m
Suspension:
  (front) progressive acting semi-elliptic leaf springs with rubber stops, telescopic shock-absorbers and anti-roll bar
  (rear) slide shackle springs with anti-roll bar
Tyres: 24R 21
Brakes: dual circuit, air, drums all-round with ABS and twin air dryers
Electrical system: 24 V
Batteries: 2 × 12 V, 180 Ah
Alternator: 28 V, 55A

Crossmobil STU5-70 semi-trailer
The semi-trailer used with UAE Army MAN 40.633 DFAETX is a five-axle design supplied by Crossmobil of Germany.

This is a full width (MBT width without outrigger boards or similar) trailer with steel decking and adjustable width rear loading ramps. Each of the five axles is rated at 14,000 kg; the front three axles are fixed, the rear two are self steer and lockable with a pneumatic interlock. All axles have air suspension, with approximately 280 mm of travel. Tyres match those of the tractor, being 24R 21 Michelin XZL.

Status
Production complete, replaced by equivalent model from the HX range of tactical trucks during 2005. In service with the UAE (approximately 30).

Contractor
Rheinmetall MAN Military Vehicles (RMMV)

MAN HX 81 (8 × 8) and MAN HX range of heavy equipment transporters

Development
In addition to militarised versions of its extensive commercial range, full details of which can be found elsewhere in this section, MAN also produces a selection of tactical military trucks. These are collectively referred to as the X range.

Displayed at DVD 2010, a MAN HX81 tractor truck fitted with a KMW Integrated Armour Cabin (IAC) (Shaun C Connors)   1391449

Displayed at DVD 2010, a MAN HX81 tractor truck fitted with a KMW Integrated Armour Cabin (IAC) (Shaun C Connors)   1391451

Development of the X range begins with the Kat 1/KAT 1 (Category 1) high mobility trucks, deliveries of which commenced in 1976; the usual abbreviation for Category 1 vehicles is Kat or KAT 1, although this is sometimes presented as Cat or CAT 1. The Kat 1 range are purpose designed trucks that meet the most stringent of military tactical requirements and have been the subject of continued evolution by MAN, current models carrying the SX range designation.

To compliment the high mobility SX range MAN also produces/has produced the FX, HX and LX tactical truck ranges. As all X range trucks share MAN's modular military cab, to the untrained eye they are often confused; there are in fact quite a number of distinct capability/application defining differences.

The SX range of tactical trucks are the most mobile of MAN's truck ranges and were purpose-designed to be capable of maintaining pace with tracked combat vehicles across any terrain. They are based around a purpose-designed box-section torsionally rigid (non-flexing) chassis frame design that mounts beam axles sprung by long-travel coil springs. Engines and cooling packs are located behind the cab; all SX range trucks are air-transportable by C-130 Hercules.

The LX range of lighter weight tactical trucks based on MAN's M2000 medium weight commercial range of trucks was introduced in 1988; no heavy tractor truck models were produced. The FX range of tactical trucks were introduced in 1990 and being optimised for heavy gross vehicle and combination weights, were initially based on chassis from MAN's F90 heavy commercial range, production of which ran from 1986-1992. From 1992 onwards FX range trucks were based on the F2000 heavy commercial range.

MAN confirmed development of the HX tactical range of trucks at DVD 2003 and first publicly displayed an HX tactical range truck at DSEi 2003. The company subsequently confirmed the HX range would be developed to cover the payload and mobility (both tactical and strategic) areas covered by both the FX and LX ranges. Production of the LX range was completed during 2004, production of the FX was completed during 2005. To achieve such broad coverage the HX range utilises a wide range of driveline components, including both small and big block engines and the eventual number of models will be well into double figures.

By 2002, following a lengthy period of consolidation and reorganisation, assembly of the MAN FX, LX and SX tactical truck ranges had been transferred to the former Österreichische Automobilfabrik ÖAF-Gräf und Stift AG plant in Vienna, renamed MAN Sonderfahrzeuge AG briefly but now known as MAN Nutzfahrzeuge Österreichische AG. MAN acquired truck-maker ÖAF in 1936.

Some components for the MAN tactical truck ranges, such as the torsionally rigid chassis frame of the SX range, and the MAN modular military cab fitted to all ranges, were manufactured at the Star truck plant in Poland, Star having been acquired by MAN in 1998; they are currently manufactured in Austria.

Dependant on market, essentially the same model from the MAN X range of tactical trucks may now be marketed and branded as either MAN or Steyr, or for the Austrian market only, as ÖAF. MAN Nutzfahrzeuge AG acquired an 85 per cent share of the truck-building activities of Austria's Steyr Nutzfahrzeuge AG in January 1990, and in 1993 the company exercised its option to acquire the remaining 15 per cent share of the business. Steyr Nutzfahrzeuge AG became known as MAN Steyr AG during 2002 and, during 2005, as MAN Nutzfahrzeuge Österreichische AG. Further details of the relationship between current MAN and Steyr truck ranges can be found in the MAN trucks or Steyr trucks entries in the Trucks section.

MAN Nutzfahrzeuge AG and Rheinmetall AG announced their respective intentions to form a joint wheeled military vehicles company in 2009. This alliance became a reality in January 2010 with the announcement of the founding of Rheinmetall MAN Military Vehicles (RMMV) GmbH. RMMV sees the merger of Rheinmetall's wheeled military vehicle activities with those of the military truck activities of MAN. Essentially this merger unites the complementary technological core competencies of MAN's automotive expertise in commercial-vehicle manufacture with Rheinmetall's technological know-how in the military land sector/systems field. The result is the creation of a new single-source provider for the entire range of armoured and unarmoured transport, command and role-specific wheeled vehicles. Throughout all entries MAN and/or RMMV designations and references are made to suit context.

HX 44.680 (8 × 8) tractor IAC (HX 81)

Following a competition that concluded around three years ago, MAN was awarded a contract to supply the German Army with two HX 44.680 (HX81) tractor trucks, with an option for a further 34. Currently two competing trailers are being evaluated for use with the HX 44.680. The vehicles delivered to the German Army are fitted with the KMW-developed IAC. Specifications of the HX 44.680 can be found in the Specifications table elsewhere in this entry.

Description

The HX range of trucks are essentially the continuance of the earlier FX and LX range concept; the combination of commercial driveline and chassis with a modular military-specific cab. The HX range are based on chassis and driveline components from the heavier elements of MAN's commercial TGA heavy truck range which was first introduced during 2000. MAN describes the HX range as medium mobility trucks, however there is no international standard by which mobility levels are measured, allowing considerable ambiguity and leading to the occasional ambitious claim by manufacturers. There are vehicles available described as high mobility by their manufacturers that are clearly less mobile, both tactically and strategically, than the MAN HX range of trucks.

The HX range of trucks are fitted with the latest version of MAN's modular military cab. This is 290 mm deeper than it's immediate predecessor and has >600 litres of gross stowage space in the rear, sufficient for radio equipment and the full kit of three soldiers. The air-sprung vinyl-covered seats for driver and passenger are fitted with integral seatbelts that prevent uncomfortable and potentially dangerous belt-locking on rough terrain. For severe off-road terrain the seats' suspension can be locked. The centre seat has a lap belt and the steel-backed backrest folds down to form a platform step for access to the roof hatch. The roof is reinforced to take the weight of two soldiers and the recoil forces of a 12.7 mm (.5 in) HMG in a ring-mount.

Two types of modular detachable hard top roof are available, a standard flat roof or a version with extended height for the optional air-conditioning equipment, plus an NBC filtration system for the over-pressured cab if required. A detonation blast-proof vertical split-windscreen is fitted as standard and a riotous protection kit is available.

The interior of the walk-through cab is primarily steel or washable plastic/vinyl, the bulk of the instrumentation package having been taken from MAN's TGA commercial range as this being deemed more practical and cost-effective than the purpose-designed instrumentation of earlier cabs. Where required controls and/or layout have been revised to accommodate combat or arctic clothing. A detonation blast-proof vertical split-windscreen is fitted.

To meet current and emerging requirements MAN, in conjunction with Ressenig of Austria, has developed a riotous protection kit and a small arms fire protected appliqué armouring system for the HX range of trucks. During production vehicles may be fitted for, but not with, the armouring kit. This cab is interchangeable between HX models, and known as the Modular Integrated Cab (MIC), it affords protection from Level 1 blast and Level 2 ballistic, according to Stanag 4569. Weight of the kit is around 1,300 kg and the hard-top is removable for air-transport if required.

Earlier generation Kat 1/SX range chassis of the German and Austrian armed forces have previously been fitted with armouring kits supplied by Krauss-Maffei Wegmann (KMW).

In cooperation with KMW, MAN has also developed the Integrated Armour Cabin (IAC). The IAC is an exchangeable cab and is fitted in pace of the conventional cab. The weight of the IAC precludes it from being fitted to chassis with single front axles for reasons of legality (where applicable) and mobility.

The engine is positioned conventionally - longitudinally between the chassis rails to gives a Cab-Over-Engine (COE) configuration; the cooling pack is located transversally at the rear of the cab. This location offers protection from damage and blockage of the radiator with mud etc. when operating off-road. It also allows for a larger volume radiator to be used, this enhancing hot-climate operating capability. Modern electronically-controlled engines reduce their power output as operating temperatures increase. The use of a larger rear-mounted radiator allows HX range trucks to operate at full power, at full GVW, in temperatures of +49°C for prolonged periods. Aside from the modular military cab, location of the cooling pack and a small number of military specific ancillary items and modifications (including all external compartments being watertight for an optional 1.5 m fording depth), MAN has strived for maximum commonality with the TGA commercial product, the aim being to reduce (compared to the SX range) both procurement and through life costs.

Power for HX range tractor trucks is provided by the latest generation MAN turbocharged and intercooled common rail EURO IV/V emissions compliant water-cooled diesel engines coupled to a 12F/2R ZF AS-Tronic automatic constant mesh gearbox (branded TipMatic in MAN's commercial product line) and ZF WSK 440 torque converter coupled to a new generation MAN two-speed transfer box.

Driveline of the HX range is completed by MAN's latest 'single tyre specific' hub-reduction axles. Heavy tractor trucks are full time all-wheel drive and axle ratings are 9,000 kg front axle(s), and 10,000 or 13,000 kg single wheel rear axles, or 16,000 kg double rear wheel axles.

The front steer-drive axle(s) is/are sprung by a combination of parabolic leaf springs with progressively acting rubber assistors and hydraulic telescopic shock-absorbers. Rear axles are sprung by inverted multi-leaf trapezoidal springs with radius rods and an anti-roll bar. All axles are fitted with driver-controlled cross-axle differential locks; there are longitudinal differential locks for axle pairs and the transfer box. A Central Tyre Inflation (CTI) system and run-flat inserts are options.

HX 81

Configuration: 8 × 8
Cab seating: 1 + up 5 dependent on configuration
Weight:
    (permissible GVW, EC road regulations) 32,000 kg
    (permissible GVW, design) 44,000 kg
    (chassis-cab; with IAC cab) 22,900 kg
    (fifth wheel load) 15,000 kg
    (permissible GTW) 130,000 kg
Overall length: (chassis cab) 9.303 m
Width: (cab) 2.55 m
Height: (top of cab, unladen) 3.457 m
Ground clearance: (front/rear) 453/410 mm
Wheelbase: (options available) 1.8 + 3.2 + 1.5 m
Angle of approach/departure: 39°/37°
Max speed: (limited) 88 km/h
Max gradient: (solo) 60%
Max sideslope: 40%
Fuel capacity: 1 × 880 litres
Fording: 750 mm
Engine: MAN D2868 V-8 16.16-litre EURO V emissions compliant turbocharged water-cooled 4-stroke diesel developing 680 hp (500 kW) at 1,900 rpm and 2,700 N.m torque at 1,000-1,700 rpm
Gearbox: ZF AS-Tronic automatic constant mesh gearbox (branded TipMatic in MAN's commercial product line) and ZF WSK 440 torque converter; 12 forward and 2 reverse gears
Transfer box: MAN 2-speed
Steering: ZF, hydraulic power-assistance
Turning radius: (wall) 14.5 m
Suspension: parabolic leaf springs with progressively acting rubber assistors and hydraulic telescopic shock-absorbers, front axles; inverted multileaf trapezoidal springs with radius rods and anti-roll bar on rearmost axle, rear bogie
Tyres: 1600R 20 (options available)
Brakes: dual circuit, air, drums on all axles, Electronic Brake System (EBS) with ABS with off-road logic included supplemented by air-actuated exhaust brake with additional Exhaust Valve Brake system; integral retarder in gearbox
Electrical system: 24 V
Batteries: 4 × 12 V, 100 Ah NATO batteries
Alternator: 2 × 28.5 V, 110 Ah

Status

Production as required, in service with the German Army (see text).

Contractor

Rheinmetall MAN Military Vehicles (RMMV)

Mercedes-Benz 2636AS (6 × 6) tank transporter

Development

The Mercedes-Benz 2636AS (6 × 6) heavy tractor truck is a militarised example of the Mercedes-Benz NG (New Generation) truck range, introduced commercially in 1973 and as the successor to the earlier LP

The Mercedes-Benz 2636AS (6 × 6) tank transporter has been supplied to Pakistan (100 ordered 1984) and other undisclosed countries (Mercedes-Benz) 1128757

range. The 2636AS (A - all-wheel drive; S - tractor truck) is a model from the revised NG80 range (New Generation 1980; introduced in 1980), this itself being superseded by the visually similar NG80DLO (NG80 with an upgraded driveline) before being supplemented by, later replaced by, the all new but visually quite similar SK range which was introduced commercially in 1988. The Actros range introduced commercially in 1996 was the replacement for the SK range; for tank transporter roles the Actros replaced the NG range which remained available until the introduction of the Actros. Full details of the Actros range can be found elsewhere in this section.

The first known customer for the 2636AS was Pakistan which ordered 100 examples in 1984 and for use (it is believed) with the locally produced 60 ton (60,000 kg) Tank Transport Trailer (TTL). Details of other users of the 2636AS and other NG range tank transporters have not been released by Mercedes-Benz.

The Mercedes-Benz 3250/3850AS (6 × 6) and 4050/4850AS (8 × 8) are heavier tractor NG range trucks and full details of these can be found elsewhere in this section.

Description
The Mercedes-Benz 2636AS (6 × 6) tank transporter is entirely conventional in design and is based on a reinforced C-section chassis. The vehicle is designed to operate at a GCW of up to 105,000 kg; quoted as 95,000 kg for earlier models.

Three versions of the commercially-based forward control cab were available, standard, medium and extra length, the largest of these having sufficient space for a tank transporter crew of two, a full tank crew and all associated stowage. The standard centre seat doubles as a platform when the circular roof hatch is in use; air conditioning, an engine pre-filter for dry/dusty environments, left- or right-hand drive, and a front brush guard were options. Maintenance flaps facilitate day-to-day work on the vehicle, and for major maintenance the cab tilts forward through 70°.

Motive power is provided by a JP4 fuel compatible V-10 diesel, this driving all three leaf sprung axles via a 16-speed manual gearbox and two-speed transfer box; an optional torque convertor and clutch unit was available. All driveline components are mud/splash protected. The hub-reduction axles are fitted with cross-axle differential locks, and there are two longitudinal differential locks, one in the transfer box and one for the rear axle pair. Axle ratio options were available.

The 2636AS was supplied to Pakistan fitted with a pair of mechanically controlled ITAG Type 241 winches capable of pulling up to 65,000 kg using 60 m of 26 mm diameter cable; single or twin drum winches were available, a pair of Rotzler 25,000 kg capacity 20000H winches being a stated option.

Specifications
Mercedes-Benz 2636AS
Cab seating: 1 + 2 (options available)
Configuration: 6 × 6
Weight:
  (unladen, tractor without winch) 11,900 kg
  (GVW, tractor) 38,000 kg
  (max front axle load) 7,500 kg
  (max rear axle load, each) 16,000 kg
  (5th wheel load) 24,000 kg
  (GCW) 105,000 kg
Length: (tractor unit) 7.075 m
Width: 2.5 m
Height: (unladen) 3.195 m
Ground clearance: (front axle) 427 mm
Track:
  (front) 1.987 m
  (rear) 1.804 m
Wheelbase: 3.5 m + 1.45 m
Angle of approach/departure: 35°/47°
Max speed: 79 km/h
Fuel capacity: 400 litres
Range: 1,000 km (approx)

Gradient: (with torque convertor)
  (GCW 38,000 kg) 80%
  (GCW 80,000 kg) 38%
  (GCW 105,000 kg) 20%
Engine: Mercedes-Benz OM 423 V-10 18.273-litre water-cooled 4-stroke diesel developing 355 hp (265 kW) at 2,300 rpm and 1,304 N.m torque at 1,200 rpm
Gearbox: ZF 16 S S-130 16-speed fully synchronised manual with 16 forward and 2 reverse gears; optional ZF 4 S 150 fully synchronised manual with 8 forward and 1 reverse gears
Transfer box: VG2000-3W/1.4 2-speed with differential lock
Clutch: GF 240 single dry disc; torque converter with ZF 4 S 150 gearbox option
Steering: LS 7F power-assisted
Turning radius: 10.15 m
Tyres: 14.00R × 20
Brakes: dual circuit, dual line, air, drums all-round, supplementary engine exhaust brake
Electrical system: 24 V
Batteries: 2 × 12 V, 110 Ah
Alternator: 28 V, 55 A

Status
Production complete. In service with Pakistan (approximately 100) and other undisclosed countries. Replaced in production by the Mercedes-Benz Actros range of heavy tractor trucks.

Contractor
Daimler AG

Mercedes-Benz 3250AS and 3850AS (6 × 6) tank transporters

Development
The Mercedes-Benz 3250AS and 3850AS (6 × 6) heavy tractor trucks are militarised examples of the Mercedes-Benz NG (New Generation) truck range, introduced commercially in 1973 as the successor to the earlier LP range. The 3250AS and 3850AS (A - all-wheel drive; S - tractor truck) are models from the revised NG80 range (New Generation 1980; introduced in 1980), this itself being superseded by the visually similar NG80DLO (NG80 with an upgraded driveline) before being supplemented by, and later replaced by, the all new but visually quite similar SK range which was introduced commercially in 1988. The Actros range introduced commercially in 1996 was the replacement for the SK range; for tank transporter roles the Actros replaced the NG range which remained available until the introduction of the Actros. Full details of the Actros range can be found elsewhere in this section.

The Mercedes-Benz 3250AS and 3850AS (6 × 6) tractor trucks are essentially a further development of the Mercedes-Benz 2636AS (6 × 6) tractor truck, full details of which can be found elsewhere in this section. The 3250AS and 3850AS, which differ primarily in axle ratio and the use of single or dual tyres on the rear drive axles, use the same engine as the 2636AS but use a different gearbox, have a 750 mm longer wheelbase and can operate at greater GCWs; the lower GVW and 5th wheel load of the 3250AS are dictated by the single sand-type tyres.

Mercedes-Benz 3250AS (6 × 6) tank transporter with optional 24R 20.5 tyres (Mercedes-Benz) 1128769

Mercedes-Benz 3850AS (6 × 6) tank transporter of the UAE Army
(Stefan Marx)
1128766

The Mercedes-Benz 4050AS and 4850AS (8 × 8) are four-axle versions of the 3250AS and 3850AS and full details of these can be found elsewhere in this section.

Description

The Mercedes-Benz 3250AS and 3850AS (6 × 6) tractor trucks are entirely conventional in design and are based on a reinforced C-section chassis. They are designed to operate at a GCW of 110,000 kg with a semi-trailer, but have an optional maximum GCW of 220,000 when a drawbar-type trailer is used.

The sleeper-type version of the commercially based cab was standard for these vehicles, this having sufficient space for a tank transporter crew of two, a full tank crew and all associated stowage. The cab is mounted at the front on two pivot bearings with flexible rubber sleeves and at the rear on four vibration-damped spring struts. The standard centre seat doubles as a platform when the circular roof hatch is in use; air conditioning, an engine pre-filter for dry/dusty environments, left- or right-hand drive, and a front brush guard were options. Maintenance flaps facilitate day-to-day work on the vehicle, and for major engine or transmission maintenance the cab tilts forward.

Motive power is provided by a Mercedes-Benz V-10 diesel, this driving all three leaf sprung axles via a 16-speed manual gearbox and two-speed transfer box. All driveline components are mud/splash protected. The hub-reduction axles are fitted with cross-axle differential locks, and there are two longitudinal differential locks, one in the transfer box and one for the rear axle pair. Axle ratios and GVWs differ between the 3250AS and 3850AS models.

Mechanical or hydraulic single or dual drum winches could be fitted and were capable of operation from either the cab or remotely. Other options included an automatic transmission, sand tyres and a Central Tyre Inflation (CTI) system.

Specifications

3250AS
[3850AS in square brackets where different]
Cab seating: 1 + up to 6
Configuration: 6 × 6
Weight:
    (unladen, without winch, approx.) 13,000 kg [13,000 kg]
    (permissible GVW) 33,000 kg [38,000 kg]
    (front axle load) 7,500 kg [8,000 kg]
    (rear axle load, each) 13,000 kg [16,000 kg]
    (5th wheel load, approx.) 20,000 kg [24,500 kg]
    (GCW, with semi-trailer) 110,000 kg
    (GCW, with drawbar-type trailer) up to 220,000 kg
Length: 7.685 m
Width: 2.765 m
Height: (unladen) 3.46 m
Ground clearance: (24R 20.5 tyres) 429 mm
Track:
    (front) 2.07 m
    (rear) 1.965 m
Wheelbase: 3.8 m + 1.45 m
Angle of approach/departure: 38°/62°
Max speed: 90 km/h
Fuel capacity: 600 litres
Range: approx 1,000 km
Gradient: (GCW 110,000 kg) 32%
Fording: up to 1.1 m (optional)
Engine: Mercedes-Benz OM 423 LA 18.273-litre V-10 turbocharged and intercooled, water-cooled 4-stroke diesel developing 500 hp (373 kW) at 2,300 rpm and 2,000 N.m torque at 1,200 rpm
Transmission: ZF 16 S 190 A fully synchronised manual with 16 forward and 2 reverse gears and ZF WSK 400 torque converter; optional automatic
Transfer box: integrated in main gearbox
Steering: LS 7F power-assisted

Turning radius: (tractor) 9.7 m (approx.)
Tyres: 13R 22. 5 (24R 22.5 optional) [12R 24 (14R 40 optional)]
Brakes: dual circuit, dual line, air, drums all-round. Supplementary engine exhaust brake
Electrical system: 24 V
Batteries: 2 × 12 V, 115 Ah
Alternator: 28 V/55 A

Status

Production complete, undisclosed full list of users, but known to include the UAE. Replaced in production by the Mercedes-Benz Actros range of heavy tractor trucks.

Contractor

Daimler AG

Mercedes-Benz Actros (8 × 8) heavy tractor trucks

Development

The Mercedes-Benz Actros range of (8 × 8) tractor trucks for military tank transporter and heavy equipment movement applications are based on purpose-designed heavy-duty chassis utilising driveline components and cabs from the extensive Actros range of commercial trucks. These commercially proven components are militarised as necessary and to suit specific operator requirements.

The Mercedes-Benz Actros range of heavy tractor trucks has replaced all previous military heavy tractor truck models in production.

Description

Power for the Mercedes-Benz Actros (8 × 8) heavy tractor truck range is normally provided by the latest Mercedes-Benz EURO 5 emissions compliant OM 502 LA turbocharged diesel engines with power outputs up to 609 hp; up to 800 hp in certain territories. Engines complying with EURO 3 emissions requirements are available if required. Gearbox options include a fully synchromeshed 16-speed manual, the Telligent gearshift system with clutch (electronic selection, pneumatic shifting) or the Telligent fully automatic gearshift system without clutch. An optional torque converter with integral retarder is also available. All cooling systems are thermostatically controlled and additional radiators can be fitted to suit mission and climate conditions. GCWs available range from 110,000 to approximately 250,000 kg.

All axles feature planetary hub reduction gearing and are leaf-sprung as standard. For maximum traction all-wheel drive is permanently engaged and driver controlled longitudinal and cross-axle differential locks can be engaged on the move. A Central Tyre Inflation (CTI) system that allows the driver to adjust tyre pressures to suit prevailing ground conditions is an option when single rear tyres are fitted, as is an Anti-lock Braking System (ABS). Other chassis mounted options include towing and/or lifting eyes, and assorted hydraulic winch systems.

The two-door forward-control all-steel tilt-cab is based on the civilian sleeper version and has capacity for a driver and co-driver, plus seating for four additional personnel. Driver plus co-driver and two bunks to provide sleeping facilities is an option. Other cab fitment options can include enhanced heating and air-conditioning systems and an observation hatch in the roof.

Canadian Armored Heavy Support Vehicle System (AHSVS)

The Canadian Department of Defense disclosed mid-2007 that it had awarded the then DaimlerChrysler AG an approximately CAD87 million contract for 82 Mercedes-Benz Actros (8 × 8) Armored Heavy Support Vehicle System (AHSVS) trucks for use on deployed operations.

Following a Request for Proposal (RfP) that was issued to industry during January 2007, responses from three potential contractors (DaimlerChrysler, MAN and Sisu) were received and the contract award,

Canadian Army Mercedes-Benz Actros (8 × 8) heavy tractor truck coupled to a King GTS 110/7 (manufactured in Germany by DOLL) semi-trailer
(Carl Schulze)
1391452

which includes an option for an additional 26, was made during March 2007. Deliveries were scheduled to commence late 2007, with final deliveries scheduled for March 2008.

With the exception of 15 vehicles retained in Canada for training purposes, the AHSVS fleet is used by Canadian Forces deployed on operations in Afghanistan where they have replaced Steyr-based Heavy Logistics Vehicle Wheeled (HLVW) trucks that were procured in the late 1980s, and are now considered unsuitable for a variety of reasons, such as the inability to accept the required level of blast and ballistic protection. AHSVS consists of four main variants:

- 25 cargo with material handling crane (including eight gun tractors for the M777 howitzer)
- 40 Palletized Loading System (PLS) with container handling unit variant vehicles (10 petroleum, oils, and lubricants variants and five water variants)
- five recovery variant vehicles
- 12 heavy tank transporter tractor variant vehicles.

All AHSVS vehicles are fitted with a medium-sized version of a benign in appearance armoured cab family designed by Daimler in conjunction with Land Mobility Technologies (LMT) of South Africa.

All AHSVS vehicles feature full-time (8 × 8) drive and are powered by V8 diesel engines developing in excess of 500 hp and meeting non-current EURO 3 emissions requirements on account of operational considerations - mainly fuel quality. All vehicles are fitted with a 16-speed automated (with manual option) gearbox and two-speed transfer box, and in order to cope with the combined weights of around 120,000 kg, the tractor truck variant driveline features a torque converter.

Bodies including recovery hampers, will be provided by EMPL of Austria, with PLS and materials handling equipment sub-contracted to Hiab (Multilift). Semi-trailers used with the tractor truck variants are King GTS 110/7 manufactured in Germany by DOLL.

A total of 13 AHSVS vehicles have been acquired under the contract option. The 13 vehicles were made up of three variants: four cargo, six heavy mobile repair team and three flat deck recovery system. Three DOLL 35,000 kg recovery trailers were also ordered under the option, specifically the flat deck recovery system option. Also ordered as a contract option were four protected troop transport pods from Daimler's sub contractor, Land Mobility Technologies (LMT).

Status
Production as required. In service with Canada (12).

Contractor
Daimler AG

Mercedes-Benz 4050A and 4850A (8 × 8) tank transporter

Development
The Mercedes-Benz 4050A and 4850A (8 × 8) heavy tractor trucks are militarised examples of the Mercedes-Benz NG (New Generation) truck range, introduced commercially in 1973 and as the successor to the earlier LP range. The 4050A and 4850A are models from the revised NG80 range (New Generation 1980; introduced in 1980), this itself being superseded by the visually similar NG80DLO (NG80 with an upgraded driveline) before being supplemented by, later replaced by, the all new but visually quite similar SK range which was introduced commercially in 1988. The Actros range introduced commercially in 1996 was the replacement for the SK range; for tank transporter roles the Actros replaced the NG range which remained available until the introduction of the Actros. Full details of the Actros range can be found elsewhere in this section.

The Mercedes-Benz 4050A and 4850A (8 × 8) tank transporter models may be regarded as (8 × 8) versions of the Mercedes Benz 3250AS and 3850AS (6 × 6) tank transporters, full details of which can be found elsewhere in this section.

The 4050A and 4850A are essentially similar vehicles and share the majority of driveline components, the primary differences being tyres which then dictates maximum permissible fifth wheel load, rear axle loads and tractor GVW.

Description
The Mercedes-Benz 4050A and 4850A (8 × 8) tractor trucks are entirely conventional in design and are based on a reinforced C-section chassis. They are designed to operate at a GCW of 110,000 kg with a semi-trailer, but have an optional maximum GCW of 220,000 when a drawbar-type trailer is used. When used with a low-bed drawbar-type trailer a ballast platform for the tractor is required.

The sleeper-type version of the commercially based cab was standard for these vehicles, this having sufficient space for a tank transporter crew of two, a full tank crew and all associated stowage. The cab is mounted at the front on two pivot bearings with flexible rubber sleeves and at the rear on four vibration-damped spring struts. The standard centre seat doubles as a platform when the circular roof hatch is in use; air conditioning, an engine pre-filter for dry/dusty environments, left- or right-hand drive, and a front brush guard were options. Maintenance flaps facilitate day-to-day work on the vehicle, and for major engine or transmission maintenance the cab tilts forward through 70°.

Mercedes-Benz 4050A (8 × 8) heavy tractor truck (Mercedes-Benz) 1128767

Motive power is provided by a Mercedes-Benz V-10 diesel, this driving all four leaf sprung axles via a 16-speed manual gearbox and two-speed transfer box; an automatic transmission was optional. All driveline components are mud/splash protected. The leaf sprung hub-reduction axles are fitted with cross-axle differential locks, and there are three longitudinal differential locks, one in the transfer box and one each for the front and rear axle pairs.

Mechanical or hydraulic drum winches could be fitted behind the cab and were capable of operation from either the cab or remotely. Other options included fuel tank capacities ranging from 400 to 1,000 litres and a Central Tyre Inflation (CTI) system.

Specifications
4050A
[Data for the 4850A in square brackets where different]
Cab seating: 1 + up to 6
Configuration: 8 × 8
Weight:
(unladen, with winches) 18,100 [17,200] kg (approx)
(permissible front axle load, each) 9,000 kg
(permissible rear axle load, each) 13,500 [16,000] kg
(permissible 5th wheel load) 25,000 [31,000] kg
(GCW, with semi-trailer) 110,000 kg
(GCW, with drawbar-type trailer) up to 220,000 kg
Length: 8.435 m
Width: 2.765 m
Height: 3.46 m
Ground clearance: (rear axle) 390 mm
Track:
(front) 2.07 m
(rear) 1.965 m
Wheelbase: 1.6 m + 2.935 m + 1.48 m
Angle of approach/departure: 35°/60°
Max speed: 90 km/h
Fuel capacity: 400 to 1,000 litres
Range: variable according to fuel capacity
Gradient: (GCW 110,000 kg) 32%
Engine: Mercedes-Benz OM 423 LA 18.273-litre V-10 water-cooled 4-stroke diesel with 2 exhaust gas turbochargers and intercooling developing 500 hp (373 kW) at 2,300 rpm 2,000 N.m torque at 1,200 rpm
Gearbox: ZF 16 S 190 fully synchromesh manual with 16 forward and 2 reverse gears coupled to a ZF WSK 400 torque converter; optional Allison CLBT 754 automatic with integrated retarder
Transfer box: VG2000 3W, single-speed; 2-speed with automatic gearbox option
Steering: dual circuit, power-assisted
Turning radius: (tractor) 13.1 [11.25] m
Tyres: 24R 21 [14.00R 20]
Brakes: dual circuit, air, drums all-round
Electrical system: 24 V
Batteries: 2 × 12 V, 115 Ah
Alternator: 28 V/55 A

Status
Production complete. Replaced in production by the Mercedes-Benz Actros range of heavy tractor trucks.

Contractor
Daimler AG

Mercedes-Benz Actros (6 × 6) heavy tractor truck range

Development

The Mercedes-Benz Actros range of (6 × 6) heavy tractor trucks for military tank transporter and heavy equipment movement applications are based on purpose-designed heavy-duty chassis utilising driveline components and cabs from the extensive Actros range of commercial trucks. These commercially proven components are militarised as necessary and to suit specific operator requirements.

The Mercedes-Benz Actros range of heavy tractor trucks have replaced all previous military heavy tractor trucks in production.

Description

Power for the Mercedes-Benz Actros (6 × 6) heavy tractor truck range is provided by Mercedes-Benz 502 series EURO 5 (optional EURO 3) emissions compliant turbocharged diesel engines, with power outputs up to 609 hp. Gearbox options include a fully synchromeshed 16-speed manual, the Telligent gearshift system with clutch (electronic selection, pneumatic shifting) or the Telligent fully automatic gearshift system without clutch. An optional ZF WSK 400 torque converter with integral retarder is also available. All cooling systems are thermostatically controlled and additional radiators can be fitted to suit mission and climate conditions. Various GCWs are available, ranging to a maximum of approximately 250,000 kg, although military application maximums are likely to be no more than 110,000 kg.

All axles feature planetary hub reduction gearing and are leaf-sprung as standard. For maximum traction, all-wheel drive is permanently engaged and driver controlled longitudinal and cross-axle differential locks can be engaged on the move. Rear axles can be fitted with either single or dual wheels and a Central Tyre Inflation (CTI) system that allows the driver to adjust tyre pressures to suit prevailing ground conditions is an option when single wheels are fitted. Other options include an Anti-lock Braking System (ABS) and various chassis mounted towing and/or lifting eyes, and assorted hydraulic winch systems.

The two-door forward-control all-steel tilt-cab is based on the civilian sleeper version and has seating capacity for a driver and co-driver, plus four additional personnel. Driver plus co-driver and two bunks to provide sleeping facilities is an option. Other cab fitment options can include enhanced heating and air-conditioning systems and an observation hatch in the roof. A high-roof version of the cab is also available.

The model 3353AS, a predecessor of the current model 3361AS, is in service with the Polish Army. The 3361AS is powered by the OM 502 LA V-8 engine developing 609 hp and 2,400 N.m torque. Details of this variant can be found in the Specifications table.

Specifications

3361AS model
Cab seating: 1 + 1 (+ 4 or 2 bunks)
Configuration: 6 × 6
Weight:
(tractor, kerb) 14,500 kg (approx.)
(max permissible GVW) 33,000 kg
(max permissible front axle load) 9,000 kg
(max permissible rear axle load (each)) 13,000 kg
(fifth wheel load) 18, 500 kg (approx)
(GCW) 110,000 kg (250,000 kg optional)
Length: 8.15 m
Width: 2.5 m
Height: (with high-roof cab) 3.71 m
Wheelbase: 4.2 m
Max speed: 85 km/h
Fuel capacity: up to 900 litres
Engine: Mercedes-Benz OM 502 LA EURO 4 V-8 15.928-litre turbocharged and intercooled, water-cooled 4-stroke direct injection diesel developing 609 hp (448 kW) at 1,800 rpm and 2,400 N.m torque at 1,080 rpm
Gearbox: Mercedes-Benz G240-16/11,7 16-speed
Transfer box: Mercedes-Benz VG 2400-3W single-speed
Steering: Mercedes-Benz hydraulic power-assisted LS8 with emergency power supply
Turning radius: (tractor) 9.65 m
Axles: planetary gear hub reduction with differential locks
(front) AL7
(rear) HD7/HL7
Tyres: 315/80R 22.5 (options available)
Brakes:
(main) dual circuit, air, drums all-round, automatic load sensing on rear axles
(parking) spring loaded rear axle, trailer brake optional
Electrical system: 24 V
Batteries: 2 × 12 V 165 Ah
Alternator: 28 V, 80 A

Prior to shipping, a Mercedes-Benz Actros heavy tractor truck destined for Pakistan (Ian C Young) 1391037

Rear three-quarter view of a Mercedes-Benz Actros model 3454AS heavy tractor truck destined for Yemen (Shaun C Connors) 1391039

Mercedes-Benz Actros model 3454AS heavy tractor truck destined for Yemen (Shaun C Connors) 1391038

Mercedes-Benz Actros model 3353AS (6 × 6) heavy tractor truck of the Polish Army (Ian C Young) 1128783

Mercedes-Benz Actros model 3353AS (6 × 6) heavy tractor trucks are in service with Polish Armed Forces (Daimler)   0121918

Status

In production. Known users of Mercedes-Benz Actros heavy tractor trucks are Canada, Botswana (model 3348), Pakistan, Poland (model 3353AS) and Yemen (model 3454AS).

Contractor

Daimler AG

FAUN FS 42.75/42 (8 × 6) FRANZISKA (SLT-56) tractor truck

Development

The FAUN SLT 50-2, or Elefant, as it is more commonly known, entered service with the German Army between 1976-1979. In total 324 SLT 50-2 Elefants and associated Kässbohrer (licence build from Krupp) 52,000 kg payload four-axle trailers were delivered. Tractor and trailer combinations were upgraded between 1982-2000, the tractor truck being designated SL 50-3 post-upgrade.

From 1989, the SLT 50-2/50-3 was supplemented in German Army service by the FAUN FS 42.75/42 FRANZISKA tractor truck and Kässbohrer 56,000 kg six-axle semi-trailer combinations. The FS 42.75/42 FRANZISKA is unofficially known as the SLT-56.

The FAUN FS 42.75/42 (8 × 6) tractor truck was never intended to replace the earlier SLT 50-3/50-3, its primary use being the movement of over-heavy loads such as the Leopard 2A5/A6 MBTs on prepared surfaces. As a result of these requirements, all-wheel drive was not required (hence the (8 × 6) drive configuration) and a multi-axle 'road friendly' legislative compliant semi-trailer could be procured. The full-width trailer was manufactured by Kässbohrer and has 24 wheels on six axles, the rear four of which are steered. An upgrade has seen these trailers uprated from 56,000 kg payload to a 59,700 kg payload.

The FS 42.75/42 can operate with the SLT-50/3's four-axle semi-trailer, and the SLT 50-3 can operate with FS 42.75/42's six-axle semi-trailer.

Description

The FS 42.75/42 follows the same overall layout as the SLT 50-2 and has a FAUN forward control cab constructed from steel and synthetic materials. Apart from the adjustable driver's seat, there is seating for three passengers. There is a roof hatch with provision for a machine gun mounting and internally there is a stowage compartment. All walls are double-skinned and, laminated glass is used for all windows. The

FAUN FS 42.75/42 (8 × 6) tractor truck towing trailer carrying Leopard 2 MBT over Leguan bridge (FAUN)   0511852

windscreen is angled forward at an angle of 5°. An engine-driven heater is used to heat the cab interior and a Webasto heater, independent of the engine, can be used for heating and ventilation when the engine is switched off.

The chassis is of a die-pressed construction with C-section members. Lateral and longitudinal supports are bolted or riveted.

The area behind the cab is mainly occupied by a dual 18,600 kg capacity winch assembly provided with a 28 mm diameter cable. The winch speed is adjustable from zero to 24 m/min for loads up to 8,500 kg and up to 9 m/min for heavier loads. The fifth wheel is a Jost JSK 38 GL.

The two front axles are used for steering but only the front axle is driven. The rear-driven Starr planetary axles are fitted with a longitudinal and cross-axle differential locks.

Specifications

Cab seating: 1 + 3
Configuration: 8 × 6
Weight:
  (laden) 36,000 or 39,700 kg
  (unladen) 19,700 kg
  (load on 5th wheel) 16,300 or 20,000 kg
  (gross train weight) 95,000 kg
Length: 8.835 m
Width: 3.07 m
Height: 3.02 m
Track:
  (front) 2.585 m
  (rear) 2.612 m
Wheelbase: 1.5 m + 2.7 m + 1.5 m
Angle of approach/departure: 30°/45°
Max speed: 72 km/h
Fuel capacity: 800 litres
Gradient: 50%
Engine: KHD BF 12 L 513 C 19.144 litre 12-cylinder air-cooled diesel developing 525 hp (386 kW) at 2,300 rpm
Gearbox: ZF Transmatic with torque converter drive clutch ZF WSK 400 and Ecosplit-gearbox 16 S 190 A with 16 forward and 2 reverse gears
Steering: ZF semi-block hydraulic, dual circuit
Turning radius: 11.2 m
Suspension: semi-elliptic leaf springs and telescopic shock-absorbers, front and rear
Tyres: 18.00 × 22.5 XS PR 20
Brakes:
  (main) dual-circuit, air
  (parking) pneumatically operated exhaust valve
Electrical system: 24 V
Batteries: 4 × 12 V
Alternator: 95 A

Status

Production complete. In service with the German Army (49 delivered from 1989).

Contractor

Tadano FAUN GmbH

FAUN HZ 40.45/45 (6 × 6) tractor truck

Development

The FAUN HZ 40.45/45 (6 × 6) tractor truck is a militarised version of a commercial tractor truck in the FAUN range adapted for the tank transporter role. The FAUN Model Number is 2144.93 Version B.

Description

The FAUN HZ 40.45/45 (6 × 6) tractor truck has a conventional layout, with the engine forward under a steel frame and reinforced glass fibre panel bonnet, the crew cab placed just to the rear of the front axle and the fifth wheel placed over the two rear axles. The steel cab has three doors, one on the left and two on the right, providing access to two rows of seating for the driver and six passengers. The front row has seating for the driver and two

FAUN HZ 40.45/45 (6 × 6) tractor truck (T J Gander)   0511854

FAUN HZ 40.45/45 (6 × 6) tractor truck of the Turkish Army (T J Gander)

1391448

passengers, all on single seats. The rear seating consists of a single padded bench with the central portion tiltable allowing access to a centrally positioned 800 mm diameter roof hatch.

The chassis frame consists of pressed segments having a U-profile design and with cross members bolted or riveted to the longitudinal girders. Towing eyes are provided at the front and a NATO trailer coupling with a towing capacity up to 55,000 kg is located at the rear.

Optional equipment available for the vehicle included a hydraulic twin-winch providing 2 × 18,000 kg drawbar pull on the first layer. The winches operate to the front or rear and each drum is provided with 55 m of 24 mm diameter cable. Cross-axle differential locks could be specified on both rear axles. Also available were: a set of six snow chains; up to four spare fuel cans; combined oil bath air filter; two 6 kg fire extinguishers; compressed air hose connection for slave filling of the brake system; slave starting device with 6 m of cable; and sliding rails to facilitate connecting a trailer to the fifth wheel.

Specifications
Cab seating: 1 + 6
Configuration: 6 × 6
Weight:
 (laden) 45,000 kg
 (unladen) 19,000 kg
Max fifth wheel load: 26,000 kg
Length: 9 m
Width: 2.75 m
Height: 3.4 m
Wheelbase: 5.4 m
Max speed: 63.6 km/h
Fuel capacity: 2 × 450 litres
Max gradient: 44.6%
Engine: Deutz Type BF 12 L 513 C 19.14-litre V-12 air-cooled direct-injection diesel developing 525 hp (386 kW) at 2,300 rpm

Gearbox: Allison CL T 754 with 5 forward and 1 reverse gears
Torque converter: Allison TC 496
Transfer box: 2-speed
Steering: ZF semi-block steering with working cylinder, primary pump and secondary pump
Turning radius: approx 12.5 m
Suspension: semi-elliptic leaf springs, longitudinal guide struts for thrust transmission, telescopic shock-absorbers, front; semi-elliptic leaf springs in floating arrangement, longitudinal guide struts for thrust transmission, rear
Tyres: 14.00 × 24
Brakes:
 (main) dual circuit, air, supplementary exhaust brake
 (parking) operating on rear axles
Electrical system: 24 V
Batteries: 2 × 12 V, 170 Ah

Status
Production complete. Supplied to Chad (38), Libya (69) and Turkey (40).

Contractor
Tadano FAUN GmbH

FAUN SLT 50-2/50-3 (8 × 8) tractor truck

Development
The development of the FAUN SLT 50-2, or Elefant, as it is more commonly known, can be traced back to 1965, when the former West Germany and the US decided to design a tank transporter known as the Heavy Equipment Transporter (HET) to carry the MBT-70 then under development by both countries. In the US, the Chrysler Corporation was the prime contractor for the tractor while in Germany FAUN was responsible for the tractor and Krupp for the trailer. In 1970 the MBT-70 and the HET were cancelled. Further development in the US resulted in the XM746, which was standardised as the M746 and production was undertaken by Ward La France.

Development continued in Germany and following successful evaluation of two prototypes from 1971, between 1976-1979 324 FAUN SLT 50-2 Elefants and associated Kässbohrer (licence build from Krupp) 52,000 kg payload four-axle trailers were delivered.

From 1982 all 324 trailers were modernised during a period of overhaul by FAUN. A major upgrade of all 324 tractor trucks was also carried out by FAUN between 1993-2000 as part of the major maintenance cycle. Following the upgrade, the designation SLT 50-3 was applied and 100 vehicles were prepared for long-term storage. Six vehicles were transferred to Poland as part of a package of vehicles, including Leopard 2 MBTs, and for deployment to the former Yugoslavia nine vehicles were fitted with a modular add-on armour package developed by Krauss-Maffei Wegmann (KMW).

From 1989, the SLT 50-2/50-3 was supplemented in German Army service by 49 FAUN FS 42.75/42 tractor truck and 56,000 kg six-axle semi-trailer combinations, full details of which can be found elsewhere in this section.

FAUN SLT 50-3 (8 × 8) Elefant tractor truck and dedicated 52,000 kg payload four-axle semi-trailer (Michael Jerchel)

1047624

FAUN SLT 50-3 (8 × 8) Elefant tractor truck and 59,000 kg payload (upgraded from an initial 56,000 kg payload rating) six-axle semi-trailer (Michael Jerchel)   1047623

Description

The SLT 50-2/50-3 is an (8 × 8) vehicle with powered steering on the front two axles. The fully enclosed cab is of steel and glass fibre construction and has seats for the driver and three passengers. The upgrade programme included the fitting of air-sprung seats for the driver and co-driver.

The drive train consists of a diesel engine coupled to a ZF 4 PW 200 H2 gearbox, W 500 10 torque converter and two-speed transfer box. The original engine was a 29.92-litre Mercedes-Benz MB 837 Ea-500 turbocharged V-8 unit developing 730 hp at 2,100 rpm and 2,650 N.m torque at 2,650 rpm. This was replaced during the SL 50-2 to SL 50-3 upgrade by a more modern, more powerful, and more efficient 21.6 litre Deutz MWM TBD 234 V-12 unit developing 734 hp at 2,100 rpm and 2,799 N.m torque at 1,650 rpm.

Axles are FAUN Type 17 and both front and rear bogies are fitted with a inter-axle lockable differential and each axle has a cross-axle lockable differential. The front and rear bogies are suspended by torque rods and taper leaf springs arranged in parallel with progressive springing.

Airbrakes are provided for both the tractor and semi-trailer and an automatic load-sensitive brake valve ensures equal braking under all load conditions. The parking brake consists of spring-loaded cylinders mounted to the rear wheel brakes. A retarder is connected directly to the gearbox and is also connected via an electric control line to the service brakes of the semi-trailer.

Mounted to the rear of the cab is a dual winch unit, each winch with a capacity of 18,600 kg (17,000 kg prior to upgrade). Both winches have a winch-up mechanism and the right winch can also be used to the front of the vehicle for self-recovery operations. Each winch is provided with 43 m of 28 mm diameter rope; maximum winding speed is 24 m/min at a capacity of 8,500 kg or 12 m/min at a capacity of 18,600 kg.

The spare wheel is mounted on the right side of the tractor and a small winch is provided to facilitate handling of the wheel.

Specifications

FAUN SLT 50-2
[SL 50-3 in square brackets where different]
Cab seating: 1 + 3
Configuration: 8 × 8
Weight:
  (unladen) 22,800 kg
  (on 5th wheel, laden) 18,300 kg
  (GCW) 92,000 kg
Length:
  (tractor) 8.83 m
  (with trailer) 18.82 m
Width: 3.07 m
Height:
  (cab) 3 m
  (to 5th wheel) 1.55 m
Ground clearance: 283 mm
Track:
  (front) 2.535 m
  (rear) 2.593 m
Wheelbase: 1.5 + 2.7 + 1.5 m
Angle of approach/departure: 30/50°

Max speed:
  (road, without semi-trailer) 65 km/h
  (road, with laden semi-trailer) 40 km/h
  (15% gradient with laden semi-trailer) 9 km/h
Range: 600 km
Fuel capacity: 800 litres
Max gradient: (87,500 kg GCW) 30%
Fording: 800 mm
Engine: Mercedes-Benz MB 837 Ea-500 29.92-litre V-8 twin turbocharged water-cooled 4-stroke precombustion injection diesel developing 730 hp (537 kW) at 2,100 rpm and 2,650 N.m torque at 2,650 rpm. [Deutz MWM TBD 234 21.6-litre V-12 water-cooled 4-stroke direct injection diesel developing 734 hp (538 kW) at 2,100 rpm and 2,799 N.m torque at 1,650 rpm]
Gearbox: ZF 4 PW 200H2 with 4 forward and 2 reverse gears
Torque converter: ZF 500-10
Transfer box: 2-speed
Steering: ZF semi-block hydraulic with emergency back-up
Turning radius: (without trailer) 11.2 m
Tyres: 18R 22.5 XS
Brakes: air, drums all-round
Electrical system: 24 V

Status

Production complete. 324 delivered to the German Army between 1976 and 1979. 100 prepared for long-term storage following upgrade (see text); six examples transferred to Poland.

Contractor

Tadano FAUN GmbH

Greece

ELBO 26S31/S38/6×6 (6 × 6) tractor truck

Development

The ELBO 26S31/S38 (6 × 6) tractor truck was produced in Greece under licence from Steyr Nutzfahrzeuge AG (later MAN Steyr AG, now MAN Nutzfahrzeuge Österreichische AG) of Austria. The associated semi-trailer was developed and produced in Greece by Nik Kioleides SA and can carry MBTs, APCs, AIFVs and construction equipment. The ELBO 26S31 was replaced in production by the Steyr 33 M 41, initial deliveries of which (badged ELBO) were made during 2002. The Steyr/ELBO 33 M 41 has now been replaced in production by an equivalent model from the current MAN TGA range.

Description

The ELBO 26S31/S38/6×6 tractor truck is entirely conventional in design, being based on a channel section chassis with conventional beam-type drive axles fitted with leaf spring suspension. The commercial design cab has seating for the driver and two passengers. Options included a 9,000 kg capacity hydraulic front winch mounted behind the front bumper for self-recovery and a 20,000 kg capacity hydraulic rear winch mounted behind the cab for the loading of disabled tanks or construction equipment.

The companion semi-trailer has a capacity of 35,000 kg, a steel frame and a timber load area.

Specifications

ELBO 26S31/S38
Cab seating: 1 + 2
Configuration: 6 × 6
Weight:
(kerb, with winches) 14,000 kg
(GVW) 32,000 kg
(max front axle load) 7,500 kg
(max rear axle load) 13,000 kg (each)
(towed load) 57,000 kg
(max load on 5th wheel) 18,000 kg
Length: (complete train) 18.5 m
Width: (overall) 3 m
Height: 3.5 m
Ground clearance: 330 mm
Wheelbase: 3.8 m + 1.35 m
Track:
(front) 1.958 m
(rear) 1.8 m
Angle of approach/departure: 30°/40°
Max speed: 80 km/h
Fuel capacity: 400 litres
Range: 500 km
Max gradient: 35%
Side slope: 30°
Fording: 800 mm
Engine: Steyr WD 615.78 9.73 litre turbocharged and intercooled water-cooled 4-stroke direct injection diesel developing 306 hp (225 kW) at 2,200 rpm
Transmission: ZF Transmatic WSK400+4S150GP with torque converter, 8 forward and 1 reverse gears
Transfer box: Steyr VG 1200 2-speed
Steering: ZF 8046 power assisted
Turning radius: 10.2 m
Suspension:
(front) semi-elliptic leaf springs with telescopic shock-absorbers
(rear) inverted semi-elliptic leaf springs with torsion bars
Tyres: 12.00 R 20
Brakes: dual-circuit air
Electrical system: 24 V
Batteries: 2 × 12 V, 143 Ah

Status

Production complete. In service with the Greek Armed Forces.

Contractor

Hellenic Vehicle Industry SA

Italy

IVECO (ASTRA) tactical range heavy equipment transporters

Development

IVECO's Defence Vehicles (IVECO DV) produces a wide range of vehicles that offer GVWs from around 5,000 kg for the lightest 4 × 4, through to a GCW of 130,000 kg for the heaviest tank transporter.

For the majority of heavy equipment transporter applications IVECO offers militarised versions of its commercial Trakker (EuroTrakker until late 2004) heavy truck range, full details of which can be found elsewhere in this section. Militarised commercial designs suit the operating needs of many armed forces and can be suited to a wide variety of military and/or peacekeeping/enforcing type roles, depending on a number of factors including the base chassis in use and degree of militarisation required. For certain applications a purpose-designed tactical truck is better suited and to meet such requirements IVECO also offers a range of tactical heavy equipment transporters. These are designed for purpose and while utilising commercially available driveline components offer far higher levels of strategic and tactical mobility than any commercially based design.

The IVECO tactical range of trucks are produced by ASTRA Veicoli Industriali SpA ASTRA was formed in 1946 in Cagliari as a refurbisher of military vehicles and the name ASTRA is taken from Azienda Sarda TRasformazione Autoveicoli. In 1951 the company transferred its headquarters to its current 135,200 m² site (43,500 m² of which is covered) in Piacenza. In 1986 IVECO bought the company. ASTRA military truck production is branded IVECO for export applications, the ASTRA name being retained for the domestic market only as this is a leading brand in Italy. For the Spanish market, ASTRA-produced military trucks are branded IVECO-Pegaso. For the purpose of clarity and continuity the brand

name IVECO and IVECO designations are used throughout *Jane's Military Vehicles and Logistics*, however where appropriate (Italian market-specific designs for example) any ASTRA designations will also be provided.

The IVECO tactical range of trucks can be split in to two families, these being referred to by the company as the tactical family and the logistic family. The differences between these two families of trucks are outlined elsewhere in this entry.

IVECO is part of the Fiat Group. IVECO came into being following the partnering of Fiat's truck-building activities with Germany's Magirus-Deutz, the truck manufacturing division of Klockner Humboldt Deutz (KHD). In the early 1970s Fiat had a virtual monopoly in its home market, commanding around 80 per cent of truck sales. It had absorbed most of the major Italian truck manufacturers over the years (including OM and Lancia), and owned Unic of France, but needed to increase its share of the world market if it were to survive, hence the January 1975 merger with KHD. IVECO stands for Industrial VEhicle COrporation.

After five years KHD pulled out of IVECO, but IVECO retained the Magirus name. By the mid-1980s the IVECO brand name had replaced all others.

In 1986 IVECO and Ford's UK truck division merged to form IVECO Ford Truck Ltd, and four years later IVECO added Spain's Pegaso (ENASA) to its ranks. This acquisition saw IVECO become parent to Seddon Atkinson of the UK, Seddon Atkinson having become part of ENASA in 1983 when International Harvester sold off its European truck interests.

In 1992 IVECO acquired International Trucks Australia Ltd.

Description

In keeping with most manufacturers, IVECO has a model designation system, a basic knowledge of which will greatly assist understanding of product ranges. There are exceptions, but in general the tactical range designations follow the following pattern: Taking model M1100.50WTM as an example: M - Military (used for export only); 1100 - GTW in tonnes (1100 - 110-tonnes); 50 - engine power output (50 - 500 hp); W - all-wheel drive; T - tractor; M - multipurpose. This designation is then completed by either tactical or logistical, depending on family. When branded ASTRA designations are different, and the same truck for the domestic market would be the ASTRA SM88.50. The tactical family are Standard Military (SM); 88 - drive type (88 - 8 × 8); 50 - engine power output (50 - 500 hp). Three additional letters can follow, these define (in order) wheelbase, gearbox type and brake type. The logistic range is known as Standard Military Heavy (SMH).

The ASTRA SMH88.50 (IVECO M1100.50 WTM for export applications) tractor truck is based on the M320.42WM. In addition to automotive enhancements the 2nd to 3rd and 3rd to 4th axle wheelbases have been revised, the rear axles are uprated, and dual rear wheels and 1400R 20 tyres are fitted (Shaun C Connors)   1047605

The SMH66.45 tractor truck was developed for a very specific Italian Army requirement and combines components from both the tactical and logistic families; this is the shorter 3.5 m wheelbase tractor (Shaun C Connors)
1047604

The ASTRA SMH66.45 was designed to meet a very specific Italian Army requirement for the road haul of the Centauro 8 × 8 tank destroyer; this is the longer 4.25 m wheelbase tractor (Shaun C Connors) 1391416

Tactical family models commenced delivery to the Italian Army during 1996. Logistic family models commenced delivery to the Italian Army during 2003.

As a builder of specialist trucks in relatively small numbers, ASTRA can meet, without the unacceptable levels of disruption such requirements would create on lines mass-producing commercial trucks, the individual requirements of individual customers with relative ease. This enables IVECO DVD to tailor the tactical range to meet a wide range of requirements, examples of this flexibility being the Italian Army's latest tank and light equipment transporters, both being a blend of tactical/logistic family components.

The ASTRA SMH88.50 (IVECO designation M1100.50WTM) 8 × 8 tractor truck operates at a GCW of 110,000 kg; maximum technically permissible is 130,000 kg. The SMH88.50 is based on a heavily modified M320.42WM chassis (IVECO designation) on which the rear suspension and drive axles have been uprated, rear axles now fitted with twin wheels and 1400R 20 tyres. Fifth wheel load is 24,000 kg, giving a GVW for a laden combination of 43,000 kg.

In Italian Army service the SMH88.50 (and derivatives) will eventually replace the earlier IVECO 320.45. Deliveries commenced and 10 examples of the SMH88.50 were delivered during 2003 and a further 18 during 2004. Development of the uprated SMH88.56 (with a revised driveline) commenced during 2009 and the type is currently under a development contract.

Also currently available is the ASTRA SMH66.45 which was designed to meet a very specific Italian Army requirement for the road haul of the Centauro 8 × 8 tank destroyer. Designated SMH (Standard Military Heavy - logistic family), the SMH66.45 features the militarised version of the 450 hp Cursor 13 engine (coupled to a ZF 6HP902 automatic gearbox) and other SM (Standard Military - tactical family) components, including single tyres on the rear drive axles. As of late 2005 some 36 examples had been ordered and delivered to the Italian Army. Two variants of the SMH66.45 have been delivered, one with a wheelbase of 3.5 m, the other with a wheelbase of 4.25 m. The longer wheelbase version is fitted with twin recovery winches.

Prior to the 2003 introduction of the logistic family (SMH), militarised versions of ASTRA's then commercial range of HD6 trucks were produced. To meet the changing demands of Italian (and other) armed forces, particularly for ever-increasing levels of tactical and strategic mobility, upon the introduction of the HD7 commercial range (now HD8/HHD8 with the latest IVECO Cursor engines), the decision was taken to develop and offer the logistic family for applications where previously HD range models would have been offered. HD6-based heavy equipment transporters are known to be in service with Algeria.

Visually the only significant difference between IVECO's tactical and logistic families is tyre size and the use of dual rear wheels for the latter. Standard tyre size for the tactical family is 14.00R 20, standard tyre size for the logistic family is 12.00R 20; HETs are the exception. Both families share IVECO's tactical flat-panelled GRP cab, a cab designed from the outset to meet military requirements. The driver and front-seat passenger are provided with air-sprung seats separated by an engine tunnel down the centreline of the cab. While lacking the interior space of a commercially derived contemporary, the use of this cab ensures both families are rail transportable on a standard rail flatcar (without preparation) and (tyre/wheel track-dependant) air-transportable by C-130 Hercules aircraft (with minimal preparation) and the optional low-roof cab. Added benefits of a flat-panelled cab are ease of field-repair, concealment and camouflage, and such a cab is more adaptable to the now almost essential appliquè armour kit.

Both families also share a similar purpose-designed C-section chassis which is constructed from special high yield strength 530 N/mm² steel (450 N/mm² is the commercial norm) that is imported from Sweden for all ASTRA trucks. This steel, plus the careful design of the chassis contribute to enabling the high levels of twist (torsion) and flex (bending moment) required by a military off-road vehicle, without any associated stress or damage.

The vast majority of driveline components for both families are commercially proven and taken from the Trakker/EuroTrakker range of commercial trucks, however many components for the tactical family will be militarised to considerably higher levels than comparable components for logistic family trucks.

Specifications

	ASTRA SMH88.50 (IVECO M1100.50WTM for export applications)	ASTRA SMH88.56 (IVECO M1100.56WTM for export applications)
Cab seating:	1 + 3 (can vary with armour package)	1 + 3 (can vary with armour package)
Configuration:	8 × 8	8 × 8
Weights:		
(kerb)	19,000 kg	19,000 kg
(GVW)	43,000 kg	43,000 kg
(GCW)	105,000 up to 130,000 kg	105,000 up to 130,000 kg
(5th wheel load)	24,000 kg	24,000 kg
Length:	8.64 m	8.64 m
Width:	2.88 m	2.88 m
Height: (top of cab)	3.035 m	3.035 m
Ground clearance: (tractor)	435 mm	435 mm
Wheelbase:	1.955 + 3.02 + 1.4 m	1.955 + 3.02 + 1.4 m
Angle of approach/ departure:	45°/35°	45°/35°
Max speed: (at 105,000 kg GCW)	80 km/h	80 km/h
Range:	800 km	800 km
Fuel capacity:	600 litres	600 litres
Max. gradient: (at 105,000 kg GCW)	>20%	>20%
Engine:	IVECO 8210 13.8-litre 6-cylinder in-line Euro II emissions compliant turbocharged and aftercooled water-cooled 4-stroke diesel developing 500 hp at 1,900 rpm	IVECO Cursor 13 12.9-litre 6-cylinder in-line Euro 5 emissions compliant variable geometry turbocharged and aftercooled water-cooled 4-stroke diesel developing 560 hp at 1,900 rpm and 2,500 N.m torque
Gearbox/ Transmission:	ZF 16 S 221 16-speed manual with ZF WSK 400 torque converter	Allison HD4700 fully automatic transmission with 6 forward and 1 reverse gears coupled to a Steyr VG2700 2-speed transfer box
Steering:	ZF Servocom Type 8099, dual circuit with auxiliary cylinder and 3 pumps (2 on engine, 1 on transfer box)	ZF Servocom Type 8099, dual circuit with auxiliary cylinder and 3 pumps (2 on engine, 1 on transfer box)
Turning: (kerb)	20.6 m	20.6 m
Suspension:	semi-elliptic leaf springs	semi-elliptic leaf springs
Tyres:	14.00R 20 (run flat optional)	14.00R 20 (run flat optional)
Brakes:		
(main)	dual circuit, air, discs all-round, (ABS optional)	dual circuit, air, discs all-round, (ABS)
(parking)	mechanical on rear axles	mechanical on rear axles
Electrical system:	24 V	24 V
Batteries:	4 × 12 V, 110 A	4 × 12 V, 110 A
Alternator:	80 A	100 A

Status

Production as required. Models SMH88.50 (M1100.50WTM) and SMH66.45 are in service with the Italian Army; model SMH88.56 entering production for the Italian Army.

Contractor

IVECO SpA
ASTRA Veicoli Industriali SpA

ASTRA HD 66.45 TIM (6 × 6) tractor truck

Development
ASTRA Veicoli Industriali S.p.A. was formed in 1946 in Cagliari as a refurbisher of military vehicles and the name ASTRA is taken from Azienda Sarda TRasformazione Autoveicoli. In 1951 the company transferred its headquarters to its current 135,200 m² (43,500 m² of which is covered) in Piacenza, Italy. In 1986 IVECO acquired the company.

In 1994, ASTRA introduced a range of 6 × 6 trucks known as the HD series to replace the earlier ASTRA 300 series. The ASTRA HD 66.45 TIM (6 × 6) tractor truck is a development of the ASTRA HD series.

From mid-2003 the HD series have no longer been offered for military applications. To meet the changing demands of Italian (and other) armed forces, particularly for ever-increasing levels of tactical and strategic mobility, and upon the introduction of the HD7 commercial range, the decision was taken to develop and offer the ASTRA/IVECO logistic family for applications where previously HD range models would have been offered.

Visually the logistic family is very similar to ASTRA/IVECO's established tactical family, the only significant visual difference between the two families of trucks being tyre size and the use of dual rear wheels for the latter. Full details of both families, branded ASTRA for the domestic market, and IVECO for the export market, can be found elsewhere in this section.

Description
The ASTRA HD 66.45 TIM (6 × 6) tractor truck is a development of the ASTRA HD series with the necessary modifications to upgrade it to a tractor truck. It is provided with a ZF torque converter between the engine and gearbox and wider axles have been installed to permit the fitting of dual 1400R 20 tyres. An oscillating fifth wheel is provided along with two 20,000 kg winches (25,000 kg winches were an option). The forward control cab has space for two crew beds and is air conditioned.

Current HD series models are the HD8, these available in a variety of drive configurations from 4 × 2 to 8 × 8 and fitted with a revised cab and options of EURO 3 or EURO 5 emissions compliant engines. The HHD8 (Heavy Heavy Duty), fitted with EURO 3 engine options, are also available, these having GVWS of up to 150,000 kg.

Specifications
HD 66.45 TIM
Cab seating: 1 + 2
Configuration: 6 × 6
Weight:
 (kerb) 15,500 kg
 (GVW) 40,500 kg
 (GCW) 100,000 kg
 (load on 5th wheel) 25,000 kg
Length: 7.64 m
Width: 2.34 m
Height: 3.22 m
Track:
 (front) 2.053 m
 (rear) 2.017 m
Wheelbase: 3.8 m + 1.4 m
Max speed: 67 km/h
Fuel capacity: 400 + 400 litres
Engine: IVECO 8280 TCA turbocharged and intercooled water-cooled 4-stroke diesel developing 440 hp (328 kW) at 1,900 rpm
Transmission: ZF 16S 221 gearbox with ZF WSK 400.90 torque converter; 16 forward and 2 reverse gears
Steering: ZF Servocom 8099 dual circuit with 2 pumps (1 on engine, 1 on transfer box)
Turning diameter: 18.9 m
Suspension:
 (front) semi-elliptic springs with shock-absorbers and torsion bar
 (rear) reinforced oscillating springs with pivot system and torsion bar

Tyres: 1400R 20
Brakes:
 (main) air, drums all-round
 (parking) mechanical on rear axles
Electrical system: 24 V
Batteries: 2 × 12 V, 170 Ah
Alternator: 80 A

Status
Production complete (see text). In service with Algeria (125).

Contractor
ASTRA Veicoli Industriali SpA
IVECO SpA

IVECO 320-45 WTM (6 × 6) tractor truck

Development
The IVECO 320-45 WTM (6 × 6) tractor truck was designed to meet an Italian Army requirement for a vehicle capable of towing a semi-trailer carrying a Leopard 1 MBT both on and off road as well as having the capability to recover damaged and disabled vehicles. The first prototype was completed in 1978 and the vehicle remains in service with the Italian Army as the ATC/81.

Description
The IVECO 320-45 WTM (6 × 6) tractor truck tows an OTO Melara-designed (now OTO Breda), Bartoletti-manufactured trailer, designated the Mod TCS 50 BO. The forward control four-passenger cab can be tilted forward giving access to the engine for maintenance. Two types of cab were available, one with a fully enclosed hardtop and the other with a windscreen that can be folded forward through 180°, removable door tops and side screens and a canvas roof that folds to the rear.

To the rear of the cab are two winches, each rated at 20,000 kg and with 50 m of cable. The standard 89 mm diameter king-pin is positioned over the two rear axles. The vehicle can be delivered with either single or dual rear wheels.

A variant was designed to operate over sandy terrain. It has a revised wheelbase (3.565 m + 1.45 m) and uses single tyres on all axles (14.00 × 24 at the front and 24 × 20.5 at the rear). Kerb weight is 14,700 kg. This variant was supplied to the UAE.

Specifications
IVECO 320-45 WTM
Cab seating: 1 + 3
Configuration: 6 × 6
Weight:
 (kerb) 15,400 kg
 (max load on 5th wheel) 21,000 kg
 (GCW) 93,420 kg
Length: 7.52 m
Width: 2.775 m
Height:
 (overall) 3.051 m
 (5th wheel) 1.647 m
Ground clearance: 360 mm
Track:
 (front) 1.985 m
 (rear) 1.97 m
Wheelbase: 3.6 m + 1.38 m
Angle of approach/departure: 41°/60°
Max speed: >65 km/h

ASTRA HD 66.45 TIM (6 × 6) tractor truck (ASTRA)   0512525

IVECO 320.45 WTM (6 × 6) (IVECO)   1296226

Range: >600 km
Fuel capacity: 500 litres
Gradient: >30% with semi-trailer
Side slope: 20%
Fording: 850 mm
Engine: Model 8280.22 17.174-litre V-8 turbocharged water-cooled 4-stroke diesel developing 450 hp (331 kW) at 2,400 rpm
Transmission: 8 forward and 1 reverse gears, torque converter, transfer box with lockable torque divider
Steering: power-assisted
Turning radius: 9.5 m
Suspension: leaf springs
Tyres: 14.00 × 20
Brakes:
  (main) air, drums all-round
  (parking) acting on rear axles
  (exhaust) pneumatic
Electrical system: 24 V
Number of batteries: 2 × 12 V, 143 Ah
Generator: 650 W

Status
Production complete. In service with the Italian and UAE armed forces.

Contractor
IVECO SpA

IVECO Trakker/EuroTrakker range of heavy tractor trucks

Description
IVECO's extensive range of trucks for military logistic applications is based on the company's range of civilian trucks, militarised to varying degrees to suit specific operator requirements. The range consists of the EuroCargo medium range of rigid chassis and the EuroTrakker heavy off-road range of tractor trucks and rigid chassis, the latter having been rebranded Trakker following a late 2004 product upgrade that included a new cab from the current IVECO Stralis range of trucks. The IVECO Stralis range has recently replaced the earlier EuroTech heavy on-road range of tractor trucks and rigid chassis and the EuroStar heavy on-road range of tractor trucks. The Stralis, EuroTech and EuroStar heavy on-road ranges are best described as suited to third-line road-haul logistical support roles and are only available in conventional 4 × 2, 6 × 2 or 6 × 4 drive configurations. For most military logistic applications variants of the heavier duty Trakker range are better suited and it is on the Trakker/chassis that this range of heavy tractor trucks are built.

IVECO produce a range of tactical heavy equipment transporters (full details of which can be found elsewhere in this section) but made the decision to launch a complimentary range derived from the commercial Trakker heavy truck range. Cabs and driveline components are shared with the civilian range and are all commercially available and proven, but items such as engines, gearboxes, transfer boxes and cooling systems have been upgraded considerably. Engine power outputs range from 310 to 500 hp with exhaust emissions meeting either EURO II, III, IV or V, depending on territory, specification and power output. Engines of up to 800 hp are available as a specialist option. Gearbox options include traditional manual gearboxes such as the ZF 16S 221 coupled to the ZF WSK 400 torque converter, through to the ZF EuroTronic family which utilises a conventional gear-box coupled to an electronic gear auto-selection lever. Allison fully automatic transmissions are also available.

Two-, three- and four-axle chassis are available and with single or dual wheels on the rear axles. Extra-wide sand-tyres can be fitted as an option. Longitudinal and cross-axle differential locks are available for and between all axles, with Automatic Driveline Management (ADM) as an

Danish Army IVECO MP720E42WT (6 × 6) tractor truck in Kosovo (Shaun C Connors)   1185437

Side view of a Danish Army IVECO MP720E42WT (6 × 6) tractor truck in Kosovo (Shaun C Connors)   1185436

IVECO EuroTrakker M1100E80WT (8 × 8) tractor truck fitted with extra-wide 24R 21 sand tyres undergoing hot-climate trials. The camouflaged load is a Giat Leclerc MBT (IVECO)   0126600

option. All-wheel drive is full-time and an IVECO or ZF two-speed transfer box is fitted to all models. An Anti-lock Braking System (ABS), Electronic Braking System (EBS) and either central or external tyre inflation systems are optional.

Maximum GCWs are 72,000 kg for the three-axle tractor and 121,000 kg for the four-axle tractor. All axles are leaf-sprung and there are currently two wheelbase options for three-axle tractor, 3.5 or 3.82 m (first to second axle) and 1.385 m (second to third axle), in both cases. The four-axle tractor has a tyre size driven wheelbase of 1.875 + 2.825 + 1.46 m. The conventional C-section chassis is strengthened and can mount a selection of recovery winches between the cab and fifth wheel assembly.

The two-door forward-control all-steel cab is based around the civilian sleeper cab model and seats up to three (including driver), with the option of additional stowage space, a bench seat for the tank crew or up to two bunks. Options can include add-on armoured protection from small arms fire in varying levels up to 7.62 mm AP, mine blast protection, air-conditioning, a roof-hatch with or without integral machine gun ring-mount. An all-steel interchangeable armoured cab is currently being developed for the Trakker range by IVECO in conjunction with Krauss-Maffei Wegmann (KMW).

EuroTrakker (6 × 6) tractor trucks are known to be in service with Algeria, Argentina, Denmark, Malaysia and Poland in the tank and heavy equipment transporter role.

The largest user of the EuroTrakker in the tank/heavy equipment transport role is Algeria. The last five from a batch of 146 MP720E44WT 6 × 6 tractor trucks were delivered mid-2006 and for use with locally procured semi-trailers. Twin Rotzler winches were fitted to 22 examples. Algeria also operates the IVECO/ASTRA HD 66.45 TIM tractor truck in the tank/heavy equipment transport role.

The Danish Army procured 10 model MP720E42W tractor trucks from 1996 for use with Swedish VM four-axle trailers (12) and German Goldhofer six-axle trailers (10). The MP720E42 W, powered by a 420 hp six-cylinder turbocharged diesel engine (the 42 in the type designation denoting nominal engine hp), is fitted with dual rear wheels and mounts two 15,000 kg Sepson winches. In service the MP720E42WT supplements earlier MAN 40.400 tractor trucks, 24 of which were procured from 1982 and of which 14 remained in service as of January 2007.

Argentina received nine vehicles to broadly the same specification as the Danish vehicles. These were delivered circa 2001 and with trailers supplied by Achleitner of Austria.

In 2001 Poland took delivery of two EuroTrakker MP720E47WT (6 × 6) tractor trucks and ZREMB 50,000 kg semi-trailers, and subsequently ordered EuroTrakker MP720E48WT tractor trucks fitted with the latest Cursor family diesel engine (rated at 480 hp), and coupled to a ZF EuroTronic semi-automatic gearbox. Deliveries continue, although exact quantities (believed to be around 45) involved have not been disclosed.

EuroTrakker model	MP720E54WT	MP1100E80WT
Cab seating:	1 + 2 + bench or twin bunks	1 + 2 + bench or twin bunks
Configuration:	6 × 6	8 × 8
Weight:		
(tractor, kerb)	14,500 kg	17,000 kg
(fifth wheel load)	22,000 kg	25,000 kg
(GCW)	85,000 kg	110,000 kg
Length:	wheelbase dependant	8.678 m
Width:	2.55 m	2.95 m (with sand tyres)
Height:	3.48 m	3.545 m
Ground clearance:	wheel/tyre dependent	wheel/tyre dependent
Track:		
(front)	axle, wheel/tyre dependant	axle, wheel/tyre dependant
(rear)	axle, wheel/tyre dependant	axle, wheel/tyre dependant
Wheelbase:	3.5 or 3.82 + 1.38 m	1.875 + 2.825 + 1.46 m
Angle of approach/departure:	wheelbase, wheel/tyre dependant	wheelbase, wheel/tyre dependant
Max speed:	driveline dependant	driveline dependant
Max range:	driveline, fuel capacity dependant	driveline, fuel capacity dependant
Fuel capacity:	600 litres (max)	1,000 litres (max)
Max gradient: (at GCW)	22%	n/avail
Side slope: (at GCW)	20%	n/avail
Fording:	800 mm	800 mm
Engine:	IVECO turbocharged water-cooled 4-stroke diesel developing 370 to 500 hp (272 to 367 kW) at Euro IV	IVECO turbocharged water-cooled 4-stroke diesel developing 500 hp (367 kW) (at EURO IV) to 800 hp (588 kW) (at Euro II)
Gearbox:	manual with torque converter, optional semi or fully-automatic	manual with torque converter, optional semi or fully-automatic
Transfer box:	IVECO full-time all-wheel drive	IVECO full-time all-wheel drive
Steering:	servo-assisted	servo-assisted
Turning radius:	wheelbase dependant	wheelbase dependant
Suspension:	semi-elliptic, parabolic leaf springs	semi-elliptic, parabolic leaf springs
Tyres:	395/85R 20 (options)	24R 21 (options)
Brakes:		
(main)	dual circuit air, drums, ABS optional	dual circuit air, drums, ABS optional
(parking)	spring-loaded on rear wheels	spring-loaded on rear wheels
Electrical system:	24 V	24 V
Batteries:	170 Ah	170 Ah

During 2002 Malaysia ordered an undisclosed quantity (thought to be around 50 including a contract option) of EuroTrakker (6 × 6) tractor trucks for the tank transporter role. These are fitted with a 600 hp V-8 diesel engine, Allison HD4070 automatic transmission, and Rotzler winches. During 2004 it was reported that an initial 25 examples had been delivered, the current figure is 27.

A customised 8 × 8 model, the EuroTrakker M 1100E80 WT (the 80 in the type designation denoting nominal (×10) engine hp), has undergone extensive trials in the UAE. For trials the tractor was coupled to a five-axle 77,000 kg payload semi-trailer with third, fourth and fifth axle steering, hydropneumatic suspension and the same 24R 21 tyres as the tractor. This tractor has subsequently been sold to a commercial operator.

Based on an in-production range of commercial trucks, throughout their production run the IVECO Trakker/EuroTrakker range of heavy equipment transporters are likely to reflect the many minor design changes and specification upgrades associated with civilian truck production.

SpecificationsSee table above

Status
In production. In service with Algeria (146, MP720E44WT), Argentina (nine, MP720E42WT), Denmark (17, MP720E42W), Poland (MP720E47WT and MP720E48WT) and Malaysia (27, MP720E52WT). See text for full details.

Contractor
IVECO SpA

Mitsubishi Model FW455LRS2 (6 × 6) tractor truck (M Kadota)   1296114

Japan

Mitsubishi Model FW455LRS2 (6 × 6) tractor truck

Description
The Mitsubishi Model FW455LRS2 (6 × 6) tractor truck is known to the Japanese Ground Self-Defence Force as the Type 84 truck tractor. It is designed to tow a three-axle semi-trailer carrying a tank with a maximum weight of 40,000 kg.

The Model FW455LRS2 uses a forward control cab of all-steel welded construction with seating for the driver and two passengers. The cab doors have extra vision panels and a ladder is provided for access to stowage space on the cab roof. A flat area behind the cab may be used for more stowage and carries the spare wheel and the fuel tank. The fifth wheel is located directly over the dual rear axles.

Specifications
Cab seating: 1 + 2
Configuration: 6 × 6
Weight:
  (empty) 9,500 kg
  (laden) 26,240 kg
  (on 5th wheel) 16,500 kg
Length: 7.16 m
Width: 2.49 m
Height:
  (cab) 3.51 m
  (5th wheel) 1.47 m
Track:
  (front) 2.005 m
  (rear) 1.845 m
Wheelbase: 3.73 m + 1.3 m
Max speed: 59 km/h

Engine: Mitsubishi 8DC9T2 turbocharged and intercooled diesel developing 430 hp (316 kW) at 2,200 rpm
Turning radius: 9.6 m
Tyres: 10.00 × 20

Status
In service with the Japanese Ground Self-Defence Force.

Contractor
Mitsubishi Motors Corporation

Korea, South

KM1002 (8 × 8) tractor truck

Development
Kia Motors was founded in 1944 as Kyomgseong Precision, changing its name to Kia Industry Co Ltd in 1952, changing it again in 1990 to Kia Motors Corporation. Kia's bankruptcy in 1997, part of the Asian financial crisis, resulted in 51 per cent of the company being acquired in 1998 by Hyundai Motor Company. Currently the Hyundai Kia Automotive Group owns less than 40 per cent of the company.

The Kia Motors KM1002 (8 × 8) tractor truck forms part of the KM100 series of 8 × 8 trucks and is similar in configuration to the KM1001 10 ton (8 × 8) recovery vehicle. The KM100 series of (8 × 8) trucks was reported to be in volume production as of late 2001.

Kia Motors is the sole provider of tactical military trucks to Korea's armed forces, currently supplying around 2,000 vehicles per year. Around 50,000 Kia military vehicles of all types are currently believed to be in service with Korea's Armed Forces.

Description
The Kia Motors KM1002 (8 × 8) tractor truck which appears to be entirely conventional in design is powered by a 450 hp turbocharged and intercooled diesel engine. Details of the transmission and many other mechanical aspects have not been generally released.

Two 25 ton recovery and load winches are located behind the forward control crew cab which has seating for the driver and five passengers. The fifth wheel has a load capacity of 20,000 kg.

In addition to the known specifications given in this entry the KM1002 (8 × 8) tractor truck is stated as having a climatic operational range of –32°C to +50°C and noise emissions of below 85 dB.

Specifications
KM1002
Cab seating: 1 + 5
Configuration: 8 × 8
Weight:
　(kerb) 16,800 kg
　(max load on 5th wheel) 20,000 kg
　(gross) 38,300 kg
Length: 9.053 m
Width: 2.574 m
Height: (overall) 3.426 m
Ground clearance: 267 mm
Track:
　(front) 2.014 m
　(rear) 1.891 m
Wheelbase: 1.692 + 3.208 m + 1.35 m
Angle of approach/departure: 31.6°/64.8°
Max speed: 74.7 km/h
Range: (cruising) 1,340 km
Gradient: 28%
Side slope: 20%
Fording: 760 mm
Engine: turbocharged and intercooled diesel developing 450 hp (336 kW) at 1,900 rpm
Turning radius: 11.63 m

Status
In production. In service with South Korea's Armed Forces.

Contractor
Kia Motors Corporation

Netherlands

DAF YTZ95.480 and DAF YTZ95.530 TROPCO heavy equipment transporters

Development
In December 2002, and following a competitive tender process, the Dutch Ministry of Defence (MoD) awarded DAF Trucks N.V. a EUR47.1 million (USD60 million) contract for the delivery of 112 DAF XF95-based (6 × 6) heavy equipment transporter tractor trucks, 102 semi-trailers and 56 add-on ballistic and mine blast protection kits. The combination is sometimes referred to as TROPCO, an abbreviation of the Dutch words Trekker (TR), Oplegger (OP), Combination (CO), or tractor, trailer, combination.

The Dutch MoD had expressed a strong preference for a commercially based 6 × 6 tractor truck that could be supported by established infrastructure, plus insisted on full legislative compliance. The contract award includes a full repair-and-maintenance element. Full development commenced by DAF Trucks and the company's partners for the project (Broshuis BV and Plasan Sasa) immediately after contract signing, and the first prototype vehicles were available for development tests by mid-2003. In February 2004 four pre-series combinations were handed over to the Dutch MoD for an extensive seven-month functional and durability test phase. Two each of the two Gross Combination Weights (GCWs) required were involved in these tests, the results of which were shared between the Dutch MoD and prime contractor DAF Trucks N.V., and resulted in some minor modifications to the product.

Series production commenced in January 2005, with initial deliveries to the Dutch MoD being made in April 2005. The final combinations were delivered in December 2005.

Description
DAF YTZ95.480 and DAF YTZ95.530 tractor truck models are based the commercial DAF XF95, albeit extensively modified from the basic commercial product to meet the Dutch Army's requirements.

The DAF YTZ95 is entirely conventional in design and is based around a standard C-section chassis that mounts a 3½ inch (89 mm) Jost 38G 5th wheel. Two NATO standard recovery eyes and a towing pin are fitted to the front and rear of the chassis. The standard DAF Space Cab is mounted to the chassis via coil springs, and all cabs are supplied fitted for the installation of an add-on ballistic protection kit developed and supplied by Israel's Plasan Sasa; 56 kits were procured.

Twin main and a single auxiliary remotely-controlled winch are mounted between the cab and 5th wheel. YTZ95.480 tractor trucks are fitted with twin Braden HP35A main winches with 54 m of cable and rated at a first line pull of 13,180 kg. YTZ95.530 tractor trucks are fitted with twin Braden HP55A main winches with 53 m of cable and rated at a first line pull of 24,500 kg. Both models are fitted with a single Braden HP2A auxiliary winch with 110 m of cable and rated at a first line pull of 1,000 kg.

The main automotive differences between the two tractor truck models are power output from the common DAF engine (480 hp, YTZ95.480; 530 hp, YTZ95.530), gearbox (ZF AS-Tronic, YTZ95.480; ZF TC-Tronic, YTZ95.530) and the gear ratio of the rear bogie drive axles.

On both models the front axle is a Sisu-supplied FSDP-14-G hub reduction unit rated at 14,000 kg, the rear bogie consisting of a pair of DAF HR1355T hub reduction units, each rated at 13,000 kg. Axle ratio for the YTZ95.480 is 4.88:1, axle ratio for the YTZ95.530 is 5.48:1.

Kia Motors KM 1002 (8 × 8) tractor truck (Kia Motors)　　0100370

DAF YTZ95.530 tractor truck fitted with appliqué protection kit supplied by Israel's Plasan Sasa. All 112 tractor trucks involved in the Dutch order are fitted for but not with protection; 56 kits were procured (DAF)　　1156045

Side view of a DAF YTZ95.480 tractor truck (DAF) 1156046

For use on deployed operations, DAF has converted five YTZ95.480 TROPCO heavy equipment transporters into recovery vehicles. As part of the conversion process, the vehicle wheelbase is lengthened and the recovery crane/hamper (which is uprated) is taken from DAF YBZ wreckers delivered during 1992-93 (Rob Dragt) 1391475

Variants

Heavy wrecker
For use on deployed operations, DAF has converted five YTZ95.480 TROPCO heavy equipment transporters into recovery vehicles. As part of the conversion process, the vehicle wheelbase is lengthened and the recovery crane/hamper (which is uprated) is taken from DAF YBZ wreckers delivered during 1992-93. Full details of the DAF YBZ can be found in the Recovery vehicles section.

Specifications

DAF TROPCO heavy equipment transporters

Model	YTZ95.480 (with Broshuis 4 AO-16-40 semi-trailer where stated)	YTZ95.530 (with Broshuis 7 ABSD-95 semi-trailer where stated)
Cab seating:	1 + 3	1 + 3
Configuration:	6 × 6	6 × 6
Weight:		
(tractor unit, solo)	14,740 kg	15,530 kg
(semi-trailer, solo)	14,000 kg	21,500 kg
(5th wheel load)	21,560 kg	20,770 kg
(combination, unladen)	28,740 kg	37,030 kg
(combination, laden, legal)	70,000 kg	100,000 kg
(combination, laden, design)	70,000 kg	102,000 kg
(payload, legal)	40,000 kg	63,000 kg
Length:		
(tractor unit)	7.837 m	7.837 m
(combination)	20.35 m	20.35 m
Width: (tractor unit)	2.5 m	2.5 m
Height:		
(max)	3.85 m	3.85 m
(5th wheel)	1.5 m	1.5 m
Wheelbase:	4.8 m	4.8 m
Max speed:	85 km/h	85 km/h

Model	YTZ95.480 (with Broshuis 4 AO-16-40 semi-trailer where stated)	YTZ95.530 (with Broshuis 7 ABSD-95 semi-trailer where stated)
Min range:	900 km	900 km
Fuel capacity:	2 × 445 litres	2 × 445 litres
Max gradient: (combination)		
(laden, up)	24%	20%
(laden, down)	24%	20%
Side slope:	50%	50%
Engine:	DAF XE-355C EURO 3 emissions compliant 12.6-litre 6-cylinder inline turbocharged and intercooled, water-cooled 4-stroke diesel developing 480 hp (353 kW) at 1,900 rpm and 2,100 N.m torque at 1,200 rpm	DAF XE-390C EURO 3 emissions compliant 12.6-litre 6-cylinder inline turbocharged and intercooled, water-cooled 4-stroke diesel developing 530 hp (390 kW) at 1,900 rpm and 2,350 N.m torque at 1,100-1,500 rpm
Gearbox:	ZF 16 AS 2601 AS-Tronic automated semi-automatic with 16 forward and 2 reverse gears; ratio spread: 14.12 - 0.83	ZF EA 3001 TC-Tronic automated semi-automatic with torque converter; ratio spread 12.93 - 0.78
Transfer box:	Steyr VG 2700/400 2-speed, selectable front-wheel drive	
Clutch:	430 mm dry plate clutch	ZF WSK 440 torque converter
Steering:	dual-circuit, hydraulic power-assisted, model TRW TAS92 steering box	
Turning radius: (combination, wall)	12 m	12.3 m
Suspension: (tractor)	parabolic leaf springs, telescopic shock-absorbers and anti-roll bar with a design rating of 11,500 kg, front; 8-rod with trapezium springs with a design rating of 26,000 kg, rear	
Tyres: (tractor)	425/65R 22.5, front axle; 13R 225 rear axles and spare	
Brakes:		
(main)	dual circuit air with EBS and ABS, drum brakes all-round supplemented by a DAF engine, brake rated at 292 kW at 2,400 rpm and ZF intarder rated at 420 kW	dual circuit air with EBS and ABS, drum brakes all-round supplemented by a DAF engine, brake rated at 292 kW at 2,400 rpm and ZF WSK440 torque converter with 1,600 N.m brake torque
(parking)	spring brake cylinders on both rear axles	
Electrical system:	24 V	24 V
Batteries:	4 × 12 V, 125 Ah	4 × 12 V, 125 Ah
Alternator:	100 A	100 A

Trailers
The Dutch MoD procured a separate semi-trailer for each version of the DAF YTZ95 tractor truck. The YTZ95-480 normally operates with a Broshuis 4 AO-16-14 four-axle semi-trailer, while the YTZ95-530 normally operates with a Broshuis 7 ABSD-95 seven-axle semi-trailer; if required either tractor truck may operate with either trailer. These trailers are designed for use on roads and prepared tracks only.

Both trailer designs are based around a torsion-free chassis on which the air reservoirs, valves and airlines are housed in the central beam to protect from damage wherever possible. Both designs have a central self-lubrication system to reduce daily maintenance demands and are fitted with a 3½ (89 mm) kingpin with a design load capacity of 22,500 kg. The trailer gooseneck is fitted with fairleads, pulleys and four lashing points, the 7 ABDS-95 trailer featuring a gooseneck which compensates hydraulically with first pair of axles.

The loadbeds are constructed of 8-10 mm checker-plate steel, the use of outriggers enabling the unladen trailers to operate without escort. Each loadbed is fitted with six pairs of detachable twistlocks (for ISO loads), 10,000 kg-rated lashing rings (seven on the 4 AO-16-40, nine on the 7 ABSD-95), plus an additional two pairs of 20,000 kg-rated lashing rings on the 7 ABSD-95. The rear-mounted power-operated loading ramps are laterally adjustable in width and detachable.

Both trailers use Gigant axle units rated at 12,000 kg, four on the 4 AO-16-10, seven on the 7 ABSD-95, giving maximum axle loadings of 48,000 and 84,000 kg respectively. The 4 AO-16-10 is equipped with two self-tracking (rear pair) and two rigid (front pair) axles; axles two and four are lift axles equipped with a load sensing lift mechanism and all axles are air-sprung with +100/-70 mm ride height control. The 7 ABSD-95 is equipped with a single self-tracking axle (1), a pair of rigid axles (2 and 3), and four steering axles (4, 5, 6 and 7), the steering axles being hydraulically controlled via rods from the 5th wheel. Axles one to four are lift axles, lifting in pairs, and equipped with a load sensing lift mechanism; all axles are hydraulically suspended with a +150/–110 mm ride height control. Power assisted steering by remote control below 15 km/h is possible. If either trailer exceeds 15 km/h the suspension will automatically revert to ride height.

Specifications

Broshuis semi-trailers

Model	Broshuis 4 AO-16-40	Broshuis 7ABSD-95
Length:		
(incl ramps)	14.61 m	14.61 m
(from rear of gooseneck)	10.539 m	10.539 m
Width:		
(trailer)	2.79 m	2.984 m
(over outriggers)	3.22 m	3.414 m
Kingpin height:	1.5 m	1.5 m
Deck height:	900 mm	1 m (1.06 m for bridging)
Max king-pin load:		
(design)	22,500 kg	22,500 kg
(legal)	15,000 kg	15,000 kg
Max axle assembly load:		
(design)	48,000 kg	84,000 kg
(legal)	40,000 kg	70,000 kg
Unladen weight:	14,000 kg	21,500 kg
Capacity:		
(design)	56,500 kg	85,000 kg
(legal)	41,000 kg	63,500 kg
Suspension:	air plus telescopic shock-absorbers	hydraulic
Tyres:	Goodyear 235/75R 17.5 G114T (18 incl 2 spare)	Goodyear 235/75R 17.5 G114T (30 incl 2 spare)
Brakes:	air, spring-type on axles 1-2	air, spring-type on axles 4-5-6-7
Electrical system:	24 V	24 V

Status
A total of 112 tractor trucks and 102 semi-trailers delivered to the Royal Netherlands Army between April and December 2005 (see text for details).

Contractor (prime)
DAF Trucks NV

Contractor (semi-trailers)
Broshuis BV

Romania

ROMAN 33.460 DFAS (6 × 6) heavy tractor truck

Development
The ROMAN 33.460 DFAS (6 × 6) tractor truck has been developed to prototype stage. It is a heavy equipment tractor truck and has been offered coupled to a Broshuis seven axle semi-trailer that has a payload capacity of 65,000 kg.

It was announced in 2003 that Pesaka Astana of Malaysia had acquired a 94.27 per cent stake in ROMAN SA, including a 100 per cent take over of two of ROMAN SA's subsidiaries which control the assembly plant and axle parts manufacturing facilities. The takeover did not involve any liabilities or debts of ROMAN SA. After one week Pesaka Astana gave up its share of ROMAN SA to SC PRO ROMAN SA, Brasov. The current privatised company began trading in 2004.

Between 1995 and early-2007 ROMAN SA supplied around 1,300 assorted trucks to the Romanian Army and around 200 assorted trucks to the Malaysian Army (1995-2003) under the AMDAC name and in conjunction with Pesaka Astana. In support of operations in Iraq the company has also received 13 contracts from TACOM for 15 different types of trucks for civilian and logistic support of the Iraqi Army.

Following privatisation in 2004 the decision was taken to use ROMAN as the primary brand name. ROMAN designations are based around the same system as earlier DAC/AMDAC designations and define approximate GVW (tonnes) and approximate engine power output (hp), with the additional lettering defining a variety of things including cab type, drive configuration, wheel/tyre fit, body/chassis type.

Description
The chassis frame of the 33.460 DFAS is of conventional channel section design with riveted or bolted cross-members. A 3½ inch (87 mm) JOST fifth wheel is fitted and a TH 10 winch with 50 m of rope is optional.

Full time all-wheel-drive is provided, conventional beam type axles and leaf spring suspension being employed. The front steer-drive axle is fitted with single wheels/tyres, the rear drive axles with dual wheels/tyres. Anti-lock Brake System (ABS) is fitted as standard.

Motive power is provided by a MAN 12-litre water-cooled diesel engine developing 460 hp. The engine is capable of operation with NATO F34/F54 fuels and is coupled to an automatic transmission. A single 410 litre capacity fuel tank is chassis mounted.

The all steel cab is a MAN design that is now fitted throughout the ROMAN military truck range in a variety of configurations. A flat-panelled cab fabricated with a two piece flat windscreen, also fitted throughout the ROMAN military truck range in a variety of configurations, is an option. Both cabs tilt forward hydraulically for engine maintenance and checks and are fitted with a high performance heating and ventilation system. An observation hatch is fitted in the cab roof for the passenger.

Climatic operational range is –s33 to +52°C.

Specifications
ROMAN 33.460 DFAS
Cab seating: 1 + up to 3
Configuration: 6 × 6
Weight:
  (GVW, tractor) 33,000 kg
  (payload, trailer) 65,000 kg
  (GCW) 105,000 kg
Length:
  (tractor) 8.93 m
Width:
  (tractor) 2.5 m
  (trailer with outriggers) 3.5 m
Height: 3.45 m
Ground clearance: 330 mm
Angle of approach/departure:
  (tractor) 20°/45°
Max speed: 90 km/h (60 km/h at GCW)
Max gradient: 33%
Fuel capacity: 410 litres
Fording: 800 mm
Side slope: 22%
Engine: MAN 12-litre 6 cylinder inline water-cooled diesel developing 460 hp (338 kW)
Gearbox: automatic
Transfer box: 2 speed
Steering: hydraulic power assisted
Turning radius:
  (kerb) 12 m
Suspension: semi-elliptic leaf springs, telescopic shock-absorbers and anti-roll bar, front; semi-elliptic leaf springs, inverted, rear bogie
Tyres: 315/80R 22.5
Brakes: dual circuit, air, drums all-round
Electrical system: 24 V

Status
Prototype.

Contractor
ROMAN SA

Russian Federation

KZKT-7428 family of 8 × 8 tractor trucks

Description
The KZKT-7428 family of 8 × 8 tractor trucks may be considered the replacement vehicles for the earlier MAZ-537 family of 8 × 8 tractor trucks. Only basic information is available regarding the KZKT-7428 family, and as

KZKT-74287 (8 × 8) tractor truck (KZKT) 0056397

Designation	KZKT-7428-011	KZKT-7428-013	KZKT-74286	KZKT-74287
Cab seating:	5 + 1 seated; sleeper configuration with 2 bunks	5 + 1 seated; sleeper configuration with 2 bunks	5 + 1 seated; sleeper configuration with 2 bunks	5 + 1 seated; sleeper configuration with 2 bunks
Configuration:	8 × 8	8 × 8	8 × 8	8 × 8
Weight:				
(tractor unit)	25,000 kg	25,000 kg	22,800 kg	25,000 kg
(semi-trailer)	70,000 kg	70,000 kg	70,000 kg	90,000 kg
(GCW)	95,000 kg	95,000 kg	92,800 kg	115,000 kg
(fifth wheel load)	27,000 kg	27,000 kg	27,000 kg	30,000 kg
Max speed:	65 km/h	65 km/h	55 km/h	45 km/h
Fuel capacity:	900 litres	900 litres	900 litres	900 litres
Cruising range:	700 km	700 km	680 km	700 km
Max gradient: (GCW)	27-31%	27-31%	27-31%	27-31%
Fording:	1.1 m	1.1 m	1.1 m	1.1 m
Engine:	YaMZ-8401.10-14 developing 650 hp (478 kW)	Cummins KTTA19-C650 developing 650 hp (478 kW)	YaMZ-240 NM 1B developing 500 hp (367 kW)	YaMZ-8401.10-14 developing 650 hp (478 kW)
Turning radius:	15.5 m	15.5 m	15.5 m	15.5 m

far as is known only the heaviest component, the KZKT-74287, is in current production. The KZKT-74287 tractor truck has been demonstrated coupled to a KZKT-9102 tank transporter semi-trailer with twin four-wheeled rear axles (eight wheels) and hydraulically raised loading ramps.

It is understood that increasing numbers of KZKT-74287 tractor trucks are entering service with the Russian Army, replacing MAZ-537 tractor trucks.

The KZKT-7428 range is currently made up of four vehicles designated 7428-001, 7428-013, 74286 and 74287, the primary differences (from available data) being engine power outputs and GCW figures.

Specifications - See table above

Status
KZKT-74287 in production and service with the Russian Army. KZKT-7428-001, 7428-013 and 74286, available.

Contractor
Strategia. (previously known as Kurgan (Rusich) Wheeled Tractor Plant (KZMT).)

MAZ-535 and MAZ-537 (8 × 8) series

Development
What is now the Minsk Wheel Tractor Plant can trace its history back to 1954 when the facility was set up to design and develop new heavy artillery systems and tractor vehicles for the Russian military. Work on the first vehicle, the MAZ-528 (4 × 4), began in 1955. Work on the first MAZ-535 prototype commenced in 1956, with the first MAZ-537 (MAZ-537G) prototype commencing in 1959. These vehicles were first seen publicly during a parade held in Moscow in 1964.

The MAZ-535 and MAZ-537 are used for a wide variety of roles by the armed forces of the Russian Federation and are closely related to the MAZ-543 (8 × 8) series of trucks, the first prototype of which was constructed during 1962.

The now independent Minsk Wheeled Tractor Plant (MWKT, Cyrillic МЗКТ, English conversion MZKT) was established in 1991 from a special-purpose wheeled tractor division of the Minsk Automobile Plant (MAZ). MAZ, in which MAN of Germany now has a controlling interest, continues to manufacture commercial and conventionally-styled military trucks with up to three axles. What became the Minsk Wheeled Tractor Plant had previously specialised in the production of heavy vehicles for mobile

A time-served MAZ-537 (8 × 8) tractor truck of the Afghan Army (MZKT)
1391476

Ukrainian Army MAZ-537 (8 × 8) tractor truck (Shaun C Connors) 0059684

MAZ-537 tractor truck and semi-trailer of the Ukrainian Army (Shaun C Connors)
1120422

missile systems and continues to concentrate on speciality multi-axle chassis, but the new concern has diversified into heavy construction plant and multiwheel drive configurations for tasks such as oil drilling and exploration or construction applications. This has led to the 'Volat' series of commercial 8 × 8 vehicles which utilise chassis and many components originally intended for military purposes but having mechanical transmissions in place of the hydromechanical equivalents used by military vehicles; they also have lower powered engines.

Description
The MAZ-535 and MAZ-537 are both full-time 8 × 8 drive with torsion bar-type independent wheel suspension. The front two pairs of wheels steer, and a central tyre pressure regulation system is standard. All models are fitted with a cab heater and an engine pre-heater. All models are powered by the same V-12 diesel, this used in some Russian Federation tanks and other armoured vehicles. In the case of the MAZ-535 the engine has been derated to deliver 375 hp instead of 525 hp in the MAZ-537.

The MAZ-535A, MAZ-537A and MAZ-537K (which has a small crane) are cargo trucks but are also used to tow trailers or heavy artillery. The other models are used to tow semi-trailers carrying missiles or armoured fighting vehicles. The tractor trucks are normally used with the ChMZAP-5247, ChMZAP-5247G and ChMZAP-9990 semi-trailers.

Variants
MAZ-535A: cargo/ballast truck
MAZ-537: tractor truck
MAZ-537A: cargo/ballast truck with a self-recovery winch

Designation	MAZ-535A	MAZ-537A	MAZ-537
Type:	truck	truck	tractor truck
Configuration:	8 × 8	8 × 8	8 × 8
Weight:			
(unladen)	18,975 kg	22,500 kg	21,600 kg
(laden)	25,975 kg	37,500 kg	n/app
(weight on front axles, laden)	n/app	14,890 kg	17,375 kg
(weight on rear axles, laden)	n/app	22,610 kg	29,425 kg
(payload)	6,000 kg	15,000 kg	n/app
(towed load, road)	50,000 kg	75,000 kg	65,000 kg
(towed load, dirt road)	15,000 kg	30,000 kg	25,000 kg
Load area:	4.5 × 2.595 m	4.562 × 2.53 m	n/app
Length:	8.78 m	9.13 m	8.96 m
Width:	2.805 m	2.885 m	2.885 m
Height:			
(cab)	2.915 m	2.8 m	3.1 m
(load area)	1.4 m	1.875 m	n/app
Ground clearance:	475 mm	500 mm	500 mm
Track:	2.15 m	2.2 m	2.2 m
Wheelbase:	1.7 + 2.35 + 1.7 m	1.7 + 2.65 + 1.7 m	1.8 + 2.65 + 1.7 m
Angle of approach/departure:	38°/60°	38°/52°	38°/52°
Max speed: (road)	60 km/h	60 km/h	55–60 km/h
Range:	650 km	650 km	600 km
Fuel capacity:	760 litres	840 litres	840 litres
Fuel consumption:	110 litres/100 km	125 litres/100 km	125 litres/100 km
Max gradient:	30°	8° (laden)	8° (laden)
Fording:	1.3 m	1.3 m	1.3 m
Engine model:	D12A-375	D12A-525	D12A-525
Engine type:	V-12 water-cooled diesel developing 375 hp (276 kW) at 1,650 rpm	V-12 water-cooled diesel developing 525 hp (386 kW) at 2,100 rpm	
Gearbox:	planetary, 3 speeds forward and 1 speed reverse, with smooth start device on low gear and reverse		
Transfer box:	manual, 2 speed, with direct drive and reduction gears, pneumatic and manual back-up control		
Auxiliary reduction gear transmission:	manual, with inter-axle self-locking differential, consisting of spur gear pair		
Torque converter:	single stage	single stage	single stage
Overdrive:	single-row 3-shaft reduction gear with spur skew gears		
Steering:	hydraulic, screw with nut on moving balls and rack engaged with gear quadrant		
Suspension:	MAZ-535A, independent, individual, lever torsion bar (rear suspension equaliser, springless on MAZ-537), with hydraulic shock-absorbers on all wheels. MAZ-537A, independent, individual, lever torsion bar, with hydraulic shock-absorbers on both sides of front axle; rear: springless equaliser		
Tyres:	18.00 × 24	18.00 × 24	18.00 × 24
Brakes:	air/hydraulic	air/hydraulic	air/hydraulic
Electrical system:	24 V	24 V	24 V
Batteries:	4 × 12-ST-70	4 × 12-ST-70	4 × 12-ST-70
Generator:	1,500 W	1,500 W	1,500 W

MAZ-537D: tractor truck with a recharger for the truck's batteries plus an additional generator between the rear of engine compartment and the fifth wheel. The MAZ-537D was used to tow electrically powered strategic missile trailers (produced from 1964 onwards)

MAZ-537E: tractor truck similar to the 537V but with an additional gearbox to drive a generator. Some sources state this model could be used with a powered semi-trailer (produced from 1965 onwards)

MAZ-537G: tractor truck with winch behind the cab for disabled AFV recovery (produced from 1964 onwards)

MAZ-537K: prototypes only. Fitted with a crane to handle missile containers and associated heavy cargo

MAZ-537L: ballast truck similar to the 537G but with a fixed-side cargo body replacing the fifth wheel. Introduced as a tow tractor for aircraft of up to 200 tonnes

MAZ-537P: cargo/ballast truck similar to the 537A but with without the self-recovery winch. Primarily used by the strategic missile forces

MAZ-537V: tractor truck with the fifth wheel moved 345 mm to the rear of the chassis (produced from 1965 onwards)

KET-T: heavy recovery version of the MAZ-537G fitted with recovery crane, winches, stabilisers and towing gear

A version of the MAZ-537 carrying a turntable crane has been observed.

Specifications - See table above

Status
Production complete. Limited numbers of the MAZ-535 may remain in service within the former Soviet Union. The MAZ-537 remains in service with members of the former Warsaw Pact as well as Afghanistan, Cambodia, Egypt, Finland, Iran, Syria, the former Yugoslavia and possibly others.

Contractor
Minsk Wheeled Tractor Plant

MZKT Volat 74135 (8 × 8) tractor truck

Development
The MZKT Volat 74135 (8 × 8) tractor truck was developed by the Minsk Wheeled Tractor Plant specifically for the Middle East market. Many tropicalised features are included to accommodate heavy carrying and recovery operations over sand. Numerous parts, including the engine and drive train make use of parts with Western origins.

MZKT Volat 74135 (8 × 8) tractor truck, 99942 semi-trailer and 83721 trailer combination, each trailer transporting a UAE Army Leclerc MBT at IDEX 2003 (Shaun C Connors)   0567954

The semi-trailer proposed for use with this tractor truck is the three-axle MWTP-99942 (originally designated MWTP-99941) with permissible axle load on each axle of 21,700 kg and a payload capacity of 70,000 kg.

Description

The MZKT Volat 74135 (8 × 8) tractor truck has a fifth wheel loading of 23,000 kg and was originally powered by a 21.6-litre Deutz diesel developing 788 hp and coupled to an Allison M6600 fully automatic transmission. Components such as the transfer box and axles are manufactured by the Minsk Wheeled Tractor Plant. A Central Tyre Inflation (CTI) system is standard.

The cab is set behind a sizeable bonnet, with a single spare wheel stowage point and handling crane at the right rear. The cab is suspended on shock absorbers and is thermal and sound insulated. Air conditioning is provided for the driver and up to six passengers.

The fifth wheel has a maximum rated capacity of 30,000 kg and is manufactured by Jost. The main winch is manufactured by Itag of Germany and has a capacity of 25,000 kg and 100 m of cable. Among other items of standard equipment are two fire extinguishers. Optional equipment includes a stainless steel drinking water tank, black-out lights, a working spotlight, and Hutchinson beadlocks for the wheel rims.

MZKT Volat 74135 (8 × 8) tractor truck, 99942 semi-trailer and 83721 trailer combination, each trailer transporting a UAE Army Leclerc MBT at IDEX 2003 (Shaun C Connors)   1047663

MZKT Volat 74135 (8 × 8) tractor truck at IDEX 2003 (Shaun C Connors)   1047664

MZKT Volat 74135 (8 × 8) tractor truck at IDEX 2005; note the new cab and the curved bonnet under which is the current Mercedes-Benz power plant (Patrick Allen)   1138094

Specifications

MZKT Volat 74135
Cab seating: 1 + 6
Configuration: 8 × 8
Weight:
  (kerb) 26,450 kg
  (GCW) 118,450 kg
Axle loads with 70,000 kg load:
  (1st axle) 11,320 kg
  (2nd axle) 10,390 kg
  (3rd axle) 13,100 kg
  (4th axle) 13,100 kg
Fifth wheel load: (nominal) 23,000 kg
Length:
  (MZKT-74135) 10.83 m
  (MZKT-74135 + MWTP-99941) 26.805 m
Width: 3.07 m
Height: (top of cab) 4.05 m
Track: (front and rear) 2.375 m
Wheelbase: 2.2 m + 2.75 m + 1.7 m
Angle of approach: 22°
Max speed: (road) 90 km/h
Range: (road, 60 km/h) 1,100 km
Fuel capacity: 1,150 litres
Gradient: 35%
Engine: Mercedes-Benz OM444LA V-12 turbocharged water-cooled 4-stroke diesel developing 796 hp (585 kW) at 2,100 rpm (at +55°C air temperature)
Transmission: Allison M6610 AR automatic and torque converter with 6 forward and 2 reverse gears
Transfer box: MZKT 2-speed
Steering: hydraulic power-assisted
Suspension:
  (front) independent, torsion bar with shock-absorbers
  (rear) independent, leaf springs with shock-absorbers
Brakes: dual circuit air/hydraulic
Tyres: 23.5R 25 XLB TL 188E TL with pressure control system
Electrical system: 24 V
Batteries: 2 × 12 V 190 Ah
Alternator: 140 A

Status

Production as required. Supplied to the UAE from around 2000 (est. 20-40).

Contractor

Minsk Wheeled Tractor Plant

Serbia and Montenegro

FAP 3232 BDST/AV (8 × 8) tractor truck

Description

First shown in 1985, the FAP 3232 BDST/AV (8 × 8) tractor truck is a variant of the FAP 2832 (8 × 8) 9,000 kg truck, full details of which can be found in the Trucks section. The main change is that in place of the usual truck cargo body there is a fifth wheel coupling for towing semi-trailers weighing up to 65,000 kg and with a payload of 50,000 kg. There are two winches located on the platform behind the cab, one for forward use. In all other respects the FAP 3232 BDST/AV and FAP 2832 truck are identical.

Any further production of the FAP 3232 BDST/AV (8 × 8) tractor truck would likely involve the use of current generation driveline components and result in a designation change.

FAP 3232 BDST/AV (Fabrika automobila Priboj)   1296225

Specifications

FAP 3232 BDST/AV
Cab seating: 1 + 1
Configuration: 8 × 8
Weight:
   (laden, on road) 34,000 kg
   (unladen) 16,000 kg
   (load on 5th wheel) 18,000 kg
Towed load: 65,000 kg
Length: 8.612 m
Width:
   (over tractor unit) 2.5 m
   (over towed load) 3.5 m
Height:
   (cab) 3.335 m
   (5th wheel) 1.9 m
Ground clearance: 380 mm
Track: 2.02 m
Wheelbase: 1.5 m + 3.2 m + 1.4 m
Angle of approach: 41°
Max speed: 60 km/h
Range: over 600 km
Max gradient: (tractor unit) 32%
Fording: 1.2 m
Engine: OM 403 15.95 litre V-10 water-cooled 4-stroke diesel developing 320 hp (235 kW)
Gearbox: synchronised with auxiliary drive, 8 forward and 1 reverse gears
Clutch: single dry plate
Transfer box: 2-speed
Steering: hydraulic, ball and joint
Turning radius: 13 m
Tyres: 15.00 × 21 T-101
Brakes:
   (main) dual circuit, air, drums all-round, supplementary exhaust brake
   (parking) mechanical
Electrical system: 24 V
Batteries: 2 × 12 V, 210 Ah
Alternator: 85 A

Status

In service with the former Yugoslav Army. Production as required. Available for export.

Contractor

FAP Korporacija a.d.

Enquiries to

Yugoimport SDPR

South Africa

Cavallo (8 × 8) extra heavy recovery system

Development

During 1994, the South African concern Armscor decided to procure the Spanish Kynos Aljaba (8 × 8) truck tractor, full details of which can be found elsewhere in this section, for the South African National Defence Force (SANDF). It entered service under the name Cavallo.

The Cavallo/Aljaba has been used as the basis for several special purpose vehicles, including a heavy recovery vehicle, full details of which can be found in the Trucks section.

Description

With the SANDF the Cavallo is used more as a tank recovery vehicle than as a tank transporter. The cross-country performance and winches of the Cavallo are used to haul a stranded vehicle to a level surface where longer hauls are then made using MAN tractor trucks and semi-trailers. To assist in the recovery role, each Cavallo has a foldable 15,000 kg lift capacity towing system which can be erected behind the fifth wheel when a semi-trailer is not connected. This is employed for the suspended tow of casualties such as the G6 and Rooikat. A 60,000 kg payload semi-trailer can be used to transport casualties such as the G6 or Olifant MBT.

The base Cavallo chassis are obtained from Spain and once in South Africa they are fitted with mine-protected cabs.

Status

Production as required. In service with the South African National Defence Force (72 of all variants).

Enquiries to

FAF Engineering

Spain

Kynos Aljaba (8 × 8) tractor truck

Development

The Kynos Aljaba (8 × 8) tractor truck was originally developed as a private venture by Kynos SA, commencing in 1982 - Kynos SA, which no longer trades, was a subsidiary of the Agroman Group and normally specialised in construction equipment. The Spanish Ministry of Defence provided some funding and one prototype and three pre-series vehicles were produced. The Spanish Army carried out field trials with one vehicle in May 1985, near Toledo. The first two production vehicles were delivered to the Spanish Marines during mid-1987 with another vehicle going to the Spanish Army in the same year. In total some 10 vehicles have been delivered to Spanish Armed Forces.

A single vehicle with a Spanish-produced four-axle semi-trailer was supplied to the UAE for extensive trials, although no orders have yet been placed.

It is understood that prior to its liquidation, Kynos SA received an order for Aljaba tractor trucks from Iran. No vehicles are known to have been produced or delivered.

It was announced, in November 2003, that Group Servicios Y Proyectos Avanzados (SPA) had acquired the assets, technology and contracts of Kynos SA.

This Aljaba was selected by the South African National Defence Force (SANDF) as their tank transporter, named the Cavallo.

Description

The Aljaba (Quiver) was designed to tow and retrieve MBTs up to a weight of 60,000 kg. It is built on a flexible rectangular chassis that is resistant to the stresses imparted when travelling over uneven terrain. The chassis is reinforced by longitudinal members with special cross-members attached. A swing-arm suspension with leaf springs and trailing arms is employed. The forward control cab is formed from a steel frame mounted on elastic shock-absorbers and has seating for the driver, crew member and three passengers.

The Aljaba is powered by a Deutz 19-litre V-12 turbocharged diesel and uses a ZF semi-automatic gearbox with torque converter. All four Rockwell (now ArvinMeritor) 13,000 kg axles are driven, the front two being steered with power assistance. Each wheel hub has a planetary reduction gear and each pair of axles can be pneumatically locked. The dual-circuit pneumatic brakes act on all wheels and the brake circuits are also used to provide air for the de-icing, protection and alarm systems. An air take-off is provided each side of the vehicle for tyre inflation. The special 24.00R 20.5XS-PR16 tyres may be fitted with chains for extra traction and the spare wheel is provided with handling gear.

Cavallo (8 × 8) tractor truck and semi-trailer (Shaun C Connors)   1296219

Kynos Aljaba (8 × 8) tank transporter as displayed at IDEX 2003 (Shaun C Connors)   0544866

For recovery the Aljaba is equipped with two 25,000 kg winches with 26 mm cable that normally operate to the rear, but the left-hand winch cable may be routed forward using a pulley fixed to the chassis. Operating speed is 8 m/min.

It was proposed that the Aljaba could also be used to carry out a number of other roles including that of a missile system carrier, artillery tractor, logistics carrier, bridging equipment carrier, shelter/container for command and communications or hospitals and other such roles.

Variants

Kynos SA also developed the Aljaba (6 × 6) tractor truck K15-100 and a complimentary six-axle semi-trailer, model GP6CHS13T, to meet a requirement for the recovery and transport of Spanish Army Leopard 2 MBTs. Full details of the K15-100 and GP6CHS13T semi-trailer can be found elsewhere in this section.

Specifications

Kynos Aljaba
Cab seating: 1 + 4
Configuration: 8 × 8
Weight:
(empty) 22,100 kg
(max load on chassis) 46,100 kg
(weight on front axles) 14,500 kg
(weight on rear axles) 7,600 kg
(GCW) 98,600 kg
Length:
(tractor) 9.875 m
(tractor and trailer) 22.269 m
Width:
(tractor) 3.3 m
(tractor and trailer) 4.025 m
Height: (overall) 3.63 m
Ground clearance: 365 mm
Track: 2.6 m
Wheelbase: 1.524 m + 3.476 m + 1.524 m
Angle of approach/departure: 30°/75°
Max speed: 80 km/h
Fuel capacity: 1,000 litres (2 × 500 litres)
Range:
(road) 1,000 km
(off-road) 700-1,000 km
Vertical obstacle: 500 mm
Trench: 2.1 m
Gradient: (fully laden) 31%
Side slope: 25%
Fording: 800 mm
Engine: Deutz BF 12 L 513 C 19.144-litre V-12 turbocharged and aftercooled diesel developing 525 hp (386 kW) at 2,300 rpm
Transmission: ZF 16S-190A manual with ZF WSK 400 torque converter; 16 forward and 2 reverse gears
Transfer box: ZF, single-speed
Steering: power-assisted on front 2 axles
Turning radius: 13.407 m
Suspension: Hendrikson swing arm with leaf springs and trailing arms; anti-roll bars on front axle
Tyres: 24.00R 20.5XS-PR16
Brakes: dual circuit, air, drums all-round
Electrical system: 24 V
Batteries: 2 × 12 V, 120 Ah

Status

Production as required. In service with Spanish (10) and South African (72) armed forces.

Contractor

Servicios Y Proyectos Avanzados SA (SPA)

Kynos Aljaba K15-100 (6 × 6) tractor truck and GP6CHS13T semi-trailer

Development

The requirement for a tank transporter capable of transporting the Spanish Army's then to be acquired Leopard 2 MBT and Buffel armoured recovery vehicle fleets was announced in 1997. A number of companies expressed an interest in the requirement, these including IVECO (Italy), Kynos (Spain), MAN (Germany), Mercedes-Benz (Germany), Renault (France) and Scania (Sweden). Two companies, Kynos and Mercedes-Benz were subsequently invited to furnish vehicles for technical evaluation and trials, and during late 2000, following two years of assessment of the Kynos K15-100 and Mercedes-Benz 2636AS, a production contract was awarded to Kynos SA.

The initial contract award called for 32 combinations of K15-100 tractor trucks and associated GP6CHS13T semi-trailers, with a further 15 combinations ordered during 2001. Deliveries were scheduled at seven combinations between contract award and May 2001, a further 10 during

Kynos (now SPA) K15-100 (6 × 6) tractor truck (Kynos(SPA)) 0587983

2001, five during 2002, 10 during 2003, 13 during 2004 and the final two combinations during 2005. A further two combinations were subsequently ordered, bringing total requirements to 49.

It was announced in November 2003 that Group Servicios Y Proyectos Avanzados (SPA) had acquired the assets, technology and contracts of Kynos S.A. The final 14 K15-100 tractor trucks and semi-trailers ordered were produced by Group SPA.

Description

K15-100 tractor truck

The K15-100 (6 × 6) tractor truck is of conventional design and is intended for heavy-duty haulage operations on a mix of roads and prepared tracks at a ratio of 70 (roads)/30 (tracks).

The C-section chassis is fitted with bolt-in cross-members and mounts beam-type axles sprung by multileaf springs, an anti-roll bar and shock-absorbers being fitted to the front steer-drive axle. All axles are fitted with hub-reduction gearing and the rear drive axle bogie is fitted with dual wheels and tyres.

The six-seat all-steel purpose-designed cab is a two-door flat-panelled design. Located immediately behind the cab is a spare wheel for the tractor truck, plus the driveline cooling pack. Between these and the fifth wheel are a pair of Rotzler 25 kN winches, each fitted with 50 m of 26 mm cable.

Motive power is provided by a four-stroke Deutz diesel engine coupled to a ZF manual gearbox with integral retarder and single-speed transfer box. All drive axles are fitted with differential locks.

The standard semi-trailer is a GP6CHS13T, the laden combination meeting all current relevant traffic legislation. In addition to a single Leopard MBT, the trailer has been designed to accept a variety of other loads, including other MBTs, two APCs or a selection of shelters and containers. Full details of the GP6CHS13T semi-trailer can be found in the Trailers section.

GP6CHS13T semi-trailer

The GP6CHS13T six-axle semi-trailer is of steel construction and is fitted with a hydraulically operated articulating gooseneck, hydraulic supporting legs front and rear and a pair of one-piece hydraulically-controlled rear loading ramps. Suspension is hydraulic and all six axles steer, being controlled by movement of the trailer kingpin and fifth wheel. A Jost 89 mm (3½ inch) fifth wheel is fitted. Two gooseneck-mounted spare wheels are carried.

In addition to a single Leopard MBT or Buffel ARV this trailer has been designed to readily accept a variety of other loads including: a single M60 MBT, a single M48 MBT, a single AMX-30 MBT, a pair of M113 APCs, a pair of Pizarro IFVs, a pair of BMR-600 IFVs, a pair of ISO 10 or 20 ft containers, a single ISO 30 or 40 ft container or a single NATO II shelter.

Specifications

K15-100 tractor truck
Cab seating: 1 + 5
Configuration: 6 × 6
Weight:
(unladen without winches) 14,225 kg
(unladen with winches fitted) 16,600 kg
Length: 6.255 m
Height:
(cab roof) 3.06 m
(roof-mounted beacons) 3.25 m
(fifth wheel, laden) 1.607 m
(fifth wheel, unladen) 1.647 m
Track:
(front) 2.07 m
(rear) 1.829 m
Wheelbase:
(1st to 2nd axles) 2.972 m
(2nd to 3rd axles) 1.143 m

Angle of approach/departure: 30°/47°
Max speed: 90 km/h
Fuel capacity (at 108,000 kg GCW): 2 × 400 litres
Gradient: 24%
Engine: Deutz 15.874-litre V-8 turbocharged water-cooled 4-stroke diesel developing 540 hp (397 kW) at 2,100 rpm
Gearbox: ZF 16S 251 manual with 16 forward and 2 reverse gears; integral ZF WSK 400 retarder
Transfer box: single-speed with longitudinal differential lock
Steering: power assisted
Turning radius (wall to wall): 9.636 m
Suspension: multileaf springs, telescopic shock-absorbers and anti-roll bar, front; multi-leaf springs (inverted) and traction rods (rear)
Brakes: dual circuit, air, drums all-round. ABS fitted
Electrical system: 24 V

Specifications

GP6CHS13T semi-trailer
Weight: 23,500 kg
Max load: 70,000 kg
Length:
  (overall) 16.982 m
  (loadbed) 13 m
  (gooseneck) 3.982 m
  (kingpin to first axle centreline) 7.417 m
Wheelbase (per axle): 1.52 m
Height:
  (kingpin) 1.56 m
  (loadbed, unladen) 1.04 m
  (ramps, raised) 3.299 m
Width: 3.6 m
Tyres: Michelin, 285/70R 19.5, 24 + 2 spare
Electrical system: 24 V

Status
Production as required. In service with Spanish Armed Forces (49).

Contractor
Servicios Y Proyectos Avanzados SA (SPA)
(For further details see text.)

Sweden

Scania T144 GB6×4NZ 530 tractor truck

Development
The first of 31 Scania T144 GB6×4NZ 530 tractor trucks for the Swedish Army was handed over for testing in March 1997. Full production started in summer 1998 and, in service, the tractors tow a five-axle semi-trailer produced by VW-Trailer of Gothenbourg, Sweden. They are used to carry the Swedish Army's Leopard 2 (Stridsvagn 121/122) MBTs.

The original Swedish order called for 60 tractor trucks to replace the Volvo N1233 fleet of tractor trucks procured in 1997, which, it was decided, should be replaced, not life-extended, during FY 94/95. The production quantity of Scania T144 GB6x4NZ 530 tractor trucks was reduced to 31 units during production due to changes in Swedish road regulations. The Volvo N1233 vehicles and their associated VM-Trailer four-axle semi-trailers remain in service. Full details of the Volvo N1233 tractor truck can be found elsewhere in this section.

The Swedish Army also uses the Scania T14 3E6×4 tractor truck and Hafo/VM-Trailer semi-trailer combination in the tank transport role. These tractor trucks are fitted with winches and the combinations were procured in the late 1980s, primarily for the transport of damaged combat vehicles.

In addition to Sweden, the Scania T144 GB6x4NZ 530 tractor truck is also used by Belgium and France. Equipment levels on all three models differ, although they are essentially the same base tractor truck.

The first of 26 tractor trucks for the Belgian Army was handed over for testing in October 1998. Deliveries commenced in June 2000 and, in service, these vehicles are coupled to a six-axle semi-trailer produced by SOFRAME Industries of Hangenbieten, France. They are used to carry armoured vehicles including the Leopard 2A5 MBT.

An order for 12 examples for use by the French Army was announced in June 2000. In service, these tractor trucks are coupled to a ACTM (*Ateliers de Construction et Travaux Mécaniques*) model S94615 60,000 to 74,000 kg payload six-axle (four steering) semi-trailer.

Description
The Scania T144 GB6x4NZ 530 tractor truck is a military version of a Scania T-cabbed 4-series tractor truck. Scania trucks for defence applications are built around the modular use of components from Scania's extensive range of heavy commercial trucks, and with the absolute minimum of non-standard components. Bonneted (T-cab; later T series) trucks were withdrawn from the Scania product line during 2005.

The T144 GB6x4NZ 530 is entirely conventional in design and uses a ladder-type C-section chassis, beam-type axles and leaf spring suspension. The cab is a Scania CT19 two-door safety sleeper cab, minus bunks, these having been replaced with sufficient seating for a tank crew of four.

Swedish Army Scania T144 GB6×4NZ 530 tractor truck (T J Gander) 0056395

Scania T144 GB6x4NZ 530 tractor truck of the French Army coupled to a SOFRAME SRPB 60 six-axle semi-trailer. The payload is a component of the RSD Chubby mine detection and clearing system (Pierre Touzin)
1120413

The vehicle has a kerb weight of 13,365 kg and can be loaded to a Gross Vehicle Weight (GVW) of 38,000 kg and a Gross Combination Weight (GCW) of 150,000 kg (124,000 kg on the French Army vehicle). In all cases the technical GCW of the vehicle exceeds the maximum peacetime limited for the axle configuration within the EU.

On the Swedish Army model two Sepson H120P recovery winches are fitted, each with a capacity of 150 kN and equipped with 50 m of 19 mm diameter cable and remote control. Other equipment includes a connector for engine heating, heat exchanger, blow torch, electric engine heater, 24 V emergency connector for starting the tractor or another truck/armoured vehicle, provision for carrying camouflage equipment, two working lights, two rotating beacons, an illuminated wide transport sign, sanding equipment and snow chains.

On the Belgian Army model two Rotzler HZ 200 recovery winches are fitted, each with a capacity of 200 kN and equipped with 45 m of 7 mm diameter cable. Other equipment includes the possibility to use the rear part of the cab as two beds instead of seating, air conditioning, cab heater, connector for engine heating, 24 V emergency connector for starting the tractor or another truck/armoured vehicle, provision for carrying camouflage equipment, two working lights, two rotating beacons, an illuminated wide transport sign, sanding equipment and snow chains.

Specifications

T144 GB6×4NZ 530
Cab seating: 1 + 5 (driver, co-driver + 4 tank crew)
Configuration: 6 × 4
Weight:
  (kerb) 13,365 kg
  (GVW) 38,000 kg
  (GCW) 150,000 kg (124,000 kg, French vehicles)
Length: 8.128 m
Width: 2.6 m
Height: 3.57 m
Ground clearance:
  (front) 247 mm
  (bogie) 237 mm
Track:
  (front) 2.083 m
  (rear) 1.83 m
Wheelbase: 4.3 m + 1.445 m
Fuel capacity: 500 litres
Engine: Scania EURO II DSC1413 V-8 electronically controlled turbocharged water-cooled 4-stroke diesel developing 530 hp (390 kW) at 1,900 rpm
Gearbox: Scania GRS900R 9 speed with Scania torque converter and Scania integrated retarder
Turning radius: (with semi-trailer, total length 22.096 m) 13.5 m
Tyres: 315/80R 22.5
Brakes: dual circuit, air, drums all-round, ABS

Electrical system: 24 V
Batteries: 2 × 12 V, 180 Ah
Alternator: 90 A

Status
Production complete. In service with the Belgian (26), French (12) and Swedish (31) armies. Bonneted trucks were phased out of the Scania portfolio during 2005.

Contractor
Scania CV AB

Scania R143EK and T143E (6 × 6) and (6 × 4) tractor trucks

Development
The Scania R143EK (6 × 6) tractor truck has a forward control cab and the Scania T143E (6 × 4) tractor truck has a bonnet. Both are a development of commercial products and were designed for towing tank transporter semi-trailers. They are similar in weight, capability and overall dimensions, but differ in detail according to cab type and the engine fitted.

The Scania R143EK (6 × 6) tractor truck is in service with the Norwegian Army, the Scania T143E (6 × 4) tractor truck is in service with the Swedish Army.

The first of 19 Scania T143E tractors for the Swedish Army was handed over in March 1990; production of the rest of the batch continued until 1991. These tractor trucks were fitted with winches and were supplied with semi-trailers supplied by HAFO/VM-Trailer. The combinations are intended primarily for the transport of damaged combat vehicles.

Also in service with the Swedish Army for tank and heavy equipment transportation are Volvo N1233 (60 supplied from 1977) tractor trucks coupled to four-axle VM-Trailer semi-trailers (ordered in 1992 as a replacement for earlier Kalmar-produced DAF two-axle semi-trailers), and Scania T144 GB6x4NZ 530 (31 supplied from 1998) tractor trucks coupled to five-axle VM-Trailer semi-trailers.

Full details of the Volvo N1233 and Scania T144 GB6x4NZ 530 tractor trucks can be found elsewhere in this section.

Norway and Sweden are expected to make a joint purchase of future trucks in this category.

Scania R143EK (6 × 6) tractor truck of the Norwegian Army coupled to a Maur six-axle semi-trailer (Carl Schulze)   1391221

Scania R143EK (6 × 6) tractor truck of the Norwegian Army coupled to a Maur six-axle semi-trailer (Shaun C Connors)   1296227

Scania R143EK (6 × 6) tractor truck of the Norwegian Army coupled to a Maur six-axle semi-trailer (Shaun C Connors)   1296228

Description
Both vehicles are of entirely conventional design and employ C-section ladder-type chassis and leaf sprung beam-type axles. The T143E has a (6 × 4) driveline (an undriven front axle), the R143EK has a (6 × 6) driveline. Commercial production of both types was completed some time ago. The cabs, forward control (type CR27) on the T143E and bonneted on the R143EH, seat a driver and five passengers.

Two Sepson MAS 30/30 recovery winches are fitted, each with a capacity of 20,000 kg and equipped with 40 m of 24 mm cable. Other equipment includes two snatch blocks, an electric engine heater, 12-pin trailer connector, 24 V emergency connection, fuel heater, battery master switch, reversing lights, 24 V sockets front and rear, 20-tonne hydraulic jack, two working lights and a rotating beacon.

Specifications
Scania R143EK
Cab seating: 1 + 5
Configuration: 6 × 6
Weight:
  (kerb) 14,800 kg
  (GVW) 31,200 kg
  (GTW) 100,000 kg
  (5th wheel) 16,500 kg
Length: 7.725 m
Width: 2.49 m
Height: 3.44 m
Ground clearance:
  (front) 315 mm
  (bogie) 277 mm
Track:
  (front) 2.086 m
  (rear) 1.83 m
Wheelbase: 3.93 m + 1.45 m
Fuel capacity: 400 litres
Engine: Scania DSC 1403 water-cooled 4-stroke diesel developing 450 hp (331 kW) at 1,900 rpm
Gearbox: GRH880 10-speed with torque converter
Transfer box: GT 811
Turning radius: 9.8 m
Tyres: 315/80 × 22.5
Axles: AMD105/RP630, front; AD100/RBP830, rear
Brakes: dual circuit, air, drums all-round
Electrical system: 24 V
Batteries: 2 × 12 V, 160 Ah
Alternator: 55 A

Status
Production complete. T143E in service with the Swedish Army (19). R143EK in service with the Norwegian Army.

Contractor
Scania CV AB

Volvo FH16 (6 × 6) tank transporter

Development
The Volvo FH16 (6 × 6) tank transporter tractor truck is intended for the towing of heavy loads under extreme climatic conditions. It is based around the Volvo FH16 heavy commercial tractor truck and, being based on a commercial product, minor specification changes will be a regular occurrence as commercial truck ranges are continually revised by manufacturers.

The only known user of the Volvo FH16 tank transporter tractor truck is the Israel Defence Force (IDF). The data given in the Specification table is for IDF vehicles.

Volvo FH16 (6 × 6) tank transporter of the Israeli Army loading a Merkava MBT (Volvo)
0524735

Volvo FL12 (6 × 6) tank transporter as supplied to Poland in 2000 for trials (Volvo)
0056363

It was disclosed during 2005 that Israel's Plasan Sasa was developing a protection kit for the IDFs Volvo FH16 fleet.

The IDF also uses a number of MAN (6 × 6) tractor trucks in the tank transport role.

Description

The Volvo FH16 (6 × 6) tank transporter tractor truck has a commercial range-topping Volvo Globetrotter high-roof sleeper specification forward control all-steel cab with seating for a driver and up to five passengers. The cab may be air-conditioned and provided with a roof hatch in various sizes and positions.

Power is currently provided by a Volvo D16G six-cylinder turbocharged and intercooled diesel developing 540 (D16G540), 600 (D16G600) or 700 (D16G700) hp. This is coupled to either a Volvo I-Shift or 14-speed range change and splitter manual gearbox with or without overdrive. Maximum commercial GTW rating for the FH16 tractor truck is 100,000 kg.

IDF vehicles are powered by a 520 hp Volvo D16A-520 six-cylinder turbocharged and intercooled diesel, coupled to a ZF manual 16-speed gearbox and torque converter. GTW rating is 110,000 kg. Two 310-litre fuel tanks are provided although other capacities are an option. IDF vehicles are provided with two 25,000 kg winches. These are powered by hydraulic pumps and may be operated separately. The winches work at two speeds: high speed with a 2,000 kg traction force and low speed for 25,000 kg. High- and low-speed power take-offs are provided.

Volvo has also produced the FL12 (6 × 6) tank transporter with a gross combination weight of 100,000 kg. A single example was supplied to Poland - coupled to a ZREMB semi-trailer - in 2000 for trials.

Full details of the Volvo FL12 range can be found in the Trucks section.

Specifications

IDF vehicle
Cab seating: 1 + 5
Configuration: 6 × 6
Weight:
 (kerb) 13,000 kg
 (GVW) 41,000 kg
 (front axle load) 9,000 kg
 (max bogie load) 32,000 kg
Length: 7.985 m
Width: (over cab) 2.467 m
Height: (cab roof, unladen) 3.545 m
Wheelbase: 4.425 m + 1.37 m
Fuel capacity: 2 × 310 litres
Engine: Volvo D16A-520 16-litre electronically controlled 6-cylinder in-line water-cooled turbocharged and intercooled 4-stroke diesel developing 520 hp (382 kW) at 1,800 rpm and 2,400 N.m torque at 1,000 rpm
Gearbox: ZF 16 S 251 with 16 forward and 2 reverse gears
Transfer box: Volvo FD7 2-speed
Steering: power assisted
Tyres: 12.00R 24

Brakes: dual circuit, air, drums all-round
Suspension: front, parabolic springs; rear, multileaf springs
Electrical system: 24 V

Status
In commercial production. In service with Israel (55).

Contractor
Volvo Truck Corporation

Volvo N1233 (6 × 4) tractor truck

Development
The Volvo N1233 (6 × 4) tractor truck was developed from a commercial vehicle to meet a Swedish Army requirement for a vehicle capable of carrying out (primarily) the strategic movement of combat vehicles such as the Centurion or S-tank.

The prototype Volvo N1233 was delivered to the Swedish Army in October 1975 for field trials and the first of 60 production tractor trucks were delivered in April 1977. The two-axle semi-trailers procured with the Volvo N1233 tractor trucks were a DAF design, designated DAF YTS 10050. They were licence-produced by Kalmar of Sweden.

Upon introduction into Swedish Army service the Volvo N1233/DAF YTS 10050 combination supplemented 30 Scania LT110S 42A (6 × 4) tractor trucks with winches and DAF semi-trailers procured in the late 1960s. These earlier DAF semi-trailers were similar to those used with the Volvo N1233 tractor trucks, although the Scania-fronted combinations, these tractor trucks being winch-equipped, were used primarily for the transport of damaged combat vehicles.

The Scania LT110S 42A tractor trucks and both batches of DAF semi-trailers have been withdrawn from Swedish Army service, the last of the semi-trailers being replaced following an order placed with VM-Trailer of Gothenburg in 1992 for a batch of more road-friendly four-axle semi-trailers.

Subsequent Swedish Army tank transporter procurements have included various trailers, plus 19 Scania T143E6×4 (6 × 4) tractor trucks with semi-trailers supplied by HAFO/VM-Trailer in 1990/91, and most recently (from 1998) 31 Scania T144GB6×4NZ530 (6 × 4) tractor trucks with semi-trailers supplied by VM-Trailer.

The Volvo N1233 tractor trucks remain in service but are overdue for replacement, the decision not to extend the service life of these vehicles having been taken during FY 94/95. The procurement of the Scania T144GB6×4NZ530/VM-Trailer combination was the intended start of the replacement process.

Full details of the Scania T143E6×4 and T144GB6×4NZ530 tractor trucks can be found elsewhere in this section.

Description
The layout of the Volvo N1233 tractor truck is entirely conventional, with the engine at the front, a fully enclosed four-door all-steel cab in the centre and the fifth wheel at the rear. The crew-type cab is large enough to accommodate a tank crew of three or four in addition to the crew of the truck.

The chassis sides are of rolled C-section steel and reinforced. The vehicle is not fitted with a winch and so cannot recover disabled or damaged vehicles. The fifth wheel is a Jost JSK 25 pivoting type.

The rear drive axles are leaf sprung, the axles being of the single reduction with hub reduction type. A driver-actuated differential lock is fitted. The front steer axle is leaf sprung and 1200R 20 tyres are fitted.

Specifications
Configuration: 6 × 4
Cab seating: 5
Max weight on front axle: 6,500 kg
Max weight on rear axles: 26,000 kg (13,500 kg per axle)
Length: 7.6 m
Width: 2.5 m
Height: (overall) 3.1 m
Track:
 (front) 1.945 m
 (rear) 1.82 m
Wheelbase: 4.2 m + 1.37 m

Volvo N1233 (6 × 4) tractor truck towing a DAF YTS 10050 semi-trailer carrying a Centurion MBT; the trailers and MBTs are no longer in service, the tractor trucks are due for replacement (Volvo)
0511860

Fuel capacity: 400 litres
Engine: Volvo TP 120 A 6-cylinder water-cooled turbocharged OHV diesel developing 330 hp (243 kW) at 2,200 rpm
Gearbox: manual, 8-speed with splitter, giving 16 forward and two reverse speeds
Clutch: twin dry plate
Steering: recirculating ball and nut with built-in servo
Tyres: 12.00 × 20
Brakes:
(main) air, dual circuit
(parking) air-operated spring brakes operating directly on front and rear wheels
Suspension:
(front) semi-elliptic leaf springs with threaded spring bolt in front mounting and slipper-type anchorage at rear. Shock-absorbers and hollow rubber springs
(rear) multileaf springs with rubber springs at both ends

Status
Production complete. Sixty units delivered to the Swedish Army (1977).

Contractor
Volvo Truck Corporation

United Kingdom

Unipower M Series tank transporters

Development
The Unipower M Series tank transporters were designed to carry tanks weighing up to 75,000 kg at speeds up to 80 km/h. Two models were available, the MH8875 8 × 8 750 hp tractor and the MH6660 6 × 6 600 hp tractor.

The MH6660 6 × 6 tractor entered service with the Royal Army of Oman in 1995 to carry the Challenger 2 main battle tank and a single trials and demonstration example of the MH8875 8 × 8 tractor was built and trialed. This model never entered series production and the prototype is currently in use as a commercial heavy hauler.

Alvis Vehicles (Alvis was acquired by BAE Systems in 2004) acquired Unipower in 1994 and by 2000 had effectively ceased active marketing of the M Series and was looking to divest the assets of the former Unipower.

Future production of M Series tank transporters is now considered unlikely.

Description
The MH6660 6 × 6 tractor is powered by a 19-litre six-cylinder Cummins diesel engine rated at 600 hp. The automatic transmission consists of a ZF 5HP 1500 five-speed gearbox with an integral two-speed transfer box and hydrodynamic torque converter with integral retarder.

The rear bogie comprises two Unipower axles while the front steer-drive axle is GKN. All axles have differential locks, both cross-axle and inter-axle. The rear suspension is a centrally pivoted spring pack providing equal axle loading over uneven ground. Front suspension is by taper-leaf springs.

The engine-behind-cab configuration ensures there is no engine intrusion into the cab, maximising space for occupants and their equipment. The cab can be configured as either a six-seat crew cab or a twin sleeper cab. The cab is also low, facilitating rapid entry and exit and ease of camouflage. The ergonomically designed interior is comfortable and minimises driver fatigue.

Heavy tank casualties can be winched on to the transporter trailer with full lateral control by two Reynolds Boughton 25,000 kg hydraulic winches mounted behind the engine. The cast steel fifth wheel is of the double oscillating type.

Specifications
Model-MH6660
Cab seating: 1 + 6
Configuration: 6 × 6

Weight:
(front axle) 10,000 kg
(1st rear axle) 18,000 kg
(2nd rear axle) 18,000 kg
(GVW) 46,000 kg
(tractor, kerb) 18,200 kg
(king-pin load) 27,000 kg
Length: 9.36 m
Width: 2.89 m
Height: 2.7 m
Wheelbase: 5.5 m
Max speed: 80 km/h
Fuel capacity: 900 litres
Range: 1,000 km
Engine: Cummins KTA-19-600 19-litre turbocharged water-cooled 4-stroke diesel developing 600 hp (441 kW) at 2,100 rpm
Transmission: ZF HP1500 fully automatic, 5 forward and 1 reverse gears
Transfer box: 2-speed
Steering: power-assisted, ZF 8098
Brakes: dual circuit, air
Tyres: 395/85R 20
Electrical system: 24 V

Status
MH6660 in service with Oman (nine).

Contractor
BAE Systems

(Scammell) Unipower S24 Contractor Range (6 × 4) and (6 × 6) transporter tractors

Development
The S24 range was introduced in 1981 by Scammell, its design based on military and civilian experience gained with the earlier Contractor models.

In May 1988, Unipower Vehicles Limited acquired the design, manufacturing and support rights for the Scammell S24 range, their rear engined crash tenders, Commander, Contractor, Explorer, Super Constructor, Crusader, LDSS, Nubian Major and Thornycroft Antar models. Unipower Vehicles Limited were subsequently acquired by Alvis Vehicles Limited who were subsequently acquired by BAE Systems. BAE Systems no longer actively market the product range.

Description
The S24 Contractor range was available in 6 × 4 and 6 × 6 configuration with left- and right-hand normal control power-assisted steering.

Power outputs ranged from 400 to 600 hp utilising Cummins N & K in-line series and Perkins RF CV8 power units, coupled to manual, semi- and fully automatic transmissions. Sustained performance figures up to 32 km/h on 1 in 40 gradients at 110,000 kg GTW were available with top speeds in the 74 to 80 km/h range.

King-pin imposed loads of 25 to 28,000 kg at unrestricted speeds were available with 12.00R 24 and 14.00R 20 tyre equipment on standard and wide track axles. All driving axles of the spiral bevel epicyclic hub reduction type are equipped with inter- and cross-lockable differentials actuated by air pressure from the cab. Front-wheel drive variants can be disengaged from the cab via the single-speed transposing box as dictated by terrain considerations.

Dual circuit primary air braking with secondary spring and parking brakes are provided, while manual transmission vehicles are equipped with engine brakes and the semi-automatic variants have integral hydraulic retarders.

Suspension is of the semi-elliptic leaf spring type with telescopic hydraulic damping at the front. High ground clearance is achieved by the fully articulating centre trunnion mounted rear springs.

An all-steel bonneted cab accommodates the driver and two passengers whilst the optional extended version can accommodate five seated passengers.

Unipower MH6660 (6 × 6) 600 hp (441 kW) tank transporter in service with the Royal Army of Oman (Unipower) 0009770

Scammell S24 Contractor (6 × 6) HET (Scammell) 1391003

Dual hydraulically driven, independently operated 20,000 kg winches are fitted behind the cab and are supplied with 50 m of 24 mm rope in an end drum.

A full set of tools and equipment associated with the transporter role are provided, together with up to two spare wheels and tyres.

Specifications

CA45
Cab seating: 1 + 2 or 1 + 5
Configuration: 6 × 6
Weight:
  (front axle, laden) 9,000 kg
  (rear bogie, laden) 36,000 kg
  (GVW) 45,000 kg
  (GCW) 100,000 kg
Length: 8.475 m
Width: 2.868 m
Height: 3.298 m
Wheelbase: 5.42 m
Max speed: 80 km/h
Fuel capacity: 900 litres
Engine: Cummins NTE 400 turbocharged and aftercooled, water-cooled 4-stroke diesel developing 400 hp (294 kW) at 2,100 rpm
Transmission: Eaton Fuller RTX 14615, 15 forward speeds
Clutch: twin plate (394 mm)
Transfer box: Unipower single-speed
Tyres: 14.00R 20
Brakes: dual circuit, air
Electrical system: 24 V

Status
Production complete. In service in the Middle East.

Contractor
BAE Systems (This company no longer markets this product.)

Scammell Commander (6 × 4) tractor truck

Development
The Scammell Commander tractor truck was developed to meet the requirements of the British Army for a new tractor truck to replace its ageing Thornycroft Antars and to carry the Challenger 1 MBT. Design work on the Commander began in 1976 with the first three prototypes being completed in 1978. Two of these were powered by the Rolls-Royce CV12 TCE diesel and the third by an American Cummins KTA 600 diesel.

In 1981, there was a General Staff Requirement (GSR) for a vehicle similar to the Commander but, as a result of defence spending cuts, the GSR was not endorsed at the time. However, in late 1982 an order for 125 Commanders for the British Army was placed. The first examples were delivered in late 1983, with production continuing into 1985. By 1999 the fleet had reduced to 120 vehicles.

In January 1992 Unipower (later Alvis Vehicles, now BAE Systems) was awarded a contract for the in-depth repair of an undisclosed pilot quantity of Commander tractor trucks. The contract involved total strip-down and refurbishing, where necessary, with new parts.

A later contract was awarded to the then Army Base Repair Organisation (ABRO) for an In-Depth Repair (IDR) programme for the full Commander fleet. This took place at ABRO's Bovington facility. Numbers were subsequently reduced and only 81 vehicles were refurbished, later examples to a standard below that of full In-Depth Repair (IDR). The programme concluded during 2002.

Although designed for towing semi-trailers carrying AFVs weighing up to 65,000 kg, the Commander can also be used for high-speed haulage of heavy indivisible loads. A small number were sold commercially.

During 1999 it was announced that as the British Army's Commanders were nearing the end of their planned life, a Private Finance Initiative (PFI) project would be used to select the replacement. Four bids were invited of which two were selected for further consideration. The two consortia concerned were FASTTRAX composed of Brown and Root teamed with the Oshkosh Truck Corporation, and DHT, a team of SERCo Military and MAN.

In January 2001 it was announced that the FASTTRAX consortium were to be awarded the GBP300 million whole-life cost contract to replace the Commander fleet. The tractor-trailer combination selected consists of an Oshkosh 1070F (8 × 8) based on the US Army 1070 variant of which around 2,700 examples are currently in service, the majority (around 2,500) with the US Army. The semi-trailer selected is a King GTS 100 seven axle design, capable of carrying 72,000 kg payload in peacetime while meeting all known and proposed legislation. Full details of both types can be found elsewhere in this section.

Following withdrawal from service with UK Armed Forces the bulk of the Scammell Commander fleet were transferred to Jordan. The first batch of 39 vehicles, freed up from British Army service in Iraq, were driven from Iraq to Kuwait and shipped by sea to Aqaba in Jordan for driver and maintenance training in JAF service late 2003. A further 20 vehicles were later shipped from Iraq as the new Oshkosh 1070F HET was introduced into British Army service in-country.

All the vehicles from the UK were supplied to the JAF in a roadworthy condition with a package of spares. Where repairs were required, vehicles from the UK and units in Germany were put through an inspection and repair process at the then ABRO facility at Bovington and the Ashchurch vehicle depot. The first batch of seven refurbished JAF Commanders from the UK, which retained their British Army paint scheme, were shipped from Marchwood Military Port to Aqaba, Jordan, in June 2004.

ABRO sent a mobile support team to the King Hussein Main Workshops in Zarqa where the Commanders are to be maintained. The UK also supplied specialist support equipment and spares to support the JAF Commander tank transporter fleet, which is understood to supplement a current JAF fleet of older Scammell Contractor 6 × 4 tank transporters.

The JAF Commander tank transporter programme is part of the UK's Al Hussein Project, which is under the leadership of the UK's Disposal Services Agency, part of the Defence Export Services Organisation of the UK Ministry of Defence. Under the first phase of the Al Hussein Project, 402 Challenger 1 MBTs were supplied to the JAF, with the first batch of 14 being delivered late in 1999 following their overhaul by ABRO. In JAF service, these are known as the Al Hussein and replace the older Tariq (upgraded Centurion MBT) and some Khalid MBTs (Chieftain/Challenger hybrids originally designed for Iran in the 1970s).

Description
The Scammell Commander tractor truck has the engine at the front, an all-steel cab in the centre, a winch located to the rear of the cab and the fifth wheel over the bogie at the rear.

The cab is arranged for left-hand drive and incorporates noise-insulating material. A two-piece flat glass windscreen with an electric heating element on the driver's side is provided. For crew access, large steps are fitted and full interior heating and ventilating equipment is standard. The cab has individual seats for the commander and driver, behind which is a bench seat for two personnel which can be positioned to form two individual bunks, one above the other.

The chassis is of steel channel side members with bolted-in, fabricated and tubular cross members. There are heavy-duty members at the front and rear for towing, lifting and recovery.

The front axle is a Scammell 12,200 kg capacity steer-only unit. Lock angles of 40° give high manoeuvrability. The rear axle is a Scammell 40,700 kg capability double drive bogie comprising two hub reduction axles linked by a lockable third differential for increased traction on poor surfaces. The fully articulated fifth wheel has an imposed load capacity of 34,600 kg.

A heavy-duty Rotzler winch is standard for the Commander for self-loading dead loads and the tractor is fully equipped with recovery fittings. The 20,300 kg line pull horizontal winch has 110 m of 26 mm diameter rope. The winch is fitted with an automatic pay-on gear and has a fail-safe brake. A high rope warning and an automatic overload cut-out is provided. The rope can be led out over the neck of the semi-trailer or through fairleads at the rear of the chassis. Winch controls are mounted behind the cab in a weatherproof enclosure.

Scammell Commander (6 × 4) tractor truck and semi-trailer
(Shaun C Connors)   0109606

The first ABRO-prepared Scammell Commander (6 × 4) tractor truck and
semi-trailer destined for Jordan (Christopher F Foss)   0577752

Specifications

Scammell Commander
Cab seating: 1 + 3 or 4
Configuration: 6 × 4
Weight:
(tractor unit) 19,920 kg
(weight on front axle, tractor unit solo) 9,680 kg
(weight on rear bogie, tractor unit solo) 10,240 kg
(GCW) 104,000 kg
Length: 9.01 m
Width: 3.25 m
Height: 3.5 m
Wheelbase: 5.03 m
Max speed: (with semi-trailer and 65,000 kg load) 61 km/h
Fuel capacity: 817 litres
Gradient: 20%
Fording: 760 mm
Engine: Rolls-Royce CV12 TCE 60° V-12 turbocharged and water-cooled 4-stroke diesel developing 625 hp (459 kW) at 2,100 rpm
Gearbox: Allison CLBT 6061 6 speed epicyclic with torque converter permitting gear changes to be made under power. Hydraulic retarder for speed control on hills to supplement wheel brakes
Steering: hydraulic power-assisted
Suspension: leaf springs front and rear with telescopic dampers to front; 2-spring high-articulation rear bogie suspension ensures equal wheel loads
Tyres: 14.00 × 24
Brakes: twin leading shoe wedge brakes with automatic adjustment on all wheels, operated by 2 air circuits; 2-line couplings for trailer connections and additional couplings for double heading
Electrical system: 24 V
Batteries: 6 × 12 V, 100 Ah

Status

Withdrawn from British Army service (120 delivered); transferred to Jordan (approx. 100).

Contractor

Scammell Motors

Enquiries to:
BAE Systems, Land Systems UK - Weapons and Vehicles

United States

Oshkosh 1070F (8 × 8) Heavy Equipment Transporter (HET)

Development

Production of the Oshkosh M1070 Heavy Equipment Transporter (HET) began in 1992 and more than 2,800 examples have so far been manufactured, primarily for the US Army. The more powerful M1070E model was developed in conjunction with the US Army as a possible Technology Insertion Programme (TIP) for their M1070 fleet. In 1997, as the M1070E1, this vehicle was offered to the UK MoD for the British Army's Heavy Equipment Transporter requirement as a Private Finance Initiative (PFI) solution by the FASTTRAX consortium consisting of Brown & Root (later Kellogg Brown & Root, now KBR), Deutsche Bank and the then Oshkosh Truck Corporation. At this stage seven consortia were bidding for the UK contract. This was subsequently short-listed to two, FASTTRAX and Defence Heavy Equipment (Serco Military teamed with MAN). The FASTTRAX consortia was awarded the GBP290 million whole-life cost 20-year PFI contract for 92 tractor trucks, 89 King GTS 110/7 semi-trailers, three Tru-Hitch recovery systems, plus staff to operate them as Sponsored Reserves in January 2001. The contract award included an option, to be exercised by June 2003, for an additional 28 systems. The option was not exercised. The original UK requirement called for 120 HET systems.

A pair of British Army 1070F HETs with additional armour protection shown on deployed operations (Carl Schulze) 1391135

The tractor truck selected by the UK MoD is the Oshkosh 1070F model, a much-revised M1070E1. The UK requirement stated that in both unladen and laden condition the combination (tractor and trailer) should be fully compliant with all current and known pending relevant legislation. This included meeting EURO 3 exhaust emission levels. The M1070E1 model is powered by a Detroit Diesel Series 60 DDEC III 14-litre six-cylinder turbocharged and aftercooled diesel, that can produce a maximum of 630 hp within EURO 3 emission levels. At the UK MoD's original 64,000 kg payload requirement a 630 hp engine was sufficient to meet performance requirements, but when it became clear the programme would develop to require a 72,000 kg payload, a more powerful engine was needed. The resultant 1070F is powered by a Caterpillar EURO 3 emissions compliant diesel, driving through an Allison seven-speed automatic gearbox and Oshkosh single-speed transfer box.

The first production model came to the UK in 2002 where Ricardo Vehicle Engineering handled final Type Approval issues. The new HET system has been issued to three regiments, two in the UK and one in Germany. The first UK HET lift was an AS90 self-propelled artillery system in July 2003. The first system was delivered to Germany in August 2003.

Oshkosh completed the last of the 92 1070F vehicles in December 2003, with final deliveries to the UK made early 2004. Some vehicles were immediately deployed to Iraq and by late 2005 some of these had covered in excess of 45,000 km. One complete system (tractor and trailer) has been lost.

Oshkosh supplied a quantity of riot protection kits with these vehicles, and during 2005 Permali Gloucester supplied 17 ballistic protection kits. Protection for the 1070F has since been further upgraded and includes a bar armour package, a protected weapon station and electronic countermeasures equipment.

The latest armouring package fitted to the 1070F is Tarian. An alternative to RPG-protecting bar armour, Tarian remains classified but is described as consisting of a range of complex interlaced fabrics and other undisclosed materials inside a protective outer coating. According to its manufacturer, it is 85 per cent lighter than steel bar armour and half the weight of aluminium systems. The UK MoD ordered an initial 20 sets during 2009 and these have since been fitted and deployed.

Description

The Oshkosh 1070F HET shares a common chassis and axle set-up with the M1070 model, but the cab and all major driveline components have been substantially revised to meet both performance and legislative requirements.

Oshkosh 1070F HET clearly showing the fifth wheel arrangement and steering third axle of the tridem rear bogie (Shaun C Connors) 0567961

Oshkosh 1070F HET (Patrick Allen) 1067543

Oshkosh 1070F HET and King GTS110/7 semi-trailer laden with a pair of Warrior IFVs (Shaun C Connors)   0567960

The all-steel two-door cab seats six, the driver and front passenger on suspension seats, the rear four passengers on a fixed bench seat that converts into bunks for two.

The in-service M1070 has a rated GCW of 104,961 kg and is powered by a Detroit Diesel Model 8V92TA DDEC 12.1-litre V8 turbocharged and aftercooled diesel developing 500 hp at 2,100 rpm and 1,993 N.m torque at 1,200 rpm. A prime requirement of the US Army's TIP was improved performance, particularly gradeability, and the M1070E1 was fitted with a Detroit Diesel Series 60 DDEC 14-litre six-cylinder in-line turbocharged and aftercooled diesel developing 600 hp at 2,300 rpm. The Allison CLT-754 5F/1R automatic transmission, TC-496 torque converter and Oshkosh 55000 two-speed transfer box of the M1070 were replaced by the more driver-friendly and efficient Allison HD 4070PR 7F/1R automatic transmission, TC-551 torque converter and Oshkosh 30000 single-speed transfer box on the E1 model.

The 1070F is fitted with the Caterpillar C18 engine, an 18.1 litre six-cylinder in-line turbocharged and aftercooled diesel unit developing 700 hp and 2,576 N.m torque at 1,300 rpm. This provides more than sufficient power to meet the MoD's performance requirements and the 1070F, at its 118,050 kg GCW, is capable of maintaining 80 km/h on primary roads, 38 km/h on a 2.5 per cent gradient, can climb a continuous 15 per cent gradient, and stop, hold and restart on a 20 per cent gradient. The transmission has been further upgraded, now consisting of an Allison HD 4076P automatic transmission and TC-561 torque converter, coupled to the Oshkosh 30000 single-speed transfer box proven in the E1 model. Cooling is provided by an eight-blade 864 mm diameter thermostatically controlled fan and 11,845 cm² fin and tube type radiator core.

The 1070F shares it chassis, axles and suspension with the M1070 model, the conventional 9.6 m long 356 × 89 × 9.5 mm C-section chassis being constructed from SAE 1027 modified, heat treated carbon manganese steel with a minimum yield strength of 110,000 psi (758 MPa). This mounts a 3.5 in (89 mm) fully floating kingpin with a maximum load of 23,600 kg, and twin dp Manufacturing 24,947 kg capacity hydraulic winches, each with 67 m of 25 mm cable. A single dp Manufacturing 1,216 kg capacity auxiliary winch with 106 m of 6 mm cable is also fitted.

The front Rockwell SVI 5MR steer-drive axle is rated at 10,886 kg and sprung by Hendrickson parabolic taper leaf springs. The rear Tridem unit is made up of Rockwell SVI 5MR units rated at 11,340 kg each and is sprung by Hendrickson-Turner air suspension. The rearmost axle is a steer-drive unit, and all four axles feature planetary hub reduction. Drum brakes are fitted on all axles, a Bendix Anti-lock Braking System (ABS) being provided for on-road use.

Unlike the (6 × 4) Scammell Commander it has replaced, the 1070F was designed to be capable of negotiating unimproved roads or tracks at its GCW. Full-time (8 × 8) drive is provided, torque being split 30/70 on axle

Oshkosh 1070F HET of the British Army fitted with bar armour (Nick Brown)   1330791

two. To prevent wheelspin on slippery surfaces an Automatic Traction Control (ATC) system that works via the ABS by applying braking force to any spinning wheel, is fitted. Michelin 16.00R 20 XZLT tyres are standard fit and when the Central Tyre Inflation (CTI) system (which allows the driver to adjust tyre pressures to suit the terrain being crossed) is engaged, the ABS adopts off-road mode and ATC is disengaged. Longitudinal and cross axle differential are then automatically engaged progressively throughout the CTI system's cross-country, mud-sand-snow, and emergency settings. The driver retains full manual override of the system.

The 1070F is capable of operating throughout a −45°C to +49°C temperature range. The 950-litre (250 gallon) fuel capacity gives a cruising range (at GCW) of 480 km and a Battlefield Mission range of 745 km. The UK requirement calls for a minimum of 500 km between mission failures; 70 per cent on-road, 30 per cent on prepared tracks.

Oshkosh M1070A1 (8 × 8) Heavy Equipment Transporter (HET)
To meet the ongoing needs of the US Army, in March 2008 Oshkosh Defense announced it had been awarded a single source contract valued at more than USD11 million (for Phase 1) from the US Army to begin engineering and initial production of the next-generation of Heavy

King GTS110/7 semi-trailer coupled to a Oshkosh 1070F. The outriggers that are required when transporting wider loads such as the AS90 (shown) or Challenger 2 MBT are in use (Patrick Allen) 1067528

Equipment Transporter (HET). The HET A1 programme is based around a power increase for the current M1070 as the US Army recognises that payload requirements for the M1A1 Abrams have increased considerably in recent years. The first production HET A1s rolled out in December 2010.

The M1070A1 is similar to the British Army's 1070F, sharing an essentially common driveline with it, however, for the purpose of continuity available details of the M1070A1 (and Global HET (6 × 6)) can be found in the M1070 entry elsewhere in this section.

King GTS110/7 stepframe semi-trailer

In 1997, in conjunction with the Oshkosh M1070E1, this trailer as a six-axle design (the GTS100/6) was offered to the UK MoD as the trailer component of the British Army's Heavy Equipment Transporter requirement. At the UK MoD's original 64,000 kg payload requirement, a six-axle trailer was sufficient to meet European axle loading requirements, but when it became clear the programme would develop to require a 72,000 kg payload, a seven-axle trailer became needed.

The first 20 production trailers became available to the British Army mid-2003 and deliveries of the 89 trailers required were complete by mid-2004.

The King GTS110/7 is one of a range of stepframe Main Battle Tank (MBT) transporters offered by King, specifically designed to comply with EC legislation applicable to military operations in Europe. The seven-axle GTS110/7 has a 75,000 kg capacity for carrying MBTs at highway speeds over metalled roads. The deck length design allows for the transport of two lighter armoured vehicles, such as the Warrior Infantry Fighting Vehicle (IFV), as an option to a single MBT.

The trailer can be designed to be compatible with all main truck/tractors and features a high articulation neck for operations in off-highway conditions. The heavy-duty frame construction incorporates a 'live' gooseneck to enable full truck traction and load equalisation to be maintained.

Adjustable track guides and stops are provided to suit a wide variety of military armoured and engineering equipment, and loading is via a pair of hydraulic side-shift adjustable loading ramps. Manual override is available for the loading ramps. Heavy-duty outriggers allow loading of the wide and heavy load, but their retraction then allows an unladen combination to travel without escort and convoy restrictions.

The trailer suspension is designed to have the capacity to allow the laden combination to maintain convoy speeds with at least one tyre station damaged. Wider tyres can be fitted for use over soft surfaces. The first and fourth to seventh axles steer.

King GTS110/7 semi-trailer, unladen and uncoupled. The outriggers (required when transporting wider loads such as the Challenger 2 MBT) are folded away (Shaun C Connors) 0547594

Following a number of tyre/suspension, stability and mobility failings on deployed operations, it was disclosed late-2008 that a project to procure a fleet of trailers better suited to conditions on current deployed operations had commenced. Three trailer types not hindered by the design compromises brought about by full legislative compliance were believed to be under consideration.

It was disclosed late-2009 that Broshuis of Holland had been selected to supply 20 heavy-duty 45-tonne payload full-width two-axle trailers.

Specifications

1070F
Cab seating: 1 + 1 + 4
Configuration: 8 × 8
Weights:
  (kerb) 20,100 kg
  (GVW) 44,900 kg
  (GCW) 118,050 kg
  (typical load on 5th wheel) 16,000 kg
  (max load on 5th wheel) 23,600 kg
Length: 9.603 m
Width: 2.67 m
Height: 3.975 m
Height: (5th wheel) 1.616 m
Track: 2.083 m
Wheelbase: 3.937 + 1.524 + 1.524 m
Max speed:
  (primary road at GCW) 80.4 km/h
  (2.5% gradient at GCW) 38 km/h
Range: (cruising) 724 km
Fuel capacity: 946 litres
Gradient: (at GCW) 15%
Fording: 750 mm
Engine: Caterpillar C18 EURO 3 emissions compliant 18.1-litre 6-cylinder in-line turbocharged and aftercooled, water-cooled 4-stroke diesel developing 700 hp (522 kW) and 2,576 N.m torque at 1,300 rpm
Transmission: Allison HD 4076P 7-speed with TC-561 torque converter, allowing second gear start
Transfer box: Oshkosh 30000 single-speed, full-time all-wheel drive with air-activated lock-up
Steering: power assisted with front and rear axle co-ordinated steer
Turning radius: (wall) 30.5 m
Suspension:
  (front) springs and hydraulic shock-absorbers front
  (rear) air ride
Tyres: 16.00R 20 XLZT with CTI system
Brakes: dual circuit, air-actuated S-cam, drums all-round. ABS fitted
Electrical system: 24 V
Batteries: 4 × 12 V
Alternator: 28 V, 260 Ah

GTS110/7
Weights:
  (approx unladen) 26,500 kg
  (max load, approx) 75,000 kg
Length: (overall) 17 m
Width: 2.9 m
Tyres: 285/70R 19.5 (Michelin XTE 2)

Status

Oshkosh 1070F: Production as required. In service with the British Army (92 supplied).

King GTS110/7: Production as required. In service with the British Army (89 supplied).

Broshuis 45-tonne semi-trailer: Production as required. In service with the British Army (20).

Contractor

Oshkosh Truck Corporation
King Trailers Ltd

Oshkosh M911 (8 × 6/6 × 6) heavy equipment transporter and 604N and 635NL tank transport semi-trailers

Development

Early in 1976 the US Army issued a requirement for a tractor truck that - among other things - at 190,034 lbs (86,183 kg) could stop and restart on a 20 per cent gradient, maintain 14 mph (22.5 km/h) on a three per cent gradient, and 45 mph (71 km/h) on level ground. It was also to be capable of operation throughout a –32°C to +52°C temperature range without the need for additional preparation, and down to –46°C with preparation. The requirement also called for the base design to have been in production as a standard model for at least one year.

In September 1976 the US Army awarded the then Oshkosh Truck Corporation contract DAAE07-76-C-4405 for a total of 774 vehicles designated M911 and based on the Oshkosh F2365 commercial tractor. A total of 747 of these were for the US Army, the remaining 27 ordered as Foreign Military Sales (FMS) through the US Army for various countries including Yemen and possibly Oman and Thailand.

In US Army service the M911 would be coupled to a M747 four-axle semi-trailer manufactured by the now defunct Consolidated Diesel Electric Company. The M747 (Condec C2288) had originally been designed as part of the to-be-cancelled Heavy Equipment Transporter for the 1970s (HET-70) project and was a joint development by Chrysler (US) and Faun and Krupp of Germany. Small numbers (66 as of late-2008) of the M747 remain in US Army service.

The M911 remains in US Army service with National Guard units and the US Army Reserve, although numbers are reducing and by late-2008 no more than 50 remained. The original US Army contract, for which production concluded in November 1980, contained an option for a further 445 vehicles. This was not exercised by the time production of the M911 ceased in May 1992.

The US Air Force ordered 2 M911s under contract F08651-85-C-0016 awarded in February 1985. These were delivered by December 1985.

The M911 tractor truck was replaced in the Oshkosh product line-up by the purpose-designed M1070 HET, full details of which can be found elsewhere in this section.

At least 1,722 M911s had been produced when production ceased and the type is known to have seen service with more than nine different armed forces.

In addition to US armed forces and the undisclosed FMS recipients under the original US Army contract, other M911 users include:

- Thailand: received 12 tractor trucks, without trailers, in 1981.
- Oman: received 15 tractor trucks, without trailers, in 1985. Mid-2005 Oman received three Oshkosh/Fontaine 635NL semi-trailers and disclosed plans to refurbish its M911 fleet with the probable assistance of Oshkosh Truck. Full details of the Oshkosh/Fontaine 635NL trailer can be found elsewhere in this entry.
- Morocco: ordered 20 vehicles complete with Oshkosh/Fontaine 604N trailers in 1988. The trailers were optimised for the transport of the M60 Main Battle Tank (MBT), of which around 300 are currently in service with the Moroccan Army. Full details of the Oshkosh/Fontaine 604N trailer can be found elsewhere in this entry.
- Taiwan: received 16 tractor trucks, without trailers, in 1989.
- Thailand: received a further 26 tractor trucks and 13 Oshkosh/Fontaine 604N trailers in 1989. Thirteen tractor trucks and the trailers supplied under US Army FMS (Foreign Military Sales) contract DAAE07-89-C-0939.

- Taiwan: received a further 11 tractor trucks, without trailers, in 1992.
- Saudi Arabia: received 760 tractor trucks and 760 Oshkosh/Fontaine 635NL trailers under FMS contract DAAE07-91-C-0987 valued at USD195.7 million and awarded by the US Army in March 1991. Production was completed in May 1992.
- Greece: received 71 vehicles, without trailers, in 1991/92 under FMS contract DAAE07-91-C-0987. Greece also received a further 16 vehicles as US surplus. The Hellenic Army is known to use the NK AP-140/58T semi-trailer with the Oshkosh M911. The NK AP-140/58T tank transporter semi-trailer was shown for the first time at the Defendory '96 exhibition in Greece, and can be described as a further development of the earlier 60,000 kg payload NK AP-130/60 T semi-trailer. The NK AP-140/58 T was designed to carry tanks and heavy engineering plant weighing up to 58,000 kg, and improvements included a longer loadbed than the earlier NK AP-130/60 T design. An order was placed for approximately 80 trailers to be delivered during 1998. In 2001, Greece transferred an unspecified (but small) number of M911s to Cyprus for use as tractor trucks with the Russian-built TOR M1 SAM system; these were later returned.
- Oman: received a further 15 vehicles, without trailers, under the same FMS contract as the original Greek deliveries.

A minimum of 1,722 M911s were produced throughout the 1976 to 1992 production run.

Description

The layout of the Oshkosh M911 tractor truck is entirely conventional, being based on a C-section chassis manufactured from carbon manganese heat-treated steel with a yield strength of 110,000 psi (758 MPa). The power unit is mounted at the front of the chassis under a large bonnet, the three-person all-steel cab is in the centre, twin Braden 20,412 kg ea. capacity winches and 914 mm (36 in) fully oscillating fifth wheel with 89 mm (3.5 in) kingpin, towards the rear. The prominent front grille shields 12,904 cm² of radiator, the eight-blade thermostatically-controlled fan also providing the cooling for the transmission and torque converter oil coolers.

Motive power is provided by a Detroit Diesel 8V92TA-90 12.06-litre V-8 two-stroke water-cooled diesel developing 435 hp (450 hp in later vehicles, and certainly those supplied to Saudi Arabia) at 2,100 rpm and peak torque of 1,684 N.m at 1,400 rpm. An Allison CLBT-750 automatic transmission (CLBT-754 in vehicles supplied to Saudi Arabia) giving five forward and one reverse gears is coupled to an Allison TC-499 torque converter and Oshkosh single-speed transfer box with 30/70 torque proportioning and a driver-controlled planetary differential lock. Built-in inhibitors prevent downshift or reverse shift at excessive speeds.

Oshkosh M911 (8 × 6) tractor truck of the US Army clearly showing the second undriven lift-axle specific to the 747 vehicles delivered to the US Army under the first (and only) US Army contract. With the possible exception of the 27 FMS vehicles involved in the original US Army contract, all other M911 deliveries featured a 6 × 6 driveline (Oshkosh)
0524746

Oshkosh M911 (6 × 6) tractor truck of the Moroccan Army coupled to an Oshkosh/Fontaine 604N semi-trailer (Oshkosh)   1128709

Oshkosh M911 (6 × 6) tractor truck of the Moroccan Army. Note the extra wide sand-type tyres on the front axle (Oshkosh)   1128706

Oshkosh M911 (6 × 6) tractor truck pre-delivery to the Royal Army of Oman (Oshkosh)   1156029

Oshkosh M911 (6 × 6) tractor truck of the Royal Army of Oman coupled to a separately procured semi-trailer (Oshkosh)   1128707

Saudi Arabian Oshkosh M911 (6 × 6) tractor truck coupled to an Oshkosh/Fontaine 635NL semi-trailer carrying an M1A1 Abrams MBT (Oshkosh)   0524747

A pair of Hellenic Army Oshkosh M911 tank transporters coupled to Nik Kioleides NK AP-140/58 T tank transport semi-trailers (Periklis Zorzovilis)   1128206

Maximum geared speed is 45 mph and unladen the M911 has a maximum range (on 757 litres (200 US gallons)) of 1,344 km. At a GCW of 86,183 kg up to 990 km can be covered at economical cruising speed. US Army vehicles are fitted with a 100 US gallon tank (RH-side) and a 50 US gallon tank (LH-side).

Three axles are driven, the M911s supplied to the US Army (and possibly the 27 supplied via FMS under the original contract) are fitted with an additional 'pusher axle' rated at 9,072 kg. This is air-suspended, undriven and when lowered (and depending on payload and 5th wheel load) reduces the loading on the rear bogie to approximately 11,340 kg per axle. All other M911s manufactured were of standard 6 × 6 configuration.

The front Oshkosh-designed steer-drive axle is rated at 10,433 kg, the rear bogie axles are Eaton DPRP-650 units on US Army vehicles (Eaton DP651-P on most others), the bogie being rated at 29,484 kg. There is a driver-controlled inter-axle differential lock. Suspension is by 760 mm × 219 mm Hotchkiss semi-elliptic leaf springs, front, and Hendrickson RT500 multi-leaf with 1.524 m equalising beam, rear. Standard tyres are 14R 24 18-ply, although there were options available.

Drum brakes are fitted all-round, these having a dual air supply system, one for the front and one for the rear axles. If the air system that supplies the front brakes fails, the rear brakes can be operated normally. If the rear system fails, the front system as well as the rear spring chamber will still remain pressurised. The main braking system is supplemented by a foot pedal-controlled hydraulic retarder in the transmission that can absorb up to 80 per cent of the engine's horsepower.

Oshkosh 604N and 635NL tank transport semi-trailers

The Oshkosh 604N and 635NL tank transport semi-trailers are the most common trailers used with the Oshkosh M911 tank transporter, and approaching 1,000 examples of these two trailers have been built to date. Production of the 604N trailer is now considered complete, but could be resumed on receipt of further orders. Production of the 635NL trailer is on an 'as required' basis.

The 604N and 635NL trailers are manufactured by Fontaine Specialized Inc, part of the Marmon Herrington Group, but were designed by Oshkosh Truck Corporation. Original deliveries were manufactured by Liddell Birmingham prior to this company's acquisition by the Marmon Herrington Group in 1993.

The 604N and 635NL trailers are of all-steel construction with ASTMA 514 main beams and steel treadplate decking. The 604N has a shorter loadbed than the 635NL, which, with its longer loadbed, was designed to be capable of transporting two lighter armoured vehicles (M113 APCs or similar) as an option to a single MBT. Loading ramps are 2.69 m in length and spring assisted. Both designs are suitable for on- and off-road use, the 604N being a four-axle design, the 635NL a five-axle design on which the rearmost axle steers. The four main axles common to both designs are rated at 13,608 kg each and sprung by Neway 4120 spring suspension. The fifth steer-axle on the 635NL model is rated at 11,340 kg and has Turner air suspension.

In addition to the Oshkosh M911 tractor truck, Saudi Arabia also operates 50 Oshkosh M1070 tractor trucks, delivered during 1993 in the tank transporter role, and the 635NL trailers delivered include a number of specific design modifications that enable them to operate with both types of tractor truck.

In addition to users already covered, the 635NL trailer has also been supplied to Egypt, Oman and Jordan.

Since early 2003 and an initial order for 100, Egypt has ordered around 250 examples purchased under a US Foreign Military Funding (FMF) contract, with additional follow-on orders expected in the future.

Prior to original contract award, a prototype trailer was produced and tested in various stages in Egypt. Testing included: 3,000 km with the maximum payload of 70,000 kg on paved roads; 1,500 km with the maximum payload of 63,500 kg on unpaved secondary roads; 1,000 km with the maximum 63,500 kg on trails; load and unload M1A1 Main Battle Tank (MBT) with all accessories - 10 iterations; load and unload M88A2 ARV - 20 iterations; lower and raise ramps - 25 iterations; loaded 635NL left to stand on landing legs for 10 hours; 25 U-turns to the left and 25 U-turns to the right; 50 repetitive starts and stops on a 15 per cent gradient; load and unload M1A1 MBT by the use of the recovery winches ten - 10 iterations, and 25 sudden brake stops from 50 km/h on paved roads, all in a laden condition.

These trailers were co-produced and supplied in Semi-KnockDown kits (SKD). Insertion of 30 per cent local content, final assembly, final paint and final test took place at the Egyptian Tank Plant. Final testing was performed on a single random 635NL from a monthly production lot. Each selected trailer was loaded and unloaded - 10 iterations, loaded and unloaded utilising the M1070 recovery winches - 10 iterations; each underwent five sudden-brake tests in a loaded condition, and was road-tested over 250 km in a loaded condition. All loaded conditions were performed utilising an M88A2 currently in production at the Egyptian Tank Plant.

Egyptian 635NL trailers are used with Oshkosh M1070 tractor trucks, acquired on a one-for-one basis under the same contract.

Oshkosh Truck won an order early 2003 for the supply of 50 635NL trailers (on a one-to-one basis with M1070 tractor trucks) to Jordan. These were delivered during 2004 and have part-replaced a quantity of time-served Scammell vehicles.

Three 635NL trailers were supplied to Oman mid-2005.

During 2010 it was disclosed that Oshkosh had been awarded a contract through the US Army's TACOM Life Cycle Managemnet Command (LCMC) worth in excess of USD40 million to supply the Iraqi Army with 60 M1070A0 HETs complete with Oshkosh 635NL trailers. Deliveries under this contract, which includes operator training, spare parts and manuals, should be complete by May 2011.

Specifications
M911 Saudi Arabian specification
Cab seating: 1 + 2
Configuration: 6 × 6
Weight:
(kerb) 18,144 kg
(GVW) 39,463 kg
(max GCW) 102,514 kg
(nominal load on 5th wheel) 20,866 kg
Length: 9.373 m
Width:
(over bumpers) 2.438 m
(rear wheels) 2.896 m
Height:
(overall) 3.404 m
(cab) 3.175 m
(5th wheel, no load) 1.626 m
Track:
(front) 2.083 m
(rear) 2.057 m
Wheelbase: 5.207 + 1.524 m
Max speed:
(road, at max GCW) 72 km/h
(3% gradient, at max GCW) 23 km/h
Range:
(no payload, maximum speed) 1,344 km
(at 86,183 kg GCW, economical speed) 990 km
Fuel capacity: 757 litres
Max gradient: (at max GCW) 20%
Fording: 711 mm
Engine: Detroit Diesel model 8V92TA-90 12.06-litre V-8 water-cooled 2-stroke diesel developing 450 hp (336 kW) at 2,100 rpm and 1,684 N.m torque at 1,400 rpm

Transmission: Allison CLBT-754 automatic with 5 forward and 1 reverse gears and hydraulic retarder, plus Allison TC-499 torque converter
Transfer case: Oshkosh Model 7038 single-speed
Auxiliary transmission: Fuller AT 1202 2-speed
Steering: hydraulic, dual power-assisted at front
Turning radius: 13.72 m
Suspension:
  (front) Hotchkiss type with 760 × 219 mm semi-elliptic main springs with Berlin eye and semi-elliptic auxiliary spring
  (rear) Hendrickson RT-500 multi leaf, equalising beam design with 1.524 m spread
Tyres: 14R 24 (options were available)
Brakes: dual-circuit, air, S-type drums all-round
Electrical system: 24 V
Batteries: 4 × 12 V, 100 Ah
Alternator: 65 A

635NL
Max load:
  (on-road) 70,000 kg
  (off-road) 63,500 kg
Length:
  (overall) 14.85 m
  (deck) 10.237 m
Height:
  (deck) 1.2 m
  (5th wheel) 1.57 m
Tyres: (18 + 2 spare) 315/80R 22.5
Max speed:
  (on-road, 72,000 kg payload) 45 km/h
  (off-road, 63,500 kg payload) 24 km/h

Status
M911 tractor truck: Production complete. Supplied to Greece (71 + 16, some examples transferred to Cyprus, 2001 onwards), Morocco (20), Oman (30 confirmed) Saudi Arabia (760), Taiwan (27 confirmed), Thailand (38), US Army (747 delivered, 47 remained as of late-2008). US Air Force (two delivered, status uncertain), Yemen (small number), plus small numbers to one or more other undisclosed countries, possibly Oman and Taiwan.

604N and 605NL trailers: 604N: Production complete, but could be resumed. In service with Morocco (20) and Thailand (13). 635NL: Production as required. In service with Egypt (approx 250), Iraq (60, ordered 2010), Jordan (50), Oman (3, 2005) and Saudi Arabia (760).

Contractor
Oshkosh Truck Corporation

Oshkosh M1070 and M1070A1 (8 × 8) heavy equipment transporters (HETs) and M1000 semi-trailer

Development
As the result of a US Army requirement to transport the M1A1 Abrams MBT, the then Oshkosh Truck Corporation (now Oshkosh Defense) was awarded a contract to produce 1,044 M1070 Heavy Equipment Transporters (HET), with an option for a further 522 units and production commenced in July 1992. The full contract, with spares, was worth USD275 million. Production for export customers began during 1993, and including further follow-on contracts for the US Army, over 2,800 HETs had been produced prior to January 2010. The final US Army A0 contract required 195 vehicles to be delivered between March 2001 and March 2003.

Following an initial two separate contracts awarded during 2004, Oshkosh Truck is currently overhauling service-worn M1070s. Reset to original build standard and with zero miles/zero hours and a full 1 year warranty, cost to the US DoD per vehicle is around 75 per cent of that of new build.

Production of new-build M1070s continues on an as required basis for export customers and by early 2007 export sales had been made to Egypt, Jordan and Saudi Arabia. From early 2010 the M1070A1 will be available for export sales.

Saudi Arabia was the first export customer for the M1070, receiving 50 examples during 1993. The largest export user to date is Egypt, which received an initial 170 examples on a one-for-one basis with Oshkosh 635NL five-axle semi-trailers under a US Foreign Military Funding (FMF) contract. Deliveries were completed in December 2004. The M1070 tractor trucks involved under this contract were supplied complete, the 635NL trailers as semi-knockdown kits for insertion of 30 per cent local content. Final assembly took place at the Egyptian Tank Plant. Further have been placed, and by late 2009 around 250 systems had been ordered, with further orders anticipated to meet the projected transportation requirements of the Egyptian Army's future main battle tank fleet.

During 2003, Oshkosh Truck won an order for the supply of 50 M1070/635NL combinations to Jordan. These were delivered during 2004.

During 2010 it was disclosed that Oshkosh had been awarded a contract through the US Army's TACOM Life Cycle Management Command (LCMC) worth in excess of USD40 million to supply the Iraqi Army with 60 M1070A0 HETs complete with Oshkosh 635NL trailers. Deliveries under this contract, which includes operator training, spare parts and manuals, should be complete by May 2011.

The more powerful M1070E1 model was developed in conjunction with the US Army as a possible Technology Insertion Programme (TIP) for their current M1070 model. Evaluation took place and a report was submitted. In 1999 this vehicle was offered to the UK MoD for the British Army's Heavy

US Army Oshkosh M1070 HETs complete with M1000 semi-trailers laden with Bradley IFVs (Oshkosh)   1128710

Equipment Transporter (HET) requirement by a team consisting of Brown and Root (now Kellogg Brown & Root (KBR)), Deutsche Bank and Oshkosh Truck Corporation. The main change from the original M1070 model is the use of a more powerful Detroit Diesel Series 60 DDEC III 14-litre, six-cylinder turbocharged and aftercooled diesel, developing 600 hp. This is coupled to an Allison HD 4070PR seven-speed automatic transmission.

At the maximum 630 hp (available from the engine while meeting the required EURO 3 exhaust emissions levels), the M1070E1 model could not meet the UK MoD's finalised performance requirements, so the much-revised 1070F model powered by a 700 hp EURO 3 compliant Caterpillar diesel engine was offered. This vehicle was subsequently selected for the British Army's requirement and deliveries of the 92 vehicles required was completed early 2004. Full details of the 1070F can be found elsewhere in this section.

To meet the ongoing needs of the US Army, in March 2008 Oshkosh Defense announced it had been awarded a single source contract valued at more than USD11 million (for Phase 1) from the US Army to begin engineering and initial production of the next-generation of Heavy Equipment Transporter (HET). The HET A1 programme is based around a power increase as the US Army recognises that payload requirements for the M1A1 Abrams have increased considerably in recent years.

The M1070A1 is equipped with similar automotive systems to the British Army's 1070F and is powered by a Caterpillar C-18 diesel engine developing 700 hp. Other improvements to the HET A1 include a new Allison 4800SP transmission, Oshkosh 30000 Series transfer box, a heavier-rated front axle and an upgraded electrical system. A new deeper bonnet (to accommodate the new engine and ancillaries) is used, and a selection of ergonomic improvements have been made to the cab. The cab is also Long Term Armor Strategy (LTAS) compliant and comes off the assembly line fitted with integral composite (A-kit) armour, and ready to receive add-on (B-kit) armour.

These upgrades were delivered on six pilot vehicles for testing. Phase II involved production verification testing and Oshkosh announced in July 2009 that it had received a USD9.4 million contract modification to begin durability and performance testing of the HET A1 at Yuma Proving Ground.

Oshkosh announced in October 2010 that it had received its first delivery order under the October 2008 awarded FHTV 3 contract for the M1070A1 HET. This delivery order is valued at over USD440 million and calls for in excess of 1,000 vehicles, deliveries of which will be completed by June 2010. The first vehicles were rolled in December 2010.

Global HET
In October 2008 Oshkosh Defense unveiled the Global HET (6 × 6) at Defendory International 2008 show in Athens, Greece. The Oshkosh Global HET (6 × 6) is similar in many ways to the M1070A1 currently in production for the US Army. The main design difference is configuration, the Global HET being a (6 × 6), the M1070A1 an (8 × 8) with a rear tridem as opposed to the more conventional twin axle bogie set-up. Global HET has a kerb weight of 18,371 kg uses wider 24R21 tyres, giving an overall width of 2.896 m.

Description
Layout of the M1070 is conventional, with a rounded sloping bonnet in front of a fully enclosed cab which has seating for the driver, one crewman and up to four passengers. Armor Holdings (now BAE Systems) had delivered 796 add-on armour kits for the M1070 HET cab by mid-2006, meeting the US Army's current protection requirements for this vehicle. The cab of the M1017A1 is Long Term Armor Strategy (LTAS) compliant and comes off the assembly line fitted with integral composite (A kit) armour, and ready to receive add-on (B-kit) armour.

The M1070 has full-time (8 × 8) drive and is powered by a Detroit Diesel 8V-92TA diesel engine developing 500 hp and coupled to an Allison five-speed automatic transmission. The M1070A1 is powered by a Caterpillar diesel developing 700 hp and coupled to an uprated Allison automatic transmission.

The conventional 9.6 m long 356 × 89 × 9.5 mm C-section chassis is constructed from SAE 1027 modified, heat treated carbon manganese steel with a minimum yield strength of 110,000 psi (758 MPa). This mounts a 3.5 in (89 mm) fully floating kingpin with a maximum load of 20,411 kg (20,865 kg; A1), and twin dp Manufacturing 55K 24,947 kg capacity hydraulic winches, each with 51.8 m of 25 mm cable. A single dp Manufacturing 3GN 1,360 kg capacity auxiliary winch with 91.4 m of 6 mm cable is also fitted.

On the A0 model the front Rockwell SVI 5MR (now AxelTech International) steer-drive axle is sprung by Hendrickson parabolic taper leaf springs. The rear Tridem unit is made up of Rockwell SVI 5MR units and is sprung by Hendrickson-Turner air suspension. The rearmost axle is a steer-drive unit, and all four axles feature planetary hub reduction. Rockwell drum brakes are fitted on all axles. A Central Tyre Inflation (CTI) system is fitted as standard. The A1 model features an uprated AxleTech 5000 Series front axle.

The M1070 HET tows the M1000 semi-trailer in service with the US Army and the Oshkosh/Fontaine 635NL trailer with the known overseas customers, Egypt, Jordan and Saudi Arabia. Full details of the M1000 semi-trailer can be found elsewhere in this entry, full details of the Oshkosh/Fontaine 635NL trailer can be found elsewhere in this section.

The M1070A0/A1 HET is transportable in C-5A and C-17 transport aircraft.

M1000 semi-trailer
The semi-trailer, Heavy Equipment Transporter (HET), M1000, with automatically steered axles, was originally developed as a private venture by Southwest Mobile Systems (later Systems & Electronics Inc (SEI), now DRS Technologies) as a response to a possible US Army requirement for transporting M1 and M1A1 MBTs. This requirement materialised as the M1000 and the HET was involved in US Army trials, completed during 1986.

A production order for 1,066 M1000 units was placed by the US Army in 1989 with the then Southwest Mobile Systems. An additional 111 units were ordered in 1992. First article approval for the US Army was given in February 1994. In January 1996, an additional contract was awarded to the then SEI, which increased via the option award to a total of 768 units. By mid-1998, over 1,650 units (from 1,830 ordered) had been delivered to the US Army, US Army Reserve, National Guard and the US Marine Corps. The total US Army requirement at the time was for 2,452 units. The then SEI received an additional contract in January 2001 for 120 additional M1000s. This contract contained an option provision for approximately 100 additional units. As of October 2001, over 2,000 M1000s had been delivered. Deliveries were completed during 2003, by which time over 2,300 units had been delivered.

US Army Oshkosh M1070 HET complete with M1000 semi-trailers laden with an Abrams MBT (Oshkosh)
1128225

Egyptian Army Oshkosh M1070 (8 × 8) heavy equipment transporter; Egypt has received 249 M1070s (Oshkosh)
1128711

The former Armor Holdings has developed an add-on armour kit for the M1070 cab (BAE Systems)
1190250

In July 2009 DRS Technologies, Inc. announced it received an order valued over USD100 million to manufacture 270 M1000 trailers for the US Army. The order was a follow-on production contract associated with the low-rate initial production of six trailers delivered in June 2009 for test and evaluation. At the completion of this order, DRS Technologies will have manufactured more than 2,600 M1000 trailers for the US Army.

The now DRS Technologies recently completed a five-year Indefinite Delivery/Indefinite Quantity (IDIQ) reset contract awarded in October 2004 by the US Army's Tank-Automotive and Armaments Command (TACOM) that called for up to 1,063 trailers to be refurbished (rebuilt to new standard (zero hours/zero miles)) over a period ending October 2008. At the completion of the final award under this contract, in excess of 700 M1000 trailers had been refurbished.

As part of a December 2010 award under the company's ongoing Theatre-Provided Equipment Refurbishment (TPER) work, Oshkosh Defense will refurbishment an unspecified quantity of M1000 semi-trailers.

There is a single known export user of the M1000 semi-trailer. In July 1997, the then SEI received a USD11.2 million contract to supply 37 M1000 HETs to the Israel Defence Force (IDF); the contract was completed by the end of 1998. These units, known as the M1000W, have a deck 3.66 m wide and are understood to be towed by a MAN tractor truck.

On 26 January 2006 DRS Technologies announced that it had completed its acquisition of Engineered Support Systems, Inc. In the transaction, a wholly-owned subsidiary of DRS was merged with Engineered Support Systems (ESSI), forming DRS's third operating segment – the Sustainment Systems & Services Group. SEI is an Engineered Support Systems (ESSI) company. In October 2008 Finmeccanica S.p.A. announced the completed acquisition of DRS Technologies, Inc.. DRS Technologies is now known as DRS Technologies, a Finmeccanica Company.

The M1000 semi-trailer uses hydraulic/mechanical steering on four of the five axles (axles 2, 3, 4 and 5); steering is automatically controlled by the tractor-trailer angle. The semi-trailer has a maximum on- and off-road

	M1070 [M1070E1 in square brackets where different]	M1070A1	Global HET
Cab seating:	1 + 1 + 4	1 + 1 + 4	1 + 1 + 4
Configuration:	8 × 8	8 × 8	6 × 6
Weight:			
(kerb)	18,598 kg	20,208 kg	18,370 kg
(GVW)	39,009 kg [43,998 kg]	n/avail	n/avail
(GCW)	104,961 kg [116,573 kg]	n/avail	n/avail
(load on 5th wheel, nominal)	20,411 kg [21.320 kg]	20,865 kg	n/avail
Length:	9.093 m	9.677 m	9.174 m
Width:	2.591 m	2.591 m	3.04 m
Height:			
(overall)	3.962 m	3.708 m	3.733 m
(5th wheel)	1.616 m	1.625 m	1.625 m
Track:	2.083 m	2.083	2.278 m
Wheelbase:	5.461 m	5.461 m	5.588 m
Max speed:			
(primary road at GCW)	72 km/h	80 km/h	80 km/h
(secondary road at GCW)	52 km/h	n/avail	n/avail
Range: (cruising)	724 km	n/avail	n/avail
Fuel capacity:	946 litres	n/avail	n/avail
Gradient: (at full GCW)	15%	n/avail	n/avail
Fording:	711 mm	711 mm	800 mm
Engine:	Detroit Diesel Model 8V-92TA DDEC II 12.06-litre turbocharged and aftercooled, water-cooled 2-stroke diesel developing 500 hp (373 kW) at 2,100 rpm and 1,993 N.m torque at 1,200 rpm [Detroit Diesel Series 60 DDEC III 14-litre 6-cylinder turbocharged and aftercooled, water-cooled 2-stroke diesel developing 600 hp (447 kW) at 2,300 rpm and 2,576 N.m torque at 1,200-1,500 rpm]	Caterpillar C-18 18.01-litre 6-cylinder in-line turbocharged and aftercooled, water-cooled 4-stroke diesel developing 700 hp (522 kW)	Caterpillar C-18 18.01-litre 6-cylinder in-line turbocharged and aftercooled, water-cooled 4-stroke diesel developing 700 hp (522 kW)
Transmission:	Allison CLT-754 automatic with 5 forward gears and TC-496 torque converter with second gear start [Allison HD 4070PR automatic with 7 forward and 1 reverse gears and TC-551 torque converter with second gear start]	Allison 4800SP fully automatic	Allison 4800SP fully automatic
Transfer box:	Oshkosh 55000 2-speed, air-operated front axle disconnect [Oshkosh 30000 single-speed, full-time all-wheel drive]	Oshkosh 30000	Oshkosh 30000
Steering:	power-assisted with front and rear axle co-ordinated steer	power-assisted with front and rear axle co-ordinated steer	power-assisted on front axle only
Turning radius: (wall)	11.1 m	11.1 m	n/avail
Suspension:			
(front)	springs and hydraulic shock-absorbers	springs and hydraulic shock-absorbers	taper leaf springs
(rear)	air ride	air ride	air ride
Tyres:	16.00R 20 XLZT with CTI system	16.00R 20 XLZT with CTI system	24.00R 21 XZL with CTI system
Brakes:	dual circuit air-actuated S-cam, drums all-round. Wabco ABS and ATC on M1070E1	dual circuit air-actuated	dual circuit air-actuated
Electrical system:	24 V start, 12 V lighting	24 V, 12 V accessory	24 V, 12 V accessory
Batteries:	4 × 12 V	n/avail	n/avail

payload of 80,000 kg and is compatible with a variety of prime movers such as the M911, MK48/16, M1070, MAN, Mercedes-Benz, Volvo and German Faun SLT 50-2 tractors. The M1000 is air-transportable in a C-5 Galaxy, complete with tractor and the C-17 Globemaster (semi-trailer only).

When coupled to an M911 the HET can negotiate 90° intersections of 9.144 m roads in a single pass. Manual steering is available for low-speed manoeuvring in tight-clearance locations.

There are five axle lines with two half-width axles per line. Each axle is mounted on a hydraulic pendular suspension providing a ±254 mm stroke, fully equalised. There is lateral oscillation provided to accommodate crowned roads and rough terrain. A hydraulic suspension system is also provided on the pivoting gooseneck to equalise fifth wheel loads. Hydraulics are used for the control of the deck height, gooseneck angle and axle jacking. Spring-assisted loading ramps can be manually lowered or raised by one person. An auxiliary diesel power pack is mounted on the gooseneck for loading, unloading and maintenance. Any axle may be raised by one person, without having to remove the payload, and the axles can be rotated to allow access to the inboard tyres for ease of changing punctured tyres. Time for one person to change any tyre is 30 minutes. There are 40 tyres in all plus two spares.

Specifications - See also table on previous page

M1000 semi-trailer
Weight: 22,860 kg
Payload: 80,000 kg (at reduced speeds)
Length:
   (overall, standard deck) 15.8 m
   (overall, wide deck) 15.7 m
   (deck) 10.2 m
Deck width:
   (standard) 3.05 m
   (wide) 3.66 m
Height:
   (deck) 1.1 m ± 0.250 m
   (5th wheel) 1.6 m - variable
King-pin: 88.9 mm (3½ in)
Max speed:
   (road) 72 km/h
   (secondary road) 64 km/h
   (cross-country) 24 km/h
Tyres: 215/75 R 17.5
Loading ramp angle: 18° (can be reduced to 14°)

Status

M1070: Production as required. In service with Egypt (249), Iraq (60, ordered 2010), Jordan (50, 2004), Saudi Arabia (50, 1993) and the US Army 2,488 delivered, July 1992 to March 2003).

M1070A1: In production for the US Army (>1,000).

M1000: Production as required. In service with the US Army, US Army Reserve, National Guard and US Marine Corps (over 2,600 units ordered in total). In service with the Israel Defence Force (37).

Global HET: Ready for production on receipt of orders.

Contractor

Oshkosh Truck Corporation
DRS Technologies

Oshkosh MK31 Medium Tactical Vehicle Replacement (MTVR) Medium Equipment Transporter (MET)

Development

The Oshkosh Defense MK31 Medium Tactical Vehicle Replacement (MTVR) Medium Equipment Transporter (MET) is a fifth wheel tractor truck variant of the standard MK23 Oshkosh MTVR. The MK31 MET was designed to meet a US Navy Seabees requirement, and following user evaluation entered production early 2005. The initial US Navy requirement called for up to 460 vehicles to be delivered by 2009 US Navy vehicles are used with a variety of commercially based semi-trailers. From late 2005, the USMC has also received vehicles. These are used primarily with the M870 flatbed and M969 and M970 fuel tankers and are fitted with a sliding fifth wheel.

The MTVR design has its origins in two US military programmes, the 5TTR (5-ton Tactical Truck Replacement) for the US Army, and the MTVR for the US Marines. The aim of these programmes was to upgrade, refurbish and prolong the effective service life of around 3,400 US Army M923 series 5-ton (6 × 6) trucks, and 8,100 US Marines M809 and M939 series 5-ton (6 × 6) trucks.

In 1996 both Oshkosh and the then AM General Corporation (now AM General LLC) were awarded prototype and development contracts for both the 5TTR and MTVR programmes, however the US Army's 5TTR programme was terminated early for financial reasons. The MTVR programme continued and at this stage it remained the intention of the Marines not to replace with new vehicles but to upgrade their ageing M809 and M939 fleets from 5-ton (4,536 kg) into dual-rated 7.1-ton (6,441 kg)

off-road, 15-ton (13,608 kg) on-road capacity trucks. In addition to an 80 per cent more powerful approximate 425 hp engine, anti-lock brakes and a traction control system, the biggest single improvement planned for the MTVR was the fitting of fully independent coil-spring suspension. With only the bonnet, cab and loadbed of the original vehicles proving salvageable - and these all requiring structural enhancements to meet the revised payload and off-road performance requirements, plus extensive anti-corrosion treatments to meet the Marines' requirement for a 22-year service life from their upgraded vehicles - it soon became clear to Oshkosh that a complete new-build option would be a far more cost-effective route to take and development of the MTVR commenced.

In February 1999 the US Department of Defense (DoD) awarded the then Oshkosh Truck a multiyear production contract with the first 20 of 5,666 MTVRs scheduled for delivery by the end of the year. The first vehicles were fielded by the USMC in July 2001. The initial contract called for up to 8,168 MTVRs (including options for 2,502) in four cargo truck variants over five program years. Three further MTVR variants were subsequently added, two dump and a wrecker, and a total of 6,931 vehicles (6,393 to the USMC, 538 to the Seabees (Navy)) would be delivered under the initial contract, deliveries concluding during August 2005.

A follow-on FY05-FY10 MTVR production contract was awarded to Oshkosh in July 2004. Production commenced in March 2005, with this Requirements-type contract initially covering just potential FMS sales plus the continuing requirements of the US Navy. The USMC and US Navy combined will now receive in excess of 2,000 vehicles under this contract, the most recent announced modification for which was awarded in January 2010 and calls for more than 90 additional MTVRs. MTVR variants to be produced under this contract modification include MK31 tractors, the modification including an armouring element and being valued at USD31.5 million.

In addition to the MK31, the US Navy currently has under contract the following MTVR variants: MK25, MK28, MK28C, MK30 and MK36. The US Navy also has a requirement to replace a fleet of assorted Special Purpose Vehicle (SPV) types based on a mix of tactical and commercial truck chassis. These are replaced by an MTVR chassis-cab variant, the MK28C.

Under a separate contract, Oshkosh commenced production in July 2004 of the MK37. Based on the MK27 and fitted with a rear-mounted Hiab material handling crane, the MK37 has been designed as a resupply vehicle for the US Marines High Mobility Artillery Rocket System (HIMARS).

The 10,000th MTVR was completed in May 2008. Full details of the MTVR family can be found in the Trucks section.

The then Oshkosh Truck was awarded the UK MoD's Wheeled Tanker contract in 2003. An articulated combination, the Wheeled Tanker requirement included a total of 348 tractor trucks based on a modified MK23 MTVR. Modifications include a 330 mm reduction in wheelbase and a 660 mm cab extension. Automotive changes include the Caterpillar C-12

Oshkosh MTVR MK31 Medium Equipment Transporter (MET) tractor trucks (Shaun C Connors)   1296269

Oshkosh MTVR MK31 Medium Equipment Transporter (MET); note the all-wheel steer of the tractor unit (Oshkosh Defense)   1128758

six-cylinder diesel uprated from 425 to 445 hp and upgraded to meet EURO III emissions regulations. The 7F/1R Allison HD 4070P automatic transmission of the standard MTVR is replaced by a 6F/1R 'wide ratio' Allison HD 4560P unit.

For use on deployed operations a small number of Wheeled Tanker tractor trucks were modified for a Light Equipment Transporter (LET) role mid-2007, and late-2008 it was suggested that Oshkosh Defense had been selected as preferred bidder for the UK's now under revision Future Light Equipment Transporter (FLET) requirement, with a Wheeled tanker based design. Further details of the Wheeled Tanker vehicles can be found in the Bulk fuel storage and distribution systems and Water supplies sections.

Description

The MK31 MTVR is essentially a tractor truck variant of the standard MK23 MTVR. Modifications include a 469 mm shorter chassis (a shorter rear overhang), a revised suspension set-up on the rear axles and an all-wheel steer system for enhanced manoeuvrability. The Holland Kompensator fully oscillating fifth wheel with 50.8 mm (2 in) SAE kingpin capability (88.9 mm optional (3.5 in)) used is the same as fitted to the Oshkosh M983 Heavy Expanded Mobility Tactical Truck (HEMTT) tractor truck.

All versions of the MTVR are based on the same (6 × 6) drive configuration with the engine under a forward non-corroding and weight-saving fibreglass bonnet. The three-seat cab is of welded aluminium extrusion construction with adhesive bonded aluminium skins. The aluminium hinged windscreen, roof, side-walls, door frames and rear wall can be folded down to reduce overall height to 2.489 m. The chassis frame is constructed using bolted/huck bolted formed channel (248 × 76 × 9.7 mm) made of heat-treated carbon manganese steel with a yield strength of 758 MPa. Both chassis and cab feature extension corrosion protection as the Marines required that MTVR should have sufficient corrosion protection to ensure an effective service life of 22 years.

With the exception of the UK's Wheeled tanker variants (and some proposed 4 × 4 variants), all MTVRs are powered by a Caterpillar C12, Advanced Diesel Engine Management (ADEM) III 11.9-litre six-cylinder inline turbocharged and water-cooled four-stroke diesel that develops a maximum 425 hp at 1,800 rpm and 2,101 N.m of torque at 1,200 rpm. Maximum sustainable speed on paved roads is 105 km/h and cruising range is 483 km. A three-stage (two-, four- or six-cylinder) manually selected, automatically applied engine compression brake is fitted to assist the braking system.

The engine is coupled to an Allison HD 4070SP automatic 7F/1R transmission, TC-541 torque converter and an Oshkosh 30000 Series single-speed transfer box. The combination of torque converter and an extra low ratio (7.63:1) first gear allows for a single-speed transfer box to replace the more complex two-speed unit more commonly associated with off-road vehicles. Full-time all-wheel drive is employed and under highway driving conditions the torque split is 32 per cent front, 68 per cent rear.

The suspension uses a system known as the Oshkosh TAK-4 independent suspension. For the MK31 the standard coil springs are used on the front axle, Hendrickson hydraulic on the rear axles. This system provides each front wheel with a total vertical travel of 406 mm and a travel of 325 mm on the rear axles. The front axle is rated at 7,257 kg, the rear axle pair at 10,432 kg each. For enhanced manoeuvrability a mechanical all-wheel steer system is fitted. This gives the solo tractor truck a turning radius (kerb to kerb) of 9.14 m. The system is designed to allow 3° of steering on the front wheels before operating on the rear axles and has a self-centre failsafe in the event of failure.

MTVR is fitted with 1600R 20 Michelin XZL super singles tyres. With the exception of the MK36 wrecker variant, no spare wheel or tyre are carried, the loss of 463 kg afforded to this removal allows the MK23 MTVR vehicle to keep below the 12,700 kg maximum value permissible for underslung transport by CH-53 helicopter. Compensating for no spare wheel is a runflat setting option on the CTI system.

The CTI system allows the driver to adjust tyre pressures to suit both payload and terrain conditions, from the driving seat. In an emergency the MTVR system can be directed to continuously inflate one tyre only. The 508 × 254 mm two-piece bolt-together steel wheel rims are fitted with beadlocks for extreme low-pressure operations and tyres will remain seated at pressures down to 10 psi. In the event that any one tyre should fail totally, a limp-home facility allows for a second axle suspension unit to be raised and secured, its wheel then rolled and fitted in the position of the damaged tyre.

The CTI system has four terrain settings; highway, cross-country, mud/sand/snow, and emergency. At the highway setting an Automatic Traction Control (ATC) system operates via the anti-lock brakes (ABS), applying braking force to any wheel detected as slipping, thus allowing torque to transfer to the non rotating opposite wheel. From cross-country through to emergency settings the ABS operates in off-road mode and the ATC is automatically disconnected and differential locks are automatically engaged in stages up to full cross and inter-axle lock-up in the emergency setting. The driver retains full control over these systems and at any time may disconnect the ATC or manually engage the differential locks in three stages; transfer box, rear inter-axle and full cross axle locks.

Obstacle surmounting requirements specified by the US Marine Corps called for the ability to climb both a vertical step of 0.61 m and ford water to a depth of 1.52 m without preparation.

To assist with vehicle repairs and diagnosis the On Board Diagnostic System (OBDS) features an information display screen and fault indicators

from the engine, transmission, ABS, ATC and CTI. It also has a laptop interface that allows access to the full MTVR database for in-the-field maintenance, diagnostics and repair.

Optional equipment includes an arctic kit for the engine, cargo and personnel arctic kit, a machine gun mounting kit, NBC alarm and decontamination apparatus mounting kits, a pioneer tool kit and a tow bar adapter kit. An Armor Protection Kit (APK) developed by Plasan Sasa of Israel is available for the MTVR.

The MTVR is air-transportable in C-5, C-17, C-130 and C-141 aircraft. The MK23 and MK31 are transportable as an underslung load by CH-53 helicopter.

MTVR has a climatic operational range of between –32° (with kits from –46°) and +52°C.

Protection kit

Oshkosh now promotes the current MTVR armour packages as the MTVR Armor Systems (MAS). The current Standard MAS with Survivability Upgrade (MAS-SU) kit is available for a variety of models including the MK31, the MK31 kit designated AMK31. The Reducible Height MAS (MAS-RH) is also available for the MK31.

Initial development of an MTVR protection kit began in 2003, and following a redesign to address the current increased threat requirement, particularly that posed by Improvised Explosive Devices (IEDs), an initial production contract was awarded late 2004. Under a contract valued at USD100 million, Israeli light armour solutions manufacturer Plasan Sasa (as a subcontractor for the now BAE Systems of the US) supplied between April and December 2005 some 920 baseline appliqué APKs for the MTVR cab and wheel arch sections, plus 460 modular armoured rear troop-carrier compartments. The cab and troop carrier kits, while complimentary, are separate units and can be installed as such.

A follow-on contract for the supply of additional APKs for the USMC's MTVRs was awarded late 2005. Also valued at USD100 million, this follow-on contract called for the supply of 930 appliqué kits for the MTVR cab and wheel arch sections and 465 modular armoured rear troop-carrier compartments. Deliveries began early 2006, with full deployment scheduled for the end of that year.

Two further contracts for a total of 293 additional kits for dump, wrecker and tractor truck MTVRs were awarded early- and mid-2007, with deliveries complete by late-2007.

The APK, which uses a composite metal armour solution to provide protection to no less than STANAG level 2, offers protection to both vehicle and crew from IEDs, mine blast and other assorted other threats. Installation of the APK requires a vehicle front axle and cab suspension mount upgrade, plus a revision to the cab roof gun mount. Air-conditioning is also fitted. From mid-2007 all production MTVRs have been armour ready, these modifications now forming part of the standard vehicle specification.

According to the USMC, since the MTVR is at the beginning of its economic life cycle, the decision was taken to integrate armour into the body of the truck, this task requiring a full stripdown and rebuild operation that takes a five-man team some 300 hours to complete.

Oshkosh announced early-2008 that it had completed the development of a height reducible armour kit for the MTVR. In August 2008 the company announced an initial contract award, valued at USD11.7 million, to install height reducible armour kits on MVTRs. An award for 200 kits was made in September 2008 and in October 2008 Oshkosh Defense announced that it had been awarded a contract valued at more than USD180 million for more than 1,500 height reducible armour kits for MTVRs. Further smaller orders have followed, these including a >USD10 million 400-kit award in April 2009 (this including some standard wrecker kits), and a 300-vehicle award in January 2010.

In April 2010 Oshkosh announced it had received an award from the USMC valued at more than USD44 million (but not to exceed USD89 million) for in excess of 5,750 armour/protection-related upgrade kits for the MTVR. Under this award Oshkosh was contracted to deliver in excess of 950 weapons mount kits that allow the installation of motorised Marine Corps Transparent Armor Gun Shields (MCTAGS), these replacing the gunner protection kits on up-armoured vehicles. Oshkosh was also contracted to supply 2,000 door-upgrade kits to support MTVR non-reducible height armour kits used on trucks that were armoured during 2005-2007. These kits make the doors common with those on MTVRs using the reducible-height armour kits, which Oshkosh began producing in 2008. Additionally, Oshkosh was contracted to deliver MTVR Troop Carrier upgrades. Work under this award was scheduled for completion in September 2010.

Plasan Sasa, in cooperation with Permali Gloucester of the UK, has also developed a small arms fire and mine blast protection kit for the UK MoD's MTVR-fronted Wheeled Tanker fleet. Fitted vehicles have been deployed by the British Army to Afghanistan and Iraq.

Specifications

MK31 MTVR MET
Cab seating: 1 + 2
Configuration: 6 × 6
Weight:
(tractor) 12,701 kg
(towed load) 42,638 kg
(GCW) 55,339 kg
Length: 7.554 m

Width: 2.489 m
Height:
   (cab) 3.065 m (reducible to 2.489)
   (5th wheel) 1.46 m
Track: 2.052 m
Wheelbase: 4.674 m
Max speed: (primary roads) 105 km/h
Range: (cruising) 483 km
Fuel capacity: 295 litres
Fording 1.52 m
Engine: Caterpillar C12 Advanced Diesel Engine Management (ADEM) III 11.9-litre 6-cylinder in-line turbocharged and water-cooled diesel 4-stroke diesel developing 425 hp (317 kW) at 1,800 rpm and 2,101 N.m torque at 1,200 rpm
Transmission: Allison HD 4070SP with 7 forward and 1 reverse gears; TC-541 torque convertor
Transfer box: Oshkosh 30000 three-shaft single-speed with torque proportioning differential and manual differential lock
Steering: all-wheel mechanical steer, power-assisted
Turning radius: (kerb) 9.14 m

Suspension: Oshkosh TAK-4 independent suspension, coil spring upper/lower control arms, front; Hendrickson hydraulic, rear. Front axle rated at 7,257 kg, rear axles at 10,432 kg each
Tyres: 1600R 20 Michelin XZL with CTI system
Brakes: dual circuit, air, drums on all axles. ABS with off-road programme. Supplementary three-stage (2-, 4- or 6-cylinder) manually selected, automatically applied engine compression brake
Electrical system: 24 V
Batteries: 2 × 12 V
Alternator: 150 A, 24 V

Status
MK31 MET entered production for the US Navy early 2005, the USMC late 2005. Tractor truck variants of the MK23/25 MTVR are also in service with the British Army. Rigid chassis (6 × 6) MTVR variants are in service with, and production for, the US Marines and Navy, and Greece.

Contractor
Oshkosh Defense

AMPHIBIANS

Introduction

This section covers vehicles designed specifically for amphibious operations, such as crossing inland waterways or carrying cargo from ships offshore on to the beach, or inland. It does not include vehicles which require preparation to make them amphibious nor does it include amphibious over-snow vehicles or tracked prime movers, details of which will be found in their respective sections.

Italy

ARIS ARK tracked amphibious support vehicle

Description

The ARK is based on the lower hull and running gear of the now BAE Systems M548 tracked cargo carrier, details of which will be found in the all-terrain carriers and prime movers section.

To improve the relatively limited amphibious capability of the M548, the ARK features an extended light alloy bow on the front of the vehicle and the engine compartment is now completely watertight. The extended bow was designed to offer the minimum of hydrodynamic drag. The cab has also been redesigned and a new snorkel-type device has been fitted to the cab rear to provide air for the engine. Hydraulic power for water propulsion is generated by two variable displacement hydraulic pumps powered by a Detroit Diesel 6V-53 six-cylinder diesel engine via an electromagnetic clutch. The motors generate propulsion through the four ducted propellers (thrusters). The ARK has a watercraft-towing capability of up to 30,000 kg and can be launched into the sea from Landing Platform Dock (LPD) vessels. The ARK has an available payload space of 8.5 m³ and can transport up to 5,200 kg when afloat. The cargo is loaded via a rear tailgate and a tarpaulin cover over removable bows can be used to cover the cargo area. Steering when afloat is carried out using a joystick control lever and the usual crew of driver and co-driver occupy a forward crew compartment that can be covered by a canvas roof when required.

The ARK can operate in open sea, lakes, rivers and marshland, and for land operations runs on the standard M548 running gear, with steering via a conventional steering wheel.

The ARK is suitable for rescue operations in case of flooding and as support to landing operations. An hydraulic power system may be fitted to power assorted equipment including a trackway dispenser, a materials handling crane or a hoist.

For use in high threat environments a ballistic protection kit has been developed for the cab and is available.

If required, the ARK can be carried inside a transport aircraft or slung under a heavy lift helicopter.

A new COTS powerpack consisting of a EURO III/IV emissions compliant diesel engine developing 275 hp (205 kW) and coupled to a new automatic transmission, plus new steering and brake systems have been developed by ARIS and are available.

Specifications

ARIS ARK
Cab seating: 1 + 2
Weight:
(unladen) 7,600 kg
(laden) 12,800 kg
Max load: 5,200 kg
Power to weight ratio: 16.4 hp/t (12.3 kW/t)
Length: 6.96 m
Width: 2.45 m
Height: (unladen) 2.767 m
Ground clearance: 410-450 mm
Max speed:
(road) 60 km/h
(water) 6 knots
Range: (road) >500 km
Max gradient: 60%
Max side slope: 30%
Fording: amphibious
Engine: Detroit Diesel 6V-52 6-cylinder water-cooled 2-stroke diesel developing 210 hp (157 kW)
Gearbox: Allison fully automatic with 4 forward and 1 reverse gears

Status
Available.

Contractor
Applicazioni Rielaborazioni Impianti Speciali (ARIS) SpA

ARIS ARK tracked amphibious support vehicle demonstrating its cross-country capability (ARIS SpA)
1121039

ARIS ARK tracked amphibious support vehicle in Italian emergency service colours (ARIS SpA)
1121040

IVECO Model 6640 H 4 × 4 2,000 kg amphibious cargo carrier

Description

The IVECO Model 6640 H 4 × 4 amphibious cargo carrier is essentially a re-powered IVECO Model 6640 G, this being based on the earlier IVECO Model 6640 A. Compared to the earlier 6640 A, both the G and H models are heavier (due primarily to stronger construction), have a slightly longer wheelbase and are fitted with a more powerful diesel engine that is coupled to an automatic transmission; propulsion in water is by water-jet.

The hull of the vehicle is of all-welded aluminium construction with a maximum thickness of 4 mm. The engine compartment is at the front of the hull and is separated from the crew compartment by a fireproof bulkhead. The two-person fully enclosed cab is heated and ventilated. The cargo area is to the rear of the cab and is provided with removable bows and a tarpaulin cover. Folding bench seats for 14 personnel run along both sides of the cargo area.

IVECO Model 6640 H 4 × 4 2,000 kg amphibious cargo carrier (IVECO)
1340285

The vehicle is propelled in water by its wheels or the water-jet mounted under the hull at the rear; steering in the water is by a rear-mounted rudder linked to the steering wheel. In an emergency the rudder can be operated by hand. There are three bilge pumps, one in the bottom of the engine compartment and two below the cargo area.

Specifications

IVECO Model 6640 G
Cab seating: 1 + 2
Configuration: 4 × 4
Weight:
  (unladen) 6,700 kg
  (laden) 8,700 kg
  (on front axle, laden) 3,400 kg
  (on rear axle, laden) 5,300 kg
Max Load: 2,000 kg
Load area: 3.21 × 1.95 m
Length: 8.2 m
Width: 2.5 m
Height:
  (cab) 2.7 m (approx.)
  (tarpaulin) 3.16 m
Ground clearance: 350 mm
Track: 1.96 m
Wheelbase: 3.1 m
Angle of approach/departure: 30°/25°
Max speed:
  (road) 100 km/h
  (water, propelled by water-jet) 11 km/h
Range:
  (road) >600 km
  (water, propelled by water-jet) >5 h
Max gradient: 60%
Max side slope: 30%
Fording: amphibious
Engine: IVECO 6-cylinder in-line turbocharged water-cooled 4-stroke diesel developing 220 hp (164 kW) at 3,000 rpm (6640 G, 195 hp (145 kW) at 3,200 rpm)
Gearbox: automatic, 3 forward and 1 reverse gears with power take-off for water-jet
Transfer box: 2-speed
Axle differential carriers: single reduction, spiral bevel drive. Air-operated cross-axle differential lock on front and rear axles
Planetary drives: (front and rear) epicyclic gear train in wheel hubs
Steering: power-assisted
Turning radius: (land) 7.5 m
Suspension: independent strut and link type with coil spring and rubber bump stop plus hydraulic shock-absorbers, front and rear
Tyres: 14.5R 20
Brakes:
  (main) dual circuit, air-over-hydraulic, discs front and rear
  (parking) drum type, mounted on transfer rear output shaft
Electrical system: 24 V
Batteries: 2 × 12 V, 110 Ah

Status

Production complete. During 1984, a total of 17 were sold to Italian Ministry of Interior (Direction of Civil Protection), plus a further 21 for Civil Defence.

Contractor

IVECO SpA

Russian Federation

PTS, PTS-M and PTS-2 tracked amphibious vehicles

Development

The PTS tracked amphibious vehicle entered service in the mid-1960s as the replacement for the earlier K-61 (GPT) vehicle. The main improvements over the K-61 were its higher water speed and its ability to transport 10,000 kg on land for 3 km in order to reach the water. The PTS-M, which first appeared in 1969, is a modified version while the later (1985) PTS-2 is the replacement for the PTS-M.

Wojskowe Zaklady Inzynieryjne of Poland offers a repair, overhaul and rebuild service for the PTS-M. Also on offer are modifications to make the PTS-M more adaptable for operations in extremely cold regions.

Belvneshpromservice of Belarus are one of a number of companies throughout the former Soviet Union continuing to offer surplus Soviet-era equipment for export sale, in either 'as is' condition or refurbished and overhauled to customer requirements. In addition to the PTS-M tracked amphibious carrier, Belvneshpromservice offer a selection of other bridge and ferry related equipment, including the GSP heavy amphibious ferry, PMM-2 amphibious bridging and ferry system, PMP and PMP-M pontoon equipment sets, MTU-20 and MT-55A mechanised bridges and the TMM-3 heavy mechanised bridge.

Description

PTS and PTS-M

These two vehicles are essentially similar and are based on the elongated chassis of the ATS-59 tracked artillery tractor (full details of which can be found in the All-terrain carriers and prime movers section). The crew compartment is at the front of the vehicle and is fully sealed against NBC attack. The crew enter the cab via two circular hatches in the roof. The cargo area is at the rear of the vehicle and vehicles are loaded via the hinged tailgate, which also has integral loading ramps. Tie-down points are fitted for securing the vehicle or other cargo. The engine is under the centre of the cargo compartment with the exhaust exits just above the top of the cargo compartment on each side. The vehicles are propelled in the water by two three-bladed propellers in tunnels under the rear of the hull and steering is by two rudders at the rear of the hull.

The suspension is of the torsion bar type and consists of six roadwheels with the idler at the rear and the drive sprocket at the front.

A winch is mounted at the front of the vehicle and before entering the water, a trim vane is erected at the front and the bilge pumps are switched on. The cargo area can be covered by bows and a tarpaulin cover and is sometimes used as an ambulance vehicle. Standard equipment includes infra-red night vision equipment, intercom, radios and a searchlight mounted on the top of the crew compartment. A special kit permits sea operations in wave heights up to 1.25 m.

These vehicles were designed to carry 5,000 kg on land or 10,000 kg on water, or up to 70 personnel. In the ambulance role, up to 12 stretchers can be carried in the open cargo area. The PTS-M has also been used to lay portable trackway across beach areas.

The PKP is a two-wheeled boat-shaped trailer designed specifically for use with the PTS/PTS-M. The foam-filled watertight hull of the PKP is fitted with loading ramps and two (one each side) small folding pontoons that improve trim and buoyancy in the water. These pontoons rest on top of the trailer when travelling on land and are swung through 180° and locked in position before entering the water. In use, the PKP trailer allows for the transport of an artillery prime mover and the towed gun in a single lift. The PTS would normally transport the gun tractor, for example a Ural 375D or 4320 truck, and the trailer a gun such as the 122 mm howitzer. Recesses for the wheels of artillery pieces are provided in the deck of the PKP trailer. Basic specifications of the trailer are: unladen weight 3,600 kg, overall length 10.3 m, width (travelling) 2.82 m, height 2.2 m, ground clearance (laden) 400 mm and track 1.89 m. Payload on land is 2,500 kg and 5,000 kg on water. The PKP can be towed at a speed of between 20 and 25 km/h laden or 25 to 30 km/h unladen.

PTS-2

Introduced in 1985, the PTS-2 is based on the chassis of the MT-T heavy tracked transporter which uses suspension components of the T-64 MBT. Full details of the MT-T heavy tracked transporter can be found in the All-terrain carriers and prime movers section. It is powered by a V-64-4 diesel derived from that used in the T-72 MBT, developing 710 hp. The PTS-2 is understood to be the intended eventual replacement for the PTS-M and has been in service for some time.

Ukrainian Army PTS-2 with trim vane erected ready for amphibious operation (Shaun C Connors)   0109603

Polish Army PTS tracked amphibious vehicle (Gregorz Holdanowicz)
0561203

The PTS-2 has revised running gear consisting of seven roadwheels and four track-return rollers; the track links have rubber pads. The driving cab is enlarged, lightly armoured and features an NBC protection system, while the trim vane at the bow is slightly curved. The sponson is higher than on earlier models and there is a rectangular exhaust outlet on both sides to accommodate the turbocharged engine mounted amidships. A ramp-like stern is provided.

The cargo space is enlarged to 8.3 × 2.6 m and, at 12,000 kg, the PTS-2 has a higher payload capacity than earlier models. Road speed is increased to 60 km/h and water speed is 12 km/h. PTS-2 can operate in both fresh and salt water, and in conditions up to Sea State 3. Road range is 500 km and the vehicle can operate up to 10 hours in the water. Dimensions are given as length 12 m, width 3.3 m and height 3.17 m.

Optional equipment available for the PTS-2 includes a multipurpose shovel, dozer blade, water-jet, air conditioning equipment and a self-recovery winch. It is possible to install radio location and navigation systems to ensure safe round-the-clock operations.

OMAR-M and OMAR-C minelayers
The OMAR-M and OMAR-C are Bulgarian amphibious warfare minelaying systems, which can be installed on any PTS vehicle.

Variants
Polish variant
The Polish Army has used a number of PTS tracked amphibious vehicles including some fitted with rocket-propelled mineclearing equipment in the rear.

In 2003, Poland announced the transfer of equipment worth USD1.4 million to the Latvian National Armed Forces. This equipment included 10 PTS-M tracked amphibious vehicles.

Specifications
PTS-M
Cab seating: 1 + 1 (up to 70 troops in rear)
Weight:
    (laden, land) 22,700 kg
    (laden, water) 27,700 kg
    (unladen) 17,700 kg
Max load:
    (land) 5,000 kg
    (water) 10,000 kg
Load area: 7.9 × 2.6 m
Length: 11.426 m
Width: 3.3 m
Height: 2.65 m
Ground clearance: (laden) 400 mm
Track: 2.8 m
Track width: 480 mm
Length of track on ground: 5.63 m
Ground pressure:
    (unladen) 0.382 kg/cm^2
    (with 5,000 kg load) 0.483 kg/cm^2
    (with 10,000 kg load) 0.582 kg/cm^2
Max speed:
    (dirt road, with 5,000 kg load) 25–27 km/h
    (road, with 5,000 kg load) 42 km/h
    (water, with 10,000 kg load) 10.6 km/h
    (water, towing 5,000 kg trailer) 8.5 km/h
Range:
    (land, 5,000 kg load) up to 380 km
    (water, 10,000 kg load) 12 km
Fuel capacity: 705 litres
Max gradient:
    (laden) 20%
    (unladen) 60%
Vertical obstacle: 650 mm
Trench: 2.5 m
Engine: V-54P V-12 4-stroke diesel developing 350 hp (261 kW) at 1,800 rpm
Electrical system: 24 V
Batteries: 4 × 12 V, 280 Ah

Status
PTS-2, production as required, offered for export sales. PTS and PTS-M in service with members of the former Warsaw Pact, including Bulgaria, Hungary and Poland. Supplied to Algeria, Angola, Congo, Cuba, Egypt, India, Iran, Latvia (Polish surplus), Libya, Serbia and Montenegro, Tanzania, Vietnam and Yemen.

Contractor
Krasnoyarsk Shipbuilding Yard

Marketing agency
Rosoboronexport

Spain

VAP 3550/1 4 × 4 3,000 kg amphibious vehicle

Development
The VAP 3550/1 4 × 4 3,000 kg amphibious vehicle was developed by ENASA, to meet Spanish Navy requirements for a vehicle to be launched from LSTs and other amphibious craft offshore, reach the coast under its own power and then travel inland over rough country. VAP is the export name of this vehicle, within Spain it is known as the Pegaso 3550, with the first production batch known as the 3550/1.

The vehicle used many automotive components of the ENASA (Pegaso) range of 3045 4 × 4 3,000 kg and 3050 6 × 6 6,000 kg trucks, of which over 6,000 were supplied to the Spanish Army.

Description
The boat-shaped hull of the VAP 3550/1 is made of all-welded 6 mm thick steel plates and is divided into watertight compartments. The driver sits in the semi-enclosed cab, which has an open back towards the front, with two passengers seated on his right. A searchlight that can be operated from within the cab is mounted over the top of the cab. Immediately behind the cab is a hydraulic crane with a maximum lifting capacity of 350 kg.

The cargo area in the centre of the vehicle can be covered with removable bows and a tarpaulin cover. Removable bench seats for troops can be fitted down either side of the cargo compartment.

The engine compartment is at the rear with the air outlet/inlet louvres and exhaust pipe mounted in the top.

The VAP is fully amphibious, propelled in the water by two water-jets at the rear of the hull immediately behind the second axle. The two single water-jets are driven by a hydraulic system composed of a pump directly connected to the vehicle's engine and two hydraulic motors acting directly on the hydrojets. It features a pressurising system for the mechanical units in contact with the water, which operates as soon as the VAP enters the water. When afloat, pivot turns can be accomplished.

The load compartment is equipped with two pumps which have a maximum capacity of 6,000 l/h and there are two automatic bilge pumps in the hull with a maximum capacity of 3,600 l/h. Mounted at the front is an optional winch with a maximum capacity of 4,500 kg.

Specifications
VAP 3550/1
Cab seating: 1 + 2 (rear, up to 18)
Configuration: 4 × 4
Weight:
    (laden) 12,500 kg
    (unladen) 9,500 kg
Max load: 3,000 kg
Load area: 3.2 × 2.05 m
Length: 8.85 m
Width: 2.5 m
Height:
    (cab) 2.5 m
    (crane) 2.83 m
Ground clearance: 320 mm
Track: 1.927 m
Wheelbase: 3.45 m
Angle of approach/departure: 33°/27°

VAP 3550/1 4 × 4 3,000 kg amphibious vehicle (IVECO Pegaso)　　1340286

Max speed:
  (road) 87 km/h
  (water) 5.5 kt
Range:
  (road) 800 km
  (water) 80 km
Fuel capacity: 250 litres
Max gradient: 60%
Max side slope: 30%
Fording: amphibious
Engine: Pegaso 9135/5 6.55 litre 6-cylinder in-line turbocharged water-cooled 4-stroke diesel developing 170 hp (127 kW) at 2,600 rpm
Gearbox: Pegaso manual with 6 forward and 1 reverse gears
Clutch: single dry plate
Transfer box: Pegaso 2-speed
Steering: recirculating ball, power-assisted
Turning radius: 9 m
Suspension: semi-elliptic springs and hydraulic double acting shock-absorbers; both axles have a self-locking differential
Tyres: 13.00 × 20
Brakes: dual circuit, air, drums all-round
Electrical system: 24 V
Batteries: 2 × 12 V, 99 Ah
Alternator: 1.5 kW

Status

Production complete. In service with the Spanish Marines. Reported as supplied to and in service with Egypt. Seven delivered to Mexico in 1982.

Contractor

IVECO Pegaso SA

United Kingdom

Aquatrack tracked 8,000 kg amphibious vehicle

Development

The Aquatrack tracked amphibious vehicle was developed by GKN Defence (later Alvis Vickers Limited, now BAE Systems Land Systems) to provide a fully amphibious vehicle capable of operating across a wide variety of terrain, including opens seas.

Only two examples of the Aquatrack were sold. These were to the Civil Defense Office of the Department of Defense, Philippines. They are now operated and maintained by the Philippine Marines.

Description

The Aquatrack tracked 8,000 kg amphibious vehicle is capable of carrying up to 8,000 kg of payload or 40 seated personnel in a fully amphibious environment and over a wide variety of terrain. Power is provided by a single diesel engine driving twin variable-pitch propellers in Kort nozzles. Twin rudders assist in allowing the vehicle to manoeuvre and operate fully laden in Sea State 5 at water speeds up to 13 km/h. The vehicle can operate in up to 3.05 m of plunging surf.

The Aquatrack has a nickel-chrome steel hull which incorporates five separate watertight compartments. The driver's cab is set well forward just behind the bow with seating for the driver, a deck-master and two passengers. An open load area behind the cab, with a non-slip deck and multiple lashing points, can carry vehicles the size of a Land Rover. The 'proven' suspension uses M113 running gear.

Aquatrack tracked 8,000 kg amphibious vehicle
(BAE Systems Land Systems)   0044384

Specifications

Aquatrack
Cab seating: 1 + 1 plus 2
Weight:
  (laden) 21,750 kg (approx.)
  (unladen) 13,750 kg (approx.)
Max load: 8,000 kg
Length: 9.6 m
Width: (min) 3.2 m
Height: 3.7 m (approx.)
Deck height: 1.43 m
Load area: 4.45 × 2.6 m
Ground clearance: (at centre) 410 mm
Angle of approach/departure: 40°/40°
Max speed:
  (land) 75 km/h
  (water) 13 km/h
Range:
  (road) 500 km
  (water, cruising) 70 km
Fuel capacity: 400 litres
Max gradient: 50%
Vertical obstacle: 500 mm
Trench: 2 m
Fording: amphibious
Engine: Deutz BF 6M 1015 11.9-litre V-6 water-cooled diesel developing 322 hp (240 kW) at 2,300 rpm
Transmission: Allison X200-6 fully automatic with 4 forward and 1 reverse gear; with torque converter
Turning circle: pivot turn

Status

Production complete, no longer marketed. In service in the Philippines (2).

Contractor

BAE Systems

United States

LARC-5 (4 × 4) 4,545 kg amphibious cargo carrier

Development

The LARC-5 (Lighter, Amphibious, Resupply, Cargo, 5 ton) (4 × 4) was developed by the Borg Warner Corporation from 1958 under the direction of the US Transportation Engineering Command at Fort Eustis, Virginia. The first production contract was awarded to the Adams Division of Le Tourneau Westinghouse in June 1961 and between 1962 and 1968 950 LARC-5s were built. The last manufacturer was ConDiesel Mobile Equipment of Waterbury, Connecticut.

The LARC-5 was designed to carry 4,545 kg of cargo, or 15 to 20 fully equipped troops from ships offshore to the beach or, if required, farther inland. It was issued on the scale of 34 per Army light amphibious company.

In mid-2004 it was announced that Power Dynamics LLC had been awarded a USD12,384,271 firm fixed price contract, consisting of a base year of USD428,677 and five options, to refurbish 37 LARC-5s. Work under this contract is part of the Naval Facilities Engineering Command's, Sealift Support Program Office's (SSPO) Service Life Extension Project (SLEP) for the LARC amphibious craft

A LARC-5 in service with Portuguese armed forces
(Victor Manuel Saraiva Barreira)   1296214

A LARC-5 from the Australian Army 10 Force Support Battalion, 35 Water Transport during Exercise Croix du Sud 2006 (Australian DoD)   1296249

It was announced in March 2006 that Power Dynamics LLC had been awarded the first contract option to repair and overhaul 13 LARC craft for the SSPO. Delivery of the first craft was scheduled for October 2006 and would continue monthly until all 13 craft were delivered against the contract option.

Option 0005 under this contract was awarded in December 2008 and called for 10 LARC craft to be to be refurbished, with work to be completed by late 2010.

Description

The hull of the LARC-5 is of all-welded 5000-series aluminium construction with reinforced aluminium frames. The cab is at the front of the vehicle and contains, in addition to the operating controls: a heater and windscreen defroster; portable lamp and cable; fire extinguisher; fabric cover for the back of the cab; radio; adjustable seat for the driver; two fixed seats for the other crew members and a magnetic compass. The cargo area is in the centre of the vehicle. Fabric curtains reinforced with stranded wire rope can be installed on each side of the cargo deck to protect the cargo.

The transfer transmission compartment is below the cargo deck and contains the transfer transmission, front wheel disconnects, drive shafts and service brakes.

The engine compartment is at the rear and is covered by two watertight hatches. Air is blown out of the compartment through a small grille between the two hatch covers. A fixed fire extinguisher is installed in the engine compartment and is controlled by a pull of a handle on the cargo deck rear bulkhead. Two manual bilge pumps are installed for use if the main hydraulic pump fails. The vehicle is propelled in the water by a three-bladed propeller under the rear of the hull.

Power is transmitted from the engine to a torque converter and hydraulic retarder installed on the flywheel end of the engine. The driver selects either forward or reverse by shifting the forward/reverse transmission lever. The main drive shaft connects the output of the forward/reverse transmission to the transfer transmission. This transmission has two gear ratios (high and low) for land operations and one gear ratio (marine) for water operations. The differential transmission transmits power to the four wheels. With the transmission in low or high range, power is always transmitted to the wheels. A mechanical disconnect can be used to apply power to the rear wheels only for two-wheel drive. Four drive shafts connect the differential transmission to the wheels. A right-angle drive assembly is installed at each wheel to apply the driving power to the wheels. The gearbox is used to apply the rotation of the four-drive shaft to the axle ends of the wheels.

Some vehicles were fitted with a hydraulically operated boom designed by the ConDiesel Mobile Equipment Division. The boom is 4.51 m long and can lift a maximum load of 2,500 kg.

Power Dynamics Service Life Extension Program (SLEP)

The Power Dynamics Service Life Extension Program (SLEP), the contract for which was awarded June 2004, consists of improving the propulsion system by installing a new John Deere turbocharged diesel engine which develops 375 hp and powers a hydraulic system made up of pumps, driving wheel and propeller motors; engine speed is constant with the hydraulic transmission controlling speed. Ancillary improvements are also be made to control, steering, and passenger carrying systems; towing capability and watertight integrity are also improved, as is technical documentation and integrated logistic support and provisions for spare parts and repairs.

Specifications

LARC-5
Cab seating: 1 + 2
Configuration: 4 × 4
Weight:
(laden) 14,053 kg
(unladen) 9,508 kg
Max load: 4,545 kg
Load area: 4.876 × 2.971 m
Length: 10.07 m
Width: 3.05 m
Height:
(overall) 3.1 m
(reduced) 2.41 m
Ground clearance: 406 mm
Track: 2.565 m
Wheelbase: 4.876 m
Angle of approach/departure: 27°/20.7°
Max speed:
(road) 48.2 km/h
(water) 13.9 km/h
Range:
(land, laden) 322 km
(land, unladen) 400 km
(water, laden) 56 km
(water, unladen) 65 km
Fuel capacity: 547.2 litres
Max gradient: 60%
Max side slope: 25%
Fording: amphibious
Engine:
(early vehicles) 8-cylinder petrol developing 300 hp (224 kW) at 3,000 rpm
(late production vehicles) Cummins V-8 water-cooled 4-stroke diesel developing 300 hp (224 kW)
Turning radius: 13.26 m
Suspension: rigid
Tyres: 18.00 × 25

Status

Production complete. Supplied to Argentina, Australia (87 delivered, all de-activated by late-94, some re-activated 98/99 of which 56 remained in service as of December 2001), Philippines, Portugal, Singapore, Thailand and the US (42 SLEP).

Contractor

ConDiesel Mobile Equipment, Connecticut (this company is no longer trading).

US SLEP contractor

Power Dynamics LLC - Entach Systems

ALL-TERRAIN CARRIERS AND PRIME MOVERS

Australia

Thales Australia Bushmaster Utility Vehicle

Development
Based on their experience in the design, development and production of the Bushmaster Infantry Mobility Vehicle (IMV) for the Australian Army, Thales Australia have developed, as a private venture, the Bushmaster Utility Vehicle which in the past has also been referred to as the Copperhead Armoured Logistic Support Vehicle.

This has been developed from the combat proven Thales Australia Bushmaster Protected Mobility Vehicle (PMV) that was originally developed to meet the requirements of the Australian Army.

This has seen extensive operational use in Afghanistan, East Timor and Iraq and provides its occupants with a very high level of protection from small arms fire, shell splinters, mine blasts and Improvised Explosive Devices (IED).

As of December 2010 the total Bushmaster PMV order book was:

Country	Quantity	Comment
Australia	737	deliveries still under way
Netherlands	86	final deliveries late 2009
UK	24	ordered and delivered for UOR in 2008
US	2	for US Army trials

Description
The Australian Army currently deploys six versions of the Bushmaster PMV, troop carrier, ambulance, assault pioneer, command, direct fire and 81 mm mortar.

Thales Australia have developed two logistics load carrier variants called the Bushmaster Utility vehicle.

They are in the single door cab arrangement (Bushmaster Utility Single Cab) and four door cab (Bushmaster Utility Dual Cab) and up to five tonnes can be carried on the flat bed at the rear.

Development of the Bushmaster Utility Vehicle is complete but as of late 2010 no production orders had been placed for this vehicle.

The Bushmaster Utility Vehicle is based on the Bushmaster PMV concept with a fully armour protected powerpack and air conditioned crew compartment at the front.

The crew compartment is provided with a large bulletproof window to the front, a door in either side with a bulletproof window in its upper part as well as hatches in the roof. The example shown in the mid-2008 was fitted with roof mounted wire cutters.

To the rear of the fully protected cab is the flatbed cargo area on which loads of up to five tonnes can be carried.

A mechanical handling system could be fitted to allow rapid unloading. The load area could also be fitted with removable sides and a tailgate at the rear.

Current Bushmaster Utility Vehicle gross vehicle weight is being quoted as 15 tonnes but this could be increased with an upgraded suspension system.

The all welded armoured steel monocoque hull is protected to STANAG 4569 Level 1 small arms fire, but mine protection is greater than STANAG 4569 Level 3.

Thales Australia also offers an enhanced range of additional armour packages as well as spall liners for the front crew compartment.

Thales Australia Bushmaster Utility Vehicle in two door cab configuration clearly showing the flatbed load area at the rear (Christopher F Foss)
1403710

The complete Thales Australia Bushmaster family of vehicles with the baseline Bushmaster Protected Patrol Vehicle at the front, Bushmaster Utility Vehicle in centre (with two door cab version on the left and four door cab version on the right) and Bushmaster ambulance to the rear (Thales Australia)
1365184

Variants
Upgraded Bushmaster suspension
Thales Australia have completed an engineering assessment to upgrade Bushmaster with new axles and suspension thus increasing the gross vehicle weight to 18 tonnes.

Bushmaster 6 × 6
This first example of the Bushmaster in a 6 × 6 configuration was completed in 2009 with a significant increase in volume and payload. It has a gross vehicle weight of up to 26 tonnes.

Specifications
Bushmaster Utility Vehicle
Crew: 2 - 3
Configuration: 4 × 4
Combat weight: 15,000 kg
Unloaded weight: 11,000 kg
Payload: (including crew) 5,000 kg
Power-to-weight ratio: 20 hp/tonne
Length: 7.33 m
Width: 2.50 m
Height: 2.66 m
Ground clearance:
  (hull) 0.43 m
  (axle housing) 0.43 m
Track: 2.1 m
Wheelbase: 3.9 m
Max road speed: 100 km/h
Fuel capacity: 292 + 19 l
Max road range: 800 km
Fording: 1.2 m
Gradient: 60%
Side slope: 30%
Trench: n/applicable
Vertical obstacle: 0.56 m
Turning radius: 9.25 m
Engine: Caterpillar 3126 ATAAC 6-cylinder, turbocharged and air-to-air after cooled diesel developing 300 hp at 2,400 rpm with 25% torque rise
Transmission: ZF 7HP502 full automatic with 6 forward and 1 reverse gears and with front end retarder providing controlled descent of 60% slopes
Steering: power assisted
Tyres: 395/85 R20 with beadlocks or optional run flat central tyre pressure regulation system
Brakes: Rockwell air-operated disc, dual circuit
Suspension: coil spring and short-long arm wishbone with double acting hydraulic shock-absorbers and bump-stock rubbers
Electrical system: 24 V
NBC system: no

Status
Development complete. Ready for production.

Contractor
Thales Australia

Belarus

Minotor Service Mule Forward Area Supply Carrier

Development
In 2003, the Minotor Service company of Belarus announced that it had developed, as a private venture, the Mule Forward Area Supply Carrier based on a much modified Russian designed and built Armoured Command and Reconnaissance Vehicle (ACRV) chassis.

As production of the ACRV has been completed, it is expected that any Mule Forward Area Supply Carrier vehicles built would be conversions of existing vehicles.

As of December 2010, it is understood that production of the Mule Forward Area Supply Carrier had not commenced although it was still being marketed.

Description
The hull of the Mule is of all-welded steel armour that provides the occupants with protection from small arms fire and shell splinters.

The vehicle commander and driver are seated at the front of the vehicle and in the upper part of the hull front, which slopes to the rear, are two large windows which can be rapidly covered by an armoured shutter hinged at the top.

The driver is seated at the front on the left and above his position is a single-piece hatch cover that opens to the rear and can be locked in the vertical position.

The vehicle commander is seated on the right and above his position is a single-piece hatch cover that opens to the rear which can be locked in the vertical position.

The driver is provided with three roof-mounted day periscopes with the vehicle commander being provided with a roof-mounted swivelling day periscope.

The diesel engine compartment is located to the rear of the commander and driver with air inlet and outlet louvres located in the roof. The exhaust outlet is located on the roof and extends to the rear of the hull.

This hull arrangement with the vehicle commander, driver and powerpack compartment at the front leaves the whole of the rear of the hull clear for its specialised role.

Suspension is of the torsion bar type with either side having seven single rubber-tyred road wheels with the drive sprocket at the front and idler at the rear. There are no track return rollers.

Mule is fully amphibious, being propelled in the water by its tracks. Before entering the water, the bilge pump is switched on, the trim vane erected at the front of the hull, shrouds are fitted to the hull above the drive sprocket and the road wheels are covered.

Any water that enters the hull during amphibious operations is removed via the exhaust outlet using the bilge pump.

Cargo can be loaded into the vehicle via hatches in the roof or through a door in the left side of the hull at the rear, which is also provided with a firing port and associated vision device.

In addition, there is a cargo platform on the roof. The latter has a capacity of 6.5 m². The internal cargo compartment has a volume of 6.5 m³ and a payload of four tonnes.

There are also stowage racks on the sides of the Mule and the main cargo area can be covered by bows and a tarpaulin cover.

Standard equipment for the Mule includes an NBC system and night vision requirement.

Variants
Belarus has also developed a number of other versions of the ACRV, including the SM-120 self-propelled mortar and the TZM-122 ammunition resupply vehicle. Both of these are understood to remain at the prototype stage.

The Mule Forward Area Supply Carrier is based on a much modified ACRV chassis (Minotor)   0567113

Specifications
Mule Forward Area Supply Carrier
Crew: 2 + 4
Combat weight: 11,300 kg
Power-to-weight ratio: 26.54 hp/tonne
Length: 7.475 m
Width: 2.85 m
Height: 2.435 m
Ground clearance: 0.40 m
Track width: 400 mm
Max speed:
  (road) 60 km/h
  (water) 4 to 6 km/h
Fuel capacity: 550 litres
Road range: 500 km
Fording: amphibious
Gradient: 77%
Side slope: 55%
Vertical obstacle: 0.70 m
Engine: YaMZ-238 V-8 water-cooled 4-stroke diesel developing 300 hp
Transmission: (manual) 4 forward and 1 reverse gears
Steering: clutch and brake
Armament: 1 × 12.7 mm externally mounted machine gun (optional)
Armour:
  (hull) 15 mm (estimate)
NBC system: yes
Night vision equipment: yes

Status
Prototype. Not yet in production or service.

Contractor
Minotor Service

Canada

General Dynamics Land Systems - Canada LAV (8 × 8) 2,470 kg armoured logistics carrier (LAV-L)

Development
The now General Dynamics Land Systems - Canada LAV (8 × 8) 2,470 kg armoured logistics carrier, or LAV-L, is one component in a series of vehicles known to the US Marine Corps as Mission-Role Vehicles (MRVs).

These are variants of the basic LAV light armoured vehicle, which is based on the Swiss MOWAG Piranha family of 8 × 8 LAV. These have now gone through a Service Life Extension Programme (SLEP) carried out by Metric Systems.

The first LAV-L was handed over to the US Marine Corps in September 1985. The delivery of a batch of 94 vehicles began in November 1985 and was completed by August 1986.

In 2006 the US Marine Corps placed an order with General Dynamics Land Systems for an additional 130 brand new vehicles which have been designated as the LAV-A2 in order to allow additional units to be equipped with the vehicle.

Under the terms of this contract five different versions of the LAV-A2 have been supplied and these are anti-tank, armoured personnel carrier, command-and-control, logistics and mortar carrier and these have now been delivered.

While US Army vehicles are all powered by a Caterpillar diesel engine all of the latest USMC vehicle are powered by the older Detroit Diesel 6V-53T diesel developing 275 hp coupled to an Allison MT653 fully automatic transmission. This will ensure commonality with existing fleet of US Marine Corps vehicles. It is planned to increase engine output to 300 hp.

These LAV-A2 will also have a number of detailed improvements such as upgraded suspension, fire detection and suppression and enhanced armour protection.

The latter will include the Ballistic Protection Upgrade which is a three kit system (A,B and C) which provides enhanced protection against a variety of threats including improvised explosive devices.

Description
The LAV-L provides the US Marine Corps with mobile logistic support in the field. It uses many components of the basic LAV light armoured vehicle, including the suspension, drive train and hull. On the LAV-L the driver is seated forward to the left of the engine compartment, under an armoured hatch. When this is in the closed down position, the driver is provided with three wide-vision periscopes.

The centre one can be replaced by a passive periscope for night driving. Behind the driver is the raised commander's position, which is provided with all-round vision devices when the armoured hatch is closed down. This position may be equipped with a pintle for a 7.62 mm machine gun. There are also two four-barrel M257 electrically-operated smoke grenade launchers controlled from the commander's position. There is seating behind the commander for a third crew member.

The main cargo-carrying compartment has an unobstructed level floor measuring 2.59 × 1.65 m. Access to the area is via two outward-opening rear doors or through two-roof hatches each with dimensions of 1.07 × 1.28 m.

FAMAE/MOWAG Piranha (8 × 8) armoured logistics carrier showing loading crane, roof hatches and power operated ramp at hull rear 0511870

General Dynamics Land Systems - Canada LAV (8 × 8) 2,470 kg armoured logistics carrier (LAV-L) 0512244

To the left rear of the roof hatch is a 500 kg telescopic crane operated from a folding platform over the left rear wheel. When the rear doors are open it is possible to load the cargo area using forklift trucks, internal net stowage and lashing points are also provided.

The LAV-L is amphibious and may be airlifted by a heavy helicopter. Extra internal seating can be provided, as can internal hoists and powered tailgates. A standard NATO towing hook is provided.

The US Army has a complete family of 8 × 8 vehicles based on the LAV-III series called the Stryker. At present, there is not a logistics version of this vehicle. General Dynamics Land Systems - Canada is currently in full scale production of the Stryker Infantry Carrier Vehicle (ICV) for the US Army.

By late 2010 the US Army had ordered over 4,000 Stryker ICV and variants with production still underway.

Variants

Chilean production of Piranha
FAMAE of Brazil has built a logistics version of the MOWAG Piranha for the Chilean Army. This is very similar to the LAV-L but has a power operated ramp at the rear rather than twin doors as in all US Marine Corps vehicles. A telescopic crane is fitted for loading and unloading purposes.

Specifications

LAV-L
Crew: 3
Configuration: 8 × 8
Weight: (combat) 12,730 kg
Max load: 2,470 kg
Length: 5.448 m
Width: 2.5 m
Height: 2.194 m
Max speed:
  (road) 100 km/h
  (water) 10 km/h
Range: 660 km
Gradient: 60%
Side slope: 30%
Vertical obstacle: 0.50 m
Trench: 2.057 m
Fording: amphibious
Engine: Detroit Diesel 6V-53T 6-cylinder diesel developing 275 hp at 2,800 rpm
Transmission: Allison MT-653 DR automatic, 5 forward and 1 reverse gears

Transfer case: Rockwell AG-VST (modified)
Steering: power-assisted on front 2 axles
Turning circle: 15.5 m
Suspension:
  (front four wheels) independent coil springs and shock-absorbers
  (rear four wheels) independent torsion bars and shock-absorbers
Tyres: 11.00 × 16 with Hutchinson run-flat inserts
Brakes:
  (main) 8-wheel dual airbrake, transmission brake and transfer case lock
  (parking) transmission brake and transfer case lock
Electrical system: 24 V
Batteries: 4 × 12 V
Alternator: 200 A
Armament:
  1 × 7.62 mm MG
  2 × 4-barrel smoke grenade dischargers
Ammunition: 7.62 mm - 1,000 rounds; smoke grenades - 8 in launchers, 8 spare
Armour:
  (hull front) 8 mm
  (hull sides) 10 mm

Status
Production complete. In service with US Marine Corps (94). The US Marine Corps has taken delivery of an additional 130 LAV-A2 vehicles which include some logistics versions as mentioned in the Development section.

Contractor
General Dynamics Land Systems - Canada

China

NORINCO PCZ45 Ammunition Support Vehicle

Development
To support the China North Industries Corporation (NORINCO) 155 mm/PLZ45 self-propelled artillery system. NORINCO has developed a complete family of supporting vehicles including the PCZ45 ammunition support vehicle.

In many respects this carries out a similar function to the now BAE Systems, US Combat Systems M992 Field Artillery Ammunition Support Vehicle (FAASV) which supports the BAE Systems, US Combat Systems M109A6 Paladin 155 mm self-propelled artillery system of the US Army.

The first customer for the PCZ45 Ammunition Support Vehicle was Kuwait who took delivery of 27 systems to support 27 155 mm PLZ45 self-propelled artillery systems. Since then a repeat order has been placed.

NORINCO has been awarded a contract by Saudi Arabia for the supply of at least 27 155 mm/45 calibre PLZ45 self-propelled artillery systems. It is believed that the PCZ45 Ammunition Support Vehicle does not form part of this contract.

It is understood that Saudi Arabia has taken delivery of a batch of NORINCO PLZ45 self-propelled gun-howitzers with Panhard General Defense of France supplying the wheeled support vehicles.

At this stage it is not known as to whether Saudi Arabia has taken delivery of any PCZ45 ammunition support vehicles.

Description
The PCZ45 ammunition support vehicle is based on a modified 155 mm PLZ45 self-propelled artillery system chassis.

The hull and superstructure is of all-welded steel armour that provides the occupants with protection from small arms fire and shell splinters.

Production standard PCZ45 ammunition support vehicle with hydraulic crane traversed to the rear and roof mounted 12.7 mm machine gun fitted for local defence (NORINCO) 1365002

The driver is seated at the front of the hull on the left side and has a single-piece hatch above his position that opens to the rear. In front of this are three periscopes. The middle one can be replaced by a passive periscope for driving at night.

The diesel powerpack is to the right of the driver's position with the air inlet and outlet louvres in the top and the exhaust outlet on the right side.

Mounted on the roof, to the rear of the driver's position is a hydraulically-operated crane with a telescopic jib. This has a maximum lifting weight of 600 kg.

The hydraulically-operated crane installed on the PCZ45 can be traversed through to a full 360° and the jib can be extended from 1.2 to 4.5 m. Maximum lifting height is 4 m.

A total of 90 × 155 mm projectiles and associated charges are carried. These are rapidly transferred through the rear of the vehicle to the 155 mm PLZ45 self-propelled artillery system at the rate of six to eight projectiles a minute.

The suspension is of the torsion bar type and either side consists of six dual rubber-tyred road wheels with the drive sprocket at the front, idler at the rear and track return rollers. The first and last road wheel stations are provided with a hydraulic shock absorber.

Standard equipment includes a 155 mm projectile transfer control system, Global Positioning System (GPS), communications system, auxiliary power unit, NBC protection system and a fire detection and suppression system. The PLZ45 and PCZ45 vehicles supplied to Kuwait is also fitted with an air conditioning system.

According to NORINCO, the main features of the PCZ45 Ammunition Support Vehicle are greater survivability, safer and convenient ammunition delivery, high mobility, rapid delivery rate and rapid replenishment of projectiles.

Armament comprises a 12.7 mm mounted machine gun plus a bank of eight electrically operated smoke grenade launchers mounted on the forward part of the superstructure.

Specifications

PCZ45 Ammunition Support Vehicle
Crew: 3
Combat weight: 33,000 kg
Power-to-weight ratio: 15.93 hp/tonne
Length: 7.15 m
Width: 3.33 m
Height:
  (top of superstructure) 3.05 m
  (top of machine gun) 3.42 m
Ground clearance: 0.45 m
Max speed: 55 km/h
Max range: 450 km
Fording: 1.20 m
Gradient: 58%
Side slope: 47%
Vertical obstacle: 0.70 m
Trench: 2.7 m
Engine: Deutz BF12 L413FC air-cooled supercharged diesel developing 526 hp
Gearbox: manual with dual power take off with 6 forward and 1 reverse gears
Steering: hydraulic
Suspension: torsion bars and hydraulic shock absorbers
Armament: 1 × 12.7 mm MG
Ammunition: 480 × 12.7 mm
NBC system: yes
Night vision equipment: optional

Status
Production as required. Known to be in service with Kuwait.

Contractor
China North Industries Corporation (NORINCO)

NORINCO Type 59 artillery tractor

Development
The Type 59 artillery tractor was designed to tow artillery systems used by the People's Liberation Army (PLA), such as the China North Industries Corporation (NORINCO) 122 mm Type 54 howitzer or the 122 mm Type 60 gun.

NORINCO Type 59 artillery tractor towing 57 mm Type 59 anti-aircraft gun
0511871

It has also been used to tow a NORINCO 57 mm Type 59 (this is a copy of the Russian 57 mm S-60) anti-aircraft gun. This weapon has been exported by NORINCO and some Type 59 artillery tractors may have been supplied with the weapons.

Production of the Type 59 artillery tractor has been completed and it is no longer being marketed by NORINCO.

Description
The fully enclosed unarmoured cab at the front of the vehicle has sufficient seats for most of the crew of the gun and has a circular observation hatch in the left side of the roof. The rear cargo area has a stake-type body and a drop tailgate, removable bows and a tarpaulin cover.

The suspension is believed to be of the torsion bar type and consists either side of five roadwheels with the drive sprocket at the front and the idler at the rear. The Type 59 may be powered by a V-12 diesel truck engine coupled to a manual transmission.

Status
Production complete. In service with China and Vietnam. No longer marketed.

Contractor
China North Industries Corporation (NORINCO)

NORINCO Type 60-1 tracked artillery tractor

Development
Recent information has indicated that the Type 60 tracked artillery tractor was developed by the Luoyang Tractor facility in Henan and uses automotive components of the NORINCO Type 63 full tracked armoured personnel carrier. Production of the Type 63 APC has been completed and NORINCO has ceased all marketing.

The original Type 60 has the industrial designation of the WZ420, while the latter Type 60-1 has the industrial designation of the WZ421.

The Type 60-1 was developed from 1975 with development being completed in 1977, after which production commenced.

When compared to the older Type 60 tracked artillery tractor, the more recent Type 60-1 has a number of improvements including upgraded manual transmission, tracks with rubber pads and heater to assist in starting the diesel engine in cold weather.

Production of the NORINCO Type 60-1 tracked artillery tractor has been completed and is no longer marketed by NORINCO.

Description
The Type 60-1 can carry up to 5,000 kg of cargo and tow artillery or trailers weighing up to 15,000 kg. The forward-control all-steel unarmoured cab accommodates a driver and an artillery detachment. The roof is equipped with a hatch mounting a 12.7 mm Type 54 machine gun, the Chinese version of the built model of the older Russian DShK.

There is stowage for the crew's personal equipment in lockers behind the cab and the main cargo area may be covered by bows and a canvas tarpaulin.

A winch may be fitted, adding 1,000 kg to the vehicle's weight. This has a maximum capacity of 17,000 kg and is equipped with 75 m of cable. The engine starting time in winter with the ambient temperature at −35°C is stated to be 18 minutes.

The Type 60-1 is used as the carrier for the 273 mm Type 83 multiple rocket system, which has four of these large calibre rockets in the ready-to-launch position. As far as it is known, this is only used by the People's Liberation Army. It is no longer marketed by NORINCO. Details of this are provided in *Jane's Armour and Artillery*.

Variants
The Type 60 is also used to carry radar systems and to tow missiles and other specialised equipment. A version with a radar system has been referred to as the R914B while a radar version of the later Type 60-1 is called the R421. A cable laying vehicle has also been reported.

NORINCO Type 60-1 tracked artillery tractor with roof mounted 12.7 mm machine gun
0511872

Specifications

Type 60-1 tracked artillery tractor
Weight:
  (with winch) 12,500 kg
  (without winch) 11,500 kg
Payload: 5,000 kg
Towed load: 15,000 kg
Length: 6.117 m
Width: 2.6 m
Height:
  (top of cab) 2.81 m
  (top of tilt) 3.015 m
  (to horizontal machine gun) 3.26 m
Ground clearance: 0.40 m
Track: 2.15 m
Length of track on ground: 3.248 m
Max speed: 48.8 km/h
Range: 400 km
Max gradient:
  (with 5,000 kg load) 30°
  (with 5,000 kg load and 15,000 kg trailer) 15°
Gradient: 26°
Side slope: 40 %
Fording: 1 m
Engine: 12150L-1 V-12 water-cooled 4-cycle direct injection diesel developing 300 hp at 1,600 rpm

Status

In service with China and possibly other countries. Production completed. No longer marketed.

Contractor

China North Industries Corporation (NORINCO)

NORINCO Type 77 Light Tracked Artillery Tractor

Development

The China North Industries Corporation (NORINCO) Type 77 Light Tracked Artillery Tractor was developed from the late 1970s by the Luoyang Tractor facility, who also designed and built a number of other vehicles of this type for the Peoples Liberation Army, including the Type 60 and Type 60-1 tracked artillery tractors.

Production of the Type 60/Type 60-1 light tracked artillery tractors has been completed and they are no longer marketed. Details are provided in a separate entry in *Jane's Military Vehicles and Logistics.*

Following trials with eight prototype vehicles, it was type classified as the Type 77 Light Tracked Artillery Tractor and entered service with the Peoples Liberation Army in 1977.

As well as carrying up to 3,500 kg of cargo it is also used to tow artillery weapons. As far as It is known, it has not been exported outside of China and has not recently been offered on the export market.

As far as it is known, production of the Type 77 Light Tracked Artillery Tractor has now been completed.

It is possible that some of these vehicles could be upgraded to extend their operational life.

Description

The layout of the Type 77 Light Tracked Artillery Tractor is similar to other Chinese vehicles of this type with the fully enclosed cab at the front and the load area at the rear.

The fully enclosed cab has two doors in either side which open to the front with a searchlight mounted on the left side. As far as it is known the cab is not armoured.

The load area is at the rear and provided with drop sides and a drop tailgate and bows and a tarpaulin cover can be quickly erected if required over the load area which is provided with seats to enable people to be carried if required. These can be folded up to allow cargo to be carried.

Standard equipment includes a winch for self-recovery operations and an engine pre-heater for use in cold weather.

Specifications

Type 77 Light Tracked Artillery Tractor
Crew: 1 + 4
Weight:
  (loaded) 8,800 kg
  (empty) 5,300 kg
Payload: 3,500 kg
Length: 5.5 m
Width: 2.4 m
Height:
  (without bows) 2.4 m
  (with bows) 2.8 m
Max speed: 54 km/h
Max range: 700 km
Fuel capacity: 510 litres
Gradient: 70%
Side slope: 40%

Fording: 1 m
Engine: Model V8-135 four-stroke diesel developing 260 hp
Transmission: manual
Suspension: torsion bar with hydraulic shock absorbers

Status

Production complete. In service with China. The Type 77 light tracked artillery tractor is no longer marketed.

Contractor

China North Industries Corporation (NORINCO)

Finland

Patria Land & Armament NA series all-terrain vehicle

Development

The Patria Land & Armament NA series all-terrain vehicle was developed for military use in extreme terrain. Testing of the first prototype began in 1985. Pre-production of 11 units started in Autumn 1986 with full-scale production commencing during 1988.

During 1988 the Finnish Defence Ministry placed an order worth USD35 million for 112 units, with first deliveries made during 1988. It is estimated that total production of the NA series amounted to at least 700 vehicles.

The Finnish Defence Force have a requirement for a new all-terrain vehicle with the two competitors being the Swedish BAE Systems Global Combat Systems (previously BAE Systems Hägglunds) BvS 10 (currently in service with the Netherlands and the UK and on order for France) and the Singapore Technologies Kinetics Bronco (in service with Singapore, Thailand and the UK).

An upgraded version of the Bronco entered service in 2010 called the Warthog which has been improved in a number of areas for operation in Afghanistan including an enhanced armour package.

As of December 2010, the Finnish Defence Force had not announced the procurement of either of these two vehicles to meet its future requirements.

Description

The Patria Land & Armament NA series all-terrain vehicle is a two-compartment vehicle with articulated steering. Each compartment has two wide and flexible rubber band tracks reinforced with composite cross members and longitudinal cords. The tracks have a guaranteed 7,500 km running life.

NA series all-terrain vehicle used by Finland and armed with a Patria Land & Armament 120 mm mortar (Christopher F Foss)   0121620

NA series all-terrain vehicle used by Finland (Richard Stickland)   1044348

Standard versions manufactured before 1994 were powered by a General Motors V-8 diesel engine, coupled to a General Motors 3L89 HD 3+1 automatic transmission. Later examples are based on a L57 6.5 litre heavy-duty Detroit Diesel V-8 unit coupled to a Hydra-Matic 4L80-E 4+1 transmission.

The engine is located in the front compartment and the compartments are connected by a flexible coupling which also accommodates the steering assembly through which the drive is transmitted to the rear unit.

The axle system is based on Sisu BTN type drive axles. The main brake is a disc unit located in the coupling assembly and operating on the drive train. Track and roadwheel assemblies are interchangeable. The vehicle is fully amphibious, being propelled in the water by its tracks.

The standard bodywork for both compartments is a single composite materials element on a light alloy frame. The front unit has four doors with space for the driver and five passengers or 700 kg of cargo; the rear unit can carry up to 12 personnel or 1,300 kg of cargo. A tow hook at the rear allows the towing of light weapons or a sledge.

The basic NA series all-terrain vehicle chassis can be adapted to a wide variety of special bodies or optional equipment. Proposed variants have included: a logistics/cargo carrier with the rear unit configured as a load area; ambulance container carrier; fuel transport vehicle; container carrying vehicle and 81 mm or 120 mm mortar carrier. Civil versions have been delivered as firefighting and rescue vehicles.

Optional accessories include: a winch; hydraulic power take-off; heavy machine gun mounting; add-on protection; large rear cabin side windows; navigation system; night vision equipment; various communications systems; air conditioning and/or NBC filtration system; and an AC electrical system.

Variants in service with the Finnish Defence Force include a 120 mm mortar carrier and its associated ammunition resupply vehicle. The latter has a Patria Land & Armament 120 mm smooth bore mortar installed in the rear unit that fires to the rear.

Specifications
NA series all terrain vehicle
Cab seating: 1 + 5 (front unit - up to 12 in rear unit)
Weight:
(empty) 5,400 kg
(GVW) 7,400 kg
Max load: 2,000 kg
Towed load: 2,500 kg
Length:
Cargo space:
(front unit) 1.8 m³
(rear unit) 6.0 m³
(total, overall) 7.67 m³
(front unit) 3.3 m³
(rear unit) 3.45 m³
Width: 1.91 m
Height: 2.35 m
Ground clearance:
(loaded) 0.30 m
Track width: 620 mm
Max speed:
(road) 60 km/h
(water) 3.6–6 km/h (depending on equipment)
Range: 500 km
Fuel capacity: 280 litres
Max gradient: 45°
Side slope: 35°
Fording: amphibious when loaded
Engine:
(until 1994) GM Powertrain 6.2 litre 4-stroke V-8 diesel
(final production) Detroit Diesel 6.5 litre L57 four-stroke V-8 diesel developing 159 hp at 3,400 rpm
Transmission:
(until 1994) GM Hydra-Matic 3L80 HD automatic with 3 forward and 1 reverse gears
(final production) GM Hydra-Matic 4L80-E automatic with 4 forward and 1 reverse gears
Transfer box: Sisu L175 2-speed manual
Steering: articulated hydrostatic
Turning radius: 6 m
Suspension: transverse leaf springs
Brakes: single circuit, disc
Electrical system: 12/24 V
Batteries: 2 × 12 V

Status
Production complete. In service with China, the Finnish Defence Forces, Russia, Turkey and the UN. No longer marketed.

Contractor
Patria Land & Armament Oy

Iran

DIO Boraq Armoured Ammunition Carrier

Development
The Boraq Armoured Ammunition Carrier (AAC) was developed by the Iranian Defence Industries Organisation (DIO), Shahid Kolahdooz Industrial Complex, Vehicle and Equipments Group.

It uses many automotive components of the Boraq full tracked armoured personnel carrier that has been in service with Iran for many years.

It is expected that the AAC will be used to support towed and self-propelled artillery systems with the former including the locally developed 122 mm Raad-1 and 155 mm Raad-2 which are already in service with Iran.

As of late 2010 it is understood that quantity production of the DIO AAC has yet to commence.

Description
The hull of the Boraq AAC is of all welded steel armour that provides the occupants with protection from small arms fire and shell splinters with the highest level of protection being over the frontal arc.

The driver is seated in raised compartment at the front left side of the chassis with another person to the rear. They can enter the vehicle via hatches in the roof.

The diesel engine compartment is to the right of the crew compartment with the air inlet and outlet louvres in the roof and the exhaust pipe on the right side of the hull.

Suspension is of the torsion bar type and either side consists of six dual rubber tyred road wheels with the drive sprocket at the front and the idler at the rear, there are also at least two return rollers.

The road wheels are understood to be the same as those fitted to the BAE Systems, US Combat Systems M113 series armoured personnel carrier which has been in service with Iran for many years. Iran has been manufacturing tracks and road wheels for the M113 for many years.

The upper part of the running gear either side, is covered by a rubber skirt which not only helps to keep down dust but also improves water flow during amphibious operations.

The cargo area is at the rear and cargo can be rapidly loaded and unloaded via the ramp in the hull rear that folds downwards. The cargo area is normally covered by bows and a tarpaulin cover.

The vehicle can typically carry a load of 4,000 kg and is fully amphibious being propelled in the water by its tracks at a speed of 7 km/h

Specifications
Boraq Armoured Ammunition Carrier
Crew: 1 + 1
Power-to-weight ratio: 28 hp/t
Ground pressure: 0.57 kg/cm²
Weight: 11,000 kg
Payload: 4,000 kg
Length: 6.2 m
Width:
(over tracks) 3.05 m
(overall) 3.165 m
Height:
(crew compartment) 2.162 m
(with bows) 2.264 m
Ground clearance: 0.42 m
Track: 2.597 m
Track width: 397 mm
Length of track on ground: 3.60 m
Max speed:
(road) 75 km/h
(water) 7 km/h
Max range: 430 km
Fuel capacity: 450 litres
Gradient: 60%
Side slope: 40%
Fording: amphibious

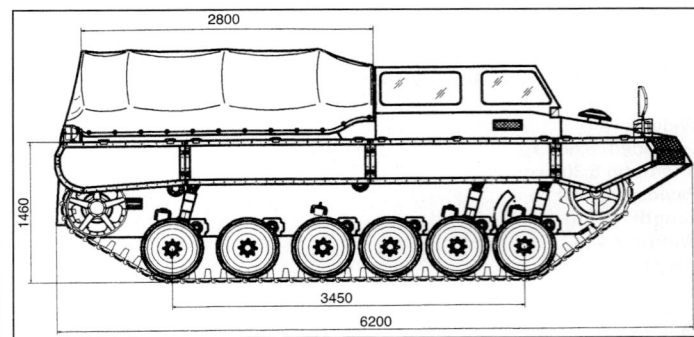

Side drawing of Boraq Armoured Ammunition Carrier (DIO)   1044350

Vertical obstacle: 0.70 m
Trench: 2.30 m
Engine: Deutz BF8L 513 4-stroke V-8 air cooled turbo charged diesel developing 330 hp at 2,300 rpm
Transmission: manual, 5 forward and 1 reverse gears
Steering: clutch and brake
Final drive: planetary/single stage
Suspension: torsion bar with hydraulic shock absorbers
Electrical system: 24 V
Batteries: 2
Armament: nil

Status
Development complete. Ready for production.

Contractor
Defence Industries Organisation

Japan

Type 73 tracked artillery tractor and Type 87 tracked ammunition carrier

Development
The Type 73 tracked artillery tractor was developed from 1969 as the replacement for the US-designed and built M4 and M8 high-speed tractors used by the Japanese Ground Self-Defence Force.

Trials with prototype vehicles were successfully completed in 1972 and the following year it was standardised as the Type 73 tracked artillery tractor, or tractor (prime mover). Production began in 1974 but only a small number were built owing to defence budget restrictions.

Neither of these two vehicles was ever offered on the export market by Japan.

Description
The Type 73 has a fully enclosed four-door cab at the front with the engine in the centre and the ammunition stowage area at the rear. The suspension is believed to be of the torsion bar type with either side consisting of six roadwheels with the drive sprocket at the front, the sixth roadwheel acting as the idler. A .50 (12.7 mm) M2 HB machine gun is mounted on the roof for anti-aircraft defence.

Type 87 tracked ammunition carrier 1334276

Type 73 tracked artillery tractor 1334278

Some Type 73s have been fitted with a hydraulically-operated dozer blade at the front of the hull for clearing obstacles and preparing fire positions.

The Type 87 tracked ammunition carrier is based on the Type 73 tracked artillery tractor. Following the switch from towed to self-propelled artillery by the Japanese Ground Self-Defence Force, over 100 Type 73s have been converted to Type 87 carriers.

The Type 87 can carry up to 50 rounds of 203 mm ammunition and is equipped with a crane. The Type 87 has a combat weight of 23.5 tonnes and a maximum road speed of 50 km/h. It is 7.17 m long, 2.99 m wide and has a height of 3 m.

Production of the Type 87 was undertaken at a very low rate with three being procured in FY1999 and just one in FY2000. The most recent orders were placed in FY2003 and FY2004, with one unit being ordered in each year.

Specifications
Type 73 tracked artillery tractor
Cab seating: 1 + 11
Weight: 19,800 kg
Max towed load: 16,000 kg
Length: 6.13 m
Width: 2.95 m
Height: 2.3 m
Max speed: (road) 45 km/h
Range: 300 km
Gradient: 60%
Engine: Mitsubishi ZF6 6-cylinder air-cooled diesel developing 400 hp at 2,200 rpm

Status
Production complete. In service with the Japanese Ground Self-Defence Force. Over 100 Type 73 tractors have been converted to Type 87 tracked ammunition carriers. The Type 73 tracked artillery tractor was never offered on the export market.

Contractor
Hitachi Manufacturing Company

Special tracked prime mover

Development
This special tracked prime mover is based on the Mitsubishi Type 73 armoured personnel carrier and is used to tow special equipment such as the Type 76 artillery locating radar (JMPQ-P7). This is mounted on a special four wheeled trailer with antenna lowered for travelling.

Description
The special tracked prime mover has a fully enclosed crew compartment towards the front of the vehicle and carries an electrical generator at the rear, but few details are available.

There is also a version of this radar mounted on a 6 × 6 truck. It should be noted that in addition to this special tracked prime mover and the Type 73 tracked artillery tractor and Type 87 tracked ammunition carrier, Japan also uses the full tracked Type 99 ammunition support vehicle.

Status
Production complete. In service with the Japanese Ground Self-Defence Force. This has never been offered on the export market.

Contractor
Mitsubishi Heavy Industries

Special tracked prime mover towing Type 76 gun-locating radar 1334279

Korea, South

Doosan Military Logistic Support Vehicle

Development

The Doosan (previously Daewoo) Military Logistic Support Vehicle (MLSV) is based on the same chassis as the Flying Tiger (Biho) twin 30 mm self-propelled anti-aircraft gun system which is now operational with the Republic of Korea Army.

The chassis is also used as the basis for the Pegasus all-weather surface-to-air missile system that has eight missiles in the ready-to-launch position.

Both of these mobile air defence systems have been offered on the export market, but as of late 2010 there are no known export sales.

Development of the Doosan Military Logistic Support Vehicle is complete but it is understood that as of late 2010 production had yet to commence.

Description

The MLSV is designed to support 155 mm self-propelled artillery systems and carries 139 155 mm projectiles, 146 charges and 167 fuzes. It uses a torsion bar suspension with either side having six dual rubber-tyred roadwheels with the drive sprocket at the front, idler at the rear and track-return rollers. The track is of the steel double-pin type with detachable rubber pads.

The raised ammunition compartment is at the rear of the hull. In the forward part of the roof is a forward-opening hatch for ammunition resupply, while to the centre of the crew cab is a cupola with facilities for an externally-mounted .50 (12.7 mm) M2 HB machine gun.

At the rear of the hull is a two-part hatch with the lower part opening to the right with the upper part opening upwards. Ammunition, both projectiles and charges, is transferred to the receiver vehicle via a conveyor belt at the rate of 6 rds/min.

Specifications

Logistic Support Vehicle
Crew: 3
Weight:
    (combat) 29,380 kg
    (empty) 18,400 kg
Ground pressure: 0.7 kg/cm^2
Power to weight ratio: 17.69 hp/t
Length: 6.9 m
Width: 3.2 m
Height: 3.2 m
Track width: 458 mm
Max speed: 65 km/h
Range: (cruising) 400 km
Fuel capacity: 500 litres
Gradient: 60%
Side slope: 30%
Vertical obstacle: 0.8 m
Trench: 2 m
Fording: 1.1 m
Engine: Doosan D2840L V-10 turbocharged diesel developing 520 hp
Transmission: L3 Propulsion Systems HMPT 500-3 EK hydromechanical
Steering: hydrostatic
Suspension: torsion bar
Brakes: multidisc, oil cooled
Electrical system: 28 V
Batteries: 4 × 6 V, 100 Ah
Generator: 100 A
Armament: 1 × .50 (12.7 mm) M2 HB MG

Doosan Field Artillery Ammunition Support Vehicle without roof-mounted .50 (12.7 mm) M2 HB machine gun installed (Daewoo)   1044351

Status

Development complete. Ready for production.

Contractor

Doosan Infracore Defense Products BG

Samsung Techwin K10 Thunder Ammunition Resupply Vehicle

Development

The K10 Thunder Ammunition Resupply Vehicle (ARV) was developed from 1999 by Samsung Techwin, Defense Program Division, and the Agency for Defence Development (ADD).

While under development the K10 Thunder ARV system was called the XK10 and the prototypes were put through over 10,000 km of extensive automotive trials over various types of terrain.

To prove the advanced automated ammunition resupply system, over 70,000 rounds of 155 mm ammunition were transferred and reloaded into the K10 Thunder ARV.

Following these extensive trials the K10 Thunder ARV was accepted for service with the Republic of Korea Army and first production vehicles were completed at the Changwon production facility of Samsung Techwin, Defense Products Division, late in 2006.

The K10 Thunder ARV has been developed to be deployed together with the K9 Thunder 155 mm/52-calibre Self-Propelled (SP) system of which about 500 are understood to be in service with the Republic of Korea Army.

The deployment of the K10 Thunder ARV has, according to Samsung Techwin Defense, improved the overall tactical effectiveness of the K9 Thunder SP artillery system.

Key Republic of Korea Army requirements were to supply substantially increased amounts of ammunition to the K9 Thunder SP system to meet its tactical requirements for a higher rate of fire, shoot and scoot tactics, a fully automated re-supply system to maximise the efficiency of artillery forces and the use of the K9 Thunder SP chassis, power pack and suspension to provide efficiency in logistic support and tactical movements.

Production of the K9 Thunder 155 mm self-propelled artillery system will continue for some years as in early 2009 MTU stated that it had been awarded a contract for the supply of engine kits and drive components for a total of 428 155 mm/52-calibre Thunder self-propelled artillery systems. These will be delivered over a four-year period.

This brought the total number of K9 engine kits up to 1,206 which includes those for new build vehicles as well as replacement engines.

This would indicate that at least 1,000 155 mm/52-calibre K9 Thunder self-propelled artillery systems and their associated K10 Ammunition Resupply Vehicle will be built.

The K10 Thunder Ammunition Resupply Vehicle has been offered on the export market but as of late 2010 there are no known sales.

Description

Chassis of the K10 Thunder ARV is identical to that of the K9 Thunder SP artillery system. This has been fitted with a new fully enclosed armour-protected superstructure at the rear. This provides the crew with protection from small arms fire and shell splinters.

The chassis is of all-welded steel armour construction with a maximum thickness of 19 mm. The driver is seated at the front of the chassis on the left with the power pack to his right and the remainder of the chassis being taken up with ammunition stowage. Mounted on the forward part of the roof is a .50 (12.7 mm) M2 HB machine gun with a shield.

K10 Thunder Ammunition Resupply Vehicle is now in service with the RoK Army to support the K9 Thunder 155 mm/52-calibre SP artillery system (Samsung Techwin)   1146708

Suspension system is of the hydropneumatic type with each side having six dual rubberised road wheels with the drive sprocket at the front, idler at the rear and three track return rollers. Track is of the double pin type with replaceable rubber pads.

The electrically driven fully automatic transfer system includes magazines for ammunition storage, loading and reloading, manipulators and movers for transferring and a mechanically extendible telescopic conveyor as well as an automated inventory management system.

It allows any type of 155 mm ammunition to be transferred to the K9 Thunder SP artillery system at the rate of more than ten rounds a minute.

The flow of charges and projectiles is carried out on the same conveyor path while coming from different storage magazines through manipulators and movers. The armour-protected extendible conveyor can be remotely controlled at the driver's seat by using the jog switch.

The conveyor is located at the front of the vehicle to facilitate fast alignment with the K9 Thunder SP artillery system under harsh terrain conditions such as narrow and rough fields.

A total of 104 × 155 mm projectiles plus 504 charges are carried. For emergency access to ammunition, the charge and projectile storage compartment have separate rear access doors for loading or reloading with manual assistance.

The K10 ARV is normally operated by a crew of three and weighs 46.7 tonnes. The ammunition compartment is provided with a fire detection and suppression system.

This would be used to feed 155 mm projectiles and charges directly into the K9 Thunder SP artillery system so allowing the K9 Thunder platform to always deploy with a full ammunition load.

The latter typically consists of 48 projectiles and associated charges. No details of the scale of issue of the K10 ARV have been revealed but it could be one per K9 Thunder SP artillery system or one per troop.

In addition to carrying older bag type 155 mm charge systems, the K9 Thunder 155 mm self-propelled artillery system can also use modular charge systems.

Specifications

K10 Thunder Ammunition Resupply Vehicle
Crew: 3
Weight: (combat) 46,700 kg
Power-to-weight ratio: 21.41 hp/tonne
Length:
  (chassis) 7.0 m
  (with conveyor) 8.5 m
Width: 3.4 m
Height:
  (including MG) 3.7 m
  (vehicle roof) 2.85 m
Ground clearance: 0.41 m
Track width: 548 mm
Length of track on ground: 4.72 m
Max road speed: 67 km/h
Fuel capacity: 850 litres
Range: 360 km plus (cruising)
Fording: 1.5 m
Max gradient: 60%
Max side slope: 30%
Vertical obstacle: 0.75 m
Trench: 2.8 m
Engine: MTU MT 881 Ka-500 water-cooled diesel developing 1,000 hp at 2,700 rpm
Transmission: Allison X1100-5 A3 automatic with 4 forward and 2 reverse gears
Suspension: hydropneumatic
Electrical system:
  (generator) 28 V DC
  (battery) 24 V DC
Armament: 1 × .50 (12.7 mm) M2 HB MG
Ammunition:
  (projectiles) 104 × 155 mm
  (charges) 504
Armour: 19 m max
Armour type: steel
NBC system: yes
Night vision equipment: yes

Status

Production. In service with Republic of Korea Army.

Contractor

Samsung Techwin, Defense Program Division

Norway

Natech P6-300M all-terrain vehicle

Development

The Natech P6-300M all-terrain vehicle was developed by Narvik Technology AS and the Finnish concern Hydrolink in co-operation with the Norwegian Armed Forces.

The first prototype was tested at the Norwegian Army Material Command's Testing and Trials unit at Helgelandsmoen in 1997. The first six production units were delivered to the Norwegian Army for use as electronic warfare system carriers. Conversions for the electronic warfare role were carried out by the now EADS and involved the SGS 2000 Hummel tactical communications jammer. The latter is also installed in armoured vehicles, such as the German Rheinmetall Landsysteme Transportpanzer 1 Fuchs (6 × 6).

Production of the P6-300M all-terrain vehicle has been completed and it is no longer marketed as the Natech company is no longer trading.

It should be noted that Norway uses large numbers of now BAE Systems Global Combat Systems Bv 206 all terrain vehicles.

Description

The Natech P6-300M all-terrain vehicle differs from most other military tracked carriers by having a total payload capacity of 7,000 kg. It also has a fully hydrostatic transmission with two variable hydraulic pumps and two variable hydraulic motors, one in each drive axle with planetary gear. There is a differential lock in both units. Drive controls involve stepless speed control, digital steering and digital load control.

The four-door front tractor unit is fully enclosed, having seating for the driver and four to five passengers. The towed rear unit has a quick-change attachment system for rapid reconfiguration of the carried load. Units such as a personnel transport cabin, hook lift load handling systems, system shelter/containers, command posts could be accommodated by the attachment system. Automatic levelling of the load area is accomplished using the hydro-pneumatic suspension.

The tracks were developed by Trelleborg/Viking. Enhanced cold start facilities are provided for the main power unit, a Cummins 6CTA8.3 diesel developing 260 hp coupled to a hydrostatic transmission.

Natech P6-300M all-terrain vehicle with rear unit being fitted with a load handling unit   0044577

Natech P6-300M all-terrain vehicle carrying a German SGS 2000 Hummel tactical communications jammer system with antennas raised in the operating position   0056308

Variants

In addition to the troop carrier and EW versions the P6-300M has also been used in the cargo role with the rear unit being fitted with a tilt-bed cargo area.

Specifications

P6-300M all terrain vehicle
Cab seating: 1 + 4 or 5 (up to 16 in rear)
Weight: 7,850 kg
Max load:
(front unit) 2,350 kg
(rear unit) 4,650 kg
Length:
(overall) approx 8.24 m
Width: 2.4 m
Height: 2.6 m
Track width: 660 mm
Max speed: 50 km/h
Fuel capacity: 300 litres
Engine: Cummins 6CTA8.3 8.3 litre 6-cylinder in-line diesel developing 260 hp at 2,200 rpm
Transmission: hydrostatic
Suspension: hydro-pneumatic
Steering: digital electronic
Turning radius: 4 m

Status

Production complete. No longer marketed. In service with the Norwegian Army.

Contractor

Narvik Technology AS (This company is no longer trading.)

Pakistan

Heavy Industries Taxila Al Qaswa Logistic Vehicle

Development

The Al Qaswa logistic vehicle was developed by Heavy Industries Taxila (HIT) who have considerable experience in the design, development and production of armoured fighting vehicles.

The first prototype of the Al Qaswa was completed in 2002 but as far as it is known the vehicle has yet to enter quantity production.

This is the latest in an increasing number of variants of the BAE Systems, US Combat Systems M113 which have been developed in Pakistan to meet local operational requirements. HIT has also developed the Talha APC of which 44 have already been supplied to Iraq.

Some of these vehicles have five dual rubber tyred road wheels either side while other versions, such as the Al Qaswa logistic vehicle has six road wheels either side which gives the vehicle greater volume and payload.

As of late 2010 it is understood that production of the Al Qaswa logistic vehicle had yet to start.

Description

The Al Qaswa is based on a stretched BAE Systems, US Combat Systems, M113A2/M113A3 series armoured personnel carrier chassis with a modified rear. The baseline M113 has five road wheel stations either side while the Al Qaswa has a total of six for increased volume and payload.

The hull of the Al Qaswa is of all welded aluminium armour plate which provides the occupants with protection from small arms fire and shell splinters.

Heavy Industries Taxila Al Qaswa logistic vehicle showing cargo area at rear and armed with pintle mounted 12.7 mm MG (HIT)   1333503

The driver is seated at the front of the vehicle on the left side and has a single piece hatch cover above his position. In front of this are day vision periscopes. The centre day periscope can be replaced by a passive night-driving device.

The power pack is to the right of the driver with the air entry and exit louvres in the roof. The commander is seated to the rear of the driver in a raised compartment and is provided with cupola with a single piece hatch cover and periscopes. A large rectangular door is provided in the left side of the hull for the commander and this opens to the rear. In addition there is a smaller access door in the lower right side of the hull that opens to the front.

A 12.7 mm machine gun can be mounted on the forward part of the cupola for local and air defence purposes. A bank of electrically operated smoke grenade launchers are mounted either side of the hull front and these cover the frontal arc.

The diesel fuel tanks are to the rear of the engine compartment and to the right of the commanders position. The load area is at the rear and is provided with sides and a drop tailgate.

If required, the rear cargo area can be fitted with bows and a tarpaulin cover to protect the cargo being carried.

Running gear either side consists of six dual rubber tyred road wheels with the drive sprocket at the front and idler at rear. There are no track return rollers. A rubber side skirt can be fitted to cover the upper part of the suspension.

The baseline M113 series is fully amphibious being propelled in the water by its tracks but the Al Qaswa logistic vehicle is not amphibious.

Variants

Although the first application of the Al Qaswa is that of a logistic vehicle carrying up to 6,116 kg of stores, HIT have suggested that its design is such that it can be adopted for a wide range of other roles such as carrying weapon systems, missiles, radar or maintenance equipment. It can also carry specialised containers for command post and ambulance roles.

Specifications

Al Qaswa logistic vehicle
Al Qaswa
Crew: 1 + 1
Weight:
(loaded) 14,829 kg
(empty) 8,713 kg
Payload: 6,116 kg
Length: 5.568 m
Width: 2.54 m
Height: 2.171 m
Ground clearance: 0.43 m
Track: 2.159 m
Track width: 381 mm
Max speed: 60 km/h
Max range: 480 km (estimate)
Fuel capacity: 360 litres (estimate)
Gradient: 60%
Side slope: 40%
Fording: 1 m
Engine: Detroit Diesel 6V-53T diesel developing 265 hp at 2,800 rpm
Transmission: Allison TX-100-1A automatic with 3 forward an 1 reverse gears
Suspension: torsion bar with hydraulic shock absorbers
Electrical system: 24 V
Armament: 1 × 12.7 mm MG
Armour type: aluminium
NBC system: yes
Night vision: yes

Status
Prototype.

Contractor
Heavy Industries Taxila

Poland

Bumar Labedy Type 668 tractor

Development
The Type 668 tractor, developed and produced by the Zaklady Mechaniczne 'Bumar Labedy' SA at Gliwice as a general purpose tractor unit, is capable of fulfilling numerous logistic and other support tasks.

It can carry a maximum load of 3,000 kg, tow artillery pieces or trailers weighing up to 14,000 kg and carry up to 12 troops in the rear cargo area. The Type 668 appears to be a close relative of the RFAS ATS-59G medium tracked artillery tractor. Details of this vehicle are given in a separate entry in *Jane's Military Vehicles and Logistics*.

Production of the Type 668 tractor has been completed by Bumar Labedy and is not currently being marketed by the company. It is possible that quantities of surplus Type 668 tractors are available for sale.

Bumar Labedy Type 668 tractor with rear cargo fitted with bows and a tarpaulin cover   0511881

Description

The Type 668 has an all-steel forward control cab located over the power pack. Seating is provided for the driver and up to five passengers. A roof-hatch is provided on the right-hand side. The cabin is kept at an overpressure for operations in NBC-contaminated environments and extra defrosting equipment can be installed for use in cold environments.

The steel-sided load area located over the engine is used to carry supplies only. Only the rear part of the load area can be configured to carry passengers or supplies. The load area can be covered by a canvas tilt over bows. The towing position at the rear is equipped with shock-absorbers.

Suspension either side consists of five rubber-tyred road wheels with the drive sprocket at the front and idler at the rear. The first and last road wheel stations are provided with a hydraulic shock absorber but there are no track return rollers.

Power is provided by a V-12 A-650-G diesel coupled to a five-speed gearbox. The exhaust outlet is on the right side of the hull to the cab rear. An engine preheater system is provided and the engine may be started by electrical or compressed air systems.

The Type 668 is provided with a recovery winch with a capacity of 14,700 kg. A version of this vehicle without the winch is known as the 668 BL.

A version of the Type 668, known as the Type 668 S, is equipped with a front-mounted lattice crane with a lift capacity of 7,500 kg and an operating radius of 2.5 m. When fully raised, the crane has a height of 7.8 m. The crane can be disassembled into three sections for transport on the cargo area.

Specifications

Type 668 tractor
Cab seating: 1 + 5 (up to 12 in rear)
Weight:
   (combat) 13,750 kg
Max load: 3,000 kg
Towed load: up to 14,000 kg
Length: 6.28 m
Width: 2.78 m
Height:
   (top of tilt) 2.62 m
   (cab) 2.58 m
   (load area) 1.27 m
Ground clearance:
   (loaded) 0.42 m
Max speed:
   (cruising) 39 km/h
   (cross-country with towed load) 22-27 km/h
Range: (cross-country with towed load) 500 km
Fuel capacity: 580 litres (plus optional 240 litres)
Fording:
   (normal) 1.1 m
   (with preparation) 1.5 m
Gradient:
   (without towed load) 35°
   (with towed load) 18°
Side slope: 25°
Engine: A-650-G V-12 diesel developing 295 hp
Transmission: synchromesh, 5 forward and 1 reverse gears
Suspension: independent torsion bar
Electrical system: 24 V
Batteries: 3 × 12 V, 210 Ah
Generator: 2,200 W

Status

Production as required. In service with Poland. It is understood that there has been no recent production of the Type 668 tractor in Poland.

Contractor

Zaklady Mechaniczne 'Bumar Labedy' SA

Russian Federation

ATS-59G medium tracked artillery tractor

Development

The ATS-59G medium tracked artillery tractor was first seen during 1972, towing a 130 mm M-46 field gun. Until its correct designation became known, the vehicle was called the M1972 in the West.

Production of the ATS-59G has been completed and it is no longer in service in large numbers with the Russian Army.

Description

It is essentially an improved version of the earlier ATS-59 with a redesigned cab. The ATS-59G has a much larger forward control type cab with the cargo area at the rear. The vertical sides are fixed with cargo being loaded via the drop-down tailgate.

Suspension either side consists of five rubber tyred road wheels with the drive sprocket at the front and idler at the rear. The first and last road wheel stations are provided with a hydraulic shock absorber but there are no track return rollers.

In Egypt, ATS-59G tractors have been adapted as carriers for the Egyptian SAKR Factory for Developed Industries SAKR 122 mm RL-21 30-round multiple rocket launcher role.

The Polish Bumar Labedy 668 tractor appears to be a close development of the ATS-59G. As far as it is known, there has been no recent production of the ATS-59G in Poland. Full details of the Polish Bumar Labedy Type 668 tractor are provided in a separate entry in *Jane's Military Vehicles and Logistics*. Production of the Type 668 tractor has been completed in Poland.

Variants

Although the primary role of the ATS-59G medium tracked artillery tractor has been to carry cargo and tow a variety of artillery systems, it can also be used for a variety of other roles.

Specifications

ATS-59G medium tracked artillery tractor
Weight:
   (empty) 13,750 kg
   (loaded) 16,750 kg
Max load: 3,000 kg
Max towed load: 14,000 kg
Fuel capacity: 580 litres
Ground pressure: 0.55 kg/cm²
Fording: 1.5 m

ATS-59G medium tracked artillery tractor   0512245

Egyptian Model RL 21 (30-round) 122 mm rocket launcher mounted on the rear of ATS-59G medium tracked artillery tractor with launcher traversed left   0500648

Status
Production complete. In service with a number of countries including Egypt, Russian Federation, Serbia and Montenegro and other countries. No longer marketed.

Contractor
State factories.

GT-SM-1D light tracked transporter

Description
The GT-SM-1D light tracked transporter is described as a multipurpose transporter tractor that can act as a light weapon carrier or tractor, cargo transport and ambulance.

Towed loads may weigh up to 2,000 kg. It is powered by a GAZ-5441 air-cooled, turbocharged diesel developing 123 hp which is coupled to a manual transmission. Independent suspension is provided for each of the six roadwheels each side. There are no track return rollers. The short link, steel tracks are rubber bushed and padded.

The GT-SM-1D can operate over a temperature from −50°C to +45°C at altitudes up to 4,500 m above sea level. The GT-SM-1D is fully amphibious and when afloat is propelled in the water by its tracks.

It is understood that there has been no recent production of the GT-SM-1D light tracked transporter for the home or export markets.

Specifications
GT-SM-1D light tracked transporter
Cab seating: 1 + 1
Weight: 3,250 kg
Max payload: 1,250 kg
Towed load: 2,000 kg
Ground pressure: 0.19 kg/cm^2
Length: 5.31 m
Width: 2.6 m
Height: 1.842 m
Range:
 (road) 900 km
Max speed:
 (road) 60 km/h
 (water) 5-6 km/h
Gradient: 35°
Fording: amphibious
Engine: GAZ-5441 4-cylinder air-cooled turbocharged diesel developing 123 hp
Transmission: mechanical, 5 speed
Suspension: torsion bars with telescopic shock absorbers
Steering: planetary

Status
Production as required. In service with Russian Federation in civil and military applications. This vehicle is still being offered on the export market. There are however no recent sales of this vehicle.

Cab area of GT-SM-1D light tracked transporter showing fully enclosed crew compartment at front of vehicle   0056406

MT-S medium tracked transporter

Development
The MT-S medium tracked transporter was developed around the same time as the MT-T heavy tracked transporter, but it does not appear to have been produced in very large numbers in the transporter form. It was replaced in production by the MT-SM.

Details of the MT-SM are provided in a separate entry in *Jane's Military*

MT-S medium tracked transporter   0511873

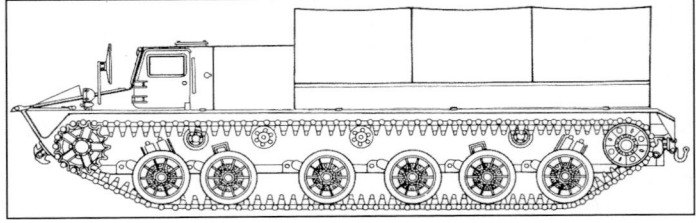

MT-S medium-tracked transporter (not to 1/76th scale) (Steve Zaloga)
                    0511874

Vehicles and Logistics. Production of this is undertaken on an as required basis.

Description
Few details regarding this vehicle have been released but it is believed to be powered by a diesel engine similar to that used by the MT-T. The basic chassis is derived from that used for the 152 mm self-propelled gun-howitzer 2S3 (S-152) Akatsiya.

It has been used for a number of other applications, including the GMZ minelayer. It is also used as a carrier for components of the 9K37 Buk (NATO SA-11 'Gadfly') surface-to-air missile system including the associated radar vehicles. The latter is used by a number of countries, including Belarus, the Russian Federation, Syria and the Ukraine. Production of this missile system is now complete.

Specifications
MT-S medium tracked transporter
(Provisional)
Cab seating: 1 + 3
Weight: 23,500 kg
Max payload: 10,200 kg
Length: 7.8 m
Width: 3.34 m
Height: 1.846 m
Engine: diesel developing 710 hp

Status
Production complete. Replaced in production by the MT-SM. In service with the Russian Federation. There are no recent export sales of the MT-S as far as it is known.

Contractor
Metrowagonmash JSC (Mytishchi Engineering Plant) (Not confirmed.)

MT-SM medium tracked transporter

Development
The MT-SM medium tracked transporter is a modernised version of the earlier MT-S which used a basic chassis derived from the 152 mm self-propelled gun-howitzer 2S3 (S-152) Akatsiya. Production of the 2S3 was completed some time ago, and it is no longer marketed, although some weapons are available from surplus Russian Army stocks.

MT-SM medium tracked transporter   0009949

Description

The MT-SM follows the same general lines as the MT-S, but shares many components with the GM-569A tracked vehicle, which is covered in detail in a separate entry in *Jane's Military Vehicles and Logistics*.

The MT-SM utilises a two-stage positive displacement hydraulic steering mechanism. Power is provided by a V-84Zh 780 hp multifuel diesel fitted with a pre-heater. The powerpack is located at the front of the vehicle with the crew of two seated in a tandem semi-armoured cab on the left-hand side. This is fully enclosed and has bullet proof windows to its front and sides.

The load area, which can carry loads up to 10 tonnes, is at the rear and can be covered by a tarpaulin over bows.

The vehicle can also be used to tow artillery or similar loads and may be fitted with radar shelters or artillery rocket systems. Among combat engineer equipment that can be carried is a hydraulically powered entrenching tool system. Maximum towed load is being quoted as 15 tonnes.

The MT-SM can operate over a temperature from –50°C to +50°C at altitudes up to 4,500 m above sea level.

Specifications

MT-SM medium tracked transporter
Cab seating: 1 + 1
Weight: 34.000 kg
Ground pressure: 0.75 kg/cm²
Max payload: 10,000 kg
Towed load: 15,000 kg
Length: 8.53 m
Width: 3.25 m
Height: 2.93 m
Range:
  (road) 600 km
Max speed:
  (road) 65 km/h
  (tracks) 35-45 km/h
Gradient: 35°
Fording: 1 m
Turning: pivot
Engine: V-84Zh multifuel diesel developing 780 hp (582 kW)
Transmission: hydromechanical
Suspension: torsion bars with telescopic shock absorbers
Steering: positive displacement hydraulic

Status

Production complete. No longer marketed. In service with the Russian Federation. There are no known recent export sales of this vehicle.

Contractor

Metrowagonmash JSC (Mytischi Engineering Plant)

AT-T heavy tracked artillery tractor

Development

The AT-T heavy tracked artillery tractor appeared in 1950. It was originally used to tow heavy artillery such as the 180 mm S-23 gun-howitzer, the 130 mm KS-30 anti-aircraft gun and the 130 mm SM-4-1 mobile coastal gun.

While none of these artillery systems are now in front line service with the Russian Army, quantities of these are still to be found in service with other countries in declining numbers.

It is now mainly relegated to the general purpose towing role for various systems and in specialised logistic roles towing heavy loads on trailers. It is also employed to carry specialised loads such as radar and other electronic shelters.

Lengthened version of AT-T heavy tracked artillery tractor with 'Long Hand' radar (T J Gander)   0512530

Description

The 415 hp diesel powerpack is under the floor of the four-person fully enclosed cab, which is of all-steel construction, having a door either side. The cargo compartment is at the rear and is provided with a drop tailgate, removable bows and a tarpaulin cover. The diesel fuel tanks are under the rear behind the engine and the winch is mounted at the very back.

The suspension is of the torsion bar type and either side consists of five large roadwheels with the drive sprocket at the front and the idler at the rear. There are no track-return rollers.

Variants

BAT and BAT-M Dozers
Full details of this are given in *Jane's Military Vehicles and Logistics*. Production of this has been completed.

Radar
The AT-T with a fully enclosed van-type body is used to mount the Track Dish (ARSOM-1). A lengthened version of the AT-T with seven roadwheels mounts the Long Track artillery surveillance radar. Production of this has been completed. It is also used to mount the Russian 'Long Hand' radar used with air defence systems.

BTM and MDK-2 Ditching Machines
Full details of this are given in *Jane's Military Vehicles and Logistics*. Production has been completed.

AT-TA
This is a special version of the basic AT-T with extra wide tracks and other modifications for polar exploration. The wider tracks improve traction and lower ground pressure which is essential when the AT-T is operating in marginal terrain. Production of this vehicle has been completed.

Specifications

AT-T heavy tracked artillery tractor
Cab seating: 1 + 3 (up to 16 in rear)
Weight:
  (empty) 20,000 kg
  (loaded) 25,000 kg
Max load: 5,000 kg
Towed load: 25,000 kg
Length: 7.043 m
Width: 3.154 m
Height: (cab) 2.845 m
Ground clearance: 0.425 m
Track: 2.64 m
Track width: 500 mm
Length of track on ground: 3.836 m
Ground pressure:
  (empty) 0.52 kg/cm²
  (loaded) 0.68 kg/cm²
Max speed: 38 km/h
Range: (with towed load) 1,100 km
Fuel: 1,415 litres
Fuel consumption:
  (not towing) 140 litres/100 km
  (towing) 190 litres/100 km
Max gradient: 60%
Vertical obstacle: 1 m
Trench: 2.1 m
Fording: 750 mm (some can ford to 1 m)
Engine: V-401 V-12 water-cooled diesel developing 415 hp (309 kW) at 1,600 rpm

Status

Production complete. In service with members of the former Warsaw Pact, former Yugoslavia, countries in the Middle East and North Africa. No longer marketed.

Contractor

State Enterprise Malyshev Plant

MT-T heavy tracked transporter

Development

The MT-T heavy tracked transporter first appeared during the early 1980s and uses suspension components from the T-64 MBT, which was designed and built in the Ukraine. Production of the T-64 MBT was completed many years ago.

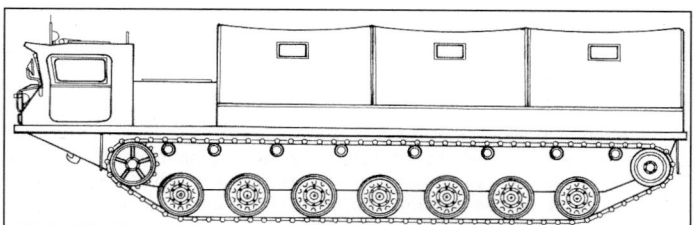

MT-T heavy tracked transporter (Steve Zaloga)   0511876

MT-T heavy tracked transporter   0511875

The Antey S-300V (NATO SA-12 'Gladiator'/'Giant') air defence missile system chassis is based on the MT-T heavy tracked transporter (Christopher F Foss)   1296057

The T-64 MBT was nver exported and in 2010 it remained in service with declining numbers with the Russian Army. The Ukraine is upgrading some of its T-64 MBT's to extend their operational lives.

The engine is the V-64-4 diesel derived from that used in the T-72 tank. On the MT-T a forward control cab is located in front of the main drive gear and the large cargo area to the rear can be covered by bows and a tarpaulin cover.

Description

The chassis of the MT-T is used as the basis for several other vehicles, including the PTS-2 amphibious tracked vehicle, the MDK-3 trenching machine and the BAT-2 tractor-mounted bulldozer and the PMM-2 amphibious bridging and ferry system. Derivatives of the MT-T are used as the basis for the Antey S-300V SA-12 'Gladiator'/'Giant' missile system transporter and launcher vehicle. The chassis carries key sub-systems such as radars and missile launchers.

Specifications

MT-T heavy tracked transporter
(Provisional)
Cab seating: 1 + 4 (up to 18 in rear)
Weight: (approx.) 25,000 kg
Max load: 12,000 kg
Towed load: 12,000 kg
Length: 8.711 m
Width: 3.277 m
Height: 3.065 m
Engine: V-64-4 diesel developing 710 hp (529 kW)

Status

Production complete. No longer marketed. In service with the Russian Federation and other countries.

Contractor

Russian state factories.

GM-569A tracked tractor

Development

During 1990, the first reports of a GM-569A tracked tractor appeared in technical reports, mainly referring to the vehicle's novel hydromechanical transmission. The main role of the GM-569A is as the platform for the Buk-M1 series of surface-to-air missiles which are currently in service with a number of countries including Belarus, Russia, Syria and Ukraine. Production of this air defence system is now complete.

Description

The GM-569A tracked tractor has a low superstructure over the forward part of the upper hull and a built-up diesel engine compartment at the rear. The driving and crew compartment extends the full width of the front hull. Suspension is of the torsion bar type, with either side having six roadwheels, with the drive sprocket at the front, idler at the rear and four track return rollers.

2S6M Tunguska self-propelled air defence system is based on a modified GM-355 series tracked chassis (Christopher F Foss)   0069230

The GM-569A's hydromechanical transmission is considered to be a significant improvement over mechanical transmissions and involves a reduction mechanism, hydraulic torque converter, planetary gearbox, an equalising block and a hydraulic steering mechanism imparting good manoeuvrability.

Pivot turns are possible on hard surfaces. Hydraulically operated and self-adjusting dry plate disc brakes are used when on the move, although a mechanical brake is used for parking.

To provide power supplies for the vehicle's various electrical and electronic control systems, two AC generators can be powered by a gas-turbine engine and there is a reserve system, used only when halted, powered by a reduction take-off from the main engine.

Variants

GM-355 tracked chassis

This is very similar to the GM-569 and is used as the basis for the Tor (NATO SA-15 'Gauntlet') self-propelled surface-to-air missile system which is used by a number of countries including Belarus, China, Cyprus, Greece, India, Russia and Ukraine.

The GM-355A is used for the Tor-M while the GM-355M is used for the export version of the system.

A similar chassis is used as the basis for the 2K22M 2S6 Tunguska self-propelled gun/missile air defence system currently in service with Algeria, China, India, Morocco and Russian Federation.

Specifications

GM-355 tracked chassis
Cab seating: 1 + 1 or 2
Weight: 37,000 kg
Ground pressure: 0.75 kg/cm^2
Max payload: 11,000 kg
Length: 8.892 m
Width: 3.26 m
Height: 2.098 m
Range: (road) 500 km
Max speed:
  (road) 65 km/h
  (tracks) 35–45 km/h
Gradient: 35°
Fording: 1 m

Tor (SA-15 'Gauntlet') mobile surface-to-air missile system is based on a GM-355 tracked chassis (Steven Zaloga)   0080391

Engine: V-84DT multifuel diesel developing 710, 780 or 840 hp (529, 582 or 626 kW)
Transmission: hydromechanical
Suspension: torsion bars with telescopic shock-absorbers
Steering: positive displacement hydraulic

Status
Production as required. The 2S6 series is in service with Algeria, China, India, Morocco and Russia. The latest version is designated the 2S6M and is the current production model.

Contractor
Metrowagonmash JSC (Mytishchi Engineering Plant)

DT-30P tracked all-terrain transporter   0056415

DT-10P, DT-30P and DT-30 tracked all-terrain transporters

Description
The DT-10P and DT-30 Vityaz (Knight) tracked all-terrain transporters have been in production, on an as-required basis, since 1982, and the DT-30P since 1986.

They are intended for carrying heavy loads over all manner of off-road terrain, including marsh and snow.

All three vehicles have twin unit articulated configuration and are powered by a V-46-5 multifuel diesel developing 710 hp. The diesel engine has a pre-heater as the vehicles are intended for use over a temperature range of –50°C to +40°C. All three vehicles have the same forward control fully enclosed cab for five personnel with the engine compartment behind.

All three vehicles have wide one-piece rubber band tracks with steel-welded cross-pieces. On the DT-10P the tracks are 960 mm wide. The DT-30P and DT-30 tracks are 1.1 m wide. The wider tracks have a number of advantages including improved traction and lower ground pressure.

An independent torsion bar suspension is employed. Steering is hydraulic, using double-acting power cylinders acting on a double-hinged steering and coupler unit.

In addition to being used for military applications, these vehicles can also be used for a number of civilian applications in rough terrain.

DT-10P
The DT-10P is the smallest of the three vehicles, being a twin-unit vehicle carrying 10 tonnes or 10 passengers, including the crew of five. There are two load-carrying areas, one on the front section behind the cab and power pack and the other including the total platform area of the second unit. Both load areas may be covered by a tarpaulin.

On the DT-10P the front load area measures 2.2 m long by 2.81 m wide. The rear area measures 6.2 × 2.81 m. Both load areas are waterproofed allowing the complete vehicle to be amphibious. The front unit has four roadwheels each side and the rear unit five. The road wheels are rubber-tyred with a sponge rubber inner tube.

DT-30P
The DT-30P is an enlarged version of the DT-10P with the load capacity increased to 30 tonnes or 30 passengers, including the crew of five. The front load area measures 4.5 m long by 3.1 m wide. The rear area measures 6.6 × 3.1 m. Both load areas are waterproofed allowing the complete vehicle to be amphibious. Both the front and rear units have six roadwheels on each side. The road wheels are rubber-tyred with a sponge rubber inner tube. Typical loads include front-line refuelling systems. A self-loading hydraulic crane is an option.

DT-30
The DT-30 also has a load capacity of 30 tonnes although it is not amphibious. On this vehicle, in place of the usual cargo bodies there is a single long cargo flatbed measuring 10.51 × 3.1 m supported by the front unit, which is structurally the same as that on the DT-30P apart from the cargo body. On the rear unit, again the same as that on the DT-30P, there is a gimbal arrangement on which the cargo area can pivot.

Production of the DT-10PM and DT-30PM is undertaken on an as required basis.

DT-10PM and DT-30PM
These are upgraded versions of the DT-10P and DT-30P tracked all terrain transporters are covered in detail in a separate entry in *Jane's Military Vehicles and Logistics*.

They have a more powerful diesel engine, higher road speed and greater operating range but have similar load carrying capabilities to the earlier generation vehicles.

Specifications - See table below

Status
Production complete. No longer marketed. Replaced in production by DT-10PM/DT-30PM vehicles. In service with the Russian Federation. DT-30 no longer in production. There are no known exports of this vehicle.

Contractor
Ishimbaytransmash JSC

DT-10PM and DT-30PM tracked all-terrain transporters

Description
The DT-10PM and DT-30PM Vezdesushchy (Ubiquitous) amphibious tracked all-terrain transporters may be regarded as upgraded versions of the DT-10P and DT-30P tracked transporters which are covered in detail in a separate entry in *Jane's Military Vehicles and Logistics* and have similar load carrying capabilities but as they are powered by a more powerful diesel engine they have a higher road speed and greater operating range.

Model	DT-10P	DT-30P	DT-30
Cab seating:	5	5	5
Weight:			
(empty)	22,500 kg	28,000 kg	29,000 kg
Max load:	10,000 kg	30,000 kg	30,000 kg
Length:			
(total, overall)	13.726 m	15.59 m	15.67 m
Width:	2.81 m	3.1 m	3.1 m
Height:	2.7 m	3.3 m	3.6 m
Track width:	960 mm	1.1 m	1.1 m
Max speed:			
(road)	36 km/h	36 km/h	37 km/h
(water)	5 km/h	4 km/h	n/a
Range:	500 km	500 km	500 km
Max gradient:	35°	30°	30°
Side slope:	20°	15°	15°
Engine:	V-46-5 multifuel liquid-cooled diesel developing 710 hp (529 kW)		
Transmission:	4 forward and 1 reverse gears		
Steering:	articulated hydrostatic		
Suspension:	torsion bars	torsion bars	torsion bars
Brakes:	air	air	air
Electrical system:	24 V	24 V	24 V

They follow the same general lines and are visually similar to the earlier vehicles but differ mainly in being powered by the more powerful YaMZ-847.10 800 hp diesel engine coupled to a hydromechanical transmission with a torque converter. Front and rear units are provided with a cargo area that is normally covered by bows and tarpaulin cover.

These are also referred to as the 'Knight' family. The DT-10PM has a maximum water speed of 5-6 km/h while the DT-30PM has a maximum water speed of 4-5 km/h. For amphibious operations it is propelled in the water by its tracks.

In addition to being used for military applications, these vehicles can also be used for a number of civilian applications in rough terrain.

Specifications

Model	DT-10PM	DT-30PM
Cab seating:	5	5
Weight: (loaded)	27,500 kg	30,200 kg
Max load:	10,000 kg	30,000 kg
Length:	14.21 m	16.15 m
Width:	3.1 m	3.1 m
Height:	3.325 m	3.3 m
Track width:	960 mm	1.1 m
Max speed:	44 km/h	43 km/h
Range:	700 km	700 km
Max gradient:	35°	30°
Engine:	YaMZ-847.10 diesel developing 800 hp (597 kW)	
Transmission:	hydromechanical with torque converter	

Status

Production as required. In service with the Russian Federation. There are no known exports of this vehicle.

Contractor

Ishimbaytransmash JSC

DT-30PM tracked all-terrain carrier with front and rear units covered by bows and a tarpaulin cover   0056416

Singapore

Singapore Technologies Kinetics Bronco All Terrain Tracked Carrier (ATTC)

Development

First announced during February 2000, the Singapore Technologies Kinetics (ST Kinetics) Bronco All Terrain Tracked Carrier (ATTC) is a multipurpose armoured articulated tracked carrier that can be configured to meet a wide range of payload requirements, from personnel or cargo carrier to command post and weapon platform.

Development began during 1995. In May 2001, Singapore Technologies Kinetics delivered the first of an undisclosed quantity of BRONCO AATC to the Singapore Armed Forces.

A batch of Bronco ATTC have been sold to Thailand and in late 2008 the UK placed an order for 115 modified versions of the Bronco to meet the Warthog Urgent Operational Requirement (OUR).

The first vehicles came off the Singapore production line in September 2009 and details are given later in this entry.

Description

The Bronco ATTC can accommodate a payload of up to 5,000 kg and is stated to have considerable growth potential. It was designed to traverse any type of terrain, including mud, snow and swamps. The vehicle can ford water obstacles up to 1.2 m deep and can float and swim following a minimum of preparation.

The Bronco ATTC travels on heavy-duty seamless rubber band tracks for low noise level running, with 12 420 mm roadwheels each side, plus two support rollers. The vehicle is equipped with a four-sprocket drive and fully articulated steering. A differential lock is optional.

Inside the front module, the driver is provided with what is described as an intuitive man-machine interface designed for minimum training and supervision. Preparing the vehicle for amphibious operations takes only a few minutes. Power is provided by an electronically-controlled Caterpillar 3126B 350 hp diesel coupled to an Allison MD3560P automatic transmission. Two bilge pumps are provided in each module.

The rear module may be fully enclosed to act as a personnel carrier or mobile command post, or it can be configured in flatbed form for numerous applications. Modular passive armour can be added if required.

Variants

In addition to the basic troop carrier, three specialised versions of the Bronco ATTC were revealed in 2001, armoured engineer, resupply and ambulance. The Bronco ATTC can also be used as a weapons platform for a variety of weapons such as ATGW.

Engineer

In addition to its crew, this version has sufficient space to carry explosives and obstacle clearing equipment and can also be configured to carry and launch rocket-propelled mineclearing equipment. This is in service with the Singapore Armed Forces (SAF).

Resupply

This has a rear unit fitted with a mechanical handling system and can carry pods of fuel or cargo weighing up to 3,000 kg.

Ambulance

The rear cabin of the ambulance can carry four stretcher or nine seated patients and utilises a swing out stretcher system for ease of loading/unloading and an integrated tentage system for additional workspace.

120 mm mortar carrier

The Bronco ATTC has been used for the Singapore Technologies Kinetics 120 mm Super Raid Advanced Mortar System (SRAMS). The design of SRAMS is such that it can be integrated onto a wide range of other chassis, tracked and wheeled.

In 2007 the United Arab Emirates ordered 48 SRAMS integrated on a South African, now BAE Systems Land Systems South Africa, RG31. As of late 2010 it is understood that only four units had been delivered to the United Arab Emirates.

It has been confirmed that the first customer for the SRAMS was the Singapore Armed Forces who deploy the system integrated onto the rear of the Bronco ATTC.

Active Articulation Vehicle

A Bronco ATTC is being used as a trials vehicle for the Active Articulation Vehicle, which has been developed as a private venture by STK.

Primus 155 mm ammunition resupply vehicle

The STK 155 mm/39-calibre Primus self-propelled artillery system used by the SAF is supported by an ammunition vehicle based on a modified Bronco ATTC. The rear unit has been modified to carry a total of 48 × 155 mm artillery projectiles and their associated propelling charges.

UK Warthog programme

In December 2008 the UK MoD awarded Singapore Technologies Kinetics a contact worth GBP150 million for the supply of 115 Bronco ATTC to meet the Warthog Urgent Operational Requirement (UOR).

Under the terms of this contract, the UK is procuring four versions of the Bronco ATTC, ambulance, command vehicle, repair and recovery vehicle and troop carrier.

First production vehicles were completed in late September 2009. These are then sent to Thales in the UK to be fitted with specific UK equipment such as General Dynamics Bowman Digital communications equipment, wire cutters, smoke grenade launchers, bar armour and devices to counter Improved Explosive Devices (IEDs).

There have been some delays in the programme but first Warthog vehicles were deployed to Afghanistan in 2010 and all will be delivered from the Singapore production line to the Thales facility in the UK by the end of 2010.

Standard Bronco All Terrain Tracked Carrier in basic troop carrying configuration (Stefan Marx)   1333666

First Warthog repair and recovery vehicle for British Army
(Christopher F Foss)   1334230

First Warthog ATTC for the British Army complete with bar armour, Platt Protected Weapon Station armed with .50 M2 HB MG, banks of 76 mm smoke grenade launchers and forward facing cameras (STK)   1365170

The Warthog award was one of a number of new protected patrol vehicles being ordered by the MoD under a GBP700 million package announced the UK MoD late in October 2008.

Specifications

Bronco All Terrain Tracked Carrier
Cab seating:
   (front module) 1 + 5
   (rear module) 10
Weight:
   (enclosed version, kerb, total) 11,200 kg
   (flatbed version, kerb, total) 10,700 kg
   (GVW, both versions) 16,000 kg
Payload:
   (enclosed version) 4,800 kg
   (flatbed version) 5,300 kg
Length: 8.6 m
Width: (over track) 2.3 m
Height: (overall) 2.2 m
Track width: 600 mm
Max speed:
   (road) 60 km/h
   (cross country) 25 km/h
   (water) 5 km/h
Gradient: 60%
Side slope: 30%
Vertical obstacle: 0.60 m
Trench: 1.5 m
Fording: 1.2 m; amphibious with preparation
Engine: Caterpillar 3126B turbocharged diesel developing 350 hp (261 kW) at 2,400 rpm
Transmission: Allison MD3560P fully automatic
Steering: hydraulic, articulated
Suspension: rubber bush
Brakes: hydraulic, disc

Status
Production. In service with:

County	Quantity	Comment
Singapore	730	estimate
Thailand	n/k	
UK	115	delivery 2009/2010

Contractor
Singapore Technologies Kinetics

South Africa

BAE Systems Land Systems South Africa
Blesbok (4 × 4) 5,000 kg armoured freighter

Development
The Blesbok (4 × 4) 5,000 kg armoured freighter is a member of the Casspir Mark II armoured personnel carrier series. It was designed to carry supplies to military and paramilitary forces operating in remote areas. The main user was the Southwest African (now Namibian) Police which operated along mechanised infantry lines when on counter-insurgency operations. In total, 160 units were produced. Most vehicles are now operated by the South African National Defence Force (SANDF).

This was previously marketed by a variety of companies, but as a result of restructuring, the current design authority is now BAE Systems Land Systems South Africa (previously BAE Systems Land Systems OMC).

Some of these vehicles are now surplus to requirements and are for sale. In recent years surplus Casspir vehicles have been sold to Angola, Djibouti, India, Indonesia, Mozambique and Nepal. As far as it is known there have been no export sales of the Blesbok armoured freighter.

Description
The Blesbok is built on the same chassis as the Casspir Mark II derived from that of a 15 ton commercial truck. The Blesbok also uses the same fully enclosed mine protected cab for the driver and passenger and has many other components of the Casspir.

The cab has seating for two personnel and houses the vehicle's 185-litre fuel tank. The cab has sloped armoured undersides for mine protection and the cab armour is proof against 5.56 and 7.62 mm NATO ball ammunition.

The cab roof has a hatch and a small turret for a 7.62 mm machine gun. All windows use 52 mm thick laminated glass. These provide the same level of protection as the armoured cab. The cab interior is cooled by two impeller fans and both adjustable seats have safety belts.

The open cargo area has drop sides and a tailgate and a tow hook is provided at the rear. Equipment carried includes a 200-litre drinking water tank and two 2.5 kg fire extinguishers. A towing pintle is provided at the front. An optional 1,000-litre fuel tank may be carried at the rear.

Variants
Duiker armoured tanker
The Duiker armoured tanker is a Blesbok with the cargo area replaced by a 5,000-litre diesel fuel tank fitted with a gravity feed system for dispensing fuel, with an electrical pump as an option. Loaded weight is 13,490 kg. A total of 30 units were produced.

Gemsbok recovery vehicle
This is similar to the Blesbok but the rear is configured for the recovery role. Details of this are given in a separate entry in *Jane's Military Vehicles and Logistics*. Production of this vehicle is complete and it is no longer marketed.

Weapons platforms
It was announced in 1996 that the Casspir range had been extended by the introduction of two armoured weapon platforms, one carrying an 81 mm mortar and the other a 106 mm M40-series recoilless rifle.

Both of these versions of the Casspir remain in service with the South African National Defence Force. Both versions feature a shorter protected cab with the weapon mounted in the rear.

Blesbok (4 × 4) 5,000 kg armoured freighter   0511882

Casspir (4 × 4) vehicle fitted with 106 mm recoilless rifle with sides folded down   0005395

In the case of the 106 mm recoilless rifle version the sides and rear fold down to allow the weapon to be rapidly laid onto a new target.

In the case of the 81 mm mortar carry the weapon fires through the open roof with the armour protected sides and rear being provided with bulletproof glass windows for enhanced situational awareness.

Specifications

Blesbok armoured freighter
Cab seating: 1 + 1
Configuration: 4 × 4
Weight:
  (empty) 9,400 kg
  (loaded) 14,400 kg
Max load: 5,000 kg
Length: 7 m
Width: 2.5 m
Height: 3.12 m
Ground clearance: 0.355 m
Wheelbase: 4.3 m
Angle of approach: 46°
Max speed: 87 km/h
Range:
  (road) 850 km
  (cross-country) 560 km
Fuel capacity: 185 litres
Max gradient: 60%
Side slope: 30°
Vertical obstacle: 0.50 m
Trench crossing: 0.95 m
Fording: 1 m
Engine: ADE 352 T 5.675 litre 6-cylinder vertical in-line direct injection diesel developing 162.5 hp (121 kW) at 2,800 rpm
Gearbox: Mercedes-Benz DB 6/3/60 - 5/7.5 synchromesh with 5 forward and 1 reverse gears
Clutch: single dry plate
Transfer box: Mercedes-Benz 2 speed
Steering: ball and nut, power-assisted
Turning radius: 9.15 m
Suspension: semi-elliptic leaf springs mounted on to needle roller bearings with telescopic shock-absorbers front and rear (double spring pack at rear)
Tyres: 14.00 × 20
Brakes:
  (main) dual-circuit pneumatic with engine-mounted exhaust brake
  (parking) mechanical
Electrical system: 12 V
Battery: 1 × 12 V
Alternator: 55 A
Armament: 1 × 7.62 mm MG
Armour: steel

Status
Production complete. In service with the Namibian Police and South African National Defence Force (SANDF). No longer marketed.

Contractor
BAE Systems Land Systems South Africa (previously BAE Systems Land Systems OMC).

Sweden

BAE Systems Global Combat Systems Bandvagn Bv 206 all-terrain carrier

Development
In 1974, the Swedish Defence Matériel Administration awarded Hägglund and Söner (now BAE Systems Global Combat Systems) a contract for the development of a new over-snow/all-terrain vehicle to succeed the Volvo Bv 202 in the Swedish Army. Three batches of Bv 206 vehicles were delivered to the Swedish Army for trials in 1976, 1977 and 1978.

Bv 206 acting as a carrier for the Saab Microwave Systems Arthur weapon locating radar (Bv 206)   0009954

Bv 206 in service with the German Army (Michael Jerchel)   1133746

BAE Systems Global Combat Systems Bv 206 all-terrain carrier (BAE Systems Global Combat Systems)   1333660

The company was awarded a first production contract in June 1979 from the Swedish Defence Administration. Under this SEK800 million contract the company delivered pre-production vehicles late in 1980 and began full-scale production in early 1981. Full rate deliveries were made from mid-1981 until 1988.

In September 1981, the Norwegian Army ordered 220 units, followed in August 1985 by a further 2,004 Bv 206 vehicles in various configurations.

In September 1981, the British Army purchased four Bv 206s for trials in a variety of forms and a further number was purchased to replace Bv 202 vehicles then in service with the Army and Royal Marines. A further order (worth USD40 million) for diesel-engined vehicles for the Royal Marines was placed in March 1990; these are known as the Bv 206D6. The UK MoD planned to upgrade about 200 of its Bv 206s by replacing their petrol engines with diesel units to bring them up to Bv 206D6 standard. In Royal

Marines service, the Bv 206 has now been supplemented by the new BAE Systems Global Combat Systems BvS 10 armoured all-terrain carrier with first two examples being delivered in mid-2001.

The first of a batch of 12 Bv 206Ds for the German Bundeswehr was delivered in mid-1985. A second order for 63 vehicles was awarded during 1989. The Royal Netherlands Marines ordered its first batch of Bv 206 vehicles in 1989 and continued to order vehicles with differing configurations during 1991 and 1992 (the total was approximately 200 units by 1992).

In October 1992, it was announced that the French Defence Ministry had awarded a contract worth SEK20 million for an initial batch of Bv 206 vehicles, mainly provided with load handling systems, for use by the French Army's 27th Mountain Division.

In early 1993 Singapore ordered a batch of 300 Bv 206s with first deliveries made during early 1994.

In November 1993 the 10,000th series produced Bv 206 was formally delivered to the Swedish Defence Matériel Administration (FMV). By late 2004, total production of the Bv 206 and its variants amounted to over 11,000 units, with production being undertaken on an as required basis.

Production of the Bv 206 S is undertaken on a required basis and by late 2009 over 500 had been built, mostly for the export market.

BAE Systems Global Combat Systems continues to market the Bv 206S alongside their latest BvS 10 vehicle.

Production of the Bv 206 family of all terrain vehicles is undertaken on an as required basis for the export market.

With the reduction in overall force levels in some countries there are a number of surplus Bv 206 vehicles for sale.

In 2010 it was stated that the Swedish Army deployed a total of 93 Bv 206S under the designation of the Bv 309 with the earlier Bv 308 being used for training.

Marketing is now being concentrated on the larger and fully armour protected BvS 10 tracked all terrain carrier.

This is already in service with the Netherlands (74) and the UK (190) with the latest customer being France who is taking delivery of a total 53 units from 2010.

Description

The Bv 206 consists of two tracked units linked together with a steering unit, each unit consisting of a chassis with the body mounted on four rubber elements.

Each chassis consists of a central beam, a final drive assembly and two track assemblies. The chassis of the front and rear units are identical, except that a two-step drop-down gearbox is mounted in the rear end of the front chassis. The track assemblies are mounted to the central beam by two transversal leaf springs. Each track assembly is built up around a tubular bar which carries the sprocket assembly, roadwheels and idler. In each track assembly there are four pairs of roadwheels on trailing arms sprung by rubber tension springs. The idler at the rear with a tensioning device is also supported by a rubber spring. All four track assemblies of the vehicle are identical and interchangeable. The tracks are rubber with longitudinal textile cord and integral steel profile reinforcements.

Steering is accomplished by changing the direction between the front and rear unit by two hydraulic cylinders, servo-controlled from a conventional steering wheel. The hydraulic system is built up of commercially available components. The steering unit is designed to permit a large freedom of movement between the two bodies.

The engine and transmission are mounted in the front unit. A shaft connects the gearbox with the drop-down gearbox. A disc brake is mounted on this shaft in front of the drop-down gearbox inside the body. Cardan shafts transmit power to the final drives on the front end of both chassis. Early units were fitted with petrol engines but later production examples are fitted with Mercedes-Benz 136 hp diesel engines.

The bodies are made of Glass-Reinforced Plastic (GRP), which is fire resistant, with PVC foam insulation. Each body is built like a closed box with integrated roll-over protection. Heating of the units is by heat exchangers and the de-icing capacity in the front unit is sufficient to keep the windscreen clear down to a temperature of −40°C. The bodies have holders for lashing cargo in the rear unit and also in the rear part of the front unit. The rear unit is also provided with brackets for carrying four stretchers. The Singapore Armed Forces employ special rear bodies containing water tanks.

The Bv 206 is fully amphibious, being propelled in the water by its tracks.

Variants

Flatbed vehicle

This variant accommodate the driver and five passengers in the front unit. The load capacity is increased to 2,350 kg. This variant is available in amphibious and non-amphibious versions.

Anti-tank vehicle

Anti-tank vehicles may be armed with a TOW, MILAN, Saab Bofors Dynamics RBS 56 BILL or other ATGW on a pivot mount which can be hydraulically raised to the required level. The open-front body is provided with roll bars, which can be quickly lowered. The low-profile rear body is designed to withstand the backblast of the weapon when it is fired and is used for storing ammunition.

The Bv 206S all-terrain armoured vehicle without weapons installed on front unit (BAE Systems Global Combat Systems)   1403711

Command Post/Radio vehicle

This can accommodate up to six operators in the rear body and the driver plus four personnel in the front body. Door arrangements are identical to the standard carrier version. The vehicle has VHF transceivers in the rear body and all the radios can be operated from the front unit.

Radar and C3I vehicles

The high payload of the Bv 206 permits the installation of a very wide range of specialist equipment. For instance, a radar vehicle has a special generator and a Saab Microwave Systems Giraffe 50 AT C-band search radar with an instrumented range of 50 km and a mast height of 7 m. A radio jamming vehicle is equipped with a separate jamming generator driven by the main engine, generating 15 kVA. The antenna is mounted on an 18 m rapidly erected mast.

A radio locating vehicle is equipped with radio intelligence and direction-finding systems. The antenna is mounted on an 18 m telescopic mast. Equipment in a radio relay vehicle consists of either VHF or UHF multichannel radios for automatic relay transmission. The rear vehicle carries spare batteries and a 3 kVA diesel-driven power unit. There is also a 20 m antenna mast for ground or vehicle mounting.

The Bv 206 is also used as a carrier for the Saab Microwave Systems Arthur weapon locating radar system. This is now used by at least six countries. Some use the Bv 206 while others use a truck.

Mortar carriers

Special shock-absorbing flatbeds in various forms enable mortars to be fired from the rear unit of a Bv 206. Mortars tested with this system include TDA and BAE Systems Global Combat Systems L16 81 mm mortars, with each vehicle carrying approximately 100 rounds of ammunition. A 107 mm/4.2 in mortar version carries 60 rounds of ammunition while a 120 mm mortar variant (in both smoothbore and rifled versions) can carry approximately 30 rounds.

Firefighting version

The Royal Air Force has three special fire and rescue Bv 206 variants based at RAF Mount Pleasant in the Falkland Islands. The rear units of these vehicles are occupied by fire and rescue equipment and are utilised as rapid intervention vehicles in the event of airfield accidents.

Bv 206D

Bv 206 all-terrain carriers used by the German Army are fitted with Mercedes-Benz OM 603.950 six-cylinder diesel engines developing 136 bhp at 4,600 rpm. This engine is the current standard installation for new vehicles. The diesel-powered models are referred to by the manufacturer as the Bv 206 D6.

Bv 208

This is the Swedish Army designation for vehicles fitted with diesel engines.

Skorpion-AB

This is an airborne open-topped version of the Bv 206, with the rear unit accommodating a Skorpion mine-launching system.

South Korean Bv 206

The Bv 206 is licence-produced in South Korea By Kia Motors. For many years the Republic of Korea (RoK) has been using the Bv 206 all-terrain vehicle. First Bv 206 vehicles were purchased direct from Sweden but the vehicle was then manufactured under licence by the local company of Kia Motors.

Early in 2002, the then company was awarded a contract worth SEK150 million from Kia Motors of the RoK for the supply of a further batch of 93 Bv 206 all-terrain vehicle kits.

These kits were delivered to Kia Motors between 2002 through to 2005 who then assembled them for the Korean Armed Forces.

Under early contracts, the company delivered about 300 Bv 206 kits to Kia Motors. It is understood that the Korean Armed Forces use a number of variants of the Bv 206 including: mortar carrier; weapons carrier and command post vehicle.

The 4.2 inch mortar carrier is designated the K532, and has a turntable mounted mortar in the rear unit with a baseplate being carried at the rear to allow the mortar to be dismounted and deployed away from the vehicle. There is also the K53X used for specialised electronics roles.

Ring Mount NM 165

When equipped with a Ring Mount NM 165 the Bv 206 can be armed with either a .50 (12.7 mm) M2 HB machine gun or a 40 mm automatic grenade launcher.

Ambulance/first aid station vehicle

This variant carries a crew of five, four stretchers, a medical specialist and medical equipment. It is provided with a tent which folds on to the rear unit allowing the vehicle to be used as a first aid station. The front unit serves as a surgery while the tent acts as a treatment area for up to eight casualties.

Forward repair team vehicle

A typical example of this variant is provided with a hydraulic crane with a lifting capacity of 1,500 kg. A 3,600 kg capacity hydraulic winch is mounted at the front. The vehicle carries a repair crew and sufficient spares, tools and so on, to remain operational for several days. The example quoted is used by the British Army and Royal Marines.

Armoured variants

Bv S7 - Also marketed as the Bv 206S, T his variant first appeared in mid-1990 and is an armoured personnel carrier version of the basic Bv 206. It is used by a number of countries including France, Germany, Italy, Spain and Sweden.

Bv S10 - Launched in mid-1998, this is a totally new vehicle. It remains based on the same design concept as the Bv 206 but has a higher payload and road speed.

SUSV

During 1983, the US Army Tank Automotive Command (TACOM) awarded a USD24.2 million contract for 268 Bv 206 all-terrain carriers (plus an option for a further 34, later exercised) known as the Small Unit Support Vehicle (SUSV). The contract followed a period of extensive trials carried out using a small batch of vehicles at the Cold Regions Test Center at Fort Greely, Alaska. Most of the vehicles involved in the contract, delivered from Sweden in 1983 and 1984, were issued to the US Army's 172nd Infantry Brigade in Alaska and the Alaskan National Guard. Early M973 SUSVs were powered by three-litre four-stroke, five-cylinder in-line diesel engines developing 125 hp at 4,500 rpm. Vehicles delivered after 1987 are powered by a Mercedes-Benz six-cylinder turbocharged diesel engine developing 136 hp at 4,500 rpm.

There are four basic SUSV variants: M973/M973A1 cargo carrier, M1066 ambulance, M1067 flatbed, and M1067 command-and-control vehicle. The M973/M973A1 has a payload of 1.5 tonnes (US), while the M1067 has a payload of two tonnes (US).

In 1988 the US Army ordered a further 390 M973 SUSVs, and these were delivered from 1989. Continued purchases until 1992 resulted in a total fleet of approximately 1,100 vehicles.

Other variants

The Bv 206 has been used for a variety of other roles, not all of them military. Using a hydraulically-operated load changer arm the Bv 206 can be used to carry a variety of containers, shelters and various load bodies. The trailer can also be used to carry a light crane or lifting platform and may be configured for a number of special purposes such as a remote area firefighting vehicle, as a mobile workshop or as a field ambulance.

Specifications

Bv 206 all-terrain carrier
[Cargo carrier variant]
Cab seating:
(front unit) 5–6
(rear unit) 11
Weight:
(empty) 4,490 kg
(loaded) 6,740 kg
(front unit - empty) 2,740 kg
(rear unit - empty) 1,730 kg
Max load:
(total) 2,250 kg
(front unit) 610 kg
(rear unit) 1,640 kg
Towed load: 2,500 kg

Load area:
(front unit) 0.81 × 1.4 m
(rear unit) 2.5 × 1.4 m
Length: 6.9 m
Width: 1.87 or 2 m
Height: 2.4 m
Ground clearance: 0.35 m
Track width: 620 mm
Max speed:
(road) 52 km/h
(water) 3 km/h
Max gradient:
(hard surface) 100%
(snow) 30%
Max side slope: 90%
Fording: amphibious
Range: (roads) 300 km
Engine:
(current) Mercedes-Benz OM 603.950 2.996-litre 6-cylinder diesel developing 136 hp (101 kW) at 4,600 rpm
(early production) Ford Model 2658 E V-6 water-cooled petrol developing 136 bhp (101 kW) at 5,200 rpm (could also be fitted with Mercedes-Benz 5-cylinder in-line turbocharged diesel engine developing 125 bhp (93 kW) at 4,500 rpm)
Gearbox: Daimler-Benz W4A-040 fully automatic with torque converter, with 4 forward and 1 reverse gears
Transfer box: Hägglunds 2-speed
Steering: articulated hydrostatic
Turning radius: 8 m (6 m with pitch control)
Electrical system: 24 V
Batteries: 2 × 12 V, 105 Ah
Alternator: 55 or 100 A

Status

Production as required. More than 11,000 ordered or in military service with 16 countries. In service with Brazil, Canada (100), Chile, China, Finland (400), France, Germany, Italy (90), South Korea, Malaysia, Netherlands (200), Norway (2,200), Pakistan, Singapore (300), Spain, Sweden (4,500), UK (600 for Army, Royal Marines and Royal Air Force) and US Army (approximately 1,100). The armoured Bv 206 S is used by France, Germany, Italy, Spain and Sweden.

Contractor

BAE Systems Global Combat Systems

Turkey

FNSS Savunma Sistemleri Armoured Combat Vehicle - Stretched Tracked Load Carrier (ACV-S TLC)

Development

Based on their experience in the design, development and quantity production of the Armoured Combat Vehicle (ACV) family of full tracked Armoured Personnel Carriers (APC) and variants, FNSS Savunma Sistemleri AS developed the Armoured Combat Vehicle - New Generation (ACV - NG).

Development of this originally commenced as a private venture in response to a US Army requirement for a new vehicle to equip its Interim Brigade Combat Teams (IBCT).

While the ACV - NG was not successful in this competition, FNSS continued development under the name of the Armoured Combat Vehicle - Stretched (ACV - S).

As well as the original prototype used in the US Army trials, other vehicles have been built to production standard including an infantry combat vehicle, and anti-tank missile team carrier and a Tracked Load Carrier (TLC).

The latter was developed to meet the potential requirements of Malaysia with the first prototype being completed early in 2003. The Malaysian Army already operates a fleet of 211 ACV.

Late in 2006 the company was awarded a contract from an undisclosed country in the Middle East for the supply of 10 ACV-S in a Tactical Command Post Vehicle (TCPV) configuration.

This was the first production contract for the ACV-S and the vehicles were delivered in 2007.

These were fitted with additional mine protection to meet STANAG 4569 2a, appliqué ballistic protection to meet STANAG 4569 3 and spall liners.

Armament consists of a roof mounted .50 (12.7 mm) M2 HB machine gun in a protected mount.

For its specialised role the TCPV is fitted with an air conditioning system, positive pressure NBC system, data terminals, VHF, HF and UHF radios and an Auxiliary Power Unit (APU) fitted as standard.

The latter allows all of the on board equipment to be run with the main diesel engine switched off, To provide additional working area a tent can be rapidly erected at the rear of the vehicle.

Armoured Combat Vehicle - Stretched Tracked Load Carrier (ACV-S TLC) has a payload of six tonnes and shown here fitted with a .50 (12.7 mm) M2 HB machine gun (FNSS)   0563980

In April 2008 it was announced that Malaysia had ordered eight ACV-S and that these would be fitted with TDA 120 mm Recoilling Rifled Mounted Mortar (2R2M) system.

The order for the eight mortars to go with these vehicles were not however ordered until early 2010.

Description

The hull of the ACV-S is of all-welded aluminium armour to which another layer of appliqué armour has been added, which provides protection against 14.5 mm armour piercing attack and 155 mm artillery projectiles bursting overhead.

FNSS also offers an additional armour kit which increases protection through the frontal arc against 30 mm attack. Increased protection is also available against anti-tank weapons with a HEAT warhead as well as anti-tank mines.

When compared to the original ACV, the ACV-S has a stretched hull with an additional road wheel either side which gives a 30 per cent increase in internal volume in the APC version.

The driver is seated at the front of the vehicle on the left side with the power pack to his right. The driver has a single piece hatch cover that opens to the right and in front of this are three day periscopes that give observation to the front and sides of the vehicle. The middle one can be replaced by a passive night vision device.

There is additional space to the rear of the power back and the driver for two people, one of whom is normally the vehicle commander. This person is provided with a standard commanders rotating hatch cover that is provided with periscopes and an externally mounted .50 (12.7 mm) M2 HB machine gun.

Other armament installations are possible. Mounted at the front of the hull is a bank of eight electrically operated 76 mm smoke grenade launchers that fire to the front of the vehicle.

To the immediate rear of the crew compartment is a flatbed complete with tie down points as well as drop sides and a drop tailgate that can be quickly removed if required.

The TLC can carry a maximum payload of six tonnes and a HIAB 182R hydraulic crane is fitted on the roof of the crew compartment to assist in loading and unloading cargo. This is operated by remote control up to 15 m away and can lift 1.6 tonnes at a reach of 3.26 m.

The suspension is of the torsion bar type with either side having six dual rubber tyred road wheels with the drive sprocket at the front and idler at the rear. There are no return rollers.

When compared to earlier vehicles the suspension has been upgraded with stronger torsion bars, greater road-wheel travel and the front driving sprocket has been raised for greater obstacle climbing ability. This all contributes to increased cross-country mobility and a better ride.

Unlike other members of the ACV and ACV-S, the TLC is not fully amphibious. In addition to the hydraulic crane, standard equipment includes a self-recovery winch, NBC system and an air conditioning system. It is also fully airportable in a Lockheed Martin C-130 Hercules transport aircraft.

Variants

Other FNSS support vehicles

Amphibious Armoured Combat Earthmover

The Turkish Land Forces Command has awarded FNSS a contract for a total of 12 Amphibious Armoured Combat Earthmovers (AACE) with the first of these to be delivered in 2012. The contract covers one prototype vehicle and 11 production vehicles.

Armoured Ammunition Resupply Vehicles

FNSS is also bidding to supply the TLFC with 71 armoured ammunition resupply vehicles. These will supply 155 mm ammunition (projectiles and charges) for TLFC 155 mm self-propelled artillery systems.

Their proposal is based on the latest Armoured Combat Vehicle – Stretched design that has already been produced for the export market.

Specifications

ACV-S tracked load carrier
Crew: 2 + 1
Combat weight: 18,500 kg
Power-to-weight ratio: 18.92 hp/tonne (14.11 kW/tonne)
Ground pressure: n/avail
Length: 6.38 m
Width: 2.946 m
Height:
   (overall) 3.15 m
   (hull roof) 2.01 m
Ground clearance: 0.40 m
Track width: 325 mm
Length of track on ground: 3.75 m
Fuel capacity: 445 litres
Max road speed:
   (forwards) 65 km/h
   (reverse) 11 km/h
Max acceleration: 22 seconds (0 to 48 km/h)
Max road range: 490 km
Fording: 1.10 m
Gradient: 60%
Side slope: 30%
Vertical obstacle: 0.74 m
Trench: 1.83 m
Engine: Detroit Diesel 6V-53T developing 350 hp (261 kW) with a 400 hp (298 kW) option
Transmission: Allison X200-4 automatic, 4 forward and 1 reverse gears
Steering: hydrostatic
Suspension: upgraded torsion bar
Electrical system: 24 V
Armament: 1 × 7.62 mm or .50 (12.7 mm) M2 HB
Smoke-laying equipment: 8 smoke grenade launchers
Ammunition: n/avail
NBC system: yes
Night vision equipment: yes

Status

Development complete. Ready for production. Baseline ACV-S is in service with Saudi Arabia (10) and Malaysia (eight in 120 mm mortar configuration).

Contractor

FNSS Savunma Sistemleri AS

Ukraine

GT-T tracked amphibious over-snow vehicle

Development

The GT-T tracked amphibious over-snow vehicle was developed in the late 1950s at the now Ordzhonikidze Kharkov Tractor Plant JSC, Ukraine, and was the largest in the GT range of tracked amphibious over-snow vehicles. It can carry a maximum of 2,000 kg of cargo and tow a trailer weighing up to 4,000 kg.

The KLP-2 wheeled/ski trailer was designed for use with the GT-T. Production of the GT-T tracked amphibious over-snow vehicle was completed some time ago and it is no longer marketed.

Description

The IZ6 six-cylinder diesel engine is at the front of the hull and extends rearwards into the crew compartment. The driver is seated on the left side and the vehicle commander on the right, both with a side door and the commander has a circular hatch in the roof.

Troops boarding GT-T tracked amphibious over-snow vehicles during Winter exercises   0511888

The load area is at the rear and is usually covered by a tarpaulin cover. Up to 10 personnel can be seated in the rear. An unusual feature of the GT-T is that the diesel fuel tanks are positioned externally above the tracks on each side at the rear.

The torsion bar suspension consists of six roadwheels on either side, with the idler at the rear and the drive sprocket at the front. The roadwheels are similar to those used on the PT-76 light amphibious tank family, and are also used as the basis for the more recent MT-LB armoured multipurpose tracked vehicle.

This was built in large numbers for the Russian Army and numerous export customers. Production is now complete and it is still in service with many countries with a number of contractors offering upgrades to improve its automotive performance.

The GT-T is fully amphibious. Most sources state that it is propelled in the water by its tracks at a speed between 5 and 6 km/h.

Variants
A number of GT-Ts have had a fifth wheel mounted to the rear of the cab for towing semi- trailers carrying air defence missiles, such as the Volga-M (NATO SA-2 'Guideline'); they were designated as GT-TS but most have now been withdrawn from service.

A number of specialised civilian models have been developed, with a fully enclosed cabin at the rear. In 1965 the GT-T maintenance vehicle entered service with the designation MTO-SG. Mounted at the front of the vehicle is an A-frame for changing components and inside the hull rear is a workshop with a petrol driven power generator, electric drill, electric grinder, arc welding equipment, compression pressure meter and a full set of tools. The A-frame can lift a maximum load of 1,500 kg. Radios are fitted as standard on all repair vehicles.

A field kitchen version was produced and a version has been reported carrying a modified aircraft jet engine to carry out NBC decontamination of equipment and vehicles.

Specifications
GT-T tracked amphibious over-snow vehicle
Cab seating: 1 + 2 (up to 10 in rear)
Weight:
　(empty) 8,200 kg
　(loaded) 10,200 kg
Max load: 2,000 kg
Towed load: 4,000 kg
Length: 6.34 m
Width: 3.14 m
Height: 2.16 m
Ground clearance: 0.45 m
Track width: 540 mm
Length of track on ground: 3.914 m
Ground pressure: (loaded) 0.24 kg/cm^2
Max speed:
　(road) 45.5 km/h
　(water) 6 km/h
Range: 500 km
Max gradient: 60%
Engine: 1Z-6 6-cylinder water-cooled diesel developing 192 hp (143 kW)

Status
Production complete. No longer marketed. In service with the Russian Federation. Numbers reducing.

Contractor
Ordzhonikidze Kharkov Tractor Plant JSC
(Original design, production would likely have been undertaken in state-owned factories.)

MT-L tracked amphibious over-snow vehicle

Development
Development of the MT-L family of full-tracked vehicles began at the now Ordzhonikidze Kharkov Tractor Plant JSC in the early 1960s and shortly after the GT-T vehicle.

Unlike the GT-T which is specifically an over-snow vehicle also used in swampy areas, the MT-L is not strictly an over-snow vehicle, as its ground pressure is 0.428 kg/cm^2.

Two special variants of the MT-L, the MT-LBV and MT-LBVM, each have a ground pressure of 0.28 kg/cm^2, which puts them in almost the same class as the GT-T.

The basic vehicle of the MT-L family is known as the MT-LB multipurpose tracked vehicle with production for the Russian Army being undertaken in Ukraine.

The MT-LB and its many variants, are still used by about 30 countries all over the world. As of late 2010 the MT-LB series of full tracked multipurpose tracked vehicle remained in service with some 20 countries for a wide range of roles.

Production of the MT-LB was undertaken in Bulgaria, Poland and Ukraine, and a number of facilities now market upgrades for this vehicle.

MT-L tracked amphibious over-snow vehicle　　　0511889

MT-LB multipurpose tracked vehicle　　　0064797

Description
The fully enclosed cab is at the front of the hull and can seat eight personnel including the vehicle commander and the driver. The diesel engine of the MT-L is in the rear part of the cab. Normal means of entry is through the doors in either side of the hull, but there is also a roof hatch.

The load area is at the rear and is provided with drop tailgate, bows and a tarpaulin cover. The torsion bar suspension either side consists of six roadwheels with the drive sprocket at the front and the idler at the rear. The MT-L can be fitted with extra wide 565 mm tracks and an aggressive grouser to facilitate over-snow and soft terrain operations.

Models so-fitted are designated either MT-LBV or MT-LBVM and have a ground pressure of 0.28 kg/cm^2. There are no track-return rollers. The roadwheels are similar to those used on members of the PT-76 light amphibious tank family and are also used on the MT-LB. A hydraulic shock absorber is mounted at the first and last roadwheel stations.

The MT-L is fully amphibious without preparation, being propelled in the water by its tracks at a maximum speed of 6 km/h. A bilge pump is fitted as standard.

Specifications
MT-L tracked amphibious over-snow vehicle
Cab seating: 1 + 7 (up to 10 in rear)
Weight:
　(laden, without trailer) 13,000 kg
　(laden, with trailer) 11,000 kg
　(unladen) 8,500 kg
Max load:
　(without trailer) 4,500 kg
　(laden, with trailer) 2,500 kg
Towed load: 7,000 kg
Length: 6.364 m
Width: 2.85 m
Height: 2.013 m
Ground clearance: 0.40 m
Track width: 350 mm
Length of track on ground: 3.7 m
Track: 2.5 m
Ground pressure:
　(MT-L) 0.428 kg/cm^2
　(MT-LBV/MT-LBVM) 0.28 kg/cm^2
Max speed:
　(road, without trailer) 61.5 km/h
　(road, with trailer) 46.8 km/h
　(water) 5–6 km/h
Range: 500 km
Max gradient:
　(without trailer) 60%
　(with trailer) 40%
Side slope: 40%
Engine: YaMZ-238V V-8 diesel developing 230 hp (172 kW) at 2,100 rpm
Transmission: manual with 6 forward and 1 reverse gears
Steering: clutch and brake
Suspension: torsion bar
Electrical system: 24 V

Status
Production complete. No longer marketed. In service with the Russian Federation. Numbers reducing.

Contractor
Ordzhonikidze Kharkov Tractor Plant JSC

United Kingdom

BAE Systems Global Combat Systems Stormer High-Mobility Load Carrier (HMLC)

Development
The Stormer High-Mobility Load Carrier was originally developed by Alvis Vehicles of Coventry as a member of the Stormer family of armoured personnel carriers which was originally developed for the export market but subsequently adopted by the British Army.

It is a flatbed tracked cargo carrier which can be used in a variety of forms, including a platform for scatterable mine systems.

Following a competition the British Army selected the Stormer APC as the basis for its Thales Air Defence High Velocity Missile (HVM) systems. A total of 135 Stormer HVM were supplied plus ten troop reconnaissance vehicles.

Other Stormer customers include Indonesia (many variants including TLC), Malaysia (25 in APC configuration) and Oman (10 in command post role).

All production of the Stormer was undertaken at the Alvis Vehicles facility at Coventry which has now closed.

Alvis Vehicles no longer exists and the overall design authority is now BAE Systems Global Combat Systems with Newcastle-upon-Tyne today being the only remaining armoured fighting vehicle production facility in the company.

Description
The hull of the Stormer HMLC is of all welded aluminium armour which provides the occupants with protection from small arms fire and shell splinters.

The driver is seated at the front left with the diesel powerpack to the right. The driver has a single piece hatch cover that opens forward plus a wide angle day periscope that can be replaced by a passive periscope for driving at night.

To the rear of the driver is the commander who is normally provided with a cupola with day periscopes for all round observation. This is provided with a 7.62 mm machine gun for self defence purpose. The vehicle is also fitted with banks of electrically operated smoke grenade launchers.

The flatbed area is to the immediate rear of the commanders position and can be fitted with removable drop sides and a drop tailgate or specialised applications.

Suspension is of the torsion bar type with each side having six dual rubber-tyred road wheels with the drive sprocket at the front and the idler at the rear and two track return rollers.

Variants
It was proposed that the Stormer HMLC could be fitted with a hydraulic crane for use in the logistics carrier role, or as a Barmine laying vehicle.

A variant has been sold to Indonesia as the carrier for a 15 m version of the SEI Light Assault Bridge. Production of this combination is complete and it is no longer manufactured or marketed.

The British Army has taken delivery of 30 modified versions of the Stormer HMLC as the platform for the Shielder anti-tank minelaying system. Final deliveries were made in mid-2001. Development work and first prototypes of the Streaker were built in Coventry, but the main production run was undertaken at the Telford facility.

Prime contractor for the Shielder Vehicle Launched Scatterable Mine System (VLSMS) is ATK of the US with BAE Systems Global Combat Systems supplying the carrier vehicle   0080335

Stormer flatbed as used by Indonesia
(BAE Systems Global Combat Systems)   1133745

Specifications
Stormer high mobility load carrier
Crew: 1 + 1 or 2
Weight: (combat laden) 13,200 kg
Payload: 4,000 kg
Length: 2.624 m
Width: 2.7 m
Height: (overall) 2.236 m
Ground clearance: (approx) 0.406 m
Track: 2.505 m
Track width: 425 mm
Length of track on ground: 3.575 m
Max speed: 80 km/h
Range: (road) >644 km
Fuel capacity: 300 litres
Gradient: 60%
Vertical obstacle: 0.60 m
Trench: 1.75 m
Fording: 1.15 m
Angle of approach/departure: 30°/28°
Engine: Perkins T6.3544 5.8 litre 6-cylinder in-line turbocharged diesel developing 250 hp (186 kW) at 2,600 rpm
Transmission: David Brown Gear Systems T300 semi-automatic with 6 forward speeds
Suspension: transverse torsion bars with trailing arm geometry and lever type hydraulic dampers
Electrical system: 28 V
Batteries: 4 ×12 V 6TN, 100 Ah
Generator: 28 V, 220 A

Status
Production complete. No longer marketed. 30 have been built for the Vehicle-Launched Scatterable Mine System (VLSMS) known as Shielder. Procured by Indonesia in flatbed form and as Light Assault Bridge carrier. Stormer flatbed is in service with Indonesia.

Contractor
BAE Systems Global Combat Systems
(Production of the Stormer was undertaken at Telford which has now closed.)

United States

BAE Systems US Combat Systems M992 Series Field Artillery Ammunition Support Vehicles (FAASV)

Development
In 1979, prototypes of three armoured artillery resupply vehicles were tested during Human Engineering Laboratory, Battalion Artillery Test (HELBAT) trials. The BMY Combat Systems (today BAE Systems US Combat Systems) vehicle was based on the chassis of the proven M109 155 mm self-propelled howitzer chassis, as was the HEL/AAI vehicle, and was named the M109 Ammunition Delivery System by the company.

Following completion of the initial trials and the Concept Evaluation Test, it was decided that the M109 chassis was most suitable for the Field Artillery Ammunition Support Vehicle. In August 1980 Tank Automotive Command (TACOM) issued a request for proposals for the design, construction, test and integrated logistics support of the FAASV.

In March 1981 BMY was awarded a contract, by TACOM, for the supply of five prototype FAASVs under the designation of XM992. These were delivered during November and December 1981 and underwent DT/OT II trials at Yuma Proving Ground and at Fort Sill until March 1982. Following these trials the XM992 was type classified as the M992 FAASV in the Autumn of 1982.

Research, development, test and evaluation costs for the FAASV up to Fiscal Year 1982 amounted to USD5.6 million and in FY83 procurement costs totalled USD29.7 million for 54 vehicles. FY84 procurement costs were USD60 million for 120 vehicles and FY85 costs were USD78.2 million for 170 vehicles. The FY86 figures were USD70.2 million for 142 vehicles and for FY87 they were USD62.5 million for 141 vehicles. FY88 planning called for USD28.7 million for 48 vehicles. Production ceased for a while until 1991 when it was restarted to meet an order for 60 FAASVs, believed to be for Saudi Arabia and worth more than USD50 million. In September 1991, a contract for 125 US Army and 20 FMS FAASVs was announced; the contract was worth USD42,340,041. In May 1993 an option for an additional 65 vehicles was awarded. Production of all these vehicles was completed in April 1994.

The following components are common to the M992 FAASV and the standard M109: aluminium armour hull structure; engine and auxiliary equipment; transmission and final drive; complete suspension; commander's and driver's hatches and controls; heating and ventilation system; electrical components; internal communications equipment; and towing provisions.

The M992A1 and M992A2 are basically similar to the M992 but are configured for the support of the 155 mm M109A6 Paladin self-propelled howitzer. See entry under Variants for details. The 155 mm M109A6 Paladin is only used by the US Army with a total of 975 units delivered.

In consultation with the US Army, BAE Systems US Combat Systems, designed and built the prototype of the M109A6 Paladin Integrated Management (PIM) SP artillery system in just nine months and this was rolled out in September 2007.

M109A6 PIM integrates an upgraded current M109A6 Paladin turret with a brand new chassis developed by BAE Systems US Combat Systems.

The new all welded aluminium armour chassis incorporates a Cummins 600 hp diesel and L3 Combat Propulsion Systems HMPT-500 series automatic transmission which are already used in the US Army's Bradley infantry combat vehicle. This powerpack will improve the power-to-weight ratio as well as the top speed of the M109A6 PIM.

It also uses Bradley final drives and torsion bars and the upgraded electrical system includes a 70 kW generator. A HUMS will be installed as standard.

In October 2009 it was announced that the US Army Tank Automotive & Armaments Command had awarded the company a contract worth USD63.9 million for the procurement and fabrication of five prototype M109A6 PIM and two M992A2 FAASV.

Under the vehicle terms of this contact, design and engineering analysis work for the vehicle structure, automotive systems and electrical vehicle electronics was performed by BAE Systems facilities in California, Michigan, Minnesota, New York and Pennsylvania and at US Government facilities at the US Army Research and Development Center in Picatinny, New Jersey.

The remanufacture programme for the M109A6 PIM will be performed in partnership with the Anniston Army Depot and at BAE Systems facilities in New York, Pennsylvania and Elgin, Oklahoma.

Funding permitting, it is possible that a total of 600 M109A6 Paladin will be upgraded to the M109A6 PIM standard together with a similar number of associated M992A2 FAASV.

Of these 600 units, 447 will be in the Heavy Brigade Combat Team (HBCT) and the remaining 153 in the Training and Doctrine Command (TRADOC) and repair/cycle floats.

The first batch could include a total of 177 M109A6 PIM and a similar quantity of M992A2 FAASV.

In mid-2010 the US Army was considering a lower figure of 400 M109A6 PIM with a potential Low Rate Initial Production (LRIP) in FY13 (against an original expected FY11) followed by Full Rate Production (FRP) in FY17 (against an earlier potential FY15).

Description

The hull of the M992 is made of all-welded 5083 aluminium armour with the driver at the front of the hull on the left, the power pack to his right and 155 mm ammunition stowage at the rear.

The export version of the M992 FAASV is normally fitted with an hydraulic crane for loading ammunition (BAE Systems US Combat Systems) 0567109

M99A2 FAASV supporting an M109A6 Paladin self-propelled artillery system (Richard Stickland)   1164671

The driver has a hinged hatch cover that opens to the rear, in front of which are three M45 day periscopes which can be covered by small metal flaps to prevent damage. The centre periscope can be replaced by an image intensification or thermal device for driving at night.

The Detroit Diesel Model 8V-71T Low Heat Rejection (LHR) is coupled to the Allison Division XTG-411-4 crossdrive automatic transmission which is at the front of the hull.

The torsion bar suspension either side consists of seven dual rubber-tyred road wheels with the drive sprocket at the front and the idler at the rear. There are no track-return rollers. The tracks are of the single-pin, centre-guide type with replaceable rubber pads.

In the forward part of the roof there is a three-part 155 mm projectile rack removal hatch and behind it is the commander's cupola. This can be traversed through 360° and has a single-piece hatch cover. A .50 (12.7 mm) M2 HB machine gun can be mounted at this station.

Prototype FAASVs had a 626 kg capacity crane mounted at the front of the hull but this crane was not fitted to full production vehicles for the US Army (it was, however, fitted to vehicles supplied to Egypt). The 155 mm projectiles are handled in racks of 10 projectiles, for example two horizontal layers of five projectiles each. If required, projectiles can also be loaded individually using the powered conveyor to feed the empty racks.

The charges are located in containers on either side of the FAASV at the rear with fuzes being stowed in the left side of the hull. Ammunition is transferred to the M109 through its lower rear door by a power-operated conveyor at a rate of 6-8 rds/min, which is higher than the M109 rate of fire.

Overhead protection is provided by the large upward-opening powered door of the vehicle. The conveyor has lateral protection from the M109 and M992 lower rear doors. When not in use the conveyor folds up and is stowed inside the vehicle.

The 155 mm projectiles are transferred from their stowed position in the forward part of the vehicle to the conveyor belt by the X-Y stacker which is part of the ammunition handling system and can be moved vertically and horizontally. The tray of the stacker serves as a working platform for installing fuzes on to the projectiles.

The upward-swinging rear door is hydraulically powered, with the smaller lower door opening manually to the right. The commander' adjustable seat is over the rear part of the conveyor belt.

US Army FAASVs are configured to carry storage racks each holding 10 × 155 mm projectiles plus charges, fuzes and other cargo. For export the following maximum quantities can be carried:

Calibre	155 mm	203 mm
Projectiles:	90 + 3 M712 CLGP	48
Propelling charges:	96	53
Fuzes:	104	56

In the US Army FAASV space was allocated for special projectiles such as the M712 Copperhead Cannon Launched Guided Projectile (three), the Remote Anti-Armor Mine System (M718/M741) and the Area Denial Artillery Munitions (M692/M731).

The auxiliary power unit is located in the forward part of the FAASV's superstructure and supplies hydraulic and electrical power to the vehicle systems as well as charging the batteries. In addition, it can also provide power to the M109A6 Paladin self-propelled howitzer for service during silent stealth operations.

The FAASV also incorporates a number of improvements which are included in the M109A6 Paladin. These include: an automatic fire suppression system; NBC VFP protection system; simplified test equipment as fitted to more recent AFVs such as the M1 MBT, M2 IFV and M3 CFV; AN/VIC-1 intercom; and an AN/PRC-68 small unit radio. Also fitted are chemical detection and alarm units and chemical decontamination units.

Variants

M992A1 and M992A2

A series of product improvements was incorporated into the FAASV, leading to the type classification of the M992A1 and M992A2. These improvements include: electrical system enhancements; the integration of a low-heat rejection engine and T-154 Track Assembly; removal of the X-Y stacker, plus container stowage and conveyor enhancements; and modification of the upward-swinging rear door, adding two small doors to allow conveyor interface with the M109A6 Paladin with the rear door closed. These improvements were generated by the US Army' Initial Operational Test and Evaluation (IOTE) of the M109A6 HIP, later named Paladin. The improvements increase the operational capabilities of the FAASV with all versions of the M109 series.

M992 vehicles have now been converted to M992A2 standard using kits supplied by the now BAE Systems US Combat Systems. A total of 164 M992 vehicles used by the US Army in Europe were upgraded in Belgium by the now BAE Systems US Combat Systems using EMI as the major subcontractor. BAE Systems, Ground Systems produced 48 new production M992A2s from FY96 dollars, additional 48 vehicles in FY97 and 36 vehicles in FY98. Cost savings generated from the FY98 vehicles being produced from used M109 howitzer chassis generated enough money to produce six additional FAASVs, which were delivered late in 2000.

M1050

The M1050 is a version of the FAASV for use with 203 mm/8 in howitzer ammunition and fitted with a stacker device. It has not yet been produced as M110A1/M110A2 has been phased out of US Army service.

Fire Direction Centre Vehicle/Command Post Vehicle (FDCV/CPV)

BMY (now part of BAE Systems US Combat Systems) delivered a Fire Direction Centre Vehicle/Command Post Vehicle (FDCV/CPV) based on the chassis of the FAASV to the US Army for trials.

The US Army has carried out extensive tests of this vehicle but there are no plans for it to enter production or service with the US Army.

Specifications

M992A2 FAASV
Cab seating: 2 (plus 6 passengers)
Weight: (combat loaded) 26,105 kg
Max load: (ammunition) 5,454 kg
Load area: 3.38 × 3.05 × 2.21 m
Length: 6.6 m
Width: 3.15 m
Height: 3.276 m
Ground clearance: 0.368 m
Track width: 381 mm
Length of track on ground: 3.962 m
Max speed: (road) 64 km/h
Range: (approx.) 354 km
Fuel capacity: 511 litres
Max gradient: 60%
Max side slope: 40%
Fording: 1.07 m
Vertical obstacle: 0.53 m
Trench: 1.83 m
Engine: Detroit Diesel Model 8V-71TLHR 9.3-litre turbocharged, 2-stroke, liquid-cooled, 8-cylinder diesel developing 440 bhp (328 kW) at 2,350 rpm
Transmission: Allison Transmission XTG-411-4 crossdrive with 4 forward and 2 reverse gears
Suspension: torsion bar with high-capacity shock-absorbers
Electrical system: 24 V
Batteries: 4 × 12 V 6TN
Alternator: 180 A

Status

Production as required. In service with Egypt (51 FAASV, 72 FDCV/CPV), Greece (41 FDCV/CPV), Spain (six FAASV), Saudi Arabia (60 FAASV), Taiwan (six FDCV/CPV), Thailand (20 FAASV), and US Army (927 FAASV). Part of the US Army fleet is expected to be upgraded under the M109A6 PIM programme covered in development.

Contractor

BAE Systems US Combat Systems

BAE Systems US Combat Systems Fighting Vehicle Systems Carrier

Development

The Fighting Vehicle Systems Carrier (XM987) is part of the Bradley Fighting Vehicle Systems (BFVS) family, which also includes: the M2 Infantry Fighting Vehicle; the M3 Cavalry Fighting Vehicle; and the M993 Multiple Launch Rocket System (MLRS) carrier, all of which were developed by FMC Corporation (now BAE Systems US Combat Systems) under contract to the US Army.

The vehicle is a highly mobile armoured carrier used for a wide range of requirements. Major features of the vehicle are its component commonality with the IFV and CFV, overpressure ventilation system, nuclear hardened electrical system, air transportability in the Lockheed C-141 Starlifter transport aircraft, tilt cab to facilitate maintenance and a current payload of 12,700 kg.

For some applications the vehicles has been upgraded with the M2A2 Bradley power train and suspension which provides an increased payload of 15,812 kg while maintaining mobility characteristics.

Prototypes of the Fighting Vehicle Systems Carrier were originally built by FMC specifically for use with the General Support Rocket System (now known as the Multiple Launch Rocket System (MLRS). The first prototype vehicles, under the designation XM993, were delivered to the two competing contractors late in 1978. After trials, the Vought system was selected and in June 1980 Vought was awarded an initial USD26.9 million contract for 1,374 missiles packed in launch containers and 16 self-propelled launcher loaders, to be built by FMC/United Defense. The M270 Multiple Launch Rocket System, of which well over 1,000 have been built, consists of the M993 carrier and the M269 launcher.

BAE Systems Global Combat Systems have completed production of the Fighting Vehicle Systems Carrier.

In US Army service the tracked MLRS is now being supplemented by the Lockheed Martin Missiles and Fire-Control High Mobility Artillery Rocket System based on a protected 6 × 6 truck chassis.

Description

The basic Fighting Vehicle Systems (FVS) Carrier has a cab-over-power pack arrangement with the cargo area at the rear.

The aluminium armour plate cab is fitted with noise attenuation materials and large ballistic windows to provide forward and side vision. The front windows are fitted with exterior louvres providing protection during rocket firing and for nuclear survivability.

The louvres can be opened or closed individually with levers inside the cab. In a tactical situation the louvres may be rotated to a stowed position on the cab roof.

The cab has accommodation for the crew of three, an overpressure ventilation system, space for radios and provisions and an instrument panel for operating the vehicle. Sufficient space is provided to add a second control panel for weapon system operation.

An overhead hatch above the right-hand seat can be fully opened for use as an airguard, or fixed partially open for additional ventilation. As an option the cab roof can be fitted with a NATO mount for a 7.62 mm M240 machine gun.

The complete power pack, which is centred in the vehicle, is interchangeable with that of the IFV and CFV. It consists of a Cummins VTA-903 (500 hp) or VTA-903T (600 hp) diesel engine coupled to a L3 Propulsion Systems HMPT 500 series automatic crossdrive transmission. The power pack can be removed or installed without breaking cooling or hydraulic lines and this arrangement enables the power pack to be operated on the ground outside the vehicle.

The power pack is wired to accommodate built-in test equipment for rapid fault isolation using Simplified Test Equipment/Fighting Vehicle System (STE/FVS), the same test equipment as used in the General Dynamics Land Systems M1A1/M1A2 Abrams MBT.

The power pack has a negative pressure system where cooling air is drawn through the radiator and discharged through the exhaust grille above the right sponson. The diesel fuel is carried in integral tanks under the floor plates at the rear of the vehicle.

The suspension is an elongated version of the IFV/CFV system and each side consists of six dual rubber-tyred road wheels, two dual support rollers, two single support rollers, front drive sprocket, raised rear idler and a high return track.

The single-pin track has forged steel blocks, rubber bushings and detachable rubber pads. Track tension is adjusted by a grease-filled cylinder between the hull and idler wheel.

Vertical roadwheel travel is controlled by high-strength steel torsion bars splined to trailing road arms forming a fully independent suspension. Linear hydraulic shock-absorbers at the first, second and sixth roadwheels stabilise the vehicle on rough terrain.

A suspension lockout system is provided for the MLRS application of the carrier. The lockout is a hydraulically actuated, multidisc brake mounted concentric with the torsion bar. Lockout units can be installed at some or all the torsion bar stations depending on the level of suspension stiffness required. The lockouts provide platform stability during both launching and loading operations.

Multiple Launch Rocket System (MLRS) deployed in firing position and with launcher traversed right (Lockheed Martin)   1296058

M270B1 MLRS upgraded for operations in Afghanistan and clearly showing additional armour fitted to three person cab
(Christopher F Foss)
1308385

In the left rear corner of the cab is the overpressure ventilation system. It consists of a five micron dust filter, three micron particulate filter, charcoal filter, bypass valve and an axial flow fan. Dual positioning of the bypass valve permits air to pass through all three filters or just through the dust filter, depending on the mission. As an option this system can be converted to a hybrid system. The present design has an M13A1 NBC unit in the cab. This secondary system provides for the crew's safety if the cabin air inadvertently becomes contaminated during the course of a mission.

Variants

MLRS carrier
This was the first application for the FVS Carrier, the chassis being designated the M993 for this purpose. In addition to being used by the US Army, MLRS is also used by many other countries. Licensed production of the chassis was also undertaken in Europe for France, Germany, Italy and the UK.

M270A1 launcher survivability enhancement
Late in 2009 it was revealed that BAE Systems US Combat Systems, had developed, using Independent Research And Development (IR&D) funding, a redesigned cab for the M270A1 MLRS.

This has been designed in conjunction with the US Army who intends to retain a fleet of 225 full tracked M270A1 227 mm (12-round) launchers through to 2050 alongside its expanding fleet of M142 227 mm (6-round) High Mobility Artillery Rocket System.

Development of the redesigned cab commenced in January 2009 at the BAE Systems US Combat Systems facility in Santa Clara, California.

When compared to the existing cab, the redesigned cab for the latest M270A1 MLRS launcher not only has an additional 40 per cent internal volume, but also an integrated armour and mine protection package for enhanced crew survivability which meets the latest armour protection requirements.

The wider and higher welded aluminium armour cab features three new mine blast and shock resistant seats. To enhanced crew survivability, the seats are now attached to the sides of the vehicle, rather than being attached to the floor.

This cab also features a Blue Force Tracker (BFT), Driver Vision Enhancement (DVE) with two flat panel displays (for driver and commander) and long range communications equipment.

In the future the US Army expects to upgrade the Fire-Control System (FCS) of the M270A1.

Some of the sub-systems used in the redesigned cab can also used in other currently deployed US Army platforms including HIMARS and Mine Resistant Ambush Protected (MRAP) vehicles. HIMARS is based on a BAE Systems Family of Medium Tactical Vehicle (FMTV) (6×6) five-tonne cross-country chassis with a protected cab.

The M270A1 is an improved version of the original M270 MRLS and features an Improved FCS, improved launcher mechanical system and 600 hp Cummins diesel engine.

The power pack of the M270A1 is retained which consists of a Cummins VTA-903 series diesel developing 600 hp coupled to an L3 Combat Propulsion Systems HMPT-500 automatic transmission.

With a combat weight of about 30 tonnes this gives a power to weight ratio of 20 hp/tonne. The new generation cab also features a power assisted device that tilts the cab forwards to allow access to the power pack located below the cab.

Cargo carrier
This was designated the XM987 but never entered production.

Armored, Forward-Area, Rearm Vehicle (AFARV)
The US Army tested the prototype of an Armored, Forward-Area, Rearm Vehicle (AFARV) to resupply armoured and infantry units in the forward battlefield area.

M270A1 Multiple Launch Rocker System (MLRS) upgraded with a new BAE Systems redesigned cab for enhanced crew survivability
(IHS Jane's/Rupert Pengelley)
1347674

A modified MLRS chassis is used as the basis for the private venture Krauss-Maffei Wegmann Armoured Gun System that is armed with a 155 mm/52-calibre weapon as used in the PzH 2000 self-propelled artillery system (Krauss-Maffei Wegmann)
1333529

There are no plans for this to enter production for the US Army.

Artillery Rearm Module (ARM)
A prototype of the ARM was delivered for US Army trials commencing in October 1990. This system is not expected to enter volume production.

Armored Maintenance Vehicle
A prototype Armored Maintenance Vehicle (AMV) fitted with a 10-tonne crane was built and evaluated by the US Army in 1985. The vehicle was leased to the US Army. This system is not expected to enter volume production.

M4 Command-and-Control Vehicle
During an initial Engineering and Manufacturing Development (EMD) phase, five prototypes of a Command-and-Control Vehicle (C2V) were built with an armoured module housing equipment and personnel for battle commander's staff. The enclosure is a self-contained unit which includes an NBC protection system, environmental control system (air conditioning and heating), a 43 kW, 60 Hz primary power unit and a 10 m telescopic mast, all remotely controlled from within the enclosure. The M4 is completely self-contained and configured to accommodate Command-and-Control (C2) mission equipment. With a change in software it may also be used as an artillery fire direction centre or an air defence battle management operations centre. The Command-and-Control (C2) Vehicle is equipped with a Cummins 600 hp engine, L3 Propulsion Systems transmission and BFVA2 final drives, steel road wheels, improved track and torsion bars. The MLRS suspension lockout system is removed. These changes are stated to provide significant growth capability for up-armoured alternatives.

During 1996 and 1997, four pre-production prototypes underwent government testing. Low Rate Initial Production (LRIP) commenced with the first production deliveries made during mid-1998. The first option under the LRIP for five added systems was awarded in December 1997. The second option added five systems and a third option an additional 10 systems with final deliveries taking place in June 2001.

In early 2003, it was revealed that the US Army had proceeded with the fielding of at least one of its recently terminated legacy systems, M4 Command-and-Control System.

In the end, a total of 25 M4 Command-and-Control Vehicles were built before the programme was terminated and the now BAE Systems US Combat Systems agreed to store them at their York facility and try to sell them overseas with US Government approval.

Late in 2002, the US Army asked the now BAE Systems US Combat Systems if these vehicles could be re-fielded. In the end, the company and Army planners mutually agreed to set aside 10 vehicles for spare parts, while re-issuing the 15 remaining vehicles for possible combat service.

Beginning in October 2002, the 15 systems were fielded to US Fifth Corps (three M4s), Third Infantry Division (three M4s), First Cavalry Division (4 M4s), Third Armored Cavalry Regiment (two M4s), and the First Armored Division (three M4s). Some of these units were subsequently deployed to the Middle East and took part in the invasion of Iraq.

XM5 Electronic Fighting Vehicle System (EFVS)
The XM5 Electronic Fighting Vehicle System (EFVS) is similar to the M4 Command-and-Control Vehicle (see preceding text) and uses the same chassis and superstructure. There are no plans for this system to enter quantity production.

Armored Medical Treatment Vehicle (AMTV)
The Armored Medical Treatment Vehicle (AMTV) is intended to be positioned well forward in battle areas to act as the Battalion Aid Station treatment facility. It protects the casualties and medical attendants while carrying out close combat medical missions and is completely self-contained. Onboard support subsystems provide power for mission equipment and maintain an NBC contamination-free treatment environment. A surgical table and one triage position are provided along with stowage for medical equipment and kits. Emergency medical procedures can be performed inside the enclosure to stabilise casualties for transport to rear area treatment facilities. A prototype has been produced and has been undergoing government evaluation. The system has yet to enter quantity production although other systems may be re-roled for this application.

Proposed variants

MLRS resupply vehicle
This vehicle can carry four pods of MLRS rockets. The load handling system is similar to that used by the Palletized Loading System (PLS). There are no plans for this version to enter production.

Fuel resupply vehicle
This vehicle can deliver 7,570 litres of fuel in one mission, sufficient to supply a company of Abrams MBTs or Bradley Fighting Vehicles in forward tactical areas. This unit can also provide oil and lubrication services during refuelling. There are no plans for this version to enter production.

Crotale NG vehicle
This vehicle mounts the Thales Air Defence Crotale New Generation (NG) air defence module. It is similar to the US Army C2V, the module being a self-contained unit. There are no plans for this to enter production.

Upgraded UK MLRS
Under the leadership of Lockheed Martin UK, a batch of M270 Multi-Launch Rocket Systems (MLRS) have been upgraded with the Lockheed Martin Missiles and Fire-Control Improved Fire-Control System (IFCS). This brings them up to the M270B1 standard.

Some M270B1 have been upgraded and deployed to Afghanistan under an Urgent Operational Requirement (UOR) with much of this work being done by the Defence Support Group.

These include appliqué armour and bar armour to the three person cab, mine protection, new energy absorbing seats, situational awareness system, wire cutter, roof mounted machine gun, ECU and upgraded suspension to take into account the increased weight of the vehicle.

An initial batch of 24 M270 are being converted to the enhanced M270B1 standard.

Following the cancellation of the Lightweight Mobile Artillery Weapon System (Rocket) programme in early 2008 the MoD has decided to upgrade another 12 M270 to the enhanced M270B1 standard.

The UK Royal Artillery have deployed five of the upgraded M270B1 MLRS to Afghanistan where they have seen extensive use firing Guided MLRS (GMLRS) which provide a precision strike capability out to over 60 km.

UK Repair and Recovery Vehicle
The now Lockheed Martin UK has converted four surplus MLRS carriers of the British Army into Repair and Recovery Vehicles for the British Army.

Full details of this vehicle, which is used by the Royal Electrical and Mechanical Engineers, are given in a separate entry in *Jane's Military Vehicles and Logistics*.

Armoured Gun Module
A modified MLRS chassis is also used as the basis for the private venture Krauss-Maffei Wegmann 155 mm/52-calibre Artillery Gun Module (AGM) which as of late 2010 remains at the prototype stage.

Specifications
Fighting Vehicle Systems Carrier
Cab seating: 1 + 1 or 1 + 2

Weight:
   (empty) 14,636 or 14,818 kg
   (loaded) 25,545 or 30,630 kg
Load area:
   (cargo bed between sponsons) 3.96 × 1.78 m
   (above sponsons) 3.96 × 2.97 m
Length: 6.97 m
Width: 2.97 m
Height:
   (cab) 2.59 m
   (chassis) 1.206 m
   (top of load area) 1.09 m
Ground clearance: 0.43 m
Track width: 533 mm
Length of track on ground: 4.33 m
Max speed:
   (road) 65 km/h
   (10% gradient) 26 km/h
Range:
   (at 40 km/h) 483 km
Fuel capacity: 726 litres
Max gradient: 60%
Max side slope: 40%
Fording: 1.02 m
Vertical obstacle: 0.91 m
Trench: 2.36 m
Engine: Cummins VTA-903 14.8-litre turbocharged 8-cylinder diesel developing 500 hp (373 kW) at 2,400 rpm or Cummins VTA-903T 14.8-litre turbocharged 8-cylinder diesel developing 600 hp (447 kW) at 2,400 rpm
Transmission: L3 Propulsion Systems HMPT 500-3EC hydromechanical with electronic controller
Steering: hydrostatic
Suspension: steel torsion bar
Brakes: multidisc, oil-cooled
Electrical system: 28 V
Batteries: 4 × 12 V 6TN, 100 Ah
Alternator: 2 × 300 A

Status
Production complete but can be resumed.

Country	Quantity
Bahrain	9
Denmark	12
Egypt	26
France	57
Finland	22 (from Netherlands)
Germany	154
Greece	36
Israel	48
Italy	22
Japan	45
Korea, South	29
Norway	not deployed
Turkey	12
United Kingdom	63
US	857

Contractor
BAE Systems US Combat Systems Division
(Also produced under licence in Europe for MLRS application.)

BAE Systems US Combat Systems M548 tracked cargo carrier

Development
The XM548 cargo carrier was designed for the US Army Signal Corps in 1960, using the basic automotive components of the M113 tracked armoured personnel carrier. At that time its primary purpose was to serve as a highly mobile transport carrier for the AN/MPQ-32 Hostile Artillery Radar System.

This application did not reach production and a modified version with a Detroit Diesel 6V-53 engine, designated the XM548E1, was designed using the power pack and automotive components common to the M113A1 APC.

Engineer and service tests on three prototype vehicles were completed late in 1964 and the vehicle was type classified the following year. First production vehicles were completed early in 1966 by the now BAE Systems US Combat Systems (the then FMC Corporation).

The US Army did not procure any vehicles in Fiscal Year 1976 to 1978 but 193 vehicles were bought with FY79 funding of USD15.6 million and 242 with 1980 funding of USD30 million. The FY82, request was for a further 160 vehicles at USD20.9 million. In FY83, 29 M548A1 carriers were produced for the US Army plus six for other countries. As of March 1987,

M548 tracked cargo carrier complete with bows, tarpaulin cover and armed with .50 (12.7 mm) M2 HB machine gun (US Army)   1296060

This Armoured Vehicle Logistic has a flatbed at the rear on which containers or pallets of supplies can be carried (BAE Systems Australia)   1334205

3,683 M548s had been purchased by the US Army. Another 1,295 were produced for export. In total 254 M548A1s were purchased by the US Army with another 18 produced for export.

Total production of all versions of the M548 series was over 6,000 vehicles. Production of this was completed some time ago and it is no longer offered by the now BAE Systems US Combat Systems.

According to the United Nations Arms transfer lists, the following quantities of M548 tracked cargo carriers were exported by the US Army between 1992 and 2008. It is understood that these were ex-US Army vehicles.

From	To	Quantity	Comment
US	Argentina	11	M548A2, delivered 1999
US	Chile	14	M548A2, delivered 1999

The M548 was used to act as an ammunition re-supply vehicle for US Army 155 mm M109 series self-propelled artillery systems but this role has now been taken over by the armoured BAE Systems US Combat Systems M992 Field Artillery Ammunition Support Vehicle (FAASV).

Production of the now BAE Systems Global Combat Systems M992 FAASV is complete but the company has the potential to commence production again if required. Details of the M992 FAASV and its potential upgrades are provided in a separate entry in *Jane's Armour and Artillery*.

Description

The power pack and crew compartment are at the front of the vehicle and the cab roof, sides, front and rear can be removed for air transport. The cargo compartment has a rear opening that can be secured by two watertight doors. Six hollow aluminium extruded plates bolted in place in either an upper or lower position form the cargo deck. The lower position allows more cargo to be carried or provides leg room for seated passengers. Tiedowns are available for both cargo deck positions. The cargo area can be enclosed using a standard vinyl-coated nylon cover supported by bows.

Standard production M548 tracked cargo carrier complete with bows and tarpaulin cover and ring mount over cab armed with a .50 M2 HB machine gun (BAE Systems US Combat Systems)   1403712

If required, an M66 ring mount for an air and local defence machine gun can be mounted over the top of the cab. If this is fitted with a 7.62 mm machine gun, 660 rounds of ammunition are carried, or if fitted with a .50 (12.7 mm) M2 HB heavy machine gun, 300 rounds of ammunition are carried.

The suspension is of the torsion bar type and either side consists of five roadwheels with the drive sprocket at the front and the idler at the rear. (The M548A1 has hydraulic shock-absorbers on the first, second and last roadwheel stations.)

There are no track-return rollers. The first and last roadwheel stations are provided with a hydraulic shock-absorber and the tops of the tracks are covered by a rubber skirt.

The vehicle has the same wheels, sprocket, sprocket carrier, track adjuster, idler, idler wheel, shock-absorber and mount, wheels and track as the M113A1 but has a larger diameter torsion bar and the final drive assembly has a different gear ratio.

The M548 is fully amphibious and propelled in the water by its tracks. On US Army vehicles, however, the amphibious capability was removed.

A winch with a 9,072 kg capacity is mounted at the front of the vehicle. Optional equipment includes a heater (personnel and cargo areas), heater (engine coolant and battery), an airbrake kit to actuate brakes on the towed trailer and a materials handling hoist.

Variants

Stretched M548A1E1

In 1977 the company completed the prototype of a stretched M548A1E1, about 0.66 m longer than the basic model with an additional set of roadwheels. The standard 210 hp engine was replaced by a turbocharged model developing 300 hp. Other improvements included a transmission that featured hydrostatic steering and a modified cooling system.

M730 Chaparral

This has four Chaparral SAMs on a launcher at the rear of the cab. Although this system has been phased out of the US Army service, it remains in service with a number of other countries.

Recovery vehicles

A recovery version, known as the XM696, was developed to the prototype stage.

The Norwegian firm of Alvis Moelv AB (this company no longer exists) fitted one of its NM84 wrecker cranes on to an M548 for the Norwegian Army. This crane has a maximum lift capacity of 5,000 kg at 3.5 m and a maximum winch pulling capacity of 18,000 kg. Maximum outreach is 5.3 m at which 3,400 kg can be lifted.

Radar vehicles

Many countries use the M548 for carrying radars: for example, the then Oerlikon Contraves (which is today known as Rheinmetall Air Defence) of Switzerland fitted its Skyguard anti-aircraft radar in the rear of the vehicle for trials.

M548A1

Introduced in 1982, this version has improved suspension and cooling systems. Both new production and depot rebuild versions were involved.

M548A3

In 1993 a prototype of an M548A3 was produced and tested. The vehicle is based on the M548A1 standard, fitted with a Detroit Diesel 6V-53T turbocharged diesel developing 275 hp, a new alternator and hydrostatic steering, all part of the M113A3 Reliability Improved Selected Equipment (RISE) package. Basic specifications, where different from those of the M548A1, are:

Width:	2.69 m (2.54 m reduced)
Height:	2.68 m
Max road speed:	58.2 km/h
Range:	458 km
Engine:	Detroit Diesel Model 6V-53T turbocharged diesel developing 275 hp (205 kW)
Transmission:	Allison X200-4 hydrokinetic

The M548A3 also features an NBC crew protection system. Initial conversions were carried out in the US (at the Red River Army Depot) and in Korea during 1994 and more were planned.

M548 options
Upgrade and re-equipment options envisaged for the M548 series included: an armoured cab (adding 1,360 kg to the vehicle weight); a material handling crane; drop side enhancements; a NBC decontamination apparatus; a global positioning system; ammunition racks (possibly from the M992 Series FAASV); a winch; and trailer brakes. Not all of these options are expected to come to fruition.

M548GA1
This is a low-sided vehicle that mounts a platform for the German Skorpion mine dispensing system.

XM1118 Universal Carrier
This was developed as a private venture by the now BAE Systems US Combat Systems and was previously known as the M113A3 Universal Carrier and was proposed for a wide range of roles and missions. It remains at the prototype stage but is not currently marketed.

ARIS ARK
The running gear and lower hull of the M548 is used as the basis for the Italian ARIS ARK amphibious support vehicle, which remains at the prototype stage.

Australian Armoured Vehicle Logistic
BAE Systems Australia has now converted a total of 50 M113 series full tracked APC's into the Armoured Logistic Vehicle. This has a stretched chassis with a total of six road wheels either side and a flatbed to the rear of the drivers and commanders compartment.

This is designated to the M113AS4 Armoured Vehicle Logistic by the Australian Army and details are provided in *Jane's Armour Artillery*.

Pakistan A1 Qaswa logistic vehicle
Details of this vehicle, developed by the Heavy Industries Taxila facility are provided in a separate entry in *Jane's Military Vehicles and Logistics*. It is understood that as of late 2010 this remains at the prototype stage.

Specifications

M548 tracked cargo carrier
Cab seating: 1 + 3
Weight:
  (empty) 7,439 kg
  (loaded) 12,882 kg
Max load: 5,443 kg
Towed load: 6,350 kg
Load area: 3.32 × 2.45 m
Length: 5.892 m
Width:
  (max) 2.69 m
  (over tracks) 2.54 m
Height:
  (excl. MG) 2.71 m
  (reduced) 1.94 m
  (load area) 1.21 m
Ground clearance: 0.43 m
Track: 2.159 m
Track width: 381 mm
Length of track on ground: 2.82 m
Ground pressure: 0.6 kg/cm^2
Angle of approach/departure: 57°/35°
Max speed:
  (road) 53.1 km/h
  (10% gradient) 18.2 km/h
Range: 483 km
Fuel capacity: 397 litres
Max gradient: 60%
Max side slope: 30%
Fording: 1 m
Vertical obstacle: 0.609 m
Trench: 1.68 m
Engine: Detroit Diesel Model 6V-53 6-cylinder liquid-cooled diesel developing 215 hp (160 kW) at 2,800 rpm
Gearbox: Allison TX-100-1 3 speed; a torque converter gives 6 forward and 2 reverse speeds
Suspension: torsion bar
Electrical system: 24 V
Batteries: 2 × 12 V, 6TN, 100 Ah

Status
Production ceased 1994. In service with Argentina (11), Australia, Chile (14), Egypt, Germany, Greece, Israel, Italy, Norway, Spain, Switzerland, Tunisia and the US.

Contractor
BAE Systems US Combat Systems

Force Protection Cougar Tactical Support Vehicle (TSV)

Development
The US company of Force Protection are well known for their extensive range of Mine Protected Vehicle (MPV) that have been built in large quantities for the home and export markets.

In 2010 the company expanded its product portfolio with the introduction of the Cougar Tactical Support Vehicle (TSV) which has been developed as a private venture to meet a perceived gap in the market.

As of late 2010 development of the Cougar TSV was regarded as complete and production could commence when firm orders are placed.

Description
TSV is a further development of the combat proven Cougar (4 × 4) MPV but has a slightly shorter wheelbase and features a two door fully enclosed cab and a load area at the rear. Maximum payload, including crew, is nine tonnes, but this depends on the level of protection.

The cab can seat up to five people on special blast attenuation seats being fitted as standard with crew entry via a door in either side that opens towards the front of the vehicle. Bulletproof windows provide enhanced situational awareness through a full 360°.

The Cougar TSV shown in October 2009 in Washington DC was fitted with a Northrop Grumman Venom mast mounted sensor pod with the operator being provided with a flat panel display inside the cab.

The sensor pod is fitted with a day/thermal optronics and a laser rangefinder/designator which would typically be used in the target acquisition/battlefield surveillance role with the system having the capability to pass information to other platforms.

It is powered by a Caterpillar C7 developing 370 hp coupled to an Allison 3500 SP series automatic transmission which that gives a maximum road speed of up to 112 km/h (sprint) or 96 km/h for normal.

Cougar Tactical Support Vehicle features a two-door fully protected cab with a flatbed to the rear which allows it to be used for a wide range of roles (Force Protection)   1364432

Baseline Wolfhound Tactical Support Vehicle (Heavy) for British Army clearly showing load area at the rear before the protected crew compartment is fitted with its enhanced armour package including bar armour (Christopher F Foss)   1403713

Standard equipment includes run flat tyres and dual air conditioning and heating systems. Baseline vehicle is fitted with a roof mounted M1114 ring mount that is typically armed with a .50 M2 HB machine gun.

As usual a host of options are available for the TSV including arctic kit, central tyre inflation system, fire detection and suppression system, independent suspension for improved cross-country mobility, seating increased to six, self-recovery winch and a slightly narrower version.

Variants
In addition to the surveillance version of the Cougar TSV mentioned in the development, Force Protection are marketing the Cougar TSV for a wide range of roles including cargo carrier, fitted with a special shelter, refuelling vehicle and maintenance support vehicle.

UK Wolfhound Tactical Support Vehicle (Heavy)
The British Army has taken delivery of a batch of 97 Tactical Support Vehicle (Heavy) Wolfhound vehicles which is based on the Mastiff Heavy Protected Patrol Vehicle (HPPV) already in service with the British Army in significant numbers.

This 6 × 6 vehicle has the protected engine compartment at the front, fully enclosed cab and a load area at the rear.

There are two baseline versions of the TSV(H) Utility and Military Working Dog/Explosive Ordnance Disposal. They are fitted with Bowman communications equipment and electronic devices to counter improved explosive devices.

Specifications
Cougar TSV
Crew: 1 + 4
Configuration: 4 × 4
Weight:
  (combat) 12,727 kg
  (unloaded) 21,818 kg
Payload: 9,090 kg
Power-to-weight ratio: 16,95 hp/tonne

Length: 5.99 m
Width: 2.56 m
Height: 2.71 m
Ground clearance: 0.38 m
Track: n/avail
Wheelbase: n/avail
Angle of approach: 40°
Angle of departure: 50°
Max road speed: 96 km/h
Fuel capacity: n/avail
Max range: 676 km
Fording: 1.016 m
Gradient: 60%
Side slope: 40%
Trench: n/avail
Vertical obstacle: n/avail
Turning radius: n/avail
Engine: Caterpillar C7 diesel developing 370 hp (276 kW) at 2,700 rpm
Transmission: Allison 3500 SP series automatic
Front axle: Marmon-Herrington MT-22
Rear axle: Marmon-Herrington R-22
Steering: power-assisted
Tyres: Michelin ZXL 395/85R20 with Hutchinson VFI run flats
Brakes: pneumatic
Electrical system: 24 V, 570 amp
NBC system: no
Air conditioning: yes
Armament: 1 × 50 M2 HB MG

Status
Prototype. Not yet in production or service.

Contractor
Force Protection Inc.

MATERIALS HANDLING EQUIPMENT

Czech Republic

CTS-servis container handling and transport systems

Development

CTS-servis is the oldest and largest manufacturer of automotive container systems in the Czech Republic. The Company was founded in 1992 by the privatisation of the originally state-owned Machinery and Tractor Centre (STS) at Okřínek.

CTS-servis has been supplying equipment to Czech armed forces since 1998 and currently manufactures four main types of military-specific transport platforms, plus load handling systems for 4 × 4 and 6 × 6 TATRA trucks for the Czech Army. In addition to those systems detailed elsewhere in this entry, CTS also offers the Flatrack 20 Model Mx and the Flatrack KSSK.

Description

Transport Platform Flatrack 20 Model T

The Transport Platform Flatrack 20 Model T has been designed to be capable of handling and transport by any load handling system-equipped truck that meets DIN 30722 or STANAG 2413 MH standards. The primary purpose of this flatrack is the transport of vehicles, either damaged or in 'ready to role' conditions.

Two manually operated fold-down width-adjustable steel ramps facilitate loading and unloading, and fold-down side extensions and adjustable and removable wheel chocks enable a wide variety of wheeled and tracked vehicles to be transported; the list including: UAZ-452; UAZ-469; Mercedes-Benz G-Class; Land Rover Defender; Ross R210.12VP; TATRA T815 4 × 4; BRDM; BRDM-2; BVP-1 and BVP-2.

Unladen racks may stacked when folded and can be handled by any suitable capacity forklift or materials handling crane. Unladen racks are rail-transportable on standard flat car rolling stock.

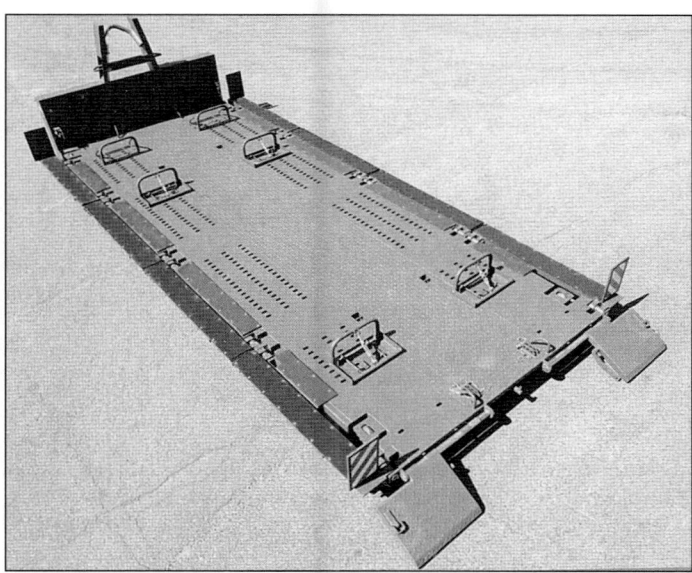

CTS Transport Platform Flatrack 20 Model T showing adjustable/removable wheel chocks. The drop-down side extensions are lowered; the adjustable loading ramps are down (CTS)   0587648

CTS Transport Platform Flatrack 20 Model T being handled by a Multilift LHS-equipped TATRA T815 series truck (CTS)   0587641

The Transport Platform Flatrack 20 Model T has been in service with the Czech Army since 1999.

Transport Platform Flatrack 20 Model M

The Transport Platform Flatrack 20 Model M has been designed to be capable of handling and transport by any load handling system-equipped truck that meets DIN 30722 or STANAG 2413 MH standards. The primary purpose of this flatrack is the transport of containers and six ISO 1D container twistlocks along each side of the platform allow for the handling of ISO 1C, ISO 1D or KSSK type containers. Other loads including pallets may be transported.

This flatrack can be fitted with folding side and rear panels, and may also be fitted with a tarpaulin and bows. Unladen racks may stacked when folded and can be handled by any suitable capacity forklift or materials handling crane. Unladen racks are rail-transportable on standard flat car rolling stock.

The Transport Platform Flatrack 20 Model M has been in service with the Czech Army since 1999.

Transport Platform Flatrack 20 models Mx, M1, M2, M3, M4 are also available.

Transport Platform 20 - VP

The Transport Platform 20 - VP was specifically designed for mounting on the TATRA T815 VNN 8 × 8 truck chassis, and when mounted the truck is known as the TATRA T815 26265 8×8.1R - Transport Platform 20' - VP.

One primary purpose of this flatrack is the transport of containers and six ISO 1D container twistlocks along each side of the platform allow for the handling of one ISO 1C, one or two ISO 1D or one KSSK type containers. Other loads including up to 28 pallets may be transported.

This platform can be fitted with folding side and rear panels, and may also be fitted with a tarpaulin and bows.

The Transport Platform 20 - VP has been in service with the Czech Army since 1999.

TATRA T815-26WR45 17 255 4x4.1/11T and /12T model NKSSK

These are two models of TATRA ARMAX family trucks fitted with a CTS-servis-supplied superstructure specifically designed for the transport of KSSK or ISO 1D containers.

The TATRA T815-26WR45 17 255 4x4.1/11T model NKSSK entered Czech Army service in 1999, the TATRA T815-26WR45 17 255 4x4.1/12T model NKSSK entered Czech Army service in 2000.

CTS 14155-VP and CTS 14255-VP load handling systems

These load handling systems are essentially the same, the designation change reflecting a different host vehicle. The TATRA T815-26WR45 17 255 4x4.1 4 × 4 ARMAX family chassis-cab mounts the CTS 14155-VP system,

The CTS Transport Platform 20 - VP was specifically designed for mounting on the TATRA T815 VNN 8 × 8 truck chassis (CTS)   0587645

These are two models of TATRA ARMAX family trucks fitted with a CTS-servis-supplied superstructure specifically designed for the transport of KSSK or ISO 1D containers (CTS)   0587644

Rear three-quarter view of a TATRA T815-26WR45 17 255 4×4.1 4 × 4 ARMAX family chassis-cab mounting the CTS 14155-VP load handling system (CTS) 0587639

Front three-quarter view of a TATRA T815 VPR8 20.235 6×6.1R 6 × 6 T815 series chassis-cab mounting the a CTS 14255-VP load handling system and handling a container-mounted flatrack (CTS) 0587643

while the TATRA T815 VPR8 20.235 6×6.1R 6 × 6 T815 series chassis cab mounts the CTS 14255-VP system. The CTS 14155-VP system entered service with the Czech Army in 1999, the CTS 14255-VP system entered service in 2000.

These systems are designed to handle containers complying with DIN 30722 and STANAG 2413 MH standards. Containers with or without an intermediate flatrack may handled.

Specifications

Model	Flatrack 20 Model T	Flatrack 20 Model M	Transport Platform 20 - VP (platform)
Weight:	3,400 kg	2,800 kg	1,960 kg
Max load:	14,100 kg	14,100 kg	12,300 kg
Length:	6.809 m	6.77 m	7.024 m
Width:	2.55 m (3 m with side extensions)	2.492 m	2.491 m
Height:	1.68 m	1.96 m	1.742 m
Height of load platform:	270 mm	265 mm	292 mm

Model	NKSSK/11T		NKSSK/12T
Weight: (incl. front auxiliary platform)	302 kg		308 kg
Max load:	18,000 kg		18,000 kg
Length: (incl. front auxiliary platform)	4.747 m		4.747 m
Width of front auxiliary platform:	2.5 m		2.5 m
Height of rear container section:	250 mm		250 mm
Height of front container section:	250 mm		250 mm

CTS 14155/14255-VP
Weight: 1,380 kg
Max load: 18,000 kg
Length: 5.067 m

Width: 1.514 m
Height: 1.918 m
Cycle time: (load/unload) 60/60 secs
Lifting capacity: 14,000 kg

Status
In production. In service the Czech Army. Offered for export sale.

Contractor
CTS-servis spol. s r.o.

Finland

Kalmar high-speed lift trucks

Development
Kalmar (Sisu) high-speed lift trucks originated from a French Army requirement for special convoy capability forklift trucks for handling palletised loads. However, most of the machines subsequently delivered now handle military containers.

Originally there was only one model in the range, the TD1612HS. During 1997 to 1998 two new models were introduced, the TD1712HS, with a 17,000 kg container capacity under a fixed 6.096 m (20 ft) frame, and the TD912-1712HS, a forklift with a 9,000 to 17,000 kg capacity. Common to all three models is their convoy speed capability and ability to ford water obstacles 1 m deep.

Vehicles delivered to the French armed forces carry a Nicolas badge.

Description
Kalmar 4 × 4 lift trucks have a top speed on roads of 70 km/h and can handle general cargo or containers weighing up to 17,000 kg at a load distance of 1.2 m. While working, the forklift mechanism is at the front of

Kalmar high-speed lift truck of the British Army following refurbishment (Shaun C Connors) 1391260

Kalmar high-speed lift truck of the British Army following refurbishment (Shaun C Connors) 1391261

the vehicle with steering on the rear axle. For high-speed travelling the seat and steering wheel are rotated through 180°. For forklift operation the hydro-pneumatic suspension is lowered and placed out of use although, as an option, it is possible to operate loads up to 8,000 kg with the suspension raised providing more ground clearance over rough terrain. For normal travelling without a load, the suspension is raised to an intermediate position and, when travelling over rough terrain, the suspension can be fully raised providing a ground clearance of nearly 500 mm.

The standard lift mast is duplex with a 3.2 m lift height. Also available were 2 or 2.5 m single section simplex masts with lift carriages an approximate 1 m front face distance from the drive axle. The standard lift carriage has hydraulic side shift and fork side shifting and tilting.

French machines were fitted with a Renault diesel engine but the standard engine option was a Cummins 6CTA8.3C 8.3 litre turbocharged diesel.

Specifications

TD1612HS
Cab seating: 1
Configuration: 4 × 4
Weight: (unladen) 24,680 kg
Axle weight: (laden)
  (front) 40,500 kg
  (rear) 3,180 kg
Length:
  (forks lowered) 8.12 m
  (forks raised) 5.6 m
Width: 2.5 m
Height: 3.1 m
Ground clearance: (laden) 260 mm
Track:
  (front) 1.816 m
  (rear) 2.05 m
Wheelbase: 3.65 m
Max speed: 70 km/h
Road range: 800 km
Fuel capacity: 560 litres
Max gradient: 33%
Engine: Renault MIDS 06.20.45 9.8 litre 6-cylinder turbocharged water-cooled direct injection 4-stroke diesel developing 270 hp (201 kW) at 2,200 rpm
Transmission: Clark 36000 series hydro-dynamic power shift with torque converter lock-up providing 4 forward and 2 reverse speeds
Turning radius: 5.2 m
Tyres:
  (dual, front) 12.00R 20 Michelin XZL
  (rear) 395/85R 20 Michelin XZL
Max load: 16,000 kg

Status
Production complete, marketing ceased in 2003. Supplied to Canada, Belgium, France (Army and Air Force), Malaysia, Sweden and the UK.

Contractor
Kalmar Industries AB

France

Marrel Ampliroll system

Description
The Marrel Ampliroll system is a load handling system designed to fit any type of truck with a load capacity from 3,000 to 25,000 kg. To meet military requirements, the systems selected for 6 × 4, 6 × 6 and 8 × 8 trucks generally have a load capacity of between 12,000 and 20,000 kg.

Marrel load handling system fitted to a French Army Renault G290.26 6 × 4 truck, part of the French Army's Véhicule de Transport Logistique (VTL) system (Shaun C Connors)   1156060

The Ampliroll system consists of: a chassis reinforcing subframe; central beam to which the tipping rams are hinged; short hinged connecting arm framework which controls the extent of rearward movement; telescopic jib sliding in the main arm and carrying at its upper end the unit front lifting hook and rear hinges and incorporating flanged rollers on bronze bushes to centralise the unit. The hydraulic system contains: a pump complete with a safety valve and transmission; two main arms providing the normal tipping action and for lowering the platform; double-acting ram to actuate the sliding jib beam; and a direction and braking valve block actuated from the vehicle cab by a remote servo-control.

Military applications include: ammunition handling, either on a flatrack or in an ISO container; fuel handling using the Marrel 9,000 or 12,000 litre roll-off fuel tank and filling unit, complete with a hydraulic pump serving five discharge points; mobile shelter handling for field hospitals; and general cargo handling, using flatracks with suitable cargo bodies and covers. The system may also be used for vehicle recovery using a multipurpose flatrack with adjustable track guides allowing for the recovery of light armoured vehicles such as the M113 APC. With some additional components the Ampliroll system can be used to launch floating bridge components (such as the Ribbon Bridge) and their associated bridging boats. Flatracks may also be used to carry engineer equipment or may be converted to carry weapon systems such as air or

Marrel load handling system fitted to a French Army Renault TRM 10000 6 × 6 truck (Shaun C Connors)   1156061

Mercedes-Benz Actros 8 × 8 truck fitted with a Marrel Ampliroll system and Marrel Amplitainer container handling unit; one of two competitors for a Royal Netherlands armed forces LHS requirement awarded to a Scania/Hiab combination of truck/LHS (Marrel)   0525600

Prototype of a Marrel Ampliroll system and Marrel Amplitainer container handling unit fitted to a Volvo FH 12 truck for a Belgian Army requirement (Marrel)   0525599

Austrian Army OAF (MAN) 6 × 6 truck fitted with a Marrel load handling system (Marrel)　0589059

coastal defence weapons. Other flatrack loads could include electrical generators, desalination plant and communication centres. There is also an Ampliroll platform configured to carry personnel on fitted benches.

If required, the lifting hook can be used as a crane both to lift loads and to haul disabled vehicles on to a flatrack ready for loading.

The most recent deliveries of Marrel LHS-equipped vehicles have included 12 OAF (MAN) 6 × 6 chassis to Austria and 104 Mercedes-Benz Actros 6 × 6 chassis to Turkey.

Status
In production. In service with the French Army (>2,800 units) and the armed forces of 11 other countries including Austria, Switzerland and Turkey.

Contractor
Marrel SA

SOFRAME PLM 17 logistic transport system

Description
The SOFRAME PLM 17 logistic transport system is composed of a hydraulic hook load handling system (LHS) (similar to the Hiab/Multilift or Marrel Ampliroll systems) fitted to any suitable capacity truck, and coupled to any LHS-compatible trailer. It is designed to be capable of transporting vehicles (wheeled or tracked) and for the logistic transport of ammunition and other combat supplies using 20 ft/6.096 m ISO flatracks.

The system can be mounted on all types of three- or four-axle trucks having a GVW of 26,000 kg or greater, and engine power outputs of around 300 hp, minimum. It has been fitted to the Renault G290 26 and TRM 10 000 6 × 6 10,000 kg trucks in conjunction with a SOFRAME RM 19 trailer, to which flatrack loads can be transferred and unloaded by the PLM 17 system.

The system uses hydraulics to either load a platform (flatrack) on to a truck or unload it on to the ground. It utilises a two-part subframe, which bolts on to the vehicle chassis. Two conical rollers, located at the rear, centre the platform during loading operations. The loading arm is constructed using two rectangular and longitudinal beams braced by cross members and is articulated round the rear part of the frame. A bracket assembly on the loading platform completes the structural system.

The hydraulic system is based on a Leduc L 65 pump operating at a maximum pressure of 400 bar (5800 psi). The pump is mounted on the vehicle gearbox and is directly driven. The hydraulic circuit has three parts for blocking the vehicle suspension, controlling the lifting bracket and the lifting arm. Two cylinders are used, one for the bracket, one for the arm. A tank associated with the hydraulic system contains 100 litres of oil.

The platform is a standard 20 ft/6.096 m DIN unit and is made of beams braced by cross members. Payload is dependent on the carrying vehicle (13,000 kg for a Renault 290.26). Net weight is 2,000 kg. A total of 12 lashing rings are provided, and forklift pockets are included for handling by all standard suitable capacity forklift trucks. Load covers are available.

SOFRAME PLM 17 materials handling system in use on Renault G290.26 6 × 4 VTL truck coupled to a SOFRAME RM 19 trailer (SOFRAME)　0056318

Specifications
PLM 17 system on Renault TRM 10 000 6 × 6 truck
Weight:
　(front axle, laden) 7,480 kg
　(rear axle, laden) 18,520 kg
　(total) 26,000 kg
　(flatrack) 2,000 kg
Loading capacity: 17,000 kg
Payload: 15,000 kg
Length: (overall) 9.2 m
Width: 2.5 m
Height:
　(overall) 3.7 m
　(platform, loaded) 1.7 m

RM 19 trailer
GVW: 19,000 kg
Payload: 13,400 kg
Length: (with flatrack) 8.37 m
Width: 2.5 m
Height: (with laden flatrack) 1.475 m

Status
Available.

Contractor
SOFRAME

Germany

Terex-Demag MAC 50 all-terrain crane

Development
Terex Corporation, through a number of acquisitions since 1996, has developed one of the most extensive range of cranes of any manufacturer. The Terex crane portfolio currently consists of all-terrain, crawler, pick-and-carry, rough-terrain, tower, and truck-mounted products. A brief overview of the Terex crane range, together with full details of Terex brand all-terrain, pick-and-carry, rough-terrain, and truck-mounted cranes can be found elsewhere in this section

The MAC 50 all-terrain crane was developed by Terex-Demag to meet a particularly demanding US Marine Corps requirement. The MAC 50, although based around commercial components to meet the USMC requirement for a 'commercial product', is a military specific design as no current commercial product could meet these especially demanding requirements.

The USMC awarded Terex-Demag an initial delivery order valued at USD5.9 million for the production of four MAC 50 cranes with accessories, factory testing, limited logistics support and training in August 2005. Four prototype examples were delivered to the USMC in July 2006 for approximately three months of verification testing at Aberdeen Proving Grounds. An additional fifth crane was built and retained for associated company trials at Terex-Demag.

Following the successful completion of these trials, an initial 100 machines were ordered and by June 2009 102 had been delivered, with a further 65 scheduled for delivery during the remainder of 2009 and 2010. The production contract includes a warranty and training package.

Terex completed its acquisition of Demag (then a 100% subsidiary of Siemens AG) of Germany in August 2002. Terex-Demag designs, manufactures and markets telescope and lattice boom cranes with load capacities ranging between 30 and 3,200 tonnes (33 - 3,527 US tons). These are built at two plants in Zweibrücken, Germany. In excess of 80 per cent of production is exported worldwide. Terex had previously acquired all-terrain crane manufacturer PPM of France in 1995, this acquisition

Pre-production example of the Terex-Demag MAC 50 all-terrain crane as displayed at Eurosatory 2006. The Terex-Demag MAC 50 is fitted with hydropneumatic suspension with ±130 mm travel, and is of 8 × 8 × 8 configuration; all-wheel drive, all-wheel steer (Shaun C Connors)　1156051

Pre-production example of the Terex-Demag MAC 50 all-terrain crane during trials (Terex-Demag)   1156053

including Italy's Bendini SpA, a manufacturer of rough-terrain cranes. The former Demag and PPM brands and product lines have merged and Terex brand all-terrain mobile cranes are now branded Terex-Demag.

Description
The Terex-Demag MAC 50 is based around Terex-Demag's commercial product line components, however to meet the requirements of the USMC, a military specific machine was developed as a standard commercial machine could not meet the combination of performance and legislation compliance required. A conventional European specification commercial all-terrain crane of this lift capacity would have a three-axle chassis, operating legally at up to 12,000 kg per axle. This does not meet the more restrictive US road regulations, and could also have soft ground mobility implications.

The MAC-50 is based on a purpose-designed box-type torsion-resistant high-tensile steel multi-axle chassis with integral outrigger housings. The outriggers are two-stage and hydraulically controlled from both sides of the vehicle, and have a maximum spread of 6.7 m.

The two-man full-width cab is for road use and is constructed of sheet steel. The standard commercial cab is used. When operating, the crane is controlled from a separate, one-man, all-steel cab; 'free on wheels' operation is possible. A small number of add-on-armor (AOA) kits have been produced for the MAC-50 by American Defense Systems Incorporated (ADSI).

The crane is constructed from torsion-resistant steel and is connected to the carrier chassis by a slewing ring allowing for 360° continuous rotation at continuously variable speeds. The four-section box-type boom consists of a base section and three telescopic sections. All sections are hydraulically extendable under load.

All Terex-Demag all-terrain cranes for commercial applications are powered by Mercedes-Benz diesel engines, coupled to a selection of automated or automatic transmissions supplied by Allison, Mercedes-Benz or ZF; the MAC 50 is powered by a Cummins diesel engine coupled to an Allison automatic transmission and, for improved off-road mobility and gradability, a two-speed transfer box. Standard Terex-Demag axles manufactured by Kessler and hydropneumatically suspended are retained, although modifications include a provision for wading. For the USMC requirement the commercial options of all-wheel drive, all-wheel steer and full cross- and longitudinal differential locking are standard.

Approach and departure angles that allow ramp access for air-transport by Airbus A400M, Lockheed C-5 and Lockheed C-17 aircraft were specified. The MAC 50 is also certified for rail and marine transport in accordance with the relevant MIL-STDs.

Other USMC requirements dictated the axle spacing arrangement and the use of 1600R 25 tyres. The crane is capable of fording 1.5 m of salt water, requiring the modification of axles and other associated components; extensive corrosion protection measures are also taken. The crane is required to be capable of starting and operating throughout a −32/+52°C temperature range.

Specifications
MAC 50
Cab seating:
  (carrier) 2
  (crane) 1
Configuration: 8 × 8 × 8
Weight: 31,600 kg
Axle load: (each) 7,900 kg
Length:
  (crane assembly) 9.482 m
  (overall) 11.58 m
Width:
  (chassis) 2.59 m
  (outriggers extended) 4.57 or 6.7 m
Height: 3.61 m
Ground clearance: 380 mm
Wheelbase:
  (1st to 2nd axle) 2.26 m
  (2nd to 3rd axle) 3.812 m
  (3rd to 4th axle) 1.7 m

Angle of approach/departure: 23°/23°
Max speed: 76 km/h
Range: 480 km
Gradient: (on-/off-road) 50%/30%
Fording: (unprepared) 1.52 m
Engine: Cummins QSC FR91506 Tier 3 8.3-litre 6-cylinder turbocharged charge air-cooled, water-cooled diesel developing 333 hp (248 kW) at 2,100 rpm and 1,383 N.m torque at 1,300 rpm
Gearbox: Allison MD 3060 fully automatic with 6 forward and 1 reverse gears
Transfer box: Kessler 2-speed
Suspension: hydropneumatic with self-locking, ±130 mm travel
Axles: Kessler steer-drive with hub-reduction gearing and differential locking
Tyres: 1600R 25 on/off-road type
Brakes: dual circuit, air
Electrical system: 24 V

Status
4 USMC verification vehicles delivered July 2006. 102 machines delivered by June 2009; additional 65 on order.

Contractor
Terex-Demag GmbH & Co.KG
Terex Corporation

Klaus Kranmobil mobile container handling system
In September 2001 the Klaus SLT product range, patents and brandname were acquired by Steelbro New Zealand Ltd, and came under the Steelbro Container Handling Solutions umbrella. All production is now undertaken in Christchurch, New Zealand.

Full details of the former Klaus SLT range can now be found in the Steelbro container handling systems entry elsewhere in this section.

Klaus Kranmobil KM 32 container handling system of the US Air Force in the UK (Shaun C Connors)   0109490

Liebherr mobile cranes

Development
Liebherr-Werk Ehingen GmbH is one of the world's leading manufacturers of mobile cranes. The company was established in 1949, by Hans Liebherr, with the development of tower cranes, and has remained a family-owned business that has steadily grown into a group of over 100 companies, with established operations on all continents, and employing over 32,000 employees. Today, Liebherr is not only one of the world's leading manufacturers of mobile cranes but is also a supplier of advanced products and services including aerospace, concrete mixing technology, construction equipment, container and mobile dock cranes, machine tools, diesel engines and material flow technology.

Liebherr LTM 1070/1 70-tonne all-terrain mobile crane of the Netherlands Army (Shaun C Connors)   1156079

Liebherr mobile cranes
(Cranes up to 160 tonnes capacity)

	Lift capacity at extension	Boom length (without extensions)	Boom extensions	Power output (carrier)	Power output (crane)	Configuration (option in brackets) [1]	Max gradient	Max speed
LTM 1030-2.1	35 tonnes at 3 m	9.2-30 m	8.6-15 m	278 hp (207 kW)	n/app	4 × 4 × 4	60%	80 km/h
LTM 1040-2.1	40 tonnes at 2.7 m	10.5-30 m	9.5 m	278 hp (207 kW)	n/app	4 × 4 × 4	60%	80 km/h
LTM 1050-3.1	50 tonnes at 3 m	11.3-38 m	9-16 m	367 hp (274 kW)	n/app	6 × 4 × 6 (6 × 6 × 6)	60%	80 km/h
LTM 1055-3.2	55 tonnes at 2.5 m	10.2-40 m	9.5-16 m	367 hp (274 kW)	n/app	(6 × 6 × 6)	60%	80 km/h
LTM 1070-4.2	70 tonnes at 2.5 m	11-50 m	9.5-16 m	367 hp (274 kW)	n/app	(8 × 6 × 8)	60%	80 km/h
LTM 1090-4.1	90 tonnes at 2.5 m	11.1-50 m	10.5-19 m	460 hp (343 kW)	202 hp (151 kW)	8 × 6 × 8 (8 × 8 × 8)	60%	80 km/h
LTM 1095-5.1	25 tonnes at 3 m	12.5-58 m	10.5-26 m	503 hp (375 kW)	197 hp (147 kW)	10 × 6 × 10 (10 × 8 × 10)	60%	80 km/h
LTM 1100-4.2	100 tonnes at 3 m	11.5-60 m	10.8-33 m	469 hp (350 kW)	175 hp (130 kW)	8 × 6 × 8 (8 × 8 × 8)	71%	80 km/h
LTM 1100-5.2	100 tonnes at 2.7 m	11.5-52 m	10.8-33 m	496 hp (370 kW)	194 hp (145 kW)	10 × 6 × 8 (10 × 8 × 8)	60%	80 km/h
LTM 1130-5.1	130 tonnes at 3 m	12.7-60 m	10.8-33 m	503 hp (375 kW)	197 hp (147 kW)	10 × 8 × 10 (10 × 10 × 10)	60%	80 km/h
LTM 1150-6.1	150 tonnes at 3 m	13.7-66 m	10.8-33 m	544 hp (406 kW)	175 hp (130 kW)	12 × 8 × 12 (12 × 10 × 12)	57%	75 km/h
LTM 1160-5.1	160 tonnes at 3 m	13.2-62 m	5.4-43 m	503 hp (375 kW)	197 hp (147 kW)	10 × 6 × 10 (10 × 8 × 10)	>60%	75 km/h

[1] Configuration example: 8 × 6 × 8 denotes eight wheels (four axles), six-wheel drive, eight-wheel steer

Liebherr FKL 10-tonne mobile crane, 251 of which were supplied to the German Army between 1991 and 1994 (Liebherr)   1121069

Liebherr 1060/2 60-tonne all-terrain mobile crane. This model has been supplied to a number of countries, including France, Malaysia, Russia and Saudi Arabia (Liebherr)   1121067

Full details of the Liebherr range of construction equipment can be found in the Field fortifications and related emplacements section.

The Liebherr Group's holding company is Liebherr-International AG, in Bulle, Switzerland, and is entirely owned by members of the Liebherr family.

Liebherr LTM 1055-3.1 55-tonne all-terrain mobile cranes awaiting delivery to the French Army (Stefan Marx)   1043783

Operating in the former Yugoslavia, one of 27 Liebherr FKM 20-tonne cranes supplied to the Netherlands Army in 1991; 208 similar vehicles were supplied to the German Army between 1991 and 1994 (Shaun C Connors)   1120427

Description
Liebherr-Werk Ehingen GmbH currently produces a range of 19 all-terrain cranes, two compact mobile cranes, a single lattice boom crane and three series of crawler track cranes. The accompanying specification table relates to the compact mobile crane and all-terrain cranes with maximum lift capacities of up to 160 tonnes. It should be noted that while cranes of up to 500 tonnes lift capacity have been supplied to military customers by Liebherr for specific roles, the bulk of military crane sales are for machines with lift capacities ranging from 30-70 tonnes.

Cranes supplied by Liebherr for military applications are essentially commercial products with varying degrees of militarisation.

The full range of Liebherr compact and all-terrain cranes are equipped with Liebherr-produced diesel engines. Cranes of up to 70 tonnes lift capacity have a single engine, cranes of ≥90 tonnes lift capacity have two; one for the carrier vehicle and one for the crane itself. Chassis have two to eight axles, and in a variety of steer and drive configurations.

Full details of the LTM 1055-3.1 AF all-terrain crane, 50 examples of which have been supplied to the French Ministry of Defence, can be found elsewhere in this section.

Liebherr-Werk Ehingen GmbH introduced a new designation system for its mobile cranes during 2004. The new designation system continues to indicate lifting capacity and generation, as before, but also now indicates the number of axles. At this time all current production cranes were given the generation (or version) name '.1'. Under this revised system, the LTM 1055/1, for example, became the LTM 1055-3.1. The 1055 indicates the 55-tonne lifting capacity (as before) the 'dash 3' indicates that it has three axles, and the 'point 1' indicates the version. If a new three-axle 55-tonne crane is introduced, it will be designated LTM 1055-3.2.

It should also be noted that as with other commercial crane manufacturers, Liebherr regularly updates its product range.

Status

In production. Since 1977, Liebherr has supplied around 800 cranes to at least 20 armed forces, including: Austria (LTF 1030, 30-tonne (1) 1981; LTM 1040/1, 40-tonne (1) 1999), Denmark (LTM 1120, 120-tonne, (2) 1994; LTM 1055-3.1, 55-tonne (1) 2004), Egypt (LTM 1500, 500-tonne (1) 2001; LTM 1030/2, 30-tonne (1) 2003), Finland (LTM 1090-4.1, 90-tonne (1) 2004), France (LTM 1060, 60-tonne (2) 1985; LTM 1045/1, 45-tonne (1) 2002; LTM 1055/1, 55-tonne (1) 2003; LTM 1055/1 (49) 2004-2005), Germany (FKL, 10-tonne (251) 1991-1994; FKM, 20-tonne (208) 1991-1994; LI 1012, 12-tonne (5) 1994), Greece (AUK 40, 24-tonne (7) 1967), Iran (LT 1090, 90-tonne (1) 1986; LTM 1050/1, 50-tonne (1) 1986; LTL 1080, 80-tonne (1) 1986; LTM 1070, 70-tonne (5) 1989; LTM 1035, 35-tonne (26) 1991; LTM 1030/2, 30-tonne (1) 1992); Iraq (LI 1012, 12-tonne (48) 1980; LTM 1030, 30-tonne (40) 1980; LT 1120, 120-tonne (6) 1981; LTM 1022, 22-tonne (7) 1982; LTL 1080, 80-tonne (12) 1983; Libya (LT1025, 25-tonne (10) 1977; LT1050, 50-tonne (10) 1977); Malaysia (LTL 1060, 60-tonne (1) 1989), Netherlands (FKM, 20-tonne (27) 1991; LTM 1070, 70-tonne (4) 1997; LTM 1070/1, 70-tonne (1) 2002), Nigeria (LTM 1030, 30-tonne (2) 1981), Russian Federation (LTM 1060, 60-tonne (12) 1993), Saudi Arabia (LTM 1060, 60-tonne (5) 1983; LTM 1050/1, 50-tonne (2) 1999; LTM 1070/1, 70-tonne (1) 1999; LTS 1030, 30-tonne (1) 1999), South Korea (LTM 1070, 70-tonne (2) 1993), Turkey (LTM 1030, 30-tonne (1) 1993), UAE (LTM 1160/2, 160-tonne (1) 1997; LTS 1030, 30-tonne (9) 1999; LTM 1070/1, 70-tonne (1) 1999; LTM 1050/1, 50-tonne (3) 1999; LTM 1045/1, 45-tonne (1) 2003), UK (LTM 1050, 50-tonne (1) 1991; LTM 1040, 40-tonne (3) 1993; LTM 1080/1, 80-tonne (1) 1999; LTM 1050/1, 50-tonne (1) 2000) and the US (LTM 1040/1, 40-tonne (1) 1996; LTM 1050/1, 50-tonne (1) 1998; LTM 1030/2, 30-tonne (1) 1999; LTM 1160/2, 160-tonne (1) 2001).

Contractor

Liebherr-Werk Ehingen GmbH

Liebherr LTM 1055-3.1 all-terrain crane

Development

Liebherr-Werk Ehingen GmbH is one of the world's leading manufacturers of mobile cranes. The company was established in 1949, by Hans Liebherr, with the development of tower cranes, and has remained a family-owned business that has steadily grown into a group of over 100 companies, with established operations on all continents, and employing over 32,000 employees. Today, Liebherr is one of the world's leading manufacturers of mobile cranes, Liebherr-Werk Ehingen GmbH currently produces a range of 20 all-terrain cranes, a single compact mobile crane, two lattice boom cranes and a range of five crawler track cranes. Full details of the compact mobile crane and all-terrain cranes with lift capacities of 35 to 160 tonnes can be found elsewhere in this section. The Liebherr Group is also a supplier of advanced products and services including aerospace, concrete-mixing technology, construction equipment, container and mobile dock cranes, machine tools, diesel engines and material flow technology.

Full details of the Liebherr range of construction equipment can be found in the Field fortifications and related emplacements section.

The Liebherr Group's holding company is Liebherr-International AG in Bulle, Switzerland, and is entirely owned by members of the Liebherr family.

Description

The Liebherr LTM 1055-3.1 is typical of the Liebherr all-terrain crane range and is based on a box-type torsion-resistant high tensile steel multi-axle chassis with integral outrigger housings. The outriggers are two-stage and hydraulically controlled from both sides of the vehicle, and have a maximum spread of 6.3 m.

The two-man full-width cab is for road use and is constructed of sheet steel. When operating, the crane is controlled from a separate one-man all-steel cab; 'free on wheels' operation is possible.

Liebherr LTM 1055-3.1 55-tonne all-terrain of the French Army operating in Kosovo (Shaun C Connors)   1156080

The crane is constructed from torsion-resistant steel and is connected to the carrier chassis by a three-row roller slewing ring with central greasing for 360° continuous rotation at continuously variable speeds from 0-1.6 rpm (with 7-tonne counterweight). The four-section box-type boom consists of a base section and three telescopic sections. All sections are hydraulically extendable under load.

Following a competitive tender, in 2002, the Liebherr company, Grues Mobiles SAS was awarded a EUR40 million contract for the supply of 50 LTM 1055-3.1 (designated LTM 1055/1 AF at the time) to the French Ministry of Defence. The first 30 cranes were delivered between September and December 2004, with the remaining 20 cranes to be delivered during 2005.

Liebherr-Werk Ehingen GmbH introduced a new designation system for its mobile cranes during 2004. The new designation system continues to indicate lifting capacity and generation, as before, but also now indicates the number of axles. At this time, all current production cranes were given the generation (or version) name ,'1'. Under this revised system, the LTM 1055/1, for example, became the LTM 1055-3.1. The 1055 indicates the 55-tonne lifting capacity (as before) the 'dash 3' indicates that it has three axles, and the 'point 1' indicates the version. When the current three-axle 55-tonne crane was introduced it was designated LTM 1055-3.2.

In service, these cranes are used by the French Air Force, Army and Navy and for a variety of roles, including vehicle repair and the handling of assorted loads, including 20 and 40 ft ISO containers.

To reduce logistic support requirements, each crane is supplied with a single 20 ft ISO-footprint container for the transport of assorted accessories and support equipment, including the hook block, ballast, spare wheel, spacers, lifting tackle in light and heavy configurations, various hooks and expanding struts, plus a 20 ft spreader. When used in conjunction with an adapter for the expanding struts and heavy lifting tackle, the 20 ft spreader can be used to handle 30 or 40 ft ISO containers weighing up to 30.5 tonnes.

To meet the requirements of the French military, a number of modifications were carried out compared to standard commercial LTM 1055-3.1 cranes. These include a Semi-automatic Tyre Inflation System (STIS) that allows for the inflation or deflation of all tyres simultaneously when the vehicle is stationary. The standard road pressure of 9 bar can be reduced to 4 bar in five minutes, this increasing tyre contact surface by up to 60 per cent. Inflation is via the braking system air compressor.

Additionally, and to meet a requirement for operator protection, Liebherr developed armoured driver and crane operator cabs for the LTM 1055-3.1. These cabs provide protection to STANAG 4569 level 1; five sets were involved in the contract. Also supplied were five sets of tyres with runflat inserts and five hydraulic emergency sets that, in the event of diesel engine failure, allow the crane to be derigged into the driving position. Armoured cabs are transported on a special 20 ft ISO footprint container; the runflat tyres and hydraulic emergency sets are also each transported on special containers. All transport containers are provided with weather-protecting tarpaulins.

It should also be noted that as with other commercial crane manufacturers, Liebherr regularly updates its product range.

Specifications

LTM 1055-3.1
Cab seating:
  (carrier) 2
  (crane) 1
Configuration: 6 × 6 × 6
Weight: (transport, with 7,000 kg ballast) 36,000 kg
Axle weight: (each) 12,000 kg
Length:
  (carrier chassis) 9.697 m
  (overall) 11.36 m
Width:
  (standard) 2.68 m
  (outriggers extended) 4.5 or 6.3 m

Height: (with standard tyres) 3.75 m
Wheelbase:
  (1st to 2nd axle) 3 m
  (2nd to 3rd axle) 1.65 m
Angle of approach/departure: 15°/15°
Max speed: 80 km/h
Engine: Liebherr D 926 TI-E A5 6-cylinder water-cooled 4-stroke diesel developing 367 hp (274 kW) at 2,100 rpm and 1,650 N.m torque at 1,400 rpm
Gearbox: ZF AS-TRONIC, 12-speed
Suspension: hydro-pneumatic with self-locking
Axles:
  (1st) steer-drive with hub-reduction gearing and differential lock
  (2nd) steer-drive with hub-reduction gearing and differential lock
  (3rd) steer-drive with hub-reduction gearing and differential lock
Tyres: 1600R 25 on/off-road type (20.5 R25 option)
Brakes: dual circuit, air, supplemented by exhaust retarder. ABS
Electrical system: 24 V
Batteries: 2 × 12 V, 170 Ah

Crane
Maximum lift capacity: 55 tonnes
Maximum lift height:
  (standard boom) 32.5 m
  (with extensions) 48.5 m
Counterweights:
  (travel) 7,000 kg
  (operating) 4,700, 7,000 or 12,100 kg

Status
Production as required. In service with France; 50 delivered between 2004-2005.

Contractor
Liebherr-Werk Ehingen GmbH

Tadano FAUN ATF 70-4 all-terrain crane

Development
The now Tadano FAUN of Germany can trace its origins back to 1845 and its founding to Justus Christian Braun. In addition to an extensive range of mobile cranes, the company has also manufactured a wide range of specialist heavy trucks, tractor trucks and fire appliances. Details of FAUN-produced heavy equipment tractor trucks that remain in service with German and some other armed forces can be found in the Heavy equipment transports section.

FAUN AG was acquired by Tadano Ltd of Japan in 1990. Tadano Ltd was founded in 1948 as a manufacturer of cargo handling equipment and, prior to the acquisition of FAUN, specialised in truck-mounted and four-wheel rough terrain cranes. In 1991 Tadano Ltd founded the wholly owned German subsidiary company of Tadano FAUN GmbH. Tadano FAUN all-terrain cranes are manufactured in Germany.

Cranes supplied by Tadano FAUN for military applications are essentially commercial products with limited militarisation. It should also be noted that as with other commercial crane manufactures, Tadano FAUN regularly updates its product range. The company currently produces a range of ten all-terrain cranes for sale within Europe, some of which, with differing designations and specification alterations, are available elsewhere.

Description
The Tadano FAUN ATF 70-4 is typical of the Tadano FAUN all-terrain crane range and is based on a box-type torsion-resistant high tensile steel multi-axle chassis with integral outrigger housings. The outriggers are two-stage and hydraulically controlled from both sides of the vehicle, and have a maximum spread of 7.2 m.

Tadano FAUN ATF 70-4 all-terrain crane of the German Army (Stefan Marx)
0587654

The two-man full-width cab is for road use and is constructed of sheet steel and fibreglass. When operating the crane is controlled from a separate one-man all-steel cab.

The crane is constructed from torsion-resistant steel and is connected to the carrier chassis by a triple roller bearing slewing ring for 360° continuous rotation at continuously variable speeds from 0-2 rpm. The five-section box-type boom consists of a base section and four telescopic sections. All sections are hydraulically extendable under load.

The 70 tonne capacity Tadano FAUN ATF 70-4 is no longer available, the closest current cranes to it in the Tadano FAUN range being the 65 tonne capacity ATF 65G-3 or the 90 tonne capacity ATF 90G-4.

Specifications
ATF 70-4
Cab seating:
  (carrier) 2
  (crane) 1
Configuration: 8 × 8 × 8
Weight: (transport) 47,000 kg
Axle weight:
  (1st and 2nd) 11,700 kg
  (2nd and 3rd) 11,800 kg
Length:
  (carrier chassis) 10.778 m
  (overall) 12.87 m
Width:
  (carrier) 2.75 m
  (travelling, outriggers retracted) 2.75 m
  (outriggers extended) 7.2 m
Height: 3.73 m (−120 mm to +150 mm, adjustable)
Wheelbase:
  (1st to 2nd axle) 1.99 m
  (1st axle to 2nd/3rd axle centreline) 5.145 m
  (3rd to 4th axle) 1.7 m
Angle of approach/departure: 19.5°/22°
Max speed: 80 km/h
Engine:
  (carrier) Mercedes-Benz OM 501LA EURO 1 6-cylinder in-line water-cooled 4-stroke diesel developing 394 hp (294 kW) at 1,800 rpm and 1,850 N.m torque at 1,080 rpm
  (crane) Mercedes-Benz OM 904LA 4-cylinder in-line water-cooled 4-stroke diesel developing 123 hp (92 kW) at 2,300 rpm
Gearbox: Allison HD 4060P automatic with 6 forward and 2 reverse gears; hydrodynamic torque converter with lock-up and integral retarder
Transfer box: Steyr VG 1200, 2-speed
Suspension: hydro-pneumatic with −120 mm to +150 mm levelling adjustment
Axles:
  (1st) steer-drive with hub-reduction gearing and differential lock
  (2nd) steer-drive with hub-reduction gearing and differential lock (non-driven option)
  (3rd) steer-drive with hub-reduction gearing and differential lock
  (4th) steer-drive with hub-reduction gearing and differential lock
Tyres: 1600R 25 on/off-road type
Brakes: dual circuit, air
Electrical system: 24 V
Batteries: 2 × 12 V

Crane
Maximum lift capacity: 70 tonnes
Maximum lift height:
  (standard boom) 40.5 m
  (with extensions) 56.5 m
Counterweights:
  (travel) 8,900 kg
  (operating) up to 12,100 kg

Status
Production complete, replaced by revised models. In service with the German Army.

Contractor
Tadano FAUN GmbH

Tadano FAUN ATF 120-5 all-terrain crane

Development
The now Tadano FAUN of Germany can trace its origins back to 1845 and founding to Justus Christian Braun. In addition to an extensive range of mobile cranes, the company has also manufactured a wide range of specialist heavy trucks, tractor trucks and fire appliances. Details of FAUN-produced heavy equipment tractor trucks that remain in service with German and some other armed forces can be found in the Heavy equipment transports section.

FAUN AG was acquired by Tadano Ltd of Japan in 1990. Tadano Ltd was founded in 1948 as a manufacturer of cargo handling equipment and, prior to the acquisition of FAUN, specialised in truck-mounted and four-wheel

Tadano FAUN ATF 120-5 all-terrain crane of the German Army. The crane is shown unloading its own counterweights from their transport location (Michael Jerchel) 0587653

rough terrain cranes. In 1991 Tadano Ltd founded the wholly owned German subsidiary company of Tadano FAUN GmbH. Tadano FAUN all-terrain cranes are manufactured in Germany.

Cranes supplied by Tadano FAUN for military applications are essentially commercial products with limited militarisation. It should also be noted that as with other commercial crane manufactures, Tadano FAUN regularly updates its product range. The company currently produces a range of ten all-terrain cranes for sale within Europe, some of which, with differing designations and specification alterations, are available elsewhere.

Description

The Tadano FAUN ATF 120-5 is typical of the Tadano FAUN all-terrain crane range and is based on a box-type torsion-resistant high-tensile steel multi-axle chassis with integral outrigger housings. The outriggers are two-stage and hydraulically controlled from both sides of the vehicle, and have a spread of 5.4 or 8 m.

The two-man full-width cab is for road use and is constructed of sheet steel and fibreglass. When operating the crane is controlled from a separate one-man all-steel cab.

The crane is constructed from torsion-resistant steel and is connected to the carrier chassis by a triple roller bearing slewing ring for 360° continuous rotation at continuously variable speeds from 0-1.5 rpm. The five-section box-type boom consists of a base section and four telescopic sections. All sections are hydraulically extendable under load.

The 130 tonne capacity Tadano FAUN ATF 120-5 is no longer available, the closest current cranes to it in the Tadano FAUN range being the 110 tonne capacity ATF 110G-5 or the 160 tonne capacity ATF 160G-5.

Specifications

ATF 120-5
Cab seating:
  (carrier) 2
  (crane) 1
Configuration:
  (on-road) 10 × 6 × 10
  (off-road) 10 × 8 × 10
Weight: (transport) 60,000 kg
Axle weight: 5 × 12,000 kg
Length:
  (carrier chassis) 12 m
  (overall) 14.55 m
Width:
  (carrier) 2.95 m
  (travelling, outriggers retracted) 3.05 m
  (outriggers extended, 1st stage) 5.4 m
  (outriggers extended, 2nd stage) 8 m
Height: 3.89 m (−116 mm to +152 mm, adjustable)

Wheelbase:
  (1st to 2nd axle) 2.56 m
  (2nd to 3rd axle) 1.7 m
  (3rd to 4th axle) 1.75 m
  (4th to 5th axle) 1.65 m
Angle of approach/departure: 26°/21°
Max speed: 80 km/h
Engine:
  (carrier) Mercedes-Benz OM 442LA EURO 1 8-cylinder in-line water-cooled 4-stroke diesel developing 503 hp (375 kW) at 2,100 rpm and 2,020 N.m torque between 1,100-1,600 rpm
  (crane) Mercedes-Benz OM 366A 6-cylinder in-line water-cooled 4-stroke diesel developing 153 hp (114 kW) at 2,000 rpm
Gearbox: ZF 16 S 220A with 16 forward and 2 reverse gears; hydrodynamic torque converter with lock-up and integral retarder
Steering: ZF dual-circuit; transmission-mounted emergency pump
Suspension: hydro-pneumatic with −116 mm to +152 mm levelling adjustment
Axles:
  (1st) steered, non-driven
  (2nd) steer-drive with hub-reduction gearing and differential lock
  (3rd) steer-drive with hub-reduction gearing and differential lock; integrated transfer gear
  (4th) steer-drive with hub-reduction gearing and differential lock
Tyres: 1600 R25 on/off-road type
Brakes:
  (main) dual circuit, air
  (parking) spring-loaded on 3rd, 4th and 5th axles
Electrical system: 24 V
Batteries: 2 × 12 V

Crane
Maximum lift capacity: 130 tonnes
Maximum lift height:
  (standard boom) 49 m
  (with extensions) 79.1 m
Counterweights:
  (travel) 4,600 kg
  (operating) up to 29,500 kg

Status

Production complete, replaced by revised models. In service with the German Army.

Contractor

Tadano FAUN GmbH

FAUN FUG container handler vehicle

Description

The FAUN FUG container handler vehicle is designed to load, reload and transport 20 ft/6.096 m ISO containers weighing up to 24,000 kg. It has a 6 × 6 or 6 × 2 hydropneumatic drive configuration and is designed to operate on rough or soft terrain. A central tyre-inflation (CTI) system is provided. Only one driver/operator is required, with full control of loading and unloading possible from a remote position using a radio control unit. Containers can be stacked two high and the vehicle can be used to load containers onto suitable trucks; the maximum lift height is 2.7 m. Due to the drive system employed, the vehicle can manoeuvre in confined areas and the overall dimensions are such that the vehicle can be carried inside C-17 or similar transport aircraft.

The FUG is available from Tadano FAUN GmbH, Military Technology & Logistics, under an arrangement from Drehtainer GmbH of Hamburg.

Side view of the FAUN FUG container handler vehicle demonstrating a stacking capability (FAUN) 0100379

FAUN FUG container handler vehicle demonstrating its relatively low height when handling a standard ISO container (FAUN)   0533621

Specifications

FUG container handler vehicle
Crew: 1
Configuration: 6 × 6 or 6 × 2
Weight:
 (kerb) 22,000 kg
 (GVW) 46,000 kg
Max load: 24,000 kg
Length: 9.4 m
Width:
 (without container) 2.98 m
 (with container) 4.14 m
Height : (overall) 3.34 m
Max speed:
 (on-road) 50 km/h
 (off-road) 25 km/h

Gradient: >30%
Fording: >1.5 m
Engine: water-cooled diesel developing 225 hp (168 kW)
Transmission: hydrostatic
Tyres: 20.5R 25

Status
Available.

Contractor
Tadano FAUN GmbH

Tadano FAUN mobile cranes

Development
The now Tadano FAUN of Germany can trace its origins back to 1845 and its founding to Justus Christian Braun. In addition to an extensive range of mobile cranes, the company has also manufactured a wide range of specialist heavy trucks, tractor trucks and fire appliances. Details of FAUN-produced heavy equipment tractor trucks that remain in service with German and some other armed forces can be found in the Heavy equipment transports section.

FAUN AG was acquired by Tadano Ltd of Japan in 1990. Tadano Ltd was founded in 1948 as a manufacturer of cargo handling equipment and, prior to the acquisition of FAUN, specialised in truck-mounted and four-wheel rough terrain cranes. In 1991 Tadano Ltd founded the wholly owned German subsidiary company of Tadano FAUN GmbH.

Tadano of Japan and Tadano FAUN of Germany currently produce a range of 16 truck-mounted, all-terrain and rough terrain cranes for sale within Europe. The accompanying specification table relates to all but the heaviest (and commercial application focused) of these machines, some of which, with differing designations and minor specification alterations, are available elsewhere. For certain markets, other specific machines are also available.

Cranes supplied by Tadano FAUN for military applications are essentially commercial products with varying degrees of militarisation. Recent deliveries have included the following: The Australian Army

Model	Origin	Type	Lift capacity	Maximum boom length (with extensions)	Power output (carrier)	Power output (crane)	Configuration[1]	Length	Width	Height	Travel weight	Axle loads (front)	Axle loads (rear)	Max speed
ATF 40G-2	Germany	AT	40 tonnes	10.5-35.2 m	279 hp	n/app	4 × 4 × 4	11.3 m	2.55 m	3.55 m	24 tonnes	12 tonnes	12 tonnes	85 km/h
ATF 50G-3	Germany	AT	50 tonnes	10-50 m	326 hp	n/app	6 × 6 × 6	11.37 m	2.55 m	3.72 m	36 tonnes	12 tonnes	2 ×12 tonnes	85 km/h
ATF 60-3	Germany	AT	60 tonnes	10.4-56.2 m	326 hp	n/app	6 × 6 × 6	11.78 m	2.66 m	3.68 m	36 tonnes	12 tonnes	2 × 12 tonnes	80 km/h
ATF 65G-4	Germany	AT	65 tonnes	11-44 m	394 hp	122 hp	8 × 6 (or 8) × 8	12.39 m	2.55 m	3.74 m	48 tonnes	2 × 12 tonnes	2 × 12 tonnes	85 km/h
ATF 90G-4	Germany	AT	90 tonnes	11.1-51.2 m	428 hp	174 hp	8 × 6 (or 8) × 8	13.05 m	2.75 m	3.92 m	48 tonnes	2 × 12 tonnes	2 × 12 tonnes	85 km/h
ATF 110G-5	Germany	AT	110 tonnes	12.8-83.1 m	517 hp	177 hp	10 × 6 (or 8) × 8	15.1 m	2.75 m	3.9 m	60 tonnes	2 × 12 tonnes	3 × 12 tonnes	80 km/h
ATF 130G-5	Germany	AT	130 tonnes	12.8-60 m	530 hp	175 hp	10 × 6 × 10	14.9 m	2.75 m	3.99 m	60 tonnes	2 × 12 tonnes	3 × 12 tonnes	80 km/h
ATF 160G-5	Germany	AT	160 tonnes	13.2-97.2 m	517 hp	184 hp	10 × 8 × 8	15.248 m	3 m	3.99 m	60 tonnes	2 × 12 tonnes	3 × 12 tonnes	85 km/h
BKF 35-4	Germany		35 tonnes	6.9-22.5 m		394 hp	8 × 6 × 4	11.85 m	2.66 m	3.7 m	31.9 tonnes	2 × 9.1 tonnes	2 × 6.9 tonnes	80 km/h
BKF 40-4	Germany		40 tonnes	6.9-28.5 m		428 hp	8 × 6 (or 8) × 8	12.8 m	2.66 m	3.65 m	30.2 tonnes	2 × 9.9 tonnes	2 × 5.2 tonnes	80 km/h
BKF 40-4L	Germany		40 tonnes	8.6-28.5 m		428 hp	8 × 6 (or 8) × 8	12.8 m	2.66 m	3.65 m	32 tonnes	2 × 10.5 tonnes	2 × 5.5 tonnes	80 km/h
HK 40	Germany	TC	40 tonnes	10.45-35.2 m			4 × [2] × 2	11.025 m	2.55 m					
HK 60	Germany	TC	60 tonnes	10.4-40.2 m			4 × [2] × 2	11.9 m	2.55 m					
HK 70	Germany	TC	70 tonnes	11-44 m			4 × [2] × 2	12.46 m	2.55 m					
GR-300EX	Japan	RT	30 tonnes	9.1-41.4 m	215 hp	n/app	4 × 4 × 4	11 m	2.62 m	3.53 m	27 tonnes	13.5 tonnes	13.75 tonnes	47 km/h
GR-550EX	Japan	RT	55 tonnes	11.1-42 m	272 hp	n/app	4 × 4 × 4	13.69 m	3.315 m	3.86 m	43.7 tonnes	23.975 tonnes	19.715 tonnes	20 km/h
GR-700EXL	Japan	RT	70 tonnes	11.5-61.7 m	225 hp	n/app	4 × 4 × 4	14.23 m	3.315 m	3.8 m	48.2 tonnes	24.7 tonnes	23.5 tonnes	40 km/h

[1] for cranes with a single steer axle this is denoted by axle count (1); for cranes with multiple steer axles this is denoted by wheel count, a four-wheel drive, four-wheel steer crane being 4 × 4 × 4
[2] dependant on truck chassis
AT - all-terrainTC - truck cranesRT - rough terrainIt should also be noted that as with other commercial crane manufactures, Tadano FAUN regularly updates its product range

received six ATF 30-2 models, Egypt received two ATF 70-4, France (Navy) received a single ATF 100-5, the German Army received ATF 70-4 and 120-5 models and two BKF 35-4 recovery vehicles for use with KFOR, plus eight ATF 100-5 models, some of which are in use in Afghanistan. Two BKF 35-4 recovery vehicles have also been supplied to Hungary.

Italy ordered 15 ATF 60-3 S (S - Special) models in 2003. In conjunction with Italy's ISOLI S p A, Tadano FAUN redesigned the FAUN ATF 60-3 to meet specific Italian Army requirements. The standard ATF 60-3 has a 40.2 m boom and 6.1-tonne counterweight, giving axles loads of 13.2 tonnes. To meet the lifting requirements and 13-tonne axle load limit of the Italian Army the ATF 60-3 S is fitted with a 32.7 m boom and 7.2-tonne counterweight.

All-terrain cranes
The entire Tadano FAUN all-terrain crane fleet is equipped with Mercedes-Benz engines. Cranes of up to three axles and 60 tonnes capacity have a single engine, cranes of four axles and >60 tonnes capacity have two; one for the carrier vehicle, one for the crane itself. Chassis have two to six axles, and in a variety of steer and drive configurations. All-terrain cranes are manufactured by FAUN GmbH in Germany.

Full details of the FAUN ATF 70-4 and ATF 120-5 all-terrain cranes supplied to the German Army for use in the former Yugoslavia and Afghanistan with KFOR can be found elsewhere in this section.

Truck-mounted cranes
Tadano FAUN currently produces three truck-mounted cranes for mounting on commercial truck chassis of customer preference. These are manufactured by FAUN GmbH in Germany. The choice of chassis has a bearing on certain specifications.

Rough terrain cranes
Tadano FAUN offers three rough terrain cranes with capacities of 30, 55 and 70 tonnes. These are manufactured in Japan by Tadano.

BKF 35-4 recovery vehicle
Tadano FAUN also currently produces the BKF 35-4, models 40-4 and 40-4 L, recovery vehicles - 40-tonne, 2.25 m boom; Long (L), 2.85 m boom. These are based on a four-axle Tadano FAUN all-terrain crane chassis. Full details of the BKF 35-4, which is in service with the German and Hungarian armies can be found in the recovery vehicles section.

Specifications - See table on previous page

Status
In production. Current and previously produced cranes are in service with the armed forces of Australia, Egypt, France, Hungary, Italy, Japan, Germany and others.

Contractor
Tadano FAUN GmbH

Italy

Merlo materials handling equipment

Development
Merlo Spa was created in 1964, and in 1966 the company produced its first dumper and self-loading concrete mixer. The first Merlo telescopic handler, the SM 30, was launched in 1982. In 1987 the Panoramic telescopic handler was launched as the world's first telescopic handler to feature a side-mounted engine together with a hydrostatic transmission. In 1991 Merlo introduced the ROTO 25.11, the world's first fully slewing telescopic handler. Merlo is the third largest producer of telescopic handlers in Europe and the largest producer of slewing handlers.

In addition to the ROTO range of 360° telescopic handlers and two ranges of conventional telescopic handlers (Panoramic and Turbofarmer), Merlo also produces the DBM range of self-loading concrete mixers with mixing capacities of up to 3,500 litres, the Cingo range of tracked multipurpose platforms with capacities of 400-1,000 kg, and the multipurpose Multifarmer machine. The Multifarmer combines the concepts of a telescopic handler and tractor, and is fitted with a telescopic boom to the front, and a three-point linkage at the rear.

Machines supplied by Merlo for military applications are essentially commercial products, however these can be modified and militarised as required to suit specific customer requirements. Militarisation can include armoured protection for the cabin and/or essential driveline components; remote control, EMC packages and screening to allow for weapons and explosive handling.

Recent military sales of Merlo materials handling equipment are known to include 128 Panoramic P35.9 EVA machines to the Australian Army, and during early 2004 some 80 Panoramic P40.9 KATF machines to the French Army. A small number (thought to be 15) of French Army machines were fitted with a small-arms-fire-protected cabin manufactured by Cabines Sarrazin of France. Orders for a further 20 machines were placed in August 2004, followed late 2005 by orders for five DBM 2500EV-ATF self-loading concrete mixers for the Corps of Engineers.

Brief details of the current Merlo ranges of Panoramic, Turbofarmer and

Merlo Panoramic P 35.9 EVA telescopic load handler of the Australian Army in Afghanistan (Carl Schulze)　　　1296247

Merlo P.40.9KATF telescopic handler of the French Army (Shaun C Connors)　　　1156078

ROTO telescopic handlers follow[1].
[1] It should be noted that in line with the majority of manufacturers of such equipment, Merlo regularly updates/revises its model range. These updates/revisions can be minor, often cosmetic and involve minimal mechanical changes, but can result in product designation changes.

Description
Panoramic range
The current Merlo Panoramic range of telescopic handlers includes 19 basic models. Some, mostly lower lift height products, have fixed front axles but most feature Merlo's unique integral sideshift front axle, offering plus or minus 110 mm of shift with boom retracted and frame levelling (up to 9°). Most machines lifting above 11 m are also fitted with Merlo's compact stabilisers, increasing stability without extra width. The periphery of all Merlo Panoramic handlers is protected by a cold-bent-to-shape 70 mm (diameter), 40 kgf.m high-tensile steel bar. This so-called 'Ring of Steel' acts as a counterweight for lifting and stability and forms the cab mount.

Merlo Panoramic machines can be split into five categories: compact; medium lift; high lift; ultra high lift, and high capacity.

The Panoramic Compact series machines were introduced to provide a narrow, low machine. Available with two lift heights (P28.8 models lift to 8.2 m, P32.6 models to 6.4 m), they use the same turbocharged 100 hp (75 kW) Deutz diesel engine as most smaller Panoramic machines, have the same power train and full-size cab as other Panoramic machines, but are only 2 m wide and have overall heights of 2.15 m (standard model) or 2 m (low profile 'L' models).

The Medium lift range is made up of four base machines, all powered by a Deutz 102 hp (76 kW) turbocharged diesel engine. The simplest are the P34.7 and P34.10 with a fixed front axle. The P36.7 and P36.10 models have side shift and frame levelling (up to 9°), which allow them to maximise their lift capacities by assuring a true vertical lift.

Four High lift machines with lift heights ranging from 11.5 to 13.6 m are powered by a Perkins 86 hp (64 kW) naturally aspirated diesel engine. The P37.12 is fitted with side shift and frame levelling, while the P38.12, P38.13 and P38.14 have side shift, frame levelling and stabilisers. A 'Plus' option has the 100 hp (75 kW) turbocharged engine and 40 km/h transmission.

The Ultra high lift range consists of three machines, the P40.14, P40.16 and P40.17. All share a Deutz naturally aspirated diesel engine developing 100 hp (75 kW) and a maximum travel speed of 40 km/h.

The higher capacity range consists of seven machines, the P45.18HM, P55.9CS, P60.10, P65.14 HM, P72.10, P80.9 HM and P101.10. All feature sideshift and frame levelling. These products are not designed for rough terrain use but offer capacities of up to 10,000 kg. The newly-introduced P55.9CS is unique in being the only telehandler in the world to feature a suspended cab to greatly reduce whole body vibration levels for the driver.

Merlo P.40.9KATF telescopic handler of the French Army. 80 of these machines, some with a small arms fire protected cab, were supplied during 2004. Orders for a further 20 machines were placed in August 2004 (Merlo)   0587635

Side view of a Merlo Panoramic P 35.9 EVA telescopic load handler of the Australian Army (Ron Fry)   1124772

Rear three-quarter view of a Merlo Panoramic P 35.9 EVA telescopic load handler of the Australian Army. Maximum reach is 5.4 m; lifting capacity at that distance is 1,250 kg; lift height is up to 6.7 m. For Australian Army requirements, a spare wheel carrier is fitted to the rear of the machine (Ron Fry)   1124771

Turbofarmer range

The Merlo Turbofarmer range is a development of the Panoramic, but with a 40 km/h transmission and other adaptations to suit farm use. The machines can be split into three categories: compact machines, those with rigid front axles, and those with side shift and frame levelling front axle.

The Turbofarmer Compact series machines were introduced to satisfy demands for a narrow, low machine. Available with two lift heights (P28.8 models lift to 8.2 m, P32.6 models to 6.4 m), they use the same turbocharged 100 hp (75 kW) Deutz diesel engine as most smaller Panoramic machines, have the same power train and full size cab as other Panoramic machines, but are only 2 m wide and have overall heights of 2.15 m (standard model) or 2 m (low profile 'L' models). There are eight models, offering various speed ranges and hydraulic equipment.

A range of eight standard Turbofarmer machines with Rigid front axles are offered, providing lift heights of 7 m and 9.7 m with lift capacities from 3,400-4,000 kg. All are powered by Deutz turbocharged diesel engines, four by 100 hp (75 kW) units and four by aftercooled 140 hp (104 kW) units. There are also eight machines with sideshift and frame levelling, again offering lift heights of 7 m and 9.7 m and lift capacities from 3,400-

4,000 kg. All are powered by Deutz turbocharged diesel engines, four by 100 hp (75 kW) units and four by aftercooled 140 hp (104 kW) units. Frame levelling (plus or minus 9°) allows the operator to obtain best use of the machine's capacity when lifting on uneven ground.

Machines such as materials handling equipment, that relies on an oscillating, unsprung axle to account for ground undulations tend to be speed-restricted when operating in rough terrain. This lack of genuine suspension also reduces effective road speed, in many cases restricting any degree of self-deployability. This can be an issue for military users. Merlo handlers may now be fitted with one of three types of suspension system. Machines featuring frame levelling can be fitted with a front axle Electronic Active Suspension (EAS) system, absorbing shock loads when travelling on rough ground at the axle. The EAS uses the frame levelling cylinders to support the front axle. A series of nitrogen/oil accumulators are controlled by electronics and provide full axle suspension. Merlo are now developing models with full cab suspension.

Fixed front axle models can utilise a simpler Boom Suspension System. A nitrogen/oil accumulator is fitted into the boom lift circuit. When the system is activated, it acts as a suspension damper, smoothing out the ride over rough surfaces.

For 2008 onwards, cab suspension will be available, first on the P55.9CS and later on other selected models in the range.

Status

In production. In service with Australia (128 P35.9 EVA), France (100 P40.9 KATF delivered 2004/2005), Sweden and possibly other undisclosed armed forces.

Contractor

Merlo Spa

Netherlands

Cargotec (Moffett) rough terrain portable forklifts

Development

The former Kooiaap and Moffett Mounty brands of rough terrain portable forklifts have merged and are now part of the Hiab group of companies, Hiab being owned by the Finnish Kone Corporation. Production facilities

The Moffett Kooi rough terrain portable forklift is in service with the British Army Air Corp in the role of ammunition tender for the Apache attack helicopter (Cargotec)   0121896

A Moffett Kooi rough terrain portable forklift truck of the Royal Army of Oman showing optional wider sand-type tyres (Cargotec)   0525611

remain in Ireland and the Netherlands, with government and military sales being handled by Hiab's UK-based Cargotec Government Business Operations. Full details of the Moffett range of rough terrain portable forklifts can now be found under United Kingdom in this section.

New Zealand

Steelbro container handling equipment

Development
Steelbro New Zealand Ltd has manufactured and exported (to over 100 countries worldwide) container Self-Loading Trailers or Sidelifters since 1978, predominantly for civilian applications. In September 2001, Steelbro acquired the German company Klaus along with its focus on armed forces container handling solutions. Klaus mobile container handling systems have been in production for over 20 years, during which time in excess of 1,000 units have been manufactured, with over of 20 per cent of these having been supplied to a number of military users. Steelbro New Zealand Ltd currently supply Steelbro Sidelifters and Truckmount Sidelifters to various NATO armed forces within Europe and Australasia.

Description
A Sidelifter has a set of independently operating crane lifting arms, and retractable stabilising legs that can lift containers from the ground, a rail wagon or another truck or trailer onto itself. The system can be used with toplift container spreaders, rope slings or chains. Control is usually carried out remotely by means of a portable control box. The ability to self-load and unload a container eliminates the need for forklifts or other heavy equipment to be available at both ends of the containers route. When not in use, the system arms can be folded down or to the side to lower the overall height for air transport in C-130 Hercules (or larger) aircraft.

A variety of Sidelifter models have been developed. The Sidelifter is primarily a semi-trailer-based container handling system, however truck-mount Sidelifters are available; these have extended operational capabilities over the normal semi-trailer set-up, especially when mounted to an all-wheel drive or tracked platform.

Sidelifters are suitable for use with a variety of payloads and can handle modules varying in size from 20 to 48 ft in length, and with weights of up to 36,000 kg.

A truck-mounted Steelbro Sidelifter mounted on a Renault Kerax truck and demonstrated at Eurosatory 2008 (Shaun C Connors)   1296215

Klaus-produced Klaus Kranmobil KM 32 container handling system of the US Air Force in the UK (Shaun C Connors)   0109490

Klaus-produced Klaus Kranmobil KM 24 E-293/S container handling system in use (Steelbro)   0044595

Klaus-produced Klaus Kranmobil KM 292 container handling system in use. The mounting vehicle is a Czech Army TATRA T815 (Shaun C Connors)   0568453

Status
In production. Klaus Kranmobil and Sideloader models are in service with the armed forces of Australia, the Czech Republic, France, Germany, Russian Federation, Sweden, UK, US, and the UN.

Contractor
Steelbro New Zealand Ltd

Swing Thru STLA 20,000 kg military container handling system

Description
Double-sided Swing Thru systems are capable of transporting and transferring containers, lifting and swinging the container over the load bearing deck to another deck or the ground. The Swing Thru system was first deployed in a military role by the New Zealand Army who, before their October 1999 deployment to East Timor, placed an order for two 10,000 kg capacity container handling systems. These were mounted on Mercedes-Benz 6 × 4 chassis. Since this deployment further developments in consultation with the British, New Zealand and US military forces has led to the development of a specialist 20,000 kg (44,000 lbs) Military Swing Thru system.

Major considerations in the development of this system were: C130 transportability; ability to operate on JP8 fuel; the ability to mount on any suitably sized and/or capacity truck or trailer using standard ISO twistlocks, avoiding the need and cost of specialist vehicles; interoperability with other systems in the supply chain; flexibility in the stabilising legs for pick-up-and-carry and transfer operations on rough terrain, and low training time and reduction of personnel requirements within the logistics chain.

In operation, unlike some similar commercial systems which drop the container at a 30° angle, the Swing Thru system lifts and delivers the container level which avoids the possibility of shifting and damage to the contents of the container.

For operational safety the stabilising legs are fitted so that a minimum leg pressure is required prior to boom operation. This ensures leg deployment is carried out prior to the commencement of lifting. At 90 per

Swing Thru STLA 20,000 kg military container handling system in use (Swing Thru) 0525598

cent of maximum rated lift, amber light will illuminate; at 100 per cent partial system cut out will activate along with an audible alarm and red light. When an overload is detected the operator can reset the machine by retracting the boom load.

Specifications

(STDA 20 tonne Swing Thru)
Lift capacity: 20,000 kg
Configuration: fixed 20 ft detachable or sliding to handle containers from 20 to 48 ft in length
Power supply: 41 hp diesel engine
Controls: manual, positioned on both sides at rear
Hydraulic pressure: 3,600 psi
Hydraulic pump: double gear pump
Hydraulic hoses: crimp type one piece fittings
Pins: steel grade 4140 or better
Lifting chains: 13 mm grade 100 complete with shortening clutches
Swing boom speed: (side to side) approx. 64 s

Status
Production as required. Earlier model in service with the New Zealand Army (2).

Contractor
Swing Thru International Limited

Romania

ROMAN truck mounted mobile field cranes

Development
The company produces a wide variety of truck mounted mobile cranes for commercial applications. Many of these are suitable for military use with little modification and ROMAN truck-mounted mobile cranes have been supplied to a number of armed forces including those of Malaysia and Romania.

Brief details of two current models, one supplied to Malaysia and the other Romania, are included here.

It was announced during 2003 that Pesaka Astana of Malaysia had acquired a 94.27 per cent stake in ROMAN SA, including a 100 per cent takeover of two of ROMAN SA's subsidiaries which control the assembly plant and axle parts manufacturing facilities. The takeover did not involve any liabilities or debts of ROMAN SA. After one week Pesaka Astana gave up its share of ROMAN SA to SC PRO ROMAN SA, Brasov. From 2004 the current privatised company began trading. Following privitisation in 2004, a decision was taken to use ROMAN as the primary brand name.

ROMAN designations are based on the same system as earlier DAC/AMDAC designations and define approximate GVW (tonnes) and approximate engine power output (hp), with the additional lettering defining a variety of things including cab type, drive configuration, wheel/tyre fit, body/chassis type and so on.

Description

ROMAN 15.220 DFAEG HTA-7 mobile crane
ROMAN 15.220 DFAEG HTA-7 mobile crane is based on a conventional channel section design truck chassis with rivet or bolted cross-members. The chassis has all-wheel drive, conventional beam-type axles and leaf spring suspension. The front steer drive and rear drive axles are fitted with single wheels/tyres. Anti-lock brakes (ABS) are fitted as standard.

ROMAN 15.220 DFAEG HTA-7 mobile crane (ROMAN) 1323548

ROMAN 26.360 DFAE AMT-950 mobile crane (ROMAN) 1323551

Motive power is by a MAN 6.87-litre six-cylinder inline water-cooled diesel engine developing 220 hp (164 kW). This is coupled to a six-speed manual gearbox and two-speed transfer box. An automatic transmission is optional. Two 220-litre capacity diesel tanks are chassis mounted.

The forward control all steel flat panelled cab is fitted with a two-piece flat glass windscreen as standard throughout the ROMAN military truck range in various configurations with two to six seats, and two or four doors. The cab tilts forward hydraulically for engine maintenance and checks and is fitted with a high performance heating and ventilation system. An observation hatch is fitted in the cab roof for the passenger.

The crane is operated from a separate cabin and the boom has three stages, the base and two telescopic. The four hydraulic stabiliser legs are chassis mounted.

The ROMAN 15.220 DFAEG HTA-7 mobile crane is in service with Romania.

ROMAN 26.360 DFAE AMT-950 mobile crane
ROMAN 26.360 DFAE AMT-950 mobile crane is based on the chassis of the ROMAN 26.360 DFAEG (6 × 6) truck, full details of which can be found in the Trucks section.

The 26.360 DFAEG is a specialist application military vehicle that forms the prototype of the launcher and resupply vehicles for the LAROM 160 Multiple Artillery Rocket System and ATROM 155 mm/52 cal self-propelled artillery system in addition to being in production as an artillery limber/tractor for the Malaysian Army.

The vehicle employs a conventional channel section chassis with riveted or bolted cross members. The chassis has all wheel drive and the conventional beam type axles have leaf spring suspension. The front steer drive and rear drive axles are fitted with single wheels/tyres. Anti-lock brakes (ABS) are fitted as standard.

Motive power is by a MAN 12-litre six-cylinder inline water-cooled diesel developing 360 hp (268 kW) and coupled to an automatic transmission. A single 310-litre capacity diesel tank is chassis mounted.

The forward control all steel flat-panelled cab is a MAN design now fitted as standard throughout the ROMAN military truck range in various configurations with two to six seats, and two or four doors. A flat panelled all-steel cab with a two piece flat glass windscreen (also fitted to certain ROMAN military models) is an option for this chassis. The cab tilts forward hydraulically for engine maintenance and checks and is fitted with a high performance heating and ventilation system. An observation hatch is fitted in the cab roof for the passenger.

The crane is operated from a separate heated cabin and is equipped with the full range of safety warning and overload devices. The boom has eight stages, the base and seven telescopic. The four hydraulic stabiliser legs are chassis mounted.

The ROMAN 26.360 DFAE AMT-950 mobile crane is in service with Malaysia.

Specifications
ROMAN truck mounted mobile field cranes

	ROMAN 15.220 DFAEG HTA-7	ROMAN 26.360 DFAE AMT-950
Cab seating:	1 + 1	1 + 1
Configuration:	6 × 6 (full time)	6 × 6 (full time)
GVW:	16,500 kg	26,000 kg
Length:	8.2 m	8.2 m
Width:	2.5 m	2.5 m
Height:	2.95 m	2.95 m
Ground clearance:	430 mm	430 mm
Angle of approach/departure:	38°/35°	30°/30°
Max speed:	76 km/h	90 km/h
Fuel capacity:	220 litres	310 litres
Max gradient:	56%	56%
Max sideslope:	33%	33%
Engine:	MAN 6.87-litre six-cylinder inline water-cooled diesel engine developing 220 hp (164 kW)	MAN 12-litre six-cylinder inline water-cooled diesel developing 360 hp (268 kW)
Turning radius: (kerb)	10.6 m	11.1 m
Electrical system:	24 V	24 V
Max lift height:	13.5 m	30 m
Max lift weight:	7,000 kg	20,000 kg

	ROMAN 15.220 DFAEG HTA-7	ROMAN 26.360 DFAE AMT-950
Max boom length:	5.87-12.7 m	5.87-12.7 m
Climatic operational range:	-33 to +52°C	-33 to +52°C

Status
In production. Supplied to Malaysia, Romania and other undisclosed countries. Recent deliveries include models 26.230, 26.260, 26.280 and 26.360.

Contractor
Roman SA

Russian Federation

Former Soviet Union truck-mounted cranes

Description
A selection of former Soviet Union truck-mounted cranes are described briefly here. Many of these have been supplied to the armed forces of the former Soviet Union and those of other former Warsaw Pact countries, but given the current situation in many of these countries, the exact status of many models is uncertain. Newer models may also have been introduced, some of which may have been manufactured/procured in small numbers.

Specifications - See tables below and on following page
[chassis designations in brackets are older or less common variants]

Model	KC-55712	KS-6973B	LAZ-690	KS-1571	K-67	K-68	KS-2571
Operation:	hydraulic	hydraulic	mechanical	360°	electric	electric	hydraulic
Traverse:	360°	360°	360°	hydraulic	360°	360°	360°
Chassis:	KrAZ-65053 (6 × 4)	BAZ-69098	ZIL-164A (ZIL-130, ZIL-150)	GAZ-53A	MAZ-500 (MAZ-200)	MAZ-200 (MAZ-500)	ZIL-130
Capacity:	25 t	50 t (most probably at 1 m)	3 t/2.5 m	4 t/3.3 m	6.3 t/3.5 m	6.3 t/5.5 m	6.3 t/3.3 m
Load: (at max radius)	-	-	1 t/5.5 m	- /9.35 m	2 t/7.5 m	2 t/7.5 m	- /9.8 m
Length:	12.5 m	-	8.88 m	-	8.2 m	8.9 m	-
Width:	2.5 m	-	2.4 m	-	2.6 m	2.71 m	-
Height:	3.65 m	-	3.45 m	-	3.35 m	3.3 m	-
Speed:	50 km/h	60 km/h	45 km/h	-	40 km/h	40 km/h	-
Remarks:	currently offered for military/ commercial applications	currently offered for military/ commercial applications	obsolete	military use not confirmed	180 hp engine	also K-68A	military use not confirmed

Model	8T210	9T31M1	AK-75	KS-3562A	KS-3571	KS-357	K-162
Operation:	hydraulic	-	mechanical	electric	hydraulic	hydraulic	electric
Traverse:	360°	360°	360°	360°	360°	360°	360°
Chassis:	Ural-375D	Ural-375D	ZIL-164A (ZIL-130)	MAZ-500A	MAZ-500A	KrAZ-255B	KrAZ-219 (KrAZ-257)
Capacity:	6.3 t/3.5 m	-	7.5 t/2.8 m	10 t/4 m	10 t/4 m	10 t/4 m	16 t/3.9 m
Load: (at max radius)	1.8 t/7.5 m	-	1.65 t/7 m	-	- /13.2 m	- /9.1 m	2.35 t/10 m
Length:	8.3 m	-	10.1 m	-	-	-	14 m
Width:	2.45 m	-	2.5 m	-	-	-	2.75 m
Height:	-	-	3.56 m	-	5 m	-	3.96 m
Speed:	70 km/h	-	40 km/h	60 km/h	75 km/h	70 km/h	30 km/h
Remarks:	special military crane originally for missile units	special military crane for missile units	97 hp engine	-	military use not confirmed	-	also K-162M

Model	KS-4571	KS-45717-1	KS-45721	KS-55713-3	KS-35714	KS-55722-1	KS-35719-3-02
Operation:	hydraulic	hydraulic	hydraulic	hydraulic	hydraulic	hydraulic	hydraulic
Traverse:	360°	360°	360°	360°	360°	360°	360°
Chassis:	KrAZ-257	Ural-4320-30	Ural-4320-40	Ural-4320-40	Ural-5557-40	Ural-5557-40	Ural-5557-40
Capacity:	16 t/3.8 m	25 t/2 m	75 t/1 m	80 t/1 m	48 t/1 m	80 t/1 m	51.2 t/1 m
Load: (at max radius)	- /20.25 m	n/avail	n/avail	n/avail	n/avail	n/avail	n/avail
Length:	-	10.9 m	12.0 m	12.0 m	10.0 m	9.98 m	10.1 m
Width:	-	2.5 m	2.5 m	2.5 m	2.5 m	2.5 m	2.5 m
Height:	-	3.6 m	3.62 m	3.65 m	3.4 m	3.59 m	3.8 m
Speed:	70 km/h	60 km/h	80 km/h	80 km/h	60 km/h	60 km/h	60 km/h
Remarks:	military use not confirmed	240 hp YaMZ-238M2 engine	230 hp YaMZ-236NE2 engine	230 hp YaMZ-236NE2 engine	230 hp YaMZ-236NE2 engine	230 hp YaMZ-236NE2 engine	230 hp YaMZ-236NE2 engine

Model	KS-45719-3A	KS-45717-1	MKT-25.5	KS-55713-3K	MPK-30	8T26	KM-61
Operation:	hydraulic	hydraulic	hydraulic	hydraulic	electric	-	mechanical
Traverse:	360°	360°	360°	360°	360°	-	80°
Chassis:	Ural-5557-40	Ural-4320-40	Ural-4320-40	Ural-5557-40	MAZ-529V	-	KrAZ-214
Capacity:	64 t/1 m	75 t/1 m	75 t/1 m	80 t/1 m	30 t/3.7 m	10 t/4.5 m	3.2 t/2 m
Load: (at max radius)	n/avail	n/avail	n/avail	n/avail	6 t/27 m	2 t/9.5 m	2 t/2.8 m
Length:	11.1 m	10.9 m	12 m	11.1 m	12.8 m	-	-
Width:	2.5 m	2.5 m	2.5 m	2.5 m	4 m	-	-
Height:	3.8 m	3.65 m	3.65 m	3.71 m	4.2 m	-	-
Speed:	60 km/h	60 km/h	60 km/h	80 km/h	25 km/h	40 km/h	-
Remarks:	230 hp YaMZ-236NE2 engine	230 hp YaMZ-236NE2 engine	230 hp YaMZ-236NE2 engine	230 hp YaMZ-236NE2 engine	articulated, with 2-wheel tractor	special military crane for missile units	used with KMT-5 mineclearing apparatus

Model	KS-2561D	8T26	KTA-28
Operation:	-	-	hydraulic
Traverse:	360°	-	360°
Chassis:	KrAZ-255B	-	Kraz-65053-02
Capacity:	6.3 t/ -	10 t/4.5 m	28 t/1 m
Load: (at max radius)	1.5 t/ -	2 t/9.5 m	n/avail
Length:	-	-	-
Width:	-	-	-
Height:	-	-	-
Speed:	-	40 km/h	50 km/h
Remarks:	150 hp engine	special military crane for missile units	330 hp YaMZ-238D engine

Sweden

HAMMAR Sideloaders

Description
HAMMAR sideloaders have been in production since 1974. They allow one operator only to lift, transfer and transport fully loaded ISO containers and flatracks without recourse to other handling equipment or devices. The sideloaders can travel both on- and off-road and it is possible to stack two loaded containers high.

Any suitable truck or special chassis can be employed to carry and operate the sideloaders. All operational controls are located in a portable control box, so the operator can have a full view of the load area. A load or off-load cycle takes 3.5 minutes.

Power is provided by a power take-off, with a double piston pump as standard. Separate diesel power packs are available.

Using common components and modules the HAMMAR sidelifters comprise a total of five different models on three types of chassis. The main items in the HAMMAR Defence Line are as follows.

HAMMAR 150 Series
The HAMMAR 150 Series of sideloaders are semi-trailer integrated. They incorporate stabiliser legs allowing easy access even under low-built trailer chassis and railway wagons. Maximum Safe Work Load (SWL) is 36,000 kg, with 42,000 kg being an option. Stacking capacity is 30,000 kg, with a capability to stack containers two high on the ground.

The 151 HS is the main model, with the 152 HS having folding tip stabilisers and automatic twistlocks as additional features.

HAMMAR 160 Series
The 160 Series includes heavy-duty models primarily intended for ground-to-ground lifting operations. Based on a semi-trailer chassis, the 160 HS is able to stack containers two high on the ground. Maximum lifting capacity (SWL) is 33,000 kg, and stacking capacity is 30,000 kg.

HAMMAR 180 Series
The HAMMAR 180 Series are fixed 20 ft units mounted on a rigid truck or special chassis. A typical example is the 183 HB mounted on a Volvo A25C (6 × 6) articulated chassis with a lift and stack capacity of 20,000 kg. The generally similar 184 HB on a three- or four-axle truck has a lifting capacity of 25,000 kg and a stacking capacity of 20,000 kg (SWL). Both models can stack containers two high. Each lifting unit consists of one upper arm, one

HAMMAR 150 Series sideloader in operation. This is Danish Army equipment (Hammar Maskin)   0052779

HAMMAR 190 HB sideloader on a Royal Netherlands Air Force (RAF) Scania P124 CB8x8HZ 420 truck, seven of which were procured as part of the Wissel Laad Systemen (WLS) package (Shaun C Connors)   1128231

Rear view of a HAMMAR 184 HB sideloader of the Danish Air Force mounted on a Scania R113 (6 × 6) truck (Hammar Maskin)   0525613

From the rear, a good view of a HAMMAR 190 HB sideloader mounted on a Royal Netherlands Air Force (RAF) Scania P124 CB8x8HZ 420 truck, seven of which were procured as part of the Wissel Laad Systemen (WLS) package (Shaun C Connors) 1128230

HAMMAR 183 HB sideloader on a Volvo A25C (6 × 6) articulated chassis (Hammar Maskin) 0056317

lower arm and two hydraulic cylinders mounted on a heavy-duty crane base on a frame of hollow U-profile beams. Telescopic legs with over-sized foot plates act as stabilisers. An extra pair of support legs is mounted on the non-lifting side of the lifting side on each unit to provide extra stability when stacking containers.

HAMMAR 190 Series

The 190 Series is the latest addition to the HAMMAR range. Lifting capacities vary from 25,000 to 33,000 kg. The 195 HC, HF and HS models are semi-trailer integrated and can handle 20 to 45 ft ISO containers, while the 190 HB and 195 HB models are vehicle mounted units for handling 20 ft ISO containers and can stack loaded 8 ft 6 in containers. All models feature a new design of articulated stabiliser legs.

Status

In production. The 183 HB is in service with the Colombian Navy, Danish Army and Air Force. The 184 HB is in service with the Danish and Israeli armies. The 160 Series is in service with Egyptian and UAE armed forces. The 190 Series, in both truck-mounted and trailer-integrated configurations, is in service with Danish, Dutch, Egyptian, Hungarian and Swedish armed forces.

Contractor

HAMMAR Maskin AB

Kalmar forklift trucks

Description

Kalmar Limited supplies a wide range of both engine-powered and electric front-loading forklift trucks from 1,000 to 50,000 kg lifting capacity. Kalmar also supplies a range of container handling and stacking machines with capacities ranging from 7,000 to 45,000 kg.

Status

In production. Models are in service with the defence forces of Belgium, Canada, Denmark, Egypt, Norway, United Kingdom, United States and others.

Contractor

Kalmar Industries AB

Kalmar Rough Terrain Container Handler (RTCH)

Development

From the late 1980s and with the shift in military doctrines towards rapid deployment-type operations, many armies around the world have embraced the ISO container concept for the transport and storage of supplies. Further to this, field accommodation, field hospitals, command centres and support infrastructure of all types are also now built around the ISO container concept or ISO footprint.

The majority of military flatbed cargo trucks adapt easily to the transport of ISO-dimensioned containers, and while a DROPS/PLS-type truck has the additional benefit of being able to load/off-load an ISO container (up to 20 ft), specialist machines are required to load non-DROPS/PLS trucks and to generally handle/stack ISO containers, especially the larger 40 ft variant.

Procurement of commercially produced container handling equipment, as manufactured by a number of companies worldwide, accompanied the embracing of the ISO concept and such equipment is in day-to-day use at military bases, depots, port facilities and so on. However, with armed forces increasingly deploying to areas with little or no supporting infrastructure, the need for a machine capable of operating on surfaces other than hard standing soon became apparent.

Rough terrain or all-terrain cranes can handle ISO containers, however a dedicated container handler is more flexible and has a far greater workrate. An early dedicated container handler with a rough terrain capability was the Boss G Series, a 4 × 4 design adopted by the British Army. The G Series is a mast-type design and retains the conventional dual-tyred front wheels of commercial container handlers, this set-up limiting mobility in certain conditions. The approach adopted by the US Army was to modify a Caterpillar wheeled loader by the addition of wide flotation-type tyres, a lifting mast and container handling attachment. These machines have proved adequate in the handling role (and have been refurbished by Caterpillar for extended service), but for road transport the mast and handling attachment must be removed; refitting is time-consuming and requires the assistance of a mobile crane. Furthermore, these machines are not adaptable for air-transport.

In the late 1990s Kalmar RT Centre developed an entirely new Rough Terrain Container Handler (RTCH) based on the latest generation of reach stacker-type container handlers. The concept was originally conceived for construction sites that had a growing need to handle containerised stores and accommodation modules.

Two of the first Kalmar RT reach stackers were leased, with an option to buy, by the US Army's Tank Automotive and Armaments Command (TACOM) for a six-to-eight-month evaluation period. Following a period of development and militarisation, in April 2000, Kalmar RT Centre LLC was awarded a US Army contract for the delivery of RTCHs. The contract, a requirements-type contract, had yearly releases and called for up to

A USMC Kalmar Rough Terrain Container Handler (RTCH) working in Camp Bastion, Afghanistan (US DoD (Lcpl Jeremy Harris)) 1391361

A USMC Kalmar Rough Terrain Container Handler (RTCH) working in Port-au-Prince, Haiti (US DoD) 1391362

A Kalmar Rough Terrain Container Handler (RTCH) reach stacker of the US Army at work in Afghanistan (Carl Schulze) 1296216

A USMC Kalmar Rough Terrain Container Handler (RTCH) working in Camp Bastion, Afghanistan (US DoD (Lcpl Jeremy Harris)) 1391363

A Kalmar Rough Terrain Container Handler (RTCH) reach stacker on a King semi-trailer with MAN tractor unit in use with the British Army (Shaun C Connors) 1186177

between 400 and 500 machines delivered during 2001-2005. Deliveries began in June 2001, and by January 2003 over 160 machines had been delivered. Two additional contracts were awarded for production through October 2008, and by the Summer of 2009, 715 machines had been delivered to all users (including FMS sales).

In October 2008, Kalmar RT Center LLC received a five-year Indefinite Delivery/Indefinite Quantity (IDIQ) follow-on contract. Production was relocated to Cibolo, Texas to support this contract. A limited re-qualification first article test was completed in June 2009 with deliveries set to begin shortly thereafter. As of September 2010, 499 vehicles were on order with deliveries extending into the Spring of 2012. These deliveries will bring the fleet size to 1,214 (including FMS sales), with additional orders anticipated.

TACOM has the sole rights to the RTCH and the awarded contracts include provisions for making sales of the RTCH to defence forces approved by the US Army.

In August 2002 it was announced that two RTCHs had been supplied to Australia. The UK MoD has also received 20 RTCHs. Other users include Denmark (three) and Iraq (three).

Description
The RTCH is based on a new cutaway chassis of high torsional stiffness. The front and rear rigid and unsprung Kessler axles are the same width and unlike conventional reach stackers with dual tyres on the front, these are fitted with single 29.5-35 tyres for improved mobility in soft and boggy ground conditions. Both axles are driven and steered; crab-steer is possible and all steering is computer controlled for precise tracking. Axles are unsprung, ground undulations being accounted for by an oscillating rear axle.

Two-wheel drive and single-axle steer is possible for road travel. Both axles are fitted with oil-immersed multidisc brakes.

The military RTCH differs from its commercial counterpart in a number of key areas, the primary driver for these being the requirement for air-transportability. TACOM initially specified the RTCH should be able to be transported within 14 hours of notice to move; this was later reduced to four hours. The RTCH can be prepared for air-transport in less than 30 minutes by one person with no external assistance, and without removing or dismantling any part of the machine.

In developing the commercial RT machine, Kalmar RT Centre identified a growing requirement for such a machine to be readily transportable by road. To achieve the necessary reduction to an overall 4 m height (including low loader) for road transport, the cab of the Kalmar RTCH slides sideways onto a hydraulically operated elevator at the side of the chassis. This then lowers the cab to allow the boom to be lowered flat onto the deck of the reach stacker. To allow the boom to fold flat, a special

double articulated boom support was developed. Prior to this operation the spreader is retracted to the 20 ft position and swung through 90° so that it is in line with the boom. The spreader is then placed flat on the ground. In transport mode the Kalmar RTCH has a total height of 3 m. The machine can be driven at slow speeds with the cab in the lowered position using safety interlocks. This feature, necessary for RO-RO transport where hold height is an issue, is also required to meet the US Army's requirement for air-transportability.

Originally designed as a commercial machine, it was not envisaged that air-transport would be a requirement for the Kalmar RTCH, and as such individual wheel loads for a machine that weighs 53,300 kg exceed the floor strength of transport aircraft. To solve this problem, a special cage has been fitted to the rear of the chassis. This is equipped with a pair of hydraulically controlled bogie wheels. When lowered and the load between these bogie wheels and the rear axle has been balanced by a pressure sensing system, they are locked in position. Similarly, the front axle wheel loading also requires lowering, and a system to fit dolly wheels to the front and rear ISO twistlock positions of the spreader will reduce front axle loading and enable the Kalmar RTCH to be transported by aircraft such as the C-5 and C-17.

Specifications
Cab seating: 1
Configuration: 4 × 4, 4 × 2 for highway use
Weight: (unladen) 53,000 kg
Towed load: n/app
Length: (self-deploy configuration) 12 m
Width: 3.65 m
Height:
 (lowered operating position) 4 m
 (transport configuration) 3 m
Ground clearance: 450 mm
Track: 2.9 m
Wheelbase: 5.5 m
Approach/departure angle: >20°
Max road speed:
 (laden) 24 km/h
 (unladen) 38 km/h
Endurance: 10 hours
Fuel capacity: 378.5 litres (341 litres useable)
Gradient: (at rated capacity) 30%
Fording: up to 1.5 m, salt water

Engine: Cummins QSM 450 10.81-litre 6-cylinder in-line turbocharged and charge air-cooled water-cooled direct injection 4-stroke diesel developing 450 hp (336 kW) at 1,800 rpm and 1,898 N.m torque at 1,400 rpm
Transmission: ZF WG 310 automatic
Steering: two wheel, four-wheel or crab-steer
Turning radius: (outer) 10 m
Axles: Kessler with planetary hub-reduction gearing
Suspension: rear axle oscillation
Tyres: 29.5 × 35R
Brakes:
　(main) enclosed oil-immersed disc with forced cooling
　(parking) disc on input shaft front and rear
Electrical system: 24 V
Battery: 4 × 6TL
Alternator: 100 A
Lift performance:
　(lift capacity to full height) 24,000 kg
　(lift capacity at full reach) 8,000 kg
　(lift height) 9.5 ft ISO containers, 3 high
　(reach at max lift height) 2 m
　(max forward reach) 2nd row at 3 high

Status

In production; 1,214 ordered (including FMS sales). In service with Australia (10), Canada (one), Denmark (three), United Kingdom (20), Iraq (three), and United States (including at least 109 USMC and 18 Navy).

Contractor

Kalmar RT Centre LLC

United Kingdom

JCB materials handling equipment

Development

JCB was founded on 23 October 1945, when the late Joseph Cyril Bamford (known universally as Mr JCB) made his first product in a rented lock-up garage in Uttoxeter, Staffordshire, United Kingdom. Today JCB, which remains a privately owned company, is one of the world's top three construction-equipment manufacturers with 18 plants: 11 in the UK and others in Brazil, China, Germany, India and the United States. There are also subsidiary companies in Belgium, France, Germany, Italy, the Netherlands, Singapore and Spain. The company's worldwide headquarters are in Rocester, Staffordshire, UK.

JCB has a supporting dealer network covering over 150 countries, with 1,500 dealer depot locations. The company employs around 7,000 people and manufactures more than 300 different machines in 13 primary product ranges including backhoe loaders, telescopic handlers, tracked and wheeled excavators, vibratory and drum compactors, wheeled loading shovels, articulated dump trucks, rough terrain fork lifts, mini excavators, Robot skid steers loaders, and Robot tracked skid steer loaders. In addition, for agricultural markets, the company produces a range of telescopic handlers and the high-speed Fastrac tractor. JCB also manufactures the Teletruk forklift for the industrial sector.

Details of backhoe loaders; tracked and wheeled excavators; wheeled loading shovels; articulated dump trucks; mini excavators and Robot skid steers loaders and Robot tracked skid steer loaders can be found in the Field fortifications and related emplacements section; details of the JCB Fastrac tractor (which is in service with the UK Royal Air Force) can be found in the Trucks section.

In 2004, JCB celebrated the production of the 500,000th JCB machine. JCB exports 75 per cent of its UK-made products to 150 countries worldwide. The company has previously stated that it maintains parts support for all JCB machines back to 1965 models, it is now stated that as long as a JCB remains in use it will be supported.

JCB 540 70 telescopic handler of the Luxembourg Army in Kosovo (Shaun C Connors) 1186165

JCB recorded pre-tax pre-exceptional profits of GBP39 million during 2008 on a turnover of GBP2 billion. With total sales of 57,000 machines and a global market share of 10.8 per cent, JCB remained the world's third largest construction equipment brand. The company also retained its position as the world's number one manufacturer of backhoe loaders, with more than a third of the market. In 2010 JCB stated that it had a 41 per cent market share for backhoe loaders.

In 2003, JCB announced GBP80 million plans to develop and manufacture its own diesel engines and a new company, JCB Power Systems Ltd, was formed to produce the engines and acquired a new manufacturing plant in Derbyshire, England. By the beginning of 2007 over 50,000 engines had been produced and over 50 per cent of JCB's current products are powered by JCB-produced engines.

In addition to supplying what are essentially commercial-off-the-shelf products JCB will design, develop and carry out militarisation of these commercial products to meet specific requirements.

Additionally, the company is one of a few within the materials handling equipment vehicle sector which will undertake the design, development and manufacture of military-specific equipment. Examples of this are the High Mobility Rough Terrain Forklift (HMRTF) and the High Mobility Variable Reach Truck (HMVRT), both of which combine the attributes of the Fastrac tractor and HMEE with those of a telescopic handler. The HMRTF was developed to UK MoD specifications and is in service with the UAE, the HMVRT was designed to meet the emerging logistic/materials handling needs of deployable forces. Full details of the HMRTF can be found elsewhere in this section.

Since 1984, JCB has supplied over 3,500 machines to around 54 different military/government organisations around the world.

The following is a brief overview of the current JCB materials handling equipment range. [1]. Full details of certain specific items of equipment (as indicated in respective sub sections) can be found elsewhere in the section.

[1] It should be noted that in line with the majority of manufacturers of such equipment, JCB regularly updates/revises its model range. These updates/revisions can be minor, often cosmetic and involve minimal mechanical changes, but can result in product designation changes.

Description

Telescopic handlers

JCB is the second largest producer of variable reach handling machines (referred to as the Loadall range by JCB or generically, by type, as telehandlers or telescopic handlers) in the world. Production of the first model, the JCB 520, began in 1977. The current line-up of models has

A JCB telescopic handler of the Finnish Army in Kosovo (R Stickland) 1124751

A JCB telescopic handler of the Royal Navy at work aboard HMS Ocean (Ian C Young) 0564290

The JCB Teletruk combines the attributes of a counterbalanced forklift truck with those of a telescopic handler (JCB)   0587663

JCB 930-4WD rough terrain forklift of the USAF (US DoD)   1391304

maximum lift capacities ranging from 2,000 to 4,537 kg and maximum lift heights ranging from 4.35 to 17.07 m. The range includes two-, three- or four-stage telescopic booms, with some machines being fitted with stabiliser legs.

Telescopic handlers have the features of conventional rough terrain trucks combined with the advantage of forward reach, which permits 'one side' loading and unloading of road and rail trucks. The use of telescopic booms also enables machines to load/unload an ISO container without entering, or to stand back from hazardous areas or soft ground and still lift or place a load accurately.

There are 30 models in the current JCB Loadall range, these and all recent models having four equal-sized wheels that, in addition to offering better off-road mobility than earlier designs, enable steering in three modes: all-wheel steer, front-wheel steer and crab steer.

All JCB telescopic handlers are powered by side or rear-mounted four-cylinder JCB diesel engines currently ranging in power outputs from 50 to 140 hp, and in most cases drive via a torque converter through a JCB synchromesh gearbox and JCB drive axles, which incorporate oil-immersed multidisc brakes. Some of the latest machines to be introduced at the smaller end of the range are fitted with hydrostatic transmissions.

The single operator all-weather cab meets all ROPS/FOPS requirements.

The JCB TM310 Telemaster is a specialised machine that combines the articulated steering attribute of a wheeled loader with the telescopic boom of a telescopic handler. The TM310 is powered by a (model dependant) 130 or 145 hp turbocharged diesel engine and has a maximum lifting capacity of 3,100 kg and a maximum lift height of 5.2 m.

Considerable numbers of assorted JCB telescopic handler models are known to be in service with all branches of UK armed forces.

E C Hallam Engineering (Leicester) Limited produce a range of aircraft tow tractors based on the Loadall range, a number of which are in service with the Royal Air Force.

JCB Teletruk

The JCB Teletruk is essentially a compact counterbalanced industrial forklift trick with a telescopic handler-type forwards reach telescopic boom. It packages the combination of small size, four-wheel drive, 2,500-3,500 kg lift capacity, quick-change attachments and variable reach. It is, according to JCB, the world's smallest 4 × 4 forklift with a turning radius less than 3 m in the 2,500-3,500 kg lift class.

The JCB Teletruck is also available in 4 × 2 configuration. There are over 100 build options available.

Rough terrain forklifts

JCB produces three rough terrain forklift truck models, the JCB 926, 930 and 940. All are built around a specially designed chassis and can be fitted with Clearview or Freelift (heights of 3.6, 4.5, 5.5 and 6.55 (926 and 930) 6.55 m (940)) masts and are available in 4 × 2 and 4 × 4 configurations. Access to the one-person cab is from either side.

The following table provides basic specifications.

Specifications
Rough terrain forklifts
	JCB 926	JCB 930	JCB 940
Weight: (operating, approx.)	5,910 kg	6,340 kg	6,360 kg
Length: (to carriage)	3.6 m	3.6 m	3.6 m
Width: (over tyres)	2.2 m	2.2 m	2.2 m
Height:	2.57 m	2.57 m	2.57 m
Engine:	JCB 444 4-litre 4-cylinder in-line water-cooled naturally aspirated diesel developing 84 hp (63 kW)		
Transmission:	JCB four-speed Syncro Shuttle with integral torque converter		

Status
In production. JCB materials handling equipment is in service with the armed forces of Australia, Egypt, Finland, India, Italy, Kuwait, Luxembourg, Mexico, Netherlands, Norway, Oman, Portugal, South Africa, Spain, UK, US and others.

Contractor
JCB Defence Products

JCB High Mobility Rough Terrain Forklift (HMRTF)

Development
In addition to customising its commercial range of construction and materials handling equipment, JCB is one of a small number of companies which design and develop machines to meet military requirements. The JCB High Mobility Rough Terrain Forklift (HMRTF) is one such machine.

The HMRTF, was previously known as the JCB 523M Loadall, combines JCB's considerable experience with telescopic handlers and their Fastrac range of high-speed tractors.

The HMRTF was originally developed by JCB to meet demanding UK MoD requirements for a vehicle with an ability to maintain the highest convoy speeds. The HMRTF was, as the Tractor Wheeled Forklift Rough Terrain (TWFRT), a competitor for the contract to replace the JCB 410M rough terrain forklift, full details of which can be found elsewhere in this section. The 410M replacement programme subsequently became part of the Private Finance Initiative (PFI) package for the MoD's C vehicle fleet.

The then Amey Lex Consortium (ALC) was announced as preferred bidder for the C vehicle fleet PFI in early 2004, and in June 2005 was awarded the contract by the Ministry of Defence. ALC was an equal partnership between Amey and Lex Defence Ltd and was established for the sole purpose of delivering the C vehicle PFI capability; the awarded contract is estimated to be worth in the region of GBP600 million over a 15 year period. Lex Defence Ltd was acquired by VT Group during 2006. The C vehicle PFI provides a worldwide fleet of construction plant and field mechanical handling equipment operated typically by the Royal Engineers and Royal Logistic Corps respectively. This fleet includes cranes, dump trucks, excavators, bulldozers, container handlers and rough-terrain forklifts. The JCB HMRTF was not selected by ALC as the replacement for the 410M, a more conventional telescopic handler option being preferred.

Description
Unlike conventional telescopic handlers which are unsprung and rely on a single oscillating rear axle to accommodate ground undulations, the HMRTF has all-round suspension with three operating modes. Travel mode - fully suspended for on and off-road travel; work raised - front suspension raised and locked for load handling; work lowered - front suspension lowered and locked for entry into a standard ISO container: the

Prototype JCB High Mobility Rough Terrain Forklift (HMRTF) during the mobility demonstration at IDEX 2005 (Patrick Allen)   1138054

Prototype JCB High Mobility Rough Terrain Forklift (HMRTF) demonstrating lift reach during the mobility demonstration at IDEX 2005 (Patrick Allen)   1138050

Prototype JCB High Mobility Rough Terrain Forklift (HMRTF) in travel configuration (Shaun C Connors)   1120441

Prototype JCB High Mobility Rough Terrain Forklift (HMRTF) in travel configuration; note the four-wheel steer (Shaun C Connors)   1120442

Prototype JCB High Mobility Rough Terrain Forklift (HMRTF) fitted with a bucket (Shaun C Connors)   1186160

standard 620 mm from centre side-shift fork frame allowing for the placement or recovery of loads from either side of an ISO container. The quick hitch tool carrier allows for the rapid change of front-end attachments and the HMRTF may also be fitted with an optional 1 m³ bucket for handling loose material.

A six-speed fully automatic and programmable gearbox and torque converter with lock-up in third to sixth gears are fitted. Maximum road speeds in the six forward and two reverse gears are: 8.8, 13.6, 20.9, 32.3, 57.6, 85.1 km/h forward, and 10 and 23.8 km/h reverse. Two- or four-wheel drive is selectable.

Operator selected four wheel steer is available, with a speed dependant safety interlock and mechanical centre lock for on-highway operation. Front wheel steering is power-assisted mechanical, rear wheel steering is hydraulic. Braking is by outboard dry discs on all wheels with twin callipers front, single callipers rear. Brake circuits are split; single front, twin rear. An anti-lock braking system (ABS) is standard. Standard tyre equipment (which includes a side-mounted spare) are Michelin on/off-road XZLs. A tyre inflation system is fitted.

The HMRTF is air transportable by C-130 Hercules aircraft without preparation, and can be transported underslung by heavy lift helicopter. For strategic mobility, and by the nature of requirements it meets, the machine is able to be transported inside a 20 ft ISO container. Front and rear lifting points, recovery points, a NATO towing pintle and underbody tie-down points are fitted.

Other standard equipment required for the MoD application included an inter-vehicle start socket, brush guards for all external lighting and a convoy/blackout lighting system.

Specifications
HMRTF
Cab seating: 1
Configuration: 4 × 4
Weight:
  (max operational) 8,060 kg
Length: (overall) 5.56 m
Width: (over tyres) 2.103 m
Height:
  (suspension raised) 2.181 m
  (suspension travel) 2.096 m
  (suspension kneel) 2.011 m
Ground clearance: (travel) 299 m
Track: 1.782 m
Wheelbase: 2.7 m
Approach/departure angle: 40°/40°
Max road speed: 84 km/h
Range: 400 km (highway)
Fuel capacity: 180 litres
Gradient: 44% (laden)
Fording: 500 mm (fresh water)
Engine: Cummins QSB 6.7-165 6.7-litre 6-cylinder in-line turbocharged water-cooled 4-stroke diesel developing 165 hp (123 kW) at 2,300 rpm
Transmission: ZF 6WG 160 with fully automatic or powershift control modes and 6 forward and 2 reverse gears
Steering: 2 or 4 wheel steering, power-assisted mechanical front, hydraulic rear
Turning radius:
  (over fork tips, 4 wheel steer) 4.62 m
  (over wheels, 4 wheel steer) 3.936 m
Tyres: 13R 22.5 Michelin XZL
Brakes:
  (main) outboard dry discs all-round, ABS
  (parking) transmission-mounted

Electrical system: 24 V
Battery: 2 × 12 V
Alternator: 55 A
Lift performance:(at 610 mm load centre)
    (lift capacity to full height) 2,311 kg
    (lift capacity at full reach) 1,000 kg
    (lift height) 5 m
    (reach at max lift height) 500 mm
    (max forward reach) 3 m
    (reach with 1,000 kg load) 3 m

Status:
Production as required. Nine machines are in service with the United Arab Emirates (UAE) land forces.

Contractor
JCB Defence Products

JCB 525-50M Loadall telescopic handler

Development
The 525-50M (M - Military) Loadall is a militarised variation of a JCB commercial telescopic handler. Full details of the current JCB telescopic handler range (together with other construction or materials handling equipment manufactured by JCB) can be found elsewhere in this section or the Field fortifications and related emplacements section.

Following a competitive tender, in a deal worth around GBP1 million, the UK Royal Air Force took delivery of 27 JCB 525-50M machines during 2002. Further orders for 13 and 20 machines followed. Over a period of two years the JCB 525-50 replaced the bulk of the earlier JCB 410M machines, 936 of which were supplied to the Army and Royal Air Force, beginning in 1984. Full details of the JCB 410M can be found elsewhere in this section.

The Netherlands armed forces received 38 JCB telescopic handlers during 2005 to 2006, these consisting of 29 model 525-50 and nine model 535-95 machines.

In addition to customising commercial machines such as the 525-50M, JCB also offers dedicated military machines such as the High Mobility Rough Terrain Forklift (HMRTF), full details of which can be found elsewhere in this section.

Description
For UK RAF service the JCB 525-50M was required to be capable of deployment worldwide to support Out of Area operations and is primarily used in Explosive Storage Areas (ESAs) for the movement and transit of ammunition and weapon loads, so all machines are fitted with Category 'C' protection. Most such loads are received in containers and a necessary part of the RAF requirement was the ability to operate with containerised loads. All machines are fitted with side-shift forks that enable load/unloading from inside a standard ISO container.

Other RAF requirements included all lights to be guarded, a search light that could be operated from inside the cab, an externally-mounted fire extinguisher, an inter-vehicle start socket, a NATO tow hitch, the ability to be transported underslung by helicopter, rear and side heated windscreens, and a mounted spare wheel and large tool box.

In addition, two of the initial 27 machines were supplied 'winterised' for operations at temperatures down to –40°C. Winterisation included additional cab and engine bay heating (with a programmable timer), snow blinds and operator protection from frost burns.

The 525-50 machines supplied to the Netherlands armed forces are fitted with 24 V electrical systems and some are spark protected for use in ammunition and weapons handling roles.

Specifications
525-50M Loadall
Cab seating: 1
Configuration: 4 × 4
Weight: 5,400 kg
Towed load: 5,000 kg
Length: (to front of fork carriage) 3.62 m
Width: 1.82 m
Height: (to top of cab) 2.19 m
Ground clearance: (min) 360 mm
Track: (front) 1.49 m
Wheelbase: 2 m
Departure angle: (with/without Quickhitch) 30°/58°
Max road speed: 32 km/h
Fuel capacity: 90 litres
Engine: Perkins 4.40 3.99-litre in-line 4-cylinder water-cooled naturally aspirated 4-stroke diesel developing 71 hp (53 kW) and 282 N.m torque at 2,000 rpm (SAE J1349)
Transmission: JCB Syncro Shuttle incorporating torque converter, reversing shuttle and all-synchromesh 4-speed gearbox
Steering: twin ram hydrostatic power on each axle with 3 steer modes: all-wheel, front-wheel and crab. 32° lock on both axles
Turning radius: (outer, over tyres) 3.71 m
Axles: epicyclic hub reduction with drop box on front axle
Suspension: unsprung, rigid front, oscillating rear
Tyres: (front and rear) 152.5 × 18

The JCB 525-50M telescopic handler (front) can be transported on a DROPS/PLS-type flatrack (Patrick Allen)   1097582

JCB 525-50M of the Royal Netherlands Army (Shaun C Connors)   1186161

The Royal Air Force has received 60 JCB 525-50M telescopic handlers (Patrick Allen)   1034690

Part of the UK RAF's requirement was for the 525-50M to be fully interoperable with standard ISO containers (JCB)   0587659

Brakes:
(main) hydraulically-activated, power-assisted multi-disc oil immersed within the planetary hub
(parking) electro/hydraulically-operated oil immersed multi-disc on the transmission output shaft. Will hold the machine on a 25% gradient
Electrical system: 24 V UK RAF; Netherlands armed forces, 12 V UK Army
Battery: 1 or 2 × 12 V, 92 Ah
Alternator: 62 A
Lift performance:
(lift capacity to full height) 2,500 kg
(lift capacity at full reach) 1,000 kg
(lift height) 5 m
(reach at max lift height) 500 mm
(max forward reach) 2.82 m
(reach with 1,000 kg load) 2.82 m
(placing height) 4.6 m
Cycle times:
(boom raise) 7.4 s
(boom lower) 5.3 s
(extend) 5.7 s
(retract) 3.2 s
(bucket dump[1]) 2.3 s
(bucket crowd[1]) 3.2 s

[1] As with all JCB Loadall telescopic handlers the 525-50M can be fitted with a wide variety of attachments including buckets.

Status
Production complete, replaced by a revised model during 2006. In service with the Royal Air Force (60), and the Netherlands Armed Forces (29).

Contractor
JCB Defence Products

JCB 410M rough terrain forklift truck

Development
The JCB 410M is a military rough terrain forklift based on a modified wheeled loader platform. The machine was designed by JCB specifically for military use and was optimised for the handling of NATO pallets.

Early 2004 it was announced that the Amey Lex Consortium (ALC) had been selected as preferred bidder for the UK MoD's Private Finance Initiative (PFI) to provide heavy plant equipment for the UK's armed forces. A programme to replace the JCB 410M rough terrain forklift truck within the British Army was delayed by this PFI. In June 2005 it was announced that ALC had been awarded the C vehicle Private Finance Initiative (PFI) contract by the Ministry of Defence, worth in the region of GBP600 million, over a 15 year period. ALC was an equal partnership between Amey and Lex Defence Ltd; Lex Defence Ltd was acquired by VT Group during 2006. The C vehicle PFI programme provides a worldwide fleet of construction plant and field mechanical handling equipment, operated typically by the Royal Engineers and Royal Logistic Corps respectively. This fleet includes cranes, dump trucks, excavators, bulldozers, container handlers and rough terrain forklifts.

The 410M was one of the first machines to be replaced by the ALC PFI. Following downselection by ALC to the preferred supplier, 329 model 524-50 telescopic handlers were supplied by JCB to replace the Army's 410M fleet. As part of the same contract award JCB also supplied ALC with 91 model 541-70 telescopic handlers. These are used for general palletised stores handling roles, having allowed some of the Case 721A and 721 BXT wheeled loaders to be re-roled from materials handling to a more general engineering role. These Case machines are now to be replaced by a fleet of JCB 436 wheeled loaders, 98 of which will be delivered during 2010.

British Army JCB 410M rough terrain forklift in travel configuration
(Shaun C Connors) 0109491

British Army JCB 410Ms, the right-hand machine being ready for deployment (Shaun C Connors) 0587652

Description
The JCB 410M is a military rough terrain forklift based on a modified wheeled loader platform and designed specifically to handle NATO pallets. It has a lift capacity of 1,815 kg. Developed for military use, the 410M has a low profile cab for air-portability and a higher travel speed to keep pace with military vehicles on the move; it can also be towed at convoy speeds. It has a forward-reach capability to allow loading and unloading from one side of a cargo truck or rail wagon. The operator's cab is on the front module to provide good visibility with minimum engine noise and vibration.

The JCB 410M is powered by a Perkins diesel engine developing 102 hp and coupled to a three-speed powershift transmission. Steering is by power-operated centre pivot articulation for increased manoeuvrability, this giving a 9.26 m maximum turning circle.

The JCB 410M can be fitted with a range of attachments such as buckets, crane hooks, sweepers and so on, to increase the machine's versatility. A NATO tow hitch is fitted as standard. Fully winterised and waterproofed versions were supplied.

Specifications
410M
Cab seating: 1
Configuration: 4 × 4
Weight: 6,850 kg
Length:
(overall) 5.625 m
(without forks) 4.5 m
Height: (top of cab) 2.67 m
Ground clearance: 400 mm
Track: 1.8 m
Wheelbase: 2.7 m
Angle of approach/departure: 45°/45°
Max speed: 57 km/h
Fuel capacity: 95 litres
Max gradient: 100%
Fording: 750 mm
Engine: Perkins T4.236 3.86-litre 4-cylinder in-line direct injection water-cooled diesel developing 102 hp (76 kW) at 2,600 rpm
Transmission: Clark 18000 series full power shift with 3 forward and 3 reverse gears
Steering: power-assisted
Turning radius: (outside tyres) 9.26 m
Tyres: 15.5/80R 20 Michelin XL
Brakes:
(main) hydraulic multidisc
(parking) axle-mounted disc on front differential shaft
Electrical system: 24 V
Batteries: 2 × 12 V, 96 Ah
Alternator: 40 A
Operating load: 1,815 kg at 610 mm

Status
Production complete. Previously supplied to the British Army (which have since been replaced) and the Royal Air Force (just a handful remain). Small numbers were exported to Oman, the USMC and other undisclosed customers.

Contractor
JCB Defence Products

Cargotec (Multilift) load handling systems

Development
Cargotec UK Limited, Government Business Operations, designs, manufactures supplies and supports a variety of loads handling solutions for military applications. The Hiab range includes Hiab cranes, Moffett

rough terrain portable forklifts, Multilift hooklift-type load handling systems and Zepro taillifts. This entry covers only Multilift load handling systems; details of Moffett rough terrain portable forklifts can be found elsewhere in this section.

Multilift was formed in 1949 in Finland. Multilift UK was set up in 1967 and the UK is currently home to the now Cargotec Limited's Government Business Operations. The Finnish Partek Corporation acquired Multilift in 1976; in 2002 the Finnish Kone Corporation acquired the group and renamed it Hiab.

Cargotec, with the brand Multilift, is a clear market leader for military application hooklift-type load handling systems. The generic term/acronym of load handling system/LHS is often used when referring to all types of hooklift-type load handling system.

Description

Multilift military hooklift-type load handling systems (14,000 - 20,000 kg capacity)

The Multilift range of military hooklift-type load handling systems has been developed specifically to meet the needs of the military end user. Consisting of two main types, pivoting and sliding, each type has its own specific advantages depending on the proposed usage profile. In 2005 Multilift changed and simplified the designations of its hooklift ranges, pivoting hooklifts now having the designation MPH (Military Pivoting Hooklift) and sliding hooklifts now having the designation MSH (Military Sliding Hooklift).

The Multilift MPH165, previously known as the Multilift Mark 4, is a high-performance pivoting load handling system for military vehicles of all mobility levels that, following an extensive trials programme, was selected for the British Army's DROPS (Demountable Rack Off-loading and Pick-up System) programme. DROPS entered service with the British Army in time to be combat tested and proven during Operation Desert Storm.

In response to US Army requirements, the then Multilift Mark 4 LHS was modified and fitted to the Oshkosh (10 × 10) PLS (Palletized Load System) chassis, becoming the Multilift Mark 5 LHS (now designated MPH165-PLS). The Mark 5/MPH165-PLS designation denotes the use of imperial measurements and sizes and not the standard metric. Further enhancements compared to the Mark 4 included a folding hook arm to bring the system within C-130 Hercules air transportable height constraints and a hydraulic system integrated with the chassis. The MPH165-PLS system is produced under licence by Oshkosh Truck and is currently fitted to the M1074 and M1075 PLS, M1120 HEMTT (Heavy Expanded Mobility Tactical Truck) and LVSR (Logistic Vehicle System Replacement).

A Mark 4 system modified with a folding hook arm for C-130 transport has been supplied to Ireland; this model retains the Mark 4/MPH165 designation.

The Mark 6 LHS (now designated MPH165-CBT) is a further development of the MPH165-PLS and has additional fixings and hydraulic couplings for the Bridge Adapter Pallet (BAP). This is fitted to M1977 CBT (Common Bridge Transporter) HEMTTs. By late 2006, around 5,800 MPH165-PLS (Mark 5) and (MPH165-CBT (Mark 6) systems, had been produced for the US Army's requirements.

The Multilift MPH range is based around commercially proven technologies, the overall system performance being improved by enhancing both below ground pick up and the ability to load misaligned flatracks, both important military operational requirements. The complete system is designed to be used in all operational conditions, including darkness or whilst wearing NBC protective equipment. An automatic, fully sequenced control system mounted in the cab aids operational safety and maximises speed, even under battle conditions.

The MPH range was designed and optimised to load, transport and unload flatracks conforming to the NATO standard (STANAG 2413). Flatracks can be pre-loaded at base with any military payload ready for dispersal to their required location. Payloads such as MLRS rockets, light armoured vehicles and command/control shelters can also be transported by using purpose built flatracks with the correct locking systems built in.

When, as with the British Army's DROPS or US Army's PLS, a prime mover of suitable capacity is used, the Multilift MPH165 LHS can transfer fully loaded flatracks to and from a suitable trailer, thus doubling the prime mover's payload, to up to 30,000 kg in the case of DROPS or PLS. The 165 of the Mark 4/5/6 revised designations denotes a 16,500 kg handling capacity, that figure including any flatrack or Container Handling Unit (CHU).

As of mid 2010, in excess of 12,000 Multilift MPH LHS were in service worldwide. In addition to small numbers supplied to other users, the company currently has fleets of vehicles in service with the following countries: Australia (from 2010); Canada (Kenworth (6 × 6) (withdrawn), Western Star (6 × 6), Steyr (6 × 6) and Mercedes-Benz Actros (8 × 8)); Czech and Slovak Republics (TATRA (6 × 6) and (8 × 8)); Estonia (MAN Cat 1 (8 × 8)); Ireland (ASTRA (8 × 8) and Scania (8 × 8)); Italy (ASTRA (8 × 4) and (8 × 8)); Malaysia (Roman (6 × 6)); Norway (Scania (8 × 6) and Mercedes-Benz (6 × 6)); Poland (Jelcz (8 × 4) and Volvo (6 × 6)); Singapore (Mercedes-Benz (8 × 8)); Spain (ASTRA (8 × 8)); UK (Foden (8 × 6) and Leyland (8 × 6)); US (Oshkosh HEMTT (8 × 8), PLS (10 × 10), LVSR (10 × 10) and Freightliner (6 × 4)).

A Dutch Army Scania R124CB8x8HZ420 (8 × 8) truck fitted with a Multilift MSH165SC Load Handling System (LHS) which includes integrated stowage for a Container Handling Unit (CHU) (Scania) 1116634

Sisu ETP (8 × 8) of the Lithuanian Army fitted with a Multilift MIH165SCA Load Handling System (LHS) (Shaun C Connors) 1296299

A Dutch Army Scania R124CB8x8HZ420 (8 × 8) truck fitted with a Multilift MSH165SC Load Handling System (LHS) which includes integrated stowage for a Container Handling Unit (CHU) (Scania) 1128244

A Canadian Army Western Star (6 × 6) Heavy Engineering Support Vehicle (HESV) fitted with a Multilift MPH165SC load handling system and dump module (Cargotec) 1128291

A Danish Army MAN F2000 family (8 × 8) truck fitted with a Multilift MSH165SC Load Handling System (LHS) (Cargotec)   1128293

A Polish Army Jelcz (8 × 6) truck fitted with a Multilift MPH165 Load Handling System (LHS) (Cargotec)   1128294

Cargotec now also produces military variants of its sliding type hooklift system, the MSH range. This solution gives the lowest possible installation height whilst maintaining most of the key military operating requirements, giving the best possible chance to carry ISO 668 1C and 1CC containers on a military chassis within the 4 m European road regulations height limit.

Recent deliveries of the MSH range systems have included 122 MSH165 systems (delivery ongoing) to Denmark, 157 MSH165SC systems to Germany (from early 2008), MSH165 systems to Switzerland on a framework contract between 2007-2013, 41 MIH165SCA to Lithuania during (2007-2009), 548 examples to the Netherlands (MSH165SC) during 2004/2005, and most recently, around 170 examples to the UK on the MAN HX55 (8 × 8) chassis under three separate UOR procurements. Previous deliveries of MSH range systems under the earlier designation system are known to have been made to Belgium (TSH230) and Denmark (TSH230), the 230 denoting depth of the LHS frame.

In total, around 2,200 MSH LHS examples are in service with a number of countries including: Belgium (IVECO (8 × 4)); Denmark (IVECO (8 × 8) and MAN (8 × 8)); Finland (Sisu (8 × 8)); Netherlands (Scania (8 × 8) and DAF (6 × 6)); Switzerland (IVECO (6 × 6) and (8 × 8)); Sweden (Scania (6 × 6), (8 × 6), (8 × 8) and Volvo (6 × 6)); UK (MAN 8 × 8).

Recent enhancements to both Multilifts' ranges of military hooklifts include the ability to specify an ISO container handling unit as standard along with a stowage system for the container lifting frame giving a true dual purpose load carrier. Where necessary this assembly can also be made to fold to meet air transportability requirements. Using the MPH165 as an example, so-equipped hooklifts carry the following designations: MPH165S allows for stowage of the CHU behind the cab; MPH165C includes a CHU and rear roller assembly as standard; MPH165A has a folding hook arm with the possibility to, for air-transport, transport a CHU as a lie-flat load. MIH denotes the hooklift is integrated into the chassis frame rails for reduced overall height.

Various combinations can be specified.

Multilift medium and small military hooklift-type load handling systems (2,000 - 14,000 kg capacity)

Multilift has also developed and produced a series of specialist medium and small hooklift LHS to compliment the larger 16,500, 19,000 and 20,000 kg capacity systems. These systems allow lighter payloads to be introduced into the logistic system on vehicles with lower capacity.

The Multilift MPH080 is an 8,000 kg capacity military load handling system that can be specified either with or without integrated CHU, this system is designed to handle the same size standard payload modules as

An Oshkosh M1120 (8 × 8) Heavy Expanded Mobility Tactical Truck (HEMTT) fitted with a Multilift Mark 5 Load Handling System (LHS) on which the folding hook arm (to enable air-transport by C-130 Hercules transport aircraft) is clearly visible. Following a 2005 redesignation by the company the Mark 5 LHS is now known as the MPH165-PLS, this defining Military Pivoting Hooklift (MPH), 16,500 kg handling capacity, including any flatrack or Container Handling Unit (CHU), and Palletized Load System (PLS) (Shaun C Connors)   0126577

IVECO EuroTrakker (6 × 6) truck of the Swiss Army fitted with a Multilift HLZ Load Handling System (LHS) cross-loading a drawbar-type trailer. The HLZ is a commercial system with a limited amount of militarisation (Cargotec)   0121899

the larger MPH165 on lower capacity chassis. Developed by Multilift as an additional variant for the US Army FMTV programme on the Stewart and Stevenson (now BAE Systems and Oshkosh) chassis its interface means it can also be installed on any other suitable vehicle.

A Multilift 2,000 kg capacity hooklift, the HL2M, has been produced for Canada, Norway, and Sweden to be installed on the Hägglunds Bv 206. This small hooklift handles a standardised NATO payload module described in STANAG 2413, which is one-third the size of the standard NATO flatrack.

Other load sizes evaluated by Multilift include one-quarter and two-third length modules allowing hooklift systems to be fitted to chassis with any known axle configuration or payload requirement.

Container Handling Unit (CHU)

Multilift pioneered the development of the ISO Container Handling Unit (CHU) and, when used in conjunction with a Multilift LHS (either MSH or MPH), the Container Handling Unit (CHU) allows the transportation of 20 ft (6 m) ISO 668 1C and 1CC freight containers.

The Multilift Container Handling Units (CHU) consists of a lifting frame and rear roller assembly. The lifting frame attaches to the front or rear of a container using self-aligning locking pins providing the load handling system (LHS) with the correct loading interface. The lifting frame is height adjustable to cater for both 8 ft (2.438 m) and 8 ft 6 in (2.59 m) containers. The CHU rear roller assembly is designed to guide and support the container during the loading and unloading operations. The design of the rollers enables a wide variety of containers and containerized facilities that have been designed around the ISO footprint to be handled, while recognizing the many different configurations available. Fixed twistlocks at the rear and flexible couplings at the front secure the container during transit so that overall vehicle mobility is not degraded.

The CHU eliminates the requirement for an intermediate flatrack to be used when carrying an ISO container; therefore, lower overall height and increased payload is achieved. A Multilift LHS when fitted with a CHU can still handle standard military flatracks. The configuration between container and flatrack mode is quick and simple and can be carried out by one man without the assistance of specialized tools.

The latest military load handling systems from the Multilift range allow the CHU to be specified as an integrated function; this allows flatracks to be handled while the container lifting frame is stowed on the chassis adding even more flexibility to vehicles within the logistic fleet.

Irish Army IVECO 8 × 8 chassis fitted with a Multilift Mark 4 LHS (load handling system); following a 2005 redesignation by the company the Mark 4 LHS is now known as the MPH165, this defining Military Pivoting Hooklift (MPH) and 16,500 kg handling capacity, including any flatrack or Container Handling Unit (CHU). The Irish Army also operates 15 Scania 8 × 8 chassis fitted with a Multilift MPH165SC LHS. The MPH165SC features an integral CHU and stowage (between LHS and cab) for the CHU when not in use (Cargotec) 0121900

Multilift Mark 6 LHS (load handling system) and BAP (Bridge Adapter Pallet) launching a Ribbon Bridge module from an Oshkosh Heavy Expanded Mobility Tactical Truck (HEMTT) (8 × 8). Following a 2005 redesignation by the company the Mark 6 LHS is now known as the MPH165-CBT, this defining Military Pivoting Hooklift (MPH), 16,500 kg handling capacity, including any flatrack or Container Handling Unit (CHU), and Common Bridge Transporter (CBT) (Cargotec) 0121903

Over 4,000 Multilift military LHS units are now in service fitted with a CHU system.

Hooklift-based Ribbon Bridge deployment and retrieval systems
Cargotec have supplied a number of Multilift MPH165-CBT (previously designated Mark 6) LHS equipped with Ribbon Bridge launch and retrieval modules for the Canadian and US military. This hooklift system is modified from the standard Multilift MPH165 (Mark 4) equipment to allow it to interface with a Multilift Bridge Adapter Pallet (BAP). The BAP is an interface flatrack with all the necessary guides, rollers, locks and winches for Ribbon Bridge unit handling.

Mounted on the Oshkosh M1977 (8 × 8) HEMTT in the US, the system is in service with the US Army's Improved Ribbon Bridge Program. Using the Multilift LHS combined with the BAP, full bridge and combat support boat launching and retrieval capability is possible.

Cargotec supplied 48 MSH165 systems to the Netherlands adapted to carry Bridge Adapter Pallets (BAPs) for use with the Royal Netherlands Army Ribbon Bridge system and Damen bridge erection boats.

Full flatrack handling functionality is retained by vehicles equipped with the BAP system.

Tipping load handling systems
A total of 75 Multilift High Capacity Tipping Hooklift MPH165T (previously designated Mark 4T) LHS were supplied to the UK Royal Engineers. This enhanced product combines the performance characteristics and interoperability of the Multilift MPH165 LHS with an additional 20,000 kg tipping capability. The chassis-mounted double-acting cylinders provide speed and performance comparable with specialised earthmoving vehicles, tipping the engineer skip-body to angles in excess of 60 degrees in less than 15 seconds.

Multilift commercial load handling systems
Multilift also has an extensive range of commercial load handling systems. The Multilift range of hooklift load handling systems are suitable for 2-, 3- and 4-axle rigid chassis mounting and have lifting capacities from 2,000 to

Detail view of a Multilift Mark 4 LHS as fitted to a British Army Leyland DROPS (8 × 6) Medium Mobility Load Carrier (MMLC). Following a 2005 redesignation by the company the Mark 4 LHS is now known as the MPH165, this defining Military Pivoting Hooklift (MPH) and 16,500 kg handling capacity, including any flatrack or Container Handling Unit (CHU) (Shaun C Connors) 1124788

Bv 206S fitted with a Multilift HL2M Load Handling System (LHS) (Cargotec) 0121902

40,000 kg. These systems lend themselves to being modified to meet more specific military requirements. The range includes hooklifts with both sliding and pivoting actions, with both tipping and non-tipping variants. All systems are hydraulically operated from within the cab, with full locking, warning and fail-safe facilities.

Status
In production. In excess of 15,000 Multilift load handling systems of all types (including around 200 HL2M 2,000 kg capacity systems) have been supplied to at least 23 armed forces since deliveries of the Mark 4 DROPS system commenced to the British Army prior to Operation Desert Storm in 1991. The bulk of those delivered, around 12,000 systems, are military-specific (MPH - Military Pivoting Hooklift) systems. Multilift LHS are known to have been supplied (or are being supplied) to the armed forces of: Australia; Belgium (IVECO (8 × 4) 24); Bulgaria (Mercedes-Benz 12 est.); Canada (Kenworth (6 × 6), Western Star (6 × 6), Steyr (6 × 6) >250, Mercedes-Benz (8 × 8) 43); Czech and Slovak Republics (TATRA (6 × 6) (8 × 8) 220 est.); Denmark (IVECO (8 × 8) 20 est. and MAN (8 × 8) 130 est.); Estonia (MAN Cat 1 (8 × 8)) ; Finland (Scania/Sisu 225 est.); Germany (MAN SX); Hungary; Indonesia (UN-supplied Leyland DROPS 7); Ireland (ASTRA (8 × 8) 22 and Scania (8 × 8) 15); Italy (ASTRA (8 × 4) and (8 × 8) >435); Kuwait; Lithuania (Sisu (8 × 8) 41); Malaysia (Roman (6 × 6) <20 and UN-supplied Leyland DROPS 10); Netherlands (Scania (8 × 8) 548 including 48 BAPs and DAF (6 × 6) 64); Norway (Mercedes-Benz (6 × 6) 40 est., Scania (8 × 6) 25 est., and Volvo (6 × 6) 15 est.); Pakistan (Renault); Poland (Jelcz (8 × 4) >40 and Volvo >35); Romania; Singapore (Mercedes-Benz (8 × 8) 130); Spain (ASTRA (8 × 8) 3); Sweden (Scania (6 × 6) (8 × 6) (8 × 8) and Volvo (6 × 6) >1,000); Switzerland (IVECO (6 × 6) (8 × 8)); UK (Leyland (8 × 6) 1,613, Foden (8 × 6) 404, and Terex (6 × 6) 75); US (Oshkosh HEMTT (8 × 8), LVSR (10 × 10) and PLS (10 × 10) 5,800 est., FMTV (6 × 6) and Freightliner (6 × 4)).

Contractor
Hiab Limited, Government Business Operations

Cargotec (Moffett) rough terrain portable forklifts

Development
Moffett rough terrain portable forklifts are a military adaptation of the commercially available Moffett truck mounted forklifts.

Moffett forklifts are widely used by defence forces and are deployed on peacekeeping/enforcing type operations and in areas inaccessible to conventional forklift trucks; they also have a towing capacity.

A Moffett E2-3T of the Danish Army (Shaun C Connors)   1296298

The Moffett rough terrain portable forklift is in service with the British Army Air Corp in the role of ammunition tender for the Apache attack helicopter (Cargotec)   1128729

Description

The manufacturer states that Moffett machines are simple to drive and easy to operate; all wheels can be hydrostatically driven and automatic differential locking can be fitted to ensure a rough terrain capability. A fully enclosed ROPS/FOPS cab with heating and ventilation can also be fitted, although open, roll-cage variants are the more common requirement.

Power is normally provided by Kubota diesel engines that can be specified to be capable of operating on Avtur F34 if required. Standard lifting capacities range from 1,500 to 3,500 kg, engines up to 50 hp, and it can lift up to heights of 3 m. Special models to meet specific customer requirements may also be produced.

Since 1998 one specialist type of Moffett has been in service with the British Army Air Corps as the ammunition tender and towing tractor for the Apache Attack Helicopter. It is designed to Explosive Safety and Transport Committee Guidelines (Category C) for handling ammunition in bunker areas. General material and pallet handling tasks can be carried out along with many more specialist duties. In use, the load is retracted within the truck footprint to give maximum overall stability. For transportation the machine can self-mount/de-mount to a grounded NATO flatrack. It can also self-mount to the rear of a truck fitted with a simple modification kit. In either case the machine can easily be transported at convoy speed. Forklifts in the Moffett range are also air transportable by the majority of NATO helicopters and transport aircraft.

Multidirectional (four-way) Moffet's are in service with the RAF and RNAF for the handling of missile containers and/or missiles in and around airfield ammunition storage bunkers. They are also available for the distribution and handling of missiles in the field.

In 1996 the RNAF began using Moffett's for logistic duties in the former Yugoslavia, these carried by the DAF YAC 2300 (6 × 6) 10,000 kg truck. In service with the Royal Netherlands Navy, the vehicle is used for the distribution and handling of gas bottle racks.

The Swedish Air Force has been using machines for tactical services since 1983 where they have also been used to tow mortars and supply ammunition from carrier trucks to the mortar.

Recent innovations have allowed a model to be designed specifically to fill and empty containers. The Moffett M9S with its low overall carriage height and all-wheel drive, has the unique ability to work inside ISO containers. This dramatically increases efficiency and reduces transport complexity. With a high proportion of front line stores and munitions being supplied in 6 or 12 meter containers, unloading heavy items from inside can prove to be an arduous task. Using a Moffett M9S Destuffer allows unloading to take place safely and quickly.

The Moffett MS9 container de-stuffer (Cargotec)   1128727

Status

In production. In service with the British Army Air Corps, Denmark, Malaysia, Netherlands (Army, Navy and Air Force), Norway, Oman and Sweden (Air Force).

Contractor

Hiab Limited, Government Business Operations.

Hyster forklift trucks

Development

Hyster started as a small manufacturer of winches and lifting machines used in the logging and timber industry of the United States' Pacific Northwest. In 1989 Hyster was purchased by NACCO Industries Ltd. In 2009 Hyster celebrated it 80th anniversary.

Hyster tailors its range offering to the preferences of major world markets, so the selection of models and configurations proposed will depend on the region of sale. The following text is relevant to European market.

Description

Hyster materials handling equipment comprises over 80 models of forklift truck, reach stackers for container and swap-body handling. The lift trucks have capacities from 1,000 to 48,000 kg, using electric and internal combustion engine power. The trucks covered in this entry are manufactured at three plants in Europe: Irvine and Craigavon in the UK and Nijmegen in the Netherlands.

The Fortens and Fortens Advance ranges of trucks comprises LPG or diesel engine powered pneumatic-tyred trucks. The range extends from the H1.6FT, which can handle loads up to 1,600 kg at 500 mm, to the H9.0FT6 which can handle loads up to 9,000 kg at 600 mm. Above this is the diesel-powered Big Trucks range which can handle anything from 8,000 kg up to fully laden containers, swap-bodies and semi-trailers weighing up to 48,000 kg. Included in the range are trucks with dedicated laden and empty containers handling attachments.

The Electric Range has capacities of from 1,000 to 5,500 kg. Trucks in the 1,500 to 3,200 kg capacity range have the option of cushion or pneumatic shaped tyres. For extra manoeuvrability, 1,000 to 2,000 kg models are available in three-wheel configuration. The SpaceSaver range of LPG powered trucks, running on cushion tyres, is specially designed to operate in confined spaces. Capacities are from 1,500 to 7,000 kg.

Hyster forklift truck of the US Air Force (US DoD)   1391287

Hyster forklift on the flight deck of the Nimitz-class aircraft carrier USS Dwight D. Eisenhower (CVN 69) (US DoD (Rafael Figueroa Medina)) 1391288

A range of over 40 warehouse trucks is also available, forming a complete line from pallet trucks and reach trucks to man-up VNA trucks for high-density storage.

Status
In production. Hyster has provided the British armed forces with some 1,200 trucks from its range during the last 16 years. Hyster trucks are in service with the US military and other defence forces.

Enquiries to
Hyster Europe Limited

Linde forklift trucks

Description
Linde Material Handling (UK) Limited is part of the Linde Group which is one of the leading manufacturers of forklift trucks and warehouse equipment in the world. Linde has factories in France, Germany, Italy and the UK.

Linde Material Handling (UK) manufactures an extensive range of materials handling equipment, ranging from 1,000 to 52,000 kg capacity in both battery electric and internal combustion engine forms. Products cater for virtually every form of materials handling from hand pallet trucks to the stacking of heavy ISO containers.

Several models have been the subject of UK MoD 'Best Buy' agreements, the reach truck, sea-going counterbalanced forklift truck and the shipboard pallet truck being the prime examples. Linde Material Handling remains an approved supplier to the UK MoD under the terms of the current Enabling Arrangement for engine-powered trucks.

The company has production plants in the UK as well as in Germany and France. In the UK, the factories are registered to BS EN ISO 9001:2000 in quality-control systems. Maintenance and spares support services are available, as are training courses for operators, engineers and instructors.

Status
Numerous models in production and in service worldwide, including with the British armed forces and the US Army, Navy and Air Force.

Contractor
Linde Material Handling (UK) Limited

Reynolds Boughton DROPS/PLS

Description
Reynolds Boughton Limited produces a wide range of DROPS/PLS hooklift-type load handling system equipment, including flatracks, trailers and load handling systems. Reynolds Boughton load handling systems are currently available in three equipment sizes with lift capacities ranging from 12,000 to 22,000 kg. Current systems feature the latest sliding jib technology for a better centre of gravity positioning leading to greater stability during loading and unloading, and are compatible with the in-service Reynolds Boughton MLRS trailer and latest tandem- and tri-axle trailer designs

All variants can accommodate a ground height difference of 500 mm between the load and the loading vehicle, and are available with rear support jacks as an option for high load operations, or when operating on extreme ground conditions. All variants are capable of carrying out cross-loading between truck and trailer.

In addition to palletised/flatrack loads all variants can accommodate a variety of load types to either DIN or CHEM standards including tipper bodies. When used in conjunction with the Reynolds Boughton tandem axle trailer a 40,000 kg gross train weight (GTW) can be achieved, or when used with the Reynolds Boughton tri-axle trailer a 44,000 GTW can be achieved.

The 8/32 22,000 kg lift capacity variant has been mounted on a frame-steer all-terrain chassis for final deliveries of palletised loads in extreme conditions.

Specifications

	8/32 variant	6/26 variant	4/19 variant
Lift capacity	22,000 kg	16,000 kg	12,000 kg
Installed weight	3,300 kg	3,000 kg	2,170 kg
Max flatrack length	7 m	6.1 m	6.1 m
Load cycle time	40 seconds	35 seconds	35 seconds

Status
In production. Supplied to Ireland (withdrawn from service), Tanzania, Thailand and the United States .

Contractor
Reynolds Boughton Limited

United States

Case rough-terrain forklift trucks

Development
The Case Corporation no longer manufactures purpose-designed military vehicles such as those covered in this entry, now specialising in the customising of their commercial equipment range to meet military requirement. Full details of the current Case commercial range of products and details of specific customisation contracts can be found elsewhere in this section.

The Case Corporation is currently resetting at least 300 M4K rough terrain forklifts for TACOM, and has previously supplied 500 engine re-power kits for the M4K rough terrain forklift.

A program to replace the Case M4K rough-terrain forklift truck is currently running.

Description
The Case M4K rough-terrain forklift truck was designed to load and unload material from ISO containers. The fork free lift, side shift and vehicle dimensions allow the forklift to enter a container and pick or place loads. Adequate side shift is provided to place loads against either wall of a container. The M4K-B is towable with standard drawbar and safety equipment. Canopies or cabs were provided with ROPS and FOPS meeting the then latest international requirements. Lift and tie-down brackets are standard equipment and designed for parachute delivery or helicopter transport. The vehicle is fitted with high-flotation tyres and standard driving and blackout lights. Other features include hydraulic fork rotation and front and rear axle disconnects for towing.

The M6K articulated rough-terrain forklift has reach for loading trucks from one side. Features include power rotation, side shifting and fork spacing. The unit has been tested and is in service in saltwater applications, both onshore and shipboard.

The M13K articulated rough-terrain forklift is designed with the primary mission of loading and unloading cargo aircraft such as the C-130. The forks can be equipped with conveyor ramps that match aircraft cargo systems. The cab, load guard and counterweight may be removed enabling the unit to be transported by C-130 aircraft.

The M6K-B and M13K have a parallel linkage system, which ensures that the forks remain in a level position throughout the lift arc. The M13K is also equipped with the necessary safety equipment for handling nuclear systems.

A Case M4K (MHE-237) rough-terrain forklift of the US Army operating in Afghanistan (Carl Schulze)   1391283

Specifications

M4K
Cab seating: 1
Configuration: 4 × 4
Weight: (without load) 4,536 kg
Length: 5.35 m
Height: (cab/canopy) 2.03 m
Width: 2.01 m
Ground clearance: 334 mm
Wheelbase: 2.34 m
Engine: Case 4-390 water-cooled 4-stroke diesel developing 66 hp (49 kW) at 2,200 rpm
Gearbox: fully automatic powershift with 3 forward and 3 reverse gears
Max road speed: 35.9 km/h
Brakes: hydraulic disc
Tyres: 15 × 19.5
Electrical system: 24 V
Forklift capacity rated: 1,814 kg at 610 mm
Max lift height: 2.54 m
Tilt:
(forward) 11°
(back) 22°
Side shift: (left/right) 559/559 mm
Fork rotation: (total) 22°

Status

M4K (MHE-237), M6K and M13K, production complete; over 3,000 Case M-series military rough-terrain forklifts were supplied to US armed forces. The M4K (MHE-237) remains in service with the US Army (at least 670 in 2004). The M6K and M6K-B were supplied to the US Navy. The M13K and M10K were supplied to the US Air Force.

Contractor

Case Corporation

Caterpillar 988 50K/50,000 lb (22,680 kg) Rough Terrain Container Handler (RTCH)

Development

The 50K Rough Terrain Container Handler (RTCH) is a non-developmental item that is a military unique integration of commercial components. The base vehicle is a Caterpillar 988B wheeled loader (later 988F) mated with a Caterpillar model AH60 60,000 lb capacity forklift mast. The RTCH is used in conjunction with assorted top handler attachments for handling standard dimension ISO containers weighing up to 25 US tons (22,680 kg). The primary use of the RTCH is in holding and marshalling areas and by supply, ammunition and transportation units.

In competition with three other manufacturers, Caterpillar was awarded a USD89 million contract from the then US Army Mobility Equipment Research and Development Command (MERADCOM) in September 1978 for initial production of the 50K RTCH. Under this contract 320 examples at a unit cost of USD159,138 were delivered to the US Army between late 1981 and early 1985. The top handlers used in conjunction with the RTCH were produced by ROPCO under subcontract to Caterpillar and were fielded concurrently.

As options to the original RTCH contract the USAF procured three machines for use with the Containerized Ammunition Distribution System (CADS) shipments, and the USMC purchased 21 machines initially, increasing their quantity to a total of 106 by awarding a contract for additional RTCHs that were fielded in FY 88. These later machines are slightly different to the original Army vehicles. In FY 89 the USAF received nine additional vehicles.

In March 1997, TACOM exercised a further contract option and purchased an additional 43 RTCHs based on the Caterpillar model 988F wheeled loader. Twenty-five of these vehicles were supplied with 40 ft top handlers, 18 with 20 ft top handlers.

An 11 year estimated useful life span was initially forecast for the RTCH. This was revised to 15 years in 1992 based on continued reliability and supportability of the RTCH at that time as well as experience from other rough terrain material handling equipment. As of mid-2005 Caterpillar had refurbished the entire fleet of 988B machines for the US Army and Marines.

The US Army placed an initial order with Kalmar RT Centre LLC in April 2000 for the delivery of up to 500 purpose-designed Kalmar Rough Terrain Container Handlers (RTCH); deliveries under a follow-on contract continue. By the summer of 2009, 715 machines had been delivered to all users (including FMS transactions). Full details of the Kalmar RTCH can be found elsewhere in this section.

Description

The original 50K RTCH is based on the commercial Caterpillar model 988B wheeled loader, later models are based on the Caterpillar 988F wheeled loader. The base wheeled loader, minus lifting arms and bucket, is mated to a Caterpillar model AH60 (60,000 lb capacity) forklift mast. The mast is used in conjunction with assorted top handlers for the handling of 20 ft (6.096 m), 35 ft (10.67 m) and 40 ft (12.19 m) ISO-width (8 ft) containers, up

Caterpillar 988B RTCH operating on deployed operations (Carl Schulze)
1391293

Caterpillar 988B RTCH following a complete rebuild by Caterpillar (Caterpillar)
0536664

to 9 ft (2.74 m) high and 50,000 lb (22,680 kg) in weight. In its standard configuration, the RTCH can stack containers two high or place them on rail or transport trucks. The RTCH's mast is equipped with carriage side shift, as well as mast tilt; lifting pins are locked in place when a container is being handled.

Two non-standard variants of the RTCH have also been supplied to the US Army. A forklift kit was issued during the initial fielding that enabled so-equipped machines to operate as a 50K rough terrain forklift. Only one US Army facility, Fort Eustis, is known to have operated so-modified RTCHs. The second RTCH variant involves the installation of a low mount fork assembly that enables the RTCH to lift half-height (4 ft 3 in) containers. A contract for the low mount fork assembly was awarded to Caterpillar in March 1992 by Volpe National Transportation System Center and 62 kits were fielded between April and September 1992.

Being based on a conventional machine the RTCH follows the general concept of a wheeled loading shovel; i.e. steering by frame articulation, unsprung with an oscillating rear axle being employed to maintain ground contact on undulating terrain. One specific military requirement called for the modification of the base machine to operate in seawater up to 1.52 m (60 in) deep, as it may have to operate at beachheads. Non-standard radial tyres are fitted to provide the compromise of flotation on sand and traction in mud.

Specifications

Caterpillar 988F Series II
Cab seating: 1
Configuration: 4 × 4
Weight:
(with 40 ft top handler) 53,050 kg
Length: 10.731 m
Width:
(over tyres) 3.555 m
Height:
(top of cab) 4.115 m
Ground clearance: 403 mm
Fuel capacity: 624.5 litres
Engine: Caterpillar 3408E HEUI water-cooled 4-stroke diesel developing 430 hp at 2,000 rpm
Steering: centre-point frame articulation, hydraulic, steering angle 30°
Tyres: 35/65-30PR
Brakes: hydraulic on all wheels

Status

In service with the US Air Force, Army and Marine Corps (see text for details).

Contractor

Caterpillar Inc.

Entwistle model 8909 and 9609 rough terrain forklift trucks

Development
These rough terrain forklift trucks were developed by The Entwistle Company of the United States primarily for the specialist mission of loading and unloading ISO containers in a variety of adverse operating conditions. The model 9609 is essentially an improved version of the model 8909. An earlier machine, the Entwistle 8606 (manufactured by Defense Technology Corporation) was supplied to the USMC.

Over 900 model 8909 and 9609 machines have been produced, this figure including some 200 machines manufactured for export. A total of 600 model 8909 have been supplied to US armed forces, and over 130 model 9609 have been supplied to the US Navy. These machines are air-transportable by C-130 Hercules.

Description
Motive power for the model 9609 is provided by a diesel engine driving two or all four (selectable) wheels through a full powershift transmission. Steering modes include two or four-wheel, or crab-steer. Fording depth is 910 mm.

Kerb weight is 5,750 kg, maximum lift is 2,000 kg at a 600 mm load centre, and maximum lift height is 3 m; the carriage has a 1.12 m side-shift capability.

Status
Model 8909, production complete. Model 9609, production as required. In service with US and other armed forces. Over 900 machines have been produced, over 200 of these for export customers.

Contractor
The Entwistle Company

An Entwistle rough terrain forklift at Sharana Airfield, Forward Operating Base Sharana, Paktika province, Afghanistan during 2010 (US DoD (Russell Hampsey))   1391285

An Entwistle rough terrain forklift of the US Army's 4th Battalion, 9th Infantry Regiment at Nasar Wasalam, Iraq during December 2009 (US DoD (Advin Illa-Medina))   1391286

Grove TMS300-5 25 ton crane

Development
Grove Manufacturing Company, the predecessor to Grove Worldwide, was founded in 1947. It's first products were by rubber-tired farm wagons. Cranes were introduced into the commercial marketplace in 1952. In 2002 the then Grove Worldwide was acquired by the Manitowoc Company, Inc.

Grove TMS300-5 25 ton crane (Grove)   0525658

Manitowoc is one of the world's largest producers of mobile cranes and access equipment, and is a supplier of cranes and lifting equipment to the military worldwide. The company currently produces an extensive range of truck-mounted, all-terrain, rough terrain and industrial cranes. Full details of the current range can be found elsewhere in this section.

Cranes supplied by Manitowoc for military applications are essentially commercial products with limited militarisation. It should also be noted that as with other commercial crane manufactures, Manitowoc regularly updates its product range.

The USMC equivalent to the Grove TMS300-5, is known as the High Speed High Mobility Crane (HSHMC) 25-ton. This was manufactured by the Harnischfeger Corporation and 130 examples were acquired during the mid-1980s.

Description
The Grove TMS300-5 25 ton crane is an example of a truck-mounted crane modified for military applications. This particular model is no longer available, the four current truck-mounted cranes offered by Manitowoc being the; 40 tonne capacity three-axle (6 × 4) TM500E-2, the 40-tonne capacity Scania four-axle (8 × 4) (with rear tridem) TMC540, the 50-55 tonne capacity four-axle (8 × 4) TMS700E, the 70 tonne capacity four-axle (8 × 4) TMS800E and the 90 tonne capacity four-axle (8 × 4) TMS9000E.

The TMS300-5 consists of a hydraulically-operated telescopic crane with a full 360° traverse mounted on an eight wheeled (8 × 4) carrier vehicle. The operator controls the crane from an electric control panel in the superstructure cab. Four outriggers are used to stabilise the crane in operation. The crane is used by engineer units in the construction and repair of roads, airfields, pipelines and bridges and can also be used for port, marine and beach facilities. In addition to lifting, it can also be used for pile-driving and clamshell operations.

Specifications
TMS300-5
Weight: 28,250 kg
Length: (travelling) 12.8 m
Width : (travelling) 2.44 m

Crane
Boom length: 2-section hydraulically-extended boom with third lattice section, giving total length of 24.4 m
Counterweight: 4,310 kg
Capacity: (max) 25,400 kg

Carrier
Configuration: 8 × 4, front 2 axles steer only
Engine: GM 6-71N 4-stroke diesel, developing 203 hp (151 kW) at 2,100 rpm
Transmission: Fuller Roadranger RTO 613, providing 13 forward and 3 reverse gears
Tyres:
  (front) 11.00 × 20, 14 ply
  (rear) 11.00 × 20, 12 ply

Status
Production complete. 133 delivered to the US Army.

Contractor
Grove Worldwide

JLG All-Terrain Lifter Army System (ATLAS) and ATLAS II

Development
In May 1995 the former TRAK International Inc. announced that it had been awarded a contract by the now Tank-automotive and Armaments COMmand (TACOM) to supply the US Army's then next-generation of

	ATLAS	ATLAS II
Cab seating:	1	1
Configuration:	4 × 4	4 × 4
Weight: (operating with driver and max fuel)		
(with 6K carriage)	13,920 kg	n/avail
(with 10K carriage)	14,520 kg	n/avail
Length:	9.1 m	9 m
Width:	2.6 m	2.4 m
Height:	2.7 m	2.6 m
Ground clearance:	360 mm	360 mm
Track:	2 m	2 m
Wheelbase:	3.2 m	3.2 m
Fuel capacity:	167 litres	227 litres
Fuel:	diesel, JP-5 or JP-8	diesel, JP-5, JP-8, Jet A, Jet A-1, NATO F-34
Gradient:	100%	100%
Fording:	910 mm	910 mm
Climatic operational range:	−32 to +49°C	−32 to +49°C
Engine:	Cummins 6BT 5.9-C165-litre 6-cylinder in-line turbocharged water-cooled 5.9-litre 4-stroke diesel developing 165 hp (123 kW) at 2,500 rpm	John Deere PE4045 HF485 4-cylinder turbocharged and water-cooled diesel developing 173 hp (129 kW) at 2,500 rpm
Transmission:	Funk Power Shift 1700 Series with 3 forward and 3 reverse speeds	Funk Power Shift 1744M110B with 4 forward and 3 reverse speeds
Steering:	3 steer modes: all-wheel, front-wheel and crab	3 steer modes: all-wheel, front-wheel and crab
Turning radius:	4.1 m	4.6 m
Axles:	Rockwell PSC-205, no-spin differential, front	Axletech PSOC 205 HOB, no-spin differential, front
Suspension:	unsprung, rigid front, oscillating rear	unsprung, rigid front, oscillating rear
Tyres:	17.5 × 25, 16-ply	17.5 × 25, 20-ply
Brakes:	discs, dry	discs, dry
Lift performance:		
(lift capacity)	4,536 kg	4,536 kg
(reach below grade)	800 mm	840 mm
(reach from front tyres to 609 mm load centre)	7.4 m	7.9 m

TRAK All-Terrain Lifter Army System (ATLAS) of the US Army in Iraq; this vehicle is fitted with a cab armouring kit (Carl Schulze) 1296248

TRAK All-Terrain Lifter Army System (ATLAS) (Shaun C Connors) 1296167

military variable reach rough terrain forklift trucks. The US Army defines the forklift as an 'All-Terrain Lifter Army System' (ATLAS). Between 1990 and 1995, TRAK International supplied the US armed forces' with over 2,200 of the previous generation vehicle, the TRAK 6000M Variable Reach Rough Terrain Fork-Lift Truck (VRRFLT). The ATLAS is a further development of the 6000M design, full details of which can be found elsewhere in this section.

The primary military mission requirement of the ATLAS is the unloading, transporting and loading containers, boxes and palletised ammunition loads. The ATLAS is capable of mobility over rough terrain and in addition to rail or sea transport, is transportable in C-130 Hercules aircraft. The ATLAS forklift is specifically designed to handle the US Air Force 463L pallet and other large size payloads. It also has the capability of accepting dual carriages, 2,724 kg (6,000 lb) at a 609 mm load centre, and 4,540 kg (10,000 lb) at 1.219 m load centre, utilising a quick attach feature.

Production of the ATLAS commenced in 1997 and by June 2008, over 2,500 vehicles had been fielded to US Army and Army Reserve units. During that period, OmniQuip International Inc. (a management buy out of TRAK International) merged with Textron Inc. (in 1999), and in August 2003, JLG Industries Inc. announced the acquisition of the OmniQuip business unit.

In addition to US armed forces', ATLAS machines have been supplied to Afghanistan (more than 100), and small numbers to Egypt, Korea and Turkey. From around June 2006 an undisclosed number of machines were supplied to Iraq. A number of US Army machines have been up-armoured for use in Iraq and later Afghanistan.

JLG industries Inc. announced the acquisition of the OmniQuip business unit of Textron Inc. in August 2003.

In August 2004, JLG Industries Inc. was awarded a three-year, 700-machine contract to reset to pre-deployment (to Afghanistan and Iraq) condition US armed forces' ATLAS and TRAK 6000M machines.

The then Oshkosh Truck Corporation announced in October 2006 that it would purchase JLG Industries Inc. for around USD3.2 billion.

The US Army's next-generation military variable reach rough terrain forklift requirement contract award, known as ATLAS II, was made in January 2007 to JLG Industries Inc.. Valued at USD102.2 million, the award called for 566 machines to be delivered over five years.

Description

The ATLAS vehicle has a one-person enclosed cab that provides the operator with protection from roll-over and falling objects. Air-conditioning is standard. There is a full-time planetary 4 × 4 drive with dry disc brakes and the front axle is equipped with a 'no-spin' differential and parking brake. The vehicle is unsprung, an oscillating rear axle accounting for ground undulations.

The hydraulically actuated forks are located at the articulating end of a telescopic three stage welded box-section boom constructed from high-strength alloy steel. The maximum reach from the front tyres to the load centre is 7.4 m for ATLAS, 7.9 m for ATLAS II, and maximum lift capacity is 4,536 kg. The frame tilt angle is 9° left or right.

For air-transportability by C-130 Hercules aircraft, the detachable rear-mounted three-piece counterweight allows for flight preparation in under 15 minutes.

As with the vast majority of telescopic handler-type vehicles, the ATLAS can accept a variety of alternative attachments including a fork-mounted bucket.

Specifications - See table on previous page

Status
ATLAS production complete, over 2,500 delivered to the US Army. ATLAS also supplied to Afghanistan (more than 100), Egypt, Iraq, South Korea and Turkey. Contract award for follow-on ATLAS II machine, made in January 2007.

Contractor
JLG Industries Inc.

JLG Millennia Military Vehicle (MMV)

Development
In April 2001, the then OmniQuip International was awarded a contract by the US Marine Corps System Command to supply the US Marine Corps' next generation of Extended Boom ForkLifts (EBFLs). A Commercial Off-The-Shelf (COTS) procurement programme took place, vehicles were tested, minor modifications implemented and the first vehicles delivered in less than one year from the contract award date.

The primary military mission requirement of the MMV is the unloading, transporting and loading of containers, boxes and palletised ammunition loads. The MMV is capable of operating over rough terrain and is certified for rail, sea and air transport. It is air-transportable by various aircraft including the CH-53 helicopter and C-130 Hercules transport aircraft.

Capable of handling the US Air Force 463L pallet, the MMV has the capability of accepting dual carriages, 3,178 kg (7,000 lb) at a 1.219 m load centre and 4,994 kg (11,000 lb) at a 609 mm load centre, utilising a quick attach feature.

Production commenced during 2001 and the first production MMVs were delivered in April 2002. The initial delivery contract ran until April 2006, and allowed for deliveries of up to 1,500 vehicles valued in excess of USD135 million. The initial batch of 137 (five test vehicles + 132) MMVs delivered during 2002 was followed by another 593 vehicles over four years. It was announced, during April 2004, that the original 132 vehicles would be upgraded by JLG over a two-year period to current production standard during a refurbishment programme. JLG subsequently purchased these machines back from the US Marine Corps (USMC) in a deal that involved the supply of production-standard machines.

By early 2008 the USMC and Navy had received over 800 machines in total, and under a USD24.7 million award in February 2008, the US Navy Seabees Construction Battalion received an additional 199 machines.

JLG Industries Inc. announced the acquisition of the OmniQuip business unit of Textron Inc. in August 2003. In 1999 OmniQuip International Inc. (a management buy out of TRAK International) merged with Textron Inc.. The then Oshkosh Truck Corporation announced in October 2006 that it would purchase JLG Industries Inc. for around USD3.2 billion.

Description
The MMV is fitted with a one-person enclosed cab that provides the operator with protection from roll-over and falling objects. Air conditioning is standard, and the operator is provided with a suspension seat and safety belt. An armoured cab has been developed for the MMV and is in use on deployed operations.

ZF rigid unsprung axles are used, the front axle being equipped with a 'no-spin' differential. Both axles oscillate to take into account the ground undulations.

The hydraulically actuated forks are located at the articulating end of a telescopic three-stage welded box-section boom constructed from high-strength alloy steel. The maximum reach from the front tyres is 8.99 m. Maximum lift height is 12.9 m. The hydraulically-controlled frame tile angle is 10° left or right.

As with the vast majority of telescopic handler-type vehicles, the MMV can accept a variety of alternative attachments including a fork-mounted bucket, concrete hopper, personnel platform and so on.

Variants
Engine Installation/Removal Vehicle (EIRV)
JLG was awarded a contract in October 2007 for the supply of 67 EIRVs to the Naval Air Command. At the completion of testing, deliveries commenced late 2009. The EIRV is designed to meet a requirement to remove and install T-56 engines and/or propellers from P-3, C-130, and E-2C aircraft.

The EIRV is based on the MMV, but with a number of role-specific modifications that include:
- Fine mode hydraulics for precision engine placement
- Creep Mode for driving while carrying a load
- Self-removable counterweight for optimal C-130 transport
- Horizontal movement jib for straight forward movement
- Active Load Moment Indicator (LMI) limits to 90 per cent of load
- Optional emergency shut-off
- Optional seat kill switch
- Halogen and LED lights.

Specifications
Millennia Military Vehicle (MMV)
Cab seating: 1
Configuration: 4 × 4
Weight: 13,154 kg
Length: (max) 6.3 m
Width: (max) 2.545 m
Height: (boom lowered) 2.39 m
Ground clearance: (axle) 380 mm
Track: 2.13 m
Wheelbase: 3.3 m
Angle of approach/departure: 20°/20°
Speed: 34 km/h
Fuel capacity: 170 litres
Fording depth: 630 mm
Engine: Cummins QSB4.5T 4-cylinder in-line 4.5-litre turbocharged water-cooled 4-stroke diesel developing 110 hp (82 kW)
Transmission: ZF 4WG 98 TS automatic with 4 forward and 3 reverse speeds
Steering: 3 steer modes: all-wheel, front-wheel and cab
Turning radius: kerb, 4.95 m; wall, 7.02 m
Axles/suspension: ZF, unsprung, oscillating front and rear; no-spin differential, front
Tyres: 15.5 × 25, radial
Brakes: oil immersed discs
Lift performance:
    (max lift height, boom extended) 12.9 m
    (max lift height, boom retracted) 6.197 m
    (max below grade depth, boom extended) 510 mm
    (max reach at max lift angle, boom extended) 1.626 m
    (max reach an max lift angle, boom retracted) 940 mm
    (max reach at min lift angle, boom extended) 8.839 m
    (max boom lift angle) +69°
    (min boom lift angle) –3°
    (fork tilt angle at max boom angle up) +84°
    (fork tilt angle at max boom angle down) –23.4°
    (fork tilt angle at min boom angle up) +12.2°
    (fork tilt angle at min boom angle down) –30.3°

Status
In production (see text). Deliveries to USMC and Navy commenced in 2002; deliveries to Naval Air Command (EIRV variant) commenced in late-2009.

Contractor
JLG Industries Inc.

Manitowoc (Grove) mobile cranes

Development
Grove Manufacturing Company, the predecessor to the now Grove Worldwide, was founded in 1947. It's first products were rubber-tired farm wagons, cranes being introduced into the commercial marketplace in 1952.

In 1967, Grove was acquired by Kidde, Inc. In 1978, Grove acquired the National Crane Corporation of Waverly, Nebraska, US, a leading manufacturer of telescoping and articulating truck-mounted hydraulic cranes. In 1979, Grove completed the acquisition of Manlift, Inc., adding a complete line of boom and scissor-type aerial work platforms to its

JLG Millenia Military Vehicle (MMV) (JLG)   1296159

Grove RT875 rough terrain crane undergoing maintenance somewhere in Southwest Asia (US DoD) 1391292

Grove All Terrain Crane (ATEC) AT422T seen in Iraq early 2004. Note the unit-made add-on armour kit fitted to the crane operator's cabin (Carl Schulze) 1296221

portfolio. In 1984, Grove acquired Coles Cranes Limited, then Europe's largest crane manufacturer. In 1987, Kidde, Inc. was acquired by the Hanson Trust PLC of the UK and in 1990 the corporate identity, Grove Worldwide, was announced.

In 1993, Grove Worldwide was reorganised into three operating businesses: Grove Crane, Grove Manlift and National Crane. In 1995 Grove acquired the Krupp mobile hydraulic crane business based in Wilhelmshaven, Germany. That same year, Grove acquired Delta Systems of Tonneins, France, which added a line of vertical mast work platforms to the Grove Manlift line. Grove Worldwide produced its 50,000th crane during 1997. In 2002, Grove was acquired by the Manitowoc Company Inc., where it was integrated in to the Manitowoc Crane Group. In 2004, the group divested the Manlift and Delta divisions and focused on lifting equipment. Thus today the Grove product sits within the Manitowoc Crane Group alongside the Manitowoc range of mobile lattice boom crawler cranes, the Potain range of tower cranes and the National range of truck mounted cranes.

Manitowoc is one of the world's largest producer of mobile cranes and access equipment, and is a supplier of cranes and lifting equipment to the military worldwide. Manitowoc, under the Grove brand, currently produces a range of >30 assorted truck-mounted, all-terrain, rough terrain and industrial cranes.

The accompanying specification table provides basic specifications for the majority of currently produced machines. Not included however are industrial cranes or some of the heavier (150 to 550 tonne capacity) all-terrain cranes as these are unlikely to be used for military applications.

All-terrain or rough terrain cranes of 15 to 40 tonnes lift capacity are the norm for military field applications, although smaller numbers of larger cranes are in service with some armed forces.

Cranes supplied by Manitowoc for military applications are essentially commercial products with limited militarisation. It should also be noted that as with other commercial crane manufactures, the company regularly updates its product range.

Description

All-terrain cranes

The entire Grove all-terrain crane fleet is equipped with Mercedes-Benz engines. Cranes of up to 100 tonnes capacity have a single engine, cranes in excess of 100 tonnes capacity have two; one for the carrier vehicle, one for the crane itself. Chassis have two to seven axles, and in a variety of steer and drive configurations. Grove all-terrain cranes are manufactured in Germany.

Recent all-terrain crane sales to the military have included over 400 AT422T cranes to the US military between 1997 and 2006. The AT422T is an all-terrain (4 × 4 × 4) 20 tonne capacity crane with a 21.4 m three-section main boom.

Truck cranes

Grove currently produces five truck-mounted cranes with lifting capacities ranging from 40 to 90 tonnes. Four of these are manufactured in the United States and are mounted on a specialist truck chassis with a one-man cab; engines are Cummins. The recently introduced GSK55 combines the lift ability of Grove all-terrain cranes with the flexibility and mobility of a

Specifications

Model	GMK2035E	GMK3050-1	GMK3055	GMK4100B	TM500E2	TMS700E	TMS800E	TMS9000E
Origin:	Germany	Germany	Germany	Germany	United States	United States	United States	United States
Type:	AT	AT	AT	AT	TM	TM	TM	TM
Lift capacity:	35 t	50 t	55 t	100 t	40 t	50-60 t	80 t	90 r
Boom length:	29 m	38 m	43 m	51 m	29 m	33.5 m	39 m	43.3 m
Power output:								
(carrier)	279 hp (208 kW)	354 hp (264 kW)	349 hp (260 kW)	390 hp (291 kW)	300 hp (224 kW)	450 hp (336 kW)	450 hp (336 kW	450 hp (336 kW)
(crane)	n/app	n/app	n/app	n/app	82 kW (110 hp)	n/app	n/app	n/app
Configuration:	4 × 4 × 4	6 × 4 (or 6) × 6	6 × 4 (or 6) × 6	8 × 6 (or 8) × 8	6 × 4 × 1 (optional pusher axle)	8 × 4 × 4	8 × 4 × 4	8 × 4 × 4
Weight: (travel)	24 t	36 t	36 t	44 t	26 t	33.9 t	36.2 t	38 t
Gradient:	60%	82%	82%	70%	32%	70%	70%	70%
Max speed:	84 km/h	80 km/h	85 km/h	85 km/h	105 km/h	105 km/h	105 km/h	105 km/h

Model	RT530E-2	RT540E	RT600E	RT700E	RT880E	RT890E	RT9130E
Origin:	United States	United States	United States	United States	United States	United States	United States
Type:	RT	RT	RT	RT	RT	RT	RT
Lift capacity:	27 t	35 t	40-45 t	50-55 t	75 t	80 t	120 t
Boom length:	29 m	31 m	32 m	33.5 m	39 m	43.2 m	48.8 m
Power output:							
(carrier)	160 hp (119 kW)	160 hp (119 kW)	173 hp (129 kW)	218 hp (163 kW)	275 hp (205 kW)	275 hp (205 kW)	300 hp (224 kW)
(crane)	n/app	n/app	n/app	n/app	n/app	n/app	n/app
Configuration:	4 × 4 × 4	4 × 4 × 4	4 × 4 × 4	4 × 4 × 4	4 × 4 × 4	4 × 4 × 4	4 × 4 × 4
Weight: (travel)	25.9 t	27.3 t	32.5 t	38.6 t	49.1 t	52.1 t	78.9 t
Gradient:	119%	119%	78%	75%	75%	75%	73%
Max speed:	40 km/h	40 km/h	39 km/h	37 km/h	35 km/h	35 km/h	24 km/h

standard on-road truck. It merges the upperworks from Grove's GMK3055 all-terrain crane (produced in Germany) with a specially-designed truck chassis that acts as a trailer. The customer can use the tractor of their choice to haul the crane to job-sites.

Rough terrain cranes

Grove offers a range of seven rough terrain cranes with lifting capacities ranging from 27 to 120 tonnes. All have four-wheel drive and steer, are unsprung and fitted with an oscillating rear axle to account for ground undulations.

In June 2002 Grove Worldwide announced the award of a refurbishment contract from the US Army's Tank Automotive and Armaments Command (TACOM). This called for the refurbishment of up to 180 Grove RT875 rough terrain cranes over a five-year period. Between 1989 and 1991 the US Army received 289 Grove RT875 rough terrain cranes, and these are used primarily for the handling of 40 ft ISO containers.

Industrial cranes

Grove industrial cranes carry the Yardboss and Shuttlelift Carrydeck brand names and are compact machines for use in confined spaces. Yardboss industrial cranes are used for plant maintenance and material handling jobs. They feature carry decks and multi-mode steering for operation in tight quarters. Nine models are currently available with carrying capacities from 7.7- to 22.7-tonnes. The Shuttlelift Carrydeck line of industrial cranes are designed for both indoor and outdoor job-sites and feature telescoping booms and a load deck for material handling. Eight models are currently offered, these having carrying capacities that range from 7.7- to 22.7-tonnes.

Notes:

The GSK55 model combines the lift ability of Grove all-terrain cranes with the flexibility and mobility of a standard on-road truck. It merges the upperworks from Grove's GMK3055 all-terrain crane with a specially-designed truck chassis that acts as a trailer. The customer can use the tractor of their choice to haul the crane to job-sites

Configuration for cranes with a single steer axle this is denoted by axle count (1); for cranes with multiple steer axles this is denoted by wheel count, a four-wheel drive, four-wheel steer crane being 4 × 4 × 4.

Type is denoted by the codes as follows: AT - all-terrain; TC - truck cranes; and RT - rough terrain.

Status

Various models of Grove cranes are in service with a number of armed forces worldwide including those of Belgium, Egypt, the UK, the US and the former Yugoslavia.

Contractor

Grove Worldwide

Terex mobile cranes

Development

Terex Corporation can trace its origins back to 1925 and Northwest Engineering, a manufacturer of cranes, power shovels and draglines. The current Terex Corporation has evolved mainly from numerous acquisitions made between 1983 and 1995, starting with the acquisition of the declared bankrupt Northwest Engineering in 1983.

In 1986 Northwest Engineering acquired Terex USA, a distributor of heavy duty earthmoving equipment, from General Motors Corporation. In 1987 Northwest Engineering exercised an option to acquire Terex Equipment Limited, the manufacturing sister of Terex USA. At the same time the company acquired Koehring Cranes and Excavators, through which it entered the crane market. In 1988 Northwest Engineering changed its name to Terex Corporation.

The current Terex Corporation designs, manufactures, and markets a broad range of heavy machinery for the construction, infrastructure, and mining industries. Product lines include telescopic mobile cranes, tower cranes, mobile crushing and screening equipment, off-highway trucks, surface mining trucks, and hydraulic mining shovels. Terex also produces light construction equipment, such as floodlighting systems, concrete mixers, and traffic control products. Details of Terex construction equipment can be found in the Field fortifications and related emplacements section.

Terex Cranes was formed in 1995 following the acquisition of PPM Cranes from Legris Industries SA of France. Crane operations were bolstered in 1997 with the purchase of Simon Engineering plc's Simon Access division and Baraga Products Inc., Terex Cranes' range now including hydraulic cranes, aerial work platforms, and rough-terrain lift trucks. The July 1998 purchase of the American Crane Corporation brought Terex a maker of lattice boom cranes. Two tower crane manufacturers, Peiner HTS of Germany and Gru Comedi SpA of Italy, were acquired in the final two months of 1998. Terex acquired the Demag crane division from the Bosch-Siemens consortium in 2002 and integrated the company into the global Terex Cranes group as Terex Demag. The current Terex-Demag can trace its origins back to 1827 and the manufacturing of oil press and flour mill machinery.

Terex is currently the world's second largest manufacturer of cranes, with manufacturing facilities in Australia, France, Germany, Italy, and the US. The most common types of crane employed for military operations are

all-terrain or rough-terrain, although other types can be used in limited numbers, and primarily on third line or support duties. This entry focuses on Terex all-terrain and rough-terrain cranes, but also includes details of truck-mounted and all-terrain pick & carry-type cranes as these are considered suitable for military use.

Description

All-terrain cranes

Terex all-terrain cranes are manufactured in France and Germany and are branded Terex Demag. Terex all-terrain cranes, of which 19 models are currently offered, have maximum lift capacities ranging from 40 to 1,200 tonnes. All-terrain cranes used for military applications are increasing in size and weight, one factor behind this trend being an increase in usage of portable accommodation and ISO dimensioned logistic support infrastructure on deployed operations, however, cranes with more than five axles and maximum lift capacities greater than around 100 tonnes remain quite rare in the military environment.

Truck cranes

Terex Demag currently produces eight truck-mounted cranes with lifting capacities ranging from 36 to 60 tonnes. These are manufactured in France and the United States and are mounted on specialist truck chassis.

Rough-terrain cranes

Terex rough-terrain cranes are manufactured in Italy and the US and are branded Terex Brandini (from Italy) and Terex (from the US). Terex Brandini can trace its origins back to 1968 and in 1989 the company became part of the PPM group, PPM also having origins dating back to 1968. Terex offers a range of 16 rough-terrain cranes with lift capacities ranging from 27.3 to 118 tonnes, this range including a cab-front series - the CD 200 Series which is used by the US Navy as a Heavy Maintenance Crane (HMC).

Pick & Carry mobile all-terrain cranes

Terex Franna all-terrain Pick & Carry mobile cranes are manufactured in Australia. Three models are currently available, all being four-wheel drive and steered by chassis articulation.

Status

Various models of Terex mobile cranes are in service with a number of armed forces worldwide.

Contractor

Terex-Demag GmbH & Co KG
Terex Corporation

Terex TX51-19M/19MD Rough Terrain Telescopic Boom Material Handler

Development

Terexlift s.r.l. (part of the Terex Corporation) supplied the US Marine Corps (USMC) with four essentially commercial rough terrain telescopic handlers for trials in June 2000. These trials lasted over 12 months, during which over 300,000 tonnes of material was handled. Following trials, and to better meet the USMC requirements, a number of modifications were carried out, resulting in the delivery of a fully redesigned military-specific machine. The frame, engine mount and operator cab were all raised to increase ground clearance and to meet the USMC fording requirement, and to improve mobility larger all-terrain wheels and tyres were adopted. The Perkins 700 Series engine was originally rated at 63 hp (47 kW), and this was uprated to 80 hp (60 kW).

The standard commercial plastic mudguards were replaced by steel units, corrosion resistance was increased, a 24 V electrical system adopted, and a –40°C cold start ability in-built. The full range of modifications resulted in a weight increase from 4,300 kg to 6,100 kg. The production contract for 569 machines worth USD30 million was awarded to Terexlift s.r.l. in September 2001, with production deliveries running from December 2001 until September 2002.

The primary USMC role of the Terex TX51-19M is to load and unload palletised cargo from trucks, trailers, aircraft, ships and ISO containers. In service, the machine has replaced a mast-type forklift which had been in service for more than 10 years.

In May 2005 the USMC placed an order for a further 82 machines. Designated TX51-19MD, these differ from the original machines primarily in power unit, the original Perkins option having been replaced by a Deutz option; D-Deutz.

Terexlift subsequently introduced a commercial machine based on the military TX51-19M specifications.

Description

The Terex TX51-19M/19MD is fitted with a one-person enclosed cab that provides the operator with protection from roll-over and falling objects. The operator is provided with a suspension seat and safety belt.

Motive power for the TX51-19M model is provided by a Perkins 700 Series turbocharged diesel engine developing 80 hp (60 kW), while motive power for the more recent TX51-19MD model is provided by a Deutz

Terex TX51-19MD Rough Terrain Telescopic Boom Material Handler as displayed at EuroSatory 2006 (Shaun C Connors) 1156050

turbocharged diesel engine developing 81.5 hp (61 kW). Transmission is hydrostatic (with disconnect for towing) with a mechanical dropbox. Rigid unsprung axles are used, the front axle being equipped with a self-locking differential. The rear axle oscillates to take account of ground undulations.

As with the vast majority of telescopic handler-type vehicles, the Terex TX51-19M/19MD can accept a variety of alternative attachments including a bucket.

Specifications

TX51-19M/19MD Rough Terrain Telescopic Boom Material Handler
Cab seating: 1
Configuration: 4 × 4
Weight: 6,100 kg
Length: (to front wheels) 3.81 m
Length: (to fork holder plate) 4.47 m
Width: (max) 1.98 m
Height: (boom lowered) 2.28 m
Ground clearance: 410 mm
Track: 1.5 m
Wheelbase: 2.39 m
Angle of approach/departure: 90°/70°
Max speed: 32 km/h
Fuel capacity: 95 litres
Climatic operational range: –32°C to +46°C
Fording depth: 915 mm
Engine: Perkins 700 Series 2.955 litre 4-cylinder in-line turbocharged water-cooled 4-stroke diesel developing 80 hp (60 kW) at 2,600 rpm [Deutz BF4L2011 3.108 litre 4-cylinder in-line turbocharged water-cooled 4-stroke diesel developing 81.5 hp (61 kW) at 2,500 rpm]
Transmission: hydrostatic, Bosch Rexroth: model A4VG56DA2D2 pump, model A6VM107DA1 motor
Steering: 3 steer modes: all-wheel, front-wheel and crab
Turning radius: (wall) 8.01 m
Axles/suspension: unsprung, rigid front, oscillating rear; self-locking differential, front
Tyres: 375/75R 20
Brakes: oil immersed multi disc on front axle
Lift capacity: 2,300 kg
 (max lift height, boom extended) 5.71 m
 (max reach an max lift angle, boom retracted) 375 mm
 (max forward reach) 3.27 m
 (max boom lift angle) +70°
 (min boom lift angle) –3°

Status
Production as required. 569 TX51-19M, delivered to the USMC 2001-2002; 82 TX51-19MD delivered to the USMC 2005.

Contractor
TerexLift s.r.l.
Terex Corporation

TRAK 6000M Variable Reach Rough Terrain Fork-Lift Truck (VRRTFLT)
Deliveries of the TRAK International 6000M Variable Reach Rough Terrain Fork-Lift Truck (VRRTFLT) to the US Army began in 1990, following the types 1988 selection after competitive testing against two other vehicles at Aberdeen Proving Grounds, Maryland. Over 300 units had been delivered in time for use during Operation Desert Storm. Over 2,200 vehicles had been delivered when production concluded in 1995, by which time the type had also been adopted for use by the US Air Force which received around 400 examples.

The 6000M VRRTFLT was superseded in production by the updated TRAK All Terrain Lifter Army System (ATLAS), 2,500 of which were supplied to the US Army.

The primary military mission requirement of the 6000M 6,000 lb (2,722 kg) capacity VRRTFLT was for the handling of ammunition pallets unloaded from standard 20 ft (6.096 m) containers. The vehicle was required to be capable of mobility over rough terrain and was to be transportable in C-130 Hercules aircraft.

In 1993, TRAK International Inc. provided the New Zealand Army with a 2,722 kg (6,000 lb) forklift modified to accept a 4,536 kg (10,000 lb) load centre.

In August 2004, JLG Industries Inc. was awarded a three year, 700-machine contract to reset to pre-deployment (to Afghanistan and Iraq) condition US armed forces TRAK 6000M and ATLAS machines.

JLG industries Inc. announced the acquisition of the OmniQuip business unit of Textron Inc., in August 2003. In 1999 OmniQuip International Inc. (a management buyout of TRAK International) merged with Textron Inc..

The then Oshkosh Truck Corporation announced in October 2006 that it would purchase JLG Industries Inc. for approximately USD3.2 billion.

Description
The 6000M is fitted with a one-person enclosed cab that provides the operator with protection from roll-over and falling objects. There is a full-time planetary 4 × 4 drive with dry disc brakes and the front axle is equipped with a 'no-spin' differential and parking brake. The vehicle is unsprung, the rear axle oscillating to take account of ground undulations.

The hydraulically actuated forks are located at the articulating end of a telescopic three stage welded box-section boom constructed from high-strength alloy steel. The maximum reach from the front tyres to the 609 mm load centre is 7.35 m and maximum lift capacity is 4,536 kg. Maximum lift height is 10.2 m. The frame tile angle is 9° left or right.

For air-transportability by C-130 Hercules aircraft flight preparation takes under 15 minutes.

Specifications
6000M VRRTFLT
Cab seating: 1
Configuration: 4 × 4
Weight: (operating with driver, max fuel and 10K carriage) 12,338 kg
Length: (with forks) 7.93 m
Width: 2.59 m
Height: 2.57 m
Ground clearance: (axle) 356 mm
Track: 2.06 m
Wheelbase: 3.15 m
Speed: 37 km/h

TRAK International 6000M Variable Reach Rough Terrain Fork-Lift Truck (VRRTFLT) (TRAK) 0525659

Fuel capacity: 166.6 litres
Climatic operational range: −32 to +49°C
Engine: Cummins 6BT 5.9 in-line 6-cylinder turbocharged water-cooled 5.9-litre 4-stroke diesel developing 152 hp (113 kW) at 2,500 rpm
Transmission: power shift with 3 forward and 3 reverse speeds
Steering: 3 steer modes: all-wheel, front-wheel and crab
Turning radius: 4.67 m
Axles/suspension: unsprung, rigid front, oscillating rear; no-spin differential, front
Tyres: 17.5 × 25, 12-ply
Brakes: discs, dry

Lift performance:
  (lift capacity) 4,536 kg
  (lift height) 10.5 m
  (reach below grade) 635 mm
  (reach from front tyres to 609 mm load centre) 7.35 m
  (reach at max height to 609 mm load centre) 4.2 m

Status
Production complete. Over 2,200 supplied to the US air force and Army.

Contractor
JLG Industries Inc.

MISCELLANEOUS EQUIPMENT

FIELD FORTIFICATIONS AND RELATED EMPLACEMENTS EQUIPMENT

Australia

Thales Australia High Mobility Engineering Vehicle (HMEV)

Development

The High Mobility Engineering Vehicle (HMEV), previously marketed as the High Speed Engineering Vehicle (HSEV), is a high-speed, all-terrain, multipurpose engineer vehicle, capable of performing a variety of military field engineering and logistic tasks. The HMEV was designed and is manufactured by Thales Australia, previously known as ADI, Thales having completed its acquisition of ADI in October 2006.

Delivery of 27 machines (designated HSEV) to the Australian Army concluded in November 2001. The Australian Army has subsequently deployed HSEVs to East Timor (1, 2000–2004), Solomon Islands (2, 2004) and Indonesia for Tsunami relief (3, 2005–2006).

For field trials and evaluation, a single machine was supplied to the Canadian Department of National Defense (DND) in 1998. Operational trials included operations with Canadian peacekeeping forces with the UN in East Timor. In November 2002, Canada's DND announced the selection of a competing bid to meet its Multi-Purpose Engineering Vehicle (MPEV) requirement.

A single HMEV that was suitably modified for operation in desert conditions was supplied to the United Arab Emirates during 2001 for trials.

Also during 2001, the US Army took delivery of a single HMEV. Following evaluation under the foreign comparative test programme, an order for 40 vehicles was placed in early 2002. This contract includes options for two additional batches of 40 vehicles. These HMEVs were supplied for the US Army's Interim High Mobility Engineering Excavator (IHMEE) programme and were understood to be for the then named Interim Brigade Combat Team. For the IHMEE programme, the then ADI teamed with Oshkosh Truck Corporation of the US, Oshkosh providing in-country support. Subsequently an order for an additional 10 units was received from the US Army. These were delivered during 2006.

It was announced early-2003 that the then ADI (teamed with Oshkosh Truck) had been selected as one of two remaining contenders for the US Army's High Mobility Engineering Excavator HMEE requirement, the other being JCB of the UK. Three trial vehicles were supplied by each of the two manufacturers with TACOM intending to publish an RFP for the production contract late 2004, and award the production contract to a single contractor mid 2005. The production contract worth up to USD140 million was awarded to JCB in September 2005 and calls for up to 1,000 machines. The initial requirement had been for up to 1,800 machines, this later reducing to up to 1,500 machines. Together with the earlier IHMEE, the HMEE programme will replace the current Unimog-based Small Emplacement Excavator (SEE).

It was announced in September 2004 that the then ADI had supplied two HMEV examples to China's People's Liberation Army (PLA) for trials that were expected to be underway by year-end. The vehicles were delivered in kit form for assembly in China to meet the PLA's requirement that the HMEV be capable of in-country manufacture. The PLA is understood to have been seeking a low-cost, multi-function engineering vehicle to undertake a range of tasks, including earth moving, lifting and drilling in

US Army IHMEE with an armoured cab on deployed operations
(Carl Schulze)   1391295

both military and civilian operations. The HMEV was the only vehicle under consideration and it is understood that the eventual PLA requirement could be in excess of 200 vehicles. Thales Australia has teamed with local wheeled and tracked excavator manufacturer, Guizhou Jonyang Kinetics Ltd, establishing a licensed manufacture agreement for the HMEV. According to Thales Australia, 30 semi-knocked down kits have been used for initial manufacturing, with increasing localisation of components for China-based production. By mid-2009 around 100 kits had been supplied. Thales Australia personnel have provided technical assistance for chassis fabrication and vehicle assembly. The PLA is understood to have specified minor modifications to the HMEV, such as cold weather kits and automotive changes to enable operation at high altitudes.

Description

The High Mobility Engineering Vehicle (HMEV) resembles a conventional backhoe loader in general appearance, but this is effectively where the similarities start and stop, in that the HMEV has a much faster maximum speed of 100 km/h, plus it can maintain 80 km/h over long distances. These speeds render the machine self-deployable in a road-going vehicle convoy. The HMEV can also achieve significantly higher speeds cross-country than conventional earth-moving equipment thanks to its unique combination of air-bag suspension and wheel size.

The standard engine is a Cummins 185 hp (138 kW) water-cooled diesel, although a more powerful version developing 149 kW (200 hp) version is available if required.

In its basic form, the High Mobility Engineering Vehicle (HMEV) is equipped with a backhoe and front-end loader that can be adapted to carry a quick-connect fork lift attachment. Other major optional accessories include an earth auger, winch, compactor, snow plough and a rock breaker. A wide range of other optional equipment is available, including a cold-weather package. If required, armour protection may be added.

The positive air pressurised cab is air conditioned and the driver's seat can be swivelled through 180°. Full roll-over and falling object protection is provided and there is space for an optional passenger seat. With a standard cab, the HMEV is air transportable by C-130 Hercules transport aircraft. It may also be transported as an underslung load by CH-47D Chinook helicopter.

The US Army took delivery of a single HMEV during 2001. Following evaluation under the foreign comparative test programme, an order for 40 vehicles was placed in early 2002. These HMEVs were supplied for the US Army's Interim High Mobility Engineering Excavator (IHMEE) programme, and subsequently an order for an additional 10 units was received from the US Army. These were delivered during 2006
(US DoD (Spc. Daniel Herrera))   1391294

Thales Australia High Mobility Engineering Vehicle (HMEV) during a mobility demonstration at IDEX 2005; note the high degree of axle travel
(Patrick Allen)   1138037

Specifications
Cab seating: 1 + 1 (optional)
Weight: (combat) 11,500 kg
Length:
　(overall) 8.541 m
　(vehicle) 5.112 m
Width: 2.49 m
Height:
　(overall) 3.487 m
　(cab roof) 2.677 m
Ground clearance: 377 mm
Track: (front) 2.073 m
Wheelbase: 3.15 m
Max speed: (road) 100 km/h
Fuel capacity: 210 litres
Range: 600 km
Gradient: 60%
Side slope: 30°
Fording: 760 mm
Vertical obstacle: 620 mm
Engine: Cummins 6BTA5.9-C185 5.9 litre in-line 6-cylinder water-cooled turbocharged and intercooled 4-stroke diesel developing 185 hp (138 kW) at 2,500 rpm
Transmission: Clark 12.5 LHR 28821 power shift with 8 forward and 4 reverse gears
Steering: power
Turning circle: 15.6 m
Suspension: multimode pneumatic spring with ride levelling, plus double-acting shock-absorbers and beam axles
Tyres: 14.00R 24 SR with beadlocks
Brakes: Dana Spicer air, drums
Electrical system: 24 V

Status
In service with the Australian (27), Chinese (>100) and US (51) armies. Evaluation vehicles delivered to Canada (2), the United Arab Emirates (1) and the US (3). Canada subsequently selected a locally produced equivalent machine; the US subsequently selected a JCB machine.

Contractor
Thales Australia

Canadian Army MPEV at work in Haiti (Canadian DND)　　1391366

Canada

ARVA MultiPurpose Engineering Vehicle (MPEV)

Development
The Australian Defence Force (ADF) and defence contractor Thales (then Australian Defence Industries - ADI) commenced the joint development of what was then termed the High Speed Engineering Vehicle (HSEV) in answer to an Australian requirement which first emerged in 1994/1995.

This requirement called for a self-deployable high-speed backhoe loader-type machine, and Australian Army HSEV trials commenced in 1996. In early 1998, 27 HSEVs were ordered, with deliveries concluding in 2001. Full details of the HSEV (now termed High Mobility Engineering Vehicle (HMEV)) can be found elsewhere in this section.

The original ADI HSEV was shipped to Canada for trials in 1998, and in 1999 the Canadian Department of National Defence (DND) ordered a second machine. Both machines were used to help the DND develop an industry tender for a high-speed backhoe loader that could maintain road speeds with the Army's 8 × 8 Light Armoured Vehicles (LAVs).

Two companies responded to that tender, ADI and Canada's ARVA Industries. In November 2002 it was announced that ARVA Industries had been awarded the MultiPurpose Engineering Vehicle (MPEV) contract for 28 vehicles. The prototype MPEV was completed in October 2003, and after requested modifications were incorporated into the design, the first machine was delivered in March 2004.

In total 30 MPEVs have been ordered, with all vehicles delivered by 2008. The first three machines delivered were Series I, the following 27 machines being Series II. ARVA currently offer the further enhanced Series III MPEV.

Description
The MultiPurpose Engineering Vehicle (MPEV) resembles a conventional backhoe loader in general appearance, but this is effectively where the similarities start and stop. Unlike a conventional backhoe loader the MPEV is based on a chassis, and one that is purpose designed to withstand the dynamic forces of both high-speed on- and off-road travel.

Compared to a conventional backhoe loader, the MPEV can attain a much faster maximum road speed of 90-110 km/h (depending on variant), this rendering the machine self-deployable in a road-going vehicle convoy. The MPEV can also achieve significantly higher speeds cross-country than conventional earth-moving equipment thanks primarily to its combination of air-suspension and wheel/tyre size. The multi-mode suspension set-up allows for full four-wheel suspension or front and/or rear axle lock-out when operating as an earthmover or loader.

The standard engine of the Series II MPEV (this version accounting for the bulk of Canadian Army deliveries) is a Cummins 205 hp water-cooled diesel, this coupled to a Funk six-speed powershift transmission.

The latest MPEV Series III features a more powerful 215 hp Cummins engine, this coupled to a Dana eight-speed automatic transmission. Other improvements include a redesigned front bonnet for improved operator visibility, improved ballistic protection and an improved steering system.

In its basic form, the MPEV is equipped with a backhoe and front-end loader. An essentially commercial backhoe supplied by Case is fitted at the rear, with the front loader arm purpose-designed to accommodate the longer bonnet dictated by the combination of a larger more powerful engine and the extended wheelbase required for stability and handling at road speeds.

The air-conditioned cab has full Roll-Over and Falling Object Protective Structures (ROPS and FOPS) and can be armoured if required. An armour package has been developed and fitted to Canadian vehicles.

The MPEV can be air transportable by C-130 Hercules transport aircraft if required, and may also be transported as an underslung load by CH-47D Chinook helicopter.

A wide variety of options are available for the MPEV, these including tyre chains, run flat inserts, camouflage net holders and rifle racks, plus a selection of engineering equipment options that include a winch, hydraulic Power Take-Off (PTO), forklift attachment, extendable rear dipper arm, a crane jib, and a selection of optional buckets.

Specifications
ARVA MPEV Series II
Cab seating: 1 + 1
Weight: (combat) 10,300 kg (without armour)
Length: (overall) 8.41 m
Width: 2.49 m
Height: (overall) 3.5 m
Ground clearance: (differential) 430 mm
Wheelbase: 3.15 m
Max speed:
　(road) 90 km/h
　(reverse) 16 km/h
Fuel capacity: 250 litres
Range: 450 km
Max gradient: 60%
Fording: 750 mm
Engine: Cummins 6BTAISB205 5.9-litre in-line 6-cylinder water-cooled turbocharged and intercooled 4-stroke diesel developing 205 hp at 2,500 rpm and 705 N.m torque at 1,600 rpm
Transmission: Funk Model 2000 6-speed long-drop powershift
Steering: power-assisted on front wheels
Turning radius: 8 m
Suspension: multimode pneumatic front and rear with reserve air tanks; selector valve permits lock up for working mode and/or front and rear axle suspension for high speed highway and off-road travel, beam axles; 17° oscillation front and rear
Axles: Dana Model SD-66 with differential lock, front; Dana Model D-66 with differential lock, rear
Tyres: 14.00R 20 Michelin XZL with beadlocks
Brakes: air, drums, ABS
Electrical system: 24 V
Alternator: 110 A

Status
Production of Series III machines as required. Thirty machines in a mix of Series I and Series II in service with Canada (see text).

Contrator
Thales Australia, formerly Australian Defence Industries (ADI)

China

NORINCO trench digger

Description

The NORINCO trench digger is based on the chassis and hull of the Type 83 152 mm self-propelled gun-howitzer, full details of which can be found in Jane's Armour and Artillery. The vehicle carries a circular trench-digging machine similar in appearance to that used on the Russian MDK-2 series of trench-digging machines. This digging machine is electro-hydraulically lifted upwards and over the hull rear for transport and lowered to behind the vehicle for digging. The top of the hull carries an armoured enclosed cab and a straight dozer blade is carried on the front of the hull.

Power for the digging operation is taken by a multipurpose gear system from the vehicle's main engine, which is mounted in the forward part of the hull together with the transmission. Mechanical and hydraulic safety devices are incorporated.

The superstructure cab is air-conditioned and the driver is provided with an infrared night vision device and an adjustable shock-absorbing seat. No armament appears to be carried other than the crew's personal weapons.

The digging machine can remove up to 300 m^3/h of soft soil and up to 150 m^3/h of harder ground. The maximum digging depth for each digging cup is 450 mm and the maximum digging depth 3.5 m. A typical finished trench can be 4.1 to 4.5 m wide at the top and 3.5 m wide at the bottom.

Specifications

NORINCO trench digger
Crew: 3
Weight: (combat) 32,000 kg
Length:
   (travelling) 8.074 m
   (operating) 10 m
Width: 3.6 m
Height:
   (top of digging equipment) 4.195 m
   (cab roof) 2.96 m
Ground clearance: 450 mm
Track: 2.62 m
Track width: 480 mm
Length of track on ground: 4.601 m
Max speed: (road) 52 km/h
Gradient: 44%
Side slope: 22%
Engine: Type 12150L diesel developing 520 hp (388 kW)

Status

Production likely to be on an as required basis. In service with the People's Liberation Army (PLA) and possibly others.

Contractor

China North Industries Corporation (NORINCO)

NORINCO trench digger (NORINCO)   0009982

NORINCO Type 82 tracked military bulldozer

Description

The Type 82 tracked military bulldozer was designed from the outset for combat engineer use. It is fitted with a dozer blade that can be angled about a central point from concave to convex. The blade is raised and lowered about a point between the second and third roadwheels on each side and is actuated vertically by a large hydraulic cylinder in front of the cab. The blade can be removed if required.

The four-person cab is armoured and provides protection from small arms fire and shell splinters and is provided with a roof hatch equipped with a mounting for a 12.7 mm AA machine gun. The cab is equipped with two infrared vision systems: one for the driver with a 30° field of view and another for the commander; a Type 85 device with a 76° horizontal field of vision and a 20° vertical field of view. A roof periscope is also provided.

The area behind the cab and over the engine and transmission covers is used as a general cargo or equipment-carrying area and is provided with steel drop sides. There is no tailgate other than a load restraint frame.

Rear three-quarter view of the NORINCO Type 82 tracked military bulldozer (NORINCO)   0137249

The Type 82 can travel at a maximum speed of 47.4 km/h to enable it to maintain station in some convoys. When operating, the minimum bulldozing speed is 2.4 km/h and when operating within a distance of 30 m the earthmoving capacity is 262 m^3/h. At an operating distance of 50 m this is reduced to 232 m^3/h. The Type 82 can operate for periods of between 20 and 25 hours. Maximum push is 16,000 kg.

Specifications

Type 82 tracked military bulldozer
Crew: 4
Weight: (combat) 20,500 kg
Length:
   (with blade) 7.17 m
   (without blade) 5.81 m
Width:
   (operating) 4.33 m
   (travelling) 3.36 m
   (without blade) 2.92 m
Height:
   (to AA MG) 3.21 m
   (top of cab) 2.76 m
Ground clearance: 450 mm
Track: 2.49 m
Length of track on ground: 3.385 m
Ground pressure: 0.7 kg/cm^2
Max speed:
   (road) 47.4 km/h
   (cruising) 32 km/h
   (reverse) 21.5 km/h
   (operating, min) 2.4 km/h
Range:
   (road) 400–450 km
   (cross-country) 350–400 km
Max operating time: 20–25 h
Fording: 1.3 m
Gradient: 30°
Vertical obstacle: 700 mm
Trench: 2.6 m
Engine: Type 12150 L-3 diesel developing 430 hp (321 kW)
Batteries: 4 × Type 65
Armament: 1 × 12.7 mm MG
Ammunition: 200 rounds

Dozer blade
Width: 4.33–4.4 m
Height: 1.1 m
Lift height: 1 m
Depth of cut: 370 mm

Status

Production likely to be on an as required basis. In service with the People's Liberation Army (PLA) and possibly others. Offered for export.

Contractor

China North Industries Corporation (NORINCO)

Czech Republic

DOK wheeled engineer tractor

Description

The DOK (dozer on wheels) is a wheeled engineer tractor designed specifically for military applications. The DOK has an articulated chassis and a rear-mounted diesel engine; drive is electric. An electrically driven

DOK-M wheeled engineer tractor (Stefan Marx)   1185418

winch is located at the rear of the cab. In addition to the normal multipurpose bucket, a snow plough attachment is also available. The cab is hermetically sealed and has a filtered ventilation system, which enables the vehicle to operate in an NBC environment.

Three variants of the DOK are known to have been produced; the DOK-L, DOK-M and DOK-R. The DOK-L has a universal shovel and the DOK-M, a modified DOK-L, has the universal shovel with the addition of a sawtooth edge and a central ridge. The DOK-M also has hydraulic steering, improved brakes and an improved hydraulic system. The DOK-R has a V-shaped blade that can be adjusted to form a straight blade for dozing.

The current quantities of these machines remaining in active service is thought to be limited.

Specifications
Cab seating: 1
Configuration: 4 × 4
Weight: 28,000 kg
Towed load: 65,000 kg
Length: 10.53 m
Width: 3.15 m
Height: 3.15 m
Ground clearance: 450 mm
Track: 2.45 m
Wheelbase: 5 m
Max speed: (road) 50 km/h
Range: (cross-country) 250 km
Fuel capacity: 500 litres
Engine: T-930-42 V-12 4-stroke diesel developing 255 hp (190 kW) at 1,800 rpm
Tyres: 21 × 28

Status
Production complete. In service in reducing numbers with the Czech and Slovak armed forces. The DOK-M appears to have been used only by the former East German Army.

Contractor
Czech state factories
Slovak state factories

Denmark

Hydrema earthmoving equipment

Development
A/S Hydrema was founded in 1959 and today the company produces a wide range of small-to-medium sized earthmoving equipment, all of which is suitable for use in military engineering and other associated tasks.

A/S Hydrema is based in Denmark, the main factory and offices being located in Stovring near Aalborg in the northern part of Denmark. In Germany, production facilities are located in Weimar.

In addition to earthmoving equipment, A/S Hydrema also manufactures the 910 MCV Mine Clearing Vehicle. This machine leverages off Hydrema's considerable experience with articulated earth moving machinery.

In addition to supplying what are essentially Commercial-Off-The-Shelf (COTS) products, Hydrema will design, develop and carry out militarisation of these commercial products on an 'as-required' basis to meet specific military requirements. Examples of this would be the small arms fire and shell splinter protection packages developed for 928D multipurpose machines, M1700 wheeled 360° excavators and R1820 tracked 360° excavators of the Swedish Army.

The following is a brief descriptive overview of the current Hydrema earthmoving range. It should be noted that in line with the majority of manufacturers of such equipment, Hydrema regularly updates/revises its model range. These updates/revisions can be minor, often cosmetic and involve minimal mechanical changes, but can result in product designation changes.

Hydrema R1820 tracked 360° excavator of the Swedish Army fitted with a small arms fire-protected cabin (A/S Hydrema)   1026869

Hydrema M1700 wheeled 360° excavator of the Swedish Army fitted with a small arms fire-protected armoured cabin (A/S Hydrema)   1026878

It should be noted that Hydrema no longer offers wheeled loaders or tracked 360° excavators.

Description
Wheeled 360° excavators
The current A/S Hydrema range of wheeled 360° excavators consists of six machines, one of which is optimised for operations on railway tracks.

All models are powered by Perkins diesel engines developing 75 to 131 hp (54 to 98 kW) and have operating weights ranging from 11,000 to 17,000 kg. All are of conventional two-axle design, having four-wheel drive and front-axle steer. Axles are unsprung, an oscillating front axle taking account of ground undulations. A front- or rear-mounted dozer blade acts as a stabiliser when operating. In common with tracked machines, wheeled 360° excavators can be used for lifting purposes, with or without interchangeable buckets attached.

Hydrema wheeled 360° excavators differ from the majority of other such machines on the market in the configuration of their digging arms, theirs allowing for movement in more than the normal four planes of: slew; boom raise and lower; dipper in and out; and bucket crowd and dump.

The previously available Hydrema tracked 360° excavator range consisted of two models which were essentially wheeled models but with a tracked undercarriage replacing the wheeled undercarriage for applications where a level of self-deployability was not an issue and where superior all-terrain mobility was required.

A number of Hydrema 360° excavators have been modified for mine clearance operations. For this role they can be armoured and then used as the basis for fitting a bushcutter/vegetation clearing device to clear areas of bush or vegetation before carrying out manual or other de-mining operations. The Hydrema M1700 is a specific example of such a machine; the 360° working radius for the bushcutter attachment is approximately

Swedish Army Hydrema 928C multipurpose machine fitted with a small arms fire-protected cabin (A/S Hydrema)   1026877

Swedish Army Hydrema 928C multipurpose machine fitted with a small arms fire-protected cabin (A/S Hydrema)   1170882

Danish Army Hydrema 908B multipurpose machine in Kosovo (Shaun C Connors)   1190220

Front three-quarter view of a Hydrema 910 MCV-2 mineclearing vehicle of the Indian Army prior to shipment. The MCV/MCV-2 leverages off Hydrema's considerable experience with articulated earth moving machinery (A/S Hydrema)   0587568

Danish Air Force Hydrema 900 MPV tool carriers (A/S Hydrema)   1170883

7 m and protection from 7.62 mm NATO ball is recommended for the cabin, although other protection levels are an option. Added weight for the armoured cabin when offering protection from 7.62 mm NATO ball is 500 kg.

The M1700 is powered by a Perkins 1004 series turbocharged, water-cooled diesel developing 131 hp and weighs 17,000 kg. A dozer blade and single tyres are fitted as standard. Double tyres are an option. The wheel and tyre configuration was chosen over caterpillar tracks because the former offers higher road speed, lower maintenance costs and requirements, and ease of transport. Machines fitted with caterpillar tracks were available if required, and these carried the prefix 'R'. From mid-2006 Hydrema ceased the production of tracked 360° excavators. With the bushcutter removed and when used in an engineering support role the M1700 has a maximum digging depth of 6.4 m and a maximum reach (with bucket) of 10 m. Bucket volume is 0.9 m³. Breakout force of the dipper is 102 kN, breakout force of the bucket is 115 kN. Maximum lifting capacity is 10,000 kg.

Dump trucks
A/S Hydrema produces a range of articulated dump trucks; a 4 × 4 and two 6 × 6 models. The 912 4 × 4 is based on the major components of the Hydrema multipurpose machine range, full details of which can be found elsewhere in this entry.

The Hydrema 912D 10,000 kg articulated dump truck is based around the major components used in the 900D series multipurpose machines and this replaced the earlier 910 and 912 10,000 kg articulated dump trucks in production. From June 2009 the 912HM (High Mobility) became available, the main differences between this and the 921D being larger wheels and a suspended front axle.

The British Army procured and continues to operate 10 Hydrema 910 machines. These have been deployed to Afghanistan as part of the Airfield Damage Repair Team.

There are four base models in the current 900 series-based dump truck range; the 912D, the 912D Multitip, the 912HM, and the 912HM Multitip. The 912D and 912HM Multitip versions being fitted with a 180° Multitip body. Unladen weight of the Multitip versions increases slightly, but payload remains 10,000 kg for all versions, this carried in a high-tensile steel tip body fitted with double-acting tip cylinders.

Motive power is provided by a Perkins 1100 series turbocharged and intercooled water-cooled diesel developing 131 hp (98 kW). A road speed of 40 km/h can be achieved with a maximum load. All four wheels are permanently driven via a six-speed ZF Ergopower powershift automatic transmission. Rigid unsprung beam axles are fitted to the 912D, ground undulations being accounted for by oscillation about the central pivot on the articulated chassis. Four equal-sized wheels are fitted, tyre options including earth moving or flotation types. Brakes are inboard, oil-immersed discs.

Equipment options include winterised versions for use in temperatures down to -40°C, cabins offering 7.62 mm AP small arms fire-protection and the front-mounting of tools including a snow plough.

The 912 dump truck series is air portable in C-130 Hercules transport aircraft and can be carried underslung by CH-47D Chinook helicopters.

The larger 922C 6 × 6 machine was introduced commercially during 2002, this replaced by the 922D in April 2010. A conventional machine, steering is by frame articulation. The single front axle is sprung, the rear axles are unsprung and of the walking beam type. Unladen weight of the 922C is 14,300 kg; maximum payload is 20,000 kg. Motive power is provided by a Cummins QSB engine developing 274 hp (201 kW). A road speed of 50 km/h can be achieved with a maximum load.

For on-road use in certain countries the narrower 2.55 m wide 922C-2.55 is available.

Hydrema multipurpose machines
Hydrema multipurpose machines can be used for a variety of combat engineering and logistics tasks and combine the attributes of a wheeled loader and a conventional backhoe loader. There are four main machines in the current 900D series range, all of which feature high cross-country mobility due to a patented pivot steer system with oscillation in the centre pivot providing automatic load distribution to the four equally-sized wheels.

Hydrema 900D series multipurpose machines

Model	906D	908D	926D	928D
Weight:	8,200 kg	8,100 kg	9,400 kg	9,400 kg
Engine power output:	102 hp (76 kW)	102 hp (76 kW)	131 hp (98 kW)	131 hp (98 kW)
Loader, bucket volume:	1.3 m³	1.3 m³	1.6 m³	1.6 m³
Loader, lift capacity:	4,000 kg	4,000 kg	4,700 kg	4,700 kg
Loader, breakout force:	66.3 kN	66.3 kN	73 kN	73 kN
Loader, dump clearance:	2.84 m	2.84 m	2.845 m	2.845 m
Excavator, slew:	280°	200-250°	280°	200-250°
Excavator, reach:	6.2 m	6.5 m	6.25 m	6.3 m
Excavator, lift capacity:	1,400 kg	1,650 kg	1,450 kg	1,550 kg
Excavator, breakout force, bucket	53 kN	53 kN	55 kN	55 kN
Excavator, breakout force, dipper	36 kN	35 kN	36 kN	36 kN

Various types of buckets, shovels and other ancillaries can be fitted, including a forklift placed on the loader. The machines are air portable in C-130 Hercules transport aircraft and can be carried underslung by CH-47D Chinook helicopters. A road speed of 40 km/h can be achieved.

The 900D series replaced the earlier 900C series models in production. The Hydrema 906B, a hydraulic side shift model offering 280° of slew with the excavator, was recently withdrawn from British Army service. Currently in service with the Danish Army are Hydrema models 807 (39), 906 (1), 908 (12), 908B (10), 908ESB (6) and 908C (8). Model 928C has been supplied to Swedish armed forces.

Options include winterised versions for use in temperatures down to -40°C and cabins offering 7.62 mm AP small arms fire-protection. Swedish Army 928C models are fitted with armoured cabins.

More technical information on the series can be found in the table labelled 'Hydrema 900D series multipurpose machines'.

Hydrema 900 MPV tool carrier
In addition to earthmoving equipment, A/S Hydrema has also produced the 900 MPV tool carrier. This machine can be used for a wide variety of earthmoving, construction and materials handling roles. The Hydrema 900 MPV tool carrier is used by the Danish Air Force. Full details of the Hydrema 900 MPV, which is no longer in commercial production, can be found elsewhere in this section.

Hydrema 910 MCV-2 mineclearing vehicle
A/S Hydrema also manufactures the 910 MCV-2 mineclearing vehicle. This machine leverages off Hydrema's considerable experience with articulated earthmoving machinery. The original machine, the 910 MCV - mineclearing vehicle - was based on technology from the Hydrema 910 10,000 kg dump truck; the more recent 910 MCV-2 - mineclearing vehicle-series 2 - machine is based on the 912C 10,000 kg dump truck. Full details of the MCV/MCV-2 can be found in *Jane's Mines and Mine Clearance*.

It is understood that the MCV/MCV-2 is in service with (or has been supplied to) the Danish Army (14), Emercon (1), India (24 MCV-2 machines were delivered to the Indian Army during 2003), Norwegian Peoples Aid Organisation in Angola (2), Norwegian Army (9, two of which are MCV-2), Singapore (2 MCV-2, 2004), the US Army (1) and others. 910 MCVs have been deployed operationally to Afghanistan (operated by the US Army), Angola, Bosnia, Croatia, Eritrea, Iraq, Kosovo and Russia.

Specifications
See table above

Status
In production. Earthmoving equipment is in service with Danish (>70), Swedish, UK and possibly other armed forces.

Contractor
A/S Hydrema.

Hydrema 900 MPV tool carrier

Development
A/S Hydrema was founded in 1959 and today the company produces a wide range of small-to-medium sized earthmoving equipment, all of which is suitable for use in military engineering and other associated tasks. The 900 MPV is an extension of that range. It was disclosed during 2005 that the Danish Air Force had received a small number of Hydrema 900 MPV tool carriers for use by the Air Force's Task Force for Restoration of Aircraft Operating Surface (RAOS) and for multiple tasks at the Mestersvig airbase in Greenland.

In addition to supplying what are essentially Commercial-Off-The-Shelf (COTS) earthmoving products, Hydrema will design, develop and carry out militarisation of these commercial products on an 'as-required' basis to meet specific military and/or demining requirements. An example of this would be the small arms fire and shell splinter protection package developed for Hydrema's 360° excavators when used in the mineclearing role. A/S Hydrema also manufactures the 910 MCV-2 mineclearing vehicle. Full details of the Hydrema range of earthmoving equipment, and outline details of the 910 MCV-2 mineclearing vehicle, can be found in the Field fortifications and related emplacements section.

A/S Hydrema is based in Denmark, the main factory and offices being located in Stovring near Aalborg in the northern part of Denmark. In Germany, production facilities are located in Weimar.

A/S Hydrema announced in 2010 that the 900 MPV was no longer being marketed.

Description
The Hydrema 900 MPV is a multipurpose vehicle that can accept a variety of hydraulically controlled implements, making it suitable for a wide selection of engineering, construction and logistic support tasks. Attachments can include a telescopic loader, with the arm also accepting forks for handling palletised loads. A backhoe and snow plough or snow blower are other options with attachment changes taking only a few minutes. Five hydraulic quick-couplings are mounted both at the front and rear of the vehicle.

One further option for the Hydrema 900 MPV is for a bushcutter to be fitted to the excavator arm, allowing the machine to clear bush or vegetation from an area prior to de-mining. Operating radius for this operation is approximately 5 m through a 280° arc. An armoured cabin is available for this role which provides protection from 7.62 mm NATO ball and weighs 500 kg. Increased protection levels are available.

The Hydrema 900 MPV is powered by a turbocharged water-cooled diesel engine developing 123 hp (92 kW); this is located under the cab. Drive is hydrostatic and speeds range from 0 to 40 km/h. Steering is by articulation of the two machine halves. Overall machine width (over tyres) is 2.25 m.

Hydrema 900 MPV tool carrier prepared for transport by C-130 Hercules transport aircraft (A/S Hydrema) 1170884

Hydrema 900 MPV tool carrier of the Danish Air Force (Shaun C Connors) 1340283

Status
Commercial production is now complete. In service with the Danish Air Force (see text).

Contractor
A/S Hydrema.

France

Case 988 wheeled excavator

Description
The French Army took delivery of 40 customised Case 988 wheeled excavators during 2000, an unspecified number of these being fitted with an armoured cab supplied by Cabines Sarrazin and providing small arms fire and shell splinter protection for the operator. The French Army machines were also fitted with the optional air-conditioning system, offset digging arm, hydraulic quick-coupler and high-flotation single wheels and tyres.

Case 988 wheeled excavator of the French Army fitted with an armoured cab supplied by Cabines Sarrazin and offering protection from shell splinters and small arms fire. This vehicle (shown with superstructure rotated through 180°) is fitted with single tyres and a front-mounted dozer blade (Shaun C Connors)   0525605

Case 988 wheeled excavator of the French Army fitted with an armoured cab supplied by Cabines Sarrazin and offering protection from shell splinters and small arms fire (Shaun C Connors)   1120468

The Case 988 was a commercially available machine (now superseded in the Case product line-up by a revised design) available in a number of configurations and is of conventional design, the main superstructure containing engine, operator cabin and digging arm, rotating through 360° on a four-wheel undercarriage. All four wheels drive and steer, the axles are rigid and unsprung, the front axle oscillating plus or minus 7°.

Power is provided by a six-cylinder turbocharged diesel developing 170 hp (127 kW), which using an average of 16.2 litres of fuel per hour, allows the machine to operate for 15 hour shifts on a single tank of fuel. The modular design of the undercarriage allows for stabilisers or a dozer blade to be fitted front and rear. A variety of digging arms and buckets - including clamshells and grabs - are available, the maximum digging depth with a conventional earthmoving bucket being 6.3 m, the maximum dump height being 10 m. When used in the lifting role (depending on a number of factors including digging arm and bucket option) the Case 988 can handle a maximum of 10,450 kg at a below ground level depth of 3 m, reducing to a minimum of 1,300 kg at 2 m height and maximum reach throughout 360°. If required the Case 988 can be configured to operate on railway lines.

Details of current construction equipment manufactured by the Case Construction Equipment can be found elsewhere in this section.

Specifications
Case 988 wheeled excavator
[base machine]
Cab seating: 1
Configuration: 4 × 4
Weight: 18,500 kg
Length: (shipping) 9.45 m
Width:
  (stabilisers raised) 2.5 m
  (stabilisers down) 3.71 m
Height: (cab roof) 3.26 m
Ground clearance: 330 mm
Wheelbase: 2.6 m
Max speed:
  (low range) 7.5 km/h
  (high range) 25 km/h
Fuel capacity: 249 litres
Operation: 15.4 h at 16.2 litres/h
Max continuous gradient: 47%
Engine: Case 6T 590 5.88 litre, 6-cylinder in-line turbocharged water-cooled 4-stroke diesel developing 170 hp (127 kW)
Transmission: hydro-mechanical with variable displacement hydraulic motor with range selector supplying continuous speed variation
Steering: hydraulic power assisted on all four wheels
Turning radius: 7.28 m
Suspension: rigid rear, oscillating front (±7°)
Tyres: 18-19.5 XF (4 wheels), 10.00-20 (8 wheels with twinning rings)
Brakes:
  (main) hydraulic, multidisc oil immersed
  (parking) electro-hydraulic on all four wheels
Electrical system: 24 V
Batteries: 2 × 12 V, 120 Ah

Status
Production of current generation model continues. In service with the French Army (40).
Case Corporation

Manufacturing plant
Case Poclain SA

Matenin trench digger

Development
This machine was designed to meet a French Army requirement for the rapid excavation of trenches and defences in forward areas by Matenin SA of France. Matenin SA no longer trades and in 2003, CEFA obtained the project management of the Matenin range of carriers.

Description
The Matenin trench digger is based on a 4 × 4 cross-country platform with a forward control cab and trench digging equipment mounted on the rear of the chassis. Essentially the same chassis is used as the basis for the Matenin mine burier and the Nexter (previously Giat) Minotaur anti-tank minelaying system.

The trench-digging equipment can dig straight or curved trenches or one-person foxholes. It operates in the vertical position and can be swung into the horizontal position for travelling. Digging can be controlled from within the cab of the vehicle or by means of a remote-control system. Sufficient fuel is carried for up to 12 hours of digging operations at a fuel consumption of 22 l/hr while digging.

The excavator itself consists of chain-driven buckets made of moulded steel with tilting bases, mounted on a boom. A conveyor belt is provided to discharge earth to the right or the left and the boom is fitted with a scraper to clean the bottom of the trench.

Matenin trench digger of the French Army (Pierre Touzin)   0589067

Matenin trench digger of the French Army (Pierre Touzin)   1120414

The power-shift hydromechanical transmission has four ranges, allowing for road travel, cross-country, digging and winch drive.

There are two models of the Matenin trench digger: the MXD, which digs a trench 850 mm wide and up to 2 m deep; and the Model NX 7B3, which digs a trench 600 mm wide and 400 mm 1.6 m deep. Both models can dig a vertical trench on a 15 per cent side slope and have a typical capacity of 260 m³/h.

Specifications

Matenin trench digger
Cab seating: 1 + 2
Configuration: 4 × 4, with locking differentials
Weight:
   (NX 7B3) 14,600 kg
   (MXD) 15,500 kg
Length: 7.55 m
Width: 2.48 m
Height:
   (over cab) 2.77 m
   (travelling) 3.56 m
Ground clearance: 500 mm
Wheelbase: 3 m
Track: 1.98 m
Angle of approach/departure: 38°/34°
Max speed: (road) 65 km/h (50 km/h average)
Max range: (road) 600 km
Fuel consumption:
   (road) 43.5 l/hr
   (digging) 22 l/hr
Max gradient: 50%
Max side slope: 20% (15% when digging)
Fording: 1.2 m
Engine: 6-cylinder water-cooled diesel developing 180 hp (134 kW) at 2,200 rpm
Transmission: powershift hydromechanical, with torque converter and two 4-gear ranges
Steering: power assisted
Tyres: 16.00 × 25, low pressure
Brakes: air
Electrical system: 24 V
Winch: driven by hydraulic motor; 6,000 kg capacity line pull

Status
In service with the French and other undisclosed armies.

Contractor
Matenin SA (this company is no longer trading)

Enquiries to
CEFA

MFRD/F1 mobile drilling machine

Description
The MFRD/F1 (Moyen de Forage Rapide de Destruction (MFRD)) is the combination of drilling equipment supplied by Constructions Industrielles d'Anjou mounted on a high mobility Pinguely RTC10 rough terrain carrier. The MFRD/F1 can be used for a variety of field engineering purposes but the primary role is for drilling holes into which demolition charges can be placed. The French Army ordered 122 examples of this system. Production is complete, with the now Pinguely-Haulotte having progressively abandoned its manufacture of such equipment to concentrate on the design, manufacture and sale of personnel aerial work platforms.

The drilling equipment can be used at any angle from the vertical to the horizontal at 7.5° intervals. The drill uses an auger in soft soils, but in rock, a bottom hammer is employed. Both have a working diameter of 220 mm. Maximum drilling depth is 6 m. When drilling through rock the following drilling speeds can be attained:

Limestone	12 m/h
Granite	17 m/h
Schist	32 m/h

The RCT10 rough terrain carrier has a 4 × 4 configuration with a forward control all-steel cab with seating for a driver/operator and one passenger. The drilling rig is carried on the area behind the cab with the gantry pivot overhanging the rear of the vehicle. An air compressor, driven from a power take-off on the gearbox, delivers 19 m³/minute at 7 bar. A 6,000 to 8,000 kg winch can be fitted.

Specifications
MFRD/F1 mobile drilling machine
Cab seating: 1 + 1
Configuration: 4 × 4
Weight:
   (total) 16,800 kg
   (front axle) 8,300 kg
   (rear axle) 8,500 kg
Length:
   (overall, travelling) 9.75 m
   (chassis) 7.565 m
Width: 2.49 m
Height:
   (overall) 2.384 m
   (cab) 2.68 m
Ground clearance: 520 mm
Wheelbase: 4.1 m
Track:
   (front) 1.971 m
   (rear) 2.038 m
Angle of approach/departure: 42°/35°
Fording: 1 m
Vertical obstacle: 500 mm
Gradient: 50%
Max speed: (road) 70-75 km/h
Range: (road) 600 km
Engine: turbocharged water-cooled diesel developing 260 hp (194 kW) at 2,200 rpm
Transmission: torque converter semi-automatic hydromechanical gearbox with 3 forward and 3 reverse gears
Suspension: double-action leaf springs and hydraulic shock-absorbers
Turning radius: 11 m
Tyres: 16.00 × 25

Status
In service with the French Army (122 delivered).

Contractor
Haulotte-Pinguely
(This company is no longer involved in the manufacture of such equipment.)

MFRD/F1 mobile drilling machines (Pierre Touzin)   0589068

India

BEML construction equipment

Development

BEML was previously known as Bharat Earth Movers Limited and was formed in 1964. BEML was wholly owned and operated by India's Ministry of Defense until 1992, when the government divested 25 per cent of its holdings in the company. According to the company, it is the second largest manufacturer of earth moving products in Asia.

In addition to construction equipment BEML also produces railway products, TATRA trucks under licence, trailers, high-power diesel engines and hydraulic aggregates. Approximately 10 per cent of BEML sales are defence-related, and the company commands a 70 per cent share of the commercial home market for construction equipment.

BEML currently manufactures more than 70 different construction-related machines in 19 product ranges. Brief details of BEML product ranges likely to be found in the inventory of military engineer regiments are included here and include: backhoe loaders; tracked excavators; wheeled loading shovels and dozers, and graders.

Construction-related equipment supplied to the military by BEML are essentially commercial-off-the-shelf (COTS) products with limited militarisation.

Description

Wheeled loaders

BEML currently produces a range of four wheeled loaders with engine power outputs, standard bucket capacity and operational weights ranging from 123 hp (92 kW), 1.7 m³ and 9,890 kg for the BL 636 through to 420 hp (313 kW), 6.3 m³ and 43,300 kg for the BL 34.

The earlier model BL 1420 which is powered by a 126 hp (94 kW) diesel engine, has a bucket capacity of 1.6 to 3 m³ and an operating weight of 14,500 kg is known to be in service with the Indian Army in numbers.

All BEML wheeled loaders are conventional in design, being four-wheel drive with equal-sized wheels. All are steered by frame articulation, an unsprung rear axle accounting for ground undulations.

Wheeled dozers

BEML currently produces a range of three wheeled dozers, all fitted with straight blades. Engine power outputs and operational weights range from 126 hp (94 kW) and 15,000 kg for the BD 14 W through to 460 hp (343 kW) and 38,700 kg for the BD 46 W.

All BEML wheeled dozers are conventional in design, being four-wheel drive with equal-sized wheels. All are steered by frame articulation, an unsprung rear axle accounting for ground undulations.

Model BD 14 W is in service with the Indian Army.

360° excavators

BEML has produced both wheeled and tracked 360° excavators, but currently offers only tracked variants, the current range consisting of ten machines.

Engine power outputs range from 63 to 404 hp (47 to 301 kW); there is also an electric model. Operating weights range from 7,100 kg for the BE 71 through to 162,000 kg for the BE 1600. For most military applications, machines with operating weights ranging from 16,000 to 26,000 kg are the norm.

Model BE 220 LC which is powered by a 148 hp (110 kW) diesel engine, has a bucket capacity of 0.44 to 1.26 m³ and an operating weight of 22,800 kg is known to be in service with the Indian Army in numbers.

BEML BL 9 H backhoe loader powered by a KOEL 4R1040 diesel engine developing 76 hp (57 kW) and driving through 4F/4R power shuttle-type transmission with integral torque convertor. Maximum travel speed is 36 km/h (Shaun C Connors) 1156183

Track-type tractors

BEML currently produces a range of 11 track-type tractors. These range from the BD 31 powered by a 66 hp (49 kW) diesel engine and with an operating weight of 6,150 kg, through to the BD 475 powered by a 770 hp (574 kW) diesel engine and with an operating weight of 95,340 kg.

The Indian Army is known to use at least three models of BEML track-type tractor, the BD 50, BD 65 and BD 80. These are powered by 90, 165 and 180 hp (67, 123 and 134 kW) diesel engines and have operating weights of 11,000, 16,770 and 21,550 kg, respectively.

Graders

BEML currently produces four motor graders, the BG 605, BG 606BX, BG 605A and BG 825. Models BG 605 and BG 825 are known to have been supplied to the Indian Army. Model BG 605 has an operating weight of 12,650 kg, a blade width of 3.71 m and is powered by a 145 hp (108 kW) diesel engine. Model BG 825 has an operating weight of 25,750 kg, a blade width of 4.928 m and is powered by a 280 hp (209 kW) diesel engine.

Backhoe loaders

Until the introduction in 2004 of new models BEML produced two backhoe loaders, the BL 8 H and BL 8 H (4 × 4), the BL 8 H being powered by a larger 90 hp (67 kW) diesel engine, compared to the previous 72 hp (54 kW) model and being an all-wheel drive machine. In all other respects, these two machines are the same. In May 2004 BEML launched the BL 9 H which was followed by the BL 9 H (4 × 4). These machines have engine power outputs, standard bucket capacity and operating weights of 76 hp (57 kW), 1 m³ and 7,600 kg (BL 9 H) and 96 hp (72 kW), 1 m³ and 8,000 kg (BL 9 H (4 × 4). The BL 9 H is in service with the Indian Army.

Status

In production. BEML construction equipment is in service with the armed forces of India, and possibly other countries.

Contractor

Bharat Earth Movers Limited (BEML)

Telcon construction equipment

Development

Telco Construction Equipment Company (Telcon) is a joint venture company between the Indian automobile company Tata Engineering Ltd and Hitachi Construction Machinery Co Ltd, Japan. In December 2005 it was announced that Hitachi had signed an agreement to increase its stake in Telcon from 20 to 40 per cent. Telcon also collaborates with John Deere of the US with regard to backhoe loader technology, Lebrero of Spain for compactors and CESAN of Turkey for asphalt plants.

The Telcon product range (branded Tata Hitachi or Tata) includes hydraulic excavators, crawler cranes, wheel loaders, backhoe loaders, off-highway dumpers, motor graders, skid steer loaders, cane loaders and truck loader cranes.

Telcon is the market leader in India. The company was the first to introduce mini-excavators in India and is the largest manufacturer of hydraulic excavators in India, with over 6,000 machines produced.

The following sections cover Telcon-produced hydraulic excavators, backhoe loaders and wheeled loaders. Equipment supplied by Telcon for military purposes are essentially commercial-off-the-shelf (COTS) products with limited militarisation.

BEML type BD 80 track-type tractor powered by a BEML B6D125 diesel engine developing 180 hp (134 kW) and driving through a manual gearbox with five forward and four reverse gears. Maximum speed is 10 km/h forward, 9.6 km/h reverse. Maximum drawbar pull is 19,600 kg (Shaun C Connors) 1156182

Description

360° tracked excavators

Telcon is the largest manufacturer of 360° tracked excavators in India and the current offered range consists of 19 machines. These range in size from the 2,200 kg TMX20 to the 84,000 kg 870 LCH. With the exception of mini-excavators, for most military applications, machines with operating weights ranging from 16,000 to 26,000 kg are the norm. Within this weight range Telco offers four machines, the 20,150 kg EX200i LC and the 20,550 kg EX210 LCH-V. The EX200 LC is available configured as a backhoe or shovel (operating weight increases when configured as a shovel) and is powered by a Tata Cummins 6BT5.9C diesel engine developing 125 hp (93 kW). This engine is an option for the EX210 LCH-V which in standard configuration is powered by a Isuzu A-6BG1T diesel engine developing 135 hp (101 kW). Also offered are the 19,900 kg ZAXIS 200LC and the 21,000 kg ZAXIS 210LCH.

Tata 315-V backhoe loader

Telcon produces a single backhoe loader model, the Tata J315-V, for which the company has a technology transfer arrangement with John Deere of the US since 1996. This licence expired in July 2006 and the machine in question was previously designated Tata JD 315-V.

The JD 315-V is a conventional two-wheel drive, front axle steer backhoe loader. Axles are unsprung, the oscillating front axle taking account of ground undulations.

Motive power, previously supplied by a Perkins 1004.4 THR diesel engine developing 98 hp (73 kW) at 2,200 rpm, is now provided by a Tata 497TC diesel engine developing 92 hp (69 kW) at 2,200 rpm. This drives the rear axle via a four-speed ZF gearbox. Maximum travel speed is 41.5 km/h. Operating weight is 7,340 kg. A 4 × 4 version is also available.

TWL 3034 and 3036 wheeled loaders

Telcon produces two wheeled loaders, model TWL 3034 and TWL 3036. These are conventional four-wheeled machines which steer through frame articulation, 40° left and right. Axles are unsprung, the oscillating rear axle (24° - TWL 3034; 27° TWL 3036) taking account of ground undulations.

Motive power for the TWL 3034 is provided by a Tata 697 NA diesel engine developing 105 hp (78 kW) at 2,400 rpm. This drives via a hydrostatic transmission to Dana planetary drive axles. Maximum travel speed is 34.6 km/h. Operating weight is 10,720 kg.

Motive power for the TWL 3036 is provided by a Tata 697 TC diesel engine developing 135 hp (101 kW) at 2,400 rpm. This drives via a ZF automatic transmission and ZF axles. Maximum travel speed is 24.5 km/h. Operating weight is 11,580 kg.

Telcon also offers the ZW 220, a 17,800 kg machine that is powered by a 223 hp (164 kW) engine and imported directly from Hitatchi of Japan.

Status

In production. Telcon construction equipment is known to be in service with Indian armed forces.

Contractor

Telcon Construction Equipment Company Ltd

Korea, South

Doosan construction equipment

Development

Doosan construction equipment is manufactured by Doosan Infracore Ltd. The company was founded in 1937 as the Chosun Machine Works and following the 1976 merger with the Daewoo Machinery Corp was renamed Daewoo Heavy Industries Ltd.

Daewoo Heavy Industries & Machinery was acquired by Doosan in 2005 and is now known as Doosan Infracore. Doosan began in 1936 as a small store in Baeogae, Seoul. During 2007 Doosan Infracore acquired the Bobcat compact machinery equipment business from Ingersoll-Rand. Doosan Infracore announced in August 2008 that it had acquired Norway's Moxy Engineering AS for USD81 million.

Doosan manufactures a wide range of construction equipment at its worldwide production facilities, the vast majority of which is suitable for military applications. This equipment is supplied to commercial specification, although limited militarisation can be carried out in-country by Doosan agents, dealerships or military workshop facilities. Militarisation can include: climatic operational range enhancements; the fitting of small arms fire and shell splinter-protecting cabs, and the fitting of winches or other hydraulically-powered ancillary equipment.

In line with most manufacturers of commercial construction equipment the Doosan range is continually updated, new models and minor design changes (often cosmetic) being made on a regular basis. The current construction equipment range (excluding Bobcat skid-steer loaders) features in excess of 35 base machines.

Description

Wheeled loaders

The Doosan wheeled loader range consists of 13 machines with operating weights ranging from 8,500 kg to 30,600 kg and bucket capacities ranging from 1.5 to 5.2 m³. With the exception of the largest two machines (the

Norwegian Army Moxy MT31. Doosan Infracore announced in August 2008 that it had acquired Norway's Moxy Engineering AS for USD81 million (Carl Schulze)   1391296

DL-400 and DL-500) which are powered by 280 and 335 hp (209 to 250 kW) Cummins diesel engine respectively, all are powered by Doosan diesel engines with power outputs ranging from 110 to 235 hp (76 to 172 kW).

All machines in the range are of conventional design, being steered by articulation and having rigid unsprung axles, the oscillating rear axle accounting for ground undulations.

Tool carrier variants of the smallest wheeled loaders (the Mega 160 and Mega 200) are also available.

360° excavators

Doosan produces ranges of both wheeled and tracked 360° excavators, the current number of basic variants totalling 40. Maximum weight of the wheeled range vary from 5,550 to 20,900 kg and engine power outputs range from 57 to 162 hp (43 to 121 kW). All are of conventional two-axle design, having four-wheel drive and steer. Axles are unsprung, an oscillating front axle compensating for ground undulations.

The Doosan range of tracked excavators has maximum weights ranging from 8,000 to 50,700 kg. Engine power outputs range from 95 to 329 hp (71 to 245 kW), with all engines being produced in-house by Doosan. In common with the wheeled excavator range, the tracked excavator range has a wide range of optional buckets or clamshells that can be fitted, and the machines can be used to lift, with or without any bucket attachment.

Compact equipment

Doosan produces a selection of compact construction equipment that comprises ranges of mini tracked 360° excavators and skid-steer loaders. The Bobcat range of skid-steer loaders has now been added to the Doosan portfolio.

The current range of mini excavators consists of ten machines with transport weights ranging from 1,540 to 8,300 kg. Engine power outputs range from 17 to 51 hp (13 to 38 kW).

The current range of skid-steer loaders (excluding Bobcat machines) consists of five machines with weights of 2,587 and 3,392 kg and engine power outputs of 45 to 75 hp (34 to 56 kW).

Articulated dumptrucks

Doosan Infracore announced in August 2008 that it had acquired Norway's Moxy Engineering AS for USD81 million. Moxy Engineering is a manufacturer of articulated dump trucks (ADTs) for off-road use in the earth moving and construction industries and the company is now known as Doosan Moxy AS.

Four base ADT models are currently available, these powered by Scania diesel engines developing between 306 and 444 hp (228 and 331 kW). Payloads range from 24,100 to 38,000 kg.

Status

In production. In service with a number of armed forces.

Contractor

Doosan Infracore Ltd

Combat Multi-Purpose Excavator (CMPE)

Description

The Combat Multi-Purpose Excavator (CMPE) is designed to perform a number of battlefield field engineering and construction tasks, and while a military-specific machine utilises commercially proven design concepts. It is intended to operate with mechanised forces.

The base platform is essentially a small (12,000 kg class), rear-engined, four-wheel drive wheeled loader that steers by frame articulation, and with an oscillating rear axle compensating for ground undulations. However, whereas on a conventional wheeled loader the front lifting arms are fixed, on the CMPE the lifting arms are turntable-mounted and may traverse 90° left or right of centre, thereby allowing a considerable degree of operational flexibility and enabling operations in confined areas.

By means of a quick-change mechanism the 1.5 m³ capacity front loading bucket can be replaced by a selection of attachments, further enhancing the operational flexibility of the CMPE. Forks, a backhoe attachment or a rock-breaker may be fitted. With forks attached maximum lift capacity is 2,500 kg; the backhoe attachment has a bucket capacity of 0.3 m³, and the rock-breaker operates at 80 kg/m. A chainsaw with a 48 cm blade is also carried as standard equipment. The vehicle deploys with these attachments stowed in the loader bucket.

The cab seats two, although only one person is required to operate the machine.

Specifications
Seating: 1 + 1
Configuration: 4 × 4
Combat weight: 12,300 kg
Length: 6.69 m
Width: 2.59 m
Height: 3.07 m
Max speed: 45 km/h
Max gradient: 60%
Sideslope: 40%
Fording: 950 m m
Engine: Deutz BF6L913 air-cooled diesel developing 148 hp
Transmission: hydrostatic
Suspension: rigid unsprung axles, rear axle oscillates about a central pivot
Electrical system: 24 V

Status
In production. In service with ROK armed forces.

Contractor
Samsung Techwin Co Ltd

Poland

HSW SL-34C loader-dozer

Development
Huta Stalowa Wola (HSW) is Poland's largest manufacturer of construction equipment. The SL-34C loader-dozer is the continuing evolution of the SL-34 series and is based on a commercial machine, but includes a number of military-specific features in its design. The SL-34C replaced the earlier SL-34B in production.

Wojskowe Zaklady Inzynieryjne of Poland offers a full overhaul and modernisation service for time-served L-34 loader-dozers, bringing them up to SL-34 standard.

Description
The HSW SL-34C loader-dozer is entirely conventional in design, being based on an articulating frame-steer chassis with four equal-sized driven wheels. The front axle is rigid and unsprung, the rear axle oscillates ±13° around a central pivot point to take account of ground undulations.

The standard bucket is a CZ-5 four-in-one Drott-type of 3 m³ capacity. This allows the machine to perform a variety of earthmoving, loading, dozing, grading/scraping and pick-and-carry tasks. A quick-couple device allows for the rapid exchange of buckets and a side-shift-capable forklift attachment or a hydraulic grab may also be used.

A Rockinger 561E towing attachment with dual line air and 24 V electrical connectors at the rear of the machine allows loads of up to 60,000 kg to be towed on paved roads.

Motive power is provided by a Cummins diesel engine developing 215 hp. The engine is equipped with a pre-heat system for starting at low ambient temperatures. The one-person cab is heated and also equipped with an overpressure system.

Specifications

	SL-34B	SL-34C
Cab seating:	1	1
Configuration:	4 × 4	4 × 4
Operating weight:		
(with bucket)	22,970 kg	22,830 kg
(with forks)	22,600 kg	22,310 kg
Length:		
(with bucket)	8.39 m	8.38 m
(with forks)	9.8 m	9.595 m
Width:		
(over tyres)	2.73 m	2.725 m
(over cab)	1.6 m	1.8 m
(over bucket)	2.885 m	2.982 m
Height:		
(top of cab)	3.645	3.607 m
(beacon)	3.87 m	3.95 m
Ground clearance:	450 mm	450 mm
Track:	2.1 m	2.09 m
Wheelbase:	3.14 m	3.145 m
Departure angle:	23°	19°
Max road speed:	(forward and reverse ±10%)	(forward and reverse ±10%)
(1st)	6 km/h	8 km/h
(2nd)	12 km/h	16 km/h
(3rd)	20 km/h	27 km/h
(4th)	35 km/h	39 km/h
Gradient:		
(with fully loaded forks)	25%	55%
(with 60,000 kg towed load)	16%	16%
Engine:	SW680/59/7 water-cooled 4-stroke diesel developing 220 hp	Cummins 6CTAA-215 8.3 litre 6-cylinder inline water-cooled 4-stroke diesel developing 215 hp at 2,200 rpm and 975 Nm torque at 1,500 rpm
Transmission:	automatic, 4 forward and 4 reverse gears	automatic powershift type with 4 forward and 4 reverse gears
Steering:	by articulation, angle of articulation ±40°	by articulation, angle of articulation ±40°
Turning radius (dependant on tyre size, ground conditions and front ancillaries):	6.7 m	6.98 m (with bucket), 7.135 m (with forks)
Axles:	rigid	rigid
Suspension:	unsprung, oscillating rear (±13°)	unsprung, oscillating rear (±13°)
Electrical system:	24 V	24 V
Loader dimensions (with CZ-5 bucket):		
(dump height)	2.95 m	2.95 m
(load over height)	3.53 m	3.53 m
(dig depth)	360 mm	360 mm
Loader performance (with CZ-5 bucket):		
(breakout force)	120 kN ±10%	120 kN ±10%
(rated load)	76 kN	80 kN
(bucket grip force)	40-65 kN	40-65 kN

Huta Stalowa Wola SL-34B loader dozer (HSW)   0587657

Status
Production as required (SL-34C), commercial variant in mass production. SL-34B (approx 20) in service with the Polish Army. Considerable numbers of earlier SL-34 machines remain in service.

Contractor
Huta Stalowa Wola SA

HSW UMI Backhoe Loader 9.50

Development
Huta Stalowa Wola (HSW) is Poland's largest manufacturer of construction equipment. The UMI Backhoe Loader 9.50 is based on the commercial model 9.50 backhoe loader introduced in 2004.

A small number of machines have been supplied to the Polish Army, and some are known to have been deployed operationally.

Description
The UMI Backhoe Loader 9.50 is entirely conventional in design and complies with the latest relevant commercial legislation. By means of a hydraulic quick connection system, the front arm may be fitted with assorted buckets, a dozer blade, a snow plough, a grab for handling tree trucks or similar, or various forks for lifting. The rear backhoe may also be fitted with assorted buckets, a hydraulic hammer or may also be used for lifting operations.

For military applications the vehicle is supplied with rifle brackets in the cab (for PM-63 or similar), an electrical system for installation of a radio telephone type R3501 and passive night-vision goggles, a compressor with air-line, a set of sapper tools, facilities to locate camouflage netting, catches to locate a riotous protection kit, and a rear convoy light.

Climatic operational range is –30°C to +40°C. Time to switch from transportation mode to operational mode is a maximum of 10 minutes. The standard vehicle may be transported by rail and may be adapted to fit inside a C-130 Hercules transport aircraft.

Specifications
Cab seating: 1
Configuration: 4 × 4
Operational weight: 7,700 kg; 8,280 kg with forks, 8,850 kg with bucket
Length (travel): 6.28 m
Width (over wheels): 2.3 m
Operational slope: gradient 25°, sideslope 15°
Engine: IVECO 4-cylinder water-cooled Tier II diesel developing 101 hp
Suspension: unsprung, oscillating front, rigid rear

HSW UMI Backhoe Loader 9.50 (Shaun C Connors)   1148966

Loader performance and dimensions:
  (bucket capacity) 1 m³
  (dig depth, horizontal bucket) 80 mm
  (dump height) 2.7 m
Forklift performance and dimensions:
  (lift height with forks) 3.2 m
  (diameter of lifted tree trunks) 350 mm
  (lift capacity to full height) 2,000 kg
Backhoe performance and dimensions:
  (maximum dig depth) 4.74 m
  (maximum reach) 5.79 m
  (maximum load over height) 3.6 m
  (bucket rotation) 180°
  (lift capacity at full reach) 660 kg

Status
In production. In service with the Polish Army.

Contractor
Huta Stalowa Wola SA

Russian Federation

BKT-RK2 wheeled bulldozer

Development
The BKT-RK2 wheeled bulldozer was developed as a multi-purpose machine capable of performing a wide variety construction and other associated engineer work.

Description
The BKT-RK2 wheeled bulldozer is designed to carry out airfield construction, road construction and other engineer work. It can also be used for surface scraping tasks, making crossings over ditches, trenches or other obstacles, digging of entrenchment pits for armoured vehicles or artillery, snow removal, soil loosening (route denial) and stump pulling.

A dozer blade (front) and combined ripper and stump pulling assembly (rear) are mounted to the base chassis. The dozer blade can work in conjunction with a ski that allows the blade to follow ground contours during dozing operations. The ski can also regulate the thickness of the soil layer being scraped. The soil ripper and stump puller are mounted at the rear of the machine. Soil ripping and stump pulling work can be carried out down to -15°C, with the soil freezing depth being 100 to 150 mm.

When working in earthmoving roles such as filling in trenches or levelling ground areas, capacity is around 100 to 120 m³/h. When stump pulling, around 20 stumps of 200 to 400 mm diameter can be pulled per hour, and when loosening soil (route denial) in class 3 to 4 soil to a depth of 400 mm, 4 to 7 km/h can be covered.

The BKT-RK2 has a crew of two and both are seated in an all-steel cab equipped with heating, heated glass, radiation warning and navigation equipment plus an air filtration system. The machine is right-hand drive.

Maximum road speed of the BKT-RK2 is 45 km/h, and road range is 800 km. Motive power is provided by a 376 hp diesel engine.

Status
Production likely to be on an as required basis. In service with the armed forces of the Russian Federation and other members of the former Warsaw Pact.

Contractor
Dmitrov Excavator Plant
JSC Budshliakhmash

Marketed by
Rosoboronexport

UDM multipurpose road construction machine

Development
The UDM multipurpose road construction machine was developed for the rapid preparation/repair of roadways for troop movement and is based on a commercial wheeled tractor chassis. The product is considered civil-related, or dual use, by its manufacturer.

Description
The UDM multipurpose road construction machine is based on the K-702M commercial wheeled tractor chassis, this very similar to the K-703M commercial wheeled tractor on which the TMK-3 trench-digging machine is based. Full details of the TMK-3 trench-digging machine can be found elsewhere in this section.

Motive power is provided by a YaMZ-8423 eight-cylinder turbocharged diesel engine fitted with a preheat system that allows for starting at temperatures down to –40°C. Transmission is hydromechanical. The front axle oscillates to account for ground undulations, the rear load-bearing axle is rigid. Steering is by articulation.

In common with the TMK-3, a hydraulically-operated dozer blade is fitted to one end of the machine and this is intended for earth moving, grading and general dozing operations. The blade can be angled to the left or right if required. Working capacity is quoted as up to 2 km/h when constructing trail roads in moderate terrain, or between 2 to 4 km/h when constructing trail roads through snow cover of up to 1 m deep. When dozing operations such as slope creation, or pit or hole filling are being undertaken, work rate is quoted as 100 to 120 m³/h. Ditch digging rate is quoted as 70 to 90 m³/h.

The front of the UDM machine is fitted with loader equipment. This is designed to excavate, load and move bulk materials over short distances. The standard bucket has a capacity of 3 m³ and maximum bucket emptying height at an empty angle of 45° is 3.2 m. The standard bucket can be replaced by a four-in-one-type bucket, this allowing limited pick-and-carry operations. Maximum lifting capacity when cargo handling is 6,000 kg.

Specifications

UDM multipurpose road construction machine
Base chassis: K-702MV
Cab seating: 2
Configuration: 4 × 4
Weight: 21,000 kg
Length: (travel configuration) 10.12 m
Width: (travel configuration) 3.365 m
Height: (travel configuration) 3.97 m
Max speed: 40 km/h
Engine: YaMZ 8-cylinder turbocharged water-cooled diesel developing 335 hp (250 kW)

Status

Production as required. Available for export.

Enquiries to

Rosoboronexport

TMK-3 trench-digging machine

Development

The TMK-3 trench-digging machine was designed for the rapid digging of troop trenches, although unlike the military specific TMK-2, which is similar in role and based on the IKT prime mover chassis, the TMK-3 is based on a commercial tractor chassis (with modifications) and is promoted by its manufacturer as a civil-related, dual use machine.

Description

The base chassis of the TMK-3 is the K-703M, this being essentially a commercial wheeled tractor with limited modifications, the engine, hydraulic torque converter, gearbox, cab and main operating controls of the military product being shared with the commercial K-703M.

For trenching operations, the transmission features GST-90 hydraulic reduction gear, enabling the machine to infinitely vary speeds within the limits of 0 to 2,000 m/h. The circular trenching rotor blade is fitted with twelve cutting tools. The rotor is driven mechanically by the tractor's power take-off shaft. The rotor drive comprises a gearbox offering rotor rotation speeds of 2 and 3.5 m/s, a turning reduction gear, torque-limiting clutch with shear pins, and rotor side and central reduction gears.

The TMK-3 trench-digging machine is designed for the rapid digging of troop trenches in both frozen and non-frozen soils and working capacity is quoted as 90 to 150 m/h in frozen soils, and 360 to 800 m/h in class 2 and class 3 non-frozen soils. Trench depths in frozen soils are 1.1 or 1.5 m; width is 600 mm. Trench depths in non-frozen soils are 1.1 or 1.5 m; width is 600 mm at the bottom of the trench, 1.1 m at the top of the trench.

A hydraulically-operated dozer blade is fitted to the front of the machine. This is intended for earth moving, grading and general dozing operations. The blade can be angled to the left or right if required.

Specifications

TMK-3
Base chassis: K-703MV
Cab seating: 2
Configuration: 4 × 4
Weight: 22,577 kg
Length: (travel configuration) 9.675 m
Width: (travel configuration) 3.37 m
Height: (travel configuration) 4.16 m
Max speed: 44 km/h
Engine: water-cooled diesel developing 335 hp (250 kW)

Status

Production as required. Available for export.

Contractor

Rosoboronexport

PKT-2 road-building machine

Description

The PKT-2 road-building machine is designed to rapidly create roads and carry out expedient repair/clearance work on existing roads. It can also be used to make crossings over ditches, trenches or other obstacles, clear ground of shrubs, small trees and rocks, construct approach roads for river crossings and bridges, snow removal and the digging of entrenchment pits for armoured vehicles or artillery.

The PKT-2 is based on the chassis of the IKT prime mover to which a front-mounted V-type dozer blade is fitted. The two-piece (left and right 'wings') of the blade enable it to be hydraulically-configured as a convex or concave blade, plus doze either left or right. For some operations the blade will also tilt 10° left or right. When lowered, the ski attachment allows the blade to follow ground contours dozing operations.

The PKT-2 has a crew of two and both are seated in an all-steel cab equipped with heating, heated glass, radiation warning and navigation equipment plus an air filtration system.

When road-building across virgin land with bushes and small trees operating speeds vary from 3 to 6 km/h. When clearing deep snow operating speeds vary from 3 to 10 km/h. When working in earthmoving roles such as building approach roads to bridging sites, filling in trenches or levelling ground areas, capacity is around 150 to 160 m³/h. When digging pits in soils of type 3 or 4 capacity is around 100 to 130 m³/h.

Maximum road speed of the PKT-2 is 45 km/h, and road range is 800 km. Motive power is provided by a 376 hp diesel engine.

A number of other similar machines are also based on the IKT prime mover chassis. These include the TMK-2 road-building machine and the BKT-RK2 bulldozer.

Status

In service with the armed forces of the Russian Federation and other members of the former Warsaw Pact.

Contractor

Dmitrov Excavator Plant
JSC Budshliakhmash

Marketed by

Rosoboronexport

Hungarian Army TMK-2 road-building machine in the former Yugoslavia (Shaun C Connors)   0109483

BTM series of high-speed ditching machines

Description

The BTM trenching machine consists of the ETR-409 ditching machine mounted on the rear of the AT-T heavy tracked artillery tractor. The equipment can dig a trench 800 mm wide to a maximum depth of 1.5 m at a rate of 1.12 km/h. The BTM-TMG is a variant of the basic BTM designed to dig trenches in frozen ground. Once a special cable and anchor assembly has been deployed it can dig a trench 600 mm wide at 100 m/h in frozen soil. A further model, the BTM-3 weighing 27,300 kg, is unable to dig trenches in frozen ground. There is also a BTM-TMG2S model, which has a larger ditching machine.

Belvneshpromservice of Belarus are one of a number of companies throughout the former Soviet Union now offering surplus Soviet-era equipment for export sale in either 'as is' condition or refurbished and overhauled to customer requirements. In addition to BTM series ditching machines, Belvneshpromservice also offers a selection of other related equipment including the TMK-2 trench-digging machine, MDK-2, MDK-2M and MDK-3 trench digging machines, BAT-2 and BAT-M route clearing machines, and the PZM-2 regimental trench-digging machine.

From 1992 onwards, the above models were joined by the BTM-4 based on the chassis of the MT-T general purpose tracked carrier. This model weighs 41,000 kg, has a two-person crew and is powered by a 710 hp

BTM series of high-speed ditching machines

	BTM	BTM-TMG	BTM-TMG2S
Crew:	2	2	2
Weight:	26,500 kg	30,000 kg	32,000 kg
Length:			
(travelling)	7.35 m	7.6 m	11.5 m
(operating)	10.85 m	-	11.5 m
Width:	3.2 m	3.2 m	4.6 m
Height:			
(travelling)	4.3 m	4.3 m	4.6 m
(operating)	3.5 m	-	3.2 m
Speed:	35 km/h	36 km/h	36 km/h
Cruising range:	500 km	400 km	400 km
Fuel capacity:	810 litres	-	-
Trench-crossing ability:	2.1 m	2.1 m	2.1 m
Max vertical obstacle:	1 m	1 m	1 m
Gradient:	36°	36°	36°
Side slope:	17°	17°	17°
Fording depth:	750 mm	750 mm	750 mm
Working capacity: (800 mm trench)	1,120 m/h	1,120 m/h (summer)	-
Depth of trench:	1.5 m	-	3 m
Width of trench:			
(top)	1.1 m	600 mm	1.1 m
(bottom)	600 mm	600 mm	-
Height of parapet:	400 mm	-	-

(529 kW) diesel engine. For transport, the BTM-4 can carry its trench-digging machine lowered on to the cargo bed behind the forward control armoured cab. When digging, spoil is dispensed to either side of the trench. The BTM-4 can dig trenches in frozen soil at increased speeds without any need for prior preparation. In unfrozen ground the BTM-4 can dig a 1.1 m wide trench at a rate of 1.2 km/h; in frozen ground the rate is 400 m/h. When a 1.5 m wide trench is dug in unfrozen ground the rate is 1 km/h; in frozen ground the rate is 300 m/h.

The latest machine in the series is the BTM-4M Tundra based on the tracked chassis of the 203 mm 2S7M Malka self-propelled gun with which it shares engine, gearboxes, final drives and so on. Compared to the 2S7M chassis, the crew seats are raised by 400 mm to improve operational view, plus the glazed area of the cabin has been enlarged. The track and suspension system is identical to that fitted to the T-80 MBT and is claimed to have a 10,000 km operational life. Full details of the 2S7M and T-80 can be found in *Jane's Armour and Artillery*.

Development of the BTM-4M was carried out by the Mobile Vehicle Special Design Bureau (JSC Spetsmash) in St Petersburg. The general layout of the BTM-4M follows that of the earlier models, but the digger at the rear is of a new type. It is driven by two sets of the GST-90 hydrostatic transmission which enable it to operate in frozen ground. The BTM-4M can cut trenches 1.5 m deep at up to 250 m/h in frozen soil, or up to 1,000 m/h in non-frozen class 2 or 3 soil, or 1.1 m deep at up 300 m/h in frozen soil, or up to 1,200 m/h in non-frozen class 2 or 3 soil. Without providing associated depth figures, some sources quote maximum digging rates as up to 800 m in frozen soil, and at speeds of up to 2 km/h. The digging rotor has a diameter of 3.3 m, and at a maximum digging depth of 1.5 m, creates a trench 600 mm wide at the bottom and 1.1 m wide at the top, leaving a 600 mm high parapet. In frozen ground, trench width reduces to 600 mm at the top, parapet height and bottom width both remaining at 600 mm.

The digging rotor is adjustable ±7° relative to the ground surface during digging operations, and ±15° relative to the vehicles' longitudinal axis when excavating curved trenches. The rear (seventh) roadwheel station suspension units can be locked for trenching operations.

A dozer blade is fitted to the front of the vehicle and earthmoving speeds are quoted as 4 to 10 km/h. The front (first) roadwheel station suspension units can be locked for dozing operations.

The BTM-4M Tundra has a crew of two, weighs 43,900 kg (although most recently weight has been quoted as 47,800 kg) and is powered by a V-94T diesel powerpack. The engine is multifuel and is provided with a preheater and combined supercharging. The fuel pump features a two-position maximum fuel feed limiter to obtain two levels of maximum power; 780 hp (582 kW) at level 1, 840 hp (626 kW) at level 2. Cruising speed is up to 50 km/h. The vehicle carries 2,200 litres of fuel and is 10.7 m long, 3.38 m wide and 3.71 m high.

Performance characteristics include the ability to climb a maximum gradient of 55 per cent, traverse a maximum sideslope of 33 per cent, cross a trench of 2.5 m and ford to 1.2 m without preparation. Time taken to switch from travel to operational mode, and vice-versa, is five minutes.

Specifications
See table above
Note: automotive details are as for the basic AT-T tractor in the All terrain carriers and prime movers section.

BTM-4M digging deploying its trench digging wheel (JSC Spetsmash)
0525660

BTM-3 in operation (Belvneshpromservice)
0589129

BTM-3 in travel configuration (Belvneshpromservice)   0589130

Status
BTM-4M is the only model in production (with production likely to be on an as required basis) and is offered for export sales. Most of the other models are in service with members of the former Warsaw Pact and some Middle Eastern and North African countries.

BTM-4M
Mobile Vehicle Special Design Bureau (JSC Spetsmash)

MDK-2 series of trench-digging machines

Description
The MDK-2 trench-digging machine *(maschina dorozhnoy kopatelnoy)* is based on the chassis of the AT-T heavy tracked artillery tractor, with which it shares the same all-steel four-man cab. Details of the AT-T can be found

MDK-2M of the Ukrainian Army commencing trenching operation (Shaun C Connors)   0109499

MDK-2M of the Ukrainian Army clearly showing front-mounted dozer blade (Shaun C Connors)   0109500

Surplus Soviet era equipment including the MDK-2 /MDK-2M remains available from a variety of sources including Belvneshpromservice of Belarus (Belvneshpromservice)   0589131

MDK-2M of the Ukrainian Army engaged in trenching operations (Shaun C Connors)   1120430

in the All-terrain carriers and prime movers section. The circular digging machine is carried horizontally on the rear of the chassis and is swung 90° into the vertical for trenching operations. The MDK-2 is used for digging weapon trenches and pits for vehicles, guns and other equipment. Depending on the soil conditions, the MDK-2 can dig a maximum of 300 m³/h. The dug ditch has a maximum depth of 4.5 m and is 3.5 m wide at the bottom and 4 m wide at the top. An OTT hydraulically operated dozer blade is mounted at the front of the vehicle. There is also an MDK-2M model.

Specifications
MDK-2 series of trench-digging machines
[data in square brackets relates to MDK-2M where different from MDK-2]
Crew: 2
Weight: 27,000 [28,000] kg
Length:
    (travelling) 8 m
    (operating) 10.23 m
Width:
    (travelling) 4 [3.4] m
    (operating) n/avail [4.05] m
Height:
    (travelling) 3.95 m
    (operating) 3.48 m
Speed: 35 km/h
Max vertical obstacle: 1 m [650 mm]
Max gradient: 80%
Side slope: 22%
Working speed: (class 1 and 2 soil) 300 [387] m³/h
Depth of ditch: 4.5 m
Width of ditch:
    (top) 4 m
    (bottom) 3.5 m

Status
Production complete. In service with members of the former Warsaw Pact and some countries in North Africa and the Middle East.

Contractor
Russian State factories

High-speed tractor-mounted bulldozers BAT-1, BAT-M, OLT, OST and OTT

Development
Most of the Russian Federation full-tracked artillery tractors described in the All-terrain carriers and prime movers section can be fitted with bulldozer blades. One vehicle, the BAT, has been specifically modified as a bulldozer and it is covered in this entry.

The BAT tractor dozers should not be confused with the OTT dozer blade mounted on the AT-T tractor, for which data is also given here.

A number of organisations continue to offer surplus Soviet-era equipment, such as the BAT-M in as-is or refurbished conditions. Wojskowe Zakłady Inzynieryjne of Poland is one of these.

Description
The BAT tractor dozer consists of the AT-T heavy tractor with a large dozer blade mounted at the front of the hull. It is designed for the hasty preparation of roads and approaches to bridges and crossing sites, and also for filling in ditches and similar obstacles. It can also fell trees, uproot stumps and boulders and dig emplacements. The basic demolition blade can be fitted with attachments to form a V-blade, bulldozer and angledozer and is provided with routers and a float.

The more recent BAT-M is an improved model and is electro-hydraulically operated, whereas the BAT (also known as the BAT-1) is electro-pneumatically operated. The BAT-M also has a hydraulic crane that can be used for a variety of uses, plus the dozer blade may be swung rearwards to improve the vehicle's load distribution when travelling.

Specifications
See table below

Display example of the BAT-M tractor-mounted dozer (Ian C Young) 1391297

Status
All of the above mentioned tractor-mounted bulldozers have been supplied to the former Warsaw Pact nations. The BAT tractor dozer has also been supplied to some North African and Middle Eastern countries.

Contractor
Former Russian state factories

MDK-3 trench-digging machine

Development
The MDK-3 trench-digging machine *(maschina dorozhnoy kopatelnoy)* was developed as the Russian Army's intended replacement of the MDK-2 and MDK-2M, full details of which can be found elsewhere in this section. It is understood that the machine was designed by the Kharkiv Morozov Machine Building Design Bureau (KMDB), a state-owned enterprise of the now Ukraine.

Description
The MDK-3 trench-digging machine is based on the chassis of the MT-T tracked carrier, full details of which can be found in the All-terrain carriers and prime movers section.

The MDK-3 chassis, known as the Kharkov engineer chassis, uses suspension elements from the T-64 tank and is powered by a V-64-4 V-12 diesel engine. The cab is armoured, fitted with a radio and may be fitted with an NBC protection system. At the front of the vehicle is a hydraulically operated dozer blade which can be tilted. Mounted at the rear of the vehicle is a six-blade digging wheel, capable of excavating a trench just under 3 m in depth in a single pass. Hydraulic rams allow the digging wheel to be positioned for excavating; when travelling, the digging wheel is positioned horizontally over the chassis rear. When digging, the vehicle is driven slowly backwards and spoil is pushed out to one side to form a loose berm alongside the ditch. Digging blades on the wheel are bolted into position and can be changed.

MDK-3 trench-digging machine
(Kharkiv Morozov Machine Building Design Bureau)   0512008

High-speed tractor-mounted bulldozers

	BAT (BAT-1)	BAT-M	OLT	OST	OTT
Tractor:	(integral)	(integral)	AT-L, AT-LM	AT-S[1], ATS-59	AT-T
Weight: (with blade)	25,300 kg	27,500 kg	7,000 kg	13,392 kg	22,000 kg
Length: (with blade)	10 m	7 m (travelling)	n/avail	n/avail	n/avail
Width: (with blade)	4.78 m	4.85 m	2.5 m	2.8 m	3.5 m
Height (travelling)	2.95 m	-	2.18 m	2.54 m	2.58 m
Max speed:	35 km/h	35 km/h	42 km/h	35 km/h	35 km/h
Cruising range:	700 km	550 km	300 km	380 km	700 km
Fuel consumption:	140-190 litres/100 km	140-190 litres/100 km	140-190 litres/100 km	140-190 litres/100 km	140-190 litres/100 km
Trench:	1.58 m	2.1 m	1 m	1.45 m	2.1 m
Max vertical obstacle:	1 m	1 m	600 mm	600 mm	1 m
Max gradient:	45%	n/avail	60°	53°	60°
Fording depth	750 mm	750 mm	600 mm	1 m	750 mm
Ground pressure:	0.65 kg/cm²	0.71 kg/cm²	0.45 kg/cm²	0.58 kg/cm²	0.68 kg/cm²
Working speed:	1.5-10 km/h (moderate terrain)	1.5-10 km/h	4-6 km/h (moderate terrain)	4 km/h	n/avail
Working capacity: (soil condition dependant)	120-140 m³/h	max 150 m³/h (excavation); max 200 m³/h (dozing)	40 m³/h	80-90 m³/h (light soil); 40-50 m³/h (medium soil)	100 m³/h
Crane capacity:	n/app	2,000 kg	n/app	n/app	n/app
Winch capacity:	n/app	25,000 kg (100 m cable)	n/app	n/app	n/app
Blade control:	electropneumatic	electrohydraulic	n/avail	cable operated	n/avail
Blade angle:	n/avail	straight (5 m wide); 55° (4 m wide); 110° (4.5 m wide)	n/avail	n/avail	n/avail
Tractive effort:	n/avail	16,300 kg	n/avail	n/avail	n/avail

[1] Data refers to OST dozer on AT-S tractor.

Specifications

MDK-3
Crew: 2
Weight: 40,000 kg
Length:
(digger raised) 10 m
(digger lowered to ground level) 12 m
Width:
(over hull) 3.2 m
(over digger) 3.5 m
Height: (digger raised or lowered) 4 m
Max speed: 50 km/h
Range: (approx.) 500 km
Engine: V-64-4 V-12 4-stroke water-cooled diesel developing 737 hp (550 kW)
Trench digging speed: 200 m/h
Trench width: 3.5 m
Trench depth: 2.9 m

Status

Production likely to be on an as required basis. Believed to be in service with the armed forces of Russia (and possibly the Ukraine) in small numbers.

Contractor

Kharkiv Morozov Machine Building Design Bureau (KMDB).

TMK-2 trench-digging machine

Development

The TMK-2 trench-digging machine was developed to dig trenches in frozen and thawed soils and is based on the chassis of the IKT prime mover. A number of other similar machines are also based on the IKT prime mover chassis, these including the PKT-2 road-building machine and the BKT-RK2 bulldozer. Full details of these machines can be found elsewhere in this section.

Description

The TMK-2 trench digging machine is based on the chassis of the IKT prime mover to which a front-mounted dozer blade and rear-mounted trenching equipment is fitted. It has a crew of two; a driver and a digger assembly operator. Both are seated in an all-steel cab equipped with heating, heated glass, radiation warning and navigation equipment plus an air filtration system. One seat faces forward, the other rearward. External equipment stowage space is provided on the cab roof.

The TMK-2 is capable of digging trenches in frozen and thawed soils up to class 4. The main trench-digging assembly is located to the rear of the vehicle and consists of a circular cutter that is raised and lowered hydraulically. The assembly has no digging shovels but relies upon cutting teeth that produce a specific pressure on their cutting edges. Excavated earth is lifted upwards and adheres to the wheel assembly by friction before being discharged to both sides once clear of the trench. The fastest trench-digging speed possible in soft soil is 1.3 km/h, controlled by a hand wheel in the cab. Maximum digging depth is 1.5 m and the width of the trench can vary from 900 mm to 1.1 m.

In addition to its trench-digging function, the TMK-2 can be used to clear bush and scrub, scrape topsoil from contaminated areas and cut approaches and exits for water crossings using the hydraulically operated front-mounted dozer blade.

It takes three minutes to switch from travel to operational modes. For road transport the front axle drive can be disengaged. The engine has a pre-heating facility enabling it to start at temperatures below −15°C. The primary electric starting system for the engine is supplemented by an compressed air starting system should the electrical system fail.

TMK-2 trench-digging machine (Belvneshpromservice)   0589132

TMK-3

The TMK-3 is similar in concept to the TMK-2 and is produced by the Spetsmash JSC of St Petersburg. Powered by a 335 hp (250 kW) diesel engine, it is based on the chassis of the commercial K-703M wheeled tractor. Full details of the TMK-3 can be found elsewhere in this section.

Specifications

TMK-2
Base vehicle: IKT prime mover
Crew: 2
Weight: 27,200 kg
Length:
(transport) 9.745 m
(working, digging a 1.5 m deep trench) 12.215 m
Width: (transport) 3.33 m
Height:
(transport) 4.175 m
(working, digging a 1.5 m deep trench) 3.1 m
Max speed:
(road) 36–40 km/h
(track) ≤20 km/h
Range: (road) 500 km
Fuel consumption: (when digging) 50 litres/h
Engine: D 12 A 375 A 12-cylinder diesel developing 375 hp (280 kW)
Transmission: hydraulic with 3 forward and 1 reverse gears
Electrical system: 24 V
Batteries: 4 × 24 V, 280 Ah
Trench digging speed:
(1.1 m depth) 300–400 m/h
(1.5 m depth) 250–300 m/h
Trench dimensions, normal soils:
(width, top) 900 mm to 1.1 m
(width, bottom) 600 mm
(depth) ≤1.5 m
Trench dimensions, frozen soils:
(width, top and bottom) 600 mm
(depth) 1.1–1.5 m

Status

Production likely to be on an as required basis. In service with the armed forces of the Russian Federation.

Contractor

Dmitrov Excavator Plant
JSC Budshliakhmash

Marketed by
Rosoboronexport

Slovakia

DOK wheeled engineer tractor

Description

The DOK (dozer on wheels) wheeled engineer tractor was produced in the state-owned factories of the former Czechoslovakia and remains in service with the armies of the Czech Republic and Slovakia. Full details of the DOK wheeled engineer tractor can be found under Czech Republic in this section.

Ukraine

PZM and PZM-2 regimental trench-digging machines

Description

The PZM regimental trench-digging machine is built on the basis of the T-150K wheeled tractor. The more recent PZM-2 is based on the T-155 or T-151K wheeled tractor powered by a SMD-62 turbocharged diesel engine developing 165 hp. This engine is started by a 'donkey engine', a single-cylinder two-stroke petrol engine, Type P-350. The transmission provides six forward and two reverse speeds, plus six slower speeds for use when trench-digging. Steering is by articulation, all four rubber-tyred wheels drive. To obtain the required tractive force when operating in certain conditions, a hydromechanically driven winch that exerts a 5,000 kg pull at a rate of 60 m/s is front-mounted and can be used.

The PZM-2 has a roller chain with digging buckets driven mechanically from the main tractor engine. A front-mounted dozer blade is provided. This can be used to prepare sites for trenching, or for general earthmoving and dozing tasks.

PZM-2 at work in soft soil (Shaun C Connors)   0109501

PZM-2 in travelling configuration; steering is by articulation (Shaun C Connors)   1120432

Variants

ETC-200
The ETC-200 is powered by the same 165 hp (123 kW) diesel engine as the PZM-2. A roller chain carrying digger buckets is used to dig trenches up to 2 m deep and is powered from the main engine. Maximum trench digging speed is up to 200 m/h. A front-mounted dozer blade can be changed to the left or right position by hand. The ETC-200 weighs 13,700 kg.

Specifications

PZM-2
Crew: 2
Weight: 13,200 kg
Length:
  (travelling) 7 m
  (operating) 9.75 m
Width: 2.52 m
Height:
  (travelling) 3.75 m
  (operating) 2.82 m
Speed: 45 km/h
Range: 500 km
Engine: SMD-62 4-stroke diesel developing 165 hp (123 kW)

Trench digging speed:
  (normal soils) 180 m/h
  (frozen soils) 35 m/h
Trench dimensions, normal soils:
  (width, top) 900 mm
  (width, bottom) 650 mm
  (depth) ≤1.2 m
Trench dimensions, frozen soils:
  (width, top and bottom) 650 mm
  (depth) ≤1.2 m
Winch pull capacity: 5,000 kg

Status
Both the PZM-2 and the ETC-200 are in service with the Ukraine. Offered for export sales.

Contractor

Agency
Ukrspetsexport

United Kingdom

Hesco Bastion Concertainer

Development
The original Hesco Bastion Concertainer product was designed to counteract the effects of coastal erosion, but it was quickly identified to be a suitable replacement for conventional field fortification materials such as sandbags. Following successful use by UK armed forces in the 1991 Gulf War, Concertainer is now an important component of the force protection package on deployed operations.

The Hesco Bastion Concertainer, plus a selection of specialised designs based around Concertainer units, is now used extensively around the world for the protection of personnel, vehicles, equipment and facilities in military and peacekeeping/enforcing operations. Typical applications include perimeter security and defence walls, equipment revetments, ammunition compounds, personnel and material bunkers, observation points, defensive firing positions, guard posts, explosives and contraband search areas, highway checkpoints, border crossing checkpoints, and protecting existing structures.

Structures built from Concertainer units have been subjected to testing with charges up to 9,071 kg (20,000 lb). Correctly configured, a wall made from Concertainer units will mitigate the effects of truck bomb attack. Concertainer units have also been tested and proven against small arms fire, shell/bomb-fragmentation and rocket-propelled grenades (RPGs).

In addition to the standard Hesco Concertainer system, several specialised off-the-shelf products based on the patented design of Concertainer units are also available, these providing rapidly deployable protective structures for specific requirements.

The most recent Concertainer development is that of a rapidly deployable version of the system, RAID (RApid In-theatre Deployment), that can be deployed quickly and with minimal manpower from a specially fitted 20ft ISO container. Outline details of RAID and other specialised off-the-shelf products based on Concertainer units can be found elsewhere in this entry.

In addition to the military environment, the Hesco Bastion Concertainer product continues to be widely used in the civilian sphere, and for a wide variety of tasks including humanitarian and environmental missions.

Concertainer is the brand name for the barrier product, however, it is commonly referred to as Hesco Bastion or just Hesco, with Hesco usually presented as HESCO.

British troops in Afghanistan using a Volvo SLDT (Self-Loading Dump Truck) to fill a Hesco-based structure (USMC)   1391332

US troops at work in Afghanistan finalising the fill of a Hesco Concertainer unit wall (US DoD)   1391331

US Marines completing the fill of a Hesco Concertainer unit-based wall in Afghanistan (USMC)   1391333

Description

Hesco Concertainer is a prefabricated multi-cellular system of various sizes and capacities that is made of coated steel welded mesh and lined with a non-woven polypropylene geotextile to contain the infill material.

Individual units, or cells, are manufactured with an aluminium-zinc coated welded wire mesh. The square-celled mesh has an opening size of 76.2 mm by 76.2 mm and is made from 8-gauge (4 mm) steel wire, except for Mil 7 and Mil 10 products, which are 6-gauge (5 mm) steel wire. The aluminium-zinc coating is 95 per cent zinc, 5 per cent aluminium.

Coil hinges and joining pins are manufactured from 8-gauge aluminium-zinc coated steel wire. The geotextile is a 2 mm heavy-duty non-woven polypropylene with a UV inhibitor, and is available coloured either beige or grey/green. The patented design of Hesco Concertainer unit is available in nine different sizes, dimensions of which are provided in the Specifications table below.

Hesco Concertainer units can be delivered flat-packed on standard timber skids/pallets, or in RAID configuration. The flat-pack design of Concertainer allows for efficient storage and transportation, for example over 1,640 m of Mil 1 units can be transported in a 20ft ISO container. Concertainer units are air-transportable.

For deployment, units are extended and joined using the provided joining pins to form a gabion wall. According to the manufacturer, the product has been carefully designed to make construction easy, even with an unfamiliar and untrained workforce.

US troops work at unloading Hesco Concertainer Units that will be used in the construction of an Afghan Police checkpoint
(US DoD/Tech. Sgt. Francisco V. Govea II)   1391334

Once extended and joined the Concertainer can be filled with available material using minimal manpower and commonly available equipment. Almost any infill material can be used, and while sand, rubble, rocks, locally available soil, even snow have been successfully used, the ideal fill is a sand/gravel mix. This fill offers a high degree of protection and is easily handled.

Concertainer can be built to any length and to any reasonable height. Concertainer can be installed in various configurations, and can be tailored to the specific threat and level of protection required.

Rapid construction is a key feature of the product - a typical Hesco Concertainer wall that is the equivalent to a wall of approximately 1,500 sandbags can be erected and filled by two men and a single standard loading shovel in less than twenty minutes. An equivalent wall constructed of sandbags would take ten men seven hours to build.

Variants

RAID (RApid In-theatre Deployment)

RAID (RApid In-theatre Deployment) was developed to reduce the logistical burden of supporting force protection missions on expeditionary operations, such as the construction of forward operating and patrol bases. It is essentially a simpler, more efficient and less labour/equipment intensive way of deploying Hesco Concertainer units into walls or other lengthy structures.

RAID utilises a specially designed and engineered ISO container to provide significant increases in the quantity of Concertainer Mil units that can be transported in a 20 ft ISO footprint. The container used conforms to all ISO stacking and transportation standards.

For deployment, the RAID container is either delivered to site by the vehicle that will deploy it, or if previously delivered, is connected to a suitable towing vehicle. The doors are opened, all transportation strapping is removed, the first cell is filled/secured and the deploying vehicle moves forward. Deployment would normally be at walking pace, however, in recent trials, RAID 7 deployed approximately 333 m of units in just under one minute.

The unit being deployed can be split by the removal of two pins, these pins placed every five cells. This ability to split allows flexibility during construction. Corners can be formed, more units can be joined, gaps in the wall can be created (for entry points etc). Splitting units also provides the benefit of only having to deploy what is required - the remainder is left on board the secure RAID container for future use.

Currently three sizes of RAID are available: RAID 1, RAID 7, and RAID 10, these denominations based on width. RAID 1 and RAID 7 are in use with around 30 units sold to military contractors. Outline details of RAID can be found in the Specifications table below.

Hesco Lightweight Bunker Roof (HLBR)

The Hesco Lightweight Bunker Roof (HLBR) is a rapid and easily erectable lightweight roof specifically designed to provide protection against indirect fire weapons. The roof can be built on almost any wall/walls capable of taking the load that the roof will impose upon it/them. It is used in situations where there is a requirement for protection typically satisfied using timber or steel roofs. Shipped in a single wooden crate, HLBR has a maximum span of 3.3 m and can be built by four men in around five hours.

Hesco Concertainer units

Unit	Mil 1	Mil 2	Mil 3	Mil 4	Mil 5	Mil 6	Mil 7	Mil 8	Mil 9	Mil 10
Height:	1.37 m	0.61 m	1 m	1 m	0.61 m	1.68 m	2.21 m	1.37 m	1 m	2.12 m
Width:	1.06 m	0.61 m	1 m	1.5 m	0.61 m	0.61 m	2.13 m	1.22 m	0.76 m	1.52 m
Length:	10 m	1.21 m	10 m	10 m	3.05 m	3.05 m	27.74 m	10 m	9.14 m	30.5 m

Hesco Accommodation Bunker (HAB)

The Hesco Accommodation Bunker (HAB) was developed as a result of the ever increasing threat to deployed personnel from indirect fire weapons. The bunker is designed to provide safe living accommodation for up to eight persons, each having around 2 m² space. There is up to 2.16 m of headroom inside the bunker. HAB will provide protection from weapons systems up to and including large mortar rounds. It has side walls formed from Mil 6 Concertainer units and a specifically engineered roof structure to combat the effects of indirect fire weapons.

HAB is provided in air-transportable kit form and is delivered in two wooden crates. These crates hold all the components for the bunker and ultimately form part of the structure themselves. Two bunkers can be built in two days by one section of soldiers assisted by a loading shovel. The bunker can be fitted out for air-conditioning, heating and other services by using the factory formed aperture placed at one end.

The modular design of the HAB allows more complex structures to be built. In its most simplistic form this would entail joining units end to end. A single HAB has a footprint of 12.4 × 6.2 × 3.5 m (L × W × H) and an overall height of around 3.5 m. In excess of 450 HABs are currently in service in Afghanistan with International Security Assistance Force (ISAF).

Extended Overhead Protection System (EOPS)

The EOPS concept provides a roof structure with defined overhead protection for larger facilities. EOPS is built around existing ISO container-buildings such as Mobile Expandable Container Configurations (MECCs), or even basic sea container units. The frames of such ISO units combined with a steel superstructure provide the necessary support for the roof. An EOPS installation forms, as a minimum, a triple wide structure. Because EOPS is essentially modular, there is no limit to the area of the installation to be protected.

Guard Post/Sanger

The components of this set provide a small emplacement with 696 mm (2 ft) thick walls and 457 mm (18 inches) of overhead cover. Embrasure (firing/observation point) forms are included in the set as are roof joists and roofing material. The interior space is 1.22 m × 1.83 m (4 ft × 6 ft) with 1.98 m (6 ft 6 in) of headroom. The complete set is delivered on a single pallet weighing 375 kg. To construct a two-man Sanger kit will take approx. 20 m³ of fill material.

Personnel and Material Bunkers

Bunkers sets have been developed to utilise standard 40 ft and 20 ft ISO containers. Walls are constructed using appropriate Mil 1 sections providing a wall thickness of 1.066 m (3 ft 6 in). The roof design provides 610 mm (2 ft) of overhead cover. Material bunkers provide access from one end of the bunker, while personnel bunkers provide access from both ends.

While the containers are not absolutely necessary, they do provide enhanced protection, by acting as a spall-liner; and can, if properly ventilated, provide environmental protection to the occupants. Bunker kits are available in both 20 ft and 40 ft single and double entry. To construct a 20 ft single entry bunker will typically take 170 m³ of fill material.

Containerised Bunker Kit

Hesco Bastion has developed a containerised kit which provides a means of transporting all the components required to construct a bunker. The ISO container has a fully opening side, facilitating rapid deployment of all components. The container also comes complete with a prefabricated personnel door and a rear escape hatch, both of which can be opened from inside.

Specifications

See table above

RAID (RApid In-theatre Deployment)

	RAID 1	RAID 7	RAID 10
Length:			
(deployed)	406 m	333 m	-
(5-cell segment)	5.5 m	10.65 m	-
Height: (deployed)	2.1 m	2.21 m	2.21 m
Width: (deployed)	1.06 m	2.13 m	1.52 m
Weight: (gross, approx.)	12,000 kg	14,000 kg	-
No of 5-cell segments:	74	31	-

Status

In production and use worldwide by numerous armed forces, governmental and other agencies.

Contractor

HESCO Bastion Ltd

Defencell deployable protection and infrastructure

Development

Defencell (also a product range trade name) is a joint-venture established in 2006 between J&S Franklin Ltd and Terram Ltd. J&S Franklin market the Defencell product, Terram Ltd produce the geotextile material the Defencell product is manufactured from.

A US affiliate company of Terram Ltd, Fiberweb Inc, manufacture and market the product in the United States.

Defencell is a geotextile-based cellular containment system that can be used for force protection roles, but can also be used for various civil engineering purposes. The product is in widespread use by armed forces, governmental agencies and civil concerns.

Description

All Defencell products are made from the same geotextile material, the minimum field life of which is stated to be three years.

When used in force protection roles five primary sizes of Defencell are available, these designated LITE, DT1, T2, T3 and T4. LITE (Lightweight Individual Tactical Emplacement) is essentially a man-portable variant and while deployment mirrors that of the larger products, key dimensions are different.

The key difference between the larger products (DT1, T2, T3 and T4) is width, these four products having a common single length and overall height, but varying in width and quantity of individual cells.

Broadly speaking (excluding LITE), per cubic meter of filled product, when empty Defencell weighs around ten per cent of the equivalent required number of sandbags. A single 40 ft ISO container will provide well over 1 km of wall, this 2 m wide and 2 m high, or 2.5 km of 1.25 m wide, 1.50 m high, with 50 m³ of raw packed Defencell equating to in excess of 5,000 m³ filled.

A single DT1 unit makes a wall section 4.9 m long, 600 mm high and 700 mm wide, the equivalent of 160 sandbags. This unit (and text) are on Defencell Stabilisation. (Defencell)   1391317

Defencell T2 is two cells wide (totalling 24 cells in an offset pattern) and provides a minimum of 1.1 m of protection when filled (Defencell)   1391318

Being of a geotextile construction, the Defencell material itself would not contribute to any secondary fragmentation or spallation related injuries (Defencell)
1391319

Once the required size Defencell has been selected the required number of units are deployed, with all sizes deploying by essentially the same method. Once opened out, a honeycomb-like structure is formed into which fill material is placed. A detachable filling frame is provided (optional with the man-portable LITE) to expedite the filling process, which can be done either manually or mechanically. Fill material can be earth, sand, gravel or even small rocks. Compaction during the fill process is recommended.

Depending on product used, the primary uses of Defencell in force protection roles are; the building of walls, protective positions, bunkers, guard posts and road barriers/chicanes. The product can also be used to protect critical equipment and facilities, and for tent compartmentalisation and general blast/explosion containment within compounds.

For enhanced protection, units can be placed alongside each other, or on top of each other to build vertical walls or small structures up to eight metres high. Being of a geotextile construction, the Defencell material itself would not contribute to any secondary fragmentation or spallation related injuries and causes no RF interference.

LITE (Lightweight Individual Tactical Emplacement)

Defencell LITE is a man-portable variant of the Defencell concept. A single wall section that weighs 3.6 kg unfilled and occupies the space of a single filled sandbag, will fill to provide a 3.2 m long, 700 mm wide and 600 mm high wall, this equivalent to about 100 sandbags. LITE can be stacked up to three high when filled.

Defencell DT1

Defencell DT1 is the lightest of the four main Defencell force protection products. A single unfilled 16-cell unit occupies approximately the same space as a filled sandbag, and when filled makes a wall section 4.9 m long, 600 mm high and 700 mm wide, the equivalent of 160 sandbags.

A standard pallet will transport 70 DT1, these weighing 335 kg and allowing for a single layer wall 343 m to be created, this the equivalent of 11,200 sandbags. A single 20 ft ISO container will transport 1,400 DT1, these weighing 6,700 kg and allowing for a single layer wall 6,860 m to be created, this the equivalent of 224,000 sandbags.

Defencell T2

Defencell T2 is two cells wide (totalling 24 cells in an offset pattern) and provides a minimum of 1.1 m of protection when filled. A single T2 unit weighs 6.8 kg and when filled makes a wall section 4.9 m long, 600 mm high and 1.3 m wide, the equivalent of 300 sandbags.

Profile 500 in use in Camp Bastion (Defencell)
1391321

A standard pallet will transport 24 T2, these weighing 205 kg and allowing for a single layer wall 117 m to be created, this the equivalent of 7,200 sandbags. A single 20 ft ISO container will transport 480 T2, these weighing 4,100 kg and allowing for a single layer wall 2,352 m to be created, this the equivalent of 144,000 sandbags.

Defencell T3

Defencell T3 is three cells wide (totalling 48 cells in an offset pattern) and provides a minimum of 1.65 m of protection when filled. A single T3 unit weighs just under 9 kg and when filled makes a wall section 4.9 m long, 600 mm high and 1.9 m wide. When stacked three units high at 1.6 m this equates to the equivalent of over 1,300 sandbags.

A standard pallet will transport 18 T3, these weighing 200 kg and allowing for a single layer wall 88 m to be created, this the equivalent of 8,100 sandbags. A single 20 ft ISO container will transport 360 T3, these weighing 4,000 kg and allowing for a single layer wall 1,764 m to be created, this the equivalent of 162,000 sandbags.

Defencell T4

Defencell T4 is four cells wide (totalling 64 cells) and provides a minimum of 2.25 m of protection when filled. A single T4 unit weighs just under 12 kg and when filled makes a wall section 4.9 m long, 600 mm high and 2.5 m wide.

A standard pallet will transport 12 T4, these weighing 172 kg and allowing for a single layer wall 59 m to be created, this the equivalent of 7,200 sandbags. A single 20 ft ISO container will transport 240 T4, these weighing 3,440 kg and allowing for a single layer wall 1,176 metres in length to be created, this the equivalent of 144,000 sandbags.

Profile 300 and Profile 500

These products can be used to construct semi-permanent protective barriers, berms or bunds, that can be landscaped and/or traversed by vehicles if required when complete. The designation 300 and 500 refers to the nominal diameter of the cell, the two products having a common cell height of 250 mm.

Stabilisation

Defencell Stabilisation is intended to provide surface stabilisation for roads and pathways, ensuring that supply routes are maintained. It can also be used for the creation of hardstanding and camp winterisation that

Defencell T4, which is four cells wide (totalling 64 cells) and provides a minimum of 2.25 m of protection when filled, in use as a perimeter wall (Defencell)
1391320

Defencell Stabilisation laid out and being filled (Defencell)
1391322

includes the building of elevated platforms for assorted structures. With stabilisers added to the fill material to prevent dust and downdraught erosion, helicopter landing sites can also be constructed.

In wet or unstable conditions the cell systems, which are available in various sizes, are simply deployed, filled and compacted.

Status
In production. In service with the Italian Air Force, Irish Army, Spanish Army, UK armed forces, US armed forces, the UN and numerous governmental and aid agencies.

Contractor
J & S Franklin Ltd

JCB construction equipment

Development
JCB was founded on 23 October 1945, when the late Joseph Cyril Bamford (known universally as Mr JCB) made his first product in a rented lock-up garage in Uttoxeter, Staffordshire, England. Today JCB, which remains a privately owned company, is one of the world's top three construction equipment manufacturers and has 18 plants: 11 in the UK and others in Brazil, China, Germany, India and the US. There are also subsidiary companies in Belgium, France, Germany, Italy, the Netherlands, Singapore and Spain. The company's worldwide headquarters is in Rocester, Staffordshire, England.

JCB has a supporting dealer network covering over 150 countries, with 1,500 dealer depot locations. The company employs around 7,000 people and manufactures more than 300 different machines in 13 primary product ranges including backhoe loaders, telescopic handlers, tracked and wheeled excavators, vibratory and drum compactors, wheeled loading shovels, articulated dump trucks, rough terrain fork lifts, mini excavators, skid steers loaders, and tracked skid steer loaders. In addition, for agricultural markets, the company produces a range of telescopic handlers and the high-speed Fastrac tractor. JCB also manufactures the Teletruk forklift for the industrial sector.

Details of rough terrain forklifts, telescopic handlers and the Teletruck forklift can be found in the Materials handling equipment section; details of the JCB Fastrac tractor (which is in service with the UK Royal Air Force) can be found in the Trucks section.

JCB exports 75 per cent of its UK-made products to 150 countries worldwide. The company stated that it maintained parts support for all JCB machines back to 1965 models, but now states that it will support a JCB machine for as long as it remains in use.

JCB recorded pre-tax pre-exceptional profits of GBP39 million during 2008 on a turnover of GBP2 billion. With total sales of 57,000 machines and a global market share of 10.8 per cent, JCB remained the world's third largest construction equipment brand. The company also retained its position as the world's number one manufacturer of backhoe loaders, with more than one third of the market. In 2010 JCB stated that it had a 41 per cent market share for backhoe loaders.

In 2003, JCB announced GBP80 million plans to develop and manufacture its own diesel engines and a new company, called JCB Power Systems Ltd, was formed to produce the engines and a new manufacturing plant in Derbyshire, England, acquired. The first engines were produced in 2005, with over 70,000 now in use. Over 50 per cent of JCB's current products are powered by JCB-produced engines, as was the Dieselmax world land-speed record car.

One of 30 JCB 426HTM wheeled loaders supplied to the Italian Army during 2003 (JCB)   0587676

JCB's trademark yellow backhoe loaders and excavators have become part of the global construction landscape and part of the English language; the name JCB is somewhat generic (globally) for a backhoe loader and as such is listed in the Oxford and Collins' Dictionaries, as a type of construction machine with a hydraulically operated shovel on the front and an excavator arm the rear.

In addition to supplying what are essentially commercial-off-the-shelf products JCB will design, develop and carry out militarisation of these commercial products to meet specific military requirements. Examples are the winterisation/deep wading package developed for the JCB 4CXM backhoe loader of the British Army, the development of armoured options by Penman Engineering for the Singapore armed forces, and the armouring package developed in cooperation with Cabines Sarrazin of France for the French Army's 4CXM backhoe loaders ordered mid 2006.

Additionally, the company is one of a few within the construction equipment sector that will undertake the design, development and manufacture of military specific equipment. Examples of this are the High Mobility Variable Reach Truck (HMVRT), the High Mobility Utility Vehicle (HMUV), the High Mobility Rough Terrain Forklift (HMRTF) and the High Mobility Engineering Excavator (HMEE). JCB was awarded a contract for the HMEE in October 2005 by the US Army's TACOM. Full details of the JCB HMEE can be found elsewhere in this section. Full details of the HMRTF can be found in the Materials handling equipment section, and outline details of the HMUV can be found in the Trucks section.

Since 1984 JCB has supplied 54 countries' military organisations with over 3,500 machines.

The following is a brief descriptive overview of the current JCB construction range[1]. Full details of certain specific items of equipment (as indicated in respective sub-sections) can be found elsewhere in this section.

[1] It should be noted that in line with the majority of manufacturers of construction equipment, JCB regularly updates/revises its model range. These updates/revisions can be minor, often cosmetic and involve minimal mechanical changes, but can result in product designation changes.

Description
Wheeled loaders
JCB currently produces 12 models of wheeled loader (including three compact models) in 35 primary variants. Operating weights for these machines range from 2,115 kg (compact) or 7,637 kg (standard) to 21,089 kg, and engine power outputs range from 36 hp for the smallest compact model through to 229 hp for the largest model that, for most military applications, would be termed a heavy wheeled loader or tractor.

JCB 426HTM wheeled loader of the Italian Army; 426 wheeled loaders supplied to the US Air Force (15 in 2003) retain their original JCB yellow paint finish are commercial specification machines (JCB)   0587675

JCB 456ZX wheeled loader, the militarisation of which is limited to a coat of green paint (JCB)   1034685

JCB JS330 360° tracked excavator, the militarisation of which is limited to a coat of green paint (JCB)   1034687

JCB 3CX backhoe loaders destined for the British Army via ALC (Shaun C Connors)   1186162

JCB skid-steer loader (JCB)   1034693

An aging Vibromax compactor of the Portuguese Army; JCB acquired Vibromax during 2005 (Victor Barreira)   1391237

All models are conventional in design, being four-wheel drive with equal-sized wheels and steered by frame articulation.

JCB wheeled loaders are in service with a number of armed forces worldwide, with recent deliveries including machines to the Austrian (436 HTM), Italian (426 HTM), UK (436) and US (426 HT and 416 HT) Armed Forces. Full details of the JCB 426 HTM can be found elsewhere in this section.

360° excavators

JCB produces both wheeled and tracked 360° excavators. The current range consists of 37 tracked (in four size ranges) and five wheeled machines.

Tracked models, for which there are a wide variety of boom and undercarriage variations, have engine power outputs ranging from 12 to 306 hp and operating weights ranging from 950 to 51,408 kg. For most military applications machines with operating weights ranging from 16,000 to 26,000 kg are the norm.

Wheeled models have engine power outputs ranging from 98 to 172 hp and operating weights ranging from 14,645 to 23,214 kg. All are of conventional two-axle design, having four-wheel drive and front-axle steering. Axles are unsprung, an oscillating front axle taking account of ground undulations. A front-mounted dozer blade and rear-mounted stabiliser legs are options regularly fitted to enhance the capabilities and

JCB 714 articulated dump truck; one of a range of three articulated dump trucks offered by JCB (JCB)   0587677

versatility of these machines. In common with tracked machines, wheeled 360° excavators can be used for lifting purposes, with or without interchangeable buckets attached.

Articulated dump trucks

The JCB Articulated Dump Truck (ADT) range consists of three models, two 4 × 4 and one 6 × 6, the 6 × 6 being introduced in March 2004. All are of conventional design, being steered by frame articulation. The front axle on all models is sprung, the rear axle(s) being unsprung; the tandem rear bogie of the 6 × 6 being of the walking beam type.

Operating weights (unladen) are 10,140, 12,450 and 17,970 kg respectively for models 714, 718 and 722, while payloads are 12,700, 16,300 and 19,970 kg respectively. All models are powered by a JCB 5.9 litre engine developing 150 (714), 173 (718) or 260 hp (722). Maximum road speed is 40 km/h for a model 714, 50 km/h for a model 718, and 46 km/h for a model 722.

Skid-steer loaders

JCB produces a range of eight skid-steer machines, five wheeled and three tracked. Operating weights for the two smallest wheeled machines are 2,650 and 3,680 kg, and capacities are 630 and 860 kg. Skid-steer machines are ideal for working in confined spaces or urban areas, and all can be trailer-transported behind either a light utility vehicle or standard 4,000 kg-class truck.

A remote control variant, essentially a technology demonstrator, has been developed by JCB.

Backhoe loaders

The commercial backhoe loader is in use worldwide for a number of military purposes as the design combines the capabilities of a loader and excavator, with the additional benefit that both the loader arms and excavator arm can be fitted with special attachments to perform the functions of a forklift, crane, grader, bulldozer, rock breaker, grab and other special functions.

The current JCB backhoe loader range consists of four product ranges[1], the 1CX, 2CX, 3CX, and 4CX.

The 1.4 m wide 1CX is a compact design based on a skid-steer platform; it is capable of turning on its own axis. The Italian Army operates a quantity of JCB 1CXM (M - Military) backhoe loaders and full details of this variant can be found elsewhere in this section.

JCB 3CX of the Portuguese Army (Victor Barreira)   1391235

The 2CX is a compact machine with four equal sized wheels, four wheel drive and four-wheel steer. A versatile 6-in-1 shovel, which will dig, load, doze, grade, backfill and grab, is fitted as standard. An optional side-tip shovel allows the operator to fill a trench parallel to the machine, while a 1.4 m wide 0.6 m³ shovel, another option, is available for hopper loading. An optional Extradig extending dipper for increased dig depth and reach is available for the backhoe. Six models are currently available.

The 3CX is the archetypal JCB backhoe loader. There are currently ten 3CX models available, all differing slightly in terms of performance and specification.

The 4CX range, of which there are currently 11 models available are fitted with equal-sized wheels, have four-wheel drive and four-wheel steer (including crab-steer), and are generally of a higher overall specification than 3CX models. JCB 3CX and 4CX backhoe loaders are in service with a number of armed forces including those of Austria, Croatia, France, Netherlands, New Zealand, Pakistan, Portugal, the UAE and the UK.

Options for militarised JCB backhoe loaders include armoured cabs which can be provided for front-line operations such as digging vehicle scrapes, combat trenches, command and first-aid posts. Riot(ous) protection kits are also available. Military models have been supplied for cold-climate and deep wading applications, and to meet air-portability requirements. Machines have also been specially prepared for airdrop operations. Remote-control facilities can be fitted. JCB is the global market leader for backhoe loaders, and in 2010 stated that the company had a 41 per cent market share.

[1] Machines produced at JCB's facility in North America have some design differences (primarily backhoe configuration) to suit local market preferences and carry different model designations.

Vibratory compactors

JCB acquired German Vibromax Equipment GmbH during 2005 and currently offers a full range of pedestrian operated, self-propelled and towed compaction equipment. The most common choice for military construction or engineer use is the self-propelled vibratory compactor. JCB currently offers a range of seven self-propelled vibratory compactors, and these range from 4,600 to 19,700 kg operating weights, and are powered by Cummins diesel engines with output powers ranging from 60 to 173 hp.

Status

In production. JCB construction equipment has been supplied to at least 54 armed forces worldwide, some users procuring standard commercial machines through local suppliers. Recent sales are known to have been made to Austria (436M wheeled loaders and 4CXM), Croatia (4CXM), Italy (1CXM backhoe loaders (156) and 426 wheeled loaders (45)), Netherlands (4CXM and 535-95), Pakistan (3CX backhoe loaders (38; 2006)), UK (3CXM (31; 21) and 4CXM (150) backhoe loaders; >13 HMEE) India (3DX and 4CX backhoe loaders), Spain (3CX backhoe loaders, and during 2005 and 2006 JS200 tracked and JS175W wheeled 360° excavators), the US Air Force (416 HT and 426HT wheeled loaders), the US Army (>636 HMEE), and small quantities to a selection of Latin American countries including Argentina, Brazil and Chile.

Contractor

JCB Defence Products

JCB 1CXM skid-steer backhoe loader

Development

The commercially available JCB 1CX is the smallest model in a range of five JCB backhoe loaders, and the only model available with skid-steer. The militarised 1CXM (M - Military) was designed and developed by JCB especially to meet an Italian Army requirement. Orders for 156 vehicles have been received to date with deliveries being made between 2000 and 2003.

Full details of the JCB range of backhoe loaders can be found elsewhere in this section.

JCB 1CXM (JCB)   1034691

Description

The JCB ICX is a genuine skid-steer machine, the four driving wheels being fixed and non-steering, with all manoeuvring being achieved by either braking or contrarotation of the drive wheels: the 1CX can turn on its own axis.

Standard operating equipment includes a ROPS/FOPS canopy, working lights, hand and foot throttle, seat-mounted ISO pattern servo controls, seatbelt, mechanical loader Quickhitch. Options in addition to militarisation include JCB pattern excavator controls, auxiliary hydraulic supply to the loader, auxiliary hand tool circuit, excavator, Quickhitch and JCB Airboss tyres. Militarisation options include paint finish, rifle mount, fire extinguisher(s) and blackout lighting.

The JCB 1CXM is air-transportable by CH-47 Chinook helicopter.

Specifications

1CXM
Cab seating: 1
Configuration: 4 × 4
Operational weight: 2,850 kg (with Quickhitch, standard shovel, full fuel tank, canopy and 450 mm excavator bucket)
Length:
  (travel) 3.4 m
  (shovel in carry position) 3.31 m
Width: (over standard tyres) 1.58 m
Height: (top of cab) 2.26 m
Ground clearance:
  (kingpost) 330 mm
  (stabiliser) 270 mm
Wheelbase: 1.07 m
Approach/departure angle: 52°/23°
Max road speed: (tyre dependant) 11 km/h
Fuel capacity: 45 litres
Engine: Perkins 4-cylinder 2.2-litre in-line naturally aspirated water-cooled 4-stroke diesel developing 50 hp (37 kW) at 2,800 rpm and 143 N.m torque at 1,800 rpm
Transmission: servo-controlled hydrostatic giving full power and maximum speed both forward and reverse; independent transmission systems for each side
Steering: skid-steer
Turning radius: (dependant on tyre size, ground conditions and front ancillaries) 3.31 m (neutral turn (turning in own axis)) possible
Suspension: unsprung, suspension by pneumatic tyres
Tyre size: (front and rear) 7 × 15 NHS 6PR, standard; 10 × 16.5 NHS 6PR, optional
Brakes:
  (main) provided by the hydrostatic transmission
  (parking) spring on, hydraulic pressure off oil-immersed multi-disc
Electrical system: 24 V (12 V for commercial applications)
Batteries: 2 × 12 V
Alternator: 40 A (50 A for commercial applications)
Loader dimensions:
  (dump height) 2.10 m
  (loadover height) 2.51 m
  (dig depth) 50 mm
  (dump angle) 50°
Loader performance:
  (rated capacity, loader) 610 kg
  (rated capacity, pallet fork) 480 kg
  (shovel breakout) 2,350 kg
  (lift capacity to full height) 2,400 kg
Backhoe dimensions:
  (maximum dig depth) 2.55 m
  (maximum reach, ground level to slew centre) 3.38 m
  (slide reach, to machine centre line) 3.83 m
  (maximum loadover height) 2.35 m
  (bucket rotation) 202°

Backhoe performance:
(max bucket tearout) 2,200 kg
(dipper tearout) 1,488 kg

Status
Commercial variant in production. Military variant in service with the Italian Army (156)

Contractor
JCB Defence Products

JCB 426 HTM wheeled loader

Development
The commercially available JCB 426 is one of a range of 14 JCB wheeled loaders. The militarised 426 HTM (M- Military) was designed and developed by JCB especially to meet an Italian Army requirement and following an initial delivery of 15 machines, a further 30 machines were delivered during 2003 increasing the total in service to 45.

The US Air Force received 15 machines during 2003, plus a further 25 machines in 2004. These were commercial products retaining their original JCB yellow paint finish. The US Air Force has also recently received eight of the slightly smaller JCB 416 wheeled loaders.

It is understood that during 2010 three of the slightly larger 436 wheeled loader will be delivered to the Italian military, a further 98 machines will be delivered to the British Army via ALC, and the USAF will receive 76 machines.

Full details of the JCB range of wheeled loaders can be found elsewhere in this section.

Description
The JCB 426HT is a conventional wheeled loader, being steered by frame articulation and with unsprung axles, an oscillating rear axle taking account of ground undulations. Militarisation options, which can vary to suit individual customer requirements, include paint finish, rifle mount, fire extinguisher(s), blackout lighting, spare wheel and remote axle breathers for deep wading operations.

Specifications
426 HTM
(with 1.9 m³ bucket with bolt-on toeplates and 20.SR25 XHA (L3) tyres)
Cab seating: 1
Configuration: 4 × 4
Weight: 12,450 kg
Max operating weight: 14,210 kg
Length: 6.75 m
Width:
(over tyres) 2.482 m
(wheel track) 1.955 m
(over cab) 1.310 m
Height (top of cab) 3.315 m
Ground clearance: 442 mm
Wheelbase: 3 m
Max road speed:
(forward) 38.5 km/h
(reverse) 24.3 km/h
Fuel capacity: 230 litres
Engine: Cummins BTAA5.9C 5.9-litre 6-cylinder in-line turbocharged water-cooled 4-stroke diesel developing 152 hp (113 kW) at 2,000 rpm and 617 N.m torque at 1,600 rpm
Transmission: ZF 4WG 160 with integral torque converter; 4 forward and 3 reverse gears
Steering: by articulation, angle of articulation ±40°
Turning radius: (dependant on tyre size, ground conditions and front ancillaries) 5.79 m
Axles: rigid, JCB PR12, front; JCB PR10, rear; limited slip differentials optional
Suspension: unsprung, oscillating rear (25°)
Tyres: (front and rear) 20.SR25 XHA (L3) (numerous options all of which affect operating specifications)
Brakes:
(main) outboard multidisc, oil immersed multi disc
(parking) mechanical disc-type operating on the transmission output shaft.
Electrical system: 24 V
Batteries: 2 × 12 V, 126 Ah
Alternator: 70 A
Loader dimensions: (variable according to bucket and tyres)
(dump height) 2.831 m
(loadover height) 3.627 m
(dig depth) 320 mm
(dump angle) 49°
Loader performance: (variable according to bucket and tyres)
(breakout force) 139 kN
(tipping load, straight) 8,690 kg
(tipping load, full turn) 7430 kg
(payload) 3,715 kg

JCB 426HTM wheeled loader of the Italian Army. The US Air Force operates similar machines, but without militarisation and supplied in their original JCB yellow paint finish (JCB)   0587676

Loader performance with forks: (variable according to tyres)
(tipping load, straight) 6,700 kg
(tipping load, full turn) 5,745 kg
(payload) 4,600 kg

Status
Current equivalent (426 EHT/426 EHT-HL/426 ZX-WM) in production. In service with the Italian Army (45) and the US Air Force (40; 15 in 2003; 25 in 2004).

Contractor
JCB Defence Products

JCB 4CX and 4CXM/4CXMA backhoe loaders

Development
The JCB 4CX is one of a range of commercial backhoe loaders produced by JCB. The JCB 4CXM (M - Military) is a militarised variant of the JCB 4CX, and when designated 4CXMA denotes a cab armouring package is fitted. The 4CX range of backhoe loaders has recently been supplied to Austrian, British, Croatian, Dutch, French, New Zealand, Netherlands and Singaporean armed forces.

Following a competitive tender, in 2002 the JCB 4CXM was selected by the British Army to become the new standard Light Wheeled Tractor (LWT), replacing a fleet of Hydrema 906B machines. Full details of the Hydrema range of backhoe loaders can be found elsewhere in this section. 150 4CXM machines were involved in the order, with production running from October 2002 until February 2003. Of the 150 machines delivered eight were fitted with protection kits for Northern Ireland by Penman Engineering, and five were waterproofed and winterised by RDS.

These machines are currently being replaced by ALC as part of that company's 16-year Private Finance Initiative (PFI). This intention of this initiative is to provide heavy plant equipment for the UK's armed forces for which the then Amey Lex Consortium was selected as preferred bidder in early 2004. Deliveries run from September 2009 until early 2010 and cover 136 mildly militarised machines, five of which will be waterproofed and winterised.

In June 2006 JCB disclosed the sale of 91 4CXMA backhoe loaders to the French Army. These are currently being delivered, with completion due during 2010. These machines are fitted for but not with armoured cabins developed in conjunction with Cabines Sarrazin of France.

Also in June 2006 JCB delivered four 4CXMs to the New Zealand Army.

In June 2007 the United Arab Emirates (UAE) Land Forces received five 4CXs.

The Dutch MoD placed an order for seven 4CX machines in 2007.

The Singapore Armed Forces received four 4CXMA machines in 2008, these fitted with armoured cabins supplied by Penman Engineering.

Austria ordered four 4CX machines in 2009, these retaining their standard yellow JCB paint finish.

The above listing should not be considered complete as some armed forces and/or governmental agencies, usually non-NATO grade, will procure standard commercial specification machines directly through a local supplier or agent.

Description
To meet the requirements of various defence procurement agencies, differing degrees of militarisation to the standard 4CX base machine have been undertaken. The standard militarised JCB 4CXM combines the current JCB 4CX platform with the P12 JCB backhoe loader cab, this being both C130 compatible and adaptable to meet armouring requirements.

For the non-ALC UK and New Zealand requirements militarisation included a 24 V electrical system with a convoy lighting/blackout system, inter-vehicle start socket, guarded lighting, rifle stowage, diesel refuelling

In June 2006 JCB disclosed the sale of 91 4CXMA backhoe loaders to the French Army. These are currently being delivered, with completion due during 2010. These machines are fitted for but not with armoured cabins developed in conjunction with Cabines Sarrazin of France
(Shaun C Connors)
1391289

JCB 4CXMA with armoured cab by Penman Engineering destined for Singapore (Shaun C Connors)
1391149

As displayed at Eurosatory 2003, a JCB 4CXM backhoe loader of the British Army with full CES kit stowed and ready for deployment
(Shaun C Connors)
1120443

system, tyre inflation system, the option for an internal NBC kit stowage box, 1.5 m fording depth (1 m optional), and the option for a shovel-mounted 7,000 kg winch. The machine is also air transportable by C-130 Hercules and underslung by Chinook helicopter. To ensure C-130 air transportability the P12 cab is fitted and to achieve the required 2.67 m transport height, tyres are reduced in pressure to 1.6 bar (23 psi). Additionally, five of the UK machines (in the latest ALC purchase) have been winterised for operations at temperatures down to –40°C.

For the French requirement militarisation included a 24 V electrical system, rifle stowage, additional equipment stowage, C-130 transportability, and fitting for but not with a small arms fire and blast protection kit. To meet a requirement for a sustainable 40 km/h road speed French Army machines also feature the commercial option of a lock-up torque converter.

JCB also produces the 1CX, 2CX and 3CX ranges of backhoe loaders, full details of which can be found elsewhere in this section.

Specifications

4CXM

Cab seating: 1
Configuration: 4 × 4 × 4
Operational weight: 10,000 kg (with 800 mm excavator bucket, standard dipper with mechanical quickhitch, 1.3 m³/2.450 m wide 6 in-1 quickhitch mounted shovel, side-shifting forks, spare wheel, stowage box, 300 mm excavator bucket and full fuel tank)
Length: (with full ancillaries) 7.25 m
Width:
  (bucket) 2.45 m
  (frame) 2.35 m
Height:
  (top of cab - standard) 2.7 m
  (top of cab - reduced) 2.67 m (see text)
Ground clearance:
  (kingpost) 520 mm
  (stabiliser) 370 mm
Wheelbase: 2.22 m
Approach/departure angle: 74°/21.5°
Max road speed: (tyre dependant) 38.8 km/h
Fuel capacity: 150 litres
Fording: 750 mm standard, 1 m optional
Engine: JCB 1004-40T 3.99-litre 4-cylinder in-line turbocharged water-cooled 4-stroke diesel developing 100 hp (75 kW) at 2,200 rpm and 403 N.m torque at 1,400 rpm
Transmission: JCB Powershift with 4 forward and 4 reverse gears
Steering: hydrostatic power on each axle with 3 steer modes: all-wheel, front-wheel and crab
Turning radius: (dependant on tyre size, ground conditions and front ancillaries)
  (kerb) 9.8 m braked, 10.5 m unbraked
  (wall) 11.3 m braked, 12.6 m unbraked
Axles: rigid, fitted with JCB Max-Trac torque proportioning differential
Suspension: unsprung, oscillating front (16°), rigid rear
Tyres: (front and rear) 440/80R 28 (options)
Brakes:
  (main) vacuum servo assisted inboard multidisc, oil immersed. 220 mm disc diameter inboard
  (parking) over-centre type on the transmission output shaft. Will hold the machine on a 33% gradient. 280 mm disc diameter
Electrical system: 24 V
Batteries: 2 × 12 V
Alternator: 55 A
Loader dimensions: (6-in-1)
  (dump height) 2.69 m
  (loadover height) 3.18 m
  (dig depth) 4.32 m
  (dump angle) 45°
  (jaw opening width) 950 mm
Loader performance: (6-in-1)
  (shovel breakout) 6,130 kgf
  (loader arm breakout) 5,590 kgf
  (lift capacity to full height) 3,425 kg
  (clamping force) 2,945 kg
Backhoe dimensions:
  (maximum dig depth) 4.67 m
  (maximum reach, ground level to slew centre) 5.4 m
  (side reach, to machine centre line) 6.02 m
  (maximum loadover height) 3.84 m
  (bucket rotation) 201°
Backhoe performance:
  (maximum bucket tearout) 5,700 kgf
  (dipper tearout) 3,630 kgf
  (lift capacity of bucket pivot at full reach) 1,795 kg

Status:
In production. Recent deliveries have been made to Austria (4), Croatia (4), France (91, from 2006), Netherlands (7), New Zealand (4, 2006), Singapore (2008) and the UK (150, 2002 to 2003) (136, 2010 to 2011 - see text).

Contractor
JCB Defence Products

Case 721A, 721 BXT and 721 CXT wheeled loaders

Development

In March 1992, the UK MoD placed a GBP5.6 million order with Case Europe Limited for 63 model 721A wheeled loaders, the primary functions of which would be earthmoving and excavations, although they would also be required to perform general material handling duties. 721A machines have been deployed by the British Army in Bosnia, Kosovo, Germany and elsewhere.

Following the delivery of the 721A machines, and to meet the demanding specifications of the UK Royal Marines, Case winterised and waterproofed 17 of its 721 BXT wheeled loaders. Case also secured the

Case 721A wheeled loader in the materials handling role
(Shaun C Connors)   1124732

British Army contract for the provision of 29 trackway dispensers for fitting to Case 721 BXT wheeled loaders to allow them to carry, deploy and recover a 32 m length of Class 30 trackway. These dispensers were manufactured by Ulrich Attachments Limited.

In late 2000 the UK MoD placed an order with Case International Limited for 103 model 721 CXT wheeled loaders for use by the Royal Engineers. Designated Medium Wheeled Tractor (MWT) by the British Army, they are used for a variety of roles from earthmoving and excavation to general materials handling and heavy lifting. Based around a commercial machine built in the US by the Case Corporation, the 721 CXT machines have been customised in the UK to meet British Army specifications.

Penman Engineering Limited of Dumfries have designed and manufactured a cab protected against ballistic attack for vehicles such as the Case 721A. Details of these can be found in the Other equipment section.

It was disclosed in 2010 that as part of their agreement under the UK MoD's C vehicle PFI programme, that ALC had awarded JCB a contract to supply 98 mildly militarised JCB 436 wheeled loaders, these to replace the remaining Case 721 series machines in service.

Description
The Case 721 series of machines are a commercial range of wheeled loaders, the 721E being the current model.

The 721A machines involved in the UK MoD's 1992 order were essentially standard production machines customised by Case in the UK to British Army specifications. Customisation included the fitting of a Boughton (now Ulrich Attachments Limited) 2.1 m³ multipurpose four-in-one bucket, front loader mounted ripper and pallet fork attachments, and a 10,000 kg capacity hydraulic winch on the rear of the chassis. The hydraulic systems were adapted to supply power on demand for hand operated tools, including a jack and bead breaker used with a loader mounted tyre handling system.

The 17 721 BXT machines supplied to the UK Royal Marines were customised by Case in the UK to operate in salt water up to 1.5 m deep. Eight were also winterised for operations in Arctic climates. The machines were required to be capable of transportation by seagoing vessels and then by landing craft, to carry out applications such as the preparation of beachheads and laying trackway underwater to facilitate vehicle landings. The 29 trackway dispensers involved in the requirement were manufactured by Ulrich attachments and allow the machines to carry, deploy and recover a 32 m length of Class 30 trackway.

The 103 721 CXT wheeled loaders were procured by the UK MoD for a variety of roles from earthmoving and excavation to general materials handling and heavy lifting. Modifications to the base commercial machine include a front chassis mounted 10,000 kg capacity hydraulic winch, a

Case 721A wheeled loader showing rear-mounted 10,000 kg capacity hydraulic winch (Shaun C Connors)   0109485

Case 721 CXT wheeled loader in travel configuration and clearly showing spare wheel and pallet fork stowage arrangements (Case International)
0547272

Case 721 BXT wheeled loader laying Class 30 trackway during a beach landing demonstration (Shaun C Connors)   0525607

multipurpose 2.1 m³ four-in-one bucket, side-shift pallet forks and a front loader mounted ripper, all supplied by Ulrich Attachments Limited. Each MWT was designed to deploy carrying its own spare wheel and tyre and was equipped with sufficient dry storage space for a full CES kit and the operator's personal equipment. The electrical and hydraulic systems were adapted to supply power for a variety of ancillary tools including trackway dispensers. Eight machines were further modified to allow for operations at temperatures down to –40°C and salt water up to 1.5 m deep.

Penman Engineering Limited of Dumfries designed and manufactured a cab protected against ballistic attack for the Case 721A.

Status
Commercial production of updated model continues. All remaining 721 series machines in British Army service are currently being replaced.

Contractor
Case Corporation
(Customised and supplied by Case International Limited)

JCB High Mobility Engineer Excavator (HMEE)

Development
The JCB High Mobility Engineer Excavator (HMEE) was developed by JCB to meet the US Army's requirement for a self-deployable engineering excavator to provide direct support to the Stryker Brigades. This in addition to replacing the in-service fleet of Unimog-based machines, the Small Emplacement Excavator (SEE).

The US Army's Tank Automotive and Armaments Command (TACOM) issued a Request For Proposal (RFP) in third quarter FY2002, following which a two year R&D contract was awarded in first quarter FY2003 to JCB and one other (ADI Limited of Australia). First Unit Equipped was anticipated in third quarter FY2006. The production contract, worth up to USD140 million, was awarded to JCB in September 2005 and calls on a requirements type contract for up to 636 machines for the US Army.

JCB supplied six machines for Production Verification Testing (PVT) in June 2006. Following successful completion of these trials, production of an initial 636 machines (including 20 to permit trials with an A and B kit armour solution devised by American Defense Systems Inc. (ADSI)) began at JCB's Savannah, Georgia facility in early 2007. The first units were delivered in September 2008, with deliveries under this first contract running until 2012. As of June 2010, around 260 machines have been provided and deployed on operations with the US Army.

JCB HMEE during the mobility demonstration at IDEX 2007
(Shaun C Connors)   1186164

JCB HMEE to US Army spec (Shaun C Connors)   1391316

The HMEE is a self-deployable, high mobility, protected, excavation system with attachments to execute a wide range of mobility, counter-mobility, survivability, and general engineering missions All HMEEs are air-transportable by C130 or equivalent and larger aircraft.

The design fundamentals of the HMEE, high mobility, high speed and protection, enable it to be deployed with main forces and therefore to provide immediate, direct support to main forces, thereby reducing the numbers of deployed personnel and equipment. The HMEE is not designed as an armoured engineer vehicle, but is a fully protected engineer plant vehicle. It provides high levels of operator protection and the ability to undertake obstacle breaching missions.

To supplement the HMEE, it was announced in July 2005 that the US Army had placed an order worth over USD50 million for 511 High Mobility Engineer Excavator (HMEE) Type III backhoe loaders. Deliveries of these, essentially commercial, backhoe loaders commenced during 2006 and is scheduled for completion during 2010.

Most recently JCB has sold HMEEs to the British Army (17), New Zealand (6), and an undisclosed Middle Eastern country (<10), this believed to be the UAE. A further three countries are understood to be showing genuine interest in acquiring the HMEE.

Description

The HMEE has been designed to meet the needs of deploying and deployed main forces and was developed to combine safe operation at high speeds over long distances, while still performing effectively as a backhoe loader, and loadall, in all terrain conditions. The machine is based on technology developed for and proven in the JCB Fastrac high-speed tractor, combined with elements of the JCB High Mobility Rough Terrain Forklift (HMRTF) high speed and high mobility telescopic handler and the JCB 4CXM backhoe loader. Full details of all these machines can be found in their respective sections.

There are currently three separate HMEE variants based on protection levels. The least protected variant being the A Kit, which is principally designed for, and used for, training and non-deployed units. The B Kit, with a fully protected cab, is for use on operations. Finally, the TRE variant, with enhanced levels of operator protection designed to meet the increasing levels of protection required by deployed forces. Engineering outputs remain the same as initially developed but the TRE variant has a governed top speed in order to meet EU road legal requirements and only one operator station.

Motive power for the HMEE is provided by a Cummins 6.7-litre turbocharged diesel engine coupled to a ZF Ergopower automatic six-speed gearbox with torque converter lock up. Manual or fully automatic gear changes are possible, with an electrically operated forward/reverse shuttle for enhanced loading cycle times. JCB axles are fitted, and these feature four wheel drive (selectable), three steering modes (front wheel, four wheel, crab steer), JCB 'soft-engage' differential locks, an anti-lock braking system and a multimode suspension system.

JCB HMEE to UK spec displayed at Eurosatory 2010 (Shaun C Connors)
1391315

Maximum road speed is 88 km/h (except for the TRE variant); maximum wading depth is 1 m to provide a capability for use with landing craft.

The cab is fully air-conditioned and configured for C-130 transportability.

Variants

Based on experience gained with the development of the HMEE and the evolving needs of deployable forces, JCB announced in June 2006 that it had developed to prototype stage the High Mobility Variable Reach Truck (HMVRT). The HMVRT is based around components, including the chassis, of the HMEE and is optimised for a balance of on-road speed and off-road mobility. The HMVRT is a telescopic handler specifically designed for use with 20 ft ISO containers with the ability to load and unload containers whether mounted on a truck or on the ground. Development work on the HMVRT is currently halted.

Specifications

High Mobility Engineer Excavator (HMEE)
Cab seating: 2 (1 in TRE variant)
Configuration: 4 × 4
Weight:
(A kit) 14,125 kg
(B kit) 15,959 kg
(TRE) n/avail
Length: (with full ancillaries) 10.10 m
Width: (bucket) 2.44 m
Height: (top of cab; prepared for air transport) 2.67 m
Ground clearance: (kingpost) 850 mm
Wheelbase: 3.06 m
Approach/departure angle: 36.5°/31.5°
Max road speed: (forward/reverse) 88.5/30.6 km/h
Fuel capacity: 265 litres
Fording: 1 m
Engine: Cummins QSB 02 6.7-litre in-line 6 cylinder turbocharged with charge-air-cooling 4-stroke water cooled diesel developing 200 hp (149 kW) at 2,300 rpm and 705 N.m torque at 1,600 rpm
Transmission: ZF Ergopower with 6 forward and 2 reverse gears, manual or automatic gear change. Selectable 4 wheel drive incorporating torque converter, reversing shuttle and all synchromesh 4 speed gearbox
Steering: power assisted mechanical front steering, synchronised hydrostatic rear steering. 3 steer modes, front wheel, 4 wheel and crab
Turning radius:
(kerb 4WS/2WS) 10.38/18.4 m
(wall 4WS/2WS) 13.1/20.1 m
Axles: JCB steer drive with differential locks
Suspension: four modes: travel mode (full suspension); transport/maintenance mode (lowers suspension for tie-down etc.); Loader mode (front axle locked); backhoe mode (rear axle locked)
Tyres: (front and rear) 445/80R 25 (runflat inserts optional)
Brakes:
(main) air-over-oil, outboard dry 460 mm discs, twin callipers front, single calliper rear, ABS
(parking) 380 mm discs on transmission output shafts. Capable of holding vehicle on 48% gradient
Electrical system: 24 V
Battery: 2 × 12 V
Alternator: 200 A, 28 V
Loader performance: (with 0.93 m³ 4-in-1 on quick-hitch)
(shovel breakout) 43,568 kgf
(loader arm breakout) 2,300 kgf
(lift capacity to full height) 2,041 kg
(dump height) 2 m
(loadover height) 3.79 m
(reach at full height) 2.02 m
(rollback/dump angles) 40.1°/45°

Backhoe performance:
(bucket tearout, speed) 4,378 kgf
(bucket tearout, power) 5131 kgf
(dipper tearout) 3,164 kgf
(lift capacity) 1,300 kg
(max dig depth) 3.94 m
(max reach, ground level to rear wheel centre) 6.54 m
(side reach, to centre line of machine) 5.25 m
(max operating height) 5.63 m
(max loadover height) 3.86 m
(bucket rotation) 187.5°

Status
In service with the US Army (see text), the British Army, the New Zealand Army, and the United Arab Emirates (UAE) land forces. Under evaluation by other armed forces.

Contractor
JCB Defence Products

United States

Case construction equipment

Description
The Case Corporation manufactures an extensive range of construction, earth moving and materials handling equipment at their worldwide production facilities. Much of the Case product range is suitable for military applications. The Case Corporation now specialises in customising commercial equipment to meet military requirements but it no longer designs or manufactures specialist military equipment. Customising operations can be carried out either at the point of manufacture, in-country by Case agents or dealerships, or by military workshop organisations. Customising can include: climatic operational range enhancements; the fitting of armour protection ranging from small arms fire and shell splinter protection for the operator, through to a full mine blast protection kit; a deep salt-water wading ability; the fitting of hydraulic-powered winches or other ancillary equipment.

Case 580 Super LE backhoe loader of the Portuguese Army
(Victor Barreira)   1391239

Case MW24C Scoop Loader of the US Army operating in Baghdad early 2007 (Carl Schulze)   1340300

In line with most manufacturers of commercial construction equipment, the Case range is continually being updated, new models and minor design changes are made on a regular basis. The current range features approximately 60 different products (with regional variance in specifications) and the company has service/support facilities in around 150 countries worldwide.

US Army
In 2005 the US Army awarded Case Construction Equipment a five-year contract valued at over USD50 million for more than 500 High Mobility Engineer Excavator (HMEE) Type III militarised commercial backhoe loaders that will be delivered either armoured or armour-ready. Approaching 700 machines were delivered, with an initial 50 armoured machines delivered late-2008. Production concluded mid 2010.

In 2007 the US Army awarded Case Construction Equipment a contract valued at in excess of USD160 million to build nearly 1,500 M400T compact track loaders and as many as 1,900 M400W skid steer loaders over a ten-year period, with deliveries scheduled to conclude during 2017.

Case 821C of the French Army mounting a dispenser for the MOBI MAT tactical matting (Shaun C Connors)   0525927

Case 580E backhoe loader of the Australian Army fitted with a four-in-one front bucket (Ron Fry)   0547274

Case MW24C Scoop Loader operating in Baghdad and fitted with a Crew Protection Kit (CPK) and additional Red Dot air-conditioning system (Carl Schulze)   1340299

Each M400W skid steer loader and M400T compact track loader will be supplied with an auger, a four-in-one multi-purpose bucket, pallet forks and a hydraulic hammer. These machines are similar in specification and capability to the commercial 420 Series 3 skid steer loader and 420CT Series 3 compact track loader, but do feature a degree of militarisation that includes: four tie-down and lift points for transport that includes underslung by helicopter and air-drop by parachute; a weapons rack; 24 V starting and charging system that provides the ability to power auxiliary equipment; necessary adaptation to run on JP-8 fuel; NATO slave receptacle; and removable steel crawler tracks for the skid steer machine.

In addition to these contract awards, Case has also earned several other US Military contracts in recent years, these including the remanufacture/refurbishment of at least 565 Case MW24C wheel loaders, the reset/refurbishment of at least 300 M4K rough terrain forklifts, and the re-powering of 500 Case M4K forklifts. Full details of the M4K and other similar Case rough terrain forklifts can be found in the Materials handling equipment section.

Status
In production. Case construction equipment is in service with numerous armed forces and governmental organisations including the Australian Army, Belgian Army, British armed forces, Canadian Army, French Air Force and Army, Netherlands Marines, US armed forces, the UN and the HALO trust.

Contractor
Case Corporation

Caterpillar M105 Deployable Universal Combat Earthmover (DEUCE)

Development
The M105 Deployable Universal Combat Earthmover (DEUCE - originally known as the Caterpillar 30/30 Engineer Support Tractor) was developed as a private venture by Caterpillar to act as a high-speed combat support machine and intended for use in several forward area roles.

Following an initial USD3.3 million development contract issued during 1995, two test machines were delivered to the US Army in June 1996. An initial order for 15 units with a total value of USD8.7 million was placed during late 1996, with the first examples delivered during May 1997. Fielding commenced during 1999. By July 2000, the initial 136 machines contracted had been delivered to the US Army and, in October 2000, a follow-on contract for an additional 91 machines was awarded to Caterpillar. By December 2002, a total of 227 machines had been manufactured. Final fielding of the M105 DEUCE occurred in mid-2004 with the delivery of machines to the third Stryker brigade combat team (SBCT).

A package of four modification upgrades began in December 2003. These focused on enhancements to operation and maintenance and were installed as part of a fleet-wide inspection process.

The UK MoD took delivery of an Engineer Support Tractor for testing in July 1998. A further 14 were delivered to Royal Engineer Units during 1999 for the support of the Joint Rapid Reaction Force. The total cost for the 15 vehicles was approximately GBP5 million.

Description
The M105 DEUCE is a self-deployable unit capable of traversing rough terrain and is fitted with a hydraulically operated angled dozer blade at the front. The driver/operator is seated in an air-conditioned forward control cab. Approximately 80 per cent of DEUCE components are standard commercial items.

The tracks use the Caterpillar Mobil-trac System with a rubber track hydropneumatic undercarriage that allows on- and off-road travel at speeds up to 53 km/h. The sound signature is stated to be low.

M105 Deployable Universal Combat Earthmover (DEUCE) of the US Army with add-on armour (Carl Schulze)   1340303

Engineer Support Tractor of the British Army (Patrick Allen)   1067397

Engineer Support Tractor of the British Army (Patrick Allen)   1067396

Power is provided by a Caterpillar 3126 7.2-litre diesel coupled to a Caterpillar planetary power shift. The engine has two outputs, 265 hp for the self-deployable mode for travelling on roads or cross-country and 185 hp for earthmoving. Sufficient fuel is carried for 10 hours of earthmoving or 322 km of road travel.

For drive-on, drive-off transport in a C-130 aircraft, the overall height can be hydraulically lowered by collapsing the two front suspension cylinders. Preparation for C-130 loading takes less than 10 minutes. For low-velocity airdrops (LVAD) the entire cab shell can be removed to lower the overall height to 2.286 m. LVAD preparation takes two mechanics under 20 minutes. Re-assembly takes under 30 minutes.

Accessories include a 10,000 kg capacity winch, pintle hook, towing lugs and a hydraulic hand tool connection.

Specifications
M105 DEUCE
Cab seating: 1
Weight: 16,100 kg
Length:
    (dozer blade angled) 6.591 m
    (dozer blade straight) 5.956 m
Width:
    (dozer blade angled) 2.718 m
    (dozer blade straight) 2.946 m
Height:
    (working) 2.794 m
    (air transport) 2.565 m
    (airdrop) 2.286 m
Ground clearance: 310 mm
Track gauge: 1.91 m
Length of track on ground: 2.438 m
Max speed:
    (self-deployable) 53 km/h
    (earthmoving) 11.7 km/h
    (reverse, both modes) 20.3 km/h
Range:
    (on road) 322 km
Gradient: 60%
Side slope: 30%
Vertical obstacle: 305 mm
Fording: 914 mm

Engine: Caterpillar Model 3126 7.2-litre water-cooled diesel developing 265 hp (198 kW) in self-deployable mode or 138 kW (185 hp) in earthmoving mode

Transmission: Caterpillar planetary power shift automatic providing (self-deployable) 6 forward and 2 reverse gears or (earthmoving) 3 forward and 2 reverse gears

Suspension: (self-deployable) hydropneumatic with 254 mm vertical travel; (earthmoving) rigid

Electrical system: 24 V

Status

Production as required. In service with UK (15) and US armed forces (227).

Contractor

Caterpillar Inc.

Caterpillar construction equipment

Description

Caterpillar offers the largest and most comprehensive range of construction and construction related equipment in the world. As of mid-2009, the Caterpillar product line-up consisted of more than 300 machines, the vast majority of these suitable for military engineering applications.

In addition to supplying what are essentially 'off-the-shelf' commercial products, Caterpillar will design/develop and carry out militarisation of these commercial products on an 'as required' basis and to meet specific military requirements, such as armour kits and mine clearing rakes for track-type tractors. In addition, the company is one of few in the construction equipment sector that will undertake the design, development and manufacture of military-specific equipment, such as the Deployable Universal Combat Earthmover (DEUCE), currently in service with British (15) and US (>220) armed forces. In addition to manufacturing new equipment, Caterpillar also runs an extensive rebuild and remanufacture programme, details of which can be found elsewhere in this entry.

To manage the company's business with the US Government, its contractors and with US and non-US military, Caterpillar set up a dedicated group, the Defense & Federal Products group, based in Mossville, Illinois and Washington, DC. To support its products in the field, Caterpillar has a worldwide network of 178 dealers with 135,000 employees.

Caterpillar type 621 wheeled tractor-scraper of US Armed Forces in Kosovo (Patrick Allen)   0547263

US Navy Naval Mobile Construction Battalion 135H motor grader at work carving out a drainage ditch (US DoD)   1391399

Caterpillar 933 tracked loader of the Australian Army. The current production model is the 933C Hystat powered by a 70 or 90 hp diesel engine and with operating weights ranging from 8,485 to 9,484 kg. The backhoe attachment shown is not standard fit or option and is most likely some form of local adaptation (Ron Fry)   0547268

Front view of an Australian Army Caterpillar 130G motor grader (Ron Fry)   0589065

The following is a brief overview of the Caterpillar product range (with the exception of forestry and waste handling equipment) as of late 2010. Included are items of equipment that technically fall outside the remit of the Field fortifications and related emplacements section, but some of which would likely be found in the inventory of better-equipped engineer regiments.

Articulated trucks (frame-steer dump trucks):	6 models with power outputs ranging from 301 to 453 hp, and capacity ranging from 22,260 to 35,610 kg
Backhoe loaders:	4 models with power outputs ranging from 88 to 124 hp, and operating weights ranging from 6,792 to 10,950 kg
Cold planers:	3 models with power outputs ranging from 225 hp to 650 hp with cutting widths from 1 to 2.1 m
Compactors:	39 models for soil, landfill and paving applications
Hydraulic excavators (360°):	42 models, further details of which can be found elsewhere in this section
Material handlers:	18 models
Motor graders:	10 models with power outputs ranging from 138 to 533 hp, and maximum gross vehicle weights ranging from 14,093 to 62,457 kg. In November 2007 TACOM awarded Caterpillar a contract for 600 120M model motor graders
Multiterrain loaders:	5 models with power outputs ranging from 56 to 90 hp
Compact track loaders:	3 models with power outputs ranging from 82 to 90 hp
Off highway trucks:	10 models with power outputs ranging from 476 to 3,370 hp
Articulated trucks:	6 models with power outputs ranging from 301 to 453 hp
Paving equipment:	9 models

Pipelayers:	4 models ranging in lifting capacity from 18,160 to 91,625 kg
Road reclaimers:	2 models
Scrapers:	11 models. In September 2010 the US DoD awarded Caterpillar a contract for up to 909 wheeled tractor scrapers. These machines will include modifications called for by the USMC and Army, these including lift and tie-down provisions and keyless engine start
Skid steer loaders:	10 models with power outputs ranging from 47 to 90 hp
Telescopic handlers:	7 models with power outputs ranging from 99 to 142 hp and with rated capacities ranging between 2,948 and 5,443 kg
Track loaders:	7 models
Track-type tractors:	25 models, further details of which can be found elsewhere in this entry
Wheeled dozers:	5 models
Wheeled Loaders:	19 models, further details can be found elsewhere in this entry

The following sub-sections include further details of ranges of Caterpillar equipment that have, or are likely to be procured by military organisations in the greatest numbers. Unless otherwise stated, any specifications given are for commercial variants, and in addition to changes likely to occur throughout any commercial products production run, these could be subject to change for military applications.

Track-type tractors
The number of military users of Caterpillar track-type tractors is extensive. Caterpillar currently produces 25 models of track-type tractor and is the world market leader for this type of machine. The D3K model is the lightest with the D11T models being the heaviest. The current D3 model is powered by a 74 hp diesel engine and has an operating weight of 7,795 kg. The two current D11 models are powered by an 850 hp diesel engine and have operating weights (with a rear-mounted ripper) of 104,590 kg.

CAT 420D backhoe loader of US Navy Seabees at work during relief operations in Haiti 2010
(US DoD (Mass Communication Spec. 1st Class Monique Hilley)) 1391400

Caterpillar D6H dozer of the Portuguese Army (Victor Barreira) 1391238

Seventeen of Caterpillar's medium- and large-size track-type tractors are fitted with an exclusive elevated sprocket design. The elevated sprocket raises final drives and associated power train components out of the work environment to extend drive train life and reduce downtime. The use of modular components is intended to simplify maintenance and further reduce downtime.

The most prevalent Caterpillar track-type tractor in military use is the D7 model. The largest users of this model are the US Army and US Marine Corps. Current D7 models are powered by a 240 hp diesel engine and have operating weights ranging from 25,304 to 27,920 kg (configuration dependant). The D7R is currently being militarised, modifications including transport provisions, blackout lights and MIL standard paint.

Caterpillar produces a Mine Clearing/Armour Protection (MCAP) kit for US Armed Forces D7 models.

In November 2005 the US Army's Tank-automotive and Armaments COMmand (TACOM) awarded American Defense Systems, Inc. (ADSI) a USD7.6 million IDIQ contract for the supply of Crew Protection Kits (CPK) for the US Army's D7G Mine-Clearing/Armour Protection (MCAP) fully tracked, low- speed, medium drawbar pull bulldozer.

In June 2008 TACOM awarded Caterpillar a contract for 152 D6K and 1,255 D7R-II track-type tractors. Both models have Type I (with winch) and Type II (with ripper) configurations.

Australian Army Caterpillar D3C dozer fitted with a power angle tilt blade and rear-mounted rippers (Gordon Arthur) 1391305

US Naval Mobile Construction Battalion D8T track-type tractor at work moving material for use as fill for HESCO Concertainer units in Al Qaim, Iraq (US DoD) 1391388

US Navy Naval Mobile Construction Battalion CAT D7 track-type tractor with armoured cab at work in Helmand province, Afghanistan
(US DoD (Mass Communications Spec. 2nd Class) Michael Lindsey) 1391401

Wheeled loaders

Caterpillar currently produces 19 models of wheeled loader. All are of conventional design, being steered by articulation and having rigid unsprung axles, an oscillating rear axle compensating for ground undulations. The lightest of the range is the model 904, powered by a 52 hp diesel engine and having an operating weight of 4,490 kg. The heaviest of the range is the model 994F, powered by a 1,463 hp diesel engine and having an operating weight of 191,899 kg. For most military applications, machines ranging from 16,000 to 26,000 kg operating weights are the norm. An example of specialised militarisation of commercial machines would be the 972G wheeled loader, of which 25 were delivered to the UK MoD during 2001. Full details of the Armoured Heavy Wheeled Tractor (AHWT) can be found elsewhere in this section.

In August 2005 TACOM awarded Caterpillar a contract for 375 966H and 350 924H wheeled loaders.

360° excavators

Caterpillar produces both wheeled and tracked 360° excavators. The current range being made up of 42 models, all but five of which are tracked. Tracked models range in size from the 1,558 kg 301.6 model powered by a 18.1 hp diesel engine, to the 84,980 kg 385C L model powered by a 513 hp diesel engine. For most military applications, machines with operating weights ranging from 16,000 to 26,000 kg are the norm.

The wheeled machines are of conventional two-axle design, having four-wheel drive and front axle steer. Axles are unsprung, an oscillating front axle accounting for ground undulations. In common with the tracked range, these machines can accept a variety of arm attachments. They may also be used for lifting purposes, with or without any bucket attached.

US Army CAT D7G track-type tractor with armoured cab at work near the Tigris River in Baghdad, Iraq (US DoD)   1391402

Caterpillar CS-433 compactor of the US Army (Caterpillar)   0589049

Caterpillar 215B LC 360° tracked excavator of the Italian Army operating in Iraq (Patrick Allen)   1033179

Compactors

Caterpillar currently produces a range of 39 different compactors, with models optimised for soil, waste and paving.

800 Series models are of wheeled loader configuration and are non-vibratory. US Armed Forces use the 20,879 kg 815F model. This is powered by a 220 hp diesel and is fitted with the optional levelling blade.

There are currently 15 machines in the vibratory soil compactor range. These have operating weights ranging from 4,400 kg to 18,620 kg. US Armed Forces have recently taken delivery of models CS-433C and CS-563C. The CS-433C weighs 6,770 kg, is powered by 105 hp diesel engine and is equipped with a smooth drum, hydraulically operated hinge pin articulated steering mechanism, a levelling blade, RollOver Protective Structure (ROPS), pad foot shell kit, 24 V electrical system, and single or dual amplitude variable frequency vibratory system. The machine is capable of compacting a 0.305 m lift at the rate of 561 m³ per hour to a level of 95 on the Proctor scale. Military modifications include the addition of lifting eyes/tie-downs to permit military transport, a rifle bracket, and an MIL standard paint finish.

The CS-563C is essentially a larger version of the previously described CS-433C, weighing 11,275 kg and powered by a 153 hp diesel engine. It is capable of compacting a 10.305 m lift at the rate of 1,458 m³ per hour at a level of 95 on the Proctor scale.

Caterpillar CS-563C compactor of the US Army (Caterpillar)   0536666

Caterpillar 800 Series (Model 815F) wheeled loader-based non-vibratory compactor of the US Army (Caterpillar)   0589050

Rebuilt Caterpillar D7F track-type tractor of the US Army (Caterpillar)   0536665

Both models are air transportable and have C-130 Hercules drive-on/drive-off capabilities. The CS-433C can also be deployed by Low Velocity Air Drop (LVAD). To build-in this capability, some changes, such as increasing weld size compared to the standard machine were required.

Rebuild or Service Life Extension Program (SLEP)
It is not uncommon for an item of commercial construction equipment to undergo a rebuild or refurbishment especially at the end of its life cycle. Therefore, in addition to new or purpose-designed machinery, Caterpillar offers an extensive rebuild and refurbishment service for some of its previously manufactured machines. The stated advantages of rebuilding an existing machine are: rebuilt to 'zero' hours; a new machine warranty; updated ILS; lower price compared to new equipment, and faster fleet modernisation.

Caterpillar currently performs military machine rebuild activities at over 45 dealer locations within the continental United States, plus the Far East, Europe and Middle East. Machines are rebuilt and returned within 60 days of approvals.

As of mid-2010, Caterpillar was rebuilding the following machines for US Armed Forces: D7F and D7G track-type tractors; 130G motor graders; 621B wheel tractors-scraper. Refurbishment of the 988B Rough Terrain Container Handler (RTCH) fleet was completed during 2005. Full details of the 988B RTCH can be found in the Materials handling equipment section.

During the past 14 years, a total of approximately 3,800 machines have been rebuilt for the US Army, US Marine Corps, and the US Army Reserves and National Guard.

Status
In production. In service worldwide (see text for details).

Contractor
Caterpillar Inc

Caterpillar DV104 Armoured Heavy Wheeled Tractor (AHWT)

Development
The Caterpillar DV104 Armoured Heavy Wheeled Tractor (AHWT) was developed specifically to meet a UK MoD requirement for a vehicle to be used in the airfield support role. It can be used in conjunction with the Flush Capping System (FCS) which is used in the Airfield Damage Repair (ADR) Mission. The AHWT is based on a commercial wheeled loader, customised as required in the UK.

Caterpillar DV1049 Armoured Heavy Wheeled Tractor (AHWT) with the full range of ancillary equipment used in the airfield damage repair role (Caterpillar)   0587571

Armouring of the Caterpillar DV104 Armoured Heavy Wheeled Tractor (AHWT) was carried out by Penman Engineering (Penman Engineering)
0098697

The GBP14 million firm fixed-price contract was awarded to Caterpillar during 2000 and called for the delivery, by spring 2001, of 25 machines and a range of ancillary equipment. However, since the award to Amey Lex Consortium (ALC) of the UK MoD's C Vehicle PFI program, the number of machines in service has been reduced.

Under the C Vehicle PFI program a fleet of 4,000 vehicles largely operated by the Royal Engineers and Royal Logistics Corps was purchased by ALC and a replacement program commenced to supply and manage a smaller fleet, including cranes, dump trucks, excavators, bulldozers, rough terrain forklifts and container handlers. ALC will gradually rationalise the MoD's fleet to approximately 2,000 assets using Whole Fleet Management techniques and will procure over 1,700 new assets during the contract, worth in excess of GBP110 million. In addition to the procurement and disposal of equipment, the agreement provides a broad range of support services.

Description
The AHWT can be used for roles normally associated with a heavy wheeled loader such as earthmoving, barricade clearance, and route clearing and denial and, however it was primarily designed to keep RAF airfields open during wartime. Its job is to act as a pathfinder, clearing debris from the runway and filling in bomb craters, before using its dynamic compactor to compress the spoil enough to allow a final concrete cap to be applied.

The 40,300 kg AHWT is based on a commercial wheeled loader, and is a significant redesign of the Caterpillar 972G model. The customised machine incorporates additional rear counterweights and 966G lift arms with a hydraulic bucket quick coupler which allows various front ancillaries such as a rock bucket, armoured bulldozer or dynamic compactor to be fitted in a short to facilitate the rapid repair of runways.

The major threat to the machine's operator is unexploded bomblets on the runway, so the vehicle has urethane foam-filled tyres and an armoured cab. The armoured cab is a split design so the upper portion can be removed within 20 minutes to transport the machine. Other armoured areas include the axles, axle hubs, bellyguard, articulated hitch and front and rear sides.

The base machines were manufactured at Caterpillar's Gosselies facility in Belgium, the armouring was carried out by the UK's Penman Engineering, while remaining customising and finishing work was carried out by Caterpillar's UK agent.

Status
Production as required. In service with the UK (25 delivered).

Enquiries to
Caterpillar Inc

BULK FUEL STORAGE AND DISTRIBUTION SYSTEMS

Australia

Project JP 2059 - Bulk Liquid Distribution

Development
Project JP 2059 is a joint-service procurement project being managed by the Defence Materiel Division (DMD). The aim of the project is to address both known and recently identified Australian Defence Force (ADF) shortfalls in bulk liquid distribution, both fuel and water.

Description
The ADF has a mature and functional bulk fuel (and water) distribution capability, which was initially enhanced to meet the requirements of the East Timor deployment. There were, however, a number of critical bulk liquid deficiencies identified during the ADF deployment to East Timor; the specification and fit of much in-service equipment reflecting 1960–70s technology and not taking full advantage of developments such as modern OH&S principles, containerisation and palletised load systems. Much of the equipment in use also fails to meet current industry standards. In addition, some of the in-service systems are approaching life-of-type and require enhancement, replacement or supplementation, if emerging requirements are to be met.

Phase 1 of the project delivered enhanced bulk fuel and storage and bulk fuel transfer systems in response to the requirements of the ADF East Timor deployment.

Current phases of Project JP 2059 (as of May 2006) are:

Phase 2 - Bulk Liquid Distribution
The aim of JP 2059 Phase 2 is to provide a bulk fuel (and water) storage and distribution capability to support the concurrent deployment of:
- A brigade-based Joint Task Force
- A Battalion Group deployed on independent operations including their supporting attachments
- A unit-line refuelling capability for the Armed Reconnaissance Helicopter (ARH).

Acquisition under Phase 2 is expected to address these requirements, with other deficiencies to be met through subsequent project phases of JP 2059 or JP 126 Joint Theatre Distribution.

As of July 2010 contracts had been signed with the following suppliers:
- Ebsray Pumps Pty Ltd in July 2004, for the supply of (37) V-35 Fuel Pumps and (34) V-15 Potable Water Pumps
- Trelleborg in November 2004, for the supply of a Tank Fabric Collapsible Marine
- Amfuel in November 2004, for the supply of (170) 1,800 litre capacity drum fabric collapsible water storage tanks
- Crusader Hose Pty Ltd in December 2004, for the supply of 12 km of 150 mm hose assemblies
- Dunlop Fabrications in December 2004, for the supply of (74) 136,000 litre fuel tanks
- Ebsray pumps Pty Ltd in February 2005, for the supply of (3) fuel flow metres
- Dunlop Fabrications in September 2005, for the supply of (9) Towed Flexible Barges
- Ebsray Pumps Pty Ltd in March 2006, for the supply of (4) V-40 fuel pumps
- Crusader Hose Pty Ltd in September 2005, for the supply of 13.5 km of 150 mm pipeline hose assemblies
- Metcalfe Pty Ltd in February 2006, for supply of (10) Vacuum Recovery Kits
- Ebsray Pumps Pty Ltd in March 2006, for the supply of (4) V-40 fuel pumps
- Flight Refuelling Ltd (United Kingdom) in March 2007, for the supply of (3) sets of barge discharge systems

- Royal Wolf Containers Pty Ltd in August 2008, for the supply of container modifications
- Ebsray Pumps Pty Ltd in December 2009, for the modification and upgrade of the Tank and Pump Assembly fleet (quantity 130 units)
- Logistic Solutions Australasia in March 2010 via DMO Support Services Panel for the provision of Through Life Support documentation for the Towed Flexible Barge Discharge System
- Gill Engineering in July 2010 for the Towed Flexible Barge Discharge System replacement Mooring Pontoons.

All significant sub-projects planned for Phase 2 have either been completed or are in contract, with the scope for the remaining acquisitions (detailed below), expected to transition to Land 121 Project Overlander for completion:
- Refuelling module and vehicle for the Armed Reconnaissance Helicopter (ARH)
- Fuel and water vehicle storage modules.

Phase 3
Phase 3 relates specifically to water purification and supply and full details can be found in the Water supplies section.

Status
See text.

Contractor
Defence Materiel Organisation

Canada

SEI Industries fuel storage and distribution systems

Development
SEI Industries is a single source for the engineering, manufacturing and on-site installation of fuel and water distribution systems. The company has completed tank-farm designs and installations for the UN, the Canadian Department of National Defense (DND) and oil and gas

SEI Industries has been supporting militaries around the world with rapidly deployable fuel and water storage, transferring, transportation and pumping systems for over 20 years. SEI Industries manufactures a wide selection of military specification products for both NATO and non-NATO countries (SEI Industries)
1421489

Arctic King collapsible fuel tanks. The tanks sit inside an above ground earth in secondary containment berm with an oil water separator to prevent ground contamination in the event of a spill (SEI Industries)
1421487

Project JP 2059 is a joint-service procurement project being managed by the Defence Materiel Division (DMD). The aim of the project is to address both known and recently identified Australian Defence Force (ADF) shortfalls in bulk liquid distribution - fuel and water (Gordon Arthur)
1391306

SEI Industries supplied Repsol Exploration in Peru with 26 × 25,000 US gallons Jungle King tanks to store 650,000 US gallons of fuel at their Nuevo Mundo Site (SEI Industries)   1421488

SEI Industries provided a turn key temporary fuel farm and deployed it in far eastern Siberia, Russia. The system was designed to store 2 million US gallons of fuel (SEI Industries)   1421486

operations in Ecuador, Myanmar, Nigeria and other countries. Applications have included fuel storage and supply in remote areas and support of drilling operations and fuel logistics in Arctic areas.

Description
The following sub-sections include brief details of specific ranges of SEI Industries fuel storage and distribution systems.

Tank and pump systems
SEI Industries can customise fuel transfer systems to meet specific requirements with respect to pumping capacity, filtration and metering.

Systems extend to portable fuel filtration and pumping units for helicopters and light aircraft operating from the aircrafts' own power supply.

SEI Industries also provides several berm liners for the secondary containment of hazardous materials, including fuel, for temporary or permanent installations. The self-supporting Insta-Berm is available in a range of sizes and can be custom-produced. The frameless design makes the system easy for one person to deploy without using tools and the berm is collapsible for storage and transport.

King series collapsible fuel tanks
SEI Industries manufactures the King series, a trio of collapsible pillow tanks ranging in capacity from 100 US gallons (379 litres) up to 50,000 US gallons (189,270 litres); larger sizes can also be produced.

The Arctic King range is designed to store fuels in arctic environments. It can be deployed on temperatures as low as –50°C with high levels of Ultra-Violet (UV) and has been designed to meet Environment Canada – Technical Requirements for Collapsible Fabric Storage Tanks (Bladders) 17 December 2009. The Desert King range is designed to store fuels in high temperatures with high levels of UV, or for fuels that have a high aromatic content. The Jungle King range is designed to store fuel in tropical climates with high temperatures, high levels of UV and high humidity.

All King series tanks are made from proprietary materials and are 100 per cent radio frequency welded, seam seals and pressure tested.

Each tank is provided with a fill/drain fitting, plus a second fitting at the centre of the tank for vent/overfill protection. A wide range of other valves, flanges and fittings in several sizes can be supplied. Optional items include camouflage covers, sunshades, berm liners, ground sheets, flow-meters and pumping systems.

Fuel-Easy helicopter-transportable tank system
The SEI Industries Fuel-Easy helicopter-transportable tank system is a fully collapsible, modular external load fuel carrier intended to support helicopter operations. The system involves a flexible fuel container carried

inside a frame which remains aerodynamic during flight, even when partially filled and is stable on the ground. Filling is via the top of the tank and emptying through the bottom, so utilising all available volume.

Fuel-Easy tanks are available in six sizes, from 180 US gallons (680 litres) to 1,260 US gallons (4,775 litres). Each tank is cradled within a collapsible high-strength aluminium frame (steel and bronze frames are available) which can be assembled without tools in about five minutes. The tank fabric is puncture-resistant but if punctured, can be repaired easily using a field repair kit.

Special Fuel-Easy tanks are available for chemicals or potable water.

Status
In production. In service with the armed forces of Canada, the US, South America, Middle East and elsewhere.

Contractor
SEI Industries

Finland

Jet Tekno refuelling systems and equipment

Development
Jet Tekno are designers and manufacturers of a wide range of vehicle and aircraft refuelling equipment and associated accessories including pumpsets, filter systems and trailers. In addition to numerous civil organisations, Jet Tekno equipment is used by China (PLA), Estonian Army and Air Force, Finnish Army, Air Force and Border Guard, Lithuanian Air Force and the Swedish Air Force.

Description
A brief description of certain items of Jet Tekno equipment follows.

Vehicle refuellers
Jet Tekno manufacturers a vehicle refuelling system consisting of a 20,300 litre tank complete with all associated pumping equipment that is suitable for mounting on a wide variety of military on- or off-road truck chassis, Sisu being the current chassis choice for Finnish military applications.

The all-aluminium tank is a five-compartment design and the twin vane-type pumps have a maximum capacity of 500 litres/min each. Six 25.4 mm diameter spring-rewind hose reels and a single 38 mm diameter hydraulic-rewind hose reel are fitted, allowing for the simultaneous refuelling of up to six vehicles or items of static equipment. Maximum delivery rates are 80 litres/min through each of the six reels or 250

Jet Tekno 20,300 litre vehicle refueller of the Finnish armed forces, based on a Sisu 8 × 4 truck chassis (Jet Tekno)   0524748

Jet Tekno 25,000 litre three-axle drawbar-type tank trailer of the Finnish armed forces (Jet Tekno)   0524749

Jet Tekno single-axle off-road refuelling trailer (Jet Tekno)   0524750

litres/min through a single reel. The single 38 mm reel is of additional length to facilitate to refuelling of static distribution tanks. All hoses are equipped with a self-closing nozzle and a litre counter. All pipework is AISI 304 stainless steel.

The compartmentalised tank allows for two fuel types to be handled simultaneously, effectively allowing for both petrol and diesel-powered vehicles and equipment to be serviced.

Also available is an all-aluminium transportable refuelling container that has a capacity of 11,400 litres in three separate 3,800 litre compartments. Diesel, diesel substitutes and patrol (gasoline) can be carried and supplied simultaneously through six refuelling pistols, each of which has a 15 m hose reel.

Aircraft refuellers
Jet Tekno manufactures an aircraft and/or helicopter refuelling system consisting of a 13,100 litre tank complete with all associated pumping and filtration equipment that is suitable for mounting on a wide variety of truck chassis, Sisu being the current chassis choice for Finnish Air Force applications, Scania for Swedish Air Force applications.

The all-aluminium tank is a three-compartment design and the single self-priming hydraulically operated centrifugal pump has a capacity of 1,100 litres/min. Both underwing and overwing refuelling is possible for aircraft, and at rates of between 900 and 1,000 litres/min for overwing, and 250 and 500 litres/min for underwing. Pressure control is pneumatic. All pipework is AISI 304 stainless steel.

Also available is a system consisting of a 12,600 litre tank complete with all associated pumping and filtration equipment that is suitable for mounting on a wide variety of truck chassis.

The all-aluminium tank is a three-compartment design, each compartment having a capacity of 4,200 litres. Two refuelling nozzles with a 35 m hydraulic rewind hosereels are fitted, these having a capacity of 300 litres/min each. All pipework is AISI 304 stainless steel.

Also available is an aircraft and/or helicopter refuelling system consisting of a 22,500 litre tank complete with all associated pumping and filtration equipment that is suitable for mounting on a wide variety of four-axle truck chassis with a capacity of around 32-tonnes GVW.

The all-aluminium tank is a four-compartment design and both underwing and overwing refuelling is possible for aircraft, and at rates of up to 1,000 litres/min for underwing, and 300 litres/min for overwing.

25,000 litre tank trailer
Jet Tekno produces a three-axle drawbar-type tank trailer with a capacity of up to 25,000 litres. For refuelling either aircraft or vehicles, dependant on role, the trailer may be used in conjunction with a hydrant truck, tanker or independent pump unit. It may also be used as the storage tank component of the Jet Tekno Field Pipe System.

The five-compartment tank is of aluminium construction, pipework being constructed of stainless steel. Two 76 mm diameter, 6 m length discharge hoses are fitted.

The trailer is sprung by conventional leaf spring suspension, axle loadings (full) being 10,000 kg on the single front axle, 16,000 kg on the rear bogie pair. The trailer measures 9 × 2.58 × 3 m (L × W × H).

Off-road refuelling trailer
This Jet Tekno single-axle trailer is specifically designed for pumping fuel in off-road or tactical situations. The trailer is outfitted for purpose but can be used as the refuelling station for a field fuel distribution system or for pumping from fuel cells, bladders, or tank trailers such as the Jet Tekno 25,000 litre tank trailer. It may also be fitted out for aircraft or helicopter refuelling.

The single vane-type pump has a maximum capacity of 600 litres/min. Six 25.4 mm diameter spring-rewind hose reels are fitted, allowing for the simultaneous refuelling of up to six items of equipment. Maximum delivery rates are 480 litres/min using all six hoses or 50 to 80 litres/min through a single hose. Five of the six hoses are 15 m in length, the sixth being 20 m. Each hose is fitted with a self-closing nozzle.

All rigid pipework is stainless steel, the flexible suction pipe being 76 mm diameter. At flow rates of 500 litres/min, the filter/water separator filters to 1 micron.

Mobile refuelling trailer
This refuelling trailer is specifically designed for the refuelling of helicopters or tactical aircraft in deployed scenarios. In the case of aircraft it can refuel underwing or overwing. The trailer is light enough to be handled by a single person and can be towed by the smallest of 4 × 4 light utility vehicles.

The pumping and filtration equipment is mounted on a single-piece steel plate trailer body running on a single leaf sprung axle. The tubular support frame has a single lifting eye top-centre, this support frame also acting as bows for a tarpaulin cover. It also offers protection to the unit in the case of a roll-over accident.

The self-priming centrifugal pump has a capacity of 1,100 litres/min, a pumping performance of 800 litres/min and is powered by a two-cylinder diesel engine. The suction hose is 5 m long and 63.5 mm diameter, the refuelling hose is 15 m long and 51 mm diameter. At a flow rate of 800 litres/min the filter/water separator filters to 1 micron.

Status
In production. Jet Tekno equipment is in service with China, Estonian Army and Air Force, Finnish Army, Air Force and Border Guard, Lithuanian Air Force and the Swedish Air Force.

Contractor
Jet Tekno

France

AÉRAZUR flexible fuel storage and transport tanks

Development
AÉRAZUR has been involved in the design, development and manufacture of safety and survival equipment, mainly to the aerospace industry, the armed forces and the armament industry, for over 60 years. AÉRAZUR produces a wide range of products made of fabrics including flexible fuel cells, de-icing systems, flexible tanks, composites parts and elastomer products. Details of bulk fuel-related products follow.

Description
Flexible fuel storage and transport tanks
AÉRAZUR manufactures a range of flexible tanks for transport (capacity 500 to 10,000 litres) and for storage (capacity 1,000 to 300,000 litres). They are made of high-performance synthetic fabrics coated with elastomer to store fuel and other liquids such as water and chemicals. The tanks are provided with standard equipment according to French and US specifications but can be equipped to suit customer requirements. All the tanks in the range can be folded when empty and are easy to set up on site. They are suitable for a wide range of climatic conditions. Transport tanks are designed for a service life of greater than 10 years.

Helisup helicopter-transportable tanks
The Helisup heli-transportable tank is used to transport fuel or drinking water underslung by helicopter. These tanks are manufactured from synthetic fabric coated on each side with elastomer and have a standard capacity of 1,500 litres.

A standard fitting is a 76 mm fill/drain flange on the top but other equipment can be fitted to suit customer specifications. Tanks are supplied complete with a heli-transport envelope, slinging equipment, transport handles, stowing straps and an emergency repair kit. The necessary equipment to pump and dispense potable water is also available.

AÉRAZUR fuel transport tank and associated containment berm and liner as displayed at Eurosatory 2006 (Shaun C Connors)   1156102

Flexible fuel storage and transport tanks

Capacity:	Dimensions: (empty)	Dimensions: (full)	Weight: (empty, approx)
25 m³	8.11 × 4.05 m	7.48 × 3.42 × 1.10 m	112 kg
30 m³	9.53 × 4.05 m	8.90 × 3.42 × 1.10 m	131 kg
35 m³	8.10 × 5.43 m	7.47 × 4.80 × 1.10 m	148 kg
40 m³	8.47 × 5.43 m	7.79 × 4.75 × 1.20 m	155 kg
45 m³	7.16 × 6.81 m	6.45 × 6.10 × 1.25 m	163 kg
50 m³	7.79 × 6.81 m	7.08 × 6.10 × 1.25 m	177 kg
60 m³	9.10 × 6.81 m	8.39 × 6.10 × 1.25 m	206 kg
70 m³	9.00 × 8.19 m	8.29 × 7.48 ×1.25 m	243 kg
80 m³	9.51 × 8.19 m	8.77 × 7.45 × 1.30 m	256 kg
90 m³	10.00 × 8.19 m	9.26 × 7.45 × 1.30 m	269 kg
100 m³	11.65 × 8.19 m	10.91 × 7.45 × 1.30 m	312 kg
120 m³	11.60 × 9.57 m	10.86 × 8.84 × 1.30 m	361 kg
150 m³	11.99 × 10.95 m	11.22 × 10.18 × 1.35 m	425 kg
200 m³	15.67 × 10.95 m	14.90 × 10.18 × 1.35 m	551 kg
300 m³	17.65 × 13.71 m	16.85 × 12.91 × 1.40 m	769 kg

A part-filled AÉRAZUR fuel transport tank carried by a French Army Renault G290.26 VTL (6 × 4) transport truck (Pierre Touzin)   0589069

Addisup 100 litre fuel tank

This self-contained 100 litre fuel tank is intended to increase the range of cargo- or troop-carrying vehicles by a factor of about 3.5. The principle is that each vehicle can carry up to four of these tanks hooked on the vehicle side rails. Each tank can be placed in position by two personnel using the integral carrying handles provided and the tank can be filled through a filling port on the top of the tank. The tank is emptied by using a drain hose placed directly into the vehicle main tank.

The tanks are manufactured using a coated fabric which is resistant to hydrocarbons, with an interchangeable abrasion-resistant cover on the side next to the carrier vehicle. The tank has a self-bracing system allowing it to hold its position when on the ground, even at decreased capacity. The drain hoses can be connected and disconnected to provide the correct refuelling lengths.

GILEP

AÉRAZUR is a member of GILEP (Groupement Interprofessionnel de Logistic et Equipments Pétroliers), a consortium composed of the main contractors to the French armed forces Joint Petroleum Service (SEA). Full details of GILEP can be found elsewhere in this section.

Specifications

Status
In production. In service with France's armed forces, NATO, and a number of armed forces in the Middle East and North Africa, including Chad and Gabon.

Contractor
AÉRAZUR

GILEP (Groupement Interprofessionnel de Logistique et d'Equipement Pétroliers)

Development
GILEP (Groupement Interprofessionnel de Logistique et d'Equipement Pétroliers) is a syndicate of various industry-related manufacturers that was created some 20 years ago under the auspices of the director at that time of the French Joint Military Service in charge of supplying the armed forces with fuels and lubricants, the SEA.

The CCP 10 Multipurpose Field Refueller Tank Truck demonstration refuelling simultaneously a towable tank and two vehicles (Patrick Allen)
1066447

The basic idea of what would become GILEP was to federate a related group of companies that had demonstrated a capability to provide the SEA with all of its required POL logistics equipment. GILEP would remain a civilian entity, but under the supervision of the military.

In addition to core fuel storage and distribution equipment, GILEP members can also provide all essential related equipment needed.

In a typical requirements scenario one GILEP member will act as project manager and integrate the components of others to deliver a final product. GILEP members have a close working relationship, however, on occasion they can also compete against one another for French or other requirements.

In addition to French armed forces, GILEP members also operate autonomously in the supply of other nations, predominantly NATO but also in the Middle East and Latin America.

The very nature of the products offered by GILEP members ensures that some member companies also produce water supplies equipment.

Product groups
The core fuel-related items/products supplied by GILEP members can be grouped into five main categories:
- Tankers solutions (including those for aviation) covering all sizes from those based on light all-terrain vehicles to maximum length semi-trailers, with or without metered distribution
- Storage equipment ranging from flexible rubber jerrycans through to the bladders as part of the complete infrastructure for a fuel farms

The CCP 10 Multipurpose Field Refueller Tank Truck showing the pump equipment (Patrick Allen)
1066449

The GILEP Leclerc MBT refuelling system is discreetly transported by TRM 10 000 (6 × 6) 10,000 kg truck (Pierre Touzin)   1120415

- Servicing units and components, distribution components such as pumps, hoses, metering devices, filters and couplings. These can be either permanent, semi-permanent; or fully autonomous that includes air-portability
- General logistics and environment material including: all products related to the operational equipment mentioned previously; air-land-sea bulk transportation services; shelters; vehicle platforms; fire-fighting vehicles, antipollution devices including floating booms
- Fluids and lubricants for all applications, including aviation servicing; NATO-grade resins, sealants, paints and coatings for all type of equipment.

GILEP member companies and competencies
The following is a list of current GILEP members and their core fuel-related competencies:
- AERAZUR (Zodiac Aerospace) - bladders; aircraft systems and equipment (specific details of certain AERAZUR products can be found elsewhere in this section)
- Cornut - customized heavy vehicles for hauling and recovery
- Daher - project management; field shelters equipped; international logistics services
- Desautel - fire-fighting trucks and equipment; airport and tactical refuellers
- Dukes Titan Aviation - aircraft refuelling equipment (refuellers; hydrant dispensers; fuelling modules and skids; bowsers)
- ERI - fuel farms building and maintenance
- Faure-Herman - volume and mass flowmeters for aeronautic use
- Haar France - pumps; autonomous servicing units
- Lafon - tank trucks; containerised service stations; metering devices
- Magyar SA - tank trucks; bowsers; tank wagons
- Maisonneuve - tank trucks; field waste water treatment units; potable water units
- Mouvex Blackmer - pumps and compressors for transfer of liquids and dry bulk products
- NYCO - lubricants and hydraulic fluids for air and land vehicles
- Pernin Equipment - servicing units; metering devices
- PPG Coatings - resins, paints, coatings and lubricants
- PRONAL - bladders; autonomous servicing units (specific details of certain PRONAL products can be found elsewhere in this section)
- Renault Trucks - tank trucks; logistic vehicles (full details of the Renault Trucks vehicle ranges can be found in the Trucks section)
- Satam - industrial metering systems
- Staubli - quick disconnect couplings for all types of fluids and electricity
- Trelleborg - assembled industrial hoses; rubber products for all applications
- Unil Opal - lubricants for industry and transport.

French Army Eurocopter Tiger/Tigre being field-refuelled with equipment supplied by GILEP members (GILEP)   1391325

Description
The following descriptive text and images provide details and examples of the range of equipment provided by GILEP.

CCP 10 Multipurpose Field Refueller Tank Truck
The CCP 10 Multipurpose Field Refueller Tank Truck is an example of a collaborative GILEP project. Most GILEP members contributed to the vehicle, providing filters, meters, couplings, hoses, and the protective/camouflaging tarpaulin. The base vehicle is a customised Scania P114CB6 × 6HZ340 (6 × 6) manufactured at Scania's Angers (France) facility, while the tank and general assembly was the responsibility of Lafon Industries.

On entering French Army service during 2004-2005, the CCP 10 progressively replaced the GILEP Leclerc MBT refuelling system. This in itself was then re-roled to replace the Trailor 5,000 litre bowser equipment for AFVs, the vast majority of which have been phased out of service.

The requirement called for 300 systems, 242 of which were ordered and were delivered by late 2005. The follow-on order for the remaining 58 systems, subject to budgets, could be placed at a later date. The base system is understood to have been evaluated by other armed forces.

The CCP-10 Field Refueller Tank Truck is an all-terrain, conventional-looking truck with a single compartment 10,000 litre capacity stainless steel tank equipped with a 60 m³/h pump and four supply lines that can be operated simultaneously to refuel up to four helicopters/vehicles in a single batch, and giving a return to operational status time of around 15 minutes.

Each line is individually filtered and electronically measured, and a fifth meter indicates the amount remaining in the tank. The various nozzles and dry-break coupling required to fill an assortment of aircraft, vehicles and equipment (including jerrycans) are interchangeable in a few moments without any specialist tools; in principle by hand. The vehicle cab accommodates a crew of five, including the driver, but the standard crew is two.

GILEP Leclerc refuelling system
Ordered by the Service des Essences des Armées (SEA), the GILEP Leclerc MBT refuelling system is based on a Renault TRM 10 000 (6 × 6) truck chassis. The single compartment 11,000 litre capacity main tank, supplied by the now defunct General Trailers, can be used to refuel four helicopters or four combat vehicles simultaneously, either by gravity or under pressure.

The service flow rate of the pumping unit is 60 m³/h, giving a certified refuelling capability of at least 12 m³/h when four vehicles, helicopters or aircraft are fed simultaneously, giving an approximate return to operational status time of 15 minutes per batch (vehicles or helicopters).

GILEP member Desautel is the key contractor for the Unimog-based CCP 3.6, deliveries of which commenced in 2010 (Shaun C Connors)   1391309

Renault Trucks Defense which supplied the (4 × 4) tractor units for these bulk fuel tankers is a key member of GILEP (GILEP)   1391324

French Army Leclerc MBT being field-refuelled with equipment supplied by GILEP members (GILEP)   1391326

GILEP member Magyar SA specialises in tank trucks; bowsers and tank wagons (Shaun C Connors)   1391310

Following the introduction into service during 2004/2005 of the GILEP CCP 10 Multipurpose Field Refueller Tank Truck (as detailed elsewhere in this entry) it is understood the GILEP Leclerc refuelling system has been re-roled to replace Trailor 5,000 litre bowser systems, the vast majority of which (possibly all) have been phased out of service.

CCP 3.6 multipurpose tactical refueller

The CCP 3.6 multipurpose tactical refueller is a further recent example of a collaborative GILEP project. Most GILEP members contributed to the vehicle, providing filters, meters, couplings, hoses, and the protective/camouflaging tarpaulin. The tank and general assembly was the responsibility of Desautel. The vehicle is a customised Mercedes-Benz Unimog U5000 (4 × 4) chassis.

The CCP 3.6 entered French Army service during 2010, its primary role being the tactical field refuelling of helicopters. It can, however, refuel a wide variety of other equipment including vehicles and jerrycans. The requirement called for 32 vehicles, 10 of which will be fitted with ballistic attack protected cabs.

The CCP 3.6 multipurpose tactical refueller is an all-terrain, conventional-looking truck with a single compartment 3,600 litre capacity stainless steel tank. Deployability was the key factor in the design of the CCP 3.6, this driving the capacity and overall pump equipment specification. The CCP 3.6 measures 6.8 × 2.47 × 2.75 m (L × W × H), has a GVW of 14.000 kg, and is transportable by C-130 transport aircraft.

The CCP 3.6 can be used throughout a -20°C to +40°C temperature range, and at altitudes of up to 1,000 m.

Status
Production as required. In service with the French and other armed forces.

Enquiries to:
Groupement Interprofessionnel de Logistique et d'Equipement Pétroliers (GILEP)

Pronal flexible tanks for fuel

Development
Pronal produces an extensive range of flexible tanks for both storage and transport of fuel. These tanks may also be used for various other liquids including water. Pronal tanks are constructed from a nitrile rubber-coated nylon fabric, and depending on application may be reinforced with high strength fabric.

Pronal flexible fuel storage tanks in use (Pronal)   0125398

A typical Pronal flexible fuel storage tank on static display at Eurosatory 2006 (Shaun C Connors)   1156103

A typical Pronal helicopter-transportable and towable flexible tank on static display (Shaun C Connors)   0589080

Pronal is a member of GILEP (Groupement Interprofessionnel de Logistic et Equipments Pétroliers), a consortium composed of the main contractors to the French armed forces Joint Petroleum Service (SEA). Full details of GILEP can be found elsewhere in this section.

Description

Flexible storage and transport tanks
Storage tanks with capacities ranging from 1,000 to 10,000 litres are fitted with a 51 mm (2 in) inlet/outlet valve; tanks with capacities ranging from 15,000 to 150,000 litres are fitted with two 76.2 mm (3 in) inlet/outlet valves (one only on 15,000 and 30,000 litre tanks). All tanks are fitted with an inspection hole with vent and vapour release system.

Transport tanks are known as Liquitank transport tanks and are generally similar to storage tanks, but are fitted with longitudinal skirts and adjustable straps for lashing/fixing to the load area of a wide variety of transport vehicles. When not full, these tanks may be rolled up leaving space available for the transport of other loads.

The figures provided in the specifications table are not comprehensive as Pronal can produce tanks to suit individual customer requirements. Heavy duty reinforced rubber tanks of up to 300,000 litres capacity are also available.

Flexible storage tanks

Capacity:	1,000 litres	2,000 litres	5,000 litres	10,000 litres	15,000 litres	20,000 litres	25,000 litres	30,000 litres	35,000 litres	40,000 litres
Length: (empty)	2.44 m	2.4 m	4.6 m	8.2 m	4.97 m	6.29 m	6.01 m	6.99 m	7.98 m	8.96 m
Width: (empty)	1.37 m	2.12 m	2.12 m	2.12 m	4.13 m	4.13 m	4.96 m	4.96 m	4.96 m	4.96 m
Height: (full)	650 mm	1.1 m	1.1 m	1.1 m	1.2 m	1.2 m	1.3 m	1.3 m	1.3 m	1.3 m
Weight: (empty)	25 kg	35 kg	55 kg	85 kg	90 kg	115 kg	135 kg	155 kg	175 kg	190 kg
Volume: (folded)	0.15 m³	0.2 m³	0.25 m³	0.4 m³	0.45 m³	0.55 m³	0.65 m³	0.75 m³	0.85 m³	0.95 m³

Flexible storage tanks (continued)

Capacity:	45,000 litres	50,000 litres	60,000 litres	70,000 litres	80,000 litres	100,000 litres	125,000 litres	150,000 litres	200,000 litres	300,000 litres
Length: (empty)	8.65 m	9.49 m	8.88 m	8.47 m	9.14 m	11.15 m	13.66 m	16.17 m	21 m	17 m
Width: (empty)	5.63 m	5.63 m	6.97 m	8.14 m	8.47 m	8.47 m	8.47 m	8.47 m	8.39 m	14.6 m
Height: (full)	1.3 m	1.3 m	1.3 m	1.35 m	1.35 m	1.35 m	1.35 m	1.35 m	1.35 m	1.35 m
Weight: (empty)	210 kg	230 kg	265 kg	300 kg	330 kg	420 kg	510 kg	595 kg	681 kg	900 kg
Volume: (folded)	1.05 m³	1.15 m³	1.3 m³	1.5 m³	1.65 m³	2.1 m³	2.55 m³	2.95 m³	3.50 m³	3.90 m³

Flexible transport tanks

Capacity:	1,000 litres	2,000 litres	3,000 litres	4,000 litres	5,000 litres	6,000 litres
Length: (empty)	1.8 m	2.4 m	3.15 m	3.85 m	4.6 m	5.3 m
Width: (empty)	1.8 m	2.12 m	2.12 m	2.12 m	2.12 m	2.12 m
Height: (full)	700 mm	1.1 m	1.1 m	1.1 m	1.1 m	1.1 m
Weight: (empty)	30 kg	40 kg	50 kg	60 kg	70 kg	80 kg
Volume: (folded)	0.15 m³	0.2 m³	0.25 m³	0.3 m³	0.35 m³	0.4 m³

Flexible transport tanks (continued)

Capacity:	7,000 litres	8,000 litres	9,000 litres	10,000 litres	11,000 litres	12,000 litres
Length: (empty)	6 m	6.75 m	7.45 m	8.2 m	8.9 m	9.65 m
Width: (empty)	2.12 m	2.12 m	2.12 m	2.12 m	2.12 m	2.12 m
Height: (full)	1.1 m	1.1 m	1.1 m	1.1 m	1.1 m	1.1 m
Weight: (empty)	90 kg	100 kg	110 kg	120 kg	130 kg	140 kg
Volume: (folded)	0.45 m³	0.5 m³	0.55 m³	0.6 m³	0.65 m³	0.7 m³

Helicopter-transportable and towable flexible tanks

Capacity:	200 litres	1,000 litres	1,900 litres
Diameter:	600 mm	1.1 m	1.35 m
Length:	1 m	1.3 m	1.6 m
Weight: (empty)	20 kg	85 kg	135 kg
Dimensions: (folded)	850 × 950 × 250 mm	1.2 × 1.5 m × 25 mm	1.5 × 1.8 m × 250 mm
Working pressure:	0.3 bar	0.3 bar	0.3 bar

RSH helicopter-transportable tanks

Model	0.5 RSH	1.0 RSH	1.5 RSH
Capacity:	500 litres	1,000 litres	1,500 litres
Weight: (tank and fittings)	25 kg	32 kg	40 kg
Dimensions:			
(empty)	1.4 × 1.4 × 0.15 m	1.8 × 1.8 × 0.15 m	2.2 × 2.2 × 0.15 m
(loaded hanging)	1.01 × 1.01 × 1.2 m	1.4 × 1.4 × 1.55 m	1.7 × 1.7 × 1.9 m

A typical Pronal flexible storage and transport tank being transported by a MAN F2000 range truck of the UAE Army during a demonstration at IDEX 2005 (Patrick Allen)   1138147

Helicopter-transportable and towable flexible tanks

These drum-shaped tanks are used to transport hydrocarbon fuels, oils or water and are made of nylon fabric coated with synthetic nitrile rubber, which is anti-ultraviolet radiation treated. There are three capacities - 200, 1,000 and 1,900 litres - with the material thickness of the two smaller tanks being five mm and the largest nine mm.

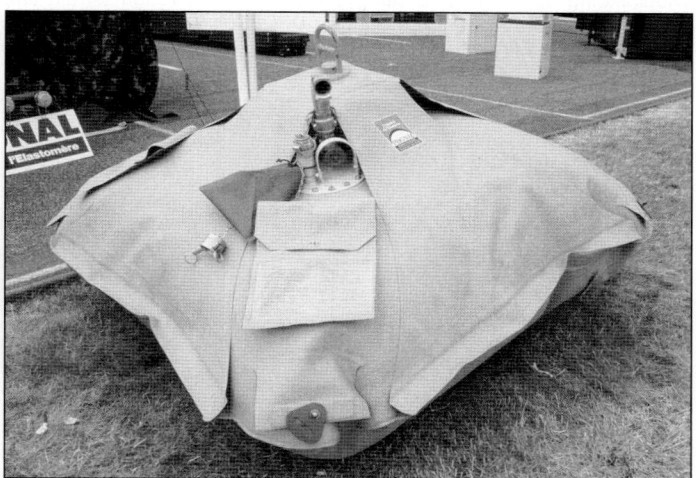

A typical Pronal RSH tank on static display (Shaun C Connors)   0589082

The 200 litre tank can be dropped from a height of 12 m and, once on the ground, is rollable. The two largest tanks can be towed. All three can be carried slung under helicopters. The 200 litre tank has a 19 mm (0.75 in) adapter and vent; a filling pipe with a 19 mm (0.75 in) coupling and semi-symmetrical DN 40 connection or Kamlock coupling. The larger tanks have a self-plugging DN 50 adapter and there is also a filling and emptying pipe 1.6 m in length - this is fitted with DN 40 Kamlock connections and caps. Also available for the larger tanks are towing, pushing or lifting bars and turning plates with lift rings.

The 200 litre tank can be dropped when full from a helicopter at heights up to 12 m from the ground. Larger capacity tanks may be dropped when full from the loadbed of trucks. When empty, the volume of these tanks represents approximately 15 per cent of filled volume.

RSH helicopter-transportable tanks

Pronal RSH (RSH - *reservoirs souples heliportables*) tanks are produced in three sizes: 500, 1,000 and 1,500 litres. A patented design is used, in which the tank is supported in a Maltese cross-shaped skirt that immediately spreads the load of the vehicle once it is lifted from its single clip-on ring. Once in flight, the skirt passes air through its panels and acts as a drogue to prevent the tank from revolving beneath the carrying helicopter. Each tank has one slinging ring, an outlet with a 51 mm (2 in) valve coupling and plug and a symmetrical Guillemin system. These tanks may also be used to carry water.

Specifications

Status
In production. Pronal products have been supplied to more than 50 nations.

Contractor
Pronal SA

Germany

WEW Westerwälder Eisenwerk GmbH Special Tank Containers

Development
WEW Westerwälder Eisenwerk GmbH has focused on the development, production and worldwide licensing of Special Tank Containers for the chemical industry for over 40 years. However, WEW also provides solutions for the transportation of liquid foods and other liquid products, including automotive fuels and potable water. WEW has been supplying fuel tank containers to the German Army since 1998. In total, WEW has supplied several hundred military fuel (and water) ISO-sized containers to the German Army. Other users of WEW Special Tank Containers include the Belgian, Irish, Lithuanian, Slovenian, UK and US armies.

Description
Unless specific contract requirements specify otherwise, all WEW Special Tank Containers are designed to be compatible with the commercial ISO transport envelope. All WEW Special Tank Containers are fully legal for global commercial transport and handling (including China, Japan and the US), and have been designed to ISO 1496-3 with prototype and impact tests.

Each tank container has a six-fold welded ring system for increased stability and for protection from corrosion, and also a low tare weight, for example, the 20 ft container with 26,000-litre capacity has a tare weight of 2,900 kg.

Tanks for specific military usage are purpose-designed to be capable of withstanding operational handling and transport in rough terrain and maybe designed for use with military DROPS/PLS-type load handling systems. For German Army applications, certain examples are

WEW tank container fitted with the Hutchinson protection system (WEW Westerwälder Eisenwerk GmbH)   1431253

A full height fuel storage optimised tank container of the Lithuanian Army that is equipped with two pumps, each having a pumping capacity of 150 litres/min (Shaun C Connors)   1340297

A reduced height tank container with a non-cylindrical double shell tank that is operable by DROPS. The system includes a pump with a pump capacity of 400 litres/min. The UK MoD received 25 of these tanks during 2009, and by late 2009 the first examples had been deployed to Afghanistan (Shaun C Connors)   1340295

transportable by a load handling system-equipped vehicle, such as the MAN SX range Multi (8 × 8). The Belgian Army transports its 16,000-litre capacity containers on low-mobility IVECO EuroTrakker (8 × 4) chassis.

WEW has also developed modular ISO-compatible pumping/stowage and tank units in lengths of 5, 10, 15 and 20 ft, and while the 5 and 15 ft lengths are not standard ISO lengths, all other dimensions of these units remain ISO compatible so when they are used modularly with certain other components, full ISO handling/transport is possible.

At Eurosatory 2010 WEW displayed for the first time concepts for protected versions of fuel tanks. In cooperation with Hutchinson a self-sealing layer is applied to the outside of the tank. In ballistic tests this has successfully demonstrated protection against 14.5 × 114 mm projectiles. A system of removable protection has been developed in conjunction with IBD Deisenroth, offering up to Level 4 protection.

Status
In production. Approximately 500 assorted tank containers in service (fuel and/or water) with Belgian, German, Irish, Lithuanian, Slovenian, UK and US armed forces.

Contractor
WEW Westerwälder Eisenwerk GmbH

Israel

Achidatex collapsible fuel containers

Development
Since 1977 Achidatex has produced the Achidatank range of collapsible containers suitable for the storage, distribution and transport of fuels, chemicals and other liquids intolerant of contamination, including water. Full details of products suited to water transportation and distribution can be found in the Water supplies section.

Description
The Achidatex pillow tank is produced in sizes ranging from 1,000 to 100,000 US gallons (3,758 to 378,500 litres) and the collapsible Drop Container range has capacities ranging from 50 to 500 US gallons (189 to 1,892 litres).

A typical Achidatex pillow tank (Achidatex)   1047910

Achidatank collapsible containers are produced in three material types, as follows:

ACH-5, with a base fabric of tyre cord strength polyester yarn. This has a high temperature resistant, tough, resilient coating with a non-extractable plasticiser.

Urethane-coated polyester ACH-7714, a specially formulated and produced membrane fabric for containing leaded or unleaded petrol, jet fuels, methanol and ethanol.

Polyester membrane fabrics ACH-8028 and 8424, approved by the US Food and Drug Administration for the containment of potable water and other liquids.

Status
Pillow tanks in production, Drop Containers no longer produced. Pillow tanks and Drop Containers in service with Israeli armed forces.

Contractor
Achidatex

Chemoplast collapsible fuel storage and transport tanks

Development
Chemoplast Industries Ltd produced a range of collapsible storage and transport tanks, plus a range of dry storage systems that are detailed in the Other equipment section. Chemoplast Industries Ltd was acquired by Defense Industries International in 2005. Achidatex, a subsidiary of Defense Industries International also produces ranges of storage and transport tanks, plus a range of dry storage systems. Details of Achidatex products, which now encompass Chemoplast products, can be found in their related sections.

Description
Chemoplast Industries Ltd produced a range of collapsible storage and transport tanks with capacities from 500 to 300,000 litres. These tanks are made from a variety of coated flexible plastic materials and are suitable for the storage and/or transport of a wide range of liquids including fuels (including gasoline, diesel, oil and kerosene) and potable water. Details of those tanks suited to the transport and/or storage of water can be found in the Water supplies section.

Chemoplast stationary collapsible fuel tanks were available in sizes ranging from 500 to 300,000 litres, while mobile collapsible tanks were available in sizes ranging from 500 to 20,000 litres. All tanks were supplied with filling and emptying fittings to suit customer requirements and contents.

Status
In service with the Israeli Air Force, Army and Navy.

Contractor
Defence Industries International Inc. (previously known as Chemoplast Industries Limited)

Poland

Container-based fueling station (KSP)

Development
The container-based fuelling station (KSP) consists of three modules and was developed for the storing of liquid fuels and other oil-based products of fire hazard categories I, II, III, plus other explosive, toxic or highly flammable substances.

The container-based fuelling station (KSP) consists of three modules, a tank module with technical room, a fuel dispensing module, and an office and staff room module (WZINZ)   1148057

The container-based fuelling station (KSP) consists of three modules, a tank module with technical room, a fuel dispensing module, and an office and staff room module (WZINZ)   1148058

Description
The container-based fuelling station (KSP) consists of three modules, a tank module with technical room, a fuel dispensing module, and an office and staff room module. The standard power supply of the container-based fuel station is 3 × 380/230 V. The container-based fuel station wiring meets Occupational Health and Safety (OHS) and fire regulations. It is equipped with a protective earth installation and a lightning protection system; the electrical system is explosion proof. Hatches in the roof of the container allow access to storage tank chambers and make it possible to measure the fuel level manually with a dip pole. All compartments of the station are fitted with locks to protect the facility from unauthorised access and/or use.

The container-based fuelling station modules comprise the following:

Tank module with technical room
- 20 m³ double-skinned steel fuel storage tank consisting of two chambers, 15 m³ for diesel and 5 m³ for petrol
- Tank level monitoring system in both chambers and a leak detection system with display unit and printer
- Drain pipe and sounding pipe, through which fuel level can be measured in each chamber, using the dip pole supplied
- Fill and drain system consisting of a self-suction pump with the maximum capacity of 500 litres per minute; pipe fitting construction allows by-passing the pump during the filling of the fuel storage tank chambers
- Adapter to a tanker truck (male)
- Evaporative loss control device preventing noxious vapour loss during filling operations
- Aeration and de-aeration system – each independent fuel storage chamber has a shifting valve and an internal emergency valve

Fuel dispensing module
- Fuel dispensing room
- Fuel dispenser pumps (fitted with quantity meters) with a maximum capacity of 90 litres of diesel fuel and 50 litres of petrol per minute
- 9 m fuel dispenser hoses on reels

Office and staff room module
- Office and staff room with electric heater
- Bathroom with wash-bowl
- WC

- Electric water heater
- Cold water system
- Sewerage system

Specifications

Container-based fueling station (KSP)
Storage capacity:

(petrol)	5 m³
(diesel)	15 m³
Pump output:	500 litres/min
Distributor I:	90 litres/min
Distributor II:	50 litres/min
Crew:	2
Hose drum:	9 m
Water connection:	Storz (1 inch (25.4 mm))
External dimensions:	
(length)	12.192 m
(width)	2.438 m
(height)	2.896 m
Total weight:	approx 13,000 kg

Status

Production as required.

Contractor

Wojskowe Zaklady Inzynieryjne (WZINZ)

Russian Federation

Bulk fuel transport, storage and distribution equipment

Description

The armed forces of the former Soviet Union, the former Warsaw Pact and those who received equipment from the former Soviet Union operated, and still operate, a considerable variety of bulk fuel transport, storage and distribution equipment. Much of this equipment is now technically obsolete although available in such vast quantities, much of it is likely to remain in use and/or storage for some time.

In addition to certain items covered in greater detail elsewhere in this section, the items covered briefly in this entry (unless otherwise stated) are some of those currently offered for export sale. Many of these items are likely to be in service with the armed forces of the Russian Federation and its allies.

ATZ-22 fuelling truck

The ATZ-22 fuelling truck is intended for the refuelling of aircraft on paved airfields. A 22,000 litre capacity tank semi-trailer is coupled to a Ural-44202-0611-30 (6 × 6) tractor truck, or most recently a Ural-44202-31 (6 × 6) tractor truck. The total weight of the laden combination is 38,260 kg.

The semi-trailer is fitted with four hoses and two liquid meters, the pumping equipment allowing for both pressure or overwing refuelling and defuelling operations. The tank may also be bypassed to allow for filtered refuelling or defuelling to or from an external source.

The filter-water separator ensures a water content 'downstream' of the filter not exceeding 0.0015 per cent when fuel prior to filtration has a water content not exceeding 0.05 per cent.

The trailer is fitted with an automatic brake-locking system that will not release the vehicles' parking brakes while any hose remains connected to an aircraft. A 'dead man' system is also fitted, cutting in should the operator lose control of the fuelling operation.

ATZ-10-4320 fuelling truck

The ATZ-10-4320 fuelling truck is intended for the refuelling of aircraft, the transportation of aviation fuel, plus short-term fuel storage. The base chassis is a Ural-4320-30 (6 × 6) truck, an earlier designation being Ural-4320-1863-30. Maximum GVW is 20,100 kg.

The elliptical tank, which has a single, large centre-mounted manhole has a capacity of 10,000 litres. Pumping equipment is mounted at the rear of the tank, and in a unit that matches the curvature of the main tank. Access is via a single, large upward-lifting door. A self-priming STsN-75/70 fuel pump is fitted and fuel flow rates are quoted at 1,000 litres/minute when pressure fuelling, or 500 litres/minute through a conventional nozzle.

Tank filling takes not more than 15 minutes, while tank depletion takes not more than 11 minutes with its own pump, and not more than 32 minutes by gravity.

The current version of this fuelling truck is based on the Ural-4320-1912-40 chassis, the GVW of which is 19,600 kg.

ATs-10-4320M tank truck

The ATs-10-4320M tank truck is intended for the transportation and short-term storage of fuel. The base chassis is a Ural-4320-30 (6 × 6) truck, an earlier designation being Ural-4320-1812-30. Maximum GVW is 19,830 kg. In appearance the ATs-10-4320M tank truck is very similar to the ATZ-10-4320 fuelling truck.

The elliptical tank, which has a single, large centre-mounted manhole has a capacity of 10,000 litres. Pumping equipment is mounted at the rear of the tank, and in a unit that matches the curvature of the main tank. Access is via a single, large upward-lifting door. A 1STsL-20-24G suction pump with a rated capacity of not less than 500 litres/minute is fitted.

Tank filling takes not more than 25 minutes, while tank depletion takes not more than 11 minutes with its own pump, and not more than 24 minutes by gravity.

ATZ-7-5557 fuelling truck

The ATZ-7-5557 fuelling truck is intended for the fuelling of automotive equipment, including armoured vehicles. It can also be used to transport and the short-term storage of fuel. A Ural-5557 (6 × 6) truck is the base chassis for the system, the GVW of which is 16,775 kg.

The tank has a capacity of 7,000 litres. Pumping equipment is mounted at the rear of the tank, which is covered by a tarpaulin and bows, giving the vehicle the appearance of a conventional General Service (GS) truck. A STsL-20-24G pump with a delivery rate of 200 litres/minute through a single hose, 400 litres/minute through two hoses, or 600 litres/minute through four hoses is fitted.

Tank filling takes not more than 16 minutes, while tank depletion takes not more than 15 minutes with its own pump, and not more than 19 minutes by gravity. Overall dimensions are quoted as: 7.65 × 2.5 × 3.55 m (L × W × H).

The latest version of this fuelling truck is the ATZ-7.5, this based on a 17,000 kg GVW Ural-5557-1112-40 chassis, and having a capacity of 7,500 litres.

ATMZ-5-4320/B fuel and oil servicing truck

The ATMZ-5-4320/B fuel and oil servicing truck is intended for the fuelling and oiling of automotive equipment, including armoured vehicles. A Ural-4320-series (6 × 6) truck is the base chassis for the system, the GVW of which is 13,800 kg.

The fuel tank has a capacity of 5,000 litres. A STsL-20-24A pump with a capacity of 750 l/min is fitted. Fuel is supplied through eight hoses, four delivery hoses of 9 m × 38 mm and four delivery/suction hoses of

ATZ-10-4320 fuelling truck (James Kinnear)   1120470

Former East German Army ATMZ-5.5 4310 fuel and oil servicing truck (Stefan Marx)   0587656

Former East German Army ATMZ-5 4320/B fuel and oil servicing truck
(Stefan Marx)   0587655

3 m × 75 mm. Delivery rates of not less than 220 litres/minute through a single hose, 440 litres/minute through two hoses, 650 litres/minute through three hoses, or 750 litres/minute through four hoses are quoted.

The oil tank has a capacity of 250 litres. A Sh8-25 pump with a capacity of 40 litres/minute is fitted. Oil, which may be heated prior to dispensing, is dispensed through a single 10 m × 25 mm hose. A single 3 m × 75 mm suction hose is also fitted. Time required to heat oil from 0 to 60°C at an air temperature of -30°C is 60 minutes.

Overall vehicle dimensions are quoted as: 7.365 × 2.5 × 2.68 m (L × W × H). Setting up time is three minutes.

ATMZ-5.5-4310 fuel and oil servicing truck

The ATMZ-5.5-4310 fuel and oil servicing truck is intended for the fuelling and oiling of automotive equipment, including armoured vehicles. It is essentially the same system as the ATMZ-5-4320/B, but mounted on a KAMAZ and not a Ural track chassis. The quoted truck chassis in published literature is the KAMAZ-4310, and while weights are dimensions provided here relate to this version, the KAMAZ-4310 (although in service in numbers) has been replaced in production by the revised KAMAZ 43114; for which figures would vary slightly.

Quoted GVW is 14,950 kg, and overall vehicle dimensions are given as: 7.88 × 2.5 × 2.875 m (L × W × H). Setting up time is five minutes. Time required to heat oil from 0 to 60°C at an air temperature of -30°C is quoted as 35 minutes.

ATZ-7-4310 fuelling truck

The ATZ-7-4310 fuelling truck is intended for the field fuelling of automotive equipment, including armoured vehicles. It can also be used to transport and the short-term storage of fuel. A KAMAZ-43114 (6 × 6) truck is the base chassis for the system, the GVW of which is 15,340 kg. Previously the KAMAZ-43101 (6 × 6) was the base vehicle, and when used the system was known as the ATZ-7-43101.

The tank has a capacity of 7,000 litres and overall dimensions are quoted as: 7.85 × 2.5 × 3.1 m (L × W × H). Setting up time for operations is five minutes. A 1SVN-80A pump with a capacity of 580 litres/minute is fitted. Fuel is supplied through five hoses, two 9 m × 38 mm and three 3 m × 75 mm. Delivery rates of not less than 200 litres/minute through a single hose and not less than 350 litres/minute through two hoses are quoted.

ATs-9-5337 fuel tanker

The ATs-9-5337 fuel tanker is designed for the transport of aviation fuel. A MAZ-5337 truck is the base chassis for the system, the GVW of which is 16,500 kg.

The fuel tank has a capacity of 9,000 litres. It may be emptied by the on-board pump, an external pump or by gravity. The pump can also be used to transfer fuel from one tank or reservoir to another, bypassing the vehicle-mounted tank in the process if required.

A STsL-20-24A pump with a capacity of 750 litres/minute is fitted. Fuel is supplied through four hoses, two delivery hoses of 9 m × 38 mm and two delivery/suction hoses of 3 m × 75 mm.

Overall vehicle dimensions are quoted as: 7.115 × 2.47 × 3.065 m (L × W × H). Setting up time is five minutes.

TZ-2-66D fuel servicing truck

The TZ-2-66D fuel servicing truck is intended for the fuelling of armoured vehicles operating with airborne formations and has been designed for air-transport (by AN-124 and IL-76 aircraft) and para-dropping. The now obsolete GAZ-66-14 (4 × 4) truck is the base chassis for the system.

Total weight is quoted as 5,800 kg, and the flat-topped and sided tank has a capacity of 2,000 litres. A SVN-80 pump with a capacity of 500 litres/minute is fitted. Fuel is supplied through five hoses, two delivery hoses of 9 m × 25 mm and three delivery/suction hoses of 3 m × 65 mm. Delivery rates of not less than 120 litres/minute through a single hose and 240 litres/minute through two hoses are quoted.

Overall vehicle dimensions are quoted as: 5.655 × 2.322 × 2.48 m (L × W × H). Setting up time is four minutes, closing down time is five minutes.

PSG-300 fuel transfer equipment

The PSG-300 fuel transfer equipment is a vehicle-mounted system that can be used for a variety of fuel pumping requirements including: transfer of fuel from bulk tankers into fuel depot storage facilities, and vice-versa; pump fuel from depot storage facilities to the initial pumping points of field pipeline systems; transfer fuel from one depot area to another; fill fuel servicing trucks, fuel tankers and other fuel storage/transport containers; be used as part of field fuelling stations and single-point pressure aircraft refuelling systems; transfer light petroleum products at fuel depots.

The equipment is contained within an all-steel rectangular body with a number of access hatches along each side. Overall weight of the equipment is quoted as 6,000 kg. The base chassis is currently listed as a KAMAZ-4310 (6 × 6) truck, however this truck has recently been replaced in production by a revised model, the KAMAZ-43114. Weights and dimensions provided relate to a KAMAZ-4310-mounted system.

Pumping equipment consists of a TsN-500/65 main pump (TsN-240-140 in the most recent literature) with a capacity of 300 m³/hour, and a STsN-75/70 booster pump with a capacity of 75 m³/hour. Fuel is pumped through eight hoses, two delivery hoses of 10 m × 100 mm and six suction hoses of 4 m × 150 mm.

The equipment can operate continuously (with refuelling) for no less than 22 hours. Overall vehicle dimensions are quoted as: 8.222 × 2.5 × 3.09 m (L × W × H). Setting up time is 40 minutes, closing down time is 20 minutes.

PNU-100/200M transfer pumping equipment

The PNU-100/200M transfer pumping unit is intended for the transfer of fuel via main field pipelines. The base trailer is a two-axle 2-PN-2M on to which a YaMZ-238G engine and 120 m³/hour capacity type 4NG-2A pump are located within an all-steel body fitted with upward opening access panels.

Max weight is 3,860 kg, and dimensions are 5.75 × 1.89 × 2.235 m (L × W × H). Three units can be transported by one four-axle rail flatcar.

PPU-500 mobile pumping unit

The PPU-500 mobile pumping unit is intended to carry out pumping operations in field conditions with pumped liquid temperatures ranging from –40 to +40° C, and at ambient air temperatures ranging from –50 to +45°C and at altitudes of up to 3,000 m above sea level. The base trailer is a two-axle 2-PN-2M (SMZ-8326).

Pumping equipment consists of a TsN-500/65 main pump with a capacity of 500 m³/hour. Fuel is pumped through four delivery/suction hoses of 4 m × 150 mm. The equipment can operate continuously (with refuelling) for no less than 50 hours. Overall dimensions are quoted as: 6.17 (incl. towbar) × 2.23 × 2.575 m (L × W × H).

PTs-6.7-8925 tank trailer

The PTs-6.7-8925 tank trailer is designed for the bulk road transportation of fuel. The base chassis is a MAZ-8925 two-axle dolly-type trailer, the elliptical tank has a capacity of 6,700 kg. The unladen trailer weighs 4,350 kg. Overall dimensions are: 6.7 × 2.5 × 2.52 m (L × W × H). A pair of 3 m × 75 mm delivery/suction hoses are carried. The tank takes 25 minutes to empty by gravity.

PZP field fuelling stations

These sets are intended for the refuelling of all vehicles involved in long-distance overland movement. The PZP-10A has 10 refuelling points with two dispensing cocks at each point, the PZP-14 has 14 refuelling points with two dispensing cocks at each point, while the PZP-20 has 20 refuelling points with two dispensing cocks at each point. In all cases, refuelling points are 10 m apart.

Fuel storage containers for each set are the 8,500 litre-capacity KrAZ-255B-mounted ATs-8.5-255B for the PZP-10A and PZP-14 (one or two), and two 25,000 litre-capacity MR-25 fabric reservoirs for the PZP-20.

Fuel pumping equipment is STsN-60 for the PZP-10A and PZP-14. This has a dispensing rate of 1,000 litres/minute, giving 100 litres/minute (PZP-10A) and 70 litres/minute (PZP-14) at each fuelling point. Fuel pumping equipment is PSG-160 for the PZP-20. This has a dispensing rate of 2,600 litres/minute, giving 130 litres/minute at each fuelling point.

Sets, minus pumping and storage equipment, weigh 1,395 kg (PZP-10A), 2,140 kg (PZP-14) and 1,600 kg (PZP-20). Set up and closing down times are 10/10 minutes (PZP-10A), 7-10/15-20 minutes (PZP-14) and 60/40 minutes (PZP-20).

PMTP-100 field pipeline set

This set is designed for the rapid transfer of bulk petrol, diesel, aviation fuel and other petroleum products to frontline units. Operational limits are –40 to +50°C.

Pipes are laid either manually or mechanically by a MST-100 pipe-laying machine. The laying rate with a single MST-100 machine is 12 km in 10 hours (summer) and 10 km in 10 hours (winter). Manual laying rates are 10 km in 10 hours (summer) and 8 km in 10 hours (winter). Dismantling rate is 10 km in 10 hours (summer) and 8 km in 10 hours (winter).

Each pipe is 6 m in length, has an internal diameter of 97.6 mm, a wall thickness of 2.2 mm, weighs 36.2 kg and is constructed from 161S steel. Each pipe holds 46 litres of liquid, this equating to 7.5 m³ per km. One set of pipes weighs 1,100 tonnes.

PMT-150 field pipeline set

This set is designed for the rapid transfer of bulk petrol, diesel, aviation fuel and other petroleum products to frontline units.

Pipes are laid manually, the laying rate being 5 km in 10 hours (summer) and 4 km in 10 hours (winter). Dismantling rate is 10 km in 10 hours (summer) and 8 km in 10 hours (winter).

Each pipe is 6 m in length, has an internal diameter of 145.5 mm, a wall thickness of 3.25 mm, weighs 78 kg and is constructed from steel 10. Each pipe holds 100 litres of liquid, this equating to 16.6 m³ per km. One set of pipes weighs 2,470 tonnes.

PMTP-150 field pipeline set

This set is designed for the rapid transfer of bulk petrol, diesel, aviation fuel and other petroleum products to frontline units and appears to be a variant of the PMT-150 field pipeline set that is capable of being laid mechanically as well as manually.

The laying rate with a single TUM-150V machine is 12 km in 10 hours (summer) and 10 km in 10 hours (winter); the TUM-150 pipe-laying machine may also be used. Manual laying rates are 8 km in ten hours (summer) and 6 km in ten hours (winter). Dismantling rate is 8 km in 10 hours (summer) and 6 km in 10 hours (winter).

Each pipe is 6 m in length, has an internal diameter of 145.5 mm, a wall thickness of 3.25 mm, weighs 80.9 kg and is constructed from steel 16GS. Each pipe holds 100 litres of liquid, this equating to 16.6 m³ per km. One set of pipes weighs 2,500 tonnes.

Status

All the above equipment is, or has recently been, offered for export sale. Production would likely be on an as required basis, with much of the featured equipment likely to be in service with the Armed Forces of the Russian Federation and its allies, past and present.

Contractor

Strommashina Zavod JSC

Enquiries to (excluding the listed equipment above)
Rosoboronexport

Fabric-reinforced rubber fuel tanks

Description

This type of fuel tank was introduced into service in 1961 and since then many variants have been produced. The first family of tanks comprised the MR-2.5, MR-4, MR-10 and MR-12. These were all orthodox reinforced rubber fuel tanks and all, except the MR-10, were used to convert flatbed trucks into mobile fuel carriers. The MR-10 was used primarily as a storage tank, not having the internal baffles fitted to the other types.

The latest in-service family of fabric-reinforced rubber fuel tanks comprises the MR-4, MR-6, MR-25, MR-50, MR-150 and MR-250. Only the MR-4 and MR-6 are now used for the mobile carriage of fuel and other liquids and are fitted with metal loading brackets on all corners and diagonal partitions internally. All the tanks have an inspection manhole, filling/draining and air connections, T-pipes and air pipes. Handles are provided for folding, unfolding and handling of each and these are situated around the periphery of each tank. The MR-150 and MR-250 have underside connectors with elbows and flexible pipes for flushing residual liquids from the tank. When folded, each tank has an external pocket into which the various fittings can be stowed. When transported, each tank is carried inside a cover fitted with loading loops. For storage, the tanks may be kept either folded or unfolded under cover, or outdoors under canvas.

The MR-50 is known to be available for export sales and is described as having an inner gasoline-proof rubber layer, a strengthening capron layer, and an outer weather-proof rubber layer. In addition to the information provided in the accompanying table, setting up time is quoted as 12 mins and closing down time as 15 mins, both instances with a crew of five. The total weight of the MR-50 is 580 kg.

Specifications

See table below

Status

The original MR-2.5, MR-10 and MR-12 are no longer in production but may be held in reserve. The later MR-4, MR-6, MR-25, MR-50, MR-150 and MR-250 are in service. The MR-50 (and possibly other models) is offered for export sales.

Contractor

Marketing agency
Rosoboronexport

South Africa

World Focus Flexitanks collapsible fuel storage and transport bladders

Description

World Focus Flexitanks manufactures rubber collapsible fuel storage tanks and transport bladders for commercial, military and aid agency applications and ranging in capacity from 400 to 100,000 litres. A variety of liquids can be stored or transported, these ranging from potable water to petrol, diesel or aircraft fuels.

Temperature tolerance ranges from –30°C to +70°C. Specific-to-application tank sizes are available, as are a variety of fittings for filling, discharge, transport and handling purposes.

Status

In production. In service with the South African National Defence Force (SANDF) and possibly other undisclosed countries. Similar products have been produced by a number of legacy companies.

Contractor

World Focus Flexitank

Turkey

BMC refuelling vehicles

Development

BMC Sanayi ve Ticaret AS has developed a range of refuelling vehicles on the company's commercial chassis range. These have been developed in conjunction with Hatehof of Israel. Basic specifications of current models are included in the Specifications table which follows.

BMC Sanayi ve Ticaret AS was originally established in 1964, in partnership with the then British Motor Corporation (BMC) of the UK. Since 1989, BMC Sanayi ve Ticaret AS has been wholly owned by Cukurova Holding of Turkey.

The BMC 827 (6 × 4) 20,000 litre aircraft refueller is air-transportable by C-130 aircraft (BMC)　　1391311

BMC 827 (6 × 4) 20,000 litre aircraft refueller (BMC)　　1391312

Tank type	MR-4	MR-6	MR-25	MR-50	MR-150	MR-250
Rated capacity	4,000 litres	6,000 litres	25,000 litres	50,000 litres	150,000 litres	250,000 litres
Length (filled)	3.6 m	3.5 m	9.2 m	17.6 m	18 m	18 m
Width (filled)	2.6 m	2.4 m	3.7 m	3.7 m	7 m	10 m
Height (filled)	650 mm	900 mm	1 m	1 m	1.4 m	1.4 m
Weight (w/o cover)	110 kg	120 kg	255 kg	515 kg	1,000 kg	1,400 kg
Number of filling/draining connectors	1	1	2	2	2	2
Number of air connectors	1	1	1	2	2	2

BMC 832 (6 × 4) 5,000 US gallon aircraft refueller (BMC)   1391313

BMC 827 (6 × 4) aircraft refueller (BMC)   1391314

Specifications

BMC refuelling vehicles

Model	BMC 827 20,000 litre aircraft refueller	BMC 832 5,000 US gallon aircraft refueller	BMC 827 20,000 litre aircraft refueller	BMC 625 15,000 litre refueller	BMC 827 20,000 litre refueller
Capacity:	20,000 litres	5,000 US gallons (5,282 litres)	20,000 litres	15,000 litres	20,000 litres
Pump rate:	2,271 litres/min	600 US gallons/min (2,271 litres/min)	1,000 litres/min	350 litres/min	350 litres/min
Engine:	Cummins C 8.3-260 Euro 1 8.3-litre six-cylinder turbo-charged diesel engine developing 263 hp	Cummins C 8.3-300 Euro 2 8.3-litre six-cylinder turbo-charged diesel engine developing 300 hp	Cummins C 8.3-260 Euro 1 8.3-litre six-cylinder turbo-charged diesel engine developing 263 hp	Cummins B 235-20 Euro 2 8.3-litre six-cylinder turbo-charged diesel engine developing 235 hp	Cummins C 8.3-260 Euro 1 8.3-litre six-cylinder turbo-charged diesel engine developing 263 hp
Gearbox:	ZF 9S 109 nine-speed	ZF 9S 109 nine-speed	ZF 9S 109 nine-speed	ZF 9S 109 nine-speed	ZF 9S 109 nine-speed
Configuration:	6 × 4	6 × 4	6 × 4	6 × 2	6 × 2
Transportability:	C-130	C-130	rail	rail	rail
Primary role:	under- and over-wing fuelling and defuelling of combat and civilian aircraft and helicopters; fuel supply with hand-held pistol			refuelling of land systems	

Status
In production. In service with Pakistan (Air Force) and Turkey (air, land and naval forces).

Contractor
BMC Sanayi ve Ticaret AS

Ukraine

PMTP-100 and PMTP-150 tactical pipelines

Development
PMTP-100 and PMTP-150 tactical POL pipelines are used by the Russian Army's pipeline regiments. Only the greater capacity PMTP-150 set is currently offered for export sale.

Description
PMTP-100 and PMTP-150 tactical POL pipelines are used by the Russian Army's pipeline regiments. Only the greater capacity PMTP-150 set is currently offered for export sale.

The pipe is laid in 6 m lengths, each with quick-connect junctions, from tractor-towed TUM-150V machines (full details of which can be found elsewhere in this section) which automatically lay the pipes at the rate of 1.3 to 3.5 km/h. The pipes can also be connected manually at a much slower rate. Once connected, the pipes are designed to be easily removed and replaced if damaged and the entire pipeline can be retrieved for later use.

Both pipelines are issued in sets sufficient to lay 150 km of pipeline, each set containing 27,000 pipes. The PMTP-100 set contains pipes with a diameter of 100 mm. Pipe diameter for the PMTP-150 is 150 mm. An assembled PMTP-100 set has a capacity of 1,200 tonnes of fuel per day while the PMTP-150 can handle 2,600 tonnes per day.

Also included with both sets of pipelines are 32 PNU-100/200M transfer pumping unit, six PSG-160 fuel pumping stations and four ZIF-55 compressor stations. Details of the PNU-100/200M transfer pumping unit can be found elsewhere in this section.

Status
In service with former Warsaw Pact forces. PMTP-150 offered for export sales.

Contractor
63 Boiler-Welding Plant

Marketed by
Progress

TUM-150V pipelaying machine

Development
The TUM-150V pipelaying machine was developed for use by pipelaying brigades assigned to each Russian Army Front to lay PMTP-100 and PMTP-150 tactical pipelines during offensive operations; it can also be used at divisional level in static situations. Full details of the PMTP-100 and PMTP-150 tactical pipelines can be found elsewhere in this section.

Description
The TUM-150V is a trailer-mounted system and lays pipes 6 m long while travelling at a speed of 1.3 km/h. A complete load of 70 pipes is placed on the machine by an onboard hydraulic crane mounted on the forward part of the trailer. The pipes are loaded from the left-hand side in layers of 10 and are unloaded into a shallow trench to the rear via a chute located at the lower right-hand side and extending to the rear. A full load of 70 pipes with a total length of 427 m can be laid in approximately 8.5 minutes. Pipes may be loaded into the machine while it is in operation and on tow.

With its towing vehicle, the TUM-150V has approximate overall dimensions of 16.2 × 3.25 × 3.78 m (L × W × H) and weighs (in running order) 31,000 kg. The towing vehicle may be a crawler tractor or a 4 × 4 wheeled tractor such as the K-701 (K-700A) tractor. The base chassis is a KrAZ-257 with active wheel drive.

Status
In service with former Warsaw Pact forces. Offered for export sales.

Contractor
63 Boiler-Welding Plant

Marketed by
Progress

United Kingdom

Fluid Transfer International Limited refuelling systems and equipment

Description
Fluid Transfer International Limited are designers and manufacturers of aircraft refuelling vehicles, portable refuellers, pumpsets and a wide range of components and systems associated with the above equipment. Since a move into the military side of the business in 1983, Fluid Transfer International Limited has become the major supplier of such equipment to the UK MoD.

In 1994, Fluid Transfer International Limited took over the design percentage of the Simon Gloster Saro-produced bulk fuel dispensing, is undertaking a refurbishment of the fuel dispensing pack and is currently handling seven-year contracts to refurbish these and the product tanks and associated fuel equipment.

In addition to numerous smaller contract awards, since the late 1990s, Fluid Transfer has completed the refurbishment of the pumping equipment and systems of 10 Hydrant Dispenser aircraft refuelling vehicles for the Royal Air Force, and in a separate tri-service programme for the UK MoD, valued at GBP7.785 million, the top hamper of 170 Bedford MK/MJ (4 × 4) 4,000 kg truck-based 4,500-litre Tactical Aircraft Refuellers (TARs) was made more legislative compliant, through an extensive refurbishment programme. The chassis/cab element of the programme, which included the fitting of new cabs from the Bedford MT range of trucks, was carried out by ABRO Stirling. Full details of the Bedford MK/MJ (4 × 4) 4,000 kg truck can be found in the Trucks section.

To supplement the refurbished TARs in Europe, a new vehicle was designed. Fully legislative compliant and based on the chassis of the Leyland Trucks (4 × 4) 5,000 kg truck (full details of which can be found in the Trucks section), 18 of these vehicles were delivered to the Army Air Corps during 2000.

Also on the Leyland Trucks (4 × 4) 5,000 kg truck chassis were the 17 and eight (delivered in two batches) 5,000-litre Tank Truck Fueller (TTF), delivered to the Royal Air Force during 1997 and 2000. Primarily for the fuelling of ground equipment, this system can dispense two products (such as diesel and gasoline) by means of the two-compartment tank and twin pumping/fuel delivery and tank filling systems.

During 1999 some 16 Air portable Fuel Dispense Vehicles (AFDV) were delivered to the Royal Air Force. The near GBP2 million contract called for the AFDV to be air portable both by C-130 Hercules and underslung by Chinook helicopter. Replacing earlier less flexible and mobile trailer-mounted equipment the AFDV is primarily designed for the close support of helicopters or tactical aircraft in the field. It can refuel these from a wide variety of sources including tankers or pillow tanks. The AFDV is based on the Leyland Trucks (4 × 4) 5,000 kg truck chassis. During 2009/10 eight of these vehicles were refurbished on their original chassis to prolong their working life for a further five years.

Fluid Transfer International Limited also designed and manufactured the pumping equipment for the Dennis Eagle Out Of Areas Refueller, 55 of which are in service with the Royal Air Force. Other recent deliveries to the UK Royal Air Force have included 175,000-litre aircraft refuellers designed for airfield refuel/defuel use and based on a modified commercial Renault Trucks (4 × 2) truck chassis. For use with AVGAS only, a further 16 vehicles were delivered to the RAF during 2001, with a follow-on batch of 16 vehicles being delivered throughout 2002. These vehicles, based on the then current generation Renault (4 × 2) chassis, are EURO III emissions compliant, fully road legal and comply with ADR legislation. The contract value was GBP2.5 million and in service these vehicles are used in support

The Unit Support Tanker (UST) formed part of the Support Vehicle (SV) contract awarded to MAN ERF UK Ltd in 2005. This MAN HX58 UST has been fitted with a number of enhancements (including bar armour) for operational deployment (Shaun C Connors)   1296261

One of 14 MAN M2000 (4 × 4) chassis-based 9,000-litre aircraft refuellers supplied to the UK Royal Air Force during 2005 for use with Search And Rescue (SAR) helicopters (Patrick Allen)   1183119

In July 2004 Fluid Transfer Limited was awarded a contract to supply 50 MAN TGA (6 × 4) chassis-based 20,000-litre aircraft refuellers and 49 associated 24,000-litre drawbar-type two-axle trailers to the RAF. Contract options for an additional 50 and 24 trucks and 20 trailers have since been exercised (Fluid Transfer Limited)   1156126

Leyland 5,000 kg truck-based 5,000-litre Tank Truck Fueller (TTF) (Fluid Transfer Limited)   0109617

Mid-2003 Fluid Transfer Limited announced it had been awarded a contract to supply 12 MAN M2000 18,000 kg (4 × 2) chassis-based 9,000-litre aircraft refuellers to the UK Royal Navy (Fluid Transfer Limited)   1156129

One of 18 Leyland 5,000 kg truck-based 5,000-litre Tactical Aircraft Refuellers (TAR) delivered to the Army Air Corps during 2000 (Fluid Transfer Limited)   0525606

One of the first of two batches of 16 each Renault (4 × 2) 5,000-litre refuelling vehicles delivered to the Royal Air Force during 2001-2002 (Fluid Transfer Limited)   0525581

In 1994 Fluid Transfer International Limited took over the design percentage of the Simon Gloster Saro-produced bulk fuel dispensing unit, full details of which can be found elsewhere in this section (Shaun C Connors)   1124731

A refurbished Bedford MK/MJ 4,500-litre Tactical Aircraft Refueller (TAR) fitted with a new Bedford MT range cab as part of the refurbishment programme (Shaun C Connors)   1124785

of the Elementary Flying Training Units, University Air Squadron, and so on. A total of 50 vehicles similarly specified to the original batch (but on a Leyland Trucks chassis) have also been supplied, as have 38 Leyland Trucks-based 9,000-litre tankers, to support land-based operations by the Royal Navy.

A small number of 7,200-litre Tactical Aircraft Refuellers used by the Royal Marines Commando helicopter force and based on the Bedford TM (4 × 4) 8,000 kg truck chassis (full details of which can be found in the Trucks section) underwent an extensive refurbishment to prolong their effective service life. This was completed in February 2001.

In January 2003, and in response to a UK MoD Urgent Operational Requirement (UOR) for a deployable bulk refuelling asset for use in the Gulf region, Fluid Transfer developed a DROPS flatrack-based Unit Bulk Refuelling Equipment (UBRE) system. This system consists of four tanks and two pumping units, one at each of the flatrack. A total of 20 racks were produced during January/February 2003.

Mid-2003 Fluid Transfer announced it had been awarded a contract to supply 12 MAN M2000 18,000 kg (4 × 2) chassis-based 9,000-litre aircraft refuellers to the UK Royal Navy. These were delivered between January and April 2004, and have replaced some of the oldest Leyland Freighter-based refuellers, delivered by Fluid Transfer in two batches during 1988 and 1990. The contract contained two options, which had to be (and were not) exercised during 2005.

In June 2004 Fluid Transfer was awarded a contract to supply 14 MAN M2000 (4 × 4) chassis-based 9,000-litre aircraft refuellers to the UK Royal Air Force. These will be used with Search And Rescue (SAR) helicopters. Deliveries commenced in December 2004, with completion by March 2005.

Also in July 2004, Fluid Transfer was awarded a contract to supply 50 MAN TGA (6 × 4) chassis-based 20,000-litre aircraft refuellers and 49 associated 24,000-litre drawbar-type two-axle trailers. On entering service, these replaced the remaining Leyland Bison vehicles and a small number of the oldest Scammell S26 fleet.

The truck component of this latest contract award was required to be air transportable by C-17 Globemaster, however it was not required to have a snow-ploughing capability (like the Scammell S26 fleet), nor was it required to be air-transportable by C-130 Hercules. The associated trailer, which, unlike the truck, is classed as a deployable asset, was required to be C-130 transportable and as such, is compatible with the Dennis Eagle air portable aircraft refueller. In addition, the trailer is also compatible with the Scammell S26.

Deliveries under this contract were completed during 2006. A contract option for an additional 50 trucks was subsequently exercised by the UK MoD, with deliveries completed March 2007. A further 24 vehicles and 20, 24,000-litre drawbar-type trailers were ordered in 2007 for delivery by March 2008, bringing totals delivered under this contract to 124 trucks and 69 trailers. Four vehicles were ordered by defence contractor QinetiQ for use at Boscombe Down, these were delivered in January 2008. Two of these vehicles have been modified to accommodate a permanent overwing hose and trigger nozzle on the forward hose reel.

In July 2004, Fluid Transfer was awarded a contract to supply the UK Royal Air Force with 17 MAN M2000 (4 × 4) chassis-based 5,000-litre ground refuellers for the dispensing of fuel to ground support equipment and vehicles. These vehicles are similar in configuration to the earlier-delivered Leyland-based Tank Truck Fueller (TTF). Deliveries were scheduled for completion by April 2005.

Fluid Transfer, as a subcontractor to MAN ERF UK Ltd, supplied the tanks and pumping equipment for the Unit Support Tanker (UST) component of the Support Vehicle (SV) contract. The UST will replace the present Unit Bulk Refuelling Equipment (UBRE), and a total of 312 vehicles were delivered between 2007 and May 2010. Of these, 230 are on MAN HX58 (6 × 6) chassis and 81 on MAN SX44 (6 × 6) chassis. The UST has a 7000-litre product tank that is certified to ADR and International Maritime Dangerous Goods (IMDG) codes, the fuel delivery system can deliver bulk off-loading at rates up to 1000 litres/minute and also through two open line trigger nozzles at up to 250 litres/minute. The system is also equipped with two dedicated jerry can filling lines delivering 50 litres/minute.

Status
Available. In use by the armed forces of Sri Lanka, Tanzania and the UK. Used in support of the Norwegian Air Force.

Contractor
Fluid Transfer International Limited

Oshkosh Wheeled Tanker, Close Support Tanker (CST) and Tactical Aircraft Refueller (TAR)

Development

Oshkosh Truck Corporation announced in January 2003 that it had been selected as the preferred bidder, by the then UK Defence Procurement Agency (DPA), to supply the MoD's Wheeled Tanker fleet. The contract was valued at approximately GBP160 million (USD250 million) for initial vehicle acquisition and support for the next 15 years. It was originally stated by the DPA that the Wheeled Tanker fleet would replace all existing tri-service vehicle types used for the bulk distribution of fuel on deployed operations.

The Wheeled Tanker programme can trace its origins back to the earlier Future Fuel Vehicle (FFV) programme which was proposed for procurement under the terms of the UK government's Private Finance Initiative (PFI). The Future Cargo Vehicle (FCV) and Future Wheeled Recovery Vehicle (FWRV) projects were also proposed as PFI programmes. FFV was advertised as a PFI in January 1998, with FCV following in August 1998 and FWRV in September 1999. FFV and FCV went through a pre-qualification phase in order to select a shortlist of potential bidders who would be invited to submit outline proposals. At the time of the outline proposal assessment (early 2000) the projected in-service date for FFV was 2003.

On 21 March 2001 the relevant government minister formally announced in a press release that PFI options would not be pursued for the FFV, FCV or FWRV programmes, thus clarifying that in these cases, PFI would not be appropriate and was unlikely to provide best value for money. Under the proposed PFI procurement, there were three potential bidders for FFV: Fastflow (Brown & Root (now KBR) and Volvo); Excalibur Logistics (Multidrive, Excel Logistics, BAE Systems - Lex had previously

A signature management kit manufactured by GMA Cover Corp has been procured for Wheeled Tanker (Shaun C Connors) 1340294

All Wheeled Tankers are fitted for but not with an appliqué protection kit developed by Israel's Plasan Sasa. Additional protection including bar armour, a protected weapon station and the installation of electronic countermeasures equipment has been installed on vehicles operating in Afghanistan and Iraq (Shaun C Connors) 1340282

withdrawn from this consortium), and Tactacon (Oshkosh Truck Corporation and Ryder - the now BAE Systems, after acquiring Unipower and having sold the then Alvis Unipower place to Oshkosh).

Following the March 2001 announcement to abandon PFI procurement, in April 2001 the FFV, FCV and FWRV programmes were re-launched along with a number of amendments as conventional asset-based procurements. FFV now included an operations highlighted requirement for bulk potable water tankers and was renamed as the Wheeled Tanker requirement, while the FCV and FWRV were merged to form the Support Vehicle requirement. Following the announcement that asset-based procurement was to be adopted, Volvo withdrew from the Wheeled Tanker and Support Vehicle programmes.

The original intention was that Wheeled Tanker would replace all existing tri-service vehicle types used for the bulk distribution of fuel and on deployed operations. This did not include airfield-based aircraft refuellers or the truck-transportable UBRE (Unit Bulk Refuelling Equipment) system (full details of which can be found elsewhere in this section), which was replaced by the Unit Support Tanker element of the Support Vehicle programme. Additionally, the Foden low mobility tanker fleet, the General Support Tanker (GST) fleet, and the then Tactical Aircraft Refueller (TAR), would be replaced.

The Foden low mobility fleet originally consisted of 250 (8 × 4) 22,500 litre low mobility and 183 (6 × 4) 12,000 litre improved low mobility tankers delivered during the late 1970s, early 1980s. As of May 2001, 137 (8 × 4)s and 160 (6 × 4)s remained in service and use; all have now been withdrawn from service. The current GST is a road-going 32,500 litre capacity articulated vehicle tractored by a (6 × 4) Seddon Atkinson unit. The then 170 vehicle TAR fleet was 2,000 litre capacity Bedford MJ-based (4 × 4)s that had been refurbished and fitted with improved cabs from the Bedford MT range of trucks. These vehicles did not have the capacity to service the British Army's Apache attack helicopter. Further details of the TAR can be found elsewhere in this section; full details of the GST can be found in the Trucks section.

At the time of shortlisting the Wheeled Tanker requirement called for a total of 437 vehicles made up of: 259 × 20,000 litre Close Support Tanker (CST); 86 × 12,000 litre Tactical Aircraft Refueller (TAR); 43 × 18,000 litre Close Support Tanker (Water) (CST(W)), and 49 × 30,000 litre General Support Tanker (GST). It was also stated by the DPA that should additional tankers be justified, and funds made available, totals could rise to 742 vehicles made up of: 355 CST; 104 TAR; 43 CST(W), and 240 GST. Contract award figures would be 218 × 20,000 litre CST; 82 × 15,000 litre TAR, and 48 × 18,000 litre CST(W).

Deliveries of Wheeled Tanker commenced in February 2005 and were scheduled for completion by November 2006. A contract option for an additional nine CST (W) has subsequently been exercised. The requirement for a 30,000-litre GST was not filled as part of the Wheeled Tanker contract, due to the in-service Seddon Atkinson vehicles remaining compliant with legislation and had not yet reached the end of their anticipated service lives.

The other major fuel asset of the British Army was the Foden-fronted Multidrive tanker fleet. These have since been withdrawn from service.

For all three variants involved in the Wheeled Tanker contract Oshkosh Truck, as prime contractor, is supplying a frameless monocoque stainless steel semi-trailer tanker manufactured by Magyar SA of France with pumping equipment supplied by Magyar (water) or Alfons Haar of Germany (fuel). Oshkosh Truck also supplied a quantity of riotous protection kits, and all vehicles are fitted for but not with an appliqué protection kit developed by Israel's Plasan Sasa. This kit is similar to the one developed for the USMC MTVRs. Additional protection including bar armour, a protected weapon station and the installation of electronic countermeasures equipment has been installed on vehicles operating in Afghanistan and Iraq. A signature management kit manufactured by GMA Cover Corp has also been procured.

Wheeled Tanker tractor trucks are a variant of the Oshkosh MTVR (Medium Tactical Vehicle Replacement), full details of which can be found in the Trucks section.

Description

All versions of the Oshkosh (6 × 6) Medium Tactical Vehicle Replacement (MTVR) are based on the same 6 × 6 drive configuration with the engine under a forward non-corroding and weight-saving fibreglass bonnet. The standard three-seat cab is of welded aluminium extrusion construction with adhesive bonded aluminium skins. The aluminium hinged windscreen, roof, side-walls, door frames and rear wall can be folded down to reduce overall height to 2.489 m. A larger crew-type cab (extended by 660 mm) in which a rear that doubles up as additional seating or a bunk for two is fitted to the Wheeled Tanker.

The MTVR chassis frame is constructed by using bolted/Huck-fastened channel (248 × 76 × 9.7 mm) made of heat-treated carbon manganese steel with a yield strength of 758 MPa. Wheeled Tanker variants are based on the MK23 MTVR with a 330 mm reduction in the wheelbase and 1.018 m reduction in the overall length. Both chassis and cab feature extensive corrosion protection. The US Marines requiring the MTVR should have sufficient corrosion protection in order to ensure an effective service life of 22 years.

All MTVR variants are powered by a Caterpillar C-12, ADEM (Advanced Diesel Engine Management) III 11.9-litre six-cylinder in-line turbocharged and water-cooled four-stroke, diesel. For the UK requirement this has been uprated from 425 hp (317 kW) to develop 445 hp (332 kW) at 1,700 rpm and upgraded to meet EURO III emissions requirements. Peak torque remains 2,101 N.m at 1,200 rpm. Maximum sustainable speed on paved roads is restricted to 85 km/h; cruising range is 500 km. A three-stage (two-, four- or six-cylinder) manually selected, automatically applied engine compression brake is fitted to assist the braking system.

The engine is coupled with a Wheeled Tanker specific Allison HD 4560P 6F/1R 'wide ratio' unit (this replaces the standard Allison HD 4070P 7F/1R unit) and Oshkosh 30000 series single-speed transfer box. The combination of torque converter and a low ratio first gear allows for a single-speed transfer box to replace the more complex two-speed unit more commonly associated with off-road vehicles. Full-time all-wheel drive is employed and under highway driving conditions, the torque split is 32 per cent front, 68 per cent rear.

The combination of Oshkosh TAK-4 independent coil spring suspension, a central tyre inflation (CTI) system, and a traction control system supplemented by manually-controlled differential locks on all axles, enables the tractor unit (while towing an undriven and laden semi-trailer) to achieve a level of off-road mobility acceptable to the UK MoD. The tractor truck can ford 1.5 m of water (with kits), climb a 34 per cent gradient with a laden trailer and has a climatic operational range of between -32°C (with winterisation kits from -46°C) and +49°C. A purpose-designed 88.9 mm (3.5 in) fully oscillating fifth wheel (40° forward; 25° after; 5° each side) supplied by Holland Neway is fitted. This enables the required angles of articulation to be achieved between the tractor truck and semi-trailer for operations such as embarking/disembarking a landing craft.

The MTVR is fitted with 1600R 20 Michelin XZL super singles tyres. The trailer-mounted spare wheel will fit either truck or trailer. There is also a emergency runflat setting option on the MTVR's CTI system (there is no CTI system for the trailer). A CTI system allows the driver to adjust tyre pressures to suit terrain conditions, there being four settings available: highway; cross-country; mud/sand/snow; and emergency. In an emergency the MTVR system can be directed to continuously inflate one tyre only. The 508 × 254 mm two-piece bolt-together steel wheel rims are fitted with beadlocks for extreme low-pressure operations and tyres will remain seated at pressures down to 69 kPa (10 psi). In the event that any one tyre should totally fail, a limp-home facility allows for a second axle suspension unit to be raised and secured, its wheel rolled and fitted in the position of the damaged tyre.

The Wheeled Tanker requirement called for 218 × 20,000 litre Close Support Tanker (CST) (shown), 82 × 15,000 litre Tactical Aircraft Refueller (TAR) and 57 × 18,000 litre Close Support Tanker (Water) (CST(W). Deliveries ran from February 2005 until November 2006. A contract option for 9 additional CST(W) has been exercised; other contract options remain (Patrick Allen) 1067546

To assist with vehicle repairs and diagnosis, an On Board Diagnostic System (OBDS) features an information display screen and fault indicators from the engine, transmission, ABS, ATC and CTI. It also has a laptop interface that allows access to the full MTVR database for in-the-field maintenance, diagnostics and repair.

Wheeled Tanker is air-transportable in C-5, C-17, A400M and AN-124 aircraft.

20,000 litre Close Support Tanker (CST)

The 20,000 litre capacity tank is manufactured by Magyar SA of France and is fitted with pumping equipment supplied by Alfons Haar of Germany.

The single compartment tank is ADR and IMDG Type II certified and is manufactured from 4.5 mm hot-rolled AISI 304 stainless steel and fitted with three lateral and two longitudinal baffles. Standard equipment includes a contents gauge with external reading display and an overfill protection system. A single 250 mm diameter hinged fill cover with 500 mm diameter tank flange is fitted. All piping is stainless steel, welded, and with flanged or threaded connections.

Two BPW Model 10110 E36.1 Eco Plus tubular non-driving axles are used. These are rated at 10,000 kg each and have a track width of 2.095 m. Tyres are 1600R 20 Michelin XZLs; a single spare is carried. Air-operated drum-type brakes are fitted, the parking brake working on the first axle. The braking system is interlocked with the fuel handling system.

The Alfons Haar pumping module features a self-priming FPOS 100/1308A142R payload pump with a 1,350 l/min capacity, twin 15 m hosereels with hydraulic rewind, each terminating with a 2 in Unisex coupler, and an Alfons Haar MKA 2290 fuel meter.

Winterised variants have a climatic operational range (pumping) of -37 to +49°C.

Overall semi-trailer length is 10.7 m, gross weight is 26,900 kg.

15,000 litre Tactical Aircraft Refueller (TAR)

The 15,000 litre capacity tank is manufactured by Magyar SA of France and is fitted with pumping equipment supplied by Alfons Haar of Germany.

The single compartment tank is ADR and IMDG Type II certified and is manufactured from 4.5 mm hot-rolled AISI 304 stainless steel and fitted with two lateral and two longitudinal baffles. Standard equipment includes a contents gauge with external reading display and an overfill protection system. A single 250 mm diameter hinged fill cover with 500 mm diameter tank flange is fitted. All piping is of stainless steel, welded, and with flanged or threaded connections.

Two BPW Model 10110 E36.1 Eco Plus tubular non-driving axles are used. These are rated at 10,000 kg each and have a track width of 2.095 m. Tyres are 1600R 20 Michelin XZLs; a single spare is carried. Air-operated drum-type brakes are fitted, the parking brake working on the first axle. The braking system is interlocked with the fuel handling system.

From the rear and showing the pumping equipment locker, a Wheeled Tanker 15,000 litre Tactical Aircraft Refueller (TAR) (Patrick Allen) 1067551

The Alfons Haar pumping module features a self-priming FPOS 100/1308A142R payload pump with a 1,350 l/min capacity, twin 30 m hosereels with hydraulic rewind, each terminating with a 2 in Unisex coupler, and Alfons Haar MKA 2290 and MKA 800 fuel meters.

Winterised variants have a climatic operational range (pumping) of -32 to +49°C.

Overall semi-trailer length is 10.8 m, gross weight is 23,330 kg.

Specifications

Oshkosh Wheeled Tanker
Cab seating: 1 + 1 + twin bunks
Configuration: 6 × 6
Weight:
(tractor) 12,050 kg
(tractor, GVW) 25,000 kg
(GCW, legislative) 40,000 kg
(GCW, design) 44,000 kg
Length:
(tractor) 6.98 m
(CST) 10.39 m
(TAR) 10.5 m
Width: 2.55 m
Height: 3.365 m (reducible to 2.489 m)
Track: 2.052 m
Wheelbase: 4.343 m
Max speed: (primary roads, restricted) 85 km/h
Range: (cruising) 500 km
Fuel capacity: 400 litres
Gradient: (at GCW) 34%
Fording: 1.5 m
Engine: Caterpillar C-12 ADEM (Advanced Diesel Engine Management) EURO III emissions compliant 11.9 litre 6-cylinder in-line turbocharged and water-cooled diesel 4-stroke diesel developing 445 hp (332 kW) at 1,700 rpm and 2,101 N.m torque at 1,200 rpm
Transmission: Allison HD 4560P with 6 forward and 1 reverse gears; TC-541 torque convertor
Transfer box: Oshkosh 30000 three-shaft single-speed with torque proportioning differential and manual differential lock
Steering: RH-drive, Shepard integral power steering with booster and separate fluid reservoir
Turning radius: (kerb) 9.14 m
Suspension: Oshkosh TAK-4 independent suspension, coil spring upper/lower control arms, anti-roll bar on second and third axles. Front axle rated at 7,500 kg, rear axles at 9,000 kg each
Tyres: 1600R 20 Michelin XZL with CTI system
Brakes: dual circuit, air, drums on all axles. ABS with off-road programme. Supplementary three-stage (2-, 4- or 6-cylinder) manually selected, automatically applied engine compression brake
Electrical system: 24 V
Batteries: 4 × 12 V
Alternator: 150 A, 24 V

Status

Production as required. In service with the UK, 218 × 20,000 litre CST and 82 × 15,000 litre TAR. Deliveries ran from February 2005 until November 2006. Also covered by the Wheeled Tanker contract were 57 × 18,000 litre CST(W).

Contractor

Oshkosh Truck Corporation

Demountable bulk fuel dispensing unit

Development

Fluid Transfer International Limited took over the design parentage of the Simon Gloster Saro-produced bulk fuel dispensing unit in 1994 and are currently refurbishing the equipment in service with the British Army. This equipment is being replaced by the Unit Support Tanker (UST) element of the current Support Vehicle (SV) procurement programme, for which MAN ERF UK Ltd (a subsidiary of Germany's MAN Nutzfahrzeuge AG) was announced preferred bidder for, in October 2004; the contract award followed in March 2005. Fluid Transfer is a sub-contractor of MAN ERF UK Ltd for the Support Vehicle contract.

Early 2003, and in answer to a UK MoD UOR (Urgent Operational Requirement) for a deployable bulk refuelling system for use in the Gulf region, Fluid Transfer International Limited developed and subsequently constructed 20 UBRE-equipped DROPS flatracks. Each rack mounts four tanks and a pumping unit at each end of the rack.

Description

The demountable bulk fuel dispensing unit comprises two tanks, one pumping and dispensing pack, a two-tier rack and mounting beams.

The unit was designed for mounting on a Bedford MK/MJ, or Leyland Trucks (4 × 4) 4,000 kg payload flatbed truck, but can be adapted to fit other chassis with suitable capacity. The unit can be removed from the vehicle by a forklift truck, crane or, in an emergency, by hand.

Rear view of a demountable bulk fuel dispensing unit on the rear of a Bedford British Army TM 4-4 (4 × 4) 8,000 kg truck (Shaun C Connors)
0109494

Rear view of a demountable bulk fuel dispensing unit on the rear of a British Army Leyland 4,000 kg (4 × 4) truck (Shaun C Connors)   0109495

The tanks are manufactured from AA5454 aluminium sheet and each tank has a capacity of 2,100 litres. Access to the tank interior is through a 406 × 356 mm collar in the top skin. The filler cap assembly incorporates a 254 mm diameter EMCO open-fill quick-release manhole and a single pressure/vacuum vent. A dip point containing a captive dipstick is provided and the filler cap and dip point are contained within a spillage band. An automatic bottom-loading facility fitted to each tank enables loading rates up to 682 litres/minute and off-loading rates of 455 litres/minute to be achieved. A drain plug is provided in the tank bottom skin and each tank is pressure tested to 69 kPa (10 psi).

The dispensing equipment may be operated independently of the tanks if desired. The pump set is resiliently mounted inside the dispensing pack frame and is adequately protected against spillage by a firescreen and boxed-in exhaust which meets MoD (Army) safety requirements.

A two-tier rack fitted with a drip tray and drain plug is provided. The lower tier of the rack is designed as a roller carriage, which can be withdrawn from either side of the vehicle. An Alan Cobham filter/water separator with differential pressure gauge is incorporated in the design.

Two 12.192 m long 32 mm diameter smoothbore delivery hoses terminating in automatic shut-off nozzles are stowed on a self-rewind Dean hose reel. Also 10 m of 63.5 mm layflat hose is provided. A cross pumping off-take complete with an Avery Hardoll 63.5 mm self-sealing coupling for cross pumping to a tanker vehicle is connected to a secondary discharge outlet.

A rigid suction pipe connects at one end to the pump and at the other to bifurcated suction hoses, which connect to the two tanks via the CC41 coupling units. The suction hoses have a bore of 63.5 mm.

The whole system is retained on two longitudinal beams mounted on the vehicle platform. The equipment is fully bonded to the vehicle and is capable of being earthed. Two Dean bonding reels are provided, each with 12.2 m of bonding cable terminating with crocodile clip-type clamps. Two fire extinguishers are mounted on the nearside and offside of the two-tier rack.

Optional equipment includes a manifold assembly box for can filling, comprising 63.5 mm Avery Hardoll hose unit type CC40, 10 m of 38 mm bore hose to BS 3158, five-way manifold, 5 m of 19 mm bore hose to BS 3395 (five off) and 19 mm automatic shut-off nozzles (five off).

The lid of the stowage box acts as holder for the cans during filling.

Specifications

Demountable bulk fuel dispensing unit
Weight: 1,798 kg
Payload: 2,967 kg
Length: 3.66 m
Width: 2.44 m
Height: 1.22 m

Status

Available. In service with the British Army (being replaced) and other unspecified armed forces.

Contractor

Simon Gloster Saro Limited
(Original)

Enquiries to

Fluid Transfer International Limited

Dunlop collapsible containers

Description

Dunlop collapsible containers can be used to store a wide variety of liquids ranging from potable water to fuels with aromatic content up to 40 per cent and in temperatures ranging from –30 to +70°C. The range produced is wide and capacities range from 225 to 250,000 litres. All containers are constructed from a flexible textile and polymer laminate with both sides of the laminate being treated to ensure long life and resistance to abrasions and hard knocks. For extra strength each corner is reinforced by metal clamping bars. Joint reinforcing straps fabricated from panels of vulcanised polymer-coated textiles add extra strength to the main structure and all the ports and fittings are constructed from either steel or brass. The filled tanks may be either placed on prepared surfaces or laid on earth or sand foundations. The smaller tanks may be carried on flatbed trucks or the decks of ships. When not in use the collapsible tanks may be cleaned and rolled up for storage ready for reuse.

Specifications

See table below

Status

In production. In service with several armed forces.

Contractor

Dunlop GRG Holdings Limited

Dunlop collapsible container in use for fuel storage with British armed forces at Basra airport, Iraq, 2004 (Patrick Allen)   1023554

Tank capacity	225 litres	1,125 litres	2,250 litres	4,500 litres	9,000 litres	11,250 litres	22,500 litres	45,000 litres	90,000 litres	135,000 litres	225,000 litres
Length	2.06 m	1.52 m	2.59 m	4.72 m	4.88 m	5.49 m	9.76 m	10.21 m	11.58 m	17.15 m	18.59 m
Width	690 mm	2.06 m	2.06 m	2.06 m	3.43 m	3.43 m	3.43 m	4.8 m	7.45 m	8.92 m	11.66 m
Height (filled)	380 mm	790 mm	790 mm	790 mm	910 mm	910 mm	910 mm	1.22 m	1.22 m	1.07 m	1.22 m

Dunlop Dracone barges

Development
The idea of the Dracone barge dates from 1956, with the concept of transporting liquids having lower specific gravity than the surrounding water through which the cargo is towed, in specially designed flexible containers. Dunlop became involved in the programme during 1963. Since 1965 it has developed the Dracone towed flexible barge (TFB) to the stage where it is now widely used by both military and civil concerns.

Description
The Dracone towed flexible barge TFB combines strength of construction with good towing capabilities in open waters. Each Dracone TFB has a tapered nose and rounded tail section and is moulded in individual seamless units joined to the parallel centre section by circumferential seams. The nose section will withstand a pull of 30,000 kg without damage. The high-tensile nylon fabrics used are coated with neoprene for the outer proofing giving resistance to abrasion, sunlight, oils and seawater. On the inside, nitrile rubber is normally used for proofing.

Dracone TFBs can be used to carry a wide range of liquids ranging from water to petroleum. Being flexible, the TFBs can slide over obstructions without friction when wet and the barge acts as its own shock absorber. For open sea towing a length of tow of approximately 100 m is usual, although this can be shortened for towing in sheltered waters or moving in confined anchorages. Nylon tow ropes are used. The towing hose, through which the barge is loaded and discharged, is designed to accept the maximum towing loads with ample safety margins. The smaller sizes can be towed at speeds up to 10 kt and the largest can travel at 7 kt. From size D5 and upwards all Dracone TFBs are fitted with a rear stabiliser to prevent snaking. The power required to tow a Dracone is considerably less than that required for a conventional barge of similar capacity.

Dracones can be launched in a number of ways, including dropping a rolled unit from a cargo net, pulling a rolled unit from a slipway by a small launch, rolling bodily from a beach or launching over the stern of a vessel. Built-in buoyancy panels keep the barge afloat even when it is completely empty.

Cargo is loaded and discharged through a length of flexible hose fitted to the nose as an integral part of the tow to make handling easier. Small barges (up to and including the D5) are fitted with a 50 mm bore hose, while the larger sizes have a 100 mm hose as standard. Larger bore hoses are available on request. All hoses are supplied in standard lengths of 4.57 m that are bolted together to suit. At the end of the hose is a lightweight corrosion-resistant float to which the loading/discharge connection is fitted. A quick-acting coupling can be fitted. Loading can be by gravity or pump.

Empty Dracone TFBs may be carried as deck cargo but are normally left afloat once launched. A special gripper bar has been developed for recovering empty barges. Little or no maintenance, other than cleaning, is normally required.

Dracone TFBs can also be used as alternatives to ship-to-shore pipelines and can be employed as floating fuel reservoirs.

Specifications
See table below

Status
In production and widespread service.

Contractor
Dunlop GRG Holdings Limited

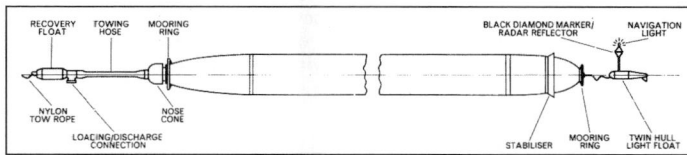

Main components of a typical Dracone towed flexible barge (TFB)
(Dunlop)
                                                                        0512037

Dennis Eagle (6 × 4) 15,500 litre air portable aircraft refueller

Development
The Dennis Eagle (6 × 4) 15,500-litre air portable aircraft refueller was developed for the UK Royal Air Force and is deployable within a C-130 Hercules transport aircraft with the minimum of preparation. The unit is based on the civilian Dennis Eagle Elite chassis cab, designed to undertake a multirole refuelling capability. The complete vehicle is capable of a stand-alone 24/7 role in ambient temperatures of −30 to +50°C. The unit meets the requirements of European and International legislation governing the carriage of dangerous goods by roads (ADR) in all respects. The vehicles were developed and produced in response to an international competitive contract and were delivered on time and to cost.

Description
The seven-seat cab is manufactured from Cromweld stainless steel and approximately one third of the 55 vehicles ordered by the Royal Air Force are winterised. The winterised vehicles feature an additional cab battery and fuel heating systems.

The chassis is designed with a reduced rail height, allowing for increased vehicle stability, improved handling characteristics and air transportability. Other driveline options could be made available to suit customer requirements, but the Royal Air Force vehicles are fitted with a Cummins C245 8.268 litre in-line six-cylinder water-cooled diesel engine developing 245 hp (183 kW). This is coupled to an Allison MD3060 six-speed automatic transmission. Axles are a GKN S75 steer axle (front), with Eaton (now DANA) units used for the double-drive rear bogie.

The 15,500 litre bulk fuel tank, supplied by General Trailers UK Ltd (later GT Fruehauf and Crane Fruehauf Ltd, now Fruehauf), is manufactured from aluminium and is of a single compartment monocoque construction. The ladder underframe is mounted through a central pivoted sprung frame at the front and low impact rubber interfaces to the rear so as to extend the fatigue life to the maximum. The tank is baffled transversely and longitudinally to give minimal surge characteristics.

The tank is configured to discharge fuel to the pumping unit, bottom load and gravity discharge to both sides of the vehicle. The tank top is fitted with two manhole covers, a dip tube and cap, retaining a captive type dip rod. The tank is fitted with suitable internal pipework to allow fuel to be drawn from a draw-bar trailer tank.

The vehicle is fitted with a pumping unit supplied by Fluid Transfer International Limited. This comprises a main fuel pump capable of 2,250 litres/min self-loading from an outside suction supply, defuelling at up to 450 litres/min, self loading from an outside source, use with open line or pressure fuelling. A filter water separator is fitted providing clean, water-free fuel and is fitted with filter elements with throughput rates up to but not exceeding 3.03 litres/min/cm. The filter incorporates an automatic air eliminator and high water automatic shut down devices. Also a fuel metering system comprising of two meters one for each dispensing hosereel fitted with non-resettable counter and a resettable register. The unit is fitted with a covered control station enclosing the functional controls, the water separator and the hose reels. The main fuel pump is mounted on the chassis cab and is PTO driven.

Full details of the Fluid Transfer range of refuelling systems and equipment will be found elsewhere in this section.

Specifications
(6 × 4) 15,500 litre air portable aircraft refueller
Crew: 1 + 6 or 1 + 3 sleeping
Configuration: 6 × 4
Weight:
  (laden) 26,000 kg
  (unladen) 12,130 kg
Length: 10.4 m
Width: 2.55 m
Height: 2.65 m
Angle of approach: 15°
Angle of departure: 15°
Max road speed: (governed) 56 mph
Fuel capacity: 164 litres
Engine: Cummins C245 8.268 litre 6-cylinder in-line water-cooled diesel developing 245 hp (183 kW)
Transmission: Allison MD3060, 6-speed automatic
Steering: integrally powered recirculating ball
Turning radius: 22 m

Dunlop Dracone barges

Model	A1	A2	D5	D10	E	F	J	L	O
100% capacity:	4.55 m³	9.1 m³	22.75 m³	45.5 m³	100 m³	191 m³	385 m³	519 m³	1,100 m³
85% capacity:	3.9 m³	7.8 m³	19.3 m³	38.6 m³	85 m³	162 m³	327.25 m³	441 m³	935 m³
Length:	7.5 m	14.1 m	15.07 m	31 m	37.64 m	49.2 m	66 m	66 m	91.45 m
Diameter:	940 mm	940 mm	1.42 m	1.42 m	1.87 m	2.347 m	2.82 m	3.28 m	4.225 m
Weight empty:	270 kg	310 kg	430 kg	780 kg	1,000 kg	2,275 kg	3,540 kg	4,060 kg	6,500 kg
Towing hose bore:	50 mm	50 mm	100 mm	100 mm	100 mm	100 mm	100 mm	100 mm	100 mm
Stabiliser:	no	no	yes	yes	yes	yes	yes	yes	yes

Dennis Eagle (6 × 4) 15,500 litre air portable aircraft refueller at RAF Coltishall (Shaun C Connors)   0137701

Axles:
(front) Dana (GKN) S75
(rear) Eaton (now Dana) 401/400
Wheels and tyres: pressed steel, spigot mounted 10-stud wheels, 22.5 in diameter
Brakes: dual circuit, air, drums all-round
Electrical system: 24 V

Status
Production as required. In service with the UK Royal Air Force (55).

Contractor
Dennis Eagle Limited

Scammell S26 (6 × 4) 4,000 gallon aircraft refueller

Development
The Scammell S26 (6 × 4) 4,000 gallon aircraft refueller was designed for aircraft refuelling (and defuelling on later batches) and open line refuelling.

The UK Royal Air Force ordered 178 vehicles which were delivered in five batches between 1987 and 1991. As of May 2000 174 remained in service. At some stage during the Royal Air Force production run a further 50 vehicles were ordered by an unspecified North African government. The first two Royal Air Force batches (25 and 30 vehicles) were built at the Scammell Motors of Watford facility. The remaining three batches (65, 10 and 48 vehicles) were built by Leyland DAF trucks at their Preston facility. The final 58 vehicles have a defuel capability.

A quantity of these vehicles have been replaced by a MAN TGA-based 20,000 litre tanker.

Description
The Scammell S26 (6 × 4) 4,000 gallon aircraft refueller is capable of aircraft pressure refuelling (and defuelling on later batches) and can also open line refuel if required. It can tow a 20,450 litre (4,500 gallon) tanker trailer and utilise the trailer tank capacity for refuelling operations. Secured to the front of chassis members are drop frames to accommodate a snow plough blade or other snow clearing attachments.

The Scammell S26 is powered by a water-cooled six-cylinder Rolls-Royce Eagle Mk3 turbocharged diesel engine developing 265 hp (198 kW). This drives the rear bogie only (6 × 4) through an Allison MT 654 CR automatic gearbox with five forward and one reverse gears. The front

Late production Scammell S26 (6 × 4) 4,000 gallon aircraft refueller fitted with snow plough (Shaun C Connors)   0137702

heavy I-section beam axle is sprung by semi-elliptic leaf springs and telescopic shock-absorbers, the rear 30,000 kg rated bogie has fully articulating semi-elliptic multi-leaf springs in slipper-mounted trunnions. Cross and inter-axle differential locks are fitted and double hub reduction gearing is employed.

Low profile 12R 22.5 tyres are fitted to allow the vehicle (with booms removed) to enter a hardened aircraft shelter. Its wheelbase precludes transport by C-130 Hercules aircraft. The two-seat all-steel cab is of non-sleeper, forward control design and tilts forward hydraulically 65° to allow for engine removal.

The tank and pumping compartment are separate assemblies, the front wall of the pumping compartment forming a fire screen. The tank is constructed of aluminium alloy with internal baffles and stiffeners, which brace the structure and divide the fuel space into interconnected compartments. Two underwing hose assemblies are fitted with 30 m of 2.5 in (63.5 mm) bore hose, and two overwing hoses of 1.5 in (38.1 mm) bore are fitted.

Status
In service with the UK Royal Air Force (187 ordered) and one other unspecified North African country (50 ordered).

Contractor
Scammell Motors Ltd
(This company is no longer trading)

Enquiries to
Leyland Trucks

United States

Amfuel static storage tanks and Sealdrums

Development
Amfuel (American Fuel Cells and Coated Fabrics) produces a wide range of products to store an equally wide range of liquids, including fuel and water. Amfuel is part of the Zodiac Aerospace Group. Full details of Amfuel products for water can be found in the Water supplies section.

Description
Amfuel static storage tanks
Amfuel static storage tanks intended for fuel use are made from a polymer-coated nylon fabric. Chafing patches at all fitting and hard-wearing locations provide double-wall thickness and protection. Handles are moulded on to each tank to assist positioning. All the tanks are free-standing. When not in use, the tanks can be stored and carried in wooden crates.

Amfuel Sealdrums
Amfuel Sealdrums are portable, collapsible rubber containers for storing and transporting POL products, water, liquid chemicals and other fluids. They are circular drums with metal 'hubs' with the bulk of the container being constructed of elastomeric-coated rayon cord. The outer cover is neoprene with the inner lining being a nitrile material. This casing is puncture-resistant and can withstand a minimum of three successive free-fall drops from a height of 3.8 m. Once filled, the Sealdrums are non-vented and hermetically sealed, with extremely low permeability. When empty, Sealdrums collapse to about 15 per cent of their filled size. When filled, they can be transported by truck, aircraft or helicopter and dropped off the rear of a truck or paradropped, being Low Altitude Parachute Extraction System (LAPES) delivery capable. They are the main item in the AAFARS, FARE and other US forces fuel systems. Full details of the AAFARS and FARE can be found elsewhere in this section.

There is an Amfuel range of similar containers known as Sealdbins, which are used for the storing and carrying of dry materials.

Specifications
See table on facing page

Static storage tanks

Capacity: (US)	Capacity: (metric)	Width:	Length:	Height:
1,000 gal	3,785 litres	2.388 m	3.073 m	610 mm
2,000 gal	7,570 litres	3.353 m	3.353 m	813 mm
3,000 gal	11,355 litres	3.581 m	4.267 m	914 mm
5,000 gal	18,925 litres	4.47 m	4.623 m	1.118 m
10,000 gal	37,850 litres	6.096 m	6.096 m	1.219 m
15,000 gal	56,775 litres	7.468 m	7.315 m	1.219 m
20,000 gal	75,700 litres	6.7 m	8.23 m	1.727 m
25,000 gal	94,625 litres	6.7 m	10.363 m	1.727 m
50,000 gal	189,250 litres	6.7 m	19.2 m	1.727 m
100,000 gal	378,500 litres	18.136 m	18.212 m	1.219 m

Sealdrums

Capacity:				
(US)	55 gal	250 gal	500 gal	515 gal
(metric)	208 litres	946 litres	1,893 litres	1,949 litres
Length:	876 mm	1.524 m	1.575 m	2.032 m
Diameter:	597 mm	1.016 m	1.349 m	1.168 m
Weight:				
(empty)	22.68 kg	113.4 kg	129.3 kg	129.3 kg

Status
In production. In service with US and other unspecified armed forces.

Contractor
American Fuel Cell and Coated Fabrics Company

Angus Chemicoil System

Description
The Angus Chemicoil System was designed for the delivery of multipurpose fuels and chemicals overland in bulk from fixed pipelines and storage points. The system may be used over long distances and may be laid by helicopters or vehicles using a minimum of manpower. It may also be used for ship-to-shore deliveries, aircraft refuelling and marine fuel bunkering. The system can be used with JP-4, JP-5 and JP-8 aircraft fuels, AVGAS, COMBATGAS and DF-2 and AM-2 diesel fuels.

The pipes used with the Chemicoil system have a high-quality, polyurethane inner lining and a circular woven and rot-proof reinforcement, which may use copper-coated textile strands for static protection. The cover uses high-quality polyurethane that is abrasion-, ozone- and weather-resistant. The covers may be coloured camouflage sand, black, or NATO green. Pipes up to 200 m long may be supplied, with diameters of 25, 38, 45, 51, 63.5, 76, 102 and 152 mm. Pipe with a diameter of 25 mm weighs 0.138 kg/m and 152 mm pipe weighs 1.558 kg/m.

Status
In service with US and other unspecified armed forces.

Contractor
Angus Fire Armour Corporation

Assault Hoseline System (AHS) and Hoseline Outfit

Description
The Assault Hoseline System (AHS) and Hoseline Outfit are cross-country distribution systems designed to move bulk fuel forward rapidly, reducing and in some cases eliminating the need for conventional fuel tankers. Both are based on 102 mm nominal (4 in) hoseline and are designed to operate in cold, moderate, and hot temperature ranges; –31.5°C to +49°C.

With the newer AHS, the hoseline can be mechanically deployed and retrieved across all types of terrain at speeds of up to 4.02 km/h (2.5 mph) and 1.21 km/h (0.75 mph), respectively, when the hoseline is empty. The earlier Hoseline Outfit is manually deployed and retrieved back into horizontal 'flaking boxes'. Once deployed, both can be connected to the Inland Petroleum Distribution System (IPDS), full details of which can be found elsewhere in this section.

The basic AHS and Hoseline Outfit comprises of not less than 4,276 m (14,000 ft) of 4 in (102 mm) collapsible hoseline in multiple connected sections, a manual (Hoseline Outfit) or powered (AHS) deployment/retrieval system, a 1,591 litres (350 US gallons) per minute diesel-powered pump unit, appropriate safety and spill containment/clean-up items, roadway crossing guards and a suspension kit allowing for gap obstacles of up to 61 m (200 ft), hoseline repair kit; additional hoses, the ability to evacuate all fuel from the deployed hoseline, and necessary couplings, clamps, slings and valves.

The Assault Hoseline System (AHS) is a cross-country fuel distribution system (TACOM (PMPAWS))   1147537

The Assault Hoseline System (AHS) is a cross-country fuel distribution system (TACOM (PMPAWS))   1147536

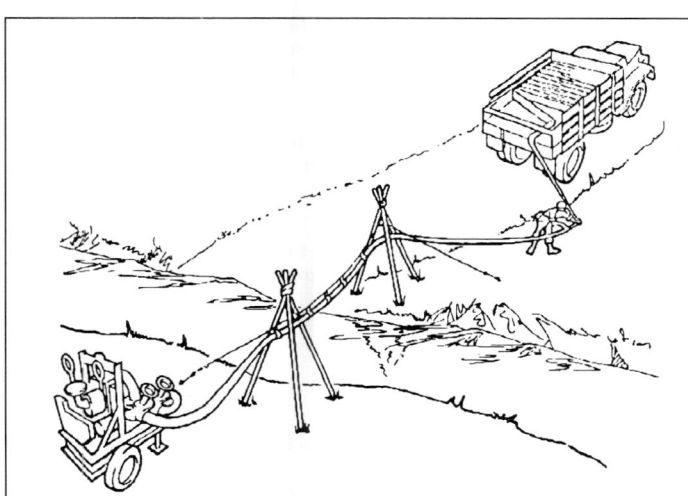

The Assault Hoseline System (AHS) and Hoseline Outfit are cross-country distribution systems (TACOM (PMPAWS))   0121804

The Assault Hoseline System (AHS) is a cross-country fuel distribution system (TACOM (PMPAWS))   1147535

The Assault Hoseline System (AHS) and Hoseline Outfit are cross-country distribution systems (TACOM) 0121803

A 210,000 US gallon (794,850 litres) tank being tested at Sierra, California (AEF) 1186175

The AHS (only) is required to be stored and transported in not more than nine TRICON containers. The maximum design system weight is 32,659 kg (72,000 lb) and the transport weight (including TRICONs) is 40,824 kg (90,000 lb). The AHS and Hoseline Outfit are air-transportable by C-130 aircraft, and any other container-capable transport of suitable capacity, including ISO standard flatracks.

Status
In excess of 200 Hoseline Outfits were bought and fielded by the then AVSCOM (St Louis) from EASI (now DRS Sustainment Systems Inc), between 1993 and 1995. Initial AHS contract awarded to LaBarge Products Inc. for up to 390 units.

Contractor
Development agency
US Army Tank-automotive and Armaments Command (TACOM)

Current Production
LaBarge Products Inc.

Avon Engineered Fabrications (AEF) 200,000 US gallon fuel tank undergoing testing prior to delivery to the US military (AEF) 1186203

Avon Engineered Fabrications

Development
Based in Mississippi, United States, Avon Engineered Fabrications (AEF) is a subsidiary of Avon Rubber and specialises in manufacturing flexible structures from coated fabrics and other specially formulated materials. Originally known as Bell Avon Inc, the company was founded in 1985 to manufacture skirts for hovercraft and air cushion vehicles. AEF has since expanded into other areas where high performance fabrications and extrusions are needed, products including assorted storage and transport tanks for fuel.

Description
210,000 US gallon collapsible fabric tank for fuel
This 210,000 US gallon (794,850 litres) collapsible fabric tank for fuel is known to the US Army as a Bulk Fuel Tank Assembly (BFTA). It was developed during the early 1980s as part of the Inland Petroleum Distribution System (IPDS) (full details of which can be found elsewhere in this section) and is used by the US Army as a component of the Tactical Petroleum Terminal.

The tank is made from a woven nylon cloth coated on both sides with an elastomer (usually polyester polyurethane). A typical installation would entail a berm with a liner.

Flexible tanks
Avon Engineered Fabrications (AEF) flexible tanks are made from a high strength, durable polymer-coated fabric specific to application, and are available in a wide range of sizes from 5 to 500,000 US gallons (18.9 to 1,892,500 litres).

When not in use, or for ease of shipping, the tanks can be folded, transported and packed into a convenient crate. They are suitable for operation throughout a wide temperature range.

Specifications
210,000 US gallon collapsible fabric tank for fuel
Capacity: 210,000 US gallons (794,850 litres)
Weight: (crated) 1,361 kg
Length: 20.73 m
Width: 20.73 m
Height: 2.03 m

Status
Production as required. In service with the US Army.

Contractor
Avon Engineered Fabrications Inc
European sales: Avon Technical Products

Avon Engineered Fabrications (AEF) 1,000 US gallon custom manufactured fuel tanks (AEF) 1186205

Flexcel liquid containers

Description

The basis of the Flexcel container is a cylindrical storage tank manufactured from acrylonitrile-butadiene synthetic rubber reinforced with nylon cords for the interior bladder and polychloroprene for the strong outer cover. The exterior is fitted with straps enabling the container to be carried in or on almost any type of vehicle or slung under a helicopter. One end of the container has a shroud containing a hose and a dispensing nozzle plus junctions and refuelling fittings.

There are various sizes of Flexcel container, with the most usual being 2.6 m long, 356 mm wide and weighing 56.7 kg empty. The storage capacity of this version is 55 US gallons (207 litres). Also available is a 30 US gallons (113 litres) version.

The Flexcel container is strong enough to be free-dropped from a helicopter even when full. It has been demonstrated being dropped from a helicopter flying at a height of 12.2 m at a speed of 80 knots. When the Flexcel has been dropped from a helicopter or vehicle it is ready for immediate use. The dispenser hose and nozzle are removed from within the shroud and are attached to the Flexcel by a quick-connect device. The vehicle or AFV to be refuelled is then driven on to the Flexcel to provide the pressure needed to force the liquid from the Flexcel as the nozzle is placed in the vehicle fuel tank. The complete process can take as little as five minutes. After use the Flexcel container can be retrieved and used again. The Flexcel can be used for liquids other than fuel such as water, decontaminants, oil and other fluids.

The Flexcel was manufactured from 1995 by the then FMW Rubber Products under contract to Teledyne Vehicle Systems and later General Dynamics Corporation. FMW Rubber Products, now FMW Composite Systems Inc., purchased the entire Flexcel programme from General Dynamics Corporation in 1998.

The most recent known Flexcel order was awarded in May 2000 and was for 43 bladders valued at USD298,000. These were supplied to the Egyptian Army, a user of the M1 Abrams MBT.

Status

Production as required. In service with Egypt and the US Army and Marine Corps.

Contractor

FMW Composite Systems Inc.

Flexcel fuel container in operation with M1 Abrams MBT (FMW Composite Systems Inc.)   0009994

Forward Area Refuelling Equipment (FARE)

Description

Forward Area Refuelling Equipment (FARE) is a lightweight, air mobile/air-transportable, 50.8 mm (2 in) nominal inside diameter refuelling system intended primarily for refuelling helicopters in forward area combat operations. As a secondary function FARE can provide a means for rapid refuelling of all US Army aircraft, ground vehicles and other equipment. FARE was type classified as Standard A, replacing the Pumping Assembly, Flammable Liquid, Bulk Transfer and Pump Centrifugal, Gas Driven, Base Mounted, 1.5 inch (38 mm), 100 US gallons/min (378.5 litres). FARE is currently being replaced by the Advanced Aviation Forward Area Refuelling System (AAFARS) only in the helicopter support role on a one for two basis. Full details of AAFARS can be found elsewhere in this section.

FARE includes a petrol or diesel engine-driven centrifugal pump with a rated capacity of 378.5 litres (100 US gallons) per minute; lightweight, military-design filter-separator rated at 378.5 litres (100 US gallons) per minute; two closed-circuit refuelling nozzles with adapters for conventional gravity fuelling; 60.96 m (200 ft) of lightweight discharge hose and 18.28 m (20 ft) of suction hose; and miscellaneous fittings, valves and accessories. FARE is capable of dispensing fuel through two nozzles simultaneously at flow rates up to 189.25 litres (50 US gallons) per minute

FARE being used in conjunction with standard 1,892.5 litre (500 US gallon) collapsible drums to refuel Bell UH-1 Iroquois helicopter (US Army) 0512041

through each nozzle. With appropriate adapters, any available bulk fuel storage tank may be used to supply fuel to the FARE, but US Army standard 1,892.5 litre (500 US gallon) collapsible drums are used as the primary bulk fuel supply.

Status

In limited service with the US Army.

Development agency

US Army Tank-automotive and Armaments Command (TACOM)

Forward Area Self-contained Transportable (FAST) fuel system

Development

FMW Rubber Products was founded in 1993 and in 1995 commenced the manufacture, under subcontract from the then Teledyne Vehicle Systems, of the Flexcel fuel bladder system for the M1 Abrams MBT. Manufacture continued under a sub-contract from General Dynamics Corporation, and in 1998 the company purchased the entire Flexcel programme from General Dynamics Corporation. That same year, FMW Rubber products became FMW Composite Systems Inc. Full details of the Flexcel system can be found elsewhere in this section.

The FAST (Forward Area Self-contained Transportable) is a next generation Flexcel with greater capacity and flexibility.

In 2000, the US DoD ordered an initial 246 FAST for the US Army and USMC under a USD1.99 million contract.

Description

FMW Composite Systems developed the FAST system from the technology perfected in its manufacture of the Flexcel fuel system, which was developed for the M1 Abrams MBT and is in service with Egyptian and US armed forces. The FAST system is air-deliverable to forward areas and is designed to provide for the transfer of liquids from a storage/transport unit to vehicles without the necessity of pumps or motors. Unlike Flexcel, which relies on vehicle pressure to force fuel out of the bladder, the larger FAST is self-contained and uses compressed air or gas to pressurise the unit in lieu of pumps or track-applied pressure.

The FAST system is described as rugged, re-usable and collapsible and, being fully contained and enclosed, the opportunities for contamination are reduced. Furthermore, since the fuel or liquid does not contact air within the unit, condensation of water is minimised. The FAST System can be used to refuel any vehicle and can be used with other liquids including potable water.

FAST bladders are available in a variety of sizes up to 500 US gallons (1,893 litres); US Army and Marine Corps FASTs are 300 US gallon (1,136 litres) capacity.

Status

Production as required. In service with the US Army and US Marine Corps.

Contractor

FMW Composite Systems Inc.

GTA collapsible containers

Development

GTA Containers Inc manufactures a complete system of collapsible containers (drums and pillow tanks) to handle the temporary storage transportation and delivery of drinking water, fuel, liquid food products, and fluid solids (grains, rice, etc). Capacities range from 55 US gallons to 225,000 US gallons (5,000 barrels).

GTA Containers Inc also supplies equipment for forward area fuel systems, the Advanced Aviation Forward Area Re-fuelling System (AAFARS) being an example, this providing a complete system for transporting and dispensing diesel jet-fuel and gasoline to forward areas in difficult terrain. GTA can also supply complete fuel transfer systems, including adaptors, hoses, pumps and monitoring equipment. Systems often include multi-tank installations used as fuel tank storage farms such as the 800K FSSP used by the US Army.

A typical GTA 210,000 US gallon static fuel tank during testing (GTA Containers Inc)

1410024

GTA Superdrum (GTA Containers Inc)

1410025

The following is a brief overview of the various containers produced by GTA Containers Inc.

Description

Fuel drums and Superdrums
GTA manufactures drums for the storage and transportation of fuel, drinking water, fluid food products and so on. Two types of fuel drum are available; a standard drum constructed using rubber-coated fabric, and the GTA Superdrum which is constructed of elastomeric coated fabric. The GTA Superdrum is significantly lighter but is more rugged and durable.

Three standard sizes are available; 55 US gallons (208 litres), 250 US gallons (946 litres) and 500 US gallons (1,893 litres). The fabric used in all types of construction is puncture- and tear-resistant and each drum is subjected to a hydraulic pressure test following assembly. Empty drums collapse to 10 per cent of their original volume for transport or storage, while filled drums can be rolled, floated, towed or lifted by helicopter. Drums can also be dropped free-fall (the 250 US gallon drum can be dropped free-fall from 4.5 m) or by parachute.

GTA fuel drums are coloured black and can be temporarily or permanently repaired in the field when necessary. Hoses, nozzles and valves have quick-connect/disconnect fittings.

These drums have numerous alternative applications including flotation devices (surface or submerged, for example for the construction of temporary bridges), as pneumatic lifting devices or ship fenders and for the underground storage of fuel supplies.

Static fuel storage pillow tanks
GTA Containers Inc manufactures a range of static fuel storage pillow tanks that are available in sizes from 3,000 US gallons (11,355 litres) to 225,000 US gallons (851,625 litres). All tanks are manufactured in accordance with US military requirements and are thus lightweight, rugged and durable with high abrasion and puncture resistance.

Each tank is constructed using tear-resistant fabric with an elastomeric coating on both sides. Chafing patches are included as part of the standard design. These are located on the interior surface directly opposite each fitting, providing a double-wall thickness supporting every piece of hardware. Handles, each capable of lifting 454 kg, are moulded on to the tank.

All tanks are equipped with standard 4 in (101.6 mm) quick-disconnect filler/discharge fittings. Bottom discharge fittings are provided for gravity unloading. A 4 in (101.6 mm) reinforced hose with quick-disconnects is also provided.

Each tank is fully collapsible and folds down into a package that occupies two per cent of the volume of the filled tank.

Specifications

Fuel drums and Superdrums

Capacity:

(US)	55 gal	250 gal	500 gal
(metric)	208 litres	946 litres	1,893 litres

Weight:

(drum)	22.7 kg	81.8 kg	104.5 kg
(Superdrum)	13.6 kg	63.6 kg	72.7 kg
Length:	0.876 m	1.524 m	1.524 m
Diameter:	0.597 m	1.016 m	1.27 m

Pillow Tanks

Capacity:

(US)	10,000 gal	20,000 gal	50,000 gal	210,000 gal
(metric)	37,850 litres	75,700 litres	189,250 litres	794,936 litres
Length:	6.71 m	7.32 m	7.62 m	19.81 m
Width:	6.71 m	8.53 m	19.81 m	19.81 m
Weight: (empty)	140.9 kg	187.2 kg	415.9 kg	1.306 kg

Status
In production. In service with US Armed Forces.

Contractor
GTA Containers Inc

Inland Petroleum Distribution System (IPDS)

Description
The Inland Petroleum Distribution System (IPDS) consists of multiple Tactical Petroleum Terminals (TPT), each of which consists of three fuel units (FU) and related equipment. This includes 3,028 litres (800 US gallons) per minute pipeline pump stations; 8.05 km (5 mile) pipeline sets, pipeline connection assemblies (PLCA), pressure reducing stations, critical gap crossings/suspension bridges of varying lengths exceeding 30.5 m (100 ft), IPDS recovery equipment and pipeline support equipment including fire suppression, configured and assembled according to individual mission requirements. In addition, the IPDS may operate with other systems based on mission requirements.

The system is capable of receiving, storing and supplying bulk fuel in an undeveloped theatre of operations, beginning at a port of disembarkation. The IPDS is installed and retrieved by engineer units, and operated and maintained by quartermaster units. Fuel is unloaded into one or more TPTs from either ship-to-shore hoselines, tanker trucks, rail tankers or the national fuel supply of the host nation, then stored or pumped through a dedicated pipeline system for dispensing.

Current pipeline deployment speed is 4.8 km (3 miles) per day and set-up and recovery time for each TPT is 72 hours. Storage capacity of each TPT is 14.06 million litres (3.7 million US gallons) and fuel can be received/discharged at a continuous rate of 2,271 litres (600 US gallons) per minute, 20 hours per day, giving an average daily fuel transfer rate of 2,725,200 litres (720,000 US gallons).

The complete system is modular-based, packed as required into a combination of TRICON and ISO standard 20 ft containers for storage and shipment. The number of containers is dependent on each mission requirement for total storage capacity and pipeline distances.

The IPDS is designed to operate and survive in high-altitude electromagnetic pulse (HEMP) and NBC contaminated environments and to operate effectively at high altitude; and in hot, moderate, and cold climates through a −31.5 to +49°C temperature range. Packaged or containerised, the system can be stored through a −40 to +49°C temperature range.

A section of Inland Petroleum Distribution System (IPDS) assault pipeline demonstrating its ability to circumnavigate an obstruction (TACOM)

0121801

A section of the Inland Petroleum Distribution System (IPDS) 680 miles of 4 in (102 mm) diameter assault pipeline (TACOM) 0121802

The IPDS was type classified in July 1984. A detailed procurement history is not available but the original IPDS procurement exercise is known to have involved 17 TPTs, 1,384 km (860 miles) of 102 mm (4 in) assault pipeline, 172 mainline pumps and associated support equipment.

Status
In service with US armed forces.

Development agency
US Army Tank-automotive and Armaments Command (TACOM)

Load Handling System Modular Fuel Farm (LMFF)

Description
The Load Handling System Modular Fuel Farm (LMFF) is part of an advanced non-developmental item test and demonstration effort to provide a flatrack-based tactical fuel and water distribution system in less time than currently required for collapsible (non-rigid) tank-based systems. The LMFF system includes two pump modules and 14 tank modules. The LMFF can be operational in less than one hour from arrival at the selected distribution point and is capable of receiving, storing and distributing fuel to vehicles, support equipment and US Army aircraft. On entering US Army service the LMFF will replace the current Fuel System Supply Point (FSSP) equipment at division level and below (only).

The LMFF tank and pump modules are built on ISO standard flatracks and in US Army service will be transported by either the Oshkosh Palletised Load System (PLS) (10 × 10) truck or Heavy Expanded Mobility Tactical Truck-Load Handling System (HEMTT-LHS) (8 × 8) truck. The LMFF ISO-compatible modules can also be handled by appropriately sized forklift trucks (>4,535 kg (10,000 lb)) or container handling equipment, and are stackable within standard 20 ft (6.1 m) ISO containers.

The pump module is a fuel pumping and filtration system powered by an integral diesel engine, weighing 3,864 kg (8,500 lb) empty of fuel and can flow fuel at up to 1,136 litres/min (400 US gallons/min). Each pump module carries four 4.57 m (15 ft) long 102 mm (4 inch) diameter suction hoses for its four inlet ports, and sufficient hoses and nozzles for its eight 76.2 mm (3 inch) outlet ports. Each refuelling point can support D1 nozzle single point refuelling, open port refuelling, and closed circuit refuelling.

Component parts of the Load handling system Modular Fuel Farm (LMFF) during trials (Oshkosh) 0137248

The tank modules are 9,463 litres (2,500 US gallons) stainless steel tanks and each module comes complete with sufficient 102 mm (4 inch) suction hoses and connectors to join it into the system. If required the tank modules can gravity discharge or hand-pump fuel through two 38.1 mm (1.5 inch) connections for vehicles, or through a single 19 mm (0.75 inch) connection to refuel stationary equipment such as a generator.

Status
Contract awarded to Systems & Electronics Incorporated (SEI, an Engineered Support Systems Incorporated (ESSI) company) in April 2005 for 6 pumpracks and 19 tankracks to support Product Qualification Test. Project now cancelled.

Development agency
US Army Tank-automotive and Armaments Command (TACOM)

Contractor
Systems & Electronics Inc.

M100/M100A1 Advanced Aviation Forward Area Refuelling System (AAFARS)

Description
The Advanced Aviation Forward Area Refuelling System (AAFARS) is a lightweight, diesel-powered, modular, air mobile/Low-Velocity Air-Drop (LVAD) capable refuelling system for primary use by US Army helicopter units that can also be used to refuel ground vehicles and equipment. With twice the capability of the earlier FARE system which it will replace, AAFARS is capable of austere area refuelling for all US Army helicopters, ground vehicles, and most other ground equipment. Full details of the FARE system can be found elsewhere in this section.

The AAFARS is designed to provide filtered fuel in configurations of up to four nozzles simultaneously at spacings of 30.48 m (100 ft) apart at flow rates up to 208.2 litres (55 US gallons) per minute per nozzle. AAFARS consists of several man-portable modules (pump/engine, filter/separator, control panel/battery, and an auxiliary pump for defuelling operations) plus appropriate nozzle assemblies, various fittings and adapters, discharge and suction hoses, drum fittings/adapter kits, other safety/environmental control items, and component transport bags. Four or more 1,892 litres (500 US gallons) capacity collapsible fuel drums were added to complete the M100 system by the user; the M100A1 version comes with 12 of these drums included as part the system. Total system

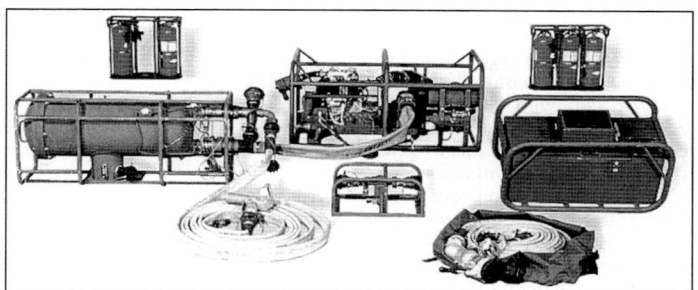

Components of the Advanced Aviation Forward Area Refuelling System (AAFARS) (minus the 1,892 litres (500 US gallons) collapsible fuel drums) (TACOM) 0121806

The Advanced Aviation Forward Area Refuelling System (AAFARS) is capable of refuelling through up to four nozzles simultaneously at 30.48 m (100 ft) apart at flow rates of up to 208.2 litres (55 US gallons) per minute (TACOM) 0121805

and individual module weights are design limited by the purchasing documents. AAFARS is designed to operate in cold, moderate, and hot temperature ranges; –31.5°C to +49°C, and is air-transportable by C-130 aircraft and UH-60 and CH-47 helicopters. Both the M100 and M100A1 versions are suitable for helicopter operations and certified for LVAD, both without TRICON's. The M100 version was packed in crates; the M100A1 version uses TRICON containers.

The initial AAFARS contract was awarded to Lear Astronics (now part of BAE Systems) during 1993 and increased in 1999 to a total of 48 systems. In September 2001, Tank-automotive and Armaments Command (TACOM) awarded an Indefinite Delivery/Indefinite Quantity (ID/IQ) contract to BAE Systems for a number of systems over an eight-year time frame, the first of which was to be fielded FY05.

In December 2006, BAE Systems announced a USD31.6 million contract from the US Army's Tank Automotive and Armament Command (TACOM) to deliver 119 additional units of the second-generation Advanced Aviation Forward Area Refuelling System (AAFARS). This 14th production order is part of the eight-year ID/IQ contract. The contract then covered 362 systems, bringing the total contract value to USD94.3 million and by late 2006 more than 200 AAFARS had been fielded, this figure including 48 M100 systems. Deliveries under the December 2006 award were scheduled to conclude in October 2007 and December 2008.

Status
In production and service. A total of 48 first-generation M100 systems were delivered; 362 second-generation M100A1 systems on contract as of December 2006. As of December 2006 over 200 M100/M100A1 AAFARS had been fielded.

Contractor
BAE Systems Platform Solutions

Development agency
US Army Tank-automotive and Armaments Command (TACOM)

Rapidly Installed Fluid Transfer System (RIFTS)

Description
The Rapidly Installed Fluid Transfer System (RIFTS) was a proposed system to address some current issues with the Inland Petroleum Distribution System (IPDS), full details of which can be found elsewhere in this section. It was anticipated that the now cancelled RIFTS would be adopted as the primary US Army system for transferring large quantities of bulk petroleum (and water) to the battlefield. The system was being designed to be capable of deployment across all types of terrain and at a minimum rate of 32.2 km (20 miles) per day, rising to an objective of 48.3 km (30 miles) per day in favourable conditions. Retrieval rates were set at a minimum of 16.1 km (10 miles) per day.

Once deployed the RIFTS had a proposed fluid throughput of 3,217,250 litres (850,000 US gallons) per day and was to have a built-in leak detection system capable of detecting any leakage greater than 37.9 litres (10 US gallons) per minute.

The RIFTS was designed to operate through a –31.5°C to +49°C temperature range and was required to have a 15-year shelf life when stored between –40°C and + 49°C, and a ten-year useful life once wetted. Components of the system were to be air-transportable by C-130 aircraft, and may have been ISO flatrack compatible for road transport.

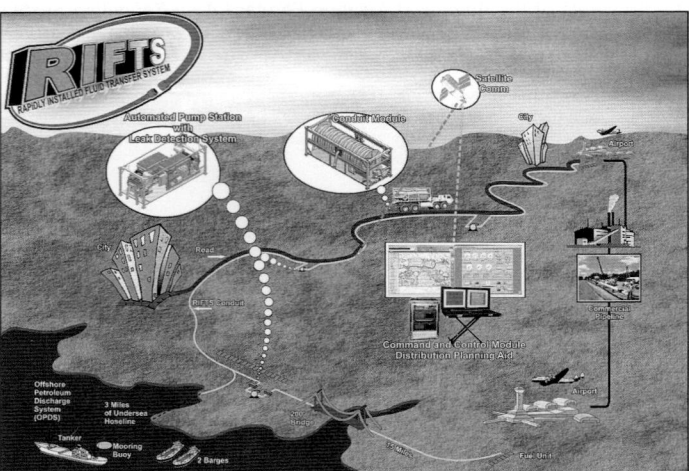

The Rapidly Emplaced Fluid Transfer System (RIFTS) concept (TACOM)
1147534

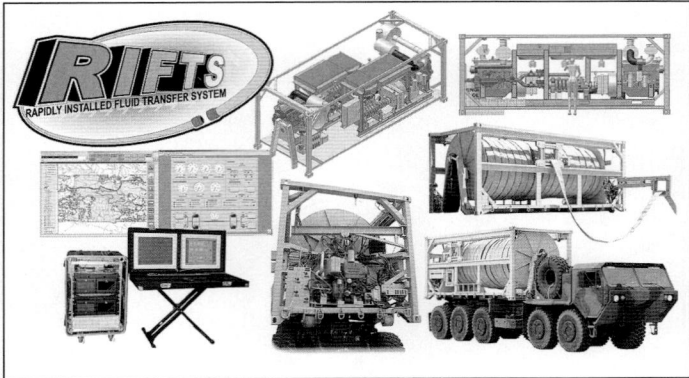

Collage of the complete Rapidly Emplaced Fluid Transfer System (RIFTS) concept (TACOM (PMPAWS))   1147539

It was announced in July 2003 that Southwest Research Institute (SwRI) had been awarded a two-year, USD4.65 million contract by TACOM to build and demonstrate a prototype Rapidly Installed Fluid Transfer System (RIFTS). It was disclosed early-2008 that the development of RIFTS had been terminated.

Status
Project terminated.

Development agency
US Army Tank-automotive and Armaments Command (TACOM)

Tank and Pump Units (TPU), high and low-profile; Tank Unit, Liquid Dispensing (TULD)

Description
The Tank and Pump Units (TPU), both high and low profile models, and the Tank Unit, Liquid Dispensing (TULD) are systems mounted on the loadbed of US Army 5 ton cargo trucks and selected trailers to convert them from general purpose cargo vehicles into fuel-dispensing units for refuelling military vehicles, ground equipment, aircraft, storage drums and 18.9 litre (5 US gallon) jerrycans. The older 'high-profile' model has two 2,271 litre (600 US gallon) tanks and the newer, 'low-profile' model is internally baffled and contains two 1,987 litre (525 US gallons) tanks. The TULD can have tank sets of either capacity. All utilise an electric motor-driven pump, hose reel assemblies, together with the related fuel-dispensing equipment mounted on a frame. The TPUs have an additional device/meter to measure and display quantities dispensed, and aluminium tanks.

Specific contract information or details of quantities of TPU or TULD in current service is not available. The first units entered US Army service over 30 years ago, the most recent during FY90, and additional quantities are not required, a replacement system for all three systems is under development.

Status
In service with the US Army.

Contractor

Development agency
US Army Tank Automotive Command Mobility Technology Center - Belvoir.

Enquiries to
US Army Tank-Automotive and armaments Command (TACOM)

Tank and Pump Unit (TPU), low profile, mounted on a US Army M809 series 5 ton truck (Michael Jerchel)   1128203

WATER SUPPLIES

Australia

Project JP 2059 - Bulk Liquid Distribution

Development
Project JP 2059 is a joint-service procurement project being managed by the Defence Materiel Division (DMD). The aim of the project is to address both known and recently identified Australian Defence Force (ADF) shortfalls in bulk liquid distribution, both water and fuel.

Description
The ADF has a mature and functional bulk water (and fuel) distribution capability, which was initially enhanced to meet the requirements of the East Timor deployment. There were, however, a number of critical bulk liquid deficiencies identified during the ADF deployment to East Timor; the specification and fit of much in-service equipment reflecting 1960–70s technology and not taking full advantage of developments such as modern OH&S principles, containerisation and palletised load systems. Much of the equipment in use also fails to meet current industry standards. In addition, some of the in-service systems are approaching life-of-type and require enhancement, replacement or supplementation, if emerging requirements are to be met.

Phase 1 of the project delivered enhanced bulk fuel and storage and bulk fuel transfer systems in response to the requirements of the ADF East Timor deployment.

Current phases of Project JP 2059 (as of May 2006) are:

Phase 2 - Bulk Liquid Distribution
The aim of JP 2059 Phase 2 is to provide a bulk water (and fuel) storage and distribution capability to support the concurrent deployment of:
- A brigade-based Joint Task Force
- A Battalion Group deployed on independent operations including their supporting attachments
- A unit-line refuelling capability for the Armed Reconnaissance Helicopter (ARH).

Acquisition under Phase 2 is expected to address these requirements, with other deficiencies to be met through subsequent project phases of JP 2059 or JP 126 Joint Theatre Distribution.

As of July 2010 contracts had been signed with the following suppliers:
- Ebsray Pumps Pty Ltd in July 2004, for the supply of (37) V-35 Fuel Pumps and (34) V-15 Potable Water Pumps
- Trelleborg in November 2004, for the supply of a Tank Fabric Collapsible Marine
- Amfuel in November 2004, for the supply of (170) 1,800 litre capacity drum fabric collapsible water storage tanks
- Crusader Hose Pty Ltd in December 2004, for the supply of 12 km of 150 mm hose assemblies
- Dunlop Fabrications in December 2004, for the supply of (74) 136,000 litre fuel tanks
- Ebsray pumps Pty Ltd in February 2005, for the supply of (3) fuel flow metres
- Dunlop Fabrications in September 2005, for the supply of (9) Towed Flexible Barges
- Ebsray Pumps Pty Ltd in March 2006, for the supply of (4) V-40 fuel pumps
- Crusader Hose Pty Ltd in September 2005, for the supply of 13.5 km of 150 mm pipeline hose assemblies
- Metcalfe Pty Ltd in February 2006, for supply of (10) Vacuum Recovery Kits
- Ebsray Pumps Pty Ltd in March 2006, for the supply of (4) V-40 fuel pumps
- Flight Refuelling Ltd (United Kingdom) in March 2007, for the supply of (3) sets of barge discharge systems
- Royal Wolf Containers Pty Ltd in August 2008 for the supply of container modifications
- Ebsray Pumps Pty Ltd in December 2009 for the modification and upgrade of the Tank and Pump Assembly fleet (Quantity 130 units).
- Logistic Solutions Australasia in March 2010 via DMO Support Services Panel for the provision of Through Life Support documentation for the Towed Flexible Barge Discharge System
- Gill Engineering in July 2010 for the Towed Flexible Barge Discharge System replacement Mooring Pontoons

All significant sub-projects planned for Phase 2 have either been completed or are in contract, with the scope for the remaining acquisitions (detailed below), expected to transition to Land 121 Project Overlander for completion:
- Refuelling module and vehicle for the Armed Reconnaissance Helicopter (ARH)
- Water and fuel vehicle storage modules.

Phase 3 - Water Purification
Phase 3 will provide a water purification and desalination capability to support the concurrent deployment of a brigade-based joint task force and a battalion group. The capability provided will produce potable water from a wide range of poor quality source water.

Phase 3 will provide a water purification and desalination capability to support the concurrent deployment of a brigade-based Joint Task Force and a battalion group. A contract was signed with Pall Corporation Australia in April 2003 to provide the Australian Defence Force with a suite of new water purification systems. Details of legacy water purification equipment can be found elsewhere in this section.
- 14 water purification units (Army) delivered
- Four additional water purification units; all 18 units now delivered
- 13 reverse osmosis water purification units (Army) delivered
- Five additional reverse osmosis water purification units; all 18 units now delivered
- operator and maintainer train-the-trainer and conversion training management packages, in progress
- Initial introduction into service courses
- Initial three years through life support.

Provision of bulk water storage bladders from Fabric Solutions Australia Pty Ltd is now complete. Storage bladders provided were: 22,500 litre water storage bladders (25) and 136 litre water storage bladders (30).

Status
See text.

Contractor
Defence Materiel Organisation

Australian water purification units, legacy and current

Description
The then Permutit Australia (now United KG Water Projects) manufactured 59 CPC 7.5 and CPC 20 trailer-mounted water purification equipment for the Australian Defence Forces and later supplied 16 air-transportable MRO 10 units, used to supply up to 10,000 litres/hour.

The CPC units use a process of chemical coagulation, settling and filtration to clarify water using a high-rate settling technique, and they operate on the concept of a low head clarifier using corrugated interceptor plates. Filtration after settling polishes the water while chlorine sterilises it. The units will make any naturally occurring dirty, muddy, unsafe and undrinkable water potable.

The units are self-contained and on arrival on site require levelling, using the jacks mounted on the equipment. After hose connection to the water source, potable water is available within one hour.

The CPC 20 unit is mounted on a two-axle trailer and can produce 20,000 litres/hour. The CPC 7.5 unit is mounted on a single-axle trailer and can produce 7,500 litres/hour.

As part of the Defence Materiel Organisation (DMO) project JP 2059 - Bulk Liquid Distribution (full details of which can be found elsewhere in this section) - a contract was signed with Pall Corporation Australia, in April 2003, to provide the Australian Defence Force with a suite of new deployable water purification systems. The contract will also provide for spare parts, training and technical documentation. An initial production version was scheduled for trial mid-2004, with the remainder planned to commence delivery late 2004-05. The final CPC 7.5 and CPC 20 units were withdrawn from service during 2009.

Status
MRO, CPC 7.5 and CPC 20 were in service with the Australian Army; replacement system now delivered.

Water purification trailer, Permutit-Boby (now United KG Water Projects) CPC 20   0512046

Contractor

MRO, CPC 7.5 and CPC 20
United KG Water Projects (part of the United Group)
(This company has stated it is no longer involved with this equipment.)

Replacement systems
Pall Corporation Australia

Stand-alone example of Mini-ROWPU water purification modules
(GE Water & Process Technologies)   0009996

Canada

GE/ZENON Advanced Double pass Reverse Osmosis Water Purification Unit (ADROWPU) and Mini-ROWPU

Development
The GE/ZENON Advanced Double pass Reverse Osmosis Water Purification Unit (ADROWPU) was designed for field use and can be used to treat water that has been contaminated by NBC agents, as well as fresh, brackish and seawater. The ADROWPU is in service with the Canadian and Taiwanese armies, the UN and the US Federal Emergency Management Association (FEMA). The ADROWPU has been deployed operationally to Angola, Cambodia, Haiti, Honduras, Marshall Islands, Qatar, Rwanda, Saudi Arabia, Somalia, and the former Yugoslavia.

The Mini-ROWPU (Mini-Reverse Osmosis Water Purification Unit) family of water purification modules was designed to meet the water purification requirements of smaller and more mobile rapid-deployment forces. These units are in service with the UN, the Canadian, Hungarian and Mexican armies, and have been deployed operationally to Haiti and Honduras.

On March 14, 2006, GE (General Electric Company) Water & Process Technologies, a unit of GE agreed to acquire ZENON Environmental for USD758 million. This deal was successfully completed in early June 2006.

Description
ADROWPU
The ADROWPU is a fully integrated self-contained system with its own diesel power generator (40 kW), automatic control system, digital controls and instrumentation. Automatic self-cleaning and pre-treatment features are built-in and are provided with each system along with onboard spares for a six month operational period. Installation by two operators takes around 30 minutes. The system is arranged in a self-contained palletised enclosure measuring 5.823 × 2.283 × 2.157 m (L × W × H) enabling it to be transported via all modes of military transport, including NATO-standard palletised load handling systems. Weight of the system is 8,618 kg and it may be transported internally by C-130 Hercules transport aircraft, or as an underslung load by CH-47 Chinook helicopter. The ADROWPU can also fit inside standard 20 or 40 ft (6.096 or 12.192 m) ISO containers, in which form it is known as the Containerized Reverse Osmosis Water Purification System, or CROWPU.

Purification is by reverse osmosis in either a single pass (using one membrane bank) or double pass (using two membrane banks) depending on the type and quality of water being purified. Two-stage water pre-treatment is provided by a 50 micron self-cleaning filter and a 5 micron cartridge filter. Post-treatment is by chlorination.

Raw water intake can reach 10,000 litres/hour, with outputs varying from 5,000 litres/hour (at +8°C water temperature) in single pass mode to 2,400 litres/hour in double pass mode.

Operational temperature ranges are −40 to +49°C (air), and +3 to +40°C (water). From a daily operational cycle, four hours are required for maintenance.

Mini-ROWPU
The Mini-ROWPU system is compact and lightweight and can be used in any terrain to treat fresh, brackish and seawater without the extensive use of chemicals. The modular system can be configured for double-pass operation to treat water contaminated with NBC agents.

The system consists of three modules which can be utilised in various configurations depending on the mission profile. The three modules are Pre-treatment, Reverse Osmosis Single Pass and Control. The Pre-treatment module employs GE/ZENON's ZeeWeed microfiltration membrane to remove bacteria and large suspended particles prior to the reverse osmosis stage.

The Mini-ROWPU has a typical output of 159 (sea water) to 340 (brackish water) litres per hour depending on the mission and customer requirements. The Mini-ROWPU is equipped with all the ancillary equipment necessary for self-contained operation including a lightweight diesel generator set (power requirement is 5 kW), water storage tanks, hoses and spare parts. The system's total transport weight is 564 kg. Transport dimensions (less power supply) are 1.549 × 1.219 × 1.251 m (L × W × H).

Specifications
ADROWPU
Weight: 8,618 kg
Length: 5.823 m
Width: 2.283 m
Height: 2.157 m
Water processing rate:
  (sea) 2,400 litres/h
  (brackish) 5,000 litres/h
Power requirements: 40 kW

Mini-ROWPU
Weight: 564 kg
Length: 1.549 m
Width: 1.219 m
Height: 1.251 m
Water processing rate:
  (sea) 159 litres/h
  (brackish) 340 litres/h
Power requirements: 5 kW

Status
ADROWPU in service with the Canadian and Taiwanese armies, the UN and the US Federal Emergency Management Association (FEMA). Has been deployed operationally to Angola, Cambodia, Haiti, Honduras, Marshall Islands, Qatar, Rwanda, Saudi Arabia, Somalia, and the former Yugoslavia. Mini-ROWPU in service with the Canadian, Hungarian and Mexican armies, and the UN. Has been deployed operationally to Haiti and Honduras.

Contractor
GE Water & Process Technologies

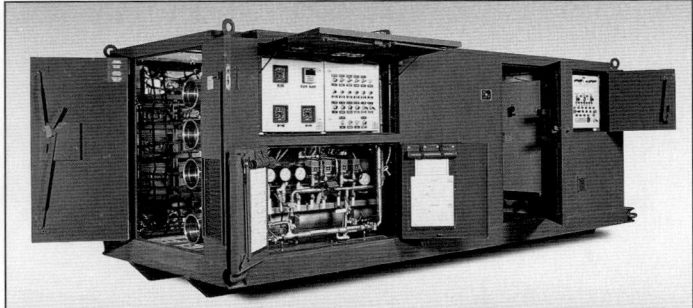

Stand-alone version of GE/ZENON Advanced Double pass Reverse Osmosis Water Purification Unit (ADROWPU)
(GE Water & Process Technologies)   0009995

SEI Industries Pick-up Truck water tank

Description
SEI Industries produces flexible water tanks that can be carried in the back of pick-up trucks to convert them into water supply vehicles for a number of purposes. The tanks can be used for potable or non-potable water, or for other non-hazardous fluids.

Two sizes of tank are available. The PT90 is for small pickup or ½-tonne trucks, while the PT150 is for ¾- or one-tonne trucks. When empty, both sizes of tank can be folded and stowed behind a cab seat.

Status
In production.

SEI Industries Pick-up Truck water tank in use (SEI Industries)   1034943

Contractor
SEI Industries

Pronal flexible water storage tanks in use (Pronal)   0125397

A Pronal open vat water storage tank in use (Pronal)   0125396

France

Pronal water storage and transport tanks

Development
Pronal produces an extensive range of flexible tanks for both storage and transport of water. These tanks may also be used for various other liquids including fuel. Pronal tanks are constructed from a nitrile rubber-coated nylon fabric, and depending on application may be reinforced with high strength fabric. Pronal is a member of GILEP (Groupement Interprofessionnel de Logistic et Equipments Pétroliers), a consortium composed of the main contractors to the French armed forces Joint Petroleum Service (SEA). Full details of GILEP can be found in the Bulk fuel storage and distribution systems section.

Description

Open vat tanks
These open vat tanks are used for the large-scale storage of water and other liquids such as NBC decontamination fluids. They have an advantage over conventional storage tanks in that the tank may be filled and emptied very quickly and more than one user point may be employed at any one time. The tanks are placed on circular groundsheets and are filled from an over standpipe or hose which is usually a 51 mm (2 in) diameter component. The sides of the tank rise with the volume contained and, if required, a tarpaulin may be used to cover the contents. The tanks are constructed of polyester fabric coated with PVC.

Flexible water storage tanks

Capacity:	1,000 litres	2,000 litres	5,000 litres	10,000 litres	15,000 litres	20,000 litres	25,000 litres	30,000 litres
Length: (empty)	2.76 m	2.76 m	3.32 m	5.14 m	4.55 m	5 57 m	6 69 m	7 82 m
Width: (empty)	1.21 m	1.83 m	2.76 m	2.96 m	4.44 m	4.44 m	4.44 m	4.44 m
Height: (full)	600 mm	900 mm	1.1 m	1.2 m	1.2 m	1.3 m	1.3 m	1.3 m
Weight: (empty)	20 kg	25 kg	35 kg	50 kg	65 kg	75 kg	85 kg	100 kg
Volume: (folded)	0.09 m³	0.11 m³	0.17 m³	0.25 m³	0.3 m³	0.4 m³	0.45 m³	0.5 m³

Flexible water storage tanks (continued)

Capacity:	35,000 litres	40,000 litres	45,000 litres	50,000 litres	60,000 litres	70,000 litres	80,000 litres	100,000 litres
Length: (empty)	6.32 m	7.06 m	7.81 m	8.55 m	7.78 m	8.88 m	9.98 m	10.07 m
Width: (empty)	5.92 m	5.92 m	5.92 m	5.92 m	7.4 m	7.4 m	8.88 m	8.88 m
Height: (full)	1.4 m	1.4 m	1.4 m	1.4 m	1.45 m	1.45 m	1.45 m	1.45 m
Weight: (empty)	110 kg	120 kg	130 kg	140 kg	160 kg	180 kg	200 kg	245 kg
Volume: (folded)	0.55 m³	0.6 m³	0.65 m³	0.7 m³	0.8 m³	0.9 m³	1 m³	1.2 m³

Flexible water storage tanks (continued)

Capacity:	125,000 litres	150,000 litres	200,000 litres	250,000 litres	300,000 litres	350,000 litres
Length: (empty)	12.3 m	14.53 m	18.98 m	19.8 m	23.6 m	27.3 m
Width: (empty)	8.88 m	9.88 m	9.88 m	10.36 m	10.36 m	10.36 m
Height: (full)	1.45 m	1.45 m	1.45 m	1.45 m	1.45 m	1.45 m
Weight: (empty)	295 kg	345 kg	445 kg	485 kg	570 kg	655 kg
Volume: (folded)	1.5 m³	1.75 m³	2.25 m³	2.5 m³	2.7 m³	3 m³

Pick-up transportable tanks

Capacity:	500 litres	1,000 litres	1,500 litres	2,000 litres	2,500 litres	3,000 litres	4,000 litres
Length: (full)	1.25 m	1.4 m	1.8 m	2.4 m	2.2 m	2.3 m	2.6 m
Width: (full)	800 mm	1.2 m	1.4 m	1.4 m	1.9 m	2.2 m	2.2 m
Height: (full)	500 mm	600 mm	600 mm	600 mm	600 mm	600 mm	700 mm
Compartments:	0	0	1	2	3	4	4
Weight: (empty)	12 kg	15 kg	21 kg	29 kg	32 kg	40 kg	n/avail

Flexible water storage tanks

Pronal produces a wide range of flexible water storage tanks to suit specific customer requirements, therefore examples given in the Specifications table should be regarded as typical rather than applicable to individual cases. The usual fittings are 51 mm (2 in) filling/discharging valves and caps, which can be connected by adapters to 51 or 76 mm (2 or 3 in) hoses.

The material used for the tanks is a PVC-coated polyester fabric with a surface area weight of 1,100 g/m² (± 50 g/m²). Tensile strength is ≥350 daN/5 cm; tearing strength is ≥35 daN; water impermeability is ≥10 m.

Pick-up transportable tanks

These small capacity pick-up transportable tanks are made with a rectangular section and are assembled by high-frequency welding. They are produced in capacities from 500 to 4,000 litres and from 1,500 litres upwards are divided internally into separate compartments by flexible walls to reduce the movement of liquids and to help ensure stability of the transporting vehicle.

All are fitted with a vent and 51 mm (2 in) filling and emptying valve and Guillemin symmetrical coupling.

Specifications

See tables on page 887 and above

Open vat tanks

Capacity:	2,000 litres	5,000 litres	10,000 litres	20,000 litres
Diameter:	2.2 m	3 05 m	4.25 m	6.05 m
Height:	750 mm	1 m	1 m	1 m
Weight:	30 kg	40 kg	62 kg	110 kg
Volume: (folded)	0.30 m³	0.45 m³	0.7 m³	1 m³

Status

In production. In service with the French and other undisclosed armed forces.

Contractor

Pronal SA

Aérazur water transport and storage tanks

Development

Aérazur has been involved in the design, development and manufacture of safety and survival equipment, mainly to the aerospace industry, the armed forces and the armament industry, for over 60 years. Aérazur produces a wide range of products made of fabrics including flexible fuel cells, de-icing systems, flexible tanks, composites parts and elastomer products. Details of bulk fuel-related products follow.

Description

Flexible water storage and transport tanks

Aérazur manufactures a range of flexible tanks for transport (capacity 500 to 10,000 litres) and for storage (capacity 1,000 to 300,000 litres). They are made of high-performance synthetic fabrics coated with elastomer to store a selection of fluids ranging from water to fuel and chemicals. The tanks are provided with standard equipment according to French and US specifications but can be equipped to suit customer requirements. All the tanks in the range can be folded when empty and are easy to set up on site. They are suitable for a wide range of climatic conditions. Transport tanks are designed for a service life of greater than 10 years.

Helisup helicopter-transportable tanks

The Helisup heli-transportable tank is used to transport water or fuel underslung by helicopter. These tanks are manufactured from synthetic fabric coated on each side with elastomer and have a standard capacity of 1,500 litres.

A standard fitting is a 76 mm fill/drain flange on the top but other equipment can be fitted to suit customer specifications. Tanks are supplied complete with a heli-transport envelope, slinging equipment, transport handles, stowing straps, an emergency repair kit, and the necessary equipment to pump and dispense potable water.

Specifications - See table below

Status

In production. In service with France's armed forces, NATO, and a number of armed forces in the Middle East and North Africa, including Chad and Gabon.

Contractor

Aérazur

Germany

WEW Westerwälder Eisenwerk GmbH Special Tank Containers

Development

WEW Westerwälder Eisenwerk GmbH has focused on the development, production and worldwide licensing of Special Tank Containers for the chemical industry for over 40 years. However, WEW also provides solutions for the transportation of liquid foods and other liquid products, including potable water and automotive fuels.

WEW has been supplying potable water tank containers to the German Army since 1997, when 18,000-litre tank containers for potable water were designed, built, tested and approved. In total, WEW has supplied around 400 military water (and fuel) ISO-sized containers to the German Army. One specific German Army example would be the 10,000-litre Multi water tank container, developed for the supply of potable water to soldiers in Afghanistan.

A German Army half-height water tank. The German Army is steadily increasing the number of half-height water (and fuel) tanks used on deployed operations (WEW Westerwälder Eisenwerk GmbH)   1391126

Flexible water storage and transport tanks

Capacity:	Dimensions: (empty)	Dimensions: (full)	Weight: (empty, approx)
25 m³	8.11 × 4.05 m	7.48 × 3.42 × 1.10 m	112 kg
30 m³	9.53 × 4.05 m	8.90 × 3.42 × 1.10 m	131 kg
35 m³	8.10 × 5.43 m	7.47 × 4.80 × 1.10 m	148 kg
40 m³	8.47 × 5.43 m	7.79 × 4.75 × 1.20 m	155 kg
45 m³	7.16 × 6.81 m	6.45 × 6.10 × 1.25 m	163 kg
50 m³	7.79 × 6.81 m	7.08 × 6.10 × 1.25 m	177 kg
60 m³	9.10 × 6.81 m	8.39 × 6.10 × 1.25 m	206 kg
70 m³	9.00 × 8.19 m	8.29 × 7.48 ×1.25 m	243 kg
80 m³	9.51 × 8.19 m	8.77 × 7.45 × 1.30 m	256 kg
90 m³	10.00 × 8.19 m	9.26 × 7.45 × 1.30 m	269 kg
100 m³	11.65 × 8.19 m	10.91 × 7.45 × 1.30 m	312 kg
120 m³	11.60 × 9.57 m	10.86 × 8.84 × 1.30 m	361 kg
150 m³	11.99 × 10.95 m	11.22 × 10.18 × 1.35 m	425 kg
200 m³	15.67 × 10.95 m	14.90 × 10.18 × 1.35 m	551 kg
300 m³	17.65 × 13.71 m	16.85 × 12.91 × 1.40 m	769 kg

As part of the US Army's Hippo programme, WEW is currently under contract to supply in excess of 60 2,000 US gallon (7,570-litre) capacity Load Handling System (LHS) compatible tank racks to prime contractor Mil-Mar Century Corporation of the US. This Hippo tank rack is being transported by a MAN SX range Multi (8 × 8) truck at DVD 2006 (Shaun C Connors)   1156030

During 2004, Belgium received in excess of 20 16,000-litre storage optimised potable water Special Tank Containers, and these are transported on low-mobility IVECO EuroTrakker (8 × 4) chassis (WEW Westerwälder Eisenwerk GmbH)   1156044

Other users of WEW Special Tank Containers include Belgium, Ireland, the US and the UK. As part of the US Army's Hippo programme, WEW is currently under contract to supply in excess of 470 × 2,000 US gallon (7,570-litre) capacity load handling system compatible tank racks to prime contractor Mil-Mar Century Corporation of the US. Full details of the Hippo system can be found in the Load Handling System (LHS) compatible water tank rack system (Hippo) entry elsewhere in this section.

Description

Unless specific contract requirements specify otherwise, all WEW Special Tank Containers are designed to be compatible with the commercial ISO transport envelope. All WEW Special Tank Containers are fully legal for global commercial transport and handling (including China, Japan and the US), and have been designed to ISO 1496-3, with prototype and impact tests. Each tank container has a six-fold welded ring system for increased stability and for protection from corrosion and also a low tare weight, for example, the 20 ft container with 26,000-litre capacity has a tare weight of 2,900 kg.

Tanks for specific military usage are purpose-designed to be capable of withstanding operational handling and transport in rough terrain. For German Army applications, certain examples are transportable by a load handling system-equipped vehicle, such as the MAN SX range Multi (8 × 8). For US Army applications, the water tank container Hippo is designed for handling by (8 × 8) M1120 (HEMTT-LHS) and (10 × 10) M1074/M1075 PLS trucks and M1076 PLS trailers. The Belgian Army transports its 16,000-litre capacity containers on low-mobility IVECO EuroTrakker (8 × 4) chassis.

WEW potable water tanks can be equipped with electrical heating, chlorination units, a UV radiation unit and pressure increasing units (double pump) to provide for both the transport and storage of potable water and the independent supply of medical, sanitary and kitchen components in a field camp.

WEW has also developed modular ISO-compatible pumping/stowage and tank units in lengths of 5, 10, 15 and 20 ft, and while the 5 and 15 ft lengths are not standard ISO lengths, all other dimensions of these units remain ISO compatible, so when they are used modularly with certain other components, full ISO handling/transport is possible.

Status

In production. Approximately 500 assorted tank containers in service (fuel and/or water) with Belgian, German, Irish, Lithuanian, Slovenian, UK and US armed forces.

Contractor

WEW Westerwälder Eisenwerk GmbH

India

DRDO (Engineers) water purification equipment

Development

This water purification equipment was designed and developed to meet Indian defence force requirements by the Defence Research and Development Organisation (Engineers), Dighi, Pune and as a mobile unit it is in service with the armed forces of India.

Once set up, the system can supply up to 13,500 litres of filtered and chlorinated potable water per hour to troops directly from natural sources including rivers, canals, wells and ponds.

Description

The equipment is skid-mounted and may be transported by any suitable capacity truck or trailer. It has been designed to be operable in a variety of terrain extremes including desert and marshland, and at altitudes of up to 4,400 m above sea level. It takes 30 minutes for the equipment to become operational after positioning at a suitable water source.

The equipment consists of a pumping set, a filter unit, filter-aider and sterilisation unit and is capable of removing all coliform bacteria and reducing the turbidity of raw water from 50 ppm to 5 ppm.

Raw water is first sterilised by electrolysis with the help of platinised titanium electrodes. The water is then passed through a filter. Suspended impurities are removed and clear water is available. Removal of entrapped particles from the filter is achieved by reversal of water flow; by monitoring back-pressure.

Status

In service with the Indian Army.

Development agency

Research and Development Establishment (Engineers)

Tank Fabric Collapsible Mk 1

Description

Tank Fabric Collapsible Mk 1 is available is three differing sizes and is intended for the storage of water in field areas. The main body of the tank is made from canvas flax (tow), with the tank base being reinforced with 610 g duck cotton. The rim of the tank is provided with pockets filled with Kapok so that the rim floats at any level of water in the tank. A cover made of canvas flax (tow) is provided.

Specifications

Capacity	Base diameter	Cover diameter
6,140 litres	3.6 m	3.5 m
2,300 litres	2.57 m	2.3 m
230 litres	914 mm	760 mm

Status

In production. In service with the Indian Army. Offered for export.

Contractor

Not known

Enquiries to

Ordnance Factory Board

Israel

Achidatex collapsible water containers

Development

Since 1977 Achidatex has produced the Achidatank range of collapsible containers suitable for the storage, distribution and transport of water, fuels, chemicals and other liquids intolerant of contamination. Full details of products suited to fuel transportation and distribution can be found in the Bulk fuel storage and distributions systems section.

Description

The Achidatex pillow tank is produced in sizes ranging from 1,000 to 100,000 US gallons (3,758 to 378,500 litres) and is constructed from a polyester reinforced membrane fabric that conforms to US military specifications and is approved by the US Food and Drug Administration.

A typical Achidatex pillow tank (Achidatex)   1047910

The collapsible Drop Container range is constructed from a reinforced, coated fabric and has capacities ranging from 50 to 500 US gallons (189 to 1,892 litres). These collapsible cylinders can be pressure-filled with water (or gasoline, jet fuel and avgas) and can be transported by a variety of methods, including helicopters. When empty Drop Containers collapse to approximately 15 per cent of their filled size. Drop Containers are no longer manufactured by Achidatex.

Status
Pillow tanks in production, Drop Containers no longer produced. Pillow tanks and Drop Containers in service with Israeli armed forces.

Contractor
Achidatex

Chemoplast collapsible water storage and transport tanks

Development
Chemoplast Industries Ltd produced a range of collapsible storage and transport tanks, plus a range of dry storage systems that are detailed in the Other equipment section. Chemoplast Industries Ltd was acquired by Defense Industries International in 2005. Achidatex, a subsidiary of Defense Industries International also produces ranges of storage and transport tanks, plus a range of dry storage systems. Details of Achidatex products, which now encompass Chemoplast products, can be found in their related sections.

Description
Chemoplast Industries Ltd produced a range of collapsible storage and transport tanks with capacities from 500 to 300,000 litres. These tanks are made from a variety of coated flexible plastic materials and are suitable for the storage and/or transport of a wide range of liquids including fuels (including gasoline, diesel, oil and kerosene) and potable water. Details of those tanks suited to the transport and/or storage of fuel can be found in the Bulk fuel storage and distribution systems section.

Chemoplast stationary collapsible fuel tanks were available in sizes ranging from 500 to 300,000 litres, while mobile collapsible tanks were available in sizes ranging from 500 to 20,000 litres. All tanks were supplied with filling and emptying fittings to suit customer requirements and contents.

Status
In service with the Israeli Air Force, Army and Navy.

Contractor
Defense Industries International Inc. (previous known as Chemoplast Industries Limited)

Korea, South

Mobilised Reverse Osmosis Water Purification Unit (ROWPU)

Development
KyongChang Inc. was established in December 1984 and completed its first commercial reverse osmosis system in October 1985. In 1993, the ROK Navy granted type-approval for a reverse osmosis fresh water generator and in 1998 the ROK Army granted type-approval for the ROWPU. KyongChang Inc was renamed KROSYS Inc. in May 2000. In June 2002, KROSYS became a ROK government designated defence item exporter.

Description
KROSYS Inc. ROWPU systems are the standard system of their type employed by the ROK Army and Marines and in excess of 50 units have been supplied.

ROWPU is designed to be capable of supplying reliable drinking water from all sources and with a variety of contaminants ranging from natural through to nuclear, biological or chemical.

Three systems are available, the KRO-060-MM, KRO-150-MM and the KRO-300-MM. Designations refer to the product flow rate per hour. i.e. KRO-060-MM, 600 gallons per hour. Each system is deployed, operated, maintained and packed by two personnel.

The KRO-060-MM is installed on a KM25 Series 2.5 ton (6 × 6) truck and the KRO-150-MM is installed on a KM50 Series 5 ton (6 × 6) truck. Each truck tows a power-supplying generator set on a two-wheel, single-axle trailer. The KRO-300-MM is a containerised system and comes with an integral power supply. The KRO-300-MM may also be installed on a semi-trailer.

KROSYS Mobilised Reverse Osmosis Water Purification Unit (ROWPU) of the South Korean Army (Gordon Arthur)   1296198

	KRO-060-MM/TD	KRO-150-MM	KRO-300-MM
Weight: (drained)	2,900 kg	4,500 kg	6,700 kg
Length:	3.7 m	4.5 m	6.1 m
Width:	2.4 m	2.4 m	2.4 m
Height:	2.5 m	2.5 m	2.5 m
Crew:	2	2	2
Product flow rate:[1]	2,300 litres/h	5,700 litres/h	113,500 litres/h
Energy consumption:	2.5 kW-h/m^3	2.1 kW-h/m^3	1.8 kW-h/m^3
Power requirement: (220 V, 3-phase, 60 Hz)	8 kW	15 kW	28 kW
Max gradient:	10°	10°	10°
Max sideslope:	10°	10°	10°

[1] At feed water of 25°C and 1,500 ppm TDS.

KROSYS Mobilised Reverse Osmosis Water Purification Unit (ROWPU) of the South Korean Army (Gordon Arthur) 1296199

Specifications
See table at bottom of previous page

Status
In production. In service with the ROK Army and Marines (>50 units)

Contractor
KROSYS Inc.

Netherlands

Promac Aquaset MLT mobile drinking water units

Description
The Promac Aquaset MLT mobile drinking water units use a specially developed and patented combination of membrane separation and other purification techniques to produce high-quality water from any source of contaminated surface water. Two sets are available.

Set 1, the Aquaset MLT MDI was designed to produce clean water from sources polluted by NBC agents and systems are also available for brackish and seawater feed sources. The first unit was designed and built in co-operation with the TNO PML Royal Netherlands Army Research Laboratory and underwent an initial two-year period of laboratory and field testing. In 2001 a new mobile drinking water unit was developed by Promac. This used the latest technology in pretreatment and process control. Several of these later units are currently operational with Dutch forces in UN-Peacekeeping areas worldwide.

Set 2, the Aquaset Mini-Modu was developed for the Royal Netherlands Navy. This Aquaset is derived from the Aquaset MLT MDI but produces 600 litres/h and measures 2.5 × 1.32 × 1.36 m. The unit is supplied in an insulated container for operations in cold environments.

Status
In service with Royal Netherlands armed forces.

Contractor
Promac BV

Poland

Container-based water purification unit KSUW-6/8

Description
The KSUW-6/8 (Kontenerowa Stacja Uzdatniania Wody) is designed to treat and return to potable quality raw water containing both natural contaminants and NBC agents. The system is STANAG compliant, and is therefore suited for use not only by armed forces but also by fire departments and other emergency relief units/organisations. It can also be used as an emergency water source for hospitals and so on. The produced water meets the standards of STANAG 2136 (MED).

The KSUW-6/8 is contained in standard 14 or 20 ft PN-83/K-4610 containers with lifting eyes. The 20 ft container variant can be transported

Demonstration use of the Water Purification Station KSUW-6/8 (Wojskowe Zaklady Inzynieryjne) 1180259

on suitable capacity flatbed trucks, a DROPS/PLS-type flatrack or a flatbed trailer, while the 14 ft container version is compact enough for transport by a Star 200 series (4 × 4) truck or similar 4,500 kg truck. The 20 ft container variant comes complete with a crew rest area.

The KSUW-6/8 consists of the following sub-components:
- Container
- Stainless steel filtration/coagulation columns
- Stainless steel absorption columns
- Flow control board
- Treatment agents dosing tanks
- Stainless steel piping
- Stainless steel jet pump
- A set of ¾-inch (19 mm) suction/pumping hoses
- A set of 2-inch (50.8 mm) suction/pumping hoses
- Main control panel
- Accessory storage cabinet
- Equipment storage cabinet
- Heater
- Power generator Ü220/230 V; N = 2.2 kW
- Internal combustion engine driven water pump Q = 500 l/m; Ht = 50 m; Hs 8 m
- Electrical circuits (utility and lighting)
- Air circulation system

Accessories available include:
- Raw/product water testing kit ZOST-90
- A set of suction hoses with brass connectors
- A set of pumping hoses with brass connectors
- A stainless steel branched connector with brass fittings
- 7552 fire fighting-type brass connectors
- Suction baskets and floats
- Connector wrench set
- Lighting support mast, 3.5 m

The Unit complies with STANAG 2136 (MED), STANAG 2885 (ENGR), Polish Ministry of Health Regulation of April 5, 1990 and container standards PN-ISO 1496 and PN-ISO-668.

Specifications
Number of filtration/coagulation columns: 5
Number of absorption columns: 2
Product water flow rate: 6-8 m³/h
Type of purification process: flow, continuous
Operating pressure: 0.35 MPa
Suction line length: up to 15 m
Pumping line length: up to 60 m
Fuel usage: 1 l/h
Set-up time: approx 30 min
Time from set-up to initial water flow: 20-30 min
Break-down time: approx 40 min
Crew: 2
External dimensions:
(length) 4.265 m (14 ft ISO)
(length) 6.085 m (20 ft ISO)
(width) 2.438 m
(height) 2.591 m
Operating temperatures:
(raw water) +1 to +30°C (274-303°K)
(ambient air) -30 to +50 C (243-323°K)
Operating weight: 4,260 kg (14 ft ISO)

Status
Production as required.

Contractor
Wojskowe Zaklady Inzynieryjne (WZINZ)

Russian Federation

Mobile well-drilling equipment

Description
These mobile drilling rig sets are currently available for export sale and are most likely in service with Russian Federation armed forces, and others. Designations identify the maximum well depth that can be drilled, that is, 50 m for the PBU-50m set.

PBU-50m mobile drilling rig set
PBU-50m mobile drilling rig set is used to drill temporary and permanent water supply boreholes and wells. The complete set includes: a drilling rig with mud pump and two compressors mounted on a Ural-4320 series (6 × 6) truck chassis (previously the Zil-131 chassis has been used), two trailers with a set of spares, drilling tools and jigs; an auxiliary truck with a set of pipes, spares and accessories. Transport speed is restricted to 70 km/h.

Boreholes are drilled using augers. Temporary and permanent drill wells of up to 200 mm diameter in ground of up to category IV density, and shaft wells of up to 1 m diameter in ground of up to category III density can be created.

A number of upgrades to improve the overall performance of the PBU-50m system are known to be available.

PBU-150m mobile drilling rig set
The PBU-150m mobile drilling rig set is essentially a larger and more capable variant of the PBU-50m mobile drilling rig set. Like the PBU-50m set, the PBU-150m set is used to drill temporary and permanent water supply boreholes and wells.

The complete PBU-150m set includes: a drilling rig with mud pump and two compressors mounted on a Ural-4320 series (6 × 6) truck chassis, two trailers with a set of spares, drilling tools and jigs; an auxiliary truck with a set of pipes, spares and accessories

PBU-200m mobile drilling rig
The PBU-200m mobile drilling rig provides underground water production by completing temporary and permanent drill wells in rocks of up category VI density. The complete rig includes: a drilling unit, a pumping unit, a pumping and compressor unit, a hydraulic crane, a generating unit, water intake and welding equipment, drilling and auxiliary equipment, and three KrAZ-260G LWB (6 × 6) trucks.

The rig design relies on the use of a combined drilling and temporary well completion technology that involves using drill pipes as casings. The drill design allows both cable tool and rotation drilling with clay drilling mud flushing.

Specifications

	PBU-50m	PBU-100m	PBU-200m
Weight	18,050 kg	67,500 kg	87,400 kg
Crew	4	3	5
Drilling depth			
(well)	50 m	100 m	200 m
(abyssinian well)	15 m	20 m	n/app
Drilling time (to max depth) (h)			
(well)	5–15 h	n/avail	72-120 h
(abyssinian well)	10–15 h	n/avail	n/app
Closure time	2–3 h	2	2
Pumping out capacity (m³/h)	9.5	pump dependant	10–12

Part of a PBU-50m mobile drilling rig set (James Kinnear)   0400003

LBU-200 mobile well-drilling equipment
The LBU-200 mobile well-drilling equipment is known to be in service with the armed forces of the Russian Federation, and possibly others, and is it is believed the PBU-200m mobile drilling rig is an improvement of this system.

The LBU-200 is capable of drilling for water, testing its purity and providing limited storage capacity. The equipment is mounted on three KrAZ-255B (6 × 6) 7,500 kg trucks and three 2-PN-6M trailers. One truck is fitted with the drilling rig, while a second carries the LGR-3 laboratory. The third truck, fitted with a hydraulic loading crane, carries hose, purification equipment and other ancillaries. RBD-5000 water tank components are carried on the trailers.

Status
PBU-50m, PBU-150m and PBU-200m are available for export sales and are likely to be in service with the armed forces of the Russian Federation and others. LBU-200 is in service with the armed forces of the Russian Federation and possibly others.

Contractor
Not known.

Enquiries to:
Rosoboronexport.

SKO-03, SKO-1 and SKO-8 integrated water treatment plants

Description
These treatment plants are designed to clean water from natural impurities, toxic, radioactive and bacterial agents and strong poisons. Designations reflect the capacity per hour of respective units: that is, SKO-1, 1 m³/h.

The complete equipment set of one plant (SKO-1 and SKO-8) includes: a water intake, ultrafiltration unit, pump, germicidal lamp unit, absorption filter, microfiltration unit, and SPTA set. Water is purified by passing through the ultrafiltration unit, absorption filter, the microfiltration unit, and is disinfected in a germicidal lamp unit. Power is supplied from an external source, usually a mobile generator. Power requirements are 380 V, 5 kW (SKO-1) and 12 kW (SKO-8). The entire plant is housed in a purpose-designed ISO-dimensioned container and is stated to be transported by a KAMAZ-4310 (6 × 6) truck, however the KAMAZ-3410 has been replaced in production by the similar but revised KAMAZ-43114 (SWB) and KAMAZ-43118 (LWB) (6 × 6) trucks. The weights and overall dimensions of the SKO-1 integrated water treatment plant suggest that it could be carried by a smaller, possibly 4 × 4, truck such as the KAMAZ-4326 or GAZ-3308 Sadko.

Specifications

	SKO-1	SKO-8
Weight	1,600 kg	4,400 kg
Length	2.5 m	4.7 m
Width	1.140 m	2.23 m
Height	1.8 m	2.25 m
Capacity (m³/h)	1	8
Crew	2	2–4
Deployment time	12 min	12 min
Closure time	12 min	12 min
Concentration reduction ratio		
(toxic agents)	100	100
(radioactive agents)	1,000	1,000
(bacterial agents)	106	106
(strong poisons)	10	10
Service life (h)		
(ultrafiltration units, raw water with a turbidity of up to 100 mg/dm³/h)	1,000	2,500
(absorption filter)	600	1,000
Replacement times (h)		
(sorbent)	3	4
(ultrafiltration units)	1	2.5

SKO-03 integrated water treatment plant
Limited information is available on a smaller system, the SKO-03. This has a capacity of 0.3 m³/h and a power requirement of 0.5 kW. Deployment and closure times are 12 minutes each, and a crew of two is required. Time between filter element changes is 200 to 600 h dependent on a number of factors. No other information is available.

Status
These systems are currently offered for export and some or all may be in service with Russian Federation armed forces.

Contractor
Not known.

Enquiries to
Rosoboronexport.

Water filtering and purifying plants

Description
The armed forces of the Russian Federation, former members of the Warsaw Pact and its allies employ a number of water filtering and purifying systems supplied by the former Soviet Union. Many of these are now technically obsolete or will be reaching the end of their usable/storage life in the near future.

Limited details are available on a number of systems that are currently being offered for export sale, and some of these systems are likely to be in service with the armed forces of the Russian Federation and possibly others.

Filtering plants
The MAFS-3, VFS-2.5 and VFS-10 filtering plants are mobile plants mounted on cross-country truck chassis for autonomy, with respective weights of 10,700, 2,800 and 14,400 kg dictating the likely transport vehicle. All required ancillary equipment, spare parts and accessories are carried in an accompanying trailer. The complete plant set includes a motor-driven pump, reservoirs, chemical water treatment reagents, and field water quality laboratories.

These filtering plants are described as offering the capability for water purification of natural contaminants and its disinfection and neutralisation of toxic compounds in field conditions.

Specifications

	MAFS-3	VFS-2.5	VFS-10
Weight	10,700 kg	2,800 kg	14,400 kg
Capacity	7–8 m³/h	2.5 m³/h	10 m³/h
Crew	5	3	4
Deployment time	90–150 min	30 min	90–120 min
Closure time	60–90 min	15 min	42 min
Time between filter element changes (h)	20–100	100	100

PVU-300 portable water purifying plant
The PVU-300 is described as a portable water purifying plant, although at a weight of 87 kg would require transport either in a trailer or a light vehicle. It also requires a 0.95 kW electrical power supply to operate.

The system is capable of purifying water in field conditions from natural impurities, toxic and radioactive agents, as well as bacterial agents and strong poisons. Basic specifications are as follows:

Specifications
Weight: 87 kg
Capacity: 300 l/h
Crew: 2
Deployment time: 12 min
Closure time: 12 min
Time between filter element changes: 600 h

Status
These systems are currently offered for export and some or all may be in service with Russian Federation armed forces or others (see text).

Contractor
Not known.

Enquiries to
Rosoboronexport

Mobile water desalination plants OPS and POU

Description
These mobile water desalination plants were produced mainly for use in desert and coastal regions and both are deployed/transported on truck chassis.

The OPS has a capacity of 1,800 to 2,200 litres/h and water salt content is reduced to acceptable drinking, manufacturing and sanitary levels by water vaporisation followed by condensation. Deployment time, with a standard crew of three, is quoted as varying between 90 and 360 minutes, with a closure time of 30 minutes. Filter elements require changing every 200 to 300 hours of operation. Power for the OPS is provided by a towed generator.

It is understood that the later OPS-5 mobile water desalinating plant is the intended eventual replacement for the OPS. Full details of the OPS-5 can be found elsewhere in this section.

The POU is the smaller of the two units; this is powered by a petrol engine and has an output capacity of 320 litres/h.

Status
In service with the armed forces of the Russian Federation.

Contractor
Former state factories.

Mobile water desalination plant OPS-5

Description
The OPS-5 mobile water distillation plant is intended to purify, desalinate, neutralise and disinfect water. It is understood OPS-5 is to eventually replace the earlier OPS (and possibly POU), details of which can be found elsewhere in section.

The complete equipment is carried in a special purpose van body mounted on a KrAZ-260 (6 × 6) truck. Included is a 17 kW generator, driven by the engine of the carrier vehicle, water purification and desalination units, filters, pumps, RDV-5000 storage tanks and auxiliary equipment, including spares, tools and accessories. On arrival at a site, the equipment is quoted to take 12 minutes to prepare for use; strip-down time is one hour. OPS-5 can be operated for 100 hours using the equipment carried on the vehicle; time between filter element replacements is quoted as 5,000 hours. At 22 litres/h fuel consumption, OPS-5 requires four to five times less fuel to operate than the earlier OPS, while producing a purer end product.

Water is purified and desalinated in a system of tanks. Raw water is chlorinated and, after sedimentation, is forced by pumps through a purification unit, an absorption filter and a water desalination unit; reverse osmosis techniques are involved.

The output capacity varies according to the salt or other impurity level of the raw water source. Water with a salt content of 2 to 6 g/litre will result in a capacity of 5 to 6 m³/h. This will drop to 1.8 to 3 m³/h when the raw water salt content is as large as 18 to 35 g/litre.

Specifications
Crew: 4
Weight: 21,600 kg
Length: 10.13 m
Width: 2.875 m
Height: 3.34 m
Fuel consumption: 22 litres/h

Status
In service with the armed forces of the Russian Federation.

Contractor
Polymerfiltr JSC

Marketing agency
Rosoboronexport.

Mobile water distillation plant OPS-5 mounted on a KrAZ-260 (6 × 6) truck
0009997

South Africa

World Focus Flexitanks collapsible water storage and transport bladders

Description
World Focus Flexitanks manufactures storage tanks and transport bladders for commercial, military and aid agency applications. These rubber storage and transport bladders range in capacity from 400 to 100,000 litres. A variety of liquids can be transported, these ranging from potable water to petrol, diesel or aircraft fuels.

Temperature tolerance ranges from −30°C to +70°C. Specific-to-application tank sizes are available, as are a variety of fittings for filling, discharge, transport and handling purposes.

Similar products have been produced by a number of legacy companies

Status
In service with the South African National Defence Force (SANDF) and possibly other undisclosed countries.

Contractor
World Focus Flexitank

Waterbuffel water treatment system

Description
The Waterbuffel (Water Buffalo) water treatment system is carried in a standard 3 m container and can be placed on level ground next to a source of raw water to generate up to 3,500 litres/h of fresh water. The system includes pretreatment, filtering and chlorination stages. Processed water can be stored within storage tanks until it is required.

For transportation the system can be carried on a SAMIL 20 (4 × 4) 2,000 kg truck or any 3,000 kg flatbed truck. It can also be towed using a set of transporter wheels. The container is equipped with lifting eyes for handling.

Status
In service with the South African National Defence Force (SANDF).

Enquiries to
Armscor

United Kingdom

PDTM Water Carriage Packs (WCP)

Development
PDTM Water Carriage Packs (WCP) were developed to carry drinking water to British Army units in the field, replacing all previous tanks in service.

Description
The basic unit of a WCP is a 680 litre polyethylene tank which can be provided with a variety of delivery hoses, a restraint frame, dispenser manifolds and lashing arrangements. The tank includes a manhole for cleaning.

The WCP can be used on standard 750 kg and 1,750 kg trailers, Land Rovers and 4,000/6,000 kg trucks as well as other vehicles. An empty WCP can be lifted by two people.

Status
In production. In service with the British Army.

Contractor
PD Rotomouldings

A PDTM Water Carriage Pack in use (PD Rotomouldings)   0044600

Pre-Mac water purification equipment

Development
Pre-Mac designs and manufactures water purification equipment ranging from personal survival units right up to containerised bulk systems for civil, military, aid agencies and emergency rescue services.

Example of a Pre-Mac Water Storage Tank (WST) (Pre-Mac)   0101931

Interior of a Pre-Mac Water Control Centre (WCC) (Pre-Mac)   1111157

Pre-Mac Water Control Centre (WCC) (Pre-Mac)   1344641

Description

Bulk water treatment systems
Pre-Mac International has developed systems to treat and store water in bulk to cater for large camps and communities. The Water Control Centre (WCC) is a self-contained water treatment, purification and distribution plant, based on a standard 20 ft ISO platform. It employs 'plug and play' technology to permit rapid deployment and re-deployment and requires minimal ground preparation before siting. The Water Storage Tank (WST) is fully complementary to the WCC and is also based on a standard 20 ft ISO platform. The 24,000-litre capacity WST is fully insulated and can be supplied with a thermostatically controlled heating system to accommodate extreme temperature environments. The WST can be used as a stand-alone item for the storage of raw, treated and waste water, or can be used in multiples forming tank farms.

Group water purifiers, models JWP4, JWP8 and SW8
Pre-Mac International's group water purifiers have been designed to provide safe, clean potable water from any contaminated freshwater source. The complete range is NATO codified and are portable and

Pre-Mac group water purifier model JWP8 in use (Pre-Mac)   0101923

suitable for use by mobile groups and early entry deployments. They can be set up quickly and easily by a single person. In standard format, the JWP models are fitted with a high-performance hand pump and the Dual version is equipped with an electric pump for use where power is available as well as a hand pump. These units can be specified for both AC and DC supplies with voltages to suit available power supplies. The SW8 model is powered by four solar panels incorporating photovoltaic cells providing 12 V power and is also equipped with the high-performance hand pump to allow operation in low-light situations. These models can be supplied with a water meter to allow monitoring of throughput.

Safe drinking water can be produced from sources contaminated with high levels of bacteria, viruses and parasites. These units also remove organic matter, improving the taste, smell and appearance of treated water. In use they treat water via filtration and an additional disinfection process.

A range of hand-held units, employing similar technology to the group range, is also available for emergency water treatment by the individual soldier when away from camp.

Status
In production. In service with UK Armed Forces.

Contractor
Pre-Mac International Limited.

Oshkosh Wheeled Tanker (Close Support Tanker (Water))

Development
Oshkosh Truck Corporation announced in January 2003 that it had been selected as the preferred bidder by the UK's then Defence Procurement Agency (DPA) to supply the MoD's Wheeled Tanker fleet. The contract was valued at approximately GBP160 million (USD250 million) for initial vehicle acquisition and support over 15 years. It was originally stated by the DPA that the Wheeled Tanker fleet would replace all existing tri-service vehicle types used for the bulk distribution of fuel on deployed operations.

The Wheeled Tanker programme can trace its origins back to the earlier Future Fuel Vehicle (FFV) programme which was proposed for procurement under the terms of the UK government's Private Finance Initiative (PFI). The Future Cargo Vehicle (FCV) and Future Wheeled Recovery Vehicle (FWRV) projects were also proposed as PFI programmes. FFV was advertised as a PFI in January 1998, with FCV following in August 1998 and FWRV in September 1999. FFV and FCV went through a pre-qualification phase to select a shortlist of potential bidders who would then be invited to submit outline proposals. At the time of the outline proposal assessment (early 2000) the projected in-service date for FFV was 2003.

On 21 March 2001, a government press release announced that PFI options would not be pursued for the FFV, FCV or FWRV programmes, making it clear that in these cases PFI would not be appropriate and was unlikely to provide best value for money. Under the proposed PFI procurement there were three potential bidders for FFV: Fastflow (Brown & Root (now KBR) and Volvo); Excalibur Logistics (Multidrive, Excel Logistics, BAE Systems - Lex had previously withdrawn from this consortium), and Tactacon (Oshkosh Truck Corporation and Ryder - the now BAE Systems, after acquiring Unipower, having sold the then Alvis Unipower place to Oshkosh).

Following the March 2001 announcement to abandon PFI procurement, in April 2001 the FFV, FCV and FWRV programmes were re-launched with

a number of amendments as conventional asset-based procurements. FFV now included a highlighted operations requirement for bulk potable water tankers and was renamed as the Wheeled Tanker requirement, while the FCV and FWRV were merged to form the Support Vehicle requirement. Following the announcement that asset-based procurement was to be adopted, Volvo withdrew from the Wheeled Tanker and Support Vehicle programmes.

The original intention was that Wheeled Tanker would replace all existing tri-service vehicle types used for the bulk distribution of fuel and deployed operations. This did not include airfield-based aircraft refuellers or the truck-transportable UBRE (Unit Bulk Refuelling Equipment) system (full details of which can be found elsewhere in this section). The latter to be replaced by the Unit Support Tanker (UST) element of the Support Vehicle programme. In a replacement process were also engaged the Foden low mobility tanker fleet, the General Support Tanker (GST) fleet, and the then Tactical Aircraft Refueller (TAR).

The Foden low mobility fleet originally consisted of 2508 × 422,500 litre low mobility and 1836 × 412,000 litre improved low mobility tankers delivered during the late 1970s and early 1980s. As of May 2001, 137 (8 × 4)s and 160 (6 × 4)s remained serviceable and in use; all have now been withdrawn from service. The current GST is a road-going 32,500 litre capacity articulated vehicle tractored by a (6 × 4) Seddon Atkinson unit. The then 170 vehicle TAR fleet was 2,000 litre capacity Bedford MJ-based (4 × 4)s and had recently been refurbished and fitted with improved cabs from the Bedford MT range of trucks. These vehicles did not have the capacity to service the British Army's Apache attack helicopter. Further details of the GST can be found in the Trucks section.

At the time of shortlisting the Wheeled Tanker requirement called for a total of 437 vehicles made up of: 259 × 20,000 litre Close Support Tanker (CST); 86 × 12,000 litre Tactical Aircraft Refueller (TAR); 43 × 18,000 litre Close Support Tanker (Water) (CST(W)), and 49 × 30,000 litre General Support Tanker (GST). It was also stated by the DPA that should additional tankers be justified, funds made available, totals could rise to 742 vehicles made up of: 355 CST; 104 TAR; 43 CST(W), and 240 GST. Contract award figures would be 218 × 20,000 litre CST; 82 × 15,000 litre TAR, and 48 × 18,000 litre CST(W).

Deliveries of the Wheeled Tanker commenced in February 2005 and were scheduled for completion by November 2006. A contract option for an additional nine CST(W) was subsequently exercised. The requirement for a 30,000-litre GST was not received as part of the Wheeled Tanker contract due to the fact that the in-service Seddon Atkinson vehicles remained compliant with legislation and had not yet reached the end of their anticipated service lives.

The other current major fuel asset of the British Army is the Foden-fronted Multidrive tanker fleet. The British Army also operated a fleet of seven 20,000 litre Multidrive potable water tankers procured in 1999. These, and the fuel tankers, have now been withdrawn from service.

For all three variants involved in the Wheeled Tanker contract, Oshkosh Truck as prime contractor is supplying a frameless monocoque stainless steel semi-trailer tanker manufactured by the Magyar SA of France with pumping equipment supplied by Magyar (water) or Alfons Haar of Germany (fuel). Oshkosh Truck also supplied a quantity of riot protection kits, and all vehicles are fitted for but not with an appliqué protection kit developed by Israel's Plasan Sasa. This kit is similar to the one developed for the USMC MTVRs. Additional protection including bar armour, a protected weapon station and electronic countermeasures equipment have been fitted to vehicles deployed to Afghanistan and Iraq. A signature management kit manufactured by GMA Cover Corp has also been procured.

Wheeled Tanker tractor trucks are a variant of the Oshkosh MTVR (Medium Tactical Vehicle Replacement). Full details can be found in the Trucks section.

Description
All versions of the Oshkosh (6 × 6) Medium Tactical Vehicle Replacement (MTVR) are based on the same 6 × 6 drive configuration with the engine under a forward non-corroding and weight-saving fibreglass bonnet. The standard three-seat cab is of welded aluminium extrusion construction with adhesive bonded aluminium skins. The aluminium hinged windscreen, roof, side-walls, door frames and rear wall can be folded down to reduce overall height to 2.489 m. A larger crew-type cab (extended by 660 mm) in which a rear that doubles up as additional seating or bunks for two is fitted to the Wheeled Tanker.

The MTVR chassis frame is constructed by using bolted/Huck fastener-bolted formed channel (248 × 76 × 9.7 mm) made of heat-treated carbon manganese steel with a yield strength of 758 MPa. Wheeled Tanker variants are based on the MK23 MTVR with a 330 mm reduction in wheelbase and 1.018 m reduction in overall length. Both cab and chassis feature extensive corrosion protection, while the US Marines requiring the MTVR, should have sufficient corrosion protection to ensure an effective service life of 22 years.

All MTVR variants are powered by a Caterpillar C-12, ADEM (Advanced Diesel Engine Management) III 11.9-litre six-cylinder in-line turbocharged and water-cooled four-stroke, diesel. For the UK requirement this has been uprated (from 425 hp) to develop 445 hp at 1,700 rpm and upgraded to meet EURO III emissions requirements. Peak torque remains 2,101 N.m at 1,200 rpm. Maximum sustainable speed on paved roads is restricted to 85 km/h; cruising range is 500 km. A three-stage (two-, four- or six-

From the rear, an Oshkosh Wheeled Tanker 18,000 litre Close Support Tanker (Water) (CST(W)) variant (Patrick Allen)   1067550

cylinder) manually selected, automatically applied engine compression brake is fitted to assist the braking system.

The engine is coupled to a Wheeled Tanker specific Allison HD 4560P 6F/1R 'wide ratio' unit (this replaces the standard Allison HD 4070P 7F/1R unit) and Oshkosh 30000 series single-speed transfer box. The combination of torque converter and a low ratio first gear allows for a single-speed transfer box to replace the more complex two-speed unit more commonly associated with off-road vehicles. Full-time all-wheel drive is employed and under highway driving conditions the torque split is 32 per cent front, 68 per cent rear.

The combination of Oshkosh TAK-4 independent coil spring suspension, a central tyre inflation (CTI) system, and a traction control system supplemented by manually-controlled differential locks on all axles, enables the tractor unit (while towing an undriven and laden semi-trailer) to achieve a level of off-road mobility acceptable to the UK MoD. The tractor truck can ford 1.5 m of water (with preparation), climb a 34 per cent gradient with a laden trailer and has a climatic operational range of between -32°C (with winterisation kits from -46°C) and +49°C. A purpose-designed 88.9 mm (3.5 in) fully oscillating fifth wheel (40° forward; 25° after; 5° each side) supplied by Holland Neway is fitted. This enables the required angles of articulation to be achieved between the tractor truck and the semi-trailer for operations such as embarking/disembarking a landing craft.

MTVR is fitted with 1600R 20 Michelin XZL super singles tyres. The trailer-mounted spare wheel will fit either truck or trailer. There is also an emergency runflat setting option on the MTVR's CTI system (there is no CTI system for the trailer). A CTI system allows the driver to adjust tyre pressures to suit terrain conditions while there are four settings available: highway; cross-country; mud/sand/snow; and emergency. In an emergency, the MTVR system can be directed to continuously inflate one tyre only. The 508 × 254 mm two-piece bolt-together steel wheel rims are fitted with beadlocks for extreme low-pressure operations and tyres remain seated at pressures down to 10 psi. In the event that any one tyre should totally fail , a limp-home facility allows for a second axle suspension unit to be raised and secured, while its wheel is rolled and fitted in the position of the damaged tyre.

To assist with vehicle repairs and diagnosis an On Board Diagnostic System (OBDS) features an information display screen and fault indicators from the engine, transmission, ABS, ATC and CTI. It also has a laptop interface that allows access to the full MTVR database for in-the-field maintenance, diagnostics and repair.

Wheeled Tanker is air-transportable in C-5, C-17, A400M and AN-124 aircraft.

18,000 litre Close Support Tanker (Water) (CST(W))
The 18,000 litre capacity tank and its associated pumping equipment are manufactured by Magyar SA of France.

The single compartment tank is manufactured from 4.5 mm hot-rolled AISI 316L stainless steel and fitted with two lateral and two longitudinal baffles. Standard equipment includes a contents gauge with an external reading display. A single 500 mm diameter hinged fill cover is fitted. In addition, a rear access door is fitted for inspection and cleaning purposes. All piping is of stainless steel, welded with flanged or threaded connections.

Two BPW Model 10110 E36.1 Eco Plus tubular non-driving axles are used. These are rated at 10,000 kg each and have a track width of 2.095 m. Tyres are 1600R 20 Michelin XZLs and a single spare is carried. Air-operated drum-type brakes are fitted with the parking brake working on the first axle. The braking system is interlocked with the water handling system.

The Magyar pumping system features a self-priming stainless steel water pump with a 1,000 l/min capacity.

Winterised variants have a climatic operational range (pumping) of -32 to +49°C.

Overall semi-trailer length is 10.5 m and gross weight is 26,500 kg.

Specifications
Wheeled Tanker
Cab seating: 1 + 1 + twin bunks
Configuration: 6 × 6
Weight:
  (tractor) 12,050 kg
  (tractor, GVW) 25,000 kg
  (GCW, legislative) 40,000 kg
  (GCW, design) 44,000 kg
Length:
  (tractor) 6.98 m
  (semi-trailer) 10.37 m
Width: 2.55 m
Height: 3.365 m (reducible to 2.489 m)
Track: 2.052 m
Wheelbase: 4.343 m
Max speed: (primary roads, restricted) 85 km/h
Range: (cruising) 500 km
Fuel capacity: 400 litres
Gradient: (at GCW) 34%
Fording: 1.5 m
Engine: Caterpillar C-12 ADEM (Advanced Diesel Engine Management) EURO III emissions compliant 11.9 litre 6-cylinder in-line turbocharged and water-cooled diesel 4-stroke diesel developing 445 hp at 1,700 rpm and 2,101 N.m torque at 1,200 rpm
Transmission: Allison HD 4560P with 6 forward and 1 reverse gears; TC-541 torque convertor
Transfer box: Oshkosh 30000 three-shaft single-speed with torque proportioning differential and manual differential lock
Steering: RH-drive, Shepard integral power steering with booster and separate fluid reservoir
Turning radius: (kerb) 9.14 m
Suspension: Oshkosh TAK-4 independent suspension, coil spring upper/lower control arms, anti-roll bar on second and third axles. Front axle rated at 7,500 kg, rear axles at 9,000 kg each
Tyres: 1600R 20 Michelin XZL with CTI system
Brakes: dual circuit, air, drums on all axles. ABS with off-road programme. Supplementary three-stage (2-, 4- or 6-cylinder) manually selected, automatically applied engine compression brake
Electrical system: 24 V
Batteries: 4 × 12 V
Alternator: 150 A, 24 V

Status
Production as required. In service with the UK, 57 × 18,000 litre CST(W). Deliveries ran from February 2005 until November 2006. Also delivered were 218 × 20,000 litre CST and 82 × 15,000 litre TAR.

Contractor
Oshkosh Truck Corporation

Stella-Meta water purification and associated equipment

Development
Stella-Meta specialises in military water purification and supplies the British Army and other armed forces (plus a number of governmental/aid agencies) with a full range of products enabling the delivery of safe drinking water in theatre.

Stella-Meta is part of Rolwey Group.

Stella-Meta Stellaflex onion tanks in use (Stella-Meta)   0102996

Description

The following descriptions give a brief overview of a range of Stella-Meta water purification and associated supply equipment.

Stellaflex flexible water tank systems

Stella-Meta has developed a complete flexible water tank system enabling the treatment, storage and distribution of drinking water on a totally mobile basis. The Stellaflex flexible tank range is manufactured in materials approved to international standards for drinking water and has been extensively field proven and climatically tested to UK MoD standard 001/issue 2 A1 and B3.

Available sizes range from 2,500 to 20,000 litres in the following types:
- Onion tanks or open top tanks where access to stored water is required
- Pillow tanks, sealed to prevent contamination of stored water
- Flexible tanks for instant transport of stored water on flatbed vehicles.

The tanks are lightweight, foldable and fully transportable when not in use and are manufactured from chemically resistant material.

Stella-Meta Small Group Unit (SGU) water purification unit

The Stella-Meta Small Group Unit (SGU) water purification unit is designed to provide up to 500 litres of potable water per hour from any freshwater source, including those containing chemical and biological contaminants. Contained within the main frame unit is the cleanable

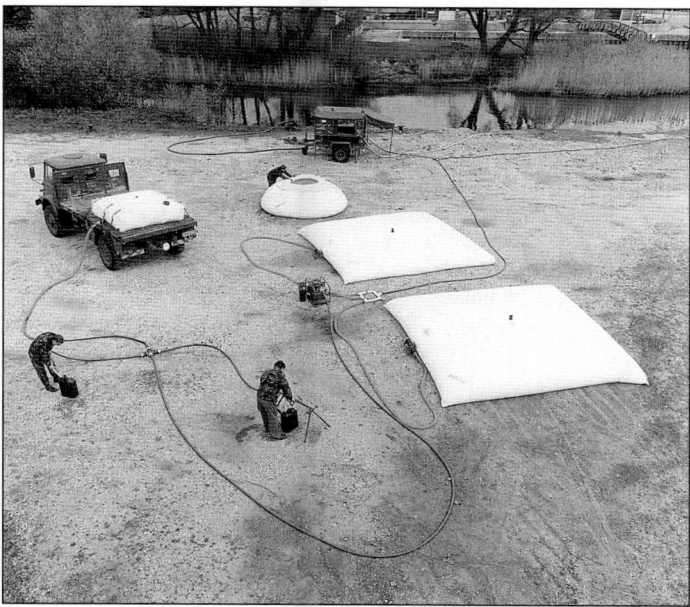

Stella-Meta Stellaflex onion, pillow and flexible water tanks in use (Stella-Meta) 0102997

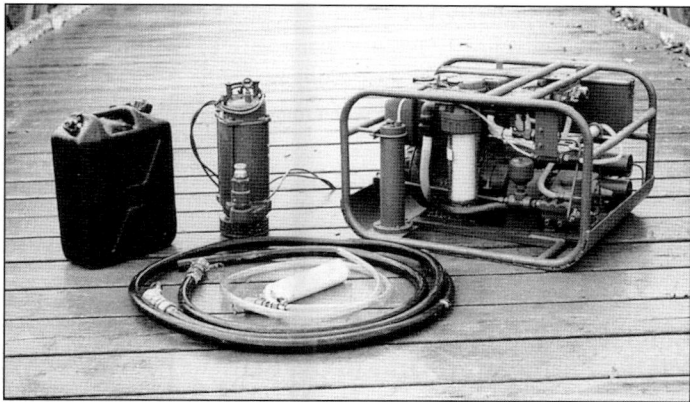

Stella-Meta WPU7 (F) water purification unit complete equipment schedule (Stella-Meta) 0121905

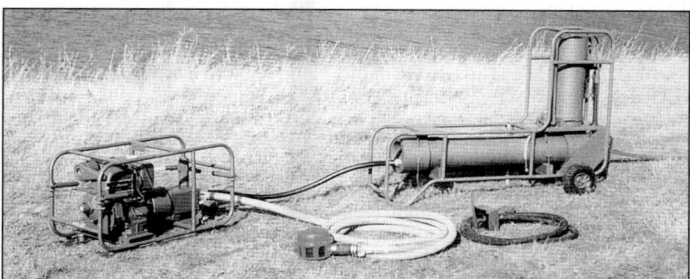

Stella-Meta Stella desalting module model DM1 complete equipment schedule (Stella-Meta) 0121907

pre-filter that removes particles down to 25 micron, replaceable cartridge filters that further remove particles down to 10 micron, carbon absorption filters, UV steriliser and the source pump, which can either be fitted or supplied loose. The unit is mains or generator powered but an optional hand-operated pump allows for operation in the event of power source failure.

Other options can include a supplied generator, drinking water storage tanks or a spares package, while accessories can include a suction strainer, a suction hose, delivery hoses and a distribution manifold.

Stella-Meta WPU7 (F) water purification unit

The Stella-Meta WPU7 (F) is a portable, skid-mounted unit producing 50 litres per hour of clean drinking water from a naturally contaminated freshwater source, being capable of removing pesticides and biological contaminants. The WPU7 (S) is a portable, skid-mounted, membrane water treatment unit that produces up to 50 litres per hour of clean drinking water from seawater or any brackish water source, being capable of removing salts, pesticides and heavy metals. Both units are mounted

Stellar Type 10A/5 trailer-mounted water purification equipment (Stella-Meta) 0102999

Stellar Type DS9 saline water treatment unit in use (Stella-Meta) 0102993

Stellar Type NBC Saline NBC water purification equipment complete equipment schedule (Stella-Meta) 0102995

within a single tubular frame that contains a pre-filter and a single-cylinder diesel engine that drives a triple-cylinder high-pressure pump. For filtration the model WPU7 (F) uses nano-filtration elements and a single carbon column, while the model WPU7 (S) uses two reverse osmosis elements. Both units supply water that meets STANAG 2136.

Both models are supplied with suction and delivery hoses, reject and drain hose, and options can include a battery-driven source pump, jerry can or other water storage systems, and a spares pack.

Stellar Type 10A/5 trailer-mounted water purification set

The Stellar Type 10A/5 trailer-mounted water purification set has a nominal rated capacity of 23 m³/hour of drinking water. It is a self-contained unit with its own diesel engine/pump/alternator set, incorporating a filter powder pretreatment plant, hypochlorite steriliser and a Stellar pressure filter with its own cleaning system.

Accessories, tools and spares are stowed within the trailer and bins are provided for storing the filter powder and hypochlorite, an efficient sterilising agent which takes immediate effect in the water.

The unit is so arranged that the pump can be used alone, the pump and filter can be used without the steriliser, or the pump and steriliser can be used without the filter. This saves filter powder and sterilant where filtration and/or sterilising is unnecessary, for example for washing water and similar domestic purposes.

All the equipment is mounted on a four-wheel trailer with suitable bodywork, side and end screens. The side and end screens are mounted on metal frames which are hinged to give protection to the operator.

The Type 10A/5 weighs 2,520 kg, with dimensions of 4.8 × 2.3 × 2.2 m.

Stellar DM desalting modules

The Stellar DM desalting modules constitute a new range of products designed to enhance the performance of the ST1 unit (full details of which can be found elsewhere in this section) whenever the source water is badly contaminated with dissolved chemicals. Each product comprises two hand-portable units and a high pressure diesel-powered pump coupled to a filtration module. These add a further two purification stages to the filtered water supplied from the ST1. The models DM1/2 feature a high-reject RO membrane and carbon absorption columns, while the model DM3 features a nano-filtration membrane and optional Stellarcarb column.

Each DM product is designed for a specific duty, as follows:
- Seawater desalination DM1 output 400 litres/hour
- NBC purification DM2 output 700 litres/hour
- Civil contaminants DM3 output 1,500 litres/hour

Stellar fresh water purification equipment

Stella-Meta manufactures mobile fresh water purification equipment with capacities ranging from the hand-portable AB1A producing 2.7 m³/hour through to the Type 10/A5 trailer-mounted unit producing 23 m³/hour.

Each Stellar unit typically comprises a pump set module, a precoat filtration module and a sterilising module. The individual units can be used separately when required to provide greater mobility in use.

Equipment is either tubular frame-mounted hand-portable with separate filtration, power and sterilisation modules, or two-wheel trailer-mounted as an option. Sterilisation is carried out with either a stand-alone hypochlorite powder dosing module, or is incorporated into the power source in the form of an electro-chlorinator.

Stellar saline water treatment units

When brackish or seawater has to be used as a water source, Stella-Meta Filters offers equipment to pump and desalinate water direct from the sea or salt lakes. Stellar units will convert saline waters to potable fluid that is in accordance with World Health Organisation standards. The complete equipment comprises a low-pressure pump, pretreatment filtration, a high-pressure pump, reverse osmosis modules and post sterilisation. All the equipment is mounted on a single trailer chassis and a diesel unit provides the motive power

Stellar NBC decontamination water purification equipment

The Stellar range of Military Transportable Water Purification Equipment has been augmented to cope with Nuclear, Biological and Chemical (NBC) contamination removal. The treatment process, designed to UK MoD specifications, includes precoat filtration, reverse osmosis, activated carbon treatment and post-disinfection, capable of removing ionic, organic and bacterial contaminants.

The range of equipment is capable of achieving output capacities of 8.2 m³/hour from fresh water or 2.2 m³/hour of NBC-contaminated water. Variants are available that will also treat seawater. The units can either be fully integral self-contained modules or 'add-on' modules compatible with non-Stellar water purification sets.

The latest equipment in service with the British armed forces is the Type NBC Saline with a capacity up to 2.2 m³/hour. The Type NBC Saline employs a modular construction incorporating a demountable transfer pump, Stellasep crossflow microfilter, slurry feed pump, diesel-driven high-pressure pump, reverse osmosis module, final trap activated carbon unit and a post-chlorination system. A demountable pump and a pillow tank complete the equipment. The Type NBC Saline is mounted in a self-contained space frame unit that can be carried on a truck, trailer, skid base or pallet.

Specifications

Stellar DM desalting modules

Model	DM1/2	DM3
Type:		
(Membrane module)	spiral (HR)	spiral (nano)
(Pump set)	positive displacement	positive displacement
Weight:		
(Membrane module)	95 kg	90 kg
(Pump set)	110 kg	115 kg
Volume:		
(Membrane module)	1.17 m³	1.17 m³
(Pump set)	0.35 m³	0.35 m³

Stellar fresh water purification equipment - Filter

Model	AB1A	AB3MA	ST1
Max rated capacity:	2.7 m³/hr	4.5 m³/hr	6.8 m³/hr
Type:	precoat	precoat	precoat
Weight:	41 kg	81 kg	78 kg
Volume:	0.23 m³	0.27 m³	0.49 m³

Stellar fresh water purification equipment - Power Module

Model	AB1A	AB3MA	ST1
Pump type:	positive displacement	centrifugal	centrifugal
Engine type:	petrol	diesel	diesel
Weight:	61 kg	98 kg	98 kg
Volume:	0.25 m³	0.21 m³	0.21 m³

Stellar fresh water purification equipment - Sterilisation

Model	AB1A	AB3MA	ST1
Type:	sterilant doser	sterilant doser	sterilant doser
Weight:	33 kg	33 kg	33 kg
Volume:	0.22 m³	0.22 m³	0.22 m³
Frame:	tubular	tubular	tubular
Option:	trailer	trailer (an be dropped by parachute)	trailer

Stellar saline water treatment unit DS9
Sea water flow rate: 2 m³/hr
Weight: 2,000 kg excluding trailer
Length: 2.4 m
Width: 2.1 m
Height: 1.7 m

Stellar NBC decontamination water purification equipment

Model	NBC6(F)	NBC Saline
Flow rate:	2.2 m³/hr	2.2 m³/hr
Weight:	2,300 kg	2,300 kg
Length:	2.4 m	2.4 m
Width:	2.1 m	2.1 m
Height:	1.7 m	1.7 m

Status
Production as required. In service with armed forces worldwide.

Contractor
Stella-Meta Limited (part of the Rolwey Group)

United States

600 GPH (gallons per hour) Reverse Osmosis Water Purification Unit (ROWPU)

Development
MECO and the now DRS Sustainment Inc have both produced this Reverse Osmosis Water Purification Unit (ROWPU) for use by the US military. The 1,500 GPH ROWPU has been developed to replace the 600 GPH ROWPU.

Description
The 600 GPH ROWPU is capable of providing potable water at up to 600 US gallons (2,270 litres) per hour (GPH) from raw water that is highly polluted, turbid, coloured, saline, or contaminated with nuclear, biological or chemical warfare agents. Up to 950 US gallons (3,590 litres) of water per hour (1,000 ppm TDS (total dissolved solids) or less) can be purified from fresh water sources (1,000 ppm TDS or less) and up to 750 US gallons (2,840 litres) of water from saline water sources (35,000 ppm TDS or more) at a temperature of +25°F. As with all reverse osmosis purification units, production capacity drops with decreasing temperature and increasing turbidity and contamination. Power for the unit can be drawn through either the standard commercial electric power supply or through a 30 kW generator set.

Two raw water, backwash, and distribution pumps are utilised to provide an integrated system with the main ROWPU unit that allows installation flexibility high mobility, and reliable (potable) water output. The 600 GPH ROWPU is available in two basic configurations: trailer or skid-mounted.

Transportation is normally trailer-mounted and behind a 5-ton truck, although the unit is transportable as an underslung load by CH-47 Chinook helicopter.

Specifications

600 GPH ROWPU
Product water: 600 US GPH (2,270 litres/h), up to 950 GPH (3,600 litres/h) depending on source water and other factors
Feedwater flow: 1,800 GPH (6,810 litres/h)
Weight:
   (skid mounted) 3,311 kg
   (30 kW generator) 1,293 kg
   (trailer) 3,095 kg
Length: (skid-mounted) 3.12 m
Width: (skid-mounted) 2.29 m
Height: (skid-mounted) 1.87 m
Overall length: (trailer-mounted) 6.25 m
Overall width: (trailer-mounted) 2.62 m
Overall height: (trailer-mounted) 2.62 m

Component specification

Description	Quantity	Capacity
Raw water pump	2	
(centrifugal)		30 US gallons/min (114 litres/min)
(motor drive)		2 hp
Backwash pump	1	
(centrifugal)		120 US gallons/min (454 litres/min)
(motor drive)		10 hp
Distribution pump	1	
(centrifugal)		30 US gallons/min (114 litres/min)
(motor drive)		1 hp

Status
Production as required. In service with US armed forces.

Contractor
DRS Sustainment Systems Inc
MECO

---

600 ft water well drilling system

Description
The US Army's 600 ft (182.9 m) well drilling system supports rapid deployment forces during operations in arid areas of the world where no surface water sources exist. The system includes a drilling machine, support vehicle, well completion kit and accessories. The system can be loaded for long-range transport into three C-130 transport aircraft. International-based trucks are used to transport the system by road.

The system is used by US Army active, reserve and National Guard drilling units and by US Navy Construction Battalions (Seabees).

Although still available as specified by the US Army, more modern drilling systems are now available to meet military needs. One such example was designed and built by the George E Failing Company (GEFCo) for the US Air Force (Red Horse Battalion) in 2001 and delivered in 2002.

GEFCo recently completed the refurbishment of two Model LP-12 drilling machines for the US Air Force.

Following refurbishment, a LP-12 drilling system mounted on a carrier-type vehicle platform. These vehicles were built for supporting operation Desert Storm and for use by the Army and Marines (GEFCo)   1173985

US Air Force (Red Horse Battalion) SD-300 well drilling system built for the US Air Force's Red Horse Battalion and mounted on an International Model F-1954 (6 × 6) truck (GEFCo)   1139548

Following refurbishment, a LP-12 drilling system mounted on a conventional truck platform and to the specifications of the US Air Force's Red Horse Battalion (GEFCo)   1173986

Prior to refurbishment, the LP-12 drilling system shown above (GEFCo)   1173984

GEFCo is currently in detailed negotiations with the US military for a new concept, low-profile, carrier-mounted top, head-type drilling machine.

Status
In service with the US Army and Navy.

Contractor
George E Failing Company (GEFCo)

3,000 gph Reverse Osmosis Water Purification Unit (ROWPU)

Development
In August 1984, the then Belvoir Research, Development and Engineering Center awarded a contract for the design, fabrication, assembly and testing of prototype Reverse Osmosis Water Purification Units (ROWPUs) capable of purifying water at a rate of 3,000 US gallons (11,355 litres) per hour (gph). This contract was awarded to Aqua-Chem Inc., Water

Aqua-Chem 3,000 US gph Reverse Osmosis Water Purification Unit (ROWPU) (Gordon Arthur)   1296265

Technologies Division and valued at USD3,309,099. Three prototype units were produced by December 1984 for testing at Aberdeen Proving Ground (Developmental) and Forts Story and Eustis (Operational) during 1985. Testing was completed by late 1986.

In November 1987, it was announced that Aqua-Chem Inc had been awarded a contract for 98 units with deliveries commencing during 1990. An option contract for 51 additional units followed a few years later.

In 1992 Keco Industries (now part of DRS Technologies) was awarded a five-year contract for up to 184 ROWPUs.

Description
Specifications of the 3,000 gph Reverse Osmosis Water Purification Unit (ROWPU) call for the purification of 3,000 US gph at +25°C using fresh and brackish water sources and 2,000 US gph (7,570 litres/h) at +25°C using seawater sources, both including NBC contamination. The units are mounted in standard ISO containers with the NBC treatment unit outside and may be transported by truck, rail or aircraft. The units are designed to be installed or packed up in 90 minutes.

Status
In service with the US Army.

Contractor
Aqua-Chem Inc.

AMFUEL static water tanks and collapsible drums

Development
AMFUEL (American Fuel Cell and Coated Fabrics Company) produces a wide range of static flexible water tanks for both military and commercial purposes. AMFUEL is a member of the Zodiac Group, and as such is a sister company to France's AERAZUR. Details of the AERAZUR range of products can be found elsewhere in this section.

Description

Static water tanks
AMFUEL static tanks produced for water and water-based products are free-standing and made from a chlorobutyl rubber-based material that is fully vulcanised and reinforced with tough nylon basket-weave fabric. These tanks can be placed at almost any location and have double-thickness panels at handling points and positions where hardware is attached. Positioning handles are provided. For transport and storage the tanks can be placed into wooden crates.

US armed forces currently employ three main types of these tanks, with capacities of 10,000 US gallons (37,850 litres), 20,000 US gallons (75,700 litres) and 50,000 US gallons (189,250 litres). They are used as part of the Tactical Water Distribution System (TWDS).

Collapsible drums
The US Army uses two main types of AMFUEL collapsible water drum that are similar in form to the AMFUEL Sealdrum tanks, full details of which can be found in the Bulk fuel storage and distribution systems section. The two models in service have a 55 US gallon (208 litre) capacity and a 250 US gallon (946 litre) capacity. Both are cylindrical tanks constructed of water-resistant synthetic rubber-coated fabric and can be towed at slow speeds over smooth surfaces for short distances. Both can be airlifted by helicopter. The 250 US gallon (946 litre) capacity drum forms the water storage component of the Forward Area Water Point Supply System (FAWPSS), full details of which can be found elsewhere in this section.

Specifications
See table below

Collapsible drums

	55 US gal	250 US gal
Capacity	208 litres	946 litres
Length	876 mm	1.524 m
Diameter	597 mm	1.016 m
Weight		
(full)	211.4 kg	1,043 kg
(empty)	22.68 kg	93 kg

Status
In production. In service with US armed forces.

Contractor
American Fuel Cell and Coated Fabrics Company (AMFUEL)

Avon Engineered Fabrications flexitanks for water

Development
Based in Mississippi, United States, Avon Engineered Fabrications (AEF) is a subsidiary of Avon Rubber and specialises in manufacturing flexible structures from coated fabrics and other specially formulated materials. Originally known as Bell Avon Inc, the company was founded in 1985 to manufacture skirts for hovercraft and air cushion vehicles. AEF has since expanded into other areas where high performance fabrications and extrusions are needed, products including a range of flexible tanks for transporting and storing water and fuel.

Avon Engineered Fabrications (AEF) US military 3,000 US gallon open top water tanks being tested prior to shipment (AEF)   1186204

**Static water tanks
(dimensions when filled)**

Capacity (US gal):	Capacity (litres):	Width:	Length:	Height:
1,000 US gal	3,785 litres	2.388 m	3.073 m	610 mm
2,000 US gal	7,570 litres	3.353 m	3.353 m	813 mm
3,000 US gal	11,355 litres	3.581 m	4.267 m	914 mm
5,000 US gal	18,295 litres	4.47 m	4.623 m	1.118 m
10,000 US gal	37,850 litres	6.096 m	6.096 m	1.219 m
15,000 US gal	56,775 litres	7.468 m	7.315 m	1.219 m
20,000 US gal	75,700 litres	6.7 m	8.23 m	1.727 m
25,000 US gal	94,625 litres	6.7 m	10.363 m	1.727 m
50,000 US gal	189,250 litres	6.7 m	19.2 m	1.727 m
100,000 US gal	378,500 litres	18.136 m	18.212 m	1.219 m

Description
Avon Engineered Fabrications (AEF) flexible tanks for the transport and storage of water are made from a high-strength, durable polymer-coated fabric specific to application, and are available in a wide range of sizes from 5 to 500,000 US gallons (18.9 to 1,892,500 litres). Bell Avon Inc also produces open top 'onion' tanks.

When not in use, or for ease of shipping, the tanks can be folded, transported and packed into a convenient crate. They are suitable for operations throughout a wide temperature range.

Status
In production. In service with US and other unspecified armed forces.

Contractor
Avon Engineered Fabrications (AEF) Inc

Forward Area Water Point Supply System (FAWPSS)

Description
The Forward Area Water Point Supply System (FAWPSS) is intended to provide large volumes of potable water to troops in remote areas where no water supplies of any type are available. Water is delivered to a central point by air, truck or any other local method and from there is distributed as required through a network of tanks, pumps and hose-lines. The complete system consists of six 1,892 litre (500 US gallons) collapsible water drums, one 473 litre (125 US gallons)/min water pump assembly, three suction hose assemblies, six discharge hose assemblies, two valve assemblies, four 'Y' junctions, four dispensing nozzles, one towing and lifting yoke and the associated hoses. The complete system is air-transportable and can be set up by two personnel. Once in use only one person is required for operation.

Status
In service with the US Army.

Contractor
American Fuel Cell and Coated Fabrics Company (AMFUEL)

Development Agency
Army Tank-automotive and Armaments Command (TACOM)

The Forward Area Water Point Supply System (FAWPSS) is intended to provide large volumes of potable water to troops in remote areas where no water supplies of any type are available (TACOM (PMPAWS))   1323201

GTA containers for water

Development
GTA Containers Inc manufactures a complete system of collapsible containers (drums and pillow tanks) to handle the temporary storage transportation and delivery of drinking water, fuel, liquid food products, and fluidic solids (grains, rice, etc). Capacities range from 55 US gallons to 225,000 US gallons (5,000 barrels).

GTA Containers Inc also supplies equipment for forward area water systems, the Forward Area Water Point Supply System (FAWPSS) being an example, this including 500-gallon drums, two-inch hoses pumps and dispensing nozzles. GTA can also supply complete water transfer systems, these including adaptors, hoses, pumps and monitoring equipment. Systems often include multitank installations used as water tank storage farms.

GTA tanks can also be supplied as a complete system with pumps hoses and chlorinators to transport and distribute water when established local sources are either interrupted or contaminated due to natural disasters or similar events.

The following is a brief overview of the various containers produced by GTA Containers Inc.

Description

Drums and Superdrums
GTA Containers Inc manufactures two types of water drum, a standard drum constructed using rubber-coated fabric and the GTA Superdrum constructed of elastomeric coated fabric. The GTA Superdrum is significantly lighter, but is more rugged and durable.

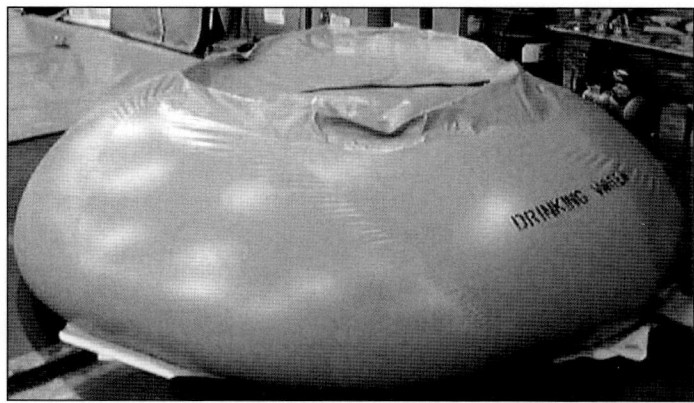

A GTA Containers Inc 3,000 US gallon 'Onion Tank' in use (GTA Containers Inc)   0134148

Three standard sizes are available; 55 US gallons (208 litres), 250 US gallons (946 litres) and 500 US gallons (1,893 litres). The fabric used in all types of construction is puncture- and tear-resistant and each drum is subjected to a hydrostatic pressure test following assembly. The inside surface of the potable water drum meets US Food and Drug Administration requirements and imparts neither taste nor odour to the water.

Empty drums collapse to 10 per cent of their original volume for transport or storage, while filled drums can be rolled, floated, towed or lifted by helicopter. Drums can also be dropped free-fall, the 250 US gallon drum can be dropped free-fall from 4.5 m (15 ft) or by parachute.

GTA drums are sand coloured and they can be temporarily or permanently repaired in the field when necessary. Hoses, nozzles and valves have quick-connect/disconnect fittings.

These drums have numerous alternative applications including flotation devices (surface or submerged, for example for the construction of temporary bridges), as pneumatic lifting devices or ship fenders and for the underground storage of water supplies.

Specifications

Drums and Superdrums

Capacity:	55 US gal	250 US gal	500 US gal
	(208 litres)	(946 litres)	(1,893 litres)
Weight:			
(drum)	22.7 kg	81.8 kg	104.5 kg
(Superdrum)	13.6 kg	63.6 kg	72.7 kg
Length:	0.876 m	1.524 m	1.524 m
Diameter:	0.597 m	1.016 m	1.27 m

Static storage tanks
GTA Containers Inc manufactures a range of static water-storage pillow tanks that are available in sizes from 3,000 US gallons (11,355 litres) to 225,000 US gallons (851,625 litres). All tanks are manufactured in accordance with US military requirements and are thus lightweight, rugged and durable with high abrasion and puncture resistance.

Each tank is constructed using tear-resistant fabric with an elastomeric coating on both sides. The inside surface of the potable water drum meets US Food and Drug Administration requirements and imparts neither taste nor odour to the water. Chafing patches are included as part of the standard design and are located on the interior surface directly opposite each fitting to provide a double-wall thickness supporting every piece of hardware. Handles, each capable of lifting 454 kg, are moulded on to the tank.

All tanks are equipped with standard 4 in (101.6 mm) quick-disconnect filler/discharge fittings. Bottom discharge fittings are provided for gravity unloading. A 4 in (101.6 mm) reinforced hose with quick-disconnects is also provided.

Each tank is fully collapsible and folds down into a package that occupies two per cent of the volume of the filled tank.

Specifications

Static storage tanks

Capacity:	3,000 US gal	10,000 US gal	20,000 US gal	50,000 US gal
	(11,355 litres)	(37,850 litres)	(75,700 litres)	(189,250 litres)
Length:	4.27 m	6.71 m	7.32 m	7.62 m
Width:	4.27 m	6.71 m	8.53 m	19.81 m
Weight: (empty)	61.8 kg	140.9 kg	187.2 kg	415.9 kg

3,000 US gallon capacity 'Onion Tank'
The Tank, Fabric, Collapsible, Self-Supporting, Sealed Top, Water Storage 3,000 US Gallon Capacity, 'Onion Tank' is manufactured by GTA Containers Inc for use by the US Army. The US national stock number is 5430-01-469-8744 and the GTA model number is GTA-Z60TPW.

The tank is a 3,000 US gallon (11,355 litres) capacity collapsible onion-type tank for the temporary storage of potable water. It is manufactured from a coated fabric and is designed for operational use throughout a 0 to less >+50°C temperature range. It can withstand folded storage throughout a –13 to +71°C temperature range. The tank is self-supporting in design and is stable on slopes of up to 10 per cent when filled to its rated 3,000 US gallon capacity.

The empty tank weighs 61.2 kg and outside dimensions when packaged are 35.56 cm (H) and 106.68 cm (W). Dimensions when filled to capacity are a height of 1.143 m, a base diameter of 3.988 m and a top diameter of 2.4 m. Each tank is supplied equipped with a 2 in (51 mm) filler/discharge fitting with female cam-lock coupling, a repair kit and a ground cloth/valise.

GTA mini-tanks
The GTA Mini-Tank is a flexible pillow tank that may be carried by a pick-up truck or light van. Three standard sizes are available; 120 US gallons (454 litres), 250 US gallons (946 litres) and 500 US gallons (1,893 litres). The fabric used is puncture- and tear-resistant and each tank is subjected to a hydrostatic pressure test following assembly. Empty tanks collapse to 10 per cent of their original volume for transport or storage.

The US Army employs a 140-US gallon (530-litre) mini-tank which is transported on a HMMWV or a towed ¾-tonne trailer.

Each tank is constructed using puncture-resistant fabric with an elastomeric coating on both sides. The inside surface of the potable water tanks meets US Food and Drug Administration requirements and imparts neither taste nor odour to the water. Chafing patches are part of the standard design and handles are bonded on to the tank. A tie-down webbing assembly consists of a nylon/polyester harness with four galvanised D-rings attached. Tanks are equipped with a manual pressure relief valve and one inlet/outlet fitting and a quick-connect male adaptor with a dust cap.

Optional equipment includes a 51 mm × 2.44 m hose assembly and a field repair kit.

Specifications

GTA mini-tanks

Capacity:	120 US gal	250 US gal	500 US gal
	(454 litres)	(946 litres)	1,893 litres)
Weight: (empty)	9.1 kg	12.7 kg	17.7 kg
Length:	1.22 m	1.83 m	3.35 m
Width:	1.52 m	1.52 m	1.52 m

Trailer tanks
The GTA Trailer Tank converts an open (flatbed-type) or closed trailer, truck or van into a tanker unit; the tanks may also be installed in barges or ships. Two personnel can unroll a flatbed tank and convert a trailer or vehicle into a tanker in approximately 15 minutes. Empty tanks collapse to two per cent of their original volume for transport or storage.

Each tank is constructed using abrasion- and puncture-resistant fabric. The inside surface of the potable water tank meets US Food and Drug Administration requirements and imparts neither taste nor odour to the water.

These tanks may be carried on highways at speeds up to 105 km/h when full. Braking from that speed will not cause shifting or leaking. The tanks can be transported off-road over unimproved terrain and gradients of up to 30 per cent without shifting or leaking while maintaining trailer stability.

GTA trailer tanks can be unloaded using a gravity drain system to empty the tank in 30 minutes or less.

Specifications

Trailer tanks

Capacity:	3,000 US gal	5,000 US gal
	(11,355 litres)	(18,925 litres)
Weight: (empty)	200 kg	250 kg
Length:	8.53 m	12.19 m
Width:	2.44 m	2.44 m

Status
In production. In service with the US Army, US Marine Corps and other undisclosed users.

Contractor
GTA Containers Inc

Lightweight Water Purification System (LWP)

Development
The Lightweight Water Purification System (LWP) was developed to support ground, amphibious, air mobile, special operations forces and temporary medical facilities during a range of contingency operations. The LWP is also capable of supporting small units that are detached from the main body of forces and can produce sufficient water to support a small platoon or company.

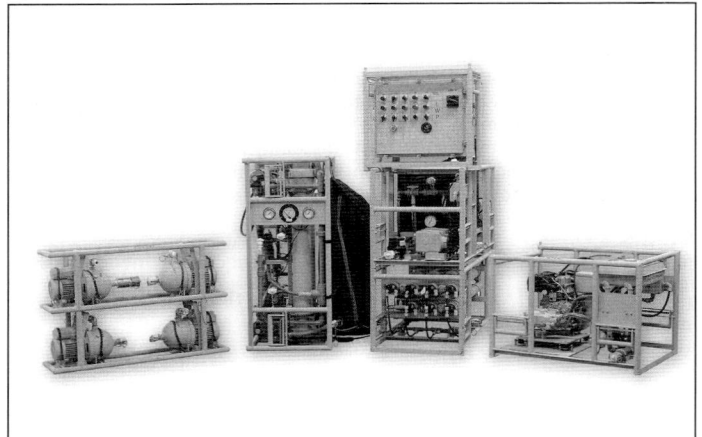

Component parts of the Lightweight Water Purification (LWP) system (TACOM (PMPAWS)) 1128235

The complete Lightweight Water Purification (LWP) system stowed in an M1097 series HMMWV (TACOM (PMPAWS)) 1128234

Demonstration use of the Lightweight Water Purification (LWP) system (TACOM (PMPAWS)) 1128236

The initial contract award was awarded to MECO in 2002 for up to 236 units. First Unit Equipped (FUE) was in Q105.

Description
The Lightweight Water Purification System (LWP) utilises the latest state-of-the-art reverse osmosis technology to produce up to 473 litres (125 US gallons) per hour of potable water from any water source including brackish, salt, nuclear, biological or chemical (NBC) contaminated supplies and throughout a -32 to +49°C temperature range. The system is designed to be set-up by four persons and operated by one person, it is modular and is designed to be both light and mobile.

A complete LWP consists of five modules: pretreatment, chemical injection, high-pressure pump, reverse osmosis elements and control panel. The system also includes a distribution point, 3,785 litres (1,000 US gallons) capacity onion tank, connecting hoses, valves and associated hardware. Weighing 907 kg (including a 3 kW generator set) and with dimensions of 1.3 × 0.71 × 1.22 m (L × W × H), LWP is designed to be transportable by the M1037/M1097 series HMMWV and is air-transportable by UH-60 helicopter, C-130 and C-17 transport aircraft.

The complete Lightweight Water Purification System (LWP) is designed to be transportable by M1037/M1097 series HMMWV vehicles (TACOM (PMPAWS)) 0126823

The complete Lightweight Water Purification System (LWP) stowed in an M1011 series High Mobility Trailer (HMT) (TACOM (PMPAWS)) 0126824

Status
Initial contract awarded 2002 to MECO for approximately 236 units. First Unit Equipped (FUE) Q105.

Contractor
MECO

Development agency
US Army Tank-automotive and Armaments Command (TACOM)

Load handling system compatible water tank rack system (Hippo)

Development
The prime role of the Load Handling System (LHS) compatible water tank rack system (Hippo) is to provide a mobile hard-wall water tanker for the bulk distribution of potable water. The Hippo system is designed around a flat-track platform and is transportable by a load handling system equipped truck.

A contract was awarded by TACOM to the Mil-Mar Century Corporation, with the first systems fielding 2Q FY07. The most recent contract award was made in September 2008, was valued at USD27,489,878 and called for 470 Hippo Water System. Estimated completion date was August 31, 2010.

A further intended award for a follow-on five-year contract was announced mid-2010. At the time of writing (January 2011) no award had been made.

Description
The Load Handling System (LHS) compatible water tank rack system (Hippo) is designed around a The US Army's Palletized Load System (PLS) flatrack platform and is transportable by the LHS equipped version of the Oshkosh Heavy Expanded Mobility Tactical Truck (HEMTT) and the Oshkosh M1074/M1075 PLS trucks and M1076 trailer.

The system operates either floor or truck/trailer-mounted and stores and distributes potable water within a brigade or company. In service the Hippo replaces the 3,000 litre and 5,000 litre Semi-trailer Mounted Fabric Tanks (SMFT). Maximum tank capacity is 7,570 litres (2,000 US gallons) and the tank racks are designed to be transportable at various stages of fill. Each tank rack is outfitted with a 2,271 litres (125 US gallons)/min centrifugal, diesel belt-driven water pump, hose reel, filling station, and heater to be used during cold weather operations. The tank rack can be

Hippo tank rack (TACOM (PMPAWS)) 1128237

Hippo tank rack (TACOM (PMPAWS)) 1128238

Under contract to prime contractor Mil-Mar Century Corporation, WEW of Germany is currently supplying tank racks, the most recent award calling for 470 units to be delivered by 2010. The rack shown here is being transported by a MAN SX range truck, in US Army service the prime mover will be either a Oshkosh HEMTT or PLS truck (Shaun C Connors) 1156030

handled by any suitable capacity forklift truck or crane and is ISO-compatible for transport and storage purposes. When required, tank racks can be stacked to reduce storage footprint.

Status
Contract awarded. First fielding during 2Q FY07.

Contractor
Mil-Mar Century Corporation

Development agency
US Army Tank-automotive and Armaments Command (TACOM)

Tactical Water Distribution System (TWDS)

Description
In service since 1981 and intended for use in a rapid deployment force-type situation, the Tactical Water Distribution System (TWDS) is a flexible distribution, storage and receiving system. It can issue a maximum of 2,725,200 litres (720,000 US gallons) of water during the course of a 20 hour working day.

A complete TWDS set includes 16.1 km (10 miles) of hoseline, six pump stations, two collapsible tanks, two distribution points plus the connecting hoses, valves and hardware. Each TWDS is manned by 30 personnel.

Tactical Water Distribution System undergoing 30-day trials in California (TACOM (PMPAWS))   0512070

The TWDS is designed to distribute water up to 112.4 km (70 miles). Working pressure is 150 to 200 psi. The basic hardware, apart from the various smaller accessories, consists of a 152.4 mm (6 inch) lightweight layflat hose, 75,700 to 189,250 litre (20,000 to 50,000 US gallon) collapsible tanks and 2,271 litre (600 US gallons)/min centrifugal, diesel-driven pumps.

Status
Further complete set procurement is considered unlikely. Over 100 10-mile sets delivered.

Contractor
Avon Engineered Fabrications (AEF) Inc (tanks)
American Fuel Cell and Coated Fabrics Company (AMFUEL)
Angus Fire Armour Corporation (hoses)

Development agency
US Army Tank-automotive and Armaments Command (TACOM)

Tactical Water Purification System (TWPS) (1,500 GPH)

Development
The 1,500 GPH (gallons (US) per hour) Tactical Water Purification System (TWPS) has been developed to replace the 600 GPH ROWPU (Reverse Osmosis Water Purification System).

It was announced in 2002 that the then SFA Inc had been awarded a contract for the production of the TWPS. The immediate value of the contract was quoted as USD17,747,394; the estimated cumulative value of the contract was quoted as USD185,911,498. Under the contract, SFA produced 221 TWPS units for the Army and 243 for the Marine Corps.

Global Strategies Group (North America) Inc announced in February 2009 that under a contract valued at in excess of USD44 million it will provide a further 87 TWPS to the US Army TACOM Life Cycle Command.

For the TWPS requirement SFA/Global Strategies Group teamed with Aqua-Chem. Aqua-Chem's role as subcontractor is in the area of system design and fabrication.

Description
The 1,500 GPH (gallons per hour) Tactical Water Purification System (TWPS) utilises the latest state-of-the-art reverse osmosis technology to produce up to 5,677 litres (1,500 US gallons) per hour of potable water from any water source including brackish, salt, nuclear, biological or chemical (NBC) contaminated supplies and throughout a –32 to +49°C temperature range. It has the capacity to provide sufficient drinking water for division and brigade ground units and its mobility will allow the TWPS to support ground, amphibious, air mobile and airborne units in both peacetime and war scenarios.

The 1,500 GPH (gallons (US) per hour) Tactical Water Purification System (TWPS) has been developed to replace the 600 GPH ROWPU (Reverse Osmosis Water Purification System) (TACOM (PMPAWS))   1323539

It was announced in 2002 that the then SFA Inc had been awarded a contract for the production of the TWPS (TACOM (PMPAWS))   1323538

The 1,500 GPH Tactical Water Purification System (TWPS) uses the latest state-of-the-art reverse osmosis technology to produce up to 5,677 litres (1,500 US gallons) per hour of potable water from any water source including brackish, salt, Nuclear, Biological or Chemical (NBC) contaminated supplies and throughout a –32 to +49°C temperature range (TACOM (PMPAWS))   1323537

The then SFA produced 221 TWPS units for the US Army and 243 for the Marine Corps under the initial production contract (TACOM (PMPAWS))   1323536

The TWPS incorporates micro-filtration technology to filter out silt and biological materials, including disease-causing micro-organisms such as Cryptosporidium. It produces 1,500 US gallons of potable water each hour when operated on water with less than 1,000 parts per million (ppm) of total dissolved solids (TDS). If the raw water has more than 45,000 ppm TDS, it will produce 1,200 US gallons per hour. Operating from normal seawater, the TWPS produces 1,200 US gallons per hour of potable water at any temperature. The system includes high salt rejection reverse osmosis technology to produce drinking water from the extremely salty seawater sources in the Middle East, and from extremely salty seawater sources (containing up to 60,000 mg/l dissolved salts), potable water production is 900 UD gallons per hour.

The system is mounted on two different platforms, one platform being skid-based for conventional truck/trailer transport (for the US Marines), the other having the system installed in an 8 × 8 × 20 ft load handling system (LHS) compatible ISO-dimensioned container, enabling the TWPS to be transported by any current US Army LHS-equipped truck.

The system can be set up by three people and operated by one, and in addition to conventional truck transport can be transported by rail, sea or by air in C-130 transport aircraft. The skid-based system is designed to fit

The 1,500 GPH Tactical Water Purification System (TWPS) as an LHS compatible load. There will be two versions of the system, the other will be skid-based and designed to fit inside any conventional ISO container (TACOM (PMPAWS))   0130073

inside a standard ISO container and weighs 4,536 kg; the total system, which consists of the basic system plus a 60 kW Tactical Quiet Generator (TQG) generator and add-on kits, weighs 11,340 kg. The complete system includes a pre-treatment system, chemical injection, high-pressure pump, reverse osmosis elements, control panel, valves, piping, cold weather protection module, waste water collection module, NBC treatment module, five 11,355 litre (3,000 US gallon) onion tanks, ocean intake system, distribution points, connecting hoses, valves and associated hardware.

Both versions are NBC warfare survivable and both can purify water that has been contaminated with NBC warfare agents. The TWPS is constructed from corrosion-resistant materials and is expected to have a minimum service life of 20 years.

Status
In service with the US Army (221) and US Marines (243). Further 87 units ordered early-2009.

Contractor
SFA Inc, part of Global Strategies Group Inc (North America)

Development agency
US Army Tank-automotive and Armaments Command (TACOM)

Unit Water Pod System - Camel and Camel II

Description

Camel
The Unit Water Pod System, Camel, was to be the primary US Army system for receiving, storing and issuing water and was to be used at all echelons throughout the battlefield. Upon entering service the Camel was to replace current M107, M149 and M1112 water trailers and had been designed to mount onto the M1095 Medium Tactical Vehicle (MTV) trailer. Full details of the M1095 MTV trailer can be found in the Family of Medium Tactical Vehicles (FMTV) entry in the Trucks section. Camel was designed to store and distribute a maximum of 3,406 litres (900 US gallons), 90 per cent of which could be dispensed by gravity flow. The system could be operated by one person and 3,406 litres is sufficient to provide (under the Stryker Brigade Combat Team (SBCT) concept) a manoeuvre company operating in a temperate environment at a minimum sustaining consumption rate with three days supply of potable water.

The system was designed to be transported either full or partially full and was to be outfitted with water pump, hose reel, filling station, and heating/chilling facilities so it could be used during cold or hot weather operations.

Camel II
TACOM is currently conducting market research to gather information on capable and experienced companies that are interested in producing 800 gallon Unit Water Pod Systems, Camel II, for the Army. Responses were sought by 10th August 2009.

The Unit Water Pod System (Camel) was to be the primary US Army system for receiving, storing and issuing water and was to be used at all echelons throughout the battlefield (TACOM (PMPAWS))   1323200

The Camel II will be the primary system for providing a more flexible and efficient way of receiving, storing, and issuing potable water. The Camel II will be used by units at all echelons throughout the battlefield and will replace the M149 and M1112 400 gallon potable water trailers.

The Camel II will be procured in two increments. The first increment (the basic unit) will consist of an 800-gallon capacity tank, mounted on a Government Furnished Family of Medium Tactical Vehicle (FMTV) M1095 trailer, and includes all of the hoses and fittings necessary to gravity flow water from the tank and/or to a fill stand. The first increment will also include integrated freeze protection that can be powered by external sources. The second increment will consist of modular components and/or an integral unit that will provide chilling, pumping and recirculation, and on-board power generation add-on capabilities for the Camel II. These add-on capabilities will be pursued after the basic unit is produced. The capabilities may be acquired on a separate contract.

Status
Camel; Initial contract award to Chenega Integrated Systems LLC, contract cancelled.
Camel II; at market research stage.

Contractor

Development agency
US Army Tank-automotive and Armaments Command (TACOM)

Water Storage and Distribution System (WSDS)

Description
The Water Storage and Distribution System (WSDS) is a flexible distribution, storage and receiving system intended for use in a rapid deployment force-type situation. Potable water is pumped from a Tactical Water Distribution System (TWDS) (full details of which can be found elsewhere in this section) or other suitable source into collapsible fabric water storage tanks for dispensing into tanker trucks, trailer-mounted water tanks or individual water containers. One WSDS can issue a maximum of 3,028,000 litres (800,000 US gallons) of water during the course of a 20 hour working day and one complete WSDS set includes (packaged in TRICON containers) 75,700 litre (20,000 US gallon) or 189,250 litre (50,000 US gallon) fabric collapsible tanks, 473 litres/min (125 US gpm) pumps, 1,325 litres/min (350 US gpm) pumps, pump connection kits, hypo chlorination units, dual-tank connection kits, hose connection kits, hose nozzle kits, bag filler connection kits and hoseline and nozzle kits. Quantities, and in some cases items, will vary with capacity and location. Each WSDS is manned by 30 personnel.

Status
Production as required. In service with US armed forces.

Contractor
Avon Engineered Fabrications (AEF) Inc
American Fuel Cell and Coated Fabrics Company (Amfuel)
(Hoses) Angus Fire Armour Corporation

Development agency
US Army Tank-automotive and Armaments Command (TACOM)

PORTABLE ROADWAYS

Czech Republic

Truck-mounted roadway laying system

Description
This system consists of a TATRA 815 (8 × 8) truck chassis (originally TATRA 813 (8 × 8) trucks were employed) with two cassettes, each loaded with 40 linked steel plates, behind the cab. Dimensions of each plate is 1 × 1.3 m. The roadway is laid with the vehicle travelling in reverse. As the truck travels backwards, the trackways unfold into the horizontal, pass over rollers and are laid under each of the rear wheels. This system is used to prepare the exit points of bridges such as the PMP/PMS pontoon bridging system. For this latter application the truck may be fitted with a front-mounted dozer blade.

Laying time with a crew of six is 10 minutes, retrieval time is 30 minutes. Once emplaced, the roadway can carry wheeled vehicles weighing up to 25,000 kg or tracked vehicles weighing up to 40,000 kg. Fully laden, the truck carrying the roadway system weighs 26,400 kg. Overall length carrying a dozer blade is 10.42 m.

Status
Production likely to be on an as required basis. In service with the armies of the Czech Republic and Slovakia. Produced in India by BEML for use with the Indian Army's licence-produced PMS pontoon bridging system.

Contractor
State factories of the former Czechoslovakia.

Contractor
BEML Ltd

Truck-mounted roadway laying system on a TATRA T 815 truck (BEML)
1185421

France

MOBI-MAT tactical mobility systems

Development
Deschamps & Sons is a family-owned business that has been manufacturing specialised fabrics since 1860. The fabric used as the basis for MOBI-MAT systems was developed and patented by the company in 1994.

Flatrack 100 mounted on an IVECO (6 × 6) truck (Deschamps)   1391113

French Army Case 821C wheeled loader fitted with a Front-end Loader launching Recovery Unit (FLRU) (Shaun C Connors)   0524732

MOBI-MAT is used by, or has been or is being evaluated by a number of armed forces including the Australian, Belgian, British, French, Greek, Italian, Norwegian, Portuguese, Singaporean, Spanish, Swiss, Swedish, Taiwanese, Turkish and unspecified Middle Eastern armies, the US Marine Corps and Army, the French, UK and US air forces, the Brazilian, French, Italian and Japanese navies.

MOBI-MAT tactical deployable mobility matting has previously been marketed as TEMP-TRAIL.

Description
MOBI-MAT is constructed using a woven polyester-based monofilament method that is light enough to place in position by hand but is capable of withstanding the weight of a Main Battle Tank (MBT) or transport aircraft. MOBI-MAT can be laid over almost any type of terrain - including longitudinal slopes of up to 20 per cent - without prior ground preparation, being particularly suited to grassland, marsh, sand or snow. According to the manufacturer it is flexible, strong and resistant to puncturing.

Three grades of MOBI-MAT are available; light grade, type LX; medium grade, type A2X; heavy grade (reinforced with fibreglass or carbon bars), types MM3V25 or C25.

MOBI-MAT, dependant on roll size, weight and surface conditions etc, can be laid in a number of ways including manually, the manual method with or without the assistance of basic recovery straps for leverage. Mechanical laying options include the Front-end Loader launching Recovery Unit (FLRU), a DROPS/PLS-type flatrack dispenser, a simple trailer, or by fluid or gas.

A Front-end Loader launching Recovery Unit (FLRU) by laying MOBI-MAT can be installed on almost any wheeled loader or all-terrain forklift truck. Laying is controlled by the operator with the usual operating controls and the laying vehicle simply drives forward onto deploying mat. The basic FLRU unit has the capacity for a 100 m roll of MM3V25 matting or a 150 m roll of A2X matting. The unladen FLRU unit weighs 1,500 kg at 4.2 m width, but is also available for 3.4 m width MOBI-MAT.

Laying from a flatrack that complies with STANAG 2413 can be carried out from any suitable truck equipped with a load-handling system of the Ampliroll, DROPS or PLS types. The roll is rotated through 90° from

Demonstration laying of MOBI-MAT by a Norwegian Army Bv206. In 2002 Deschamps received a EUR650,000 order from the Norwegian procurement agency for sufficient MOBI-MATs and associated laying mechanisms for the conversion of 50 Bv206 vehicles (Patrick Allen) 1181966

MOBI-MAT Beach Access in use during Joint Logisitics Over The Shore (JLOTS) 2009 (US Army) 1391116

Norwegian Army Bv206 converted for the transport and deployment of MOBI-MAT mobility matting (Shaun C Connors) 0524730

transport to laying position and the laying vehicle simply reverses onto deploying mat. The basic flatrack unit has the capacity for a 100 m roll of MM3V25 matting or a 150 m roll of A2X matting. The basic unit without matting weighed 3,000 kg.

Between 2007 and 2009, Deschamps developed a custom made flatrack, designated Flatrack 100", for the deployment of more than 100 m of MM3V25 MOBI-MAT. Total weight of the system is 10,600 kg, this including flatrack structure, 100 m of MOBI-MAT and mat fixing accessories. Flatrack 100 can be transported by any suitable capacity (6 × 6) truck equipped with a standard hooklift system. An unspecified number of units will be introduced into service by an unspecified customer early-2010.

A variation of the flatrack laying system has been developed for the rear section of the Hägglunds Bv206 all-terrain vehicle (or other similar vehicle) and is in service with the Norwegian Army.

MOBI-MAT, normally supplied in a white finish, is laid from rolls, which are anchored, to the ground with stakes or ground anchors through stainless steel grommets in the mat. Lengths can also be joined sideways on to create hard standing or storage and distribution areas. Once laid MOBI-MAT can be used throughout a −40 to +80°C temperature range, requires no maintenance and can be quickly pressure-washed and rolled up for movement, future use or storage. The matting is resistant to ultra-violet rays, while being weatherproof, rot-proof and unaffected by salt or sea water, oil or fuel spillage.

Temporary Roadway Quick Access (heavy duty MM3)
This is the standard grade used for temporary roadways. Standard width is 4.2 m, with standard roll lengths being 12.5 and 25 m; lengths of up to 100 m are available. A typical 4.2 × 25 m (W × L) mat reinforced with carbon

Australian Army MOBI-MAT Beach Access in use and deployed from a Front-end Loader launching Recovery Unit (FLRU) (Australian DoD) 1391114

Demonstration laying of Fast Composite Roadway (FCR) (Deschamps) 1391117

bars weighs 659 kg and has a rolled dimensions of diameter 850 mm; surface area covered is 105 m². Quick Access is suitable for all types of vehicles, wheeled or tracked. Up to 1,200 crossings without damage to the material are possible.

Beach Access
Beach Access is primarily for use during cross-beach landing operations and enables both wheeled and tracked vehicles to move freely in sand or pebble/shingle-type beach conditions. A 4.2 × 10 m (W × L) mat has rolled dimensions of diameter 450 mm and weighing 83 kg can be manually installed in five minutes; surface area covered is 42 m². Beach Access is available in standard lengths ranging from 10 to 40 m, and in 4.2 and 3.4 m widths. Lengths of up to 100 m are available on request. Fluorescent or reflective edging strips are an option. Up to 1,200 crossings without damage to the material are possible.

Beach Access normally uses medium duty A2X MOBI-MAT, however Deschamps does offer Beach Access in heavier grade MM3V25.

Traction Mat
Traction Mat is essentially 500 or 800 mm widths of A2X grade Beach Access matting in 5 or 8 m lengths. These are carried on vehicles and can be used as a preventative measure in areas known to be soft or difficult, or as a recovery aid for a bogged vehicle. A stainless steel eyelet at each end allows the matting to be secured to the ground by means of stakes or ground anchors supplied. A 500 mm × 5 m (W × L) mat has rolled dimensions of diameter 300 mm and weighs 4.5 kg; surface area covered is 2.5 m².

Fast Composite Roadway (FCR)
The Fast Composite Roadway (FCR) is a heavy duty roll-out aluminium mat system designed for supporting off road mobility requirements in adverse terrains and suitable for Joint Logistics Over The Shore (JLOTS) operations. Commercial-Off-The-Shelf (COTS), the FCR is composed of non-skid aluminium plates linked by connectors which allow a reduction in weight and volume and offer the possibility of rolling the FCR into a compact roll. Rapid deployment and recovery can be achieved with the Front-end Loader Roadway Dispenser or flatrack.

The US Army Corps of Engineers has ranked the FCR as the best performer solution under traffic.

Helipad (medium duty A2X)
Helipads are constructed using two or three rolls of medium grade A2X MOBI-MAT. Using three rolls a 12 × 12 m pad can be constructed by two people in approximately 10 minutes. Each roll weighs 85 kg. Once laid the

MOBI-MAT A2X matting in use as a helipad (Deschamps) 0538470

MOBI-MAT A2X matting in use as a helipad (US DoD)   1391115

helipad is suitable for all types of helicopters fitted with either wheeled or skid landing gear. MOBI-MAT is normally supplied in a white finish, although for helipad applications requiring higher visibility, with a black border. Helipads are currently in use in Afghanistan.

Tentfloor and Recpath (light duty LX)
Tentfloor and Recpath are supplied in 2.2 and 4.2 m widths and in lengths ranging from 6 to 25 m. This type of matting is used within temporary or semi-permanent expeditionary-type camps and can be supplied in green or brown if required.

Mobi-Deck
Mobi-Deck is an adjustable in height rigid flooring system that enables a dry floor environment to be preserved with any type of tent, offering protection to both personnel and equipment from flooding. Made of composite panels, Mobi-Deck uses a raised connecting frame which supports the composite decking material and assists with cable distribution and integration.

Tow-Mat (heavy duty MM3)
Heavy duty MM3 matting is suited for heavy aircraft crash recovery operations and for such usage is available in 1.05, 2.1 or 3 m widths.

Status
In production. In service. In addition to numerous civil applications worldwide, MOBI-MAT is, or has been, used, or is being evaluated by, the Australian, Belgian, British, French, Greek, Italian, Norwegian, Portuguese, Singaporean, South Korean, Spanish, Swedish, Swiss and unspecified Middle Eastern armies, the US Marine Corps and Army, the French, UK and US air forces, and the Brazilian, French, Italian and Japanese navies.

Contractor
Deschamps.

Subsidiary
DMS Inc.

Germany

Krauss-Maffei Wegmann folding roadway system

Development
During the late 1960s France, Germany and Italy undertook a study to improve the crossing of rough terrain by heavy vehicles. In 1974, these studies led to a concept and definition phase conducted by France and Germany. This was completed in late 1982. By then, 24 proposals had been submitted, of which four were selected for further study. The decision ultimately favoured a system of loosely interlocked hexagonal plates forming a temporary roadway capable of compensating for longitudinal and lateral inclinations without suffering damage, the Krauss-Maffei Wegmann (KMW) folding roadway system.

Description
The Krauss-Maffei Wegmann folding roadway system is made up of loosely interlocked hexagonal plates in sections 4.2 m wide and 2.77 m long, these sections being joined by a special joint. A 50 m standard logistic roadway is made up of 18 sections which can be rapidly disconnected or connected to form shorter or longer roadways.

The laying mechanism developed to lay and recover the roadway can be mounted on any type of truck with a payload greater than 10,000 kg.

During 1989 Krauss-Maffei Wegmann, the prime contractor, commenced series production. Subcomponents are produced in France by SOFRAME (formerly known as LOHR) and Fonderie Brea.

The equipment is carried on Austrian, German and the Royal Netherlands army MAN (8 × 8) 15,000 kg high-mobility trucks while the French Army uses Renault TRM 10000 (6 × 6) 10,000 kg trucks. The MAN

Krauss-Maffei Wegmann folding roadway of the Royal Netherlands Army in use, the section joints clearly visible at the front of the image (Shaun C Connors)   1128232

Folding Roadway System being deployed from a German Army MAN (8 × 8) high mobility truck (Krauss-Maffei Wegmann (KMW))   0059702

truck carries approximately 50 m of roadway while the Renault vehicle originally carried 40 m and used shorter (2.2 m) sections. A revised version of the TRM 10000 that could carry the same 50 m length as the MAN vehicle was being considered; it is not known if this was adopted. The French system is known as MATS (*Moyen d'Aide a la Traficabilite des Sols*). The carrying and laying equipment can also be mounted on other existing truck chassis.

The laying mechanism, which weighs 3,600 kg, is constructed of welded steel and is supported at three points. A swivel arm is erected hydraulically to guide the belt during the laying and/or recovery process. The laying mechanism can be lowered for rail transport. The main frame is the base for the roadway carrier. It is constructed of torsional elastic steel and consists of individual cross members. These are hinged to the vehicle chassis and support rails, which are bolted to the cross members. The roadway sits directly on the roadway carrier, which has an upper and lower cradle. To position the roadway the lower cradle can be moved longitudinally and the upper cradle can rotate 90° in either direction. Both assemblies are of welded steel construction and the lower cradle has a jointed cross-shaft axle to compensate for chassis distortion. The launching guide is a tubular steel lattice framework hydraulically pivoted over the top of an upright support. Rollers are mounted on the framework to reduce friction. The upright support is a welded aluminium two-part unit.

Folding Roadway System being deployed from a German Army MAN (8 × 8) high mobility truck (Krauss-Maffei Wegmann (KMW))   0059703

MATS/DEP-96 flatrack version of the Folding Roadway System on a Renault TRM 10000 (6 × 6) high mobility truck (Pierre Touzin)   0589078

MATS/DEP-96 flatrack version of the Folding Roadway System on a Renault TRM 10000 (6 × 6) high mobility truck (Pierre Touzin)   0056356

In use, the carrying truck is backed up to the site to be covered by the roadway. The roadway carrier is then rotated and moved into the laying position before a belt is attached to the beginning of the folding roadway. The laying operation starts as the vehicle moves on to the roll-on lanes attached to the first roadway section, which have first been passed to the rear wheels over the launching guide. The roadway is launched by continuously backing up the equipment. Unfolding of the roadway is stabilised and braked by the guide belt running off the winch.

The hexagonal roadway plates are plated chilled aluminium castings while joints and locks are aluminium.

The laying process takes approximately three minutes for every 50 m of roadway and the roadway can be laid on longitudinal slopes of up to 30 per cent and 15 per cent transverse slopes, as well as under water. The recovery process, using the central belt and rear winch is the reverse of the laying procedure with the carrying truck moving forward one section of plates at a time. The recovery process takes 20 minutes. Laying and recovery involves a vehicle driver and one other person.

Introduced in 1996, a variant known as the MATS/DEP-96 became available. This involves the same folding roadway system as described above but the entire system is mounted on a flatrack and is thus able to be carried on and deployed from, any truck with a 13,000 kg capacity (or upwards) fitted with a hydraulic load handling system. The French Army deploys this system from a Renault TRM 10 000 truck.

Specifications

Folding roadway system
Total length: 50 m
Length of each section: 2.77 m
Width: (nominal) 4.2 m
Weight:
(each plate) 10 kg (approx.)
(each section) 520 kg (approx.)
(50 m roadway) 9,400 kg (approx.)

Continuous load capacity:
(wheeled) MLC 30
(tracked) MLC 70

Status
Production as required. In service with the Austrian, French, German and Royal Netherlands armies.

Contractor
Krauss-Maffei Wegmann GmbH & Co Ltd

Portable roadway - Thyssen system

Description
The basis of this heavy portable roadway system is a hexagonal steel plate, which is connected to adjoining plates by angled iron brackets. Each plate weighs 23 kg and a standard truck width can be formed by joining nine plates which form a roadway 4.2 m wide. The roadway is constructed by hand and up to eight personnel can lay 1 m of roadway per minute. To support a 5,000 kg truck, a mat of 200 plates is necessary and for a 7,000 kg truck, 288 plates. To enable the system to be used for water crossings, a method has been evolved in which a completed mat is towed across the water obstacle by a vehicle with a winch. One of the advantages of this system is that it can be assembled under cover and then dragged by winch across the ground to be covered, enabling heavy concentrations to be built up rapidly in forward areas.

Status
Supplied to the Danish, German and Royal Netherlands armies (and possibly others); exact operational status unclear. Any further production of this product by the now ThyssenKrupp is highly unlikely as the technology used has been superseded.

Royal Netherlands Army Thyssen portable roadway in use late 2006 (Shaun C Connors)   1128233

Greece

MICROTECH Class 60 trackway

Description
The MICROTECH Class 60 trackway is used to support armoured and other vehicles over soft ground. It uses the same components and general construction methods as the MICROTECH Runway Repair Decking described in the Rapid runway repair equipment/portable runways section. The trackway is designed for both tracked and wheeled vehicles and is constructed from extruded sections made of heat-treated aluminium alloy. The trackway consists of a number of panels with a

tongue on one side and a groove in the other. Each panel has a corrugated shape which, together with additional grooves on the section faces, provides an anti-slip surface. The panels are provided in 2.3 and 4.6 m lengths which can be easily handled by one person or, more conveniently, by two people using special handling tools. Two end ramp panel sections are supplied enabling vehicles to get on to the trackway easily.

The tongue-and-groove connecting method joins panels together. The panels are locked in place with special aluminium alloy bolts which may be removed for disassembly, cleaning and storage. If the trackway is to be laid on a slope it should be anchored in place using a special chain and shackle assembly. Eight section-handling tools are supplied for ease of carrying and assembly of the panels as well as placement of the locking bolts. Optional accessories include towing adaptors.

To produce a standard trackway 40.4 m long and 4.6 m wide a full set as supplied will consist of the following: 176 4.6 m long panels, eight 2.3 m long panels, two ramp panels, eight handling tools, four towing adaptors, 400 locking bolts, four strap assemblies, four 18-link welded chains, 24 steel guy stakes and 12 shackles. Recovery of the mat is facilitated by the use of a strong 50 m long recovery strap.

The trackway can also be used to construct a mat to cover an area of soft ground for depot, maintenance area and other uses. A standard set can be produced to construct a mat 18.4 m wide and 11.7 m long. The tools and accessories supplied are the same as those used for a standard trackway set but the mat requires 185 4.6 m panels, 54 2.3 m panels and eight ramp panels.

Specifications

MICROTECH Class 60 trackway
Main section width:
(overall) 242 mm
(effective) 225 mm
Length:
(long panel) 4.6 m
(short panel) 2.3 m
Weight:
(long panel) 32 kg
(short panel) 16 kg
Ramp section width:
(overall) 184 mm
(effective) 152 mm
Ramp section length: (long panel) 4.6 m
Ramp section weight: (long panel) 37 kg
Breaking load: 150 kg/cm of length of standard panel

Status
In service with the Greek armed forces (an inventory of 74 sets in 2004).

Contractor
MICROTECH Limited (this company is no longer trading)

India

Mat Ground Surfacing-CL 70 (MGS-70)

Description
The Mat Ground Surfacing-CL 70 (MGS-70) was developed by the Research and Development Establishment (Engineers) at Dighi, Pune, and was previously referred to as Mat Fording. It is intended for deployment at the approaches to water obstacle fording points and in waterlogged areas and may be used at water depths up to 1 m. It can support vehicles up to MLC 70 and provides a firm roadway 4.8 m wide.

Mat Ground Surfacing is formed by laterally joining a series of 4 m wide extruded aluminium planks, which are interlocked to form a standard length of 50 m which is rolled on to a spool. A swivelling platform supports

Mat Ground Surfacing-CL 70 (MGS-70) in the launch position and showing detail of the launch platform and spool (Shaun C Connors)   0525925

the spool and is mounted on a Bharat Earth Movers Limited (BEML) licence-produced TATRA 815 (8 × 8) truck. Other similar vehicles with a ≥9,000 kg payload capability could be employed.

The system is operated by a hydraulic unit powered by a power take-off on the vehicle. In the transport mode, the spool is locked in position along the chassis. In operation, the spool is turned through 90° to position the spool across the chassis.

For laying, the vehicle is positioned with the rear wheels just ahead of the position where laying is to commence. The mat is laid over the rear of the vehicle and placed under the rear wheels. As the vehicle reverses, the mat rolls off the spool until the full 50 m length is in position. More 50 m lengths can be laid if required.

The mat is recovered in the reverse sequence.

Specifications
MGS-70
Areal density: (of mat) 34 kg/m^2
Weight:
(mat, 50 m length) 8,500 kg
Length: 50 m
Width 4.8 m

Status
In production. In service with the Indian Army and offered for export sales.

Development agency
Research and Development Establishment (Engineers)

Trackway Heavy

Description
Trackway Heavy was developed by the Research and Development Establishment (Engineers) at Dighi, Pune. It is a trackway expedient suitable for negotiating marginal terrain at bridge or ferry sites where it is essential to avoid the formation of ruts to maintain continuous traffic. It can also be used to cross loose desert sand.

The Trackway Heavy consists of a 50 m long series of extruded aluminium alloy planks each 3.35 m wide. It is rolled on to a spool mounted on a swivelling platform and carried on a wheeled vehicle. Trackway Heavy can support MLC 30 traffic over sandy or marshy terrain and can be laid over the vehicle cab and in front of the carrier vehicle at the rate of 1,000 m/h by one platoon of engineers.

The system can be configured for mounting on any vehicle with a payload capacity of 5,000 kg and a load area measuring 4 × 2 m.

Status
In production. In service with the Indian Army and offered for export sales.

Development agency
Research and Development Establishment (Engineers)

Trackway Heavy in the transport position on a Shaktiman truck (DRDO)
0044607

Trackway Light

Description
Trackway Light was developed by the Research and Development Establishment (Engineers) at Dighi, Pune. It is a trackway expedient suitable for enabling light wheeled traffic (MLC 12) to travel over very soft sandy or marshy ground, deserts and ploughed fields.

Trackway Light consists of aluminium alloy planks 1 m wide supplied in rolls 25 m long. Rolls can be joined and spread with a gap of 0.75 m between two rolls, thereby forming a trackway for light vehicles. The trackway can be laid manually or by mechanical means.

Laying rolls of Trackway Light (DRDO)   0010149

1,000 m of Trackway Light can be laid in eight hours by one engineer section. Eight rolls of the trackway can be carried by a single 3,000 kg Shaktiman truck.

Status
In production. In service with the Indian Army and offered for export sales.

Development agency
Research and Development Establishment (Engineers)

Japan

JGSDF trackway

Description
The Japanese Ground Self-Defence Force uses at least two locally produced types of trackway. These are both transported by Isuzu SKW series 3,500 kg (6 × 6) dump trucks. It is probable the difference between the two types is load classification, although what appears to be the lighter trackway is constructed of larger (widthways) planks.

Demonstration laying of JGSDF trackway by its transport/laying vehicle, an Isuzu SKW series 3,500 kg (6 × 6) dump truck. This is probably the heaviest (MLC class) of the two trackway types known to be used by the JGSDF (Mitsuhiro Kadota)   0587593

Japanese GSDF trackway is transported/laid by an Isuzu SKW series 3,500 kg (6 × 6) dump truck. This is probably the lightest (MLC class) trackway which differs primarily from the heavier trackway in the type of planks used (Mitsuhiro Kadota)   1156105

Spools of trackway are transported lengthways in the dump body of the transport/laying truck, the spool platform swivelling through 90° for laying operations. The free end of the mat is placed under the rear wheels of the carrying vehicle, which then reverses to roll the trackway off the spool. It is likely that individual rolls of trackway can be joined to form extended roadways.

No technical details regarding trackway used by the JGSDF have been made available, although weight of the trackway, spool and platform is unlikely to be more than 5,000 kg, the on-road payload rating of the Isuzu SKW series dump truck.

Status
Production likely to be on an as required basis. In service with the JGSDF.

Contractor
Not known.

Netherlands

Robusta Trackway Mats and Bog Strips

Development
The original Mammoth Mat was developed by Robusta under the supervision of the Royal Netherlands Army as a temporary roadway to allow the operation of vehicles, wheeled or tracked, in areas that were or would very quickly become difficult or impossible to traverse. Mammoth Mat may also be used to construct temporary helicopter landing pads and for the recovery of off-runway aircraft.

The lighter Bog Strips were developed to be used to facilitate the passage of wheeled vehicles across ground that would otherwise be impassable to them; they may also be used to assist in the recovery of a bogged vehicle, including in conjunction with a self-recovery winch or towing vehicle in the case of badly bogged vehicles.

Description
Trackway Mats
Robusta currently offers a Light Trackway Mat, a Heavy Trackway Jumbo Mat, and a Heavy Trackway Mammoth Mat, in standard sizes of 100 × 300 cm, 2,500 × 400 cm, 2,500 × 400 cm, and weighing 145 kg, 400 kg, and 1,500 kg, respectively. Other sizes are available to meet specific user requirements.

These mats can be used on a variety of soft soil types including fine non-cohesive sand, clay, loam or peat in marshland or swamp-like areas. Wheeled vehicles can climb gradients of approximately 55 per cent on the laid mat. These mats require no maintenance and are constructed from a chemical and UV resistant woven polypropylene fabric that is reinforced lengthwise by galvanised steel wires. In addition to the lengthwise steel wires, Heavy Trackway Mammoth Mat is reinforced by transverse spring steel bars that work to provide the mat with a so-called membrane action that enables the transfer of high wheel loads to the sub-soil without significant rutting of the soil or permanent deformation of the mat.

Light Trackway Mat can be carried by a team of six, and laid by a team of two people. Jumbo and Mammoth mats, while heavier remain relatively light in weight and easy to handle. Rolls are reusable and can be handled by most cargo vehicle-mounted materials handling cranes and can be laid and retrieved by four to five people.

Bog Strips
Bog Strips are manufactured from a woven synthetic fabric composed of deltaflex yarns, which are specially made to reduce the risk of overheating the fabric under spinning wheel conditions. For reinforcement, Bog Strips

Four Bog Strips allow 'leap-frogging', an operation that enables this Australian Army Land Rover to make a climb up through some sand dunes; a climb it would otherwise be unable to make due to the combination of gradient and loose, soft sand (Robusta)   0524768

Mammoth Mat being unrolled on soft ground to provide a track for a UK Royal Air Force aircraft (Robusta)   0524769

Class 30 trackway ready to be launched (MVRDE)   0512428

include transversely located flexible steel rods of high yield stress. Four types are presently available: Bog Strips Classic (550 × 50 cm; 16.5 kg), Bog Strips Classic Light Weight (550 × 50 cm; 8 kg); Bog Strips Special (400 × 100 cm; 25 kg); Bog Strips Special Light Weight (400 × 100 cm; 10 kg). Other sizes are also available to meet specific requirements.

Bog Strips may be used in a variety of terrain including loose sand and soft mud where they can facilitate the passage of wheeled vehicles across ground that would otherwise be impassable to them. Bog Strips may also be used to assist in the recovery of a bogged vehicle, including in conjunction with a self-recovery winch or towing vehicle in the case of badly bogged vehicles. After use they are easily cleaned and may be stored or transported folded or rolled for future use.

Individual strips are light enough to be handled by one person and using four strips allows 'leap-frogging', enabling a vehicle, for example, to make a climb up through sand dunes or across a wide expanse of soft mud. A simple steel anchor or peg can be used to fix Bog Strips to the ground in particularly slippery surface conditions.

Status
In production. In service with the British Army and Royal Air Force and being, or has been evaluated by the armed forces of Australia, Canada, France and the Netherlands.

Contractor
Robusta BV

Pakistan

Trackway, Class 30 and Class 60

Development
The Military Vehicles Research and Development Establishment at Rawalpindi has developed two forms of trackway, Class 30 and Class 60. These trackways are designed to allow the negotiation of impassable terrain and to enable the continuous transit of marginal terrain by a variety of wheeled and tracked vehicles. They are similar in appearance and construction to the FAUN Class 30 and Class 60/Class 70 Portable Trackways which are in service with around 30 countries.

Description

Vehicle Launched Assault Trackway Class 30
The Vehicle Launched Assault Trackway Class 30 is assembled from a number of high-tensile extruded aluminium alloy planks, 3.352 m long and 257 mm wide, with interlocking tongue and groove joints, forming a continuous non-skid surface 3.352 m wide and 50 m long. The trackway can be used by wheeled vehicles and tracked vehicles with suitable running gear. Heavier vehicles can use the trackway when ground conditions are favourable. Tanks up to Class 50 may cross at an angle provided they do not slew when negotiating the trackway.

The Class 30 trackway can be launched and recovered by its transport vehicle. A spool carrying 50 m of trackway is mounted on a 5,000 kg forward control cab truck. The carriage assembly comprises a swivel-type turntable on which a steel stand carrying a three-flanged spool and steel wire rope spool drum is fitted. The trackway is wrapped around the spool and, using the turntable, can be turned to the appropriate position for launching the trackway. The spool can be rotated mechanically in either direction while laying or retrieving the trackway using a 7,000 kg pull capacity winch, powered through an auxiliary drive from the carrier vehicle's transmission. A manual handbrake on one side of the spool is used to control the speed during the uncoiling of the spool.

The launching assembly consists of a structural steel frame to carry the trackway over the carrier vehicle cab during the launching operation. The assembly can be removed for carrying on the vehicle body during moves and can be replaced within minutes.

The leading edge of the Class 30 trackway is first laid on the ground by hand with the trackway passing above the vehicle cab and with the leading edge placed under the front wheels. The vehicle then moves forward so that the trackway unwinds and passes under the truck wheels. Recovery is over the rear of the vehicle. The preparation and launching operation can be carried out in 10 to 20 minutes by a crew of three. Recovery takes approximately the same time.

Vehicle Launched Tank Access Class 60
This heavy-duty trackway is intended for both wheeled and tracked vehicles and can support MBTs up to 60,000 kg over very soft ground. Its construction is similar to that of the Class 30 trackway except that each panel in 4.572 m long and 228 mm wide. Each panel weighs 33 kg and is 6.35 mm thick.

This trackway is launched and recovered hydraulically by its transporter vehicle. A complete 45 m length set is carried on two Yasoob 6 × 6 (or similar) trucks, each carrying a 22.5 m length.

For this trackway the launching assembly consists of a steel framework which carries the trackway over the vehicle platform during a launching operation. The assembly can be removed and carried on the vehicle body during moves and can be replaced within minutes.

For launch, a spool carrying the two joined halves of the trackway is carried towards the rear of the carrier vehicle. The swivelling stand carrying the spool is hydraulically powered to the lateral operational position and a short length of trackway is fed off the spool and tucked under the rear wheels. The vehicle then reverses and launches the trackway as it proceeds. Recovery is carried out in the opposite direction using a winch to position the trackway back on the spool. The preparation and launching operation can be carried out in 10-20 minutes by a crew of three. Recovery takes approximately the same time.

Specifications

Type	Class 30	Class 60
Length:	50.292 m	45 m
Weight:		
(each set of 220 planks)	3,400 kg	7,350 kg
(each plank)	16 kg	33 kg
Width:	3.352 m	4.572 m
Carrying vehicle:	5 ton truck	6 ton truck
Launch system:	vehicle	hydraulic

Status
In production. In service with Pakistani armed forces.

Contractor
Development agency
Military Vehicles Research and Development Establishment, (MVRDE)

Russian Federation

Glued plywood roadway sections - SRDP

Description
The lightest of the Russian Federation types of portable roadway is the SRDP (*Sborno-Razbornoye-Dorozhnoye Pokrytiye*). The basic element of this system is a glued plywood panel measuring 2.5 m × 1 m × 700 mm and weighing between 100 and 120 kg. Each panel is held in place by wooden inserts placed into butt-brackets at each end. The panels can be laid to form either strips or wider roadways. They are normally laid by hand by teams of 10 to 12 personnel, but a mechanical laying method has been developed which enables strips to be laid from amphibious PTS vehicles.

SRDP glued plywood roadway sections forming the operating base for a KrAZ 255B crane truck during bridge-building operations
(James Kinnear)   0567946

This method replaces the wooden end inserts with steel cables and the panels are pre-prepared as they are loaded on to the PTS.

The panels are prepared using methods that have been specially developed taking advantage of the large timber resources of the Russian Federation. The wooden sheets that make up each panel are joined together by phenol-formaldehyde glues and are then rapidly passed to a further process, which pressure-coats the panels with a layer of Bakelite material. The ends are covered by strips of similarly treated plywood and surface gripping strips are added. The panels then require no further maintenance and can be stored in the open if necessary.

Specifications

SRDP
Panel dimensions: 2.5 × 1.0 × 0.7 m
Wearing quality: 40,000-50,000 vehicles
Weight:
 (single panel) 100-120 kg
 (panels for 1 km road) 80,000-100,000 kg
Number of ZIL-164 trucks: (to transport 1 km of road) 25-30
Rate of laying: 100-150 running m/h

Status
Production likely to be on an as required basis. In service with the armed forces of the Russian Federation.

Contractor
State factories.
(Simplified versions may be assembled in army workshops)

Heavy portable roadway sections

Description
There are three basic forms of portable heavy roadway used by the armed forces of the Russian Federation, two of which make use of the great timber resources of the Russian Federation with timber girders and planks on timber ribs. As such there are many different forms and sizes and many are made either by local state (or former state) factories, or by Army workshops. Although the sizes may vary, for supply purposes, each section using wood planks is estimated to weigh between 160 and 220 kg less crosspieces and the girders are estimated to weigh between 250 and 300 kg. Roadways using such timber sections are laid either by hand or by cranes and the rate of laying can vary between 40 and 60 m/h.

Portable roadway sections with KrAZ-255B (6 × 6) truck acting as carrying and laying vehicle (James Kinnear)   0589079

The third form of roadway section is manufactured from corrugated steel sheets, each weighing between 100 and 110 kg. Each section measures 2 m × 1.05 m × 800 mm, although this may vary. Roadways using these steel sheets can be assembled either by hand or by crane.

Specifications

Heavy portable roadway sections
Dimensions: 2.0 × 1.05 × 0.8 m
Wearing quality: 50,000-70,000 vehicles
Weight:
 (single section) 100-110 kg
 (section for 1 km road) 100,000-120,000 kg
Number of trucks: (to transport 1 km of road) 30-35
Rate of laying: up to 100 m/h

Status
Production likely to be on an as required basis. In service with the former Warsaw Pact forces.

Contractor
State factories.
Can be assembled in army workshops.

Slovakia

Truck-mounted roadway laying system

Description
This system was produced in the state factories of the former Czechoslovakia and remains in service with the armies of the Czech Republic and Slovakia. It is understood to be in use in India with PMS bridging sets licence produced by BEML limited. Full details of the system can be found under Czech Republic in this section.

Sweden

Columbus Mat

Description
The Columbus Mat was designed by Curt F Lundin and is used for a wide variety of civilian and military applications. These include the reinforcement of soft ground to enable tracked or wheeled vehicles to cross difficult country, at river exit points and as military bridge access mats. It is also used as recovery tracks for aircraft recovery after abortive take-offs and landing overruns. (The Royal Thai Air Force and Scandinavian airports purchased sets for this purpose.) The standard 5 m mat consists of polythene tubing held together by 15 steel cables. At the ends of the mats there are three tubes 65 mm in diameter and 15 mm thick. The other tubes (71 in all) have an external diameter of 65 mm and are 5.8 mm thick. The cables have 171 threads and a diameter of 8 mm and the cable ends are drawn in a loop back through the heavy end tube. Coupling links at the cable ends enable mats to be joined end-to-end to form a roadway of any length.

Laying and recovery require no special tools or equipment and the mat can be transported by truck either flat, rolled or folded.

For use by heavy vehicles at water crossings, a special system called the Vehicle Mat 2MT was developed. The complete system consists of: four mats, each with 140 mm outside diameter end tubes and heavy-duty cables with coupling links, two steel anchoring beams, four climbing frames, 12 chains, 10 soil anchor frames, 20 soil rod sets plus cables and other accessories. Weight of the complete equipment is 5,600 kg. The system was developed in close co-operation with the Swedish Army.

The basic idea is that the mats and the climbing frames, which consist of four Bailey bridge panels, are assembled on the bank on one side of the river and then winched down the river bank by a winch on the far bank. Once in place, the mats are held firmly in position by the soil anchor frames that are staked to the ground and connected to the anchoring beam by chains.

Specifications

Basic mat
Width: 4.5 m (other widths were available in 300 mm multiples)
Length: max 15 m (normal standard 5 m)
Weight: 20 kg/m²

Status
Production complete. Supplied to the armed forces of Germany, Norway, Sweden, Switzerland, Thailand, UK and the US. Used with aircraft recovery kits by many countries.

Contractor
Vårgårda Plast AB

United Kingdom

FAUN Portable Trackways

Development

The Military Load Class (MLC) 30 and 60 (now MLC 70) Portable Trackways made by FAUN MV Ltd's Trackway Division were originally designed for the British Army by the then Military Engineering Experimental Establishment (MEXE). Later development was by Laird (Anglesey) Limited (subsumed into FAUN Municipal Vehicles Ltd in 1996) in conjunction with the British Aluminium Company (now Alcan Inc).

The most recent Trackway development by FAUN is the Medium/Heavy Ground Mobility Systems (MGMS)/(HGMS). The MGMS/HGMS is essentially Class 30 or Class 70 Trackway, but adapted for use in a single mechanised operation and available as a complete system.

FAUN Portable Trackway in all forms continues to be supplied to armed forces (and others) worldwide, with around 40 current military users.

The same basic technology is used in FAUN MVs Rapid Runway Repair (RRR), Aircraft Landing Mat (ALM) and Helicopter Landing Mat (HLM) products. Full details of these products can be found in the Rapid runway repair equipment/portable runways section.

Description

FAUN Trackway products consist of a number of interlocking, captive tongue-and-groove jointed, extruded aluminium alloy planks, these able to be unwound from a spool to provide non-skid surfaces which are firm enough for going over ground that is, or would quickly become, impassable to vehicles. After use Trackway products can be recovered, rewound, relocated and reused many times.

MGMS/HGMS, the latest Trackway development, differ from conventional Trackway in that they are carried on and deployed from a Fastrack (MGMS) or Trackrack (HGMS).

The following subsections detail individual Trackway and MGMS/HGMS products:

Class 30 Trackway

Class 30 Trackway is stated to have an almost unlimited life when used by military vehicles up to MLC 30. This includes most wheeled logistic vehicles and tracked vehicles with rubber-blocked tracks. It can also be used by heavier wheeled and tracked vehicles, up to MLC 50, when ground conditions are favourable, although some damage to the trackway may occur.

Prior to the recent introduction of the MGMS the standard truck-mounted laying and recovery system for Trackway was known as the Laying and Recovery Equipment (LRE), and this could be transported by any typical 4,000 kg flatbed military truck. Carried along the length of the truck during road delivery, the spool is rotated through 90° on its turntable

32 m lengths of Class 30 Trackway; the Case 721 BXT wheeled loader is fitted with an empty Trackway spool and a Trackway dispenser (Carl Schulze)   1391223

A MAN SX range truck of the Norwegian Army on a length of Class 30 Trackway (Carl Schulze)   1391224

British Army Leyland Trucks (4 × 4) 4,000 kg truck carrying Class 30 Trackway (Richard Stickland)   0056304

A Grove Coles 315M Medium Field Crane removing a recently recovered roll of Class 30 Trackway from a British Army Bedford MJ (4 × 4) 4,000 kg truck (Shaun C Connors)   0525926

assembly so that Trackway can be laid either over the front of the truck or over the rear. Preparation on site and launching of standard 32 m spools can be completed by a team of five in 10 minutes. Trackway is recovered over the rear of the truck using ratchet spanners by a team of five in about 15 minutes.

When unwound a standard roll of Class 30 Trackway will form a continuous non-skid surface that is 32 m long and 3.35 m wide. When a Trackway longer than 32 m is required, a vehicle-mounted LRE can be reloaded with further spools delivered by general-purpose transport or hydraulic recover over the rear. Once laid, the second and subsequent lengths of Trackway can be clamped to those already laid. Anchorage stores are provided for use on steeply sloping ground.

An important application of Class 30 Trackway is beach landing. The Trackway on its carrier frame, matched to a waterproofed rough terrain fork lift truck or wheeled loader, is unrolled on to the beach as the fork lift or loader moves through the shallows from a landing craft on to the beach.

Case UK Limited secured a British Army contract for the provision of Trackway Dispensers for fitment to Case 721 BXT wheeled loaders to allow them to carry, deploy and recover a 32 m length of Class 30 Trackway. The dispenser is manufactured by Ulrich Attachments Limited. A total of nine were delivered to the Royal Marines, 40 to the Royal Engineers, with a further two units having been supplied to the Royal Netherlands Marines.

The dispenser is fitted with free-wheel for deployment of the Trackway and a hydraulic motor rewind for recovery. A manually operated brake controls free-wheel when laying and prevents rotation when travelling. The dispenser's carriage frame incorporates an hydraulically operated side shift and rotation which allows a 175 mm movement either side to assist alignment during recovery, as well as loading and unloading on Landing Craft Utility Mark 10.

Class 70 Trackway

Heavy-duty Class 70 Trackway, originally designed to carry tracked and wheeled vehicles up to MLC 60 has also been approved for use by MLC 70 vehicles.

When used to reinforce any heavily used route, such as defiles at a bridge approach and exit, Class 70 Trackway is usually delivered in a roll and unwound at the site. The Trackway can be laid as a roll up to 15 m long from under armour when carried by tanks or other combat vehicles, power-laid from a roll up to 50 m long from 10,000 to 16,000 kg payload logistic vehicles, or laid by hand either as a 15 m roll or as an area mat.

Class 70 Trackway has other applications for the rapid repair of battle damage to runways for fast jet aircraft or for the rapid construction of extra hardstandings and dispersals for aircraft.

Typical military vehicles can carry rolls up to 30 m on 8,000 kg, 45 m on 10,000 kg and 50 m on 16,000 kg trucks. A standard Class 70 plank weighs 33.1 kg, is 4.6 m long and provides an effective width of 200 mm. Half planks are used to stagger the joints during mat assembly and to allow easy subdivision of long (50 m) rolls.

A roll of Class 30 Trackway on a Danish Army IVECO Magirus 110-16 AWM 5,000 kg truck (Martin Pagh)   1156193

Demonstration laying of FAUN Class 30 Trackway (Shaun C Connors)   0116242

FAUN Class 30 Trackway in use to facilitate the transfer of wheeled vehicles from MEXEFLOAT to shore (Shaun C Connors)   1124783

Demonstration laying of FAUN Class 60 Trackway (Shaun C Connors)   0116243

When transported on suitably equipped logistic vehicles, 50 m of Class 70 Trackway can be laid or recovered by a team of two in five to 10 minutes.

As with the lighter Class 30 Trackway, the Trackway is carried on a detachable spool supported by a swivelling stand with a hydraulic power unit. The LRE can be mounted directly on the vehicle chassis or clamped to the vehicle deck. Trackway is laid or recovered over the rear of the vehicle.

Heavy Ground Mobility System (HGMS)
The HGMS is essentially Class 70 Trackway, but adapted for use in a single mechanised operation and available as a complete system. No dedicated vehicle is required and the concept offers essentially an autonomous mechanised laying and retrieval system.

Initially the HGMS consisted of four subsystems: the Trackrack, spool, Trackway and accessories. A recent addition to the product is the Spoolrack, a Trackway transfer system.

The key component of the HGMS is the Trackrack, this capable of transport by any DROPS/PLS-type truck or trailer, and operated by any DROPS-PLS-type truck with the necessary hydraulic adaptations.

Mounted on the Trackrack is a turntable carrying a spool stand on which is wound the Trackway. The Trackway consists of a number of full and half panels linked together to form a track 4.57 m wide. When laid on the ground the Trackway can bear up to MLC 70 loads (wheeled vehicles up to MLC 60). At 5 m intervals along the Trackway, half panels help divide the Trackway into shorter sections or to enable the removal of damaged panels at any position. If required, one length of Trackway can be joined to another, with the ends overlapping by about 1 m.

For deployment, the mounting vehicle comes to a halt and the turntable is traversed through 90°. The vehicle then moves slowly backwards as the Trackway unwinds over the rear. Trackway can be laid and recovered without the driver leaving the cab. On level terrain and under typical daylight conditions, the HGMS can launch 50 m of Trackway within six minutes of the vehicle coming to a halt. The actual laying time is under three minutes.

Complete launch/recover cycle times in ideal daylight conditions are less than 10 minutes, these increasing to less than 15 minutes when dark.

Total weight of a Trackrack is 4,020 kg, the spool weighs approximately 740 kg, 50 m clean Trackway approximately 7,950 kg (33.11 kg per full panel; 159 kg per linear m), giving a total weight of around 12,710 kg. Overall Trackrack dimensions are 5.89 × 2.44 × 2.36 m (L × W × H).

The transport vehicle, which would ideally be a four-axle (preferably 8 × 8) DROPS/PLS-type truck. should have a rated payload of at least 2,000 kg greater than the 12,700 kg figure, 2,000 kg being the estimated weight increase of a 'dirty' 50 m length of Trackway.

The recently introduced Spoolrack is a simplified version of the Trackrack. The Spoolrack is described as a force multiplier. It is demountable, designed to carry 50 m of Trackway, and can be operated by two people. The Spoolrack carrying an additional 50 m of Trackway weighs 10,700 kg and is transported on a DROPS/PLS or flatbed trailer (or another DROPS/PLS or flatbed truck). ISO Twistlock fitting locations are to ISO 668 Series 1 freight containers type 1C, and tie down restraints to STANAG 3400 & 3548.

After laying the first roll of Trackway the empty truck is parked alongside the trailer (or other truck) and the two connected with quick release hydraulic couplings. Chains on the Trackrack are attached to the end of the Trackway on the Spoolrack to pull the Trackway across, the Trackway being transferred across to the Trackrack in a constant tension mode. The complete operation takes two people less than 15 minutes in daylight conditions (less than 20 when dark) with one set of controls. The transfer system is completely reversible to recover the Trackway.

The Spoolrack has been tested in extreme conditions including operating temperatures down to −40 °C.

The Norwegian Army was the initial customer for the HGMS, with the first deliveries made during late 1998. The Norwegian Army currently has 8 racks and 16 rolls of Trackway, using a Scania P113 HK (8 × 6) truck to carry and deploy the system.

Sweden, Switzerland and Turkey have also procured the HGMS. Sweden and Switzerland jointly procured a total of 32 HGMS, with first deliveries (of nine HGMS) to Sweden during 2009. Turkey received 40 HGMS mounted on IVECO (8 × 8) Trakker chassis during 2008-2010, the order valued at EUR19.5 million.

Medium Ground Mobility System (MGMS)
The recently introduced MGMS is essentially Class 30 Trackway, but as with the earlier HGMS, is adapted for use in a single mechanised operation and available as a complete system.

The key components and operating concept of the MGMS are similar to those of the HGMS, there are however weight, dimensional, operating and capability differences.

When laid on the ground the Trackway can bear up to MLC 30 loads (wheeled vehicles up to MLC 60). At 5 m intervals along the Trackway, half panels help divide the Trackway into shorter sections or to enable the removal of damaged panels at any position. If required, one length of Trackway can be joined to another, with the ends overlapping by about 1 m.

For deployment, the mounting vehicle comes to a halt and the turntable is traversed through 90°. The vehicle then moves slowly backwards as the Trackway unwinds over the rear. Trackway can be laid and recovered without the driver leaving the cab. On level terrain and under typical daylight conditions, the MGMS can launch 32 m of Trackway within 10 minutes of the vehicle coming to a halt. The actual laying time is five minutes.

Total weight of a Fastrack is 537 kg, the Turntable weighs 324 kg, the Spool weighs approximately 320 kg, which with a 32 m roll of Trackway gives a total weight of 5,000 kg. Overall Trackrack dimensions are 4.6 × 2.15 × 1.85 m (L × W × H).

The transport vehicle, which would ideally be a two-axle (preferably 4 × 4) truck should have a rated payload of at least 5,000 kg, the Fastrack (which includes an integral hydraulic powerpack) being fitted to either the standard flatbed body by either ISO twistlocks or side clamps, or direct to the truck chassis if required.

MGMS Beach Dispenser

The MGMS can also be deployed and recovered using a medium weight (>13,000 kg GVW) wheeled tractor. The Beach Dispenser was specifically designed to meet a UK Royal Marines requirement for beach landings.

The Beach Dispenser requires three minutes 30 seconds to lay a 32 m roadway in daylight conditions, this increasing to six minutes when dark. Recovery takes eight minutes 30 seconds in daylight, 11 minutes when dark; in all instances three personnel are required.

The Beach Dispenser is fitted with free-wheel for deployment of the Trackway and a hydraulic motor rewind for recovery. A manually operated brake controls free-wheel when laying and prevents rotation when travelling. The dispenser's carriage frame incorporates an hydraulically operated side shift and rotation which allows a 175 mm movement either side to assist alignment during recovery, as well as loading and unloading on landing craft.

Status

In production. Supplied to around 40 armed forces worldwide.

Contractor

FAUN MV Ltd

United States

BRAVO mat system

Description

The BRAVO mat system is a temporary surface for access and staging over soft soils or delicate surfaces. Individual BRAVO mats weigh 22.68 kg each and measure 1.22 × 1.22 m, with 1.07 × 1.07 m of useable surface per mat. Each mat includes four integrated twist lock fasteners permanently retained within the unit, and require a simple waist-high tool to lock the mats in place. A two-person crew can install a 6.10 × 15.24 m area in less than one hour.

The BRAVO mat system is made of a durable and lightweight thermoplastic formulation that can be configured in multiple patterns for a wide variety of uses and is capable of support normal vehicle traffic. Compressive load capacity is at present 2.07 MPa (21.1 kg/cm²), testing is ongoing. Rubberised surfaces on both sides of the mat provide traction as well as resistance to weather, oil, and chemicals. Tests are ongoing, although a five-year active service life is projected.

Status

In production. In service with the US Army.

Contractor

Newpark Mats & Integrated Services LLC

The BRAVO mat system in use as a temporary field workshop floor (Newpark Mats & Integrated Services)   1036526

DURA-BASE composite mat system

Development

The DURA-BASE composite mat system was developed as a quickly assembled, semi-permanent surface, to allow for the continued movement of both wheeled and tracked vehicles across marginal terrain or surfaces that would rapidly become difficult to negotiate due to heavy traffic flow. The DURA-BASE composite mat system is suitable for both military and civil applications.

Description

Individual DURA-BASE mat sections are constructed of high-density polythene (HDPE) and the standard size is 2.44 × 4.27 m (8 × 14 ft), allowing them to be transported on a suitable capacity conventional flatbed truck. Each mat consists of two HDPE parts heat-welded together for added strength and durability and has a nominal weight of 476 kg (1,050 lb). Thickness is 108 mm (4 ¼ in) and an overlapping lip and 16-hole pin system provides a solid interlocking system to reduce slippage and movement on uneven or loose surfaces. To enhance the grip and traction of traversing vehicles, the surface has an embossed tread pattern that has a friction coefficient comparable to a metalled road surface.

DURA-BASE is fully reversible, providing two identical surfaces for extended wear and utility. Once deployed, DURA-BASE can withstand a fixed track or neutral turn by tracked armour, such as the 30,000 kg Bradley infantry fighting vehicle.

The mat's ability to dissipate static charge equals that of typical two-ply wooden matting, while structural and performance tests indicate five times the life expectancy of such a system. Specific traffic tests have shown the mats to have a life expectancy in excess of 15 years and fatigue tests have shown no appreciable damage at 60,000 cycles (203 mm (6 in) deflection of 2.44 m (8 ft) span).

The DURA-BASE composite mat system can be used on sand, mud, gravel, snow and ice, and in addition to forming roadways for transport purposes, the modular design of the systems allows mat sections to be configured in the support role where sections can be configured for use as maintenance, storage or work surfaces, these including those used in temporary medical facilities. DURA-BASE can also be used in the airfield support role and is in use providing a suitable platform for landing and manoeuvring the AH-64 Apache helicopter, for which 12 mat sections are normally used.

No special tools or equipment are required to handle DURA-BASE mat sections in the construction of a roadway or other surfaces.

Status

In production. In service with the US Air Force, Army and Navy.

Contractor

Newpark Mats & Integrated Services

Causeway created using the DURA-BASE composite mat system (Newpark Mats & Integrated Services)   0116894

MO-MAT roadway system

Description

MO-MAT was designed for laying over terrain such as mud, sand and snow to allow the passage of wheeled vehicles. It is also used for a variety of other roles including use as a helicopter pad.

MO-MAT is fabricated from a glass fibre-reinforced plastic called Stratoglas, developed by the Stratoglas Division of the Air Logistics Corporation. MO-MAT is moulded into a structural shape resembling that of a waffle with an overall thickness of 16 mm. It was also available in thicknesses of 2.2 and 3.2 mm forming a lattice cross-section 16 mm thick overall and has a durable non-skid material bound to the top surface.

The standard duty MO-MAT (2.2 mm) weighs 4.9 kg/m² and the heavy-duty MO-MAT (3.2 mm) 7.3 kg/m². MO-MAT was supplied in standard panels 3.709 m wide and 14.782 m long. Utility panels 3.709 m wide and 6.6 m long and sheets 3.6 m long and 1.8 m wide were also available. Precision holes are provided around the periphery for interconnecting panels or sheets to any desired length or width. Panels or sheets may also be attached to frames to form a variety of structures.

The MO-MAT panels reduce the ground pressure by spreading the wheel loads over a wider surface area. Excessive crowning of the roadway caused by heavy traffic can be mitigated by doubling the thickness of the roadway - laying one panel on top of the other by/or increasing the width of the roadway and spreading the traffic pattern.

The sheets are supplied rolled up on a pallet for ease of transport and can be manually deployed, re-rolled or assembled without the use of special tools or equipment.

Status

Production complete. In service with US and other armed forces including Greece (an inventory of 92 sets in 2004) and Spain.

Contractor

Air Logistics Corporation

Spanish Navy using a 10K-AT forklift to unload a roll of MO-MAT roadway system (US DoD (SSGT Cherie A. Thurlby USAF)) 1391290

Spanish Marines manually un-roll a roll of MO-MAT roadway system while on exercise in Egypt (US DoD (SSGT Patricia Bunting USAF)) 1391291

RAPID RUNWAY REPAIR EQUIPMENT/PORTABLE RUNWAYS

France

DALLEXPRESS emergency runway repair system for runways and taxiways

Development
The DALLEXPRESS emergency runway repair system for runways and taxiways was developed by the then Lafarge Fondu International, a subsidiary of Lafarge. It is distributed by Automatismes & Techniques Nouvelles (ATN), a subsidiary of Sofinfra. The DALLEXPRESS system was introduced in 1984.

According to the manufacturer, over 300 craters have been repaired worldwide using the DALLEXPRESS system.

Description
The DALLEXPRESS system employs quick-setting concrete technologies to produce a concrete slab in 30 minutes. With this process a binder in the form of a liquid grout is pumped on to a course of aggregates through which it percolates to occupy all voids and spaces. At the end of the operation the liquid grout entirely covers the aggregate course. The thickness of the finished slab (corresponding to the thickness of the aggregate course) can be adjusted according to traffic requirements. The resultant surface is flat and even and can be matched to the surrounding material by using a broom. Traffic can be resumed in 30 to 40 minutes after the application of the grout.

The process can be used over a temperature range of –20 to +50°C. As an example, a transport aircraft of the C-130 Hercules type will require a slab thickness of 370 mm on an aggregate course.

Status
In use. Current generation versions of the systems are available on an as required basis.

Contractor
ATN SA

Greece

MICROTECH runway repair decking

Description
MICROTECH runway repair decking provides a rapid repair system to create a firm running surface over bomb damaged runways. The decking is constructed from extruded sections of heat-treated aluminium alloy and consists of panels and accessories that fit together to form a mat. The main sections have been designed to join with a tongue at one end and a groove at the other. Once in position, the connections are locked in place using special aluminium alloy bolts. The sections are supplied in two sizes, each size being man-portable. Each section is corrugated in cross-section and has an non-slip upper surface. Ramp sections can be fitted to the sides or ends of the mat. Special handling tools are supplied for carrying, assembly and disassembly of the decking. Other accessories include towing adaptors and expansion bolts to anchor the decking.

To form a standard runway repair decking 18.4 m wide and 11.7 m long the following items are required: 185 long panels, 54 short panels, eight long ramp panels, eight handling tools, four towing adaptors, 500 locking devices and 40 expansion bolts. The resultant mat may be rolled for stowage if required.

The MICROTECH runway repair decking can be used, without anchoring, to form a forward area helicopter landing pad that can be rolled up and moved to new locations as required.

The components used for the MICROTECH runway repair decking are the same as those used for the MICROTECH Class 60 Trackway described in the Portable roadways section.

Specifications

MICROTECH runway repair decking
Main section width:
  (overall) 242 mm
  (effective) 225 mm
Length:
  (long panel) 4.6 m
  (short panel) 2.3 m
Weight:
  (long panel) 32 kg
  (short panel) 16 kg
Ramp section width:
  (overall) 184 mm
  (effective) 152 mm

Ramp section length: (long panel) 4.6 m
Ramp section weight: (long panel) 37 kg
Breaking load: 150 kg/cm of length of standard panel

Status
In service with the Greek Air Force.

Contractor
MICROTECH Limited (this company is no longer trading).

United Kingdom

FAUN Airfield Landing Mat (ALM) and Helicopter Landing Mat (HLM)

Development
Designed and developed by the then Military Vehicles Engineering Establishment (MVEE) (Christchurch) in conjunction with the then British Aluminium Company Limited, the Airfield Landing Mat (ALM) is usually referred to as the Prefabricated Surface Aluminium (PSA).

The Airfield Landing Mat (ALM) and Helicopter Landing Mat (HLM) are based on areas of interlocking Class 70 Trackway aluminium alloy panels, a full description of which is given in the entry for FAUN Portable Trackways in the Portable roadways section.

The Airfield Landing Mat (ALM) and Helicopter Landing Mat (HLM) are in service with the UK (Royal Air Force) and other undisclosed countries.

A new panel design, suitable for use as a runway and a forward operating pad is currently in development.

Description
The standard mat, known as the PSA1 (which stands for Prefabricated Surface Aluminium) and which weighs 15 kg/m², is suitable for most freight and passenger aircraft and for combat aircraft with low-pressure tyres; the maximum tyre pressure being 5.62 kg/cm². The mats are made from aluminium panels and, apart from their general use for aircraft landing strip assembly, can be used as operating pads for aircraft such as the Harrier and also for rapid runway repair.

The Airfield Landing Mat (ALM) and Helicopter Landing mat (HLM) uses six basic components, as follows:
Basic panel - This is 2.74 m long with an effective width of 250 mm. It is light enough to be carried by one person as the PSA1 panel weighs 9.5 kg. Each panel has slots and lugs to connect it with its neighbouring panels in a brickwork pattern at an angle of 45° to the line of the runway.
Double female panel - This panel is 2.7 m long and 44.5 mm wide. It forms the centreline of the runway from which panels can be laid on both sides.
End anchor panel - This is the same as the basic panel apart from six 25 mm picket holes which provide anchorage.
Picket - The picket is 1.2 m long and 22 mm in diameter. It is made from galvanised steel rod and is used to anchor the end anchor panel. It has a T-shaped head that fits flush into the panel corrugation.
Repair panel - This is a two-part basic panel with a longitudinal interlocking joint. The two halves can be held in place by nine countersunk screws.
Edge restraint device - To prevent the ripple effect that forms when aircraft land and brake on airfield surface mats, the edge restraint device is fitted to the edge of all airfield landing mats. It consists of a fabric strip filled with earth or sand and with the fabric tied around the filling to form a long flexible cylinder. The fabric is laid on a connected plywood strip 305 mm wide.

To build a runway, some site preparation is needed to ensure the area is reasonably flat and drained. In wet areas, a layer of neoprene-coated nylon fabric (PSN) may be laid. The airfield landing mat can be used by unskilled

Demonstration laying of FAUN Airfield Landing Mat (ALM)
(FAUN MV Ltd)
    1391367

labour under engineer supervision and it is possible to lay a complete airfield runway in one or two days. Once laid, the mat requires only a minimum of maintenance, but a well-laid and maintained runway can be recovered and re-used with only a minimum of panels needing replacement.

Status
In service with the UK (Royal Air Force) and other undisclosed countries.

Contractor
FAUN MV Ltd

FAUN rapid runway repair system (BDRM/BDRP)

Development
The FAUN rapid runway repair system is NATO approved and underwent extensive trials with both the Royal and US air forces. It was accepted for service by the UK in 1970 and entered service in 1972.

Description
The FAUN rapid runway repair system (BDRM/BDRP) is based on the rapid runway repair mat or patch which consists of an area of interlocking Class 70 Trackway aluminium alloy panels, a full description of which is given in the FAUN Portable Trackways entry in the Portable roadways section.

The mat (Bomb Damaged Repair Mat - BDRM) or patch (Bomb Damaged Repair Patch - BDRP) can be built to any desired size, although the 22 × 16 m mat is the accepted size for the repairing of bomb craters caused by 340 to 450 kg bombs.

The mat is stowed rolled on special chocks and when required is lifted and transported on a runway repair mat trolley, enabling the mat to be positioned at the crater site without additional lifting equipment. The laden trolley can be towed by a Medium Wheeled Tractor (MWT) or the Armoured Heavy Wheeled Tractor (AHWT).

Following a strike on a runway, the first task of the repair team is to locate the damage and transfer the information to a runway plan. A minimum operating strip, possibly 1,500 m long and 15 m wide, is then plotted to establish the least amount of initial repair work necessary to restart operations.

The area around the bomb crater is first cleared of debris and fallback material is taken from inside the crater. The crater is then filled with selected aggregate, stockpiled within the perimeter of the airfield. If aggregate is not available, crater debris may be used and pushed back into the crater.

Once the fill has been compacted, the damaged area is levelled with a purpose-built screed beam and the repair mat is moved to the site, lowered to the ground and unrolled over the levelled fill. The mat is then tensioned and fastened to the undamaged section of the runway by expanding foundation bolts which pass through the fairing panels. Special fairing panels which enable aircraft to run on to and off the repair mat are connected to each end.

The final stage is to clear the area of all loose material with a motorised roller. The complete operation can take as little as one hour and 30 minutes from the time tractors start clearing debris.

To aid concealment, the trackway and fairing panels are treated with pylumin, a chemical dip producing a grey/green finish. The Class 70 mat can also be used for aircraft dispersal pads and portable runways.

A new style end fairing panel has recently been developed to enable the Eurofighter aircraft to use the BDRM/BDRP.

Status
Available. In service with the UK (Royal Engineers and Royal Air Force - RAF) and other armed forces.

Contractor
FAUN MV Ltd

RAF Harrier on FAUN BDRM/BDRP (FAUN MV Ltd)   1374853

Flush Capping System

Development
The Flush Capping System (FCS) was developed to meet a British Army requirement for a system to perform the Airfield Damage Repair (ADR) Mission. It was procured through a competitive tender process and is operated by specific Army Royal Engineer Regiments whose role it is to furnish engineering support to the Royal Air Force. 23 systems were procured, however, since the award to Amey Lex Consortium (ALC) of the UK MoD's C Vehicle PFI program, the number of systems in service has been reduced and some of the equipment used has been revised.

Under the C Vehicle PFI program a fleet of 4,000 vehicles largely operated by the Royal Engineers and Royal Logistics Corps was purchased by ALC and a replacement program commenced to supply and manage a smaller fleet, including cranes, dump trucks, excavators, bulldozers, rough terrain forklifts and container handlers. ALC will gradually rationalise the MoD's fleet to approximately 2,000 assets using Whole Fleet Management techniques and will procure over 1,700 new assets during the contract, worth in excess of GBP110 million. In addition to the procurement and disposal of equipment, the agreement provides a broad range of support services.

Description
The Flush Capping System (FCS) consists of four main elements: the mixer unit, the water bowser, DROPS transport flatracks (2) and cementitious material. The primary purpose of the system is to perform the Airfield Damage Repair (ADR) Mission, being capable of the rapid repair of scab, spall or crater damage. In addition to the ADR mission the FCS can be used to mix and dispense Portland Cement in support of civil engineering requirements.

The FCS consists of two 6.9 m tri-axle trailers, one dedicated to the mixer and its sub-systems, the other a water bowser and pumping unit. The DROPS flatracks are used for the transport of bagged cementitious material. Brief details of the water bowser, which is manufactured by Reynolds Boughton Ltd are in the following paragraphs.

A core crew of five are required to operate the system, although this does not include support personnel and equipment for crater preparation and finishing or the resupply of material to the proximity of the system.

Mixer unit
The full designation of the mixer unit is Mixer Unit, Flush Capping System. The unit is produced by The Entwistle Company of the US (Entwistle model 9610) and is derived from the US Air Force's Deployable Pavement Repair System (DPRS), details of which can be found elsewhere in this section.

The primary role of the FCS mixer unit is the repair of craters and adjacent scabs on battle damaged runway surfaces. It operates as an autonomous production and delivery unit capable of producing various slurry and concrete mixes. The system is capable of continuous and variable mixing by weight to within 1 per cent of the required amounts, with a delivery rate of up to 1 m³ per minute. In its peacetime role, the FCS mixer is capable of transporting sufficient unmixed cement, sand, crushed stone or gravel and admixes to a job site to produce up to 6 m³ of concrete when supported by the bowser.

The mixer consists of the following major trailer-mounted components:
- A tri-axle trailer
- Large material bin for fine and coarse aggregates or cement material
- Capacity 3 m³ (5.7 m³ with extensions)
- Water tank, capacity 756 litres
- Small material bin, capacity 1 m³ (1.7 m³ with extensions)
- Two material conveyors and proportioning system capable of metering all components of mix (exclusive of aggregate) to ±1 per cent by weight
- A Perkins 1004-40t diesel engine and drive train
- Vibrators
- A compressed air subsystem
- A hydraulic subsystem
- A mixing subsystem
- A mix discharge subsystem capable of horizontal movement through 180°, 90° left and right of centreline
- All necessary controls
- An integral 1,850 kg capacity crane.

The design and layout of the components and subsystems of the mixer considers passive survivability in a hostile combat environment. These considerations include locating and protecting vital components and systems to minimise system vulnerability to weapon effects such as blast, fragmentation and small arms fire.

The mixer is capable of operation throughout a −25 to +47°C temperature range without modification. It may be towed on improved roads at up to 50 km/h, and on unimproved roads at 10 km/h. It is not designed for cross-country travel.

Following a degree of preparation the mixer is air-transportable by C-130 transport aircraft. It is rail transportable without preparation.

From May 2011 an initial six Nurock mixers mounted on an IVECO Trakker chassis are being supplied.

Reynolds Boughton 8,000 litre heated water bowser
This 8,180 litre capacity heated tank is provided with an onboard pumping system capable of discharge through a 30 m reeled hose at up to 727 litres/min, or self-loading from below ground level water source through a 12 m suction hose. The onboard heating system can raise water temperature to a maximum of +70°C.

The road-going three-axle turntable type chassis is fitted with Hendrickson 2000 Series axles sprung by leaf springs. The two leading axles are fitted with an Anti-lock Braking System (ABS).

Specifications

Flush Capping System - 8,000 litre heated water bowser
Weight:
   (laden) 25,000 kg
   (unladen) 12,500 kg
Length :
   (transport including drawbar) 7.645 m
   (transport drawbar stowed) 6.251 m
   (operating including drawbar) 8.602 m
   (operating drawbar stowed) 7.108 m
Width:
   (transport) 2.483 m
   (operating) 3.251 m
Height:
   (transport) 2.438 m
   (operating) 3.542 m
Track: 2.037 m
Wheelbase:
   (first to third axle) 3.668 m
   (first to second axle) 2.184 m
Angle of approach/departure:
   (transport) 62°/23°
   (operating) 62°/9°
Max towing speed:
   (improved roads) 50 km/h
   (unimproved roads) 10 km/h
Fuel capacity: 189 litres
Sideslope:
   (unladen, left side) 73%
   (unladen, right side) 92%
Fording: 750 mm
Axles:
   (front) Hendrickson Type SM10/K H2000 Series with ABS and Y800501 suspension
   (second) Hendrickson Type SM10/K H2000 Series with Ridewell Dynaflex Model RDX-2045 suspension and ABS fittings
   (rear) Hendrickson Type SM10/K H2000 Series with Ridewell Dynaflex Model RDX-2045 suspension; no ABS
Wheels: one-piece steel, 10-stud
Tyres: Goodyear 385/65 R22.5 G165T/L
Brakes: air, drums all-round. ABS on 1st and 2nd axles
Electrical system: 24 V

Status

Production as required. In service with the UK (23 supplied).

Contractor

(Mixer Unit, Flush Capping System)
The Entwistle Company

United States

Deployable Pavement Repair System (DPRS)

Development
The Deployable Pavement Repair System (DPRS) was developed by The Entwistle Company for use by the US Air Force as part of the Rapid Runway Repair program; 14 systems were delivered.

The Flush Capping System (FCS) runway repair system used by the UK's armed forces is based around a mixer unit manufactured by The Entwistle Company and based on the DPRS. Full details of the FCS can be found elsewhere in this section.

Description
The DPRS (Entwistle model 9310) is a semi-trailer-mounted mobile concrete system with the primary mission of proportioning, mixing and pouring of fast-setting cements. It may also be used for the proportioning, mixing and pouring of Portland cement. Power is provided by an integral diesel engine.

The DPRS is designed around commercial technology, but incorporates a number of unique military features to provide a full multi-mission capability. The DPRS is air-transportable by C-130 Hercules aircraft.

Kerb weight of the system is 16,000 kg.

Status
Production as required. In service with the US Air Force (14). A system based around the DPRS is in service with the UK's armed forces.

Contractor
The Entwistle Company

SHELTERS AND CONTAINERS

Austria

CHV Container shelters and containers

Description
CHV Container has been a supplier of container and modular solutions to both the government and military for 20 years. The company has offices in Austria and production facilities in Romania and Slovakia.

CHV manufacturers and supplies a wide selection of shelters, containers and modular containerised solutions for a variety of roles including; field camp infrastructure, medical usage, command-and-control roles and basic logistic support applications. These shelters and containers can be supplied to standard ISO dimensions and be fully CSC approved, or to specific requirements-meeting dimensions if required.

Forklift pockets or fixings to enable handling by the hook arm of a DROPS/PLS-type truck can be included in any specification.

Shelters and containers can be provided insulated and equipped with air-conditioning/heating, ECUs and power systems to suit individual requirements. They can also be supplied with EMP/NEMP protection if required, a further option being certified ballistic and blast effect protection which can either be fitted internally, or externally as an appliqué kit.

Status
In production. In service in Europe, Africa and the Middle East.

Contractor
CHV Container

Belgium

MODULMED containerised medical, logistical and tactical mobile systems

Development
MODULMED has been producing integrated mobile container systems since 1981. MODULMED systems were originally centred around the provision of mobile field hospitals and their associated medical and logistic units, however the company now produces a full range of container systems for all medical, logistical and tactical applications.

Description
MODULMED produces solutions based on single volume containers or the MODULMED patented one-side and two-side expandable containers. All MODULMED containers conform to ISO standards when in transportation mode. They may be handled by all conventional ISO container transport and handling equipment and may be stacked, for storage, up to nine high. They may also be transported underslung by any suitable capacity helicopter. EMC shielding and NBC protection is available for the full range of container systems. Ballistic protection is a further option.

Construction is based around a framed steel structure made of mild and CORTEN steel, using sandwich panels made of galvanised steel, GRP or aluminium, and filled with fire retardant thermal and acoustic insulation varying in thickness between 70 and 100 mm.

A typical MODULMED application is the modular surgical unit deployed by the Italian Army. This consists of a fully equipped surgical unit in one expandable 20 ft ISO 1C container, a services module in one 10 ft ISO 1C container and the connections between the two. The internal floor area available is about 24 m^2 and the total internal volume is more than 50 m^3. The internal height within the expanded area is 2.1 m. Other MODULMED mobile medical facilities are much larger. A Belgian Army mobile field hospital consists of an operating theatre, a pre-operating unit, a laboratory and a post-operating ward. The basic hospital can be operational with four modules.

CHV 200 camp containers of the Austrian Army (CHV Container)   1375406

A typical MODULMED shelter being handled by a forklift (MODULMED)
1345945

A ballistically protected container during a demonstration; protection levels from B6 (EN 1063) up to NATO STANAG (4569) Level 3 are available (CHV Container)   1375405

MODULMED command post (MODULMED)   1345944

In conjunction with a number of armed forces, MODULMED has also developed a purpose-designed range of expandable containers for mobile command post duties. These come complete with integrated air conditioning, lights and electrical and telecommunication interfaces. EMI, EMPNBC and ballistic protection is optional.

Status
In production. In service with a number of armed forces including those of Belgium (mobile field hospital), Botswana, Italy (mobile surgical hospital), Portugal (mobile field hospital), Saudi Arabia (100-bed mobile field hospital) and Switzerland (medical units). Other MODULMED medical and surgical containerised solutions are in use by governmental and aid organisations in the Balkans (Kosovo), Benin, Ethiopia, Germany, Kenya, Malawi, Romania, Russia and Slovenia.

Contractor
MODULMED Patented Systems SA

Canada

Weatherhaven portable shelters and camp systems

Development
Weatherhaven has over 25 years of experience in the global deployment of prefabricated structures, and offers a full range of military products from individual shelters to complete turnkey camps, including camp systems and services. The company has manufacturing facilities on three continents.

Weatherhaven specialises in rugged fabric structures and the expandible MECC and ERSA container shelters. Weatherhaven's fabric shelters are designed to be lightweight and highly portable, while for more complex deployments Weatherhaven offers a range of semi-permanent ISO-dimensioned products. These can serve as command posts, technical centres, engineering workshops and so on. Kitchens and ablutions for personnel camps are also available.

Complementing a wide range of shelter and infrastructure products, the company also offers a complete site service that can include power generation, water and waste treatment, distribution, and collection.

Description

Mobile Expandable Container Configuration (MECC)
The Weatherhaven Mobile Expandable Container Configuration (MECC) is a expandible shelter system combining fold-out soft-wall fabric 'wings' with a standard 20 ft ISO container. Once deployed the MECC gives the user up to three times the useable floor area of a conventional rigid structure with the same transport footprint.

A single MECC takes two people approximately 10-15 minutes to deploy, requires no special training and using in-built hand-winches requires no external electrical or hydraulic power supply. MECCs can be handled by crane or forklift and can be transported commercially by truck, trailer, rail or sea, being fully ISO compatible. MECCs may also be transported by C-130 transport aircraft or underslung by any suitable capacity helicopter. For the transport/handling of MECCs, Weatherhaven offers an on/off-highway trailer that has a maximum highway speed of 88.5 km/h and a payload of 6,804 kg (15,000 lbs), and for either 10 or 20 ft (3.05 or 6.10 m) MECCs, a low-speed mobilizer capable of handling up to 10,886 kg (24,000 lbs) is also available.

Once off-loaded from its transport platform the MECC can function as an individual unit, or utilising MECC-to-MECC interconnecting kits can be mated using core to core, wing to wing or core to wing, to form complexes of any size. Various jacking systems have been developed for deployment on uneven ground. If required MECCs can be fully deployed and complexed from the load platform of their transport truck, trailer or mobilizer. MECCs may also be fully deployed and interconnected while stacked two high, and for transport or storage purposes may be stacked nine high. An aluminium version, which can be stacked up to three-high, is available where weight is an issue.

The base MECC container is, in addition to the standard 8 ft × 20 ft (2.44 × 6.10 m) ISO configuration, also available in 8 ft 6 in × 20 ft (2.59 × 6.10 m) ISO configuration. During transportation the standard configuration MECC offers 25 m³ of storage space and a 6,800 kg carrying capacity. The empty weight is 3,360 kg for the standard 8 ft MECC. A 10 ft (3.05 m) long ISO-certified version is available in steel or aluminium for applications requiring less space.

The steel container frame and exterior panels are provided with marine grade or military specification coatings and the ceiling and fold-out floors have rigid foam insulation. Floor surfaces have a 2 mm PVC covering over 15 mm marine ply boarding and 37.5 mm of rigid foam insulation. Chequer-plate steel or aluminium flooring are options. A single aluminium-skinned door is usually fitted. Additional doors or windows are optional.

The wings are constructed from 500 g/m² UV and mildew resistant, fire retardant and weatherproof vinyl-coated polyester with an opaque insulation layer and inner liner. Climatic operational range is –55 to +65°C. Insect netting and infrared reflective fabrics can be used if required.

Weatherhaven Mobile Expandable Container Configuration (MECC) mounted on a Oshkosh MK 48 series LVS of the US Marine Corps (Weatherhaven)   0524743

Personnel access ports and/or interconnecting kits and double-glazed slide-type window units complete with insect screens are also available. For especially hot climates a sunshade is available.

Command Post
When the MECC is used in a command post role, sensitive equipment can be stored and transported in the centre core of the MECC and does not need to be removed from the unit, thereby eliminating the risk of handling, or external weather damage. In a command post role the MECC offers various electrical and mechanical interfaces, and can be connected to other MECC and MTS shelters to create a tactical command centre. Custom electrical packages are available, with outlets for radios, computers, and other similar equipment.

Containerized Kitchen
The US Army has purchased over 600 Weatherhaven containerised kitchens for field use. These were supplied by US prime contractor Global Strategies Group (North America) Inc. (GLOBAL), formerly known as SFA Inc.. These kitchens use stainless-steel furnishings and combine 25.2 m² (280 ft²) of food preparation space, 7.2 m² (80 ft²) of serving-line space, and a 2.7 m² (30 ft²) mechanical room. Kitchen staff can prepare three fresh, basic meals daily for at least 650 soldiers. The Containerized Kitchen can be used as a stand-alone unit, or linked to a dining hall.

Deployable Field Kitchen 500 (DFK 500)
The semi-permanent Deployable Field Kitchen 500 is commonly used in military camps and deployed with a corridor and dining halls. Kitchen staff can prepare three full fresh meals daily for 500 persons. The DFK 500 is a full-service kitchen with the capability to bake, broil, and cook various types of meals. The DFK 500 comes with an integrated fire suppression system and full electrical and mechanical interfaces.

Deployable Field Ablution - 5 and 5
This ablution configuration is a preferred design by the military and is often used in conjunction with accommodation for up to 100 persons as a deployment module. Commonly referred to as the 5 and 5, it includes five showers, five toilets, two urinals, one washtub and six sinks. The unit includes an internal mechanical room which allows for rapid setup. The unit is available for use within 45 minutes of deployment.

Laundry - self serve or batch
The MECC laundry is available in two configurations. Both can be used as stand-alone units and both are pre-wired and pre-plumbed which allows for rapid setup. The unit is available for use within 45 minutes of deployment. The self-serve laundry version comes with ten industrial-grade, heavy-duty washing machines and dryers for soldiers to do their own laundry and folding. The batch laundry can be configured with two commercial-grade 22 kg washers and two 34 kg dryers for dedicated personnel to do laundry and folding for the entire camp.

Deployable Field Workshop Series
The MECC can be customised for various workshop configurations. Some of the more common workshops that Weatherhaven manufactures are:
- Tool Crib (this comes complete with a jib crane to support maintenance operations on deployments. Provides power, air conditioning, air compressor, repair-parts cabinets, and tool cabinets in a readily assembled format)
- Tire Maintenance Facility (TMF)
- Tire Storage Facility (complements the Tire Maintenance Facility)
- Electronic Repair Facility (includes furnishings, special equipment, and electrical and mechanical details custom-designed to meet specific repair requirements. Equipment is stored and shipped in the centre core, so sensitive equipment is not exposed to external weather conditions)

Rear view of two Weatherhaven Mobile Expandable Container Configuration (MECCs) mounted on Oshkosh MK 48 series LVS trucks of the US Marine Corps and joined wing-to-wing using a complexing kit (Weatherhaven)   0524744

Fabric shelters

Weatherhaven designs and manufactures a wide range of tensioned fabric shelters that are suitable for use in all climates. In addition to its standard product line, brief details of which follow, Weatherhaven can provide larger front line and second-line aircraft-hangar shelters. These large tactical hangars are spacious enough for repair and refuelling. The aircraft hangars can be linked to one or more MECCs and a generator to provide a turnkey stand-alone system when deployed. Weatherhaven sunshades can be used in combination with a Weatherhaven fabric shelter when deployed in areas of extreme direct solar radiation. Use of a sunshade reduces exposure to harmful UV radiation and solar gain, thereby extending the life of all materials. Use of a sunshade also reduces the demands on climate control systems, such as air conditioning.

Modular Tentage System (MTS)

The Modular Tentage System (MTS) is available in a selection of sizes and is predominantly used by military forces that need to connect shelters to form larger complexes. Common uses for the MTS are accommodation, ablutions, kitchens, laundries, command posts, workshops, and medical facilities. The MTS is fully insulated, so it may be sued in all weather conditions, has a variety of mechanical and electrical interfaces, and is available with several optional floor systems for various types of deployment.

Base Transient Shelter (BTS)

The Base Transient Shelter (BTS) is a semi-permanent structure that is ideal for transient personnel on military bases. This shelter is installed directly on a concrete pad or hard standing and is commonly used for long-term accommodation, offices, mess halls and classrooms. The BTS is provided with an aluminium frame, fabric cover, and inner liner, and is designed and engineered to meet national and provincial building codes in Canada.

Series 4

The Series 4 is the original Weatherhaven shelter. It is a high-performance shelter that is in use worldwide in all climates, including polar regions. This shelter is widely used by military forces for accommodation, recreation and first aid units. For military applications, the Series 4 is insulated and is available in a number of sizes with a broad range of options.

Series 4 Shop

The Series 4 Shop is an extended-height Series 4 shelter. The Series 4 Shop s designed for semi-permanent applications and is used primarily for helicopter and vehicle maintenance. The Series 4 Shop offers several vehicle-door options, can be equipped with workshop-specific electrical packages, and if required can be fully insulated.

MEX-26

The MEX-26 (Maintenance Extended Height 26′ wide) is the upgrade version of the Series 4 Shop. The MEX-26 is a modular structure designed specifically for tactical front line and second-line applications such as armoured vehicle and helicopter maintenance. The frame pieces are all aluminium to reduce weight. The MEX-26 shelter comes with several door options and special pre-assembled electrical kits and packaging options for shipping. One packaging option is the roto-moulded Titan Cases, which are specifically designed with interior compartments to accommodate the complete shelter frame and cover components. Each case is equipped with packing load lists and is individually marked to facilitate air or ground deployments and inventory management.

Series 8

The Series 8 shelter is a lightweight version of the Series 4. The Series 8 designed for locations that do not have high winds or snow loads. This shelter is used for accommodation, offices and first aid shelters. In warmer locations it is typically used with a thermal cap, this covers the top half of the shelter and reduces solar gain. A tropical version with side ventilation openings, complete with insect mesh and awnings is also available.

Series 8 Shop

The Series 8 Shop is a 20-foot (6.10 m) width extended height version of the Series 8. The Series 8 can be used for vehicle maintenance, storage and other ancillary activities. A tropical model with side ventilation openings, complete with insect mesh and awnings, and an optional thermal cap insulation is also available.

Status

In production. In service with a number of armed forces worldwide.

Contractor

Weatherhaven

Denmark

Container Load Trailer (CLT)

Description

The Container Load Trailer (CLT), developed by Danish Container Supply ApS in co-operation with the Danish Army. Around 150 examples were produced between 1980 and 2008. The 20,600 kg capacity CLT system is now being manufactured for special US and European military requirements by CDK Mobile Systems under a license from Danish Container Supply of Denmark. Full details of this product can be found elsewhere in this section.

Status
See text.

Contractor
Danish Container Supply ApS

Container Load Trailer (CLT) of the Australian Army coupled and configured for road use (Ron Fry)   1156110

France

SOFRAME container handling and carrying trailers

Development

These trailers were designed and developed for the autonomous logistic handling and transport of ISO shelters/containers on roads or over rough terrain. They are of similar design and configuration, the SLCT 8 differing primarily in having two and not a single axle.

SOFRAME RMTS 7.5 Rl container handling and carrying trailer, unladen (SOFRAME)   0056430

Description

For loading and unloading, these trailers remain attached to the towing vehicle, while the towing bar is hydraulically driven downwards to lower the rear end of the trailer to the ground at an angle of 14°. Containers are loaded on to the trailer using an electrical winch with a pull force of 3,500 kg (RMTS 7.5) or 5,440 kg (SLCT 8).

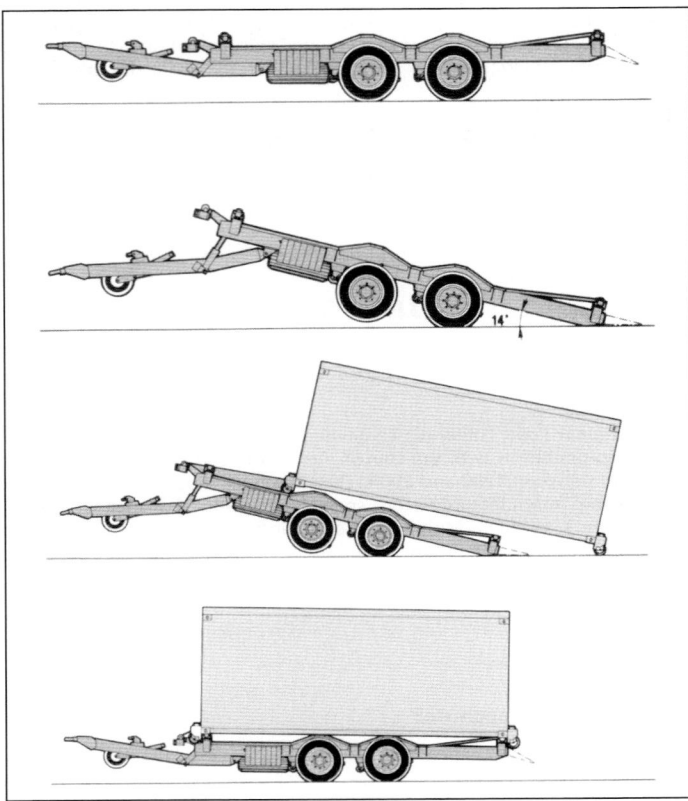

The loading/unloading process of the SOFRAME SLCT 8 Self Loading and Carrying Trailer (SOFRAME)   1128220

SOFRAME RMTS 7.5 RI container handling and carrying trailer transporting French Army mobile field hospital shelters (Pierre Touzin)
0536759

SOFRAME SLCT 8 Self Loading and Carrying Trailer, unladen (SOFRAME)   1128218

SOFRAME SLCT 8 Self Loading and Carrying Trailer in loading/unloading position (SOFRAME)   1128219

The RMTS 7.5 RI trailer can handle 10 and 20 ft ISO shelters and can be used to load and unload containers into and from C-130 or C-160 transport aircraft. The French Army uses this trailer with mobile field hospital shelters.

There is also an RMTS 10 with a payload of 10,000 kg.

The SLCT 8 Self Loading and Carrying Trailer follows the same general lines as the RMTS 7.5 but uses two air-sprung carrying axles. It is intended primarily for the transport and handling of 20 ft/6.09 m ISO containers.

Depending on aircraft, two or three trailers can be stacked for air transport.

The SOFRAME RPC 8500 is a similar trailer with an 8,500 kg carrying capacity.

Specifications

	RMTS 7.5 RI	SLCT 8
Weight:		
(unladen)	3,000 kg	3,500 kg
(GVW)	11,000 kg	11,500 kg
Payload:	8,000 kg	8,000 kg
Length:		
(overall)	8.9 m	8.68 m
(air transport)	6.512 m	n/avail
Width:	2.5 m	2.42 m
Height:	1.136 m	920 mm
Ground clearance:(laden)	385 mm	n/avail
Max towing speed:(road)	70 km/h	n/avail
Tyres:	9.5 R 17.5 Michelin XTA	307/70R 19.5

Status

Production as required. In service with the French Army.

Contractor

SOFRAME

SOFRAME UMC multipurpose container

Description

The SOFRAME UMC (*Unité Mobile de Campagne*) multipurpose 20 ft container was designed to withstand a variety of environments while providing an effective facility for various systems and/or equipment. The UMC container is constructed using insulated aluminium-skinned sandwich panels and stands on four retractable legs, one at each corner and extending 500 mm. The interior can be extended by lowering one or both side walls to extend the floor area. Tarpaulins can be used to protect the interior and access platforms are available. The UMC can be handled by forklift or various load handling systems such as the SOFRAME PLM 17.

Two or more containers can be joined to compose a field kitchen unit (ELC 500R) or a field bakery unit (UMBC). The ELC 500R field kitchen uses two UMC containers and caters for 500 people. One container is equipped for food preparation and washing, the other for cooking and meal distribution. Power is supplied by a 130 kVA generator integral to the food preparation and washing container. Total floor space is 52 m².

The UMBC field bakery uses one or more UMC containers and can produce 250-5,000 kg of bread per day.

Other uses for UMC containers can include command post, mobile office, communications, workshop, medical post or field laundry.

The ELC 500R mobile kitchen uses two SOFRAME UMC shelters (SOFRAME)   1128224

SOFRAME UMC shelter (SOFRAME)   0056431

Specifications
Weight: (empty) 2,900 kg
Length:
  (closed) 6.055 m
  (open) 6.055 m
Width:
  (closed) 2.435 m
  (open) 4.486 m
Height:
  (closed) 2.591 m
  (open) 2.591 m

Status
Production as required. In service with the French Army and other undisclosed armies.

Contractor
SOFRAME

Marrel Amplitainer CHU system

Description
The Marrel Amplitainer CHU (container handling unit) system is a container handling unit which operates as a complement to the Marrel Ampliroll Load Handling System (full details of which can be found in the Materials handling equipment section). It enables autonomous loading and transport of standard ISO 20 ft (6.096 m) containers without using any interface flatrack, skid, or specialised container handling equipment.

The Amplitainer consists of an 'H' frame, adjustable in height to take both standard height containers, that throughout loading and transport operations holds the container by its four front ISO-standard corner fittings. When not in use the 'H' frame is stored behind the host vehicles' cab, requiring 200 mm of space, and allowing the vehicle to transport a conventional flatrack. A support beam and rear roller assembly centres and tilts during loading, locking it in place with the rear ISO corners during transport.

The Amplitainer is adaptable to any kind or make of truck and is compatible with all types of 20 ft (6.096 m) container. No special tools are required during use. The system, including the rear beam and roller assembly, weighs <1,200 kg and has a nominal capacity of 16,500 kg. Operating temperature range is –32 to +55°C. Time for configuration is less than one minute, and time for loading a container is less than five minutes.

The Amplitainer system is known to be used by the Austrian Army on OAF chassis, the French Army on Renault chassis, and the Turkish Army on Mercedes-Benz Actros chassis.

Marrel Amplitainer CHU system fitted to a Marrel LHS-equipped Turkish Army Mercedes-Benz Actros (6 × 6) truck (Marrel)   0589048

Marrel Amplitainer CHU system fitted to a Marrel LHS-equipped Turkish Army Mercedes-Benz Actros (6 × 6) truck (Marrel)   0525713

Status
In production. In service with a number of armed forces including the Austrian (12), French, Swiss and Turkish (104). Evaluated by the Belgian and Royal Netherlands armed forces.

Contractor
Marrel SA

Multi-Trans air-portable handling units for mobile technical shelters

Description
There are 10 models in the family of Multi-Trans air-portable handling units for mobile technical shelters. They range in useful load capacity from 6,000 to 25,000 kg and weigh from 500 to 800 kg with accessories that can include a triangular tow frame, jacks, sand support plates and protective covers for example. The units can be attached to any shelter using existing attachment points and when in position they can be used to move the shelter by means of 24 V electric motors in the handling units. The same motors can also be used to raise and lower the shelters although the means to effect both raising and movement can be obtained manually. The lifting height can be between 0 and 1.865 m and the load lifting performance times are:

- 6,000 kg manual, approx 20 minutes
- 6,000 kg electrical, approx 3 minutes
- 10,000 kg manual, approx 30 minutes
- 10,000 kg electrical, approx 4 minutes
- 25,000 kg, manual, approx 30 minutes.

Loaded shelters can be towed across flat firm surfaces at speeds up 40 km/h.

Status
In production and widespread use.

Contractor
Henri Blanc SA

Model HB 1/6-tonne motorised Multi-Trans air-portable handling unit in use loading a shelter into a C-160 Transall transport aircraft (Henri Blanc SA)   0056372

Germany

Drehtainer shelters and containers

Development
Drehtainer GmbH was founded in 1974 as a service company DT, the company developing and manufacturing specialised containers for the commercial, governmental (including nuclear) and defence sectors since 1982.

The Drehtainer Watchtower is a transportable ISO-dimensioned container/structure that can be used for surveillance and protection purposes, particularly at camps and military installations with limited or single-point access (Drehtainer)   1391335

Tactical Operation Centre (TOC) is a modular building, built up from up to 152 specialised 20 ft ISO-dimensioned containers (Drehtainer)   1391336

The company now specialises in the development and manufacture of protected shelters and containers.

Since 1999 Drehtainer has supplied more than 3,500 specialist containers to the German Bundeswehr, and over 1,500 protective units/containers to the Australian and Dutch armed forces.

Drehtainer also offers a dedicated container handling vehicle, this also offered under licence by FAUN as the FUG. Full details of this vehicle can be found in the Materials handling equipment section.

Description

Drehtainer offers a full range of shelters and containers conforming to ISO dimensions, these being either 10, 20 or 40 ft, and either conventional or single or double expandable in construction.

Conventional, non-armoured shelters and containers are also available, however, Drehtainer now specialises in protected shelters and containers with protection afforded against side-blast, anti-tank mine blast and various ballistic threats.

Outline details of a selection of key Drehtainer products follow:

Protected mobile containers

Drehtainer protective mobile containers are designed for use either mounted on trucks, trailers or as free-standing units on the ground. These containers can be either 10 or 20 ft ISO dimensioned and used for a wide variety of roles that include:
- personnel transport (16 to 20 seats)
- ambulances (two to six stretchers)
- mobile rescue containers
- protected communication shelters
- independent surveillance post.

Drehtainer protected mobile containers can be fitted with a proprietary anti-shock wall and floor system, this outlined elsewhere in this entry.

Protected three-in-one containers

Drehtainer has recently launched a three-in-one expandable protected container. This can be used for a variety of roles including an emergency room (or other medical installations), as a training facility, a kitchen container, or a mission control centre. Protection up to STANAG Level 3 is available.

Tactical Operations Centre (TOC)

The Tactical Operation Centre (TOC) is a modular building, built up from up to 152 specialised 20 ft ISO-dimensioned containers. The side and/or front wall elements of individual containers can be removed to combine the required number of containers and in the desired configuration.

The coupling technology adopted ensures that no concrete foundations are required, and once coupled the containers, which are supplied with over-pressure ventilation, are weatherproof.

TOCs can be built to two stories high if required, and a protective roof that affords protection against 107 and 122 mm rocket threats, plus artillery and motor fire can be fitted if required.

The TOC, also referred to as the modular protected building or modular chalets, can be used for a wide variety of roles that include:
- mission control centre
- medical centre
- operations centre
- armoured accommodation centre
- communication centre
- surveillance centre.

The containers used for the TOC can be fitted with a proprietary anti-shock wall and floor system, this outlined elsewhere in this entry.

Watchtower

The Drehtainer Watchtower is a transportable ISO-dimensioned container/structure that can be used for surveillance and protection purposes, particularly at camps and military installations with limited or single-point access.

The basic protected Watchtower weighs around 6,000 kg and has a 2,000 kg payload. The Watchtower can be mounted on a conventional ISO container to increase overall height if required. A purpose-designed second unprotected 10 ft ISO-dimensioned unit is also available, the two units capable of joining if required for transport within the 20 ft ISO envelope.

Roof platforms, ancillary equipment such as searchlights and so on, and external staircases can be fitted as required.

Zero Shock

Zero Shock is the trade name given to a system developed by Drehtainer to offer those (or expensive/sensitive materials) inside of so-equipped structures additional protection from vertical and/or horizontal blast effects.

In principle the floor of the living/work space involved is suspended from the ceiling of the structure in question, which can also be a vehicle. In the event of a blast, acceleration sensors detect this and within 0.4 milliseconds so-called Pin-Pullers (pyrotechnics) sever the cables that connect the floor to the ceiling. The floor then drops with a force of 1G, the fall to cushioned by shock absorbers some 10 to 15 milliseconds later, the shock wave and any momentum from the blast having meanwhile petered out.

Protection from side blasts would be offered in a similar way.

Status

Drehtainer products are in service with the armed forces of Australia, Canada, Chile, Germany and Switzerland.

DOLL shelters and containers

Development

DOLL Fahrzeugbau GmbH offers a wide range of non-tactical container/shelter-type bodies for a variety of truck, trailer or semi-trailer mounting purposes. In addition to military, these are suitable for use by a variety of governmental or civil organisations.

Description

Applications for DOLL non-tactical container/shelter-type bodies range from truck-mounted catering facilities to semi-trailer-mounted decontamination units with an example of the latter in service with the

Typical Doll 20 ft/6.096 m ISO shelter/container converted for workshop use (DOLL)   0512107

German Bundeswehr. The decontamination unit (produced in co-operation with the now Kärcher Futuretech) consists of a two-container set-up that is mounted on a two-axle semi-trailer, this usually being coupled to a MAN LX range 4 × 4 tractor truck; hence the entire set-up has a degree of off-highway mobility. This two-shelter system has a capacity of 50 personnel per hour. The first (front of the semi-trailer) 10 ft container is equipped with the air-conditioning and heating systems, the water supply and an independent power unit. The second 30 ft container is equipped with a contaminant detection unit and a shower line.

In cooperation with MAN Nutzfahrzeuge GmbH, DOLL combined to produce a series of special shelters/containers for use on the full range of MAN high-mobility military vehicles. These are understood to be in service with an unspecified country. The basic shelter/container was fitted out to suit customer requirements and was built around a steel framework with steel covering panels insulated by 50 mm thick sandwich-type foam. A hydraulic or electrically operated material handling could be installed in front of the shelter. The shelter/container roof may be folded backwards for loading and unloading and the entire shelter/container and crane may be lifted by an overhead crane or gantry.

DOLL has also produced two smaller trailer-borne aluminium shelter/containers. One has dimensions of 2.5 × 2.2 × 2 m and can be transported on a single-axle trailer, the other has dimensions of 3.5 × 2.2 × 2 m and is transported on a twin-axle trailer. Both units can be carried underslung by helicopter. The larger unit can be fitted with stabilising jacks at each corner.

Status

Production as required. In service with German and other unspecified armed forces.

Contractor

DOLL Fahrzeugbau GmbH

EADS Defence & Security TransHospital mobile medical systems

Description

EADS Defence & Security is the prime contractor for the TransHospital mobile medical system, a system that was developed for, and is now in service with, German armed forces operating in support of various international missions involved in humanitarian disaster and other relief operations. The system has also been delivered to Libya's Military Medical Service, the Slovenian Army, Spanish Air Force, Thai Air Force and United Arab Emirates (UAE) armed forces. Naval versions have also been delivered to the German and Singapore navies as add-ons for supply ships.

The TransHospital is based on a modular system consisting of laterally expandible and non-expandible containers. The complete mobile hospital can fulfil the same tasks as a stationary hospital with a capacity for up to 200 patients. It contains modules dedicated to specific medical tasks such as emergency ward, diagnostics (X-ray and computer tomography), specialist sections (e.g. internal medicine, ENT, urology, dental, gynaecology), surgery, intensive care, as well as sterilisation, laboratories and pharmacy modules. Also provided are all necessary services, including electrical power supplies, water supply and disposal, laundry, kitchen, workshop and satellite communication services.

The smallest unit is an emergency rescue station (corresponding to NATO Role 1) consisting of one container and one tent. The minimum configuration of a complete mobile hospital for 100 beds (corresponding to NATO Role 3) can consist of 18 containers. All containers can be easily combined with tents; the maximum configuration uses 60 containers.

EADS Defence & Security is a corporate unit of the EADS European Aeronautic Defence and Space Company.

EADS Defence & Security TransHospital (EADS)   1391097

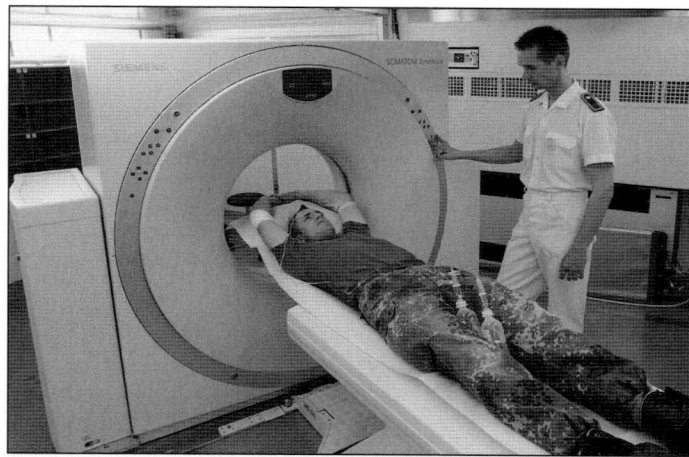

Interior view of an EADS Defence & Security TransHospital computer tomography container (EADS)   1391098

Status

In production. Systems are maintained and upgraded/modified in situ or in the field. Since 1996 EADS has delivered more than 400 medical shelters and these are currently in use worldwide, including Afghanistan, Congo, Indonesia, Kosovo and Pakistan.

Contractor

EADS Deutschland GmbH.

EADS Defence & Security TransProtec protected transport container

Development

The proliferation of suicide and roadside bomb attacks on military forces in Afghanistan has led to a growing interest in technologies to protect vehicles and their occupants.

To address this, Defence Electronics, an integrated business unit of EADS Defence & Security, accelerated efforts to promote its TransProtec protected transport container concept. TransProtec is designed to provide protected transportation of soldiers and civilians outside the combat zone.

The German military acquired an initial four TransProtec containers in 2004 for testing and initial operational use. Of the four TransProtec containers ordered by Germany, two have been used for off-road driving and destructive explosive blast-load testing. The explosive tests involved underbody mine detonations and (lateral) blasts to simulate an Improvised Explosive Device (IED) or suicide bomb scenario.

In addition to Germany acquisitions, four units were also ordered by the Danish Army.

TransProtec has been developed by EADS in partnership with Krauss-Maffei Wegmann (KMW). EADS Defence & Security has responsibility for the design of the container interior, air conditioning, NBC (Nuclear, Biological And Chemical) protection and power supply, while KMW has developed the armour protection. EADS Defence & Security, as system leader, is also responsible for logistic support, training and maintenance.

Description

The TransProtec container has 18 seats plus space for personal equipment and weapons. There is one main door at the rear, plus two additional exits; one in the side and one in the roof. There are 13 armoured-glass windows

EADS Defence & Security TransProtec protected transport container on a MAN SX range Multi (8 × 8) truck (Shaun C Connors)   1391328

The EADS Defence & Security TransProtec container has 18 seats plus space for personal equipment and weapons (Shaun C Connors)   1391327

EADS Defence & Security TransProtec protected transport container on a MAN SX range Multi (8 × 8) truck (Shaun C Connors)   1391329

are fitted as standard, although the container can also be supplied windowless. The latter option making it less obvious to the casual observer that people may be inside.

TransProtec has been stated as offering ballistic protection against B-32 projectiles fired from the 7.62 x 54 R calibre Dragunov sniper rifle, anti-tank mines, 20 mm Fragment Simulating Projectiles (FSPs) and blasts from lateral detonations of IEDs or suicide bombs.

Ideally any truck transporting the container should protected with add-on armour to ensure the safety of driver and guard. An intercom connection would also be advised to allow for communication between the driving cab and the container.

TransProtec and can be used in all climate zones, from -32ºC to greater than +55ºC, as well as in dusty environments. As such it is claimed to offer a cost-effective and flexible alternative to conventional armoured personnel carriers, while its protection and comfort levels are higher.

A modified version of TransProtec is capable of transporting up to nine casualties (six on stretchers, three in seats) and nursing staff together with the necessary treatment facilities. This configuration combines two options: one setup for low care users, four on stretchers, six in seats, two

health personnel. The other setup is for intermediate-care users, six on stretchers, three in seats, two health personnel. Alternation between low and intermediate care configurations is possible.

Other possible applications for the TransProtec container include using it as a protected mobile command post, a protected fire-control unit for weapons systems, or to transport sensitive equipment or essentials.

Status
Production as required. Supplied to Denmark (4) and Germany (4).

Contractor
EADS Defence & Security

---

haacon lifting, rolling and loading systems for mobile tactical shelters and containers

Description
There are two base models in the haacon range of lifting, rolling and loading systems for mobile tactical shelters and containers and they differ primarily in their maximum handling capacity. The type 1350.10 system has a maximum handling capacity of 10,000 kg; the type 1350.6.5 system has a maximum handling capacity of 6,500 kg.

In operation, if required, the shelter or container to be handled can be lifted directly from its transporting vehicle (maximum loadbed height of 1.75 m), to then be lowered to a rolling height of 460 mm. The tug or other suitable towing vehicle is then attached for movement to the carrying aircraft, where the aircraft's integral winch system is used to pull the shelter or container into the load area.

The COBRA (COunter Battery RAdar) system transport vehicle has moved clear to leave the COBRA unit free-standing and ready for movement by the haacon lifting, rolling and loading system (haacon)   1173892

Detail shot of a COBRA-specific (COunter Battery RAdar) haacon lifting, rolling and loading system unit (haacon)   1173891

haacon's lifting, rolling and loading system moving one part of the COBRA (COunter Battery RAdar) system (the antenna is a separate unit for transport) towards its transport aircraft (haacon) 1173894

Both systems will load in to the transport aircraft without any dismantling and remain fully operational at wind speeds of up to 64 km/h and throughout a –30 to +50°C temperature range. Maximum rolling speed is 24 km/h and both systems will operate on slopes of up to 2°. Options include an automatic brake (in case of winch failure) and electric motor drive. For motor operation 2 × 700 W motors at 24 V DC give a lifting time of approximately six minutes. The type 1350.6.5 set weighs 1,056 kg and the type 1350.10 set weighs 1,300 kg.

On behalf of Krauss-Maffei Wegmann (KMW), haacon has developed a suitable lifting and transport rack for the load/unload of the COBRA (COunter Battery RAdar) to and from trucks, aircraft and rail flatcars. Following testing, the system was accepted into service in July 2005.

Status

In production. In service with the armed forces of Australia (32), Belgium (15), Brazil (under evaluation), Canada (under evaluation), Denmark (17), Egypt (under evaluation), Finland (over 100), France (over 120), Germany (over 1,000), Greece (10), India (5), Israel (7), Italy (1,200), Netherlands (over 400), New Zealand (50), Norway (45), Poland (1), Portugal (37), Spain (50), Sweden (over 30), Switzerland (8), Turkey (12), UK (over 140) and the US (over 250), plus others as integral parts of various shelter and containerised systems.

Contractor

haacon hebetechnik GmbH

Zeppelin Mobile Systeme shelters

Description

Zeppelin Mobile Systeme produces a wide range of shelters for a wide variety of purposes ranging from ISO-compatible designs to vehicle-mounted bodies and specialist electronics and radar cabins. The entire range is constructed from basic sandwich monocoque with the side walls, roof and floor units all having aluminium skins as standard, with a stainless steel option. The core material is CFC-free polyurethane foam. The joints of the exterior cover sheets at the edges of the door are welded to the door profiles all round. An insulating layer is interposed between the framing sections. All external riveting is air and watertight and the corner fittings are replaceable.

Zeppelin Mobile Systeme FM1 (ACE 1) tactical shelter (Zeppelin Mobile System) 0134041

ISO shelters

Zeppelin ISO-compatible shelters are available in three standard sizes, 10, 15 and 20 ft. Expandable shelters giving twice or three times the floor space of a standard shelter are also available. Erection time for the expandable-type shelter is around 30 minutes, depending on configuration.

Zeppelin-supplied shelters form part of this truck-based mobile radar system (Zeppelin Mobile Systeme) 1114561

COBRA (COunter Battery RAdar) system fitted Zeppelin-produced shelters fitted with integrated splinter protection (Zeppelin Mobile Systeme) 1114563

Zeppelin Mobile Systeme ISO shelters in MobilMediCare configuration (Zeppelin Mobile Systeme) 1114575

The majority of Zeppelin ISO shelters are suitable for transport by air or sea, some can be underslung by helicopter and they can be handled by conventional materials handling cranes and stacked for storage/transport purposes. The company also produces telescopic legs and wheel sets for loading/unloading operations and for shelters likely to be used in extreme off-road conditions, the torsion-free Zeppelin System Frame can be installed on carrier vehicles that do not have a torsionally rigid chassis.

In most cases the shelter door is located in one end wall and mounted on the right-hand side by three heavy-duty hinge units. All four corners are rounded and there is a three-point locking device fitted. Various optional

doors, hatches and windows can be fitted to either side wall or end, and to suit individual user requirements. Flooring is constructed from 20 mm thick marine plywood and skids are mounted lengthwise under the floor unit with each skid being 51 mm high and approximately 100 mm wide. These skids are riveted or bolted to the integral stiffening members of the floor unit.

Conventional or expandable shelters can be interlinked together to form a modular network. Shelters are located together by their respective ISO corners and can be joined end to end or side on, dependent on configuration. Uses for such a modular network are extensive, but the Zeppelin MobilMediCare which utilises 20 ft shelters is in service with the armed forces of Germany and Chile, a single system being delivered to the Chilean Army in 2001.

In MobilMediCare configuration, Zeppelin shelters are fitted with air-conditioning units and individual shelters can be raised or lowered by self-levelling electro-mechanical jacks. The main surgery shelter is

Zeppelin Mobile Systeme LMOG-26 ambulance shelter mounted on a Mercedes-Benz G-Wagon of the Royal Netherlands Army
(Shaun C Connors)   0137097

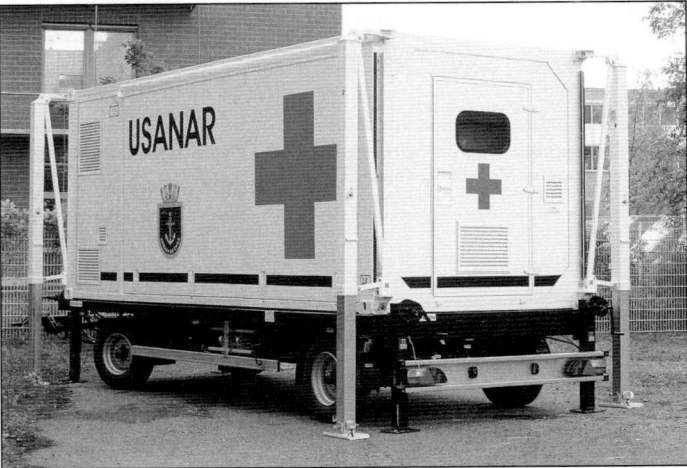

Zeppelin Mobile Systeme ISO-configured mobile medical facility pre-delivery to the Chilean Army (Zeppelin Mobile System)   0134049

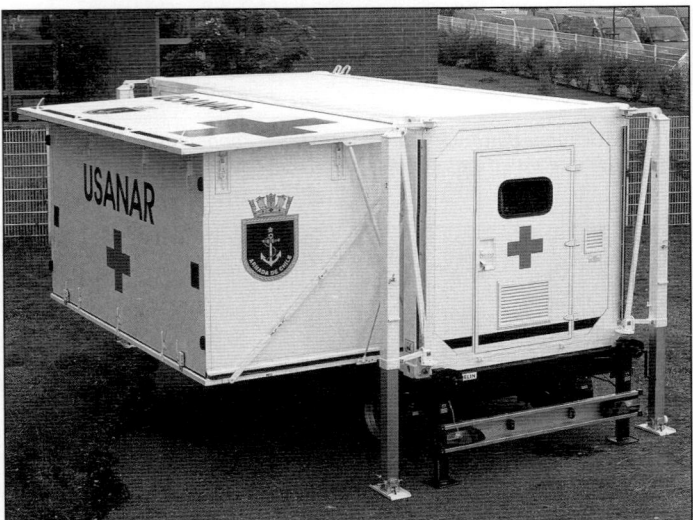

Zeppelin Mobile Systeme ISO-configured mobile medical facility (expanded) pre-delivery to the Chilean Army (Zeppelin Mobile System)
0134044

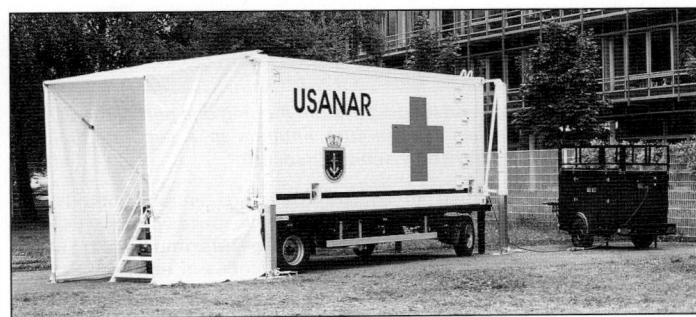

Deployed and ready for use, a Zeppelin Mobile Systeme ISO-configured mobile medical facility pre-delivery to the Chilean Army
(Zeppelin Mobile Systeme)   0134042

Zeppelin Mobile Systeme ISO shelters configured as a field hospital
0010155

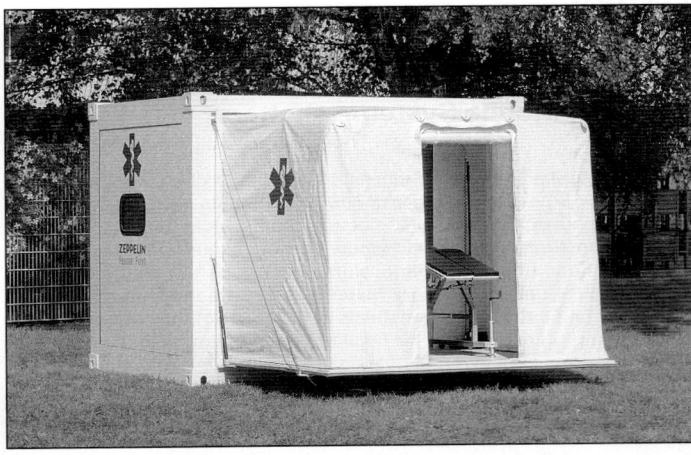

A one-sided expandable 10 ft shelter for mobile operations
(Zeppelin Mobile Systeme)   1114574

A four-sided expandable 10 ft shelter for mobile operations
(Zeppelin Mobile Systeme)   1114573

FM1 and FM2 shelters

	FM1 (ACE 1)	FM2 (ACE II)
Height:		
(external)	1.82 m	2.08 m
(internal)	1.66 m	1.91 m
Length:		
(external)	2.99 m	4.25 m
(internal)	2.76 m	4.11 m
Width:		
(external)	2.05 m	2.20 m
(internal)	1.91 m	2.06 m
Weight:		
(empty)	570 kg	960 kg
(maximum permissible)	2,000 kg	5,000 kg
(maximum payload)	1,250 kg	3,960 kg

normally supplied as an expandable shelter with a 35 m² floor area. The system can be configured, or reconfigured, to suit individual user or operational requirements and is guaranteed to have a minimum service life of 20 years.

Series FM1 (ACE 1) and FM2 (ACE II) shelters
The Series FM1 and FM2 shelters are available in two types. Type A is for general requirements, while type B has integral HF screening. However, the design of the type A shelter is such that HF screening can easily be retro-fitted if required. FM shelters are designed to the BWB test programme K35-1,5, and FM shelters with HF screening meet NATO specification 6516.

Over 6,000 FM shelters have been manufactured for military and civilian use.

Specifications - See table above
Shelter LMOG-26
This shelter is designed for mounting on chassis-cab variants of light 4 × 4 vehicles, primarily the Mercedes-Benz G-Wagon and Land Rover Defender. Sizes and weights will vary slightly according to shelter

dimensions and the wheelbase of the host vehicle. The figures given in the table below are for ambulance shelters of three varying sizes for installation on the Mercedes-Benz G-Wagon with a 3.4 m wheelbase.

The LMOG-26 shelter design can be adapted for a wide variety of uses and is constructed from materials common to the Zeppelin ISO and FM shelter ranges. One application in widespread use is the previously mentioned ambulance body, produced in either two- or four-stretcher configurations. Over 350 examples are in use with German armed forces, the Netherlands operates around 950 vehicles, while Norway received around 500 vehicles.

Another user of the G-Wagon chassis mounting Zeppelin shelters is Slovenia who recently received around 70 LMOG-26 shelters configured for the command post role and fitted with radio equipment.

Specifications
See table on page 932

Shelter LBMU-32
This shelter was designed for mounting on the Mercedes-Benz Unimog U1550L with a 3.25 m wheelbase, but could be adapted to suit the current production Unimog or any similar chassis. The base design is integrated

Zeppelin Mobile Systeme K-type (shielded) shelter on a Mercedes-Benz G-Class chassis (Zeppelin Mobile Systeme)   1114567

A Zeppelin C-130 transportable shelter mounted complete with a torsion free subframe to a Mercedes-Benz Unimog chassis (Zeppelin Mobile Systeme)   1114564

From the rear, a C-130 transportable Zeppelin shelter mounted via a torsion free subframe to a Mercedes-Benz Unimog truck (Zeppelin Mobile Systeme)   1114565

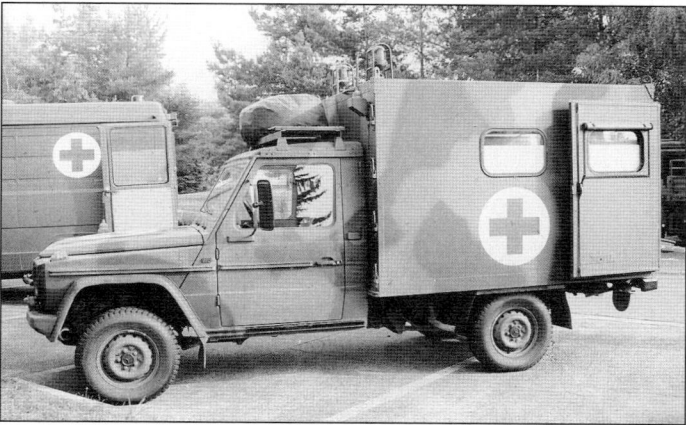

Zeppelin Mobile Systeme LMOG-26 ambulance shelter mounted on a Mercedez-Benz (Michael Jerchel)   1124729

LMOG

	LMOG-26 option 1	LMOG-27 option 2	LMOG-29 option 3
Length:			
(external)	2.57 m	2.65 m	2.85 m
(internal)	2.47 m	2.55 m	2.75 m
Width:			
(external)	1.93 m	2.1 m	2.1 m
(internal)	1.83 m	2.0 m	2.0 m
Height:			
(external)	1.78 m	1.9 m	1.9 m
(internal)	1.66 m	1.77 m	1.77 m
Weight:			
(without internal equipment or options)	430 kg	460 kg	520 kg

with the torsionally rigid Unimog chassis and has internal dimensions of 3.32 × 2.2 × 1.44 m (l × w × h) and weighs approximately 800 kg empty. The complete vehicle is transportable by C-130 Hercules transport aircraft.

The LBMU-32 shelter is not HF screened. It is available configured to suit individual requirements and has been produced in maintenance, command post and ambulance versions. The ambulance version weighs approximately 1,200 kg fully equipped and can accommodate four stretcher patients, six sitting patients or a combination of two stretcher and three sitting patients.

Over 450 LBMU-32 shelters have been manufactured and tests have shown the type to have an expected 15-year service life.

Shelter type K2
This shelter was designed for mounting on the Mercedes-Benz Unimog U4000 with a 3.8 m wheelbase. The shelter is integrated with the torsionally rigid Unimog chassis but is designed to be easily removable should the need arise. The K2 shelter can be mounted with or without a generator and air-conditioning unit located between it and the host vehicle cab. The shelter-fitted Unimog vehicle is air-transportable by C-130 Hercules transport aircraft.

The standard K2 shelter is shielded, but versions without shielding are an option. Internal dimensions are 3.08 × 2.12 × 1.57 m (l × w × h) and the empty shelter weighs approximately 600 kg, giving a payload allowance of approximately 1,900 kg.

Status
In production. In service with the armed forces of Chile, Germany, Netherlands, Norway, Slovenia and other undisclosed countries.

Contractor
Zeppelin Mobile Systeme GmbH

Greece

NK military shelters

Description
Nik Kioleides SA produces a multipurpose 4,000 kg shelter based on the dimensions of a standard 20 ft ISO container fitted with eight ISO corners.

Construction is of lightweight sandwich material, with the outer skin being primarily aluminium. The rear panel is fitted with a left-hanging door and three 300 × 300 mm input/output panels to accommodate power supply and communication sockets. A 600 × 600 mm emergency escape hatch is located in the right sidewall just above floor level.

Options include an air-conditioning unit and a heater, mounted on the front wall and within the ISO envelope.

NK MSS-20 shelter (Nik Kioleides SA)   1035117

In standard configuration this shelter is designated MSS-20, but as an alternative it may be supplied with EMI shielding in which case it is designated MS-20E.

Specifications
Weight:
(fully equipped) 7,000 kg (± 10%)
(empty) 3,000 kg (± 10%)
Max load: 4,000 kg
Length: (external) 6.058/6.055 m
Width: (external) 2.438/2.435 m
Height: (external) 2.438/2.589 m

Status
In production for the Hellenic Army.

Contractor
Nik Kioleides SA.

International

Euro-Shelter shelters and containers

Description
Euro-Shelter was a 50/50 joint venture between the former Giat Industries (now Nexter) and INSYS Ltd (formerly Hunting Engineering Ltd, now Lockheed Martin UK), however Lockheed Martin did not acquire the former INSYS' 50 per cent share of Euro-Shelter when it acquired the company in 2006. Euro-Shelter is now a 100 per cent subsidiary of the Nexter Group.

Euro-Shelter produces a wide range of military containers and shelters for tactical, medical and logistical use. As a prime contractor it can provide complete logistic complexes such as hospitals, laundries and kitchens, fully equipped and ready for use, and as a supplier of shelters to other prime contractors, it can provide either bare shelters or shelters pre-equipped with utilities such as electrical power generators, distribution systems, lighting and air conditioning.

Euro-Shelter produces shelters to meet the severest of defence requirements including Nuclear Biological and Chemical (NBC) protection, Electro-Magnetic (EM) and TEMPEST shielding, extremes of climate and all forms of transportation including carriage within tactical transport aircraft. Shelters can be of non-ISO or ISO dimensions, with full UIC/SCS certification if required. They can also be given varying degrees of EM attenuation depending on requirement.

Euro-Shelter uses folding, sliding and inflatable technologies to produce a variety of single and double-expandable shelters, for the maximisation of working space with the minimisation of transport volume. The company makes and assembles all the major components of its products, including composite panels and, for all its products, the company provides full customer support, including documentation, training and maintenance.

Status
In production. In service with numerous armed forces.

Contractor
Euro-Shelter

Euro-Shelter NG2 shelter

Description
The Euro-Shelter NG2 mobile technical shelter is designed to take military or civil equipment requiring both mobility and in-built protection from electro-magnetic interference or other hostile environments. It can be used for a variety of applications including command post, radio transmission centre or electronic workshop. The shelter can be

Dimensions	External			Internal			Mass	
	L	W	H	L	W	H	Empty	Payload
10 ft	2.991	2.438	2.100 or 2.330 or 2.438 or 2.591	4.524	2.438	1.953 or 2.183 or 2.291 or 2.444	810 kg	2,500 kg
15 ft	4.524	as above		4.390	as above		1,000 kg	4,000 kg
20 ft	6.058	as above		5.924	as above		1,400 kg	6,000 kg
30 ft	9.125	as above		8.991	as above		2,400 kg	6,600 kg

A Euro-Shelter EM-protected 4.524 m (15 ft) shelter   0121895

A French Army hospital complex formed from Euro-Shelter MTS 0020 20 ft (6.058 m) Single Expandable Shelters (Euro-Shelter)   0121894

transported by road, rail, sea or air and can be used either on a vehicle or free-standing on the ground. The level of EM protection can be varied to suit individual requirements and the shelter is available in the ISO standard dimensions listed here.

Specifications
See table above
Construction: composite panel structure, continuously welded seams, watertight exterior, assembled on light alloy frame, with internal riveted angle strips. Upper and lower ISO corners in cast alloy, providing an ISO interface for handling and mounting on a carrier vehicle, using quarter-turn twist-lock systems
Thermal characteristics: overall thermal transmission coefficient on panels <0.8 W/(m^2.°C)
Sound attenuation: from the outside 20 dB
Electrical continuity between interior walls: earthing continuity <0.5 m Ω under 10 A
Roof loading: temporary load of 150 kg over 0.18 m^2 or 3.6 kPa uniformly spread without causing permanent distortion
Wind loading: maximum wind speed 230 km/h (door and hatches closed)
Salt spray: resistance 96 hours in compliance with French Standard EG13. Document 4
Frost: complies with French Standard EG13, Document 22, Severities 1, 2, 3 and 4

Status
Production as required. In service with the French armed forces and used in numerous civil applications.

Contractor
Euro-Shelter

Euro-Shelter MTS 0020 20 ft Single Expandable Shelter

Description
The Euro-Shelter MTS 20 ft (6.058 m) Single Expandable Shelter can be transported as a simple 20 ft container and then extended for operational use. It has been designed to provide an aseptic internal environment and to give protection from biological and chemical attack. Normally fitted out for medical purposes, the shelter can be equipped with a variety of medical equipment, fulfilling roles including surgical theatre, intensive care ward or X-ray unit. Several MTS shelters can be combined in a protected network, using the concertina-type interconnection system and thereby providing a complete hospital complex. The shelters have integral jacks and spirit levels to provide a simple levelling system. The extending module is extended and retracted by a manually operated winch. This also extends the floor, which folds up within the main module. When deployed the floor is perfectly plane. The MTS shelter is transportable by road, rail, sea or air, although it is normally designed to be carried on vehicles using Ampliroll or DROPS/PLS self-loading equipment, MTS 20 ft Expandable Shelters can be fully operational in the hospital role within two hours of arrival on site.

Specifications
Dimensions	Closed	Deployed
External		
(length)	6.058 m	6.058 m
(width)	2.438 m	3.938 m
(height)	2.438 m	2.438 m
Internal		
(length)	5.758 m	5.758 m
(width)	2.338 m	3.878 m
(height)	2.153 m	2.153 m
Weight		
(pre-fitted container)	<3,000 kg	–
(payload)	5,500 kg	–

Usable access: both main doors open (height 1.25 m, width at bottom 1.494 m, at top, 1.384 m)
Construction: composite panel structure, continuously welded seams, watertight exterior, assembled on light alloy frame, with internal riveted angle strips.
Thermal characteristics: overall thermal transmission coefficient on panels < 0.9 W/(m^2°C)
Electrical continuity between interior wall: earthing continuity <0.5 m Ω under 10 A
Roof loading: UDL of 2,700 kg on main module, UDL of 1,350 kg on extending module without causing permanent distortion
Floor loading: 400 kg on any given area of 500 × 500 mm in main module. Total static load of 1,000 kg in extending main module
Salt spray: resistance 96 hours in compliance with French Standard EG13, Document 4
Frost: complies with French Standard EG13, Document 22, Severities 1, 2, 3 and 4

Status
In production. Over 70 units in service with the military medical services of France and the UK.

Contractor
Euro-Shelter

Euro-Shelter double expandable APS shelter

Description
The Euro-Shelter double expandable APS shelter is composed of a steel frame with ISO corners and base, fitted with two drop-down side panels, which form an extended floor, and two inflatable structures attached to the drop-down sides and the body of the container, which form the walls and roofs of the extensions. The composite wall and roof panels consist of aluminium alloy sheet skins on a PVC foam core. Expanding and retracting the side walls requires only two operators and the integral winch. The drop-down floors ensure a flush floor surface when deployed. The APS inflatable wall system provides total sealing of the extension. It is inflated and the pressure is maintained (0.2 to 0.4 bar) by an air compressor and automatic regulation system. The inflatable panels are composed of a multilayer PVC and polyester fibre envelope, providing strength, rigidity

A Euro-Shelter double expandable APS shelter closed up for transport and showing the winching and jacking mechanisms stowed within the ISO envelope (Euro-Shelter)   0121807

A deployed Euro-Shelter double expandable APS shelter (Euro-Shelter)
0121809

and thermal insulation. Doors and windows are incorporated into the APS walls. The four jacks needed for levelling the container on deployment are fitted to an outer end wall within the ISO dimension. The container can be fully operational within two hours of deployment and has a variety of uses, one being a sterilisation facility within a mobile hospital complex. An APS extension unit is being used within the Integrated Biological Detection System (IBDS) as used by the British Army.

Specifications

Dimensions	Closed	Deployed
External		
(length)	6.058 m	6.058 m
(width)	2.438 m	6.230 m
(height)	2.438 m	2.090 m
Internal		
(length)		5.566 m
(width)		5.910 m
(height)		2.090 m
Weight		
(pre-fitted container)	<4,010 kg	–
(max gross weight)	10,000 kg	–

Status
In production.

Contractor
Euro-Shelter

Euro-Shelter Double Expandable Rigid Walled (DERW) shelter

Description
The Euro-Shelter Double (or single) Expandable Rigid-Walled shelter is fitted with rigid, fold-out roofs and side walls. These shelters can be interconnected to form large working areas, ideal for such use as a kitchen

Interior of a Euro-Shelter Double Expandable Rigid-Walled (DERW) ISO shelter fitted out as an ELC 500-man kitchen (Euro-Shelter)   0121893

Two Euro-Shelter Double Expandable Rigid Walled (DERW) ISO shelters fitted out and deployed as an ELC 500-man kitchen (Euro-Shelter) 0121892

facility. The linking kit provides a level floor, a fully waterproof roof with gutter, and simple connections for electricity and water. The container has an integrated DROPS/PLS or Ampliroll facility to allow rapid and simple loading and unloading onto the ground.

The framework is made from welded steel profiles. The one-piece roof, consisting of a sandwich panel with an exterior skin of steel, is continuously welded on to the frame in order to prevent any ingress of water. The composite panels consist of an aluminium sheet interior skin, with a centre of alveolar foam (class M1) of closed cells (non-hygroscopic) and an exterior sheet steel skin. The floor panels are finished with a poured covering of non-slip polyurethane resin. All the panels are designed for the direct fitting on both faces of bolts or blind rivets (NF-E-25701, NF-25702, NF-E-25703). The external skin of the panels is glued and riveted onto a welded metal strip on the frame.

When used as a kitchen, one of the two containers is fitted with a 125 kVA continuous/137.5 kVA short period generator in an integral electrical compartment. The electrical system is managed by a Sicotronic power management system which monitors power usage by the various electrical cooking systems and directs or shuts off power as required, thereby allowing a much greater installed capacity than the size of the generator would normally allow.

Specifications
Maximum external
(length) 6.058 m
(width) 2.438 m
(height) 2.591 m
Minimum internal
(length) 5.740 m
(width) 2.269 m
(height) 2.200 m
Weights
(bare structure) 3,200 kg
(empty container) 5,000 kg
Permissible roof loading: the roof of the container can withstand, without permanent deformation, a load of 300 kg uniformly spread over an area of 0.18 m²
Salt spray: resistance to 96 hours in compliance with French Standard EG13, Document 4
Frost: the container meets the French Standard EG13, Document 22, Severities 1, 2, 3 and 4
Electrical continuity: electrical continuity between all the major components of the container is <0.5 m Ω (current of 10 A), French Standard EG13, Part 61, Test 61 MA, Severity 1

Status
In production.

Contractor
Euro-Shelter

Dimensions	External			Internal			Mass	
	L	W	H	L	W	H	Empty	Payload
10 ft	2.991	2.438	0.849 1.204 1.527	2.640	2.090	0.765 1.124 1.440	800 kg	3,500 kg

Pressurised containers

Description
Pressurised containers are used for the long-term storage and handling of high-value spares and assemblies such as tank engines and gearboxes, providing an inert, dust-free and humidity-controlled environment. The light alloy container consists of a welded, drawn aluminium strip base, a dome and an adapter cradle specific to the particular assembly being stored or transported. The container is pressurised with inert gas via two Staubli unions. Three pressure regulation valves, in compliance with MIL 27166A, allow for automatic regulation during air transport. An integral control panel enables the pressure and humidity to be monitored. The containers conform to the ISO 10 ft (2.991 m) standard and are available in three heights. Cast light alloy ISO corners provide an ISO interface for handling operations

Specifications
See table above
Thermal characteristics
   operating range: −25 to +52°C with solar radiation <1,120 W/m²
   storage range: −40 to +70°C
   relative humidity range: 20–93%
Pressure differential: 0.2 bars
Safety release pressure: safety valves actuate before differential reaches 0.3 bar
Waterproofing: maintains water tightness when immersed in water at 0.3 bar
Salt spray: resistance 96 hours in compliance with French Standard EG13, Document 4

Status
In production. In service with the French armed forces.

Contractor
Euro-Shelter

Euro-Shelter pressurised logistics containers for the transport/storage of high-value spares and assemblies   0121891

Israel

Achidatex Lightweight All Purpose Shelter

Development
This lightweight shelter was developed by Achidatex to be a portable all-purpose structure with the minimum possible packed volume for ease of transportation.

Description
The Achidatex All Purpose Shelter is light in weight and described as man-portable, having a total weight when broken down into component parts of 345 kg, without floor, or 400 kg with floor. Dimensions when packed are 1.05 × 1.05 × 0.8 m (L × W × H) for the cover, and 5.5 × 0.3 m (L × W) for the frames.

Erection time from unpacking is less than 30 minutes with 4-6 people, and once erected six people can manhandle a shelter. The erected shelter has dimensions of 10 × 7 × 3.95 m (L × W × H).

The fabric used is Seaman Corporation Style 8217 Military, while the frame consists of fibreglass reinforced rods. This Achidatex All Purpose Shelter meets all Israeli military requirements for this type of shelter.

Proposed uses include a forward shelter for tracked and wheeled vehicles, a tactical shelter and/or command post, a first aid post or small forward hospital, a modular tentage system. It is possible to adapt the structure to become a controlled dry storage shelter or a NBC protected equipment and personal shelter system.

Demonstration erection of a Achidatex Lightweight All Purpose Shelter (Achidatex)   0589046

Component parts (minus floor) of an Achidatex Lightweight All Purpose Shelter ready for transport/erection (Achidatex)   0589043

Specifications
Lightweight All Purpose Shelter
Dimensions:
   (cover - packed) 1.05 × 1.05 × 0.8 m (L × W × H)
   (frames - packed) 5.5 × 0.3 m (L × W)
   (erected shelter) 10 × 7 × 3.95 m (L × W × H)
Weight:
   (without floor) 345 kg
   (with floor) 400 kg

Status
In production. In service with unspecified armed forces outside of Israel.

Contractor
Achidatex

Italy

ARIS Airlift Global Carrier (AGC)

Development
The ARIS Airlift Global Carrier (AGC) is a prime mover which was designed specifically for transport, with cargo, by C-130 Hercules transport aircraft. The vehicle is in service with the Italian Air Force for the NATO Rapid Reaction Force. It is used for the rapid deployment of the MBDA Spada low to medium-altitude surface-to-air missile system, although it can be used for the transport/handling of a variety of other systems.

Description
The ARIS AGC 170 is capable of C-130 Hercules transport aircraft drive-on/drive-off operations complete with cargo and requires no assistance from any form of loading or unloading equipment. A variety of equipment

*ARIS Airlift Global Carrier (AGC) as displayed at Eurosatory 2006
(Shaun C Connors)*   1185424

ARIS Airlift Global Carrier (AGC) (ARIS)   1196999

types can be transported between the two-axle short wheelbase tractor
and the rear axle assembly, these including 20 ft ISO containers, assorted
shelters or purpose-designed flatbeds mounting missile launchers, radar
antenna and sheltered modules.

The purpose-designed tractor is available in 4 × 2 or 4 × 4 configuration,
the 4 × 4 having independent suspension and a more powerful engine. A
new four-wheel drive flatbed semi-trailer has been produced. This item
connected to the TPA towing tractor gives the system an all-terrain 8 × 8
capability.

The fifth wheel of the tractor is fitted with a jib-type assembly that not
only locates the container or other load, but also raises and lowers it to
facilitate the load and unload process. The cab of the towing tractor is an
adapted light commercial vehicle product. A purpose designed protected
cab has been developed and is in production for the new AGC series.

Specifications

	Three-axle configuration	Four-axle configuration (8 × 8)
Max load:		
(for C130 transport)	8,000 kg	8,1000 kg
(on-road)	10,000 kg	12,000 kg
(off-road)	9,000 kg	12,000 kg
Max speed:	110 km/h	110 km/h
Range:	500 km	500 km
Max gradient:	30%	45%
Fording:		
(without preparation)	750 mm	750 mm
Engine:	6-cylinder turbocharged and intercooled water-cooled 4-stroke diesel developing 170 hp (127 kW) at 3,200 rpm (275 hp (205 kW) at 2,300 rpm for the 6 × 4)	6-cylinder turbocharged and intercooled water-cooled 4-stroke diesel developing 275 hp (205 kW) at 2,300 rpm

Status
In production. Used by the Italian air force for the NATO Rapid Reaction
Force for the rapid deployment of the MBDA Spada low to medium-
altitude surface-to-air missile system.

ARIS Airlift Global Carrier (ACG) (ARIS)   1196996

Contractor
Applicazioni Rielaborazioni Impianti Speciali (ARIS) SpA

Eurovinil (EV) inflatable tents and shelters

Development
Eurovinil began producing life-saving equipment in 1977 when the
company produced its first life raft. Eurovinil has been manufacturing
inflatable tents and shelters for military, governmental and leisure
indusrty use since 1985. Eurovinil products have been used on operational
deployments since Somalia in 1993.

Description
Each tent or shelter is inflated to its full working pressure by using a
portable electrically-powered air blower. Once inflated the tent supporting
structure is airtight, therefore there is no need for a continuously running
compressor.

As modular structures, Eurovinil inflatable shelters can be constructed
in a variety of configurations such as field hospitals, troop
accommodation, storage shelters, vehicle garages or repair facilities and
so on.

All Eurovinil products are manufactured from the same patented
material named EV Marine Compound (E.M.C.). EMC is a fabric formed by
a polyester support with a high tenacity (from 275 to 3.300 decitex) that
grants a very high resistance to traction, tearing and puncture, which is
plastomer coated on both sides to make it water and airproof. It is qualified
to resist in a range of temperatures between -50ºC and +66ºC.

The Eurovinil Multifunction Medium-Sized Tent (MMST) is part of the
Eurovinil range of modular, self-supporting pneumatic shelters and can be
interlinked with other structures in the same range. The MMST consists of
three basic modular sections and can be increased in size by adding one or
more central sections in order to achieve the required dimensions.
Shelters from 60 to 140 m² can be erected in less than one hour, using
unskilled personnel. Accessories include an insulation sheet, electrical
plant, air conditioning, a heater and cases and pallets for transport.

Specifications
Weights:
(rear section) 198 kg
(central section) 187 kg
(front section) 181 kg
(standard accessories) 202 kg
Dimensions:
(rear section) 8.25 × 4.5 × 4.1 m
(central section) 8.25 × 4.75 × 4.1 m
(front section) 8.25 × 3.25 × 4.1 m

Status
In production.

Contractor
EUROVINIL SpA

A typical EV Multifunction Medium-Sized Tent (MMST)   0010156

Piaggio Aero Industries shelters

Development
Piaggio Aero Industries came into being in 1998, following the acquisition
of the assets of IAM Rinaldo Piaggio. The now Piaggio Aero Industries
started building military shelters in 1964 and since then has produced
shelters for both military and civilian purposes.

Type	ACE1	ACE2	ACE3	UEO1	UEO2	S250
Length	2.9 m	4.25 m	5 m	2.71 m	3.983 m	2.16 m
Width	2.05 m	2.2 m	2.2 m	1.74 m	1.915 m	1.254/2 m
Height	1.881 m	2.131 m	2.131 m	1.9 m	2.1 m	1.75 m
Weight	700 kg	900 kg	1,200 kg	600 kg	750 kg	500 kg
Capacity (useful load)	1,300 kg	3,600 kg	4,300 kg	1,400 kg	3,250 kg	1,000 kg

Description

There are now 10 basic Piaggio shelter types with a far larger number being produced for special purposes, although the overall construction remains the same.

Each shelter has eight horizontal angles and four vertical angles in light alloy. The corner blocks may be standard ISO container types and all the wall and floor or ceiling panels are constructed from a sandwich formed from light-alloy sheets 0.8 to 2 mm thick with a core of 50 mm thick honeycomb or polyurethane foam. Internal strengthening ribs are fitted and there are three underside skids. The floor has a drain plug and the end access door is built in several dimensions according to customer requirements. Other standard fittings are access steps, roof reinforcement in the centre and an electrical earthing point.

A wide range of accessories is available and numerous sizes can be produced to suit customer requirements. Piaggio was the first manufacturer to comply with NATO's requirements for EMP shelters (shelters protected against electromagnetic pulse from nuclear blast).

Piaggio EMP shelters differ from conventional shelters in that the outer skin of the cabin is fusion welded, which according to the company guarantees flawless electrical continuity.

Besides the above mentioned types, Piaggio has developed and manufactured, on its own or in co-operation with other companies, a full range of special shelters including shelters with bulletproof protection, nuclear-hardened shelters, modular shelters and expandable shelters.

Specifications

See table above

Status

In production. Piaggio shelters have been supplied to the armed forces of Denmark, France, Germany, Italy, Spain, Turkey, the US and possibly other undisclosed countries.

Contractor

Piaggio Aero Industries SpA

Piaggio shelters (Piaggio)　0587974

A Piaggio shelter (Piaggio Aero Industries)　0587977

Piaggio shelters (Piaggio Aero Industries)　0587976

Piaggio shelters (Piaggio Aero Industries)　0587975

SAI Ambrosini shelters and containers

Development

SAI Ambrosini began manufacturing containers and shelters in 1970 and produced a wide range of specialist containers for military purposes. The company ceased to trade in 1992, although the brand/tradename is now used by T.A. Tecnologie d' Avanguardia, a manufacturer of timepieces.

Description

SAI Ambrosini containers are constructed from a sandwich material made up of light aluminium alloy, heat-bonded to a polyurethane core. Watertight rivets and stainless steel bolts and nuts are used to hold the panels together. All panels have a special lattice of light aluminium struts to absorb stresses from internal and external loads and to provide lashing anchors for internal loads.

SAI Ambrosini also produced a range of air conditioned containers for special purposes. There were three main models in this range, the smallest with a 4 kW conditioner, then a 9 kW conditioner and the largest with a 20 kW conditioner unit. These units could be used to provide refrigeration if required.

Both standard and cooled containers were supplied with a range of accessories that included jacks for lifting and loading, ladders, special or emergency exits and hatches, special electrical looms or lighting and RF suppression.

SAI Ambrosini shelters were available built to standard dimensions or to special requirements. Air conditioning units were usually installed and the units could be equipped with mechanical systems for loading and unloading from trucks, including over the sides of drop side trucks. Lifting points were provided and the shelters could be carried on special SAI Ambrosini trailers and trailer systems.

Shelters could be supplied in armoured, RF screened, EMP- and NBC-protected forms.

Wheel-coupled shelter and platform transporters

To complete its shelter and container systems, SAI Ambrosini designed and constructed a wheel-coupled trailer for the transport of shelters and platforms. The wheel-coupling system meets Mil-M-8090F with reference to Mobility Type III, Group C.

The system can be towed by a number of types of military vehicle. The two rolling trains can be coupled independently at the front or rear of the shelter or platform and lift the load for towing. If necessary, the load can be lifted to a height of 700 mm for towing through fords or over rough terrain.

When not carrying a load, the transporter sections can be connected to form a compact unit for towing.

Specifications
Containers

Capacity	3,000 kg	5,000 kg	8,000 kg
Weight	1,600 kg	2,700 kg	2,800 kg
Length	3.25 m	4.55 m	4.55 m
Width	2.1 m	2.2 m	2.3 m

Specifications
Wheel coupled shelter and platform transports

Model	TP-3	TP-5	TP-8
Length	2.45 m	3.4 m	3.4 m
Width	2.25 m	2.3 m	2.3 m
Height	1.43 m	1.47 m	1.47 m
Track	1.93 m	2.01 m	2.01 m
Weight	1,300 kg	2,700 kg	2,800 kg
Max capacity	3,500 kg	7,500 kg	7,500 kg

Status
Production complete. In service with the Italian Army.

Contractor
SAI Ambrosini - Società Aeronautica Italiana SpA

Poland

Wojskowe Zaklady Inzynieryjne (WZINZ) containers

Development
The Wojskowe Zaklady Inzynieryjne (WZINZ) Military Engineering Works specialises in the repair, upgrade and production of technical equipment for the Polish Army, but also supplies other armed forces and commercial concerns. As part of its product range the company produces a range of 10, 15 and 20 ft ISO-dimensioned containers that are suitable for a variety of general military uses, including power supply stations, water purification plants, fuel and lubricant handling and cookhouses.

Basic outline specifications for WZINZ 10, 15 and 20 ft containers are included in this entry.

Description
Containers supplied by WZINZ conform to ISO norms, can be transported or mounted to any standard load-carrying truck and may be handled by cranes, container stackers or forklift trucks. They may be transported by sea, on or under decks.

As with all steel containers of ISO dimensions, options available in terms of fixtures, fittings, doors/hatches and so on are extensive, but basic dimensions and capacities may be found in the accompany table below.

Mounted on a Star 1466 6,000 kg (6 × 6) truck, this specialist container produced by Wojskowe Zaklady Inzynieryjne has a number of role-specific fixtures and fittings including doors, power connection points, an environmental control unit, and external fittings (WZINZ)   1156118

A specific example of a WZINZ supplied and equipped container would be the Containerized Kitchen. The Containerized Kitchen is a self-sufficient catering complex intended for the preparation and supply of 100 all-day meals in field conditions. It can also supply meals in areas without, or with interrupted, infrastructure, and in various climatic conditions, including high humidity and high ambient temperatures.

The Containerized Kitchen can be transported by any DROPS/PLS-type truck or trailer, on railway platforms equipped with hooks for handling 20-feet ISO 1CC containers, sea-going vessels (provided the kitchen container is placed on the top layer in the vessel's hold), and by air in an air-tight hold where pressure is compensated to prevent damage to the air conditioning unit and refrigeration cabinet.

Outline specifications for the Containerized Kitchen are included in this entry.

Specifications
Containerized Kitchen
Length: 6.058 m
Width: 2.438 m
Height: 2.591 m
Weight: 5,000 kg
Useable area: 14.8 m^2
Volume: 38.2 m^3
Power rating of installed equipment: 75 kW
Max power consumption: 135 A
Electrical installation: 400/230 V
Staffing: 2 required

Status
In production. In service with the Polish Army.

Contractor
Wojskowe Zaklady Inzynieryjne (WZINZ)

Singapore

Mobile field hospital

Description
This mobile field hospital was designed to provide a full range of medical facilities in any field or emergency environment. It is based on a specially designed container that can be configured as an operating theatre, X-ray unit, laboratory, blood bank, dental clinic, nursing ward, casualty clearing unit, kitchen, laundry or for other specialised medical purposes.

Each container is fully equipped for its purpose and can be carried into position using a platform truck or a tractor truck with a flatbed semi-trailer. On-site the containers are placed on the ground in a suitable formation although each unit can be used independently if required. Power is supplied by towed generators. When not in use, the containers can be stacked up to five high.

Each container has external dimensions of 6.058 × 2.438 × 2.438 m.

Status
Understood to be in service with Singapore armed forces.

Contractor
Singapore Technologies Kinetics

Spain

SPA shelters

Description
SPA shelters are built to military standards and have been certified to comply with the applicable MIL specifications (such as MIL-STD-907B) and their NATO equivalent (SHCPE 6516).

The shelters feature a foam and beam structure together with several innovative features such as ISO-type corner fittings and a door locking device that provides them with a distinctive appearance.

WZINZ ISO containers

	10 ft ISO	15 ft ISO	20 ft ISO
Length:	2.991 m	4.572 m	6.058 m
Width:	2.438 m	2.438 m	2.438 m
Height:	2.438 m	2.438 m	2.438 m
Weight:			
(max gross operating)	10,160 kg	17,500 kg	24,000 kg
(tare)	1,000 kg	1,700 kg	2,200 kg
(payload)	9,160 kg	15,800 kg	21,800 kg

A typical Servicios y Protectos Avanzados SA (SPA) shelter
(Servicios y Protectos Avanzados SA (SPA))   1156062

A model S-788 shelter produced by Servicios y Protectos Avanzados SA (SPA) and mounted on an AM General HMMWV
(Servicios y Protectos Avanzados SA (SPA))   1156063

A typical shelter produced by Servicios y Protectos Avanzados SA (SPA) and transported by a Spanish Army URO MT 2,000 kg (4 × 4) truck
(Servicios y Protectos Avanzados SA (SPA))   1156064

Applications include telecommunications, radar control, command post, medical centre, air traffic control and field laboratory. Versions include RFI shielding to MIL-STD-285, nuclear hardening and various types of other protection, including EMP, NBC TEMPEST and ballistic. Available models include the most widely used, both in the military field (S-280/E, S-788 (for HMMWV), NATO ACE types I, II and III) and in the commercial (ISO 10, 15 and 20 ft); expandable shelters are also available.

The two types mainly used by the Spanish Army are the NATO II, with internal dimensions of 3.645 × 1.915 × 1.9 m and the S-250E with internal dimensions of 1.864 × 1.834/0.954 × 1.627 m.

Accessories available include shelter lifting and fastening slings, lifting and levelling devices, a platform for the entry door, air conditioners of varying capacities and NBC filters and output valves.

Status
In service with the Spanish and other undisclosed armed forces.

Contractor
Servicios y Protectos Avanzados SA (SPA)

Switzerland

RUAG Mobile Expandable Container 1:3

Development
In response to the Swiss armed forces XXI (the Swiss Army's transformation plans), from 2004 RUAG Land Systems developed and introduced the RUAG Mobile Expandable Container 1:3. This and other RUAG Land Systems containers are in service with the Swiss armed forces.

Description
The RUAG Mobile Expandable Container 1:3 is an expandable shelter system combining fold-out walls with a standard 20 ft ISO container (20 × 8 × 8 ft; optional 20 × 8.5 × 8.5 ft). When expanded, the container offers approaching 36 m² of floor space (almost three times that of a standard 20 ft ISO container which offers around 12 m²) combined with a headroom of 1.95 m. Side walls are constructed of aluminium sandwich elements for optimal insulation; the container is designed for a –35 to +71°C climatic operational range. Full autonomy with a field power supply, or supply by means of conventional external power-supply socket are possible. The use of modular interior fittings allow for the container to be fitted out to suit a variety of customer requirements and uses. The use of modular interior fittings allows for the container to be re-roled as required. Proposed uses include conference, command and control, medical, catering or field accommodation. The container is CSC-approved and corresponds with the applicable standards for truck, sea and rail transportation. In addition to the usual forklift or crane handling methods, if required the RUAG Mobile Expandable Container can be fitted for handling by a load handling system-equipped (LHS) truck fitted with a container handling unit (CHU). Once deployed on concrete, tarmac, gravel or other suitable hard ground, the container is ready for use in a few minutes. Containers may be stacked nine-high.

Specifications
RUAG Mobile Expandable Container 1:3

Maximum gross weight:	11,000 kg
Length:	
(closed)	6.058 m
(expanded)	6.058 m
Width:	
(closed)	2.438 m
(expanded)	6.600 m
Height:	
(closed)	2.438 m
(expanded)	2.438 m

Status
Production as required. In service with the Swiss Army.

Contractor
RUAG Land Systems

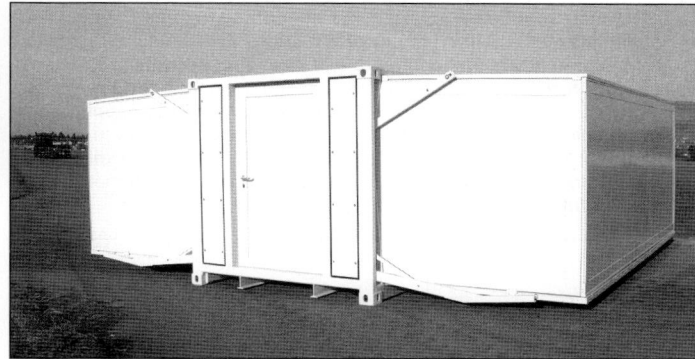

RUAG Mobile Expandable Container 1:3 in use (RUAG Land Systems)
                                                              1173036

RUAG NEMP-protected containers (1:1 and 1:2)

Description
RUAG Land Systems NEMP-protected containers are designed to combine a NEMP-protected environment with the logistically compatible ISO container footprint.

These containers are CSC-approved and correspond with the applicable standards for truck, sea and rail transportation. In addition to the usual forklift or crane-handling methods, if required RUAG NEMP-protected Containers can be fitted for handling by a Load-Handling System-equipped (LHS) truck fitted with a Container Handling Unit (CHU).

RUAG Land Systems NEMP-protected Container 1:2, expanded
(RUAG Land Systems)   1173031

Once deployed on concrete, tarmac, gravel or other suitable hard ground these containers are ready for use in a few minutes. Containers maybe stacked nine-high.

Two versions are offered, the 1:1 and the expandable 1:2. Both versions are supplied as standard with air-conditioning, an electrical supply, prepared for interior fitting, and with NEMP protection of >60 dB at 1 GHz. The 1:1 has 12 m^2, the 1:2 with its slide-out extension has a two-third increase in floor space to 20 m^2.

Side walls of these containers are steel or aluminium sandwich elements. The use of modular interior fittings allows for these container to be re-roled as required. In addition to the standard telecommunication role, other proposed uses for these shelters include communication or surveillance systems units.

Specifications
RUAG NEMP-protected containers

Max gross weight:	11,000 kg
Length:	6.058 m
Width:	2.438 m (1:2 expanded: 3.9 m)
Height:	2.438 m

Status
Production as required. In service with the Swiss Army.

Contractor
RUAG Land Systems, Logistic Vehicles & Containers

RUAG material container (MAC)

Description
The RUAG Land Systems material container (MAC) is a purpose-designed ISO container. The layout of the container is flexible and can be varied to suit customer requirements, however the concept of the idea remains constant, easy access in a variety of ways to a wide selection (small or large) of stored items. The container and its sliding drawers are lockable. Weather protection for opened drawers is integral in the design.

The RUAG material container is CSC-approved and corresponds with the applicable standards for truck, sea and rail transportation. In addition to the usual forklift or crane-handling methods, if required this RUAG container can be fitted for handling by a Load-Handling System-equipped (LHS) truck fitted with a Container Handling Unit (CHU).

RUAG Land Systems material container (MAC) clearly showing storage arrangements and integral weather protection for the open drawers
(RUAG Land Systems)   1173033

Once deployed on concrete, tarmac, gravel or other suitable hard ground the container is ready for use in a few minutes. Containers maybe stacked nine-high.

Specifications
Unladen weight:	6,000 kg
Max laden weight:	15,000 kg
Load carrying capacity:	9,000 kg
Length:	6.058 m
Width:	2.438 m
Height:	2.438 m

Status
Production as required. In service with the Swiss Army.

Contractor
RUAG Land Systems, Logistic Vehicles & Containers

Turkey

Ibrahim Örs military shelters

Description
Ibrahim Örs AS offers a range of military tactical shelters and associated equipment from its Kirikkale facility, including the following:
- S-250
- S-280
- NATO I
- NATO II
- NATO III
- ACE 1
- ACE II
- ACE III

These shelters are produced to full military standards and are all capable of being configured for a wide range of military applications. Construction is aluminium. Ibrahım Örs produces tactical shelters with RFI, EMI, EMP and NBC shielding.

Ibrahim Örs also produces stainless steel, aluminium and steel bodied double-walled containers and ISO-type shelters for a variety of special uses.

A typical Ibrahim Örs AS NATO-type shelter (Ibrahim Örs)   1325700

A shielded shelter produced by Ibrahim Örs AS (Ibrahim Örs)   1325699

Model	S-250	S-280	NATO I	NATO II	NATO III
Length	2.16 m	3.734 m	2.9 m	4.25 m	5 m
Width	2 m	2.21 m	2.05 m	2.2 m	2.2 m
Height	1.254/1.75 m	2.022 m	1.825 m	2.075 m	2.075 m
Weight empty	500 kg	850 kg	700 kg	900 kg	1,200 kg
Payload	1,000 kg	3,650 kg	1,300 kg	3,600 kg	4,300 kg

The following specifications for tactical shelters are from Ibrahim Örs AS literature.

Specifications
See table above

Status
Production as required. In service with Turkish and other armed forces.

Contractor
Ibrahim Örs AS

United Kingdom

CSC demountable shelters, shelters and containers

Description
CSC (Specialised Vehicles) is part of the Paneltex Group. CSC has considerable experience with conventional shelters, shelter-type vehicle bodies and containers, and has designed, manufactured and supplied the UK MoD and others with a number of assorted solutions over a 30 year timeframe. CSC bodies are built of composite construction aluminium faced one piece panels. RFI screening and NBC protection can be provided if required.

Recent CSC projects have included the production of prototype shelters for UK MoD evaluation. One unit was built in conjunction with MSI Defence Systems Ltd and Racal Defence Electronics, and comprises a demountable shelter mounted on the chassis of a MOWAG DURO (6 × 6) truck. A second unit was built in conjunction with Dytecna Ltd and BAE Systems and comprises a demountable unit mounted onto a Supacat HMT (6 × 6) chassis-cab.

Demountable shelters provided are designed to accept in-service standard lifting and mobility equipment as applicable. However, the system provided for the HMT Supacat project was designed and built specifically for it, as the shelter body was such that it could not accept standard lifting equipment.

Other units supplied by CSC include medical facilities, workshops, command posts and field kitchens.

CSC demountable shelter body fitted on an HMT Supacat (6 × 6) truck (CSC) 0522418

CSC body on a Reynolds Boughton RB-44 TUH (Truck Utility Heavy) (Shaun Connors) 0536657

Status
In production. In service with the UK MoD and others.

Contractor
CSC (Specialised Vehicles) Limited

Douglas SPD Mobiliser shelter and container transport system

Description
The Douglas SPD Mobiliser system utilises a pair of road-legal axle bogies which, using pneumatics and hydraulics, can lift an ISO container, NATO shelter or any similar container and immediately convert it into a road-going drawbar trailer. When a shelter or container is carried, the bogies are mounted to the ends of the shelter or container using standard ISO twistlock connectors or other similar fixings. Twin hydraulic rams and hand-operated pumps on each bogie provide the load raise/lower facility. Small lateral adjustments may be made by operating the rams individually, via a control valve. The hydraulic system can be used in combination with the air suspension to provide additional ground clearance when required as the unit has a full cross-country capability.

The intrinsic geometry of the Mobiliser ensures that the payload container or shelter stays horizontal at all times during the pick-up operation. This negates any possible need for the specialist containers or shelters that may be required when handling fuel or ammunition with more conventional load handling and transport systems.

The chassis and lifting frames of the unit are constructed from high tensile rolled hollow section plate with welds to BS5135, shot-blasted to BS4232 Type 2. The front bogie incorporates an Ackerman-type steering axle, the rear bogie is normally non-steering, although steering is an option.

Suspension is by Hendrickson rolling diaphragm air suspension with twinleaf quarter elliptic spring location and hydraulic shock absorbers. Standard wheel and tyre equipment is 11R 22.5 non-traction/open tread tyres (options are available) mounted on 7.5 × 22.5 10-stud, spigot location wheels. The Mobiliser is road legal throughout the EU and is fitted with a dual-line air brake system, load sensing valves on each bogie, an anti lock braking system (ABS) and a full lighting array. When not in use, the two bogie units are coupled together to create their own drawbar unit.

The Mobiliser can be towed behind any suitable capacity truck and with a standard ISO container or shelter is air-transportable by C-130 Hercules transport aircraft.

Operational parameters are 5 to 99 per cent relative humidity, a –30 to +52°C operational range, and –30 to +70°C storage range.

Specifications
Length: 9.405 m (with 20 ft ISO container)
Width: 2.44 m
Height:
(lowered) 2.44 m
(raised) 945 mm (under container)
(under axle) 330 mm
Ground clearance:
(ride) 550 mm
(raised) 945 mm (under container)
(under axle) 330 mm
Turning radius: model dependant
Brakes: dual circuit air, drums on both bogies, ABS
Tyres: 11R 22.5
Electrical system: 24 V

Douglas SPD Mobiliser shelter and container transport system transporting RAF generator 0114042

Status
In production. In service with the Saudi Arabia and the UK Royal Air Force.

Contractor
Douglas Equipment Limited

Dytecna Engineering military shelters

Description
GEL Engineering Ltd was founded in 1931. It was announced in April 2008 that Dytecna had acquired GEL Engineering Ltd, the company renamed to Dytecna Engineering Ltd and reporting to Dytecna's Malvern-based defence systems division.

Dytecna Engineering Ltd supplies a range of standard and custom-built military shelters for communications, radar management, training and other associated operations. These military shelters are supplied to the MoD and electronics industry for service in all three armed forces, for the UK and overseas.

Dytecna military shelters can be supplied in a range of standard sizes or custom built to any size and shape. They may be single standalone units or complexes, standard ISO or custom built, RFI, EMC, EMP, TEMPEST, NBC-protected with full systems installation.

Protected military shelters are also available.

Status
Production as required. In service with the armed forces of the UK and others.

Contractor
Dytecna Engineering Ltd, previously known as GEL Engineering Limited.

KUDOS Kabin system

Development
The KUDOS Kabin system (previously known as the UBK Kabin system) was developed specifically for the military to meet rapid deployment demands in all parts of the world. It is now used by a wide variety of armed forces, plus governmental and aid agencies.

In July 1999 it was announced that a GBP110 million, three-year contract had been awarded to the now Lockheed Martin UK Ltd (then INSYS Ltd; prior to that Hunting Engineering Ltd) to support UK armed forces personnel operating in Kosovo. As part of this contract Kudos 2000 Limited supplied approximately 2,600 folding UBK Kabins as sleeping accommodation units. These were supplied complete with emergency lighting, a heater, air-conditioning units, fly screens, blackout blinds and furniture. The flat-folding furniture included bunk beds and mattresses, lockers and kit lockers. Folding desks and seating were supplied for office accommodation.

KUDOS cabins are known to be deployed in Afghanistan, Algeria, Belize, Bosnia, Cambodia, Chad, Cyprus, Ethiopia, Ghana, Guatemala, Indonesia, Iraq, Kosovo, Kuwait, Oman, Pakistan, Poland, Russia, Siberia, Somalia, Sudan, United Arab Emirates (Dubai), United Kingdom, and the US, by armed forces and various governmental and aid agencies.

Description
The KUDOS system is designed to convert from a flat-pack to a rigid, weatherproof structure in about 30 minutes without the need for tools or lifting gear. Up to four complete cabins measuring 5.2 × 2.4 m can be carried on a DROPS flatrack. Whether packed or deployed the standard cabin is DROPS compatible and can be transported using most military vehicles, medium helicopters and transport aircraft.

A complete KUDOS Kabin (Lockheed Martin INSYS UK Ltd)   1185479

KUDOS Kabins in Belize (Lockheed Martin INSYS UK Ltd)   1185480

KUDOS Kabins in Kosovo (Lockheed Martin INSYS UK Ltd)   1185481

The KUDOS system can be finished to suit operations in arctic, European, tropical or desert regions and is certified to operate between -31°C to +50°C. The modularity of the system allows for easy extension and expansion to meet most operational requirements, as side and end walls can be easily removed to create larger areas. Modules can be added creating longer buildings or removed for smaller applications. Rapid repairs can be easily effected without recourse to a workshop by replacing damaged panels. All components are either interchangeable or replaceable.

KUDOS cabins are supplied as specified or with a basic 'fitted for role' facility, from field accommodation to offices and conference rooms, stores, security post or medical facility. Basic cabins are supplied with a built-in electrical system complete with lighting, light switches, power points and consumer unit, one lockable door and two windows. Alternative materials, fittings and colours can be utilised to meet customer specifications. A wide range of folding equipment, including folding bunk beds, lockers, cages and furniture, is available to support the system.

Cabin panels are formed from a nominal 51 mm thick rigid extruded Styrofoam core encapsulated by one outer UV stabilised glass reinforced plastic colour co-ordinated high impact layer and one colour co-ordinated high impact inner layer. The panels are fire rated inside and out. The central frame and all pressed steel sections are fabricated from Zintec-coated mild steel sheet grade 43. Floor panels, which are waterproof and non-slip, have an overall thickness of 62 mm. They are steel braced, reinforced, insulated, reversible sandwich panels with glass reinforced plastic facing on both sides. Floor is capable of carrying a uniformly distributed load of 2.5 kN/m². Double glazed windows can be provided and may be fitted with blackout blinds and fly screens. The roof is manufactured using a 63 mm-thick extruded polystyrene foam core encapsulated by colour co-ordinated high impact glass reinforced plastic skins. As an extra precaution against severe weather conditions and as an extra layer of insulation, a one-piece 'weathershield' can be supplied to fit over the roof of a standard Kabin. The roof is capable of withstanding uniformly distributed load greater than the equivalent of 2 m of snow (1.5 kN/ m²).

Status
In production. In use worldwide.

Contractor
Lockheed Martin INSYS UK Ltd

Marconi ISOLATOR electronic equipment shelters

Description

The Marconi ISOLATOR shelter is a high-strength, low-weight transportable shelter for both military and commercial applications. It protects electronic equipment from the adverse effects of the environment including the elements, EMI, RFI and NEMP and is provided with TEMPEST shielding if required. Construction utilised sandwich panel technology and offered the end-user total flexibility in the location of doors, apertures, escape hatches and interface panels.

ISOLATOR shelters were supplied to the UK's armed forces, and others, for a variety of applications.

Status

Production complete. In service with the British Army, NATO and some overseas defence organisations.

Contractor

Former GEC-Marconi Defence Systems.

Marconi ISOLATOR sandwich panel technology adapted for a hardtop application on a Reynolds Boughton RB-44 Truck Utility Heavy (TUH) (Shaun C Connors)   0536657

Marshall Land Systems range of shelters

Description

Since 1946, Marshall Land Systems (MLS) group and its predecessor companies has supplied the international defence market with more than 5,000 tactical shelters in over 200 different configurations. Currently the sub-group Marshall Specialist Vehicles (MSV) offers a wide range of shelters, these range from simple ISO steel container based solutions, through to more complex expanding single or double MATRIX shelters, configured as field hospitals and so on.

Recently three fully transportable self-contained shelter-based field hospitals, consisting of CBRN, EMP, EMC and EMI protected MATRIX and steel ISO shelters, were delivered to Norway. In addition a fully deployable and similarly protected HQ based on MATRIX shelters has just been delivered to FMV Sweden. Both projects featured a high degree of systems integration.

Shelter-based ground-control station shelters have included Watchkeeper UAV and ASTOR programmes for the UK MoD, and the BAE Systems Herti UAV. Similar vehicle based ground-control station shelters include those for Watchkeeper and ASTOR.

Shown under construction are four battery charging units for the RAF which were delivered in 2010. These units have been designed to maintain all in-service batteries including specialist batteries for Typhoon aircraft. The shelters are designed to meet all current health and safety requirements and include a drench shower (Shaun C Connors)   1391339

All MSV ground deployable shelters are based on ISO 20 ft footprints and are CSC plated, making them suitable for transportation by sea, land or air. Similarly all MSV shelters have inbuilt forklift pockets and are DROPS/palletized load handling system compatible, enabling them to be rapidly deployed from or reloaded onto transport systems.

MSV expandible shelters have simple to operate with automatic, powered shelter expansion systems and in-built levelling jacks. This enables the shelters to be deployed from a transport system and brought into operation in approximately 90 seconds.

A feature of MSV shelters is their extensive usable internal wall space. This is achieved by the basic design of the shelter expansion system. Integral power sources and climatic conditioning systems make MSV's shelter systems suitable for medical and C3I systems. Typically MSV

A Marshall Matrix 150 compatible shelter (Marshall Land Systems) 0121858

The General Purpose Thermal Imaging Repair Facility (GPTIRF) developed originally by Racal Instruments, now part of EADS, has been refurbished and housed in a self-contained shelter by Marshall Land Systems. Included in the shelter are air conditioning units and a generator (Shaun C Connors)   1391341

Marshall Land Systems built the original Power Pack Repair Facility (PPRF) in 1999. These units have been returned to the company for a full refurbishment. Shown here is the engine run up facility which has a protected operator area in case of an unexpected incident with the power pack. Fitted inside this area are all the controls for managing the engine (Shaun C Connors)   1391340

shelters maintain an internal noise level of less than 65dB even with integral generators and attain RFI screening levels of 80dB. Coupled with high levels of thermal protection to maintain internal temperatures of between +16 to +25°C (+61 to +77°F). MSV shelters are also capable of full humidity control depending on individual shelter use within a shelter complex.

Provided the weight penalty is acceptable, armour, to differing standards, can be applied as required. Alternatively appliqué armour can be fitted to protect shelters whilst being transported. All MSV shelters are constructed to the appropriate MIL-STD, DEF STAN or NATO STANAG.

Status
In production. In service with the UK and other armed forces.

Contractor
Marshall Land Systems

MSI-Defence Systems shelters

Development
MSI-Defence Systems Ltd (MSI-DSL) designs and manufactures a wide variety of shelters for rapid response and high mobility applications. The company has 80 years of experience in defence markets and on a six acre site at its production headquarters in the UK has 20,000 ft² dedicated to the production shelters.

Description
The basic MSI-Defence Systems shelter is of standard 20 ft ISO configuration, although a variety of lengths up to 40 ft (12.19 m) are available. Non-ISO dimensions are also available. Shelters are constructed from either steel, aluminium composite panels or screened GRP. RFI, EMP/NEMP, EMI and TEMPEST protection can be incorporated, as can NBC filtration or ballistic protection. Air conditioning, a fire detection/suppression system, various power generating or electrical systems and special-to-purpose equipment may also be installed.

DROPS/PLS inter-operability can be in-built and a number of lifting, jacking and mobilisation options are available. Fork pockets can be in-built into the base frame to allow handling by any suitable capacity fork lift truck. ISO compatibility also ensures handling by commercial container handling equipment is possible.

MSI-Defence Systems also produces 1:2 or 1:3 expandable tactical shelters. Complexes are formed by either side-to-side or end-to-end direct coupling or joining by the use of door-to-door butting kits. The use of butting kits does not affect any RFI or NBC integrity.

NATO ACE 6516/SHCPE/86 standard tactical shelters offering environmental, EMC/RFI and NBC protection are also available from MSI-Defence Systems.

Variants
Employing shelter/container manufacturing techniques and materials, MSI-Defence Systems offers a wide range of vehicle bodies for platforms ranging in size from 6 × 6 ATV through to four-axle rigid truck chassis or semi-trailers, and that range from basic ISO dimension containers to fully tactical shelter-type constructions.

Status
In production. In service with British and other unspecified armed forces.

Contractor
MSI-Defence Systems Limited

United States

AAR Mobility Systems Mobility Wheel Sets, Mobilizers and accessories

Development
AAR Mobility Systems (formerly AAR Cadillac Manufacturing) produces a range of mobility wheel sets, mobilizers and adapters for use with the AAR Mobility Systems range of shelters and containers, standard 20 ft ISO shelters and containers, ISU containers, and the MECC range of shelters.

Description
High Speed Mobility Wheel Set (HSMWS)
The High Speed Mobility Wheel Set (HSMWS) provides for the towed transport of ELAMS (Expandable Light Air Mobile Shelter), HELAMS (Hardside Expandable Light Air Mobile Shelter) and LAMS (Light Air Mobile Shelter) at highway speeds of up to 93 km/h. In conjunction with the optional 2.74 m support beams, the set can also transport ISU four-way containers, the beams being installed through the forklift tubes. The HSMWS lifting system utilises the standard military 24 V DC electrical system; a 12 V DC system is optional. Tare weight is 1,588 kg, maximum axle loads are 3,629 kg front and rear, and the maximum gross weight is 7,031 kg. Standard trailer lighting is provided, all wheels are braked and the air-ride suspension provides for 102 mm of wheel travel. Shock-absorbers and transverse anti-roll bars are fitted both front and rear. Minimum ground clearance at maximum weight is 330 mm and the HSMWS is suitable for off-highway operation.

Low Speed Mobility Wheel Set (LSMWS)
The Low Speed Mobility Wheel Set (LSMWS), previously designated Standard Speed Mobility Wheel Sat (SSMWS), is designed for use with either two- or four-way ISU containers. For use with four-way ISU containers, 2.74 and 2.24 m length support beams are available and for use with two-way ISU containers, a 2.74 m H-bar allows the container to be transported in the 2.24 m configuration. The LSMWS lifting system utilises the standard military 24 V DC electrical system. The LSMWS can also be used with standard 463L pallets and can be used as a helicopter or aircraft loading device.

The LSMWS has a maximum speed of 16 km/h and a maximum tare weight of 612 kg. Maximum load capacity is 5,443 kg.

ISO High Speed Mobility Wheel Set/Mobilizer (HSMWS/M)
The ISO High Speed Mobility Wheel Set/Mobilizer (HSMWS/M) allows for the towing of standard 20 ft ISO shelters/containers and the MECC range of shelters. Full details of the MECC range of shelters can be found elsewhere in this section.

The HSMWS/M is suitable for both on- and off-road use and for the former options including anti-lock brakes, mudguards/flaps and running lights to enable the varying legislative requirements for road use to be met. The HSMWS/M may also be used as a transport aircraft loading device.

Tare weight is 2,867 kg; gross weight rating is 13,835 kg. Maximum axle loads are 6,917 kg, front and rear. Maximum speed on roads is 88.5 km/h. Ground clearance at ride height is 508 mm; suspension is of the air-ride type with additional transverse anti-roll bars and levering valves, front and rear. All four wheels are braked (anti-lock is an option), the air-operated system having temporary use air tanks and a spring-applied parking brake that automatically activates (rear axle only) following the loss of system air.

The hydraulic system for raising/lowering the shelter has a three-way power cord allowing for the simultaneous lifting of each end during aircraft loading operations. Integral mobilizer/shelter levelling jacks are built into the mobilizer structure. A 24 V DC electrical system with standard NATO connectors operates the lift system via on-board batteries and charger (110 or 230 V), vehicle connection or in emergency, a hand-operated pump.

An MSI-Defence Systems expandable shelter housing a training theatre (MSI)   0126683

High Speed Mobility Wheel Set (HSMWS) attached to a Light Air Mobile Shelter (LAMS) (AAR Mobility Systems)   0126565

M1022 Mobilizer Adapter

The M1022 Mobilizer Adapter is a 6.03 × 2.39 × 2.54 m (L × W × H) dimensioned cradle that allows the M1022 dolly set to be used as a general purpose flatbed trailer in addition to its normal container handling role. The cradle has a tare weight of 1,470 kg and has a load capacity of 10,887 kg. This allows it to transport two fully loaded ISU-90 containers. The decking has a non-slip treadplate surface and 340 kg capacity cargo tie-down rings are located around the periphery and are positioned to suit standard 463L configured loads.

Status

Either available for production, or in production and in service with US armed forces.

Contractor

AAR Mobility Systems

AAR Mobility Systems range of shelters

Description

AAR Mobility Systems (formerly AAR Cadillac Manufacturing) produces a wide range of transportable shelter systems suitable not only for military applications, but also for civil use where temporary accommodation facilities are required. These shelter systems are available in varying sizes and configurations and can be tailored to a user's specific requirements. They can be fully operational in time frames ranging from minutes to hours depending on various factors including the system, its size and the deployment site. The complete range are fully transportable and in addition to road and transport aircraft, most are certified for external helicopter lift operations.

In addition to the items detailed elsewhere in this section, AAR Mobility Systems also manufacture the Weatherhaven Mobile Expandable Container Configuration (MECC) for the US market, full details of which can also be found elsewhere in this section.

Status

In production. In widespread use, primarily by all branches of US armed forces.

Contractor

AAR Mobility Systems

In addition to manufacturing a wide range of shelters and containers, AAR Mobility Systems also market the Weatherhaven Mobile Expandable Container Configuration (MECC) (AAR Mobility Systems)   0126574

AAR Mobility Systems range of ISU containers

Description

AAR Mobility Systems (formerly AAR Cadillac Manufacturing) produce an extensive range of air-transportable and helicopter slingable ISU containers. There are two sizes available, the standard being 2.74 × 2.23 m (L × W) and the half-size 2.74 × 1.22 m, with heights varying from 1.53 to 2.44 m. The height is distinguished by the nomenclature in the description of the container; for example the ISU-90 base-model being 2.23 m (90 in). Weight, cubic capacity and payload are very much dependent on individual configuration but the standard ISU-90 container, which itself can fitted out to suit a variety of requirements, has a tare weight of 780 kg and maximum payload (including fittings) of 4,536 kg (5 tons). It has four doors, two each side and is certified for transport in C130, C141, C5, C17, KC10, Boeing 747 and DC10 aircraft. It can also be helicopter underslung.

The full range have a structure that is weather, dust and sand proof and an extruded aluminium base that is liftable by either four- or two-way forklift(s). Winching rings are fitted at each lower corner to facilitate easier handling and aircraft loading and where applicable, laden containers can be stacked two-high. They can also be lifted and handled by crane. For

Four of the ISU-80 model will fit directly inside a standard 40 ft ISO container, two will fit directly inside a standard 20 ft ISO container (AAR Mobility Systems)   0126566

road transport the ISU range of containers can be carried on any standard military transport vehicle and two/four of the ISU-80 model will fit directly inside a standard 20 ft/40 ft ISO container. To further enhance handling and mobility AAR Cadillac also manufacture two types of quick-attach mobility wheel sets that, when used with support beams, can be used to transport and handle ISU four-way containers. Full details of these can be found elsewhere in this section.

Door configurations and internal fixture permutations are numerous and can be adapted to suit individual requirements. These can also include fitting out for specialist uses such as a self-contained laundry unit, animal transport containers, computer room or an environmentally controlled 'clean room'.

The latest addition to the range is the Expandable ISU Container (EISU). This follows the configuration of a conventional expandable container in that when expanded it occupies and provides approximately three times the floor space of the closed product. In the case of the EISU, the wing walls of the base unit fold down to form the floor of the expanded container, the 'side rooms' formed from fabric walls and ceilings. Two personnel can deploy an EISU in less than 15 minutes.

Dimensions of the closed EISU mirror those of the standard ISU at 2.74 × 2.23 m; height of the EISU is 2.324 m. Expanded the EISU measures 6.3 × 2.74 m, and has a internal ceiling height of 1.84 to 2.13 m. Floor space expanded is 14.77 m². Tare weight is 1,134 kg, payload is 3,402 kg.

The ISU range of containers are in production at a rate of between 3,000 and 5,000 units per year. Over 35,000 units are in service with US armed forces and over 2,000 with other armed forces including the Royal Air Force.

AAR Mobility Systems also produces the SAMS (Small Air Mobile Shelter) and ESAMS (Expandable Small Air Mobile Shelter), both based around standard ISU container dimensions. Full details of SAMS and ESAMS can be found elsewhere in this section.

Status

In production. In service with US (35,000) and other armed forces (2,000), including the Royal Air Force.

Contractor

AAR Mobility Systems

Accordion Expandable Shelter (AES)

Development

The AAR Mobility Systems (formerly AAR Cadillac Manufacturing) Accordion Expandable Shelter (AES) is a weather-tight shelter designed primarily to house personnel in a variety of climatic environments and extremes. The AES has been in production for around 35 years and several thousand units have been delivered to the US armed forces, and others, throughout that time. Those units remaining in service with US forces (estimated to be several hundred) are primarily in the Middle East and South America. The AES remains available and the most recent known US forces order featured an updated specification.

Description

The AES is weather-tight and was designed primarily to house personnel in a variety of climatic environments and extremes. The most recent known delivery featured an updated specification that included heating and air-conditioning equipment.

Integrated jack levelling and ground anchor systems allow the AES to be erected and secured on unprepared ground and once erected, the AES can withstand windspeeds in excess of 36 m/s (70 kt). Set up time for the basic shelter by four people is 90 minutes. A single unit weighs 1,500 kg and expands from 0.813 × 3.96 × 2.44 m (L × W × H) to form a hard-floored shelter with doors and windows at either end and with interior dimensions of 9.6 × 3.4 × 2.13 m.

Accordion Expandable Shelter (AES) deployed (expanded) with the optional 5 ton ECU kit attached (AAR Mobility Systems)   0126573

The packaged shelter's two-way forkliftable pallet-type base allows for forklift capability using a standard 5-ton (4,536 kg) fork truck with 1.8 m tines. The AES was designed to fit the loadbed of the US Army's 2.5- and 5-ton trucks. In addition to fitting any truck of similar size, it is also transportable by the FMTV family and PLS (or similar systems) flatracks. It can be transported as a single unit or connected in double or triple modes. Each unit is fitted with lift-ring assemblies that allow helicopter sling lifting and facilitate lifting/moving by crane. For air-transportability when loaded on standard 463L pallets, three systems (nine units) take up five 463L pallet positions in a C-130 transport aircraft.

Status
Production as required. In service with US and other undisclosed armed forces.

Contractor
AAR Mobility Systems

Army Standard Family (ASF) shelters

Development
The Army Standard Family (ASF) of relocatable/expandible shelters was developed by the US Army and is used by all branches of the US armed forces and military services worldwide.

The most recent ASF shelters contract was awarded to Gichner Shelter Systems in July 2005. The US Army's RDECOM (Natick) awarded a five-year requirements type contract to Gichner for up to six different types of expandible and non-expandible ASF shelters on an as needed basis. The latest announced award under this contract was placed in April 2010 and called for the production of 48 Single-Side Army Standard Family Expandable Shelters, 28 Single-Side 60 AMP Expandable Shelters and 20 Single-Side 100 AMP Expandable Shelters, for a total contract value of USD8.2 million.

Previously ASF shelters had been supplied by Marion Composites, part of the now General Dynamics Armament and Technical Products (GDATP).

Gichner was founded in 1967. The company currently employs around 1,000 employees and is primarily involved in the design, manufacture, integration and test of shelters, containers and their sub-systems.

It was announced in April 2010 that Kratos Defense & Security Solutions, Inc. would acquire Gichner Holdings, Inc.

Description
Army Standard Family (ASF) shelters are available in three configurations: non-expandible; single-side expandible; and double-side expandible. All three configurations measure 2.4 × 2.4 × 6 m when in the shipping mode. When deployed the single and double-side expandible units expand to 4.43 × 5.82 m and 6.55 × 5.82 m respectively providing up to 37.2 m² of floor space.

The shelters, constructed of honeycomb core with aluminium-faced panels, are highly mobile and can be set up on ground slopes up to 7.5 per cent. The shelters conform to ISO shipping container standards and can be transported by ship, rail, truck, cargo air, sea and helicopter lift.

Primary uses for ASF shelters include deployable repair and maintenance facilities, communications systems, command posts, hospitals and kitchens.

Specifications
See table below

Status
In production. More than 3,300 units are in service with the US armed forces and other military services worldwide.

Contractor
Gichner Shelter Systems

CDK Mobile Systems Inc 5th Wheel Mobilizer System

Development
CDK Mobile Systems Inc. developed the 5th Wheel Mobilizer System for the handling and transport of standard ISO containers and shelters behind either standard commercial or military specification tractor trucks. The system is produced in partnership with Gichner Shelter Systems and Wenzlau Engineering. The first nine systems were fielded by the US Navy during 2004.

Description
Unlike the lunette ring/pintle connection associated with the vast majority of shelter mobilisers (or dolly sets), the 5th Wheel Mobilizer System utilises the standard fifth wheel assembly of tractor trucks. Use of a 5th wheel connection enhances mobility, the system being able to turn with the rear inside wheel remaining virtually stationary.

The front portion of the 5th Wheel Mobilizer System consists of a rigid frame, which connects to the four ISO corner castings on the front end of the container. This half also includes the lifting jacks for raising of the container up to kingpin height, and electrical and air brake connections to the tow vehicle. The front part also includes removable castor wheels to assist with positioning and connection to the container. The frame attaches to the tractor in the same way as any commercial trailer.

The rear portion of the 5th Wheel Mobilizer System is the rear half of the standard US Army M1022A1 Dolly Set. This half includes a diesel engine hydraulic system for attachment to the shelter and for lifting up to ride height.

The rear portion also includes shock-absorbers and an air bag suspension set-up; the system is rough terrain capable. Air brakes are included on the rear unit, as is a parking brake system capable of holding the weight of the entire system when disconnected from the tow vehicle. Further details of the M1022A1 Dolly Set can be found elsewhere in this section.

Specifications
Tare Weight: 2,136 kg
Capacity: 9,090 kg
Length:
    (with 20 ft ISO shelter) 10.34 m
Width: 2.44 m
Height: 2.44 m
Ground clearance: 250 mm
Speed:
    (on-road) 90 km/h
    (off-road) 25 km/h
Tyres: 12R 22.5

ASF shelters

Type	non-expandible	single-side expandible	double-side expandible
Military specification:	MIL-S-44196	MIL-S-44197	MIL-S-44195
Weight: (empty)	1,751 kg	2,504 kg	3,153 kg
Payload:	5,053 kg	4,300 kg	3,652 kg
Dimensions:			
(exterior, shipping)	6.06 × 2.44 × 2.44 m	6.06 × 2.49 × 2.49 m	6.06 × 2.49 × 2.49 m
(interior, shipping)	5.82 × 2.17 × 2.31 m	5.82 × 2.14 × 2.17 m	5.82 × 1.98 × 2.17 m
(interior, deployed)	5.82 × 2.17 × 2.31 m	5.82 × 4.43 × 2.17 m	5.82 × 6.55 × 2.17 m
Volume:			
(shipping)	28.3 m³	27.2 m³	24.9 m³
(deployed)	28.3 m³	53.8 m³	79.2 m³
Floor area:			
(shipping)	13.5 m²	12.4 m²	11.5 m²
(deployed)	13.5 m²	25.3 m²	37.2 m²

CDK Mobile Systems 5th Wheel Mobiliser System in use, the tow vehicle being a standard commercial tractor truck (CDK Mobile Systems) 1136163

CDK Mobile Systems 5th Wheel Mobiliser System disconnected from a tractor truck (CDK Mobile Systems) 1136164

Status
In production. The first nine units were delivered to the US Navy during 2004.

Contractor
CDK Mobile Systems Inc

CDK Mobile Systems Inc C-130 Loading Kits

Description
The CDK Mobile Systems Inc C-130 Loading Kits are man-portable kits designed to be assembled onto the end of an ISO container or tactical shelter within 15 minutes to facilitate the loading of C-130 and other transport aircraft. The kits can be disassembled inside the aircraft and stored on board, or removed through a side door to save payload or space so that two 6.096 m/20 ft containers can be loaded onto a single C-130.

The kits are assembled onto the front end of the container while the M1022-A1 or CLT Dolly Set (full details of which can be found elsewhere in this section) is attached to the rear during loading. The single-axle C-130 system can load a single container weighing up to 9,072 kg.

Specifications
Weight:
(kit capacity) 5,897 kg
(max container) 9,072 kg
(kit) 408 kg
Steering: manual
Lifting: manual

Single-axle CDK Mobile Systems Inc C-130 Loading Kit in position (CDK Systems) 0100590

Status
Production as required. In service with military agencies in Canada, Denmark, Germany, Italy, Netherlands, Thailand and the US.

Contractor
CDK Mobile Systems Inc

CDK Mobile Systems Inc M1022-A1 Dolly Set and CLT Dolly Set

Description
The CDK Mobile Systems Inc M1022-A1 Dolly Set and CLT Dolly Set are combined handling and transport devices for ISO containers and military shelters. They are designed to perform three military-related mission functions, as follows:

ISO shelter/container transport - end lifting permits the mobilisation of ISO containers and tactical shelters at highway speeds in excess of 100 km/h, or 30 km/h over rough terrain

ISO shelter/container handling - side lifting permits containers to be loaded on and off trucks, trailers or railway wagons at their origin, destination or intermediate points

Transport aircraft loading - when attached to the end of ISO containers or tactical shelters with heights of 2.438 m/8 ft or 2.59 m/8.5 ft, the M1022-A1 and CLT Dolly Set systems permit roll-on and roll-off loading of containers weighing up to 9,072 kg/20,000 lb.

The 9,072 kg/20,000 lb capacity M1022-A1 system is the US Army standard system for the handling and transport of tactical shelters. The 9,072 kg/ 20,000 lb capacity CLT Dolly Set is the European NATO standard mobiliser system certified for EU Road Use per Framework Directive 7-/156/EEC. Each system includes diesel-powered hydraulic systems to perform all connection and lift functions within a matter of minutes. Each system includes a unique three-wheel handling mode, which permits the unloaded movement of each half by one person.

A S-280 adapter kit has been developed to permit the CLT Dolly Set to operate with S-280 shelters, and an ACE Adapter is also available for the handling and transport of NATO ACE shelters.

Gichner Systems Group manufactured around 1,500 of the earlier M1022 dolly sets between 1985 and 1990.

M1022-A1 Dolly Set carrying a US Army tactical shelter (CDK Mobile Systems) 0100588

M1022-A1 Dolly Set in use loading a C-130 Hercules transport aircraft (CDK Mobile Systems) 0100585

CLT Dolly Set system being used on container for side lift handling onto a Canadian Armed Forces truck (CDK Mobile Systems)   0100587

Specifications

M1022-A1 + CLT Dolly Set
Weight: (empty) 2,790 kg
Lift capacity: 9,072 kg
Transport capacity:
  (at 80.5 km/h) 9,072 kg
  (at 88.5 km/h) 6,804 kg
Max lift height 1.27 m
Length: 10.97 m (with 6.096 m container)
Width: 2.438 m
Height: adjustable
Tyres: 12.00R 22.5
Suspension: air/spring
Engine: diesel 5.5 hp

Status

More than 850 M1022-A1 Dolly Sets have been fielded by military forces in Algeria, Belgium, Canada, China, Taiwan, Thailand, UK and US (754). More than 150 CLT Dolly Set systems (including the recently EU Road Certified system) have been fielded in Australia, Denmark, Germany, Italy, Japan, Netherlands and the UK.

Contractor

CDK Mobile Systems Inc

CDK Mobile Systems Container Load Trailer (CLT)

Development

The CDK Mobile Systems Inc Container Load Trailer (CLT) system was developed as a combined handling and transport device for ISO containers and military shelters. The original version of the CLT was developed by Danish Container Supply (DCS) of Denmark and in co-operation with the Danish Army.

DCS manufactured around 150 earlier CLT systems between 1980 and 2008, these supplied to military forces in Australia, Brazil, Canada, Denmark, Italy, Spain, UK and the US.

The 20,600 kg capacity CLT system is now being manufactured by CDK Mobile Systems for special US and European military requirements under license from DCS, and recent fieldings by CDK include NASA, US Navy SeaBees, US Army, and the USN Joint High Speed Vessel (JHSV) programme.

Description

The CDK Mobile Systems Inc Container Load Trailer (CLT) system is a combined handling and transport device for ISO containers and military shelters. The CLT is designed to perform three military-related mission functions:
- ISO shelter/container transport - end lifting permits the mobilisation of ISO containers and tactical shelters at highway speeds in excess of 100 km/h, or 30 km/h over rough terrain

CDK CLT loading a C-17 aircraft with a NASA Orion crew module   1421144

CDK CLT of the US Navy SeaBees   1421147

Container Load Trailer (CLT) produced by DCS (CDK Mobile Systems)   1421143

- ISO shelter/container handling - side lifting permits containers to be loaded on and off trucks, trailers or railway wagons at their origin, destination or intermediate points
- Transport aircraft loading - when attached to the end of ISO containers or tactical shelters with heights of 2.438 m/8 ft or 2.59 m/8.5 ft, the CLT systems permit roll-on and roll-off loading of containers.

Each system includes diesel-powered hydraulic systems to perform all connection and lift functions within a matter of minutes. Each system includes a unique three-wheel handling mode, which permits the unloaded movement of each half by one person.

Specifications

Weight: (empty) 6,375 kg
Lift capacity: 24,000 kg
Transport cpacity: (at 85 km/h) 20,600 kg
Lift height: (max) 1.8 m
Length: 12.7 m (with 6.096 m container)
Width: 2.55 m
Height: adjustable
Tyres: 65R × 22.5
Suspension: hydraulic
Engine: diesel 5.5 hp

Status

In excess of 150 CLT Systems have previously been supplied by DCS to the armed forces of Australia, Brazil, Canada, Denmark, Italy, Spain , UK and the US. Recent fieldings by CDK include NASA, US Navy SeaBees, US Army, and the USN Joint High Speed Vessel (JHSV) Programme.

Contractor

CDK Mobile Systems Inc.

Craig Systems Shelters and Containers

Description

Craig Systems was one of the largest manufacturers of mobile shelters in the US and produced a wide range of standard mobile shelters, shelter vans and accessories. The company was acquired by the AAR Cadillac Corporation (now AAR Mobility Systems) in 1998. AAR Mobility Systems continues to produce the US DoD Standard Family of Tactical Shelters S-250, S-280 and S-350 tactical shelters, but the remainder of the range, as produced by Craig Systems, is no longer in production. Examples of Craig Systems shelters do, however, remain in service with US armed forces and possibly others .

Status
Production complete, numbers in service reducing.

Contractor
Craig Systems
(This company is no longer trading - see text)

Deployable Rapid Assembly Shelter (DRASH)

Description
DRASH is a Commercial-Off-The-Shelf (COTS) shelter and mobile support system. All products are manufactured by DHS Systems LLC. DRASH is a series of tactical soft walled, quick-erect/strike shelters providing usable interior floor space per single shelter ranging from approximately 10 m² up to 116 m². A family of tactical Utility Shelter Transporter Trailers (USTs) provides mobile electrical power and environmental control to the shelters when in the field. Both shelters and trailers have been tested by Aberdeen Proving Grounds and are certified to meet all US mil-standards for shelters (wind, rain, snow and blackout) and trailers (safety, towing and air lift). The shelter technology and trailer designs are patented. In 2008 over 16,000 shelters and 5,000 trailers were in service with US and NATO forces.

DRASH meets the requirements for a rugged, man-portable shelter system that can operate in any climate and be deployed by as few as four persons in less than 15 minutes. No field assembly is required and no special tools are needed. There are no loose parts or locking devices. There are only three basic components: an expandable frame with pre-attached interior and exterior covers; a ground cover which sets the ground plan; and a floor that seals the interior of the shelter.

There are five basic series of shelters, the C, S, XB, M and J. Each series is defined by its interior width. The model size is determined by the shelter's length. Speciality shelters include the EMI Shelter, Satellite Antenna Shelter (SAS), the Arctic Tent, the Mobile Hygiene System and Self Enclosed Lobby Annex (SEAL).

The S Series, of which there are six models, measures 3.5 m wide and extends up to 11.7 m long. The XB Series measures 4.2 m wide and extends up to 10.8 m long. The XB Series also has six models. Both the S and XB come in three basic variants. The full variant can be used as a stand alone shelter or easily connected to other DRASH shelters using a Universal Connector Set. The Truncated or T variant can connect one end to another T variant to extend the length of the shelter. The TI variant comes with two open ends that can be used to further extend the shelters' length or provide an entrance way to the shelter.

The M Series come in three basic models of varying lengths, all with an interior width of 5.5 m that can be lengthened to increase an operating area by removing the shelters' end sections and adding additional centre sections.

The C Series shelter, or DRASH Small Command Post, is 3.4 m wide and 3 m long.

DRASH J Series shelter with a M6XBT shelter in use as a command post during Operation Iraqi Freedom (DHS Systems)   1029197

A tan MX Shelter pictured with the HP-2C/185 trailer (DHS Systems) 1173675

The DRASH Model HP-2C/185 trailer which is HMMWV towable seen mounting a 18 kW generator that offers 60,000 Btu of cool air; 50,000 Btu of heat with a 17,000 Btu pre-heater (DHS Systems)   1173674

DRASH UST Trailer model HP-2C. This trailer is certified for towing behind a HMMWV (DHS Systems)   1029196

A packed J Series shelter on the J Trailer tiltbed ready to be off-loaded (DHS Systems)   1140328

A complex of J Series and various other models of DRASH shelters of the US Army (DHS Systems)   1029198

The largest single shelter is the J Series. The J series shelter is 9 m wide and 15.6 m long. All shelters can interconnect for interoperability and to create large complexes.

Each basic DRASH shelter series includes the following standard components: advanced composite Titanite tubing frame, pre-attached interior and exterior covers to provide thermal insulation along with interior and exterior flooring, screen windows with flaps, built-in screen doors, ground stake loops and wind lines; interior loops for hanging map boards, lighting and other items; field repair kit; operators manual and PVC push poles to give a mechanical advantage when erecting the shelter. The larger J Series uses a low pressure air blower to give mechanical advantage when erecting. All covers, flooring and ground covers are manufactured from lightweight specially coated polyester and nylon fabrics, which are fire retardant, mildew resistant, water repellent and have high abrasion and ultra-violet resistance. The fabrics also include blackout in the visual and near infra-red spectrum.

Mobile Integrated Support Systems also make up the DRASH product line. These are a family of Utility Shelter Transport (UST) trailers with a 5 to 33 kW tactically quiet generator sets integrated with ECUs, cargo space and designed to work with the shelters. The trailers have been tested by the US Army at Aberdeen and certified as safe for towing behind HMMWVs, FMTVs, MTVs and non-tactical vehicles. DRASH UST trailers have also been tested at the Nevada Automotive Test Center and have met military criteria during environmental, EMI and EMP testing. The trailers have design patents. Over 5,000 are in service with US Forces and NATO.

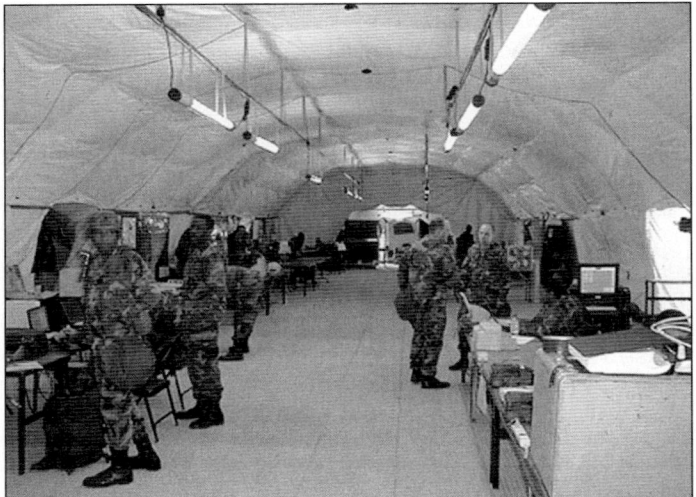

Inside two J Series shelters connected end-to-end. Each J series shelter provides 334.4 sq.m of usable space (DHS Systems) 0134462

Two XB Series Model 6XB shelters in use as part of a command centre (DHS Systems) 0134465

DRASH Model HP-2C trailer (DHS Systems) 1140327

A comparison between an XB Series DRASH shelter (left) and an S Series shelter (right); the XB model is wider and has a larger doorway (DHS Systems) 0056440

DRASH also offers a complete line of support products. Vehicle boots are used to connect wheeled or tracked vehicles to the shelters, while lighting, power distribution units, wiring, cabling, flooring and fuel fired heaters are used for operations as required.

DHS Systems has been manufacturing DRASH since 1984 and is ISO9001:2008 registered. All DRASH products are fully supported 24 hours a day, seven days a week through a comprehensive logistics program.

Specifications

DRASH S Series shelters

Model:	Area: (erected internal)	Dimensions: (erected external)	Dimensions: (stowed)	Weight:
1S	10.4 m²	4.1 × 4.1 × 3.4 m	1.68 × 0.61 × 0.74 m	112 kg
2S	15.6 m²	4.1 × 5.6 × 3.4 m	1.68 × 0.71 × 0.76 m	142 kg
3S	21 m²	4.1 × 7.2 × 3.4 m	1.68 × 0.84 × 0.79 m	173 kg
4S	26.3 m²	4.1 × 8.7 × 3.4 m	1.68 × 0.89 × 0.80 m	200 kg
5S	31.7 m²	4.1 × 10.2 × 3.4 m	1.68 × 0.91 × 0.81 m	228 kg
6S	37.7 m²	4.1 × 11.7 × 3.4 m	1.68 × 0.94 × 0.84 m	261 kg

DRASH XB Series shelters

Model:	Area: (erected internal)	Dimensions: (erected external)	Dimensions: (stowed)	Weight:
1XB	13.0 m²	4.7 × 4.7 × 3.2 m	1.32 × 0.93 × 0.64 m	110.2 kg
2XB	18.0 m²	4.7 × 5.9 × 3.2 m	1.32 × 0.98 × 0.67 m	146.5 kg
3XB	23.0 m²	4.7 × 7.1 × 3.2 m	1.32 × 1.04 × 0.70 m	182.8 kg
4XB	28.2 m²	4.7 × 8.3 × 3.2 m	1.32 × 1.09 × 0.74 m	219.1 kg
5XB	33.3 m²	4.7 × 9.5 × 3.2 m	1.32 × 1.18 × 0.77 m	255.4 kg
6XB	38.4 m²	4.7 × 10.8 × 3.2 m	1.32 × 1.27 × 0.80 m	292.1 kg

DRASH M Series

Model:	Area: (erected internal)	Dimensions: (erected external)	Dimensions: (stowed)	Weight:
MX centre	28.0 m²	6.0 × 9.4 × 3.4 m	1.42 × 1.13 × 0.80 m	222.0 kg
MX5 centre	36.0 m²	6.0 × 10.6 × 3.4 m	1.4 × 1.07 × 0.74 m	267.3 kg
M centre	57.0 m²	6.0 × 14.5 × 3.4 m	1.42 × 1.13 × 0.80 m	443.9 kg
M end cap	6.3 m²	6.0 × 2.1 × 3.4 m	1.3 × 0.58 × 0.58 m	31.7 kg

Each shelter system consists of one centre section and two end caps. The centre section on the M model is stowed as two packages, dimensions shown are for each package.

DRASH J Series

Model:	Area: (erected internal)	Dimensions: (erected external)	Dimensions: (stowed)	Weight:
J	98.0 m²	10.4 × 10.3 × 5.5 m	1.35 × 1.42 × 2.39 m	726 kg
1XBTJ end cap	9.0 m²	4.7 × 2.9 × 2.9 m	1.32 × 0.86 × 0.61 m	97.8 kg
J maintenance	98.0 m²	10.4 × 10.3 × 5.5 m	1.35 × 1.42 × 2.39 m	726 kg
J maintenance door	17.1 m²	5.0 × 3.8 × 4.2 m	N/A	266.3 kg

Each shelter system consists of one centre section and two end caps (J shelter), or doors (J maintenance shelter).

Status

In production. In service with the Australian, Austrian, German, Israeli, Japanese, Norwegian, Spanish, Singapore and UK armed forces, all branches of the US armed forces plus non-US Department of Defense customers including the FBI Hostage Rescue Team, Crisis Response Unit and Evidence Recovery Teams, the Department of Alcohol, Tobacco and Firearms, the National Disaster Medical System and many Federal and State government offices throughout the US.

Contractor

DHS Systems LLC

Expandable Light Air Mobile Shelter (ELAMS)

Description

The AAR Mobility Systems (formerly AAR Cadillac Manufacturing) Expandable Light Air Mobile Shelter (ELAMS) entered production in 1999 alongside the Light Air Mobile Shelter, full details of which can be found elsewhere in this section. ELAMS is a weather-tight tactical shelter designed to be configured for a variety of support missions that can include medical facilities, shops, office or command and control space. Integral self-levelling jacks allow deployment on unprepared ground. Deployment time from arrival on site in secure transportable format, to expanded operational configuration, can be under 10 minutes. ELAMS is designed to function either on the ground or from the load bed of any suitable transport vehicle. An infinite number of units can be joined together, although each unit is designed to be self sufficient. It comes complete with an environmental control system, permanently mounted 110 V electrical outlets and an input panel for communications and computer lines. A dehumidification system is an option.

A single unit weighs 1,724 kg empty and with the side walls stowed, has exterior dimensions of 4.52 × 2.44 × 2.74 m (L × W × H) and internal dimensions of 3.56 × 2.06 × 2.13 m. With side walls deployed, exterior dimensions are 3.71 × 6.12 × 2.21 m and internal dimensions 3.56 × 5.97 × 2.13 m, giving the user up to three times the useable floor area of a conventional rigid structure with the same transport footprint. Maximum payload capacity is 4,536 kg (5 short tons) and ELAMS has inbuilt two-way forklift guides and, payload dependant, can be lifted by a standard 5 ton (4,536 kg) fork truck with 1.8 m tines. ELAMS can be transported on a wide variety of trucks or trailers, including commercial models, and can also be transported on PLS, or similar systems, flatracks. Tie down/lifting rings allow for lifting by crane or sling lifting by helicopter. A detachable air mobility rail systems allows ELAMS to be loaded into most transport aircraft without the need for specialised material handling equipment. To further enhance handling and mobility, AAR Mobility Systems also manufacture two types of quick-attach mobility wheel sets that connect to special points at either end of the container. Full details of these can be found elsewhere in this section.

The ELAMS TOC (Tactical Operations Centre) are a range of ELAMS available optimised for the command and control role.

ELAMS is in current production for US armed forces, and unspecified quantities have also been supplied to two other undisclosed countries.

Status

In production. In service with US and at least two other undisclosed armed forces.

Contractor

AAR Mobility Systems

A pair of joined Expandable Light Air Mobile Shelters (ELAMS) fitted with High Speed Mobility Wheel Sets (HSMWS) (AAR Mobility Systems) 0126571

Expandable Mobility Shop Container/Shelter (EMSC)

Description

The AAR Mobility Systems (formerly AAR Cadillac Manufacturing) Expandable Mobility Shop Container/Shelter (EMSC) is an air-portable environmentally controlled shelter. It is designed for a variety of tactical uses including operations or command and control centre, medical, repair, communication or a field bunking unit. Each unit is equipped with an

The Expandable Mobility Shop Container (EMSC) shown in expanded mode (AAR Mobility Systems) 0126570

environmental control unit for all-weather operations that provides up to 22,000 BTU/h (6.4 kW) cooling or 20,500 BTU/h (6 kW) heating, door-activated blackout lighting and an integral panel for communications equipment. Options include a dehumidifier and, to allow for complete stand-alone operations, a 12.5 kVA diesel-powered generator set with fuel capacity for 14 hours at full load output, remote start panel and carbon monoxide alarm.

Deployment from transport configuration to being fully operational can be accomplished by a team of two in 8 to 10 minutes. Standard equipment transported inside the unit includes a levelling jack kit that allows the EMSC to be deployed fully from the loadbed of its transport vehicle, or independent of any transport vehicle and on unprepared ground. Weighing 1,724 kg empty EMSC is transportable on a variety of trucks including standard US Army 2.5- and 5-ton payload vehicles and PLS (or similar systems) flatracks. Maximum payload capacity is 4,536 kg (5 tons) and dependant on payload, EMSC can be lifted by a standard fork truck with 1.8 m tines. Tie down/lifting rings allow for lifting by crane or sling lifting by helicopter and EMSC can be air-transported on standard 463L aircraft pallets. To further enhance handling and mobility AAR Mobility Systems also manufacture two types of quick-attach mobility wheel sets that connect to special points at either end of the shelter. Full details of these can be found elsewhere in this section.

With the side walls stowed, the EMSC has exterior dimensions of 3.71 × 2.21 × 2.21 m (L × W × H) and internal dimensions of 3.56 × 2.06 × 2.13 m. With side walls deployed, exterior dimensions are 3.71 × 6.12 × 2.21 m and internal dimensions 4.98 × 5.97 × 2.13 m. This gives the user up to three times the useable floor area of a conventional non-expandable structure with the same transport footprint.

Status

Available. In service with US armed forces (500), predominantly in Europe and South Korea.

Contractor

AAR Mobility Systems

Expandable Small Air Mobile Shelter (ESAMS)

Description

The AAR Mobility Systems (formerly AAR Cadillac Manufacturing) Expandable Small Air Mobile Shelter (ESAMS) became available in 2003. ESAMS is an expandable version of the SAMS (Small Air Mobile Shelter) and provides an insulated and climate-controlled workspace for a variety of missions.

When closed, ESAMS occupies one pallet position, being based around the dimensions of a standard 2.74 × 2.23 (L × W) AAR ISU container (height is 2.44 m). It expands to offer 15.7 m² of floor space when fully deployed with internal ceiling height ranging from 2.18 (max) to 1.9 (min) m. All perimeter walls, ceiling and floor are insulated. The R-10 wing-walls of the closed container fold down to serve as floors in the expanded mode. The side 'rooms' are enclosed within R-4 fabric walls and ceiling, which are supported by simple struts; the ceiling is R-12.

ESAMS is four-way forkliftable and has a tare weight of 1,134 kg. Payload is 3,402 kg. Interior space is 10.33 m³. Standard equipment includes a 20,000 BTU/h (5.85 kW) environmental control unit and 13,660 BTU/h (4 kW) heating.

Full details of the non-expandable SAMS (Small Air Mobile Shelter) can be found elsewhere in this section.

Status

In production.

Contractor

AAR Mobility Systems

Gichner Shelter Systems

Description
Gichner Shelter Systems has been involved in the design, development and manufacture of lightweight mobile shelter systems since its founding in 1967, supplying shelters to every branch of the United States Armed Forces and its Allies. The company claims to be the world's largest manufacturer of military shelters, electronic equipment enclosures and ancillary products.

Gichner Shelter Systems specific product entries, which can be found elsewhere in this section, provide details and specifications of the company's core products; those currently available or in production, or those currently remaining in service in the most significant roles or substantial numbers. As a bespoke shelter manufacturer, many of these core products will have been, or can be, manufactured to meet specific operational requirements.

Gichner Shelter Systems has also manufactured transportable materials handling pallets and mobiliser dolly sets. The company also produces trailers or trailer mounting bodies utilising shelter panel technology and materials.

A European division of Gichner Shelter Systems was originally based in Brussels, Belgium and during 2004, the division moved to Toulouse, France. This division is no longer operational. Gichner's European operation manufactured and delivered NATO ACE II and ACE III shelters to unspecified European customers. These shelters were designed and tested to the requirements of Allied Command Europe's Standard Shelter Technical Specification 6516/SHCPR/88.

It was announced in April 2010 that Kratos Defense & Security Solutions, Inc. would acquire Gichner Holdings, Inc.

Status
In production. In widespread use, primarily by US armed forces.

Contractor
Gichner Shelter Systems

Gichner MERWS/GRASS shelters

Development
Gichner was founded in 1967. The company currently employs around 1,000 employees and is primarily involved in the design, manufacture, integration and test of shelters, containers and their sub-systems.

It was announced in April 2010 that Kratos Defense & Security Solutions, Inc. would acquire Gichner Holdings, Inc.

The Modular Extendable Rigid Wall Shelter (MERWS) is one of an extensive range of shelter- and container-based products offered by the company.

Description
The Modular Extendable Rigid Wall Shelter (MERWS) is a modular shelter assembled from 40 individual paper honeycomb and aluminium skin panels. The shelter serves as an expansion kit for the Army Standard Expandable ISO shelter. The MERWS provides 106.8 m² of open workspace for command, hospital, maintenance or other similar applications when attached to a two-sided ISO.

The MERWS can be unpacked from the 20 ft ISO in which it is stored, transported and erected by four soldiers in less than four hours. Included with the shelter are lights, a circuit breaker panel, a single personnel door and ECU interface and levelling jacks. Individual panels can be removed and replaced with custom designed panels for specific applications.

The MERWS was designed to strict US Army performance requirements and for applications not requiring some or all of these, Gichner also offers the Gichner Re-locatable Accommodations Shelter System (GRASS). GRASS is a further development of MERWS that utilises the same assembly principles but differing construction techniques. The end result is a lower cost alternative to MERWS that can include in its user specific specifications any required number of MERWS features.

The standard GRASS is stored and transported in a 20 ft ISO, to which it may be joined when assembled giving a total workspace of 75.7 m² (65 m² (GRASS) + 13.7 m² (ISO)) and headroom of 2.1 m. As with MERWS, GRASS shelters can be erected by four soldiers in less than four hours.

Additional sections may be added, each adding an additional 13.7 m² of unobstructed workspace.

Uses for GRASS include operations centres/command posts, accommodations shelters, mess halls, medical clinics/wards, briefing rooms and so on.

Status
In production. In service with US armed forces (MERWS).

Contractor
Gichner Shelter Systems

Gichner Navair range of ISO shelters

Development
Gichner was founded in 1967. The company currently employs around 1,000 employees and is primarily involved in the design, manufacture, integration and test of shelters, containers and their sub-systems.

It was announced in April 2010 that Kratos Defense & Security Solutions, Inc. would acquire Gichner Holdings, Inc.

Gichner Shelter Systems announced in November 2006 that it had been awarded a USD42 million firm-fixed-price, indefinite-delivery, indefinite-quantity contract for up to 1,000 mobile maintenance facilities for the Naval Air Warfare Center Aircraft Division, for use in the testing and operation of various avionics systems. Work is expected to be completed in November 2011.

Gichner Shelter Systems has produced more than 8,000 of these shelters under numerous contracts with the US Navy and various prime contractors.

Description
The Gichner Navair range of shelters were designed in accordance with military specification MIL-M-81957(AS) and meet ISO/ANSI specification 1496/1 and ANSI MH5.1, 5.1.1, and 5.4. Over 7,000 of these shelters have been supplied to the US Navy.

The basic Navair range shelters are constructed with aluminium skins over a core of rigid closed cell foam. Aluminium structural members within the panels provide added structural strength and provide locations for the mounting of equipment using rivnut-type mounting hardware. The end bands and base frame are fabricated from steel resulting in a strong and rigid overall structure.

A significant benefit of this type of shelter is its ability to be complexed, which can accomplished in a number of ways. Shelters can be connected via personnel doors using special butting kits that provide an environmental shield between complexed shelters. Multiple side removable shelters can be joined into larger complexes providing large open interior spaces.

The Navair range of shelters are available in six standard Mobile Facility configurations, although Gichner can combine features to create a custom design shelter to meet specific user requirements. Within the Gichner shelter range the base model shelter is known as the GMS-459.

The following is a brief description of the six available standard configurations in the Navair Mobile Facility range of shelters:

Basic Mobile Facility Type A (BMFA)
This is a basic 20 ft ISO shelter with a 1.22 × 1.93 m (W × H) personnel door at each end. It is wired for 100 A 60 Hz power and is capable of transferring this power as well as 400 Hz power to another shelter. Interior lighting is provided via ceiling-mounted fluorescent lights. The shelter contains provisions for the installation of a 36,000 BTU heat pump, which can be integrally mounted through the side of the shelter.

Basic Mobile Facility Type B (BMFB)
This shelter is essentially similar to Type A, but is wired to operate on both 60 and 400 Hz power.

Side Opening Mobile Facility Type A (SOMFA)
This shelter is similar to the Basic Mobile Facility Type B except that it has provisions for two ECUs on one side. The other side is removable to permit complexing with either a Side Opening Mobile Facility Type B or a Side Opening Mobile Facility Type C shelter.

Side Opening Mobile Facility Type B (SOMFB)
This shelter is similar to the Basic Mobile Facility Type A except that it has no end doors. It has a small personnel door located between the ECU opening on the non-removable side. This shelter is generally used in complexes with other side removable shelters.

Side Opening Mobile Facility Type C (SOMFC)
This shelter contains no power distribution or lighting, but has two removable sides and a single end personnel door. It is generally used in complexes with other side removable shelters to provide increased workspace.

Gichner Navair range ISO shelters (Gichner Shelter Systems)   1344693

Integration Unit Mobile Facility
This shelter is used as a junction for up to six other Mobile Facility shelters. It contains power distribution capabilities that allow it to transfer 200 A 60 Hz and 100 A 400 Hz power to the attached Mobile Facilities.

Status
In production. In service with US (greater than 8,000) and other armed forces.

Contractor
Gichner Shelter Systems

Gichner S-530A/G expandable shelter

Development
Gichner was founded in 1967. The company currently employs around 1,000 employees and is primarily involved in the design, manufacture, integration and test of shelters, containers and their sub-systems.

It was announced in April 2010 that Kratos Defense & Security Solutions, Inc. would acquire Gichner Holdings, Inc.

The S-530A/G shelter is one of the US DoD's Standard Family of Tactical Shelters; it is not currently in production.

Description
The S-530A/G is constructed of aluminium skins over a Nomex honeycomb core and its primary use is for mobile maintenance or repair facilities. The EMI shielding package provides at least 60 dB EMI attenuation over 150 kHz to 10 GHz for electric and magnetic fields and plane waves.

In its transport/storage configuration the S-530A/G has exterior dimensions of 3.708 × 2.209 × 2.286 m (L × W × H).

Interior dimensions are 3.479 × 2.007 × 2.057 m.

In use, two shelters are linked together to form a single larger shelter. Each shelter provides a roof or floor panel and a side wall to the expanded shelter, resulting in a single enclosure that is three times the size of either single shelter. Interior dimensions of the expanded shelter are 3.479 × 6.198 × 2.057 m. Six soldiers can accomplish assembly of this shelter in 45 minutes. The S-530A/G shelter weighs 907 kg and has a payload of 2,041 kg, giving a maximum gross weight of 2,948 kg.

Status
Not currently in production. In service with the US Air Force.

Contractor
Gichner Shelter Systems

General Purpose (GP) shelter

Description
The AAR Mobility Systems (formerly AAR Cadillac Manufacturing) General Purpose (GP) shelter is an air-transportable unit which can be assembled in a variety of configurations including dining halls, storage, assembly, administrative or central command areas. Other configurations such as emergency hospitals are possible with the use of options such as lightweight flooring and using larger single doors creates a secure and weather-protected vehicle maintenance area.

The in-use shelter expands to dimensions of 14.6 × 9.45 × 3.66 m (L × W × H) from an air-transportable container measuring 3 × 2.74 × 2.44 m (L × W × H). Prepared ground is not required and a shelter can be set-up by six people in 14 hours. Each shelter comes complete with a built-in power distribution system and environmental control ports.

The AAR Mobility Systems General Purpose shelter remains available and in excess of 1,000 units have been supplied to the US Air Force. Of these an estimated 400 currently remain in service.

Specifications
GP shelter
Length:
   (container) 14.6 m
   (shelter) 3.0 m
Width:
   (container) 9.45 m
   (shelter) 2.74 m
Height:
   (container) 3.66 m
   (shelter) 2.44 m

Status
Available. In service with the US Air Force (400 approx).

Contractor
AAR Mobility Systems

Gichner 20 ft ISO shelters/containers

Development
Gichner was founded in 1967. The company currently employs around 1,000 employees and is primarily involved in the design, manufacture, integration and test of shelters, containers and their sub-systems.

It was announced in April 2010 that Kratos Defense & Security Solutions, Inc. would acquire Gichner Holdings, Inc.

Description
The standard Gichner 20 ft ISO product is a rigid, rectangular, non-expansible shelter/container of adhesive-bonded sandwich panelling consisting of seamless aluminium exterior skins, extruded aluminium framework structure and a polyurethane foam core. It has integral ISO corner fittings that meet ANSI MH 5.1 requirements. It is used as a multipurpose electronic equipment enclosure (radar, communication, maintenance, housing, laboratory and so on), with a special butting kit feature and slide-in/slide-out air conditioner unit optional. Large doors are provided for the installation and removal of equipment. EMI shielded versions provide EMI protection of 60 dB.

The shelter/container meets military specification MIL-M-81957 and can be transported by truck, transporter (M1022 end mount or van undercarriage type), fixed-wing aircraft, rail and ship. It can be stacked via ISO couplers. All external dimensions of the containers conform to the IAW ISO 668 designation 1C standard.

Gicher also now offers a composite 20 ft ISO shelter, this a lightweight, high-strength, insulated enclosure constructed of non-corrosive composite materials. The Composite ISO Shelter has been designed and developed as a low-maintenance alternative to standard aluminium ISO shelters. Constructed of lightweight TYCOR composite panels and steel end-bands and base-frame, when compared to conventional shelters, this shelter is stated to provide superior corrosion resistance and durability. Optional polyurethane coatings are available on interior and exterior surfaces for added corrosion resistance and increased durability.

Specifications

Shelter base material	Aluminium	Composite
Length:		
(interior)	5.897 m	5.893 m
(exterior)	6.057 m	6.057 m
Width:		
(interior)	2.23 m	2.26 m
(exterior)	2.438 m	2.438 m
Height:		
(interior)	2.141 m	2.13 m
(exterior, less skids)	2.438 m	2.438 m
(exterior, with skid)	2.514 m	n/app
Weight:	1,906 kg	2,132 kg
Payload:	7,196 kg	6,895 kg

Status
In production. In service with the US and other armed forces.

Contractor
Gichner Shelter Systems

Gichner HMMWV compatible shelters

Development
Gichner Shelter Systems produces a wide range of shelters that are compatible with all versions of the AM General HMMWV. The models covered in this entry are either in current production, in service or available

Gichner was founded in 1967. The company currently employs around 1,000 employees and is primarily involved in the design, manufacture, integration and test of shelters, containers and their sub-systems.

It was announced in April 2010 that Kratos Defense & Security Solutions, Inc. would acquire Gichner Holdings, Inc.

S-788/G (LMS)
The S-788/G shelter is also known as the Lightweight, Multipurpose Shelter (LMS) and is lightweight, high-strength enclosure specifically for use on the HMMWV. LMS construction involves aluminium-faced, honeycomb core, hot-bonded panels on the walls, roof and floor.

With approximately 8.35 m³ of useable interior space (50 per cent more than the S-250 shelter), the S-788 LMS has been selected by the US Army as its primary electronics platform for wheeled tactical vehicles. The S-788 is one of the DoD Standard Family of Tactical Shelters and is available in four standard configurations: Type 1 is the basic S-788; Type II has a generator tunnel, escape hatch and CB purge valve; Type III has the generator tunnel only; Type V is the basic Type 1 S-788 with double door endwall - non-EMI. There is also a version designed for the General Motors Commercial Utility Cargo Vehicle (CUCV) available. This, and the HMMWV version, are C-130 Hercules transportable without preparation.

Model	S-710	GSS-1497	S-788/G (LMS)
Length:			
(exterior)	2.678 m	2.59 m	2.59 m
(interior)	2.604 m	2.47 m	2.53 m
Width:			
(exterior)	n/app	2.24 m	2.13 m
(exterior, upper section)	2.132 m	n/app	n/app
(exterior, lower section)	1.268 m	n/app	n/app
(interior)	n/app	2.06 m	2.07 m
(interior, upper section)	2.057 m	n/app	n/app
(interior, lower section)	1.194 m	n/app	n/app
Height:			
(exterior)	1.726 m	1.74 m	1.70 m
(interior)	1.297 m	1.65 m	1.64 m
(interior, centre section)	1.651 m	n/app	n/app
Weight:	308 kg	248 kg	275, 295 and 287 kg (Type I, Type II and Type III)
Usable internal volume:	n/avail	n/avail	8.35 m^3
Payload:	862 kg	1,497 kg	1,510 kg
Floor loading: (without permanent deformation)		1,627 kg/m^2 (1,000 lb over 3ft^2)	
Roof loading: (snow and ice)		1,611 kg/m^2 (660 lb over 2 ft^2)	
Heat transfer:	U-factor 0.40 BTU/hr/sq.ft/°F	U-factor 0.46 BTU/hr/sq.ft/°F	0.50, 0.56 and 0.56 BTU/hr/sq.ft/°F (Type I, Type II and Type III)
RFI shielding:	60 dB minimum attenuation over 150 kHz to 10 GHz range for electric and magnetic fields and plane waves as for IAW MIL-STD-285		
Temperature range:			
(operating)		-54 to +52°C (plus solar load)	
(non-operating)		-62 to +71°C	
Watertightness:	tested to 762 mm fording depth and to simulated rainfall	tested to 534 mm fording depth and to simulated rainfall	tested to 762 mm fording depth (Type I only) and to simulated rainfall

In September 2004 The US Army's RDECOM (Natick) selected Gichner Shelter Systems as its supplier for the S-788 shelter. The 5-year contract included the development, build and First Article Test of three Type I and three Type III shelters.

The most recent announced related award was placed in August 2008 and called for the test and production of Double Door Endwall (DDE) shelters by the US Army. These shelters are similar to the standard S-788 HMMWV shelter except that they have double doors on the rear instead of the standard single personnel door. While not armoured themselves, the shelters are specifically designed to be installed on armoured HMMWVs. The initial award called for the design and First Article Test of three of the shelters. Production orders for up to 400 shelters over three years could take the value of the program to more than USD7 million.

S-832/G (SICPSV4)
The S-832/G or Standardised Integrated Command Post Shelter (Version 4) is designed to provide an interior environment that is shielded from environmental, electronic, and chemical/biological threats. The basic shelter, constructed of paper honeycomb bonded to aluminium skins, is a derivative of the DoD Standard Family of Tactical Shelters S-788 shelter and mounts to a HMMWV using a flexible mounting kit. Gichner incorporated several enhancements to the basic shelter during the development of the SICPSV4 to improve the design. The door and escape hatch jams have been redesigned to improve maintainability and EMI performance of the shelter. With these modifications the basic shelter now provides greater than 70 dB of shielding. This improvement is available on all Gichner S-788 type shelters.

The SICPSV4 is designed to be configurable to provide systems for planning, co-ordinating and controlling tactical operations. Equipment includes an onboard 10 kW generator, 18,500 BTU ECU, Gas Particulate Filter Unit (GPFU), full power distribution and control, equipment racks, lighting, power and signal interface panels, a Quick Erect Antenna Mast (QEAM), Vehicle Intercom System (VIS) and an operator chair.

GSS-1497
The GSS-1497 electronic equipment shelter was designed for dedicated use with the HMMWV and attaches to the vehicle via a bolt-on attachment kit. At 248 kg the GSS-1497 is the lightest weight HMMWV shelter offered by Gichner. The GSS-1497 utilises the same construction method applied in the S-280 shelters; sandwich panel construction consisting of a polyurethane foam core, aluminium skins, and a framework of high-strength welded and riveted aluminium alloy extrusions. A generator tunnel and an escape hatch in the roof are optional.

The dimensions of the GSS-1497 shelter allow for a C-130 transport aircraft drive-on/back-off capability.

S-710
The S-710 lightweight shelter has the largest internal volume of the Gichner HMMWV shelter range. It was developed specifically for the M1037 HMMWV, although it can also be fitted to subsequent heavy HMMWVs such as the M1113 ECV (Expanded Capacity Vehicle) and all current production models, but may also be fitted to the older M1028 CUCV. Fixing is via bolt-on adapter kits, negating the need for tie-down slings. The construction techniques and materials are the same as those

Gichner S-788 shelter on a HMMWV (Gichner Shelter Systems) 1344695

Gichner GSS-1497 shelter on a HMMWV (Gichner Shelter Systems) 1344692

used for the S-280 (C)/G shelter per MIL-S-55286E, being bonded sandwich construction consisting of a polyurethane foam core, aluminium skins, and a framework of high-strength welded and riveted aluminium alloy extrusions.

A generator tunnel, an escape hatch in the roof and an over-cab equipment pod are optional. The dimensions of the shelter allow C-130 transport aircraft drive-on/back off capability when used with either vehicle.

Specifications

Status
In production and/or service; predominantly with US armed forces.

Contractor
Gichner Shelter Systems

Gichner shelter, electrical equipment S-250G

Development
Gichner was founded in 1967. The company currently employs around 1,000 employees and is primarily involved in the design, manufacture, integration and test of shelters, containers and their sub-systems.

It was announced in April 2010 that Kratos Defense & Security Solutions, Inc. would acquire Gichner Holdings, Inc.

Description
The S-250 is a T-shape, non-expandable shelter of foam and beam bonded sandwich construction, this consisting of a polyurethane foam core, aluminium skins and a framework of aluminium alloy extrusions. It is one of the DoD Standard Family of Tactical Shelters. The S-250 is primarily used to carry communications, radar, teletype and maintenance electronic equipment and is usually mounted on an HMMWV, although it may also be mounted on the older M1028 CUCV. The S-250 can be transported by fixed- and rotary-wing aircraft, rail and ship.

The shelter meets military specifications MIL-S-55541 and is available with RFI shielding.

Specifications
S-250G
Length:
(interior) 1.981 m
(exterior) 2.108 m
Width:
(interior, upper section) 1.905 m
(interior, lower section) 1.143 m
(exterior, upper section) 2.000 m
(exterior, lower section) 1.232 m
Height:
(interior, centre section) 1.625 m
(interior, incl skid) 1.778 m
Weight:
(without RFI kit) 349±9 kg
(with RFI kit) 355±9 kg
Payload: 862 kg
Floor loading: 454 kg over a 0.279 m² area without permanent deformation
Roof loading:
(snow and ice) 195 kg/m²
(personnel and equipment) 299 kg over a 0.186 m² area
Heat transfer: U-factor 0.50 BTU/hr/sq.ft/°F (designed to meet MIL-S-55541)

RFI shielding: with addition of RFI modification kit, attenuation 60 dB minimum over 150 kHz to 10 GHz for electric and magnetic fields and plane waves measured IAW MIL-STD-285
Temperature range:
(operating) -54 to +52°C (plus solar load)
(non-operating) -62 to +71°C
Watertightness: tested to 762 mm and to simulated rainfall

Status
In service with the US and other armed forces.

Contractor
Gichner Shelter Systems

Gichner shelter, general purpose S-749

Development
Gichner was founded in 1967. The company currently employs around 1,000 employees and is primarily involved in the design, manufacture, integration and test of shelters, containers and their sub-systems.

It was announced in April 2010 that Kratos Defense & Security Solutions, Inc. would acquire Gichner Holdings, Inc.

Description
The S-749 is a rigid, non-expandable, insulated, all-weather shelter that satisfies general-purpose applications for housing communications and other transportable electronic equipment. The S-749 shelter is of the same foam-and-beam sandwich panel construction as the Gichner S-280C/G shelter, that being a polyurethane core, seamless aluminium skins and a framework of aluminium alloy extrusions. The inner and outer floor skins are 1.25 mm thick, the three full-length, shock-absorbing underside skids are replaceable. Structural strength is assured by the 'barrel hoop' transverse orientation of the floor and roof beams. The shelter corners are reinforced to accept levelling jacks and to withstand side loads imposed by high wind velocities.

The S-749 is considered a mid-sized shelter within the family of transportable shelters. Its design dimensions are such that the interior will accommodate standing personnel, while the overall length of the shelter allows for transverse location on the load platform of either a standard 2.5- or 5-ton truck. The S-749 may also be transported by a fixed-wing aircraft, helicopter, rail or ship.

The shelter meets military specification MIL-S-55286E and is available with RFI integrity. Other options include a combination lifting/tie-down sling to facilitate handling.

Specifications
S-749
Length:
(interior) 1.981 m
(exterior) 2.210 m
Width:
(interior) 2.070 m
(exterior) 2.210 m
Height:
(interior) 1.959 m
(exterior, incl skid) 2.194 m
Weight: 476 kg
Payload: 1,587 kg
Floor loading: 1,134 kg over a 0.279 m² area without permanent deformation

Gichner S-250 shelters (Gichner Shelter Systems)   1344694

A typical Gichner S-749 shelter (Gichner Shelter Systems)   1175919

Roof loading:
(snow and ice) 195 kg/m^2
(personnel and equipment) 299 kg over a 0.186 m^2 area
Heat transfer: U-factor 0.35 BTU/hr/sq.ft/°F
RFI shielding: with addition of RFI modification kit, attenuation 60 dB minimum over 150 kHz to 10 GHz for electric and magnetic fields and plane waves measured IAW MIL-STD-285
Temperature range:
(operating) -54 to +52°C (plus solar load)
(non-operating) -62 to +71°C
Watertightness: tested to 533 mm and to simulated rainfall

Status
In production. In service with US armed forces.

Contractor
Gichner Shelter Systems

Hardside Expandable Light Airmobile Shelter (HELAMS)

Description
The AAR Mobility Systems (formerly AAR Cadillac Manufacturing) Hardside Expandable Light Air Mobile Shelter (HELAMS) became available in 2003 and is based on the soft-walled Expandable Light Air Mobile Shelter (ELAMS) that entered production in 1999.

HELAMS is a weather-tight shelter designed to be configured for a variety of support missions that can include medical facilities, shops, office or command and control space. Four main and six side levelling jacks allow deployment on unprepared surfaces. HELAMS is self sufficient and comes complete with a slide in/slide out 36,000 BTU/h (10.5 kW) environmental control unit.

Payload of a single unit is 6,804 kg, and with the side walls stowed the unexpanded exterior dimensions are 4.52 × 2.44 × 2.44 m (L × W × H). To enhance handling and mobility, AAR Mobility Systems manufactures the quick-attach HSMWS (High Speed Mobility Wheel Set) that connect to special points at either end of the HELAMS. Full details of the HSMWS can be found elsewhere in this section.

Status
Available.

Contractor
AAR Mobility Systems

General Dynamics Armament and Technical Products (GDATP) general purpose rigid ISO shelter

Development
General Dynamics Armament and Technical Products (GDATP) was formed in June 2002 and combines the former General Dynamics Armaments Systems and the four companies of the former Advanced Technical Products Inc: Intellitec, Lincoln Composites, Lunn Industries, and Marion Composites. The general purpose rigid ISO shelter was produced by Marion Composites.

In January 2009, General Dynamics announced that it completed the acquisition of AxleTech International from The Carlyle Group. AxleTech International is a global manufacturer and supplier of axles, axle components, planetary axles, independent suspensions, brakes and after market parts for military vehicles, commercial speciality trucks, and off-highway machines used in the construction, material handling, forestry, mining and agricultural markets. Axletech is now part of the General Dynamics Armaments and Technical Products business unit, which is based in Charlotte, N.C.

Description
Designed and developed for the US Marine Corps, these lightweight honeycomb-constructed 2.4 and 6 m general purpose rigid ISO shelters with their 'mount anywhere' capability, can be combined into large suites by removing the side walls and connecting the units with a dedicated kit. ISO fittings and forklift tunnels assure handling and transport under maximum ISO load conditions.

Construction involves aluminium-faced, honeycomb sandwich panels hot bonded with epoxy adhesives. There are electrical service entry and distribution panels for 120/208 V, 60 Hz, 60 A, three-phase, five-wire power supplies. Also provided are 15 A utility outlets, while ceiling-mounted fluorescent fixtures are standard.

Accessories include blackout curtains, levelling jacks, dedicated connection kit, exhaust fan and a joining corridor.

The shelters can be mounted at any location using high-strength threaded inserts providing up to 726 kgf pull-out and 43 N m torque. The shelters are US Coast Guard certified (ISP 1496/1) for sea transport including six high stacking. The units can also be transported by rail, truck and air.

Specifications
Rigid 10 ft ISO
Military specification: MIL-S-29434(MC)
Weight: (empty) 1,080 kg
Payload: 2,322 kg
Dimensions:
(exterior) 2.99 × 2.44 × 2.44 m
(interior) 2.72 × 2.25 × 2.14 m

Rigid 20 ft ISO
Military specification: MIL-S-29410(MC)
Weight: (empty) 1,724 kg
Payload: 5,080 kg
Dimensions:
(exterior) 6.06 × 2.44 × 2.44 m
(interior) 5.78 × 2.25 × 2.14 m

Status
In service with the US Armed Forces.

Contractor
General Dynamics Armament and Technical Products (GDATP)

General Dynamics Armament and Technical Products (GDATP) relocatable hospitals

Development
General Dynamics Armament and Technical Products (GDATP) was formed in June 2002 and combines the former General Dynamics Armaments Systems and the four companies of the former Advanced Technical Products Inc: Intellitec, Lincoln Composites, Lunn Industries, and Marion Composites. The relocateable hospital was produced by Marion Composites.

In January 2009, General Dynamics announced that it completed the acquisition of AxleTech International from The Carlyle Group. AxleTech International is a global manufacturer and supplier of axles, axle components, planetary axles, independent suspensions, brakes and after market parts for military vehicles, commercial speciality trucks, and off-highway machines used in the construction, material handling, forestry, mining and agricultural markets. Axletech is now part of the General Dynamics Armaments and Technical Products business unit, which is based in Charlotte, N.C.

Description
Developed in conjunction with the US armed forces, this modular hospital system was designed for use in outlying or remote locations. It has a full spectrum of uses, from primary care and emergency/disaster relief to a semi-permanent hospital installation capable of offering a wide range of medical services. Modules may be configured in various combinations and layouts to meet the needs of a particular site or hospital service requirements. Configurations ranging from mobile medical clinics to 200-bed hospital systems are available.

Basic modules include an operating room, emergency receiving area, eight-bed ward, laboratory, pharmacy and x-ray options, a central material supply room, dental surgery, post-operative or intensive care units and a power and water supply module. Optional units include a kitchen, dining area and a laundry.

All units are constructed using aluminium-faced honeycomb sandwich panels.

Specifications
Basic unit
Weight: (max, equipped) 6,804 kg
Dimensions:
(shipping mode, external) 6.06 × 2.44 × 2.44 m
(deployed, internal) 5.59 × 6.55 × 2.16 m

Status
In service with the US armed forces. Deployed worldwide.

Contractor
General Dynamics Armament and Technical Products (GDATP)

General Dynamics Armament and Technical Products (GDATP) HMMWV compatible shelters

Development
General Dynamics Armament and Technical Products (GDATP) was formed in June 2002 and combines the former General Dynamics Armaments Systems and the four companies of the former Advanced Technical Products Inc: Intellitec, Lincoln Composites, Lunn Industries, and Marion Composites. HMMWV-compatible shelters are produced by

the former Marion Composites and are deployed worldwide in applications including communications, command, surveillance, electronics, maintenance and medical systems.

In January 2009, General Dynamics announced that it completed the acquisition of AxleTech International from The Carlyle Group. AxleTech International is a global manufacturer and supplier of axles, axle components, planetary axles, independent suspensions, brakes and after market parts for military vehicles, commercial speciality trucks, and off-highway machines used in the construction, material handling, forestry, mining and agricultural markets. Axletech is now part of the General Dynamics Armaments and Technical Products business unit, which is based in Charlotte, N.C.

Description

The S-788 Lightweight Multipurpose Shelter (LMS) offers lightweight, high-strength environmental and EMI protection. Three types of LMS are available, Type I (basic shelter), Type II (with tunnel, CB and hatch) and Type III (with tunnel). Standard equipment includes an access ladder, roof access steps, HMMWV mounting kit and a pintle extension.

GDATP owns patents on the unique fabrication processes involved in the LMS and on manufacturing details enhancing EMI performance.

An advanced version of the LMS is the Standardised Integrated Command Post Shelter (SICPS). The SICPS shelter provides an interior environment that is shielded from environmental, electronic, and chemical/biological threats and is designed to be configurable to provide systems for planning, co-ordinating and controlling tactical operations. The latest version is the S842/G (SICPSV5), full details of which can be found elsewhere in this section.

Construction of these shelters involves aluminium facing sheets bonded to a honeycomb core. EMI shielding involves a minimum of 60 dB attenuation for electromagnetic radiation over a frequency range of 150 kHz to 10 GHz.

Specifications

LMS Type 1 (basic)
Weight:
    (empty) 265 kg
    (mounting kit) 40 kg
Payload: 1,837 kg
Dimensions:
    (external) 2.59 × 2.13 × 1.7 m
    (internal) 2.53 × 2.07 × 1.64 m
    (height on prime mover) 2.59 m
Volume: 8.07 m³
Floor area: 5.2 m²

Status

In production. In service with the US armed forces.

Contractor

General Dynamics Armament and Technical Products (GDATP)

General Dynamics Armaments and Technical Products (GDATP) S-842/G (SICPSV5) HMMWV shelter

Development

General Dynamics Armament and Technical Products (GDATP) was formed in June 2002 and combines the former General Dynamics Armaments Systems and the four companies of the former Advanced Technical Products Inc: Intellitec, Lincoln Composites, Lunn Industries, and Marion Composites. The S-842/G (SICPSV5) HMMWV shelter was produced by Marion Composites.

In January 2009, General Dynamics announced that it completed the acquisition of AxleTech International from The Carlyle Group. AxleTech International is a global manufacturer and supplier of axles, axle components, planetary axles, independent suspensions, brakes and after market parts for military vehicles, commercial speciality trucks, and off-highway machines used in the construction, material handling, forestry, mining and agricultural markets. Axletech is now part of the General Dynamics Armaments and Technical Products business unit, which is based in Charlotte, N.C.

Description

The S-842/G (SICPSV5) HMMWV shelter is the latest version of the SICPS (Standardised Integrated Command Post Shelter) range to be produced by GDATP. The SICPS range of shelters provides an interior environment that is shielded from environmental, electronic, and chemical/biological threats, designed to be configurable to provide systems for planning, co-ordinating and controlling tactical operations.

Improvements made over earlier versions to the base SICPSV5 include improved, patented, built-in RFI shielding (60 dB minimum attenuation over 150 kHz to 10 GHz); a payload compatible with the carrying capacity of the M1113 ECV HMMWV; increased fibre optic connectivity (up to 12

GDATP SICPSV5 shelter (D Sheerar)   0536667

TFOCA II connectors); increased tent interface connectivity giving four UTP CAT 5 LAN connections; moisture sealed tent interface; signal interface; and power entry panels/vaults. Operator enhancements include a new and lighter ECU (75 kg) with an increased 20,200 BTU/hr (5.9 kW) cooling and 12,000 BTU/hr (3.5 kW) heating capacity; a variable speed ventilation fan with gas particle filter unit (GPFU) interlock, a CO monitor and an active air flow indicator; new low-profile cool lighting system; adjustable and dimming work station lighting; a quick-release removable operators chair, and a redesigned access ladder.

Standard equipment also includes an onboard 10 kW, 120 V/240 V single-phase power supply, a vehicle intercom system (VIS), and a secondary roof exit.

Status

In production. In service with the US armed forces.

Contractor

General Dynamics Armament and Technical Products (GDATP)

Light Air Mobile Shelter (LAMS)

Description

The AAR Mobility Systems (formerly AAR Cadillac Manufacturing) Light Air Mobile Shelter (LAMS) entered production in 1999. It was designed to provide air mobile and other forces with a rigid walled shelter to house encampment support facilities such as latrines, showers, laundry, catering, and general maintenance and supply facilities. Operational dimensions of the LAMS are 4.47 × 2.44 × 2.74 m (L × W × H), with a height reduction to 2.29 m for road transport. Each LAMS has inbuilt two-way forklift guides and can be lifted by a standard 4,536 kg fork truck with 1.8 m tines. Tare weight is 2,869 kg; maximum payload is 6,804 kg. It can be transported on a wide variety of trucks or trailers, including commercial models with a payload capacity of 5 tons (4,536 kg) or more. It can also be transported on PLS, or similar systems, flatracks. Tie down/lifting rings allow for lifting by crane or sling lifting by helicopter. A detachable air-mobility rail system allows LAMS to be loaded into most transport aircraft without the need for specialised material handling equipment. To further enhance handling and mobility, AAR Cadillac also manufacture two types of quick-attach mobility wheel sets that connect to special points at either end of the shelter. Full details of these can be found elsewhere in this section.

Light Air Mobile Shelter (LAMS) fitted with a quick-attach Mobility Caster Set for handling purposes (AAR Mobility Systems)   0126572

A standard LAMS is equipped with an environmental control unit, lights and power distribution panel, with power being provided by an external compartment fitted generator of either 7.5 or 12.5 kW. Other internal fittings are to suit user requirements.

Status
In production. In service with US armed forces.

Contractor
AAR Mobility Systems

M-832 and B-832 mobilisers

Development
The M-832 mobiliser provides mobility for medium range shelter payloads. The type, which remains in use by US armed forces (and possibly others), has been produced by a number of companies including Turtle Mountain Manufacturing Co. and Craig Systems, the latter having been acquired by the AAR Cadillac Corporation (now AAR Mobility Systems) in 1998. AAR Mobility Systems produces its own range of shelter transporters (details of which can be found elsewhere in this section) and production of the M-832 (along with a selection of other models produced by Craig Systems) has ceased.

CDK Mobile Systems Inc. has developed the B-832 mobiliser to replace the older, and now technically obsolete, M-832 mobiliser.

Description
The M-832 mobiliser (or dolly set) provides mobility for medium-range shelter payloads up to 4,763 kg. The front and rear dolly assemblies are attached to the payload. Hydraulic cylinders permit lowering and raising of the shelter suspension bars and strut assemblies lock the trailer in the raised position for transport. Air over hydraulic brakes are provided on all four wheels of the dolly set. Tail, stop and blackout lights are mounted on the rear trailer.

The B-832 produced by CDK Mobile Systems operates in a similar manner to CDK's B-720 mobiliser, which is in production as the current generation M-720 mobiliser. Full details of the M-720/B-720 mobiliser systems can be found elsewhere in this section.

The B-832 is a commercial, improved version of the earlier M-832 system. The B-832 system provides the same form, fit and function as the obsolete M-832, but has been re-engineered and improved with commercial off-the-shelf components and stronger materials. The B-832 is rated for highway or off-road transport of S-280 or similar style shelters when pulled behind a suitable tow vehicle. The B-832 can also load S-280 shelters onto C-130 transport aircraft (either pulled on-board with aircraft winch, or pushed on by a tow vehicle).

The front B-832 dolly includes a drawbar with 3 inch (76.2 mm) lunette eye and safety chains. The drawbar is spring loaded and can be stored in the vertical position. The front part also includes an electrical connector to MS 75020-1 and two Gladhand Fittings to attach to the light and brake connections on the tow vehicle.

The B-832 includes air-over-hydraulic brakes, lights and reflectors to meet US road regulations. The unit also incorporates a hand parking brake lever at the rear axle.

CDK Mobile Systems Inc B-832 mobiliser (CDK Mobile Systems)   1136169

CDK Mobile Systems Inc B-832 mobiliser (CDK Mobile Systems)   1136168

Specifications

Model	M-832	B-832
Weight	1,665 kg	2,322 kg
Payload(max)	4,763 kg	5,897 kg
Length	3.038 m	
(towbar lowered)		4.67 m
(towbar raised)		3.23 m
Width	2.438 m	2.43 m
Height	1.321 m	1.55 m
Track width	2.134 m	n/avail
Road speed	n/avail	80 km/h
Road clearance	432 mm	380 mm
Shelter levelling capability	0–305 mm	n/avail
Mobility		Type V, rough terrain
Shelter lift capability	0–432 mm	
Suspension	n/avail	air
Brakes	n/avail	air/hydraulic
Tyres	9.00 × 20	11R 22.5

Status
M-832; production complete. In service with US and possibly other armed forces. B-832; available for production.

Contractor
M-832 - see text
B-832 - CDK Mobile Systems Inc.

M720 and B720 mobiliser sets for S-280 shelters

Development
The M720 Mobiliser Dolly Set was manufactured by the now defunct Mobile Frame Structures Inc. (and possibly others) as the dedicated transport vehicle for the US armed forces range of S-280 tactical shelters. The current variant is the B720 Mobiliser Dolly Set manufactured by CDK Mobile Systems. The B720 and heavier B720HD are essentially re-engineered versions of the now obsolete M720.

Description
The M720 and B720 dolly sets are used for the deployment and movement of S-280 shelters enabling the user to position these items in the field as required. They can be coupled/de-coupled in minutes and negate the need for specialised materials handling equipment. When not attached to a shelter, two complete dolly sets coupled together may be towed by a

Rear section of a B720 Mobiliser Dolly Set attached to a S-280 shelter (CDK Mobile Systems)   0593101

CDK B-720 mobiliser, uncoupled (CDK Mobile Systems)   1136167

The Shop Van Shelter mounts directly to the chassis of the 2.5-ton FMTV (Shaun C Connors)   1391338

single vehicle at highway speeds. The normal tow vehicle is an M939 series 5 ton truck.

The M720 can be mounted to a shelter by two people, and the hydraulic lift mechanism can be operated independently at each end to mount the shelter. Braking is air-over-hydraulic on all four wheels and automotive type steering is used. The M720 weighs 1,000 kg unladen and has a capacity of 2,721.6 kg (6,000 lb, 3 tons). Dimensions are (L × W × H) 2.35 × 2.43 × 2.43 m (790 mm reduced). Although technically obsolete the M720 remains in US Army service and is likely to do so for some time.

The current B720 dolly set is produced by CDK Mobile Systems. It is a commercial, improved version of the old military designated M720 system. It provides the same fit, form and function as the obsolete M720, but has been re-engineered and improved with commercial off-the-shelf components and stronger materials.

The B720 is rated for both highway and off-highway transport of the S280 shelter when pulled by a suitable tow vehicle. The B720 can also load an S-280 shelter onto a C-130 Hercules transport aircraft, either pulled on board by the aircraft's winch, or pushed on by a tow vehicle.

There are two versions of the B720 available: the B720 and the heavier B720HD. The B720 has a tare weight of 1,179 kg and a capacity of 2,721.6 kg (6,000 lb, 3 tonnes); the B720HD has a tare weight of 1,293 kg and a capacity of 3,628.8 kg (8,000 lb, 4 tonnes). Dimensions are (L × W × H) 2.362 (drawbar vertical) or 3.81 (drawbar down) × 2.413 × 1.245 m.

The front B720 dolly includes a drawbar with a 76.2 mm (3 in) lunette eye and safety chains. The drawbar is spring-loaded and can stored in the vertical position. The front dolly also includes an electrical connector to MS 75020-1 and two Gladhand fittings to attach to the light and brake connections on the tow vehicle. The B720 is fitted with air suspension complemented by telescopic shock-absorbers to enable the effective transport of shelters containing shock-sensitive electronic equipment.

Once attached to the shelter, the B720 is raised for transport by means of two hydraulic cylinders on each section operated by a lever-operated manual hand pump. Mechanical lockout struts are provided for safety during transport operations and a rear pintle to MS 51335-2 is provided to allow for tandem towing of empty dolly sets.

The B720 is provided with air-over-hydraulic brakes and lights and reflectors that meet current US road regulations. A hand parking brake lever is fitted to each corner. Tyres are 7.50 × 16, 10-ply rating.

Status
In production. In service with US armed forces.

Contractor
CDK Mobile Systems Inc

Mobility Shop Containers (MSC) and other truck-mounted shelters

Description
AAR Mobility Systems (formerly AAR Cadillac Manufacturing) produce a range of three differently sized Mobility Shop Containers (MSC). Of these the larger two are truck-mounted, one of these being specifically for the now BAE Systems 2.5-ton FMTV.

The larger of the two truck-mounted MSCs has external dimensions of 4.22 × 2.21 × 2.13 m (L × W × H). These dimensions ensure that while this MSC is transportable by a wide variety of military trucks and trailers, including PLS (and other similar systems) flatracks, it can be transported by standard US Army 2.5- and 5-ton payload trucks (including the FMTV range), with their body drop sides still in place. There are two models of this MSC currently in service with US armed forces and both are fitted out primarily to support mobile military maintenance functions, although the base structure is suitable for a variety of other applications.

The Expandable Shop Van Shelter (EVAN) mounts directly to the chassis of the long wheelbase 5-ton FMTV (Shaun C Connors)   1391337

The smaller truck-mounted MSC became available during 2003. This has been designed specifically for the 2.5-ton variant of the FMTV family and has dimensions of 3.66 × 2.21 × 2.13 m (L × W × H).

Both truck-mounted MSCs may be operated either truck-mounted or free on the ground and are two-way liftable by a standard 4,536 kg forklift truck with 1.83 m tines. Tie-down/lifting rings enable lifting by a materials handling crane. Standard equipment includes an electrical power distribution panel that controls the permanently mounted 110 V AC electrical outlets, 110 V AC fluorescent lights, 12 V DC emergency and blackout lighting system, an environmental control system and a dehumidification unit.

The smallest MSC, the M105 Trailer Shop Van, is configured specifically to fit the load area of the in-service M105 trailer. It has external dimensions of 2.72 × 1.86 × 2.13 m (L × W × H) and internal dimensions of 2 × 1.8 × 1.98 m. The M105 Trailer Shop Van can be fitted out to suit user requirements and standard equipment includes lighting, power distribution and storage facilities. Like the larger MSCs, the unit can be handled by either forklift truck or crane, and is deployable either trailer-mounted or free on the ground.

The Shop Van Shelter mounts directly to the chassis of the 2.5-ton FMTV, but can be customised to fit other similar trucks. It has dimensions of 4.75 × 2.41 × 2.16 m (L × W × H) and tare and GVWs of 1,842 and 3,790 kg. Standard equipment includes transportable stairs for entry and exit, an electrical power distribution panel that controls the permanently mounted 120 V AC electrical outlets, 120 V AC fluorescent lights and 24 V DC emergency and blackout lighting system. Optional equipment includes an environmental control system, a dehumidification unit and various interior fitments.

The Expandable Shop Van Shelter (EVAN) mounts directly to the chassis of the long wheelbase 5-ton FMTV, but can be customised to fit other similar trucks. It has dimensions of 7.06 × 2.44 × 2.44 m (L × W × H), width increasing to 4.17 m when fully expanded. Tare and GVWs are 4,271 and 6,804 kg. Standard equipment includes an electrical power distribution panel that controls the permanently mounted 120 V AC electrical outlets, 120 V AC fluorescent lights and 24 V DC emergency and blackout lighting system. Optional equipment includes an environmental control system, a dehumidification unit and various interior fitments.

Status
In production. In service with US armed forces.

Contractor
AAR Mobility Systems

S-250, S-280 and S-530 shelters

Description

These shelters were part of a wide range of tactical shelters originally produced by Craig Systems of Massachusetts, US, until that company's acquisition by AAR Cadillac Manufacturing (now AAR Mobility Systems) in 1998.

The S-250 and S-280 models are mobile tactical rigid wall, all-weather insulated shelters designed primarily for communications and electronic equipment. They are of panel construction; the panels being of the sandwich type and filled with closed-cell rigid polyurethane foam hot-bonded between the two skins. The single-piece door, with an integral 'kick-out' emergency panel, provides a watertight seal for deep-fording operations. Options include EMI shielding, fittings to suit user requirements, and on the larger S-280 model additional openings can be introduced. The EMI shielding package provides at least 60 dB EMI attenuation in the frequency range from 150 KHz to 10 GHz. It is also available as an upgrade package for current in-service non-shielded shelters.

The S-250 has external dimensions of 2.2 × 2 × 1.78 m (L × W × H), weighs 349 kg, has a maximum payload of 1,148 kg and a gross weight of 1,497 kg. It is primarily transported by the HMMWV but can also be transported by the M1028 CUCV. The larger S-280 is normally deployed on a 5-ton payload truck and has external dimensions of 3.7 × 2.2 × 2.18 m. It weighs 635 kg, has a maximum payload of 3,221 kg and a gross weight of 3,856 kg. Both models are air-transportable on suitable cargo pallets and can be slung under helicopters of suitable capacity. To enhance its mobility, the S-280 can be used with either the Craig Systems-produced M832 dolly set or the AAR High Speed Mobility Wheel Set (HSMWS). Full details of these can be found elsewhere in this section.

The S-530 shelter is an air-transportable, truck or trailer deployable, self-contained structure of similar construction to the S-250 and S-280 models. Its primary use is as an electrical maintenance shop.

S-250 shelter shown loaded into a HMMWV (AAR Mobility Systems)

0126569

S-280 shelter shown loaded into an M939 series 5-ton cargo track (AAR Mobility Systems)   0126568

Status

Current generation versions remain available. In service with US and possibly other undisclosed armed forces.

Contractor

AAR Mobility Systems

Small Air Mobile Shelter (SAMS)

Description

The AAR Mobility Systems (formerly AAR Cadillac Manufacturing) Small Air Mobile Shelter (SAMS) became available in 2003. SAMS is an environmentally controlled shelter designed for a variety of uses. Based around the dimensions of a standard 2.74 × 2.23 (L × W) AAR ISU container (height is 2.29 m) SAMS is sized for transport on most of the worlds' transport aircraft and is certified for transport on C-130, C-5, C-17, KC-10, Boeing 747 and DC-10 aircraft. It is also helicopter slingable.

The structure is weather and dust proof and features a four-way forkliftable base making SAMS forkliftable from any side by a standard 5 ton (4,536 kg) capacity forklift truck with 1.83 m tines. A single securable door is fitted. Interior walls are bright white and non-permeable for easy cleaning. The floor is covered with 3 mm diamond tread plate aluminium flooring. Payload is 4,536 kg; tare weight is 1,134 kg. Interior space is 10.8 m³, and interior fittings can include shelves, racks, specialised lighting or dehumidification equipment. Standard equipment includes a 208 V, 3-phase, 60 A power distribution kit and a 18,000 BTU/h (5.3 kW) environmental control unit.

AAR Mobility Systems also produces the ESAMS (Expandable Small Air Mobile Shelter), full details of which can be found elsewhere in this section.

Status

In production.

Contractor

AAR Mobility Systems

OTHER EQUIPMENT

Austria

Achleitner logistic support products

Development
Within its specialist field of vehicle bodies, trailers, drivelines and specialist vehicles, Franz Achleitner Fahrzeugbau und Reifenzentrum GmbH is one of a small number of companies specialising in military logistic support products.

Achleitner currently offers vehicle bodies, trailers, recovery systems and a selection of purpose designed vehicles, some using company developed and produced driveline modifications.

These vehicles include the MANTRA (based on the Mercedes-Benz Sprinter or similar light vans) and the armoured Survivor range, this consisting of the Survivor 1 Light (up to 3,250 kg GVW), Survivor 1 Basic (up tp 5,000 kg GVW), RCV Survivor 1 (up to 8,000 kg GVW), and the PMV Survivor II (up to 15,000 kg GVW). Early Survivor models (based on the Mercedes-Benz G-Class) and the Protector (based on the Pinzgauer) are no longer available.

Brief details of the MANTRA are included in this entry, with full details available in the Light vehicles section. Details of the Survivor range can be found in *Jane's Armour and Artillery*.

Description

Vehicle bodies
Achleitner offers a full range of vehicle bodies. These can range from troop carrying/cargo-type bodies with drop sides, a tarpaulin and bows, to fully enclosed sandwich panel office or shelter-type bodies. Winches, cranes, 5th wheels and other equipment can also be installed to truck chassis.

Trailers
Achleitner offers a full range of semi-trailers including tank and heavy equipment transport trailers. Achleitner trailers have been supplied to Argentina, Iraq, Iran, Kuwait and Nigeria. Recent heavy equipment transport models produced for customers or trials include the following.
- **Type 3STA71** This three-axle semi-trailer has an unladen weight of 16,000 kg, a technical maximum weight of 71,000 kg which gives a permissible payload of 55,000 kg. The three dual-wheeled axles are fitted with 1400R 20 tyres and rated at 16,000 kg each; imposed 5th wheel load is 21,000 kg. This trailer is fitted with two hand-winch operated spare wheel carriers and mechanical landing gear. Hydraulic

Steyr (MAN) (8 × 8) truck fitted with an Achleitner dropside body (MAN)
0122604

A MANTRA all-terrain vehicle as displayed at Eurosatory 2008 (Shaun C Connors)
1296222

An Achleitner three-axle heavy equipment transport semi-trailer and Steyr (6 × 6) tractor truck (Rotzler)
1185450

landing gear is an option, and up to three axles can be hydraulically steered.
- **Type 3STA72** This three axle semi-trailer is similar to the Type 3STA71, but has a technical maximum weight of 72,000 kg.
- **Type 5STA88** This five-axle semi-trailer follows the same general lines as the 3STA71 and 3STA72 semi-trailers, but has five and not three axles. 1400R 20 tyres are standard and up to three axles may be hydraulically steered.
- **Type 5STA92** This five-axle semi-trailer is similar in appearance to the Type 5STA88. It has an unladen weight of 29,000 kg and a technical maximum weight of 92,000 kg which gives a permissible payload of 62,000 kg. The five single-wheeled axles are rated at 13,000 kg each; imposed 5th wheel load is 27,000 kg. This trailer is fitted with two hand-winch operated spare wheel carriers and hydraulic landing gear.

MANTRA 4 × 4 light vehicle
The MANTRA was developed from around 1998 to meet the requirements of the Saudi Arabian National Guard (SANG) for multipurpose light all-terrain vehicles. An initial 200 vehicles were delivered 2000-2002 as the first stage of a proposed Pinzgauer replacement project. With the exception of around 10 vehicles, all are fitted with a DROPS/PLS-type load handling system.

Gabon is understood to have acquired around 30 vehicles in 2001 (possibly 2002) in GS troop carrying/cargo configuration. Oman ordered 355 vehicles in 2007 Romania received 18 vehicles in ambulance configuration during 2008.

Vehicles sold to military customers, along with a selection of commercial sales to fire departments and municipalities are based on the Mercedes-Benz Sprinter 416, but using Achleitner-designed axles, suspension, steering and four-wheel drive system. This system can be used with any similar vehicle and the MANTRA is also available based on the IVECO Daily or Volkswagen Crafter light vans.

Various wheelbases and body configurations are available. Full details of the MANTRA can be found in the Light vehicles section.

Status
Achleitner products have been supplied to a number of countries with recent deliveries of assorted products made to Argentina (trailers, truck bodies), Gabon (MANTRA), Iraq (trailers), Iran (trailers), Kuwait (trailers), Montenegro (Survivor), Nigeria (trailers), Oman (MANTRA), Romania (MANTRA) and Saudi Arabia (trailers, truck bodies, MANTRA).

Contractor
Franz Achleitner Fahrzeugbau und Reifenzentrum GmbH

EMPL logistic support products

Development
Within its specialist field of vehicle bodies, trailers and recovery equipment, EMPL Fahrzeugwerk GmbH is one of a small number of companies specialising in military logistic support products.

EMPL offers vehicle bodies, trailers and assorted lifting, loading and recovery systems and has supplied military equipment to a wide range of customers, predominantly (but not always) on or in conjunction with European truck manufacturers, and predominantly MAN (MAN, OAF, Steyr) or Mercedes-Benz chassis.

EMPL products can be supplied Completely Built Up (CBU), Semi-Knocked Down (SKD) or Completely Knocked Down (CKD) and with appropriate technology transfer if required.

Mercedes-Benz Zetros truck fitted with an EMPL torsion-free platform; this vehicle had recently returned from Australia's Land 121 trials (Shaun C Connors) 1391345

MAN HX 77 fitted with an EMPL torsion-free platform and a materials handling crane (Shaun C Connors) 1391346

Mercedes-Benz Actros trucks fitted with EMPL platform/troop carrying bodies (EMPL) 1296207

Mercedes-Benz Actros fitted with EMPL load handling equipment (EMPL) 1186197

EMPL military products has recently been delivered to Algeria, Austria, Bahrain, Bulgaria, Canada, Denmark, Estonia, Ethiopia, Gabon, Germany, Greece, Hungary, Ireland, Kuwait, Libya, Lithuania, Nigeria, Oman, Pakistan, Qatar, Saudi Arabia, Singapore, Tunisia, Venezuela and other undisclosed users.

Mercedes-Benz Actros (6 × 6) destined for Gabon and fitted with an EMPL tipping body and rear-mounted crane (EMPL) 1296208

Volvo FM range truck destined for Kuwait and fitted with an EMPL cargo body (EMPL) 1296209

Scania R420 CB (6 × 6) truck of the Irish Army fitted with an EMPL troop carrying body (EMPL) 1296206

Gabon Army Mercedes-Benz Actros 1831 (4 × 4) fitted with an EMPL specialist rear body (EMPL) 1186195

Description
Vehicle bodies
EMPL offers a full range of vehicle bodies. These can range from the more complex torsion free platforms to basic troop carrying/cargo-type bodies with drop sides, a tarpaulin and bows. Such bodies can be configured for a variety of purposes and kitted out for various roles including field

Austrian Army Mercedes-Benz Unimog U4000 fitted with an EMPL interchangeable body system (EMPL)   1296251

MAN TGA 18.310 (4 × 4) BB truck destined for Yemen and fitted with a mobile workshop (EMPL)   1296212

Mercedes-Benz Actros 1832 (4 × 4) truck destined for Bulgaria and fitted with an EMPL tanker body (EMPL)   1296213

Canadian Army Mercedes-Benz Actros 3750 fitted with EH/W 200 Heavy Duty Bison recovery equipment and front-mounted crane (EMPL)   1296201

service/lubrication or repair. Fully enclosed office, ambulance or shelter-type bodies are also available, and these can shielded or configured for C-130 Hercules transport as required.

EMPL also produces interchangeable torsion free body systems and has recently supplied the Austrian Army with 1,014 such bodies configured as troop carrier, field communications unit, ambulance, flatbed or mobile workshop unit, and for use with Mercedes-Benz Unimog and MAN TGM range trucks.

Tanker bodies

EMPL produces a full range of tanker bodies and in a variety of capacities. Water or fuel bodies are available, and with an assortment of pumping options.

Austrian Army OAF truck fitted with an EMPL installed load handling system (EMPL)   1186189

Destined for Bulgaria, a Mercedes-Benz Actros (6 × 6) fitted with EMPLEH/TC 53.000 recovery equipment (EMPL)   1190229

MAN TGA 41.530 destined for the UAE Armed Forces and fitted with EMPL EH/W 200 Slewing Boom Version (SBV) recovery equipment (EMPL)   1296204

Mercedes-Benz Actros of the Estonian Army fitted with EMPL EH/W SBV 1000 recovery equipment (EMPL)   1296205

Load handling systems

EMPL offers a full range of DROPS/PLS-type equipment including a recently developed Container Handling Unit (CHU). In addition to installing proprietary load handling systems on various chassis, EMPL produces its

An EMPL produced riot-control vehicle (EMPL)   1190224

A tandem axle trailer complete with flatrack. The load handling system of the towing vehicle can load/unload the trailer (EMPL)   1296210

own wide range of specialist flatracks. These include racks for light armoured vehicle transport, bridge component transport, and specialist fuel transport and distribution, all of which are in service with the Austrian Army.

Recovery vehicles

EMPL offers a wide range of recovery vehicles in four basic types, EH/W (underlift), EH/W Type SBV (crane with underlift), EW/R winch vehicle, EH/TC salvage crane. These are available as kits.

A sliding platform recovery vehicle is also produced. EMPL has also produced a recovery variant of the MOWAG DURO. This vehicle is fitted with hampers for recovery equipment stowage and is adapted to take a fifth wheel for towing a single-axle EMPL-supplied recovery trailer.

Trailers

EMPL also produces a wide range of trailers. These can vary from small single-axle trailers compatible with lightweight Land Rover-sized vehicles to three-axle flatbed semi-trailers for tank and heavy equipment transport. Specialist recovery, fuel or water tank trailers, as well as trailers with shelter or office-type bodies are also available.

Other equipment

Chassis-mounted cranes, winches, tail lifts, specialist riot control vehicles, fire-fighting vehicles, decontamination bodies and mobile medical treatment centres are further examples of the range of equipment offered by EMPL.

Status

EMPL military products have recently been delivered to Algeria, Austria, Bahrain, Bulgaria, Canada, Denmark, Estonia, Ethiopia, Gabon, Germany, Greece, Hungary, Ireland, Kuwait, Libya, Lithuania, Nigeria, Oman, Pakistan, Qatar, Saudi Arabia, Singapore, Tunisia, Venezuela and other undisclosed users.

Contractor

EMPL Fahrzeugwerk GmbH

Germany

DOLL vehicle bodies and trailers

Development

The now DOLL Fahrzeugbau AG was established in 1878 as Dollenschmiede (DOLL's forging shop), the first products offered including carriages and logging tools. The company remains a family-owned business. Early international military business included a French Army contract in 1950 for 396 platform trailers. From the mid-1980s DOLL has focused on three core business areas, logging transport, special haulage and mobile systems. Military products include vehicle bodies of all types and semi-trailers of all types.

DOLL produces a wide range of low-torsion and torsion-free bodies (DOLL)   0583254

Description

Vehicle bodies

DOLL produces a wide range of low-torsion and torsion-free flatbed bodies for mounting on a variety of truck chassis. Platform lengths can vary between 5 and 8 m, and cranes may be mounted at either end of the body platform.

The basic flatbed body platform can be fitted with a number of fixing/fitting systems thereby allowing the transport of shelters, containers or a selection of quick-release seating. Dropsides and tailifts are further options.

The low-torsion flatbed design is mounted directly to the truck chassis and an auxiliary frame, whereas the torsion-free body is fixed via a three-point mounting system.

These body types allow bodies to maintain a relatively horizontal position during cross-country operations, thus protecting loads such as shelters/containers from potentially damaging torsional stresses.

Semi-trailers

DOLL produces a wide range of flatbed, low bed or drop bed semi-trailers for the transport of heavy or outsize loads. These trailers can have up to seven axles, all of which may be steered hydraulically if required. Remote steering is optional. With single, double or triple extensions these trailers have a maximum length of up to 45 m.

The DOLL Vario T3H from the Vario series of semi-trailers is just one example of DOLL semi-trailers in current service with a number of armed forces. The Vario T3H is a three-axle drop bed-type semi-trailer for heavy haulage applications. All three trailer axles steer, the angle on the rearmost axle being 45°. Overall trailer length is 15.37 m, with a dropped length of 7 m. Outriggers provide an increase in overall width of 270 mm for the transport of wider loads. The hydraulically operated side-shift capable loading ramps are 1 m wide and 2.7 m long and are rated at 36,000 kg.

In addition to complete semi-trailers, DOLL also designs, develops and manufactures specialist components for heavy haulage semi-trailers. One example of such components would be the swivel axles and detachable gooseneck fitted to the King GTS110/7 seven-axle semi-trailer, 89 of which were manufactured for the UK's tank transporter trailer.

DOLL subsequently manufactured eight of these trailers during 2008 for the Canada Army for use with Mercedes-Benz Actros (8 × 8) Armoured Heavy Support Vehicle System (AHSVS) trucks in Afghanistan. DOLL also supplied the Canadian Army with three, three-axle 25,000 kg payload recovery semi-trailers for use in Afghanistan.

DOLL low-torsion bodies fitted to Mercedes-Benz Actros (6 × 6) trucks and destined for an Asian customer (DOLL)   0583252

One of three three-axle 25,000 kg payload recovery semi-trailers supplied to the Canadian Army for use in Afghanistan (Carl Schulze) 1391342

One of eight GTS110/7 trailers supplied to the Canada Army for use with Mercedes-Benz Actros (8 × 8) Armoured Heavy Support Vehicle System (AHSVS) trucks in Afghanistan (Carl Schulze) 1391343

Currently the DOLL HET semi-trailer VARIO S7P-0S2, an evolution of the UK/Canadian trailers, is being evaluated by the German Bundeswehr.

Status
In production. In service with a number of armed forces.

Contractor
DOLL Fahrzeugbau AG

Israel

Rabintex dry storage systems

Description
Rabintex produces two basic types of dry storage system, one passive (known as CONRASS), the other active.

CONRASS passive dry storage systems
CONRASS (CONstant Readiness Advanced Storage System) passive dry storage systems are claimed to be an effective and simple method of storing ordnance and other military equipment including vehicles for long periods of time.

A tough and highly impermeable envelope, from which air and moisture have been extracted, is used to provide protection. Since the equipment is stored in vacuum conditions, problems with corrosion - even when items are stored for long periods out of doors and under a variety of adverse environmental conditions - are practically eliminated. Additionally there is little or no risk of damage from chaffing in high winds since the vacuum draws the polymer cover tightly over the stored equipment. According to company literature, the polymer material used in CONRASS retains its physical characteristics through a –40 to +100 °C temperature range, and ageing properties are excellent, with only minimal deterioration even after 15 years exposure to extreme weather conditions.

The CONRASS system is completely self-contained and does not require base facilities or constant support. Once installed there is no need for electrical power lines or any other power source and/or dehumidification equipment. This elimination of the need for any type of support permits wide dispersal, concealment and logistic support benefits.

Rabintex CONRASS (CONstant Readiness Advanced Storage System - Stationary Type - in use (Rabintex) 0583258

Visual inspection of the cover is all that is required to ensure that environmental protection is in perfect order. Relevant data concerning the condition of the stored equipment, or air pressure and humidity inside the envelope, can be relayed via cable to indicating and recording equipment located outside the envelope.

Installation and removal are fast and simple, and require no special tools or specially trained personnel. CONRASS units are reusable.

CONRASS - Stationary Type
This provides a conditioned storage environment for wheeled or tracked vehicles, or other bulky equipment and stores. A Stationary Type CONRASS unit can be made to almost any size or shape to suit the storage requirements of a particular piece of equipment.

In use, the piece of equipment to be stored is first placed on a base sheet. A sectional slotted tube placed around the periphery of the membrane contains its edge and provides a sealing channel. Once the cover envelope is placed over the stored equipment its inflatable seal is placed into the sealing channel and inflated, thus creating a seal between the base membrane and the cover envelope. Air is then evacuated using a simple air pump, via a valve located in the envelope wall.

Preparation of a Stationary Type CONRASS unit for the storage of an armoured vehicle can be accomplished by two men in about 15 minutes.

The polymer material used in CONRASS retains its physical characteristics through a –40 to +100 °C temperature range. Ageing properties are excellent, with only minimal deterioration even after 15 years exposure to extreme weather conditions.

Active Dry Storage System
The Active Dry Storage System utilises a humidifier to maintain a consistent atmosphere inside a sealed system cover at optimum corrosion protection levels. Corrosion, degradation and moisture-induced failures (especially on sensitive components) can therefore be significantly reduced.

Status
In production. In service with Israeli and possibly other armed forces.

Contractor
Rabintex Industries Limited

Achidatex protective equipment covers

Development
Achidatex has developed a range of dry storage systems to protect outdoor equipment such as aircraft and helicopters of all sizes. In addition it provides common shell dry storage systems for vehicles, tanks and artillery, as well as standard dry storage tunnels for equipment such as engines and spare parts.

The Achidatex Common Structure Dry Storage Cell provides cover for out-sized equipment such as armoured vehicles. These may be used for temporary storage, or as cover for extended periods.

In addition to the above, Achidatex also produces multipurpose dry storage shelters, hanging liners and special containers.

Description
The Achidatex dry storage system maintains a 'climatic bubble' around a stored item, isolating it from the effects of humidity, rain, frost, sand erosion and the chemical influence of bacteria, fungi, insects and acid rain. Stored items are thus protected against rust and corrosion, thereby eliminating the need for storage sheds and reducing equipment life-cycle costs. As they are flame retardant, Achidatex covers also limit the danger from fire.

Achidatex coverings are made from PVC, urethane or other material suitable for local climatic conditions. A dehumidifier maintains dry air inside the cover at corrosion-prevention levels by absorbing and expelling excess water vapours through a regulated cycle of operations. Units can be connected to a standard electrical supply or a small generator.

Storage systems can be placed in large warehouses providing extra protection and humidity control for sensitive systems and parts.

Status
In production. In service with the Israeli armed forces, the German Army and the US Army.

Contractor
Achidatex

Chemoplast humidity controlled dry storage systems

Development
The Chemoplast humidity controlled dry storage system was designed for the long-term maintenance-free storage of a wide variety of military vehicles and their associated equipment. It can also be used for the storage of complete aircraft or helicopters. The system is based on the principle of storing equipment, ordnance or other material in a controlled humidity environment, preventing the occurrence of corrosion and fungi.

Chemoplast Industries Ltd was acquired by Defense Industries International in 2005. Achidatex, a subsidiary of Defense Industries International also produces a range of dry storage systems, plus ranges of storage and transport tanks. Details of Achidatex products, which now encompass Chemoplast products, can be found in their related sections elsewhere in this title.

Description
The Chemoplast humidity controlled dry storage system consists of two main elements, sealed storage units and the humidifying equipment. The Chemoplast humidity controlled dry storage system is available in a number of configurations that can include tailor-made covers or tunnels, mobile hanging liners, modular storage containers, multipurpose shelters, or as a dry storage modification to conventional long-term storage facilities.

A tailor-made cover, tunnel or shelter is manufactured from PVC sheeting, urethane laminated film, polyurethane, polyethylene, CPE (chlorinated polyethylene), or other materials appropriate to the climatic conditions under which the covered equipment is to be stored. These are designed to resist the effects of UV and ozone as well as attack from moisture, hydrocarbons, fungi or insects. They are also abrasion resistant and flame retardant. Seams generally overlap 20 mm and are formed by continuous heat welding for maximum strength and covers/shelters are sealed/entered by two and/or three track zips designed to be watertight, rustproof and remain flexible in extremes of climate. Zips are continuous heat-welded to the cover. The base is designed so the underside of equipment can also be protected, base size and shape being determined by the type of equipment to be stored. The base can be placed on almost any type of surface.

Dehumidification equipment maintains the air inside the protected area at a corrosion-prevention level by absorbing and expelling excess water vapour through a regulated cycle of operation. Humidifying equipment is connected to the standard electricity supply or a suitable generator. Chemical dehumidification is an option. Humidity sensing equipment and a warning system for unsafe humidity levels is included.

The Chemoplast humidity controlled dry storage tunnel system is portable, weighing only 150 kg, and measures 15 × 2.8 × 2 m and provides a covered volume of 80 m³. Other sizes are available to suit specific customer requirements. The roof and sides of the tunnel form a single unit supported on a plastic frame system of assorted GRP elements, which can be easily assembled and dismantled. Assembly takes approximately one hour. An extruded all-around closure ensures top and bottom sealing.

When the Chemoplast system is used to convert conventional long-term storage facilities into dry storage facilities the internal walls and ceiling of the structure to be converted are covered with high water vapour

Reserve equipment in a conventional storage shed converted to a controlled dry storage environment (Chemoplast)   0137706

permeability sheeting fitted with curtains that can be raised or lowered to allow vehicles to drive in or out. These curtains are zip-sealed and the internal humidity is maintained by the means of a suitable humidifier.

Status
In service with the armed forces of Brazil, Chile, Germany, Israel, the US and other undisclosed countries.

Contractor
Defense Industries International Inc. (previously know as Chemoplast Industries Limited)

Malaysia

Bry-Air dry storage systems

Description
Bry-Air has manufacturing facilities in Brazil, India, Malaysia and the US, and manufactures dehumidification equipment for humidity control in the short- or long-term storage and preservation of all types of military equipment. Bry-Air products are used by numerous armed forces, worldwide.

Flexible Barrier Storage System (FBS)
The Flexible Barrier Storage System (FBS) effectively creates a storage 'bubble' around the contained item, maintaining a relative humidity (RH) of between 30 and 40 per cent by the means of a desiccant dehumidifier which offers internal protection from the corrosive effects of humidity and humidity-associated problems. FBS is a mobile system, requiring no storage sheds. It can be set up on virtually any terrain and requires little manpower to manage or install, and once installed can be maintained by unskilled personnel. The reusable cover material used, the shroud, is resistant to the effects of moisture, bacteria, fungi, insects and rodents, temperature extremes, ultra violet rays, and oil-based liquids.

Enviroliner
The Enviroliner is essentially humidity controlled housing for items such as automotive components, ammunition, clothing or food, but it may also be used for the storage and preservation of vehicles. Enviroliner is a custom-made PVC store house that requires only a floor and ceiling for erection. The thermo-plastic barrier material is attached to walls built from a framework and zipped closed around the to-be-stored items. A small desiccant dehumidifier controls the relative humidity to the required level - between 35 and 50 per cent RH. Doors can be installed for personnel or forklift truck access, panels can be translucent to take advantage of existing lighting or internal lighting can be fitted.

Specifications

Standard Enviroliner modular sizes. Can be extended linearly by 3 m

Length	Width	Height
2.44 m	2.44 m	2.44 m
3 m	3 m	3 m
6 m	5 m	5 m
6 m	5 m	3 m

Status
In production. In service with numerous armed forces and governmental and defence-related organisations including Belgian armed forces, India, (including Navy), Malaysia, Netherlands armed forces (including Navy), Taiwan, Royal Thai Army and Navy, and defence-related organisations in the US.

Contractor
BRY-AIR Malaysia

Sweden

Munters dry air method

Description
The Munters dry air method (controlled humidity environment) was first used by the Swedish Army during the late 1950s. Since then its use has become widespread for the protection of equipment against depredations caused by moisture in the atmosphere (high humidity).

The Munters dry air method uses dehumidifiers that will operate efficiently in any climatic conditions. The essence of the system is to envelop weapons systems, subsystems, system components, logistical supplies and ammunition in dry air. This can be done by placing the systems or supplies in a dehumidified building or room or by blowing a small current of dry air into the systems (active status protection). Corrosion is thus halted, electronic malfunctions are reduced and mould and fungi growth is prevented. By using this preventive method, maintenance costs can be reduced significantly, while availability and readiness are improved.

CV 90 Infantry Fighting Vehicles (IFV) protected by the Munters dry air method; active status protection (Munters AB) 1142981

Status
In production for over 50 years. In service with most NATO countries, plus Australia, Austria, China, Finland, Israel, Japan, New Zealand, South Africa, Sweden, Switzerland, UAE and numerous other undisclosed countries.

Contractor
Munters AB

Defence business contact
Munters AB DHi

United Kingdom

Airflex protective storage system

Description
The Airflex protective storage system provides a humidity-controlled environment for the shipment and long-term storage of military vehicles, weapon systems and support hardware. The system consists of a butyl-rubber bag that stands on either a similar material or rigid palletised base. The bag can be tailored to fit equipment of any shape or size and the Airflex system is passive, requiring no permanent facilities such as electricity or heat when deployed.

Once deployed, maintenance required is little more than regular checks of the humidity indicator to ensure environmental protection integrity is being maintained. Existing installations have proven a life expectancy in excess of ten years.

Status
Production as required. Supplied to the UK Ministry of Defence, the US Air Force, Army and Marines, the defence forces of Canada and Taiwan and other undisclosed countries.

Contractor
Portsmouth Aviation Ltd

A member of the CVR(T) Combat Vehicle Reconnaissance (Tracked) family in the Airflex protective storage system (Airflex) 0116891

EPS LT protection and storage systems

Development
EPS Logistics Technology Limited produces a range of protective packaging and specialises in the design and manufacture of reusable containers and preservation systems suitable for the protection of anything from spares and electronic equipment, to vehicles, aircraft, satellites and armaments.

Driclad cover system in use protecting an armoured vehicle (EPS) 0101634

The Driclad military storage system in use (EPS) 1156107

Description
The Driclad system is the result of applied research into the causes of corrosion and deterioration of equipment during storage and in transit. It is based on the enclosure of stores or equipment in a dry and clean atmosphere within a flexible plastic cover.

Driclad was accepted into British Army service in 1965 after extensive trials in Europe and Asia lasting over two years. The system is in service with many countries all over the world.

Driclad covers are custom made from thermoplastic barrier and foil-laminate materials. They are re-sealable and reusable, indoors and outdoors and offer very low water vapour transmission rates in all climatic conditions between -35 and +60°C. A Driclad system can be designed to accommodate any shape. Equipment protected requires no special building or packing materials and maintenance requirements are greatly reduced and, in some instances, maintenance procedures become redundant.

Dripak is a range of long-life containers with polyurethane elastomer joints between panels, compliant to ATA 300 category 1. They combine flexibility with shock and climate protection.

Dricase containers give protection to DEF-STAN 81-41 up to and including level J. Dricase containers can be used to protect equipment weighing up to 20,000 kg during transport and long-term storage in open environments.

Storlina is a modular lining system using flexible barrier material and dehumidifiers to convert part, or all, of a building into a cost-effective humidity controlled environment store, protecting equipment from damaging atmospheric moisture.

Status
In production. In service worldwide.

Contractor
EPS Logistics Technology Ltd

Marshall VE vehicle bodies

Development
Marshall Vehicle Engineering (MVE), part of Marshall Land Systems (MLS), offers a complete range of military bodies and since its establishment in 1946, through the current and predecessor companies, has supplied the UK MoD and others with more than 90,000 vehicle bodies.

Description
Marshall Vehicle Engineering (MVE) offers bodies ranging from conventional general service cargo/troop carrying-type drop side bodies for trucks, through to special-purpose shelter-type bodies utilising Marshall Matrix sandwich panel technology.

Prototype artillery limber body on a MAN HX (4 × 4) truck
(Shaun C Connors)   1340298

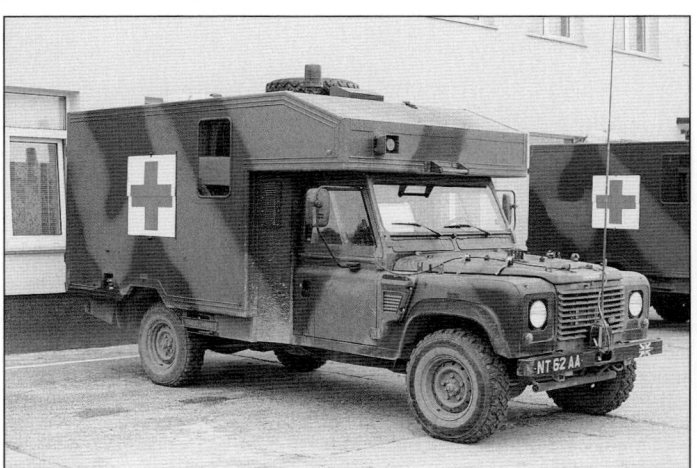

A Marshall-bodied Land Rover Defender XD-based Pulse ambulance of the
British Army; 800 of these were delivered from 1996 (R Stickland) 0121855

MAN 6,000 kg Support Vehicle trucks fitted with Marshall-produced
General Service (GS) troop-carrying/cargo bodies (Shaun C Connors)
1391349

As a sub-contractor of MAN Truck and Bus UK Ltd (a subsidiary of
Germany's MAN Nutzfahrzeuge AG) Marshall designed, manufactured
and fitted the dropside cargo/troop carrying load beds for the UK's
Support Vehicle fleet, for which MAN Truck and Bus UK Ltd was awarded
the prime contract in 2005. The Support Vehicle contract (including
exercised options) calls for in excess of 6,500 bodies in 6,000, 9,000 and
15,000 kg configurations. Marshall Vehicle Engineering is design authority
for 35 of the 39 Support Vehicle variants, and in addition to design,
manufacture and installation of Support Vehicle bodies it provides cranes,
tail lifts, technical, ILS and long term through life support. The British
Army's current legacy Bedford MK/MJ fleet are also fitted with Marshall-
produced bodies.

Marshall-produced shelter-type bodies have been fitted to a selection of
light vehicles including the Land Rover, MOWAG DURO (formerly Bucher
DURO), Pinzgauer and Supacat (6 × 6) vehicles.

Marshall-manufactured cargo body on a developmental Lockheed Martin
vehicle (Shaun C Connors)   1391348

Marshall manufacturers the cargo bodies for the Wolfhound Tactical
Support Vehicle (TSV) Heavy (Shaun C Connors)   1391347

Marshall has also produced a wide range of Land Rover-specific
ambulance bodies. In more than 25 years of production over 4,000 have
been produced for customers worldwide. Designed to fit either the 110 or
130 Land Rover chassis, specific customer design requirements can be
met. Interior arrangements offer a capability of accepting up to four
stretcher patients or two stretcher patients and four sitting patients, or
eight sitting patients. An attendant's seat is fitted and locker space for
storage of medical equipment is provided. A wide range of optional
equipment can be offered, including air conditioning, oxygen systems,
portable resuscitation equipment and emergency first aid equipment.

A wide range of other conversions have been supplied for the Land
Rover series. These have included signal vehicles, weapon platforms,
radar stations, command posts, workshops, refuelling and missile support
vehicles. A cargo-bodied version has been supplied through Land Rover to
several overseas territories.

Status
Production as required. In widespread service.

Contractor
Marshall Land Systems

Penman Engineering Limited

Description
Penman has been in business since 1859, evolving from a family business
to become part of a UK PLC, and more recently returning to private
ownership. The company operates from a secure 15 acre site in southern
Scotland and currently employs around 140 people.

Penman Engineering Limited designs and manufactures a wide variety
of vehicles and equipment for governmental and military customers, with
around 30 per cent of production being for export customers.

Penman bomb disposal vehicle based on a DAF LF series (4 x 2) chassis in service with the UK Ministry of Defence (Patrick Allen)   1067392

Penman Engineering has extensive experience with Land Rover vehicles and during 2005 (as part of an extensive package of equipment supplied by coalition forces) it was disclosed by the UK DPA that the company would refurbish 72 ex-British Army Land Rover Armoured Patrol Vehicles (APV) for the Iraqi Police (Patrick Allen)   1146287

Displayed at DVD 2006, one of the 35 MOWAG DURO vehicles supplied for Cormorant communication system 'loose stowage' items (Patrick Allen)   1183165

Displayed at DVD 2006, a Project Citizen DURO III (Shaun C Connors)   1156035

Specialist vehicles and bodies

Under the Penman Specialist Vehicles banner, the company produces/converts a selection of vehicles for a wide variety of roles including general cargo, specialist application, Explosive Ordnance Disposal (EOD), fire, long range patrol, internal security, and riot control applications.

During 2005 the UK MoD ordered a batch of 35 MOWAG DURO 6 x 6 vehicles for the Cogent Defence and Security Networks Ltd Cormorant communication system 'loose stowage' items. These vehicles had been delivered by June 2006 and are fitted with a Penman-supplied cargo-type body and a Hiab materials handling crane.

As previously mentioned Penman produces a range of EOD vehicles on two- and three-axle chassis. A number of 6 x 6 vehicles on a Penman-converted Land Rover chassis are in service with the Hong Kong Police, the most recent delivery occurring during 2008. Two ranges of 4 x 2 EOD vehicles based on DAF chassis are in service with the UK Ministry of Defence. Under Project Wedgewood, Penman supplied the UK MoD with around 150 (DAF 45 Series-based) EOD vehicles.

To meet a UK MoD UOR (Urgent Operational Requirement) for EOD vehicles for deployment to Iraq during the second Gulf War, eight DURO I 6 x 6 vehicles were fitted with EOD bodies removed from surplus pre-contract Wedgewood DAF 4 x 2 chassis. A further four DURO II 6 x 6 chassis for EOD use and fitted with Penman bodies and riot protection kits were delivered early 2004. During 2005, an initial eight DURO III chassis-cabs were fitted with Penman EOD bodies and protection kits. In service these vehicles replaced the earlier procured DURO I EOD vehicles. It was disclosed mid-2006 that in order to meet operational requirements, 14 and not 8 chassis had, under UOR Project Citizen, been fitted with Penman blast protected bodies for EOD use on deployed operations. It was disclosed in June 2006 that under UOR Project Teller, the UK MoD would procure 18 DURO III 4 x 4 chassis for EOD use by the Royal Engineers. These vehicles are fitted with protected cabs and bodies supplied by Penman Engineering and were delivered late-2006.

Additional DURO III vehicles with communications bodies have been supplied to UK, four 4 x 4 during 2008, and a further four 6 x 6 during 2009.

Delivered to the Irish Army during 2004 were six EOD vehicles on the MOWAG DURO II 6 x 6 chassis. Three of these chassis are fitted with blast-proof rear bodies and armoured cabs.

The Irish Army has also received 10 Scania 4 x 2 trucks fitted with EOD bodies. These were 2006-2007 model year chassis that were delivered during 2008.

A further specialist vehicle marketed by Penman Engineering is the Trekker ERPV (Extended Range Patrol Vehicle), full details of which can be found in the Special attack vehicles section.

A range of armoured, internal security and riot control vehicles is also available. Armoured platforms vary from discreetly armoured saloon cars or 4 x 4s through to fully armoured Land Rover (or similar) chassis. Cash In Transit vehicles are also produced. Internal security or riot control vehicles can be built onto Land Rover 4 x 4 and 6 x 6 chassis, the 4 x 4 seating six personnel and the 6 x 6 seating ten. Options such as turrets, cupolas, grenade launchers, and so on are available. Vehicle designs can be tailored to meet customer requirements.

Armoured cabs

These cabs are fitted to construction plant, agricultural tractors and on and off highway trucks. Equipped vehicles are utilised during mine clearing and disposal, heavy equipment transport, airfield damage repair and with

Lannen 90 wheeled loader fitted with a Penman armoured cab for obstacle and demining operations in service with the Finnish Army (Penman)   0127000

logistic support vehicles generally. The Penman range of armoured cabs includes specific versions providing NBC protection in addition to ballistic, ROPS/FOPS and mine protection. Penman can design tailored solutions to meet defined threats for any DEM equipment.

Recent deliveries have included 10 CAT 972 wheeled loaders and eight CAT 932 wheeled loaders to a Middle Eastern customer, and an unspecified number of JCB 4CXM backhoe loaders to Singapore, and around 30 examples each of CAT 257 skid-steer loaders, CAT 434 backhoe loaders and CAT 938 wheeled loaders.

Non-armoured cabs are also available and are generally produced for short production run specialist vehicle applications such as the Alvis Unipower BR90 series. During 2008 Penman supplied nine Alvis Unipower BR90 pattern cabs to MPI of le Havre, this company producing nine BR90 chassis for a French Army container transport vehicle requirement.

The company also supplies the armoured bodies for the Aardvark mineflail.

Other equipment
Penman also produces a range of trailers and is the current supplier of the British Army's Lightweight General Service (GS) trailer.

In October 2001 the UK MoD announced the possible refurbishment of around 1,800 FV2381 'wide track' General Service (GS) 750 kg cargo trailers to extend their service life by 18 years. Additionally the MoD would procure up to 4,600 new build trailers to comply with the latest legal requirements. A requirement for 6,450 new 750 kg General Service (GS) trailers was advertised early 2002, and following an industry day held in April 2002, the original 38 respondents were shortlisted to eight. Three companies (Bradley Doublelock, Penman Engineering and Universal Engineering) were then invited to tender and supply a single trailer, at their own expense, to QinetiQ for trials purposes. Bradley Doublelock subsequently withdrew from the competition, and in October 2002 it was announced that Penman Engineering of Dumfries had been awarded the production contract. Bradley Doublelock is a major subcontractor to Penman Engineering for this contract. During trials both Penman Engineering and Universal Engineering proposed a payload increase for the trailer, and at no increase in unladen weight or unit cost. This was accepted by the MoD. In October 2002 it was announced Penman Engineering had been awarded the production contract and deliveries of the 6,001 trailers ordered began early 2003, and were scheduled to run until 2007.

Trailers delivered under this contract comply with all current EU legislation and are replacing all versions of the FV2381 trailer currently in service. By August 2004 all 'narrow track' FV2381 trailers had been withdrawn from service, and it was intended that by 2008 (2009 at the latest) all the remaining 'wide track' trailers were to have been withdrawn from service.

During mid-2003 an additional 370 trailers were ordered under a separate contract to carry 4.5 kW mobile power generators. Further GS trailers could be ordered to meet the original Total Fleet Requirement of 6,450.

Around 200 trailers similar to those supplied to the UK MoD have been supplied to NAMSA.

Penman Engineering has also designed and manufactured a dedicated trailer for the MOWAG DURO II, selected by the British Army as the platform for the Cogent Defence and Security Networks Ltd Cormorant communication system. A total of 28 CART (Cormorant Auxiliary Ruggedised Trailer) were supplied during 2005.

The company has also produced a variety of tactical shelter-type bodies.

Aardvark Joint Service Flail Unit (JSFU)
The Aardvark Joint Service Flail Unit (JSFU) Mk 4 is a dedicated armoured mine clearance vehicle system, specifically designed to counter the threat of conventional land mines in excess of 10 kg net explosive content. Over 120 units in service with 24 countries. Aardvark Clear Mine Limited is now

owned by Penman Engineering Ltd. Penman had built the JSFU since the early/mid-90s and at the time the company was acquired by Penman, Penman was responsible for around 80 per cent of the finished product. Full details of the Aardvark JSFU can be found in *Jane's Mines and Mine Clearance.*

Status
In production. Penman military products (excluding Aardvark) are in service with the armed forces of Hong Kong, Ireland, Finland, the UK and other undisclosed countries. Aardvark; over 120 units in service with 24 countries, including Canada, Egypt, Finland, France, Italy, Jordan, Kuwait, Libya (14), Pakistan, Saudi Arabia, Sweden, UK and the US. Also used by the UN.

Contractor
Penman Engineering Ltd

Pipe fascines

Development
Pipe fascines are a modern development of an ancient combat engineering technique used to provide emergency crossings of gap-type obstacles. They were developed to their current standard by the then Royal Armament Research and Development Establishment, Christchurch (RARDE(C)) and entered service with UK armed forces in 1984.

Description
The basic pipe fascine comprises a bundle of lightweight polythene pipes, held together by a high-tensile steel chain, and in which the inner pipes are designed to enable the fascine bundle to alter its shape to the profile of the gap to be crossed. The inner pipes are held together by load nets and recovery and lifting chains are integral.

In contrast to the earlier wood fascines used until the introduction of the pipe fascine, the polythene unit is much lighter, more durable, does not create dams in wet gaps (hollow pipes) and can be recovered and reused many times. It is also easier to store for long periods, easier to handle and can withstand heavier loads. They are also easy to repair in the field and require no specialist training to maintain/repair.

The standard pipe fascine used with heavy armoured vehicles is the MAXI. This weighs 2,500 kg, is 4.6 m wide and has a diameter of approximately 2.2 m. A single MAXI pipe fascine can fill a gap 5 m wide and 3 m deep, although with additional pipe fascines gaps of up to 15 m in width can be crossed. Pipe fascines have successfully achieved over 3,000 crossings by MBTs at speeds of up to 70 km/h.

MAXI pipe fascines being handled by a Canadian Army Badger Armoured Engineer Vehicle (AEV) (Carl Schulze)   1391344

MAXI pipe fascines stacked on a Chieftain AVRE fitted with a dozer blade (Shaun C Connors)   1043789

Displayed at DVD 2005, a Lightweight General Service Trailer (Shaun C Connors)   1067421

When used to cross wet gaps, MAXI pipe fascines can be used in currents of up to 1.5 m/sec at a water depth of 1.5 m, and up to 5 m/sec at a water depth of up 750 mm. Recovery for re-use from all gap situations takes 15 to 20 minutes, less if a crane is involved.

Operational temperature range is −46 to +44°C. Pipe fascines may be open air stored for up to 15 years in extremes of temperature.

Vehicles such as the British Army's Chieftain AVRE or later Challenger Trojan ETS (Engineer Tank System) can carry up to three MAXI pipe fascines and launch two simultaneously, but many other vehicles, such as bulldozers or dump trucks, can carry and launch them.

There is also a MINI pipe fascine which weighs 210 kg, is 4.6 m wide and has a diameter of approximately 550 mm. The MINI pipe fascine is constructed from six pipes tensioned into a flexible loop by steel chains with integral lifting points. MINI pipe fascines can be carried on the sides of APCs such as the M113 and can be dropped to fill ditches or small gaps for wheeled vehicles, or used in conjunction with MAXI pipe fascines.

Status
In production. In service with the Canadian, Dutch, British, US and possibly other armies.

Contractor
PD Rotomouldings

Reynolds Boughton vehicle bodies

Description
Reynolds Boughton Limited produces a wide variety of vehicle bodies including general service cargo, tipper or special-to-role types.

General service cargo bodies can be manufactured from combinations of welded steel and aluminium, and usually with treated hardwood floors fitted with steel wearing strips. Underfloor winches or body-mounted self-loading cranes can also be fitted. Reynolds Boughton general service bodies are in service with a number of armed forces, predominantly in Asia and the Middle East.

Tipper-type bodies are manufactured from high-tensile steel, and can be fitted with either front-end or under-body tipping gear. Reynolds Boughton tipper-type bodies are in service with a number of armed forces, predominantly in Asia.

In addition to the more conventional general service and tipper-type bodies, Reynolds Boughton also produces special-to-role bodies. A typical example of these would be the 40 8 × 3 m wooden-decked flatbeds mounted on Unipower 8 × 8 vehicles for the British Army's BR90 system, and the mounting of 12 load handling systems of the DROPS/PLS type to a frame-steer all-terrain chassis for an unspecified customer. Full details of the Reynolds Boughton DROPS/PLS system can be found in the Materials handling equipment section.

Status
In production. In service (see text for details).

Contractor
Reynolds Boughton Limited

United States

Aerostar International decoys

Description
Aerostar International Inc designs and manufactures a wide range of full-size inflatable military fighting vehicle replicas for use as decoys or training aids. In addition to aircraft and airfield support vehicles, these include the likes of Scud missile launcher systems, T-72 MBTs, SA-6 Gainful low- to medium-altitude surface-to-air missile system, SA-15 Gauntlet low- to medium-altitude self-propelled surface-to-air missile system, SA-19 Grison low- to medium-altitude surface-to-air missile system and ZSU-23-4 anti-aircraft weapon system. Design features include special radar reflective materials and thermal heating systems for greater authenticity.

Status
In production. In service with the armed forces of the UK (Scud, SA-15 and SA-19) and US.

Contractor
Aerostar International Inc

Aerostar International inflatable SA-6 and Scud missile launcher decoys (Aerostar International)   1129603

General Dynamics Armament and Technical Products specialist vehicle bodies and cargo bed covers

Development
General Dynamics Armament and Technical Products (GDATP) was formed in June 2002 to combine the former General Dynamics Armaments Systems and the four companies of the former Advanced Technical Products Inc: Intellitec, Lincoln Composites, Lunn Industries, and Marion Composites.

Reynolds Boughton Ltd supplied the 8 × 3 m wooden-decked flatbeds for the British Army's BR90 bridging vehicles (BVs) (Shaun C Connors) 1120472

In January 2009, General Dynamics announced that it completed the acquisition of AxleTech International from The Carlyle Group. AxleTech International is a global manufacturer and supplier of axles, axle components, planetary axles, independent suspensions, brakes and aftermarket parts for military vehicles, commercial speciality trucks, and off-highway machines used in the construction, material handling, forestry, mining and agricultural markets. Axletech is now part of the GDATP business unit, which is based in Charlotte, N.C.

Description

Multipurpose Maintenance and Shop Van (MMSV)

GDATP Multipurpose Maintenance and Shop Van (MMSV) was designed for field maintenance personnel. The MMSV, mounted on the US Army's M1079 Light Medium Tactical Vehicle (LMTV) 2.5-ton truck, is fabricated using an aluminium skin, foam and beam core sandwich panels. Standard equipment includes power entry and distribution, lights, blackout provisions, double rear doors, windows, removable steps and provisions for an optional heater and air conditioner. The MMSV is supplied with a base frame for quick mounting and dismounting from the LMTV. Interfaces can be developed to adapt the MMSV for other applications.

Cargo Bed Covers

General Dynamics Armaments and Technical Products (GDATP) has developed a family of general-purpose truck and trailer covers that provide environmental protection for personnel and cargo, plus security, for mission equipment. The bonded aluminium skin/honeycomb enclosures are ground, rail and air transportable when mounted on the HMMWV, M105A2 cargo trailer and M35 and LMTV 2.5- ton trucks. Standard equipment includes mounting provisions, hoist fittings, a personnel access door and air vents. Enhancement kits are optional for electrical and signal entry panels, antenna mountings, internal lighting, windows and a cab access port for the HMMWV cargo bed cover.

Specifications

	Cargo Bed Cover (Type 1)	MMSV
Weight:		
(cover + mounting)	145 kg	1,887 kg
(cover only)	n/avail	1,590 kg
Width:		
(exterior)	2.14 m	2.40 m
(interior)	2.09 m	2.29 m
Height:		
(exterior)	1.61 m	2.17 m
(interior)	1.59 m	2.20 m
(on prime mover)	2.59 m	3.51 m
Length:		
(exterior)	2.10 m	3.78 m
(interior)	2.05 m	3.66 m
Volume:	6.2 m^3	17 m^3
Floor area:	4.2 m^2	8.4 m^2

Status

In production. In service with US Armed Forces.

Contractor

General Dynamics Armament and Technical Products (GDATP)

INVENTORY

INVENTORY

INVENTORY

Introduction

For ease of reference, the inventory is divided into five key sections: armoured engineer vehicles, recovery vehicles (tracked and wheeled), mechanised bridges (tracked and wheeled), light vehicles and trucks. For the purposes of this Inventory, light vehicles have a cross-country payload of no more than 1,500 kg.[1]

In addition to the vehicle type, the following additional information is provided where possible: model number(s), cross-country payload, configuration, number delivered or known to remain in service and the approximate delivery date. If a replacement programme is known to be pending or in progress, this will also be noted. It should be noted that the total number normally includes many variants. In some cases the figures are approximate. This is due to a number of factors such as reduced force levels that have taken place in many armies around the world and vehicles withdrawn from service through accidents or loss.

Some manufacturers provide payload figures for the basic chassis-cab vehicle, while others will quote payload with a standard dropside

troop/cargo body fitted. Unless otherwise stated, quoted payload figures used are for the latter.

[1] Some light vehicles, the Mercedes-Benz G-Class for example, now have a payload (for some applications) in excess of the previously stated 1,500 kg Light vehicle ceiling. However, as the G-Class is clearly a light utility vehicle in design, the type will always be listed under Light vehicles. This same methodology has been applied to a small number of other light vehicles whose payload capability has grown over the years and now brackets the 1,500 kg figure. It should also be noted that the editors have - on rare occasions - used their discretion and omitted certain vehicles from the Light vehicle category despite a 1,500 kg payload. One example would be the Dong Feng EQ2061 (4 × 4), clearly a truck and not a Light vehicle.

Abbreviations used in this section:

ABFS	Amphibious Bridge and Ferry System
AEV	Armoured Engineer Vehicle
AIL	Automotive Industries Limited
ALV	Air-Portable Light Vehicle
ATC	American Truck Company
ATL	Automotive Technik Limited
ATMP	All Terrain Mobile Platform
ARV	Armoured Recovery Vehicle
AVLB	Armoured Vehicle-Launched Bridge
BARV	Beach Armoured Recovery Vehicle
CEV	Combat Engineer Vehicle
DROPS	Demountable Rack Off-Loading and Pick-Up System
FAV	Fast Attack Vehicle
FRS-H	Forward Repair System - Heavy
HEMTT	Heavy Expanded Mobility Tactical Truck
HESV	Heavy Engineering Support Vehicle
HET	Heavy Equipment Transporter
HLVW	Heavy Logistic Vehicle Wheeled
IFAV	Interim Fast Attack Vehicle
KD	Knock-Down
LAV	Light Armoured Vehicle
LET	Light Equipment Transporter
LHS	Load Handling System
LSVW	Light Support Vehicle Wheeled
MDT	Medium Dump Truck
MTT	Medium Tactical Truck
MTVR	Medium Tactical Vehicle Replacement
OUVS	Operational Utility Vehicle System
PFI	Private Finance Initiative
PO	Phasing Out
SLDT	Self-Loading Dump Truck
SDP	Steyr-Daimler-Puch
W	Wrecker

Afghanistan

Recovery vehicles
T-54/T-55 ARV

Mechanised bridges
MTU-20 AVLB
MTU AVLB

Light vehicles
AM General HMMWV (4 × 4) est. >5,000
Ford Ranger (4 × 4) est. >5,000 (from 2005)
Mahindra Bolero (4 × 4) 80 (2004)
Mahindra MM550XD (4 × 4) 40 (2004)
UAZ-469B series 600 kg (4 × 4) (inc 1,600 possibly for UN use) January-March 2004)

Trucks
International 7000 MV (6 × 6) approx. 9,500 (from 2005)
International (various non-tactical) (from 2005)
M35 series 2½ ton (6 × 6) (US surplus)
M809 series 5 ton (6 × 6) (US surplus)
Tata LPTA 713 TC 2,500 kg (4 × 4)
Tata SD 1015 TC (4 × 4) (Field Artillery Tractor)
Ural-375D 4,000 kg (6 × 6)
ZIL-131 3,500 kg (6 × 6)

Weapons and equipment have thus far been provided to Afghanistan's new armed forces on an *ad hoc* basis by many donor nations: (including India (2004), Poland (June 2002) and Romania (December 2002), making the collation of an accurate inventory difficult at best. Procurement for the armed forces has stabilised recently, with generous purchases of Ford Ranger light vehicles and International medium/heavy trucks.

Albania

Recovery vehicles
T-54/T-55 ARV

Light vehicles
G-Class (4 × 4) (20) (2004) (from ELBO, Greece)
UAZ-469B series 600 kg (4 × 4)

Trucks
IFA W-50 3,000 kg (4 × 4) (120) (1993) (ex-German Army, sent as humanitarian aid)
MAN 7,000 kg (4 × 4) (1993) (ex-US Desert Storm)
Steyr (4 × 4?) (20) (ex-Swiss Army)

ZIL-131 3,500 kg (6 × 6)
Assorted designs of Soviet origin

In January 2000, Germany made a donation to Albania that included 58 vehicles. In addition to 20 Steyr trucks Switzerland also contributed 10 light utility vehicles.
Complete reorganisation and re-equipment of the Albanian land forces are required to provide a credible self-defence capability.

Algeria

Recovery vehicles
T-54/T-55 ARV (?)
Kader Fahd 240 RRV(?) (1992)

Light vehicles
AM General HMMWV (approx. 80)
IVECO 40.10 (4 × 4)
Land Rover (4 × 4)
M151 Mutt (4 × 4) (status uncertain)
Mercedes-Benz G-Class 750 kg (4 × 4) (90 delivered)
Nissan Patrol SUV (4 × 4) (Police/paramilitary)
Toyota Land Cruiser (4 × 4) (Police/paramilitary)
UAZ-469B series 600 kg (4 × 4)

Trucks
ASTRA HD66.45 (6 × 6) (130) (mid-1990s) (HET)
ASTRA HET (6 × 6) (110) (late-1990s)
BAZ-5937 (6 × 6) (SA-8 Gecko)
Berliet GBC 8 KT 4,000 kg (6 × 6) (status uncertain)
IVECO EuroTrakker MP720E44WT (6 × 6) (146, final deliveries mid-2006) (HET)
IVECO-Magirus 160-23 ANWM 7,000 kg (6 × 6) (final deliveries 1985, 6,000± delivered, 4,000 remain in service with around 1,300 of these refurbished/rebuilt since 1996 - project ongoing)
IVECO-Magirus 200-23 ANWM 10,000 kg (6 × 6)
IVECO-Magirus 210-32 ANWM 10,000 kg (6 × 6)
IVECO-Magirus 400M33 AS (6 × 6) (600) (1982-83) (HET)
IVECO-Magirus 400M33 AS (designated 330-40 ANWTM) (6 × 6) (90) (1985) (HET)
MAN 14.240 FAEG 6,000 kg (4 × 4); MAN 20.280 DFAEG 10,000 kg (6 × 6), (280 delivered in total) (prior to 1989)
MAN M2000 (4 × 4) (2005) (with Zeppelin mobile field hospital)
MAN F2000 range (post-2001) (small number)

MAN TGA 40.460 (6 × 6) (HET)
Mercedes-Benz Unimog (4 × 4)
Renault TRM 9000 9,000 kg (6 × 6) (500 delivered)
Renault TRM 1200 1,200 kg (4 × 4)
SNVI M120 (4 × 4) (local copy of (possibly) a Berliet design)
SNVI M210/230 (6 × 6) (local copy of Berliet GBC 8 KT)
SNVI HET (6 × 4)
Steyr 680M (1,500-2,000 delivered)

Angola

Recovery vehicles
T-54/T-55

Light vehicles
Beijing Jeep Corporation BJ212/BJ2020 series (4 × 4)
ENGESA EE-12 (4 × 4)
ENGESA EE-15 1,500 kg (4 × 4)
Jeep TJ-L (4 × 4) (4) (2004) (for trials)
Land Rover (4 × 4)
Mahindra Jeep (4 × 4) (early/mid-90s)
Pinzgauer 716 (4 × 4)
UAZ-469B series 600 kg (4 × 4) (incl 250-300 early 2002)
UMM (4 × 4) light vehicle
URO VAMTAC (4 × 4) (Police)

Trucks
BAZ-5937 (6 × 6) (SA-8 Gecko)
DAF YA-4440 4,000 kg (4 × 4) (100, 2003; 50, 2004 - ex-Netherlands MoD)
ENGESA EE-25 2,500 kg (6 × 6)
ENGESA EE-50 5,000 kg (6 × 6) (255) (ENGESA-built Scania T113 HK)
GAZ-66 2,000 kg (4 × 4)
Mercedes-Benz Unimog (4 × 4)
Renault TRM 2000 2,000 kg (4 × 4) (85)
SAMIL (4 × 4) (1997 to 1998) (ex-SANDF)
Star 266 3,500 kg (6 × 6)
Ural-375D 4,000 kg (6 × 6)
ZIL-131 3,500 kg (6 × 6)
ZIL-135 series (8 × 8) (FROG-7)

Portugal pledged logistic equipment in October 2001. Angola does not release meaningful equipment requirements but has tended to buy equipment (certainly armour) from eastern European surplus stocks.

Argentina

Recovery vehicles
SDP 4KH 7FA SB 20 Greif ARV (6)
Mercedes-Benz NG 2626 (6 × 6)
AAVR7 ARV (1) (Marines)

Mechanised bridges
AMX-13 AVLB (withdrawn from service)

Light vehicles
AGRALE Marrua (4 × 4) (18) (2008-2009)
Ford F-100 (approx. 450 remain including around 150 in ambulance role)
Ford Ranger (4 × 4) (not confirmed)
Ford F350 (4 × 4) (small number)
HMMWV (4 × 4) (>50)
Isuzu Trooper (4 × 4) (about 150; command and control roles)
Kia Asia and Kia Besta (4 × 2) (150) (mid 1990s) (used as ambulances and liaison vehicles)
LOHR (now SOFRAME) Fardier FL 500 (4 × 4) (50)
Mahindra Jeep (4 × 4) (marines)
Mercedes-Benz G-Class 750 kg (4 × 4) (1,200 delivered; approx. 900 thought to remain in service)
M151 362 kg Mutt (4 × 4) (approx 90 remain) (ex-US)
M1008 CUCV (4 × 4) (approx 65 remain, retirement pending)
Tata Sumo (4 × 4) (not confirmed)
Toyota Land Cruiser (4 × 4) (50, air force)
Toyota Hi Lux (4 × 4) (air force)
Toyota SUVs (4 × 4) (marines)
VELA Gaucho (4 × 4) (30 believed to be in service; requirement calls for 100-200)
Volvo C202 Laplander (4 × 4) (utility roles)

Trucks
Fiat 619T1
Fiat 697 (HET)
IVECO MP380E42W HET (6 × 6) (9) (2001) (Achleitner trailers)
IVECO Euro range (assorted rigid chassis)
LARC 5 (4 × 4) (10) (marines; amphibious)
Mercedes-Benz 1112 (4 × 4)
Mercedes-Benz 1113 (4 × 4)
Mercedes-Benz 1114 (4 × 4) (army and navy) (as many as 800 Mercedes-Benz 1112, 1113 and 1114 trucks may remain in service, numbers are reducing)
Mercedes-Benz 1518 (4 × 4) (152)
Mercedes-Benz Atego 1720/1720A (4 × 2/4 × 4) (total requirement is 105 1720 and 130 1720A)
Mercedes-Benz U416/421 Unimog (4 × 4) (>1,500) (short and long wheelbase) (overhaul in progress)
M35 series 2,268 kg (6 × 6) (many re-engined)
M35A3 2,268 kg (6 × 6) (approx. 50) (marines)
M52A2 (6 × 6) (re-engined) (tractor trucks, small number for plant and MBT transport)
M54A2 4,536 kg (6 × 6) (re-engined)
URO MT 18.14 2,000 kg (4 × 4) (30) (post-1996)

Australia

Recovery vehicles
M88A2 Hercules ARV (7)
LAV recovery (8 × 8)
ASLAV-F (fitters) (10)
M806A1 light ARV
Mack MC3 heavy wrecker (6 × 6) (64 upgraded vehicles from 2004)
M543/M543A1 W (6 × 6)
M816 W (6 × 6)
Mercedes-Benz Unimog U2450 (6 × 6) (55) (1997 to 1998)

Mechanised bridges
Biber AVLB (5)

Light vehicles
Land Rover Defender 110 (4 × 4) (approx 3,000) (from 1987) (various models)
Land Rover Defender Td5 (4 × 4) (50) (2000 to 2004)

Supacat HMT Nary (4 × 4) (31) (from 2008) (Special Forces)
Toyota (600) (June 2001) (inc 200 HJ78 (70 Series) troop carriers)

Trucks
ISUZU (4 × 4) (36) (2005))
HINO (4 × 4) (106) (2004-2005)
International Harvester SF2670 (6 × 4) HET (ordered 1987) (being withdrawn)
Land Rover 110 heavy-duty (6 × 6) truck (400) (1989 to 1991)
Mack Fleet-Liner CH788RS MC4 (6 × 4) (115) (2000 to 2003)
Mack Model RM6866RS 8,000 kg (6 × 6) (906) (1981-1986)
Mack Model RM6866RS 8,000 kg (6 × 6) (19) (1988)
MAN H76 TGA 41.530 (8 × 8) (14 + 4) (2006-2007) (Drake semi-trailer)
Mercedes-Benz Actros (8 × 8) (19) (2002) (Air Force)
Mercedes-Benz Unimog 1700L 4,000 kg (4 × 4) (1,295 delivered) (1982 to 1987)
Scania P114CB4x4HZ340 4-series (4 × 4) (104) (2002-2004)

Under the ongoing Project Overlander (Land 121) the Land Rover, Mack and Unimog fleets, plus a number of trailers will be replaced.

Austria

Armoured engineer vehicles
SDP 4KH 7FA AVE (19)

Recovery vehicles
M88A1 ARRV(10)
M60/M108 W (6 × 6)
M578 ARRV (21)
SDP 4KH 7FA SB 20 Greif ARV (36)
Steyr 14 M 22 (4 × 4)
Steyr 33 M 37 (6 × 6)

Light vehicles
Mercedes-Benz G-Class 750 kg (4 × 4) (approx 1,200)
Mercedes-Benz Sprinter 313 CDI 1,200 kg 3.5 m WB (4 × 4) (120) (ordered 2002)
Mercedes-Benz Sprinter 316 CDI (4 × 4) (10) (ambulance)
Jeep TJ-L (4 × 4) (1) (2005) (trials)
SDP Pinzgauer (4 × 4 and 6 × 6)

Trucks
MAN F2000 range (4 × 4) (6 × 6) (badged OAF)
MAN Kat 1/SX range (8 × 8) (usually badged OAF) (inc 24 with IAC, delivery pending)
MAN TGM 12.240 (4 × 4) (307) (deliveries from 2007)
OAF 20.320 10,000 kg (6 × 6) (410)
OAF 33.403 DFAS (with 55,000 kg semi-trailer) (HET)
Steyr 480 4,000 kg (4 × 2)
Steyr 680 M 4,500 kg (4 × 4) (replacement pending)
Steyr 680 M3 3,500 kg (6 × 6) (replacement pending)
Steyr 12 S 22 (4 × 2) (51) (2, 000) (driver training vehicle)
Steyr 12 M 18 5,000 kg (4 × 4) (>2,000)
Steyr 12 M 21 5,000 kg (4 × 4)
Unimog U4000 (4 × 4) (268) (delivery from 2006)

Bahrain

Recovery vehicles
M88A1 ARV (4)
M113A2 MRV (4) (1991)

Light vehicles
AM General HMMWV (4 × 4) (277)
Land Rover (4 × 4)
Assorted various SUV types

Trucks
Bedford TM 4-4 8,000 kg (4 × 4)
KAMAZ 43118 (6 × 6) (40) (2003)
Oshkosh HEMTT 9,979 kg (8 × 8)

Bangladesh

Recovery vehicles
Type 653 ARV
T-54/T-55 ARV
Hino (4 × 4)
Renault Kerax (6 × 6) (<10)
M1089A1 (6 × 6) RV (17)

Light vehicles
Beijing Jeep Corporation BJ212/BJ2020 (4 × 4)
Land Rover Defender (4 × 4)
Mahindra CL (4 × 4) (small number supplied)
Mitsubishi Pajero (4 × 4)
Nissan Patrol (4 × 4)
Tata SFC 407 1,000 kg (4 × 4)
Tata Sumo (4 × 4)
Toyota Land Cruiser (4 × 4)

Trucks
ACMAT VLRA (4 × 4) (approx 10) (ambulance)
Bedford MK 4,000 kg (4 × 4)
BMC 235-16 (4 × 4) (24)
BMTF Arunima Bolyan (Isuzu CKD)
DAF CF (no other details)
Dong-Feng EQ2061E
Dong-Feng EQ2082E
Isuzu (4 × 4)
IVECO Trakker (no other details)
MAN TGA 40.410
Mercedes-Benz Unimog
Mercedes-Benz 2026 (6 × 6)
North-Benz 2026 (6 × 6)
Renault GBC (6 × 6) (with LHS)
Renault Kerax (6 × 6) (small quantity)
Renault TRM 180/200 (4 × 4) (approx 500) (1996-1997)
Shaanxi SX2150 (6 × 6)
Shaanxi SX2190 (6 × 6)
Shaktiman 4,000 kg (4 × 4)
Tiema XC2030 (6 × 6)
Western Star WS/M4866S HET (small number) (2000)

Bangladesh is known to be evaluating the SOVAMAG TC10 in the gun tractor role, and the Auverland A3 light vehicle in the 106 mm recoilless rifle carrier role.

Belgium

Armoured engineer vehicles
Leopard 1 AEV (6)

Recovery vehicles
Leopard 1 ARV (20)
M113A1-B-REC ARV (PO)
Pandur (6 × 6) maintenance/recovery (4) (1999)
Renault Kerax (8 × 4) (1999-2000) (27)

Mechanised bridges
Leguan AVLB on Leopard 1 chassis (9)

Light vehicles
IVECO 40.10 1,500 kg (4 × 4) (Gendarmerie)
IVECO LMV (4 × 4) (440 + 120 appliqué protection kits) (deliveries commenced 2006) (optional 2 × 90 vehicles and 30 protection kits)
Land Rover Defender 110 (4 × 4) (status uncertain)
VW Iltis 500 kg (4 × 4) (2,673) (<900 as of 2010 - replacement pending)

Trucks
IVECO EuroTrakker MP410E37H (8 × 4) (24) (1999) (with LHS)
IVECO EuroTrakker MP410E44H (8 × 4) (150) (2004-2006) (with LHS)
IVECO M250.45WM 8,000 kg (6 × 6) (400 + 350 armour kits: 120, 2005; 120, 2006; 120, 2007; 40, 2008) (included an option for 379)

Mercedes-Benz Unimog U1350L (1,666) (4 × 4)
Mercedes-Benz 1017/1017A 5,000 kg (4 × 2/4 × 4) (status uncertain)
MAN 11.136 HA 5,000 kg (4 × 4) (approx. 500; 3,000 delivered)
MAN Kat 1 (8 × 8) (82)
Scania P124 4-series LET (6 × 4)
Scania T144GB6x4NZ530 HET (6 × 4) (26) (2000)
Volvo N10 (6 × 4) (721 delivered, some cast)
Volvo N10 (6 × 6) (500 delivered, some cast)

Belize

Light vehicles
Land Rover (4 × 4)
M1008 CUCV (4 × 4) (US surplus)

Trucks
Bedford MK 4,000 kg (4 × 4)

Following withdrawal of UK forces in 1994, a considerable quantity of surplus equipment was left behind. Details were never released, but this was thought to include Land Rover light vehicles and Bedford MK/MJ and TM trucks.

Benin

Trucks
ACMAT VLRA (4 × 4)

Most of Benin's equipment is French post-colonial or Soviet vintage, and is now obsolete.

Bolivia

Recovery vehicles
SDP 4KH 7FA SB 20 Greif ARV (2)
M578 ARV

Light Vehicles
AM General HMMWV (4 × 4) (30)
Beijing BJ2020VJ (4 × 4)
Jeep CJ-5 (4 × 4)
Jeep CJ-7 (4 × 4)
Kojak FAV (4 × 2) (10 from 60 required known to have been delivered)
M38 Jeep (4 × 4)
M151 Mutt 362 kg (4 × 4)
Suzuki Vitari (4 × 4) (non-tactical roles)
Toyota Hi Lux (4 × 4) (non-tactical roles)
Toyota Land Cruiser (4 × 4)
(other assorted SUV types)

Trucks
Dodge M37 (4 × 4) (small number)
Dong Feng EQ2081 2,500 kg (6 × 6) (2000) (Navy)
ENGESA EE-15 (4 × 4)
ENGESA EE-25 2,500 kg (6 × 6) (597 delivered)
Fiat-IVECO 619
Fiat-IVECO CL75
FAW CA1122J 2,500 kg (34) (2007)
Ford F750 (16) (2005)
IVECO Trakker (6 × 4) (small number) (2007)
Jiefang CA-1091 (C-141) 5,000 kg (4 × 2) (KD form)
M35/M44 series 2,268 kg (6 × 6) (small number)
Mercedes-Benz (from 2008) (from Argentina, USD7 million credit)
Steyr 1491 330.S34 (6 × 6) (30)
Steyr 1491 tractor trucks (20) (not confirmed)
Unimog U416 (4 × 4) (Argentine built)
Unknown (30) (2008) (Venezuelan donation worth USD4 million)

Botswana

Recovery vehicles
ACMAT VLRA (6 × 6)
Mercedes-Benz L2624 (6 × 6)
MOWAG Piranha ARV (8 × 8)
SDP 4KH 7FA SB20 Grief ARV(2)

Light vehicles
Land Rover (4 × 4) (inc 40 2003-2004 from SA)
Toyota (4 × 4)

Trucks
ACMAT VLRA (4 × 4) (at least 344, delivered in batches of 48, 168 and 128); (2000-2004) (up to 200 more 2005-2006)
Bedford TJ 10,000 kg (82) (1990 to 1991)
Bedford MT range (4 × 4) (6 × 6) (>100) (from 1995)
DAF YA 4440 4,000 kg (200-280) (mid-1990s) (ex-Dutch Army)
Mercedes-Benz LA911B/LA1113 (4 × 4) (refurbishment now complete)
Mercedes-Benz Actros (no other details available)
Mercedes-Benz Actros 3348 (6 × 6) (small number) (HET)

Brazil

Recovery vehicles
AAVR7 ARV (1) (Marines)
HART ARV
Mercedes-Benz Unimog (6 × 6) (6 or 7) (with EMPL recovery equipment)
M62 5 ton (6 × 6)
M578 ARV
M113 ARV
SDP 4KH7FA-SB 20 Greif ARV (1)

Bridging systems
XLP-10 AVLB

Light vehicles
AGRALE Marrua (4 × 4) (>100) (deliveries continue)
Bernadini Xingu BT25 500 kg (4 × 4) (small numbers remain)
Bernadini Xingu BT25 BT50 500 kg (4 × 4) (small numbers remain)
ENGESA EE-50 (6 × 6)
ENGESA EE-34 (4 × 4) (approx 30 remain in service)
ENGESA EE-15 1,500 kg (4 × 4) (approx 500 remain)
Ford U50 (4 × 4) (several hundred)
Gurgel (various models) (<100)
Jeep CJ-5 (4 × 4)
Jeep-type designs (various)
JPX (4 × 4) (approx 100)
Land Rover Defender 90 and 130 Crew Cab (4 × 4) (approx 750) (2001 to 2006) (supplied KD)
Toyota Bandeirante (4 × 4) (Marines)
UAI M1-34 750 kg (4 × 4) (small numbers remain)
VLE Gaucho LSV/FAV (deliveries underway)

Trucks
DaimlerChrysler (62) (2002) (no other details available)
ENGESA EE-25 2,500 kg (6 × 6) (>250)
ENGESA EE-50 5,000 kg (6 × 6)
Mercedes-Benz Unimog (4 × 4)
Mercedes-Benz Unimog (6 × 6) (small number)
Mercedes-Benz LAK 1418 (4 × 4) (inc 513, 1999 to 2002)
M35/M44 2,268 kg (6 × 6)
Scania T113 HK (6 × 6)
Tectran (6 × 6) (used with ASTROS saturation rocket system)
TEREX UAI M1-50 5,000 kg (6 × 6) (small number)
Volkswagen 14.210 Worker 5,000 kg (4 × 4) (small number)
Ural 3420 series (4 × 4)
Volvo NL10 (4 × 4) (small numbers)

Brunei

Recovery vehicles
Samson ARV (2)
Reynolds Boughton RV (4 × 4) (6+)

Light vehicles
IVECO 40.10 1,500 kg (4 × 4) (approx 50)
Land Rover ALV 564 kg (4 × 4) (status uncertain)
Land Rover Defender (4 × 4) (since 1999; most recent delivery 2009-2010)

Trucks
Bedford MK 4,000 kg (4 × 4)
Leyland 4,000 kg (4 × 4) (41) (1995 to 1996)
Hicom Handalan II 3,000 kg (4 × 4) (69, 2005)

Bulgaria

Recovery vehicles
T-54/T-55 ARV
MTP-1 ARV
Mercedes-Benz Actros (6 × 6) (EMPL top hamper)

Mechanised bridges
BLG-67 AVLB
TMM-3 (6 × 6)
TMM modified (6 × 6)

Light vehicles
AM General HMMWV (4 × 4) (52) (from 2007)
Mercedes-Benz G-Class (4 × 4) (deliveries ongoing)
UAZ-469B series 600 kg (4 × 4)
UAZ-452 series 800 kg (4 × 4)

Trucks
BAZ specialist chassis
GAZ-66 2,000 kg (4 × 4)
KrAZ-255 (6 × 6)
MAZ specialist chassis
Mercedes-Benz Unimog (4 × 4) (current models)
Mercedes-Benz Actros (various inc (4 × 4) and tractor units)
Mercedes-Benz Zetros (4 × 4)
Ural-4320 series (6 × 6)
ZIL-157 2,500 kg (6 × 6)
ZIL-131 2,500 kg (6 × 6)
ZIL-135 (8 × 8) (FROG-7)

Late 2004, the Bulgarian Army received the first 32 Mercedes-Benz vehicles (from a then estimated 12,900 vehicles) which will replace 15,000 current military vehicles by 2015. The first batch included 15 ×270 CDI G-Class, 6 × 1832A Actros (4 × 4) trucks, some buses, container trucks and ambulances. The EUR256 million contract was awarded in December 2003 to DaimlerChrysler and includes trucks from 1,500 to 8,500 kg, all-terrain vehicles, buses, and personnel carriers. An undisclosed Bulgarian partner is undertaking 70 per cent of the work. As of late-2009 it was reported that total deliveries of all vehicle types were around 400.

Burkina Faso

Light vehicles
Auverland/SAMO (4 × 4) (status uncertain)

Trucks
ACMAT VLRA (4 × 4)
Pegaso 3045 3,000 kg (4 × 4) (33)

Burundi

Light vehicles
Auverland/SAMO (4 × 4)
Citroën A FAF (4 × 4) (status uncertain)

Trucks
Steyr 14 M 22 (4 × 4) (14) (2001)

Cambodia

Recovery vehicles
T-54/T-55 ARV

Light vehicles
UAZ-469B series 600 kg (4 × 4)

Trucks
GAZ-662,000 kg (4 × 4)
IFA L60 LA/PVB 5,000 kg (4 × 4)
MAZ-543 (8 × 8)
ZIL-157 2,500 kg (6 × 6)
ZIL-151 2,500 kg (6 × 6)

In January 1998 it was reported that Cambodia had received (in military aid) 116 military trucks and 70 light utility vehicles from China. In August 1999 the Thai Army was reported to have formally transferred arms and other military equipment to the Cambodian Army. France is reported to have supplied Cambodia with some heavy transport trucks, although no other details are available.

Cameroon

Light vehicles
Auverland/SAMO (4 × 4)
VW Iltis 500 kg (4 × 4)

Trucks
ACMAT VLRA (4 × 4)
Dong Feng EQ1112F8D (4 × 2)
URO MT MT 18.14) (4 × 4) (25) (post 1996)
URO MT MAT 15.14 (4 × 4) (50) (post 1996)
Artillery tractors and limbers; type unknown for around 60 pieces of towed artillery of assorted calibre

Canada

Armoured engineer vehicles
Leopard AEV (Badger) (9)
M113 Engineering Specially Equipped Vehicle (28)

Recovery vehicles
Büffel ARV (2)
Leopard 1 ARV Taurus (8)
M578 ARV
Bison (8 × 8) MRTV (16)
MAN (8 × 8)
Percheron (6 × 6) (124)

Mechanised bridges
Biber AVLB (9)

Light vehicles
AM General HMMWV (4 × 4)
GM LSSV (4 × 4) (861 + 200 contract option) (2003-2005) (part-replaced Bombardier Iltis)
Mercedes-Benz 270 CDI G-Class (4 × 4) (802+ contract option of 357 + 25 additional units) (deliveries from early 2004 to mid-2006) (part-replaced Bombardier Iltis)
Western Star M1500 LSVW 1,500 kg (4 × 4) (2,815)

Trucks
Armoured Heavy Support Vehicle System (AHSVS) (8 × 8) (82 + 13) (2007-2008)
Bombardier MLVW 2,500 kg (6 × 6) (2,769) (1982) (replacement program underway; see note below)
MAN 10,000 kg (8 × 8) (42)
Medium Support Vehicle System (MSVS) (6 × 6) (1,300) (deliveries from mid-2009)
Percheron HLVW 10,000 kg (6 × 6) (1,212) (1988 to 1991)
Steyr 8,000 kg (4 × 4) (not confirmed)
Western Star M4866S HESV 15,000 kg (6 × 6) (65) (1996 to 2002)
Western Star M4900SA HESV 15,000 kg (6 × 6) (25) (2002-2004)
Western Star M4900SA (6 × 4) (5) (2002) (tractor trucks)

In January 2009 Navistar Defense received a USD231 million contract from the Canadian Department of National Defence for up to 1,300 Military Commercial off the Shelf (MILCOTS) vehicles as the first element of the Medium Support Vehicle System (MSVS) project, the Bombardier MLVW replacement program. This program will conclude with the award for the Standard Military Pattern (SMP) trucks and trailers component which is expected to call for in excess of 1,500 units. No date has been set for this award.

Cape Verde

Light vehicles
UMM (4 × 4) light vehicle

Other equipment is likely to be of French or Russian origin.

Central African Republic (CAR)

Light vehicles
Auverland/SAMO (4 × 4)
Sovamag TC-10 1,100 kg (4 × 4) (including 33 during 2004)

Trucks
Sovamag TC 24 2,500 kg (4 × 4) (47) (most recently 20 during 2005 and 5 during 2006)

France withdrew 1,400 troops from the CAR during mid-1998, transferring some equipment to the CAR Army in the process. Reports in late 2002 suggested Libya was about to provide weapons and equipment to the CAR. In 2002, it was announced that France had donated a package of equipment and vehicles worth USD3.2 million to the CAR. The CAR Army and Gendarmerie received USD3.2 million worth of donated military equipment, including 46 military vehicles and communications equipment in January 2004 as part of efforts to re-equip battalions retrained by French instructors to deal with internal security and border patrol.

Chad

Recovery vehicles
Renault Kerax (6 × 6) (2) (2009)

Light vehicles
Auverland/SAMO (4 × 4)
Beijing Jeep Corporation BJ-212/212A (4 × 4)
HMMWV (4 × 4) (20)
Toyota Land Cruiser (4 × 4)

Trucks
ACMAT VLRA (4 × 4)
M35/M44 series 2,268 kg (6 × 6)
Mercedes-Benz (6 × 4)
Renault Kerax (6 × 6) (50) (2009)
Renault Midlum 240.14 (4 × 4) (10) (2009-2010)
Renault Kerax (6 × 6) (44) (2009-2010)
Renault Kerax (8 × 8) (10) (2009-2010)

Chile

Armoured engineer vehicles
Leopard 1 (10) (3 ex-Netherlands, 7 ex-German)
Leopard mine clearing tanks (2)

Armoured Recovery Vehicles
Leopard 1 (7)

Mechanised bridges
Leopard AVLB (8) some ex-Netherlands, some local conversion)

Light vehicles
AIL M-240 Storm 850 kg (4 × 4) (approx 500)
AM General HMMWV (4 × 4) (150) (2006-2009) (some earlier ex-US surplus vehicles have also been supplied)
Daewoo KV-8 (4 × 4) (Marines) (small numbers)
Kia Motors KM450 (4 × 4)
Land Rover Series III 850 kg (4 × 4) (being retired from service)
Land Rover Defender (4 × 4) (101) (2009-2010) (further order pending)

Mahindra (4 × 4) (Marines) (small numbers)
Mitsubishi L200 (4 × 4) (Marines) (small numbers)
M151 Mutt 362 kg (4 × 4) (some US surplus) (being retired from service)
M1008 CUCV (4 × 4) (small numbers)
M1010 CUCV (4 × 4) (small numbers) (ambulance)
Nissan Pajero (4 × 4) (Marines)
Peugeot P4 750 kg (4 × 4) (23) (1991-1992) (status uncertain)

Trucks
AIL M-325 1,800 kg Commandcar (4 × 4) (approx 400)
AIL M-462 (4 × 4)
Dodge M37 (4 × 4)
International (4 × 4) (small number)
IVECO ACL70 (4 × 4) (Navy) (Italian surplus)
IVECO/Fiat TM69 (4 × 4) (Navy) (Italian surplus)
Kia Motors KM250 2,268 kg (6 × 6)
Mack HET (no other details available)
Mercedes-Benz Vario (4 × 4) (ambulance configuration)
Mercedes-Benz Unimog (4 × 4) (>160) (various, short and long wheelbase) (some bought second hand)
Mercedes-Benz Unimog U1300 (4 × 4) (>70)
Mercedes-Benz 1114 (4 × 4)
Mercedes-Benz 1418 LAK (4 × 4)
Mercedes-Benz 1017 (4 × 4) (approx 400)
Mercedes-Benz Atego 1017A (4 × 4)
Mercedes-Benz Atego 1720A (4 × 4) (replacing AIL M-325)
Mercedes-Benz 2632 (6 × 6) (small number)
Mercedes-Benz Actros 3343 (6 × 6)
Mercedes-Benz Actros 3354 (6 × 6) (HET)
M35 series 2,268 kg (6 × 6) (>120) (some US surplus)
Ural-4320 series (6 × 6) (approx 100) (1996) (status uncertain)

The is the stated intention is that HMMWVs will become the standard light vehicle in front line units, with second line units retaining AIL M-240 Storm light vehicles. The recent Land Rover Defender purchases may impact on this statement. The new Mercedes-Benz vehicles (Vario, Atego 1720A, Actros 3343, Actros 3354) will eventually replace the bulk of the older truck fleet).

China

Recovery vehicles
Type 653/653A ARV
Type 85 armoured repair vehicle

Mechanised bridges
Type 84 AVLB
TMM-3 (6 × 6)
KMM (6 × 6)
Type 84A heavy mechanised bridge (8 × 8)

Light vehicles
Beijing BJ-212/212A 425/600 kg (4 × 4)
Beijing BJ-2020S/2020SA 425/600 kg (4 × 4)
Beijing BJ-2022 Brave Warrior (4 × 4) (successor to the BJ-212/2020 series)
Dong Feng EQ2050 1,500 kg (4 × 4) (57) (from 2004)
Nanjing IVECO Motor NJ2045 1,500 kg (4 × 4) (licence-build IVECO 40.10)
Nanjing IVECO Motor NJ2046 1,500 kg (4 × 4)
NORINCO (developed by Wuhan Lingyun Co Ltd) fast attack vehicle (FAV) (4 × 4) (entered service in 2001)
Various locally produced SUV types

Trucks
CA-30 2,500 kg (6 × 6)
Dong Feng EQ1093F6D 5,000 kg (4 × 2) (and earlier variants)
Dong Feng EQ2061E 1,500 kg (4 × 4)
Dong Feng EQ2081 series 2,500 kg (6 × 6)
Dong Feng EQ2100E series 3,500 kg (6 × 6)
Dong Feng EQ2102 series 3,500 kg (6 × 6)

Hongyan CQ 261 8,250 kg (6 × 6) (being, or has been replaced by the SX2190)
HY473 (Type 82) Heavy Equipment Transporter (6 × 6) (numerous other 4 × 4, 6 × 6 and 8 × 8 derivations are available)
Jiefang CA-10 3,540 kg (4 × 2)
Jiefang CA-141 5,000 kg (4 × 2)
Jiefang CA-1091 5,000 kg (4 × 2)
North-Benz 2629A 10,000 kg (6 × 6) (from late-1990s; 1,500 ordered in 2005) (based on Mercedes-Benz designs and understood to be available in 4 × 4 and 8 × 8 derivations)
Shaanxi Automobile Corporation SX2110 3,500 kg (4 × 4) (Steyr technology-based)
Shaanxi Automobile Corporation SX2150 (previously designated SX250) 5,000 kg (6 × 6) (from 1974) (expected to be superceded by the SX2150K and SX2190 in the future)
Shaanxi Automobile Corporation SX2150K 5,000 kg (6 × 6) (essentially a second generation SX250/2150)
Shaanxi Automobile Corporation SX2190 7,000 kg (6 × 6) (Steyr 1491.6 × 6 M technology based) (from the late-90s replaced Shaanqi SX2150, Huanghe JN252, and Hongyan CQ261)
Shaanxi Automobile Corporation SX2300 15,000 kg (8 × 8) (ready for production)
Tai-an Aerospace Special Vehicle TAS5380 (8 × 8) (TEL) (2, 3 and 5 axle versions also in production/service and/or available; usually for specialist roles)
Tiema XC2030 8,000 kg (6 × 6) (suggested figures of around 2,000 per year from 1986) (reverse engineered Mercedes-Benz 2626TM-SC2030)
Wanshan Special Vehicle Factory WS2400 (8 × 8) (similar to MAZ-543) (3, 5, 6 and 7 axle chassis also produced/available)
ZIL-157 2,500 kg (6 × 6) (continued use unlikely)
ZIL-151 2,500 kg (6 × 6) (continued use unlikely)

Colombia

Light vehicles
AGRALE Marrua (4 × 4) (small number, pending)
AIL M-462 (4 × 4) (>300)
AM General HMMWV (4 × 4) (several hundreds)
ARO 750 kg (4 × 4) (status uncertain)
ENGESA EE-15 1,500 kg (4 × 4)
Jeep (various)
Land Rover (4 × 4) (not confirmed)
M715 (4 × 4)
M1008 CUCV (4 × 4)
Various commercial SUV types

Trucks
ENGESA EE-15 1,500 kg (4 × 4)
ENGESA EE-25 2,500 kg (6 × 6)
International CXT (4 × 4) (7) (2006) (with protection)
M35A2 2.5-ton (6 × 6)

A number of essentially commercial medium truck designs including the Chevrolet/Isuzu NPR, Mazda T45 and Nissan U41 are in service. Heavy transport trucks include Chevrolet B70, C70 and Kodiak commercial models

Congo-Brazzaville

Light vehicles
Auverland/SAMO (4 × 4)
UMM (4 × 4) light vehicle

No official requirements have been made public.

Croatia

Recovery vehicles
M-84A1 ARV
WZT-3 ARV

Mechanised bridges
MT-55A AVLB

Cuba

Recovery vehicles
T-54/T-55 ARV

Mechanised bridges
MTU-20 AVLB
TMM (6 × 6)
KMM (6 × 6)

Light vehicles
UAZ-469B series 600 kg (4 × 4)
GAZ-69/69A 500 kg (4 × 4)

Trucks
GAZ-51 2,000 kg (4 × 2)
GAZ-63 2,000 kg (4 × 4)
GAZ-66 2,000 kg (4 × 4)
KrAZ-214 (6 × 6)
KrAZ-255/255B (6 × 6)
Ural 375D (6 × 6)
Ural 4320 series (6 × 6)
ZIL-157 2,500 kg (6 × 6)
ZIL-151 2,500 kg (6 × 6)
ZIL-135 Series (8 × 8) (FROG-7)

Cyprus

Recovery vehicles
BREM-L (1)
AMX-30D ARV (2) (1988 to 1990)
Steyr 19 S 25 (4 × 4)
Steyr 32 S 29 (6 × 6)
Steyr 14 M 22 (4 × 4)

Light vehicles
Land Rover (4 × 4)
Mercedes-Benz/ELBO G-Class 750 kg (4 × 4) (supplied via Greece)
SDP Pinzgauer (6 × 6) (possibly 4 × 4 also)
Toyota Land Cruiser (4 × 4) (non-tactical roles)

Trucks
ACMAT VLRA (>120)
Bedford MT range (4 × 4) (15) (1995) (fire appliance bodies)
GAZ-66 (4 × 4)
Mercedes-Benz Unimog (4 × 4)
Oshkosh M911 HET (6 × 6) (ex-Greece)
Renault TRM 10000 10,000 kg (6 × 6) (small number)
Steyr/ELBO 14 M 14 8,000 kg (4 × 4) (approx 425) (supplied via Greece)
Steyr/ELBO 24 M 12,000 kg (6 × 6)
Steyr 40 M 60 HET (6 × 6) (possibly short-term loan from Greece)
Ural 375D(?) (6 × 6) (BM-21 Grad MRS and possibly other applications)

Czech Republic

Recovery vehicles
MT-55 ARV
VT-72B ARV
VT-55A ARV
VPV ARV (BMP-1 chassis)
WPT-TOPAS ARV (OT-62A chassis)
AD-90 (6 × 6)
AV-15 (8 × 8)

Mechanised bridges
MT-55A AVLB
AM-50 (6 × 6)

Light vehicles
AM General HMMWV (4 × 4) (26) (borrowed for Afghan mission)
AM General HMMWV (4 × 4) (5) (2010)
IVECO LMV (4 × 4) (approx 140) (from 2007, deliveries continue)
Land Rover Defender (4 × 4) (>600) (1996-2007)
UAZ-452 series 800 kg (4 × 4) (approx 150)
UAZ-469B series 600 kg (4 × 4) (approx 950)

Trucks
GAZ-66 (4 × 4) (replacement pending)
Praga V3S 3,000 kg (6 × 6) (approx 1,500) (replacement programme running)
ROSS R210 (6 × 6) (14) (1997 to 1999)

TATRA 148 14,580 kg (6 × 6) (approx 190)
TATRA T810 (6 × 6) (556 ordered) (2007-2010)
TATRA 813 (6 × 6) (numbers reducing)
TATRA 813 (8 × 8) (numbers reducing)
TATRA 815 5,800 kg (4 × 4)
TATRA 815 8,000 kg (6 × 6)
TATRA 815 10,000 kg (8 × 8)
TATRA 815 ARMAX family (4 × 4) (6 × 6) (8 × 8) (2003 to 2008)
TATRA T815-7 (6 × 6)

Democratic Republic of Congo

Recovery vehicles
M816 W (6 × 6)

Light vehicles
Auverland/SAMO (4 × 4)
Land Rover (4 × 4) (not confirmed)
M151 Mutt 362 kg (6 × 6)
Toyota Land Cruiser (4 × 4)

Trucks
ACMAT VLRA (4 × 4)
M35/M44 series 2,268 kg (6 × 6)
M809 series 4,536 kg (6 × 6)
MAN (4 × 4) (possibly 11.136 5,000 kg or similar)
Russian Ural and/or Zil (unconfirmed)
SAMIL 50 5,000 kg 4 × 4) (surplus SANDF)
SAMIL 100 10,000 kg (6 × 6) (surplus SANDF)
SX2150 (6 × 6)
TATRA T815 (8 × 8) (MLRS)

Denmark

Recovery vehicles
M578 ARV (24 delivered, small numbers remain)
Leopard 1 bergepanzer (14)
IVECO ASTRA M320E/W (8 × 8) (5) (recovery/crane, air force/navy)
IVECO EuroTrakker MP410E42W (8 × 8) (16) (from 1998)
MAN 35.464 VFAK (8 × 8) (4) (from 2002)

Mechanised bridges
Biber AVLB (10)

Light vehicles
HMMWV M1045 TOW (4 × 4) (30) (1999) (converted to armed light strike/recce configuration)
Mercedes-Benz G-Class 750 kg (4 × 4) (approx. 2,000) (some cast or possibly cascaded)
Mercedes-Benz G-Class 270 CDI/280 CDI (4 × 4) (>400) (deliveries continue)
Mercedes-Benz Sprinter 316 CDI (4 × 4) (7) (2006) (air force, ambulance)
Supacat HMT 4x4E (4 × 4) (>15) (2006-2007) (SRV-type)
Toyota Hilux (4 × 4) (15) (from 1994)
Toyota Land Cruiser VX100 (4 × 4) (30; 20 army, 10 air force) (protected; used in Afghanistan)
VW Transporter T5 (4 × 4) (>150) (from 2005)

Trucks
IVECO Magirus 110-16 AWM 5,000 kg (4 × 4) (>1,000) (Danish designation is 168 M 11 FAL) (numbers reducing)
IVECO Magirus 110-17 AWM 5,500 kg (4 × 4) (est. 40, ex-German Army)
(EuroTrakker numbers quoted are deliveries, in some cases vehicles have been cast)
IVECO EuroTrakker MP260E37H (6 × 4/6 × 6)
Tractor truck (6 × 4) (7) (from 1994)
fuel tanker (6 × 4) (10) (from 1996)
dump truck (6 × 4) (10) (from 1997)
tractor truck (6 × 6) (10) (from 1994)
fuel tanker (6 × 6) (2) (from 1996)
DALLADS (6 × 6) (4) (from 1996)
with HMF 1113 K1 materials handling crane (6 × 6) (51 from 1996)
with HMF 953K2 materials handling crane (6 × 6) (16 from 1996)
with HMF 823K2 materials handling crane (6 × 6) (76 from 1994)
cargo (6 × 6) (184 from 1994)

IVECO EuroTrakker MP380E42W (6 × 6) (10 from 1996) (tractor truck)
IVECO EuroTrakker MP410E42W (8 × 8) (2) (1999) (crane trucks for use with mobile field hospitals)
IVECO EuroTrakker MP410E42W (8 × 8) (1) (1999)
IVECO EuroTrakker MP410E42W (8 × 8) (21 from 1999) (LHS)
(MAN numbers (excluding HX/SX) quoted are deliveries, in some cases vehicles have been cast)
MAN 8.136 3,000 kg (4 × 4) (989) (1985 to 1991) (some cast, some cascaded - see note)
MAN 10.185 LAEC (4 × 4) (24) (2001 to 2002) (Home Guard)
MAN 16.232FAE (4 × 4) (approx. 30) (air force)
MAN 18.224 LAC (4 × 4) (1) (8,000 litre specialist helicopter refueller)
MAN 18.225 LAEC (4 × 4) (approx. 70) (from 1998)
MAN 19.403 FAC (4 × 4) (2) (fuel tanker, navy)
MAN 26.372 DFAE (6 × 6) (2) (from 1993) (fuel tanker)
MAN 27.314 DFAEC (6 × 6) (approx. 250) (from 2001)
MAN 33.464 DFLT (6 × 4) (11) (2001 to 2002) (tractor truck)
MAN TGA 33.480 BLS (6 × 4) (10) (from 2005) (tractor truck)
MAN 40.400 DFT (6 × 6) HET (1982) (24)
MAN 35.464 VFAK (8 × 8) (approx. 50 (from 2001)
MAN HX (6 × 6/8 × 8) (approx. 200) (deliveries from early 2006)
MAN SX (6 × 6/8 × 8) (30) (deliveries from early 2006)
Mercedes-Benz Unimog U416 (4 × 4) (numbers reducing)
Mercedes-Benz 1831SK-AK (4 × 4) (approx. 18) (air force)
Mercedes-Benz Unimog L1530/37 (4 × 4) (56) (Stinger Groups)
Mercedes-Benz Unimog U2150/38 (4 × 4)
MOWAG DURO IIIP (6 × 6) (29) (2008-2009) (ambulance, protected)

Denmark has, in recent years, donated surplus trucks to the Balkan states. These donations are known to have included two Mercedes-Benz 2632 crash tenders to Lithuania (2004), 58 Mercedes-Benz Unimog 416 to Lithuania (2004), 62 Land Rovers to Lithuania, 73 Mercedes-Benz Unimog 416 to Latvia (2004) and 94 Mercedes-Benz Unimog 416 to Estonia (2004). In 2006, Denmark sold 100 surplus MAN 8.136 3,000 kg (4 × 4) to Iraq for a peppercorn sum.

Djibouti

Light vehicles
AM General HMMWV (4 × 4) (18)
Mahindra Scorpio (4 × 4)
Toyota Land Cruiser (4 × 4)

Trucks
ACMAT VLRA (4 × 4)
M34/M44 series 2,268 kg (6 × 6)
M929A1 4,536 kg (6 × 6) (89)
MAN (4 × 4) (commercial pattern, 1980s vintage)

Dominican Republic

Light vehicles
Carolina Growler UV100DB (4 × 4) (80) (2002) (rebuilt M151A2 Mutt)
Carolina Wolverine Model 450 (4 × 4) (40) (2002) based on rebuilt M151A2 Mutt)
Land Rover (4 × 4) (non-tactical roles)
Nissan Patrol ML-6 (4 × 4) (non-tactical roles)
Polaris ATV (6 × 6) (several dozen)
URO VAMTAC 1,500 kg (4 × 4) (60 - 40, 2000; 20, 2001)

Trucks
M35A2 2,268 kg (6 × 6) (90) (ex-US)
Pegaso 3055 6,000 kg (6 × 6) (12) (1990s)

URO MT 15.14, MT 18.14 and MT 18.16 2,000 kg (4 × 4) (100) (post-1996)

Ecuador

Light vehicles
AGRALE Marrua AM10/AM20 (4 × 4) (30) (2008-2009)
AIL M-240 Storm (4 × 4)
AM General HMMWV (4 × 4) (approx. 360) (some US surplus)
GM CUCV II (4 × 4)
Land Rover Series III 850 kg (4 × 4)
M38 (4 × 4) (small number may remain in use)
M151 Mutt 362 kg (4 × 4)
Toyota Land Cruiser (4 × 4) (non-tactical roles)
Toyota Hilux (4 × 4) (non-tactical roles)

Trucks
Engesa EE-25 2,500 kg (6 × 6) (24)
KaMAZ 5320 series
Mercedes-Benz U416 (4 × 4) (short and long wheelbase)
Mercedes-Benz 1418 LAK (4 × 4) (acquired from Brazil)
M34/M44 series 2,268 kg (6 × 6)
M939 series 4,536 kg (6 × 6) (>100, US surplus)
Ural 375D 4,000 kg (6 × 6)
Zil-131 3,500 kg (6 × 6)

Egypt

Recovery vehicles
T-54/T-55 ARV
M88A1 ARV (221)
M88A2 ARV (87) (local assembly)
M113 ARV
M578 ARV (43)
BMR 3560.55 ARV (6 × 6)

Mechanised bridges
MTU-20 AVLB
MTU AVLB
KMM (6 × 6)

Light vehicles
AM General HMMWV (4 × 4) (est. 1,700 in service, 500 pending)
IVECO 40.10 1,500 kg (4 × 4) (100-150)
Jeep AM 720 1,135 kg (4 × 4) (1,965 inc J-20) (production ceased 1987)
Jeep J-20 (4 × 4) (1,965 inc AM 720) (production ceased 1987)
Jeep CJ-6, CJ-7, CJ-8 (4 × 4) (11,776) (1977 to 1986)
Jeep YJ-L (4 × 4) (1988 to 1998) (3,199)
Jeep TJ-L (4 × 4) (2003 onwards) (around 7,000 required)
Land Rover 1,000 kg (4 × 4) (status uncertain)
M151 Mutt 362 kg (4 × 4)
Mercedes-Benz G-Class (4 × 4) (2,900) (no confirmation of numbers)
Santana Model 88 500 kg (4 × 4)
Santana Model 109 1,000 kg (4 × 4)
Toyota Land Cruiser (4 × 4)
UAZ-469B 600 kg (4 × 4)
UAZ-452D 800 kg (4 × 4)

Trucks
FAP 1118 (4 × 4) (1,250) (no confirmation of delivery or numbers)
FAP 2026(6 × 6) (860) (no confirmation of delivery or numbers)
FAP 2228 (6 × 6) (650) (no confirmation of delivery or numbers)
GAZ-66 2,000 kg (4 × 4)
International Harvester 5070 Series (HETS)
IVECO-Magirus 75-13 AWM 2,500 kg (4 × 4)
IVECO-Magirus 160-23 ANWM 7,000 kg (or similar model) (6 × 6)
IVECO Euro range (small numbers)
KaMAZ-5320 series (since 2001)
KrAZ-255B 7,500 kg (6 × 6)
KrAZ-260 series 9,000 kg (6 × 6)
(Egypt is understood to have received around 3,000 KrAZ trucks since 1961, including close to 400 between 1996 and 1998)

KrAZ-6322 (6 × 6) (250 from 1999; no confirmation of numbers)
KrAZ-64431 (6 × 4) (at least 18 from 2006) (tractor truck)
MAZ-543 series (8 × 8)
Mercedes-Benz Unimog (4 × 4)
M35 series (6 × 6)
M54 series (6 × 6)
M939 series (6 × 6)
NASR 4,000 kg (4 × 4)
Oshkosh MTT (4 × 4) (6 × 6) (30) (from 2007) (further deliveries likely)
Oshkosh MTVR (6 × 6) (handful; evaluation?)
Oshkosh M1070 HET (8 × 8) (240) (further deliveries likely)
Oshkosh HEMTT 9,979 kg (8 × 8) (est. 100)
Pegaso 3046/10 5,000 kg (4 × 4) (11,650 delivered)
Renault TRM 9000 9,000 kg (6 × 6) (50 delivered)
Steyr 17 M 29 7,000 kg (4 × 4)
Steyr 24 M 12,000 kg (6 × 6)
Ural-375D 4,000 kg (6 × 6)
Ural-4320 series (6 × 6)
ZIL-131 3,500 kg (6 × 6)
ZIL-157 2,500 kg (6 × 6)
ZIL-135 (8 × 8) (FROG-7 and support)

El Salvador

Light vehicles
AIL M-240 Storm 850 kg (4 × 4) (38)
CJ-8 Jeep (4 × 4) (commercial M38)
M37 680 kg (4 × 4) (most have probably been used as donors for Cashuat APCs)
M151 Mutt 362 kg (4 × 4)

Trucks
M35/M44 series 2,268 kg (6 × 6)
M809 series 4,536 kg (6 × 6)
MAN 630 Series 5,000 kg (4 × 4)

Equatorial Guinea

Recovery vehicles
T-54/T-55 ARV (?)

No requirements have been made public

Ethiopia

Light vehicles
Toyota Land Cruiser (4 × 4)

Trucks
Ural-4320 series (4 × 4)
Ural-4320 series (6 × 6)
ZIL-157 2,500 kg (6 × 6)
ZIL-151 2,500 kg (6 × 6)

Mirroring Ethiopian armoured vehicle and artillery stocks, it must be assumed that a sizeable logistic fleet of Soviet-sourced equipment remains in service.

Finland

Armoured Engineer Vehicles
Heavy Mine Breaching Vehicle (6)

Recovery vehicles
T-54/T-55 ARV
Scania P113HK (6 × 6) (2)

Mechanised bridges
Leopard 2 AVLB (trials)
MTU-20 AVLB
MTU AVLB

Light vehicles
Land Rover Defender (4 × 4) (345)
Mercedes-Benz G-Class 750 kg (4 × 4) (175)
Mercedes-Benz 416 CDI Sprinter (4 × 4)
Toyota Land Cruiser (4 × 4) (approx. 200) (Military Police)

Trucks

GAZ-66 2,000 kg (4 × 4) (approx. 100)
KrAZ-255B/255B1 (6 × 6) (<300)
KrAZ-260 (6 × 6) (small number)
Mercedes-Benz Unimog (4 × 4) (88)
Mercedes-Benz Atego (4 × 4) (approx. 120) (from 2001)
Scania SBA 111 (6 × 6) (1)
Scania R144 HET (8 × 4) (6) (HET)
Scania 4 Series (approx. 180) (1999-2007)
Scania (approx. 150) (2007-2010)
Sisu SA110 3,500 kg (4 × 4)
Sisu A45 3,050 kg (4 × 4) (handful)
Sisu A2045 5,000 kg (4 × 4) (234 + optional 240) (2009-2010)
Sisu A2045 5,000 kg (4 × 4) (40) (2010-2014)
Sisu SA130 6,500 kg (4 × 4) (130)
Sisu SA150 6,500 kg (4 × 4) (237)
Sisu SA151 6,500 kg (4 × 4) (<100)
Sisu SK171 (4 × 4) (small numbers)
Sisu SK181 (4 × 2) (4 × 4) (6 × 2) (138)
Sisu SK192 (4 × 4) (36)
Sisu SA240 10,000 kg (6 × 6) (93)
Sisu SA241 10,000 kg (6 × 6) (118)
Sisu SM300 HET (8 × 4) (small numbers)
Sisu EIIT 15,000 kg (6 × 6) (215) (1998 to 2007)
Sisu EIIT 19,750 kg (8 × 8) (70) (2001 to 2006)
Sisu E13TP (6 × 6) (30) (2010-2014)
Sisu E13TP (8 × 8) (72) (2009-2014)
Sisu E13TP (10 × 10) (9) (2006-2008) (bridgelayer)
TATRA T-815 (8 × 8) (ex-East German)
Ural-375D (6 × 6) (small numbers)
Ural-4320 (6 × 6) (small numbers)
ZIL-131 3,500 kg (6 × 6) (>350)
ZIL-157 2,500 kg (6 × 6) (small numbers)

Finland has an ongoing requirement for a new vehicle of the Bv-206/BvS-10 all-terrain type.

France

Armoured engineer vehicles
AMX-30 EBG (71, 54 upgraded)

Recovery vehicles
ACMAT Type TPK 6.40 WRT
AMX-30D ARV (134)
Leclerc ARV (20)
Berliet TBC 8 KT W (6 × 6)
Renault TRM 10,000 CLD (6 × 6) (300) (delivery 1992 to 1999)
Renault Kerax (8 × 4) (17)

Mechanised bridges
EFA (4 × 4) (39)
Gillois Series 2 (60)
PAA (4 × 4) (55) (1974 to 1978)
PTA Modular Assault Bridge (18)

Light vehicles
Auverland Type A3 (4 × 4) (around 3,000) (all services incl. Gendarmerie)
Auverland Type A3F FAV (4 × 4) (106 VAL, 148 VAC) (airborne forces)
Land Rover Defender (4 × 4) (>320) (until 2006) (up to 600 over 5 years; contract award late 2006)
Panhard VPS (Le Vehicle Patrouille SAS) (4 × 4) (41 + 10) (2006-2007) (based on MB G-Class)
Peugeot P4 750 kg (4 × 4) (13,500) (1983 to 1992) (additional batch of 30 ordered 1994) (all services incl. Gendarmerie) full (replacement from approx. 2012)
Renault B110 (4 × 4) (297) (from 1994) incl. 100 Gendarmerie)
SOVAMAG TC-10 1,100 kg (4 × 4) (Air Force (342)) (Army (68)) (1999)
Toyota Land Cruiser (4 × 4) (small number)

Trucks
ACMAT VLA (4 × 4) (6 × 6) (41) (mid-1990s)
ACMAT VLRA (4 × 4) (6 × 6) (800-1,000)
Mercedes-Benz Unimog (4 × 4) (approx. 40)
Berliet GBC 8 KT 4,000 kg (6 × 6) (17,000 delivered, 5,560 to be upgraded)
Berliet GBU 15 6,000 kg (6 × 6) (status uncertain)
Renault GBC 180 5,000 kg (6 × 6) (designation of refurbished GBC 8 KT)

Renault KERAX (various configurations incl. 4 × 4, 6 × 6 and 8 × 4) (around 400 ordered/delivered as of January 2010)
Renault G 290.26 and G340.26 (6 × 4) (Véhicule de Transport Logistique (VTL)) (5,550 delivered) (replacement programme underway)
Renault R 390 HET (6 × 4)
Renault TRM 200-13 (approx. 150)
Renault TRM 1200 1,200 kg (4 × 4) (small numbers may remain in service)
Renault TRM 2000 2,000 kg (4 × 4)
Renault TRM 4000 4,000 kg (4 × 4) (7,000 delivered)
Renault TRM 10 000 10,000 kg (6 × 6) (2,500) (1987 to 1999)
Renault TRM 700-100 HET (6 × 6) (179)
Renault CBH series (6 × 4) (6 × 6)
Renault Sherpa 5 5,000 kg (6 × 6) (from 2009)
Scania R114CB6x6HZ340 (6 × 6) (242) (2003-2005) (10,000 litre tankers)
Scania R340CB6x6HHZ (6 × 6) (10) (2006)
Scania P340 (6 × 6) (161) (2008-2009) (150 dump trucks (22 converted to cargo post-delivery), 11 12,000 litre water tankers and 23 interchangeable armoured cabs)
Scania R340 (6 × 6) (11) (2006) (with armoured cabs, for use with CNIM PFM Mle F1 floating bride and ferry)
Scania T-series (6 × 4) (12) (heavy tractor trucks)
Sisu 480-35 E-Tech HET (6 × 4) (110) (from 2005)
SUMB MH 600 BS 1,500/3,000 kg (4 × 4) (1,000 refurbished by Renault)

The P4 fleet is scheduled for replacement from around 2012 onwards, however a driveline upgrade may take place in the interim. Small numbers of P4s are thought to have been cascaded to other nations. France's current major truck replacement programme is the Porteur Polyvalente Terrestre (PPT), a programme to procure around 2,500 trucks that will replace the current VTL (Véhicule de Transport Logistique) logistic package.

Gabon

Recovery vehicles
Mercedes-Benz Actros model 3331 (6 × 6) (EMPL top hamper)

Light vehicles
Achleitner Mantra (4 × 4) (approx 40) (post 2000)
Mercedes-Benz G-Class (4 × 4) (possibly Peugeot P4 incorrectly identified)
Peugeot P4 750 kg (4 × 4) (75)
ENGESA EE-15 1,500 kg (4 × 4)

Trucks
ACMAT VLRA (4 × 4)
ENGESA EE-25 2,500 kg (6 × 6)
Mercedes-Benz Atego range (4 × 4) (small numbers including model 1317)
Mercedes-Benz Actros 1831 (4 × 4)
Sovamag TC 24 2,500 kg (4 × 4) (2)

Gambia

Light vehicles
M151 Mutt 362 kg (4 × 4)

Trucks
ACMAT VLRA (4 × 4)

The Gambian Army is only around 800-strong.

Germany

Armoured engineer vehicles
Pionierpanzer 2 Dachs (149)

Recovery vehicles
Büffel ARV (75)
Leopard 1 ARV (440)
M88A1 ARV (2)
Faun BKF 30.40 RV (8 × 8) (10)
Faun RTF 15 M RV (4 × 4)
Faun RTF 30-3 M RV (6 × 6)

Mechanised bridges
Biber AVLB (104)
M3 (4 × 4) (30)
PSB 2 AVLB (35 on order)

Light vehicles
VW Iltis 500 kg (4 × 4) (8,800 delivered) (many cascaded to other nations; no more than 200 remain)
KMW Mungo (4 × 4) (388) (contract awarded early 2004)
Land Rover Discovery (4 × 4) (<10) (2006)
Mercedes-Benz G-Class 750 kg (4 × 4) (12,000)
Mercedes-Benz G-Class 270 CDI (4 × 4) (from 2003)
Mercedes-Benz G-Class 280 CDI (4 × 4) (from 2007)
Mercedes-Benz G-Class (RLS LIV) (4 × 4) (21) (2004)
Mercedes-Benz Sprinter (4 × 4)
Multicar (4 × 4) (ex-NVA)
RLS LIV (SO) (4 × 4) (21) (2003) (G-Class-based)

Trucks
FAUN SLT 50-2 (8 × 8) HET (324 delivered 1976-79)
FAUN SLT 50-3 (8 × 8) HET (new designation of SLT 50-2 following upgrade)
FAUN FS 42.75/42 (8 × 6) HET (49 delivered from 1989)
IVECO Magirus 75-13 2,500 kg (4 × 4) (numbers reducing)
IVECO Magirus 110-16 5,000 kg (4 × 4) (numbers reducing)
IVECO Magirus 110-17 5,000 kg (4 × 4) (4 × 2) (numbers reducing)
IVECO 100E21W EuroCargo 2,000 kg (4 × 4) (approx. 260) (2006-2009) (BwFuhrparkService)
IVECO Euro 140E24W EuroCargo 5,000 kg (4 × 4) (approx. 260) (2006-2009) (BwFuhrparkService)
IVECO Trakker/EuroTrakker (from 1996) (deliveries continue in batches, usually specialist or fuel-related applications)
MAN TGA 18.350 (4 × 2) (592) (2006) (driver training fleet; BwFuhrparkService)
MAN TGA 18.360 BB (4 × 4) (500) (ordered/delivered 2007; BwFuhrparkService)
Mercedes-Benz Unimog (4 × 4) various models with some estimates giving an in-service figure as high as 18,000
Mercedes-Benz Vario 2,500 kg (4 × 4)
Mercedes-Benz Model 1017 5,450 kg (4 × 2)
Mercedes-Benz Model 1017 5,450 kg (4 × 4) (between 1977-1987 a total of 15,000 MB 1017 were delivered, 95% of these (4 × 4))
Mercedes-Benz Atego range (4 × 4) (699) (2006-2009) (BwFuhrparkService)
Mercedes-Benz Axor range (4 × 4) (876) (2008) (BwFuhrparkService)
MAN Kat 1 (1977 to 1983), Kat 1A1 (1985 to 1987) 5,000 kg (4 × 4)
MAN Kat 1 (1977 to 1983), Kat 1A1 (1985 to 1987) Kat 1A1.1 (1992 to present) 7,000 kg (6 × 6)
MAN Kat 1 (1977 to 1983) 10,000 kg (8 × 8)
(by 1983 the Bundeswehr had received a total of 8,617 Kat 1 vehicles)
MAN Kat 1A1 (1985 to 1987) Kat 1A1.1 (1992 to present) 15,000 kg (8 × 8)
(From 1988 the Bundeswehr ordered 1,100 Cat 1A1 models) (from 1993 the Bundeswehr ordered around 500 MAN Category 1 A1.1 trucks)
(MAN Kat 1A1.1 trucks are now known as the SX range)
(Figures released in 2008 stated that around 6,500 Kat 1 trucks remained in service. A program to replace this fleet is currently running)
MAN FX range of (4 × 4) and (6 × 6) chassis (small numbers)
MAN LX range of (4 × 4) and (6 × 6) chassis (small numbers)

MAN (various)
MAN HX 41.680 (HX81) HET (8 × 8) (2) (2009) (optional 34)
MOWAG DURO IIIP (Yak) (6 × 6) (30 - 2003-2005; 108 ordered for delivery from October 2006)

Ghana
Recovery vehicles
Steyr 19 S 25 (4 × 4)
Steyr 32 S 29 (6 × 6)
Steyr 14 M 22 (4 × 4)

Light vehicles
Intrall Honker (4 × 4) (200) (2004) (not confirmed)
Mahindra Jeep (4 × 4)
SDP Pinzgauer (4 × 4)

Trucks
Dong Feng (4 × 4) (possibly EQ1093
SAMIL 50 5,000 kg (4 × 4) (ex-SANDF supplied via military surplus dealer)
SAMIL 100 10,000 kg (6 × 6) (ex-SANDF supplied via military surplus dealer)
Steyr 17 M 29 7,000 kg (4 × 4)

Ghana is known to have considered the Achleitner Mantra (4 × 4) in cargo/troop carrying configuration and the unconfirmed purchase of Intrall Honker light vehicles in 2004 could have been to meet this requirement.

Greece
Recovery vehicles
Leopard 1 ARV (43)
Leopard 2 Büffel ARV (12)
M48 ARV (3)
M88A1 ARV (95)
M578 ARV (113)
Oshkosh MTVR (6 × 6)
Oshkosh M984A1 (8 × 8) (8)
Steyr 33 M 97 (6 × 6)
Steyr 14 M 22 (4 × 4)

Light vehicles
AM General HMMWV (4 × 4) (654 from 1999)
Mercedes-Benz/ELBO (4 × 4) (15,500 produced) (some transferred to Cyprus)

Trucks
BAE Systems FMTV (12)
GAZ-66 2,000 kg (4 × 4) (ex-German Army surplus)
IFA W50 (4 × 4) (ex-East German Army surplus)
IFA Robur LO2002A 2,000 kg (4 × 4) (ex-East German Army surplus)
KamAZ 43101 (6 × 6) (used with TOR M1 system)
MAN SX range 15,000 kg (8 × 8) (24) (2002) (fitted with Atlas LHS)
MAN Cat 1 7,000 kg (6 × 6) (24) (2002)
M35/M44 series (6 × 6) (small number)
Oshkosh MTVR (6 × 6) (73 between 2004-2006)
Oshkosh M911 HET (6 × 6) (87)
Oshkosh HEMTT (8 × 8) (56)
Scania PH-113K (6 × 6) (87)
Steyr/ELBO 680 M 4,500 kg (4 × 4)
Steyr/ELBO 680 M3 3,500 kg (6 × 6)
Steyr/ELBO 14 M 14 8,000 kg (4 × 4) (approx. 850)
Steyr/ELBO 14 M 22 8,000 kg (4 × 4) (80) (initial production replacement for 14 M 14)
Steyr/ELBO 26 S 28 (6 × 6) (250 approx.) (some delivered to Cyprus)
Steyr/ELBO 26 S 31 MET (6 × 6)
Steyr/ELBO 33 M 41 (6 × 6) (37: 36 tractor trucks, 1 recovery) (initial production replacement for 26 S 28 and 26 S 31)
Steyr 40 M 60 HET (6 × 6) (66) (deliveries concluded 2003)
TATRA T815CA (16,000 litre tankers) (24) (ex-East German Army surplus)
TATRA T815 VVN.20.235 8,000 kg (6 × 6) (ex-East German Army surplus)
TATRA T815 VT 26.265 10,000 kg (8 × 8) (ex-East German Army surplus)

Ural 4320 series 4,000 kg (6 × 6) (used with TOR M1 system)

Grenada
Light vehicles
CUCV (4 × 4) (status uncertain)

Guatemala
Light vehicles
M151 Mutt 362 kg (4 × 4) (approx. 200) (refurbished ongoing)
Mercedes-Benz G-Class 750 kg (4 × 4) (50 delivered)

Trucks
M35/M44 series 2,268 kg (6 × 6)
M-462 Abir 1,800 kg (4 × 4)

The Guatemalan Army has a need for a sizeable quantity (put at 500 by some sources) of utility vehicles.

Guyana
Light vehicles
Land Rover ALV 564 kg (4 × 4) (status uncertain)
Mahindra Jeep (4 × 4) (Rakshak and RIV - security forces).

Haiti
Recovery vehicles
V-150 ARV(?) (4 × 4)

Light vehicles
M715 1,360 kg (4 × 4)

Trucks
M35/M44 series 2,268 kg (6 × 6)

Honduras
Light vehicles
AM General HMMWV (4 × 4) (125)
CUCV (4 × 4)
M38 (4 × 4)
M151 Mutt 362 kg (4 × 4) (approx. 30)
Toyota Land Cruiser (4 × 4)

Trucks
Ashok Leyland Stallion (4 × 4) (2009)
Ashok Leyland Topchi (4 × 4) (2009)
Mercedes-Benz LG1213 (4 × 4) (Brazilian-made)
Mercedes-Benz LA911 (4 × 4) (ex-Argentina)
M35/M44 series 2,268 kg (4 × 4)
M809 series 4,536 kg (6 × 6)

Honduras has benefited from US assistance, including training since the 1980s.

Hungary
Armoured engineer vehicles
BAT-2 CEV

Recovery vehicles
T-54/T-55 ARV
BMP-1 VPV

Mechanised bridges
BLG-60 AVLB
MTU AVLB
TMM-3 (6 × 6)

Light vehicles
Mercedes-Benz G-Class 270 CDI/G280 CDI (4 ×4) (>120) (deliveries ongoing)
UAZ-469B series 600 kg (4 × 4)

Trucks
DAC 665T 5,000 kg (6 × 6) (numbers reducing)

Csepel D-566 5,000 kg (6 × 6) (numbers reducing)
Csepel D-564 4,000 kg (4 × 4) (numbers reducing)
IFA L60 3,000 kg (4 × 4) (numbers reducing)
IFA W50 3,000 kg (4 × 4) (numbers reducing)
KrAZ-255B 7,500 kg (6 × 6) (incl. TMM truck-mounted treadway bridge)
MAN HX77 15,000 kg (8 × 8)
Mercedes-Benz Unimog (4 × 4) (ex-German Army)
Mercedes-Benz Unimog U4000 (4 × 4)
Mercedes-Benz 1017 and/or 1017A (ex-German Army)
Rába H-14 (4 × 4) (fitted with MAN engine and military cab)
Rába H-18 (6 × 6) (fitted with MAN engine and military cab)
Robur 1800 A 1,800 kg (4 × 4) (numbers reducing)
TATRA 148 14,580 kg (6 × 6) (numbers reducing)
TATRA T813 (8 × 8)
Ural-375 4,000 kg (6 × 6) (numbers reducing)
Ural-4320 4,500 kg (6 × 6) (numbers reducing)

Hungary is reported to have received 500 ex-German Army trucks. Hungarian truck manufacturer Rába was selected in January 2003 to manage a USD1.1 billion contract for the purchase of 13,000 military support vehicles through 2015. Five types of off-road vehicles are covered in a deal with German partners DaimlerChrysler and MAN. Vehicles on order are DaimlerChrysler G-Wagens, Mercedes-Benz U4000 Unimogs, MAN 15,000 kg HX77 trucks and Rába 5,000 to 8,000 kg H-14 and 10,000 to 18,000 kg H-18 trucks, plus speciality trailers. Specific orders to complete the vehicle replacement programme, including types and numbers, are announced annually. The truck part of the requirement now calls for 4,350 vehicles, the Logistic segment (awarded to IVECO) for an estimated 5,000 logistic vehicles to be delivered over a 15 year period was cancelled following two years of complex legal wrangling, by which time numbers involved had reduced to 1,500 vehicles.

India
Armoured engineer vehicles
Combat Engineer Tractor (15)
Armoured Engineer Reconnaissance Vehicle

Recovery vehicles
T-54/T-55 ARV
VT-72B ARV (>200)
WZT-3 ARV (124, including vehicles on order)
Vijayanta
Ashok Leyland LRV (4 × 4) (at least 1,056)

Mechanised bridges
BLG-60 AVLB
BLT T-72 AVLB (12)
Kartik AVLB
MT-55 AVLB
MTU-20 AVLB
AM-50 (6 × 6)

Light vehicles
Carrier 750 kg (4 × 4) (production complete)
Jonga (4 × 4) (around 1,000 remain) (production complete)
Maruti Gypsy (4 × 4) (20,000) (deliveries continue)
Mahindra Jeep CL series (4 × 4) (replaced by MM series around 1997)
Mahindra MM550XD (4 × 4)(1997 to 2002)
Mahindra (current model) (4 × 4) (2002 to present)
(India operates around 19,000 Mahindra CL/MM series vehicles in total)
Mahindra Bolero (4 × 4) (trials)
Mahindra Scorpio (4 × 4)
Tata SFC 407 1,000 kg (4 × 2/4 × 4) (approx. 9,000) (deliveries continue)
Tata Sumo (4 × 4) (around 4,000; Police and Army) (deliveries continue)

Trucks
Ashok Leyland Stallion Mk II 5,000 kg (4 × 4) (350) (1994-1996)
Ashok Leyland Stallion Mk III 5,000 kg (4 × 4) (mostly GS) (>57,000) (deliveries continue)
Ashok Leyland Topchi Field Artillery Tractor (FAT) (4 × 4) (261) (2005-2006)
KrAZ (various models incl. 255B and 255B (B1)) (>2,000)
MAZ-543 (8 × 8) (specialist role)
Shaktiman 4,000 kg (4 × 4) (production complete) (approx. 7,000 remain in use)
Scania SBAT 111S 6,000 kg (6 × 6) (600 delivered)
Swaraj Mazda (4 × 2/4 × 4)
TATA LPTA 713 TC 2,500 kg (4 × 4) (>23,000) (deliveries continue)
Tata SD 1015 TC Field Artillery Tractor (FAT) (4 × 4) (>2,000)
Tata SA 1212 TC 4,000 kg (4 × 4) (>6,000 delivered) (1999-2006) (replaced in production by Tata LPTA 1413)
TATRA T815 (4 × 4) license-build by BEML
TATRA T815 (6 × 6) license-build by BEML
TATRA T815 (8 × 8) license-build by BEML
(BEML has supplied around 11,000 TATRA trucks to the Army, with deliveries continuing at between 500-1,500 per year)
TATRA T815 (10 × 10) (for Smerch MRS)
TATRA T815 (12 × 12) (for Brahmos missile system)
(around 100 chassis (10 × 10/12 × 12) had been delivered by early 2010)
URAL 375D (6 × 6) incl. BM21 Grad)
URAL 4320 (6 × 6) (relatively small numbers)
Zil 131 3,500 kg (6 × 6) (pre-1990) (status/numbers uncertain)
Zil 157 (6 × 6) (post-1990)

India has ongoing requirements for light vehicles, high mobility trucks and heavy artillery tractors.

Indonesia
Recovery vehicles
AMX-13 ARV (2)
Stormer ARV
T-54/T-55 ARV

Mechanised bridges
AMX-13 AVLB
Stormer AVLB (2)
Leguan (8 × 8)

Light vehicles
Beijing Jeep Corporation BJ 2020SJ (4 × 4) (500) (2000 to 2001)
Cakra FAV (4 × 4) (appears SUV based)
DAF 66 YA 400 kg (4 × 2) (150 delivered) (status uncertain)
Jeep CJ-7 (4 × 4)
KM42 series (4 × 4) (140) (2003)
Land Rover ALV 564 kg (4 × 4) (812 delivered) (status uncertain)
Land Rover Defender 90 and 110 (4 × 4) (early 80s to late 90s) (about 2,100)
Land Rover (small number) (2006) (specialist versions)
Mahindra (4 × 4) (25) (donated/supplied Jan 2003)
Mercedes-Benz G-Class (4 × 4) (early 1980s)
M151 Mutt 362 kg (4 × 4)
Nissan Q4W73 750 kg (4 × 4) (600 delivered) (status uncertain)
SDP 700 AP (4 × 4) (1,000 delivered)
STK Flyer FAV (4 × 4) (2?) (some sources state 26, possibly from Australia, with a total requirement of 160)

Trucks
Bedford MK 4,000 kg (4 × 4)
Jiefang CA-1091 (C-141) 5,000 kg (4 × 2)
KM25 series 2.5-ton (6 × 6) (circa 1999)
Leyland 4,000 kg (4 × 4) (14)
Maesa PT44 2,500 kg (4 × 4)
MAN/Leguan (8 × 8) (bridging)
Mercedes-Benz Unimog (4 × 4)

Steyr 680 M 4,500 kg (4 × 4) (750)
Steyr 17 M 29 7,000 kg (4 × 4) (>200)
TATRA T-815 (8 × 8) (ex-Czech Republic)
Tiema XC2030 8,000 kg (6 × 6)

Several hundred trucks were ordered from South Korea with payment via barter trade. This figure likely included the 140 KM42 series light vehicles. India donated/supplied 25 light vehicles and 10 trucks to Indonesia in January 2003. Indonesia also operates small numbers of a variety of indigenously developed fast attack-type light strike vehicles.

Iran
Recovery vehicles
Chieftain ARV
M578 ARV

Mechanised bridges
Chieftain AVLB (14)

Light vehicles
Land Rover (4 × 4)
Land Rover 1,000 kg (4 × 4)
Mahindra (4 × 4) (25,000 supplied KD from 1980, some likely in military use)
Sahand Cruiser (4 × 4) (locally-produced Toyota 40 Series clone, some likely in military use)
UAZ-469B series 600 kg (4 × 4)

Trucks
GAZ-66 2,000 kg (4 × 4)
MAZ-543 (8 × 8) (specialist roles)
M34/M44 series 2,268 kg (6 × 6)
Mercedes-Benz LA911 clone (no other details available)
Mercedes-Benz (4 × 4) (no other details available)
Mercedes-Benz (6 × 6) (no other details available)
Mercedes-Benz/Titan (6 × 6) HETS (with Achleitner trailer) (70 incl. some to Iraq)
Volvo NL10 (4 × 4)

Iraq
Recovery vehicles
VT-55A (2) (donated by Hungary) (T-55 based)
BT-55A (2) (2005) ARV
BTR-5B (3) (2006) ARV
Type 653 ARV
T-54/T-55 ARV
ENGESA EE-11 repair and recovery (6 × 6)

Mechanised bridges
BLG-60 AVLB
MT-55 AVLB

Light vehicles
AM General HMMWV (4 × 4) (>12,000)
Ford F350 Super Duty (4 × 4) (approx. 500) (2008)
Ford Ranger (4 × 4) (360) (2008)
Honker (4 × 4) (>100) (from 2005) (includes 100 ambulance and 10 Skorpion 3 patrol variants)
Jeep TJ-L (4 × 4) (100) (2005)
KM450 (4 × 4)
Land Rover (4 × 4) (incl. recent deliveries from Otokar of Turkey that include 400 ambulances)
UAZ-469B series 600 kg (4 × 4) (incl. 421 delivered March 2004)

Trucks
Ashok Leyland Stallion Mk3 (172) (2007)
BAE Systems FMTV (140) (not confirmed)
Berliet GBC 8KT 4,000 kg (6 × 6)
DAC 15.215 5,000 kg (6 × 6) (1980)
GAZ-66 2,000 kg (4 × 4)
GAZ-33081 Sadko (4 × 4) (643) (2004)
GAZ-3307 Zemlyak (4 × 2) (600) (2004) (no confirmation of delivery)
International 7000 Series MV (6 × 6) (2004-2009) (>1,500)

IVECO 6605 (6 × 6) (200) (1984)
KrAZ (6 × 6) (approx. 2,000) (figures include approx. 1,600 Model 6322 and 6322-056 from 2004)
L 60 LA/PVB 6,200 kg (4 × 4)
MAN 8.138 2,000 kg (4 × 4) (100) (2006) (Danish Army surplus)
MB Unimog (4 × 4)
Mercedes-Benz/IVECO-Magirus (100) (2004) (assorted, donated, ex-German Army)
Mercedes-Benz/Titan (6 × 6) HETS (with Achleitner trailer) (approx. 70 incl. some to Iran)
Scania (4 × 4)
Star 266 (6 × 6) (ex-Polish)
Ural-375D 4,000 kg (6 × 6)
W 50 LA/A 3,000 kg (4 × 4)

The continued serviceability of equipment (if acquired during Saddam's reign), must now be in doubt

Ireland
Recovery vehicles
ACMAT VLRA 640WRT.TD (6 × 6) (3) (1989)
ACMAT VLRA TPK640SM (6 × 6) (1) (1994)
IVECO 320.42 (8 × 8) (1) (2000)
Leyland (4 × 4) (4) (1997 to 1999) (Holmes 655 recovery gear ex-Bedford)
MAN 32.321 (6 × 6) (1) (1987) (ex-EKA demonstrator vehicle)
MAN SX45 (8 × 8) (2) (2009-2010) (UK Support Vehicle spec)

Light vehicles
Ford/Ricardo RDV (4 × 4) (12) (2004) (Ford F-350-based, Ricardo conversion)
Land Rover Defender 110 (4 × 4) (6) (ambulance bodies)
Mitsubishi Pajero (4 × 4) (from 2009) (up to 320)
Nissan Patrol 750 kg (4 × 4) (520) (procured from 1989)

Trucks
ACMAT VLRA TPK420SM3 (4 × 4) (16) (1983 to 1993)
ACMAT VLRA TPK435SM (4 × 4) (5) (1988 to 1994)
IVECO 320.42 15,000 kg (8 × 8) (22) (1997 to 2001) (fitted with Multilift LHS)
IVECO EuroCargo ML140E18W 4,000 kg (4 × 4) (20) (2003)
Leyland 4,000 kg (4 × 4) (52) (1997 to 1999)
MAN 14.240 FAEG 5,000 kg (4 × 4) (36) (1979 to 1989) (22 remain, 2003)
Mercedes-Benz 1117A 4,000 kg (4 × 4) (60) (2000 to 2002)
MOWAG DURO II (6 × 6) (6) (2003) (EOD)
Scania R124CB8x8 HZ420 (15) (2004-2005) (with LHS)
Scania R420 (6 × 6) (36) (2007-2008)
Scania (8 × 4) (2) (2007-2008)
Scania (4 × 2) (10) (2008) (EOD)

Israel
Recovery vehicles
Centurion Mk 2 ARV
M88A1 ARV (25)
M113 series ARV
EYAL (6 × 6) RV

Mechanised bridges
MTU-20 AVLB
MTU AVLB
MAB/F (4 × 4)
M48 AVLB

Light vehicles
CUCV (4 × 4)
Ford (4 × 4) (assorted, likely FMS)
HMMWV (4 × 4) (approx. 3,000)
Land Rover (4 × 4 and 6 × 6) (specialist roles)
M715 1,360 kg (4 × 4)
M151 Mutt 362 kg (4 × 4)
AIL M-240 Storm 850 kg (4 × 4) (5,000) (from 1991)

AIL M-242 Storm (4 × 4) (500)
AIL M-243 Storm (4 × 4) (from 2010)

Trucks
ATC MTT 10,000 kg (6 × 6) (302) (2004-2006) (will replace some M35s)
ATC MTT 10,000 kg (6 × 6) (2006) (small contract option exercised)
International (179) (2006) (non-tactical)
International Medium Tactical vehicles (114) (2010)
MAN F90 series (6 × 6) (HET)
Mercedes-Benz Actros (6 × 6) (est. 50) (delivered 2006) (HET)
M325 Command Car 1,800 kg (4 × 4) (9,000 delivered)
M462 ABIR 1,800 kg (4 × 4) (est. 1,500 delivered)
M35/M44 series 2,268 kg (6 × 6)
M54 series 4,536 kg (6 × 6) (numbers reducing)
Oshkosh HEMTT 9,979 kg (8 × 8) (approx. 500)
Volvo FH16 (6 × 6) (55) (HET)

Italy

Armoured engineer vehicles
Leopard 1 AEV (40)
M113 Combat Engineer Support Vehicle

Recovery vehicles
Leopard 1 ARV (137)
IVECO 6605 (6 × 6)
AAV7RAI ARV

Mechanised bridges
Biber AVLB (64)

Light vehicles
Fresia F18 400 kg (4 × 4)
IVECO LMV (4 × 4) (est. 1,300 ordered)
IVECO 40.10 WM 1,500 kg (4 × 4) (>1,400) (incl. follow-on 40.12, 40.13)
Land Rover Defender 90 (4 × 4) (2,109) (2001-2006)

Trucks
ARIS Airlift Global Carrier (AGC) 170/275 (4 × 2/4 × 4) (used with MBDA Spada low- to medium-altitude SAM)
ASTRA SM 44 tactical family 7,000 kg (4 × 4) (from 2001, deliveries continue)
ASTRA SM 66 tactical family 10,000 kg (6 × 6) (from 2001, deliveries continue)
ASTRA SM 88 tactical family 15,000 kg (8 × 8) (from 1996, deliveries continue)
ASTRA SMH 44 logistic family 9,500 kg (4 × 4) (deliveries continue)
ASTRA SMH 66 logistic family 20,000 kg (6 × 6) (deliveries continue)
ASTRA SMH 88 logistic family 25,000 kg (8 × 8) (deliveries continue)
ASTRA SMH 84 logistic family 25,000 kg (8 × 4) (deliveries continue)
(Between 1996 and mid 2005 Italian armed forces received around 800 tactical family models, and between 2003 and mid-2005, around 275 logistic family were delivered. Production and delivery of all models continues at around 150 vehicles per year)
ASTRA SMH 88.50 tactical family (8 × 8) (10, 2003; 18, 2004) (further orders anticipated) (HET)
ASTRA SMH 66.45 (6 × 6) (36) (by late-2005) (further orders anticipated) (MET)
ASTRA HD6 84.45 15,000 kg (8 × 4)
ASTRA HD 66.45/5S-C-IMT (6 × 6) (tractor truck for CNIM pontoon bridging system)
IVECO 75-14 WM 2,500 kg (4 × 4)
IVECO 90-17 WM 4,000 kg (4 × 4)
IVECO 320.45 (6 × 6) HET (being replaced by ASTRA SMH 88.50)
IVECO Cargo/EuroCargo (various configurations)
IVECO Trakker/EuroTrakker (various configurations)
IVECO M135E24WM (4 × 4) Multipurpose Medium Vehicle (MMV) (<10) (2005) (Air Force)

ASTRA products are branded IVECO for all export applications.

Jamaica

Light vehicles
CUCV (4 × 4)
Land Rover ALV 564 kg (4 × 4) (status uncertain)
M-151 Mutt (4 × 4)

Trucks
M809 series 4,536 kg (6 × 6)

Japan

Armoured engineer vehicles
Type 75 armoured dozer

Recovery vehicles
Type 70 ARV (4)
Type 78 ARV (50)
Type 90 ARV (>11)
Isuzu SKW464MR light wrecker (6 × 6)
Mitsubishi Model FW415M1 (6 × 6)
Mitsubishi Model FW419M1 (6 × 6)
Mitsubishi Model FX50MMY190 (6 × 6)
Type 90 ARV (20)

Mechanised bridges
Type 91 AVLB
Type 70 pontoon bridge (4 × 4)
Type 81 (6 × 6)

Light vehicles
HMMWV (4 × 4) (5 delivered)
Koukidosya 1,500 kg (4 × 4)
Mitsubishi Type 73 Light Truck (4 × 4) (Jeep CJ3B body style) (until 1998)
Mitsubishi Type 73 Light Truck (4 × 4) (Mitsubishi Pajero-based) (from 1998)
Nissan Q4W73 750 kg (4 × 4) (probably in reserve or limited use)
Toyota 2FQ15L 750 kg (4 × 4) (probably in reserve or limited use)

Trucks
Hino 4,000 kg (6 × 6)
Isuzu SKW series 3,500 kg (6 × 6))
Mitsubishi W121P 6,000 kg (6 × 6)
Mitsubishi FW415 series 7,000 kg (6 × 6) (production complete)
Mitsubishi FW419 series 5,800 kg (6 × 6) (replaced FW415 series in production)
Mitsubishi 7,000 kg (6 × 6) (replaced FW419 series in production)
Mitsubishi FW115 10,000 kg (6 × 6)
Mitsubishi (8 × 8) (specialist applications)
Toyota 2,500 kg (6 × 6)
Type 73 2,000 kg (4 × 4)
Type 74 10,000 kg (6 × 6)

With a wealth of indigenous light 4 × 4 manufacturers (including Daihatsu, Mitsubishi, Nissan, Suzuki and Toyota) it is likely that examples of most marques are in use performing non-tactical roles.

Jordan

Recovery vehicles
AB1 M47 ARRV (20) (delivery 2001)
Centurion Mk 2 ARV
Chieftain ARV
M578 ARV
M88A1 ARV (32)
Chieftain AARV (6) (2004)
M1089A1 (6 × 6) RV (10)

Light vehicles
AB3 Black Iris 500 kg (4 × 2) (limited numbers)
AB5 Desert Iris >500 kg (4 × 4) (est. 450)
AB5 1,000 kg (4 × 4) (Land Rover-based special forces vehicle)
Dodge Ram (4 × 4)
HMMWV (4 × 4) (approx. 700)
JLVM Al-Thalab (Fox) Long Range Patrol Vehicle (LRPV) (approx. 200)
Land Rover (4 × 4) (incl. 1,500 Defender 110 between 2000 and 2003 as KD kits)

Pinzgauer (4 × 4)
Toyota Land Cruiser (4 × 4)

Trucks
DAF YA4440 4,000 kg (4 × 4) (18) (circa 2002)
IVECO Trakker (small quantity)
M35/M44 series 2,268 kg (6 × 6)
M809 series 4,536 kg (6 × 6)
Oshkosh M1070 HET (8 × 8) (50) (2004)
Oshkosh M977 Heavy Expanded Mobility Tactical Truck (HEMTT)
Scammell Commander (6 × 4) (95) (from 2003) (ex-British Army) (HET)
Scammell Contractor HET (6 × 4) (replacement programme underway) (HET)
FMTV (6 × 6) (55, 2005-2006; 45, 2006; further order mid-2008)

Kenya

Recovery vehicles
Vickers ARV (7)

Light vehicles
Land Rover Defender (4 × 4) incl. FFR)
Pinzgauer (4 × 4)

Trucks
Mercedes-Benz Unimog (4 × 4)
Bedford MK 4,000 kg (4 × 4)
Leyland 4,000 kg (4 × 4) (approx. 50) (2000 to 2001)
Mack (6 × 6) (HET)
Mercedes-Benz LA911B/LA1113
Shaanxi SX2151 (4 × 4) (2005)

Korea, South

Armoured engineer vehicles
M9 armoured combat earthmover (207)

Recovery vehicles
AAVR7 ARV (8) (Marines)
K-1 ARV (200)
K288A1 ARV
M47 ARV
M88A1 ARV (38)
KM502 W (6 × 6)
M816 W (6 × 6)
KM 1001 10 Ton (8 × 8) wrecker

Mechanised bridges
K-1 AVLB (56)

Light vehicles
KM41 (or 410) series (4 × 4) (produced until 1997) (numbers reducing)
KM42 (initially 420) series (4 × 4) (approx. 23,000) (1997 to 2006) (replaced KM41 series from 1997)
KM45 family 1,530 kg (4 × 4)
M151 Mutt 362 kg (4 × 4) (replaced, or replacement imminent)
Nissan Q4W73 750 kg (4 × 4) (replaced, or replacement imminent)
Ssangyong Rexton SUV (4 × 4) (small number) (Air Force)
Toyota 2FQ15L 750 kg (4 × 4) (replaced, or replacement imminent)

Trucks
KM25 family 2,500 kg (6 × 6)
KM50 family 5,000 kg (6 × 6)
KM1000 family (8 × 8) (recovery and HET versions)
M35/M44 series 2,268 kg (6 × 6)
M54 series 4,536 kg (6 × 6)
M809 series 4,536 kg (6 × 6)
Oshkosh HEMTT 9,979 kg (8 × 8)

Kuwait
Recovery vehicles
M88A1 (6)
M88A2 (14)

Type 653A ARV
Warrior mechanised recovery vehicle
Warrior mechanised combat repair vehicle
Pandur (6 × 6) ARV
Western Star M4900SA (6 × 6) (1) (2003)
Mercedes-Benz Actros (6 × 6) (with EMPL top hamper)

Light vehicles
Ford SUV-types (4 × 4)
GMC SUV-types (4 × 4)
HMMWV (4 × 4) (approx. 770)
Jeep (YJ) (4 × 4)
Land Rover Defender (4 × 4)
Mercedes-Benz G-Class 750 kg (4 × 4) (400)

Trucks
MAN M2000 (4 × 4) (small number)
MAN TGM (4 × 4)
MAN TGA (6 × 6)
Mercedes-Benz (4 × 4) (pre-Atego/Axor generation)
Mercedes-Benz Actros (6 × 6)
Mercedes-Benz Unimog (4 × 4)
M35A3 series 2.5-ton (6 × 6)
M939 series 5-ton (6 × 6)
MAZ-543M (8 × 8)
Oshkosh HEMTT (8 × 8) (specialist applications)
Steyr 5,000 kg (4 × 4)
Tata SD 1015 TC (4 × 4) (gun tractor)
Tata SA 1212 TC 4,000 kg (4 × 4)
Volvo FL6 5,000 kg (4 × 4)
Volvo FH12 (6 × 6) (2007-2008)
Western Star M4800 series (4 × 4) (45)
Western Star M4900SA (4 × 4) (28?) (2003)
Western Star M4900SA (6 × 6) (17?) (2003)

Kuwait received around 90 HETs between 1993 and 1996. The tractor is not known, the trailers were 80 tonne full off-highway capable five-axle designs supplied by Achleitner.

Lebanon
Recovery vehicles
AMX-13 ARV (18)
M113 ARV
Steyr 32 S 29 (6 × 6)

Light vehicles
Land Rover (4 × 4)
asstd US surplus 'jeeps'.

Trucks
Berliet GBC-8KT (6 × 6)
M35/M44 series 2,268 kg (6 × 6)
M809 series 4,536 kg (6 × 6)

Although specific details have not been made available, more than 3,000 tactical wheeled vehicles were supplied ex-US from stocks in Belgium, Germany and the Netherlands. France has also supplied surplus equipment including Berliet GBC-8KT trucks.

Liberia
Light vehicles
CUCV (4 × 4)
M151 Mutt 362 kg (4 × 4)

Trucks
M35/M44 series 2,268 kg (6 × 6)
M809 series 4,536 kg (6 × 6)

The UN arms embargo, imposed on Liberia since 1992, the country's dire economic situation, and the dissolution of its residual armed forces at the end of 2004 mean that Liberia is not currently in a position to engage in military procurement. Whatever the small new army does require in terms of uniforms, infrastructure, basic infantry and support equipment will almost certainly be provided by the US under its commitment to train and re-equip 4,000 Liberian personnel.

Libya
Recovery vehicles
T-54/T-55 ARV

Light vehicles
AB3 Black Iris LSV (4 × 2) (25 ordered)
Land Rover (4 × 4) (inc 200 during 1999)
UAZ-469B series 600 kg (4 × 4)

Trucks
ACMAT VLRA (600 delivered)
BAZ-5937 (6 × 6) (SA-8 system)
ENGESA EE-25 2,500 kg (6 × 6)
FAUN HZ 40.45/45 (6 × 6) (69) (HET)
GAZ-66 2,000 kg (4 × 4)
IVECO 6605 (6 × 6)
Mercedes-Benz Unimog (4 × 4)
TATRA 148 (4 × 4) (6 × 6) (large quantities were delivered)
Ural-375D 4,000 kg (6 × 6)
Zil-135 (8 × 8) (FROG-7)

Luxembourg
Recovery vehicles
MAN LX (6 × 6)
MAN SX (8 × 8) (1) (not confirmed)

Light vehicles
HMMWV (4 × 4) (69 inc M1114)
Land Rover 1,000 kg (4 × 4) (57)
Mercedes-Benz G-Class 750 kg (4 × 4) (38)

Trucks
MAN (assorted including LX range) (4 × 4 and 6 × 6)

Madagascar
Light vehicles
Auverland/SAMO (4 × 4)

No requirements have been publicised and there is almost no likelihood of new equipment being ordered in the short term. The best chance of additional equipment is likely to be cascaded French surplus equipment.

Malaysia
Recovery vehicles
FNSS ARV
Hicom Handalan TFS33H (4 × 4) (67) (1999 to 2004)
K288A1 (>4)
SIBMAS ARV (6 × 6) (22)
Volvo F10 (4 × 4) (30)
Doosan K288A1 ARV (4)
WZT- 4 ARV (6)

Light vehicles
Ford SUVs (4 × 4)
Gomba Stonefield (4 × 4) (33) (1983 to 1986) (refurbished)
IVECO 40.10/12 1,500 kg (4 × 4) (approx. 25)
Land Rover Defender (4 × 4) (incl. 343 GS and 550 FFR as KD kits; the latter being local conversions) (2002 to 2003)
Mercedes-Benz G-Class 290 GDT 750 kg (4 × 4) (est. 84) (2003)
Mercedes-Benz G-Class 270 CDI (4 × 4) (2003 onwards)
Pinzgauer (4 × 4) (168) (post 1996)
Pinzgauer (6 × 6) (164) (post 1996)
Ssangyong Rexton II SUV (4 × 4) (est. 200) (2008-2010)
Supacat ATMP (6 × 6) (at least 6) (2001 onwards)
Toyota Hilux (4 × 4)
URO VAMTAC (4 × 4) (85) (2008-2009)

Trucks
Avibras Astros II (6 × 6) (from 2002)
Hicom Handalan Mk1 3,000 kg (4 × 4) (approx. 1,870)

Hicom Handalan Mk2 3,000 kg (4 × 4) (242 as of April 2003, 1,000 more understood to be required)
Hicom Handalan Mk2 3,000 kg (4 × 4) (100) fire and rescue bodies
IVECO EuroTrakker (8 × 4) (2)
IVECO EuroTrakker MP750E52 WT (6 × 6) HET (27) (up to 100 could be required) (Hicom DT.TT1.5-60 semi-trailer)
Leyland 4,000 kg (4 × 4) (40) (status uncertain)
MAN (6 × 6) (gun tractor role?)
MAN (8 × 8) (for BR90 bridging system) (delivered 2003 to 2004)
Mercedes-Benz (4 × 4) (no other information available)
MOWAG DURO 1 (6 × 6) (2003) (57)
MOWAG DURO II (4 × 4/6 × 6) (licence production from 2005)
ROMAN 8.140 FAE 2,200 kg (4 × 4) (6)
ROMAN 16.310 FAEG 6,000 kg (4 × 4)
ROMAN 26.360 DFAEG (6 × 6)
ROMAN 26.360 DFAES (6 × 6) (tractor truck for CNIM PFM SIR)
ROMAN 33.320 DFA 19,400 kg (6 × 6) (10)
ROMAN 33.360 DFA (6 × 6) tractor truck (HET)
ROMAN 33.360 DFAS (6 × 6) tractor truck
Tata 1613 (4 × 4)
TATRA T815 ARMAX family
Volvo FL10 (4 × 4)
Volvo FL7 (prime mover)
Volvo 4140 (4 × 4) (status uncertain)
Volvo 4140 (6 × 6) (status uncertain)

Malta
Light vehicles
Land Rover (4 × 4)

Trucks
Bedford RL 4,000 kg (4 × 4)

Malta has a military co- operation agreement with Italy.

Mexico
Light vehicles
AM General HMMWV (4 × 4) (3,600)
Chenowth LSV (4 × 2)
CJ-8 (4 × 4) (being replaced by HMMWV)
Dodge RAM (4 × 4)
Ford F250 (4 × 4)
General Motors CUCV (4 × 4) (FMS)
Land Rover Series III (4 × 4) (Marines)
Land Rover Defender (4 × 4)
M38 Jeep (4 × 4)
M151 Mutt 362 kg (4 × 4)
M561 Gama Goat (6 × 6)
Supacat (6 × 6)
Volkswagen-based LSV (>50) (from 2000)

Trucks
Commando (4 × 4) (est. 300)
Freightliner (6 × 4) tractor truck
Freightliner commercial pattern (4 × 2(
General Motors Medium (4 × 4) and Heavy (6 × 6) Duty Service Support vehicles (MDSSV/HDSSV) (from 2002)
International 4000 series (4 × 2) (4 × 4)
Kenworth (6 × 4) (heavy tractor trucks)
Mack (6 × 4)
Mercedes-Benz Unimog (4 × 4) (includes recent deliveries)
Mini-Commando (4 × 4)
M-35 2,268 kg (6 × 6)
M939 (6 × 6)
M520 GOER (4 × 4) (specialist design; articulated frame steer)
URAL 4320 (6 × 6) (approx. 100) (2005)

Mongolia
Recovery vehicles
T-54/T-55 ARV

Light vehicles
UAZ-469B series 600 kg (4 × 4)

Trucks
Ural-375D 4,000 kg (6 × 6)

China, Turkey and the US have all supplied military aid packages to Mongolia. No procurement requirements have been announced, but this does not mean that none exist.

Montenegro

Armoured engineer vehicles
IWT CEV (equivalent to Russian IMR)

Recovery vehicles
M-84A1 ARV
T-54/T-55 ARV

Mechanised bridges
MT-55 AVLB
TMM-3 (6 × 6)

Light vehicles
FIAT Campagnola 1,107 AD 750 kg (4 × 4)
IMR A-0.75 750/1,000 kg (4 × 4)
IMR TARA 1,200 kg (4 × 4)
Mercedes-Benz G-Class 750 kg (4 × 4) (500)
SDP Pinzgauer
Zastava AR-51 500 kg (4 × 4)

Trucks
TAM 110 T7 BV 1,500/2,500 kg (4 × 4)
TAM 150 T11 BV 3,000/5,000 kg (6 × 6)
TAM 4500 4,500 kg (4 × 4)
TAM 5000 5,000 kg (4 × 4)
TAM 5500 5,500 kg (4 × 4)
TAM 6500 6,500 kg (4 × 4)
FAP 2220 BDS (6 × 4)
FAP 2026 BS/AV 10,000 kg (6 × 6)
FAP 2832 BS/AV 9,000 kg (6 × 6)
FAP 3232 BDST/AV (8 × 8) HET

Morocco

Recovery vehicles
M578 ARV
M88A1 ARV (18)
SDP 4KH 7FA SB 20 Greif ARV (10)

Light vehicles
AM General HMMWW (4 × 4)
Nissan Patrol (4 × 4)
Santana Model 88 500 kg (4 × 4)
Santana Model 109 1,000 kg (4 × 4)
URO VAM-TL (4 × 4) (650 approx.) (2004-2009)
URO VAMTAC (4 × 4) (1,200 est.) (2007-2009)

Trucks
ACMAT VLRA (4 × 4) (150-200)
ACMAT VLA 8,000 kg (8 × 8) (50)
Berliet GBC 8 KT 4,000 kg (6 × 6)
IVECO tractor trucks (probably Trakker) (see notes)
Mercedes-Benz Unimog (4 × 4)
M35/M44 series 2,268 kg (6 × 6) (additional deliveries from US surplus during 2001)
M809 series 4,536 kg (6 × 6) (US surplus)
Oshkosh M911 HET (6 × 6) (20) (1988)
Pegaso 3046 3,000 kg (4 × 4)
Pegaso 7323 6,000 kg (6 × 6) (>1,000) (1987-1988)
RENAULT TRM 1200 1,200 kg (4 × 4)
RENAULT TRM 2000 2,000 kg (4 × 4) (190)
RENAULT TRM 9000 9,000 kg (6 × 6) (1,500)
Renault KERAX tractor trucks (4?) (2003)
URO 18.14 2,000 kg (4 × 4) (>100) (delivered post-1996)
URO (4 × 4) (see notes)
Volvo NL10 (4 × 4)

Early 2006 it was disclosed that Morocco had ordered a large package of military transport equipment from URO of Spain. Official details have not been released but the order is understood to consist of around 1,200 VAMTAC

and <800 other assorted vehicles that include additional VAM-TL light vehicles, URO (4 × 4) trucks and some tractor trucks supplied by IVECO. Deliveries commenced in 2007 and were completed early 2009.

Mozambique

Light vehicles
Jonga (4 × 4) (200)
UAZ-469B series 600 kg (4 × 4)

Trucks
Mercedes-Benz Unimog (4 × 4)
SAMIL 20 2,000 kg (4 × 4) (4) (ex-SANDF)
SAMIL 50 5,000 kg (4 × 4) (30) (ex-SANDF)
Ural-375D 4,000 kg (6 × 6)
Ural-4320 series (6 × 6)
Zil-131 (6 × 6)

No procurement plans have been published, however, the most obvious requirement is for spare parts to repair key systems from a dilapidated Soviet-era inventory.

Myanmar

Recovery vehicles
Type 72 ARV

Light vehicles
Mitsubishi (4 × 4) (probably Pajero and L200)
Nissan Patrol (4 × 4)

Trucks
Dong Feng 6,500 kg (4 × 2)
Jiefang 5,000 kg (4 × 2)
Lan Jian 2,000 kg
Kungi 2,000 kg
Hanyang (tank transporter tractors)
Nissan 5,000 kg
Star 266 (6 × 6) crane trucks
Star 12,500 kg

In recent years a major effort has been made to mechanise a number of the Myanmar Army's infantry battalions, for which purpose the SPDC has purchased 3,000 2.5 tonne Chinese trucks and in August 2005, 400 military trucks were supplied to the army. Earlier information (from 2003) had stated that deliveries of Dong Feng 6,500 kg (4 × 2), Jiefang 5,000 kg (4 × 2), Lan Jian 2,000 kg and Kungi 2,000 kg trucks had collectively totalled approximately 1,000 since 1988.

Namibia

Trucks
Renault TRM 2000 2,000 kg (4 × 4) (50)
SAMIL 50 5,000 kg (4 × 4) (ex-SANDF) (no other details)
SAMIL 100 10,000 kg (6 × 6) (150) (ex-SANDF, refurbished and delivered 1998 to 1999)

By 2011-2012 the Ministry of Defence aims to carry out research into modern equipment, acquire 10 per cent of defence equipment and replace 10 per cent of obsolete equipment with at least 10 per cent of latest technology items.

Netherlands

Armoured engineer vehicles
Kodiak AEV (10 ordered 2008)
Leopard 1 AEV (25) (some sold)

Recovery vehicles
Büffel ARV (25)
Leopard 1 ARV (52) (reduced number)
Leopard 1 BARV
M113 ARV
M578 ARV
DAF YBZ 3300 DKX (6 × 6) HRV (255) (1991 to 1993)

Mechanised bridges
Biber AVLB (17)
Leopard 2 AVLB (14) (on order)

Light vehicles
Mercedes-Benz G-Class 750 kg (4 × 4) (3,300 est.) (to be replaced from around 2010)
Mercedes-Benz G-Class G280 CDI (4 × 4) (128) (ordered 2007) (armed patrol variant - Army and Marines)
Land Rover Defender (4 × 4) (Marines only)
Land Rover Defender XD (4 × 4) (Marines only)
LOHR (SOFRAME) VLA (179)

Trucks
DAF YA 4440 4,000 kg (4 × 4) (7,612 delivered) (1977 to 1983) (most sold as surplus or cast)
DAF YA 4442 DNT 4,000 kg (4 × 4) (5,125 delivered) (1986 to 1993)
DAF YA 5442 5,000 kg (4 × 4) (195) RNAF
DAF YA 5444 (4 × 4) (5,000 kg)
DAF YA 2300 DHTD 7,000 kg (6 × 6) (85) (NATO)
DAF YAZ 2300 10,000 kg (6 × 6) (1,500 delivered)
DAF XF95 HET (6 × 6) (102) (ordered 2002, deliveries 2005-2006)
Mercedes-Benz Unimog (4 × 4) (small quantity of (6 × 6) to Air Force also)
Mercedes-Benz Atego range (4 × 4) small numbers
Scania P124CB8x8HZ420 (8 × 8) (533) (with LHS) (contract award late 2003)

No
A program to replace the Mercedes-Benz G-Class, Land Rover and LOHR light vehicle fleets, the DAF truck fleets (with the exception of the XF95 HET) and a selection of other current in-service types was officially launched mid-2008

New Zealand

Recovery vehicles
FMTV (6 × 6) (5) (mid-1990s)

Light vehicles
Nissan Navara (4 × 4) (>240)
Nissan Patrol (4 × 4) (10)
Pinzgauer (6 × 6) (321) (two tranches 2004-07)

Trucks
Mercedes-Benz U1300L 1,500 kg (4 × 4) (210 delivered)
Mercedes-Benz UL1700L 4,000 kg (4 × 4) (412 delivered)
Mercedes-Benz 2228/4 8,000 kg (6 × 4) (118 delivered)
Mercedes-Benz 2636AS tractor truck (4) (1982)

The refurbishment of 429 Unimogs was completed in 2001. The refurbishment was expected to give a further 10 years of service life. The Land Transport Capability Program, formerly known as the General Service Vehicle Replacement project, is a program to replace the NZDF's general service vehicle fleet, including medium and heavy vehicles, trailers and mechanical handling equipment. Preliminary work is underway on this project and a progressive vehicle replacement program is expected to begin from 2011.

Nicaragua

Recovery vehicles
T-54/T-55 ARV

Mechanised bridges
TMM-3

Light vehicles
UAZ-469B series 600 kg (4 × 4)
VW Iltis 500 kg (4 × 4) (ex-German army stocks)

Trucks
GAZ-66 (4 × 4)
KrAZ-255B 7,500 kg (6 × 6)
M35 series (6 × 6)
Mercedes-Benz Unimog U1300 (4 × 4) (possibly ex-German army stocks)
Pegaso 3045 3,000 kg (4 × 4)
Ural-375D 4,000 kg (6 × 6) (60 retrofitted with MB diesel engines; 375 transferred to Ecuador)
Ural-4320 5,000 kg (6 × 6) (possibly)

As a result of an agreement signed early in 2004, the US was to provide USD9 million in equipment (mainly wheeled transport vehicles and other equipment) as compensation for the Nicaraguan Army's decision to destroy part of its MANPADS arsenal. The status of this agreement is uncertain after a 2008 decision to halt the MANPADS destruction.

Nigeria
Recovery vehicles
SDP 4KH 7FA SB 20 Greif ARV (2)
Vickers ARV (15)
Steyr 19 S 25 (4 × 4)
Steyr 32 S 29 (6 × 6)
Steyr 14 M 22 (4 × 4) (1998)

Mechanised bridges
MTU-20 AVLB
Vickers AVLB (18)

Light vehicles
Land Rover (4 × 4)
Mahindra Jeep (4 × 4) (most recent delivery 30-40 MM540, 2004)
SDP 700 AP (4 × 4)
SDP Pinzgauer (4 × 4)
Tata SFC 407 1,000 kg (4 × 4)

Trucks
DAF YAK 4440 4,000 kg (4 × 4) (10) (ex-Dutch Army)
DAF YA 4440 4,000 kg (4 × 4) (90) (ex-Dutch Army)
KrAZ (4 × 4) (recent delivery; Police)
MAN F2000 (6 × 6) (EMPL tanker body)
Mercedes-Benz (various; Police)
Mercedes-Benz Unimog (4 × 4)
Steyr 680 M 4,500 kg (4 × 4)
Steyr 14 M 14 8,000 kg (4 × 4)
Steyr 1491.330.S34 (6 × 6) (approx. 50) (mid-to-late 1980s) (HET)
TATA (approx. 2,000) (1997 to 1998) (other deliveries likely)

From 1995 Achleitner supplied 90 three-axle, 60-tonne off-highway HET trailers to Nigeria.

Norway
Armoured engineer vehicles
Leopard AEV (22) (1999 to 2002)

Recovery vehicles
Leopard 1 ARV (6)
M88A1 ARV (3)
M578 ARV
Scania P113 HK (6 × 6)

Mechanised bridges
Leguan (8 × 8) (26) (MAN chassis)
Leopard 1 Leguan (9)

Light vehicles
IVECO LMV (4 × 4) (108) (2006-2009) (all armoured)
Land Rover (4 × 4) (small number)
Mercedes-Benz G-Class 750 kg (4 × 4) (3,500 delivered)
Mercedes-Benz G-Class 270 CDI (4 × 4)
Toyota Land Cruiser (4 × 4) (small number)

Trucks
MAN SX (8 × 8) (approx. 40)

MAN SX (8 × 8) (small number) (2007 delivery) (with IAC)
Mercedes-Benz Vario 815 DA 2,500 kg (4 × 4)
Mercedes-Benz Actros (8 × 8) (small number) (with LHS)
Scania 3 series (4 × 4) (6 × 6) (8 × 6) (>1,700) (1986 to 1995)

Oman
Recovery vehicles
Pinzgauer (6 × 6) (2001 to 2003) (<10)
Challenger ARV (4)
M88A1 (2)
MOWAG Piranha ARV (8 × 8) (2)
MOWAG Piranha repair and recovery (8 × 8)
Samson ARV (3)
IVECO EuroTrakker (6 × 6) (1)
MAN M2000 (4 × 4) (with EMPL tiltbed recovery body)
MAN M2000 (4 × 4) (with EMPL underlift top hamper)
MAN F2000 (6 × 6) (various models with EMPL top hamper)
MAN LX range (6 × 6) (with EMPL top hamper)
Reynolds Boughton 6 tonne (4 × 4)

Light vehicles
AM General HMMWV (4 × 4) (>100)
Chenowth Light Strike Vehicle (LSV)
Jeep (CJ) (4 × 4)
Jeep TJ-L (4 × 4) (4) (trials)
Land Rover Defender (4 × 4) (>1,100 incl. 100 soft top Defender 110 delivered 2001-03)
Mercedes-Benz G-Class 750 kg (4 × 4)
Pinzgauer (6 × 6) (2001 to 2003)
SDP Pinzgauer (4 × 4 and 6 × 6) (>1,200) (mostly 6 × 6)
Toyota Land Cruiser 70 Series (4 × 4)
Toyota Land Cruiser 80 or 105 Series (4 × 4)
VW Iltis 500 kg (4 × 4) (status uncertain)

Trucks
ACMAT VLRA (4 × 4) (small number; not confirmed)
Bedford TM 4-4 8,000 kg (4 × 4)
IVECO Trakker (small numbers)
MAN LX range (6 × 6)
MAN TGA range (no details)
MAN TGM range (approx. 100) (2009)
MAN Cat II (6 × 6) (95)
MAN 16.284 LAE (4 × 4) (approx. 600) (deliveries commenced 2004)
MAN 18.284 LAE (4 × 4)
MAN F2000-based (8 × 8) (with torsion-free rear body)
MAN LX range (400-500) (1992 onwards)
Oshkosh M977 HEMTT (8 × 8) (no other details available)
Oshkosh M911 (6 × 6) (15; 1985) (15; 1991-92) (refurbishment scheduled)
Unipower MH6660 HET (6 × 6) (9) (1995)

Pakistan
Recovery vehicles
M88A1 ARV (52)
Type 653 ARV

Mechanised bridges
M47M AVLB (trials)
M48 AVLB

Light vehicles
Beijing BJ-212/212A (4 × 4)
IVECO 40-10 WM 1,500 kg (4 × 4) (2,200)
KM450 (4 × 4) (is, or has, replaced the visually almost identical M715)
Land Rover Defender (4 × 4) (approx. 1,800) (1999-00) (BU)
Land Rover Defender 90/110 (4 × 4) (3,750) (2000-05) (civilian spec for local conversion) (Army) (KD)
Land Rover Defender 90/110/130 (4 × 4) 2,800 (from 2006; around 1,000 supplied by January

2007 - deliveries post-2007 will be 2007 model year specification) (Army) (KD)
Land Rover Defender 90/110 (4 × 4) (808)
M880 series 1,133 kg (4 × 4) (4 × 2)
M151 Mutt 362 kg (4 × 4) (>1,000 delivered) (1988)
M715 (4 × 4) (being, or has been, replaced by the visually almost identical KM450)
Nispak 400 kg (4 × 4) (production status uncertain, probably complete)
Toyota Land Cruiser 70 Series (4 × 4)

Trucks
Hino (various; no other details)
Isuzu (various; no other details)
IVECO 90.17 4,000 kg (4 × 4) (final deliveries 2001)
KrAZ-260 9,000 kg (6 × 6)
MAN M2000 (4 × 4) (small number, no details available)
Mercedes-Benz Unimog (4 × 4)
M35/M44 series 2,268 kg (6 × 6)
M809 series 4,536 kg (6 × 6)
Mercedes-Benz 2028A 10,000 kg (6 × 6)
Mercedes-Benz 2636AS (6 × 6) HET (100 ordered 1984)
Mercedes-Benz Actros (6 × 6) (500) (2005-2009)
Mercedes-Benz Actros (6 × 6) (40) (2008) (HET)
Steyr 5,000 kg (4 × 4)
Tiema XC2030 8,000 kg (6 × 6)
Yasoob Mk1/Mk2 6,000 kg (6 × 6) (approx. 450) (1993-95) (production complete)
Yasoob 4,000 kg (4 × 4) (approx. 250) (1993-95) (production complete)

Beijing Jeep Corporation BJ2020 series light vehicles are known to be assembled from KD kits in Pakistan by Adam Motor Co. under the local name of Zabardast.

Panama
Light vehicles
CUCV (4 × 4)

Trucks
M35/M44 series 2,268 kg (6 × 6)
M809 series 4,536 kg (6 × 6)

Panama has no army *per se*. The >10,000 strong Panamanian National Police (PNP) is the equivalent force.

Papua New Guinea
Light vehicles
Land Rover (4 × 4)

The strength of the Army is approximately 1,800 personnel; the PNGDF is badly in need of new equipment.

Peru
Recovery vehicles
M578 (small number)

Light vehicles
AIL M-240 Storm (4 × 4) (Police, small number)
AM General HMMWV (4 × 4) (<50) (2009)
Gurgel X-12 (40) (used by special forces)
Jeep Cherokee (4 × 4) (small numbers, MP and VIP transport)
Jeep Wrangler (4 × 4) army, navy and air force, special forces and MPs)
Kia K-3000 2,500 kg (60) (acquired as part-replacement for aging donated Japanese light vehicles)
M38 Jeep (4 × 4) (second line units, numbers reducing)
M151 Mutt 362 kg (4 × 4)
Peugeot P4 (4 × 4) (<20)
Toyota Hi-Ace and Hi-Lux (small numbers)
VW Beetle-based fast-attack buggies (4 × 2) (assorted designs)
Assorted donated Japanese- used light vehicles (>300 delivered mid-1990s, of which most are FAW CA1020LF)

Trucks

AIL M325 1,800 kg Commandcar (4 × 4) (approx. 300) (air force (special forces), army and navy)
AIL M462 1,890 kg Abir tactical truck (4 × 4) (approx. 200; army approx. 100, Police >100)
Dong Feng (EQ2081E 2,500 kg) (6 × 6) (approx. 200)
Kenworth T600 (low-mobility) (few dozen, used by engineer battalions)
Kia Motors KM25 2.5-ton (6 × 6) (38) (2006)
KrAZ-255B (6 × 6)
Magirus Deutz 310M32 ANWTM and 320D24 (6 × 6) (at least 70) (HET)
MAN Cat II 14.240 6,000 kg (6 × 6) (> 100 remain in service) (known locally as MAN M20/280 DF)
Mercedes-Benz U416 Unimog (4 × 4) (short and long wheelbase) (army, numbers reducing)
Mercedes-Benz S404 Unimog (4 × 4) (navy and air force)
Mercedes-Benz LA-1113 (4 × 4) (>100 remain in service) (army)
M35 series 2,268 kg (6 × 6) (small number may remain)
NORINCO (4 × 4) (2010)
NORINCO (6 × 6) (2010)
Pegaso 3046/10 3,000 kg (4 × 4) (navy, refurbished)
Pegaso 3050 6,000 kg (6 × 6) (navy)
Ural 375 4,000 kg (6 × 6) (>100)
Ural 4320 4,000 kg (6 × 6) (army)
Volvo N1020 low-mobility (few dozen, used by engineer battalions)
Volvo N1027 low mobility (few dozen, used by engineer battalions)
Volvo NL10 (6 × 4) (few dozen, used by engineer battalions)
Volvo NL12 (6 × 4) (few dozen, used by engineer battalions)
Zil-131 3,500 kg (6 × 6)

Philippines

Recovery vehicles
M578 ARV
M816 W (6 × 6) (36)
Freightliner M916 series (6 × 6) (10)

Light vehicles
AM General HMMWV (4 × 4) (440)
CM-125 1,250 kg (4 × 4)
Delta Explorer (4 × 4) (Toyota 40 Series clone)
Kia Motors KM45 (4 × 4) (650) (2007-2009)
M151 Mutt 362 kg (4 × 4)

Trucks
LARC-5 4,545 kg (4 × 4) (amphibious)
M35/M44 series 2,268 kg (6 × 6)
M809 series 4,536 kg (6 × 6)
Freightliner M917 (6 × 6) (4)
Freightliner M916A1 (6 × 6) (4) (tractor trucks)

Poland

Armoured engineer vehicles
IWT CEV (T-55 chassis)
MT-LB engineer reconnaissance vehicle

Recovery vehicles
Leopard 1 ARV (10)
MT-LB technical support vehicle
T-54/T-55 ARV
WZT-3 ARV
WPT-TOPAS ARV

Mechanised bridges
BLG-67M2 AVLB
SMT-1 (6 × 6)

Light vehicles
AM General HMMWV (4 × 4) (229) (2004-2008)
Honker Skorpion RDV (4 × 4) (31) (ordered 2004)
Honker (4 × 4) (2,000 est.)
IVECO 40.12 (4 × 4) (50) (ambulance bodies only)
IVECO 40.13 (4 × 4) (43) (2007-2009) (ambulance bodies only)

Jeep J-8 (4 × 4) (2009) (MoI)
Land Rover Defender (4 × 4) (>180 including some special forces and 138 × 110 (2005-10) for the Zandarmeria Wojskowa (ZW - Military Police) (BU)
Mercedes-Benz G-Class (4 × 4) (small number)
Pinzgauer (4 × 4) (small number) (status uncertain)
SCAM SM55 (4 × 4) (115) (2002-04) (ambulance bodies only)
Toyota Hilux (4 × 4)
UAZ-469B series 600 kg (4 × 4)

Trucks
FAUN SLT 50-3 (8 × 8) (transferred from German Army stocks) (HET)
IVECO EuroTrakker MP720E47WT HET (2), MP720E48WT HET (approx. 45) (6 × 6) (2000 to 2008)
IVECO Stralis (commercial pattern)
Jelcz (various) (<300) (2005-2009)
Jelcz (various) (pre-2004)
KrAZ 255 (6 × 6) (to be replaced as soon as funds permit)
MAN (various) (>20) (1999-2003)
Mercedes-Benz Actros 3353AS HET (6 × 6) (9) (2002 to 2002)
Robur LO 1800 A 1,800 kg (4 × 4)
Star 66 2,500 kg (6 × 6)
Star 266 3,500 kg (6 × 6)
Star 266M 3,500 kg (6 × 6) (upgraded Star 266)
Star 244 5,000 kg (4 × 4) (small number)
Star 944 5,000 kg (4 × 4) (650) (2001-2007)
Star 1466 6,000 kg (6 × 6) (<30) (production complete)
TATRA T813/T815 (8 × 8) (to be replaced as soon as funds permit)
Volvo FM12 (6 × 6) (small number with LHS)
Zil 131 3,500 kg (6 × 6) (to be replaced as soon as funds permit)

Portugal

Armoured engineer vehicles
M728 CEV

Recovery vehicles
M88A1 (6)
SDP Pandur II (8 × 8) (7) (ordered 2004; deliveries 2006-09)
Mercedes-Benz Actros 3340/41 (6 × 6) (EMPL top hamper)

Light vehicles
AM General HMMWV (4 × 4) (approx 50)
Chenowth Light Strike Vehicle (LSV)
IVECO 40.10 1,500 kg (4 × 4)
Land Rover Defender 90/110 (4 × 4) incl.. small number during 2009)
Mercedes-Benz G-Class (4 × 4) (small number)
Mercedes-Benz Sprinter 313CDI (4 × 4) (small number)
Mitsubishi L200 (4 × 4)
MWG 1,500 kg (6 × 6) (6)
Toyota Land Cruiser (4 × 4)
Toyota Hilux (4 × 4)
UMM Alter (4 × 4)
UMM 490 1,000 kg (4 × 4)

Trucks
Berliet GBC 8 KT 4,000 kg (6 × 6)
Berliet GBC 8 4,000 kg (4 × 4)
DAF YA 4440 4,000 kg (4 × 4) (300) (1984 to 1985)
IVECO 90-17 WM 4,000 kg (4 × 4)
IVECO EuroCargo
IVECO-Magirus (6 × 4) (6 × 6)
LARC-5 4,545 kg (4 × 4) (amphibious cargo carrier)
MAN 10.224 LAEK (4 × 4) (small numbers)
MAN (6 × 4) (6 × 6)
Mercedes-Benz Unimog (4 × 4)
Mercedes-Benz 1017 (4 × 2)/1017A (4 × 4) 5,000 kg trucks
Mercedes-Benz Atego (4 × 2) (4 × 4)
Mercedes-Benz Actros (tractor truck)
M35 series (6 × 6)

M809 series (6 × 6)
Scania 4-series (4 × 4) (13) (with dump bodies)
Volvo FH12 (tractor trucks)

Qatar

Recovery vehicles
AMX-30D ARV (1)
Piranha repair and recovery vehicles (2)
MAN F2000-based (6 × 6) (6) (2003) (EMPL recovery hamper)
Mercedes-Benz 2632 (6 × 6) (EMPL recovery equipment)
Mercedes-Benz Actros 3348 (6 × 6) (EMPL recovery hamper)

Light vehicles
AM General HMMWV (40)
Land Rover (4 × 4)
Toyota Land Cruiser 70 series (4 × 4)

Trucks
Avibras ASTROS MRS (6 × 6) (3 batteries) (Mercedes-Benz truck based)
Berliet TBH280 (6 × 6) (HET)
Berliet (6 × 4)
KaMAZ (various)
MAN F2000 range (post-2001) (no other details available)
Mercedes-Benz LK range (4 × 4)
Mercedes-Benz 2632 (6 × 6)
Mercedes-Benz Actros range
Oshkosh HEMTT (8 × 8)
Renault TRM 2000 2,000 kg (4 × 4) (10)
Zil-131 (6 × 6)

Romania

Recovery vehicles
T-54/T-55 ARV

Mechanised bridges
MT-55A AVLB
BLG-67M AVLB
BLG-67M2 AVLB

Light vehicles
Achleitner MANTRA (4 × 4) (16) (2008) (ambulance)
AM General HMMWV (4 × 4) (20) (2006-2007)
ARO range (4 × 4) (est. 1,000)
UAZ-469B series 600 kg (4 × 4)
URO VAMTAC (4 × 4) (2006) (<70 - incl. 20 armoured)

Trucks
DAC 8.120 FAEG 2,380 kg (4 × 4)
DAC 8.140 FAE 2,200 kg (4 × 4) (not confirmed)
DAC 11.154 FAEG 2,500 kg (4 × 4) (small number)
DAC 13.215 FAEG 5,000 kg (4 × 4)
DAC 14.250 (4 × 4) (small number)
DAC 15.215 DFAEG 5,000 kg (6 × 6)
DAC 15.240 DFAEG 5,000 kg (6 × 6)
DAC 16.215 FA 6,765 kg (4 × 4) (>900) (1985-1994)
DAC 16.230 (4 × 4) (approx. 300) (1995-2000)
DAC 16.240 FA 7,000 kg (4 × 4)
DAC 21.410 VFAEG 7,000 kg (8 × 8) (not confirmed)
DAC 23.210 (6 × 6) DFAEG (2007) (small number)
DAC 33.360 DFA 19,400 kg (6 × 6)
ROMAN 26.360 DFAEG (6 × 6) (basis for a number of prototype platforms)
ROMAN 33.360 DFA (6 × 6) (tractor truck for light armour)
ROMAN 33.460 DFAS (6 × 6) (heavy tractor truck) (prototype)
TATRA-T815 series (8 × 8)
Ural-375D 4,000 kg (6 × 6)

DAC models (produced by ROMAN) are now branded ROMAN)

Russian Federation

Armoured engineer vehicles
BAT-2 CEV
IMR-2 CEV (T-72 chassis)
IMR CEV (T-55 chassis)
IRM engineer reconnaissance vehicle
MT-LB engineer vehicle

Recovery vehicles
BMP-1 light ARV
BREM-K ARV
BREM-D ARV
BTR-50PK (B) amphibious ARV
BREM-1 ARV (T-72 chassis)
BREhM-D repair and recovery vehicle
BREM-L ARV
M1977 ARV
MTP-LB technical support vehicle
RM-G tracked repair vehicle
T-54/T-55 ARV
VT-72B ARV
VPV ARV (BMP-1 chassis)
KET-L (6 × 6) (Ural chassis)
Ural MTP-A2 (6 × 6)
Ural-375D (6 × 6)
Ural-4320 (6 × 6)

Mechanised bridges
Gusenitsa-2 (trials)
MT-55 AVLB
MTU-72 AVLB
MTU-20 AVLB
MTU AVLB
PMM-2 ABFS
TMM-6 (trials)

Light vehicles
GAZ-2330 series (4 × 4) (developed as the Tiger (AB17) for UAE/Jordan)
LuAZ-967M (4 × 4)
LuAZ-969 series (4 × 4)
UAZ-469B series 600 kg (4 × 4)
UAZ-3151/Hunter series (4 × 4)
UAZ-452D 800 kg (4 × 4)

Trucks
BAZ-5937 (6 × 6) (specialist applications)
BAZ-5939 (6 × 6) (specialist applications)
BAZ (6 × 6) (8 × 8) (specialist applications; essentially the long term replacement for the earlier BAZ-5937/5939 and similar chassis)
GAZ-63 2,000 kg (4 × 4) (numbers reducing)
GAZ-66 2,000 kg (4 × 4) (numbers reducing)
GAZ-3308 Sadko 2,000 kg (4 × 4) (replacement for GAZ-66)
GAZ-3307/3309 (4 × 2) (4 × 2 commercial version of GAZ-3308)
GAZ 3937 (4 × 4) (usually protected)
GAZ-53 3,000 kg (4 × 2) (numbers reducing)
KaMAZ-5320 series 8,000 kg (6 × 4/6 × 6) (original KamAZ series models from which all current designs evolved)
KamAZ-4310 series 6,000 kg (4 × 4) (followed by 4326, 43114 and 43118)
KamAZ-43101 series (6 × 6) (followed by 4326, 43114 and 43118)
KamAZ-4326 series (4 × 4) (later 43261)
KamAZ-43114 (6 × 6)
KamAZ-43118 (6 × 6)
KamAZ-44108 (6 × 6) (tractor truck)
KamAZ-4350 Mustang series (4 × 4) (followed by 43501 and 43502)
KamAZ-5350 Mustang series (6 × 6) (followed by 53501)
KamAZ-6350 Mustang series (8 × 8) (followed by 63501 and 63502)
KamAZ-53504 Mustang series (6 × 6) (tractor truck)
KamAZ-6520 series (6 × 4) (base for a heavy family in 6 × 6 configuration with single or twin rear tyres)
KrAZ-214 7,000 kg (6 × 6) (numbers reducing)
KrAZ-255B/B17,500 kg (6 × 6) (numbers reducing)
KrAZ-260 9,000 kg (6 × 6)

MAZ-543 (now MZKT-543) series (8 × 8) (specialist applications incl. HETs)
MZKT-7930 (8 × 8) (small numbers, specialist applications)
MZKT-74287 (8 × 8) (small numbers, replacement HET for MAZ 543)
MZKT-8022 (4 × 4) (small numbers, specialist applications)
Ural-375/375D 4,000 kg (6 × 6) (numbers reducing)
Ural-4320 series (6 × 6) (current base chassis designated Ural-4320-31)
Ural-43206 series (4 × 4)
Ural-5323 series (8 × 8)
Ural-377 7,500 kg (6 × 6) (numbers reducing)
YaAZ-214 7,000 kg (6 × 6) (numbers reducing)
ZIL-130 (4 × 2) (numbers reducing)
ZIL-131 3,500 kg (6 × 6) (numbers reducing)
ZIL-433420 series (6 × 6) (replacement series for ZIL-131; entered series production in 1995)
ZIL-135 (8 × 8) (specialist applications)
ZIL-151 2,500 kg (4 × 4) (numbers reducing)
ZIL-157 2,500 kg (6 × 6) (numbers reducing)
ZIL-432720 series (4 × 4) (production commenced in 1998)

Saudi Arabia

Armoured engineer vehicles
M728 CEV (15)

Mechanised bridges
AMX-30 AVLB (12)

Recovery vehicles
AMX-10 ECH RV
AMX-30D ARV (57)
M88A1 ARV (139)
M578 ARV (88)
Leclerc ARV
BMR 3560.55 ARV (6 × 6)
LAV (8 × 8) (67)
LAV-150 ARV (4 × 4)
Steyr 19 S 25 (4 × 4) RV (EMPL top hamper)
Steyr 32 S 29 (6 × 6) RV (EMPL top hamper)
M984A1 HEMTT (8 × 8)

Light vehicles
AB3 Desert Iris LSV (4 × 4) (est. 150) (ordered confirmed 2004)
Achleitner Mantra (4 × 4) (200) (2000-2002)
AM General HMMWV (4 × 4) (3,829) (deliveries ongoing)
ATL Pinzgauer (6 × 6) (approx. 50) (2000 to 2001)
Land Rover APV 564 kg (4 × 4) (numbers reducing)
Land Rover Defender 110 (4 × 4)
Light Tactical Vehicle (LTV) (4 × 4) (380) (2007)
M151 Mutt 362 kg (4 × 4)
Panhard (Auverland A3) (4 × 4) (50) (2005)
Panhard (Auverland A3L) (4 × 4) (84) (not confirmed)
Panhard (Sovamag TC-10) 1,100 kg (4 × 4) (32) (not confirmed)
Panhard (Sovamag TC-24) (4 × 4) (34) (not confirmed)
SDP Pinzgauer (4 × 4) (6 × 6) (est. 3,200)
Toyota Land Cruiser (4 × 4)

Trucks
ACMAT VLRA (4 × 4) (approx. 80)
ACMAT VLRA (6 × 6) (approx. 120)
Avibras ASTROS MRS (6 × 6) (est. 10 batteries) (Mercedes-Benz truck based)
BAE Systems (Stewart & Stevenson) FMTV (6 × 6) (Patriot support vehicles)
FAP 2026 BS (6 × 6)
IVECO Cargo (4 × 4) (from 2006) (incl. Trakker est. 800)
IVECO Trakker (6 × 6) (from 2006) (incl. Cargo est. 800)
Jiefang CA-1091 (C-141) 5,000 kg (4 × 2) (military use not confirmed)
KamAZ 43101 (6 × 6) (500 delivered) (1991) (cargo) (possibly cast)
KamAZ 55288 (6 × 6) (500 delivered) (1991) (tankers) (possibly cast)

MAN M2000 (4 × 4) (>200) (2000-2003)
MAN F2000 (6 × 6) (8 × 8) (>200) (1999-2003)
Mercedes-Benz Unimog (4 × 4)
Mercedes-Benz Actros (6 × 6) (2007-2008)
M35/M44 2,268 kg (6 × 6)
M809 4,536 kg (6 × 6)
M939A2 4,536 kg (6 × 6) (2,633) (1991-1992)
Oshkosh HEMTT 9,979 kg (8 × 8) (est. 200)
Oshkosh M911 (6 × 6) (760) (1991-92) (HET)
Oshkosh M1070 (8 × 8) (50) (1993) (HET)
Panhard TC-54 (4 × 4) (133) (not confirmed)
RENAULT TRM 9000 9,000 kg (6 × 6) (38)
RENAULT TRM 10,000 10,000 kg (6 × 6) (67 delivered)
Steyr 18 M 28 (4 × 4) (>100)
Steyr 17M series (4 × 4)
Steyr 24M series (6 × 6)
Steyr 26 M 42 (8 × 8)
Steyr M2000 series (4 × 4) (various)
Steyr 3891/6 × 6 (6 × 6) (approx. 40) (mid-to-late 1980) (HET)
TAM 110 T7 BV 1,500/2,500 kg (4 × 4)
TAM 140 T11 BV 3,000/5,000 kg (6 × 6)
Tata SA1212 TC (4 × 4)
TATRA T-815 series (8 × 8) (not confirmed)
Tata SA 1212 TC 4,000 kg (4 × 4)
TATRA T-815 series (no other details)

Senegal

Light vehicles
M151 Mutt 362 kg (4 × 4)
Peugeot P4 750 kg (4 × 4) (10)

Trucks
ACMAT VLRA (4 × 4)
Jiefang CA 1121 (4 × 2)
M35/M44 series 2,268 kg (6 × 6)
M809 series 4,536 kg (6 × 6)
Sovamag TC 24 2,500 kg (4 × 4) (1)

In 2001, the US offered Senegal USD5 million worth of surplus equipment for use by Senegalese peacekeepers in Sierra Leone. French military assistance almost certainly means that some of Senegal's requirements will be met by 'cascaded' French equipment. A little more than two years after Senegal restored diplomatic ties with China, in December 2007 Beijing gave Senegal's Army, trucks, ambulances, communication and mine clearance equipment worth EUR1.5 million to help with peacekeeping missions. An agreement for a second shipment of military goods of equivalent value was also signed between the two countries. In October 2008 Senegal received 82 trucks worth USD6 million from the United States prior to their peacekeeping deployment to Darfur.

Serbia

Armoured engineer vehicles
IWT CEV (equivalent to Russian IMR)

Recovery vehicles
T-54/T-55 ARV
M-84A1 ARV

Mechanised bridges
MT-55 AVLB
TMM-3 (6 × 6)

Light vehicles
AM General HMMWV (4 × 4) (small number; special forces)
FIAT Campagnola 1,107 AD 750 kg (4 × 4)
IMR A-0.75 750/1,000 kg (4 × 4)
IMR TARA 1,200 kg (4 × 4)
Land Rover Defender (4 × 4) (commercial spec)
Mercedes-Benz G-Class (4 × 4) (500 delivered)
SDP Pinzgauer
Zastava AR-51 500 kg (4 × 4)

Trucks
TAM 110 T7 BV 1,500/2,500 kg (4 × 4)
TAM 150 T11 BV 3,000/5,000 kg (6 × 6)

TAM 4500 4,500 kg (4 × 4)
TAM 5000 5,000 kg (4 × 4)
TAM 5500 5,500 kg (4 × 4)
TAM 6500 6,500 kg (4 × 4)
FAP 2220 BDS (6 × 4)
FAP 2026 BS/AV 10,000 kg (6 × 6)
FAP 2832 BS/AV 9,000 kg (6 × 6)
FAP 3232 BDST/AV (8 × 8) HET

Singapore

Armoured engineer vehicles
M728 CEV (8)
Combat Engineer Tractor (36)

Recovery vehicles
Bionix ARV
M806A1 ARV
M113A1 fitters
V-200 ARV (4 × 4)

Mechanised bridges
AMX-13 AVLB
Bionix AVLB
M60 AVLB (12)
M2 system (4 × 4) (36) (upgraded)

Light vehicles
Ford Everest (4 × 4) (870) (from 2007)
Mercedes-Benz G-Class 750 kg (4 × 4) (311)
Land Rover 110 (4 × 4) (approx. 3,000) (being replaced)
M151 Mutt 362 kg (4 × 4)
STK Flyer LSV (4 × 4) (79)

Trucks
BAE Systems FMTV (6 × 6) (18) (2009) (HIMARS)
IVECO 90-17/90-16 4,000 kg (4 × 4) (1990 to 1991) (3,000)
LARC-5 4,545 kg (4 × 4) (amphibious cargo carrier)
MAN Cat II 10,000 kg (6 × 6) (165)
MAN 16.284 LAERC (4 × 4) (>1,100) (deliveries concluded 2002)
MAN (6 × 6) and (8 × 8) (2008-2009)
Mercedes-Benz Unimog (4 × 4)
Mercedes-Benz 911 (4 × 4) (status uncertain)
Mercedes-Benz Actros with Multilift LHS (8 × 8) (130) (2000 to 2002)
Mercedes-Benz (8 × 8) (transporters for Eurobridge)
MOWAG DURO (4 × 4) (61) (2000-02)

Slovakia

Recovery vehicles
MT-55 ARV
VT-55A ARV
VT-72B ARV
VPV ARV (BMP-1 chassis)
WPT-TOPAS ARV (OT-62A chassis)
AD-90 (6 × 6)
TATRA AV-15 (8 × 8)

Mechanised bridges
MT-55A AVLB
AM-50 (6 × 6)

Light vehicles
Mercedes-Benz G-Class (4 × 4) (approx. 60) (from mid-1990s)
UAZ-469B series 600 kg (4 × 4) (approx. 400)

Trucks
BAZ SNA 4,000 kg (6 × 6) (approx. 400) (original Czechoslovak replacement for Praga V3S)
KrAZ-255B (6 × 6) (small number)
KrAZ-260 (6 × 6) (including SA-10 Grumble support vehicles)
MAZ-543 (8 × 8) (SA-10 Grumble)
Praga V3S 3,000 kg (6 × 6) (<1,000) (to be replaced by the TATRA Sipox Aktis)
TATRA 148 14,580 kg (6 × 6)

TATRA 138 11,850 kg (6 × 6)
TATRA 813 7,900 kg (8 × 8)
TATRA 815 8,000 kg (8 × 8)
TANAX Aktis 4 × 4.1R 3,500 kg (4 × 4) (>100) (from 2001) (deliveries continue)
ZIL-131 3,500 kg (6 × 6) (to be replaced by the TANAX Aktis)

Somalia

Light vehicles
Commercial SUV and pick-ups (various)
M151 Mutt 362 kg (4 × 4)
M825 Mutt 362 kg (4 × 4) (25 converted from M151) (1987)

Trucks
ACMAT VLRA (4 × 4)
IVECO 90-17 WM 4,000 kg (4 × 4) (100)
IVECO 75-14 WM 2,500 kg (4 × 4)
IVECO 6605 (6 × 6) (291)
M35/M44 series 2,268 kg (6 × 6)
M809 series 4,536 kg (6 × 6)
Pegaso 3046/10 3,000 kg (4 × 4)
Pegaso 3050 and/or 3055 6,000 kg (6 × 6)

Following the overthrow of Major General Siad Barre by the United Somali Congress (USC) on 27 January 1991, Somalia ceased to have a functioning central government, and, consequently, has not had a formal national army per se. The Transitional Federal Government (TFG) has an army, however, much like the government, until recently has been an army mostly in name only.

South Africa

Recovery vehicles
Olifant ARV (Centurion chassis)
Ratel (6 × 6)
SAMIL 50 (4 × 4) (to be replaced/part-replaced under Project Vistula)
SAMIL 100 (6 × 6) (to be replaced/part-replaced under Project Vistula)

Mechanised bridges
Olifant AVLB (28)

Light vehicles
BAE Systems Wasp/Hornet (4 × 4) (25) (delivered 2004-05)
Gecko 880 kg (8 × 8) (106 (75 + 31)) (2003)
Jakkals 350 kg (4 × 4) (replaced by Gecko)
Land Rover LWB (4 × 4) (tactical roles)
Tata SFC 407 1,000 kg (4 × 4)
Toyota Land Cruiser (4 × 4) (semi/non-tactical roles)
Toyota Hilux (4 × 4) (semi/non-tactical roles)

Trucks
Kynos Aljaba (8 × 8) (72) (specialist applications)
Kynos Cavallo HET (8 × 8)
MAN (6 × 6) (HET)
Mercedes-Benz Unimog (4 × 4)
MOWAG DURO (4 × 4) (14) (2000-02)
SAKOM/SAMAG (not all-wheel drive) (to be replaced/part-replaced under Project Vistula; announcement pending)
SAMIL 20 2,000 kg (4 × 4) (to be replaced/part-replaced under Project Vistula; announcement pending)
SAMIL 50 5,000 kg (4 × 4) (to be replaced/part-replaced under Project Vistula; announcement pending)
SAMIL 100 10,000 kg (6 × 6) (to be replaced/part-replaced under Project Vistula; announcement pending)
Tata LPTA 713 TC 2,500 kg (4 × 4)

Spain

Armoured engineer vehicles
CZ-10/25E (38)

Recovery vehicles
AAVR7 (1)
Büffel ARV (16)
GEMESA M47VR ARV (22) (1996 to 1997)
M88A1 ARV (1)
M578 ARV
BMR 3560.55 (6 × 6) ARV
M543 W (6 × 6)

Mechanised bridges
M60 AVLB (12)

Light vehicles
AM General HMMWV (4 × 4) (est. 150) (Marines)
Chenowth Light Strike Vehicle (LSV)
Citroën Méhari Armée (4 × 2) (status uncertain)
EINSA Model MM-1A MATV 1,200 kg (4 × 4) (14) (army and navy)
Fresia 1,000 kg (4 × 4) (48) (airborne forces)
IVECO 40.10 1,500 kg (4 × 4)
LOHR (SOFRAME) Fardier (4 × 4) (status uncertain)
M151 Mutt 362 kg (4 × 4) (status uncertain)
M37 680 kg (4 × 4) (status uncertain)
Nissan Patrol ML-6 (4 × 4) (local build)
Santana Model 88 500 kg (4 × 4) (replacement underway)
Santana Model 109 1,000 kg (4 × 4) (replacement underway)
Santana PS-10 (4 × 4) (75) (2003) (navy)
Santana PS-10 (4 × 4) (>3,300) (2005-2009)
URO VAMTAC T3 1,500 kg (4 × 4) (approx. 720) (1998-2006)
URO VAMTAC I3 1,500 kg (4 × 4) (from late 2006; up to 1,000 incl. S3 required)
URO VAMTAC T5 1,500 kg (4 × 4) (approx. 500) (1998-2006)
URO VAMTAC S3 1,500 kg (4 × 4) (from late 2006; up to 1,000 incl. I3 required)

Trucks
IVECO 250.37 12,000 kg (6 × 6) (approx. 400) (2000-2002) (superseded by IVECO 250.40)
IVECO 250.40 12,000 kg (6 × 6) (approx. 500) (from 2003)
IVECO 320.42 15,000 kg (8 × 8) (8) (2000-2002) (superseded by IVECO 320.45)
IVECO 320.45 15,000 kg (8 × 8) (approx. 50) (from 2003)
IVECO Euro range (various)
IVECO-Pegaso VAP 3550/1 3,000 kg (4 × 4) (amphibious vehicle; Marines)
Kynos Aljaba HET (8 × 8) (10)
Kynos Aljaba K15-100 HET (6 × 6) (49) (2000-06)
M35/M44 series 268 kg (6 × 6)
M54 series 4,356 kg (6 × 6)
M809 series 4,536 kg (6 × 6)
Mercedes-Benz Unimog (4 × 4) (small number)
Pegaso 3046 3,000 kg (4 × 4) (>4,000 delivered)
Pegaso 3055 6,000 kg (6 × 6)
Pegaso 7323 6,000 kg (6 × 6) (>1,000 delivered) (1987 to 1988)
Pegaso 7217 4,000 kg (4 × 4) (>200) (from 1987)
Pegaso 7223 4,000 kg (4 × 4)
Pegaso 7226 4,000 kg (4 × 4) (est. 400) (from 2001)
Santana S-2000 2,000 kg (4 × 4) (status uncertain)
URO MT and MAT range 2,000 kg (4 × 4) (approx. 1000) (1984 to 2003)
URO MT (4 × 4) (15) (2009)

Sri Lanka

Armoured recovery vehicles
Type 653 ARV
VT-55A ARV

Light vehicles
Land Rover (4 × 4)
Mahindra Jeep (4 × 4) (regular deliveries)
Mahindra Scorpio (4 × 4)
Tata SFC 407 1,000 kg (4 × 4)
Tata Sumo (4 × 4)

Trucks

Ashok Leyland Comet 10,000 kg (4 × 4) (approx. 200) (2004)
M35 series (6 × 6)
Tata SD 1015 TC (4 × 4) (Field Artillery Tractor (FAT))
Tata SA 1212 TC 4,000 kg (4 × 4)
TATRA (8 × 8) (MLRS)
Tiema XC2030 8,000 kg (6 × 6)

The Sri Lankan Army is reported to have secured a deal with the US government to purchase 200 reconditioned Army trucks; it is not known if deliveries occurred. In May 2000, the Czech Republic supplied the Sri Lanka Army with a package of equipment including six tank recovery vehicles and six tank transporters, the latter likely a TATRA design.

Sudan

Recovery vehicles
M113 ARV
M88A1 ARV (2)
T-54/T-55 ARV
M3 repair vehicle (4 × 4)

Light vehicles
Beijing BJ212 series Jeep (4 × 4)
Land Rover ALV 564 kg (4 × 4)
SDP Pinzgauer
Toyota Land Cruiser (4 × 4)

Trucks
IVECO-Magirus 75-13 AWM 2,500 kg (4 × 4)
IVECO-Magirus 90-13 ANWM 4,000 kg (4 × 4)
IVECO-Magirus 120-19 ANWM 5,000 kg (4 × 4)
IVECO-Magirus 160-23 ANWM 7,000 kg (6 × 6)
IVECO-Magirus 260-23 ANWM (6 × 6) (tippers)
IVECO-Magirus 330-32 ANWTM (6 × 6) HET
KrAZ (6 × 6 - probable) (2005) (no other details)
MAN 16.220 LE M2000 (4 × 4) (2,700) (ordered late-2005; deliveries likely to include follow-on TGM variant)
MAN TGA 26.410 (6 × 6) (300) (ordered late-2005)
M35/M44 series 2,268 kg (6 × 6)
M809 series 4,536 kg (6 × 6)
SAMIL 50 5,000 kg (4 × 4) (ex-SANDF)
SAMIL 100 10,000 kg (6 × 6) (ex-SANDF)
URAL-4320 (6 × 6) (not confirmed)

Sweden

Armoured engineer vehicles
Kodiak (6 ordered 2008)

Recovery vehicles
Bgbv 82 ARV (24)
Bgbv 81 ARV (Centurion Mk 2)
Büffel ARV (14)
CV 90 ARV (26)
Scania 3-series (6 × 6)
Scania P124CB6x6HZ 4-series (6 × 6)

Mechanised bridges
Brobv AVLB (17)

Light vehicles
Mercedes-Benz G-Class 750 kg (4 × 4)
Mercedes-Benz Sprinter 313 CDI/413 CDI (4 × 4)
Toyota Land Cruiser (4 × 4)
Volvo L3314 Laplander (4 × 4) (numbers reducing)

Trucks
MAN SX range (8 × 8) (approx. 30)
Scania SBA 111 4,500 kg (4 × 4) (numbers reduced, some cascaded)
Scania SBAT 111S 6,000 kg (6 × 6) (numbers reduced, some cascaded)
Scania 3-series (various configurations)
Scania 4-series (>400) (1996-2005) (various configurations)
Scania T144GB6x4NZ530 HET (6 × 4) (31) (1998)

Scania T143E HET (6 × 4) (19) (1990 to 1996)
Volvo 4140 (4 × 4) (numbers reducing)
Volvo 4140 (6 × 6) (numbers reducing)
Volvo BM A25C (6 × 6) (articulated steering)
Volvo FL6 5,000 kg (4 × 4)
Volvo FL10 and FL12 (6 × 6) (approx. 200)
Volvo FM9 (various support roles) (not all-wheel drive)
Volvo FM12 (4 × 4)
Volvo FM12 (6 × 6) (incl. 40 or use with pontoon bridging equipment and 30 with Quick Lock mounting system, 2003)
Volvo N10 (various support roles) (not all-wheel drive)
Volvo NL10 (4 × 4)
Volvo N12 HET (6 × 4) (60 delivered) (from 1977)
The Scania SBA 111 4,500 kg (4 × 4) and the Scania SBAT 111S 6,000 kg (6 × 6) make a total of 2,500 delivered.

Switzerland

Armoured Engineer Vehicles
Kodiak (12 ordered 2007)

Recovery vehicles
Büffel (25)
Saurer Gottwald (6 × 6) (100 delivered) (1982 to 1986)

Mechanised bridges
Bru Pz 68/88 AVLB

Light vehicles
AM General HMMWV (5) (delivered)
Mercedes-Benz G-Class 750 kg (4 × 4) (5,300) (1988 to 1996) (as Puch GE 230)
Mercedes-Benz Sprinter 313 CDI 1,200 kg (4 × 4) (150) (2000 to 2001)
Mercedes-Benz Sprinter 413 CDI 2,300 kg (4 × 4) (250) (2000 to 2001)
SDP Pinzgauer (4 × 4) (6 × 6) (6,300 delivered) (1971 onwards (4 × 4)) (1973 onwards (6 × 6))
Toyota Land Cruiser 450 GX 780 kg (4 × 4) (22) (1995)

Trucks
IVECO EuroTrakker MP190E35W 9,000 kg (4 × 4) (250) (2000 to 2001)
IVECO EuroTrakker MP260E44W 11,000 kg (6 × 6) (75) (2000 to 2001)
IVECO EuroTrakker (4 × 4) (6 × 6) (8 × 8) (150) (2003) (follow-on to previous order)
IVECO Trakker (4 × 4) (6 × 6) (8 × 8) (up to 357 over 5 years from 2007)
MOWAG DURO 1 (4 × 4) (6 × 6) (3,007) (1994 to 2001)
MOWAG DURO III (6 × 6) (7) (2006-07)
Saurer 6 DM 6,000 kg (4 × 4) (800 delivered) (1982 to 1986)
Saurer 10 DM 10,000 kg (6 × 6) (300 delivered) (1982 to 1986)
Steyr 680 M 4,500 kg (4 × 4) (approx. 1,800 delivered) (1968 to 1974) (replacement programme pending)
Steyr 1291.320P43 5,600 kg (4 × 4) (250) (1997 to 1998)
Steyr 1491.320P40 9,600 kg (6 × 6) (60) (1997 to 1998)
Steyr 12 S 18 2,300 kg (4 × 4) (1998) small numbers
Steyr 12 S 23 5,200 kg (4 × 4) (1998) small numbers
Steyr 1291.320 7,900 kg (4 × 4) (6) (1995)
Steyr 19 S 32 8,300 kg (4 × 4) (29) (1995 to 1998)
By 2010 the Swiss Army was operating a figure approaching 1,000 IVECO vehicles of all types. The Swiss Army has no HETs, all heavy armoured vehicle movement being by rail.

Syria

Recovery vehicles
T-54/T-55 ARV

Mechanised bridges
MTU-20 AVLB
MTU AVLB

Light vehicles
GAZ-69/69A 500 kg (4 × 4)
UAZ-469B series 600 kg (4 × 4)

Trucks
GAZ-66 2,000 kg (4 × 4)
GAZ-3308 (4 × 4)
KAMAZ (2006) (understood to be licence production)
KrAZ-6322 (6 × 6) (70) (2006)
MAZ-537 (8 × 8)
Mercedes-Benz Unimog (4 × 4)
Mercedes-Benz (6 × 4) HET (various generations)
TATRA 148
TATRA T-815 series incl.. (6 × 6))
Ural-375D (6 × 6)
Ural-4320 (6 × 6)
Zil-131 (6 × 6)
Zil-130 (4 × 2)

Taiwan

Armoured engineer vehicles
M9 ACE

Recovery vehicles
M88A1 ARV (33)

Mechanised bridges
M48 AVLB
M3 (4 × 4) (modified) (being delivered)

Light vehicles
AM General HMMWV (4 × 4) (5,429) (ongoing)
CUCV (4 × 4)
M151 Mutt 362 kg (4 × 4)

Trucks
FMTV (6 × 6) (small number) (1996) (Patriot)
International 7400 (4 × 4) (>4,800) (2006-2009)
KM25 2.5-ton (6 × 6) (est. 150)
M35/M44 series 2,268 kg (6 × 6)
M809 series 4,536 kg (6 × 6)
Mercedes-Benz Atego (4 × 4) (small numbers)
Mercedes-Benz Actros (6 × 6) (<50)
Oshkosh M911 (6 × 6) (16) (1989); (11) (1992)
Oshkosh M977 HEMTT 9,979 kg (8 × 8)

Tanzania

Recovery vehicles
Vickers ARV (4) (1990)

Light vehicles
Land Rover (4 × 4)

Trucks
IVECO Cargo (4 × 4) (approx. 600) (2006-08)
IVECO Trakker (approx. 200) (2006-08)
Jiefang CA-1091 (C-141) 5,000 kg
Mercedes-Benz Unimog (4 × 4)
SAMIL 50 5,000 kg 4 × 4) (ex-SANDF) (not confirmed)

Thailand

Recovery vehicles
AAVR7 ARV (1) (Marines)
M88A1 ARV (21)
M88A2 ARV (6)
WZT-4 ARV
AAVR7 ARV (1)
M113A3 maintenance/recovery (10)
Samson ARV
Type 653 ARV

Mechanised bridges
Type 84 AVLB

Light vehicles
AM General HMMWV (4 × 4)
Kia KM450 (4 × 4) (est. 200) (2005-2006)
Mitsubishi SUV (4 × 4)
M151 Mutt 362 kg (4 × 4)
M37 680 kg (4 × 4)
Pinzgauer 716 (4 × 4) and 718 (6 × 6) (approx. 100)
Pinzgauer (older models)

Trucks
Ashok Leyland Stallion (6 × 6) (approx. 75) (2008-2009)
Bedford MT range (6 × 6) (8) (1995) (bridging vehicles)
Dong Feng EQ2061E 1,500 kg (4 × 4)
Dong Feng EQ2080E4DY 2,500 kg (6 × 6) (235)
FMTV
Isuzu TW (4 × 4) (6 × 6)
Jiefang CA-1091 (C-141) 5,000 kg
Kia KM25 2.5-ton (6 × 6) (est. 150)
LARC-5 4,545 kg (4 × 4) (amphibious)
M35/M44 series 2,268 kg (6 × 6)
M809 series 4,536 kg (6 × 6)
MAN L2000/M2000 (4 × 4) (small numbers, no other details)
Mercedes-Benz Unimog (4 × 4) (including small numbers of U5000)
Mercedes-Benz (6 × 4)
Oshkosh M911 (6 × 6) (12) (1981); (26) (1989)
Renault (about 100 incl. 8 Kerax tractor trucks and 66 R385ti tractor trucks)
Scania 113E 360 (6 × 4) (HET)
Tiema XC2030 8,000 kg (6 × 6)

Togo

Light vehicles
Assorted commercial spec SUVs/pick-up designs
Peugeot P4 750 kg (4 × 4) (20)

Trucks
ACMAT VLRA (4 × 4)
Panhard TC-54 (4 × 4) (30 to 80) (2009-2010)

Tunisia

Armoured engineer vehicles
SDP 4KH 7FA AVE (3)

Recovery vehicles
M88A1 ARV (6)
SDP 4KH 7FA 20 Grief ARV (2)

Light vehicles
AM General HMMWV (4 × 4) (341)
FIAT Campagnola 1107 AD 750 kg (4 × 4) (200 delivered)
LOHR (SOFRAME) Fardier (4 × 4)
SDP Pinzgauer

Trucks
IVECO EuroTrakker (no other details)
IVECO-Magirus 75-12 AWM 2,500 kg (4 × 4)
IVECO-Magirus 90-13 ANWM 4,000 kg (4 × 4)
IVECO-Magirus 110-16 AWM 5,000 kg (4 × 4)
IVECO-Magirus 120-19 ANWM 5,000 kg (4 × 4)
IVECO-Magirus 160-23 ANWM 7,000 kg (6 × 6) (approx. 600 delivered, 500 remain as of late 2006) (rebuild project from 1996; project ongoing)
IVECO-Magirus 260-23 ANWM (6 × 6) (tippers)
IVECO-Magirus 330-32 ANWTM (6 × 6) (HET)
Mercedes-Benz Unimog (4 × 4)

Turkey

Armoured Engineer Vehicles
M48 AEV

Armoured Engineering Squad Vehicles
M113A2T2

Recovery vehicles
Leopard 1 ARV (12)
M47 ARV

Light vehicles
HMMWV (4 × 4) (2)
Land Rover Defender 110 (4 × 4) (est. 16,000 delivered)
Land Rover Defender 130 (4 × 4)
M151 Mutt 362 kg (4 × 4)
M37 680 kg (4 × 4)

Trucks
Bedford MK 4,000 kg (4 × 4) (300 delivered) (status uncertain)
BMC 215-09 2,500 kg (4 × 4) (>180) (2003-2008))
BMC 185-09 B 2,500 kg (4 × 4) (706) (2009-2010)
BMC 235-16 5,000 kg (4 × 4) (approx. 500) (2003-2008)
BMC 235-16 P 5,000 kg (4 × 4) (282) (2009-2010)
BMC 380-26 10,000 kg (6 × 6) (small number)
BMC 380-26 P 10,000 kg (6 × 6) (403) (2009-2010)
BMC (6 × 4) (fuel tankers)
FAUN HZ 40.45/45 (6 × 6) (40) (HET)
IVECO-Magirus 160-23 ANWM/232 D 16 AL series 7,000 kg (6 × 6) (deliveries around mid-1980s)
IVECO Trakker (8 × 8) (>40) (2008-2010)
M35/M44 series 2,268 kg (6 × 6)
M54 series 4,536 kg (6 × 6)
MAN (some badged MANAS) (various)
Mercedes-Benz Unimog (4 × 4)
Mercedes-Benz Unimog U5000 (4 × 4) (40; further deliveries likely) (2006) (CKD)
Mercedes-Benz Atego (4 × 4) (50) (2006)
Mercedes-Benz Actros with LHS (6 × 6) (104) (2001 to 2002)
Mercedes-Benz HET (approx. 100) (mid-1990s)
MZKT-79091/92 (8 × 8) (est. 300) (circa 2000)
Oshkosh HEMTT (8 × 8) (deliveries including M997 and M984A2 - 42, 2005; 36, 2006)

Uganda

Light vehicles
Land Rover (4 × 4)

Trucks
Bedford MK 4,000 kg (4 × 4)
Jiefang CA-1091 (C-141) 5,000 kg
Steyr 14 M 14 8,000 kg (4 × 4)

Since 2001, a substantial number of basic trucks have been delivered, including over 100 donated by China's People's Liberation Army, which has undertaken military construction projects in Uganda.

Ukraine

Armoured Engineer Vehicles
BAT-2 CEV

Light Vehicles
UAZ-469B series 600 kg (4 × 4)
UAZ-452D 800 kg (4 × 4)

Trucks
BAZ (6 × 6) (specialist applications)
GAZ-66 2,000 kg (4 × 4) (numbers reducing)
KamAZ-5320 series 8,000 kg (6 × 4/6 × 6) (original KamAZ series models from which all current designs evolved)
KrAZ-214 7,000 kg (6 × 6) (numbers reducing)
KrAZ-255B/B 17,500 kg (6 × 6) (numbers reducing)
KrAZ-260 9,000 kg (6 × 6)
KrAZ-6322 series 10,000 kg (6 × 6)
MAZ-543 (now MZKT-543) series (8 × 8) (specialist applications incl. HETs)
Ural-375/375D 4,000 kg (6 × 6) (numbers reducing)
Ural-4320 series (6 × 6)
Ural-43206 series (4 × 4)
ZIL-130 (4 × 2) (numbers reducing)
ZIL-131 3,500 kg (6 × 6) (numbers reducing)
ZIL-157 2,500 kg (6 × 6) (numbers reducing)

United Arab Emirates

Armoured engineer vehicles
ACV - AESV

Recovery vehicles
AMX-30D ARV (4)
Leclerc ARV (46) (1995 to 1999)
BREM-L ARV (85)
Renault TRM 9,000 (6 × 6)

Light vehicles
AB3 Black Iris LSV (4 × 4) (45) (ordered 2003)
AM General HMMWV (4 × 4)
BMW X3 (4 × 4) (60)
IVECO 40.10 (1,500 kg) (4 × 4)
Land Rover (4 × 4)
Mercedes-Benz G-Class 750 kg (4 × 4) (25)
NIMR (4 × 4) (est. 500) (from 2008)
Nissan Patrol (4 × 4)
Toyota Land Cruiser

Trucks
Bedford MK 4,000 kg (4 × 4)
Bedford MT range (4 × 4) (50) (1995)
Bedford TM 4-4 8,000 kg (4 × 4)
Bedford TM 6-6 14,000 kg (6 × 6)
Bedford TM 30-30 18,000 kg (6 × 6)
Berliet GBU 15 6,000 kg (6 × 6)
FMTV (6 × 6) (20) (2009) (HIMARS)
IVECO 320.45 WTM (6 × 6) HET (numbers reducing)
IVECO 230-35 WM 10,000 kg (6 × 6)
KamAZ 4326 4,000 kg (4 × 4) (approx. 300) (1997-2003)
KamAZ 43114 6,000 kg (6 × 6) (2003)
MAN M2000 range (4 × 4) (including 16.284)
MAN 33.423 (6 × 6) (100)
MAN 41.464 (8 × 8) (280)
MAN 40.633 DFAETX HET (6 × 6) (35)
Mercedes-Benz LA 911 4,500 kg (4 × 4)
Mercedes-Benz 2028A 10,000 kg (6 × 6)
Mercedes-Benz NG/NG80 range
Mercedes-Benz Unimog (4 × 4)
Mercedes-Benz Actros (6 × 6)
MZKT Volat HET (8 × 8) (est. 40) (circa 2000)
NIMR (6 × 6) (on order)
Oshkosh HEMTT (8 × 8) (>40) (2010) (Patriot)
Renault TRM 9000 (6 × 6)
TATRA T816 (8 × 8) (1,100) (1996 to 1997)
TATRA T816 (8 × 8) (26) (1998) (Matenin minelaying equipment)

United Kingdom

Armoured engineer vehicles
Terrier CET (65 on order)
Titan ETS (33)
Trojan ETS (33)

Recovery vehicles
Challenger ARV (81) (1990 to 1993)
MLRS ARV (4)
Beach Recovery Vehicle (4)
Chieftain ARV (47)
FV434 armoured repair vehicle
Samson ARV
Saxon ARV (4 × 4)
Warrior mechanised combat repair vehicle (101)
Warrior mechanised recovery vehicle (39)
Reynolds Boughton 6 tonne (4 × 4) (19) (being replaced by Support Vehicle)
Foden (6 × 6) (333 delivered) (being replaced by Support Vehicle)
FBRV (4) (2002 to 2003)
MAN SX45 Heavy Recovery Vehicle (Heavy) Improved Medium Mobility (288 (plus 69 associated trailers)) (from June 2007 as part of the Support Vehicle contract award)

Mechanised bridges
BR90 (1995 to 1998)
M3 ABFS (4 × 4) (38)

Light vehicles

SDP Pinzgauer (4 × 4/6 × 6) (approx. 1,000) (1994 to 2002)
Pinzgauer (4 × 4/6 × 6) (> 600 ordered (not including armoured Pinzgauer Vector PPV) since 2002)
Land Rover Defender 90 TUL (4 × 4)
Land Rover Defender 110 TUM (4 × 4)
Land Rover Defender 130 (4 × 4) (small numbers)
(3,700 Land Rover Defenders (est. <200 TUL/<3,500 TUM) remained as of late 2008; TUM fleet being refurbished)
Land Rover Defender XD (4 × 4) (8,800) (1997 to 2001)
Supacat ATMP Mk III (6 × 6) (65) (from 2000) (55 Army, 10 RM)
Supacat HMT SRV (4 × 4) (65) (2002-2004)
Supacat HMT MWMIK/Jackal (4 × 4) (>350) (2007-2010)

Trucks

ACMAT VLRA (4 × 4) (small number) (specialist application)
Bedford MJ 4,000 kg (4 × 4) (to be replaced by Support Vehicle)
Bedford TM 6-6 14,000 kg (1,045 delivered) (1986 to 1990) (to be replaced by Support Vehicle)
Bedford TM 4-4 8,000 kg (4 × 4) (2,099 delivered) (to be replaced by Support Vehicle)
Dennis Eagle 15,500 litre air portable aircraft refueller (6 × 4) (55) (1998-99) (RAF)
Foden DROPS (8 × 6) (404)
Foden (6 × 6) MDT (55) (2001 to 2003) (being replaced under the ALC C-fleet PFI)
IVECO 150.30WM 7,000 kg (4 × 4) (3) (2001) (specialist application) (being replaced under the ALC C-fleet PFI)
IVECO EuroCargo (4 × 4) (small numbers, incl. RAF)
IVECO EuroTrakker (6 × 6) (2) (2001) (specialist application) (being replaced under the ALC C-fleet PFI)
JCB 150M (4 × 4) (26) (RAF)
Leyland 4,000 kg (4 × 4) (approx. 4,400 delivered) (1990 onwards) (to be replaced by Support Vehicle)
Leyland DROPS (8 × 6) (in depth repair programme completed mid 2006)
MAN HX60 Cargo (Light) Medium Mobility 6 tonne (4 × 4) (5213) (from June 2007 as part of the Support Vehicle contract award)
MAN HX60 (4 × 4) (107) (2009) (Falcon)
MAN HX58 Cargo (Medium) Medium Mobility 9 tonne (6 × 6) (606 (including 230 Unit Support Tankers)) (from June 2007 as part of the Support Vehicle contract award)
MAN HX77 Cargo (Heavy) Medium Mobility 15 tonne (8 × 8) (923) (from June 2007 as part of the Support Vehicle contract award)
MAN HX77 EPLS 15 tonne (8 × 8) (87) (2009-2010)
MAN SX44 Cargo (Medium) Improved Medium Mobility 9 tonne (6 × 6) (186 (including 81 Unit Support Tankers)) (from June 2007 as part of the Support Vehicle contract award)
MAN LE18.220 (4 × 4) (14) (2004-05) (9,000 litre fuel tanker, RAF)
MAN TGA 26.310 (6 × 4) (124) (20,000 litre tankers) (some with 24,000 litre trailers) (RAF)
MAN TGA 26.430 (6 × 4) (6) (2005-2006) (tractor truck with 42,500 litre semi-trailer for RAF)
MAN TGA 26.530 (6 × 4) (2) (2006) (STGO3 tractor truck and specialist trailer)
Mercedes-Benz Unimog (4 × 4) (small numbers)
MOWAG DURO I (6 × 6) (8) (late 2003) (EOD) (UOR for Operation Telic)
MOWAG DURO II (6 × 6) (4) (early 2004) (EOD) (UOR for Operation Telic)
MOWAG DURO II (6 × 6) (83) (Cormorant system)
MOWAG DURO II (6 × 6) (35) (2005-06) (Cormorant system loose stowage)
MOWAG DURO III (6 × 6) (>65) (2005-06)
MOWAG DURO III (4 × 4) (18) (2006-07) (specialist application)
MOWAG DURO III (4 × 4) (small number) (2008) (specialist application)
Oshkosh 1070F HET (8 × 8) (92) (2003) (PFI)

Oshkosh MTVR tankers (6 × 6) (348 + 9 option) (2004-06) (fuel and water)
Reynolds Boughton RB-44 2,000 kg (4 × 4) (840 delivered)
Seddon Atkinson LET (6 × 4) (approx. 120)
Scammell S26 (6 × 4) (187 delivered) (4,000 gallon aircraft refueller) (some cast) (RAF)
Volvo FL12 (6 × 6) SLDT (144) (being replaced under the ALC C-fleet PFI)

United States

Armoured engineer vehicles

M9 armored combat earthmover (485)
Assault Breacher Vehicle (6+42) (USMC)
Stryker Engineer Squad Vehicle

Recovery vehicles

AAVR7 ARV (54) (Marines)
M88A1 ARV (81) (Marines)
M88A1 ARV (2,470) (Army)
M88A2 ARV (>100) (Army)
M88A2 ARV (44) (Marines)
M578 ARV
LAV repair and recovery (46) (Marines)
Oshkosh MTVR MK36 wrecker (6 × 6) (Marines)
FMTV M1089 (6 × 6)
M816/M819 (6 × 6)
Oshkosh FRS-H (10 × 10)
M984A0/A1/A2 (8 × 8)

Mechanised bridges

M48/M60 AVLB
Rapidly Emplaced Bridge System (20)
Wolverine HAB (41)

Light vehicles

AM General HMMWV (4 × 4) (>175,000 delivered; around 130,000 thought to be in service) (from 1983)
AM General/GM Light Service Support Vehicle (LSSV) (2000-2005) (Air Force and Navy)
Chenowth fast attack vehicle (4 × 2) (4 × 4) (some refurbished for deployment to Afghanistan)
Chenowth advanced light strike vehicle (4 × 4)
CUCV (4 × 4) (approx. 60,000 delivered, considerably smaller number remain in service)
JLTV (projected HMMWV replacement)
John Deere Gator light utility vehicle (6 × 6) (>2,500 delivered)
Land Rover RSOV (4 × 4) (60) (Rangers) (upgraded)
Land Rover Defender 110 (4 × 4) (75) (2003) (delivered for Operation Enduring Freedom)
Mercedes-Benz G-Class 750 kg (4 × 4) (480)
Mercedes-Benz G-Class 750 kg IFAV (4 × 4) (approx. 90) (Marines)
Toyota Tacoma (4 × 4) (special forces use in Afghanistan)
Toyota Land Cruiser (4 × 4) (US forces in Japan)

Trucks

AM General M915 series (1977 to 1985)
FMTV family (LMTV 2,268 kg (4 × 4), MTV 4,536 kg (6 × 6) and trailers) (>48,000) (1991 to 2009) (deliveries continue) (contract now with Oshkosh)
Freightliner M915 series (1988 to 2009) (current contract extended)
M35/M44 series 2,268 kg (6 × 6) (16,587 late 2007; numbers reducing)
M809 series 4,536 kg (6 × 6) (6,405 late 2007; numbers reducing)
M939 series 4,536 kg (6 × 6) (28,268 late 2007)
Oshkosh M977A0/A2/A4 series HEMTT 9,979 kg (8 × 8) (>21,000) (FHTV 3 contract awarded late 2008) (life extension programmes underway)
Oshkosh MK48 Logistic Vehicle System (LVS) 9,072 kg (8 × 8) (>1,700) (Marines) (replacement contract awarded to Oshkosh Defense May 2006)
Oshkosh Logistic Vehicle System replacement (LVSR) (8 × 8) (up to 1,900) (deliveries from 2007-2012)
Oshkosh MTVR 13,608 kg (6 × 6) (around 10,000) (Marines) (deliveries continue)

Oshkosh PLS (10 × 10) (approx. 6,000) (FHTV 3 contract awarded late 2008) (life extension programmes underway)
Oshkosh M911 (8 × 6) HET (747 delivered; 47 remained as of late 2008)
Oshkosh M1070 (8 × 8) HET (>2,488) (1992 to 2003) (FHTV 3 contract awarded late 2008) (life extension programme underway)

Venezuela

Recovery vehicles

AAVR7 ARV (1) (marines)
AMX-30D ARV (4)
Samson ARV
DURO 1 (6 × 6) (5th wheel conversion for use with EMPL single-axle semi-trailer)
IVECO 90 PM 16 W (4 × 4) (60)
M816 (6 × 6)
Steyr (4 × 4) (EMPL top hamper)

Light vehicles

AIL M325 CommandCar (4 × 4)
AM General HMMWV (4 × 4)
Cenareca UR-53AR50 Tiuna (4 × 4) (approx. 1,600))
Chevrolet pick-up (<100)
Ford Explorer (4 × 4) (late 1990s)
IVECO 40.10 1,500 kg (4 × 4)
Jeep Wrangler (4 × 4) (120)
Land Rover Defender 90 hardtop (4 × 4) (25)
Land Rover Defender 110 station wagon (4 × 4) (est. 50) (Marines)
M38 Jeep (4 × 4)
M151 Mutt 362 kg (4 × 4)
SDP Pinzgauer 710M/K (4 × 4) (upgraded)
SDP Pinzgauer 712M/K (6 × 6) (upgraded)
Toyota Land Cruiser (4 × 4) (>700) (late 1990s)
URO VAMTAC (4 × 4) (Police)

Trucks

IVECO 90 PM 4,000 kg (4 × 4)
M35/M44 2,268 kg (6 × 6)
MAN CAT III 6000/10,000 kg (405)
MAN 14.224 FAC (4 × 4) (450)
MAN (various)
Mercedes-Benz Actros
Mercedes-Benz Actros HET (6 × 6)
MOWAG DURO 1 (4 × 4) (358) (2001 to 2003)
Steyr 10 M 22 (4 × 4)

From the late 1990s, Venezuela received as many as 1,700 light vehicles, including more than 700 Toyota Land Cruisers and a few hundred Ford Explorers. Quantities of various commercial pattern trucks are also in use.

Vietnam

Recovery vehicles

T-54/T-55 ARV

Light vehicles

UAZ-69/69A 500 kg (4 × 4)
UAZ-469B series 600 kg (4 × 4)

Trucks

KrAZ (6 × 6)
ZIL-151 2,500 kg (6 × 6)
ZIL-157 2,500 kg (6 × 6)

Yemen

Recovery vehicles

T-54/T-55 ARV (?)

Light vehicles

AM General HMMWV (4 × 4)
Dodge Ram (4 × 4)
Land Rover (4 × 4)
Toyota Land Cruiser (4 × 4)
UAZ-469B 600 kg (4 × 4)
UAZ-69/69A 500 kg (4 × 4)

Trucks
International AFMTV (6 × 6) (43) (circa 2006)
KaMAZ (500) (ordered 2005; delivery not confirmed)
MAN (approx. 120) (2006-2008)
Mercedes-Benz Actros (approx. 120) (2006-2008)
Star 266 3,500 kg (6 × 6) (400) (1999 to 2000)
Ural-4320 series (6 × 6)

Zambia
Recovery vehicles
T-54/T-55 ARV (?)

Light vehicles
Beijing BJ212 (4 × 4)
Mercedes-Benz G-Class 750 kg (4 × 4) (50)
Land Rover (4 × 4)

Trucks
ACMAT VLRA (4 × 4) incl. 20) (2004)
Tata SA 1212 TC 4,000 kg (4 × 4)

Zimbabwe
Recovery vehicles
T-54/T-55 ARV (?)
ACMAT VLRA (6 × 6)
Steyr 33 M 97 (6 × 6)

Light vehicles
Land Rover (4 × 4)
SAMO (Auverland A2) (4 × 4)

Trucks
ACMAT VLRA (4 × 4)
Bedford MK 4,000 kg (4 × 4)
Dong Feng (>100) (2005)
MAN 33.373 (6 × 6) (7) 2001)
Steyr 12 M 22 (4 × 4) (105)
Steyr 14 M 22 (4 × 4) (59) (2001)

Contractors

Australia

Defence Material Organisation (DMO)
Land Systems
(a subsidiary of Headquarters Australian Defence Force, Australia)
Victoria Barracks, 256 - 310 St Kilda Road, Southbank, Melbourne, Victoria, 3006, Australia
Tel: (+61 3) 92 82 64 86
(+61 2) 61 27 19 99
Fax: (+61 3) 92 82 64 77
e-mail: mediaops@defence.gov.au
Web: www.defence.gov.au/dmo

Defence Materiel Organisation (DMO)
Land Systems
Land Manoeuvre Systems Branch, Engineer Systems Program Off ce, 256-310 St Kilda, Victoria Barracks, Southbank, Melbourne, Victoria, 3006, Australia
Tel: (+61 3) 92 82 49 02
(+61 2) 61 27 19 99
Fax: (+61 3) 92 82 67 15
e-mail: mediaops@defence.gov.au
Web: www.defence.gov.au

Jaguar Land Rover Australia
Defence Engineering
32 Birnie Avenue, Lidcombe, New South Wales, 2141, Australia
Tel: (+61 2) 90 20 15 00
(+61 2) 90 43 97 01
Fax: (+61 2) 96 49 71 96
e-mail: landrover@customers1to1.com.au
Web: www.landrover.com.au

John Holland Group Pty Ltd
Level 6 235 Pyrmont Street, Pyrmont, Sydney, New South Wales, 2009, Australia
Tel: (+61 2) 95 52 42 88
Fax: (+61 2) 95 52 47 52
Web: www.johnholland.com.au

Mack Trucks Defence - Volvo Commercial Vehicles Australia Pty Ltd (VCV)
Sumner Park,
PO Box 1047 Queensland, 4074, Australia
20 Westgate Street, Wacol, Queensland, 4076, Australia
Tel: (+61 7) 37 18 35 00
(+61 7) 37 18 34 15
Freephone: (+61 1800) 80 34 27
Fax: (+61 7) 37 18 33 92
Web: www.macktrucks.com
www.volvo.com

Minelab Electronics Pty Ltd
Countermine
118 Hayward Avenue,
PO Box 537 Torrensville, South Australia, 5031, Australia
Tel: (+61 8) 82 38 08 88
Fax: (+61 8) 82 38 08 90
e-mail: corporate@minelab.com
countermine@minelab.com.au
Web: www.minelab.com

Pall Corporation Australia
6 Chivers Road, Somersby, New South Wales, 2250, Australia
Tel: (+61 2) 43 40 89 00
Fax: (+61 2) 43 40 89 99
Web: www.pall.com

Austria

CHV Container
Lastenstrasse 30, A-1230, Wien, Austria
Tel: (+43 1) 86 52 05 00
Fax: (+43 1) 865 24 47
e-mail: office@chv.at
Web: www.chv.at

General Dynamics European Land Systems-Steyr GmbH
2 Haidequerstrasse 3, A-1111, Wien, Austria
Tel: (+43 1) 760 64
Fax: (+43 1) 769 81 49
e-mail: info.wheeledvehicles@gdels.com
office@steyr-ssf.com
Web: www.steyr-ssf.com

MAN Nutzfahrzeuge Österreich AG
(a subsidiary of MAN Nutzfahrzeuge AG, Germany)
Schönauer Strasse 5, A-4400, Steyr, Austria
Tel: (+43 1) 86 63 10
Fax: (+43 1) 86 63 12 78
(+43 1) 86 63 11 08
Web: www.man-mn.at

Belarus

Minotor Service Enterprise
40 Radialnaya Street, 220070, Minsk, Belarus
Tel: (+375 17) 230 68 52
Fax: (+375 17) 287 53 61
e-mail: info@minotor-service.com
Web: www.minotor-service.com

Minsk Wheel Tractor Plant (MWTP)
Marketing
Minsky Zavod Kalyosnikh Tyagecsey (MZKT)
150 Partizanski Avenue, 220021, Minsk, Belarus
Tel: (+375 17) 246 10 44
(+375 17) 291 31 63
(+375 17) 291 31 78
Fax: (+375 17) 291 31 93
(+375 17) 291 31 95
e-mail: volat@mzkt.by
Web: www.mzkt.by

Belgium

Meuse & Sambre SA (MeuSam)
16 Rue de Namur, B-5000, Namur, Beez, Belgium
Tel: (+32 81) 22 02 33
Fax: (+32 81) 22 59 20
e-mail: info@meusam.com
Web: www.meusam.com

Sabiex International SA
(a subsidiary of Sofema, France)
Chaussée de Tubize 65, B-B-1420, Braine l'Alleud, Belgium
Tel: (+32 2) 384 80 15
Fax: (+32 2) 384 17 10
e-mail: mail@awex.wallonies.be
Web: www.sabiex.com

Bulgaria

Kintex
66 James Baucher Boulevard, 1407, Sofiya, Bulgaria
Tel: (+359) 866 23 11
Fax: (+359) 963 16 12
(+359) 963 11 23
e-mail: minkin@mbox.contact.bg
Web: www.bdia-bg.com

Canada

GE Water & Process Technologies
Zenon Membrane Solutions
3239 Dundas Street West, Oakville, Ontario, L6M 4B2, Canada
Tel: (+1 905) 465 30 30
Fax: (+1 905) 465 30 50
Web: www.gewater.com

General Dynamics Canada
Calgary Operations
1020-68th Avenue Northeast, Calgary, Alberta, T2E 8P2, Canada
Tel: (+1 403) 295 67 00
(+1 403) 295 67 50
Fax: (+1 403) 295 67 90
e-mail: info@gdcanada.com
busdev.calgary@gdcanada.com
Web: www.gdcanada.com

General Dynamics Land Systems - Canada (GDLS-C)
(a subsidiary of General Dynamics Land Systems, US)
1991 Oxford Street East, Building 15, London, Ontario, N5V 2Z7, Canada
Tel: (+1 519) 964 59 00
Fax: (+1 519) 964 52 10
e-mail: gdlscanada@gdls.com
Web: www.gdlscanada.com
www.gdls.com
www.generaldynamics.com

Kamma & Blake Industries Ltd
5406 Argyle Street, Port Alberni, British Columbia, V9Y IT7, Canada
Tel: (+1 250) 723 62 63
Freephone: (+1 877) 827 98 19
Fax: (+1 250) 723 15 01
e-mail: info@quaycraft.com
Web: www.quaycraft.com

SEI Industries Ltd
7400 Wilson Avenue, Delta, British Columbia, V4G 1E5, Canada
Tel: (+1 604) 946 31 31
Fax: (+1 604) 940 95 66
e-mail: seisales@sei-ind.com
Web: www.sei-ind.com

Weatherhaven
8355 Riverbend Court, Burnaby, British Columbia, V3N 5E7, Canada
Tel: (+1 604) 451 89 00
Fax: (+1 604) 451 89 99
e-mail: info@weatherhaven.com
Web: www.weatherhaven.com

Chile

Fábricas y Maestranzas del Ejercito (FAMAE)
Manuel Rodriguez 02, Talagante, Chile
Tel: (+56 2) 510 74 00
Fax: (+56 2) 510 77 72
Web: www.famae.cl

China

Baotou Bei Ben Heavy-Duty Truck Co Ltd
PO Box 2 014032, Baotou, Inner Mongolia Municpality, China
Tel: (+86 472) 311 73 04
(+86 472) 311 89 72
Fax: (+86 472) 311 73 04
(+86 472) 311 89 72
Web: www.beiben.cn
btbfbc.en.alibaba.com

China DongFeng Motor Industry Import & Export Corporation
Dongfeng International Building, No 317, Yuanshen Road, 200135, Wuhan, Hubei, China
Tel: (+86 21) 68 75 37 00
Fax: (+86 21) 68 75 26 77
(+86 21) 58 20 15 05
e-mail: dfm@chinadfm.com
Web: www.chinadfm.com

China North Industries Corporation (NORINCO)
Headquarters
12A Guang An Men Nan Jie,
PO Box 2932 100053, Beijing, China
Tel: (+86 10) 63 52 99 88
Fax: (+86 10) 63 54 03 98
e-mail: norinco@norinco.com.cn
Web: www.norinco.com

China Shipbuilding Trading Co Estate Ltd
(a subsidiary of China Shipbuilding Trading Co Ltd, China)
8th-12th floor, Bldg.1, No.9 Shouti South Road, 100048,
Haidan District, China
Tel: (+86 10) 88 57 36 88
Fax: (+86 10) 88 57 36 00
Web: www.chinaships.com

Chongqing Tiema Industries Corporation
No. 43 Yangjiaping Street, 400050, Chongqing, China
Tel: (+86 23) 68 44 72 19
Fax: (+86 23) 68 42 20 92
Web: www.tiematruck.com.cn
www.cqtiema.en.alibaba.com

DongFeng Motor Corporation (DFM)
430015, Wuhan, Hubei, China
Web: www.dfmc.com.cn

First Automobile Works
FAW
No.3025, Dong Feng Street, 130011, Changchung, Jilin,
China
Tel: (+86 431) 590 54 07
Fax: (+86 431) 761 47 80
e-mail: cfagiec@public.cc.jl.cn
Web: www.faw.com

Shaanxi Automobile Group Co Ltd
No 1. Shan Qi Road, Jing Wei Industrial Park, 710200,
Xi Xian, China
Tel: (+86 029) 8695 55 55
Fax: (+86 029) 8695 50 00
Web: www.sxqc.com

Croatia

Agencija Alan doo
Nike Grskovca 15, 10000, Zagreb, Croatia
Tel: (+385 1) 378 08 06 (export)
(+385 1) 378 08 05 (import)
(+385 1) 378 08 02 (gm office)
Fax: (+385 1) 378 08 40 (export)
(+385 1) 378 08 32 (import)
(+385 1) 378 08 38 (gm office)
e-mail: export.dep1@aalan.hr
Web: www.aalan.hr

Czech Republic

Avia Ashok Leyland Motors sro
Beranových 140, CZ-199 03, Praha, 18, Letnany, Czech
Republic
Tel: (+420 225) 14 11 11
e-mail: info@aal.cz
Web: www.avia.cz

CTS-Servis spol sro
Okrinek 53, Podebrady, CZ-290 01, Czech Republic
Tel: (+420 325) 60 81 11
(+420 325) 65 30 81
Fax: (+420 325) 65 30 97
e-mail: info@cts-servis.cz
Web: www.cts-servis.cz

Omnipol AS
Nekázanka 11, CZ-112 21, Praha, 1, Czech Republic
Tel: (+420 2) 24 01 11 11
(+420 2) 24 01 11 76 (defence equipment)
Fax: (+420 2) 24 01 22 41
(+420 2) 24 01 21 99 (defence equipment)
e-mail: omnipol@omnipol.cz
Web: www.omnipol.cz

Tatra AS
Areál Tatry 1450/1, CZ-742 21, Koprivnice, Czech
Republic
Tel: (+420 556) 49 23 98
(+420 556) 49 11 11
(+420 556) 49 37 77
Fax: (+420 556) 49 20 50
(+420 556) 49 26 72
e-mail: tatra@tatra.cz
fu@tatra.cz (finance)
ou@tatra.cz (commercial)
pu@tatra.cz (personnel)
tu@tatra.cz (technical)
rju@tatra.cz (quality)
informatika@tatra.cz (information technology)
servisni.skola@tatra.cz (service school)
projects@tatra.cz (defence programmes)
marketing@tatra.cz (marketing)
Web: www.tatra.cz

VOP 025 Novy Jicín sp
Dukelská 102, CZ-742 42, Senov u Nového Jicina,
Czech Republic
Tel: (+420 556) 78 31 11
(+420 556) 78 33 16
Fax: (+420 556) 70 17 34
e-mail: marketing@vop025.cz
Web: www.vop025.cz

Denmark

Danish Container Supply AS
Virkelyst 8, DK-9400, Norresundby, Denmark
Tel: (+45 7023) 13 80
Fax: (+45 7023) 13 81
Web: www.danishcontainersupply.dk

Hydrema AS
Gl Kirkevej 16, DK-9530, Støvring, Denmark
Tel: (+45 98) 37 13 33
(+45 98) 37 26 00 (sales and service)
Fax: (+45 98) 37 19 96
(+45 98) 37 39 66 (sales and service)
e-mail: hydrema@hydrema.com
Web: www.hydrema.com

Egypt

Arab American Vehicles Co (AAV)
(a joint venture between the Arab Organisation for Industrialisation, Egypt (51 per cent) and Chrysler, Egypt (49 per cent))
4.5 Km Suez Road,
PO Box 2419 Heliopolis, Cairo, Egypt
Tel: (+20 2) 526 38 00
(+20 2) 25 29 70 00
(+20 2) 529 91 00
(+20 2) 22 69 32 00
(+20 2) 22 69 22 85
Fax: (+20 2) 524 67 00
(+20 2) 25 29 70 05
(+20 2) 22 69 35 62
(+20 2) 226 92 47 72
e-mail: dcegypt@daimlerchrysler.com
Web: www.aav.com.eg

Kader Factory for Developed Industries
(a subsidiary of the Arab Organisation for Industrialisation, Egypt)
Orouba Street,
PO Box 287 Heliopolis, Cairo, Egypt
2 El Tayaran Street, Nasr, Cairo, Egypt
Tel: (+20 2) 61 11 42
(+20 2) 24 02 43 24
(+20 2) 24 02 43 19
Fax: (+20 2) 22 67 19 78
(+20 2) 22 67 12 20
e-mail: aoikader@aoi.com.eg
Web: www.aoi.com.eg

Finland

Jet-Tekno Oy
Nuutisarankatu 12, FI-33900, Tampere, Finland
Tel: (+358 3) 233 88 00
Fax: (+358 3) 233 88 77
e-mail: jet-tekno@jet-tekno.fi
Web: www.jet-tekno.fi

Patria Land and Armament Oy
(a subsidiary of Patria Oyj, Finland)
Autotehtaantie 6,
PO Box 186 FI-13101, Hämeenlinna, Finland
Tel: (+358 20) 46 91
Fax: (+358 20) 469 66 86
e-mail: land.armament@patria.fi
Web: www.patria.fi

Sisu Defence Oy
PO Box 68 FI-10301, Karjaa, Finland
Tammisaarentie 45, FI-10300, Karjaa, Finland
Tel: (+358 10) 275 46 72
(+358 10) 27 51
Fax: (+358 19) 23 30 01
Web: www.sisuauto.com

France

Aérazur (Aerazur DPE)
Department Elastomer Products (DTES)
(a subsidiary of Zodiac, France)
4 rue Lesage Maille, F-76320, Caudebec-les-Elbeuf,
France
Tel: (+33 2) 32 96 59 08
(+33 2) 32 96 49 23
Fax: (+33 2) 32 96 56 92
(+33 2) 32 96 56 01
(+33 2) 32 96 56 90
Web: www.zodiacaerospace.com

Ateliers de Constructions Mécaniques de l'Atlantique (ACMAT)
ALM
Le Point du Jour, F-44600, Saint-Nazaire, France
Tel: (+33 2) 40 22 69 98
(+33 2) 40 22 33 71
Fax: (+33 2) 40 66 30 96
e-mail: sa@acmat.fr
Web: www.acmat.fr

ATN SA
102 Bureaux de la Colline, F-92213, Saint Cloud, France
Tel: (+33 1) 49 11 49 11
Fax: (+33 1) 47 71 16 82
e-mail: info@sofinfra.fr
Web: www.sofinfra.fr

Automobiles Peugeot
75 avenue de la Grande Armée,
PO Box 0116 F-75116, Paris, Cedex, France
Tel: (+33 1) 40 66 55 11
Fax: (+33 1) 45 62 70 20
Web: www.peugeot.com

CEFA
Route de Woerth,
PO Box 11 F-67250, Soultz-sous-Forêts, France
Tel: (+33 3) 88 63 35 00
Fax: (+33 3) 88 80 50 05
e-mail: cefa@cefa.fr
Web: www.cefa.fr

Constructions Industrielles de la Méditerranée (CNIM)
Head Office
35 rue de Bassano, F-75008, Paris, France
Tel: (+33 1) 44 31 11 53
(+33 1) 44 31 11 00
Fax: (+33 1) 53 57 86 98
(+33 1) 44 31 11 30
e-mail: dircom.dds@cnim.com
Web: www.cnim.com
www.cnim.fr

Constructions Industrielles de la Méditerranée (CNIM)
Zone Industrielle de Bregaillon,
PO Box 208 F-83507, La Seyne sur Mer, Cedex, France
Tel: (+33 4) 94 10 30 00
Fax: (+33 4) 494 11 15 91
(+33 4) 94 30 31 00
e-mail: dircom.dds@cnim.com

Deschamps SAS
Usine de Bourisson,
BP 20 F-16400, La Couronne, France
Tel: (+33 5) 45 67 70 30
Fax: (+33 5) 45 67 81 60
e-mail: deschamps@deschamps.fr
events-deschamps@deschamps.fr
Web: www.mobi-mat.com
www.deschamps.fr

Euro Shelter
72 rue Claude Bernard, CS 64338, F-35043, Rennes,
Cedex, France
Tel: (+33 2) 99 01 73 73
Fax: (+33 2) 99 01 73 91
(+33 2) 99 01 73 96
e-mail: commerce@euro-shelter.com
Web: www.euro-shelter.com

Gilep
27 Boulevard de Stalingrad, F-92240, Malakoff, France
Tel: (+33 1) 55 58 80 30
Fax: (+33 1) 55 58 80 01
e-mail: contact@gilep.com
Web: www.gilep.com

Henri Blanc SA
30-32 Avenue de la Republique, F-78640, Neauphle le
Chateau, France
Tel: (+33 134) 89 61 62
Fax: (+33 134) 89 22 88

Nexter
Headquarters
13 route de la Minière, F-78034, Versailles, Cedex,
France
Tel: (+33 1) 30 97 37 37
(+33 1) 30 97 36 41
Fax: (+33 1) 30 97 39 78
(+33 1) 39 24 16 93
(+33 1) 30 97 39 00
Web: www.nexter-group.fr

Nexter Systems
13 route de la Minière, F-78034, Versailles, Cedex,
France
Tel: (+33 1) 30 97 37 37
Fax: (+33 1) 30 97 39 78
Web: www.giat-industries.fr

Panhard General Defense
Head Office
2 rue Panhard et Levassor, F-91630,
Marolles-en-Hurepoix, France
Tel: (+33 1) 60 82 48 48
(+33 1) 60 82 49 87
Fax: (+33 1) 60 85 08 20
(+33 1) 60 82 48 05
Web: www.panhard.fr

Pronal SA
Zone Industrielle Roubaix Estate, rue du Trieu du
Quesnoy,
BP 18 F-59115, Leers, France
Tel: (+33 3) 20 99 75 00
Fax: (+33 3) 20 99 75 20
e-mail: pronal@pronal.com
contact@pronal.com
Web: www.pronal.com

Renault Trucks
Head Office
TER B50001, 99 Route de Lyon, F-69802, Lyon, St
Priest, France
Tel: (+33 4) 72 96 81 11
Fax: (+33 4) 72 96 67 25
Web: www.renault-trucks.com

Renault Trucks Defense
Communications
(a subsidiary of Renault Trucks, France)
15bis allée des marronniers, F-78008, Versailles, Satory,
France
Tel: (+33 134) 49 26 40
(+33 134) 49 22 50
Fax: (+33 134) 49 23 23
Web: www.renault-trucks-defense.com

Société Nouvelle des Automobiles Auverland (SNAA)
PO Box 12 F-42260, Saint Germain-en-Laye, France
Tel: (+33 4) 77 65 58 71
Fax: (+33 4) 77 65 58 84
Web: www.auverland.fr
www.auverland.com

Soframe
29 rue du 14 Juillet,
BP 1 Hangenbieten F-67838, Tanneries Cedex, France
Tel: (+33 3) 88 38 98 00
Fax: (+33 3) 88 96 06 36
Web: www.soframe.com

Germany

Ahlmann Baumaschinen GmbH
(a wholly owned subsidiary of Mecalac, France)
Postfach 964 D-24758, Rendsburg, Germany
Am Friedrichsbrunnen, D-24782, Büdelsdorf, Germany
Tel: (+49 4331) 35 10
(+49 4331) 3 5 13 19
Fax: (+49 4331) 35 13 03
e-mail: info@ahlmann.com
Web: www.ahlmann.com
www.mecalac-ahlmann.com

Daimler AG
Mercedes-Benz Unterturkheim Plant (]#)
Mercedesstrasse 137, D-70327, Stuttgart, Germany
Tel: (+49 711) 170
Web: www.daimlerchrysler.com

Daimler AG
Mercedes-Benz Wörth Plant
Daimlerstraße 1, D-76742, Wörth, Germany
Tel: (+49 7271) 711
Web: www.daimler.com

Doll Fahrzeugbau AG
Industriestrasse 13, D-77728, Oppenau, Germany
Tel: (+49 7804) 490
Fax: (+49 7804) 491 77
(+49 7804) 491 57
e-mail: info@doll-oppenau.com
Web: www.doll-oppenau.com

Dynamit Nobel Defence GmbH
Dr Hermann-Fleck-Allee 8, D-57299, Burbach, Germany
Tel: (+49 2736) 46 20 14
Fax: (+49 2736) 46 21 07
e-mail: info@dn-defence.com
Web: www.dn-defence.com

EADS Deutschland GmbH
Cassidian Electronics
Wörthstraße 85, D-89007, Ulm, Germany
Tel: (+49 731) 39 20
Fax: (+49 731) 392 33 93
Web: www.eads.com

Faun GmbH
Faunberg 2,
Postfach 10 01 08 D-91205, Lauf an der Pegnitz,
Germany
Tel: (+49 9123) 18 50
Fax: (+49 9123) 18 51 15
(+49 9123) 18 53 49 (military sales)
e-mail: info@faun.de
Web: www.faun.de

Flensburger Fahrzeugbau GmbH (FFG)
PO Box 1564 D-24905, Flensburg, Germany
Werftstrasse 24, D-24939, Flensburg, Germany
Tel: (+49 461) 481 20
Fax: (+49 461) 481 22 18
(+49 461) 481 21 00
e-mail: info@ffg-flensburg.de
Web: www.ffg-flensburg.de

General Dynamics European Land Systems Germany GmbH
**(a subsidiary of General Dynamics European
Land Systems, Austria)**
Barbarossastrasse 30, D-67655, Kaiserslautern,
Germany
Tel: (+49 631) 361 60
Fax: (+49 631) 361 63 00
e-mail: info@gdels.com
Web: www.gdels.de
www.generaldynamics.com

Haacon Hebetechnik GmbH
Josef-Haamann Strasse 6, D-97896, Freudenberg,
Germany
Tel: (+49 9375) 840
Fax: (+49 9375) 84 66
e-mail: haacon@haacon.com
Web: www.haacon.com
www.haacon.de

Iveco Magirus Brandschutztechnik GmbH
(a subsidiary of Iveco Fiat SpA, Italy)
Graf-Arco-Strasse 30, D-89079, Ulm, Germany
Tel: (+49 731) 40 80
(+49 731) 408 44 09
Fax: (+49 731) 408 24 10
(+49 731) 408 38 83
(+49 731) 408 23 95
e-mail: magirus@iveco.com
Web: www.iveco-magirus.de

Kärcher Futuretech GmbH
Max-Eyth Strasse 35, D-71364, Winnenden, Germany
Tel: (+49 7195) 14 24 52
(+49 7195) 14 24 57
Fax: (+49 7195) 14 27 80
e-mail: futuretech@de.kaercher.com
Web: www.kaercher-futuretech.com

Krauss Maffei Wegmann GmbH & Co KG (KMW)
Headquarters
Krauss-Maffei-Strasse 11, D-80997, München, Germany
Tel: (+49 89) 81 49 50
(+49 89) 81 40 48 20
Fax: (+49 89) 81 40 49 00
e-mail: info@kmweg.de
Web: www.kmweg.com
www.kmweg.de

Krauss-Maffei Wegmann GmbH & Co KG
PO Box 3151 D-55021, Mainz, Germany
Wilhelm-Theodor-Romheld Strasse 24, D-55130, Mainz,
Germany
Tel: (+49 6131) 215 52 88
Fax: (+49 6131) 215 53 83
e-mail: info@kmweg.de
bridges@kmweg.de
Web: www.kmweg.com

Liebherr-Werk Ehingen GmbH
Postfach 1361 D-89582, Ehingen, Germany
Dr Hans-Liebherr-Strasse 1, D-89584, Germany
Tel: (+49 7391) 502 36 63
Fax: (+49 7391) 502 34 03
e-mail: info.lwe@liebherr.com
Web: www.liebherr.com

MAN Nutzfahrzeuge AG
(a subsidiary of MAN SE, Germany)
Postfach 50 06 20 D-80976, München, Germany
Dachauer Strasse 667, D-80995, München, Germany
Tel: (+49 89) 15 80 20 01
Fax: (+49 89) 15 80 91 24 85
e-mail: info@man-mn.com
militarytrucks@man.eu
Web: www.man-mn.com/militarytrucks

Military Mobile Bridges GmbH
PO Box 3480 D-55024, Mainz, Germany
Wilhelm-Theodor-Römheld-Strasse 24, D-55130, Mainz,
Germany
Tel: (+49 6131) 215 52 88
Fax: (+49 6131) 215 53 83
e-mail: bridges@kmweg.de
Web: www.kmweg.de

Rheinmetall Landsysteme GmbH
Headquarters
(a subsidiary of Rheinmetall AG, Germany)
Dr Hell-Strasse 6, D-24107, Kiel, Germany
Tel: (+49 431) 21 85 01
Fax: (+49 431) 21 85 27 86
e-mail: rls-info@rheinmetall.com
Web: www.rheinmetall-defence.com

Telerob Gesellschaft für Fernhantierungstechnik mbH
Vogelsangstrasse 8, D-73760, Ostfildern, Germany
Tel: (+49 711) 34 10 21 20
(+49 711) 34 10 20
Fax: (+49 711) 34 10 25 55
e-mail: telerob@telerob.de
Web: www.telerob.de

Terex Demag GmbH
Postfach 1552 D-66465, Zweibrücken, Germany
Dinglerstrasse 24, D-66482, Zweibrücken, Germany
Tel: (+49 6332) 830
Fax: (+49 6332) 167 15
e-mail: info.cranes@terex.com
Web: www.terexcranes.com

WEW Westerwälder Eisenwerk GmbH
Ringstrasse 65a, D-57586, Weitefeld, Germany
Tel: (+49 2743) 922 20
Fax: (+49 2743) 34 11
e-mail: wew@wew-tankcontainer.de
Web: www.wew.de

Greece

Nik Kioleides SA
17 Km Athens - Thessaloniki Road, Deiradon &
Korinthou 47 strs, GR-145 64, Kifissia, Athens, Greece
Tel: (+30 210) 818 00 00
Fax: (+30 210) 818 00 01
e-mail: info@kioleides.gr
Web: www.kioleides.com

India

Ashok Leyland Ltd
1 Sardar Patel Road, Guindy, Chennai (Madras), 600
032, India
Tel: (+91 44) 22 20 60 00
Fax: (+91 44) 22 20 60 01
Web: www.ashokleyland.com

BEML Limited
Corporate
Beml Soudha, 23/1 4th Main Road,
Sampangiramanagar, Bangalore, Karnataka, 560 027,
India
Tel: (+91 80) 22 96 32 40
(+91 80) 22 96 32 50
Fax: (+91 80) 22 96 32 78
(+91 80) 22 96 31 56
(+91 80) 22 96 31 64
(+91 80) 22 96 32 80
e-mail: office@cmd.beml.co.in
Web: www.bemlindia.com

Mahindra Defence Systems
Head Office
Mahindra Towers, 2-A Bhikaji Cama Place, New Delhi,
110 066, India
Tel: (+91 11) 41 22 03 00
Fax: (+91 11) 41 45 85 05
(+91 11) 41 45 85 85
e-mail: defencesystems@mahindra.com
Web: www.mahindra.com

Maruti Suzuki India Limited
(a subsidiary of Suzuki Motor Corporation, Japan)
Nelson Mandela Road, Vasant Kunj, New Delhi, 110070,
India
Tel: (+91) 01 80 01 80
Fax: (+91) 46 15 02 75
(+91) 46 15 02 76
Web: www.marutisuzuki.com

Ministry of Defence (MoD)
Defence Research and Development Organisation (DRDO)
Research & Development Establishment (R&DE Engrs),
Alandi Road, Pune, 411015, India
Tel: (+91 20) 27 15 08 81
(+91 20) 27 15 08 84
(+91 20) 27 15 08 88
Fax: (+91 20) 27 15 07 83
(+91 20) 27 15 03 30
e-mail: rde@vsnl.com
Web: www.drdo.org

Ordnance Factory Board (OFB)
(a subsidiary of Ministry of Defence, India)
Ayudh Bhawan, 10-A S K Bose Road, Kolkata
(Calcutta), 700001, India
Tel: (+91 33) 22 48 90 27
(+91 33) 22 48 21 03
(+91 33) 22 48 50 77
(+91 33) 22 48 50 80
(+91 33) 22 48 12 09
(+91 33) 22 48 97 44
Fax: (+91 33) 22 48 17 48
(+91 33) 22 10 82 35
(+91 33) 22 48 29 27
e-mail: ofbtrade@vsnl.net
ofbtrade@dataone.in
ofboard@giascl01.vsnl.net.in
Web: ofbindia.gov.in

Telco Construction Equipment Company Limited
Jubilee Building, 45 Museum Road, Bangalore, 560025,
India
Tel: (+91 80) 25 58 33 45
Web: www.seekandsource.com/telco

Vehicle Factory
Indian Ordnance Factories
Jabalpur, 482009, India
Tel: (+91 761) 233 05 20
Fax: (+91 761) 233 04 36
(+91 761) 233 02 57
e-mail: vfj.ofb@nic.in
Web: ofbindia.gov.in

Israel

Achidatex Nazareth Elite Ltd
PO Box 2156 IL-52121, Ramat Gan, Israel
12 Hamefalsim Street, Petach Tikva, Israel
Tel: (+972 3) 921 34 31
Fax: (+972 3) 921 34 36
e-mail: achidatex@achidatex.co.il
Web: www.achidatex.co.il

Automotive Industries Ltd (AIL)
PO Box 535 IL-17105, Nazareth Illit, Israel
Tel: (+972 4) 655 81 11
(+972 4) 655 81 04
Fax: (+972 4) 655 81 03
Web: www.ail.co.il

Defense Industries International Inc
PO Box 779 IL-78101, Ashkelon, Israel
Tel: (+972 8) 689 16 11
Fax: (+972 8) 689 92 87
e-mail: exportez@zahav.net.il
Web: www.defense-industries.com

ELTA Systems Ltd (IAI/ELTA)
(a subsidiary of Israel Aircraft Industries Ltd, Israel)
100 Yitzhak, Hanasi Boulevard,
PO Box 330 IL-77102, Ashdod, Israel
Tel: (+972 8) 857 21 55
(+972 8) 857 23 12 (international marketing)
Fax: (+972 8) 856 18 72 (international marketing)
(+972 8) 856 45 68
e-mail: market@elta.co.il
Web: www.iai.co.il
www.elta-iai.com

IDE Technologies Ltd
Hamatechet Street, Hasharon Industrial Park,
PO Box 5016 IL-60920, Kadima, Israel
Tel: (+972 9) 892 97 77
Fax: (+972 9) 892 97 15
e-mail: contact@ide-tech.com
Web: www.ide-tech.com

Israel Aerospace Industries Ltd (IAI)
Ramta
(a subsidiary of Israel Aerospace Industries Ltd, Israel)
PO Box 323 IL-84102, Beer-Sheeva, Israel
Tel: (+972 8) 627 22 31
Fax: (+972 7) 640 22 52
(+972 8) 627 67 70
e-mail: mktg@iai.co.il
Web: www.iai.co.il

Israel Military Industries (IMI)
PO Box 1044 IL-47100, Ramat Hasharon, Israel
Tel: (+972 3) 548 56 19
Fax: (+972 3) 548 61 25
e-mail: imimrktg@imi-israel.com
Web: www.imi-israel.com

Israel Military Industries Ltd (IMI)
Rocket Systems (RSD)
PO Box 1044/6044 IL-47100, Ramat Hasharon, Israel
Tel: (+972 3) 548 56 17
(+972 8) 924 26 84
(+972 8) 927 74 47
(+972 8) 927 74 49
Fax: (+972 3) 548 61 25
(+972 8) 925 28 96
e-mail: imimrktg@imi-israel.com
Web: www.imi-israel.com

Rafael Advanced Defense Systems Ltd
Rafael Systems (RSD)
PO Box 2250 IL-31021, Haifa, Israel
Tel: (+972 4) 879 44 44
(+972 4) 879 20 02
Fax: (+972 4) 879 46 81
e-mail: intl-mkt@rafael.co.il (marketing)
esdmrkt@rafael.co.il
Web: www.rafael.co.il

SIBAT - Foreign Defence Assistance and Defence Export

Ministry of Defence, IL-61909, Hakirya, Tel Aviv, Israel
Tel: (+972 3) 697 55 85
Fax: (+972 3) 697 67 24
e-mail: sibat@mod.gov.il
Web: www.sibat.mod.gov.il

Urdan Metal and Casting Industries Ltd

(a subsidiary of Clal Industries and Investments Ltd, Israel)
Haplada Street 11, Industrial Area, IL-42378, Netanya, Israel
Tel: (+972 9) 862 45 25
(+972 9) 884 63 78
Fax: (+972 9) 861 02 46
e-mail: rkm@urdan.co.il
sales@urdan.co.il
Web: www.urdan.co.il

Italy

ARIS SpA

Strada Cascina Bertola 10, Regione Poligono, I-10040, Lombardore Turin, Italy
Tel: (+39 11) 995 61 50
Fax: (+39 11) 995 62 05
e-mail: info@aris-spa.it
Web: www.aris-spa.it

Astra Veicoli Industriali SpA

Via Caorsana 79, I-29100, Piacenza, Italy
Tel: (+39 523) 54 31 11
Fax: (+39 0523) 59 32 93
(+39 523) 59 17 73
e-mail: info@astraspa.com
Web: www.astraspa.com

Avio SpA

Headquarters
Via I Maggio, 99, I-10040, Torino, Rivalta, Italy
Tel: (+39 11) 008 21 11
Fax: (+39 11) 008 41 63
Web: www.aviogroup.com

Farid Industrie SpA

Head Office
Via Moncalieri 109,LOC, Tetti Caglieri, Vinovo, I-10048, Italy
Tel: (+39 011) 640 03 11
Fax: (+39 011) 973 73 99
Web: www farid.it

Fresia SpA

Head Office
Via Trento e Trieste 30, I-17017, Millesimo, Savona, Italy
Tel: (+39 19) 560 00 05
Fax: (+39 19) 560 00 09
e-mail: fresia@fresia.it
Web: www.fresia.it

Iveco SpA

Defence Vehicles
Via Volta 6, I-39100, Bolzano, Bolzano, Italy
Tel: (+39 471) 90 53 14
(+39 471) 90 51 11
Fax: (+39 471) 90 54 33
(+39 471) 90 54 44
e-mail: dvdbzcom@iveco.com
Web: www.iveco.com

Merlo SpA

Via Nazionale 9, South Defendente di Cervasca, I-12020, Cuneo, Italy
Tel: (+39 171) 61 41 11
(+39 171) 61 43 54 (service)
(+39 171) 61 41 40 (help desk)
(+39 171) 61 42 02 (spare parts)
Fax: (+39 171) 61 41 00
e-mail: info@merlo.com
service@merlo.com
spare.parts@merlo.com
Web: www.merlo.it

Oto Melara SpA

Main
(a subsidiary of Finmeccanica SpA, Italy)
Via Valdilocchi, 15, I-19136, La Spezia, Italy
Tel: (+39 0187) 58 11
Fax: (+39 0187) 58 27 95
e-mail: marketing&sales@otomelara.it
press-office@otomelara.it
communication@otomelara.it
Web: www.otomelara.it

Piaggio Aero Industries SpA

Via Cibrario 4, I-16154, Genoa, Italy
Tel: (+39 10) 648 11 (operator)
(+39 10) 648 19 87 (press office)
Fax: (+39 10) 648 12 53 (press office)
(+39 10) 648 13 09 (marketing and commercial)
(+39 10) 652 01 60 (marketing and commercial)
(+39 10) 650 33 78 (human resources)
(+39 10) 648 13 74 (product support)
(+39 10) 648 13 18 (general)
e-mail: marketing@piaggioaero.it
info@piaggioamerica.com
comunicazione@piaggioaero.it
mediarelations@piaggioaero.it
Web: www.piaggioaero.com

TerexLift Srl

(a subsidiary of Terex Corporation, US)
Zona Industriale, Umbertide, I-06019, Perugia, Italy
Tel: (+39 75) 94 18 11
(+39 75) 941 81 29 (technical)
(+39 75) 941 81 47 (spare parts)
(+39 75) 941 81 26 (sales)
(+39 75) 941 81 09
Fax: (+39 75) 941 81 01
(+39 75) 941 81 46 (spare parts)
(+39 75) 941 81 46 (technical)
e-mail: terexlift@terexlift.it
im.sales@terexlift.it
im.service@terexlift.it (technical)
im.export@terexlift.it
Web: www.terexlift.it

Japan

Hitachi Zosen Corporation

Maizuru Works
(a subsidiary of Hitachi Zosen Corporation, Japan)
1180 Amarube-Shimo Maizuru, Kyoto, 625-8501, Japan
Tel: (+81 773) 62 89 25
Fax: (+81 773) 62 88 27
Web: www.hitachizosen.co.jp

Isuzu Motors Limited

Head Office
6-26-1 Minami-Oi, Shinagawa-ku, Tokyo, 140-8722, Japan
Tel: (+81 3) 54 71 11 41
Web: www.isuzu.co.jp/world

Kawasaki Heavy Industries Ltd (KHI)

Head Office
World Trade Centre Building, 4-1 Hamamatsu-cho 2-chome, Minato-ku, Tokyo, 105-6116, Japan
Tel: (+81 3) 34 35 21 11
(+81 3) 34 35 21 81
Fax: (+81 3) 34 36 30 37
(+81 3) 34 36 30 38
Web: www.khi.co.jp

Komatsu Ltd

Head Office
2-3-6 Akasaka, Minato-ku, Tokyo, 107-8414, Japan
Tel: (+81 3) 55 61 26 16
Web: www.komatsu.com

Mitsubishi Fuso Truck and Bus Corporation (MFTBC)

890-12, Kashimada, Saiwai-ku, Kawasaki, Kanagwa, 212-0058, Japan
Tel: (+81 44) 330 77 00
Fax: (+81 3) 67 19 01 11
Web: www.mitsubishi-fuso.com

Mitsubishi Heavy Industries Ltd (MHI)

Head Office
Mitsubishi Jukogyo Kabushiki Kaisha
16-5 Konan, 2-Chome, Minato-ku, Tokyo, 108-8215, Japan
Tel: (+81 3) 67 16 31 11
(+81 3) 67 16 30 22
Fax: (+81 3) 67 16 58 00
e-mail: qq2100@hq.mhi.co.jp
jjk200@mail.smw.mhi.co.jp
Web: www.mhi.co.jp

Mitsubishi Motors Corporation

Head Office
33-8, Shiba 5-chome, Minato-ku, Tokyo, 108-8410, Japan
Tel: (+81 033) 456 11 11
Web: www.mitsubishi-motors.com

Jordan

King Abdullah II Design and Development Bureau (KADDB)

PO Box 928125 11190, Amman, Jordan
Tel: (+962 6) 625 60 24
(+962 6) 460 32 30
Fax: (+962 6) 562 72 03
(+962 6) 460 32 43
e-mail: info@kaddb.com
sales@kaddb.com
Web: www.kaddb.mil.jo

Korea, South

Doosan Infracore Co Ltd

Seoul
Doosan Tower 22-26th Floor, 18-12 Euljiro-6Ga, Jung Gu, Seoul, Korea, South
Tel: (+82 233) 98 81 14
Fax: (+82 233) 98 81 17
Web: www.doosaninfracore.co.kr

Hyundai Rotem Company

Headquarters
231 Yangjae-dong, Seocho-gu, Seoul, 137-938, Korea, South
Tel: (+82 2) 34 64 11 14
(+82 2) 34 64 74 30
(+82 2) 34 64 74 39
(+82 2) 34 64 46 45
(+82 2) 34 64 48 70
(+82 2) 34 64 48 74
Fax: (+82 2) 34 64 75 86
(+82 2) 34 64 49 75
(+82 2) 34 64 47 92
(+82 2) 34 64 47 91
Web: www.hyundai-rotem.co.kr
www.rotem.co.kr

Kia Motors Corporation

231 Yangjae-Dong, Seocho-Gu, Seoul, 137-938, Korea, South
Tel: (+82 2) 34 64 11 14
Fax: (+82 2) 34 64 68 00
Web: www.kia.co.kr
www.kiamotors.com

Krosys Inc

3 Ra. 726 Shiwha Industrial Complex, Shihung, Kyongki, 429-854, Korea, South
Tel: (+82 31) 496 53 60
(+82 31) 496 53 00
Fax: (+82 31) 496 54 00
e-mail: krosys@krosys.com
Web: www.krosys.com

Samsung Techwin Co Ltd

Head Office
19th Floor, Samsung Life Seocho Tower 1321-15, Seocho 2-dong, Seocho-Gu, Seoul, 137-955, Korea, South
Tel: (+82 2) 34 67 71 83
Fax: (+82 2) 34 67 71 84
Web: www.samsungtechwin.com

Samsung Techwin Co Ltd
Defense Program
14th Floor, Samsung Yok, 647-9 Yoksam-Dong
Kangnam Ku, Seoul, Korea, South
Tel: (+82 2) 34 67 71 14
(+82 2) 34 67 76 88
(+82 2) 34 67 70 00
Fax: (+82 2) 34 67 76 60
(+82 2) 34 67 70 80
e-mail: techwin@samsung.com
Web: www.samsungtechwin.com

Malaysia

Bry-Air (Malaysia) Sdn Bhd
Lot 11 Jalan P/7, Bangi Industrial Estate, Bandar Baru
Bangi, 43650, Selangor Darul Ehsan, Malaysia
Tel: (+60 3) 89 25 66 22
Fax: (+60 3) 89 25 99 57
e-mail: bryair@bryair.com.my
marketing@bryair.com.my
Web: www.bryair.com.my

DRB HICOM Defence Technologies Sdn Bhd (DEFTECH)
Headquarters
Lot 26, Jalan Pengapit 15/19, Section 15, 40200, Shah
Alam, Selangor, Malaysia
Tel: (+60 3) 55 22 88 00
(+60 3) 55 22 88 88
(+60 3) 55 12 31 00
(+60 3) 55 22 88 08
(+60 9) 426 57 00 (pekan, plant)
Fax: (+60 3) 55 22 89 99
(+60 3) 55 22 89 96
(+60 9) 426 58 00 (pekan, plant)
e-mail: enquiries@deftech.com.my
Web: www.deftech.com.my

Netherlands

DAF Trucks NV
PO Box 90065 NL-5600 PT, Eindhoven, Netherlands
Hugo van der Goeslaan 1, NL-5643 TW, Eindhoven,
Netherlands
Tel: (+31 40) 214 91 11
Fax: (+31 40) 214 43 25
e-mail: info@daftrucks.com
Web: www.daftrucks.com
www.daf.com

Damen Shipyards Group
PO Box 1 NL-4200 AA, Gorinchem, Netherlands
Avelingen West 20, NL-4202 MS, Gorinchem,
Netherlands
Tel: (+31 183) 63 99 22
(+31 183) 63 98 20
(+31 183) 63 99 62
Fax: (+31 183) 63 21 89
(+31 183) 63 95 05
e-mail: info@damen.nl
info.group@damen.nl
Web: www.damen.nl

Munters AB
Defence Marketing
(a subsidiary of Munters AB, Sweden)
PO Box 229 NL-2400 AE, Alphen aan den Rijn,
Netherlands
Tel: (+31 172) 43 32 31
Fax: (+31 172) 44 29 60
e-mail: defence@munters.com
Web: www.munters.com
www.munters.nl

Promac BV
Water Treatment
PO Box 22 NL-5300 AA, Zaltbommel, Netherlands
Van Voordenpark 14, NL-5301 KP, Zaltbommel,
Netherlands
Tel: (+31 418) 68 33 33
Fax: (+31 418) 68 33 55
e-mail: info@promac.nl
Web: www.promac.nl

Robusta Technical and Industrial Fabrics
PO Box 41 NL-8280 AA, Genemuiden, Netherlands
Sasdijk 4, NL-8281 BM, Genemuiden, Netherlands
Tel: (+31 38) 385 48 66
Fax: (+31 38) 385 65 41
e-mail: info@robusta.nl
Web: www.robusta.nl

New Zealand

Steelbro New Zealand Ltd
1-31 Treffers Road,
PO Box 11-077 Christchurch, New Zealand
Tel: (+64 3) 348 84 99
Fax: (+64 3) 348 57 86
e-mail: marketing@steelbro.com
Web: www.steelbro.com

Norway

Natech NSV AS
N-8512, Narvik, Norway
Teknologiveien 4, N-8517, Narvik, Norway
Tel: (+47 769) 228 00
Fax: (+47 769) 228 99
e-mail: natech@natech.no
Web: www.natech.no

Norwegian Demining Consortium AS (NoDeCo)
Oscarsgate 42,
PO Box 2521 Solli N-0202, Oslo, Norway
Tel: (+47 22) 43 82 80
Fax: (+47 22) 43 42 17
Web: www.ndrf.dk

Pakistan

Heavy Industries Taxila (HIT)
(a subsidiary of Defence Export Promotion Organisation, Pakistan)
APC Factory, Taxila Cantt, Pakistan
Tel: (+92 596) 92711 55
(+92 596) 925 11
(+92 51) 927 05 71
(+92 51) 927 05 71 (ext. 2131)
(+92 51) 927 05 72
(+92 51) 927 05 73
(+92 51) 927 05 74
Fax: (+92 596) 931 41 51
(+92 596) 31 99

Poland

DZT Tyminscy sp. J
20-952 Zaklad produkcji samochodow Honker,
Melgiewska, PL-7 9 20 952, Lublin, Poland
Tel: (+48 81) 749 32 76
Fax: (+48 81) 749 32 09
e-mail: dzt.lublin@dzt.com.pl
Web: www.dzt.com.pl

Huta Stalowa Wola SA (HSW SA)
Military Production Centre (CPW)
Ulica Kwiatkowskiego 1, PL-37-450, Stalowa Wola,
Poland
Tel: (+48 15) 813 42 12
(+48 15) 813 53 10
Fax: (+48 15) 813 49 84
(+48 15) 843 41 20
e-mail: cpw@hsw.pl
Web: www.hsw.pl

Mechanical Works Bumar Labedy SA
ZM Bumar-Labedy SA
Zaklady Mechaniczne Bumar-Labedy SA
ulitsa Mechaników 9, PL-44-109, Gliwice, Poland
Tel: (+48 32) 734 51 11
(+48 32) 734 58 00
(+48 32) 733 62 56 (marketing)
Fax: (+48 32) 234 24 43
(+48 32) 734 69 75 (marketing)
(+48 32) 734 65 11
e-mail: hr@bumar.gliwice.pl (marketing)
Web: www.bumar.gliwice.pl

Research and Development Centre of Mechanical Appliances
Osrodek Badawczo-Rozwojowy Urzaden Mechanicznych
ulitsa Toszecka 102, PL-44-117, Gliwice, Poland
Tel: (+48 32) 231 72 14
(+48 32) 279 39 30
Fax: (+48 32) 231 58 87
e-mail: info@obrum.gliwice.pl
Web: www.obrum.gliwice.pl

Wojskowe Zaklady Inzynieryjne (WZInz)
Military Engineering Works
ul 15 Pulku Piechoty Wilków 3, PL-08-530, Deblin,
Poland
Tel: (+48 81) 880 15 00
(+48 81) 880 15 01
Fax: (+48 81) 880 15 02
e-mail: info@wzinz.com.pl
Web: www.wzinz.com.pl

Romania

ARO SA
223 Traian Street, R-115100, Campulung Muscel, Arges,
Romania
Tel: (+40 48) 21 70 99
(+40 248) 51 03 22
(+40 48) 21 28 00
Fax: (+40 48) 21 74 00
(+40 248) 51 03 22
(+40 48) 212 80 00
e-mail: officearo@yahoo.com
Web: www.aro.ro

Roman SA
5 Poienelor Street, R-500419, Brasov, Romania
Tel: (+40 268) 31 28 50
(+40 268) 30 21 20
(+40 268) 30 21 23
Fax: (+40 268) 31 17 36
(+40 268) 30 21 22
e-mail: info@roman.ro
vanzari@roman.ro
Web: www.roman.ro

Romtehnica
(a subsidiary of Ministry of Defence, Romania)
5C Timisoara Boulevard, R-61301, Bucharest, 6,
Romania
Tel: (+40 21) 318 50 04
Fax: (+40 21) 318 50 35
(+40 21) 318 50 00
e-mail: marketing@romtehnica.com.ro
Web: www.romtehnica.com.ro

Russian Federation

Arzamas Machine Plant
2/9 May Street, 607220, Arzamas, Nizhni Novgorod
Region, Russian Federation
Tel: (+7 83147) 967 50
(+7 83147) 407 80
Fax: (+7 83147) 431 40
(+7 83147) 448 33
e-mail: ovs@arzamas.nnov.ru
Web: www.amz.ru

Bryansk Motor Vehicle Plant JSC
Ul 1st Mytischinskaya 3, Building 1, 129626, Moskva, Russian Federation
Tel: (+7 495) 741 01 58
Fax: (+7 495) 741 01 59
Web: www.bzkt.ru

Concern of Medium and Small Tonnage Shipbuilding (KCMK)
5 floor, 1 entrance, 2 Slavanskaya Square, 109074, Moskva, Russian Federation
Tel: (+7 095) 755 82 69
Fax: (+7 095) 784 69 63
e-mail: info@kcmk.ru
Web: www.kcmk.ru

Dmitrov Excavator Plant
1 Pushkin Street, 141800, Dmitrov, Moscow Region, Russian Federation
Tel: (+7 495) 993 80 52
     (+7 495) 993 82 46
     (+7 495) 993 91 26
Fax: (+7 495) 993 80 48
e-mail: explan@mcomm.ru
Web: www.dez.dmitrow.ru

GAZ Group (OJSC GAZ)
Open Joint-Stock Company GAZ
88 Lenina Prospect, 603950, Nizhnyi Novgorod, Russian Federation
Tel: (+7 831) 299 09 90
e-mail: general@atom.gaz.ru
Web: eng.gazgroup.ru

Kurganmashzavod Joint Stock Company
Kurgan Machine Construction Plant
17 Mashinostroitley Avenue, 640027, Kurgan, Russian Federation
Tel: (+7 3522) 53 22 44
     (+7 3522) 23 20 83
     (+7 3522) 47 13 39
     (+7 3522) 47 15 86
Fax: (+7 3522) 53 39 96
     (+7 3522) 23 20 71
e-mail: root@kurganmash.ru
Web: www.kurganmash.ru
     www.kmz.ru

Metrowagonmash JSC
4 Kolontsov Street, Mytishchi, 141009, Moskva, Russian Federation
Tel: (+7 095) 586 62 77
     (+7 495) 582 56 51 (directorate)
     (+7 495) 582 56 77
     (+7 495) 586 25 55 (sales)
Fax: (+7 495) 581 53 66
e-mail: info@metrowagonmash.ru
Web: www.metrowagonmash.ru

Mobile Vehicle Special Design Bureau JSC Specsmash
Stachek pr. 47, korp. 2, 198097, St Petersburg, Russian Federation
Tel: (+7 812) 784 98 73
     (+7 812) 183 86 29
Fax: (+7 812) 184 19 64
e-mail: specmash@specmash-kb.com
Web: www.specmash-kb.com

Open Joint Stock Company KAMAZ (OJSC KAMAZ)
Avtozavodsky pr 2, Naberezhnye Chelny,
PO Box 423827 Tatarstan, Russian Federation
Tel: (+7 8552) 45 21 35
     (+7 8552) 37 18 16 (export)
Fax: (+7 8552) 45 29 36
     (+7 8552) 53 24 04 (export)
e-mail: export@kamaztrade.ru (export)
     cso@kamaz.net
Web: www.kamaz.net

Polymerfilter JSC
Kalinin str, 341, 350000, Krasnodar, Russian Federation
Tel: (+7 861) 259 05 62
     (+7 861) 255 43 78
Fax: (+7 861) 255 90 43
e-mail: waterpf@mail.kubtelekom.ru
Web: www.polymerfilter.ru

Rosoboronexport State Corporation
27 Stromynka Street, 107076, Moskva, Russian Federation
Tel: (+7 495) 964 83 11
Fax: (+7 495) 963 26 13
e-mail: rv@post.rusarm.ru
Web: www.rusarm.ru

Stankomash JSC
Peer Street 8, 454010, Chelyabinsk, Russian Federation
e-mail: stankom@mail.ru (marketing)
Web: www.stankomash74.ru

Strategia
3D, Nevezhina Street, 640003, Kurgan, Russian Federation
Tel: (+7 3522) 44 30 99
     (+7 3522) 44 71 11
e-mail: stategia@infocentr.ru
Web: www.kzkt.ru

Ulyanovsky Avtomobilny Zavod
Moskovskoye shosse, 86, 432008, Ulyanovsk, Russian Federation
Tel: (+7 8422) 40 61 68
Fax: (+7 8422) 40 61 69
e-mail: export@uaz.ru
Web: www.uaz.ru

Ural Automobile Plant
1 Avtozavodtsev Avenue, 456300, Chelyabinsk, Russian Federation
Tel: (+7 35135) 335 70
     (+7 3513) 55 16 37
     (+7 3513) 29 11 09 (press)
Fax: (+7 35135) 55 16 37
     (+7 35135) 29 11 54 (press)
e-mail: press@mail.uralaz.ru
     gdural@mail.uralaz.ru
     tdurlz@miass.ru
     export@tduralaz.ru
Web: www.uralaz.ru

Uralvagonzavod
Vostochnoye Chaussee 28, 622007, Nizhniy Tagil, Sverdlovsk Region, Russian Federation
Tel: (+7 3435) 23 17 74
     (+7 3435) 33 66 17
     (+7 3435) 34 50 00
Fax: (+7 3435) 34 53 14
     (+7 3435) 23 34 92
     (+7 3435) 34 53 57
e-mail: press@uvz.ru
     web@uvz.ru
     vned@uvz.ru
Web: www.uvz.ru

Serbia

FAP Korporacija a d
Priboj Radnicka bb, 31330, Priboj, Serbia
Tel: (+381 33) 513 31
Fax: (+381 33) 552 41
e-mail: fap@eunet.rs
Web: www.fap.co.rs

Industrija Motora Rakovica DD (IMR)
Patrijarha Dimitrija 7, 13, 11090, Beograd, Rakovica, Serbia
11090, Rakovica, Montenegro
Tel: (+381 11) 59 11 11
     (+381 11) 356 40 13 (sales)
     (+381 11) 356 40 34 (spare parts sales)
     (+381 11) 356 40 33 (service)
     (+381 11) 356 40 81 (manufacturing service)
     (+381 11) 356 41 63 (manufacturing service)
     (+381 11) 356 40 35 (manufacturing service)
Fax: (+381 11) 58 10 50
e-mail: imr-q@infosky.net (quality)
     imr_fin@infosky.net (finance)
     imrkb@eunet.yu (research and development)
Web: www.imr-rakovica.com

Yugoimport SDPR
2 Bulevar Umetnosti, 11150, Beograd, Serbia
Tel: (+381 11) 222 44 44
Fax: (+381 11) 222 45 99
e-mail: fdsp@eunet.rs
     office@yugoimport.com
Web: www.yugoimport.com

Singapore

Singapore Technologies Kinetics Ltd (ST Kinetics)
Headquarters
(a subsidiary of Singapore Technologies Engineering Ltd, Singapore)
249 Jalan Boon Lay, 619523, Singapore
Tel: (+65) 64 73 63 11
Fax: (+65) 64 71 06 62
e-mail: comms.kinetics@stengg.com
Web: www.stengg.com

Singapore Technologies Marine Ltd (ST Marine)
Headquarters
51 Cuppage Road, 09-08 Starhub Centre, 229469, Singapore
Tel: (+65 6722) 18 18
Fax: (+65 6720) 22 93
e-mail: comms.marine@stengg.com
     mktg.marine@stengg.com
     commercial@stengg.com
Web: www.stengg.com

Slovakia

CSM Tisovec as
Daxnerova 756, SK-980 61, Tisovec, Slovakia
Tel: (+421 47) 549 44 00
Fax: (+421 47) 549 43 11
e-mail: csm@csmtisovec.sk
Web: www.csmtisovec.sk

Kerametal AS
Jasikova 2, SK-826 05, Bratislava, Slovakia
Tel: (+421 2) 48 29 11 11 (switchboard)
Fax: (+421 2) 48 29 15 81
     (+421 2) 48 29 15 68
     (+421 2) 48 29 15 63
e-mail: kerametal@kerametal.sk
Web: www.kerametal.sk

Konstrukta Industry AS
Kvystavisku 13, SK-912 50, Trencín, Slovakia
Tel: (+421 831) 53 58 50
     (+421 831) 346 82
     (+421 32) 743 57 31
     (+421 32) 650 75 28
Fax: (+421 32) 743 19 30
e-mail: kotadef@kotadef.sk
Web: www.kotadef.sk

PPS Group as
Podpolianske Stromjárne Detva
Tajovského 7, SK-962 12, Detva, Slovakia
Tel: (+421 45) 521 91 02
     (+421 45) 521 91 41 (marketing and strategy)
     (+421 45) 521 93 11 (business)
     (+421 855) 95 51 11
Fax: (+421 45) 521 91 10
     (+421 45) 521 93 50 (business)
     (+421 855) 95 53 27
e-mail: pps@ppsgroup.sk
Web: www.ppsgroup.sk

Tanax as
Partizánska 73, SK-957 11, Banovce Nad Beravou, Slovakia
Tel: (+421 38) 760 36 93 (sales)
     (+421 832) 760 38 46
Fax: (+421 832) 760 33 35 (sales)
e-mail: odbyt@tanax.sk
Web: www.tanax.sk

Technopol International AS
Kutlikova 17, SK-852 50, Bratislava, Slovakia
Tel: (+421 2) 68 28 62 84
Fax: (+421 2) 68 28 62 12
e-mail: os3@technopol.sk
military@technopol.sk
Web: www.technopol.sk

VSS as Kosice
Jusná trieda 82, SK-040 01, Kosice, Slovakia
Tel: (+421 55) 611 52 12
Fax: (+421 55) 611 52 93
e-mail: vss@vss.sk
Web: www.vss.sk

Slovenia

**Tovarna Vozil Maribor doo
(TVM)**
Cesta k Tamu 33,
P O Box 188 SI-2000, Maribor, Slovenia
Tel: (+386 2) 460 11 00 (finance)
(+386 2) 460 11 02
(+386 2) 460 11 11 (marketing)
(+386 2) 460 11 16 (development, technology and
production)
Fax: (+386 2) 460 11 18 (head office and finance)
(+386 2) 460 12 59 (marketing, development and
technology)
(+386 2) 460 11 22 (production)
e-mail: marketing@tvm.si
Web: www.tvm.si

South Africa

**Armaments Corporation of
South Africa Ltd (ARMSCOR)**
Private Bag X337 0001, Pretoria, South Africa
370 Nossob Street, 0001, Pretoria, South Africa
Tel: (+27 12) 428 19 11
Fax: (+27 12) 428 56 35
e-mail: info@armscor.co.za
Web: www.armscor.co.za

**BAE Systems Land &
Armaments**
Global Tactical Systems, Land Systems OMC
**(a part of BAE Systems Land & Armaments,
South Africa)**
12 Barnsley Road, Industrial Sites, 1501, Benoni,
Gauteng, South Africa
Tel: (+27 11) 747 33 00
Fax: (+27 11) 845 13 79
e-mail: marketing@baesystemsomc.co.za
Web: www.baesystems.com/landarmaments
www.baesystems.com/southafrica

CSIR
Defence, Peace, Safety and Security
Meiring Naude Road,
PO Box 395 0001, Pretoria, South Africa
Tel: (+27 12) 841 29 11
(+27 12) 841 27 80
Fax: (+27 12) 841 11 58
(+27 12) 349 11 53
e-mail: callcentre@csir.co.za
Web: www.csir.co.za

DCD-Dorbyl (Pty) Ltd
Rolling Stock (RSD)
Victor Street Industrial Sites, Boksburg East,
PO Box 229 1460, Boksburg, Gauteng, South Africa
Tel: (+27 11) 914 14 00
Fax: (+27 11) 914 38 85
Web: www.dcd-dorbyl.com

Denel (Pty) Ltd
Head Office
PO Box 8322 0046, Centurion, South Africa
Nellmapius Drive, Irene, Pretoria, South Africa
Tel: (+27 12) 671 27 00
(+27 12) 671 28 58
Fax: (+27 12) 671 27 51
(+27 12) 67 12 79 31
e-mail: marketing@denel.co.za
Web: www.denel.co.za

**Mechem (Pty) Ltd
(a subsidiary of Denel (Pty) Ltd, South
Africa)**
PO Box 14864 0140, Lyttelton, South Africa
368B Selbourne Avenue, 0157, Lyttelton, South Africa
Tel: (+27 12) 640 30 00
(+27 12) 664 39 31
(+27 12) 664 39 06
Fax: (+27 12) 664 35 28
e-mail: marketing@mechem.co.za
Web: www.mechemdemining.com

**World Focus Flexitanks
(a subsidiary of IDE Technologies Ltd, Israel)**
Induna Mills Road,
PO Box 1240 3290, Howick, Kwa-Zulu Natal, South
Africa
Tel: (+27 33) 239 72 15
(+27 33) 239 72 34
Freephone: (+27 33) 866 93 68 11
Fax: (+27 33) 330 46 39
e-mail: worldfocus1001@telkomsa.net
Web: www.worldfocusflexitanks.com

Spain

**Equipos Industriales de
Manutención SA (EINSA)**
Carretera M-300, Kilometer 29, E-28802, Alcalá de
Henares, Madrid, Spain
Tel: (+34 91) 880 90 00
Fax: (+34 91) 880 90 86
e-mail: info@einsa.es
Web: www.einsa.es

**Explosivos Alaveses SA
(EXPAL SA)**
Avenida del Partenon 16, 5a Planta, E-28042, Madrid,
Spain
Tel: (+34 91) 722 02 35
Fax: (+34 91) 722 02 95

**General Dynamics European
Land Systems-Santa Bárbara
Sistemas**
Headquarters
**(a part of General Dynamics European Land
Systems, Austria)**
Parque Empresarial Cristalia, Edificio 7/8, Vía de los
Poblados 3, E-28033, Madrid, Spain
Tel: (+34 91) 585 01 10
(+34 91) 585 03 90
Fax: (+34 91) 585 02 68
e-mail: info.sbs@gdels.com
sales.sbs@gdels.com
Web: www.gdsbs.com
www.generaldynamics.com
www.gdels.com

Iveco Pegaso SA
Avenida de Aragón 402, E-28022, Madrid, Spain
Tel: (+34 91) 325 27 35
(+34 91) 325 10 00
Fax: (+34 91) 747 47 32
(+34 91) 325 28 11
Web: www.iveco.com

Santana Motor SA
Avenida 1 de Mayo, Linares, E-23700, Jaen, Spain
Tel: (+34 953) 64 92 00
(+34 91) 428 24 10
(+34 91) 428 24 20
Fax: (+34 953) 69 70 03
(+34 953) 69 35 63
(+34 91) 746 39 60
(+34 91) 746 38 16
e-mail: informatica@santana-motor.es
atencion.clientes@santana-motor.es
marketing@santana-motor.es
Web: www.santana-motor.es

**URO Vehiculos Especiales SA
(UROVESA)**
Factory
Via Edison 17, Poligono Ind del Tambre, E-15890,
Santiago de Compostela, Spain
Tel: (+34 981) 58 03 22
Fax: (+34 981) 56 53 70
e-mail: info@urovesa.com
Web: www.urovesa.com

Sweden

**BAE Systems Land &
Armaments**
Global Combat Systems Vehicles
SE-891 82, Örnsköldsvik, Sweden
Tel: (+46 660) 800 00
Fax: (+46 660) 809 95
Web: www.baesystems.com/landandarmaments

**BAE Systems Land &
Armaments**
Global Combat Systems Weapons
SE-691 80, Karlskoga, Sweden
Tel: (+46 0586) 73 30 00
Fax: (+46 0596) 73 30 12
Web: www.baesystems.com/landandarmaments

Hammar Maskin AB
Government Sales
Olsfors, SE-517 95, Sweden
Tel: (+46 33) 29 00 00
Fax: (+46 33) 29 00 01
e-mail: government@hammar.eu
info@hammar.eu
Web: www.hammar.eu

Kockums AB
Head Office
**(a subsidiary of Howaldtswerke Deutsche
Werft GmbH, Germany)**
SE-205 55, Malmö, Sweden
Stora Varvsgatan 11, SE-211 19, Malmö, Sweden
Tel: (+46 40) 34 80 00
Fax: (+46 40) 97 32 81
e-mail: information@kockums.se
Web: www.kockums.com
www.kockums.se

**Kockums AB
(a subsidiary of Kockums AB, Sweden)**
SE-371 82, Karlskrona, Sweden
Tel: (+46 455) 68 30 00
Fax: (+46 455) 179 34
e-mail: information@kockums.se
Web: www.kockums.se

**Saab Dynamics AB
(a subsidiary of Saab AB, Sweden)**
Boforsvägen 1, SE-691 80, Karlskoga, Sweden
Tel: (+46 586) 810 00
Fax: (+46 586) 857 00
e-mail: bofors@dynamics.saab.se
Web: www.saabgroup.com

Volvo Truck Corporation
Headquarters
Gropegårdsgatan, SE-405 08, Göteborg, Sweden
Tel: (+46 31) 66 00 00
Fax: (+46 31) 51 04 65
Web: www.volvo.com

Switzerland

**General Dynamics European
Land Systems-Mowag
(GDELS-MOWAG)**
Mowag Motorwagenfabrik AG
**(a subsidiary of General Dynamics European
Land Systems, US)**
Unterseestrasse 65, CH-8280, Kreuzlingen, Switzerland
Tel: (+41 71) 677 55 00 (switchboard)
(+41 71) 677 55 59 (main)
Fax: (+41 71) 672 81 42 (marketing and sales)
(+41 71) 672 28 86 (main)
(+41 71) 672 55 14
e-mail: purchasing@mowag.ch
info@gdels.com
Web: www.mowag.ch

Modulmed Patented Systems SA
Rue de la Grotte 6,
PO Box 687 CH-1001, Lausanne, Switzerland
Tel: (+41 21) 825 56 66
Fax: (+41 23) 825 56 67
e-mail: modulmed@modulmed.com
info@modulmed.com
Web: www.modulmed.com

RUAG Land Systems Ltd
(a subsidiary of RUAG Holding, Switzerland)
Allmendstrasse 86, CH-3602, Thun, Switzerland
Tel: (+41 332) 28 21 11
(+41 332) 28 21 57
(+41 33) 228 47 60
(+41 33) 228 20 76
Fax: (+41 33) 228 47 83
e-mail: info.landsystems@ruag.com
marketing.landsystems@ruag.com
info@ruag.com
Web: www.ruag.com

Turkey

FNSS Savunma Sistemleri AS (FNSS)
(a joint venture between BAE Systems Land & Armaments, US and NUROL Holding, Turkey)
PO Box 37 TR-06830, Gölbasi, Ankara, Turkey
Tel: (+90 312) 497 43 00
Fax: (+90 312) 497 43 01
(+90 312) 497 43 02
e-mail: marketing@fnss.com.tr
info@fnss.com.tr
Web: www.fnss.com.tr

Ibrahim ORS Agricultural & Military Equipment Factories (ORS)
Head Office
Samsun yolu 8 km, TR-71600, Kirikkale, Turkey
Tel: (+90 318) 284 14 14 (5 lines)
Fax: (+90 318) 284 14 19
e-mail: ibrahimors@superonline.com.tr
Web: www.ibrahimors.com.tr

Makine ve Kimya Endüstrisi Kurumu (MKEK)
General Directorate
Tandogan Medyani, TR-06330, Ankara, Turkey
Tel: (+90 312) 296 10 00
(+90 312) 296 11 70 (marketing)
(+90 312) 212 66 80 (central operator)
(+90 312) 296 11 30 (procurement)
(+90 312) 296 11 69 (marketing)
(+90 312) 296 11 82 (marketing)
(+90 312) 296 11 74 (marketing)
(+90 312) 223 20 11 (marketing)
(+90 312) 223 13 46 (procurement)
(+90 312) 296 11 30 (procurement)
(+90 312) 296 10 36 (human resource)
(+90 312) 223 12 00 (personnel)
Fax: (+90 312) 222 22 51
(+90 312) 212 33 15 (human resource)
(+90 312) 222 22 41 (marketing)
(+90 312) 223 01 40 (procurement)
e-mail: mkekexport@mkek.gov.tr
mkekpazarlama@mkek.gov.tr
mkekexp@mkek.gov.tr
mkek@mkek.gov.tr
Web: www.mkek.gov.tr

MAN Turkiye AS
(a subsidiary of MAN Nutzfahrzeuge Group, Germany)
Esenboga Havalimani Yolu 22 Km, TR-06750, Ankara, Akyurt, Turkey
Tel: (+90 312) 398 02 20
Fax: (+90 312) 398 01 69
Web: www.man-mn.com
www.man.com.tr

Ukraine

Foreign Trade Firm KrAZ
2 Proyezd Yaroslavskiy Street, 39631, Kremenchug, Poltava Region, Ukraine
Tel: (+380 536) 76 62 10
Fax: (+380 536) 77 16 73
e-mail: market@ftfkraz.poltava.ua
office@ftfkraz.poltava.ua
Web: www.autokraz.com.ua

Kharkov Morozov Machine Building Design Bureau (KMDB)
126 Plekhanovskaya Street, 61001, Kharkov, Ukraine
Tel: (+380 572) 28 31 90
(+380 577) 57 41 67
(+380 577) 57 41 44
(+380 577) 57 41 43 (marketing)
Fax: (+380 572) 26 33 21
(+380 577) 57 41 01
(+380 577) 57 41 68
e-mail: marketing@morozov.com.ua
morozov@morozov.com.ua
Web: www.morozov.com.ua

Kraz
Joint Stock Company Foreign Trade Firm Kraz
2 Yaroslavskiy proyezd street, Kremenchuck, 39631, Kremenchug, Poltava region, Ukraine
Tel: (+380 536) 76 62 10
Fax: (+380 536) 77 16 73
e-mail: office@ftfkraz.poltava.ua
Web: www.autokraz.com.ua

Kryukovsky Railway Car Building Works (KCBW)
139 Prikhodko Street, 39621, Kremenchug, Ukraine
Tel: (+380 536) 76 95 05
(+380 536) 76 94 09
Fax: (+380 536) 74 36 20
e-mail: kvsz@kvsz.com
Web: www.kvsz.com

PJSC Automobile Company Bogdan Motors
WOS Assembly Plant #2
8/2 Sumgaitskiaya Street, Cherkassy, Ukraine
Tel: (+380 47) 265 10 94

Progress
**Specialised Foreign Trade Firm Progress (FTF)
(a subsidiary of Ukrspetsexport, Ukraine)**
10a Rileeva Street, 04073, Kiyev, Ukraine
Tel: (+380 44) 568 50 42
Fax: (+380 44) 568 51 98
(+380 44) 461 92 53
e-mail: progress@progress.gov.ua
Web: www.progress.gov.ua

State Enterprise Malyshev Plant
SOE Kharkiv Morozov Machine Building Design Bureau
Plekhanovskaya Street 126, 61001, Kharkov, Ukraine
Tel: (+380 57) 795 09 59 (marketing and advertising)
Fax: (+380 57) 766 87 33 (marketing and advertising)
e-mail: marketing@malyshev.kharkov.ua
Web: www.malyshevplant.com

Ukrspetsexport
36 Dehtyarivska Street, 04119, Kiyev, Ukraine
Tel: (+380 44) 458 46 81
(+380 44) 461 95 03
Fax: (+380 44) 489 07 58
(+380 44) 461 97 59
e-mail: aira@ukrspetsexport.com
Web: www.ukrspetsexport.com
www.use-weapon.astral.kiev.ua

United Arab Emirates

Adcom Systems
Industrial City of Abu Dhabi,
PO Box 25298 Abu Dhabi, United Arab Emirates
Tel: (+971 2) 550 06 30
Fax: (+971 2) 550 06 31
e-mail: adcom@eim.ae

United Kingdom

Aardvark Clear Mine Ltd
Shevock Estate, Insch, Aberdeenshire, AB52 6XQ, United Kingdom
Tel: (+44 1464) 82 01 22
Fax: (+44 1464) 82 09 85
e-mail: info@aardvarkclearmine.com
Web: www.landmineclearance.com

Amethyst Group
Headquarters
Lodge Road, Staplehurst, Tonbridge, Kent, TN12 0QW, United Kingdom
Tel: (+44 1580) 89 56 63
(+44 1580) 89 22 11
Fax: (+44 1580) 89 58 58
(+44 1580) 89 37 37
e-mail: info@amethystgroup-uk.com
sales@amethystgroup-uk.com
Web: www.amethystgroup-uk.com

Avon Protection
Hampton Park West, Semington Road, Melksham, Wiltshire, SN12 6NB, United Kingdom
Tel: (+44 1225) 89 67 05
Fax: (+44 1225) 89 63 01
e-mail: enquiries@avon-rubber.com
protection@avon-rubber.co.uk
Web: www.avon-protection.com

BAE Systems Land & Armaments
Global Combat Systems Vehicles
Armstrong Works, Scotswood Road, Newcastle-upon-Tyne, NE99 1BX, United Kingdom
Tel: (+44 191) 273 88 88
Fax: (+44 191) 273 23 24
Web: www.baesystems.com/landandarmaments

BAE Systems Land & Armaments
Global Combat Systems Vehicles
Spring Road, Ettingshall,
PO Box 37 Wolverhampton, West Midlands, WV4 6YN, United Kingdom
Tel: (+44 1902) 40 50 50
Web: www.baesystems.com/landandarmaments

Cargotec UK Ltd
Government Business Operations
Partek Cargotec Ltd
Cargotec Industrial Park, Ellesmere Port, Shropshire, SY12 9JW, United Kingdom
Tel: (+44 16 91) 62 31 00
Fax: (+44 16 91) 62 64 39
e-mail: gboenquiries@hiab.com
enquiries.uk@hiab.com
Web: www.hiab.co.uk

CSC Specialised Vehicles
Somerden Road, Kingston-upon-Hull, HU9 5PE, United Kingdom
Tel: (+44 1482) 78 72 36
(+44 1482) 79 84 00
Fax: (+44 1482) 78 72 38
e-mail: sales@paneltex.co.uk
Web: www.paneltex.co.uk

Dennis Eagle Ltd
Heathcote Way, Heathcote Industrial Estate, Warwick, CV34 6TE, United Kingdom
Tel: (+44 1926) 45 85 00
Fax: (+44 1926) 31 65 50
e-mail: enquiries@dennis-eagle.co.uk
Web: www.dennis-eagle.co.uk

Douglas Equipment Ltd
Douglas House, Village Road, Arle, Cheltenham, Gloucestershire, GL51 0AB, United Kingdom
Tel: (+44 1242) 52 79 21
Fax: (+44 1242) 22 11 98
e-mail: sales@douglas-equipment.com
spares@douglas-tugmaster.co.uk
Web: www.douglas-equipment.com

Douglas Equipment Ltd
Special Products
Douglas House, Village Road, Arle, Cheltenham,
Gloucestershire, GL51 0AB, United Kingdom
Tel: (+44 1242) 53 12 54
(+44 1242) 52 79 21
Fax: (+44 1242) 22 11 98
e-mail: spd@douglas-equipment.com
Web: www.douglas-equipment.com

Dytecna Ltd
Aspen House, Malvern Hills Science Park, Malvern,
Hereford and Worcestershire, WR14 3SZ, United
Kingdom
Tel: (+44 1684) 57 90 00
Fax: (+44 1684) 57 53 06
Web: www.dytecna.com

Enhanced Protection Systems (EPS) UK Ltd
Unit 1, Machine House, Newfields, Moira, Derbyshire,
DE12 6EG, United Kingdom
Tel: (+44 1283) 22 49 99
Web: www.enhancedpro.com

EPS Logistics Technology Ltd
152 Staplehurst Road, Sittingbourne, Kent, ME10 1XS,
United Kingdom
Tel: (+44 1795) 42 44 33
Fax: (+44 1795) 43 60 35
e-mail: sales@epslt.co.uk
Web: www.epslt.co.uk

Faun Municipal Vehicles Ltd
Trackway
(a subsidiary of Faun GmbH, Germany)
Llangefni, Anglesey, LL77 7XA, United Kingdom
Tel: (+44 1248) 72 53 09
(+44 1248) 72 27 77
Fax: (+44 1248) 75 02 20
e-mail: sales@fauntrackway.co.uk
Web: www.fauntrackway.co.uk

FBM Babcock Marine
The Courtyard, Saint Cross Business Park, Monks
Brook, Newport, Isle of Wight, PO30 5BF, United
Kingdom
Tel: (+44 1983) 82 57 00
Fax: (+44 1983) 82 41 80
e-mail: fbm@babcock.co.uk
Web: www.fbmuk.com
www.babcock.co.uk

Fluid Transfer International Ltd
Nailsworth Mills Estate, Avening Road, Nailsworth,
Gloucestershire, GL6 0BS, United Kingdom
Tel: (+44 1453) 83 33 81
Fax: (+44 1453) 83 35 29
e-mail: sales@fluid-transfer.co.uk
Web: www.fluid-transfer.co.uk

Hesco Bastion Ltd
Unit 37, Knowsthorpe Gate, Cross Green Industrial
Estate, Leeds, West Yorkshire, LS9 0NP, United
Kingdom
Tel: (+44 113) 248 66 33
Fax: (+44 113) 248 35 01
e-mail: hescob@aol.com
Web: www.hesco.com

HMT Vehicles Ltd
The Airfield, Dunkeswell, Honiton, Devon, EX14 4LF,
United Kingdom
Tel: (+44 1404) 89 17 77
Fax: (+44 1404) 89 17 76
e-mail: generalenquiries@supacat.com
Web: www.supacat.com

Hyster Europe
Marketing and Communication
Flagship House, Reading Road North, Fleet, Hampshire,
GU51 4WD, United Kingdom
Tel: (+44 1252) 81 02 61
Fax: (+44 1252) 77 07 02
e-mail: infoeurope@hyster.com
Web: www.hyster.co.uk

ITT PCI Membranes Ltd
PCI Membranes
Jays Close, Viables Estate, Basingstoke, Hampshire,
RG22 4BA, United Kingdom
Tel: (+44 1256) 30 38 00
Fax: (+44 1256) 30 38 01
e-mail: aquious@itt.com
Web: www.aquious.itt.com
www.pcimem.com

J&S Franklin Ltd
Franklin House, 151 Strand, London, WC2R 1HL, United
Kingdom
Tel: (+44 20) 78 36 57 46
Fax: (+44 20) 78 36 27 84
e-mail: defence@franklin.co.uk
Web: www.franklin.co.uk

Jankel Armouring Ltd
PO Box 1 Weybridge, Surrey, KT13 8XR, United
Kingdom
Tel: (+44 1932) 85 77 66
Fax: (+44 1932) 85 56 94
e-mail: info@jankel.co.uk
Web: www.jankel.com

JCB Sales Ltd
Military Products
Rocester, Staffordshire, ST14 5JP, United Kingdom
Tel: (+44 1889) 59 03 12
Web: www.jcb.com

King Trailers Ltd
Riverside, Market Harborough, Leicestershire, LE16 7PX,
United Kingdom
Tel: (+44 1858) 46 73 61
Fax: (+44 1858) 46 71 61
e-mail: sales@kingtrailers.co.uk
Web: www.kingtrailers.co.uk

Land Rover UK
Gaydon
Banbury Road, Gaydon, Warwickshire, CV35 0RR,
United Kingdom
Tel: (+44 1926) 64 92 60
(+44 1926) 64 92 61
(+44 8705) 00 05 00 (customer service)
Freephone: (+44 800) 11 01 10
Fax: (+44 1926) 64 91 03
e-mail: enquiries@landrover-militarysales.co.uk
Web: www.landrover.com
www.landrover.co.uk

Leyland Trucks Ltd
Croston Road Leyland, Preston, Lancashire, PR26 6LZ,
United Kingdom
Tel: (+44 1772) 62 14 00
Fax: (+44 1772) 62 57 70
Web: www.leylandtrucksltd.co.uk

Linde Material Handling (UK) Ltd
Kingsclere Road, Basingstoke, Hampshire, RG21 6XJ,
United Kingdom
Tel: (+44 845) 608 50 00
(+44 1256) 34 20 00
Fax: (+44 845) 609 33 34
(+44 1256) 34 29 23
e-mail: enquiries@linde-mh.co.uk
Web: www.linde-mh.co.uk

Lockheed Martin UK INSYS Ltd (LMUK)
(a subsidiary of Lockheed Martin UK Ltd, UK)
Reddings Wood, Ampthill, Bedfordshire, MK45 2HD,
United Kingdom
Tel: (+44 1525) 84 10 00
Fax: (+44 1525) 40 58 61
Web: www.lockheedmartin.co.uk

Mabey & Bridge Ltd
(a subidiary of Mabey Holdings Ltd, UK)
Chepstow, NP16 5YL, United Kingdom
Tel: (+44 1291) 62 38 01
Fax: (+44 1291) 62 54 53
e-mail: mail@mabeybridge.co.uk
Web: www.mabeybridge.co.uk

Manitowoc Crane Group
Sales
1 Azure Court, Doxford International Business Park,
Sunderland, Tyne and Wear, SR3 3BE, United Kingdom
Tel: (+44 191) 522 20 00
(+44 191) 565 62 81
Fax: (+44 191) 564 04 42
(+44 191) 515 74 75
Web: www.manitowoccranes.com

Marshall Land Systems (MLS)
Marshall SV
Airport House, The Airport, Cambridge, CB5 8RX, United
Kingdom
Tel: (+44 1223) 37 39 00
(+44 1223) 37 39 09 (sales and marketing)
(+44 1223) 37 37 37
Fax: (+44 1223) 37 30 64
(+44 1223) 32 10 32
e-mail: info@marshalls-ls.com
Web: www.marshall-ls.com

Merlo UK Ltd
(a subsidiary of Merlo SpA, Italy)
The Paddocks, Headlands Business Park, Salisbury
Road, Ringwood, Hampshire, BH24 3PB, United
Kingdom
Tel: (+44 1425) 48 08 06
(+44 1425) 47 07 01 (parts and service)
(+44 1507) 52 31 80 (marketing)
Fax: (+44 1425) 47 74 78
(+44 1425) 47 32 73 (parts and service)
(+44 1507) 52 26 05 (marketing)
(+44 1507) 52 58 88
e-mail: sales@merlo.co.uk
info@merlo.co.uk
parts@merlo.co.uk
pmg@merlo.co.uk (marketing)
Web: www.merlo.co.uk

MSI-Defence Systems Ltd
Headquarters
(a division of MS International plc, UK)
Salhouse Road, Norwich, Norfolk, NR7 9AY, United
Kingdom
Tel: (+44 1603) 48 40 65
Fax: (+44 1603) 41 56 49
e-mail: contact@msi-dsl.com
Web: www.msi-dsl.com

PD Rotomouldings
Maes Yclawdd Industry Estate, Maesbury Road,
Oswestry, Shropshire, SY10 8NN, United Kingdom
Tel: (+44 1691) 65 99 05
Fax: (+44 1691) 65 93 44
e-mail: sales@pdrotomouldings.co.uk
Web: www.defence.pdrotomouldings.co.uk
www.pdrotomouldings.co.uk

Penman Engineering Ltd
Heathhall, Dumfries and Galloway, DG1 3NY, United
Kingdom
Tel: (+44 1387) 25 27 84
e-mail: sales@penman.co.uk
admin@penman.co.uk
info@penman.co.uk
Web: www.penman.co.uk

Pre-Mac International Ltd
Unit 5, Morewood Close, Sevenoaks, Kent, TN13 2HU,
United Kingdom
Tel: (+44 1732) 46 03 33
Fax: (+44 1732) 46 02 22
e-mail: office@pre-mac.com
Web: www.pre-mac.com

Reynolds Boughton (Devon) Ltd
Winkleigh Airfield, Winkleigh, Devon, EX19 8DR, United
Kingdom
Tel: (+44 1837) 835 55
Fax: (+44 1837) 837 68
e-mail: winkleignenquiries@reynoldsboughton.com
Web: www.reynolds-boughton.com

Reynolds Boughton Ltd (RBL)

Graycar Business Park, Barton-Under-Needwood,
Burton-on-Trent, Staffordshire, DE13 8EN, United
Kingdom
Tel: (+44 1283) 71 17 71
Fax: (+44 1283) 71 16 70
e-mail: salesoffice@reynoldsboughton.com
enquiries@reynoldsboughton.com
engineering@reynoldsboughton.com
Web: www.reynoldsboughton.com

Ricardo Vehicle Engineering (RVE)

Special Vehicle Operations
Ricardo plc
(a subsidiary of Ricardo MTC Ltd, UK)
8 Cecil Pashley Way, Shoreham Airport, Shoreham by
Sea, West Sussex, BN43 5FG, United Kingdom
Tel: (+44 1273) 79 44 51
(+44 1273) 44 14 45
(+44 1273) 45 56 11
Fax: (+44 1273) 79 40 67
(+44 1273) 46 41 24
e-mail: special.vehicles@ricardo.com
Web: www.ricardo.com

Supacat Limited

The Airfield, Dunkeswell, Honiton, Devon, EX14 4LF,
United Kingdom
Tel: (+44 1404) 89 17 77
Fax: (+44 1404) 89 17 76
e-mail: generalenquiries@supacat.com
salesandservices@supacat.com
Web: www.supacat.com

Trelleborg Dunlop GRG UK Ltd

Dunlop Fabrications
(a subsidiary of Invensys plc, US)
Unit 62, Touchet Hall Road, Stakehill Industrial Park,
Middleton, Manchester, M24 2RW, United Kingdom
Tel: (+44 161) 653 59 64
Fax: (+44 161) 643 01 84
e-mail: enquiries@dunlopgrg.co.uk
Web: www.trelleborg.com

WFEL Ltd

Crossley Road, Heaton Chapel, Stockport, Cheshire,
SK4 5BB, United Kingdom
Tel: (+44 161) 975 57 00
Fax: (+44 161) 432 02 81
(+44 161) 431 35 75
e-mail: info@wfel.com
Web: www.wfel.com

United States

AAR Mobility Systems

**(a division of AAR Manufacturing Group Inc,
US)**
201 Haynes Street, Cadillac, Michigan, 49601, United
States
Tel: (+1 231) 779 48 12
Freephone: (+1 800) 355 20 15
Fax: (+1 231) 779 48 04
e-mail: milsales@aarcorp.com
Web: www.aarcorp.com

Acrow Corporation of America

Suite 202, 181 New Road, Parsippany, New Jersey,
07054-5625, United States
Tel: (+1 973) 244 00 80
Fax: (+1 973) 244 00 85
e-mail: sales@acrowusa.com
Web: www.acrowusa.com

Air Logistics Corporation

World Headquarters
Strength Elements and Mechanical Groups, 146 Railroad
Avenue, Monrovia, California, 91016, United States
Tel: (+1 626) 256 12 57
Fax: (+1 626) 359 16 89
Web: www.airlog.com

Alliant Techsystems Inc

Corporate Headquarters
7480 Flying Cloud Drive, Minneapolis, Minnesota, 55344,
United States
Tel: (+1 952) 351 30 00
e-mail: atk.corporate@atk.com
Web: www.atk.com

Allison Transmission

Headquarters
PO Box 894 - L7 Indianapolis, Indiana, 46206-0894,
United States
4700 West 100th Street, Indianapolis, Indiana, 46222,
United States
Tel: (+1 317) 242 50 00
(+1 317) 242 27 15
Fax: (+1 317) 242 51 39
Web: www.allisontransmission.com

AM General LLC

Headquarters
105 North Niles Avenue,
PO Box 7025 South Bend, Indiana, 46634, United
States
Tel: (+1 574) 237 67 22
Fax: (+1 574) 284 29 59
Web: www.amgeneral.com

American Fuel Cells and Coated Fabrics Co (AMFUEL)

(a part of Zodiac Aerospace Group, France)
601 Firestone Drive,
PO Box 887 Magnolia, Arkansas, 71753, United States
Tel: (+1 870) 234 33 81
Fax: (+1 870) 235 72 70
e-mail: sales@amfuel.com
Web: www.amfuel.com

Aqua-Chem Inc

Water Technologies Division
3001 East John Sevier Highway, Knoxville, Tennessee,
37914, United States
Tel: (+1 865) 544 20 65
Freephone: (+1 800) 964 70 35
Fax: (+1 865) 546 43 30
e-mail: milsales@aqua-chem.com
Web: www.aqua-chem.com

ATK Advanced Weapons

4700 Nathan Lane, Plymouth, Minnesota, 55442-2890,
United States
Tel: (+1 763) 744 53 12
Fax: (+1 763) 744 58 16
Web: www.atk.com

ATK Launch Systems

Headquarters
PO Box 707 Brigham City, Utah, 84302, United States
9160 North Highway 83, Corinne, Utah, 84307, United
States
Tel: (+1 435) 863 35 11
Fax: (+1 435) 863 23 91
e-mail: businessdevelopment@atk.com
Web: www.atk.com

Avon Engineered Fabrications Inc (AEF)

(a subsidiary of Avon Rubber plc, UK)
1200 Martin Luther King Junior Boulevard, Picayune,
Mississippi, 39466-5427, United States
Tel: (+1 601) 799 12 17
Fax: (+1 601) 799 13 60
(+1 601) 799 01 48 (sales)
e-mail: enquiries@avon-rubber.com
Web: www.avon-rubber.com

BAE Systems Electronic Solutions

(E&IS)
6500 Tracor Lane, Austin, Texas, 78725, United States
Tel: (+1 659) 26 07
Web: www.baesystems.com/eis

BAE Systems Land & Armaments

Headquarters
1101 Wilson Boulevard, Suite 2000, Arlington, Virginia,
22209-2444, United States
Tel: (+1 703) 312 61 00
Fax: (+1 703) 312 61 11
Web: www.baesystems.com/landarmaments

BAE Systems Land & Armaments

US Combat Systems
1205 Coleman Avenue, Santa Clara, California, 95050,
United States
Tel: (+1 408) 289 01 11
Fax: (+1 408) 289 27 45
Web: www.baesystems.com/landandarmaments

BAE Systems Land & Armaments

Global Tactical Systems
5000 I-10 West, Sealy, Texas, 77474, United States
Tel: (+1 979) 885 29 77
Fax: (+1 979) 885 79 10
Web: www.baesystems.com/gts

BAE Systems Land & Armaments

US Combat Systems
1100 Bairs Road, York, Pennsylvania, 17405-1512,
United States
Tel: (+1 717) 225 80 00
Fax: (+1 717) 225 80 03
Web: www.baesystems.com/landandarmaments

BAE Systems Platform Solutions

Headquarters
(EI&S)
(a subsidiary of BAE Systems Inc, US)
600 Main Street, Johnson City, New York, 13790, United
States
Tel: (+1 607) 770 20 00
Fax: (+1 607) 770 35 24
Web: www.baesystems.com

BAE Systems Platform Solutions

(E&IS)
1930 South Vineyard Avenue, Ontario, California, 91761,
United States
Tel: (+1 909) 947 76 00
Fax: (+1 310) 673 84 57
e-mail: ps.communications@baesystems.com
Web: www.baesystems.com

Bailey Bridges Inc

119 40th Street Northeast, Fort Payne, Alabama, 35967,
United States
PO Box 1186, San Luis Obispo, California, 93406,
United States
Tel: (+1 256) 845 75 75
Freephone: (+1 800) 477 73 20
Fax: (+1 256) 845 77 75
e-mail: sales@baileybridge.com
Web: www.baileybridge.com

Caterpillar Inc

Defence and Federal Products
100 North East Adams Street, Peoria, Illinois, 61629,
United States
Tel: (+1 309) 675 10 00
Fax: (+1 309) 578 73 29
e-mail: cat_power@cat.com
Web: www.cat-engines.com
www.catdfp.com
www.cat.com

CDK Mobile Systems Inc

PO Box 7631 Wilmington, Delaware, 19803-0631, United
States
Tel: (+1 302) 475 66 96
Fax: (+1 302) 475 66 18
e-mail: company@cdkmobile.com
Web: www.cdkmobile.com

Chenega Integrated Systems LLC
5911 Kingstowne Village Parkway, Alexandria, Virginia, 22315, United States
Tel: (+1 904) 861 04 00
Web: www.cis-llc.net

Choctaw Manufacturing and Development Corporation (CMDC)
203 Choctaw Industrial Drive, Hugo, Oklahoma, 74743-4743, United States
Tel: (+1 580) 326 83 65
Web: www.choctawdefense.com

Chrysler LLC
PO Box 21-8004 Auburn Hills, Michigan, 48321-8004, United States
Freephone: (+1 800) 247 97 53
Web: www.chryslerllc.com

Commercial & Military Systems Co Inc (CMS)
2950 Mike Padgett Highway, PO Box 6766 Augusta, Georgia, 30906, United States
Tel: (+1 706) 798 60 20
Fax: (+1 706) 790 44 08
Web: www.cms-us.com

Daimler Trucks North America LLC (DTNA)
(a wholly owned subsidiary of Daimler AG, Germany)
4435 North Channel Avenue, PO Box 3849 Portland, Oregon, 97217, United States
Tel: (+1 803) 578 34 14
(+1 503) 745 88 55
(+1 803) 578 34 09
Freephone: (+1 800) FTL HELP (385 43 57)
Fax: (+1 803) 578 37 20
(+1 503) 745 71 00
e-mail: info@freightliner.com
Web: www.freightlinertrucks.com
www.daimler-trucksnorthamerica.com

DHS Systems LLC
33 Kings Highway, Orangeburg, New York, 10962-1802, United States
Tel: (+1 845) 359 60 66
Fax: (+1 845) 365 21 14
e-mail: drash@drash.com
Web: www.dhssystemsllc.com
www.dhstechnologiesllc.com

DRS Environmental Systems Inc
7375 Industrial Road, Florence, Kentucky, 41042, United States
Tel: (+1 859) 525 21 02
Fax: (+1 859) 795 14 75
Web: www.drs.com

DRS Technologies Ltd
Corporate Headquarters
(a wholly owned subsidiary of Finmeccanica, Italy)
5 Sylvan Way, Parsippany, New Jersey, 07054, United States
Tel: (+1 973) 898 15 00
(+1 973) 451 35 84
Fax: (+1 973) 898 47 30
(+1 973) 451 35 46
(+1 973) 898 71 84
e-mail: info@drs.com
Web: www.drs.com

Flyer Defense LLC
(a subsidiary of Marvin Land Systems Inc and Marvin Engineering Co Inc, US)
261 West Beach, Inglewood, California, 90302, United States
Tel: (+1 310) 674 50 30
Fax: (+1 310) 324 56 46
e-mail: flyerdefensellc@aol.com

Force Protection Inc
9801 Highway 78, Ladson, South Carolina, 29456, United States
Tel: (+1 843) 574 70 00
(+1 843) 740 70 15
Fax: (+1 843) 329 03 80
e-mail: info@forceprotection.net
Web: www.forceprotection.net

Ford Worldwide Direct Market Operations
Fairlane Business Park III, Room 130, MD74, 1555 Fairland Drive, Allen Park, Michigan, 48101, United States
Tel: (+1 313) 322 42 88
Fax: (+1 313) 845 36 59
Web: www.motorcraft.com

General Dynamics Armament & Technical Products
Headquarters
(a subsidiary of General Dynamics Corp, US)
Four Lake Pointe Plaza, 2118 Water Ridge Parkway, Charlotte, North Carolina, 28217, United States
Tel: (+1 704) 714 80 00
Fax: (+1 704) 714 80 04
Web: www.gdatp.com
www.generaldynamics.com

General Dynamics Land Systems (GDLS)
Headquarters & Sterling Heights Complex
(a wholly owned subsidiary of General Dynamics Corporation, US)
PO Box 2074 Warren, Michigan, 48090-2074, United States
38500 Mound Road, Sterling Heights, Michigan, 48310-3200, United States
Tel: (+1 586) 825 40 00
Fax: (+1 586) 825 40 13
e-mail: info@gdls.com
Web: www.gdls.com
www.generaldynamics.com

George E Failing Company (GEFCO)
(a division of Blue Tee Corp, US)
2215 South Van Buren, Enid, Oklahoma, 73702, United States
Tel: (+1 580) 234 41 41
Freephone: (+1 800) 759 74 41
Fax: (+1 580) 233 68 07
(+1 580) 548 27 16
e-mail: intsales@gefco.com
Web: www.gefco.com

Gichner Shelter Systems
Gichner Mobile Systems
490 East Locust Street, Dallastown, Pennsylvania, 17313-1902, United States
Tel: (+1 717) 246 54 53 (sales)
(+1 717) 244 76 11
(+1 717) 246 54 79
Fax: (+1 717) 246 54 96
e-mail: info@gichnerss.com
Web: www.gichner.us

Global Strategies Group (North America) Inc
Headquarters
2200 Defense Highway, Suite 405, Crofton, Maryland, 21114, United States
Tel: (+1 301) 858 12 30
Fax: (+1 301) 858 12 33
e-mail: info@globalgroup.us.com
Web: www.globalgroup.us.com
www.globalgroup.com

Grove Worldwide
Headquarters
Manitowoc Crane Group, 1565 Buchanan Trail East, PO Box 21 Shady Grove, Pennsylvania, 17256-0021, United States
Tel: (+1 717) 597 81 21
Web: www.groveworldwide.com
www.manitowoccranegroup.com

JLG Industries Inc
Headquarters
(a subsidiary of Oshkosh Corporation, US)
1 JLG Drive, McConnellsburg, Pennsylvania, 17233-9533, United States
Tel: (+1 717) 485 51 61
Freephone: (+1 877) 554 54 38
(+1 877) 554 73 55
Fax: (+1 717) 485 64 17
e-mail: comments@jlg.com
Web: www.jlg.com

Kalmar RT Center LLC
103 Guadalupe Drive, PO Box 1028 Cibolo, Texas, 78108-1028, United States
Tel: (+1 210) 599 65 41
Freephone: (+1 800) 232 12 36
Fax: (+1 210) 599 40 09
Web: www.kalmarrt.com

Kidde Fire Fighting
Headquarters
180 Sheree Boulevard, Suite 3900 Exton, Pennsylvania, 19341-0695, United States
Tel: (+1 919) 639 61 51
(+1 610) 363 14 00
Fax: (+1 919) 639 85 19
(+1 610) 524 90 73
Web: www.kidde-fire.com

LaBarge Inc
Corporate Headquarters
9900 Clayton Road, St Louis, Missouri, 63124, United States
Tel: (+1 314) 997 08 00
Fax: (+1 314) 812 94 38
Web: www.labarge.com

Mack Trucks Inc
World Headquarters
7825 National Service Road, Greensboro, North Carolina, 27409, United States
Tel: (+1 336) 393 33 46
(+1 336) 291 92 01
Freephone: (+1 800) 866 11 77
Fax: (+1 336) 291 92 52
(+1 336) 291 93 02
(+1 336) 291 92 02
e-mail: customer.satisfaction@macktrucks.com
mktg.comm@macktrucks.com
govt.comm.relations@macktrucks.com
Web: www.macktrucks.com

Marion Metal Works Inc
4750 South Pine Avenue, Ocala, Florida, 34475, United States
Tel: (+1 352) 351 42 21
Fax: (+1 352) 622 29 22
e-mail: info@marionmetalworks.com
Web: www.marionmetalworks.com

Marvin Land Systems Inc (MLS)
260 West Beach Avenue, Inglewood, California, 90302, United States
Tel: (+1 310) 674 50 30
Fax: (+1 310) 673 94 72
e-mail: sales@marvinland.com
Web: www.marvinland.com

Mechanical Equipment Co Inc (MECO)
12505 Reed Road, Suite 100, Sugar Land, Texas, 77478, United States
Tel: (+1 281) 276 76 00
Freephone: (+1 800) 421 17 98
Fax: (+1 281) 313 06 43
Web: www.meco.com
www.mecomilitary.com

Mil-Mar Century Inc (MMC)
8641 Washington-Church Road, Miamisburg, Ohio, 45342, United States
Tel: (+1 937) 275 48 60
Fax: (+1 937) 275 49 04
e-mail: info@milmarcentury.com
Web: www.milmarcentury.com

Navistar Defense LLC
4201 Winfield Road, Warrenville, Illinois, 60555, United States
Tel: (+1 630) 753 50 00
Freephone: (+1 800) 448 78 25
Web: www.navistardefense.com

Newpark Mats and Integrated Services
(dba Dura-Base)
207 Town Center Parkway, Lafayette, Louisiana, 70506-7524, United States
Tel: (+1 337) 981 50 58
Freephone: (+1 877) MAT-ROAD (628 76 23)
Fax: (+1 337) 984 92 41
Web: www.newpark.com
www.newparkmats.com

Oshkosh Corporation
PO Box 2566 Oshkosh, Wisconsin, 54903-2566, United States
2307 Oregon Street, Oshkosh, Wisconsin, 54902, United States
Tel: (+1 920) 235 91 50
Fax: (+1 920) 233 96 24
(+1 920) 233 95 06
Web: www.oshkoshcorp.com

Power Dynamics LLC
Entech Systems
MSAAP, Building 9166, Stennis Space Center, Mississippi, 39529, United States
Tel: (+1 228) 689 85 60
Fax: (+1 228) 689 85 70
e-mail: sales@pdi-entech.com
Web: www.pdi-entech.com

Schiebel Technology Inc (STI)
(a subsidiary of Schiebel Industries AG, Austria)
70 Main Street, Suite 11, Warrenton, Virginia, 20186, United States
Tel: (+1 540) 351 17 31
Fax: (+1 540) 351 17 36
e-mail: info@schiebel.net
Web: www.schiebel.net

Talbert Manufacturing Inc
1628 West State Road 114, Rensselaer, Indiana, 47978-9169, United States
Tel: (+1 219) 866 71 41
Freephone: (+1 800) 348 52 32
Fax: (+1 219) 866 54 37
e-mail: sales@talbertmfg.com
Web: www.talbertmfg.com

Terex Corporation
200 Nyala Farm Road, Westport, Connecticut, 06880, United States
Tel: (+1 203) 222 71 70
Fax: (+1 203) 222 70 76
(+1 203) 222 79 76
e-mail: info@terex.com
Web: www.terex.com

Textron Marine & Land Systems (TMLS)
(a subsidiary of Textron Defense Systems and Textron Inc, US)
19401 Chef Menteur Highway, New Orleans, Louisiana, 70129, United States
Tel: (+1 504) 245 66 00
Fax: (+1 504) 254 80 09
Web: www.textronmarineandland.com

The Entwistle Company
6 Bigelow Street, Hudson, Massachusetts, 01749-2697, United States
Tel: (+1 508) 481 40 00
Fax: (+1 508) 481 40 04
Web: www.entwistleco.com

US Army Tank-Automotive & Armament Command (TACOM)
Armament Research, Dev and Engineering Centre (ARDEC)
US Army, ARDEC
AMSRD-AAR-AO, Building 59, Picatinny Arsenal, New Jersey, 07806-5000, United States
Tel: (+1 973) 724 40 21
Fax: (+1 201) 724 30 44
Web: www.pica.army.mil

US Army Tank - Automotive & Armament Command (TACOM)
PM Petroleum & Water Systems
6501 East, 11 Mile Road, Warren, Michigan, 48397-5000, United States
Tel: (+1 586) 574 41 49
(+1 586) 574 42 00
(+1 586) 786 42 00 (dsn)
Fax: (+1 586) 574 41 23
(+1 586) 574 39 88
e-mail: pmpaws@tacom.army.mil
Web: peocscss.tacom.army.mil

INDEXES

Alphabetical Index

For details of the latest updates to *Jane's Military Vehicles and Logistics* online and to discover the additional information available exclusively to online subscribers please visit
jmvl.janes.com

For details of the latest updates to *Jane's Military Vehicles and Logistics* online and to discover the additional information available exclusively to online subscribers please visit

jmvl.janes.com

For details of the latest updates to *Jane's Military Vehicles and Logistics* online and to discover
the additional information available exclusively to online subscribers please visit
jmvl.janes.com

For details of the latest updates to *Jane's Military Vehicles and Logistics* online and to discover
the additional information available exclusively to online subscribers please visit

jmvl.janes.com

For details of the latest updates to *Jane's Military Vehicles and Logistics* online and to discover
the additional information available exclusively to online subscribers please visit
jmvl.janes.com

Manufacturers' Index

For details of the latest updates to *Jane's Military Vehicles and Logistics* online and to discover
the additional information available exclusively to online subscribers please visit
jmvl.janes.com

For details of the latest updates to *Jane's Military Vehicles and Logistics* online and to discover
the additional information available exclusively to online subscribers please visit
jmvl.janes.com

For details of the latest updates to *Jane's Military Vehicles and Logistics* online and to discover
the additional information available exclusively to online subscribers please visit
jmvl.janes.com

Former state factories
BMK-130 *bridging boats* (Russian Federation)..235
BMK-150 *bridging boats* (Russian Federation)..235
LVM light suspension bridge *non-floating bridges* (Russian Federation) 214
MO-108 *bridging boats* (Slovakia)..237
MO-111 *bridging boats* (Slovakia)..237
OPS and POU *water supplies* (Russian Federation)..............................893
PPS heavy girder floating bridge *floating bridges/ferries*
　(Russian Federation)..198
PVM foot suspension bridge *non-floating bridges* (Russian Federation) 214
TVM heavy suspension bridge *non-floating bridges*
　(Russian Federation)..214
Underwater bridge set *non-floating bridges* (Russian Federation)..............214

Franz Achleitner Fahrzeugbau und Reifenzentrum GmbH
Achleitner logistic support products *other equipment* (Austria) 961

Freightliner LLC
6966XD series *heavy transporters* (Canada) 704
Freightliner *recovery vehicles* (United States) 132
M915 Series *trucks* (United States)..675
M 1500 LSVW *trucks* (Canada)..392
M4866S *heavy transporters* (Canada)..704
M4866S HESV *trucks* (Canada)..393

Fresia SpA
Fresia *light vehicles* (Italy) 279
Fresia F18 *light vehicles* (Italy)..278

G

GAMESA International
GAMESA M-47 VR *armoured recovery vehicles* (Spain) 71

GEC Engineering (Accrington) Limited
MEXEFLOTE *floating bridges/ferries* (United Kingdom)............................201

General Dynamics Armament and Technical Products
GDATP Specialist vehicle bodies and cargo bed covers *other equipment*
　(United States) 971
General purpose rigid OSP shelter *shelters/containers* (United States)..........956
HMMWV compatible shelters *shelters/containers* (United States)................956
Relocatable hospitals *shelters/containers* (United States) 956
S-842/G (SICPSV5) HMMWV shelter *shelters/containers*
　(United States) 957

General Dynamics European Land Systems - Germany GmbH
Bundeswehr Faltschwimmbrucke (FSB) *floating bridges/ferries*
　(Germany)..187
Improved Ribbon Bridge (IRB) *floating bridges/ferries* (Germany) 188
Infantry Assault Bridge *non-floating bridges* (Germany)............................210
M2 amphibious bridging and ferrying system *mechanised bridges*
　(Germany)..150
M3 amphibious bridging and ferrying system *mechanised bridges*
　(Germany)..149
Piranha III Armoured Vehicle Launched Bridge *mechanised bridges*
　(International)..156
Rapidly Emplaced Bridge System (REBS) *mechanised bridges*
　(Germany) 151

General Dynamics European Land Systems - MOWAG GmbH
Piranha *armoured repair vehicles* (Switzerland)............................99

General Dynamics European Land Systems Santa Bárbara Sistemas
Pizarro Recovery Combat Vehicle *armoured recovery vehicles* (Spain)..........72

**General Dynamics European Land Systems - Steyr GmbH (previously
Steyr-Daimler-Puch Spezialfahrzeug AG & Co KG)**
Bergepanzer 4KH7FA-SB 20 Greif *armoured recovery vehicles*
　(Austria)..39

**General Dynamics European Land Systems - Steyr GmbH (previously
Steyr-Daimler-Puch Spezialfahrzeug AG & Co KG**
Pandur I ARRV *armoured recovery vehicles* (Austria) 39

General Dynamics Land Systems
M48 AVLB *mechanised bridges* (United States)............................180
M60 AVLB *mechanised bridges* (United States) 180
M728 CEV *armoured engineer vehicles* (United States) 31
Wolverine HAB *mechanised bridges* (United States)............................178

General Dynamics Land Systems - Canada
Bison *armoured repair vehicles* (Canada)............................94
Engineer Squad Vehicle *armoured engineer vehicles* (United States) 32
LAV *armoured repair vehicles* (Canada) 94

General Dynamics Santa Bárbara Sistemas
BMR 3560.55 *armoured recovery vehicles* (Spain)............................73

General Dynamics Santa Bárbara Sistemas - MOWAG GmbH
Piranha III Armoured Vehicle Launched Bridge *mechanised bridges*
　(International)..156

George E Failing Company (GEFCo)
600 ft water well drilling system *water supplies* (United States) 899

GE Water & Process Technologies
ADROWPU *water supplies* (Canada) 886
Mini-ROWPU *water supplies* (Canada)............................886

Gichner Shelter Systems
20 ft ISO shelter/container *shelters/containers* (United States)......................953
ASF shelters *shelters/containers* (United States)............................946
GRASS *shelters/containers* (United States) 952
GSS-1497 *shelters/containers* (United States) 953
HMMWV compatible shelters *shelters/containers* (United States)................953
MERWS *shelters/containers* (United States) 952
Navair range of ISO shelters *shelters/containers* (United States)................952
S-250G *shelters/containers* (United States) 955
S-530A/G *shelters/containers* (United States)............................953
S-710 *shelters/containers* (United States)............................953
S-749 *shelters/containers* (United States)............................955
S-788/G (LMS) *shelters/containers* (United States) 953
Shelter Systems *shelters/containers* (United States)............................952

Global Strategies Group Inc
Tactical Water Purification System (TWPS) (1,500 GPH) *water supplies*
　(United States) 904

Global Tactical Systems, Land Systems OMC
Wasp RDRV *special attack vehicles* (South Africa)............................362

GM Defense
Commercial Utility Cargo Vehicles II (CUCV II) *light vehicles*
　(United States) 343
Commercial Utility Cargo Vehicles (CUCV) *light vehicles*
　(United States) 341
GM CEMMV *trucks* (United States)............................656

Gorky Automobile Plant (GAZ Joint Stock Company)
GAZ-66 *trucks* (Russian Federation)..572
GAZ medium truck series *trucks* (Russian Federation)............................571

Government of India
Kartik *mechanised bridges* (India) 152
Vijayanta *armoured recovery vehicles* (India)............................54

Groupement Interprofessionnel de Logistique et d'Equipement Pétroliers
CCP 10 *fuel storage/distribution* (France) 862

Grove Worldwide
Manitowoc (Grove) Mobile cranes *materials handling* (United States).........818
TMS300-5 *materials handling* (United States)............................816

GTA Containers Inc
3,000 US gallon capacity 'Onion tank' *water supplies* (United States).........901
Drums and Superdrums *water supplies* (United States) 901
GTA fuel drums and Superdrums *fuel storage/distribution*
　(United States) 881
GTA mini-tanks *water supplies* (United States)............................901
GTA static fuel storage pillow tanks *fuel storage/distribution*
　(United States) 881
Static storage tanks *water supplies* (United States)............................901
Trailer tanks *water supplies* (United States) 901

H

haacon hebetechnik GmbH
Lifting, rolling and loading systems for mobile tactical shelters and containers
　shelters/containers (Germany)..928

HAMMAR Maskin AB
HAMMAR Sideloaders *materials handling* (Sweden) 802

Hanyang Special Auto Works
HY 473A *heavy transporters* (China) 705
HY 4390 *heavy transporters* (China) 705

HARSCO BMY-Wheeled Vehicles Division
M939 *trucks* (United States)..679

Haulotte-Pinguely
MFRD/F1 mobile drilling machine *field fortifications* (France)....................832

Heavy Industries Taxila
Al Hadeed Armoured Repair and Recovery Vehicle
　armoured recovery vehicles (Pakistan)..61
Al Qaswa *all-terrain carriers/movers* (Pakistan)..766

For details of the latest updates to *Jane's Military Vehicles and Logistics* online and to discover
the additional information available exclusively to online subscribers please visit
jmvl.janes.com

For details of the latest updates to *Jane's Military Vehicles and Logistics* online and to discover
the additional information available exclusively to online subscribers please visit
jmvl.janes.com

For details of the latest updates to *Jane's Military Vehicles and Logistics* online and to discover
the additional information available exclusively to online subscribers please visit
jmvl.janes.com

For details of the latest updates to *Jane's Military Vehicles and Logistics* online and to discover the additional information available exclusively to online subscribers please visit
jmvl.janes.com

For details of the latest updates to *Jane's Military Vehicles and Logistics* online and to discover
the additional information available exclusively to online subscribers please visit
jmvl.janes.com

NOTES

NOTES

NOTES

NOTES

NOTES